THE ROYAL & ANCIENT

GOLFER'S HANDBOOK 2004

EDITOR RENTON LAIDLAW

MACMILLAN

First published 1984 by Macmillan
This edition published 2003 by Macmillan
an imprint of Pan Macmillan Ltd
Pan Macmillan, 20 New Wharf Road, London N1 9RR
Basingstoke and Oxford
Associated companies throughout the world
www.panmacmillan.com

ISBN 1 405 02126 8   (Hardback)
ISBN 1 405 02127 6   (Paper laminate case)

Note
Whilst every care has been taken in compiling the information contained in
this book, the Publishers, Editor and Sponsors accept no responsibility for
any errors or omissions.

Correspondence
Letters on editorial matters should be addressed to:
The Editor, Royal & Ancient Golfer's Handbook, Pan Macmillan,
20 New Wharf Road, London N1 9RR

The information on golf courses and clubs contained in
this Handbook is available for purchase on disk as
mailing labels. For further information please
e-mail golfmailing@macmillan.co.uk

9 8 7 6 5 4 3 2 1

A CIP catalogue record for this book is available from the British Library

Typeset by Penrose Typography, Maidstone, Kent

Printed and bound in Great Britain by Mackays of Chatham plc, Chatham, Kent

Contents

The Captain of The R&A, 2003–2004   6

Prince Urges Members to Encourage Juniors *John Hopkins*   7

Annika and the men who made it into the Top Six *Renton Laidlaw*   10

Four First-Time Winners in a Season of Surprises *David Davies*   13

Impressive Last Day Rally makes Walker Cup History *Mark Garrod*   19

Farcical, Capricious and Down-right Incredulous *Furman Bisher*   21

Barsebäck Triumph Raises Profile of Women's Golf *Lewine Mair*   25

The Handshake that gave Birth to a Golfing Empire *Ian Wooldridge*   27

Royal Troon – a Constant Battle for Survival *Keith Mackie*   29

How a Successful Open helps the Global Game *Mike Aitken*   31

The Royal and Ancient and the modern game   33

Dates and Venues for all Majors and Cup Matches   35

R&A Championship Dates, 2004–2006   36

Schedules and Dates for 2004   37

Part I The Major Championships

The Open Championship   42

The US Open Championship   52

The Masters   60

US PGA Championship   67

Men's Major Title Table   75

Weetabix Women's British Open Championship   76

US Women's Open Championship   83

McDonald's LPGA Championship   91

Nabisco Dinah Shore   99

du Maurier Classic   106

Women's Major Title Table   107

Part II Men's Professional Tournaments

Official World Rankings   110

European Tour – 2003 and Past Results   111

European Senior Tour, 2003   131

European Challenge Tour, 2003   134

US PGA Tour, 2003   136

US Champions Tour, 2003   147

US Nationwide Tour, 2003   150

Japanese Tour, 2003   152

Davidoff Asian PGA Tour, 2003   154

Australasian Tour, 2003   155

South African Tour, 2003   156
Canadian Tour, 2003   157
Tour de Las Americas, 2003   158
World Championship Events   160
Other International Events   167
International Team Events   168
National and Regional Championships   184
Overseas National Championships   191

Part III Women's Professional Events

Golf Weekly Official World Rankings   194
Evian Ladies' Tour   195
US LPGA Tour   199
Futures Tour   206
Japan LPGA Tour   207
International Team Events   209
Professional Women's Overseas Championships   214

Part IV Men's Amateur Events

National and International Amateur Championships   218
Team Events   235
Principal 72-hole Tournaments   257
National District Championships   264
Other Men's Amateur Tournaments   268
Foursomes Events   273
University and School Events   276
County and Other Regional Championships   281
Overseas Amateur Championships   286
Callaway Handicapping   291

Part V Women's Amateur Events

National and International Tournaments   294
Team Events   309
Other Women's Amateur Tournaments   324
Irish Ladies District Championships   327
Foursomes Events   327
Regional Amateur Championships   328
Amateur Championships Overseas   333

Part VI Junior Tournaments and Events

Boys and Youths' Tournaments   338
Girls and Junior Ladies' Tournaments   350
Golf Foundation Events   357

Part VII Awards

                                                           361

Part VIII Who's Who in Golf

British, Irish and Continental Players, Men	370
British, Irish and Continental Players, Women	382
Overseas Players, Men	387
Overseas Players, Women	403
British Isles International Players, Professional Men	407
British Isles International Players, Professional Women	412
British Isles International Players, Amateur Men	413
British Isles International Players, Amateur Women	427

Part IX Governing the Game

Rules get major revision	438
The Rules of Golf	441
Professional Governing Bodies	503
Amateur Governing Bodies	505
Championship and International Match Conditions	508
Golf Associations	513
Directory of Golfing Organisations Worldwide	515
Royal clubs	532

Part X Golf History

History of Championships and Team Events	536
Famous personalities of the Past	542
Interesting Facts and Unusual Incidents	551
Record Scoring	579

Part XI Guide to Golfing Services and Places to Stay in the British Isles and Ireland

Golf Club Facilities	590
Buyer's Guide	599
Golfing Hotel Compendium	616
Professional Associations	622

Part XII Clubs and Courses in the British Isles and Europe

Club Centenaries	626
Golf Clubs and Courses in the British Isles and Europe	627
How to Use this Section	627
Great Britain and Ireland County Index	628
Continent of Europe Country and Region Index	829

General Index	919

The Duke of York – R&A Captain

HRH the Duke of York, the captain of the Royal and Ancient Golf Club of St Andrews, in full regalia. The Duke, who has a low single figure handicap, holds the captaincy during the year that the club celebrates its 250th anniversary. The Duke is the sixth member of the Royal Family to captain the club.

Prince Urges Members To Encourage Juniors

John Hopkins meets the R&A Captain

His Royal Highness The Duke of York, the Captain of the R&A, was in his office in Buckingham Palace telling a story. As he spoke, sunlight streamed in through the windows and a murmur of traffic rose from ground level. It was just a couple of days after the excitement of the Open at Sandwich, an Open won by an outsider, perhaps the greatest surprise winner for a century. For a few minutes the conversation was all about the young American Ben Curtis and how well he had played but then it turned to another aspect of golf.

'Has Doug ever told you the story of my first lesson?' HRH Prince Andrew asked. 'Doug [McLelland] had been told to come to Windsor Castle and to report to a particular gate, which he did. From there he was directed to a place underneath the battlements of the castle. His wife sat reading in the car. I came out to meet him and there and then, he started to give me a lesson.

'He had his back to the castle about ten yards away from some steps leading down from the castle and I was facing him. We'd been going for a few minutes when some dogs appeared on the steps. Doug couldn't see them because he was facing me and anyway he didn't know their significance so he carried on teaching me and I carried on listening. I knew what the dogs meant, however, and I was trying to tell him but I couldn't seem to find a moment to interrupt him. Finally, Doug noticed a corgi and just as he did so I said to him: "Doug, may I introduce you to The Queen?"'

Doug has taught the Prince well. Prince Andrew drove into office at St Andrews on a windy morning last September with one of the best tee shots hit by any captain in recent memory, one unofficially measured at 265 yards, into the wind. When he assumed office, the Duke of York became the sixth member of the Royal Family to hold this position, happily at a time when the Royal and Ancient Golf Club of St Andrews is celebrating its 250th anniversary.

Racing may be the sport of kings but, clearly, there has been a long historic link between golf and the R&A. The first member of the Royal Family to captain the R&A was HRH the Prince of Wales, later to become Edward VII, in 1863. Prince Leopold became captain in 1876, the Prince of Wales, later Edward VIII, in 1922 and the Duke of York, later to become King George VI, in 1930,

seven years before the Duke of Kent. Though the Duke of Kent was the oldest member of the royal family to captain the R&A, Prince Andrew is the youngest captain since 1937. Prince Andrew was 43 years, seven months and 30 days old when he drove in.

'I want it [my year of captaincy] to be a celebration of golf,' Prince Andrew said on this July morning. 'The Open was an example. Its a game in which all those who have done their preparation can win.

'I also want to encourage young people to play golf. I don't want them to feel that they cannot play or feel intimidated. I want to see people who join clubs early in their lives stay in the game. Juniors bring a vibrancy to golf clubs. I look at some clubs and I wonder why they are so orientated towards older members. Whenever I visit a new club I say to them: "how many juniors have you got?"

'It seems to me there are two simple things clubs could do for younger members. I was at a golf club in the US not long ago and I noticed they had tee markers very near the edge of the fairway. I asked what they were for because they seemed an awfully long way forward. I was told they were for the under 12's. Children in those age groups play the course and have their own cards. Why shouldn't they have their own tees? – they can compete with one another. The second thing I think clubs could do is give juniors more competition. I want juniors to be included not excluded.'

Young Champions' Trophy

Junior golfers are a subject close to the heart of the Duke of York. In an earlier interview he had stressed the importance of juniors and explained that was why he had started his Young Champions' Trophy for some of the best young boy and girl golfers in Europe.

'I want junior golf to be a stepping stone to allow them to play good golf later. I want to encourage them to stay amateur longer. Those who turn pro are few and far between when measured against all the young people who play golf. When we started the competition the idea was to try and get together all the winners of the other junior events in Europe so they could get an idea of where the pinnacle of golf for that year was. It is not designed as a junior Open. It is designed as fun but at the same time it is an

opportunity to get people to realise that junior golf needs encouragement particularly at club level to allow younger people to play and give them the same playing privileges as full members. Some clubs will, some clubs won't.

'There are excellent clubs around that give their juniors a good time and encourage them. Of course it is not that the juniors should be given *carte blanche*, just that I think that younger members should be encouraged by older members and mentored by them in the folklore of the game and the etiquette. Things such as "you should keep up to the game in front, not keep ahead of the game behind". When you teach somebody how to play a foursome there should never be more than two people on the tee at any one time. The people out front should act as forecaddies.'

At times like this as you listen to the Duke talking animatedly about golf in general and junior golf in particular, you forget you are at Buckingham Palace. You forget that you have had to give your name to policemen at the entrance who have checked your name off against a list. You forget you have walked on a 100-yard-long red carpet to a waiting room on the ground floor of the Palace, where a young man in a white jacket offers you a seat until an aide comes down in a creaky old lift to escort you upstairs. You forget how, having got out of the lift, you have walked along a long corridor lined with antiques and oil paintings and have glimpsed rooms used as offices at the front of Buckingham Palace.

You forget even how, as you walked along the corridor, you wondered whether the Duke of Edinburgh would come charging out of one room or you might overhear the voice of the Queen down the corridor. You forget all this in the kinship of golf. You forget you are talking to the man who is in line to the throne. Instead you get caught up in his enthusiasm for the game, and for a few moments it is as if a small knot of golfers have met in a corner of the bar at their local club and simply talked golf.

The Duke of York has become a respectable amateur golfer. Ask him his handicap and this is what he says: 'I am off 5.5 and until Sunday I was dreadful. Now I'm a good 4. I saw Doug on Sunday and he said I was hitting everything off the toe of my club. I had no power. He said I had too short a backswing. He told me to take my left hand off the club and to try and feel as though I was hitting the back of the ball with authority. I am now. It's much better.'

There was no visible sign of golf in his office. It contained the inevitable fax machine, a mobile telephone, a desk, a lamp and family portraits. He was asked whether he had a putter lying around in order to put in a little practice on the carpet between appointments. He smiled at the thought. 'I used to,' he said. He looked around. 'I think someone must have half-inched [pinched] it.' He smiled.

'Golf for me is an opportunity to relax, to unburden myself, to make the most of what is around me. There are the things I have to do as a member of the Royal Family. When I am playing golf I am among

A large crowd watched the Duke of York drive himself into office and win the Queen Adelaide Medal at the traditional ceremony which is marked by the firing of a canon. The Club's honorary professional John Panton was in attendance and the Duke later played in the autumn medal partnered by his predecessor John Whitmore and former USGA president Bill Campbell. At the driving-in ceremony the Duke hit a magnificent drive which flew over the heads of the caddies who were waiting to retrieve the ball but it was eventually returned to the new captain by 37-year-old Ian Reddie who received the traditional gold sovereign.

friends, people who are of a like mind who enjoy playing a game with a little white ball.'

The Duke of York is a Special Representative for International Trade and Investment and the duties that he must fulfil in his role as captain of the R&A must fit in around these commitments. Fortunately, planning for his year of captaincy of the R&A began months ago. That was an absolute necessity.

'Michael Bonallack came to me and asked me privately if it would be possible for me to be captain for the 250th anniversary of the R&A. Then I was formally asked in 2000 by the past captains. I started to have everything put into my diary. I shall do only limited speaking engagements and have asked some of the past captains to help me in that regard.

'When my diary is plotted I put the R&A alongside my other schedules. For instance, I shall be at Augusta for The Masters next year and play at a nearby course. In fact I shall play more golf over my year in office than I did in the previous year.

'It was a clever move to mark the 250th anniversary of the R&A in this way. It might have been controversial for me to have been Captain at some other time. I think those in the game will appreciate having a member of the Royal Family involved. It is like Princess Anne and horses. I am doing the same thing on behalf of golf. Other members of the Royal Family have represented the country in the Olympics and that is not a question of advantage. They have done so because of their ability. In this respect my handicap is not a nonsense handicap.'

Then he told another story. He was playing in the R&A's spring meeting on the Old Course and as he came up the 18th hole he noticed a lot of men in the Bay window of the clubhouse. 'Who are they and what are they doing?' he asked a playing companion. 'They are the old captains' was the reply. Then the speaker risked being banished to the Tower or even a beheading by adding: 'You'll be one soon'.

Honorary Membership for Jacklin and Trevino

Tony Jacklin, winner of the 1969 Open Championship and 1970 US Open, and Lee Trevino winner of six majors including the Open in 1971 at Royal Birkdale and in 1972 at Muirfield, have both been elected honorary members of the Royal and Ancient Golf Club of St Andrews.

Jacklin and Trevino battled for the Open in 1972 coming to the 17th, where 'Supermex' chipped in for an unexpected birdie 4 and Jacklin three putted for 6. The list of honorary members now stands at 13.

The other Open champions who have been so honoured are Kel Nagle (1960), Jack Nicklaus (1966, 1970, 1978), Arnold Palmer (1961, 1962), Gary Player (1959, 1968, 1974), Peter Thomson (1954, 1955, 1956, 1958 and 1965), Roberto de Vicenzo (1967) and Tom Watson (1975, 1977, 1980, 1982 and 1983). His Royal Highness The Duke of Edinburgh KG KT, His Royal Highness The Duke of York CVO ADC and His Royal Highness The Duke of Kent KG GCMG GCVO are also honorary members as is President George Herbert Walker Bush KGCB.

Annika and the men who made it into the Top Six

Renton Laidlaw makes his 2003 selection

It was Tim Yeo MP who echoed the voice of many of you when he wrote last year to suggest that we revive the feature in the *Golfer's Handbook* which names the best six golfers of the year. But how to choose? Do you select the best golfers on what events they have won, how much money they have amassed, how international their schedule has been or how big an impact they have had on the golfing world? There are no hard and fast rules, so the six I have chosen for 2003 are my own personal choice. Ladies first.

It was not difficult to list the lady golfer who once again dominated the golfing scene. Annika Sörenstam does not like to be referred to as the Tiger of ladies golf but she is breaking all sorts of records. In 2003 she was inducted into the LPGA Hall of Fame having completed ten years on Tour. She inspired her team mates to a memorably successful victory over the United States in the Solheim Cup and won two more majors. Her victory at Royal Lytham and St Annes in the Weetabix British Women's Open gave her her first complete set of major titles.

'Every year,' she says, 'I have a simple goal. I want to win the LPGA money list, the Vare Trophy, which rewards the low average scorer for the season, and the Player of the Year.' She missed out only on the Vare Trophy because she did not play enough rounds to qualify.

Her most high-profile performance came at the Bank of America Colonial event when she took on the men on their home ground. Many of the men were openly hostile to her in the weeks leading up to the occasion but she handled the pressure impressively throughout, made many new friends and, in the end, disappointed herself and many golfing fans by failing narrowly to make the halfway cut. The ultimate accolade of her performance? – praise from Jack Nicklaus.

A dedicated athlete she had scored her 46th LPGA Tour win when she won the Mizuno Classic in Japan for a third time in a row in November, becoming the first person to complete a second 'three-peat' as the Americans call it.

It was not difficult to include Annika in my top six nor was it difficult to add in Ernie Els and Vijay Singh – the men who finished No.1 on the European and American money lists.

Ernie is a truly international performer who, unlike so many of the top Americans, takes his impressive game around the world like a modern golfing missionary. He won seven times during the year which began for him so dramatically. He won four of the first five events in which he played, pipped only in the other by Chinese golfer Lian-Wei Zhang in Singapore. He set new under-par winning totals on the European, American, Australasian and Asian Tours by shooting 31-under-

Annika Sörenstam – another dominating year for the hugely successful record-breaking Swede.

Ernie Els – the quiet international achiever impressed wherever he played.

Vijay Singh – he promised to head Tiger in the 2003 US money list and did.

photos © Phil Sheldon

photos © Phil Sheldon

Tiger Woods – by his own high standards a disappointing 2003 but he is still 'the man'.

Tom Watson – the senior golfer who continues to impress both on and off the course.

Ben Curtis – the unknown whose victory in the Open captured everybody's imagination.

par at the Mercedes Championship in Hawaii in January and 29-under-par in the Johnnie Walker Classic which was played at Lake Karrinyup in Perth, Australia, in February. His other victories comprised the Sony Open in Hawaii, the Heineken Classic, the Barclays Scottish Open, the Omega European Masters and the HSBC World Match Play Championship at Wentworth for a record-equalling fifth time, matching the feat of Gary Player and Seve Ballesteros. Few would bet against golf's 'Big Easy' winning this event several more times in the next few years.

Despite all that he did not win a major which some may feel puts him behind Mike Weir, the Canadian who won The Masters. Jim Furyk who took the US Open title, Ben Curtis, the Open champion, and Shaun Micheel whose victory in the US PGA Championship was highlighted by one of the finest last-hole recovery shots since Sandy Lyle hit that towering 7-iron from a fairway bunker to make a birdie at the last and become the first British golfer to collect a Green Jacket, in 1988.

Powerful finish

That may be true but Els is on my list anyway as is Vijay Singh who at the end of 2002 set a personal goal – to head Tiger Woods at the top of the American money list … a goal he achieved with the help of victories in the Phoenix Open, the EDS Byron Nelson Championship, the John Deere Classic and the Funai Classic – victories spread throughout the season. He had top 10 finishes in 10 of his last 11 events to take top spot with $7,573,907. Few players work as hard on their games, spend as long on the practice range as Singh who has come such a long way since struggling to make a living on the Australian Tour and for a time acting as club professional in a remote Borneo resort. Like Els he did not win a major, all of which in 2003 went to first-time winners but he relentlessly went after Tiger, preventing the American from taking the

No.1 spot on the US Tour for a record fifth year in a row and setting himself up for an off-the-course battle with Furyk. Davis Love III, winner of The Players' Championship, Woods and Weir for American Player of the Year. That vote was not in when we went to print.

Standard bearer

I know that by his own high standards it was not a year Tiger may wish to remember with particular delight because he did not add to his majors tally and did not finish top money earner despite winning another two of those World Championship events which bring together the best in the world four times a year – make that three times! Fifteen of the top 20 in the world turned down the opportunity of playing for their countries in the WGC World Cup at Kiawah Island which, putting it mildly, was disappointing!

Yet Woods is still the standard bearer, still the golfer who brings the crowds in wherever he plays, although mostly in America. Unlike Els or Singh the Tiger is less inclined to pack his bags too often and leave home. Throughout the year the multi-millionaire struggled with his driving. Hitting too many off-line was the real reason he missed out on the majors. Neither could he quite lift his game to win the Tour Championship at season's end in America and foil the charging Singh but despite that I would have been uncomfortable at leaving the modern golfing icon off the list.

Sörenstam, Els, Singh, Woods and now I need two more from my own short list which comprises the four major winners, Darren Clarke, who became only the second golfer to win two World Championship events (Tiger is the other!); Kenny Perry who was unbeatable in mid-season winning three times in eight US Tour weeks; Frederick Jacobsen, the first Swede to win three titles on the European Tour and who had a fifth and sixth place finish in the US Open and the Open; senior golfer Tom Watson who

topped the US Champions Tour's money list and Lee Westwood, who produced the comeback of the year. It ws good to have him back.

One of my last two votes goes to Watson who impressed me with his continuing dedication to the game and his work off course in aid of charity. His long-time caddie Bruce Edwards has contracted a wasting disease for which there is no cure at this time. When they appeared together for the last time at the US Open in June at Olympia Fields it was one of the season's most emotional moments. Later, Watson donated $1 million of his earnings to research into the disease. Watson may have missed the cut in the dreadful weather at The Masters and failed to play four rounds at Oak Hill in the US PGA Championship, a title, incidentally, he never managed to win but he played well in the US Open and Open and won two and finished second twice in four of the five senior majors.

Left-handed brilliance

Choosing the last of my six was more difficult. Mike Weir, the Masters winner, impressed by keeping his cool and his deadly putting touch in the closing stages when others stumbled. In addition the first Canadian to win a Green Jacket and only the second left-hander to win a major (Bob Charles was the other back in 1963 at Lytham St Annes), won the Bob Hope Chrysler Classic and the Nissan Open.

Jim Furyk, the US Open champion who also won the Buick Open, was in total control of his game throughout the week at Olympia Fields and, as one top professional put it, gave hope to all those of us whose swings are not as rhythmical or as smooth as Ernie Els or Colin Montgomerie. Furyk's swing is one of the least impressive but the bottom line is that it works for him every time and his father, himself a professional, was wise enough not to try and change it. Furyk's major title victory was applauded by many as was that of the two 'unlikely lads' – Micheel and Curtis – and it is the latter who makes it into the top six.

Curtis's performance at Royal St George's was nothing short of miraculous. He had never won in America (still has not done so), had never been in Britain, had seldom if ever played links golf, did not bring his regular US Tour caddie and only qualified because he had finished tied 13th in the 100th Western Open from which spots at Royal St George's were available.

The scenario of the young man from Kent, Ohio, coming to Kent, England and taking on the world's best on one of the toughest of courses is akin to the feats of Roy of the Rovers in the adventure comics. Roy always got that last minute winner … and Curtis's winner was an 11 foot putt on the last which helped him nail Woods, Thomas Bjørn, Singh and Love.

It couldn't happen, it shouldn't happen but it did and the name Ben Curtis was engraved on golf's most famous trophy – the Claret Jug. Curtis's success was the fairy-tale of the year and we wish him success. Nobody wants him to be a one-title wonder and watching him in action at the HSBC World Match-play Championship I do not think he will be. So there it is – Sörenstam. Els, Singh, Woods, Watson and Curtis – my top six.

Elsewhere in this edition we celebrate with Mark Garrod the tremendous victory of the Great Britain and Ireland Walker Cup side at Ganton and with Lewine Mair the staggering performance of the Europeans in the Solheim Cup at Barsebäck – two team performances which did much to enhance the reputation of golf, although I am glad the rules are being changed to ensure that all games are played to a finish. The Solheim event did end in a farcical way when the players still on the course after the impressive and under-rated Catriona Matthew had clinched victory just walked off.

The 2003 season saw the continuation of the changing of the guard. There had been no wins by mid November, for the former Big Five – Bernhard Langer, Ian Woosnam, Nick Faldo, Sandy Lyle and Seve Ballesteros, the latter only a shadow of his former self and who, in the Seve Trophy, lost more holes in a row to Colin Montgomerie than he had ever done in his whole career. José María Olazábal did not win and Colin Montgomerie only managed to do so after a play-off at Macau in an Asian PGA Tour event.

Roe impressed

There were, however, 17 first time winners in Europe but not so many in America where as, Furman Bisher points in his article, the over 40's hit back including Fred Couples and Peter Jacobsen. There were first time wins in Japan for Jyoti Randhawa and Yeh Wei-Tzi and young Adam Scott, coached by Butch Harmon, won on both of the sides of the Atlantic – at Malmo and Boston – a feat worth recording.

It was the year that saw the passing of Mark McCormack about whom Ian Wooldridge writes elsewhere and of veteran Ryder Cuppers Sam King, Ted Jarman and Ralph Moffitt but any mini-review of the year would not be complete without mentioning Mark Roe whose disqualification in the Open when he had played himself into contention was a personal tragedy. He and fellow competitor Jesper Parnevik had failed to change cards, signed for each other's scores and were disqualified. They did not cheat and such an incident may never happen again but the manner in which Roe accepted the situation and the blame was impeccable. Ben Curtis may have won the Open in 2003 but Mark Roe, with his mature behaviour in the most upsetting of circumstances, upheld the traditions of our great game.

Four First-Time Winners in a Season of Surprises

David Davies looks back at the 2003 majors

Consider for a moment some of those who did not win a major championship in the year 2003. Tiger Woods, the world no. 1 didn't; Ernie Els, the no. 2 didn't; Davis Love III, Vijay Singh, Padraig Harrington and Phil Mickelson didn't and neither did Sergio García.

Consider instead those who did. Mike Weir won the Masters, Jim Furyk won the US Open, Ben Curtis won the Open and Shaun Micheel won the US PGA. The first two might be considered slightly surprising, the second two were a massive shock in what was the topsiest and turveyest season in living memory.

The old certainties no longer obtained, and the fear-of-Tiger factor diminished to the point that it almost disappeared. Woods has not now won in his last six majors, which, while a statistic that is surprising only when applied to him, nevertheless hurt the man concerned. That old adage that a man must challenge before he can win at the highest level was completely destroyed, first at Royal St George's and then at Oak Hill. Things can never be the same again.

Rain, rain, rain

It was a miserable Masters week even before the gates opened at 8am on Monday. Half an hour before that, as people formed long queues to get in, loudspeakers began to boom out the warning: 'Dangerous weather is approaching. We recommend that you go back to your cars and go home'.

Sure enough, there was a deluge, the Masters officials decided that it would be dangerous underfoot for the would-be spectators, and decided not to allow anyone in. For many of those denied entry it would have been their one chance to see the Augusta National course. They were desperately disappointed.

Yet there was no doubt the right decision had been made and as the week progressed the weather continued to be atrocious. By Thursday 3.85 inches of rain had fallen on the Augustan acres and that was too much even for a course with some of the most sophisticated draining equipment in the world.

The first round had to be called off and even though that meant the players would have to try and play 36 holes on Friday, conditions were so obviously impossible that there were no complaints.

Indeed there may have been no play on Friday had it not been for SubAir, a machine that is buried under several of the more susceptible greens at Augusta and, in effect, sucks the water down from the surface, out, and away from the area. It got the greens fit for play but there was one consequence with which not everybody coped.

Although the fairways were still wet, the greens were dry and firm, which meant that the players were ending up further from the greens than usual because of the soft conditions, and so were hitting longer irons than usual into greens that were just as hard as usual.

Sandy Lyle, a former Masters champion, took 82, so did Chris DiMarco who had just missed making the Ryder Cup team of 2002; Craig Perks, a winner of the Players Championship took 80 and Fred Funk and Thomas Levet both shot 79.

Crucially, so did Ernie Els. He had been irresistible in the early season, winning four of his first five tournaments and coming second in the other one, but that was in January and February and by April the well had run dry. He was all over the place in that first round and when he came in offered the inexplicable explanation that he had 'no feel with

© Phil Sheldon

Mike Weir became the first Canadian and only the second left-hander to win a Major when he held off a challenge from Len Mattiace to win the Masters at Augusta.

the putter'. The poor old putter gets blamed for a lot by the pros but rarely for delivering its boss into the rough and the trees!

That, in effect, was the end of Ernie, although he fought back with a 66 in the second round and was going well in the third until he got to the 14th. He hit a monster drive there, had only a half-shot with a 9-iron for his second, pitched it by the pin ... and saw it spin back some 60 feet, off the green and into a near-impossible place.

Lost concentration

Instead of a tap-in birdie, Els had to write down a bogey on his card and said afterwards: 'I was screwed at the 14th. I lost concentration after that'. Not the kind of comment you want to hear from a world no. 2 and indicative of the fact that his sports psychologist, Jos Vanstiphout, still had work to do.

Thanks to that delayed start, the Masters proceeded piecemeal. Darren Clarke opened up with a magnificent 66 to take the lead briefly, but because he had to start the second round an hour after the first, soon lost it. 'Are you looking forward to the second round?' he was asked and by way of reply patted his ample stomach and said: 'Does it look like it?'

Tiger Woods, the perpetual favourite was going for what the Americans call a 'three-peat' and a further place in history, given that no one has ever won three Masters in a row. His opening 76, however, was his worst in 24 rounds at Augusta and he only scraped into the weekend by getting up and down from a bunker to make the cut on the limit.

Jim Furyk may have one of the most idiosyncratic of golf swings but he handled the pressure well at the US Open at Olympia Fields to win his first Major.

© Phil Sheldon

Relieved, he produced a superb 66 in the third round and found himself only four behind Jeff Maggert and two behind Canadian left-hander Mike Weir, going into the final round. From nowhere, he was suddenly the popular pick to win.

Maggert duly self-destructed but, to everyone's astonishment, so did Woods. He hit a driver into the trees at the 350 yards long third, had to play left-handed from the edges of an azalea bush, thinned a pitch, duffed another and there was an ugly double bogey 6 on his card.

Tiger loses out

Inside quarter of an hour there was also a 4 on his card instead of a par 3 at the fourth, where he left a 30-foot birdie putt fully nine feet short. Out of form, out in 39, he was also out of contention for a third Masters Green Jacket in a row.

Ahead of him, though, an almost unknown journeyman Len Mattiace was going crazy. While Weir was moving steadily on, Mattiace holed an outrageous blind chip shot from 60 yards at the eighth for an eagle, a 60-foot slider at the 10th and he needed to par the 18th for a 64. Had he done so, he would have won the Masters.

Instead he drove into the trees, had to hack out sideways and his bogey 5 enabled Weir to force a play-off. The Canadian left-hander, one of the pre-tournament favourites, was odds-on to win, given that this was rarefied air for Mattiace. In fact the American hooked his second to the 10th, the first play-off hole, deep into the trees, could only recover to the last place he needed to be, 30 feet above the hole. His par putt actually ran off the green.

When he missed the return, Weir, who had played some wonderfully steadfast golf, not least on the greens, while all the explosions and implosions were going on around him, had two putts for the Masters. It was typical that he took them, and fitting that it should be Woods who draped the green jacket around the shoulders of the first Canadian to win the title.

Patience the key

The venue for the US Open, Olympia Fields, just outside Chicago, was dressed in the usual green straightjacket imposed on their Championship courses by the United States Golf Association. Before the start Padraig Harrington suggested that the way to win the US Open was 'to be the most boring golfer around' meaning that caution and patience would win over attack and aggression.

No less a player than Woods agreed, saying that 'you've got to plod your way along' and in a slightly different manner, Darren Clarke agreed with both of them. He decided that as the rough was so thick everywhere, he may as well take the driver as often as possible, on the grounds that if he hit the fairway, fine, and if not, then he would at least be nearer the green than if he'd taken a 1-iron.

The course itself lacked drama. Undoubtedly a good members course it was damned by faint praise from Tiger, who said: 'It's not as easy as people might think.' It was a strange choice and one local paper asked a number of competitors to name their favourite course in the Chicago area. Not one named Olympia Fields.

For all that, in USGA-mode, it was too tough for Tiger. In his first nine holes of the Championship Woods hit only two fairways and went on to hit only five of the 14 available. He is such a superb scrambler that he managed to get round in 70, but inaccuracy on such a monumental scale will always catch up in a major, and Woods, who was celebrating his 200th week as the world no.1, eventually paid an appropriate price.

It was to be a memorable week for Brian Davis, the Hertfordshire-based golfer who had made the effort to go to the States to qualify for the Championship, returned to the UK to play in the British Masters and then headed straight back to America. His reward was to startle everyone at Olympia Fields when he began with an eagle, followed by 3 successive birdies, to be 5-under after only 4 holes. It couldn't last, of course, but that brief spurt gave him quite a bit more than the standard 15 minutes of fame.

The course was a perfect fit for those who specialise in fairways and greens and Jim Furyk has always been good at that. If you were a talent scout and decided to spend time on the practice range looking for a player with an obviously good swing, the first golfer to be crossed off the list would be Furyk. His swing goes out, up, around at the top, inside and down. The legs, meantime, are doing something akin to the Charleston, and the effect, if it wasn't so effective, would be comical.

Furyk has the gift, however, of muscle memory and brings the club back to the ball square and pointing in the right direction every time. It came naturally to him and his golf professional father has to be commended for realising that and not even attempting to change it.

Furyk's fast start

At Olympia Fields the unorthodox swing proved, too, that it can stand up to the pressures of a major – although it has to be said that no one really made a run at him in the final round. Leading by three overnight he began with five straight pars which had the surprising effect of separating him completely from his challengers.

Vijay Singh, for instance, had a double bogey at the third, bogied the fifth and eighth and disappeared. Nick Price was three over par after eight and Furyk was able to switch on the cruise control.

By the time he reached the 18th green he could have five-putted and won. He did three-putt, but having won his first major, he fell into the arms of his wife and their one-year old daughter, Caleigh Lynne. It was the first emotion he had shown all week.

Thomas Bjørn had victory within his grasp in the Open at Royal St George's but saw his dream shattered in a bunker at the 16th.

If the season had opened with two slightly surprising winners it was nothing compared with what was to come at Royal St George's in the Open Championship. Even weeks later it was almost impossible to comprehend that a golfer ranked 396th in the world, a rookie on the US Tour, a 750-1 shot with the bookies, playing his first major championship, in alien conditions and with no expectations beyond making the cut, should actually stand up at the presentation ceremony and be acclaimed by the R&A secretary Peter Dawson as 'the Champion golfer of 2003'.

Yet that is what happened to a modest 26-year old from Columbus, Ohio called Ben Curtis. It was easily the biggest shock in modern Open history – a surprise victory probably assisted by the course conditions that week. Royal St George's was bone hard, fast running and bouncy – true links conditions, admittedly, but a bit too much in places. The first and 17th fairways in particular came in for criticism as being fluky or unfair as the world's best players hit their best shots down the middle and saw them ricochet into the rough. 'You have to accept', said Tiger Woods, 'that some good shots will get bad bounces and some marginal shots great bounces'.

Tiger's first lost ball

Patience is the buzz word in modern golf and it was needed in bucket loads for this particular Open, given that the rough itself was penal. Ask Woods, who, for the first time in his seven seasons as a professional, lost a ball. Furthermore he did it with his first tee shot of the Championship after hitting it into

© Phil Sheldon

He had never before been in England and had never finished in the top 10, far less won an event on the US Tour, but 26-year-old Ohio-based Ben Curtis took on the superstars at the Open at Royal St George's and beat them.

a patch of Cocksfoot, Yorkshire Fog and Common Bent grass so dense that it defied around 30 people searching for the statutory five minutes.

He had to go back, and proceeded to hit his second into almost precisely the same place – but this time 30 pairs of eyes watched it land and it was safely located. The original wasn't for about 30 minutes, until a marshall, Terry Bennett, stepped on it. It was a fortunate find. The *Sun* newspaper later bought it from him for a reputed £7,500.

That day Woods hit just three of the 14 fairways and yet contrived to get round in 72, a remarkable demonstration of his all-round ability. The wind blew hard, too, a steady 25, gusting to 35mph and Woods' score was in fact 4.5 shots below the average for the field on this par 71 course. No one who went out after midday broke par and Phil Mickelson said of the weather: 'You couldn't land an aeroplane in that cross-wind, it would tip over'.

Hennie Otto joined a list of journeymen who have led the first round of an Open, and Colin Montgomerie the list of those who have had to retire during a round. A bizarre stumble while on the way to breakfast caused him to injure a thumb and although he made an effort to play, he had to give up after seven holes.

Davis Love III led after two rounds and Thomas Bjørn after three but Saturday's story was less to do with the Dane than with an Englishman who was

only two strokes behind him. Mark Roe, three times a winner on the European tour, three times a World Cup player, had played one of the rounds of his life to record a 67 ... except that ultimately he failed to record it.

Roe was playing with Jesper Parnevik and, quite unbelievably, the pair managed to get round the whole course and then through a rigorous checking and recording process, without having exchanged cards. That meant that under the name Mark Roe there was a score of 81, which was Parnevik's score, and, of course, vice versa. The cards were signed and, once they had left the recording area there was nothing for it, under the rules, but to disqualify both of them.

There was uproar. Roe, while obviously a good player is not normally a contender in the majors and this might have been his only chance of a championship. That he should be denied it on what some deemed a technicality was simply awful and the sympathy for him was massive. There were demands from all quarters that if this was the rule, then it was silly and should be changed immediately and even retrospectively.

The R&A, while being just as sympathetic as the critics if not more so had to stay calm. They pointed out that the rule has to apply to all of golf, not just players in televised championships. David Rickman, the R&A's rules executive, said: 'I'm sure there will be an extensive review of the recording procedures, but I sense that a rule change as such is not the answer. If you cannot rely on the absolute accuracy of the scorecard, what can you rely on? It is the only true testimony of what the player has done that day'.

The 2003 Open was not done with drama just yet. There were players such as Woods and Love on the leader board on the final day but in the early stages Bjørn seemed able to ignore them and cope well with the pressures of leading a major. In fact the challenge to Bjørn came from a totally unexpected quarter in the shape of Ben Curtis who found himself in the lead after 12 holes.

Talk about an unknown, all the British journalists were rushing to their American counterparts – and there were 111 US golf writers in the media centre – to try and find out something, anything, about the fellow. Said one: 'You could ask us all and the sum total you would get would be nothing'.

Title-winning putt

Yet no sooner had Curtis gone to the front than he shot into reverse. It was hardly unexpected, for he had so little professional or championship experience. When he dropped four shots over the next five holes the view was that it would all have been good experience for him and that anyway you have to contend before you can win.

Meanwhile Curtis looked likely to drop another shot on the 18th when he chipped 11-feet past the hole from the back of the green. The man himself said later of the putt: 'I thought if I holed it I might

have a chance'. Well it did go in and it won him the Open.

As the American had slipped on the back nine, Bjørn had been catching up, playing well enough to build up a three shot lead with four to play. Even though he dropped one on the 15th, he appeared calm enough to survive the closing holes but appearances, of course, can be deceptive, and when his tee shot to the short 16th drifted into a bunker it was the beginning of the end.

Twice the Dane tried and failed to get the ball over a crest in front of him but the ball rolled back into the sand. The third time he succeeded, but it was an ugly double bogey 5 and now not only had he no margin at all, he must have been in bits. Another bogey, after a wild drive, followed at the 17th and golf's oldest Championship had been presented to its rawest recruit.

There was a nasty surprise for the players when they turned up at Oak Hill Country Club in Rochester, New York for the US PGA Championship. They found a US Open course.

The PGA have previously taken pride in presenting a challenge that allows the players to move the ball forwards from the rough, whereas the USGA seem to prefer the hack out sideways. The rough at Oak Hill was supposed to be four inches tall, a claim that caused Woods to laugh out loud. 'Just show me the spot where that is', he said.

Oak Hill – a survival test

Fred Funk said the tournament would be 'a survival test' and Mark Calcavecchia thought that 'there could be a bunch of guys in hospital with broken wrists'.

It was fearsome stuff and was to lead to a 36-hole cut at eight-over par. Some big names missed it, including Colin Montgomerie who had handed in a 12-over par 82 in the first round – a total that matched both the temperature and the humidity that day.

Woods, languishing in 128th spot in the driving accuracy category of statistics on the US Tour, dumped his Nike driver for an old Titleist, although it hardly seemed to make any difference. He opened up with a 74, followed with a 72 and was tied for 39th with nine other players.

The leader after 36 holes was a golfer of whom the Rochester Democrat and Chronicle carried a full tabloid page picture with the caption, 'Who is this man?' It was indeed Shaun Micheel who had scores of 69, 68, to be three-under, two ahead of Billy Andrade and Mike Weir. The rough had done for the likes of Davis Love III, Sergio García, Darren Clarke, Retief Goosen, the defending champion Rich Beem and the new Open champion, Ben Curtis.

Up among the leaders, however, was Alex Cejka, the Czech-born German who had finished second in the 2002 US Tour Qualifying school and was doing well in his rookie season. He was to go on and finish fourth on his own, earning a cheque that took him to $1,033,000 after only 6½ months of the year.

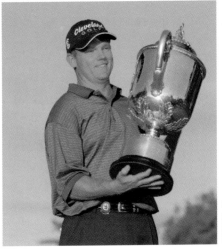

© Phil Sheldon

When Shaun Micheel won the US PGA Championship at Oak Hill in August he became the fourth of four first-time Major winners in a year in which Tiger Woods failed to add to his Majors tally.

The par 70 Oak Hill course continued to win its battle with the golfers easily enough through the third round, after which, in a week where there had been no wind, the field averaged 74.3. Micheel, too, continued his unlikely journey with his third successive round under par and when he then went on to birdie the first hole of the final round, he had the outright lead.

He then played like the veteran championship contender he definitely was not. He was helped by the fact that Weir bogeyed his first 5 holes, that Singh was three-over for the front nine and Ernie Els two-over after 12 and when Micheel arrived on the 17th tee he had a two stroke lead.

Brilliant recovery

He duly dropped a shot at the most dangerous hole on the course but then got the kind of break winners usually need. His tee shot off the last was heading for the rough on the left when it kicked kindly to the right and came to rest in the fringe of the fairway.

He had 174 yards to go, about 160 of it carry and he took a 7-iron. He then proceeded to hit a shot that will go down in major championship history as one of the finest of all time. The ball pitched on the front edge of the green and ran slowly but very surely towards the hole. It stopped 2 inches away and when eventually Micheel climbed the slope to the green and saw where it was he said to his caddie: 'I think even I can manage that one'.

So the 169th man in the world rankings, Micheel followed the 369th man Curtis to a major championship success rounding off, in suitable fashion, what had been a quite extraordinary year.

Smiles all round after Cup Success

© Phil Sheldon

Two wins in 67 years: Five in last 15!

It was smiles all round at Ganton after Great Britain and Ireland's amateur golfers rallied to take the last day singles and complete a second successive successful defence of the Walker Cup last September. Great Britain and Ireland's amateur golfers had little success in the early history of the Walker Cup. In fact they won the match only twice and drew once between 1921 when the fixture was inaugurated and 1987. Now it is all so different. The Great Britain and Ireland teams have won five of the last eight encounters with the Americans.

The Great Britain and Ireland victories have come in 1989 at Peachtree, Atlanta when Geoffrey Marks was captain, at Porthcawl in Wales when Cliff Brown was in charge of the side. Peter McEvoy captained the winning side at Nairn in 1999 and at Ocean Forest, Sea Island, Georgia, two years later. Garth McGimpsey, who captained the side that scored the historic third win in a row at Ganton in 2003, has been given control again when the GB&I men defend the Cup at the Chicago Golf Club, Wheaton, Illinois, in August 2005.

Impressive Last Day Rally makes Walker Cup History

Mark Garrod on a notable triumph at Ganton

An historic third successive win by Great Britain and Ireland over the United States in the Walker Cup was the obvious highlight of the amateur season in Britain.

Captain Garth McGimpsey had a tough act to follow in Peter McEvoy, who guided the 1999 and 2001 sides to record 15-9 victories at Nairn in Scotland and at Sea Island in Georgia. America, after all, still led by 31 wins to six in a series dating back to 1922 and, on paper, the home team were, with the notable exception of the experienced Gary Wolstenholme, an unknown quantity on such a big stage.

Yet how well they rose to the occasion at Ganton. On a dramatic second afternoon they grabbed a 12½-11½ victory – only the second time since 1926 that a single point has separated the sides.

As with the two previous matches the United States led after the first day, this time by a 7-5 margin but unlike 1999 and 2001 the two point difference remained the same after the second series of foursomes, leaving Britain and Ireland trailing 7-9 with the huge and daunting task of winning five and halving one of the eight concluding singles to win the Cup again.

Wolstenholme, who at Royal Troon in June had regained the Amateur Championship title he had first won at Ganton in 1991, hit back from two first day defeats to contribute two points on the Sunday, his 3 and 2 victory over US Amateur Championship runner-up Casey Wittenberg giving him the ninth Walker Cup win of his career – one more than previous Great Britain and Ireland points record-holder Sir Michael Bonallack.

The 43-year-old Wolstenholme then waited to discover if he would be part of a fourth winning team – in itself significant. No other Walker Cup player on this side of the Atlantic has featured on more than two winning teams.

In the top singles Oliver Wilson produced a brilliant closing par 4 to beat Bill Haas, whose father professional Jay Haas had just earned selection for America's Presidents Cup team at the age of 49. In deep rough off the tee the Mansfield player smashed it over trees to just short of the green, chipped to seven feet and made it for the half he required to win the point. Now the overall score was 9-9.

Middlesbrough's Michael Skelton, at 19 the baby of the side, made it 10-9 for Great Britain and Ireland with a 3 and 2 success over Adam Rubinson,

but then Scot Stuart Wilson and Ireland's Colm Moriarty were unable to repeat earlier successes and so America led 11-10.

There was, however, to be one more dramatic swing of the pendulum. Wilson's fellow Scot David Inglis was a spectacular seven-under-par in beating Ryan Moore 4 and 3. Now it was 11-11 and the stage was set for Welsh pair Stuart Manley and Nigel Edwards to finish the job off and deliver the crucial knock-out blows.

Manley faced one of America's stars, the big-hitting Trip Kuehne, but beat him 3 and 2 to ensure the Cup was retained and as he did that Edwards, having chipped in to win the 14th, holed an outrageous 60-foot birdie putt on the short 17th to draw level with Lee Williams. Edwards needed a half point to give the team overall victory and he got it with a rock-solid par on the last. McGimpsey's men had written another chapter of glorious Walker Cup history. The win meant that for the first time Great Britain and Ireland had completed a hat-trick of wins just two years after a first-ever successful defence of the Cup.

'I don't know why we leave it so late,' said a jubilant McGimpsey. 'I was a shattered man yesterday and not in my wildest dreams did I think we could pull it off but I put Nigel and Stuart out last because we [Peter McEvoy and myself] thought they were real street-fighters. They were and they produced the goods.'

Edwards finished unbeaten with two wins and two halves. To be the team's top scorer meant so much more to him because in the previous victory at Sea Island he had played just one game and lost it.

'I was down all the way and just kept digging in,' said Edwards, suddenly finding himself another Welsh golfing star just a year after the Ryder Cup heroics of Phillip Price, who, co-incidentally, had been best man at his wedding.

McEvoy, now chairman of selectors, commented: 'It's not very often you have the chance to make some history in your life and this was the hardest of the lot but it's easier to keep winning than to start winning. We've now won five out of the last eight matches. That's a pattern and most of these lads (only Wolstenholme and Edwards were over 30) cannot remember the days when we were expected to lose'.

© Phil Sheldon

Gary Wolstenholme had a marvellous year winning the Amateur Championship for a second time, the Scottish stroke play title, the Sherry Cup and he played his part in the WalkerCup triumph.

To be able to produce your best in the weeks when you want it most is a priceless gift and Wolstenholme, still famous for his 1995 victory over Tiger Woods in that year's Cup match at Royal Porthcawl, managed it during 2003.

In an era dominated by the power-hitters the Amateur Championship gave a timely reminder that there is still a place for those who rely on accuracy, consistency and a cool head under pressure when the heat really is on.

'Gary Grinds Them Down' was the apt headline for Wolstenholme's achievement in becoming the oldest winner of the Amateur title in modern times.

Only once all week at Troon was he taken to the 18th and in the 36-hole final he demolished promising Swiss player Raphael de Sousa 6 and 5 guaranteeing that the season would be remembered by him for more than just taking over from McEvoy as England's record cap-holder.

'I do hit the ball straight and it's hard for young guys to beat me because they have to make birdies,' he said. He is right. It was not easy to make birdies on a Royal Troon lay-out measuring 7,126 yards.

'It's a thinking man's course,' he added, 'and to win this title again is particularly gratifying. If you win this title twice you've got to be a good player.'

That victory, of course, gives him another chance next April to display his skills in the Masters at Augusta. On his first visit there in 1992 he led after going to the turn in 33 in the first round when paired with Arnold Palmer no less!

The race for places in the Walker Cup team was particularly keen and some candidates must have felt real disappointment at missing out, not least a list of impressive winners. Jack Doherty just missed out on selection despite becoming the first Scot to capture the Australian Amateur Championship title, while Jon Lupton, Richard Finch and Richard Walker who won the Brabazon Trophy, the St Andrews Links Trophy and the Portuguese Amateur Championship respectively did not receive the nod either.

Stuart Wilson secured his spot by landing the Lytham Trophy and then reaching the final of the Scottish Amateur Championship before losing to Walker Cup teammate Graham Gordon, while Skelton, European boy champion last year, won the Welsh Stroke Play Championship and was runner-up in the English Amateur Championship to Gary Lockerbie. Manley stormed to the Welsh Amateur Championship title by thrashing Rhys Davies 8 and 7 in the final.

The European team title went to Spain – they beat England 5-2 in the final only two months after losing 18½-5½ in an international match between the two at Lindrick – but Donegal's Brian McElhinney earned himself a place in the 2004 Open Championship at Royal Troon in July by lifting the European Individual Championship title.

Youngest players in European Tour events

13 years 280 days – Lo Shih-Kai (Chi)	2003 Omega Hong Kong Open
15 years 45 days – Sergio García (Esp)	1995 Turespaña Open Mediterraneo.
15 years 223 days – Ronan Rafferty (NI)	1979 Carrolls Irish Open
15 years 241 days – Sergio García (Esp)	1995 Trophée Lancôme
15 years 241 days – Reinier Saxton (Ned)	2003 Dutch Open
15 years 251 days – Nicolas Colsaerts (Bel)	1998 TNT Dutch Open

Youngest players in European Challenge Tour events

14 years 99 days – Eduardo de la Riva (Esp)	1996 Eulen Open Galea Spain

Youngest players recently in the Open Championship

16 years 151 days – Sandy Lyle (Sco)	1974 Royal Lytham and St Annes
16 years 151 days – Sergio García (Esp)	1996 Royal Lytham and St Annes

Farcical, Capricious and Down-right Incredulous

Furman Bisher on an entertaining year in the US

There was much more to golf in America than one woman's attempt to crash the male preserve of Augusta National Golf Club, home of the hallowed Masters Tournament, though for a very long time that story was tougher to shake than a case of shingles. The game itself, however, provided plenty of surprises.

The four majors were won by players who had never won a major tournament, one left-handed, one with a cranky swing, and two who had never won any kind of tournament on the PGA Tour. It was like something out of the pages of a manuscript so unbelievably unlikely that no sensible publisher would have ever touched it.

It was the left-handed player who won the Masters, and a world that had once been conceded to Tiger Woods took a sharp turn into the great unknown. Mike Weir, the smallish Canadian, became the first southpaw – as we colonists have bastardized the term – to win a major championship since Bob Charles, who beat portly Phil Rogers in a playoff for the Open Championship in 1963. Weir won his title with an inscrutable putting performance. Before the tournament, Phil Mickelson, himself rather left-handed, was asked who the next great left-handed player might be. When it was Weir being helped into the green jacket by Tiger Woods that Sunday afternoon rather than himself, it was the signal of a barren year ahead in the major championships for the last great player never to have won one – a burdensome cross to bear.

That was only the introductory shock to the televised class, which feasts on a diet of Woods to the fore, or starves without him. Jim Furyk, who swings at a golf ball as if he were about to kill a snake, won the US Open at Olympia Fields, but stand by if you have a taste for anomaly.

Ever hear of the Hooters Tour? Probably not, considering that neither have most of the 200 million Americans. It's rock bottom golf, where the desperate go just trying to find a game. They once took flight to Asia, or South Africa, or to the bush-league tours, but now they have one last haven at home.

About 40 per cent of PGA Tour players have played the Hooters, Scott McCarron, Tom Lehman and Lee Janzen, for example. The Hooters began as the TC Jordan Tour, because Mr Jordan was a golf addict who put up the money. He then sold out to Bob Brooks, who planted on it the name of his restaurant chain, which features scantily-clad waitresses.

Well, Ben Curtis played the Hooters Tour. You recognize the name of the unlikely winner of The Open at Royal St George's. Ben Curtis, a mild-mannered, 750-to-1 shot barely known outside his hometown of Ostrander, Ohio, a refugee from rock bottom.

That was just the opening act. The Sunday round of the PGA Championship at Oak Hill, Pittsford,

'The Walrus' Craig Stadler turned 50, won a senior major title right away then returned briefly to the main Tour and won again!

© Phil Sheldon

NY, paired Shaun Micheel and Chad Campbell, both alumni of the Hooters Tour, in the final group. Not Woods or Mickelson or Love or Els but Campbell and Micheel. Now, Campbell ranked in the top 10 on the US Tour, is a force to be reckoned with – he won the Tour Championship at the end of the Year – but Micheel was far up the track. Yet, it was Micheel, the longshot, who won with a 7-iron approach shot which, with a rapier-like thrust, finished within two inches of the cup on the 18th hole on the final day.

Forties fling

The year in general had taken some quirky turns on this side of the pond. Whereas, 18 winners of PGA Tour tournaments in 2002 were taking their first bow, 2003 was the year of the veteran, the seasoned warriors, who didn't have to be told where to stand when the camera was on the man presenting the cheque.

Woods would not win a major, but he won often enough on Tour including two World Championship events bringing his tally since those events began to eight in 15 attempts. Davis Love took several first time cheques and, in and out of the USA, Ernie Els won regularly especially at the start of the year and – don't go away – those in their forties were having a fling. Kenny Perry, 42, won three times. Fred Couples, Scott Hoch, Peter Jacobsen, 49, who hadn't won since 1995, and had retired apparently to host a comedy show on the Golf Channel, and Kirk Triplett all won. Jay Haas, also 49, never won but he was a frequent nuisance to those who did.

Craig Stadler, a rookie in the 50-year class, gave the regular tour a kiss goodbye when he won the BC

Classic a week after winning the Players Championship on the Seniors Tour.

Stand by now for late news on the women's front. The ladies came on strong in a strangely coincidental incursion of male tours, and in numbers – step forward Annika Sörenstam, Suzy Whaley, Se Ri Pak, Laura Davies, Jan Stephenson and the 13-year-old Michelle Wie. The last female to crash the men's tour had been Babe Didrikson (Zaharias), who made the cut in the Los Angeles Open in 1945.

This time it came off like a carnival act, when Sörenstam accepted a sponsor's exemption to play in the Colonial at Fort Worth, Texas, an event played on ground sacred to Ben Hogan. It was, indeed, something to savour, or to bash, as one saw fit.

Sörenstam played well, handled herself majestically, and finally came to tears as she finished her 36 holes, short of making the cut. She drew the gallery, she drew television ratings, and she was, as they say, a credit to the game. Kenny Perry won the tournament.

Winning personality

Whaley, a teaching professional in Connecticut, earned her way into the Greater Hartford Open, winning a sectional tournament. Her sparkling personality was a winner, but her game was not up to it. She, too, missed the cut. Peter Jacobsen was the shock winner.

Stephenson's challenge was mystifying considering she had not been able to win on the LPGA Tour since 1987, but she still decided to test the waters of the Seniors Tour, now re-christened the

Fred Couples, whose career has been affected so much with back trouble, delighted his fans by joining the 'over 40's' in the winner's circle on the US Tour in 2003.

Champions Tour and finished last. Young Miss Wie would take her game to the Canadian Tour, in a tournament played in Michigan.

Such was the course of professional golf in the United States in 2003. It covered a broad span of moods and at times, left its followers scratching their heads. From the capricious to the incredulous, from acrimony to comedy, and in the end, if there was a trend, it was that there was none but as always it was as enjoyable as ever.

Huge crowds followed Annika Sörenstam for the first two days of the Colonial event in Texas. The Swedish star, taking on the men on equal terms, missed the half-way cut – but only by a shot. That week she made a host of new friends and silenced those who had criticised her for playing in the event.

© Phil Sheldon

New Young Winners on the LPGA Tour

When Korean golfer Shi Hyun Ahn, took first prize in the CJ Nine Bridges Classic at the age of 19 years 1 month and 18 days she became the youngest international winner and the sixth youngest winner in LPGA history behind Marlene Haage (two teenage wins), Amy Alcott and Sandra Haynie (two wins). The list of young winners is:

Marlene Haage	1952 Sarasota Open	18 years 16 days
Marlene Haage	1952 Bakersfield Open	18 years 2 months 18 days
Amy Alcott	1975 Orange Blossom Classic	19 years 1 day.
Sandra Haynie	1962 Austin Civitan Open	19 years 6 days
Sandra Haynie	1962 Cosmopolitan Open	19 years 13 days
Shi Hyun Ahn	2003 CJ Nine Bridges Classic	19 years 1 month 18 days
Dorothy Delasin	2000 Giant Eagle LPGA Classic	19 years 11 months 4 days

In addition Ahn became only the 13th non-LPGA member to win a Tour event and the first to do so since Karrie Webb took the 1995 Weetabix Women's British Open. Among the other non-Tour members who earned LPGA cards by winning Tour tournaments are French golfer Catherine Lacoste at the 1962 US Women's Open – she is still the only amateur to have won that title – and England's Laura Davies who won the 1987 US Women's Open.

Cup Heroines in Swedish Rhapsody

Europeans in control on last day

On a sunny afternoon in Sweden, Europe's Solheim Cup side won back the trophy with a dramatic last day charge giving golf on this side of the Atlantic a tremendous boost. With World No.1 Annika Sörenstam in the side, the Europeans, captained by Catrin Nilsmark, played with tremendous courage and spirit in the final series of singles to score only their third win since the fixture was started in 1990 at Lake Nona in Florida. The Americans won that match and 2003 captain Nilsmark was in the team that won the match at Dalmahoy two years later. The Americans won in 1994, 1996 and 1998 but in a dramatic match at Loch Lomond in 2000 Europe regained the Cup only to lose it again in 2002 at Interlachen. English golfer Laura Davies has played in all eight matches.

Barsebäck Triumph Raises Profile of Women's Golf

Lewine Mair salutes the Solheim Superstars

It was America's Beth Daniel who, at the end of the 2003 Solheim Cup at Barsebäck, said she detected 'the wind of change' in the women's game. For years, the women professionals had had the feeling that they were small beer *vis-a-vis* the men but in that week in Sweden, they were walking tall. 'I guarantee,' said Daniel, 'that there is not a men's tournament in the world this week which has been playing in front of galleries as big as the ones we have known.'

Well in excess of 90,500 spectators were in hot pursuit as Europe defeated the Americans 17½-10½. What is more, the fans watched no less avidly than had they been following a Ryder Cup, the explanation being that Swedes see golf as golf rather than men's golf and women's golf. It was this way even before Lotta Neumann, Annika Sörenstam and Helen Alfredson captured eight majors among them to the men's none. Intriguingly, there were no men standing outside the ropes at Barsebäck insisting that they could do better.

This was the Europeans' third Solheim Cup win in eight starts. In 1992, when they won the second match at Dalmahoy, the Americans suspected they had taken the fixture too lightly. In several instances, their players had tacked a family holiday on to the trip and failed to put enough emphasis on the match itself.

In 2000, when the Europeans won again at Loch Lomond, the Americans repaired to their homeland with the feeling that they were lucky that they had endured nothing worse than a beating. They could have drowned, so dark and dire was the loch-side weather that week.

Gracious tribute

In 2003 with the match brought forward a year in order to escape another clash with the Ryder Cup, there were no excuses made by or on behalf of the Americans. Patty Sheehan, their captain, came up with the most gracious of all tributes when she said that she had just witnessed 'the most beautiful golf ever played by a winning side in a Solheim Cup'.

The Europeans, thanks to an order of merit system which may lean too heavily on the European Tour rather than what their players are doing globally, were one, maybe two players light of being at their best. Theirs was a team, however, which gelled mag-

nificently under the captaincy of Catrin Nilsmark, even though the Swede was unable to be the ubiquitous soul she would have wished to be because of a painful back injury which confined her to a buggy.

As is usually the case, the Europeans proved themselves the better at foursomes. On the first morning they won by 3½-½, on the second by 3-1. They wasted much of their advantage on the Friday when they picked up just the one point from the afernoon fourballs but, second time around, they did rather better to bed down with a 9½-6½ lead going into the Sunday singles.

The last match on Saturday night had stood out above the rest and is one which will be recalled whenever the subject of the 2003 Solheim Cup is raised. Annika Sörenstam and Norway's Suzann Pettersen were playing Kelly Robbins and Laura Diaz and the four of them were taking forever – five and a half hours to be precise. If the Americans were the winners, they would go into the singles just one point behind with the score 7½- 8½. If the Europeans were to win, they would have that three-point lead.

Everything pointed to the former scenario as the Americans, whose Kelly Robbins was the furthest from the hole in two on the 17th green, used the format to have Diaz tackle her four-footer first for the birdie. Diaz holed, seemingly to put America one up, only for Sörenstam to follow her in from 22 feet. 'It was one of those occasions which was made for Annika and she seized it,' said David Earl, her understandably proud spouse.

Much the same happened at the 18th, only this time Diaz had her concentration diluted after questions were asked as to whether or not she would be treading on Europe's line as she putted. She missed and Pettersen rammed home a 15 footer to give Europe their three-point lead. 'It was absolutely fantastic to get a point there,' said Nilsmark.

Nilsmark's singles line-up was not too different from Sam Torrance's in the Ryder Cup at The Belfry the previous autumn. Her strongest players were out first, though Janice Moodie, rather than Sörenstam was at the top and off at 8 am, a ridiculously early hour born of the fact that the Lancôme, the European Tour men's event being played in Paris, was to have pride of place on afternoon television. On the one hand, Nilsmark had wanted to give Sörenstam

a later tee-off time following her Saturday evening exploits; on the other, she knew that Moodie had the personality to make waves at the front.

The plan worked to perfection, with Moodie having blue or European figures plastered on the board from the start as she went four up on Kuehne over the front nine. The crowd responded with a chant of 'Eur-Up, Eur-Up, Eur-Up' which spread through the Barsebäck trees. Carin Koch never really got going against Juli Inkster in the second of the singles, but there was plenty more to cheer in match number 3 as Sophie Gustafsson romped home against Heather Bowie; and in the fourth as Iben Tinning, all grit, defeated Wendy Ward.

For a while, it looked as if Annika Sörenstam would be the one to hole the winning putt tor Europe. As it was, she defeated Angela Stanford five minutes too soon, paving the way for Scotland's Catriona Matthew to shine. Two up with two to play against Rosie Jones, Matthew sensed she was safe when she struck a breathtaking second to nine feet at the 17th. The match was soon conceded.

Amid the ensuing celebrations, there was chaos as those matches still out on the course thought they had the option not to continue. It was a spur of the moment thing and one to have significant repercussions as the players concerned were made to see that they had not only spoiled things for spectators but rendered hard-earned individual records more than a little meaningless. The likelihood is that a clause is going to be written into the players' contracts saying that in future matches,

no-one would be allowed to concede a game until the 18th green. The wind of change to which Daniel had referred at Barsebäck had its origins at the Colonial in May, when Sörenstam played among the men. There were those who had said that it would be a disaster for women's golf if the Swede were to play badly but, in the event, she was outstanding, particularly in an opening 71. Jack Nicklaus, for long determinedly unimpressed with the women's game, was just one to be won over. 'Of course I was impressed with Annika. It was impossible not to be,' he said.

Sörenstam went on to win two majors in the wake of that Colonial outing, with the second of them the Weetabix Women's British Open at Royal Lytham and St Annes. An unprecedented 75,000 came to watch, with the result everything the sponsors could have hoped for as Sörenstam defeated Se Ri Pak by a single shot to complete her career Grand Slam. One way and another, it was arguably the best year for women's golf since the 1920's when the late Joyce Wethered dominated the game. Wethered won five English women's championships and four British and was described by Bobby Jones as having 'the best swing, man's or woman's, I've ever seen.'

Fingers were crossed that the buzz would not die down over the winter and that 2003 would pave the way for a less skeletal European tour in 2004. The professionals deserve it and so, too, do the younger fry. Players such as Wales' Becky Brewerton who are pouring their all into the amateur game in a bid to become the Solheim Cup golfers of the future.

Carly – Champion three times over

Carly Booth with a handicap of 6, became the youngest club champion in Britain when she won the Dunblane Ladies Championship on her 11th birthday. She was just two-over-par when she beat another youngster – 14 year old Sally Kettlewell.

Carly, just five feet tall and virtually self taught although she has had coaching recently at Gleneagles and at the Scottish National Golf centre at Drumoig, then went on to win the Comrie and Auchterarder Golf Club Championships as well. She beat Elaine Davidson by 6 and 5 at Comrie and beat Joan Ritchie, the previous year's ladies' captain, at Auchterarder. Carly now plays off 5.

Carly comes from a well-known sporting family. Her father Wally was a former Scottish and Commonwealth Games champion and her 17-year-old brother, Wallace, who has a handicap of plus 2, plays for Scotland and has accepted a PE scholarship at the University of Augusta, Georgia. When he was 14 he represented Scotland concurrently in three sports – golf, squash and wrestling.

© David Phillips

The Handshake that gave Birth to a Golfing Empire

Ian Wooldridge on Mark McCormack's legacy

The irony of the late Mark McCormack's meteoric career – America's prestigious *Sports Illustrated* magazine unequivocally front-covered him as 'The Most Powerful Man in World Sport' – is that it wasn't at all the destiny he had mapped out for himself as a young man.

Born to a comfortable middle-class education and country-club lifestyle near Chicago and suffocated by the boredom of his early days as a small town contracts lawyer, all he yearned to be was a professional golfer.

Golf, literally, had come to him by accident. Aged six, he was struck by a car when crossing the street and suffered a fractured skull. Forthwith he was banned from all body-contact sports. His publisher father suggested golf, to which Mark's competitive nature responded. By his early teens he was down to scratch, periodically better. He was certainly good enough to compete in four US Amateur championships, four British Amateurs and the national Open Championships of Canada, South Africa and Australia. His greatest achievement was to qualify

©IMG

Mark McCormack with Arnold Palmer. Their friendship lasted a lifetime.

for the US Open in 1958. The problem was that he was an also-ran in all of them.

'I was smart enough to realise', he told me one afternoon on a cruise liner between Australia and Bali, 'that I was two shots off the pace. I was never going to become the next Bobby Jones or Ben Hogan'.

His luxurious floating apartment was filled with trunks of fascinating memorabilia since, flatteringly, he had invited me to co-write his autobiography. Back in London the prospective publishers hosted a sumptious lunch attended by chairman, directors, editors and circulation-pushers. 'You realise, Mark, that this has to be *the* book. The inside story of what all your clients are really like.'

There was a deafening silence for many seconds. Mark then replied: 'That I will never do'. The project was dead in the water. There may have been other publishers less demanding but unfortunately Mark never met one before his shocking death. Shocking because one week after his annual checkup at the Mayo Clinic had declared him in full health, he underwent a minor cosmetic operation for a skin blemish and never woke up from the anaesthetic. After three months in a coma, he died in May 2003. He was 72.

Mark McCormack was one of the most influential entrepreneurs of the last third of the 20th century. It began with the most famous handshake in the history of sport. Mark had recognised Arnold Palmer as charismatic dynamite when they had played together in inter-collegiate matches. Intuition plus a smart business brain led him to ask Palmer if he could handle his business affairs. Wihin a year Palmer's income, boosted by commercial endorsements, had risen by 1000 per cent. The handshake was the only contract they ever had. Inside five years both were multi-millionaires.

It was McCormack who persuaded Palmer to revive American competition, sadly flagging in the 1950s, in the Open Championships in Britain. Palmer, winning at Royal Birkdale in 1961 and at Royal Troon the following year, injected sensation with his go-for-broke style of golf. Shortly after, Mark had Jack Nicklaus and Gary Player on his client roster: the Big Three.

By 1969 Tony Jacklin was another client. He won at Royal Lytham, the first British winner since Max

Faulkner in 1951. Someone presented Jacklin with a bottle of champagne. 'Turn the bottle round and show the maker's name', yelled McCormack as Jacklin faced the television cameras. No opportunity was too small to miss to attract another commercial endorsement fee. The Royal & Ancient Golf Club were soon to acknowledge this, allowing him to mastermind their commercial enterprises at Open Championships, as did the All England Tennis Championships at Wimbledon. He made millions for both.

Meanwhile, he was writing books about entrepreneurial business. I read his first, *What They Don't Teach You at Harvard Business School*, in manuscript and dismissed it as garbage. At the last count, still in print, it has sold more than two million copies. He extended his empire all over the world with more than 4000 employees running not only sports events but world-class orchestras, international solo musicians and modelling agencies. His only big failure was in the shady world of European football. He wasn't prepared to risk his name in so many dodgy deals.

Mark, who reputedly took 20 per cent of the earnings of those for whom he made fortunes, had enemies who envied his astonishing lifestyle.

He rarely slept more than four hours a night, logged every mile he travelled and was so compulsively addicted to recording his overseas travels that he hung his hotel keys, from hotels he'd visited, on a ceiling-to-floor wall of his Cleveland office. This he discontinued after being accused of theft.

I was fortunate to know Mark well for personal reasons. He was the hardest conceivable negotiator on a business level but an amazingly soft touch to his friends who had fallen on hard times. Unfortunately it will not appear in his never-written autobiography.

Langer to lead Europe's defence

Bernhard Langer will lead Europe into action against the Americans captained by Hal Sutton when the 35th Ryder Cup takes place at Oakland Hills CC, Bloomfield Hills, Michigan from September 17–19 next year.

The 45-year-old is the 19th captain taking over from Sam Torrance who was in charge of the European side at The Belfry in September 2002. Langer has played under five different captains – John Jacobs, Tony Jacklin, Bernard Gallacher, Severiano Ballesteros and Sam Torrance. Mark James did not give him a wild card spot in 1999 or he would have matched Nick Faldo's 11 appearances between 1977 and 1997. Langer played in his first Ryder Cup in 1981 and was a member of the team that won the Cup for the first time in 28 years in 1985. He has played 42 games in the Cup match, won 21 times and halved on six other occasions.

'It is a fabulous honour. I have always enjoyed being part of the Ryder Cup,' said Langer. 'I am well aware of the responsibility of captaining the side – it's a real challenge but I know American captain Hal Sutton well and both of us have a great respect for the traditions of the game. Both of us want it to be another great sporting contest.'

Royal Troon – a Constant Battle for Survival

Keith Mackie looks at the 2004 Open venue

It is doubtful if any championship course has suffered more from the relentless forces of nature and the comparatively puny yet still destructive weapons of war devised by man than the rugged links of Royal Troon where the 133rd Open Championship will be played in July 2004.

Bombardment from land, sea and air threatened the first century of the club's existence. Floods and sand storms, crashing aircraft, unexploded hand grenades, runaway tanks and mysterious ice bombs falling from clear skies made golf at Troon a frustrating and often dangerous sport. There were no fatalities, but many near misses.

Visitors in the modern era, subjected to nothing more scary than fierce winds off the Irish Sea and deafeningly close encounters with jumbo jets leaving and approaching nearby Prestwick airport, enjoy the uncompromising challenge and perfect condition of Troon's links with scarcely a thought for its early traumas.

It was in 1878 that local doctor John Highet and Glasgow builder James Dickie conceived the idea of forming a small golf club on a large area of rough duneland owned by the Duke of Portland. Surveyors poured cold water on the idea with huge estimates for the cost of clearing and draining the land and finally five modest holes were laid out and a disused railway carriage hauled into place as a makeshift clubhouse for the 24 original members.

Within eight years the course had been extended, first to six, then 12 and eventually 18 holes, and a substantial stone clubhouse erected. Carved out through dunes covered with whins and brambles and hollows that were soft and marshy with casual water, the course quickly acquired a reputation for the fine quality of its greens, which it retains to this day. Bobby Locke, the 1950 Open champion at Troon, sent the club a Christmas card each year which always bore the same message: 'Still the best greens in the world'.

Yet in those early days nature did its best to thwart Troon's golfers. Gale force winds off the sea regularly covered the course in a thick layer of hundreds of tons of sand, a problem that lasted 80 years until the erection of protective fences and the planting of marram grasses in the dunes.

Storms also overwhelmed the wall that guarded the spot where the Pow Burn meets the sea in 1896. Two new groynes were built at considerable expense, but again in 1913 and 1936 the sea encroached two hundred yards into the golf course. More than 2000 sand bags had to be laid in 1950 and further sea defence measures in the 1990s cost a quarter of a million pounds.

Man teamed up with nature to frustrate Troon's early members. Local farmers drove carts across the course to harvest seaweed for fertiliser and then dumped it on the fairways to dry. The coastal area was also popular for weekend picnics and many a non-golfing family gratefully spread out their fare on the finely groomed greens.

But worse was to come from man-made hazards. During the first World War part of the links area was used as a hand-grenade practice range and well into the last decade of the 20th century greenkeepers cutting turf would hear the heart-stopping clink of metal on metal as another unexploded grenade wormed its way towards the surface.

Renegade tank

The second world conflict brought further danger and destruction to the links. Tank training for the Normandy invasion was taking place across the beaches and through the dunes. Access across the golf course was strictly controlled through clearly defined lanes, but who can argue with a renegade tank?

Certainly not the young schoolboy who was cutting the 12th green. A tank suddenly appeared behind him and charged into the heart of the green. With flailing tracks cutting a deep swathe in the immaculate surface it executed a sharp right turn and disappeared into the dunes. The schoolboy was Norman Fergusson who was subsequently to become the club's highly respected greens superintendent.

An even closer encounter was to befall caddiemaster Bob Manson when a Mustang dropped out of the sky, skimmed over his head and made an emergency landing which ripped out the fourth green. The pilot stepped unharmed from the wreckage and, presumably with thoughts of a restorative whisky in mind, asked calmly: 'Was that the Marine Hotel I just passed?'

With the return of peace, the scars in Troon's fine turf quickly healed, but a mysterious aerial bombardment came literally out of the blue. Great chunks of ice started to rain down on the course from cloudless skies, thudding into the turf and upsetting many a tentative putting stroke.

Prestwick airport was being extensively developed to serve the increasing trans-Atlantic traffic. Arriving from the west at high altitude, planes were shedding ice that had built up on wing edges as they came in to land, dropping their potentially lethal missiles at the far end of the links. There were, luckily, no direct hits, but the nerves of many members were put to a severe test. The development of de-icing equipment finally put an end to the rain of terror.

Now only an occasional, almost silent, appearance of a jumbo jet from behind the sandhills, rapidly followed by the thunder of its engines as some 300 tons of machinery, flaps and undercarriage lowered like a giant eagle swooping on its prey, intrudes on an otherwise tranquil game.

Yet none of the problems faced by Troon over many years have detracted from its championship record. When first selected to host the Open in 1923, the ferocious weather was best mastered by tall English professional Arthur Havers. His strong, four-knuckle left-hand grip helped him punch the ball low in the wind and he holed a bunker shot at the last hole to beat defending champion Walter Hagen by a single stroke. It was to be the last British victory for 10 years.

Despite the success of that championship and the enlightened attitude of Troon in becoming the first to open its clubhouse doors to competing professionals, there was a gap of 27 years before Bobby Locke won the second of his four Opens, successfully defending the title he had won the year before at Royal St George's.

Swashbuckling Arnie

Troon's next appearance in the spotlight was in 1962, a championship which marked a watershed in the history of the Open. Arnold Palmer, in full swashbuckling mode, won by six strokes from Kel Nagle, with the rest of the field trailing 13 shots in his wake. He had fired the imagination of the golf-watching public in the previous two Opens at St Andrews and Birkdale and huge crowds followed him at Troon. The stewarding arrangements that had been perfectly adequate for years just couldn't cope. From that point on the R&A has fenced the perimeter of all Open courses and roped off the fairways.

Palmer also started an American take-over of championships played at Troon. Tom Weiskopf was next in line in 1973. He opened with rounds of 68-67 in a week plagued by rain, a start that gave him sufficient strokes in hand to withstand a last round challenge of 66 from Neil Coles and 65 from Jack Nicklaus. It was to prove the only major success for a man of such supreme golfing talent.

Tom Weiskopf won his only Major at Troon in 1973, five years before the club celebrated its centenary and was afforded royal status by Her Majesty the Queen.

Although Tom Watson captured the fourth of his five Open titles at Royal Troon (the club had been granted the all-important prefix to commemorate its centenary in 1978), it was not one of his regal performances. Watson ground out a 284 total and then watched from the clubhouse as those who led going into the final round failed to hang on to their advantage.

For the first time in 1989 the title was decided by a four-hole play-off. Previously nothing less than a full round had been played to resolve ties, but in order to complete the championship within four days the new mini-round play-off had been introduced. Greg Norman's final round 64 set a club-house target of 275 that survived for two hours and was finally matched by fellow Australian Wayne Grady and American Mark Calcavecchia. The matter was resolved when the American hit a five-iron to six feet from the right rough at the 18th with Grady trailing and Norman under the lip of a bunker 310 yards from the tee.

Troon's reputation for superb greens was further enhanced in 1997 when young American Justin Leonard had only 25 putts in a final round of 65 to beat Darren Clarke and Jesper Parnevik by three shots and third-placed Jim Furyk by seven. In a masterful display he holed four putts between 10 and 36 feet in the closing nine holes. Perhaps like Bobby Locke, he should add Royal Troon to his Christmas card list.

How a Successful Open helps the Global Game

Mike Aitken highlights where the money goes

It may come as a shock to those only familiar with the outdated myth of the Royal and Ancient golf club of St Andrews as an elitist body to learn that the organisers of the Open Championship have also become the good Samaritans of the game around the world.

While the commercial success of the Open is well documented, the story of how the profits are dispersed from the annual staging of the game's oldest championship is rarely mentioned in dispatches. Far from disappearing into the R&A's coffers each year, the money is scattered like seed capital to develop the game among emerging golf nations as well as helping young people follow their dream of one day lifting aloft the Claret Jug.

Thanks to the funds generated by the Open, the R&A is able to distribute three million in grants each year and one million in interest free loans. Much of this aid now goes abroad rather than being spent within the UK and Ireland. In fact, golf clubs which successfully applied for financial aid ten years ago would have less chance of getting it today.

'The truth is that in the past we were probably doing too much domestically and not enough internationally,' admits Duncan Weir, the R&A's golf development secretary. 'The point needs to be made first and foremost that we wouldn't be able to carry out any of this work if the Open wasn't so successful. The change in emphasis from domestic to international was made because there was a feeling that perhaps we were subsidising projects which in the end would only benefit a few club members.

'Don't get me wrong, this change isn't to the detriment of the game in the four home countries. We still make a grant of £500,000 each year to the Golf Foundation and also assist with coaching at home union level. We also needed to develop and promote golf more around the world, however, and our work in emerging countries, whether it is building a driving range in Bolivia or public access courses in Argentina and Brazil, makes the game available for all newcomers.'

As the body responsible for the governance of golf outside America, it is fitting the R&A's work

Alasdair Barr with young golfers in Ecuador in an initiative supported by an R&A grant.

© R&A

should be so far reaching, delving into the shanty towns of Brazil as well as launching a programme specifically aimed at assisting the indigenous population of Australia.

The completion of the first public golf course outside Rio de Janeiro in late 2003 thanks to a grant of £50,000 from the R&A was a particularly praiseworthy scheme which prompted *The Scotsman* to pen an effusive editorial. 'The Royal and Ancient is to be congratulated on its initiative, which is in the true spirit of the game,' the newspaper applauded. 'It will not be long before the golfing equivalent of Pele is whipping round the Old Course under par'.

If most Brazilian teenagers are more likely to lie awake at night with aspirations to emulate Ronaldo, at least the construction of the country's first public golf course in the suburb of Japeri, 50 miles from Rio, prompted some to dwell on the possibility of matching the achievements of Tiger Woods.

As is the case throughout most of South America, golf is a game for the haves rather than the have-nots: every one of the 55 clubs across Brazil is privately owned. In a country more than twice the size of the entire European Union, that equates to three million people per course.

What started as a poignant imitation of the real thing, a shanty course built by caddies for their own amusement using bamboo sticks and plastic bags as flags and old tin cans as holes, began to evolve into a much more serious introduction to the game when the Mayor of Japeri gifted 170 acres of land for the project and the R&A came in to provide some financial help.

The decision to offer assistance was taken after Weir and Noel Stephens, the chairman of the external funds supervisory committee, visited Japeri in 2002 when attending the Copa Los Andes, the continent's international amateur team championship. Having spent £25,000 on helping that event to take place, Weir and Stephens made the contacts there which eventually made the course in Japeri possible.

'Our feeling in Brazil was that they could and should be doing more,' Weir explained. 'Oddly enough, there aren't the resort courses in that part of the world which would normally attract American investment and involvement. We were happy to get involved in these ground-breaking projects and should they turn out to be successful we'll be delighted to go back and help with other facilities and projects such as investing in coaching and equipment for youngsters'.

In Africa, the R&A also support an international amateur team tournament with Kenya, Tanzania, Botswana, Lesotho, Malawi, Mozambique, Namibia, South Africa, Swaziland, Uganda, Zambia and Zimbabwe all participating. Malawi, with only 1000 registered players, hosted the event in 2003 at their only 18 hole course. In addition to giving them a grant to stage the competition, the R&A also sent an agronomist to advise on course preparation as

© R&A

Duncan Weir pictured in 2003 with greenkeeping staff at Lilangwe Golf Club in Malawi, who received machinery donated by the R&A.

well as providing mowing equipment for the tees and greens at Lilongwe golf club. Moreover, a teaching professional from Zimbabwe has been enlisted to help prepare the Malawian players for the 2004 competition.

In Asia, the main drive is to foster the growth of the game in China. There are currently a meagre 150 courses in a country with a population of 1.2 billion. The Chinese hope to expand the number of courses to 500 by 2010. Another way in which the R&A is trying to assist is through education. Finance has been set up for a partnership with Elmwood College at Cupar near St Andrews in Scotland which will take greenkeeper education into China's universities. Young Chinese come to Elmwood initially to learn the rudiments of good greenkeeping.

In Europe, the needs of individual countries are, if anything, even more diverse. The Czech Republic, for example, has a population of 11 million but only 20 courses. Here the R&A put up money to build the country's first public course at Brno. And in Portugal, which has the same population but double the number of courses, the challenge is to attract more young Portuguese nationals to take up the sport. So Portugal's 'Drive' programme, which hopes to encourage champions, has been assisted by an interest free loan from the R&A.

'We want to work even more closely with the 127 Golf Federations around the world in future and will be asking the various overseas unions to let us know exactly what their needs are,' adds Weir. 'Whether it be providing range balls used during the Open or building a public access course, we are here to help'.

The Royal and Ancient and the modern game

The Royal and Ancient Golf Club of St Andrews holds a unique position within the game. Formed in 1754 as a private members' club, it has evolved through two and a half centuries as golf's senior authority. There are now three distinct areas of responsibility within the framework of administration undertaken by the R&A.

At international level, outside North America, the club has been the governing authority for the Rules of Golf since 1897, with more than 120 countries, unions and associations affiliated to it.

The running of the Open and Amateur Championships has also been part of the R&A remit since 1920, a national commitment now enlarged with the running of the Boys, Mid-Amateur and Seniors Championships and, more recently, the Junior Open. The R&A selects teams to represent Great Britain & Ireland in events such as the Walker Cup (GB&I v USA) and the St Andrews Trophy (GB&I v Europe), and organises these events when they are played in Britain and Ireland.

As a private club the R&A has 2400 members throughout the world, many of whom are leading administrators within their own country's golf authority. With representatives on the International Golf Federation, the R&A also is involved in the running of the Eisenhower Trophy (the world amateur men's team championship) and the Espirito Santo Trophy (the world amateur women's team championship). Both these tournaments are held every two years. This wealth of expertise makes a wide range of experience available to all R&A committees.

In 2002, the new Golf Course Committee replaced the Golf Course Advisory Panel and is concerned with all aspects of the golf course, paying particular attention to environmental and ecological issues; the use of water and chemicals; climate change; planning of new courses and levels of play. It also offers best-practice professional advice and information to architects, golf associations and federations, planners, government agencies, golf clubs, greenkeepers and other relevant groups.

Promoting the game

Another major aspect of the R&A's leadership is the allocation of funds from Open Championship revenues to help finance projects large and small which promote and expand the game worldwide. Many millions have been ploughed back into grassroots golf in this way.

The Royal and Ancient Golf Club staged the first international golf conference in 1970 bringing together representatives from Britain and Europe. This developed ten years later into a truly international gathering at which 33 affiliated countries were represented. At the sixth conference in 2001, more than 150 delegates from 69 organisations around the world were involved in discussing topics vital to the growth and development of the game.

Judgements made by the R&A on all aspects of the game are made against a background of history and tradition established over six centuries, but always with an understanding of modern demands.

Refining the laws of the ancient game

During a 10-year period towards the end of the 19th century, when the number of golf clubs in Britain rose from fewer than 200 to almost 1000, the need for a governing body to bring conformity to the rules became a matter of serious debate. Until that time each club could set and administer its own regulations for playing the game.

The R&A was already recognised as something of a father figure and eventually agreed to pressure from the leading clubs to take responsibility for the laws of the game. On September 28, 1897, the Rules of Golf Committee was formed and the R&A moved from its position as a highly regarded advisor to a firmly established governing authority with well-defined powers.

With the exception of the United State and Mexico, whose allegiance lies with the United States Golf Association, and Canada, which is self-governing but affiliated to the R&A, every country where the game is played has affiliated to the Royal and Ancient and accepts the club's authority over the laws of the game and the regulation on amateur status. Following a four-day meeting in the House of Lords between the R&A and the USGA, a uniform code of rules has been applied world-wide since 1952. Yet, even today, the R&A does not impose the Rules of Golf, but rather governs by consent.

The main thrust of the work of the Rules of Golf Committee is in the area of interpretation and constant review, revision and simplification of the laws. To this end the R&A and USGA meet twice a year to discuss possible changes, which will then be examined at great length in consultation with amateur and professional golfing bodies worldwide. Any agreed changes to the rules are made every four years.

The Rules Committee is composed of 12 members of the R&A with up to a further 12 representatives from golfing bodies at home and abroad. In addition to the USGA, there are advisory members from Britain's Council of National Golf Unions and the Ladies Golf Union, plus delegates from Europe, Australia, New Zealand, Canada, South Africa, South America, Asia and the Pacific, and Japan.

Since the creation of the first Rules Committee in 1897, the R&A has spawned two further offspring to meet the ever-increasing pressures of administration. The Implements and Ball Committee investigates and rules on the admissibility or otherwise of newly developed clubs and golf balls, and the Amateur Status Committee defines the laws which govern acceptable levels of prizes, tournament rules, grants and scholarships and applications for reinstatement to the amateur ranks.

The Open Championship

The R&A first became involved with the Open Championship after Young Tom Morris won the original championship belt outright in 1870 and Prestwick Golf Club, which had inaugurated the event 10 years earlier, asked the Royal and Ancient and the Honourable Company of Edinburgh Golfers to join them in providing a new trophy and staging the championship.

By 1919 a total of 26 golf clubs had become involved in the organisation of the Open and Amateur Championships. It was a cumbersome and at times chaotic situation, which was resolved when the clubs invited the R&A to take full responsibility for both events from 1920.

Significant changes had taken place over the first 60 years since the first Championship in 1860. Entries had increased from eight to more than 250, qualifying rounds were introduced and play changed from three rounds of Prestwick's 12-hole course in one day to four rounds of 18 holes over two days.

Those changes pale into insignificance when set beside the modern championship. Well over 2000 entries are received each year. Prize money has reached almost £4 million and spectators number more than 200,000. The tented village is virtually a small township, with more than 7000 people involved as volunteers or paid employees.

It is not just the Open, however, which occupies the talents of Championship Committee members. They are also responsible for the Amateur, Boys, Mid-Amateur and Seniors Championships and the Junior Open. International events also come under their umbrella. These include organisation of the Walker Cup, St Andrews and Jacques Léglise Trophies when they are played in Great Britain and Ireland.

The Selection Committee, which reports directly to the General Committee, has the responsibility for teams representing Great Britain & Ireland and involves members from each of the four home countries.

Profits from the Open Championship are channelled back into the game through the External Funds Supervisory Committee which recommends grants and loans for projects throughout the world, particularly those concerned with the training and development of junior golf and encourages golf in countries where the game is in its infancy.

The R&A as a private club

Beginning in January 2004 the R&A separated the private club from its external activities. R&A Championships Ltd has been formed to administer championship management and commercial matters. R&A Rules Ltd will perform the governance functions. The new R&A Foundation with charitable status will ensure that the surpluses created at the Open Championship will be efficiently chanelled to golf development projects worlwide.

Although the worldwide membership of the R&A is 2400, those resident in St Andrews barely number three figures. Many who wear the R&A tie are also members of leading clubs in other golfing nations and bring a wealth of experience to committee discussions.

Yet despite its pre-eminent position, the club has no golf course. For many years the upkeep of the Old Course was paid for by the R&A and the New Course was built and maintained at the members' expense. This arrangement ws modified in 1953 by the creation of the Joint Links Committee which consisted of an equal number of R&A and Town Council members and took responsibility for the then four courses at St Andrews. Since 1974 the St Andrews courses, now numbering seven, have been administered by the Links Trust.

Now the St Andrews courses are administered by a Links Trust and Links Management Committee on which the R&A has the right to appoint representation and the club still makes significant contributions to the maintenance and improvement of the courses with grants and loans.

Members gather from around the world for the club's spring and autumn meetings and in September each year the new captain follows tradition by driving into office to the resounding boom of an ancient cannon.

Dates and Venues for Majors and Cup Matches

	The Masters	US Open	US PGA Championship
2004	April 8–11 Augusta National, Augusta, Georgia	June 17–20 Shinnecock Hills, Southampton, New York	August 12–15 Whistling Straits, Kohler, Wisconsin
2005	April 7–10 Augusta National, Augusta, Georgia	June 16–19 Pinehurst No.2, Pinehurst, North Carolina	August Baltusrol GC, Springfield, New Jersey
2006	April 6–9 Augusta National, Augusta, Georgia	June 15–18 Winged Foot GC, Mamaroneck, New York	August Medinah CC, Medinah, Illinois
2007	April 5–8 Augusta National, Augusta, Georgia	June 14–17 Oakmont CC, Pennsylvania	August Southern Hills, Tulsa, Oklahoma
2008	April 10–13 Augusta National, Augusta, Georgia	June 23–15 Torrey Pines GC. La Jolla, California	August Oakland Hills, Bloomfield Hills CC, Michigan
2009	April 9–12 Augusta National, Augusta, Georgia		August Hazeltine National GC, Chaska, Minnesota
2010	April 8–11 Augusta National, Augusta, Georgia		August Sahalee CC, Richmond, Washington
2011			August Atlanta AC, Deluth, Georgia

The US Masters normally begins on the Thursday following the first Sunday in April.
The US Open Championship normally begins on the Thursday following the second
Sunday in June.
The US PGA Championship normally begins on the second Thursday in August.

Ryder Cup

2004 at Oakland Hills Country Club, Birmingham, Michigan on September 17–19
2006 at The K Club, County Kildare, Ireland
2008 at Valhalla Golf Club, Louisville, Kentucky
2010 at Celtic Manor Resort, Newport, Wales
2012 at Medinah Country Club, Illinois
2014 at Gleneagles Hotel, Perthshire, Scotland
2016 at Hazeltine National GC, Chaska, Minnesota

Presidents Cup (USA v Rest of the World (but not Europe))

2003 at Fancourt Hotel and CC Estate (The Links Course), George, South Africa

R&A Championship Dates, 2004–2006

	2004	2005	2006
The Amateur Championship	**May 31–June 5** St Andrews Old & Jubilee	**May 30–June 4** Royal Birkdale Southport and Ainsdale	**June 19–24** Royal St George's Prince's
The Open Championship Regional Qualifying	**July 5**	**July 4**	**July 10**
The Open Championship Final Qualifying	**July 10–11** Glasgow (Gailes) Irvine Turnberry Kintyre Western Gailes	**July 9–10** Ladybank Leven Links Lundin Scotscraig	**July 15–16** Conwy (Caernarvonshire) Formby Wallasey West Lancashire
The Junior Open Championship	**July 12–14** Kilmarnock (Barassie)	*Not played*	TBA
The Open Championship	**July 15–18** Royal Troon	**July 14–17** St Andrews (Old Course)	**July 20–23** Royal Liverpool
The Senior British Open	**July 22–25** TBA	**July 21–24** TBA	**July 27–31** TBA
The Seniors' Open Amateur Championship	**August 4–6** The Berkshire, (Red and Blue Courses)	**August 3–5** Woburn (Dukes and Duchess Courses)	**August 9–11** Saunton (East and West Courses)
The Boys' Home Internationals	**August 3–5** Royal Dublin	**August 2–4** Woodhall Spa – Hotchkin	**August 8–10** Moray
The Boys' Amateur Championship	**August 9–14** Conwy (Caernarvonshire)	**August 8–13** Hunstanton	**August 14–19** Royal Aberdeen
The British Mid-Amateur Championship	**August 11–15** Royal Liverpool	**August 10–14** Muirfield	**August 16–20** Southport & Ainsdale
The Jacques Léglise Trophy	**August 27–28** Nairn	**August 26–27** Royal Porthcawl	**September 1–2** Continent of Europe
The St Andrews Trophy	**August 27–28** Nairn	*Not played*	**September 1–2** Continent of Europe
The Walker Cup	*Not played*	**August 13–14** Chicago GC, Wheaton, Illinois	*Not played*
The Eisenhower Trophy	**October 28–31** Hyatt Dorado Beach Resort and CC, Puerto Rico	*Not played*	**TBC** Spier, CC, South Africa
Espirito Santo Trophy	**October 20–23** Hyatt Dorado Beach Resort and CC, Puerto Rico	*Not played*	**TBC** Stellenbosch GC, South Africa

Schedules and Dates for 2004

European International Amateur Calendar

Championships in bold-type have not been confirmed yet

Mar 3–7	Spanish Ladies Amateur Championship, El Bosque G&CC (Valencia)
	Spanish Amateur Championship, Desert Springs Golf (Almeria)
Mar 10–14	Portuguese Ladies Amateur Championship, Quinta da Ria (Algarve)
	Portuguese Amateur Championship, Quinta da Ria (Algarve)
April 8–12	French Lady Juniors Championship, St Cloud
	French Boys Championship, Toulouse-Seilh
April 14–17	Spanish Lady Junior Championship, GC Lomas-Bosque (Madrid)
April 21–23	Europe *v* Asia-Pacific (Bonallack Trophy), Circolo Golf Roma, Italy
April 23–25	German Ladies Amateur Championship, GC Elfrather Mühle
	German Amateur Championship, GC Elfrather Mühle
April 24–25	Scottish Ladies' Open Stroke Play Championship, Troon – Portland
April 30–May 2	Lytham Trophy, Royal Lytham & St Annes
May 1–2	Welsh Ladies Open Amateur Stroke Play Championship, Ashburnham GC
May 3–6	**Israel Ladies Amateur Open Championship**
	Israel Amateur Open Championship
May 7–9	Irish Amateur Open Championship, Carton House GC
May 14–16	English Men's Open Stroke Play Championship (Brabazon Trophy), West Lancs GC
May 19–23	Spanish Junior Championship, G&CC La Marquesa (Alicante)
May 21–23	Swedish International Championship for Girls, TBA
	Swedish International Championship for Boys, TBA
May 21–23	Scottish Open Amateur Stroke Play Championship, Lundin
May 27–29	European Mid-Amateur, Varese, Italy
May 28–31	**Austrian Ladies Amateur Championship**
	Austrian Amateur Championship
May 29–30	Welsh Open Youths Championship, Rolls of Monmouth
May 31–June 5	The Amateur Championship, St Andrews Old/Jubilee
June 4–6	French Ladies Amateur Stroke Play Championship (Trophée Cécile Rotschild), Morfontaine
June 4–6	International Amateur Championships of Germany for Girls and Boys, St. Leon-Rot
June 10–12	European Seniors, La Baule, France
June 12–13	Curtis Cup (GB&I *v* America Ladies), Formby GC
June 18–20	French Men Amateur Stroke Play Championship (Coupe Murat), Golf de Chantilly
June 18–20	Welsh Open Stroke Play Championship, Royal Porthcawl
June 18–20	Scottish Youths Open Amateur Stroke Play Championship, Brunston Castle
June 21–24	Russian Ladies Amateur Championship, Moscow CC
	Russian Amateur Championship, Moscow CC
June 22–26	Ladies' British Open Amateur Championship Gullane GC no. 1
June 24–25	Irish Youths Amateur Open Championship, Clandeboye GC
June 26–27	Danish International Ladies Amateur Championship, Silkeborg GC
	Danish International Amateur Championship, Silkeborg GC
July 2–4	Ladies' British Open Mid Amateur Championship, Hunstanton GC
	EGA Challenge Trophy – Men, Binowo Park, Poland
July 14–18	Luxembourg Ladies Amateur Championship, Grand-Ducal
	Luxembourg Amateur Championship, Grand-Ducal
July 15–17	**Slovak Amateur Championship**
July 15–17	Dutch Junior International, Toxandria
July 20–22	English Boys (under 18) Open Amateur Stroke Play Championship (Carris Trophy)

European International Calendar *continued*

	Northumberland GC
July 22–24	European Young Masters, Styrian GC Murhof, Austria
July 24–25	Irish Ladies' Open Stroke Play Championship, Ballykisteen GC
July 29–30	Scottish Ladies' Junior Open Stroke Play Championship, Kirkcaldy GC
July 27–29	Danish Girls Championship, Smorum GC
	Danish Boys Championship, Smorum GC
Aug 4–6	British Senior Championship, The Berkshire
Aug 4–8	Girls British Open Amateur Championship, Lanark GC
Aug 5–7	Finnish Ladies Amateur Championship, Helsinki GC, Tali
	Finnish Amateur Championship, Helsinki GC, Tali
Aug 6–8	Swiss Ladies Amateur Championship, Domaine Impérial
	Swiss Amateur Championship, Domaine Impérial
Aug 9–14	British Boys Championship, Conwy (Caernarvonshire)
Aug 10–13	English Ladies' Open Intermediate Championship, Moor Park GC
Aug 11–13	British Girls Internationals, Strathaven GC
Aug 11–14	Czech International Ladies Amateur Championship, Karlovy Vary GC
	Czech International Amateur Championship, Karlovy Vary GC
Aug 11–15	British Mid-Amateur Championship, Royal Liverpool
Aug 18–21	European Amateur, Skövde, Sweden
Aug 24–28	Belgian International Lady Junior Championship, Ravenstein
	Belgian International Junior Championship, Ravenstein
Aug 25–27	Ladies' British Open Amateur Stroke Play Championship, Alwoodley GC
Aug 25–28	European Ladies, Ulzama GC (Navarra), Spain
	EGA Challenge Trophy – Boys
Aug 26–28	Hungarian Open Ladies Amateur Championship, TBA
	Hungarian Open Amateur Championship, TBA
Sep 2–5	**Slovenian Ladies Amateur Championship**
	Slovenian Amateur Championship
Sep 3–5	Estonian Open Ladies Amateur Championship, Tallinn GC (Niitvälja)
	Estonian Open Amateur Championship, Tallinn GC (Niitvälja)
Seo 8–10	British Ladies Home Internationals, Royal Porthcawl GC
Sep 8–11	**Polish Open Amateur Championship**
Sep 13–14	Irish Senior Ladies' Open Amateur Stroke Play Championship, Seapoint GC
Sep 15–19	Italian International Ladies Amateur Championship, Bogogno GC
	Italian International Amateur Championship, Villa d'Este GC
Sep 21–23	Senior Ladies' British Open Amateur Championship, Portstewart GC
Sep 23–26	**Hellenic Ladies Amateur Championship**
	Hellenic Amateur Championship
Sep 30–Oct 2	European Club Cup Trophy – Ladies, Mons Royal GC du Hainault, Belgium
Sep 30–Oct 3	**Turkish Open Amateur Championship (Men)**
Oct 5–7	British Senior Home Internationals, Kilkeel GC
Oct 22–23	Bulgarian Amateur Championship, Greyhawk GC (Sofia)
Oct 28–31	European Club Cup Trophy – Men, Greece
Oct 28–31	Cyprus Amateur Open, TBA

European Team Championships

July 6–10	Lady Juniors, Royal Cinque Ports GC, England
July 6–10	Youths, The Island GC, Ireland
July 6–10	Girls, Golf National, France
July 6–10	Boys, Kymen Golf Ry, Finland

some dates are provisional

Main US amateur dates for 2004 can be found on page 406

PGA European Tour 2004

Dec 4–7	Omega Hong Kong Open, Hong Kong GC, Hong Kong
Jan 15–18	South African Airways Open, Erinvale GC, Somerset West, Western Cape, South Africa
Jan 22–25	dunhill championship, Houghton GC, Johannesburg, South Africa
Jan 29–Feb 1	Johnnie Walker Classic, Alpine G& SC, Bangkok, Thailand
Feb 5–8	Heineken Classic, Royal Melbourne GC, Victoria, Australia
Feb 12–15	ANZ Championship, Horizons Golf Resort, Port Stephens, Australia
Feb 19–22	Carlsberg Malaysian Open, Saujana GC, Kuala Lumpur, Malaysia
Feb 25–29	WGC–Accenture Matchplay, La Costa Resort & Spa, Carlsbad, CA, USA
Mar 4–7	Dubai Desert Classic, Emirates GC, Dubai
Mar 11–14	Qatar Masters, Doha GC, Qatar
Mar 18–21	Caltex Masters presented by Carlsberg, Singapore 2004, Laguna National G & CC, Singapore
Mar 25–28	Madeira Island Open, Santo da Serra, Madeira
Apr 1 – 4	Algarve Open de Portugal, TBA
Apr 8–11	MASTERS TOURNAMENT, Augusta National, Georgia, USA
Apr 15–18	TBA
Apr 22–25	Canarias Open de España, TBA
Apr 29–May 2	61st Telecom Italia Open, Castello di Tolcinasco G & CC, Milan, Italy
May 6–9	BMW Asian Open, Tomson GC, Shanghai, China
May 13–16	The Daily Telegraph Damovo British Masters, Marriott Forest of Arden, Warwickshire
May 20–23	Deutsche Bank – SAP Open TPC of Europe, Golf Club St Leon-Rot, Heidelberg, Germany
May 27–30	VOLVO PGA CHAMPIONSHIP, Wentworth Club, Surrey
June 3–6	The Celtic Manor Resort Wales Open, The Celtic Manor Resort, City of Newport, Wales
June 10–13	Diageo Championship at Gleneagles, The Gleneagles Hotel, Perthshire, Scotland
June 17–20	US OPEN CHAMPIONSHIP, Shinnecock Hills GC, Southampton, NY, USA
June 17–20	Aa St Omer Open, Saint-Omer, Lumbres, France
June 24–27	Open de France, Le Golf National, Paris, France
July 1–4	Smurfit European Open, The K Club, Dublin, Ireland
July 8–11	The Barclays Scottish Open, Loch Lomond GC, Glasgow, Scotland
July 15–18	133rd OPEN CHAMPIONSHIP, Royal Troon GC, Ayrshire, Scotland
July 22–25	Nissan Irish Open, Co Louth GC, Baltray, Drogheda, Ireland
July 29–Aug 1	Scandinavian Masters, Barsebäck G & CC, Malmö, Sweden
Aug 5–8	Dutch Open, TBA
Aug 12–15	US PGA CHAMPIONSHIP, Whistling Straits, Kohler, Wisconsin, USA
Aug 12–15	BMW Russian Open, Le Meridien Moscow G & CC, Moscow, Russia
Aug 19–22	WGC–NEC Invitational, Firestone CC, Akron, Ohio, USA
Aug 26–29	BMW International Open, Golfclub München Nord-Eichenried, Munich, Germany
Sep 2–5	Omega European Masters, Crans-sur-Sierre, Crans Montana, Switzerland
Sep 9–12	Linde German Masters, Gut Lärchenhof, Cologne, Germany
Sep 17–19	THE 35TH RYDER CUP MATCHES, Oakland Hills CC, Bloomfield Hills, Michigan, USA
Sep 23–26	TBA
Sep 30–Oct 3	WGC–American Express Championship, Mount Juliet, Thomastown, Co Kilkenny, Ireland
Oct 7–10	dunhill links championship, Old Course St Andrews, Carnoustie & Kingsbarns, Scotland
Oct 14–17	HSBC World Match Play Championship, Wentworth Club, Surrey
Oct 14 – 17	Turespaña Mallorca Classic, Pula GC, Majorca, Spain
Oct 21 – 24	Telefonica Madrid Open, Club de Campo, Madrid, Spain
Oct 28–31	Volvo Masters Andalucia, Club de Golf, Valderrama, Spain
Nov 18–21	WGC–World Cup, Real Club de Golf Sevilla, Seville, Spain

The following players earned cards for the 2004 season: R McEvoy (Eng), W Ormsby (Aus), D McGrane (Ire), J Huldahl (Den), M Cort (Eng), N Sato (Jpn), B Banks (Eng), P Marantz (Aus), T Price (Aus), W Bennett (Eng), P Nyman (Swe), D Gaunt (Aus), F. Delamontagne (Fra), S O'Hara (Sco), D Dixon (Eng), C Gane (Eng), D Carter (Eng), M Eliasson (Swe), C Monasterio (Arg), T Whitehouse (Eng), S Jeppesen (Swe), A McLean (Eng), J Berendt (Arg), J-F Lucquin (Fra), MA Martin (Spa), J M Arruti (Esp), M Nilsson (Swe), C Spence (Aus), M Pendaries (Fra) F. Roca (Spa) C Hanell (Swe), R Rashell (USA), L Oosthuizen (RSA), E Little (Sco), D Botes (RSA).

There were also 15 qualifiers for 2004 Tour cards from the Challenge Tour. (See page 134)

Abbreviations

Alb	Albania	IoM	Isle of Man	Por	Portugal
Arg	Argentina	Irl	Ireland	Pur	Puerto Rico
Aus	Australia	Isl	Iceland	Rus	Russia
Aut	Austria	Isr	Israel	Sin	Singapore
Bel	Belgium	Ita	Italy	RSA	South Africa
Bra	Brazil	Jam	Jamaica	Sco	Scotland
Can	Canada	Jpn	Japan	Slo	Slovenia
Chi	China	Kor	Korea (South)	StL	Saint Lucia
Chl	Chile	Mal	Malaysia	Swe	Sweden
Col	Colombia	Mex	Mexico	Sui	Switzerland
Den	Denmark	Nam	Namibia	Tai	Taiwan
Eng	England	Ned	Netherlands	Tha	Thailand
Esp	Spain	NI	Northern Ireland	Tri	Trinidad and
Fij	Fiji	Nor	Norway		Tobago
Fin	Finland	NZ	New Zealand	USA	United States
Fra	France	Pan	Panama	Ven	Venezuela
Gua	Guatemala	Par	Paraquay	Wal	Wales
Ger	Germany	Per	Peru	Zim	Zimbabwe
Hun	Hungary	Phi	Philippines		
Ind	India	Pol	Poland		
(am)	Amateur	(M)	Match play	jr	Junior
(D)	Defending champion	(S)	Stroke play	sr	Senior

Where available, total course yardage and the par for a course are displayed in square brackets,
i.e. [6686–70]

* indicates winner after play-off

PART I

The Major Championships

The Open   42
US Open   52
The Masters   60
US PGA   67
Men's Major Title Table   75
Weetabix Women's British Open   76
US Women's Open   83
McDonald's LPGA   91
Nabisco Dinah Shore   99
du Maurier Classic   106
Women's Major Title Table   107

The Open Championship

2003 Open Championship (132nd) at Royal St George's (7034–71)

Prize Money £3.9 million. Entries: 2152. Regional qualifying courses: Alwoodley, Ashridge, Blackmoor, Co.Louth, Hadley Wood, Hindhead, Little Aston, Minchinhampton, Notts, Ormskirk, Orsett, Renfrew, Silloth-on-Solway, Stockport, Trentham, Wildernesse. Final qualifying courses: Littlestone, North Foreland, Prince's, Royal Cinque Ports. Final Field: 156 (3 amateurs), of whom 75 (no amateurs) made the half-way cut on 150 or less.

1	Ben Curtis (USA)	72-72-70-69—283	£700000	€1010800
2	Thomas Bjørn (Den)	73-70-69-72—284	345000	498180
	Vijay Singh (Fij)	75-70-69-70—284	345000	498180
4	Davis Love III (USA)	69-72-72-72—285	185000	267140
	Tiger Woods (USA)	73-72-69-71—285	185000	267140
6	Brian Davis (Eng)	77-73-68-68—286	134500	194218
	Fredrik Jacobson (Swe)	70-76-70-70—286	134500	194218
8	Nick Faldo (Eng)	76-74-67-70—287	97750	141151
	Kenny Perry (USA)	74-70-70-73—287	97750	141151
10	Gary Evans (Eng)	71-75-70-72—288	68000	98192
	Sergio García (Esp)	73-71-70-74—288	68000	98192
	Retief Goosen (RSA)	73-75-71-69—288	68000	98192
	Hennie Otto (RSA)	68-76-75-69—288	68000	98192
	Phillip Price (Wal)	74-72-69-73—288	68000	98192
15	Stuart Appleby (Aus)	75-71-71-72—289	49333	71237
	Chad Campbell (USA)	74-71-72-72—289	49333	71237
	Pierre Fulke (Swe)	77-72-67-73—289	49333	71237
18	Ernie Els (RSA)	78-68-72-72—290	42000	60648
	Mathias Grönberg (Swe)	71-74-73-72—290	42000	60648
	Greg Norman (Aus)	69-79-74-68—290	42000	60648
	Tom Watson (USA)	71-77-73-69—290	42000	60648
22	Angel Cabrera (Arg)	75-73-70-73—291	32917	47532
	Choi Kyung-Ju (Kor)	77-72-72-70—291	32917	47532
	Peter Fowler (Aus)	77-73-70-71—291	32917	47532
	Padraig Harrington (Irl)	75-73-74-69—297	32917	47532
	Thomas Levet (Fra)	71-73-74-73—291	32917	47532
	JL Lewis (USA)	78-70-72-71—291	32917	47532
28	Mark Foster (Eng)	73-73-72-74—292	26000	37544
	SK Ho (Kor)	70-73-72-77—292	26000	37544
	Paul McGinley (Irl)	77-73-69-73—292	26000	37544
	Andrew Oldcorn (Sco)	72-74-73-73—292	26000	37544
	Nick Price (Zim)	74-72-72-74—292	26000	37544
	Mike Weir (Can)	74-76-71-71—292	26000	37544
34	Stewart Cink (USA)	75-75-75-68—293	18778	27115
	José Coceres (Arg)	77-70-72-74—293	18778	27115
	Bob Estes (USA)	77-71-76-69—293	18778	27115
	Shingo Katayama (Jpn)	76-73-73-71—293	18778	27115
	Scott McCarron (USA)	71-74-73-75—293	18778	27115
	Adam Mednick (Swe)	76-72-76-69—293	18778	27115
	Gary Murphy (Irl)	73-74-73-73—293	18778	27115
	Marco Ruiz (Par)	73-71-75-74—293	18778	27115
	Duffy Waldorf (USA)	76-73-71-73—293	18778	27115
43	Robert Allenby (Aus)	73-75-74-72—294	14250	20577
	Rich Beem (USA)	76-74-75-69—294	14250	20577
	Tom Byrum (USA)	77-72-71-74—294	14250	20577

46	Markus Brier (Aut)	76-71-74-74—295	11864	17132
	Fred Couples (USA)	71-75-71-78—295	11864	17132
	Brad Faxon (USA)	77-73-70-75—295	11864	17132
	Mathew Goggin (Aus)	76-72-70-77—295	11864	17132
	Tom Lehman (USA)	77-73-72-73—295	11864	17132
	Ian Poulter (Eng)	78-72-70-75—295	11864	17132
	Anthony Wall (Eng)	75-74-71-75—295	11864	17132
53	Michael Campbell (NZ)	78-72-74-72—296	10200	14729
	Trevor Immelman (RSA)	77-73-72-74—296	10200	14729
	Raphaèl Jacquelin (Fra)	77-71-72-76—296	10200	14729
	David Lynn (Eng)	73-76-71-76—296	10200	14729
	Mark McNulty (Zim)	79-71-77-69—296	10200	14729
	Rory Sabbatini (RSA)	79-71-75-71—296	10200	14729
59	Darren Clarke (NI)	75-75-71-76—297	9550	13790
	Alastair Forsyth (Sco)	74-70-78-75—297	9550	13790
	Skip Kendall (USA)	73-76-73-75—297	9550	13790
	Peter Lonard (Aus)	73-73-70-81—297	9550	13790
	Phil Mickelson (USA)	74-72-73-78—297	9550	13790
	Craig Parry (Aus)	73-73-76-75—297	9550	13790
65	Charles Howell III (USA)	71-76-77-74—298	9050	13068
	Stephen Leaney (Aus)	74-76-78-70—298	9050	13068
	Len Mattiace (USA)	74-75-74-75—298	9050	13068
	Mark O'Meara (USA)	73-77-77-71—298	9050	13068
69	Katsuyoshi Tomori (Jpn)	72-77-75-76—300	8800	12707
70	John Rollins (USA)	72-76-78-75—301	8700	12563
71	Chris Smith (USA)	74-73-76-79—302	8600	12418
72	John Daly (USA)	75-74-74-80—303	8450	12202
	Ian Woosnam (Wal)	73-75-80-75—303	8450	12202
74	Jesper Parnevik (Swe)	72-75 DQ	8250	11913
	Mark Roe (Eng)	77-70 DQ	8250	11913

The following players missed the half-way cut:

76	Mark Calcavecchia (USA)	78-73—151		97T	David Toms (USA)	80-73—153
	Anders Hansen (Den)	76-75—151		107	Chris DiMarco (USA)	79-75—154
	Lee Janzen (USA)	76-75—151			Søren Hansen (Den)	80-74—154
	Justin Leonard (USA)	74-77—151			Cliff Kresge (USA)	81-73—154
	José María Olazábal (Esp)	74-77—151			Hirofumi Miyase (Jpn)	81-73—154
	Eduardo Romero (Arg)	75-76—151			Peter O'Malley (Aus)	78-76—154
	Steen Tinning (Den)	78-73—151			Mårten Olander (Swe)	79-75—154
	Lee Westwood (Eng)	76-75—151		113	Luke Donald (Eng)	76-79—155
84	Bradley Dredge (Wal)	80-72—152			Kenneth Ferrie (Eng)	74-81—155
	Niclas Fasth (Swe)	76-76—152			Fred Funk (USA)	75-80—155
	Jim Furyk (USA)	74-78—152			Dudley Hart (USA)	76-79—155
	Ignacio Garrido (Esp)	80-72—152			Paul Lawrie (Sco)	81-74—155
	Jay Haas (USA)	80-72—152			Craig Perks (NZ)	78-77—155
	Søren Kjeldsen (Den)	74-78—152			Nobuhito Sato (Jpn)	72-83—155
	Bernhard Langer (Ger)	76-76—152			Charl Schwartzel (RSA)	78-77—155
	Sandy Lyle (Sco)	73-79—152			Christopher Smith (Eng)	77-78—155
	Nick O'Hern (Aus)	82-70—152		122	Paul Casey (Eng)	85-71—156
	Corey Pavin (USA)	74-78—152			Robert-Jan Derksen (Ned)	78-78—156
	Andrew Raitt (Eng)	74-78—152			Steve Flesch (USA)	73-83—156
	Hal Sutton (USA)	76-76—152			David Howell (Eng)	77-79—156
	Scott Verplank (USA)	78-74—152			Jonathan Kaye (USA)	75-81—156
97	Ricky Barnes (USA) (am)	79-74—153			Shigeki Maruyama (Jpn)	83-73—156
	Steven Bowditch (Aus)	77-76—153			Greg Owen (Eng)	79-77—156
	Joe Durant (USA)	77-76—153			Adam Scott (Aus)	82-74—156
	Todd Hamilton (USA)	76-77—153			Simon Wakefield (Eng)	82-74—156
	Jarrod Moseley (Aus)	74-79—153			Gary Wolstenholme (Eng) [am]	74-82—156
	Rolf Muntz (Ned)	82-71—153		132	Gary Emerson (Eng)	77-80—157
	Cameron Percy (Aus)	76-77—153			Euan Little (Sco)	80-77—157
	Chris Riley (USA)	78-75—153			Jyoti Randhawa (Ind)	80-77—157
	Jeff Sluman (USA)	78-75—153			Mark Smith (Eng)	80-77—157

132nd Open Championship continued

132T	Hideto Tanihara (Jpn)	79-78—157	146T	Adam Le Vesconte (Aus)	82-80—162
	Paul Wesselingh (Eng)	79-78—157	148	Anthony Sproston (Eng)	83-80—163
138	Ben Crane (USA)	78-80—158	149	Andrew George (Eng)	79-85—164
	Iain Pyman (Eng)	81-77—158	150	Noboru Sugai (Jpn)	83-82—165
140	Justin Rose (Eng)	79-80—159	151	Toru Taniguchi (Jpn)	82-87—169
141	Scott Godfrey (Eng) (am)	82-78—160	152	Charles Challen (Eng)	86-87—173
	David Smail (NZ)	77-83—160			
143	David Duval (USA)	83-78—161		Steve Elkington (Aus)	86 WD
	Philip Golding (Eng)	83-78—161		Jerry Kelly (USA)	86 WD
	Malcolm Mackenzie (Eng)	82-79—161		Paul Azinger (USA)	Retd
146	Robert Coles (Eng)	85-77—162		Colin Montgomerie (Sco)	Retd

2002 Open Championship at Muirfield   (7034–71)

Prize Money £3.885 million. Entries: 2260. Regional qualifying courses: Alwoodley, Blackmoor, Co.Louth, Hadley Wood, Hindhead, Little Aston, Minchinhampton, Northamptonshire County, Notts, Ormskirk, Orsett, Renfrew, Silloth-on-Solway, Stockport, Trentham, Wildernesse. Final qualifying courses: Dunbar, Gullane No.1, Luffness New, North Berwick. Final Field: 156 (3 amateurs), of whom 83 (no amateurs) made the half-way cut on 144 or less.

1	Ernie Els (RSA)	70-66-72-70—278 £700000	28	Bradley Dredge (Wal)	70-72-74-68—284	24000
2	Stuart Appleby (Aus)	73-70-70-65—278 286667		Niclas Fasth (Swe)	70-73-71-70—284	24000
	Steve Elkington (Aus)	71-73-68-66—278 286667		Pierre Fulke (Swe)	72-69-78-65—284	24000
	Thomas Levet (Fra)	72-66-74-66—278 286667		Jerry Kelly (USA)	73-71-70-70—284	24000
				Bernhard Langer (Ger)	72-72-71-69—284	24000
	After a four-hole play-off, Appleby and Elkington were			Jesper Parnevik (Swe)	72-72-70-70—284	24000
	eliminated; Els won the sudden-death play-off with Levet at			Loren Roberts (USA)	74-69-70-71—284	24000
	the first extra hole.			Des Smyth (Irl)	68-69-74-73—284	24000
				Tiger Woods (USA)	70-68-81-65—284	24000
5	Gary Evans (Eng)	72-68-74-65—279 140000	37	Darren Clarke (NI)	72-67-77-69—285	16917
	Padraig Harrington (Irl)	69-67-76-67—279 140000		Andrew Coltart (Sco)	71-69-74-71—285	16917
	Shigeki Maruyama (Jpn)	68-68-75-68—279 140000		Neal Lancaster (USA)	71-71-76-67—285	16917
8	Thomas Bjørn (Den)	68-70-73-69—280 77500		Stephen Leaney (Aus)	71-70-75-69—285	16917
	Sergio García (Esp)	71-69-71-69—280 77500		Scott Verplank (USA)	72-68-74-71—285	16917
	Retief Goosen (RSA)	71-68-74-67—280 77500		Ian Woosnam (Wal)	72-72-73-68—285	16917
	Søren Hansen (Den)	68-69-73-70—280 77500	43	Trevor Immelman (RSA)	72-72-71-71—286	13750
	Scott Hoch (USA)	74-69-71-66—280 77500		Steve Jones (USA)	68-75-73-70—286	13750
	Peter O'Malley (Aus)	72-68-75-65—280 77500		Carl Pettersson (Swe)	67-70-76-73—286	13750
14	Justin Leonard (USA)	71-72-68-70—281 49750		Esteban Toledo (Mex)	73-70-75-68—286	13750
	Peter Lonard (Aus)	72-72-68-69—281 49750	47	Paul Eales (Eng)	73-71-76-67—287	12000
	Davis Love III (USA)	71-72-71-67—281 49750		Jeff Maggert (USA)	71-68-80-68—287	12000
	Nick Price (Zim)	68-70-75-68—281 49750		Rocco Mediate (USA)	71-72-74-70—287	12000
18	Bob Estes (USA)	71-70-73-68—282 41000	50	Fredrik Andersson (Swe)	74-70-74-70—288	10267
	Scott McCarron (USA)	71-68-72-71—282 41000		Warren Bennett (Eng)	71-68-82-67—288	10267
	Greg Norman (Aus)	71-72-71-68—282 41000		Ian Garbutt (Eng)	69-70-74-75—288	10267
	Duffy Waldorf (USA)	67-69-77-69—282 41000		Mikko Ilonen (Fin)	71-70-77-70—288	10267
22	David Duval (USA)	72-71-70-70—283 32000		Shingo Katayama (Jpn)	72-68-74-74—288	10267
	Toshimitsu Izawa (Jpn)	76-68-72-67—283 32000		Barry Lane (Eng)	74-68-72-74—288	10267
	Mark O'Meara (USA)	69-69-71-68—283 32000		Ian Poulter (Eng)	69-69-78-72—288	10267
	Corey Pavin (USA)	69-70-75-69—283 32000		Bob Tway (USA)	70-66-78-74—288	10267
	Chris Riley (USA)	70-71-76-66—283 32000				
	Justin Rose (Eng)	68-75-68-72—283 32000				

Other players who made the cut: Stewart Cink (USA), Joe Durant (USA), Nick Faldo (Eng), Richard Green (Aus), Kuboya Kenichi (Jpn), Paul Lawrie (Sco), Steve Stricker (USA) 289; Chris DiMarco (USA), Phil Mickelson (USA), Jarrod Moseley (Aus) 290; Stephen Ames (Tri), Jim Carter (USA), Matthew Cort (Eng), Len Mattiace (USA), Toru Taniguchi (Jpn), Mike Weir (Can) 291; Sandy Lyle (Sco), Chris Smith (USA) 292; Anders Hansen (Den), Roger Wessels (RSA) 293; David Park (Wal) 294; Mark Calcavecchia (USA), Lee Janzen (USA) 295; Colin Montgomerie (Sco) 297; David Toms (USA) 298.

2001 Open Championship *at Royal Lytham & St Annes* (6905–71)

Prize Money £3,229,748. Entries 2255. Regional qualifying courses: Alwoodley, Blackmoor, Burnham & Berrow, Carlisle, County Louth, Copt Heath, Coxmoor, Hadley Wood, Hindhead, Little Aston, Northamptonshire County, Orsett, Renfrew, Stockport, Wildernesse, Wilmslow. Final qualifying courses: Fairhaven, Hillside, St Anne's Old Links, Southport & Ainsdale. Final field comprised 156 players, of whom 70 (including one amateur) made the half-way cut on 144 or better.

1	David Duval (USA)	69-73-65-67—274	£600000
2	Niclas Fasth (Swe)	69-69-72-67—277	360000
3	Darren Clarke (NI)	70-69-69-70—278	141667
	Ernie Els (RSA)	71-71-67-69—278	141667
	Miguel Angel Jiménez (Esp)	69-72-67-70—278	141667
	Bernhard Langer (Ger)	71-69-67-71—278	141667
	Billy Mayfair (USA)	69-72-67-70—278	141667
	Ian Woosnam (Wal)	72-68-67-71—278	141667
9	Sergio García (Esp)	70-72-67-70—279	63750
	Mikko Ilonen (Fin)	68-75-70-66—279	63750
	Jesper Parnevik (Swe)	69-68-71-71—279	63750
	Kevin Sutherland (USA)	75-69-68-67—279	63750
13	Billy Andrade (USA)	69-70-70-71—280	40036
	Alex Cejka (Ger)	69-69-69-73—280	40036
	Retief Goosen (RSA)	74-68-67-71—280	40036
	Raphaël Jacquelin (Fra)	71-68-69-72—280	40036
	Colin Montgomerie (Sco)	65-70-73-72—280	40036
	Loren Roberts (USA)	70-70-70-70—280	40036
	Vijay Singh (Fij)	70-70-71-69—280	40036
	Des Smyth (Irl)	74-65-70-71—280	40036
21	Davis Love III (USA)	73-67-74-67—281	32500
	Nick Price (Zim)	73-67-68-73—281	32500
23	Michael Campbell (NZ)	71-72-71-68—282	30500
	Greg Owen (Eng)	69-68-72-73—282	30500
25	Bob Estes (USA)	74-70-73-66—283	27500
	Joe Ogilvie (USA)	69-68-71-75—283	27500
	Eduardo Romero (Arg)	70-68-72-73—283	27500
	Tiger Woods (USA)	71-68-73-71—283	27500
29	Barry Lane (Eng)	70-72-72-70—284	25000
30	Stewart Cink (USA)	71-72-72-70—285	21500
	David Dixon (Eng) (am)	70-71-70-74—285	
	Phil Mickelson (USA)	70-72-72-71—285	21500
	Justin Rose (Eng)	69-72-74-70—285	21500
	Phillip Price (Wal)	74-69-71-71—285	21500
	Nicolas Vanhootegem (Bel)	72-68-70-75—285	21500
	Scott Verplank (USA)	71-72-70-72—285	21500
37	Andrew Coltart (Sco)	75-68-70-73—286	16300
	Padraig Harrington (Irl)	75-66-74-71—286	16300
	Dudley Hart (USA)	74-69-69-74—286	16300
	Frank Lickliter (USA)	71-71-73-71—286	16300
	Toru Taniguchi (Jpn)	72-69-72-73—286	16300
42	Richard Green (Aus)	71-70-72-74—287	13500
	JP Hayes (USA)	69-71-74-73—287	13500
	Paul Lawrie (Sco)	72-70-69-76—287	13500
	Mark O'Meara (USA)	70-69-72-76—287	13500
	Steve Stricker (USA)	71-69-72-75—287	13500

Other players who made the cut: Robert Allenby (Aus), Chris DiMarco (USA), Brad Faxon (USA), Matt Gogel (USA), Peter Lonard (Aus), Adam Scott (Aus), Lee Westwood (Eng) 288; Mark Calcavecchia (USA), Paul Curry (Eng), Carlos Franco (Par), Paul McGinley (Irl), José María Olazábal (Esp), Rory Sabbatini (RSA), Duffy Waldorf (USA) 289; Stuart Appleby (Aus) 290; Gordon Brand jr (Sco), Brandel Chamblee (USA), Pierre Fulke (Swe) 291; Neil Cheetham (Eng) 295; Alexandre Balicki (Fra), Thomas Levet (Fra) 296; David Smail (NZ) 298; Scott Henderson (Sco), Sandy Lyle (Sco) 301.

2000 Open Championship *at St Andrews* (7115–72)

Prize Money £2,722,150. Entries 2477. Regional qualifying courses: Alwoodley, Beau Desert, Blackmoor, Burnham & Berrow, Camberley Heath, Carlisle, Copt Heath, County Louth, Coxmoor, Hadley Wood, Hindhead, Northamptonshire County, Ormskirk, Renfrew, Romford, Stockport, Wildernesse. Final qualifying courses: Ladybank, Leven, Lundin, Scotscraig. Final field comprised 156 players, of whom 74 (none amateur) made the half-way cut on 144 or better.

1	Tiger Woods (USA)	67-66-67-69—269	£500000
2	Ernie Els (RSA)	66-72-70-69—277	245000
	Thomas Bjørn (Den)	69-69-68-71—277	245000
4	Tom Lehman (USA)	68-70-70-70—278	130000
	David Toms (USA)	69-67-71-71—278	130000
6	Fred Couples (USA)	70-68-72-69—279	100000
7	Loren Roberts (USA)	69-68-70-73—280	66250
	Paul Azinger (USA)	69-72-72-67—280	66250
	Pierre Fulke (Swe)	69-72-70-69—280	66250
	Darren Clarke (NI)	70-69-68-73—280	66250
11	Bernhard Langer (Ger)	74-70-66-71—281	37111
	Mark McNulty (Zim)	69-72-70-70—281	37111
11T	David Duval (USA)	70-70-66-75—281	37111
	Stuart Appleby (Aus)	73-70-68-70—281	37111
	Davis Love III (USA)	74-66-74-67—281	37111
	Vijay Singh (Fij)	70-70-73-68—281	37111
	Phil Mickelson (USA)	72-66-71-72—281	37111
	Bob May (USA)	72-72-66-71—281	37111
	Dennis Paulson (USA)	68-71-69-73—281	37111
20	Steve Flesch (USA)	67-70-71-74—282	25500
	Padraig Harrington (Irl)	68-72-70-72—282	25500
	Steve Pate (USA)	73-70-71-68—282	25500
	Bob Estes (USA)	72-69-70-71—282	25500

Other players who made the cut: Eduardo Romero (Arg), Sergio García (Esp), Jesper Parnevik (Swe), Craig Parry (Aus), José Coceres (Arg), Robert Allenby (Aus) 286; Nick Faldo (Eng), Justin Leonard (USA), Stewart Cink (USA), Jim Furyk (USA), Nick O'Hern (Aus), Jarrod Moseley (Aus), Gary Orr (Sco), Jeff Maggert (USA), Retief Goosen (RSA), Lucas Parsons (Aus), Tsuyoshi Yoneyama (Jpn) 287; Mike Weir (Can), Ian Garbutt (Eng), Rocco Mediate (USA), 288; David Frost (RSA), Tom Watson (USA), Shigeki Maruyama (Jpn), Greg Owen (Eng), Andrew Coltart (Sco) 289; Christy O'Connor jr (Irl), Jeff Sluman (USA), Steve Elkington (Aus), Kirk Triplett (USA) 290; Desvonde Botes (RSA), Ian Poulter (Eng), Per-Ulrik Johansson (Swe), Lee Westwood (Eng) 291; Gordon Brand jr (Sco), Ian Woosnam (Wal), 292; Tom Kite (USA), Kazuhiko Hosokawa (Jpn) 294; Peter Senior (Aus), Lionel Alexandre (Fra) 295; Dudley Hart (USA) Retd.

1999 Open Championship *at Carnoustie* (7361-71)

Prize Money £2,009,550. Entries 2222. Regional qualifying courses: Beau Desert, Blackmoor, Burnham & Berrow, Carlisle, Copt Heath, County Louth, Coxmoor, Glenbervie, Hankley Common, Moortown, Northamptonshire County, Ormskirk, Romford, South Herts, Stockport, Wildernesse. Final qualifying courses: Downfield, Monifieth Links, Montrose Links, Panmure. Final field comprised 156 players, of whom 73 (none amateurs) made the half-way cut on 154 or better.

1	P Lawrie* (Sco)	73-74-76-67—290	£350000	18T	A Coltart (Sco)	74-74-72-77—297	20500
2	J Leonard (USA)	73-74-71-72—290	185000		F Nobilo (NZ)	76-76-70-75—297	20500
	J Van de Velde (Fra)	75-68-70-77—290	185000		P Sjöland (Swe)	74-72-77-74—297	20500
	Lawrie won four-hole play-off				L Westwood (Eng)	76-75-74-72—297	20500
4	C Parry (Aus)	76-75-67-73—291	100000		C Rocca (Ita)	81-69-74-73—297	20500
	A Cabrera (Arg)	75-69-77-70—291	100000	24	P O'Malley (Aus)	76-75-74-73—298	15300
6	G Norman (Aus)	76-70-75-72—293	70000		E Els (RSA)	74-76-76-72—298	15300
7	D Frost (RSA)	80-69-71-74—294	50000		B Watts (USA)	74-73-77-74—298	15300
	D Love III (USA)	74-74-77-69—294	50000		I Woosnam (Wal)	76-74-74-74—298	15300
	T Woods (USA)	74-72-74-74—294	50000		MA Martin (Esp)	74-76-72-76—298	15300
10	J Parnevik (Swe)	74-71-78-72—295	34800	29	P Harrington (Irl)	77-74-74-74—299	13500
	S Dunlap (USA)	72-77-76-70—295	34800	30	J Maggert (USA)	75-77-75-73—300	11557
	R Goosen (RSA)	76-75-73-71—295	34800		D Clarke (NI)	76-75-76-73—300	11557
	H Sutton (USA)	73-78-72-72—295	34800		P Stewart (USA)	79-73-74-74—300	11557
	J Furyk (USA)	78-71-76-70—295	34800		P Fulke (Swe)	75-75-77-73—300	11557
15	T Yoneyama (Jpn)	77-74-73-72—296	26000		T Bjørn (Den)	79-73-75-73—300	11557
	C Montgomerie (Sco)	74-76-72-74—296	26000		T Herron (USA)	81-70-74-75—300	11557
	S Verplank (USA)	80-74-73-69—296	26000		L Mattiace (USA)	73-74-75-78—300	11557
18	B Langer (Ger)	72-77-73-75—297	20500				

Other players who made the cut: M McNulty (Zim), D Hart (USA), P Baker (Eng), N Price (Zim), M Weir (Can), P Affleck (Wal) 301; D Waldorf (USA), M James (Eng) 302; S Pate (USA), N Ozaki (Jpn), J Sluman (USA), D Howell (Eng) 303; N Price (Eng), T Levet (Fra), K Tomori (Jpn), Kyoung-Ju Choi (Kor), B Hughes (Aus), D Robertson (Sco), B Estes (USA), S Allan (Aus), P Lonard (Aus) 304; D Paulson (USA), J Robinson (Eng), S Luna (Esp), P Price (Wal) 305; J Ryström (Swe), D Duval (USA), M Brooks (USA) 306; J Sandelin (Swe) 307; S Strüver (Ger) 308; L Thompson (Eng) 309; B Davis (Eng), J Huston (USA) 310; L Janzen (USA) 311; K Shingo (Jpn) 312; M Thompson (Eng), D Cooper (Eng) 313.

1998 Open Championship *at Royal Birkdale* (7018-70)

Prize money: £1,750,000. Entries: 2336. Regional qualifying courses: Beau Desert, Blackmoor, Burnham & Berrow, Carlisle, Copt Heath, County Louth, Coxmoor, Glenbervie, Hankley Common, Moortown, Northamptonshire County, Ormskirk, Romford, South Herts, Stockport and Wildernesse. Final qualifying courses: Hesketh, Hillside, Southport & Ainsdale and West Lancashire. Final field comprised 151 players, of whom 78 (including 3 amateurs) made the half-way cut on 146 or better.

1	M O'Meara (USA)*	72-68-72-68—280	£300000	19	C Strange (USA)	73-73-74-70—290	17220
2	B Watts (USA)	68-69-73-70—280	188000		V Singh (Fij)	67-74-78-71—290	17220
	O'Meara won four-hole play-off				S Lyle (Sco)	71-72-75-72—290	17220
3	T Woods (USA)	65-73-77-66—281	135000		R Allenby (Aus)	67-76-78-69—290	17220
4	J Furyk (USA)	70-70-72-70—282	76666		M James (Eng)	71-74-74-71—290	17220
	J Parnevik (Swe)	68-72-72-70—282	76666	24	S Torrance (Sco)	69-77-75-70—291	12480
	R Russell (Sco)	68-73-75-66—282	76666		B Estes (USA)	72-70-76-73—291	12480
	J Rose (Eng) (am)	72-66-75-69—282			S Ames (Tri)	68-72-79-72—291	12480
8	D Love III (USA)	67-73-77-68—285	49500		P O'Malley (Aus)	71-71-78-71—291	12480
9	T Bjørn (Den)	68-71-76-71—286	40850		L Janzen (USA)	72-69-80-70—291	12480
	C Rocca (Ita)	72-74-70-70—286	40850	29	S Dunlap (USA)	72-69-80-71—292	10030
11	J Huston (USA)	65-77-73-72—287	33333		N Price (Zim)	66-72-82-72—292	10030
	B Faxon (USA)	67-74-74-72—287	33333		S Maruyama (Jpn)	70-73-75-74—292	10030
	D Duval (USA)	70-71-75-71—287	33333		L Roberts (USA)	66-76-76-74—292	10030
14	G Brand jr (Sco)	71-70-76-71—288	29000		E Els (RSA)	74-74-72-72—292	10030
15	P Baker (Eng)	69-72-77-71—289	23650		S García (Esp) (am)	69-75-76-72—292	
	G Turner (NZ)	68-75-75-71—289	23650	35	M Calcavecchia (USA)	69-77-73-74—293	8900
	JM Olazábal (Esp)	73-72-75-69—289	23650		S Luna (Esp)	70-72-80-71—293	8900
	D Smyth (Irl)	74-69-75-71—289	23650		S Strüver (Ger)	75-70-80-68—293	8900

Other players who made the cut: P Sjöland (Swe), J Haeggman (Swe), P Walton (Irl), N Ozaki (Jpn), T Kite (USA), S Tinning (Den) 294; K Tomori (Jpn), D Howell (Eng), D Frost (RSA), R Davis (Aus), D Carter (Eng), N Faldo (Eng), P Stewart (USA), A Coltart (Sco) 295; S Stricker (USA), B Mayfair (USA), B Jobe (USA), L Mize (USA), F Minoza (Phi) 296; T Dodds (Nam), E Romero (Arg), S Jones (USA), J Leonard (USA), I Garrido (Esp), I Woosnam (Wal), L Westwood (Eng), C Daniel Franco (Par) 298; S Cink (USA), M Brooks (USA), M Campbell (NZ), F Couples (USA), M Long (NZ), D De Vooght (Bel) (am) 299; A Clapp (Eng) 300; G Evans (Eng) 301; B May (USA) 303; A McLardy (RSA) 304; F Jacobson (Swe) 305; K Hosokawa (Jpn) 306; R Giles (Irl) 307; P Mickelson (USA) 308; A Oldcorn (Sco) 309; D Hart (USA) 310.

1997 Open Championship *at Royal Troon*   (7079–71)

Prize money: £1,586,300. Entries: 2133. Regional qualifying courses: Beau Desert, Burnham & Berrow, Carlisle, Copt Heath, Coxmoor, Glenbervie, Hankley Common, Moortown, North Hants, Romford, South Herts, Sundridge Park, Wilmslow. Final qualifying courses: Irvine Bogside, Glasgow Gailes, Kilmarnock Barassie, Western Gailes. 156 players took part, 70 (including 1 amateur) qualified for final 36 holes.

1	J Leonard (USA)	69-66-72-65—272	£250000	20	JM Olazábal (Esp)	75-68-73-67—283	14500
2	D Clarke (NI)	67-66-71-71—275	150000		M James (Eng)	76-67-70-70—283	14500
	J Parnevik (Swe)	70-66-66-73—275	150000		B Faxon (USA)	77-67-72-67—283	14500
4	J Furyk (USA)	67-72-70-70—279	90000		S Appleby (Aus)	72-72-68-71—283	14500
5	S Ames (Tri)	74-69-66-71—280	62500	24	P Lonard (Aus)	72-70-69-73—284	10362
	P Harrington (Irl)	75-69-69-67—280	62500		C Montgomerie (Sco)	76-69-69-70—284	10362
7	F Couples (USA)	69-68-70-74—281	40666		I Woosnam (Wal)	71-73-69-71—284	10362
	E Romero (Arg)	74-68-67-72—281	40666		D A Russell (Eng)	75-72-68-69—284	10362
	P O'Malley (Aus)	73-70-70-68—281	40666		T Woods (USA)	72-74-64-74—284	10362
10	R Goosen (RSA)	75-69-70-68—282	24300		T Lehman (USA)	74-72-72-66—284	10362
	L Westwood (Eng)	73-70-67-72—282	24300		J Haas (USA)	71-70-73-70—284	10362
	T Watson (USA)	71-70-70-71—282	24300		P Mickelson (USA)	76-68-69-71—284	10362
	M Calcavecchia (USA)	74-67-72-69—282	24300	32	M McNulty (Zim)	78-67-72-68—285	8750
	R Allenby (Aus)	76-68-66-72—282	24300	33	J Lomas (Eng)	72-71-69-74—286	8283
	S Maruyama (Jpn)	74-69-70-69—282	24300		D Duval (USA)	73-69-73-71—286	8283
	T Kite (USA)	72-67-74-69—282	24300		R Davis (Aus)	73-73-70-70—286	8283
	D Love III (USA)	70-71-74-67—282	24300	36	A Magee (USA)	70-75-72-70—287	7950
	E Els (RSA)	75-69-69-69—282	24300		G Norman (Aus)	69-73-70-75—287	7950
	F Nobilo (NZ)	74-72-68-68—282	24300				

Other players who made the cut: R Russell (Sco), M O'Meara (USA), J Kernohan (USA), M Bradley (USA), B Langer (Ger), V Singh (Fij) 288; J Coceres (Arg), D Tapping (Eng), C Strange (USA), J Kelly (USA) 289; S Jones (USA), J Payne (Eng), R Boxall (Eng) 290; A Cabrera (Arg), J Maggert (USA), W Riley (Aus), P Senior (Aus), C Pavin (USA), P Mitchell (Eng), N Faldo (Eng), G Turner (NZ) 291; P Stewart (USA) 292; J Nicklaus (USA), B Howard (Sco) (am) 293; T Purtzer (USA), J Spence (Eng), S Stricker (USA), P Teravainen (USA) 294; P McGinley (Irl), P-U Johansson (Swe), G Clark (Eng) 295; T Tolles (USA) 296; B Andrade (USA) 298.

1996 Open Championship *at Royal Lytham & St Annes*   (6892–71)

Prize money: £1,400,000. Entries: 1918. Regional qualifying courses: Beau Desert, Burnham & Berrow, Carlisle, Copt Heath, Coxmoor, Glenbervie, Hankley Common, Moortown, North Hants, Romford, South Herts, Sundridge Park, Wilmslow. Final qualifying courses: Fairhaven, Formby, St Anne's Old Links, Southport & Ainsdale. Qualified for final 36 holes: 77 (including 1 amateur).

1	T Lehman (USA)	67-67-64-73—271	£200000	18T	R Mediate (USA)	69-70-69-72—280	15500
2	M McCumber (USA)	67-69-71-66—273	125000	22	M James (Eng)	70-68-75-68—281	11875
	E Els (RSA)	68-67-71-67—273	125000		J Haas (USA)	70-72-71-68—281	11875
4	N Faldo (Eng)	68-68-68-70—274	75000		T Woods (USA) (am)	75-66-70-70—281	
5	J Maggert (USA)	69-70-72-65—276	50000		C Mason (Eng)	68-70-70-73—281	11875
	M Brooks (USA)	67-70-68-71—276	50000		S Stricker (USA)	71-70-66-74—281	11875
7	P Hedblom (Swe)	70-65-75-67—277	35000	27	B Crenshaw (USA)	73-68-71-70—282	9525
	G Norman (Aus)	71-68-71-67—277	35000		T Kite (USA)	77-66-69-70—282	9525
	G Turner (NZ)	72-69-68-68—277	35000		P Broadhurst (Eng)	65-72-74-71—282	9525
	F Couples (USA)	67-70-69-71—277	35000		C Pavin (USA)	70-66-74-72—282	9525
11	A Cejka (Ger)	73-67-71-67—278	27000		P Mitchell (Eng)	71-68-71-72—282	9525
	D Clarke (NI)	70-68-69-71—278	27000		F Nobilo (NZ)	70-72-68-72—282	9525
	V Singh (Fij)	69-67-69-73—278	27000	33	E Romero (Arg)	70-71-75-67—283	7843
14	M McNulty (Zim)	69-71-70-69—279	20250		T Tolles (USA)	73-70-71-69—283	7843
	D Duval (USA)	76-67-66-70—279	20250		S Simpson (USA)	71-69-73-70—283	7843
	P McGinley (Irl)	69-65-74-71—279	20250		E Darcy (Irl)	73-69-71-70—283	7843
	S Maruyama (Jpn)	68-70-69-72—279	20250		D Gilford (Eng)	71-67-71-74—283	7843
18	M Welch (Eng)	71-68-73-68—280	15500		M O'Meara (USA)	67-69-72-75—283	7843
	P Harrington (Irl)	68-68-73-71—280	15500		H Tanaka (Jpn)	69-71-70-75—283	7843
	L Roberts (USA)	67-69-72-72—280	15500		B Faxon (USA)	67-73-68-75—283	7843

Other players who made the cut: M Calcavecchia (USA), P Mickelson (USA), K Eriksson (Swe), D Frost (RSA) 284; C Stadler (USA), B Mayfair (USA), P Jacobsen (USA), T Hamilton (Can), B Hughes (Aus), P Stewart (USA), R Boxall (Eng), J Nicklaus (USA), N Price (Zim), J Furyk (USA), J Parnevik (Swe) 285; J Payne (Eng), S Lyle (Sco), R Allenby (Aus), S Ames (Tri) 286; M Jonzon (Swe), DA Weibring (USA), J Sluman (USA), B Barnes (Sco) 287; C Suneson (Eng), C Rocca (Ita), G Law (Sco) 288; DA Russell (Eng), B Ogle (Aus), J Daly (USA) 289; H Clark (Eng) 290; B Charles (NZ) 291; D Hospital (Esp), R Todd (Can), C Strange (USA), R Chapman (Eng) 292; R Goosen (RSA) 293; A Langenaeken (Bel) 298.

1995 Open Championship *at St Andrews* (6933–72)

Prize money: £1,250,000. Entries: 1836. Regional qualifying courses: Beau Desert, Blackwell, Glenbervie, Hankley Common, Lanark, Moortown, North Hants, Romford, Sherwood Forest, South Herts, Sundridge, Wilmslow. Final qualifying courses: Ladybank, Leven Links, Lundin, Scotscraig. Qualified for final 36 holes: 103 (including 4 amateurs).

1	J Daly (USA)*	67-71-73-71—282	£125000	20	P Mitchell (Eng)	73-74-71-70—288	13500
2	C Rocca (Ita)	69-70-70-73—282	100000		D Duval (USA)	71-75-70-72—288	13500
	Daly won four-hole play-off				A Coltart (Sco)	70-74-71-73—288	13500
3	S Bottomley (Eng)	70-72-72-69—283	65666		B Lane (Eng)	72-73-68-75—288	13500
	M Brooks (USA)	70-69-73-71—283	65666	24	L Janzen (USA)	73-73-71-72—289	10316
	M Campbell (NZ)	71-71-65-76—283	65666		S Webster (USA) (am)	70-72-74-73—289	
6	V Singh (Fij)	68-72-73-71—284	40500		B Langer (Ger)	72-71-73-73—289	10316
	S Elkington (Aus)	72-69-69-74—284	40500		J Parnevik (Swe)	75-71-70-73—289	10316
8	M James (Eng)	72-75-68-70—285	33333		M Calcavecchia (USA)	71-72-72-74—289	10316
	B Estes (USA)	72-70-71-72—285	33333		B Glasson (USA)	68-74-72-75—289	10316
	C Pavin (USA)	69-70-72-74—285	33333		K Tomori (Jpn)	70-68-73-78—289	10316
11	P Stewart (USA)	72-68-75-71—286	26000	31	R Drummond (Sco)	74-68-77-71—290	8122
	B Ogle (Aus)	73-69-71-73—286	26000		JM Olazábal (Esp)	72-72-74-72—290	8122
	S Torrance (Sco)	71-70-71-74—286	26000		D Frost (RSA)	72-72-74-72—290	8122
	E Els (RSA)	71-68-72-75—286	26000		H Sasaki (Jpn)	74-71-72-73—290	8122
15	G Norman (Aus)	71-74-72-70—287	18200		J Huston (USA)	71-74-72-73—290	8122
	R Allenby (Aus)	71-74-71-71—287	18200		P Jacobsen (USA)	71-76-70-73—290	8122
	B Crenshaw (USA)	67-72-76-72—287	18200		D Clarke (NI)	69-77-70-74—290	8122
	P-U Johansson (Swe)	69-78-68-72—287	18200		D Feherty (NI)	68-75-71-76—290	8122
	B Faxon (USA)	71-67-75-74—287	18200		T Watson (USA)	67-76-70-77—290	8122

Other players who made the cut: S Ballesteros (Esp), W Bennett (Eng) (am), P Mickelson (USA), M McNulty (Zim), N Faldo (Eng), B Watts (USA), G Sherry (Sco) (am), J Cook (USA), N Price (Zim) 291; I Woosnam (Wal), A Forsbrand (Swe), M O'Meara (USA), T Nakajima (Jpn), B Claar (USA), K Green (USA) 292; J Gallagher (USA), P O'Malley (Aus), R Claydon (Eng) 293; P Senior (Aus), P Broadhurst (Eng), D Cooper (Eng), E Herrera (Col), T Kite (USA), P Lawrie (Sco), M Gates (Eng), R Floyd (USA), J Leonard (USA), D Gilford (Eng) 294; P Baker (Eng), J Maggert (USA), J Lomas (Eng), F Nobilo (NZ), G Player (RSA), O Karlsson (Swe), M Hallberg (Swe), S Hoch (USA), G Hallberg (USA), J Rivero (Esp), T Woods (USA am) 295.

1994 Open Championship *at Turnberry* (6957–70)

Prize money: £1,100,000. Entries 1701. Regional qualifying courses: Blackwell, Glenbervie, Hankley Common, Lanark, Moortown, North Hants, Orsett, Sherwood Forest, South Herts, Sundridge Park, Wilmslow. Final qualifying courses: Glasgow Gailes, Irvine Bogside, Kilmarnock Barassie, Western Gailes. Qualified for final 36 holes: 81 (including 1 amateur). Non-qualifiers after 36 holes with scores of 143 or more: 75 (71 professionals, 4 amateurs)

1	N Price (Zim)	69-66-67-66—268	£110000	20	M Brooks (USA)	74-64-71-68—277	12500
2	J Parnevik (Swe)	68-66-68-67—269	88000		V Singh (Fij)	70-68-69-70—277	12500
3	F Zoeller (USA)	71-66-64-70—271	74000		G Turner (NZ)	65-71-70-71—277	12500
4	A Forsbrand (Swe)	72-71-66-64—273	50666		P Senior (Aus)	68-71-67-71—277	12500
	M James (Eng)	72-67-66-68—273	50666	24	B Estes (USA)	72-68-72-66—278	7972
	D Feherty (NI)	68-69-66-70—273	50666		T Price (Aus)	74-65-71-68—278	7972
7	B Faxon (USA)	69-65-67-73—274	36000		P Lawrie (Sco)	71-69-70-68—278	7972
8	N Faldo (Eng)	75-66-70-64—275	30000		J Maggert (USA)	69-74-67-68—278	7972
	T Kite (USA)	71-69-66-69—275	30000		T Lehman (USA)	70-69-70-69—278	7972
	C Montgomerie (Sco)	72-69-65-69—275	30000		E Els (RSA)	69-69-69-71—278	7972
11	R Claydon (Eng)	72-71-68-65—276	19333		M Springer (USA)	72-67-68-71—278	7972
	M McNulty (Zim)	71-70-68-67—276	19333		L Roberts (USA)	68-69-69-72—278	7972
	F Nobilo (NZ)	69-67-72-68—276	19333		P Jacobsen (USA)	69-70-67-72—278	7972
	J Lomas (Eng)	66-70-72-68—276	19333		C Stadler (USA)	71-69-66-72—278	7972
	M Calcavecchia (USA)	71-70-67-68—276	19333		A Coltart (Sco)	71-69-66-72—278	7972
	G Norman (Aus)	71-67-69-69—276	19333	35	M Davis (Eng)	75-68-69-67—279	6700
	L Mize (USA)	73-69-64-70—276	19333		L Janzen (USA)	74-69-69-67—279	6700
	T Watson (USA)	68-65-69-74—276	19333		G Evans (Eng)	69-69-73-68—279	6700
	R Rafferty (NI)	71-66-65-74—276	19333				

Other players who made the cut: D Gilford (Eng), D Hospital (Esp), JM Olazábal (Esp), S Ballesteros (Esp), B Marchbank (Eng), D Clarke (NI) 280; J Van De Velde (Fra), D Love III (USA), M Ozaki (Jpn) 280; J Gallagher jr (USA), D Edwards (USA), G Kraft (USA), H Twitty (USA) 281; D Frost (RSA), M Lanner (Swe), K Tomori (Jpn), T Watanabe (Jpn) 282; P Baker (Eng), J Cook (USA), T Nakajima (Jpn), B Watts (USA), R McFarlane (Eng) 283; G Brand jr (Sco), H Meshiai (Jpn), B Langer (Ger), C O'Connor jr (Irl), P-U Johansson (Swe), R Allenby (Aus), W Grady (Aus) 284; S Elkington (Aus), M Roe (Eng), L Clements (USA), C Mason (Eng), R Alvarez (Arg) 285; W Bennett (Eng) (am), W Riley (Aus) 286; A Lyle (Sco) 287; C Ronald (Eng), C Gillies (Eng) 288; B Crenshaw (USA), C Parry (Aus), J Haeggman (Swe) 289; N Henning (RSA) 291; J Daly (USA) 292.

Open Championship History

The Belt

Year	Winner	Score	Venue	Entrants
1860	W Park, Musselburgh	174	Prestwick	8
1861	T Morris sr, Prestwick	163	Prestwick	12
1862	T Morris sr, Prestwick	163	Prestwick	6
1863	W Park, Musselburgh	168	Prestwick	14
1864	T Morris sr, Prestwick	167	Prestwick	6
1865	A Strath, St Andrews	162	Prestwick	10
1866	W Park, Musselburgh	169	Prestwick	12
1867	T Morris sr, St Andrews	170	Prestwick	10
1868	T Morris jr, St Andrews	154	Prestwick	12
1869	T Morris jr, St Andrews	157	Prestwick	14
1870	T Morris jr, St Andrews	149	Prestwick	17

Having won it three times in succession the Belt became the property of Young Tom Morris and the Championship was held in abeyance for a year. In 1872 the Claret Jug was, and still is, offered for annual competition.

The Claret Jug

Year	Winner	Score	Venue	Entrants
1872	T Morris jr, St Andrews	166	Prestwick	8
1873	T Kidd, St Andrews	179	St Andrews	26
1874	M Park, Musselburgh	159	Musselburgh	32
1875	W Park, Musselburgh	166	Prestwick	18
1876	B Martin, St Andrews	176	St Andrews	34
(D Strath tied but refused to play off)				
1877	J Anderson, St Andrews	160	Musselburgh	24
1878	J Anderson, St Andrews	157	Prestwick	26
1879	J Anderson, St Andrews	169	St Andrews	46
1880	B Ferguson, Musselburgh	162	Musselburgh	30
1881	B Ferguson, Musselburgh	170	Prestwick	22
1882	B Ferguson, Musselburgh	171	St Andrews	40
1883	W Fernie, Dumfries	158	Musselburgh	41
(After a tie with B Ferguson, Musselburgh)				
1884	J Simpson, Carnoustie	160	Prestwick	30
1885	B Martin, St Andrews	171	St Andrews	51
1886	D Brown, Musselburgh	157	Musselburgh	46
1887	W Park jr, Musselburgh	161	Prestwick	36
1888	J Burns, Warwick	171	St Andrews	53
1889	W Park Jr, Musselburgh	155	Musselburgh	42
(After a tie with A Kirkaldy)				
1890	J Ball, Royal Liverpool (am)	164	Prestwick	40
1891	H Kirkaldy, St Andrews	166	St Andrews	82

After 1891 the competition was extended to 72 holes and for the first time entry money was imposed

1892	H Hilton, Royal Liverpool (am)	305	Muirfield	66
1893	W Auchterlonie, St Andrews	322	Prestwick	72
1894	J Taylor, Winchester	326	Sandwich, R St George's	94
1895	J Taylor, Winchester	322	St Andrews	73
1896	H Vardon, Ganton	316	Muirfield	64
(Vardon won a 36 hole play-off after a tie with a score of 157 to Taylor's 161)				
1897	H Hilton, Royal Liverpool (am)	314	Hoylake, R Liverpool	86
1898	H Vardon, Ganton	307	Prestwick	78
1899	H Vardon, Ganton	310	Sandwich, R St George's	98
1900	J Taylor, Mid-Surrey	309	St Andrews	81
1901	J Braid, Romford	309	Muirfield	101
1902	A Herd, Huddersfield	307	Hoylake, R Liverpool	112
1903	H Vardon, Totteridge	300	Prestwick	127
1904	J White, Sunningdale	296	Sandwich, R St George's	144
1905	J Braid, Walton Heath	318	St Andrews	152
1906	J Braid, Walton Heath	300	Muirfield	183
1907	A Massy, La Boulie	312	Hoylake, R Liverpool	193
1908	J Braid, Walton Heath	291	Prestwick	180

Open Championship Claret Jug winners history *continued*

Year	Winner	Score	Venue	Entrants
1909	J Taylor, Mid-Surrey	295	Deal, R Cinque Ports	204
1910	J Braid, Walton Heath	299	St Andrews	210
1911	H Vardon, Totteridge	303	Sandwich, R St George's	226

(After a tie with A Massy. The play-off was over 36 holes, but Massy picked up at the 35th hole before holing out. He had taken 148 for 34 holes, and when Vardon holed out at the 35th hole his score was 143)

Year	Winner	Score	Venue	Entrants
1912	E Ray, Oxhey	295	Muirfield	215
1913	J Taylor, Mid-Surrey	304	Hoylake, R Liverpool	269
1914	H Vardon, Totteridge	306	Prestwick	194
1915–19	*No Championship owing to World War I*			

Year	Winner	Score	Venue	Qualifiers	Entrants
1920	G Duncan, Hanger Hill	303	Deal, R Cinque Ports	81	190
1921	J Hutchison, Glenview, Chicago	296	St Andrews	85	158

(After a tie with R Wethered (am). Play-off scores: Hutchison 150; Wethered 159)

Year	Winner	Score	Venue	Qualifiers	Entrants
1922	W Hagen, Detroit, USA	300	Sandwich, R St George's	80	225
1923	A Havers, Coombe Hill	295	Troon	88	222
1924	W Hagen, Detroit, USA	301	Hoylake, R Liverpool	86	277
1925	J Barnes, USA	300	Prestwick	83	200
1926	R Jones, USA (am)	291	R Lytham and St Annes	117	293
1927	R Jones, USA (am)	285	St Andrews	108	207
1928	W Hagen, USA	292	Sandwich, R St George's	113	271
1929	W Hagen, USA	292	Muirfield	109	242
1930	R Jones, USA (am)	291	Hoylake, R Liverpool	112	296
1931	T Armour, USA	296	Carnoustie	109	215
1932	G Sarazen, USA	283	Sandwich, Prince's	110	224
1933	D Shute, USA	292	St Andrews	117	287

(After a tie with C Wood, USA. Play-off scores: Shute 149; Wood 154)

Year	Winner	Score	Venue	Qualifiers	Entrants
1934	T Cotton, Waterloo, Belgium	283	Sandwich, R St George's	101	312
1935	A Perry, Leatherhead	283	Muirfield	109	264
1936	A Padgham, Sundridge Park	287	Hoylake, R Liverpool	107	286
1937	T Cotton, Ashridge	290	Carnoustie	141	258
1938	R Whitcombe, Parkstone	295	Sandwich, R St George's	120	268
1939	R Burton, Sale	290	St Andrews	129	254
1940–45	*No Championship owing to Second World War*				
1946	S Snead, USA	290	St Andrews	100	225
1947	F Daly, Balmoral	293	Hoylake, R Liverpool	100	263
1948	T Cotton, Royal Mid-Surrey	284	Muirfield	97	272
1949	A Locke, RSA	283	Sandwich, R St George's	96	224

(After a tie with H Bradshaw, Kilcroney. Play-off scores: Locke 135; Bradshaw 147)

Year	Winner	Score	Venue	Qualifiers	Entrants
1950	A Locke, RSA	279	Troon	93	262
1951	M Faulkner, England	285	R Portrush	98	180
1952	A Locke, RSA	287	R Lytham and St Annes	96	275
1953	B Hogan, USA	282	Carnoustie	91	196
1954	P Thomson, Australia	283	Birkdale	97	349
1955	P Thomson, Australia	281	St Andrews	94	301
1956	P Thomson, Australia	286	Hoylake, R Liverpool	96	360
1957	A Locke, RSA	279	St Andrews	96	282
1958	P Thomson, Australia	278	R Lytham and St Annes	96	362

(After a tie with D Thomas, Sudbury. Play-off scores: Thomson 139; Thomas 143)

Year	Winner	Score	Venue	Qualifiers	Entrants
1959	G Player, RSA	284	Muirfield	90	285
1960	K Nagle, Australia	278	St Andrews	74	410
1961	A Palmer, USA	284	Birkdale	101	364
1962	A Palmer, USA	276	Troon	119	379
1963	R Charles, New Zealand	277	R Lytham and St Annes	119	261

(After a tie with P Rodgers, USA. Play-off scores: Charles 140; Rodgers 148)

Year	Winner	Score	Venue	Qualifiers	Entrants
1964	T Lema, USA	279	St Andrews	119	327
1965	P Thomson, Australia	285	R Birkdale	130	372
1966	J Nicklaus, USA	282	Muirfield	130	310
1967	R De Vicenzo, Argentina	278	Hoylake, R Liverpool	130	326
1968	G Player, RSA	289	Carnoustie	130	309
1969	A Jacklin, England	280	R Lytham and St Annes	129	424
1970	J Nicklaus, USA	283	St Andrews	134	468

(After a tie with Doug Sanders, USA. Play-off scores: Nicklaus 72; Sanders 73)

Year	Winner	Score	Venue	Qualifiers	Entrants
1971	L Trevino, USA	278	R Birkdale	150	528
1972	L Trevino, USA	278	Muirfield	150	570
1973	T Weiskopf, USA	276	Troon	150	569
1974	G Player, RSA	282	R Lytham and St Annes	150	679

Year	Winner	Score	Venue	Qualifiers	Entrants
1975	T Watson, USA	279	Carnoustie	150	629

(After a tie with J Newton, Australia. Play-off scores: Watson 71; Newton 72)

Year	Winner	Score	Venue	Qualifiers	Entrants
1976	J Miller, USA	279	R Birkdale	150	719
1977	T Watson, USA	268	Turnberry	150	730
1978	J Nicklaus, USA	281	St Andrews	150	788
1979	S Ballesteros, Spain	283	R Lytham and St Annes	150	885
1980	T Watson, USA	271	Muirfield	151	994
1981	B Rogers, USA	276	Sandwich, R St George's	153	971
1982	T Watson, USA	284	R Troon	150	1121
1983	T Watson, USA	275	R Birkdale	151	1107
1984	S Ballesteros, Spain	276	St Andrews		1413
1985	A Lyle, Scotland	282	Sandwich, R St George's	149	1361
1986	G Norman, Australia	280	Turnberry	152	1347
1987	N Faldo, England	279	Muirfield	153	1407
1988	S Ballesteros, Spain	273	R Lytham and St Annes	153	1393
1989	M Calcavecchia, USA	275	R Troon	156	1481

(Calcavecchia won a four-hole play-off after a tie with W Grady, Australia, and G Norman, Australia)

Year	Winner	Score	Venue	Qualifiers	Entrants
1990	N Faldo, England	270	St Andrews	152	1707
1991	I Baker-Finch, Australia	272	R Birkdale	156	1496
1992	N Faldo, England	272	Muirfield	156	1666
1993	G Norman, Australia	267	Sandwich, R St George's	156	1827
1994	N Price, Zimbabwe	268	Turnberry	156	1701
1995	J Daly, USA	282	St Andrews	159	1836

(Daly won a four-hole play-off after a tie with C Rocca, Italy)

Year	Winner	Score	Venue	Qualifiers	Entrants
1996	T Lehman, USA	271	R Lytham and St Annes	156	1918
1997	J Leonard, USA	272	R Troon	156	2133
1998	M O'Meara, USA	280	R Birkdale	152	2336

(O'Meara won a four-hole play-off after a tie with B Watts, USA)

Year	Winner	Score	Venue	Qualifiers	Entrants
1999	P Lawrie, Scotland	290	Carnoustie	156	2222

(Lawrie won a four-hole play-off after a tie with J Leonard, USA, and J Van de Velde, France)

Year	Winner	Score	Venue	Qualifiers	Entrants
2000	T Woods, USA	269	St Andrews	156	2477
2001	David Duval, USA	274	R Lytham and St Annes	156	2255
2002	Ernie Els, RSA	278	Muirfield	156	2260
2003	Ben Curtis, USA	283	Sandwich, R St George's	156	2152

Royal Troon hosts its eighth Open

Royal Troon Golf Club, a happy hunting ground for American professionals, has staged seven previous Open Championships stretching back to 1923 when Arthur Havers from Coombe Hill shot a winning total of 295. The Championship did not return again until 1950 when Bobby Locke won the second of his four Opens and few will forget the scenes in 1962 when Arnold Palmer, watched by crowds walking down the fairways for the last time, successfully defended the title he had won a year earlier at Royal Birkdale. In not the best of weather Tom Weiskopf won the Open and his only Major in 1973. By the time Tom Watson took his fourth Open title in 1982 the club had achieved Royal status. More recently Mark Calcavecchia in 1989 and Justin Leonard in 1997 have taken the famous Claret Jug back to American when they won over the tough Ayrshire links. Seven Opens won by one Englishman, one South African and five Americans!

The US Open Championship

Players are of American nationality unless stated

2003 US Open Championship (103rd) *at Olympia Fields, IL*

(7190–70)

Prize Money $6 million. Entries: 7820. Final Field: 156, of whom 68 (including 2 amateurs) made the half-way cut on 143 or less.

1	Jim Furyk	67-66-67-72—272	$1080000
2	Stephen Leaney (Aus)	67-68-68-72—275	650000
3	Kenny Perry	72-71-69-67—279	341367
	Mike Weir (Can)	73-67-68-71—279	341367
5	Ernie Els (RSA)	69-70-69-72—280	185934
	Fredrik Jacobson (Swe)	69-67-73-71—280	185934
	Nick Price (Zim)	71-65-69-75—280	185934
	Justin Rose (Eng)	70-71-70-69—280	185934
	David Toms	72-67-70-71—280	185934
10	Padraig Harrington (Irl)	69-72-72-68—281	124936
	Jonathan Kaye	70-70-72-69—281	124936
	Cliff Kresge	69-70-72-70—281	124936
	Billy Mayfair	69-71-67-74—281	124936
	Scott Verplank	76-67-68-70—281	124936
15	Jonathan Byrd	69-66-71-76—282	93359
	Tom Byrum	69-69-71-73—282	93359
	Tim Petrovic	69-70-70-73—282	93359
	Eduardo Romero (Arg)	70-66-70-76—282	93359
	Higemichi Tamaka (Jpn)	69-71-71-71—282	93359
20	Mark Calcavecchia	68-72-67-76—283	64170
	Robert Damron	69-68-73-73—283	64170
	Ian Leggatt (RSA)	68-70-68-77—283	64170
	Justin Leonard	66-70-72-75—283	64170
	Peter Lonard (Aus)	72-69-74-68—283	64170
	Vijay Singh (Fij)	70-63-72-78—283	64170
	Jay Williamson	72-69-69-73—283	64170
	Tiger Woods	70-66-75-72—283	64170
28	Stewart Cink	70-68-72-74—284	41254
	John Maginnes	72-70-72-70—284	41254
	Dicky Pride	71-69-66-78—284	41254
	Brett Quigley	65-74-71-74—284	41254
	Kevin Sutherland	71-71-72-70—284	41254
	Kirk Triplett	71-68-73-72—284	41254
	Tom Watson	65-72-75-72—284	41254
35	Angel Cabrera (Arg)	72-68-73-72—285	32552
	Chad Campbell	70-70-69-76—285	32552
	Chris DiMarco	72-71-71-71—285	32552
	Fred Funk	70-73-71-71—285	32552
	Sergio García (Esp)	69-74-71-71—285	32552
	Brandt Jobe	70-68-76-71—285	32552
	Mark O'Meara	72-68-67-78—285	32552
42	Darren Clarke (NI)	70-69-72-75—286	25002
	Retief Goosen (RSA)	71-72-73-70—286	25002
	Bernhard Langer (Ger)	70-70-73-73—286	25002

42T	Steve Lowery	70-72-70-74—286	25002
	Colin Montgomerie (Sco)	69-74-71-72—286	25002
	Loren Roberts	69-72-74-71—286	25002
48	Woody Austin	74-64-76-73—287	19025
	Marco Dawson	72-71-75-69—287	19025
	Niclas Fasth (Swe)	75-68-73-71—287	19025
	Dan Forsman	71-67-73-76—287	19025
	Darron Stiles	71-68-72-76—287	19025
53	Charles Howell III	70-73-74-71—288	17004
	John Rollins	73-70-68-77—288	17004
55	Lee Janzen	72-68-72-77—289	16199
	Phil Mickelson	70-70-75-74—289	16199
57	Trip Kuehne (am)	74-67-76-73—290	
	Len Mattiace	69-73-77-71—290	15643
59	Ricky Barnes (am)	71-71-79-70—291	
	Olin Browne	72-70-74-75—291	15347
61	Chris Anderson	72-70-78-72—292	14810
	Alexander Cejka (Ger)	73-66-76-77—292	14810
	Brian Davis (Eng)	71-72-74-75—292	14810
64	Jay Don Blake	66-77-75-75—293	14200
	JP Hayes	70-73-79-71—293	14200
66	Fred Couples	70-72-73-80—295	13711
	Brian Henninger	76-67-76-76—295	13711
68	Ryan Dillon	72-68-81-80—301	13334

The following players missed the half-way cut. All professionals received $1000 each:

69	Stuart Appleby (Aus)	75-69—144
	Rob Bradley	73-71—144
	Tim Clark (RSA)	69-75—144
	Joe Durant	72-72—144
	Steve Flesch	73-71—144
	Tom Gillis	68-76—144
	Neal Lancaster	72-72—144
	Spike McRoy	71-73—144
	Joe Ogilvie	70-74—144
	José María Olazábal (Esp)	74-70—144
	Craig Parry (Aus)	70-74—144
	Adam Scott (Aus)	72-72—144
81	Thomas Bjørn (Den)	71-74—145
	Craig Bowden	76-69—145
	Paul Casey (Eng)	76-69—145
	Dudley Hart	72-73—145
	John B Holmes	76-69—145
	Richard S Johnson (Swe)	71-74—145
	Geoff Ogilvy (Aus)	74-71—145
	Jesper Parnevik (Swe)	74-71—145
	Jeff Sluman	74-71—145
90	Robert Allenby (Aus)	75-71—146
	Christopher Baryla (am)	72-74—146
	Brian Gay	77-69—146
	Scott Hoch	70-76—146
	Trevor Immelman (RSA)	72-74—146
	Jeff Maggert	74-72—146
	Hunter Mahan (am)	74-72—146

90T	Hiroshi Matsuo (Jpn)	72-74—146
	Bryce Molder	74-72—146
	Geoffrey Fisk	76-70—146
	David Smail (NZ)	74-72—146
	Roland Thatcher	73-73—146
	Grant Waite (NZ)	74-72—146
	Dean Wilson	76-70—146
104	Doug Dunakey	73-74—147
	Bob Estes	70-77—147
	Jay Haas	75-72—147
	Jerry Kelly	75-72—147
	Bill Lunde	74-73—147
	Sean McCarty	78-69—147
	Rocco Mediate	73-74—147
	Toru Taniguchi (Jpn)	79-68—147
	Bob Tway	74-73—147
113	Bret Guetz	75-73—148
	Tom Kite	72-76—148
	Doug LaBelle II	72-76—148
	Maarten Lafeber (Ned)	75-73—148
	Shigeki Maruyama (Jpn)	75-73—148
	Larry Mize	76-72—148
	Corey Pavin	72-76—148
	Chris Riley	76-72—148
	Rory Sabbatini (RSA)	73-75—148
	Warren Schutte	77-71—148
	Mark Wurtz	76-72—148
124	Tommy Armour III	76-73—149
	Bob Burns	78-71—149
	Brad Elder	75-74—149

124T	Bill Haas	73-76—149
	Kent Jones	76-73—149
	Paul Lawrie (Sco)	75-74—149
	Luke List (am)	75-74—149
	Sean Murphy	78-71—149
	Rod Pampling	72-77—149
133	Billy Andrade	78-72—150
	Rich Beem	74-76—150
	David Duval	78-72—150
	Nick Faldo (Eng)	75-75—150
	Brad Faxon	73-77—150
138	Davis Love III	76-75—151
139	Steve Gotsche	76-76—152
	Rick Reinsberg	76-76—152
	Matt Seppanen	76-76—152
142	Anthony Arvidson	75-78—153
	Cortney Brisson	75-78—153
	Choi Kyoung-Ju (Kor)	79-74—153
	Scott McCarron	74-79—153
	Alan Morin	79-74—153
	Chez Reavie (am)	75-78—153
148	Michael Campbell (NZ)	74-80—154
	Chris Smith	77-77—154
150	Greg Hiller	78-77—155
151	Jason Knutzon	75-81—156
152	Don Pooley	81-76—157
	Joey Sindelar	76-81—157
154	Roy Biancalana	75-84—159
	Tom Glissmeyer (am)	80-79—159

2002 US Open at Bethpage Black Course, Farmingdale, NY (7214–70)

Prize money: $5.5 million. Entries: 8468

1	Tiger Woods	67-68-70-72—277	$1000000	24	Jim Carter	77-73-70-71—291	47439
2	Phil Mickelson	70-73-67-70—280	585000		Darren Clarke (NI)	74-74-72-71—291	47439
3	Jeff Maggert	69-73-68-72—282	362356		Chris DiMarco	74-74-72-71—291	47439
4	Sergio García (Esp)	68-74-67-74—283	252546		Ernie Els (RSA)	73-74-70-74—291	47439
5	Nick Faldo (Eng)	70-76-66-73—285	182882		Davis Love III	71-71-72-77—291	47439
	Scott Hoch	71-75-70-69—285	182882		Jeff Sluman	73-73-72-73—291	47439
	Billy Mayfair	69-74-68-74—285	182882	30	Jason Caron	75-72-72-73—292	35639
8	Tom Byrum	72-72-70-72—286	138669		Kyoung-Ju Choi		
	Padraig Harrington				(Kor)	69-73-73-77—292	35639
	(Irl)	70-68-73-75—286	138669		Paul Lawrie (Sco)	73-73-73-73—292	35639
	Nick Price (Zim)	72-75-69-70—286	138669		Scott McCarron	72-72-70-78—292	35639
11	Peter Lonard (Aus)	73-74-73-67—287	119357		Vijay Singh (Fij)	75-75-67-75—292	35639
12	Robert Allenby (Aus)	74-70-67-77—288	102338	35	Shingo Katayama		
	Jay Haas	73-73-70-72—288	102338		(Jpn)	74-72-74-73—293	31945
	Dudley Hart	69-76-70-73—288	102338		Bernhard Langer		
	Justin Leonard	73-71-68-76—288	102338		(Ger)	72-76-70-75—293	31945
16	Shigeki Maruyama			37	Stuart Appleby (Aus)	77-73-75-69—294	26783
	(Jpn)	76-67-73-73—289	86372		Thomas Bjørn (Den)	71-79-73-71—294	26783
	Steve Stricker	72-77-69-71—289	86372		Niclas Fasth (Swe)	72-72-74-76—294	26783
18	Luke Donald (Eng)	76-72-70-72—290	68995		Donnie Hammond	73-77-71-73—294	26783
	Charles Howell III	71-74-70-75—290	68995		Franklin Langham	70-76-74-74—294	26783
	Steve Flesch	72-72-75-71—290	68995		Rocco Mediate	72-72-74-76—294	26783
	Thomas Levet (Fra)	71-77-70-72—290	68995		Kevin Sutherland	74-75-70-75—294	26783
	Mark O'Meara	76-70-69-75—290	68995		Hidemichi Tanaka		
	Craig Stadler	74-72-70-74—290	68995		(Jpn)	73-73-72-76—294	26783

Other players who made the cut: Tom Lehman, Frank Lickliter, Kenny Perry, David Toms, Jean Van de Velde (Fra) 295; Craig Bowden, Tim Herron, Robert Karlsson (Swe), José María Olazábal (Esp) 296; Harrison Frazar, Ian Leggatt (Can), Jesper Parnevik (Swe), Corey Pavin 297; Brad Lardon 298; John Maginnes, Greg Norman (Aus), Bob Tway 299; Andy Miller, Jeev Milkha Singh (Ind), Paul Stankowski 300; Spike McRoy 301; Angel Cabrera (Arg), Brad Faxon 302; Kent Jones, Len Mattiace 303; John Daly, Tom Gillis 304; Kevin Warrick (am) 307.

2001 US Open at Southern Hills CC, Tulsa, OK (6874–71)

Prize money: $5,000,000. Entries: 8300

1	Retief Goosen* (RSA)	66-70-69-71—276	$900000	22T	Scott Verplank	71-71-73-71—286	54813
2	Mark Brooks	72-64-70-70—276	530000		Thomas Bjørn (Den)	72-69-73-72—286	54813
	(in play-off: Goosen 70, Brooks 72)			24	Mark Calcavecchia	70-74-73-70—287	42523
3	Stewart Cink	69-69-67-72—277	325310		Hal Sutton	70-75-71-71—287	42523
4	Rocco Mediate	71-68-67-72—278	226777		Tom Lehman	76-68-69-74—287	42523
5	Tom Kite	73-72-72-64—281	172912		Olin Browne	71-74-71-71—287	42523
	Paul Azinger	74-67-69-71—281	172912		Steve Lowery	71-73-72-71—287	42523
7	Davis Love III	72-69-71-70—282	125172		Joe Durant	71-74-70-72—287	42523
	Vijay Singh (Fij)	74-70-74-64—282	125172	30	Dean Wilson	71-74-72-71—288	30055
	Angel Cabrera (Arg)	70-71-72-69—282	125172		Bob Estes	70-72-75-71—288	30055
	Phil Mickelson	70-69-68-75—282	125172		Steve Jones	73-73-72-70—288	30055
	Kirk Triplett	72-69-71-70—282	125172		Gabriel Hjertstedt (Swe)	72-74-70-72—288	30055
12	Tiger Woods	74-71-69-69—283	91734		Padraig Harrington (Irl)	71-73-71-73—288	30055
	Sergio García (Esp)	70-68-68-77—283	91734		Jesper Parnevik (Swe)	73-73-74-68—288	30055
	Michael Allen	77-68-67-71—283	91734		Darren Clarke (NI)	74-71-71-72—288	30055
	Matt Gogel	70-69-74-70—283	91734		Bob May	72-72-69-75—288	30055
16	David Duval	70-69-71-74—284	75337		Bryce Molder (am)	75-71-68-74—288	
	Scott Hoch	73-73-69-69—284	75337		JL Lewis	68-68-77-75—288	30055
	Chris DiMarco	69-73-70-72—284	75337	40	Bernhard Langer (Ger)	71-73-71-74—289	23933
19	Corey Pavin	70-75-68-72—285	63426		Tim Herron	71-74-73-71—289	23933
	Chris Perry	72-71-73-69—285	63426		Briny Baird	71-72-70-76—289	23933
	Mike Weir (Can)	67-76-68-74—285	63426		Shaun Micheel	73-70-75-71—289	23933

Other players who made the cut: Fred Funk, Toshimitsu Izawa (Jpn), Brandel Chamblee, Jeff Maggert, Duffy Waldorf, Kevin Sutherland, Tom Byrum 290; Eduardo Romero (Arg) 291; Loren Roberts, Colin Montgomerie (Sco), Mark Wiebe, Bob Tway, Hale Irwin, José Coceres (Arg), Scott Dunlap, Brandt Jobe, Frank Lickliter, Jimmy Walker 292; Jim Furyk, Dudley Hart, Richard Zokol (Can), Tim Petrovic 293; Ernie Els (RSA), Peter Lonard (Aus), Dan Forsman, David Toms, Harrison Frazer, David Peoples 294; Nick Faldo (Eng), Franklin Langham 295; Anthony Kang (Kor), Mathias Grönberg (Swe), Gary Orr (Sco), Thongchai Jaidee (Tha) 296; Jim McGovern 297; Stephen Gangluff 301.

2000 US Open *at Pebble Beach, CA* (6874–71)

Prize money: $4,500,000. Entries: 8457 (record high)

1	Tiger Woods	65-69-71-67—272	$800000	22	Notah Begay III	74-75-72-73—294	53105
2	Miguel Angel Jiménez			23	Hal Sutton	69-73-83-70—295	45537
	(Esp)	66-74-76-71—287	391150		Bob May	72-76-75-72—295	45537
	Ernie Els (RSA)	74-73-68-72—287	391150		Tom Lehman	71-73-78-73—295	45537
4	John Huston	67-75-76-70—288	212779		Mike Brisky	71-73-79-72—295	45537
5	Padraig Harrington			27	Tom Watson	71-74-78-73—296	34066
	(Irl)	73-71-72-73—289	162526		Nick Price (Zim)	77-70-78-71—296	34066
	Lee Westwood (Eng)	71-71-76-71—289	162526		Steve Stricker	75-74-75-72—296	34066
7	Nick Faldo (Eng)	69-74-76-71—290	137203		Steve Jones	75-73-75-73—296	34066
8	Loren Roberts	68-78-73-72—291	112766		Hale Irwin	68-78-81-69—296	34066
	David Duval	75-71-74-71—291	112766	32	Tom Kite	72-77-77-71—297	28247
	Stewart Cink	77-72-72-70—291	112766		Chris Perry	75-72-78-72—297	28247
	Vijay Singh (Fij)	70-73-80-68—291	112766		Richard Zokol (Can)	74-74-80-69—297	28247
12	José María Olazábal				Rocco Mediate	69-76-75-77—297	28247
	(Esp)	70-71-76-75—292	86223		Lee Porter	74-70-83-70—297	28247
	Paul Azinger	71-73-79-69—292	86223	37	Woody Austin	77-70-78-73—298	22056
	Retief Goosen (RSA)	77-72-72-71—292	86223		Jerry Kelly	73-73-81-71—298	22056
	Michael Campbell				Larry Mize	73-72-76-77—298	22056
	(NZ)	71-77-71-73—292	86223		Craig Parry (Aus)	73-74-76-75—298	22056
16	Justin Leonard	73-73-75-72—293	65214		Bobby Clampett	68-77-76-77—298	22056
	Mike Weir (Can)	76-72-76-79—293	65214		Angel Cabrera (Arg)	69-76-79-74—298	22056
	Fred Couples	70-75-75-73—293	65214		Lee Janzen	71-73-79-75—298	22056
	Scott Hoch	73-76-75-69—293	65214		Ted Tryba	71-73-79-75—298	22056
	Phil Mickelson	71-73-73-76—293	65214		Charles Warren	75-74-75-74—298	22056
	David Toms	73-76-72-72—293	65214				

Other players who made the cut: Rick Hartmann, Sergio García (Esp), Colin Montgomerie (Sco), Scott Verplank, Thomas Bjørn (Den) 299; Warren Schutte (SA), Mark O'Meara 300; Darren Clarke (NI), Keith Clearwater, Jeff Coston 301; Kirk Triplett 302; Dave Eichelberger, Jimmy Green 303; Jeffrey Wilson (am) 304; Jim Furyk 305; Brandel Chamblee, Carlos Daniel Franco (Par) 306; Robert Damron 313.

1999 US Open *at Pinehurst No. 2, NC* (7175–70)

Prize money: $3,500,000. Entries: 7889 (record high)

1	P Stewart	68-69-72-70—279	$625000	17T	S Verplank	72-73-72-74—291	46756
2	P Mickelson	67-70-73-70—280	370000	23	MA Jiménez (Esp)	73-70-72-77—292	33505
3	V Singh (Fij)	69-70-73-69—281	196791		N Price (Zim)	71-74-74-73—292	33505
	T Woods	68-71-72-70—281	196791		T Scherrer	72-72-74-74—292	33505
5	S Stricker	70-73-69-73—285	130655		B Watts	69-73-77-73—292	33505
6	T Herron	69-72-70-75—286	116935		DA Weibring	69-74-74-75—292	33505
7	D Duval	67-70-75-75—287	96260	28	D Berganio jr	68-77-76-72—293	26185
	J Maggert	71-69-74-73—287	96260		T Lehman	73-74-73-73—293	26185
	H Sutton	69-70-76-72—287	96260	30	B Estes	70-71-77-76—294	23804
10	D Clarke (NI)	73-70-74-71—288	78862		G Sisk	71-72-76-75—294	23804
	B Mayfair	67-72-74-75—288	78862	32	S Cink	72-74-78-71—295	22448
12	P Azinger	72-72-75-70—289	67347		S Strüver (Ger)	70-76-75-74—295	22448
	P Goydos	67-74-74-74—289	67347	34	B Fabel	69-75-78-74—296	19083
	D Love III	70-73-74-72—289	67347		C Franco (Par)	69-77-73-77—296	19083
15	J Leonard	69-75-73-73—290	58214		G Hjertstedt (Swe)	75-72-79-70—296	19083
	C Montgomerie (Sco)	72-72-74-72—290	58214		R Mediate	69-72-76-79—296	19083
17	J Furyk	69-73-77-72—291	46756		C Parry (Aus)	69-73-79-75—296	19083
	J Haas	74-72-73-72—291	46756		S Pate	70-75-75-76—296	19083
	D Hart	73-73-76-69—291	46756		C Pavin	74-71-78-73—296	19083
	J Huston	71-69-75-76—291	46756		E Toledo (Mex)	70-72-76-78—296	19083
	J Parnevik (Swe)	71-71-76-73—291	46756				

Other players who made the cut: S Allan (Aus), G Hallberg, L Mattiace, C Perry 297; R Allenby (Aus), B Chamblee, L Janzen, D Lebeck, 298; S Elkington (Aus), C Tidland 299; G Kraft, S McRoy, P Price (Wal), J Tyska 300; J Kelly, T Watson, K Yokoo (Jpn) 301; J Cook, T Kite 302; C Smith, B Tway 303; L Mize 304; H Kuehne (am) 306; B Burns, T Tryba 308; J Daly 309.

1998 US Open at The Olympic Club, San Francisco, CA   (6797–70)

Prize money: $3,000,000. Entries: 7117

1	L Janzen	73-66-73-68—280	$535000	18T	JM Olazábal (Esp)	68-77-71-74—290	41833
2	P Stewart	66-71-70-74—281	315000		T Woods	74-72-71-73—290	41833
3	B Tway	68-70-73-73—284	201730	23	C Martin	74-71-74-72—291	34043
4	N Price (Zim)	73-68-71-73—285	140597		G Day	73-72-71-75—291	34043
5	S Stricker	73-71-69-73—286	107392	25	DA Weibring	72-72-75-73—292	25640
	T Lehman	68-75-68-75—286	107392		P-U Johansson (Swe)	71-75-73-73—292	25640
7	D Duval	75-68-75-69—287	83794		E Romero (Arg)	72-70-76-74—292	25640
	L Westwood (Eng)	72-74-70-71—287	83794		C Perry	74-71-72-75—292	25640
	J Maggert	69-69-75-74—287	83794		V Singh (Fij)	73-72-73-74—292	25640
10	J Sluman	72-74-74-68—288	64490		T Bjørn (Den)	72-75-70-75—292	25640
	P Mickelson	71-73-74-70—288	64490		M Carnevale	67-73-74-78—292	25640
	S Appleby (Aus)	73-74-70-71—288	64490	32	A Magee	70-76-78-69—293	18372
	S Cink	73-68-73-74—288	64490		P Harrington (Irl)	73-72-76-72—293	18372
14	P Azinger	75-72-77-65—289	52214		B Zabriski	74-71-74-74—293	18372
	J Parnevik (Swe)	69-74-76-70—289	52214		S Pate	72-75-73-73—293	18372
	M Kuchar (am)	70-69-76-74—289			J Huston	73-72-72-76—293	18372
	J Furyk	74-73-68-74—289	52214		J Durant	68-73-76-76—293	18372
18	C Montgomerie (Sco)	70-74-77-69—290	41833		C DiMarco	71-71-74-77—293	18372
	L Roberts	71-76-71-72—290	41833		L Porter	72-67-76-78—293	18372
	F Lickliter II	73-71-72-74—290	41833				

Other players who made the cut: J Leonard, S McCarron, F Nobilo (NZ) 294; D Clarke (NI), J Sindelar, T Kite, J Acosta jr, O Browne, J Nicklaus 295; E Els (RSA), M Reid, B Faxon, S Verplank 296; F Couples, T Herron, J Johnston, J Daly 297; M Brooks 298; S Simpson 300; R Walcher 303; T Sipula 305.

1997 US Open at Congressional CC, Bethesda, MD   (7213–70)

Prize money: $2,600,000. Entries: 7013

1	E Els (SA)	71-67-69-69—276	$465000	19T	P Stankowski	75-70-68-73—286	31915
2	C Montgomerie (Sco)	65-76-67-69—277	275000		H Sutton	66-73-73-74—286	31915
3	T Lehman	67-70-68-73—278	172828	24	L Mattiace	71-75-73-68—287	24173
4	J Maggert	73-66-68-74—281	120454		E Fryatt	72-73-73-69—287	24173
5	B Tway	71-71-70-70—282	79875		S Dunlap	75-66-75-71—287	24173
	O Browne	71-71-69-71—282	79875		S Elkington (Aus)	75-68-72-72—287	24173
	J Furyk	74-68-69-71—282	79875	28	P Goydos	73-72-74-69—288	17443
	J Haas	73-69-68-72—282	79875		P Azinger	72-72-74-70—288	17443
	T Tolles	74-67-69-72—282	79875		P Stewart	71-73-73-71—288	17443
10	S McCarron	73-71-69-70—283	56949		M McNulty (Zim)	67-73-75-73—288	17443
	S Hoch	71-68-72-72—283	56949		H Kase	68-73-73-74—288	17443
	D Ogrin	70-69-71-73—283	56949		F Zoeller	72-73-69-74—288	17443
13	L Roberts	72-69-72-71—284	47348		K Gibson	72-69-72-75—288	17443
	S Cink	71-67-74-72—284	47348	28	J Sluman	69-72-72-75—288	17443
	B Andrade	75-67-69-73—284	47348	36	J Leonard	69-72-78-70—289	13483
16	B Hughes (Aus)	75-70-71-69—285	40086		G Waite	72-74-72-71—289	13483
	JM Olazábal (Esp)	71-71-72-71—285	40086		S Stricker	66-76-75-72—289	13483
	D Love III	75-70-69-71—285	40086		M O'Meara	73-73-71-72—289	13483
19	N Price (Zim)	71-74-71-70—286	31915		S Appleby (Aus)	71-75-70-73—289	13483
	L Westwood (Eng)	71-71-73-71—286	31915		F Nobilo (NZ)	71-74-70-74—289	13483
	T Woods	74-67-73-72—286	31915		J Cook	72-71-71-75—289	13483

Other players who made the cut: D Clarke (NI), P Mickelson, F Funk, C Perry, C Parry (Aus) 290; J Parnevik (Swe), D Duval, N Faldo (Eng) 291; D White 292; L Janzen, J Nicklaus, H Irwin, F Couples, P Teravainen, P Broadhurst (Eng) 293; L Mize, C Rose 294; C Smith, D Waldorf, R Butcher, S Jones 295; T Watson 296; D Schreyer, B Crenshaw, B Faxon 297; T Kite, M Hulbert, G Kraft, J Morse, S Ames (Tri), T Björn (Den) 298; J Green 299; R Wylie, A Coltart (Sco) 300; D Mast, G Towne, V Singh (Fij), P Parker, D Hammond 301; J Ferenz 303; M Dawson 304; S Adams 306.

1996 US Open *at Oakland Hills, Birmingham, MI* (6990-70)

Prize money: $2,400,000. Entries: 5925

1	S Jones	74-66-69-69—278	$425000	16T	S Cink	69-73-70-73—285	33188
2	D Love III	71-69-70-69—279	204801		S Torrance (Sco)	71-69-71-74—285	33188
	T Lehman	71-72-65-71—279	204801	23	B Bryant	73-71-74-68—286	23806
4	J Morse	68-74-68-70—280	111235		P Jacobsen	71-74-70-71—286	23806
5	E Els (RSA)	72-67-72-70—281	84964		B Andrade	72-69-72-73—286	23806
	J Furyk	72-69-70-70—281	84964		W Austin	67-72-72-75—286	23806
7	S Hoch	73-71-71-67—282	66294	27	C Strange	74-73-71-69—287	17809
	V Singh (Fij)	71-72-70-69—282	66294		P Jordan	71-74-72-70—287	17809
	K Green	73-67-72-70—282	66294		J Nicklaus	72-74-69-72—287	17809
10	L Janzen	68-75-71-69—283	52591		P Stewart	67-71-76-73—287	17809
	G Norman (Aus)	73-66-74-70—283	52591		J Daly	72-69-73-73—287	17809
	C Montgomerie (Sco)	70-72-69-72—283	52591	32	M Swartz	72-72-74-70—288	14070
13	D Forsman	72-71-70-71—284	43725		T Purtzer	76-71-71-70—288	14070
	T Watson	70-71-71-72—284	43725		B Mayfair	72-71-74-71—288	14070
	F Nobilo (NZ)	69-71-70-74—284	43725		B Ogle (Aus)	70-75-72-71—288	14070
16	N Faldo (Eng)	72-71-72-70—285	33188		S Gotsche	72-70-74-72—288	14070
	D Begganio	69-72-72-72—285	33188		M Campbell (NZ)	70-73-73-72—288	14070
	M Brooks	76-68-69-72—285	33188		A Forsbrand (Swe)	74-71-71-72—288	14070
	M O'Meara	72-73-68-72—285	33188		S Murphy	71-75-68-74—288	14070
	J Cook	70-71-71-73—285	33188				

Other players who made the cut: L Parsons, JL Lucas, B Ford, S Simpson, W Riley (Aus), S Elkington (Aus), T Tolles, C Pavin, K Triplett, L Roberts 289; W Westner (RSA), B Gilder, K Perry, J Sluman, J Gullion, H Irwin, A Cejka (Ger), M Bradley, K Gibson, J Leonard 290; S Stricker, S Lowery, B Porter, W Murchison, R Leen (am), D Gilford (Eng), D Harrington 291; D Duval, A Morse, P Azinger, F Linklater II, M Ozaki (Jpn), C Rocca (Ita), W Grady (Aus), D Ogrin, P O'Malley (Aus), C Byrum, J Gallagher jr, B Tway 292; T Kuehne (am), M Christie, I Woosnam (Wal) 293; T Woods (am), J Huston, K Jones, S Kendall, S McCarron, T Kite, B Faxon, N Lancaster 294; C Parry (Aus), J Sanchez, J O'Keefe, J Haas 295; A Rodriguez, T Pernice jr, P Mickelson 296; J Maggert, J Thorpe, B McCallister (Aus), P Walton (Irl) 297; O Uresti, O Browne 298; G Trevisonno 299; M Wiebe 300; S Scott (am), R Yokota (Jpn) 301; M Burke jr 302; S Kelly 309.

1995 US Open *at Shinnecock Hills, NY* (6944-70)

Prize money: $2,000,000. Entries: 6,001

1	C Pavin	72-69-71-68—280	$350000	21T	B Ogle (Aus)	71-75-72-69—287	20085
2	G Norman (Aus)	68-67-74-73—282	207000		P Jordan	74-71-71-71—287	20085
3	T Lehman	70-72-67-74—283	131974		B Andrade	72-69-74-72—287	20085
4	N Lancaster	70-72-77-65—284	66633		S Verplank	72-69-71-75—287	20085
	J Maggert	69-72-77-66—284	66633		I Woosnam (Wal)	72-71-69-75—287	20085
	B Glasson	69-70-76-69—284	66633	28	C Montgomerie (Sco)	71-74-75-68—288	13912
	J Haas	70-73-72-69—284	66633		MA Jiménez (Esp)	72-72-75-69—288	13912
	D Love III	72-68-73-71—284	66633		M Hulbert	74-72-72-70—288	13912
	P Mickelson	68-70-72-74—284	66633		M Ozaki (Jpn)	69-68-80-71—288	13912
10	F Nobilo (NZ)	72-72-70-71—285	44184		S Simpson	67-75-74-72—288	13912
	V Singh (Fij)	70-71-72-72—285	44184		D Duval	70-73-73-72—288	13912
	B Tway	69-69-72-75—285	44184		JM Olazábal (Esp)	73-70-72-73—288	13912
13	M McCumber	70-71-77-68—286	30934		G Hallberg	70-76-69-73—288	13912
	D Waldorf	72-70-75-69—286	30934	36	B Porter	73-70-79-67—289	9812
	Brad Bryant	71-75-70-70—286	30934		R Floyd	74-72-76-67—289	9812
	J Sluman	72-69-74-71—286	30934		H Sutton	71-74-76-68—289	9812
	M Roe (Eng)	71-69-74-72—286	30934		C Strange	70-72-76-71—289	9812
	L Janzen	70-72-72-72—286	30934		G Boros	73-71-74-71—289	9812
	N Price (Zim)	66-73-73-74—286	30934		S Elkington (Aus)	72-73-73-71—289	9812
	S Stricker	71-70-71-74—286	30934		C Byrum	70-70-76-73—289	9812
21	F Zoeller	69-74-76-68—287	20085		B Langer (Ger)	74-67-74-74—289	9812
	P Stewart	74-71-73-69—287	20085				

Other players who made the cut: B Lane (Eng) 290; J McGovern, C Pena, O Uresti, J Daly, N Faldo (Eng), B Hughes 291; B Burns, E Romero (Arg), T Tryba, P Jacobsen, M Gogel 292; B Faxon, T Watson, C Perry, S Lowery, S Hoch, G Bruckner 293; J Gallagher, J Cook, B Jobe, D Edwards, P Goydos 294; T Kite, M Brisky, T Armour III 295; J Connelly 296; B Crenshaw, J Maginnes 297; J Gullion 301.

1994 US Open *at Oakmont, PA* (6946–71)

Prize money: $1,700,000. Entries: 6010

1	E Els (RSA)*	69-71-66-73—279	$320000
2	L Roberts	76-69-64-70—279	141828
	C Montgomerie (Sco)	71-65-73-70—279	141828

*Els won at second sudden-death play-off hole against Roberts after both shot 74 in 18-hole play-off. Montgomerie shot 78.

4	C Strange	70-70-70-70—280	75728
5	J Cook	73-65-73-71—282	61318
6	C Dennis	71-71-70-71—283	49485
	G Norman (Aus)	71-71-69-72—283	49485
	T Watson	68-73-68-74—283	49485
9	D Waldorf	74-68-73-69—284	37179
	J Maggert	71-68-75-70—284	37179
	J Sluman	72-69-72-71—284	37179
	F Nobilo (NZ)	69-71-68-76—284	37179
13	J McGovern	73-69-74-69—285	29767
	S Hoch	72-72-70-71—285	29767
	D Edwards	73-65-75-72—285	29767
16	F Couples	72-71-69-74—286	25899
	S Lowery	71-71-68-76—286	25899

18	S Verplank	70-72-75-70—287	22477
	S Ballesteros (Esp)	72-72-70-73—287	22477
	H Irwin	69-69-71-78—287	22477
21	S Torrance (Sco)	72-71-76-69—288	19464
	S Pate	74-66-71-77—288	19464
23	B Langer (Ger)	72-72-73-72—289	17223
	K Triplett	70-71-71-77—289	17223
25	M Springer	74-72-73-71—290	14705
	C Parry (Aus)	78-68-71-73—290	14705
	C Beck	73-73-70-74—290	14705
28	D Love III	74-72-74-72—292	11514
	J Furyk	74-69-74-75—292	11514
	L Clements	73-71-73-75—292	11514
	J Nicklaus	69-70-77-76—292	11514
	M Ozaki (Jpn)	70-73-69-80—292	11514
33	M Carnevale	75-72-76-70—293	9578
	T Lehman	77-68-73-75—293	9578
	F Allen	73-70-74-76—293	9578
	T Kite	73-71-72-77—293	9578
	B Crenshaw	71-74-70-78—293	9578

Other players who made the cut: B Hughes, P Baker (Eng), G Brand Jr (Sco), B Jobe 294; F Quinn jr 295; P Goydos, F Funk, D Walsworth 296; T Dunlavey, O Browne, B Lane (Eng), M Emery, D Bergano, J Gallagher jr, W Levi, P Mickelson 297; T Armour III, H Royer III, S Simpson 298; S Richardson (Eng), F Zoeller 299; D Rummells, D Martin 301; E Humenik, M Smith, M Aubrey 302.

US Open Championship History

Year	Winner	Runner-up	Venue	Score
1894	W Dunn	W Campbell	St Andrews, NY	2 holes

After 1894 decided by stroke play

Year	Winner	Venue	Score
1895	HJ Rawlins	Newport	173
1896	J Foulis	Southampton	152
1897	J Lloyd	Wheaton, IL	162
1898	F Herd	Shinnecock Hills	328
72 holes played from 1898			
1899	W Smith	Baltimore	315
1900	H Vardon (Eng)	Wheaton, IL	313
1901	W Anderson	Myopia, MA	315
(After a tie with A Smith. Play-off: Anderson 85, Smith 86)			
1902	L Auchterlonie	Garden City	305
1903	W Anderson	Baltusrol	307
(After a tie with D Brown Play-off: Anderson 82, Brown 84)			
1904	W Anderson	Glenview	304
1905	W Anderson	Myopia, MA	335
1906	A Smith	Onwentsia	291
1907	A Ross	Chestnut Hill, PA	302
1908	F McLeod	Myopia, MA	322
(After a tie with W Smith. Play-off: McLeod 77, Smith 83)			
1909	G Sargent	Englewood, NJ	290
1910	A Smith	Philadelphia	289
(After a tie with J McDermott and M Smith)			
1911	J McDermott	Wheaton, IL	307
(After a tie with M Brady and G Simpson.			
Play-off: McDermott 80, Brady 82, Simpson 85)			
1912	J McDermott	Buffalo, NY	294
1913	F Ouimet (am)	Brookline, MA	304
(After a tie with H Vardon and E Ray)			
1914	W Hagen	Midlothian	297
1915	J Travers (am)	Baltusrol	290

Year	Winner	Venue	Score
1916	C Evans (am)	Minneapolis	286
1917-18	*No Championship*		
1919	W Hagen	Braeburn	301
(After a tie with M Brady. Play-off: Hagen 77, Brady 78)			
1920	E Ray (Eng)	Inverness	295
1921	J Barnes	Washington	289
1922	G Sarazen	Glencoe	288
1923	R Jones jr (am)	Inwood, LI	295
(After a tie with R Cruikshank.. Play-off: Jones 76,			
Cruikshank 78)			
1924	C Walker	Oakland Hills	297
1925	W MacFarlane	Worcester	291
(After a tie with R Jones jr. Play-off: MacFarlane 75-72,			
Jones 75-73)			
1926	R Jones jr (am)	Scioto	293
1927	T Armour	Oakmont	301
(After a tie with H Cooper. Play-off: Armour 76, Cooper 79)			
1928	J Farrell	Olympia Fields	294
(After a tie with R Jones jr. Play-off: Farrell 143, Jones 144)			
1929	R Jones jr (Am)	Winged Foot, NY	294
(After a tie with A Espinosa. Play-off: Jones 141,			
Espinosa 164)			
1930	R Jones jr (am)	Interlachen	287
1931	B Burke	Inverness	292
(After a tie with G von Elm. Play-off: Burke 149-148,			
von Elm 149-149)			
1932	G Sarazen	Fresh Meadow	286
1933	J Goodman (am)	North Shore	287
1934	O Dutra	Merion	293

Year	Winner	Venue	Score
1935	S Parks	Oakmont	299
1936	T Manero	Springfield	282
1937	R Guldahl	Oakland Hills	281
1938	R Guldahl	Cherry Hills	284
1939	B Nelson	Philadelphia	284
(After a tie with C Wood and D Shute)			
1940	W Lawson Little	Canterbury, OH	287
(After a tie with G Sarazen. Play-off: Little 70, Sarazen 73)			
1941	C Wood	Fort Worth, TX	284
1942–45	No Championship		
1946	L Mangrum	Canterbury	284
(After a tie with B Nelson and V Ghezzie)			
1947	L Worsham	St Louis	282
(After a tie with S Snead. Play-off: Worsham 69, Snead 70)			
1948	B Hogan	Los Angeles	276
1949	Dr C Middlecoff	Medinah, IL	286
1950	B Hogan	Merion, PA	287
(After a tie with L Mangrum and G Fazio. Play-off: Hogan 69, Mangrum 73, Fazio 75)			
1951	B Hogan	Oakland Hills, MI	287
1952	J Boros	Dallas, TX	281
1953	B Hogan	Oakmont	283
1954	E Furgol	Baltusrol	284
1955	J Fleck	San Francisco	287
(After a tie with B Hogan. Play-off: Fleck 69, Hogan 72)			
1956	Dr C Middlecoff	Rochester, NY	281
1957	D Mayer	Inverness	282
(After a tie with Dr C Middlecoff. Play-off: Mayer 72, Middlecoff 79)			
1958	T Bolt	Tulsa, OK	283
1959	W Casper	Winged Foot, NY	282
1960	A Palmer	Denver, CO	280
1961	G Littler	Birmingham, MI	281
1962	J Nicklaus	Oakmont	283
(After a tie with A Palmer. Play-off: Nicklaus 71, Palmer 74)			
1963	J Boros	Brookline, MA	293
(After a tie. Play-off: J Boros 70, J Cupit 73, A Palmer 76)			
1964	K Venturi	Washington	278
1965	G Player (RSA)	St Louis, MO	282
(After a tie with K Nagle. Play-off: Player 71, Nagle 74)			
1966	W Casper	San Francisco	278
(After a tie with A Palmer. Play-off: Casper 69, Palmer 73)			
1967	J Nicklaus	Baltusrol	275
1968	L Trevino	Rochester, NY	275
1969	O Moody	Houston, TX	281

Year	Winner	Venue	Score
1970	A Jacklin (Eng)	Hazeltine, MN	281
1971	L Trevino	Merion, PA	280
(After a tie with J Nicklaus. Play-off: Trevino 68, Nicklaus 71)			
1972	J Nicklaus	Pebble Beach	290
1973	J Miller	Oakmont, PA	279
1974	H Irwin	Winged Foot, NY	287
1975	L Graham	Medinah, IL	287
(After a tie with Mahaffey. Play-off: Graham 71, Mahaffey 73)			
1976	J Pate	Atlanta, GA	277
1977	H Green	Southern Hills, Tulsa	278
1978	A North	Cherry Hills	285
1979	H Irwin	Inverness, OH	284
1980	J Nicklaus	Baltusrol	272
1981	D Graham (Aus)	Merion, PA	273
1982	T Watson	Pebble Beach	282
1983	L Nelson	Oakmont, PA	280
1984	F Zoeller	Winged Foot	276
(After a tie with G Norman. Play-off: Zoeller 67, Norman 75)			
1985	A North	Oakland Hills, MI	279
1986	R Floyd	Shinnecock Hills, NY	279
1987	S Simpson	Olympic, San Francisco	277
1988	C Strange	Brookline, MA	278
(After a tie with N Faldo. Play-off: Strange 71, Faldo 75)			
1989	C Strange	Rochester, NY	278
1990	H Irwin	Medinah	280
(After a tie with M Donald. Won at 1st extra hole after 18-hole play-off tie)			
1991	P Stewart	Hazeltine, MN	282
(After a tie with S Simpson. Play-off: Stewart 75, Simpson 77)			
1992	T Kite	Pebble Beach, FL	285
1993	L Janzen	Baltusrol	272
1994	E Els (RSA)	Oakmont, PA	279
(After a tie with L Roberts and C Montgomerie. Play-off: Els 74, Roberts 74, Montgomerie 78. Els then defeated Roberts at the second hole of a sudden death play-off)			
1995	C Pavin	Shinnecock Hills, NY	280
1996	S Jones	Oakland Hills, MI	278
1997	E Els (RSA)	Congressional, Bethesda	276
1998	L Janzen	Olympic, San Francisco	280
1999	P Stewart	Pinehurst No. 2, NC	279
2000	T Woods	Pebble Beach, CA	272
2001	R Goosen (RSA)	Southern Hills CC, OK	276
2002	T Woods	Farmingdale, NY	277
2003	J Furyk	Olympia Fields, IL	272

World Championship Dates 2004

Feb 25–29   Accenture Match Play Championship, La Costa Resort and Spa, California, USA

Aug 19–22   NEC Invitational, Firestone CC, Akron, Ohio., USA

Sept 30–Oct 3   American Express Championship, Mount Juliet, Kilkenny, Ireland.

Nov 18–21   World Cup, Real Club de Golf de Seville, Seville, Spain.

The Masters

Players are of American nationality unless stated.   Held annually at Augusta National GC, GA

2003 Masters (67th)   (7290–72)

Prize Money: $6,000,000.   Final field of 93 of whom 49 (with 3 amateurs) survived the half-way cut on 149 or better.

1	Mike Weir (Can)*	70-68-75-68—281	$1080000
2	Len Mattiace	73-74-69-65—281	648000
	(Weir won at first extra hole of play-off)		
3	Phil Mickelson	73-70-72-68—283	408000
4	Jim Furyk	73-72-71-68—284	288000
5	Jeff Maggert	72-73-66-75—286	240000
6	Ernie Els (RSA)	79-66-72-70—287	208500
	Vijay Singh (Fij)	73-71-70-73—287	208500
8	Jonathan Byrd	74-71-71-72—288	162000
	José María Olazábal (Esp)	73-71-71-73—288	162000
	Mark O'Meara	76-71-70-71—288	162000
	David Toms	71-73-70-74—288	162000
	Scott Verplank	76-73-70-69—288	162000
13	Tim Clark (RSA)	72-75-71-71—289	120000
	Retief Goosen (RSA)	73-74-72-70—289	120000
15	Rich Beem	74-72-71-73—290	93000
	Angel Cabrera (Arg)	76-71-71-72—290	93000
	Choi Kyoung-Ju (Kor)	76-69-72-73—290	93000
	Paul Lawrie (Sco)	72-72-73-73—290	93000
	Davis Love III	77-71-71-71—290	93000
	Tiger Woods	76-73-66-75—290	93000
21	Ricky Barnes (am)	69-74-75-73—291	
22	Bob Estes	76-71-74-71—292	72000
23	Brad Faxon	73-71-79-70—293	57600
	Scott McCarron	77-71-72-73—293	57600
	Nick Price (Zim)	70-75-72-76—293	57600
	Chris Riley	76-72-70-75—293	57600
	Adam Scott (Aus)	77-72-74-70—293	57600
28	Darren Clarke (NI)	66-76-78-74—294	43500
	Fred Couples	73-75-69-77—294	43500
	Sergio García (Esp)	69-78-74-73—294	43500
	Charles Howell III	73-72-76-73—294	43500
	Hunter Mahan (am)	73-72-73-76—294	
33	Nick Faldo (Eng)	74-73-75-73—295	36375
	Rocco Mediate	73-74-73-75—295	36375
	Loren Roberts	74-72-76-73—295	36375
	Kevin Sutherland	77-72-76-70—295	36375
37	Shingo Katayama (Jpn)	74-72-76-74—296	31650
	Billy Mayfair	75-70-77-74—296	31650
39	Robert Allenby (Aus)	76-73-74-74—297	27000
	Craig Parry (Aus)	74-73-75-75—297	27000
	Kenny Perry	76-72-78-71—297	27000
	Justin Rose (Eng)	73-76-71-77—297	27000
	Philip Tataurangi (NZ)	75-70-74-78—297	27000
44	Jeff Sluman	75-72-76-75—298	23400
45	Ryan Moore (am)	73-74-75-79—301	
	Pat Perez	74-73-79-75—301	22200
47	John Rollins	74-71-80-77—302	21000

| 48 | Jerry Kelly | 72-76-77-79—304 | 19800 |
| 49 | Craig Stadler | 76-73-79-77—305 | 18600 |

The following players missed the half-way cut. Each professional player received $5000:

50	Padraig Harrington (Irl)	77-73—150
	Scott Hoch	77-73—150
	Shigeki Maruyama (Jpn)	75-75—150
	Eduardo Romero (Arg)	74-76—150
	Toru Taniguchi (Jpn)	71-79—150
55	Steve Elkington (Aus)	75-76—151
	Lee Janzen	78-73—151
	Tom Lehman	75-76—151
58	Larry Mize	78-74—152
	Tom Watson	75-77—152
60	Stuart Appleby (Aus)	77-76—153
	Miguel Angel Jiménez (Esp)	76-77—153
62	Chad Campbell	77-77—154

62T	Niclas Fasth (Swe)	81-73—154
	Toshimitsu Izawa (Jpn)	78-76—154
	Steve Lowery	78-76—154
	Colin Montgomerie (Sco)	78-76—154
	Kirk Triplett	82-72—154
	Ian Woosnam (Wal)	80-74—154
69	Michael Campbell (NZ)	78-77—155
	Ben Crenshaw	79-76—155
	Fred Funk	79-76—155
	Jay Haas	79-76—155
	Bernhard Langer (Ger)	79-76—155
	Justin Leonard	82-73—155
	Sandy Lyle (Sco)	82-73—155
	Craig Perks (NZ)	80-75—155
	Fuzzy Zoeller	77-78—155

78	John Cook	78-78—156
	John Huston	73-83—156
	Thomas Levet (Fra)	79-77—156
81	Tom Byrum	82-75—157
	Raymond Floyd	77-80—157
83	Peter Lonard (Aus)	78-82—160
84	Seve Ballesteros (Esp)	77-85—162
	David Duval	79-83—162
	Jack Nicklaus	85-77—162
	Gary Player	82-80—162
88	Alejandro Larrazabal (Esp) (am)	82-81—163
89	Charles Coody	83-81—164
90	Arnold Palmer	83-83—166
91	George Zahringer (am)	82-85—167
92	Tommy Aaron	92-80—172
93	Chris DiMarco	82-W/D

2002 Masters

Prize money: $5,600,000. Entries: 89, of whom two withdrew and 45 (with no amateurs) made the half-way cut.

1	Tiger Woods	70-69-66-71—276	$1008000
2	Retief Goosen (RSA)	69-67-69-74—279	604800
3	Phil Mickelson	69-72-68-71—280	380800
4	José María Olazábal (Esp)	70-69-71-71—281	268800
5	Ernie Els (RSA)	70-67-72-73—282	212800
	Padraig Harrington (Irl)	69-70-72-71—282	212800
7	Vijay Singh (Fij)	70-65-72-76—283	187600
8	Sergio García (Esp)	68-71-70-75—284	173600
9	Angel Cabrera (Arg)	68-71-73-73—285	151200
	Miguel Angel Jiménez (Esp)	70-71-74-70—285	151200
	Adam Scott (Aus)	71-72-72-70—285	151200
12	Chris DiMarco	70-71-72-73—286	123200
	Brad Faxon	71-75-69-71—286	123200
14	Nick Faldo (Eng)	75-67-73-72—287	98000
	Davis Love III	67-75-74-71—287	98000
	Shigeki Maruyama (Jpn)	75-72-73-67—287	98000
	Colin Montgomerie (Sco)	75-71-70-71—287	98000
18	Thomas Bjørn (Den)	74-67-70-77—288	81200
	Paul McGinley (Irl)	72-74-71-71—288	81200
20	Darren Clarke (NI)	70-74-73-72—289	65240
	Jerry Kelly	72-74-71-72—289	65240
20T	Justin Leonard	70-75-74-70—289	65240
	Nick Price (Zim)	70-76-70-73—289	65240
24	Mark Brooks	74-72-71-73—290	46480
	Stewart Cink	74-70-72-74—290	46480
	Tom Pernice	74-72-71-73—290	46480
	Jeff Sluman	73-72-71-74—290	46480
	Mike Weir (Can)	72-71-71-76—290	46480
29	Robert Allenby (Aus)	73-70-76-72—291	38080
	Charles Howell III	74-73-71-73—291	38080
	Jesper Parnevik (Swe)	70-72-77-72—291	38080
32	John Daly	74-73-70-75—292	32410
	Bernhard Langer (Ger)	73-72-73-74—292	32410
	Billy Mayfair	74-71-72-75—292	32410
	Craig Stadler	73-72-76-71—292	32410
36	Fred Couples	73-73-76-72—294	26950
	Rocco Mediate	75-68-77-74—294	26950
	Greg Norman (Aus)	71-76-72-75—294	26950
	David Toms	73-74-76-71—294	26950
40	Steve Lowery	75-71-76-73—295	22960
	Kirk Triplett	74-70-74-77—295	22960
	Tom Watson	71-76-76-72—295	22960
43	Scott Verplank	70-75-76-75—296	20720
44	Lee Westwood (Eng)	75-72-74-76—297	19600
45	Bob Estes	73-72-75-78—298	18480

2001 Masters

Prize money: $5,574,920. Entries: 93, of whom 47 made the half-way cut.

	Player	Scores	Prize
1	Tiger Woods	70-66-68-68—272	$1008000
2	David Duval	71-66-70-67—274	604800
3	Phil Mickelson	67-69-69-70—275	380800
4	Toshimitsu Izawa (Jpn)	71-66-74-67—278	246400
	Mark Calcavecchia	72-66-68-72—278	246400
6	Bernhard Langer (Ger)	73-69-68-69—279	181300
	Jim Furyk	69-71-70-69—279	181300
	Ernie Els (RSA)	71-68-68-72—279	181300
	Kirk Triplett	68-70-70-71—279	181300
10	Brad Faxon	73-68-68-71—280	128800
	Steve Stricker	66-71-72-71—280	128800
	Miguel Angel Jiménez (Esp)	68-72-71-69—280	128800
	Angel Cabrera (Arg)	66-71-70-73—280	128800
	Chris DiMarco	65-69-72-74—280	128800
15	José María Olazábal (Esp)	70-68-71-72—281	95200
	Paul Azinger	70-71-71-69—281	95200
	Rocco Mediate	72-70-66-73—281	95200
18	Vijay Singh (Fij)	69-71-73-69—282	81200
	Tom Lehman	75-68-71-68—282	81200
20	Mark O'Meara	69-74-72-68—283	65240
	Jesper Parnevik (Swe)	71-71-72-69—283	65240
	John Huston	67-75-72-69—283	65240
	Jeff Maggert	72-70-70-71—283	65240
24	Darren Clarke (NI)	72-67-72-73—284	53760
25	Tom Scherrer	71-71-70-73—285	49280
26	Fred Couples	74-71-73-68—286	44800
27	Padraig Harrington (Irl)	75-69-72-71—287	40600
	Justin Leonard	73-71-72-71—287	40600
	Mike Weir (Can)	74-69-72-72—287	40600
	Steve Jones	74-70-72-71—287	40600
31	Stuart Appleby (Aus)	72-70-70-76—288	33208
	Mark Brooks	70-71-77-70—288	33208
	Duffy Waldorf	72-70-71-75—288	33208
	Lee Janzen	67-70-72-79—288	33208
	David Toms	72-72-71-73—288	33208
36	Hal Sutton	74-69-71-75—289	28840
37	Loren Roberts	71-74-73-72—290	26320
	Chris Perry	68-74-74-74—290	26320
	Scott Hoch	74-70-72-74—290	26320
40	Steve Lowery	72-72-78-70—292	22960
	Shingo Katayama (Jpn)	75-70-73-74—292	22960
	Franklin Langham	72-73-75-72—292	22960
43	Dudley Hart	74-70-78-71—293	19600
	Bob May	71-74-73-75—293	19600
	Jonathan Kaye	74-71-74-74—293	19600
46	Carlos Franco (Par)	71-71-77-75—294	17360
47	Robert Allenby (Aus)	71-74-75-75—295	16240

2000 Masters

Prize money: $4,617,000. Entries: 95, of whom 57 made the half-way cut.

	Player	Scores	Prize
1	Vijay Singh (Fij)	72-67-70-69—278	$828000
2	Ernie Els (RSA)	72-67-74-68—281	496800
3	Loren Roberts	73-69-71-69—282	266800
	David Duval	73-65-74-70—282	266800
5	Tiger Woods	75-72-68-69—284	184000
6	Tom Lehman	69-72-75-69—285	165600
7	Davis Love III	75-72-68-71—286	143367
	Carlos Franco (Par)	79-68-70-69—286	143367
	Phil Mickelson	71-68-76-71—286	143367
10	Hal Sutton	72-75-71-69—287	124200
11	Greg Norman (Aus)	80-68-70-70—288	105800
	Nick Price (Zim)	74-69-73-72—288	105800
	Fred Couples	76-72-70-70—288	105800
14	Chris Perry	73-75-72-69—289	80500
	Jim Furyk	73-74-71-71—289	80500
	John Huston	77-69-72-71—289	80500
	Dennis Paulson	68-76-73-72—289	80500
18	Jeff Sluman	73-69-77-71—290	69000
19	Padraig Harrington (Irl)	76-69-75-71—291	53820
	Steve Stricker	70-73-75-73—291	53820
	Jean Van de Velde (Fra)	76-70-75-70—291	53820
	Colin Montgomerie (Sco)	76-69-77-69—291	53820
	Bob Estes	72-71-77-71—291	53820
	Glen Day	79-67-74-71—291	53820
25	Larry Mize	78-67-73-74—292	37567
	Craig Parry (Aus)	75-71-72-74—292	37567
	Steve Jones	71-70-76-75—292	37567
28	Nick Faldo (Eng)	72-72-74-75—293	28673
	Bernhard Langer (Ger)	71-71-75-76—293	28673
28T	Justin Leonard	72-71-77-73—293	28673
	Stewart Cink	75-72-72-74—293	28673
	Mike Weir (Can)	75-70-70-78—293	28673
	Dudley Hart	75-71-72-75—293	28673
	Paul Azinger	72-72-77-72—293	28673
	Masashi Ozaki (Jpn)	72-72-74-75—293	28673
	Thomas Bjørn (Den)	71-77-73-72—293	28673
37	Fred Funk	75-68-78-73—294	21620
	Jay Haas	75-71-75-73—294	21620
	Notah Begay III	74-74-73-73—294	21620
40	Ian Woosnam (Wal)	74-70-76-75—295	17480
	Sergio García (Esp)	70-72-75-78—295	17480
	Jesper Parnevik (Swe)	77-71-70-77—295	17480
	Darren Clarke (NI)	72-71-78-74—295	17480
	Mark Brooks	72-76-73-74—295	17480
	Retief Goosen (RSA)	73-69-79-74—295	17480
46	Shigeki Maruyama (Jpn)	76-71-74-75—296	13800
	Scott Gump	75-70-78-73—296	13800
48	Brandt Jobe	73-74-76-74—297	12604
49	Miguel Angel Jiménez (Esp)	76-71-79-72—298	11623
	Steve Pate	78-69-77-74—298	11623
	David Toms	74-72-73-79—298	11623
52	Steve Elkington (Aus)	74-74-78-73—299	10948
	Rocco Mediate	71-74-75-79—299	10948
54	Jack Nicklaus	74-70-81-78—303	10672
	David Gossett (am)	75-71-79-78—303	10672
56	Skip Kendall	76-72-77-83—308	10580
57	Tommy Aaron	72-74-86-81—313	10488

1999 Masters

Prize money: $3,200,000. Entries: 96, of whom 56 made the half-way cut.

	Player	Score	Prize		Player	Score	Prize
1	JM Olazábal (Esp)	70-66-73-71—280	$720000	27T	E Els (RSA)	71-72-69-80—292	29000
2	D Love III	69-72-70-71—282	432000		R Mediate	73-74-69-76—292	29000
3	G Norman (Aus)	71-68-71-73—283	272000	31	T Lehman	73-72-73-75—293	23720
4	B Estes	71-72-69-72—284	176000		S Maruyama (Jpn)	78-70-71-74—293	23720
	S Pate	71-75-65-73—284	176000		M O'Meara	70-76-69-78—293	23720
6	D Duval	71-74-70-70—285	125200		J Sluman	70-75-70-78—293	23720
	C Franco (Par)	72-72-68-73—285	125200		B Watts	73-73-70-77—293	23720
	P Mickelson	74-69-71-71—285	125200	36	J Huston	74-72-71-77—294	20100
	N Price (Zim)	69-72-72-72—285	125200		A Magee	70-77-72-75—294	20100
	L Westwood (Eng)	75-71-68-71—285	125200	38	B Andrade	76-72-72-75—295	18800
11	S Elkington (Aus)	72-70-71-74—287	92000		M Brooks	76-72-75-72—295	18800
	B Langer (Ger)	76-66-72-73—287	92000		R Floyd	74-73-72-76—295	18800
	C Montgomerie (Sco)	70-72-71-74—287	92000		C Stadler	72-76-70-77—295	18800
14	J Furyk	72-73-70-73—288	70000		S Stricker	75-72-69-79—295	18800
	L Janzen	70-69-73-76—288	70000		S García (Esp) (am)	72-75-75-73—295	
	B Jobe	72-71-74-71—288	70000	44	J Haas	74-69-79-75—297	14000
	I Woosnam (Wal)	71-74-71-72—288	70000		T Herron	75-69-74-79—297	14000
18	B Chamblee	69-73-75-72—289	52160		S Hoch	75-73-70-79—297	14000
	B Glasson	72-70-73-74—289	52160		T McKnight (am)	73-74-73-77—297	
	J Leonard	70-72-73-74—289	52160	48	S Lyle (Sco)	71-77-70-80—298	12000
	S McCarron	69-68-76-76—289	52160		C Parry (Aus)	75-73-73-77—298	12000
	T Woods	72-72-70-75—289	52160	50	C Perry	73-72-74-80—299	10960
23	L Mize	76-70-72-72—290	41600		M Kuchar (am)	77-71-73-78—299	
24	B Faxon	74-73-68-76—291	35200	52	O Browne	74-74-72-80—300	9980
	P-U Johansson (Swe)	75-72-71-73—291	35200		J Daly	72-76-71-81—300	9980
	V Singh (Fij)	72-76-71-72—291	35200		P Stewart	73-75-77-75—300	9980
27	S Cink	74-70-71-77—292	29000		B Tway	75-73-78-74—300	9980
	F Couples	74-71-76-71—292	29000	56	T Immelman (RSA) (am)	72-76-78-79—305	

1998 Masters

Prize money: $3,200,000. Entries: 88, of whom 46 made the half-way cut.

	Player	Score	Prize		Player	Score	Prize
1	M O'Meara	74-70-68-67—279	$576000	23T	J Huston	77-71-70-71—289	33280
2	D Duval	71-68-74-67—280	281600		J Maggert	72-73-72-72—289	33280
	F Couples	69-70-71-70—280	281600	26	D Frost (RSA)	72-73-74-71—290	26133
4	J Furyk	76-70-67-68—281	153600		S Jones	75-70-75-70—290	26133
5	P Azinger	71-72-69-70—282	128000		B Faxon	73-74-71-72—290	26133
6	J Nicklaus	73-72-70-68—283	111200	29	M Bradley	73-74-72-72—291	23680
	D Toms	75-72-72-64—283	111200	30	S Elkington (Aus)	75-75-71-71—292	22720
8	D Clarke (NI)	76-73-67-69—285	89600	31	A Magee	74-72-74-73—293	21280
	J Leonard	74-73-69-69—285	89600		J Parnevik (Swe)	75-73-73-72—293	21280
	C Montgomerie (Sco)	71-75-69-70—285	89600	33	L Janzen	76-74-72-72—294	18112
	T Woods	71-72-72-70—285	89600		F Zoeller	71-74-75-74—294	18112
12	J Haas	72-71-71-72—286	64800		P Blackmar	71-78-75-70—294	18112
	P-U Johansson (Swe)	74-75-67-70—286	64800		J Daly	77-71-71-75—294	18112
	P Mickelson	74-69-69-74—286	64800		D Love III	74-75-67-78—294	18112
	JM Olazábal (Esp)	70-73-71-72—286	64800	38	T Kite	73-74-74-74—295	15680
16	M Calcavecchia	74-74-69-70—287	48000	39	B Langer (Ger)	75-73-74-74—296	14720
	E Els (RSA)	75-70-70-72—287	48000		P Stankowski	70-80-72-74—296	14720
	S Hoch	70-71-73-73—287	48000	41	C Pavin	73-77-72-75—297	13440
	I Woosnam (Wal)	74-71-72-70—287	48000		C Stadler	79-68-73-77—297	13440
	S McCarron	73-71-72-71—287	48000	43	J Cook	75-73-74-76—298	12480
21	W Wood	74-74-70-70—288	38400	44	L Westwood (Eng)	74-76-72-78—300	11840
	M Kuchar (am)	72-76-68-72—288			J Kribel (am)	74-76-76-75—301	
23	S Cink	74-76-69-70—289	33280	46	G Player (RSA)	77-72-78-75—302	11200

1997 Masters

Prize money: $2,500,000. Entries: 86, of whom 46 made the half-way cut.

1	T Woods	70-66-65-69—270	$486000	24	N Price (Zim)	71-71-75-74—291	24840
2	T Kite	77-69-66-70—282	291600		L Westwood (Eng)	77-71-73-70—291	24840
3	T Tolles	72-72-72-67—283	183600	26	L Janzen	72-73-74-73—292	21195
4	T Watson	75-68-69-72—284	129600		C Stadler	77-72-71-72—292	21195
5	C Rocca (Ita)	71-69-70-75—285	102600	28	P Azinger	69-73-77-74—293	19575
	P Stankowski	68-74-69-74—285	102600		J Furyk	74-75-72-72—293	19575
7	F Couples	72-69-73-72—286	78570	30	S McCarron	77-71-72-74—294	17145
	B Langer (Ger)	72-72-74-68—286	78570		L Mize	79-69-74-72—294	17145
	J Leonard	76-69-71-70—286	78570		C Montgomerie (Sco)	72-67-74-81—294	17145
	D Love III	72-71-72-71—286	78570		M O'Meara	75-74-70-75—294	17145
	J Sluman	74-67-72-73—286	78570	34	A Lyle (Sco)	73-73-74-75—295	14918
12	S Elkington (Aus)	76-72-72-67—287	52920		F Zoeller	75-73-69-78—295	14918
	P-U Johansson (Swe)	72-73-73-69—287	52920	36	D Waldorf	74-75-72-75—296	13905
	T Lehman	73-76-69-69—287	52920	37	D Frost (SA)	74-71-73-79—297	13230
	JM Olazábal (Esp)	71-70-74-72—287	52920	38	S Hoch	79-68-73-78—298	12690
	W Wood	72-76-71-68—287	52920	39	J Nicklaus	77-70-74-78—299	11610
17	M Calcavecchia	74-73-72-69—288	39150		S Torrance (Sco)	75-73-73-78—299	11610
	E Els (RSA)	73-70-71-74—288	39150		I Woosnam (Wal)	77-68-75-79—299	11610
	F Funk	73-74-69-72—288	39150	42	M Ozaki (Jpn)	74-74-74-78—300	10530
	V Singh (Fij)	75-74-69-70—288	39150	43	C Pavin	75-74-78-74—301	9720
21	S Appleby (Aus)	72-76-70-71—289	30240		C Rose	73-75-79-74—301	9720
	J Huston	67-77-75-70—289	30240	45	B Crenshaw	75-73-74-80—302	8910
	J Parnevik (Swe)	73-72-71-73—289	30240	46	F Nobilo (NZ)	76-72-74-81—303	8370

1996 Masters

Prize money: $2,500,000. Entries: 92, of whom 44 made the half-way cut.

1	N Faldo (Eng)	69-67-73-67—276	$450000	23	L Mize	75-71-77-68—291	25000
2	G Norman (Aus)	63-69-71-78—281	270000		L Roberts	71-73-72-75—291	25000
3	P Mickelson	65-73-72-72—282	170000	25	R Floyd	70-74-77-71—292	21000
4	F Nobilo (NZ)	71-71-72-69—283	120000		B Faxon	69-77-72-74—292	21000
5	S Hoch	67-73-73-71—284	95000	27	B Estes	71-71-79-72—293	18900
	D Waldorf	72-71-69-72—284	95000		J Leonard	72-74-75-72—293	18900
7	D Love III	72-71-74-68—285	77933	29	J Furyk	75-70-78-71—294	15571
	J Maggert	71-73-72-69—285	77933		J Gallagher jr	70-76-77-71—294	15571
	C Pavin	75-66-73-71—285	77933		H Irwin	74-71-77-72—294	15571
10	S McCarron	70-70-72-74—286	65000		S Simpson	69-76-76-73—294	15571
	D Frost (RSA)	70-68-74-74—286	65000		C Stadler	73-72-71-78—294	15571
12	B Tway	67-72-76-72—287	52500		J Daly	71-74-71-78—294	15571
	L Janzen	68-71-75-73—287	52500		I Woosnam (Wal)	72-69-73-80—294	15571
	E Els (RSA)	71-71-72-73—287	52500	36	F Funk	71-72-76-76—295	12333
15	F Couples	78-68-71-71—288	43750		J Haas	70-73-75-77—295	12333
	M Calcavecchia	71-73-71-73—288	43750		B Langer (Ger)	70-72-76-77—295	12333
17	J Huston	71-71-71-76—289	40000	39	C Montgomerie (Sco)	72-74-75-75—296	11050
18	P Azinger	70-74-76-70—290	32600		V Singh (Fij)	69-71-74-82—296	11050
	M O'Meara	72-71-75-72—290	32600	41	S Lowery (Sco)	71-74-75-77—297	10050
	T Lehman	75-70-72-73—290	32600		J Nicklaus	70-73-76-78—297	10050
	N Price (Zim)	71-75-70-74—290	32600	43	S Ballesteros (Esp)	73-73-77-76—299	9300
	D Duval	73-72-69-76—290	32600	44	A Cejka (Ger)	73-71-78-80—302	8800

1995 Masters

Prize money: $2,132,000. Entries: 86, of whom 47 made the half-way cut.

1	B Crenshaw	70-67-69-68—274	$396000	24T	D Edwards	69-73-73-71—286	18260
2	D Love III	69-69-71-66—275	237600		L Roberts	72-69-72-73—286	18260
3	J Haas	71-64-72-70—277	127600		N Faldo (Eng)	70-70-71-75—286	18260
	G Norman (Aus)	73-68-68-68—277	127600		D Waldorf	74-69-67-76—286	18260
5	S Elkington (Aus)	73-67-67-72—279	83600	29	B Estes	73-70-76-68—287	15300
	D Frost (RSA)	66-71-71-71—279	83600		M Ozaki (Jpn)	70-74-70-73—287	15300
7	S Hoch	69-67-71-73—280	70950	31	B Lietzke	72-71-71-74—288	13325
	P Mickelson	66-71-70-73—280	70950		P Jacobsen	72-73-69-74—288	13325
9	C Strange	72-71-65-73—281	63800		B Langer (Ger)	71-69-73-75—288	13325
10	F Couples	71-69-67-75—282	57200		M O'Meara	68-72-71-77—288	13325
	B Henninger	70-68-68-76—282	57200	35	D Forsman	71-74-74-71—290	10840
12	K Perry	73-70-71-69—283	48400		W Grady (Aus)	69-73-74-74—290	10840
	L Janzen	69-69-74-71—283	48400		J Nicklaus	67-78-70-75—290	10840
14	JM Olazábal (Esp)	66-74-72-72—284	39600		C Beck	68-76-69-77—290	10840
	T Watson	73-70-69-72—284	39600		M McCumber	73-69-69-79—290	10840
	H Irwin	69-72-71-72—284	39600	40	T Lehman	71-72-74-75—292	9500
17	C Montgomerie (Sco)	71-69-76-69—285	28786	41	M Calcavecchia	70-72-78-73—293	8567
	P Azinger	70-72-73-70—285	28786		T Woods (am)	72-72-77-72—293	
	B Faxon	76-69-69-71—285	28786		J Sluman	73-72-71-77—293	8567
	I Woosnam (Wal)	69-72-71-73—285	28786		P Stewart	71-72-72-78—293	8567
	R Floyd	71-70-70-74—285	28786	45	S Ballesteros (Esp)	75-68-78-75—296	7500
	C Pavin	67-71-72-75—285	28786		J Daly	75-69-71-81—296	7500
	J Huston	70-66-72-77—285	28786	47	R Fehr	76-69-69-83—297	6800
24	D Gilford (Eng)	67-73-75-71—286	18260				

1994 Masters

Prize money: $1,960,000. Entries: 86, of whom 51 made the half-way cut.

1	JM Olazábal (Esp)	74-67-69-69—279	$360000	27	S Simpson	74-74-73-73—294	14800
2	T Lehman	70-70-69-72—281	216000		V Singh (Fij)	70-75-74-75—294	14800
3	L Mize	68-71-72-71—282	136000		C Strange	74-70-75-75—294	14800
4	T Kite	69-72-71-71—283	96000	30	L Janzen	75-71-76-73—295	13300
5	J Haas	72-72-72-69—285	73000		C Parry (Aus)	75-74-73-73—295	13300
	J McGovern	72-70-71-72—285	73000	32	N Faldo (Eng)	76-73-73-74—296	12400
	L Roberts	75-68-72-70—285	73000	33	R Cochran	71-74-74-79—297	11500
8	E Els (RSA)	74-67-74-71—286	60000		S Torrance (Sco)	76-73-74-74—297	11500
	C Pavin	71-72-73-70—286	60000	35	D Frost (RSA)	74-71-75-78—298	10300
10	I Baker-Finch (Aus)	71-71-71-74—287	50000		N Price (Zim)	74-73-74-77—298	10300
	R Floyd	70-74-71-72—287	50000		F Zoeller	74-72-74-78—298	10300
	J Huston	72-72-74-69—287	50000	38	F Allem (RSA)	69-77-76-77—299	9000
13	T Watson	70-71-73-74—288	42000		F Funk	79-70-75-75—299	9000
14	D Forsman	74-66-76-73—289	38000		A Lyle (Sco)	75-73-78-73—299	9000
15	C Beck	71-71-75-74—291	34000	41	W Grady (Aus)	74-73-73-80—300	7400
	B Faxon	71-73-73-74—291	34000		A Magee	74-74-76-76—300	7400
	M O'Meara	75-70-76-70—291	34000		H Meshiai (Jpn)	71-71-80-78—300	7400
18	S Ballesteros (Esp)	70-76-75-71—292	24343		C Rocca (Ita)	79-70-78-73—300	7400
	B Crenshaw	74-73-73-72—292	24343		M Standly	77-69-79-75—300	7400
	D Edwards	73-72-73-74—292	24343	46	J Cook	77-72-77-75—301	6000
	B Glasson	72-73-75-72—292	24343		I Woosnam (Wal)	76-73-77-75—301	6000
	H Irwin	73-68-79-72—292	24343	48	J Daly	76-73-77-78—304	5250
	G Norman (Aus)	70-70-75-77—292	24343		H Twitty	73-76-74-81—304	5250
	L Wadkins	73-74-73-72—292	24343	50	J Maggert	75-73-82-75—305	5000
25	B Langer (Ger)	74-74-72-73—293	16800		J Harris (am)	72-76-80-77—305	
	J Sluman	74-75-71-73—293	16800				

The Masters History

Year	Winner	Score	Year	Winner	Score
1934	H Smith	284	1971	C Coody	279
1935	G Sarazen*	282	1972	J Nicklaus	286
1936	H Smith	285	1973	T Aaron	283
1937	B Nelson	283	1974	G Player (RSA)	278
1938	H Picard	285	1975	J Nicklaus	276
1939	R Guldahl	279	1976	R Floyd	271
1940	J Demaret	280	1977	T Watson	276
1941	C Wood	280	1978	G Player (RSA)	277
1942	B Nelson*	280	1979	F Zoeller*	280
1946	H Keiser	282	1980	S Ballesteros (Esp)	275
1947	J Demaret	281	1981	T Watson	280
1948	C Harmon	279	1982	C Stadler*	284
1949	S Snead	283	1983	S Ballesteros (Esp)	280
1950	J Demaret	282	1984	B Crenshaw	277
1951	B Hogan	280	1985	B Langer (Ger)	282
1952	S Snead	286	1986	J Nicklaus	279
1953	B Hogan	274	1987	L Mize*	285
1954	S Snead*	289	1988	A Lyle (Sco)	281
1955	C Middlecoff	279	1989	N Faldo (Eng)*	283
1956	J Burke	289	1990	N Faldo (Eng)*	278
1957	D Ford	283	1991	I Woosnam (Wal)	277
1958	A Palmer	284	1992	F Couples	275
1959	A Wall	284	1993	B Langer (Ger)	277
1960	A Palmer	282	1994	JM Olazábal (Esp)	279
1961	G Player (RSA)	280	1995	B Crenshaw	274
1962	A Palmer*	280	1996	N Faldo (Eng)	276
1963	J Nicklaus	286	1997	T Woods	270
1964	A Palmer	276	1998	M O'Meara	279
1965	J Nicklaus	271	1999	JM Olazábal (Esp)	280
1966	J Nicklaus*	288	2000	V Singh (Fij)	278
1967	G Brewer	280	2001	T Woods	272
1968	R Goalby	277	2002	T Woods	276
1969	G Archer	281	2003	M Weir (Can)*	281
1970	W Casper*	279			

Watson made over $1 million in majors

Tom Watson played in nine majors in 2003 and banked $1,128,747 in prize-money. This was how he performed:

The Masters	missed cut	75-77—152	
US Open	28th	65-72-75-72—284	$41,254
The Open	18th	71-77-73-69—290	$66,763
US PGA	missed cut	75-75—154	
Senior PGA	17th	71-73-73-67—284	$24,000
US Senior	2nd	66-72-70-71—279	$228,000
Senior Players	2nd	70-64-71-69—274	$183,000
Senior British Open	1st	66-67-66-64—263	$255,730
Jeld-Wen Tradition	1st	68-62-73-70—273	$330,000

US PGA Championship

Players are of American nationality unless stated

2003 US PGA Championship (85th) *at Oak Hill CC, Rochester, NY*   (7134–70)

Prize money: $6million. Final field: 156, of whom 70 made the half-way cut on 148 or better.

1	Shaun Micheel	69-68-69-70—276	$1080000
2	Chad Campbell	69-72-65-72—278	648000
3	Tim Clark (RSA)	72-70-68-69—279	408000
4	Alex Cejka (Ger)	74-69-68-69—280	288000
5	Ernie Els (RSA)	71-70-70-71—282	214000
	Jay Haas	70-74-69-69—282	214000
7	Fred Funk	69-73-70-72—284	175667
	Loren Roberts	70-73-70-71—284	175667
	Mike Weir (Can)	68-71-70-75—284	175667
10	Billy Andrade	67-72-72-74—285	135500
	Niclas Fasth (Swe)	76-70-71-68—285	135500
	Charles Howell III	70-72-70-73—285	135500
	Kenny Perry	75-72-70-68—285	135500
14	Robert Gamez	70-73-70-73—286	98250
	Tim Herron	69-72-74-71—286	98250
	Scott McCarron	74-70-71-71—286	98250
	Rod Pampling (Aus)	66-74-73-73—286	98250
18	Carlos Franco (Par)	73-73-69-72—287	73000
	Jim Furyk	72-74-69-72—287	73000
	Toshimitsu Izawa (Jpn)	71-72-71-73—287	73000
	Rocco Mediate	72-74-71-70—287	73000
	Kevin Sutherland	69-74-71-73—287	73000
23	Stuart Appleby (Aus)	74-73-71-70—288	52000
	Luke Donald (Eng)	73-72-71-72—288	52000
	Phil Mickelson	66-75-72-75—288	52000
	Adam Scott (Aus)	72-69-72-75—288	52000
27	Woody Austin	72-73-69-75—289	43000
	Geoff Ogilvy (Aus)	71-71-77-70—289	43000
29	Todd Hamilton	70-74-73-73—290	36600
	Padraig Harrington (Irl)	72-76-69-73—290	36600
	Frank Lickliter II	71-72-71-76—290	36600
	Peter Lonard (Aus)	74-74-69-73—290	36600
	David Toms	75-72-71-72—290	36600
34	Fred Couples	74-71-72-74—291	29000
	Lee Janzen	68-74-72-77—291	29000
	JL Lewis	71-75-71-74—291	29000
	Jesper Parnevik (Swe)	73-72-72-74—291	29000
	Vijay Singh (Fij)	69-73-70-79—291	29000
39	Robert Allenby (Aus)	70-77-73-72—292	22000
	Briny Baird	73-71-67-81—292	22000
	Mark Calcavecchia	73-71-76-72—292	22000
	Joe Durant	71-76-75-70—292	22000
	Hal Sutton	75-71-67-79—292	22000
	Tiger Woods	74-72-73-73—292	22000
45	Angel Cabrera (Arg)	71-76-72-74—293	17500
	Tom Pernice jr	70-71-72-80—293	17500
	Duffy Waldorf	70-75-72-76—293	17500
48	Ben Crane	73-73-76-72—294	14733
	Trevor Immelman (RSA)	74-70-77-73—294	14733

85th US PGA Championship *continued*

48T	Shigeki Maruyama (Jpn)	75-72-73-74—294	14733
51	José Coceres (Arg)	73-68-78-76—295	13320
	Gary Evans (Eng)	74-74-71-76—295	13320
	Brian Gay	74-74-75-72—295	13320
	Len Mattiace	74-70-75-76—295	13320
	José María Olazábal (Esp)	74-74-76-71—295	13320
56	Chris DiMarco	74-71-78-73—296	12700
57	Aaron Baddeley (Aus)	69-77-73-78—297	12450
	Bob Estes	71-76-73-77—297	12450
	Scott Hoch	75-72-73-77—297	12450
	Bernhard Langer (Ger)	75-72-75-75—297	12450
61	Jonathan Kaye	74-73-72-79—298	12000
	Billy Mayfair	76-72-78-72—298	12000
	Ian Poulter (Eng)	72-75-72-79—298	12000
	Eduardo Romero (Arg)	77-71-76-74—298	12000
	Philip Tataurangi (NZ)	72-71-78-77—298	12000
66	Paul Casey (Eng)	79-69-75-76—299	11700
67	Bob Burns	72-76-70-82—300	11600
68	Rory Sabbatini (RSA)	71-75-75-81—302	11500
69	Michael Campbell (NZ)	74-71-80-79—304	11350
	Choi Kyoung-Ju (Kor)	74-74-80-76—304	11350

The following players missed the half-way cut. Each received $2000:

71	Paul Azinger	73-76—149	94T	Brian Davis (Eng)	73-78—151	126T	Colin Montgomerie		
	Thomas Bjørn			Alastair Forsyth			(Sco)	82-74—156
	(Den)	78-71—149		(Sco)	73-78—151	128	Rich Beem	82-85—157
	Darren Clarke (NI)	79-70—149		Ignacio Garrido			Dino Lucchesi	79-78—157
	Steve Flesch	79-70—149		(Esp)	75-76—151		Craig Parry (Aus)	79-78—157
	Dan Forsman	75-74—149		Retief Goosen (RSA)	77-74—151		Tim Petrovic	82-75—157
	Sergio García (Esp)	72-77—149		Hank Kuehne	70-81—151		Steve Schneite	77-80—157
	Stephen Leaney			Rob Labritz	76-75—151	133	Michael Combs	79-79—158
	(Aus)	73-76—149		Chris Riley	73-78—151		Mike Schuchart	77-81—158
	Davis Love III	74-75—149		John Rollins	78-73—151		Cary Sciorra	76-82—158
	Paul McGinley (Irl)	73-76—149		Bob Tway	78-73—151		Andre Stolz	75-83—158
	Greg Norman (Aus)	79-70—149		Lee Westwood (Eng)	73-78—151	137	Jonathan Byrd	80-79—159
	Gene Sauers	72-77—149	108	JC Anderson	76-76—152		Skip Kendall	80-79—159
	Scott Verplank	77-72—149		Stewart Cink	79-73—152		Rick Schuller	79-80—159
83	Don Berry	74-76—150		Jeff Maggert	79-73—152		Bob Sowards	81-78—159
	Bradley Dredge			Scott A Porter	80-72—152	141	Sean Farren	79-81—160
	(Wal)	75-75—150		Phillip Price (Wal)	77-75—152		Ricardo Gonzalez	77-83—160
	Mathias Grönberg			Chip Sullivan	74-78—152		Ron A Philo jr	82-78—160
	(Swe)	76-74—150	114	Jerry Kelly	78-75—153	144	Brad Faxon	82-79—161
	Peter Jacobsen	73-77—150	115	Robert Karlsson			Pierre Fulke (Swe)	81-80—161
	Fredrik Jacobson			(Swe)	75-79—154		John Guyton	80-81—161
	(Swe)	76-74—150		Jeffrey Lankford	78-76—154		Dave Spengler	81-80—161
	Shingo Katayama			Justin Leonard	79-75—154		Toru Taniguchi (Jpn)	82-79—161
	(Jpn)	75-75—150		Ken Schall	80-74—154	149	Alan Morin	84-79—163
	Tom Lehman	75-75—150		Jeff Sluman	75-79—154	150	Terry Hatch	84-81—165
	Steve Lowery	75-75—150		Tim Thelen	75-79—154	151	Tim Fleming	84-83—167
	Greg Owen (Eng)	77-73—150	121	Anders Hansen				
	Carl Petterson (Swe)	74-76—150		(Den)	78-77—155		Kirk Triplett	76 WD
	Tom Watson	75-75—150		Mark O'Meara	73-82—155		John Huston	79 WD
94	Mark Brooks	77-74—151		Justin Rose (Eng)	77-78—155		Wayne DeFrancesco	79 WD
	Kevin Burton	78-73—151		Dave Tentis	79-76—155		David Duval	80 WD
	Ben Curtis	75-76—151		Dean Wilson	78-77—155		John Jacobs	87 WD
	John Daly	76-75—151	126	Stephen Ames (Tri)	82-74—156			

2002 US PGA Championship at *Hazeltine Naional, Chaska, MN* (7360–72)

Prize money: $5,500,000. Entries: 156 (one amateur), of whom 72 made the half-way cut.

1	Rich Beem	72-66-72-68—278	$990000	22	Heath Slocum		73-74-75-69—291	57000
2	Tiger Woods	71-69-72-67—279	594000	23	Michael Campbell (NZ)	73-70-77-72—292	44250
3	Chris Riley	71-70-72-70—283	374000		Retief Goosen (RSA)		69-69-79-75—292	44250
4	Fred Funk	68-70-73-73—284	235000		Bernhard Langer (Ger)	70-72-77-73—292	44250
	Justin Leonard	72-66-69-77—284	235000		Justin Rose (Eng)		69-73-76-74—292	44250
6	Rocco Mediate	72-73-70-70—285	185000		Adam Scott (Aus)		71-71-76-74—292	44250
7	Mark Calcavecchia	70-68-74-74—286	172000		Jeff Sluman		70-75-74-73—292	44250
8	Vijay Singh (Fij)	71-74-74-68—287	159000	29	Brad Faxon		74-72-75-72—293	33500
9	Jim Furyk	68-73-76-71—288	149000		Tom Lehman		71-72-77-73—293	33500
10	Robert Allenby (Aus)	76-66-77-70—289	110714		Craig Perks (NZ)		72-76-74-71—293	33500
	Stewart Cink	74-74-72-69—289	110714		Kenny Perry		73-68-78-74—293	33500
	José Coceres (Arg)	72-71-72-74—289	110714		Kirk Triplett		75-69-79-70—293	33500
	Pierre Fulke (Swe)	72-68-78-71—289	110714	34	David Duval		71-77-76-70—294	26300
	Sergio García (Esp)	75-73-73-68—289	110714		Ernie Els (RSA)		72-71-75-76—294	26300
	Ricardo Gonzalez (Arg)	74-73-71-71—289	110714		Neal Lancaster		72-73-75-74—294	26300
	Steve Lowery	71-71-73-74—289	110714		Phil Mickelson		76-72-78-68—294	26300
17	Stuart Appleby (Aus)	73-74-74-69—290	72000		Mike Weir (Can)		73-74-77-70—294	26300
	Steve Flesch	72-74-73-71—290	72000	39	Chris DiMarco		76-69-77-73—295	21500
	Padraig Harrington (Irl)	71-73-74-72—290	72000		Joel Edwards		73-74-77-71—295	21500
	Charles Howell III	72-69-80-69—290	72000		John Huston		74-74-75-72—295	21500
	Peter Lonard (Aus)	69-73-75-73—290	72000		Scott McCarron		73-71-79-72—295	21500

Other players who made the cut: Briny Baird, Søren Hansen (Den), Shigeki Maruyama (Jpn), Loren Roberts, Kevin Sutherland 296; Angel Cabrera (Arg), Steve Elkington (Aus), Davis Love III, Len Mattiace, Tom Watson 297; Cameron Beckman, Tim Clark (RSA), Brian Gay, Toshimitsu Izawa (Jpn), Lee Janzen, Greg Norman (Aus), Chris Smith 298; Joe Durant, Nick Faldo (Eng), Hal Sutton 299, JJ Henry 301; Don Berry, Matt Gogel, JP Hayes, Joey Sindelar 302; Dave Tentis 304; José María Olazábal (Esp) 305; Pat Perez 309; Thomas Levet (Fra) 310; Stephen Ames (Tri) W/D

2001 US PGA Championship at *Atlanta Athletic Club, Atlanta, Georgia*

Prize money: $5,205,049. Entries: 150, of whom 76 made the half-way cut. (7213–70)

1	David Toms	66-65-65-69—265	$936000	16T	Chris DiMarco	68-67-71-71—277	70666
2	Phil Mickelson	66-66-66-68—266	562000	22	Mark O'Meara	72-63-70-73—278	44285
3	Steve Lowery	67-67-66-68—268	354000		Shigeki Maruyama		
4	Mark Calcavecchia	71-68-66-65—270	222500		(Jpn)	68-72-71-67—278	44285
	Shingo Katayama (Jpn)	67-64-69-70—270	222500		Paul Azinger	68-67-69-74—278	44285
6	Billy Andrade	68-70-68-66—272	175000		Paul McGinley (Irl)	68-72-71-67—278	44285
7	Jim Furyk	70-64-71-69—274	152333		Briny Baird	70-69-72-67—278	44285
	Scott Verplank	69-68-70-67—274	152333		J Brian Gay	70-68-69-71—278	44285
	Scott Hoch	68-70-69-67—274	152333		Charles Howell III	71-67-69-71—278	44285
10	David Duval	66-68-67-74—275	122000	29	Greg Norman (Aus)	70-68-71-70—279	29437
	Justin Leonard	70-69-67-69—275	122000		Tiger Woods	73-67-69-70—279	29437
	Kirk Triplett	68-70-71-66—275	122000		Nick Price (Zim)	71-67-71-70—279	29437
13	Steve Flesch	73-67-70-66—276	94666		Kyoung-Ju Choi (Kor)	66-68-72-73—279	29437
	Jesper Parnevik (Swe)	70-68-70-68—276	94666		Bob Tway	69-69-71-70—279	29437
	Ernie Els (RSA)	67-67-70-72—276	94666		Carlos Franco (Par)	67-72-71-69—279	29437
16	Stuart Appleby (Aus)	66-70-68-73—277	70666		Niclas Fasth (Swe)	66-69-72-72—279	29437
	Mike Weir (Can)	69-72-66-70—277	70666		Christopher Smith	69-71-68-71—279	29437
	Dudley Hart	66-68-73-70—277	70666		José María Olazábal		
	José Coceres (Arg)	69-68-73-67—277	70666		(Esp)	70-70-68-71—279	29437
	Robert Allenby (Aus)	69-67-73-68—277	70666				

Other players who made the cut: Fred Couples, Davis Love III, Bob Estes, Angel Cabrera (Arg), Andrew Coltart (Sco), Retief Goosen (RSA) 280; Andrew Oldcorn (Sco), Greg Chalmers (Aus), Jerry Kelly, Hal Sutton, Kenny Perry, Lee Westwood (Eng), Rick Schuller 281; Nick Faldo (Eng), Ian Woosnam (Wal), Joe Durant, Vijay Singh (Fij), Scott Dunlap, Tom Pernice, Chris Riley, Frank Lickliter 282; Brad Faxon, Stewart Cink, Phillip Price (Wal), Grant Waite (NZ) 283; Skip Kendall, Thomas Bjørn (Den), Jonathan Kaye, Rocco Mediate 284; Tom Watson, Steve Stricker, Robert Damron 285; Fred Funk, Scott McCarron 286; John Huston 287; Bob May 291; Paul Stankowski 293; Steve Pate 294; Colin Montgomerie (Sco) DQ

2000 US PGA Championship at Valhalla GC, Louisville, Kentucky   (7167–72)

Prize money: $5,000,000. Entries: 150, of whom 80 made the half-way cut.

1	Tiger Woods	66-67-70-67—270	$900000		19T	JP Hayes	69-68-68-86—281	56200
2	Bob May	72-66-66-66—270	540000			Angel Cabrera (Arg)	72-71-71-67—281	56200
Woods won after play-off						Robert Allenby (Aus)	73-71-68-69—281	56200
3	Thomas Bjørn (Den)	72-68-67-68—275	340000			Lee Janzen	76-70-70-65—281	56200
4	Greg Chalmers (Aus)	71-69-66-70—276	198667		24	Paul Azinger	72-71-66-73—282	41000
	José María Olazábal					Steve Jones	72-71-70-69—282	41000
	(Esp)	76-68-63-69—276	198667			Jarmo Sandelin (Swe)	74-72-68-68—282	41000
	Stuart Appleby (Aus)	70-69-68-69—276	198667		27	Brad Faxon	71-74-70-68—283	34167
7	Franklin Langham	72-71-65-69—277	157000			Skip Kendall	72-72-69-70—283	34167
8	Notah Begay III	72-66-70-70—278	145000			Tom Pernice	74-69-70-70—283	34167
9	Tom Watson	76-70-65-68—279	112500		30	Mike Weir (Can)	76-69-68-71—284	28875
	Fred Funk	69-68-74-68—279	112500			Jean Van de Velde		
	Davis Love III	68-69-72-70—279	112500			(Fra)	70-74-69-71—284	28875
	Darren Clarke (NI)	68-72-72-67—279	112500			Stephen Ames (Tri)	69-71-71-73—284	28875
	Scott Dunlap	66-68-70-75—279	112500			Kenny Perry	78-68-70-68—284	28875
	Phil Mickelson	70-70-69-70—279	112500		34	Sergio García (Esp)	74-69-73-69—285	24000
15	Stewart Cink	72-71-70-67—280	77500			Chris Perry	72-74-70-69—285	24000
	Lee Westwood (Eng)	72-72-69-67—280	77500			Mark Calcavecchia	73-74-71-67—285	24000
	Chris Dimarco	73-70-69-68—280	77500			Ernie Els (RSA)	74-68-72-71—285	24000
	Michael Clark II	73-70-67-70—280	77500			Blaine McCallister	73-71-70-71—285	24000
19	Tom Kite	70-72-69-70—281	56200					

Other players who made the cut: Toshimitsu Izawa (Jpn), Colin Montgomerie (Sco) 286; Jeff Sluman, Justin Leonard, Paul Stankowski, Steve Pate, David Toms 287; Bernhard Langer (Ger), Mark O'Meara, Shigeki Maruyama (Jpn), Duffy Waldorf, Brian Henninger 288; Nick Faldo (Eng), Jesper Parnevik (Swe), Steve Lowery, Brian Watts, Glen Day, Andrew Coltart (Sco), Jonathan Kaye 289; Padraig Harrington (Irl), Loren Roberts, Curtis Strange, Carlos Franco (Par), Dennis Paulson, Joe Ogilvie 290; Wayne Grady (Aus), Craig Stadler, Bill Glasson, Miguel Angel Jiménez (Esp), Jay Haas 291; Greg Kraft, Kirk Triplett 292; John Huston 293; Jim Furyk, Paul Lawrie (Sco) 294; Robert Damron, Billy Mayfair, Scott Hoch 297; Masashi Ozaki (Jpn), Rory Sabbatini 299; Hidemichi Tanaka (Jpn) 301; Frank Dobbs 313

1999 US PGA Championship at Medinah, Illinois   (7401–72)

Prize money: $3,000,000. Entries: 149, of whom 74 made the half-way cut.

1	T Woods	70-67-68-72—277	$630000		21	D Frost (RSA)	75-68-74-71—288	33200
2	S García (Esp)	66-73-68-71—278	378000			S Hoch	71-71-75-71—288	33200
3	S Cink	69-70-68-73—280	203000			S Kendall	74-65-71-78—288	33200
	J Haas	68-67-75-70—280	203000			JL Lewis	73-70-74-71—288	33200
5	N Price (Zim)	70-71-69-71—281	129000			K Wentworth	72-70-72-74—288	33200
6	B Estes	71-70-72-69—282	112000		26	F Couples	73-69-75-72—289	24000
	C Montgomerie (Sco)	72-70-70-70—282	112000			C Franco (Par)	72-71-71-75—289	24000
8	J Furyk	71-70-69-74—284	96500			J Kelly	69-74-71-75—289	24000
	S Pate	72-70-73-69—284	96500			H Sutton	72-73-73-71—289	24000
10	D Duval	70-71-72-72—285	72166			J Van de Velde (Fra)	74-70-75-70—289	24000
	MA Jiménez (Esp)	70-70-75-70—285	72166		31	P Goydos	73-70-71-76—290	20000
	J Parnevik (Swe)	72-70-73-70—285	72166			M James (Eng)	70-74-79-67—290	20000
	C Pavin	69-74-71-71—285	72166			T Tryba	70-72-76-72—290	20000
	C Perry	70-73-71-71—285	72166		34	S Flesch	73-71-72-75—291	15428
	M Weir (Can)	68-68-69-80—285	72166			P Lawrie (Sco)	72-73-74-72—291	15428
16	M Brooks	70-73-70-74—287	48600			T Lehman	70-74-76-71—291	15428
	G Hjertstedt (Swe)	72-70-73-72—287	48600			B Mayfair	75-69-75-72—291	15428
	B Jobe	69-74-69-75—287	48600			K Perry	74-69-72-76—291	15428
	G Turner (NZ)	73-69-70-75—287	48600			S Verplank	73-72-73-73—291	15428
	L Westwood (Eng)	70-68-74-75—287	48600			L Wadkins	72-69-74-76—291	15428

Other players who made the cut: P Azinger, Angel Cabrera (Arg), C DiMarco, N Faldo (Eng), H Irwin, R Karlsson (Swe), D Waldorf, B Watts 292; O Browne, D Love III, R Mediate, V Singh (Fij), K Triplett 293; JP Hayes, A Magee, J Sluman 294; P Mickelson, M O'Meara, P Stewart, B Tway 295; M Calcavecchia, B Faxon, G Kraft, B Langer (Ger) 296; A Cejka (Ger), A Coltart (Sco), M Reid 297; S Dunlap, B Zabriski 298; R Beem, T Bjørn (Den), N Ozaki (Jpn) 299; F Funk 300

1998 US PGA Championship at Sahalee, Seattle, Washington   (6906–70)

Prize money: $3,000,000. Entries: 150, of whom 75 made the half-way cut.

1	V Singh (Fij)	70-66-67-68—271	$540000	21	E Els (RSA)	72-72-71-66—281	32000
2	S Stricker	69-68-66-70—273	324000		A Magee	70-68-72-71—281	32000
3	S Elkington (Aus)	69-69-69-67—274	204000	23	P-U Johansson (Swe)	69-74-71-68—282	26000
4	F Lickliter	68-71-69-68—276	118000		F Funk	70-71-71-70—282	26000
	M O'Meara	69-70-69-68—276	118000		S Gump	68-69-72-73—282	26000
	N Price (Zim)	70-73-68-65—276	118000		G Kraft	71-73-65-73—282	26000
7	B Mayfair	73-67-67-70—277	89500	27	J Sluman	71-73-70-69—283	20500
	D Love III	70-68-69-70—277	89500		H Sutton	72-68-72-71—283	20500
9	J Cook	71-68-70-69—278	80000	29	G Day	68-71-75-70—284	17100
10	K Perry	69-72-70-68—279	69000		T Lehman	71-71-70-72—284	17100
	T Woods	66-72-70-71—279	69000		I Woosnam (Wal)	70-75-67-72—284	17100
	S Kendall	72-68-68-71—279	69000		L Rinker	70-70-71-73—284	17100
13	B Faxon	70-68-74-68—280	46000		S Hoch	72-69-70-73—284	17100
	F Couples	74-71-67-68—280	46000	34	P Mickelson	70-70-78-67—285	14250
	B Tway	69-76-67-68—280	46000		B Estes	68-76-69-72—285	14250
	P Azinger	68-73-70-69—280	46000		P Goydos	70-70-72-73—285	14250
	B Glasson	68-74-69-69—280	46000		R Cochran	69-71-70-75—285	14250
	S Flesch	75-69-67-69—280	46000	38	C Stadler	69-74-71-72—286	12750
	J Huston	70-71-68-71—280	46000		D Waldorf	74-70-70-72—286	12750
	R Allenby (Aus)	72-68-69-71—280	46000				

Other players who made the cut: J Sindelar, J Haas, J Durant, C Franco (Par) 287; J Ozaki (Jpn), J Maggert, S Lowery, D Ogrin, K Sutherland, C Montgomerie (Sco), PH Horgan III, M Calcavecchia, D Hart, B Andrade 288; N Faldo (Eng), S Verplank 289; T Tryba, M Brooks, B Watts, J Carter, D Frost (RSA), JD Blake 290; T Dodds (Nam), T Byrum, O Browne 291; R Karlsson (Swe), S Maruyama (Jpn), L Roberts 292; S Leaney (Aus) 293; A Coltart (Sco) 294; D Sutherland 295; B Geiberger, C Parry (Aus), B Fabel 296; C Perry 297; T Herron 298

1997 US PGA Championship at Winged Foot CC, New York   (6987–70)

Prize money: $2,600,000. Entries: 150, of whom 77 made the half-way cut.

1	D Love III	66-71-66-66—269	470000	13T	B Tway	68-75-72-69—284	35100
2	J Leonard	68-70-65-71—274	280000		M O'Meara	69-73-75-67—284	35100
3	J Maggert	69-69-73-65—276	175000	23	M Calcavecchia	71-74-73-67—285	22500
4	L Janzen	69-67-74-69—279	125000		B Langer (Ger)	73-71-72-69—285	22500
5	T Kite	68-71-71-70—280	105000		D Martin	69-75-74-67—285	22500
6	P Blackmar	70-68-74-69—281	85000		S Maruyama (Jpn)	68-70-74-73—285	22500
	J Furyk	69-72-72-68—281	85000		K Perry	73-68-73-71—285	22500
	S Hoch	71-72-68-70—281	85000		J Cook	71-71-74-69—285	22500
9	T Byrum	69-73-70-70—282	70000	29	P Azinger	68-73-71-74—286	13625
10	T Lehman	69-72-72-70—283	60000		R Black	76-69-71-70—286	13625
	S McCarron	74-71-67-71—283	60000		F Couples	71-67-73-75—286	13625
	J Sindelar	72-71-71-69—283	60000		J Daly	66-73-77-70—286	13625
13	D Duval	70-70-71-73—284	35100		P Goydos	70-72-71-73—286	13625
	T Herron	72-73-68-71—284	35100		H Irwin	73-70-71-72—286	13625
	C Montgomerie (Sco)	74-71-67-72—284	35100		P Mickelson	69-69-73-75—286	13625
	G Norman (Aus)	68-71-74-71—284	35100		F Nobilo (NZ)	72-73-67-74—286	13625
	N Price (Zim)	72-70-72-70—284	35100		D Pooley	72-74-70-70—286	13625
	V Singh (Fij)	73-66-76-69—284	35100		P Stewart	70-72-72-74—286	13625
	T Tolles	75-70-73-66—284	35100		L Westwood (Eng)	74-68-71-73—286	13625
	K Triplett	73-70-71-70—284	35100		T Woods	70-70-71-75—286	13625

Other players who made the cut: I Garrido (Esp), S Jones, D Ogrin, E Romero (Arg) 287; T Bjørn (Den), S Elkington (Aus), J Parnevik (Swe), S Torrance (Sco) 288; R Allenby (Aus), B Henninger, C Perry, L Roberts 289; O Browne, E Els (RSA), B Mayfair, T Smith, C Stadler 290; S Lowery, L Mize, L Wadkins 291; S Appleby (Aus), J Haas, R Cochran, F Funk, R Goosen (RSA), L Rinker 292; P Jacobsen, P-U Johansson (Swe), P Stankowski 293; C Franco (Par) 294; M Bradley, Y Kaneko (Jpn), L Nelson, C Rocca (Ita) 295; A Magee 296; P Jordan, K Sutherland 297.

1996 US PGA Championship *at Valhalla, Louisville, Kentucky*   (7144–72)

Prize money: $2,400,000. Entries: 150, of whom 87 made the half-way cut.

1	M Brooks*	68-70-69-70—277	$430000	17T	D Edwards	69-71-72-70—282	27285
2	K Perry	66-72-71-68—277	260000		J Furyk	70-70-73-69—282	27285
Brooks won play-off at extra hole					G Norman (Aus)	68-72-69-73—282	27285
3	S Elkington (Aus)	67-74-67-70—278	140000	24	E Aubrey	69-74-72-68—283	21500
	T Tolles	69-71-71-67—278	140000		MA Jiménez (Esp)	71-71-71-70—283	21500
5	J Leonard	71-66-72-70—279	86666	26	F Funk	73-69-73-69—284	18000
	J Parnevik (Swe)	73-67-69-70—279	86666		M O'Meara	71-70-74-69—284	18000
	V Singh (Fij)	69-69-69-72—279	86666		C Pavin	71-74-70-69—284	18000
8	L Janzen	68-71-71-70—280	57500		C Strange	73-70-68-73—284	18000
	P-U Johansson (Swe)	73-72-66-69—280	57500		S Stricker	73-72-72-67—284	18000
	P Mickelson	67-67-74-72—280	57500	31	P Azinger	70-75-71-69—285	13000
	L Mize	71-70-69-70—280	57500		M Bradley	73-72-70-70—285	13000
	F Nobilo (NZ)	69-72-71-68—280	57500		P Burke	71-72-69-73—285	13000
	N Price (Zim)	68-71-69-72—280	57500		J Haas	72-71-69-73—285	13000
14	M Brisky	71-69-69-72—281	39000		T Herron	71-73-68-73—285	13000
	T Lehman	71-71-69-70—281	39000	36	M Calcavecchia	70-74-70-72—286	9050
	J Sindelar	73-72-69-67—281	39000		R Mediate	71-72-67-76—286	9050
17	B Faxon	72-68-73-69—282	27285		D Ogrin	75-70-68-73—286	9050
	T Watson	69-71-73-69—282	27285		I Woosnam (Wal)	68-72-75-71—286	9050
	D A Weibring	71-73-71-67—282	27285		F Zoeller	76-67-72-71—286	9050
	R Cochran	68-72-65-77—282	27285				

Other players who made the cut: G Day, D Duval, G Morgan, J Morse 287; J Sluman, F Couples 287; P Blackmar, J Cook, S McCarron, P Stankowski, B Watts 288; J Adams, B Boyd, A Cejka (Ger), J Gallagher Jr, L Rinker, C Rocca (Ita), N Lancaster, B Mayfair, T Nakajima (Jpn) 289; E Els (RSA), D Forsman, S Hoch, M Wiebe 290; N Faldo (Eng), W Grady (Aus), C Parry (Aus), W Wood 291; W Austin, B Crenshaw, N Henke, P Stewart 292; P Goydos, J Maggert 293; M Dawson 294; B Langer (Ger) 295; J Edwards 296; S Higashi (Jpn), S Ingraham 297; H Clark (Eng), J Reeves 298.

1995 US PGA Championship *at Riviera, Los Angeles, California*   (6956–71)

Prize money: $2,000,000. Entries: 150, of whom 72 made the half-way cut.

1	S Elkington (Aus)*	68-67-68-64—267	$360000	20	G Norman (Aus)	66-69-70-72—277	21000
2	C Montgomerie (Sco)	68-67-67-65—267	216000		J Parnevik (Swe)	69-69-70-69—277	21000
Elkington won at first play-off hole					D Waldorf	69-69-67-72—277	21000
3	E Els (RSA)	66-65-66-72—269	116000	23	W Austin	70-70-70-68—278	15500
	J Maggert	66-69-65-69—269	116000		N Henke	68-73-67-70—278	15500
5	B Faxon	70-67-71-63—271	80000		P Jacobsen	69-67-71-71—278	15500
6	B Estes	69-68-68-68—273	68500		L Janzen	66-70-72-70—278	15500
	M O'Meara	64-67-69-73—273	68500		B Lietzke	73-68-67-70—278	15500
8	J Haas	69-71-64-70—274	50000		B Mayfair	68-68-72-70—278	15500
	J Leonard	68-66-70-70—274	50000		S Stricker	75-64-69-70—278	15500
	S Lowery	69-68-68-69—274	50000		S Torrance (Sco)	69-69-69-71—278	15500
	J Sluman	69-67-68-70—274	50000	31	P Azinger	70-70-72-67—279	8906
	C Stadler	71-66-66-71—274	50000		M Brooks	67-74-69-69—279	8906
13	J Furyk	68-70-69-68—275	33750		F Couples	70-69-74-66—279	8906
	MA Jiménez (Esp)	69-69-67-70—275	33750		N Faldo (Eng)	69-73-70-67—279	8906
	P Stewart	69-70-69-67—275	33750		G Morgan	66-73-74-66—279	8906
	K Triplett	71-69-68-67—275	33750		JM Olazábal (Esp)	72-66-70-71—279	8906
17	M Campbell (NZ)	71-65-71-69—276	26000		Joe Ozaki (Jpn)	71-70-65-73—279	8906
	C Rocca (Ita)	70-69-68-69—276	26000		DA Weibring	74-68-69-68—279	8906
	C Strange	72-68-68-68—276	26000				

Other players who made the cut: L Clements, F Funk, A Lyle (Sco) 280; N Price (Zim), P Walton (Eng) 280; C Beck, B Crenshaw, J Gallagher jr, G Sauers, P Senior (Aus) 281; J Adams, B Claar, R Freeman, Jumbo Ozaki (Jpn), K Perry 282; M Bradley, H Irwin, T Kite, S Simpson 283; E Dougherty, P-U Johansson (Swe), S Pate, L Roberts, T Watson 284; B Lane (Eng), M Sullivan, L Wadkins 285; D Pruitt 286; D Frost (RSA), J Nicklaus 287; F Zoeller 288; B Kamm 289; C Byrum, W Defrancesco 291.

1994 US PGA Championship *at Southern Hills, Tulsa, Oklahoma*   (6834–70)

Prize money: $1,750,000. Entries: 151, of whom 76 made the half-way cut.

Pos	Player	Score	Prize	Pos	Player	Score	Prize
1	N Price (Zim)	67-65-70-67—269	$310000	19T	M McCumber	73-70-71-68—282	18666
2	C Pavin	70-67-69-69—275	160000		F Zoeller	69-71-72-70—282	18666
3	P Mickelson	68-71-67-70—276	110000		B Glasson	71-73-68-70—282	18666
4	N Faldo (Eng)	73-67-71-66—277	76666		C Strange	73-71-68-70—282	18666
	G Norman (Aus)	71-69-67-70—277	76666		C Parry (Aus)	70-69-70-73—282	18666
	J Cook	71-67-69-70—277	76666	25	B Lane (Eng)	70-73-68-72—283	13000
7	S Elkington (Aus)	73-70-66-69—278	57500		B Langer (Ger)	73-71-67-72—283	13000
	JM Olazábal (Esp)	72-66-70-70—278	57500		D Frost (RSA)	70-71-69-73—283	13000
9	I Woosnam (Wal)	68-72-73-66—279	41000		E Els (RSA)	68-71-69-75—283	13000
	T Kite	72-68-69-70—279	41000		J Sluman	70-72-66-75—283	13000
	T Watson	69-72-67-71—279	41000	30	B Faxon	72-73-73-66—284	8458
	L Roberts	69-72-67-71—279	41000		W Grady (Aus)	75-68-71-70—284	8458
	B Crenshaw	70-67-70-72—279	41000		B Boyd	72-71-70-71—284	8458
14	J Haas	71-66-68-75—280	32000		L Clements	74-70-69-71—284	8458
15	K Triplett	71-69-71-70—281	27000		S Torrance (Sco)	69-75-69-71—284	8458
	L Mize	72-72-67-70—281	27000		R Zokol (Can)	77-67-67-73—284	8458
	M McNulty (Zim)	72-68-70-71—281	27000	36	C Beck	72-70-72-71—285	7000
	G Day	70-69-70-72—281	27000		B McAllister	74-64-75-72—285	7000
19	C Stadler	70-70-74-68—282	18666		C Montgomerie (Sco)	67-76-70-72—285	7000

Other players who made the cut: F Couples, B Mayfair, G Morgan, T Lehman, H Irwin 286; N Lancaster, D Edwards, D Gilford (Eng) 287; B Andrade, F Allem (RSA), B Estes, A Magee, F Nobilo (NZ), G Kraft, J Ozaki (Jpn), DA Weibring 288; D Hart, F Funk, H Sutton, T Dolby, K Perry, M Springer 289; R Floyd, T Nakajima (Jpn), R McDougal, L Wadkins, B Fleisher 290; L Janzen, JD Blake, P Stewart, J Inman, T Smith 291; D Hammond, P Senior (Aus) 292; A Lyle (Sco), D Pride 297; B Henninger, H Meshiai (Jpn) 298.

US PGA Championship History

Year	Winner	Runner-up	Venue	By
1916	J Barnes	J Hutchison	Siwanoy	1 hole
1919	J Barnes	F McLeod	Engineers' Club	6 and 5
1920	J Hutchison	D Edgar	Flossmoor	1 hole
1921	W Hagen	J Barnes	Inwood Club	3 and 2
1922	G Sarazen	E French	Oakmont	4 and 3
1923	G Sarazen	W Hagen	Pelham	38th hole
1924	W Hagen	J Barnes	French Lick	2 holes
1925	W Hagen	W Mehlhorn	Olympic Fields	6 and 4
1926	W Hagen	L Diegel	Salisbury	4 and 3
1927	W Hagen	J Turnesa	Dallas, TX	1 hole
1928	L Diegel	A Espinosa	Five Farms	6 and 5
1929	L Diegel	J Farrell	Hill Crest	6 and 4
1930	T Armour	G Sarazen	Fresh Meadow	1 hole
1931	T Creavy	D Shute	Wannamoisett	2 and 1
1932	O Dutra	F Walsh	St Paul, MN	4 and 3
1933	G Sarazen	W Goggin	Milwaukee	5 and 4
1934	P Runyan	C Wood	Buffalo	38th hole
1935	J Revolta	T Armour	Oklahoma	5 and 4
1936	D Shute	J Thomson	Pinehurst	3 and 2
1937	D Shute	H McSpaden	Pittsburgh	37th hole
1938	P Runyan	S Snead	Shawnee	8 and 7
1939	H Picard	B Nelson	Pomonok	37th hole
1940	B Nelson	S Snead	Hershey, PA	1 hole
1941	V Ghezzie	B Nelson	Denver, CO	38th hole
1942	S Snead	J Turnesa	Atlantic City, NJ	2 and 1
1943	*No Championship*			
1944	B Hamilton	B Nelson	Spokane, WA	1 hole
1945	B Nelson	S Byrd	Dayton, OH	4 and 3
1946	B Hogan	E Oliver	Portland	6 and 4
1947	J Ferrier	C Harbert	Detroit	2 and 1
1948	B Hogan	M Turnesa	Norwood Hills	7 and 6
1949	S Snead	J Palmer	Richmond, VA	3 and 2

United States PGA Championship History *continued*

Year	Winner	Runner-up	Venue	By
1950	C Harper	H Williams	Scioto, OH	4 and 3
1951	S Snead	W Burkemo	Oakmont, PA	7 and 6
1953	W Burkemo	F Lorza	Birmingham, MI	2 and 1
1954	C Harbert	W Burkemo	St Paul, MN	4 and 3
1955	D Ford	C Middlecoff	Detroit	4 and 3
1956	J Burke	T Kroll	Boston	3 and 2
1957	L Hebert	D Finsterwald	Miami Valley, Dayton	3 and 1

Changed to stroke play

Year	Winner	Venue	Score	Year	Winner	Venue	Score
1958	D Finsterwald	Llanerch, PA	276	1981	L Nelson	Atlanta, GA	273
1959	B Rosburg	Minneapolis, MN	277	1982	R Floyd	Southern Hills, OK	272
1960	J Hebert	Firestone, Akron, OH	281	1983	H Sutton	Pacific Palisades, CA	274
1961	J Barber*	Olympia Fields, IL	277	1984	L Trevino	Shoal Creek, AL	273
1962	G Player (RSA)	Aronimink, PA	278	1985	H Green	Cherry Hills, Denver, CO	278
1963	J Nicklaus	Dallas, TX	279	1986	R Tway	Inverness, Toledo, OH	276
1964	B Nichols	Columbus, OH	271	1987	L Nelson*	PGA National, FL	287
1965	D Marr	Laurel Valley, PA	280	1988	J Sluman	Oaktree, OK	272
1966	A Geiberger	Firestone, Akron, OH	280	1989	P Stewart	Kemper Lakes, IL	276
1967	D January*	Columbine, CO	281	1990	W Grady (Aus)	Shoal Creek, AL	282
1968	J Boros	Pecan Valley, TX	281	1991	J Daly	Crooked Stick, IN	276
1969	R Floyd	Dayton, OH	276	1992	N Price (Zim)	Bellerive, MS	278
1970	D Stockton	Southern Hills, OK	279	1993	P Azinger*	Inverness, Toledo, OH	272
1971	J Nicklaus	PGA National, FL	281	1994	N Price (Zim)	Southern Hills, OK	269
1972	G Player (RSA)	Oakland Hills, MI	281	1995	S Elkington (Aus)*	Riviera, LA	267
1973	J Nicklaus	Canterbury, OH	277	1996	M Brooks*	Valhalla, Kentucky	277
1974	L Trevino	Tanglewood, NC	276	1997	D Love III	Winged Foot, NY	269
1975	J Nicklaus	Firestone, Akron, OH	276	1998	V Singh (Fij)	Sahalee, Seattle, WA	271
1976	D Stockton	Congressional, MD	281	1999	T Woods	Medinah, IL	277
1977	L Wadkins*	Pebble Beach, CA	287	2000	T Woods*	Valhalla, Louisville KY	270
1978	J Mahaffey*	Oakmont, PA	276	2001	D Toms	Atlanta Athletic Club, GA	265
1979	D Graham (Aus)*	Oakland Hills, MI	272	2002	R Beem	Hazeltine National, MN	278
1980	J Nicklaus	Oak Hill, NY	274	2003	S Micheel	Oak Hill, NY	276

Top performances in the 2003 Majors

Name	The Masters	US Open	The Open	USPGA
Played Four rounds in all four 2003 majors:				
Mike Weir	1	T3	T28	T7
Ernie Els	T6	T5	T18	T5
Vijay Singh	T6	T20	T2	T34
Kenny Perry	T39	T3	T8	T10
Len Mattiace	2	T57	T65	T51
Phil Mickelson	3	T55	T59	T23
Tiger Woods	T15	T20	T4	T39
Charles Howell III	T28	T53	T65	T10
Angel Cabrera	T15	T35	T15	T45
Other 2003 Major winners:				
Jim Furyk	4	1	MC	T18
Ben Curtis	DNP	DNP	1	MC
Shaun Micheel	DNP	DNP	DNP	1
Other notables:				
Darren Clarke	T28	T42	T59	MC
Colin Montgomerie	MC	T42	Ret	MC
Padraig Harrington	MC	T10	T22	T29
Thomas Bjørn	DNP	MC	T2	MC
Nick Faldo	T33	MC	T8	DNP
Nick Price	T23	T5	T28	DNP

Men's Major Title Table

Jack Nicklaus

Bobby Jones

Walter Hagen

	Open	US Open	Masters	US PGA	Amateur	US Amateur	*Total Titles*
Jack Nicklaus	3	4	6	5	0	2	20
Bobby Jones	3	4	0	0	1	5	13
Walter Hagen	4	2	0	5	0	0	11
Tiger Woods	1	2	3	2	0	3	11
John Ball	1	0	0	0	8	0	9
Ben Hogan	1	4	2	2	0	0	9
Gary Player	3	1	3	2	0	0	9
Arnold Palmer	2	1	4	0	0	1	8
Tom Watson	5	1	2	0	0	0	8
Harold Hilton	2	0	0	0	4	1	7
Gene Sarazen	1	2	1	3	0	0	7
Sam Snead	1	0	3	3	0	0	7
Harry Vardon	6	1	0	0	0	0	7
Lee Trevino	2	2	0	2	0	0	6
Nick Faldo	3	0	3	0	0	0	6

Weetabix Women's British Open Championship

2003 Weetabix Women's British Open Championship
at Royal Lytham & St Annes, England (6308–72)

Prize money: £1.05 million. Final field of 144, of whom 68 (1 amateur) made the half-way cut on 147 or under.

1	Annika Sörenstam (Swe)	68-72-68-70—278	£160000	€228720
2	Se Ri Pak (Kor)	69-69-69-72—279	100000	142950
3	Grace Park (Kor)	74-65-71-70—280	62500	89344
	Karrie Webb (Aus)	67-72-70-71—280	62500	89344
5	Patricia Meunier-Lebouc (Fra)	70-69-67-76—282	45000	64327
6	Vicki Goetze-Ackerman (USA)	73-71-68-71—283	37000	52891
	Wendy Ward (USA)	67-71-69-76—283	37000	52891
8	Sophie Gustafson (Swe)	73-69-71-71—284	32000	45744
9	Young Kim (Kor)	73-70-72-70—285	29000	41455
10	Candie Kung (Tai)	73-71-69-73—286	25000	35737
	Gloria Park (Kor)	70-75-69-72—286	25000	35737
12	Paula Marti (Esp)	71-70-70-76—287	21000	30019
	Karen Stupples (Eng)	69-74-70-74—287	21000	30019
14	Lynnette Brooky (NZ)	70-74-75-69—288	16150	23086
	Beth Daniel (USA)	74-71-67-76—288	16150	23086
	Laura Diaz (USA)	73-74-71-70—288	16150	23086
	Jeong Jang (Kor)	76-69-72-71—288	16150	23086
	Cristie Kerr (USA)	74-71-71-72—288	16150	23086
19	Heather Bowie (USA)	70-66-74-79—289	12500	17869
	Laura Davies (Eng)	75-70-70-74—289	12500	17869
	Hee Won Han (Kor)	75-71-70-73—289	12500	17869
	Lorie Kane (Can)	69-75-70-75—289	12500	17869
	Becky Morgan (Wal)	72-70-71-76—289	12500	17869
24	Brandie Burton (USA)	76-69-69-76—290	8996	12860
	Moira Dunn (USA)	70-74-74-72—290	8996	12860
	Michiko Hattori (Jpn)	78-69-71-72—290	8996	12860
	Pat Hurst (USA)	73-71-74-72—290	8996	12860
	Soo-Yun Kang (Kor)	70-75-72-73—290	8996	12860
	Emilee Klein (USA)	72-70-74-74—290	8996	12860
	Lorena Ochoa (Mex)	74-65-77-74—290	8996	12860
	Dottie Pepper (USA)	71-75-71-73—290	8996	12860
	Jennifer Rosales (Phi)	69-72-76-73—290	8996	12860
	Iben Tinning (Den)	71-73-73-73—290	8996	12860
	Hiroko Yamaguchi (Jpn)	72-71-75-72—290	8996	12860
	Young-A Yang (Kor)	71-75-71-73—290	8996	12860
36	Georgina Simpson (Eng)	69-73-74-75—291	7000	10006
37	Christine Kuld (Den)	69-76-75-72—292	6375	9113
	Meg Mallon (USA)	71-72-71-78—292	6375	9113
	Michele Redman (USA)	71-69-76-76—292	6375	9113
	Nadina Taylor (Aus)	71-74-72-75—292	6375	9113
41	Elisabeth Esterl (Ger)	72-75-75-71—293	5250	7505
	Akiko Fukushima (Jpn)	72-67-79-75—293	5250	7505
	Johanna Head (Eng)	76-71-71-75—293	5250	7505
	Juli Inkster (USA)	74-71-77-71—293	5250	7505
	Catrin Nilsmark (Swe)	73-72-74-74—293	5250	7505

46	Kelli Kuehne (USA)	73-69-69-83—294	£4300	€6147
	Elisa Serramia (Esp) (am)	72-75-74-73—294		
	Rachel Teske (Aus)	70-77-70-77—294	4300	6147
	Karen Weiss (USA)	73-73-76-72—294	4300	6147
50	Kasumi Fujii (Jpn)	71-76-71-77—295	3600	5146
	Angela Jerman (USA)	74-72-73-76—295	3600	5146
	Carin Koch (Swe)	70-74-75-76—295	3600	5146
	Kelly Robbins (USA)	72-74-74-75—295	3600	5146
54	Cherie Byrnes (Aus)	71-75-76-74—296	2812	4020
	Michelle Ellis (Aus)	71-73-78-74—296	2812	4020
	Woo-Soon Ko (Kor)	72-72-78-74—296	2812	4020
	Shani Waugh (Aus)	69-78-74-75—296	2812	4020
58	Heather Daly-Donofrio (USA)	72-75-74-76—297	2250	3216
	Susan Parry (USA)	74-72-73-78—297	2250	3216
	Kirsty Taylor (Eng)	73-74-75-75—297	2250	3216
61	Helen Alfredsson (Swe)	70-75-75-78—298	1950	2788
	Alison Nicholas (Eng)	73-74-75-76—298	1950	2788
63	Beth Bauer (USA)	73-74-73-79—299	1800	2573
64	Silvia Cavalleri (Ita)	75-72-77-76—300	1617	2311
	Sophie Sandolo (Ita)	73-71-80-76—300	1617	2311
	Angela Stanford (USA)	72-69-74-85—300	1617	2311
67	Suzanne Strudwick (Eng)	75-72-80-76—303	1000	1429
68	Marnie McGuire (NZ)	72-74-85-77—308	1000	1429

The following 78 players missed the cut. Each professional player received £300 (€429):

69	Mandy Adamson (RSA)	75-73—148	103T	Lora Fairclough (Eng)	75-76—151
	Danielle Ammaccapane (USA)	70-78—148		Tracy Hanson (USA)	75-76—151
	Dorothy Delasin (USA)	76-72—148		Marlene Hedblom (Swe)	77-74—151
	Kate Golden (USA)	74-74—148		Diane Irvin (USA)	79-72—151
	Samantha Head (Eng)	72-76—148		Ludivine Kreutz (Fra)	76-75—151
	Maria Hjörth (Swe)	74-74—148		Jung Yeon Lee (Kor)	71-80—151
	Trish Johnson (Eng)	72-76—148		Laurette Maritz (RSA)	76-75—151
	Christina Kim (USA)	72-76—148		Mhairi McKay (Sco)	78-73—151
	Mi Hyun Kim (Kor)	74-74—148		Charlotta Sörenstam (Swe)	74-77—151
	Leta Lindley (USA)	74-74—148		Rebecca Stevenson (Aus)	74-77—151
	JoAnne Mills (Aus)	76-72—148	117	Rachel Bailey (Eng)	78-74—152
	Miriam Nagl (Ger)	75-73—148		Karen Davies (Wal)	76-76—152
	Liselotte Neumann (Swe)	74-74—148		Karen Margrethe Juul (Den)	78-74—152
	Kim Saiki (USA)	73-75—148		Hilary Lunke (USA)	78-74—152
	Ana Belen Sanchez (Esp)	74-74—148		Yun Jye Wei (PRC)	73-79—152
	Gina Scott (NZ)	73-75—148	122	Florence Descampe (Bel)	85-68—153
	Giulia Sergas (Ita)	70-78—148	123	Amy Fruhwirth (USA)	76-78—154
	Sherri Steinhauer (USA)	76-72—148		Yu Ping Lin (Tai)	79-75—154
87	Beth Bader (USA)	72-77—149		Janice Moodie (Sco)	77-77—154
	Tina Barrett (USA)	73-76—149		Vibeke Stensrud (Nor)	74-80—154
	Asa Gottmo (Swe)	76-73—149		Vicky Uwland (Aus)	76-78—154
	Natalie Gulbis (USA)	75-74—149	128	Jean Bartholomew (USA)	77-78—155
	Sarah Heath (Eng)	78-71—149		Betsy King (USA)	74-81—155
	Alexandra Keighley (Eng) (am)	70-79—149		Anne-Marie Knight (Aus)	76-79—155
	Denise Killeen (USA)	76-73—149		Joanne Morley (Eng)	76-79—155
	Kathryn Marshall (Sco)	77-72—149		Lara Tadiotto (Bel)	79-76—155
	Catriona Matthew (Sco)	78-71—149	133	Deb Richard (USA)	77-79—156
	Kimberley Williams (USA)	75-74—149	134	Marisa Baena (Col)	80-77—157
97	Becky Brewerton (Wal) (am)	75-75—150		Wendy Dicks (Eng)	81-76—157
	Corinne Dibnah (Aus)	72-78—150		Veronica Zorzi (Ita)	78-79—157
	Jackie Gallagher-Smith (USA)	73-77—150	137	Virginie Auffret (Fra)	78-81—159
	Tamara Hyett (Aus)	77-73—150		Karen Lunn (Aus)	83-76—159
	Stephanie Louden (USA)	71-79—150		Filippa Helmersson (Swe)	81-78—159
	Suzann Pettersen (Nor)	74-76—150	140	Ana Larraneta (Esp)	83-80—163
103	Stephanie Arricau (Fra)	72-79—151	141	Karine Icher (Fra)	85-79—164
	Federica Dassu (Ita)	75-76—151	142	Diana Luna (Ita)	76-95—171
	Wendy Doolan (Aus)	83-68—151	143	Alison Munt (Aus)	80 retd
	Cecilia Ekelundh (Swe)	76-75—151		Amy Read (USA)	78 retd

2002 Weetabix Women's British Open at Turnberry, Ayrshire   (6407-72)

Prize money: £1,000,000

1	Karrie Webb (Aus)	66-71-70-66—273	£154982	24	Patricia Meunier			
2	Michelle Ellis (Aus)	69-70-68-68—275	84990		Lebouc (Fra)	69-71-69-76—285	10249	
	Paula Marti (Esp)	69-68-69-69—275	84990		Suzann Pettersen (Nor)	72-71-72-70—285	10249	
4	Jeong Jang (Kor)	73-69-66-69—277	42308	26	Dorothy Delasin (USA)	70-71-70-75—286	9366	
	Candie Kung (Tai)	65-71-71-70—277	42308		Elisabeth Esterl (Ger)	67-71-72-76—286	9366	
	Catrin Nilsmark (Swe)	70-69-69-69—277	42308		Emilee Klein (USA)	68-71-72-75—286	9366	
	Jennifer Rosales (Phi)	69-70-65-73—277	42308	29	Brandie Burton (USA)	71-70-71-75—287	7949	
8	Beth Bauer (USA)	70-67-70-71—278	25164		Cristie Kerr (USA)	72-71-69-75—287	7949	
	Carin Koch (Swe)	68-68-68-74—278	25164		Kelli Kuehne (USA)	75-67-71-74—287	7949	
	Meg Mallon (USA)	69-71-68-70—278	25164		Yu Ping Lin (Tai)	73-69-74-71—287	7949	
11	Sophie Gustafson (Swe)	69-73-69-68—279	19748		Iben Tinning (Den)	71-69-71-76—287	7949	
	Se Ri Pak (Kor)	67-72-69-71—279	19748	34	Toshimi Kimura (Jpn)	74-70-70-74—288	7249	
13	Natalie Gulbis (USA)	69-70-67-74—280	16581	35	Kathryn Marshall (Sco)	70-71-76-72—289	6499	
	Pat Hurst (USA)	69-70-69-72—280	16581		Catriona Matthew (Sco)	73-71-70-75—289	6499	
	Angela Stanford (USA)	69-70-69-72—280	16581		Liselotte Neumann			
16	Tina Barrett (USA)	67-70-70-76—283	14348		(Swe)	70-71-71-77—289	6499	
	Beth Daniel (USA)	73-68-68-74—283	14348		Kelly Robbins (USA)	70-75-68-76—289	6499	
18	Jean Bartholomew				Shani Waugh (Aus)	70-73-74-72—289	6499	
	(USA)	71-72-72-69—284	12099	40	Helen Alfredsson (Swe)	70-75-71-74—290	5249	
	Wendy Doolan (Aus)	70-69-71-74—284	12099		Lora Fairclough (Eng)	71-69-73-77—290	5249	
	Jane Geddes (USA)	71-69-70-74—284	12099		Becky Iverson (USA)	69-76-72-73—290	5249	
	Marine Monnet (Fra)	71-70-70-73—284	12099		Karen Lunn (Aus)	73-71-72-74—290	5249	
	Fiona Pike (Aus)	72-73-67-72—284	12099		Sophie Sandolo (Ita)	71-74-68-77—290	5249	
	Rachel Teske (Aus)	67-74-68-75—284	12099					

Other players who made the cut: Asa Gottmo (Swe), Mhairi McKay (Sco) 291; Heather Daly-Donofrio (USA), Federica Dassu (Ita), Tracy Hanson (USA), Johanna Head (Eng), Becky Morgan (Wal), Giulia Sergas (Ita) 292; Heather Bowie (USA), Grace Park (Kor), Suzanne Strudwick (Eng) 293; Raquel Carriedo (Esp), Karen Stupples (Eng), Wendy Ward (USA) 294; Betsy King (USA) 295; Vicki Goetze-Ackerman (USA) 296; Mi Hyun Kim (Kor), Charlotta Sörenstam (Swe) 297; Tonya Gill (USA) 298; Riikka Hakkarainen (Fin) 299; Marina Arruti (Esp) 301; Ana Larraneta (Esp) 302

2001 Weetabix Women's British Open at Sunningdale, Berkshire

Prize money: £730,000   (6245-72)

1	Se Ri Pak (Kor)	71-70-70-66—277	£155000	21T	Emilee Klein (USA)	71-70-71-73—285	11125	
2	Mi Hyun Kim (Kor)	72-65-71-71—279	100000		Lora Fairclough (Eng)	71-70-67-77—285	11125	
3	Laura Diaz (USA)	74-70-69-67—280	51813	25	Danielle Ammaccapane			
	Iben Tinning (Den)	71-69-72-68—280	51813		(USA)	75-68-74-69—286	9071	
	Janice Moodie (Sco)	67-70-71-72—280	51813		Dina Ammaccapane			
	Catriona Matthew (Sco)	70-65-72-73—280	51813		(USA)	72-71-74-69—286	9071	
7	Kristal Parker (USA)	72-71-71-67—281	25600		Silvia Cavalleri (Ita)	71-73-72-70—286	9071	
	Marina Arruti (Esp)	71-73-70-67—281	25600		Maria Hjörth (Swe)	72-73-71-70—286	9071	
	Kathryn Marshall (Sco)	75-71-68-67—281	25600		Gloria Park (Kor)	71-73-71-71—286	9071	
	Kelli Kuehne (USA)	71-70-71-69—281	25600		Lee Ji Hee (Kor)	75-71-69-71—286	9071	
	Kasumi Fujii (Jpn)	71-71-69-70—281	25600		Laura Davies (Eng)	68-73-69-76—286	9071	
12	Raquel Carriedo (Esp)	73-70-70-69—282	17750	32	Annika Sörenstam (Swe)	70-74-74-69—287	6767	
	Tracy Hanson (USA)	72-69-70-71—282	17750		Marisa Baena (Col)	72-74-72-69—287	6767	
	Rosie Jones (USA)	70-69-71-72—282	17750		Suzann Pettersen (Nor)	78-64-74-71—287	6767	
15	Brandie Burton (USA)	72-71-73-67—283	14400		Wendy Doolan (Aus)	72-68-75-72—287	6767	
	Pearl Sinn (USA)	74-70-72-67—283	14400		Grace Park (Kor)	70-71-74-72—287	6767	
	Jill McGill (USA)	70-70-72-71—283	14400		Kelly Robbins (USA)	69-72-73-73—287	6767	
	Karrie Webb (Aus)	74-67-68-74—283	14400		Mhairi McKay (Sco)	70-72-72-73—287	6767	
19	Becky Morgan (Wal)	73-68-71-72—284	12575		Hee Won Han (Kor)	72-73-69-73—287	6767	
	Trish Johnson (Eng)	70-67-72-75—284	12575		Hiromi Kobayashi (Jpn)	72-70-71-74—287	6767	
21	Johanna Head (Eng)	70-74-69-72—285	11125		Rebecca Hudson (Eng)			
	Marlene Hedblom (Swe)	70-74-69-72—285	11125		(am)	71-70-70-76—287		

Other players who made the cut: Sophie Gustafson (Swe), Kellee Booth (USA), Joanne Morley (Eng), Vicki Goetze-Ackerman (USA) 288; Lorie Kane (Can), Suzanne Strudwick (Eng), Tina Barrett (USA), Cindy Schreyer (USA), Elisabeth Esterl (Ger), Riikka Hakkarainen (Fin) 289; Joanne Mills (Aus) 290; Becky Iverson (USA), Yu Ping Lin (Tai) 291; Liselotte Neumann (Swe) 292; Carin Koch (Swe), Jenny Lidback (Per), Marine Monnet (Fra), Diane Barnard (Eng) 293; Kaori Harada (Jpn), Laurette Maritz (RSA), Karin Icher (Fra), Lisa Hed (Swe) 294; Nicola Moult (Eng), Helen Alfredsson (Swe), Patricia Meunier-Lebouc (Fra) 295; Kirsty Taylor (Eng) 296; Judith Van Hagen (Ned), Claire Duffy (Eng) 297; Dorothy Delasin (USA) 298

2000 Women's British Open Championship *at Royal Birkdale* (6285–73)

Prize money: £730,000

1	Sophie Gustafson (Swe)	70-66-71-75—282	£120000	20	Kelly Robbins (USA)	73-74-73-70—290	8475
2	Kirsty Taylor (Eng)	71-74-72-67—284	50713		Karen Weiss (USA)	73-70-75-72—290	8475
	Becky Iverson (USA)	70-70-75-69—284	50713		Rachel Hetherington		
	Liselotte Neumann (Swe)	71-73-71-69—284	50713		(Aus)	71-74-73-72—290	8475
	Meg Mallon (USA)	74-69-71-70—284	50713		Brandie Burton (USA)	72-74-71-73—290	8475
6	Laura Philo (USA)	72-73-72-68—285	27500	24	Michele Redman (USA)	74-73-73-71—291	7275
7	Karrie Webb (Aus)	68-75-72-71—286	23250		Alicia Dibos (Per)	72-73-74-72—291	7275
8	Janice Moody (Sco)	73-74-73-67—287	19500		Marine Monnet (Fra)	72-73-74-72—291	7275
	Vicki Goetze-Ackerman				Raquel Carriedo (Esp)	76-71-72-72—291	7275
	(USA)	77-69-73-68—287	19500	28	Riko Higashio (Jpn)	74-72-76-70—292	6313
10	Maggie Will (USA)	74-72-76-66—288	13250		Susan Redman (USA)	70-78-71-73—292	6313
	Michelle McGann (USA)	72-76-69-71—288	13250		Jill McGill (USA)	71-71-76-74—292	6313
	Juli Inkster (USA)	70-69-77-72—288	13250		Mhairi McKay (Sco)	74-71-71-76—292	6313
	Jenny Lidback (Per)	71-71-73-73—288	13250	32	Shani Waugh (Aus)	73-74-76-70—293	5400
	Trish Johnson (Eng)	71-72-72-73—288	13250		Michelle Estill (USA)	72-75-75-71—293	5400
	Kellee Booth (USA)	73-71-71-73—288	13250		Sofia Grönberg		
	Kathryn Marshall (Sco)	72-69-73-74—288	13250		Whitmore (Swe)	80-69-73-71—293	5400
17	Pat Bradley (USA)	74-71-74-70—289	9850		Gail Graham (Can)	79-71-71-72—293	5400
	Rosie Jones (USA)	72-72-73-72—289	9850		Betsey King (USA)	74-73-73-73—293	5400
	Annika Sörenstam (Swe)	70-76-71-72—289	9850				

Other players who made the cut: Giulia Sergas (Ita), Maria Hjörth (Swe), Tina Barrett (USA), Leigh Ann Mills (USA), Julie Forbes (Sco), Wendy Daden (Eng), Pernilla Sterner (Swe), Laura Davies (Eng) 294; Anna Berg (Swe), Yu Ping Lin (Tai), Aki Takamura (Jpn), Karen Pearce (Aus) 295; Silvia Cavalleri (Ita), Stephanie Arricau (Fra), Sara Eklund (Swe), Karen Stupples (Eng), Sandrine Mendiburu (Fra), Jenifer Feldott (USA), Helen Alfredsson (Swe), Anne-Marie Knight (Aus) 296; Federica Dassu (Ita) 297; Kristal Parker-Gregory (USA), Elizabeth Esterl (Ger) 298; Catrin Nilsmark (Swe), Smriti Mehra (Ind), Johanna Head (Eng) 299; Mardi Lunn (Aus), Mandy Adamson (RSA), Dale Reid (Sco) 300; Hiromi Kobayashi (Jpn), Lisa De Paulo (USA) 301; Hsui Feng Tseng (Chn), Nina Karlsson (Swe), Judith Van Hagen (Ned) 303; Emilee Klein (USA), Gina Marie Scott (NZ), Laurette Maritz (RSA) 304; Lora Fairclough (Eng) 306

1999 Weetabix Women's British Open *at Woburn G&CC* (6463–73)

Prize money: £575,000

1	S Steinhauer (USA)	71-71-68-73—283	£100000	17T	C Figg-Currier (USA)	69-76-72-73—290	6614
2	A Sörenstam (Swe)	69-71-72-72—284	60000		V Van		
3	H Dobson (Eng)	71-72-72-70—285	31666		Ryckeghem (Bel)	72-75-70-73—290	6614
	C Flom (USA)	71-74-69-71—285	31666		K Taylor (Eng)	73-71-72-74—290	6614
	F Pike (Aus)	70-70-71-74—285	31666	24	G Sergas (Ita) (am)	71-73-74-73—291	
6	E Klein (USA)	72-70-73-71—286	16000		J Morley (Eng)	70-75-73-73—291	5300
	S Gustafson (Swe)	73-69-72-72—286	16000		A Nicholas (Eng)	73-71-73-74—291	5300
	M Lunn (Aus)	71-72-70-73—286	16000		M Hjörth (Swe)	71-68-77-75—291	5300
	I Tinning (Den)	68-69-75-74—286	16000		S Lowe (Eng)	72-74-70-75—291	5300
	C McCurdy (USA)	73-70-68-75—286	16000		P Meunier-		
11	S Mehra (Ind)	70-70-76-71—287	11000		Lebouc (Fra)	73-70-72-76—291	5300
12	C Koch (Swe)	74-72-72-70—288	9625		M Yoneyama (Jpn)	73-70-72-76—291	5300
	S Strudwick (Eng)	71-70-76-71—288	9625	31	C Nilsmark (Swe)	72-71-76-73—292	4150
14	R Jones (USA)	73-71-73-72—289	8033		M Hirase (Jpn)	73-72-74-73—292	4150
	L Philo (USA)	69-71-75-74—289	8033		D Barnard (Eng)	73-72-74-73—292	4150
	L Neumann (Swe)	72-70-72-75—289	8033		K Marshall (Sco)	72-75-72-73—292	4150
17	D Richard (USA)	72-73-73-72—290	6614		S Cavalleri (Ita)	73-72-73-74—292	4150
	L Navarro (Esp)	70-70-77-73—290	6614		Yu Chen Huang (Tai)	71-75-72-74—292	4150
	M McNamara (Aus)	72-70-75-73—290	6614		R Hudson (Eng) (am)	72-69-75-76—292	
	T Kimura (Jpn)	69-74-74-73—290	6614				

Other players who made the cut: L Davies (Eng), T Barrett (USA), M McKay (Sco), C Dibnah (Aus), K Webb (Aus) J Head (Eng), R Higashio (Jpn) 293; C Sörenstam (Swe), J Moodie (Sco), L Hackney (Eng), J Forbes (Sco), J McGill (USA), K Orum (Den), F Dassu (Ita), A Belen Sanchez (Esp) 294; N Scranton (USA), M Baena (Col), H Kobayashi (Jpn), L Lambert (Aus), T Johnson (Eng), A Takamura (Jpn), E Poburski (Ger), M Dunn (USA), B Pestana (RSA) 297; J Mills (Aus), M Sutton (Eng), B Morgan (Wal) (am), C Schmitt (Fra) 299; P Wright (Sco), S Croce (Ita) 300; N Nijenhuis (Ned) (am), C Matthew (Sco) 301; M Hageman (Ned) 302; Le Kreutz (Fra), V Stensrud (Nor) 303

1998 Weetabix Women's British Open *at Royal Lytham & St Annes*

Prize money: £575,000   (6355–72)

1	S Steinhauer	81-72-70-69—292	£100000	20T	J Gallacher-Smith	76-74-74-79—303	6300
2	S Gustafson	78-71-74-70—293	50000		K Marshall	79-74-71-79—303	6300
	B Burton	71-74-77-71—293	50000	24	D Andrews	81-72-76-75—304	5600
4	J Moodie	75-72-72-75—294	30000		J Morley	79-74-74-77—304	5600
5	K Webb	76-76-71-73—296	25000		P Hurst	76-77-70-81—304	5600
6	L Spalding	76-70-75-76—297	17000	27	C Johnstone-Forbes	78-76-79-72—305	5100
	W Ward	76-71-74-76—297	17000		S Strudwick	75-72-75-83—305	5100
	S Mehra	73-77-71-76—297	17000	29	C Koch	79-74-76-77—306	4700
	B King	71-77-72-77—297	17000		K Saiki	80-76-73-77—306	4700
10	C Nilsmark	77-77-69-75—298	12000	31	C McCurdy	80-77-75-75—307	4216
11	T Johnson	72-77-77-73—299	9687		F Dassu	82-72-77-76—307	4216
	J Inkster	75-75-76-73—299	9687		A Nicholas	79-72-76-80—307	4216
	A Sörenstam	75-73-77-74—299	9687	34	L Fairclough	77-77-78-76—308	3300
	ML de Lorenzi	79-70-76-74—299	9687		SR Pak	78-74-79-77—308	3300
15	M McKay	75-74-75-76—300	8000		W Doolan	83-72-76-77—308	3300
16	M Murray	81-76-69-75—301	7300		L Baugh	77-80-74-77—308	3300
	D Reid	73-79-73-76—301	7300		C Dibnah	77-80-74-77—308	3300
	H Wadsworth	79-74-72-76—301	7300		H Dobson	80-71-79-78—308	3300
19	H Kobayashi	77-74-75-76—302	6800		C McMillan	76-78-76-78—308	3300
20	M Hjörth	82-73-76-72—303	6300		C Figg-Currier	78-78-74-78—308	3300
	K Tschetter	79-75-73-76—303	6300		V Odegard	82-73-74-79—308	3300

Other players who made the cut: E Klein, C Sörenstam, R Carriedo, S Lowe 309; S Dallongeville, L Philo 310; A Munt, C Hall, T Fischer 311; K Pearce, L Kane, B Whitehead, J Forbes, D Barnard 312; I Tinning, L Neumann 313; L Maritz, T Barrett, H Stacy 314; R Hakkerainen, A Berg 316; M Hirase 317; C Johnson 318; M Spencer-Devlin 319; E Knuth 321

1997 Weetabix Women's British Open *at Sunningdale*   (6255–72)

Prize money: £525,000

1	K Webb	65-70-63-71—269	£82500	19T	C Dibnah	72-71-70-73—286	5837
2	R Jones	70-70-66-71—277	52000		A Dibos	71-72-70-73—286	5837
3	A Sörenstam	72-70-69-67—278	36750	23	L Davies	74-73-69-71—287	5300
4	B Burton	73-69-71-67—280	27000		R Hetherington	75-70-71-71—287	5300
5	L Hackney	74-69-67-71—281	20000		K Tschetter	73-70-72-72—287	5300
	C Matthew	70-70-70-71—281	20000	26	E Klein	69-74-70-75—288	5000
7	W Doolan	74-70-68-70—282	14000	27	S Farron	72-75-75-67—289	4475
	T Barrett	70-72-70-70—282	14000		B Whitehead	71-74-77-67—289	4475
9	C Johnson	71-71-73-68—283	11500		J Morley	75-69-76-69—289	4475
10	C Sörenstam	71-70-72-71—284	10100		L Brooky	72-73-72-72—289	4475
	B King	71-72-68-73—284	10100		H Alfredsson	69-76-72-72—289	4475
12	J Lidback	71-74-70-70—285	7414		J Moodie	74-71-71-73—289	4475
	M Hirase	76-65-74-70—285	7414	33	K Lunn	74-71-75-70—290	3875
	L Neumann	68-75-71-71—285	7414		P Hurst	76-72-70-72—290	3875
	J Inkster	69-71-73-72—285	7414		S Cavalleri (am)	70-73-73-74—290	
	B Mucha	72-67-73-73—285	7414	36	S Maynor	72-74-74-71—291	3650
	H Dobson	73-69-69-74—285	7414	37	S Strudwick	72-74-74-72—292	3350
	K Marshall	70-68-73-74—285	7414		D Richard	71-72-75-74—292	3350
19	C Koch	76-71-71-68—286	5837		G Graham	73-73-71-75—292	3350
	L Lambert	70-73-73-70—286	5837				

Other players who made the cut: M Estill, S Steinhauer, K Parker-Gregory 293; P Meunier Lebouc, A Gottmo, S Prosser, A Fruhwirth, S Waugh 294; M Spencer-Devlin, H Kobayashi, F Dassu 295; T Green, A Yamaoka, T Johnson, E Esterl (am) 296; S Croce, C Pierce, J Lee, W Dicks 297; M Koch, K Taylor, H Wadsworth, L Fairclough, L Kane, M Murray 298; C Figg-Currier 299; N Moult, D Barnard, S Gustafson 301; S Dallongeville 302.

1996 Weetabix Women's British Open at Woburn G&CC   (6309-73)

Prize money: £500,000

1	E Klein	68-66-71-72—277	£80000	19T	D Reid	68-74-74-72—288	5675
2	P Hammel	71-70-72-71—284	42500		K Yamazaki	71-70-74-73—288	5675
	A Alcott	72-70-70-72—284	42500		H Alfredsson	69-76-69-74—288	5675
4	J Geddes	72-73-70-70—285	20416		J Lidback	68-73-73-74—288	5675
	L Hackney	71-69-73-72—285	20416	25	J Morley	72-71-74-72—289	4850
	A Nicholas	68-71-74-72—285	20416		K Marshall	71-72-73-73—289	4850
7	B Whitehead	76-70-71-69—286	9571		T Abitbol	70-75-70-74—289	4850
	D Richard	71-73-71-71—286	9571		T Barrett	71-74-69-75—289	4850
	ML de Lorenzi	74-72-68-72—286	9571		M Hjörth	70-70-71-78—289	4850
	P Bradley	70-75-69-72—286	9571	30	S Grönberg-Whitmore	75-73-71-71—290	4100
	C Johnson	72-69-73-72—286	9571		A Fukushima	74-74-69-73—290	4100
	R Jones	69-71-73-73—286	9571		C Sörenstam	76-70-71-73—290	4100
	T Kerdyk	70-70-72-74—286	9571		V Goetze	74-70-72-74—290	4100
14	B Mucha	73-71-74-69—287	6600		J Piers	68-73-72-77—290	4100
	D Eggeling	69-77-71-70—287	6600	35	B Daniel	77-71-71-72—291	3300
	C Nilsmark	72-76-68-71—287	6600		C Matthew	71-73-75-72—291	3300
	K Webb	69-70-74-74—287	6600		S Maynor	73-73-71-74—291	3300
	A Sörenstam	69-70-73-75—287	6600		T Fischer	72-71-74-74—291	3300
19	D Andrews	80-65-74-69—288	5675		D Pepper	71-72-72-76—291	3300
	L Davies	72-75-71-70—288	5675		W Doolan	72-74-67-78—291	3300

Other players who made the cut: H Kobayashi, T Hanson, M Hirase 292; E Knuth, K Parker-Gregory 293; M Mallon, S Strudwick, L Brooky, S Croce, E Orley, L Navarro 294; A-M Knight, P Sterner, S Redman, C Dibnah, P Rigby-Jinglov, M Figueras-Dotti, M Berteotti, C Figg-Currier 295; R Hetherington, J Crafter, B Hackett (am) 296; R Carriedo, J Forbes, X Wunsch-Ruiz, M Estill 297; S Farwig, J Mcgill, C Hj Koch 298; N Harvey 300; K Weiss 302; M Sutton, K Harada 303.

1995 Weetabix Women's British Open at Woburn G&CC   (6257-73)

Prize money: £360,000

1	K Webb	69-70-69-70—278	£60000	19T	A Gottmo	70-73-74-74—291	4032
2	J McGill	71-73-71-69—284	30000		B Burton	72-70-74-75—291	4032
	A Sörenstam	70-72-71-71—284	30000	23	R Hetherington	74-76-76-66—292	3710
4	M Berteotti	73-71-71-70—285	14333		J Morley	72-72-74-74—292	3710
	C Pierce	70-70-72-73—285	14333		E Orley	71-73-74-74—292	3710
	V Skinner	74-68-67-76—285	14333	26	V Michaud	76-73-75-69—293	3215
7	S Strudwick	73-68-71-74—286	9500		A Nicholas	73-72-76-72—293	3215
8	ML de Lorenzi	68-74-73-73—288	6937		S Dallongeville	76-72-72-73—293	3215
	W Doolan	73-71-70-74—288	6937		M McGuire	68-78-73-74—293	3215
	N Lopez	71-73-70-74—288	6937		T Fischer	76-66-77-74—293	3215
	L Neumann	67-74-71-76—288	6937		L Hackney	74-74-70-75—293	3215
12	K Tschetter	73-75-74-67—289	4957		L Fairclough	76-68-72-77—293	3215
	C Matthew	74-71-73-71—289	4957		M Lunn	73-67-73-80—293	3215
	V Goetze	73-72-71-73—289	4957	34	M McNamara	76-73-74-71—294	2585
	P Meunier	73-71-71-74—289	4957		T Johnson	75-74-74-71—294	2585
16	J Forbes	69-73-77-71—290	4430		Li Wen-Lin	74-71-75-74—294	2585
	S Prosser	70-74-74-72—290	4430		L West	73-75-71-75—294	2585
	H Kobayashi	72-70-74-74—290	4430		S Waugh	68-75-72-79—294	2585
19	L Brooky	69-74-76-72—291	4032		S Croce	71-71-73-79—294	2585
	K Pearce	74-71-72-74—291	4032				

Other players who made the cut: D Barnard, C Hall, T Hanson, C Hjalmarsson, P Hammel 296; L Davies, LA Mills, S Burnell, P Wright, W Dicks, E Klein, K Peterson-Parker 297; C Duffy, E Knuth, A Brighouse, K Orum, J Geddes 298; A Rogers, K Marshall, L Weima, C Eliasson-Wharton, S Gr-Whitmore 299; A Arruti, A Shapcott, T Barrett, K Davies 300; G Stewart, L Dermott (am) 301; S Moon, D Reid 302; J Soulsby, P Sterner 303; H Hopkins, C Evelyn Louw 304; K Stupples (am) 305; N Buxton 307.

1994 Weetabix Women's British Open *at Woburn G&CC*　　(6224-73)

Prize money: £335,000

1	L Neumann	71-67-70-72—280	£52500	17T	E Knuth	78-69-72-73—292	4100
2	D Mochrie	73-66-74-70—283	27250	21	P Wright	68-75-78-72—293	3740
	A Sörenstam	69-75-69-70—283	27250		K Pearce	70-74-75-74—293	3740
4	L Davies	74-66-73-71—284	14625		K Tschetter	68-76-75-74—293	3740
	C Dibnah	75-70-67-72—284	14625	24	K Cockerill	71-77-73-73—294	3425
6	C Figg-Currier	69-74-68-74—285	10750		A Alcott	74-74-75-71—294	3425
7	H Alfredsson	71-76-71-68—286	9250		B King	73-74-69-78—294	3425
8	T Hanson	74-73-66-74—287	8000		A Ritzman	69-76-75-74—294	3425
9	S Strudwick	71-71-71-75—288	6250	28	S Moon	72-78-74-71—295	2930
	V Skinner	77-71-66-74—288	6250		A Nicholas	72-73-70-80—295	2930
	C Pierce	70-75-71-72—288	6250		D Reid	76-72-75-72—295	2930
12	H Kobayashi	73-73-69-74—289	5100		M Lunn	73-75-75-72—295	2930
13	S Gautrey	69-74-72-75—290	4800		K Marshall	76-72-75-72—295	2930
14	T Abitbol	76-68-75-72—291	4526		L Fairclough	75-72-72-76—295	2930
	P Grice-Whittaker	77-72-72-70—291	4526		S Redman	74-71-76-74—295	2930
	M McGuire	71-73-78-69—291	4526	35	T Johnson	75-75-72-74—296	2480
17	S Grönberg-Whitmore	71-69-74-78—292	4100		E Orley	73-76-74-73—296	2480
	Li Wen-Lin	73-70-73-76—292	4100		K Albers	75-67-78-76—296	2480
	J Geddes	74-72-72-74—292	4100				

Other players who made the cut: LA Mills, H Person, C Hall, L Navarro, L West 297; T Barrett 298; M Figueras-Dotti, K Orum, W Doolan, T Fischer (am), J Forbes 299; ML de Lorenzi, C Hjalmarsson, I Maconi 300; X Wunsch-Ruiz, LR Sugg, K Noble 301; F Dassu, M De Boer, G Steward, F Descampe, C Nilsmark, S Prosser, M Spencer-Devlin, S Waugh, H Wadsworth, S Mendiburu, S Robinson 302; N Scranton 303; D Barnard, L Hackney, E Crosby 304; M Hageman 306; B New, M Burstrom, N Moult, M Lawrence Wengler 307; J Lawrence, S Gustafson 309.

Women's British Open History

Year	Winner	Country	Venue	Score
1976	J Lee Smith	England	Fulford	299
1977	V Saunders	England	Lindrick	306
1978	J Melville	England	Foxhills	310
1979	A Sheard	South Africa	Southport and Ainsdale	301
1980	D Massey	USA	Wentworth (East)	294
1981	D Massey	USA	Northumberland	295
1982	M Figueras-Dotti	Spain	Royal Birkdale	296
1983	*Not played*			
1984	A Okamoto	Japan	Woburn	289
1985	B King	USA	Moor Park	300
1986	L Davies	England	Royal Birkdale	283
1987	A Nicholas	England	St Mellion	296
1988	C Dibnah*	Australia	Lindrick	296
* *Won play-off after a tie with S Little*				
1989	J Geddes	USA	Ferndown	274
1990	H Alfredsson*	Sweden	Woburn	288
* *Won play-off at fourth extra hole after a tie with J Hill*				
1991	P Grice-Whittaker	England	Woburn	284
1992	P Sheehan	USA	Woburn	207
Reduced to 54 holes by rain				
1993	K Lunn	Australia	Woburn	275
1994	L Neumann	Sweden	Woburn	280
1995	K Webb	Australia	Woburn	278
1996	E Klein	USA	Woburn	277
1997	K Webb	Australia	Sunningdale	269
1998	S Steinhauer	USA	Royal Lytham & St Annes	292
1999	S Steinhauer	USA	Woburn	283
2000	S Gustafson	Sweden	Royal Birkdale	282
2001	SR Pak	Korea	Sunningdale	277
2002	K Webb	Australia	Turnberry	273
2003	A Sörenstam	Sweden	Royal Lytham & St Annes	278

US Women's Open Championship

Players are of American nationality unless stated

2003 US Women's Open Championship (58th)
at Pumpkin Ridge GC, North Plains, OR (6509–71)

Prize Money: $3.1 million. Final field 156, of whom 59 (including 7 amateurs) made the cut at 149 or under.

1	Hilary Lunke*	71-69-68-75—283	$560000
2	Kelly Robbins	74-69-71-69—283	272004
	Angela Stanford	70-70-69-74—283	272004

(play-off rounds: Hilary Lunke 70, Angela Stanford 71, Kelly Robbins 73)

4	Annika Sörenstam (Swe)	72-72-67-73—284	150994
5	Aree Song (am)	70-73-68-74—285	
6	Jeong Jang (Kor)	73-69-69-75—286	115333
	Mhairi McKay (Sco)	66-70-75-75—286	115333
8	Juli Inkster	69-71-74-73—287	97363
9	Rosie Jones	70-72-73-73—288	90241
10	Grace Park (Kor)	72-76-73-68—289	79243
	Suzann Pettersen (Nor)	76-69-69-75—289	79243
12	Donna Andrews	69-72-72-77—290	71362
13	Laura Diaz	71-71-74-76—292	56500
	Natalie Gulbis	73-69-72-78—292	56500
	Cristie Kerr	72-73-73-74—292	56500
	Patricia Meunier-Lebouc (Fra)	73-69-74-76—292	56500
	Lorena Ochoa (Mex)	71-75-72-74—292	56500
	Jennifer Rosales (Phi)	74-69-76-73—292	56500
	Rachel Teske (Aus)	71-73-72-76—292	56500
20	Beth Daniel	73-69-77-74—293	43491
	Yuri Fudoh (Jpn)	74-72-75-72—293	43491
22	Lorie Kane (Can)	73-75-73-73—294	36575
	Christina Kim	74-74-72-74—294	36575
	Leta Lindley	73-69-77-75—294	36575
	Catriona Matthew (Sco)	74-70-76-74—294	36575
26	Danielle Ammaccapane	74-74-73-74—295	28354
	Dorothy Delasin	79-70-76-70—295	28354
	Kelli Kuehne	72-74-75-74—295	28354
	Paula Marti (Esp)	71-76-76-72—295	28354
30	Ashli Bunch	71-73-77-75—296	22678
	Annette DeLuca	71-73-78-74—296	22678
	Elizabeth Janangelo (am)	75-73-73-75—296	
	Mi-Hyun Kim (Kor)	73-73-73-77—296	22678
	Jane Park (am)	76-73-74-73—296	
35	Candy Hannemann	75-69-73-80—297	20360
	Stephanie Louden	71-74-77-75—297	20360
	Guilia Sergas (Ita)	70-74-79-74—297	20360
	Kirsty Taylor (Eng)	71-75-73-78—297	20360
39	Michele Redman	71-74-74-79—298	18783
	Michelle Wie (am)	73-73-76-76—298	
41	Heather Bowie	76-71-72-80—299	17840
	Karen Stupples (Eng)	71-75-72-81—299	17840
43	Beth Bauer	75-73-76-76—300	15338

2003 US Women's Open Championship *continued*

43T	Hee-Won Han (Kor)	79-69-74-78—300	15338
	Jamie Hullett	71-76-77-76—300	15338
	Emilee Klein	73-75-74-78—300	15338
	Becky Morgan (Wal)	72-77-75-76—300	15338
	Karen Weiss	74-74-78-74—300	15338
49	Sherri Turner	73-75-72-81—301	13152
50	Se Ri Pak (Kor)	77-72-71-82—302	12527
51	Leigh Ann Hardin (am)	75-68-86-74—303	
52	Morgan Pressel (am)	70-78-78-78—304	
53	Alison Nicholas (Eng)	75-67-83-80—305	11276
	Suzanne Strudwick (Eng)	72-73-83-77—305	11276
	Michelle Vinieratos	75-74-76-80—305	11276
56	Yu Ping Lin (Tai)	73-75-76-82—306	10028
57	Mollie Fankhauser (am)	77-72-80-78—307	
58	Irene Cho (am)	71-75-75-87—308	
59	Mardi Lunn (Aus)	74-72-82-81—309	9759

The following players missed the cut:

60	Beth Bader	76-74—150
	Laura Davies (Eng)	79-71—150
	Alicia Dibos (Per)	76-74—150
	Moira Dunn	72-78—150
	Kate Golden	75-75—150
	Angela Jerman	75-75—150
	Soo-Yun Kang (Kor)	77-73—150
	Carin Koch (Swe)	76-74—150
	Candie Kung (Tai)	79-71—150
	Meg Mallon	76-74—150
	Liselotte Neumann (Swe)	77-73—150
	Virada Nirapathpongporn (am)	78-72—150
	Karrie Webb (Aus)	78-72—150
73	Jackie Gallagher-Smith	76-75—151
	Tracy Hanson	72-79—151
	Pamela Kerrigan	76-75—151
	Kim Saiki	72-79—151
	Annie Thurman (am)	78-73—151
78	Lori Atsedes	78-74—152
	AJ Eathorne (Can)	79-73—152
	Michelle Ellis (Aus)	75-77—152
	Katherine Hull (Aus)	77-75—152
	Pat Hurst	75-77—152
	Soo Young Moon (Kor)	76-76—152
	Joanne Morley (Eng)	77-75—152
	Miriam Nagl (Ger)	77-75—152
	Namika Omata (Jpn)	76-76—152
	Naree Song (am)	76-76—152
	Maggie Will	75-77—152
89	Audra Burks	80-73—153
	Raquel Carriedo (Esp)	78-75—153
	Lisa Chang	78-75—153
89T	Liz Earley (Can)	77-76—153
	Akika Fukushima (Jpn)	78-75—153
	Sophie Gustafson (Swe)	78-75—153
	Jung Yeon Lee (Kor)	74-79—153
	Kris Lindstrom	73-80—153
	Kim Williams	80-73—153
98	Katie Bakken	77-77—154
	Jimin Kang (Kor)	82-72—154
	Denise Killeen	76-78—154
	Becky Lucidi (am)	79-75—154
	Gloria Park (Kor)	76-78—154
	Abby Pearson	75-79—154
	Stacy Prammanasudh	76-78—154
	Wendy Ward	75-79—154
	Young-A Yang (Kor)	79-75—154
107	Brandie Burton	76-79—155
	Paula Creamer (am)	75-80—155
	Kathryn Marshall (Sco)	78-77—155
	Marianne Morris	78-77—155
	Cheryl Musser	77-78—155
	Cindy Shin (am)	78-77—155
	Sherri Steinhauer	79-76—155
114	Diana D'Alessio	84-72—156
	Wendy Doolan (Aus)	78-78—156
	Brandi Jackson (am)	78-78—156
	Alice Kim (am)	78-78—156
	Laura Korus	81-75—156
	Jill McGill	75-81—156
	Janice Moodie (Sco)	81-75—156
	Charlotta Sörenstam (Swe)	75-81—156
	Erika Wicoff	79-77—156
123	Vicki Goetze-Ackerman	78-79—157
	Michelle Murphy	79-78—157
	Cindy Schreyer	79-78—157
126	Kasumi Fujii (Jpn)	82-76—158
	Maria Hjörth (Swe)	79-79—158
	Betsy King	78-80—158
129	Michelle Bell	75-84—159
	Tammie Green	79-80—159
	Penny Hammel	76-83—159
	Shani Waugh (Aus)	79-80—159
133	Kathy Choi-Rogers	82-78—160
	Vickie Linkous	88-72—160
	Adele Snyder	79-81—160
	Whitney Wade (am)	81-79—160
137	Jean Bartholomew	79-82—161
	Lynnette Brooky (NZ)	76-85—161
	Heather Daly-Donofrio	84-77—161
	Susan Ginter-Brooker	79-82—161
141	Kimberly Adams	73-89—162
	Allison Fouch (am)	78-84—162
	Val Skinner	79-83—162
144	Rachel Bates	81-82—163
	Seol An Jeon (Kor)	76-87—163
	Salimah Mussani	86-77—163
	Amy Read	81-82—163
148	Stacey Bergman	85-80—165
149	Cara Bateman	74-92—166
	Sidney Burlison (am)	81-85—166
151	Kelly Schaub (am)	84-84—168
152	Leah Hart (am)	86-83—169
153	Kathryn Cusick	93-81—174
	Kellee Booth	84-84 WD
	Dottie Pepper	72-70 WD
	Helen Alfredsson (Swe)	76-80 DQ

2002 US Women's Open Championship at *Prairie Dunes, Hutchinson, KS*

Prize money: $3,000,000   (6253–70)

Pos	Player	Scores	Prize
1	Juli Inkster	67-72-71-66—276	$535000
2	Annika Sörenstam (Swe)	70-69-69-70—278	315000
3	Shani Waugh (Aus)	67-73-71-72—283	202568
4	Raquel Carriedo (Esp)	75-71-72-66—284	141219
5	Se Ri Pak (Kor)	74-75-68-68—285	114370
6	Mhairi McKay (Sco)	70-75-71-70—286	101421
7	Beth Daniel	71-76-71-69—287	78016
	Laura Diaz	67-72-77-71—287	78016
	Kelli Kuehne	70-76-72-69—287	78016
	Janice Moodie (Sco)	71-72-71-73—287	78016
	Jennifer Rosales (Phi)	73-72-74-68—287	78016
12	Lynnette Brooky (NZ)	73-73-69-73—288	54201
	Stephanie Keever	72-71-73-72—288	54201
	Jill McGill	71-70-69-78—288	54201
	Joanne Morley (Eng)	78-68-73-69—288	54201
	Kelly Robbins	71-74-74-69—288	54201
	Rachel Teske (Aus)	75-71-72-70—288	54201
18	Donna Andrews	74-74-70-71—289	40738
	Beth Bauer	74-72-71-72—289	40738
	Lorie Kane (Can)	69-77-69-74—289	40738
	Grace Park (Kor)	71-77-71-70—289	40738
22	Danielle Ammaccapane	74-71-73-72—290	26894
	Michelle Ellis (Aus)	71-71-75-73—290	26894
	Susan Ginter-Brooker	74-72-70-74—290	26894
	Jeong Jang (Kor)	73-73-74-70—290	26894
	Rosie Jones	71-77-69-73—290	26894
	Mi Hyun Kim (Kor)	74-72-70-74—290	26894
	Meg Mallon	73-75-73-69—290	26894
	Catriona Matthew (Sco)	69-80-72-69—290	26894
	Stacy Prammanasudh	75-74-72-69—290	26894
	Michele Redman	71-69-73-77—290	26894
32	Brandie Burton	70-74-76-71—291	18730
	Laura Davies (Eng)	75-73-68-75—291	18730
	Hee-Won Han (Kor)	72-77-70-72—291	18730
	Cristie Kerr	74-71-72-74—291	18730
	Charlotta Sörenstam (Swe)	73-70-77-71—291	18730
37	Jenna Daniels	72-70-77-73—291	15209
	Wendy Doolan (Aus)	73-76-75-68—292	15209
	Jackie Gallagher-Smith	70-76-73-73—292	15209
	Carin Koch (Swe)	73-72-70-77—292	15209
	Liselotte Neumann (Swe)	72-74-70-76—292	15209
	Karen Stupples (Eng)	80-68-72-72—292	15209
	Kris Tschetter	72-77-72-71—292	15209

Other players who made the cut: Jean Bartholomew, Audra Burke, Mitzi Edge, Jung Yeon Lee (Kor), Gloria Park (Kor), Cindy Schreyer, Leslie Spalding 293; Alicia Dibos (Per), Vicki Goetze-Ackerman, Angela Jerman (am), Ara Koh (Kor), Sherri Steinhauer, Karen Weiss, Aree Song Wongluekiet (Tha) 294; Amy Fruhwirth, Kim Saiki; Sherri Turner 295; Heather Bowie, Soo Young Moon (Kor) 296; Patricia Meunier-Lebouc (Fra) 297; Dawn Coe-Jones (Can), Dorothy Delasin, Pearl Sin (Kor) 298; Allison Finney 299; Tracy Hanson 300; Michele Vinieratos 301

2001 US Women's Open Championship at *Southern Pines, NC* (6256–70)

Prize money: $2,700,000

Pos	Player	Scores	Prize
1	Karrie Webb (Aus)	70-65-69-69—273	$520000
2	Se Ri Pak (Kor)	69-70-70-72—281	310000
3	Dottie Pepper	74-69-70-69—282	202580
4	Cristie Kerr	69-73-71-70—283	118697
	Sherri Turner	72-70-71-70—283	118697
	Catriona Matthew (Sco)	72-68-70-73—283	118697
7	Lorie Kane (Can)	75-68-72-69—284	80726
	Kristi Albers	71-69-74-70—284	80726
	Kelli Kuehne	70-71-72-71—284	80726
	Wendy Doolan	71-70-70-73—284	80726
11	Sophie Gustafson (Swe)	74-66-74-71—285	66581
12	Kelly Robbins	72-68-76-70—286	57088
	AJ Eathorne (Can)	67-71-75-73—286	57088
	Juli Inkster	68-72-71-75—286	57088
	Yuri Fudoh (Jpn)	73-68-70-75—286	57088
16	Emilee Klein	72-69-75-71—287	46885
	Michele Redman	70-72-73-72—287	46885
	Annika Sörenstam (Swe)	70-72-73-72—287	46885
19	Maria Hjörth (Swe)	70-71-77-70—288	37327
	Marisa Baena (Col)	71-72-75-70—288	37327
	Jill McGill	68-76-72-72—288	37327
19T	Wendy Ward	70-71-74-73—288	37327
	Dorothy Delasin	75-70-70-73—288	37327
24	Beth Daniel	73-70-71-75—289	30091
	Audra Burks	70-72-72-75—289	30091
26	Brandie Burton	73-70-77-70—290	24649
	Helen Alfredsson (Swe)	71-73 74-72—290	24649
	Mi Hyun Kim (Kor)	68-76-72-74—290	24649
	Janice Moodie (Sco)	71-70-73-76—290	24649
30	Kris Tschetter	72-74-77-68—291	20472
	Michelle Ellis	75-69-75-72—291	20472
	Candy Hannemann (am)	73-73-72-73—291	
	Meg Mallon	72-70-76-73—291	20472
34	Pat Hurst	73-71-76-72—292	18408
	Natalie Gulbis (am)	73-71-75-73—292	
	Catrin Nilsmark (Swe)	70-76-72-74—292	18408
	Dina Ammaccapane	69-73-75-75—292	18408
	Karen Weiss	74-71-71-76—292	18408
39	Marcy Newton	74-72-74-73—293	16061
	Liselotte Neumann (Swe)	70-73-76-74—293	16064
	Rosie Jones	73-68-75-77—293	16061
	Grace Park (Kor)	76-70-69-78—293	16061

Other players who made the cut: Leta Lindley, Paula Marti (Esp), Amy Fruhwirth, Aki Nakano, Cindy Figg-Currier, Alison Nicholas (Eng) 294; Pearl Sinn (Kor) 295; Stephanie Keever (am), Christina Kim (am), Sherri Steinhauer 296; Smriti Mehra (Ind), Jean Bartholamew, Raquel Carriedo (Esp) 297; Terry-Jo Myers; Yu Ping Lin (Twn), Jamie Hullett 299, Lynnette Brooky, Lisa Strom 299

2000 US Women's Open Championship at Merit Club, Libertyville, IL

Prize money: $2,700,000   (6540–72)

1	Karrie Webb (Aus)	69-72-68-73—282	$500000	21T	Wendy Doolan (Aus)	77-69-74-75—295	34113
2	Cristie Kerr	72-71-74-70—287	240228	23	Donna Andrews	73-75-79-70—297	28404
	Meg Mallon	68-72-73-74—287	240228		Kristi Albers	71-77-73-76—297	28404
4	Rosie Jones	73-71-72-72—288	120119		Michele Redman	74-74-73-76—297	28404
	Mi Hyun Kim (Kor)	74-72-70-72—288	120119		Juli Inkster	70-74-73-80—297	28404
6	Grace Park (Kor)	74-72-73-70—289	90458	27	Charlotta Sörenstam		
	Kelli Kuehne	71-74-73-71—289	90458		(Swe)	75-74-76-73—298	21740
8	Beth Daniel	71-74-72-73—290	79345		AJ Eathorne (Can)	73-77-73-75—298	21740
9	Annika Sörenstam				Silvia Cavalleri (Ita)	72-73-75-78—298	21740
	(Swe)	73-75-73-70—291	67369		Joanne Morley (Eng)	73-72-74-79—298	21740
	Kelly Robbins	74-73-71-73—291	67369	31	Tina Barrett	72-78-75-74—299	17067
	Laura Davies (Eng)	73-71-72-75—291	67369		Danielle Ammaccapane	72-73-79-75—299	17067
12	Jennifer Rosales (Phi)	75-75-69-73—292	55355		Emilee Klein	77-72-75-75—299	17067
	Pat Hurst	73-72-72-75—292	55355		Fiona Pike (Aus)	72-74-77-76—299	17067
	Dorothy Delasin	76-68-72-76—292	55355		Kate Golden	75-72-76-76—299	17067
15	Se Ri Pak (Kor)	74-75-75-69—293	47846		Jenny Lidback (Per)	73-74-76-76—299	17067
	Kellee Booth	70-78-75-70—293	47846		Carin Koch (Swe)	75-73-73-78—299	17067
17	Janice Moodie (Sco)	73-77-75-69—294	40586		Sophie Gustafson		
	Kathryn Marshall (Sco)	72-72-77-73—294	40586		(Swe)	72-78-71-78—299	17067
	Shani Waugh (Aus)	69-75-73-77—294	40586		Hiromi Kobayashi		
	Lorie Kane (Can)	71-74-72-77—294	40586		(Jpn)	77-72-70-80—299	17067
21	Jackie Gallagher Smith	71-77-73-74—295	34113				

Other players who made the cut: Michelle Ellis (Aus), Valerie Skinner, Mary Beth Zimmerman, Naree Wongluekiet (am) 300; Catriona Matthew (Sco), Jill McGill 301; Leta Lindley, Nancy Scranton, Nancy Lopez, Jan Stephenson (Aus), Jae Jean Ro (am), Betsy King, Sara Sanders 302; Jean Zedlitz 304; Marisa Baena (Col), Anna Macosko 305; Hilary Homeyer (am) 306; Carri Wood 307; Barb Mucha 308; Pearl Sinn (Kor) 310; Michelle McGann 311

1999 US Women's Open Championship at Old Waverley, West Point, MS

Prize money: $1,750,000   (6421–72)

1	J Inkster	65-69-67-71—272	$315000	20T	L Lindley	72-72-73-70—287	21832
2	S Turner	69-69-68-71—277	185000		S Gustafson (Swe)	72-72-70-73—287	21832
3	K Kuehne	64-71-70-74—279	118227		D Andrews	69-71-72-75—287	21832
4	L Kane (Can)	70-64-71-75—280	82399		H Fukushima (Jpn)	69-70-71-77—287	21832
5	C Koch (Swe)	72-69-68-72—281	62938	25	K Saiki	70-71-73-74—288	16006
	M Mallon	70-70-69-72—281	62938		S Croce (Ita)	71-71-71-75—288	16006
7	K Webb (Aus)	70-70-68-74—282	53132		R Jones	71-70-72-75—288	16006
8	H Dobson (Eng)	71-70-73-69—283	45244		L Kiggens	71-67-73-77—288	16006
	M Hjörth (Swe)	73-69-70-71—283	45244		S Steinhauer	68-69-73-78—288	16006
	C Matthew (Sco)	69-68-74-72—283	45244	30	M Lunn (Aus)	72-71-74-72—289	11652
	G Park (Kor) (am)	70-67-73-73—283			J Zedlitz	75-67-75-72—289	11652
12	H Alfredsson (Swe)	72-68-70-74—284	37666		M McKay (Sco)	73-68-76-72—289	11652
	B Iverson	72-64-73-75—284	37666		N Scranton	69-72-75-73—289	11652
14	M Redman	72-71-75-67—285	32389		D Coe Jones	73-71-71-74—289	11652
	Se Ri Pak (Kor)	68-70-74-73—285	32389		A Acker Macosko	73-71-71-74—289	11652
	D Pepper	68-69-72-76—285	32389		K Robbins	70-70-74-75—289	11652
17	L Neumann (Swe)	73-71-69-73—286	27422	37	H Kobayashi (Jpn)	74-70-76-70—290	10078
	AJ Eathorne (Can)	69-71-71-75—286	27422		D Dormann	74-70-73-73—290	10078
	C Nilsmark (Swe)	69-71-70-76—286	27422		K Booth (am)	71-73-70-76—290	
20	C McCurdy	72-72-74-69—287	21832				

Other players who made the cut: M Estill, M Berteotti, K Tschetter, W Ward, M Dunn 291; P Kerrigan, S Strudwick (Eng) 292; B King, B Daniel, B Mucha, A Munt, W Doolan, V Odegard 293; M Will, R Hetherington (Aus) 294; J Lidback, L Hackney, C Figg-Currier, A Nicholas (Eng) 295; P Rizzo 296; J Feldott, P Hammel 297; K Millies 298; T Green 299

1998 US Women's Open Championship at Blackwolf Run, Wisconsin, WI

Prize money: $1,500,000

(6412-1)

1	Se Ri Pak* (Kor)	69-70-75-76—290	$267500	19T	J Lidback (Per)	71-73-79-75—298	18998
2	J Chuasiriporn (am)	72-71-75-72—290			A Fukushima (Jpn)	72-71-79-76—298	18998
	*Se Ri Pak won at second extra hole after both had shot 73				R Jones	74-74-74-76—298	18998
	in the play-off				W Ward	76-69-75-78—298	18998
3	L Neumann (Swe)	70-70-75-76—291	157500		D Andrews	70-75-75-78—298	18998
4	Dani Ammaccapane	76-71-74-71—292	77351		L Walters (Can)	76-70-74-78—298	18998
	P Hurst	69-75-75-73—292	77351	26	D Dormann	72-76-79-72—299	12972
	C Johnson	72-70-76-74—292	77351		N Scranton	76-72-78-73—299	12972
7	S Croce (Ita)	74-71-76-72—293	46737		M Estill	75-74-76-74—299	12972
	T Green	73-71-76-73—293	46737		H Dobson (Eng)	71-75-77-76—299	12972
	M McKay (Sco)	72-70-73-78—293	46737		L Rinker Graham	75-71-77-76—299	12972
10	T Johnson (Eng)	73-71-77-73—294	39015	31	K Williams	68-81-79-72—300	10093
11	L Davies (Eng)	68-75-78-74—295	34929		P Hammel	71-79-77-73—300	10093
	D Pepper	71-71-78-75—295	34929		B Daniel	77-69-78-76—300	10093
13	C Koch (Swe)	72-74-77-73—296	30684		D Eggeling	71-72-79-78—300	10093
	H Alfredsson (Swe)	75-75-73-73—296	30684		K Webb (Aus)	76-73-73-78—300	10093
15	H Stacy	76-68-82-71—297	25871	36	D Coe Jones	71-74-83-73—301	8897
	A Acker Macosko	74-74-76-73—297	25871		I Blais (am)	74-73-78-76—301	
	Dina Ammaccapane	75-70-78-74—297	25871		K Tschetter	75-72-77-77—301	8897
	B Burton	74-72-77-74—297	25871		B Corrie Kuehn (am)	70-72-80-79—301	
19	L Kane (Can)	74-72-82-70—298	18998		L Spalding	69-74-78-80—301	8897

Other players who made the cut: H Wadsworth, E Klein, N Bowen, A Sörenstam, B Mucha 302; P Bradley, P Rizzo, P Sinn 304; K Albers, M Redman, M Lovander, K Booth (am), A De Luca 305; H Kobayashi 306; ML de Lorenz 307; S Lowe 308; J Stephenson, TJ Myers 309; JJ Robertson (am) 310; C Kerr 311; K Parker 314; K Baue 316

1997 US Women's Open Championship at Pumpkin Ridge GC, Cornelius, OR

Prize money: $1,300,000

(6365-71)

1	A Nicholas (Eng)	70-66-67-71—274	$232500	21	K Kuehne	72-73-74-67—286	13800
2	N Lopez	69-68-69-69—275	137500		K Weiss	74-72-72-68—286	13800
3	K Robbins	68-69-74-66—277	86708		Se Ri Pak (Kor)	68-74-75-69—286	13800
4	K Webb (Aus)	73-72-65-68—278	60432		P Hurst	72-74-70-70—286	13800
5	S Croce (Ita)	72-69-71-67—279	46159		L Bemvenuti	73-71-72-70—286	13800
	L Hackney (Eng)	71-70-67-71—279	46159		C Pierce	71-71-73-71—286	13800
7	T Green	74-70-71-65—280	37542	27	C Matthew (Sco)	76-69-70-72—287	10961
	M Redman	74-67-70-69—280	37542	28	S Smyers	71-71-75-71—288	9188
9	P Sheehan	72-71-71-68—282	28769		P Bradley	72-71-73-72—288	9188
	C Johnson	72-68-73-69—282	28769		K Marshall (Sco)	72-71-73-72—288	9188
	D Coe-Jones	72-67-73-70—282	28769		B King	74-72-69-73—288	9188
	D Andrews	74-71-66-71—282	28769		J Pitcock	71-69-75-73—288	9188
	A Fukushima (Jpn)	71-71-69-71—282	28769	33	D Eggeling	71-74-76-70—291	7392
14	B Burton	73-72-69-70—284	21287		E Makings	72-73-75-71—291	7392
	D Pepper	72-70-72-70—284	21287		V Fergon	72-75-71-73—291	7392
	J Inkster	72-66-76-70—284	21287		M Morris	75-69-74-73—291	7392
	L Neumann (Swe)	67-70-76-71—284	21287		R Jones	70-74-73-74—291	7392
	D Richard	68-70-73-73—284	21287		P Sinn	70-73-74-74—291	7392
19	T Johnson (Eng)	69-74-71-71—285	17407		M McGann	73-70-73-75—291	7392
	K Williams	71-71-67-76—285	17407		C Nilsmark (Swe)	76-70-69-76—291	7392

Other players who made the cut: A Dibos, J McGill 292; N Bowen, M McGeorge, M Mallon, J Lidback, E Wicoff 293; J Stephenson, H Alfredsson, L Kane 294; B Iverson, B Mucha 295; E Klein, J Gallagher-Smith, M Spencer-Devlin 296; T Hanson, S Redman, J Chuasiriporn (am) 297; D Dormann, N Harvey 298; M Edge, R Walton 299; B Corrie Kuehn (am) 302; P Dunlap 303.

1996 US Women's Open Championship

at Pine Needles Lodge & GC, Southern Pines, NC (6207–70)

Prize money: $1,200,000

1	A Sörenstam (Swe)	70-67-69-66—272	$212500		19T	K Webb (Aus)	74-73-68-72—287	14374
2	K Tschetter	70-74-68-66—278	125000			B Daniel	69-78-68-72—287	14374
3	P Bradley	74-70-67-69—280	60372			W Ward	76-68-71-72—287	14374
	J Geddes	71-69-70-70—280	60372			M Hirase	74-69-69-75—287	14374
	B Burton	70-70-69-71—280	60372		25	M Hattori	74-71-74-69—288	10482
6	L Davies (Eng)	74-68-70-69—281	40077			K Williams	69-78-69-72—288	10482
7	C Nilsmark (Swe)	72-73-68-69—282	35995			B Iverson	73-71-71-73—288	10482
8	C Rarick	73-70-72-68—283	29584			N Harvey	72-71-69-76—288	10482
	L Neumann (Swe)	74-69-70-70—283	29584		29	K Weiss	74-72-73-70—289	8134
	V Skinner	74-68-71-70—283	29584			S Redman	73-73-71-72—289	8134
	T Green	72-70-69-72—283	29584			R Jones	71-70-76-72—289	8134
12	J Lidback	70-76-68-70—284	24654			T Kerdyk	73-72-69-75—289	8134
13	A Nicholas (Eng)	74-70-74-67—285	23243			E Klein	71-69-73-76—289	8134
14	P Sheehan	74-71-72-69—286	19664		34	C Pierce	72-75-73-70—290	7294
	S Croce (Ita)	72-70-74-70—286	19664			J Inkster	74-71-71-74—290	7294
	C Schreyer	74-70-70-72—286	19664		36	G Graham	72-70-76-73—291	6479
	M Will	71-72-70-73—286	19664			H Kobayashi (Jpn)	77-71-69-74—291	6479
	M Redman	70-73-69-74—286	19664			S Steinhauer	72-73-71-75—291	6479
19	C Johnston-Forbes	72-75-71-69—287	14374			K Saiki	73-70-73-75—291	6479
	M Mallon	77-68-72-70—287	14374			B Mucha	74-71-70-76—291	6479

Other players who made the cut: K Albers, C Mockett, J Piers, M McGeorge, M McGann, I Shiotani, J Pitcock 292; J McGill, K Golden, T Johnson 293; Dani Ammaccapane, C Matthew 294; S Farwig, J Stephenson, M Bell, M Baena (am) 295; K Robbins, S Turner, C Johnson 296; E Dahllof, N Foust 300.

1995 US Women's Open Championship

at The Broadmoor, Colorado Springs, CO (6398–70)

Prize money: $1,000,000

1	A Sörenstam (Swe)	67-71-72-68—278	$175000		21	L Neumann (Swe)	70-71-75-71—287	11154
2	M Malon	70-69-66-74—279	103500			A Okamoto	70-73-71-73—287	11154
3	B King	72-69-72-67—280	56238			A Ritzman	75-69-69-74—287	11154
	P Bradley	67-71-72-70—280	56238		24	C Hill	74-73-70-71—288	9287
5	L Lindley	70-68-74-69—281	35285			J Pitcock	72-73-72-71—288	9287
	R Jones	69-70-70-72—281	35285			L Davies (Eng)	72-73-69-74—288	9287
7	T Green	68-70-75-69—282	28009			MB Zimmerman	72-72-68-76—288	9287
	D Coe-Jones	68-70-74-70—282	28009		28	A Fruhwirth	75-72-72-70—289	6841
	J Larsen	68-71-68-75—282	28009			B Burton	72-74-73-70—289	6841
10	M Morris	73-73-70-67—283	22190			N Lopez	72-73-74-70—289	6841
	P Sheehan	70-73-71-69—283	22190			M Hirase	70-74-73-72—289	6841
	V Skinner	68-72-72-71—283	22190			C Walker	69-73-75-72—289	6841
13	D Mochrie	73-70-69-72—284	18007			P Wright (Sco)	72-73-71-73—289	6841
	K Tschetter	68-74-69-73—284	18007			D Miho Koyama	74-68-73-74—289	6841
	K Robbins	74-68-68-74—284	18007			J Bartholomew	67-71-77-74—289	6841
16	C Johnson	71-70-74-70—285	14454			G Graham	71-72-71-75—289	6841
	J Briles-Hinton	66-72-74-73—285	14454		37	S Strudwick	75-70-73-72—290	5218
	T Abitbol	67-72-72-74—285	14454			J Inkster	72-73-72-73—290	5218
	D Eggeling	70-68-73-74—285	14454			H Stacy	69-72-75-74—290	5218
20	M Redman	70-75-71-70—286	12449					

Other players who made the cut: H Alfredsson, J Dickinson, M McGann, A Dibos, C Hjalmarsson, J Geddes 291; K Peterson-Parker 292; L Kean, M McGeorge, P Hurst, A Nicholas 293; S Turner, J Stephenson, S Lebrun Ingram (am) 294; K Marshall, E Hayashida, V Goetze 295; K Albers, L Rinker-Graham, M Nause, K Noble, W Ward (am), K Booth (am) 296; A Alcott, E Crosby, A Benz, M Will, L Rittenhouse, M Estill, G Park (am) 297; S Rule, S Maynor, C Keggi 298; B Mucha, A Acker-Macosko 299; M Platt 303; A Munt 306.

1994 US Women's Open Championship
at Indianwood G&CC, Lake Orion, MI   (6244-71)

Prize money: $850,000

1	P Sheehan	66-71-69-71—277	$155000	25	K Tschetter	71-73-72-73—289	8089
2	T Green	66-72-69-71—278	85000		D Richard	68-74-72-75—289	8089
3	L Neumann (Swe)	69-72-71-69—281	47752		P Bradley	72-69-70-78—289	8089
4	T Abitbol	72-68-73-70—283	31132		P Wright (Sco)	74-65-71-79—289	8089
	A Dibos	69-68-73-73—283	31132	29	K Lunn (Aus)	72-72-77-69—290	7371
6	M Mallon	70-72-73-69—284	21486		V Goetze	71-73-73-73—290	7371
	H Alfredsson (Swe)	63-69-76-77—285	16445	31	D Eggeling	67-73-79-72—291	6929
12	L Merten	74-68-75-69—286	12805		J Carner	69-74-75-73—291	6929
	D Mochrie	72-72-71-71—286	12805		A Read	68-72-76-75—291	6929
	L Grimes	72-73-69-72—286	12805		C Semple Thompson		
	J Dickinson	66-73-73-74—286	12805		(am)	66-75-76-74—291	
	M Estill	69-68-75-74—286	12805	35	C Walker	73-73-75-71—292	6048
	L Davies (Eng)	68-68-75-75—286	12805		H Vaughn	74-70-76-72—292	6048
18	M McGann	71-70-77-69—287	10202		K Williams	72-74-72-74—292	6048
	J Inkster	75-72-69-71—287	10202		J Geddes	73-72-73-74—292	6048
	B Daniel	69-74-71-73—287	10202		D Coe-Jones	73-73-71-75—292	6048
	J Pitcock	74-72-67-74—287	10202		N Lopez	73-71-73-75—292	6048
22	S Maynor	73-70-76-69—288	9011		M McGeorge	69-73-75-75—292	6048
	L Walters	72-73-72-71—288	9011		K Monaghan	75-69-72-76—292	6048
	S Steinhauer	68-72-74-74—288	9011				

Other players who made the cut: V Fergon, M Berteotti, E Crosby, M Hirase, B Burton, S Little 293; N Bowen, A Okamoto 294; S Turner, D Dormann, E Klein (am) 295; J Stephenson, H Kobayashi, N Ramsbottom 296; C Pierce, T Fleming, A Ritzman, M Edge, S LeBrun Ingram (am) 297; T Kimura, L Kiggens 298; P Sinn, P Dunlap 300; J Sams 303; S McGuire 304

US Women's Open History

Year	Winner	Runner-up	Venue	Score
1946	P Berg	B Jamieson	Spokane	5 and 4

Changed to strokeplay

Year	Winner	Venue	Score
1947	B Jamieson	Greensboro	300
1948	B Zaharias	Atlantic City	300
1949	L Suggs	Maryland	291
1950	B Zaharias	Wichita	291
1951	B Rawls	Atlanta	294
1952	L Suggs	Bala, PA	284
1953	B Rawls*	Rochester, NY	302

* *Won play-off after a tie with J Pung 71-77*

1954	B Zaharias	Peabody, MA	291
1955	F Crocker	Wichita	299
1956	K Cornelius*	Duluth	302

* *Won play-off after a tie with B McIntire (am) 75-82*

1957	B Rawls	Mamaroneck	299
1958	M Wright	Bloomfield Hills, MI	290
1959	M Wright	Pittsburgh, PA	287
1960	B Rawls	Worchester, MA	292
1961	M Wright	Springfield, NJ	293
1962	M Lindstrom	Myrtle Beach	301
1963	M Mills	Kenwood	289
1964	M Wright*	San Diego	290

* *Won play-off after a tie with R Jessen, Seattle 70-72*

1965	C Mann	Northfield, NJ	290

US Women's Open Championship History *continued*

Year	Winner	Venue	Score
1966	S Spuzich	Hazeltine National, MN	297
1967	C Lacoste (Fra) (am)	Hot Springs, VA	294
1968	S Berning	Moselem Springs, PA	289
1969	D Caponi	Scenic-Hills	294
1970	D Caponi	Muskogee, OK	287
1971	J Gunderson-Carner	Erie, PA	288
1972	S Berning	Mamaroneck, NY	299
1973	S Berning	Rochester, NY	290
1974	S Haynie	La Grange, IL	295
1975	S Palmer	Northfield, NJ	295
1976	J Carner*	Springfield, PA	292

* Won play-off after a tie with S Palmer 76-78

Year	Winner	Venue	Score
1977	H Stacy	Hazeltine, MN	292
1978	H Stacy	Indianapolis	299
1979	J Britz	Brooklawn, CN	284
1980	A Alcott	Richland, TN	280
1981	P Bradley	La Grange, IL	279
1982	J Alex	Del Paso, Sacramento, CA	283
1983	J Stephenson (Aus)	Broken Arrow, OK	290
1984	H Stacy	Salem, MA	290
1985	K Baker	Baltusrol, NJ	280
1986	J Geddes*	NCR	287

* Won play-off after a tie with S Little 71-73

1987	L Davies (Eng)*	Plainfield	285

* Won play-off after a tie with J Carner and A Okamoto – Davies 71, Okamoto 73, Carner 74

Year	Winner	Venue	Score
1988	L Neumann (Swe)	Baltimore	277
1989	B King	Indianwood, MI	278
1990	B King	Atlanta Athletic Club, GA	284
1991	M Mallon	Colonial, TX	283
1992	P Sheehan*	Oakmont, PA	280

* Won play-off after a tie with J Inkster 72-74

Year	Winner	Venue	Score
1993	L Merton	Crooked Stick	280
1994	P Sheehan	Indianwood, MI	277
1995	A Sörenstam (Swe)	The Broadmore, CO	278
1996	A Sörenstam (Swe)	Pine Needles Lodge, NC	272
1997	A Nicholas (Eng)	Pumpkin Ridge, OR	274
1998	SR Pak (Kor)*	Blackwolf Run, WI	290

* Won play-off after a tie with J Chausiriporn (am). Both shot 73 then Pak 5, 3 to 5, 4

Year	Winner	Venue	Score
1999	J Inkster	Old Waverley, West Point, MS	272
2000	K Webb (Aus)	Merit Club, Libertyville, IL	282
2001	K Webb (Aus)	Pine Needles Lodge & GC, NC	273
2002	J Inkster	Prairie Dunes, KS	276
2003	H Lunke*	Pumpkin Ridge GC, OR	283

McDonald's LPGA Championship

Players are of American nationality unless stated.   *Held annually at Du Pont CC, DE*

2003 McDonald's LPGA Championship   (6408–71)

Prize Money: $1.6 million. Field of 144 players, of whom 70 made the half-way cut on 148 or less.

1	Annika Sörenstam (Swe)*	70-64-72-72—278	$240000
2	Grace Park (Kor)	69-72-70-67—278	147934
3	Beth Daniel	71-71-70-72—284	85718
	Rosie Jones	73-68-72-71—284	85718
	Rachel Teske (Aus)	69-70-74-71—284	85718
6	Kate Golden	72-70-68-75—285	41873
	Young Kim (Kor)	70-73-72-70—285	41873
	JoAnne Mills (Aus)	68-73-75-69—285	41873
	Becky Morgan (Wal)	73-70-70-72—285	41873
	Young-A Yang (Kor)	73-74-69-69—285	41873
11	Akiko Fukushima (Jpn)	72-68-74-72—286	24037
	Hee-Wan Han (Kor)	67-69-74-76—286	24037
	Jeong Jang (Kor)	72-73-69-72—286	24037
	Angela Jerman	73-72-69-72—286	24037
	Patricia Meunier-Lebouc (Fra)	75-69-72-70—286	24037
	Suzann Pettersen (Nor)	70-71-75-70—286	24037
	Michele Redman	74-70-69-73—286	24037
	Jennifer Rosales (Phi)	74-68-74-70—286	24037
	Wendy Ward	68-69-75-74—286	24037
20	Donna Andrews	73-70-70-74—287	16719
	Tina Barrett	76-69-71-71—287	16719
	Michelle Ellis (Aus)	73-70-71-73—287	16719
	Natalie Gulbis	71-69-78-69—287	16719
	Kelli Kuehne	73-73-65-76—287	16719
	Lorena Ochoa (Mex)	72-72-71-72—287	16719
	Karen Stupples (Eng)	73-73-71-70—287	16719
27	Danielle Ammaccapane	74-72-74-68—288	13769
	Meg Mallon	74-69-70-75—288	13769
	Angela Stanford	72-73-71-72—288	13769
30	Laura Diaz	73-70-75-71—289	11987
	Tracy Hanson	71-77-70-71—289	11987
	Mi-Hyun Kim (Kor)	72-72-71-74—289	11987
	Deb Richard	75-71-74-69—289	11987
34	Moira Dunn	78-70-72-70—290	10367
	Lorie Kane (Can)	72-75-70-73—290	10367
	Cristie Kerr	74-69-75-72—290	10367
37	Juli Inkster	71-72-71-77—291	8970
	Hilary Lunke	72-70-75-74—291	8970
	Catriona Matthew (Sco)	72-73-75-71—291	8970
	Jan Stephenson (Aus)	74-72-69-76—291	8970
41	Jill McGill	76-72-71-73—292	7937
	Terry-Jo Myers	74-73-75-70—292	7937
43	Vicki Goetze-Ackerman	73-74-72-74—293	7154
	Pat Hurst	73-73-74-73—293	7154
	Giulia Sergas (Ita)	73-72-75-73—293	7154

2003 McDonald's LPGA Championship *continued*

46	Marisa Baena (Col)	73-74-77-70—294	6155
	Brandie Burton	77-70-75-72—294	6155
	Jung Yeon Lee (Kor)	76-70-75-73—294	6155
	Se Ri Pak (Kor)	72-74-72-76—294	6155
	Leslie Spalding	72-73-76-73—294	6155
51	Yu Ping Lin (Tai)	74-74-74-73—295	5346
	Kathryn Marshall (Sco)	77-70-75-73—295	5346
	Joanne Morley (Eng)	74-72-77-72—295	5346
54	Dorothy Delasin	71-71-79-75—296	4941
	Kim Saiki	72-74-80-70—296	4941
56	Dawn Coe-Jones (Can)	74-74-76-73—297	4374
	Jane Crafter (Aus)	70-76-80-71—297	4374
	Wendy Doolan (Aus)	72-75-74-76—297	4374
	Jackie Gallagher-Smith	72-72-77-76—297	4374
	Karrie Webb (Aus)	72-72-78-75—297	4374
61	Fiona Pike (Aus)	73-74-76-75—298	3969
62	Heather Bowie	74-73-76-76—299	3888
63	Marnie McGuire (NZ)	74-72-78-76—300	3807
64	Mitzi Edge	73-74-76-78—301	3645
	Marcy Hart	71-75-79-76—301	3645
	Michelle McGann	72-76-77-76—301	3645
67	Marilyn Lovander	74-74-77-79—304	3402
	Liselotte Neumann (Swe)	74-73-81-76—304	3402
	Dottie Pepper	73-74-80-77—304	3402
70	Kim Williams	73-72-78-83—306	3240

The following players missed the cut:

71	Laura Davies (Eng)	75-74—149
	Tammie Green	76-73—149
	Johanna Head (Eng)	79-70—149
	Maria Hjörth (Swe)	75-74—149
	Christina Kim	76-73—149
	Hiromi Kobayashi (Jpn)	73-76—149
	Charlotta Sörenstam (Swe)	74-75—149
	Shani Waugh (Aus)	75-74—149
79	Jean Bartholomew	74-76—150
	Annette DeLuca	75-75—150
	AJ Eathorne (Can)	75-75—150
	Cindy Figg-Currier	74-76—150
	Lisa Grimes	75-75—150
	Candie Kung (Tai)	77-73—150
	Leta Lindley	75-75—150
	Mardi Lunn (Aus)	74-76—150
	Gloria Park (Kor)	77-73—150
	Kelly Robbins	74-76—150
	Karen Weiss	75-75—150
90	JoAnne Carner	77-74—151
	Amy Fruhwirth	74-77—151
	Sophie Gustafson (Swe)	75-76—151
	Chris Johnson	78-73—151
	Soo-Yun Kang (Kor)	77-74—151
	Betsy King	76-75—151
	Mhairi McKay (Sco)	75-76—151

90T	Janice Moodie (Sco)	78-73—151
	Catrin Nilsmark (Swe)	76-75—151
	Namika Omata (Jpn)	75-76—151
	Kris Tschetter	78-73—151
101	Kristi Albers	74-78—152
	Helen Alfredsson (Swe)	76-76—152
	Heather Daly-Donofrio	78-74—152
	Kristal Parker-Manzo	73-79—152
	Suzanne Strudwick (Eng)	78-74—152
106	Anna Acker-Macosko	78-75—153
	Beth Bader	76-77—153
	Beth Bauer	79-74—153
	Silvia Cavalleri (Ita)	80-73—153
	Stephanie Louden	74-79—153
	Barb Mucha	78-75—153
	Miriam Nagl (Ger)	76-77—153
	Carrie Roberts	79-74—153
114	Tina Fischer (Ger)	76-78—154
	Suzy Green-Roebuck	81-73—154
	Loraine Lambert (Aus)	78-76—154
	Nancy Scranton	77-77—154

114T	Sherri Steinhauer	79-75—154
	Sherri Turner	80-74—154
120	Diana D'Alessio	81-75—156
	Emilee Klein	76-80—156
	Ara Koh (Kor)	76-80—156
	Sally Little	71-85—156
	Nancy Lopez	77-79—156
	Georgina Simpson (Eng)	77-79—156
126	Gail Graham (Can)	78-79—157
	Laurel Kean	78-79—157
128	Nancy Harvey (Can)	80-78—158
129	DeDe Cusimano	79-82—161
	Eva Dahllof (Swe)	79-82—161
	Dana Dormann	82-79—161
	Smriti Mahra (Ind)	82-79—161
	Suzy Whaley	79-82—161
134	Shannon Hanley	80-82—162
135	Dale Eggeling	85-78—163
136	Kellee Booth	80-84—164
	Denise Killeen	82-82—164
	Connie Ross	74-90—164
139	Nancy Henderson	82-86—168
	Raquel Carriedo (Esp)	84-84 WD
	Jane Geddes	83-83 WD
	Minni Yeo (Kor)	79-79 WD
	Soo Young Kim	WD
	Pat Bradley	DQ

2002 McDonald's LPGA Championship

Prize money: $1,400,000

1	Se Ri Pak (Kor)	71-70-68-70—279	$225000	20T	Barb Mucha	70-73-75-75—293	16950
2	Beth Daniel	67-70-68-77—282	136987	22	Silvia Cavalleri (Ita)	72-73-73-76—294	15450
3	Annika Sörenstam				Maria Hjörth (Swe)	78-70-75-71—294	15450
	(Swe)	70-76-73-65—284	99375		Kelly Robbins	70-75-74-75—294	15450
4	Juli Inkster	69-75-70-71—285	69375	25	Danielle Ammaccapane	73-76-73-73—295	12543
	Karrie Webb (Aus)	68-71-72-74—285	69375		Brandie Burton	74-76-74-71—295	12543
6	Carin Koch (Swe)	68-73-73-72—286	46500		Vicki Goetze-Ackerman	72-72-74-77—295	12543
	Michele Redman	74-69-70-73—286	46500		Tammie Green	70-78-73-74—295	12543
8	Catriona Matthew				Leta Lindley	72-77-71-75—295	12543
	(Sco)	70-73-75-70—288	37125		Kathryn Marshall (Sco)	73-73-72-77—295	12543
9	Kristi Albers	74-73-73-70—290	30625		Gloria Park (Kor)	75-72-73-75—295	12543
	Michelle McGann	71-72-72-75—290	30625		Kris Tschetter	74-75-75-71—295	12543
	Karen Stupples (Eng)	75-70-70-75—290	30625	33	Eva Dahllof (Swe)	75-73-75-73—296	9056
12	Meg Mallon	73-72-76-70—291	24650		Dorothy Delasin	79-68-73-76—296	9056
	Kim Saiki	71-71-69-80—291	24650		Moira Dunn	74-75-75-72—296	9056
	Karen Weiss	70-74-75-72—291	24650		Michelle Ellis (Aus)	72-77-74-73—296	9056
15	Akiki Fukushima (Jpn)	71-71-76-74—292	19650		Lorie Kane (Can)	70-74-76-76—296	9056
	Natalie Gulbis	72-72-75-73—292	19650		Mi Hyun Kim (Kor)	77-71-72-76—296	9056
	Kelli Kuehne	71-75-74-72—292	19650		Charlotta Sörenstam		
	Grace Park (Kor)	72-73-73-74—292	19650		(Swe)	75-73-74-74—296	9056
	Rachel Teske (Aus)	72-71-77-72—292	19650		Sherri Turner	74-73-76-73—296	9056
20	Laura Diaz	73-71-71-78—293	16950				

Other players who made the cut: Jane Crafter (Aus), Heather Daly-Donofrio, Tracy Hanson, Pat Hurst, Cristie Kerr, Mhairi McKay (Sco) 297; Angela Buzminski, Jackie Gallagher-Smith, Betsy King, Joanne Morley (Eng), Jennifer Rosales (Phi) 298; Beth Bauer, Jenna Daniels, Michelle Estill, Liselotte Neumann (Swe), Susie Parry 299; Hee-Won Han (Kor), Jeong Jang (Kor) 300; Stephanie Keever, Angela Stanford 301; Denise Killeen, Marnie McGuire (NZ), Patricia Meunier-Lebouc 302; Emilee Klein 303; Becky Iverson, Val Skinner 304; Chris Johnson 305; AJ Eathorne (Can) 307; Karen Pearce 308; Alicia Dibos (Per), Shiho Katano (Jpn) 309.

2001 McDonald's LPGA Championship

Prize money: $1,500,000

1	Karrie Webb (Aus)	67-64-70-69—270	$225000	17T	Dottie Pepper	71-72-71-68—282	16819
2	Laura Diaz	67-71-66-68—272	139639		Kelly Robbins	69-74-71-68—282	16819
3	Maria Hjörth (Swe)	71-67-66-70—274	90577		Rachel Teske (Aus)	68-72-70-72—282	16819
	Wendy Ward	65-69-71-69—274	90577	26	Heather Daly-Donofrio	75-68-71-69—283	13162
5	Annika Sörenstam (Swe)	68-69-71-67—275	64157		Beth Daniel	71-71-70-71—283	13162
6	Laura Davies (Eng)	67-68-70-71—276	48684		Akiko Fukushima (Jpn)	66-72-73-72—283	13162
	Becky Iverson	66-73-67-70—276	48684		Nancy Scranton	73-68-70-72—283	13162
8	Mi Hyun Kim (Kor)	70-70-68-69—277	39250	30	Dawn Coe-Jones	72-69-71-72—284	11603
9	Helen Alfredsson (Swe)	68-66-74-70—278	35476		Catriona Matthew (Sco)	71-72-72-69—284	1 603
10	Michele Redman	69-66-73-71—279	30245		Grace Park (Kor)	71 72-71-70—284	11633
	Maggie Will	68-74-67-70—279	30245	33	Danielle Ammaccapane	69-71-71-74—285	10257
12	Rosie Jones	71-69-71-69—280	25013		Jane Crafter (Aus)	71-71-69-74—285	10257
	Lorie Kane (Can)	69-71-71-69—280	25013		Patricia Meunier-Lebouc		
	Liselotte Neumann (Swe)	69-72-68-71—280	25013		(Fra)	70-73-71-71—285	10257
15	Wendy Doolan (Aus)	70-71-72-68—281	21239		Sherri Turner	71-72-72-70—285	10257
	Juli Inkster	71-71-69-70—281	21239	37	Brandie Burton	69-74-68-75—286	9125
17	Pat Hurst	72-68-72-70—282	16819		Hee Won Han (Kor)	70-75-72-69—286	9125
	Carin Koch (Swe)	69-73-71-69—282	16819	39	Kathryn Marshall (Sco)	71-73-71-72—287	8011
	Leta Lindley	71-71-70-70—282	16819		Se Ri Pak (Kor)	71-73-69-74—287	8011
	Meg Mallon	71-74-67-70—282	16819		Deb Richard	72-71-73-71—287	8011
	Mhairi McKay (Sco)	68-72-70-72—282	16819		Kris Tschetter	71-74-69-73—287	8011
	Terry-Jo Myers	70-71-69-72—282	16819				

Other players who made the cut: Alicia Dibos, Vicki Goetze-Ackerman, Gloria Park (Kor), Kristal Parker 288; Suzy Green, Jenny Lidback (Per), Marnie McGuire 289; Mitzi Edge, Jackie Gallagher-Smith, Emilee Klein, Sara Sanders 290; Amy Alcott, Donna Andrews, Marisa Baena (Col), Susan Ginter, Betsy King, Charlotta Sörenstam (Swe), Leslie Spalding 291; Dorothy Delasin, Alison Nicholas (Eng) 292; Jean Bartholomew, Gail Graham (Can), Joanne Morley (Eng) 293; Janice Moodie (Sco), Barb Mucha, Joan Pitcock 294; Annette DeLuca 296; Michelle McGann 299.

2000 McDonald's LPGA Championship

Prize money: $1,400,000

1	Juli Inkster*	72-69-65-75—281	$210000
	Winner after second play-off hole		
2	Stefania Croce (Ita)	72-67-74-68—281	130330
3	Se Ri Pak (Kor)	73-69-69-71—282	76319
	Nancy Scranton	72-70-67-73—282	76319
	Wendy Ward	69-69-68-76—282	76319
6	Heather Bowie	74-70-70-69—283	42503
	Jane Crafter (Aus)	72-69-69-73—283	42503
	Laura Davies (Eng)	70-66-75-72—283	42503
9	Akiko Fukushima (Jpn)	71-72-71-70—284	29839
	Jan Stephenson (Aus)	70-69-69-76—284	29839
	Karrie Webb (Aus)	72-70-69-73—284	29839
12	Amy Fruhwirth	74-71-70-70—285	21885
	Mi Hyun Kim (Kor)	70-73-70-72—285	21885
	Leta Lindley	71-73-71-70—285	21885
	Kelly Robbins	72-72-73-68—285	21885
	Annika Sörenstam (Swe)	70-73-70-72—285	21885
17	Dawn Coe-Jones	71-73-72-70—286	16602
	Wendy Doolan (Aus)	69-71-71-75—286	16602
	Jane Geddes	66-74-73-73—286	16602
	Pat Hurst	71-70-71-74—286	16602
	Meg Mallon	72-73-69-72—286	16602
	Michele Redman	70-70-70-76—286	16602
23	Pat Bradley	68-76-67-76—287	13304
23T	Betsy King	68-78-67-74—287	13304
	Janice Moodie (Sco)	72-73-71-71—287	13304
	Alison Nicholas (Eng)	72-72-71-72—287	13304
	Dottie Pepper	71-73-69-74—287	13304
28	Rosie Jones	70-74-74-70—288	11191
	Jenny Lidback (Per)	75-71-71-71—288	11191
	Gloria Park (Kor)	68-75-75-70—288	11191
	Karen Weiss	73-71-70-74—288	11191
	Barb Whitehead	73-72-70-73—288	11191
33	Beth Daniel	72-72-70-75—289	9698
	Emilee Klein	74-71-71-73—289	9698
	Kim Saiki	77-69-71-72—289	9698
36	Jean Bartholomew	71-71-74-74—290	8464
	Alicia Dibos (Per)	72-74-74-70—290	8464
	Cindy McCurdy	73-74-71-72—290	8464
	Maggie Will	74-72-67-77—290	8464
40	Sophie Gustafson (Swe)	76-70-69-76—291	6820
	Carin Koch (Swe)	74-70-73-74—291	6820
	Barb Mucha	72-72-70-77—291	6820
	Laura Philo	72-74-73-72—291	6820
	Jennifer Rosales (Phi)	71-73-74-73—291	6820
	Sherri Steinhauer	70-75-68-78—291	6820

Other players who made the cut: Cindy Flom, Kathryn Marshall (Sco), Leigh Ann Mills, Patty Sheehan, Kris Tschetter, Mary Beth Zimmerman 292; Cindy Figg-Currier, Yu Ping Lin (Tre), 293; Jill McGill, Joanne Morley (Eng) 293; Marisa Baena (Col), AJ Eathorne (Can), Vicki Goetze-Ackerman, Kate Golden, Tracy Hanson, Catrin Nilsmark (Swe) 294; Ashli Bunch, Val Skinner, Leslie Spalding 295; Pamela Kerrigan, Nancy Lopez, Shani Waugh (Aus) 296; Danielle Ammaccapane, Debbi Koyama (Jpn) 298; Moira Dunn 299; Carmen Hajjar 300; Julie Piers 301; Dina Ammaccapane 305

1999 McDonald's LPGA Championship

Prize money: $1,400,000

1	J Inkster	68-66-69-65—268	$210000
2	L Neumann (Swe)	67-67-70-68—272	130330
3	M Lunn (Aus)	68-74-65-66—273	84538
	N Scranton	69-68-66-70—273	84538
5	R Jones	64-72-68-70—274	54596
	C Kerr	70-64-69-71—274	54596
7	E Klein	72-68-67-68—275	35224
	J McGill	70-69-68-68—275	35224
	L Davies (Eng)	65-71-71-68—275	35224
	Se Ri Pak (Kor)	68-69-67-71—275	35224
11	M Hirase	70-73-68-65—276	23487
	S Sanders	70-68-68-70—276	23487
	T Green	68-70-68-70—276	23487
	J Lidback	67-67-72-70—276	23487
	M Mallon	70-71-63-72—276	23487
16	A Sörenstam (Swe)	73-68-68-68—277	18415
	S Redman	70-68-70-69—277	18415
	J Stephenson	69-69-69-70—277	18415
19	D Pepper	71-72-68-67—278	16301
	S Steinhauer	74-69-65-70—278	16301
	H Kobayashi (Jpn)	70-67-71-70—278	16301
22	L Kiggens	68-74-69-68—279	14063
	A Fukushima (Jpn)	70-70-69-70—279	14063
	V Odegard	69-70-70-70—279	14063
	A Finney	67-69-71-72—279	14063
26	P Sinn	71-71-70-68—280	11087
	Mi Hyun Kim (Kor)	70-70-71-69—280	11087
	V Fergon	67-73-70-70—280	11087
	J Crafter	70-69-71-70—280	11087
	L Lindley	70-72-67-71—280	11087
	B Mucha	70-70-69-71—280	11087
	K Kuehne	68-67-72-73—280	11087
	A Nicholas (Eng)	67-73-66-74—280	11087
	T Johnson (Eng)	67-70-69-74—280	11087
	L Kane	70-66-70-74—280	11087
36	T Tombs	71-71-69-70—281	8164
	H Stacy	73-68-70-70—281	8164
	C Koch	68-73-70-70—281	8164
	N Bowen	70-72-68-71—281	8164
	S Waugh	70-69-71-71—281	8164
	C Figg-Currier	71-70-67-73—281	8164

Other players who made the cut: Dana Dormann, W Doolan, J Moodie (Sco), R Hetherington (Aus), M Spencer-Devlin 282; C Flom, M Nause, B Iverson, M McGann, D Eggeling, S Croce (Ita), T Barrett 283; K Coats, K Tschetter, P Hammel, C Nilsmark (Swe), K Saiki, D Richard, S Little, C Johnson, S Gustafson (Swe) 284; M Hjörth (Swe), M Will 285; P Bradley 286; K Robbins 287; D Barnard 288; M McGeorge 289; B King, D Killeen 290; K Lunn (Aus) 299

1998 McDonald's LPGA Championship

Prize money: $1,300,000

1	Se Ri Pak (Kor)	65-68-72-68—273	$195000	21T	H Dobson (Eng)	76-70-70-68—284	13558
2	D Andrews	71-67-69-69—276	104666		P Hurst	71-73-68-72—284	13558
	L Hackney (Eng)	70-66-69-71—276	104666		J Lidback	70-73-68-73—284	13558
4	K Webb (Aus)	71-73-67-66—277	62145	25	D Dormann	71-74-74-66—285	11579
	W Ward	71-67-69-70—277	62145		M McGann	68-74-73-70—285	11579
6	M Mallon	71-69-68-70—278	39467		N Scranton	73-73-67-72—285	11579
	C Johnson	69-71-67-71—278	39467		S Redman	68-76-69-72—285	11579
	E Klein	72-67-68-71—278	39467		D Eggeling	68-69-74-74—285	11579
9	C Nilsmark (Swe)	69-73-70-67—279	29110	30	W Doolan	73-72-71-70—286	9365
	K Robbins	69-71-68-71—279	29110		V Odegard	69-74-73-70—286	9365
11	J Pitcock	69-75-70-66—280	23180		A Sörenstam (Swe)	73-71-71-71—286	9365
	A DeLuca	70-71-69-70—280	23180		R Hetherington	71-71-72-72—286	9365
	J Geddes	69-69-70-72—280	23180		L Kane (Can)	72-73-68-73—286	9365
14	T Green	72-68-70-71—281	19691		K Tschetter	71-71-71-73—286	9365
	L Walters	66-69-73-73—281	19691		J Morley	73-69-69-75—286	9365
16	M Hjörth (Swe)	71-70-73-68—282	17402	37	S Steinhauer	73-73-71-70—287	7093
	J Inkster	70-71-69-72—282	17402		B King	71-73-72-71—287	7093
18	M Redman	70-71-74-68—283	15767		M Spencer-Devlin	74-71-70-72—287	7093
	C Koch (Swe)	71-73-69-70—283	15767		L Neumann (Swe)	73-69-73-72—287	7093
	C Johnston-Forbes	71-70-70-72—283	15767		M Halpin	73-73-68-73—287	7093
21	J Moodie (Sco)	75-69-73-67—284	13558		M Estill	72-70-72-73—287	7093

Other players who made the cut: D Coe-Jones, S Little, N Lopez, L Davies, C McCurdy, M Figueras-Dotti, P Bradley 288; C Figg-Currier, K Saiki, B Mucha, D Barnard, H Alfredsson 289; E Dahllof, C Sörenstam 290; C McMillan, K Albers, K Monaghan, B Daniel, M Berteotti 291; H Stacy, M Dobek, P Hammel 292; G Graham, T Hanson 293; M McGeorge, B Burton 295; J Gallagher-Smith, M Morris 297; H Daly-Donofrio 298

1997 McDonald's LPGA Championship

Prize money: $1,200,000

1	C Johnson*	68-73-69-71—281	$180000	16T	K Saiki (Jpn)	68-75-69-77—289	15397
2	L Lindley	72-69-69-71—281	111711	20	A Fruhwirth	72-75-73-70—290	13586
Johnson won play-off at second extra hole					J Wyatt	73-75-71-71—290	13586
3	A Sörenstam (Swe)	70-73-72-67—282	81519	22	M Lunn (Aus)	72-77-75-67—291	12176
4	L Davies (Eng)	67-75-74-68—284	57365		M Mallon	72-76-73-70—291	12176
	S Steinhauer	68-71-73-72—284	57365		T Barrett	69-77-75-70—291	12176
6	G Graham	69-79-71-66—285	38947	25	D Reid (Sco)	74-75-73-70—292	10446
	D Coe-Jones	72-75-71-69—285	38947		W Ward	72-78-71-71—292	10446
8	T Johnson (Eng)	70-73-72-71—286	31400		C Matthew (Sco)	71-75-75-71—292	10446
9	K Webb (Aus)	71-79-70-67—287	26871		M McGeorge	73-74-73-72—292	10446
	B Mucha	68-73-72-74—287	26871		A Dibos	71-76-73-72—292	10446
11	K Robbins	73-74-74-67—288	20047		C Figg-Currier	71-76-72-73—292	10446
	P Bradley	70-75-76-67—288	20047	31	S Strudwick (Eng)	72-74-77-70—293	8423
	B Burton	71-73-76-68—288	20047		M McGann	74-76-71-72—293	8423
	D Dormann	70-73-75-70—288	20047		H Dobson (Eng)	78-72-69-74—293	8423
	J Dickinson	75-72-68-73—288	20047		K Weiss	73-75-71-74—293	8423
16	W Doolan	74-72-74-69—289	15397		C Walker	72-74-73-74—293	8423
	L Kane (Can)	73-74-71-71—289	15397		N Bowen	73-72-73-75—293	8423
	D Andrews	73-71-73-72—289	15397				

Other players who made the cut: N Lopez, K Monaghan, D Richard, N Ramsbottom, D Pepper, M Edge, M Estill, K Parker-Gregory, B Whitehead 294; A Miller, K Albers, A Finney, K Marshall, J Lidback, M Morris, J Pitcock 295; B King, H Stacy, CH Koch, M Berteotti, S Redman, J Inkster 296; MB Zimmerman 297; J McGill, V Goetze-Ackerman, H Kobayashi, J Crafter, R Hetherington, K Peterson-Parker, N Scranton 298; C Mockett, H Alfredsson, Danielle Ammaccapane, J Geddes, D Killeen, A Alcott, J Gallagher-Smith, E Klein 299; M Hirase, M Spencer-Devlin, C Johnston-Forbes, A-M Palli, P Hurst 300; L Walters, V Skinner 301; Vickie Odegard 302.

1996 McDonald's LPGA Championship

Prize money: $1,200,000   Rain reduced event to 54 holes

1	L Davies (Eng)	72-71-70—213	$180000	18T	S Steinhauer	74-71-74—219	13080
2	J Piers	72-72-70—214	111711		D Richard	74-70-75—219	13080
3	P Hammel	73-72-70—215	72461		A Benz	73-71-75—219	13080
	J Crafter (Aus)	75-68-72—215	72461		N Lopez	70-73-76—219	13080
5	J Dickinson	71-74-71—216	37800		K Robbins	69-71-79—219	13080
	J Inkster	70-73-73—216	37800	26	J McGill	76-70-74—220	9744
	S Furlong	70-73-73—216	37800		S Redman	74-72-74—220	9744
	V Skinner	73-69-74—216	37800		D Pepper	70-76-74—220	9744
	H Kobayashi (Jpn)	71-70-75—216	37800		T-J Myers	74-71-75—220	9744
10	M Dobek	72-75-70—217	22342		J Geddes	71-74-75—220	9744
	P Sheehan	72-74-71—217	22342		C Pierce	75-69-76—220	9744
	M Mallon	69-75-73—217	22342		M McGeorge	74-70-76—220	9744
	K Albers	72-71-74—217	22342		B Daniel	72-72-76—220	9744
14	L Kiggens	75-70-73—218	17058	34	B Mucha	76-72-73—221	7366
	B King	72-72-74—218	17058		P Hurst	76-72-73—221	7366
	J Briles-Hinton	73-69-76—218	17058		T Johnson (Eng)	75-73-73—221	7366
	A Sörenstam (Swe)	69-73-76—218	17058		C Figg-Currier	73-74-74—221	7366
18	CH Koch (Swe)	73-74-72—219	13080		L Grimes	74-70-77—221	7366
	K Tschetter	75-71-73—219	13080		E Dahllof	72-72-77—221	7366
	K Marshall (Sco)	73-73-73—219	13080		R Hood	71-73-77—221	7366

Other players who made the cut: T Kerdyk, A Dibos, M Redman, K Monaghan, K Webb, M McGann, M Hirase, L Neumann, S Croce, T Hanson 222; D Dormann, P Bradley, G Graham, MB Zimmerman, B Whitehead, A Nicholas, M Nause 223; M Lunn, E Klein, S Maynor, S Strudwick, C Johnson 224; L West, D Andrews, B Iverson, B Burton, T Green, K Parker-Gregory 225; K Williams, R Jones, M Dunn 226; M Will, M Berteotti 227; M Morris, C Johnston-Forbes 228; A-M Palli, V Goetze 229; M Spencer-Devlin 231; M Estill 232.

1995 McDonald's LPGA Championship

Prize money: $1,200,000

1	K Robbins	66-68-72-68—274	$180000	18T	S Redman	73-71-71-71—286	13080
2	L Davies (Eng)	68-68-69-70—275	111711		L Garbacz	71-71-72-72—286	13080
3	J Larsen	71-68-70-71—280	65416		K Tschetter	73-69-71-73—286	13080
	M Morris	67-71-70-72—280	65416		N Lopez	73-71-68-74—286	13080
	P Sheehan	67-68-72-73—280	65416		C Walker	70-70-72-74—286	13080
6	B Thomas	70-66-73-72—281	38947		A Finney	71-68-70-77—286	13080
	D Mochrie	67-70-71-73—281	38947	26	S Turner	73-74-70-70—287	10626
8	P Bradley	71-70-70-71—282	29890		K Guadagnino	72-73-68-74—287	10626
	T Green	69-72-70-71—282	29890		N Bowen	71-71-71-74—287	10626
10	A Sörenstam (Swe)	71-71-72-69—283	25362	29	K Williams	72-71-75-70—288	9374
11	K Albers	71-71-72-70—284	20681		M Redman	75-68-72-73—288	9374
	D Eggeling	72-72-68-72—284	20681		J Geddes	71-71-75-75—288	9374
	J Pitcock	75-66-71-72—284	20681		M Estill	72-73-67-76—288	9374
	B King	69-71-72-72—284	20681	33	P Hurst	74-72-74-69—289	7970
15	L Kiggens	70-70-75-70—285	16504		K Peterson-Parker	74-73-71-71—289	7970
	M Mallon	70-72-71-72—285	16504		V Fergon	73-71-74-71—289	7970
	B Mucha	71-69-71-74—285	16504		E Gibson	73-69-74-73—289	7970
18	B Daniel	71-73-72-70—286	13080		R Jones	72-71-68-78—289	7970
	N Scranton	71-75-69-71—286	13080				

Other players who made the cut: J Carner, S Little, J Lidback, R Heiken, L Neumann, H Alfredsson, C Johnson, B Iverson, T Johnson 290; D Coe-Jones, A Nicholas, L Walters, T Kerdyk, J Inkster, M Edge, K Noble, V Skinner 291; A Ritzman, M Berteotti, J Dickinson, C Hill, J Crafter, M Figueras-Dotti 292; C Pierce, M McGeorge, C Johnston-Forbes, H Dobson, MB Zimmerman 293; D Massey, V Goetze, B Scherbak, C Mockett, A Benz 294; C Rarick 295; E Klein, T Hanson 296; J Briles-Hinton 297; E Dahllof 298; S Strudwick 299; L Tatum 300.

1994 McDonald's LPGA Championship

Prize money: $1,100,000

1	L Davies (Eng)	70-72-69-68—279	$165000	17T	D Andrews	73-76-69-71—289	12257
2	A Ritzman	68-73-71-70—282	102402		B King	74-73-71-71—289	12257
3	E Crosby	76-71-69-67—283	54660		M McGeorge	75-71-70-73—289	12257
	P Bradley	73-73-70-67—283	54660		K Monaghan	72-72-72-73—289	12257
	H Kobayashi (Jpn)	72-73-71-67—283	54660		M Lunn (Aus)	70-75-70-74—289	12257
	L Neumann (Swe)	74-73-67-69—283	54660		R Walton	70-70-75-74—289	12257
7	S Steinhauer	75-70-72-68—285	27676	26	J Carner	73-75-74-68—290	9907
	A Alcott	71-75-70-69—285	27676		M McGann	70-76-75-69—290	9907
	B Daniel	72-74-68-71—285	27676	28	J Lidback	73-73-74-71—291	8460
	P Sheehan	72-68-72-73—285	27676		M Berteotti	75-70-75-71—291	8460
11	D Mochrie	68-78-70-70—286	20203		G Graham	73-71-76-71—291	8460
	M Mallon	71-71-69-75—286	20203		B Burton	76-70-73-72—291	8460
13	V Skinner	74-69-72-72—287	18266		A Okamoto (Jpn)	74-72-73-72—291	8460
14	J Inkster	69-76-74-69—288	16051		J Wyatt	72-74-73-72—291	8460
	D Dormann	71-76-71-70—288	16051		T Barrett	73-77-68-73—291	8460
	C Johnson	70-74-73-71—288	16051	35	D Eggeling	76-74-71-71—292	6891
17	B Mucha	73-74-75-67—289	12257		P Dunlap	71-74-75-72—292	6891
	N Bowen	73-75-73-68—289	12257		A Arruti (Esp)	75-73-71-73—292	6891
	T Green	71-76-74-68—289	12257		H Alfredsson (Swe)	73-74-71-74—292	6891

Other players who made the cut: J Dickinson, C Schreyer, M Spencer-Devlin, L Kiggens, K Guadagnino, L West 293; H Stacy 294; B Bunkowsky, L Merton, MB Zimmerman 295; M Morris, N Daghe, N Scranton, N Foust, K Tschetter 296; A Finney, L Walters, C Figg-Currier 297; P Sinn, K Noble, P Allen, M Estill, M Figueras-Dotti, J Anschutz 298; J Stephenson, A Benz, C Rarick 299; J Larsen, N Ramsbottom, C Johnston-Forbes, K Saiki, A Miller, C Keggi, M Edge 300; S Hamlin, N Harvey, V Goetze, M Will 301; D Coe-Jones 303; K Marshall 304; L Rinker-Graham, S Biago 305.

LPGA Championship History

The Championship was known simply as the LPGA Championship from its inauguration in 1955 until 1987. It was sponsored by Mazda from 1988 until 1993 when the sponsorship was taken over by McDonald's.

Year	Winner	Venue	Score
1955	B Hanson	Orchard Ridge	4 and 3
1956	M Hagg	Forest Lake	291
(After a tie with P Berg)			
1957	L Suggs	Churchill Valley	285
1958	M Wright	Churchill CC	288
1959	B Rawls	Churchill CC	288
1960	M Wright	French Lick	292
1961	M Wright	Stardust	287
1962	J Kimball	Stardust	282
1963	M Wright	Stardust	294
1964	M Mills	Stardust	278
1965	S Haynie	Stardust	279
1966	G Ehret	Stardust	282
1967	K Whitworth	Pleasant Valley	284
1968	S Post	Pleasant Valley	294
(After a tie with K Whitworth)			
1969	B Rawls	Concord	293
1970	S Englehorn	Pleasant Valley	285
(After a tie with K Whitworth)			
1971	K Whitworth	Pleasant Valley	288
1972	K Ahern	Pleasant Valley	293
1973	M Mills	Pleasant Valley	288
1974	S Haynie	Pleasant Valley	288

LPGA Championship History *continued*

Year	Winner	Venue	Score
1975	K Whitworth	Pine Ridge	288
1976	B Burfeindt	Pine Ridge	287
1977	C Higuchi (Jpn)	Bay Tree	279
1978	N Lopez	Kings Island	275
1979	D Caponi	Kings Island	279
1980	S Little (SA)	Kings Island	285
1981	D Caponi	Kings Island	280
1982	J Stephenson (Aus)	Kings Island	279
1983	P Sheehan	Kings Island	279
1984	P Sheehan	Kings Island	272
1985	N Lopez	Kings Island	273
1986	P Bradley	Kings Island	277
1987	J Geddes	Kings Island	275
1988	S Turner	Kings Island	281
1989	N Lopez	King's Island	274
1990	B Daniel	Bethesda	280
1991	M Mallon	Bethesda	274
1992	B King	Bethesda	267
1993	P Sheehan	Bethesda	275
1994	L Davies (Eng)	Wilmington, Delaware	275
1995	K Robbins	Wilmington, Delaware	274
1996	L Davies (Eng)	Wilmington, Delaware	213
(Reduced to 54 holes – bad weather)			
1997	C Johnson	Wilmington, Delaware	281
1998	Se Ri Pak (Kor)	Wilmington, Delaware	273
1999	J Inkster	Wilmington, Delaware	268
2000	J Inkster	Wilmington, Delaware	281
(After a tie with Stefania Croce (Ita))			
2001	K Webb (Aus)	Wilmington, Delaware	270
2002	Se Ri Pak (Kor)	Wilmington, Delaware	279
2003	A Sörenstam (Swe)*	Wilmington, Delaware	278

Nabisco Dinah Shore

Players are of American nationality unless stated. *Held annually at Mission Hills CC, CA*

2003 Nabisco Dinah Shore   (6520–72)

Prize Money $1.6 million. Final field comprised 99 players, of whom 79 (including 4 amateurs) made the half-way cut on 154 or less.

1	Patricia Meunier Lebouc (Fra)	70-68-70-73—281	$240000
2	Annika Sörenstam (Swe)	68-72-71-71—282	146120
3	Lorena Ochoa (Mex)	71-70-74-68—283	106000
4	Laura Davies (Eng)	70-75-69-70—284	82000
5	Beth Daniel	75-74-68-70—287	51200
	Laura Diaz	76-71-69-71—287	51200
	Maria Hjörth (Swe)	72-72-73-70—287	51200
	Catriona Matthew (Sco)	71-74-72-70—287	51200
9	Jennifer Rosales (Phi)	74-70-72-72—288	35600
	Michelle Wie (am)	72-74-66-76—288	
11	Juli Inkster	75-74-66-75—290	29160
	Cristie Kerr	74-71-74-71—290	29160
	Woo-Soon Ko (Kor)	74-73-70-73—290	29160
	Rosie Jones	71-75-72-72—290	29160
15	Dawn Coe-Jones (Can)	72-74-72-73—291	22080
	Dorothy Delasin	71-71-76-73—291	22080
	Catrin Nilsmark (Swe)	71-78-73-69—291	22080
	Se Ri Pak (Kor)	71-72-71-77—291	22080
	Karen Stupples (Eng)	71-71-76-73—291	22080
20	Hee-Won Han (Kor)	73-74-75-70—292	19040
21	Danielle Ammaccapane	75-68-78-72—293	17440
	Jeong Jang (Kor)	75-73-76-69—293	17440
	Virada Nirapathpongporn (am)	76-72-72-73—293	
	Michele Redman	70-72-76-75—293	17440
	Aree Song (am)	72-77-73-71—293	
	Karrie Webb (Aus)	70-79-71-73—293	17440
27	Leta Lindley	76-70-75-73—294	15840
28	Tammie Green	77-71-73-74—295	14160
	Christina Kim	72-76-71-76—295	14160
	Betsy King	75-74-70-76—295	14160
	Candie Kung (Tai)	74-75-74-72—295	14160
	Charlotta Sörenstam (Swe)	73-74-71-77—295	14160
33	Heather Bowie	72-78-72-74—296	11373
	Heather Daly-Donofrio	74-77-72-73—296	11373
	Moira Dunn	74-80-73-69—296	11373
	Amy Fruhwirth	73-75-75-73—296	11373
	Vicki Goetze-Ackerman	75-74-74-73—296	11373
	Meg Mallon	72-76-73-75—296	11373
39	Beth Bauer	74-76-70-77—297	9440
	Jackie Gallagher-Smith	75-74-74-74—297	9440
	Lorie Kane (Can)	72-72-78-75—297	9440
42	Brandie Burton	74-78-72-74—298	7840
	Raquel Carriedo (Esp)	78-76-71-73—298	7840
	Michelle Ellis (Aus)	71-75-74-78—298	7840
	Liselotte Neumann (Swe)	75-73-73-77—298	7840
	Gloria Park (Kor)	73-74-74-77—298	7840
	Kelly Robbins	72-79-74-73—298	7840
48	Natalie Gulbis	77-75-78-69—299	6560
	Rachel Teske (Aus)	75-76-70-78—299	6560

2003 Nabisco Dinah Shore *continued*

48T	Wendy Ward	74-74-74-77—299	6560
51	Sophie Gustafson (Swe)	74-76-74-76—300	5560
	Pat Hurst	76-73-77-74—300	5560
	Kelli Kuehne	74-78-79-69—300	5560
	Barb Mucha	76-75-73-76—300	5560
	Dottie Pepper	74-76-76-74—300	5560
	Angela Stanford	75-75-76-74—300	5560
57	Nanci Bowen	77-74-76-74—301	4560
	Akiko Fukushima (Jpn)	74-72-75-80—301	4560
	Laurel Kean	75-75-77-74—301	4560
	Mi-Hyun Kim (Kor)	75-76-73-77—301	4560
	Joanne Morley (Eng)	73-76-76-76—301	4560
	Kim Saiki	71-77-76-77—301	4560
	Lindsey Wright (am)	74-78-75-74—301	
64	Helen Alfredsson (Swe)	76-74-72-80—302	3800
	Donna Andrews	72-73-79-78—302	3800
	Emilee Klein	80-74-73-75—302	3800
	Stephanie Louden	75-74-77-76—302	3800
	Janice Moodie (Sco)	74-75-76-77—302	3800
	Shani Waugh (Aus)	73-75-81-73—302	3800
70	Mhairi McKay (Sco)	75-79-78-71—303	3480
	Patty Sheehan	73-74-75-81—303	3480
72	Suzanne Strudwick (Eng)	76-75-77-76—304	3360
73	Tina Fischer (Ger)	75-79-74-77—305	3280
74	Tracy Hanson	72-75-81-78—306	3200
75	Kasumi Fujii (Jpn)	73-75-77-82—307	3140
	Yu Ping Lin (Tai)	78-76-78-75—307	3140
77	Pat Bradley	76-76-81-75—308	3080
78	Dale Eggeling	79-74-79-78—310	3040
79	Mardi Lunn (Aus)	80-74-78-79—311	3000

The following players missed the cut:

Grace Park (Kor)	76-79—155	Kris Tschetter	79-79—158
Naree Song (am)	78-77—155	Kate Golden	77-82—159
Hiromi Kobayashi (Jpn)	84-72—156	Sally Little	77-82—159
Jill McGill	76-80—156	Nancy Lopez	78-83—161
Paula Marti (Esp)	79-77—156	Becky Lucidi (am)	81-81—162
Sherri Steinhauer	79-77—156	Alison Nicholas (Eng)	78-85—163
Amy Alcott	76-81—157	Nancy Scranton	83-80—163
Wendy Doolan (Aus)	79-78—157	Marnie McGuire (NZ)	83-81—164
Pearl Sinn-Bonanni	81-76—157	Alice Miller	79-85—164
Silvia Cavalleri (Ita)	77-81—158	JoAnne Carner	85-81—166

2002 Nabisco Dinah Shore

Prize money: $1,500,000

1	Annika Sörenstam (Swe)	70-71-71-68—280	$225000		21T	Janice Moodie (Sco)	73-73-73-70—289	16350
2	Liselotte Neuman (Swe)	69-70-73-69—281	136987		25	Sophie Gustafson (Swe)	77-69-71-73—290	13800
3	Rosie Jones	72-69-72-69—282	88125			Hee-Won Han (Kor)	74-74-73-69—290	13800
	Cristie Kerr	74-70-70-68—282	88125			Laurel Kean	79-74-71-66—290	13800
5	Akiko Fukushima (Jpn)	73-76-68-66—283	56250			Suzann Pettersen (Nor)	74-71-73-72—290	13800
	Carin Koch (Swe)	73-73-71-66—283	56250			Michele Redman	75-70-72-73—290	13800
7	Karrie Webb (Aus)	75-70-67-72—284	42375		30	Laura Diaz	74-73-73-71—291	12225
8	Lorena Ochoa (am)	75-69-71-70—285				Aree Song Wongluekiet		
9	Becky Iverson	71-74-68-73—286	31050			(am)	71-74-73-73—291	
	Lorie Kane (Can)	73-72-70-71—286	31050		32	Heather Daly-Donofrio	74-73-72-73—292	11100
	Leta Lindley	72-72-72-70—286	31050			Kathryn Marshall (Sco)	75-72-73-72—292	11100
	Se Ri Pak (Kor)	74-71-71-70—286	31050			Alison Nicholas (Eng)	76-71-70-75—292	11100
	Grace Park (Kor)	75-73-70-68—286	31050			Gloria Park (Kor)	70-76-75-71—292	11100
14	Vicki Goetze-Ackerman	74-73-68-72—287	21900		36	Marisa Baena (Col)	79-74-68-72—293	8524
	Heather Bowie	75-71-72-69—287	21900			Maria Hjörth (Swe)	76-73-69-75—293	8524
	Beth Daniel	71-70-75-71—287	21900			Pat Hurst	78-72-71-72—293	8524
	Dorothy Delasin	72-73-69-73—287	21900			Chris Johnson	75-71-76-71—293	8524
	Kris Tschetter	74-69-73-71—287	21900			Betsy King	71-75-73-74—293	8524
19	Juli Inkster	73-76-71-68—288	18225			Kelli Kuehne	74-73-73-73—293	8524
	Mhairi McKay (Sco)	73-72-73-70—288	18225			Meg Mallon	75-73-74-71—293	8524
21	Laura Davies (Eng)	75-75-69-70—289	16350			Sherri Steinhauer	73-78-70-72—293	8524
	Wendy Doolan (Aus)	78-70-72-69—289	16350			Wendy Ward	77-74-73-69—293	8524
	Mi Hyun Kim (Kor)	74-75-69-71—289	16350					

Other players who made the cut: Helen Alfredsson (Swe), Yuri Fudoh (Jpn), Jeong Jang (Kor), Yu Ping Lin (Tai) 294; Donna Andrews, Barb Mucha 295; Penny Hammel, Karin Icher (Fra), Catriona Matthew (Sco), Deb Richard 296; Tina Barrett, Amy Fruhwirth, Jill McGill 298; Moira Dunn, Kelly Robbins, Pearl Sinn (Kor), Naree Song Wongluekiet (am) 299; Brandie Burton, Charlotta Sörenstam (Swe), Sherri Turner 300; Dina Ammaccapane, Rachel Teske (Aus), Karen Weiss 301; Amy Alcott, Kate Golden 302; Emilee Klein 303; Patty Sheehan 305; Tammie Green 306; Meredith Duncan (am) 307; Hiromi Kobayashi (Jpn) 312

2001 Nabisco Dinah Shore

Prize money: $1,250,000

1	Annika Sörenstam (Swe)	72-70-70-69—281	$225000		21T	Loreno Ochoa (Mex) (am)	72 71-74-73—290	
2	Karrie Webb (Aus)	73-72-70-69—284	87557		23	Becky Iverson	75-70-72-74—291	15955
	Janice Moodie (Sco)	72-72-70-70—284	87557		24	Maria Hjörth	73-72-75-72—292	14540
	Dottie Pepper	71-71-71-71—284	87557			Tammie Green	72-73-75-72—292	14540
	Akiko Fukushima (Jpn)	74-68-70-72—284	87557			Kelly Robbins	75-72-72-73—292	14540
	Rachel Teske (Aus)	72-73-66-73—284	87557			Penny Hammel	70-75-72-75—292	14540
7	Sophie Gustafson (Swe)	72-74-70-69—285	41891		28	Meg Mallon	74-71-78-70—293	12063
	Brandie Burton	74-69-72-70—285	41891			Grace Park (Kor)	75-75-72-71—293	12063
9	Laura Diaz	71-74-69-72—286	33589			Dina Ammaccapane	74-74-73-72—293	12063
	Pat Hurst	70-68-74-74—286	33589			Rosie Jones	73-73-75-72—293	12063
11	Laura Davies (Eng)	71-73-75-68—287	25957			Alison Nicholas (Eng)	71-75-75-72—293	12063
	Dorothy Delasin	73-70-74-70—287	25957			Stefania Croce (Ita)	74-72-73-74—293	12063
	Se Ri Pak (Kor)	73-69-73-72—287	25957			Emilee Klein	72-74-72-75—293	12063
	Tina Barrett	71-73-70-73—287	25957		35	Kelli Kuehne	75-70-75-74—294	10446
15	Mi Hyun Kim (Kor)	74-71-70-73—288	20736		36	Jan Crafter (Aus)	78-73-74-70—295	9124
	Carin Koch (Swe)	70-69-75-74—288	20736			Heather Bowie	77-73-74-71—295	9124
	Juli Inkster	70-75-68-75—288	20736			Charlotte Sörenstam		
18	Liselotte Neumann (Swe)	70-74-74-71—289	18220			(Swe)	78-71-75-71—295	9124
	Jeong Jang (Kor)	74-71-71-73—289	18220			Nancy Scranton	72-75-75-73—295	9124
	Michele Redman	71-72-71-75—289	18220			Moira Dunn	78-73-70-74—295	9124
21	Jill McGill	75-71-70-74—290	16711			Wendy Ward	76-73-70-76—295	9124

Other players who made the cut: Amy Fruhwirth, Joanne Morley (Eng), Danielle Ammaccapane, Lorie Kane (Can) 296; Helen Alfredsson (Swe), Aree Wongluekiet (am) 297; Jenny Lidback (Per), Cindy Figg Currier, Nanci Bowen, Leta Lindley, Chris Johnson, Cathy Johnston Forbes, Donna Andrews 298; Beth Daniel, Laurie Kean, Pearl Sinn (Kor) 299; Jackie Gallagher Smith, Vickie Goetze Ackerman, Caroline McMillan, Vicki Fergon, Naree Wongluekiet (am) 300; Wendy Doolan (Aus), Nancy Lopez, Hiromi Kobayashi (Jpn) 301; Cristie Kerr, Susie Redman 302; Joan Pitcock, Catrin Nilsmark (Swe), Kellee Booth 303; Ok Hee Ku (Jpn) 305; Dawn Coe-Jones, Marine Monnet (Fra) 306; Betsy King 309

2000 Nabisco Dinah Shore
Prize money: $1,250,000

1	Karrie Webb (Aus)	67-70-67-70—274	$187500	17T	Kaori Higo (Jpn)	76-72-73-71—292	14321
2	Dottie Pepper	68-72-72-72—284	116366		Sherri Steinhauer	73-71-77-71—292	14321
3	Meg Mallon	75-70-73-67—285	84916		Charlotta Sörenstam		
4	Cathy Johnston-				(Swe)	75-75-70-72—292	14321
	Forbes	74-71-71-70—286	59755		Juli Inkster	76-71-73-72—292	14321
5	Michele Redman	73-73-69-71—286	59755		Nancy Bowen	75-72-73-72—292	14321
6	Helen Dobson (Eng)	73-74-72-68—287	40750		Carin Koch (Swe)	79-70-70-73—292	14321
	Chris Johnson	73-68-73-73—287	40750		Nancy Scranton	78-70-71-73—292	14321
8	Rosie Jones	74-71-74-69—288	31135		Barb Mucha	77-71-70-74—292	14321
	Kim Saiki	72-77-68-71—288	31135	27	Jane Geddes	74-72-78-69—293	10969
10	Jenny Lidback (Per)	75-72-74-68—289	24170		Leta Lindley	73-76-73-71—293	10969
	Wendy Doolan (Aus)	73-73-69-74—289	24170		Catriona Matthew		
	Pat Hurst	72-72-70-75—289	24170		(Sco)	72-77-73-71—293	10969
	Aree Song				Alison Nicholas (Eng)	71-74-74-74—293	10969
	Wongluekiet (am)	75-71-68-75—289		31	Susie Redman	73-75-74-72—294	9507
14	Kristi Albers	77-71-72-70—290	20845		Caroline McMillan		
	Se Ri Pak (Kor)	73-71-77-70—291	18957		(Eng)	73-74-74-73—294	9507
	Janice Moodie (Sco)	74-72-70-75—291	18957		Gail Graham (Can)	71-75-75-73—294	9507
17	Kelly Robbins	79-69-73-71—292	14321		Brandie Burton	74-75-71-74—294	9507
	Annika Sörenstam						
	(Swe)	76-72-73-71—292	14321				

Other players who made the cut: Akiko Fukushima (Jpn), Tina Barrett, Dawn Coe Jones, Laura Davies (Eng), Cristie Kerr, Fumiko Muraguchi (Jpn), Lorie Kane (Can), Beth Bauer (am) 295; Pearl Sinn (Kor), Nancy Lopez, Wendy Ward, Barb Whitehead 296; Cindy McCurdy, Becky Iverson, Mi Hyun Kim (Kor), Jill McGill, Patty Sheehan, Beth Daniel 297; Kris Tschetter, Donna Andrews, Mary Beth Zimmerman, Jan Stephenson (Aus) 298; Helen Alfredsson (Swe), Eva Dahlloff (Swe), Jackie Gallagher Smith, Catrin Nilsmark (Swe), Amy Fruhwirth 299; Mayumi Hirase (Jpn), Penny Hammel, Tammie Green, Sherri Turner, Rachel Hetherington (Aus) 300; Maggie Will, Ayako Okamoto (Jpn), Julie Piers, Kathryn Marshall (Sco) 301; Marnie McGuire (NZ) 302; Liselotte Neumann (Swe) 306; Dale Eggeling 309

1999 Nabisco Dinah Shore
Prize money: $1,000,000

1	D Pepper	70-66-67-66—269	$150000	13T	K Tschetter	68-70-73-75—286	13712
2	M Mallon	66-69-71-69—275	93093	21	M Spencer-Devlin	72-69-77-69—287	9692
3	K Webb (Aus)	73-71-70-66—280	67933		H Stacy	74-74-69-70—287	9692
4	K Robbins	69-73-67-72—281	52837		M Estill	70-76-71-70—287	9692
5	C Sörenstam (Swe)	72-68-76-66—282	42772		R Hetherington (Aus)	70-74-71-72—287	9692
6	J Inkster	72-66-71-74—283	35224		N Lopez	72-73-69-73—287	9692
7	C Matthew (Sco)	72-73-69-70—284	26502		D Eggeling	73-70-70-74—287	9692
	A Sörenstam (Swe)	70-73-71-70—284	26502		H Kobayashi (Jpn)	70-69-74-74—287	9692
	J Moodie (Sco)	69-68-75-72—284	26502		D Andrews	70-69-74-74—287	9692
10	S Steinhauer	70-72-72-71—285	19289	29	H Dobson (Eng)	74-72-74-68—288	7812
	M Hjörth (Swe)	77-68-68-72—285	19289		D Dormann	74-73-71-70—288	7812
	H Alfredsson (Swe)	69-71-73-72—285	19289		L Kane (Can)	73-74-71-70—288	7812
13	R Jones	73-70-73-70—286	13712		J Pitcock	77-68-73-70—288	7812
	M Will	72-71-73-70—286	13712	33	W Ward	74-73-72-70—289	6516
	M Redman	71-74-69-72—286	13712		A Alcott	74-71-71-73—289	6516
	P Bradley	73-69-72-72—286	13712		J Geddes	73-72-71-73—289	6516
	C McCurdy	70-74-69-73—286	13712		T Green	70-75-71-73—289	6516
	Se Ri Pak (Kor)	73-69-69-75—286	13712		B Mucha	73-75-67-74—289	6516
	M Hirase	70-72-69-75—286	13712		J Crafter (Aus)	70-74-71-74—289	6516

Other players who made the cut: K Saiki, T Tombs, N Bowen, G Park (am) 290; K Marshall (Sco), E Klein, M Nause, P Hurst, B Daniel 291; G Graham, T Johnson, C Figg-Currier 292; T Barrett, C Johnson, M McGeorge, D Coe-Jones, K Albers, S Turner, A Nicholas (Eng) 293; L Neumann (Swe), M McGann, T Hanson, M Hattori 294; C Johnston-Forbes, P Sinn, L Kiggens 295; V Fergon, Dina Ammaccapane 296; D Richard, J Piers, J Chuasiriporn (am) 297; E Crosby, C Flom, L Davies (Eng) 298; P Sheehan, TJ Myers, Dani Ammaccapane, K Harada 299; B King 300; B Iverson 301; V Skinner, S Gustafson 302

1998 Nabisco Dinah Shore

Prize money: $1,000,000

1	P Hurst	68-72-70-71—281	$150000	18T	M Spencer-Devlin	72-70-76-73—291	12147
2	H Dobson (Eng)	70-74-71-67—282	93093		L Hackney (Eng)	71-71-73-76—291	12147
3	L Davies (Eng)	75-70-70-68—283	60385	23	G Park (Kor) (am)	77-73-71-71—292	
	H Alfredsson (Swe)	70-73-70-70—283	60385	24	E Klein	76-74-73-70—293	9256
5	D Andrews	71-72-71-70—284	38998		J Inkster	74-75-74-70—293	9256
	L Neumann (Swe)	69-71-71-73—284	38998		C Figg-Currier	74-72-77-70—293	9256
7	A Sörenstam (Swe)	76-71-69-70—286	27928		B Iverson	74-72-77-70—293	9256
	K Webb (Aus)	71-72-70-73—286	27928		B Mucha	72-75-74-72—293	9256
9	D Pepper	73-72-74-68—287	22393		T Green	72-72-76-73—293	9256
	S Steinhauer	69-76-71-71—287	22393		Dani Ammaccapane	75-73-71-74—293	9256
11	A Fruhwirth	73-71-73-71—288	18438		M McGann	74-71-72-76—293	9256
	D Coe-Jones	70-72-74-72—288	18438		M Hirase	73-69-73-78—293	9256
13	C Matthew (Sco)	75-74-70-70—289	15670	33	H Kobayashi (Jpn)	77-71-77-69—294	6964
	P Hammel	73-72-71-73—289	15670		T Barrett	76-73-74-71—294	6964
	N Lopez	71-71-73-74—289	15670		M Halpin	72-77-74-71—294	6964
16	M Mallon	75-69-76-70—290	13658		G Graham	71-75-74-74—294	6964
	B Bauer (am)	76-70-72-72—290			A Nicholas (Eng)	75-70-75-74—294	6964
18	L Kane (Can)	76-71-74-70—291	12147		J Geddes	73-75-71-75—294	6964
	R Jones	75-66-78-72—291	12147		D Dormann	73-74-72-75—294	6964
	J Carner	73-72-73-73—291	12147				

Other players who made the cut: A Alcott, J Stephenson 295; C McCurdy, K Saiki, J Crafter, P Sheehan, M Redman, J Pitcock, P Bradley, K Robbins 296; V Skinner, D Richard, D Eggeling, J Piers, R Burton 297; J Lidback, MB Zimmerman, K Marshall, L Walters 298; T Tombs, R Hetherington 299; C Rarick, B King, K Weiss 300; V Skinner 301; S Redman, P Rizzo, N Bowen 302; S Hamlin, T Johnson 303; M Morris 304; L Kiggens 305; B Daniel 306

1997 Nabisco Dinah Shore

Prize money: $900,000

1	B King	71-67-67-71—276	$135000	16T	L Davies (Eng)	70-70-74-72—286	10898
2	K Tschetter	66-76-66-70—278	83783		K Marshall (Sco)	66-73-73-74—286	10898
3	A Fruhwirth	69-70-68-72—279	54346	23	C Schreyer	72-74-73-68—287	8690
	K Robbins	70-67-68-74—279	54346		M Baena (am)	74-71-73-69—287	
5	N Bowen	70-74-70-68—282	35097		P Hammel	76-72-67-72—287	8690
	L Hackney (Eng)	70-72-72-68—282	35097		T Johnson (Eng)	70-72-73-72—287	8690
7	T Barrett	70-71-70-72—283	26720		N Lopez	70-74-69-74—287	8690
8	MB Zimmerman	75-74-72-63—284	21285	28	B Mucha	71-72-73-72—288	8000
	H Kobayashi (Jpn)	72-69-71-72—284	21285	29	K Webb (Aus)	69-74-71-75—289	7728
	A Sörenstam (Swe)	70-72-68-74—284	21285	30	M Hirase	70-77-72-71—290	6940
11	M Morris	71-75-72-67—285	15065		M Estill	72-73-73-72—290	6940
	D Andrews	73-71-72-69—285	15065		D Coe-Jones	73-72-72-73—290	6940
	J Geddes	68-75-72-70—285	15065		D Richard	68-75-74-73—290	6940
	J Crafter (Aus)	70-71-72-72—285	15065		D Eggeling	68-72-75-75—290	6940
	D Pepper	69-70-71-75—285	15065	35	J Briles-Hinton	72-76-74-69—291	5668
16	T Green	72-73-71-70—286	10898		C Johnson	75-72-72-72—291	5668
	J Inkster	72-74-69-71—286	10898		E Klein	73-74-71-73—291	5668
	M McGann	74-70-71-71—286	10898		A-M Palli (Fra)	73-74-70-74—291	5668
	L Neumann (Swe)	74-71-69-72—286	10898		H Stacy	72-73-72-74—291	5668
	P Hurst	74-69-71-72—286	10898		P Bradley	69-72-73-77—291	5668

Other players who made the cut: A Nicholas, C Walker 292; V Skinner, J Lidback, C Rarick, B Iverson, L Walters 293; S Turner, B Burton, S Steinhauer, K Harada, J Pitcock, V Goetze-Ackerman 294; J Piers, R Hood, H Alfredsson 295; T Hanson, A Finney, A Alcott, K Monaghan 296; N Ramsbottom, R Walton 298; P Sheehan 299; A Okamoto 300; M Spencer-Devlin 301; A Ritzman, TJ Myers 302; B Bunkowsky-Scherbak, A Fukushima, L Kiggens 303; V Fergon, B Whitehead 304; T Kerdyk, A Benz 305.

1996 Nabisco Dinah Shore

Prize money: $900,000

1	P Sheehan	71-72-67-71—281	$135000	19T	T Kerdyk	67-72-77-72—288	10189
2	K Robbins	71-72-71-68—282	64158		J Inkster	70-70-74-74—288	10189
	M Mallon	71-70-71-70—282	64158	23	P Bradley	73-76-71-69—289	8111
	A Sörenstam (Swe)	67-72-73-70—282	64158		J Geddes	74-72-74-69—289	8111
5	A Fruhwirth	71-73-68-71—283	32305		D Andrews	74-70-76-69—289	8111
	K Webb (Aus)	72-70-70-71—283	32305		A Fukushima (Jpn)	74-68-78-69—289	8111
	B Burton	75-67-68-73—283	32305		A Alcott	68-78-71-72—289	8111
8	H Stacy	69-71-74-70—284	23550		P Hammel	75-69-73-72—289	8111
9	K Tschetter	71-74-70-70—285	21285		D Pepper	71-71-75-72—289	8111
10	D Richard	73-71-73-69—286	16212		N Bowen	76-70-70-73—289	8111
	L Neumann (Swe)	73-69-75-69—286	16212	31	B Iverson	76-71-73-70—290	6544
	V Skinner	74-71-71-70—286	16212		S Redman	73-75-71-71—290	6544
	R Jones	72-67-75-72—286	16212		A Nicholas (Eng)	75-72-72-71—290	6544
	T Hanson	69-69-74-74—286	16212		H Kobayashi (Jpn)	72-74-72-72—290	6544
15	N Lopez	73-72-73-69—287	12114	35	C Pierce	72-71-75-73—291	5411
	M McGeorge	74-70-74-69—287	12114		T Johnson (Eng)	74-72-71-74—291	5411
	J Pitcock	71-74-71-71—287	12114		D Coe-Jones	72-73-72-74—291	5411
	L Davies (Eng)	72-70-70-75—287	12114		P Sinn	73-73-70-75—291	5411
19	M Morris	76-71-71-70—288	10189		C Schreyer	72-71-73-75—291	5411
	S Farwig	71-73-73-71—288	10189		S Little (RSA)	69-73-71-78—291	5411

Other players who made the cut: C Johnston-Forbes, K Parker-Gregory, N Ramsbottom, R Walton, B Mucha, G Graham, M Nause 292; J Piers, H Alfredsson, A Okamoto, T Barrett, J Wyatt, S Furlong 293; I Shiotani, L Lindley, V Fergon, M Redman 294; C Walker, K Marshall, M Estill, K Albers 295; J Dickinson, M McGann, MB Zimmerman, Dani Ammaccapane, A Ritzman 296; K Shipman, L Rinker-Graham 297; J Crafter 298; A Dibos, A Finney, S Strudwick, P Wright 299; A Benz, K Guadagnino, 301; S Palmer, E Klein 302; J Stephenson 303; J Carner, C Mackey 305.

1995 Nabisco Dinah Shore

Prize money: $850,000

1	N Bowen	69-75-71-70—285	$127500	16T	P Bradley	74-75-71-72—292	10056
2	S Redman	75-70-70-71—286	79129		J Inkster	76-70-73-73—292	10056
3	B Burton	76-71-71-69—287	42237		T-J Myers	77-68-73-74—292	10056
	S Turner	72-74-71-70—287	42237		M Estill	72-72-74-74—292	10056
	L Davies (Eng)	75-69-70-73—287	42237		M Mallon	74-72-71-75—292	10056
	N Lopez	74-71-68-74—287	42237	24	A Sörenstam (Swe)	76-74-74-69—293	8040
7	C Walker	74-73-69-72—288	23738		M Spencer-Devlin	69-79-74-71—293	8040
	T Green	71-70-70-77—288	23738		K Albers	76-72-72-73—293	8040
9	D Coe-Jones	71-75-71-72—289	20103	27	J Geddes	76-75-74-69—294	7014
10	C Pierce	77-71-73-69—290	17964		K Tschetter	75-74-73-72—294	7014
11	B King	77-75-71-68—291	14200		L West	74-75-71-74—294	7014
	D Mochrie	78-73-70-70—291	14200		K Robbins	76-67-76-75—294	7014
	B Mucha	74-74-72-71—291	14200		B Thomas	79-69-70-76—294	7014
	S Palmer	72-73-74-72—291	14200	32	D Eggeling	72-78-75-70—295	5859
	D Massey	71-75-72-73—291	14200		C Rarick	74-73-78-70—295	5859
16	A Dibos	77-74-75-66—292	10056		L Neumann (Swe)	75-74-74-72—295	5859
	S Steinhauer	78-74-72-68—292	10056		J Larsen	74-76-72-73—295	5859
	A Nicholas (Eng)	75-74-73-70—292	10056		K Noble	71-77-71-76—295	5859

Other players who made the cut: C Keggi, V Skinner, H Kobayashi, A Okamoto, N Ramsbottom, L Merten 296; P Sheehan, A Benz, L Walters, MB Zimmerman 297; Danielle Ammaccapane, C Schreyer, A Ritzman, B Daniel, P Jordan 298; R Jones, F Descampe, J Crafter, J Briles-Hinton, M McNamara 299; Jean Zedlitz, M McGann, I Shiotani, T Johnson, C Johnson, P Hammel 300; K Guadagnino, M Figueras-Dotti 301; L Kiggens, C Johnston-Forbes 302; P Sinn 303; A Finney, T Barrett, K Peterson-Parker, S Farwig, C Hill 304; J Stephenson, M Nause, D Andrews 305; M Berteotti 307; J Anschutz 311.

1994 Nabisco Dinah Shore

Prize money: $700,000

1	D Andrews	70-69-67-70—276	$105000	19T	C Keggi	72-73-72-71—288	7204
2	L Davies (Eng)	70-68-69-70—277	65165		C Johnson	74-73-69-72—288	7204
3	T Green	70-72-69-68—279	47553		P Sheehan	73-71-72-72—288	7204
4	J Stephenson	70-69-70-71—280	36985		D Mochrie	74-73-68-73—288	7204
5	M McGann	70-68-70-73—281	29940		A Okamoto (Jpn)	69-74-72-73—288	7204
6	G Graham	73-71-71-68—283	21251		M McGeorge	72-71-70-75—288	7204
	K Robbins	73-70-69-71—283	21251	28	T Tombs	73-74-72-70—289	5670
	B Burton	73-73-65-72—283	21251		S Turner	72-74-71-72—289	5670
9	H Stacy	72-72-70-70—284	15674		V Skinner	72-72-72-73—289	5670
	N Lopez	68-72-73-71—284	15674		M Berteotti	71-73-72-73—289	5670
11	M Mallon	72-75-69-69—285	12064	32	T-J Myers	76-73-71-70—290	4913
	L Neumann (Swe)	76-71-68-70—285	12064		H Kobayashi (Jpn)	72-77-71-70—290	4913
	D Dormann	73-71-70-71—285	12064		K Tschetter	73-69-76-72—290	4913
	D Eggeling	71-71-71-72—285	12064		S Steinhauer	76-68-72-74—290	4913
15	K Monaghan	70-76-70-70—286	9862	36	J Larsen	76-70-75-70—291	3949
	V Fergon	69-74-72-71—286	9862		K Albers	77-73-70-71—291	3949
17	L Merten	74-74-71-68—287	8982		C Rarick	72-74-74-71—291	3949
	N Scranton	75-70-69-73—287	8982		D Coe-Jones	74-70-75-72—291	3949
19	B Daniel	76-72-70-70—288	7204		Toshimi Kimura	71-74-73-73—291	3949
	J Geddes	70-77-71-70—288	7204		M Nause	74-71-72-74—291	3949
	P Bradley	71-75-71-71—288	7204		A Miller	68-71-77-75—291	3949

Other players who made the cut: M Spencer-Devlin, E Crosby, Danielle Ammaccapane, D Richard, T Johnson 292; J Crafter, J Carner, K Noble, S Strudwick, H Alfredsson, C Schreyer, J Dickinson, L Kean, B King, L Walters 293; C Figg-Currier, A Alcott 294; S Redman, M McNamara, T Kerdyk, L Garbacz 295; A Ritzman, M Will, R Hood, A Benz 296; M Estill 297; B Mucha, S Little, K Guadagnino 298; S Palmer, C Walker, P Wright 299; E Klein (am) 300; C Mackey 305; S Farwig 306; A-M Palli 307

Nabisco Dinah Shore History

This event was inaugurated in 1972 as the Colgate Dinah Shore and continued to be sponsored by Colgate until 1981. Nabisco took over the sponsorship in 1982; and the Nabisco Dinah Shore was designated a Major Championship in 1983. Mission Hills CC, Rancho Mirage, California, is the event's permanent venue.

Year	Winner	Score
1972	J Blalock	213
1973	M Wright	284
1974	J Prentice	289
1975	S Palmer	283
1976	J Rankin	285
1977	K Whitworth	289
1978	S Post	283
1979	S Post	276
1980	D Caponi	275
1981	N Lopez	277
1982	S Little	278
1983	A Alcott	282
1984	J Inkster*	280
Won play-off after a tie with P Bradley		
1985	A Miller	278
1986	P Bradley	280
1987	B King*	283
Won play-off after a tie with P Sheehan		

Year	Winner	Score
1988	A Alcott	274
1989	J Inkster	279
1990	B King	283
1991	A Alcott	273
1992	D Mochrie*	279
Won play-off after a tie with J Inkster		
1993	H Alfredsson (Swe)	284
1994	D Andrews	276
1995	N Bowen	285
1996	P Sheehan	281
1997	B King	276
1998	P Hurst	281
1999	D Pepper	269
2000	K Webb (Aus)	274
2001	A Sörenstam (Swe)	281
2002	A Sörenstam (Swe)	280
2003	P Meunier Labourc	281

du Maurier Classic History

The du Maurier Classic was inaugurated in 1973 and designated a Major Championship in 1979. It was discontinued after 2000 and was replaced as a major on the US LPGA schedule by the Weetabix Women's British Open.

Players are of American nationality unless stated

Year	Winner	Venue	Score
1973	J Bourassa*	Montreal GC, Montreal	214
Won play-off after a tie with S Haynie, J Rankin			
1974	CJ Callison	Candiac GC, Montreal	208
1975	J Carner*	St George's CC, Toronto	214
Won play-off after a tie with C Mann			
1976	D Caponi*	Cedar Brae G&CC, Toronto	212
Won play-off after a tie with J Rankin			
1977	J Rankin	Lachute G&CC, Montreal	214
1978	J Carner	St George's CC, Toronto	278
1979	A Alcott	Richelieu Valley CC, Montreal	285
1980	P Bradley	St George's CC, Toronto	277
1981	J Stephenson (Aus)	Summerlea CC, Dorian, Quebec	278
1982	S Haynie	St George's CC, Toronto	280
1983	H Stacy	Beaconsfield CC, Montreal	277
1984	J Inkster	St George's CC, Toronto	279
1985	P Bradley	Beaconsfield CC, Montreal	278
1986	P Bradley*	Board of Trade CC, Toronto	276
Won play-off after a tie with A Okamoto			
1987	J Rosenthal	Islesmere GC, Laval, Quebec	272
1988	S Little (RSA)	Vancouver GC, Coquitlam, BC	279
1989	T Green	Beaconsfield GC, Montreal	279
1990	C Johnston	Westmount G&CC, Kitchener, Ontario	276
1991	N Scranton	Vancouver GC, Coquitlam, BC	279
1992	S Steinhauer	St Charles CC, Winnipeg, Manitoba	277
1993	B Burton*	London H&CC, Ontario	277
Won play-off after a tie with B King			
1994	M Nause	Ottawa Hunt Club, Ontario	279
1995	J Lidback	Beaconsfield CC, Montreal	280
1996	L Davies (Eng)	Edmonton CC, Edmonton, Alberta	277
1997	C Walker	Glen Abbey GC, Toronto	278
1998	B Burton	Essex G&CC, Ontario	270
1999	K Webb (Aus)	Priddis Greens G&CC, Calgary, Alberta	277
2000	M Mallon	Royal Ottawa GC, Aylmer, Quebec	282

Women's Major Title Table

Juli Inkster

Karrie Webb

Mickey Wright

All photographs © Phil Sheldon

	#British Open	US Open	LPGA	†Dinah Shore	*du Maurier	British Amateur	US Amateur	*Total Titles*
Juli Inkster	0	2	2	2	1	0	3	10
Karrie Webb (Aus)	3	2	1	1	1	0	0	8
Mickey Wright	0	4	4	0	0	0	0	8
Jo Anne Carner	0	2	0	0	0	0	5	7
Betsy King	1	2	1	3	0	0	0	7
Pat Bradley	0	1	1	1	3	0	0	6
Betsy Rawls	0	4	2	0	0	0	0	6
Annika Sörenstam (Swe)	1	2	1	2	0	0	0	6
Glenna Collett Vare	0	0	0	0	0	0	6	6
Louise Suggs	0	2	1	0	0	1	1	5
Babe Zaharias	0	3	0	0	0	1	1	5
Amy Alcott	0	1	0	3	1	0	0	5
Laura Davies (Eng)	1	1	2	0	1	0	0	5

 # Designated a major on the US LPGA circuit from 2001   † Designated a major in 1983
* Designated a major in 1979, discontinued after 2000

PART II

Men's Professional Tournaments

Official World Rankings	110
European Tour	111
European Senior Tour	131
European Challenge Tour	134
US PGA Tour	136
US Champions Tour	147
US Nationwide Tour	150
Japan PGA Tour	152
Asian PGA Tour	154
Australasian Tour	155
South African Sunshine Tour	156
Canadian Tour	158
Tour de Las Americas	159
World Championship Events	160
Other International Events	167
International Team Events	168
National and Regional Championships	184
Overseas National Championships	191

Official World Rankings,
Top 50 (at end US and European Tours 2003)

Ranking		Name	Country	Points Average	Total Points	No. of Events	2001/2002 Pts Lost	2003 Pts Gained
1	(1)	Tiger Woods	USA	16.82	672.72	40	−488.89	+501.37
2	(8)	Vijay Singh	Fij	10.37	601.45	58	−275.81	+550.87
3	(3)	Ernie Els	RSA	9.01	495.62	55	−350.98	+477.13
4	(9)	Davis Love III	USA	8.14	398.81	49	−235.30	+412.39
5	(11)	Jim Furyk	USA	7.67	398.92	52	−198.69	+392.70
6	(46)	Mike Weir	Can	7.13	327.76	46	−181.65	+390.81
7	(5)	Retief Goosen	RSA	6.22	372.90	60	−300.44	+303.62
8	(28)	Kenny Perry	USA	5.73	303.81	53	−159.50	+301.42
9	(6)	David Toms	USA	5.65	299.35	53	−278.88	+247.10
10	(7)	Padraig Harrington	Ire	5.40	259.02	48	−209.00	+191.92
11	(23)	Darren Clarke	NI	4.86	267.55	55	−149.82	+238.28
12	(13)	Nick Price	Zim	4.83	193.39	40	−135.47	+158.91
13	(2)	Phil Mickelson	USA	4.37	222.96	51	−286.79	+131.59
14	(165)	Chad Campbell	USA	4.17	258.46	62	−65.61	+269.37
15	(32)	Stuart Appleby	Aus	3.97	242.29	61	−124.24	+196.93
16	(17)	Justin Leonard	USA	3.85	192.57	50	−157.19	+149.80
17	(25)	Robert Allenby	Aus	3.84	218.98	57	−151.01	+166.59
18	(48)	Brad Faxon	USA	3.76	199.30	53	−109.57	+182.05
19	(83)	Fredrik Jacobson	Swe	3.71	166.88	45	−67.45	+149.89
20	(41)	Choi Kyoung–Ju	Kor	3.66	230.28	63	−110.96	+191.99
21	(20)	Charles Howell III	USA	3.61	238.58	66	−157.41	+184.95
22	(40)	Adam Scott	Aus	3.37	198.72	59	−111.10	+154.90
23	(33)	Scott Verplank	USA	3.34	173.71	52	−135.00	+166.55
24	(137)	Jonathan Kaye	USA	3.31	182.05	55	−57.61	+173.20
25	(104)	Paul Casey	Eng	3.28	170.56	52	−79.57	+179.74
26	(126)	Jay Haas	USA	3.27	160.32	49	−72.52	+178.48
27	(12)	Chris DiMarco	USA	3.24	181.16	56	−213.65	+152.37
28	(88)	Bob Tway	USA	3.23	174.34	54	−79.74	+162.91
29	(44)	Chris Riley	USA	3.18	184.53	58	−109.64	+146.09
30	(35)	Thomas Bjørn	Den	3.13	153.25	49	−107.55	+120.39
31	(34)	Fred Funk	USA	3.12	202.75	65	−125.85	+151.48
32	(26)	Rocco Mediate	USA	3.12	146.56	47	−116.22	+117.54
33	(27)	Jerry Kelly	USA	3.10	182.94	59	−155.46	+143.49
34	(4)	Sergio García	Esp	3.07	162.67	53	−230.90	+71.60
35	(60)	Stephen Leaney	Aus	2.96	148.06	50	−74.81	+119.82
36	(145)	Fred Couples	USA	2.93	117.31	40	−52.54	+128.87
37	(21)	Rich Beem	USA	2.84	164.47	58	−121.54	+70.30
38	(24)	Bob Estes	USA	2.81	143.27	51	−152.54	+121.73
39	(10)	Colin Montgomerie	Sco	2.75	151.39	55	−154.37	+77.52
40	(29)	Shigeki Maruyama	Jpn	2.74	145.46	53	−115.96	+100.70
41	(55)	Alex Cejka	Ger	2.73	152.97	56	−68.21	+118.09
42	(43)	Peter Lonard	Aus	2.72	176.55	65	−113.97	+129.39
43	(245)	Shaun Micheel	USA	2.67	157.67	59	−32.64	+150.91
44	(18)	Michael Campbell	NZ	2.67	136.25	51	−119.66	+75.06
45	(19)	Eduardo Romero	Arg	2.66	116.91	44	−83.04	+61.31
46	(37)	Justin Rose	Eng	2.64	153.38	58	−106.98	+103.72
47	(53)	Loren Roberts	USA	2.62	128.39	49	−72.17	+92.28
48	(1269)	Ben Curtis	USA	2.60	103.93	40	−14.60	+118.54
49	(76)	Ian Poulter	Eng	2.59	147.58	57	−75.66	+123.86
50	(71)	Stewart Cink	USA	2.50	140.00	56	−93.04	+130.24

Ranking in brackets indicates position at 31st December 2002

European Tour –
2003 and Past Results

2003 Volvo Order of Merit (at end of season)

1	Ernie Els (RSA)	€2,975,374	59	Gary Murphy (Ire)	386,419
2	Darren Clarke (NI)	2,210,051	60	Nick Dougherty (Eng)	385,077
3	Padraig Harrington (Irl)	1,555,623	61	Mårten Olander (Swe)	349,701
4	Fredrik Jacobson (Swe)	1,521,302	62	David Park (Wal)	342,676
5	Ian Poulter (Eng)	1,500,855	63	Arjun Atwal (Ind)	335,855
6	Paul Casey (Eng)	1,360,455	64	Peter O'Malley (Aus)	335,122
7	Lee Westwood (Eng)	1,330,712	65	Stephen Scahill (NZ)	313,986
8	Thomas Bjørn (Den)	1,327,148	66	James Kingston (RSA)	312,081
9	Brian Davis (Eng)	1,245,512	67	Mark Foster (Eng)	306,101
10	Phillip Price (Wal)	1,234,017	68	Henrik Stenson (Swe)	300,463
11	Adam Scott (Aus)	1,152,526	69	Christian Cévaër (Fra)	294,147
12	Retief Goosen (RSA)	1,115,886	70	Raymond Russell (Sco)	293,271
14	Stephen Leaney (Aus)	1,099,806	71	Charl Schwartzel (RSA)	291,533
15	Trevor Immelman (RSA)	1,000,777	72	Rolf Muntz (Ned)	288,132
16	Michael Campbell (NZ)	881,999	73	Hennie Otto (RSA)	286,522
17	David Howell (Eng)	881,600	74	Jean-Francois Remesy (Fra)	281,579
18	Ignacio Garrido (Esp)	854,005	75	Ian Woosnam (Wal)	278,598
19	Peter Lonard (Aus)	850,491	76	Richard Sterne (RSA)	277,634
18	Alastair Forsyth (Sco)	850,179	77	Nicolas Colsaerts (Bel)	275,331
20	Raphaël Jacquelin (Fra)	834,814	78	Thomas Levet (Fra)	274,432
21	Greg Owen (Eng)	808,179	79	Gary Orr (Sco)	267,138
22	Niclas Fasth (Swe)	784,444	80	Stephen Dodd (Wal)	261,591
23	Miguel Angel Jiménez (Esp)	781,351	81	Santiago Luna (Esp)	261,464
24	Carlos Rodiles (Esp)	780,256	82	Fredrik Andersson (Swe)	256,701
25	Justin Rose (Eng)	767,900	83	Richard Green (Aus)	254,775
26	Mathias Grönberg (Swe)	748,117	84	Martin Maritz (RSA)	251,664
27	Søren Kjeldsen (Den)	743,848	85	Jonathan Lomas (Eng)	249,162
28	Colin Montgomerie (Sco)	730,773	86	Simon Khan (Eng)	246,718
29	Maarten Lafeber (Ned)	726,788	87	Anthony Wall (Eng)	243,514
30	Gary Evans (Eng)	688,137	88	Pierre Fulke (Swe)	232,797
31	Andrew Coltart (Sco)	647,277	89	Paul Broadhurst (Eng)	232,041
32	Philip Golding (Eng)	643,258	90	Bernhard Langer (Ger)	231,139
33	Paul McGinley (Irl)	637,521	91	Mark Roe (Eng)	225,943
34	Kenneth Ferrie (Eng)	628,539	92	Miles Tunicliff (Eng)	225,191
35	Peter Hedblom (Swe)	623,112	93	José Manuel Lara (Esp)	225,165
36	Eduardo Romero (Arg)	607,761	94	Matthew Blackey (Eng)	223,475
37	Nick O'Hern (Aus)	604,445	95	Marcel Siem (Ger)	223,159
38	John Bickerton (Eng)	583,048	96	Graeme McDowell (NI)	221,909
39	Darren Fichardt (RSA)	574,137	97	Patrik Sjöland (Swe)	219,455
40	Robert-Jan Derksen (Ned)	547,721	98	Steve Webster (Eng)	217,129
41	David Lynn (Eng)	543,315	99	Simon Wakefield (Eng)	214,435
42	Bradley Dredge (Wal)	543,050	100	Jarmo Sandelin (Swe)	209,297
43	Mark McNulty (Zim)	540,047	101	Emanuele Canonica (Ita)	206,834
44	Jarrod Moseley (Aus)	532,623	102	Gregory Havret (Fra)	206,816
45	Peter Fowler (Aus)	527,549	103	David Gilford (Eng)	205,275
46	Nick Faldo (Eng)	503,858	104	Mikko Ilonen (Fin)	197,872
47	Ricardo Gonzalez (Arg)	503,752	105	Andrew Oldcorn (Sco)	196,788
48	Robert Karlsson (Swe)	501,539	106	Julien Clement (Swi)	192,535
49	Sergio García (Esp)	496,521	107	Andrew Marshall (Eng)	189,928
50	Stephen Gallacher (Sco)	479,995	108	Jamie Spence (Eng)	188,081
51	Paul Lawrie (Sco)	477,247	109	Klas Eriksson (Swe)	180,493
52	José Maria Olazábal (Esp)	467,710	110	Markus Brier (Aut)	177,269
53	Angel Cabrera (Arg)	463,541	111	Henrik Bjornstad (Nor)	175,527
54	Barry Lane (Eng)	449,411	112	Brett Rumford (Aus)	169,924
55	Søren Hansen (Den)	424,472	113	Roger Chapman (Eng)	167,735
56	Peter Lawrie (Ire)	422,816	114	Mads Vibe-Hastrup (Den)	166,796
57	Anders Hansen (Den)	386,419	115	Luke Donald (Eng)	165,079
58	Jamie Donaldson (Wal)	397,806	116	Robert Rock (Eng)	165,036

Career Money List (at end of 2003 season)

1	Colin Montgomerie (Sco)	€16,242,768	51	Paul Broadhurst (Eng)	3,043,387
2	Darren Clarke (NI)	12,254,090	52	Jean Van Der Valde (Fra)	3,020,502
3	Ernie Els (RSA)	11,837,097	53	José Coceres (Arg)	2,973,485
4	Bernhard Langer (Ger)	11,210,207	54	Jarmo Sandelin (Swe)	2,884,467
5	Retief Goosen (RSA)	9,908,362	55	Miguel Angel Martin (Esp)	2,869,109
6	Padraig Harrington (Irl)	9,421,355	56	Justin Rose (Eng)	2,830,682
7	Lee Westwood (Eng)	9,323,993	57	Tony Johnstone (Zim)	2,804,726
8	Ian Woosnam (Wal)	8,855,820	58	Mark Roe (Eng)	2,802,910
9	José María Olazábal (Esp)	8,680,906	59	Peter Mitchell (Eng)	2,747,567
10	Thomas Bjørn (Den)	7,828,254	60	Patrik Sjöland (Swe)	2,725,270
11	Vijay Singh (Fij)	7,714,326	61	Joakim Haeggman (Swe)	2,684,544
12	Nick Faldo (Eng)	7,572,646	62	Thomas Levet (Fra)	2,663,594
13	Miguel Angel Jiménez (Esp)	7,042,104	63	Greg Norman (Aus)	2,658,192
14	Eduardo Romero (Arg)	6,740,006	64	Greg Owen (Eng)	2,641,312
15	Michael Campbell (NZ)	6,334,123	65	Paul Casey (Eng)	2,596,996
16	Paul Lawrie (Sco)	5,499,000	66	Des Smyth (Irl)	2,588,803
17	Sam Torrance (Sco)	5,429,805	67	Ricardo Gonzalez (Arg)	2,575,399
18	Phillip Price (Wal)	5,416,366	68	Santiago Luna (Esp)	2,509,253
19	Mark McNulty (Zim)	5,362,075	69	Howard Clark (Eng)	2,507,193
20	Seve Ballesteros (Esp)	5,328,216	70	John Bickerton (Eng)	2,506,716
21	Paul McGinley (Irl)	5,136,593	71	Peter Lonard (Aus)	2,499,138
22	Angel Cabrera (Arg)	4,900,418	72	Sven Strüver (Ger)	2,464,141
23	Barry Lane (Eng)	4,662,492	73	Anders Hansen (Den)	2,401,573
24	Sergio García (Esp)	4,617,471	74	Andrew Oldcorn (Sco)	2,389,808
25	Mark James (Eng)	4,597,599	75	Peter Fowler (Aus)	2,343,975
26	Andrew Coltart (Sco)	4,532,763	76	Russell Claydon (Eng)	2,333,481
27	Robert Karlsson (Swe)	4,471,830	77	Trevor Immelman (RSA)	2,307,587
28	Peter O'Malley (Aus)	4,318,815	78	Raphaël Jacquelin (Fra)	2,238,018
29	Costantino Rocca (Ita)	4,285,661	79	Søren Hansen (Den)	2,197,200
30	Gordon Brand jr (Sco)	3,888,399	80	Raymond Russell (Sco)	2,144,057
31	Niclas Fasth (Swe)	3,846,922	81	Malcolm Mackenzie (Eng)	2,130,416
32	Pierre Fulke (Swe)	3,729,150	82	Peter Senior (Aus)	2,122,118
33	Mathias Grönberg (Swe)	3,703,308	83	Steve Webster (Eng)	2,101,861
34	Stephen Leaney (Aus)	3,651,578	84	Steen Tinning (Den)	2,045,059
35	Fredrik Jacobson (Swe)	3,620,274	85	David Carter (Eng)	2,014,835
36	David Gilford (Eng)	3,579,903	86	Jonathan Lomas (Eng)	2,001,765
37	Adam Scott (Aus)	3,559,047	87	Mark Mouland (Wal)	2,000,948
38	Gary Orr (Sco)	3,551,348	88	Søren Kjeldsen (Den)	1,985,314
39	Ian Poulter (Eng)	3,517,382	89	Jarrod Moseley (Aus)	1,983,237
40	Peter Baker (Eng)	3,516,790	90	Richard Green (Aus)	1,953,759
41	David Howell (Eng)	3,498,764	91	Bradley Dredge (Wal)	1,950,897
42	Ignacio Garido (Esp)	3,485,043	92	Steven Richardson (Eng)	1,876,238
43	Sandy Lyle (Sco)	3,435,226	93	Nick O'Hern (Aus)	1,844,885
44	Jamie Spence (Eng)	3,191,995	94	Dean Robertson (Sco)	1,843,773
45	Ronan Rafferty (NI)	3,165,250	95	Alastair Forsyth (Sco)	1,829,908
46	Greg Turner (NZ)	3,152,518	96	Wayne Riley (Aus)	1,806,180
47	Roger Chapman (Eng)	3,121,462	97	Paul Eales (Eng)	1,724,171
48	Brian Davis (Eng)	3,087,337	98	Mats Lanner (Swe)	1,719,398
49	Anders Forsbrand (Swe)	3,086,484	99	Carl Mason (Eng)	1,717,708
50	Gary Evans (Eng)	3,060,165	100	Roger Wessels (RSA)	1,671,780

2003 Tour Statistics (Reuters Performance Data)

Stroke averages

Pos	Name	Avg
1	Ernie Els (RSA)	68.95
2	Marcus Fraser (Aus)	69.85
3	Paul Casey (Eng)	70.06
4	Retief Goosen (RSA)	70.15
5	Brian Davis (Eng)	70.35
6	Miguel Angel Jiménez (Esp)	70.37
7	Thomas Levet (Fra)	70.39
8	Padraig Harrington (Irl)	70.46
9	Darren Clarke (NI)	70.48
10	Nick O'Hern (Aus)	70.50
11	Thomas Bjørn (Den)	70.51
12	David Howell (Eng)	70.58
13	Peter Fowler (Aus)	70.69
14	Dean Robertson (Sco)	70.70
15	Maarten Lafeber (Ned)	70.72
16	John Bickerton (Eng)	70.73
17T	Fredrik Jacobson (Swe)	70.77
	Bradley Dredge (Wal)	70.77
19	Gary Orr (Sco)	70.79
20	Sergio García (Esp)	70.83

Driving accuracy

Pos	Name	%
1	Jarrod Moseley (Aus)	78.1
2	Richard Green (Aus)	74.2
3	Gary Murphy (Irl)	73.5
4	Peter O'Malley (Aus)	73.4
5	Hennie Otto (RSA)	71.6
6	Simon Wakefield (Eng)	71.1
7	Stephen Leaney (Aus)	70.2
8	Ian Garbutt (Eng)	70.1
9T	Gary Orr (Sco)	70.0
	Dean Robertson (Sco)	70.0

Average putts per round

Pos	Name	Avg
1	Padraig Harrington (Irl)	28.2
2	Pierre Fulke (Swe)	28.4
3	Robert Karlsson (Swe)	28.5
4	Angel Cabrera (Arg)	28.6
5T	Marcel Siem (Ger)	28.7
	Richard Bland (Eng)	28.7
7T	Jarmo Sandelin (Swe)	28.8
	Jamie Spence (Eng)	28.8
	David Lynn (Eng)	28.8
	Ian Poulter (Eng)	28.8
	Retief Goosen (RSA)	28.8
	Michael Campbell (NZ)	28.8

Driving distance

Pos	Name	Yds
1	Titch Moore (RSA)	316.7
2	Emanuele Canonica (Ita)	316.5
3	Jean Hugo (RSA)	314.5
4	Ernie Els (RSA)	310.0
5	Marcel Siem (Ger)	307.0
6	Paul Casey (Eng)	304.0
7	François Delamontagne (Fra)	303.0
8	Ricardo Gonzalez (Arg)	302.9
9	Richard Sterne (RSA)	302.5
10	Angel Cabrera (Arg)	301.7

Sand saves

Pos	Name	%
1T	Charlie Wi (Kor)	73.3
	Sebastien Delagrange (Fra)	73.3
3	Joakim Haeggman (Swe)	70.0
4	Padraig Harrington (Irl)	69.4
5	Mikael Lundberg (Swe)	69.2
6	Patrik Sjöland (Swe)	67.0
7	Warren Bennett (Eng)	66.7
8	Justin Rose (Eng)	66.1
9	Robert Karlsson (Swe)	66.0
10T	Ernie Els (RSA)	65.0
	Jorge Berendt (Arg)	65.0

Greens in regulation

Pos	Name	%
1	Ernie Els (RSA)	80.2
2	Peter O'Malley (Aus)	78.3
3	Darren Clarke (NI)	76.8
4	Thomas Levet (Fra)	76.5
5T	Gary Evans (Eng)	73.7
	Stephen Leaney (Aus)	73.7
7	Richard Green (Aus)	72.9
8	Paul Lawrie (Sco)	72.8
9	Stuart Little (Eng)	72.7
10	Raymond Russell (Sco)	72.4

Putts per green in regulation

Pos	Name	Avg
1	Ernie Els (RSA)	1.699
2	Retief Goosen (RSA)	1.718
3	Fredrik Jacobson (Swe)	1.724
4	Niclas Fasth (Swe)	1.729
5	Thomas Bjørn (Den)	1.733
6	Robert Karlsson (Swe)	1.734
7	Padraig Harrington (Irl)	1.736
8	Paul Casey (Eng)	1.740
9	Ian Poulter (Eng)	1.742
10	Arjun Atwal (Ind)	1.745

Tour Results (in chronological order)

BMW Asian Open

2002   J Sandelin (Swe)   278

2003 *at Ta Shee, Taiwan*   (7101–72)

1	Padraig Harrington (Irl)	66-70-68-69—273	£158328	€247967
2	Jyoti Randhawa (Ind)	65-75-70-64—274	105548	165305
3	Trevor Immelman (RSA)	69-67-68-72—276	49082	76870
	Maarten Lafeber (Ned)	66-66-71-73—276	49082	76870
	Andrew Pitts (USA)	67-70-69-70—276	49082	76870

Omega Hong Kong Open

2002   JM Olazábal (Esp)   262

2003 *at Hong Kong GC*   (6463–69)

1	Fredrik Jacobson (Swe)	68-65-63-64—260	£71619	€113385
2	Jorge Berendt (Arg)	68-65-62-67—262	38417	60822
	Henrik Nystrom (Swe)	64-68-63-67—262	38417	60822

South African Airways Open

1903	LB Waters	1930	SF Brews	1958	AA Stewart (am)	1980	R Cole
1904	LB Waters	1931	SF Brews	1959	D Hutchinson (am)	1981	G Player
1905	AG Gray	1932	C McIlvenny	1960	G Player	1982	*Not played*
1906	AG Gray	1933	SF Brews	1961	R Waltman	1983	C Bolling
1907	LB Waters	1934	SF Brews	1962	HR Henning	1984	T Johnstone (Zim)
1908	G Fotheringham	1935	AD Locke (am)	1963	R Waltman	1985	G Levenson
1909	J Fotheringham	1936	CE Olander	1964	A Henning	1986	D Frost
1910	G Fotheringham	1937	AD Locke (am)	1965	G Player	1987	M McNulty
1911	G Fotheringham	1938	AD Locke	1966	G Player	1988	W Westner
1912	G Fotheringham	1939	AD Locke	1967	G Player	1989	S Wadsworth
1913	JAW Prentice (am)	1940	AD Locke	1968	G Player	1990	T Dodds
1914	G Fotheringham	1946	AD Locke	1969	G Player	1991	W Westner
1919	WH Horne	1947	RW Glennie (am)	1970	T Horton (Eng)	1992	E Els
1920	LB Waters	1948	JM Janks (am)*	1971	S Hobday	1993	C Whitelaw
1921	J Brews	1949	SF Brews	1972	G Player	1994	T Johnstone (Zim)
1922	F Jangle	1950	AD Locke	1973	RJ Charles (NZ)	1995	R Goosen
1923	J Brews	1951	AD Locke	1974	R Cole	1996	E Els
1924	BH Elkin	1952	SF Brews	1975	D Hayes	1997	V Singh (Fij)
1925	SF Brews	1953	JR Boyd (am)	1976	G Player	1998	E Els
1926	J Brews	1954	RC Taylor (am)	1976	G Player	1999	D Frost
1927	SF Brews	1955	AD Locke	1977	G Player	2000	M Grönberg (Swe)
1928	J Brews	1956	G Player	1978	H Baiocchi	2001	M McNulty (Zim)
1929	A Tosh	1957	HR Henning*	1979	G Player	2002	T Clark

2003 *at Erinvale, Cape Town, RSA*   (7087–72)

1	Trevor Immelman (RSA)*	70-71-66-67—274	£79000	€121669
2	Tim Clark (RSA)	67-67-71-69—274	57500	88557
3	Jean Hugo (RSA)	66-73-65-73—277	22480	34622
	Bobby Lincoln (RSA)	71-68-69-69—277	22480	34622
	Charl Schwartzel (RSA)	75-69-68-65—277	22480	34622
	Tjaart Van Der Walt (RSA)	69-76-64-68—277	22480	34622
	Bradford Vaughan (RSA)	69-71-68-69—277	22480	34622

Alfred Dunhill Championship

(1959–99 combined with South African PGA Championship)

1995	E Els	Wanderers Club	271	1999	E Els	Houghton GC	273
1996	S Strüver	Houghton GC	202 (54)	2000	A Wall	Houghton GC	204
1997	N Price	Houghton GC	269	2001	A Scott	Houghton GC	267
1998	T Johnstone	Houghton GC	271	2002	J Rose	Houghton GC	268

2003 *at Houghton, Johannesburg, RSA* (7284–72)

1	Mark Foster (Eng)*	70-66-69-68—273	£79000	€120574
2	Anders Hansen (Den)	70-65-69-69—273	31030	47360
	Trevor Immelman (RSA)	69-67-70-67—273	31030	47360
	Paul Lawrie (Sco)	68-73-67-65—273	31030	47360
	Doug McGuigan (Sco)	69-67-69-68—273	31030	47360
	Bradford Vaughan (RSA)	70-66-66-71—273	31030	47360

Caltex Singapore Masters

2001	V Singh (Fij)	263	2002	A Atwal (Ind)	274

2003 *at Laguna National, Singapore* (7145–72)

1	Zhang Lian-wei (PRC)	68-71-69-70—278	£92747	€140713
2	Ernie Els (RSA)	69-67-70-73—279	61831	93809
3	Prayad Marksaeng (Tha)	73-67-69-71—280	34836	52852

Heineken Classic

1996	I Woosnam (Wal)	277	2000	M Campbell (NZ)	268
1997	MA Martin (Esp)	273	2001	M Campbell (NZ)	270
1998	T Bjørn (Den)	280	2002	E Els (RSA)	271
1999	Jarrod Moseley (Aus)	274			

2003 *at Royal Melbourne GC, Victoria, Australia* (6981–72)

1	Ernie Els (RSA)	70-72-66-65—273	£137508	€207309
2	Nick Faldo (Eng)	69-71-65-69—274	64743	97608
	Peter Lonard (Aus)	67-72-67-68—274	64743	97608

The ANZ Championship

2002	R Johnson (Swe)	46 points

2003 *at NSW GC, Sydney, Australia* (6816–72)

1	Paul Casey (Eng)	8-10-21-6—45 points	£118133	€180934
2	Stuart Appleby (Aus)	16-2-15-8—41	55621	85190
	Nick O'Hern (Aus)	10-12-8-11—41	55621	85190

Johnnie Walker Classic

1992	I Palmer	Bangkok	268	1998	T Woods*	Blue Canyon CC, Phuket	279
1993	N Faldo	Singapore Island	269	1999	*Not played*		
1994	G Norman	Blue Canyon, Phuket	277	2000	M Campbell	Ta Shee, Taiwan	276
1995	F Couples	Orchard GC, Manila	277	2001	T Woods	Bangkok	263
1996	I Woosnam	Tanah Merah, Singapore	272	2002	R Goosen	Perth, Australia	274
1997	E Els	Hope Island, Queensland	278				

Johnnie Walker Classic *continued*

2003 *at Lake Karrinyup, Perth, Australia* (7014–72)

1	Ernie Els (RSA)	64-65-64-66—259	£166660	€251263
2	Stephen Leaney (Aus)	68-67-68-66—269	86855	130946
	André Stolz (Aus)	68-68-67-66—269	86855	130946

Carlsberg Malaysian Open

1992	V Singh	1996	S Fiesch	2000	Y Wei Tze
1993	G Norquist	1997	L Westwood	2001	V Singh
1994	J Haegmann	1998	E Fryatt	2002	A Forsyth*
1995	C Devers	1999	G Norquist		

2003 *at The Mines Resort, Kuala Lumpur, Malaysia* (6785–71)

1	Arjun Atwal (Ind)	62-65-67-66—260	£113834	€169765
2	Retief Goosen (RSA)	66-64-66-68—264	59323	88471
	Brad Kennedy (Aus)	68-66-66-64—264	59323	88471

WGC Accenture Match Play

2003 *at La Costa, Carlsbad, CA, USA*

Final: Tiger Woods (USA) (£651,875, €973394) beat David Toms (USA) (£378,214, €556225)

Consolation match: Adam Scott (Aus) (£302,571, €444980) beat Peter Lonard (Aus) (£245,839, €361546)

Fuller details of this event are to be found on p.159

Dubai Desert Classic

1989	M James*	Emirates	277	1996	C Montgomerie	Emirates	270
1990	E Darcy	Emirates	276	1997	R Green	Emirates	272
1991	*Not played*			1998	JM Olazábal	Emirates	269
1992	S Ballesteros*	Emirates	272	1999	D Howell	Dubai Creek	275
1993	W Westner	Emirates	274	2000	J Coceres	Dubai Creek	274
1994	E Els	Emirates	268	2001	T Bjørn	Emirates	266
1995	F Couples	Emirates	268	2002	E Els	Emirates	272

2003 *at Emirates GC, Dubai* (7201–72)

1	Robert-Jan Derksen (Ned)	67-72-67-65—271	£200000	€291994
2	Ernie Els (RSA)	66-68-69-69—272	133330	194658
3	Alastair Forsyth (Sco)	65-69-69-71—274	62000	90518
	David Lynn (Eng)	68-66-69-71—274	62000	90518
	Ian Woosnam (Wal)	69-66-70-69—274	62000	90518

Qatar Masters *at Doha, Qatar*

1998	A Coltart	270	2001	T Johnstone	274
1999	P. Lawrie	268	2002	A Scott	269
2000	R Muntz	280			

2003 (7110–72)

1	Darren Fichardt (RSA)*	71-69-66-69—275	£156055	€226983
2	James Kingston (RSA)	68-67-71-69—275	104032	151316
3	Paul McGinley (Irl)	68-72-70-67—277	58614	85255

Madeira Island Open

1993	M James	Campo de Golf da Madeira	281		1998	M Lanner	Santo de Serra GC	277
1994	M Lanner	Campo de Golf da Madeira	206 (54)		1999	P Linhart	Santo da Serra GC	276
1995	S Luna	Campo de Golf da Madeira	272		2000	N Fasth	Santo de Serra GC	279
1996	J Sandelin	Campo de Golf da Madeira	279		2001	D Smyth	Santo de Serra GC	270
1997	P Mitchell	Santo de Serra GC	204 (54)		2002	D Borrego	Santo de Serra GC	281

2003 at Santo da Serra, Madeira (6826–72)

1	Bradley Dredge (Wal)	69-72-60-71—272	£67790	€100000
2	Fredrik Andersson (Swe)	73-68-70-69—280	30329	44740
	Brian Davis (Eng)	74-70-68-68—280	30329	44740
	Andrew Marshall (Eng)	71-70-69-70—280	30329	44740

The MASTERS at Augusta National, GA, USA (7290–72)

1	Mike Weir (Can)*	70-68-75-68—281	£692441	€1008312
2	Len Mattiace	73-74-69-65—281	£415464	€604986
3	Phil Mickelson	73-70-72-68—283	£261588	€380917

Fuller details of this event are included in Part I The Majors page 60

Algarve Open de Portugal

1953	EC Brown	Estoril	260		1978	H Clark	Penina	291
1954	A Miguel	Estoril	263		1979	B Barnes	Vilamoura	287
1955	F van Donck	Estoril	267		1982	S Torrance	Penina	207 (54)
1956	A Miguel	Estoril	268		1983	S Torrance	Troia	286
1958	P Alliss	Estoril	264		1984	A Johnstone	Quinta do Lago	274
1959	S Miguel	Estoril	265		1985	W Humphreys	Quinta do Lago	279
1960	K Bousfield	Estoril	268		1986	M McNulty	Quinta do Lago	270
1961	K Bousfield	Estoril	263		1987	R Lee	Estoril	195 (54)
1962	A Angelini	Estoril	269		1988	M Harwood	Quinta do Lago	280
1963	R Sota	Estoril	204 (54)		1989	C Montgomerie	Quinta do Lago	264
1964	A Miguel	Estoril	279		1990	M McLean	Quinta do Lago	274
1966	A Angelini	Estoril	273		1991	S Richardson	Estela	283
1967	A Gallardo	Estoril	214 (54)		1992	R Rafferty	Vila Sol	273
1968	M Faulkner	Estoril	273		1993	D Gilford*	Vila Sol	275
1969	R Sota	Estoril	270		1994	P Price	Penha Longa	278
1970	R Sota	Estoril	274		1995	A Hunter*	Penha Longa	277
1971	L Platts	Estoril	277		1996	W Riley	Aroeira	271
1972	G Garrido	Estoril	196 (54)		1997	M Jonzon	Aroeira	269
1973	J Benito*	Penina	294		1998	P Mitchell	Algarve	274
1974	BGC Huggett	Estoril	272		1999	V Phillips*	Penina	276
1975	H Underwood	Penina	292		2000	G Orr	Penina	275
1976	S Balbuena	Quinta do Lago	283		2001	P Price	Algarve	273
1977	M Ramos	Penina	287		2002	C Pettersson*	Vale do Lobo	142 (36)

2003 at Vale do Lobo, Portugal (7125–72)

1	Fredrik Jacobson (Swe)	64-76-71-72—283	£142541	€208330
2	Brian Davis (Eng)	70-71-71-72—284	63775	93210
	Bradley Dredge (Wal)	69-73-74-68—284	63775	93210
	Jamie Donaldson (Wal)	72-71-73-68—284	63775	93210

Canarias Open de España

1912	A Massy (Fra)	Polo, Madrid		1925	A de la Torre	Puerta de Hierro
1916	A de la Torre	Puerta de Hierro		1926	J Bernardino	Puerta de Hierro
1917	A de la Torre	Puerta de Hierro		1927	A Massy (Fra)	Puerta de Hierro
1919	A de la Torre	Puerta de Hierro		1928	A Massy (Fra)	Puerta de Hierro
1921	E Lafitte	Puerta de Hierro		1929	E Lafitte	Puerta de Hierro
1923	A de la Torre	Puerta de Hierro		1930	J Bernardino	Puerta de Hierro

Canarias Open de España continued

1932	G Gonzalez	Puerta de Hierro		1972	A Garrido*	Pals
1933	G Gonzalez	Puerta de Hierro		1973	NC Coles (Eng)	La Manga
1934	J Bernardino	Puerta de Hierro		1974	J Heard	La Manga
1935	A de la Torre	Puerta de Hierro		1975	A Palmer (USA)	La Manga
1941	M Provencio	Puerta de Hierro		1976	E Polland (NI)	La Manga
1942	G Gonzalez	Sant Cugat		1977	B Gallacher (Sco)	La Manga
1943	M Provencio	Puerta de Hierro		1978	B Barnes (Sco)	El Prat
1944	N Sagardia	Pedrena		1979	D Hayes (RSA)	Torrequebrada
1945	C Celles	Puerta de Hierro		1980	E Polland (NI)	Escorpion
1946	M Morcillo	Pedrena		1981	S Ballesteros	El Prat
1947	M Gonzalez (am)	Puerta de Hierro		1982	S Torrance (Sco)	Club de Campo
1948	M Morcillo	Negun		1983	E Darcy (Irl)	Las Brisas
1949	M Morcillo	Puerta de Hierro		1984	B Langer (Ger)	El Saler
1950	A Cerda	Cedana		1985	S Ballesteros	Vallromanos
1951	M Provencio	Puerta de Hierro		1986	H Clark (Eng)	La Moraleja
1952	M Faulkner (Eng)	Puerta de Hierro		1987	N Faldo (Eng)	La Brisas
1953	M Faulkner (Eng)	Puerta de Hierro		1988	M James (Eng)	Pedrena
1954	S Miguel	Puerta de Hierro		1989	B Langer (Ger)	El Saler
1955	H de Lamaze (Fra) (am)	Puerta de Hierro		1990	R Davis (Aus)	Club de Campo
1956	P Alliss (Eng)	El Prat		1991	E Romero* (Arg)	Club de Campo
1957	M Faulkner (Eng)	Club de Campo		1992	A Sherborne (Eng)	RACE, Madrid
1958	P Alliss (Eng)	Puerta de Hierro		1993	J Haeggman (Swe)	RACE, Madrid
1959	PW Thomson (Aus)	El Prat		1994	C Montgomerie (Sco)	Club de Campo
1960	S Miguel	Club de Campo		1995	S Ballesteros	Club de Campo
1961	A Miguel	Puerta de Hierro		1996	P Harrington (Irl)	Club de Campo
1963	R Sota	El Prat		1997	M James* (Eng)	La Moraleja II
1964	A Miguel	Tenerife		1998	T Bjørn (Swe)	El Prat
1966	R de Vicenzo (Arg)	Sotogrande		1999	J Sandelin (Swe)	El Prat
1967	S Miguel	Sant Cugat		2000	B Davis	PGA Golf de
1968	R Shaw	La Galea				Catalunya
1969	J Garaialde	RACE, Madrid		2001	R Karlsson (Swe)	El Saler
1970	A Gallardo	Nueva Andalucia		2002	S García (Esp)	El Cortij
1971	D Hayes (RSA)	El Prat				

2003 at Golf Costa Adeje, Tenerife   (6816–72)

1	Kenneth Ferrie (Eng)*	67-65-65-69—266	£201732	€291660
2	Peter Hedblom (Swe)	64-70-65-67—266	105130	151995
	Peter Lawrie (Irl)	67-64-69-66—266	105130	151995

60th Italian Open Telecom Italia

1925	F Pasquali	Stresa	154	1959	P Thomson	Villa d'Este	269
1926	A Boyer	Stresa	147	1960	B Wilkes	Venice	285
1927	P Alliss	Stresa	145	1961	R Sota	Garlenda	282
1928	A Boyer	Villa d'Este	145	1961–1971	Not played		
1929	R Golias	Villa d'Este	143	1972	N Wood	Villa d'Este	271
1930	A Boyer	Villa d'Este	140	1973	A Jacklin	Rome	284
1931	A Boyer	Villa d'Este	141	1974	P Oosterhuis	Venice	249 (63)
1932	A Boomer	Villa d'Este	143	1975	W Casper	Monticello	286
1934	N Nutley	San Remo	132	1976	B Dassu	Is Molas	280
1935	P Alliss	San Remo	262	1977	A Gallardo*	Monticello	286
1936	H Cotton	Sestriere	268	1978	D Hayes	Pevero	293
1937	M Dallemagne	San Remo	276	1979	B Barnes*	Monticello	281
1938	F van Donck	Villa d'Este	276	1980	M Mannelli	Rome	276
1947	F van Donck	San Remo	263	1981	J M Canizares*	Milan	280
1948	A Casera	San Remo	267	1982	M James	Is Molas	280
1949	H Hassanein	Villa d'Este	263	1983	B Langer*	Ugolino	271
1950	U Grappasonni	Rome	281	1984	A Lyle	Milan	277
1951	J Adams	Milan	289	1985	M Piñero	Molinetto	267
1952	E Brown	Milan	273	1986	D Feherty*	Albarella, Venice	270
1953	F van Donck	Villa d'Este	267	1987	S Torrance*	Monticello	271
1954	U Grappasonni	Villa d'Este	272	1988	G Norman	Monticello	270
1955	F van Donck	Venice	287	1989	R Rafferty	Monticello	273
1956	A Cerda	Milan	284	1990	R Boxall	Milan	267
1957	H Henning	Villa d'Este	273	1991	C Parry	Castelconturbia	279
1958	P Alliss	Varese	282	1992	A Lyle	Monticello	270

1993	G Turner	Modena	267	1999	D Robertson	Circolo GC, Torino	271
1994	E Romero	Marco Simone	272	2000	I Poulter	Is Molas	267
1995	S Torrance	Le Rovedine	269	2001	G Havret	Is Molas	268
1996	J Payne	Bergamo GC	275	2002	I Poulter	Olgiata GC	197
1997	B Langer	Gardagolf	273			*(reduced to 56 holes because of rain)*	
1998	JM Olazábal	Castelconturbia	195 (54)				

2003 *at Gardagolf, Brescia, Italy*   (7112–72)

1	Mathias Grönberg (Swe)	71-67-68-65—271	£127173	€183330
2	Ricardo Gonzalez (Arg)	67-70-66-70—273	56901	82027
	José Manuel Lara (Esp)	69-68-71-65—273	56901	82027
	Colin Montgomerie (Sco)	70-67-71-65—273	56901	82027

Benson and Hedges International Open

1971	A Jacklin*	Fulford	279	1987	N Ratcliffe	Fulford	275
1972	J Newton	Fulford	281	1988	P Baker*	Fulford	271
1973	V Baker	Fulford	276	1989	G Brand jr	Fulford	272
1974	P Toussaint*	Fulford	276	1990	JM Olazábal	St Mellion	279
1975	V Fernandez	Fulford	266	1991	B Langer	St Mellion	286
1976	G Marsh	Fulford	272	1992	P Senior*	St Mellion	287
1977	A Garrido	Fulford	280	1993	P Broadhurst	St Mellion	276
1978	L Trevino*	Fulford	274	1994	S Ballesteros	St Mellion	281
1979	M Bembridge	St Mellion	272	1995	P O'Malley	St Mellion	280
1980	G Marsh	Fulford	272	1996	S Ames	The Oxfordshire	283
1981	T Weiskopf	Fulford	272	1997	B Langer	The Oxfordshire	276
1982	G Norman	Fulford	283	1998	D Clarke	The Oxfordshire	273
1983	J Bland	Fulford	273	1999	C Montgomerie	The Oxfordshire	273
1984	S Torrance	Fulford	270	2000	JM Olazábal	The Belfry	275
1985	A Lyle	Fulford	274	2001	H Stenson	The Belfry	275
1986	M James*	Fulford	274	2002	A Cabrera	The Belfry	278

2003 *at The Belfry, Sutton Coldfield, England*   (7118–72)

1	Paul Casey (Eng)	71-69-66-71—277	£183330	€262228
2	Padraig Harrington (Irl)	67-68-71-75—281	122220	174819
3	Paul Lawrie (Sco)	71-72-70-69—282	56833	81292
	Rolf Muntz (Ned)	70-71-69-72—282	56833	81292
	Stephen Scahill (NZ)	71-70-65-76—282	56833	81292

Deutsche Bank – SAP Open TPC of Europe

1977	N Coles	Foxhills	288	1990	M McLean	Quinta do Lago	274
1978	B Waites	Foxhills	286	1991	*not played*		
1979	M King	Moor Park	281	1992	*not played*		
1980	B Gallacher	Moortown	268	1993	*not played*		
1981	B Barnes*	Dalmahoy	276	1994	*not played*		
1982	N Faldo	Notts	270	1995	B Langer	Gut Kaden	270
1983	B Langer	St Mellion	269	1996	F Nobilo	Gut Kaden	270
1984	J Gonzalez*	St Mellion	265	1997	R McFarlane	Gut Kaden	282
1985	*Not played*			1998	L Westwood	Gut Kaden	265
1986	I Woosnam	The Belfry	277	1999	T Woods	St Leon-Rot	273
1987	*Not played*			2000	L Westwood	Gut Kaden, Hamburg	273
1988	*Not played*			2001	T Woods	St Leon-Rot	266
1989	C Montgomerie	Quinta do Lago	264	2002	T Woods*	St Leon-Rot	268

2003 *at Gut Kaden, Hamburg, Germany*   (7215–72)

1	Padraig Harrington (Irl)*	65-66-70-68—269	£322474	€450000
2	Thomas Bjørn (Den)	71-70-65-63—269	214983	300000
3	Retief Goosen (RSA)	65-69-70-66—270	121121	169020

Volvo PGA Championship

1955	K Bousfield	Pannal	277		1979	V Fernandez	St Andrews	288
1956	CH Ward	Maesdu	282		1980	N Faldo	R St George's	283
1957	P Alliss	Maesdu	286		1981	N Faldo	Ganton	274
1958	H Bradshaw	Llandudno	287		1982	A Jacklin*	Hillside	284
1959	DJ Rees	Ashburnham	283		1983	S Ballesteros	R St George's	278
1960	AF Stickley	Coventry	247 (63)		1984	H Clark	Wentworth Club	204 (54)
1961	BJ Bamford	R Mid-Surrey	266		1985	P Way*	Wentworth Club	282
1962	P Alliss	Little Aston	287		1986	R Davis*	Wentworth Club	281
1963	PJ Butler	R Birkdale	306		1987	B Langer	Wentworth Club	270
1964	AG Grubb	Western Gailes	287		1988	I Woosnam	Wentworth Club	274
1965	P Alliss	Prince's	286		1989	N Faldo	Wentworth Club	272
1966	GB Wolstenholme	Saunton	278		1990	M Harwood	Wentworth Club	271
1967	BGC Huggett	Thorndon Park	271		1991	S Ballesteros*	Wentworth Club	271
1967	ME Gregson	Hunstanton	275		1992	T Johnstone	Wentworth Club	272
1968	PM Townsend	R Mid-Surrey	275		1993	B Langer	Wentworth Club	274
1968	D Talbot	Dunbar	276		1994	JM Olazábal	Wentworth Club	271
1969	B Gallacher	Ashburnham	293		1995	B Langer	Wentworth Club	279
1972	A Jacklin	Wentworth Club	279		1996	C Rocca	Wentworth Club	274
1973	P Oosterhuis	Wentworth Club	280		1997	I Woosnam	Wentworth Club	275
1974	M Bembridge	Wentworth Club	278		1998	C Montgomerie	Wentworth Club	274
1975	A Palmer	R St George's	285		1999	C Montgomerie	Wentworth Club	270
1976	NC Coles*	R St George's	280		2000	C Montgomerie	Wentworth Club	271
1977	M Piñero	R St George's	283		2001	A Oldcorn	Wentworth Club	272
1978	N Faldo	R Birkdale	278		2002	A Hansen	Wentworth Club	269

2003 *at Wentworth Club, Surrey, England* (7072–72)

1	Ignacio Garrido (Esp)*	70-69-66-65—270	£414556	€583330
2	Trevor Immelman (RSA)	69-69-64-68—270	276366	388880
3	Mathias Grönberg (Swe)	72-67-67-67—273	155708	219100
4	Ernie Els (RSA)	69-69-67-69—274	124368	175000
5	Kenneth Ferrie (Eng)	70-67-70-68—275	96260	135450
	Barry Lane (Eng)	72-68-68-67—275	96260	135450
7	Søren Kjeldsen (Den)	68-72-69-67—276	68402	96250
	Thomas Levet (Fra)	74-69-66-67—276	68402	96250
9	Paul Casey (Eng)	70-72-64-71—277	46812	65870
	Nick Faldo (Eng)	71-68-68-70—277	46812	65870
	Colin Montgomerie (Sco)	69-70-69-69—277	46812	65870
	Gary Orr (Sco)	69-72-66-70—277	46812	65870
	Phillip Price (Wal)	71-69-67-70—277	46812	65870
14	Darren Clark (NI)	66-69-72-71—278	34367	48358
	Paul Eales (Eng)	74-69-67-68—278	34367	48358
	Niclas Fasth (Swe)	69-67-68-74—278	34367	48358
	David Gilford (Eng)	70-69-71-68—278	34367	48358
	Kevin Na (Kor)	69-70-68-71—278	34367	48358
	Eduardo Romero (Arg)	72-71-65-70—278	34367	48358
20	Peter Fowler (Aus)	70-71-70-68—279	28936	40717
	Stephen Leaney (Aus)	69-73-65-72—279	28936	40717
	Adam Scott (Aus)	68-73-71-67—279	28936	40717
23	John Bickerton (Eng)	72-69-71-68—280	25868	36400
	Henrik Bjornstad (Nor)	71-71-71-67—280	25868	36400
	Sandy Lyle (Sco)	75-68-67-70—280	25868	36400
	Martin Maritz (RSA)	71-71-68-70—280	25868	36400
	Robert Rock (Eng)	69-68-70-73—280	25868	36400
28	Stephen Dodd (Wal)	71-72-69-69—281	22511	31675
	Peter Hedblom (Swe)	69-74-69-69—281	22511	31675
	Mårten Olander (Swe)	73-67-69-72—281	22511	31675
	Mikko Ilonen (Fin)	69-70-72-70—281	22511	31675
32	Emanuele Canonica (Ita)	71-69-69-73—282	18500	26031
	Andrew Coltart (Sco)	68-71-70-73—282	18500	26031
	Fredrik Jacobson (Swe)	72-69-70-71—282	18500	26031
	Paul McGinley (Irl)	70-69-71-72—282	18500	26031
	Mark McNulty (Zim)	69-71-68-74—282	18500	26031
	Ronan Rafferty (NI)	69-72-72-69—282	18500	26031

32T	Justin Rose (Eng)	68-73-70-71—282	18500	26031
	Miles Tunnicliff (Eng)	69-73-71-69—282	18500	26031
40	Gordon Brand, jr (Sco)	68-70-68-77—283	15422	21700
	Jamie Donaldson (Wal)	69-71-68-75—283	15422	21700
	Alastair Forsyth (Sco)	67-71-71-74—283	15422	21700
	Henrik Stenson (Swe)	71-72-70-70—283	15422	21700
44	James Kingston (RSA)	67-76-67-74—284	13432	18900
	Raymond Russell (Sco)	74-67-73-70—284	13432	18900
	Jean Van De Velde (Fra)	71-70-70-73—284	13432	18900
	Ian Woosnam (Wal)	68-69-72-75—284	13432	18900
48	Matthew Blackey (Eng)	70-73-71-71—285	11193	15750
	Michael Campbell (NZ)	69-74-69-73—285	11193	15750
	David Drysdale (Sco)	72-71-71-71—285	11193	15750
	Ricardo Gonzales (Arg)	69-73-70-73—285	11193	15750
	José María Olazábal (Esp)	68-71-74-72—285	11193	15750
53	Peter Baker (Eng)	68-73-70-75—286	8706	12250
	Anders Hansen (Den)	70-72-70-74—286	8706	12250
	Henrik Nystrom (Swe)	73-69-74-70—286	8706	12250
	Jean-François Remesy (Fra)	73-69-75-69—286	8706	12250
	Sam Torrance (Sco)	70-71-70-75—286	8706	12250
58	Roger Chapman (Eng)	71-69-79-68—287	6840	9625
	Pierre Fulke (Swe)	71-72-70-74—287	6840	9625
	Santiago Luna (Esp)	72-71-71-73—287	6840	9625
	Greg Owen (Eng)	68-71-73-75—287	6840	9625
	Steen Tinning (Den)	74-69-70-74—287	6840	9625
	Greg Turner (NZ)	72-70-71-74—287	6840	9625
64	Darren Fichardt (RSA)	69-73-77-69—288	5472	7700
	Thongthai Jaidee (Tha)	67-72-76-73—288	5472	7700
	Mikael Lundberg (Swe)	72-69-73-74—288	5472	7700
	Nick O'Hern (Aus)	73-69-71-75—288	5472	7700
	Peter Senior (Aus)	68-73-76-71—288	5472	7700
69	Søren Hansen (Den)	69-68-77-75—289	4634	6520
	Carlos Rodiles (Esp)	70-73-73-73—289	4634	6520
71	Arjun Atwal (Ind)	68-74-72-77—291	3731	5250
72	Barry Austin (Eng)	73-68-77-74—292	3728	5245
	David Orr (Sco)	72-71-75-74—292	3728	5245
74	Christian Cévaèr (Fra)	73-70-77-75—295	3725	5241
75	Ben Willman (Eng)	73-68-77-79—297	3722	5238

81 missed the cut on 144

The Celtic Manor Resort Wales Open

at Celtic Manor Resort, Newport, Wales (7355–72)

2000	S Tinning	Newport	223	2002	P Lawrie	Newport	272
2001	P McGinley	Newport	138				

2003

1	Ian Poulter (Eng)	65-67-68-70—270	£250000	€347360
2	Darren Fichardt (RSA)	68-67-70-68—273	111853	155413
	Jonathan Lomas (Eng)	66-71-68-68—273	111853	155413
	Jarrod Moseley (Aus)	74-67-63-69—273	111853	155413

Daily Telegraph Damovo British Masters

1946T	AD Locke	Stoneham	286	1951	M Faulkner	Wentworth Club	281
	J Adams			1952	H Weetman	Mere	281
1947	A Lees	Little Aston	283	1953	H Bradshaw	Sunningdale	272
1948	N Von Nida	Sunningdale	272	1954	AD Locke	Prince's	291
1949	C Ward	St Andrews	290	1955	H Bradshaw	Little Aston	277
1950	D Rees	Hoylake	281	1956	C O'Connor	Prestwick	277

Daily Telegraph Damovo British Masters *continued*

1957	E Brown	Hollinwell	275	1980	B Langer	St Pierre	270
1958	H Weetman	Little Aston	276	1981	G Norman	Woburn	273
1959	C O'Connor	Portmarnock	276	1982	G Norman	St Pierre	267
1960	J Hitchcock	Sunningdale	275	1983	L Woosnam	St Pierre	269
1961	P Thomson	Porthcawl	284	1985	L Trevino	Woburn	278
1962	D Rees	Wentworth Club	278	1986	S Ballesteros	Woburn	275
1963	B Hunt	Little Aston	282	1987	M McNulty	Woburn	274
1964	C Legrange	Royal Birkdale	288	1988	A Lyle	Woburn	273
1965	B Hunt	Portmarnock	283	1989	N Faldo	Woburn	267
1966	N Coles	Lindrick	278	1990	M James	Woburn	270
1967	A Jacklin	R St George's	274	1991	S Ballesteros	Woburn	275
1968	P Thomson	Sunningdale	274	1992	C O'Connor jr*	Woburn	270
1969	C Legrange	Little Aston	281	1993	P Baker	Woburn	266
1970	B Huggett	R Lytham & St Annes	293	1994	I Woosnam	Woburn	271
1971	M Bembridge	St Pierre	273	1995	S Torrance	Collingtree Park	270
1972	R J Charles	Northumberland	277	1996	R Allenby*	Collingtree Park	284
1973	A Jacklin	St Pierre	272	1997	G Turner	Forest of Arden	275
1974	B Gallacher*	St Pierre	282	1998	C Montgomerie	Forest of Arden	281
1975	B Gallacher	Ganton	289	1999	B May	Woburn	269
1976	B Dassu	St Pierre	271	2000	G Orr	Woburn	267
1977	G Hunt*	Lindrick	291	2001	T Levet*	Woburn	274
1978	T Horton	St Pierre	279	2002	J Rose	Woburn	26
1979	G Marsh	Woburn	283				

2003 *at Forest of Arden, England*   (7213–72)

1	Greg Owen (Eng)	68-68-67-71—274	£250000	€348312
2	Christian Cévaèr (Fra)	73-70-66-68—277	130280	181513
	Ian Poulter (Eng)	71-73-63-70—277	130280	181513

US OPEN CHAMPIONSHIP

2003 *at Olympian Fields, Matteson, IL, USA*   (7190–70)

1	Jim Furyk (USA)	67-66-67-72—272	£649741	€923471
2	Stephen Leaney (Aus)	67-68-68-72—275	391048	555793
3	Kenny Perry (USA)	72-71-69-67—279	205371	291891
	Mike Weir (Can)	73-67-68-71—279	205371	291891

Fuller details of this event are included in Part I The Majors page 52

Aa St Omer Open   *at St Omer, France*   (6799–71)

2000	P Edmond	274	2001	S Delagrange	272	2002	N Vanhootagem	277

2003

1	Brett Rumford (Aus)	64-70-68-67—269	£46901	€66660
2	Ben Mason (Eng)	70-69-66-69—274	31267	44440
3	Federico Bisazza (Ita)	68-72-68-70—278	17618	25040

Diageo Championship   *at Gleneagles Hotel, Scotland*   (7060–72)

1999	W Bennett	282	2001	P Casey	274
2000	P Fulke	271	2002	A Scott	262

2003

1	Søren Kjeldsen (Den)	72-68-67-72—279	£200000	€281928
2	Alastair Forsyth (Sco)	70-73-69-69—281	133330	187947
3	Paul Broadhurst (Eng)	73-68-71-70—282	75120	105892

Open de France

1906	A Massy	La Boulie	292		1960	R De Vicenzo	St Cloud	275
1907	A Massy	La Boulie	294		1961	KDG Nagle	La Boulie	271
1908	JH Taylor	La Boulie	300		1962	A Murray	St Germain	274
1909	JH Taylor	La Boulie	290		1963	B Devlin	St Cloud	273
1910	J Braid	La Boulie	298		1964	R de Vicenzo	Chantilly	272
1911	A Massy	La Boulie	284		1965	R Sota	St Nom-la-Bretêche	268
1912	J Gassiat	La Boulie	284		1966	DJ Hutchinson	La Boulie	274
1913	G Duncan	Chantilly	304		1967	BJ Hunt	St Germain	271
1914	JD Edgar	Le Touquet	284		1968	PJ Butler	St Cloud	272
1920	W Hagen	La Boulie	298		1969	J Garaialde	St Nom-la-Bretêche	277
1921	A Boomer	Le Touquet	284		1970	D Graham	Chantaco	268
1922	A Boomer	La Boulie	284		1971	Lu Liang Huan	Biarritz	262
1923	J Ockenden	Dieppe	284		1972	B Jaeckel*	Biarritz & La Nivelle	265
1924	CJH Tolley (am)	La Boulie	290		1973	P Oosterhuis	La Boulie	280
1925	A Massy	Chantilly	291		1974	P Oosterhuis	Chantilly	284
1926	A Boomer	St Cloud	280		1975	B Barnes	La Boulie	281
1927	G Duncan	St Germain	290		1976	V Tshabalaia	Le Touquet	272
1928	CJH Tolley (am)	La Boulie	283		1977	S Ballesteros	Le Touquet	282
1929	A Boomer	Fourqueux	283		1978	D Hayes	La Baule	269
1930	ER Whitcombe	Dieppe	282		1979	B Gallacher	Lyons	284
1931	A Boomer	Deauville	291		1980	G Norman	St Cloud	268
1932	AJ Lacey	St Cloud	296		1981	A Lyle	St Germain	270
1933	B Gadd	Chantilly	283		1982	S Ballesteros	St Nom-la-Bretêche	278
1934	SF Brews	Dieppe	284		1983	N Faldo*	La Boulie	277
1935	SF Brews	Le Touquet	292		1984	B Langer	St Cloud	270
1936	M Dallemagne	St Germain	277		1985	S Ballesteros	St Germain	263
1937	M Dallemagne	St Cloud	278		1986	S Ballesteros	La Boulie	269
1938	M Dallemagne	Fourqueux	282		1987	J Rivero	St Cloud	269
1939	M Pose	Le Touquet	285		1988	N Faldo	Chantilly	274
1946	TH Cotton	St Cloud	269		1989	N Faldo	Chantilly	273
1947	TH Cotton	Chantilly	285		1990	P Walton*	Chantilly	275
1948	F Cavalo	St Cloud	287		1991	E Romero	National GC	281
1949	U Grappasonni	St Germain	275		1992	MA Martin	National GC	276
1950	R De Vicenzo	Chantilly	279		1993	C Rocca*	National GC	273
1951	H Hassanein	St Cloud	278		1994	M Roe	National GC	274
1952	AD Locke	St Germain	268		1995	P Broadhurst	National GC	274
1953	AD Locke	La Boulie	276		1996	R Allenby*	National GC	272
1954	F van Donck	St Cloud	275		1997	R Goosen	National GC	271
1955	B Nelson	La Boulie	271		1998	S Torrance	National GC	276
1956	A Miguel	Deauville	277		1999	R Goosen*	Golf du Médoc	272
1957	F van Donck	St Cloud	266		2000	C Montgomerie	Le Golf National	272
1958	F van Donck	St Germain	276		2001	JM Olazábal	Lyon GC	268
1959	DC Thomas	La Boulie	276		2002	M Mackenzie	Le Golf National	279

2003 at Le Golf National, Paris, France (7105–72)

1	Phil Golding (Eng)	66-70-68-69—273	£290791	€416660
2	David Howell (Eng)	71-65-69-69—274	193858	277770
3	Peter O'Malley (Aus)	70-69-66-70—275	98231	140750
	Justin Rose (Eng)	68-69-73-65—275	98231	140750

Smurfit European Open

1978	B Wadkins*	Walton Heath	283		1991	M Harwood	Walton Heath	277
1979	A Lyle	Turnberry	275		1992	N Faldo	Sunningdale	262
1980	T Kite	Walton Heath	284		1993	G Brand jr	E. Sussex National	275
1981	G Marsh	Royal Liverpool	275		1994	D Gilford	E. Sussex National	275
1982	M Piñero	Sunningdale	266		1995	B Langer*	The K Club	280
1983	L Aoki	Sunningdale	274		1996	P-U Johansson	The K Club	277
1984	G Brand jr	Sunningdale	270		1997	P-U Johansson	The K Club	267
1985	B Langer	Sunningdale	269		1998	M Grönberg	The K Club	275
1986	G Norman*	Sunningdale	269		1999	L Westwood	The K Club	271
1987	P Way	Walton Heath	279		2000	L Westwood	The K Club	276
1988	I Woosnam	Sunningdale	260		2001	D Clarke	The K Club	273
1989	A Murray	Walton Heath	277		2002	M Campbell	The K Club	282
1990	P Senior	Sunningdale	267					

Smurfit European Open continued

2003 at The K Club, Dublin, Ireland   (7337–72)

1	Phillip Price (Wal)	66-69-67-70—272	£333330	€481245
2	Alastair Forsyth (Sco)	66-70-69-68—273	173710	250794
	Mark McNulty (Zim)	68-69-68-68—273	173710	250794

The Barclays Scottish Open

1986	D Feherty*	Haggs Castle	270	1995	W Riley	Carnoustie	276
1987	I Woosnam	Gleneagles	264	1996	I Woosnam	Carnoustie	289
1988	B Lane	Gleneagles	271	1996	T Bjørn	Loch Lomond	277
1989	M Allen	Gleneagles	272	1997	T Lehman	Loch Lomond	265
1990	I Woosnam	Gleneagles	269	1998	L Westwood	Loch Lomond	276
1991	C Parry	Gleneagles	268	1999	C Montgomerie	Loch Lomond	268
1992	P O'Malley	Gleneagles	262	2000	E Els	Loch Lomond	273
1993	J Parnevik	Gleneagles	271	2001	R Goosen	Loch Lomond	268
1994	C Mason	Gleneagles	265	2002	E Romero	Loch Lomond	273

2003 at Loch Lomond, Glasgow, Scotland   (7095–71)

1	Ernie Els (RSA)	64-67-67-69—267	£366660	€532889
2	Darren Clarke (NI)	69-70-64-69—272	191080	277708
	Phillip Price (Wal)	67-68-68-69—272	191080	277708

The 132nd OPEN CHAMPIONSHIP

2003 at Royal St George's, Sandwich, Kent, England   (7106–71)

1	Ben Curtis (USA)	72-72-70-69—283	£700000	€1010800
2	Thomas Bjørn (Den)	73-70-69-72—284	345000	498180
	Vijay Singh (Fij)	75-70-69-70—284	345000	498180

Past results and fuller details in Part I The Majors page 42

Nissan Irish Open

1927	G Duncan	Portmarnock	312	1980	M James	Portmarnock	284
1928	E Whitcombe	Newcastle	288	1981	S Torrance	Portmarnock	276
1929	A Mitchell	Portmarnock	309	1982	J O'Leary	Portmarnock	287
1930	C Whitcombe	Portrush	289	1983	S Ballesteros	Royal Dublin	271
1931	E Kenyon	Royal Dublin	291	1984	B Langer	Royal Dublin	267
1932	A Padgham	Cork	283	1985	S Ballesteros*	Royal Dublin	278
1933	E Kenyon	Malone	286	1986	S Ballesteros	Portmarnock	285
1934	S Easterbrook	Portmarnock	284	1987	B Langer	Portmarnock	269
1935	E Whitcombe	Newcastle	292	1988	I Woosnam	Portmarnock	278
1936	R Whitcombe	Royal Dublin	281	1989	I Woosnam*	Portmarnock	278
1937	B Gadd	Portrush	284	1990	JM Olazábal	Portmarnock	282
1938	A Locke	Portmarnock	292	1991	N Faldo	Killarney	283
1939	A Lees	Newcastle	287	1992	N Faldo*	Killarney	274
1946	F Daly	Portmarnock	288	1993	N Faldo*	Mount Juliet	276
1947	H Bradshaw	Portrush	290	1994	B Langer	Mount Juliet	275
1948	D Rees	Portmarnock	295	1995	S Torrance*	Mount Juliet	277
1949	H Bradshaw	Belvoir Park	286	1996	C Montgomerie	Druid's Glen	279
1950	H Pickworth	Royal Dublin	287	1997	C Montgomerie	Druid's Glen	269
1953	E Brown	Belvoir Park	272	1998	D Carter	Druid's Glen	278
1975	C O'Connor Jr	Woodbrook	275	1999	S García	Druid's Glen	268
1976	B Crenshaw	Portmarnock	284	2000	P Sjöland	Ballybunion	270
1977	H Green	Portmarnock	283	2001	C Montgomerie	Fota Island	266
1978	K Brown	Portmarnock	281	2002	S Hansen	Fota Island	270
1979	M James	Portmarnock	282				

2003 at Portmarnock, Dublin, Ireland   (7363–72)

1	Michael Campbell (NZ)*	66-69-71-71—277	£212498	€300000
2	Thomas Bjørn (Den)	64-74-68-71—277	110740	156340
	Peter Hedblom (Swe)	70-71-68-68—277	110740	156340

Scandic Carlsberg Scandinavian Masters

1991	C Montgomerie	Drottningholm	270	1997	J Haeggman	Barsebäck	270
1992	N Faldo	Barsebäck	277	1998	J Parnevik	Kungsängen	273
1993	P Baker*	Forsgårdens	278	1999	C Montgomerie	Barsebäck	268
1994	V Singh	Drottningholm	268	2000	L Westwood	Kungsängen	270
1995	J Parnevik	Barsebäck	270	2001	C Montgomerie	Kungsängen	274
1996	L Westwood	Forsgårdens	281	2002	G McDowell (NI)	Kungsängen	270

2003 *at Kungsängen, Stockholm, Sweden*   (6761-71)

1	Adam Scott (Aus)	70-71-67-69—277	£225072	€316660
2	Nick Dougherty (Eng)	67-69-74-69—279	150050	211110
3	Andrew Coltart (Sco)	67-76-69-68—280	69774	98167
	Luke Donald (Eng)	71-68-71-70—280	69774	98167
	Robert Karlsson (Swe)	71-69-71-69—280	69774	98167

Nordic Open   *at Simon's GC, Copenhagen, Denmark*   (7027-72)

2003

1	Ian Poulter (Eng)	68-67-65-66—266	£187003	€266660
2	Colin Montgomerie (Sco)	70-65-64-68—267	124666	177770
3	Stephen Gallacher (Sco)	71-65-69-63—268	57972	82667
	Søren Hansen (Den)	71-66-62-69—268	57972	82667
	Gregory Havret (Fra)	68-63-69-68—268	57972	82667

US PGA CHAMPIONSHIP

2003 *at Oak Hill, Rochester, NY, USA*   (7134-70)

1	Shaun Micheel	69-68-69-70—276	£671642	953980
2	Chad Campbell	69-72-65-72—278	402985	572388
3	Tim Clark (RSA)	72-70-68-69—279	253731	360392

Past results and fuller details in Part I The Majors page 67

BMW Russian Open

1996	C Watts	203	1999	I Pyman	273	2002	I Pyman	269
1997	M Reale	280	2000	M Bernardini	269			
1998	W Bennett	270	2001	J Donaldson	270			

2003 *at Le Meridien, Moscow, Russia*   (7174-72)

1	Marcus Fraser (Aus)*	68-65-68-68—269	£46931	€66660
2	Martin Wiegele (Aut)	68-66-67-68—269	31288	44440
3	Peter Hanson (Swe)	71-68-67-66—272	17629	25040

WGC: NEC Invitational   *at Firestone CC, Akron, OH, USA*   (7283-70)

1	Darren Clarke (NI)	65-70-66-67—268	£657977	€932920
2	Jonathan Kaye (USA)	68-69-65-70—272	344655	488672
3	David Love III (USA)	66-70-68-69—273	225592	319858

Fuller details of this event are included in World Championship Events on page 160

BMW International Open

1989	D Feherty	Golfplatz, Munich	269					*(36 holes only)*
1990	P Azinger*	Golfplatz, Munich	277	1997	R Karlsson	GC München	264	
1991	A Lyle	Golfplatz, Munich	268	1998	R Claydon	GC München	270	
1992	P Azinger*	Golfplatz, Munich	266	1999	C Montgomerie	GC München	268	
1993	P Fowler	Golfplatz, Munich	267	2000	T Bjørn	GC München	368	
1994	M McNulty	St Eurach L&GC	274	2001	J Daly	GC München	261	
1995	F Nobilo	St Eurach L&GC	272	2002	T Bjørn	GC Munchen	264	
1996	M Farry	St Eurach L&GC	132					

2003 *at Golfclub München Nord-Eichenried, Munich* (6963–72)

1	Lee Westwood (Eng)	65-68-70-66—269	£207001	€300000
2	Alex Cejka (Ger)	69-66-70-67—272	138001	200000
3	Paul Casey (Eng)	65-69-70-69—273	54648	79200
	Andrew Coltart (Sco)	70-70-65-68—273	54648	79200
	Gary Evans (Eng)	66-68-68-71—273	54648	79200
	Peter Hedblom (Swe)	66-66-74-67—273	54648	79200
	Raphaèl Jacquelin (Fra)	62-69-71-71—273	54648	79200

Omega European Masters *at Crans-sur-Sierre, Switzerland* (6857–71)
(since 1939)

1923	A Ross	Engen	149	1969	R Bernardini	277
1924	P Boomer	Engen	150	1970	G Marsh	274
1925	A Ross	Engen	148	1971	PM Townsend	270
1926	A Ross	Lucerne	145	1972	G Marsh	270
1929	A Wilson	Lucerne	142	1973	H Baiocchi	278
1930	A Boyer	Samedan	150	1974	RJ Charles	275
1931	M Dallemagne	Lucerne	145	1975	D Hayes	273
1934	A Boyer	Lausanne	133	1976	M Piñero	274
1935	A Boyer	Lausanne	137	1977	S Ballesteros	273
1936	F Francis (am)	Lausanne	134	1978	S Ballesteros	272
1937	M Dallemagne	Samedan	138	1979	H Baiocchi	275
1938	J Saubaber	Zumikon	139	1980	N Price	267
1939	F Cavalo	Crans-sur-Sierre	273	1981	M Piñero*	277
1948	U Grappasonni		285	1982	I Woosnam*	272
1949	M Dallemagne		270	1983	N Faldo*	268
1950	A Casera		276	1984	J Anderson	261
1951	EC Brown		267	1985	C Stadler	267
1952	U Grappasonni		267	1986	JM Olazábal	262
1953	F van Donck		267	1987	A Forsbrand	263
1954	AD Locke		276	1988	C Moody	268
1955	F van Donck		277	1989	S Ballesteros	266
1956	DJ Rees		278	1990	R Rafferty	267
1957	A Angelini		270	1991	J Hawkes	268
1958	K Bousfield		272	1992	J Spence*	271
1959	DJ Rees		274	1993	B Lane	270
1960	H Henning		270	1994	E Romero	266
1961	KDG Nagle		268	1995	M Grönberg	270
1962	RJ Charles*		272	1996	C Montgomerie	260
1963	DJ Rees*		278	1997	C Rocca	266
1964	HR Henning		276	1998	S Strüver	263
1965	HR Henning		208 (54)	1999	L Westwood	270
1966	A Angelini		271	2000	E Romero	261
1967	R Vines		272	2001	R Gonzalez	268
1968	R Bernardini		272	2002	R Karlsson	270

2003

1	Ernie Els (RSA)	65-69-68-65—267	£185730	€266660
2	Michael Campbell (NZ)	67-67-73-66—273	123818	177770
3	Eduardo Romero (Arg)	66-67-67-74—274	69762	100160

Trophée Lancôme *at Saint-Nom-La-Bretèche, Paris* (6712–71)

1970	A Jacklin	206	(54)	1987	I Woosnam	264	
1971	A Palmer	202	(54)	1988	S Ballesteros	269	
1972	T Aaron	279		1989	E Romero	266	
1973	J Miller	277		1990	JM Olazábal	269	
1974	W Casper	283		1991	F Nobilo	267	
1975	G Player	278		1992	M Roe	267	
1976	S Ballesteros	283		1993	I Woosnam	267	
1977	G Marsh*	273		1994	V Singh	263	
1978	L Trevino	272		1995	C Montgomerie	269	
1979	J Miller	281		1996	J Parnevik	268	
1980	L Trevino	280		1997	M O'Meara	271	
1981	D Graham	280		1998	MA Jiménez	273	
1982	D Graham	276		1999	P Fulke	270	
1983	S Ballesteros	269		2000	R Goosen	271	
1984	A Lyle*	278		2001	S García	266	
1985	N Price*	275		2002	A Cejka	272	
1986T	S Ballesteros*	274					
	B Langer*						

2003

1	Retief Goosen (RSA)	63-65-68-70—266	£209043	€300000
2	Paul McGinley (Irl)	66-67-66-71—270	139362	200000
3	Raphaèl Jacquelin (Fra)	69-67-68-67—271	70615	101340
	Ian Poulter (Eng)	67-69-65-70—271	70615	101340

Linde German Masters

1987	A Lyle*	Stuttgart	278	1995	A Forsbrand	Motzener See	264	
1988	JM Olazábal	Stuttgart	279	1996	D Clarke	Motzener See	264	
1989	B Langer	Stuttgart	276	1997	B Langer	Berliner G & CG	267	
1990	S Torrance	Stuttgart	272	1998	C Montgomerie	Gut Lärchenhof	266	
1991	B Langer*	Stuttgart	275	1999	S García	Gut Lärchenhof	277	
1992	B Lane	Stuttgart	272	2000	M Campbell	Gut Lärchenhof	197	
1993	S Richardson	Stuttgart	271	2001	B Langer	Gut Lärchenhof	266	
1994	S Ballesteros*	Motzener See	270	2002	S Leaney	Gut Lärchenhof	266	

2003 *at Gut Lärchenhof, Cologne* (6665–72)

1	Choi Kyoung-ju (Kor)	63-68-64-67—262	£351979	€500000
2	Miguel Angel Jiménez (Esp)	67-62-67-68—264	234650	333330
3	Niclas Fasth (Swe)	68-67-65-65—265	118898	168900
	Ian Poulter (Eng)	65-63-69-68—265	118898	168900

dunhill links championship

2001	P Lawrie	270	2002	P Harrington	269

2003 *at St Andrews (Old Course), Carnoustie, Kingsbarns*

1	Lee Westwood (Eng)	70-68-62-67—267	£490346	€705093
2	Ernie Els (RSA)	72-65-67-64—268	326895	470059
3	Raphaèl Jacquelin (Fra)	69-68-64-69—270	184174	264833

WGC: American Express Championship

2003 *at Capital City, Woodstock, GA* (7209–70)

1	Tiger Woods (USA)	67-66-69-72—274	£632644	€914475
2	Stuart Appleby (Aus)	71-68-69-68—276	244020	352726
	Tim Herron (USA)	66-72-67-71—276	244020	352726
	Vijay Singh (Fij)	70-70-64-72—276	244020	352726

Fuller details of this event can be found in World Championship Events on page 163

Dutch Open

1919	D Oosterveer	The Hague	158	1964	S Sewgolum	Eindhoven	275
1920	H Burrows	Kennemer	155	1965	A Miguel	Breda	278
1921	H Burrows	Domburg	151	1966	R Sota	Kennemer	276
1922	G Pannell	Noordwijk	160	1967	P Townsend	The Hague	282
1923	H Burrows	Hilversumsche	153	1968	J Cockin	Hilversumsche	292
1924	A Boomer	The Hague	138	1969	G Wolstenholme	Utrecht	277
1925	A Boomer	The Hague	144	1970	V Fernandez	Eindhoven	279
1926	A Boomer	The Hague	151	1971	R Sota	Kennemer	277
·1927	P Boomer	The Hague	147	1972	J Newton	The Hague	277
1928	ER Whitcombe	The Hague	141	1973	D McClelland	The Hague	279
1929	JJ Taylor	Hilversumsche	153	1974	B Barnes	Hilversumsche	211 (54)
1930	J Oosterveer	The Hague	152	1975	H Baiocchi	Hilversumsche	279
1931	F Dyer	Kennemer	145	1976	S Ballesteros	Kennemer	275
1932	A Boyer	The Hague	137	1977	R Byman	Kennemer	278
1933	M Dallemagne	Kennemer	143	1978	R Byman	Noordwijkse	21 (54)
1934	SF Brews	Utrecht	286	1979	G Marsh	Noordwijkse	285
1935	SF Brews	Kennemer	275	1980	S Ballesteros	Hilversumsche	280
1936	F van Donck	Hilversumsche	285	1981	H Henning	The Hague	280
·1937	F van Donck	Utrecht	286	1982	P Way	Utrecht	276
1938	AH Padgham	The Hague	281	1983	K Brown	Kennemer	274
1939	AD Locke	Kennemer	281	1984	B Langer	Rosendaelsche	275
1946	F van Donck	Hilversumsche	290	1985	G Marsh	Noordwijkse	282
1947	G Ruhl	Eindhoven	290	1986	S Ballesteros	Noordwijkse	271 (70)
1948	C Denny	Hilversumsche	290	1987	G Brand jr	Hilversumsche	272
1949	J Adams	The Hague	294	1988	M Mouland	Hilversumsche	274
1950	R De Vicenzo	Breda	269	1989	JM Olazábal*	Kennemer	277
1951	F van Donck	Kennemer	281	1990	S McAllister	Kennemer	274
1952	C Denny	Hilversumsche	284	1991	P Stewart	Noordwijkse	267
1953	F van Donck	Eindhoven	286	1992	B Langer*	Noordwijkse	277
·1954	U Grappasonni	The Hague	295	1993	C Montgomerie	Noordwijkse	281
1955	A Angelini	Kennemer	280	1994	MA Jiménez	Hilversumsche	270
1956	A Cerda	Eindhoven	277	1995	S Hoch	Hilversumsche	269
1957	J Jacobs	Hilversumsche	284	1996	M McNulty	Hilversumsche	266
1958	D Thomas	Kennemer	277	1997	S Strüver	Hilversumsche	266
1959	S Sewgolum	The Hague	283	1998	S Leaney	Hilversumsche	266
1960	S Sewgolum	Eindhoven	280	1999	L Westwood	Hilversumsche	269
1961	BBS Wilkes	Kennemer	279	2000	S Leaney	Nordwijkse	269
1962	BGC Huggett	Hilversumsche	274	2001	B Langer*	Nordwijkse	269
1963	R Waltman	Wassenaar	279	2002	T Dier	Hilversum	263

2003 *at Hilversum, Netherlands*   (6634–70)

1	Maarten Lafeber (Ned)	67-69-64-67—267	£116211	€166660
2	Mathias Grönberg (Swe)	70-66-67-65—268	60564	86855
	Søren Hansen (Den)	68-65-66-69—268	60564	86855

HSBC World Match Play Championship

1964	A Palmer	N Coles	2 and 1	1984	S Ballesteros	B Langer	2 and 1
1965	G Player	P Thomson	3 and 2	1985	S Ballesteros	B Langer	6 and 5
1966	G Player	J Nicklaus	6 and 4	1986	G Norman	A Lyle	2 and 1
1967	A Palmer	P Thomson	1 hole	1987	I Woosnam	A Lyle	1 hole
1968	G Player	R Charles	1 hole	1988	A Lyle	N Faldo	2 and 1
1969	R Charles	G Littler	37th hole	1989	N Faldo	I Woosnam	1 hole
1970	J Nicklaus	L Trevino	2 and 1	1990	I Woosnam	M McNulty	4 and 2
1971	G Player	J Nicklaus	5 and 4	1991	S Ballesteros	N Price	3 and 2
1972	T Weiskopf	L Trevino	4 and 3	1992	N Faldo	J Sluman	8 and 7
1973	G Player	G Marsh	40th hole	1993	C Pavin	N Faldo	1 hole
1974	H Irwin	G Player	3 and 1	1994	E Els	C Montgomerie	4 and 2
1975	H Irwin	A Geiberger	4 and 2	1995	E Els	S Elkington	2 and 1
1976	D Graham	H Irwin	38th hole	1996	E Els	V Singh	3 and 2
1977	G Marsh	R Floyd	5 and 3	1997	V Singh	E Els	1 hole
1978	I Aoki	S Owen	3 and 2	1998	M O'Meara	T Woods	1 hole
1979	W Rogers	I Aoki	1 hole	1999	C Montgomerie	M O'Meara	3 and 2
1980	G Norman	A Lyle	1 hole	2000	L Westwood	C Montgomerie	38th hole
1981	S Ballesteros	B Crenshaw	1 hole	2001	I Woosnam	P Harrington	2 and 1
1982	S Ballesteros	A Lyle	37th hole	2002	E Els	S García	2 and
1983	G Norman	N Faldo	3 and 2				

2003 *at Wentworth, Surrey, England* (7072–72)

First Round
Tim Clark (RSA) beat Stephen Leaney (Aus) 3 and 2
Vijay Singh (Fij) beat Alex Cejka (Ger) 8 and 7
Chad Campbell (USA) beat Fredrik Jacobson (Swe) 6 and 5
Thomas Bjørn (Den) beat Len Mattiace (USA) 4 and 3

Quarter Finals
Ernie Els (RSA) beat Tim Clark 2 holes
Vijay Singh beat Shaun Micheel (USA) at 38th
Ben Curtis (USA) beat Chad Campbell 5 and 3
Thomas Bjørn beat Mike Weir (Can) 5 and 4

Semi-Finals
Ernie Els beat Vijay Singh 5 and 4
Thomas Bjørn beat Ben Curtis 2 holes

Final
Ernie Els beat Thomas Bjørn 4 and 3

Prize Money: Els £1m, €1,409,920;
Bjørn £400,000, €563, 988; Singh and
Curtis £120,000, €169,190

Turespaña Mallorca Classic

2003 *at Pula GC, Majorca, Spain* (6568–70)

1	Miguel Angel Jiménez (Esp)	72-67-65—204	£47279	€66660
2	José María Olazábal (Esp)	66-69-70—205	31520	44440
3	Gary Emerson (Eng)	73-64-69—206	15973	22520
	Jamie Spence (Eng)	71-66-69—206	15973	22520

Telefonica Open de Madrid
(formerly BBVA Open Turespaña Masters de la Communidad de Madrid)

1968	G Garrido	1977	A Garrido	1986	H Clark	1995	A Cejka
1969	R Soto	1978	H Clark	1987	I Woosnam	1996	D Borrego
1970	M Cabrera	1979	S Hobday	1988	D Cooper	1997	JM Olazábal
1971	V Barrios	1980	S Ballesteros	1989	S Ballesteros	1998	MA Jiménez
1972	J Kinsetta	1981	M Pineto	1990	B Langer	1999	MA Jiménez
1973	G Garrido	1982	S Ballesteros	1991	A Sherborne	2000	P Harrington
1974	M Pineto	1983	A Lyle	1992	D Feherty	2001	R Goosen
1975	K Shearer	1984	H Clark	1993	D Smyth	2002	S Tinning
1976	F Abreu	1985	M Pineto	1994	C Mason		

2003 *at Club de Campo, Madrid, Spain* (6967–71)

1	Ricardo Gonzales (Arg)	69-70-66-65—270	£162288	€233330
2	Padraig Harrington (Irl)	65-73-68-65—271	64780	93137
	Mårten Olander (Swe)	69-65-70-67—271	64780	93137
	Nick O'Hern (Aus)	67-67-69-68—271	64780	93137
	Paul Casey (Eng)	63-65-71-72—271	64780	93137

Volvo Masters Andalucia

1988	N Faldo	Valderrama	284	1996	M McNulty	Valderrama	276
1989	R Rafferty	Valderrama	282	1997	L Westwood	Montecastillo	200 (54)
1990	M Harwood	Valderrama	286	1998	D Clarke	Montecastillo	271
1991	R Davis	Valderrama	280	1999	MA Jiménez	Montecastillo	269
1992	A Lyle	Valderrama	287	2000	P Fulke	Montecastillo	272
1993	C Montgomerie	Valderrama	274	2001	P Harrington	Montecastillo	204 (54)
1994	B Langer	Valderrama	276	2002	B Langer	Valderrama	281
1995	A Cejka	Valderrama	282				

2003 *at Valderrama, Cadiz, Spain* (7006–72)

1	Fredrik Jacobsen (Swe)*	64-71-71-70—276	£406703	€583330
2	Carlos Rodiles (Esp)	68-69-69-70—276	271131	388880
3	Brian Davis (Eng)	71-73-69-66—279	158615	227500.

The Seve Trophy (Instituted 2000)

2000	Continental Europe 13½	GB&I 12½
2002	GB&I 14½	Continental Europe 11½

2003 *at Campo de Golf Parador El Saler, Valencia, Spain*

Captains: Seve Ballesteros (Europe), Colin Montgomerie (GBI)

First Day – Fourball

Olazábal & Ballesteros	0	Westwood & Howell (2 holes)	1
Garrido & Jiménez	0	Davis & Casey (2 and 1)	1
Cejka & Jacquelin (4 and 3)	1	Rose & Poulter	0
Jacobson & Fasth	½	Lawrie & Montgomerie	½
Bjørn & García	0	Price & Harrington (2 holes)	1
	1½		3½

Second Day – Fourball

Bjørn & García	0	Westwood & Howell (5 and 3)	1
Cejka & Jacquelin (2 and 1)	1	Lawrie & Montgomerie	0
Garrido & Jiménez	0	Davis & Casey (2 holes)	1
Jacobson & Fasth (1 hole)	1	Price & Harrington	0
Olazábal & Ballesteros	0	Rose & Poulter (3 and 1)	1
	2		3

Match position: Continental Europe 3½, GB&I 6½

Third Day: Morning – Greensomes

Jacobson & Fasth (5 and 4)	1	Harrington & Lawrie	0
Bjørn & Olazábal	½	Rose & Montgomerie	½
Cejka & Jacquelin (3 and 2)	1	Davis & Casey	0
García & Ballesteros	0	Westwood & Poulter (3 and 1)	1
	2½		1½

Match position: Continental Europe 6, GB&I 8

Afternoon – Foursomes

Garrido & Jiménez	0	Harrington & Montgomerie (2 and 1)	1
Jacobson & Fasth (3 and 2)	1	Lawrie & Casey	0
Cejka & Jacquelin (5 and 3)	1	Howell & Westwood	0
García & Bjørn	0	Rose & Poulter (2 and 1)	1
	2		2

Match position: Continental Europe 8, GB&I 10

Fourth Day – Singles

Seve Ballesteros (Esp)	0	Colin Montgomerie (Sco) (5 and 4)	1
Alex Cejka (Ger)	0	David Howell (Eng) (1 hole)	1
Ignacio Garrido (Esp) (3 and 2)	1	Paul Lawrie (Sco)	0
Fredrik Jacobson (Swe) (2 and 1)	1	Lee Westwood (Eng)	0
José María Olazábal (Esp)	½	Padraig Harrington (Irl)	½
Niclas Fasth (Swe)	½	Ian Poulter (Eng)	½
Thomas Bjørn (Den) [conceded]	0	Paul Casey (Eng)	1
Raphaël Jacquelin (Fra)	0	Justin Rose (Eng) (3 and 2)	1
Miguel Angel Jiménez (Esp) (2 and 1)	1	Brian Davis (Eng)	0
Sergio García (Esp) (4 and 3)	1	Phillip Price (Wal)	0
	5		5

Result: Continental Europe 13, GB&I 15

World Cup of Golf *at Kiawah Island, SC*

Result: 1 South Africa; 2 England; 3 France

Full results can be found on page 166

European Senior Tour 2003

Final Ranking (Top 15 earn full Tour card)

1	Carl Mason (Eng)	€350,242	41	Eddie Polland (NI)	44,504
2	Bill Longmuir (Sco)	253,667	42	Priscillo Diniz (Bra)	43,905
3	Terry Gale (Aus)	195,727	43	Bob Lendzion (USA)	41,053
4	John Chillas (Sco)	190,003	44	Hank Woodrome (USA)	40,496
5	Denis Durnian (Eng)	146,604	45	Seiji Ebihara (Jpn)	39,349
6	Guillermo Encina (Chl)	145,388	46	John Irwin (Can)	38,447
7	David Oakley (USA)	142,933	47	Manuel Velasco (Esp)	37,856
8	Denis O'Sullivan (Irl)	130,427	48	Bob Larratt (Eng)	36,282
9	Jerry Bruner (USA)	128,039	49	Liam Higgins (Irl)	34,933
10	David Good (Aus)	125,316	50	Alan Mew (Tri)	34,876
11	Nick Job (Eng)	124,648	51	John Mashego (RSA)	33,934
12	Delroy Cambridge (Jam)	124,031	52	Ian Stanley (Aus)	33,318
13	Noel Ratcliffe (Aus)	120,141	53	John McTear (Sco)	30,784
14	Brian Jones (Aus)	111,480	54	Tommy Horton (Eng)	28,581
15	Bob Cameron (Eng)	109,333	55	Christy O'Connor jr (Irl)	28,079
			56	Bob Shearer (Aus)	28,005
16	Horacio Carbonetti (Arg)	104,280	57	Jeff Van Wagenen (USA)	27,387
17	Giuseppe Cali (Ita)	101,365	58	Robbie Stewart (RSA)	25,603
18	Jim Rhodes (Eng)	89,007	59	Neville Clarke (RSA)	23,188
19	Keith Macdonald (Eng)	83,676	60	Sam Torrance (Sco)	19,782
20	John Morgan (Eng)	78,938	61	Bill Hardwick (Can)	19,658
21	Alan Tapie (USA)	78,302	62	George Burns (USA)	19,539
22	Paul Leonard (NI)	74,512	63	Alberto Croce (Ita)	18,021
23	Ian Mosey (Eng)	72,696	64	Peter Townsend (Eng)	16,352
24	Mike Miller (Sco)	68,592	65	Bernard Gallacher (Sco)	14,558
25	Eamonn Darcy (Irl)	66,153	66	Craig Maltman (Sco)	14,424
26	Baldovino Dassu (Ita)	62,919	67	David Jones (NI)	13,001
27	Manuel Piñero (Esp)	62,718	68	Martin Foster (Eng)	12,648
28	Ray Carrasco (USA)	62,035	69	John Benda (USA)	12,644
29	Martin Gray (Sco)	61,465	70	Noboru Sugai (Jpn)	12,625
30	Simon Owen (NZ)	60,240	71	Steve Wild (Eng)	12,585
31	Malcolm Gregson (Eng)	60,039	72	Hisao Inoue (Jpn)	12,435
32	Dragon Taki (Jpn)	57,856	73	Keith Ashdown (Eng)	12,423
33	Steve Stull (USA)	56,284	74	Craig Defoy (Wal)	12,174
34	David Creamer (Eng)	54,361	75	John Fourie (RSA)	11,722
35	Gary Wintz (USA)	54,044	76	Joe McDermott (Irl)	10,663
36	John Grace (USA)	53,265	77	Geoff Tickell (Wal)	10,587
37	Maurice Bembridge (Eng)	49,782	78	Bill Brask (USA)	9,177
38	Neil Coles (Eng)	48,349	79	David Huish (Sco)	9,173
39	Russell Weir (Sco)	47,718	80	Antonio Garrido (Esp)	8,808
40	Barry Vivian (NZ)	46,051			

Career Money List

1	Tommy Horton (Eng)	€1,358,059.24
2	Noel Ratcliffe (Aus)	937,067.31
3	Neil Coles (Eng)	865,938.12
4	John Morgan (Eng)	824,270.30
5	David Oakley (USA)	715,533.15
6	Denis Durnian (Eng)	714,300.87
7	Malcolm Gregson (Eng)	707,812.76
8	Denis O'Sullivan (Irl)	688,259.06
9	Jim Rhodes (Eng)	669,080.05
10	Seiji Ebihara (Jpn)	658,164.64
11	Brian Huggett (Eng)	638,782.76
12	Jerry Bruner (USA)	629,304.90
13	Terry Gale (Aus)	613,987.09
14	Ian Stanley (Aus)	592,102.45
15	David Creamer (Eng)	583,570.63
16	Maurice Bembridge (Eng)	580,654.26
17	Eddie Polland (NI)	540,284.50
18	Antonio Garrido (Esp)	529,606.97
19	David Huish (Sco)	508,019.95
20	Bob Charles (NZ)	504,503.53
21	David Good (Aus)	503,258.60
22	Bobby Verwey (RSA)	494,360.28
23	Delroy Cambridge (Jam)	486,070.29
24	Brian Waites (Eng)	482,279.68
25	Nick Job (Eng)	456,158.84
26	Alberto Croce (Ita)	446,959.09
27	Liam Higgins (Irl)	415,194.38
28	Christy O'Connor jr (Irl)	410,533.68
29	John Grace (USA)	406,165.35
30	Bob Shearer (Aus)	405,891.16
31	Bernard Gallacher (Sco)	377,984.13
32	Gary Player (RSA)	371,214.63
33	David Jones (NI)	368,956.99
34	John Fourie (RSA)	368,661.52
35	Alan Tapie (USA)	365,275.36
36	Priscillo Diniz (Bra)	361,947.26
37	Carl Mason (Eng)	350,241.61
38	Paul Leonard (NI)	347,017.71
39	John Chillas (Sco)	342,434.64
40	Bill Hardwick (Can)	320,562.28
41	Renato Campagnoli (Ita)	317,192.41
42	Simon Owen (NZ)	309,159.14
43	Bob Lendzion (USA)	298,490.71
44	Keith Macdonald (Eng)	297,834.04
45	Craig Defoy (Wal)	296,615.25
46	Ray Carrasco (USA)	295,936.54
47	Barry Vivian (NZ)	271,478.00
48	Ross Metherell (Aus)	254,732.78
49	Bill Longmuir (Sco)	253,666.95
50	Jeff Van Wagenen (USA)	248,728.03

51	John Bland (Eng)	238,889.82
52	Mike Miller (Sco)	236,911.75
53	Brian Barnes (Sco)	234,975.31
54	Tom Watson (USA)	233,619.79
55	John Irwin (Can)	233,536.14
56	Peter Dawson (Eng)	223,142.11
57	Guillermo Encina (Chl)	222,325.59
58	Bill Brask (USA)	221,406.07
59	John McTear (Sco)	219,198.68
60	Jay Horton (Eng)	217,676.19
61	Peter Townsend (Eng)	216,829.24
62	Steve Stull (USA)	193,752.35
63	Joe McDermott (Irl)	185,362.90
64	Norman Wood (Sco)	181,961.22
65	Ian Mosey (Eng)	179,130.69
66	Brian Jones (Aus)	177,555.56
67	Russell Weir (Sco)	168,380.63
68	Peter Butler (Eng)	155,984.85
69	Hugh Inggs (RSA)	153,047.98
70	John Garner (Eng)	142,685.87
71	Noboru Sugai (Jpn)	142,488.47
72	Chick Evans (USA)	141,711.67
73	David Butler (Eng)	141,202.30
74	Ian Richardson (Eng)	135,191.62
75	Steve Wild (Eng)	133,975.19
76	Eamonn Darcy (Irl)	128,907.61
77	David Snell (Eng)	128,125.56
78	Jay Dolan III (USA)	126,901.31
79	Dragon Taki (Jpn)	122,916.08
80	Vincent Tshabalala (RSA)	122,877.42
81	Gary Wintz (USA)	119,413.94
82	Deray Simon (USA)	118,695.26
83	Agim Bardha (Alb)	118,051.27
84	Michael Murphy (Irl)	114,308.87
85	JR Delich (USA)	113,165.12
86	Geoff Parslow (Aus)	112,714.36
87	Doug Dalziel (USA)	112,220.00
88	Tony Grubb (Eng)	111,240.20
89	Hank Woodrome (USA)	110,712.42
90	Barry Sandry (Eng)	109,740.67
91	Bob Cameron (Eng)	109,333.17
92	Tony Jacklin (Eng)	109,224.24
93	Randall Vines (Aus)	104,772.63
94	Horacio Carbonetti (Arg)	104,280.32
95	Roger Fidler (Eng)	103,628.58
96	Joe Carr (USA)	102,745.32
97	Snell Lancaster (USA)	101,667.55
98	Giuseppe Cali (Ita)	101,364.81
99	George Burns (USA)	100,733.54
100	Tienie Britz (RSA)	94,886.73

Tour Results

Digitel Jamaica Classic	Montego Bay, Jamaica	Ray Carrasco (USA)	211 (-5)
Royal Westmoreland Barbados Open	Royal Westmoreland, Barbados	Terry Gale (Aus)	206 (-10)
Tobago Plantations Seniors Classic	Tobago Plantations	Terry Gale (Aus)	203 (-13)
AIB Irish Seniors Open	Adare Manor, Ireland	Noel Ratcliffe (Aus)	211 (-5)
Wallonia Open	Pierpont, Belgium	Hank Woodrome (USA)*	210 (-6)
USPGA Seniors Championship	Aronimink, PA	John Jacobs (USA)	276 (-4)
Irvine Whitlock Jersey Seniors Classic	La Moye, Jersey	Malcolm Gregson (Eng)	203 (-13)
De Vere Northumberland Seniors Classic	Slaley Hall, England	Jerry Bruner (USA)	202 (-14)
US Senior Open	Inverness, Toledo, OH	Bruce Lietzke (USA)	277 (-7)
Ryder Cup Wales Seniors Open	Royal St David's, Wales	Bill Longmuir (Sco)	199 (-8)
The Mobile Cup	Stoke Park, England	Carl Mason (Eng)	203 (-10)

Senior British Open   Turnberry, Scotland
1   Tom Watson (USA)*   66-67-66-64—263 (-17)
2   Carl Mason (Eng)   67-64-65-67—263
3   Bruce Summerhays (USA)   68-65-66-65—264

De Vere PGA Seniors Championship	Carden Park, England	Bill Longmuir (Sco)	271 (-17)
Bad Ragaz PGA Seniors Open	Bad Ragaz, Switzerland	Horacio Carbonetti (Arg)	197 (-13)
Travis Perkins Senior Masters	Wentworth, England	John Chillas (Sco)	209 (-7)
Nigel Mansell Classic	Woodbury Park, England	Mike Miller (Sco)	205 (-11)
Charles Church Scottish Seniors Open	The Roxburghe, Scotland	Terry Gale (Aus)	205 (-11)
European Senior Masters	Woburn, England	Paul Leonard (NI)	208 (-8)
Seniors Match Play Championship	Los Flamingos, Spain	Carl Mason (Eng) beat Denis O'Sullivan (Irl)	1 hole
Merseyside English Seniors Open	Hillside, England	Carl Mason (Eng)	208 (-8)
Tunisian Seniors Open	Port El Kantaoui, Tunisia	David Good (Aus)	198 (-18)
Estoril Seniors Tour Championship	Oitavos, Portugal	Carl Mason (Eng)	202 (-11)

Nicklaus times five

The BMW Charity Classic played at the Cliffs Valley and Cliffs at Keowee Vineyards in Greenville, South Carolina had a special significance for the golfing Nicklaus's last year. The Golden Bear (63) was in the field for the Nationwide Tour event but so, too, were his four sons – Gary (34) who like his father is a professional, Jack II (41) who caddied for his father when he won The Masters at age 46, Michael (30) and Steve (39). It was the first time that five members of the one family had played together in a PGA affiliated Tour event.

European Challenge Tour 2003

Final Order of Merit (top 15 earn full Tour cards)

1	Johan Edfors (Swe)	€94,509		51	Erol Simsek (Ger)	22,100
2	Martin Lemesurier (Eng)	88,643		52	Alvaro Salto (Esp)	21,393
3	José Manuel Carriles (Esp)	86,603		53	Marco Soffietti (Ita)	21,311
4	Martin Wiegele (Aut)	86,057		54	Juan Abbate (Arg)	21,100
5	Peter Hanson (Swe)	83,662		55	Jesus Maria Arruti (Esp)	20,878
6	Martin Erlandsson (Swe)	80,426		56	Michele Reale (Ita)	20,307
7	Scott Drummond (Sco)	79,773		57	Edward Rush (Eng)	20,279
8	Stuart Little (Eng)	75,553		58	Chris Gane (Eng)	19,122
9	Sebastian Fernandez (Arg)	72,115		59	Didier De Vooght (Bel)	19,027
10	Jamie Elson (Eng)	70,551		60	Benoit Teilleria (Fra)	18,998
11	James Hepworth (Eng)	67,970		61	Tony Edlund (Swe)	17,810
12	Michael Jonzon (Swe)	66,307		62	David Patrick (Sco)	17,589
13	Robert Coles (Eng)	65,869		63	André Bossert (Swi)	17,423
14	Ivo Giner (Esp)	60,635		64	Olivier David (Fra)	17,416
15	Ben Mason (Eng)	59,828		65	Ryan Reid (RSA)	17,111
16	Cesar Monasterio (Arg)	57,782		66	Oskar Bergman (Swe)	16,945
17	Greig Hutcheon (Scot)	55,664		67	Paul Dwyer (Eng)	16,800
18	Sion E Bebb (Wal)	51,399		68	Philip Archer (Eng)	16,663
19	Richard McEvoy (Eng)	51,259		69	Hennie Otto (RSA)	16,519
20	Michael Kirk (RSA)	51,010		70	Neil Cheetham (Eng)	16,466
21	Peter Gustafsson (Swe)	45,631		71	Stephen Browne (Ire)	16,398
22	Damien McGrane (Irl)	44,667		72	Massimo Florioli (Ita)	16,329
23	Marc Pendaries (Fra)	37,944		73	Leif Westerberg (Swe)	16,205
24	Kalle Brink (Swe)	37,229		74	Gianluca Baruffaldi (Ita)	15,719
25	Louis Oosthuizen (RSA)	36,382		75	Marcello Santi (Ita)	15,222
26	Graeme Storm (Eng)	36,293		76	Allan Hogh (Den)	15,144
27	Sam Walker (Eng)	35,888		77	Daren Lee (Eng)	14,284
28	Euan Little (Scot)	35,287		78	Raphael Pellicioli (Fra)	14,146
29	Daniel Vancsik (Arg)	35,028		79	Fredrik Henge (Swe)	14,031
30	Sam Little (Eng)	34,726		80	Pehr Magnebrant (Swe)	13,456
31	Titch Moore (RSA)	34,664		81	Jimmy Kawalec (Swe)	13,281
32	Garry Houston (Wal)	34,588		82	Magnus Persson Atlevi (Swe)	12,885
33	Gregory Bourdy (Fra)	34,261		83	Marcel Haremza (Ger)	12,738
34	Steven O'Hara (Scot)	31,946		84	Regis Gustave (StL)	12,522
35	Mark Sanders (Eng)	31,879		85	Gareth Paddison (NZ)	12,472
36	David J Geall (Eng)	31,619		86	Carlos Quevedo (Esp)	11,615
37	Federico Bisazza (Ita)	31,127		87	Johan Skold (Swe)	11,410
38	Mattias Eliasson (Swe)	30,050		88	Marco Bernardini (Ita)	11,203
39	Craig Williams (Wal)	29,261		89	Ilya Goroneskoul (Fra)	11,051
40	Pasi Purhonen (Fin)	29,236		90	Thomas Norret (Den)	11,010
41	Christopher Hanell (Swe)	29,038		91	Sebastien Delagrange (Fra)	10,980
42	Joakim Rask (Swe)	28,393		92	José Trauwitz (Mex)	10,337
43	Jamie Little (Eng)	28,392		93	Fredrik Orest (Swe)	10,236
44	Alexandre Balicki (Fra)	27,083		94	Francesco Guermani (Ita)	10,068
45	Tim Milford (Eng)	26,541		95	Paolo Terreni (Ita)	9,791
46	Steven Bowditch (Aus)	25,100		96	Joakim Kristiansson (Swe)	9,641
47	Gary Ckark (Eng)	24,973		97	Richard Dinsdale (Wal)	9,463
48	Mark Mouland (Wal)	24,473		98	Stefano Reale (Ita)	9,327
49	Kariem Baraka (Ger)	23,412		99	Adam Crawford (Aus)	9,152
50	David Ryles (Eng)	23,216		100	Paul McKechnie (Sco)	9,070

Tour Results

Costa Rica Open	Cariari, San Jose, Costa Rica	Sebastian Fernandez (Arg)*	278 (-6)
Telefonica Centro America Abierto de Guatemala	Hacienda Nueva, Guatemala	Daniel Vancsik (Arg)*	274 (-10)
American Express Los Encinos Open	Los Encinos, Toluca, Mexico	James Hepworth (Eng)	275 (-13)
Stanbic Zambia Open	Lusaka, Zambia	Johan Edfors (Swe)	206 (-13)
Madeira Island Open	Santo da Serra, Madeira	Bradley Dredge (Wal)	272 (-16)
Panalpina Banque Commerciale du Maroc Classic	Royal Dar Es Salam, Rabat, Morocco	Greig Hutcheon (Sco)	284 (-8)
Tessali-Metaponto Open di Puglia e Basilicata	Riva dei Tessali, Italy	Martin LeMesurier (Eng)*	273 (-12)
Izki Challenge de España	Urturi, Vittoria, Spain	Martin Erlandsson (Swe)	273 (-45)
Fortis Challenge Open	Burggolf Purmerend, Netherlands	Johan Edfors (Swe)	273 (-15)
Nykredit Danish Open	Gilleleje, Helsingor, Denmark	Marcus Fraser (Aus)	276 (-12)
Aa Open de Saint Omer	Aa Saint Omer, France	Brett Rumford (Aus)	269 (-15)
Clearstream International Luxembourg Open	Kikuoka, Canach, Luxembourg	Martin LeMesurier (Eng)	265 (-23)
Galeria Kaufhof Pokal Challenge	Rittergut Birkhof, Germany	Michael Jonzon (Swe)	263 (-25)
Volvo Finnish Open	Espoon, Finland	Jamie Elson (Eng)	264 (-24)
Open des Volcans Challenge de France	Golf des Volcans, France	Ivo Giner (Esp)	269 (-15)
Kitzbühel Golf Alpin Open	Kitzbühel-Schwarzsee, Austria	David J Geall (Eng)	261 (-23)
GC Padova Terme Euganee International Open	Padova, Valsansibio, Italy	Ivo Giner (Esp)	259 (-29)
Talma Finnish Challenge	Talma, Finland	Marcus Fraser (Aus)*	275 (-13)
BMW Russian Open	Le Meridien, Moscow, Russia	Marcus Fraser (Aus)*	269 (-19)
Rolex Trophy	GC Genève, Switzerland	Michael Jonzon (Swe)	267 (-21)
Skandia PGA Open	Falsterbo, Sweden	Titch Moore (RSA)	273 (-11)
BA CA Telekom Golf Open	Fontana, Vienna, Austria	Robert Coles (Eng)*	275 (-13)
Northern Ireland Masters	Clandeboye, Belfast, N Ireland	Darren Clarke (NI)	273 (-11)
Telia Grand Prix	Ljunghusens, Sweden	Euan Little (Sco)	276 (-8)
Open de Toulouse	Toulouse-Palmola, France	Scott Drummond (Sco)	269 (-19)
Ryder Cup Wales Challenge	Northop, Wales	Craig Williams (Wal)	267 (-17)
Turespaña Mallorca Classic	Pula Majorca, Spain	Miguel Angel Jimenez (Esp)	204 (-6)
Challenge Tour Grand Final	Médoc, Bordeaux, France	José Manuel Carriles (Esp)*	273 (-11)

US PGA Tour 2003

Players are of US nationality unless stated

Final Ranking

The top 125 on the money list retained their cards for the 2004 season. The top 40 earned a spot at The Masters.

1	Vijay Sing (Fij)	$7,573,907	42	John Huston	1,565,119	83	Harrison Frazar	776,876
2	Tiger Woods	6,673,413	43	Robert Gamez	1,519,804	84	David Gossett	769,840
3	Davis Love III	6,081,896	44	Woody Austin	1,518,707	85	Darren Clarke (NI)	763,931
4	Jim Furyk	5,182,865	45	Geoff Ogilvy (Aus)	1,477,246	86	Jeff Maggert	747,166
5	Mike Weir (Can)	4,918,910	46	Ben Curtis	1,434,911	87	Cliff Kresge	734,667
6	Kenny Perry	4,400,122	47	Jonathan Byrd	1,430,538	88	Paul Goydos	734,284
7	Chad Campbell	3,912,064	48	Ben Crane	1,419,070	89	Paul Stankowski	719,436
8	David Toms	3,710,905	49	Frank Lickliter II	1,340,436	90	Luke Donald (Eng)	705,121
9	Ernie Els (RSA)	3,371,237	50	Peter Lonard (Aus)	1,323,594	91	Brandt Jobe	691,604
10	Retief Goosen		51	Brenden Pappas		92	Joey Sindelar	691,328
	(RSA)	3,166,373		(RSA)	1,307,809	93	David Peoples	674,222
11	Brad Faxon	2,718,445	52	Loren Roberts	1,297,739	94	Carlos Franco (Col)	672,022
12	Stuart Appleby		53	Tim Clark (RSA)	1,253,690	95	Sergio García (Esp)	666,386
	(Aus)	2,662,538	54	Scott McCarron	1,250,849	96	JJ Henry	660,341
13	Bob Tway	2,601,600	55	Adam Scott (Aus)	1,238,736	97	Billy Andrade	659,694
14	Charles Howell III	2,568,955	56	Len Mattiace	1,221,476	98	Dean Wilson	654,345
15	Jay Haas	2,563,545	57	Tom Pernice jr	1,210,541	99	Jeff Brehaut	650,019
16	Jonathan Kaye	2,474,837	58	Duffy Waldorf	1,206,005	100	Craig Barlow	638,721
17	Justin Leonard	2,450,525	59	Scott Hoch	1,198,250	101	Jay Williamson	627,132
18	Chris DiMarco	2,350,630	60	Alex Cejka (Ger)	1,182,883	102	Todd Fischer	621,398
19	Scott Verplank	2,306,714	61	Tom Lehman	1,173,237	103	Arron Oberholser	619,865
20	Nick Price (Zim)	2,271,111	62	Peter Jacobsen	1,162,726	104	Patrick Sheehan	618,019
21	Steve Flesch	2,269,630	63	Dan Forsman	1,140,209	105	Steve Allan (Aus)	616,325
22	Briny Baird	2,202,519	64	Lee Janzen	1,132,001	106	Cameron Beckman	608,981
23	Chris Riley	2,178,133	65	Mark Calcavecchia	1,121,069	107	Marco Dawson	601,729
24	Robert Allenby		66	Joe Durant	1,119,002	108	John Senden (Aus)	601,670
	(Aus)	2,176,452	67	Kevin Sutherland	1,092,918	109	Tom Byrum	590,720
25	Tim Herron	2,176,390	68	Rod Pampling		110	Neal Lancaster	590,627
26	Jerry Kelly	2,158,342		(Aus)	1,064,974	111	Brent Geiberger	588,533
27	Fred Funk	2,144,653	69	Hidemichi Tanaka		112	JP Hayes	585,331
28	JL Lewis	2,039,259		(Jpn)	1,024,678	113	Craig Stadler	584,830
29	Kirk Triplett	2,001,561	70	Skip Kendall	1,022,244	114	David Frost (RSA)	583,177
30	Choi Kyoung-Ju		71	Rich Beem	1,013,950	115	Robert Damron	580,087
	(Kor)	1,999,663	72	Stephen Ames		116	Andrew Magee	578,558
31	Rocco Mediate	1,832,656		(Tri)	1,005,959	117	Pat Perez	578,141
32	Shaun Micheel	1,827,000	73	Aaron Baddeley		118	Jesper Parnevik	
33	Bob Estes	1,824,414		(Aus)	989,168		(Swe)	570,587
34	Fred Couples	1,820,495	74	Carl Pettersson		119	Notah Begay III	565,572
35	Stewart Cink	1,781,885		(Swe)	977,076	120	Richard Johnson	
36	Tim Petrovic	1,739,349	75	Hal Sutton	939,719		(Swe)	559,021
37	Shigeki Maruyama		76	Tommy Armour III	932,984	121	Bernhard Langer	
	(Jpn)	1,669,292	77	Steve Lowery	932,293		(Ger)	555,981
38	Phil Mickelson	1,623,137	78	Matt Gogel	897,410	122	Kent Jones	539,737
39	John Rollins	1,612,314	79	Billy Mayfair	842,186	123	Pat Bates	496,978
40	Jeff Sluman	1,609,748	80	Heath Slocum	815,812	124	Glen Hnatiuk	488,429
41	Rory Sabbatini		81	Glen Day	788,557	125	Esteban Toledo	
	(RSA)	1,604,701	82	Brett Quigley	786,294		(Mex)	487,495

Career Money List (at end of 2003 season)

1	Tiger Woods	$39,777,265	51	David Frost (RSA)	8,584,414
2	Davis Love III	26,132,746	52	Mark Brooks	8,123,182
3	Vijay Singh (Fij)	25,845,923	53	Steve Flesch	8,024,835
4	Phil Mickelson	23,773,106	54	Tim Herron	7,961,913
5	Jim Furyk	19,039,707	55	Andrew Magee	7,959,025
6	Nick Price (Zim)	18,919,447	56	Sergio García (Esp)	7,806,269
7	Ernie Els (RSA)	18,679,767	57	Steve Pate	7,806,237
8	Scott Hoch	17,216,624	58	Dan Forsman	7,686,555
9	David Toms	16,585,384	59	Scott McCarron	7,656,128
10	David Duval	16,235,305	60	Curtis Strange	7,599,951
11	Justin Leonard	16,108,759	61	Joey Sindelar	7,451,769
12	Mark Calcavecchia	15,694,587	62	Steve Stricker	7,392,146
13	Fred Couples	15,148,465	63	Peter Jacobsen	7,340,119
14	Hal Sutton	15,145,667	64	Retief Goosen (RSA)	7,233,886
15	Jeff Sluman	14,494,507	65	Dudley Hart	7,221,318
16	Brad Faxon	14,310,795	66	Ben Crenshaw	7,091,166
17	Tom Lehman	14,130,264	67	Charles Howell III	7,055,867
18	Kenny Perry	13,957,135	68	Larry Mize	6,967,713
19	Greg Norman (Aus)	13,931,929	69	Chris Perry	6,866,671
20	Mark O'Meara	13,143,679	70	Shigeki Maruyama (Jpn)	6,852,705
21	Loren Roberts	13,083,271	71	Frank Lickliter II	6,745,125
22	Fred Funk	12,915,575	72	Kevin Sutherland	6,625,693
23	Mike Weir (Can)	12,845,208	73	José Maria Olazábal (Esp)	6,583,445
24	Paul Azinger	12,680,533	74	Scott Simpson	6,551,731
25	Bob Estes	12,240,269	75	Glen Day	6,479,938
26	Bob Tway	12,150,183	76	Jonathan Kaye	6,476,174
27	John Huston	12,131,701	77	Bruce Lietzke	6,474,794
28	Payne Stewart	11,737,008	78	Chris Riley	6,437,849
29	Jay Haas	11,720,183	79	Lanny Wadkins	6,355,681
30	Scott Verplank	11,281,259	80	Bernhard Langer (Ger)	6,353,515
31	Lee Janzen	11,263,976	81	Bill Glasson	6,330,231
32	Rocco Mediate	11,104,130	82	Len Mattiace	6,222,248
33	John Cook	11,084,705	83	Chip Beck	6,199,550
34	Tom Kite	10,920,309	84	Craig Parry (Aus)	6,173,390
35	Jeff Maggert	10,753,185	85	Steve Jones	6,052,026
36	Chris DiMarco	10,637,535	86	Hale Irwin	5,966,031
37	Stuart Appleby (Aus)	10,284,272	87	Jim Gallagher jr	5,860,720
38	Kirk Triplett	10,284,090	88	Fuzzy Zoeller	5,803,343
39	Corey Pavin	10,257,093	89	Jack Nicklaus	5,722,901
40	Steve Elkington (Aus)	10,018,932	90	Skip Kendall	5,681,383
41	Billy Mayfair	9,980,493	91	Joe Durant	5,624,641
42	Tom Watson	9,881,778	92	Jay Don Blake	5,513,915
43	Jesper Parnevik (Swe)	9,846,860	93	Russ Cochran	5,344,387
44	Stewart Cink	9,654,318	94	Raymond Floyd	5,323,075
45	Craig Stadler	9,593,493	95	Carlos Franco (Col)	5,322,039
46	Steve Lowery	9,350,137	96	Choi Kyoung-Ju (Kor)	5,310,642
47	Robert Allenby (Aus)	9,253,571	97	Mark McCumber	5,309,688
48	Jerry Kelly	8,831,176	98	Rich Beem	5,273,317
49	Billy Andrade	8,808,559	99	Gil Morgan	5,259,164
50	Duffy Waldorf	8,695,756	100	Robert Gamez	5,246,201

Tour Statistics

Scoring averages

Pos	Name	Avg
1	Tiger Woods	68.41
2	Vijay Singh (Fij)	68.65
3	Mike Weir (Can)	68.97
4	Ernie Els (RSA)	68.99
5	Jim Furyk	69.10
6	Retief Goosen (RSA)	69.20
7	Davis Love III	69.41
8	Kenny Perry	69.57
9	Chad Campbell	69.68
10	Robert Allenby (Aus)	69.75

Sand saves

Pos	Name	%
1	Stuart Appleby (Aus)	62.1
2	Arron Oberholser	60.2
3	Kevin Sutherland	60.1
4	Jay Williamson	60.0
5	Jay Haas	59.5
6	Justin Leonard	59.1
7	Geoff Ogilvy (Aus)	58.8
8	Vijay Singh (Fij)	58.6
9	Scott Verplank	58.2
10T	Gavin Coles	57.9
	Jeff Sluman	57.9

Driving accuracy
(Percentage of fairways in regulation)

Pos	Name	%
1	Fred Funk	77.9
2	Glen Hnatiuk	77.7
3	Hal Sutton	75.8
4	Jim Furyk	75.7
5	Robert Damron	74.9
6	Mike Grob	74.6
7T	Skip Kendall	74.2
	Jeff Maggert	74.2
9	Peter Jacobsen	74.1
10T	Tim Clark (RSA)	74.0
	Joe Durant	74.0

Greens in regulation

Pos	Name	%
1	Joe Durant	72.9
2	Briny Baird	72.2
3	Dan Forsman	71.9
4	Chad Campbell	71.8
5	Tom Lehman	70.5
6	Jim Furyk	70.3
7	John Senden (Aus)	70.0
8	Mike Heinen	69.9
9T	Retief Goosen (RSA)	69.8
	David Sutherland	69.8

Driving distance
(Average yards per drive)

Pos	Name	Yds
1	Hank Kuehne	321.4
2	John Daly	314.3
3	Phil Mickelson	306.0
4	Darren Clarke (NI)	304.9
5	Ernie Els (RSA)	303.3
6	Vijay Singh (Fij)	301.9
7	Sergio García (Esp)	300.9
8	Mike Heinen	300.8
9	Brenden Pappas (RSA)	300.3
10	Mathew Goggin (Aus)	299.8

Putting averages
(Average per hole)

Pos	Name	Avg
1	John Huston	1.713
2	Justin Leonard	1.718
3T	Aaron Baddeley (Aus)	1.723
	Chris DiMarco	1.723
5T	Stewart Cink	1.728
	Paul Goydos	1.728
7T	David Frost (RSA)	1.729
	Scott Verplank	1.729
9	Greg Chalmers (Aus)	1.731
10	Tiger Woods	1.732

Tour Results (in chronological order)

Players are of American nationality unless stated

Mercedes Championships
Plantation Course, Kapalua, HI   (7263–73)

1	Ernie Els (RSA)	64-65-65-67—261	$1000000
2	Choi Kyoung-Ju (Kor)	67-67-62-73—269	450000
	Rocco Mediate	72-69-65-63—269	450000

Sony Open
Waialae CC, Honolulu, HI   (7060–70)

1	Ernie Els (RSA)*	66-65-66-67—264	$810000
2	Aaron Baddeley (Aus)	66-64-65-69—264	486000
3	Chris DiMarco	65-66-69-66—266	306000

Phoenix Open
TPC Scottsdale, AZ   (7059–71)

1	Vijay Singh (Fij)	67-66-65-63—261	$720000
2	John Huston	64-67-66-67—264	432000
3	Harrison Frazar	62-67-67-69—265	192000
	Robert Gamez	70-65-64-66—265	192000
	Retief Goosen (RSA)	65-68-65-67—265	192000
	Tim Petrovic	66-63-68-68—265	192000

Bob Hope Chrysler Classic
PGA West, La Quinta   (6931–72)

1	Mike Weir (Can)	67-64-65-67-67—330	$810000
2	Jay Haas	67-61-67-68-69—332	486000
3	Chris DiMarco	64-68-66-66-70—334	261000
	Tim Herron	69-64-61-65-75—334	261000

AT&T Pebble Beach National Pro-Am
Pebble Beach, CA   (6816–72)

1	Davis Love III	72-67-67-68—274	$900000
2	Tom Lehman	68-70-70-67—275	540000
3	Tim Herron	69-69-72-66—276	290000
	Mike Weir (Can)	67-74-67-68—276	290000

Buick Invitational
Torrey Pines (South), San Diego, CA   (S7208–72)

1	Tiger Woods	70-66-68-68—272	$810000
2	Carl Petterson (Swe)	69-68-70-69—276	486000
3	Brad Faxon	70-64-71-72—277	306000

Nissan Open
Riviera CC, Pacific Palisades, CA   (7078–71)

1	Mike Weir (Can)*	72-68-69-66—275	$810000
2	Charles Howell III	69-65-68-73—275	486000
3	Fred Funk	65-74-70-68—277	261000
	Nick Price (Zim)	68-67-70-72—277	261000

WGC Accenture Match Play
La Costa, Carlsbad, CA

Final: Tiger Woods (USA) ($1,050,000) beat David Toms (USA) ($600,000) 2 and 1

Consolation match: Adam Scott (Aus) ($480,000) beat Peter Lonard (Aus) ($390,000) 1 hole

Fuller details of this event are to be found on page 160

Chrysler Classic
Tucson, AZ   (7109–72)

1	Frank Lickliter	67-63-70-69—269	$540000
2	Chad Campbell	70-71-63-67—271	324000
3	Brenden Pappas (RSA)	71-66-67-68—272	204000

Ford Championship
Doral, Miami, FL   (7125–72)

1	Scott Hoch*	66-70-66-69—271	$900000
2	Jim Furyk	68-66-69-68—271	540000
3	Bob Tway	65-68-69-71—273	340000

Honda Classic
Heron Bay, Coral Springs, FL   (7157–72)

1	Justin Leonard	63-70-64-67—264	$900000
2	Chad Campbell	69-65-66-65—265	440000
	Davis Love III	66-65-65-69—265	440000

Bay Hill Invitational
Orlando, FL   (7207–72)

1	Tiger Woods	70-65-66-68—269	$810000
2	Stewart Cink	69-69-70-72—280	297000
	Brad Faxon	70-71-65-74—280	297000
	Kenny Perry	72-68-69-71—280	297000
	Kirk Triplett	73-69-68-70—280	297000

The Players Championship
TPC, Sawgrass, Ponte Vedra Beach, FL   (7093-72)

1	Davis Love III	70-67-70-64—271	$1170000
2	Jay Haas	68-70-67-72—277	572000
	Padraig Harrington (Irl)	67-68-70-72—277	572000

BellSouth Classic
TPC Sugarloaf, Duluth, GA   (7259–72)

1	Ben Crane	73-72-64-63—272	$720000
2	Bob Tway	70-66-69-71—276	432000
3	Retief Goosen (RSA)	68-70-74-65—277	208000
	Hank Kuehne	71-69-67-70—277	208000
	Jay Williamson	68-72-70-67—277	208000

THE MASTERS
Augusta National, GA   (7290–72)

1	Mike Weir (Can)*	70-68-75-68—281	$1080000
2	Len Mattiace	73-74-69-65—281	648000
3	Phil Mickelson	73-70-72-68—283	408000

Fuller details of this event are be found in Part I The Majors page 72

MCI Heritage
Harbour Town, Hilton Head Island, SC   (6916–71)

1	Davis Love III*	66-69-69-67—271	$810000
2	Woody Austin	68-70-65-68—271	486000
3	David Gossett	71-67-68-66—272	216000
	Geoff Ogilvy	68-67-70-67—272	216000
	Chris Riley	69-70-66-67—272	216000
	Hal Sutton	67-66-71-68—272	216000

Shell Houston Open
Redstone, Humble, TX   (7508–72)

1	Fred Couples	65-68-67-67—267	$810000
2	Stuart Appleby (Aus)	66-70-66-69—271	336000
	Mark Calcavecchia	68-65-68-70—271	336000
	Hank Kuehne	69-64-72-66—271	336000

HP Classic of New Orleans
English Turn, New Orleans, LA   (7116–72)

1	Steve Flesch*	67-70-65-65—267	$900000
2	Bob Estes	66-66-66-69—267	540000
3	Scott Verplank	65-63-67-74—269	340000

Wachovia Championship
Quail Hollow, Charlotte, NC   (7396–72)

1	David Toms	70-69-66-73—278	$1008000
2	Robert Gamez	72-67-71-70—280	418133
	Brent Geiberger	71-69-71-69—280	418133
	Vijay Singh (Fij)	73-72-67-68—280	418133

Verizon Byron Nelson Classic
TPC Cottonwood Valley, Irving, TX   (7017–70; 6846–70)

1	Vijay Singh (Fij)	65-65-69-66—265	$1008000
2	Nick Price (Zim)	66-70-66-65—267	604800
3	Robert Allenby (Aus)	67-67-69-65—268	380800

Bank of America Colonial
Colonial CC, Fort Worth, TX   (7080–70)

1	Kenny Perry	68-64-61-68—261	$900000
2	Justin Leonard	68-72-66-61—267	540000
3	Jeff Sluman	68-68-67-65—268	340000

Memorial Tournament
Muirfield Village, Dublin, OH   (7224–72)

1	Kenny Perry	65-68-70-72—275	$900000
2	Lee Janzen	67-67-71-72—277	540000
3	Mike Weir (Can)	72-70-71-65—278	340000

FBR Capital Open
TPC Avenal, Potomac, MD   (7005–71)

1	Rory Sabbatini (RSA)	68-66-68-68—270	$810000
2	Joe Durant	69-70-69-66—274	336000
	Fred Funk	70-70-66-68—274	336000
	Duffy Waldorf	71-68-66-69—274	336000

US OPEN
Olympian Fields, Matteson, IL   (7190–70)

1	Jim Furyk	67-66-67-72—272	$1080000
2	Stephen Leaney (Aus)	67-68-68-72—275	650000
3	Kenny Perry	72-71-69-67—279	341367
	Mike Weir (Can)	73-67-68-71—279	341367

Fuller details of this event are to be found in Part I The Majors page 64

Buick Classic
Westchester CC, Harrison, NY   (6722–71)

1	Jonathan Kaye*	70-66-68-67—271	$900000
2	John Rollins	70-67-67-67—271	540000
3	Joey Sindelar	66-69-70-68—273	640000

FedEx St Jude Classic
TPC Southwind, Memphis, TN   (7030–71)

1	David Toms	68-67-65-64—264	$810000
2	Nick Price (Zim)	73-67-65-62—267	486000
3	Bob Estes	67-70-66-65—268	234000
	Fredrik Jacobson (Swe)	66-67-68-67—268	234000
	Richard S Johnson (Swe)	64-66-69-69—268	234000

100th Western Open
Cog Hill, Lemont, IL   (7073–72)

1	Tiger Woods	63-70-65-69—267	$810000
2	Rich Beem	69-71-65-67—272	486000
3	Jim Furyk	71-66-72-65—274	234000
	Jerry Kelly	66-72-68-68—274	234000
	Mike Weir (Can)	67-70-69-68—274	234000

Greater Milwaukee Open
Brown Deer Park, Milwaukee, WI   (6739–70)

1	Kenny Perry	69-67-66-66—268	$630000
2	Steve Allan (Aus)	69-66-68-66—269	308000
	Heath Slocum	72-63-68-66—269	308000

OPEN CHAMPIONSHIP
Royal St George's, Sandwich, Kent, England   (7106–71)

1	Ben Curtis (USA)	72-72-70-69—283	$1112720
2	Thomas Bjørn (Den)	73-70-69-72—284	548412
	Vijay Singh (Fij)	75-70-69-70—284	548412

Fuller details of this event are to be found in Part I The Majors page 54

BC Open
En-Joie, Endicott, NY   (6974–72)

1	Craig Stadler	67-69-68-63—267	$540000
2	Alex Cejka (Ger)	66-66-69-67—268	264000
	Steve Lowery	64-64-68-72—268	264000

Greater Hartford Open
TPC River Highlands, Cromwell, CT   (6820–70)

1	Peter Jacobsen	63-67-69-67—266	$720000
2	Chris Riley	72-65-63-68—268	432000
3	Todd Fischer	66-69-69-69—273	272000

Buick Open
Warwick Hills, Grand Blanc, MI   (7127–72)

1	Jim Furyk	68-66-65-68—267	$720000
2	Briny Baird	70-68-65-66—269	264000
	Chris DiMarco	67-64-71-67—269	264000
	Geoff Ogilvy (Aus)	70-65-69-65—269	264000
	Tiger Woods	69-65-69-66—269	264000

The International
Castle Pines, Castle Rock, CO   (7594–72)

1	Davis Love III	19-17-5-5—46 points	$900000
2	Retief Goosen (RSA)	2-15-9-8—34 points	440000
	Vijay Singh (Fij)	4-15-9-6—34 points	440000

Modified Stableford

US PGA CHAMPIONSHIP
Oak Hill CC, Rochester, NY   (7134–70)

1	Shaun Micheel	69-68-69-70—276	$1080000
2	Chad Campbell	69-72-65-72—278	648000
3	Tim Clark (RSA)	72-70-68-69—279	408000

Fuller details of this event are included in Part I The Majors page 79

WGC: NEC Invitational
Firestone CC, Akron, OH   (7283–70)

1	Darren Clarke (NI)	65-70-66-67—268	$1050000
2	Jonathan Kaye (USA)	68-69-65-70—272	550000
3	David Love III (USA)	66-70-68-69—273	360000

Fuller details of this event are to be found on page 161

Reno-Tahoe Open
Montreux GCC, Reno, NV   (7472–72)

1	Kirk Triplett	67-68-73-63—271	$540000
2	Tim Herron	69-65-69-71—274	324000
3	Rod Pampling (Aus)	67-73-67-68—275	174000
	Dennis Paulson	68-66-73-68—275	174000

Deutsche Bank US Championship
TPC Boston, Norton, MA   (7178–71)

1	Adam Scott (Aus)	69-62-67-66—264	900000
2	Rocco Mediate	67-70-66-65—268	540000
3	Justin Rose (Eng)	63-71-68-67—269	340000

Bell Canadian Open
Hamilton, ON   (6946–70)

1	Bob Tway*	70-70-66-66—272	$756000
2	Brad Faxon	67-72-66-67—272	453600
3	Tom Pernice jr	68-72-65-68—273	285600

John Deere Classic
TPC Deere Run, Silvas, IL   (6762-71)

1	Vijay Singh (Fij)	66-68-69-65—268	$630000
2	Jonathan Byrd	65-67-72-68—272	261333
	JL Lewis	65-65-71-71—272	261333
	Chris Riley	66-69-66-71—272	261333

84 Lumber Classic of Pennsylvania
Farmington PA   (7032-72)

1	JL Lewis	69-67-68-62—266	$720000
2	Stuart Appleby (Aus)	69-68-64-67—268	298667
	Frank Lickliter II	70-67-65-66—268	298667
	Tim Petrovic	67-69-65-67—268	298667

Valero Texas Open
La Cantera, San Antonio, TX   (6881-70)

1	Tommy Armour III	64-62-63-65—254	$630000
2	Loren Roberts	64-66-69-62—261	308000
	Bob Tway	61-69-67-64—261	308000

WGC American Express Championship
Capital City, Woodstock GA   (7209-70)

1	Tiger Woods	67-66-69-72—274	$1050000
2	Stuart Appleby (Aus)	71-68-69-68—276	405000
	Tim Herron	66-72-67-71—276	405000
	Vijay Singh (Fij)	70-70-64-72—276	405000

Southern Farm Bureau Classic
Annandale GC, Madison, MA   (7199-72)

1	John Huston	66-66-68-68—268	$540000
2	Brenden Pappas (RSA)	72-69-66-62—269	324000
3	Shigeki Maruyama (Jpn)	68-68-68-66—270	204000

Las Vegas Invitational
TPCs Summerlin (7243-72), The Canyons (7381-71), Southern Highlands (7193-72), Las Vegas NV

1	Stuart Appleby (Aus)*	62-68-63-66-69—328	$720000
2	Scott McCarron	69-62-64-67-66—328	432000
3	Steve Lowery	65-64-70-65-67—331	272000

Chrysler Classic of Greensboro
Forest Oaks, Greensboro NC   (7062-72)

1	Shigeki Maruyama (Jpn)	65-64-70-67—266	$810000
2	Brad Faxon	67-67-68-69—271	486000
3	Matt Gogel	70-67-68-68—273	306000

Funai Classic at Walt Disney World
Disney's Magnolia and Palm Courses, Lake Buena Vista

(6967–72)

1	Vijay Singh (Fij)	64-65-69-67—265	$720000
2	Tiger Woods	66-67-71-65—269	298666
	Scott Verplank	66-66-66-71—269	298666
	Stewart Cink	67-65-66-71—269	298666

Chrysler Championship
Westin, Innisbrook Resort, FL

(7230–71)

1	Retief Goosen (RSA)	69-66-67-70—272 (-12)	$860000
2	Vijay Singh (Fij)	70-70-65-67—275	518400
3	Briny Baird	72-66-66-72—276	326400

The Tour Championship
Champions GC, Houston, TX

(6980–71)

1	Chad Campbell	70-69-61-68—268	$1080000
2	Charles Howell III	67-67-67-70—271	648000
3	Retief Goosen (RSA)	69-67-67-69—272	414000

World Cup of Golf *at Kiawah Island, SC*

Result: 1 South Africa; 2 England; 3 France

Full results can be found on page 166

Franklin–Templeton Shoot Out
Tiburon GC, Naples, FL

(7288–72)

1	Jeff Sluman and Hank Kuehne*	193	$275000
2	Brad Faxon and Scott McCarron	193	142000
	Chad Campbell and Shaun Micheel	193	142000

Unofficial money event

Why Americans love Royal Troon

The last five of the seven Open Championships played at Royal Troon have been won by American golfers. The honours list at the course which was designated Royal to mark its 100th anniversary in 1978 is:

1923	Arthur Havers (England)	73-73-73-76—295
1950	Bobby Locke (South Africa)	69-72-70-68—279
1962	Arnold Palmer (USA)	71-69-67-69—276
1973	Tom Weiskopf (USA)	68-67-71-70—276
1982	Tom Watson (USA)	69-71-74-70—284
1989	Mark Calcavecchia (USA)	71-68-68-68—275
1997	Justin Leonard (USA)	69-66-72-65—272

US Champions Tour 2003

Players are of American nationality unless stated

Final Ranking

1	Tom Watson	$1,853,108
2	Jim Thorpe	1,830,306
3	Gil Morgan	1,620,206
4	Bruce Lietzke	1,610,826
5	Hale Irwin	1,607,391
6	Tom Kite	1,549,819
7	Tom Jenkins	1,415,503
8	Larry Nelson	1,365,973
9	Allen Doyle	1,349,272
10	Bruce Fleisher	1,306,013
11	Dana Quigley	1,303,304
12	Bob Gilder	1,278,247
13	Doug Tewell	1,237,681
14	Craig Stadler	1,192,278
15	Morris Hatalsky	1,150,584
16	Tom Purtzer	1,043,977
17	Vicente Fernandez (Arg)	1,038,339
18	Des Smyth	959,600
19	Bobby Wadkins	942,109
20	Wayne Levi	935,241
21	Mike McCullough	887,434
22	Rodger Davis	885,781
23	David Eger	851,217
24	John Jacobs	785,181
25	Graham Marsh (Aus)	745,152
26	Fuzzy Zoeller	741,830
27	Dave Barr (Can)	731,726
28	DA Weibring	729,852
29	Jay Sigel	721,989
30	José Maria Canizares (Esp)	680,895
31	Jim Ahern	626,958
32	Walter Hall	578,806
33	Ed Dougherty	565,146
34	Stewart Ginn	553,941
35	Hubert Green	514,575
36	Bruce Summerhays	509,194
37	Eamonn Darcy (Irl)	498,181
38	Don Pooley	491,012
39	Hugh Baiocchi (RSA)	475,512
40	Mark McCumber	475,021
41	James Mason	465,985
42	Isao Aoki (Jpn)	449,231
43	Mike Hill	388,410
44	Leonard Thompson	372,079
45	Jim Colbert	344,011
46	John Bland	343,642
47	Dave Stockton	339,468
48	Bobby Walzel	328,129
49	John Harris	324,304
50	Jim Dent	304,812

Career Money List

1	Hale Irwin	$24,523,599
2	Gil Morgan	17,971,963
3	Tom Kite	16,700,518
4	Tom Watson	15,598,471
5	Larry Nelson	14,422,995
6	Raymond Floyd	13,959,972
7	Lee Trevino	13,166,291
8	Jim Colbert	12,737,520
9	Bruce Fleisher	12,166,537
10	Dave Stockton	11,378,562
11	Craig Stadler	10,785,771
12	Bruce Lietzke	10,732,870
13	George Archer	10,196,507
14	Jim Thorpe	9,629,214
15	Isao Aoki (Jpn)	9,621,586
16	Bob Charles (NZ)	9,421,688
17	Dana Quigley	9,164,882
18	JC Snead	9,133,654
19	Jim Dent	9,085,264
20	Allen Doyle	9,063,479
21	Jack Nicklaus	8,989,613
22	Doug Tewell	8,730,956
23	Mike Hill	8,693,214
24	Bob Murphy	8,517,250
25	Bob Gilder	8,466,630
26	Jay Sigel	7,988,376
27	Hubert Green	7,847,570
28	Graham Marsh (Aus)	7,763,760
29	Chi Chi Rodriguez (Pur)	7,671,844
30	Gary Player (RSA)	7,646,763
31	Ben Crenshaw	7,527,206
32	Fuzzy Zoeller	7,490,384
33	Dale Douglass	7,442,035
34	Lanny Wadkins	7,378,639
35	Tom Jenkins	7,183,602
36	John Jacobs	7,120,482
37	Bruce Summerhays	7,062,241
38	John Mahaffey	7,025,277

US Champions Tour *continued*

39	Mike McCullough	6,757,468	45	Leonard Thompson	6,364,292
40	Tom Wargo	6,749,448	46	Wayne Levi	6,349,743
41	Vicente Fernandez (Arg)	6,634,796	47	John Bland	6,213,125
42	Al Geiberger	6,548,182	48	Bruce Crampton	6,028,877
43	Dave Eichelberger	6,522,301	49	Jim Albus	6,009,823
44	Ed Dougherty	6,433,701	50	Mark McCumber	5,996,737

Tour Statistics

Scoring average

Pos	Name	Rounds	Avg
1	Tom Watson	48	68.81
2	Craig Stadler	48	69.38
3	Hale Irwin	69	69.59
4	DA Weibring	46	69.70
5	Gil Morgan	79	69.71
6	Tom Kite	86	69.79
7	Larry Nelson	74	69.82
8	Tom Jenkins	94	69.99
9	Bruce Fleisher	91	70.02
10	Bruce Lietzke	67	70.04

Driving accuracy

Pos	Name	%
1	Doug Tewell	81.5
2	Allen Doyle	80.9
3	John Bland	79.1
4	Wayne Levi	78.2
5	Hale Irwin	77.1
6	Jim Albus	76.1
7	Isao Aoki (Jpn)	76.0
8	Seiji Ebihara (Jpn)	75.8
9T	Ed Dougherty	75.6
	DA Weibring	75.6

Driving distance

(Average yards per drive)

Pos	Name	Yds
1	Tom Purtzer	298.3
2	Andy Bean	297.9
3	Rodger Davis	288.9
4	Jim Ahern	288.2
5	Craig Stadler	287.0
6	Gil Morgan	286.0
7	Bruce Lietzke	285.4
8	Tom Watson	284.0
9	John Harris	282.7
10	Terry Dill	282.6

Putting leaders

(Average putts per hole)

Pos	Name	Avg
1	Rodger Davis	1.726
2	Tom Watson	1.736
3	Bob Gilder	1.745
4	Hubert Green	1.750
5	Larry Nelson	1.752
6	Walter Hall	1.758
7	Bruce Fleisher	1.759
8	Jim Thorpe	1.760
9	Jay Overton	1.765
10	Bruce Lietzke	1.768

Sand saves

Pos	Name	%
1	Rodger Davis	60.0
2	Mike McCullough	58.9
3	Vicente Fernandez (Arg)	58.8
4	Ed Fiori	56.6
5	Doug Tewell	56.3
6T	Stewart Ginn	55.3
	Dana Quigley	55.3
8	Larry Nelson	54.8
9T	Mike Hill	53.6
	Jay Overton	53.6

Greens in regulation

Pos	Name	Rounds	%
1	Tom Kite	86	74.3
2	Hale Irwin	69	73.6
3	Tom Purtzer	73	73.1
4	Craig Stadler	48	73.0
5	Doug Tewell	84	72.8
6	DA Weibring	46	72.4
7T	Tom Jenkins	94	72.2
	Tom Watson	48	72.2
9	Gil Morgan	79	72.1
10T	Bruce Fleisher	91	71.7
	Bruce Lietzke	67	71.7

Tour Results

Tournament	Location	Winner	Score
Senior Skins Game	Wailea, Maui, HI	Lee Trevino	(skins)
MasterCard Championship	Hualalai, Kaupulehu-Kona, HI	Dana Quigley	198 (-18)
Royal Caribbean Classic	Crandon Park, Key Biscayne, FL	Dave Barr (Can)	207 (-9)
ACE Group Classic	Twin Eagles, Naples, FL	Vicente Fernandez (Arg)	202 (-14)
Verizon Classic	TPC Tampa Bay, Lutz, FL	Bruce Fleisher	205 (-8)
The Bosque Real Championship	Col Lomas Altas, Mexico City	David Eger	204 (-12)
SBC Classic	Valencia, Santa Clarita, CA	Tom Purtzer	135 (-9)
Toshiba Senior Classic	Newport Beach, CA	Rodger Davis (Aus)	197 (-16)
Emerald Coast Classic	The Moors, Milton, Pensacola, FL	Bob Gilder	193 (-17)
Liberty Mutual Legends of Golf	Savannah GA	Bruce Lietzke	206 (-10)
Bruno's Memorial Classic	Greystone, Birmingham, AL	Tom Jenkins	200 (-16)
Kinko's Classic of Austin	The Hills, Austin TX	Hale Irwin	208 (-8)
Bayer Advantage Invitational	Kansas City MO	Jay Sigel	205 (-11)
Columbus Southern Open	Green Island, Columbus GA	Morris Hatalsky	198 (-12)
Music City Championship	Nashville TN	Jim Ahern	196 (-20)
SENIOR PGA CHAMPIONSHIP	Newtown Square PA	John Jacobs	276 (-4)
Farmers Charity Classic	Egypt Valley, Ada, MI	Doug Tewell	201 (-15)
US SENIOR OPEN	Inverness, Toledo OH	Bruce Lietzke	277 (-7)
Ford Senior Players Championship	TPC Michigan, Dearborn MI	Craig Stadler	271 (-17)
SENIOR BRITISH OPEN	Turnberry, Scotland	Tom Watson	263 (-17) ·
FleetBoston Classic	Nashawtuc, Concord, MA	Allen Doyle	198 (-15)
3M Championship	TPC Twin Cities, Blaine, MN	Wayne Levi	205 (-11)
Long Island Classic	Eisenhower Park, Long Island NY	Jim Thorpe	195 (-15)
Allianz Championship	Glen Oaks, West Desmoines IA	Don Pooley	200 (-13)
JELD-WEN Tradition	Reserve Vineyards, Aloha OR	Tom Watson	273 (-15)
Kroger Classic	Rivers' Bend, Maineville OH	Gil Morgan	200 (-16)
Constellation Energy Classic	Hayfields Baltimore MD	Larry Nelson	207 (-9)
SAS Championship	Prestonwood, Cary NC	DA Weibring	203 (-13)
Greater Hickory Classic	Rock Barn, Conover NC	Craig Stadler	201 (-15)
Turtle Bay Championship	Kahuku, Oahu HI	Hale Irwin	208 (-8)
SBC Championship	Oak Hills, San Antonio TX	Craig Stadler	198 (-15)
Charles Schwab Cup Championship	Sonoma CA	Jim Thorpe	268 (-20)

US Nationwide Tour 2003

Players are of American nationality unless stated

Final Ranking (Top 15 earned US Tour Card)

Pos	Name	Events	Prize $	Pos	Name	Events	Prize $
1	Zach Johnson	20	$494,882	51	Steve Haskins	26	94,911
2	Joe Ogilvie	23	392,337	52	Bobby Gage	23	94,202
3	Tom Carter	22	360,990	53	Scott Sterling	28	94,017
4	Chris Couch	21	342,874	54	Hunter Haas	26	93,125
5	Bo Van Pelt	24	289,248	55	Michael Allen	24	89,201
6	Ryan Palmer	24	286,066	56	Shane Bertsch	26	85,558
7	Mark Hensby	23	276,519	57	Nick Cassini	10	84,552
8	Tripp Isenhour	21	262,646	58	Mike Brisky	23	82,558
9	Jason Bohn	18	255,191	59	Andrew McLardy	25	82,342
10	Jason Dufner	26	237,637	60	Fran Quinn	25	82,327
11	Vaughn Taylor	17	223,988	61	Shane Tait	22	81,150
12	Blaine McCallister	18	223,232	62	John Paul Curley	25	80,345
13	Andre Stolz	16	218,867	63	Bubba Watson	21	79,854
14	Guy Boros	20	210,461	64	Stephen Gangluff	25	77,898
15	Ted Purdy	25	206,584	65	Franklin Langham	22	75,831
16	D.J. Brigman	23	195,941	66	Danny Briggs	16	75,550
17	Lucas Glover	26	193,989	67	Boo Weekley	23	74,149
18	David Morland IV	22	190,284	68	Keoke Cotner	28	72,611
19	Craig Bowden	19	180,238	69	Russ Cochran	16	72,505
20	Tommy Tolles	29	179,963	70	Eduardo Herrera	21	72,380
21	Daniel Chopra	22	178,799	71	Rick Price	23	70,307
22	Roger Tambellini	17	177,963	72	Rob Bradley	25	70,014
23	Tjaart Van der Walt (RSA)	24	175,967	73	Scott Petersen	25	69,972
24	Brett Wetterich	22	174,805	74	Trevor Dodds (Nam)	20	65,728
25	Kyle Thompson	24	174,008	75	Brian Wilson	26	65,103
26	Scott Gutschewski	12	172,103	76	Steve Ford	17	62,855
27	Paul Claxton	28	171,594	77	Mark Wurtz	21	60,892
28	Charles Warren	26	155,837	78	Robin Freeman	15	59,756
29	Roland Thatcher	25	151,477	79	Brad Ott	17	58,909
30	Wes Short	28	146,997	80	Emlyn Aubrey	24	58,367
31	Jimmy Walker	18	146,516	81	Sonny Skinner	26	55,371
32	Chris Tidland	24	140,848	82	Scott Dunlap	23	55,173
33	Ken Duke	26	133,167	83	Jeff Gove	26	54,643
34	Jeff Klauk	25	132,912	84	Jason Schultz	23	53,463
35	Michael Long	26	131,644	85	Zoran Zorkic	27	53,280
36	Omar Uresti	28	127,961	86	Bill Glasson	8	50,928
37	Ryuji Imada (Jpn)	24	127,861	87	David McKenzie	7	49,014
38	Jeff Freeman	29	123,397	88	Rob McKelvey	25	47,382
39	David Branshaw	26	120,808	89	Lee Porter	25	46,370
40	Jess Daley	27	119,593	90	Victor Schwamkrug	18	46,339
41	Doug LaBelle II	25	115,786	91	Chris Downes	9	45,272
42	Todd Demsey	22	109,951	92	Jimmy Green	19	45,259
43	John Elliott	30	107,802	93	Kelly Gibson	15	44,418
44	Bob Heintz	25	104,903	94	Ryan Howison	21	44,369
45	Rich Barcelo	27	98,146	95	Kevin Pendley	23	43,743
46	James Oh	8	97,334	96	Mike Sullivan	21	41,752
47	Kevin Johnson	27	97,295	97	Todd Rose	24	41,717
48	Craig Lile	16	96,937	98	Kevin Durkin	18	41,236
49	Scott Gump	25	95,721	99	Jaxon Brigman	16	39,925
50	DA Points	24	95,613	100	Barry Cheesman	24	39,156

Tour Results

Jacob's Creek Open Championship	Kooyonga, Adelaide, S Australia	Joe Ogilvie	279 (-5)
Holden Clearwater Classic	Christchurch, NZ	Ryan Palmer	271 (-17)
Louisiana Open	Le Triomphe, Broussard, LA	Brett Wetterich	264 (-24)
Arkansas Classic	Diamante CC, Hot Springs Village, AR	Ted Purdy	275 (-13)
Rheem Classic	Hardscrabble, Fort Smith, AR	Zach Johnson*	272 (-8)
BMW Charity Pro-Am	Cliffs Valley, Travelers Rest, SC	Tripp Isenhour	269 (-19)
Virginia Beach Open	Virginia Beach, VA	Michael Long	277 (-11)
SAS Carolina Classic	Raleigh, NC	David Morland	268 (-16)
LaSalle Bank Open	Glen Club, Chicago, IL	Andre Stolz	276 (-12)
NE Pennsylvania Classic	Glenmaura National, Scranton, PA	Blaine McCallister	265 (-19)
Lake Erie Charity Classic	Findley Lake, NY	Guy Boros	275 (-13)
Knoxville Open	Fox Den, Knoxville, TN	Vaughn Taylor	268 (-20)
Samsung Canadian PGA Championship	DiamondBack, Toronto, ON	Tom Carter	275 (-9)
Reese's Cup	Hershey, OP	Joe Ogilvie	274 (-10)
Henrico County Open	Dominion Club, VA	Mark Hensby	268 (-20)
Dayton Open	Centerville, OH	Guy Boros	265 (-23)
Chattanooga Classic	Black Creek, Chattanooga, TN	Jason Bohn	265 (-23)
Omaha Classic	Champions Club, Omaha, NE	Bo Van Pelt	262 (-26)
Price Cutter Charity Championship	Highland Springs, Springfield, MO	Tom Carter	267 (-21)
Preferred Health Systems Wichita Open	Crestview, Wichita, KS	Jeff Klauk	265 (-19)
Alberta Calgary Classic	Cochrane, Alberta	Tom Carter	263 (-17)
EnvirocareUtah Classic	Salt Lake City, UT	Zack Johnson	267 (-21)
Oregon Classic	Shadow Hills, Eugene, OR	Chris Couch	274 (-14)
Albertsons Boise Open	Hillcrest, Boise, ID	Roger Tambellini	267 (-17)
Mark Christopher Charity Classic	Rancho Cucamonga, CA	James Oh	268 (-16)
Monterey Peninsula Classic	Seaside, CA	Scott Gutschewski	276 (-12)
Gila River Classic	Wild Horse Pass, Chandler, AZ	Lucas Glover	270 (-18)
Permian Basin Charity Golf Classic	Midland/Odessa, TX	DJ Brigman	272 (-16)
Miccosukee Championship	Miami, FL	Craig Bowden	270 (-14)
Nationwide Tour Championship	Capitol Hill, Prattville, AL	Chris Couch	270 (-18)

Japan PGA Tour

Players are of Japanese nationality unless stated

Results 2002

Mitsui Sumitomo VISA Taiheiyo Masters	Taiheiyo, Shizuoka	Tsuneyuki Nakajima	272 (-16)
Dunlop Phoenix Tournament	Phoenix CC, Miyazaki	Kaname Yokoo	269 (-15)
Casio World Open	Ibusuki, Kagoshima	David Smail (NZ)	200 (-16)
Golf Nippon Series JT Cup	Tokyo Yomiuri CC, Tokyo	Shingo Katayama	261 (-19)
Okinawa Open	Southern Links, Naha	Hiroyuki Fujita	202 (-14)

Final Ranking 2002

1 Toru Tamaguchi	¥145,440,341	6 Tsuneyuki Nakajima	89,788,484
2 Nobuhito Sato	130,825,969	7 Kenichi Kuboya	83,654,013
3 Shingo Katayama	129,258,019	8 Brendan Jones (Aus)	80,771,735
4 Dean Wilson (USA)	97,116,100	9 Yasuharu Imano	76,309,705
5 David Smail (NZ)	94,173,576	10 Toshi Izawa	75.906,757

including WGC events and majors

Results 2003

Token Homemate Cup	Tado GC, Mieq	Andre Stolz	278 (-6)
Tsuruya Open	Sports Shinko CC, Hyogo	Hirofumi Miyase	270 (-14)
The Crowns	Nagoya, Aichi	Hidemasa Hoshino	270 (-10)
Fujisankei Classic	Kawana, Shizuoka	Todd Hamilton (USA)	267 (-17)
JPGA Championship	Caledonian GC, Chiba	Shingo Katayama	271 (-17)
Munsingwear Open KSB Cup	Ayutaki, Kagawa	Hirofumi Miyase	275 (-13)
Diamond Cup Tournament	Sayama	Todd Hamilton (USA)	276 (-10)
JCB Classic Sendai	Omotezao Kokusai, Miyagi	Katsuyoshi Tomori	264 (-20)
Mandom Lucido Yomiuri Open	Yomiuri, Hyogo	Hideto Tanihara	200 (-16)
Mizuno Open	Setonaikai, Okayama	Todd Hamilton (USA)	278 (-10)
JGT Championship	Horai, Tochigi	Toshimitsu Izawa	270 (-14)
Woodone Open Hiroshima	Hiroshima	Toshimitsu Izawa	275 (-13)
NST Niigata Open	Nakamine, Niigata	Katsumasa Miyamoto	271 (-17)
Aiful Cup	Twin Fields, Ishikawa	Taichi Teshima	269 (-19)
Sun Chlorella Classic	Sapporo Bay, Hokkaido	Brendan Jones	280 (-8)
Hisamitsu-KBC Augusta	Keya, Fukuoka	Soshi Tajima	269 (-19)
JPGA Match Play Championship	Nidom, Hokkaido	Todd Hamilton (USA) beat David Smail (NZ)	
Suntory Open	Sobu CC, Chiba	Jyoti Randhawa (Ind)	276 (-8)
ANA Open	Sapporo, Hokkaido	Yeh Wei-tze	277 (-11)
Acom International	Shioka, Ibaragi	Masuhiro Kuramoto	271 (-13)
Tokai Classic	Miyoshi CC, Aichi	Nozomi Kawahara	275 (-13)
JAPAN OPEN	Saitama, Tokyo	Keiichiro Fukaboro	276 (-5)
Bridgestone Open	Sodegaura, Chiba	Naomichi ('Joe') Ozaki	267 (-21)
ABC Championship	Hyogo	Shingo Katayama	265 (-23)
Mitsui Sumitomo Taiheyo Masters	Taiheiyo, Shizuoka	Kiyoshi Murota	272 (-16)
Dunlop Phoenix	Phoenix CC, Miya	Kaname Yokoo	(D)
Casio World Open	Ibusuki, Kagoshima	David Smail (NZ)	(D)
Golf Nippon Series JT Cup	Tokyo Yomiuri	Shingo Katayama	(D)

Latest Ranking (after Matsui Sumitomo Taiheyo Masters and with four events still to play. Totals include major and WGC event prize money)

1	Todd Hamilton (USA)	¥115,907,151	6	Hirofumi Miyase	65,189,986
2	Toshimitsu Izawa	113,874,300	7	Brendan Jones (Aus)	62,471,561
3	Shingo Katayama	103,686,413	8	Hiroyuki Fujita	62,150,222
4	Taichi Toshima	85,534,731	9	Katsumasu Miyamoto	59,634,671
5	Tetsuji Hiratsuka	76,687,033	10	Kiyoshi Murota	58,776,873

A Magical 59 from Kuramoto

Masahiro Kuramoto set a new Japanese Tour record when he fired the first sub-60 score on the Japanese Tour in the ACOM International. Kuramoto, a 48-year-old from Hiroshima, had seven successive birdies on his card and holed a 30 footer on the final green for his 59. There have been several 59's on the US Tour but nobody has ever beaten 60 on the European Tour.

Other 59's on the main Tours:

American PGA Tour: Sam Snead (Greenbrier Open, 1959); Al Geiberger* (Danny Thomas Memphis Classic, 1977); Chip Beck (Las Vegas Invitational, 1991); David Duval (Bob Hope Chrysler Classic, 1999).

European Tour: Nobody has ever shot 59.

Australasian Tour: No records kept.

Japanese Tour: Masahiro Kuramoto (Acom International, 2003).

South African Sunshine Tour: It is understood that nobody has shot 59.

LPGA Tour: Annika Sörenstam (Standard Register Ping, 2002).

Ladies European Tour: Nobody has shot 59.

Asian PGA Tour: Nobody has shot 59.

Others: Gary Player (Brazilian Open, Rio, 1974); Miguel Angel Martin (South Argentine Open, 1987).

Only one player, Jason Bohn, has shot a score better than 59. When playing in the Bayer Championship on the Canadian Tour in 2001 he returned a 13-under-par 58.

Asian PGA Tour

Results 2002

Okinawa Open	Southern Links Golf Club, Japan	Hiroyuki Fujita (Jpn)	202 (-14)
TLC Classic	Harbour Plaza, Dongguan, China	Colin Montgomerie (Sc0)	272 (-16)
BMW Asian Open	Ta Shee, Taiwan	Padraig Harrington (Ire)	273 (-15)
Omega Hong Kong Open	Hong Kong GC	Frederik Jacobsen (Swe)	260 (-16)
Volvo Masters of Asia	Kota Permai, Malaysia	Kevin Na (Kor)	276 (-16)

Final Ranking 2002

1	Jyoti Randhawa (Ind)	US$266264	11	Charlie Wi (Kor)		119220
2	Thongchai Jaidee (Tha)	242558	12	Lian Wen-chong (Chi)		106090
3	Arjun Atwal (Ind)	207625	13	Kang Wook-soon (Kor)		103655
4	Kevin Na (Kor)	171574	14	Arjun Singh (Ind)		100521
5	Thammanoon Srirot (Tha)	168782	15	Pablo Delomo (Mex)		100300
6	Simon Yates (Sco)	158431	16	James Kingston (RSA)		99489
7	Andrew Pitts (USA)	146107	17	Tsai Clu-huang (Tai)		93771
8	Rick Gibson (Can)	139594	18	Zhang Lian-Wei (Chi)		93468
9	Anthony Kang (Kor)	124491	19	Brad Kennedy (Aus)		93368
10	David Geeson (Aus)	120194	20	Prayad Marksaeng (Tha)		90457

Results and Fixtures 2003–2004

Caltex Singapore Masters	Laguna	Zhang Lian-Wei (Chi)	278 (-10)
Johnnie Walker Classic	Lake Karrinyup, Australia	Ernie Els (RSA)	259 (-29)
Carlsberg Malaysian Open	Kuala Lumpur	Arjun Atwal (Ind)	260 (-24)
Myanmar Open	Yangon, Myanmar	Lin Keng-Chi (Tai)	275 (-13)
Phoenix Dynasty Cup	Shenzhen, China	Asia beat Japan 16½–7½	
Royal Challenge Indian Open	New Delhi	Mike Cunning (USA)	270 (-18)
Tailand Open	Krisada City Golf Hills	Edward Loar (USA)	269 (-19)
Maekyung Open	Seoul, Korea	Chung Joon (Kor)	275 (-13)
SK Telecom Open	Baekahmvista CC, Korea	Choi Kyung-Ju (Kor)	201 (-15)
Mercuries Masters	Taipei Taiwan	Lin Wen-Ko (Tai)	280 (-8)
Davidoff Nations Cup*	Singapore	Myanmar	
Kolon Cup, Korean Open	Woo Jung Hills CC	John Daly (USA)	282 (-6)
Macau Open	Macau	Colin Montgomerie (Sco)	273 (-11)
		(after play-off with Scott Barr (Aus))	
Sanyo Open	Yalong Bay GC, China	Marcus Both (Aus)	275 (-13)
Hero Honda Masters	New Delhi, India	Arjun Atwal (Ind)	281 (-7)
Volvo China Open	Silport, Shanghai	Zhang Lian-Wei (Chi)	277 (-11)
Acer Taiwan Open	Sunrise GCC, Taiwan	Danny Chia (Mal)	(D)
Omega Hong Kong Open	Hong Kong GC	Fredrik Jacobsen (Swe)	(D)
Volvo Masters of Asia	Bangkok GC, Thailand	Kevin Na (Kor)	(D)

* Fuller details on page 182

Latest Ranking (after Volvo China Open and with three events to play)

1	Arjun Atwal (Ind)	US$282,193	6	Chung Joon (Kor)	104,019
2	Zhang Lian-Wei (Chi)	245,569	7	Simon Yates (Sco)	103,351
3	Thaworn Wiratchant (Tha)	143,265	8	Thammanoon Srirot (Tha)	100,927
4	Thongchai Jaidee (Tha)	138,786	9	Lin Wen-Ko (Tai)	85,187
5	Brad Kennedy (Aus)	128,808	10	Rick Gibson (Can)	81,700

Australasian Tour

Results 2002–2003

Players are of Australian nationality unless stated

Australian MasterCard Masters	Huntingdale, Melbourne	Peter Lonard (Aus)	279 (-9)
Australian PGA	Hyatt Coolum, Queensland	Peter Lonard (Aus) & Jarrod Moseley (Aus)	271 (-17)
Holden Australian Open	Victoria GC, Melbourne	Steve Allan (Aus)	198 (-12)
Holden New Zealand Open	Auckland, NZ	Mahal Pearce (NZ)	278 (-10)
Heineken Classic [1]	Royal Melbourne, Victoria	Ernie Els (RSA)	273 (-15)
ANZ Championship [1]	The Lakes, Sydney, NSW	Paul Casey (Eng)	45 pts
Johnnie Walker Classic [2]	Lake Karrinyup, Perth	Ernie Els (RSA)	259 (-29)
Jacob's Creek Open Championship [3]	Kooyonga	Joe Ogilvie (USA)	279 (-5)
Clearwater Classic [3]	Clearwater Resort	Ryan Palmer (USA)	271 (-17)
MasterCard Masters	Huntingdale GC, Victoria	Peter Lonard (Aus)	(D)
Australian PGA	Hyatt Coolum, Queensland	Peter Lonard (Aus) & Jarrod Moseley (Aus)	(D)
Australian Open	Moonah Links, Victoria	Steve Allan (Aus)	(D)

Latest Ranking 2002–2003

(after Clearwater Classic and with three events still to be played before end of season)

1	Andre Stolz (NSW)	AUS$403480	11	David Smail (NZ)	137668
2	Paul Casey (Eng)	365257	12	Chris Downes (Qld)	127341
3	Peter Lonard (NSW)	259474	13	Nathan Green (NSW)	120456
4	Nick O'Hern (WA)	255904	14	Shane Tait (Qld)	118747
5	Stephen Leaney (WA)	245902	15	Brett Rumford (WA)	113078
6	Joe Ogilvie (USA)	218246	16	Peter Senior (Qld)	110553
7	Mahal Pearce (NZ)	202273	17	Robert Allenby (Vic)	100496
8	Stuart Appleby (Vic)	156118	18	Peter O'Malley (NSW)	98162
9	Jarrod Moseley (WA)	143692	19	Robert Karlsson (Swe)	95580
10	Peter Fowler (NSW)	141025	20	Greg Turner (NZ)	87789

Fixtures 2004

New Zealand Open	Grange, NZ	Mahal Pearce (NZ)	(D)
Johnnie Walker Classic [2]	Alpine G & SC, Bangkok	Ernie Els (RSA)	(D)
Heineken Classic [1]	Royal Melbourne, Victoria	Ernie Els (RSA)	(D)
ANZ Championship [1]	Horizons GC	Paul Casey (Eng)	(D)
Jacob's Creek Open Championship [3]	Kooyonga GC	Joe Ogilvie (USA)	(D)
NZ PGA Championship [3]	Clearwater Resort	Ryan Palmer (USA)	(D)

The remaining 2004 fixtures are not yet finalised

[1] joint venture with Asian PGA Tour and European Tour
[2] joint venture with European Tour
[3] joint venture with US Nationwide Tour

South African Sunshine Tour

Players are of South African nationality unless stated

Later results 2002–2003 (not in 2003 edition)

Telkom PGA Championship	Woodhill CC	Michiel Bothma	273 (-15)
Nedbank Golf Challenge	Gary Player GC, Sun City	Ernie Els	267 (-21)
Nashua Masters	Wild Coast Sun CC	Hennie Otto	279 (-1)
Vodacom Players Championship	Royal Cape GC	Mark McNulty (Zim)	272 (-16)
SAA South African Open	Erinvale	Trevor Immelman	274 (-14)
Dunhill Championship	Houghton	Mark Foster (Eng)*	273 (-15)
Dimension Data Pro-Am	Gary Player CC	Trevor Immelman	271 (-17)
The Tour Championship	Leopard Creek CC	Hennie Otto	271 (-17)

Final Order of Merit 2002–2003

1	Trevor Immelman	SAR 2,044,279	11	Andrew McLardy	411,433
2	Mark Foster (Eng)	1,110,935	12	Tjaart van der Walt	388,175
*	Tim Clark	901,037	13	Titch Moore	366,434
3	Hennie Otto	877,188	14	Craig Lile	356,105
4	Bradford Vaughan	854,746	15	Charl Schwarzel	352,402
5	Mark McNulty (Zim)	580,960	*	Justin Rose (Eng)	337,659
6	Doug McGuigan (Sco)	547,200	16	Michiel Bothma	326,369
7	Scott Dunlap (USA)	475,247	17	Marc Cayeux (Zim)	304,522
8	Bobby Lincoln	437,547	18	Simon Hurd (Eng)	296,735
9	Jean Hugo	427,469	19	Nic Henning	258,319
10	Richard Sterne	419,761	20	Louis Oosthuizen	233,682

* played in 3 events only and did not qualify for place in Order of Merit

Trevor Immelman won the 2003 South African Airways Open and topped the Sunshine Tour's 2002/2003 Order of Merit.

Ernie Els won the Nedbank Golf Challenge for the third time in 2002.

Results and Fixtures 2003–2004

2003

Stanbic Zambia Open	Lusaka GC, Zambia	Johan Edfors (Swe)	206 (-13)
FNB Botswana Open	Phakalane GC, Gabarone	Trevor Fisher jr	201 (-15)
Limpopo Industrelek Classic	Pietersburg GC	Marc Cayeux (Zim)	197 (-19)
Capital Alliance Royal Swazi Sun Open	Royal Swazi Sun, Mbabne	Des Terblanche	36 points
Devonvale Championship	Devonvale Conference Centre and Golf Estate	Hendrik Buhrmann	198 (-18)
Canon Classic	Bramble Hill GC, Fancourt, George	Tyrol Auret	200 (-13)
Royal Swazi Sun Classic	Royal Swazi Sun CC	Nic Henning	198 (-18)
Parmalat Classic	Silver Lakes CC, Pretoria	Desvonde Botes	207 (-9)
Seekers Travel Pro-Am	Dainfern CC, Sandton	Chris Williams (Eng)	203 (-13)
Bearingman Highveld Classic	Witbank cc	Dion Foorie	201 (-15)
Platinum Classic	Mooinooi CC, Rustenburg	Doug McGuigan (Sco)	199 (-17)
Nedbank Golf Challenge[1]	Gary Player GC, Sun City	Ernie Els	(D)

2004

South African Airways Open	Erinvale GC, Somerset West	Trevor Immelman	(D)
dunhill championship	Houghton GC, Johannesburg	Mark Foster (Eng)	(D)
Dimension Data Pro-Am	Gary Player and Lost City GC, Sun City	Trevor Immelman	(D)
Nashua Masters	Wild Coast CC, Port Edward	Hennie Otto	(D)
Telkom PGA Championship	Woodhill CC, Tschwane, Pretoria	Michiel Bothma	(D)
Tour Championship	Leopard Creek, Malelane	Hennie Otto	(D)

[1] *unoffical event*

Latest Ranking (after Platinum Classic and with six offical events to go before the end of the season)

1 Johan Edfors (Swe)	SAR134,664	
2 Des Terblanche	102,027	
3 Ashley Roestoff	97,914	
4 Michael Kirk	95,815	
5 Doug McGuigan (Sco)	93,266	
6 Desvonde Botes	87,197	
7 Tyrol Auret	86,424	
8 Marc Cayeux (Zim)	84,316	
9 Nic Henning	79,670	
10 Scott Drummond (Sco	69,684	

South African brothers make history

South Africa has long been noted for its famous golfing families. Sid and Jock Brews both won the South African Open during that period in the 1920's and 1930's when they dominated the local scene, and there have been the Hennings – Harold, Brian, Allan and Graham, and the Pappas – Dean, Sean and Brendan. More recently there have been Mike and Alan Michell and Bradford and Jason Vaughan but now there is a new double act in South African golf and this time the golfers are black. Charley (29) and Peter Misiza (28) from the Daveyton Golf Club near Johannesburg, are the first black brothers to play on the Sunshine Tour. Following an amateur career in which he played for the South African President's team for development golfers twice, Charley has now joined Peter on the professional circuit and in the process has continued a long family tradition in South African golf.

Canadian Tour 2003

Players are of Canadian nationality unless stated

Travel Tex.com Canadian Tour Classic	Austin TX	Anders Hultman (Swe)	272 (-8)
Travel Tex.com Canadian Tour Challenge	Austin TX	Rob Johnson (USA)	134 (-10)
Michelin Guadalajara Classic	Guadalajara, Mexico	Erik Compton (USA)	270 (-14)
Corona Ixtapa Classic	Ixtapa, Mexico	Derek Gillespie (USA)	265 (-23)
Northern Ontario Open	Sault Ste Marie ON	Mario Tiziani	271 (-9)
MTS Classic	Pine Ridge, Winnipeg, MB	Jon Mills	275 (-9)
Telus Edmonton Open	Windermere, Edmonton AB	Rob Johnson (USA)	273 (-11)
Victoria Open	Royal Colwood, Victoria, BC	Patrick Damron (USA)	269 (-11)
Greater Vancouver Classic	Swan-e-set Bay, Vancouver, BC	James Lepp (Can) (am)	269 (-19)
Lewis Chitengwa Memorial Championship	Stoney Creek, Wintergreen VA	Nick Watney	268 (-20)
Bay Mills Open Players Championship	Wild Bluff, Brimley, MI	Rodney Butcher	278 (-10)
Casino de Charlesvoix Cup	Le Manoir Richelieu, Pointe-au-Pic	Bryn Parry and Alex Rocha	

Final Order of Merit 2003

1	Jon Mills	CAN$55,321	21	Jim Salinetti (USA)	18,782
2	Rob Johnson (USA)	54,164	22	Jason Enloe (USA)	18,275
3	Derek Gillespie	47,844	23	Stephen Woodard (USA)	17,792
4	Mark Johnson (USA)	47,451	24	Bryan DeCorso	17,591
5	Michael Harris (USA)	47,012	25	Matt Bettencourt (USA)	17,356
6	Mario Tiziani (USA)	44,260	26	Kris Mikkelsen (USA)	16,766
7	Chris Wall (USA)	41,356	27	Paul Devenport, Paul (NZ)	16,759
8	Anders Hultman (Swe)	38,926	28	Wes Martin	16,712
9	Patrick Damron (USA)	38,120	29	Conrad Ray (USA)	15,707
10	David McKenzie (Aus)	36,804	30	Clint Jensen (USA)	15,525
11	Brad Sutterfield (USA)	33,361	31	Josh Habig (USA)	15,396
12	Erik Compton (USA)	32,012	32	Dustin Risdon	15,174
13	Robert Hamilton (USA)	31,926	33	Darren Griff	14,935
14	Alex Quiroz (Mex)	26,487	34	Jim Lemon (USA)	14,928
15	Lee Williamson (USA)	26,461	35	Bryan Wright (USA)	13,809
16	David Hearn	24,860	36	Craig Kanada (USA)	13,505
17	Dave Christensen (USA)	23,527	37	Roger Tambellini (USA)	13,500
18	Chris Wisler (USA)	20,430	38	Doug McGuigan	12,751
19	Alan McLean (RSA)	19,918	39	Craig Matthew	12,462
20	Tony Carolan (Aus)	19,640	40	Wes Heffernan	11,479

Tour de las Americas

Results 2002–2003

Medellin Open	El Rodeo, Medellin, Colombia	Jesus Amaya (Col)*	280 (-8)
Serrezuela Masters	Serrezuela, Bogota, Colombia	Jesus Amaya (Col)	275 (-13)
Venezuela Open	Lagunita, Caracas, Venezuela	Jesus Amaya (Col)	266 (-14)
Argentine Open	Hurlingham, Buenos Aires, Argentina	Angel Cabrera	269 (-11)
Caribbean Open	Our Lucaya, Freeport, Bahamas	Rafael Gomez (Arg)	275 (-13)
Samsung Panama Open	Coronado, Panama	Charles Warren (USA)	278 (-10)
Cable and Wireless Master Panama	Summit, Panama	Andres Romero (Arg)	274 (-14)
Costa Rica Open	Cariari, San Jose	Sebastian Fernandez (Arg)*	278 (-6)
Telefonica CA Guatemala Open	Hacienda Nueva, Guatemala	Daniel Vancsik (Arg)*	274 (-10)
American Express Open	Toluca, Mexico	James Hepworth (Eng)	275 (-13)
Acapulca Fest Invitational		Octavio Gonzalez (Mex)	263 (-17)

Final Ranking 2002–2003

1	Juan Abbate (Arg)	US$33,691	11	Rodolfo Gonzalez (Arg)	9,207
2	Sebastian Fernandez (Arg)	21,505	12	Octavio Gonzalez (Mex)	9,000
3	Daniel Vancsik (Arg)	21,199	13	Alex Balicki (Fra)	8,730
4	Rafael Gomez (Arg)	21,166	14	Francesco Guermani (Ita)	8,600
5	Cesar Monasterio (Arg)	15,274	15	Richard Terga (USA)	8,170
6	Pedro Martinez (Par)	15,184	16	Andres Romero (Arg)	8,080
7	Jose Trauwitz (Mex)	14,258	17	Gustavo Mendoza (Col)	7,994
8	Julio Zapata (Arg)	12,088	18	Eduardo Argiro (Arg)	7,674
9	Miguel Fernandez (Arg)	10,322	19	Raul Fretes (Par)	6,846
10	John Bloomfield (Jam)	9,994	20	Mauricio Molina (Arg)	6,499

Fixtures 2003–2004 (subject to alteration)

2003

Nations Cup [1]	Paradise Village, Nueva Vallarta, Mexico	Chile (Roy Mackenzie and Felipe Aguilar)	270
Serrezuela Masters	Serrezuela CC, Bogota, Colombia		
Abierto de Medellin Open	Club Campestre, Medellin, Colombia		
Abierto de Brasil	San Fernando GC		

2004

Caribbean Open	Our Lucaya, Freeport, Bahamas	Rafael Gomez	(D)
Panama Open	Coronado, Panama		
Venezuela Open	Caracas	Rafael Harcon	(D)
Panama Masters	Summit GC, Panama City	Pedro Martinez	(D)
Summit Masters	Summit GC, Panama City	Rafael Gomez	(D)
Costa Rica Open	Valle del Sol GC, Santa Ana	Sebastian Fernandez	(D)
Telefonica de Centroamerica Abierti de Guatemala	Guatemala City	Daniel Vancsik	(D)
Brisas de Chicureo	Brisas de Chicureo		
Puerto Rico Open	San Juan, Puerto Rico		

[1] Full details on page 183

World Championship Events

Accenture Match Play Championship
(formerly Anderson Consulting Match Play Championship)

2000   Darren Clarke (NI) beat Tiger Woods (USA) 4 and 3 at La Costa, Carlsbad, CA, USA
2001   Steve Stricker (USA) beat Pierre Fulke (Swe) 4 and 3 at Metropolitan GC, Melbourne, Australia
2002   Kevin Sutherland (USA) beat Scott McCarron (USA) 1 hole at La Costa, Carlsbad, CA, USA

2003 *at La Costa, Carlsbad, CA, USA*   (7029–72)

First Round
Tiger Woods (USA) beat Carl Pettersson (Swe) 2 and 1
Choi Kyung-ju (Kor) beat Fred Funk (USA) 1 hole
Justin Leonard (USA) beat José María Olazábal (Esp) 2 holes
Stephen Leaney (Aus) beat Bob Estes (USA) 2 and 1
Padraig Harrington (Irl) beat John Cook (USA) 4 and 3
Scott Hoch (USA) beat Tom Lehman (USA) 3 and 1
Toshimitsu Izawa (Jpn) beat Chris DiMarco (USA) 2 and 1
Eduardo Romero (Arg) beat John Huston (USA) 2 and 1

Jay Haas (USA) beat Retief Goosen (RSA) 5 and 3
Shigeki Maruyama (Jpn) beat Scott McCarron (USA) 4 and 3
Nick Price (Zim) beat Paul Lawrie (Sco) 4 and 3
Niclas Fasth (Swe) beat Charles Howell III (USA) 1 hole
Kevin Sutherland (USA) beat Sergio García (Esp) 2 and 1
Justin Rose (Eng) beat David Duval (USA) at 20th
Rocco Mediate (USA) beat Shingo Katayama (Jpn) 1 hole
Adam Scott (Aus) beat Bernhard Langer (Ger) 3 and 2

Phil Tataurangi (NZ) beat Ernie Els (RSA) at 20th
Peter Lonard (Aus) beat Kenny Perry (USA) 2 and 1
Robert Allenby (Aus) beat Trevor Immelman (RSA) 4 and 2
Jeff Sluman (USA) beat Michael Campbell (NZ) 3 and 2
Davis Love III (USA) beat Paul Casey (Eng) 5 and 4
Darren Clarke (NI) beat Tim Clark (RSA) 4 and 3
Jim Furyk (USA) beat Len Mattiace (USA) 2 and 1
Steve Lowery (USA) beat Rich Beem (USA) 2 holes

Phil Mickelson (USA) beat Robert Karlsson (Swe) 1 hole
Brad Faxon (USA) beat Craig Parry (Aus) 2 and 1
Mike Weir (Can) beat Loren Roberts (USA) at 26th
Jerry Kelly (USA) beat Thomas Bjørn (Den) 5 and 4
David Toms (USA) beat Anders Hansen (Den) 3 and 1
Chris Riley (USA) beat Stuart Appleby (Aus) 1 hole
Alex Cejka (Ger) beat Colin Montgomerie (Sco) 4 and 2
Angel Cabrera (Arg) beat Scott Verplank (USA) 3 and 2

Second Round
Woods beat Choi 4 and 3
Leaney beat Leonard 6 and 5
Hoch beat Harrington 3 and 2
Izawa beat Romero 3 and 1
Haas beat Maruyama 1 hole
Price beat Fasth 2 and 1
Sutherland beat Rose 1 hole
Scott beat Mediate 1 hole
Lonard beat Tataurangi 5 and 4
Allenby beat Sluman 1 hole
Clarke beat Love 7 and 6
Furyk beat Lowery 6 and 5
Mickelson beat Faxon 3 and 2
Kelly beat Weir 2 and 1
Toms beat Riley 1 hole
Cejka beat Cabrera 4 and 2

Third Round
Woods beat Leaney 7 and 6
Hoch beat Izawa 4 and 3
Haas beat Price at 20th
Scott beat Sutherland 2 and 1
Lonard beat Allenby 1 hole
Clarke beat Furyk 1 hole

Kelly beat Mickelson 3 and 2
Toms beat Cejkz 4 and 3

Quarter-finals
Woods beat Hoch 5 and 4
Scott beat Haas 2 and 1
Lonard beat Clarke 2 holes
Toms beat Kelly 4 and 3

Semi-finals
Woods beat Scott at 19th
Toms beat Lonard 1 hole

Final (36 holes)
Tiger Woods beat David Toms 2 and 1

Consolation Match
Adam Scott beat Peter Lonard 1 hole

Winner:	$1050000	€973394
Runner-up:	$600000	556225
3rd place:	$480000	444980
4th place:	$390,000	361546
QF:	$200000	185408
3rd round:	$95000	88069
2nd round:	$60000	55622
1st round:	$30000	27811

NEC Invitational

1999	T Woods (USA)	66-71-62-71—270	at Firestone CC, Akron, OH
2000	T Woods (USA)	64-61-67-67—259	at Firestone CC, Akron, OH
2001	T Woods (USA)	66-67-66-69—268	at Firestone CC, Akron, OH
2002	C Parry (Aus)	72-65-66-65—268	at Sahalee, Redmond, WA

2003 *at Firestone CC (South Course), Akron, OH*   (7283–70)

1	Darren Clarke (NI)	65-70-66-67—268	$1050000
2	Jonathan Kaye (USA)	68-69-65-70—272	550000
3	Davis Love III (USA)	66-70-68-69—273	360000
4	Chris Riley (USA)	66-67-70-71—274	235000
	Tiger Woods (USA)	65-72-67-70—274	235000
6	Robert Allenby (Aus)	69-69-68-69—275	163333
	Jim Furyk (USA)	69-69-68-69—275	163333
	Vijay Singh (Fij)	69-65-72-69—275	163333
9	Brad Faxon (USA)	68-67-70-71—276	116750
	Trevor Immelman (RSA)	70-68-70-68—276	116750
11	Steve Flesch (USA)	71-67-67-72—277	91667
	Dan Forsman (USA)	69-68-70-70—277	91667
	Bernhard Langer (Ger)	71-73-65-68—277	91667
14	Fred Funk (USA)	72-62-72-72—278	75000
	Toshimitsu Izawa (Jpn)	70-71-68-69—278	75000
	Peter Jacobsen (USA)	73-64-71-70—278	75000
17	Paul Casey (Eng)	72-66-71-70—279	59250
	Ernie Els (RSA)	67-70-71-71—279	59250
	Retief Goosen (RSA)	67-69-69-74—279	59250
	Jay Haas (USA)	72-69-73-65—279	59250
21	Fred Couples (USA)	67-71-71-71—280	52500
	Charles Howell III (USA)	72-68-74-66—280	52500
23	Angel Cabrera (Arg)	70-71-70-70—281	48000
	Justin Leonard (USA)	75-69-69-68—281	48000
	Peter Lonard (Aus)	70-73-72-66—281	48000
	Shaun Micheel (USA)	71-69-70-71—281	48000

NEC Invitational *continued*

23T	Phil Mickelson (USA)	68-73-70-70—281	48000
	Colin Montgomerie (Sco)	68-70-70-73—281	48000
	Mike Weir (Can)	71-72-69-69—281	48000
30	Ben Curtis (USA)	64-76-72-70—282	43000
	Sergio García (Esp)	64-76-69-73—282	43000
	Len Mattiace (USA)	72-69-69-72—282	43000
33	Chris DiMarco (USA)	71-68-73-71—283	38583
	Ian Poulter (Eng)	73-68-67-75—283	38583
	Eduardo Romero (Arg)	70-74-68-71—283	38583
	Justin Rose (Eng)	72-73-69-69—283	38583
	Hal Sutton (USA)	68-69-68-78—283	38583
	David Toms (USA)	66-67-76-74—283	38583
39	Paul Azinger (USA)	72-69-67-76—284	35500
	Padraig Harrington (Irl)	73-71-70-70—284	35500
	Jeff Sluman (USA)	67-74-75-68—284	35500
42	Alex Cejka (Ger)	72-68-71-74—285	33750
	Ben Crane (USA)	71-75-68-71—285	33750
	Robert-Jan Derksen (Ned)	73-70-70-72—285	33750
	Nick Price (Zim)	73-67-71-74—285	33750
46	Stephen Allan (Aus)	74-68-76-68—286	31500
	Stuart Appleby (Aus)	70-75-68-73—286	31500
	Bob Estes (USA)	68-74-70-74—286	31500
	Scott Verplank (USA)	66-73-70-77—286	31500
	Lee Westwood (Eng)	70-70-73-73—286	31500
51	Rory Sabbatini (RSA)	73-72-70-72—287	29750
	Scott Hoch (USA)	69-72-72-74—287	29750
53	Mark Calcavecchia (USA)	70-68-73-77—288	28150
	Chad Campbell (USA)	73-71-72-72—288	28150
	Choi Kyoung-Ju (Kor)	73-71-71-73—288	28150
	Jerry Kelly (USA)	68-71-76-73—288	28150
	Kenny Perry (USA)	72-76-68-72—288	28150
58	Niclas Fasth (Swe)	67-76-74-72—289	27000
	Paul McGinley (Irl)	70-71-73-75—289	27000
	Kaname Yokoo (Jpn)	73-71-70-75—289	27000
61	Thomas Bjørn (Den)	72-72-75-71—290	26250
	Stewart Cink (USA)	70-71-74-75—290	26250
	Philip Golding (Eng)	76-69-73-72—290	26250
64	Tim Clark (RSA)	73-69-73-76—291	25500
	Craig Parry (Aus)	69-75-71-76—291	25500
	Adam Scott (Aus)	72-70-69-80—291	25500
67	Rich Beem (USA)	69-69-78-76—292	24625
	Pierre Fulke (Swe)	72-72-75-73—292	24625
	Phillip Price (Wal)	68-75-75-74—292	24625
	John Rollins (USA)	75-72-71-74—292	24625
71	Jonathan Byrd (USA)	71-77-73-72—293	23375
	Michael Campbell (NZ)	74-71-70-78—293	23375
	Stephen Leaney (Aus)	75-69-72-77—293	23375
	Kevin Na (Kor)	71-80-69-73—293	23375
	Jesper Parnevik (Swe)	69-72-75-77—293	23375
	Steen Tinning (Den)	71-74-76-72—293	23375
77	Bob Burns (USA)	74-70-75-75—294	22000
	Ignacio Garrido (Esp)	74-74-72-74—294	22000
	Robert Karlsson (Swe)	72-72-77-73—294	22000
	Rocco Mediate (USA)	78-73-69-74—294	22000
	Hennie Otto (RSA)	72-69-75-78—294	22000
82	Nick Faldo (Eng)	74-67-79-75—295	21125
	Jarrod Moseley (Aus)	76-74-72-73—295	21125
84	Fredrik Jacobson (Swe)	75-71-77-73—296	20750
85	Gene Sauers (USA)	73-76-77-82—308	20500

American Express Championship

1999	Tiger Woods* (USA)	71-69-70-68—278	at Valderrama GC, Cadiz, Spain
	(after play-off with Miguel Angel Jimenez)		
2000	Mike Weir (Can)	68-75-65-69—277	at Valderrama GC, Cadiz, Spain
2001	*Cancelled*		
2002	Tiger Woods (USA)	65-65-67-66—263	at Mount Juliet, Kilkenny, Ireland

2003 *at Capital City, Atlanta GA*   (7209–70)

1	Tiger Woods (USA)	67-66-69-72—274	$1050000
2	Stuart Appleby (Aus)	71-68-69-68—276	405000
	Tim Herron (USA)	66-72-67-71—276	405000
	Vijay Singh (Fij)	70-70-64-72—276	405000
5	David Toms (USA)	73-72-67-65—277	235000
6	Choi Kyoung-ju (Kor)	67-71-68-73—279	182500
	Padraig Harrington (Irl)	71-73-69-66—279	182500
8	Paul Casey (Eng)	73-71-66-71—281	137500
	Retief Goosen (RSA)	73-69-67-72—281	137500
10	Fred Couples (USA)	71-73-70-68—282	111250
	Ignacio Garrido (Esp)	68-71-69-74—282	111250
12	Alec Cejka (Ger)	70-76-72-65—283	89375
	Ernie Els (RSA)	71-74-71-67—283	89375
	Jim Furyk (USA)	70-74-69-70—283	89375
	Sergio García (Esp)	65-73-70-75—283	89375
16	Niclas Fasth (Swe)	68-76-70-70—284	71000
	Brad Faxon (USA)	75-71-66-72—284	71000
	Rocco Mediate (USA)	66-72-73-73—284	71000
	Loren Roberts (USA)	69-75-70-70—284	71000
20	Jonathan Kaye (USA)	73-69-73-70—285	65000
21	Robert Allenby (Aus)	72-76-73-65—286	60000
	Steve Flesch (USA)	71-75-72-68—286	60000
	Charles Howell III (USA)	76-75-65-70—286	60000
	Jerry Kelly (USA)	70-72-69-75—286	60000
25	Bob Estes (USA)	77-74-68-68—287	53000
	Toshimitsu Izawa (Jpn)	70-74-72-71—287	53000
	Eduardo Romero (Arg)	72-74-68-73—287	53000
28	Thomas Bjørn (Den)	74-73-67-74—288	46071
	David Howell (Eng)	74-75-71-68—288	46071
	Fredrik Jacobson (Swe)	75-74-70-69—288	46071
	Kenny Perry (USA)	70-74-70-74—288	46071
	Chris Riley (USA)	74-73-70-71—288	46071
	Justin Rose (Eng)	75-69-74-70—288	46071
	Mike Weir (Can)	69-73-72-74—288	46071
35	Brian Davis (Eng)	71-77-68-73—289	41500
	Lee Westwood (Eng)	72-71-71-75—289	41500
37	Peter Lonard (Aus)	75-74-70-71—290	40000
38	Darren Clarke (NI)	69-82-72-68—291	38500
	Phil Mickelson (USA)	73-77-70-71—291	38500
40	Alastair Forsyth (Sco)	71-77-71-73—292	36250
	Fred Funk (USA)	73-74-69-76—292	36250
	Davis Love III (USA)	74-77-70-71—292	36250
	Adam Scott (Aus)	70-73-75-74—292	36250
44	Trevor Immelman (RSA)	70-77-71-75—293	34250
	Shaun Micheel (USA)	72-75-71-75—293	34250
	Peter O'Malley (Aus)	69-74-70-80—293	34250
	Ian Poulter (Eng)	73-74-68-78—293	34250
48	Arjun Atwal (Ind)	76-72-72-74—294	32500
	Hennie Otto (RSA)	76-73-73-72—294	32500
	Nick Price (Zim)	71-73-73-77—294	32500
51	Colin Montgomerie (Sco)	74-75-70-76—295	31083
	Taichi Teshima (Jpn)	77-75-70-73—295	31083
	Scott Verplank (USA)	75-75-68-77—295	31083
54	Jay Haas (USA)	74-72-75-75—296	30000
	Len Mattiace (USA)	70-74-74-78—296	30000
	Craig Parry (Aus)	76-72-75-73—296	30000

American Express Challenge *continued*

54T	Phillip Price (Wal)	70-79-72-75—296	30000
	Jyoti Randhawa (Ind)	69-77-74-76—296	30000
59	Rich Beem (USA)	76-75-73-73—297	28625
	Chad Campbell (USA)	74-76-73-74—297	28625
	Raphaèl Jacquelin (Fra)	77-80-68-72—297	28625
	Søren Kjeldsen (Den)	70-75-74-78—297	28625
	JL Lewis (USA)	72-74-77-74—297	28625
	Bob Tway (USA)	73-80-70-74—297	28625
65	Kirk Triplett (USA)	74-72-70-82—298	27750
66	Ben Curtis (USA)	76-76-72-75—299	27375
	Thongchai Jaidee (Tha)	73-72-72-82—299	27375
68	Michael Campbell (NZ)	82-76-75-67—300	26875
	Mark Foster (Eng)	76-77-73-74—300	26875
70	Chris DiMarco (USA)	76-74-76-75—301	26375
	Scott Hoch (USA)	75-79-75-72—301	26375
72	Todd Hamilton (USA)	78-81-72-71—302	26000

World Cup of Golf (Known as the Canada Cup until 1966)

Year	Winner	Runners-up	Venue	Score
1953	Argentina	Canada	Montreal	287
	(A Cerda and R De Vincenzo)	(S Leonard and B Kerr)		
	(Individual: A Cerda, Argentina, 140)			
1954	Australia	Argentina	Laval-Sur-Lac	556
	(P Thomson and K Nagle)	(A Cerda and R De Vincenzo)		
	(Individual: S Leonard, Canada, 275)			
1955	United States	Australia	Washington	560
	(C Harbert and E Furgol)	(P Thomson and K Nagle)		
	(Individual: E Furgol, USA, after a play-off with P Thomson and F van Donck, 279)			
1956	United States	South Africa	Wentworth	567
	(B Hogan and S Snead)	(A Locke and G Player)		
	(Individual: B Hogan, USA, 277)			
1957	Japan	United States	Tokyo	557
	(T Nakamura and K Ono)	(S Snead and J Demaret)		
	(Individual: T Nakamura, Japan, 274)			
1958	Ireland	Spain	Mexico City	579
	(H Bradshaw and C O'Connor)	(A Miguel and S Miguel)		
	(Individual: A Miguel, Spain, after a play-off with H Bradshaw, 286)			
1959	Australia	United States	Melbourne	563
	(P Thomson and K Nagle)	(S Snead and C Middlecoff)		
	(Individual: S Leonard, Canada, 275, after a tie with P Thomson, Australia)			
1960	United States	England	Portmarnock	565
	(S Snead and A Palmer)	(H Weetman and B Hunt)		
	(Individual: F van Donck, Belgium, 279)			
1961	United States	Australia	Puerto Rico	560
	(S Snead and J Demaret)	(P Thomson and K Nagle)		
	(Individual: S Snead, USA, 272)			
1962	United States	Argentina	Buenos Aires	557
	(S Snead and A Palmer)	(F de Luca and R De Vicenzo)		
	(Individual: R De Vicenzo, Argentina, 276)			
1963	United States	Spain	St Nom-La-Breteche	482
	(A Palmer and J Nicklaus)	(S Miguel and R Sota)		
	(Individual: J Nicklaus, USA, 237 [63 holes])			
1964	United States	Argentina	Maui, Hawaii	554
	(A Palmer and J Nicklaus)	(R De Vicenzo and L Ruiz)		
	(Individual: J Nicklaus, USA, 276)			
1965	South Africa	Spain	Madrid	571
	(G Player and H Henning)	(A Miguel and R Sota)		
	(Individual: G Player, South Africa, 281)			
1966	United States	South Africa	Tokyo	548
	(J Nicklaus and A Palmer)	(G Player and H Henning)		
	(Individual: G Knudson, Canada, and H Sugimoto, Japan, each 272; Knudson won play-off)			
1967	United States	New Zealand	Mexico City	557
	(J Nicklaus and A Palmer)	(R Charles and W Godfrey)		
	(Individual: A Palmer, USA, 276)			
1968	Canada	United States	Olgiata, Rome	569
	(A Balding and G Knudson)	(J Boros and L Trevino)		
	(Individual: A Balding, Canada, 274)			

Year	Winner	Runners-up	Venue	Score
1969	United States (O Moody and L Trevino) (Individual: L Trevino, USA, 275)	Japan (T Kono and H Yasuda)	Singapore	552
1970	Australia (B Devlin and D Graham) (Individual: R De Vicenzo, Argentina, 269)	Argentina (R De Vicenzo and V Fernandez)	Buenos Aires	545
1971	United States (J Nicklaus and L Trevino) (Individual: J Nicklaus, USA, 271)	South Africa (H Henning and G Player)	Palm Beach, Florida	555
1972	Taiwan (H Min-Nan and LL Huan) (Individual: H Min-Nan, Taiwan, 217 [3 rounds only])	Japan (T Kono and T Murakami)	Melbourne	438
1973	United States (J Nicklaus and J Miller) (Individual: J Miller, USA, 277)	South Africa (G Player and H Baiocchi)	Marbella, Spain	558
1974	South Africa (R Cole and D Hayes) (Individual: R Cole, South Africa, 271)	Japan (I Aoki and M Ozaki)	Caracas	554
1975	United States (J Miller and L Graham) (Individual: J Miller, USA, 275)	Taiwan (H Min-Nan and KC Hsiung)	Bangkok	554
1976	Spain (S Ballesteros and M Pinero) (Individual: EP Acosta, Mexico, 282)	United States (J Pate and D Stockton)	Palm Springs	574
1977	Spain (S Ballesteros and A Garrido) (Individual: G Player, South Africa, 289)	Philippines (R Lavares and B Arda)	Manila, Philippines	591
1978	United States (J Mahaffey and A North) (Individual: J Mahaffey, USA, 281)	Australia (G Norman and W Grady)	Hawaii	564
1979	United States (J Mahaffey and H Irwin) (Individual: H Irwin, USA, 285)	Scotland (A Lyle and K Brown)	Glyfada, Greece	575
1980	Canada (D Halldorson and J Nelford) (Individual: A Lyle, Scotland, 282)	Scotland (A Lyle and S Martin)	Bogota	572
1981	*Not played*			
1982	Spain (M Pinero and JM Canizares) (Individual: M Pinero, Spain, 281)	United States (B Gilder and B Clampett)	Acapulco	563
1983	United States (R Caldwell and J Cook) (Individual: D Barr, Canada, 276)	Canada (D Barr and J Anderson)	Pondok Inah, Jakarta	565
1984	Spain (JM Canizares and J Rivero) (Individual: JM Canizares, Spain, 205. Played over 54 holes due to storm)	Scotland (S Torrance and G Brand Jr)	Olgiata, Rome	414
1985	Canada (D Halidorson and D Barr) (Individual: H Clark, England, 272)	England (H Clark and P Way)	La Quinta, Calif.	559
1986	*Not played*			
1987	Wales (won play-off) (I Woosnam and D Llewelyn) (Individual: I Woosnam, Wales, 274)	Scotland (S Torrance and A Lyle)	Kapalua, Hawaii	574
1988	United States (B Crenshaw and M McCumber) (Individual: B Crenshaw, USA, 275)	Japan (T Ozaki and M Ozaki)	Royal Melbourne, Australia	560
1989	Australia (P Fowler and W Grady) (Individual: P Fowler. Played over 36 holes due to storms.)	Spain (JM Olazábal and JM Canizares)	Las Brisas, Spain	278
1990	Germany (B Langer and T Giedeon) (Individual: P Stewart, USA, 271)	T England (M James and R Boxall) Ireland (R Rafferty and D Feherty)	Grand Cypress Resort, Orlando, Florida	556
1991	Sweden (A Forsbrand and P-U Johansson) (Individual: I Woosnam, Wales, 273)	Wales (I Woosnam and P Price)	La Querce, Rome	563
1992	USA (F Couples and D Love III) (Individual: B Ogle, Australia, 270 after a tie with I Woosnam, Wales)	Sweden (A Forsbrand and P-U Johansson)	La Moraleja II, Madrid, Spain	548
1993	USA (F Couples and D Love III) (Individual: B Langer, Germany, 272)	Zimbabwe (N Price and M McNulty)	Lake Nona, Orlando, FL	556
1994	USA (F Couples and D Love III) (Individual: F Couples, USA, 265)	Zimbabwe (M McNulty and T Johnstone)	Dorado Beach, Puerto Rico	536

World Cup of Golf continued

Year	Winner	Runners-up	Venue	Score
1995	USA	Australia	Mission Hills, Shenzhen,	543
	(F Couples and D Love III)	(B Ogle and R Allenby)	China	
	(Individual: D Love III, USA, 267)			
1996	South Africa	USA	Erinvale, Cape Town	547
	(E Els and W Westner)	(T Lehman and S Jones)	South Africa	
	(Individual: E Els, S. Africa, 272)			
1997	Ireland	Scotland	Kiawah Island, SC	545
	(P Harrington and P McGinley)	(C Montgomerie and R Russell)		
	(Individual: C Montgomerie, Scotland, 266)			
1998	England	Italy	Gulf Harbour, Auckland	568
	(N Faldo and D Carter)	(C Rocca and M Florioli)	New Zealand	
	(Individual: Scott Verplank, USA, 279)			
1999	USA	Spain	The Mines Resort, KL	545
	(T Woods and M O'Meara)	(S Luna and MA Martin)	Malaysia	
	(Individual: Tiger Woods, USA, 263)			
2000	USA	Argentina	Buenos Aires GC	254
	(T Woods and D Duval)	(A Cabrera & E Romero)	Argentina	
2001	South Africa	New Zealand	The Taiheiyo Club,	254
	(E Els and R Goosen)	(Michael Campbell and David Smail)	Japan	
		USA		
		(David Duval and Tiger Woods)		
		Denmark		
		(Thomas Bjørn and Søren Hansen)		
2002	Japan	USA	Puerto Vallarta, Mexico	252
	(S Maruyama and T Izawa)	(P Mickelson and D Toms)		

2003 at The Ocean Course, Kiawah Island, SC   (7296–72)

			per player
1	South Africa (Trevor Immelman and Rory Sabbatini)	70-69-63-73—275	$700,000
2	England (Justin Rose and Paul Casey)	73-73-66-67—279	350,000
3	France (Thomas Levet and Raphaël Jacquelin)	69-72-68-71—280	200,000
4	Germany (Alex Cejka and Marcel Siem)	67-77-67-71—282	100,000
5	USA (Jim Furyk and Justin Leonard)	71-70-68-75—284	67,500
	Ireland (Paul McGinley and Padraig Harrington)	74-77-66-67—284	67,500
7	Japan (Shigeki Maruyama and Hidemichi Tanaka)	74-71-71-69—285	51,250
	Sweden (Niclas Fasth and Fredrik Jacobson)	72-72-67-74—285	51,250
9	Paraguay (Carlos Franco and Marco Ruiz)	70-75-70-71—286	35,833
	Scotland (Paul Lawrie and Alastair Forsyth)	71-73-68-74—286	35,833
	South Korea (KJ Choi and SK Ho)	71-75-71-69—286	35,833
12	Wales (Ian Woosnam and Bradley Dredge)	68-74-71-75—288	30,000
13	Argentina (Eduardo Romero and Angel Cabrera)	70-73-70-76—289	27,500
14	Spain (Miguel Angel Jimenez and Ignacio Garrido)	71-75-66-81—293	25,000
15	Trinidad and Tobago (Stephen Ames and Robert Ames)	75-81-67-71—294	24,000
	Australia (Stuart Appleby and Stephen Leaney)	72-76-71-75—294	24,000
	New Zealand (Michael Campbell and David Smail)	71-74-72-77—294	24,000
18	Mexico (Alejandro Quiroz and Antonio Maldonado)	71-78-70-79—298	23,000
19	Denmark (Anders Hansen and Søren Kjeldsen)	72-84-72-73—301	22,500
20	Myanmar (Kyi Hla Han and Aung Win)	72-83-73-74—302	22,000
21	Hong Kong (Derek Fung and James Stewart)	76-80-69-78—303	21,500
22	India (Gaurav Ghei and Digvijay Singh)	81-83-70-70—304	21,000
23	Thailand (Jamnian Chitprasong and Pornsakon Tipsanit)	76-78-76-84—314	20,500

Chile (Roy MacKenzie and Felipe Aguilar) did not finish because of injury to Felipe Aguilar

World Cup qualifiers (Nations Cup tournaments at Singapore and Mexico) can be found on page 183.

Other International Events

Hassan II Trophy

1971	O Moody (USA)	1981	B Eastwood (USA)	1995	N Price (Zim)
1972	R Cerrudo (USA)	1982	F Connor (USA)	1996	I Garrido (Esp)
1973	W Casper (USA)	1983	R Streck (USA)	1997	C Montgomerie (Sco)
1974	L Ziegler (USA)	1984	R Maltbie (USA)	1998	S Luna (Esp)
1975	W Casper (USA)	1985	K Green (USA)	1999	D Toms (USA)*
1976	S Balbuena (USA)	1986–90	*Not played*	2000	R Chapman (Eng)
1977	L Trevino (USA)	1991	V Singh (Fij)	2001	J Haegmann (Swe)
1978	P Townsend (Eng)	1992	P Stewart (USA)	2002	Santiago Luna (Esp)
1979	M Brannan (USA)	1993	P Stewart (USA)		
1980	E Sneed (USA)	1994	M Gates (Eng)		

2003 event not yet played

Nedbank Golf Challenge *at Sun City, Bophutatswana, South Africa* (7597–72)

1982 (Jan)	J Miller (USA)	277	1990	D Frost (RSA)	284	1998	N Price* (Zim)	273
1982 (Dec)	R Floyd (USA)	280	1991	B Langer (Ger)	272	1999	E Els (RSA)	263
1983	S Ballesteros (Esp)	274	1992	D Frost (RSA)	276	2000	E Els (RSA)	268
1984	S Ballesteros (Esp)	279	1993	N Price (Zim)	264	2001	S García* (Esp)	268
1985	B Langer (Ger)	278	1994	N Faldo (Eng)	272	2002	E Els (RSA)	267
1986	M McNulty (Zim)	282	1995	C Pavin (USA)	276			
1987	I Woosnam (Wal)	274	1996	C Montgomerie				
1988	F Allem (RSA)	278		(Sco)	274			
1989	D Frost (RSA)	276	1997	N Price (Zim)	275			

2003 event being played November 20–23

Tiger Woods Sets Records

Tiger Woods ended the 2003 professional golf season without a major championship, but headed to the 'off-season' with two additional records in his pocket. He captured an unprecedented fifth straight PGA Player of the Year Award and Vardon Trophy.

Tiger concluded the year with 88 points, while Vijay Singh – the season's top money-winner – finished with 78 points in a tie for second with Masters Champion Mike Weir. Woods' winning total was based on five tournament wins worth 50 points, 20 points for capturing the Vardon Trophy and 18 points for finishing second in money earnings.

Four-event winner Davis Love III finished fourth in the PGA Player of the Year race with 74 points. US Open Champion Jim Furyk was fifth with 66.

Woods tied Tom Watson with a record six career PGA Player of the Year titles and tied Billy Casper and Lee Trevino with five career Vardon Trophies. Woods completed his season with a 68.41 adjusted scoring average through 68 rounds, his second lowest adjusted average since finishing with a record 67.79 in 2000.

Singh was runner-up at 68.65 based on 102 rounds, Weir was third at 68.97 based on 75 rounds and Ernie Els fourth at 68.99 through 60 rounds.

Since joining the PGA Tour in 1996, Woods has won PGA Player of the Year honours in 1997, 1999, 2000, 2001, 2002 and 2003. He has won the Vardon Trophy – which showcases a player's adjusted scoring average – every year since 1999.

International Team Events

Ryder Cup

Great Britain v USA

1921 *at Gleneagles*
Result: GBI 10½, USA 4½

1926 *at Wentworth*
Result: GBI 13½, USA 1½
Singles
Abe Mitchell beat Jim Barnes 8 and 7
George Duncan beat Walter Hagen 6 and 5
Aubrey Boomer beat Tommy Armour 2 and 1
Archie Compston lost to Bill Mehlhorn 1 hole
George Gadd beat Joe Kirkwood 8 and 7
Ted Ray beat Al Watrous 6 and 5
Fred Robson beat Cyril Walker 5 and 4
Arthur Havers beat Fred McLeod 10 and 9
Ernest Whitcombe halved with Emmett French
Herbert Jolly beat Joe Stein 3 and 2
Foursomes
Mitchell & Duncan beat Barnes & Hagen 9 and 8
Boomer & Compston beat Armour & Kirkwood 3 and 2
Gadd & Havers beat Mehlhorn & Watrous 3 and 2
Ray & Robson beat Walker & McLeod 3 and 2
Whitcombe & Jolly beat French & Stein 3 and 2

RYDER CUP – Inaugurated 1927

1927 *at Worcester, MA*
Result: USA 9½, GBI 2½
Captains: W Hagen (USA), E Ray (GBI)
Foursomes
Hagen & Golden beat Ray & Robson 2 and 1
Farrell & Turnesa beat Duncan & Compston 8 and 6
Sarazen & Watrous beat Havers & Jolly 3 and 2
Diegel & Mehlhorn lost to Boomer & Whitcombe 7 and 5
Singles
Bill Mehlhorn beat Archie Compston 1 hole
Johnny Farrell beat Aubrey Boomer 5 and 4
Johnny Golden beat Herbert Jolly 8 and 7
Leo Diegel beat Ted Ray 7 and 5
Gene Sarazen halved with Charles Whitcombe
Walter Hagen beat Arthur Havers 2 and 1
Al Watrous beat Fred Robson 3 and 2
Joe Turnesa lost to George Duncan 1 hole

1929 *at Moortown*
Result: GBI 7, USA 5
Captains: George Duncan (GBI),
Walter Hagen (USA)
Foursomes
C Whitcombe & Compston halved with Farrell &
Turnesa
Boomer & Duncan lost to Diegel & Espinosa 7 and 5

Mitchell & Robson beat Sarazen & Dudley 2 and 1
E Whitcombe & Cotton lost to Golden & Hagen 2 holes
Singles
Charles Whitcombe beat Johnny Farrell 8 and 6
George Duncan beat Walter Hagen 10 and 8
Abe Mitchell lost to Leo Diegel 9 and 8
Archie Compston beat Gene Sarazen 6 and 4
Aubrey Boomer beat Joe Turnesa 4 and 3
Fred Robson lost to Horton Smith 4 and 2
Henry Cotton beat Al Watrous 4 and 3
Ernest Whitcombe halved with Al Espinosa

1931 *at Scioto, Columbus, OH*
Result: USA 9, GBI 3
Captains: Walter Hagen (USA),
Charles Whitcombe (GBI)
Foursomes
Sarazen & Farrell beat Compston & Davies 8 and 7
Hagen & Shute beat Duncan & Havers 10 and 9
Diegel & Espinosa lost to Mitchell & Robson 3 and 1
Burke & Cox beat Easterbrook & E Whitcombe 3 and 2
Singles
Billy Burke beat Archie Compston 7 and 6
Gene Sarazen beat Fred Robson 7 and 6
Johnny Farrell lost to William H Davies 4 and 3
Wilfred Cox beat Abe Mitchell 3 and 1
Walter Hagen beat Charles Whitcombe 4 and 3
Densmore Shute beat Bert Hodson 8 and 6
Al Espinosa beat Ernest Whitcombe 2 and 1
Craig Wood lost to Arthur Havers 4 and 3

1933 *at Southport & Ainsdale*
Result: GBI 6½, USA 5½
Captains: JH Taylor (GBI), Walter Hagen (USA)
Foursomes
Alliss & Whitcombe halved with Sarazen & Hagen
Mitchell & Havers beat Dutra & Shute 3 and 2
Davies & Easterbrook beat Wood & Runyan 1 hole
Padgham & Perry lost to Dudley & Burke 1 hole
Singles
Alf Padgham lost to Gene Sarazen 6 and 4
Abe Mitchell beat Olin Dutra 9 and 8
Arthur Lacey lost to Walter Hagen 2 and 1
William H Davies lost to Craig Wood 4 and 3
Percy Alliss beat Paul Runyan 2 and 1
Arthur Havers beat Leo Diegel 4 and 3
Syd Easterbrook beat Densmore Shute 1 hole
Charles Whitcombe lost to Horton Smith 2 and 1

1935 *at Ridgewood, NJ*
Result: USA 9, GBI 3
Captains: Walter Hagen (USA),
Charles Whitcombe (GBI)
Foursomes
Sarazen & Hagen beat Perry & Busson 7 and 6
Picard & Revolta beat Padgham & Alliss 6 and 5

Runyan & Smith beat Cox & Jarman 9 and 8
Dutra & Laffoon lost to C Whitcombe & E Whitcombe
  1 hole

Singles
Gene Sarazen beat Jack Busson 3 and 2
Paul Runyon beat Dick Burton 5 and 3
Johnny Revolta beat Charles Whitcombe 2 and 1
Olin Dutra beat Alf Padgham 4 and 2
Craig Wood lost to Percy Alliss 1 hole
Horton Smith halved with Bill Cox
Henry Picard beat Ernest Whitcombe 3 and 2
Sam Parks halved with Alf Perry

1937 *at Southport & Ainsdale*
Result: USA 8, GBI 4
Captains: Charles Whitcombe (GBI),
  Walter Hagen (USA)

Foursomes
Padgham & Cotton lost to Dudley & Nelson 4 and 2
Lacey & Bill Cox lost to Guldahl & Manero 2 and 1
Whitcombe & Rees halved with Sarazen & Shute
Alliss & Burton beat Picard & Johnny Revolta 2 and 1

Singles
Alf Padgham lost to Ralph Guldahl 8 and 7
Sam King halved with Densmore Shute
Dai Rees beat Byron Nelson 3 and 1
Henry Cotton beat Tony Manero 5 and 3
Percy Alliss lost to Gene Sarazen 1 hole
Dick Burton lost to Sam Snead 5 and 4
Alf Perry lost to Ed Dudley 2 and 1
Arthur Lacey lost to Henry Picard 2 and 1

1947 *at Portland, OR*
Result: USA 11, GBI 1
Captains: Ben Hogan (USA),
  Henry Cotton (GBI)

Foursomes
Oliver & Worsham beat Cotton & Lees 10 and 9
Snead & Mangrum beat Daly & Ward 6 and 5
Hogan & Demaret beat Adams & Faulkner 2 holes
Nelson & Herman Barron beat Rees & King 2 and 1

Singles
Dutch Harrison beat Fred Daly 5 and 4
Lew Worsham beat Jimmy Adams 3 and 2
Lloyd Mangrum beat Max Faulkner 6 and 5
Ed Oliver beat Charlie Ward 4 and 3
Byron Nelson beat Arthur Lees 2 and 1
Sam Snead beat Henry Cotton 5 and 4
Jimmy Demaret beat Dai Rees 3 and 2
Herman Keiser lost to Sam King 4 and 3

1949 *at Ganton*
Result: USA 7, GBI 5
Captains: Charles Whitcombe (GBI),
  Ben Hogan (USA)

Foursomes
Faulkner & Adams beat Harrison & Palmer 2 and 1
Daly & Ken Bousfield beat Hamilton & Alexander 4 and 2
Ward & King lost to Demaret & Heafner 4 and 3
Burton & Lees beat Snead & Mangrum 1 hole

Singles
Max Faulkner lost to Dutch Harrison 8 and 7
Jimmy Adams beat Johnny Palmer 2 and 1
Charlie Ward lost to Sam Snead 6 and 5
Dai Rees beat Bob Hamilton 6 and 4
Dick Burton lost to Clayton Heafner 3 and 2
Sam King lost to Chick Harbert 4 and 3

Arthur Lees lost to Jimmy Demaret 7 and 6
Fred Daly lost to Lloyd Mangrum 1 hole

1951 *at Pinehurst, NC*
Result: USA 9½, GBI 2½
Captains: Sam Snead (USA), Arthur Lacey (GBI)

Foursomes
Heafner & Burke beat Faulkner & Rees 5 and 3
Oliver & Henry Ransom lost to Ward & Lees 2 and 1
Mangrum & Snead beat Adams & Panton 5 and 4
Hogan & Demaret beat Daly & Bousfield 5 and 4

Singles
Jack Burke beat Jimmy Adams 4 and 3
Jimmy Demaret beat Dai Rees 2 holes
Clayton Heafner halved with Fred Daly
Lloyd Mangrum beat Harry Weetman 6 and 5
Ed Oliver lost to Arthur Lees 2 and 1
Ben Hogan beat Charlie Ward 3 and 2
Skip Alexander beat John Panton 8 and 7
Sam Snead beat Max Faulkner 4 and 3

1953 *at Wentworth*
Result: USA 6½, GBI 5½
Captains: Henry Cotton (GBI),
  Lloyd Mangrum (USA)

Foursomes
Weetman & Alliss lost to Douglas & Oliver 2 and 1
Brown & Panton lost to Mangrum & Snead 8 and 7
Adams & Hunt lost to Kroll & Burke 7 and 5
Daly & Bradshaw beat Burkemo & Middlecoff 1 hole

Singles
Dai Rees lost to Jack Burke 2 and 1
Fred Daly beat Ted Kroll 9 and 7
Eric Brown beat Lloyd Mangrum 2 holes
Harry Weetman beat Sam Snead 1 hole
Max Faulkner lost to Cary Middlecoff 3 and 1
Peter Alliss lost to Jim Turnesa 1 hole
Bernard Hunt halved with Dave Douglas
Harry Bradshaw beat Fred Haas jr 3 and 2

1955 *at Palm Springs, CA*
Result: USA 8, GBI 4
Captains: Chick Harbert (USA),
  Dai Rees (GBI)

Foursomes
Harper & Barber lost to Fallon & Jacobs 1 hole
Ford & Kroll beat Brown & Scott 5 and 4
Burke & Bolt beat Lees & Weetman 1 hole
Snead & Middlecoff beat Rees & Bradshaw 3 and 2

Singles
Tommy Bolt beat Christy O'Connor 4 and 2
Chick Harbert beat Syd Scott 3 and 2
Cary Middlecoff lost to John Jacobs 1 hole
Sam Snead beat Dai Rees 3 and 1
Marty Furgol lost to Arthur Lees 3 and 1
Jerry Barber lost to Eric Brown 3 and 2
Jack Burke beat Harry Bradshaw 3 and 2
Doug Ford beat Harry Weetman 3 and 2

1957 *at Lindrick*
Result: GBI 7½, USA 4½
Captains: Dai Rees (GBI), Jack Burke (USA)

Foursomes
Alliss & Hunt lost to Ford & Finsterwald 2 and 1
Bousfield & Rees beat Art Wall jr & Hawkins 3 and 2

1957 *continued*

Faulkner & Weetman lost to Kroll & Burke 4 and 3
O'Connor & Brown lost to Mayer & Bolt 7 and 5
Singles
Eric Brown beat Tommy Bolt 4 and 3
Peter Mills beat Jack Burke 5 and 3
Peter Alliss lost to Fred Hawkins 2 and 1
Ken Bousfield beat Lionel Hebert 4 and 3
Dai Rees beat Ed Furgol 7 and 6
Bernard Hunt beat Doug Ford 6 and 5
Christy O'Connor beat Dow Finsterwald 7 and 6
Harry Bradshaw halved with Dick Mayer

1959 *at Palm Desert, CA*

Result: USA 8½, GBI 3½
Captains: Sam Snead (USA),
Dai Rees (GBI)
Foursomes
Rosburg & Souchak beat Hunt & Brown 5 and 4
Ford & Wall lost to O'Connor & Alliss 3 and 2
Boros & Finsterwald beat Rees & Bousfield
   2 holes
Snead & Middlecoff halved with Weetman & Thomas
Singles
Doug Ford halved with Norman Drew
Mike Souchak beat Ken Bousfield 3 and 2
Bob Rosburg beat Harry Weetman 6 and 5
Sam Snead beat Dave Thomas 6 and 5
Dow Finsterwald beat Dai Rees 1 hole
Jay Hebert halved with Peter Alliss
Art Wall jr beat Christy O'Connor 7 and 6
Cary Middlecoff lost to Eric Brown 4 and 3

1961 *at Royal Lytham & St Anne's*

Result: USA 14½, GBI 9½
Captains: Jerry Barber (USA),
Dai Rees (GBI)
First Day: **Foursomes – Morning**
O'Connor & Alliss beat Littler & Ford 4 and 3
Panton & Hunt lost to Wall & Hebert 4 and 3
Rees & Bousfield lost to Casper & Palmer 2 and 1
Haliburton & Coles lost to Souchak & Collins 1 hole
Foursomes – Afternoon
O'Connor & Alliss lost to Wall & Hebert 1 hole
Panton & Hunt lost to Casper & Palmer 5 and 4
Rees & Bousfield beat Souchak & Collins 4 and 2
Haliburton& Coles lost to Barber & Finsterwald
   1 hole
Second Day: **Singles – Morning**
Harry Weetman lost to Doug Ford 1 hole
Ralph Moffitt lost to Mike Souchak 5 and 4
Peter Alliss halved with Arnold Palmer
Ken Bousfield lost to Billy Casper 5 and 3
Dai Rees beat Jay Hebert 2 and 1
Neil Coles halved with Gene Littler
Bernard Hunt beat Jerry Barber 5 and 4
Christy O'Connor lost to Dow Finsterwald 2 and 1
Singles – Afternoon
Weetman lost to Wall 1 hole
Alliss beat Bill Collins 3 and 2
Hunt lost to Souchak 2 and 1
Tom Haliburton lost to Palmer 2 and 1
Rees beat Ford 4 and 3
Bousfield beat Barber 1 hole
Coles beat Finsterwald 1 hole
O'Connor halved with Littler

1963 *at Atlanta, GA*

Result: USA 23, GBI
Captains: Arnold Palmer (USA),
John Fallon (GBI)
First Day: **Foursomes – Morning**
Palmer & Pott lost to Huggett & Will 3 and 2
Casper & Ragan beat Alliss & O'Connor 1 hole
Boros & Lema halved with Coles & B Hunt
Littler & Finsterwald halved with Thomas & Weetman
Foursomes – Afternoon
Maxwell & Goalby beat Thomas & Weetman 4 and 3
Palmer & Casper beat Huggett & Will 5 and 4
Littler & Finsterwald beat Coles & G Hunt 2 and 1
Boros & Lema beat Haliburton & B Hunt 1 hole
Second Day: **Fourball – Morning**
Palmer & Finsterwald beat Huggett & Thomas
   5 and 4
Littler & Boros halved with Alliss & B Hunt
Casper & Maxwell beat Weetman & Will 3 and 2
Goalby & Ragan lost to Coles & O'Connor 1 hole
Fourball – Afternoon
Palmer & Finsterwald beat Coles & O'Connor 3 and 2
Lema & Pott beat Alliss & B Hunt 1 hole
Casper & Maxwell beat Haliburton & G Hunt 2 and 1
Goalby & Ragan halved with Huggett & Thomas
Third Day: **Singles – Morning**
Tony Lema beat Geoffrey Hunt 5 and 3
Johnny Pott lost to Brian Huggett 3 and 1
Arnold Palmer lost to Peter Alliss 1 hole
Billy Casper halved with Neil Coles
Bob Goalby beat Dave Thomas 3 and 2
Gene Littler lost to Tom Haliburton 6 and 5
Julius Boros lost to Harry Weetman 1 hole
Dow Finsterwald lost to Bernard Hunt 2 holes
Singles – Afternoon
Arnold Palmer beat George Will 3 and 2
Dave Ragan beat Neil Coles 2 and 1
Tony Lema halved with Peter Alliss
Gene Littler beat Tom Haliburton 6 and 5
Julius Boros beat Harry Weetman 2 and 1
Billy Maxwell beat Christy O'Connor 2 and 1
Dow Finsterwald beat Dave Thomas 4 and 3
Bob Goalby beat Bernard Hunt 2 and 1

1965 *at Royal Birkdale*

Result: GBI 12½, USA 19½
Captains: Harry Weetman (GBI),
Byron Nelson (USA)
First Day: **Foursomes – Morning**
Thomas & Will beat Marr & Palmer 6 and 5
O'Connor & Alliss beat Venturi & January 5 and 4
Platts & Butler lost to Boros & Lema 1 hole
Hunt & Coles lost to Casper & Littler 2 and 1
Foursomes – Afternoon
Thomas & Will lost to Marr & Palmer 6 and 5
Martin & Hitchcock lost to Boros & Lema 5 and 4
O'Connor & Alliss beat Casper & Littler 2 and 1
Hunt & Coles beat Venturi & January 3 and 2
Second Day: **Fourball – Morning**
Thomas & Will lost to January & Jacobs 1 hole
Platts & Butler halved with Casper & Littler
Alliss & O'Connor lost to Marr & Palmer 5 and 4
Coles & Hunt beat Boros & Lema 1 hole
Fourball – Afternoon
Alliss & O'Connor beat Marr & Palmer 1 hole
Thomas & Will lost to January & Jacobs 1 hole

Platts & Butler halved with Casper & Littler
Coles & Hunt lost to Lema & Venturi 1 hole

Third Day: Singles – Morning
Jimmy Hitchcock lost to Arnold Palmer 3 and 2
Lionel Platts lost to Julius Boros 4 and 2
Peter Butler lost to Tony Lema 1 hole
Neil Coles lost to Dave Marr 2 holes
Bernard Hunt beat Gene Littler 2 holes
Peter Alliss beat Billy Casper 1 hole
Dave Thomas lost to Tommy Jacobs 2 and 1
George Will halved with Don January

Singles – Afternoon
Butler lost to Palmer 2 holes
Hitchcock lost to Boros 2 and 1
Christy O'Connor lost to Lema 6 and 4
Alliss beat Ken Venturi 3 and 1
Hunt lost to Marr 1 hole
Coles beat Casper 3 and 2
Will lost to Littler 2 and 1
Platts beat Jacobs 1 hole

1967 at Houston, TX
Result: USA 23½, GBI 8½
*Captains: Ben Hogan (USA),
    Dai Rees (GBI)*
First Day: Foursomes – Morning
Casper & Boros halved with Huggett & Will
Palmer & Dickinson beat Alliss & O'Connor
    2 and 1
Sanders & Brewer lost to Jacklin & Thomas
    4 and 3
Nichols & Pott beat Hunt & Coles 6 and 5

Foursomes – Afternoon
Boros & Casper beat Huggett & Will 1 hole
Dickinson & Palmer beat Gregson & Boyle 5 and 4
Littler & Geiberger lost to Jacklin & Thomas
    3 and 2
Nichols & Pott beat Alliss & O'Connor 2 and 1

Second Day: Fourball – Morning
Casper & Brewer beat Alliss & O'Connor 3 and 2
Nichols & Pott beat Hunt & Coles 1 hole
Littler & Geiberger beat Jacklin & Thomas 1 hole
Dickinson & Sanders beat Huggett & Will 3 and 2

Fourball – Afternoon
Casper & Brewer beat Hunt & Coles 5 and 3
Dickinson & Sanders beat Alliss & Gregson
    4 and 3
Palmer & Boros beat Will & Boyle 1 hole
Littler & Geiberger halved with Jacklin & Thomas

Third Day: Singles – Morning
Gay Brewer beat Hugh Boyle 4 and 3
Billy Casper beat Peter Alliss 2 and 1
Arnold Palmer beat Tony Jacklin 3 and 2
Julius Boros lost to Brian Huggett 1 hole
Doug Sanders lost to Neil Coles 2 and 1
Al Geiberger beat Malcolm Gregson 4 and 2
Gene Littler halved with Dave Thomas
Bobby Nichols halved with Bernard Hunt

Singles – Afternoon
Palmer beat Huggett 5 and 3
Brewer lost to Alliss 2 and 1
Gardner Dickinson beat Jacklin 3 and 2
Nichols beat Christy O'Connor 3 and 2
Johnny Pott beat George Will 3 and 1
Geiberger beat Gregson 2 and 1
Boros halved with Hunt
Sanders lost to Coles 2 and 1

1969 at Royal Birkdale
Result: USA 16, GBI 16
Captains: Eric Brown (GBI), Sam Snead (USA)
First Day: Foursomes – Morning
Coles & Huggett beat Barber & Floyd 3 and 2
Gallacher & Bembridge beat Trevino & Still 2 and 1
Jacklin & Townsend beat Hill & Aaron 3 and 1
O'Connor & Alliss halved with Casper & Beard

Foursomes – Afternoon
Coles & Huggett lost to Hill & Aaron 1 hole
Gallacher & Bembridge lost to Trevino & Littler 2 holes
Jacklin & Townsend beat Casper & Beard 1 hole
Hunt & Butler lost to Nicklaus & Sikes

Second Day: Fourball – Morning
O'Connor & Townsend beat Hill & Douglass 1 hole
Huggett & Alex Caygill halved with Floyd & Barber
Barnes & Alliss lost to Trevino & Littler 1 hole
Jacklin & Coles beat Nicklaus & Sikes 1 hole

Fourball – Afternoon
Townsend & Butler lost to Casper & Beard 2 holes
Huggett & Gallacher lost to Hill & Still 2 and 1
Bembridge & Hunt halved with Aaron & Floyd
Jacklin & Coles halved with Trevino & Barber

Third Day: Singles – Morning
Peter Alliss lost to Lee Trevino 2 and 1
Peter Townsend lost to Dave Hill 5 and 4
Neil Coles beat Tommy Aaron 1 hole
Brian Barnes lost to Billy Casper 1 hole
Christy O'Connor beat Frank Beard 5 and 4
Maurice Bembridge beat Ken Still 1 hole
Peter Butler beat Ray Floyd 1 hole
Tony Jacklin beat Jack Nicklaus 4 and 3

Singles – Afternoon
Barnes lost to Hill 4 and 2
Bernard Gallacher beat Trevino 4 and 3
Bembridge lost to Miller Barber 7 and 6
Butler beat Dale Douglass 3 and 2
O'Connor lost to Gene Littler 2 and 1
Brian Huggett halved with Casper
Coles lost to Dan Sikes 4 and 3
Jacklin halved with Nicklaus

1971 at St Louis, MO
Result: USA 18½, GBI 13½
*Captains: Jay Hebert (USA),
    Eric Brown (GBI)*
First Day: Foursomes – Morning
Casper & Barber lost to Coles & O'Connor 2 and 1
Palmer & Dickinson beat Townsend & Oosterhuis
    2 holes
Nicklaus & Stockton lost to Huggett & Jacklin 3 and 2
Coody & Beard lost to Bembridge & Butler 1 hole

Foursomes – Afternoon
Casper & Barber lost to Bannerman & Gallacher 2 and 1
Palmer & Dickinson beat Townsend & Oosterhuis
    1 hole
Trevino & Rudolph halved with Huggett and Jacklin
Nicklaus & Snead beat Bembridge & Butler 5 and 3

Second Day: Fourball – Morning
Trevino & Rudolph beat O'Connor & Barnes 2 and 1
Beard & Snead beat Coles & John Garner 2 and 1
Palmer & Dickinson beat Oosterhuis & Gallacher 5 and 4
Nicklaus & Littler beat Townsend & Bannerman 2 and 1

Fourball – Afternoon
Trevino & Casper lost to Oosterhuis & Gallacher
    1 hole

1951 *continued*

Littler & Snead beat Huggett & Jacklin 2 and 1
Palmer & Nicklaus beat Townsend & Bannerman 1 hole
Coody & Beard halved with Coles & O'Connor

Third Day: **Singles – Morning**
Lee Trevino beat Tony Jacklin 1 hole
Dave Stockton halved with Bernard Gallacher
Mason Rudolph lost to Brian Barnes 1 hole
Gene Littler lost to Peter Oosterhuis 4 and 3
Jack Nicklaus beat Peter Townsend 3 and 2
Gardner Dickinson beat Christy O'Connor 5 and 4
Arnold Palmer halved with Harry Bannerman
Frank Beard halved with Neil Coles

Singles – Afternoon
Trevino beat Brian Huggett 7 and 6
JC Snead beat Jacklin 1 hole
Miller Barber lost to Barnes 2 and 1
Stockton beat Townsend 1 hole
Charles Coody lost to Gallacher 2 and 1
Nicklaus beat Coles 5 and 3
Palmer lost to Oosterhuis 3 and 2
Dickinson lost to Bannerman 2 and 1

1973 *at Muirfield*
Result: USA 19, GBI 13
Captains: Bernard Hunt (GBI), Jack Burke (USA)
First Day: **Foursomes – Morning**
Barnes & Gallacher beat Trevino & Casper 1 hole
O'Connor & Coles beat Weiskopf & Snead 3 and 2
Jacklin & Oosterhuis halved with Rodriguez & Graham
Bembridge & Polland lost to Nicklaus & Palmer 6 and 5

Fourball – Afternoon
Barnes & Gallacher beat Aaron & Brewer 5 and 4
Bembridge & Huggett beat Nicklaus & Palmer 3 and 1
Jacklin & Oosterhuis beat Weiskopf & Casper 3 and 1
O'Connor & Coles lost to Trevino & Blancas 2 and 1

Second Day: **Foursomes – Morning**
Barnes & Butler lost to Nicklaus & Weiskopf 1 hole
Jacklin & Oosterhuis beat Palmer & Hill 2 holes
Bembridge & Huggett beat Rodriguez & Graham
  5 and 4
O'Connor & Coles lost to Trevino & Casper 2 and 1

Fourball – Afternoon
Barnes & Butler lost to Snead & Palmer 2 holes
Jacklin & Oosterhuis lost to Brewer & Casper
  3 and 2
Clark & Polland lost to Nicklaus & Weiskopf 3 and 2
Bembridge & Huggett halved with Trevino &
  Blancas

Third Day: **Singles – Morning**
Brian Barnes lost to Billy Casper 2 and 1
Bernard Gallacher lost to Tom Weiskopf 3 and 1
Peter Butler lost to Homero Blancas 5 and 4
Tony Jacklin beat Tommy Aaron 3 and 1
Neil Coles halved with Gay Brewer
Christy O'Connor lost to JC Snead 1 hole
Maurice Bembridge halved with Jack Nicklaus
Peter Oosterhuis halved with Lee Trevino

Singles – Afternoon
Brian Huggett beat Blancas 4 and 2
Barnes lost to Snead 3 and 1
Gallacher lost to Brewer 6 and 5
Jacklin lost to Casper 2 and 1
Coles lost to Trevino 6 and 5
O'Connor halved with Weiskopf
Bembridge lost to Nicklaus 2 holes
Oosterhuis beat Arnold Palmer 4 and 2

1975 *at Laurel Valley, PA*
Result: USA 21, GBI 11
Captains: Arnold Palmer (USA),
Bernard Hunt (GBI)
First Day: **Foursomes – Morning**
Nicklaus & Weiskopf beat Barnes & Gallacher 5 and 4
Littler & Irwin beat Wood & Bembridge 4 and 3
Geiberger & Miller beat Jacklin & Oosterhuis 3 and 1
Trevino & Snead beat Horton & O'Leary 2 and 1

Fourball – Afternoon
Casper & Floyd lost to Jacklin & Oosterhuis 2 and 1
Weiskopf & Graham beat Darcy & Christy O'Connor jr
  3 and 2
Nicklaus & Murphy halved with Barnes & Gallacher
Trevino & Irwin beat Horton & O'Leary 2 and 1

Second Day: **Fourball – Morning**
Casper & Miller halved with Jacklin & Oosterhuis
Nicklaus & Snead beat Horton & Wood 4 and 2
Littler & Graham beat Barnes & Gallacher 5 and 3
Geiberger & Floyd halved with Darcy & Hunt

Foursomes – Afternoon
Trevino & Murphy lost to Jacklin & Barnes 3 and 2
Weiskopf & Miller beat O'Connor & O'Leary 5 and 3
Irwin & Casper beat Oosterhuis & Bembridge 3 and 2
Geiberger & Graham beat Darcy & Hunt 3 and 2

Third Day: **Singles – Morning**
Bob Murphy beat Tony Jacklin 2 and 1
Johnny Miller lost to Peter Oosterhuis 2 holes
Lee Trevino halved with Bernard Gallacher
Hale Irwin halved with Tommy Horton
Gene Littler beat Brian Huggett 4 and 2
Billy Casper beat Eamonn Darcy 3 and 2
Tom Weiskopf beat Guy Hunt 5 and 3
Jack Nicklaus lost to Brian Barnes 4 and 2

Singles – Afternoon
Ray Floyd beat Jacklin 1 hole
JC Snead lost to Oosterhuis 3 and 2
Al Geiberger halved with Gallacher
Lou Graham lost to Horton 2 and 1
Irwin beat John O'Leary 2 and 1
Murphy beat Maurice Bembridge 2 and 1
Trevino lost to Norman Wood 2 and 1
Nicklaus lost to Barnes 2 and 1

1977 *at Royal Lytham & St Anne's*
Result: USA 12½, GBI 7½
Captains: Brian Huggett (GBI),
Dow Finsterwald (USA)
First Day: **Foursomes**
Gallacher & Barnes lost to Wadkins & Irwin 3 and 1
Coles & Dawson lost to Stockton & McGee 1 hole
Faldo & Oosterhuis beat Floyd & Graham 2 and 1
Darcy & Jacklin halved with Sneed & January
Horton & James lost to Nicklaus & Watson 5 and 4

Second Day: **Fourball**
Barnes & Horton lost to Watson & Green 5 and 4
Coles & Dawson lost to Sneed & Wadkins 5 and 3
Faldo & Oosterhuis beat Nicklaus & Floyd 3 and 1
Darcy & Jacklin lost to Hill & Stockton 5 and 3
James & Brown lost to Irwin & Graham 1 hole

Third Day: **Singles**
Howard Clark lost to Lanny Wadkins 4 and 3
Neil Coles lost to Lou Graham 5 and 3
Peter Dawson beat Don January 5 and 4
Brian Barnes beat Hale Irwin 1 hole

Tommy Horton lost to Dave Hill 5 and 4
Bernard Gallacher beat Jack Nicklaus 1 hole
Eamonn Darcy lost to Hubert Green 1 hole
Mark James lost to Ray Floyd 2 and 1
Nick Faldo beat Tom Watson 1 hole
Peter Oosterhuis beat Jerry McGee 2 holes

From 1979 GBI became a European team

1979 at Greenbrier, WV
Result: USA 17, Europe 11
Captains: Billy Casper (USA),
*   John Jacobs (Eur)*
First Day: Fourball – Morning
Wadkins & Nelson beat Garrido & Ballesteros 2 and 1
Trevino & Zoeller beat Brown & James 3 and 2
Bean & Elder beat Oosterhuis & Faldo 2 and 1
Irwin & Mahaffey lost to Gallacher & Barnes 2 and 1

Foursomes – Afternoon
Irwin & Kite beat Brown & Smyth 7 and 6
Zoeller & Green lost to Garrido & Ballesteros 3 and 2
Trevino & Morgan halved with Lyle & Jacklin
Wadkins & Nelson beat Gallacher & Barnes 4 and 3

Second Day: Foursomes – Morning
Elder & Mahaffey lost to Lyle & Jacklin 5 and 4
Bean & Kite lost to Oosterhuis & Faldo 6 and 5
Zoeller & Hayes halved with Gallacher & Barnes
Wadkins & Nelson beat Garrido & Ballesteros 3 and 2

Fourball – Afternoon
Wadkins & Nelson beat Garrido & Ballesteros 5 and 4
Irwin & Kite beat Lyle & Jacklin 1 hole
Trevino & Zoeller lost to Gallacher & Barnes 3 and 2
Elder & Hayes lost to Oosterhuis & Faldo 1 hole

Third Day: Singles
Lanny Wadkins lost to Bernard Gallacher 3 and 2
Larry Nelson beat Seve Ballesteros 3 and 2
Tom Kite beat Tony Jacklin 1 hole
Mark Hayes beat Antonio Garrido 1 hole
Andy Bean beat Michael King 4 and 3
John Mahaffey beat Brian Barnes 1 hole
Lee Elder lost to Nick Faldo 3 and 2
Hale Irwin beat Des Smyth 5 and 3
Hubert Green beat Peter Oosterhuis 2 holes
Fuzzy Zoeller lost to Ken Brown 1 hole
Lee Trevino beat Sandy Lyle 2 and 1
Gil Morgan, Mark James: injury; match a half

1981 at Walton Heath
Result: USA 18½, Europe 9½
Captains: John Jacobs (Eur), Dave Marr (USA)
First Day: Foursomes – Morning
Langer & Pinero lost to Trevino & Nelson 1 hole
Lyle & James beat Rogers & Lietzke 2 and 1
Gallacher & Smyth beat Irwin & Floyd 3 and 2
Oosterhuis & Faldo lost to Watson & Nicklaus 4 and 3

Fourball – Afternoon
Torrance & Clark halved with Kite & Miller
Lyle & James beat Crenshaw & Pate 3 and 2
Smyth & Canizares beat Rogers & Lietzke 6 and 5
Gallacher & Darcy lost to Irwin & Floyd 2 and 1

Second Day: Fourball – Morning
Faldo & Torrance lost to Trevino & Pate 7 and 5
Lyle & James lost to Nelson & Kite 1 hole
Langer & Pinero beat Irwin & Floyd 2 and 1

Smyth & Canizares lost to Watson & Nicklaus
    3 and 2
Foursomes – Afternoon
Oosterhuis & Torrance lost to Trevino & Pate 2 and 1
Langer & Pinero lost to Watson & Nicklaus 3 and 2
Lyle & James lost to Rogers & Floyd 3 and 2
Gallacher & Smyth lost to Nelson & Kite 3 and 2

Third Day: Singles
Sam Torrance lost to Lee Trevino 5 and 3
Sandy Lyle lost to Tom Kite 3 and 2
Bernard Gallacher halved with Bill Rogers
Mark James lost to Larry Nelson 2 holes
Des Smyth lost to Ben Crenshaw 6 and 4
Bernhard Langer halved with Bruce Lietzke
Manuel Pinero beat Jerry Pate 4 and 2
José Maria Canizares lost to Hale Irwin 1 hole
Nick Faldo beat Johnny Miller 2 and 1
Howard Clark beat Tom Watson 4 and 3
Peter Oosterhuis lost to Ray Floyd 2 holes
Eamonn Darcy lost to Jack Nicklaus 5 and 3

1983 at PGA National, FL
Result: USA 14½, Europe 13½
Captains: Jack Nicklaus (USA),
*   Tony Jacklin (Eur)*
First Day: Foursomes – Morning
Watson & Crenshaw beat Gallacher & Lyle 5 and 4
Wadkins & Stadler lost to Faldo & Langer 4 and 2
Floyd & Gilder lost to Canizares & Torrance 4 and 3
Kite & Peete beat Ballesteros & Way 2 and 1

Fourball – Afternoon
Morgan & Zoeller lost to Waites & Brown 2 and 1
Watson & Haas beat Faldo & Langer 2 and 1
Floyd & Strange lost to Ballesteros & Way 1 hole
Crenshaw & Peete halved with Torrance & Woosnam

Second Day: Foursomes – Morning
Floyd & Kite lost to Faldo & Langer 3 and 2
Wadkins & Morgan beat Canizares & Torrance 7 and 5
Gilder & Watson lost to Ballesteros & Way 2 and 1
Haas & Strange beat Waites & Brown 3 and 2

Fourball – Afternoon
Wadkins & Stadler beat Waites & Brown 1 hole
Crenshaw & Peete lost to Faldo & Langer 2 and 1
Haas & Morgan halved with Ballesteros & Way
Gilder & Watson beat Torrance & Woosnam 5 and 4

Third Day: Singles
Fuzzy Zoeller halved with Seve Ballesteros
Jay Haas lost to Nick Faldo 2 and 1
Gil Morgan lost to Bernhard Langer 2 holes
Bob Gilder beat Gordon J Brand 2 holes
Ben Crenshaw beat Sandy Lyle 3 and 1
Calvin Peete beat Brian Waites 1 hole
Curtis Strange lost to Paul Way 1 hole
Tom Kite halved with Sam Torrance
Craig Stadler beat Ian Woosnam 3 and 2
Lanny Wadkins halved with José Maria Canizares
Ray Floyd lost to Ken Brown 4 and 3
Tom Watson beat Bernard Gallacher 2 and 1

1985 at The Belfry
Result: Europe 16½, USA 11½
Captains: Tony Jacklin (Eur),
*   Lee Trevino (USA)*
First Day: Foursomes – Morning
Ballesteros & Pinero beat Strange & O'Meara 2 and 1
Faldo & Langer lost to Kite & Peete 3 and 2
Brown & Lyle lost to Floyd & Wadkins 4 and 3
Clark & Torrance lost to Stadler & Sutton 3 and 2

1985 *continued*

Fourball – Afternoon
Way & Woosnam beat Green & Zoeller 1 hole
Ballesteros & Pinero beat Jacobsen & North 2 and 1
Canizares & Langer halved with Stadler & Sutton
Clark & Torrance lost to Floyd & Wadkins 1 hole

Second Day: Fourball – Morning
Clark & Torrance beat Kite & North 2 and 1
Way & Woosnam beat Green & Zoeller 4 and 3
Ballesteros & Pinero lost to O'Meara & Wadkins
 3 and 2
Langer & Lyle halved with Stadler & Strange

Foursomes – Afternoon
Canizares & Rivero beat Kite & Peete 7 and 5
Ballesteros & Pinero beat Stadler & Sutton 5 and 4
Way & Woosnam lost to Jacobsen & Strange 4 and 3
Brown & Langer beat Floyd & Wadkins 3 and 2

Third Day: Singles
Manuel Pinero beat Lanny Wadkins 3 and 1
Ian Woosnam lost to Craig Stadler 2 and 1
Paul Way beat Ray Floyd 2 holes
Seve Ballesteros halved with Tom Kite
Sandy Lyle beat Peter Jacobsen 3 and 2

Bernhard Langer beat Hal Sutton 5 and 4
Sam Torrance beat Andy North 1 hole
Howard Clark beat Mark O'Meara 1 hole
Nick Faldo lost to Hubert Green 3 and 1
José Rivero lost to Calvin Peete 1 hole
José Maria Canizares beat Fuzzy Zoeller 2 holes
Ken Brown lost to Curtis Strange 4 and 2

1987 *at Muirfield Village, OH*
Result: Europe 15, USA 13
Captains: Jack Nicklaus (USA),
 Tony Jacklin (Eur)
First Day: Foursomes – Morning
Kite & Strange beat Clark & Torrance 4 and 2
Pohl & Sutton beat Brown & Langer 2 and 1
Mize & Wadkins lost to Faldo & Woosnam 2 holes
Nelson & Stewart lost to Ballesteros & Olazábal 1 hole

Fourball – Afternoon
Crenshaw & Simpson lost to Brand & Rivero 3 and 2
Bean & Calcavecchia lost to Langer & Lyle 1 hole
Pohl & Sutton lost to Faldo & Woosnam 2 and 1
Kite & Strange lost to Ballesteros & Olazábal 2 and 1

Second Day: Foursomes – Morning
Kite & Strange beat Brand & Rivero 3 and 1
Mize & Sutton halved with Faldo & Woosnam
Nelson & Wadkins lost to Langer & Lyle 2 and 1
Crenshaw & Stewart lost to Ballesteros & Olazábal
 1 hole

Fourball – Afternoon
Kite & Strange lost to Faldo & Woosnam 5 and 4
Bean & Stewart beat Brand & Darcy 3 and 2
Mize & Sutton beat Ballesteros & Olazábal 2 and 1
Nelson & Wadkins lost to Langer & Lyle 1 hole

Third Day: Singles
Andy Bean beat Ian Woosnam 1 hole
Dan Pohl lost to Howard Clark 1 hole
Larry Mize halved with Sam Torrance
Mark Calcavecchia beat Nick Faldo 1 hole
Payne Stewart beat José Maria Olazábal 2 holes
Scott Simpson beat José Rivero 2 and 1
Tom Kite beat Sandy Lyle 3 and 2
Ben Crenshaw lost to Eamonn Darcy 1 hole
Larry Nelson halved with Bernhard Langer
Curtis Strange lost to Seve Ballesteros 2 and 1

Lanny Wadkins beat Ken Brown 3 and 2
Hal Sutton halved with Gordon Brand jr

1989 *at The Belfry*
Result: Europe 14, USA 14
Captains: Tony Jacklin (Eur), Ray Floyd (USA)
First Day: Foursomes – Morning
Faldo & Woosnam halved with Kite & Strange
Clark & James lost to Stewart & Wadkins 1 hole
Ballesteros & Olazábal halved with Beck & Watson
Langer & Rafferty lost to Calcavecchia & Green 2 and 1

Fourball – Afternoon
Brand & Torrance beat Azinger & Strange 1 hole
Clark & James beat Couples & Wadkins 3 and 2
Faldo & Woosnam beat Calcavecchia & McCumber
 1 hole
Ballesteros & Olazábal beat O'Meara & Watson 6 and 5

Second Day: Foursomes – Morning
Faldo & Woosnam beat Stewart & Wadkins 3 and 2
Brand & Torrance lost to Azinger & Beck 4 and 3
O'Connor & Rafferty lost to Calcavecchia & Green
 3 and 2
Ballesteros & Olazábal beat Kite & Strange 1 hole

Fourball – Afternoon
Faldo & Woosnam lost to Azinger & Beck 2 and 1
Canizares & Langer lost to Kite & McCumber 2 and 1
Clark & James beat Stewart & Strange 1 hole
Ballesteros & Olazábal beat Calcavecchia & Green
 4 and 2

Third Day: Singles
Seve Ballesteros lost to Paul Azinger 1 hole
Bernhard Langer lost to Chip Beck 3 and 1
José Maria Olazábal beat Payne Stewart 1 hole
Ronan Rafferty beat Mark Calvecchia 1 hole
Howard Clark lost to Tom Kite 8 and 7
Mark James beat Mark O'Meara 3 and 2
Christy O'Connor jr beat Fred Couples 1 hole
José Maria Canizares beat Ken Green 1 hole
Gordon Brand jr lost to Mark McCumber 1 hole
Sam Torrance lost to Tom Watson 3 and 1
Nick Faldo lost to Lanny Wadkins 1 hole
Ian Woosnam lost to Curtis Strange 1 hole

1991 *at Kiawah Island, SC*
Result: USA 14½, Europe 13½
Captains: Dave Stockton (USA),
 Bernard Gallacher (Eur)
First Day: Morning – Foursomes
Ballesteros & Olazábal beat Azinger & Beck 2 and 1
Langer & James lost to Floyd & Couples 2 and 1
Gilford & Montgomerie lost to Wadkins & Irwin 4 and 2
Faldo & Woosnam lost to Stewart & Calcavecchia 1 hole

Afternoon – Fourball
Torrance & Feherty halved with Wadkins & O'Meara
Ballesteros & Olazábal beat Azinger & Beck 2 and 1
Richardson & James beat Pavin & Calcavecchia 5 and 4
Faldo & Woosnam lost to Floyd & Couples 5 and 3

Second Day: Morning – Foursomes
Torrance & Feherty lost to Irwin & Wadkins 4 and 2
James & Richardson lost to Calcavecchia & Stewart
 1 hole
Faldo & Gilford lost to Azinger & O'Meara 7 and 6
Ballesteros & Olazábal beat Couples & Floyd 3 and 2

Afternoon – Fourball
Woosnam & Broadhurst beat Azinger & Irwin 2 and 1
Langer & Montgomerie beat Pate & Pavin 2 and 1

James & Richardson beat Wadkins & Levi 3 and 1
Ballesteros & Olazábal halved with Couples & Stewart

Third Day – Singles
Nick Faldo beat Ray Floyd 2 holes
David Feherty beat Payne Stewart 2 and 1
Colin Montgomerie halved with Mark Calcavecchia
José Maria Olazábal lost to Paul Azinger 2 holes
Steven Richardson lost to Corey Pavin 2 and 1
Seve Ballesteros beat Wayne Levi 3 and 2
Ian Woosnam lost to Chip Beck 3 and 1
Paul Broadhurst bat Mark O'Meara 3 and 1
Sam Torrance lost to Fred Couples 3 and 2
Mark James lost to Lanny Wadkins 3 and 2
Bernhard Langer halved with Hale Irwin
David Gilford (withdrawn) halved with Steve Pate
  (withdrawn – injured)

1993 *at The Belfry*
Result: Europe 13, USA 15
Captains: Bernard Gallacher (Eur)
  Tom Watson (USA)

First Day: Morning – Foursomes
Torrance & James lost to Wadkins & Pavin 4 and 3
Woosnam & Langer beat Azinger & Stewart 7 and 5
Ballesteros & Olazábal lost to Kite & Love 2 and 1
Faldo & Montgomerie beat Floyd & Couples 4 and 3

Afternoon – Fourball
Woosnam & Baker beat Gallagher & Janzen 1 hole
Lane & Langer lost to Wadkins & Pavin 4 and 2
Faldo & Montgomerie halved with Azinger & Couples
Ballesteros & Olazábal beat Kite & Love 4 and 3

Second Day: Morning – Foursomes
Faldo & Montgomerie beat Wadkins & Pavin 3 and 2
Langer & Woosnam beat Couples & Azinger 2 and 1
Baker & Lane lost to Floyd & Stewart 3 and 2
Ballesteros & Olazábal beat Kite & Love 2 and 1

Afternoon – Fourball
Faldo & Montgomerie lost to Beck & Cook 2 holes
James & Rocca lost to Pavin & Gallacher 5 and 4
Woosnam & Baker beat Couples & Azinger 6 and 5
Olazábal & Haeggman lost to Floyd & Stewart 2 and 1

Third Day – Singles
Ian Woosnam halved with Fred Couples
Barry Lane lost to Chip Beck 1 hole
Colin Montgomerie beat Lee Janzen 1 hole
Peter Baker beat Corey Pavin 2 holes
Joakim Haeggman beat J Cook 1 hole
Sam Torrance (withdrawn at start of day) halved with
  Lanny Wadkins (withdrawn at start of day)
Mark James lost to Payne Stewart 3 and 2
Constantino Rocca lost to Davis Love III 1 hole
Seve Ballesteros lost to Jim Gallagher jr 3 and 2
José Maria Olazábal lost to Ray Floyd 2 holes
Bernhard Langer lost to Tom Kite 5 and 3
Nick Faldo halved with Paul Azinger

1995 *at Oak Hill, Rochester, NY*
Result: USA 13½, Europe 14½
Captains: Lanny Wadkins (USA),
  Bernard Gallacher (Eur)

First Day: Morning – Foursomes
Faldo & Montgomerie lost to Pavin & Lehman
  1 hole
Torrance & Rocca beat Haas & Couples 3 and 2
Clark & James lost to Love & Maggert 4 and 3
Langer & Johansson beat Crenshaw & Strange 1 hole

Afternoon – Fourball
Gilford & Ballesteros beat Faxon & Jacobsen 4 and 3
Torrance & Rocca lost to Maggert & Roberts 6 and 5
Faldo & Montgomerie lost to Couples & Love 3 and 2
Langer & Johansson lost to Pavin & Mickelson 6 and 4

Second Day: Morning – Foursomes
Faldo & Montgomerie beat Haas & Strange 4 and 2
Torrance & Rocca beat Love & Maggert 6 and 5
Woosnam & Walton lost to Roberts & Jacobsen 1 hole
Langer & Gilford beat Pavin & Lehman 4 and 3

Afternoon – Fourball
Torrance & Montgomerie lost to Faxon & Couples
  4 and 2
Woosnam & Rocca beat Love & Crenshaw 3 and 2
Ballesteros & Gilford lost to Haas & Mickelson 3 and 2
Faldo & Langer lost to Pavin & Roberts 1 hole

Third Day – Singles
Seve Ballesteros lost to Tom Lehman 4 and 3
Howard Clark beat Peter Jacobsen 1 hole
Mark James beat Jeff Maggert 4 and 3
Ian Woosnam halved with Fred Couples
Costantino Rocca lost to Davis Love III 3 and 2
David Gilford beat Brad Faxon 1 hole
Colin Montgomerie beat Ben Crenshaw 3 and 1
Nick Faldo beat Curtis Strange 1 hole
Sam Torrance beat Loren Roberts 2 and 1
Bernhard Langer lost to Corey Pavin 3 and 2
Philip Walton beat Jay Haas 1 hole
Per-Ulrik Johansson lost to Phil Mickelson 2 and 1

1997 Ryder Cup *at Valderrama, Spain*
Result: Europe 14½, USA 13½,
Captains: Seve Ballesteros (Eur),
  Tom Kite (USA)

First Day: Morning – Fourball
Olazábal & Rocca beat Love & Mickelson 1 hole
Faldo & Westwood lost to Couples & Faxon 1 hole
Parnevik & Johansson beat Lehman & Furyk 1 hole
Montgomerie & Langer lost to Woods & O'Meara 3 and 2

Afternoon – Foursomes
Rocca & Olazábal lost to Hoch & Janzen 1 hole
Langer & Montgomerie beat O'Meara & Woods 5 and 3
Faldo & Westwood beat Leonard & Maggert 3 and 2
Parnevik & Garrido halved with Lehman & Mickelson

Second Day: Morning – Fourball
Montgomerie & Clarke beat Couples & Love 1 hole
Woosnam & Bjørn beat Leonard & Faxon 2 and 1
Faldo & Westwood beat Woods & O'Meara 2 and 1
Olazábal & Garrido halved with Mickelson & Lehman

Afternoon – Foursomes
Montgomerie & Langer beat Janzen & Furyk 1 hole
Faldo & Westwood lost to Hoch & Maggert 2 and 1
Parnevik & Garrido halved with Leonard & Woods
Olazábal & Rocca beat Love & Couples 5 and 4

Third Day – Singles
Ian Woosnam lost to Fred Couples 8 and 7
Per-Ulrik Johansson beat Davis Love III 3 and 2
Costantino Rocca beat Tiger Woods 4 and 2
Thomas Bjørn halved with Justin Leonard
Darren Clarke lost to Phil Mickelson 2 and 1
Jesper Parnevik lost to Mark O'Meara 5 and 4
José Maria Olazábal lost to Lee Janzen 1 hole
Bernhard Langer beat Brad Faxon 2 and 1
Lee Westwood lost to Jeff Maggert 3 and 2
Colin Montgomerie halved with Scott Hoch
Nick Faldo lost to Jim Furyk 3 and 2
Ignacio Garrido lost to Tom Lehman 7 and 6

1999 Ryder Cup at Brookline, MA
Result: USA 14½, Europe 13½
Captains: Ben Crenshaw (USA),
    Mark James (Eur)
First Day: Morning – Foursomes
Montgomerie & Lawrie beat Duval & Mickelson 3 and 2
Parnevik & García beat Lehman & Woods 2 and 1
Jiménez & Harrington halved halved with Love &
    Stewart
Clarke & Westwood lost to Sutton & Maggert 3 and 2
Afternoon – Fourball
Montgomerie & Lawrie halved with Love & Leonard
Parnevik & García beat Mickelson & Furyk 1 hole
Jiménez & Olazábal beat Sutton & Maggert 2 and 1
Clarke & Westwood beat Duval & Woods 1 hole
Second Day: Morning – Foursomes
Montgomerie & Lawrie lost to Sutton & Maggert 1 hole
Clarke & Westwood beat Furyk & O'Meara 3 and 2
Jiménez & Harrington lost to Pate & Woods 1 hole
Parnevik & García beat Stewart & Leonard 3 and 2
Afternoon – Fourball
Clarke & Westwood lost to Mickelson & Lehman 2 and 1
Parnevik & García halved with Love & Duval
Jiménez & Olazábal halved with Leonard & Sutton
Montgomerie & Lawrie beat Pate & Woods 2 and 1
Third Day – Singles
Lee Westwood lost to Tom Lehman 3 and 2
Darren Clarke lost to Hal Sutton 4 and 2
Jarmo Sandelin lost to Phil Mickelson 4 and 3
Jean Van de Velde lost to Davis Love III 6 and 5
Andrew Coltart lost to Tiger Woods 3 and 2
Jesper Parnevik lost to David Duval 5 and 4
Padraig Harrington beat Mark O'Meara 1 hole
Miguel Angel Jiménez lost to Steve Pate 2 and 1
José María Olazábal halved with Justin Leonard
Colin Montgomerie beat Payne Stewart 1 hole
Sergio García lost to Jim Furyk 4 and 3
Paul Lawrie beat Jeff Maggert 4 and 3

2001 *event cancelled*

2002 Ryder Cup at The Belfry
Result: Europe 13½, UAS 12½
Captains: Sam Torrance (Eur),
    Curtis Strange (USA)
First Day, Morning – Fourball
Bjørn & Clarke beat Azinger & Woods 1 hole
García & Westwood beat Duval & Love 4 and 3
Langer & Montgomerie Beat Furyk & Hoch 4 and 3
Fasth & Harrington lost to Mickelson & Toms (1 hole)
Afternoon – Foursomes
Bjørn & Clarke lost to Sutton & Verplank 2 and 1
García & Westwood beat Calcavecchia & Woods 2 and 1
Langer & Montgomerie halved with Mickelson & Toms
Harrington & McGinley lost to Cink & Furyk 3 and 2
Second Day, Morning – Foursomes
Fulke & Price lost to Mickelson & Toms 2 and 1
García & Westwood beat Cink & Furyk 2 and 1
Langer & Montgomerie beat Hoch & Verplank 1 hole
Bjørn & Clarke lost to Love & Woods 4 and 3
Afternoon – Fourball
Fasth & Parnevik lost to Calcavecchia & Duval 1 hole
García & Westwood lost to Love & Woods 1 hole
Harrington & Montgomerie beat Mickelson & Toms
    2 and 1
Clarke & McGinley halved with Furyk & Hoch
Third Day – Singles
Colin Montgomerie (Sco) beat Scott Hoch 5 and 4
Sergio García (Esp) lost to David Toms 1 hole
Darren Clarke (NI) halved with David Duval
Bernhard Langer (Ger) beat Hal Sutton 4 and 3
Padraig Harrington (Irl) beat Mark Calcavecchia
    5 and 4
Thomas Bjørn (Den) beat Stewart Cink 2 and 1
Lee Westwood (Eng) lost to Scott Verplank 2 and 1
Niclas Fasth (Swe) halved with Paul Azinger
Paul McGinley (Irl) halved with Jim Furyk
Pierre Fulke (Swe) halved with Davis Love III
Phillip Price (Wal) beat Phil Mickelson 3 and 2
Jesper Parnevik (Swe) halved with Tiger Woods

INDIVIDUAL RECORDS

Matches were contested as Great Britain *v* USA from 1927–71; as Great Britain & Ireland *v* USA from 1973–77; and as Europe *v* USA from 1979. Bold type indicates captain; non-playing in brackets.

Europe

Name	Year	Played	Won	Lost	Halved
Jimmy Adams	*1939-47-49-51-53	7	2	5	0
Percy Alliss	1929-33-35-37	6	3	2	1
Peter Alliss	1953-57-59-61-63-65-67-69	30	10	15	5
Laurie Ayton	1949	0	0	0	0
Peter Baker	1993	4	3	1	0
Severiano Ballesteros (Esp)	1979-83-85-87-89-91-93-95-(97)	37	20	12	5
Harry Bannerman	1971	5	2	2	1
Brian Barnes	1969-71-73-75-77-79	25	10	14	1
Maurice Bembridge	1969-71-73-75	16	5	8	3
Thomas Bjørn (Den)	1997-2002	6	3	2	1
Aubrey Boomer	1927-29	4	2	2	0
Ken Bousfield	1949-51-55-57-59-61	10	5	5	0
Hugh Boyle	1967	3	0	3	0
Harry Bradshaw	1953-55-57	5	2	2	1
Gordon J Brand	1983	1	0	1	0
Gordon Brand jr	1987-89	7	2	4	1
Paul Broadhurst	1991	2	2	0	0

* In 1939 a GB&I team was named but the match was not played because of the Second World War

Eric Brown	1953-55-57-59-**(69)**-**(71)**	8	4	4	0
Ken Brown	1977-79-83-85-87	13	4	9	0
Stewart Burns	1929	0	0	0	0
Dick Burton	1935-37-*39-49	5	2	3	0
Jack Busson	1935	2	0	2	0
Peter Butler	1965-69-71-73	14	3	9	2
José Maria Canizares (Esp)	1981-83-85-89	11	5	4	2
Alex Caygill	1969	1	0	0	1
Clive Clark	1973	1	0	1	0
Howard Clark	1977-81-85-87-89-95	15	7	7	1
Darren Clarke	1997-99-2002	12	4	6	2
Neil Coles	1961-63-65-67-69-71-73-77	40	12	21	7
Andrew Coltart	1999	1	0	1	0
Archie Compston	1927-29-31	6	1	4	1
Henry Cotton	1929-37-*39-**47**-**(53)**	6	2	4	0
Bill Cox	1935-37	3	0	2	1
Allan Dailey	1933	0	0	0	0
Fred Daly	1947-49-51-53	8	3	4	1
Eamonn Darcy	1975-77-81-87	11	1	8	2
William Davies	1931-33	4	2	2	0
Peter Dawson	1977	3	1	2	0
Norman Drew	1959	1	0	0	1
George Duncan	1927-**29**-31	5	2	3	0
Syd Easterbrook	1931-33	3	2	1	0
Nick Faldo	1977-79-81-83-85-87-89-91-93-95-97	46	23	19	4
John Fallon	1955-**(63)**	1	1	0	0
Niclas Fasth (Swe)	2002	3	0	2	1
Max Faulkner	1947-49-51-53-57	8	1	7	0
David Feherty	1991	3	1	1	1
Pierre Fulke (Swe)	2002	2	0	1	1
George Gadd	1927	0	0	0	0
Bernard Gallacher	1969-71-73-75-77-79-81-83-**(91)**-**(93)**-**(95)**	31	13	13	5
Sergio García (Esp)	1999-2002	10	6	3	1
John Garner	1971-73	1	0	1	0
Antonio Garrido (Esp)	1979	5	1	4	0
Ignacio Garrido (Esp)	1997	4	0	1	3
David Gilford	1991-95	6	3	3	0
Eric Green	1947	0	0	0	0
Malcolm Gregson	1967	4	0	4	0
Joakim Haeggman (Swe)	1993	2	1	1	0
Tom Haliburton	1961-63	6	0	6	0
Jack Hargreaves	1951	0	0	0	0
Padraig Harrington	1999-2002	7	3	3	1
Arthur Havers	1927-31-33	6	3	3	0
Jimmy Hitchcock	1965	3	0	3	0
Bert Hodson	1931	1	0	1	0
Reg Horne	1947	0	0	0	0
Tommy Horton	1975-77	8	1	6	1
Brian Huggett	1963-67-69-71-73-75-**(77)**	25	9	10	6
Bernard Hunt	1953-57-59-61-63-65-67-69-**(73)**-**(75)**	28	6	16	6
Geoffrey Hunt	1963	3	0	3	0
Guy Hunt	1975	3	0	2	1
Tony Jacklin	1967-69-71-73-75-77-79-**(83)**-**(85)**-**(87)**-**(89)**	35	13	14	8
John Jacobs	1955-**(79)**-**(81)**	2	2	0	0
Mark James	1977-79-81-89-91-93-95-**(99)**	24	8	15	1
Edward Jarman	1935	1	0	1	0
Miguel Angel Jiménez (Esp)	1999	5	1	2	2
Per-Ulrik Johansson (Swe)	1995-97	5	3	2	0
Herbert Jolly	1927	2	0	2	0
Michael King	1979	1	0	1	0
Sam King	1937-*39-47-49	5	1	3	1
Arthur Lacey	1933-37-**(51)**	3	0	3	0
Barry Lane	1993	3	0	3	0
Bernhard Langer (Ger)	1981-83-85-87-89-91-93-95-97-2002	42	21	15	6
Paul Lawrie	1999	5	3	1	1
Arthur Lees	1947-49-51-55	8	4	4	0
Sandy Lyle	1979-81-83-85-87	18	7	9	2
Paul McGinley (Irl)	2002	3	0	1	2
Jimmy Martin	1965	1	0	1	0
Peter Mills	1957-59	1	1	0	0
Abe Mitchell	1929-31-33	6	4	2	0
Ralph Moffitt	1961	1	0	1	0
Colin Montgomerie	1991-93-95-97-99-2002	28	16	7	5
Christy O'Connor jr	1975-89	4	1	3	0

* In 1939 a GB&I team was named but the match was not played because of the Second World War

Ryder Cup European Individual Records *continued*

Name	Year	Played	Won	Lost	Halved
Christy O'Connor sr	1955-57-59-61-63-65-67-69-71-73	36	11	21	4
José Maria Olazábal (Esp)	1987-89-91-93-97-99	28	15	8	5
John O'Leary	1975	4	0	4	0
Peter Oosterhuis	1971-73-75-77-79-81	28	14	11	3
Alf Padgham	1933-35-37-*39	6	0	6	0
John Panton	1951-53-61	5	0	5	0
Jesper Parnevik (Swe)	1997-99-2002	11	4	3	4
Alf Perry	1933-35-37	4	0	3	1
Manuel Pinero (Esp)	1981-85	9	6	3	0
Lionel Platts	1965	5	1	2	2
Eddie Polland	1973	2	0	2	0
Phillip Price	2002	2	1	1	0
Ronan Rafferty	1989	3	1	2	0
Ted Ray	1927	2	0	2	0
Dai Rees	1937-*39-47-49-51-53-**55-57-59-61**-(67)	18	7	10	1
Steven Richardson	1991	4	2	2	0
José Rivero (Esp)	1985-87	5	2	3	0
Fred Robson	1927-29-31	6	2	4	0
Costantino Rocca (Ita)	1993-95-97	11	6	5	0
Jarmo Sandelin (Swe)	1999	1	0	1	0
Syd Scott	1955	2	0	2	0
Des Smyth	1979-81	7	2	5	0
Dave Thomas	1959-63-65-67	18	3	10	5
Sam Torrance	1981-83-85-87-89-91-93-95-**2002**	27	7	15	5
Peter Townsend	1969-71	11	3	8	0
Jean Van de Velde (Fra)	1999	1	0	1	0
Brian Waites	1983	4	1	3	0
Philip Walton	1995	2	1	1	0
Charlie Ward	1947-49-51	6	1	5	0
Paul Way	1983-85	9	6	2	1
Harry Weetman	1951-53-55-57-59-61-63-(**65**)	15	2	11	2
Lee Westwood	1997-99-2002	10	5	5	0
Charles Whitcombe	1927-29-**31**-33-**35**-**37**-*39-(**49**)	9	3	2	4
Ernest Whitcombe	1929-31-35	6	1	4	1
Reg Whitcombe	1935-*39	1	0	1	0
George Will	1963-65-67	15	2	11	2
Norman Wood	1975	3	1	2	0
Ian Woosnam	1983-85-87-89-91-93-95-97	31	14	12	5

United States of America

Name	Year	Played	Won	Lost	Halved
Tommy Aaron	1969-73	6	1	4	1
Skip Alexander	1949-51	2	1	1	0
Paul Azinger	1989-91-93-2002	16	5	8	3
Jerry Barber	1955-**61**	5	1	4	0
Miller Barber	1969-71	7	1	4	2
Herman Barron	1947	1	1	0	0
Andy Bean	1979-87	6	4	2	0
Frank Beard	1969-71	8	2	3	3
Chip Beck	1989-91-93	9	6	2	1
Homero Blancas	1973	4	2	1	1
Tommy Bolt	1955-57	4	3	1	0
Julius Boros	1959-63-65-67	16	9	3	4
Gay Brewer	1967-73	9	5	3	1
Billy Burke	1931-33	3	3	0	0
Jack Burke	1951-53-55-**57**-59-(**73**)	8	7	1	0
Walter Burkemo	1953	1	0	1	0
Mark Calcavecchia	1987-89-91-2002	14	6	7	1
Billy Casper	1961-63-65-67-69-71-73-75-(**79**)	37	20	10	7
Stewart Cink	2002	3	1	2	0
Bill Collins	1961	3	1	2	0
Charles Coody	1971	3	0	2	1
John Cook	1993	2	1	1	0
Fred Couples	1989-91-93-95-97	20	7	9	4
Wilfred Cox	1931	2	2	0	0
Ben Crenshaw	1981-83-87-95-(**99**)	12	3	8	1
Jimmy Demaret	*1941-47-49-51	6	6	0	0
Gardner Dickinson	1967-71	10	9	1	0

* US teams were selected in 1939 and 1941, but did not play because of the Second World War

Name	Year	Played	Won	Lost	Halved
Leo Diegel	1927-29-31-33	6	3	3	0
Dale Douglass	1969	2	0	2	0
Dave Douglas	1953	2	1	0	1
Ed Dudley	1929-33-37	4	3	1	0
Olin Dutra	1933-35	4	1	3	0
David Duval	1999-2002	7	2	3	2
Lee Elder	1979	4	1	3	0
Al Espinosa	1927-29-31	4	2	1	1
Johnny Farrell	1927-29-31	6	3	2	1
Brad Faxon	1995-97	6	2	4	0
Dow Finsterwald	1957-59-61-63-(77)	13	9	3	1
Ray Floyd	1969-75-77-81-83-85-(89)-91-93	31	12	16	3
Doug Ford	1955-57-59-61	9	4	4	1
Ed Furgol	1957	1	0	1	0
Marty Furgol	1955	1	0	1	0
Jim Furyk	1997-99-2002	11	3	6	2
Jim Gallagher jr	1993	3	2	1	0
Al Geiberger	1967-75	9	5	1	3
Vic Ghezzi	*1939-*41	0	0	0	0
Bob Gilder	1983	4	2	2	0
Bob Goalby	1963	5	3	1	1
Johnny Golden	1927-29	3	3	0	0
Lou Graham	1973-75-77	9	5	3	1
Hubert Green	1977-79-85	7	4	3	0
Ken Green	1989	4	2	2	0
Ralph Guldahl	1937-*39	2	2	0	0
Fred Haas jr	1953	1	0	1	0
Jay Haas	1983-95	8	3	4	1
Walter Hagen	**1927-29-31-33-35-(37)**	9	7	1	1
Bob Hamilton	1949	2	0	2	0
Chick Harbert	1949-**55**	2	2	0	0
Chandler Harper	1955	1	0	1	0
EJ (Dutch) Harrison	1947-49-51	3	2	1	0
Fred Hawkins	1957	2	1	1	0
Mark Hayes	1979	3	1	2	0
Clayton Heafner	1949-51	4	3	0	1
Jay Hebert	1959-61-(71)	4	2	1	1
Lionel Hebert	1957	1	0	1	0
Dave Hill	1969-73-77	9	6	3	0
Jimmy Hines	*1939	0	0	0	0
Scott Hoch	1997-2002	7	2	3	2
Ben Hogan	*1941-**47**-(49)-51-(67)	3	3	0	0
Hale Irwin	1975-77-79-81-91	20	13	5	2
Tommy Jacobs	1965	4	3	1	0
Peter Jacobsen	1985-95	6	2	4	0
Don January	1965-77	7	2	3	2
Lee Janzen	1993-97	5	2	3	0
Herman Keiser	1947	1	0	1	0
Tom Kite	1979-81-83-85-87-89-93-(97)	28	15	9	4
Ted Kroll	1953-55-57	4	3	1	0
Ky Laffoon	1935	1	0	1	0
Tom Lehman	1995-97-99	10	5	3	2
Tony Lema	1963-65	11	8	1	2
Justin Leonard	1997-99	8	0	3	5
Wayne Levi	1991	2	0	2	0
Bruce Lietzke	1981	3	0	2	1
Gene Littler	1961-63-65-67-69-71-75	27	14	5	8
Davis Love III	1993-95-97-99-2002	21	8	9	4
Jeff Maggert	1995-97-99	11	6	5	0
John Mahaffey	1979	3	1	2	0
Mark McCumber	1989	3	2	1	0
Jerry McGee	1977	2	1	1	0
Harold McSpaden	*1939-*41	0	0	0	0
Tony Manero	1937	2	1	1	0
Lloyd Mangrum	*1941-47-49-51-**53**	8	6	2	0
Dave Marr	1965-(81)	6	4	2	0
Billy Maxwell	1963	4	4	0	0
Dick Mayer	1957	2	1	0	1
Bill Mehlhorn	1927	2	1	1	0
Dick Metz	*1939	0	0	0	0
Phil Mickelson	1995-97-99-2002	16	8	5	3
Cary Middlecoff	1953-55-59	6	2	3	1
Johnny Miller	1975-81	6	2	2	2

US teams were selected in 1939 and 1941, but did not play because of the Second World War

Ryder Cup American Individual Records *continued*

Name	Year	Played	Won	Lost	Halved
Larry Mize	1987	4	1	1	2
Gil Morgan	1979-83	6	1	2	3
Bob Murphy	1975	4	2	1	1
Byron Nelson	1937-*39-*41-47-(65)	4	3	1	0
Larry Nelson	1979-81-87	13	9	3	1
Bobby Nichols	1967	5	4	0	1
Jack Nicklaus	1969-71-73-75-77-81-(83)-(87)	28	17	8	3
Andy North	1985	3	0	3	0
Ed Oliver	1947-51-53	5	3	2	0
Mark O'Meara	1985-89-91-97-99	14	4	9	1
Arnold Palmer	1961-**63**-65-67-71-73-(75)	32	22	8	2
Johnny Palmer	1949	2	0	2	0
Sam Parks	1935	1	0	0	1
Jerry Pate	1981	4	2	2	0
Steve Pate	1991-99	4	2	2	0
Corey Pavin	1991-93-95	8	5	3	0
Calvin Peete	1983-85	7	4	2	1
Henry Picard	1935-37-*39	4	3	1	0
Dan Pohl	1987	3	1	2	0
Johnny Pott	1963-65-67	7	5	2	0
Dave Ragan	1963	4	2	1	1
Henry Ransom	1951	1	0	1	0
Johnny Revolta	1935-37	3	2	1	0
Loren Roberts	1995	4	3	1	0
Chi Chi Rodriguez	1973	2	0	1	1
Bill Rogers	1981	4	1	2	1
Bob Rosburg	1959	2	2	0	0
Mason Rudolph	1971	3	1	1	1
Paul Runyan	1933-35-*39	4	2	2	0
Doug Sanders	1967	5	2	3	0
Gene Sarazen	1927-29-31-33-35-37-*41	12	7	2	3
Densmore Shute	1931-33-37	6	2	2	2
Dan Sikes	1969	3	2	1	0
Scott Simpson	1987	2	1	1	0
Horton Smith	1929-31-33-35-37-*39-*41	4	3	0	1
JC Snead	1971-73-75	11	9	2	0
Sam Snead	1937-*39-*41-47-49-**51**-53-55-**59**-(69)	13	10	2	1
Ed Sneed	1977	2	1	0	1
Mike Souchak	1959-61	6	5	1	0
Craig Stadler	1983-85	8	4	2	2
Payne Stewart	1987-89-91-93-99	19	7	10	2
Ken Still	1969	3	1	2	0
Dave Stockton	1971-77-(**91**)	5	3	1	1
Curtis Strange	1983-85-87-89-95-**2002**	20	6	12	2
Hal Sutton	1985-87-99-2002	16	7	5	4
David Toms	2002	5	3	1	1
Lee Trevino	1969-71-73-75-79-81-(**85**)	30	17	7	6
Jim Turnesa	1953	1	1	0	0
Joe Turnesa	1927-29	4	1	2	1
Ken Venturi	1965	4	1	3	0
Scott Verplank	2002	3	2	1	0
Lanny Wadkins	1977-79-83-85-87-89-91-93-(**95**)	33	20	11	2
Art Wall jr	1957-59-61	6	4	2	0
Al Watrous	1927-29	3	2	1	0
Tom Watson	1977-81-83-89-(**93**)	15	10	4	1
Tom Weiskopf	1973-75	10	7	2	1
Craig Wood	1931-33-35-*41	4	1	3	0
Tiger Woods	1997-99-2002	15	5	8	2
Lew Worsham	1947	2	2	0	0
Fuzzy Zoeller	1979-83-85	10	1	8	1

US teams were selected in 1939 and 1941, but did not play because of the Second World War

The Seve Trophy (Instituted 2000)

2000 Sunningdale, England	GBI 12½, Europe 13½	2002 Druid's Glen, Ireland	Europe 12½, GBI 14½

2003 *at El Saler, Valencia, Spain*
GB&I 15, Continental Europe 13
Full results can be found on page 130

PGA Cup (Instituted 1973)

Great Britain and Ireland Club Professionals v United States Club Professionals

1973	USA	Pinehurst, NC	13–3	*Played alternate years from 1984*			
1974	USA	Pinehurst, NC	11½–4½	1986	USA	Knollwood, Lake Fore, IL	16–9
1975	USA	Hillside, Southport, England	9½–6½	1988	USA	The Belfry, England	15½–10½
1976	USA	Moortown, Leeds, England	9½–6½	1990	USA	Turtle Point, Kiawah Island, SC	19–7
1977	Halved	Mission Hills, Palm Springs	8½–8½	1992	USA	K Club, Ireland	15–11
1978	GB&I	St Mellion, Cornwall	10½–6½	1994	USA	Palm Beach, Florida	15–11
1979	GB&I	Castletown, Isle of Man	12½–4½	1996	Halved	Gleneagles, Scotland	13–13
1980	USA	Oak Tree, Edmond, OK	15–6	1998	USA	The Broadmoor, Colorado	
1981	Halved	Turnberry Isle, Miami, FL	10½–10½			Springs, CO	11½–4½
1982	USA	Holston Hills, Knoxville, TN	13–7	2000	USA	Celtic Manor, Newport, Wales	13½–12½
1983	GB&I	Muirfield, Scotland	14½–6½	2002	*Cancelled.*		
1984	GB&I	Turnberry, Scotland	12½–8½				

2003 *at South Course, Port St Lucie, FL*

Captains: (USA) Jack Connelly (Huntingdon Valley, PA) & Will Mann (Swepsonville, NC) [joint];
(GBI) David Jones (Templepatrick)

First Day – Morning: Foursomes
Evans & Thelen beat Cameron & Longmuir 2 and 1
DeFrancesco & Labritz beat Edwards & Wesselingh 1 hole
Berry & Morin beat Dwyer & Hare 3 and 1
Gilmore & Weinhart beat Law & McGovern 4 and 3

Afternoon: Fourball
Stevens & Thelen beat Longmuir & Wesselingh 4 and 2
Berry & Morin beat Edwards & McGovern 3 and 2
Gilmore & Zabriski halved with Arnott & Dwyer
Labritz & Weinhart beat Bell & Hare 4 and 3

Second Day – Morning: Foursomes
Evans & Thelen beat Arnott & Edwards 6 and 5
Gilmore & Weinhart beat Dwyer & Hare 4 and 3
DeFrancesco & Labritz beat Cameron & Law 4 and 3
Berry & Stevens beat Longmuir & Wesselingh 3 and 2

Afternoon: Fourball
DeFrancesco & Labritz beat Cameron & McGovern
4 and 2
Evans & Morin halved with Edwards & Wesselingh
Berry & Thelen beat Hare & Law 4 and 3
Stevens & Zabriski beat Arnott & Dwyer 5 and 3

Third Day: Singles
Craig Stevens (Brookstone, Acworth, GA) lost to
Bill Longmuir (London GC, Ash, Kent) 4 and 2
Mike Gilmore (Piping Rock, Locust Valley, NY) lost to
Paul Wesselingh (Kedleston Park) 2 and 1
Tim Weinhart (River Pines, Alpharetta, GA) lost to
Simon Edwards (Bannal DR, Wrexham) 2 and 1
Alan Morin (The Falls, Lake Worth, FL) beat
John Dwyer (Ashbourne, Co.Meath) 3 and 2
Don Berry (Edinburgh, Brooklyn Park, MN) lost to
Andrew Hare (Cold Ashby, Northampton) 2 and 1
Wayne DeFrancesco (Woodholme, Baltimore, MD) lost to
Robert Arnott (Bishopbriggs, DR) 3 and 2
Barry Evans (Berry Hills, Charleston, WV) beat
Graeme Bell (Eaglescliffe, Stockton-on-Tees) 2 and 1
Tim Thelen (Baywood, Pasadena, TX) beat
Gordon Law (Uphall, West Lothian) 8 and 6
Rob Labritz (Glen Arbor, Bedford Hills, NY) beat
Brendan McGovern (Headfort, Co. Meath) 4 and 3
Bruce Zabriski (Old Palm,Palm Beach Gardens, FL) lost to
Bob Cameron (Sundridge Park) 3 and 2

Result: USA 19, Great Britain & Ireland 7

Presidents Cup (Instituted 1994)

1994	USA	Lake Manassas, Virginia	20–12
1996	USA	Lake Manassas, Virginia	16½–15½
1998	International	Royal Melbourne, Australia	20½–11½
2000	USA	Robert Trent Jones GC, Gainsville	20½–11½

The match scheduled for 2002 was postponed and the event was played on 18–23 November 2003 at Fancourt Hotel and CC, George, South Africa, and will continue in odd-numbered years

Praia d'el Rey Rover European Cup

(European Seniors v Ladies' European PGA, instituted 1997)

at Praia d'el Rey, Obidos, Portugal

1997	European PGA Seniors beat ELPGA	13–7
1998	European PGA Seniors halved with ELPGA	10–10
1999	Ladies' European Tour beat European PGA Seniors	11–9

Discontinued

Alfred Dunhill Cup (Held at St Andrews from 1985 to 2000)

Year	Winner	Runner-up	Score
1985	Australia (G Norman, G Marsh, D Graham)	USA (M O'Meara, R Floyd, C Strange)	3–0
1986	Australia (R Davis, D Graham, G Norman)	Japan (T Ozaki, N Ozaki, T Nakajima)	3–0
1987	England (N Faldo, G Brand, H Clark)	Scotland (S Lyle, S Torrance, G Brand jr)	2–1
1988	Ireland (D Smyth, R Rafferty, E Darcy)	Australia (R Davis, D Graham, G Norman)	2–1
1989	USA (M Calcavecchia, T Kite, C Strange)	Japan (H Meshiai, N Ozaki, K Suzuki)	3½–2½
1990	Ireland (P Walton, R Rafferty, D Feherty)	England (M James, R Boxall, H Clark)	3½–2½
1991	Sweden (A Forsbrand, P-U Johansson, M Lanner)	South Africa (J Bland, D Frost, G Player)	2–1
1992	England (S Richardson, J Spence, D Gilford)	Scotland (G Brand Jr, C Montgomerie, S Lyle)	2–0
1993	USA (P Stewart, F Couples, J Daly)	England (M James, N Faldo, P Baker)	2–1
1994	Canada (D Barr, R Gibson, R Stewart)	USA (T Kite, C Strange, F Couples)	2–1
1995	Scotland (A Coltart, C Montgomerie, S Torrance)	Zimbabwe (T Johnstone, M McNulty, N Price)	2–1
1996	USA (M O'Meara, P Mickelson, S Stricker)	New Zealand (F Nobilo, G Turner, G Waite)	2–1
1997	South Africa (R Goosen, D Frost, E Els)	Sweden (J Parnevik, P-U Johansson, J Haeggman)	2–1
1998	South Africa (R Goosen, D Frost, E Els)	Spain (MA Jiménez, S Luna, JM Olazábal)	2–1
1999	Spain (S García, JM Olazábal, MA Jiménez)	Australia (C Parry, PO'Malley, S Leaney)	2–1
2000	Spain (MA Martin, MA Jiménez, JM Olazábal)	South Africa (D Frost, R Goosen, E Els)	2–1

Discontinued

UBS Cup (Instituted 2001)

2001	USA	2002	USA

2003 *at Sea Island, St Simons Island, GA – November 21–23*

Dynasty Cup (Instituted 2003)

at Mission Hills, Shenzhen, China

Captains: Hsieh Min-nan (Tai) (Asia); Isao Aoki (Japan)

First Day – **Foursomes**

Zhang & Liang	1	Meshiai & Sato	0
Atwal & Singh	0	Fujita & Miyamoto	1
Lin & Kang	0	Teshima & Fukabori	1
Jaidee & Marksaeng	1	Suzuki & Kuwabara	0
Srirot & Wiratchant	0	Nakajima & Kondo	1
Randhawa & Wi	1	Murota & Imano	0
	3		3

Second Day – **Fourball**

Srirot & Wiratchant	0	Nakajima & Meshiai	1
Jaidee & Marksaeng	1	Miyamoto & Suzuki	0
Lin & Kang	1	Sato & Imano	0
Atwal & Singh	1	Fujita & Keiichiro Fukabori	0
Zhang & Liang	1	Murota & Kondo	0
Randhawa & Wi	1	Teshima & Kuwabara	0
	5		1

Match position: Asia 8, Japan 4

Third Day – **Singles**

Prayad Marksaeng (Tha)	1	Taichi Teshima	0
Kang Wook-soon (Kor)	1	Tohru Suzuki	0
Jyoti Randhawa (Ind)	1	Hirofumi Miyase	0
Thaworn Wiratchant (Tha)	0	Katsunori Kuwabara	1
Charlie Wi (Kor)	1	Hajime Meshiai	0
Liang Wen-chong (Chi)	1	Yasuharu Imano	0
Lin Keng-chi (Tai)	0	Kiyoshi Murota	1
Thammanoon Srirot (Tha)	1	Hiroyuki Fujita	0
Arjun Atwal (Ind)	0	Tommy Nakajima	1
Thongchai Jaidee (Tha)	½	Tomohiro Kondo	½
Jeev Milkha Singh (Ind)	1	Katsumasa Miyamoto	0
Zhang Lian-wei (Chi)	1	Nobuhito Sato	0
	8½		3½

Result: Asia 16½, Japan 7½

WGC – World Cup Qualifiers

Nations Cup (Asian Qualifer)

2000   Korea   2001   China   2002   Switzerland

2003 *at Singapore*

1	Myanmar	Kyi Hla Han and Aung Win	66-70-68-73—277
2	India	Digvijay Singh and Gaurav Ghei	70-73-68-71—282
	China[1]	Lian Wen-chong and Zheng Wen-gen	69-70-67-76—282
4	Hong Kong	Derek Fung and James Stewart	69-73-72-70—284

The above four teams qualify for the World Cup

Other finishers: 5 Sri Lanka, Thailand; 7 Malaysia, Philippines; 9 Finland; 10 Taiwan; 111 Guam; 11 Netherlands; 12 Mauritius; 13 Indonesia; 14 Nigeria

[1]China finished second but withdrew because of dates clashes with the Japan Tour School which affected Lian Wen-chong. Thailand (J Chitprasong and P Tipsanit) had earned the first reserve spot.

Nations Cup (Latin American Qualifer)

2003 *at Paradise Village, Nueva Vallarta, Nayarit, Mexico*

1	Chile	Roy Mackenzie and Felipe Aguilar	270
2	Mexico	Alejandro Quiroz and Antonio Maldonado	271

The above two teams qualify for the World Cup

Other finishers: 3 Costa Rica; 4 Colombia, Venezuela, Puerto Rico; 7 Bermuda; 8 Brazil, Bahamas; 10 Jamaica; 11 Israel; 12 Peru; 13 Poland, Guatemala

National and Regional Championships

National Championships

Glenmuir Club Professionals' Championship

Year	Player	Venue	Score	Year	Player	Venue	Score
1973	DN Sewell	Calcot Park	276	1988	R Weir	Harlech	269
1974	WB Murray	Calcot Park	275	1989	B Barnes	Sandwich, Prince's	280
1975	DN Sewell	Calcot Park	276	1990	A Webster	Carnoustie	292
1976	WJ Ferguson	Moortown	283	1991	W McGill	King's Lynn	285
1977	D Huish	Notts	284	1992	J Hoskison	St Pierre	275
1978	D Jones	Pannal	281	1993	C Hall	Coventry	274
1979	D Jones	Pannal	278	1994	D Jones	North Berwick	278
1980	D Jagger	Turnberry	286	1995	P Carman	West Hill	269
1981	M Steadman	Woburn	289	1996	B Longmuir	Co Louth	280
1982	D Durnian	Hill Valley	285	1997	B Rimmer	Northop	268
1983	J Farmer	Heaton Park	270	1998	M Jones	Royal St David's	280
1984	D Durnian	Bolton Old Links	278	1999	S Bebb*	Kings Lynn	283
1985	R Mann	The Belfry	291	2000	R Cameron*	St Andrews	295
1986	D Huish	R Birkdale	278	2001	S Edwards	County Louth	275
1987	R Weir	Sandiway	273	2002	B Cameron	Saunton	280

2003 *at St Andrews Bay*

1	Gordon Law (Uphall)		68-73-68-71—280
2	Scott Henderson (Kings Links)		69-77-69-69—284
3	Ian Keenan (Royal Liverpool)		71-72-69-73—285

The De Vere PGA Seniors' Championship

Year	Player	Venue	Score	Year	Player	Venue	Score
1970	M Faulkner	Longniddry	288	1987	N Coles	Turnberry	279
1971	K Nagle	Elie	269	1988	P Thomson	North Berwick	287
1972	K Bousfield	Longniddry	291	1989	N Coles	West Hill	277
1973	K Nagle	Elie	270	1990	B Waites	Brough	269
1974	E Lester	Lundin	282	1991	B Waites	Wollaton Park	277
1975	K Nagle	Longniddry	268	1992	T Horton	R Dublin	290
1976	C O'Connor	Cambridgeshire Hotel	284	1993	B Huggett	Sunningdale	204 (54)
1977	C O'Connor	Cambridgeshire Hotel	288	1994	J Morgan	Sunningdale	203
1978	P Skerritt	Cambridgeshire Hotel	288	1995	J Morgan	Sunningdale	204
1979	C O'Connor	Cambridgeshire Hotel	280	1996	T Gale	The Belfry	284
1980	P Skerritt	Gleneagles Hotel	286	1997	W Hall	The Belfry	277
1981	C O'Connor	North Berwick	287	1998	T Horton	The Belfry	277
1982	C O'Connor	Longniddry	285	1999	R Metherall	The Belfry	276
1983	C O'Connor	Burnham and Berrow	277	2000	J Grace*	The Belfry	282
1984	E Jones	Stratford-upon-Avon	280	2001	I Stanley	Carden Park	278
1985	N Coles	Pannal, Harrogate	284	2002	S Ebihara	Carden Park	267
1986	N Coles	Mere, Cheshire	276				

2003 *at Carden Park*

1	Bill Longmuir (Sco)		68-67-69-67—271
2	Carl Mason (Eng)		71-69-64-69—273
	Denis O'Sullivan (Ire)		65-71-70-67—273

PGA British Assistants Championship

1984	G Weir	Coombe Hill	286	1994	M Plummer	Burnham & Berrow	278
1985	G Coles	Coombe Hill	284	1995	I Sparkes	The Warwickshire	285
1986	J Brennand	Sand Moor	280	1996	S Purves	Moor Allerton	281
1987	J Hawksworth	Coombe Hill	282	1997	P Sefton	De Vere, Blackpool	273
1988	J Oates	Coventry	284	1998	A Raitt	Bearwood Lakes	280
1989	C Brooks	Hillside	291	1999	I Harrison	Bearwood Lakes	274
1990	A Ashton	Hillside	213 (54)	2000	T Anderson	St Annes Old Links	273
1991	S Wood	Wentworth	288	2001	C Goodfellow	St Annes Old Links	207
1992	P Mayo	E Sussex National	285	2002	D Orr	St Annes Old Links	271
1993	C Everett	Oaklands	280				

2003 *at St Annes Old Links, Lytham*

1	Matthew Tottey (North Wales)*		67-68-69—204
2	Neil Ridewood (Hartswood)		67-69-68—204
3	Iain Ferrie (Bowood)		68-71-66—205
	John Wells (Beverley & East Riding)		69-66-70—205

Smurfit Irish PGA Championship

1944	H Bradshaw	Hermitage	291	1974	E Polland	Portstewart	277
1945	J McKenna	Newlands	283	1975	C O'Connor	Carlow	275
1946	F Daly	Clandeboye	285	1976	P McGuirk	Waterville	291
1947	H Bradshaw	County Louth	291	1977	P Skerritt	Woodbrook	281
1948	J McKenna	Galway	285	1978	C O'Connor	Dollymount	286
1949	C Kane	Portrush	301	1979	D Smyth	Dollymount	215 (54)
1950	H Bradshaw	Grange	277	1980	D Feherty	Dollymount	283
1951	H Bradshaw	Balmoral	280	1981	D Jones	Woodbrook	283
1952	F Daly	Mullingar	284	1982	D Feherty	Woodbrook	287
1953	H Bradshaw	Dundalk	272	1983	L Higgins	Woodbrook	275
1954	H Bradshaw	Newcastle	300	1984	M Sludds	Skerries	277
1955	E Jones	Castleroy	276	1985	D Smyth	Co Louth	204 (54)
1956	C Greene	Clandeboye	281	1986	D Smyth	Waterville	282
1957	H Bradshaw	Ballybunion	286	1987	P Walton	Co Louth	144 (36)
1958	C O'Connor	Royal Belfast	279	1988	E Darcy	Castle, Dublin	269
1959	NV Drew	Mullingar	282	1989	P Walton	Castle, Dublin	266
1960	C O'Connor	Warrenpoint	271	1990	D Smyth	Woodbrook	271
1961	C O'Connor	Lahinch	280	1991	P Walton	Woodbrook	277
1962	C O'Connor	Bangor	264	1992	E Darcy	K Club	285
1963	C O'Connor	Little Island	271	1993	M Sludds	K Club	285
1964	E Jones	Knock	279	1994	D Clarke	Galway Bay	285
1965	C O'Connor	Mullingar	283	1995	P Walton	Belvoir Park	273
1966	C O'Connor	Warrenpoint	269	1996	D Smyth	Slieve Russell GC	281
1967	H Boyle	Tullamore	214 (54)	1997	P McGinley	Fota Island	285
1968	C Greene	Knock	282	1998	P Harrington*	Powerscourt	216 (54)
1969	J Martin	Dundalk	268	1999	N Manchip	The Island	271
1970	H Jackson	Massareene	283	2000	P McGinley	Co Louth	270
1971	C O'Connor	Galway	278	2001	D Smyth	Castle Rock	273
1972	J Kinsella	Bundoran	289	2002	P McGinley	Westport	213
1973	J Kinsella	Limerick	284				

2003 *at Adare Manor*

1	Paul McGinley (K Club)		71-68-69-72—280
2	Gary Murphy (unattached)		74-66-73-72—285
3	Michael Hoey (unattached)		71-70-73-72—286

Irish Club Professionals' Championship

1993	D Mooney	Royal Tara	208	1998	L Robinson	Nuremore	140
1994	K O'Donnell	Knockanally	216	1999	N Manchip	Nuremore	139
1995	D Jones	Fota Island	145	2000	L Walker	Nuremore	134
1996	B McGovern	Headfort	140	2001	M Allen*	Nuremore	142
1997	N Manchip	Mount Wolseley	141	2002	N Manchip	Nuremore	135

2003 *at Tulfarris*

1	Damian Mooney (Laganview Centre)*	71-72—143
2	Geoff Loughrey (unattached)	72-71—143
3	Jimmy Heggarty (Spawell DR)	74-70—144

Young Professionals Scottish Championship
(formerly Macallan Spey Scottish Assistant's Championship)

1980	F Mann	Dunbar	294	1992	E McIntosh	Turnberry Hotel	266
1981	M Brown	West Kilbride	290	1993	J Wither	Alloa	280
1982	R Collinson	West Kilbride	294	1994	S Henderson	Newmacher	283
1983	A Webster	Stirling	285	1995	A Tait	Newmacher	276
1984	C Elliott	Stirling	285	1996	S Thompson	Newmacher	278
1985	C Elliott	Falkirk Tryst	284	1997	M Hastie	Balbirnie Park	275
1986	P Helsby	Erskine	295	1998	D Orr	Balbirnie Park	272
1987	C Innes	Hilton Park	284	1999	A Forsyth	Balbirnie Park	269
1988	G Collinson	Turnberry	289	2000	C Lee	Balbirnie Park	275
1989	C Brooks	Windyhill	282	2001	C Kelly	Spey Bay	275
1990	P Lawrie	Cruden Bay	279	2002	C Kelly	Spey Bay	277
1991	G Hume	Kilmarnock Barassie	299				

2003 *at Balbirnie Park*

1	Gary Dingwall (Royal Dornoch)	74-71-68-68—281
2	Derek Watters (Largs)	69-73-73-68—283
	Euan Cameron (Esporta Dougalston)	69-70-74-70—283

Scottish Match Play Championship
Sponsored by Aberdeen Asset Management at Meldrum House, Aberdeen

2002   Paul Lawrie

2003 *not played*

Scottish Professionals' Championship

1965	EC Brown	Forfar	271	1984	I Young	Dalmahoy	276
1966T	EC Brown	Cruden Bay	137 (36)	1985	S Torrance	Dalmahoy	277
	J Panton			1986	R Drummond	Glenbervie	270
1967	H Bannerman	Montrose	279	1987	R Drummond	Glenbervie	268
1968	EC Brown	Monktonhall	286	1988	S Stephen	Haggs Castle	283
1969	G Cunningham	Machrihanish	284	1989	R Drummond	Monktonhall	274
1970	RDBM Shade	Montrose	276	1990	R Drummond	Deer Park	278
1971	NJ Gallacher	Lundin Links	282	1991	S Torrance	Erskine	274
1972	H Bannerman	Strathaven	268	1992	P Lawrie	Cardross	273
1973	BJ Gallacher	Kings Links	276	1993	S Torrance	Dalmahoy	269
1974	BJ Gallacher	Drumpellier	276	1994	A Coltart	Dalmahoy	281
1975	D Huish	Duddingston	279	1995	C Gillies	Dalmahoy	278
1976	J Chillas	Haggs Castle	286	1996	B Marchbank	Dalmahoy	276
1977	BJ Gallacher	Barnton	282	1997	G Law	Downfield	284
1978	S Torrance	Strathaven	269	1998	C Gillies	Newmacher	273
1979	AWB Lyle	Glasgow Gailes	274	1999	G Hutcheon	Gleneagles	288
1980	S Torrance	East Kilbride	273	2000	A Forsyth	Gleneagles	255
1981	B Barnes	Dalmahoy	275	2001	J Chillas	Gleneagles	284
1982	B Barnes	Dalmahoy	286	2002	F Mann	Gleneagles	280
1983	B Gallacher	Dalmahoy	276				

2003 *at Gleneagles*

1	Chris Kelly (Scotscraig)	67-70-69-69—275
2	Scott Henderson (Kings Links)	72-69-71-70—282
3	Ross Drummond (Jim Farmer Golf)	66-75-70-72—283

Craigielaw Classic *at Craigielaw*

2003

1	Chris Kelly (Scotscraig)	67-69-66-68—270
2	Scott Henderson (Kings Links)	66-66-74-66—272
	Mark King (Kingsfield)	71-70-63-68—272

Welsh National Championships

Year	Winner	Venue	Score		Year	Winner	Venue	Score
1960	RH Kemp jr	Llandudno	288		1982	C DeFoy	Cardiff	137
1961	S Mouland	Southerndown	286		1983	S Cox	Cardiff	136
1962	S Mouland	Porthcawl	302		1984	K Jones	Cardiff	135
1963	H Gould	Wrexham	291		1985	D Llewellyn	Whitchurch	132
1964	B Bielby	Tenby	297		1986	P Parkin	Whitchurch	142
1965	S Mouland	Penarth	281		1987	A Dodman	Cardiff	132
1966	S Mouland	Conway	281		1988	I Woosnam	Cardiff	137
1967	S Mouland	Pyle and Kenfig	219 (54)		1989	K Jones	Royal Porthcawl	140
1968	RJ Davies	Southerndown	292		1990	P Mayo	Fairwood Park	136
1969	S Mouland	Llandudno	277		1991	P Mayo	Fairwood Park	138
1970	W Evans	Tredegar Park	289		1992	C Evans	Asburnham	142
1971	J Buckley	St Pierre	291		1993	P Price	Caerphilly	138
1972	J Buckley	Porthcawl	298		1994	M Plummer	Northop	133
1973	A Griffiths	Newport	289		1995	S Dodd	Northop	139
1974	M Hughes	Cardiff	284		1996	M Stanford	Northop	137
1975	C DeFoy	Whitchurch	285		1997	M Ellis	Vale of Glamorgan	139
1976	S Cox	Radyr	284		1998	L Bond	Vale of Glamorgan	69 (18)
1977	C DeFoy	Glamorganshire	135		1999	R Dinsdale	Vale of Glamorgan	134
1978	BCC Huggett	Whitchurch	145		2000	M Plummer	Newport	136
1979	*Cancelled*				2001	S Dodd	Ashburnham	214
1980	A Griffiths	Cardiff	139		2002	S Edwards	Pyle & Kenfig	210
1981	C DeFoy	Cardiff	139					

2003 *at Porthmadog*

1	Simon Edwards (Wrexham)	64-65-67—196 (-17)
2	Ian Harrison (Woodlake Park)	66-63-68—197
3	Paul Mayo (Newport)	68-69-64—201

PGA of Europe Championship

1983	Cees Renders (Ned)		1989	Russell Weir (Sco)	1997	Claude Grenier (Aut)
1984	Donald Armour (Ned)		1990	John Woof (Ned)	1998	Simon Brown (Eng)
1985	John Woof (Ned)		1991	Paul Carman (Eng)	1999	Richard Dinsdale (Wal)
1986	Stuart Brown (Eng)		1992	Tim Giles (Eng)	2000	Sion Bebb (Wal)
1987	Jim Rhodes (Eng)		1993	Russell Weir (Sco)	2001	A George (Eng)
1988	Russell Weir (Sco)		1994/1996 – *not played*		2002	P Wesselingh (Eng)

2003 *not played*

PGA of Europe Team Championship

1990	Scotland	1995	Spain	2000	Wales
1991	Netherlands	1996	Scotland	2001	Spain
1992	Scotland	1997	Scotland	2002	Spain
1993	Scotland	1998	Ireland		
1994	*Not played*	1999	England		

2003 *being played at Atalaya Park, Spain, in December*

Regional Championships

Bedford & Cambridge PGA

1994	R Robertson	1999	P Simpson
1995	D Armor	2000	F Kiddie
1996	J Boast	2001	P Abbott
1997	M Roberts	2002	P Abbott
1998	A George	2003	M Litton

Berks, Bucks & Oxon

2003	S Wells

Cheshire & North Wales

2003	S Edwards

Derbyshire Professionals

1994	D Stafford	1999	D Russell
1995	A Carnall	2000	M Smith
1996	C Cross	2001	M Smith
1997	A Carnall	2002	M Poxon
1998	J Mellor	2003	P Wesselingh

Devon Open

1994	I Higgins	1999	J Langmead
1995	B Austin	2000	B Austin
1996	J Langmead	2001	B Austin
1997	J Langmead	2002	B Austin
1998	D Sheppard	2003	R Knott

East Anglian Open

1994	R Mann	1999	P Curry
1995	N Brown	2000	J Bevan
1996	N Brown	2001	D Parker
1997	I Poulter	2002	I Ellis
1998	P Curry	2003	I Ellis

East Region PGA

1995	*Not Played*	1999	S Khan
1995	L Fickling	2000	I Ellis
1996	T Charnley	2001	P Barham
1997	R Mann	2002	D Parker
1998	T Charnley	2003	P Cherry

Essex Open

1994	D Jones	1999	P Joiner
1995	J Robson	2000	S Khan
1996	S Khan	2001	R Coles
1997	V Cox	2002	D Parker
1998	J Robson	2003	S Cipa/M Stokes

Essex Professionals

1994	V Cox	1999	P Curry
1995	M Stokes	2000	W McColl
1996	P Joiner	2001	J Fryatt
1997	M Stokes	2002	R Green
1998	G Carter	2003	M Stokes

Hampshire PGA

1994	G Hughes	1999	J Barnes
1995	I Benson	2000	K Saunders
1996	R Bland	2001	S Cowle
1997	J Lovell	2002	K Saunders
1998	G Hughes	2003	J Barnes

Hampshire Match Play

1994	M Wheeler	1999	J Lovell
1995	M Wheeler	2000	M Robbins
1996	J Le Roux	2001	P Bryden
1997	D Harris	2002	J Barnes
1998	D Harris	2003	R Tate

Hampshire, Isle of Wight and Channel Islands Open

1994	R Bland	1999	R Bland
1995	R Bland	2000	R Bland
1996	G Hughes	2001	S Cowle
1997	M Blackey	2002	R Tate
1998	R Bland	2003	M Treleaven

Herts Professionals

1994T	N Brown	1999	L Jones
	D Tapping	2000	R Mitchell
1995	N Brown	2001	A Bailey
1996	R Hurd	2002	D Field
1997	P Winston	2003	D Tapping
1998T	R Mitchell		
	I Parker		

Kent Open

1994	T Berry	1999	R Cameron
1995	T Milford	2000	M McLean
1996	S Green	2001	J Marshall
1997	S Page	2002	M Day
1998	D Parris	2003	M McLean

Kent PGA

1994	M Lawrence	1999	R Cameron
1995	T Poole	2000	B Coomber
1996	A Butterfield	2001	S Wood
1997	P Lyons	2002	S Stevens
1998	T Milford	2003	S Green

Lancashire Open

1994	A Lancaster	1999	C Corrigan
1995	G Furey	2000	G Furey
1996	G Furey	2001	M Hollingsworth
1997	G Furey	2002	S Astin
1998	J Cheetham	2003	D Shacklady

Leicestershire & Rutland Open

1994	J Herbert	1999	I Ball
1995	I Lyner	2000	M Cort
1996	D Gibson	2001	I Ball
1997	N Bland	2002	G Shaw
1998	J Caylis (am)	2003	G Shaw

Lincolnshire Open

1994	S Brewer	1999	M King (am)
1995	S Cox	2000	M King (am)
1996	S Bennett	2001	S Emery
1997	M King (am)	2002	S Emery
1998	M King (am)	2003	D Greenwood

Middlesex PGA

1994	L Fickling	1999	N Wichelow
1995	S Whiffin	2000	S Whiffin
1996	N Wichelow	2001	N Wichelow
1997	L Jones	2002	P Winston
1998	L Jones	2003	S Whiffin

Middlesex Open

2003	L Curling

Midland Professionals

1996	S Bennett (M) DJ Russell (S)	2000	R Rock (M) DJ Russell (S)
1997	J Higgins (M and S)	2001	J Robinson (M) T Rouse (S)
1998	J Robinson (M) S Webster (S)	2002	I Lyner (M) R Rock (S)
1999	I Ball (M) C Hall (S)	2003	P Edwards (S)

Norfolk Open

1994	J Hill	1999	P Little
1995	M Barrett	2000	M Jubb
1996	M Barrett	2001	D Henderson (am)
1997	N Lythgoe	2002	A Varney
1998	R Wilson	2003	A Varney

Norfolk Professionals

1994	A Collison	1999	I Ellis
1995	P Briggs	2000	M Jubb
1996	P Bower	2001	A Collison
1997	T Varney	2002	A Varney
1998	R Wilson	2003	A Varney

Northern Region PGA

1994	P Wesselingh	1999	R Wragg
1995	G Furey	2000	C Hislop
1996	S Townend	2001	B Sharrock
1997	G Furey	2002	P Archer
1998	P Carman	2003	J Cheetham

Northern Open

1994	K Stables	1999	A Forsyth
1995	J Higgins	2000	J Payne
1996	S Henderson	2001	G Rankin
1997	D Thomson	2002	F Mann
1998	L James	2003	G Law

Northumberland & Durham Open

2002	B Rumney	2003	S McKenna

South West PGA

1994	G Emerson	1999	G Ryall
1995	G Howell	2000	K Spurgeon
1996	M Stanford	2001	M Wiggett
1997	M Stanford	2002	B Austin
1998	S Little	2003	*Not played*

Southern Assistants

1994	M Wheeler	1999	C Fromant
1995	P Lyons	2000	N Reilly
1996	D Parris	2001	C Roake
1997	A Lovelace	2002	P Schunter
1998	D Parris	2003	N Reilly

Southern Assistants Match Play

1994	M Groombridge	1999	M Nichols
1995	M Groombridge	2000	S Wells
1996	A Butterfield	2001	S Crooks
1997	B Hodkin	2002	G Lingard
1998	B Hodkin	2003	R Campbell

Southern Professionals

1994	R Edwards	1999	S Wood
1995	P Sefton	2000	P Robshaw
1996	P Hughes	2001	K Saunders
1997	P Sherman	2002	A Lovelace
1998	P Simpson	2003	M Hazelden

Staffordshire Open

1994	D Scott	1999	G Beddow
1995	I Proverbs	2000	J Cookson (am)
1996	B Rimmer	2001	R Maxfield (am)
1997	A Roger	2002	I Proverbs
1998	R Peace	2003	I Benson

Staffordshire and Shropshire

1994	J Rhodes	2000	P Wesselingh
1995	B Stevens	2001	S Russell
1996	J Higgins	2002	G Gilligan (S)
1997	R Fisher		J Harrold (M)
1998	A Feriday	2003	*Not played*
1999	P Wesselingh		

Suffolk Open

1994	L Patterson	1999	S MacPherson
1995	R Mann	2000	J Keeley
1996	S MacPherson	2001	J Moul (am)
1997	P Wilby	2002	A Lucas
1998	J Wright	2003	S Keeley

Suffolk Professionals

1994	C Jenkins (M)		S MacPherson (S)
	L Patterson (S)	1999	R Mann (M)
1995	C Jenkins (M)		S MacPherson (S)
	R Mann (S)	2000	R Hitchcock (M)
1996	K Vince (M)		J Bevan (S)
	T Cooper (S)	2001	J Moul (am) (M)
1997T	A Cotton (M)		A Cotton (S)
	A Lucas (S)	2002	R Mann
	C Jenkins (S)	2003	S Keeley
1998	K Golding (M)		

Surrey Open

1994	M Nichols	1999	H Stott
1995	A Wall	2000	C Gane
1996	P Hughes	2001	N Reilly
1997	M Nichols	2002	M Nichols
1998	P Sefton	2003	R Humphrey

Sussex Open

1994	K Hinton	1999	P Lyons
1995	J Blamires	2000	P Lyons
1996	K Macdonald	2001	G Murray
1997	K Macdonald	2002	T Spence
1998	J Doherty (am)	2003	J Harris

Ulster Professionals

1994	P Russell	1999	D Mooney
1995	R Burns	2000	P Collins
1996	J Heggarty	2001	J Dwyer
1997	D Mooney	2002	L Walker
1998	D Mooney	2003	L Walker

Warwickshire Open

1994	D White	1999	D Clayton
1995	C Dowling	2000	T Whitehouse (am)
1996	P Chalkley	2001	A Carey
1997	D Barton	2002	M Morris
1998	SJ Walker	2003	A Carey

Warwickshire Professionals

1994	C Wicketts (M)	1999	D Clayton (M)
	S Webster (am)		A Bownes (S)
	(S)	2000	A Carey (M)
1995	J Cook		A Stokes (S)
	(M and S)	2001	A Stokes (M)
1996	C Phillips (M)		A Bownes (S)
	S Edwards (S)	2002	M Morris (M and
1997	L Bashford (M)		S)
	C Phillips (S)	2003	A Bownes (M)
1998	C Phillips (M)		A Carey (S)
	J Corns* (S)		

West Region PGA

1994	S Little	1999	S Little
1995	M Thompson	2000	M Higley
1996	M McEwan	2001	I Ferrie
1997	M Thompson	2002	M Thompson
1998	J Taylor	2003	B Austin

Hills Wiltshire Pro Champ

1994	S Robertson	1999	S McDonald
1995	G Laing	2000	A Beal
1996	B Sandry	2001	S Robertson
1997	M Smith	2002	D Hutton
1998	R Blake	2003	D Hutton

Worcestershire Open

1994	S Edwards	1999	S Edwards
1995	C Clark	2000	N Turley
1996	D Clee	2001	N Turley
1997	P Scarrett	2002	R Wassell
1998	D Eddiford*	2003	M Butler

Worcestershire PGA

1994	C Clark	1999	F Clark
1995	I Clark	2000	J Jones
1996	F Clark	2001	N Turley
1997	I Clark	2002	M Toombes
1998	D Eddiford	2003	M Quigley

Yorkshire Professionals

1994	L Turner	1999	G Brown
1995	R Golding	2000	G Walker
1996	N Ludwell	2001	A Ambler
1997	S Robinson	2002	A Ambler
1998	G Brown	2003	A Wainwright

Overseas National Championships

(Excluding European Tour or Affiliated Events)

Australian Open

1904 Hon Michael Scott (am)	1959 Kel Nagle
1905 Dan Soutar	1960 Bruce Devlin (am)
1906 Carnegie Clark (am)	1961 Frank Phillips
1907 Hon Michael Scott (am)	1962 Gary Player
1908 Clyde Pearce (am)	1963 Gary Player
1909 C Felstead (am)	1964 Jack Nicklaus
1910 Carnegie Clark (am)	1965 Gary Player
1911 Carnegie Clark (am)	1966 Arnold Palmer
1912 Ivo Whitton (am)	1967 Peter Thomson
1913 Ivo Whitton (am)	1968 Jack Nicklaus
1914-1919 not played	1969 Gary Player
1920 Joe Kirkwood	1970 Gary Player
1921 A Le Fevre	1971 Jack Nicklaus
1922 C Campbell	1972 Peter Thomson
1923 T Howard	1973 J C Snead
1924 A Russell (am)	1974 Gary Player
1925 Fred Popplewell	1975 Jack Nicklaus
1926 Ivo Whitton (am)	1976 Jack Nicklaus
1927 R Stewart	1977 David Graham
1928 Fred Popplewell	1978 Jack Nicklaus
1929 Ivo Whitton (am)	1979 Jack Newton
1930 F Eyre	1980 Greg Norman
1931 Ivo Whitton (am)	1981 Bill Rogers
1932 Mick Ryan (am)	1982 Bob Shearer
1933 M Kelly	1983 Peter Fowler
1934 Bill Bolger	1984 Tom Watson
1935 F McMahon	1985 Greg Norman
1936 Gene Sarazen	1986 Rodger Davis
1937 George Naismith	1987 Greg Norman
1938 Jim Ferrier (am)	1988 Mark Calcavecchia
1939 Jim Ferrier (am)	1989 Peter Senior
1940-1945 not played	1990 John Morse
1946 Ossie Pickworth	1991 Wayne Riley
1947 Ossie Pickworth	1992 Steve Elkington
1948 Ossie Pickworth	1993 Brad Faxon
1949 Eric Cremin	1994 Robert Allenby
1950 Norman Von Nida	1995 Greg Norman
1951 Peter Thomson	1996 Greg Norman
1952 Norman Von Nida	1997 Lee Westwood
1953 Norman Von Nida	1998 Greg Chalmers
1954 Ossie Pickworth	1999 Aaron Baddeley (am)
1955 Bobby Locke	2000 Aaron Baddeley
1956 Bruce Crampton	2001 Stuart Appleby
1957 Frank Phillips	2002 Stuart Appleby
1958 Gary Player	2003 Steve Allan

Austrian Open

1993 R Rafferty	1999 J Ciola
1994 M Davis	2000 Not played
1995 A Cejka	2001 C Gane
1996 P McGinley	2002 M Brier
1997 E Simsek	2003 M Brier
1998 K Carissimi	

Canadian Open

1904 J H Oke	1956 D Sanders (am)
1905 G Cumming	1957 G Bayer
1906 C Murray	1958 W Ellis jr
1907 P Barrett	1959 D Ford
1908 A Murray	1960 A Wall jr
1909 K Keffer	1961 J Cupit
1910 D Kenny	1962 T Kroll
1911 C Murray	1963 D Ford
1912 G Sargent	1964 KDG Nagle
1913 A Murray	1965 G Littler
1914 K Kesser	1966 D Massengale
1915-1918 not played	1967 W Casper
1919 J D Edgar	1968 RJ Charles
1920 J D Edgar	1969 T Aaron
1921 W H Trovinger	1970 D Zarley
1922 A Watrous	1971 L Trevino
1923 C W Hackney	1972 G Brewer jr
1924 L Diegel	1973 T Weiskopf
1925 L Diegel	1974 B Nichols
1926 M Smith	1975 T Weiskopf
1927 T Armour	1976 J Pate
1928 L Diegel	1977 L Trevino
1929 L Diegel	1978 B Lietzke
1930 T Armour	1979 L Trevino
1931 W Hagen	1980 B Gilder
1932 H Cooper	1981 P Oosterhuis
1933 J Kirkwood	1982 B Lietzke
1934 T Armour	1983 J Cook
1935 G Kunes	1984 G Norman
1936 L Little	1985 C Strange
1937 H Cooper	1986 B Murphy
1938 S Snead	1987 C Strange
1939 H McSpaden	1988 K Green
1940 S Snead	1989 S Jones
1941 S Snead	1990 W Levi
1942 C Wood	1991 N Price
1943-1944 not played	1992 G Norman
1945 B Nelson	1993 D Frost
1946 G Fazio	1994 N Price
1947 AD Locke	1995 M O'Meara
1948 CW Congdon	1996 D Hart
1949 E J Harrison	1997 S Jones
1950 J Ferrier	1998 B Andrade
1951 J Ferrier	1999 H Sutton
1952 J Palmer	2000 T Woods
1953 D Douglas	2001 S Verplank
1954 P Fletcher	2002 J Rollins
1955 A Palmer	2003 R Tway

Hong Kong Open

1993	B Watts	1999	P Sjöland
1994	D Frost	2000	S Dyson
1995	G Webb	2001	J M Olazábal
1996	G Webb	2002	F Jacobson
1997	F Nobilo	2003	*To be played*
1998	WS Kang		

Korean Open

1993	Y Kun Han	1999	Choi Kyung Ju
1994	M Cunning	2000	T Jaidee
1995	B Jobe	2001	DS Kim (am)
1996	Choi Kyung-Ju	2002	S García
1997	K Jong-Duck	2003	J Daly (USA)
1998	DS Kim (am)		

Indian Open

1993	A Sher	1999	A Atwal
1994	E Aubrey	2000	J Randhawa
1995	J Rutledge	2001	T Jaidee
1996	H Shirakata	2002	V Kumar
1997	E Fryatt	2003	M Cunning
1998	A Firoz		

New Zealand Open

1993	P Fowler	1999	M Lane
1994	C Jones	2000	M Campbell
1995	L Parsons	2001	C Parry
1996	M Long	2002	C Parry
1997	G Turner	2003	M Pearce
1998	G Turner		

Japanese Open

1993	S Okuda	1999	N Ozaki
1994	M Ozaki	2000	N Ozaki
1995	T Izwa	2001	T Teshima
1996	P Teravainen	2002	D Smail
1997	C Parry	2003	K Fukabori
1998	H Tanaka		

Singapore Open

1993	P Maloney	1999	J Milkha Singh
1994	KH Han	2000	J Randhawa
1995	S Conran	2001	T Warachant
1996	J Kernohan	2002	*Not played*
1997	Z Moe	2003	*Not played*
1998	S Micheel		

Kenya Open

1993	C Maltman	1999	M Lafeber
1994	P Carman	2000	T Immelman
1995	J Lee	2001	A Roestoff
1996	M Miller	2002	I James
1997	J Berendt	2003	*Not played*
1998	R Gonzalez		

Zambian Open

1993	P Harrison	1999	*Not played*
1994	*Not played*	2000	J Loughnane
1995	*Not played*	2001	M Foster
1996	D Botes	2002	M Cayeux
1997	*Not played*	2003	J Edfors
1998	M Cayeux		

Other 2003 Overseas National Championships

Caribbean Open	R Gomez	Malaysian Open	A Atwal
Danish Open	M Fraser	Portuguese Open	F Jacobson
Finnish Open	J Elson	Russian Open	M Fraser
French Open	P Golding	South African Open	T Immelman
Italian Open	M Grönberg	Spanish Open	K Ferrie

PART III

Women's Professional Tournaments

Golf Weekly World Ranking	194
Evian Ladies' European Tour	195
US LPGA Tour	199
Futures Tour	206
Japan LPGA Tour	207
International Team Events	209
Professional Women's Overseas Championships	214

Golf Weekly World Ranking for Women's Professional Golf

Latest ranking after Mobile LPGA Tournament of Champions

1	Annika Sorenstam (Swe)	821.08
2	Se Ri Pak (Kor)	629.71
3	Grace Park (Kor)	474.98
4	Karrie Webb (Aus)	406.47
5	Juli Inkster (USA)	357.75
6	Rachel Teske (Aus)	343.75
7	Hee-Won Han (Kor)	339.17
8	Sophie Gustafson (Swe)	294.71
9	Beth Daniel (USA)	288.81
10	Rosie Jones (USA)	288.39
11	Candie Kung (Tai)	263.83
12	Lorie Kane (Can)	262.26
13	Laura Davies (Eng)	260.78
14	Cristie Kerr (USA)	234.99
15	Lorena Ochoa (Mex)	234.69
16	Patricia Meunier-Lebouc (Fra)	221.12
17	Meg Mallon (USA)	220.00
18	Mi Hyun Kim (Kor)	203.31
19	Yuri Fudoh (Jpn)	201.80
20	Catriona Matthew (Sco)	191.89
21	Michele Redman (USA)	176.39
22	Laura Diaz (USA)	166.20
23	Becky Morgan (Wal)	141.15
24	Angela Stanford (USA)	137.10
25	Dorothy Delasin (USA)	135.78
26	Suzann Pettersen (Nor)	135.52
27	Jennifer Rosales (Phi)	132.70
28	Elisabeth Esterl (Ger)	130.04
29	Jeong Jang (Kor)	128.29
30	Mhairi McKay (Sco)	127.50
31	Wendy Ward (USA)	126.19
32	Carin Koch (Swe)	121.31
33	Gloria Park (Kor)	119.00
34	Soo Yun Kang (Kor)	115.26
35	Woo-Soon Ko (Kor)	114.24
36	Pat Hurst (USA)	112.98
37	Iben Tinning (Den)	106.21
38	Toshimi Kimura (Jpn)	101.35
39	Kelly Robbins (USA)	101.10
40	Shani Waugh (Aus)	96.20
41	Heather Bowie (USA)	94.51
42	Ok-Hee Ku (Kor)	89.83
43	Helen Alfredsson (Swe)	86.58
44	Lynnette Brooky (NZ)	86.10
45	Akiko Fukushima (Jpn)	85.70
46	Kasumi Fujii (Jpn)	83.66
47	Michelle Ellis (Aus)	82.50
48	Danielle Ammaccapane (USA)	80.45
49	Ana Belen Sanchez (Esp)	78.24
50	Karen Stupples (Eng)	76.61
51	Paula Marti (Esp)	75.88
52	Jung Yeon Lee (Jpn)	71.90
53	Wendy Doolan (Aus)	69.92
54	Hilary Lunke (USA)	68.50
55	Young Kim (Kor)	66.00
56	Ji-hee Lee (Kor)	66.00
57	Tammie Green (USA)	63.50
58	Trish Johnson (Eng)	61.88
59	Kate Golden (USA)	61.60
60	Janice Moodie (Sco)	59.25
61	Ikuyo Shiotani (Jpn)	59.00
62	Leta Lindley (USA)	58.80
63	Beth Bauer (USA)	58.25
64	Kelli Kuehne (USA)	57.42
65	Kaori Higo (Jpn)	56.71
66	Vicki Goetze Ackerman (USA)	56.52
67	Donna Andrews (USA)	56.10
68	Kirsty Taylor (Eng)	55.38
69	Emilee Klein (USA)	55.21
70	Junko Omote (Jpn)	55.10
71	Miho Koga (Jpn)	54.40
72	Ludivine Kreutz (Fra)	52.25
73	Maria Hjorth (Swe)	51.80
74	Gina Scott (NZ)	51.25
75	Karine Icher (Fra)	50.58
76	Corinne Dibnah (Aus)	50.54
77	Kim Saiki (USA)	50.25
78	Johanna Head (Eng)	50.00
79	Alison Nicholas (Eng)	49.14
80	Marisa Baena (USA)	49.00
81	Orie Fujino (Jpn)	47.00
82	Christina Kim (USA)	46.16
83	Liselotte Neumann (Swe)	45.68
84	Silvia Cavalleri (Ita)	44.63
85	Catrin Nilsmark (Swe)	44.09
86	Joanne Mills (Aus)	44.00
87	Kaori Suzuki (Jpn)	43.20
88	Yun Jye Wei (Jpn)	43.16
89	Marlene Hedblom (Swe)	43.08
90	Michiko Hattori (Jpn)	42.41
91	Brandie Burton (USA)	41.64
92	Shi Hyun Ahn (Kor)	40.00
93	Natalie Gulbis (USA)	39.35
94	Hsiu-Feng Tseng (Jpn)	39.20
95	Vibeke Stensrud (Nor)	37.25
96	Stephanie Arricau (Fra)	36.83
97	Samantha Head (Eng)	36.00
98	Betsy King (USA)	35.50
99	Young-A Yang (Kor)	35.10
100	Raquel Carriedo (Esp)	34.56

Evian Ladies' European Tour, 2003

Final Order of Merit (The top 90 players retain a full card)

1	Sophie Gustafson (Swe)	917.95		52	Laurette Maritz (RSA)	87.41
2	Elisabeth Esterl (Ger)	702.46		53	Cherie Byrnes (Aus)	85.90
3	Laura Davies (Eng)	681.25		54	Marina Arruti (Esp)	84.84
4	Iben Tinning (Den)	466.15		55	Georgina Simpson (Eng)	84.80
5	Lynnette Brooky (NZ)	391.85		56	Maria Hjorth (Swe)	83.23
6	Ludivine Kreutz (Fra)	388.36		57	Julie Forbes (Sco)	81.84
7	Shani Waugh (Aus)	386.55		58	Asa Gottmo (Swe)	81.21
8	Ana Belen Sanchez (Esp)	372.70		59	Joanne Mills (Aus)	80.80
9	Trish Johnson (Eng)	372.45		60	Nicole Stillig (Ger)	77.85
10	Stephanie Arricau (Fra)	326.34		61	Christina Kuld (Den)	76.38
11	Suzann Pettersen (NOR)	307.98		62	Lara Tadiotto (Bel)	76.08
12	Marlene Hedblom (Swe)	306.86		63	Eleanor Pilgrim (Wal)	74.53
13	Alison Nicholas (Eng)	304.68		64	Sara Beautell (Esp)	72.60
14	Rebecca Stevenson (Aus)	293.73		65	Carina Vagner (Den)	71.63
15	Gina Scott (NZ)	292.30		66	Marine Monnet (Fra)	69.30
16	Corinne Dibnah (Aus)	287.80		67	Valerie Van Ryckeghem (Bel)	69.10
17	Patricia Meunier Lebouc (Fra)	272.03		68	Maria Boden (Swe)	68.37
18	Kirsty Taylor (Eng)	268.26		69	Laura Cabanillas Gomez (Esp)	67.90
19	Karine Icher (Fra)	267.40		70	Jackie Kebbell (MNX)	65.98
20	Paula Marti (Esp)	250.64		71	Charlotta Sorenstam (Swe)	65.03
21	Alison Munt (Aus)	250.60		72	Marieke Zelsmann (NL)	63.65
22	Becky Morgan (Wal)	246.78		73	Mandy Adamson (SA)	60.95
23	Vibeke Stensrud (Nor)	241.00		74	Anna Becker (Swe)	60.11
24	Johanna Head (Eng)	208.26		75	Nienke Nijenhuis (NL)	56.62
25	Mhairi McKay (Sco)	207.65		76	Emma Zackrisson (Swe)	54.20
26	Sophie Sandolo (Ita)	205.43		77	Johanna Westerberg (Swe)	53.40
27	Federica Dassu (Ita)	198.52		78	Amanda Moltke-Leth (Den)	51.50
28	Ana Larraneta (Esp)	190.71		79	Martina Eberl (Ger)	50.86
29	Carin Koch (Swe)	183.53		80	Wendy Dicks (Eng)	48.64
30	Nadina Taylor (Aus)	176.77		81	Claire Duffy (Eng)	45.97
31	Diana Luna (Ita)	172.02		82	Riikka Hakkarainen (Fin)	44.89
32	Karen Lunn (Aus)	169.88		83	Sarah Heath (Eng)	43.80
33	Samantha Head (Eng)	146.65		84	Dale Reid (Sco)	42.10
34	Helen Alfredsson (Swe)	144.90		85	Florence Descampe (Bel)	40.04
35	Anne-Marie Knight (Aus)	144.38		86	Jane Leary (Aus)	39.70
36	Veronica Zorzi (Ita)	137.44		87	Filippa Helmersson (Swe)	39.60
37	Cecilia Ekelundh (Swe)	136.16		88	Tamara Hyett (Aus)	37.60
38	Alexandra Armas (Esp)	136.10		89	Esther Poburski (Ger)	36.88
39	Vicky Uwland (Aus)	129.98		90	Pam Sowden (NZ)	35.40
40	Natascha Fink (Aut)	129.47				
41	Karen Margrethe Juul (Den)	127.15		91	Nicola Moult (Eng)	31.56
42	Marta Prieto (Esp)	126.77		92	Tina Schneeberger (Aut)	30.48
43	Silvia Cavalleri (Ita)	106.08		93	Suzanne Dickens (Eng)	29.70
44	Susan Parry (USA)	104.27		94	Helena Svensson (Swe)	28.89
45	Rachel Bailey (Eng)	97.86		95	Anna Berg (Swe)	27.84
46	Nina Karlsson (Swe)	97.61		96	Sara Eklund (Swe)	26.90
47	Lora Fairclough (Eng)	94.75		97	Cecilie Lundgreen (Nor)	25.76
48	Marie-Laure de Lorenzi (Fra)	94.00		98	Lesley Nicholson (Sco)	24.40
49	Virginie Auffret (Fra)	91.50		99	Ellen Smets (Bel)	23.22
50	Catrin Nilsmark (Swe)	91.21		100	Sandrine Mendiburu (Fra)	22.85
51	Gwladys Nocera (Fra)	87.78				

Tour Results (in chronological order)

ANZ Ladies' Masters
Royal Pines, Gold Coast, Queensland   (6397–72)

1	Laura Davies (Eng)	67-68-68—203	€73264
2	Rebecca Stevenson (Aus)	68-68-68—204	41516
	Karrie Webb (Aus)	68-66-70—204	41516

AAMI Women's Australian Open
Terrey Hills, Sydney, NSW, Australia   (6379–72)

1	Mhairi McKay (Sco)	72-67-71-67—277	€46580
2	Laura Davies (Eng)	65-68-73-72—278	31053
3	Rachel Teske (Aus)	68-72-70-69—279	21737

Tenerife Ladies Open
Golf Las Americas, Tenerife   (6237–72)

1	Elisabeth Esterl (Ger)	71-69-67-69—276	€30000
2	Becky Brewerton (Wal) (am)	69-67-68-73—277	
3	Karine Icher (Fra)	70-69-70-70—279	17150
	Ana Belen Sanchez (Esp)	70-67-72-70—279	17150

La Perla Italian Open
Poggio dei Medici, Florence, Italy   (6273–73)

1	Ludivine Kreutz (Fra)	76-68-68-70—282	€26362
2	Elisabeth Esterl (Ger)	72-73-67-71—283	13211
	Anne-Marie Knight (Aus)	73-68-69-73—283	13211
	Karen Lunn (Aus)	69-71-70-73—283	13211

Ladies' Open of Costa Azul
Aroeira (New), Costa da Caparica, Portugal   (6147–72)

1	Alison Munt (Aus)*	69-72-68—209	€24750
2	Elisabeth Esterl (Ger)	70-73-66—209	16747
3	Ana Belen Sanchez (Esp)	71-70-69—210	10230
	Vicky Uwland (Aus)	72-67-71—210	10230

Open de España Femenino
Campo de Golf, Salamanca, Spain   (6201–72)

1	Federica Dassu (Ita)	67-73-72-70—282	€37500
2	Corinne Dibnah (Aus)	67-71-73-73—284	18792
	Ana Belen Sanchez (Esp)	71-73-69-71—284	18792
	Sophie Sandolo (Ita)	72-70-71-71—284	18792

Ladies' Irish Open

Mahoney's Point, Killarney, Ireland (6171–73)

1	Sophie Gustafson (Swe)	66-63-73—202	€24750
2	Laura Davies (Eng)	66-68-71—205	16747
3	Trish Johnson (Eng)	67-71-69—207	11550

Arras Open de France Dames

Anzin St Aubin, France (6195–72)

1	Lynnette Brooky (NZ)	68-70-69-67—274	€41250
2	Trish Johnson (Eng)	71-67-70-67—275	23581
	Vibeke Stensrud (Nor)	72-67-68-68—275	23581

Evian Masters

Evian Les Bains, France (6091–72)

1	Juli Inkster (USA)	66-72-64-65—267	€279462
2	Hee-Won Han (Kor)	71-68-65-69—273	182957
3	Rosie Jones (USA)	67-68-67-73—275	117697
	Lorena Ochoa (Mex)	66-70-71-68—275	117697

WEETABIX WOMEN'S BRITISH OPEN

Royal Lytham & St Annes, Lancashire, England (6308–72)

1	Annika Sörenstam (Swe)	68-72-68-70—278	€228720
2	Se Ri Pak (Kor)	69-69-69-72—279	142950
3	Grace Park (Kor)	74-65-71-70—280	89344
	Karrie Webb (Aus)	67-72-70-71—280	89344

Fuller details of this event are included in Part I The Majors page 88

HP Open

Drottningholm, Stockholm, Sweden (6921–72)

1	Sophie Gustafson (Swe)*	67-71-63-68—269	€70346
2	Suzann Pettersen (Nor)	70-67-70-62—269	47601
3	Annika Sörenstam (Swe)	68-68-67-68—271	32828

BT Ladies Open

Warrenpoint, Newry, Ireland (5908–72)

1	Sophie Gustafson (Swe)	66-69-68-72—275	€32332
2	Alison Nicholas (Eng)	67-69-67-73—276	21878
3	Iben Tinning (Den)	72-67-67-74—280	15088

The Wales WPGA Championship of Europe

Royal Porthcawl, Wales   (5653–73)

1	Shani Waugh (Aus)	73-71-73-69—286	€86190
2	Becky Brewerton (Wal) (am)	73-72-73-70—288	
3	Stephanie Arricau (Fra)	69-72-74-74—289	58322

The Solheim Cup *Barsebäck, Malmo, Sweden*   (6518–72)

Europe defeated the USA 17½–10½

Full details of this event can be found on page 209

Biarritz Ladies' Classic

Biarritz Le Phare, France   (5681-70)

1	Marlene Hedblom (Swe)	66-69-65—200	€24750
2	Gina Scott (NZ)	66-68-68—202	16747
3	Ludivine Kreutz (Fra)	65-68-70—203	10230
	Marta Prieto (Esp)	70-66-67—203	10230

Women golfers in men's events in 2003

Annika Sörenstam became the first woman professional since Babe Zaharias to play in a men's competition when she teed up in the Colonial event on the PGA Tour. She missed the half-way cut but others followed her lead.

Suzy Whaley had qualified to play in the US PGA Club Championship and missed the half-way cut as did Michelle Wie when she played in the Nationwide and Canadian Tour events. Jan Stephenson finished last in a US Champions Tour event in which there was no cut.

After Laura Davies missed the half-way cut in the Korean Open it was Se Ri Pak who finally became the first woman in 58 years to make the half-way cut in a men's event when she finished 10th in the SBS Super tournament in Korea, 11 shots behind winner Chang Ik-je.

Babe Zaharias played in three men's events in 1945 in America and made the cut in all three.

LPGA Tour 2003

Players are of American nationality unless stated

Money List
(position after Mobile LPGA Tournament of Champions with one 2003 season event still to be played)

Rank	Name	Money Won	Events
1	Annika Sörenstam (Swe)	$1,914,506	16
2	Se Ri Pak (Kor)	1,543,893	24
3	Grace Park	1,339,217	24
4	Hee-Won Han (Kor)	1,025,560	25
5	Juli Inkster	997,145	19
6	Candie Kung (Tai)	910,569	28
7	Rachel Teske (Aus)	873,432	25
8	Beth Daniel	841,349	20
9	Lorena Ochoa (Mex)	812,940	23
10	Rosie Jones	751,255	17
11	Karrie Webb (Aus)	734,209	21
12	Patricia Meunier-Labouc (Fra)	666,572	16
13	Lorie Kane (Can)	645,797	25
14	Hilary Lunke	633,433	24
15	Angela Stanford	621,637	19
16	Sophie Gustafson (Swe)	620,622	21
17	Cristie Kerr	610,097	22
18	Meg Mallon	544,070	22
19	Catriona Matthew (Sco)	483,613	25
20	Mi-Hyun Kim (Kor)	462,703	25
21	Laura Davies (Eng)	460,152	20
22	Becky Morgan (Wal)	459,844	22
23	Jeong Jang (Kor)	443,278	25
24	Michele Redman	435,918	21
25	Wendy Ward	421,234	22
26	Kelly Robbins	410,186	19
27	Pat Hurst	405,625	23
28	Laura Diaz	391,657	25
29	Heather Bowie	389,159	24
30	Suzann Pettersen (Nor)	387,920	19
31	Jennifer Rosales (Phi)	366,564	20
32	Soo-Yun Kang (Kor)	363,341	23
33	Dorothy Delasin	354,170	26
34	Karen Stupples (Eng)	325,774	25
35	Gloria Park (Kor)	317,960	28
36	Mhairi McKay (Sco)	282,954	23
37	Jung Yeon Lee (Jpn)	261,587	25
38	Danielle Ammaccapane	258,476	23
39	Natalie Gulbis	251,562	26
40	Leta Lindley	238,522	22
41	Wendy Doolan (Aus)	237,391	20
42	Helen Alfredsson (Swe)	227,229	18
43	Tammie Green	224,507	21
44	Young Kim (Kor)	223,866	22
45	Kim Saiki	222,804	24
46	Vicki Goetz-Ackerman	219,711	25
47	Christina Kim	215,632	28
48	Donna Andrews	211,242	26
49	Janice Moodie (Sco)	209,845	24
50	Kate Golden	208,300	24

Tour Results (in chronological order)

Conagra LPGA Skins Game
Waileai, Maui, HI

Winner: Karrie Webb (Aus)   12 skins

Welch's/Fry's Championship

	Randolph Park, Tucson, AZ		(6176–70)
1	Wendy Doolan (Aus)	65-62-67-65—259	$120000
2	Lorie Kane (Can)	61-66-65-70—262	62592
	Betsy King	67-65-65-65—262	62592

Safeway PING

	Moon Valley, Phoenix, AZ		(6473–72)
1	Se Ri Pak (Kor)	65-68-68-64—265	$150000
2	Grace Park (Kor)	67-67-67-65—266	90488
3	Hee-Won Han (Kor)	68-69-66-66—269	52432
	Patricia Meunier-Lebouc (Fra)	67-66-67-69—269	52432
	Annika Sörenstam (Swe)	67-66-65-71—269	52432

KRAFT NABISCO CHAMPIONSHIP

	Mission Hills, Rancho Mirage, CA		(6520–72)
1	Patricia Meunier Labouc (Fra)	70-68-70-73—281	$240000
2	Annika Sörenstam (Swe)	68-72-71-71—282	146120
3	Lorena Ochoa (Mex)	71-70-74-68—283	106000

Fuller details of this event are included in Part I The Majors page 99

The Office Depot Championship

	El Caballero, Tarzana, CA		(6394–72)
1	Annika Sörenstam (Swe)	68-72-71—211	$225000
2	Heather Bowie	72-70-73—215	104917
	Pat Hurst	75-68-72—215	104917
	Se Ri Pak (Kor)	73-71-71—215	104917

LPGA Takefuji Classic

	Las Vegas CC, NV		(6494–72)
1	Candie Kung (Tai)	67-67-70—204	$165000
2	Annika Sörenstam (Swe)	72-67-67—206	77129
	Soo-Yun Kang (Kor)	69-70-67—206	77129

Chick-a-fil-A Charity Championship

Eagle's Landing, Stockbridge, GA   (6368–72)

1	Se Ri Pak (Kor)*	71-65-64—200	$202500
2	Shani Waugh (Aus)	69-66-65—200	123000
3	Suzann Petterson (Nor)	69-68-67—204	89228

Michelob Light Open

Kingsmill, Williamsburg, VA   (6285–71)

1	Grace Park (Kor)	67-68-69-71—275	$240000
2	Cristie Kerr	69-68-68-71—276	110601
	Lorena Ochoa (Mex)	66-69-72-69—276	110601
	Karrie Webb (Aus)	70-71-68-67—276	110601

Asahi Ryokuken International Championship

Mount Vintage, North Augusta, SC   (6426–72)

1	Rosie Jones	66-68-69-70—273	$195000
2	Wendy Ward	68-67-71-70—276	118443
3	Laura Diaz	68-68-69-73—278	68630
	Patricia Meunier-Labouc (Fra)	70-74-67-67—278	68630
	Lorena Ochoa (Mex)	68-71-69-70—278	68630

LPGA Corning Classic

Corning CC, NY   (6062–72)

1	Juli Inkster	68-66-68-62—264	$150000
2	Lorie Kane (Can)	67-65-69-67—268	90090
3	Catriona Matthew (Sco)	68-64-67-70—269	65354

Kellogg-Keebler Classic

Stonebridge, Aurora, IL   (6413–72)

1	Annika Sörenstam (Swe)	62-66-71—199	$180000
2	Mhairi McKay (Sco)	66-64-72—202	109590
3	Mi-Hyun Kim (Kor)	66-71-67—204	70500
	Becky Morgan (Wal)	67-69-68—204	70500

McDONALDS LPGA CHAMPIONSHIP

DuPont CC, Wilmington, DE   (6408–71)

1	Annika Sörenstam (Swe)*	70-64-72-72—278	$240000
2	Grace Park (Kor)	69-72-70-67—278	147934
3	Beth Daniel	71-71-70-72—284	85718
	Rosie Jones	73-68-72-71—284	85718
	Rachel Teske (Aus)	69-70-74-71—284	85718

Fuller details of this event are included in Part I The Majors page 91

Giant Eagle LPGA Classic

Squaw's Creek, Vienna, OH (6466–72)

1	Rachel Teske (Aus)*	70-65-69—204	$150000
2	Lorie Kane (Can)	70-71-63—204	69945
	Jennifer Rosales (Phi)	72-64-68—204	69945
	Annika Sörenstam (Swe)	71-65-68—204	69945

Wegmans Rochester International

Locust Hill, Pittsford, NY (6192–72)

1	Rachel Teske (Aus)	69-68-72-68—277	$180000
2	Lorena Ochoa (Mex)	73-70-72-66—281	110392
3	Grace Park (USA)	69-72-73-68—282	80081

ShopRite LPGA Classic

Bay Course, Marriott, Galloway Township, NJ (6051–71)

1	Angela Stanford	65-67-65—197	$195000
2	Becky Morgan (Wal)	68-66-66—200	120196
3	Juli Inkster	66-67-68—201	77323
	Lorie Kane (Can)	68-67-66—201	77323

US WOMEN'S OPEN CHAMPIONSHIP

Pumpkin Ridge, North Plains, OR (6550–71)

1	Hilary Lunke*	71-69-68-75—283	$560000
2	Kelly Robbins	74-69-71-69—283	272004
	Angela Stanford	70-70-69-74—283	272004

Fuller details of this event are included in Part I The Majors page 83

BMO Financial Group Canadian Women's Open

Point Grey, Vancouver, BC, Canada (6408–72)

1	Beth Daniel	69-69-69-68—275	$195000
2	Juli Inkster	68-72-67-69—276	118169
3	Grace Park (Kor)	68-75-69-67—279	76019
	Kim Saiki	70-70-70-69—279	76019

Sybase Big Apple Classic

Wykagyl, New Rochelle, NY (6161–71)

1	Hee-Won Han (Kor)	68-66-68-71—273	$142500
2	Meg Mallon	70-67-65-73—275	85962
3	Cindy Figg-Currier	69-65-73-72—279	55299
	Grace Park (Kor)	69-69-73-68—279	55299

Evian Masters
Evian-les-Bains, France   (6091–72)

1	Juli Inkster (USA)	66-72-64-65—267	$315000
2	Hee-Won Han (Kor)	71-68-65-69—273	206223
3	Rosie Jones (USA)	67-68-67-73—275	132664
	Lorena Ochoa (Mex)	66-70-71-68—275	132664

WEETABIX WOMEN'S BRITISH OPEN
Royal Lytham & St Annes, England   (6308–72)

1	Annika Sörenstam (Swe)	68-72-68-70—278	$254880
2	Se Ri Pak (Kor)	69-69-69-72—279	159300
3	Grace Park (Kor)	74-65-71-70—280	99563
	Karrie Webb (Aus)	67-72-70-71—280	99563

Fuller details of this event are included in Part I The Majors page 76

Wendy's Championship for Children
Tartan Fields, Dublin, OH   (6517–72)

1	Hee-Won Han (Kor)*	68-65-66—199	$165000
2	Wendy Ward	69-67-63—199	100221
3	Michele Redman	71-63-67—201	72704

Jamie Farr Kroger Classic
Highland Meadows, Sylvania, OH   (6408–71)

1	Se Ri Pak (Kor)	69-67-64-71—271	$150000
2	Marisa Baena	68-68-67-70—273	79364
	Hee-Won Han (Kor)	68-67-66-72—273	79364

Wachovia LPGA Classic
Berkleigh, Kutztown, PA   (6381–72)

1	Candie Kung (Tai)	71-67-66-70—274	$180000
2	Meg Mallon	68-66-71-71—276	94323
	Se Ri Pak (Kor)	70-71-67-68—276	94323

State Farm Classic
Rail GC, Springfield, IL   (6558–72)

1	Candie Kung (Tai)	64-67-71—202	$180000
2	Laura Davies (Eng)	70-67-66—203	109852
3	Hee-Won Han (Kor)	66-69-69—204	79690

John Q Hammons Hotel Classic

Tulsa, OK (6269–70)

1	Karrie Webb (Aus)	65-69-66—200	$150000
2	Dorothy Delasin	68-75-66—209	61541
	Tammie Green	67-72-70—209	61541
	Jamie Hullett	70-69-70—209	61541
	Candie Kung (Tai)	71-71-67—209	61541

The Solheim Cup

Barsebäck, Malmo, Sweden (6518–72)

Europe beat the USA 17½–10½

Full details of this event can be found on page 209

Safeway Classic

Columbia Edgewater, Portland, OR (6307–72)

1	Annika Sörenstam (Swe)	67-68-66—201	$180000
2	Beth Daniel	62-73-67—202	110950
3	Cristie Kerr	66-69-69—204	80487

Longs Drugs Challenge

Twelve Bridges, Lincoln, CA (6388–72)

1	Helen Alfredsson (Swe)	72-69-64-70—275	$150000
2	Pat Hurst	70-70-66-70—276	56120
	Jung Yeon Lee (Kor)	71-69-66-70—276	56120
	Se Ri Pak (Kor)	71-64-71-70—276	56120
	Grace Park (Kor)	67-73-67-69—276	56120
	Rachel Teske (Aus)	70-70-66-70—276	56120

Samsung World Championship

TPC The Woodlands, TX (6376–72)

1	Sophie Gustafson (Swe)	72-69-69-64—274	$200000
2	Beth Daniel	70-69-67-70—276	105000
	Rachel Teske (Aus)	70-69-66-71—276	105000

Sports Today CJ Nine Bridges Classic

CJ Nine Bridges, Jeju Island, S Korea (6306–72)

1	Shi Hyun Ahn (Kor)	65-71-68—204	$187500
2	Laura Davies (Eng)	68-71-68—207	79534
	Se Ri Pak (Kor)	69-70-68—207	79534
	Gloria Park (Kor)	76-69-62—207	79534
	Grace Park (Kor)	66-73-68—207	79534

Mizuno Classic
Seta GC

1	Annika Sörenstam (Swe)	63-63-66—192	$169500
2	Se Ri Pak (Kor)	67-65-69—201	78111
	Sophie Gustafson (Swe)	68-66-67—201	78111
	Grace Park (Kor)	65-68-68—201	78111

Mobile LPGA Tournament of Champions
The Crossings GC, Mobile, AL   (6253–72)

1	Dorothy Delasin*	72-71-68-69—280	$122000
2	Hee-Won Han (Kor)	72-71-69-68—280	75500
3	Laura Davies (Eng)	71-71-70-69—281	54250

ADT Championship
West Palm Beach, FL

Annika Sörenstam (Swe)   (D)

Renee Powell is PGA of America First Lady

PGA Professional Renee Powell, the second African-American woman to compete on the LPGA Tour who went on to dedicate her career to introducing golf and life skills to the underprivileged from Africa and work tirelessly promoting golf in her hometown of East Canton, Ohio, has been named recipient of the 2003 PGA First Lady of Golf Award.

The second oldest of three children, Renee was introduced to golf at the age of three by her father, who in 1948 opened Clearview Golf Course in East Canton – the first course completely designed and built by an African-American.

Powell began her competitive career at the age of 12, and later competed at Ohio University and Ohio State University, before making her professional début in 1967 at the US Women's Open in Hot Springs, V.A.

She competed on the LPGA Tour from 1967 to 1980, living in England and spending her off-course time as a clothes designer. In 1980 she was head professional at a course outside of London before moving back to the United States where she got involved in programmes which enabled her to travel to Africa and teach golf.

She returned to the US in 1988, working to build inner-city youth programmes in Cleveland, to establish a network of celebrity and pro-am charity events, and to tour historically-black colleges attracting new players to the game.

'Renee Powell's life's work has been to open the doors to many who otherwise would not have had the opportunity to pick up a golf club and find enjoyment in their lives. Renee's tireless efforts to build opportunities for young people in golf have elevated her among her peers. She comes from one of the great families in golf,' said PGA of America President MG Orender.

'I am flattered and so honored to have been selected for this award,' said Powell. 'To be recognized by those in the golf industry in this manner is the icing on the cake. Golf has been my entire life, and my family has been my inspiration. Golf is what I do; it is who I am.'

The PGA First Lady of Golf Award, inaugurated in 1998, is presented to a woman who has made significant contributions to the promotion of the game of golf. Past recipients include Barbara Nicklaus, Judy Rankin, Judy Bell and Nancy Lopez.

FUTURES Tour 2003

Players are of American nationality unless stated

Results

Lakeland FUTURES Golf Classic	Eaglebrooke, Lakeland, FL	Soo Young Moon (Kor)	206 (-10)
Florida Hospital FUTURES Golf Classic	Sun 'N Lake, Sebring, FL	Lee Ann Walker-Cooper	211 (-5)
Tampa Bay Next Generation FUTURES Golf Classic	Tampa, FL	Colleen Cashman	209 (-7)
Frye Chevrolet Classic	Wichita, KS	Stacy Prammanasudh	207 (-9)
IOS FUTURES Golf Classic	El Paso, TX	Vicki Fergon	216 (E)
Isleta Casino FUTURES Golf Classic	Albuquerque, NM	Catherine Cartwright*	213 (-3)
Northwest Indiana FUTURES Golf Classic	Merrillville, IN	Reilley Rankin*	211 (-5)
Aurora Health Care FUTURES Charity Golf Classic	Sussex, WI	Katherine Hull (Aus)	210 (-6)
The Greater Lima FUTURES Open	Lima, OH	Katherine Hull (Aus)	205 (-11)
Michelob Light FUTURES Charity Golf Classic	Hickory Point, Forsyth, IL	Stephanie George	208 (-8)
Bank of Ann Arbor FUTURES Golf Classic	Ann Arbor, MI	Ju Kim (Kor)	209 (-7)
Lincoln FUTURES Golf Classic	Avon, CT	Stacy Prammanasudh	203 (-10)
GE FUTURES Professional Golf Classic	Orchard Creek, Altamont, NY	Lindsey Wright (Aus)*	205 (-8)
M&T Bank Loretto FUTURES Golf Classic	Erie Village, Syracuse, NY	Soo Young Moon (Kor)	207 (-6)
Hunters Oak Hospice FUTURES Golf Classic	Hunters Oak, Queenstown, MD	Candy Hannemann (Bra)	203 (-13)
Betty Puskar FUTURES Golf Classic	The Pines, Morgantown, WV	Reilley Rankin	134 (-10)
York Newspaper Company FUTURES Golf Classic	Regent's Glen, York, PA	Candy Hannemann (Bra)	207 (-9)

Final Money List

1	Stacy Prammanasudh	$57760	6	Lisa Hall (Eng)		31877
2	Soo Young Moon (Kor)	49234	7	Erika Wicoff		30775
3	Candy Hannemann (Bra)	43097	8	Catherine Cartwright		28703
4	Ju Kim (Kor)	37255	9	Katherine Hull (Aus)		27614
5	Reilley Rankin	35245	10	Isabelle Beisiegel		26597

Japan LPGA Tour

Players are of Japanese nationality unless stated

Results 2002

Itoen Ladies	Great Island Club, Chonan, Chiba	Yuri Fudoh	204 (-12)
Daio Seishi Elleair Open	Elleair, Saita, Kagawa	Hiromi Kobayashi	205 (-11)
Japan LPGA Championship (Ricoh Cup)	Hibiscus, Sadowara, Miyazaki	Woo-Soon Ko (Kor)	278 (-6)

Final Ranking 2002

1	Yuri Fudoh	¥95,690,917	6	Mikino Kubo	51,082,033
2	Kasumi Fujii	82,647,102	7	Ok-Hee Ku (Kor)	48,232,944
3	Woo-Soon Ko (Kor)	73,082,748	8	Midori Yoneyama	46,433,917
4	Toshimi Kimura	64,977,480	9	Mihoko Takahashi	43,609,536
5	Orie Fujino	51,877,305	10	Yu-Chan Huang	42,711,236

Results 2003

Daikin Orchid Ladies	Ryukyu, Tamagusuku, Okinawa	Yuri Fudoh	208 (-8)
Promise Ladies Golf Tournament	Water Hills, Hyogo	Ji-Hee Lee (Kor)	208 (-8)
Saishunkan Ladies	Kumamoto Airport	Ji-Hee Lee (Kor)	216 (0)
Katokichi Queens	Yashima, Mure, Kagawa	Kasumi Fujii	207 (-9)
Nichirei Cup World Ladies	Yomiuri, Tokyo	Annika Sörenstam (Swe)	275 (-13)
Vernal Ladies	Fukuoka Century, Amagi	Oh-hee-ku (Kor)	210 (-6)
Chukyo TV Bridgestone Open	Chukyo, Toyota, Aichi	Yuri Fudoh	207 (-9)
Kosaido Ladies Cup	Kosaido, Ichihara, Chiba	Michiko Hattori	209 (-7)
Resort Trust Ladies	The Tradition, Aichi	Yuri Fudoh	205 (-11)
Suntory Ladies Open	Japan Memorial, Yokawa, Hyogo	Ji-Hee Lee (Kor)	272 (-16)
Apita Circle K Sunks	Nakatsugawa, Gifu	Yun-Jye-Wei (Tai)	208 (-8)
Belluna Ladies Cup	Obatago, Gunma	Shiho Oyama	207 (-9)
Toyo Suisan Ladies Hokkaido	Sapporo Kitahiroshima, Hokkaido	Kaori Suzuki	210 (-6)
Stanley Ladies	Tomei, Shizuoka	Yuri Fudoh	208 (-8)
Golf 5 Ladies	Mizunami, Gifu	Mihoko Takahashi	204 (-12)
NEC Karuizawa 72	Karuizawa 72, Nagano	Akiko Fukishima	208 (-8)
New Caterpillar Mitsubishi	Daihakone, Kanagawa	Yuri Fudoh	208 (-11)
Yonex Ladies	Yonex, Nigata	Miho Koga	207 (-9)
Fuji Sankei Classic	Fujizakura, Yamanashi	Ikuyo Shiotani	202 (-11)
JLPGA Championship Konica Cup	Konan Course, Taiheiyo, Saitama	Yuri Fudoh	277 (-11)
Munsingwear Tokai Classic	Ryosen, Mie	Yuri Fudoh	206 (-10)
Miyagi TV Cup Dunlop Open	Rainbow Hills, Miyagi	Ai Miyazato	211 (-5)
Japan Women's Open	Noda Course, Chiba	Michiko Hattori	287 (-1)
SANKYO Ladies Open	Akagi, Gunma		
Fujitsu Ladies	Tokyu 700, Chiba	Yuri Fudoh	204 (-12)

Japan LPGA Tour Results *continued*

Masters GC Ladies	Masters, Hyogo	Hiromi Takesue	206 (-10)
Mizuno Classic	Seta, Shiga	Annika Sörenstam (Swe)	192 (-24)
Itoen Ladies	Great Island, Chiba	Yuri Fudoh	(D)
Daioh Seishi Elleair Open	Elleair, Matsuyama, Ehime	Hiromi Kobayashi	(D)
JLPGA Tour Championship			
Ricoh Cup	Miyazaki	Woo-Soon Ko (Kor)	(D)

Latest Ranking 2003 (after Mizuno Classic)

1	Yuri Fudoh	¥123 525 679	11	Toshimi Kimura	30 097 060
2	Ji-Hee Lee (Kor)	67 493 418	12	Ikuyo Shiotani	28 821 607
3	Ok-Hee Ku (Kor)	49 707 799	13	Junko Omote	28 702 602
4	Michiko Hattori	48 183 983	14	Kaori Suzuki	27 365 125
5	Woo-Soon Ko (Kor)	40 748 824	15	Hsiu-Feng Tseng	26 340 027
6	Miho Koga	40 535 380	16	Mihoko Takahashi	25 255 885
7	Shiho Ohyama	36 162 440	17	Midori Yoneyama	25 202 022
8	Yun-Jye Wei	34 156 202	18	Kaori Higo	24 944 641
9	Hiroko Yamaguchi	33 533 085	19	Hiromi Takesue	23 785 646
10	Kasumi Fujii	31 702 227	20	Aki Nakano	21 220 454

Three events had still to be played on the 2003 Japan LPGA circuit

International Team Events

Solheim Cup

2003 *at Barsebäck, Sweden*

Captains: Catrin Nilsmark (Swe) (Europe), Patty Sheehan (USA)

Europe		USA	
First Day – **Foursomes**			
Carin Koch & Laura Davies (halved)	½	Beth Daniel & Kelly Robbins (halved)	½
Janice Moodie & Catriona Matthew (5 and 3)	1	Juli Inkster & Wendy Ward	0
Annika Sörenstam & Suzann Pettersen			
(4 and 3)	1	beat Laura Diaz & Heather Bowie	0
Sophie Gustafson & Elisabeth Esterl (3 and 2)	1	Meg Mallon & Rosie Jones	0
	3½		½

Fourball			
Laura Davies & Catriona Matthew	0	Kelli Kuehne & Cristie Kerr (2 and 1)	1
Annika Sörenstam & Carin Koch	0	Juli Inkster & Beth Daniel (1 hole)	1
Suzann Pettersen & Patricia Meunier-Labouc			
(3 and 2)	1	Angela Stanford & Meg Mallon	0
Iben Tinning & Sophie Gustafson	0	Michele Redman & Rosie Jones (2 holes)	1
	1		3

Match Position: Europe 4½, USA 3½

Second Day – **Foursomes**			
Sophie Gustafson & Suzann Pettersen			
(3 and 1)	1	Kelli Kuehne & Cristie Kerr	0
Elisabeth Esterl & Iben Tinning (halved)	½	Angela Stanford & Michele Redman (halved)	½
Annika Sörenstam & Carin Koch (3 and 4)	1	Wendy Ward & Heather Bowie	0
Janice Moodie & Catriona Matthew (halved)	½	Meg Mallon & Kelly Robbins (halved)	½
	3		1

Fourball			
Ana Belen Sanchez & Mhairi McKay	0	Beth Daniel & Juli Inkster (5 and 4)	1
Sophie Gustafson & Laura Davies	0	Cristie Kerr & Kelli Kuehne (2 and 1)	1
Catriona Matthew & Janice Moodie (4 and 3)	1	Wendy Ward & Rosie Jones	0
Annika Sörenstam & Suzann Pettersen			
(1 hole)	1	Kelly Robbins & Laura Diaz	0
	2		2

Match Position: Europe 9, USA 6

Third Day – **Singles**			
Janice Moodie (Sco) (3 and 2)	1	Kelli Kuehne	0
Carin Koch (Swe)	0	Juli Inkster (5 and 4)	1
Sophie Gustafson (Swe) (5 and 4)	1	Heather Bowie	0
Iben Tinning (Den) (2 and 1)	1	Wendy Ward	0
Ana Belen Sanchez (Esp)	0	Michele Redman (3 and 1)	1
Catriona Matthew (Sco) (2 and 1)	1	Rosie Jones	0
Annika Sörenstam (Swe) (3 and 2)	1	Angela Stanford	0
Suzann Pettersen (Nor)	0	Cristie Kerr (conceded)	1
Laura Davies (Eng) (conceded)	1	Meg Mallon	0
Elisabeth Esterl (Ger)	0	Laura Diaz (5 and 4)	1
Mhairi McKay (Sco) (conceded)	1	Beth Daniel	0
Patricia Meunier-Labouc (Fra) (conceded)	1	Kelly Robbins	0
	8		4

Result: Europe 17, USA 10

Solheim Cup *continued*

1990 *at Lake Nona, FL*
Result: USA 11½, Europe 4½
Captains: Kathy Whitworth (USA),
  Mickey Walker (Europe)
First Day – Foursomes
Bradley & Lopez lost to Davies & Nicholas 2 and 1
Gerring & Mochrie beat Wright & Neumann 6 and 5
Sheehan & Jones beat Reid & Alfredsson 6 and 5
Daniel & King beat Johnson & de Lorenzi 5 and 4
Second Day – Fourball
Sheehan & Jones beat Johnson & de Lorenzi 2 and 1
Bradley & Lopez beat Reid & Alfredsson 2 and 1
King & Daniel beat Davies & Nicholas 4 and 3
Gerring & Mochrie lost to Neumann & Wright 4 and 2
Third Day – Singles
Cathy Gerring beat Helen Alfredsson 4 and 3
Rosie Jones lost to Laura Davies 3 and 2
Nancy Lopez beat Alison Nicholas 6 and 4
Betsy King halved with Pam Wright
Beth Daniel beat Liselotte Neumann 7 and 6
Patty Sheehan lost to Dale Reid 2 and 1
Dottie Mochrie beat Marie Laure de Lorenzi 4 and 2
Pat Bradley beat Trish Johnson 8 and 7

1992 *at Dalmahoy*
Result: Europe 11½, USA 6½
Captains: Mickey Walker (Europe),
  Kathy Whitworth (USA)
First Day – Foursomes
Davies & Nicholas beat King & Daniel 1 hole
Neumann & Alfredsson beat Bradley & Mochrie 2 and 1
Descampe & Johnson lost to Ammaccapane & Mallon
  1 hole
Reid & Wright halved with Sheehan & Inkster
Second Day – Fourball
Davies & Nicholas beat Sheehan & Inkster 1 hole
Johnson & Descampe halved with Burton & Richard
Wright & Reid lost to Mallon & King 1 hole
Alfredsson & Neumann halved with Bradley & Mochrie
Third Day – Singles
Laura Davies beat Brandie Burton 4 and 2
Helen Alfredsson beat Danielle Ammaccapane 4 and 3
Trish Johnson beat Patty Sheehan 2 and 1
Alison Nicholas lost to Juli Inkster 3 and 2
Florence Descampe lost to Beth Daniel 2 and 1
Pam Wright beat Pat Bradley 4 and 3
Catrin Nilsmark beat Meg Mallon 3 and 2
Kitrina Douglas lost to Deb Richard 7 and 6
Liselotte Neumann beat Betsy King 2 and 1
Dale Reid beat Dottie Pepper Mochrie 3 and 2

1994 *at the Greenbrier, WA*
Result: USA 13, Europe 7
Captains: JoAnne Carner (USA),
  Mickey Walker (Europe)
First Day – Foursomes
Burton & Mochrie beat 3 and 2
Daniel & Mallon lost to Nilsmark & Sörenstam 1 hole
Green & Robbins lost to Fairclough & Reid 2 and 1
Andrews & King lost to Davies & Nicholas 3 holes
Sheehan & Steinhauer beat Johnson & Wright 2 holes
Second Day – Fourball
Burton & Mochrie beat Davies & Nicholas 2 and 1
Daniel & Mallon beat Nilsmark & Sörenstam 6 and 5

Green & Robbins lost to Fairclough & Reid 4 and 3
Andrews & King beat Johnson & Wright 3 and 2
Sheehan & Steinhauer lost to Alfredsson & Neumann
  1 hole
Third Day – Singles
Betsy King lost to Helen Alfredsson 2 and 1
Dottie Pepper Mochrie beat Catrin Nilsmark 6 and 5
Beth Daniel beat Trish Johnson 1 hole
Kelly Robbins beat Lora Fairclough 4 and 2
Meg Mallon beat Pam Wright 1 hole
Patty Sheehan lost to Alison Nicholas 3 and 2
Brandie Burton beat Laura Davies 1 hole
Tammie Green beat Annika Sörenstam 3 and 2
Sherri Steinhauer beat Dale Reid 2 holes
Donna Andrews beat Liselotte Neumann 3 and 2

1996 *at St Pierre, Chepstow*
Result: USA 17, Europe 11
Captains: Juy Rankin (USA),
  Mickey Walker (Europe)
First Day – Foursomes
Sörenstam & Nilsmark halved with Robbins & McGann
Davies & Nicholas lost to Sheehan & Jones 1 hole
de Lorenzi & Reid lost to Daniell & Skinner 1 hole
Alfredsson & Neumann lost to Pepper & Burton 2 and 1
Fourball
Davies & Johnson beat Robbins & Bradley 6 and 5
Sörenstam & Marshall beat Skinner & Geddes 1 hole
Neumann & Nilsmark lost to Pepper & King 1 hole
Alfredsson & Nicholas halved with Mallon & Daniel
Second Day – Foursomes
Davies & Johnson beat Daniel & Skinner 4 and 3
Sörenstam & Nilsmark beat Pepper & Burton 1 hole
Neumann & Marshall halved with Mallon & Geddes
de Lorenzi & Alfredsson beat Robbins & McGann 4 and 3
Fourball
Davies & Hackney beat Daniel & Skinner 6 and 5
Sörenstam & Johnson halved with McGann & Mallon
de Lorenzi & Morley lost to Robbins & King 2 and 1
Nilsmark & Neumann beat Sheehan & Geddes 2 and 1
Third Day – Singles
Annika Sörenstam beat Pat Bradley 2 and 1
Kathryn Marshall lost to Val Skinner 2 and 1
Laura Davies lost to Michelle McGann 3 and 2
Liselotte Neumann halved with Beth Daniel
Lisa Hackney lost to Brandie Burton 1 hole
Trish Johnson lost to Dottie Pepper 3 and 2
Alison Nicholas halved with Kelly Robbins
Marie Laure de Lorenzi lost to Betsy King 6 and 4
Joanne Morley lost to Rosie Jones 5 and 4
Dale Reid lost to Jane Geddes 2 holes
Catrin Nilsmark lost to Patty Sheehan 2 and 1
Helen Alfredsson lost to Meg Mallon 4 and 2

1998 *at Muirfield Village, Dublin, OH*
Result: USA 16, Europe 12
Captains: Judy Rankin (USA),
  Pia Nilsson (Europe)
First Day – Foursomes
Pepper & Inkster beat Davies & Johnson 3 and 1
Mallon & Burton beat Alfredsson & Nicholas 3 and 1
Robbins & Hurst beat Hackney & Neumann 1 hole
A Sörenstam & Matthew beat Andrews & Green 3 and 2

Fourball
King & Johnson halved with Davies & C Sörenstam
Hurst & Jones beat Hackney & Gustafson 7 and 5
Robbins & Steinhauer lost to Alfredsson & de Lorenzi
  2 and 1
Pepper & Burton beat A Sörenstam & Nilsmark 2 holes

Second Day – **Foursomes**
Andrews & Steinhauer beat A Sörenstam & Matthew
  3 and 2
Mallon & Burton lost to Davies & C Sörenstam 3 and 2
Pepper & Inkster beat Alfredsson & de Lorenzi 1 hole
Robbins & Hurst beat Neumann & Nilsmark 1 hole

Fourball
King & Jones lost to A Sörenstam & Nilsmark 5 and 3
Johnson & Green lost to Davies & Hackney 2 holes
Andrews & Steinhauer beat Alfredsson & de Lorenzi
  4 and 3
Mallon & Inkster beat Neumann & C Sörenstam 2 and 1

Third Day – **Singles**
Pat Hurst lost to Laura Davies 1 hole
Juli Inkster lost to Helen Alfredsson 2 and 1
Donna Andrews lost to Annika Sörenstam 2 and 1
Brandie Burton lost to Liselotte Neumann 1 hole
Dottie Pepper beat Trish Johnson 3 and 2
Kelly Robbins beat Charlotta Sörenstam 2 and 1
Chris Johnson lost to Marie Laure de Lorenzi 1 hole
Rosie Jones beat Catrin Nilsmark 6 and 4
Tammie Green beat Alison Nicholas 1 hole
Sherri Steinhauer beat Catriona Matthew 3 and 2
Betsy King lost to Lisa Hackney 6 and 5
Meg Mallon halved with Sophie Gustafson

2000 *at Loch Lomond*

Result: Europe 14½, USA 11½
Captains: Dale Reid (Europe), Pat Bradley (USA)

First Day – **Foursomes**
Davies & Nicholas beat Pepper & Inkster 4 and 3
Johnson & Gustafson beat Robbins & Hurst 3 and 2
Nilsmark & Koch beat Burton & Iverson 2 and 1
Sörenstam & Moodie beat Mallon & Daniel 1 hole

Foursomes
Davies & Nicholas lost to Iverson & Jones 6 and 5
Johnson & Gustafson halved with Inkster & Steinhauer
Neumann & Alfredsson lost to Robbins & Hurst 2 holes
Moodie & Sörenstam beat Mallon & Daniel 1 hole

Second Day – **Fourball**
Nilsmark & Koch beat Scranton & Redman 2 and 1
Neumann & Meunier Labouc halved with Pepper & Burton
Davies & Carriedo halved with Mallon & Daniel
Sörenstam & Moodie lost to Hurst & Robbins 2 and 1
Johnson & Gustafson beat Jones & Iverson 3 and 2
Nicholas & Alfredsson beat Inkster & Steinhauer 3 and 2

Third Day – **Singles**
Annika Sörenstam lost to Juli Inkster 5 and 4
Sophie Gustafson lost to Brandie Burton 4 and 3
Helen Alfredsson beat Beth Daniel 4 and 3
Trish Johnson lost to Dottie Pepper 2 and 1
Laura Davies lost to Kelly Robbins 3 and 2
Liselotte Neumann halved with Pat Hurst
Alison Nicholas halved with Sherri Steinhauer
Patricia Meunier Labouc lost to Meg Mallon 1 hole
Catrin Nilsmark beat Rosie Jones 1 hole
Raquel Carriedo lost to Becky Iverson 3 and 2
Carin Koch beat Michele Redman 2 and 1
Janice Moodie beat Nancy Scranton 1 hole

2002 *at Interlachen CC, Madina, MN*

Result: USA 15½, Europe 12½
Captains: Patty Sheehan (USA),
  Dale Reid (Europe)

First Day – **Foursomes**
Inkster & Diaz lost to Davies & Marti 2 holes)
Daniel & Ward beat Carriedo & Tinning 1 hole
Hurst & Robbins lost to Alfredsson & Pettersen
  4 and 2
Kuehne & Mallon lost to Koch & Sörenstam 3 and 2

Fourballs
Jones & Kerr beat Davies & Marti 1 hole
Diaz & Klein beat Gustafson & Icher 4 and 3
Mallon & Redman beat Hjörth & Sörenstam 3 and 1
Inkster & Kuehne lost to Koch & McKay 3 and 2

Second Day – **Foursomes**
Kerr & Redman lost to Koch & Sörenstam 4 and 3
Klein & Ward beat McKay & Tinning 3 and 2
Inkster & Mallon beat Davies & Marti 2 and 1
Diaz & Robbins beat Alfredsson & Pettersen 3 and 1

Fourballs
Daniel & Ward lost to Koch & Sörenstam 4 and 3
Hurst & Kuehne lost to Hjörth & Tinning 1 hole
Jones & Kerr lost to Carriedo & Icher 1 hole
Klein & Robbins lost to Davies & Gustafson 1 hole

Third Day – **Singles**
Juli Inkster beat Raquel Carriedo (Esp) 4 and 3
Laura Diaz beat Paula Marti (Esp) 5 and 3
Emilee Klein beat Helen Alfredsson (Swe) 2 and 1
Kelli Kuehne lost to Iben Tinning (Den) 3 and 2
Michele Redman halved with Suzann Pettersen (Nor)
Wendy Ward halved with Annika Sörenstam (Swe)
Kelly Robbins beat Maria Hjörth (Swe) 5 and 3
Cristie Kerr lost to Sophie Gustafson (Swe) 3 and 2
Meg Mallon beat Laura Davies (Eng) 3 and 2
Pat Hurst beat Mhairi McKay (Sco) 3 and 2
Beth Daniel halved with Carin Koch (Swe)
Rosie Jones beat Karine Icher (Fra) 3 and 2

Solheim Cup – Individual Records

Brackets indicate non-playing captain

Europe

Name		Year	Played	Won	Lost	Halved
Helen Alfredsson	Swe	1990-92-94-96-98-2000-02	24	10	12	2
Raquel Carriedo	Esp	2000-02	5	1	3	1
Laura Davies	Eng	1990-92-94-96-98-2000-02-03	32	16	13	3
Florence Descampe	Bel	1992	3	0	2	1
Kitrina Douglas	Eng	1992	1	0	1	0
Elisabeth Esterl	Ger	2003	3	1	1	1
Lora Fairclough	Eng	1994	3	2	1	0
Sophie Gustafson	Swe	1998-2000-02-03	14	7	5	2
Lisa Hackney	Eng	1996-98	6	3	3	0
Maria Hjörth	Swe	2000	3	1	2	0
Karine Icher	Fra	2002	3	1	2	0
Trish Johnson	Eng	1990-92-94-96-98-2000	19	5	11	3
Carin Koch	Swe	2000-02-03	12	8	2	2
Marie Laure de Lorenzi	Fra	1990-96-98	11	3	8	0
Mhairi McKay	Sco	2002-03	5	2	3	0
Kathryn Marshall	Sco	1996	3	1	1	1
Paula Marti	Esp	2002	4	1	3	0
Catriona Matthew	Sco	1998-03	8	4	3	1
Patricia Meunier Labouc	Fra	2000-03	4	2	1	1
Janice Moodie	Sco	2000-03	8	6	1	1
Joanne Morley	Eng	1996	2	0	2	0
Liselotte Neumann	Swe	1990-92-94-96-98-2000	21	6	10	5
Alison Nicholas	Eng	1990-92-94-96-98-2000	18	7	8	3
Catrin Nilsmark	Swe	1992-94-96-98-2000-(03)	16	8	7	1
Pia Nilsson	Swe	(1998)	0	0	0	0
Suzann Pettersen	Nor	2002-03	8	5	2	1
Dale Reid	Sco	1990-92-94-96-(2000-02)	11	4	6	1
Ana Belen Sanchez	Esp	2003	2	0	2	0
Annika Sörenstam	Swe	1994-96-98-2000-02-03	27	16	8	3
Charlotta Sörenstam	Swe	1998	4	1	2	1
Iben Tinning	Den	2002-03	7	3	3	1
Mickey Walker	Eng	(1990)-(92)-(94)-(96)	0	0	0	0
Pam Wright	Sco	1990-92-94	6	1	4	1

United States

Name	Year	Played	Won	Lost	Halved
Danielle Ammaccapane	1992	2	1	1	0
Donna Andrews	1994-98	7	4	3	0
Heathert Bowie	2003	3	0	3	0
Pat Bradley	1990-92-96-(2000)	8	2	5	1
Brandie Burton	1992-94-96-98-2000	14	8	4	2
Jo Anne Carner	(1994)	0	0	0	2
Beth Daniel	1990-92-94-96-2000-02-03	23	10	8	5
Laura Diaz	2002-03	7	4	3	0
Jane Geddes	1996	4	1	2	1
Cathy Gerring	1990	3	2	1	0
Tammie Green	1994-98	6	2	4	0
Pat Hurst	1998-2000-02	11	6	4	1
Juli Inkster	1992-98-2000-02-03	19	10	7	2
Becky Iverson	2000	4	2	2	0
Chris Johnson	1998	3	0	2	1
Rosie Jones	1990-96-98-2000-02-03	19	10	9	0
Cristie Kerr	2002-03	8	4	4	0
Betsy King	1990-92-94-96-98	15	7	6	2
Emilee Klein	2002	4	3	1	0
Kelli Kuehne	2002-03	8	2	6	0
Nancy Lopez	1990	3	2	1	0
Michelle McGann	1996	4	1	1	2
Meg Mallon	1992-94-96-98-2000-02-03	26	11	9	6
Alice Miller	(1992)*	0	0	0	0
Dottie Pepper	1990-92-94-96-98-2000	20	13	5	2

Name	Year	Played	Won	Lost	Halved
Judy Rankin	(1996)-(98)	0	0	0	0
Michele Redman	2000-02-03	8	3	3	2
Deb Richard	1992	2	1	0	1
Kelly Robbins	1994-96-98-2000-02-03	24	10	10	4
Nancy Scranton	2000	2	0	2	0
Patty Sheehan	1990-92-94-96-(2002)-(03)	13	5	7	1
Val Skinner	1996	4	2	2	0
Angela Stanford	2003	3	0	2	1
Sherri Steinhauer	1994-98-2000	10	5	1	2
Wendy Ward	2002-03	8	2	5	1
Kathy Whitworth	(1990)-(92)*	0	0	0	0

Old Course to be lengthened for 2005 Open

When the golfers arrive at St Andrews in 2005 for the 27th Open Championship to be played over the famous Old Course, they will find important changes have been made to the layout over which Tiger Woods won the Millennium Open.

The lengthening of the course by 160 yards making it 7115 yards (compared to 6960 yards in 1995) is not in itself the significant factor. What is important in helping the Old Course, the most famous links in the world, cope with modern technology are the seven new tees which will be constructed – tees designed specifically to bring some of the course's famous bunkers back into play.

Peter Dawson, secretary of the Royal and Ancient Golf Club who run the Open, explains that the changes were a delicate balancing act. 'We have not gone for extreme length as they did at Augusta because we believe the Open must give an opportunity to those who do not necessarily hit it long.'

The R&A and the St Andrews Links Trust, which runs the courses, believe that the Old Course should always be hard and fast-running as it was for the 2000 Open but want the traditional hazards to be brought back in to play – bunkers such as Cheape's, the Coffins, the Beardies and Hell! The work will be completed over the next 18 months.

The changes are:
Second hole: A new Championship tee, built on an unused part of the Himalayas putting area will add 30 yards.. It will stretch the hole to 443 yards and bring Cheape's bunker more into play.

Fourth hole: A new tee lengthens the hole by 15 yards in order to restore the choice of going right or left off the tee. The hole will now play at 479 yards.

Ninth hole: A new tee built on part of the New Course will mean the drive is now partially blind although the length of 352 yards is unchanged.

Eleventh hole: It will become an even greater challenge by extending the length to 189 yards by putting in a new tee 15 yards behind the existing one.

Twelfth hole: The fairway bunkers will be brought back into play by extending the hole by 30 yards making the total length 344 yards.

Thirteenth hole: The hole is being extended to 465 yards by building a new tee 35 yards behind the existing one. This will mean the Coffins bunkers will be brought back into play. During the Dunhill Championship the top professionals were driving over them.

Fourteenth hole: There is a further 35 yards added to this hole as well making it the longest hole in Championship golf at 616 yards. This will bring the Beardies back into play, make the out-of-bounds wall more of a factor and, into a head wind, make players aware of Hell bunker when they play their second shots.

Professional Women's Overseas Championships

Australian Ladies Masters

1998	K Webb	2001	K Webb
1999	K Webb	2002	A Sörenstam
2000	K Webb	2003	L Davies

AAMI Australian Women's Open

1995	L Neumann	2000	K Webb
1996	C Matthew	2001	S Gustafson
1997	J Crafter	2002	K Webb
1998	M McGuire	2003	M McKay
1999	*Not played*		

French Ladies Open

1992	*Not played*	1998	*Not played*
1993	*Not played*	1999	T Johnson
1994	J Forbes	2000	P Meunier-Lebouc
1995	L Kreutz	2001	S Pettersen
1996	L Rolner	2002	L Brooky
1997	K Lunn	2003	L Brooky

Italian Ladies Open

1992	L Davies	1998	*Not played*
1993	A Arruti	1999	S Head
1994	C Dibnah	2000	S Gustafson
1995	D Booker	2001	P Marti
1996	L Davies	2002	I Tinning
1997	V Van Ryckegham	2003	L Kreutz

Other 2003 Overseas Championships

Canadian Open	B Daniel
Japanese Open	M Hattori
Portuguese Masters	A Munt
South African Ladies Masters	??????
Spanish Open	F Dassu

British Golf Museum
St Andrews

Willie and Laurie Auchterlonie in their workshop

Bruce Embankment, St. Andrews, Fife KY16 9AB

Phone 01334 460046 • Fax 01334 460064

Website www.britishgolfmuseum.co.uk

Opening Times:

Summer: Easter to Mid-October 9.30am–5.30pm • Open 7 days

Winter: 11am–3pm • Closed Tuesday and Wednesday

PART IV

Men's Amateur Tournaments

National and International Championships   218
Team Events   235
Principal 72-hole Championships   257
National District Championships   264
Other Men's Amateur Tournaments   268
Foursomes Events   273
University and School Events   276
County and Other Regional Championships   281
Overseas Amateur Championships   286
Callaway Handicapping System   291

National and International Championships

Amateur Championship (inaugurated 1885)

Year	Winner	Runner-up	Venue	By	Ent
1885	A MacFie	H Hutchinson	Hoylake, Royal Liverpool	7 and 6	44
1886	H Hutchinson	H Lamb	St Andrews	7 and 6	42
1887	H Hutchinson	J Ball	Hoylake, Royal Liverpool	1 hole	33
1888	J Ball	J Laidlay	Prestwick	5 and 4	38
1889	J Laidlay	L Melville	St Andrews	2 and 1	40
1890	J Ball	J Laidlay	Hoylake, Royal Liverpool	4 and 3	44
1891	J Laidlay	H Hilton	St Andrews	20th hole	50
1892	J Ball	H Hilton	Sandwich, Royal St George's	3 and 1	45
1893	P Anderson	J Laidlay	Prestwick	1 hole	44
1894	J Ball	S Fergusson	Hoylake, Royal Liverpool	1 hole	64
1895	L Melville	J Ball	St Andrews	19th hole	68
From 1896 36 holes played					
1896	F Tait	H Hilton	Sandwich, Royal St George's	8 and 7	64
1897	A Allan	J Robb	Muirfield	4 and 2	74
1898	F Tait	S Fergusson	Hoylake, Royal Liverpool	7 and 5	77
1899	J Ball	F Tait	Prestwick	37th hole	101
1900	H Hilton	J Robb	Sandwich, Royal St George's	8 and 7	68
1901	H Hilton	J Low	St Andrews	1 hole	116
1902	C Hutchings	S Fry	Hoylake, Royal Liverpool	1 hole	114
1903	R Maxwell	H Hutchinson	Muirfield	7 and 5	142
1904	W Travis (USA)	E Blackwell	Sandwich, Royal St George's	4 and 3	104
1905	A Barry	Hon O Scott	Prestwick	3 and 2	148
1906	J Robb	C Lingen	Hoylake, Royal Liverpool	4 and 3	166
1907	J Ball	C Palmer	St Andrews	6 and 4	200
1908	E Lassen	H Taylor	Sandwich, Royal St George's	7 and 6	197
1909	R Maxwell	Capt C Hutchison	Muirfield	1 hole	170
1910	J Ball	C Aylmer	Hoylake, Royal Liverpool	10 and 9	160
1911	H Hilton	E Lassen	Prestwick	4 and 3	146
1912	J Ball	A Mitchell	Westward Ho!, Royal North Devon	38th hole	134
1913	H Hilton	R Harris	St Andrews	6 and 5	198
1914	J Jenkins	C Hezlet	Sandwich, Royal St George's	3 and 2	232
1915–19 No Championship owing to the Great War					
1920	C Tolley	R Gardner (USA)	Muirfield	37th hole	165
1921	W Hunter	A Graham	Hoylake, Royal Liverpool	12 and 11	223
1922	E Holderness	J Caven	Prestwick	1 hole	252
1923	R Wethered	R Harris	Deal, Royal Cinque Ports	7 and 6	209
1924	E Holderness	E Storey	St Andrews	3 and 2	201
1925	R Harris	K Fradgley	Westward Ho!, Royal North Devon	13 and 12	151
1926	J Sweetser (USA)	A Simpson	Muirfield	6 and 5	216
1927	Dr W Tweddell	D Landale	Hoylake, Royal Liverpool	7 and 6	197
1928	T Perkins	R Wethered	Prestwick	6 and 4	220
1929	C Tolley	J Smith	Sandwich, Royal St George's	4 and 3	253
1930	R Jones (USA)	R Wethered	St Andrews	7 and 6	271
1931	E Smith	J De Forest	Westward Ho!, Royal North Devon	1 hole	171
1932	J De Forest	E Fiddian	Muirfield	3 and 1	235
1933	Hon M Scott	T Bourn	Hoylake, Royal Liverpool	4 and 3	269
1934	W Lawson Little (USA)	J Wallace	Prestwick	14 and 13	225
1935	W Lawson Little (USA)	Dr W Tweddell	R Lytham and St Annes	1 hole	232
1936	H Thomson	J Ferrier (Aus)	St Andrews	2 holes	283
1937	R Sweeney jr (USA)	L Munn	Sandwich, Royal St George's	3 and 2	223
1938	C Yates (USA)	R Ewing	Troon	3 and 2	241
1939	A Kyle	A Duncan	Hoylake, Royal Liverpool	2 and 1	167
1940–45 Suspended during Second World War					
1946	J Bruen	R Sweeny (USA)	Birkdale	4 and 3	263
1947	W Turnesa (USA)	R Chapman (USA)	Carnoustie	3 and 2	200
1948	F Stranahan (USA)	C Stowe	Sandwich, Royal St George's	5 and 4	168
1949	S McCready	W Turnesa (USA)	Portmarnock	2 and 1	204

Year	Winner	Runner-up	Venue	By	Ent
1950	F Stranahan (USA)	R Chapman (USA)	St Andrews	8 and 6	324
1951	R Chapman (USA)	C Coe (USA)	Royal Porthcawl	5 and 4	192
1952	E Ward (USA)	F Stranahan (USA)	Prestwick	6 and 5	286
1953	J Carr	E Harvie Ward (USA)	Hoylake, Royal Liverpool	2 holes	279
1954	D Bachli (Aus)	W Campbell (USA)	Muirfield	2 and 1	286
1955	J Conrad (USA)	A Slater	Royal Lytham and St Annes	3 and 2	240
1956	J Beharrell	L Taylor	Troon	5 and 4	200
1957	R Reid Jack	H Ridgley (USA)	Formby	2 and 1	200
In 1956 and 1957 the Quarter Finals, Semi-Finals and Final were played over 36 holes					
1958	J Carr	A Thirlwell	St Andrews	3 and 2	488
In 1958, Semi-Finals and Final only were played over 36 holes					
1959	D Beman (USA)	W Hyndman (USA)	Sandwich, Royal St George's	3 and 2	362
1960	J Carr	R Cochran (USA)	Royal Portrush	8 and 7	183
1961	MF Bonallack	J Walker	Turnberry	6 and 4	250
1962	R Davies (USA)	J Povall	Hoylake, Royal Liverpool	1 hole	256
1963	M Lunt	J Blackwell	St Andrews	2 and 1	256
1964	G Clark	M Lunt	Ganton	39th hole	220
1965	MF Bonallack	C Clark	Royal Porthcawl	2 and 1	176
1966	R Cole (RSA)	R Shade	Carnoustie (18 holes)	3 and 2	206
1967	R Dickson (USA)	R Cerrudo (USA)	Formby	2 and 1	
1968	MF Bonallack	J Carr	Royal Troon	7 and 6	249
1969	MF Bonallack	W Hyndman (USA)	Hoylake, Royal Liverpool	3 and 2	245
1970	MF Bonallack	W Hyndman (USA)	Newcastle, Royal Co Down	8 and 7	256
1971	S Melnyk (USA)	J Simons (USA)	Carnoustie	3 and 2	256
1972	T Homer	A Thirlwell	Sandwich, Royal St George's	4 and 3	253
1973	R Siderowf (USA)	P Moody	Royal Porthcawl	5 and 3	222
1974	T Homer	J Gabrielsen (USA)	Muirfield	2 holes	330
1975	M Giles (USA)	M James	Hoylake, Royal Liverpool	8 and 7	206
1976	R Siderowf (USA)	J Davies	St Andrews	37th hole	289
1977	P McEvoy	H Campbell	Ganton	5 and 4	235
1978	P McEvoy	P McKellar	Royal Troon	4 and 3	353
1979	J Sigel (USA)	S Hoch (USA)	Hillside	3 and 2	285
1980	D Evans	D Suddards (RSA)	Royal Porthcawl	4 and 3	265
1981	P Ploujoux (Fra)	J Hirsch (USA)	St Andrews	4 and 2	256
1982	M Thompson	A Stubbs	Deal, Royal Cinque Ports -	4 and 3	245
Qualifying round introduced					
1983	P Parkin	J Holtgrieve (USA)	Turnberry	5 and 4	288
1984	JM Olazábal (Esp)	C Montgomerie	Formby	5 and 4	291
1985	G McGimpsey	G Homewood	Royal Dornoch	8 and 7	457
1986	D Curry	G Birtwell	Royal Lytham and St Annes	11 and 9	427
1987	P Mayo	P McEvoy	Prestwick	3 and 1	373
1988	C Hardin (Swe)	B Fouchee (RSA)	Royal Porthcawl	1 hole	391
1989	S Dodd	C Cassells	Royal Birkdale	5 and 3	378
1990	R Muntz (Ned)	A Macara	Muirfield	7 and 6	510
1991	G Wolstenholme	B May (USA)	Ganton	8 and 6	345
1992	S Dundas	B Dredge	Carnoustie	7 and 6	364
1993	I Pyman	P Page	Royal Portrush	37th hole	279
1994	L James	G Sherry	Nairn	2 and 1	288
1995	G Sherry	M Reynard	Hoylake, Royal Liverpool	7 and 6	288
1996	W Bladon	R Beames	Turnberry	1 hole	288
1997	C Watson	T Immelman (RSA)	Royal St Georges, Royal Cinque Ports	3 and 2	369
1998	S García (Esp)	C Williams	Muirfield	7 and 6	537
1999	G Storm	A Wainwright	Royal County Down, Kilkeel	7 and 6	433
2000	M Ilonen	C Reimbold	Royal Liverpool and Wallasey	2 and 1	376
2001	M Hoey	I Campbell	Prestwick & Kilmarnock	1 hole	288
2002	A Larrazábal	M Sell	Royal Porthcawl and Pyle & Kenfig	1 hole	286

108th Amateur Championship *at Royal Troon and Irvine*

289 entrants from 22 countries played in the 36-hole qualifying competition, 65 of whom qualified on 148 or better for the match play stage.

Leading Qualifier: David Inglis (Glencorse) 66-68—134

First Round
Michael Thannhauser (Ger) beat Ville Karhu (Fin) 1 hole

Second Round
Peter Laws (Can) beat David Inglis (Glencorse) at 19th

Second Round *continued*
Gary Wolstenholme (Kilworth Springs) beat Tommi Laitto (Fin) 6 and 5

Craig Smith (St Mellons) beat Matjaz Gojcic (Slo) 1 hole

Richard Walker (Frodsham) beat Darryl Berry (West Bradford) at 19th

Amateur Championship *continued*

Second Round *continued*

Jean-Baptiste Gonnet (Fra) beat Claudio Blaesi
(Sui) 5 and 4
Daniel Wardrop (Didsbury) beat Wilhelm Schauman
(Swe) 2 and 1
Stuart Wilson (Forfar) beat Mark Donaldson
(Kirkcaldy) 3 and 1
Edoardo Molinari (Ita) beat Alvaro Velasco (Esp)
3 and 1

Andrew McArthur (Windyhill) beat Marc Leishman
(Aus) 4 and 2
Gareth Maybin (Ballyclare) beat Adam Stott
(Reddish Vale) 4 and 3
Alex Smith (Pyle & Kenfig) beat Richard Moir
(Aus) 1 hole
Ari Savolainen (Fin) beat Haraldur Heimisson (Isl)
3 and 2
Francesco Molinari (Ita) beat Lee Boxall (West
Surrey) 2 and 1
Paul Bradshaw (Gainsborough) beat Gian Paolo
Zanol (Ita) 7 and 6
Michael Mezei (Can) beat Alfredo García (Esp)
1 hole
Kevin Freeman (Stoke Park) beat Paul Spargo (Aus)
2 and 1

Jack Doherty (Vale of Glamorgan) beat Inaki
Alustiza (Esp) at 20th
Nigel Edwards (Whitchurch) beat Carlos Del Moral
(Esp) 2 and 1
Raphaël de Sousa (Sui) beat Andrew Lynch
(Stirling) 3 and 2
Giles Legg (Dudsbury) beat Hugo Santos (Por)
8 and 7
Colm Moriarty (Athlone) beat Brad Shilton (NZ)
1 hole
Glenn Campbell (Blairgowrie) beat Stephen Lewton
(Woburn) 5 and 4
Craig Watson (East Renfrewshire) beat Gary
Lockerbie (Penrith) 3 and 2
Nicolas Meitinger (Ger) beat Zane Scotland (Walton
Heath) 1 hole

Albert Kruger (RSA) beat Rafaël Vera (Esp) 3 and 2
Sam Osborne (Wentworth) beat Sigurpall Sveinsson
(Isl) 8 and 6
Julien Quesne (Fra) beat Heikka Mantyla (Fin)
at 19th
Sebastian García beat Peter Chalkley (Copt Heath)
1 hole

Greg Kennedy (USA) beat Graeme Clark
(Doncaster) at 19th
Martin Sell (Wrag Barn) beat Ewan Forbes (Turriff)
5 and 4
Eric Ramsay (Carnoustie) beat Graham Gordon
(Newmachar) 2 and 1
JJ Jakovac (USA) beat Michael Thannhauser (Ger)
5 and 3

Third Round

Wolstenholme beat Laws 5 and 4
C Smith beat Walker 4 and 2
Gonnet beat Wardrop 5 and 4
Wilson beat E Molinari 2 holes

McArthur beat Maybin 2 holes
Savolainen beat A Smith 1 hole
F Molinari beat Bradshaw at 19th
Freeman beat Mezei 2 and 1

Doherty beat Edwards 2 and 1
De Sousa beat Legg 8 and 7
Campbell beat Moriarty 7 and 6
Watson beat Meitinger 5 and 4

Osborne beat Kruger 5 and 4
S García beat Quesne 2 and 1
Sell beat Kennedy 2 and 1
Ramsay beat Jakovac 2 and 1

Fourth Round

Wolstenholme beat C Smith 3 and 1
Gonnet beat Wilson 4 and 2
McArthur beat Savolainen 5 and 4
F Molinari beat Freeman 1 hole
De Sousa beat Doherty at 19th
Campbell beat Watson at 19th
Osborne beat S García at 19th
Ramsay beat Sell 3 and 2

Quarter Finals

Wolstenholme beat Gonnet 4 and 3
F Molinari beat McArthur 2 and 1
De Sousa beat Campbell 3 and 2
Ramsay beat Osborne 1 hole

Semi-Finals

Wolstenholme beat F Molinari 1 hole
De Sousa beat Ramsay 1 hole

Final

Gary Wolstenholme (Kilworth Springs) beat
Raphaël de Sousa (Sui) 6 and 5

British Seniors' Open Amateur Championship (inaugurated 1969)

1969	R Pattinson	Formby	154	1977	Dr TE Donaldson	Panmure	228
1970	K Bamber	Prestwick	150	1978	RJ White	Formby	225
1971	GH Pickard	Royal Cinque Ports;		1979	RJ White	Harlech, R St David's	226
		Royal St George's	150	1980	JM Cannon	Prestwick St Nicholas	218
1972	TC Hartley	St Andrews	147	1981	T Branton	Hoylake, R Liverpool	227
1973	JT Jones	Longniddry	142	1982	RL Glading	Blairgowrie	218
1974	MA Ivor-Jones	Moortown	149	1983	AJ Swann (USA)	Walton Heath	222
1975	HJ Roberts	Turnberry	138	1984	JC Owens (USA)	Western Gailes	222
1976	WM Crichton	Berkshire	149	1985	D Morey (USA)	Hesketh	223

1986	AN Sturrock	Panmure	229
1987	B Soyars (USA)	Royal Cinque Ports	226
1988	CW Green	Royal Burgess	221
1989	CW Green	Moortown, Alwoodley	226
1990	CW Green	The Berkshire	207
1991	CW Green	Prestwick	219
1992	C Hartland	Purdis Heath	221
1993	CW Green	Royal Aberdeen	150
1994	CW Green	Formby,	
		Southport & Ainsdale	223

1995	G Steel	Hankley Common	218
1996	J Hirsch	Blairgowrie	210
1997	G Bradley (USA)	Sherwood Forest	216
1998	D Lane	Western Gailes/	
		Glasgow Gailes	221
1999	W Shean (USA)	Frilford Heath	219
2000	J Hirsch (USA)	Gullane	218
2001	K Richardson		
	(USA)	Royal Portrush	217
2002	J Baldwin (USA)	Woodhall Spa	216

2003 *at Blairgowrie (Rosemount and Lansdowne)*

1	Roy Smethurst (Crewe)*	68-76-71—215
2	Joel Hirsch (USA)	74-72-69—215
3	John Baldwin (USA)	70-74-74—218

British Mid-Amateur Championship (inaugurated 1995)

1995	GP Wolstenholme	S Vale	Sunningdale
1996	GP Wolstenholme	G Steel	Hillside, Lancs
1997	S Philipson	G Thomson	Prestwick
1998	GP Wolstenholme	S Twynholm	Ganton
1999	J Kemp	S East	Walton Heath
2000	A Farmer	J Kemp	Royal Troon
2001	S East	J McGroarty	Royal Troon
2002	J Kemp	J Williams	Formby

2003 *at St Andrews (Jubilee)*

Leading Qualifier: Bryan Norton (USA)
75-69—144

Quarter Finals
Keith Macnair (Glasgow) beat Craig Gordon
(Ratho Park) 2 and 1
John Kemp (John O'Gaunt) beat Eurig Llyr Williams
(Royal St David's) 2 and 1
Stephen East (Moortown) beat Gary Sharp
(St Andrews) 1 hole

Quarter Finals *continued*
Roger Roper (Catterick) beat Hugh Hamilton
(Seaton Carew) 1 hole

Semi-Finals
Kemp beat Macnair 4 and 3
Roper beat East 1 hole

Final
John Kemp beat Roger Roper 4 and 3

English Amateur Championship (inaugurated 1925)

1925	TF Ellison	S Robinson	Royal Liverpool	1 hole
1926	TF Ellison	Sq Ldr CH Hayward	Walton Heath	6 and 4
1927	TP Perkins	JB Beddard	Little Aston	2 and 1
1928	JA Stout	TP Perkins	R Lytham and St Annes	3 and 2
1929	W Sutton	EB Tipping	Northumberland	3 and 2
1930	TA Bourn	CE Hardman	Burnham & Berrow	3 and 2
1931	LG Crawley	W Sutton	Hunstanton	1 hole
1932	EW Fiddian	AS Bradshaw	Royal St George's	1 hole
1933	J Woollam	TA Bourn	Ganton	4 and 3
1934	S Lunt	LG Crawley	Formby	37th hole
1935	J Woollam	EW Fiddian	Hollinwell	2 and 1
1936	HG Bentley	JDA Langley	Royal Cinque Ports	5 and 4
1937	JJ Pennink	LG Crawley	Saunton	6 and 5
1938	JJ Pennink	SE Banks	Moortown	2 and 1
1939	AL Bentley	W Sutton	Royal Birkdale	5 and 4
1946	IR Patey	K Thom	Mid-Surrey	5 and 4
1947	GH Micklem	C Stow	Ganton	1 hole
1948	AGB Helm	HJR Roberts	Little Aston	2 and 1
1949	RJ White	C Stowe	Formby	5 and 4
1950	JDA Langley	IR Patey	Royal Cinque Ports	1 hole
1951	GP Roberts	H Bennett	Hunstanton	39th hole
1952	E Millward	TJ Shorrock	Burnham and Berrow	2 holes
1953	GH Micklem	RJ White	Royal Birkdale	2 and 1
1954	A Thirlwell	HG Bentley	Royal St George's	2 and 1
1955	A Thirlwell	M Burgess	Ganton	7 and 6
1956	GB Wolstenholme	H Bennett	R Lytham and St Annes	1 hole
1957	A Walker	G Whitehead	Royal Liverpool	4 and 3

English Amateur Championship *continued*

1958	DN Sewell	DA Procter	Walton Heath	8 and 7
1959	GB Wolstenholme	MF Bonallack	Formby	1 hole
1960	DN Sewell	MJ Christmas	Hunstanton	41st hole
1961	I Caldwell	GJ Clark	Wentworth	37th hole
1962	MF Bonallack	MSR Lunt	Moortown	2 and 1
1963	MF Bonallack	A Thirlwell	Burnham and Berrow	4 and 3
1964	Dr D Marsh	R Foster	Hollinwell	1 hole
1965	MF Bonallack	CA Clark	The Berkshire	3 and 2
1966	MSR Lunt	DJ Millensted	R Lytham and St Annes	3 and 2
1967	MF Bonallack	GE Hyde	Woodhall Spa	4 and 2
1968	MF Bonallack	PD Kelley	Ganton	12 and 11
1969	JH Cook	P Dawson	Royal St George's	6 and 4
1970	Dr D Marsh	SG Birtwell	R Birkdale	6 and 4
1971	W Humphreys	JC Davies	Burnham and Berrow	9 and 8
1972	H Ashby	R Revell	Northumberland	5 and 4
1973	H Ashby	SC Mason	Formby	5 and 4
1974	M James	JA Watts	Woodhall Spa	6 and 5
1975	N Faldo	D Eccleston	Royal Lytham and St Annes	6 and 4
1976	P Deeble	JC Davies	Ganton	3 and 1
1977	TR Shingler	J Mayell	Walton Heath	4 and 3
1978	P Downes	P Hoad	Royal Birkdale	1 hole
1979	R Chapman	A Carman	Royal St George's	6 and 5
1980	P Deeble	P McEvoy	Moortown	4 and 3
1981	D Blakeman	A Stubbs	Burnham & Berrow	3 and 1
1982	A Oldcorn	I Bradshaw	Royal Liverpool	4 and 3
1983	G Laurence	A Brewer	Wentworth	7 and 6
1984	D Gilford	M Gerrard	Woodhall Spa	4 and 3
1985	R Winchester	P Robinson	Little Aston	1 hole
1986	J Langmead	B White	Hillside	2 and 1
1987	K Weeks	R Eggo	Frilford Heath	37th hole
1988	R Claydon	D Curry	R Birkdale	38th hole
1989	S Richardson	R Eggo	Royal St George's	2 and 1
1990	I Garbutt	G Evans	Woodhall Spa	8 and 7
1991	R Willison	M Pullan	Formby	10 and 8
1992	S Cage	R Hutt	Royal Cinque Ports	3 and 2
1993	D Fisher	R Bland	Saunton	3 and 1
1994	M Foster	A Johnson	Moortown	8 and 7
1995	M Foster	S Jarman	Hunstanton	6 and 5
1996	S Webster	D Lucas	Hollinwell	6 and 4
1997	A Wainwright	P Rowe	Royal Liverpool	2 and 1
1998	M Sanders	S Gorry	Woodhall Spa	6 and 5
1999	P Casey	S Dyson	St Mellion	2 and 1
2000	P Casey	G Wolstenholme	Royal Lytham and St Annes	4 and 2
2001	S Godfrey	S Robinson	Saunton	4 and 3
2002	R Finch	G Legg	Walton Heath	6 and 5

2003 *at Alwoodley*

Quarter Finals

Laurence Allen (Brookmans Park) beat
Matthew Baldwin (Hesketh) 4 and 3
Gary Lockerbie (Penrith) beat Andy Town
(Northcliffe) 4 and 3
Peter Richardson (Eden) beat Richard Walker
(Frodsham) 2 holes
Michael Skelton (Middlesbrough) beat
Jonathan Young (Brokenhurst Manor) 1 hole

Semi-Finals

Lockerbie beat Allen 6 and 4
Skelton beat Richardson 4 and 3

Final

Gary Lockerbie beat Michael Skelton 6 and 5

English Open Amateur Stroke Play Championship (Brabazon Trophy) (inaugurated 1957)

1957	D Sewell	Moortown	287	1963	RDBM Shade	R Birkdale	306
1958	AH Perowne	Birkdale	289	1964	MF Bonallack	Deal, R Cinque Ports	290
1959	D Sewell	Hollinwell	300	1965T	CA Clark	Formby	289
1960	GB Wolstenholme	Ganton	286		DJ Millensted		
1961	RDBM Shade	Hoylake, R Liverpool	284		MJ Burgess		
1962	A Slater	Woodhall Spa	209	1966	PM Townsend	Hunstanton	282

1967	RDBM Shade	Saunton	299	1986	R Kaplan	Sunningdale	286
1968	MF Bonallack	Walton Heath	210	1987	JG Robinson	Ganton	287
1969T	R Foster	Moortown	290	1988	R Eggo	Saunton	289
	MF Bonallack			1989T	C Rivett	Hoylake, R Liverpool	293
1970	R Foster	Little Aston	287		RN Roderick		
1971	MF Bonallack	Hillside	294	1990T	O Edmond	Burnham and Berrow	287
1972	PH Moody	Hoylake, R Liverpool	296		G Evans		
1973	R Revell	Hunstanton	294	1991T	G Evans	Hunstanton	284
1974	N Sundelson	Moortown	291		M Pullan		
1975	A Lyle	Hollinwell	298	1992	I Garrido	Notts	280
1976	P Hedges	Saunton	294	1993	D Fisher	Stoneham	277
1977	A Lyle	Royal Liverpool	293	1994	G Harris	Little Aston	280
1978	G Brand Jr	Woodhall Spa	289	1995T	M Foster	Hillside	283
1979	D Long	Little Aston	291		CS Edwards		
1980T	R Rafferty	Hunstanton	293	1996	P Fenton	R St Georges	297
	P McEvoy			1997	D Park	Saunton	271
1981	P Way	Hillside	292	1998	P Hansson	Formby	287
1982	P Downes	Woburn	299	1999	M Side	Moortown	279
1983	C Banks	Hollinwell	294	2000	J Lupprien (Ger)	Woodhall Spa	284
1984	M Davis	Deal, R Cinque Ports	286	2001	R Walker	Royal Birkdale	280
1985T	R Roper	Seaton Carew	296	2002	C Schwartzel (RSA)	Royal Cinque Ports	282
	P Baker						

2003 *at Hunstanton*

1	Jonathan Lupton (Middlesbrough)	75-68-70-74—287
2	Jack Doherty (Vale of Glamorgan)	71-72-73-73—289
3	Gonzalo Fernandez Castaño (Esp)	70-74-74-74—292

English Seniors' Amateur Championship (inaugurated 1981)

1981	CR Spalding	Copt Heath	152	1993	G Edwards	John O'Gaunt	221
1982	JL Whitworth	Lindrick	152	1994T	G Steel	Parkstone,	
1983	B Cawthray	Ross-on-Wye	154		F Jones	Broadstone	72 (18)
1984	RL Glading	Thetford	150	1995	H Hopkinson	Copt Heath	226
1985	JR Marriott	Bristol and Clifton	153	1996T	G Edwards		
1986	R Hiatt	Northants County	153		B Berney	West Lancs	224
1987	I Caldwell	North Hants	72 (18)	1997	D Lane	West Hill	215
1988	G Edwards	Bromborough	222	1998	J Marks	Saunton	217
1989	G Clark	West Sussex	212	1999	D Lane	Shifnal	73 (18)
1990	N Paul	Enville, Bridgnorth	217	2000	R Smethurst	Moor Park	212
1991	W Williams	Gerrards Cross	217	2001	R Smethurst	Sherwood Forest	220
1992	B Cawthray	Fulford	223	2002	D Arnold	Heswall & Bromborough	224

2003 *at Frilford Heath*

1	Douglas Arnold (Copthorne)	73-73-72—218
2	David Lane (Goring & Streatley)	75-70-77—222
3	Roy Smethurst (Crewe)	77-74-75—226

English Open Mid-Amateur Championship (Logan Trophy)

(inaugurated 1988)

1988	P McEvoy	Little Aston	284	1995	C Banks	Seacroft	222
1989	A Mew	Moortown	290	19 97	C Banks	Stockport	211
1990	A Mew	Wentworth	214	1998	S East	Broadstone	216
1991	I Richardson	West Lancashire	223	1999	S East	Little Aston	217
1992	A Mew	King's Lynn	222	2000	B Downing	Ponteland	208
1993	R Godley	Southport & Ainsdale	210	2001	S East	Lindrick	206
1994T	I Richardson	Trentham	217	2002T	F Illouz	Prince's, Sandwich	217
	A McLure				S Crosby		

2003 *at Royal Birkdale*

1	John Longcake (Silloth-on-Solway)	72-71-70—213
2	John Kemp (John O'Gaunt)	73-71-70—214
3	Sandy Twynholm (Morpeth)	71-71-73—215

English County Champions' Tournament (Formerly President's Bowl)
(inaugurated 1962)

1962T	G Edwards, Cheshire	1983	N Chesses, Warwickshire
	A Thirwell, Northumberland	1984T	N Briggs, Herts/P McEvoy, Warwickshire
1963T	M Burgess, Sussex/R Foster, Yorks	1985	P Robinson, Herts
1964	M Attenborough, Kent	1986	A Gelsthorpe, Yorks
1965	M Lees, Lincs	1987T	F George, Berks, Bucks & Oxon
1966	R Stephenson, Middx		D Fay, Surrey
1967	P Benka, Surrey	1988	R Claydon, Cambridge
1968	G Hyde, Sussex	1989	R Willison, Middlesex
1969	A Holmes, Herts	1990T	P Streeter, Lincs/R Sloman, Kent
1970	M King, Berks, Bucks and Oxon	1991	T Allen, Warwickshire
1971	M Lee, Yorks	1992	L Westwood, Notts
1972	P Berry, Glos	1993	R Walker, Durham
1973	A Chandler, Lancs	1994	GP Wolstenholme, Glos
1974T	G Hyde, Sussex/A Lyle, Shrops & Hereford	1995	S Webster, Warwickshire
1975	N Faldo, Herts	1996T	J Herbert, Leics/G Wolstenholme, Glos
1976	R Brown, Devon	1997	J Herbert, Leicestershire & Rutland
1977	M Walls, Cumbria	1998	GP Wolstenholme, Leics
1978	I Simpson, Notts	1999	D Griffiths, Herts
1979	N Burch, Essex	2000	P Bradshaw, Lincolnshire
1980	D Lane, Berks, Bucks and Oxon	2001	G Wolstenholme, Leicestershire & Rutland
1981	M Kelly, Yorks	2002	G Evans, Middlesex
1982	P Deeble, Northumberland		

2003 at Woodhall Spa

1	James Crampton (Lincolnshire)	71-73—144
2	Graeme Clark (Yorkshire)	74-71—145
	Eddie Vernon (Derbyshire)	71-74—145

Irish Amateur Open Championship (inaugurated 1892)

1892	A Stuart	JH Andrew	Royal Portrush	1 hole
1893	John Ball	LS Anderson	Newcastle	8 and 7
1894	John Ball	DL Low	Dollymount	9 and 7
1895	WB Taylor	JM Williamson	Royal Portrush	13 and 11
1896	WB Taylor	D Anderson	Newcastle	9 and 8
1897	HH Hilton	LS Anderson	Dollymount	5 and 4
1898	WB Taylor	ROJ Dallmyer	Royal Portrush	at 37th
1899	John Ball	JM Williamson	Portmarnock	13 and 11
1900	HH Hilton	SH Fry	Newcastle	11 and 9
1901	HH Hilton	P Dowie	Dollymount	6 and 5
1902	HH Hilton	WH Hamilton	Royal Portrush	5 and 4
1903	G Wilkie	HA Boyd	Portmarnock	1 hole
1904	JS Worthington	JF Mitchell	Newcastle	6 and 4
1905	HA Boyd	JF Mitchell	Dollymount	3 and 2
1906	HH Barker	JS Worthington	Royal Portrush	5 and 4
1907	JD Brown	SH Fry	Portmarnock	2 and 1
1908	JF Mitchell	HM Cairnes	Newcastle	3 and 2
1909	LO Munn	R Garson	Dollymount	2 holes
1910	LO Munn	G Lockhart	Royal Portrush	9 and 7
1911	LO Munn	Hon. Michael Scott	Portmarnock	7 and 6
1912	G Lockhart	P Jenkins	Newcastle	11 and 9
1913	CA Palmer	LA Phillips	Dollymount	4 and 3
1914-1918	*Not played due to First World War*			
1919	C Bretherton	TD Armour	Royal Portrush	5 and 3
1920	GNC Martin	CW Robertson	Portmarnock	6 and 5
1921	D Smyth	J Gorry	Newcastle	2 holes
1922	A Lowe	J Henderson	Royal Portrush	6 and 4
1923	GNC Martin	CO Hezlet	Newcastle	1 hole
1924	EF Spiller	JDA McCormack	Dollymount	3 and 1
1925	TA Torrance	CO Hezlet	Royal Portrush	4 and 3
1926	CO Hezlet	RM McConnell	Portmarnock	7 and 6
1927	RM McConnell	DEB Soulby	Newcastle	5 and 3
1928	GS Moon	EF Spiller	Dollymount	1 hole
1929	CO Hezlet	JA Lang	Royal Portrush	1 hole
1930	W Sutton	DA Fiddian	Portmarnock	4 and 2

1931	EA McRuvie	DEB Soulby	Newcastle	7 and 5
1932	J McLean	JC Brown	Dollymount	9 and 8
1933	J McLean	E Fiddian	Newcastle	3 and 2
1934	H Thomson	HG Bentley	Portmarnock	3 and 2
1935	H Thomson	J McLean	Royal Portrush	5 and 4
1936	JC Brown	WM O'Sullivan	Portmarnock	at 39th
1937	J Fitzsimmons	RA McKinna	Dollymount	4 and 3
1938	J Bruen jr	JR Mahon	Newcastle	9 and 8
1939–1945	*Not played due to Second World War*			
1946	JB Carr	AT Kyle	Royal Portrush	3 and 1
1947	J Burke	JB Carr	Dollymount	1 hole
1948	RC Ewing	JB Carr	Newcastle	1 hole
1949	WM O'Sullivan	BJ Scannell	Killarney	2 holes
1950	JB Carr	RC Ewing	Rosses Point	at 40th
1951	RC Ewing	JB Carr	Portmarnock	2 and 1
1952	NV Drew	CH Beamish	Royal Portrush	5 and 4
1953	NV Drew	WM O'Sullivan	Killarney	3 and 2
1954	JB Carr	RC Ewing	Dollymount	6 and 4
1955	JF Fitzgibbon	JW Hulme	Royal County Down	1 hole
1956	JB Carr	JR Mahon	Portmarnock	1 hole
1957	JL Bamford	W Meharg	Royal Portrush	at 37th

from 1958 decided by Stroke Play

1958	T Craddock	Dollymount	484
1959	J Duncan	Newcastle	313

not played 1960–1994

1995	P Harrington	Fota Island	283
1996	K Nolan	Fota Island	286
1997	K Nolan	Fota Island	279
1998	M Hoey	Royal Dublin	286
1999	G Cullen	Royal Dublin	282
2000	N Fox	Royal Dublin	284
2001	R McEvoy*	Royal Dublin	277
2002	L Oosthuizen (RSA)	Royal Dublin	283

2003 *at Royal Dublin*

1	Noel Fox (Portmarnock)	68-70-70-74—282
2	Stuart Manley (Mountain Ash)	71-70-74-69—284
3	Jamie Moul (Stoke by Nayland)	72-71-71-72—286

Irish Amateur Close Championship (inaugurated 1893)

1893	T Dickson	G Combe	Royal Portrush	2 holes
1894	R Magill jr	T Dickson	Newcastle	3 and 1
1895	WH Webb	J Stevenson	Dollymount	10 and 9
1896	J Stewart-Moore jr	HAS Upton	Royal Portrush	8 and 7
1897	HE Reade	WH Webb	Newcastle	2 and 1
1898	WH Webb	J Stewart-Moore jr	Dollymount	9 and 8
1899	HE Reade	JP Todd	Royal Portrush	3 and 2
1900	RGN Henry	J McAvoy	Portmarnock	4 and 3
1901	WH Boyd	HE Reade	Newcastle	7 and 5
1902	FB Newett	R Shaw	Dollymount	1 hole
1903	HE Reade	DRA Campbell	Royal Portrush	5 and 4
1904	HA Boyd	JP Todd	Portmarnock	4 and 2
1905	FB Newett	B O'Brien	Newcastle	6 and 5
1906	HA Boyd	HM Cairnes	Dollymount	at 38th
1907	HM Cairnes	HA Boyd	Royal Portrush	7 and 6
1908	LO Munn	A Babbington	Portmarnock	10 and 9
1909	AH Patterson	EF Spiller	Newcastle	at 37th
1910	JF Jameson	LO Munn	Dollymount	2 and 1
1911	LO Munn	HA Boyd	Royal Portrush	7 and 6
1912	AH Craig	P Halligan	Castlerock	13 and 11
1913	LO Munn	HA Boyd	Portmarnock	6 and 5
1914	LO Munn	Earl Annesley	Hermitage	10 and 8
1915–1918	*Not played due to First World War*			
1919	E Carter	WG McConnell	Portmarnock	9 and 7
1920	CO Hezlet	CL Crawford	Castlerock	12 and 11
1921	E Carter	G Moore	Portmarnock	9 and 8
1922	EM Munn	WK Tillie	Royal Portrush	3 and 1

Irish Amateur Close Championship *continued*

1923	JD McCormack	LE Werner	Milltown	2 and 1
1924	JD McCormack	DEB Soulby	Newcastle	4 and 2
1925	CW Robertson	HM Cairnes	Portmarnock	4 and 3
1926	AC Allison	OW Madden	Royal Portrush	7 and 6
1927	JD McCormack	HM Cairnes	Cork	at 37th
1928	DEB Soulby	JO Wisdom	Castlerock	7 and 5
1929	DEB Soulby	FP McConnell	Dollymount	4 and 3
1930	J Burke	FP McConnell	Lahinch	6 and 5
1931	J Burke	FP McConnell	Rosses Point	6 and 4
1932	J Burke	M Crowley	Royal Portrush	6 and 5
1933	J Burke	GT McMullan	Cork	3 and 2
1934	JC Brown	RM McConnell	Rosslare	6 and 5
1935	RM McConnell	J Burke	Galway	2 and 1
1936	J Burke	RM McConnell	Castlerock	7 and 6
1937	J Bruen jr	J Burke	Ballybunion	3 and 2
1938	J Bruen jr	R Simcox	Rathfarnham Castle	3 and 2
1939	GH Owens	RM McConnell	Rosses Point	6 and 5
1940	J Burke	WM O'Sullivan	Dollymount	4 and 3
1941–1945	*Not played due to Second World War*			
1946	J Burke	RC Ewing	Dollymount	2 and 1
1947	J Burke	J Fitzsimmons	Lahinch	2 holes
1948	RC Ewing	BJ Scannell	Royal Portrush	3 and 2
1949	J Carroll	P Murphy	Galway	4 and 3
1950	B Herlihy	BC McManus	Baltray	4 and 3
1951	M Power	JB Carr	Cork	3 and 2
1952	TW Egan	JC Brown	Royal Belfast	at 41st
1953	J Malone	M Power	Rosses Point	2 and 1
1954	JB Carr	I Forsythe	Carlow	4 and 3
1955	JR Mahon	G Crosbie	Lahinch	3 and 2
1956	AGH Love	G Crosbie	Malone	at 37th
1957	JB Carr	G Crosbie	Galway	2 holes
1958	RC Ewing	GA Young	Ballybunion	5 and 3
1959	T Craddock	JB Carr	Portmarnock	at 38th
1960	M Edwards	N Fogarty	Portstewart	6 and 5
1961	D Sheahan	J Brown	Rosses Point	5 and 4
1962	M Edwards	J Harrington	Baltray	42nd hole
1963	JB Carr	EC O'Brien	Killarney	2 and 1
1964	JB Carr	A McDade	Co Down	6 and 5
1965	JB Carr	T Craddock	Rosses Point	3 and 2
1966	D Sheahan	J Faith	Dollymount	3 and 2
1967	JB Carr	PD Flaherty	Lahinch	1 hole
1968	M O'Brien	F McCarroll	Royal Portrush	2 and 1
1969	V Nevin	J O'Leary	Co Sligo	1 hole
1970	D Sheahan	M Bloom	Grange	2 holes
1971	P Kane	M O'Brien	Ballybunion	3 and 2
1972	K Stevenson	B Hoey	Co Down	2 and 1
1973	RKM Pollin	RM Staunton	Rosses Point	1 hole
1974	R Kane	M Gannon	Portmarnock	5 and 4
1975	MD O'Brien	JA Bryan	Cork	5 and 4
1976	D Brannigan	D O'Sullivan	Royal Portrush	2 holes
1977	M Gannon	A Hayes	Westport	19th hole
1978	M Morris	T Cleary	Carlow	1 hole
1979	J Harrington	MA Gannon	Ballybunion	2 and 1
1980	R Rafferty	MJ Bannon	Co Down	8 and 7
1981	D Brannigan	E McMenamin	Co Sligo	19th hole
1982	P Walton	B Smyth	Woodbrook	7 and 6
1983	T Corridan	E Power	Killarney	2 holes
1984	CB Hoey	L McNamara	Malone	20th hole
1985	D O'Sullivan	D Branigan	Westport	1 hole
1986	J McHenry	P Rayfus	Dublin	4 and 3
1987	E Power	JP Fitzgerald	Tranmore	2 holes
1988	G McGimpsey	D Mulholland	Royal Portrush	2 and 1
1989	P McGinley	N Goulding	Rosses Point	3 and 2
1990	D Clarke	P Harrington	Baltray	3 and 2
1991	G McNeill	N Goulding	Ballybunion	3 and 1
1992	G Murphy	JP Fitzgerald	Portstewart	2 and 1
1993	E Power	D Higgins	Enniscrone	3 and 2
1994	D Higgins	P Harrington	Portmarnock	20th hole
1995	P Harrington	D Coughlan	Lahinch	3 and 2
1996	P Lawrie	G McGimpsey	Royal Co Down	3 and 2
1997	K Kearney	P Lawrie	Fota Island	5 and 4
1998	E Power	B Omelia	The Island	1 hole

1999	C McMonagle	M Sinclair	Killarney	2 and 1
2000	G McDowell	A McCormick	Royal Portrush	7 and 6
2001	G McNeill	S Browne	Co Sligo	20th hole
2002	J McGinn	K Kearney	Carlow	3 and 1

2003 *at Tramore*

Leading Qualifiers: Noel Fox (Portmarnock), Gareth Maybin (Ballyclare) 136
Match Play: 64 qualified on 148 or better (9 out of 14 on 148)

Quarter Finals

David Carroll (Grange) beat Justin Kehoe (Birr)
  2 and 1
Michael Brett (Portmarnock) beat Greg Bowden
  (Hermitage) at 24th
Desmond Morgan (Mullingar) beat Peter O'Keeffe
  (Douglas) 2 and 1
Mark O'Sullivan (Galway) beat Gareth Maybin
  (Ballyclare) 3 and 2

Semi-Finals

Carroll beat Brett 2 and 1
O'Sullivan beat Morgan 2 and 1

Final

Mark O'Sullivan beat David Carroll 1 hole

Irish Seniors' Open Amateur Championship (inaugurated 1970)

1970	RC Ewing	Lahinch	153	1987	J Murray	Castleroy	150
1971	J O'Sullivan	Rosslare	159	1988	WB Buckley	Westport	154
1972	BJ Scannell	Co. Sligo	152	1989	B McCrea	Royal Belfast	150
1973	JW Hulme	Warrenpoint	147	1990	C Hartland	Cork	149
1974	P Walsh	Cork	155	1991	C Hartland	Mullingar	147
1975	SA O'Connor	Woodbrook	152	1992	C Hartland	Athlone	145
1976	BJ Scannell	Athlone	150	1993	P Breen	Bangor	147
1977	DB Somers	Warrenpoint	150	1994	B Buckley	Tramore	151
1978	DP Herlihy	Limerick	150	1995	B Hoey	Dundalk	151
1979	P Kelly	Royal Tara	153	1996	E Condren	Oughterard	148
1980	GN Fogarty	Galway	144	1997	B Wilson	The Knock	152
1981	GN Fogarty	Bundoran	149	1998	J Harrington	Thurles	149
1982	J Murray	Douglas	141	1999	A Lee	Thurles	150
1983	F Sharpe	Courtown	153	2000	D Jackson	Westport	151
1984	J Boston	Connemara	147	2001	D Jackson	Clandeboye	153
1985	J Boston	Newcastle	155	2002	T Fox	Limerick	146
1986	J Coey	Waterford	141				

2003 *at Mullingar*

1	Phil Jones (Bromborough)	73-77—150 (won after countback on back nine)
2	P Cowley (Cork)	73-77—150
3	J O'Donoghue (Tipperary)	72-78—150

Scottish Amateur Championship (inaugurated 1922)

1922	J Wilson	E Blackwell	St Andrews	19th hole
1923	TM Burrell	Dr A McCallum	Troon	1 hole
1924	WW Mackenzie	W Tulloch	Aberdeen	3 and 2
1925	JT Dobson	W Mackenzie	Muirfield	3 and 2
1926	WJ Guild	SO Shepherd	Leven	2 and 1
1927	A Jamieson jr	Rev D Rutherford	Gailes	22nd hole
1928	WW Mackenzie	W Dodds	Muirfield	5 and 3
1929	JT Bookless	J Dawson	Aberdeen	5 and 4
1930	K Greig	T Wallace	Carnoustie	9 and 8
1931	J Wilson	A Jamieson Jr	Prestwick	2 and 1
1932	J McLean	K Greig	Dunbar	5 and 4
1933	J McLean	KC Forbes	Aberdeen	6 and 4
1934	J McLean	W Campbell	Western Gailes	3 and 1
1935	H Thomson	J McLean	St Andrews	2 and 1
1936	ED Hamilton	R Neill	Carnoustie	1 hole
1937	H McInally	K Patrick	Barassie	6 and 5
1938	ED Hamilton	R Rutherford	Muirfield	4 and 2
1939	H McInally	H Thomson	Prestwick	6 and 5
1946	EC Brown	R Rutherford	Carnoustie	3 and 2
1947	H McInally	J Pressley	Glasgow Gailes	10 and 8

Scottish Amateur Championship *continued*

1948	AS Flockhart	G Taylor	Royal Aberdeen	7 and 6
1949	R Wright	H McInally	Muirfield	1 hole
1950	WC Gibson	D Blair	Prestwick	2 and 1
1951	JM Dykes	J Wilson	St Andrews	4 and 2
1952	FG Dewar	J Wilson	Carnoustie	4 and 3
1953	DA Blair	J McKay	Western Gailes	3 and 1
1954	JW Draper	W Gray	Nairn	4 and 3
1955	RR Jack	AC Miller	Muirfield	2 and 1
1956	Dr FWG Deighton	A MacGregor	Troon	8 and 7
1957	JS Montgomerie	J Burnside	Balgownie	2 and 1
1958	WD Smith	I Harris	Prestwick	6 and 5
1959	Dr FWG Deighton	R Murray	St Andrews	6 and 5
1960	JR Young	S Saddler	Carnoustie	5 and 3
1961	J Walker	ST Murray	Western Gailes	4 and 3
1962	SWT Murray	R Shade	Muirfield	2 and 1
1963	RDBM Shade	N Henderson	Troon	4 and 3
1964	RDBM Shade	J McBeath	Nairn	8 and 7
1965	RDBM Shade	G Cosh	St Andrews	4 and 2
1966	RDBM Shade	C Strachan	Western Gailes	9 and 8
1967	RDBM Shade	A Murphy	Carnoustie	5 and 4
1968	GB Cosh	R Renfrew	Muirfield	4 and 3
1969	JM Cannon	A Hall	Troon	6 and 4
1970	CW Green	H Stuart	Royal Aberdeen	1 hole
1971	S Stephen	C Green	St Andrews	3 and 2
1972	HB Stuart	A Pirie	Prestwick	3 and 1
1973	IC Hutcheon	A Brodie	Carnoustie	3 and 2
1974	GH Murray	A Pirie	Western Gailes	2 and 1
1975	D Greig	G Murray	Montrose	7 and 6
1976	GH Murray	H Stuart	St Andrews	6 and 5
1977	A Brodie	P McKellar	Troon	1 hole
1978	IA Carslaw	J Cuddihy	Downfield	7 and 6
1979	K Macintosh	P McKellar	Prestwick	5 and 4
1980	D Jamieson	C Green	Royal Aberdeen	2 and 1 (18)
1981	C Dalgleish	A Thomson	Western Gailes	7 and 6
1982	CW Green	G Macgregor	Carnoustie	1 hole
1983	CW Green	J Huggan	Gullane	1 hole
1984	A Moir	K Buchan	Renfrew	3 and 3
1985	D Carrick	D James	Southerness	4 and 2
1986	C Brooks	A Thomson	Monifieth	3 and 2
1987	C Montgomerie	A Watt	Nairn	9 and 8
1988	J Milligan	A Coltart	Kilmarnock (Barassie)	1 hole
1989	A Thomson	A Tait	Moray	1 hole
1990	C Everett	M Thomson	Gullane	7 and 5
1991	G Lowson	L Salariya	Downfield	4 and 3
1992	S Gallacher	D Kirkpatrick	Glasgow Gailes	37th hole
1993	D Robertson	R Russell	Royal Dornoch	2 holes
1994	H McKibben	A Reid	Renfrew	39th hole
1995	S Mackenzie	H McKibben	Southerness	8 and 7
1996	M Brooks	A Turnbull	Dunbar	7 and 6
1997	C Hislop	S Cairns	Carnoustie	5 and 3
1998	G Rankin	M Donaldson	Prestwick	6 and 5
1999	C Heap	M Loftus	Cruden Bay	7 and 5
2000	S O'Hara	C Heap	Royal Dornoch	1 hole
2001	B Hume	C Watson	Downfield	4 and 3
2002	A McArthur	S Jamieson	Western Gailes	2 and 1

2003 *at The Duke's Course, St Andrews*

Quarter Finals

Neil MacRae (Cawder) beat Keith Hamilton
(Whitecraigs) 3 and 2

Graham Gordon (Newmachar) beat
Andrew McArthur (Windyhill) 5 and 4

Stuart Wilson (Forfar) beat Scott Jamieson
(Cathkin Braes) 3 and 1

David Inglis (Glencorse) beat Thomas Gilchrist
(Falkirk Tryst) 2 and 1

Semi-Finals

Gordon beat MacRae 2 holes

Wilson beat Inglis 5 and 4

Final

Graham Gordon beat Stuart Wilson 4 and 3

Scottish Open Amateur Stroke Play Championship

(inaugurated 1967)

1967	BJ Gallacher	Muirfield and Gullane	291
1968	RDBM Shade	Prestwick and Prestwick St Nicholas	282
1969	JS Macdonald	Carnoustie and Monifieth	288
1970	D Hayes	Glasgow Gailes and Barassie	275
1971	IC Hutcheon	Leven and Lundin	277
1972	BN Nicholas	Dalmahoy and Ratho Park	290
1973T	DM Robertson/GJ Clark	Dunbar and North Berwick	284
1974	IC Hutcheon	Blairgowrie and Alyth	283
1975	CW Green	Nairn and Nairn Dunbar	295
1976	S Martin	Monifieth and Carnoustie	299
1977	PJ McKellar	Muirfield and Gullane	299
1978	AR Taylor	Cawder	281
1979	IC Hutcheon	Blairgowrie	286
1980	G Brand jr	Musselburgh and R Musselburgh	207 (54 holes)
1981	F Walton	Erskine and Renfrew	287
1982	C Macgregor	Downfield and Camperdown	287
1983	C Murray	Irvine and Irvine Ravenspark	291
1984	CW Green	Blairgowrie	287
1985	C Montgomerie	Dunbar and North Berwick	274
1986	KH Walker	Carnoustie	289
1987	D Carrick	Lundin and Ladybank	282
1988	S Easingwood	Cathkin Braes and East Kilbride	277
1989	F Illouz	Blairgowrie	281
1990	G Hay	Royal Aberdeen and Murcar	133 (36 holes)
1991	A Coltart	Royal Troon and Troon Portland	291
1992	D Robertson	Mortonhall and Bruntsfield Links	281
1993	A Reid	St Andrews Jubilee and New	289
1994	D Downie	Letham Grange	288
1995	S Gallacher	Paisley and Renfrew	284
1996	A Forsyth	Cardross and Helensburgh	279
1997	DB Howard	Monifieth and Panmure	271
1998	L Kelly	Moray and Elgin	275
1999	G Rankin	St Andrews Old and Jubilee	286
2000	S McKenzie*	Letham Grange	278
2001	J Sutherland*	Nairn and Nairn Dunbar	279
2002	B Hume	Southerness	277

2003 *at Turnberry Kintyre*

1	Gary Wolstenholme (Kilworth Springs)	69-67-68-69—273
2	Richard Walker (Frodsham)	74-67-69-67—277
3	Marc Leishman (Aus)	69-68-72-70—279

Scottish Senior Championship (inaugurated 1978)

1978T	JM Cannon	Glasgow	149	1989	AS Mayer	Glasgow	139
	GR Carmichael			1990	C Hartland	Royal Burgess	146
1979	A Sinclair	Glasgow	143	1991	CW Green	Glasgow	140
1980	JM Cannon	Royal Burgess	149	1992	G Clark	Royal Burgess	148
1981T	IR Harris	Glasgow	146	1993	J Maclean	Glasgow	141
	Dr J Hastings			1994	DM Lawrie	Ladybank	149
	AN Sturrock			1995	CW Green	Glasgow	141
1982T	JM Cannon	Royal Burgess	143	1996	CW Green	Western Gailes	146
	J Niven			1997	CW Green	Glasgow	137
1983	WD Smith	Glasgow	145	1998	CW Green	Ladybank	146
1984	A Sinclair	Royal Burgess	148	1999	G Steel*	Glasgow	145
1985	AN Sturrock	Glasgow	143	2000	N Grant	Falkirk Tryst	142
1986	RL Glading	Royal Burgess	153	2001	D Lane	Glasgow	140
1987	I Hornsby	Glasgow	145	2002	D Lane	Scotscraig	142
1988	J Hayes	Royal Burgess	143				

2003 *at Glasgow*

1	Ian Hutcheon (Monifieth)	74-72-75—221
2	Anthony Gresham (Pennant Hills)	78-73-79—230
3	Charles Green (Cardross)	76-72-83—231
	Tony McIntyre (Lundin)	74-75-82—231

Scottish Champion of Champions (inaugurated 1970) *at Leven*

1970	A Horne	1981	I Hutcheon	1992	D Robertson
1971	D Black	1982	G Macgregor	1993	R Russell
1972	R Strachan	1983	D Carrick	1994	G Sherry
1973	*Not held*	1984	S Stephen	1995	S Gallacher
1974	M Niven	1985	I Brotherston	1996	M Brooks
1975	A Brodie	1986	I Hutcheon	1997	G Rankin
1976	A Brodie	1987	G Shaw	1998	G Rankin
1977	V Reid	1988	I Hutcheon	1999	D Patrick
1978	D Greig	1989	J Milligan	2000	G Fox
1979	B Marchbank	1990	J Milligan	2001	M Loftus
1980	I Hutcheon	1991	G Hay	2002	S Carmichael

2003

1	Stuart Wilson (Forfar)	66-69-64-66—265
2	Glenn Campbell (Blairgowrie)	73-68-65-67—273
3	Steven Armstrong (Turnhouse)	66-69-68-71—274
	Barry Scott (Dumfries & Galloway)	70-69-68-67—274

Scottish Mid-Amateur Championship (inaugurated 1994)

1994	C Watson	1997	H McDonald	2000	J Cameron
1995	M Thomson	1998	G Campbell	2001	M Thompson
1996	B Smith	1999	G Crawford	2002	C Elliot

2003 *at Renfrew*

Leading Qualifier: Frank McCarron (Stonehaven) 72-73—145

Semi-Finals
Mike Thomson (Torwoodlee) beat Ross Hinshelwood (East Kilbride) 2 and 1
Craig Gordon (Ratho Park) beat James Smart (Paisley) 3 and 1

Final
Craig Gordon beat Mike Thomson 2 holes

Welsh Amateur Championship (inaugurated 1895)

Year	Winner	Runner-up	Venue	Score
1895	J Hunter	TM Barlow	Aberdovey	2 holes
1896	J Hunter	P Plunkett	Rhyl	1 hole
1897	FE Woodhead	J Hunter	Penarth	4 and 3
1898	FE Woodhead	Dr E Reid	Aberdovey	5 and 4
1899	FE Woodhead	TD Cummins	Conway	6 and 5
1900	TM Barlow	H Ludlow	Royal Porthcawl	2 and 1
1901	Major Green	P Plunkett	Aberdovey	8 and 7
1902	J Hunter	H Ludlow	Penarth	5 and 4
1903	J Hunter	TM Barlow	Rhos-on-Sea	2 holes
1904	H Ludlow	RM Brown	Ashburnham	13 and 11
1905	J Duncan jr	AP Cary Thomas	Conway	6 and 5
1906	G Renwick	WT Davies	Radyr	9 and 7
1907	LA Phillips	LH Gottwaltz	Royal Porthcawl	3 and 1
1908	G Renwick	LA Phillips	Southerndown	7 and 5
1909	J Duncan jr	EJ Byrne	Rhyl	9 and 8
1910	G Renwick	RM Brown	Swansea	2 holes
1911	HM Lloyd	TC Mellor	Conway	4 and 2
1912	LA Phillips	CH Turnbull	Royal Porthcawl	4 and 3
1913	HN Atkinson	CJ Hamilton	Chester	at 38th
1914–1919	*Not played due to First World War*			
1920	HR Howell	J Duncan jr	Southerndown	2 holes
1921	CEL Fairchild	E Rowe	Aberdovey	1 hole
1922	HR Howell	EDSN Carne	Tenby	12 and 11
1923	HR Howell	CEL Fairchild	Rhyl	3 and 1
1924	HR Howell	CH Turnbull	Radyr	2 and 1
1925	CEL Fairchild	GS Emery	Rhyl	10 and 8
1926	DR Lewis	K Stoker	Royal Porthcawl	1 hole
1927	DR Lewis	JL Jones	Tenby	4 and 3

Year	Winner	Runner-up	Venue	Score
1928	CC Marston	DR Lewis	Royal St David's	at 37th
1929	HR Howell	R Chapman	Southerndown	4 and 3
1930	HR Howell	DR Lewis	Tenby	2 and 1
1931	HR Howell	WG Morgan	Aberdovey	7 and 6
1932	HR Howell	HE Davies	Ashburnham	7 and 6
1933	JL Black	AA Duncan	Royal Porthcawl	2 and 1
1934	SB Roberts	GS Noon	Prestatyn	4 and 3
1935	R Chapman	GS Noon	Tenby	1 hole
1936	RM de Lloyd	G Wallis	Aberdovey	1 hole
1937	DH Lewis	R Glossop	Porthcawl	2 holes
1938	AA Duncan	SB Roberts	Rhyl	2 and 1
1939–1945 *Not played due to Second World War*				
1946	JV Moody	A Marshman	Porthcawl	9 and 8
1947	SB Roberts	G Breen Turner	Royal St David's	8 and 7
1948	AA Duncan	SB Roberts	Porthcawl	2 and 1
1949	AD Evans	MA Jones	Aberdovey	2 and 1
1950	JL Morgan	DJ Bonnell	Southerndown	9 and 7
1951	JL Morgan	WI Tucker	Royal St David's	3 and 2
1952	AA Duncan	JL Morgan	Ashburnham	4 and 3
1953	SB Roberts	D Pearson	Prestatyn	5 and 3
1954	AA Duncan	K Thomas	Tenby	6 and 5
1955	TJ Davies	P Dunn	Royal St David's	38th hole
1956	A Lockley	WI Tucker	Southerndown	2 and 1
1957	ES Mills	H Griffiths	Royal St David's	2 and 1
1958	HC Squirrell	AD Lake	Conway	4 and 3
1959	HC Squirrell	N Rees	Porthcawl	8 and 7
1960	HC Squirrell	P Richards	Aberdovey	2 and 1
1961	AD Evans	J Toye	Ashburnham	3 and 2
1962	J Povall	HC Squirrell	Royal St David's	3 and 2
1963	WI Tucker	J Povall	Southerndown	4 and 3
1964	HC Squirrell	WI Tucker	Royal St David's	1 hole
1965	HC Squirrell	G Clay	Porthcawl	6 and 4
1966	WI Tucker	EN Davies	Aberdovey	6 and 5
1967	JK Povall	WI Tucker	Asburnham	3 and 2
1968	J Buckley	J Povall	Conway	8 and 7
1969	JL Toye	EN Davies	Porthcawl	1 hole
1970	EN Davies	J Povall	Royal St David's	1 hole
1971	CT Brown	HC Squirrell	Southerndown	6 and 5
1972	EN Davies	JL Toye	Prestatyn	40th hole
1973	D McLean	T Holder	Ashburnham	6 and 4
1974	S Cox	EN Davies	Caernarvonshire	3 and 2
1975	JL Toye	WI Tucker	Porthcawl	5 and 4
1976	MPD Adams	WI Tucker	Royal St David's	6 and 5
1977	D Stevens	JKD Povall	Southerndown	3 and 2
1978	D McLean	A Ingram	Caernarvonshire	11 and 10
1979	TJ Melia	MS Roper	Ashburnham	5 and 4
1980	DL Stevens	G Clement	Prestatyn	10 and 9
1981	S Jones	C Davies	Porthcawl	5 and 3
1982	D Wood	C Davies	Royal St David's	8 and 7
1983	JR Jones	AP Parkin	Southerndown	2 holes
1984	JR Jones	A Llyr	Prestatyn	1 hole
1985	ED Jones	MA Macara	Ashburnham	2 and 1
1986	C Rees	B Knight	Conwy	1 hole
1987	PM Mayo	DK Wood	Porthcawl	2 holes
1988	K Jones	RN Roderick	Royal St David's	40th hole
1989	S Dodd	K Jones	Tenby	2 and 1
1990	A Barnett	A Jones	Prestatyn	1 hole
1991	S Pardoe	S Jones	Ashburnham	7 and 5
1992	H Roberts	R Johnson	Pyle & Kenfig	3 and 2
1993	B Dredge	M Ellis	Southerndown	3 and 1
1994	C Evans	M Smith	Royal Porthcawl	5 and 4
1995	G Houston	C Evans	Royal St David's	3 and 2
1996	Y Taylor	DH Park	Ashburnham	3 and 2
1997	JR Donaldson	M Pilkington	Pyle & Kenfig	5 and 4
1998	M Pilkington	K Sullivan	Prestatyn	2 and 1
1999	M Griffiths	R Brookman	Tenby	7 and 6
2000	JG Jermine	R Brookman	Royal St David's	1 hole
2001	C Williams	L Harpin	Royal Porthcawl	1 hole
2002	D Price	L Harpin	Conwy	20th hole

Welsh Amateur Championship *continued*

2003 *at Southerndown*

Quarter Finals
Rhys Davies (Royal Porthcawl) beat Stuart Clark
(Whitchurch) 4 and 3
Gareth Wright (West Linton) beat Craig Smith
(St Mellons) 1 hole
Nigel Edwards (Whitchurch) beat Carl Wakely
(Whitchurch) 2 and 1
Stuart Manley (Mountain Ash) beat Brian Lee
(Newport) at 23rd

Semi-Finals
Davies beat Wright 2 and 1
Manley beat Edwards 3 and 2

Final
Stuart Manley beat Rhys Davies 8 and 7

Welsh Open Amateur Stroke Play Championship (inaugurated 1967)

1967	EN Davies	Harlech	295	1986	M Calvert	Pyle & Kenfig	299
1968	JA Buckley	Harlech	294	1987	MA Macara	Llandudno (Maesdu)	290
1969	DL Stevens	Tenby	288	1988	RN Roderick	Tenby	283
1970	JK Povall	Newport	292	1989	SC Dodd	Conwy	304
1971T	EN Davies	Harlech	296				
	JL Toye				*Open event since 1990*		
1972	JR Jones	Pyle & Kenfig	299	1990	G Houston	Pyle & Kenfig	288
1973	JR Jones	Llandudno (Maesdu)	300	1991	A Jones	Royal Porthcawl	290
1974	JL Toye	Tenby	307	1992	AJ Barnett	Royal St David's	278
1975	D McLean	Wrexham	288	1993	M Macara	Maesdu	280
1976	WI Tucker	Newport	282	1994	N Van Hootegem	St Pierre	290
1977	JA Buckley	Prestatyn	302	1995	M Peet	Prestatyn	282
1978	HJ Evans	Pyle & Kenfig	300	1996	M Blackey	Tenby	276
1979	D McLean	Holyhead	289	1997	G Wolstenholme	Conwy	286
1980	TJ Melia	Tenby	291	1998	DAJ Patrick	Southerndown	279
1981	D Evans	Wrexham	270	1999	C Williams	Northop	288
1982	JR Jones	Cradoc	287	2000	J Donaldson	Ashburnham	283
1983	G Davies	Aberdovey	287	2001	J Lupton	Maesdu	266
1984	RN Roderick	Newport	292	2002	J Doherty	Pyle & Kenfig	282
1985	MA Macara	Harlech	291				

2003 *at Prestatyn*

1	Michael Skelton (Middlesbrough)	71-72-67-68—278
2	Cennydd Mills (Vale of Glamorgan)	70-68-72-71—281
	Richard Moir (Aus)	71-72-70-68—281

Welsh Seniors' Amateur Championship (inaugurated 1975) *at Aberdovey*

1975	A Marshman	77 (18)	1990	I Hughes	159	
1976	AD Evans	156	1991	RO Ward	155	
1977	AE Lockley	154	1992	I Hughes	150	
1978	AE Lockley	75 (18)	1993	G Perks	149	
1979	CR Morgan	158	1994T	G Perks/I Hughes/		
1980	ES Mills	152		A Prytherch	157	
1981	T Branton	153	1995	I Hughes	147	
1982	WI Tucker	147	1996	G Isaac	152	
1983	WS Gronow	153	1997	I Hughes	148	
1984	WI Tucker	150	1998	D Reidford	158	
1985	NA Lycett	149	1999	G Isaac	150	
1986	E Mills	154	2000	JR Jones*	145	
1987	WS Gronow	146	2001	W Stowe	222	
1988	NA Lycett	150	2002	B Cramb	221	
1989	WI Tucker	160				

2003

1	Phil Jones (Bromborough)	71-72-70—213
2	John Roger Jones (Conwy)	76-70-75—221
3	John Whitcutt (Burnham & Berrow)	77-72-75—224

Welsh Tournament of Champions (inaugurated 1979) at Cradoc

1979	J L Toye (Radyr)	1987	J R Jones (Langland Bay)	1995	G Houston (Flint)
1980	J M Morrow (Porthmadog)	1988	S C Dodd (Brynhill)	1996	M H Peat (Pyle & Kenfig)
1981	A P Vicary (St Pierre)	1989	P Sykes (Pontypridd)	1997	M Pilkington (Nefyn)
1982	P M Mayo (Newport)	1990	G Houston (Flint)	1998	M Gwyther (Morlais Castle)
1983	P M Mayo (Newport)	1991	G Houston (Flint)	1999	R Williams (Conwy)
1984	M Bearcroft (St Pierre)	1992	B Dredge (Bryn Meadows)	2000	J Davidson (Llanwern)
1985	S C Dodd (Brynhill)	1993	B Dredge (Bryn Meadows)	2001	N Oakley (St Mellons)
1986	S C Dodd (Brynhill)	1994	B Dredge (Bryn Meadows)	2002	T Hayward (Pontnewydd)

2003

1	Lewis James (Brynhill)*	70-74—144
2	Peter Bowen (Aberdare)	73-71—144
3	Simon Langford (Fairwood Park)	71-74—145

European Amateur Championship (inaugurated 1986)

1986	A Haglund (Swe)	Eindhoven, Netherlands	1996	D Olsson (Swe)	Karlstad, Sweden
1988	D Ecob (Aus)	Falkenstein, Germany	1997	D de Vooght (Bel)	Domaine Imperial,
1990	K Erikson (Swe)	Aalborg, Denmark			Switzerland
1991	J Payne (Eng)	Hillside, England	1998	P Gribben (Irl)	Golf du Medoc, France
1992	M Scarpa (Ita)	Le Querce, Italy	1999	G Havret (Fra)	Ascona, Switzerland
1993	M Backhausen (Den)	Dalmahoy, Scotland	2000	C Pettersson (Swe)	Murhof, Austria
1994	S Gallacher (Sco)	Aura, Finland	2001	S Browne (Irl)	Odense, Denmark
1995	S García (Esp)	El Prat, Spain	2002	R Pellicioli (Fra)	Tróia, Portugal

2003 *at Nairn*

1	Brian McElhinney (Irl)	72-68-76-67—283
2	Pablo Martin Benavides (Esp)	71-74-73-66—284
	Matthew Richardson (Eng)	71-67-75-71—284
	Michael Thannhauser (Ger)	67-68-73-76—284

European Seniors' Championship (inaugurated 1999)

1999	H-J Ecklebe (Ger)	Switzerland	216	2001	G Steel (Eng)	Spain	216
2000	HH Giesen (Ger)	Spain	217	2002	A Morrison (Eng)	Spain	212

2003 *at Chantaco, France*

1	David J. Smith (Sco)	73-73-70—216 (win after play-off 6 holes)
2	Luis Javier Trenor (Esp)	73-73-70—216
	Douglas Arnold (Eng)	74-75-67—216

European Mid-Amateur Championship (inaugurated 1999)

1999	H-G Reiter (Ger)	Luxembourg	215	2001	B Downing (Eng)	Turkey	216
2000	F Illouz (Fra)	England	221	2002	H-G Reiter (Ger)	Austria	210

2003 *at Mosjö Golf Club, Sweden*

1	Hans-Günther Reiter (Ger)	70-75-71—216
2	Roger Roper (Eng)	74-74-70—218
3	François Illouz (Fra)	79-71-69—219

National Orders of Merit

England – 2003

1	Gary Wolstenholme (Kilworth Springs)	964	6	Paul Bradshaw (Gainsborough)	444.17
2	Richard Walker (Frodsham)	522	7	Richard Finch (Hull)	425
3	Michael Skelton (Middlesbrough)	476.1	8	Lee Corfield (Burnham & Berrow)	382
4	Jon Lupton (Middlesbrough)	474	9	Sam Osborne (Wentworth)	369.14
5	Matthew Richardson (Pinner Hill)	462.68	10	Martin Sell (Wrag Barn)	356.17

Ireland – Willie Gill Award 2003

1	Noel Fox (Portmarnock)	90	5T	Mark O'Sullivan (Galway)	85
2	Brian McElhinney (North West)	90		Michael Sinclair (Knock)	85
	Michael McGeady (City of Derry)	90	8	Justin Kehoe (Birr)	80
	Colm Moriarty (Athlone)	90	9	Darren Crowe (Dunmurry)	70
5	John Foster (Ballyclare)	85		Desmond Morgan (Mullingar)	70

Scotland – Order of Merit 2003

1	Stuart Wilson (Forfar)	700.00	6	Craig Watson (East Renfrewshire)	320.00
2	Jamie McLeary (Leven GS)	523.50	7	Neil MacRae (Cawder)	281.16
3	Graham Gordon (Newmachar)	500.71	8	Eric Ramsay (Carnoustie)	257.50
4	Glenn Campbell (Blairgowrie)	390.83	9	Andrew McArthur (Windyhill)	255.00
5	George Murray (Earlsferry Thistle)	325.83	10	Jonathan King (Cardross)	240.00

Scottish Golf Ranking 2003

1	Stuart Wilson (Forfar)	-2.88	6	Steven Armstrong (Turnhouse)	-0.56
2	Jamie McLeary (Leven GS)	-1.19	7	Neil MacRae (Cawder)	-0.47
3	Glenn Campbell (Blairgowrie)	-1.18	8	Jonathan King (Cardross)	-0.37
4	Graham Gordon (Newmachar)	-0.92	9	Eric Ramsay (Carnoustie)	-0.29
5	Craig Watson (East Renfrewshire)	-0.58	10	George Murray (Earlsferry Thistle)	-0.26

Wales – Konica Order of Merit 2003

1	Stuart Manley (Mountain Ash)	832.77	6	Richard Scott (Haverfordwest)	217.50
2	Nigel Edwards (Whitchurch)	681.83	7	Alex Smith (Kyle & Penfig)	193.00
3	Gareth Wright (West Linton)	422.83	8	James Williams (Pontypridd)	182.87
4	Rhys Davies (Royal Porthcawl)	313.87	9	Cennydd Mills (Vale of Glamorgan)	178.00
5	Craig Smith (St Mellons)	305.96	10	Tim Dykes (Wrexham)	141.99

Daily Telegraph/JJB Order of Merit 2003

1	Gary Wolstenholme (Kilworth Springs)	3518	11	Brian McElhinney (North West)	1390
2	Colm Moriarty (Athlone)	2037	12	Richard Finch (Hull)	1348
3	Stuart Wilson (Forfar)	1998	13	Gareth Wright (West Linton)	1303
4	Richard Walker (Frodsham)	1957	14	Graham Gordon (Newmachar)	1285
5	Nigel Edwards (Whitchurch)	1934	15	Jon Lupton (Middlesbrough)	1260
6	Stuart Manley (Mountain Ash)	1916	16	Jamie Moul (Stoke by Nayland)	1160
7	Noel Fox (Portmarnock)	1771	17	Paul Bradshaw (Gainsborough)	1135
8	Jack Doherty (Vale of Glamorgan)	1595	18	Justin Kehoe (Birr)	1106
9	Michael Skelton (Middlesbrough)	1475	19	David Inglis (Glencorse)	1104.50
10	Ross Fisher (Wentworth)	1450	20	Craig Smith (St Mellons)	1104.16

Team Events

Walker Cup *(home team names first)*

2003 *at Ganton*

Captains: Garth McGimpsey (GBI), Bob Lewis (USA)

First Day *Foursomes*

GP Wolstenholme & M Skelton	0	W Haas & T Kuehne	1
S Wilson & D Inglis	1	L Williams & G Zahringer	0
NB Edwards & S Manley	1	C Nallen & R Moore	0
N Fox & C Moriarty	1	A Rubinson & C Wittenberg	0
	3		1

Singles

GP Wolstenholme (Kilworth Springs) (Eng)	0	W Haas	1
O Wilson (Coxmoor) (Eng)	½	T Kuehne	½
D Inglis (Glencorse) (Sco)	0	B Mackenzie	1
S Wilson (Forfar) (Sco)	½	M Hendrix	½
NB Edwards (Whitchurch) (Wal)	1	George Zahringer	0
C Moriarty (Athlone) (Irl)	0	Chris Nallen	1
Noel Fox (Portmarnock) (Irl)	0	A Rubinson	1
Graham Gordon (Newmachar) (Sco)	0	C Wittenberg	1
	2		6

Match position: GBI 5, USA 7

Second Day *Foursomes*

GP Wolstenholme & O Wilson	1	W Haas & T Kuehne	0
N Fox & C Moriarty	0	B Mackenzie & M Hendrix	1
S Wilson & D Inglis	½	C Wittenberg & A Rubinson	½
NB Edwards & S Manley	½	L Williams & G Zahringer	½
	2		2

Match position: GBI 7, USA 9

Singles

Oliver Wilson	1	Bill Haas	0
Gary Wolstenholme	1	Casey Wittenberg	0
Michael Skelton (Middlesbrough) (Eng)	1	Adam Rubinson	0
Colm Moriarty	0	Brock Mackenzie	1
Stuart Wilson	0	Matt Hendrix	1
David Inglis	1	Ryan Moore	0
Nigel Edwards	½	Lee Williams	½
Stuart Manley (Mountain Ash) (Wal)	1	Trip Kuehne	0
	5½		2½

Result: Great Britain and Ireland 12½, USA 11½

21 May 1921 *at Hoylake*
Unofficial match — GBI v USA
Result: USA 9, GBI 3
Foursomes
Simpson & Jenkins lost to Evans & Jones 5 and 3
Tolley & Holderness lost to Ouimet & Guilford 3 and 2
de Montmorency & Wethered lost to Hunter & Platt
  1 hole
Aylmer & Armour lost to Wright & Fownes 4 and 2
Singles
CJH Tolley beat C Evans jr 4 and 3
JLC Jenkins lost to FD Ouimet 6 and 5
RH de Montmorency lost to RT Jones jr 4 and 3
JG Simpson lost to JP Guilford 2 and 1
CC Aylmer beat P Hunter 2 and 1
TD Armour beat JW Platt 2 and 1
EWE Holderness lost to F Wright 2 holes
RH Wethered lost to WC Fownes jr 3 and 1

1922 *at National Golf Links, New York*
Officially named the Walker Cup
Result: USA 8, GBI 4
Captains: WC Fownes (USA), R Harris (GBI)
Foursomes
Guilford & Ouimet beat Tolley & Darwin 8 and 7
Evans & Gardner lost to Wethered & Aylmer 5 and 4
Jones & Sweetser beat Torrance & Hooman 3 and 2
Marston & Fownes beat Caven & Mackenzie 2 and 1
Singles
JP Guilford beat CJH Tolley 2 and 1
RT Jones jr beat RH Wethered 3 and 2
C Evans jr beat J Caven 5 and 4
FD Ouimet beat CC Aylmer 8 and 7
RA Gardner beat WB Torrance 7 and 6
MR Marston lost to WW Mackenzie 6 and 5
WC Fownes jr lost to B Darwin 3 and 1
JW Sweetser lost to CVL Hooman at 37th

1923 *at St Andrews*
Result: USA 6½, GBI 5½
Captains: R Harris (GBI), RA Gardner (USA)
Foursomes
Tolley & Wethered beat Ouimet & Sweetser 6 and 5
Harris & Hooman lost to Gardner & Marston 7 and 6
Holderness & Hope beat Rotan & Herron 1 hole
Wilson & Murray beat Johnston & Neville
  4 and 3
Singles
RH Wethered halved with FD Ouimet
CJH Tolley beat JW Sweetser 4 and 3
R Harris lost to RA Gardner 1 hole
WW Mackenzie lost to GV Rotan 5 and 4
WL Hope lost to MR Marston 6 and 5
EWE Holderness lost to FJ Wright jr 1 hole
J Wilson beat SD Herron 1 hole
WA Murray lost to OF Willing 2 and 1

1924 *at Garden City, New York*
Result: USA 9, GBI 3
Captains: RA Gardner (USA), CJH Tolley (GBI)
Foursomes
Marston & Gardner beat Storey & Murray 3 and 1
Guilford & Ouimet beat Tolley & Hezlet 2 and 1
Jones & Fownes jr lost to Scott & Scott jr 1 hole
Sweetser & Johnston beat Torrance & Bristowe 4 and 3

Singles
MR Marston lost to CJH Tolley 1 hole
RT Jones jr beat CO Hezlet 4 and 3
C Evans jr beat WA Murray 2 and 1
FD Ouimet beat EF Storey 1 hole
JW Sweetser lost to Hon M Scott 7 and 6
RA Gardner beat WL Hope 3 and 2
JP Guilford beat TA Torrance 2 and 1
OF Willing beat DH Kyle 3 and 2

1926 *at St Andrews*
Result: USA 6½, GBI 5½
Captains: R Harris (GBI), RA Gardner (USA)
Foursomes
Wethered & Holderness beat Ouimet &
  Guilford 5 and 4
Tolley & Jamieson lost to Jones & Gunn 4 and 3
Harris & Hezlet lost to Von Elm & Sweetser 8 and 7
Storey & Brownlow lost to Gardner & MacKenzie
  1 hole
Singles
CJH Tolley lost to RT Jones jr 12 and 11
EWE Holderness lost to JW Sweetser 4 and 3
RH Wethered beat FD Ouimet 5 and 4
CO Hezlet halved with G Von Elm
R Harris beat JP Guilford 2 and 1
Hon WGE Brownlow lost to W Gunn 9 and 8
EF Storey beat RR MacKenzie 2 and 1
A Jamieson jr beat RA Gardner 5 and 4

1928 *at Wheaton, Chicago, IL*
Result: USA 11, GBI 1
Captains: RT Jones jr (USA),
  W Tweddell (GBI)
Foursomes
Sweetser & Von Elm beat Perkins & Tweddell 7 and 6
Jones & Evans beat Hezlet & Hope 5 and 3
Ouimet & Johnston beat Torrance & Storey 4 and 2
Gunn & MacKenzie beat Beck & Martin 7 and 5
Singles
RT Jones jr beat TP Perkins 13 and 12
G Von Elm beat W Tweddell 3 and 2
FD Ouimet beat CO Hezlet 8 and 7
JW Sweetser beat WL Hope 5 and 4
HR Johnston beat EF Storey 4 and 2
C Evans jr lost to TA Torrance 1 hole
W Gunn beat RH Hardman 11 and 10
RR MacKenzie beat GNC Martin 2 and 1

1930 *at St George's, Sandwich*
Result: USA 10, GBI 2
Captains: RH Wethered (GBI),
  RT Jones jr (USA)
Foursomes
Tolley & Wethered beat Von Elm & Voigt 2 holes
Hartley & Torrance lost to Jones & Willing 8 and 7
Holderness & Stout lost to MacKenzie & Moe 2 and 1
Campbell & Smith lost to Johnston & Ouimet 2 and 1
Singles
CJH Tolley lost to HR Johnston 5 and 4
RH Wethered lost to RT Jones jr 9 and 8
RW Hartley lost to G Von Elm 3 and 2
EWE Holderness lost to GJ Voigt 10 and 8
JN Smith lost to OF Willing 2 and 1
TA Torrance beat FD Ouimet 7 and 6
JA Stout lost to DK Moe 1 hole
W Campbell lost to RR MacKenzie 6 and 5

1932 at Brookline, MA
Result: USA 9½, GBI 2½
Captains: FD Ouimet (USA), TA Torrance (GBI)

Foursomes
Sweetser & Voigt beat Hartley & Hartley 7 and 6
Seaver & Moreland beat Torrance & de Forest
   6 and 5
Ouimet & Dunlap beat Stout & Burke 7 and 6
Moe & Howell beat Fiddian & McRuvie 5 and 4

Singles
FD Ouimet halved with TA Torrance
JW Sweetser halved with JA Stout
GT Moreland beat RW Hartley 2 and 1
J Westland halved with J Burke
GJ Voigt lost to LG Crawley 1 hole
MJ McCarthy jr beat WL Hartley 3 and 2
CH Seaver beat EW Fiddian 7 and 6
GT Dunlap jr beat EA McRuvie 10 and 9

1934 at St Andrews
Result: USA 9½, GBI 2½
Captains: Hon M Scott (GBI), FD Ouimet (USA)

Foursomes
Wethered & Tolley lost to Goodman & Little 8 and 6
Bentley & Fiddian lost to Moreland & Westland 6 and 5
Scott & McKinlay lost to Egan & Marston 3 and 2
McRuvie & McLean beat Ouimet & Dunlap 4 and 2

Singles
Hon M Scott lost to JG Goodman 7 and 6
CJH Tolley lost to WL Little jr 6 and 5
LG Crawley lost to FD Ouimet 5 and 4
J McLean lost to GT Dunlap jr 4 and 3
EW Fiddian lost to JW Fischer 5 and 4
SL McKinlay lost to GT Moreland 3 and 1
EA McRuvie halved with J Westland
TA Torrance beat MR Marston 4 and 3

1936 at Pine Valley, NJ
Result: USA 10½, GBI 1½
*Captains: FD Ouimet (USA),
   W Tweddell (GBI)*

Foursomes
Goodman & Campbell beat Thomson & Bentley
   7 and 5
Smith & White beat McLean & Langley 8 and 7
Yates & Emery halved with Peters & Dykes
Givan & Voigt halved with Hill & Ewing

Singles
JG Goodman beat H Thomson 3 and 2
AE Campbell beat J McLean 5 and 4
JW Fischer beat RC Ewing 8 and 7
R Smith beat GA Hill 11 and 9
W Emery beat GB Peters 1 hole
CR Yates beat JM Dykes 8 and 7
GT Dunlap jr halved with HG Bentley
E White beat JDA Langley 6 and 5

1938 at St Andrews
Result: GBI 7½, USA 4½
Captains: JB Beck (GBI), FD Ouimet (USA)

Foursomes
Bentley & Bruen halved with Fischer & Kocsis
Peters & Thomson beat Goodman & Ward 4 and 2
Kyle & Stowe lost to Yates & Billows 3 and 2
Pennink & Crawley beat Smith & Haas 3 and 1

Singles
J Bruen jr lost to CR Yates 2 and 1
H Thomson beat JG Goodman 6 and 4
LG Crawley lost to JW Fischer 3 and 2
C Stowe beat CR Kocsis 2 and 1
JJF Pennink lost to MH Ward 12 and 11
RC Ewing beat RE Billows 1 hole
GB Peters beat R Smith 9 and 8
AT Kyle beat F Haas jr 5 and 4

1947 at St Andrews
Result: USA 8, GBI 4
Captains: JB Beck (GBI), FD Ouimet (USA)

Foursomes
Carr & Ewing lost to Bishop & Riegel 3 and 2
Crawley & Lucas beat Ward & Quick 5 and 4
Kyle & Wilson lost to Turnesa & Kammer 5 and 4
White & Stowe beat Stranahan & Chapman 4 and 3

Singles
LG Crawley lost to MH Ward 5 and 3
JB Carr beat SE Bishop 5 and 3
GH Micklem lost to RH Riegel 6 and 5
RC Ewing lost to WP Turnesa 6 and 5
C Stowe lost to FR Stranahan 2 and 1
RJ White beat AF Kammer jr 4 and 3
JC Wilson lost to SL Quick 8 and 6
PB Lucas lost to RD Chapman 4 and 3

1949 at Winged Foot, New York
Result: USA 10, GBI 2
Captains: FD Ouimet (USA), PB Lucas (GBI)

Foursomes
Billows & Turnesa lost to Carr & White 3 and 2
Kocsis & Stranahan beat Bruen & McCready 2 and 1
Bishop & Riegel beat Ewing & Micklem 9 and 7
Dawson & McCormick beat Thom & Perowne
   8 and 7

Singles
WP Turnesa lost to RJ White 4 and 3
FR Stranahan beat SM McCready 6 and 5
RH Riegel beat J Bruen jr 5 and 4
JW Dawson beat JB Carr 5 and 3
CR Coe beat RC Ewing 1 hole
RE Billows beat KG Thom 2 and 1
CR Kocsis beat AH Perowne 4 and 2
JB McHale jr beat GH Micklem 5 and 4

1951 at Birkdale
Result: USA 7½, GBI 4½
*Captains: RH Oppenheimer (GBI),
   WP Turnesa (USA)*

Foursomes
White & Carr halved with Stranahan & Campbell
Ewing & Langley halved with Coe & McHale
Kyle & Caldwell lost to Chapman & Knowles jr
   1 hole
Bruen jr & Morgan lost to Turnesa & Urzetta 5 and 4

Singles
SM McCready lost to S Urzetta 4 and 3
JB Carr beat FR Stranahan 2 and 1
RJ White beat CR Coe 2 and 1
JDA Langley lost to JB McHale jr 2 holes
RC Ewing lost to WC Campbell 5 and 4
AT Kyle beat WP Turnesa 2 holes
I Caldwell halved with HD Paddock jr
JL Morgan lost to RD Chapman 7 and 6

1953 at Kittansett, MA
Result: USA 9, GBI 3
Captains: CR Yates (USA), AA Duncan (GBI)

Foursomes
Urzetta & Venturi beat Carr & White 6 and 4
Ward & Westland beat Langley & AH Perowne 9 and 8
Jackson & Littler beat Wilson & MacGregor 3 and 2
Campbell & Coe lost to Micklem & Morgan 4 and 3

Singles
EH Ward jr beat JB Carr 4 and 3
RD Chapman lost to RJ White 1 hole
GA Littler beat GH Micklem 5 and 3
J Westland beat RC MacGregor 7 and 5
DR Cherry beat NV Drew 9 and 7
K Venturi beat JC Wilson 9 and 8
CR Coe lost to JL Morgan 3 and 2
S Urzetta beat JDA Langley 3 and 2

1955 at St Andrews
Result: USA 10, GBI 2
Captains: GA Hill (GBI), WC Campbell (USA)

Foursomes
Carr & White lost to Ward & Cherry 1 hole
Micklem & Morgan lost to Patton & Yost 2 and 1
Caldwell & Millward lost to Conrad & Morey
  3 and 2
Blair & Cater lost to Cudd & Jackson 5 and 4

Singles
RJ White lost to EH Ward jr 6 and 5
PF Scrutton lost to WJ Patton 2 and 1
I Caldwell beat D Morey 1 hole
JB Carr lost to DR Cherry 5 and 4
DA Blair beat JW Conrad 1 hole
EB Millward lost to BH Cudd 2 holes
RC Ewing lost to JG Jackson 6 and 4
JL Morgan lost to RL Yost 8 and 7

1957 at Minikahda, MN
Result: USA 8½, GBI 3½
Captains:CR Coe (USA), GH Micklem (GBI)

Foursomes
Baxter & Patton beat Carr & Deighton 2 and 1
Campbell & Taylor beat Bussell & Scrutton 4 and 3
Blum & Kocsis lost to Jack & Sewell 1 hole
Robbins & Rudolph halved with Shepperson &
  Wolstenholme

Singles
WJ Patton beat RR Jack 1 hole
WC Campbell beat JB Carr 3 and 2
R Baxter jr beat A Thirlwell 4 and 3
W Hyndman III beat FWG Deighton 7 and 6
JE Campbell lost to AF Bussell 2 and 1
FM Taylor jr beat D Sewell 1 hole
EM Rudolph beat PF Scrutton 3 and 2
H Robbins jr lost to GB Wolstenholme 2 and 1

1959 at Muirfield
Result: USA 9, GBI 3
Captains:GH Micklem (GBI), CR Coe (USA)

Foursomes
Jack & Sewell lost to Ward & Taylor 1 hole
Carr & Wolstenholme lost to Hyndman & Aaron
  1 hole
Bonallack & Perowne lost to Patton & Coe 9 and 8
Lunt & Shepperson lost to Wettlander & Nicklaus
  2 and 1

Singles
JB Carr beat CR Coe 3 and 1
GB Wolstenholme lost to EH Ward jr 9 and 8
RR Jack beat WJ Patton 5 and 3
DN Sewell lost to W Hyndman III 4 and 3
AE Shepperson beat TD Aaron 2 and 1
MF Bonallack lost to DR Beman 2 holes
MSR Lunt lost to HW Wettlander 6 and 5
WD Smith lost to JW Nicklaus 5 and 4

1961 at Seattle, WA
Result: USA 11, GBI 1
Captains: J Westland (USA),
  CD Lawrie (GBI)

Foursomes
Beman & Nicklaus beat Walker & Chapman 6 and 5
Coe & Cherry beat Blair & Christmas 1 hole
Hyndman & Gardner beat Carr & G Huddy 4 and 3
Cochran & Andrews beat Bonallack & Shade
  4 and 3

Singles
DR Beman beat MF Bonallack 3 and 2
CR Coe beat MSR Lunt 5 and 4
FM Taylor jr beat J Walker 3 and 2
W Hyndman III beat DW Frame 7 and 6
JW Nicklaus beat JB Carr 6 and 4
CB Smith lost to MJ Christmas 3 and 2
RW Gardner beat RDBM Shade 1 hole
DR Cherry beat DA Blair 5 and 4

1963 at Turnberry
Result: USA 14, GBI 10
Captains: CD Lawrie (GBI),
  RS Tufts (USA)

First Day – **Foursomes**
Bonallack & Murray beat Patton & Sikes 4 and 3
Carr & Green lost to Gray & Harris 2 holes
Lunt & Sheahan lost to Beman & Coe 5 and 3
Madeley & Shade halved with Gardner &
  Updegraff

Singles
SWT Murray beat DR Beman 3 and 1
MJ Christmas lost to WJ Patton 3 and 2
JB Carr beat RH Sikes 7 and 5
DB Sheahan beat LE Harris 1 hole
MF Bonallack beat RD Davies 1 hole
AC Saddler halved with CR Coe
RDBM Shade beat AD Gray jr 4 and 3
MSR Lunt halved with CB Smith

Second Day – **Foursomes**
Bonallack & Murray lost to Patton & Sikes 1 hole
Lunt & Sheahan lost to Gray & Harris 3 and 2
Green & Saddler lost to Gardner & Updegraff
  3 and 1
Madeley & Shade lost to Beman & Coe 3 and 2

Singles
Murray lost to Patton 3 and 2
Sheahan beat Davies 1 hole
Carr lost to Updegraff 4 and 3
Bonallack lost to Harris 3 and 2
Lunt lost to Gardner 3 and 2
Saddler halved with Beman
Shade beat Gray 2 and 1
Green lost to Coe 4 and 3

1965 at Five Farms, MD
Result: USA 12, GBI 12
Captains: JW Fischer (USA), JB Carr (GBI)

First Day – Foursomes
Campbell & Gray lost to Lunt & Cosh 1 hole
Beman & Allen halved with Bonallack & Clark
Patton & Tutwiler beat Foster & Clark 5 and 4
Hopkins & Eichelberger lost to Townsend & Shade
2 and 1

Singles
WC Campbell beat MF Bonallack 6 and 5
DR Beman beat R Foster 2 holes
AD Gray jr lost to RDBM Shade 3 and 1
JM Hopkins lost to CA Clark 5 and 3
WJ Patton lost to P Townsend 3 and 2
D Morey lost to AC Saddler 2 and 1
DC Allen lost to GB Cosh 2 holes
ER Updegraff lost to MSR Lunt 2 and 1

Second Day – Foursomes
Campbell & Gray beat Saddler & Foster 4 and 3
Beman & Eichelberger lost to Townsend & Shade 2 and 1
Tutwiler & Patton beat Cosh & Lunt 2 and 1
Allen & Morey lost to CA Clark & Bonallack 2 and 1

Singles
Campbell beat Foster 3 and 2
Beman beat Saddler 1 hole
Tutwiler beat Shade 5 and 3
Allen lost to Cosh 4 and 3
Gray beat Townsend 1 hole
Hopkins halved with CA Clark
Eichelberger beat Bonallack 5 and 3
Patton beat Lunt 4 and 2

1967 at St George's, Sandwich
Result: USA 15, GBI 9
Captains: JB Carr (GBI), JW Sweetser (USA)

First Day – Foursomes
Shade & Oosterhuis halved with Murphy & Cerrudo
Foster & Saddler lost to Campbell & Lewis 1 hole
Bonallack & Attenborough lost to Gray & Tutwiler
4 and 2
Carr & Craddock lost to Dickson & Grant 3 and 1

Singles
RDBM Shade lost to WC Campbell 2 and 1
R Foster lost to RJ Murphy jr 2 and 1
MF Bonallack halved with AD Gray jr
MF Attenborough lost to RJ Cerrudo 4 and 3
P Oosterhuis lost to RB Dickson 6 and 4
T Craddock lost to JW Lewis jr 2 and 1
AK Pirie halved with DC Allen
AC Saddler beat MA Fleckman 3 and 2

Second Day – Foursomes
Bonallack & Craddock beat Murphy & Cerrudo 2 holes
Saddler & Pirie lost to Campbell & Lewis 1 hole
Shade & Oosterhuis beat Gray & Tutwiler 3 and 1
Foster & Millensted beat Allen & Fleckman 2 and 1

Singles
Shade lost to Campbell 3 and 2
Bonallack beat Murphy 4 and 2
Saddler beat Gray 3 and 2
Foster halved with Cerrudo
Pirie lost to Dickson 4 and 3
Craddock beat Lewis 5 and 4
Oosterhuis lost to Grant 1 hole
Millensted lost to Tutwiler 3 and 1

1969 at Milwaukee, WI
Result: USA 13, GBI 11
Captains: WJ Patton (USA),
MF Bonallack (GBI)

First Day – Foursomes
Giles & Melnyk beat Bonallack & Craddock
3 and 2
Fleisher & Miller halved with Benka & Critchley
Wadkins & Siderowf lost to Green & A Brooks
W Hyndman III & Inman jr beat Foster & Marks
2 and 1

Singles
B Fleisher halved with MF Bonallack
M Giles III beat CW Green 1 hole
AL Miller III beat B Critchley 1 hole
RL Siderowf beat LP Tupling 6 and 5
S Melnyk lost to PJ Benka 3 and 1
L Wadkins lost to GC Marks 1 hole
J Bohmann beat MG King 2 and 1
ER Updegraff beat R Foster 6 and 5

Second Day – Foursomes
Giles & Melnyk halved with Green & Brooks
Fleisher & Miller lost to Benka & Critchley
2 and 1
Siderowf & Wadkins beat Foster & King 6 and 5
Updegraff & Bohmann lost to Bonallack & Tupling
4 and 3

Singles
Fleisher lost to Bonallack 5 and 4
Siderowf halved with Critchley
Miller beat King 1 hole
Giles halved with Craddock
Inman beat Benka 2 and 1
Bohmann lost to Brooks 4 and 3
Hyndman halved with Green
Updegraff lost to Marks 3 and 2

1971 at St Andrews
Result: GBI 13, USA 11
Captains: MF Bonallack (GBI),
JM Winters jr (USA)

First Day – Foursomes
Bonallack & Humphreys beat Wadkins & Simons
1 hole
Green & Carr beat Melnyk & Giles 1 hole
Marsh & Macgregor beat Miller & Farquhar
2 and 1
Macdonald & Foster beat Campbell & Kite
2 and 1

Singles
CW Green lost to L Wadkins 1 hole
MF Bonallack lost to M Giles III 1 hole
GC Marks lost to AL Miller III 1 hole
JS Macdonald lost to S Melnyk 3 and 2
RJ Carr halved with W Hyndman III
W Humphreys lost to JR Gabrielsen 1 hole
HB Stuart beat J Farquhar 3 and 2
R Foster lost to T Kite 3 and 2

Second Day – Foursomes
Marks & Green lost to Melnyk & Giles 1 hole
Stuart & Carr beat Wadkins & Gabrielsen 1 hole
Marsh & Bonallack lost to Miller & Farquhar
5 and 4
Macdonald & Foster halved with Campbell & Kite

1971 continued

Singles
Bonallack lost to Wadkins 3 and 1
Stuart beat Giles 2 and 1
Humphreys beat Melnyk 2 and 1
Green beat Miller 1 hole
Carr beat Simons 2 holes
Macgregor beat Gabrielsen 1 hole
Marsh beat Hyndman 1 hole
Marks lost to Kite 3 and 2

1973 at Brookline, MA

Result: USA 14, GBI 10
Captains: JW Sweetser (USA), DM Marsh (GBI)

First Day – **Foursomes**
Giles & Koch halved with King & Hedges
Siderowf & Pfeil beat Stuart & Davies 5 and 4
Edwards & Ellis beat Green & Milne 2 and 1
West & Ballenger beat Foster & Homer 2 and 1

Singles
M Giles III beat HB Stuart 5 and 4
RL Siderowf beat MF Bonallack 4 and 2
G Koch lost to JC Davies 1 hole
M West lost to HK Clark 2 and 1
D Edwards beat R Foster 2 holes
M Killian lost to MG King 1 hole
W Rodgers lost to CW Green 1 hole
M Pfeil lost to WT Milne 4 and 3

Second Day – **Foursomes**
Giles & Koch beat Homer & Foster 7 and 5
Siderowf & Pfeil halved with Clark & Davies
Edwards & Ellis beat Hedges & King 2 and 1
Rodgers & Killian beat Stuart & Milne 1 hole

Singles
Ellis lost to Stuart 5 and 4
Siderowf lost to Davies 3 and 2
Edwards beat Homer 2 and 1
Giles halved with Green
West beat King 1 hole
Killian lost to Milne 2 and 1
Koch halved with Hedges
Pfeil beat Clark 1 hole

1975 at St Andrews

Result: USA 15½, GBI 8½
*Captains: DM Marsh (GBI),
    ER Updegraff (USA)*

First Day – **Foursomes**
James & Eyles beat Pate & Siderowf 1 hole
Davies & Poxon lost to Burns & Stadler
    5 and 4
Green & Stuart lost to Haas & Strange 2 and 1
Macgregor & Hutcheon lost to Giles & Koch 5 and 4

Singles
M James beat J Pate 2 and 1
JC Davies halved with C Strange
P Mulcare beat RL Siderowf 1 hole
HB Stuart lost to G Koch 3 and 2
MA Poxon lost to J Grace 3 and 1
IC Hutcheon halved with WC Campbell
GRD Eyles lost to J Haas 2 and 1
G Macgregor lost to M Giles III 5 and 4

Second Day – **Foursomes**
Mulcare & Hutcheon beat Pate & Siderowf 1 hole
Green & Stuart lost to Burns & Stadler 1 hole
James & Eyles beat Campbell & Grace 5 and 3
Hedges & Davies lost to Haas & Strange 3 and 2

Singles
Hutcheon beat Pate 3 and 2
Mulcare lost to Strange 4 and 3
James lost to Koch 5 and 4
Davies beat Burns 2 and 1
Green lost to Grace 2 and 1
Macgregor lost to Stadler 3 and 2
Eyles lost to Campbell 2 and 1
Hedges halved with Giles

1977 at Shinnecock Hills, NY

Result: USA 16, GBI 8
*Captains: LW Oehmig(USA),
    AC Saddler (GBI)*

First Day – **Foursomes**
Fought & Heafner beat Lyle & McEvoy 4 and 3
Simpson & Miller beat Davies & Kelley 5 and 4
Siderowf & Hallberg lost to Hutcheon & Deeble 1 hole
Sigel & Brannan beat Brodie & Martin 1 hole

Singles
L Miller beat P McEvoy 2 holes
J Fought beat IC Hutcheon 4 and 3
S Simpson beat GH Murray 7 and 6
V Heafner beat JC Davies 4 and 3
B Sander lost to A Brodie 4 and 3
G Hallberg lost to S Martin 3 and 2
F Ridley beat AWB Lyle 2 holes
J Sigel beat P McKellar 5 and 3

Second Day – **Foursomes**
Fought & Heafner beat Hutcheon & Deeble 4 and 3
Miller & Simpson beat McEvoy & Davies 2 holes
Siderowf & Sander lost to Brodie & Martin 6 and 4
Ridley & Brannan lost to Murray & Kelley 4 and 3

Singles
Miller beat Martin 1 hole
Fought beat Davies 2 and 1
Sander lost to Brodie 2 and 1
Hallberg beat McEvoy 4 and 3
Siderowf lost to Kelley 2 and 1
Brannan lost to Hutcheon 2 holes
Ridley beat Lyle 5 and 3
Sigel beat Deeble 1 hole

1979 at Muirfield

Result: USA 15½, GBI 8½
Captains: R Foster (GBI), RL Siderowf (USA)

First Day – **Foursomes**
McEvoy & Marchbank lost to Hoch & Sigel 1 hole
Godwin & Hutcheon beat West & Sutton
    2 holes
Brand jr & Kelley lost to Fischesser & Holtgrieve
    1 hole
Brodie & Carslaw beat Moody & Gove 2 and 1

Singles
P McEvoy halved with J Sigel
JC Davies lost to D Clarke 8 and 7
J Buckley lost to S Hoch 9 and 7
IC Hutcheon lost to J Holtgrieve 6 and 4
B Marchbank beat M Peck 1 hole
G Godwin beat G Moody 3 and 2
MJ Kelley beat D Fischesser 3 and 2
A Brodie lost to M Gove 3 and 2

Second Day – **Foursomes**
Godwin & Brand lost to Hoch & Sigel 4 and 3
McEvoy & Marchbank beat Fischesser & Holtgrieve
    2 and 1
Kelley & Hutcheon halved with West & Sutton
Carslaw & Brodie halved with Clarke & Peck

Singles
McEvoy lost to Hoch 3 and 1
Brand lost to Clarke 2 and 1
Godwin lost to Gove 3 and 2
Hutcheon lost to Peck 2 and 1
Brodie beat West 3 and 2
Kelley lost to Moody 3 and 2
Marchbank lost to Sutton 3 and 1
Carslaw lost to Sigel 2 and 1

1981 at Cypress Point, CA
Result: USA 15, GBI 9
*Captains: J Gabrielsen (USA),
   R Foster (GBI)*

First Day – Foursomes
Sutton & Sigel lost to Walton & Rafferty 4 and 2
Holtgrieve & Fuhrer beat Chapman & McEvoy
   1 hole
Lewis & von Tacky beat Deeble & Hutcheon 2 and 1
Commans & Pavin beat Evans & Way 5 and 4

Singles
H Sutton beat R Rafferty 3 and 1
J Rassett beat CR Dalgleish 1 hole
R Commans lost to P Walton 1 hole
B Lewis lost to R Chapman 2 and 1
J Mudd beat G Godwin 1 hole
C Pavin beat IC Hutcheon 4 and 3
D von Tacky lost to P Way 3 and 1
J Sigel beat P McEvoy 4 and 2

Second Day – Foursomes
Sutton & Sigel lost to Chapman & Way 1 hole
Holtgrieve & Fuhrer lost to Walton & Rafferty 6 and 4
Lewis & von Tacky lost to Evans & Dalgleish 3 and 2
Rassett & Mudd beat Hutcheon & Godwin 5 and 4

Singles
Sutton lost to Chapman 1 hole
Holtgrieve beat Rafferty 2 and 1
Fuhrer beat Walton 4 and 3
Sigel beat Way 6 and 5
Mudd beat Dalgleish 7 and 5
Commans halved with Godwin
Rassett beat Deeble 4 and 3
Pavin halved with Evans

1983 at Hoylake
Result: USA 13½, GBI 10½
Captains: CW Green (GBI), J Sigel (USA)

First Day – Foursomes
Macgregor & Walton beat Sigel & Fehr 3 and 2
Keppler & Pierse lost to Wood & Faxon 3 and 1
Lewis & Thompson lost to Lewis & Holtgrieve
   7 and 6
Mann & Oldcorn beat Hoffer & Tentis 5 and 4

Singles
P Walton beat J Sigel 1 hole
SD Keppler lost to R Fehr 1 hole
G Macgregor halved with W Wood
DG Carrick lost to B Faxon 3 and 1
A Oldcorn beat B Tuten 4 and 3
P Parkin beat N Crosby 5 and 4
AD Pierse lost to B Lewis jr 3 and 1
LS Mann lost to J Holtgrieve 6 and 5

Second Day – Foursomes
Macgregor & Walton lost to Crosby & Hoffer 2 holes
Parkin & Thompson beat Faxon & Wood 1 hole
Mann & Oldcorn beat Lewis & Holtgrieve 1 hole
Keppler & Pierse halved with Sigel & Fehr

Singles
Walton beat Wood 2 and 1
Parkin lost to Faxon 3 and 2
Macgregor lost to Fehr 2 and 1
Thompson lost to Tuten 3 and 2
Mann halved with Tentis
Keppler lost to Lewis 6 and 5
Oldcorn beat Holtgrieve 3 and 2
Carrick lost to Sigel 3 and 2

1985 at Pine Valley, NJ
Result: USA 13, GBI 11
Captains: J Sigel (USA), CW Green (GBI)

First Day – Foursomes
Verplank & Sigel beat Montgomerie & Macgregor
   1 hole
Waldorf & Randolph lost to Hawksworth & McGimpsey 4
   and 3
Sonnier & Haas lost to Baker & McEvoy 6 and 5
Podolak & Love halved with Bloice & Stephen

Singles
S Verplank beat G McGimpsey 2 and 1
S Randolph beat P Mayo 5 and 4
R Sonnier halved with J Hawksworth
J Sigel beat CS Montgomerie 5 and 4
B Lewis lost to P McEvoy 2 and 1
C Burroughs lost to G Macgregor 2 holes
D Waldorf beat D Gilford 4 and 2
J Haas lost to AR Stephen 2 and 1

Second Day – Foursomes
Verplank & Sigel halved with Mayo & Montgomerie
Randolph & Haas beat Hawksworth & McGimpsey
   3 and 2
Lewis & Burroughs beat Baker & McEvoy 2 and 1
Podolak & Love beat Bloice & Stephen 3 and 2

Singles
Randolph halved with McGimpsey
Verplank beat Montgomerie 1 hole
Sigel lost to Hawksworth 4 and 3
Love beat McEvoy 5 and 3
Sonnier lost to Baker 5 and 4
Burroughs lost to Macgregor 3 and 2
Lewis beat Bloice 4 and 3
Waldorf lost to Stephen 2 and 1

1987 at Sunningdale
Result: USA 16½, GBI 7½
Captains: GC Marks (GBI), F Ridley (USA)

First Day – Foursomes
Montgomerie & Shaw lost to Alexander & Mayfair
   5 and 4
Currey & Mayo lost to Kite & Mattice 2 and 1
Macgregor & Robinson lost to Lewis & Loeffler 2 and 1
McHenry & Girvan lost to Sigel & Andrade 3 and 2

Singles
D Currey beat B Alexander 2 holes
J Robinson lost to B Andrade 7 and 5
CS Montgomerie beat J Sorenson 3 and 2
R Eggo lost to J Sigel 3 and 2
J McHenry lost to B Montgomery 1 hole
P Girvan lost to B Lewis 3 and 2
DG Carrick lost to B Mayfair 2 holes
G Shaw beat C Kite 1 hole

Second Day – Foursomes
Currey & Carrick lost to Lewis & Loeffler 4 and 3
Montgomerie & Shaw lost to Kite & Mattice 5 and 3
Mayo & Macgregor lost to Sorenson & Montgomery
   4 and 3
McHenry & Robinson beat Sigel & Andrade 4 and 2

1987 *continued*

Singles
Currey lost to Alexander 5 and 4
Montgomerie beat Andrade 4 and 2
McHenry beat Loeffler 3 and 2
Shaw halved with Sorenson
Robinson beat Mattice 1 hole
Carrick lost to Lewis 3 and 2
Eggo lost to Mayfair 1 hole
Girvan lost to Sigel 6 and 5

1989 *at Peachtree, GA*

Result: GBI 12½, USA 11½
Captains: F Ridley (USA), GC Marks (GBI)
First Day – **Foursomes**
Gamez & Martin beat Claydon & Prosser 3 and 2
Yates & Mickelson halved with Dodd & McGimpsey
Lesher & Sigel lost to McEvoy & O'Connell 6 and 5
Eger & Johnson lost to Milligan & Hare 2 and 1
Singles
R Gamez beat JW Milligan 7 and 6
D Martin lost to R Claydon 5 and 4
E Meeks halved with SC Dodd
R Howe lost to E O'Connell 5 and 4
D Yates lost to P McEvoy 2 and 1
P Mickelson beat G McGimpsey 4 and 2
G Lesher lost to C Cassells 1 hole
J Sigel halved with RN Roderick
Second Day – **Foursomes**
Gamez & Martin halved with McEvoy & O'Connell
Sigel & Lesher lost to Claydon & Cassells 3 and 2
Eger & Johnson lost to Milligan & Hare 2 and 1
Mickelson & Yates lost to McGimpsey & Dodd
    2 and 1
Singles
Gamez beat Dodd 1 hole
Martin halved with Hare
Lesher beat Claydon 3 and 2
Yates beat McEvoy 4 and 3
Mickelson halved with O'Connell
Eger beat Roderick 4 and 2
Johnson beat Cassells 4 and 2
Sigel halved with Milligan

1991 *at Portmarnock*

Result: USA 14, GBI 10
Captains: G Macgregor (GBI),
*   JR Gabrielsen (USA)*
First Day – **Foursomes**
Milligan & Hay lost to Mickelson & May 5 and 3
Payne & Evans lost to Duval & Sposa 1 hole
McGimpsey & Willison lost to Voges & Eger 1 hole
McGinley & Harrington lost to Sigel & Doyle 2 and 1
Singles
A Coltart lost to P Mickelson 4 and 3
J Payne beat F Langham 2 and 1
G Evans beat D Duval 2 and 1
R Willison lost to B May 2 and 1
G McGimpsey beat M Sposa 1 hole
P McGinley lost to A Doyle 6 and 4
G Hay beat T Scherrer 1 hole
L White lost to J Sigel 4 and 3
Second Day – **Foursomes**
Milligan & McGimpsey beat Voges & Eger 2 and 1
Payne & Willison lost to Duval & Sposa 1 hole
Evans & Coltart beat Langham & Scherrer 4 and 3
White & McGinley beat Mickelson & May 1 hole

Singles
Milligan lost to Mickelson 1 hole
Payne beat Doyle 3 and 1
Evans lost to Langham 4 and 2
Coltart beat Sigel 1 hole
Willison beat Scherrer 3 and 2
Harrington lost to Eger 3 and 2
McGimpsey lost to May 4 and 3
Hay lost to Voges 3 and 1

1993 *at Interlachen, Edina, MN*

Result: USA 19, GBI 5
Captains: M Giles III (USA), G Macgregor (GBI)
First Day – **Foursomes**
Abandoned – rain & flooding
Singles
A Doyle beat I Pyman 1 hole
D Berganio lost to M Stanford 3 and 2
J Sigel lost to D Robertson 3 and 2
K Mitchum halved with S Cage
T Herron beat P Harrington 1 hole
D Yates beat P Page 2 and 1
T Demsey beat R Russell 2 and 1
J Leonard beat R Burns 4 and 3
B Gay lost to V Phillips 2 and 1
J Harris beat B Dredge 4 and 3
Second Day – **Foursomes**
Doyle & Leonard beat Pyman & Cage 4 and 3
Berganio & Demsey beat Stanford & Harrington 3 and 2
Sigel & Mitchum beat Dredge & Phillips 3 and 2
Harris & Herron beat Russell & Robertson 1 hole
Singles
Doyle beat Robertson 4 and 3
Harris beat Pyman 3 and 2
Yates beat Cage 2 and 1
Gay halved with Harrington
Sigel beat Page 5 and 4
Herron beat Phillips 3 and 2
Mitchum beat Russell 4 and 2
Berganio lost to Burns 1 hole
Demsey beat Dredge 3 and 2
Leonard beat Stanford 5 and 4

1995 *at Royal Porthcawl*

Result: GBI 14, USA 10
Captains: C Brown (GBI),
*   AD Gray jr (USA)*
First Day – **Foursomes**
Sherry & Gallacher lost to Harris & Woods 4 and 3
Foster & Howell halved with Bratton & Riley
Rankin & Howard lost to Begay & Jackson 4 and 3
Harrington & Fanagan beat Cox & Kuehne 5 and 3
Singles
G Sherry beat N Begay 3 and 2
L James lost to K Cox 1 hole
M Foster beat B Marucci 4 and 3
S Gallacher beat T Jackson 4 and 3
P Harrington beat J Courville jr 2 holes
B Howard halved with A Bratton
G Rankin lost to J Harris 1 hole
GP Wolstenholme beat T Woods 1 hole
Second Day – **Foursomes**
Sherry & Gallacher lost to Bratton & Riley 4 and 2
Howell & Foster beat Cox & Kuehne 3 and 2
Wolstenholme & James lost to Marucci & Courville
    6 and 5
Harrington & Fanagan beat Harris & Woods 2 and 1

Singles
Sherry beat Riley 2 holes
Howell beat Begay 2 and 1
Gallacher beat Kuehne 3 and 2
Fanagan beat Courville 3 and 2
Howard halved with Jackson
Foster halved with Marucci
Harrington lost to Harris 3 and 2
Wolstenholme lost to Woods 4 and 3

1997 at Quaker Ridge, NY
Result: USA 18, GBI 6
Captains: AD Gray jr (USA), C Brown (GBI)
First Day – **Foursomes**
Howard & Young lost to Elder & Kribel 4 and 3
Rose & Brooks lost to Courville & Marucci 5 and 4
Wolstenholme & Nolan lost to Gore & Harris 6 and 4
Coughlan & Park lost to Leen & Wollman 1 hole
Singles
S Young beat D Delcher 5 and 4
C Watson beat S Scott 1 hole
B Howard lost to B Elder 5 and 4
J Rose beat J Kribel 1 hole
K Nolan lost to R Leen 3 and 2
G Rankin lost to J Gore 3 and 2
R Coughlan halved with C Wollman
GP Wolstenholme lost to J Harris 1 hole
Second Day – **Foursomes**
Young & Watson lost to Harris & Elder 3 and 2
Howard & Rankin lost to Courville & Marucci 5 and 4
Coughlan & Park lost to Delcher & Scott 1 hole
Wolstenholme & Rose beat Leen & Wollman 2 and 1
Singles
Young beat Kribel 2 and 1
Watson halved with Gore
Rose lost to Courville 3 and 2
Nolan lost to Elder 2 and 1
Brooks lost to Harris 6 and 5
Park lost to Marucci 4 and 3
Wolstenholme lost to Delcher 2 and 1
Coughlan lost to Scott 2 and 1

1999 at Nairn
Result: GBI 15, USA 9
Captains: P McEvoy (GBI), D Yates jr (USA)
First Day – **Foursomes**
Rankin & Storm lost to Haas & Miller 1 hole
Casey & Donald beat Byrd & Scott 5 and 3
Gribben & Kelly lost to Gossett & Jackson 3 and 1
Rowe & Wolstenholme beat Kuchar & Molder 1 hole
Singles
G Rankin lost to E Loar 4 and 3
L Donald beat T McKnight 4 and 3
G Storm lost to H Haas 5 and 3
P Casey beat S Scott 4 and 3
D Patrick lost to J Byrd 6 and 5
S Dyson halved with D Gossett
P Gribben halved with B Molder
L Kelly lost to T Jackson 3 and 1

Second Day – **Foursomes**
Rankin & Storm beat Loar & McKnight 4 and 3
Dyson & Gribben lost to Haas & Miller 1 hole
Casey & Donald beat Gossett & Jackson 1 hole
Rowe & Wolstenholme beat Kuchar & Molder 4 and 3
Singles
Rankin beat Scott 1 hole
Dyson lost to Loar 5 and 4
Casey beat Miller 3 and 2
Storm beat Byrd 1 hole
Donald beat Molder 3 and 2
Rowe beat Kuchar 1 hole
Gribben beat Haas 3 and 2
Wolstenholme beat Gossett 1 hole

2001 at Ocean Forest, Sea Island, GA
Result: GBI 15, USA 9
*Captains: D Yates jr (USA),
          P McEvoy (GBI)*
First Day – **Foursomes**
D Green & DJ Trahan lost to S O'Hara & GP
Wolstenholme
   5 and 3
N Cassini & L Glover beat L Donald & N Dougherty
   4 and 3
D Eger & B Molder halved with J Elson & R McEvoy
J Driscoll & J Quinney lost to G McDowell & M Hoey
   3 and 1
Singles
E Compton beat G Wolstenholme 3 and 2
DJ Trahan beat S O'Hara 2 and 1
J Driscoll lost to N Dougherty 2 and 1
N Cassini beat N Edwards 5 and 4
J Harris lost to M Warren 5 and 4
J Quinney lost to L Donald 3 and 2
B Molder beat G McDowell 2 and 1
L Glover beat M Hoey 1 hole
Second Day – **Foursomes**
E Compton & J Harris lost to L Donald & N Dougherty
   3 and 2
N Cassini & L Glover lost to G McDowell & M Hoey
   2 and 1
D Eger & B Molder beat S O'Hara & M Warren
   7 and 6
D Green & DJ Trahan lost to J Elson & R McEvoy
   1 hole
Singles
L Glover lost to L Donald 3 and 2
J Harris lost to S O'Hara 4 and 3
DJ Trahan lost to N Dougherty 1 hole
J Driscoll lost to M Warren 2 and 1
B Molder beat G McDowell 1 hole
D Green lost to M Hoey 1 hole
E Compton halved with J Elson
N Cassini lost to GP Wolstenholme 4 and 3

Walker Cup – INDIVIDUAL RECORDS

Notes: Bold type indicates captain; in brackets, did not play
† indicates players who have also played in the Ryder Cup

Great Britain and Ireland

Name		Year	Played	Won	Lost	Halved
MF Attenborough	Eng	1967	2	0	2	0
CC Aylmer	Eng	1922	2	1	1	0
†P Baker	Eng	1985	3	2	1	0
JB Beck	Eng	1928-(38)-(47)	1	0	1	0
PJ Benka	Eng	1969	4	2	1	1
HG Bentley	Eng	1934-36-38	4	0	2	2
DA Blair	Sco	1955-61	4	1	3	0
C Bloice	Sco	1985	3	0	2	1
MF Bonallack	Eng	1957-59-61-63-65-67-**69-71-73**	25	8	14	3
†G Brand jr	Sco	1979	3	0	3	0
OC Bristowe	Eng	(1923)-24	1	0	1	0
A Brodie	Sco	1977-79	8	5	2	1
A Brooks	Sco	1969	3	2	0	1
M Brooks	Sco	1997	2	0	2	0
C Brown	Wal	**1995**-(97)	0	0	0	0
Hon WGE Brownlow	Eng	1926	2	0	2	0
J Bruen	Irl	1938-49-51	5	0	4	1
JA Buckley	Wal	1979	1	0	1	0
J Burke	Irl	1932	2	0	1	1
R Burns	Irl	1993	2	1	1	0
AF Bussell	Sco	1957	2	1	1	0
S Cage	Eng	1993	3	0	2	1
I Caldwell	Eng	1951-55	4	1	2	1
W Campbell	Sco	1930	2	0	2	0
JB Carr	Irl	1947-49-51-53-55-57-59-61-63-(65)-67	20	5	14	1
RJ Carr	Irl	1971	4	3	0	1
DG Carrick	Sco	1983-87	5	0	5	0
IA Carslaw	Sco	1979	3	1	1	1
P Casey	Eng	1999	4	4	0	0
C Cassells	Eng	1989	3	2	1	0
JR Cater	Sco	1955	1	0	1	0
J Caven	Sco	1922	2	0	2	0
BHG Chapman	Eng	1961	1	0	1	0
R Chapman	Eng	1981	4	3	1	0
MJ Christmas	Eng	1961-63	3	1	2	0
†CA Clark	Eng	1965	4	2	0	2
GJ Clark	Eng	1965	1	0	1	0
†HK Clark	Eng	1973	3	1	1	1
R Claydon	Eng	1989	4	2	2	0
†A Coltart	Sco	1991	3	2	1	0
GB Cosh	Sco	1965	4	3	1	0
R Coughlan	Irl	1997	4	0	3	1
T Craddock	Irl	1967-69	6	2	3	1
LG Crawley	Eng	1932-34-38-47	6	3	3	0
B Critchley	Eng	1969	4	1	1	2
D Curry	Eng	1987	4	1	3	0
CR Dalgleish	Sco	1981	3	1	2	0
B Darwin	Eng	1922	2	1	1	0
JC Davies	Eng	1973-75-77-79	13	3	8	2
P Deeble	Eng	1977-81	5	1	4	0
FWG Deighton	Sco	(1951)-57	2	0	2	0
SC Dodd	Wal	1989	4	1	1	2
L Donald	Eng	1999-01	8	7	1	0
N Dougherty	Eng	2001	4	3	1	0
B Dredge	Wal	1993	3	0	3	0
†NV Drew	Irl	1953	1	0	1	0
AA Duncan	Wal	**(1953)**	0	0	0	0
JM Dykes	Sco	1936	2	0	1	1
S Dyson	Eng	1999	3	0	2	1
NB Edwards	Wal	2001-03	5	2	1	2
R Eggo	Eng	1987	2	0	2	0

Name		Year	Played	Won	Lost	Halved
J Elson	Eng	2001	3	1	0	2
D Evans	Wal	1981	3	1	1	1
G Evans	Eng	1991	4	2	2	0
RC Ewing	Irl	1936-38-47-49-51-55	10	1	7	2
GRD Eyles	Eng	1975	4	2	2	0
J Fanagan	Irl	1995	3	3	0	0
EW Fiddian	Eng	1932-34	4	0	4	0
J de Forest	Eng	1932	1	0	1	0
M Foster	Eng	1995	4	2	0	2
R Foster	Eng	1965-67-69-71-73-(**79**)-(**81**)	17	2	13	2
N Fox	Irl	2003	3	1	2	0
DW Frame	Eng	1961	1	0	1	0
S Gallacher	Sco	1995	4	2	2	0
†D Gilford	Eng	1985	1	0	1	0
P Girvan	Sco	1987	3	0	3	0
G Godwin	Eng	1979-81	7	2	4	1
G Gordon	Sco	2003	1	0	1	0
CW Green	Sco	1963-69-71-73-75-(**83**)-(**85**)	17	4	10	3
P Gribben	Irl	1999	4	1	2	1
RH Hardman	Eng	1928	1	0	1	0
A Hare	Eng	1989	3	2	2	0
†P Harrington	Irl	1991-93-95	9	3	5	1
R Harris	Sco	(**1922**)-**23-26**	4	1	3	0
RW Hartley	Eng	1930-32	4	0	4	0
WL Hartley	Eng	1932	2	0	2	0
J Hawksworth	Eng	1985	4	2	1	1
G Hay	Sco	1991	3	1	2	0
P Hedges	Eng	1973-75	5	0	2	3
CO Hezlet	Irl	1924-26-28	6	0	5	1
GA Hill	Eng	1936-(**55**)	2	0	1	1
M Hoey	Irl	2001	4	3	1	0
Sir EWE Holderness	Eng	1923-26-30	6	2	4	0
TWB Homer	Eng	1973	3	0	3	0
‡CVL Hooman	Eng	1922-23	3	†1	2	†0
WL Hope	Sco	1923-24-28	5	1	4	0
DB Howard	Sco	1995-97	6	0	4	2
D Howell	Eng	1995	3	2	0	1
G Huddy	Eng	1961	1	0	1	0
W Humphreys	Eng	1971	3	2	1	0
IC Hutcheon	Sco	1975-77-79-81	15	5	8	2
D Inglis	Sco	2003	4	2	1	1
RR Jack	Sco	1957-59	4	2	2	0
L James	Eng	1995	2	0	2	0
†M James	Eng	1975	4	3	1	0
A Jamieson jr	Sco	1926	2	1	1	0
MJ Kelley	Eng	1977-79	7	3	3	1
L Kelly	Sco	1999	2	0	2	0
SD Keppler	Eng	1983	4	0	3	1
†MG King	Eng	1969-73	7	1	5	1
AT Kyle	Sco	1938-47-51	5	2	3	0
DH Kyle	Sco	1924	1	0	1	0
JA Lang	Sco	(1930)	0	0	0	0
JDA Langley	Eng	1936-51-53	6	0	5	1
CD Lawrie	Sco	(**1961**)-(**63**)	0	0	0	0
ME Lewis	Eng	1983	1	0	1	0
PB Lucas	Eng	(1936)-47-(**49**)	2	1	1	0
MSR Lunt	Eng	1959-61-63-65	11	2	8	1
†AWB Lyle	Sco	1977	3	0	3	0
AR McCallum	Sco	1928	1	0	1	0
SM McCready	Irl	1949-51	3	0	3	0
JS Macdonald	Sco	1971	3	1	1	1
G McDowell	Irl	2001	4	2	2	0
P McEvoy	Eng	1977-79-81-85-89-(**99**)-(**01**)	18	5	11	2
R McEvoy	Eng	2001	2	1	0	1
G McGimpsey	Irl	1985-89-91-(**03**)	11	4	5	2
P McGinley	Irl	1991	3	1	2	0
G Macgregor	Sco	1971-75-83-85-87-(**91**)-(**93**)	14	5	8	1
RC MacGregor	Sco	1953	2	0	2	0
J McHenry	Irl	1987	4	2	2	0
P McKellar	Sco	1977	1	0	1	0

‡*In 1922 Hooman beat Sweetser at the 37th – on all other occasions halved matches have counted as such.*

Walker Cup Individual Records continued

Name		Year	Played	Won	Lost	Halved
WW Mackenzie	Sco	1922-23	3	1	2	0
SL McKinlay	Sco	1934	2	0	2	0
J McLean	Sco	1934-36	4	1	3	0
EA McRuvie	Sco	1932-34	4	1	2	1
JFD Madeley	Irl	1963	2	0	1	1
S Manley	Wal	2003	3	2	0	1
LS Mann	Sco	1983	4	2	1	1
B Marchbank	Sco	1979	4	2	2	0
GC Marks	Eng	1969-71-(87)-(89)	6	2	4	0
DM Marsh	Eng	71-(73)-(75)	3	2	1	0
GNC Martin	Irl	1928	1	0	1	0
S Martin	Sco	1977	4	2	2	0
P Mayo	Wal	1985-87	4	0	3	1
GH Micklem	Eng	1947-49-53-55-(57)-(59)	6	1	5	0
DJ Millensted	Eng	1967	2	1	1	0
JW Milligan	Sco	1989-91	7	3	3	1
EB Millward	Eng	(1949)-55	2	0	2	0
WTG Milne	Sco	1973	4	2	2	0
†CS Montgomerie	Sco	1985-87	8	2	5	1
JL Morgan	Wal	1951-53-55	6	2	4	0
C Moriarty	Irl	2003	4	1	3	0
P Mulcare	Irl	1975	3	2	1	0
GH Murray	Sco	1977	2	1	1	0
SWT Murray	Sco	1963	4	2	2	0
WA Murray	Sco	1923-24-(26)	4	1	3	0
K Nolan	Irl	1997	3	0	3	0
E O'Connell	Irl	1989	4	2	0	2
S O'Hara	Sco	2001	4	2	2	0
A Oldcorn	Eng	1983	4	4	0	0
†PA Oosterhuis	Eng	1967	4	1	2	1
R Oppenheimer	Eng	(1951)	0	0	0	0
P Page	Eng	1993	2	0	2	0
D Park	Wal	1997	3	0	3	0
P Parkin	Wal	1983	3	2	1	0
D Patrick	Sco	1999	1	0	1	0
J Payne	Eng	1991	4	2	2	0
JJF Pennink	Eng	1938	2	1	1	0
TP Perkins	Eng	1928	2	0	2	0
GB Peters	Sco	1936-38	4	2	1	1
V Phillips	Eng	1993	3	1	2	0
AD Pierse	Irl	1983	3	0	2	1
AH Perowne	Eng	1949-53-59	4	0	4	0
AK Pirie	Sco	1967	3	0	2	1
MA Poxon	Eng	1975	2	0	2	0
D Prosser	Eng	1989	1	0	1	2
I Pyman	Eng	1993	3	0	3	0
†R Rafferty	Irl	1981	4	2	2	0
G Rankin	Sco	1995-97-99	8	2	6	0
D Robertson	Sco	1993	3	1	2	0
J Robinson	Eng	1987	4	2	2	0
RN Roderick	Wal	1989	2	0	1	1
J Rose	Eng	1997	4	2	2	0
P Rowe	Eng	1999	3	3	0	0
R Russell	Sco	1993	3	0	3	0
AC Saddler	Sco	1963-65-67-(77)	10	3	5	2
Hon M Scott	Eng	1924-34	4	2	2	0
R Scott, jr	Sco	1924	1	1	0	0
PF Scrutton	Eng	1955-57	3	0	3	0
DN Sewell	Eng	1957-59	4	1	3	0
RDBM Shade	Sco	1961-63-65-67	14	6	6	2
G Shaw	Sco	1987	4	1	2	1
DB Sheahan	Irl	1963	4	2	2	0
AE Shepperson	Eng	1957-59	3	1	1	1
G Sherry	Sco	1995	4	2	2	0
AF Simpson	Sco	(1926)	0	0	0	0
M Skelton	Eng	2003	2	1	1	0
JN Smith	Sco	1930	2	0	2	0
WD Smith	Sco	1959	1	0	1	0

Name		Year	Played	Won	Lost	Halved
M Stanford	Eng	1993	3	1	2	0
AR Stephen	Sco	1985	4	2	1	1
EF Storey	Eng	1924-26-28	6	1	5	0
G Storm	Eng	1999	4	2	2	0
JA Stout	Eng	1930-32	4	0	3	1
C Stowe	Eng	1938-47	4	2	2	0
HB Stuart	Sco	1971-73-75	10	4	6	0
A Thirlwell	Eng	1957	1	0	1	0
KG Thom	Eng	1949	2	0	2	0
MS Thompson	Eng	1983	3	1	2	0
H Thomson	Sco	1936-38	4	2	2	0
CJH Tolley	Eng	1922-23-**24**-26-30-34	12	4	8	0
TA Torrance	Sco	1924-28-30-**32**-34	9	3	5	1
WB Torrance	Sco	1922	2	0	2	0
†PM Townsend	Eng	1965	4	3	1	0
LP Tupling	Eng	1969	2	1	1	0
W Tweddell	Eng	**1928**-(36)	2	0	2	0
J Walker	Sco	1961	2	0	2	0
†P Walton	Irl	1981-83	8	6	2	0
M Warren	Sco	2001	3	2	1	0
C Watson	Sco	1997	3	1	1	1
†P Way	Eng	1981	4	2	2	0
RH Wethered	Eng	1922-23-26-**30**-34	9	5	3	1
L White	Eng	1991	2	1	1	0
RJ White	Eng	1947-49-51-53-55	10	6	3	1
R Willison	Eng	1991	4	1	3	0
J Wilson	Sco	1923	2	2	0	0
JC Wilson	Sco	1947-53	4	0	4	0
O Wilson	Eng	2003	3	2	0	1
S Wilson	Sco	2003	4	1	1	2
GB Wolstenholme	Eng	1957-59	4	1	2	1
GP Wolstenholme	Eng	1995-97-99-01-03	17	9	8	0
S Young	Sco	1997	4	2	2	0

United States of America

Name	Year	Played	Won	Lost	Halved
†TD Aaron	1959	2	1	1	0
B Alexander	1987	3	2	1	0
DC Allen	1965-67	6	0	4	2
B Andrade	1987	4	2	2	0
ES Andrews	1961	1	1	0	0
D Ballenger	1973	1	1	0	0
R Baxter, jr	1957	2	2	0	0
N Begay III	1995	3	1	2	0
DR Beman	1959-61-63-65	11	7	2	2
D Berganio	1993	3	1	2	0
RE Billows	1938-49	4	2	2	0
SE Bishop	1947-49	3	2	1	0
AS Blum	1957	1	0	1	0
J Bohmann	1969	3	1	2	0
M Brannan	1977	3	1	2	0
A Bratton	1995	3	1	0	2
GF Burns	1975	3	2	1	0
C Burroughs	1985	3	1	2	0
J Byrd	1999	3	1	2	0
AE Campbell	1936	2	2	0	0
JE Campbell	1957	1	0	1	0
WC Campbell	1951-53-(**55**)-57-65-67-71-75	18	11	4	3
N Cassini	2001	4	2	2	0
RJ Cerrudo	1967	4	1	1	2
RD Chapman	1947-51-53	5	3	2	0
D Cherry	1953-55-61	5	5	0	0
D Clarke	1979	3	2	0	1
RE Cochran	1961	1	1	0	0
CR Coe	1949-51-53-(**57**)-**59**-61-63	13	7	4	2
R Commans	1981	3	1	1	1

Walker Cup Individual Records *continued*

Name	Year	Played	Won	Lost	Halved
E Compton	2001	3	1	1	1
JW Conrad	1955	2	1	1	0
J Courville jr	1995-97	6	4	2	0
K Cox	1995	3	1	2	0
N Crosby	1983	2	1	1	0
BH Cudd	1955	2	2	0	0
RD Davies	1963	2	0	2	0
JW Dawson	1949	2	2	0	0
D Delcher	1997	3	2	1	0
T Demsey	1993	3	3	0	0
RB Dickson	1967	3	3	0	0
A Doyle	1991-93	6	5	1	0
J Driscoll	2001	3	0	3	0
GT Dunlap jr	1932-34-36	5	3	1	1
†D Duval	1991	3	2	1	0
D Edwards	1973	4	4	0	0
HC Egan	1934	1	1	0	0
D Eger	1991-01	5	3	1	1
HC Eger	1989	3	1	2	0
D Eichelberger	1965	3	1	2	0
B Elder	1997	4	4	0	0
J Ellis	1973	3	2	1	0
W Emery	1936	2	1	0	1
C Evans jr	1922-24-28	5	3	2	0
J Farquhar	1971	3	1	2	0
†B Faxon	1983	4	3	1	0
R Fehr	1983	4	2	1	1
JW Fischer	1934-36-38-**(65)**	4	3	0	1
D Fischesser	1979	3	1	2	0
MA Fleckman	1967	2	0	2	0
B Fleisher	1969	4	0	2	2
J Fought	1977	4	4	0	0
WC Fownes jr	**1922-24**	3	1	2	0
F Fuhrer	1981	3	2	1	0
JR Gabrielsen	1977-**(81)**-**(91)**	3	1	2	0
R Gamez	1989	4	3	0	1
RA Gardner	1922-**23-24-26**	8	6	2	0
RW Gardner	1961-63	5	4	0	1
B Gay	1993	2	0	1	1
M Giles	1969-71-73-75	15	8	2	5
HL Givan	1936	1	0	0	1
L Glover	2001	4	2	2	0
JG Goodman	1934-36-38	6	4	2	0
J Gore	1997	3	2	0	1
D Gossett	1999	4	1	2	1
M Gove	1979	3	2	1	0
J Grace	1975	3	2	1	0
JA Grant	1967	2	2	0	0
AD Gray jr	1963-65-67-**(95)**-**(97)**	12	5	6	1
D Green	2001	3	0	3	0
JP Guilford	1922-24-26	6	4	2	0
W Gunn	1926-28	4	4	0	0
†F Haas jr	1938	2	0	2	0
H Haas	1999	4	3	1	0
†J Haas	1975	3	3	0	0
J Haas	1985	3	1	2	0
W Haas	2003	4	2	2	0
G Hallberg	1977	3	1	2	0
GS Hamer jr	(1947)	0	0	0	0
J Harris	1993-95-97-01	14	10	4	0
LE Harris jr	1963	4	3	1	0
V Heafner	1977	3	3	0	0
M Hendrix	2003	3	2	0	1
SD Herron	1923	2	0	2	0
T Herron	1993	3	3	0	0
†S Hoch	1979	4	4	0	0
W Hoffer	1983	2	1	1	0
J Holtgrieve	1979-81-83	10	6	4	0

Name	Year	Played	Won	Lost	Halved
JM Hopkins	1965	3	0	2	1
R Howe	1989	1	0	1	0
W Howell	1932	1	1	0	0
W Hyndman	1957-59-61-69-71	9	6	1	2
J Inman	1969	2	2	0	0
JG Jackson	1953-55	3	3	0	0
T Jackson	1995-99	6	3	2	1
K Johnson	1989	3	1	2	0
HR Johnston	1923-24-28-30	6	5	1	0
RT Jones jr	1922-24-26-**28-30**	10	9	1	0
AF Kammer	1947	2	1	1	0
M Killian	1973	3	1	2	0
C Kite	1987	3	2	1	0
†TO Kite	1971	4	2	1	1
RE Knepper	(1922)	0	0	0	0
RW Knowles	1951	1	1	0	0
G Koch	1973-75	7	4	1	2
CR Kocsis	1938-49-57	5	2	2	1
J Kribel	1997	3	1	2	0
M Kuchar	1999	3	0	3	0
T Kuehne	1995-03	7	1	5	1
F Langham	1991	3	1	2	0
R Leen	1997	3	2	1	0
†J Leonard	1993	3	3	0	0
G Lesher	1989	4	1	3	0
B Lewis jr	1981-83-85-87-**(03)**	14	10	4	0
JW Lewis	1967	4	3	1	0
WL Little jr	1934	2	2	0	0
†GA Littler	1953	2	2	0	0
E Loar	1999	3	2	1	0
B Loeffler	1987	3	2	1	0
†D Love III	1985	3	2	0	1
B Mackenzie	2003	3	3	0	0
RR Mackenzie	1926-28-30	6	5	1	0
MJ McCarthy jr	(1928)-32	1	1	0	0
BN McCormick	1949	1	1	0	0
T McKnight	1999	2	0	2	0
JB McHale	1949-51	3	2	0	1
MR Marston	1922-23-24-34	8	5	3	0
D Martin	1989	4	1	1	2
B Marucci	1995-97	6	4	1	1
L Mattiace	1987	3	2	1	0
R May	1991	4	3	1	0
B Mayfair	1987	3	3	0	0
E Meeks	1989	1	0	0	1
SN Melnyk	1969-71	7	3	3	1
†P Mickelson	1989-91	8	4	2	2
AL Miller	1969-71	8	4	3	1
J Miller	1999	3	2	1	0
L Miller	1977	4	4	0	0
K Mitchum	1993	3	2	0	1
DK Moe	1930-32	3	3	0	0
B Molder	1999-01	8	3	3	2
B Montgomery	1987	2	2	0	0
G Moody	1979	3	1	2	0
R Moore	2003	2	0	2	0
GT Moreland	1932-34	4	4	0	0
D Morey	1955-65	4	1	3	0
J Mudd	1981	3	3	0	0
†RJ Murphy	1967	4	1	2	1
C Nallen	2003	2	1	1	0
JF Neville	1923	1	0	1	0
†JW Nicklaus	1959-61	4	4	0	0
LW Oehmig	(1977)	0	0	0	0
FD Ouimet	1922-23-24-26-30-**32-34**-(36)-(38)-(47)-**(49)**	16	9	5	2
HD Paddock jr	1951	1	0	0	1
†J Pate	1975	4	0	4	0
WJ Patton	1955-57-59-63-65-**(69)**	14	11	3	0
†C Pavin	1981	3	2	0	1
M Peck	1979	3	1	1	1

Walker Cup Individual Records *continued*

Name	Year	Played	Won	Lost	Halved
M Pfeil	1973	4	2	1	1
M Podolak	1985	2	1	0	1
SL Quick	1947	2	1	1	0
J Quinney	2001	2	0	2	0
S Randolph	1985	4	2	1	1
J Rassett	1981	3	3	0	0
F Ridley	1977-(87)-(89)	3	2	1	0
RH Riegel	1947-49	4	4	0	0
C Riley	1995	3	1	1	1
H Robbins jr	1957	2	0	1	1
†W Rogers	1973	2	1	1	0
GV Rotan	1923	2	1	1	0
A Rubinson	2003	4	1	3	0
†EM Rudolph	1957	2	1	0	1
B Sander	1977	3	0	3	0
T Scherrer	1991	3	0	3	0
S Scott	1997-99	6	2	4	0
CH Seaver	1932	2	2	0	0
RL Siderowf	1969-73-75-77-(79)	14	4	8	2
J Sigel	1977-79-81-83-85-87-89-91-93	33	18	10	5
RH Sikes	1963	3	1	2	0
JB Simons	1971	2	0	2	0
†S Simpson	1977	3	3	0	0
CB Smith	1961-63	2	0	1	1
R Smith	1936-38	4	2	2	0
R Sonnier	1985	3	0	2	1
J Sorensen	1987	3	1	1	1
M Sposa	1991	3	2	1	0
†C Stadler	1975	3	3	0	0
FR Stranahan	1947-49-51	6	3	2	1
†C Strange	1975	4	3	0	1
†H Sutton	1979-81	7	2	4	1
‡JW Sweetser	1922-23-24-26-28-32-(67)-(73)	12	7	†4	†1
FM Taylor	1957-59-61	4	4	0	0
D Tentis	1983	2	0	1	1
DJ Trahan	2001	4	1	3	0
RS Tufts	(1963)	0	0	0	0
WP Turnesa	1947-49-51	6	3	3	0
B Tuten	1983	2	1	1	0
EM Tutweiler	1965-67	6	5	1	0
ER Updegraff	1963-65-69-(75)	7	3	3	1
S Urzetta	1951-53	4	4	0	0
K Venturi	1953	2	2	0	0
S Verplank	1985	4	3	0	1
M Voges	1991	3	2	1	0
GJ Voigt	1930-32-36	5	2	2	1
G Von Elm	1926-28-30	6	4	1	1
D von Tacky	1981	3	1	2	0
†JL Wadkins	1969-71	7	3	4	0
D Waldorf	1985	3	1	2	0
EH Ward	1953-55-59	6	6	0	0
MH Ward	1938-47	4	2	2	0
M West	1973-79	6	2	3	1
J Westland	1932-34-53-(61)	5	3	0	2
HW Wettlaufer	1959	2	2	0	0
E White	1936	2	2	0	0
L Williams	2003	3	0	1	2
OF Willing	1923-24-30	4	4	0	0
JM Winters jr	(1971)	0	0	0	0
C Wittenberg	2003	4	1	3	0
C Wollman	1997	3	1	1	1
W Wood	1983	4	1	2	1
†T Woods	1995	4	2	2	0
FJ Wright	1923	1	1	0	0
CR Yates	1936-38-(53)	4	3	0	1
D Yates jr	1989-93-(99)-01	6	3	2	1
RL Yost	1955	2	2	0	0
G Zahringer	2003	3	0	2	1

World Amateur Team Championship (Eisenhower Trophy)

Year	Winners	Runners-up	Venue	Score
1958	Australia	United States	St Andrews	918

(After a tie, Australia won the play-off by two strokes: Australia 222, United States 224)

Year	Winners	Runners-up	Venue	Score
1960	United States	Australia	Ardmore, USA	834
1962	United States	Canada	Kawana, Japan	854
1964	Great Britain & Ireland	Canada	Olgiata, Rome	895
1966	Australia	United States	Mexico City	877
1968	United States	Great Britain & Ireland	Melbourne	868
1970	United States	New Zealand	Madrid	857
1972	United States	Australia	Buenos Aires	865
1974	United States	Japan	Dominican Rep.	888
1976	Great Britain & Ireland	Japan	Penina, Portugal	892
1978	United States	Canada	Fiji	873
1980	United States	South Africa	Pinehurst, USA	848
1982	United States	Sweden	Lausanne	859
1984	Japan	United States	Hong Kong	870
1986	Canada	United States	Caracas, Venezuela	860
1988	Great Britain & Ireland	United States	Ullva, Sweden	882
1990	Sweden	New Zealand	Christchurch, New Zealand	879
1992	New Zealand	United States	Capilano, Canada	823
1994	United States	Great Britain & Ireland	Paris, France	838
1996	Australia	Sweden	Manila, Philippines	838
1998	Great Britain and Ireland	Australia	Los Leones/La Dehesa, Chile	852
2000	United States	Great Britain & Ireland	Sporting Club, Berlin	841
2002	United States	France	Saujana, Malaysia	568

Copa de las Americas (Inaugurated 2003)

at Dorado Beach, Puerto Rico

1   Canada

Men:

Peter Laws	70	69	75	75	289
James Lepp	75	73	72	75	295
	145	142	147	150	584

Team total: 1176

Women:

Laura Mathews	76	72	75	68	291
Lisa Meldrum	75	78	75	73	301
	151	150	150	141	592

2   United States

Men:

Ricky Barnes	74	78	77	72	301
Ryan Moore	75	76	74	69	294
	149	154	151	141	595

Team total: 1188

Women:

Kathy Hartwiger	75	72	72	76	295
Becky Lucidi	78	75	72	73	298
	153	147	144	149	593

3   Mexico

Men:

Enrique Llaguno	75	75	79	75	304
Mauricio Mendez	73	71	76	80	300
	148	146	155	155	604

Team total: 1230

Women:

Tanya Dergal	83	80	71	78	312
Violeta Retamoza	73	78	82	81	314
	156	158	153	159	626

4T Peru, Argentina; 5 Puerto Rico; 6 Chile; 7 Ecuador; 8 Dominican Republic

Europe v Asia-Pacific (Bonallack Cup)

2000	Europe	Puerta de Hierro, Spain	2002	Asia-Pacific	Hirono GC, Japan

European Amateur Team Championship

Year	Winner	Runner-up	Venue
1959	Sweden	France	Barcelona, Spain
1961	Sweden	England	Brussels, Belgium
1963	England	Sweden	Falsterbo, Sweden
1965	Ireland	Scotland	St George's, England
1967	Ireland	France	Turin, Italy
1969	England	Germany	Hamburg, Germany
1971	England	Scotland	Lausanne, Switzerland
1973	England	Scotland	Penina, Portugal
1975	Scotland	Italy	Killarney, Ireland
1977	Scotland	Sweden	The Haagsche, Netherlands
1979	England	Wales	Esbjerg, Denmark
1981	England	Scotland	St Andrews, Scotland
1983	Ireland	Spain	Chantilly, France
1985	Scotland	Sweden	Halmstad, Sweden
1987	Ireland	England	Murhof, Austria
1989	England	Scotland	Royal Porthcawl, Wales
1991	England	Italy	Puerta de Hierro, Spain
1993	Wales	England	Marianske Lasne, Czech Republic
1995	Scotland	England	Royal Antwerp, Belgium
1997	Spain	Scotland	Portmarnock, Ireland
1999	Italy	Germany	Monticello, Italy
2001	Scotland	Ireland	Ljunghusens, Sweden
2003	Spain	Sweden	Royal Hague, Netherlands

European Club Cup (Albacom Trophy)

1975	Club de Campo, Spain	Club de Campo	1990	Ealing, England	Aloha
1976	Växjö Golfklub, Sweden	El Prat	1991	Club de Golf Terramar, Spain	La Quinta
1977	Chantilly, France	RC Belgique	1992	Hillerod, Denmark	La Quinta
1978	Hamburger, Germany	Deauville	1993	Lahden, Finland	La Quinta
1979	Hamburger, Germany	Santa Ponsa	1994	Kilmarnock (Barassie),	
1980	Limerick, Ireland	Santa Ponsa		Scotland	Vilamoura
1981	El Prat, Spain	Aloha	1995	Racing C de France, France	Vilamoura
1982	El Prat, Spain	Aloha	1996	Racing C de France, France	Vilamoura
1983	Rapallo, Italy	Aloha	1997	Racing C de France, France	Parco de Medici
1984	Hamburger, Germany	Aloha	1998	Aalborg, Denmark	Parco de Medici
1985	El Prat, Spain	Aloha	1999	Aalborg, Denmark	Parco de Medici
1986	Hamburger, Germany	Aloha	2000	Shandon Park,	
1987	Puerto de Hierro, Spain	Aloha		Northern Ireland	Parco de Medici
1988	Brokenhurst Manor, England	Aloha	2001	Shandon Park	La Boulie
1989	Ealing, England	Aloha	2002	Bordelais, France	Parco de Medici

2003 *at Antalyn, Turkey*

1	Deauville (Fra)	440 (Gregoire Brizay, Julien Duclos Grenet, Marc Mauret)
2	Puerta de Hiero (Esp)	441
3	Bordelais (Fra)	442

Best individual: Gonzales Castaño (Esp) 215

St Andrews Trophy (Great Britain & Ireland v Continent of Europe) *Match instituted 1956, trophy presented 1962*

1956	Great Britain & Ireland	Wentworth	12½–2½
1958	Great Britain & Ireland	St Cloud, France	10–5
1960	Great Britain & Ireland	Walton Heath	13–5
1962	Great Britain & Ireland	Halmstead, Sweden	18–12
1964	Great Britain & Ireland	Muirfield	23–7
1966	Great Britain & Ireland	Bilbao, Spain	19½–10½
1968	Great Britain & Ireland	Portmarnock	20–10
1970	Great Britain & Ireland	La Zoute, Belgium	17½–12½
1972	Great Britain & Ireland	Berkshire	19½–10½
1974	Continent of Europe	Punta Ala, Italy	16–14
1976	Great Britain & Ireland	St Andrews	18½–11½

1978	Great Britain & Ireland	Bremen, Germany	20½–9½
1980	Great Britain & Ireland	Sandwich, Royal St George's	19½–10½
1982	Continent of Europe	Rosendaelsche, Netherlands	14–10
1984	Great Britain & Ireland	Saunton, Devon	13–11
1986	Great Britain & Ireland	Halmstead, Sweden	14½–9½
1988	Great Britain & Ireland	St Andrews	15½–8½
1990	Great Britain & Ireland	El Saler, Spain	13–11
1992	Great Britain & Ireland	Royal Cinque Ports	14–10
1994	Great Britain & Ireland	Chantilly, France	14–10
1996	Great Britain & Ireland	Woodhall Spa	16–8
1998	Continent of Europe	Villa d'Este, Italy	14–10
2000	Great Britain & Ireland	The Ailsa Course, Turnberry	13–11
2002	Great Britain & Ireland	Lausanne, Switzerland	14–10

Home Internationals

1932	Scotland	1959T	England/Ireland/Scotland	1979	No Internationals held
1933	Scotland	1960	England	1980	England
1934	Scotland	1961	Scotland	1981	Scotland
1935T	England/Ireland/Scotland	1962T	England/Ireland/Scotland	1982	Scotland
1936	Scotland	1963T	England/Ireland/Scotland	1983	Ireland
1937	Scotland	1964	England	1984	England
1938	England	1965	England	1985	England
1939–46	No Internationals held	1966	England	1986	Scotland
1947	England	1967	Scotland	1987	Ireland
1948	England	1968	England	1988	England
1949	England	1969	England	1989	England
1950	Ireland	1970	Scotland	1990	Ireland
1951T	Ireland and Scotland	1971	Scotland	1991	Ireland
1952	Scotland	1972T	Scotland/England	1992T	England and Ireland
1953	Scotland	1973	England	1993	England
1954	England	1974	England	1994	England
1955	Ireland	1975	Scotland	1995	England
1956	Scotland	1976	Scotland	1996	England
1957	England	1977	England	1997	England
1958	England	1978	England		

1998 at Royal Porthcawl

Ireland beat Scotland	11 matches to 4
England beat Wales	11 matches to 4
Ireland halved with Wales	7½ matches each
England beat Scotland	9 matches to 6
England beat Ireland	8 matches to 7
Wales beat Scotland	11½ matches to 3½

Winners: England

1999 at Royal County Down

England beat Scotland	10 matches to 5
Ireland beat Wales	8 matches to 7
England beat Wales	11½ matches to 3½
Ireland beat Scotland	10½ matches to 4½
Scotland beat Wales	10½ matches to 4½
England beat Ireland	8½ matches to 6½

Winners: England

2000 at Carnoustie

England halved with Wales	7½ matches to 7½
Ireland halved with Scotland	7½ matches to 7½
England halved with Scotland	7½ matches to 7½
Wales beat Ireland	8 matches to 7
Scotland beat Wales	8½ matches to 6½
Ireland beat England	9½ matches to 5½

Winners: Scotland

2001 at Woodhall Spa

England beat Scotland	9 matches to 6
Ireland beat Wales	10½ matches to 4½
England halved with Wales	7½ matches to 7½
Scotland beat Ireland	8½ matches to 6½
Scotland beat Wales	10½ matches to 4½
England beat Ireland	11½ matches to 3½

Winners: England

2002 at Royal St David's

Wales beat England	8 matches to 7
Ireland halved with Scotland	7½ matches to 7½
Wales beat Ireland	8½ matches to 6½
Scotland beat England	10 matches to 5
England beat Ireland	10 matches to 5
Wales beat Scotland	9 matches to 6

Winners: Wales

2003 at Ballybunion

Ireland beat Wales	8 matches to 7
Scotland halved with England	7½ matches to 7½
Ireland beat England	8 matches to 7
Scotland beat Wales	9½ matches to 5½
Wales beat England	11 matches to 4
Ireland halved with Scotland	7½ matches to 7½

Winners: Ireland

Winning team: Mark Campbell (Stackstown), Darren Crowe (Dunmurry), John Foster (Ballyclare), Noel Fox (Portmarnock), Justin Kehoe (Birr), Michael Sinclair (Knock), Richard Kilpatrick (Banbridge), Brian McElhinney (North West), Michael McGeady (City of Derry), Mark O'Sullivan (Galway), Mervyn Owens (Mallow)

Senior Home Internationals

2002   England   Nairn Dunbar

2003 at Seaton Carew

Wales beat England	4 matches to 3	Ireland beat England	5 matches to 2
Ireland beat Scotland	4 matches to 3	England beat Scotland	5½ matches to 1½
Scotland beat Wales	5 matches to 2	Wales beat Ireland	5 matches to 2

Result: 1 Ireland & Wales 2 points,   3 England 1 point,   4 Scotland 1 point

Winning teams: Ireland: Edward Condren, Peter Cowley, Patrick Harrington, Michael Malone, John O'Donoghue, Robert Wallace. **Wales:** Brian Cramb, Roger Floyd, John Gottwaltz, John Roger Jones, Phil Jones, George Stowe, John Whitcutt

English County Championship

1928	Warwickshire	1958	Surrey	1982	Yorkshire
1929	Lancashire	1959	Northumberland	1983	Berks, Bucks, Oxon
1930	Lancashire	1961	Lancashire	1984	Yorkshire
1931	Yorkshire	1962	Northumberland	1985T	Devon/Hertfordshire
1932	Surrey	1963	Yorkshire	1986	Hertfordshire
1933	Yorkshire	1964	Northumberland	1987	Yorkshire
1934	Worcestershire	1965	Northumberland	1988	Warwickshire
1935	Worcestershire	1966	Surrey	1989	Middlesex
1936	Surrey	1967	Lancashire	1990	Warwickshire
1937	Lancashire	1968	Surrey	1991	Middlesex
1938	Staffordshire	1969	Berks, Bucks, Oxon	1992	Dorset
1939	Worcestershire	1970	Gloucestershire	1993	Yorkshire
1947	Staffordshire	1971	Staffordshire	1994	Middlesex
1948	Staffordshire	1972	Berks, Bucks, Oxon	1995	Lancashire
1949	Lancashire	1973	Yorkshire	1996	Hampshire
1950	*Not played*	1974	Lincolnshire	1997	Yorkshire
1951	Lancashire	1975	Staffordshire	1998	Yorkshire
1952	Yorkshire	1976	Warwickshire	1999	Yorkshire
1953	Yorkshire	1977	Warwickshire	2000	Surrey
1954	Cheshire	1978	Kent	2001	Yorkshire
1955	Yorkshire	1979	Gloucestershire	2002	Yorkshire
1956	Staffordshire	1980	Surrey		
1957	Surrey	1981	Surrey		

2003 at Formby

Leics & Rutland halved with BBO	4½ matches to 4½	Leics & Rutland beat Yorkshire	6½ matches to 2½
Devon beat Yorkshire	6 matches to 3	BBO beat Yorkshire	6 matches to 3
Devon beat BBO	5½ matches to 3½	Devon beat Leics & Rutland	5 matches to 4

Result: 1 Devon 3,   2 Leicestershire & Rutland 1½,   3 Berks, Bucks & Oxon 1½,   4 Yorkshire 0

Winning team: Adam Bridgewater, Alan Gawman, Damion Gee, Kevin Harper, Paul Hendriksen, James Ruth, Craig Townsend

English Club Championship

1989	Ealing	Southport and Ainsdale	1996	Hartlepool	Frilford Heath
1990	Ealing	Goring and Streatley	1997	Royal Mid-Surrey	Sandiway
1991	Trentham	Porters Park	1998	Moor Park	Northumberland
1992	Bristol & Clifton	South Staffs	1999	Royal Mid-Surrey	Moor Park
1993	Worksop	Rotherham	2000	Coxmoor	Berkhampstead
1994	Sandmoor	Coxmoor	2001	St Mellion	Minchinhampton
1995	Sandmoor	Ipswich	2002	Woodcote Park	Northamptonshire County

2003 at King's Lynn

1   Southern Valley (Kent)   287   (Ed Richardson, Will Richardson, Ricky Neil-Jones)
2   John O'Gaunt (Bedfordshire) 288
      Drayton Park (Staffordshire) 288

Scottish Club Championship

1985	Cochrane Castle	Helensburgh	1994	Kilmarnock Barassie	North Berwick
1986	Thornhill	Dunblane New	1995	Kelso	Cochrane Castle
1987	Alloa	Cruden Bay	1996	Cochrane Castle	Alloa
1988	Cowglen	Tulliallan	1997	Blairgowrie	Burnstone Castle
1989	Cowglen	Crieff	1998	Turvill	Boat of Garven
1990	Haggs Castle	Haggs Cstle	1999	Tulliallan	Kilmarnock Barassie
1991	Cochrane Castle	Ranfurley Castle	2000	Cowglen	Crow Wood
1992	Kilmarnock Barassie	Scotscraig	2001	Blairgowrie	North Berwick
1993	Troon Wellbeck	Helensburgh	2002	Tulliallan	Tulliallan

2003 *at Powfoot*

1	Dumfries & Galloway	285 (John Power, Ian Reid, Barry Scott)
2	Bon Accord	287
3	Tulliallan	289

Scottish Area Team Championship

1990	North East	1996	Renfrewshire	2002	Perth and Kinross
1991	Glasgow	1997	Lothians		
1992	North East	1998	Lanarkshire		
1993	Lothians	1999	Lothians		
1994	Lothians	2000	North		
1995	North	2001	Perth and Kinross		

2003 *at Alloa*

Semi-finals
Clackmannanshire beat Angus 5-4
Lothians beat South 8-1

Final
Lothians beat Clackmannanshire 5-4

Winning team: John Gallacher, Steven Armstrong, Keith Nicholson, Simon Mckenzie, Craig Gordon, Tom Caldwell, Lloyd Saltman

Scottish Foursomes Tournament –
Glasgow Evening Times Trophy

1923 Gullane Comrades	1949 Troon Portland	1968 Troon St Meddans	1986 Hamilton
1924 St Andrews New	1950 '36 Club	1969 Irvine	1987 Drumpellier
1925 St Andrews New	1951 Troon Portland	1970 Cardross	1988 Irvine Ravenspark
1926 Pollok	1952 Western Gailes	1971 Airdrie	1989 Cochrane Castle
1927 Erskine	1953 Irvine	1972 Scottish Building	1990 Pitreavie
1928 Earlsferry Thistle	1954 Glasgow University	Contractors	1991 Irvine Ravenspark
1929 Pollok	1955 Haggs Castle	1973 Glasgow Insurance	1992 Cochrane Castle
1930 Mortonhall	1956 Prestonfield	1974 Baberton	1993 Baberton
1931 Royal Burgess	1957 Falkirk Tryst	1975 Prestwick St Cuthbert	1994 Standard Life
1932 Hayston	1958 Troon St Meddans	1976 Wishaw	1995 Ratho Park
1933 Lothianburn	1959 Cambuslang	1977 Stirlingshire Jun.&	1996 Cardross
1934 Ayr Academy FP	1960 Irvine	Youth Society	1997 Cardross
1935 Ayr Academy FP	1961 Falkirk Tryst	1978 Helensburgh	1998 Haggs Castle
1936 Ayr Academy FP	1962 Irvine	1979 Helensburgh	1999 Scottish Life
1937 Ayr Academy FP	1963 Clydebank & Dist	1980 Helensburgh	2000 Colville Park
1938 Western Gailes	1964 Scottish Building	1981 Duddingston	2001 Hamilton
1939–45 *Not played*	Contractors	1982 Haggs Castle	2002 Wishaw
1946 St Andrews New	1965 Falkirk Tryst	1983 Haggs Castle	
1947 Western Gailes	1966 Bathgate	1984 Royal Musselburgh	
1948 Melville College FP	1967 Prestonfield	1985 East Renfrewshire	

2003 *at Drumpelier*

Final: Whitecraigs (Keith Hamilton and Chris Rossi) beat Drumpelier (Alan Ferguson and Guy Shanks)
1 hole

Scottish Clubs Handicap Championship

2001   Dunbar   2002   Newmachar

2003 *at Cardrona, Peebleshire*

1	Galashiels	
	(Bruce Currie and Keith Donaldson)	64 points
2	Wishaw	65 points
3	Cruden Bay	67 points

Welsh Inter-Counties Championship

2003 *at Aberdovey*

1	Gwent	695
2	Denbigh	709
3	Dyfed	714

Best individual: Craig Smith (Gwent)   66-64—130

Winning team: Leon Clark, Chris Cole, Brian Lee, Phil Rees, Mark Skinner, Craig Smith

Welsh Team Championship

2003 *at Newport*

Semi-Finals:
Newport beat St Mellons 4-1
Pontnewydd beat Tredegar Park 3½-1½

Final
Pontnewydd beat Newport 3-2

Winning team: T Hayward, L Clark, S Cameron, L Hayward, M Skinner

Principal 72 hole Tournaments

Including the National District Championships

Aberconwy Trophy (Inaugurated 1976) at Conwy/Llandudno (Maesdu), Gwynedd

1976	JR Jones	1985	MA Macara	1994	G Marsden
1977	EN Davies	1986	JR Berry	1995	S Andrew
1978	MG Mouland	1987	M Sheppard	1996	R Williams
1979	JM Morrow	1988	MG Hughes	1997	I Campbell
1980	JM Morrow	1989	JN Lee	1998	J Donaldson
1981	D Evans	1990	S Wilkinson	1999	J Donaldson
1982	G Tuttle	1991	S Wilkinson	2000	J Donaldson
1983	GH Brown	1992	MJ Ellis	2001	L Harpin*
1984	D McLean	1993	S Wilkinson	2002	R Scott

2003

1	Richard Scott (Haverfordwest)	75-71-72-72—290
2	James Huw Williams (Pontypridd)	71-72-71-79—293
3	Neil Oakley (St Mellons)	73-77-72-78—300
	Gareth Dobson-Jones (Porthmadoc)	72-74-77-77—300

Berkshire Trophy (Inaugurated 1946) at The Berkshire

1946	R Sweeney	148	1965	MF Bonallack	278	1985	P McEvoy	279
1947	PB Lucas	298	1966	P Oosterhuis	287	1986	R Muscroft	280
1948	LG Crawley	301	1967	DJ Millensted	283	1987	J Robinson	275
1949	PB Lucas	300	1968	MF Bonallack	273	1988	R Claydon	276
1950	PF Scrutton	296	1969	JC Davies	278	1989	J Metcalfe	272
1951	PF Scrutton	301	1970	MF Bonallack	274	1990	J O'Shea	271
1952	PF Scrutton	286	1971T	MF Bonallack	277	1991	J Bickerton	280
1953	JL Morgan	289		J Davies		1992	V Phillips	274
1954T	Ft Lt K Hall	303	1972	DP Davidson	280	1993	V Phillips	271
	E Bromley-Davenport		1973	PJ Hedges	278	1994T	J Knight	274
1955	GH Micklem	282	1974	J Downie	280		A Marshall	
1956	GB Wolstenholme	285	1975	N Faldo	281	1995	G Harris	275
1957	MF Bonallack	291	1976	PJ Hedges	284	1996	GP Wolstenholme	274
1958T	GB Wolstenholme	284	1977	A Lyle	279	1997	GP Wolstenholme	275
	AH Perowne		1978	PJ Hedges	281	1998	M Hilton	284
1959	JB Carr	279	1979	D Williams	274	1999	D Henley	275
1960	GB Wolstenholme	276	1980	P Downes	280	2000	C Edwards	281
1961	MF Bonallack	275	1981	D Blakeman	280	2001	G Evans	283
1962	SC Saddler	279	1982	SD Keppler	278	2002	G Wolstenholme	267
1963	DW Frame	289	1983	S Hamer	288			
1964	R Foster	281	1984	JL Plaxton	276			

2003

1	Ross Fisher (Wentworth)	68-68-71-68—275
	Adam Blyth (Aus)	68-70-67-70—275
3	Ross McGowan (Banstead Downs)	68-70-68-71—277

Cameron Corbett Vase (Inaugurated 1897) at Haggs Castle, Glasgow

1897	AF Duncan	1933	W Tulloch	1970T	J McTear	
1898	AF Duncan	1934	JM Dykes		D Hayes	
1899	W Laidlaw	1935	H Thomson	1971	G Macgregor	
1900	GH Hutcheson	1936	J Gray	1972	HB Stuart	
1901	G Fox jr	1937	TI Craig jr	1973	MJ Miller	
1902	AF Duncan	1938	JS Logan	1974	M Rae	
1903	G Fox jr	1939	A Steel	1975	D Barclay Howard	
1904	R Bone	1940–41	No competition	1976	GH Murray	
1905	R Bone	1942	AC Taylor	1977	MJ Miller	
1906	W Gemmill	1943–45	No competition	1978	GH Murray	
1907	G Wilkie	1946	JS Montgomerie	1979	KW Macintosh	
1908	AF Duncan	1947	W Maclaren	1980	IA Carslaw	
1909	EB Tipping	1948	J Pressley	1981	GH Murray	
1910	JH Irons	1949	GB Peters	1982	GH Murray	
1911	G Morris	1950	J Gray	1983	AS Oldcorn	
1912	R Scott jr	1951	GB Peters	1984	D Barclay Howard	
1913	R Scott jr	1952	J Stewart Thomson	1985	J McDonald	
1914	D Martin	1953	J Orr	1986	JW Milligan	
1915–18	Not played due to First	1954	JR Cater	1987	J Semple	
	World War	1955	RC Macgregor	1988	C Everett	
1919	HR Orr	1956	RC Macgregor	1989	AG Tait	
1920	DJ Murray Campbell	1957	I Rennie	1990	D Robertson	290
1921	HM Dickson	1958	DH Reid	1991	K Gallacher	285
1922	WS Macfarlane	1959	AS Kerr	1992	D Kirkpatrick	284
1923	JO Stevenson	1960	J Mackenzie	1993	R Russell	278
1924	JO Stevenson	1961	GB Cosh	1994	J Hodson	280
1925	A Jamieson jr	1962	JH Richmond	1995	D Barclay Howard	268
1926	G Chapple	1963	JA Davidson	1996	C Watson	282
1927	RS Rodger	1964	IA MacCaskill	1997	C Watson	268
1928	SL McKinlay	1965	H Frazer	1998	E Wilson	140 (36)
1929	D McBride	1966	D Black	1999	W Bryson	278
1930	HM Dickson	1967	JRW Walkinshaw	2000	P McKechnie	277
1931	HM Dickson	1968	CW Green	2001	P Gault	291
1932	W Stringer	1969	A Brooks	2002	B Hume*	275

2003

1	James McLeary (Leven GS)	71-65-72-68—276
2	Neil MacRae (Cawder)	70-69-70-70—279
	Neil Mitchell (Murcar)	70-69-70-70—279
	David Roger (Windyhill)	73-68-68-70—279

Clwyd Open (Inaugurated 1991) at Prestatyn/Wrexham

1991	G Houston	1995	M Ellis	1999	L Harpin
1992	C O'Carrol	1996	M Ellis	2000	K Sullivan
1993	M Ellis	1997	D Park	2001	A Campbell
1994	G Houston	1998	R Donovan	2002	G Wright

2003

1	Tim Dykes (Wrexham)	66-70-74-72—282
2	Gareth Wright (West Linton)	68-71-75-73—287
3	David Price (Vale of Glamorgan)	69-73-71-75—288

Craigmillar Park Open (Inaugurated 1961) at Craigmillar Park, Edinburgh

1961	RDBM Shade	1968	RDBM Shade	1975	IC Hutcheon
1962	A Sinclair	1969	GB Cosh	1976	NA Faldo
1963	HM Campbell	1970	PJ Smith	1977	CW Green
1964	RDBM Shade	1971	CW Green	1978	DM McCart
1965	GB Cosh	1972	CW Green	1979	IC Hutcheon
1966	RDBM Shade	1973	DF Campbell	1980	JB Dunlop
1967	RDBM Shade	1974	GH Murray	1981	GK MacDonald

1982	AS Oldcorn	1989	RM Roper	1996	GW Tough
1983	G Macgregor	1990	SJ Bannerman	1997	CD Hislop
1984	G Macgregor	1991	N Walton	1998	G Rankin
1985	C Bloice	1992	SJ Knowles	1999	S Mackenzie
1986	SR Easingwood	1993	R Russell	2000	M Warren
1987	RM Roper	1994	BW Collier	2001	S O'Hara
1988	B Shields	1995	C Watson	2002	M Warren

2003

1	Graham Gordon (Newmachar)	66-69-72-64—271
2	Jonathan King (Cardross)	68-69-68-69—274
	Jamie McLeary (Leven GS)	70-66-71-67—274

Duncan Putter (Inaugurated 1959) at Southerndown, Bridgend, Glamorgan

1959	G Huddy	301	1974	S Cox	302	1988	S Dodd	290
1960	Wl Tucker	289	1975	JG Jermine	295	1989	RN Roderick	280
1961T	G Huddy	295	1976T	Wl Tucker	286	1990	R Willison	311
	WI Tucker			H Stott		1991	R Willison	267
1962	EN Davies	297	1977	H Stott	295	1992	R Dinsdale	213
1963	Wl Tucker	296	1978	P McEvoy	295	1993	M Thomson	289
1964	JL Toye	293	1979	HJ Evans	292	1994	GP Wolstenholme	226
1965	P Townsend	305	1980	P McEvoy	296	1995	B Dredge	293
1966	MF Attenborough	291	1981T	R Chapman	294	1996	GP Wolstenholme	291
1967	D Millensted	297		PG Way		1997	M Pilkington	283
1968	JL Morgan	299	1982	D McLean	283	1998	M King	291
1969	Wl Tucker	304	1983	JG Jermine	297	1999	GP Wolstenholme	216 (54)
1970	JL Toye	305	1984	JP Price	284	2000	J Donaldson	285
1971	W Humphreys	295	1985	P McEvoy	299	2001	N Edwards	140 (36)
1972	P Berry (3 rounds)	230	1986	D Wood	300	2002T	S Manley	286
1973	JKD Povall	299	1987	P McEvoy	278		N Oakley	

2003

1	Stuart Manley (Mountain Ash)	73-74-75-68—290
2	Colm Moriarty (Athlone)	74-75-70-72—291
3	Rhys Davies (Royal Porthcawl)	77-74-75-72—298
	Nigel Edwards (Whitchurch)	77-75-71-75—298

Hampshire Salver (Inaugurated 1979) at North Hants/Blackmoor

1979	P McEvoy	280	1987	A Rogers	286	1995	M Treleaven	275
1980	J Morrow	282	1988	N E Holman	279	1996	J Knight	272
1981	A P Sherborne	211*	1989	P Dougan	286	1997	J P Rose	275
1982	I Gray	293	1990	J Metcalfe	272	1998	S J Dyson	275
1983	D G Lane	281	1991	G Evans	281	1999	B Mason	273
1984	D H Currie	283	1992	S R Cage	276	2000	M Young	207*
1985	A J Clapp	285	1993	D J Hamilton	281	2001	G Wolstenholme	271
1986	D Gilford	287	1994	W Bennett	279	2002	J Moul	277

2003

1	Martin Sell (Wrag Barn)	71-67-69-71—278
2	Ross Fisher (Wentworth)	69-72-66-73—280
3	Jonathan Lupton (Middlesbrough)	72-73-71-69—285

Lagonda Trophy (Inaugurated 1975) at Camberley Heath; from 1990 at Gog Magog

1975	WJ Reid	143	1985	J Robinson	283	1995	P Nelson	274
1976	JC Davies	142	1986	D Gilford	282	1996	S Collingwood	283
1977	WS Gronow	145	1987	DG Lane	290	1997	L Donald	279
1978	JC Davies	135	1988	R Claydon	275	1998	K Ferrie	284
1979	JG Bennett	142	1989	T Spence	280	1999	Z Scotland	284
1980	P McEvoy	139	1990	L Parsons	273	2000	M Young	279
1981	N Mitchell	138	1991	J Cook	277	2001	D Skinns	271
1982	A Sherborne	290	1992	L Westwood	279	2002	G Wolstenholme	275
1983	I Sparkes	216 (54)	1993	L James	279			
1984	MS Davis	289	1994	S Webster	276			

2003

1	Steven Tiley (Royal Cinque Ports)	66-66-67-70—269
2	Lee Yearn (Ely City)	67-69-67-67—270
3	Lloyd Campbell (Rochester & Cobham)	70-65-71-65—271
	Robert Dinwiddie (Barnard Castle)	67-67-70-67—271
	Sam Osborne (Wentworth)	65-66-71-69—271

Standard Life Leven Gold Medal (Inaugurated 1870) at Leven Links, Fife

1870	J Elder	85	1913	W Whyte	73	1964	A Cunningham	68
1871	R Wallace	91	1914	GB Rattray	76	1965	PG Buchanan	71
1872	P Anderson	91	1915–18 *No competition*			*Two rounds played from 1966*		
1873	R Armit	95	1919	G Wilkie	77			
1874	D Campbell	93	1920	JJ Smith	76	1966	GM Rutherford	144
1875	AM Ross	90	1921	GV Donaldson	77	1967	AO Maxwell	140
1876	AM Ross	88	1922	SO Shepperd	72	1968	A Cunningham	140
1877	J Wilkie	88	1923	GV Donaldson	73	*Four rounds played from 1966*		
1878	R Wallace	90	1924	JN Smith	76			
1879	C Anderson	89	1925	A Robertson	73	1969	P Smith	284
1880	C Anderson	89	1926	T Ainslie	75	1970	JC Farmer	277
1881	J Foggo	91	1927	EA McRuvie	72	1971	J Scott Macdonald	207
1882	J Wilkie	89	1928	EA McRuvie	70	1972	J Rankine	282
1883	J Foggo	86	1929	EA McRuvie	72	1973	S Stephen	288
1884	C Anderson	89	1930	EA McRuvie	68	1974	P Smith	282
1885	R Adam	84	1931	A Dunsire	71	1975	HB Stuart	286
1886	R Adam	87	1932	J Ballingall	72	1976	IC Hutcheon	266
1887	J Foggo	81	1933	CA Danks	73	1977	IC Hutcheon	289
1888	DA Leitch	86	1934	EA McRuvie	67	1978	R Wallace	287
1889	R Adam	81	1935	EG Stoddart	71	1979	B Marchbank	274
1890	W Marshall	80	1936	GA Buist	73	1980	J Huggan	279
1891	DM Jackson	80	1937	JY Strachan	75	1981	IC Hutcheon	282
1892	Col DW Mackinnon	85	1938	S Macdonald	71	1982	IC Hutcheon	272
1893	HS Colt	79	1939	D Jamieson	72	1983	J Huggan	274
1894	J Bell jr	82	1940–45 *No competition*			1984	S Stephen	278
1895	C Wllkie jr	80	1946	EA McRuvie	77	1985	AD Turnbull	281
1896	J Bell jr	78	1947	JE Young	74	1986	P-U Johansson	275
1897	J Bell jr	79	1948	J Imrie	77	1987	G Macgregor	271
1898	G Wilkie jr	82	1949	WM Ogg	76	1988	CE Everett	280
1899	G Wilkie jr	78	1950	E McRuvie	77	1989	AJ Coltart	280
1900	W Henderson	78	1951	J Imrie	72	1990	CE Everett	280
1901	R Simpson	76	1952	HVS Thomson	69	1991	GA Lowson	284
1902	J Bell	76	1953	O Rolland	70	1992	D Robertson	279
1903	W Henderson	76	1954	JW Draper	73	1993	L Westwood	276
1904	W Henderson	77	1955	JW Draper	72	1994	B Howard	265
1905	G Wilkie	76	1956	R Dishart	72	1995	S Mackenzie	273
1906	G Wilkie	78	1957	I Pearson	72	1996	M Eliasson	267
1907	M Goodwillie	73	1958	W McIntyre	71	1997	S Carmichael	278
1908	W Henderson	77	1959	W Moyes	71	1998	G Rankin	268
1909	W Henderson	77	1960	T Taylor	69	1999	J Mathers	291
1910	W Whyte	76	1963	W Moyes	68	2000	G Gordon	269
1911	G Wilkie	73	1961	A Cunningham	69	2001	P Whiteford*	271
1912	G Wilkie	73	1962	W Moyes	71	2002	J Doherty	263

2003

1	Jim White (Leven Thistle)	65-66-68-63—262
2	Ronnie Brechin (Murcar)	67-69-67-68—271
	Neil Mitchell (Murcar)	69-67-67-68—271
	George Murray (Earlsferry Thistle)	68-73-64-66—271

Lytham Trophy (Inaugurated 1965) at Royal Lytham & St Annes and Fairhaven

1965T	MF Bonallack	295	1975	G Macgregor	299	1990	G Evans	291
	CA Clark		1976	MJ Kelley	292	1991	G Evans	284
1966	PM Townsend	290	1977	P Deeble	296	1992	S Cage	294
1967	R Foster	296	1978	B Marchbank	288	1993	T McLure	292
1968	R Foster	286	1979	P McEvoy	279	1994	W Bennett	285
1969T	T Craddock	290	1980	IC Hutcheon	293	1995	S Gallacher	281
	SG Birtwell		1981	R Chapman	221	1996	M Carver	284
1970T	JC Farmer	296	1982	MF Sludds	306	1997	G Rankin	279
	CW Green		1983	S McAllister	299	1998	L Kelly	288
	GC Marks		1984	J Hawksworth	289	1999	T Schuster	283
1971	W Humphreys	292	1985	MPD Walls	291	2000	D Dixon	285
1972	MF Bonallack	281	1986	S McKenna	297	2001	R McEvoy	276
1973T	MG King	292	1987	D Wood	293	2002	L Corfield	283
	SG Birtwell	292	1988	P Broadhurst	296			
1974	CW Green	291	1989	N Williamson	286			

2003

1	Stuart Wilson (Forfar)	70-72-73-68—283
2	Paul Bradshaw (Gainsborough)	67-73-74-73—287
3	Colm Moriarty (Athlone)	76-74-70-71—291

St Andrews Links Trophy (Inaugurated 1989) at St Andrews (Old and Jubilee)

1989	R Claydon	284	1994	DB Howard	294	1999	D Patrick	152 (36)
1990	S Bouvier (Aus)	280	1995	G Rankin	276	2000	M King	140
1991	R Willison	289	1996	DB Howard	282	2001	S O'Hara	281
1992	C Watson	281	1997	J Rose	284	2002	S Mackenzie	289
1993	G Hay	280	1998	C Watson	276			

2003

1	Richard Finch (Hull)	71-66-69-70—276
2	Lee Corfield (Burnham & Berrow)	67-72-72-70—281
3	Jack Doherty (Vale of Glamorgan)	69-72-72-71—284

St David's Gold Cross (Inaugurated 1930) at Royal St David's, Gwynedd

1930	GC Stokoe	1951	JL Morgan	1967	MSR Lunt
1931	EW Fiddian	1952	SB Roberts	1968	AW Holmes
1932	Dr W Tweddell	1953	S Lunt	1969	AJ Thomson
1933	IS Thomas	1954	GB Turner	1970	AJ Thomson
1934	SB Roberts	1955	JL Morgan	1971	A Smith
1935	IS Thomas	1956	W Cdr CH Beamish	1972	EN Davies
1936	RMW Pritchard	1957	CD Lawrie	1973	RD James
1937	IS Thomas	1958	GB Turner	1974	GC Marks
1938	SB Roberts	1959	MSR Lunt	1975	CP Hodgkinson
1939	IS Thomas	1960	LJ Ranells	1976	JR Jones
1940–45	No competition	1961	MSR Lunt	1977	JA Fagan
1946	SB Roberts	1962	PD Kelley	1978	S Wild
1947	G Mills	1963	JKD Povall	1979	MA Smith
1948	CH Eaves	1964	MSR Lunt	1980	CP Hodgkinson
1949	SB Roberts	1965	MSR Lunt	1981	G Broadbent
1950	DMG Sutherland	1966	MSR Lunt	1982	MW Calvert

St David's Gold Cross continued

1983	RD James	1990	MA Macara	1997	M Pilkington
1984	RJ Green	1991	RJ Dinsdale	1998	L Harpin
1985	KH Williams	1992	B Dredge	1999	D Jones
1986	RN Roderick	1993	B Dredge	2000	D Price
1987	SR Andrew	1994	C Evans	2001	C Williams
1988	MW Calvert	1995	M Skinner	2002	A Smith
1989	AJ Barnett	1996	L Harpin		

2003

1	Stuart Manley (Mountain Ash)	65-68-70-70—273
2	Rhys Davies (Royal Porthcawl)	68-68-75-71—282
	Nigel Edwards (Whitchurch)	75-70-71-66—282

Sherry Cup

1990	Alvaro Prat	1995	José Maria Zamora	2000	G Wolstenholme
1991	Padraig Harrington	1996	Alvaro Salto	2001	G Wolstenholme*
1992	Frederic Cupillard	1997	Sergio García	2002	L Harpin
1993	Francisco Valera	1998	Sergio García		
1994	Francisco Cea	1999	Marcel Siem		

2003 at Sotogrande, Spain

1	Gary Wolstenholme (Eng)	70-72-69-67—278
2	Pablo Martin Benavides (Esp)	67-66-68-78—279
3	Zane Scotland (Eng)	69-69-70-72—280

Sutherland Chalice (Inaugurated 2000)

2000	G Gordon	275	2001	S Carmichael	274	2002	G Gordon	264

2003 at Dumfries & Galloway

1	David Sutton (Lockerbie)	68-68-69-70—275
2	Chris Heslip (Monifieth)	66-69-74-67—276
	Glenn Campbell (Blairgowrie)	67-71-68-70—276

Tennant Cup (Inaugurated 1880) at Glasgow GC

1880	AW Smith	1903	CB Macfarlane	1930	JE Dawson
1881	AW Smith	1904	WS Colville	1931	GNS Tweedale
1882	AM Ross	1905	TW Robb	1932	SL McInlay
1883	J Kirk	1906	JG Macfarlane	1933	H Thomson
1884	W Doleman	1907	R Andrew	1934	K Lindsay jr
1885	TR Lamb	1908	R Carson	1935	JM Dykes jr
1886	D Bone	1909	WS Colville	1936	JNW Dall
1887	JR Motion	1910	R Andrew	1937	WS McCleod
1888	D Bone	1911	WS Colville	1938	A Jamieson jr
1889	W Milne	1912	R Scott jr	1939	GB Peters
1890	W Marshall	1913	SO Shepherd	1940–45	No competition
1891	D Bone	1914	John Caven	1946	JB Stevenson
1892	D Bone	1915–19	No competition	1947	JC Wilson
1893	W Doleman	1920	G Lockhart	1948	J Wallace
1894	W Doleman	1921	R Scott jr	1949	W Irvine
1895	JA Shaw	1922	WD Macleod	1950	JW Mill
1896	J Thomson	1923	FW Baldie	1951	WS McCleod
1897	D Bone	1924	J Barrie Cooper	1952	GT Black
1898	R Bone	1925	R Scott jr	1953	AD Gray
1899	W Hunter	1926	W Tulloch	1954	H McInally
1900	JG Macfarlane	1927	W Tulloch	1955	LG Taylor
1901	R Bone	1928	A Jamieson jr	1956	JM Dykes
1902	CB Macfarlane	1929	R Scott jr	1957	LG Taylor

1958	Dr FWG Deighton	1973	PJ Smith	1988	C Dalgleish
1959	JF Milligan	1974	D McCart	1989	DG Carrick
1960	Dr FWG Deighton	1975	CW Green	1990	C Everett
1961	R Reid Jack	1976	IC Hutcheon	1991	C Everett
1962	WS Jack	1977	S Martin	1992	D Robertson
1963	SWT Murray	1978	IA Carslaw	1993	D Robertson
1964	Dr FWG Deighton	1979	G Hay	1994	G Rankin
1965	J Scott Cochran	1980	Allan Brodie	1995	S Gallacher
1966	AH Hall	1981	G MacDonald	1996	G Rankin
1967	BJ Gallacher	1982	LS Mann	1997	C Hislop
1968	CW Green	1983	C Dalgleish	1998	G Rankin
1969	J Scott Cochran	1984	E Wilson	1999	G Fox
1970	CW Green	1985	CJ Brooks	2000	G Fox
1971	Andrew Brodie	1986	PG Girvan	2001	C Watson
1972	Allan Brodie	1987	J Rasmussen	2002	B Hume

2003

1	Graham Gordon (Newmachar)	71-71-65-67—274
2	David Inglis (Glencorse)	70-71-69-66—276
3	Martin Laird (Hilton Park)	73-71-66-67—277

Tillman Trophy (Inaugurated 1989)

1989	J Cook	1994	*Not played*	1999	J Conteh
1990	M Wiggett	1995	P Stuart	2000	B Welch
1991	A Tillman	1996	S Wakefield	2001	R Fisher
1992	D Probert	1997	M Searle	2002	A Gee
1993	C Nowicki	1998	R Blaxhill		

2003 *at Moortown*

1	James Smith (Sundridge Park)	75-64-72-71—282
2	Ben Harvey (Ferndown)	70-72-70-71—283
3	Adam Gee (Leatherhead)	73-68-72-73—286

Trubshaw Cup (Inaugurated 1989) *at Ashburnham and Tenby*

1989	MA Macara	1996	M Ellis	1999	N Matthews
1990	TSM Wilkinson	1994	C Evans	2000	N Edwards
1991	S Pardoe	1995	B Dredge	2001	N Edwards
1992	B Dredge	1997	M Pilkington	2002	J Doherty
1993	B Dredge	1998	M Pilkington		

2003

1	Nigel Edwards (Whitchurch)	70-70-68-69—277
2	Gareth Wright (West Linton)	72-73-69-70—284
3	Richard Scott (Haverfordwest)	73-73-71-69—286

Tucker Trophy (Inaugurated 1991)

1991	C Evans (W. Monmouthshire)	1995	M Ellis (Wrexham)	1999	J Donaldson (Macclesfield)
1992	R Dinsdale (Newport)	1996	M Searle (High Post)	2000	I Campbell (Marlborough)
1993	B Dredge (Bryn Meadows)	1997	J Donaldson (Macclesfield)	2001	NB Edwards (Whitchurch)
1994	D Park (Burghill)	1998	NB Edwards (Whitchurch)	2002	NB Edwards (Whitchurch)

2003 *at Newport/Whitchurch*

1	Nigel Edwards (Whitchurch)	72-64-69-68—273
2	Alex Smith (Pyle & Kenfig)	69-68-67-74—278
3	Cennydd Mills (Vale of Glamorgan)	70-71-72-69—282

National District Championships

Midland Open (Inaugurated 1976)

1976	P Downes	1983	CA Banks	1990	J Bickerton	1997	P Streeter
1977	P Downes	1984	K Valentine	1991	P Sefton	1998	L Donald
1978	P McEvoy	1985	MC Hassall	1992	M McGuire	1999	G Davies
1979	M Tomlinson	1986	G Wolstenholme	1993	N Williamson	2000	D Dixon
1980	P Downes	1987	C Suneson	1994	D Howell	2001	M Lock
1981	P Baxter	1988	R Winchester	1995	G Harris	2002	G Wolstenholme
1982	NJ Chesses	1989	J Cook	1996	M Carver		

2003 at Woodhall Spa

1	John Kemp (John O'Gaunt)	71-70-68-69—278
2	Adam Gee (Leatherhead)	71-72-71-67—281
3	Tom Lawson (Ellesborough)	72-71-73-68—284

West of England Open Match Play (Inaugurated 1912)

at Burnham & Berrow

1912	RA Riddell	1937	O Austreng	1964	DC Allen	1986	J Bennett
1913	Hon M Scott	1938	HJ Roberts	1965	DE Jones	1987	D Rosier
1914–18	No competition	1939–45	No competition	1966	A Forrester	1988	N Holman
1919	Hon M Scott	1946	JH Neal	1967	A Forrester	1989	N Holman
1920	Hon D Scott	1947	WF Wise	1968	SR Warrin	1990	I West
1921	CVL Hooman	1948	WF Wise	1969	SR Warrin	1991	S Amor
1922	Hon M Scott	1949	J Payne	1970	C Ball	1992	K Baker
1923	D Grant	1950	EB Millward	1971	G Irlam	1993	D Haines
1924	D Grant	1951	J Payne	1972	JA Bloxham	1994	A Emery
1925	D Grant	1952	EB Millward	1973	SC Mason	1995	A March
1926	K Whetstone	1953	F Griffin	1974	CS Mitchell	1996	M Carver
1927	GC Brooks	1954	EB Millward	1975	MR Lovett	1997	SJ Martin
1928	JA Pierson	1955	SJ Fox	1976	No competition	1998	D Dixon
1929	DE Landale	1956	SJ Fox	1977	AR Dunlop	1999	D Dixon
1930	RH de	1957	D Gardner	1978	R Broad	2000	J Morgan
	Montmorency	1958	AJN Young	1979	N Burch	2001	L Corfield
1931	DR Howard	1959	DM Woolmer	1980	JM Durbin	2002	J Donaldson
1932	R Straker	1960	AW Holmes	1981	M Mouland		
1933	DM Anderson	1961	JM Leach	1982	M Higgins		
1934	Hon M Scott	1962	Sq Ldr WE	1983	C Peacock		
1935	JJF Pennink		McCrea	1984	GB Hickman		
1936	PH White	1963	KT Warren	1985	AC Nash		

2003

Quarter-Finals

Lee Corfield (Burnham & Berrow) beat Alistair Pilcher (Exeter) 6 and 4
Martin Sell (Wrag Barn) beat Justin Lane (Burnham & Berrow) 4 and 3
Ed Butler (Lansdown) beat Robert Perret (Clevedon) 3 and 2
Neil Povall (Tredegar Park) beat Rich Ackland (St Mellion) 1 hole

Semi-Finals

Corfield beat Sell at 20th
Butler beat Povall 3 and 2

Final

E Butler beat LWW Corfield at 37th

West of England Open Stroke Play (Inaugurated 1968)

1968	PJ Yeo	Saunton	297	1986	P Baker	R North Devon	282
1969	A Forrester	Saunton	304	*Won at second extra hole after play-off with P McEvoy*			
1970	PJ Yeo	R North Devon	312	1987	G Wolstenholme	Saunton	296
1971	P Berry	Saunton	303	1988	MC Evans	R North Devon	291
1972	P Berry	R North Devon	310	1989	AD Hare	Saunton	289
1973	SC Mason	Saunton	287	1990	J Payne	Saunton	290
1974	R Abbott	R North Devon	301	1991	D Lee	Saunton	286
1975	BG Steer	Saunton	290	1992	M Stanford	R North Devon	291
1976	R Abbott	R North Devon	304	1993	PR Trew	Saunton	279
1977	PE McEvoy	Saunton	298	1994	CP Nowicki	R North Devon	294
1978	JG Bennett	R North Devon	291	1995	G Clark	Saunton	141 (36)
After play-off with PE McEvoy				1996	R Wiggins	Saunton	288
1979	R Kane	Saunton	296	1997	M Reynard	R North Devon	280
1980	PE McEvoy	R North Devon	288	1998	C Edwards	R North Devon	287
1981	N Taee	Saunton	245 (54)	1999	D Griffiths	Saunton	286
1982	MP Higgins	R North Devon	286	2000	S Grewal	R North Devon	279
1983	PE McEvoy	Saunton	298	2001	R Finch	Saunton	279
1984	A Sherborne	R North Devon	288	2002	D Barnes	Royal North Devon	219
1985	PE McEvoy	Saunton	307				

2003 at Royal North Devon

1	Ed Butler (Lansdown)	74-68-70-70—282
2	Paul Bradshaw (Gainsborough)	71-73-73-70—287
	Colin Edwards (Bath)	71-77-70-69—287
	Martin Sell (Wrag Barn)	76-74-68-69—287

East of Ireland Open

1989	D Clarke	1993	R Burns	1997	S Quinlivan	2001	K Kearney
1990	D O'Sullivan	1994	G McGimpsey	1998	G McGimpsey	2002	N Fox
1991	P Hogan	1995	D Brannigan	1999	K Kearney		
1992	R Burns	1996	N Fox	2000	N Fox*		

2003 at Co Louth

1	Michael Sinclair (Knock)	69-72-72-74—287
2	Andrew McCormick (Scrabo)	70-76-69-76—291
3	Richard Kilpatrick (Banbridge)	73-76-69-75—293

North of Ireland Open

1989	N Anderson	1993	G McGimpsey	1997	M Sinclair	2001	S Paul
1990	D Clarke	1994	N Ludwell	1998	P Gribben	2002	G Maybin
1991	G McGimpsey	1995	F Nolan	1999	P Gribben		
1992	G McGimpsey	1996	M McGinley	2000	M Hoey		

2003 at Royal Portrush

Leading Qualifier: Darren Crowe (Dunmurry) 65-66—131

Quarter-Finals
Brian McElhinney (North West) beat Mark Campbell
(Stackstown) 2 holes
Clancy Bowe (Tramore) beat B Fitzsimons (Downpatrick)
4 and 3
Johnny Foster (Ballyclare) beat Gareth Maybin (Ballyclare)
4 and 2
Barry Trainor (Warrenpoint) beat Richard Kilpatrick
(Banbridge) 2 and 1

Semi-Finals
McElhinney beat Bowe 3 and 2
Foster beat Trainor 8 and 6

Final: Brian McElhinney beat
Johnny Foster 1 hole

South of Ireland Open

1989	S Keenan	1993	P Sheehan	1997	P Collier	2001	J Kehoe
1990	D Clarke	1994	D Higgins	1998	J Foster	2002	C Moriarty
1991	P McGinley	1995	J Fanagan	1999	M Campbell		
1992	L MacNamara	1996	A Morrow	2000	G McDowell		

2003 *at Lahinch*

Quarter-Finals

Colm Moriarty (Athlone) beat Michael O'Kelly (Limerick) 1 hole

Justin Kehoe (Birr) beat David Finn (Mallow) 4 and 3

Mervyn Owens (Mallow) beat Noel Kavanagh (Westport) 6 and 4

Michael McGeady (City of Derry) beat Noel Fox (Portmarnock) at 20th

Semi-Finals

Moriarty beat Kehoe 4 and 2

Owens beat McGeady 4 and 3

Final: Mervyn Owens beat Colm Moriarty 1 hole

West of Ireland Open

1989	P McInerney	1993	G McGimpsey	1997	J Fanagan	2001	M McDermott
1990	N Goulding	1994	P Harrington	1998	N Fox	2002	S Paul
1991	N Goulding	1995	E Brady	1999	M Ilonen (Fin)		
1992	K Kearney	1996	G McGimpsey	2000	E Brady		

2003 *at Co Sligo (Rosses Point)*

Leading Qualifier: Gary Wardlow (Shandon Park) 69-72—141

Quarter-Finals

Brian McElhinney (North West) beat Frank O'Donoghue (Belvoir Park) 5 and 4

Mark Ryan (Grange) beat Trevor Spence (Clandeboye) 3 and 2

Alan Dowling (Hermitage) beat Robert McCarthy (The Island) 4 and 3

Darren Crowe (Dunmurry) beat Desmond Morgan (Mullingar) 4 and 3

Semi-Finals

Ryan beat McElhinney 1 hole

Dowling beat Crowe 1 hole

Final

Mark Ryan beat Alan Dowling 3 and 1

East of Scotland Open Stroke Play

1989	K Hird	1993	S Meiklejohn	1997	S Meiklejohn	2001	J King
1990	G Lawrie	1994	A Reid	1998	B Lamb (Aus)	2002	D Inglis
1991	R Clark	1995	G Davidson	1999	R Beames		
1992	ST Knowles	1996	C Hislop	2000	C Watson		

2003 *at Lundin GC*

1	Jonathan King (Cardross)* *(won after 6 extra holes)*	68-70-68-69—275
2	Brian Innes (Murcar)	67-71-70-67—275
3	Graeme Brown (Royal Montrose)	66-69-69-72—276
	Craig Gordon (Ratho Park)	71-72-70-63—276
	Andrew Laurence (Baberton)	69-68-70-69—276
	Jamie McLeary (Leven GS)	67-66-73-70—276
	James White (Leven Thistle)	65-67-68-76—276

North of Scotland Open Stroke Play

1989	G Hickman	1993	D Downie	1997	G Crawford	2001	G Thomson
1990	S McIntosh	1994	E Forbes	1998	C Taylor	2002	W Booth
1991	S Henderson	1995	R Beames	1999	N Steven*		
1992	K Buchan	1996	C Dunan	2000	C Watson		

2003 *at Royal Dornoch*

1	George Murray (Earlsferry Thistle)	70-77-78-71—296
2	Thomas Gilchrist (Falkirk Tryst)	75-83-70-72—300
3	Glenn Campbell (Blairgowrie)	76-76-79-70—301
	Steven McIntosh (Torvean)	76-73-77-75—301

North-East Scotland District Championship

1999	BA Innes	2000	E Forbes	2001	G Gordon	2002	B Innes

2003 *at Newmachar*

1	Jamie McLeary (Leven GS)	67-68-66-79—280
2	Glenn Campbell (Blairgowrie)	70-78-71-71—290
3	George Murray (Earlsferry Thistle)	75-72-71-73—291

South-East Scotland District Championship

1999	S Carmichael	2000	J King	2001	J Doherty	2002	S Armstrong

2003 *at West Linton*

1	Stuart Wilson (Forfar)	68-64-68-67—267
2	George Murray (Earlsferry Thistle)	72-64-70-68—274
3	Craig Watson (East Renfrewshire)	65-71-71-69—276

West of Scotland Open

1989	A Elliot	1993	B Howard	1997	C Hislop	2001	B Fitzsimmons
1990	S Knowles	1994	J Hodgson	1998	L Kelly	2002	G Gordon
1991	A Coltart	1995	G Rankin	1999	L Kelly		
1992	S Henderson	1996	C Hislop	2000	S O'Hara		

2003 *at Hayston*

1	Graham Gordon (Newmachar)	69-65-71-69—274
2	Glenn Campbell (Blairgowrie)	68-74-67-68—277
	Neil MacRae (Cawder)	69-69-70-69—277
	Richard Ramsay (Royal Aberdeen)	72-67-68-70—277

Other Men's Amateur Tournaments

Berkhamsted Trophy (Inaugurated 1960)

1960	HC Squirrell	150	1975	PG Deeble	147	1990	J Barnes	144
1961	DW Frame	147	1976	JC Davies	144	1991	G Homewood	141
1962	DG Neech	149	1977	AWB Lyle	144	1992	P Page	141
1963	HC Squirrell	149	1978	JC Davies	146	1993	S Burnell	143
1964	PD Flaherty	149	1979	JC Davies	147	1994	M Treleaven	140
1965	LF Millar	153	1980	R Knott	143	1995	J Crampton	142
1966	P Townsend	150	1981	P Dennett	146	1996	L Donald	139
1967	DJ Millensted	150	1982	DG Lane	148	1997	P Streeter	143
1968	PD Flaherty	144	1983	J Hawksworth	146	1998	G Storm	69 (18)
1969	MM Niven	149	1984	R Willison	139	1999	GP Wolstenholme*	140
1970	R Hunter	145	1985	F George	144	2000	J Wormald*	141
1971	A Millar	144	1986	P McEvoy	144	2001	S Godfrey	140
1972	C Cieslewicz	148	1987	F George	141	2002	G Wolstenholme	140
1973	SC Mason	141	1988	J Cowgill	146			
1974	P Fisher	144	1989	J Payne	142			

2003

1	James Knight (Sandford Springs)	70-70—140
2	Jamie Farnworth (Coxmoor)	71-70—141
3	Paul Bradshaw (Gainsborough)	69-73—142

John Cross Bowl (Inaugurated 1957) *at Worplesdon, Surrey*

1957	DW Frame	1973	DW Frame	1989	KG Jones
1958	G Evans	1974	RPF Brown	1990	D Lee
1959	G Evans	1975	BJ Winteridge	1991	P Sefton
1960	DW Frame	1976	DW Frame	1992	R Watts
1961	DW Frame	1977	DW Frame	1993	J Collier
1962	DW Frame	1978	RPF Brown	1994	P Benka
1963	PO Green	1979	JG Bennett	1995	M Galway
1964	RL Glading	1980	JG Bennett	1996	B Barham
1965	P Townsend	1981	ME Johnson	1997	C Banks
1966	P Townsend	1982	R Boxall	1998	J Wormald
1967	MJ Burgess	1983	DG Lane	1999	M Galway
1968	PJ Benka	1984	I Gray	2000	R Mann*
1969	DW Frame	1985	M Devetta	2001	J Bint
1970	P Dawson	1986	C Rotheroe	2002	D Holmes
1971	PBQ Drayson	1987	B White		
1972	AR Kerr	1988	B White		

2003

1	D Curtis (Knole Park)	70-70—140
2	T Hunter (Ilford)	73-68—141
3	L Kennedy (Chelmsford)	70-72—142
	E Richardson (Southern Village)	68-74—142

Frame Trophy (Inaugurated 1986 for players aged 50+) at Worplesdon, Surrey

1988	DW Frame	229	1993	DW Frame	216	1998	DG Lane	211
1989	JRW Walkinshaw	219	1994	DG Lane	222	1999	NH Barnes	220
1990	WJ Williams	224	1995	M Christmas	223	2000	DW Frame	213
1991	DB Sheahan	223	1996	DG Lane	217	2001	DW Frame	217
1992	DW Frame	223	1997	B Turner	226	2002	BK Turner	209

2003

1	BK Turner (Laleham)	73-73-73—219
2	MJ Toole (Brokenhurst Manor)	75-72-73—220
3	RE Pauley (Peterborough Milton)	78-73-70—221
	DG Lane (Goring & Streatley)	70-76-75—221

Golf Illustrated Gold Vase (Inaugurated 1909)

1909	CK Hutchison	1949	RJ White	1975	MF Bonallack
1910	Abe Mitchell	1950	AW Whyte	1976	A Brodie
1911	R Harris	1951	JB Carr	1977	J Davies
1912	R Harris	1952	JDA Langley	1978	P Thomas
1913	Abe Mitchell	1953	JDA Langley	1979	KJ Miller
1914	H Hilton	1954	H Ridgeley	1980	G Brand jr
1919	D Darwin	1955	Major DA Blair	1981	P Garner
1920	DS Crowther	1956	Major DA Blair	1982	I Carslaw
1921	M Seymour	1957	GB Wolstenholme	1983	S Keppler
1922	WA Murray	1958	M Lunt	1984	JV Marks
1923	CJH Tolley	1959	A Bussell	1985	M Davis
1924	CC Aylmer	1960	D Sewell	1986	R Eggo
1925	JB Beck	1961T	DJ Harrison/MF Bonallack	1987	D Lane
1926T	CJH Tolley/TA Torrance	1962	BHG Chapman	1988	M Turner
1927	RH Wethered	1963	RH Mummery	1989	GP Wolstenholme
1928	CJH Tolley	1964	D Moffat	1990	A Rogers
1929	D Grant	1965	C Clark	1991	R Scott
1930	RT Jones (US)	1966	PM Townsend	1992	P Page
1931	WA Murray	1967T	MF Bonallack/	1993T	C Challen/V Phillips
1932	RW Hartley		RA Durrant	1994	S Burnell
1933	RW Hartley	1968	MF Bonallack	1995	A Wall
1934	WL Hartley	1969T	MF Bonallack/J Hayes	1996	Not played
1935	J Thomas	1970	D Harrison	1997	M James
1936	J Ferrier	1971	MF Bonallack	1998	R Rea*
1937	R Sweeney	1972T	H Ashby/DP Davidson/	1999	M Side
1938	CJ Anderson		R Hunter	2000	J Kemp
1939	SB Robert	1973	J Davies	2001	J Heath
1948	RD Chapman	1974	P Hedges	2002	A Inglis

2003 at Cardrona

1	Roger Roper (Catterick)	71-71—142
2	Farren Keenan (Royal Mid-Surrey)	72-72—144
3	Neil Herron (Bird Hill)	79-69—148

Hampshire Hog (Inaugurated 1957) at Northants

1957	MF Bonallack	1971	DW Frame	1985	A Clapp
1958	PF Scrutton	1972	R Revell	1986	R Eggo
1959	Col AA Duncan	1973	SC Mason	1987	A Rogers
1960	MF Attenborough	1974	TJ Giles	1988	S Richardson
1961	HC Squirrell	1975	HAN Stott	1989	P McEvoy
1962	FD Physick	1976	MC Hughesdon	1990	J Metcalfe
1963	Sqn Ldr WE McCrea	1977	AWB Lyle	1991	M Welch
1964	DF Wilkie	1978	GF Godwin	1992	S Graham
1965	T Koch de Gooreynd	1979	MF Bonallack	1993	D Hamilton
1966	Major DA Blair	1980	RA Durrant	1994	B Ingleby
1967	Major DA Blair	1981	G Brand jr	1995	J Rose
1968	MJ Burgess	1982	A Sherborne	1996	R Tate
1969	B Critchley	1983	I Gray	1997	GP Wolstenholme
1970	Major DA Blair	1984	J Hawksworth	1998	P Rowe

Hampshire Hog *continued*

| 1999 | C Rodgers | | 2001 | J Lupton |
| 2000 | M Booker | | 2002 | G Wolstenholme |

2003

1	Martin Sell (Wrag Barn)	71-67—138
	Eddie Vernon (Burton-on-Trent)	69-69—138
3	Ross Fisher (Wentworth)	66-73—139

King George V Coronation Cup *at Porters Park, Herts.*

1990	C Boal	141	1995	S Jarvis	140	2000	R Chattaway	142
1991	S Hoffman	142	1996	N Swaffield	134	2001	M Payne*	143
1992	R Watts	141	1997	J Knight	136	2002	G Evans	141
1993	D Hamilton	134	1998	M King	65 (18)			
1994	S Webster	146	1999	J Field*	141			

2003

1	L Gauthier (East Berkshire)	66-71—137
2	P Coburn (Sandy Lodge)	71-68—139
3	S Barwick (East Berkshire)	68-71—139

Prince of Wales Challenge Cup (Inaugurated 1928) *at Royal Cinque Ports*

1928	D Grant	142	1959	D Johnstone	149	1982	SG Homewood	145
1929	NR Reeves	153	1960	CG Moore	162	1983	M Davis	141
1930	R Harris	156	1961	RH Bazell	151	1984T	F Wood	146
1931	RW Hartley	149	1962	Dr J Pittar	154		DH Niven	
1932	EN Layton	151	1963	Sq Ldr WE McCrea	155	1985	RJ Tickner	141
1933	JB Nash	148	1964	NA Paul	153.	1986	JM Baldwin	149
1934	R Sweeney	304	1965T	NA Paul	150	1987	S Finch	148
1935	HG Bentley	301		VE Barton		1988	MP Palmer	144
1936	LOM Munn	301	1966	P Townsend	150	1989T	T Lloyd	146
1937	DHR Martin	291	1967	MF Bonallack	141		NA Farrell	
1938	EA Head	291	1968T	NA Paul	144	1990T	G Homewood	
1939–46	*No competition*			GC Marks			BS Ingleby	145
1947	PB Lucas	154	1969	MF Attenborough	152	1991	S Pardoe	152
1948	Capt DA Blair	151	1970	J Butterworth	153	1992	L Westwood	160
1949	C Stowe	142	1971	VE Barton	147	1993	ML Welch	143
1950	I Caldwell	151	1972	PJ Hedges	162	1994	I Hardy	149
1951	I Caldwell	151	1973	PJ Hedges	138	1995	L Ferris	152
1952	I Caldwell	150	1974	PJ Hedges	146	1996	J Maddock	142
1953	JG Blackwell	159	1975	JC Davies	150	1997	J Carter	154
1954	DLW Woon	143	1976	MJ Inglis	162	1998	G Woodman	144
1955T	C Taylor	153	1977	PJ Hedges	154	1999	A Webster (Aus)	147
	GT Duncan		1978	ER Dexter	145	2000	JM Bint	145
1956	PF Scrutton	151	1979	GF Godwin	148	2001	A Webster	140
1957	*No competition*		1980T	GM Dunsire	149	2002	G Homewood	151
1958T	KR Mackenzie	158	1980T	B Nicholson	149			
1958T	BAF Belmore	158	1981	JM Baldwin	146			

2003

1	Steven Tiley (Royal Cinque Ports)	70-72—142
2	Bryan Ingleby (Royal Cinque Ports)	73-71—144
3	Lincoln Bolsover (Sunningdale)	74-71—145
	Nicholas Olsen (Faversham)	70-75—145

Rosebery Challenge Cup (Inaugurated 1933) at Ashridge

1962	PR Johnston	1976	G Stradling	1990	C Tingey
1963	CA Murray	1977	J Ambridge	1991	M Thompson
1964	A Millar	1978	RJ Bevan	1992	R Harris
1965	EJ Wiggs	1979	JB Berney	1993	M Hooper
1966	A Holmes	1980	JA Watts	1994	P Wilkins
1967	A Holmes	1981	RY Mitchell	1995	P Wilkins
1968	A Holmes	1982	DG Lane	1996	J Kemp
1969	A Holmes	1983	N Briggs	1997	L Watcham
1970	PW Bent	1984	DG Lane	1998	S Vinnicombe
1971	AW Holmes	1985	P Wharton	1999	J Kemp
1972	AW Holmes	1986	JE Ambridge	2000	J Kemp
1973	AJ Mason	1987	HA Wilkerson	2001	J Ruebotham
1974	G Stradling	1988	N Leconte	2002	R Leonard
1975	JA Watts	1989	C Slattery		

2003

1	Dean Stockwell (The Bedford)	72-67—139
2	Ben Austin (South Beds)	70-69—139
	James Ruebotham (Welwyn Garden City)	70-69—139
	Robert Leonard (Harpenden Common)	69-70—139
	Simon Butler (South Herts)	68-71—139

St George's Grand Challenge Cup (Inaugurated 1888)
at Royal St George's, Sandwich, Kent

1888	J Ball	180	1927	WL Hartley	153	1968	MF Bonallack	142
1889	J Ball	169	1928	D Grant	146	1969	PJ Benka	150
1890	J Ball	175	1929	TA Torrance	148	1970	PJ Hedges	150
1891	J Ball	174	1930	RW Hartley	148	1971	EJS Garrett	143
1892	FA Fairlie	167	1931	WL Hartley	149	1972	JC Davies	149
1893	HH Hilton	165	1932	HG Bentley	151	1973	JC Davies	141
1894	HH Hilton	167	1933	JB Beck	151	1974	JC Davies	140
1895	E Blackwell	176	1934	AGS Penman	153	1975	JC Davies	147
1896	FG Tait	165	1935	Maj WHH Aitken	158	1976	JC Davies	158
1897	CE Hambro	162	1936	DHR Martin	150	1977	JC Davies	154
1898	FG Tait	163	1937	DHR Martin	144	1978	C Phillips	145
1899	FG Tait	155	1938	JJF Pennink	142	1979	CF Godwin	146
1900	R Maxwell	155	1939	AA McNair	153	1980	J Simmance	150
1901	SH Fry	165	1940–46	No competition		1981	MF Bonallack	151
1902	H Castle	162	1947	PB Lucas	147	1982	SJ Wood	145
1903	CK Hutchison	158	1948	M Gonzalez	144	1983	R Willison	155
1904	J Graham jr	154	1949	PF Scrutton	143	1984	SJ Wood	142
1905	R Harris	154	1950	E Bromley-Davenport	148	1985	SJ Wood	144
1906	S Mure Fergusson	155	1951	PF Scrutton	142	1986	RC Claydon	143
1907	CE Dick	161	1952	GH Micklem	148	1987	MR Coodwin	147
1908	AC Lincoln	157	1953	Major DA Blair	148	1988	T Ryan	143
1909	SH Fry	153	1954	H Berwick (Aus)	141	1989	S Green	149
1910	Capt CK Hutchison	157	1955	PF Scrutton	150	1990	P Sullivan	144
1911	E Martin Smith	148	1956	DAC Marr	148	1991	D Fisher	141
1912	Hon Michael Scott	146	1957	PF Scrutton	148	1992	L Westwood	146
1913	HD Gillies	153	1958	PF Scrutton	144	1993	P Sefton	137
1914	J Graham jr	146	1959	J Nicklaus (USA)	149	1994	M Welch	142
1915–19	No competition		1960	JG Blackwell	152	1995	J Harris	142
1920	R Harris	162	1961	Sq Ldr WE McCrea	143	1996	M Brooks	137
1921	WB Torrance	154	1962	Sq Ldr WE McCrea	145	1997	Abandoned due to rain	
1922	WI Hunter	156	1963	Sq Ldr WE McCrea	150	1998	C Gold*	145
1923	F Ouimet (USA)	153	1964	Major DA Blair	153	1999	M Williamson (Aus)	149
1924	RH Wethered	149	1965	MF Bonallack	144	2000	P Appleyard	151
1925	D Grant	149	1966	P Townsend	148	2001	A Gee	140
1926	Maj CO Hezlet	158	1967	Major DA Blair	154	2002	B St John	145

2003

1	Nicholas Olsen (Faversham)	70-71—141
2	James Heath (Combe Wood)	74-70—144
3	Ian Lewis (Kings Hill)	72-74—146

Selborne Salver (Inaugurated 1976) at Blackmoor

1976	A Miller	1985	SM Bottomley	1994	W Bennett		
1977	CS Mitchell	1986	TE Clarke	1995	S Drummond		
1978	GM Brand	1987	A Clapp	1996	J Knight		
1979	P McEvoy	1988	NE Holman	1997	R Binney		
1980	P McEvoy	1989	M Stamford	1998	M Side		
1981	A Sherborne	1990	J Metcalfe	1999	B Mason		
1982	IA Cray	1991	J Payne	2000	J Franks		
1983	DG Lane	1992	M Treleaven	2001	G Wolstenholme		
1984	D Curry	1993	M Welch	2002	G Clark		

2003

1	Zane Scotland (Walton Heath)	67-71—138
2	Martin Sell (Wrag Barn)	69-71—140
3	Lawrence Dodd (Bury St Edmunds)	67-73—140

World Championships break new ground

The World Amateur Team Championships in 2006 will be played for the first time in South Africa. The venues for the men's Eisenhower Trophy event and for the women's Espirito Santo Trophy competition will be the Spier Country Club and Stellenbosch Golf Club.

The Eisenhower Trophy, which was played for the first time at St Andrews in 1958 when Australia were successful, has been staged in America (twice), Japan, Italy, Mexico, Australia, Spain, Argentina, the Dominican Republic, Portugal, Fiji, Switzerland, Hong Kong, Venezuela, Sweden, New Zealand, Canada, France, The Philippines, Chile, Germany and Malaysia. The Espirito Santo event began in 1964 in France. The 2004 events are scheduled for Puerto Rico.

America have won the men's event 12 of the 24 tournaments, Great Britain and Ireland have been successful on four occasions, Australia three times and other winners have been Japan, Canada, Sweden and New Zealand.

In the women's competition the Americans have won the event on 13 occasions, Australia, France and Spain have taken the trophy twice and the other winning country was South Korea in 1996.

Foursomes Events

The Antlers (Inaugurated 1933) at Royal Mid-Surrey

1933	TFB Law and PWL Risdon	147	1970	JB Carr and R Carr	142
1934	GA Hill and HS Malik	153	1971	I Mosey and I Gradwell	144
1935	EF Storey and Sir WS Worthington Evans	152	1972	MJ Kelley and W Smith	144
1936	HG Bentley and F Francis	144	1973	DOJ Albutt and P Flaherty	148
1937	LG Crawley and C Stowe	145	1974	BF Critchley and MC Hughesdon	140
1938	RW Hartlev and PWL Risdon	149	1975	JC Davies and PJ Davies	140
1939	LG Crawley and H Thomson	148	1976	JK Tate and P Deeble	144
1940–47	*Not played due to Second World War*		1977	JC Davies and PJ Davies	141
1948	RC Quilter and E Bromley-Davenport	151	1978	R Chapman and R Fish	148
1949	LG Crawley and JC Wilson	143	1979	N Roche and D Williams	143
1950	L Gracey and I Caldwell	151	1980	G Coles and M Johnson	148
1951	LG Crawley and JC Wilson	147	1981	R Boxall and R Chapman	143
1952T	Major DA Blair and GH Micklem	145	1982	IA Carslaw and J Huggan	139
	LG Crawley and JC Wilson		1983	N Fox and G Lashford	147
1953	D Wilson and G Simmons	148	1984	M Palmer and M Belsham	147
1954	JR Thornhill and PF Scrutton	147	1985	S Blight and R Wilkins	143
1955	G Evans and D Sewell	147	1986	M Gerrard and B White	146
1956	GH Micklem and AF Bussell	141	1987	IA Carslaw and J Huggan	141
1957	Major DA Blair and CD Lawrie	138	1988	A Raitt and P Thornley	143
1958	D Sewell and G Evans	143	1989	A Howard and R Hunter	146
1959	HC Squirrell and P Dunn	146	1990	AC Livesey and RG Payne	143
1960	MSR Lunt and JC Behrrell	139	1991	WM Hopkinson and MR Cook	143
1961	HC Squirrell and P Dunn	145	1992	J C Davies and P J Davies	148
1962	AW Holmes and JM Leach	142	1993	M Benka and S Seman	138
1963	RC Pickering and MJ Cooper	146	1994	D Cowap and J Brant	142
1964	MF Bonallack and Dr DM Marsh	145	1995	R Neill and G Evans	141
1965	MSR Lunt and DE Rodway	146	1996	I Tottingham and R Harris	144
1966	PD Kelley and Dr DM Marsh	144	1997	S Kay and R Peacock	143
1967	Play abandoned		1998	G Willman and B Willman	142
1968	H Broadbent and G Birtwell	144	1999	D Lomas and K Staunton*	104
1969T	SR Warrin and JH Cook		2000	M Booker and R Rae	143
	J Povall and K Dabson		2001	M Booker and R Rae	142
	JC Davies and W Humphreys		2002	R Rea and M Booker	138
	RD Watson-Jones and LOM Smith	146			

2003
Not played

Burhill Family Foursomes (Inaugurated 1937) at Burhill, Surrey

1937	Captain JR Stroyan and Miss S Stroyan	1963T	GA Rowan-Robinson and
1938	W Price and Miss E Price		Miss 'Pooh' Rowan Robinson
1939–1946	*No competition*	1964	Mrs P Todhunter and T Todhunter
1947	Mrs GH Brooks and PJ Brooks	1965	Mrs WT Warrin and SR Warrin
1948	W Price and Miss E Price	1966	Mrs WT Warrin and SR Warrin
1949	Mrs EC Pepper and W Pepper	1967	Mrs WT Warrin and SR Warrin
1950	A Forbes Ilsley and Miss J Ilsley	1968	Mrs CHP Trollope and Nigel Trollope
1951	Major E Loxley Land and Miss J Land	1969	Mrs EPP D'A Walton and JF Walton
1952	CHV Elliot and Miss S Elliott	1970	JF Young and Miss EJ Young
1953	JC Hubbard and Miss A Hubbard	1971	PHA Brownrigg and Miss D Brownrigg
1954	JC Hubbard and Miss A Hubbard	1972	Mrs S Grant and NJ Grant
1955	Mrs HP Thornhill and JR Thornhill	1973	MV Blake and Miss B Blake
1956	Mrs HP Thornhill and JR Thornhill	1974	Mrs NR Bailhache and WJ Bailhache
1957	CH Young and Mrs PBK Gracey	1975	Mrs PR Williams and PM Williams
1958	Mrs HM Winckley and JB Winckley	1976	Mrs D Gotla and C Gotla
1959	Jack and Anna van Zwanenberg	1977	Mrs J Maudsley and C Maudsley
1960	Mrs M Kippax and JM Kippax	1978	Mrs H Calderwood and WR Calderwood
1961	Mrs R Sutherland Pilch and J Sutherland Pilch	1979	Dr AG Wells and Miss E Wells
1962	JC Hubbard and Miss Trudi Hubbard	1980	JL Hall and Miss Cynthia Hall

Burhill Family Foursomes *continued*

1981	Mrs J Fox and N Fox		1992	R Stocks and Miss Joanna Stocks
1982	Mrs J Fox and N Fox		1993	Mrs M Bartlett and Jerome Bartlett
1983	Mrs J Rowe and D Rowe		1994	MJ Toole and Miss SJ Toole
1984	Mrs JS Gilbert and AS Gilbert		1995	Mrs G Warner and R Warner
1985	Mrs MM Pollitt and R Pollitt		1996	Mrs AP Croft and MC Croft
1986	Mrs J Maudesley and C Maudesley		1997	Mrs J Clink and T Clink
1987	Mrs A Croft and M Croft		1998	MJ Toole and Miss SJ Toole
1988	Mrs V Hargreaves and R Hargreaves		1999	MJ Toole and Miss SJ Toole
1989	Mrs J Lawson and P Lawson		2000	Mrs V Marchbanks and R Marchbanks
1990	Mrs M Maisey and S Maisey		2001	Mrs C Warren and R Warren
1991	Mrs M Pollitt and R Pollitt		2002	GR and TG Clark

2003

Final

M Hall & R-L Hall (Basingstoke/West Byfleet) beat C Warren & G Warren (Clandon Regis) 1 hole

Sunningdale Foursomes (Inaugurated 1934) *at Sunningdale*

1934	Miss D Fishwick and EN Layton		1972	JC Davies and MG King
1935	Miss J Wethered and JSF Morrison		1973	J Putt and Miss M Everard
1936	Miss J Wethered and JSF Morrison		1974	PJ Butler and CA Clark
1937	AS Anderson and Dai Rees		1975	*Cancelled due to snow*
1938	Miss P Barton and Alf Padgham		1976	CA Clark and M Hughesdon
1939	C Rissik and EWH Kenyon		1977	GN Hunt and D Matthew
1940-47	*Not played due to Second World War*		1978	GA Caygill and Miss J Greenhalgh
1948	Miss Wanda Morgan and Sam King		1979	G Will and R Chapman
1949	RG French and SS Field		1980	NC Coles and D McClelland
1950	M Faulkner and J Knipe		1981	A Lyddon and G Brand jr
1951	Miss J Donald and TB Haliburton		1982	Miss MA McKenna and Miss M Madill
1952	PF Scrutton and Alan Waters		1983	J Davies and M Devetta
1953	Miss J Donald and TB Haliburton		1984	Miss M McKenna and Miss M Madill
1954	PF Scrutton and Alan Waters		1985	J O'Leary and S Torrance
1955	W Sharp and SS Scott		1986	R Rafferty and R Chapman
1956	G Knipe and DC Smalldon		1987	I Mosey and W Humphreys
1957	BGC Huggett and R Whitehead		1988	SC Mason and A Chandler
1958	Miss J Donald and Peter Alliss		1989	AD Hare and R Claydon
1959	MF Bonallack and D Sewell		1990	Miss D Reid and Miss C Dibnah
1960	Miss B McCorkindale and MJ Moir		1991	J Robinson and W Henry
1961	Mrs J Anderson and Peter Alliss		1992	R Boxall and D Cooper
1962	ER Whitehead and NC Coles		1993	A Beal and L James
1963	L Platts and D Snell		1994	S Webster and A Wall
1964	B Critchley and R Hunter		1995	D Cooper and R Boxall
1965	Mrs AD Spearman and T Fisher		1996	L Donald and M O'Connor
1966	RRW Davenport and A Walker		1997	Mrs J Hall and Miss H Wadsworth
1967	NC Coles and K Warren		1998	D Fisher and W Bennett
1968	JC Davies and W Humphreys		1999	Miss L Walters and R McEvoy
1969	P Oosterhuis and PJ Benka		2000	Mrs C Caldwell and R Caldwell
1970	R Barrell and Miss A Willard		2001	Miss C Lipscombe and S Little
1971	A Bird and H Flatman		2002	J Kemp and M Wharton

2003

Quarter Finals

Glenn Ralph (Camberley Heath) & Tim Spence (Battle) beat Ben St John & Zane Scotland (Woodcote Park) at 19th

Pip Elson (Henley in Arden) & Jamie Elson (Kenilworth) beat Kate Phillips (Creigiau) & Anna Highgate (Cottrell Park) 5 and 4

John Le Roux (Worldham Park) & James Ablett (Alresford) beat P Bagshaw (Ramsdale Park) & C Swinburn (Notts) 3 and 2

Ross Fisher & Simon Griffiths (Wentworth) beat Carole & Richard Caldwell (Sunningdale) 1 hole

Semi-Finals

Elson & Elson beat Ralph & Spence 3 and 2

Fisher & Griffiths beat Le Roux & Ablett at 19th

Final

Ross Fisher & Simon Griffiths beat Pip Elson & Jamie Elson 4 and 3

Fathers and Sons Foursomes *at West Hill, Surrey*

1991	DM and WK Laing	1995	J and D Niven	1999	R and K Boxall
1992	JA and R Piggott	1996	MJ and J Hickey	2000	G and M Steele
1993	B and R Groce	1997	DR and M Baxter	2001	J and D Niven
1994	RJ and P Hill	1998	SF and P Brown	2002	GR and TG Clark

2003

Final

R & T Stocks (St George's Hill) beat G & M Steel (Moor Park) 4 and 3

Worplesdon Mixed Foursomes (Inaugurated 1921) *at Worplesdon, Surrey*

1921	Miss Helme and TA Torrance	1965	Mrs G Valentine and JE Behrend
1922	Miss Joyce Wethered and R Wethered	1966	Mrs C Barclay and DJ Miller
1923	Miss Joyce Wethered and CJ Tolley	1967	JF Gancedo and Mlle C Lacoste
1924	Miss SR Fowler and EN Layton	1968	JD van Heel and Miss Dinah Oxley
1925	Miss Cecil Leitch and E Esmond	1969	Mrs R Ferguson and Alistair Wilson
1926	Mlle de la Chaume and R Wethered	1970	Miss R Roberts and RL Glading
1927	Miss Joyce Wethered and CJH Tolley	1971	Mrs D Frearson and A Smith
1928	Miss Joyce Wethered and JSF Morrison	1972	Miss B Le Garreres and CA Strang
1929	Miss M Gourlay and Maj CO Hezlet	1973	Miss T Perkins and RJ Evans
1930	Miss M Gourlay and Maj CO Hezlet	1974	Mrs S Birley and RL Glading
1931	Miss J Wethered and Hon M Scott	1975	Mr and Mrs JR Thornhill
1932	Miss J Wethered and RH Oppenheimer	1976	Mrs B Lewis and J Caplan
1933	Miss J Wethered and B Darwin beat	1977	Mrs D Henson and J Caplan
1934	Miss M Gourlay and TA Torrance	1978	Miss T Perkins and R Thomas
1935,	Miss G and J Craddock-Hartopp	1979	Miss J Melville and A Melville
1936	Miss J Wethered and Hon T Coke	1980	Mrs L Bayman and I Boyd
1937	Mrs Heppel and LG Crawley	1981	Mrs J Nicholsen and MN Stern
1938	Mrs MR Garon and EF Storey	1982	Miss B New and K Dobson
1939–45	*Not played due to Second World War*	1983	Miss B New and K Dobson
1946	Miss J Gordon and AA Duncan	1984	Mrs L Bayman and MC Hughesdon
1947	Miss J Gordon and AA Duncan	1985	Mrs H Kaye and D Longmuir
1948	Miss W Morgan and EF Storey	1986	Miss P Johnson and RN Roderick
1949	Miss F Stephens and LG Crawley	1987	Miss J Nicholson and B White
1950	Miss F Stephens and LG Crawley	1988	Mme A Larrezac and JJ Caplan
1951	Mrs AC Barclay and G Evans	1989	Miss J Kershaw and M Kershaw
1952	Mrs RT Peel and GW Mackie	1990	Miss S Keogh and A Rodgers
1953	Miss J Gordon and G Knipe	1991	J Rhodes and C Banks
1954	Miss F Stephens and WA Slark	1992	D Henson and B Turner
1955	Miss P Garvey and PF Scrutton	1993	A Macdonald and S Skeldon
1956	Mrs L Abrahams and Maj WD Henderson	1994	Mr and Mrs K Quinn
1957	Mrs B Singleton and WD Smith	1995	Mrs C Caldwell and P Carr
1958	Mr and Mrs M Bonallack	1996	Miss L Walters and M Naylor
1959	Miss J Robertson and I Wright	1997	Miss K Burton and G Wolstenholme
1960	Miss B Jackson and MJ Burgess	1998	Miss K Burton and J Smith
1961	Mrs R Smith and B Critchley	1999	Miss AM Boatman and RG Hodgkinson
1962	Viscomtesse de Saint Sauveur and DW Frame	2000	Mr and Mrs Galway
1963	Mrs G Valentine and JE Behrend	2001	Miss K Fisher and J Harper
1964	Mrs G Valentine and JE Behrend	2002	C Court and J Donaldson

2003

Semi-Finals

Andrea Downer (Bramley) and Lee Boxall (West Surrey) beat Marie Allan (Moor Park) and John Maguire (Turnhouse) at 20th

Tara Walters and James Duane (Muswell Hill) beat Samatha Lovell (Stock Brook Manor) and Marcus Stam (Royal Liverpool) 1 hole

Final

Andrea Downer and Lee Boxal beat Tara Walters and James Duane 5 and 4

University and School Events

Halford-Hewitt Cup (Inaugurated 1924) at Deal

1924	Eton	1955	Eton	1980	Shrewsbury
1925	Eton	1956	Eton	1981	George Watson's
1926	Eton	1957	George Watson's	1982	Charterhouse
1927	Harrow	1958	Harrow	1983	Charterhouse
1928	Eton	1959	Wellington	1984	Charterhouse
1929	Harrow	1960	Rossall	1985	Harrow
1930	Charterhouse	1961	Rossall	1986	Repton
1931	Harrow	1962	Oundle	1987	Merchiston
1932	Charterhouse	1963	Repton	1988	Stowe
1933	Rugby	1964	Fettes	1989	Eton
1934	Charterhouse	1965	Rugby	1990	Tonbridge
1935	Charterhouse	1966	Charterhouse	1991	Shrewsbury
1936	Charterhouse	1967	Eton	1992	Tonbridge
1937	Charterhouse	1968	Eton	1993	Shrewsbury
1938	Marlborough	1969	Eton	1994	Tonbridge
1939	Charterhouse	1970	Merchiston	1995	Harrow
1940–46	No competition	1971	Charterhouse	1996	Radley
1947	Harrow	1972	Marlborough	1997	Oundle
1948	Winchester	1973	Rossall	1998	Charterhouse
1949	Charterhouse	1974	Charterhouse	1999	George Watson's
1950	Rugby	1975	Harrow	2000	Epsom
1951	Rugby	1976	Merchiston	2001	Tonbridge
1952	Harrow	1977	George Watson's	2002	Charterhouse
1953	Harrow	1978	Harrow		
1954	Rugby	1979	Stowe		

2003

Semi-Finals	Edinburgh Academy beat Whitgift 3-2
	Charterhouse beat Oundle 3½-1½
Final	Edinburgh Academy beat Charterhouse 3½-1½

Winning team: Michael Gray, Kenneth Hannah, Oliver Lindsay, Iain MacDonald, Michael Macphee, Steven Malcolm, Charlie Maran, David Simson, Ian Smith, Christopher Tugwell. Non-playing captain: J Lang

Senior Halford-Hewitt Competitions (Inaugurated 2000)

Bernard Darwin Trophy (Original 16) at Woking GC

2000	Wellington College	2001	Malvern College	2002	Wellington College
2003	Tonbridge				

Mellin Trophy (Second 16) at West Hill GC

2000	Lansing College	2001	Cheltenham College	2002	Shrewsbury School
2003	Haileybury				

Cyril Gray Trophy (Remaining 32) at Worplesdon

2000	Stoneyhurst School	2001	Canford School	2002	George Watson's College
2003	Stowe				

Senior Halford-Hewitt Trophy (Play-off between winners of Darwin, Mellin and Gray Trophies)

2000	Wellington College beat Lansing College beat Stoneyhurst School at West Hill GC	2002	Wellington College beat George Watson's College beat Shrewsbury School at Worplesdon
2001	Canford School beat Malvern College beat Cheltenham College at Woking GC	2003	Haileybury beat Tonbridge beat Stowe

Grafton Morrish Trophy (Inaugurated 1963) *at Hunstanton and Brancaster*

1963	Tonbridge	1977	Haileybury	1991	Repton
1964	Tonbridge	1978	Charterhouse	1992	Charterhouse
1965	Charterhouse	1979	Harrow	1993	Malvern
1966	Charterhouse	1980	Charterhouse	1994	George Heriot's
1967	Charterhouse	1981	Charterhouse	1995	Repton
1968	Wellington	1982	Marlborough	1996	Coventry
1969	Sedbergh	1983	Wellington	1997	George Heriot's
1970	Sedbergh	1984	Sedbergh	1998	Solihull
1971	Dulwich	1985	Warwick	1999	George Heriot's
1972	Sedbergh	1986	Tonbridge	2000	Lancing
1973	Pangbourne	1987	Harrow	2001	King's College School
1974	Millfield	1988	Robert Gordon's	2002	George Heriot's
1975	Oundle	1989	Tonbridge		
1976	Charterhouse	1990	Clifton		

2002

Semi-Finals
Clifton beat Solihull 2–1
Glasgow Academy beat Coventry 2–1

Final
Glasgow Academy beat Clifton 2–1

Winning team: Graeme Belch (captain), David Connolly, Martin Hamilton, Douglas Hunter, Graeme Noblett, Paul Stevens

---

Oxford v Cambridge Varsity Match (Inaugurated 1878)

1878	Oxford	Wimbledon		1922	Cambridge	Prince's, Sandwich
1879	Cambridge	Wimbledon		1923	Oxford	Rye
1880	Oxford	Wimbledon		1924	Cambridge	Hoylake
1881	*Not played*			1925	Oxford	Hunstanton
1882	Cambridge	Wimbledon		1926	Cambridge	Burnham and Berrow
1883	Oxford	Wimbledon		1927	Cambridge	Hoylake
1884	Oxford	Wimbledon		1928	Cambridge	Prince's, Sandwich
1885	Oxford	Wimbledon		1929	Cambridge	Rye
1886	Oxford	Wimbledon		1930	Oxford	Hoylake
1887	Cambridge	Wimbledon		1931	Oxford	Prince's, Sandwich
1888	Cambridge	Wimbledon		1932	Oxford	Lytham St Annes
1889	Oxford	Wimbledon		1933	Cambridge	Prince's, Sandwich
1890	Cambridge	Wimbledon		1934	Oxford	Formby
1891	Cambridge	Wimbledon		1935	Cambridge	Burnham and Berrow
1892	Cambridge	Wrlmbledon		1936	Cambridge	Hoylake
1893	Cambridge	Wimbledon		1937	Cambridge	Prince's, Sandwich
1894	Oxford	Sandwich		1938	Cambridge	Westward Ho!
1895	Cambridge	Sandwich		1939	Cambridge	Royal St George's
1896	Halved	Wimbledon		1940–45	*No competitions due to Second World War*	
1897	Cambridge	Sandwich		1946	Cambridge	Royal Lytham & St Annes
1898	Cambridge	Sandwich		1947	Oxford	Rye
1899	Oxford	Sandwich		1948	Oxford	Royal St George's
1900	Oxford	Sandwich		1949	Cambridge	Hoylake
1901	Oxford	Sandwich		1950	Oxford	Royal Lytham & St Annes
1902	Oxford	Sandwich		1951	Cambridge	Rye
1903	Oxford	Sandwich		1952	Cambridge	Rye
1904	Oxford	Woking		1953	Cambridge	Rye
1905	Cambridge	Sunningdale		1954	Cambridge	Rye
1906	Cambridge	Hoylake		1955	Cambridge	Rye
1907	Cambridge	Hoylake		1956	Oxford	Formby
				1957	Oxford	Royal St George's
After 1907 the result was arrived at by matches won				1958	Cambridge	Rye
				1959	Cambridge	Burnham & Berrow
1908	Cambridge	Sunningdale		1960	Cambridge	Royal Lytham & St Annes
1909	Oxford	Royal St George's		1961	Oxford	Royal St George's
1910	Cambridge	Hoylake		1962	Halved	Hunstanton
1911	Oxford	Rye		1963	Cambridge	Royal Birkdale
1912	Halved	Prince's, Sanswich		1964	Oxford	Rye
1913	Halved	Hoylake		1965	Cambridge	Royal St George's
1914	Oxford	Rye		1966	Cambridge	Hunstanton
1915–19	*No competitions due to First World War*			1967	Cambridge	Rye
1920	Cambridge	Sunningdale		1968	Cambridge	Porthcawl
1921	Oxford	Hoylake				

Oxford v Cambridge Varsity Match *continued*

1969	Cambridge	Formby	1986	Oxford	Ganton
1970	Halved	Royal St George's	1987	Cambridge	Formby
1971	Oxford	Rye	1988	Cambridge	Royal Porthcawl
1972	Cambridge	Formby	1989	Cambridge	Rye
1973	Oxford	Saunton	1990	Cambridge	Muirfield
1974	Cambridge	Ganton	1991	Cambridge	Royal St George's
1975	Cambridge	Hoylake	1992	Oxford	Royal Cinque Ports
1976	Cambridge	Woodhall Spa	1993	Oxford	Royal Liverpool
1977	Cambridge	Porthcawl	1994	Oxford	Rye
1978	Oxford	Rye	1995	Oxford	Royal Lytham & St Annes
1979	Oxford	Harlech	1996	Oxford	Royal West Norfolk
1980	Oxford	Hoylake	1997	Oxford	Royal St George's
1981	Cambridge	Formby	1998	Cambridge	Rye
1982	Cambridge	Hunstanton	1999	Oxford	Royal Cinque Ports
1983	Cambridge	Royal St George's	2000	Cambridge	Porthcawl
1984	Cambridge	Sunningdale	2001	Oxford	Formby
1985	Oxford	Rye	2002	Cambridge	Royal St George's

2003 *at Walton Heath*

Captains: H Westall (Oxford); T Dawson (Cambridge)

Foursomes

Coker & Edwards beat Lindsay & Dawson 2 and 1
Kohansky & Westall beat Kennedy & Cumming 3 and 2
Greenhalgh & Mann beat Gold & Gobby 2 and 1
Davidson & Webster lost to Southworth & Nikolic 1 hole
Hayes & Locke beat Chepiga & Hannah 2 and 1

Singles

Harry Westall (Balliol) beat Tom Dawson (Emmanuel) 4 and 3
Robert Mann (St Edmund Hall) lost to Chris Gobby (Fitzwilliam) 1 hole
Matthew Webster (New College) beat Toby Cumming (Gonville & Caius) 6 and 5
David Hayes (Corpus Christi) beat Ken Hannah (Wolfson) 9 and 8
Gregg Kohansky (Christ Church) beat Chris Southworth (Trinity) 11 and 10
Edward Greenhalgh (New College) lost to Oliver Lindsay (Pembroke) 8 and 7
Adam Edwards (BNC) beat Geoff Chepiga (Wolfson) 3 and 2
Matthew Locke (Corpus Christi) lost to Krysto Nikolic (Queens') 1 hole
Alistair Davidson (Exeter) lost to Adam Gold (Peterhouse) 1 hole
Jonathan Coker (Christ Church) beat Graham Kennedy (Downing) 7 and 6

Result: Oxford beat Cambridge 10-5

Oxford and Cambridge Golfing Society for the President's Putter (Inaugurated 1920) *at Rye*

1920	EWE Holderness	1937	JB Beck	1961	ID Wheater
1921	EWE Holderness	1938	CJH Tolley	1962	MF Attenborough
1922	EWE Holderness	1939	JOH Greenly	1963	JG Blackwell
1923	EWE Holderness	1940–46	*No competition*	1964	DMA Steel
1924	B Darwin	1947	LG Crawley	1965	WJ Uzielli
1925	HD Gillies	1948	Major AA Duncan	1966	MF Attenborough
1926T	EF Storey	1949	PB Lucas	1967	JR Midgley
	RH Wethered	1950	DHR Martin	1968	AWJ Holmes
1927	RH Wethered	1951	LG Crawley	1969	P Moody
1928	RH Wethered	1952	LG Crawley	1970	DMA Steel
1929	Sir EWE Holderness	1953	GH Micklem	1971	GT Duncan
1930	TA Bourn	1954	G Huddy	1972	P Moody
1931	AG Pearson	1955	G Huddy	1973	AD Swanston
1932	LG Crawley	1956	GT Duncan	1974	R Biggs
1933	AJ Peech	1957	AE Shepperson	1975	CJ Weight
1934	DHR Martin	1958	Lt-Col AA Duncan	1976	MJ Reece
1935	RH Wethered	1959	ID Wheater	1977	AWJ Holmes
1936	RH Wethered	1960	JME Anderson	1978	MJ Reece

1979	Cancelled due to snow	1987	CD Meacher	1995	A Woolnough
1980	S Melville	1988	G Woollett	1996	C Rotheroe
1981	AWJ Holmes	1989	M Froggatt	1997	C Rotheroe
1982	DMA Steel	1990	G Woollett	1998	N Pabari
1983	ER Dexter	1991	B Ingleby	1999	C Dale
1984	A Edmond	1992	M Cox	2000	CJ Dale
1985	ER Dexter	1993	C Weight	2001	B Streather
1986	J Caplan	1994	S Seman	2002	T Etridge

2003

Quarter-Finals
J Fricker beat I Henderson 3 and 2
M Williamson beat S Seman 6 and 5
T Etridge beat W Jackson 2 and 1
D Hayes beat C Rotheroe 1 hole

Semi-Finals
Williamson beat Fricker 4 and 3
Hayes beat Etridge 2 and 1

Final
David Hayes beat Mark Williamson 5 and 4

Palmer Cup (USA university students v Great Britain & Ireland students)

1997	USA	19–5	Bay Hill, Orlando, Florida	2000	GB&I	12½–11½	Royal Liverpool
1998	USA	12–12	St Andrews, Scotland	2001	USA	14–2	Springfield, NJ
1999	USA	17½–6½	Honors, Tennessee	2002	USA	15½–8½	Doonbeg, Ireland

2003 at Kiawah Island, SC, USA

First Day: **Fourball**
Haas and Nallen beat Canízares and Wilson 4 and 3
Bray and Snedeker beat Castaño and Inglis 2 and 1
Rubinson and Tomasulo lost to Price and Skinns 1 hole
Hartwick and Moore beat Nilsson and Schauman 1 hole

Singles
Haas (USA) lost to Castaño (GBI) 3 and 2
Nallen (USA) lost to Wilson (GBI) 2 and 1
Bray (USA) lost to Canízares (GBI) 1 hole
Snedeker (USA) beat Inglis (GBI) 2 and 1
Tomasulo (USA) halved with Skinns (GBI)
Rubinson (USA) lost to Schauman (GBI) 7 and 6
Hartwick (USA) lost to Price (GBI) 3 and 1
Moore (USA) halved with Nilsson (GBI)

Second Day: **Foursomes**
Haas and Nallen lost to Canízares and Castaño 3 and 1
Bray and Snedeker beat Skinns and Wilson 2 and 1

Second Day: **Foursomes** *continued*
Rubinson and Tomasulo halved with Nilsson
and Schauman Hartwick and Moore lost to
Inglis and Price
1 hole

Singles
Dustin Bray beat Oliver Wilson (Eng) 2 and 1
Brandt Snedeker lost to Alejandro
Canízares (Esp) 3 and 1
Bill Haas lost to Gonzalo Castaño (Esp)
3 and 2
Peter Tomasulo lost to David Skinns (Eng)
1 hole
Chris Nallen beat Wilhelm Schauman (Swe)
2 and 1
Ryan Moore lost to Par Nilsson (Swe) 3 and 2
Jason Hartwick halved with David Inglis
(Sco)
Adam Rubinson beat David Price (Wal)
2 and 1

Result: United States 10, Great Britain & Ireland 14

Boyd Quaich (University Championship) at St Andrews

1946	AS Mayer	Glasgow	161	1958	R Mummery	London	299
1947T	H Brews	Johannesburg	148	1959-61	*Not played*		
	FWG Deighton	Glasgow	148	1962	DB Sheahan	Univ. Coll., Dublin	217
1948	JL Lindsay	St Andrews	203	1963	S MacDonald	Edinburgh	295
1949	FD Tatum	Oxford	217	1964	AJ Low	St Andrews	299
1950	GP Roberts	Liverpool	294	1965	S MacDonald	Edinburgh	295
1951	H Dooley	Nottingham	299	1966	FE McCarroll	Queen's, Belfast	291
1952	G Parker	Glasgow	297	1967	B Nicholson	Aberdeen	294
1953	JL Bamford	Trinity, Dublin	290	1968	JW Johnston	Aberdeen	291
1954	I Caldwell	London	287	1969	PH Moody	Cambride	286
1955	HC Squirrll	Birmingham	292	1970	JT Moffat	Strathclyde	297
1956	JL Bamford	Trinity, Dublin	295	1971	JW Johnston	Aberdeen	289
1957	DM Marsh	Liverpool	293	1972	D Greig	Aberdeen	288

Boyd Quaich *continued*

1973	J Rube	Sweden	285	1988	A Mathers	Stirling	289
1974	G Cairns	Edinburgh	297	1989	A Mathers	Stirling	300
1975	S Dunlop	Trinity, Dublin	291	1990	A Mathers	Stirling	297
1976	R Watson	Dundee	297	1991	C Somner	Friberg, Switzerland	302
1977	R Watson	Dundee	297	1992	L Walker	Trinity, Dublin	286
1978	R Watson	Dundee	298	1993	G Sherry	Stirling	298
1979	D McLeary	St Andrews	302	1994	C Sanderson	Stellenbosch, SA	283
1980	ME Lewis	Bath	290	1995	C Sanderson	Stellenbosch, SA	290
1981	P Gallagher	Heriot-Watt	302	1996	B Templeton	Heriot-Watt	294
1982	ME Lewis	Bath	297	1997	G Maly	St Andrews	289
1983	R Risan	Lund, Sweden	296	1998	D Simpson	Edinburgh	283
1984	J Huggan	Stirling	297	1999	O Lindsay	St Andrews	290
1985	S Elgie	W. Ontario, Canada	299	2000	G Greer	Glasgow	288
1986	A Roberts	Hull	291	2001	P Botha*	Pretoria	292
1987	M Pask	St Andrews	293	2002	G Duncan	Heriot-Watt	283

2003

1	Richard Hooper (St Andrews)*	75-70-73-69—287 (count back)
2	Rob Hyson (St Andrews)	72-70-73-72—287
	Mark Kerr (Edinburgh)	72-67-74-74—287

Queen Elizabeth Coronation Schools Trophy (inaugurated 1953)

at Royal Burgess, Barnton

1953	Watsonians	1978	Old Lorettonians
1954	Daniel Stewart's FP	1979	Gordonians
1955	Watsonians	1980	George Heriot's FP
1956	Watsonians	1981	Ayr Academicals
1957	Hillhead High School FP	1982	George Heriot's FP
1958	Watsonians	1983	Perth Academy FP
1959	Glasgow High School FP	1984	Glasgow High School FP
1960	Glasgow High School FP	1985	Glasgow High School FP
1961	Watsonians	1986	Watsonians
1962	Glasgow High School FP	1987	Daniel Stewart's/Melville FP
1963	Glasgow High School FP	1988	Watsonians
1964	Dollar Academicals	1989	Kelvinside Academicals
1965	Old Lorettonians	1990	Hutchesons' Grammar School FP
1966	Merchistonians	1991	Glasgow High School FP
1967	Merchistonians	1992	Daniel Stewart's/Melville FP
1968	Hillhead High School FP	1993	Merchistonians
1969	Kelvinside Academicals	1994	Perth Academy FP
1970	Dollar Academicals	1995	Glasgow High School FP
1971	Merchistonians	1996	Glasgow High School FP
1972	Merchistonians	1997	Old Uppinghamians
1973	Merchistonians	1998	Watsonians
1974	Old Carthusians	1999	Morrisonians
1975	Old Lorettonians	2000	Breadalbane Academicals
1976	Watsonians	2001	Old Carthusians
1977	Glasgow High School FP	2002	Old Campbellians

2003

Semi-Finals
Old Uppinghamians beat Daniel Stewart's/Melville FP 2-1
Breadalbane Academicals beat Old Campbellians 2-1

Final
Breadalbane Academicals beat Old Uppinghamians 2-1

Winning team: SF Carruthers, CP Christy, IJ Panton, MG Rose, I Taylor, AD Wilson

County and Other Regional Championships

England

Bedfordshire

1994	J Kemp	1999	J Kemp
1995	I Tottingham	2000	S Vinnecombe
1996	M Wharton	2001	J Kemp
1997	K Kemp	2002	M Wharton
1998	M Wharton	2003	G Benson

Berks, Bucks and Oxon

1994	D Fisher	1999	L Rusher
1995	D Lane	2000	K Freeman
1996	J Carlsen	2001	C Bowler
1997	L Donald	2002	A Walton
1998	L Donald	2003	L Gauthier

Cambridgeshire

1994	A Emery	1999	O Cousins
1995	S Jarvis	2000	LG Yearn
1996	P Rains	2001	LG Yearn
1997	O Cousins	2002	K Arthur
1998	L Yearn	2003	L Tearn

Channel Islands

2003	M Jones

Cheshire

1994	J Hodgson	2000	FA Bibby
1995	C Smethurst	2001	GJ Bradley
1996	D Vaughan	2002	D Wardrop
1997	N Pabari	2003	S Shaw (M)
1998	J Donaldson		M Pilling (S)
1999	SS Grewal		

Cornwall

1994	R Binney	1999	I Veale
1995	M Lock	2000	S Chapman
1996	I Veale	2001	C Llewellyn
1997	P Darlington	2002	IT Veale
1998	I Atkinson	2003	IC Veale

Cumbria

1994	B Story	1999	J Longcake
1995	N Mitchell	2000	J Carr
1996	R Secular	2001	S Young
1997	G Watson	2002	N Bell
1998	P Jack	2003	W Bowe

Derbyshire

1994	J Feeney	1999	JP Feeney
1995	G Shaw	2000	N Vowles
1996	J Feeney	2001	P Gration
1997	AS Humpston	2002	P Gration
1998	L Walley	2003	E Vernon

Devon

1994	M Crossfield	1999	G Ruth
1995	A Capping	2000	S Davey
1996	D Eva	2001	G Ruth
1997	G Ruth	2002	K Harper
1998	S Pike	2003	C Townsend

Dorset

1994	M Davies	1999	C Jessup
1995	M Davies	2000	M Davies
1996	A Lawrence	2001	A Lawrence
1997	J Baldwin	2002	T Peacock
1998	J Pounder	2003	T Peacock

Durham

1994	J Kennedy	1999	A McLure
1995	A McLure	2000	AJ McLure
1996	S Ord	2001	M Ridley
1997	J Dryden	2002	J Harper
1998	C Hamilton	2003	R Aisbitt

Essex

1994	R Coles	1999	R Blaxhill
1995	D Salisbury	2000	S Middleton
1996	G Clark	2001	R Blaxill
1997	B Taylor	2002	P Ring
1998	B Taylor	2003	L Kennedy

Gloucestershire

1994	G Wolstenholme	1999	D Young
1995	T Smith	2000	C Newman
1996	G Wolstenholme	2001	M Unwin
1997	M Unwin	2002	P Reed
1998	TP Smith	2003	M Unwin

Hampshire, Isle of Wight and Channel Islands

1994	R Bland	1999	D Henley
1995	M Le Mesurier	2000	C McLaughlin
1996	M Blackey	2001	D Henley
1997	S Stanley	2002	R Elmes
1998	C Hudson	2003	D Porter

Hertfordshire

1994	G Maly	1999	D Griffiths
1995	H Steel	2000	I Farrant
1996	S Little	2001	M Payne
1997	C Duke	2002	B Connelly
1998	R Conway-Lye	2003	B Connelly

Isle of Man

1994	R Sayle	1999	G Wilson
1995	G Wilson	2000	S Ellis
1996	G Wilson	2001	G Wilson
1997	P McMullan	2002	M Sutton
1998	P McMullan	2003	D Jones

Kent

1994	B Barham	1999	J Carter
1995	T Milford	2000	D Curtis
1996	B Barham	2001	L Godwin
1997	D Ottoway	2002	L Campbell
1998	D Ottaway	2003	M Ford

Lancashire

1994	K Wallbank	1999	A Jackson
1995	G Boardman	2000	M Cox
1996	G Boardman	2001	R Bardsley
1997	D Johnson	2002	R Walker
1998	P Wiliams	2003	R Bardsley

Leicestershire and Rutland

1994	I Lyner	1999	D Gibson
1995	P Frith	2000	N Knighton
1996	J Herbert	2001	G Wolstenholme
1997	J Herbert	2002	C Shave
1998	G Wolstenholme	2003	D Gibson

Lincolnshire

1994	J Crampton	1999	D Skinns
1995	J Crampton	2000	P Bradshaw
1996	P Streeter	2001	LJ Toyne
1997	P Streeter	2002	P Bradshaw
1998	A White	2003	J Crampton

Middlesex

1994	WJ Bennett	1999	G Evans
1995	G Clark	2000	S Samphire
1996	S Kay	2001	S Samphire
1997	C Austin	2002	G Evans
1998	R Vaney	2003	M Richardson

Norfolk

1994	J Durrant	1999	CJ Lamb
1995	I Ellis	2000	NJ Williamson
1996	P Little	2001	D Henderson
1997	G Price	2002	D Henderson
1998	CJ Lamb	2003	Austin Brydon

Northamptonshire

1994	A Print	1999	N Soto
1995	A Lord	2000	A Print
1996	I Dallas	2001	N Soto
1997	P Langrish-Smith	2002	M Peacock
1998	G Keates	2003	G Keates

Northumberland

1994	S Twynholm	2000	AR Paisley
1995	M Hall	2001	C McDonnell
1996	K Cademy-Taylor	2002	SE Phillipson
1997	D Clark	2003	A Minnikin (M)
1998	J McCallum		C McDonnell (S)
1999	SE Philipson		

Nottinghamshire

1994	D Lucas	1999	AJ Liddle
1995	H Hopkinson	2000	M Allen
1996	D McJannet	2001	D McJannet
1997	O Wilson	2002	T Payne
1998	AJ Liddle	2003	M Betteridge

Shropshire and Herefordshire

1994	M Welch	1999	K Baker
1995	D Park	2000	R Brown
1996	D Harris	2001	D McDonnell
1997	K Preece	2002	K Williams
1998	O Pughe	2003	B Ruddick

Somerset

1994	C Edwards	1999	G Legg
1995	B Whittock	2000	D Dixon
1996	D Dixon	2001	C Edwards
1997	R Swords	2002	B Porter
1998	J Morgan	2003	C Edwards

Staffordshire

1994	R Mayfield	1999	R Chattaway
1995	T Ryder	2000	C Russell
1996	R Parkes	2001	MA Payne
1997	SD Wakefield	2002	A Cheese
1998	KD Hale	2003	JJ Kendall

Suffolk

1994	J Maddock	1999	P Barnard
1995	D Quinney	2000	L Dodd
1996	J Keely	2001	L Dodd
1997	J Maddock	2002	J Wright
1998	J Wright	2003	K Day

Surrey

1994	M Ellis	1999	N Pimm
1995	A Wall	2000	J Franks
1996	M Palmer	2001	Z Scotland
1997	T Paterson	2002	D Lomas
1998	C Rodgers	2003	J Heath

Sussex

1994	P Clevely	1999	M Galway
1995	M Allen	2000	J Doherty
1996	M Harris	2001	S Nightingale
1997	M Harris	2002	C Newman
1998	M Harris	2003	J Budgen

Warwickshire

1994	N Connolly	1999	T Whitehouse
1995	S Webster	2000	T Whitehouse
1996	A Carey	2001	T Whitehouse
1997	T Whitehouse	2002	J Hemphill
1998	T Whitehouse	2003	R Steele

Wiltshire

1994	R Searle	1999	P Bicknell
1995	N Mumford	2000	S Surry
1996	A Mutch	2001	I Campbell
1997	P Bicknell	2002	J Huffam
1998	P Bicknell	2003	M Searle

Worcestershire

2003	A Norman

Yorkshire

1994	P Wood (M)	1999	GA Clark (M)
	N Ludwell (S)		SJ Dyson (S)
1995	J Ellis (M)	2000	JB Godbold (M)
	N Gibson (S)		GA Clark (S)
	J Hepworth (S)		RM Hollins (S)
1996	R Jones (M)	2001	R Finch (M)
	N Emmerson (S)		R Finch (S)
1997	R Jones (M)	2002	DJ Berry (M)
	A Wright (S)	2003	G Clark (M)
1998	S Tarplett (M)		
	M Bugg /		
	R Hodgkinson (S)		
	(tied)		

Scotland

Angus

1994	E Wilson	2001	M Lindsay (M)
1995	J Rae		A Johnston (S)
1996	G Bell	2002	GW Tough (M)
1997	P Cunningham		JA Watt (S)
1998	E Ramsay	2003	G Bell (M)
1999	J Flynn		G Brown (S)
2000	S Wilson		

Argyll and Bute

1994	G Bolton	2001	G Bolton (M)
1995	G Tyre		G Reynolds (S)
1996	L Kelly	2002	G Bolton (M)
1997	S Campbell		G Tyre (S)
1998	J Sharp	2003	I McLennan (M)
1999	G Bolton		G Bolton (S)
2000	G McMillan		

Ayrshire

1994	J Cairney (M)	1999	G Holland
	G Lawrie (S)		(M and S)
1995	A Reid (M)	2000	L Bagnall (M)
	A Gourlay (S)		A Gourlay (S)
1996	J Cairney (M)	2001	A Gourlay (M)
	G Lawrie (S)		G Bryden (S)
1997	G Fox (M)	2002	A Gourlay (M)
	B Aitken (S)		R Duncan (S)
1998	I Robertson (M)	2003	B Crawford (M)
	D Glass (S)		T McInally (S)

Borders Golfers' Association

1994	M Thomson	1999	J Paterson
1995	M Thomson	2000	M Thomson
1996	D Ballantyne	2001	M Thomson
1997	W Simpson	2002	RD Ballantyne
1998	D Ballantyne	2003	M Thomson

Clackmannshire

1994	P McLeod	2000	AC Fairbrother
1995	I Ross	2001	I Macaulay (M and S)
1996	R Stewart	2002	M Crichton (S)
1997	G Bowie		C Macaulay (M)
1998	B Stewart	2003	N Scaife (S)
1999	M Crichton		I Ross (M)

Dunbartonshire

1994	D Carrick (M)	1999	G Greer (M)
	F Hutchison (S)		J Hughes (S)
1995	T McKeown (M)	2000	J Devonney (M)
	F Jardine (S)		SR McIntosh (S)
1996	K MacNair (M)	2001	F Bone (M)
	A Leitch (S)		P Gault (S)
1997	S Carmichael (M)	2002	P Gault jr (M)
	S McLeitch (S)		K Smyth (S)
1998	S Carmichael (M)	2003	C Peddie (M)
	G Murphy (S)		J Hamilton (S)

Fife

1994	C MacDougall	2001	J McLeary (M)
1995	D Paton		S Meiklejohn (S)
1996	B Erskine	2002	R Dickson (M)
1997	S Meiklejohn		JT Bunch (S)
1998	J Bunch	2003	K McGowan (M)
1999	J McLeary		S Mackie (S)
2000	R Bremner		

Glasgow

2003	C Kerr (M)	
	J Laurie (S)	

Lanarkshire

1994	M Moir (M)		W Bryson (S)
	W Bryson (S)	2000	I Duff (M)
1995	W Bryson (M)		C Heap (S)
	K Nisbet (S)	2001	C Gibson (M)
1996	J Ralston (M)		W Bryson (S)
	K Ralston (S)	2002	G Rodger (M)
1997	W Bryson (M)		S Douglas (S)
	E Moir (S)	2003	R Hinshelwood (M)
1998	R Hinshelwood (M)		G Rodger (S)
	M Warren (S)		
1999	W Bryson		
	(M and S)		

Lothians

1994	S Smith	2001	K Nicholson (M)
1995	S Smith		D Thomson (S)
1996	N Shillinglaw	2002	B Smith (M)
1997	K Nicholson		G Corrigan (S)
1998	K Nicholson	2003	J Gallagher (M)
1999	C Swanston		K Nicholson (S)
2000	M Timmins		

North (Scotland)

2003	S McIntosh

North-East (Scotland)

2003	B Edmond (M)
	E McIntosh (S)

Perth and Kinross

1994	E Lindsay	2001	G Campbell
1995	S Herd		(M and S)
1996	M Rose	2002	S Carruthers (M)
1997	N Macdonald		G Campbell (S)
1998	K Grant	2003	G Campbell
1999	N Macdonald		(M and S)
2000	G Campbell		

Renfrewshire

1994	M Carmichael	2001	A Craig (M)
1995	R Adam		G Murphy (S)
1996	S Nicol	2002	C Rossi (M)
1997	D Owens		GW Urquhart (S)
1998	A McKay	2003	M Clark (M)
1999	A McKay		R Clark (S)
2000	S Robertson		

SE Scotland Championship

1994	I Reid	2001	I Brotherston (M)
1995	B Scott		C Haddow (S)
1996	E Little	2002	BJ Scott (S)
1997	I Brotherston		J Power (M)
1998	D Sutton	2003	B Scott (M and S)
1999	I Thomson		
2000	BJ Scott		

Stirlingshire

1994	K McArthur	2001	H Anderson (M)
1995	K Brunton		D Todd (S)
1996	G McDonald	2002	H Anderson (M)
1997	A Ellison		D Buchanan (S)
1998	JR Johnson	2003	S McLachlan (M)
1999	K McArthur		G Barrie (S)
2000	H Anderson		

Wales

Anglesey

1994	J Campbell	1999	A Williams
1995	D McLean	2000	H Hughes
1996	A Williams	2001	H Hughes
1997	M Perdue	2002	M Perdue
1998	EO Jones	2003	L Baynes

Brecon & Rador

2003   M Maddock

Caernarfon and District

1994	D McLean	1999	R Williams
1995	S Pritchard	2000	H Hughes
1996	A Williams	2001	M Tottey
1997	Not played	2002	A Williams
1998	A Clishem	2003	A Thomas

Caernarfonshire Cup

1994	J Dabecki	1999	E Angel
1995	J Dabecki	2000	M Wyn Jones
1996	M Pilkington	2001	A Thomas
1997	Not played	2002	A Thomas
1998	M Pilkington	2003	E Williams

Dyfed

2003   R Scott

Flintshire

2003   R Caldecott

Glamorgan

1994	N Edwards	1999	S Roberts
1995	S Roberts	2000	N Edwards
1996	N Edwards	2001	N Edwards
1997	Y Taylor	2002	L James
1998	C Williams	2003	J Holmes

Gwent
(Formerly Monmouthshire Amateur)

1994	B Dredge	1999	A Williams
1995	C Dinsdale	2000	CJ Dinsdale
1996	M Hayward	2001	S Westley
1997	R Price	2002	J Davidson
1998	N Povall	2003	A Mason

World Ice Golfers head for Spitzbergen

There's a new venue in 2004 for the annual Drambuie World Ice Golf Championship – the remote Arctic island of Spitzbergen. The venue, which is in Norwegian territory, was chosen by Pen Hadow, the leading polar explorer as a replacement for the venue in Greenland of the previous four Championships. Freak weather caused the event to be cancelled last year prompting sponsors Drambuie to look for a new spot which would guarantee an on-ice playing field in a visually stunning but remote location in order to provide the ultimate golfing experience. The search took in many places around the world including Siberia and Alaska.

There have been three winners of the World Ice Golf Championships to date – journalist Peter Masters won in 1999, female professional golfer Annika Ostberg from Denmark won in 2000 and 2001 and Roger Beames from Scotland, who was the winner in 2002 and who is returning with 35 contestants to defend his title in April.

Ice golf is not a relaxed experience. Play takes place despite temperatures reaching minus 30 degrees at times and the players can be exposed to the hazards of snow blindness, falling into seal holes or running into polar bears!

Overseas Amateur Championships

Australian (inaugurated 1894)

1894	LA Whyte	1924	H Sinclair	1954	P Toogood	1980	R Mackay
1895	RAA Balfour	1925	H Sinclair	1955	J Rayner	1981	O Moore
	Melville	1926	Len Nettlefold	1956	H Berwick	1982	EM Couper
1896	HA Howden	1927	WS Nankivell	1957	BH Warren	1983	WJ Smith
1897	HA Howden	1928	Len Nettlefold	1958	K Hartley	1984	BP King
1898	HA Howden	1929	MJ Ryan	1959	BW Devlin	1985	B Ruangkit (Tha)
1899	CES Gillies	1930	HW Hattersley	1960	Ted Ball	1986	DJ Ecob
1900	LA Whyte	1931	HL William	1961	T Crow	1987	B Johns
1901	HA Howden	1932	Dr RH Bettington	1962	D Bachli	1988	S Bouvier
1902	H Macneil	1933	WL Hope	1963	J Hayes (RSA)	1989	SJ Conran
1903	DG Soutar	1934	TS McKay	1964	B Baker	1990	CD Gray
1904	JD Howden	1935	J Ferrier	1965	K Donohoe	1991	LKJ Parsons
1905	Hon. Michael Scott	1936	J Ferrier	1966	W Britten	1992	MS Campbell (NZ)
1906	EA Gill	1937	HL Williams	1967	J Muller	1993	GJ Chalmers
1907	Hon. Michael Scott	1938	J Ferrier	1968	R Stott	1994	W Bennett (Eng)
1908	Clyde Pearce	1939	J Ferrier	1969	RA Shearer	1995	MC Goggin
1909	Hon. Michael Scott	1940–45	*Not played*	1970	PA Bennett	1996	DC Gleeson
1910	Hon. Michael Scott	1946	AN Waterson	1971	GR Hicks	1997	K Felton
1911	JD Howden	1947	HW Hattersley	1972	CR Kaye	1998	B Rumford
1912	Hector Morrison	1948	D Bachli	1973	RJ Jenner	1999	BM Jones
1913	AR Lempriere	1949	WD Ackland-	1974	TR Gale	2000	BP Lamb
1914–19	*Not played*		Horman	1975	C Bonython	2001	S Bowditch
1920	EL Apperley	1950	H Berwick	1976	P Sweeney	2002	K Barnes
1921	CL Winser	1951	Peter Heard	1977	AY Gresham	2003	J Doherty (Sco)
1922	Ivo Witton	1952	R Stevens	1978	MA Clayton		
1923	Ivo Witton	1953	Peter Heard	1979	J Kelly		

Canadian (inaugurated 1895)

1895	TH Harley	1924	F Thompson	1954	E Harvie Ward	1979	R Alarcon (Mex)
1896	JS Gillespie	1925	DD Carrick	1955	M Norman	1980	G Olson
1897	WAH Kerr	1926	CR Somerville	1956	M Norman	1981	R Zokol
1898	GS Lyon	1927	DD Carrick	1957	N Weslock	1982	D Roxburgh
1899	Vere C Brown	1928	CR Somerville	1958	B Castator	1983	D Milovic
1900	GS Lyon	1929	E Held	1959	J Johnston	1984	W Swartz
1901	WAH Kerr	1930	CR Somerville	1960	RK Alexander	1985	B Franklin
1902	FR Martin	1931	CR Somerville	1961	G Cowan	1986	B Franklin
1903	GS Lyon	1932	GB Taylor	1962	R Taylor	1987	B Franklin
1904	J Percy Taylor	1933	A Campbell	1963	N Weslock	1988	D Roxburgh
1905	GS Lyon	1934	A Campbell	1964	N Weslock	1989	P Major
1906	GS Lyon	1935	CR Somerville	1965	G Henry	1990	W Sye
1907	GS Lyon	1936	F Haas jr	1966	N Weslock	1991	J Kraemer
1908	Alex Wilson	1937	CR Somerville	1967	S Jones	1992	D Ritchie
1909	E Legge	1938	T Adams	1968	J Doyle	1993	G Simpson
1910	F Martin	1939	K Black	1969	Wayne McDonald	1994	W Sye
1911	GH Hutton	1940–44	*Not played*	1970	A Miller	1995	G Willis (USA)
1912	George S Lyon	1946	H Martell	1971	R Siderowf	1996	R McMillan
1913	GH Turpin	1947	FR Stranahan	1972	D Roxburgh	1997	D Goehring
1914	George S Lyon	1948	FR Stranahan	1973	G Burns	1998	C Matthew
1915–19	*Not played*	1949	RD Chapman	1974	D Roxburgh	1999	Han Lee (USA)
1920	CB Grier	1950	W Mawhinney	1975	J Nelford	2000	Han Lee (USA)
1921	F Thompson	1951	W McElroy	1976	J Nelford	2001	G Paddison
1922	CC Fraser	1952	L Bouchey	1977	R Spittle	2002	D Pruitt
1923	WJ Thompson	1953	D Cherry	1978	R Spittle	2003	R Scott

New Zealand (inaugurated 1893)

1893	JA Somerville	1922	ADS Duncan	1953	DL Woon	1979	J Durry
1894	H Macneil	1923	J Goss jr	1954	DL Woon	1980	PE Hartstone
1895	G Gosset	1924	L Quin	1955	SG Jones	1981	T Cochrane
1896	MS Todd	1925	TH Horton	1956	PA Toogood	1982	J Peters
1897	D Pryde	1926	ADS Duncan	1957	EJ McDougall	1983	C Taylor
1898	W Pryde	1927	S Morpeth	1958	WJ Godfrey	1984	J Wagner
1899	ADS Duncan	1928	TH Horton	1959	SG Jones	1985	G Power
1900	ADS Duncan	1929	S Morpeth	1960	R Newdick	1986	P O'Malley
1901	ADS Duncan	1930	HA Black	1961	SG Jones	1987	O. Kendall
1902	SH Gollan	1931	R Wagg	1962	SG Jones	1988	B Hughes
1903	K Tareha	1932	R Wagg	1963	J Durry	1989	L Peterson
1904	AH Fisher	1933	BV Wright	1964	SG Jones	1990	M Long
1905	ADS Duncan	1934	BM Silk	1965	J Durry	1991	L Parsons
1906	SH Gollan	1935	JP Hornabrook	1966	SG Jones	1992	R Lee
1907	ADS Duncan	1936	JP Hornabrook	1967	J Durry	1993	P Tatamaugi
1908	HC Smith	1937	BM Silk	1968	BA Stevens	1994	P Fitzgibbon
1909	ADS Duncan	1938	PGF Smith	1969	G Stevenson	1995	S Bittle
1910	HB Lusk	1939	JP Hornabrook	1970	EJ McDougall	1996	D Somerville
1911	ADS Duncan	1940–45	*Not played*	1971	SG Jones	1997	C Johns
1912	BB Wood	1946	WG Horne	1972	RC Murray	1998	B MacDonald
1913	BB Wood	1947	BM Silk	1973	MN Nicholson	1999	A Duffin
1914	ADS Duncan	1948	A Gibbs	1974	RM Barltrop	2000	E Burgess
1915–18	*Not played*	1949	J Holden	1975	SF Reese	2001	B Gallie
1919	H Crosse	1950	DL Woon	1976	TR Pulman	2002	M Fraser
1920	S Morpeth	1951	DL Woon	1977	TR Pulman	2003	J Nitties (Aus)
1921	AG Syme	1952	H Berwick	1978	F Nobilo		

South African (inaugurated 1892)

1892	D Walker	1922	WCE Stent	1952	M Janks	1978	EA Webber (Zim)
1893	DG Proudfoot	1923	WCE Stent	1953	R Brews	1979	L Norval
1894	DG Proudfoot	1924	AL Forster	1954	A Jackson	1980	E Grienewald
1895	DG Proudfoot	1925	TG McLelland	1955	B Keyter	1981	D Suddards
1896	DG Proudfoot	1926	WS Bryant	1956	RC Taylor	1982	N James
1897	DG Proudfoot	1927	GJ Chantler	1957	A Stewart	1983	C-C Yuan (Chi)
1898	DG Proudfoot	1928	B Wynne	1958	JR Boyd	1984	M Wiltshire
1899	DG Proudfoot	1929	C Hunter	1959	A Walker	1985	N Clarke
1900–01	*Not played*	1930	B Wynne	1960	WM Grinrod	1986	E Els
1902	DG Proudfoot	1931	C Coetzer	1961	JG Le Roux	1987	B Fouche
1903	R Law	1932	CE Olander	1962	J Hayes	1988	N Clarke
1904	JR Southey	1933	B Wynne	1963	D Symons	1989	C Rivett
1905	HCV Nicholson	1934	CE Olander	1964	JR Langridge	1990	R Goosen
1906	Lt. HM Ballinghall	1935	AD Locke	1965	P Vorster	1991	D Botes
1907	Lt. HM Ballinghall	1936	CE Olander	1966	Comrie du Toit	1992	B Davidson
1908	JAW Prentice	1937	AD Locke	1967	Derek Kemp	1993	L Chitengwa (Zim)
1909	JAW Prentice	1938	B Wynne	1968	R Williams	1994	B Vaughan
1910	Dr EL Steyn	1939	O Hayes	1969	D Thornton	1995	W Abery
1911	JAW Prentice	1940	HEP Watermeyer	1970	H Baiocchi	1996	T Moore
1912	HG Stewart	1941–45	*Not played*	1971	C Dreyer	1997	T Immelman
1913	JAW Prentice	1946	JR Boyd	1972	N Dundelson	1998	J Hugo
1914	SM McPherson	1947	C de G Watermeyer	1973	A. Oosthuizen	1999	R Sterne
1915–18	*Not played*	1948	RR Ryan	1974	T Lagerwey	2000	J Van Zyl
1919	HG Stewart	1949	RW Glennie	1975	P Vorster	2001	D Dixon (Eng)
1920	HG Stewart	1950	EADalton	1976	R Kotzen	2002	R Loubser
1921	AL Forster	1951	ES Irwin	1977	EA Webber (Zim)	2003	A Haig

South African Stroke Play (inaugurated 1969)

1969	D Hayes	1978	D Suddards	1987	B Fouchee	1996	T Moore
1970	D Hayes	1979	D Suddards	1988	N Clarke	1997	U van den Berg
1971	K Suddards	1980	E Groenewald	1989	E Els	1998	T Immelman
1972	P Dunne	1981	C-C Yuan (Chi)	1990	P Pascoe	1999	J Hugo
1973	G Harvey (Zim)	1982	Li Wen-sheng	1991	N Henning	2000	C McMonagle (Ire)
1974	N Sundelson	1983	Peter van der Riet	1992	J Nelson	2001	R Sterne
1975	G Levenson	1984	D James	1993	D Kinnear	2002	G Wolstenholme
1976	G Harvey (Zim)	1985	D van Steden	1994	N Homann		(Eng)
1977	M McNulty	1986	C-S Hsieh	1995	M Murless	2003	A Kruger

United States

Year	Winner	Runner-up	Venue	By
1895	CB Macdonald	C Sands	Newport, RI	12 and 11
1896	HJ Whigham	JG Thorp	Shinnecock Hills, NY	8 and 7
1897	HJ Whigham	WR Betts	Wheaton, IL	8 and 6
1898	FS Douglas	WB Smith	Morris County, NJ	5 and 3
1899	HM Harriman	FS Douglas	Onwentsia, IL	3 and 2
1900	WJ Travis	FS Douglas	Garden City, NY	2 holes
1901	WJ Travis	WE Egan	Atlantic City, NJ	5 and 4
1902	LN James	EM Byers	Glenview, IL	4 and 3
1903	WJ Travis	EM Byers	Nassau, NY	5 and 4
1904	HC Egan	F Herreshof	Baltusrol, NJ	8 and 6
1905	HC Egan	DE Sawyer	Wheaton, IL	6 and 5
1906	EM Byers	GS Lyon	Englewood, NJ	2 holes
1907	JD Travers	A Graham	Cleveland, OH	6 and 5
1908	JD Travers	MH Behr	Garden City, NY	8 and 7
1909	RA Gardner	HC Egan	Wheaton, IL	4 and 3
1910	WC Fownes jr	WK Wood	Brookline, MA	4 and 3
1911	HH Hilton	F Herreshof	Apawamis, NY	37th
1912	JD Travers	C Evans jr	Wheaton, IL	7 and 6
1913	JD Travers	JG Anderson	Garden City, NY	5 and 4
1914	F Ouimet	JD Travers	Ekwanok, VT	6 and 5
1915	RA Gardner	JG Anderson	Detroit, MI	5 and 4
1916	C Evans jr	RA Gardner	Merion, PA	4 and 3
1917–18 Not played due to First World War				
1919	SD Herron	RT Jones jr	Oakmont, PA	5 and 4
1920	C Evans jr	F Ouimet	Roslyn, NY	7 and 6
1921	JP Guildford	RA Gardner	Clayton, MO	7 and 6
1922	JW Sweetser	C Evans jr	Brookline, MA	3 and 2
1923	MR Marston	JW Sweetser	Flossmoor, IL	38th
1924	RT Jones jr	G Von Elm	Merion, PA	9 and 8
1925	RT Jones jr	W Gunn	Oakmont, PA	8 and 7
1926	G Von Elm	RT Jones jr	Baltusrol, NJ	2 and 1
1927	RT Jones jr	C Evans jr	Minikahda, MN	8 and 7
1928	RT Jones jr	TP Perkins	Brae Burn, MA	10 and 9
1929	HR Johnston	OF Willing	Pebble Beach, CA	4 and 3
1930	RT Jones jr	EV Homans	Merion, PA	8 and 7
1931	F Ouimet	J Westland	Beverley, IL	6 and 5
1932	CR Somerville	J Goodman	Baltimore, MD	2 and 1
1933	GT Dunlap jr	MR Marston	Kenwood, OH	6 and 5
1934	W Lawson Little jr	D Goldman	Brookline, MA	8 and 7
1935	W Lawson Little jr	W Emery	Cleveland, OH	4 and 2
1936	JW Fischer	J McLean	Garden City, NY	37th
1937	J Goodman	RE Billows	Portland, OR	2 holes
1938	WP Turnesa	BP Abbott	Oakmont, PA	8 and 7
1939	MH Ward	RE Billows	Glenview, IL	7 and 5
1940	RD Chapman	WB McCullough	Winged Foot, NY	11 and 9
1941	MH Ward	BP Abbott	Omaha, NE	4 and 3
1946	SE Bishop	S Quick	Baltusrol, NJ	37th
1947	RH Riegel	JW Dawson	Pebble Beach, CA	2 and 1
1948	WP Turnesa	RE Billows	Memphis, TN	2 and 1
1949	CR Coe	R King	Rochester, NY	11 and 10
1950	S Urzetta	FR Stranahan	Minneapolis, MN	39th
1951	WJ Maxwell	J Gagliardi	Saucon Valley, PA	4 and 3
1952	J Westland	A Mengert	Seattle, WA	3 and 2

Year	Winner	Runner-up	Venue	By
1953	G Littler	D Morey	Oklahoma City, OK	1 hole
1954	A Palmer	R Sweeney	Detroit, MI	1 hole
1955	E Harvie Ward	W Hyndman	Richmond, VA	9 and 8
1956	E Harvie Ward	C Kocsis	Lake Forest, IL	5 and 4
1957	H Robbins	FM Taylor	Brookline, MA	5 and 4
1958	CR Coe	TD Aaron	San Francisco, CA	5 and 4
1959	JW Nicklaus	CR Coe	Broadmoor, CO	1 hole
1960	DR Beman	RW Gardner	St Louis, MO	6 and 4
1961	JW Nicklaus	HD Wysong	Pebble Beach, CA	8 and 6
1962	LE Harris jr	D Gray	Pinehurst, NC	1 hole
1963	DR Beman	RH Sikes	Des Moines, IA	2 and 1
1964	WC Campbell	EM Tutweiler	Canterbury, OH	1 hole

Changed to stroke play

Year	Winner	Venue	Score
1965	RJ Murphy	Tulsa, OK	291
1966	G Cowan (Can)	Merion, PA	285
1967	RB Dickson	Broadmoor, CO	285
1968	B Fleisher	Columbus, OH	284
1969	S Melnyk	Oakmont, PA	286
1970	L Wadkins	Portland, OR	280
1971	G Cowan (Can)	Wilmington, DE	280
1972	M Giles	Charlotte, NC	285

Reverted to match play

Year	Winner	Runner-up	Venue	By
1973	C Stadler	D Strawn	Inverness, OH	6 and 5
1974	J Pate	J Grace	Ridgewood, NJ	2 and 1
1975	F Ridley	K Fergus	Richmond, VA	2 holes
1976	B Sander	CP Moore	Bel-Air, CA	8 and 6
1977	J Fought	D Fischesser	Aronimink, PA	9 and 8
1978	J Cook	S Hoch	Plainfield, NJ	5 and 4
1979	M O'Meara	J Cook	Cleveland, OH	8 and 7
1980	H Sutton	B Lewis	Pinehurst, NC	9 and 8
1981	N Crosby	B Lindley	San Francisco, CA	37th
1982	J Sigel	D Tolley	Brookline, MA	8 and 7
1983	J Sigel	C Perry	Glenview, IL	8 and 7
1984	S Verplank	S Randolph	Oak Tree, OK	4 and 3
1985	S Randolph	P Persons	Montclair, NJ	1 hole
1986	S Alexander	C Kite	Shoal Creek, AL	5 and 3
1987	W Mayfair	E Rebmann	Jupiter Hills, FL	4 and 3
1988	E Meeks	D Yates	Hot Springs, VA	7 and 6
1989	C Patton	D Green	Merion, PA	3 and 1
1990	P Mickelson	M Zerman	Cherry Hills, CO	5 and 4
1991	M Voges	M Zerman	Chattanooga, TN	7 and 6
1992	J Leonard	T Scherrer	Muirfield Village, OH	8 and 7
1993	J Harris	D Ellis	Houston, TX	5 and 3
1994	T Woods	T Kuehne	Sawgrass, FL	2 holes
1995	T Woods	G Marucci	Newport, RI	2 holes
1996	T Woods	S Scott	Pumpkin Ridge, OR	38th
1997	M Kuchar	J Kribel	Cog Hill, Lemont, IL	2 and 1
1998	H Kuehne	T McKnight	Oak Hill, Rochester, NY	2 and 1
1999	D Gossett	Sung Yoon Kim	Pebble Beach, CA	9 and 8
2000	J Quinney	J Driscoll	Springfield, NJ	39th hole
2001	B Dickerson	R Hamilton	East Lake, Atlanta, GA	1 hole
2002	R Barnes	H Mahon	Oakland Hills, MI	2 and 1

2003 at Oakmont, PA

Quarter Finals

Lee Williams (Alexander City, AL) beat Patrick Carter (Lesage, WV) 4 and 3
Casey Wittenberg (Memphis, TN) beat George Zahringer (New York, NY) 1 hole
Nick Flanagan (Aus) beat Jerry Courville (Milford, CT) 1 hole
David Oh (Cerritos, CA) beat Bill Haas (Greenville, SC) 2 and 1

Semi-Finals: Wittenberg beat Williams 5 and 4   Flanagan beat Oh 1 hole

Final: Nick Flanagan beat Casey Wittenberg at 37th

Other 2003 Overseas Amateur Championships

Austrian (Close)	Florian Praegant	Hungarian (Close)	Istvan Wilheim
Austrian	Martin Kaymer (Ger)	Hungarian	Lepori Daniel
Belgian	Pierre Relecom	Luxembourg	Benjamin Miarka
Caribbean	Sean Hartman (USA)	Netherlands	Reinier Sexton
Czech	Peter Nič	Portuguese	Richard Walker (Eng)
Danish	Jeppe Huldahl	Slovak	Peter Jusko
Finnish	Avi Savolainen	Slovak Stroke Play	Peter Wieger
French	Eric Chadouet	Spanish	Sebastian García Grout
German (Close)	Dennis Küpper	Swiss	Erik Johanson (Nor)
German	Christian Schunck	Turkish	Gencer Özcan
Hellenic	Steve Parthenis		

After 100 years an Australian winner

Nineteen-year-old Nick Flanagan became the first Australian in 100 years and the first foreign player since Canadian Gary Cowan in 1971 to win the US Amateur Championship played in 2003 at the historic Oakmont Country Club.

In a final – the first between two teenagers since the event reverted to match play in 1973 – Flanagan edged home at the 37th. hole against 18-year-old American Walker Cup golfer Casey Wittenburg from Memphis. By winning he matched Walter Travis as an Australian winner of the title, his success coming exactly a century after Travis won his third US Amateur title.

Flanagan is the second youngest winner of the Championship beaten only by Tiger Woods who was just 18 when he won the first of his three successive titles in 1994. Winner of the Tasmanian Open earlier in the year Flanagan spent the summer in America during which time he also won the Pacific Northwest Amateur title.

Callaway Handicapping

It frequently occurs in social competitions such as office or business association outings that many of the competitors do not have official handicaps. In such cases the best solution is to use the Callaway handicapping system, so called after the name of its inventor, as it is simple to use yet has proved equitable.

Competitors complete their round marking in their gross figures at every hole and their handicaps are awarded and deducted at the end of the 18 holes using the following table:

Competitor's Gross Score	Handicap Deduction
par or less	none
one over par – 75	½ worst hole
76–80	worst hole
81–85	worst hole plus ½ next worse
86–90	two worst holes
91–95	two worst holes plus ½ next
96–100	three worst holes
101–105	three worst holes plus ½ next
106–110	four worst holes
111–115	four worst holes plus ½ next
116–120	five worst holes
121–125	five worst holes plus ½ next
126–130	six worst holes

Note 1: Worst hole equals highest score at any hole regardless of the par of the hole except that the maximum score allowed for any one hole is twice the par of the hole.

Note 2: The 17th and 18th holes are not allowed to be deducted.

Example: Competitor scores 104. From the table he should deduct as his handicap the total of his three worst (i.e. highest) individual hole scores plus half of his fourth worst hole. If he scored one 9, one 8 and several 7's he would therefore deduct a total of 27½ from his gross score of 104 to give a net score of 76½.

PART V

Women's Amateur Tournaments

National and International Tournaments   294
Team Events   309
Other Women's Amateur Tournaments   324
Irish Ladies District Championships   327
Foursomes Events   327
Regional Amateur Championships   328
Overseas Amateur Championships   333

National and International Tournaments

Ladies British Amateur Championship (Inaugurated 1893)

1893	M Scott	I Pearson	St Annes	7 and 5
1894	M Scott	I Pearson	Littlestone	3 and 2
1895	M Scott	E Lythgoe	Portrush	5 and 4
1896	Miss Pascoe	L Thomson	Hoylake, Royal Liverpool	3 and 2
1897	EC Orr	Miss Orr	Gullane	4 and 2
1898	L Thomson	EC Neville	Yarmouth	7 and 5
1899	M Hezlet	Magill	Newcastle Co Down	2 and 1
1900	Adair	Neville	Westward Ho!, R North Devon	6 and 5
1901	Graham	Adair	Aberdovey	3 and 1
1902	M Hezlet	E Neville	Deal	19th hole
1903	Adair	F Walker-Leigh	Portrush	4 and 3
1904	L Dod	M Hezlet	Troon	1 hole
1905	B Thompson	ME Stuart	Cromer	3 and 2
1906	Kennon	B Thompson	Burnham	4 and 3
1907	M Hezlet	F Hezlet	Newcastle Co Down	2 and 1
1908	M Titterton	D Campbell	St Andrews	19th hole
1909	D Campbell	F Hezlet	Birkdale	4 and 3
1910	Miss Grant Suttie	L Moore	Westward Ho!, R North Devon	6 and 4
1911	D Campbell	V Hezlet	Portrush	3 and 2
1912	G Ravenscroft	S Temple	Turnberry	3 and 2

(Final played over 36 holes after 1912)

1913	M Dodd	Chubb	St Annes	8 and 6
1914	C Leitch	G Ravenscroft	Hunstanton	2 and 1

1915–18 *No Championship owing to the Great War*
1919 *Should have been played at Burnham in October, but abandoned owing to railway strike*

1920	C Leitch	M Griffiths	Newcastle Co Down	7 and 6
1921	C Leitch	J Wethered	Turnberry	4 and 3
1922	J Wethered	C Leitch	Prince's, Sandwich, Royal St George's	9 and 7
1923	D Chambers	A Macbeth	Burnham, Somerset	2 holes
1924	J Wethered	Mrs Cautley	Portrush	7 and 6
1925	J Wethered	C Leitch	Troon	37th hole
1926	C Leitch	Mrs Garon	Harlech	8 and 7
1927	T de la Chaume (Fra)	Miss Pearson	Newcastle Co Down	5 and 4
1928	N Le Blan (Fra)	S Marshall	Hunstanton	3 and 2
1929	J Wethered	G Collett (USA)	St Andrews	3 and 1
1930	D Fishwick	G Collett (USA)	Formby	4 and 3
1931	E Wilson	W Morgan	Portmarnock	7 and 6
1932	E Wilson	CPR Montgomery	Saunton	7 and 6
1933	E Wilson	D Plumpton	Gleneagles	5 and 4
1934	AM Holm	P Barton	Porthcawl	6 and 5
1935	W Morgan	P Barton	Newcastle Co Down	3 and 2
1936	P Barton	B Newell	Southport and Ainsdale	5 and 3
1937	J Anderson	D Park	Turnberry	6 and 4
1938	AM Holm	E Corlett	Burnham	4 and 3
1939	P Barton	T Marks	Portrush	2 and 1

1940–45 *No Championship owing to Second World War*

1946	GW Hetherington	P Garvey	Hunstanton	1 hole
1947	B Zaharias (USA)	J Gordon	Gullane	5 and 4
1948	L Suggs (USA)	J Donald	Lytham St Annes	1 hole
1949	F Stephens	V Reddan	Harlech	5 and 4
1950	Vicomtesse de St Sauveur (Fra)	J Valentine	Newcastle Co Down	3 and 2
1951	PJ MacCann	F Stephens	Broadstone	4 and 3
1952	M Paterson	F Stephens	Troon	39th hole
1953	M Stewart (Can)	P Garvey	Porthcawl	7 and 6
1954	F Stephens	E Price	Ganton	4 and 3

1955	J Valentine	B Romack (USA)	Portrush	7 and 6
1956	M Smith (USA)	M Janssen (USA)	Sunningdale	8 and 7
1957	P Garvey	J Valentine	Gleneagles	4 and 3
1958	J Valentine	E Price	Hunstanton	1 hole
1959	E Price	B McCorkindale	Ascot	37th hole
1960	B McIntyre (USA)	P Garvey	Harlech	4 and 2
1961	M Spearman	DJ Robb	Carnoustie	7 and 6
1962	M Spearman	A Bonallack	Royal Birkdale	1 hole
1963	B Varangot (Fra)	P Garvey	Newcastle Co Down	3 and 1
1964	C Sorenson (USA)	BAB Jackson	Sandwich, Prince's, Royal St George's	37th hole
1965	B Varangot (Fra)	IC Robertson	St Andrews	4 and 3
1966	E Chadwick	V Saunders	Ganton	3 and 2
1967	E Chadwick	M Everard	Harlech	1 hole
1968	B Varangot (Fra)	C Rubin (Fra)	Walton Heath	20th hole
1969	C Lacoste (Fra)	A Irvin	Portrush	1 hole
1970	D Oxley	IC Robertson	Gullane	1 hole
1971	M Walker	B Huke	Alwoodley	3 and 1
1972	M Walker	C Rubin (Fra)	Hunstanton	2 holes
1973	A Irvin	M Walker	Carnoustie	3 and 2
1974	C Semple (USA)	A Bonallack	Porthcawl	2 and 1
1975	N Syms (USA)	S Cadden	St Andrews	3 and 2
1976	C Panton	A Sheard	Silloth	1 hole
1977	A Uzielli	V Marvin	Hillside	6 and 5
1978	E Kennedy (Aus)	J Greenhalgh	Notts	1 hole
1979	M Madill	J Lock (Aus)	Nairn	2 and 1
1980	A Quast (USA)	L Wollin (Swe)	Woodhall Spa	3 and 1
1981	IC Robertson	W Aitken	Conway	20th hole
1982	K Douglas	G Stewart	Walton Heath	4 and 2
1983	J Thornhill	R Lautens (Sui)	Silloth	4 and 2
1984	J Rosenthal (USA)	J Brown	Royal Troon	4 and 3
1985	L Beman (Irl)	C Waite	Ganton	1 hole
1986	McGuire (NZ)	L Briars (Aus)	West Sussex	2 and 1
1987	J Collingham	S Shapcott	Harlech	19th hole
1988	J Furby	J Wade	Deal	4 and 3
1989	H Dobson	E Farquharson	Royal Liverpool	6 and 5
1990	J Hall	H Wadsworth	Dunbar	3 and 2
1991	V Michaud (Fra)	W Doolan (Aus)	Pannal	3 and 2
1992	P Pedersen (Den)	J Morley	Saunton	1 hole
1993	C Lambert	K Speak	Royal Lytham	3 and 2
1994	E Duggleby	C Mourgue d'Algue	Newport	3 and 1
1995	J Hall	K Mourgue d'Algue	Royal Portrush	3 and 2
1996	K Kuehne (USA)	B Morgan	Royal Liverpool	5 and 3
1997	A Rose	M McKay	Cruden Bay	4 and 3
1998	K Rostron	C Nocera	Little Aston	3 and 2
1999	M Monnet (Fra)	R Hudson	Royal Birkdale	1 hole
2000	R Hudson	E Duggleby	Royal Birkdale	5 and 4
2001	M Prieto (Esp)	E Duggleby	Ladybank	4 and 3
2002	R Hudson	L Wright	Ashburnham	5 and 4

2003 *at Lindrick*

Leading Qualifier: Danielle Masters (Bearsted) 72-73—145

First Round

Danielle Masters (Bearsted) beat Jenna Wilson (Strathaven) 6 and 5
Kerstin Honisch (Ger) beat Sara Garbutt (Ganton) 2 holes
Fany Schaeffer (Fra) beat Giuly Colavito (Ita) 2 and 1
Vikki Laing (Musselburgh) beat Bettina Hauert (Ger) 1 hole
Denise Simon (Ger) beat Stephanie Doering (Ger) 3 and 2
Alena Sharp (Brantford) beat Jo Pritchard (Tredegar Park) 5 and 4
Becky Brewerton (Abergele) beat Lisa Ball (Parklands) 5 and 3
Peggy Fraysse (Fra) beat Niloufar Aazam (Sui) 1 hole
Pia Odefey (Ger) beat Jo Nicolson (Wrexham) 5 and 4
Margherita Rigon (Ita) beat Martina Gillen (Beaverstown) 1 hole
Clare Queen (Drumpellier) beat Rachel Adby (Sandiway) 5 and 4
Chloe Court (Goodwood) beat Michelle Smith (Hallowes) 1 hole
Carmen Alonso (Esp) beat Karin Borjeskog (Swe) 4 and 2
Tricia Mangan (Ennis) beat Rachael Lomas (Hallowes) 4 and 3

Ladies British Amateur Championship *continued*

First Round *continued*

Louise Stahle (Swe) beat Emma Duggleby (Malton & Norton) 3 and 1
Nuria Clau (Esp) beat Dana Lacey (Aus) 2 and 1
Anne-Sophie Le Nalio (Fra) beat Marie Allen (Moor Park) 3 and 2
Elisa Serramia (Esp) beat Emma Brown (West Wilts) at 19th
Nicola Timmins (Sene Valley) beat Amparo Gala Marco (Esp) 3 and 2
Sofie Andersson (Swe) beat Elizabeth Bennett (Brokenhurst Manor) 1 hole
Kelly Hanwell (Northampton) beat Adriana Zwanck (Esp) 4 and 2
Sarah Jones (Pennard) beat Heather Nolan (Shannon) 7 and 6
Beatriz Recari Eransus (Esp) beat Karin Sjodin (Swe) at 22nd
Lynn Kenny (University of Stirling) beat Ria Denise Quiazon (USA) 3 and 2
Anne Laing (Vale of Leven) beat Lisa Holm Sorrensen (Den) 4 and 2
Minea Blomqvist (Fin) beat Elizabeth McKinnon (Nairn) 5 and 4
Sophie Giquel (Fra) beat Carolin Landmann (Ger) 4 and 3
Fame More (Chesterfield) beat Heather Macrae (Dunblane New) 6 and 4
Raphaelle Vilatte (Fra) beat Chris Kobarg (Ger) 3 and 2
Anna Highgate (Cottrell Park) beat Kelly Hutcherson (Porters Park) at 21st
Alexandra Vilatte (Fra) beat Beatrice Soubiron (Fra) 1 hole
Anja Monke (Ger) beat Marion Sapin (Fra) 1 hole

Second Round
Masters beat Honisch 3 and 2
Schaeffer beat V Laing 5 and 4
Simon beat Sharp 5 and 4
Brewerton beat Fraysse 6 and 5
Odefey beat Rigon 4 and 3
Queen beat Court at 19th
Alonso beat Mangan 4 and 2
Stahle beat Clau 4 and 3
Serramia beat Le Nalio 3 and 2
Timmins beat Andersson 2 and 1
Hanwell beat Jones 2 and 1
Kenny beat Recari Eransus 4 and 3
A Laing beat Blomqvist 7 and 5
More beat Giquel 7 and 6
Highgate beat R Vilatte 8 and 7
Monke beat A Vilatte 6 and 4

Third Round
Schaeffer beat Masters 3 and 2
Simon beat Brewerton 4 and 3

Third Round *continued*
Odefey beat Queen 4 and 3
Alonso beat Stahle 3 and 2
Serramia beat Timmins 2 and 1
Kenny beat Hanwell 3 and 2
More beat Laing 5 and 3
Monke beat Highgate 6 and 5

Quarter Finals
Schaeffer b Simon 3 and 2
Odefey beat Alonso 1 hole
Serramia beat Kenny 2 and 1
Monke beat More 5 and 4

Semi-Finals
Odefey beat Schaeffer 6 and 5
Serramia beat Monke 2 holes

Final
Elisa Serramia (Esp) beat Pia Odefey (Ger) 2 holes

Ladies British Open Amateur Stroke Play Championship

(Inaugurated 1969)

1969	A Irvin	Gosforth Park	295	1983	A Nicholas	Moortown	292
1970	M Everard	Birkdale	313	1984	C Waite	Caernarvonshire	295
1971	IC Robertson	Ayr Belleisle	302	1985	IC Robertson	Formby	300
1972	IC Robertson	Silloth	296	1986	C Hourihane	Blairgowrie	291
1973	A Stant	Purdis Heath	298	1987	L Bayman	Ipswich	297
1974	J Greenhalgh	Seaton Carew	302	1988	K Mitchell	Porthcawl	317
1975	J Greenhalgh	Gosforth Park	298	1989	H Dobson	Southerness	298
1976	J Lee Smith	Fulford	299	1990	V Thomas	Strathaven	287
1977	M Everard	Lindrick	306	1991	J Morley	Long Ashton	297
1978	J Melville	Foxhills	310	1992	J Hockley	Frilford Heath	287
1979	M McKenna	Moseley	305	1993	J Hall	Gullane	290
1980	M Mahill	Brancepeth Castle	304	1994	K Speak	Woodhall Spa	297
1981	J Soulsby	Norwich	300	1995	MJ Pons (Esp)	Princes	289
1982	J Connachan	Downfield	294	1996	C Kuld (Den)	Conwy (Caernarvonshire)	289

1997	KM Juul (Den)	Silloth-on-Solway	293	2000	R Hudson	Newcastle, NI	294
1998	N Nijenhuis	Stirling	297	2001	R Hudson	Kilmarnock	300
1999	B Brewerton	Huddersfield	294	2002	B Brewerton	Hunstanton	291

2003 *at Royal Portrush*

1	Shelley McKevitt (Reading)	75-79-81-71—306
2	Lynn Kenny (University of Stirling)	85-72-76-74—307
3	Clare Queen (Drumpellier)	79-79-75-75—308

Ladies British Open Mid-Amateur Championship (inaugurated 2002)

2002	A Laing	The Berkshire	214

2003 *at Royal Liverpool*

1	Sarah Walton (Accrington & District)*	81-74-74—229
2	Stinne Thorsen (Den)	77-77-75—229
3	Caroline Marron (Bromborough)	80-75-76—231

Senior Ladies British Open Amateur Stroke Play Championship

1981	BM King	Formby	159	1992	A Uzielli	Stratford-upon-Avon	148
1982	P Riddiford	Ilkley	161	1993	J Thornhill	Ashburnham	151
1983	M Birtwistle	Troon Portland	167	1994	D Williams	Nottingham	154
1984	O Semelaigne	Woodbridge	152	1995	A Uzielli	Blairgowrie	152
1985	Dr G Costello	Prestatyn	158	1996	V Hassett	Pyle & Kenfig	236
1986	P Riddiford	Longniddry	154	1997	T Wiesner (USA)	Frilford Heath	231
1987	O Semelaigne	Copt Heath	152	1998	A Uzielli	Powfoot	227
1988	C Bailey	Littlestone	156	1999	A Uzielli	Malone	229
1989	C Bailey	Wrexham	149	2000	B Mogensen (Den)	West Kilbride	242
1990	A Uzielli	Harrogate	153	2001	M McKenna	Aberdovy	230
1991	A Uzielli	Ladybank	154	2002	R Page	Longniddry	229

2003 *at South Staffordshire*

1	Christina Burke (Swe)	76-73-77—226
2	Sue Pidgeon (Wrekin)	80-75-77—232
3	Carole Caldwell (Sunningdale)	77-79-77—233

English Ladies Close Amateur Championship (inaugurated 1912)

1912	M Gardner	Mrs Cautley	Sandwich	at 20th
1913	FW Brown	Mrs McNair	Hollinwell	1 hole
1914	Cecil Leitch	Miss Bastin	Walton Heath	2 and 1
1915–1918	*Not played due to First World War*			
1919	Cecil Leitch	Mrs Temple Dobell	St Annes Old	10 and 8
1920	Joyce Wethered	Cecil Leitch	Sheringham	2 and 1
1921	Joyce Wethered	Mrs Mudford	Lytham St Annes	12 and 11
1922	Joyce Wethered	J Stocker	Hunstanton	7 and 6
1923	Joyce Wethered	Mrs TA Lodge	Ganton	8 and 7
1924	Joyce Wethered	DR Fowler	Cooden Beach	8 and 7
1925	DR Fowler	J Winn	Westward Ho!	9 and 7
1926	Molly Gourlay	Elsie Corlett	Woodhall Spa	6 and 4
1927	Mrs H Guedalla	Enid Wilson	Pannal	1 hole
1928	Enid Wilson	Dorothy Pearson	Walton Heath	9 and 8
1929	Molly Gourlay	Diana Fishwick	Broadstone	6 and 5
1930	Enid Wilson	Mrs RO Porter	Aldeburgh	12 and 11
1931	Wanda Morgan	Molly Gourlay	Ganton	3 and 1
1932	Diana Fishwick	Miss B Brown	Royal Ashdown Forest	5 and 4
1933	Dorothy Pearson	M Johnson	Westward Ho!	5 and 3
1934	P Wade	M Johnson	Seacroft	4 and 3
1935	Mrs M Garon	Elsie Corlett	Birkdale	at 38th
1936	Wanda Morgan	P Wade	Hayling Island	2 and 1
1937	Wanda Morgan	M Fyshe	St Enodoc	4 and 2

English Ladies Close Amateur Championship *continued*

1938	Elsie Corlett	J Winn	Aldeburgh	2 and 1
1939–1946 *Not played due to Second World War*				
1947	M Wallis	Elizabeth Price	Ganton	3 and 1
1948	Frances Stephens	Zara Bolton	Hayling Island	1 hole
1949	Diana Critchley	Lady Katharine Cairns	Burnham & Berrow	3 and 2
1950	Hon Mrs A Gee	Pamela Davies	Sheringham	8 and 6
1951	Jeanne Bisgood	A Keiller	St Annes Old	2 and 1
1952	Pamela Davies	Jacqueline Gordon	Westwood Ho!	6 and 5
1953	Jeanne Bisgood	J McIntyre	Sandwich	6 and 5
1954	Frances Stephens	Elizabeth Price	Woodhall Spa	at 37th
1955	Frances Smith	Elizabeth Price	Moortown	4 and 3
1956	Bridget Jackson	Ruth Ferguson	Hunstanton	2 and 1
1957	Jeanne Bisgood	Margaret Nichol	Bournemouth	10 and 8
1958	Angela Bonallack	Bridget Jackson	Formby	3 and 2
1959	Ruth Porter	Frances Smith	Aldeburgh	5 and 4
1960	Margaret Nichol	Angela Bonallack	Burnham & Berrow	3 and 1
1961	Ruth Porter	Peggy Reece	Littlestone	2 holes
1962	Jean Roberts	Angela Bonallack	Woodhall Spa	3 and 1
1963	Angela Bonallack	Elizabeth Chadwick	Liphook	7 and 6
1964	Marley Spearman	Mary Everard	Lytham St Annes	6 and 5
1965	Ruth Porter	G Cheetham	Whittington Barracks	6 and 5
1966	Julia Greenhalgh	Jean Holmes	Hayling Island	3 and 1
1967	Ann Irvin	Margaret Pickard	Alwoodley	3 and 2
1968	Sally Barber	Dinah Oxley	Hunstanton	5 and 4
1969	Barbara Dixon	M Wenyon	Burnham & Berrow	6 and 4
1970	Dinah Oxley	Sally Barber	Rye	3 and 2
1971	Dinah Oxley	Sally Barber	Hoylake	5 and 4
1972	Mary Everard	Angela Bonallack	Woodhall Spa	2 and 1
1973	Mickey Walker	Carol Le Feuvre	Broadstone	6 and 5
1974	Ann Irvin	Jill Thornhill	Sunningdale	1 hole
1975	Beverly Huke	Lynne Harrold	Birkdale	2 and 1
1976	Lynne Harrold	Angela Uzielli	Hollinwell	3 and 2
1977	Vanessa Marvin	Mary Everard	Burnham & Berrow	1 hole
1978	Vanessa Marvin	Ruth Porter	West Sussex	2 and 1
1979	Julia Greenhalgh	Susan Hedges	Hoylake	2 and 1
1980	Beverley New	Julie Walker	Aldeburgh	3 and 2
1981	Diane Christison	S Cohen	Cotswold Hills	2 holes
1982	Julie Walker	C Nelson	Brancepeth Castle	4 and 3
1983	Linda Bayman	C Macintosh	Hayling Island	4 and 3
1984	Claire Waite	Linda Bayman	Hunstanton	3 and 2
1985	Patricia Johnson	Linda Bayman	Ferndown	1 hole
1986	Jill Thornhill	Susan Shapcott	Sandwich	3 and 1
1987	Joanne Furby	Maria King	Alwoodley	4 and 3
1988	Julie Wade	Susan Shapcott	Little Aston	at 19t
1989	Helen Dobson	Simone Morgan	Burnham & Berrow	4 and 3
1990	Angela Uzielli	Linzi Fletcher	Rye	2 and 1
1991	Nicola Buxton	Karen Stupples	Sheringham	2 holes
1992	Caroline Hall	Joanne Hockley	St Annes Old	1 hole
1993	Nicola Buxton	Sarah Burnell	St Enodoc	2 and 1
1994	Julie Wade	S Sharpe	The Berkshire	1 hole
1995	Julie Wade	Elaine Ratcliffe	Ipswich	2 and 1
1996	Joanne Hockley	Lisa Educate	Silloth-on-Solway	4 and 3
1997	Kim Rostron	K Burton	Saunton	4 and 2
1998	Elaine Ratcliffe	Lisa Walters	Walton Heath	at 19th
1999	Fiona Brown	Kerry Smith	Ganton	2 and 1
2000	Emma Duggleby	Rebecca Hudson	Hunstanton	4 and 3
2001	Rebecca Hudson	Emma Duggleby	West Sussex	at 20th
2002	K Knowles	C Court	Littlestone	6 and 5

2003 *at Aldeburgh*

Leading Qualifier: Nicola Timmins (Sene Valley) 72-69—141

Quarter Finals

Naomi Edwards (Ganton) beat Nicola Timmins
(Sene Valley) 3 and 2
Shelley McKevitt (Reading) beat Caroline Marron
(Bromborough) at 21st
Danielle Masters (Rochester & Cobham) beat
Kerry Smith (Waterlooville) 4 and 3
Emma Duggleby (Malton & Norton) beat
Fame More (Chesterfield) 4 and 3

Semi-Finals

Edwards beat McKevitt 3 and 2
Duggleby beat Masters 4 and 3

Final

Emma Duggleby beat Naomi Edwards 2 and 1

English Ladies Close Amateur Stroke Play Championship

(Inaugurated 1984)

1984	P Grice	Moor Park	300	1994	F Brown	Ferndown	289
1985	P Johnson	Northants County	301	1995	L Walton	Hallamshire	289
1986	S Shapcott	Broadstone	301	1996	S Gallagher	Little Aston	290
1987	J Wade	Northumberland	296	1997	L Tupholme	Hankley Common	293
1988	S Prosser	Wentworth	297	1998	E Duggleby	Broadstone	306
1989	S Robinson	Notts	302	1999	C Lipscombe	Gog Magog	300
1990	K Tebbet	Saunton	299	2000	R Hudson	Silloth-on-Solway	290
1991	J Morley	Ganton	301	2001	C Marron*	Stoneham	291
1992	J Morley	Littlestone	289	2002	S Garbutt	Whittington Heath	294
1993	J Hall	King's Norton	298				

2003 *at Saunton*

1	Sophie Walker (Kenwick Park)*	71-79-80-73—303
2	Lisa Ball (Parklands)	74-75-76-78—303
	(sudden death play-off)	
3	Kerry Smith (Waterlooville)	81-76-75-75—307

English Ladies Under-23 Championship (Inaugurated 1978)

1978	S Bamford	Caldy	228	1991	J Hockley	Saunton	303
1979	B Cooper	Coxmoor	223	1992	N Buxton	Littlestone	292
1980	B Cooper	Porters Park	226	1993	R Millington	King's Norton	302
1981	J Soulsby	Willesley Park	220	1994	F Brown	Ferndown	289
1982	M Gallagher	High Post	221	1995	E Fields	Hallamshire	297
1983	P Grice	Hallamshire	219	1996	R Hudson	Little Aston	299
1984	P Johnson	Moor Park	300	1997	R Bailey	Hankley Common	306
1985	P Johnson	Northants County	301	1998	L Meredith	Broadstone	307
1986	S Shapcott	Broadstone	301	1999	C Lipscombe	Gog Magog	300
1987	J Wade	Northumberland	296	2000	R Hudson	Silloth-on-Solway	290
1988	J Wade	Wentworth	299	2001	E Weeks	Stoneham	291
1989	A Shapcott	Notts Ladies	302	2002	S Garbutt	Whittington Heath	294
1990	K Tebbet	Saunton	299				

2003 *at Saunton*

1	Sophie Walker (Kenwick Park)	71-79-80-73—303
2	Rachel Bell (Ganton)	80-77-80-71—308
3	Faye Sanderson (Heworth)	74-77-81-76—308

English Senior Ladies Stroke Play Championship (Inaugurated 1986)

1988	A Thompson	Wentworth	158	1996	A Uzielli	Royal North Devon	153
1989	C Bailey	Notts Ladies	163	1997	A Thompson	Formby Ladies	152
1990	A Thompson	Fairhaven	162	1998	E Boatman	Royal Liverpool	154
1991	C Bailey	Burnham and Berrow	155	1999	S Westall	Northants County	151
1992	A Thompson	Pleasington	154	2000	E McCombe	Formby	162
1993	A Uzielli	Hunstanton	150	2001	R Page	Woodhall Spa	159
1994	S Bassindale	Littlestone	163	2002	C Caldwell	Saunton	158
1995	V Morgan	Tandridge	151				

2003 *at Rye*

1	Carole Caldwell (Sunningdale)*	78-76—154
2	Deborah Backhouse (Colchester)	78-76—154
3	Val McFarlane (Lansdown)	75-80—155

English Senior Ladies Match Play Championship (Inaugurated 1994)

1994	E Annison	S Bassindale	Whitting Heath
1995	A Thompson	G Palmer	R Ashdown Forest
1996	R Farrow	V Morgan	Lindrick
1997	G Palmer	C Means	S Winchester
1998	E McCombe	J Thornhill	West Sussex
1999	E McCombe	V Morgan	Lindrick
2000	E McCombe	M Griffiths	Burnham & Berrow
2001	A Vine	V Morgan	Beau Desert
2002	C Stirling	C Caldwell	Ganton

2003 *at The Berkshire*

Semi-Finals
Ros Page (Henbury) beat Val McFarlane (Lansdown) at 24th
Christine Watson (Beaconsfield) beat Carole Caldwell (Sunningdale) 3 and 2

Final
Christine Watson beat Ros Page 4 and 3

English Senior Ladies Close Amateur Championship

2003 *at Ilkley*

Quarter Finals:
Geraldine Bray (Littlestone) beat Isobel Williams (Appleby) 3 and 1
Adele Mitchell (Keighley) beat Margaret Maisey (Ellesborough) 3 and 2
Sue Pidgeon (Wrekin) beat Barbara Woodham (Bearsted) 4 and 3
Vivien Saunders (Cambridge Meridian) beat Sue Westall (Copt Heath) 5 and 3

Semi-Finals:
Mitchell beat Bray at 19th
Saunders beat Pidgeon 7 and 6

Final:
Adele Mitchell beat Vivien Saunders 1 hole

English Ladies Open Intermediate Championship (Inaugurated 1982)

1982	J Rhodes	Headingley	19th hole	1993	K Speak	Seascale	2 and 1
1983	L Davies	Worksop	2 and 1	1994	J Oliver	Beaconsfield	2 up
1984	P Grice	Whittington Barracks	3 and 2	1995	K Smith	Clitheroe	5 and 4
1985	S Lowe	Caldy	2 and 1	1996	R Bailey	Sandiway	3 and 2
1986	S Moorcroft	Hexham	6 and 5	1997	K Smith	Abbotsley	2 and 1
1987	J Wade	Sheringham	2 and 1	1998	J Lamb	Hornsea	1 hole
1988	S Morgan	Enville, Staffs	20th hole	1999	K Fisher	Woodbury Park	1 hole
1989	L Fairclough	Warrington	4 and 3	2000	K Keogh	Woodbury Park	1 hole
1990	L Fletcher	Whitley Bay	7 and 6	2001	A Keighley	Pleasington	22nd hole
1991	J Morley	West Lancashire	6 and 5	2002	*Not played*		
1992	K Speak	South Staffs	3 and 1				

2003 *at Notts Ladies*

Quarter-Finals
Nicola Timmins (Sene Valley) beat Sara Garbutt (Ganton)
    1 hole
Clare Lipscombe (Cirencester) beat Tara Watters (Muswell
    Hill) 5 and 4
Lauren Hamilton (Celtic Manor) beat Jemma Wilson
    (Strathaven) 4 and 3
Laura Eastwood (Yelverton) beat Marie Allen (Moor Park)
    at 19th

Semi-Finals
Timmins beat Lipscombe 2 and 1
Eastwood beat Hamilton 2 and 1

Final
Nicola Timmins beat Laura Eastwood
    2 and 1

Irish Ladies Close Amateur Championship (Inaugurated 1894)

Year	Winner	Runner-up	Venue	Score
1894	Miss Mulligan	N Graham	Carnalea	3 and 2
1895	Miss Cox	Miss MacLaine	Portrush	3 and 2
1896	N Graham	N Brownrigg	Newcastle	4 and 3
1897	N Graham	Miss Magill	Dollymount	4 and 3
1898	Miss Magill	M Hezlet	Malone	1 hole
1899*	M Hezlet	Miss Adair	Newcastle	5 and 4
1900*	Miss Adair	V Hezlet	Portrush	9 and 7
1901	Miss Adair	F Walker-Leigh	Portmarnock	4 and 2
1902	Miss Adair	ME Stuart	Newcastle	9 and 7
1903	Miss Adair	V Hezlet	Portrush	7 and 5
1904	M Hezlet	F Walker-Leigh	Lahinch	3 and 2
1905	M Hezlet	F Hezlet	Portsalon	2 and 1
1906	M Hezlet	F Hezlet	Newcastle	2 and 1
1907	F Walker-Leigh	Mrs Fitzgibbon	Dollymount	4 and 3
1908	M Hezlet	F Hezlet	Portrush	5 and 4
1909	Miss Ormsby	V Hezlet	Lahinch	4 and 2
1910	M Harrison	Miss Magill	Newcastle	5 and 4
1911	M Harrison	F Walker-Leigh	Malahide	6 and 4
1912	M Harrison	Mrs Cramsie	Portsalon	5 and 3
1913	J Jackson	M Harrison	Lahinch	4 and 3
1914	J Jackson	Miss Meldon	Castlerock	3 and 2
1915–1918	*Not played due to First World War*			
1919	J Jackson	M Alexander	Portmarnock	5 and 4
1920	J Jackson	Mrs Cramsie	Portrush	5 and 4
1921	Miss Stuart French	M Fitzgibbon	Hermitage	4 and 3
1922	Mrs Claude Gotto	MR Hirsch	Newcastle	2 holes
1923	J Jackson	Mrs Babington	Portmarnock	5 and 4
1924	CG Thornton	Miss Hewitt	Castlerock	4 and 3
1925	J Jackson	JF Jameson	Lahinch	2 and 1
1926	P Jameson	CH Murland	Newcastle	5 and 3
1927	Miss McLoughlin	F Blake	Dollymount	2 holes
1928	Mrs Dwyer	H Clarke	Cork	3 and 2
1929	MA Hall	I Taylor	Rosapenna	1 hole
1930	JB Walker	JF Jameson	Portmarnock	2 and 1
1931	Miss Pentony	JH Todd	Rosses Point	2 and 1
1932	B. Latchford	D Ferguson	Ballybunion	7 and 5
1933	Miss Pentony	F Blacke	Newcastle	3 and 2
1934	P Sherlock Fletcher	JB Walker	Portmarnock	3 and 2
1935	D Ferguson	Miss Ellis	Rospenna	2 and 1
1936	C Tiernan	S Moore	Ballybunion	7 and 6
1937	HV Glendinning	EL Kidd	Portrush	37th hole
1938	J Beck	B Jackson	Portmarnock	5 and 4
1939	C MacGeagh	E Gikdea	Bundoran	1 hole
1940–1945	*Not played due to Second World War*			
1946	P Garvey	V Reddan	Lahinch	39th hole
1947	P Garvey	C Syme	Portrush	5 and 4
1948	P Garvey	V Reddan	Rosslare	9 and 7
1949	C Syme	J Beck	Baltray	9 and 7
1950	P Garvey	T Marks	Rosses Point	6 and 4
1951	P Garvey	D Forster	Ballybunion	12 and 10
1952	DM Forster	PG McCann	Newcastle	3 and 2
1953	P Garvey	Mrs Hegarty	Rosslare	8 and 7
1954	P Garvey	HV Glendinning	Portmarnock	13 and 12

* Final = 36 holes on these dates

Irish Ladies Close Amateur Championship *continued*

Year	Winner	Runner-up	Venue	Score
1955	P Garvey	A O'Donohoe	Rosses Point	10 and 9
1956	P O'Sullivan	JF Hegarty	Killarney	14 and 12
1957	P Garvey	K McCann	Portrush	3 and 2
1958	P Garvey	Z Fallon	Carlow	7 and 6
1959	P Garvey	H Colhoun	Lahinch	12 and 10
1960	P Garvey	PG McCann	Cork	5 and 3
1961	K McCann	A Sweeney	Newcastle	5 and 3
1962	P Garvey	M Earner	Baltray	7 and 6
1963	P Garvey	E Barnett	Killarney	9 and 7
1964	Z Fallon	P O'Sullivan	Portrush	37th hole
1965	E Purcell	P O'Sullivan	Mullingar	3 and 2
1966	E Bradshaw	P O'Sullivan	Rosslare	3 and 2
1967	G Brandom	P O'Sullivan	Castlerock	3 and 2
1968	E Bradshaw	M McKenna	Lahinch	3 and 2
1969	M McKenna	C Hickey	Ballybunion	3 and 2
1970	P Garvey	M Earner	Portrush	2 and 1
1971	E Bradshaw	M Mooney	Baltray	3 and 1
1972	M McKenna	I Butler	Killarney	5 and 4
1973	M Mooney	M McKenna	Bundoran	2 and 1
1974	M McKenna	V Singleton	Lahinch	3 and 2
1975	M Gorry	E Bradshaw	Tramore	1 hole
1976	C Nesbitt	M McKenna	Rosses Point	20th hole
1977	M McKenna	R Hegarty	Ballybunion	2 holes
1978	M Gorry	I Butler	Grange	4 and 3
1979	M McKenna	C Nesbitt	Donegal	6 and 5
1980	C Nesbitt	C Hourihane	Lahinch	1 hole
1981	M McKenna	M Kenny	Laytown & Bettystown	1 hole
1982	M McKenna	M Madill	Portrush	2 and 1
1983	C Hourihane	V Hassett	Cork	6 and 4
1984	C Hourihane	M Madill	Rosses Point	19th hole
1985	C Hourihane	M McKenna	Waterville	4 and 3
1986	T O'Reilly	E Higgins	Castlerock	4 and 3
1987	C Hourihane	C Hickey	Lahinch	5 and 4
1988	L Bolton	E Higgins	Tramore	2 and 1
1989	M McKenna	C Wickham	West Port	19th hole
1990	ER McDaid	L Callan	The Island	2 and 1
1991	C Hourihane	E McDaid	Ballybunion	1 hole
1992	ER Power	C Hourihane	Co. Louth	1 hole
1993	E Higgins	A Rogers	R Belfast	2 and 1
1994	L Webb	H Kavanagh	Rosses Point	20th hole
1995	ER Power	S O'Brien-Kenney	Cork	1 hole
1996	B Hackett	L Behan	Tullamore	3 and 2
1997	S Fanagan	ER Power	Enniscrone	4 and 3
1998	L Behan	O Purfield	Clandeboye	19th hole
1999	C Coughlan	ER Power	Carlow	4 and 3
2000	A Coffey	C Coughlan	Co Louth	3 and 2
2001	A Coffey	C Coughlan	The European Club	4 and 3
2002	R Coakley	A Coffey	Cork	4 and 3

2003 *at Donegal*

Leading Qualifier: Claire Coughlan (Cork) 73-74—147

Quarter Finals

Claire Coughlan (Cork) beat Maura Morrin (The Curragh) 1 hole

Maria Dunne (Skerries) beat Karen Delaney (Carlow) 1 hole

Helen Jones (Strabane) beat Tricia Mangan (Ennis) at 20th

Martina Gillen (Beaverstown) beat Tara Delaney (Carlow) 5 and 4

Semi-Finals

Dunne beat Coughlan 4 and 3

Gillen beat Jones 3 and 2

Final

Martina Gillen beat Maria Dunne 2 holes

Irish Ladies Open Amateur Stroke Play Championship
(Inaugurated 1993)

1993	T Eakin	Milltown	293
1994	H Kavanagh	Milltown	286
1995	N Quigg	Grange	300
1996	ER Power	Grange	218
1997	Y Cassidy	Waterford Castle	217
1998	S O'Brien	Waterford Castle	141
1999	H Kavanagh	Waterford Castle	217
2000	R Cookley	Birr	205
2001	A Laing	Birr	214
2002	R Coakley	Dundalk	214

2003 *at Rathsallagh*

1	Claire Coughlan (Cork)	72-69-74—215
2	Maura Morrin (The Curragh)	74-70-78—222
3	Sinead Keane (The Curragh)	75-71-79—225

Irish Senior Ladies Amateur Championship (Inaugurated 1988)

1988	M Magan		1993	G Costello	81	1998	M Moran	78
1989	Dr G Costello		1994	G Costello	80	1999	R Fanagan	80
1990	A Hesketh		1995	A Gaynor	81	2000	S Kearney	80
1991	C Hickey	77	1996	M Stuart	81	2001	M McKenna*	162
1992	C Hickey	79	1997	M O'Donnell	85	2002	P Williamson	157

2003 *at Seapoint*

1	Pam Williamson (Baberton)	77-76—153
2	Valerie Hassett (Ennis)	79-75—154
3	Diane Williams (USA)	84-75—159

Centenary Scottish Ladies Close Amateur Championship
(Inaugurated 1903)

Year	Winner	Runner-up	Venue	Score
1903	AM Glover	MA Graham	St Andrews	1 hole
1904	MA Graham	M Bishop	Prestwick St Nicholas	6 and 5
1905	D Campbell	MA Graham	North Berwick	at 19th
1906	D Campbell	AM Glover	Cruden Bay	3 and 1
1907	FS Teacher	D Campbell	Troon	at 21st
1908	D Campbell	MA Cairns	Gullane	7 and 6
1909	EL Kyle	D Campbell	Machrihanish	3 and 1
1910	EL Kyle	AM Glover	Nairn	4 and 3
1911	E Grant-Suttie	EL Kyle	St Andrews	1 hole
1912	DM Jenkins	M Neil Fraser	Lossiemouth	4 and 2
1913	JW McCulloch	R Mackintosh	Machrihanish	4 and 3
1914	ER Anderson	FS Teacher	Muirfield	at 20th
1915–1919	*Not played due to First World War*			
1920	Mrs JB Watson	L Scroggie	Cruden Bay	5 and 3
1921	Mrs JB Watson	Mrs M Martin	Machrihanish	1 hole
1922	Mrs JB Watson	A Kyle	St Andrews	2 and 1
1923	Mrs WH Nicholson	Mrs JB Watson	Lossiemouth	2 and 1
1924	CPR Montgomery	H Cameron	Turnberry	5 and 4
1925	J Percy	E Grant-Suttie	Gullane	2 and 1
1926	MJ Wood	Mrs J Cochrane	Cruden Bay	2 and 1
1927	B Inglis	H Cameron	Machrihanish	1 hole
1928	JW McCulloch	P Ramsay	St Andrews	3 and 1
1929	Mrs JB Watson	Doris Park	Nairn	3 and 1
1930	Helen Holm	Doris Park	Turnberry	1 hole
1931	JW McCulloch	Doris Park	Gullane	at 19th
1932	Helen Holm	Mrs G Coates	Cruden Bay	at 23rd
1933	MJ Couper	Helen Holm	Turnberry	at 22nd
1934	Nan Baird	J Anderson	North Berwick	1 hole

Centenary Scottish Ladies Close Amateur Championship *continued*

Year	Winner	Runner-up	Venue	Score
1935	M Robertson-Durham	Nan Baird	Lossiemouth	at 20th
1936	Doris Park	CPR Montgomery	Turnberry	at 19th
1937	Helen Holm	Mrs I Bowhill	Gleneagles	3 and 2
1938	Jessie Anderson	Helen Holm	Nairn	2 holes
1939	Jessie Anderson	Catherine Park	Turnberry	at 19th
1939–1946	*Not played due to Second World War*			
1947	Jean Donald	J Kerr	Elie	5 and 3
1948	Helen Holm	Vivien Falconer	Gleneagles	5 and 4
1949	Jean Donald	Helen Holm	Troon	6 and 4
1950	Helen Holm	Charlotte Beddows		
		(Mrs JB Watson)	St Andrews	6 and 5
1951	Mrs G Valentine	Moira Paterson	Nairn	3 and 2
1952	Jean Donald	Mrs RT Peel	Gullane	13 and 11
1953	Mrs G Valentine	Jean Donald	Carnoustie	8 and 7
1954	Mrs RT Peel	Mrs G Valentine	Turnberry	7 and 6
1955	Mrs G Valentine	Millicent Couper	North Berwick	8 and 6
1956	Mrs G Valentine	Helen Holm	Dornoch	8 and 7
1957	Marigold Speir	Helen Holm	Troon	7 and 5
1958	Dorothea Sommerville	Janette Robertson	Elie	1 hole
1959	Janette Robertson	Belle McCorkindale	Nairn	6 and 5
1960	Janette Robertson	Dorothea Sommerville	Turnberry	2 and 1
1961	JS Wright			
	(*née* Robertson)	AM Lurie	St Andrews	1 hole
1962	JB Lawrence	C Draper	R Dornoch	5 and 4
1963	JB Lawrence	IC Robertson	Troon	2 and 1
1964	JB Lawrence	SM Reid	Gullane	5 and 3
1965	IC Robertson	JB Lawrence	Nairn	5 and 4
1966	IC Robertson	M Fowler	Machrihanish	2 and 1
1967	J Hastings	A Laing	North Berwick	5 and 3
1968	Joan Smith	J Rennie	Carnoustie	10 and 9
1969	JH Anderson	K Lackie	West Kilbride	5 and 4
1970	A Laing	IC Robertson	Dunbar	1 hole
1971	IC Robertson	A Ferguson	R Dornoch	3 and 2
1972	IC Robertson	CJ Lugton	Machrihanish	5 and 3
1973	I Wright	Dr AJ Wilson	St Andrews	2 holes
1974	Dr AJ Wilson	K Lackie	Nairn	22nd hole
1975	LA Hope	JW Smith	Elie	1 hole
1976	S Needham	T Walker	Machrihanish	3 and 2
1977	CJ Lugton	M Thomson	R Dornoch	1 hole
1978	IC Robertson	JW Smith	Prestwick	2 holes
1979	G Stewart	LA Hope	Gullane	2 and 1
1980	IC Robertson	F Anderson	Carnoustie	1 hole
1981	A Gemmill	W Aitken	Stranraer	2 and 1
1982	J Connachan	P Wright	R Troon	19th hole
1983	G Stewart	F Anderson	North Berwick	3 and 1
1984	G Stewart	A Gemmill	R Dornoch	3 and 2
1985	A Gemmill	D Thomson	Barassie	2 and 1
1986	IC Robertson	L Hope	St Andrews	3 and 2
1987	F Anderson	C Middleton	Nairn	4 and 3
1988	S Lawson	F Anderson	Southerness	3 and 1
1989	J Huggon	L Anderson	Lossiemouth	5 and 4
1990	E Farquharson	S Huggan	Machrihanish	3 and 2
1991	C Lambert	F Anderson	Carnoustie	3 and 2
1992	J Moody	E Farquharson	R Aberdeen	2 and 1
1993	C Lambert	M McKay	Prestwick St Nicholas	5 and 4
1994	C Matthew	V Melvin	Gullane	1 hole
1995	H Monaghan	S McMaster	Portpatrick	21st hole
1996	A Laing	A Rose	R Dornoch	1 hole
1997	A Rose	H Monaghan	W Kilbride	3 and 2
1998	E Moffat	C Agnew	North Berwick	4 and 3
1999	J Smith	A Laing	Nairn Dunbar	2 and 1
2000	L Kenny	H Stirling	Machrihanish	1 hole
2001	L Morton	L Mackay	Carnoustie	6 and 4
2002	H Stirling	A Laing	Stranraer	3 and 1

2003 *at Old Course, St Andrews*

Leading Qualifiers: Lynn Kenny (73,73), Anne Laing (72,74) 146

Quarter Finals	Semi-Finals

Quarter Finals

Claire Hargan (Prestonfield) beat Lynn Kenny
(University of Stirling) 4 and 3
Laura Wells (Dumfries & County) beat
Louise Kenney (Pitreavie) 1 hole
Martine Pow (Selkirk) beat Elaine Moffat
(St Regulus) 3 and 2
Anne Laing (Vale of Leven) beat Fiona Lockhart
(St Regulus) 7 and 6

Semi-Finals

Hargan beat Wells 5 and 4
Laing beat Pow 5 and 3

Final

Anne Laing beat Claire Hargan 4 and 2

Scottish Ladies Open Stroke Play Championship (Helen Holm Trophy) (Inaugurated 1973)

1973 Belle Robertson	1981 Gillian Stewart	1989 Sara Robinson	1997 Kim Rostron
1974 Sandra Needham	1982 Wilma Aitken	1990 Catriona Lambert	1998 K-M Juul Esbjerg
1975 Muriel Thomson	1983 Jane Connachan	1991 Julie Wade	1999 L Nicholson
1976 Muriel Thomson	1984 Gillian Stewart	1992 Mhairi McKay	2000 Rebecca Hudson
1977 Beverly Huke	1985 Pamela Wright	1993 Julie Wade	2001 Fiona Brown
1978 Wilma Aitken	1986 Belle Robertson	1994 K Tebbet	2002 Heather Stirling
1979 Belle Robertson	1987 Elaine Farquharson	1995 Maria Hjörth	
1980 Wilma Aitken	1988 Elaine Farquharson	1996 J Hockley	

2003 *at Royal Troon and Troon Portland*

1	Nathalie David (La Baule, Fra)	76-74-77—227
2	Becky Brewerton (Abergele)	74-78-77—229
	Rachel Lomas (Hallowes)	75-75-79—229
	Clare Queen (Drumpellier)	70-77-82—229

Scottish Senior Ladies Amateur Championship (Inaugurated 1997)

1997	A Wilson	1999	P Williamson	2001	F Liddle
1998	I McIntosh	2000	P Hutton	2002	P Williamson

2003 *at Ballater*

1	Karen Ballantyne (Craigmillar Park)	69-70—139
2	Noreen Fenton (Merchants of Edinburgh)	70-73—143
3	Lynne Terry (Cruden Bay)	75-74—149

Welsh Ladies Amateur Championship (Inaugurated 1905)

Year	Winner	Runner-up	Venue	Score
1905	E Young	B Duncan	Penarth	2 and 1
1906	B Duncan	Mrs Storry	Radyr	5 and 4
1907	B Duncan	Mrs Wenham	Royal Porthcawl	5 and 4
1908	B Duncan	Miss Lloyd Williams	Conwy	4 and 2
1909	B Duncan	Mrs Ellis Griffiths	Southerndown	4 and 3
1910	Miss Lloyd Roberts	Miss Leaver	Rhyl	4 and 3
1911	Miss Clay	Miss Allington-Hughes	Royal Porthcawl	2 and 1
1912	B Duncan	P Williams	Llandrindod Wells	4 and 2
1913	Miss Brooke	Miss Shaw	Rhos-on-Sea	at 19th
1914	Mrs Vivian Phillips	Miss Morgan	Tenby	4 and 3
1915–1919 *Not played due to First World War*				
1920	Mrs Rupert Phillips	M Marley	Royal Porthcawl	8 and 6
1921	M Marley	I Rieben	Aberdovey	7 and 5
1922	J Duncan	H Franklyn Thomas	Llandrindod Wells	9 and 8
1923	MR Cox	M Marley	Southerndown	at 39th
1924	MR Cox	B Pyman	Rhyl	11 and 10

Welsh Ladies Amateur Championship *continued*

Year	Winner	Runner-up	Venue	Score
1925	MR Cox	J Rhys	Tenby	9 and 7
1926	MC Justice	A Smalley	Aberdovey	4 and 3
1927	J Duncan	Mrs Blake	Porthcawl	1 hole
1928	J Duncan	I Rieben	Harlech	2 and 1
1929	I Rieben	B Pyman	Tenby	2 and 1
1930	MJ Jeffreys	I Rieben	Llandudno	2 holes
1931	MJ Jeffreys	B Pyman	Southerndown	4 and 3
1932	I Rieben	MJ Jeffreys	Aberdovey	2 and 1
1933	MJ Jeffreys	Mrs Bridge	Porthcawl	2 and 1
1934	I Rieben	MJ Jeffreys	Harlech	3 and 2
1935	*Abandoned – snow*			
1936	I Rieben	M Thompson	Prestatyn	2 and 1
1937	GS Emery	Dr P Whitaker	Porthcawl	10 and 9
1938	B Pyman	GS Emery	Llandudno	1 hole
1939	B Burrell	H Reynolds	Swansea	2 and 1
1940–1946	*Not played due to Second Word War*			
1947	M Barron	E Jones	Prestatyn	1 hole
1948	N Seely	M Barron	Prestatyn	12 and 11
1949	S Bryan Smith	E Brown	Newport	3 and 2
1950	Dr Garfield Evans	Nancy Cook	Porthcawl	2 and 1
1951	E Bromley-Davenport	Nancy Cook	Harlech	1 hole
1952	Elsie Lever	Pat Roberts	Southerndown	6 and 5
1953	Nancy Cook	Elsie Lever	Llandudno	3 and 2
1954	Nancy Cook	ED Brown	Tenby	1 hole
1955	Nancy Cook	Pat Roberts	Holyhead	2 holes
1956	Pat Roberts	M Barron	Royal Porthcawl	2 and 1
1957	M Barron	Pat Roberts	Royal St David's	6 and 4
1958	Nancy Cook Wright	Pat Roberts	Newport	1 hole
1959	Pat Roberts	A Gwyther	Conwy	6 and 4
1960	M Barron	E Brown	Tenby	8 and 6
1961	M Oliver	N Sneddon	Aberdovey	5 and 4
1962	M Oliver	P Roberts	Radyr	4 and 2
1963	P Roberts	N Sneddon	Royal St David's	7 and 5
1964	M Oliver	M Wright	Southerndown	1 hole
1965	M Wright	E Brown	Prestatyn	3 and 2
1966	A Hughes	P Roberts	Ashburnham	5 and 4
1967	M Wright	C Phipps	Royal St David's	21st hole
1968	S Hales	M Wright	Royal Porthcawl	3 and 2
1969	P Roberts	A Hughes	Caernarvonshire	3 and 2
1970	A Briggs	J Morris	Newport	19th hole
1971	A Briggs	EN Davies	Royal St David's	2 and 1
1972	A Hughes	J Rogers	Tenby	3 and 2
1973	A Briggs	J John	Holyhead	3 and 2
1974	A Briggs	Dr H Lyall	Ashburnham	3 and 2
1975	A Johnson (*née* Hughes)	K Rawlings	Prestatyn	1 hole
1976	T Perkins	A Johnson	Royal Porthcawl	4 and 2
1977	T Perkins	P Whitley	Aberdovey	5 and 4
1978	P Light	A Briggs	Newport	2 and 1
1979	V Rawlings	A Briggs	Caernarvonshire	2 holes
1980	M Rawlings	A Briggs	Tenby	2 and 1
1981	M Rawlings	A Briggs	Royal St David's	5 and 3
1982	V Thomas			
	(*née* Rawlings)	M Rawlings	Ashburnham	7 and 6
1983	V Thomas	T Thomas (*née* Perkins)	Llandudno	1 hole
1984	S Roberts	K Davies	Newport	5 and 4
1985	V Thomas	S Jump	Prestatyn	1 hole
1986	V Thomas	L Isherwood	Royal Porthcawl	7 and 6
1987	V Thomas	S Roberts	Aberdovey	3 and 1
1988	S Roberts	F Connor	Tenby	4 and 2
1989	H Lawson	V Thomas	Conwy	2 and 1
1990	S Roberts	H Wadsworth	Ashburnham	3 and 2
1991	V Thomas	H Lawson	Royal St David's	4 and 3
1992	J Foster	S Boyes	Newport	4 and 3
1993	A Donne	V Thomas	Abergele & Pensarn	19th hole
1994	V Thomas	L Dermott	Royal Porthcawl	19th hole
1995	L Dermott	K Stark	Aberdovey	19th hole
1996	L Dermott	V Thomas	Tenby	4 and 3
1997	E Pilgrim	L Davis	Northop	4 and 2
1998	L Davis	R Morgan	Ashburnham	1 hole

Year	Winner	Runner-up	Venue	Score
1999	R Brewerton	R Morgan	Conwy	19th hole
2000	K Evans	K Phillips	Pyle & Kenfig	19th hole
2001	B Brewerton	S Jones	Royal St David's	2 and 1
2002	E Pilgrim	A Highgate	Newport	1 hole

2003 *at Aberdovey*

Quarter Finals

Sarah Jones (Pennard) beat Anna Highgate
(Cottrell Park) 1 hole
Kate Phillips (Creigiau) beat Jo Nicolson
(Wrexham) 3 and 1
Katie Walls (Taunton & Pickeridge) beat Lydia Hall
(Royal Porthcawl) 1 hole
Becky Brewerton (Abergele) beat Louise Davis
(Conwy) 5 and 4

Semi-Finals

Phillips beat Jones 8 and 6
Walls beat Brewerton 2 and 1

Final

Kate Phillips beat Katie Walls 2 and 1

Welsh Ladies Open Amateur Strokeplay Championship

(Inaugurated 1976)

Year	Winner	Venue	Score		Year	Winner	Venue	Score
1976	P Light	Aberdovey	227		1990	L Hackney	Newport	218
1977	J Greenhalgh	Aberdovey	239		1991	M Sutton	R Porthcawl	224
1978	S Hedges	Aberdovey	49 holes		1992	C Lambert	R Porthcawl	218
1979	S Crowcroft	Aberdovey	228		1993	J Hall	Newport	221
1980	T Thomas	Aberdovey	233		1994	A Rose	Newport	217
1981	V Thomas	Aberdovey	224		1995	F Brown	Newport	221
1982	V Thomas	Aberdovey	225		1996	E Duggleby	Whitchurch	223
1983	J Thornhill	Aberdovey	239		1997	K Edwards	Whitchurch	216
1984	L Davies	Aberdovey	230		1998	G Simpson	Rolls of Monmouth	154
1985	C Swallow	Aberdovey	219		1999	A Walker	Celtic Manor	230
1986	H Wadsworth	Aberdovey	223		2000	R Prout	Ashburnham	228
1987	S Shapcott	Newport	225		2001	V Laing	Royal Porthcawl	229
1988	S Shapcott	Newport	218		2002	V Laing	Northop Country Park	218
1989	V Thomas	Newport	220					

2003 *at Southerndown*

1 Vikki Laing (Musselburgh)   68-69-76—213
2 Becky Brewerton (Abergele)   70-67-78—215
3 Sarah Jones (Pennard)   78-71-72—221
   Jemma Wilson (Strathaven)   68-76-77—221

Welsh Senior Ladies Championship (Inaugurated 1990)

Year	Winner	Venue	Score		Year	Winner	Venue	Score
1990	E Higgs	Vale of Llangollen	171		1997	C Thomas	Fairwood Park	160
1991	H Lyall	Pyle and Kenfig	160		1998	C Thomas	Padeswood	163
1992	P Morgan	Cardigan	83		1999	V Mackenzie	St Mellons	153
1993	P Morgan	Pwllheli	157		2000	F Shehan	Carmarthen	159
1994	C Thomas	Llandudno	163		2001	F Shehan	Porthmadog	159
1995	C Thomas	Tredegar Park	157		2002	C Thomas	Creigiau	154
1996	C Thomas	Vale of Llangollen	157					

2003 *at Cardigan*

1 Chris Thomas (Holyhead)   165
2 Sue Payne (Royal St David's)   166
3 Verona MacKenzie (Whitchurch)   166
4 Jean O'Connor (Newport)   166

Ladies European Open Amateur Championship (Inaugurated 1986)

1986	M Koch (Ger)	Morfontaine, France	286
1988	F Descampe (Bel)	Pedrena, Spain	289
1990	M Koch (Ger)	Zumicon, Switzerland	295
1991	D Bourson (Fra)	Schönborn, Austria	294
1992	J Morley (Eng)	Estoril, Portugal	284
1993	V Steinsrud (Nor)	Torino, Italy	277
1994	M Fischer (Ger)	Bastad, Sweden	288
1995	M Hjörth (Swe)	Berlin, Germany	284
1996	S Cavalleri (Ita)	Furesoe, Denmark	288
1997	S Cavalleri (Ita)	Formby, England	297
1998	G Sergas (Ita)	Noordwijk, Netherlands	295
1999	S Sandolo (Ita)	Karlovy Vary, Czech Republic	284
2000	E Duggleby (Eng)	Amber Baltic GC, Poland	283
2001	M Eberl (Ger)	Biella, Italy	217
2002	B Brewerton (Wal)	Kristianstad, Sweden	288

2003 at Shannon, Ireland

1	Virginie Beauchet (Fra)	71-74-75-73—293
2	Adriana Zwanck (Esp)	72-73-77-73—295
3	Elin Ohlsson (Swe)	76-72-74-74—296
	Alexandra Vilatte (Fra)	77-73-76-70—296

European Senior Ladies Championship (Inaugurated 2000)

2000	C Mourgue d'Algue (Fra)	La Manga	226
2001	C Mourgue d'Algue (Fra)	Torremirona	219
2002	C Mourgue d'Algue (Fra)	La Manga	220

2003 at Chantaco, France

1	Claudine Cros Chatrier (Fra)	71-72-78—221 (win after play-off 1 hole)
2	Vicky Pertierra (Esp)	71-76-74—221
3	Maj-Britt Heden (Swe)	76-76-70—222

Lexus European Under 21 Championships (Inaugurated 1998)

1998	Kirsty Taylor (Eng)	2001	Emma Cabrera (Esp)
1999	Rebecca Hudson (Eng)		*Discontinued*
2000	Rebecca Hudson (Eng)		

National Orders of Merit

English Order of Merit, 2003

1	Emma Duggleby (Malton & Norton)	1144
2	Kerry Smith (Waterlooville)	936
3	Danielle Masters (Rochester & Cobham)	935

ILGU Irish Order of Merit, 2003

1	Tricia Mangan (Ennis)	1335
2	Claire Coughlan (Cork)	1195
3	Martina Gillen (Beaverstown)	1070

Dunfermline Building Society Scottish Order of Merit, 2003

1	Anne Laing (Vale of Leven)	2280
2	Clare Queen (Drumpellier)	2035
3	Lynn Kenny (University of Stirling)	1980

Welsh Order of Merit, 2003

1	Sarah Jones (Pennard)	1200
2	Becky Brewerton (Abergele)	1195
3	Anna Highgate (Cottrell Park)	1105

Team Events

Great Britain & Ireland v USA for the Curtis Cup

(home team names first)

1932 at Wentworth
Result: USA 5½, GBI 3½
Captains: J Wethered (GBI), M Hollins (USA)

Foursomes
Wethered & Morgan lost to Vare & Hill 1 hole
Wilson & JB Watson lost to Van Wie & Hicks 2 and 1
Gourlay & Doris Park lost to Orcutt & Cheney 1 hole

Singles
Joyce Wethered beat Glenna Collett Vare 6 and 4
Enid Wilson beat Helen Hicks 2 and 1
Wanda Morgan lost to Virginia Van Wie 2 and 1
Diana Fishwick beat Maureen Orcutt 4 and 3
Molly Gourlay halved with Opal Hill
Elsie Corlett lost to Leona Pressley Cheney 4 and 3

1934 at Chevy Chase, MD
Result: USA 6½, GBI 2½
Captains: Glenna Collett Vare (USA),
  Doris Chambers (GBI)

Foursomes
Van Wie & Glutting halved with Gourlay & Barton
Orcutt & Cheney beat Fishwick & Morgan 2 holes
Hill & Lucille Robinson lost to Plumpton & Walker 2 and 1

Singles
Virginia Van Wie beat Diana Fishwick 2 and 1
Maureen Orcutt beat Molly Gourlay 4 and 2
Leona Pressley Cheney beat Pamela Barton 7 and 5
Charlotte Glutting beat Wanda Morgan
Opal Hill beat Diana Plumpton 3 and 2
Aniela Goldthwaite lost to Charlotte Walker 3 and 2

1936 at Gleneagles
Result: USA 4½, GBI 4½
Captains: Doris Chambers (GBI),
  Glenna Collett Vare (USA)

Foursomes
Morgan & Garon halved with Vare & Berg
Barton & Walker lost to Orcutt & Cheney 2 and 1
Anderson & Holm beat Hill & Glutting 3 and 2

Singles
Wanda Morgan lost to Glenna Collett Vare 3 and 2
Helen Holm beat Patty Berg 4 and 3
Pamela Barton lost to Charlotte Glutting 1 hole
Charlotte Walker lost to Maureen Orcutt 1 hole
Jessie Anderson beat Leona Pressley Cheney 1 hole
Marjorie Garon beat Opal Hill 7 and 5

1938 at Essex, MA
Result: USA 5½, GBI 3½
Captains: Frances Stebbins (USA),
  Mrs RH Wallace-Williamson (GBI)

Foursomes
Page & Orcutt lost to Holm & Tiernan 2 holes
Vare & Berg lost to Anderson & Corlett 1 hole
Miley & Kathryn Hemphill halved with Walker &
  Phyllis Wade

Singles
Estelle Lawson Page beat Helen Holm 6 and 5
Patty Berg beat Jessie Anderson 1 hole
Marion Miley beat Elsie Corlett 2 and 1
Glenna Collett Vare beat Charlotte Walker 2 and 1
Maureen Orcutt lost to Clarrie Tiernan 2 and 1
Charlotte Glutting beat Nan Baird 1 hole

1948 at Birkdale
Result: USA 6½, GBI 2½
Captains: Doris Chambers (GBI),
  Glenna Collett Vare (USA)

Foursomes
Donald & Gordon beat Suggs & Lenczyk 3 and 2
Garvey & Bolton lost to Kirby & Vare 4 and 3
Ruttle & Val Reddan lost to Page & Kielty 5 and 4

Singles
Philomena Garvey halved with Louise Suggs
Jean Donald beat Dorothy Kirby 2 holes
Jacqueline Gordon lost to Grace Lenczyk 5 and 3
Helen Holm lost to Estelle Lawson Page 3 and 2
Maureen Ruttle lost to Polly Riley 3 and 2
Zara Bolton lost to Dorothy Kielty 2 and 1

1950 at Buffalo, NY
Result: USA 7½, GBI 1½
Captains: Glenna Collett Vare (USA),
  Diana Fishwick Critchley (GBI)

Foursomes
Hanson & Porter beat Valentine & Donald 3 and 2
Helen Sigel & Kirk lost to Stephens & Price 1 hole
Dorothy Kirby & Kielty beat Garvey & Bisgood 6 and 5

Singles
Dorothy Porter halved with Frances Stephens
Polly Riley beat Jessie Anderson Valentine 7 and 6
Beverly Hanson beat Jean Donald 6 and 5
Dorothy Kielty beat Philomena Garvey 2 and 1
Peggy Kirk beat Jeanne Bisgood 1 hole
Grace Lenczyk beat Elizabeth Price 5 and 4

1952 at Muirfield
Result: GBI 5, USA 4
Captains: Lady Katherine Cairns (GBI),
  Aniela Goldthwaite (USA)

Foursomes
Donald & Price beat Kirby & DeMoss 3 and 2
Stephens & JA Valentine lost to Doran & Lindsay 6 and 4
Paterson & Garvey beat Riley & Patricia O'Sullivan
  2 and 1

Singles
Jean Donald lost to Dorothy Kirby 1 hole
Frances Stephens beat Marjorie Lindsay 2 and 1
Moira Paterson lost to Polly Riley 6 and 4
Jeanne Bisgood beat Mae Murray 6 and 5
Philomena Garvey lost to Claire Doran 3 and 2
Elizabeth Price beat Grace DeMoss 3 and 2

1954 at Merion, PA
Result: USA 6, GBI 3
Captains: Edith Flippin (USA),
Mrs JB Beck (GBI)

Foursomes
Faulk & Riley beat Stephens & Price 6 and 4
Doran & Patricia Lesser beat Garvey & Valentine 6 and 5
Kirby & Barbara Romack beat Marjorie Peel & Robertson 6 and 5

Singles
Mary Lena Faulk lost to Frances Stephens 1 hole
Claire Doran beat Jeanne Bisgood 4 and 3
Polly Riley beat Elizabeth Price 9 and 8
Dorothy Kirby lost to Philomena Garvey 3 and 1
Grace DeMoss Smith beat Jessie Anderson Valentine 4 and 3
Joyce Ziske lost to Janette Robertson 3 and 1

1956 at Prince's, Sandwich
Result: GBI 5, USA 4
Captains: Zara Davis Bolton (GBI),
Edith Flippin (USA)

Foursomes
Valentine & Garvey lost to Lesser & Smith 2 and 1
Smith & Price beat Riley & Romack 5 and 3
Robertson & Veronica Anstey lost to Downey & Carolyn Cudone 6 and 4

Singles
Jessie Anderson Valentine beat Patricia Lesser 6 and 4
Philomena Garvey lost to Margaret Smith 9 and 8
Frances Stephens Smith beat Polly Riley 1 hole
Janette Robertson lost to Barbara Romack 6 and 4
Angela Ward beat Mary Ann Downey 6 and 4
Elizabeth Price beat Jane Nelson 7 and 6

1958 at Brae Burn, MA
Result: GBI 4½, USA 4½
Captains: Virginia Dennehy (USA),
Daisy Ferguson (GBI)

Foursomes
Riley & Romack lost to Bonallack & Price 2 and 1
Gunderson & Quast lost to Robertson & Smith 3 and 2
Johnstone & McIntire beat Jackson & Valentine 6 and 5

Singles
JoAnne Gunderson beat Jessie Anderson Valentine 2 holes
Barbara McIntire halved with Angela Ward Bonallack
Anne Quast beat Elizabeth Price 4 and 2
Anna Johnstone lost to Janette Robertson 3 and 2
Barbara Romack beat Bridget Jackson 3 and 2
Polly Riley lost to Frances Stephens Smith 2 holes

1960 at Lindrick
Result: USA 6½, GBI 2½
Captains: Maureen Garrett (GBI),
Mildred Prunaret (USA)

Foursomes
Price & Bonallack beat Gunderson & McIntyre 1 hole
Robertson & McCorkindale lost to Eller & Quast 4 and 2
Frances Smith & Porter lost to Goodwin & Anna Johnstone 3 and 2

Singles
Elizabeth Price halved with Barbara McIntyre
Angela Ward Bonallack lost to JoAnne Gunderson 2 and 1
Janette Robertson lost to Anne Quast 2 holes
Philomena Garvey lost to Judy Eller 4 and 3
Belle McCorkindale lost to Judy Bell 8 and 7
Ruth Porter beat Joanne Goodwin 1 hole

1962 at Broadmoor, Colorado Springs, CO
Result: USA 8, GBI 1
Captains: Polly Riley (USA),
Frances Stephens Smith (GBI)

Foursomes
Decker & McIntyre beat Spearman & Bonallack 7 and 5
Jean Ashley & Anna Johnstone beat Ruth Porter & Frearson 8 and 7
Creed & Gunderson beat Vaughan & Ann Irvin 4 and 3

Singles
Judy Bell lost to Diane Frearson 8 and 7
JoAnne Gunderson beat Angela Ward Bonallack 2 and 1
Clifford Ann Creed beat Sally Bonallack 6 and 5
Anne Quast Decker beat Marley Spearman 7 and 5
Phyllis Preuss beat Jean Roberts 1 hole
Barbara McIntyre beat Sheila Vaughan 5 and 4

1964 at Porthcawl
Result: USA 10½, GBI 1½
Captains: Elsie Corlett (GBI),
Helen Hawes (USA)

First Day: Foursomes
Spearman & Bonallack beat McIntyre & Preuss 2 and 1
Sheila Vaughan & Porter beat Gunderson & Roth 3 and 2
Jackson & Susan Armitage lost to Sorenson & White 8 and 6

Singles
Angela Ward Bonallack lost to JoAnne Gunderson 6 and 5
Marley Spearman halved with Barbara McIntyre
Julia Greenhalgh lost to Barbara White 3 and 2
Bridget Jackson beat Carol Sorenson 4 and 3
Joan Lawrence lost to Peggy Conley 1 hole
Ruth Porter beat Nancy Roth 1 hole

Second Day: Foursomes
Spearman & Bonallack beat McIntyre & Preuss 6 and 5
Armitage & Jackson lost to Gunderson & Roth 2 holes
Porter & Vaughan halved with Sorenson & White

Singles
Spearman halved with Gunderson
Lawrence lost to McIntyre 4 and 2
Greenhalgh beat Phyllis Preuss 5 and 3
Bonallack lost to White 3 and 2
Porter lost to Sorenson 3 and 2
Jackson lost to Conley 1 hole

1966 at Hot Springs, VA
Result: USA 13, GBI 5
Captains: Dorothy Germain Porter (USA),
Zara Bolton (GBI)

First Day: Foursomes
Ashley & Preuss beat Armitage & Bonallack 1 hole
Barbara McIntire & Welts halved with Joan Hastings & Robertson
Boddie & Flenniken beat Chadwick & Tredinnick 1 hole

Singles
Jean Ashley beat Belle McCorkindale Robertson 1 hole
Anne Quast Welts halved with Susan Armitage
Barbara White Boddie beat Angela Ward Bonallack
  3 and 2
Nancy Roth Syms beat Elizabeth Chadwick 2 holes
Helen Wilson lost to Ita Burke 3 and 1
Carol Sorenson Flenniken beat Marjory Fowler 3 and 1

Second Day: Foursomes
Ashley & Preuss beat Armitage & Bonallack 2 and 1
McIntire & Welts lost to Burke & Chadwick 1 hole
Boddie & Flenniken beat Hastings & Robertson 2 and 1

Singles
Ashley lost to Bonallack 2 and 1
Welts halved with Robertson
Boddie beat Armitage 3 and 2
Syms halved with Pam Tredinnick
Phyllis Preuss beat Chadwick 3 and 2
Flenniken beat Burke 2 and 1

1968 at Newcastle, Co Down
Result: USA 10½, GBI 7½
Captains: Zara Bolton (GBI),
* Evelyn Monsted (USA)*
First Day: Foursomes
Irvin & Robertson beat Hamlin & Welts 6 and 5
Pickard & Saunders beat Conley & Dill 3 and 2
Howard & Pam Tredinnick lost to Ashley & Preuss 1 hole

Singles
Ann Irvin beat Anne Quast Welts 3 and 2
Vivien Saunders lost to Shelley Hamlin 1 hole
Belle McCorkindale Robertson lost to Roberta Albers
  1 hole
Bridget Jackson halved with Peggy Conley
Dinah Oxley halved with Phyllis Preuss
Margaret Pickard beat Jean Ashley 2 holes

Second Day: Foursomes
Oxley & Tredinnick lost to Ashley & Preuss 5 and 4
Irvin & Robertson halved with Conley & Dill
Pickard & Saunders lost to Hamlin & Welts 2 and 1

Singles
Irvin beat Hamlin 3 and 2
Robertson halved with Welts
Saunders halved with Albers
Ann Howard lost to Mary Lou Dill 4 and 2
Pickard lost to Conley 1 hole
Jackson lost to Preuss 2 and 1

1970 at Brae Burn, MA
Result: USA 11½, GBI 6½
Captains: Carolyn Cudone (USA),
* Jeanne Bisgood (GBI)*
First Day: Foursomes
Bastanchury & Hamlin lost to McKenna & Oxley
  4 and 3
Preuss & Wilkinson beat Irvin & Robertson 4 and 3
Jane Fassinger & Hill lost to Everard & Greenhalgh
  5 and 3

Singles
Jane Bastanchury beat Dinah Oxley 5 and 3
Martha Wilkinson beat Ann Irvin 1 hole
Shelley Hamlin halved with Belle McCorkindale
  Robertson
Phyllis Preuss lost to Mary McKenna 4 and 2
Nancy Hager beat Margaret Pickard 5 and 4
Alice Dye beat Julia Greenhalgh 1 hole

Second Day: Foursomes
Preuss & Wilkinson beat McKenna & Oxley 6 and 4
Dye & Hill halved with Everard & Greenhalgh
Bastanchury & Hamlin beat Irvin & Robertson 1 hole

Singles
Bastanchury beat Irvin 4 and 3
Hamlin halved with Oxley
Preuss beat Robertson 1 hole
Wilkinson lost to Greenhalgh 6 and 4
Hager lost to Mary Everard 4 and 3
Cindy Hill beat McKenna 2 and 1

1972 at Western Gailes
Result: USA 10, GBI 8
Captains: Frances Stephens Smith (GBI),
* Jean Ashley Crawford (USA)*
First Day: Foursomes
Everard & Beverly Huke lost to Baugh & Kirouac 2 and 1
Frearson & Robertson beat Booth & McIntyre 2 and 1
McKenna & Walker beat Barry & Hollis Stacy 1 hole

Singles
Mickey Walker halved with Laura Baugh
Belle McCorkindale Robertson lost to Jane Bastanchury
  Booth 3 and 1
Mary Everard lost to Martha Wilkinson Kirouac 4 and 3
Dinah Oxley lost to Barbara McIntire 4 and 3
Kathryn Phillips beat Lancy Smith 2 holes
Mary McKenna lost to Beth Barry 2 and 1

Second Day: Foursomes
McKenna & Walker beat Baugh & Kirouac 3 and 2
Everard & Huke lost to Booth & McIntyre 5 and 4
Frearson & Robertson halved with Barry & Stacy

Singles
Robertson lost to Baugh 6 and 5
Everard beat McIntyre 6 and 5
Walker beat Booth 1 hole
McKenna beat Kirouac 3 and 1
Diane Frearson lost to Smith 3 and 1
Phillips lost to Barry 3 and 1

1974 at San Francisco, CA
Result: USA 13, GBI 5
Captains: Sis Choate (USA),
* Belle McCorkindale Robertson (GBI)*
First Day: Foursomes
Hill & Semple halved with Greenhalgh & McKenna
Booth & Sander beat Lee-Smith & LeFeuvre 6 and 5
Budke & Lauer lost to Everard & Walker 5 and 4

Singles
Carol Semple lost to Mickey Walker 2 and 1
Jane Bastanchury Booth beat Mary McKenna 5 and 3
Debbie Massey beat Mary Everard 1 hole
Bonnie Lauer beat Jennie Lee-Smith 6 and 5
Beth Barry beat Julia Greenhalgh 1 hole
Cindy Hill halved with Tegwen Perkins

Second Day: Foursomes
Booth & Sander beat McKenna & Walker 5 and 4
Budke & Lauer beat Everard & LeFeuvre 5 and 3
Hill & Semple lost to Greenhalgh & Perkins 3 and 2

Singles
Anne Quast Sander beat Everard 4 and 3
Booth beat Greenhalgh 7 and 5
Massey beat Carol LeFeuvre 6 and 5
Semple beat Walker 2 and 1
Mary Budke beat Perkins 5 and 4
Lauer lost to McKenna 2 and 1

1976 at Royal Lytham & St Annes
Result: USA 11½, GBI 6½
Captains: Belle McCorkindale Robertson (GBI),
Barbara McIntyre (USA)
First Day: Foursomes
Greenhalgh & McKenna lost to Daniel & Hill 3 and 2
Cadden & Henson lost to Horton & Massey 6 and 5
Irvin & Perkins beat Semple & Syms 3 and 2
Singles
Ann Irvin lost to Beth Daniel 4 and 3
Dinah Oxley Henson beat Cindy Hill 1 hole
Suzanne Cadden lost to Nancy Lopez 3 and 1
Mary McKenna lost to Nancy Roth Syms 1 hole
Tegwen Perkins lost to Debbie Massey 1 hole
Julia Greenhalgh halved with Barbara Barrow
Second Day: Foursomes
Cadden & Irvin lost to Daniel & Hill 4 and 3
Henson & Perkins beat Semple & Syms 2 and 1
McKenna & Anne Stant lost to Barrow & Lopez 4 and 3
Singles
Henson lost to Daniel 3 and 2
Greenhalgh beat Syms 2 and 1
Cadden lost to Donna Horton 6 and 5
Jennie Lee-Smith lost to Massey 3 and 2
Perkins beat Hill 1 hole
McKenna beat Carol Semple 1 hole

1978 at Apawamis, NY
Result: USA 12, GBI 6
Captains: Helen Wilson (USA),
Carol Comboy (GBI)
First Day: Foursomes
Daniel & Brenda Goldsmith lost to Greenhalgh &
Marvin 3 and 2
Cindy Hill & Smith lost to Everard & Thomson
2 and 1
Cornett & Carolyn Hill halved with McKenna &
Perkins
Singles
Beth Daniel beat Vanessa Marvin 5 and 4
Noreen Uihlein lost to Mary Everard 7 and 6
Lancy Smith beat Angela Uzielli 4 and 3
Cindy Hill beat Julia Greenhalgh 2 and 1
Carolyn Hill halved with Carole Caldwell
Judy Oliver beat Tegwen Perkins 2 and 1
Second Day: Foursomes
Cindy Hill & Smith beat Everard & Thomson 1 hole
Daniel & Goldsmith beat McKenna & Perkins 1 hole
Oliver & Uihlein beat Greenhalgh & Marvin 4 and 3
Singles
Daniel beat Mary McKenna 2 and 1
Patricia Cornett beat Caldwell 3 and 2
Cindy Hill lost to Muriel Thomson 2 and 1
Lancy Smith beat Perkins 2 holes
Oliver halved with Greenhalgh
Uihlein halved with Everard

1980 at St Pierre, Chepstow
Result: USA 13, GBI 5
Captains: Carol Comboy (GBI), Nancy Roth
Syms (USA)
First Day: Foursomes
McKenna & Nesbitt halved with Terri Moody & Smith
Stewart & Thomas lost to Castillo & Sheehan 5 and 3
Caldwell & Madill halved with Oliver & Semple

Singles
Mary McKenna lost to Patty Sheehan 3 and 2
Claire Nesbitt halved with Lancy Smith
Jane Connachan lost to Brenda Goldsmith 2 holes
Maureen Madill lost to Carol Semple 4 and 3
Linda Moore halved with Mary Hafeman
Carole Caldwell lost to Judy Oliver 1 hole
Second Day: Foursomes
Caldwell & Madill lost to Castillo & Sheehan 3 and 2
McKenna & Nesbitt lost to Moody & Smith 6 and 5
Moore & Thomas lost to Oliver & Semple 1 hole
Singles
Madill lost to Sheehan 5 and 4
McKenna beat Lori Castillo 5 and 4
Connachan lost to Hafeman 6 and 5
Gillian Stewart beat Smith 5 and 4
Moore beat Goldsmith 1 hole
Tegwen Perkins Thomas lost to Semple 4 and 3

1982 at Denver, CO
Result: USA 14½, GBI 3½
Captains: Betty Probasco (USA),
Maire O'Donnell (GBI)
First Day: Foursomes
Inkster & Semple beat McKenna & Robertson 5 and 4
Baker & Smith halved with Douglas & Soulsby
Benz & Hanlon beat Connachan & Stewart 2 and 1
Singles
Amy Benz beat Mary McKenna 2 and 1
Cathy Hanlon beat Jane Connachan 5 and 4
Mari McDougall beat Wilma Aitken 2 holes
Kathy Baker beat Belle McCorkindale Robertson
7 and 6
Judy Oliver lost to Janet Soulsby 2 holes
Juli Inkster beat Kitrina Douglas 7 and 6
Second Day: Foursomes
Inkster & Semple beat Aitken & Connachan 3 and 2
Baker & Smith beat Douglas & Soulsby 1 hole
Benz & Hanlon lost to McKenna & Robertson 1 hole
Singles
Inkster beat Douglas 7 and 6
Baker beat Gillian Stewart 4 and 3
Oliver beat Vicki Thomas 5 and 4
McDougall beat Soulsby 2 and 1
Carol Semple beat McKenna 1 hole
Lancy Smith lost to Robertson 5 and 4

1984 at Muirfield
Result: USA 9½, GBI 8½
Captains: Diane Robb Bailey (GBI),
Phyllis Preuss (USA)
First Day: Foursomes
New & Waite beat Pacillo & Sander 2 holes
Grice & Thornhill halved with Rosenthal & Smith
Davies & McKenna lost to Farr & Widman 1 hole
Singles
Jill Thornhill halved with Joanne Pacillo
Claire Waite lost to Penny Hammel 4 and 2
Claire Hourihane lost to Jody Rosenthal 3 and 1
Vicki Thomas beat Dana Howe 2 and 1
Penny Grice beat Anne Quast Sander 2 holes
Beverley New lost to Mary Anne Widman 4 and 3
Second Day: Foursomes
New & Waite lost to Rosenthal & Smith 3 and 1
Grice & Thornhill beat Farr & Widman 2 and 1
Hourihane & Thomas halved with Hammel & Howe

Singles

Thornhill lost to Pacillo 3 and 2
Laura Davies beat Sander 1 hole
Waite beat Lancy Smith 5 and 4
Grice lost to Howe 2 holes
New lost to Heather Farr 6 and 5
Hourihane beat Hammel 2 and 1

1986 *at Prairie Dunes, KS*

Result: GBI 13, USA 5
Captains: Judy Bell (USA),
*   Diane Robb Bailey (GBI)*

First Day: Foursomes
Kessler & Schreyer lost to Behan & Thornhill 7 and 6
Ammaccapane & Mochrie lost to Davies & Johnson
    2 and 1
Gardner & Scrivner lost to McKenna & Robertson 1 hole

Singles
Leslie Shannon lost to Patricia (Trish) Johnson 1 hole
Kim Williams lost to Jill Thornhill 4 and 3
Danielle Ammaccapane lost to Lillian Behan 4 and 3
Kandi Kessler beat Vicki Thomas 3 and 2
Dottie Pepper Mochrie halved with Karen Davies
Cindy Schreyer beat Claire Hourihane 2 and 1

Second Day: Foursomes
Ammaccapane & Mochrie lost to Davies & Johnson
    1 hole
Shannon & Williams lost to Behan & Thornhill 5 and 3
Gardner & Scrivner halved with McKenna & Belle
    McCorkindale Robertson

Singles
Shannon halved with Thornhill
Kathleen McCarthy Scrivner lost to Trish Johnson
    5 and 3
Kim Gardner beat Behan 1 hole
Williams lost to Thomas 4 and 3
Kessler halved with Davies
Schreyer lost to Hourihane 5 and 4

1988 *at Royal St George's*

Result: GBI 11, USA 7
Captains: Diane Robb Bailey (GBI),
*   Judy Bell (USA)*

First Day: Foursomes
Bayman & Wade beat Kerdyk & Scrivner 2 and 1
Davies & Shapcott beat Scholefield & Thompson 5 and 4
Thomas & Thornhill halved with Keggi & Shannon

Singles
Linda Bayman halved with Tracy Kerdyk
Julie Wade beat Cindy Scholefield 2 and 1
Susan Shapcott lost to Carol Semple Thompson 1 hole
Karen Davies lost to Pearl Sinn 4 and 3
Shirley Lawson beat Pat Cornett-Iker 1 hole
Jill Thornhill beat Leslie Shannon 3 and 2

Second Day: Foursomes
Bayman & Wade lost to Kerdyk & Scrivner 1 hole
Davies & Shapcott beat Keggi & Shannon 2 holes
Thomas & Thornhill beat Scholefield & Thompson
    6 and 5

Singles
Wade lost to Kerdyk 2 and 1
Shapcott beat Caroline Keggi 3 and 2
Lawson lost to Kathleen McCarthy Scrivner 4 and 3
Vicki Thomas beat Cornett-Iker 5 and 3
Bayman beat Sinn 1 hole
Thornhill lost to Thompson 3 and 2

1990 *at Somerset Hills, NJ*

Result: USA 14, GBI 4
Captains: Leslie Shannon (USA),
*   Jill Thornhill (GBI)*

First Day: Foursomes
Goetze & Anne Quast Sander beat Dobson & Lambert
    4 and 3
Noble & Margaret Platt lost to Wade & Imrie 2 and 1
Thompson & Weiss beat Farquharson & Helen
    Wadsworth 3 and 1

Singles
Vicki Goetze lost to Julie Wade 2 and 1
Katie Peterson beat Kathryn Imrie 3 and 2
Brandie Burton beat Linzi Fletcher 3 and 1
Robin Weiss beat Elaine Farquharson 4 and 3
Karen Noble beat Catriona Lambert 1 hole
Carol Semple Thompson lost to Vicki Thomas 1 hole

Second Day: Foursomes
Goetze & Sander beat Wade & Imrie 3 and 1
Noble & Platt lost to Dobson & Lambert 1 hole
Burton & Peterson beat Farquharson & Wadsworth 5 and 4

Singles
Goetze beat Helen Dobson 4 and 3
Burton beat Lambert 4 and 3
Peterson beat Imrie 1 hole
Noble beat Wade 2 holes
Weiss beat Farquharson 2 and 1
Thompson beat Thomas 3 and 1

1992 *at Hoylake*

Result: GBI 10, USA 8
Captains: Elizabeth Boatman (GBI),
*   Judy Oliver (USA)*

First Day: Foursomes
Hall & Wade halved with Fruhwirth & Goetze
Lambert & Thomas beat Ingram & Shannon 2 and 1
Hourihane & Morley beat Hanson & Thompson 2 and 1

Singles
Joanne Morley halved with Amy Fruhwirth
Julie Wade lost to Vicki Goetze 3 and 2
Elaine Farquharson beat Robin Weiss 2 and 1
Nicola Buxton lost to Martha Lang 2 holes
Catriona Lambert beat Carol Semple Thompson 3 and 2
Caroline Hall beat Leslie Shannon 6 and 5

Second Day: Foursomes
Hall & Wade halved with Fruhwirth & Goetze
Hourihane & Morley halved with Lang & Weiss
Lambert & Thomas lost to Hanson & Thompson 3 and 2

Singles
Morley beat Fruhwirth 2 and 1
Lambert beat Tracy Hanson 6 and 5
Farquharson lost to Sarah LeBrun Ingram 2 and 1
Vicki Thomas lost to Shannon 2 and 1
Claire Hourihane lost to Lang 2 and 1
Hall beat Goetze 1 hole

1994 *at Chattanooga, TN*

Result: GBI 9, USA 9
Captains: Lancy Smith (USA),
*   Elizabeth Boatman (GBI)*

First Day: Foursomes
Sarah LeBrun Ingram & McGill halved with Matthew
    & Moodie
Klein & Thompson beat McKay & Kirsty Speak
    7 and 5
Kaupp & Port lost to Wade & Walton 6 and 5

1994 *continued*

Singles
Jill McGill halved with Julie Wade
Emilee Klein beat Janice Moodie 3 and 2
Wendy Ward lost to Lisa Walton 1 hole
Carol Semple Thompson beat Myra McKinlay 2 and 1
Ellen Port beat Mhairi McKay 2 and 1
Stephanie Sparks lost to Catriona Lambert Matthew
1 hole
Second Day: Foursomes
Ingram & McGill lost to Wade & Walton 2 and 1
Klein & Thompson beat McKinlay & Eileen Rose
Power 4 and 2
Sparks & Ward lost to Matthew & Moodie 3 and 2
Singles
McGill beat Wade 4 and 3
Klein lost to Matthew 2 and 1
Port beat McKay 7 and 5
Wendy Kaupp lost to McKinlay 3 and 2
Ward beat Walton 4 and 3
Thompson lost to Moodie 2 holes

1996 *at Killarney*

Result: GBI 11½, USA 6½
Captains: Ita Burke Butler (GBI),
Martha Lang (USA)
First Day: Foursomes
Lisa Walton Educate & Wade lost to K Kuehne & Port
2 and 1
Lisa Dermott & Rose beat B Corrie Kuehn & Jemsek 3 and 1
McKay & Moodie halved with Kerr & Thompson
Singles
Julie Wade lost to Sarah LeBrun Ingram 4 and 2
Karen Stupples beat Kellee Booth 3 and 2
Alison Rose beat Brenda Corrie Kuehn 5 and 4
Elaine Ratcliffe halved with Marla Jemsek
Mhairi McKay beat Cristie Kerr 1 hole
Janice Moodie beat Carol Semple Thompson 3 and 1
Second Day: Foursomes
McKay & Moodie beat Booth & Ingram 3 and 2
Dermott & Rose beat B Corrie Kuehn & Jemsek 2 and 1
Educate & Wade lost to K Kuehne & Port 1 hole
Singles
Wade lost to Kerr 1 hole
Ratcliffe beat Ingram 3 and 1
Stupples lost to Booth 3 and 2
Rose beat Ellen Port 6 and 5
McKay halved with Thompson
Moodie beat Kelli Kuehne 2 and 1

1998 *at Minikahda, Minneapolis, MN*

Result: USA 10, GBI 8
Captains: Barbara McIntire (USA),
Ita Burke Butler (GBI)
First Day: Foursomes
Bauer & Chuasiriporn lost to Ratcliffe & Rostron
1 hole
Booth & Corrie Kuehn beat Brown & Stupples 2 and 1
Burke & Derby Grimes beat Morgan & Rose 3 and 2
Singles
Kellee Booth beat Kim Rostron 2 and 1
Brenda Corrie Kuehn beat Alison Rose 3 and 2
Jenny Chuasiriporn halved with Rebecca Hudson
Beth Bauer beat Hilary Monaghan 5 and 3
Jo Jo Robertson lost to Becky Morgan 2 and 1
Carol Semple Thompson lost to Elaine Ratcliffe
3 and 2

Second Day: Foursomes
Booth & Corrie Kuehn beat Morgan & Rose 6 and 5
Bauer & Chuasiriporn lost to Brown & Hudson 2 holes
Burke & Derby Grimes beat Ratcliffe & Rostron 2 and 1
Singles
Booth beat Rostron 2 and 1
Corrie Kuehn beat Morgan 2 and 1
Thompson lost to Karen Stupples 1 hole
Robin Burke lost to Hudson 2 and 1
Robertson lost to Fiona Brown 1 hole
Virginia Derby Grimes halved with Ratcliffe

2000 *at Ganton*

Result: USA 10, GBI 8
Captains: Claire Hourihane Dowling (GBI),
Jane Bastanchury Booth (USA)
First Day: Foursomes
Andrew & Morgan lost to Bauer & Carol Semple
Thompson 1 hole
Brewerton & Hudson lost to Keever & Stanford
1 hole
Duggleby & O'Brien halved with Derby Grimes &
Homeyer
Singles
Kim Rostron Andrew lost to Beth Bauer 3 and 2
Fiona Brown lost to Robin Weiss 1 hole
Rebecca Hudson lost to Stephanie Keever 4 and 2
Lesley Nicholson halved with Angela Stanford
Suzanne O'Brien beat Leland Beckel 3 and 1
Emma Duggleby lost to Hilary Homeyer 1 hole
Second Day: Foursomes
Brewerton & Hudson beat Bauer & Thompson
2 and 1
Duggleby & O'Brien beat Keever & Stanford
7 and 6
Andrew & Morgan lost to Derby Grimes & Homeyer
3 and 1
Singles
Hudson lost to Bauer 1 hole
O'Brien beat Weiss 3 and 2
Duggleby beat Keever 4 and 2
Becky Brewerton lost to Homeyer 3 and 2
Becky Morgan beat Stanford 5 and 4
Andrew beat Virginia Derby Grimes 6 and 5

2002 *at Fox Chapel, PA*

Result: USA 11, GBI 7
Captains: Mary Budke (USA), Pam Benka (GBI)
First Day: Foursomes
Duncan & Jerman beat Duggleby & Hudson 4 and 3
Fankhauser & Semple Thompson beat Laing & Stirling
1 hole
Myerscough & Swaim beat Coffey & Smith 3 and 2
Singles
Emily Bastel lost to Rebecca Hudson 2 holes
Leigh Anne Hardin beat Emma Duggleby 2 and 1
Meredith Duncan beat Fame More 5 and 4
Angela Jerman beat Sarah Jones 6 and 5
Courtney Swaim beat Heather Stirling 4 and 2
Mollie Fankhauser lost to Vikki Laing 1 hole
Second Day: Foursomes
Hardin & Bastel lost to Laing & Stirling 3 and 1
Myerscough & Swaim beat Hudson & Smith
4 and 2
Duncan & Jerman lost to Coffey & Dugglesby
4 and 2

Singles
Mollie Fankhauser beat Rebecca Hudson 3 and 1
Carol Semple Thompson Beat Vikki Laing 1 hole
Leigh Anne Hardin lost to Emma Duggleby 4 and 3

Singles *continued*
Laura Myerscough beat Heather Stirling 2 holes
Meredith Duncan beat Akison Coffey 3 and 1
Courtney Swaim lost to Sarah Jones 5 and 3

Curtis Cup INDIVIDUAL RECORDS

Bold print: captain; bold print in brackets: non-playing captain
Maiden name in parentheses, former surname in square brackets

Great Britain and Ireland

Name		Year	Played	Won	Lost	Halved
Jean Anderson (Donald)	Sco	1948	6	3	3	0
Kim Andrew (Rostron)	Eng	1998-2000	8	2	6	0
Diane Bailey [Frearson] (Robb)	Eng	1962-72-**(84)**-**(86)**-**(88)**	5	2	2	1
Sally Barber (Bonallack)	Eng	1962	1	0	1	0
Pam Barton	Eng	1934-36	4	0	3	1
Linda Bayman	Eng	1988	4	2	1	1
Baba Beck (Pym)	Irl	**(1954)**	0	0	0	0
Charlotte Beddows [Watson] (Stevenson)	Sco	1932	1	0	1	0
Lilian Behan	Irl	1986	4	3	1	0
Veronica Beharrell (Anstey)	Eng	1956	1	0	1	0
Pam Benka (Tredinnick)	Eng	1966-68 **(2002)**	4	0	3	1
Jeanne Bisgood	Eng	1950-52-54-**(70)**	4	1	3	0
Elizabeth Boatman (Collis)	Eng	**(1992)**-**(94)**	0	0	0	0
Zara Bolton (Davis)	Eng	1948-**(56)**-**(66)**-**(68)**	2	0	2	0
Angela Bonallack (Ward)	Eng	1956-58-60-62-64-66	15	6	8	1
Becky Brewerton	Wal	2000	3	1	2	0
Fiona Brown	Eng	1998-2000	4	2	2	0
Ita Butler (Burke)	Irl	1966-**(96)**	3	2	1	0
Lady Katherine Cairns	Eng	**(1952)**	0	0	0	0
Carole Caldwell (Redford)	Eng	1978-80	5	0	3	2
Doris Chambers	Eng	**(1934)**-**(36)**-**(48)**	0	0	0	0
Alison Coffey	Irl	2002	3	1	2	0
Carol Comboy (Grott)	Eng	**(1978)**-**(80)**	0	0	0	0
Jane Connachan	Sco	1980-82	5	0	5	0
Elsie Corlett	Eng	1932-38-**(64)**	3	1	2	0
Diana Critchley (Fishwick)	Eng	1932-34-**(50)**	3	1	2	0
Alison Davidson (Rose)	Sco	1996-98	7	4	3	0
Karen Davies	Wal	1986-88	7	4	1	2
Laura Davies	Eng	1984	2	1	1	0
Lisa Dermott	Wal	1996	2	2	0	0
Helen Dobson	Eng	1990	3	1	2	0
Kitrina Douglas	Eng	1982	4	0	3	1
Claire Dowling (Hourihane)	Irl	1984-86-88-90-92-**(2000)**	8	3	3	2
Marjorie Draper [Peel] (Thomas)	Sco	1954	1	0	1	0
Emma Duggleby	Eng	2000	4	2	1	1
Lisa Educate (Walton)	Eng	1994-96	6	3	3	0
Mary Everard	Eng	1970-72-74-78	15	6	7	2
Elaine Farquharson	Sco	1990-92	6	1	5	0
Daisy Ferguson	Irl	**(1958)**	0	0	0	0
Marjory Ferguson (Fowler)	Sco	1966	1	0	1	0
Elizabeth Price Fisher (Price)	Eng	1950-52-54-56-58-60	12	7	4	1
Linzi Fletcher	Eng	1990	1	0	1	0
Maureen Garner (Madill)	Irl	1980	4	0	3	1
Marjorie Ross Garon	Eng	1936	2	1	0	1
Maureen Garrett (Ruttle)	Eng	1948-**(60)**	2	0	2	0
Philomena Garvey	Irl	1948-50-52-54-56-60	11	2	8	1
Carol Gibbs (Le Feuvre)	Eng	1974	3	0	3	0
Jacqueline Gordon	Eng	1948	2	1	1	0
Molly Gourlay	Eng	1932-34	4	0	2	2
Julia Greenhalgh	Eng	1964-70-74-76-78	17	6	7	4
Penny Grice-Whittaker (Grice)	Eng	1984	4	2	1	1
Caroline Hall	Eng	1992	4	2	0	2
Marley Harris [Spearman] (Baker)	Eng	1960-62-64	6	2	2	2
Dorothea Hastings (Sommerville)	Sco	1958	0	0	0	0
Lady Heathcoat-Amory (Joyce Wethered)	Eng	**1932**	2	1	1	0

Curtis Cup Individual Records *continued*

Name		Year	Played	Won	Lost	Halved
Dinah Henson (Oxley)	Eng	1968-70-72-76	11	3	6	2
Helen Holm (Gray)	Sco	1936-38-48	5	3	2	0
Ann Howard (Phillips)	Eng	1956-68	2	0	2	0
Rebecca Hudson	Eng	1998-2000-02	11	5	5	1
Shirley Huggan (Lawson)	Sco	1988	2	1	1	0
Beverley Huke	Eng	1972	2	0	2	0
Ann Irvin	Eng	1962-68-70-76	12	4	7	1
Bridget Jackson	Eng	1958-64-68	8	1	6	1
Patricia Johnson	Eng	1986	4	4	0	0
Sarah Jones	Wal	2002	2	1	1	0
Vikki Laing	Sco	2002	4	2	2	0
Susan Langridge (Armitage)	Eng	1964-66	6	0	5	1
Joan Lawrence	Sco	1964	2	0	2	0
Wilma Leburn (Aitken)	Sco	1982	2	0	2	0
Jenny Lee Smith	Eng	1974-76	3	0	3	0
Kathryn Lumb (Phillips)	Eng	1970-72	2	1	1	0
Mhairi McKay	Sco	1994-96	7	2	3	2
Mary McKenna	Irl	1970-72-74-76-78-80-82-84-86	30	10	16	4
Myra McKinlay	Sco	1994	3	1	2	0
Suzanne McMahon (Cadden)	Sco	1976	4	0	4	0
Sheila Maher (Vaughan)	Eng	1962-64	4	1	2	1
Kathryn Marshall (Imrie)	Sco	1990	4	1	3	0
Vanessa Marvin	Eng	1978	3	1	2	0
Catriona Matthew (Lambert)	Sco	1990-92-94	12	7	4	1
Tegwen Matthews [Thomas] (Perkins)	Wal	1974-76-78-80	14	4	8	2
Moira Milton (Paterson)	Sco	1952	2	1	1	0
Hilary Monaghan	Sco	1998	1	0	1	0
Janice Moodie	Sco	1994-96	8	5	1	2
Fame More	Eng	2002	1	0	1	0
Becky Morgan	Wal	1998-2000	7	2	5	0
Wanda Morgan	Eng	1932-34-36	6	0	5	1
Joanne Morley	Eng	1992	4	2	0	2
Nicola Murray (Buxton)	Eng	1992	1	0	1	0
Beverley New	Eng	1984	4	1	3	0
Lesley Nicholson	Sco	2000	1	0	0	1
Suzanne O'Brien	Irl	2000	4	3	0	1
Maire O'Donnell	Irl	**(1982)**	0	0	0	0
Margaret Pickard (Nichol)	Eng	1968-70	5	2	3	0
Diana Plumpton	Eng	1934	2	1	1	0
Elizabeth Pook (Chadwick)	Eng	1966	4	1	3	0
Doris Porter (Park)	Sco	1932	1	0	1	0
Eileen Rose Power (McDaid)	Irl	1994	1	0	1	0
Elaine Ratcliffe	Eng	1996-98	6	3	1	2
Clarrie Reddan (Tiernan)	Irl	1938-48	3	2	1	0
Joan Rennie (Hastings)	Sco	1966	3	0	1	1
Maureen Richmond (Walker)	Sco	1974	4	2	2	0
Jean Roberts	Eng	1962	1	0	1	0
Belle Robertson (McCorkindale)	Sco	1960-66-68-70-72-(**74**)-(**76**)-82-86	24	5	12	7
Claire Robinson (Nesbitt)	Irl	1980	3	0	1	2
Vivien Saunders	Eng	1968	4	1	2	1
Susan Shapcott	Eng	1988	4	3	1	0
Linda Simpson (Moore)	Eng	1980	3	1	1	1
Ruth Slark (Porter)	Eng	1960-62-64	7	3	3	1
Anne Smith [Stant] (Willard)	Eng	1976	1	0	1	0
Frances Smith (Stephens)	Eng	1950-52-54-56-58-60-(**62**)-(**72**)	11	7	3	1
Kerry Smith	Eng	2002	2	0	2	0
Janet Soulsby	Eng	1982	4	1	2	1
Kirsty Speak	Eng	1994	1	0	1	0
Gillian Stewart	Sco	1980-82	4	1	3	0
Heather Stirling	Sco	2002	4	1	3	0
Karen Stupples	Eng	1996-98	4	2	2	0
Vicki Thomas (Rawlings)	Wal	1982-84-86-88-90-92	13	6	5	2
Muriel Thomson	Sco	1978	3	2	1	0
Jill Thornhill	Eng	1984-86-88	12	6	2	4
Angela Uzielli (Carrick)	Eng	1978	1	0	1	0
Jessie Valentine (Anderson)	Sco	1936-38-50-52-54-56-58	13	4	9	0
Julie Wade	Eng	1988-90-92-94-96	19	6	10	3

Name		Year	Played	Won	Lost	Halved
Helen Wadsworth	Wal	1990	2	0	2	0
Claire Waite	Eng	1984	4	2	2	0
Mickey Walker	Eng	1972-74	4	3	0	1
Pat Walker	Irl	1934-36-38	6	2	3	1
Verona Wallace-Williamson	Sco	(1938)	0	0	0	0
Nan Wardlaw (Baird)	Sco	1938	1	0	1	0
Enid Wilson	Eng	1932	2	1	1	0
Janette Wright (Robertson)	Sco	1954-56-58-60	8	3	5	0
Phyllis Wylie (Wade)	Eng	1938	1	0	0	1

United States of America

Name	Year	Played	Won	Lost	Halved
Roberta Albers	1968	2	1	0	1
Danielle Ammaccapane	1986	3	0	3	0
Kathy Baker	1982	4	3	0	1
Barbara Barrow	1976	2	1	0	1
Beth Barry	1972-74	5	3	1	1
Emily Bastel	2002	2	0	2	0
Beth Bauer	1998-2000	7	4	3	0
Laura Baugh	1972	4	2	1	1
Leland Beckel	2000	1	0	1	0
Judy Bell	1960-62-(86)-(88)	2	1	1	0
Peggy Kirk Bell (Kirk)	1950	2	1	1	0
Amy Benz	1982	3	2	1	0
Patty Berg	1936-38	4	1	2	1
Barbara Fay Boddie (White)	1964-66	8	7	0	1
Jane Booth (Bastanchury)	1970-72-74-(2000)	12	9	3	0
Kellee Booth	1996-98	7	5	2	0
Mary Budke	1974-(2002)	3	2	1	0
Robin Burke	1998	3	2	1	0
Brandie Burton	1990	3	3	0	0
Jo Anne Carner (Gunderson)	1958-60-62-64	10	6	3	1
Lori Castillo	1980	3	2	1	0
Leona Cheney (Pressler)	1932-34-36	6	5	1	0
Sis Choate	(1974)	0	0	0	0
Jenny Chuasiriporn	1998	3	0	2	1
Peggy Conley	1964-68	6	3	1	2
Mary Ann Cook (Downey)	1956	2	1	1	0
Patricia Cornett	1978-88	4	1	2	1
Brenda Corrie Kuehn	1996-98	7	4	3	0
Jean Crawford (Ashley)	1962-66-68-(72)	8	6	2	0
Clifford Ann Creed	1962	2	2	0	0
Grace Cronin (Lenczyk)	1948-50	3	2	1	0
Carolyn Cudone	1956-(70)	1	1	0	0
Beth Daniel	1976-78	8	7	1	0
Virginia Dennehy	(1958)	0	0	0	0
Virginia Derby Grimes	1998-2000	6	3	1	2
Mary Lou Dill	1968	3	1	1	1
Meredith Duncan	2002	4	3	1	0
Alice Dye	1970	2	1	0	1
Mollie Fankhauser	2002	3	1	2	0
Heather Farr	1984	3	2	1	0
Jane Fassinger	1970	1	0	1	0
Mary Lena Faulk	1954	2	1	1	0
Carol Sorensen Flenniken (Sorensen)	1964-66	8	6	1	1
Edith Flippin (Quier)	(1954)-(56)	0	0	0	0
Amy Fruhwirth	1992	4	0	1	3
Kim Gardner	1986	3	1	1	1
Charlotte Glutting	1934-36-38	5	3	1	1
Vicki Goetze	1990-92	8	4	2	2
Brenda Goldsmith	1978-80	4	2	2	0
Aniela Goldthwaite	1934-(52)	1	0	1	0
Joanne Goodwin	1960	2	1	1	0
Mary Hafeman	1980	2	1	0	1
Shelley Hamkin	1968-70	8	3	3	2
Penny Hammel	1984	3	1	1	1
Nancy Hammer (Hager)	1970	2	1	1	0
Cathy Hanlon	1982	3	2	1	0

Curtis Cup Individual Records *continued*

Name	Year	Played	Won	Lost	Halved
Beverley Hanson	1950	2	2	0	0
Tracy Hanson	1992	3	1	2	0
Patricia Harbottle (Lesser)	1954-56	3	2	1	0
Leigh Anne Hardin	2002	3	1	2	0
Helen Hawes	(1964)	0	0	0	0
Kathryn Hemphill	1938	1	0	0	1
Helen Hicks	1932	2	1	1	0
Carolyn Hill	1978	2	0	0	2
Cindy Hill	1970-74-76-78	14	5	6	3
Opel Hill	1932-34-36	6	2	3	1
Marion Hollins	(1932)	0	0	0	0
Hilary Homeyer	2000	4	3	0	1
Dana Howe	1984	3	1	1	1
Juli Inkster	1982	4	4	0	0
Maria Jemsek	1996	3	0	2	1
Angela Jerman	2002	3	2	1	0
Ann Casey Johnstone	1958-60-62	4	3	1	0
Mae Murray Jones (Murray)	1952	1	0	1	0
Wendy Kaupp	1994	2	0	2	0
Stephanie Keever	2000	4	2	2	0
Caroline Keggi	1988	3	0	2	1
Tracy Kerdyk	1988	4	2	1	1
Cristie Kerr	1996	3	1	1	1
Kandi Kessler	1986	3	1	1	1
Dorothy Kielty	1948-50	4	4	0	0
Dorothy Kirby	1948-50-52-54	7	4	3	0
Martha Kirouac (Wilkinson)	1970-72	8	5	3	0
Emilee Klein	1994	4	3	1	0
Nancy Knight (Lopez)	1976	2	2	0	0
Kelli Kuehne	1996	3	2	1	0
Martha Lang	1992-(96)	3	2	0	1
Bonnie Lauer	1974	4	2	2	0
Sarah Le Brun Ingram	1992-94-96	7	2	4	1
Marjorie Lindsay	1952	2	1	1	0
Patricia Lucey (O'Sullivan)	1952	1	0	1	0
Mari McDougall	1982	2	2	0	0
Jill McGill	1994	4	1	1	2
Barbara McIntire	1958-60-62-64-66-72-(76)	16	6	6	4
Lucile Mann (Robinson)	1934	1	0	1	0
Debbie Massey	1974-76	5	5	0	0
Marion Miley	1938	2	1	0	1
Dottie Mochrie (Pepper)	1986	3	0	2	1
Evelyn Monsted	(1968)	0	0	0	0
Terri Moody	1980	2	1	0	1
Laura Myerscough	2002	3	3	0	0
Karen Noble	1990	4	2	2	0
Judith Oliver	1978-80-82-(92)	8	5	1	2
Maureen Orcutt	1932-34-36-38	8	5	3	0
Joanne Pacillo	1984	3	1	1	1
Estelle Page (Lawson)	1938-48	4	3	1	0
Katie Peterson	1990	3	3	0	0
Margaret Platt	1990	2	0	2	0
Frances Pond (Stebbins)	(1938)	0	0	0	0
Ellen Port	1994-96	6	4	2	0
Dorothy Germain Porter	1950-(66)	2	1	0	1
Phyllis Preuss	1962-64-66-68-70-(84)	15	10	4	1
Betty Probasco	(1982)	0	0	0	0
Mildred Prunaret	(1960)	0	0	0	0
Polly Riley	1948-50-52-54-56-58-(62)	10	5	5	0
Jo Jo Robertson	1998	2	0	2	0
Barbara Romack	1954-56-58	5	3	2	0
Jody Rosenthal	1984	3	2	0	1
Anne Sander [Welts] [Decker] (Quast)	1958-60-62-66-68-74-84-90	22	11	7	4
Cindy Scholefield	1988	3	0	3	0
Cindy Schreyer	1986	3	1	2	0
Kathleen McCarthy Scrivner (McCarthy)	1986-88	6	2	3	1
Carol Semple Thompson	1974-76-80-82-90-92-94-96-**98**-2000-02	33	16	13	4
Leslie Shannon	1986-88-90-92	9	1	6	2

Name	Year	Played	Won	Lost	Halved
Patty Sheehan	1980	4	4	0	0
Pearl Sinn	1988	2	1	1	0
Grace De Moss Smith (De Moss)	1952-54	3	1	2	0
Lancy Smith	1972-78-80-82-84-(94)	16	7	5	4
Margaret Smith	1956	2	2	0	0
Stephanie Sparks	1994	2	0	2	0
Hollis Stacy	1972	2	0	1	1
Claire Stancik (Doran)	1952-54	4	4	0	0
Angela Stanford	2000	4	1	2	1
Judy Street (Eller)	1960	2	2	0	0
Louise Suggs	1948	2	0	1	1
Courtney Swaim	2002	4	3	1	0
Nancy Roth Syms (Roth)	1964-66-76-(80)	9	3	5	1
Noreen Uihlein	1978	3	1	1	1
Virginia Van Wie	1932-34	4	3	0	1
Glenna Collett Vare (Collett)	1932-(34)-36-38-48-(50)	7	4	2	1
Wendy Ward	1994	3	1	2	0
Jane Weiss (Nelson)	1956	1	0	1	0
Robin Weiss	1990-92-2000	7	4	2	1
Donna White (Horton)	1976	2	2	0	0
Mary Anne Widman	1984	3	2	1	0
Kimberley Williams	1986	3	0	3	0
Helen Sigel Wilson (Sigel)	1950-66-(78)	2	0	2	0
Joyce Ziske	1954	1	0	1	0

Women's World Amateur Team Championship for the Espirito Santo Trophy

1964	France	United States	St Germain	588
1966	United States	Canada	Mexico	580
1968	United States	Australia	Melbourne	616
1970	United States	France	Madrid	598
1972	United States	France	Buenos Aires	583
1974	United States	GB&I, South Africa	Dominican Republic	620
1976	United States	France	Vilamoura, Portugal	605
1978	Australia	Canada	Fiji	596
1980	United States	Australia	Pinehurst, USA	588
1982	United States	New Zealand	Geneva, Switzerland	579
1984	United States	France	Hong Kong	585
1986	Spain	France	Caracas, Venezuela	580
1988	United States	Sweden	Drottningholm, Sweden	587
1990	United States	New Zealand	Christchurch, New Zealand	585
1992	Spain	GB&I	Vancouver, Canada	588
1994	United States	Korea	Paris, France	569
1996	Korea	Italy	Manila, Philippines	438
1998	United States	Italy	Santiago, Chile	558
2000	France	Korea	Sporting Club, Berlin	580
2002	Australia	Thailand	Saujana, Kuala Lumpur	578

Commonwealth Tournament (Instituted 1959)

1959	Great Britain	St Andrews
1963	Great Britain	Royal Melbourne, Australia
1967	Great Britain	Ancaster, Ontario, Canada
1971	Great Britain	Hamilton, New Zealand
1975	Great Britain	Ganton, England
1979	Canada	Lake Karrinup, Perth, Australia

1983	Australia	Glendale, Edmonton, Canada
1987	Canada	Christchurch, New Zealand
1991	Great Britain	Northumberland, England
1995	Australia	Royal Sydney, Australia
1999	Australia	Marine Drive, Vancouver, Canada

2003 at Remeura, New Zealand

First Day:
Australia beat South Africa 4½ – 1½
New Zealand beat Canada 5 – 1

Second Day:
Australia beat Great Britain 4 – 2
Canada beat South Africa 4 – 2

Commonwealth Tournament *continued*

Third Day:
Great Britain halved with South Africa 3 – 3
Australia beat New Zealand 4½ – 1½

Fourth Day:
New Zealand beat Great Britain 4 – 2
Australia beat Canada 3½ – 2½

Fifth Day:
Great Britain halved with Canada 3 – 3
New Zealand beat South Africa 4½ – 1½

Final Placings:

1	Australia	4 wins
2	New Zealand	3 wins
3	Canada	1 win, 1 halved match
4	Great Britain	2 halved matches
5	South Africa	1 halved match

Winning team: Edwina Kennedy (non-playing captain); Misun Cho, Sarah Kemp, Sarah-Jane Kenyon, Rochelle Miles, Anna Parsons

Women's European Amateur Team Championship

1967	England	France	Penina, Portugal	1987	Sweden	Wales	Turnberry, Scotland
1969	France	England	Tylosand, Sweden	1989	France	England	Pals, Spain
1971	England	France	Ganton, England	1991	England	Sweden	Wentworth, England
1973	England	France	Brussels, Belgium	1993	England	Spain	Royal Haagshe
1975	France	Spain	Paris, France	1995	Spain	Scotland	Milan, Italy
1977	England	Spain	Sotogrande, Spain	1997	Sweden	Scotland	Nordcenter, Finland
1979	Ireland	Germany	Hermitage, Ireland	1999	France	England	St Germain, France
1981	Sweden	France	Troia, Portugal	2001	Sweden	Spain	Pontevedra, Spain
1983	Ireland	England	Waterloo, Belgium	2003	Spain	Sweden	Wittelsbacher, Germany
1985	England	Italy	Stavanger, Norway				

Vagliano Trophy – Great Britain & Ireland v Continent of Europe

1959	GB & I	12–3	Wentworth	1981	Europe	14–10	P de Hierro
1961	GB & I	8–7	Villa d'Este	1983	GB & I	14–10	Woodhall Spa
1963	GB & I	20–10	Muirfield	1985	GB & I	14–10	Hamburg
1965	Europe	17–13	Cologne	1987	GB & I	15–9	The Berkshire
1967	Europe	15½–14½	Lytham	1989	GB & I	14½–9½	Venice
1969	Europe	16–14	Chantilly	1991	GB & I	13½–10½	Nairn
1971	GB & I	17½–12½	Worplesdon	1993	GB & I	13½–10½	Morfontaine
1973	GB & I	20–10	Eindhoven	1995	Europe	14–10	Ganton
1975	GB & I	13½–10½	Muirfield	1997	Europe	14–10	Halmstad
1977	GB & I	15½–8½	Malmo	1999	Europe	13–11	North Berwick
1979	Halved	12–12	R Porthcawl	2001	Europe	7–5	Venice

2003 *at Co. Louth, Ireland*

(home team names first)

*Captains: Ada O'Sullivan (GB&I),
Macarena Campomanes (Europe)*

First Day – Foursomes
V Laing & Brewerton beat Schreefel & Cabrera 2 holes
More & Queen lost to Giquel & Hauert 4 and 3
Kenny & Mangan lost to Blomquist & Sorensen 1 hole
Masters & Duggleby halved with Elosegui & Serramia

Singles
Becky Brewerton (Wal) beat Elisa Serramia (Esp) 3 and 1
Emma Duggleby (Eng) beat Fany Schaeffer (Fra) 4 and 3
Fame More (Eng) lost to Bettina Hauert (Ger) 1 hole
Anne Laing (Sco) beat Emma Cabrera (Esp) 2 and 1
Tricia Mangan (Irl) beat Lisa Holm Sorensen (Den) 4 and 3
Vikki Laing (Sco) beat Dewi Claire Schreefel (Ned) 2 and 1
Lynn Kenny (Sco) halved with Minia Blomqvist (Fin)
Danielle Masters (Eng) beat Tania Elosegui (Esp) 2 and 1

Second Day – Foursomes
V Laing & Brewerton beat Giquel & Hauert 1 hole
More & Queen lost to Schreefel & Cabrera 2 and 1
Duggleby & Masters beat Elosegui & Serramia 4 and 2
Kenny & Mangan halved with Blomquist & Sorensen

Singles
Becky Brewerton (Wal) beat Lisa Holm Sorensen (Den) 2 and 1
Emma Duggleby (Eng) halved with Sophie Giquel (Fra)
Fame More (Eng) lost to Emma Cabrera (Esp) 4 and 3
Anne Laing (Sco) lost to Bettina Hauert (Ger) 3 and 2
Tricia Mangan (Irl) lost to Dewi Claire Schreefel (Ned) 2 and 1
Vikki Laing (Sco) lost to Elisa Serramia (Esp) 2 and 1
Lynn Kenny (Sco) lost to M Blomqvist (Fin) 6 and 5
Danielle Masters (Eng) halved with Tania Elosegui (Esp)

Result: GB&I 12½, Continent of Europe 11½

Copa de las Americas

for results see page 251

European Club Cup

2003 at La Boulie, France

1	Germany (Bergisch-Land GC)	141-148-147—436	(Bettina Hauert, Katharina Schellenberg, Sibylle Gabler)
2	Spain (Puerta de Hiero)	147-149-144—440	
3	France (La Boulie)	148-149-145—442	

Women's Home Internationals

2003 at Cruden Bay

Scotland 4½	Ireland 4½	England 4½	Scotland 4½
England 4½	Wales 4½	Ireland 5	England 4
Wales 4	Ireland 5	Scotland 5½	Wales 3½

Result: 1 Ireland 2½ [14½]; 2 Scotland 2 [14½]; 3 England 1 [13]; 4 Wales ½ [12]

Winning team: Mary McKenna (captain); Claire Coughland (Cork), Tara Delaney (Carlow), Maria Dunne (Skerries), Helen Jones (Strabane), Sinead Keane (The Curragh), Tricia Mangan (Ennis), Maura Morrin (The Curragh), Heather Nolan (Shannon)

1948	England	R Lytham and St Annes	1972	England	R Lytham and St Annes
1949	Scotland	Harlech	1973	England	Harlech
1950	Scotland	Newcastle Co Down	1974T	England/Scotland/	
1951	Scotland	Broadstone		Ireland	Sandwich, Princes
1952	Scotland	Troon	1975	England	Newport
1953	England	Porthcawl	1976	England	Troon
1954T	England/Scotland	Ganton, Scotland	1977	England	Cork
1955	England	Western Gailes	1978	England	Moortown
1956	Scotland	Sunningdale	1979T	Scotland/Ireland	Harlech
1957	Scotland	Troon	1980	Ireland	Cruden Bay
1958	England	Hunstanton	1981	Scotland	Portmarnock
1959	England	Hoylake	1982	England	Burnham and Barrow
1960	England	Gullane	1983	*Matches abandoned due to weather*	
1961	Scotland	Portmarnock	1984	England	Gullane
1962	Scotland	Porthcawl	1985	England	Waterville
1963	England	Formby	1986	Ireland	Whittington Barracks
1964	England	Troon	1987	England	Ashburnham
1965	England	Portrush	1988	Scotland	Kilmarnock (Barassie)
1966	England	Woodhall Spa	1989	England	Westport
1967	England	Sunningdale	1990	Scotland	Hunstanton
1968	England	Porthcawl	1991	Scotland	Aberdovey
1969T	England/Scotland	Western Gailes	1992	England	Hamilton
1970	England	Killarney	1993	England	Dublin
1971	England	Longniddry			

1994 at Huddersfield, Yorkshire

England beat Ireland	6½ matches to 2½
Scotland beat Wales	8½ matches to ½
England beat Wales	8 matches to 1
Scotland halved with Ireland	4½ matches to 4½
England beat Scotland	6 matches to 3
Ireland beat Wales	5½ matches to 3½

Result: England 3; Scotland 1½; Ireland 1½; Wales 0

1995 at Wrexham, Clwyd

England beat Scotland	6 matches to 3
Ireland halved with Wales	4½ matches to 4½
Ireland beat Scotland	5 matches to 4
Wales beat England	5 matches to 4
England beat Ireland	9 matches to 0
Scotland beat Wales	5 matches to 4

Result: England 2; Wales 1½; Ireland 1½; Scotland 1

1996 at Longniddry

Scotland beat Ireland	5½ matches to 3½
England beat Wales	6 matches to 3
Scotland beat Wales	5 matches to 4
England beat Ireland	6 matches to 3
England beat Scotland	5 matches to 4
Ireland beat Wales	5½ matches to 3½

Result: England 3; Scotland 2; Ireland 1; Wales 0

1997 at Lahinch, Ireland

Ireland beat Wales	6½ matches to 2½
England beat Scotland	6½ matches to 2½
England beat Ireland	6 matches to 3
Scotland beat Wales	5½ matches to 3½
England beat Wales	5 matches to 4
Ireland beat Scotland	7 matches to 2

Result: England 3; Ireland 2; Scotland 1; Wales 0

Women's Home Internationals continued

1998 at Burnham & Berrow

Ireland beat Wales	6 matches to 3
England beat Scotland	6 matches to 3
England beat Ireland	5 matches to 4
Ireland halved with Scotland	4½ matches to 4½
England beat Wales	6½ matches to 2½
Scotland halved with Wales	4½ matches to 4½

Result: England 3; Ireland 1½; Scotland 1; Wales ½

1999 at Royal Dornoch

Ireland beat Scotland	5 matches to 4
England halved with Wales	4½ matches to 4½
Wales beat Ireland	7½ matches to 1½
England beat Scotland	5 matches to 4
England beat Ireland	7 matches to 2
Wales beat Scotland	5½ matches to 3½

Result: Wales 2½; England 2½; Ireland 1; Scotland 0
(Wales won on individual games countback 17½–16½)

2000 at Royal St David's

Ireland halved with Wales	4½ matches to 4½
England beat Scotland	6 matches to 3
Wales beat Scotland	8 matches to 1
England beat Ireland	8 matches to 1

2000 continued

Ireland beat Scotland	5 matches to 4
England beat Wales	5 matches to 4

Result: England 3; Wales 1½; Ireland 1½; Scotland 0

2001 at Carlow

Ireland beat Wales	6 matches to 3
England beat Scotland	5½ matches to 3½
Wales halved with Scotland	4½ matches to 4½
England beat Ireland	5½ matches to 3½
England beat Wales	5 matches to 4
Ireland beat Scotland	5½ matches to 3½

Result: England 3; Ireland 2; Scotland & Wales ½

2002 at The Berkshire

Ireland beat England	5 matches to 4
Scotland beat Wales	5 matches to 4
England beat Scotland	5½ matches to 3½
Wales beat England	5 matches to 4
England beat Wales	6½ matches to 2½
Scotland beat Ireland	6 matches to 3

Result: England 2; Scotland 2; Ireland 1; Wales 1

Senior Home Internationals at Whittington Heath

England beat Wales 4 matches to 3
Ireland beat Scotland 4 matches to 3
England beat Scotland 4½ matches to 2½

Ireland beat Wales 5 matches to 2
England beat Ireland 6 matches to 1
Wales beat Scotland 4 matches to 3

Result: 1 England 3 (14½), 2 Ireland 2 (10), 3 Wales 1 (9), 4 Scotland 0 (8½)

Winning team: Carole Caldwell (Sunningdale), Adele Mitchell (Keighley), Rosaling Page (Came Down), Vivien Saunders (Cambridge Meridien), Chris Stirling (Meon Valley), Christina Watson (Beaconsfield)

England and Wales Ladies County Championship

1908	Lancashire	1935	Essex	1964	Lancashire	1985	Surrey
1909	Surrey	1936	Surrey	1965	Staffordshire	1986	Glamorgan
1910	Cheshire	1937	Surrey	1966	Lancashire	1987	Lancashire
1911	Cheshire	1938	Lancashire	1967	Lancashire	1988	Surrey
1912	Cheshire	1947	Surrey	1968	Surrey	1989	Cheshire
1913	Surrey	1948	Yorkshire	1969	Lancashire	1990	Cheshire
1920	Middlesex	1949	Surrey	1970	Yorkshire	1991	Glamorgan
1921	Surrey	1950	Yorkshire	1971	Kent	1992	Hampshire
1922	Surrey	1951	Lancashire	1972	Kent	1993	Lancashire
1923	Surrey	1952	Lancashire	1973	Northumberland	1994	Staffordshire
1924	Surrey	1953	Surrey	1974	Surrey	1995	Hampshire
1925	Surrey	1954	Warwickshire	1975	Glamorgan	1996	Cheshire
1926	Surrey	1955	Surrey	1976	Staffordshire	1997	Surrey
1927	Yorkshire	1956	Kent	1977	Essex	1998	Yorkshire
1928	Cheshire	1957	Middlesex	1978	Glamorgan	1999	Yorkshire
1929	Yorkshire	1958	Lancashire	1979	Essex	2000	Yorkshire
1930	Surrey	1959	Middlesex	1980	Lancashire	2001	Yorkshire
1931	Middlesex	1960	Lancashire	1981	Glamorgan	2002	Lancashire
1932	Cheshire	1961	Middlesex	1982	Surrey		
1933	Yorkshire	1962	Staffordshire	1983	Surrey		
1934	Surrey	1963	Warwickshire	1984	Surrey/Yorkshire		

2003 at Pyle & Kenfig

1 Kent 19½; 2 Glamorgan 13; 3 Leicestershire & Rutland 11; 4 Cheshire 10½

Winning team: Claire Aitken, Helen Batt, Hayley Charlick, Danielle Masters, Sian Reddick, Nicola Timmins, Anne Wheble

Scottish Ladies County Championship

1992	Dunbartonshire & Argyll	1997	Dunbartonshire & Argyll	2001	Stirlingshire &
1993	East Lothian	1998	East Lothian		Clackmannanshire
1994	East Lothian	1999	East Lothian	2002	Stirlingshire &
1995	Fife	2000	Northern Counties		Clackmannanshire
1996	East Lothian				

2003 *at Scotscraig*

1 Northern Counties 3 (20); 2 Fife 2 (19); 3 Borders 1 (8); 4 Ayrshire 0 (7)

Winning team: Cara Gruber, Lesley Mackay (University of Stirling/Royal Dornoch), Pam Mackay (Royal Dornoch), Kerri Harper (Inverness), Pat McLellan (Forres), Jenny Milne (Elgin), Mary Smith (Tain)

Scottish Ladies Foursomes

1992	Haggs Castle	1996	Hilton Park	2000	Windyhill
1993	North Berwick	1997	Stirling	2001	Stirling
1994	Turnberry	1998	Prestonfield	2002	Ladies Panmure, Barry
1995	Gullane	1999	Dunblane New		

2003 *at Alyth*

1	Drumpellier (Clare Queen, Susan Wood)	69-73—142
2	Dunblane New (Heather MacRae, Lynn Kenny)	73-70—143

Welsh Ladies Team Championship

1992	Whitchurch	1996	R. St Davids	2000	Pennard
1993	Pennard	1997	St Pierre	2001	Whitchurch
1994	St Pierre	1998	Wrexham	2002	Abergele
1995	R. St Davids	1999	Pennard		

2003 *at Radyr*

Pennard beat Royal Porthcawl

Winning team: Sarah Jones, Julie Ace, Leila Jones, Laura Weatherill, Geraldine Edards, Judy Ganz

Weetabix Challenge

2003 *at Royal Birkdale*

Foursomes

B Brewerton & S Jones beat E Esterl & M Zelsmann 2 holes
K Smith & A Highgate lost to K Taylor & N Moult 6 and 5
A Laing & A Keighley lost to C Hall & J Morley 5 and 4
C Queen & F More halved with J Mills & C Duffy
S Garbutt & D Masters halved with L Fairclough & N Fink
T Mangan & N Timmins lost to KS Taylor & R Bailey 1 hole
L Mackay & L Kenny lost to D Reid & J Forbes 4 and 2

Singles

Becky Brewerton (Abergele) beat Kirsty Taylor (Eng) 1 hole
Fame More (Chesterfield) lost to Marieke Zelsmann (Ned)
  1 hole
Kerry Smith (Waterlooville) lost to Elisabeth Esterl (Ger) 5 and 3
Clare Queen (Drumpellier) lost to Nicky Moult (Eng) 5 and 3
Danielle Masters (Rochester & Cobham) lost to Lora Fairclough
  (Eng) 5 and 3

Singles *continued*

Tricia Mangan (Ennis) lost to Claire Duffy (Eng) 2 and 1
Anna Highgate (Cottrell Park) lost to Rachel Bailey (Eng)
  2 holes
Nicola Timmins (Sene Valley) lost to Kirsty S Taylor
  (Eng) 5 and 4
Lesley Mackay (University of Stirling) lost to Caroline
  Hall (Eng) 5 and 4
Alex Keighley (Lightcliffe) lost to Julie Forbes (Sco)
  4 and 3
Anne Laing (Vale of Leven) beat Natascha Fink (Aut)
  3 and 2
Sarah Jones (Pennard) lost to Dale Reid (Sco) 3 and 2
Sara Garbutt (Ganton) lost to Joanne Mills (Aus) 2 and 1
Lynn Kenny (University of Stirling) halved with Joanne
  Morley (Eng)

Result: GBI Elite Squad 4½, Ladies European Tour Professionals 16½

Other Women's Amateur Tournaments

Lady Astor Salver (Inaugurated 1951) at *The Berkshire*

1951	Jeanne Bisgood	1964	Marley Spearman	1977	Angela Uzielli	1990T	Joanne Morley,
1952	Jeanne Bisgood	1965	Marley Spearman	1978	Mary Everard		Julie Wade
1953	Jeanne Bisgood	1966	Angela Bonallack	1979	Julia Greenhalgh	1991	EJ Smith
1954	Jean Donald	1967	Mary Everard	1980	Jane Lock	1992	Lisa Walton
1955	Elizabeth Price	1968	Mary Everard	1981	Angela Uzielli	1993	S Lambert
1956T	J Barton,	1969	Julia Greenhalgh	1982	*Abandoned*	1994	S Lambert
	Elizabeth Price	1970	B Whitehead	1983	Linda Denison-	1995	J Oliver
1957	Angela Ward	1971	Angela Uzielli		Pender Bayman	1996	S Gallagher
1958	Angela Ward	1972	Jill Thornhill	1984	Linda Bayman	1997	J Lamb
	Bonallack	1973T	Linda Denison-	1985	Helen Wadsworth	1998	R Morgan
1959	Elizabeth Price		Pender, Angela	1986	Caroline Pierce	1999	*Not played*
1960	Angela Bonallack		Uzielli	1987	Vicki Thomas	2000T	C Court,
1961	Angela Bonallack	1974	Cathy Barclay	1988	Jill Thornhill		K Taylor
1962	Ruth Porter	1975	Jill Thornhill	1989	Sarah Sutton	2001	E Pilgrim
1963	Ruth Porter	1976	Heather Clifford			2002	*Abandoned – rain*

2003

1	Kerry Smith (Waterlooville)	71-70—141
2	Stephanie Evans (Vale of Llangollen)	74-73—147
	Kelly Hutcherson (Porter's Park)	76-71—147
	Claire Lipscombe (Cirencester)	76-71—147
	Shelley McKevitt (Reading)	76-71—147

Bridget Jackson Bowl (Inaugurated 1982) at *Handsworth*

1982	Julie Brown (Leek)	1990	Susan Elliott (Henbury)	1996	Rebecca Hudson (Wheatley)
1983	Julie Brown (Leek)	1991	Fiona Edmund (Frinton-on-	1997	Kate MacIntosh (Aus)
1984	Trish Johnson (Pyle & Kenfig)		Sea)	1998	Claire Dowling (Copt Heath)
1985	Trish Johnson (Pyle & Kenfig)	1992	Fiona Brown (Heswall)	1999	Shelley McKevitt (Reading)
1986	Julia Hill (Hazel Grove)	1993	Simone Morgan (Hearsall)	2000	Rebecca Hudson (Wheatley)
1987	Vicki Thomas (Pennard)	1994	Kirsty Speak (Clitheroe)	2001	Laura Wright (Stanton-on-the-
1988	Vicki Thomas (Pennard)	1995	Karen Stupples (Royal Cinque		Wolds)
1989	Helen Dobson (Seacroft)		Ports)	2002	Claire Dowling (Copt Heath)

2003

1	Shelley McKevitt (Reading)	70-71—141
2	Sara Garbutt (Ganton)	73-71—144
	F Johnston (Harborne)	73-71—144

Critchley Salver (Inaugurated 1982) at *Sunningdale*

1982	Miss H Reid	1988	Mrs JE Bayman	1993	Mr CG Watson	1997	Miss L Waters
1983	Miss K Douglas		Miss J Wade	1994	Mrs S Lambert	1998	Miss L Waters
1984	Mrs JE Bayman	1989	Miss L Fletcher		Miss K Speak	1999	Miss LC Tupholme
1985	Mrs JE Bayman	1990	Miss S Hourihane	1995	Miss K Tebbet	2000	Miss C Court
1986	Mrs K Wooldridge	1991	Miss NL Buxton		Mrs A Uzielli	2001	Miss E Duggleby
1987	Miss S Moorcraft	1992	Mrs C Caldwell	1996	Miss S Gallagher	2002	Miss E Pilgrim

2003

1	Anna Highgate (Cottrell Park)	141
2	Emma Duggleby (Malton & Norton)	143
3	Sarah Jones (Pennard)	145
	Clare Lipscombe (Cirencester)	145

Hampshire Rose (Inaugurated 1973) at North Hants

1973	Carole Redford	1979	Carol Larkin	1987	Jill Thornhill	1995	J Oliver
1974	Pru Riddiford	1980	Beverley New	1988	Jill Thornhill	1996	K Stupples
1975	Vanessa Marvin	1981	Jillian Nicolson	1989	Alison MacDonald	1997	S Sanderson
1976T	Heather Clifford,	1982	Jill Thornhill	1990	S Keogh	1998	C Court
	Wendy Pithers	1983	J Pool	1991	K Egford	1999	C Court
1977	Julia Greenhalgh	1984	Carole Redford	1992	Angela Uzielli	2000	K Fisher
1978T	Heather Clifford		Caldwell	1993	C Hourihane	2001	K Smith
	Glyn-Jones,	1985	Angela Uzielli	1994T	K Shepherd,	2002	K Smith
	Vanessa Marvin	1986	Claire Hourihane		K Egford		

2003

1	Fame More (Chesterfield)	69-73—142
2	Kerry Smith (Waterlooville)	75-71—146
3	Alex Keighley (Lightcliffe)	74-72—146

Liphook Scratch Cup (Inaugurated 1992) at Liphook

1992T	T Kernan,	1994	S Sharpe	1997	E Weeks	2000	K Smith
	K Shepherd	1995	K Shepherd	1998	K Knowles	2001	N Timmins
1993	K Egford	1996	K Shepherd	1999	R Prout	2002	F More

2003

1	Shelley McKevitt (Reading)	70-74—144
2	Kerry Smith (Waterlooville)	72-73—145
3	Emma Brown (West Wilts)	72-73—145

Roehampton Gold Cup (Inaugurated 1926) at Roehampton

1926	Mrs WM McNair	1953	Jeanne Bisgood	1973T	Ann Irvin,	1986T	Katherine
1927	Molly Gourlay	1954	Isabella Bromley		Carole Redford		Harridge,
1928	Cecil Leitch		Davenport	1974	Lyn Harrold		Patricia Johnson
1929	I Doxford	1955	Louisa Abrahams	1975T	Wendy Pithers,	1987	Diane Barnard
1930	Enid Wilson	1956	Shirley Allom		Carole Redford	1988	Alison Johns
1931	V Lamb	1957	Mary Roberts	1976T	Ann Irvin,	1989T	Catriona Lambert,
1932	Mrs A Gold	1958	Patricia Moore		Vanessa Marvin		Cathy Panton
1933	A Ramsden	1959	Mavis G lidewell	1977	Angela Uzielli	1990	Kathryn Imrie
1934	J Hamilton	1960	Elizabeth Price	1978T	Carole Redford	1991	K Hurley
1935	Pam Barton	1961	Louisa Abrahams		Caldwell,	1992	Mrs K Marshall
1936	B Newell	1962	Louisa Abrahams		Belle Robertson	1993	Beverley New
1937	Pam Barton	1963	Ruth Porter	1979	Belle Robertson	1994	C Hall
1938	Pam Barton	1964	RC Archer	1980	Angela Bonallack	1995	S Gallagher
1939	Pam Barton	1965	Marley Spearman	1981	Belle Robertson	1996T	Joanne Morley,
1940–47	Not played	1966	Gwen Brandon	1982	Belle Robertson		J Soulsby
1948	Maureen Ruttle	1967	Ann Irvin	1983T	Beverley New,	1997T	J Forbes, J Oliver
1949	Frances Stephens	1968	Ann Irvin		Vicki Thomas	1998T	K Lunn, J Head
1950	Maureen Ruttle	1969	Ann Irvin	1984	Beverley New	1999	K Taylor
	Garrett	1970	Mary Everard	1985	Vicki Thomas	2000	S Forster
1951	Jeanne Bisgood	1971	Beverly Huke			2001	T Loveys
1952	Jeanne Bisgood	1972	Ann Irvin			2002	F More

2003

1	Tracy Loveys (Broadstone)	76-71—147
2	Caroline Hall (Filton)	75-75—150
3	Kirsty Taylor (Sandford Springs)	74-77—151

St Rule Trophy (Inaugurated 1984) at St Andrews

1984	P Hammel (USA)	149	1991	A Rose	237	1998	N Clau[†]	154 (36)
1985	K Imrie	151	1992	M Wright	222	1999	L Nicholson	227
1986	T Hammond	153	1993	C Lambert	215	2000	V Laing*	153 (36)
1987	J Morley	153	1994	C Matthew	217	2001	A Coffey	221
1988	C Middleton	152	1995	M Hjörth	220	2002	H Stirling	218
1989	C Middleton	232	1996	A Laing	227			
1990	A Sörenstam	228	1997	K Rostron	217			

[†] *At 16 years, the youngest ever winner*

2003

1	Karin Borjeskog (Swe)	68-74-75—217
2	Martine Gillen (Beaverstown)	70-78-71—219
	Anne Laing (Vale of Leven)	75-70-74—219

Sherry Cup at Soto Grande, Cadiz, Spain

1991	Caterina Quintarelli	1995	Maria Hjörth	1999	Martina Eberl
1992	Estafania Knuth	1996	Maria Hjörth	2000	Martina Eberl
1993	Ana F Johansson	1997	Marieke Zelsman	2001	Carmen Alonso Fuentes
1994	Ada O'Sullivan	1998	Nicole Stillia	2002	K Evans

2003

1	Bettina Hauert (Ger)	69-71-72-75—287
2	Tania Elosegui (Esp)	71-74-72-74—291
3	Denise Simon (Ger)	71-72-75-76—294

Munross Trophy 2003 at Montrose Links

1	Anne Laing (Vale of Leven)	68-70—138
2	Clare Queen (Drumpellier)	70-70—140
3	Louise Kenney (Pitreavie)	74-67—141

Mackie Bowl 2003 at Gullane

1	Laura Wells (Dumfries & Galloway)*	73-71—144
2	Lindsey Anderson (Gullane Ladies)	72-72—144
3	Martine Pow (Selkirk)	72-73—145

Riccarton Rose Bowl 2003 at Hamilton

1	Anne Laing (Vale of Leven)	71-67—138
2	Laura Wells (Dumfries & Galloway)	72-69—141
3	Heather Macrae (Dunblane New)	69-72—141

Mary McCallay Trophy 2003 at Dumfries & Galloway

1	Lynn Kenny (University of Stirling)	71-66—137
2	Anne Laing (Vale of Leven)	67-71—138
3	Pam Mackay (Royal Dornoch)	68-72—140

Ness Open 2003 at Inverness

1	Jocelyn Carthew (Ladybank)	73-75—148
2	Cara Gruber (University of Stirling)	72-77—149
3	Elaine Cuthill (Lanark)	68-82—150

Irish Ladies District Championships

Connaught Ladies 2003 *at Co. Sligo*
Deirdre Judge (Roscommon)

Leinster Ladies 2003 *at Glen of the Downs*
Maura Morrin (The Curragh)

Midlands Ladies (Ireland) 2003 *at The Heath*
Karen Delaney (Carlow)

Munster Ladies 2003 *at Waterville*
Trish Mangan (Ennis)

Ulster Open Ladies 2003 *at Bangor*
Helen Jones (Strabane)

Women's Foursomes Events

London Ladies Foursomes

1992	Chelmsford	1996	The Berkshire	2000	Worplesdon
1993	Knebworth	1997	The Berkshire	2001	Porter's Park
1994	Knebworth	1998	The Berkshire	2002	Porter's Park
1995	The Berkshire	1999	The Berkshire		

2003

Chelmsford (Trish Wilson, Fiona Smith) beat Moor Park 3 and 2

Mothers and Daughters Foursomes *at Royal Mid-Surrey*

1992	Mrs P Carrick and Mrs A Uzielli	1997	Mrs S Lines and Miss K Lines
1993	Mrs P Carrick and Mrs A Uzielli	1998	Mrs H Joyce and Miss C Joyce
1994	Mrs P Carrick and Mrs A Uzielli	1999	Mrs E Boatman and Miss A Boatman
1995T	Mrs P Carrick and Mrs A Uzielli	2000	Lady Bonallack and Mrs G Beasley
	Mrs P Huntley and Miss J Huntley	2001	Mrs and Miss Gay
1996T	Mrs A Uzielli and Miss C Uzielli	2002	Mrs J Thornhill and Mrs C Weeks
	Mrs E Boatman and Miss A Boatman	2003	A Laughland & R Jenner
	Mrs S Lines and Miss K Lines		

Women's Regional Amateur Championships

England

Bedfordshire Ladies

1994	T Gale	1999	E Bruce
1995	A Bradley	2000	C Hoskin
1996	C Hoskin	2001	P Gale
1997	J Faris	2002	B Quinn
1998	S Cormack	2003	H Carr

Berkshire Ladies

1994	J Guntrip	1999	L Webb
1995	A Uzielli	2000	L Webb
1996	S Sanderson	2001	E Cooper
1997	L Meredith	2002	L Webb
1998	S Sanderson	2003	L Webb

Buckinghamshire Ladies

1994	P Williamson	1999	C Watson
1995	C Dowling	2000	C Watson
1996	C Watson	2001	S Mace
1997	C Watson	2002	C Watson
1998	C Watson	2003	K Platt

Cambridgeshire and Huntingdonshire Ladies

1994	T Eakin	1999	R Farrow
1995	P Parker	2000	J Walter
1996	J Walter	2001	P Parker
1997	J Walter	2002	J Walter
1998	J Walter	2003	S Attwood

Cheshire Ladies

1994	F Brown	1999	R Adby
1995	E Ratcliffe	2000	O Briggs
1996	L Dermott	2001	R Adby
1997	E Ratcliffe	2002	S Beardsall
1998	E Ratcliffe	2003	S Beardsall

Cornwall Ladies

1994	E Fields	1999	G Dowling
1995	L Simpson	2000	G Dowling
1996	L Simpson	2001	S Sanderson
1997	L Simpson	2002	S Sanderson
1998	G Dowling	2003	J Teague

Cumbria Ladies

1994	J Currie	1999	J Blaydes
1995	J Viles	2000	J Viles
1996	R Bruce	2001	J Blades
1997	J Blaydes	2002	E Woodhouse
1998	A Wood	2003	J Blaydes

Derbyshire Ladies

1994	L Walters	1999	L Walters
1995	L Holmes	2000	R Wood
1996	L Shaw	2001	L Shaw
1997	L Walters	2002	R Wood
1998	L Shaw	2003	M Reid

Devon Ladies

1994	K Tebbet	1999	K Clarke
1995	J Roberts	2000	K Clarke
1996	R Cirin	2001	K Clarke
1997	J Roberts	2002	E Frayn
1998	C Copping	2003	L Eastwood

Dorset Ladies

1994	W Russell	1999	S Phillips
1995	A Monk	2000	J Topp
1996	C Brown	2001	C Jones
1997	A Monk	2002	C Jones
1998	A Monk	2003	H Brockway

Durham Ladies

1994	P Dobson	1999	L Keers
1995	K Lee	2000	P Simpson
1996	A Dobson	2001	A Dobson
1997	K Lee	2002	D Roseberry
1998	P Dobson	2003	F Sanderson

Essex Ladies

1994	T Wilson	1999	E Gibson
1995	G Scase	2000	S Smith
1996	G Scase	2001	J Dartford
1997	S Barber	2002	J Dartford
1998	M Williams	2003	F Smith

Gloucestershire Ladies

1994	K Hamilton	1999	N Lumb
1995	N Sutton	2000	L Occleshaw
1996	J Clingan	2001	C Lipscombe
1997	C Lipscombe	2002	Z Lennox
1998	C Lipscombe	2003	R Rowntree

Hampshire Ladies

1994	K Egford	1999	K Taylor
1995	H Wheeler	2000	K Taylor
1996	C Stirling	2001	N Booth
1997	H Wheeler	2002	K Smith
1998	E Weekes	2003	K Smith

Hertfordshire Ladies

1994	J Oliver	1999	H Skinner
1995	J Oliver	2000	K Evans
1996	K Evans	2001	S Matthews
1997	K Evans	2002	K Hutcherson
1998	M Allen	2003	M Allen

Kent Ladies

1994	M Sutton	1999	N Timmins
1995	C Caldwell	2000	D Masters
1996	K Stupples	2001	N Timmins
1997	S Butchers	2002	D Masters
1998	K Stupples	2003	N Timmins

Lancashire Ladies

1994	G Nutter	1999	K Fisher
1995	G Nutter	2000	C Blackshaw
1996	A Murray	2001	K Fisher
1997	G Nutter	2002	K Fisher
1998	A Murray	2003	A Peacock

Leicestershire and Rutland Ladies

1994	M Page	1999	J Morris
1995	C Gay	2000	H Lowe
1996	H Lowe	2001	C Gay
1997	J Morris	2002	R Rowlands
1998	C Gay	2003	J Morris

Lincolnshire Ladies

1994	S Brook	1999	S Hunter
1995	A Thompson	2000	S Walker
1996	M Willerton	2001	N Chantry
1997	A Thompson	2002	S Walker
1998	M Willerton	2003	S Walker

Middlesex Ladies

1994	M Henderson	1999	P Costello
1995	J Sadler	2000	D McCormack
1996	P Ramchand	2001	C Irons
1997	J Barnett	2002	P Ranchard
1998	J Sadler	2003	T Watters

Midland Ladies

1994	J Morris	1999	S Pidgeon
1995	K Edwards	2000	S Walker
1996	S Gallagher	2001	K Hanwell
1997	R Bailey	2002	S Walker
1998	N Lawrenson	2003	M Reid

Norfolk Ladies

1994	J Wilkerson	1999	R Shubrook
1995	J Wilkerson	2000	J Wilkerson
1996	C Grady	2001	J Wilkerson
1997	T Williamson	2002	J Wilkerson
1998	T Williamson	2003	T Williamson

Northamptonshire Ladies

1994	S Sharpe	1999	S Turbayne
1995	S Sharpe	2000	C Gibbs
1996	S Carter	2001	S Carter
1997	S Carter	2002	K Hanwell
1998	C Gibbs	2003	K Jennings

Northern Ladies Close (ELGA)

1994	G Nutter	1999	C Ritson
1995	K Rostron	2000	L Mackay
1996	K Rostron	2001	N Evans
1997	G Nutter	2002	N Edwards
1998	R Lomas	2003	C Lee

Northern Ladies Counties Championship

1994	Lancashire	1999	Yorkshire
1995	Cheshire	2000	Yorkshire
1996	Lancashire	2001	Yorkshire
1997	Lancashire	2002	Cheshire
1998	Yorkshire	2003	Cheshire

Northumberland Ladies

1994	D Glenn	1999	J Ross
1995	H Wilson	2000	J Ross
1996	C Hall	2001	J Ross
1997	C Hall	2002	C Hall
1998	C Hall	2003	K McKenna

Nottinghamshire Ladies

1994	G Palmer	1999	L Wright
1995	G Palmer	2000	L Wright
1996	L Wright	2001	*Event cancelled*
1997	J Collingham	2002	L Slack
1998	J Collingham	2003	J Doleman

Oxfordshire Ladies

1994	L King	1999	K Humphris
1995	L King	2000	N Woolford
1996	L King	2001	N Woolford
1997	L King	2002	J de Vere Hunt
1998	N Woolford	2003	J Corkish

Shropshire Ladies

1994	A Johnson	1999	S Heath
1995	B Smith	2000	L Archer
1996	B Smith	2001	S Heath
1997	S Heath	2002	S Heath
1998	L Archer	2003	S Hinton

Somerset Ladies

1994	S Burnell	1999	V McFarlane
1995	L Wixon	2000	A Pitt
1996	L Wixon	2001	B New
1997	L Wixon	2002	K Walls
1998	G Pritchard	2003	K Walls

South-Eastern Ladies

1994	K Egford	1999	K Knowles
1995	K Smith	2000	A Waller
1996	J Oliver	2001	K Smith
1997	L Evans	2002	R Prout
1998	A Waller	2003	N Booth

South-Western Ladies

1994	R Morgan	1999	J Clingan
1995	E Fields	2000	E Pilgrim
1996	B Morgan	2001	C Lipsombe
1997	E Pilgrim	2002	K Walls
1998	C Lipscombe	2003	L Eastwood

Staffordshire Ladies

1994	S Gallagher	1999	C Champion
1995	K Edwards	2000	J Peacock
1996	S Gallagher	2001	R Bolas
1997	K Edwards	2002	S Spenser
1998	K Edwards	2003	D Warren

Suffolk Ladies

1994	J Hockley	1999	A Boatman
1995	J Hall	2000	L Steadman
1996	J Hockley	2001	A Boatman
1997	L Wright	2002	A Boatman
1998	J Hockley	2003	H Rees

Surrey Ladies

1994	S Lambert	1999	R Prout
1995	J Thornhill	2000	K Knowles
1996	L McGowan	2001	L McGowan
1997	J Thornhill	2002	R Prout
1998	K Burton	2003	M Bruck

Sussex Ladies

1994	J Head	1999	P Carver
1995	Z Steel	2000	C Court
1996	C Court	2001	C Court
1997	C Court	2002	A Greenfield
1998	J Galway	2003	K Sykes

Warwickshire Ladies

1994	S Westhall	1999	C Dowling
1995	S Westhall	2000	T Atkin
1996	C Dowling	2001	C Dowling
1997	C Dowling	2002	F Johnson
1998	C Dowling	2003	H Coles

Wiltshire Ladies

1994	S Sutton	1999	J Wheaton
1995	J Lamb	2000	J Wheaton
1996	J Lamb	2001	G Loughrey
1997	J Lamb	2002	G Loughrey
1998	W Martin	2003	P Abbott

Worcestershire Ladies

1994	N Lawrenson	1999	S Haslam
1995	S Tufnall	2000	S Nicklin
1996	N Lawrenson	2001	K Greenfield
1997	N Lawrenson	2002	L Day
1998	N Lawrenson	2003	W Bill

Yorkshire Ladies

1994	N Buxton	1999	R Hudson
1995	R Hudson	2000	E Duggleby
1996	J Aldersley	2001	A Keighley
1997	R Hudson	2002	E Duggleby
1998	R Hudson	2003	A Keighley

Scotland

Aberdeenshire Ladies

1994	C Hunter	1999	L Urquhart
1995	J Matthews	2000	S Wood
1996	S Wood	2001	S Wood
1997	K Moggach	2002	S Wood
1998	L Urquhart	2003	J Henderson

Angus Ladies

1994	M Summers	1999	L Fenton
1995	K Sutherland	2000	A Ramsay
1996	S Simpson	2001	K Sutherland
1997	S Raitt	2002	D Dewar
1998	L Fenton	2003	D Carcary

Ayrshire Ladies

1994	A Gemmill	1999	S Lambie
1995	R Kennedy	2000	R Kennedy
1996	A Gemmill	2001	L Keohone
1997	A Gemmill	2002	S Lambie
1998	S Lambie	2003	L Moffat

Border Counties Ladies

1994	W Wells	1999	J Anderson
1995	A Fleming	2000	M Pow
1996	K Inkpen	2001	M Pow
1997	J Anderson	2002	J Anderson
1998	A Hunter	2003	M Pow

Dumfriesshire Ladies

1994	F Watson	1999	L Wells
1995	D Douglas	2000	L Wells
1996	C Adamson	2001	K Wells
1997	L Wells	2002	F Macgregor
1998	D MacDonald	2003	D MacDonald

Dunbartonshire and Argyll Ladies

1994	V Melvin	1999	V Melvin
1995	A Laing	2000	V Melvin
1996	V Melvin	2001	A Laing
1997	K Burns	2002	C McNeil
1998	A Laing	2003	S Bishop

East Lothian Ladies

1994	C Matthew	1999	L Nicholson
1995	H Monaghan	2000	L Nicholson
1996	H Monaghan	2001	J Smith
1997	S McMaster	2002	S McMaster
1998	S McEwan	2003	J Smith

Eastern Division Ladies (Scotland)

1994	J Ford	1999	L Kenny
1995	L Nicholson	2000	H Stirling
1996	H Monaghan	2001	H Stirling
1997	S Grant	2002	H Stirling
1998	F Lockhart	2003	J Carthew

Fife County Ladies

1994	L Bennett	1999	L Fury
1995	K Milne	2000	E Moffat
1996	E Moffat	2001	L Kenney
1997	J Hall	2002	S Millar
1998	K Milne	2003	L Bennett

Galloway Ladies

1994	C Meldrum	1999	S Booth
1995	T Dodds	2000	S McMurtrie
1996	A Cairns	2001	S McMurtrie
1997	S McMurtrie	2002	S McMurtrie
1998	S McMurtrie	2003	S McMurtrie

Lanarkshire Ladies County

1994	J Gardner	1999	F Prior
1995	R Rankin	2000	A Bell
1996	A Prentice	2001	C Queen
1997	L Lloyd	2002	C Queen
1998	F Prior	2003	M Hughes

Midlothian Ladies

1994	E Bruce	1999	C Williamson
1995	P Silver	2000	B Murphy
1996	M Quigley	2001	F Hunter
1997	P Silver	2002	B Murphy
1998	V Laing	2003	C Hargan

Northern Counties (Scotland) Ladies

1994	L Roxburgh	1999	L Mackay
1995	F McKay	2000	L Mackay
1996	F McLennan	2001	C Gruber
1997	E Vass	2002	L McKinnon
1998	L Vass	2003	M Smith

Northern Division Ladies (Scotland)

1994	J Matthews	1999	L McLardy
1995	J Harrison	2000	J Yellowlees
1996	J Harrison	2001	S Wood
1997	C Hunter	2002	L Devenish
1998	J Tough	2003	A Scott

Perth and Kinross Ladies

1994	C Dunbar	1999	A Murray
1995	F Farquharson	2000	C Meir
1996	E Wilson	2001	J Yellowlees
1997	N Harding	2002	D Butchart
1998	J Yellowlees	2003	N Harding

Renfrewshire County Ladies

1994	C Agnew	1999	D Jackson
1995	D Jackson	2000	D Jackson
1996	D Jackson	2001	D Jackson
1997	L Robertson	2002	S Harman
1998	K Fitzgerald	2003	C-M Carlton

Southern Division Ladies (Scotland)

1994	D Douglas	1999	J Anderson
1995	J Anderson	2000	M Pow
1996	D Douglas	2001	A Shamash
1997	J Anderson	2002	L Fleming
1998	D MacDonald	2003	L Wells

South of Scotland Ladies

1994	F Rennie	1999	D MacDonald
1995	C Meldrum	2000	M Pow
1996	S McMurtrie	2001	M Pow
1997	J Anderson	2002	*Event cancelled*
1998	D Sutton	2003	L Wells

Stirling and Clackmannan County Ladies

1994	H Stirling	1999	H Stirling
1995	S Grant	2000	H Stirling
1996	H Hume	2001	L Kenny
1997	S Grant	2002	H Stirling
1998	L Kenny	2003	L Kenny

Western Division Ladies (Scotland)

1994	V Melvin	1999	A Laing
1995	A Hendry	2000	A Laing
1996	K Fitzgerald	2001	C Hargan
1997	C Malcolm	2002	A Laing
1998	A Laing	2003	ALaing

Wales

Caernarfonshire and Anglesey Ladies

1994	C Thomas	1999	K Evans
1995	L Davies	2000	L Davies
1996	L Davies	2001	L Davies
1997	F Vaughan-Thomas	2002	K Evans
1998	F Vaughan-Thomas	2003	F Vaughan-Thomas

Denbighshire and Flintshire Ladies

1994	A Donne	1999	R Brewerton
1995	S Lovatt	2000	S Mountford
1996	B Jones	2001	J Nicholson
1997	R Brewerton	2002	*Cancelled*
1998	B Jones	2003	S Mountford

Glamorgan County Ladies

1994	V Thomas	1999	K Phillips
1995	J Thomas	2000	V Thomas
1996	V Thomas	2001	A Highgate
1997	V Thomas	2002	A Highgate
1998	P Chugg	2003	A Highgate

Mid-Wales Ladies

1994	G Gibb	1999	S Hughes
1995	J James	2000	J Dyer
1996	L Davies	2001	J Dyer
1997	K Humphries	2002	D Tuffnell
1998	A Hubbard	2003	G Badham

Monmouthshire Ladies

1994	E Pilgrim	1999	R Morgan
1995	E Pilgrim	2000	J Pritchard
1996	C Waite	2001	L Diggle
1997	S O'Sullivan	2002	E Pilgrim
1998	S O'Sullivan	2003	L Diggle

Overseas Amateur Championships

Australian	Katy Jarochowicz
Austrian (Close)	Stefanie Endstrasser
Austrian	Stefanie Michl
Belgian	Tamara Luccioli
Canadian	Lisa Meldrum
Czech Republic	Lucie Sărochová
Danish	Mette Buus
Finnish	Ursula Tuutti
French	Peggy Fraysse
German (Close)	Pia Odefey
German	Bettina Hauert
Hellenic	Irene Krambs
Hungarian (Close)	Krisztina Batta
Hungarian	Siobhan Maguire
Italian	Anja Monke (Ger)
Luxembourg	Frédérique Seeholzer
Netherlands	Myrte Eikenaar
New Zealand (Stroke Play)	Melanie Holmes-Smith (Aus)
Portuguese	Charlotte Heeres (Ned)
Slovak	Barbora Kachlikova
Slovak (Stroke Play)	Zuzana Kamasova
South African	Tanica van As
South African (Stroke Play)	Tanica van As
Spanish	Maria Hernandez
Swiss	Anja Monke (Ger)
Turkish	Nejla Gerçek

United States Ladies Amateur Championship (Inaugurated 1895)

Year	Winner	Runner-up	Venue	By
1895	CS Brown	N Sargent	Meadowbrook, NY	132
Changed to match play				
1896	B Hoyt	A Tunure	Morristown, NJ	2 and 1
1897	B Hoyt	N Sargent	Essex County, MA	5 and 4
1898	B Hoyt	M Wetmore	Ardsley, NY	5 and 3
1899	R Underhill	M Fox	Philadelphia, PA	2 and 1
1900	FC Griscom	M Curtis	Shinnecock Hills, NY	6 and 5
1901	G Hecker	L Herron	Baltusrol, NJ	5 and 3
1902	G Hecker	LA Wells	Brookline, MA	4 and 3
1903	B Anthony	JA Carpenter	Wheaton, IL	7 and 6
1904	GM Bishop	EF Sanford	Merion, PA	5 and 3
1905	P Mackay	M Curtis	Morris County, NJ	1 hole
1906	HS Curtis	MB Adams	West Newton, MA	2 and 1
1907	M Curtis	HS Curtis	Blue Island, IL	7 and 6
1908	KC Harley	TH Polhemus	Chevy Chase, MD	6 and 5
1909	D Campbell	N Barlow	Merion, PA	3 and 2
1910	D Campbell	GM Martin	Homewood, IL	2 and 1
1911	M Curtis	LB Hyde	Baltusrol, NJ	5 and 4
1912	M Curtis	N Barlow	Essex County, MA	3 and 2
1913	G Ravenscroft	M Hollins	Wilmington, DE	2 holes

United States Ladies' Amateur Championship *continued*

Year	Winner	Runner-up	Venue	By
1914	KC Harley	EV Rosenthal	Nassau, NY	1 hole
1915	F Vanderbeck	M Gavin (Eng)	Onwentsia, IL	3 and 2
1916	A Stirling	M Caverly	Belmont Springs, MA	2 and 1
1917–1918	*Not played due to First World War*			
1919	A Stirling	M Gavin (Eng)	Shawnee, PA	6 and 5
1920	A Stirling	D Campbell Hurd	Cleveland, OH	5 and 4
1921	M Hollins	A Stirling	Deal, NJ	5 and 4
1922	G Collett	M Gavin (Eng)	Greenbrier, WV	5 and 4
1923	E Cummings	A Stirling	Westchester, NY	3 and 2
1924	D Campbell Hurd	MK Browne	Nyatt, RI	7 and 6
1925	G Collett	A Stirling Fraser	Clayton, MO	9 and 8
1926	H Stetson	E Goss	Merion, PA	2 and 1
1927	MB Horn	M Orcutt	Garden City, NY	5 and 4
1928	G Collett	V Van Wie	Hot Springs, VA	13 and 12
1929	G Collett	L Pressler	Oakland Hills, MI	4 and 3
1930	G Collett	V Van Wie	Beverly Hills, CA	6 and 5
1931	H Hicks	G Collett Vare	Williamsville, NY	2 and 1
1932	V Van Wie	G Collett Vare	Peabody, MA	10 and 8
1933	V Van Wie	H Hicks	Highland Park, IL	4 and 3
1934	V Van Wie	D Traung	Whitemarsh Valley, PA	2 and 1
1935	G Collett Vare	P Berg	Interlachen, MN	3 and 2
1936	P Barton (Eng)	M Orcutt	Canoe Brook, NJ	4 and 3
1937	EL Page	P Berg	Memphis, TN	7 and 6
1938	P Berg	EL Page	Westmoreland, IL	6 and 5
1939	B Jameson	D Kirby	Wee Burn, CT	3 and 2
1940	B Jameson	J Cochran	Pebble Beach, CA	6 and 5
1941	E Hicks Newell	H Sigel	Brookline, MA	5 and 3
1942–1945	*Not played due to Second World War*			
1946	B Zaharias	C Sherman	Tulsa, OK	11 and 9
1947	L Suggs	D Kirby	Franklin, MI	2 holes
1948	G Lenczyk	H Sigel	Pebble Beach, CA	4 and 3
1949	D Porter	D Kielty	Merion, PA	3 and 2
1950	B Hanson	M Murray	Atlanta, GA	6 and 4
1951	D Kirby	C Doran	St Paul, MN	2 and 1
1952	J Pung	S McFedters	Portland, OR	2 and 1
1953	ML Faulk	P Riley	West Barrington, RI	3 and 2
1954	B Romack	M Wright	Sewickley, PA	4 and 2
1955	P Lesser	J Nelson	Charlotte, NC	7 and 6
1956	M Stewart	J Gunderson	Indianapolis, IN	2 and 1
1957	J Gunderson	AC Johnstone	Del Paso, CA	8 and 6
1958	A Quast	B Romack	Wee Burn, CT	3 and 2
1959	B McIntyre	J Goodwin	Washington, DC	4 and 3
1960	J Gunderson	J Ashley	Tulsa, OK	6 and 5
1961	A Quast	P Preuss	Tacomac, WA	14 and 13
1962	J Gunderson	A Baker	Rochester, NY	9 and 8
1963	A Quast	P Conley	Williamstown, MA	2 and 1
1964	B McIntyre	J Gunderson	Prairie Dunes, KA	3 and 2
1965	J Ashley	A Quast	Denver, CO	5 and 4
1966	J Gunderson Carner	JD Stewart Streit	Sewickley, PA	41st hole
1967	ML Dill	J Ashley	Pasadena, CA	5 and 4
1968	J Gunderson Carner	A Quast	Birmingham, MI	5 and 4
1969	C Lacoste (Fra)	S Hamlin	Las Colinas, TX	3 and 2
1970	M Wilkinson	C Hill	Wee Burn, CT	3 and 2
1971	L Baugh	B Barry	Atlanta, GA	1 hole
1972	M Budke	C Hill	St Louis, MO	5 and 4
1973	C Semple	A Quast	Montclair, NJ	1 hole
1974	C Hill	C Semple	Seattle, WA	5 and 4
1975	B Daniel	D Horton	Brae Burn, MA	3 and 2
1976	D Horton	M Bretton	Del Paso, CA	2 and 1
1977	B Daniel	C Sherk	Cincinnati, OH	3 and 1
1978	C Sherk	J Oliver	Sunnybrook, PA	4 and 3
1979	C Hill	P Sheehan	Memphis, TN	7 and 6
1980	J Inkster	P Rizzo	Prairie Dunes, KA	2 holes
1981	J Inkster	L Goggin (Aus)	Portland, OR	1 hole
1982	J Inkster	C Hanlon	Colorado Springs, CO	4 and 3
1983	J Pacillo	S Quinlan	Canoe Brook, NJ	2 and 1
1984	D Richard	K Williams	Seattle, WA	37th hole
1985	M Hattori (Jpn)	C Stacy	Pittsburgh, PA	5 and 4
1986	K Cockerill	K McCarthy	Pasatiempo, CA	9 and 7

Year	Winner	Runner-up	Venue	By
1987	K Cockerill	T Kerdyk	Barrington, RI	3 and 2
1988	P Sinn	K Noble	Minikahda, MN	6 and 5
1989	V Goetze	B Burton	Pinehurst, NC	4 and 3
1990	P Hurst	S Davis	Canoe Brook, NJ	37th hole
1991	A Fruhwirth	H Voorhees	Prairie Dunes, KA	5 and 4
1992	V Goetze	A Sörenstam (Swe)	Kemper Lakes, IL	1 hole
1993	J McGill	S Ingram	San Diego, CA	1 hole
1994	W Ward	J McGill	Hot Springs, VA	2 and 1
1995	K Kuehne	A-M Knight	Brookline, MA	4 and 2
1996	K Kuehne	M Baena	Lincoln, NE	2 and 1
1997	S Cavalleri (It)	R Burke	Brae Burn, MA	5 and 4
1998	G Park (Kor)	J Chuasiriporn	Blackwolf Run, WI	7 and 6
1999	D Delasin	J Kang	Biltmore Forest, NC	4 and 3
2000	N Newton	L Myerscough	Biltmore Forest, NC	8 and 7
2001	M Duncan	N Perrot	Flint Hills, KS	at 37th
2002	B Lucidi	B Jackson	Sleepy Hollow, NY	3 and 2

2003 *at Philadelphia CC*

Leading Qualifier: Aree Song (Kor) 138

Quarter Finals
Virada Nirapathpongporn (Tha) beat Aree Song (Kor) 1 hole
In-Bee Park (Eustis, FL) beat Ashley Knoll (The Woodlands, TX) 3 and 1
Jane Park (Oak Valley, CA) beat Becky Lucidi (Poway, CA) 2 holes
Paula Creamer (Pleasanton, CA) beat Erica Blasberg (Corona, CA) 6 and 5

Semi-Finals
Nirapathpongporn beat I Park 3 and 1
J Park beat Creamer 2 and 1

Final
Virada Nirapathpongporn beat Jane Park 2 and 1

Open qualifying on five continents

History is being made this year with Open Championship qualifying taking place in Africa, Australia, Asia, America and Europe. The selected venues for the 36-hole qualifying competitions which will be open to any players with official world ranking points but who have not gained exemption in any other way are: Australia: Kingston Heath GC; Europe: Sunningdale GC; America: Congressional CC, Maryland; Asia: Saujana G and CC, Kuala Lumpur, Malaysia; South Africa: To be decided. The tournaments in Australia, Africa and Asia guarantee at least four spots and the European and American events guarantee at least 12 places in the Open Championship being staged at Royal Troon from July 15–18.

The new events are in addition to the existing 16 regional qualifying events in Britain and Ireland and the four local qualifying events which take place during Open week at Glasgow Gailes, Irvine, Turnberry Kintyre and Western Gailes from which only three spots will be guaranteed per venue.

Michael Tate, assistant secretary of the R&A explains: 'We have always believed that the Open was the most open of all the majors and this new system gives a greater opportunity to many fine players who would not have been able to attend final qualifying in Britain.'

Multiple Winners in Europe and America

The following players won more than once during 2003 on the European and US Tours:

Europe

5 – Ernie Els (Heineken Classic, Johnnie Walker Classic, Barclays Scottish Open, Omega European Masters, HSBC World Match Play Championship*)

3 – Frederick Jacobsen (Omega Hong Kong Open, Algarve Open de Portugal, Volvo Masters Andalucia)

2 – Paul Casey (ANZ Championship, Benson and Hedges International)

Padraig Harrington (BMW Asian Open, Deutsche Bank SAP Open TPC of Europe)

Ian Poulter (Celtic Manor Resort Wales Open, Nordic Open)

Lee Westwood (BMW International, dunhill links championship)

Tiger Woods (Accenture Match Play, American Express Championship)†

* Approved event but not official money
† World Championship events are included on the European schedule.

USA

5 – Tiger Woods (Buick Invitational, Accenture Match Play, Bay Hill Invitational, Western Open, American Express Championship)

4 – Vijay Singh (Phoenix Open, Verizon Byron Nelson Classic, John Deere Classic, Funai Classic)

Davis Love III (AT&T Pebble Beach National Pro-Am, The Players Championship, MCI Heritage, The International)

3 – Mike Weir (Bob Hope Chrysler Classic, Nissan Open, The Masters)

Kenny Perry (Bank of America Colonial, Memorial Tournament, Greater Milwaukee Open)

2 – Ernie Els (Mercedes Championships, Sony Open)

Jim Furyk (US Open, Buick Open)

David Toms (Wachovia Championship, Fedex St Jude Classic)

PART VI

Junior Tournaments and Events

Boys' and Youths' Tournaments   338
Girls' and Junior Ladies' Tournaments   350
Golf Foundation Events   357

Boys' and Youths' Tournaments

Boys Amateur Championship

Year	Winner	Runner-up	Venue	By
1921	ADD Mathieson	GH Lintott	Ascot	37th hole
1922	HS Mitchell	W Greenfield	Ascot	4 and 2
1923	ADD Mathieson	HS Mitchell	Dunbar	3 and 2
1924	RW Peattie	P Manuevrier (Fra)	Coombe Hill	2 holes
1925	RW Peattie	A McNair	Barnton	4 and 3
1926	EA McRuvie	CW Timmis	Coombe Hill	1 hole
1927	EW Fiddian	K Forbes	Royal Burgess	4 and 2
1928	S Scheftel	A Dobbie	Formby	6 and 5
1929	J Lindsay	J Scott-Riddell	Royal Burgess	6 and 4
1930	J Lindsay	J Todd	Fulwell	9 and 8
1931	H Thomson	F McGloin	Glasgow (Killermont)	5 and 4
1932	IS MacDonald	LA Hardie	Royal Lytham and St Annes	2 and 1
1933	PB Lucas	W McLachlan	Carnoustie	3 and 2
1934	RS Burles	FB Allpass	Moortown	12 and 10
1935	JDA Langley	R Norris	Royal Aberdeen	6 and 5
1936	J Bruen	W Innes	Birkdale	11 and 9
1937	IM Roberts	J Stewart	Bruntsfield	8 and 7
1938	W Smeaton	T Snowball	Moor Park	3 and 2
1939	SB Williamson	KG Thom	Carnoustie	4 and 2
1940-45	*Suspended during War*			
1946	AFD MacGregor	DF Dunstan	Bruntsfield	7 and 5
1947	J Armour	I Caldwell	Hoylake	5 and 4
1948	JD Pritchett	DH Reid	Kilmarnock (Barassie)	37th hole
1949	H MacAnespie	NV Drew	St Andrews	3 and 2
1950	J Glover	I Young	Royal Lytham and St Annes	2 and 1
1951	N Dunn	MSR Lunt	Prestwick	6 and 5
1952	M Bonallack	AE Shepperson	Formby	37th hole
1953	AE Shepperson	AT Booth	Dunbar	6 and 4
1954	AF Bussell	K Warren	Hoylake	38th hole
1955	SC Wilson	BJK Aitken	Kilmarnock (Barassie)	39th hole
1956	JF Ferguson	CW Cole	Sunningdale	2 and 1
1957	D Ball	J Wilson	Carnoustie	2 and 1
1958	R Braddon	IM Stungo	Moortown	4 and 3
1959	AR Murphy	EM Shamash	Pollok	3 and 1
1960	P Cros (Fra)	PO Green	Olton	5 and 3
1961	FS Morris	C Clark	Dalmahoy	3 and 2
1962	PM Townsend	DC Penman	Royal Mid-Surrey	1 hole
1963	AHC Soutar	DI Rigby	Prestwick	2 and 1
1964	PM Townsend	RD Gray	Formby	9 and 8
1965	GR Milne	DK Midgley	Gullane	4 and 2
1966	A Phillips	A Muller	Moortown	12 and 11
1967	LP Tupling	SC Evans	Western Gailes	4 and 2
1968	SC Evans	K Dabson	St Annes Old Links	3 and 2
1969	M Foster	M Gray	Dunbar	37th hole
1970	ID Gradwell	JE Murray	Hillside	1 hole
1971	H Clark	G Harvey	Kilmarnock (Barassie)	6 and 5
1972	G Harvey	R Newsome	Moortown	7 and 5
1973	DM Robertson	S Betti (Ita)	Blairgowrie	5 and 3
1974	TR Shannon	A Lyle	Hoylake	10 and 9
1975	B Marchbank	A Lyle	Bruntsfield	1 hole
1976	M Mouland	G Hargreaves	Sunningdale	6 and 5
1977	I Ford	CR Dalgleish	Downfield	1 hole
1978	S Keppler	M Stokes	Seaton Carew	3 and 2
1979	R Rafferty	D Ray	Kilmarnock (Barassie)	6 and 5
1980	D Muscroft	A Llyr	Formby	7 and 6

Year	Winner	Runner-up	Venue	By
1981	J Lopez (Esp)	R Weedon	Gullane	4 and 3
1982	M Grieve	G Hickman	Burnham and Barrow	37th hole
1983	JM Olazábal (Esp)	M Pendaries	Glenbervie	6 and 5
1984	L Vannett	A Mednick (Swe)	Royal Porthcawl	2 and 1
1985	J Cook	W Henry	Royal Burgess	5 and 4
1986	L Walker	G King	Seaton Carew	5 and 4
1987	C O'Carrol	P Olsson (Swe)	Barassie	3 and 1
1988	S Pardoe	D Haines	Formby	3 and 2
1989	C Watts	C Fraser	Nairn	5 and 3
1990	M Welch	M Ellis	Hunstanton	3 and 1
1991	F Valera (Esp)	R Walton	Montrose	4 and 3
1992	L Westerberg (Swe)	F Jacobson (Swe)	Royal Mid-Surrey	3 and 2
1993	D Howell	V Gustavsson (Swe)	Glenbervie	3 and 1
1994	C Smith	C Rodgers	Little Aston	2 and 1
1995	S Young	S Walker	Dunbar	7 and 6
1996	K Ferrie	M Pilkington	Littlestone	2 and 1
1997	S García (Esp)	R Jones	Saunton	6 and 5
1998	S O'Hara	S Reale (Ita)	Ladybank	1 hole
1999	A Gutierrez (Esp)	M Skelton	Royal St David's	1 hole
2000	D Inglis	D Skinns	Hillside	1 hole
2001	P Martin	R Cabrera	Ganton	3 and 2
2002	M Pilling	R Davies	Carnoustie	at 37th

2003 at Royal Liverpool

Quarter Finals

Rhys Davies (Royal Porthcawl) beat Daniel Osorio (Esp) at 21st
Wallace Booth (Crieff) beat Christopher Svendsen (Den) 2 and 1
Chris Hanson (Crosland Heath) beat Zachariah Gould (Vale of Glamorgan) at 25th
Pablo Martin (Esp) beat Victor Riu (Fra) 1 hole

Semi-Finals

Davies beat Booth 4 and 3
Martin beat Hanson 6 and 5

Final

Rhys Davies beat Pablo Martin 1 hole

British Youths Open Amateur Championship

This championship bridged the gap between the Boys and the Men's tournaments from 1954 until 1995, when it was discontinued because it was no longer needed. The date on the schedule was used to introduce the Mid-Amateur (over 25s).

Year	Winner	Club	Venue	Score
1954	JS More	Swanston	Erskine	287
1955	B Stockdale	Royal Lytham & St Annes	Pannal	287
1956	AF Bussell	Coxmoor	Royal Burgess	287
1957	G Will	St Andrews	Pannal	290
1958	RH Kemp	Glamorganshire	Dumfries & County	281
1959	RA Jowle	Moseley	Pannal	286
1960	GA Caygill	Sunningdale	Pannal	279
1961	JS Martin	Kilbirnie Place	Bruntsfield	284
1962	GA Caygill	Sunningdale	Pannal	287
1963	AJ Low	St Andrews U	Pollok	283
1964	BW Barnes	Burnham & Berrow	Pannal	290
1965	PM Townsend	Porters Park	Gosforth Park	281
1966	PA Easterhouse	Dulwich & Sydenham Hill	Dalmahoy	219 (54 holes)
1967	PJ Benka	Addington	Copt Heath	278
1968	PJ Benka	Addington	Ayr Belleisle	281
1969	JH Cook	Calcot Park	Lindrick	289
1970	B Dassu	Italy	Royal Burgess	276
1971	P Elson	Coventry	Northamptonshire County	277
1972	AH Chandler	Regent Park (Bolton)	Glasgow Gailes	281
1973	SC Mason	Goring & Streatley	Southport & Ainsdale	284
1974	DM Robertson	Dunbar	Downfield	284
1975	N Faldo	Welwyn Garden City	Pannal	278
1976	ME Lewis	Henbury	Gullane	277
1977	AWB Lyle	Hawkstone Park	Moor Park	285
1978	B Marchbank	Auchterarder	East Renfrewshire	278
1979	G Brand jr	Knowle	Woodhall Spa	291
1980	G Hay	Hilton Park	Royal Troon	303

British Youths Open Amateur Championship *continued*

Year	Winner	Club	Venue	Score
1981	T Antevik	Sweden	West Lancashire	290
1982	AP Parkin	Newtown	St Andrews New	280
1983	P Mayo	Newport	Sunningdale	290
1984	R Morris	Padeswick & Buckley	Blairgowrie	281
1985	JM Olazábal	Spain	Ganton	281
1986	D Gilford	Trentham Park	Carnoustie	283
1987	J Cook*	Leamington & County	Hollinwell	283
1988	C Cevaer*	France	Royal Aberdeen	275
1989	M Smith*	Brokenhurst Manor	Ashburnham	285
1990	M Gronberg	Sweden	Southerness	275
1991	J Payne	Sandilands	Woodhall Spa	287
1992	W Bennett	Ruislip	Northumberland	283
1993	L Westwood	Worksop	Glasgow Gailes	278
1994	F Jacobson	Sweden	Royal St Davids	277

English Boys Stroke Play Championship (formerly Carris Trophy)

1935	R Upex	75 (18)	1962	FS Morris	145	1983	P Baker	288
1936	JDA Langley	152	1963	EJ Threlfall	147	1984	J Coe	283
1937	RJ White	149	1964	PM Townsend	148	1985	P Baker	286
1938	IP Garrow	147	1965	G McKay	145	1986	G Evans	292
1939	CW Warren	149	1966	A Black	151	1987	D Bathgate	289
1946	AH Perowne	158	1967	RF Brown	147	1988	P Page	284
1947	I Caldwell	159	1968	P Dawson	149	1989	I Garbutt	285
1948	I Caldwell	152	1969	ID Gradwell	150	1990	M Welch	276
1949	PB Hine	148	1970	MF Foster	146	1991	I Pyman	284
1950	J Glover	144	1971	RJ Evans	146	1992	M Foster	286
1951	I Young	154	1972	L Donovan	143	1993	J Harris	285
1952	N Thygesen	150	1973	S Hadfield	148	1994	R Duck	280
1953	N Johnson	148	1974	KJ Brown	304	1995	J Rose	266
1954	K Warren	149	1975	A Lyle	270	1996	G Storm	281
1955	ID Wheater	151	1976	H Stott	285	1997	D Griffiths	283
1956	G Maisey	141	1977	R Mugglestone	293	1998	S Godfrey	286
1957	G Maisey	145	1978	J Plaxton	144	1999	D Porter	275
1958	J Hamilton	149	1979	P Hammond	288	2000	G Lockerbie	279
1959	RT Walker	152	1980	MP McLean	290	2001	M Richardson*	138
1960	PM Baxter	150	1981	D Gilford	290	2002	C Del Moral	282
1961	DJ Miller	143	1982	M Jarvis	298			

2003 *at Burnham & Berrow*

1	Daniel Denison (Howley Hall)	71-73-71-71—286
	Grant Slater (Carlyon Bay)	67-73-72-74—286
3	Alexander MacGregor (Killiow)	73-73-70-71—287

English Boys Under-16 Championship (McGregor Trophy)

1994	G Storm	291	1997	R Paolillo	285	2000	M Skelton	289
1995	J Rose	287	1998	MY Ali	280	2001	P Waring	212
1996	E Molinari	291	1999	J Heath	280	2002	M Baldwin	289

2003 *at Rotherham*

1	Wouter De Vries (Ned)	71-69-73-68—281
2	Oliver Fisher (West Essex)	66-73-69-74—282
3	Ben Parker (Gut Waldhof)	71-72-68-72—283

IMSL Irish Boys Championship (inaugurated 1983)

1983	J Carvill	J Farrell	Curragh	144
1984	E O'Connell	J Farrell	Mullingar	142
1985	K Kearney	D Clarke	Athlone	145
1986	D Errity	G McNeill	Royal Tara	147
1987	G McNeill	P McCartan	Warrenpoint	143
1988	D McGrane	P Harrington	Birr	219
1989	D Higgins	JWH Clark	Mullingar	221
1990	R Burns	G Murphy	Kilkenny	213
1991	R Coughlan	R Burns	Thurles	207
1992	J O'Sullivan	D Dunne	Athlone	210
1993	H Armstrong	C McMonagle/P Byrne	Warrenpoint	222
1994	P Byrne	R Leonard/A Thomas	Nenagh	209
1995	L Dalton	M McGreedy	Mullingar	222
1996	M Campbell	L Dalton	Galway	213
1997	M Hoey	D Jones	Galway	217
1998	D Jones	D O'Connor	Youghal	214
1999	M McTernan	M O'Sullivan	Kilkenny	210
2000	D McNamara	C Doran	Strandhill	268
2001	M McHugh*	K Fahey	Donaghadee	280
2002	M McNamara	G Shaw	Thurles	279

2003 at Hermitage

1	B McCarroll (Ballyliffin)	74-74-72-71—291
2	K Gilbert (Malone)	73-74-72-76—295
3	D Daly (Muskerry)	77-68-75-76—296
	N Grant (Clandeboye)	80-66-73-77—296

Irish Youths Open Amateur Championship (inaugurated 1969)

1969	D Branigan	Delgany	142	1986	JC Morris	Carlow	280
1970	LA Owens	Tullamore	286	1987	C Everett	Killarney	300
1971	MA Gannon	Athlone	277	1988	P McGinley	Malone	283
1972	MA Gannon	Mullingar	291	1989	A Mathers	Athlone	280
1973	J Purcell	Tullamore	289	1990	D Errity	Dundalk	293
1974	S Dunlop	Athlone	293	1991	R Coughlan	Lahinch	288
1975	P McNally	Mullingar	287	1992	K Nolan	Clandeboye	275
1976	R McCormack	Tullamore	294	1993	CD Hislop	Co Sligo	279
1977	B McDaid	Athlone	290	1994	B O'Melia	Tullamore	272
1978	T Corridan	Thurles	279	1995	S Young	Ballybunion	286
1979	R Rafferty	Tullamore	293	1996	S Young	Royal Portrush	291
1980	J McHenry	Clandeboye	296	1997	N Howley	Galway	284
1981	J McHenry	Westport	303	1998	A Murray	Headfort	281
1982	K O'Donnell	Mullingar	286	1999	G McDowall	Cork	284
1983	P Murphy	Cork	287	2000	G McDowall	Malone	276
1984	JC Morris	Bangor	292	2001	M Ryan	Enniscrone	298
1985	J McHenry	Co Sligo	287	2002	G Wright	Seapoint	288

2003 at Cork

1	Cennydd Mills (Vale of Glamorgan)	74-74-75-71—294
2	R McCarthy (The Island)	71-73-72-79—295
	M Staunton (Ballinasloe)	73-74-77-71—295

Scottish Boys Championship

1960	L Carver	S Wilson	North Berwick	6 and 5
1961	K Thomson	G Wilson	North Berwick	10 and 8
1962	HF Urquhart	S MacDonald	North Berwick	3 and 2
1963	FS Morris	I Clark	North Berwick	9 and 8
1964	WR Lockie	MD Cleghorn	North Berwick	1 hole
1965	RL Penman	J Wood	North Berwick	9 and 8
1966	J McTear	DG Greig	North Berwick	4 and 3
1967	DG Greig	I Cannon	North Berwick	2 and 1
1968	RD Weir	M Grubb	North Berwick	6 and 4
1969	RP Fyfe	IP Doig	North Berwick	4 and 2
1970	S Stephen	M Henry	North Berwick	38th hole

Scottish Boys Championship *continued*

1971	JE Murray	AA Mackay	North Berwick	4 and 3
1972	DM Robertson	G Cairns	North Berwick	9 and 8
1973	R Watson	H Alexander	North Berwick	8 and 7
1974	DM Robertson	J Cuddihy	North Berwick	6 and 5
1975	A Brown	J Cuddihy	North Berwick	6 and 4
1976	B Marchbank	J Cuddihy	Dunbar	2 and 1
1977	JS Taylor	GJ Webster	Dunbar	3 and 2
1978	J Huggan	KW Stables	Dunbar	2 and 1
1979	DR Weir	S Morrison	West Kilbride	5 and 3
1980	R Gregan	AJ Currie	Dunbar	2 and 1
1981	C Stewart	G Mellon	Dunbar	3 and 2
1982	A Smith	J White	Dunbar	39th hole
1983	C Gillies	C Innes	Dunbar	38th hole
1984	K Buchan	L Vannet	Dunbar	2 and 1
1985	AD McQueen	FJ McCulloch	Dunbar	1 hole
1986	AG Tait	EA McIntosh	Dunbar	6 and 5
1987	AJ Coltart	SJ Bannerman	Dunbar	37th hole
1988	CA Fraser	F Clark	Dunbar	9 and 8
1989	M King	D Brolls	Dunbar	8 and 7
1990	B Collier	D Keeney	West Kilbride	2 and 1
1991	C Hislop	R Thorton	West Kilbride	11 and 9
1992	A Reid	A Forsyth	West Kilbride	2 and 1
1993	S Young	A Campbell	West Kilbride	4 and 2
1994	S Young	E Little	Dunbar	2 and 1
1995	S Young	M Donaldson	Royal Aberdeen	7 and 6
1996	S Whiteford	I McLaughlin	West Kilbride	3 and 2
1997	M Donaldson	L Rhind	Dunbar	1 hole
1998	S O'Hara	D Sutton	Murcar	2 holes
1999	L Harper	M Syme	West Kilbride	6 and 5
2000	S Buckley	M Risbridger	Dunbar	7 and 6
2001	S Brown	R Gill	Royal Aberdeen	6 and 4
2002	J Hempstock	R Taylor	West Kilbride	4 and 2

2003 *at Dunbar*

Quarter Finals

Scott Borrowman (Dollar) beat Lewis Barclay (Kirkcaldy) 2 and 1

Paul Doherty (Vale of Glamorgan) beat Doug Considine (Banchory) at 19th

Steven Morgan (Auchterarder) beat Scott Mann (Carnoustie) at 21st

Garry Wood (Crow Wood) beat Colin Kelly (Kirkhill) 3 and 2

Semi-Finals

Doherty beat Borrowman 3 and 2

Wood beat Morgan 2 and 1

Final

Paul Doherty beat Garry Wood 7 and 5 (36 holes)

Scottish Boys Stroke Play Championship

1970	D Chillas	Carnoustie	298	1986	G Cassells	Edzell	294
1971	JE Murray	Lanark	274	1987	C Ronald	Lanark	287
1972	S Martin	Montrose	280	1988	M Urquhart	Dumfries and County	280
1973	S Martin	Royal Burgess	284	1989	C Fraser	Stirling	282
1974	PW Gallacher	Lundin Links	290	1990	N Archibald	Monifieth	292
1975	A Webster	Kilmarnock (Barassie)	286	1991	S Gallacher	Crieff	280
1976	A Webster	Forfar	292	1992	S Gallacher	Monifieth	288
1977T	J Huggan	Renfrew	303	1993	J Bunch	Powfoot	292
	L Mann			1994	S Young	Drumpellier	288
1978	R Fraser	Arbroath	283	1995	C Lee	Arbroath	284
1979	L Mann	Stirling	289	1996	M Brown	Dullatur	286
1980	ASK Glen	Forfar	288	1997	L Rhind	Downfield	287
1981	J Gullen	Bellshill	296	1998	G Holland	Burntisland	281
1982	D Purdie	Monifieth	296	1999	B Hume	Nairn Dunbar	281
1983	L Vannet	Kilmarnock (Barassie)	286	2000	C Ries (RSA)	Cawder	275
1984	K Walker	Carnoustie	280	2001	S Jamieson	Lanark	275
1985	G Matthew	Baberton	297	2002	M Lamb	Peterhead	275

2003 *at Prestwick*

1	Lloyd Saltman (Kilspindie)	73-68-73-72—286
2	Ross Duncan (Brodick)	76-69-72-74—291
3	Wallace Booth (Crieff)	72-73-74-74—293

Scottish Boys Under-16 Stroke Play Championship

1990	G Davidson	W Linton	148		1997	D Inglis	Glenbervie	139
1991	D Patrick	R Musselburgh	152		1998	D Inglis	Braehead	139
1992	*Not played*				1999	G Murray	Lundin	141
1993	S Lamond	Old Ranfurly	150		2000	W Booth	The Hirsel	138
1994	S Fraser	Crieff	142		2001	C Johnston	Edzell	143
1995	C Campbell	Shotts	73 (18)		2002	S Borrowman	Ratho Park	142
1996	P Whiteford	Bothwell	143					

2003 *at Helensburgh*

1	David Addison (Kilmarnock (Barassie)	58-70—128
2	Scott Henry (Cardross)	74-67—141
3	Scott McGrenaghan (Cochrane Castle)	74-69—143

Scottish Youths Stroke Play Championship

1979	A Oldcorn	Dalmahoy	217		1991	D Robertson	Hilton Park	273
1980	G Brand jr	Monifieth & Ashludie	281		1992	R Russell	Nairn	296
1981	S Campbell	Cawder and Keir	279		1993	CD Hislop	West Kilbride	284
1982	LS Mann	Leven and Scoonie	270		1994	S Gallacher	Crieff	275
1983	A Moir	Mortonhall	284		1995	E Little	Irvine, Ayr	280
1984	B Shields	Eastwood, Renfrew	280		1996	E Little	Stranraer & Portpatrick	280
1985	H Kemp	East Kilbride	282		1997	S Young	Cawder	269
1986	A Mednick	Cawder	282		1998	T Rice*	Bruntsfield/R. Burgess	287
1987	K Walker	Bogside	291		1999	J Hendry*	Crieff & Aucterarder	142
1988	P McGinley	Ladybank & Glenrothes	281		2000	J Hendry	Newmachar	285
1989	J Mackenzie	Longniddry	281		2001	J McLeary	Crail	287
1990	S Bannerman	Portpatrick & Stranraer	213		2002	G Bourdy	Murrayshall	276

2003 *at Letham Grange (Old)*

1	Martin Laird (Hilton Park)	77-75-72-73—297
2	Scott Jamieson (Cathkin Braes)	75-71-73-81—300
	Chris Johnston (Dunbar)	73-78-74-75—300

Welsh Boys' Championship (inaugurated 1954)

1954	JWH Mitchell	DA Rees	Llandrindod Wells	8 and 6
1955	EW Griffith	DA Rees	Llandrindod Wells	3 and 2
1956	DA Rees	JP Hales	Llandrindod Wells	2 and 1
1957	P Waddilove	JG Jones	Llandrindod Wells	2 and 1
1958	P Waddilove	J Williams	Llandrindod Wells	1 hole
1959	C Gilford	JG Jones	Llandrindod Wells	6 and 4
1960	C Gilford	JL Toye	Llandrindod Wells	5 and 4
1961	AR Porter	JL Toye	Llandrindod Wells	3 and 2
1962	RC Waddilove	W Wadrup	Harlech	20th hole
1963	G Matthews	R Witchell	Penarth	6 and 5
1964	D Lloyd	M Walters	Conway	2 and 1
1965	G Matthews	DG Lloyd	Wenvoe Castle	7 and 6
1966	J Buckley	DP Owen	Holyhead	4 and 2
1967	J Buckley	DL Stevens	Glamorganshire	2 and 1
1968	J Buckley	C Brown	Maesdu	1 hole
1969	K Dabson	P Light	Glamorganshire	5 and 3
1970	P Tadman	A Morgan	Conway	2 and 1
1971	R Jenkins	TJ Melia	Ashburnham	3 and 2
1972	MG Chugg	RM Jones	Wrexham	3 and 2
1973	R Tate	N Duncan	Penarth	2 and 1
1974	D Williams	S Lewis	Llandudno	5 and 4

Welsh Boys Championship *continued*

1975	G Davies	PG Garrett	Glamorganshire	20th hole
1976	JM Morrow	MG Mouland	Caernarvonshire	1 hole
1977	JM Morrow	MG Mouland	Glamorganshire	2 and 1
1978	JM Morrow	A Laking	Harlech	2 and 1
1979	P Mayo	M Hayward	Penarth	24th hole
1980	A Llyr	DK Wood	Llandudno (Maesdu)	2 and 1
1981	M Evans	P Webborn	Pontypool	5 and 4
1982	CM Rees	KH Williams	Prestatyn	2 holes
1983	MA Macara	RN Roderick	Radyr	1 hole
1984	GA Macara	D Bagg	Llandudno	1 hole
1985	B Macfarlane	R Herbert	Cardiff	1 hole
1986	C O'Carroll	A Salmon	Rhuddlan	1 hole
1987	SJ Edwards	A Herbert	Abergavenny	19th hole
1988	C Platt	P Murphy	Holyhead	2 and 1
1989	R Johnson	RL Evans	Southerndown	2 holes
1990	M Ellis	C Sheppard	Llandudno (Maesdu)	3 and 2
1991	B Dredge	A Cooper	Tenby	2 and 1
1992	Y Taylor	J Pugh	Wrexham	1 hole
1993	R Davies	S Raybould	Pyle and Kenfig	3 and 2
1994	R Peet	K Sullivan	Abergele & Pensarn	7 and 6
1995	M Palmer	O Pughe	Newport	4 and 3
1996	A Smith	M Griffiths	Borth & Ynyslas	at 19th hole
1997	A Lee	I Campbell	Glamorganshire	4 and 3
1998	M Setterfield	D Price	Llandudno	3 and 2
1999	C Mills	D Price	Neath	3 and 2
2000	R Narduzzo	G Dobson-Jones	Pwllheli	1 hole
2001	J Morgan	B Briscoe	St Mellons	3 and 2
2002	C Cole	J Morgan	Radyr	4 and 3

2003 *at Porthmadog*

Quarter Finals

Carl Wakely (Whitchurch) beat James Connolly (Pyle & Kenfig) 4 and 3

Tom Light (Monmouth) beat Dan Cope (Tenby) 3 and 2

Rory Young (Maesdu) beat Peter Williams (Llantrisant & Pontyclun) 1 hole

Russell Caldecott (Rhuddlan) beat Rhys Davies (Royal Porthcawl) 3 and 2

Semi-Finals

Light beat Wakely 2 and 1

Young beat Caldecott 4 and 3

Final

Tom Light beat Rory Young 7 and 6

Welsh Boys Stroke Play Championship (inaugurated 1995)

1995	M Pillangton (Nefyn & Dist.)	1998	Bennett (Cirencester)	2001	J Morgan (Alice Springs)
1996	A Lee (St Mellons)	1999	G Bennett (Cirencester)	2002	C Cole (Monmouthshire)
1997	GM James (Wrexham)	2000	C Mills (Vale of Glamorgan)		

2003 *at Porthmadog*

1	Carl Wakely (Whitchurch)	73-68—141
2	Rhys Davies (Royal Porthcawl)	69-73—142
3	Stuart Runcie (Abergele)	72-74—146

Welsh Boys Under-15 Championship (inaugurated 1985)

1985	A Wesson (Tredegar Park)	1991	M Lucas (Brynhill)	1997	RW Johnson (Cardiff)
1986	A Wesson (Tredegar Park)	1992	MC Gordon (Pyle & Kenfig)	1998	BM Briscoe (Old Colwyn)
1987	J Grundy (Radyr)	1993	G Jones (Builth Wells)	1999	L James (Brynhill)
1988	S Rees (Carmarthen)	1994	AGL Smith (Rhondda)	2000	M Jones (Pontypridd)
1989	Y Taylor (Brynhill)	1995	C Thomas (Oxley Park)	2001	P Smith (Dewston)
1990	R Morgan (Morlais Castle)	1996	J Lloyd (Southerndown)	2002	Z Goned (Vale of Glamorgan)

2003 *at Glamorganshire*

1	Tom Smith (Pontypridd)	74-71—145
2	Richard Merchant (Monmouthshire)	72-74—146
3	Kieran Davies (Peterstone)	77-72—149

Welsh Open Youths Championship (inaugurated 1993)

1993	A McKenna	Langland Bay	310	1998	M Hearne	Carmarthen	294
1994	D Quinney	Vale of Llangollen	290	1999	D Price	Rhuddlan	281
1995	R Warner	Glamorganshire	289	2000	B Welch	Cottrell Park	276
1996	D Harris	Porthmadog	295	2001	T Dykes	Wrexham	281
1997	N Matthews	Cradoc	294	2002	J Ruth	Cardiff	283

2003 *Northop Country Park*

1	Mark Laskey (Brocket Hall)	69-71-68-72—280
2	Rob Leonard (Harpenden Common)	73-68-66-75—282
3	Nicholas Olson (Faversham)	76-68-71-71—286

Peter McEvoy Trophy *at Copt Heath*

1988	P Sefton	1993	S Webster	1998	J Rose
1989	D Bathgate	1994	J Harris	1999	D Porter
1990	P Sherman	1995	C Duke	2000	Z Scotland
1991	L Westwood	1996	M Pilkington	2001	B Harvey
1992	B Davis	1997	P Rowe	2002	M Richardson

2003 *at Copt Heath*

1	Tommy Hunter (Ilford)	70-69-75-73—287
2	Rhys Davies (Royal Porthcawl)	67-74-72-75—288
	Chris Kilgannon (Royal Winchester)	71-72-69-76—288

Nick Faldo Junior Series

1997	N Dougherty			2000	N Dougherty	Royal Liverpool	140
1998	G Hyde	Loch Lomond	138	2001	G Bondarenko*	Saunton	152
1999	N Dougherty	The Belfry	109 (27 holes)	2002	J Heath	Burhill	138

2003 *at Brocket Hall*

1	Mark Pilling (Astbury)	68-66—134
2	Andrew Bradley (Doncaster)	72-66—138

Under 18 winner: Luke Collins (Mendip Spring)   70-70—140

Under 17 winner: Nicky Grant (Clandeboye)   66-71—137

Under 16 winner: Jordan Smith (Woodcote Park)   74-69—143

Under 15 winner: Oliver Fisher (West Essex)   68-70—138

Nick Faldo Junior Series (International Trophy)

1999	Etienne Bond (Fra)	The Belfry	111 (27 holes)
2000	A Kruger (RSA)	Royal Liverpool	150
2001	P Erofejeff (Fin)	Saunton	153
2002	C Westrup (Swe)	Burhill	142

2003 *at Brocket Hall*

1	Wouter De Vries (Ned)	68-66—134
2	Reinier Saxton (Ned)	70-69—139
3	Dmitri Vinogradov (Rus)	72-69—141

R&A Junior Open Championhips (Boys and Girls)

1994	Orn Aevar Hjartanson (Isl)	2000	Steven Jeppeson (Swe)
1996	Antti Hiltunen (Fin)	2001	*Not played*
1998	David Inglis (Sco)	2002	C McNamara (Irl)

Midland Boys Amateur Championship

1989	M Wilson	1994	R Duck	1998	E Vernon
1990	ML Welch	1995	C Richardson	1999	C Stevenson
1991	S Drummond	1996T	S Walker	2000	J Prince
1992	S Drummond		K Cliffe	2001	O West
1993	S Webster	1997	K Hale	2002	B Stafford

2003 *at Burton-on-Trent*

1	Christopher Evans (Maxstoke Park)	71-68—139
2	George Woolgar (Chesterfield)	71-73—144
3	David Gojka (Shifnal)	72-73—145

Bank of Scotland Junior Masters

2003 *at Gleneagles (Queen's Course)*

1	Luke Pirie (Duff House Royal)	42 pts
2	Jonathan Elliot (Milngavie)	36 pts
	Andrew Dingwall (Peterculter)	
	Christopher Barr (Eastwood)	
	Stuart King (Eastwood)	
	Jonathan Reiss (Alyth)	

Taiwanese youngster makes history

When 13-year-old Lo Shih-Kai won the Hong Kong Amateur Championship he earned the right to play in the Omega Hong Kong Open, a joint venture on the Asian and European Tours.

Lo was the youngest player by two years to play in a European event. The previous youngest player had been Spaniard Sergio García who was just 15 when he played in the Turespaña Mediterranean Open in 1995.

US Tour officials do not have details of their youngest competitor but 15-year-old Bob Panasik is the youngest to make the half-way cut when he made it through to the weekend in the 1957 Canadian Open.

The youngest player to compete on the LPGA Tour in America is Beverly Klass who played four events in 1967 at the age of 10 and made the cut in three of the tournaments missing out only at that year's US Open.

Team Events

Toyota World Junior Team Championship

1995	USA	643	1998	England	874	2001	RSA	856
1996	Japan	625	1999	England	863	2002	*Not played*	
1997	USA	864	2000	USA	859			

2003 *in Rosewood, Kobe, Japan*
1 Korea 868, 2 Japan 870, 3 Spain 880, 4 USA 888, 5 Canada 888 — 13 teams played

European Young Masters
2003 *at Golf-Club Augsburg, Germany*
1 Spain 647, 2 England 649, 3 Wales 663, 4 France 667
Individual: Boys: Ben Parker (Eng) 211; Girls: Azahara Muñoz (Esp) 216

European Youths Team Championship

1990	Italy	Sweden	Turin, Italy
1992	Sweden	England	Helsinki, Finland
1994	Ireland	Sweden	Esbjerg, Denmark
1996	Scotland	Spain	Madeira
1998	Wales	Sweden	Royal Waterloo, Belgium
2000	England	Scotland	Kilmarnock (Barassie), Scotland
2002	Sweden	England	Gdansk, Poland

European Boys Team Championship

1980	Spain	El Prat, Barcelona	1992	Scotland	Conwy, Wales
1981	England	Olgiata, Rome	1993	Sweden	Ascona, Switzerland
1982	Italy	Frankfurt, Germany	1994	England	Vilamoura, Portugal
1983	Sweden	Helsinki, Finland	1995	England	Woodhall Spa
1984	Scotland	Royal St George's, England	1996	Spain	Gut Murstatten, Austria
1985	England	Troia, Portugal	1997	Spain	Bled, Slovenia
1986	England	Turin, Italy	1998	Ireland	Gullane, Scotland
1987	Scotland	Chantilly, France	1999	England	Uppsala, Sweden
1988	France	Renfrew, Scotland	2000	Scotland	Noord Nederlandse
1989	England	Lyckoma, Sweden	2001	Sweden	Amber Baltic, Poland
1990	Spain	Reykjavik, Iceland	2002	Spain	Reykjavik, Iceland
1991	Sweden	Oslo, Norway			

2003 *at Karlovy Vary, Czech Republic*

Final Ranking:
1 Italy, 2 Austria; 3 France, 4 Netherlands, 5 England, 6 Sweden, 7 Scotland, 8 Spain
— 19 teams played

Great Britain & Ireland v Continent of Europe (Jacques Léglise Trophy)

1958	GB&I	11½–½	Moortown	1985	GB&I	7½–4½	Royal Burgess
1959	GB&I	7–2	Pollok	1986	Europe	8½–3½	Seaton Carew
1960	GB&I	8–7	Olton	1987	GB&I	7½–4½	Kilmarnock (Barassie)
1961	GB&I	11–4	Dalmahoy	1988	GB&I	5½–2½	Formby
1962	GB&I	11–4	Royal Mid-Surrey	1989	GB&I	7½–4½	Nairn
1963	GB&I	12–3	Prestwick	1990	GB&I	10–2	Hunstanton
1964	GB&I	12–1	Formby	1991	GB&I	6½–5½	Montrose
1965	GB&I	12–1	Gullane	1992	GB&I	8–7	Royal Mid–Surrey
1966	GB&I	10–2	Moortown	1993	GB&I	8–7	Glenbervie
1967–76	*Not played*			1994	GB&I	12½–2½	Little Aston
1977	Europe	7–6	Downfield	1995	GB&I	9–6	Dunbar
1978	Europe	7–6	Seaton Carew	1996	Europe	13–11	Woodhall Spa
1979	GB&I	9½–2½	Kilmarnock (Barassie)	1997	Europe	12½–11½	Aberdeen
1980	GB&I	7–5	Formby	1998	GB&I	14–10	Villa d'Este, Italy
1981	GB&I	8–4	Gullane	1999	GB&I	15–9	Burnham & Berrow
1982	GB&I	11–1	Burnham & Berrow	2000	GB&I	16–8	Turnberry
1983	GB&I	6½–5½	Glenbervie	2001	Europe	16–8	Chantilly
1984	GB&I	6½–5½	Royal Porthcawl	2002	Europe	14–10	Lausanne, Switzerland

2003 *at Lahinch, Ireland* (GBI names first):

Captains: Paul Waring (GBI); Gonzalo Fernandez-Castaño (Esp) (non-playing)

First Day, Morning – **Foursomes**

Rhys Davies & Daniel Denison beat Pablo Martin & Wouter de Vries 4 and 3

Lloyd Saltman & Aaron O'Callaghan beat Lorenzo Dagli & Federico Colombo 4 and 3

Cian McNamara & Tommy Hunter beat Matteo del Podio & Michael Lorenzo-Vera 1 hole

Paul Worthing & Gareth Shaw lost to Stefan Gross & Pierre Relecom 5 and 4

Afternoon – **Singles**

Rhys Davies (Wal) beat Bernd Wiesberger (Aut) 1 hole

Wallace Booth (Sco) halved with Pablo Martin (Esp)

Cian McNamara (Irl) beat Wouter de Vries (Ned) 1 hole

Gareth Shaw (Irl) beat Federico Colombo (Ita) 5 and 4

Tommy Hunter (Eng) beat Lorenzo Dagli (Ita) 3 and 2

Daniel Denison (Eng) lost to Stefan Gross (Ger) 6 and 5

Lloyd Saltman (Sco) beat Pierre Relecom (Bel) 6 and 5

Paul Waring (Eng) beat Matteo del Podi (Ita) 1 hole

Second Day, Morning – **Foursomes**

R Davies & D Denison beat S Gross & P Relecom 3 and 2

P Waring & G Shaw lost to P Martin & M Lorenzo-Vera 2 and 1

C McNamara & T Hunter lost to M del Podio & L Dagli 2 holes

L Saltman & A O'Callaghan beat W de Vries & B Wiesberger 2 and 1

Afternoon – **Singles**

P Waring lost to P Relecom 2 and 1

R Davies beat F Colombo 1 hole

L Saltman beat M del Podio 3 and 1

C McNamara beat S Gross 3 and 2

G Shaw beat B Wiesberger 2 and 1

W Booth beat Michael Lorenzo-Vera (Fra) 4 and 3

Aaron O'Callaghan (Irl) lost to W de Vries 2 and 1

T Hunter lost to P Martin 6 and 5

Result: GBI 16½, Europe 7½

Boys Home Internationals (R&A Trophy) (Instituted 1985)

1985T	England/Ireland	Royal Burgess	1994	England	Little Aston
1986	Ireland	Seaton Carew	1995	Scotland	Dunbar
1987	Scotland	Barassie	1996	England	Littlestone
1988	England	Formby	1997	Ireland	Royal North Devon
1989	England	Nairn	1998	England	St Andrews
1990	Scotland	Hunstanton	1999	England	Conwy
1991	England	Montrose	2000	England	Portmanock
1992T	Wales/Scotland	Royal Mid-Surrey	2001	England	Moortown
1993	England	Glenbervie	2002	England	Lansdowne

2003 at Royal St David's

England beat Scotland	13½–1½
Wales lost to Ireland	5½–9½
England halved with Wales	7½–7½
Ireland beat Scotland	9–6
Wales lost to Scotland	6½–8½
Ireland lost to England	6½–8½

Result: 1 England 29½; 2 Ireland 25; 3 Wales 19½; 4 Scotland 16

Winning Team: Paul Waring (Bromborough) (captain); Andrew Bravant, (South Herts), Daniel Denison (Howley Hall), Ben Evans (Rye), Paul Grannell (Sandiway), Martyn Hamer (Worsley Park), Tommy Hunter (Ilford), Lloyd Kennedy (Chelmsford), Alex MacGregor (Killiow), James Ruth (Tavistock), Grant Slater (Carlyon Bay).

English Boys County Finals

2000 Surrey   2001 Lancashire   2002 Yorkshire

2003 at Copthorne

1 Yorkshire, 2 Kent, 3 Lincolnshire, 4 Wiltshire

Winning Team: Daniel Denison, Daniel Dunn, Christopher Hanson, Matthew Marsh, John Parry, Thomas Robinson, Andrew Town

Scottish Boys Team Championship

2000 Lothians   355   2001 Dunbartonshire   347   2002 Lothians   370

2003 at Ballater

1	Lothians	350
2	Fife	359
3	North	360

Winning Team: Lloyd Saltman, Stuart Beattie, Chris Johnston, Kenny Glen
Niagara Cup (Best Singles): Paul O'Hara (Lanarkshire) 67

The Junior Ryder Cup

1995	Rochester, USA	Exhibition Match won by Europe
1997	San Roque & Alcaidesa, Spain	United States won 7–5
1999	Cape Cod, USA	Europe won 10½–1½
2002	K Club, Dublin, Ireland	Europe won 9½–2½

Girls' and Junior Ladies' Tournaments

Girls British Open Championship

Year	Winner	Runner–up	Venue	By
1960	S Clarke	AL Irvin	Kilmarnock (Barassie)	2 and 1
1961	D Robb	J Roberts	Beaconsfield	3 and 2
1962	S McLaren-Smith	A Murphy	Foxton Hall	2 and 1
1963	D Oxley	B Whitehead	Gullane	2 and 1
1964	P Tredinnick	K Cumming	Camberley Heath	2 and 1
1965	A Willard	A Ward	Formby	3 and 2
1966	J Hutton	D Oxley	Troon Portland	20th hole
1967	P Burrows	J Hutton	Liphook	2 and 1
1968	C Wallace	C Reybroeck	Leven	4 and 3
1969	J de Witt Puyt	C Reybroeck	Ilkley	2 and 1
1970	C Le Feuvre	Michelle Walker	North Wales	2 and 1
1971	J Mark	Maureen Walker	North Berwick	4 and 3
1972	Maureen Walker	S Cadden	Norwich	2 and 1
1973	AM Palli	N Jeanson	Northamptonshire	2 and 1
1974	R Barry	T Perkins	Dunbar	1 hole
1975	S Cadden	L Isherwood	Henbury	4 and 3
1976	G Stewart	S Rowlands	Pyle and Kenfig	5 and 4
1977	W Aitken	S Bamford	Formby Ladies	2 and 1
1978	M L de Lorenzi	D Glenn	Largs	2 and 1
1979	S Lapaire	P Smilie	Edgbaston	19th hole
1980	J Connachan	L Bolton	Wrexham	2 holes
1981	J Connachan	P Grice	Woodbridge	20th hole
1982	C Waite	M Mackie	Edzell	6 and 5
1983	E Orley	A Walters	Leeds	7 and 6
1984	C Swallow	E Farquharson	Maesdu	1 hole
1985	S Shapcott	E Farquharson	Hesketh	3 and 1
1986	S Croce	S Bennett	West Kilbride	5 and 4
1987	H Dobson	S Croce	Barnham Broom	19th hole
1988	A Macdonald	J Posener	Pyle and Kenfig	3 and 2
1989	M McKinlay	S Eriksson	Carlisle	19th hole
1990	S Cavalleri	E Valera	Penrith	5 and 4
1991	M Hjorth	J Moodie	Whitchurch	3 and 2
1992	M McKay	L Navarro	Northamptonshire	2 holes
1993	M McKay	A Vincent	Helensburgh	4 and 3
1994	A Vincent	R Hudson	Gog Magog	1 up
1995	A Lemoine	J Krantz	Northop Park	3 and 2
1996	M Monnet	C Laurens	Formby	4 and 3
1997	C Laurens	M Nagl	West Kilbride	2 and 1
1998	M Beautell	M Nagl	Holyhead	4 and 3
1999	S Pettersen	M Nagl	High Post	3 and 1
2000	T Calzavara	R Bell	Blairgowrie	1 hole
2001	C Queen	C Alonso	Brough	1 hole
2002	*Rain washed out this tournament in its later stages. Awards were made to the top qualifiers:*			
	E Cabrera	L Stable	Sandiway	

2003 *at Newport, Gwent*

Leading Qualifiers: 138 Emma Cabrera (Esp), Belen Mozo (Esp), Caroline Westrup (Swe)

Quarter-Finals
Marianne Skarpnord (Nor) beat Emma Cabrera (Esp) 2 holes
Dewi Claire Schreefel (Ned) beat Azahara Munoz (Esp)
  3 and 2
Isabel Alvarez Valcarce (Esp) beat Adriana Zwanck (Esp)
  2 holes
Beatriz Recari Eransus (Esp) beat Kelly Froelich (Fra) at 20th

Semi-Finals
Skarpnord beat Schreefel 2 holes
Recari Eransus beat Alvarez Valcarce
  at 20th

Final
Marianne Skarpnord beat
  Beatriz Recari Eransus 2 and 1

English Girls Close Championship

Year	Winner	Runner–up	Venue	By
1964	S Ward	P Tredinnick	Wollaton Park	2 and 1
1965	D Oxley	A Payne	Edgbaston	2 holes
1966	B Whitehead	D Oxley	Woodbridge	1 hole
1967	A Willard	G Holloway	Burhill	1 hole
1968	K Phillips	C le Feuvre	Harrogate	6 and 5
1969	C le Feuvre	K Phillips	Hawkstone Park	2 and 1
1970	C le Feuvre	M Walker	High Post	2 and 1
1971	C Eckersley	J Stevens	Liphook	4 and 3
1972	C Barker	R Kelly	Trentham	4 and 3
1973	S Parker	S Thurston	Lincoln	19th hole
1974	C Langford	L Harrold	Knowle	2 and 1
1975	M Burton	R Barry	Formby	6 and 5
1976	H Latham	D Park	Moseley	3 and 2
1977	S Bamford	S Jolly	Chelmsford	21st hole
1978	P Smillie	J Smith	Willesley Park	3 and 2
1979	L Moore	P Barry	Cirencester	1 hole
1980	P Smillie	J Soulsby	Kedleston Park	3 and 2
1981	J Soulsby	C Waite	Worksop	7 and 5
1982	C Waite	P Grice	Wilmslow	3 and 2
1983	P Grice	K Mitchell	West Surrey	2 and 1
1984	C Swallow	S Duhig	Bath	3 and 1
1985	L Fairclough	K Mitchell	Coventry	6 and 5
1986	S Shapcott	N Way	Huddersfield	7 and 6
1987	S Shapcott	S Morgan	Sandy Lodge	1 hole
1988	H Dobson	S Shapcott	Long Ashton	1 hole
1989	H Dobson	A MacDonald	Edgbaston	3 and 1
1990	C Hall	J Hockley	Bolton Old Links	20th hole
1991	N Buxton	C Hall	Knole Park	2 and 1
1992	F Brown	L Nicholson	Finham Park	2 and 1
1993	G Simpson	L Wixon	Cotswold Hills	7 and 5
1994	K Hamilton	S Forster	Whitley Bay	3 and 2
1995	R Hudson	G Nutter	Porters Park	2 and 1
1996	R Hudson	D Rushworth	Bedford	8 and 6
1997	S McKevitt	C Ritson	Kingsdown	3 and 2
1998	L Walters	K Lawton	Harrogate	5 and 4
1999	S Heath	A Cook	Chigwell	6 and 4
2000	S Walker	R Wood	Sheringham	1 hole
2001	A Marshall	S Walker	Long Ashton	3 and 2
2002	L Eastwood	N Haywood	Fairhaven	1 hole

2003 *at Porters Park*

Quarter Finals
Claire Aitken (Mid Kent) beat Rachel Jennings
  (Izaak Walton) 3 and 1
Joanne Hodge (Knowle) beat Hannah Coles
  (Maxstoke Park) 2 and 1
Anna Scott (Consett & District) beat Felicity Johnson
  (Harborne) 1 hole
Kerry-Anne Haskell (Broadstone) beat Kirsty Law
  (Evesham) 3 and 2

Semi-Finals
Hodge beat Aitken 3 and 2
Haskell beat Scott 3 and 2

Final
Kerry-Anne Haskell beat Joanne Hodge 4 and 3

Irish Girls Championship (inaugurated 1951)

Year	Winner	Runner–up	Venue	By
1951	J Davies	I Hurst	Milltown	3 and 2
1952	J Redgate	A Phillips	Grange	at 22nd
1953	J Redgate	I Hurst	Grange	4 and 3
1954–60	*Suspended*			
1961	M Coburn	C McAuley	Portrush	6 and 5
1962	P Boyd	P Atkinson	Elm Park	4 and 3
1963	P Atkinson	C Scarlett	Donaghadee	8 and 7
1964	C Scarlett	A Maher	Milltown	6 and 5
1965	V Singleton	P McKenzie	Ballycastle	7 and 6
1966	M McConnell	D Hulme	Dun Laoghaire	3 and 2
1967	M McConnell	C Wallace	Portrush	6 and 5
1968	C Wallace	A McCoy	Louth	3 and 1
1969	EA McGregor	M Sheenan	Knock	6 and 5
1970	EA McGregor	J Mark	Greystones	3 and 2
1971	J Mark	C Nesbitt	Belfast	3 and 2
1972	P Smyth	M Governey	Elm Park	1 hole
1973	M Governey	R Hegarty	Mullingar	3 and 1
1974	R Hegarty	M Irvine	Castletroy	2 holes
1975	M Irvine	P Wickham	Carlow	2 and 1
1976	P Wickham	R Hegarty	Castle	5 and 3
1977	A Ferguson	R Walsh	Birr	3 and 2
1978	C Wickham	B Gleeson	Killarney	1 hole
1979	L Bolton	B Gleeson	Milltown	3 and 2
1980	B Gleeson	L Bolton	Kilkenny	5 and 3
1981	B Gleeson	E Lynn	Donegal	1 hole
1982	D Langan	S Lynn	Headfort	5 and 4
1983	E McDaid	S Lynn	Ennis	20th hole
1984	S Sheehan	L Tormey	Thurles	6 and 4
1985	S Sheehan	D Hanna	Laytown/Bettystown	5 and 4
1986	D Mahon	T Eakin	Mallow	4 and 3
1987	V Greevy	B Ryan	Galway	8 and 7
1988	L McCool	P Gorman	Courtown	3 and 2
1989	A Rogers	R MacGuigan	Athlone	2 and 1
1990	G Doran	L McCool	Royal Portrush	3 and 1
1991	A Rogers	D Powell	Mallow	2 and 1
1992	M McGreevy	N Gorman	Kilkenny	2 and 1
1993	M McGreevy	E Dowdall	Strandhill	2 and 1
1994	A O'Leary	D Doyle	Mullingar	23rd hole
1995	P Murphy	G Hegarty	Douglas	5 and 4
1996	P Murphy	C Smyth	Warren Point	2 holes
1997	J Gannon	C Coughlan	Lay/Bettystown	3 and 2
1998	P Murphy	C Coughlan	Galway	5 and 4
1999	P Murphy	M Gillen	Tullamore	20th hole
2000	M Gillen	N Mullooly	Limerick	6 and 5
2001	DM Conaty	H Nolan	Belvoir Park	3 and 2
2002	K Delany	H Nolan	Athenry	4 and 3

2003 *at Ardee*

Quarter Finals

Danielle McVeigh (Royal County Down) beat Jenna
Kinnear (Belvoir Park) at 19th

Tara Delaney (Carlow) beat Louise Coffey (Warrenpoint)
5 and 4

Karen Delaney (Carlow) beat Sinead O'Sullivan
(Galway) 2 and 1

Vicki Power (Brampton Park) beat Niamh Kitching
(Claremorris) 5 and 4

Semi-Finals

Tara Delaney beat Danielle McVeigh
3 and 1

Karen Delaney beat Vicki Power 2 and 1

Final

Karen Delaney beat Tara Delaney 4 and 3

Scottish Ladies Junior Open Stroke Play Championship
(inaugurated 1955)

1955	M Fowler	Erskine	1979	A Gemmill	Royal Troon, Portland
1956	B McCorkindale	Erskine	1980	J Connachan	Kirkcaldy
1957	M Fowler	Kilmacolm	1981	K Douglas	Downfield
1958	R Porter	Ranfurly Castle	1982	J Rhodes	Dumfries & Galloway
1959	D Robb	Helensburgh	1983	S Lawson	Largs
1960	J Greenhalgh	Ranfurly Castle	1984	S Lawson	Dunbar
1961	D Robb	Whitecraigs	1985	K Imrie	Ballater
1962	S Armitage	Dalmahoy	1986	K Imrie	Dumfries and County
1963	A Irvin	Dumfries	1987	K Imrie	Douglas Park
1964	M Nuttall	Dalmahoy	1988	C Lambert	Baberton
1965	I Wylie	Carnoustie	1989	C Lambert	Dunblane New
1966	J Smith	Douglas Park	1990	J Moodie	Royal Troon
1967	J Bourassa	Dunbar	1991	C Macdonald	Alyth
1968	K Phillips	Dumfries	1992	L McCool	North Berwick
1969	K Phillips	Prestonfield	1993	J Moodie	Dumfries and County
1970	B Huke	Leven	1994	C Agnew	Dumfries and County
1971	B Huke	Dalmahoy	1995	R Hakkarainen (Fin)	Lanark
1972	L Hope	Troon, Portland	1996	L Moffat	Auchterarder
1973	G Cadden	Edzell	1997	L Nicholson	Stranraer
1974	S Lambie	Stranraer	1998	V Laing	Duff House Royal
1975	S Cadden	Lanark	1999	L Kenny	Alyth
1976	S Cadden	Prestonfield	2000	L Morton	Cardross
1977	S Cadden	Edzell	2001	L Kenny	Southerness
1978	J Connachan	Peebles	2002	K Brotherton	Baberton

2003 at Kilmacolm

1	Jenna Wilson (Strathaven)*	71-73-73—217
2	Heather MacRae (Dunblane New)	73-71-73—217
3	Kelly Brotherton (Tulliallan)	78-72-68—218

Scottish Girls Close Championship (inagurated 1960)

Year	Winner	Runner–up	Venue	By
1960	J Hastings	A Lurie	Kilmacolm	6 and 4
1961	I Wylie	W Clark	Murrayfield	3 and 1
1962	I Wylie	U Burnet	West Kilbride	3 and 1
1963	M Norval	S MacDonald	Carnoustie	6 and 4
1964	JW Smith	C Workman	West Kilbride	2 and 1
1965	JW Smith	I Walker	Leven	7 and 5
1966	J Hutton	F Jamieson	Arbroath	2 holes
1967	J Hutton	K Lackie	West Kilbride	4 and 2
1968	M Dewar	J Crawford	Dalmahoy	2 holes
1969	C Panton	A Coutts	Edzell	23rd hole
1970	M Walker	L Bennett	Largs	3 and 2
1971	M Walker	S Kennedy	Edzell	1 hole
1972	G Cadden	C Panton	Stirling	3 and 2
1973	M Walker	M Thomson	Cowal, Dunoon	1 hole
1974	S Cadden	D Reid	Arbroath	3 and 1
1975	W Aitken	S Cadden	Leven	1 hole
1976	S Cadden	D Mitchell	Dumfries and County	4 and 2
1977	W Aitken	G Wilson	West Kilbride	2 holes
1978	J Connachan	D Mitchell	Stirling	7 and 5
1979	J Connachan	G Wilson	Dunbar	3 and 1
1980	J Connachan	P Wright	Dumfries and County	21st hole
1981	D Thomson	P Wright	Kilmarnock (Barassie)	2 and 1
1982	S Lawson	D Thomson	Montrose	1 hole
1983	K Imrie	D Martin	Leven	2 and 1
1984	T Craik	D Jackson	Peebles	3 and 2
1985	E Farquharson	E Moffat	West Kilbride	2 holes
1986	C Lambert	F McKay	Nairn	4 and 3
1987	S Little	L Moretti	Stirling	3 and 2
1988	J Jenkins	F McKay	Dumfries and County	4 and 3
1989	J Moodie	V Melvin	Kilmacolm	19th hole
1990	M McKay	J Moodie	Duff House Royal	3 and 2
1991	J Moodie	M McKay	Leven Links	5 and 4
1992	M McKay	L Nicholson	Powfoot	2 and 1

Scottish Girls Close Championship *continued*

Year	Winner	Runner–up	Venue	By
1993	C Agnew	H Stirling	Baberton	19th hole
1994	C Nicholson	L Moffat	Deeside	3 and 1
1995	L Moffat	F Lockhart	Paisley	2 and 1
1996	V Laing	C Hunter	Peebles	5 and 4
1997	V Laing	A Walker	Dunfermline	5 and 4
1998	V Laing	L Moffat	Kilmarnock Barassie	at 21st hole
1999	V Laing	L Wells	Edzell	3 and 2
2000	L Kenney	F Gilbert	Dunblane New	3 and 2
2001	H MacRea	L Kenney	Glenbervie	1 hole
2002	L Walker	G Webster	Powfoot	2 and 1

2003 *at Newmachar*

Quarter Finals

Kelly Brotherton (Tulliallan) beat Gemma Webster (Hilton Park) 3 and 1

Sjavon Wilson (Murcar) beat Sally Kettlewell (Dunblane New) 7 and 5

Kate O'Sullivan (Cochrane Castle) beat Emma Fairnie (Minto) at 19th

Krystle Caithness (St Regulus) beat Laura Murray (Alford) 2 and 1

Semi-Finals

Brotherton beat Wilson 3 and 2

Caithness beat O'Sullivan 2 and 1

Final

Kelly Brotherton beat Krystle Caithness 3 and 2

Welsh Girls Championship (inaugurated 1957)

Year	Winner	Runner–up	Venue	By
1957	A Coulman	S Wynne-Jones	Newport	1 hole
1958	S Wynne-Jones	A Coulman	Conwy	3 and 1
1959	C Mason	T Williams	Glamorgan	3 and 2
1960	A Hughes	D Wilson	Llandrindod Wells	6 and 4
1961	J Morris	S Kelly	North Wales	3 and 2
1962	J Morris	P Morgan	Southerndown	4 and 3
1963	A Hughes	A Brown	Conway	8 and 7
1964	A Hughes	M Leigh	Holyhead	5 and 3
1965	A Hughes	A Reardon-Hughes	Swansea Bay	19th hole
1966	S Hales	J Rogers	Prestatyn	1 hole
1967	E Wilkie	L Humphreys	Pyle and Kenfig	1 hole
1968	L Morris	J Rogers	Portmadoc	1 hole
1969	L Morris	L Humphreys	Wenvoe Castle	5 and 3
1970	T Perkins	P Light	Rhuddlan	2 and 1
1971	P Light	P Whitley	Glamorganshire	4 and 3
1972	P Whitley	P Light	Llandudno (Maesdu)	2 and 1
1973	V Rawlings	T Perkins	Whitchurch	19th hole
1974	L Isherwood	S Rowlands	Wrexham	4 and 3
1975	L Isherwood	S Rowlands	Swansea Bay	1 hole
1976	K Rawlings	C Parry	Rhuddlan	5 and 4
1977	S Rowlands	D Taylor	Clyne	7 and 5
1978	S Rowlands	G Rees	Abergele	3 and 2
1979	M Rawlings	J Richards	St Mellons	19th hole
1980	K Davies	M Rawlings	Vale of Llangollen	19th hole
1981	M Rawlings	F Connor	Radyr	4 and 3
1982	K Davies	K Beckett	Wrexham	6 and 5
1983	N Wesley	J Foster	Whitchurch	4 and 2
1984	J Foster	J Evans	Pwllheli	6 and 5
1985	J Foster	S Caley	Langland Bay	6 and 5
1986	J Foster	L Dermott	Holyhead	3 and 2
1987	J Lloyd	S Bibbs	Cardiff	2 and 1
1988	L Dermott	A Perriam	Builth Wells	2 holes
1989	L Dermott	N Stroud	Carmarthen	4 and 2
1990	L Dermott	N Stroud	Padeswood and Buckley	6 and 4
1991	S Boyes	R Morgan	Clyne	3 and 1
1992	B Jones	S Musto	Rhuddlan	2 and 1
1993	K Stark	S Tudor-Jones	Radyr	3 and 2
1994	K Stark	J Evans	Wrexham	4 and 3
1995	E Pilgrim	L Davis	Borth and Ynyslas	2 holes
1996	K Stark	S Bourne	Monmouth	4 and 3

Year	Winner	Runner–up	Venue	By
1997	R Brewerton	K Stark	Perhos	19th hole
1998	B Brewerton	L Archer	Old Padeswood	3 and 1
1999	K Phillips	R Last	Pontardawe	6 and 5
2000	K Phillips	J Pritchard	Northop Country Park	1 hole
2001	S Jones	J Dyer	Carmarthen	3 and 2
2002	L Gould	R Vaughan-Jones	North Wales GC	4 and 3

2003 *at North Wales GC*

Quarter Finals

Lucy Gould (Bargoed) beat Samantha Birks (Wolstanton)
1 hole

Sahra Hassan (Vale of Glamorgan) beat Kimberley
Boulden (Llandudno Maesdu) 1 hole

Breanne Loucks (Wrexham) beat Melanie Peake (Rhyl)
4 and 2

Rachel Hunt (Pyle & Kenfig) beat Natasha Morgan
(Alice Springs) 4 and 3

Semi-Finals

Gould beat Hassan 4 and 3

Loucks beat Hunt 4 and 3

Final

Lucy Gould beat Breanne Loucks
4 and 2

Nick Faldo Junior Series

1998	K Philips	Loch Lomond	154
1999	A Highgate	The Belfry	114 (27 holes)
2000	A Highgate	Royal Liverpool	146
2001	O Rotmistrova	Saunton	155
2002	F Parker	Burhill	152

2003 *at Brocket Hall*

Under 18

1	Tara Delaney (Carlow)	75-70—145
2	Felicity Johnson (Harborne)	76-72—148
3	Kiran Matharu (Sand Moor)	76-74—150

Bank of Scotland Junior Masters

2003 *at Gleneagles (Queen's Course)*

1	Michelle Thomson (McDonald)	37 pts
2	Carly Booth (Auchterarder)	37 pts
	Nicole Blackie (Eyemouth)	

Team Events

European Lady Juniors Team Championship

Year	Winner	Second	Venue
1990	Sweden	England	Shannon, Ireland
1992	Spain	Sweden	St Nom–la–Breteche, France
1994	Sweden	France	Gutenhof, Vienna, Austria
1996	France	Spain	Nairn, Scotland
1998	Spain	Italy	Oslo, Norway
2000	Spain	Germany	Moscow, Russia

European Girls Team Championship

Year	Winner	Venue
1995	Sweden	Luxembourg
1997	Spain	Germany
1999	Germany	Finland
2001	Spain	Portugal

2003 *at Esjberg, Denmark*

Final Ranking: 1 Spain, 2 Sweden, 3 Norway, 4 France, 5 Germany, 6 Austria, 7 Italy, 8 England —14 teams played

European Young Masters
2003 *at Golf-Club Augsburg, Germany*

1 Spain 647, 2 England 649, 3 Wales 663, 4 France 667

Individual: Girls: Azahara Muñoz (Esp) 216; Boys: Ben Parker (Eng) 211

Girls Home Internationals (Stroyan Cup)

Year	Winner	Venue	Year	Winner	Venue
1966	Scotland	Troon (Portland)	1985	England	Hesketh GC
1967	England	Liphook	1986	England	West Kilbride
1968	England	Leven	1987	England	Barnham Broom
1969	England	Ilkley	1988	England	Pyle and Kenfig
1970	England	North Wales	1989	England	Carlisle
1971	England	North Berwick	1990	England	Penrith
1972	Scotland	Royal Norwich	1991	England	Whitchurch
1973	Scotland	Northamptonshire County	1992	Scotland	Moseley
1974	England	Dunbar	1993	Scotland	Helensburgh
1975	England	Henbury	1994	Scotland	Gog Magog
1976	Scotland	Pyle and Kenfig	1995	England	Northop
1977	England	Formby Ladies	1996	England	Formby
1978	England	Largs	1997	England	Forfar
1979	England	Edgbaston	1998	England	Mullingar
1980	England	Wrexham	1999	Wales	High Post
1981	England	Woodbridge	2000	England	Downfield
1982	England	Edzell	2001	England	Brough
1983	England	Alwoodley	2002	England	The Hermitage
1984	Scotland	Llandudno (Maesdu)			

2003 *at Pyle & Kenfig*

Ireland beat Scotland 5-4
England beat Wales 6½-2½
Wales beat Ireland 6-3

England beat Scotland 6-3
England beat Ireland 7½-1½
Scotland beat Wales 5-4

Result: 1 England 3, 2 Wales 1, 3 Scotland 1, 4 Ireland 1

Winning team: Angela Caton (captain); Claire Aitken (Mid-Kent), Kerry Anne Haskell (Knighton Heath), Joanne Hodge (Knowle), Felicity Johnson (Harborne), Alex Marshall (Toft), Kiran Matharu (Sandmoor), Melissa Reid (Chevin), Roseann Youngman (Oundle)

Golf Foundation Events

Weetabix Age Group Championships

Boys

Year	Under 16	Under 15	Under 14
1990	C Lane (Kingsthorpe)	G Harris (Broome Manor)	P Collier (Limerick)
1991	G Harris (Broome Manor)	C Richardson (Burghley Park)	J Bajcer (Church Stretton)
1992	C Leach (Gillingham)	S Walker (Walmley)	D Kirton (Worksop)
1993	K Godfrey (St Enodoc)	S Young (Seascale)	J Rose (North Hants)
1994	A Smith (Rhondda)	T Hilton (Lewes)	A Smith (Enville)
1995	G Legg (Enmore Park)	S Robinson (Seaton Carew)	D Inglis (Glencorse)
1996	S Fromant (Orsett)	D Skinns (Canwick Park)	C Smith (Cotgrave Place)
1997	M Stam (Royal Liverpool)	G Lockerbie (Keswick)	S Robinson (Thames Ditton)
1998	D Rix (Malton and Norton)	M Skelton (Hunley Hall)	L Shepherd (Cleckheaton & District)
1999	W Schucksmith (Sand Moor)	J Moul (Stoke by Nayland)	T Robinson (Middlesbrough)
2000	M Jones (Upton-by-Chester)	S Taylor (Blundells Hill)	S Hufton (Copt Heath)
2001	J Cundy (Kings Lynn)	M Baldwin (Hesketh)	T Chambers (Coxmoor)
2002	J Parry (Harrogate)	L Lewis (Fairwood Park)	M Swales (Bowood)

Year	Under 13
1990	S Walker (Boldmere)
1991	N Rossin (John O'Gaunt)
1992	D Main (Moray)
1993	S Godfrey (St Enodoc)
1994	D Tarbotton (Hull)
1995	D Porter (Wellow)
1996	J Maxwell (Muckhart)
1997	J Turner (Newmarket Links)
1998	C Paisley (Stocksfield)
1999	J Haugh (Salisbury and S Wilts)
2000	J Stevenson (Torrington)
2001	Z Gould (Vale of Glamorgan)
2002	N Eardley (Burslem)

2003 at Forest of Arden, Meriden

Under 16
Lee Lewis (Gower)	72-69—141
Adam Bates (Stressholme)	69-72—141
Steven Capper (Caldy)	70-72—142
Andrew Sullivan (Purley Chase)	75-68—143
Haminder Matharu (Sand Moor)	72-72—144

Under 15
Lewis Edmunds (West Cornwall)	73-68—141
Dean Perkes (Fleetwood)	68-75—143
Andrew Ellis (Oxley Park)	72-72—144
Shane Smyth (Co. Louth)	71-73—144

Under 14
Henry Smart (Banstead)	69-70—139
Christopher Rabbich (Crompton & Royton)	71-73—144
Joshua Lutt (Redbourn)	76-73—149

Under 13
Christopher Lloyd (Kendleshire)	73-74—147
Tommy Fleetwood (Sefton Juniors)	75-74—149
Adam Myers (Northamptonshire)	74-75—149

Girls

Year	Under 17	Under 16	Under 15
1990		T Poulton (Boyce Hill)	V Hanks (Broome Manor)
1991		G Simpson (Cleckheaton & District)	D Doyle (Lahinch)
1992		H Stirling (Bridge of Allan)	G Nutter (Prestwich)
1993		K Wrigglesworth (Hornsea)	R Hudson (Wheatley)
1994		L Meredith (Wentworth)	L Moffat (W. Kilbride)
1995	R Hudson (Wheatley)	L Moffat (W. Kilbride)	V Laing (Musselburgh)
1996	K Fisher (Leyland)	F More (Lindrick)	L Archer (Lilleshall Hall)
1997	V Laing (Musselburgh)	R Bell (Northcliff)	L Kenney (Pitreavie)
1998	J Pritchard (Tredegar Park)	L Archer (Lilleshall Hall)	A Marshall (Burghley Park)
1999	P Willett (Enfield)	H MacRae (Callander)	A Marshall (Burghley Park)
2000	C Queen (Drumpelier)	L Eastwood (Yelverton)	N Haywood (Rotherham)
2001	L Eastwood (Yelverton)	N Haywood (Rotherham)	F Johnson (Harborne)
2002	J Phipps (Gog Magog)	A Scott (Consett & District)	M Reid (Chevin)

2003 at Forest of Arden, Meriden

Under 16

Melissa Reid (Chevin)	67-68—135	
Joanne Hodge (Knowle)	66-71—137	
Rebecca Copland (Scotscraig)	76-79—155	
Catherine Baines (Shaw Hill)	77-79—156	

Under 14

Kiren Matharu (Sand Moor)	73-72—145	
Henrietta Brockway (Yeovil)	76-75—151	
Elenor Givens (Blackwell Grange)	79-77—156	

Under 15

Jodi Ewart (Catterick)	74-74—148
Lindsey Wilson (Sherwood Forest)	78-72—150
Helen Connor (Basingstoke)	79-75—154
Sarah Faller (Galway)	75-80—155

Duke of York Trophy Winners (For best 36-hole aggregate)

Year	Boys	Girls
1991	Gary Harris (Broome Manor)	Georgina Simpson (Cleckheaton)
1992	Christopher Leach (Gillingham)	Heather Stirling (Bridge of Allan)
1993	Kristian Godfrey (St Enodoc)	Katy Wrigglesworth (Hornsea)
1994	Alex Smith (Rhondda)	Lisa Meredith (Wentworth)
1995	Gavin Legg (Enmore Park)	Rebecca Hudson (Wheatley)
1996	Stuart Fromant (Orsett)	Fame More (Lindrick)
1997	Marcus Stam (Royal Liverpool)	Louise Kenney (Pitreavie)
1998	Darren Rix (Malton & Norton)	Laura Archer (Lilleshall Hall)
1999	William Shucksmith (Sand Moor)	Alexandra Marshall (Burghley Park) and Polly Willett (Enfield)
2000	Sam Hufton (Copt Heath)	Natalie Haywood (Rotherham)
2001	James Cundy (King's Lynn)	Natalie Haywood (Rotherham)
2002	John Parry (Harrogate)	Melissa Reid (Chevin)
2003	Henry Smart (Banstead)	Melissa Reid (Chevin)

Golf Foundation Schools Team Championship (for the R&A Trophy)

Year	Winner	Country	Venue
1990	Lycée Bellevue	France	St Andrews
1991	Lycée Bellevue	France	Sunningdale
1992	Lycée Bellevue	France	St Andrews
1993	Lycée Bellevue	France	Gleneagles
1994	Lycée Bellevue	France	St Andrews
1995	Kelvin Grove High School	Australia	Sunningdale
1996	Welkom Gymnasium	South Africa	Blairgowrie
1997	Lycée Bellevue	France	Loch Lomond
1998	Damelin College, Randburg	South Africa	Sunningdale
1999	Kooralbyn International School	Australia	St Andrews

Year	Winner	Country	Venue
2000	Rotorua Boys' High School	New Zealand	Royal County Down
2001	Rotorua Boys' High School	New Zealand	The Berkshire
Discontinued			

Golf Foundation Award Winners

Year	Winner	Club
1982	Lindsey Anderson	Tain
1983	Nigel Osborne Clarke	Shirehampton
1984	Wayne Henry	Redbourn
1985	David Grantham	Hull
1986	Matthew Stanford	Saltford
1987	Jane Marchant	Whittington Barracks
1988	*Boys:* Ian Garbutt	Wheatley
	Girls: Lisa Dermott	St Melyd
1989	*Boys:* Lee Westwood	Worksop
	Girls: Lynn McCool	Strabane
1990	*Boys:* Keith Law	Forfar
	Girls: Mhairi McKay	Turnberry
1991	*Boys:* Gary Harris	Broome Manor
	Girls: Nicola Buxton	Woodsome Hall
1992	*Boys:* Shaun Devenney	Strabane
	Girls: Mhairi McKay	Turnberry
1993	*Boys:* Craig Williams	Greigiau
	Girls: Georgina Simpson	Cleckheaton & Dist
1994	*Boys:* Denny Lucas	Worksop
	Girls: Rebecca Hudson	Wheatley
1995	*Boys:* Justin Rose	North Hants
	Girls: Rebecca Hudson	Wheatley
1996	*Boys:* Mark Pilkington	Nefyn & District GC and Pwllheli
	Girls: Fame More	Chesterfield GC and Lindrick GC
1997	*Boys:* Nicholas Dougherty	Shaw Hill, Lancs
	Girls: Rebecca Brewerton	Abergele & Pensarn
1998	*Boys:* Steven O'Hara	Colville Park
	Girls: Vikki Laing	Musselburgh
1999	*Boys:* Barry Hume	Haggs Castle
	Girls: Rebecca Brewerton	Abergele
2000	*Boys:* David Inglis	Glencorse
	Girls: Sophie Walker	Kenwick Park

Discontinued

PART VII

Awards

Awards

Association of Golf Writers' Trophy (Awarded to the man or woman who, in the opinion of golf writers, has done most for European golf during the year)

1951	Max Faulkner	1977	Christy O'Connor
1952	Miss Elizabeth Price	1978	Peter McEvoy
1953	Joe Carr	1979	Severiano Ballesteros
1954	Mrs Roy Smith (Miss Frances Stephens)	1980	Sandy Lyle
1955	Ladies' Golf Union's Touring Team	1981	Bernhard Langer
1956	John Beharrell	1982	Gordon Brand Jr
1957	Dai Rees	1983	Nick Faldo
1958	Harry Bradshaw	1984	Severiano Ballesteros
1959	Eric Brown	1985	European Ryder Cup Team
1960	Sir Stuart Goodwin (sponsor of international golf)	1986	GB&I Curtis Cup Team
1961	Commdr Charles Roe (ex-hon secretary, PGA)	1987	European Ryder Cup Team
1962	Mrs Marley Spearman, British Ladies' Champion 1961–1962	1988	Sandy Lyle
		1989	Great Britain & Ireland Walker Cup Team
1963	Michael Lunt, Amateur Champion, 1963	1990	Nick Faldo
1964	GB&I Eisenhower Trophy Team	1991	Severiano Ballesteros
1965	Gerald Micklem, golf administrator, President, English Golf Union	1992	European Solheim Cup Team
		1993	Bernhard Langer
1966	Ronnie Shade	1994	Laura Davies
1967	John Panton	1995	European Ryder Cup Team
1968	Michael Bonallack	1996	Colin Montgomerie
1969	Tony Jacklin	1997	Alison Nicholas
1970	Tony Jacklin	1998	Lee Westwood
1971	Great Britain & Ireland Walker Cup Team	1999	Sergio García
1972	Miss Michelle Walker	2000	Lee Westwood
1973	Peter Oosterhuis	2001	Great Britain & Ireland Walker Cup Team
1974	Peter Oosterhuis	2002	Ernie Els
1975	Golf Foundation	2003	*Not yet decided*
1976	Great Britain & Ireland Eisenhower Trophy Team		

Daily Telegraph Woman Golfer of the Year

1982	Jane Connachan
1983	Jill Thornhill
1984	Gillian Stewart and Claire Waite
1985	Belle Robertson
1986	GB&I Curtis Cup Team
1987	Linda Bayman
1988	GB&I Curtis Cup Team
1989	Helen Dobson
1990	Angela Uzielli
1991	Joanne Morley
1992	GB&I Curtis Cup Team, Captain Liz Boatman
1993	Catriona Lambert and Julie Hall
1994	GB&I Curtis Cup Team, Captain Liz Boatman
1995	Julie Hall
1996	GB&I Curtis Cup Team
1997	Alison Rose
1998	Kim Andrew
1999	Welsh International Team
2000	Rebecca Hudson
2001	Rebecca Hudson
2002	Becky Brewerton
2003	Becky Brewerton

Joyce Wethered Trophy

(Awarded to the outstanding amateur under 25)

1994	Janice Moodie	1999	Becky Brewerton
1995	Rebecca Hudson	2000	Sophie Walker
1996	Mhairi McKay	2001	Clare Queen
1997	Rebecca Hudson	2002	Sarah Jones
1998	Liza Walters	2003	Sophie Walker

LET Players' Player of the Year

1995	Annika Sörenstam (Swe)
1996	Laura Davies (Eng)
1997	Alison Nicholas (Eng)
1998	Sophie Gustafson (Swe)
1999	Laura Davies (Eng)
2000	Sophie Gustafson (Swe)
2001	Raquel Carriedo (Esp)
2002	Annika Sörenstam (Swe)
2003	Sophie Gustafson (Swe)

Evian Tour Order of Merit

1979	Catherine Panton-Lewis (Sco)
1980	Muriel Thomson (Sco)
1981	Jenny Lee-Smith (Eng)
1982	Jenny Lee-Smith (Eng)
1983	Muriel Thomson (Sco)
1984	Dale Reid (Sco)
1985	Laura Davies (Eng)
1986	Laura Davies (Eng)
1987	Dale Reid (Sco)
1988	Marie-Laure Taud (Fra)
1989	Marie-Laure de Laurenzi (Fra)
1990	Trish Johnson (Eng)
1991	Corinne Dibnah (Aus)
1992	Laura Davies (Eng)
1993	Karen Lunn (Aus)
1994	Liselotte Neumann (Swe)
1995	Annika Sörenstam (Swe)
1996	Laura Davies (Eng)
1997	Alison Nicholas (Eng)
1998	Helen Alfredsson (Swe)
1999	Laura Davies (Eng)
2000	Sophie Gustafson (Swe)
2001	Raquel Carriedo (Esp)
2002	Paula Marti (Esp)
2003	Sophie Gustafson (Swe)

Bill Johnson Trophy

Awarded to the Rookie of the Year on the Evian Tour

1984	Katrina Douglas (Eng)
1085	Laura Davies (Eng)
1986	Patricia Gonzales
1987	Trish Johnson (Eng)
1988	Laurette Maritz (USA)
1989	Helen Alfredsson (Swe)
1990	Pearl Sinn (Kor)
1991	Helen Wdsworth (Wal)
1992	Sandrine Mendiburu (Fra)
1993	Annika Sörenstam (Swe)
1994	Tracy Hansen (USA)
1995	Karrie Webb (Aus)
1996	Anne-Marie Knight (Aus)
1997	Anna Berg (Swe)
1998	Laura Philo (USA)
1999	Elaine Ratcliffe (Eng)
2000	Guila Sergas (Ita)
2001	Suzann Pettersen (Nor)
2002	Kirsty S Taylor (Eng)
2003	Rebecca Stevenson (Aus)

Vivien Saunders Trophy

		Scoring average
1991	Alison Nicholas	71.71
1992	Laura Davies	70.35
1993	Laura Davies	71.63
1994	Liselotte Neumann	69.56
1995	Annika Sörenstam	69.75
1996	Marie Laure de Lorenzi	71.39
1997	Marie Laure de Lorenzi	72.20
1998	Laura Davies	71.96
1999	Elaine Ratcliffe	73.76
2000	Laura Davies	70.50
2001	Catriona Mathew	70.08
2002	Sophie Gustafson	70.59
2003	Sophie Gustafson	69.93

US LPGA Louise Suggs Rookie of the Year

1962	Mary Mills	1986	Jody Rosenthal
1963	Clifford Ann Creed	1987	Tammi Green
1964	Susie Berning	1988	Liselotte Neumann (Swi)
1965	Margie Masters		
1966	Jan Ferraris	1989	Pamela Wright (Sco)
1967	Sharron Moran	1990	Hiromi Kobayashi (Jpn)
1968	Sandra Post		
1969	Jane Blalock	1991	Brandie Burton
1970	JoAnne Carner	1992	Helen Alfredsson (Swe)
1971	Sally Little		
1972	Jocelyne Bourassa	1993	Suzanne Strudwick (Eng)
1973	Laura Baugh		
1974	Jan Stephenson	1994	Annika Sörenstam (Swe)
1975	Amy Alcott		
1976	Bonnie Lauer	1995	Pat Hurst
1977	Debbie Massey	1996	Karrie Webb (Aus)
1978	Nancy Lopez	1997	Lisa Hackney (Eng)
1979	Beth Daniel	1998	Se Ri Pak (Kor)
1980	Myra Van Hoose	1999	Mi Hyun Kim (Kor)
1981	Patty Sheehan	2000	Dorothy Delason
1982	Patti Rizzo	2001	Hee Won Han (Kor)
1983	Stephanie Farwig	2002	Beth Bauer
1984	Juli Inkster	2003	Lorena Ochoa (Mex)
1985	Penny Hammel		

US LPGA Rolex Player of the Year

1966	Kathy Whitworth	1985	Nancy Lopez
1967	Kathy Whitworth	1986	Pat Bradley
1968	Kathy Whitworth	1987	Ayako Okamoto
1969	Kathy Whitworth	1988	Nancy Lopez
1970	Sandra Haynie	1989	Betsy King
1971	Kathy Whitworth	1990	Beth Daniel
1972	Kathy Whitworth	1991	Pat Bradley
1973	Kathy Whitworth	1992	Dottie Mochrie
1974	JoAnne Carner	1993	Betsy King
1975	Sandra Palmer	1994	Beth Daniel
1976	Judy Rankin	1995	Annika Sörenstam
1977	Judy Rankin	1996	Laura Davies
1978	Nancy Lopez	1997	Annika Sörenstam
1979	Nancy Lopez	1998	Annika Sörenstam
1980	Beth Daniel	1999	Karrie Webb
1981	Jo Anne Carner	2000	Karrie Webb
1982	Jo Anne Carner	2001	Annika Sörenstam
1983	Patty Sheehan	2002	Beth Bauer
1984	Betsy King	2003	Annika Sörenstam

LPGA Vare Trophy

		Scoring average				Scoring average
1953	Patty Berg	75.00	1979	Nancy Lopez		71.20
1954	Babe Zaharias	75.48	1980	Amy Alcott		71.51
1955	Patty Berg	74.47	1981	Jo Anne Carner		71.75
1956	Patty Berg	74.57	1982	Jo Anne Carner		71.49
1957	Louise Suggs	74.64	1983	Jo Anne Carner		71.41
1958	Beverly Hanson	74.92	1984	Patty Sheehan		71.40
1959	Betsy Rawls	74.03	1985	Nancy Lopez		70.73
1960	Mickey Wright	73.25	1986	Pat Bradley		71.10
1961	Mickey Wright	73.55	1987	Betsy King		71.14
1962	Mickey Wright	73.67	1988	Colleen Walker		71.26
1963	Mickey Wright	72.81	1989	Beth Daniel		70.38
1964	Mickey Wright	72.46	1990	Beth Daniel		70.54
1965	Kathy Whitworth	72.61	1991	Pat Bradley		70.66
1966	Kathy Whitworth	72.60	1992	Dottie Mochrie		70.80
1967	Kathy Whitworth	72.74	1993	Nancy Lopez		70.83
1968	Carol Mann	72.04	1994	Beth Daniel		70.90
1969	Kathy Whitworth	72.38	1995	Annika Sörenstam		71.00
1970	Kathy Whitworth	72.26	1996	Annika Sörenstam		70.47
1971	Kathy Whitworth	72.88	1997	Karrie Webb		70.01
1972	Kathy Whitworth	72.38	1998	Annika Sörenstam		69.99
1973	Judy Rankin	73.08	1999	Karrie Webb		69.43
1974	JoAnne Carner	72.87	2000	Karrie Webb		70.05
1975	JoAnne Carner	72.40	2001	Annika Sörenstam		69.42
1976	Judy Rankin	72.25	2002	Annika Sörenstam		68.70
1977	Judy Rankin	72.16	2003	*Not yet decided but between* Se Ri Pak (Kor)		
1978	Nancy Lopez	71.76		*and* Grace Park (Kor)		

Arnold Palmer Award

(Awarded to the US PGA Tour leading money-winner)

1981	Tom Kite	1993	Nick Price
1982	Craig Stadler	1994	Nick Price
1983	Hal Sutton	1995	Greg Norman
1984	Tom Watson	1996	Tom Lehman
1985	Curtis Strange	1997	Tiger Woods
1986	Greg Norman	1998	David Duval
1987	Paul Azinger	1999	Tiger Woods
1988	Curtis Strange	2000	Tiger Woods
1989	Tom Kite	2001	Tiger Woods
1990	Greg Norman	2002	Tiger Woods
1991	Corey Pavin	2003	Vijay Singh
1992	Fred Couples		

Payne Stewart Award

(presented to the player who respects and upholds the traditions of the game)

2000	Byron Nelson, Jack Nicklaus, Arnold Palmer
2001	Ben Crenshaw
2002	Nick Price
2003	Tom Watson

Jack Nicklaus Award

(US PGA Tour Player of the Year – decided by player ballot)

1990	Wayne Levi	1997	Tiger Woods
1991	Fred Couples	1998	Mark O'Meara
1992	Fred Couples	1999	Tiger Woods
1993	Nick Price	2000	Tiger Woods
1994	Nick Price	2001	Tiger Woods
1995	Greg Norman	2002	Tiger Woods
1996	Tom Lehman	2003	*Not yet decided*

First Lady of Golf Award

(PGA award for women who have made a significant contribution to the game)

1998	Barbara Nicklaus
1999	Judy Rankin
2000	*No award given*
2001	Judy Bell
2002	Nancy Lopez
2003	Renee Powell

The US Vardon Trophy (The award is made by the PGA of America to the member of the US Tour who completes 60 rounds or more, with the lowest scoring average over the calendar year)

1937	Harry Cooper		1962	Arnold Palmer	70.27	1983	Ray Floyd	70.61
1938	Sam Snead		1963	Billy Casper	70.58	1984	Calvin Peete	70.56
1939	Byron Nelson		1964	Arnold Palmer	70.01	1985	Don Pooley	70.36
1940	Ben Hogan		1965	Billy Casper	70.85	1986	Scott Hoch	70.08
1941	Ben Hogan		1966	Billy Casper	70.27	1987	Dan Pohl	70.25
1942–46	No Awards – World War II		1967	Arnold Palmer	70.18	1988	Chip Beck	69.46
1947	Jimmy Demarel	69.90	1968	Billy Casper	69.82	1989	Greg Norman	69.49
1948	Ben Hogan	69.30	1969	Dave Hill	70.34	1990	Greg Norman	69.10
1949	Sam Snead	69.37	1970	Lee Trevino	70.64	1991	Fred Couples	69.59
1950	Sam Snead	69.23	1971	Lee Trevino	70.27	1992	Fred Couples	69.38
1951	Lloyd Mangrum	70.05	1972	Lee Trevino	70.89	1993	Nick Price	69.11
1952	Jack Burke	70.54	1973	Bruce Crampton	70.57	1994	Greg Norman	69.81
1953	Lloyd Mangrum	70.22	1974	Lee Trevino	70.53	1995	Steve Elkington	69.82
1954	Ed Harrison	70.41	1975	Bruce Crampton	70.51	1996	Tom Lehman	69.32
1955	Sam Snead	69.86	1976	Don January	70.56	1997	Nick Price	68.98
1956	Cary Middlecoff	70.35	1977	Tom Watson	70.32	1998	David Duval	69.13
1957	Dow Finsterwald	70.30	1978	Tom Watson	70.16	1999	Tiger Woods	68.43
1958	Bob Rosburg	70.11	1979	Tom Watson	70.27	2000	Tiger Woods	67.79
1959	Art Wall	70.35	1980	Lee Trevino	69.73	2001	Tiger Woods	68.81
1960	Billy Casper	69.95	1981	Tom Kite	69.80	2002	Tiger Woods	68.56
1961	Arnold Palmer	69.85	1982	Tom Kite	70.21	2003	Tiger Woods	68.41

US PGA Player of the Year
(Decided on merit points)

1948	Ben Hogan	1976	Jack Nicklaus
1949	Sam Snead	1977	Tom Watson
1950	Ben Hogan	1978	Tom Watson
1951	Ben Hogan	1979	Tom Watson
1952	Julius Boros	1980	Tom Watson
1953	Ben Hogan	1981	Bill Rogers
1954	Ed Furgol	1982	Tom Watson
1955	Doug Ford	1983	Hal Sutton
1956	Jack Burke	1984	Tom Watson
1957	Dick Mayer	1985	Lanny Wadkins
1958	Dow Finsterwald	1986	Bob Tway
1959	Art Wall	1987	Paul Azinger
1960	Arnold Palmer	1988	Curtis Strange
1961	Jerry Barner	1989	Tom Kite
1962	Arnold Palmer	1990	Nick Faldo
1963	Julius Boros	1991	Corey Pavin
1964	Ken Venturi	1992	Fred Couples
1965	Dave Marr	1993	Nick Price
1966	Billy Casper	1994	Nick Price
1967	Jack Nicklaus	1995	Greg Norman
1968	not awarded	1996	Tom Lehman
1969	Orville Moody	1997	Tiger Woods
1970	Billy Casper	1998	Mark O'Meara
1971	Lee Trevino	1999	Tiger Woods
1972	Jack Nicklaus	2000	Tiger Woods
1973	Jack Nicklaus	2001	Tiger Woods
1974	Johnny Miller	2002	Tiger Woods
1975	Jack Nicklaus	2003	Tiger Woods

US PGA Tour Rookie of the Year

1990	Robert Gamez	1997	Stewart Cink
1991	John Daly	1998	Steve Flesch
1992	Mark Carnevale	1999	Carlos Franco
1993	Vijay Singh	2000	Michael Clark II
1994	Ernie Els	2001	Charles Howell III
1995	Woody Austin	2002	Jonathan Byrd
1996	Tiger Woods	2003	Not yet decided

Sir Henry Cotton European Rookie of the Year

1960	Tommy Goodwin	1983	Grant Turner
1961	Alex Caygill	1984	Philip Parkin
1962	No Award	1985	Paul Thomas
1963	Tony Jacklin	1986	José Maria Olazàbal
1964	No Award	1987	Peter Baker
1966	Robin Liddle	1988	Colin Montgomerie
1967	No Award	1989	Paul Broadhurst
1968	Bernard Gallacher	1990	Russell Claydon
1969	Peter Oosterhuis	1991	Per-Ulrik Johansson
1970	Stuart Brown	1992	Jim Payne
1971	David Llewellyn	1993	Gary Orr
1972	Sam Torrance	1994	Jonathan Lomas
1973	Philip Elson	1995	Jarmo Sandelin
1974	Carl Mason	1996	Thomas Bjorn
1975	No Award	1997	Scott Henderson
1976	Mark James	1998	Olivier Edmond
1977	Nick Faldo	1999	Sergio García
1978	Sandy Lyle	2000	Ian Poulter
1979	Mike Miller	2001	Paul Casey
1980	Paul Hoad	2002	Nick Dougherty
1981	Jeremy Bennett	2003	Peter Lawrie
1982	Gordon Brand Jr		

Harry Vardon Trophy (Awarded to the PGA member heading the Order of Merit at the end of the season)

1937	Charles Whitcombe	1963	Neil Coles	1984	Bernhard Langer
1938	Henry Cotton	1964	Peter Alliss	1985	Sandy Lyle
1939	Roger Whitcombe	1965	Bernard Hunt	1986	Severiano Ballesteros
1940–45	*In abeyance*	1966	Peter Alliss	1987	Ian Woosnam
1946	Bobby Locke	1967	Malcolm Gregson	1988	Severiano Ballesteros
1947	Norman Von Nida	1968	Brian Huggett	1989	Ronan Rafferty
1948	Charlie Ward	1969	Bernard Gallacher	1990	Ian Woosnam
1949	Charlie Ward	1970	Neil Coles	1991	Severiano Ballesteros
1950	Bobby Locke	1971	Peter Oosterhuis	1992	Nick Faldo
1951	John Panton	1972	Peter Oosterhuis	1993	Colin Montgomerie
1952	Harry Weetman	1973	Peter Oosterhuis	1994	Colin Montgomerie
1953	Flory van Donck	1974	Peter Oosterhuis	1995	Colin Montgomerie
1954	Bobby Locke	1975	Dale Hayes	1996	Colin Montgomerie
1955	Dai Rees	1976	Severiano Ballesteros	1997	Colin Montgomerie
1956	Harry Weetman	1977	Severiano Ballesteros	1998	Colin Montgomerie
1957	Eric Brown	1978	Severiano Ballesteros	1999	Colin Montgomerie
1958	Bernard Hunt	1979	Sandy Lyle	2000	Lee Westwood
1959	Dai Rees	1980	Sandy Lyle	2001	Retief Goosen
1960	Bernard Hunt	1981	Bernhard Langer	2002	Retief Goosen
1961	Christy O'Connor	1982	Greg Norman	2003	Ernie Els
1962	Christy O'Connor	1983	Nick Faldo		

Bobby Jones Award

(Awarded by USGA for distinguished sportsmanship in golf)

1955	Francis Ouimet	1972	Michael Bonallack	1989	Chi-Chi Rodriquez
1956	Bill Campbell	1973	Gene Littler	1990	Peggy Kirk Bell
1957	Babe Zaharias	1974	Byron Nelson	1991	Ben Grenshaw
1958	Margaret Curtis	1975	Jack Nicklaus	1992	Gene Sarazen
1959	Findlay Douglas	1976	Ben Hogan	1993	PJ Boatwright Jr
1960	Charles Evans Jr	1977	Joseph C Dey	1994	Lewis Oehmig
1961	Joe Carr	1978	Bob Hope and Bing Crosby	1995	Herbert Warren Wind
1962	Horton-Smith	1979	Tom Kite	1996	Betsy Rawls
1963	Patty Berg	1980	Charles Yates	1997	Fred Brand
1964	Charles Coe	1981	JoAnne Carner	1998	Nancy Lopez
1965	Mrs Edwin Vare	1982	Billy Joe Patton	1999	Ed Updegraff
1966	Gary Player	1983	Maureen Garrett	2000	Barbara McIntyre
1967	Richard Tufts	1984	Jay Sigel	2001	Thomas Cousins
1968	Robert Dickson	1985	Fuzzy Zoeller	2002	Judy Rankin
1969	Gerald Micklem	1986	Jess W Sweetser	2003	Carol Semple Thompson
1970	Roberto De Vicenzo	1987	Tom Watson		
1971	Arnold Palmer	1988	Isaac B Grainger		

PGA of America Distinguished Service Award

1988	Herb Graffis	1992	Gene Sarazen	1996	Frank Chirkinian	2000	Jack Nicklaus
1989	Bob Hope	1993	Byron Nelson	1997	George Bush	2001	Mark McCormack
1990	*No award*	1994	Arnold Palmer	1998	Paul Runyan	2002	Tim Finchem
1991	Gerald Ford	1995	Patty Berg	1999	Bill Dickey	2003	Vince Gill

US PGA Tour Dates 2004

Jan 5–11	Mercedes Championships, Plantation Course at Kapalua, Kapalua, HI
Jan 12–18	Sony Open in Hawaii, Waialae Country Club, Honolulu, HI
Jan 19–25	Bob Hope Chrysler Classic, Bermuda Dunes, La Quinta, CA
Jan 26–Feb 1	FBR Open, Tournament Players Club of Scottsdale, Scottsdale, AZ
Feb 2–8	AT&T Pebble Beach National Pro-Am, Pebble Beach Golf Links, Pebble Beach, CA
Feb 9–15	Buick Invitational, Torrey Pines Golf Course, San Diego, CA
Feb 16–22	Nissan Open, Riviera Country Club, Pacific Palisades, CA
Feb 23–29	WGC–Accenture Match Play Championship, La Costa Resort and Spa, Carlsbad, CA
	Chrysler Classic of Tucson, Omni Tucson National Golf Resort and Spa, Tucson, AZ
Mar 1–7	Ford Championship at Doral, Doral Golf Resort and Spa, Miami, FL
Mar 8–14	The Honda Classic, Country Club at Mirasol, Palm Beach Gardens, FL
Mar 15–21	Bay Hill Invitational Presented by MasterCard, Bay Hill Golf Club and Lodge, Orlando, FL
Mar 22–28	THE PLAYERS Championship, Tournament Players Club at Sawgrass, Ponte Vedra Beach, FL
Mar 29–4	BellSouth Classic, Tournament Players Club at Sugarloaf, Duluth, GA
Apr 5–11	The Masters, Augusta National Golf Club, Augusta, GA
Apr 12–18	MCI Heritage, Harbour Town Golf Links, Hilton Head Island, SC
Apr 19–25	Shell Houston Ope, Redstone Golf Club, Houston, TX
Apr 26–May 2	HP Classic of New Orleans, English Turn Golf and Country Club, New Orleans, LA
May 3–9	Wachovia Championship, Quail Hollow Club, Charlotte, NC
May 10–16	EDS Byron Nelson Championship, TPC at Four Seasons Resort and Cottonwood Valley, Irving, TX
May 17–23	Bank of America Colonia, Colonial Country Club, Fort Worth, TX
May 24–30	FedEx St. Jude Classic, Tournament Players Club at Southwind, Memphis, TN
May 31–June 6	The Memorial Tournament, Muirfield Village Golf Club, Dublin, OH
June 7–13	Buick Classic, Westchester Country Club, Harrison, NY
June 14–20	U.S. Ope, Shinnecock Hills Golf Club, Southampton, NY
June 21–27	Booz Allen Classic, Tournament Players Club at Avenel, Potomac, MD
June 28–July 4	Western Open, Cog Hill Golf and Country Club, Lemont, IL
July 5–11	John Deere Classic, Tournament Players Club at Deere Run, Silvis, IL
July 12–18	British Open, Royal Troon Golf Club, Royal Troon, Scotland
	B.C. Open, En Joie Golf Club, Endicott, NY
July 19–25	Greater Milwaukee Ope, Brown Deer Park Golf Course, Milwaukee, WI
July 26–Aug 1	Buick Open, Warwick Hills Golf and Country Club, Grand Blanc, MI
Aug 2–8	The INTERNATIONAL, Castle Pines Golf Club, Castle Rock, CO
Aug 9–15	PGA Championship, Whistling Straits, Kohler, WI
Aug 16–22	WGC–NEC Invitational, Firestone Country Club, Akron, OH
	Reno Tahoe Open, Montreux Golf and Country Club, Reno, NV
Aug 23–29	Buick Championship, Tournament Players Club at River Highlands, Cromwell, CT
Aug 30–Sep 6	Deutsche Bank Championship, Tournament Players Club of Boston, Norton, MA
Sep 6–12	Bell Canadian Open, Glen Abbey Golf Club, Oakville, ON, Canada
Sep 13–19	Valero Texas Open, LaCantera Golf Club, San Antonio, TX
Sep 17–19	Ryder Cup, Oakland Hills Country Club, Detroit, MI
Sep 20–26 84	Lumber Classic of Pennsylvania, Nemacolin Woodlands Resort & Spa, Farmington, PA
Sep 27–Oct 3	WGC–American Express Championship, Mount Juliet Estate, Co. Kilkenny, Ireland
	Southern Farm Bureau Classic, Annandale Golf Club, Madison, MS
Oct 4–10	TBD
Oct 11–17	Chrysler Classic of Greensboro, Forest Oaks Country Club, Greensboro, NC
Oct 18–24	FUNAI Classic, Walt Disney World Resort, Lake Buena Vista, FL
Oct 25–31	Chrysler Championship, Westin Innisbrook Resort, Palm Harbor, FL
Nov1–7	THE TOUR Championship, East Lake Golf Club, Atlanta, GA

PART VIII

Who's Who
in Golf

British, Irish and Continental Players, Men	370
British, Irish and Continental Players, Women	382
Overseas Players, Men	387
Overseas Players, Women	403
British Isles International Players, Professional Men	407
British Isles International Players, Professional Women	412
British Isles International Players, Amateur Men	413
British Isles International Players, Amateur Women	427

British, Irish and Continental Players, Men

Alliss, Peter (Eng)
Born Berlin, 28 February 1931
Turned professional 1946
Following a distinguished career as a tournament golfer in which he won 18 titles between 1954 and 1966 and played eight times in the Ryder Cup between 1953 and 1969, he turned to golf commentating. In Britain he works for the BBC and in America for the ABC network. Twice captain of the PGA in 1962 and 1987 he won the Spanish, Italian and Portuguese Opens in 1958. Author or co-author of several golf books and a novel with a golfing background, he has also designed several courses including the Brabazon course at The Belfry in association with Dave Thomas. In 2003 he was awarded Life Membership of the PGA in honour of his lifelong contribution and commitment to the game.

Baker, Peter (Eng)
Born Shifnal, Shropshire, 7 October 1967
Rookie of the year in 1987, Peter was hailed as the best young newcomer by Nick Faldo when he beat Faldo in a play-off for the Benson and Hedges International in 1988. Several times a winner since then he played in the 1993 Ryder Cup scoring three points out of four. In the singles he beat Corey Pavin.

Ballesteros, Severiano (Esp)
Born Pedrena, 9 April 1957
Turned professional 1974
Charismatic Spaniard who won 52 titles between 1976 and 1999 including three Opens (1979, 1984 at St Andrews and 1988) and The Masters at Augusta in 1980 and again in 1983. One of four brothers all of whom play golf. He was introduced to the game by big brother Manuel and first hit the headlines when he and Jack Nicklaus finished second to Johnny Miller at Royal Birkdale in 1976. He played in eight Ryder Cups and captained the side to victory at Valderrama in 2000. Never one of golf's straightest hitters his powers of recovery from seemingly impossible positions have been legendary throughout his career. He was the driving force in getting a match started between the British and Irish golfers and the Continentals in 2000. They now play annually for the Seve Trophy. Sadly has lost his game but not his hope that one day it will return.

Barnes, Brian (Sco)
Born Addington, Surrey, 3 June 1945
Turned professional 1964
Extrovert Scottish professional whose father-in-law is former Open champion Max Faulkner. He was a ten times winner on the European Tour between 1972 and 1981 and was twice British Seniors champion successfully defending the title in 1996. He played in six Ryder Cup matches most notably at Laurel Valley in 1975 when, having beaten Jack Nicklaus in the morning, he beat him again in the afternoon. Now prevented from continuing to play on the US Senior Tour because of rheumatoid arthritis he is expanding his career as a commentator.

Beharrell, John Charles (Eng)
Born Birmingham, 14 January 1935
Youngest winner of the Amateur Championship when he took the title at Troon (now Royal Troon) in 1956. Held the post of captain of the Royal and Ancient Golf Club of St Andrews in 1998/99. Married Veronica Anstey, former Curtis Cup player, Australian and New Zealand Ladies champion.

Benka, Peter (Eng)
Born London, 18 September 1946
Former Walker Cup player who won the British Youths Championship in 1967 and 1968. Now chairman of the R&A Selection Committee.

Bennett, Warren (Eng)
Born Ruislip, 20 August 1971
Turned professional 1994
Leading amateur in the 1994 Open Championship and winner of the Australian Centennial Amateur Championship the same year. A former British Youths champion, Bennett won the 1999 Scottish PGA Championship but his career has been dogged by injury.

Bjørn, Thomas (Den)
Born Silkeborg, 18 February 1971
Turned professional 1993
A former Danish Amateur champion in 1990 and 1991, he became the first Dane to play in the Ryder Cup when he made the team in 1997. Four down after four holes against Justin Leonard in the last day singles at

Valderrama he fought back to halve the match and gain a valuable half-point in the European victory. He missed out on the 1999 match because of injury but was in the 2001 side and beat Stewart Cink in the singles. Won four times in the Challenge Tour before gaining his full European card. He came joint second to Tiger Woods in the 2000 Open at St Andrews just a few weeks after finishing third behind Woods in the US Open at Pebble Beach. In Japan in 1999 he beat Sergio García at the fourth hole of a play-off for the Dunlop Phoenix title. In 2001 he beat Tiger Woods in the Dubai Desert Classic. He looked set to win the 2003 Open at Royal St George's when three shots clear with four to play but took 3 to get out of a bunker at the short sixteenth and lost to Ben Curtis, the American playing in his first Open. A week later Bjørn lost a play-off to Michael Campbell in the Nissan Irish Open at Portmarnock. He remains one of Europe's most talented players who is expected to win a Major in the next year or so.

Bonallack Kt OBE, Sir Michael (Eng)
Born Chigwell, Essex, 31 December 1934
One of only three golfing knights (the others are the late Sir Henry Cotton and Sir Bob Charles) he won the Amateur Championship five times between 1961 and 1970 and was five times English champion between 1962 and 1968. He also won the English stroke play title four times and was twice leading amateur in the Open in 1968 and 1971. In his hugely impressive career he played in nine Walker Cup matches captaining the side on two occasions. He participated in five Eisenhower Trophy matches and five Commonwealth team competitions. He scored his first national title win in the 1952 British Boys' Championship and took his Essex County title 11 times between 1954 and 1972. After serving as secretary of the R&A from 1983 to 1999 he was captain in 1999/2000. Twice winner of the Association of Golf Writers' award in 1968 and 1999, he also received the Bobby Jones award in 1972, the Donald Ross and Gerald Micklem awards in 1991 and the Ambassador of Golf award in 1995. In 2000 he was inducted into the World Hall Golf of Fame. A former chairman of the R&A selection committee, he served as chairman of the PGA from 1976 to 1981 and is now a non-executive director of the PGA European Tour. He was chairman of the Golf Foundation in 1977 and president of the English Golf Union in 1982. His wife Lady Angela is the former English champion Angela Ward.

Brown, Ken (Sco)
Born Harpenden, Hertfordshire, 9 January 1957
Turned professional 1974
Renowned as a great short game exponent, especially with his hickory-shafted putter, he won four times in Europe between 1978 and 85, and took the Southern Open on the US tour in 1987. He played in two winning Ryder Cup sides in 1985 and 1987 having previously played in the 1977, 1979 and 1983 matches. Latterly he has carved out a new career for himself as a television commentator working closely with Peter Alliss on the BBC team.

Canizares, José Maria (Esp)
Born Madrid, 18 February 1947
Turned professional 1967
A seven-time winner on the European Tour between 1972 and 1992 the popular Spaniard now plays full time on the US Senior Tour where he has won over $5 million from 164 starts through to the end of the 2002 season. A former caddie, he played in four Ryder Cup matches in the 80s winning five and halving two of his 11 games.

Carr, Joe (Ire)
Born Dublin, 18 February 1922
Winner of the Amateur Championship in 1953, 1958 and 1960, he is Ireland's most successful post-war amateur golfer. Between 1954 and 1967 he won six Irish championships, and was Irish Open Amateur champion four times between 1946 and 1956. He won the south of Ireland Open Amateur Championship three times, but took the East of Ireland title and West of Ireland title twelve times each. He played in ten Walker cups and captained the side twice. He was leading amateur in the Open in 1956 and 1958, was awarded the Association of Golf Writers' Trophy in 1953 and was presented with the Bobby Jones Award in 1961 and the Walter Hagen Award in 1967. He captained the R&A in 1991/92.

Casey, Paul (Eng)
Born Cheltenham, 21 July 1977
Turned professional 2001
Winner of the English Amateur Championship in 1999 and 2000, he attended Arizona State University where he was a three time All American in NCAA Golf. While at college he broke records set by Phil Mickelson and Tiger Woods. In the 1999 Walker Cup match, which the Great Britain and Ireland side won at Nairn, he won all of his four games. After turning professional he earned his European Tour card after just five events helped by a second-equal finish in the Great North Open 2001 and twelfth place finishes in the Compass English Open and Benson and Hedges International. He became a winner in his 11th event when taking the Gleneagles Scottish PGA title over the PGA Centenary course. His coach is Peter Kostis. In 2002 he shot a course record 62 at Gut Lärchenhof in the Linde German Masters won by Stephen Leaney. In the early part of the 2003 European season he won the ANZ Championship in Sydney and the last Benson and Hedges International at The Belfry.

Chapman, Roger (Eng)
Born Nakuru, Kenya, 1 May 1959
Turned professional 1981
After playing on the European Tour for eighteen years without success, he lost his card and had to return to the qualifying school in 1999. Regaining his playing privileges with a twelfth place finish in the six round competition, he made his break-through win by beating Padraig Harrington at the second hole of a play-off in the Brazil Rio de Janeiro Five Hundred Years Open. Later that year he won the Hassan II Trophy at Dar-Es-Salaam in Morocco. A former English Amateur Champion in 1981 he played in the Walker Cup the same year beating Hal Sutton twice in a day at Cypress Point.

Clark, Clive (Eng)
Born Winchester, 27 June 1945
Turned professional 1965
In the 1965 Walker Cup at Five Farms East in Maryland, he holed a 35-foot putt to earn a half point against Mark Hopkins and ensure a drawn match against the Americans. After turning professional he played in the 1973 Ryder Cup and was a four time winner of titles between 1966 and 1974. Following a career as commentator with the BBC he continued his golf course architecture work in America, and has received awards for his innovative designs.

Clark, Howard (Eng)
Born Leeds, 26 August 1954
Turned professional 1973
A scratch player by the age of 16 he turned professional after playing in the 1973 Walker Cup. An eleven-time winner on the European tour he played in six Ryder Cups and was in the winning team three times – in 1985 at The Belfry, 1987 at Muirfield Village, when the Europeans won for the first time on American soil, and in 1995 when he gained a vital point helped by a hole in one in the last day singles against Peter Jacobsen. In the 1985 World Cup played at La Quinta in Palm Springs he was the individual champion. He played 494 tournaments before giving up full-time competition to concentrate on his job as a golf analyst on the Sky TV commentary team.

Clarke, Darren (NI)
Born Dungannon, Northern Ireland, 14 August 1968
Turned professional 1990
He became the first European Tour player to shoot 60 twice when he returned that record low score at the European Open at the K Club in 1999. Seven years earlier he had shot a nine under par 60 at Mont Agel in the European Monte Carlo Open, but his 60 in Dublin was 12 under par. With his second 60 he also equalled two other records. With twelve birdies on the card he matched the best birdie total in a round and he also scored a record-equalling eight birdies in a row. Tied second in the 1997 Open behind Justin Leonard and third equal in 2001 at Lytham, Clarke played particularly well in the 2000 Andersen Consulting Match Play Championship at La Costa in California beating Paul Azinger, Mark O'Meara, Thomas Bjørn, Hal Sutton and David Duval to reach the final against Tiger Woods. He became the first European to win a World Golf Championship event when he beat Woods 4 and 3 and picked up the million dollar first prize. He took a second World Championship event in 2003 when he was an impressive winner of the NEC Invitational at Firestone. He will take up his US Tour card option and play 16 or 17 events in America in 2004. He played in the 1997, 1999 and 2001 Ryder Cup matches making a vital half point on the final day with David Duval in the 2001 match.

Coles MBE, Neil (Eng)
Born 26 September 1934
Turned professional 1950
Remarkably he has won golf tournaments in six decades and who is to say he will not win in seven decades. He turns 70 in September. In 2003 he did not win but in the Travis Perkins event at Wentworth's Edinburgh Course which he helped design he shot a 64 – great golf for a man who has been a prof for 54 years. In 1956 he won the Gor-Ray tournament and made golfing history when he took the Microlease Jersey Seniors Open at La Moye in 2000. From 1973 to 1979 he played in 68 events on the main European Tour without missing a half-way cut and became the then oldest winner when he won the Sanyo Open in Barcelona in 1982 at the age of 48 years and 14 days. (Des Smyth has since become an even older winner.) Coles remains, however, the oldest winner on the European Senior tour scoring his Jersey win when aged 65 years and 10 months and the following year won the Lawrence Batley Seniors Open at Huddersfield. A member of eight Ryder Cup teams, he has represented his country nineteen times since turning professional at the age of sixteen with a handicap of 14. He has been chairman of the PGA European Tour's Board of Directors since its inception in 1971 and in 2000 was inducted into the World Golf Hall of Fame. Internationally respected he might well have won more in America but for an aversion to flying caused by a bad experience on an internal flight from Edinburgh to London.

Coltart, Andrew (Sco)
Born Dumfries, 12 May 1970
Turned professional 1991
Twice Australian PGA champion in 1994 and 1997 he was the Australasian circuit's top money earner for the 1997/98 season. He made his Ryder Cup debut at Brookline in 1999 as a captain's pick and on the final day found himself up against Tiger Woods. He played well but still lost. A former Walker Cup and Eisenhower Trophy player he was a member of the only Scottish team to win the Alfred Dunhill Cup at St Andrews in 1995. His European Tour successes include the 1998 Qatar Masters and 2001 Great North Open. His sister Laurae is married to fellow professional Lee Westwood.

Darcy, Eamonn (Ire)
Born Dalgeny, 7 August 1952
Turned professional 1969
One of Ireland's best known players who has played more than 600 tournament appearances on the European Tour despite suffering for many years with back trouble. First played when he was 10 years old and is renowned for his very distinctive swing incorporating a flying right elbow. He played in four Ryder Cups including the memorable one at Muirfield Village in 1987 when Europe won for the first time in America. He scored a vital point in the last day singles holing a tricky left to right downhill seven footer for a valuable point against Ben Crenshaw. In 2002 he joined the European Senior Tour. A year later he earned his card for the US Senior Tour – the Champions Tour.

Donald, Luke (Eng)
Born Hemel Hempstead, Hertfordshire, 7 December 1977
Turned professional 2001
Member of the winning Great Britain and Ireland team against the Americans in the 1999 Walker Cup at Nairn

and again in 2001 before turning professional. In 1999 won the NCAA Championship and was named NCAA Player of the Year. Has played most of his golf in 2002 in America and he scored his first win on the US Tour when he took the rain-shortened Southern Farms Bureau title, becoming the 18th first-time winner of the season. He continued to make steady progress in 2003.

Drew, Norman (NI)
Born Belfast, 25 May 1932
Turned professional 1958
Twice Irish Open Amateur champion in 1952 and 1953 he played in the 1953 Walker Cup and six years later represented Great Britain and Ireland in the Ryder Cup.

Edwards, Nigel (Wal)
Born Caerphilly
Top scoring member of the winning Walker Cup sides in 2001 and 2003. Last year at Ganton he teamed up with fellow countryman Nigel Manley to score 1½ points in the Fourballs, beat George Zahringer in the first day singles and halved with Lee Williams on day two holing from 30 yards with the putter at the 17th to ensure victory.

Faldo MBE, Nick (Eng)
Born Welwyn Garden City, 18 July 1957
Turned professional 1976
Decided to turn professional after watching the US Masters on television and being impressed by Jack Nicklaus's performance. Europe's most successful major title winner having won three Open Championships in 1987, 1990 at St Andrews and 1992 and three Masters titles in 1989, 1990 and 1996. Of current day players only Tom Watson with eight wins has won more majors. When he successfully defended the Masters in 1990 he became only the second man (after Nicklaus) to win in successive years. Staged a dramatic last day revival to win the 1996 Masters having started the last round six behind Greg Norman. When he realised his swing was not good enough to win majors he completely revamped it with the help of coach David Leadbetter. His 31 European Tour victories include a record three Irish Open victories in a row. In 1992 became the first player to win over £1 million in prize-money during a season. He played with distinction in 11 Ryder Cup matches including the winning teams in 1985, 1987, 1995 and 1997. He holds the record for most games played in the Cup – 46 – and most points won – 25. In 1995 at Oak Hill came from behind to score a vital last day point against Curtis Strange, the American who had beaten him in a play-off for the US Open title in 1988 at The Country Club in Boston. He became the first international player to be named USPGA Player of the Year in 1990 and led the official World Golf Rankings for 81 weeks in 1993-1994. After having teamed up with Swedish caddie Fanny Sunesson for ten years they split only to be reunited as one of golf's best-known partnerships in 2001. He has indicated that he would love to play in his 12th Ryder Cup this year.

Fasth, Niclas (Swe)
Born Gothenburg, Sweden, 29 April 1972
Turned professional 1989
The studious-looking Swede tried to play both US and European tours in 1998 but found it too difficult. Made the headlines in 2001 when finishing second to David Duval in the Open. Played in the 2002 Ryder Cup side and made a half point against Paul Azinger on the final day.

Faulkner OBE, Max (Eng)
Born Bexhill, Sussex, 29 July 1916
Turned professional 1933
One of the game's most extrovert and colourful characters who played in five Ryder Cups but whose career highlight was winning the Open at Royal in 1951. After having been ignored for an honour for 50 years he was deservedly recognised in 2001 when awarded an OBE. He is father-in-law of Brian Barnes.

Feherty, David (NI)
Born Bangor, Northern Ireland, 13 August 1958
Turned professional 1976
Quick-witted Ulsterman who gave up his competitive golfing career to become a hugely successful commentator for CBS in America where his one-liners are legendary. Had five European title wins and three victories on the South African circuit before switching his golf clubs for a more lucrative career with a microphone.

Fiddian, Eric Westwood (Eng)
Born Stourbridge, Worcestershire, 28 March 1910
Best remembered for having had two holes in one during the final of the 1933 Irish Open Amateur Championship but still lost by 3 and 2 to J. McLean.

Foster, Rodney (Eng)
Born Shipley, Yorkshire, 13 October 1941
Played in the Walker Cup five times between 1965 and 1973 and captained the side in 1979. He also captained the Eisenhower Trophy team in 1980.

Fulke, Pierre (Swe)
Born Nyköping, Sweden, 21 February 1971
Turned professional 1993
Son of a Swedish swimming champion he finished runner-up to Steve Stricker in the 2001 Accenture Matchplay Championship a few weeks after winning the Volvo Masters. Played on the 2002 winning Ryder Cup side.

Gallacher CBE, Bernard (Sco)
Born Bathgate, Scotland, 9 February 1949
Turned professional 1967
For many years combined tournament golf with the club professional's post at Wentworth where he was honoured in 2000 by being appointed captain. He took up golf at the age of 11 and nine years later was European No.1. He has scored 30 victories worldwide. Gallacher was the youngest Ryder Cup player when he

made his début in the 1969 match in which he beat Lee Trevino in the singles. He played in eight Cup matches and captained the side three times losing narrowly in 1991 at Kiawah Island and 1993 at The Belfry before leading the team to success at Oak Hill in 1995. He is a member of the European Tour's Board of Directors. Now plays on the European Senior Tour and made his break-through win in 2002 when he took first prize in the Mobile Cup at Stoke Park. In 2003 was granted honorary membership of the European Tour but missed much of the season through injury.

García, Sergio (Esp)
Born Castellon, 9 January 1980
Turned professional 1999
The extrovert Spaniard having won the French and Amateur Championships in 1997 took the British title in 1998 and in both years was European Amateur Masters champion. Son of a greenkeeper/professional who now plays on the European Senior Tour, Sergio's future was always going to be in professional golf but he waited until after the 1999 Masters in which he was leading amateur before joining the paid ranks at the Spanish Open. Although only just starting to collect Ryder Cup points he easily made the 1999 team and formed an invaluable partnership with Jesper Parnevik at Brookline scoring three and a half points out of four on the first two days. Victories in the Murphy's Irish Open and Linde German Masters helped him to the 1999 Rookie of the Year title in Europe but arguably an even better performance was finishing runner-up to Tiger Woods in the US PGA Championship at Medinah outside Chicago. Although he did not win in 2000 he won the Mastercard Colonial and Buick Classic on the US Tour in 2001 and the Mercedes Championship, the Canaries Open de España and the Kolon Cup in Korea. He was in the 2002 Ryder Cup team and formed a useful partnership with Lee Westwood winning 3 out of 4 points on the first two days. He continues to play on both sides of the Atlantic.

Garrido, Ignacio (Esp)
Born Madrid, 27 March 1972
Turned professional 1993
Eldest son of Antonio Garrido who played in the 1979 Ryder Cup, Ignacio emulated his father when he made the team at the 1997 match at Valderrama having earlier that year won the Volvo German Open. In 2003 he had his most impressive win when beating Trevor Immelman in a play-off for the Volvo PGA Championship at Wentworth. Before turning professional with a handicap of 4 he won the English Amateur Stroke Play title (the Brabazon Trophy) in 1992. In the 80s used to caddie for his father who has since caddied for him on occasion.

Glover, John (NI)
Born Belfast, 3 March 1933
He was secretary of the R&A Rules of Golf committee from 1980 until his retirement in 1995. He played eight times for Ireland between 1951 and 1970.

Green OBE, Charlie (Sco)
Born Dumbarton, 2 August 1932
One of Scotland's most successful amateur golfers who was leading amateur in the 1962 Open Championship. A prolific winner he took the Scottish Amateur title three times in 1970, 1982 and 1983. He played in five and was non-playing captain in two more Walker Cups and was awarded the Frank Moran Trophy for his services to Scottish sport in 1974.

Haeggman, Joakim (Swe)
Born Kalmar, 28 August 1969
Turned professional 1989
Became the first Swedish player to play in the Ryder Cup when he made the side which lost to the Americans at The Belfry in 1993. He received one of team captain Bernard Gallacher's 'wild cards' and beat John Cook in his last day singles. Gave up ice hockey after dislocating his shoulder and breaking ribs in 1994. Realised then that ice hockey and golf do not mix but has become an enthusiastic angler when not on the links. Equalled the world record of 27 for the first nine holes in the Alfred Dunhill Cup over the Old course at St Andrews in 1997. Occasionally acts as commentator for Swedish TV and was a member of Sam Torrance's Ryder Cup back-room team at The Belfry in 2002.

Harrington, Padraig (Ire)
Born Dublin, Ireland, 31 August 1971
Turned professional 1995
A qualified accountant, he was Irish Open and Close Amateur champion (1995) and played three times in the Walker Cup player before turning professional. Played in the 1999 Ryder Cup at Brookline and beat Mark O'Meara in the singles. He was a member of the victorious European team for the postponed 2001 match beating Mark Calcavecchia in the final day singles. Remembered in 2000 for being disqualified on the final day of the Benson and Hedges International at The Belfry after having moved into a five shot lead at the 54-hole stage. It was only then discovered that one of his playing partners had signed Harrington's card on the first day and not Harrington himself. The manner in which he accepted this disappointment greatly impressed observers. In the autumn of 2002 he won the US$800,000 first prize in the Dunhill Links Championship beating Eduardo Romero at the 2nd play-off hole at St Andrews. Won the BMW Asian Open in Taiwan and the Deutsche Bank SAP Open TPC of Europe in the early part of the 2003 European season.

Horton MBE, Tommy (Eng)
Born St Helens, Lancashire, 16 June 1961
Turned professional 1957
A former Ryder Cup player who was no.1 earner on the European Seniors Tour in 1993 and for four successive seasons between 1996 and 1999. Awarded an MBE by Her Majesty the Queen for his services to golf, Tommy is a member of the European Tour Board and is chairman of the European Seniors Tour committee. A

distinguished coach, broadcaster, author and golf course architect, Tommy retired as club professional at Royal Jersey in 1999 after 25 years in the post. He continues to play on the Senior Tour.

Howard, Barclay (Sco)
Born Johnstone, Scotland, 27 January 1953
Leading amateur in the Open Championship at Royal Troon in 1997, he has successfully battled cancer which affected his golfing career after he had played in both the 1995 and 1997 Walker Cup matches. When Dean Robertson won the Italian Open at Turin in 1999 he dedicated his victory to him as a tribute to his courage in adversity.

Huggett MBE, Brian (Wal)
Born Porthcawl, Wales, 18 November 1936
Turned professional 1951
Brian won the first of his 16 European Tour titles in Holland in 1962 and was still winning in 2000 when he landed the Beko Seniors Classic in Turkey after a play-off. A dogged competitor he played in six Ryder Cup matches before being given the honour of captaining the side in 1977 – the last year the Americans took on players from only Great Britain and Ireland. A respected golf course designer, Huggett was awarded the MBE for his services to golf and in particular Welsh golf.

Hunt MBE, Bernard (Eng)
Born Atherstone, Warwickshire, 2 February 1930
Turned professional 1946
One of Britain's most accomplished professionals he won 22 times between 1953 and 1973. He was third in the 1960 Open at the Old Course behind Kel Nagle and fourth in 1964 when Tony Lema took the title at St Andrews. Among his other victories were successes in Egypt and Brazil. Having made eight appearances in the Ryder Cup he captained the side in 1973 and again in 1975. He was PGA captain in 1966 and won the Harry Vardon Trophy as leading player in the Order of Merit on three occasions.

Ilonen, Mikko (Fin)
Born Lahti, 18 December 1979
Turned professional 2001
Became the first Finnish golfer to win the Amateur Championship when he beat Christian Reimbold from Germany 2 and 1 in the final at Royal Liverpool. He has won both the Finnish match play and stroke play titles. Represented Finland in the 1998 and 2000 Eisenhower Trophy events. Now plays professionally on the European Tour and in 2001 finished ninth behind David Duval in the Open at Royal Lytham.

Jacklin CBE, Tony (Eng)
Born Scunthorpe, 7 July 1944
Turned professional 1962
Played an important and often under-rated role in the growth of the PGA European Tour after it became a self-supporting organisation in 1971. Although playing most of his golf in America he was encouraged by John Jacobs, the then executive director of the European Tour, to return to Europe to help build up the circuit. In

1969 he won the Open Championship at Royal Lytham and St Annes – the first British winner of the title since Max Faulkner in 1951. A year later he led from start to finish to win the US Open at Hazeltine – the first British player to win that event since Ted Ray had been successful in 1920 and the only one to have done so to date. He was the first player since Harry Vardon to hold the British and American Open titles simultaneously. He might well have won further Opens but a thunderstorm halted his bid for the title at St Andrews in 1970, he came third in 1971 and in 1972 Lee Trevino chipped in at the 17th at Muirfield and went on to win a title the British player had seemed set to win. He is now one of just 13 honorary members of the Royal and Ancient Golf Club of St Andrews having been elected in 2003 along with Lee Trevino.

Jacobs OBE, John (Eng)
Born Lindrick, Yorkshire, 14 March 1925
The first Executive Director of the independently run PGA European Tour, John Jacobs was awarded the OBE in 2000 for his services to golf as a player, administrator and coach. Known as 'Dr Golf' Jacobs has built up an awesome reputation as a teacher around the world and is held in high esteem by the golfing world. Top American coach Butch Harmon summed up Jacobs' contribution in this field of golf when he said: 'There is not one teacher who does not owe something to John. He wrote the book on coaching.' With 75 per cent of the votes he was inducted into the World Golf Teachers Hall of Fame and was described at that ceremony as 'the English genius'. Last year he was also, quite correctly, welcomed into the World Golf Hall of Fame in America. Having played in the 1955 Ryder Cup match he captained the side in 1979 when Continental players were included for the first time and again in 1981. Ken Schofield who succeeded him as European Tour supremo believes that Jacobs changed the face of golf sponsorship allowing, as he points out, more than 10 players a season to earn a living. In 2002 he received the Association of Golf Writers award for oustanding services to golf.

James, Mark (Eng)
Born Manchester, 28 October 1953
Turned professional 1976
Veteran of over 500 European tournaments who is now chairman of the European Tour's Tournament committee. A seven-time Ryder Cup player including the 1995 match at Oak Hill when he scored a vital early last day point against Jeff Maggert, he captained the side at Brookline in 1999. Four times a top five finisher in the Open Championship Mark has been involved in his fair share of controversy especially in the early days. He has won 18 European Tour events and four elsewhere but these days having successfully battled cancer, he is just as happy working in his Yorkshire garden. Caused some raised eyebrows with some of his comments in his book reviewing the 1999 Ryder Cup entitled 'Into the Bear Pit', then followed that up with a less controversial sequel. Affectionately known as Jesse to his friends.

Jiménez, Miguel Angel (Esp)
Born Malaga, 4 January 1954
Turned professional 1982
Talented Spaniard who was runner-up to Tiger Woods in the 2000 US Open. This was a year after making his successful début in the Ryder Cup. One of seven brothers he did not take up golf until his mid-teens. He loves cars, drives a Ferrari and has been nicknamed 'The Mechanic' by his friends. His best-remembered shot was the 3-wood he hit into the hole for an albatross 2 at the infamous 17th hole at Valderrama in the Volvo Masters but he was credited with having played the Canon Shot of the Year when he chipped in at the last to win 1998 Trophée Lancôme. In 2000 lost in a play-off at Valderrama in a World Championship to Tiger Woods. He played on both sides of the Atlantic in 2002.

Johansson, Per-Ulrik (Swe)
Born Uppsala, 6 December 1966
Turned professional 1990
A former amateur international at both junior and senior level he became the first Swede to play in two Ryder Cups when he made the 1995 and 1997 teams. In 1997 he played Phil Mickelson with whom he had studied at Arizona State University. In 1991 he was winner of the Sir Henry Cotton Rookie of the Year award in Europe but now plays most of his golf on the US Tour.

Lane, Barry (Eng)
Born Hayes, Middlesex, 21 June 1960
Turned professional 1976
After winning his way into the 1993 Ryder Cup he hit the headlines when he won the first prize of $1 million in the Andersen Consulting World Championship in beating David Frost in the final at Greyhawk in Arizona. He has played over 400 European events.

Langer, Bernhard (Ger)
Born Anhausen, 27 August 1957
Turned professional 1972
One of the game's most respected figures and consistent performers he is best known for having conquered the putting yips on more than one occasion. Twice winner of the US Masters in 1985 and 1993 he has never managed to win the Open despite coming second twice and third on three occasions. Deeply religious he was for many years Germany's only top player. He has been an inspiration to many taking his own National title on 12 occasions and winning 37 titles in Europe between 1980 and 2000. In 1979 he won the Cacherel Under 25s Championship by 17 shots. He played nine times in the Ryder Cup between 1981 and 1997 proving a mainstay in foursomes and fourballs with 11 different partners. He regained his place for the 2002 match after having been overlooked for a captain's pick in 1999 and made 3½ points – 2½ of them partnering Colin Montgomerie. Now plays both the US and European Tours. Has won 11 times in Germany including five German Opens. In 2003 was named captain of the 2004 European Ryder Cup side for Oakland Hills.

Lawrie MBE, Paul (Sco)
Born Aberdeen, 1 January 1969
Turned professional 1986
Made golfing history when he came from 10 shots back on the final day to win the 1999 Open Championship at Carnoustie after a play-off against former winner Justin Leonard and Frenchman Jean Van de Velde. With his win he became the first home-based Scot since Willie Auchterlonie in 1893 to take the title. Still based in Aberdeen he hit the opening tee shot in the 1999 Ryder Cup and played well in partnership with Colin Montgomerie in foursomes and four balls and in the singles earned a point against Jeff Maggert. Originally an assistant at Banchory Golf Club on Royal Deeside Lawrie has had a hole named after him at the club. Coached by former Tour player Adam Hunter and Scottish Rugby Union psychologist Dr Richard Cox, Lawrie has been awarded an MBE for his achievements in golf.

Lunt, Michael (Eng)
Born Birmingham, 20 May 1935
From a well-known golfing family, Lunt won the Amateur Championship in 1963 beating John Blackwell in the final then reached the final again the following year. He was English Amateur champion in 1966 and played four times in the Walker Cup.

Lyle MBE, Sandy (Sco)
Born Shrewsbury, 9 February 1958
Turned professional in 1977
With his win in the 1985 Open Championship at Royal St George's became the first British player to take the title since Tony Jacklin in 1969. He was also the first British player to win a Green Jacket in the Masters at Augusta in 1988 helped by a majestic 7-iron second shot out of sand at the last for a rare winning birdie 3. Although he represented England as an amateur at boys', youths' and senior level he became Scottish when he turned professional, something he was entitled to do at the time because his late father, the professional at Hawkstone Park, was a Scot. This is no longer allowed. He made his international début at age 14 and, two years later, qualified for and played 54 holes in the 1974 Open at Royal Lytham and St Annes. A tremendously talented natural golfer he fell a victim later in his career to becoming over-technical. Now lives in Perthshire in Scotland but still competes when possible on the US Tour and on the European Tour.

McDowell, Graeme (NI)
Born Ballymoney, Northern Ireland, 30 July 1979
Turned professional 2002
A member of the winning Great Britain and Ireland Walker Cup team in 2001, he earned his European Tour card in just his fourth event as a professional. McDowell, who had been signed up to represent the Kungsangen Golf Club in Sweden just two weeks earlier, received a last minute sponsor's invitation to play there in the Volvo Scandinavian Masters ... and not only won the event but also broke the course

record with an opening round of 64. He beat Trevor Immelman into second place with former USPGA champion Jeff Sluman third. McDowell's winning score of 270 – 14-under-par – earned him a first prize of over £200,000 and a place in the World Golf Championship NEC event at Sahalee in Washington. He was the European Tour's 12th first time winner of the season and at 23 the youngest winner of the title.

McEvoy OBE, Peter (Eng)
Born London, 22 March 1953
The most capped player for England who has had further success as a captain of Great Britain and Ireland's Eisenhower Trophy and Walker Cup sides. The Eisenhower win came in 1998 and the Walker Cup triumphs at Nairn in 1999 and at Ocean Forest, Sea Island, Georgia in 2001. On both occasions his team won 15-9. A regular winner of amateur events McEvoy was amateur champion in 1977 and 1978 and won the English stroke play title in 1980. He reached the final of the English Amateur the same year. In 1978 he played all four rounds in the Masters at Augusta and that year received the Association of Golf Writers' Trophy for his contribution to European golf. He was leading amateur in two Open Championships – 1978 and 1979. In 2003 he was awarded the OBE by Her Majesty the Queen for his services to golf

McGimpsey, Garth (Ire)
Born Bangor, 17 July 1955
A long hitter who was Irish long-driving champion in 1977 and UK long-driving title holder two years later. He was amateur champion in 1985 and Irish champion the same year and again in 1988. He played in three Walker Cup matches and competed in the home internationals for Ireland in 1978 and from 1980 to 1998. He captained the winning Great Britain and Ireland Walker Cup side who beat the US 12½–11½ at Ganton in 2003.

McGinley, Paul (Ire)
Born Dublin, 16 December 1966
Turned Professional 1991
Popular Irish golfer who turned to the game after breaking his left kneecap playing Gaelic football. With Padraig Harrington won the 1977 World Cup at Kiawah and made his Ryder Cup début when the postponed 2001 match was played in 2002. In a tense finish to his match with Jim Furyk he holed from 9 feet to get the half point the Europeans needed for victory.

Macgregor, George (Sco)
Born Edinburgh, 19 August 1944
After playing in five Walker Cup matches he captained the side in 1991 and later served as chairman of the R&A Selection committee. He won the Scottish Stroke Play title in 1982 after having been runner up three times.

Marks, Geoffrey (Eng)
Born Hanley, Stoke-on-Trent, November 1938
President of the English Golf Union in 1995 he captained the Walker Cup side in 1987 after having played on two previous occasions. He made eight appearances for England in the home internationals before captaining the team in a non-playing capacity at the start of the 1980s. He is a former England selector and was chairman of the R&A selection committee for four years from 1989.

Marsh, Dr David (Eng)
Born Southport, Lancashire, 29 April 1934
Twice winner of the English Amateur Championship in 1964 and 1970, he was captain of the R&A in 1990/1991. He played in the 1971 Walker Cup match at St Andrews and helped the home side win by scoring a vital one hole victory in the singles against Bill Hyndman. He captained the team in 1973 and 1975 and had a distinguished career as a player and then captain for England between 1956 and 1972. He was chairman of the R&A selection committee from 1979 to 1983 and in 1987 was president of the English Golf Union.

Milligan, Jim (Sco)
Born Irvine, Ayrshire, 15 June 1963
The 1988 Scottish Amateur champion had his moment of international glory in the 1989 Walker Cup which was won by the Great Britain and Ireland side for only the third time in the history of the event and for the first time on American soil. With GB&I leading by a point at Peachtree in Atlanta only Milligan and his experienced opponent Jay Sigel were left on the course. The American looked favourite to gain the final point and force a draw. The American was two up with three to play but Milligan hit his approach from 100 yards to a few inches to win the 16th with a birdie then chipped in after both had fluffed chips to square at the 17th. The last was halved leaving the Great Britain and Ireland side historic winners by a point.

Montgomerie MBE, Colin (Sco)
Born Glasgow, 23 June 1963
Turned professional 1987
Europe's most consistent golfer who topped the Volvo Order of Merit an unprecedented seven years in a row between 1993 and 1999. Although he has yet to win a major he has come close losing a play-off for the US Open to Ernie Els in 1994 and again being pipped by Els in the 1997 Championship. He was third behind Tom Kite in the 1992 US Open. In 1995 he was beaten in a play-off for the USPGA Championship by Australian Steve Elkington. He has had over 30 victories around the world and has played with distinction in six Ryder Cups. At Brookline in 1999 and at The Belfry in 2002 he was a pillar of strength for the team in difficult on-course conditions. In the 2002 match he was never down and was top points scorer making 4½ out of 5 points. He has twice won the Association of Golf Writers' Golfer of the Year award and has been three times Johnnie Walker Golfer of the Year in Europe. His low round in Europe is 61 achieved at Crans-sur-Sierre in the Canon

European Masters in 1996. He has been honoured by Her Majesty the Queen for his record-breaking golfing exploits but is troubled these days by a persistent back injury and midway through 2003 had not added to his total of victories. He did, however, take first prize toward the end of the year at the Macau Open.

O'Connor Sr, Christy (Ire)
Born Galway, 21 December 1924
Turned professional 1946
Never managed to win the Open but came close on three occasions finishing runner-up to Peter Thomson in 1965 and being third on two other occasions. Played in ten Ryder Cup matches between 1955 and 1973 and scored 24 wins in tournament play between 1955 and 1972. Known affectionately as 'Himself' by Irish golfing fans who have long admired his talent with his clubs. He is a brilliant shot maker.

O'Connor Jr, Christy (Ire)
Born Galway, 19 August 1948
Turned professional 1965
Nephew of Christy Sr, he finished third in the 1985 Open Championship. A winner on the European and Safari circuits he won the 1999 and 2000 Senior British Open – only the second man to successfully defend. Played in two Ryder Cup matches hitting a career best 2-iron to the last green at The Belfry in 1989 to beat Fred Couples and ensure a drawn match enabling Europe to keep the trophy. Now plays on the US Senior Tour but his career was interrupted when he broke a leg in a motorcycle accident.

Olazábal, José Maria (Esp)
Born Fuenterrabia, 5 February 1966
Turned professional 1985
Twice a winner of the Masters, his second triumph was particularly emotional. He had won in 1994 but had to withdraw from the 1995 Ryder Cup with a foot problem eventually diagnosed as rheumatoid polyarthritis in three joints of the right foot and two of the left. He was out of golf for eighteen months but treatment from Munich doctor Hans-Wilhelm Muller-Wohlfahrt helped him back to full fitness after a period when he was house bound and unable to walk. At that point it seemed as if his career was over, but he came back in 1999 to beat Davis Love III by two shots at Augusta. With over twenty victories in Europe and a further seven abroad, the son of a Real Sebastian greenkeeper who took up the game at the age of four has been one of the most popular players in the game. He competed in six Ryder Cups between 1987 and 1999 frequently partnering Severiano Ballesteros. He is a former British Boys Youths and Amateur champion. His best performance in the Open was third in 1992 when Nick Faldo won at Muirfield.

O'Leary, John (Ire)
Born Dublin, 19 August 1949
Turned professional 1979
After a successful career as a player including victory in the Carrolls Irish Open in 1982 he retired because

of injury and now is director of golf at the Buckinghamshire Club. He is a member of the PGA European Tour Board of Directors.

Oosterhuis, Peter (Eng)
Born London, 3 May 1948
Turned professional 1968
Twice runner up in the Open Championship in 1974 and 1982, he was also the leading British player in 1975 and 1978. He finished third in the US Masters in 1973, had multiple wins on the European tour and in Africa and won the Canadian Open on the US tour 1981. He played in six Ryder Cups partnering Nick Faldo at Royal Lytham and St Annes in 1977 when Faldo made his début. He was top earner in Europe four years in a row from 1971. Following his retirement from top-line golf he moved to Arizona and after a spell working for the Golf Channel in Europe he is now a respected member of the CBS commentary team and makes guest appearances on the Golf Channel.

Panton MBE, John (Sco)
Born Pitlochry, Perthshire, 9 October 1916
Turned professional 1935
Honorary professional since 1988 to the Royal & Ancient Golf Club of St Andrews, he is one of Scotland's best known and admired professionals. He was leading British player in the 1956 Open and beat Sam Snead for the World Senior's title in 1967. He played in three Ryder Cup matches and was twelve times a contestant in the World Cup with the late Eric Brown as his regular partner. He won the Association of Golf Writer's Trophy for his contribution to the game in 1967 and has been honoured with an MBE.

Parnevik, Jesper (Swe)
Born Danderyd, Stockholm, 7 March 1965
Turned professional 1986
Son of a well-known Swedish entertainer he is one of the most extrovert of golfers best known for his habit of wearing a baseball cap with the brim turned up and brightly coloured drain-pipe style trousers. Winner of events on both sides of the Atlantic he plays most of his golf these days in America where he has won five times since 1998 but made history in 1995 when he became the first Swede to win in Sweden when he took the Scandinavian Masters at Barseback in Malmo. Has twice finished runner-up in the Open at Turnberry in 1994 when he was two ahead but made a bogey at the last and was passed by Nick Price who finished with an eagle and a birdie in the last three holes. He led by two with a round to go in 1998 but shot 73 and finished tied second with Darren Clarke behind Justin Leonard. Played in the 1997 and 1999 Ryder Cup teaming up successfully with Sergio García to win three and a half points in 1999. Was also in the 2002 team and halved with Tiger Woods in the singles. Has had health problems suffering injuries and illness and has resorted at times to unusual remedies including eating volcanic dust to cleanse the system.

Poulter, Ian (Eng)

Born Hitchen, England, 10 January 1976
Turned professional 1994
Having failed narrowly to make the 2002 European Ryder Cup side it remains extrovert Poulter's main aim to make the side in 2004. His form in 2003 would indicate that he may not be disappointed. By mid-September he had won at Celtic Manor and in Copenhagen insisting he wishes to be noticed for the quality of his always-attacking golf as much as for his colourful but often wierd hairstyles. A real character with no shortage of talent.

Price, Phillip (Wal)

Born Pontypridd, 21 October 1966
Turned professional 1989
Winner of the 1994 Portuguese Open he abandoned plans to play the US Tour in 2002. He made his Ryder Cup début in 2002 and produced a sterling last day performance when he beat the world no.2 Phil Mickelson 3 and 2 for a vital point. He was named Asprey Golfer of the Month of July after winning the Smurfit European Open at the K-Club and finishing in the top 10 at the Barclays Scottish Open and the Open at Royal St George's.

Rafferty, Ronan (NI)

Born Newry, Northern Ireland, 13 January 1964
Turned professional 1981
Won the Irish Amateur Championship as a 16 year old in 1980 when he also won the English Amateur Open Stroke Play title, competed in the Eisenhower Trophy and played against Europe in the home internationals. Winner of the British Boys, Irish Youths' and Ulster Youths' titles in 1979, he also played in the senior Irish side against Wales that year. A regular winner on the European tour between 1988 and 1993 he was also victorious in tournaments played in South America, Australia and New Zealand. A wrist injury has curtailed his career but he is active on the corporate golf front and often commentates for Sky TV. He has an impressive wine collection.

Rivero, José (Esp)

Born Madrid, 20 September 1955
Turned professional 1973
One of only eight Spaniards who have played in the Ryder Cup he competed in the winning 1985 and 1987 sides. Worked as a caddie but received a grant from the Spanish Federation to pursue his golf career. With José Maria Canizares won the World Cup in 1984 at Olgiata in Italy.

Rocca, Costantino (Ita)

Born Bergamo, 4 December 1956
Turned professional 1981
The first and to date only Italian to play in the Ryder Cup. In the 1999 match at Valderrama he beat Tiger Woods 4 and 2 in a vital singles. Left his job in a polystyrene box making factory to become a club professional and graduated to the tournament scene

through Europe's Challenge Tour. In 1995 he fluffed a chip at the final hole in the Open at St Andrews only to hole from 60 feet out of the Valley of Sin to force a play-off against John Daly which he then lost. In recent years he has met with success in European Tour events.

Rose, Justin (Eng)

Born Johannesburg, South Africa, 30 July 1980
Turned professional 1998
Walker Cup player who shot to attention in the 1998 Open Championship when he finished top amateur and third behind winner Mark O'Meara after holing his third shot at the last on the final day for a closing birdie. Immediately after that Open he turned professional and missed his first 21 half-way cuts before finding his feet. In 2002 was a multiple winner in Europe and also won in Japan and South Africa. Delighted his father who watched him win the Victor Chandler British Masters just a few weeks before he died of leukemia. In 2003 he found winning more difficult.

Sandelin, Jarmo (Swe)

Born Imatra, Finland, 10 May 1967
Turned professional 1987
Extrovert Swede who made his début in the Ryder Cup at Brookline in 1999 although he did not play until the singles. Has always been a snazzy dresser on course where he is one of the game's longest hitters often in the early days with a 54-inch shafted driver. Five time winner on Tour he met his partner Linda when she asked to caddie for him at a Stockholm pro-am.

Smyth, Des (Ire)

Born Drogheda, Ireland, 12 February
Turned professional 1973
Became the oldest winner on the PGA European Tour when he won the Madeira Island Open in 2001. Smyth was 48 years and 34 days – 20 days older than Neil Coles had been when he won the Sanyo Open in Barcelona in 1982. One of the Tour's most consistent performers, he played in 592 events before joining the Senior Tour in Europe and qualifying for the US Seniors Tour as well. Five times Irish National Champion he was a member of the winning Irish side in the 1988 Alfred Dunhill Cup.

Thomas, Dave (Wal)

Born Newcastle-upon-Tyne, 16 August 1934
Twice runner-up in the Open Championship, Welshman Thomas lost a play-off to Peter Thomson in 1958. He played 11 times in the World Cup for Wales and four times in the Ryder Cup. In all he won 10 tournaments between 1961 and 1969 before retiring to concentrate on golf course design. Along with Peter Alliss designed the Ryder Cup course at The Belfry. Was appointed captain of the Professional Golfers' Association for 2001 – their Centenary year – and for 2002.

Torrance OBE, Sam (Sco)
Born Largs, Ayrshire, 24 August 1953
Turned professional 1970
Between 1976 and 1998 he won 21 times on the European Tour in which he has played over 680 events. Captain of the 2002 European Ryder Cup side having previously played in eight matches notably holing the winning putt in 1985 to end a 28-year run of American domination. He was an inspired captain when the 2001 match was played in September 2002. Tied 8 points each, Torrance's men won the singles for only the third time since 1979 to win 15½–12½. His father Bob, who has been his only coach, looks after the swings these days of several others on the European Tour including Paul McGinley who holed the nine foot putt that brought the Ryder Cup back to Europe. He was awarded the MBE in 1996. European Tour officials worked out that in his first 28 years Torrance walked an estimated 14,000 miles and played 15,000 shots earning at the rate of £22 per stroke. In 2003 he retired from full-time competition on the European Tour and made his début in the Charles Church Scottish Seniors at The Roxburghe in late August.

Van de Velde, Jean (Fra)
Born Mont de Marsan, 29 May 1966
Turned professional 1987
Who ever remembers who came second? Everybody will remember Jean Van de Velde, however, for finishing runner-up after a play-off with eventual winner Paul Lawrie and American Justin Leonard when the Open returned to a somewhat tricked-up Carnoustie in 1999. Playing the last hole he led by three but refused to play safe and paid a severe penalty. He ran up a triple bogey 7 after seeing his approach ricochet off a stand into the rough and his next into the Barry Burn. He appeared to contemplate playing the half-submerged ball when taking off his shoes and socks and wading in but that was never a possibility. Took up the game as a youngster when holidaying with his parents in Biarritz. Has scored only one win in Europe (the Roma Masters in 1993) and has returned to the European Tour after a spell in America. Made his Ryder Cup début at Brookline in 1999. Injury prevented him competing regularly in 2003 during which time he was part of the BBC Golf Commentary team with, among others, Peter Alliss, Sam Torrance and Ken Brown.

Walton, Philip (Ire)
Born Dublin, 28 March 1962
Turned professional 1983
Twice a Walker Cup player he is best remembered for two-putting the last to beat Jay Haas by one hole and clinch victory in the 1995 Ryder Cup at Oak Hill. He played in five Alfred Dunhill Cup competitions at St Andrews and was in the winning side in 1990.

Westwood, Lee (Eng)
Born Worksop, Nottinghamshire, 24 April 1973
Turned professional 1993
A former British Youths champion who missed out on Walker Cup honours, he quickly made the grade in

the professional ranks. In 2000 he ended the seven-year reign of Colin Montgomerie by taking the top spot in the Volvo Order of Merit. He was six-time winner that year in Europe taking five order of merit titles and beating Montgomerie at the second extra hole of the Cisco World Match Play final at Wentworth. Among his overseas victories are three successful Taiheiyo Masters titles in Japan, the Australian Open in 1997 when he beat Greg Norman in a play-off and the Freeport McDermott Classic at New Orleans on the US Tour. He has already won titles on every major circuit. He is married to Laurae Coltart, sister of fellow professional Andrew Coltart. He has been a member of the last three Ryder Cup teams and in the 2002 match won 3 points out of 4. Although he admits he had thoughts of giving up tournament play he persevered and won again for the first time in three years when he was successful in the BMW International at Nord Eichenried, Munich. A month later he picked up first prize in the Dunhill Links Championship bringing his earnings in five weeks to over $1 million. He credits David Leadbetter for sorting out his game and is now using experienced caddie Peter Coleman who worked for over 20 years for Bernhard Langer.

White, Ronnie (Eng)
Born Wallasey, Cheshire, 9 April 1921
A five times Walker Cup team member between 1947 and 1953 he was one of the most impressive players in post-war amateur golf. He won six and halved one of the 10 Walker Cup matches he played and won the English Amateur in 1949 and the English Open stroke play title the following two years.

Wolstenholme, Gary (Eng)
Born Egham, Surrey, 21 August 1960
The 1991 Amateur champion he has been one of the most regular title winners in the past 11 years and regained the Amateur title in 2003 when beating Raphael De Sousa, the first Swiss to reach the final, by 6 and 5. At 42 he was the oldest player in the field and not one of the longest hitters on a course measuring 7126 yards. In 1991 he had beaten Bob May 8 and 6 in the final. A week after his triumph at Troon he won the Scottish Stroke-Play title. Son of former professional the late Guy Wolstenholme he won the 1995 and 1996 British Mid-Amateur Championship, the Chinese Amateur title in 1993, the Emirates Amateur in 1995 and the Finnish Amateur in 1996. He also won the 2002 Australian Amateur Championship title and the 2002 and 2003 South African stroke-play title. He was England County champion of champions in 1994 and 1996 and he highlighted his appearances in Walker Cup golf by beating Tiger Woods by one hole in the first day singles of the 1995 match at Royal Porthcawl. Great Britain and Ireland won that year but Woods gained his revenge on Wolstenholme by beating him on the second day. He was named 2003 Ping English Golfer of the Year.

Woosnam MBE, Ian (Wal)
Born Oswestry, Shropshire, 2 March 1958
Turned professional 1976
Highlight of his career was winning the Green Jacket at the Masters in 1991 after a last day battle with Spaniard José Maria Olazábal who went on to win in 1994 and again in 1999. Teamed up very successfully with Nick Faldo in Ryder Cup golf and was in four winning teams in 1985, 1987, 1995 and 1997. Was vice-captain in 2001 to Sam Torrance. He has scored 28 European Tour victories and twice won the World Match Play Championship in 1987 when he beat Sandy Lyle, with whom he used to play boys' golf in Shropshire, in 1990 when his opponent was Zimbabwean Mark McNulty and in 2001 when he beat Retief Goosen, then US Open Champion, Colin Montgomerie, Lee Westwood and then Padraig Harrington in the final. In 1989 he lost a low-scoring final to Nick Faldo on the last green. His lowest round was a 60 he returned in the 1990 Monte Carlo Open at Mont Agel. Partnered by David Llewellyn he won the World Cup of Golf in 1987 beating Scotland's Sam Torrance and Sandy Lyle in a play-off. Honoured with an MBE from Her Majesty the Queen he now lives with his family in Jersey. Finished joint third in the 2001 Open at Lytham after having been penalised two shots for discovering on the second tee he had 15 clubs (one over the limit) in his bag. In 2003 he was a front runner to captain the 2004 European Ryder Cup side but lost out to Bernhard Langer.

Film to Honour Bobby Jones' Life

St Andrews, the home of golf, was transformed back to the 1930's when scenes were shot in the autumn for a new film, A Stroke of Genius, which recalls the life of arguably the greatest of all amateur golfers – Robert Tyre Jones jr – commonly referred to as Bobby Jones but as Bob by those who knew him better.

St Andrews played a very special part in Jones' life. When he first played the Old course in 1921 he got caught up in a deep bunker at the 11th hole, could not extricate himself and picked up! Five years later he won the Open Championship there and asked the town of St Andrews to keep the Claret Jug on his behalf because of his misdemeanour in 1921.

In 1930 he was back at St Andrews and won the Amateur Championship as part of his Grand Slam when he won the Amateur and Open titles on both sides of the Atlantic. When he was asked whether the course he built with architect Alister MacKenzie which hosts the Masters each year was the greatest in the world he denied it saying that the Old course at St Andrews held that honour. In 1958 when the Old course was host to the first Eisenhower Trophy, the World Amateur Team Championship for men, Jones was given the Freedom of St Andrews – an honour previously only accorded to Benjamin Franklin. It was there, crippled and in a wheelchair, that he said that were he permitted to play only one course for the rest of his life it would be the Old course. That speech was filmed and may well be used in the finished film. The flags in the town all flew at half-mast when he died in 1972.

The film, which is scheduled to be released simultaneously at St Andrews and Pebble Beach on St Patrick's Day, March 17th – exactly 102 years after Jones was born – stars James Caviezel as the great man although the actor is not a golfer. Local St Andrews professional Jim Farmer, who has studied Jones's swing, acted as advisor to Caviezel on the film and Farmer's son, himself a low-handicap amateur, was drafted in to hit most of the shots Cavaziel had to play.

The film crew were allowed to shoot scenes on the Old course on two Sundays during last autumn with locals re-enacting the welcome Jones received on earlier visits with all the enthusiasm that was shown when he once turned up to play (he thought) unexpectedly. Word had got out that he was motoring down from Gleneagles Hotel where he was staying for a game and hundreds joined him on the course.

Tom Crow, founder of the Cobra Golf Club company and a former Australian Amateur champion who helped finance the film, believes it will be as popular with film fans as *Chariots of Fire* or *Sea Biscuit*. It will, he insists, give us a feel of what the world was like in those days.

British, Irish and Continental Players, Women

Alfredsson, Helen (Swe)
Born Gothenburg, 9 April 1965
Turned professional 1989
After earning Rookie of the Year on the 1989 European Tour she won the 1992 Ladies' British Open. Two years later she was Gatorade Rookie of the Year on the American LPGA Tour. She has competed in seven Solheim Cup matches and has won titles in Europe, America, Japan and Australia.

Andrew, Kim (née Rostron) (Eng)
Born 12 February 1974
After taking the English and Scottish Ladies stroke play titles in 1997 she won the Ladies British Open Amateur a year later. She played in the 1998 and 2000 Curtis Cup matches.

Bailey MBE, Mrs Diane (Frearson née Robb) (Eng)
Born Wolverhampton, 31 August 1943
After playing in the 1962 and 1972 Curtis Cup matches she captained the side in 1984, 1986 and 1988. In 1984 at Muirfield the Great Britain and Ireland side lost narrowly to the Americans but she led the side to a first ever victory on American soil at Prairie Dunes in Kansas two years later. The result was a convincing 13-5. She was in charge again when the GB & I side held on to the Cup two years later this time by 11-7 at Royal St George's.

Bisgood CBE, Jeanne (Eng)
Born Richmond, Surrey, 11 August 1923
Three times English Ladies champion in 1951, 1953 and 1957. Having played in three Curtis Cups she captained the side in 1970. Between 1952 and 1955 she won the Swedish, Italian, German, Portuguese and Norwegian Ladies titles.

Bonallack, Lady Angela (née Ward) (Eng)
Born Birchington, Kent, 7 April 1937
Wife of Sir Michael Bonallack OBE she played in six Curtis Cup matches. She was leading amateur in the 1975 and 1976 Colgate European Opens, won two English Ladies titles and had victories, too, in the Swedish, German, Scandinavian and Portuguese Championships.

Butler, Ita (née Burke) (Ire)
Born Nenagh, County Tipperary
Having played in the Curtis Cup in 1966, she captained the side that beat the Americans by 5 points at Killarney thirty years later.

Cavalleri, Silvia (Ita)
Born Milan, 10 October 1972
Turned professional 1997
Became the first Italian to win the US Amateur when she beat Robin Burke 5 and 4 at Brae Burn in the final. She was five times Italian National Junior champion and won the British Girls title in 1990 with a 5 and 4 success over E. Valera at Penrith. As a professional her best finish to date is tied second in the 2000 Ladies' Italian Open.

Davidson, Alison (née Rose) (Sco)
Born Stirling, Scotland, 18 June 1968
Twice a Curtis Cup player in 1996 and 1998. She won the Ladies British Open Amateur in 1997.

Davies CBE, Laura (Eng)
Born 10 October 1963
Turned professional 1985
Record-breaking performer who has won over 60 events worldwide including the US and British Women's Opens. For six days in 1987 she held both titles having won the American event before joining the US Tour. Was a founder member of the Women's Tour in Europe where she has won a record 33 times. Still holds the record for the number of birdies in a round – 11 which she scored in the 1987 Open de France Feminin. Her 16-shot victory, by a margin of five shots, in the 1995 Guardian Irish Holidays Open at St Margaret's remains the biggest in European Tour history. Her 267 totals in the 1988 Biarritz Ladies Open and the 1995 Guardian Irish Holidays Open are the lowest on Tour. Other major victories include the LPGA Championship twice and the du Maurier Championship. A big-hitting 5ft 10 ins blonde she has won every year in America since 1988 except in 1990, 1992 and 1999 when her best finish was second. Between 1985 and 1990 she had won in Europe at least once a season. In 1999 she became the first European Tour player to pass through the £1 million in prize-money earnings and finished European No. 1 that year for a record fifth time. The 1996 Rolex Player of the Year in America she has won almost $5.5 million in

US prize-money. Originally honoured with an MBE by Her Majesty the Queen in 1988, she became a CBE in 2000. Enjoys all sports including soccer (she supports Liverpool FC). Among other awards she has received during her career have been the Association of Golf Writers' Trophy for her contribution to European golf in 1994 and the American version in 1994 and 1996 for her performances on the US Tour. In 1994 she became the first golfer to score victories on five different Tours – European, American, Australasian, Japanese and Asian in one calendar year. As an amateur she played for Surrey and was a Curtis Cup player in 1984. She has competed in all eight Solheim Cup matches. In 2000 was recognised by the LPGA in their top 50 players and teachers honours list.

Dowling, Clare (*née* Hourihane) (Ire)
Born 18 February 1958
Won three Irish Ladies Championships in a row – 1983, 1984 and 1985 and won the title again in 1987 and 1991. She won the 1986 British Ladies Stroke play amateur title. Two years earlier she had made the first of five playing appearances in the Curtis Cup before acting as non-playing captain in 2000.

Duggelby, Emma (Eng)
Born Fulford, York, 5 October 1971
Talented English golfer who won the British Ladies Open Amateur Championship in 1994 and the English Ladies in 2000 when she also made her Curtis Cup début.

Esterl, Elisabeth (Ger)
Born Dingolfing, 29 August 1976
Turned professional 1997
Made her début in the Solheim Cup in 2003.

Garrett, Maureen (*née* Ruttle) (Eng)
Born 22 August 1922
President of the Ladies' Golf Union from 1982 to 1985, she captained the Curtis Cup (1960) and Vagliano Trophy (1961) teams. In 1983 won the Bobby Jones award presented annually by the United States Golf Association to a person who emulates Jones' spirit, personal qualities and attitude to the game and its players.

Garvey, Philomena (Ire)
Born Drogheda, Co Louth, 27 April 1927
Turned professional 1964 but later reinstated
Winner of the Irish Ladies title 15 times between 1946 and 1970 and six times a Curtis Cup player between 1948 and 1960 she remains one of Ireland's most successful players. In 1957 she won the British Ladies Open Amateur title.

Goldschmid Isa (*née* Bevione) (Ita)
Born Italy, 15 October 1925
One of Italy's greatest amateurs she won her national title 21 times between 1947 and 1974 and was ten times Italian Open champion between 1952 and 1969. Among her other triumphs were victories in the 1952 Spanish Ladies and the 1973 French Ladies.

Gustafson, Sophie (Swe)
Born Saro, 27 December 1973
Turned professional 1992
Winner of the 2000 Weetabix Women's British Open she had studied marketing, economics and law before turning to professional golf. Credits Seve Ballesteros and Laura Davies as the two players most influencing her career. Her first European victory was the 1996 Swiss Open and her first on the USLPGA Tour was the Chick-fil-A Charity Cup in 2000. Played in the 1998, 2000, 2002 and 2003 Solheim Cups.

Harris, Marley (*née* Spearman) (Eng)
Born January 11 1982
Superb ambassadress for golf in the 1950s and 1960s whose exuberance and joie de vivre is legendary. Three times a Curtis Cup player she won the British Ladies in 1961 and again in 1962. She was English champion in 1964. In 1962 was awarded the Association of Golf Writers' Trophy for her services to golf.

Hjörth, Maria (Swe)
Born Falun, 10 October 1973
Turned professional 1996
After an excellent amateur career when she won titles in Finland, Norway and Spain (where she won the prestigious Sherry Cup), she attended Stirling University in Scotland on a golf bursary and graduated with a BA honours degree in English before turning professional. In 2002 she played in the Solheim Cup.

Hudson, Rebecca (Eng)
Born Doncaster, Yorkshire, 13 June 1979
Turned professional 2002
A member of the 1998, 2000 and 2002 Curtis Cup teams Rebecca is one of the most gifted of younger players. In 2000 she won both the British Match Play and Stroke Play titles, the Scottish and English Stroke play Championships and the Spanish Women's Open. In addition she made the birdie that ensured Great Britain and Ireland won a medal in the World Team Championship for the Espirito Santo Trophy in Berlin in 2000.

Irvin, Ann (Eng)
Born 11 April 1943
Winner of the British Ladies' title in 1973, she played in four Curtis Cup matches between 1962 and 1976. She was Daks Woman Golfer of the Year in 1968 and 1969 and has been active in administration at junior and county level.

Jackson, Bridget (Eng)
Born Birmingham, 10 July 1936
A former President of the Ladies Golf Union she played in three Curtis Cup matches and captained the Vagliano Trophy side twice after having played four times. Although the best she managed in the British Championship was runner-up in 1964 she did win the English, German and Canadian titles.

Johnson, Trish (Eng)
Born Bristol, 17 January 1966
Turned professional 1987
Another stalwart of the Women's Tour in Europe who learned the game at windy Westward Ho. Regular winner on Tour both in Europe and America, she scored two and a half points out of four in Europe's dramatic Solheim Cup win over the Americans at Loch Lomond in 2000. She has played in six Solheim Cup matches. She was European no.1 earner in 1990. A loyal supporter of Arsenal FC she regularly attends games at Highbury.

Koch, Carin (Swe)
Born Kungalv, Sweden, 2 February 1971
She has been playing golf since she was nine and in two Solheim Cups remains unbeaten. In 2000 she won 3 points out of 3 and in 2002 2½ points out of 3.

Lawrence, Joan (Sco)
Born Kinghorn, Fife, 20 April 1930
After a competitive career in which she three times won the Scottish championship and played in the 1964 Curtis Cup, she has played her part in golf administration. She had two four-year spells as an LGU selector, is treasurer of the Scottish Ladies Golf Association and has also served on the LGU executive.

Lee-Smith, Jennifer (Eng)
Born Newcastle-upon-Tyne, 2 December 1948
Turned professional 1977
After winning the Ladies British Open as an amateur in 1976 was named Daks Woman Golfer of the Year. She played twice in the Curtis Cup before turning professional and winning nine times in a six year run from 1979. For a time she ran her own driving range in southern England but now lives in Florida.

De Lorenzi, Marie-Laure (Fra)
Born Biarritz, 21 January 1961
Turned professional 1986
The stylish French golfer won 20 titles in Europe between 1987 and 1997 setting a record in 1988 when she won eight times but for family reasons never spent time on the US Tour. Jointly holds the record for 54 holes on the European Tour with her 201 total in the 1995 Dutch Open.

McKay, Mhairi (Sco)
Born Glasgow 18 April 1975
Turned professional 1997
Former British Girls Champion (1992 and 1993) she has played in the Vagliano Trophy and Curtis Cup. She was an All-American when studying at Stanford University and made her first appearance in the Solheim Cup at Barsebäck, Sweden, in 2003.

McKenna, Mary (Ire)
Born Dublin, 29 April 1949
Winner of the British Ladies Amateur Stroke play title in 1979 and eight times Irish champion between 1969 and 1989. One of Ireland's most successful golfers she played in nine Curtis Cup matches and nine Vagliano Trophy matches between 1969 and 1987. She captained the Vagliano team in 1995. Three times a member of the Great Britain and Ireland Espirito Santo Trophy side she went on to captain the team in 1986. She was Daks Woman Golfer of the Year in 1979.

Matthew, Catriona (Sco)
Born Edinburgh, 25 August 1969
Turned professional 1995
Former Scottish Girls Under-21 and Amateur champion, Catriona also won the British Amateur in 1993. She played in the 1990, 1992 and 1994 Curtis Cup matches and made her début in the Solheim Cup at Barsebäck in 2003 and had the honour of holing the winning putt. She performed impressively throughout showing considerable coolness under pressure. Now plays on both the European and American Tours.

Moodie, Janice (Sco)
Born Glasgow, 31 May 1973
Turned professional 1997
The 1992 Scottish Women's Stroke play champion played in two winning Curtis Cup teams and earned All American honours at San José State University where she graduated with a degree in psychology. She plays both the European and American Tours and in 2000 finished 17th in America and ninth in Europe. Started playing at age 11 and has been helped considerably by Cawder professional Ken Stevely. In the 2000 Solheim Cup she won three out of four points but was controversially left out of the 2002 team despite having won the Asahi Ryokuken International on the LPGA tour. She was reinstated by captain Catrin Nilsmark for the 2003 match at Barsebäck in Sweden. She teamed up well with Catriona Matthew and also won her singles.

Meunier-Lebouc, Patricia (Fra)
Born Dijon, 16 November 1972
Turned professional 1993
French amateur champion in 1992, she has been a regular winner on Europe's Evian Tour. She played in the 2000 Solheim Cup and again last year at Barsebäck. In 2003 she won the Kraft-Nabisco Championship on the US Tour.

Neumann, Liselotte (Swe)
Born Finspang, 20 May 1966
Turned professional 1985
Having won the US Women's Open in 1988 she won the Weetabix British Women's title in 1990 to become one of six players to complete the Transatlantic double. The others are Laura Davies, Alison Nicholas, Jane Geddes, Betsy King and Patty Sheehan. The 1988 Rookie of the Year on the LPGA Tour she played in the first six Solheim Cup matches.

Nicholas MBE, Alison (Eng)
Born Gibraltar, 6 February 1978
In Solheim Cup golf had a successful partnership with Laura Davies. In addition they have both won the British and US Open Championship. Alison's first win on the European Tour came in the 1987 Weetabix British Open and she added the US Open ten years later

after battling with Nancy Lopez who was trying to win her national title for the first time. Alison is a former winner of the Association of Golf Writers' Golfer of the Year award and has been honoured with an MBE.

Nilsmark, Catrin (Swe)
Born Gothenburg, Sweden, 28 Aug 1967
Holed the winning putt in Europe's Solheim Cup victory in 1992. Her early career was affected by whiplash injury after a car crash. Used to hold a private pilot's licence but now rides Harley Davidson motorcycles. She captained the European team to victory in the 2003 Solheim Cup matches at Barsebäck in Sweden..

Otto, Julie (*née* Wade) (Eng)
Born Ipswich, Suffolk, 10 March 1967
Secretary of the Ladies Golf Union from 1996 to 2000 she was one of the most successful competitors in both individual and team golf. Among the many titles she won were the English Stroke Play in 1987 and 1993, the British Ladies Stroke Play in 1993 and the Scottish Stroke Play in 1991 and 1993. She shared Britain's Golfer of the Year award in 1993 and won it again in 1995 on her own. She played in five Curtis Cups matches including the victories at Royal Liverpool in 1992 and Killarney in 1996 and the drawn match in 1994 at Chattanooga. Now works with the R&A.

Panton-Lewis, Cathy (Sco)
Born Bridge of Allan, Stirlingshire, 14 June 1955
Turned professional 1978
A former Ladies British Open Amateur Champion in 1976 when she was named Scottish Sportswoman of the year. She notched up thirteen victories as a professional on the European tour between 1979 and 1988. Daughter of John Panton, MBE.

Petterson, Suzann (Swe)
Born Oslo, April 7 1981
Turned professional 2000
Five times Norwegian Amateur champion, Suzann was World Amateur champion in 2000. She won the French Open in 2001 and made her Solheim Cup début in the 2003 match at Barsebäck. One of the best performers on the week and was unbeaten going into the singles.

Prado, Catherine (*née* Lacoste) (Fra)
Born Paris 27 June 1945
The only amateur golfer ever to win the US Women's Open she won the title at Hot Springs, Virginia in 1967. She was also the first non-American to take the title and the youngest. Two years later she won both the US and British Amateur titles. She was a four times winner of her own French Championship in 1967, 1969, 1970 and 1972 and won the Spanish title in 1969, 1972 and 1976. She comes from a well-known French sporting family.

Price Fisher, Elizabeth (Eng)
Born London, 17 January 1923
Turned professional 1968 but reinstated as an amateur
three years later
Between 1950 and 1960 she played in six Curtis Cup matches and, in addition to her 1959 victory in the

British Ladies Championship, also won national titles in Denmark and Portugal. For many years worked for the *Daily Telegraph*.

Reid MBE, Dale (Sco)
Born Ladybank, Fife, 20 March 1959
Turned professional 1979
Scored twenty-one wins in her professional career between 1980 and 1991 and was so successful in leading Europe's Solheim Cup side to victory against the Americans at Loch Lomond in 2000 that she was again captain in 2002 when the Americans won. Following the team's success in the 2000 Solheim Cup she received an MBE.

Robertson MBE, Belle (Sco)
Born Southend, Argyll, 11 April 1936
One of Scotland's most talented amateur golfers who was Scottish Sportswoman of the Year in 1968, 1971, 1978 and 1981. She was Woman Golfer of the Year in 1971, 1981 and 1985. A former Ladies British Open Amateur Champion and six times Scottish Ladies Champion, she competed in nine Curtis Cups acting as non-playing captain in 1974 and 1976.

Sanchez, Ana Belen (Esp)
Born Malaga, 16 February 1976
Turned professional 1997
As an amateur she was a member of the winning Spanish side in the 1995 European Team Championship. Now plays on the Evian Tour and made her Solheim Cup début at Barsebäck in 2003.

Saunders, Vivien (Eng)
Born Sutton, Surrey, 24 November 1946
Turned professional 1969
Founder of the Women's Professional Golfers' Association (European Tour) in 1978 and chairman for the first two years. In 1969 she was the first European golfer to qualify for the LPGA Tour in America. No longer playing top-line professional golf, she is keen to be reinstated as an amateur but not finding that easy.

Segard, Mme Patrick (de St Saveur, *née* Lally Vagliano) (Fra)
Former chairperson of the Women's Committee of the World Amateur Golf Council holding the post from 1964 to 1972. A four times French champion (1948, 50, 51 and 52) she also won the British (1950), Swiss (1949 and 1965), Luxembourg (1949), Italian (1949 and 1951) and Spanish (1951) amateur titles. She represented France from 1937 to 1939, from 1947 to 1965 and again in 1970.

Sörenstam, Annika (Swe)
Born Stockholm, 9 October 1970
Turned professional 1992
Winner of the US Open in 1995 and 1996 she and Karrie Webb of Australia have battled for the headlines on the USLPGA Tour over the past few years. A prolific winner of titles in America. She won four in a row in

early summer 2000 as she and Webb battled again for the No. 1 spot in 2001. Sörenstam was the No. 1 earner in 1995, 1997 and 1998, Webb in 1996, 1999 and 2000. At the Standard Register Ping event she became the first golfer to shoot 59 on the LPGA Tour. Her second round score 59 included 13 birdies, 11 of them in her first 12 holes. Her 36-hole total of 124 beat the previous record set by Webb the previous season by three. Her 54-hole score of 193 matched the record set by Karrie Webb and her 72-hole total of 261 which gave her victory by three shots from Se Ri Pak matched the low total on Tour set by Se Ri Pak in 1998. Sörenstam's 27-under-par winning score was a new record for the Tour beating the 26-under-par score Webb returned in the Australian Ladies' Masters in 1999. Her sister Charlotta also plays on the LPGA and Evian Tours. Before turning professional she finished runner-up in the 1992 US Women's Championship. Sörenstam continued on her winning way in 2002 when her victories included another major – the Kraft Nabisco Championship. By the end of August she had won six times in the US and once more in Europe. By the beginning of October she had won nine times on the 2002 LPGA Tour and collected her 40th LPGA title. Only four players have won more than 9 events in one LPGA season. By October she had won $2.5 million wordwide. When Annika won the Mizuno Classic in Japan she became the first player for 34 years to win 10 titles in a season. In 2003 she took up the challenge of playing on the US Men's Tour teeing up in a blaze of publicity in the Colonial event in Texas but missed the half-way cut. She won her fifth Major when she took the McDonald's LPGA Championship in June and when she won the Weetabix British Women's Open at Royal Lytham and St Annes she completed a Grand Slam of major titles. Her tally is now six Majors. Her win at Lytham was her sixth major success. By the end of August 2003 she had won 46 LPGA tournaments and was inducted into the World Golf Hall of Fame. When she won the Mizuno Classic for the third successive year she was winning her 46th LPGA title and had wrapped up the Player of the Year and top money earner award.

Thomas, Vicki (née Rawlings) (Wal)
Born Northampton, 27 October 1954
One of Wales' most accomplished players who took part in six Curtis Cup matches between 1982 and 1992. She won the Welsh Championship eight times between 1979 and 1994 as well as the British Ladies Stroke Play in 1990.

Tinning, Iben (Den)
Born Copenhagen, 4 February 1974
Turned professional 1995
Cousin of the European Tour player Steen Tinning she is Denmark's leading lady professional and made her Solheim Cup début in 2003 at Barsebäck.

Valentine MBE, Jessie (née Anderson) (Sco)
Born Perth, Scotland, 18 March 1915
Turned professional 1960
A winner of titles before and after World War II, she was an impressive competitor and was one of the first

ladies to make a career out of professional golf. She won the British Ladies as an amateur in 1937 and again in 1955 and 1958 and was Scottish champion in 1938 and 1939 and four times between 1951 and 1956. But for the war years it is certain she would have had more titles and victories. She played in seven Curtis Cups between 1936 and 1958 and represented Scotland in the Home Internationals on 17 occasions between 1934 and 1958.

Varangot, Brigitte (Fra)
Born Biarritz, 1 May 1940
Winner of the French Amateur title five times in six years from 1961 and again in 1973. Her run in the French Championship was impressive from 1960 when her finishes were 2, 1, 1, 2, 1, 1, 1, 2. She was also a triple winner of the British Championship in 1963, 1965 and 1968. One of France's most successful players she also won the Italian title in 1970.

Walker OBE, Mickey (Eng)
Born Alwoodley, Yorkshire, 17 December 1952
Turned professional 1973
Always a popular and modest competitor she followed up an excellent amateur career by doing well as a professional. Twice a Curtis Cup player she won the Ladies British Open Amateur in 1971 and 1972, the English Ladies in 1973 and had victories, too, in Portugal, Spain and America where she won the 1972 Trans-Mississippi title. She won six times as a professional but is perhaps best known for her stirring captaincy of the first four European Solheim Cup sides leading them to a five point success at Dalmahoy. In 1992 she galvanised her side by playing them tapes of the men's Ryder Cup triumphs. Now a club professional she also works regularly as a television commentator.

Wright, Janette (née Robertson) (Sco)
Born Glasgow, 7 January 1935
Another of Scotland's most accomplished amateur players she competed four times in the Curtis Cup and was four times Scottish champion between 1959 and 1973. Formerly married to the late golf professional Innes Wright her daughter Pamela plays professionally on the LPGA Tour in America.

Wright, Pamela (Sco)
Born Aboyne, Scotland, 26 June 1964
Turned professional 1988
Daughter of former Scottish champion and Curtis Cup golfer Janette Wright and the late Aboyne professional Innes Wright. She played in the first three Solheim Cup matches being a member of the winning team at Dalmahoy in 1992 and was vice-captain in 2000. She was an All-American in 1987 and again in 1988 when she also won Collegiate Golfer of the Year honours. She was LPGA Tour rookie of the year in 1989.

Overseas Players, Men

Aaron, Tommy (USA)
Born Gainesville, Georgia, 22 February 1937
Turned professional 1961
After finishing runner-up in the 1972 US PGA Championship he won the 1973 Masters. He was a member of the 1969 and 1973 Ryder Cup teams. Inadvertently marked down a 4 on Roberto de Vicenzo's card for the 17th hole in the 1968 Masters when the Argentinian took 3. De Vicenzo signed for the 4 and lost out by one shot on a play-off for the Green Jacket.

Allenby, Robert (Aus)
Born Melbourne, 12 July 1971
Turned professional 1992
Pipped by a shot from winning the Australian Open as an amateur in 1991 by Wayne Riley's birdie, birdie, birdie finish at Royal Melbourne, he won the title three years later as a professional. After competing on the European Tour and winning four times, he now plays on the US Tour. He has played in three Presidents Cup matches in 1996, 2000 and 2003.

Aoki, Isao (Jpn)
Born Abiko, Chiba, 31 August 1942
Turned professional 1964
Successful international performer whose only victory on the main US Tour came dramatically in Hawaii in 1983 when he holed a 128 yards pitch for an eagle 3 at the last at Waialae to beat Jack Renner. Only Japanese golfer to win on the main European Tour taking the European Open in 1983. He also won the World Match Play in 1978 beating Simon Owen and was runner up the following year. He holed in one at Wentworth in that event to win a condominium at Gleneagles. He was top earner five times in his own country and is the Japanese golfer who has come closest to winning a major title finishing runner-up two shots behind Jack Nicklaus in the 1980 US Open at Baltusrol.

Atwal, Arjun (Ind)
Born Asansol, India, 20 March 1973
Turned professional 1995
Learned the game at Royal Calcutta and became the first Indian to win on the European Tour when he won the Caltex Singapore Masters in 2002. He won again in 2003 when he won the Carlsberg Malaysian Open. Only the second Indian to earn a card – the first was Jeeu Milka Singh.

Azinger, Paul (USA)
Born Holyoke, Massachusetts, 6 January 1960
Turned professional 1981
Helped by a second hole play-off victory against Greg Norman in the 1993 US PGA Championship at Inverness he made almost $1.5 million to finish second on the US money list to Nick Price. The following year he played only four events after having been diagnosed with lymphoma in his right shoulder blade. Happily he made a good recovery and scored his 12th US Tour victory in 2000 and his first since his 1993 US PGA win when he opened with a 63 and led from start to finish in the Sony Open in Hawaii. He played in three Ryder Cup matches in 1989, 1991 and 1993 and was on the 2001 team making headlines by holing a bunker shot at the last to halve with Niclas Fasth. In 1987 he was joint runner-up with Rodger Davis in the Open at Muirfield won by Nick Faldo. Injury prevented his enjoying much success in the 2003 season in the States.

Baddeley, Aaron (Aus)
Born New Hampshire, USA, 17 March 1981
Turned professional 2000
Became the first amateur to win the Australian Open since Bruce Devlin in 1969 and the youngest when he took the title at Royal Sydney in 2000. Then, having turned professional he successfully defended it at Kingston Heath. He had shown considerable promise when at age 15, he qualified for the Victorian Open. Represented Australia in the Eisenhower Trophy and holds both Australian and American passports. Played a limited schedule in 2002 despite having a European Tour card.

Baiocchi, Hugh (RSA)
Born Johannesburg, 17 August 1946
Turned professional 1971
A scratch golfer when he was 15, Hugh Baiocchi joined the Senior PGA Tour after playing with distinction for 23 years on the European Tour. He has played in 31 different countries around the world winning in many of them. He gained an extra special delight at winning the 1978 South African Open emulating his long-time golfing hero Gary Player who is a multiple winner of that title.

Baker-Finch, Ian (Aus)
Born Namour, Queensland, 24 October 1960
Turned professional 1979
Impressive winner of the Open Championship in 1991 he emerged as a tremendous ambassador for golf. Sadly in attempting to hit the ball further off the tee he lost his

game completely when teeing up in Tour events and was forced, after an agonising spell, to retire prematurely. After having been given the chance by Channel Seven producer Graeme Rowland to commentate in Australia, he took up the opportunity to do a similar job for the American ABC network.

Beem, Rich (USA)

Born Phoenix Arizona 24 August 1974
Turned professional 1994.
Playing in only his fourth major championship he hit the headlines in 2002 when he held off the spirited challenge of Tiger Woods to win the US PGA Championship at Hazeltine. The 31-year-old from Phoenix who now lives in Texas admitted he was 'flabbergasted to have won' having arrived with no expectations, although a winner of two US Tour titles – the 1999 Kemper Open and the 2002 International event at Castle Pines just a few weeks before the US PGA title. Just a year after turning professional Beem had given up the game to sell car stereos and mobile phones before becoming an assistant club professional before returning once again to tournament play in 1999. On the final day at Hazeltine, Beem hit two great shots – a fairway wood to to seven feet for an eagle at the at the 587 yards 11th and a 40 foot putt for a birdie at the 16th which helped him hold off Woods who finished with four birdies in a row. Beem prevented Woods from winning three majors in a year for the second time. From 73rd in the World Rankings Beem jumped to 26th.

Brooks, Mark (USA)

Born Fort Worth, Texas, 25 March 1961
Turned professional 1983
A seven-time winner on the US Tour between 1988 and 1996 he took the US PGA Championship title in 1996 after a play-off with Kenny Perry at Valhalla. On that occasion he birdied the 72nd hole and the first extra hole to win but he was beaten by South African Retief Goosen in the 18-hole play-off for the 2000 US Open at Southern Hills in Tulsa. Goosen shot 70, Brooks 72.

Calcavecchia, Mark (USA)

Born Laurel, Nebraska, 12 June 1960
Turned professional 1981
Winner of the 1989 Open Championship at Royal Troon after the first ever four-hole play-off against Australians Greg Norman and Wayne Grady. He was runner-up in the 1987 Masters at Augusta to Sandy Lyle and came second to Jodie Mudd in the 1990 Players' Championship. He played in the 1987, 1989, 1991 and 2002 Ryder Cup sides.

Campbell, William Cammack (USA)

Born West Virginia, 5 May 1923
One of America's most distinguished players and administrators. He won the US Amateur Championship in 1964 ten years after finishing runner-up in the Amateur Championship in Britain to Australian Doug Bachli at Muirfield. One of a select group who have been both President of the United States Golf

Association (in 1983) and captain of the Royal and Ancient Golf Club of St Andrews (in 1987/1988). He played in eight Ryder Cup matches between 1951 and 1975 captaining the side in 1955.

Casper, Billy (USA)

Born San Diego, California, 24 June 1931
Turned professional 1954
A three-time major title winner he took the US Open in 1959 and 1966 and the US Masters in 1970. In 1966 he came back from seven strokes behind Arnold Palmer with nine to play to force a play-off which he then won. Between 1956 and 1975 he picked up 51 first prize cheques on the US Tour. His European victories were the 1974 Trophée Lancôme and Lancia D'Oro and the 1975 Italian Open. As a senior golf he won nine times between 1982 and 1989 including the US Senior Open in 1983. Played in eight Ryder Cups and captained the American side in 1979 at Greenbrier. He and wife Shirley have 11 children several of them adopted. He was named Father of the Year in 1966. Started playing golf aged 5 and rates Ben Hogan, Byron Nelson and Sam Snead as his heroes. Five times Vardon Trophy winner (for low season stroke-average) and twice top money earner he was US PGA Player of the Year in 1966 and 1970. He was inducted into the World Golf Hall of Fame in 1978 and the US PGA Hall of Fame in 1982.

Charles, Sir Bob (NZ)

Born Auckland, 14 March 1936
Turned professional 1960
Three years after turning professional he became the first and still the only New Zealander to win the Open Championship. He defeated Phil Rodgers in the last 36-hole play-off for the title at Royal Lytham and St Annes then was runner-up in 1968 to Gary Player at Carnoustie and in 1969 to Tony Jacklin again at Lytham. Earlier in 1954 he had won the first of his four New Zealand Opens as an amateur. Between 1954 and 1960 worked in a bank before embarking on a golf career which has seen him win extensively around the world on golf's main Tours and the US Senior Tour. He won seven times on the US Tour, nine times in Europe, 24 times in New Zealand and has also won in Canada, Japan and South Africa. He does everything right-handed except games requiring two hands. In 1972 received the OBE from Her Majesty the Queen, the CBE in 1992 and was knighted in 1999 for his services to golf. He had for many years been the only left-hander to win a major but that changed when Canadian Mike Weir won the Masters in a play-off at Augusta in 2003.

Choi, Kyoung-Ju (Kor)

Born Wando, South Korea, 19 May 1970
When his high school teacher suggested he take up golf, he studied all Jack Nicklaus' videos. Son of a rice farmer he was the first Korean to earn a US Tour card and won twice in 2002. In 2003 he became the first Korean to win on the Euopean Tour when he won the Linde German Masters. Better known as KJ Choi.

Cink, Stewart (USA)
Born Huntsville, Alabama, 21 May 1973
Turned professional 1995
The Rookie of the Year on the US Tour in 1997 when he won the Canon Greater Hartford Classic. The year before he had been top rookie on the Buy.com tour. Although he made the 2002 Ryder Cup side he missed a two foot putt on the last and, as a result, a play-off for the US Open with Mark Brooks and winner Retief Goosen.

Coe, Charles (USA)
Born Oklahoma City, 26 October 1923
Another fine American amateur golfer who finished runner-up with Arnold Palmer to Gary Player in the 1961 Masters at Augusta. Twice US Amateur champion in 1949 and 1958, he played in six Walker Cup matches and was non-playing captain in 1959. He won seven and halved two of the 13 games he played. Winner of the Bobby Jones award in 1964.

Cole, Bobby (RSA)
Born Springs, 11 May 1948
Turned professional 1966
Winner of the Amateur Championship in 1966 when he beat R.D.B.M. Shade in the final which because of haar (fog) was reduced to 18 holes. Among his victories when he turned professional were two South African Opens in 1974 and 1980.

Cook, John (USA)
Born Toledo, Ohio, 2 October 1957
Turned professional 1979
A regular winner on the US Tour he gave Nick Faldo a fright in the 1992 Open at Muirfield. Three strokes behind with eight to play Cook had moved out in front after 16 holes on the final day but finished 5,5 to Faldo's 4,4. He was also tied second that year in the US PGA Championship. Given much help in his early years by Jack Nicklaus and Tom Weiskopf. Jointly with Mark Calcavecchia holds the low first-54 holes record of 189 at the St Jude Classic in 1996.

Couples, Fred (USA)
Born Seattle, Washington, 3 October 1959
Turned professional 1980
Troubled continually with a back problem he has managed to win only one major – the 1992 US Masters but is one of the most popular of all American players. Although he has been known to say he enjoys watching television lying on the sofa, he is no stay-at-home in a golfing sense. He has always been willing to travel and his overseas victories include two Johnnie Walker World Championships, the Johnnie Walker Classic, the Dubai Desert Classic and the Tournoi Perrier de Paris. On the US Tour he won 14 times between 1983 and 1998. He played five Ryder Cup matches and three times teed up for the US in the Presidents Cup. After an absence of years he returned to the winner's circle when he won the Shell Houston Open.

Crenshaw, Ben (USA)
Born Austin, Texas, 11 January 1952
One of golf's great putters who followed up his victory in the 1984 US Masters with an emotional repeat success in 1995 just a short time after the death of his long-time coach and mentor Harvey Pennick. He played in four Ryder Cup matches between 1981 and 1995 before captaining the side in 1999 when the Americans came from four points back to win with a scintillating last day performance. Winner of the Byron Nelson award in 1976 he was also named Bobby Jones award winner in 1991. Now combines playing with an equally successful career as a golf course designer and is an acknowledged authority on every aspect of the history of the game. In 2002 he was named the Payne Stewart Award winner – an award that recognises a player's respect of and upholding of the traditions of the game.

Curtis, Ben (USA)
Born Columbus, Ohio, 26 May 1977
Turned professional 2000
Shock 750-1 outsider who played superbly at Royal St George's to get his name engraved with all the other golfing greats on the famous Claret Jug. His victory while well deserved was one of golf's biggest shocks in years. It was his first major appearance. He only qualified for the Open with a 14th place finish in the Western Open in Chicago – a designated qualifying event. He had never played in Britain nor had he any experience of links golf but he outplayed Tiger Woods, Thomas Bjørn, David Love III and Vijay Singh to take the title with a score of 283. He learned the game in Ohio at the golf course his grandfather built at Ostrander, Ohio.

Daly, John (USA)
Born Sacramento, California, 28 April 1966
Turned professional 1987
Winner of two majors – the 1991 US PGA Champion-ship and the 1995 Open Championship at St Andrews after a play-off with Costantino Rocca, his career has not been without its ups and downs. He admits he has battled alcoholism and, on occasions, has been his own worst enemy when having run-ins with officialdom but he remains one of the most popular and likeable if sometimes unorthodox players on Tour because of his long hitting. His average drive is over 300 yards. When he won the US PGA Championship at Crooked Stick he got in as ninth alternate, drove through the night to tee it up without a practice round and shot 69, 67, 69, 71 to beat Bruce Lietzke by three. Given invaluable help at times by Fuzzy Zoeller he writes his own songs and is a mean performer on the guitar. In 2001 took the BMW International Open title at Munich. In 2002 was a member of both the US and European Tours. Curiously, despite winning two majors, he has never played in the Ryder Cup. In 2003 he won the Korean Open.

Davis, Rodger (Aus)
Born Sydney, 18 May 1951
Turned professional 1974
Experienced Australian competitor who came joint second in the 1987 Open Championship behind Nick Faldo at Muirfield. A regular on the European Tour he hopes to extend his playing career on the US Senior circuit. Winner of 27 titles, 19 of them on the Australasian circuit where, in 1988, he picked up an Aus$1 million first prize in the Bicentennial event at Royal Melbourne. Gave up golf for a while but lost all his money in a hotel venture that went wrong and took up tournament play again. Usually plays in trademark 'plus twos'. Now a regular on the US Senior Tour.

Dickson, Bob (USA)
Born McAlester, Oklahoma, 25 January 1944
Turned professional 1968
Best remembered for being one of only four players to complete a Transatlantic amateur double. In 1967 he won the US Amateur Championship at Broadmoor with a total of 285 (the Championship was played over 72 holes from 1965 to 1972) and the British Amateur title with a 2 and 1 win over fellow American Ron Cerrudo at Formby. After turning professional scored two wins on the US Tour.

Duval, David (USA)
Born Jacksonville, Florida, 19 November 1971
Turned professional 1993
A regular winner on the US Tour who wears dark glasses because of an eye stigmatism which is sensitive to light, he won his first major at Royal Lytham and St Annes last year when he became only the second American professional to win the Open over that course. He was the first player in US Tour history to win titles by play-off in consecutive weeks. Played 86 events and had seven second-place finishes and four thirds before making his break-through win in the Michelob Championship then won the following week as well. His father Bob plays the US Senior Tour. He was a winner of the US Tour Championship in 1997 and the Players' Championship in 1999. In the 1998 and 2001 Masters he came second and was third in that event in 2000. He played in 1991 Walker Cup and was a member of the winning Ryder Cup side on his début in 1999 and was also a member of the 2002 Cup side halving his match with Darren Clarke in the singles. Injury and illness meant Duval did not enjoy a successful 2003 season.

Elkington, Steve (Aus)
Born Inverell, 8 December 1962
Turned professional 1985
A former Australian (1990 and 1991) and New Zealand (1990) champion he is a regular winner these days on the US Tour despite an allergy to grass. At Riviera CC in Los Angeles in 1995 he beat Colin Montgomerie in a play-off for the US PGA Championship, the only major he has won to date.

Winner of the 1992 Australian Open he has one of the finest swings in golf. He is also an accomplished artist in his spare time. He has played four times since 1994 in the Presidents Cup. In 2002 after prequalifying for the event at Dunbar he played off for the Open title at Muirfield with Thomas Levet, Stuart Appleby and eventual winner Ernie Els.

Els, Ernie (RSA)
Born Johannesburg, 17 October 1969
Turned professional 1989
Teenage winner of the South African Amateur Championship in 1996 he is renowned as one of the game's big hitters. His short game can be deadly too and when on song he is one of the most impressive international performers. He has won two US Opens – in 1994 at Oakmont after a play-off against Loren Roberts and Colin Montgomerie and at Congressional where he beat Montgomerie into second place. Although proficient at Rugby Union and cricket he decided to concentrate on golf when he played off scratch at age 14. He has matched Gary Player's record of winning three successive South African Opens and has collected the South African PGA and Masters titles as well. In 1994 equalled the European Tour record of 12 birdies in the 61 he fired en route to victory in the Dubai Desert Classic. He was made an honorary member of the PGA European Tour in recognition of his two US Open wins and his three successive World Match Play title successes round the famous West Course. Going for a fourth successive win in 1997 he lost on the last green to Vijay Singh. In 2002 Els won the Heineken Classic at Royal Melbourne, the Dubai Desert Classic and the Genuity Championship on the US Tour before realising his life-long dream by winning the Open Championship at Muirfield 43 years after Gary Player had won at the same venue. He beat Frenchman Thomas Levet in a sudden-death play-off at the first extra hole after tieing with him in a four hole play-off which also involved Australians Stuart Appleby and Steve Elkington. All had finished on six-under-par 268. Els played a brilliant recovery from an awkward lie in a greenside trap at the 18th to make the par that earned him his third major title victory. By winning he ended Tiger Woods' hopes of winning all four majors in the same year. Woods had won the Masters and US Open earlier. He made a whirlwind start of 2003 winning twice in America at the Mercedes Championship where he won with a record 31 under total and the Sony Open in Hawaii and twice on the European Tour taking the Heineken Classic at Royal Melbourne and the Johnnie Walker Classic for the second time. At the Johnnie Walker at Lake Karinyup he was at his blistering best, powering 315 yards plus drives and shooting a remarkable 29-under-par. By the start of September he had added the Barclay's Scottish Open and the Omega European Masters and the HSBC World Match Play Championship and ended up top money earner on the European Tour.

Faxon, Brad (USA)
Born Oceanport, New Jersey, 1 August 1961
Turned professional 1983
A former Walker Cup player who competed in the 1983 match he has played twice in the Ryder Cup (1995 and 1997). A seven-time winner on the US Tour he also putted superbly to win the Australian Open at Metropolitan in 1993.

Fernandez, Vicente (Arg)
Born Corrientes, 5 May 1946
Turned professional 1964
After playing on the European Tour where he won five times between 1975 and 1992 he joined the US Senior Tour competing with considerable success. In this respect he was following in the footsteps of fellow Argentinian Roberto de Vicenzo. Born with one leg shorter than the other which is why he limps, he is remembered in Europe for the 87 foot putt he holed up three tiers on the final green at The Belfry in 1992 to win the Murphy's English Open. His nickname is 'Chino'.

Finsterwald, Dow (USA)
Born Athens, Ohio, 6 September 1929
Turned professional 1951
Winner of the 1958 US PGA Championship he won 11 other competitions between 1955 and 1963. He played in four Ryder Cup matches in a row from 1957 and captained the side in 1977. He was US PGA Player of the Year in 1958.

Floyd, Raymond (USA)
Born Fort Bragg, North Carolina, 4 September 1942
Turned professional 1961
A four time major winner whose failure to win an Open Championship title prevented his completing a Slam of Majors. He won the US Open in 1986, the Masters in 1976 when he matched the then 72-hole record set by Jack Nicklaus to win by eight strokes and took the US PGA title in 1969 and 1982. In addition to coming second and third in the Open he was also runner-up three times in the Masters and in the US PGA once. After scoring 22 victories on the main US Tour he has continued to win as a senior. Inducted into the World Golf Hall of Fame in 1989 he is an avid Chicago Cubs baseball fan. Played in eight Ryder Cup matches between 1969 and 1993 making history with his last appearance by being the oldest player to take part in the match. He was 49. He was non-playing captain in 1989 when the match was drawn at The Belfry.

Ford, Doug (USA)
Born West Haven, Connecticut, 6 August 1922
Turned professional 1949
His 25 wins on the US Tour between 1955 and 1963 included the 1975 US Masters. US PGA Player of the Year in 1955, he competed in four Ryder Cup matches in succession from 1955.

Franco, Carlos (Par)
Born Asunción, 24 May 1965
Turned professional 1986
Emerged on to the international stage from humble beginnings. He was one of a family of nine who shared a one-room home at the course where his father was greens superintendent and caddie. All five of his brothers play golf and he was appointed Paraguayan Minister of Sport in 1999. Won twice in his rookie year on the US Tour and became the first player to make more than $1 million in his first two seasons. Has scored three wins on the US circuit, five times in Japan where he had 11 top 10 finishes in 1997, once in the Philippines and 19 times in South America. First made headlines at St Andrews when he beat Sam Torrance in the Alfred Dunhill Cup.

Frost, David (RSA)
Born Cape Town, 11 September 1959
Turned professional 1981
Although now based permanently in the United States has won as many titles overseas as on the US Tour. The 1993 season was his best in America when he made over $1 million in prize money and finished fifth on the money list. He has established a vineyard in South Africa growing 100 acres of vines on the 300-acre estate. He has very quickly earned a reputation for producing quality wines.

Furyk, Jim (USA)
Born West Chester, Pennsylvania, 12 May 1970
Turned professional 1992
Considered one of the best players not to have won a major, Furyk put that right when he won the US Open at Olympia Fields, Chicago. He was one of four first-time major winners in 2003. He clearly enjoys playing in Las Vegas where he has won three Invitational events in 1995, 1999 and 1998. Has teed it up in two Presidents Cups and two Ryder Cups beating Nick Faldo in the singles at Valderrama in 1997. He was also in the 2002 side. Has one of the most easily recognisable if idiosyncratic swings in top line golf. His father Mike has been his only coach.

Goosen, Retief (RSA)
Born Pietersburg, 3 February 1969
Turned professional 1990
Introduced to golf at the age of 11 he scored his first major success when leading from start to finish at the 2001 US Open at Tulsa and then beating Mark Brooks in the 18-hole play-off by two shots. Although he suffered health problems after being hit by lightning as a teenager he has enjoyed a friendly rivalry with South Africa's other talented young player Ernie Els. Winner of the 1990 South African Amateur title, he scored his first professional victory in the Iscor Newcastle Classic a year later. In Europe where he has been helped by Belgian psychologist Jos Vanstiphout, golf's quiet achiever enjoys playing in France where he has won two French Championships (1997 and 1999) and the Trophée Lancôme in 2000. Just weeks

after his US Open win in 2001 he led again from start to finish to win the Scottish Open at Loch Lomond. In 2002 he was a runaway eight shot winner in the Johnnie Walker Classic at Lake Karynup in Perth, Australia.

Grady, Wayne (Aus)

Born Brisbane, 26 July 1957
Turned professional 1973 and again in 1978

One of Australia's most popular players he won the US PGA Championship at Shoal Creek by three shots over Fred Couples. A year earlier he had tied with Greg Norman and eventual winner Mark Calcavecchia for the Open Championship losing out in the first ever four-hole play-off for the title. Took over in 2001 as chairman of the Australasian Tour from Jack Newton and was the architect of a tie up between the Australasian Tour and the US Nationwide Tour for two joint events a year. With a reduced playing schedule he was able to join the BBC TV commentary team for the 2003 Open and has been signed up for a full season in 2004.

Graham, David (Aus)

Born Windsor, Tasmania, 23 May 1946
Turned professional 1962

Played superbly for a closing 67 round Merion to win the 1981 US Open Championship from George Burns and Bill Rogers. That day he hit every green in regulation. Two years earlier he had beaten Ben Crenshaw at the third extra hole at Oakland Hills to win the US PGA Championship. When he took up the game at age 14 he played with left-handed clubs before making the switch to a right-handed set. Awarded the Order of Australia for his services to golf he is a member of the Cup and Tee committee that sets up Augusta each year for the Masters. A regular winner around the world in the 70s and 80s he won eight times on the US Tour between 1972 and 1983. Now plays on the US Senior Tour but also has gained a considerable reputation as a course designer.

Graham, Lou (USA)

Born Nashville, Tennessee, 7 January 1938
Turned professional 1962

Won the US Open at Medinah in 1975 after a play-off against John Mahaffey.

Green, Hubert (USA)

Born Birmingham, Alabama, 18 December 1946
Turned professional 1970

Beat Lou Graham for the 1977 US Open at Southern Hills despite being told with four holes to play that he had received a death threat. Three times a Ryder Cup player he also won the 1985 US PGA Championship. His only European Tour victory was the 1977 Irish Open. Best known for his unorthodox swing and distinctive crouching putting style. He is successfully beating throat cancer – an illness that has meant he has been unable to compete in the US Senior Tour.

Harper, Chandler (USA)

Born Portsmouth, Virginia, 10 March 1914
Turned professional 1934

Winner of the 1950 US PGA Championship he won over ten tournaments and was elected to the US PGA Hall of Fame in 1969. Once shot 58 (29-29) round a 6100 yards course in Portsmouth.

Hayes, Dale (RSA)

Born Pretoria, 1 July 1952
Turned professional 1970

Former South African amateur stroke play champion who was a regular winner in South Africa and Europe after turning professional. He was Europe's top money earner in 1975 but retired from competitive golf to move into business. He is now a successful television commentator in South Africa with a weekly programme of his own often working as a double act with veteran Denis Hutchinson.

Henning, Harold (RSA)

Born Johannesburg, 3 October 1934
Turned professional 1953

One of three brothers from a well-known South African golf family he was a regular winner of golf events in his home country and Europe and had two wins on the US Tour. Played ten times for South Africa in the World Cup winning the event with Gary Player in Madrid in 1965.

Hoch, Scott (USA)

Born Raleigh, North Carolina, 24 November 1955
Turned professional 1979

Ryder Cup, Presidents Cup, Walker Cup and Eisenhower Trophy player who is a regular winner on the US Tour. Has scored 10 wins on the US Tour between 1980 and 2001 and has had six more victories worldwide. In 1989 he donated $100,000 of his Las Vegas Invitational winnings to the Arnold Palmer Children's Hospital in Orlando where his son Cameron had been successfully treated for a rare bone infection in his right knee. More unfortunately remembered for missing a short putt at the first extra hole of a play-off that would have won him a Masters Green Jacket.

Irwin, Hale (USA)

Born Joplin, Montana, 3 June 1945
Turned professional 1968

A three time winner of the US Open (1974, 1979 and 1990) he has been a prolific winner on the main US Tour and, since turning 50, on the US Senior Tour. He had 20 wins on the main Tour including the 1990 US Open triumph where he holed a 45-foot putt on the final green at Medinah to force a play-off with Mike Donald then after both were still tied following a further 18 holes became the oldest winner of the Championship at 45 when he sank a 10-foot birdie putt at the first extra hole of sudden death. Joint runner-up to Tom Watson in the 1983 Open at Royal Birkdale where he stubbed the ground and missed a tap-in putt on the final day – a slip that cost him the chance of a play-off. Three times top

earner on the Senior Tour where, prior to the start of the 2001 season, he had averaged $90,573 per start in 130 events coming in the top three in 63 of those events and finishing over par in only nine of them.

Jacobsen, Frederik (Swe)
Born Moindal, Sweden, 26 September 1974

He made his European Tour winning breakthrough when he took the 2003 Omega Hong Kong Open and then followed that up with victory in the Algarve Open de Portugal. He finished fifth in the US Open, sixth in the Open and became the latest player to shoot 60 when he did so in the first round of the Linde German Masters. He won his third title of the European season when he beat Carlos Rodiles in the end-of-season Volvo Masters at Andalucia. With that win at Valderrama, Jacobsen became the first Swede to win three titles in a season and by doing so moved into the top 20 of the world rankings for the first time. He finished the European season fourth in the Volvo Order of Merit.

January, Don (USA)
Born Plainview, Texas, 20 November 1929
Turned professional 1955

Winner of the US Open in 1967 he followed up his successful main Tour career in which he had 11 wins between 1956 and 1976 with double that success as a Senior winning 22 times. Much admired for his easy rhythmical style.

Janzen, Lee (USA)
Born Austin, Minnesota, 28 August 1964
Turned professional 1986

Twice a winner of the US Open in 1993 and again in 1998 when he staged the best final round comeback since Johnny Miller rallied from six back to win the title 25 years earlier. Five strokes behind the late Payne Stewart after 54 holes at Baltusrol he closed with a 67 to beat Stewart with whom he had also battled for the title in 1993.

Jones, Steve (USA)
Born Artesia, New Mexico, 27 December 1958
Turned professional 1981

First player since Jerry Pate in 1976 to win the US Open after having had to qualify. His 1996 victory was the result of inspiration he received from reading a Ben Hogan book given to him the week before the Championship at Oakland Hills. Uses a reverse overlapping grip as a result of injury. Indeed his career was put on hold for three years after injury to his left index finger following a dirt-bike accident. He dominated the 1997 Phoenix Open shooting 62, 64, 65 and 67 for an 11 shot victory over Jesper Parnevik That week his 258 winning total was just one outside the low US Tour record set by Mike Souchak in 1955.

Kite, Tom (USA)
Born Austin, Texas, 9 December 1949
Turned professional 1972

He won the US Open at Pebble Beach in 1992 in difficult conditions when aged 42 to lose the 'best

player around never to have won a Major' tag. With 19 wins on the main Tour he was the first to top $6million, $7 million, $8 million and $9 million dollars in prize money. Has been playing since he was 11 and after a lifetime wearing glasses had laser surgery to correct acute near-sightedness. The Ryder Cup captain in 1997 he now plays the US Senior Tour.

Kuchar, Matt (USA)
Born Lake Mary, Florida, 21 June 1978
Turned professional 2002

Winner of the US Amateur in 1997 he was leading amateur in the 1998 Masters and US Open Championship. Scored his first win as a professional when he landed the 2002 Honda Classic.

Lehman, Tom (USA)
Born Austin, Minnesota, 7 March 1959
Turned professional 1982

Winner of the Open Championship at Royal Lytham and St Annes in 1996 he was runner-up in the US Open in 1996 and third in 1997. He was runner-up in the 1994 US Masters having come third the previous year. Has played in four Ryder Cup matches.

Leonard, Justin (USA)
Born Dallas, Texas, 15 June 1972
Turned professional 1994

Winner of the 1997 Open at Royal Troon when he beat Jesper Parnevik and Darren Clarke into second place with a closing 65 and nearly won the title again in 1999 when he lost a four-hole play-off with Jean Van de Velde and Paul Lawrie to the Scotsman at Carnoustie. In 1998 came from five back to beat Lee Janzen in the Players Championship and is remembered for his fight back against José Maria Olazábal on the final day of the 1999 Ryder Cup at Brookline. Four down after 11 holes he managed to share a half-point with the Spaniard to help America win the Cup.

Littler, Gene (USA)
Born San Diego, California, 21 July 1930
Turned professional 1954

Winner of the 1953 US Amateur Championship he had a distinguished professional career scoring 26 victories on the US Tour between 1955 and 1977. He scored his only major triumph at Pebble Beach in 1971 when he beat Bob Goalby and Doug Sanders at Oakland Hills. He had been runner-up in the US Open in 1954 and was runner-up in the 1977 US PGA Championship and the 1970 US Masters. A seven-time Ryder Cup player between 1961 and 1977 he is a former winner of the Ben Hogan, Bobby Jones and Byron Nelson awards. He won the Hogan award after successfully beating cancer.

Love III, Davis (USA)
Born Charlotte, North Carolina, 13 April 1964
Turned professional 1985

Son of one of America's most highly rated teachers who died in a plane crash in 1988, Love has won only

one major – the 1997 US PGA Championship at Winged Foot where he beat Justin Leonard by five shots. He has been runner-up in the US Open (1996) and the US Masters (1999). In the World Cup of Golf won the title in partnership with Fred Couples four years in a row (1992–1995). He has played in five Ryder Cups and enjoyed a superb 2003 winning four times between February and August. His victories were the AT&T Pebble Beach National Pro-Am, the Players Championship, The Heritage and The International.

McNulty, Mark (Zim)
Born Zimbabwe, 25 October 1953
Turned professional 1977
Recognised as one of the best putters in golf he was runner-up to Nick Faldo in the 1990 Open at St Andrews. Although hampered throughout his career by a series of injuries and illness he has scored 16 wins on the European Tour and 33 around the world including 23 on the South African Sunshine circuit. He won the South African Open in 1987 and again in 2001 holing an 18-foot putt on the last at East London to beat Justin Rose.

Maggert, Jeff (USA)
Born Columbia, Missouri, 20 February 1964
Turned professional 1986
A three times Ryder Cup player who competed in the 1995, 1997 and 1999 matches he won the World Golf Championship Match Play event in 1999 to land a million. A quiet achiever he has come third in the US PGA Championship twice in 1995 and 1997.

Marsh, Graham (Aus)
Born Kalgoorlie, Western Australia, 14 January 1944
Turned professional 1968
A notable Australian who followed up his international playing career by gaining a reputation for designing fine courses. Although he played in Europe, America and Australasia he spent most of his time on the Japanese circuit where he had 17 wins between 1971 and 1982 but won 11 times in Europe and scored victories also in the United States, India, Thailand and Malaysia. He now plays on the US Senior Tour.

Melnyk, Steve (USA)
Born Brunswick, Georgia, 26 February 1947
Turned professional 1971
US Amateur champion in 1969 and British champion in 1971. His professional career was cut short because of an ankle injury. Today he commentates for CBS, one of the US networks.

Micheel, Shaun (USA)
Born Orlando, Florida, 5 January 1969
Turned professional 1962
Surprise winner of the USPGA Championship at Oak Hill in 2003. He fired rounds of 69, 68, 69 and 70 for a winning total of 276. He completed his victory with one of the most brilliant approach irons from the rough to just one foot of the hole at the last. Micheel was one of four first time winners in 2003.

Mickelson, Phil (USA)
Born San Diego, California, 16 June 1970
Turned professional 1992
Plays all sports right-handed except golf and claims to have started hitting golf balls at 18 months. Although he won the 2000 Tour Championship is still without a major victory. His best finishes in Majors are second in the 2001 US PGA Championship and the 1999 US Open and third in the 1994 US PGA Championship. His 19 victories on the US Tour include a win as an amateur in the 1995 Tucson Open. His 65 at the Masters in 1996 is lowest score by a left-hander at that event. One of only three players to win the NCAA Championship and US Amateur in the same year. The others – Jack Nicklaus and Tiger Woods. He has played in two Walker Cups, four times in Presidents Cup and in four Ryder Cup matches. Like Colin Montgomerie in Europe, Mickelson remains one of golf's most successful players never to have won a major.

Miller, Johnny (USA)
Born San Francisco, California, 29 April 1947
Turned professional 1969
Dreamed of winning the Open after Tony Lema, another member of the Olympic Club in San Francisco, did so in 1964. Realised his dream when he beat Jack Nicklaus and Seve Ballesteros into second place in the 1976 Open at Royal Birkdale. His US Open win in 1973 came with the help of a brilliant last round 63 which set the record, since equalled for the lowest round in the Championship. Was involved with Tom Weiskopf and Jack Nicklaus in one of the greatest finishes to a US Masters in 1975 which Nicklaus won. He scored 24 wins between 1971 and 1984 and in 1975 shot 49 under par when winning the Phoenix and Tucson Opens in successive weeks. Now commentates for NBC.

Mize, Larry (USA)
Born Augusta, Georgia, 23 September 1958
Turned professional 1980
Only local player ever to win the Masters and he did it in dramatic style holing a 140-foot pitch and run at the second extra hole to edge out Greg Norman and Seve Ballesteros. He had made the play-off by holing a 10-foot birdie on the final green. In 1993 he beat an international field to take the Johnnie Walker World Championship title at Tryall in Jamaica. His middle name is Hogan.

Nagle, Kel (Aus)
Born North Sydney, 21 December 1920
Turned professional 1946
In the dramatic Centenary Open at St Andrews in 1960 he edged out Arnold Palmer, winner already that year of the Masters and US Open, to become champion. It was the finest moment in the illustrious career of a golfer who has been a wonderful ambassador for his country. Along with Peter Thomson he competed nine times in the World Cup winning the event in 1954. He is an

honorary member of the Royal and Ancient Golf Club of St Andrews.

Nelson, Byron (USA)

Born Fort Worth, Texas, 4 February 1912
Turned professional 1932

In the 1945 US season he won 18 times including 11 events in a row between March and August – a record unlikely ever to be broken. Between 1935 and 1946 he won 54 times but although he won the US Open in 1939, the US PGA Championship in 1940 and 1945 and the US Masters in 1937 and 1942 he never managed to complete the set of four majors. His only win in Europe was the 1955 French Open. He remains a father figure in US golf and until he retired in 2001 was one of the Masters honorary starters along with the late Gene Sarazen and the late Sam Snead.

Nelson, Larry (USA)

Born Fort Payne, Alabama, 10 September 1947
Turned professional 1971

Often underrated he learned to play by reading Ben Hogan's The Five Fundamentals of Golf and broke 100 first time out and 70 after just nine months. Active as well these days on course design he has won the Jack Nicklaus award. He has been successful in the US Open (1983 at Oakmont) and two US PGA Championships (in 1981 at the Atlanta Athletic Club and in 1987 after a play-off with Lanny Wadkins at PGA National). Three times a Ryder Cup player he has competed equally successfully as a Senior having won 15 titles (at end of July 2001). He did not play as a youngster but visited a driving range after completing his military service and was hooked. He was named Senior PGA Tour Player of the Year for finishing top earner and winning six times in 2000. At the end of his third full season on the Senior Tour and after 87 events he had won just short of $10 million.

Newton, Jack (Aus)

Born Sydney, 30 January 1950
Turned professional 1969

Runner-up to Tom Watson after a play-off in the 1975 Open at Carnoustie and runner-up to Seve Ballesteros in the 1980 Masters at Augusta, he was a popular personality on both sides of the Atlantic and in his native Australia only to have his playing career ended prematurely when he walked into the whirling propeller of a plane at Sydney airport. He lost an eye, an arm and had considerable internal injuries but the quick action of a surgeon who happened to be around probably saved his life. Learned to play one-handed and still competes in pro-ams successfully. Until his retirement in 2000 he was chairman of the Australasian Tour and remains Australia's most respected golf commentator.

Nicklaus, Jack (USA)

Born Columbus, Ohio, 21 January 1940
Turned professional 1961

The greatest golfer of the 20th century and possibly of all time depending on what Tiger Woods manages to achieve. After winning two US Amateurs he went on to win 18 professional major titles. His record is phenomenal. He won the Open in 1966, 1970 and 1978, the last two at St Andrews and was runner-up seven times and third on two further occasions. He won the US Open in 1962, 1967, 1972 and 1980 and came second four times. He won five US PGA titles in 1963, 1971, 1973, 1975 and 1980 and was runner-up four times and third on two further occasions and he won six Masters in 1963, 1965, 1966, 1972, 1975 and 1986 when at the age of 46 he became the oldest winner of a Green Jacket. In addition he was runner-up four times and third twice. In 1966 he became the first player to successfully defend the Masters (a feat later matched by Nick Faldo in 1990). He won six Australian Opens (1964, 1968, 1971, 1975, 1976 and 1978) and played in six Ryder Cups, captaining two more in 1983 at Palm Beach Gardens when America won and in 1987 at Muirfield Village where his side were losers for the first time on home soil. Credited with saving the Cup match after suggesting that Continental golfers should be included in the side from 1979. Ten years earlier he conceded the 18-inch putt that Jacklin had for a half at the last when the result of the match depended on the result of that game. The match was drawn. After winning 71 times between 1962 and 1984 on the main Tour he won a further ten times on the Senior Tour. He has won almost every honour you can win in golf including the Byron Nelson, Ben Hogan and Walter Hagen awards. He was the US top money earner in seasons 1964, 1965, 1967, 1971, 1972, 1973, 1975 and 1976 and is a honorary member of the Royal and Ancient Golf Club of St Andrews. Bobby Jones once said of Nicklaus that 'he played a game with which I am not familiar'. With the constant support of his wife Barbara, Nicklaus has been the personification of all that is good about the game. He has designed over 200 courses worldwide.

Nobilo, Frank (NZ)

Born Auckland, 14 May 1960
Turned professional 1979

Injury has affected his career in recent years but he remains one of his country's most popular players with an excellent swing. After winning regularly in Europe he moved to America where in 1997 he won the Greater Greensboro Classic. He has represented New Zealand in nine World Cup matches between 1982 and 1999, played in 11 Alfred Dunhill Cups and three Presidents Cup sides. Now a television analyst for the Golf Channel.

Norman, Greg (Aus)

Born Mount Isa, Queensland, 10 February 1955
Turned professional 1976

Australia's most prolific winner in recent years credited with 77 victories worldwide (as of July 2001) but has slowed down because of injury and trimmed his schedule in recent times. He won the Open in tough conditions at Turnberry in 1986 and again in glorious weather at Royal St George's in 1993 when he fired the lowest winning aggregate of 267 (66, 68, 69, 64). Decided to take up golf after caddying for his mother and abandoned plans to join the Australian Air

Force. One of the few golfers to have topped the official money lists on both sides of the Atlantic he received his first winner's cheque in the Westlake Classic on the Australian Tour in 1976. Has the unhappy reputation of having lost Majors in three different types of play-off – the 1987 Masters to Larry Mize and the 1993 US PGA to Paul Azinger in sudden death, the Open to Mark Calcavecchia at Royal Troon in a four-hole play-off in 1989 and the US Open over 18 holes to Fuzzy Zoeller at Winged Foot in 1984. In 1986 he led going into the final round of all four Majors that year and won only the Open. During his career he has set all kinds of money records on the US Tour but is jinxed at the US Masters where he has finished second three times. He has also been runner-up on five other occasions in Majors. Today spends as much time in the boardroom looking after his business interests as he does playing.

North, Andy (USA)
Born Thorp, Wisconsin, 9 March 1950
Turned professional 1972
Although this tall American found it difficult to win Tour events he did pick up two US Open titles. His first Championship success came at Cherry Hills in Denver in 1986 when he edged out Dave Stockton and J.C. Snead and the second at Oakland Hills in 1985 when he finished just a shot ahead of Dave Barr, T.C. Chen and Denis Watson who had been penalised a shot during the Championship for waiting longer than the regulation 10 seconds at one hole to see if his ball would drop into the cup. North is now a very successful golf commentator whose analytical comments are much admired.

O'Meara, Mark (USA)
Born Goldsboro, North Carolina, 13 January 1957
Turned professional 1980
A former US Amateur Champion in 1979 Mark was 41 when he won his first Major – the US Masters at Augusta. That week in 1998 he did not three putt once on Augusta's glassy greens. Three months later he won the Open at Royal Birkdale battling with, among others, Tiger Woods with whom he has had a particular friendship. They both live at Isleworth in Florida. He is the oldest player to win two Majors in the same year and was chosen as PGA Player of the Year that season. When he closed birdie, birdie to win the Masters he joined Arnold Palmer and Art Wall as the only players to do that and became only the fifth player in Masters history to win without leading in the first three rounds. He won his Open championship title in a four hole play-off against Brian Watts. O'Meara played in five Ryder Cups between 1985 and 1999.

Ozaki, 'Jumbo' Masashi (Jpn)
Born Kaiman Town, Tokushima, 24 January 1947
Turned professional 1980
Along with Isao Aoki is Japan's best known player, but unlike Aoki has maintained his base in Japan where he has scored over 80 victories. His only overseas win was the New Zealand Open early in his career. He is a golfing icon in his native country. His two brothers Joe (Naomichi) and Jet also play professionally.

Palmer, Arnold (USA)
Born Latrobe, Pennsylvania, 10 September 1929
Turned professional 1954
Winner of 61 titles on the US Tour between 1956 and 1980, he is one of the most charismatic players in golf who has been credited with starting the golfing boom in the latter part of the 20th century. A former US Amateur champion in 1954, his performances were always exciting to watch and for years he was followed around by his own ever-loyal army of fans ... indeed still is when he tees up on the US Senior Tour. He won eight Major titles – the 1960 US Open and the 1961 and 1962 Opens at Royal Birkdale in very stormy weather and at Royal Troon where he beat Kel Nagle by six shots and the rest of the field by 13. He won the US Masters in 1958, 1960, 1962 and 1964 but never managed to win the US PGA although he finished second three times. The first player to pass the $1 million mark in earnings he helped Keith Mackenzie the then secretary of the Royal and Ancient Golf Club of St Andrews revive the Open and is now a distinguished honorary member of the club. In 1960 having won the US Masters and US Open he came to St Andrews for the Centenary Open hoping to match three majors in a season – a record held at the time by Ben Hogan but he was beaten by Australian Kel Nagle. Son of the greenkeeper at Ligonier in the Pennsylvanian mountains – he later bought the club – he has remained a respected golfing idol noted for his remarkable strength and his attacking golf. With Jack Nicklaus and Gary Player he became a member of the modern Big Three – a concept developed by his manager – the late Mark McCormack whose first client he was.

Parry Craig (Aus)
Born Sunshine, Victoria, Australia 12 January 1966.
Turned professional 1985.
Australian Parry, winner of 18 titles internationally but never a winner on the US Tour, put that right in 2002 when he landed the World Golf Championship NEC Invitational at Sahalee in Washington to pick up his largest career cheque – $1 million. After 15 years of trying to win in America the chances of him being successful at Salahee seemed slim having missed the four previous cuts. However, the 300-1 long-shot played and putted beautifully covering the last 48 holes without making a bogey to win by four from another Australian Robert Allenby and American Fred Funk. Tiger Woods, trying to win the event for a record fourth-successive year was fourth. Only Gene Sarazen and Walter Hagen have ever won the same four titles in successive years. It was Parry's 236th tournament in the United States and moved him from 118th in the world to 45th.

Pate, Jerry (USA)

Born Macon, Georgia, 16 September 1953
Turned professional 1975
Winner of the 1976 US Open when he hit a 5-iron across water to three feet at the 72nd hole at the Atlanta Athletic Club. He was a member of what is regarded as the strongest ever Ryder Cup side that beat the Europeans at Walton Heath in 1981. Has now retired from golf and commentates occasionally on American television.

Pavin, Corey (USA)

Born Oxnard, California, 26 May 1961
Turned professional 1983
Although not one of golf's longer hitters he battled with powerful Greg Norman to take the 1995 US Open title at Shinnecock Hills. A runner-up in the 1994 US PGA Championship and third in the 1992 US Masters he won 13 times between 1984 and 1996. His only victory in Europe came when he took the German Open title in 1983 while on honeymoon.

Perry, Kenny (USA)

Born Elizabethtown, Kentucky, 10 August 1960
Turned professional 1982
After winning for times between 1991 and 2001, he had a marvellous 2003 winning the Bank of America Colonial, the Memorial Tournament and the Greater Milwaukee Open between May 25 and July 13.

Player, Gary (RSA)

Born Johannesburg, 1 November 1935
Turned professional 1953
One of the modern Big Three with Arnold Palmer and Jack Nicklaus, he has won 167 titles worldwide including nine Majors between 1959 and 1978 and nine senior Majors between 1986 and 1997. His Major wins include three Open Championships in 1959 at Muirfield, 1968 at Carnoustie and 1974 at Royal Lytham and St Annes, three US Masters in 1961, 1974 and 1978, the US Open in 1965 when he completed a Grand Slam of major titles and the US PGA Championship in 1962 and 1972. A life-long fitness fanatic who has won titles in five decades he is one of only five players to have won all four Major titles. Gene Sarazen, Ben Hogan, Jack Nicklaus and Tiger Woods are the others. He considers the greatest thrill of his life was becoming the third man in history to do so. Having never based himself full-time in the US he has travelled more miles than any other golfer during his career – an estimated 12 million by the end of 2000. He entered his first Open in 1955 and failed to qualify but finished fourth in 1956 and played for the last time at Royal Lytham and St Annes in 2001 when 66. One of his most dramatic major performances came when he went into the last round seven shots behind Hubert Green at the 1974 US Masters, came home in 30 and equalled the then record 64 to win. He scored a record seven wins in the Australian Open, took the South African Open a record 13 times and won the World Match Play title a record-equalling five times coming from seven down after 19 holes in one tie in 1965 to beat Tony Lema at the 37th. Credited as being one of the game's greatest bunker

players he remains as enthusiastic about competing today as he did when he first took up the game.

Price, Nick (Zim)

Born Durban, South Africa, 28 January 1957
Turned professional 1977
One of the game's most popular players his greatest season was 1990 when he took six titles including the Open at Turnberry when he beat Jesper Parnevik and the US PGA at Southern Hills when Corey Pavin was second. He had scored his first Major triumph two years earlier when he edged out John Cook, Nick Faldo, Jim Gallagher Jr and Gene Sauers at the US PGA at Bellerive, St Louis. Along with Tiger Woods his record of 15 wins in the 90s was the most by any player. One of only seven players to win consecutive Majors, the others being Ben Hogan, Jack Nicklaus, Arnold Palmer, Lee Trevino, Tom Watson and Tiger Woods. Four times a Presidents Cup player he jointly holds the Augusta National record of 63 with Greg Norman. One of only two players in the 90s to win two Majors in a year, the others being Nick Faldo in 1990 and Mark O'Meara in 1998. Born of English parents but brought up in Zimbabwe he played his early golf with Mark McNulty and Tony Johnstone. Winner of 41 titles by end of August 2003. In 2002 he was named recipient of the Payne Stewart Award which goes to the player who respects the traditions of the game and works to uphold them. In 2003, ten years after being named PGA Tour Player of the Year, he was inducted into the World Golf Hall of Fame.

Randhawa, Jyoti (Ind)

Born New Delhi, 4 May 1972
First Indian winner on the Japanese Tour when he triumphed in the 2003 Suntory Open. Son of an Indian general, he was top earner on the Asian PGA Tour in 2002 despite missing several events after breaking his collarbone in a motorcycle accident.

Rogers, Bill (USA)

Born Waco, Texas, 10 September 1951
Turned professional 1974
US PGA Player of the Year in 1981 when he won the Open at Royal St George's and was runner-up in the US Open. That year he also won the Australian Open but retired from top line competitive golf not long after because he did not enjoy all the travelling. A former Walker Cup player in 1973 he only entered the Open in 1981 at the insistence of Ben Crenshaw. Now a successful club professional and sometime television commentator, he is also competing on the US Champions Tour – the US Seniors Tour.

Romero, Eduardo (Arg)

Born Cordoba, Argentina, 12 July 1954
Turned professional 1982
Son of the Cordoba club professional he learned much from former Open champion Roberto de Vicenzo and has inherited his grace and elegance as a competitor. A wonderful ambassador for Argentina

he briefly held a US Tour card in 1994 but prefers to play his golf these days on the European Tour where he has won seven times including impressively at the 1999 Canon European Masters where he improved his concentration after studying Indian yoga techniques. Used his own money to sponsor Angel Cabrera with whom he finished second in the 2000 World Cup in Buenos Aires behind Tiger Woods and David Duval. Beat Frederick Andersson in a play-off in 2002 to win the Barclays Scottish Open at Loch Lomond but lost to Padraig Harrington in a play-off for the US$800,000 first prize in the Dunhill Links Championship at St Andrews. Continued playing well in 2003 and insists practising yoga helps.

Scott, Adam (Aus)

Born Adelaide, 16 July 1980
Turned professional 2000

Highly regarded young Australian who was ranked World No. 2 amateur when he turned professional in 2000. Coached in the early days by his father Phil, himself a golf professional, Scott now uses Butch Harmon whom he met while attending the University of Las Vegas. Swings very much like another Harmon client Tiger Woods. He made headlines as an amateur when he fired a 10-under-par 63 at the Lakes in the Greg Norman Holden International in 2000 but has shot 62 in the US Junior Championship at Los Coyotes CC. Made his European Tour card in just eight starts and secured his first Tour win when beating Justin Rose in the 2001 Alfred Dunhill Championship at Houghton in Johannesburg. In 2002 he won at Qatar and at Gleneagles Hotel when he won the Diageo Scottish PGA Championship by ten shots with a 26 under par total. He was 22 under par that week for the par 5 holes. In 2003 he was an impressive winner of the Scandinavian Masters at Barsebäck in Sweden and the Deutsche Bank Championship on the US Tour.

Senior, Peter (Aus)

Born Singapore, 31 July 1959
Turned professional 1978

One of Australia's most likeable and underrated performers who has been a regular winner over the years on the Australian, Japanese and European circuits. Converted to the broomstick putter by Sam Torrance – a move that saved his playing career. A former winner of the Australian Open, Australian PGA and Australian Masters titles he had considerable success off the course when he bought a share in a pawn-broking business. Senior now plays irregularly outside Australia.

Siderowf, Dick (USA)

Twice a winner of the British Amateur title in 1973 when he beat Peter Moody at Royal Porthcawl and again in 1976 when he had to go to the 37th hole to beat John Davies. He was leading amateur in the 1968 US Open and played in four Walker Cups (1969, 1973, 1975 and 1977) before captaining the winning side in 1979.

Sigel, Jay (USA)

Born Narbeth, Pennsylvania, 13 November 1943
Turned professional 1993

Winner of the Amateur Championship in 1979 when he beat Scott Hoch 3 and 2 at Hillside, he also won the US Amateur in successive years 1982 and 1983. He was leading amateur in the US Open in 1984 and leading amateur in the US Masters in 1981, 1982 and 1988. He played in nine Walker Cup matches between 1977 and 1993 and has a record 18 points to his credit. Turned professional in order to join the US Senior Tour where he has had several successes.

Simpson, Scott (USA)

Born San Diego, California, 17 September 1955
Turned professional 1977

Winner of the US Open in 1987 at San Francisco's Olympic Club, he was beaten in a play-off for the title four years later at Hazeltine when the late Payne Stewart won the 18-hole play-off.

Singh, Vijay (Fij)

Born Lautoka, 22 February 1963
Turned professional 1982

An international player who began his career in Australasia, he became the first Fijian to win a major when he won the 1998 US PGA Championship at Sahalee but may well be remembered more for his victory in the 2000 US Masters which effectively prevented Tiger Woods winning all four Majors in a year. Tiger went on to win the US Open, Open and US PGA Championship that year and won the Masters the following year to hold all four Major titles at the one time. Introduced to golf by his father, an aeroplane technician, Vijay modelled his swing on that of Tom Weiskopf. Before making the grade on the European Tour where he won the 1992 Volvo German Open by 11 shots he was a club professional in Borneo. He has won tournaments in South Africa, Malaysia, the Ivory Coast, Nigeria, France, Zimbabwe, Morocco, Spain, England, Germany, Sweden, Taiwan and the United States. He ended Ernie Els' run of victories in the World Match Play Championship when he beat him in the final by one hole in 1997 when the South African was going for a fourth successive title. One of the game's most dedicated practisers. In 2003 he won the Phoenix Open, the EDS Byron Nelson Championship, the John Deere Classic and the Funai Classic. With 10 top ten finishes in his last 15 starts, Singh ended Woods' run as top money earner when he finished with a grand total of $7,753,907 – the second largest total in Tour history.

Stadler, Craig (USA)

Born San Diego, California, 2 June 1953
Turned professional 1975

Nicknamed 'The Walrus' because of his moustache and stocky build, he was the winner of the 1982 Masters at Augusta. Winner of 12 titles on the US Tour between 1980 and 1996 he played in two Ryder Cups (1983 and

1985). As an amateur he played in the 1975 Walker Cup two years after winning the US Amateur. He won his first senior major title when he took the Ford Senior Players' Championship just a few weeks after turning 50 then went back to the main tour the following week and won the BC Open against many players half his age.

Stockton, Dave (USA)
Born San Bernardino, California, 2 November 1941
Turned professional 1964
Winner of two US PGA Championships in 1970 and 1976, he has won more Senior Tour titles (14 as of end July 2001) than he did on the main Tour (11). Captained the American Ryder Cup team controversially in the infamous 'War on the Shore' match at Kiawah Island in 1991.

Stranahan, Frank R (USA)
Born Toledo, Ohio, 5 August 1922
Turned professional 1954
One of America's most successful amateurs he won the Amateur championship at Royal St George's in 1948 and 1950. He also won the US Amateur in 1950, the Mexican Amateur in 1946, 1948 and 1951 and the Canadian title in 1947 and 1948. He was also leading amateur in the Open in 1947, 1949, 1950, 1951 and 1953 behind Ben Hogan. He played in three Walker Cups in 1947, 1949 and 1951.

Strange, Curtis (USA)
Born Norfolk, Virginia, 20 January 1955
Turned professional 1976
Winner of successive US Opens in 1988 and again in 1989 when he beat Nick Faldo in an 18-hole play-off at The Country Club Brookline after getting up and down from a bunker at the last to tie on 278. Winner of 17 US Tour titles he won at least one event for seven successive years from 1983. Having played in five Ryder Cup matches he captained the US side when the 2001 match was played at The Belfry in 2002. Now commentates for the ABC Network.

Stricker, Steve (USA)
Born Egerton, Wisconsin, 23 February 1967
Turned professional 1990
Started 2001 by winning the $1 million first prize in the Accenture Match Play Championship, one of the World Golf Championship series. In the final he beat Pierre Fulke. Was a member of the winning American Alfred Dunhill Cup side in 1996.

Sutton, Hal (USA)
Born Shreveport, Louisiana, 28 April 1958
Turned professional 1981
Winner of the 1983 US PGA Championship at the Riviera CC in Los Angeles beating Jack Nicklaus into second place. Played in the 1985 and 1987 Ryder Cup matches and returned to the side in 1999 at Brookline

when he beat Darren Clarke 4 and 2 in the singles. He made the 2001 side as well and will captain the American team at Oakland Hills in 2004.

Thomson CBE, Peter (Aus)
Born Melbourne, 23 August 1929
Turned professional 1949
He is one of only four players who have won five Open Championships. At the start of the 20th century J.H. Taylor and James Braid won five, and Tom Watson won five in eight years from 1975 while Thomson completed his five victories between 1954 and 1965. In one seven-year spell from 1952 Thomson never finished worse than second in the Championship. His run of finishes from 1952 was 2, 2, 1, 1, 1, 2, 1. His fifth victory, arguably his most impressive, came at Royal Birkdale in 1965 when more Americans were in the field. He played only three times in the US Open finishing fourth in 1956. He played in five US Masters with fifth his best finish in 1957. He won three Australian Opens and in Europe had 24 victories between 1954 and 1972. With one of the most fluent and reliable swings he made golf look easy. Instrumental in developing the game throughout Asia, Africa and the Middle East he was ready to retire from golf and pursue a career in Australian politics but he was not elected and turned instead to the US Senior Tour with great success. In 1985 he won nine Senior Tour titles. Has captained three Rest of the World Presidents Cup sides, was elected to the World Golf Hall of Fame in 1988 and is an honorary member of the Royal and Ancient Golf Club of St Andrews. After his retirement from top-line golf he concentrated on his hugely successful golf course designing business based in Melbourne completing projects in many countries around the world.

Toms, David (USA)
Born Monroe, LA, 4 January 1967
Turned professional 1989
Most important of his six wins on the US Tour was his first Major success by beating Phil Mickelson into second place in the 2001 USPGA Championship. Toms shot 66, 65, 65 and 69 for a 265 record winning aggregate at the Atlanta Athletic Club. This is the lowest aggregate in any Major. The previous year he had come joint fourth to Tiger Woods in the Open. Made his Ryder Cup début in 2001 and was the American side's top points scorer with 3½ points. In 2003 he had won twice in the Wachovia Championship and the Fedex St Jude Classic by the end of August.

Trevino, Lee (USA)
Born Dallas, Texas, 1 December 1939
Turned professional 1961
Twenty times a winner on the US Tour between 1968 and 1981 'Supermex', as he was nicknamed by his peers, hit the headlines in 1971 when he won the US Open beating Jack Nicklaus in a play-off at Merion, the Canadian Open at Montreal and the Open at Royal

Birkdale in succession. One of the most extrovert of golfers who followed up his 27 victories on the main Tour with 29 on the US Senior Tour was entirely self-taught. He won six Majors – the Open in 1971 and 1972 when he chipped in at the 71st hole to end Tony Jacklin's hopes of winning, the US Open in 1968 and 1971 and the US PGA Championship in 1974 and 1984 but he never finished better than tenth twice in the Masters at Augusta – a course with so many right to left dog-legs that he felt it did not suit his game. In 1975 he was hit by lightning while playing in the Western Open in Chicago and had to undergo back surgery in order to keep competing. He was involved in one of the low scoring matches in the World Match Play Championship with Tony Jacklin in 1972 when he again came out on top. In 2003 he was made an honorary member of the Royal & Ancient Golf Club of St Andrews.

Verplank, Scott (USA)

Born Dallas, Texas, 9 July 1964

When he won the Western Open as an amateur in 1985 he was the first to do so since Doug Sanders took the 1956 Canadian Open. Missed most of the 1991 and 1992 seasons because of an elbow injury and the injury also affected his 1996 season. He has diabetes and wears an insulin pump while playing to regulate his medication. Curtis Strange chose him as one of his two 'picks' for the 2001 US Ryder Cup side. In the singles on the final day he beat Lee Westwood 2 and 1.

De Vicenzo, Roberto (Arg)

Born Buenos Aires, 14 April 1923
Turned professional 1938

Although he won the Open in 1967 at Royal Liverpool this impressive South American is perhaps best known for the Major title he might have won. In 1968 he finished tied with Bob Goalby at Augusta or he thought he had. He had finished birdie, bogey to do so but sadly signed for the par 4 that had been inadvertently and carelessly put down for the 17th by Tommy Aaron who was marking his card. Although everyone watching on television and at the course saw the Argentinian make 3 the fact that he signed for 4 was indisputable and he had to accept that there would be no play-off. It remains one of the saddest incidents in golf with the emotion heightened by the fact that that Sunday was de Vicenzo's 45th birthday. The gracious manner in which he accepted the disappointments was remarkable. What a contrast to the scenes at Hoylake nine months earlier when, after years of trying, he finally won the Open beating Jack Nicklaus and Clive Clark in the process thanks to a pressure-packed brilliant last round 70. In fact he was runner-up in the event in 1950 and came third six times. The father of South American golf he was a magnificent driver and is credited with having won over 200 titles in his extraordinary career including nine Argentinian Opens between 1944 and 1974 plus the 1957 Jamaican, 1950 Belgian, 1950 Dutch, 1950, 1960 and 1964 French, 1964 German Open and 1966 Spanish Open titles. He played 15 times for Argentina in the World Cup and four times for Mexico. Inducted into the World Golf Hall of Fame in 1989 he is an honorary member of the Royal and Ancient Golf Club of St Andrews.

Wadkins, Lanny (USA)

Born Richmond, Virginia, 5 December 1949
Turned professional 1971

His 21 victories on the US Tour between 1972 and 1992 include the 1977 US PGA Championship, his only Major. He won that after a play-off with Gene Littler at Pebble Beach but lost a play-off for the same title in 1987 to Larry Nelson at Palm Beach Gardens. He was second on two other occasions to Ray Floyd in 1982 and to Lee Trevino in 1984. In other Majors his best finish was third three times in the US Masters (1990, 1991 and 1993), tied second in the US Open (1986) and tied fourth in the 1984 Open at St Andrews. One of the fiercest of competitors he played eight Ryder Cups between 1977 and 1993 winning 20 of his 33 games, but was a losing captain at Oak Hill in 1995.

Ward, Harvie (USA)

Born Tarboro, North Carolina 1926
Turned professional 1973

Winner of the Amateur Championship in 1952 when he beat Frank Stranahan 6 and 5 at Prestwick, he went on to win the US title in 1955 and 1956 and the Canadian Amateur in 1964. He played in the 1953, 1955 and 1959 Walker Cup matches and won all of his six games.

Watson, Tom (USA)

Born Kansas City, Missouri, 4 September 1949
Turned professional 1971

Winner of 34 career titles, he won at least three a year on the main US Tour in a six-year spell between 1977 and 1982. He is best known for having won five Open championships in eight years between 1975 and 1983 to match the feat of J.H. Taylor, James Braid and Peter Thomson. When he had a chance to win a sixth Open and tie Harry Vardon's record at St Andrews in 1984 he hit his second close to the wall through the green at the 17th and lost out to Seve Ballesteros. Watson's wins came at Carnoustie in 1975 after a play-off with Jack Newton; a memorable 1977 triumph in which he edged out Jack Nicklaus at Turnberry shooting 65, 65 over the weekend to Nicklaus' 65, 66; 1980 at Muirfield where he beat Lee Trevino; 1982 at Royal Troon where Peter Oosterhuis and Nick Price came second and 1983 when Andy Bean and Hale Irwin were runners-up. Watson also won the 1982 US Open chipping in from the rough at the 17th on the final day to go on and beat Nicklaus and two US Masters in 1977 and 1981 but he never did better than tied second in the 1977 US PGA Championship to miss out joining Gene Sarazen, Ben Hogan, Gary Player, Jack Nicklaus and Tiger Woods as a winner of all four Majors. Became the oldest winner on the US Tour when he won the Mastercard Colonial in 1998 nearly 24 years after scoring his first win in the Western Open. He was 48, two years older than the previous oldest Ben Hogan, when he won the same event for the fifth time in 1959. Six times Player of the Year he played in four Ryder

Cups and captained the side to victory in 1993 at The Belfry. Inducted into the World Golf Hall of Fame in 1988, he is an honorary member of the Royal and Ancient Golf Club of St Andrews. Now plays on the US Senior Tour and returned in triumph to Turnberry in 2003 to win the Senior British Open 26 years after his memorable shoot-out for the Open over the same course. Although Nicklaus was again in the field, Watson's main rival this time was rookie European Senior Tour player Carl Mason who let a two shot lead playing the last slip then lost the play-off to the American at the second extra hole.

Weir, Mike (Can)

Born Sarnia, Ontario, 12 May 1970
Turned professional 1992

A left-hander, he was the first Canadian to play in the Presidents Cup when he made the side in 2000 and the first from his country to win a World Golf Championship event when he took the American Express Championship at Valderrama in 2000. Wrote to Jack Nicklaus as a 13-year-old to enquire whether or not he should switch from playing golf left-handed to right-handed and was told not to switch. In 1997 he led the scoring averages on the Canadian Tour with a score of 69.29 but his greatest triumph came when he became only the second left-hander to win a major when he played beautifully and putted outstandingly to beat Len Mattiace for a Masters Green Jacket. Weir had to hole from 15 feet at the last to take the tournament into extra holes but won his first major title when Mattiace failed to par the tenth – the first extra hole. He has now assumed hero status in Canada.

Weiskopf, Tom (USA)

Born Massillon, Ohio, 9 November 1942
Turned professional 1946

Winner of only one Major – the 1973 Open Championship at Royal Troon, he lived in the shadow of Jack Nicklaus throughout his competitive career. He was runner-up in the 1976 US Open to Jerry Pate and was twice third in 1973 and 1977. His best finish in the US PGA Championship was third in 1975 – the year he had to be content for the fourth time with second place at the US Masters. He had been runner-up for a Green Jacket in 1969, 1972 and 1974 previously but played perhaps his best golf ever in 1975 only to be pipped at the post by Nicklaus. With 22 wins to his name he now plays the US Senior Tour with a curtailed schedule because of his course design work for which he and his original partner Jay Morrish have received much praise. One of their designs is Loch Lomond, venue of the revived Scottish Open. Played in just two Ryder Cup matches giving up a place in the team one year in order to go Bighorn sheep hunting in Alaska.

Woods, Eldrick 'Tiger' (USA)

Born Cypress, California, 30 December 1975
Turned professional 1996

First golfer in history to hold all four Majors simultaneously. He won the 2000 US Open, the Open at St Andrews and the US PGA Championship after a play-off with Bob May then scored his second victory at Augusta when he won the 2001 US Masters. He is rewriting the record books. As an amateur he successfully made two defences of the US Championship to win the event a record three years in a row but the meteoric start to his professional career gives rise to the view that he might beat Jack Nicklaus' 18 major title wins record. In 2000 he was 53-under-par for the four Majors with Ernie Els next best at 17-under. His nine Tour victories in a season was the most by anyone since Ben Hogan won 11 in 1950. When he won the AT and T at Pebble Beach in 2000 he became the first player since Ben Hogan in 1948 to win on six successive starts on the US Tour. At Pebble Beach in the US Open he shot 65, 69, 71, 67 to tie the US Open record of 272 but his 12-under-par score was a new sub-par record. Having won the US Masters for the first time with a record 270 total which gave him a 12 shot victory in 1997 and taken the US PGA title in 1999 he needed only to win the Open in Britain to become the youngest and only the fifth player in history (the others were Gene Sarazen, Ben Hogan, Gary Player and Jack Nicklaus) to have won all four Majors. At the Old Course at St Andrews he romped home by eight shots with a new British Open and major Championship record total of 269 – 19-under-par. He needed extra holes to beat Bob May at Valhalla to successfully defend the US PGA title a few weeks later. With that victory he joined Ben Hogan (1953) as a winner of three Majors in a season but beat that record when he took the US Masters Green Jacket for a second time in 2001. His current Majors tally is six. His chance of winning all four Majors in one season was lost when he did not successfully defend his US Open title later in the year. During the 2000 season he set or tied 27 records and his average score on the US Tour of 68.1 beat Sam Snead's record of 69.23 set in 1945. Named Tiger after a Vietnamese soldier who was a friend of his father's he was born to play golf, hitting shots on the Bob Hope Show when aged two and shooting 48 for nine holes at age three. He is the youngest player to have won 20 events on the US Tour. He is so far ahead in the World rankings that he is unlikely to be deposed for some considerable time. He played in the 1997 and 1999 Ryder Cup matches and was a member of the 2002 side. Woods won the Masters title again in 2002 beating Retief Goosen into second place at Augusta on a final day when both Ernie Els and Vijay Singh challenged strongly before the South African ran up a 7 and the Fijian a 9 on the back nine. When he also won the US Open again at Bethpage Park in New York State he was in line to win all four majors in the same year but just like Jack Nicklaus 30 years earlier he lost out at Muirfield where Ernie Els was the winner of the Open. Caught in severe weather on the third day Woods fired a career high professional score of 81 but hit back with a closing 65 to finish joint 28th. In the US PGA Championship at Hazeltine he closed with four birdies but lost his chance of a ninth major in six years when Rich Beem took the title. Although a regular winner in 2003 he did not win any of the four majors stretching his losing run to six. He created headlines

when he dediced to leave the Nike driver out of his bag in favour of his old Titleist club. He is contracted to Nike but was able to swich to the older club under the terms of his sponsorship. Woods still described telling Nike what he planned to do was one of the most difficult things he had had to do in his career. In the 2003 Open at Royal St George's he lost a ball off his opening drive when it plunged into the thick rough. At the beginning of October, Woods scored his 52nd victory in the seven years since turning pro and his fifth of the season when he won the American Express Championship, part of the WGC circuit, at the Capital City Club in Atlanta. Woods was winning his eighth GC event in 15 starts – bringing his earnings in these competitions to over $10 million. His win moved him into top spot on the US money list as he attempted to finish No. 1 for the fifth consecutive year. His victory also marked the 100th. victory of his caddie Steve Williams. Woods other victories on the US Tour up to that point had comprised the Buick Invitational, the WGC Accenture Match-play Championship, the Bay Hill Invitational and the 100th Western Open. He has played in three Ryder Cups and with David Duval won the World Cup of Golf in 2001. His bid to finish No.1 on the PGA Tour came to the very last event of the season when he needed to win the Tour Championship to have a chance of overhauling Vijay Singh who had moved over $700,000 ahead on the money list. Although Woods was again the low average scorer for the fifth successive year, he failed to catch Singh for the No.1 spot.

Yates, Charles Richard (Charlie) (USA)
Born Atlanta, Georgia, 9 September 1913
Great friend of the late Bobby Jones he was top amateur in the US Masters in 1934, 1939 and 1940. In 1938 came to Royal Troon and won the British Amateur title beating R. Ewing 3 and 2. For many years acted as chairman of the press committee at the US Masters and annually stages an overseas golf writers party in the Augusta Clubhouse.

Yeh, Wei-tze (Tai)
Born Taiwan, 20 February 1973
Turned professional 1994
Fisherman's son who became the third Asia golfer after "Mr Lu" and Isao Aoki to win on the European Tour when he won the 2000 Benson and Hedges Malaysian Open. In 2003 he won the ANA Open on the Japanese Tour.

Zoeller, Fuzzy (USA)
Born New Albany, Indiana, 11 November 1951
Turned professional 1973
Winner of the US Masters in 1979 after a play-off with Ed Sneed (who had dropped shots at the last three holes in regulation play) and Tom Watson and the US Open in 1984 at Winged Foot after an 18-hole play-off with Greg Norman. A regular winner on the US Tour between 1979 and 1986, he played in three Ryder Cups (1979, 1983 and 1985).

Zhang, Lian-Wei (Chi)
Born Shenzhen, 2 May1965
Turned professional 1994
Leading Chinese player whose victory in the 2003 Caltex Singapore Open when he edged out Ernie Els was the first by a Chinese golfer on Tour. Initially he trained as a javelin thrower before turning to golf. Self-taught he was also the first Asian golfer to win on the Canadian Tour but remains a stalwart on the Asian circuit.

R&A 250th Anniversary Celebrations

Detailed planning for the celebration in 2004 of the 250th Anniversary of the Royal & Ancient Golf Club of St Andrews has taken three years and includes local and international competition and a dinner for 1200 members and guests in a huge marquee to be built on the Bruce Embankment beside the R&A clubhouse. Representatives from all 127 of the R&A's worldwide affiliated unions and associations have been invited.

Oil paintings have been commissioned to mark the driving-in as captain of His Royal Highness The Duke of York and of the top table at the Club's annual dinner when all the club's trophies will be on display.

The Royal Bank of Scotland are issuing a £5 note with an image of the R&A clubhouse on it. In addition the third volume of the club history will be published to commemorate the founding date of the club – May 14 1754.

Overseas Players, Women

Berg, Patty (USA)
Born Minneapolis, 13 February 1918
Turned professional 1940
A founder member of the LPGA Tour in America, she won 57 times in her career including the 1946 US Women's Open. She was leading US money winner in 1954, 1955 and 1957. The first president of the LPGA she was honoured several times winning, among others, the Bobby Jones award in 1963 and the Ben Hogan award and Hall of Fame in 1976.

Bradley, Pat (USA)
Born Westford, Massachusetts, 24 March 1951
Turned professional 1974
Winner of four US LPGA majors – the Nabisco Championship, the US Women's Open, the LPGA Championship and the du Maurier Classic, she won 31 times on the American circuit. An outstanding skier and ski instructor as well, she started playing golf when she was 11. Every time she won her mother would ring a bell on the porch of the family home whatever the time of day. The bell is now in the World Golf Hall of Fame. She played in four Solheim Cup sides and captained the team in 2000 at Loch Lomond. Inducted into the LPGA Hall of Fame in 1991 she was Rolex Player of the Year in 1986 and 1991.

Caponi, Donna (USA)
Born Detroit, Michigan, 29 January 1945
Turned professional 1965
Twice winner of the US Women's Open in 1969 and 1970 she collected 24 titles between 1969 and 1981 on the LPGA Tour. Winner of the 1975 Colgate European Open at Sunningdale, she is now a respected commentator/analyst.

Carner, Jo Anne (*née* Gunderson) (USA)
Born Kirkland, Washington, 4 April 1939
Turned professional 1970
Had five victories in the US Ladies' Amateur Championship (1957, 1960, 1962, 1966 and 1968) before turning professional and winning the 1971 and 1976 US Women's Open. She remains the last amateur to win on the LPGA Tour after having taken the 1969 Burdine's Invitational. Between 1970 and 1985 scored 42 victories on the LPGA Tour and was Rolex Player of the Year in 1974, 1981 and 1982. She was inducted into the LPGA Hall of Fame in 1982 and the World Golf Hall of Fame in 1985. She won the Bobby Jones award in 1981 and the Mickey Wright award in 1974 and 1982.

Daniel, Beth (USA)
Born Charleston, South Carolina, 14 October 1956
Turned professional 1978
A member of the LPGA Hall of Fame she won 32 times between 1979 and 1995 including the 1990 US LPGA Championship. She was Rolex Player of the Year in 1980, 1990 and 1994. Before turning professional she won the US Women's Amateur title in 1975 and 1977 and played in the 1976 and 1978 Curtis Cup teams. She has played in five Solheim Cup competitions since it began in 1990, missing only the 1998 match.

Dibnah, Corinne (Aus)
Born Brisbane, 29 July 1962
Turned professional 1984
A former Australian and New Zealand amateur champion, she joined the European Tour after turning professional and won 13 times between 1986 and 1994. A pupil of Greg Norman's first coach Charlie Earp, she was Europe's top earner in 1991.

Geddes, Jane (USA)
Born Huntingdon, New York, 5 February 1960
Turned professional 1983
In 1986 she was the 13th player on the LPGA Tour to score her first victory at the US Women's Open. A year later she won the US LPGA title and took the British Women's title in 1989. She won 11 times on the US Tour between 1986 and 1994.

Haynie, Sandra (USA)
Born Fort Worth, Texas, 4 June 1943
Turned professional 1961
Twice a winner of the US Open (1965 and 1974) she won 42 times between 1962 and 1982 on the US LPGA Tour. She was elected to the LPGA Hall of Fame in 1977.

Higuchi, Hisako "Chako" (Jpn)
Born Saitama Prefecture, Japan, 13 October 1945
Turned professional 1967
A charter member and star of the Japan LPGA Tour she won 72 victories worldwide during her career. In 2003 she was elected to the World Golf Hall of Fame.

Inkster, Juli (USA)

Born Santa Cruz, California, 24 June 1960
Turned professional 1983

Winner of two majors in 1984 (the Nabisco Championship and the du Maurier) she also had a double Major year in 1999 when she won the US Women's Open and the LPGA Championship which she won for a second time in 2000. In 2002 she won the US Women's Open for a second time. In all she has won seven major titles. In her amateur career she became the first player since 1934 to win the US Women's amateur title three years in a row (1980, 81, 82). Only four other women and one man (Tiger Woods) have successfully defended their national titles twice in a row. Coached for a time by the late London-based Leslie King at Harrods Store.

King, Betsy (USA)

Born Reading, Pennsylvania, 13 August 1955
Turned professional 1977

Another stalwart of the LPGA Tour in America she has won 34 times between 1984 and 2001. Winner of the British Open in 1985 she has also won the US Open in 1989 and 1990, the Nabisco Championship three times in 1987, 1990 and 1997 and the LPGA Championship in 1990. She never managed to win the du Maurier event although finishing in the top six on nine occasions. Three times Rolex Player of the Year in 1984, 1989 and 1993 she was elected to the LPGA Hall of Fame in 1995.

Klein, Emilee (USA)

Born Santa Monica, California, 11 June 1974
Turned professional 1994

The former Curtis Cup player who played in the 1994 match scored her biggest triumph as a professional when winning the Weetabix British Women's Open at Woburn in 1996.

Kuehne, Kelli (USA)

Born Dallas, Texas, 11 May 1977
Turned professional 1998

Having won the US Women's Amateur Championship in 1995 she successfully defended the title the following year when she also won the British Women's title – the first player to win both in the same year. She was also the first player to follow up her win in the US Junior Girls Championship in 1994 with victory in the US Women's event the following year. Her brother Hank is also a professional.

Lopez, Nancy (*née* Knight) (USA)

Born Torrance, California, 6 January 1957
Turned professional 1977

One of the game's bubbliest personalities and impressive performers who took her first title – the New Mexico Women's Amateur title at age 12. Between 1978 and 1995 she won 48 times on the LPGA Tour and was Rolex Player of the Year on four occasions (1978, 79, 85 and 88). In 1978, her rookie

year, she won nine titles including a record five in a row. That year she also lost two play-offs and remains the only player to have won the Rookie of the Year, Player of the Year and Vare Trophy (scoring average) in the same season. A year later she won eight tournaments. Three times a winner of the LPGA Championship in 1978, 1985 and 1989 she has never managed to win the US Open although she was runner-up in 1975 as an amateur, in 1977, 1989 and most recently 1997 when she lost out to Britain's Alison Nicholas. She has now retired from competitive golf and in 2002 was awarded the PGA's First Lady in Golf award for the contribution she has made to the game.

Lunn, Karen (Aus)

Born Sydney, 21 March 1966
Turned professional 1985

A former top amateur she won the British Women's Open in 1993 at Woburn following the success in the European Ladies Open earlier in the year by her younger sister Mardi.

McIntire, Barbara (USA)

Born Toledo, Ohio, 1935

One of America's best amateurs who finished runner-up in the 1956 US Women's Open to Kathy Cornelius at Northland Duluth. Winner of the US Women's Amateur title in 1959 and 1964 she also won the British Amateur title in 1960. She played in six Curtis Cups between 1958 and 1962.

Mallon, Meg (USA)

Born Natwick, Maryland, 14 April 1963
Turned professional 1986

Winner of the 1991 US Women's Open, 1991 Mazda LPGA Championship, the 2000 du Maurier Classic and 11 other events between 1991 and 2002.

Mann, Carole (USA)

Born Buffalo, New York, 3 February 1940
Turned professional 1960

Winner of 38 events on the LPGA Tour in her 22 years on Tour. A former president of the LPGA she was a key figure in the founding of the Tour and received the prestigious Babe Zaharias award. In 1964 she won the Western Open, then a Major, and in 1965 the US Women's Open but in 1968 she had a then record 23 rounds in the 60s, won 11 times and won the scoring averages prize with a score of 72.04. Enjoys a hugely successful corporate career within golf.

Massey, Debbie (USA)

Born Grosse Pointe, Michigan, 5 November 1950
Turned professional 1977

Best known for winning the British Women's Open in 1980 and 1981.

Okamoto, Ayako (Jpn)
Born Hiroshima, 12 April 1951
Turned professional 1976
Although she won the British Women's Open in 1984 she managed only a runner-up spot in the US Women's Open and US LPGA Championships despite finishing in the top 20 28 times and missing the cut only four times. In the LPGA Championships she finished second or third five times in six years from 1986. She scored 17 victories in the USA between 1982 and 1992, won the 1990 German Open and was Japanese Women's champion in 1993 and 1997.

Pak, Se Ri (Kor)
Born Daejeon, 28 September 1977
Turned professional 1996
In 1998 she was awarded the Order of Merit by the South Korean government – the highest honour given to an athlete – for having won two Majors in her rookie year on the US Tour. She won the McDonald LPGA Championship matching Liselotte Neumann in making a major her first tour success. When she won the US Women's Open later that year after an 18-hole play-off followed by two extra holes of sudden death against amateur Jenny Chuasiriporn, she became the youngest golfer to take that title. By the middle of 2001 she had won 12 events on the US tour including the Weetabix Women's British Open at Sunningdale – an event included on the US Tour as well as the European Circuit for the first time. In 2002 she was again a multiple winner on the US Tour adding to her majors by winning the McDonald's LPGA Championship. As an amateur in Korea she won 30 titles and became the first lady professional to make the cut in a men's professional event for 58 years when she played four rounds in a Korean Tour event.

Pepper (Mochrie, Scarinzi), Dottie (USA)
Born Saratoga Springs, Florida, 17 August 1965
Turned professional 1987
Winner of 17 events (through to July 2001) on the US LPGA Tour including two majors. A fierce competitor she took the Nabisco Dinah Shore title in 1992 and again in 1999. She played in all Solheim Cup matches to 2000.

Rawls, Betsy (USA)
Born Spartanburg, South Carolina, 4 May 1928
Turned professional 1951
Winner of the 1951, 1953, 1957 and 1960 US Women's Open and the US LPGA Championship in 1959 and 1969 as well as two Western Opens when the Western Open was a Major, she scored 55 victories on the LPGA Tour between 1951 and 1972. One of the best shot makers in women's golf who was noted for her game around and on the greens.

Sander, Anne (Welts, Decker, *née* Quast) (USA)
Born Marysville, 1938
A three times winner of the US Ladies title in 1958, 1961 and 1963, she also won the British Ladies title in 1980. She made eight appearances in the Curtis Cup stretching from 1958 to 1990. Only Carole Semple Thompson has played more often having played ten times.

Semple Thompson, Carol (USA)
Born 1950
Winner of six USLPGA titles including the US Ladies title in 1973 and the British Ladies in 1974. She has played in 12 Curtis Cups between 1974 and 2002 and holed the 27-foot winning putt in the 2002 match. At 53 she is the oldest US Curtis Cup Player.

Sheehan, Patty (USA)
Born Middlebury, Vermont, 27 October 1956
Turned professional 1980
Scored 35 victories between 1981 and 1996 including six Majors – the LPGA Championship in 1983, 1984 and 1994, the US Women's Open in 1993 and 1994 and the Nabisco Championship in 1996. As an amateur she won all her four games in the 1980 Curtis Cup. She is a member of the LPGA Hall of Fame.

Steinhauer, Sherri (USA)
Born Madison, Wisconsin, 27 December 1962
Turned professional 1985
Winner of the Women's British Open in 1998 at Royal Lytham and St Annes and the following year at Woburn. She has played in the last three Solheim Cup matches.

Stephenson, Jan (Aus)
Born Sydney, 22 December 1951
Turned professional 1973
She won three majors on the LPGA Tour – the 1981 du Maurier Classic, the 1982 LPGA Championship and the 1983 US Women's Open. She was twice Australian Ladies champion in 1973 and 1977.

Streit, Marlene Stewart (Can)
Born Cereal, Alberta, 9 March 1934
One of Canada's most successful amateurs she won her national title ten times between 1951 and 1973. She won the 1953 British Amateur, the US Amateur in 1956 and the Australian Ladies in 1963. She was Canadian Woman Athlete of the Year in 1951, 1953, 1956, 1960 and 1963.

Suggs, Louise (USA)
Born Atlanta, Georgia, 7 September 1923
Turned professional 1948
Winner of 58 titles on the LPGA Tour after a brilliant amateur career which included victories in the 1947 US Amateur and the 1948 British Amateur

Championships. She won 11 Majors including the US Open in 1949 and 1952 and the LPGA Championship in 1957. A founder member of the US Tour she was an inaugural honoree when the LPGA Hall of Fame was instituted in 1967.

Webb, Karrie (Aus)

Born Ayr, Queensland, 21 December 1974
Turned professional 1994
Blonde Australian who is rewriting the record books with her performances on the LPGA Tour. Peter Thomson, the five times Open champion considers she is the best golfer male or female there is and Greg Norman, who was her inspiration as a teenager, believes she can play at times better than Tiger Woods although Webb herself hates comparisons. She scored her first Major win in 1995 when she took the Weetabix Women's British Open – a title she won again in 1997. When she joined the LPGA Tour she won the 1999 du Maurier Classic, the 2000 Nabisco Championship and the 2000 and 2001 US Women's Open – five Majors out of eight (by the end of July 2001) – the most impressive run since Mickey Wright won five out of six in the early 1960s. In 2002 she became the first player to complete a career Grand Slam when she won her third Weetabix British Open which had become an official major on the US LPGA Tour. It was her sixth major title in four years. Her winning total at Turnberry was 15 under par 273. Enjoys a close rivalry with Annika Sörenstam.

Whitworth, Kathy (USA)

Born Monahans, Texas, 27 September 1939
Turned professional 1958
Won 88 titles on the LPGA Tour between 1959 and 1991 – more than any one else male or female. Her golden period was in the 1960s when she won eight events in 1965, nine in 1966, eight in 1967 and 10 in 1968. When she finished third in the 1981 US Women's Open she became the first player to top $1 million in prize money on the LPGA Tour. She was the seventh member of the LPGA Tour Hall of Fame when inducted in 1975. Began playing golf at the age of 15 and made golfing history when she teamed up with Mickey Wright to play in the previously all male Legends of Golf event. Winner of six Majors – including three LPGA Championship wins in 1967, 1971 and 1975. In addition she won two Titleholders Championships (1966 and 1967) and the 1967 Western Open when they were Majors. Enjoyed a winning streak of 17 successive years on the LPGA Tour.

Wright, Mickey (USA)

Born San Diego, California, 14 February 1935
Turned professional 1954
Her 82 victories on the LPGA Tour between 1956 and 1973 was bettered only by Kathy Whitworth who has 88 official victories. One of the greatest golfers in the history of the Tour she had a winning streak of 14 successive seasons. Winner of 13 Major titles she is the only player to date to have won three in one season. In 1961 she took the US Women's Open, the LPGA Championship and the Titleholders Championship. That year she became only the second player to win both the US Women's Open and LPGA Championship in the same year having done so previously in 1958. Scored 79 of her victories between 1956 and 1969 when averaging almost eight wins a season. During this time she enjoyed a tremendous rivalry with Miss Whitworth. Truly a golfing legend.

USGA Championship Dates 2004

June 17–20	US Open Championship, Shinnecock Hills GC, Southampton, NY
July 1–4	US Women's Open Orchard GC, South Hadley, MA
July 29–Aug 1	US Senior Championship, Bellerive CC, St Louis, MO
Aug 9–14	US Women's Amateur Championship, The Kahkwa Club, Erie, PA
Aug 16–22	US Amateur Championship, Winged Foot GC, Mamaroneck, NY
Oct 20–23	Women's World Amateur Team Championship (Espirito Santo Trophy), Hyatt Dorado Beach Resort and CC, Puerto Rico
Oct 28–31	World Amateur Team Championship (Eisenhower Trophy), Hyatt Dorado Beach Resort and CC, Puerto Rico

British Isles International Players, Professional Men

Key

RC	Ryder Cup GBI till 1977; Europe thereafter.	DC	Dunhill Cup – by home country
USA	1921, 1926: pre-Ryder Cup	CC	Canada Cup
RoW	Rest of World	WbC	Warburg Cup
FT	Four Tours World Championship, Players represented European Tour; also in Nissan Cup and Kirin Cup	(S)Eur	European Seniors v Ladies European Tour
		*	indicates winning team
Eur	GBI v Continent of Europe	'to' indicates inclusive dates: e.g. '1908 to 1911' means '1908-09-10-11'; otherwise individual years are shown.	
WC	World Cup – by home country; was Canada (Cup) till 1966	Captaincy is indicated by the year printed in bold type; non-playing captaincy in brackets	

ENGLAND

Alliss, Percy
RC 1929-31-33-35-37; Sco 1932 to 1937; Irl 1932-38; Wal 1938; (GBI) Fra 1939

Alliss, Peter
RC 1953-57-59-61-63-65-67-69; CC 1954-55-57-58-59-61-62-64-66; WC 1967

Baker, Peter
RC 1993; DC 1993 (r/u)-98; WC 1999

Bamford, BJ
CC 1961

Barber, T
Irl 1932-33

Batley, JB
Sco 1912

Beck, AG
Wal, Irl 1938

Bembridge, Maurice
RC 1969-71-73-75; SA 1976; WC 1974-75; (S) Eur 1997

Bickerton, J
Eur 2000

Boomer, Aubrey
USA 1926; RC 1927-29

Bousfield, Ken
RC 1949-51-55-57-59-61; CC 1956-57

Boxall, R
WC 1990; DC 1990

Branch, WJ
Sco 1936

Brand, Gordon J
RC 1983; Nissan 1986; WC 1983; DC 1986-87*

Broadhurst, Paul
RC 1991; FT 1991-95; WC 1997; DC 1991

Burton, J
Irl 1933

Burton, R (Dick)
RC 1935-37-49; Sco 1935-36-37; Sco, Wal, Irl 1938

Busson, JH
Sco 1938

Busson, Jack J
RC 1935; Sco 1934-35-36-37

Butler, Peter J
RC 1965-69-71-73; Eur 1976; WC 1969-70-73

Carter, D
DC 1998; WC 1998*

Cawsey, GH
Sco 1906-07

Caygill, G Alex
RC 1969

Chapman, R
DC 2000

Clark, Clive
RC 1973

Clark, Howard K
RC 1977-81-85-87-89-95; Aus 1988; Eur 1978-84; Nissan 1985; WC 1978-84-85-87; DC 1985-86-87*-89-90-94-95

Claydon, R
DC 1997

Coles, Neil C
RC 1961-63-65-67-69-71-73-77; Eur 1974-76-78-80; (S) Eur 1998-99; Can 1963; WC 1968

Collinge, T
Sco 1937

Collins, JF
Sco 1903-04

Compston, Archie
USA 1926; RC 1927-29-31; Fra 1929; Sco, Irl 1932; Sco 1935

Cotton, T Henry
RC 1929-37-47; Fra 1929

Cox, WJ (Bill)
RC 1935-37; Sco 1935-36-37

Curtis, D
Sco 1934; Sco, Wal, Irl 1938

Davis, B
DC 2000

Davies, William H
RC 1931-33; Sco, Irl 1932-33

Dawson, Peter
RC 1977; WC 1977

Denny, Charles S
Sco 1936

Durnian, Denis
WC 1989; DC 1989; WbC 2001-02

Easterbrook, Syd
RC 1931-33; Sco 1932 to 35; 38; Irl 1933

Faldo, Nick A
RC 1977-79-81-83-85-87-89-91-93-95-97; Eur 1978-80-82-84; RoW 1982; Nissan 1986; Kirin 1987; FT 1990; WC 1977-91-98*; DC 1985-86-87*-88-91-93; WbC 2001-02

Faulkner, Max
RC 1947-49-51-53-57

Foster, M
Eur 1976; WC 1976

Gadd, B
Sco, Irl 1933; Sco 1935; Sco, Irl, Wal 1938

Gadd, George
USA 1926; RC 1927

Garner, John R
RC 1971-71

Gaudin, PJ
Sco 1905-06-07-09-12-13

Gilford, David
RC 1991-95; WC 1992-93; DC 1992*

Gray, E
Sco 1904-05-07

Green, Eric
RC 1947

Green, T
Sco 1935; also Wal v Sco, Irl 1937 and Sco, Eng 1938

Gregson, Malcolm
RC 1967; WC 1967; (S) Eur 1997

Hargreaves, Jack
RC 1951

Havers, AG
USA 1921-26; RC 1927-31-33; Fra 1929; Sco, Irl 1932-33; Sco 1934

Hitchcock, Jimmy
RC 1965

Horne, Reg
RC 1947

Horton, Tommy
RC 1975-77; Eur 1974-76; WC 1976; (S) Eur 1997-(98)-(99)

Howell, D
Eur 2000; DC 1999

Hunt, Bernard J
RC 1953-57-59-61-63-65-67-69; Can 1958-59-60-62-63-64; WC 1968

Hunt, Guy L
RC 1975; Eur 1974; WC 1972-75

Hunt, Geoffrey M
RC 1963

Jacklin, A (Tony)
RC 1967-69-71-73-75-77-79-(83)-(85)-(87)-(89); Eur 1976-82; RoW 1982; Can 1966; WC 1970-71-72

Jacobs, John RM
RC 1955

Jagger, D
Eur 1976

James, Mark H
RC 1977-79-81-89-91-93-95-(99); Eur 1978-80-82; RoW 1982; Aus 1988; Kirin 1988; FT 1989-90; WC 1978-79-82-84-87-88-93-97-99; DC 1988-89-90-93-95-97-99

Jarman, Edward W
RC 1935; Sco 1935

Job, Nick
Eur 1980

Jolly, Herbert C
USA 1926; RC 1927; Fra 1929

Jones, D
(S)Eur 1998-99

Jones, R
Sco 1903 to 07; 09-10-12-13

Kenyon, EWH
Sco, Irl 1932

King, Michael
RC 1979; WC 1979

King, Sam L
RC 1937-47-49; Sco 1934-36-37; Sco, Wal, Irl 1938

Lacey, Arthur J
RC 1933-37; Sco, Irl 1932-33; Sco 1934-36-37; Sco, Irl, Wal 1938

Lane, Barry
RC 1993; WC 1988-94; DC 1988-94-95-96; WbC 2002

Lees, Arthur
RC 1947-49-51-55; Sco, Wal, Irl 1938

Mason, SC
Eur 1980; WC 1980

Mayo, CH
Sco 1907-09-10-12-13

Mills, R Peter
RC

Mitchell, Abe
USA 1921-26; RC 1929-31-33; Sco 1932-33-34

Mitchell, P
WC 1996

Moffitt, Ralph
RC 1961

Morgan, J
(S)Eur 1997-99

Ockenden, J
USA 1921

Oke, WG
Sco 1932

Oosterhuis, Peter A
RC 1971-73-75-77-79-81; Eur 1974; WC 1971

O'Sullivan, DF
(S)Eur 1998

Padgham, Alf H
RC 1933-35-37; Sco, Irl 1932-33; Sco 1934 to 37; Sco, Irl, Wal 1938

Payne, J
WC 1996

Perry, Alf
RC 1933-35-37; Irl 1932; Sco 1933-36-38

Platts, Lionel
RC 1965

Rainford, P
Sco 1903-07

Ray, E (Ted)
USA 1921-26; RC 1927; Sco 1903 to 07; 09-10-12-13

Reid, W
Sco 1906-07

Renouf, TG
Sco 1903-04-05-10-13

Rhodes, J
(S)Eur 1998

Richardson, Steven
RC 1991; FT 1991; WC 1992; DC 1991-92*

Robson, F
USA1926; RC 1927-29-31; Sco 1909-10

Roe, Mark
WC 1989-94-95; DC 1994

Rowe, AJ
Sco 1903-06-07

Scott, Syd S
RC 1955

Seymour, M
(SCO) Irl 1932; (ENG): Sco, Irl 1932-33

Sherlock, JG
USA 1921; Sco 1903 to 07; 09-10-12-13

Snell, D
Canada 1965

Spence, J
DC 1992*-2000

Sutton, M
Can 1955

Taylor, JH
USA 1921; Sco 1903 to 07; 09-10-12-13

Taylor, JJ
Sco 1937

Taylor, Josh
USA 1921; Sco 1913

Tingey, A
Sco 1903-05

Townsend, Peter
RC 1969-71; Eur 1974; WC 1969-74

Twine, WT
Irl 1932

Vardon, Harry
USA 1921

Waites, Brian J
RC 1983; Eur 1980-82-84; RoW 1982; WC 1980-82-83; (S)Eur 1997-98

Ward, Charlie H
RC 1947-49-51; Irl 1932

Way, Paul
RC 1983-85; WC 1985; DC 1985-99

Weetman, Harry
RC 1951-53-55-57*-59-61-63;
Can 1954-56-60

Westwood, Lee
RC 1997-99-2002; Eur 2000; DC
1996-97-98-99

Whitcombe, Charles A
RC 1927-29-31-33-35-37; Fra
1929; Sco 1932 to 38; Irl 1933

Whitcombe, EE
Sco, Wal, Irl 1938

Whitcombe, Ernest R
USA 1926; RC 1929-31-35; Fra
1929; Sco 1932; Irl 1933

Whitcombe, Reg A
RC 1935; Sco 1933 to 38

Wilcock, P
WC 1973

Williamson, T
Sco 1904 to 07; 09-10-12-13

Wilson, RG
Sco 1913

Wolstenholme, Guy B
Can 1965

IRELAND

Boyle, Hugh F
RC 1967; WC 1967

Bradshaw, Harry
RC 1953-55-57; Can 1954 to1959;
Sco 1937-38; Wal 1937; Eng 1938

Carrol, LJ
Sco, Wal 1937; Sco, Eng 1938

Cassidy, D
Sco 1936; Sco, Wal 1937

Cassidy, J
Eng 1933; Sco 1934-35

Clarke, Darren
RC 1997-99-2002; Eur 2000; DC
1994 to 99; WC 1994-95-96

Daly, Fred
RC 1947-49-51-53; Sco 1936; Sco,
Wal 1937; Sco, Eng 1938; Can
1954-55

Darcy, Eamonn
RC 1975-77-81-87; Eur 1976-84;
SA 1976; WC 1976-77-83-84-85-
87; DC 1987-88*-91

Drew, Norman V
RC 1959; Can 1960-61

Edgar, J
Sco 1938

Fairweather, S
Eng 1932; Sco 1933; [SCO] Eng
1933-35-36; Irl, Wal 1938

Feherty, David
RC 1991; FT 1990-91; DC 1985-
86-90*-91-93; WC 1990

Greene, C
Can 1965

Hamill, J
Eng 1932; Eng, Sco 33; Sco 34-35

Harrington, Padraig
RC 1999-2002; Eur 2000; DC
1996 to 99; WC 1996-97*-98-99-
2000

Holley, W
Sco 1933-34-35-36-38; Eng 1932-
33-38

Jackson, H
WC 1970-71

Jones, E
Can 1965

Kinsella, J
WC 1968-69-72-73

Kinsella, W
Sco 1937; Sco, Eng 1938

McCartney, J
Sco 1932 to 38; Eng 1932-33-38;
Wal 1937

McDermott, M
Sco, Eng 1932

McGinley, Paul
RC 2002; WC 1993-94-97*-98-99-
2000; DC 1993-94-96-97-98-99

McGinn, John
HI 2002

McKenna, J
Sco 1936; Sco, Wal 1937; Sco,
Wal, Eng 1938

McKenna, R
Sco, Eng 1933; Sco 1935

McNeill, H
Eng 1932

Mahon, PJ
Sco 1932 to 38; Eng 1932-33-38;
Wal 1937-38

Martin, Jimmy
RC 1965; Can 1962-63-64-66; WC
1970

O'Brien, W
Sco 1934-36; Sco, Wal 1937

O'Connor, Christy
RC 1955-57-59-61-63-65-67-69-
71-73; Can 1956 to 64; 66; WC
1967-68-69-71-73

O'Connor, Christy jr
RC 1975-89; Eur 1974-84; SA
1976; (S)Eur 1998; WC 1974-75-
78-85-89-92; DC 1985-89-92

O'Connor, CJ
(S)Eur 1998

O'Connor, P
Sco, Eng 1932-33; Sco 1934-35-36

O'Leary, John E
RC 1975; Eur 1976-78-82; RoW
1982; WC 1972-80-82

O'Neill, J
Eng 1933

O'Neill, M
Sco, Eng 1933; Sco 1934

Patterson, E
Sco 1933 to 36; Eng 1933; Wal
1937

Polland, Eddie
RC 1973; Eur 1974-76-78-80;
(S)Eur 1998-99; WC 1973-74-76-
77-78-79

Pope, CW
Sco, Eng 1932

Rafferty, Ronan
RC 1989; Eur 1984; Kirin 1988;
FT 1989-90-91; Aus 1988; WC
1983-84-87-88; 90 to 93; DC
1986-87-88*-89-90*-91-92-93-95

Smyth, Des
RC 1979-81; Eur 1980-82-84;
RoW 1982; WC 1979-80-82-83-
88-89; DC 1985-86-87-88*-2000;
WbC 2001

Stevenson, P
Sco 1933 to 36; 38; Eng 1933-38

Wallace, L
Sco, Eng 1932

Walton, Philip
RC 1995; WC 1995; DC 1989-
90*-92-94-95

SCOTLAND

Adams, J
RC 1947-49-51-53; Eng 1932 to
1938; Wal 1937-38; Irl 1937-38

Ainslie, T
Irl 1936

Anderson, Joe
Irl 1932

Anderson, W
Irl 1936; Eng, Wal 1937

Ayton, LB
Eng 1910-12-13-33-34

Ayton, Laurie B jr
RC 1949; Eng 1937

Ballantine, J
Eng 1932-36

Ballingall, J
Eng, Irl, Wal 1938

Bannerman, Harry
RC 1993; WC 1967-72

Barnes, Brian
RC 1969-71-73-75-77-79; Eur
1974-76-78-80; SA 1976; WC
1974-75-76-77

Braid, James
USA 1921; Eng 1903 to 07; 10-12

Brand, Gordon jr
RC 1987-89; Aus 1988; Nissan
1985; Kirin 1988; FT 1989; WC

1984-85-88-89-90-92-94; DC 1985 to 89; 91 to 94; 97

Brown, Eric C
RC 1953-55-57-59; Can 1954 to 62; 65-66; WC 1967-68

Brown, Ken
RC 1977-79-83-85-87; Eur 1978; Kirin 1987; WC 1977-78-79-83

Burns, Stewart
RC 1929; Eng 1932

Callum, WS
Irl 1935

Campbell, J
Irl 1936

Coltart, Andrew
RC 1999; DC 1994-95*-96-98-2000; WC 1994-95-96-98

Coltart, F
Eng 1909

Dailey, Allan
RC 1933; Eng 1932 to 36; Eng, Irl, Wal 1938

Davis, W
Irl 1933 to 36; Irl, Eng, Wal 1937-38

Dobson, T
Eng, Irl 1932 to 1936; Eng, Irl, Wal 1937; Irl, Wal 1938

Don, W
Irl 1935-36

Donaldson, J
Eng 1932-35-38; Irl, Wal 1937

Dorman, R
Irl 1932

Duncan, George
USA 1921-26; **RC** 1927-29-31; Eng 1906-07-09-10-12-13-32-34 to 37

Durward, JG
Irl 1934; Eng 1937

Fairweather, S
[IRL] Eng 1932; Sco 1933; [SCO] Eng 1933-35-36; Irl, Wal 1938

Fallon, John
RC 1955; Eng 1936; Eng, Irl, Wal 1937-38

Fenton, WB
Eng, Irl 1932; Irl 1933

Fernie, TR
Eng 1910-12-13-33

Gallacher, Bernard
RC 1969-71-73-75-77-79-81-83-(91)-(93)-(95); Eur 1974-78-82-84; SA 1976; RoW 1982; WC 1969-71-74-82-83

Good, G
Eng 1934-36

Gow, A
Eng 1912

Grant, T
Eng 1913

Haliburton, Tom B
RC 1961-63; Can 1954; Irl 1935-36; Irl, Wal, Eng 1938

Hastings, W
Eng, Wal, Irl 1937-38

Hepburn, J
Eng 1903-05-06-07-09-10-12-13

Herd, A (Sandy)
Eng 1903-04-05-06-09-10-12-13-32

Houston, D
Irl 1934

Huish, D
WC 1973

Hunter, W
Eng 1906-07-09-10

Hutton, GC
Irl 1936; Irl, Eng, Wal 1937; Eng 1938

Ingram, D
WC 1973

Knight, G
Eng 1937

Laidlaw, W
Eng 1935-36-38; Irl, Wal 1937

Lawrie, Paul
RC 1999; WC 1996; DC 1999

Lockhart, G
Irl 1934-35

Lyle, AWB (Sandy)
RC 1979-81-83-85-87; Eur 1980-82-84; RoW 1982; Aus 1988; Nissan 1985-86; Kirin 1987; WC 1979-80-87; DC 1985 to 90; 92

McCulloch, D
Eng, Irl 1932 to 35; Eng 1936-37

McDowall, J
Eng 1932; Eng, Irl 1933 to 36

McEwan, P
Eng 1907

McIntosh, G
Eng, Irl, Wal 1938

McMillan, J
Eng, Irl 1933-34; Eng 1935

McMinn, W
Eng 1932-33-34

Martin, S
WC 1980

Montgomerie, Colin
RC 1991-93-95-97-99-2002; Eur 2000; FT 1991; WC 1988-91-92-93-97 (individual winner)-98-99; DC 1988; 91 to 98 (winners 95); 2000

Orr, Gary
Eur 2000; DC 1998-99-2000

Panton, John
RC 1951-53-61; Can 1955 to 66; WC 1968

Park, J
Eng 1909

Ritchie, WL
Eng 1913

Robertson, F
Irl 1933; Eng 1938

Robertson, P
Eng, Irl 1932; Irl 1934

Russell, Raymond
WC 1997; DC 1996-97

Sayers, Ben jr
Eng 1906-07-09

Seymour, M
Irl 1932; (ENG): Sco, Irl 1932-33

Shade, Ronnie DBM
WC 1970-71-72

Simpson, A
Eng 1904

Smith, CR
Eng 1903-04-07-09-13

Smith, GE
Irl 1932

Spark, W
Irl 1933; Irl, Eng 1935; Irl, Wal 1937

Thompson, R
Eng 1903 to 07; 09-10-12

Torrance, Sam
RC 1981-83-85-87-89-91-93-95-(2002); Eur 1976-78-80-82-84; RoW 1982; Nissan 1985; FT 1991; WC 1976-78-82-84-85-87-89-90-93-95; DC 1985-86-87-89-90-91-93-95*; WbC 2001-02

Walker, RT
Can 1964

Watt, T
Eng 1907

Watt, W
Eng 1912-13

White, J
Eng 1903 to 07; 09; 12-13

Will, George
RC 1963-65-67; Can 1963; WC 1969-70

Wilson, T
Irl 1932; Irl, Eng 1933-34

Wood, Norman
RC 1975; WC 1975

WALES

Affleck, P
DC 1995-96

Cox, S
WC 1975

Davies, R
WC 1968

De Foy, Craig B
WC 1971; 73 to 78

Dobson, K
WC 1972

Gould, H
Can 1954-55

Grabham, C
Eng, Sco 1938

Healing, SF
Sco 1938

Hill, EF
Sco, Irl 1937; Sco, Eng 1938

Hodson, Bert
RC 1931; Sco, Irl 1937; Sco, Eng 1938; also Eng v Irl 1933

Huggett, Brian GC
RC 1963-67-69-71-73-75; Eur 1974-78; Can 1963-64-65; WC 1968-69-70-71-76-79; (S) Eur 1998

James, G
Sco, Irl 1937

Jones, DC
Sco, Irl 1937; Sco, Eng 1938

Jones, T
Sco 1936; Irl 1937; Eng 1938

Llewellyn, D
Eur 1984; WC 1974-85-87*-88; DC 1985-88

Lloyd, F
Sco, Irl 1937; Sco, Eng 1938

Mayo, Paul
DC 1993

Mouland, Mark
Kirin 1988; WC 1988-89-90-92-93-95-96; DC 1986-87-88-89-93-95-96

Mouland, S
Can 1965-66; WC 1967

Park, D
DC 2000

Parkin, P
Eur 1984; WC 1984-89; DC 1985-86-87-89-90-91

Pickett, C
Sco, Irl 1937; Sco, Eng 1938

Price, Phillip
RC 2002; Eur 2000; WC 1994-95-97-98-2000; DC 1991-96

Rees, Dai J
RC 1937-47-49-51-53-(55)-(57)*-(59)-(61)-(67)

Smalldon, D
Can 1955-56

Thomas, Dave C
RC 1959-63-65-67; Can 1957 to 63; 66; WC 1967-69-70

Vaughan, DI
WC 1972-73-77-78-79-80

Williams, K
Sco, Irl 1937; Sco, Eng 1938

Woosnam, Ian
RC 1983-85-87-89-91-93-95-97; Eur 1982-84-2000; RoW 1982; Aus 1988; Nissan 1985-86; Kirin 1987; FT 1989-90; WC 1980; 82 to 85; 87*; 90 to 94; 96-97-98; DC 1985 to 91; 93-95-2000; WbC 2001-02

First Time Winners in Europe and US

There were first wins on the European Tour in 2003 for players from China (Lian-Wei Zhang in Singapore) and Korea (KJ Choi in Cologne)

European Tour:
Frederick Jacobsen (Swe)
Trevor Immelman (RSA)
Mark Foster (Eng)
Lian-Wei Zhang (Chi)
Robert-Jan Derksen (Ned)
Bradley Dredge (Wal)
Kenneth Ferrie (Eng)
Jim Furyk (USA)
Greg Owen (Eng)

Brett Rumford (Aus)
Søren Kjeldsen (Den)
Philip Golding (Eng)
Ben Curtis (USA)
Shaun Micheel (USA)
Marcus Fraser (Aus)
KJ Choi (Kor)
Maarten Lafeber (Ned)

US PGA Tour
Ben Crane (USA)
Steve Flesch (USA)
Ben Curtis (USA)
Sean Micheel (USA)

Jonathan Kaye (USA)
Adam Scott (Aus)
Chad Campbell (USA)

Because the major championships are included on the official European Tour and US Tour schedules, Open champion Ben Curtis and US PGA champion Sean Micheel were first-time winners on both tours and Jim Furyk, the US Open champion, was considered a first time winner on the European Tour.

British Isles International Players, Professional Women

Non-playing captaincy in brackets

ENGLAND

Davies, Laura
SOLHEIM CUP 1990-92-94-96-98-2000-2002-03

Douglas, Kitrina
SOLHEIM CUP 1992

Fairclough, Lora
SOLHEIM CUP 1994

Hackney, Lisa
SOLHEIM CUP 1996-98

Johnson, Trish
SOLHEIM CUP 1990-92-94-96-98-2000

Morley, Joanne
SOLHEIM CUP 1996

Nicholas, Alison
SOLHEIM CUP 1990-92-94-96-98-2000

Walker, Mickey
SOLHEIM CUP (1990)-(92)-(94)-(96)

SCOTLAND

McKay, Mhairi
SOLHEIM CUP 2002-03

Marshall, Kathryn
SOLHEIM CUP 1996

Matthew, Catriona
SOLHEIM CUP 1998-2003

Moodie, Janice
SOLHEIM CUP 2000-03

Reid, Dale
SOLHEIM CUP 1990-92-94-96-(2000)-(2002)

Wright, Pam
SOLHEIM CUP 1990-92-94

British Isles International Players, Amateur Men

Key

WC	Walker Cup	Scan	Scandinavia
CT	Commonweath Tournament	*	indicates winning team
ET	Eisenhower Trophy		
ETC	played in European Team Championship for home country		
HI	played in Home International matches		
NNC	Nixdorf Nations Cup		

'to' indicates inclusive dates: e.g.'1908 to 1911' means '1908-09-10-11'; otherwise individual years are shown.

Captaincy is indicated by the year printed in bold type; non-playing captaincy in brackets

ENGLAND

Ashby, H
Dominican Int 1973; Eur 1974; HI 1972-73-74

Attenborough, MF
WC 1967; Eur 1966-68; HI 1964-66-67-68; ETC 1967

Aylmer, CC
USA 1921; **WC** 1922; Sco 1911-22-23-24

Baker, P
WC 1985; Eur 1986; HI 1985

Ball, J
Sco 1902 to 12

Banks, C
HI 1983

Banks, SE
HI 1934-38

Bardsley, R
HI 1987; Fra 1988

Barker, HH
Sco 1907

Barry, AG
Sco 1906-07

Bathgate, D
HI 1990

Bayliss, RP
Irl 1929; HI 1933-34

Beck, JB
WC 1928-**(38)***-**(47)**; Sco 1926-30; HI 1933

Beddard, JB
Wal/Irl 1925; Sco 1927-28; Sco, Irl 1929

Beharrell, JC
HI 1956

Bell, RK
HI 1947

Benka, PJ
WC 1969; Eur 1970; HI 1967-68-69-70; ETC 1969

Bennett, H
HI 1948-49-51

Bennett, S
Sco 1979

Bennett, W
ET 1994; Eur 1994; HI 1992-93-94; Fra 1994

Bentley, AL
HI 1936-37; Fra 1937-39

Bentley, HG
WC 1934-36-38; Sco, Irl 1931; HI 1932 to 38; 47; Fra 1934 to 37; 39; 54

Berry, P
Eur 1972; HI 1972

Birtwell, SG
HI 1968-70-73

Blackey, M
HI 1995-96-97; ETC 1997; Fra 1994-96; Esp 1995

Bladon,W
Eur 1996; HI 1996

Blakeman, D
HI 1981; Fra 1982

Bland, R
HI 1994-95; Esp 1995

Bloxham, JA
HI 1966

Bonallack, Sir Michael F
WC 1957 to 73; **[69-71*]**; ET 1960 to 72; CT 1959-63-67-71; Eur 1958; 62 to 72; HI 1957 to 74; ETC 1969-71

Bottomley, S
HI 1986

Bourn, TA
Aus 1934; Irl 1928; Sco 1930; HI 1933-34; Fra 1934

Bowman, TH
HI 1932

Boxall, R
HI 1980-81-82; Fra 1982

Bradshaw, AS
HI 1932

Bradshaw, EI
Sco 1979; ETC 1979

Bradshaw, Paul
HI 2003

Bramston, JAT
Sco 1902

Brand, GJ
Eur 1976; HI 1976

Bretherton, CF
Sco 1922 to 25; Wal/Irl 1925

Bristowe, OC
WC 1923-24

Broadhurst. P
Eur 1988; HI 1986-87; Fra 1988

Bromley-Davenport, E
HI 1938-51

Brough, S
Eur 1960; HI 1952-55-59-60; Fra 1952-60

Brownlow, Hon WGE
WC 1926

Burch, N
HI 1974

Burgess, MJ
HI 1963-64-67; ETC 1967

Butterworth, JR
Fra 1954

Cage, S
WC 1993; HI 1992

Caldwell, I
WC 1951-55; HI 1950 to 59; 61; Fra 1950

Cannon, JHS
Irl/Wal 1925

Carman, A
Sco 1979; HI 1980

Carr, FC
Sco 1911

Carrigill, PM
HI 1978

Carver, M
HI 1996; ETC 1997

Casey, P
WC 1999; ET 2000; Eur 2000; HI 1999

Cassells, C
HI 1989

Castle, H
Sco 1903-04

Chapman, BHG
WC 1961; Eur 1962; HI 1961-62

Chapman, R
WC 1981; Eur 1980; Sco 1979; HI 1980-81; ETC 1981

Christmas, MJ
WC 1961-63; Eur 1962-64; ET 1962; HI 1960 to 64

Clark, CA
WC 1965; Eur 1964; HI 1964

Clark, Graeme
HI 1995-2002-03; ETC 2001; Esp 2001-03 Fra 2002

Clark, GJ
WC 1965; Eur 1964-66

Clark, HK
WC 1973; HI 1973

Claydon, Russell
WC 1989; HI 1988; ETC 1989

Colt, HS
Sco 1908

Cook, J
HI 1989-90

Cook, JH
HI 1969

Corfield, Lee
HI 2002

Crawley, Leonard G
WC 1932-34-38-47; Sco, Irl 1931; HI 1932-33-34-36-37-38-47-48-49-54-55; Fra 1936-37-38-49

Critchley, Bruce
WC 1969; Eur 1970; HI 1962-69-70; ETC 1969

Curry, DH
WC 1987; ET 1986; Eur 1986-88; HI 1984-86-87; Fra 1988

Darwin, Bernard
WC 1922; Sco 1902-04-05-08-09-10-23-24

Davies, JC
WC 1973-75-77-79; ET 1974-76*; Eur 1972-74-76-78; HI 1969-71-72-73-74-78; ETC 1973-75-77

Davies, M
HI 1984-85

Davison, C
HI 1989

Dawson, P
HI 1969

De Bendern, Count J (John de Forest)
WC 1932; Sco, Irl 1931

Deeble, P
WC 1977-81; Eur 1978;

Colombian Int 1978; HI 1975-76-77-78-80-81-83-84; Sco 1979; ETC 1979-81; Fra 1982

Dixon, D
HI 2000; RSA Esp 2001

Donald, Luke
WC 1999-2001; ET 1998*-2000; Eur 2000; HI 1996-97-98;ETC 1999-2001; Fra 1996

Dougherty, Nick
WC2001; Eur 2000; HI 2000; ETC 2001; Fra 2000; Esp, RSA 2001

Downes, P
Eur 1980; HI 1976-77-78-80-81-82; ETC 1977-79-81

Downie, JJ
HI 1974

Drummond, S
HI 1995

Duck, R
HI 1997

Dunn, NW
Irl 1928

Durrant, RA
HI 1967; ETC 1967

Dyson, S
WC 1999; HI 1998-99; ETC 1999; Esp 1999

Edwards, CS
Asia Pacific 2002; HI 1991 to 95; 97-98; 2003; ETC 1995-99; Fra 1992-94-96-2000; Esp 1993-95-99-2001

Eggo, R
WC 1987; Eur 1988; HI 1986 to 90; Fra 1988

Ellis, HC
Sco 1902-12

Ellison, TF
Sco 1922-25-26-27

Elson, Jamie
WC2001; HI 2000-01-02; Fra 2000-02; Esp 2001

Evans, G
HI 1961

Evans, G
WC 1991; ET 1990; HI 1990; ETC 1991

Eyles, GR
WC 1975; ET 1974; Eur 1974; HI 1974-75; ETC 1975

Fairbairn, KA
HI 1988

Faldo, N
CT 1975; HI 1975

Fenton, P
HI 1996

Ferrie, K
HI 1998

Fiddian, EW
WC 1932-34; Sco, Irl 1929-30-31; HI 1932 to 35; Fra 1934

Finch, Richard
HI 2000-02; ETC 2003; Fra 2000-02; Esp 2003

Fisher, D
Eur 1994; HI 1993-94; Fra 1994

Fisher, Ross
HI 2003; ETC 2003

Fogg, HN
HI 1933

Foster, M
WC 1995; HI 1994-95; ETC 1995; Esp 1995

Foster, MF
HI 1973

Foster, R
WC 1965-67-69-71-73-**(79)-(81)**; ET 1964-70-**80**; Eur 1964-66-68-70; CT 1967-71; HI 1963-64; 66 to 72; ETC 1967-69-71-73

Fowler, WH
Sco 1903-04-05

Fox, SJ
HI 1956-57-58

Frame, DW
WC 1961; HI 1958 to 63

Francis, F
HI 1936; Fra 1935-36

Frazier, K
HI 1938

Fry, SH
Sco 1902 to 09

Garbutt, I
Eur 1992; HI 1990-91-92; ETC 1991; Fra 1992

Garner, PF
HI 1977-78-80; Sco 1979

Garnet, LG
Aus 1934; Fra 1934

Gent, J
Irl 1930; HI 1938

Gilford, David
WC 1985; ET 1984; Eur 1986; HI 1983-84-85

Gillies, HD
Sco 1908-25-26-27

Godfrey, S
HI 2001

Godwin, G
WC 1979-81; HI 1976-77-78-80-81; Sco 1979; ETC 1979-81; Fra 1982

Gray, CD
HI 1932

Green, HB
Sco 1979

Green, PO
CT 1963; HI 1961-62-63

Griffiths, D
HI 1999-2000-01; Fra 2000; RSA, Esp 2001

Hambro, AV
Sco 1905-08-09-10-22

Hamer, S
HI 1983-84

Hardman, RH
WC 1928; Sco 1927-28

Hare, A
WC 1989; HI 1988; ETC 1989

Harris, G
HI 1994; ETC 1995; Esp 1995

Harris, M
Eur 2000; HI 1998-99

Hartley, RW
WC 1930-32; Sco 1926 to 31; Irl
1928 to 31; HI 1933-34-35

Hartley, WL
WC 1932; Irl/Wal 1925; Sco 1927-
31; Irl 1928-31; HI 1932-33; Fra
1935

Hassall, JE
Sco 1923; Irl/Wal 1925

Hawksworth, J
WC 1985; HI 1984-85

Hayward, CH
Sco 1925; Irl 1928

Heath, James
HI 2003

Hedges, PJ
WC 1973-75; ET 1976; Eur 1974-
76; HI 1970; 73 to 78;82-83; ETC
1973-75-77

Helm, AGB
HI 1948

Henriques, GLQ
Irl 1930

Henry, W
HI 1987; Fra 1988

Hill, GA
WC 1936-**(1955)**; HI 1936-37

Hilton, HH
Sco 1902 to 07; 09 to 12

Hilton, M
Esp 1999

Hoad, PGJ
HI 1978; Sco 1979

Hodgson, C
Sco 1924

Hodgson, J
HI 1994

Holderness, Sir EWE
USA 1921; WC 1923-26-30; Sco
1922 to 26; 28

Holmes, AW
HI 1962

Homer, TWB
WC 1973; ET 1972; Eur 1972; HI
1972-73; ETC 1973

Homewood, G
HI 1985-91; ETC 1991

Hooman, CVL
WC 1922-23; Sco 1910-22

Howell, D
WC 1995; HI 1994-95; ETC 1995;
Esp 1995

Huddy, G
WC 1961; HI 1960-61-62

Humphreys, W
WC 1971; Eur 1970; HI 1970-71;
ETC 1971

Hutchings, C
Sco 1902

Hutchinson, HG
Sco 1902-03-04-06-07-09

Hutt, R
HI 1991-92-93

Hyde, GE
HI 1967-68

Illingworth, G
Sco 1929; Fra 1937

Inglis, MJ
HI 1977

James, L
WC 1995; ET 1994; Eu 1994; HI
1993-94-95; ETC 1995; Fra 1994;
Esp 1995

James, M
WC 1975; HI 1974-75; ETC 1975

James, RD
HI 1974-75

Jobson, RH
Irl 1928

Jones, JW
HI 1948 to 52; 54-55

Kelley, MJ
WC 1977-79; ET 1976*; Eur
1976-78; Colombian Int 1978; HI
1974 to 78; 80-81-82-**(88)**; ETC
1977-79; Fra 1982

Kelley, PD
HI 1965-66-68

Kemp, John
HI 2003

Keppler, SD
WC 1983; HI 1982-83; Fra 1982

King, M
WC 1969-73; Eur 1970-72; CT
1971; HI 1969 to 73; ETC 1971-73

Kitchin, JE
Fra 1949

Knight, J
Fra 1996

Langley, JDA
WC 1936-51-53; HI 1950 to 53;
Fra 1950

Langmead, J
HI 1986

Lassen, EA
Sco 1909 to 12

Laurence, C
HI 1983-84-85

Layton, EN
Sco 1922-23-26; Irl/Wal 1925

Lee, M
HI 1950

Lee, MG
HI 1965

Lewis, ME
WC 1983; HI 1980-81-82-**(99)**-
(2001); Fra 1982

Lincoln, AC
Sco 1907

Lockerbie, Gary
HI 2003

Logan, GW
HI 1973

Lucas, D
HI 1996

Lucas, PB
WC 1936-47-**(49)**; HI 1936-48-49;
Fra 1936

Ludwell, N
HI 1991; Fra 1992

Lunt, MSR
WC 1959-61-63-65; ET 1964; Eur
1964; CT 1963; HI 1956 to 60; 62-
63-64-66

Lunt, S
HI 1932 to 35; Fra 1934-35-39

Lupton, Jonathan
Jonathan   HI 2001-02; ETC
2003; Fra 2002; Esp 2003

Lyle, AWB (Sandy)
WC 1977; Eur 1976; CT 1975; HI
1975-76-77; ETC 1977

Lynn, D
HI 1995

Lyon, JS
HI 1937-38

McCarthy, S
HI 1998

McEvoy, Peter
WC 1977-79-81-85-89-**(1999)***-
(2001)*; ET 1978-80-84-86-88*;
Eur 1978-80-86-88; HI 1976-77-
78; 80-81; 83 to 89; 91; **(94) to
(97)**; Sco 1979; ETC 1977-79-81-
89; Fra 1982-88-92-(02)

McEvoy, R
WC2001; HI 2000-01; ETC 2001;
Fra 2000; Esp 2001

McGuire, M
HI 1992

Marks, GC
WC 1969-71-**(87)**-**(89)***; ET 1970;
Eur 1968-70; CT 1975; Colombian
Int 1975; HI 1963; 67 to 71; 74-75-
82; ETC 1967-69-71-75; Fra
(1982)

Marsh, David M
WC 1959-71-**(73)**-**(75)**; Eur 1958;
HI 1956 to 60; 64-66; 68 to 72;
ETC 1971

Martin, DHR
HI 1938; Fra 1934-49

Mason, B
HI 1998-99; Esp 1999

Mason, SC
HI 1973

Mellin, GL
Sco 1922

Metcalfe, J
Eur 1990; HI 1989

Micklem, Gerald H
WC 1947-49-53-55-**(57)**-**(59)**; ET
1958; HI 1947 to 55

Millensted, Dudley J
WC 1967; CT 1967; HI 1966;
ETC 1967

Millward, EB
WC 1949-55; HI 1950; 52 to 55

Mitchell, Abe
Sco 1910-11-12

Mitchell, CS
HI 1975-76-78

Mitchell, FH
Sco 1906-07-08

Moffat, DM
HI 1961-63-67; Fra 1959-60

Montmorency, RH de
USA 1921; Sco 1908; Wal/Irl 1925; SA 1927

Moody, PH
Eur 1972; HI 1971-72

Morgan, J
Fra 2000

Morrison, JSF
Irl 1930

Mosey, IJ
HI 1971

Muscroft, R
HI 1986

Nash, A
HI 1988-89

Neech, DG
HI 1961

Nelson, P
Fra 1996

Newey, AS
HI 1932

Oldcorn, Andrew
WC 1983; ET 1982; HI 1982-83

Oosterhuis, Peter A
WC 1967; ET 1968; Eur 1968; HI 1966-67-68

Oppenheimer, RH
WC (1951); Irl 1928-29; Irl, Sco 1930

Page, P
WC 1993; HI 1993

Palmer, DJ
HI 1962-63

Patey, IR
HI 1925; Fra 1948-49-50

Pattinson, R
HI 1949

Payne, J
HI 1950-51

Payne, J
WC 1991; Eur 1990; HI 1989-90; ETC 1991

Pearson, AG
SA 1927

Pearson, MJ
HI 1951-52

Pease, JWB (Lord Wardington)
Sco 1903 to 06

Pennink, JJF
WC 1938; HI 1937-38-47; Fra 1937-38-39

Perkins, TP
WC 1928; Sco 1927-28-29

Perowne, AH
WC 1949-53-59; ET 1958; HI 1947 to 51; 53-54-55-57

Philipson, S
HI 1997

Phillips, V
WC 1993

Plaxton, J
HI 1983-84

Pollock, VA
Sco 1908

Powell, WA
Sco 1923-24; Wal/Irl 1925

Poxon, Martin A
WC 1975; HI 1975-76; ETC 1975

Prosser, D
ETC 1989

Pullan, M
HI 1991-92

Pyman, I
WC 1993; HI 1993

Rawlinson, D
HI 1949-50-52-53

Ray, D
HI 1982; Fra 1982

Revell, RP
HI 1972-73; ETC 1973

Reynard, M
HI 1996-97; Fra 1996

Richardson, Matthew
Esp 2003

Richardson, S
HI 1986-87-88

Risdon, PWL
HI 1935-36

Roberts, GP
HI 1951-53; Fra 1949

Roberts, HJ
HI 1947-48-53

Robertson, A
HI 1986-87; Fra 1988

Robinson, J
Irl 1928

Robinson, J
WC 1987; HI 1986

Robinson, S
Sco 1925; Irl 1928-29-30

Rodgers, C
HI 1999; Esp 1999

Rogers, A
HI 1991; Fra 1992

Roper, HS
Sco, Irl 1931

Roper, R
HI 1984 to 87

Rose, Justin
WC 1997; HI 1997; ETC 1997

Rothwell, J
HI 1947-48

Rowe, Philip
WC 1999; Asia Pacific 2000; HI 1997-98-2000; ETC 1999; Esp 1999

Ryles, D
HI 2000

Sanders, M
HI 1998-99; Esp 1999

Sandywell, A
HI 1990; ETC 1991

Scotland, Zane
HI 2000-01-02; Fra 2000-02

Scott, KB
HI 1937-38; Fra 1938

Scott, Hon Michael
WC 1924-(34); Aus 1934; Sco 1911-12; 23 to 26

Scott, Hon O
Sco 1902-05-06

Scrutton, EWHB
Sco 1912

Scrutton, PF
WC 1955-57; HI 1950-55

Sell, Martin
Esp 2003

Sewell, D
WC 1957-59; ET 1960; CT 1959; HI 1956 to 60

Shepperson, AE
WC 1957-59; HI 1956 to 60; 62

Sherborne, A
HI 1982-83-84

Shingler, TR
HI 1977

Shorrock, TJ
Fra 1952

Side, M
HI 1999

Skelton, Michael
WC 2003*; HI 2003

Skinns, David
HI 2001-02-03; Fra 2002

Slark, WA
HI 1957

Slater, A
HI 1955-62

Smith, Eric M
Sco, Irl 1931

Smith, Everard
Sco 1908-09-10-12

Smith, GF
Sco 1902-03

Smith, JR
HI 1932

Smith, LOM
HI 1963

Smith, W
Eur 1972; HI 1972

Snowdon, J
HI 1934

Stanford, M
WC 1993; ET 1992; Eur 1992; HI 1991-92-93; Fra 1992

Steel, Donald MA
HI 1970

Stevens, LB
Sco 1912

Storey, EF
WC 1924-26-28; Sco 1924 to 28; 30; HI 1936; Fra 1936

Storm, G
WC 1999; HI 1999; ETC 1999

Stott, HAN
HI 1976-77

Stout, JA
WC 1930-32; Sco 1928 to 31; Irl 1929-31

Stowe, C
WC 1938-47; HI 1935 to 38; 47-49-54; Fra 1938-39-49

Straker, R
HI 1932

Streeter, P
HI 1992; Fra 1994-96

Stubbs, AK
HI 1982

Suneson, C
HI 1988; ETC 1989

Sutherland, DMG
HI 1947

Sutton, W
Sco 1929-31; Irl 1929-30-31

Tate, JK
HI 1954-55-56

Taylor, HE
Sco 1911

Thirlwell, A
WC 1957; Eur 1956-58-64; CT 1953-64; HI 1951-52; 54 to 58; 63-64

Thirsk, TJ
Irl 1929; HI 1933 to 38; Fra 1935 to 39

Thom, KG
WC 1949; HI 1947-48-49-53

Thomas, I
HI 1933

Thompson, ASG
HI 1935-37

Thompson, MS
WC 1983; HI 1982

Timmis, CT
Irl 1930; HI 1936-37

Tipping, EB
Irl 1930

Tipple, ER
Irl 1928-29; HI 1932

Tolley, Cyril JH
USA 1921; WC 1922-23-**24**-26-30-34; SA 1927; Sco 1922 to 30; Irl/Wal 1925; HI 1936-37-38; Fra 1938

Townsend, Peter M
WC 1965; ET 1966; Eur 1966; HI 1965-66

Tredinnick, SV
HI 1950

Tupling, LP
WC 1969; HI 1969; ETC 1969

Turner A
HI 1952

Tweddell, W

WC 1928-(36); Sco 1928-29-30; HI 1935

Wainwright, A
HI 1997-99

Walker, MS
Irl/Wal 1925

Walker, Richard
ET 2002; HI 2001-02-03; ETC 2003; Fra 2002; Esp 2003

Wallbank, K
HI 1996-97; Fra 1996

Walls, MPD
HI 1980-81-85

Walters, Justin
Esp 2003

Walton, AR
HI 1934-35

Wardrop, Daniel
Esp 2003

Warren, KT
HI 1962

Watts, C
HI 1991-92; Fra 1992

Way, Paul
WC 1981; HI 1981; ETC 1981

Webster, S
HI 1995-96; ETC 1997

Weeks, K
HI 1987-88; Fra 1988

Welch, M
HI 1993-94; Fra 1994

Wells, J
HI 1999

Westwood, Lee
HI 1993

Wethered, Roger H
USA 1921; WC 1922-23-26-**30**-34; Sco 1922 to 30

White, L
WC 1991; HI 1990; ETC 1991

White, RJ
WC 1947-49-51-53-55; HI 1947-48-49-53-54

Whitehouse, Tom
HI 2000

Wiggett, M
HI 1990

Wiggins, R
Eur 1996; HI 1996; ETC 1997

Williams, DF
Sco 1979

Willison, R
WC 1991; ET 1990; Eur 1990; HI 1988-89-90; ETC 1989-91

Wilson, Oliver
WC 2003*; HI 2002; ETC 2003, Fra 2002

Winchester, R
HI 1985-87-89

Winter, G
HI 1991

Wise, WS
HI 1947

Wolstenholme, Guy G
WC 1957-59; ET 1958-60; CT 1959; HI 1953; 55 to 60

Wolstenholme, Gary P
WC 1995-97-99*-2001*-03*; ET 1996-98*-2002; Eur 1992-94; Asia Pacific 2000; HI 1988 to 2003; ETC 1995-97-99-2001-03 Fra 1988-92-94-2000-02; Esp 1989-91-95-99-2001-03; RSA 2001

Woollam, J
HI 1933-34-35; Fra 1935

Woolley, FA
Sco 1910-11-12

Worthington, JS
Sco 1905

Yasin Ali
HI 2002

Yeo, J
HI 1971

Zacharias, JP
HI 1935

Zoete, HW de
Sco 1903-04-06-07

IRELAND

Allison, A
Eng 1928; Sco 1929

Anderson, N
Eur 1988; HI 1985 to 90; 93; ETC 1989

Babington, A
Wal 1913

Baker, RN
HI 1975

Bamford, JL
HI 1954-56

Beamish, CH
HI 1950-51-53-56

Bell, HE
Wal 1930; HI 1932

Bowen, J
HI 1961

Boyd, HA
Wal 1913-23

Brady, E
HI 1995-98; ETC 1999

Branigan, D
HI 1975-76-77-80-81-82-86; ETC 1977-81; WGer, Fra, Swe 1976

Briscoe, A
Eng 1928 to 31; Sco, Wal 1929-30-31; HI 1932-33-38

Brown, JC
HI 1933 to 38; 48-52-53

Browne, S
HI 2001; ETC 2001

Bruen, J
WC 1938-49-51; HI 1937-38-49-50

Burke, J
WC 1932; Eng, Wal 1929; Eng, Wal, Sco 1930-31; HI 1932 to 38; 47-48-49

Burns, M
HI 1973-75-83

Burns, R
WC 1993; ET 1992; Eur 1992; HI 1991-92

Cairnes, HM
Sco, Eng 1904; Wal 1913-25; Sco 1927

Campbell, MK
HI 1999-2003

Carr, Joe B
WC 1947 to 63; (65)-**(67)**; ET 1958-60; Eur 1954-56-64-66-68; HI 1947 to 69; ETC 1965-67-69

Carr, JJ
HI 1981-82-83

Carr, JR
Wal 1930; Wal, Eng 1931; HI 1933

Carr, R
WC 1971; HI 1970-71; ETC 1971

Carroll, CA
Wal 1924

Carroll, JP
HI 1948-49-50-51-62

Carroll, W
Wal 1913-23-24-25; Eng 1925; Sco 1929; HI 1932

Carvill, J
Eur 1990; HI 1989; ETC 1989

Cashell, BG
HI 1978; Fra, WGer, Swe 1978

Caul, P
HI 1968-69; 1971 to 75

Clarke, D
Eur 1990; HI 1987-89

Cleary, T
HI 1976-77-78; 82 to 86; Wal 1979; Fra, WGer, Swe 1976

Corcoran, DK
HI 1972-73; ETC 1973

Corridan, T
HI 1983-84-91-92

Coughlan, R
WC 1997; HI 1991-94; ETC 1997

Crabbe, JL
Wal 1925; Sco 1927-28

Craddock, T
WC 1967-69; HI 1955 to 60; 67 to 70

Craigan, RM
HI 1963-64

Crosbie, GF
HI 1953-55-56-57-**(88)**

Crowe, Darren
HI 2002-03

Crowley, M
Eng 1928 to 31; Wal 1929-31; Sco 1929-30-31; HI 1932

Cullen, G
Asia Pacific 2000; HI 1999; ETC 1999

Davies, FE
Wal 1923

Dickson, JR
HI 1980; ETC 1977

Donellan, B
HI 1952

Dooley, Padraig
HI 2002

Drew, Norman V
WC 1953; HI 1952-53

Duncan, J
HI 1959-60-61

Dunne, D
HI 1997

Dunne, E
HI 1973-74-76-77-**(2001)**; Wal 1979; ETC 1975

Edwards, B
HI 1961-62; 64 to 69; 73

Edwards, M
HI 1956-57-58-60-61-62

Egan, TW
HI 1952-53-59-60-62-67-68; ETC 1967-69

Elliot, IA
HI 1975-77-78; ETC 1975; Fra, WGer, Swe 1978

Errity, D
HI 1990

Ewing, RC
WC 1936-38-47-49-51-55; HI 1934 to 38; 47 to 51; 53 to 58

Fanagan, J
WC 1995; Eur 1992-96; HI 1989 to 97; ETC 1995-97

Ferguson, M
HI 1952

Ferguson, WJ
HI 1952-54-55-58-59-61

French, WF
Sco 1929; HI 1932

Fitzgibbon, JF
HI 1955-56-57

Fitzsimmons, J
HI 1938-47-48

Flaherty, JA
HI 1934 to 37

Flaherty, PD
HI 1967; ETC 1967-69

Fleury, RA
HI 1974

Fogarty, GN
HI 1956-58-63-64-67

Foster, J
HI 1998-2000-01-03

Fox, Noel
WC 2003*; ET 2002; Eur 2000; HI 1996 to 99; 2001-02-03; ETC 1997-2001-03

Froggatt, P
HI 1957

Gannon, MA
Eur 1974-78; HI 1973-74-77-78-80-81-83-84; 87 to 90; ETC 1979-81-89; Fra, WGer, Swe 1978-80

Gill, WJ
Wal 1931; HI 1932 to 37

Glover, J
HI 1951-52-53-55-59-60-70

Goulding, N
HI 1988 to 92; ETC 1991

Graham, JSS
HI 1938-50-51

Greene, R
HI 1933

Gribben, P
WC 1999; ET 1998*; HI 1997-98-99

Guerin, M
HI 1961-62-63

Hanway, M
HI 1971-74

Harrington, J
HI 1960-61-74-75-76; Wal 1979; ETC 1975

Harrington, Padraig
WC 1991-93-95; Eur 1992-94; HI 1990 to 95; ETC 1991-95

Hayes, JA
HI 1977

Healy, TM
Sco, Eng 1931

Heather, D
HI 1976; Fra, WGer, Swe 1976

Hegarty, J
HI 1975

Hegarty, TD
HI 1957

Henderson, J
Wal 1923

Herlihy, B
HI 1950

Heverin, AJ
HI 1978; Fra, WGer, Swe 1978

Hezlet, CO
WC 1924-26-28; SA 1927; Wal 1923-25-27-29-31; Sco 1927 to 31; Eng 1929-30-31

Higgins, D
HI 1993-94

Higgins, L
HI 1968-70-71

Hoey, M
WC 2001; HI 1999-2000-01; ETC 1999-2001

Hoey, TBC
HI 1970 to 73; 77-84; ETC 1971-77

Hogan, P
HI 1985 to 88; ETC 1991

Hulme, WJ
HI 1955-56-57

Humphreys, AR
Eng 1957

Hutton, R
HI 1991

Jameson, JF
Wal 1913-24

Johnson, TWG
Eng 1929

Jones, D
HI 1998

Kane, RM
Eur 1974; HI 1967-68-71-72-74-78; Wal 1979; ETC 1971-79

Kearney, Ken
HI 1988-89-90-92-94-95-97-98-2002; ETC 1999

Keenan, S
HI 1989

Kehoe, Justin
ET 2002; HI 2000-01-02-03; ETC 2003

Kelleher, WA
HI 1962

Kelly, NS
HI 1966

Kilduff, AJ
Sco 1928

Kilpatrick, Richard
HI 2003

Kissock, B
HI 1961-62-74-76; Fra, WGer, Swe 1978

Lawrie, P
HI 1996; ETC 1997

Lehane, N
HI 1976; Fra, WGer, Swe 1976

Leyden, PJ
HI 1953-55-56-57-59

Long, D
HI 1973-74; 80 to 84; Wal 1979; ETC 1979

Lowe, A
Wal 1924; Eng 1925-28; Sco 1927-28

Lyons, P
HI 1986

McCarroll, F
HI 1968-69

McCarthy, L
HI 1953 to 56

McConnell, FP
Wal, Eng 1929; Wal, Eng, Sco 1930-31; HI 1934

McConnell, RM
Wal 1924-25-29-30-31; Eng 1925; 28 to 31; Sco 1927-28-29-31; HI 1934 to 37

McConnell, WG
Eng 1925

McCormack, JD
Wal 1913-24; Eng 1928; HI 1932 to 37

McCormick, Andrew
HI 1997 to 2002

McCrea, WE
HI 1965-66-67; ETC 1965

McCready, SM
WC 1949-51; HI 1947-49-50-52-54

McDaid, B
Wal 1979

McDermott, M
HI 2000-01; ETC 2001

McDowell, G
WC 2001; HI 2000; ETC 2001

McElhinney, Brian
HI 2003; ETC 2003

McGeady, Michael
HI 2003; ETC 2003

McGimpsey, G
WC 1985-89-91-(2003)*; ET 1984-86-88*; Eur 1986-88-90-92; HI 1978; 80 to 99; Wal 1979; ETC 1981-89-91-95-97-99

McGinley, M
HI 1996

McGinley, P
WC 1991; HI 1989-90; ETC 1991

McGinn, John
HI 2002

McHenry, J
WC 1987; HI 1985-86

McInally, RH
HI 1949-51

Mackeown, HN
HI 1973; ETC 1973

McMenamin, E
HI 1981

McMonagle, C
HI 1999-2000; ETC 1999

McMullan, C
HI 1933-34-35

MacNamara, L
HI 1977; 83 to 92; ETC 1977-91

McNeill, G
HI 1991-93-2001

McTernan, Sean
HI 2002

Madeley, JFD
WC 1963; Eur 1962; HI 1959 to 64

Mahon, RJ
HI 1938-52-54-55

Malone, B
HI 1959-64-69-71-75; ETC 1971-75

Manley, N
Wal 1924; Sco 1927-28; Eng 1928

Marren, JM
Wal 1925

Martin, GNC
WC 1928; Wal 1923-29; Sco 1928-29-30; Eng 1929-30

Maybin, Gareth
HI 2002; ETC 2003

Meharg, W
HI 1957

Moore, GJ
Eng 1928; Wal 1929

Moriarty, Colm
WC 2003*; ET 2002; HI 2001-02; ETC 2003

Morris, JC
HI 1993 to 98; ETC 1995

Morris, MF
HI 1978-80-82-83-84; Wal 1979; ETC 1979; Fra, WGer, Swe 1980

Morrow, AJC
HI 1975-83-92-93-96-97-99-2000

Mulcare, P
WC 1975; Eur 1972; HI 1968 to 72; 74-78-80; ETC 1975-79; Fra, WGer, Swe 1978-80

Mulholland, D
HI 1988

Munn, E
Wal 1913-23-24; Sco 1927

Munn, L
Wal 1913-23-24; HI 1936-37

Murphy, G
HI 1992 to 95; ETC 1995

Murphy, M
HI 2000

Murphy, P
HI 1985-86

Murray, P
HI 1995-96

Neill, JH
HI 1938-47-48-49

Nestor, JM
HI 1962-63-64

Nevin, V
HI 1960-63-65-67-69-72; ETC 1967-69-73

Nicholson, J
HI 1932

Nolan, K
WC 1997; ET 1996; Eur 1996; HI 1992 to 96; ETC 1995-97

O'Boyle, P
ETC 1977

O'Brien, MD
HI 1968 to 72; 75-76-77; ETC 1971; Fra, WGer, Swe 1976

O'Connell, A
HI 1967-70-71

O'Connell, E
WC 1989; ET 1988*; Eur 1988; HI 1985; ETC 1989

O'Leary, JE
HI 1969-70; ETC 1969

O'Neill, JJ
HI 1968

O'Rourke, P
HI 1980-81-82-84-85

O'Sullivan, DF
HI 1976-85-86-87-91; ETC 1977

O'Sullivan, Mark
HI 2003

O'Sullivan, WM
HI 1934 to 38; 47 to 51; 53-54

Omelia, B
HI 1994 to 97

Owens, M
HI 2003

Ownes, GH
HI 1935-37-38-47

Patterson, AH
Wal 1913

Paul, Stuart
HI 2001-02

Pierse, AD
WC 1983; ET 1982; Eur 1980; HI 1976-77-78; 80 to 85; 87-88; Wal 1979; ETC 1981; Fra, WGer, Swe 1980

Pollin, RKM
HI 1971; ETC 1973

Power, E
HI 1987-88-93-94-95-97-98-99

Power, M
HI 1947 to 52; 54

Purcell, M
HI 1973

Rafferty, Ronan
WC 1981; ET 1980; Eur 1980; Wal 1979; HI 1980-81; ETC 1981; Fra, WGer, Swe 1980

Rainey, WHE
HI 1962

Rayfus, P
HI 1986-87-88

Reade, HE
Wal 1913

Reddan, B
HI 1987

Rice, JH
HI 1947-52

Rice, T
HI 2000-01; ETC 2001

Robertson, CT
Wal, Sco 1930

Scannel, BJ
HI 1947 to 51; 53-54

Sheals, HS
Wal 1929; Eng 1929-30-31; Sco 1930; HI 1932-33

Sheahan, D
WC 1963; Eur 1962-64-67; HI 1961 to 67; 70

Simcox, R
Wal, Sco 1930; Wal, Sco, Eng 1931; HI 1932 to 36; 38

Sinclair, M
HI 1999

Slattery, B
HI 1947-48

Sludds, MF
HI 1982

Smyth, D
HI 1972-73; ETC 1973

Smyth, DW
Wal 1923-30; Eng 1930; Sco 1931; HI 1933

Smyth, V
HI 1981-82

Soulby, DEB
Sco, Wal, Eng 1929-30

Spiller, EF
Wal 1924; Eng 1928; Sco 1928-29

Spring, G
HI 1996

Staunton, R
HI 1964-65-72; ETC 1973

Stevenson, JF
Wal 1923-24; Eng 1925

Stevenson, K
HI 1972

Taggart, J
HI 1953

Timbey, JC
Sco 1928-31; Wal 1931

Waddell, G
Wal 1925

Walton, P
WC 1981-83; ET 1982; Wal 1979; HI 1980-81; ETC 1981; Fra, WGer, Swe 1980

Webster, F
HI 1949

Welch, L
HI 1936

Werner, LE
Wal 1925

West, CH
Eng 1928; HI 1932

Young, D
HI 1969-70-77

SCOTLAND

Aitken, AR
Eng 1906-07-08

Alexander, DW
HI 1958; Scan 1958

Anderson, RB
HI 1962-63; Scan 1960-62

Andrew, R
Eng 1905 to 10

Armour, A
Eng 1922

Armour, TD
USA 1921

Bannerman, SJ
HI 1988; Swe 1990

Barrie, GC
HI 1981-83; Swe 1983

Beames, Roger
Eur 1996; HI 1995-96-99; Esp 1996; Fra, Swe 1997

Beveridge, HW
Eng 1908

Birnie, J
Irl 1927

Black, D
HI 1966-67

Black, FC
Eur 1966; HI 1962-64-65-66-68; ETC 1965-67; Scan 1962

Black, GT
HI 1952-53; SA 1954

Black, WC
HI 1964-65

Blackwell, EBH
Eng 1902, 1904 to 1907, 1909-10-12, 1923-24-25

Blair, DA
WC 1955-61; CT 1954; HI 1948-49-51-52-53-55-56-57; Scan 1956-58-62

Bloice, C
WC 1985; HI 1985-86; ETC 1985; Fra 1985; Ita, Swe 1986

Blyth, AD
Eng 1904

Bookless, JT
Eng, Irl 1930; Eng, Wal 1931

Booth, Wallace
Fra 2003

Braid, HM
Eng 1922-23

Brand, Gordon jr
WC 1979; ET 1978-80; Eur 1978-80; HI 1978-80

Brock, J
Irl 1929; HI 1932

Brodie, Allan
WC 1977-79; ET 1978; Eur 1974-76-78-80; HI 1970, 1972 to 1978, 1980; Eng 1979; ETC 1973-77; Bel, Esp 1977; Fra 1978; Ita 1979

Brodie, Andrew
HI 1968-69; Esp 1974

Brooks, A
WC 1969; HI 1968-69; ETC 1969

Brooks, CJ
Eur 1986; HI 1984-85; Swe 1984; Swe, Ita 1986

Brooks, M
WC 1997; ET 1996; Eur 1996; HI 1995-96; ETC 1997; Aut 1994; Esp 1996; Fra, Swe 1997

Brotherston, IR
HI 1984-85; ETC 1985; Fra 1985

Bryson, WS
HI 1991-92-93; Swe, Ita 1992; Fra 1993; Esp 1994

Bucher, AMM
HI 1954-55-56; Scan 1956

Burnside, J
HI 1956-57

Burrell, TM
Eng 1924

Bussell, AF
WC 1957; Eur 1956-62; HI 1956-57-58-61; Scan 1956-60

Cairns, S
HI 1997

Cameron, D
HI 1938-51

Campbell, C
HI 1999

Campbell, Glenn
HI 2003

Campbell, Sir Guy, Bt
Eng 1909-10-11

Campbell, HM
Eur 1964; HI 1962-64-68; ETC 1965-(79); Scan 1962; Aus 1964

Campbell, JGS
HI 1947-48

Campbell, W
WC 1930; Irl 1927; Irl, Eng 1928-29-30; Irl, Eng, Wal 1931; HI 1933 to 36

Cannon, JM
HI 1969; Esp 1974

Carmichael, Steven
HI 1998-99-2001-02; Swe 1999; Esp, Ita 2002; Fra 2003

Carrick, DG
WC 1983-87; Eur 1986; HI 1981 to 89; ETC 1987-(89)-(91); WGer 1987; Ita 1984-86-88; Fra 1987-89; Swe 1983-84-86

Carslaw, IA
WC 1979; Eur 1978; HI 1976-77-78-80-81; ETC 1977-79; Eng 1979; Esp 1977; Fra 1978-83; Bel 1978; Ita 1979

Cater, JR
WC 1955; HI 1952 to 56; SA 1954; Scan 1956

Caven, J
WC 1922; Eng 1926

Chillas, D
HI 1971

Cochran, JS
HI 1966

Collier, B
HI 1994; Aut 1994

Coltart, Andrew
WC 1991; ET 1990; Eur 1990; HI 1988-89-90; ETC 1989-91; NNC 1990; Ita, Swe 1990; Fra 1991

Cosh, GB
WC 1965; ET 1966-68; Eur 1966-68; CT 1967; HI 1964 to 69; ETC 1965-(69)

Coutts, FJ
HI 1980-81-82; ETC 1981-83; Fra 1981-82-83

Crawford, DR
HI 1990-91; ETC 1991; Fra 1991

Crawford, G
Esp 2002

Cuddihy, J
HI 1977-78

Dalgleish, CR
WC 1981; Eur 1982; HI 81-82-83-89-(95); ETC 1981-83-(93)-(95); Fra 1982; NNC 1989

Dawson, JE
Irl 1927-29; Irl, Eng 1930; Irl, Eng, Wal 1931; HI 1932-33-34-37

Dawson, M
HI 1963-65-66

Deboys, A
HI 1956-59-60; Scan 1960

Deighton, Frank WG
WC 1951-57; CT 1954-59; HI

1950-52-53-56-58-59-60; SA 1954; NZ 1954; Scan 1956

Denholm, RB
Irl 1927-29; Irl, Wal, Eng 1931; HI 1932-33-34

Dewar, FG
HI 1952-53-55; SA 1954; ETC (1971)-(73)

Dick, CE
Eng 1902-03-04-05-09-12

Dickson, HM
Irl 1929-31

Doherty, Jack
ET 2002; ETC 2003; HI 2001-02; Swe 2001; Esp, Ita 2002

Dowie, Andrew
HI 1949

Downie, D
HI 1993-94; Esp, Ita 1994; Fra, Swe 1995

Draper, JW
HI 1954

Dundas, S
HI 1992-93

Dykes, J Morton
WC 1936; HI 1934-35-36-48-49-51

Easingwood, SR
HI 1986-87-88-90; ETC 1989; Fra 1987-89; Ita 1988-90

Elliot, A
HI 1989; ETC 1989; Fra 1989

Elliot, C
HI 1982; Fra 1983

Everett, C
HI 1988-89-90; ETC 1989-91; NNC 1989-90; Ita 1988-90; Fra 1988-89-91; Swe 1990

Fairlie, WE
Eng 1912

Farmer, A
HI 1997; Swe 1999

Farmer, JC
HI 1970

Ferguson, S Mure
Eng 1902-03-04

Fleming, J
HI 1987

Flockhart, AS
HI 1948-49

Forbes, E
HI 1996-98-2000-01; Ita 1996-2000; Fra 1997; Swe 1997-99; Esp 2002

Forsyth, A
HI 1996; ETC 1997; Ita 1996; Fra, Swe 1997

Fox, G
HI 1997-98-99; ETC 1999; Swe 1999

Gairdner, JR
Eng 1902

Gallacher, Bernard J
HI 1967

Gallacher, S
WC 1995; ET 1994; HI 1992 to 95; ETC 1993-95; Ita, Esp 1994; Fra, Swe 1995

Galloway, RF
HI 1957-58-59; Scan 1958

Garson, R
Irl 1927-28-29

Gibb, C
Eng 1927; Irl 1928

Gibson, WC
HI 1950-51

Girvan, P
WC 1987; HI 1986; ETC 1987; WGer 1987

Gordon, Graham
WC 2003*; ET 2002; ETC 2003; HI 2000-02

Graham, AJ
Eng 1925

Graham, J
Eng 1902 to 11

Green, CT
WC 1963-69-71-73-75-(83)-(85); ET 1970-72-(84)-(86);Eur 1962-66-68-70-72-74-76; CT 1971; HI 1961 to 78; Eng 1979; ETC 1965 to 83; Scan 1962; Aus 1964; Bel 1973-75-77-78; Esp 1977; Ita 1979

Greig, DG
CT 1975; HI 1972-73-75

Greig, K
HI 1933

Guild, WJ
Eng 1925; Eng, Irl 1927-28

Hall, AH
HI 1962-66-69

Hamilton, ED
HI 1936-37-38

Hare, WCD
HI 1953; NZ 1954

Harris, IR
HI 1955-56-58-59

Harris, R
WC **1922**-23-26; Eng 1905-08-10-11-12; 22 to 28

Hastings, JL
HI 1957-58; Scan 1958

Hay, G
WC 1991; Eur 1980; Eng 1979; HI 1980-88-90-91-92; ETC 1991-93; Bel 1980; Fra 1980-82-89-91-93; Ita 1988-92-94; Swe 1992; Esp 1994

Hay, J
HI 1972

Heap, Craig
HI 1999-2001; ETC 2001

Henderson, N
HI 1963-64

Hird, K
HI 1987-88-89; NNC 1989; Ita 1990

Hislop, Craig
HI 1994-96; Aut 1994; Ita 1996

Hope, WL
WC 1923-24-28; Eng 1923; 25 to 29

Horne, A
HI 1971

Horne, S
HI 1997-98

Hosie, JR
HI 1936

Howard, D Barclay
WC 1995-97; ET 1996; Eur 1980-94-96; Eng 1979; HI 1980 to 83; 93 to 96; ETC 1981-95-97; Bel 1980; Fra 1980-81-83-95-97; Ita 1984-94; Esp 1994-96; Swe 1995-97

Huggan, J
HI 1981 to 84; ETC 1981; Fra 1982-83; Swe 1983; Ita 1984

Hume, B
HI 1999-2000-01; ETC 2001; Ita 2000; Swe 2001

Hunter, NM
1903-12

Hunter, R
HI 1966

Hunter, WI
Eng 1922

Hutcheon, I
WC 1975-77-79-81; ET 1974-76*-80; Eur 1974-76; CT 1975; Dominican Int 1973; Colombian Int 1975; HI 1971 to 78; 80; ETC 1973-75-77-79-81; Bel 1973-75-77-78-80; Esp 1977; Fra 1978-80-81; Ita 1979; Swe 1983

Hutchison, CK
Eng 1904 to 12

Inglis, David
WC 2003*; ETC 2003; HI 2001-02

Innes, Brian
HI 2003

Jack, R Reid
WC 1957-59; ET 1958; Eur 1956; CT 1959; HI 1950-51; 54 to 59; 61; NZ 1954; Scan 1956-58

Jack, WS (Billy)
HI 1955

James, D
HI 1985

Jamieson, A jr
WC 1926; Eng 1927; Eng, Irl 1928; Eng, Irl, Wal 1931; HI 1932-33-36-37

Jamieson, D
HI 1980

Jamieson, Scott
HI 2002

Jenkins, JLC
USA 1921; Eng 1908-12-22-24-26-28; Irl 1928

Johnston, JW
HI 1970-71

Kelly, L
WC 1999; ET 1998*; HI 1997-98; ETC 1999; Swe 1999

Killey, GC
Irl 1928

King, Jonathan
HI 2001-02-03; Swe 2001; Esp 2002; Fra 2003

Kirkpatrick, D
HI 1992; ETC 1993; Fra 1993

Knowles, ST
HI 1990-91-92; Fra 1991

Kyle, AT
WC 1938-47-51; SA 1952; HI 1938-47; 49 to 53

Kyle, DH
WC 1924; Eng 1924-30

Kyle, EP
Eng 1925

Laidlay, JE
Eng 1902 to 11

Laird, Martin
HI 2003

Lang, JA
WC 1930; Irl, Eng 1929; Irl 1930; Irl, Eng, Wal 1931

Lawrie, CD
WC (1961)-(1963); ET (1960)-(1962); Eur (1960)-(1962); HI 1949-50; 55 to 58; Swe 1950; Scan 1956-58

Lee, IGF
HI 1958 to 62; Scan 1960

Lindsay, J
HI 1933 to 36

Little, E
Ita 1996

Lockhart, G
Eng 1911-12

Loftus, M
Eur 2000; HI 1999-2000; Ita 2000

Low, AJ
HI 1963-64; ETC 1965; Aus 1964

Low, JL
Eng 1904

Lowdon, CJ
Irl 1927

Lowson, AG
HI 1989-90-91-97; Swe 1990; Swe, Ita 1992

Lygate, M
HI 1970-75-(88); ETC 1971-85-87

McAllister, SD
HI 1983; ETC 1983; Swe 1983

McArthur, Andrew
ETC 2003; HI 2002-03

McArthur, W
HI 1952-54; SA 1954

McBeath, J
HI 1964

McBride, D
HI 1932

McCallum, AR
WC 1928; Eng 1929

McCart, DM
HI 1977-78; Bel, Fra 1978

MacDonald, GK
HI 1978-81-82; Eng 1979; Fra 1981-82-83

McDonald, H
HI 1970

Macdonald, J Scott
WC 1971; Eur 1970; HI 1969 to 72; ETC 1971; Bel 1973

Macfarlane, CB
Eng 1912

Macgregor, A
Scan 1956

Macgregor, G
WC 1971-75-83-85-87-(91)-(93); ET 1982; Eur 1970-74-84; CT 1971-75; HI 1969 to 76; 80 to 87; (99); Eng 1979; ETC 1971-73-75-81-83-85-87; Bel 1973-75-80; Fra 1981-82-85-87; Swe 1983-84-86; Ita 1984-86

MacGregor, RC
WC 1953; HI 1951 to 54; NZ 1954

McInally, H
HI 1937-47-48

McIntosh, EA
HI 1989

Macintosh, KW
Eur 1980; Eng 1979; HI 1980; Bel, Fra 1980

McKay, G
HI 1969

McKay, JR
HI 1950-51-52-54; NZ 1954

McKechnie, P
HI 1998

McKellar, PJ
WC 1977; Eur 1978; HI 1976-77-78; Eng 1979; Bel, Fra 1978

Mackenzie, F
Eng 1902-03

Mackenzie, S
ET 2002; HI 1990; 93 to 2001-03; ETC 1999-2001; Esp 1994-96-02; Ita 1994-2000; Fra 1997; Swe 1997-99

Mackenzie, WW
WC 1922-23; Eng 1923-26-27-29; Irl 1930

McKibbin, H
HI 1994-95; ETC 1995; Fra, Swe 1995; Esp 1996

Mackie, GW
HI 1948-50

McKinlay, SL
WC 1934; Eng 1929-30-31; Irl 1930; Wal 1931; HI 1932-33-35-37-47

McKinna, RA
HI 1938

McKinnon, A
HI 1947-52

McLean, J
WC 1934-36; Aus 1934; HI 1932 to 36
McLeary, Jamie
HI 2002-03
McLeod, AE
HI 1937-38
McLeod, WS
HI 1935-37-38; 47 to 51; Swe 1950
McNair, AA
Irl 1929
MacRae, Neil
HI 2003; Ita 2002
McRuvie, Eric A
WC 1932-34; Eng 1929; Eng, Irl 1930; Eng, Irl, Wal 1931; HI 1932 to 36
McTear, J
HI 1971
Manford, GC
Eng 1922-23
Mann, LS
WC 1983; HI 1982-83; ETC 1983; Swe 1983
Marchbank, Brian
WC 1979; ET 1978; Eur 1976-78; HI 1978; ETC 1979; Ita 1979
Martin, S
WC 1977; ET 1976; Eur 1976; HI 1975-76-77; ETC 1977; Bel, Esp 1977
Maxwell, R
Eng 1902 to 07; 09-10
Melville, LM Balfour
Eng 1902-03
Melville, TE
HI 1974
Menzies, A
Eng 1925
Mill, JW
HI 1953-54
Miller, AC
HI 1954-55
Miller, MJ
HI 1974-75-77-78; Bel, Fra 1978
Milligan, JW
WC 1989-91; ET 1988*-90; Eur 1988-92; HI 1986 to 92; ETC 1987-89-91; NNC 1989; Swe 1986-90-92; WGer 1987; Fra 1987-89-91; Ita 1988-90-92
Milne, WTG
WC 1973; HI 1972-73; ETC 1973; Bel 1973
Moir, A
Eur 1984; HI 1983-84; ETC 1985; Swe, Ita 1984; Fra 1985
Montgomerie, Colin S
WC 1985-87; ET 1984-86; Eur 1986; HI 1984-85-86; ETC 1985-87; Ita 1984; Swe 1984-86; Fra 1985; WGer 1987
Montgomerie, JS
HI 1957; ETC 1965; Scan 1958

Morris, FS
HI 1963
Morrison, JH
Scan 1960
Munro, RAG
HI 1960
Murdoch, D
HI 1964
Murphy, AR
HI 1961-67
Murray, GH
WC 1977; Eur 1978; HI 1973 to 78; 83; ETC 1975-77; Esp 1974-77; Bel 1975-77
Murray, SWT
WC 1963; Eur 1958-62; HI 1959 to 63; Scan 1960
Murray, WA
WC 1923-24; Eng 1923 to 27
Murray, WB
HI 1967-68-69; ETC 1969
Neill, R
HI 1936
Noon, J
HI 1987
O'Hara, Steven
WC 2001; ET 2000; Eur 2000; HI 1999-2000; ETC 2001; Ita 2000; Swe 2001
Osgood, TH
Eng 1925
Paton, DA
HI 1991
Patrick, D
WC 1999; Asia Pacific 2000; HI 1997-98-99; ETC 1999; Swe 1999
Patrick, KG
HI 1937
Peters, GB
WC 1936-38; HI 1934 to 38
Pirie, AK
WC 1967; Eur 1970; HI 1966 to 75; ETC 1967-69; Bel 1973-75; Esp 1974
Pressley, J
HI 1947-48-49
Raeside, A
Irl 1929
Ramsay, Eric
HI 2002-03, Ita 2002
Rankin, G
WC 1995-97-99; HI 1994-95-97-98; ETC 1995-97-99; Swe 1995-97-99; Fra 1995-97; Esp 1996
Reid, A
HI 1993-94-95; ETC 1993-95; Esp, Ita 1994; Fra 1995
Renfrew, RL
HI 1964
Robb, J jr
Eng 1902-03-05-06-07
Robb, WM
HI 1935

Roberts, AT
Irl 1931
Roberts, GW
HI 1937-38
Robertson, Dean
WC 1993; ET 1992; Eur 1992; HI 1991-92-93; ETC 1993; Swe, Ita 1992; Fra 1993
Robertson, DM
HI 1973-74; Esp 1974
Robertson-Durham, JA
Eng 1911
Russell, R
WC 1993; HI 1992-93; ETC 1993; Fra 1993
Rutherford, DS
Irl 1929
Rutherford, R
HI 1938-47
Saddler, AC
WC 1963-65-67-(77); ET 1962-(76)*; Eur 1960-62-64-66; CT 1959-63-67; HI 1959 to 64; 66; ETC 1965-67-(75)-(77); Scan 1962
Scott, R jr
WC 1924; Eng 1924-28
Scott, WGF
Irl 1927
Scroggie, FH
Eng 1910
Shade, Ronnie DBM
WC 1961-63-65-67; ET 1962-64-66-68; Eur 1960-62-64-66; CT 1963-67; Aus 1964; HI 1957; 60 to 68; ETC 1965-67; Scan 1960-62
Shaw, G
WC 1987; HI 1984-86-87-88-90; ETC 1987; Swe 1984; Fra, WGer 1987
Sherry, Gordon
WC 1995; ET 1994; Eur 1994; HI 1993-94-95; ETC 1995; Fra 1993-95; Esp 1994; Swe 1995
Shields, B
HI 1986
Simpson, AF
Eng 1927; Irl 1928
Simpson, JG
USA 1921; Eng 1907-08-09-11-12-22-24-26
Sinclair, A
HI 1950; ETC (1967)
Smith, JN
WC 1930; Irl 1928; Irl, Eng 1930; Irl, Eng, Wal 1931; HI 1932-33-34
Smith, S
Aut 1994
Smith, WD
WC 1959; Eur 1958; HI 1957 to 60; 63; Scan 1958-60
Stephen, AR (Sandy)
WC 1985; Eur 1972; HI 1971 to 77; 84-85; ETC 1975-85; Esp 1974; Bel 1975-77-78; Fra 1985

Stevenson, A
HI 1949

Stevenson, JB
Irl 1931; HI 1932-38-47-49-50-51

Strachan, CJL
HI 1965-66-67; ETC 1967

Stuart, HB
WC 1971-73-75; ET 1972; Eur 1968-72-74; CT 1971; HI 1967 to 74; 76; ETC 1969-71-73-75; Bel 1973-75

Stuart, JE
HI 1959

Tait, AG
HI 1987-88-89; NNC 1989

Taylor, GN
HI 1948

Taylor, JS
Eng 1979; HI 1980; Bel, Fra 1980

Taylor, LG
HI 1955-56

Thomson, AP
HI 1970; ETC 1971

Thomson, G
HI 1996

Thomson, Hector
WC 1936-38; HI 1934 to 38

Thomson, JA
HI 1981 to 89; 91-92; ETC 1983; WGer 1987; Ita 1984-86-88-90; Swe 1990

Thomson, Mike
HI 1998

Thorburn, K
Irl 1927; Eng 1928

Torrance, TA
WC 1924-28-30-**32**-34; Eng 1922-23-25-26-28-29-30; HI 1933

Torrance, WB
WC 1922; Eng 1922-23-24-26-27-28-30; Irl 1928-29-30

Tulloch, W
Eng 1927-29; Eng, Irl 1930; Eng, Irl, Wal 1931; HI 1932

Turnbull, A
HI 1995-96-97; Fra 1995; Esp 1996

Twynholm, S
HI 1990; NNC 1990

Urquhart, M
HI 1993; Ita 1996

Vannet, Lee
HI 1984

Walker, J
WC 1961; Eur 1958-60; HI 1954-55-57-58; 60 to 63; Scan 1958-62

Walker, KH
HI 1985-86

Walker, RS
HI 1935-36

Warren, Marc
WC 2001; HI 2000-01; ETC 2001; Ita 2000; Swe 2001

Watson, Craig R
WC 1997; HI 1991-92; 94 to 2000, **2001**, 2003; ETC 1997-99-2001-03; Swe 1992-97-2001; Ita 1992; Aut 1994; Esp 1996-2002; Fra 1997

Watt, AW
HI 1987

Webster, AJ
HI 1978

Wemyss, DS
HI 1937

Whyte, AW
HI 1934

Wight, R
Swe 1950

Wilkie, DF
HI 1962-63-65-67-68

Wilkie, G
Eng 1911

Williamson, SB
HI 1947-48-49-51-52

Wilson, E
HI 1985

Wilson, J
WC 1923; Eng 1922-23-24-26; Irl 1932

Wilson, JC
WC 1947-53; CT 1954; SA 1954; HI 1947-48-49-51-52-53; Swe 1950; NZ 1954

Wilson, P
HI 1976; Bel 1977

Wilson, Stuart
WC 2003*; Asia-Pacific 2002; ETC 2003; HI 2000-02-03; Esp, Ita 2002; Fra 2003

Wright, I
HI 1958 to 61; Scan 1960-62

Young, ID
Eur 1982; HI 1981-82; Fra 1982

Young, JR
Eur 1960; HI 1960-61-65; Scan 1960

Young, S
WC 1997; HI 1996; ETC 1997; Ita 1996

WALES

Adams, MPD
HI 1969 to 72; 75-76-77

Atkinson, HN
Irl 1913

Barnett, A
HI 1989-90-91; ETC 1991

Bayne, PWGA
HI 1949

Bevan, RJ
HI 1964-65-66-67-73-74

Black, JL
HI 1932 to 1936

Bonnell, DJ
HI 1949-50-51

Broad, RD
Irl 1979; HI 1980-81-82-84; ETC 1981

Brookman, R
HI 1999-2000

Brown, CT
WC (**1995**)*-(**97**); Eur [1996]; HI 1970 to 75; 77-78-80-[88]; ETC 1973; Den 1977; Irl 1979; Den, Esp, Sui 1980

Brown, D
Irl 1923-30-31; Eng 1925; Sco 1931

Buckley, JA
WC 1979; HI 1967-68-69-76-77-78; ETC 1967-69; Den 1976-77

Calvert, M
HI 1983-84-86-87-89-91

Campbell, A
HI 1996-97-2000-01

Campbell, I
HI 1998-99-2001; ETC 1999-2001

Carr, JP
Irl 1913

Chapman, JA
Irl 1923-29-30-31; Eng 1925; Sco 1931

Chapman, R
Irl 1929; HI 1932-34-35-36

Charles, WB
Irl 1924

Clark, MD
Irl 1947

Clay, G
HI 1962

Clement, G
Irl 1979

Coulter, JG
HI 1951-52

Cox, S
HI 1970 to 74; ETC 1971-73

Davies, EN
HI 1959 to 74; ETC 1969-71-73

Davies, G
HI 1981-82-83; Den 1977

Davies, HE
HI 1933-34-36

Davies, Rhys
HI 2002-03

Davies, TJ
HI 1954 to 60

Dinsdale, R
HI 1991-92-93

Disley, A
HI 1976-77-78-(**99**); Irl 1979; Den 1977

Dodd, SC
WC 1989; HI 1985-87-88-89

Donaldson, J
ET 2000; Eur 2000; HI 1996 to 2000; ETC 1997-99

Dredge, Bradley
WC 1993; ET 1992; Eur 1994; HI 1992 to 95; ETC 1995

Duffy, I
HI 1975

Duncan, AA
WC (1953); HI 1933-34-36-38; 47 to 59

Duncan, GT
HI 1952 to 58

Duncan, J jr
Irl 1913

Dykes, Tim
HI 2001-02-03

Eaves, CH
HI 1935-36-38-47-48-49

Edwards, Nigel
WC 2001*-03*; ET 2002; Asia Pacific 2002; HI 1995 to 2002; ETC 1997-99-2001-03

Edwards, S
HI 1992

Edwards, TH
HI 1947

Ellis, M
Eur 1996; HI 1992 to 96

Emerson, T
HI 1932

Emery, G
Irl 1925; HI 1933-36-38

Evans, AD
Sco, Irl 1931; Sco 1935; HI 1932 to 35; 38; 47 to 56; 61

Evans, C
1990 to 95; ETC 1995

Evans, Duncan
WC 1981; Eur 1980; HI 1978-80-81; Irl 1979; ETC 1981

Evans, HJ
HI 1976-77-78-80-81-84-85-87-88; Irl 1979; ETC 1979-81; Fra 1976; Den 1977-80; Esp, Sui 1980

Evans, M Gear
Irl 1930; Sco, Irl 1931

Fairchild, CEL
Irl 1923; Eng 1925

Fairchild, IJ
Irl 1924

Gilford, CF
HI 1963 to 67

Glossop, R
HI 1935-37-38-47

Griffiths, HGB
Irl 1923-24-25

Griffiths, HS
Eng 1958

Griffiths, JA
HI 1933

Griffiths, M
HI 1999-2000-01; ETC 2001

Hales, JP
Sco 1963

Hall, A
HI 1994

Hall, D
HI 1932-37

Hall, K
HI 1955-59

Hamilton, CJ
Irl 1913

Harpin, Lee
ET 2002; HI 1996; 1998 to 2003; ETC 1999-2001

Harrhy, A
HI 1988-89-95

Harris, D
HI 1997

Harrison, JW
HI 1937-50

Herne, KTC
Irl 1913

Houston, G
HI 1990 to 95; ETC 1991-95

Howell, HR
Irl 1923-24-25-29-30-31; Eng 1925; Sco 1931; HI 1932; 34 to 38; 47

Howell H Logan
Irl 1925

Hughes, I
HI 1954-55-56

Humphrey, JG
Irl 1925

Humphreys, DI
HI 1972

Isitt, GH
Irl 1923

Jacob, NE
HI 1932 to 36

Jermine, JG
HI 1972 to 76; 82; 2000; ETC 1975-77; Fra 1975

Johnson, R
Eur 1994; HI 1990-92-93-94; ETC 1991

Jones, A
HI 1989-90; ETC 1991

Jones, DK
HI 1973

Jones, EO
HI 1983-85-86

Jones, JG Parry
HI 1959-60

Jones, JL
HI 1933-34-36

Jones, JR
HI 1970-72-73-77-78; 80 to 85; Irl 1979; ETC 1973-79-81; Den 1976; Den, Sui, Esp 1980

Jones, KG
HI 1988

Jones, MA
HI 1947 to 51; 53-54-57

Jones, Malcolm F
HI 1933

Jones, SP
HI 1981 to 86; 88-89-91-93

Knight, B
HI 1986

Knipe, RG
HI 1953 to 56

Knowles, WR
Eng 1948

Lake, AD
HI 1958

Last, CN
HI 1975

Lee, JN
HI 1988-89; ETC 1991

Lewis, DH
HI 1935 to 38

Lewis, DR
Irl 1925-29-30-31; Sco 1931; HI 1932-34

Lewis, R Cofe
Irl 1925

Lloyd, HM
Irl 1913

Lloyd, RM de
Sco, Irl 1931; HI 1932 to 38; 47-48

Llyr, A
HI 1984-85

Lockley, AE
HI1956-57-58-62

Macara, MA
HI 1983-84-85; 87; 89 to 93

McLean, D
HI 1968 to 78; 80 to 83; 85-86-88-90; Irl 1979; ETC 1975-77-79-81; Fra 1975; Fra, Den 1976; Den, Sui, Esp 1980

Maliphant, FR
HI 1932

Manley, Stuart
WC 2003*; HI 2001-02; ETC 2003

Marsden, G
HI 1994

Marshman, A
HI 1952

Marston, CC
Irl 1929-30; Irl, Sco 1931

Mathias-Thomas, FEL
Irl 1924-25

Matthews, L
HI 2003

Matthews, N
HI 1999; ETC 1999

Matthews, RL
HI 1935-37

Mayo, PM
WC 1985-87; HI 1982-88

Melia, TJ
HI 1976-77-78-80-81-82; Irl 1979; ETC 1977-79; Den 1976; Den, Sui, Esp 1980

Mills, Cennydd
HI 2003

Mills, ES
HI 1957

Mitchell, JWH
HI 1964-65-66-67

Moody, JV
HI 1947-48-49-51-56; 58 to 61

Morgan, JL
WC 1951-53-55; HI 1948 to 62;
64-68

Morris, R
HI 1983-86-87

Morris, TS
Irl 1924-29-30

Morrow, JM
Irl 1979; HI 1980-81; ETC 1979-81; Den, Sui, Esp 1980

Moss, AV
HI 1965-66-68

Mouland, MG
HI 1978-81; Irl 1979; ETC 1979

Moxon, GA
Irl 1929-30

Newman, JE
HI 1932

Newton, H
Irl 1929

Noon, GS
HI 1935-36-37

Oakley, Neil
HI 2002

O'Carroll, C
HI 1989 to 93; ETC 1991

Owen, JB
HI 1971

Owens, GF
HI 1960-61

Palferman, H
HI 1950-53

Palmer, M
HI 1998

Pardoe, S
HI 1991

Parfitt, RWM
Irl 1924

Park, D
WC 1997; HI 1994 to 97; ETC
1995-97

Parkin, AP
WC 1983; HI 1980-81-82

Parry, JR
HI 1966-75-76-77; Fra 1976

Peet, M
HI 1995-96

Peters, JL
HI 1987-88-89

Phillips, LA
Irl 1913

Pilkington, M
HI 1997-98; ETC 1997

Pinch, AG
HI 1969

Povall, J
Eur 1962; HI 1960 to 63; 65 to 77;
ETC 1967-69-71-73-75-77; Fra
1975; Fra, Den 1976

Pressdee, RNG
HI 1958 to 62

Price, David
ET 2002; HI 1999 to 2003; ETC
2003

Price, JP
HI 1986-87-88

Price, Rhodri
HI 1994-96-97

Pugh, RS
Irl 1923-24-29

Pughe, O
HI 1997-98

Rees, CN
HI 1986-88-89-91-92; 94 to 97

Rees, DA
HI 1961 to 64

Renwick, G jr
Irl 1923

Ricardo, W
Irl 1930; Irl, Sco 1931

Rice-Jones, L
Irl 1924

Richards, PM
HI 1960 to 63; 71

Roberts, H
HI 1992-93

Roberts, J
HI 1937

Roberts, S
HI 1998-99

Roberts, SB
HI 1932 to 35; 37-38; 47 to 54

Roberts, WJ
HI 1948 to 54

Roderick, RN
WC 1989; Eur 1988; HI 1983 to
88

Rolfe, B
HI 1963-65

Roobottom, EL
HI 1967

Roper, MS
Irl 1979

Scott, Richard
HI 2003

Sheppard, M
HI 1990

Smith, Alex
HI 1998-2000-02-03; ETC 2003

Smith, Craig
HI 2002-03; ETC 2003

Smith, M
HI 1993 to 97; ETC 1995-97

Smith, VH
Irl 1924-25

Squirrel, HC
HI 1955 to 71; 73-74-75; ETC
1967-69-71-75; Fra 1975

Stevens, DI
HI 1968-69-70; 74 to 78; 80-82;
ETC 1969-77; Fra 1976; Den
1977

Stoker, K
Irl 1923-24

Stokoe, GC
Eng 1925; Irl 1929-30

Sullivan, Kyron
HI 1998 to 2001; ETC 2001

Symonds, A
Irl 1925

Taylor, TPD
HI 1963

Taylor, Y
HI 1995-96-97; ETC 1995-97

Thomas, KR
HI 1951-52

Tooth, EA
Irl 1913

Toye, JL
HI 1963 to 67; 69 to 74; 76-78;
ETC 1971-73-75-77; Fra 1975

Tucker, WI
HI 1949 to 72; 74-75; ETC 1967-
69-75; Fra 1975

Turnbull, CH
Irl 1913-25

Turner, GB
HI 1947 to 52; 55-56

Wallis, G
HI 1934-36-37-38

Walters, EM
HI 1967-68-69; ETC 1969

Wilkie, GT
HI 1938

Wilkinson, S
HI 1990-91

Willcox, FS
Sco, Irl 1931

Williams, Craig
Asia Pacific 2000; HI 1998 to
2001; ETC 1999-2001

Williams, James
HI 2001-02-03

Williams, KH
HI 1983 to 87

Williams, PG
Irl 1925

Wills, M
HI 1990

Winfield, HB
Irl 1913

Wood, DK
HI 1982 to 87

Woosnam, Ian
Fra 1976

Wright, Garwth
HI 2002-03; ETC 2003

British Isles International Players, Amateur Women

Key

Entries for the Curtis Cup, Commonwealth Tournament, World Amateur Team Championship and Vagliano Trophy, indicate that the player is representing Great Britain and Ireland. Other entries are for the home country.

CC	Curtis Cup
CT	Commonwealth Tournament
ES	World Amateur Team Championship (Espirito Santo)
VT	Vagliano Trophy
ELTC	played in European Ladies Team Championship for home country
HI	played in Home International matches
*	indicates winning team

'to' indicates inclusive dates: e.g.'1908 to 1911' means '1908-09-10-11'; otherwise individual years are shown.

Captaincy is indicated by the year printed in bold type; non-playing captaincy in brackets

[1998] indicates Espirito Santo Team selection which was subsequently advised not to travel to Chile

Maiden names are shown in brackets; other surnames and titles in square brackets

ENGLAND

Allen, F
HI 1952

Andrew, Kim (Rostron)
CC 1998-2000; HI 1996-97-99-2001; ELTC 1997-2001; (GBI) VT 1997-99-2001; ES [1998]; CT 1999

Archer, A (Rampton)
HI (1968)

Bailey [Frearson](Robb)
CC 1962-72-(84)-(86)*-(88)*; VT 1961-(83)-(85); CT 1983; HI 1961-62-71; ELTC 1968-(93)

Barber (Bonallack)
CC 1962; ES (1996); VT 1961-63-69; CT (1995); HI 1960-61-62-68-70-72-77-(78); ELTC 1969-71

Bargh Etherington, B (Whitehead)
HI 1974

Barry, L
HI 1911 to 14

Barry, P
HI 1982

Barton, Pam
CC 1934-36; HI 1935 to 39

Bastin, G
HI 1920 to 25

Bayman, Linda (Denison Pender)
CC 1988; ES 1988; VT 1971-85-87; HI 1971-72-73-83-84-85-87-88-(95)-(96); ELTC 1985-87-89-(97)-(2001)

Beharrell, Veronica (Anstey)
CC 1956; HI 1955-56-57-(61)

Benka, Pam (Tredinnick)
CC 1966-68-(2002); CT (2003); VT 1967; HI 1967

Biggs, A (Whittaker)
VT 1959

Bisgood, Jeanne
CC 1950-52-54-(70); HI 1949 to 54; 56-58

Blaymire, J
HI 1971-88-(89)

Boatman, Elizabeth A (Collis)
CC (1992)*-(94); CT (1987)-(91); HI 1974-80-(84)-(85)-(90)-(91); ELTC (1985)-(87)

Bolas, R
HI 1992

Bolton, Zara (Bonner Davis)
CC 1948-(56)-(66)-(68); CT 1967; HI 1939; 48 to 51; (55)-(56)

Bonallack, Angela (Ward) [Lady Bonallack]
CC 1956-58-60-62-64-66; VT 1959-61-63; HI 1956 to 66; 72

Bostock, M
HI (1954)

Bourn, Mrs
HI 1909-12

Brown, Fiona
CC 1998-2000; VT 1999-2001; CT 1999; HI 1994; 96 to 2001; ELTC 1997-99-2001

Brown, J
HI 1984

Burnell, S
HI 1993; ELTC 1993

Burton, M
ELTC 1997

Cairns, Lady Katherine
CC (1952)*; HI 1947-48; 50 to 54

Caldwell, Carole (Redford)
CC 1978-80; VT 1973; HI 1973-78-79-80

Cann, M (Nuttall)
HI 1966

Carrick, P (Bullard)
HI 1939-47

Cautley, B (Hawtrey)
HI 1912-13-14; 22 to 25; 27

Chambers, Doris
(1934)-(36)-(38); 1906-07; 09 to 12; 20-24-25

Christison, D
HI 1981

Clark, G (Atkinson)
HI 1955

Clarke, Mrs ML
HI 1933-35

Clarke, Nickie
HI (2002)

Clarke, P
HI 1981

Clement, V
HI 1932-34-35

Close, M (Wenyon)
VT 1969; HI 1968-69; ELTC 1969

Collett, P
HI 1910

Collingham, J (Melville)
VT 1979-87; CT 1987; HI 1978-79-81-84-86-87-92; ELTC 1989

Comboy, Carol (Grott)
CC (1978)-(80); ES (1978); VT (1977)-(79); CT (1979); HI (1975)-(76)

Corlett, Elsie
CC 1932-38-(64); HI 1927; 29 to 33; 35 to 39

Cotton, S (German)
VT 1967; HI 1967-68; ELTC 1967

Court, C
HI 2000

Critchley, Diana (Fishwick)
CC 1932-34-(50); HI 1930 to 33; 35-36-(47)

Croft, A
HI 1927

Crummack, Miss
HI 1909

Davies, Laura
CC 1984; HI 1983-84

Dobson, Helen
CC 1990; VT 1989; HI 1987-88-89; ELTC 1989

Dod, L
HI 1905

Douglas, K
CC 1982; VT 1983; HI 1981-82-83

Dowling, D
HI 1979

Duggleby, Emma
CC 2000-02; ES 2002; VT 1995-2001-03; HI 1994-95-96-99 to 2003; ELTC 1995-99-2001-03

Durrant, B [Green] (Lowe)
HI 1954

Edmond, F (Macdonald)
VT 1991; HI 1991; ELTC 1991

Educate, Lisa (Walton)
CC 1994-96; VT 1993-95; CT 1995; HI 1991-94-95; ELTC 1993-95

Egford, K
HI 1992-94

Evans, H
HI 1908

Everard, Mary
CC 1970-72-74-78; ES 1968-72-78; VT 1967-69-71-73; CT 1971; HI 1964-67-69-70-72-73-77-78; ELTC 1967-71-77

Fairclough, L
VT 1989; HI 1988-89-90; ELTC 1989

Ferguson, R (Ogden)
HI 1957

Fields, E
HI 1995-96

Fisher, Kirsty
VT 2001; HI 1998 to 2002; ELTC 1999-2001

Fletcher, Linzi
CC 1990; CT 1991; HI 1989-90; ELTC 1991

Foster, C
HI 1905-06-09

Fowler, J
HI 1928

Furby, J
HI 1987-88; ELTC 1987

Fyshe, M
HI 1938

Garbutt, Sara
HI 2002-03

Garon, Marjorie Ross
CC 1936; HI 1927-28-32-33-34-36-37-38

Garrett, Maureen (Ruttle)
CC 1948-(60); VT 1959; HI 1947-48-50-53-(59)-(60)-(63)

Gee, Hon. J (Hives)
HI 1950-51-52

Gibb, M (Titterton)
HI 1906-07-08-10-12

Gibbs, Carol (Le Feuvre)
CC 1974; VT 1973; HI 1971 to 74

Gold, N
HI 1929-31-32

Gordon, Jacqueline
CC 1948; HI 1947-48-49-52-53

Gourlay, Molly
CC 1932-34; HI 1923-24; 27 to 30; 32-33-34-38-(57)

Green, B (Pockett)
HI 1939

Grice-Whitaker, Penny (Grice)
CC 1984; ES 1984; HI 1983-84

Griffiths, M
HI 1920-21

Guadella, E (Leitch)
HI 1908-10-20-21-22; 27 to 30; 33

Hackney, L
HI 1990

Hall, Caroline
CC 1992; VT 1991; HI 1991-92; ELTC 1991

Hall, CM
HI 1985

Hambro, W (Martin Smith)
HI 1914

Hamilton, J
HI 1937-38-39

Hammond, T
HI 1985

Hampson, M
HI 1954

Harris, Marley [Spearman] (Baker)
CC 1960-62-64; ES 1964; VT 1959-61-65; HI 1955 to 65; ELTC 1965-71

Harrold, L
HI 1974-75-76

Hartill, D
HI 1923

Hartley, E
HI (1964)

Hayter, J (Yuille)
HI 1956

Heath, Sarah (Gleeson)
HI 2001-02; ELTC 2001

Heathcoat-Amory, Lady (Joyce Wethered)
CC 1932; HI 1921 to 25; 29

Hedges, S (Whitlock)
VT 1979; CT 1979; HI 1979

Helme, E
HI 1911-12-13-20

Heming Johnson, G
HI 1909-11-13

Henson, Dinah (Oxley)
CC 1968-70-72-76; ES 1970; VT 1967-69-71; CT 1967-71; HI 1967 to 70; 75 to 78; ELTC 1971-77

Hetherington, Mrs (Gittens)
HI 1909

Hill, J
HI 1986

Hockley, J
ES 1992; VT 1993; HI 1991-92-93-96

Hodge, Susan (Shapcott)
CC 1988; ES 1988; VT 1987; CT 1987; HI 1986-88; ELTC 1987

Hodgson, M
HI 1939

Holmes, A
HI 1931

Holmes [Hetherington] (McClure)
HI 1956-66-(67)

Hooman, EM (Gavin)
HI 1910-11

Howard, Ann (Phillips)
CC 1956-58; HI 1953 to 58; (79)-(80)

Hudson, Rebecca
CC 1998-2000-02; ES [1998]-2000; VT 1997-2001; CT 1999; HI 1996-2001-02; ELTC 1997-99-2001

Huke, Beverley
CC 1972; VT 1975; HI 1971-72-75-76-77

Hunter, D (Tucker)
HI 1905

Irvin, Ann
CC 1962-68-70-76; ES (1982); VT 1961 to 75; CT 1967-75; HI 1962-63-65; 67 to 73; 75; ELTC 1965-67-69-71

Jackson, Bridget
CC 1958-64-68; ES 1964; VT 1959-63-65-67-**(73)-(75)**; CT 1959-67; HI 1955 to 59; 63 to 66; **(73)-(74)**

Johns, A
HI 1987-88-89

Johnson, M
HI 1934-35

Johnson, Patricia M
CC 1986; ES 1986; VT 1985; HI 1984-85-86; ELTC 1985

Kaye, H (Williamson)
HI **(1986)-(87)**

Keighley, Alex
HI 2002-03; ELTC 2003

Keiller, G (Style)
HI 1948-49-52

Kennedy, D (Fowler)
HI 1923-24-25-27-28-29

Kennion, Mrs (Kenyon Stow)
HI 1910

Kyle, B [Rhodes] (Norris)
HI 1937-38-39-48-49

Lamb, J
HI 1998-99

Lambert, S (Cohen)
VT 1979-95; HI 1979-80-93-94-95; ELTC 1995

Langridge, Susan (Armitage)
CC 1964-66; VT 1963-65; HI 1963 to 66; ELTC 1965

Large, P (Davies)
HI 1951-52-**(81)-(82)**

Latham Hall, E (Chubb)
HI 1928

Lee Smith, Jenny
CC 1974-76; ES 1976; CT 1975; HI 1973 to 76

Leitch, C
HI 1910 to 14; 20-21-22-24-25-27-28

Lipscombe, Clare
HI 1999

Lobbett, P
HI 1922-24-27-29-30

Luckin, B (Cooper)
HI 1980

Lumb, Kathryn (Phillips)
CC 1972; VT 1969-71; HI 1968 to 71; ELTC 1969

Lyons, T (Ross Steen)
VT 1959; HI 1959

Macbeth, M (Dodd)
HI 1913-14; 20 to 25

Macdonald, F
HI 1990

McIntosh, B (Dixon)
VT 1969; HI 1969-70; ELTC 1969

McIntyre, J
HI 1949-54

McKevitt, Shelley
CT 2003

McNair, W
HI 1921

Maher, Sheila (Vaughan)
CC 1962-64; VT 1961; CT 1963; HI 1960 to 64

Marvin, Vanessa
CC 1978; VT 1977; HI 1977-78; ELTC 1977

Masters, Danielle
VT 2003; HI 2003; ELTC 2003

Merrill, Julia (Greenhalgh)
CC 1964-70-74-76-78; ES 1970-74-78; VT 1961-65-75-77; CT 1963; HI 1960-61-63-66-69-70-71; 75 to 78; ELTC 1971-77

Moorcroft, S
HI 1985-86; ELTC 1985-87

Morant, E
HI 1906-10

More, Fame
CC 2002; VT 2001-03; HI 2000-01-02-03; ELTC 2001-03

Morgan, S
HI 1989; ELTC 1989

Morgan, Wanda
CC 1932-34-36; HI 1931 to 37

Morley, Joanne
CC 1992; ES 1992; VT 1991-93; HI 1990 to 93; ELTC 1991-93

Morris, L (Moore)
HI 1912-13

Morrison, G (Cheetham)
VT 1965; HI 1965-**(69)**

Morrison, G (Cradock-Hartopp)
HI 1936

Murray, Nicola (Buxton)
CC 1992; VT 1991-93; HI 1991-92-93; ELTC 1991-93

Murray, S (Jolly)
HI 1976

Nes, K (Garnham)
HI 1931-32-33; 36 to 39

Neville, E
HI 1905-06-08-10

New, Beverley
CC 1984; VT 1983; HI 1980 to 83

Newell, B
HI 1936

Newton, B (Brown)
HI 1930; 33 to 37

Oliver, J
HI 1995

Parker, S
HI 1973

Pearson, D
HI 1928 to 32; 34

Phillips, ME
HI 1905

Pickard, Margaret (Nichol)
CC 1968-70; VT 1959-61-67; HI 1958 to 61; 67-69; **(83)**

Pook, Elizabeth (Chadwick)
CC 1966; VT 1963-67; CT 1967; HI 1963-65-66-67

Porter, M (Lazenby)
HI 1931-32

Price, M (Greaves)
HI **(1956)**

Price Fisher, Elizabeth (Price)
CC 1950-52-54-56-58-60; VT 1959; CT 1959; HI 1948; 51 to 60

Prout, Rebecca
HI 2000

Rabbidge, R
HI 1931

Ratcliffe, Elaine
CC 1998; ES 1996; VT 1997; HI 1995-96-97; ELTC 1995-97

Read, P
HI 1922

Reece, P (Millington)
HI 1966

Remer, H
HI 1909

Richardson, Mrs
HI 1907-09

Robinson, S
HI 1989

Roskrow, M
HI 1948-50

Rudgard, G
HI 1931-32-50-51-52

Sabine, Diana (Plumpton)
CC 1934; HI 1934-35

Saunders, Vivien
CC 1968; VT 1967; CT 1967; HI 1967-68; ELTC 1967

Sheppard, E (Pears)
HI 1947

Simpson, Linda (Moore)
CC 1980; HI 1979-80

Slark, Ruth (Porter)
CC 1960-62-64; ES 1964-66; VT 1959-61-65; CT 1963; HI 1959 to 62; 64-65-66-68-78; ELTC 1965

Smillie, P
HI 1985-86

Smith, Anne [Stant] (Willard)
CC 1976; VT 1975; CT **1959-63**; HI 1974-75-76

Smith, E
HI 1991

Smith, Frances (Stephens)
CC 1950-52-54-56-58-60; **(62)-(72)**; VT 1959-71; CT 1959-63; HI 1947 to 55; 59; **(62)-(71)-(72)**

Smith, Kerry
CC 2002; VT 2001; HI 1997 to 2003; ELTC 1999-2003

Soulsby, Janet
CC 1982

Speak, Kirsty
CC 1994; ES 1994; VT 1993; HI 1993-94; ELTC 1993

Steel, E
HI 1905 to 08; 11

Stocker, J
HI 1922-23

Stupples, Karen
CC 1996-98; VT 1997; HI 1995 to 98; ELTC 1995-97

Sugden, J (Machin)
HI 1953-54-55

Sumpter, Mrs
HI 1907-08-12-14-24

Sutherland Pilch, R (Barton)
HI 1947-49-50-(58)

Swallow, C
HI 1985; ELTC 1985

Tamworth, Mrs
HI 1908

Tebbet, K
HI 1990-94

Temple, S
HI 1913-14

Temple Dobell, G (Ravenscroft)
HI 1911 to 14; 20-21-25-30

Thompson, M (Wallis)
HI 1948-49

Thornhill, J (Woodside)
CC 1984-86-88; VT 1965-83-85-87-(89); CT 1983-87; HI 1965-74; 82 to 88; ELTC 1965-85-87

Thomlinson, J [Evans] (Roberts)
CC 1962; VT 1963; HI 1962-64

Timmins, Nicola
HI 2003; ELTC 2003

Turner, B
HI 1908

Uzielli, Angela (Carrick)
CC 1978; VT 1977; HI 1976-77-78-90; (92)-(93); ELTC 1977

Wade, Julie
CC 1988-90-92-94-96; ES 1988-90-94; VT 1989-91-93-95; CT 1991-95; HI 1987 to 95; ELTC 1987 to 95

Waite, Claire
CC 1984; ES 1984; VT 1983; CT 1983; HI 1981 to 84; ELTC 1985

Walker, B (Thompson)
HI 1905 to 09; 11

Walker, Mickey
CC 1972-74; VT 1971; CT 1971; HI 1970-72; ELTC 1971

Walker, Sophie
HI 2003

Walker-Leigh, F
HI 1907-08-09; 11 to 14

Walter, J
HI 1974-79-80-82-86

Walters, L
HI 1998

Watson, C (Nelson)
HI 1982

Westall, S (Maudsley)
HI 1973

Williamson, C (Barker)
HI 1979-80-81

Willock-Pollen, G
HI 1907

Wilson, Enid
CC 1932; HI 1928-29-30

Winn, J
HI 1920-21-23-25

Wragg, M
HI 1929

Wylie, Phyllis (Wade)
CC 1938; HI 1934 to 38; 47

IRELAND

Alexander, M
HI 1920-21-22-30

Arbuthnot, M
HI 1921

Armstrong, M
HI 1906

Barlow, Mrs
HI 1921

Beck, Baba (Pim)
HI 1930 to 34; 36-37; 47 to 56; 58-59-61

Beckett, J
HI 1962-66-67-68

Behan, L
CC 1986; VT 1985; HI 1984-85-86-96-98

Birmingham, M
HI (1967)

Blake, Miss
HI 1931 to 36

Boyd, J
HI 1912-13-14

Bradshaw, E
VT 1969-71; HI 1964; 66 to 71; 74-75-(80)-(81); ELTC 1969-71-75

Brandom, G
VT 1967; HI 1965 to 68; ELTC 1967

Brennan, R (Hegarty)
HI 1974 to 79; 81

Brice, Mrs
HI 1948

Brinton, Mrs
HI 1922

Brooks, E
HI 1953-54-56

Brown, B
HI 1960

Brownlow, Miss
HI 1923

Butler, I (Burke)
CC 1966-(96)*; ES 1964-66; VT 1965; 1962 to 66; 68; 70 to 73; 76 to 79; (86)-(87); ELTC 1967

Byrne, A (Sweeney)
HI 1959 to 63; (90)-(91)

Callen, L
HI 1990

Casement, M (Harrison)
HI 1909 to 14

Cassidy, Yvonne
HI 1994-95-2000-01

Clarke, Mrs
HI 1922

Coffey, Alison
CC 2002; ES 2000; VT 1999-2001; HI 1995 to 2002; ELTC 1997-99-2001

Colquhoun, H
HI 1959-60-61-63

Coote, Miss
HI 1925-28-29

Costello, G
HI 1973-(84)-(85)

Coughlan, Claire
HI 1999-2000-01-03; ELTC 1999-2001-03

Cramsie, F (Hezlet)
HI 1905 to 10; 13-20-24

Cuming, Mrs
HI 1910

Cuthell, R (Adair)
HI 1908

Delaney, Tara
HI 2003

Dering, Mrs
HI 1923

Dickson, E
HI 1999-2000; ELTC 1999

Dickson, M
HI 1909

Dowdall, Elaine
HI 1997 to 2001

Dowling, Claire (Hourihane)
CC 1984-86-88-90-92-(2000); ES 1986-90-[98]; VT 1981-83-85-87-89-91-(99); HI 1979 to 92; ELTC 1981-83-85-87-89-(97)

Dunne, Marie
HI 2003; ELTC 2003

Durlacher, Mrs
HI 1905 to 10; 14

Dwyer, Mrs
HI 1928

Eakin, P (James)
HI 1967

Eakin, T
HI 1990 to 94; ELTC 1993

Earner, M
HI 1960 to 63; 70

Ellis, E
HI 1932-35-37-38

Ferguson, A
HI 1989

Ferguson, Daisy
CC (1958); HI 1927 to 32; 34 to 38; (61)

Fitzgibbon, M
HI 1920-21; 29 to 33

Fitzpatrick, O (Heskin)
HI 1967

Fletcher, P (Sherlock)
HI 1932-34-35-36-38-39-54-55-(66)

Gardiner, A
HI 1927-29

Garvey, Philomena
CC 1948-50-52-54-56-60; VT 1959-63; HI 1947 to 53; 54-56-57-58-59-60-61-62-63-68-69

Gaynor, Z (Fallon)
ES 1964; HI 1952 to 65; 68-69-70; (72)

Gildea, Miss
HI 1936 to 39

Gillen, Martina
HI 1999-2001-02; ELTC 2001-03

Glendinning, D
HI 1937-54

Gorman, S
HI 1976; 79 to 82; (92)-(93); ELTC (1993)

Gorry, Mary
VT 1977; HI 1971 to 80; 88-(89); ELTC 1971-75

Gotto, Mrs C
HI 1923

Gotto, Mrs L
HI 1920

Graham, N
HI 1908-09-10-12

Gubbins, Miss
HI 1905

Hackett, B
HI 1993-94-96

Hall, Mrs
HI 1927-30

Hanna, D
HI 1987-88

Harrington, D
HI 1923

Hazlett, VP
HI (1956)

Healy, B
HI 1980-82

Hegarty, G
HI 1955-56-(64)

Heskin, A
HI 1968-69-70-72-75-77-(82)-(83)

Hewett, G
HI 1923-24

Hezlet, Mrs
HI 1910

Hickey, C
HI 1969-(75)-(76)

Higgins, E
HI 1981 to 88; 91 to 96; ELTC 1987-93-(2001)

Holland, I (Hurst)
HI 1958

Hulton, V (Hezlet)
HI 1905-07; 09 to 12; 20-21

Humphreys, D (Forster)
HI 1951-52-53-55-57

Hyland, B
HI 1964-65-66;

Jackson, B
HI 1937-38-39-50

Jackson, Mrs H
HI 1921

Jackson, J
HI 1912-13-14; 20 to 25; 27 to 30

Jackson, Mrs L
HI 1910-12-14-20-22-25

Jameson, S (Tobin)
HI 1913-14-20-24-25-27

Jones, Helen
HI 2003; ELTC 2003

Kavanagh, H
VT 1995; HI 1993-94-95-97-98-2001; ELTC 1997-2001

Keane, Sinead
HI 2000-02-03; ELTC 2001

Keenan, D
HI 1989

Kidd, Mrs
HI 1934-37

King, Mrs
HI 1923-25-27-29

Kirkwood, Mrs
HI 1955

Larkin, C (McAuley)
HI 1966 to 72; ELTC 1971

Latchford, B
HI 1931-33

Lauder, G
HI 1911

Lauder, R
HI 1911

Lowry, Mrs
HI 1947

MacCann, K
HI 1984-85-86

MacCann, K (Smye)
HI 1947 to 54; 56-57-58-60-61-62-64-(65)

McCarthy, A
HI 1951-52

McCarthy, D
HI 1988-90-91-95; ELTC 1993

McCool, L
HI 1993

McDaid, E (O'Grady)
HI 1959

MacGeach, C
HI 1938-39-48-49-50

McGowan, Darragh
HI 2002

McGreevy, V
HI 1987-90-92

McKenna, Mary
CC 1970 to 86; ES 1970-74-76-(86)-(90); VT 1969 to 81; 85-87; (95); HI 1968 to 91; 93; (2002); ELTC 1969-71-75-87

McNeile, CL
HI 1906

McQuillan, Y
HI 1985-86

Madeley, M (Coburn)
HI 1964-69; ELTC 1969

Madill, Maureen
CC 1980; ES 1980; VT 1979-81-85; CT 1979; HI 1978 to 85

Madill, Mrs
HI 1920-24-25-27-28-29-33

Magill, J
HI 1907-11-13

Mahon, D
HI 1989-90

Mallam, Mrs S
HI 1922-23

Mangan, Tricia
VT 2003; HI 1998-2000-02-03; ELTC 2003

Marks, Mrs T
HI 1950

Marks, Mrs
HI 1930-31-33-35

Menton, D
HI 1949

Millar, D
HI 1928

Milligan, J (Mark)
HI 1971-72-73

Mitchell, J
HI 1930

Mooney, M
VT 1973; HI 1972-73; ELTC 1971

Moore, S
HI 1937-38-39-47-48-49-(68)

Moran, V (Singleton)
HI 1970-71-73-74-75; ELTC 1971-75

Moriarty, M (Irvine)
HI 1979

Morrin, Maura
HI 2003; ELTC 2003

Morris, Mrs de B
HI 1933

Murray, Rachel
HI 1952

Nolan, Heather
HI 2002-03

Nutting, P (Jameson)
HI 1927-28

O'Brien, A
HI 1969

O'Brien, Suzanne (Fanagan)
CC 2000; ES 2000; VT 1999; HI 1995 to 2000; ELTC 1997-99

O'Brien Kenney, S
HI 1977-78; 83 to 86

O'Donnell, Maire
CC (1982); VT (1981); HI 1974-77-(78)-(79); ELTC (1980)

O'Donohue, A
HI 1948 to 51; 53; (73)-(74)

O'Hare, S
HI 1921-22

O'Reilly, T (Moran)
HI 1977-78-86-88; (95); ELTC 1987

O'Sullivan, A
HI 1982-83-84-92-94-95-96; ELTC 1993-97

O'Sullivan, P
HI 1950 to 60; 63 to 67; (69)-(70)-(71); ELTC (1971)

Ormsby, Miss
HI 1909-10-11

Orr, P (Boyd)
HI 1971

Pim, Mrs
HI 1908

Power, Eileen Rose (McDaid)
CC 1994; VT 1995-97; HI 1987 to 97; 2001-02; ELTC 1987-93-97-99

Purcell, E
HI 1965-66-67-72-73

Purfield, O
HI 1998-99

Reddan, Clarrie (Tiernan)
CC 1938-48; HI 1935-36-38-39-47-48-49

Reddan, MV
HI 1955

Rice, J
HI 1924-27-29

Riordan, Marian
HI 2002

Roberts, E (Pentony)
HI 1932 to 36; 39

Roberts, E (Barnett)
HI 1961 to 65; ELTC 1964

Robinson, C (Nesbitt)
CC 1980; VT 1979; HI 1974 to 81

Robinson, R (Bayly)
HI 1947-56-57

Roche, Mrs
HI 1922

Rogers, A
HI 1992-93; ELTC 1993

Ross, M (Hezlet)
HI 1905 to 08; 11-12

Slade, Lady
HI 1906

Smith, Deirdre
HI 1999; ELTC 2001

Smith, Mrs L
HI 1913-14-21-22-23-25

Smythe, M
HI 1947 to 56; 58-59; (62)

Starrett, L (Malone)
HI 1975 to 78; 80

Stuart, M
HI 1905-07-08

Stuart-French, Miss
HI 1922

Sweeney, L
HI 1991

Taylor, I
HI 1930

Thornhill, Miss
HI 1924-25

Thornton, Mrs
HI 1924

Todd, Mrs
HI 1931 to 36

Tynte, V
HI 1905-06-08-09; 11 to 14

Walker, Pat
CC 1934-36-38; HI 1928 to 39; 48

Walsh, R
HI 1987

Webb, L (Bolton)
HI 1981-82-88-89-91-92-94

Wickham, C
HI 1983-89

Wickham, P
HI 1976-83-87; ELTC 1987

Wilson, Mrs
HI 1931

SCOTLAND

Agnew, C
HI 1995

Aitken, E (Young)
HI 1954

Anderson, E
HI 1910-11-12-21-25

Anderson, F
VT 1987; HI 1977-79-80-81-83-84-87 to 92; ELTC 1979-83-87-91

Anderson, H
VT 1969; HI 1964-65-68-69-70-71; ELTC 1969

Anderson, Jean (Donald)
CC 1948-50-52; HI 1947 to 52

Anderson, L
HI 1986 to 89; ELTC 1987-89

Anderson, VH
HI 1907

Bald, J
HI 1968-69-71; ELTC 1969

Barclay, C (Brisbane)
HI 1953-61-68

Baynes, Mrs CE
HI 1921-22

Beddows, C [Watson] (Stevenson)
CC 1932; HI 1913-14-21-22-23-27; 29 to 37; 39; 47 to 51

Bennett, Lorna
HI 1977-80-81

Benton, MH
HI 1914

Blair, N (Menzies)
HI 1955

Bowhill, M (Robertson-Durham)
HI 1936-37-38

Broun, JG
HI 1905-06-07-21

Brown, Mrs FW (Gilroy)
HI 1905 to 11; 13-21

Brown, TWL
HI 1924-25

Burns, K
HI 1999

Burton, H (Mitchell)
VT 1961; HI 1931-55-56-(59)

Cadden, G
VT (1997); HI 1974-75-(95)-(96); ELTC (1997)

Campbell, J (Burnett)
HI 1960

Coats, Mrs G
HI 1931 to 34

Cochrane, K
HI 1924-25-28-29-30

Connachan, J
CC 1980-82; ES 1980-82; VT 1981-83; CT 1983; HI 1979 to 83

Copley, K (Lackie)
HI 1974-75

Couper, M
HI 1929; 34 to 37; 39-56

Craik, T
HI 1988

Crawford, I (Wylie)
HI 1970-71-72

Cresswell, K (Stuart)
HI 1909 to 12; 14

Cruickshank, DM (Jenkins)
HI 1910-11-12

Davidson, Alison (Rose)
CC 1996-98; VT 1995-97; CT 1995; HI 1990 to 98; 2000; ELTC 1991-93-95-97-99

Davidson, B (Inglis)
HI 1928

Draper, Marjorie [Peel] (Thomas)
CC 1954; VT **(1963)**; HI 1929-34-38; 49 to 53; **(54)-(55)**; 56-57-58; **(61)**; 62

Duncan, MJ (Wood)
HI 1925-27-28-39

Falconer, V (Lamb)
HI 1932-36-37; 47 to 56

Farie-Anderson, J
HI 1924

Farquharson-Black, Elaine (Farquharson)
CC 1990-92; VT 1989-91; CT 1991; HI 1987 to 91; 97-98; **(2002)**; ELTC 1989-91

Feggans, Pamela
HI 2002-03

Ferguson, Marjory (Fowler)
CC 1966; VT 1965; HI 1959; 62 to 67; 69-70-85; ELTC 1965-67-71

Forbes, J
HI 1985 to 89; ELTC 1987-89

Ford, J
HI 1993-94-95

Gallagher, S
HI 1983-84

Gemmill, A
HI 1981-82; 84 to 89; 91-**(97)**

Glennie, H
HI 1959

Glover, A
HI 1905-06-08-09-12

Gow, J
HI 1923-24-27-28

Graham, MA
HI 1905-06

Granger Harrison, Mrs
HI 1922

Grant-Suttie, E
HI 1908-10-11-14-22-23

Grant-Suttie, R
HI 1914

Greenlees, E
HI 1924

Greenlees, Y
HI 1928-30-31-33-34-35-38

Hamilton, S (McKinven)
HI 1965

Hargan, Claire
ELTC 2001-03; HI 1999-2000-01

Hastings, Dorothea (Sommerville)
CC 1958; VT 1963; HI 1955 to 63

Hay, J (Pelham Burn)
HI 1959

Holm, Helen (Gray)
CC 1936-38-48; HI 1932 to 38; 47-48-50-51-55-57

Hope, LA
HI 1975-76-80; 84 to 87; **(88)-(89)-(90)**

Huggan, Shirley (Lawson)
CC 1988; VT 1989; HI 1985 to 89; ELTC 1985-87-89

Hurd [Howe] (Campbell)
HI 1905-06-08-09-11-28-30

Jack, E (Philip)
HI 1962-63-64-**(81)-(82)**

Jackson, D
HI 1990

Kelway Bamber, Mrs
HI 1923-27-33

Kenny, Louise
HI 2003

Kenny, Lynn
VT 2003; **CT 2003**; ELTC 2003; HI 2000-01-03

Kerr, J
HI 1947-48-49-54

Kinloch, Miss
HI 1913-14

Knight, Mrs
HI 1922

Kyle, E
HI 1909-10

Laing, A
VT 1967; HI 1966-67-70-71-**(73)-(74)**

Laing, Anne
VT 1999-2003; CT 1999-**2003**; HI 1995 to 99; 2001-02-03; ELTC 1997-99-2001-03

Laing, Susannah
HI 2002

Laing, Vicki
CC 2002; VT 2003; HI 1997-98; ELTC 2001-03

Lambie, S
HI 1976

Lawrence, Joan B
CC 1964; ES 1964; VT 1963-65; CT 1971; HI 1959 to 70; **(77)**; ELTC 1965-67-69-71

Leburn, Wilma (Aitken)
CC 1982; VT 1981-83; HI 1978 to 83; 85

Leete, Mrs IG
HI 1933

Little, S
HI 1993

Lugton, C
HI 1968-72-73-**75-76**-77-78-80

MacAndrew, F
HI 1913-14

McCulloch, J
HI 1921 to 24; 27; 29 to 33; 35; **(60)**

Macdonald, K
HI 1928-29

MacIntosh, I
HI **(1991)-(92)-(93)**; ELTC **(1993)**

McKay, F
HI 1992-93-94; ELTC 1993

Mackay, Lesley
HI 1999 to 2003; ELTC 2001-03

McKay, Mhairi
CC 1994-96; ES 1996; VT 1993-95-97; CT 1995; HI 1991-93-94-96; ELTC 1993-95

Mackenzie, A
HI 1921

McKinlay, Myra
CC 1994; HI 1990-92-93; ELTC 1993

McLarty, E
HI **(1966)-(67)-(68)**

McMahon, Suzanne (Cadden)
CC 1976; VT 1975; HI 1974 to 77; 79

McMaster, S
HI 1994 to 97; ELTC 1995-97

McNeil, K
HI **(1969)-(70)**

MacRae, Heather
HI 2003

Main, M (Farquhar)
HI 1950-51

Maitland, M
HI 1905-06-08-12-13

Marr, H (Cameron)
HI 1927 to 31

Marshall, Kathryn (Imrie)
CC 1990; VT 1989; HI 1984-85-89; ELTC 1987-89

Mather, H
HI 1905-09-12-13-14

Matthew, Catriona (Lambert)
CC 1990-92-94; ES 1992; VT 1989-91-93; CT 1991; HI 1989 to 93; ELTC 1989-91-93

Mellis, Mrs
HI 1924-27

Melvin, V
HI 1994-96

Menzies, M
HI **(1962)**

Milton, Moira (Paterson)
CC 1952; HI 1948 to 52

Moffat, L
VT 1999; HI 1996-98-2001

Monaghan, Hilary
CC 1998; VT 1999; HI 1995 to 98; 2000; ELTC 1997-99

Moodie, Janice
CC 1994-96; ES 1996; VT 1993-95-97; CT 1995; HI 1990-91-92; ELTC 1991-93-95-97

Morton, Linzi
HI 2000-01-02; ELTC 2001

Myles, M
HI 1955-57-59-60-67

Neill-Fraser, M
HI 1905 to 14

Nicholson, J (Hutton)
CT 1971; HI 1969-70; ELTC 1971

Nicholson, Lesley
CC 2000; VT 1999; HI 1994 to 99; ELTC 1995-97-99

Nicholson, Mrs WH
HI 1910-13

Nimmo, H
HI 1936-38-39

Norris, J (Smith)
VT 1977; HI 1966 to 72; 75 to 79; **(83)-(84)**; ELTC 1971

Norwell, I (Watt)
HI 1954

Panton-Lewis, C (Panton)
ES 1976; VT 1977; HI 1972-73-76-77-78

Park, Mrs
HI 1952

Patey, Mrs
HI 1922-23

Percy, G (Mitchell)
HI 1927-28-30-31

Porter, Doris (Park)
CC 1932; HI 1922-25-27; 29 to 35; 37-38; 47-48

Provis, I (Kyle)
HI 1910-11

Purvis-Russell-Montgomery, C
HI 1921-22-23-25; 28 to 39; 47 to 50; 52

Queen, Clare
VT 2003; ELTC 2003; HI 2002-03

Rawlinson, T (Walker)
VT 1973; HI 1970-71-73-76

Reid, A (Lurie)
VT 1961; HI 1960 to 64; 66

Reid, A (Kyle)
HI 1923-24-25

Reid, D
HI 1978-79

Rennie, J (Hastings)
CC 1966; VT 1961-67; 1961-65-66-67-71-72; ELTC 1967

Richmond, M (Walker)
CC 1974; VT 1975; HI 1972 to 75; 77-78

Rigby, F (Macbeth)
HI 1912-13

Ritchie, C (Park)
HI 1939-47-48-51-52-53-**(64)**

Roberts, M (Brown)
ES 1964; HI **(1965)**

Robertson, B (McCorkindale)
CC 1960-66-68-70-72-**(74)-(76)**-82-86; ES 1964-66-**(68)**-72-80-82; VT 1959-63-69-71-81-85; CT 1971-**(75)**; HI 1958 to 66; 69-72-73-78-80-81-82-84-85-86; ELTC 1965-**67**-69-**71**

Robertson, D
HI 1907

Robertson, E
HI 1924

Robertson, G
HI 1907-08-09

Roxburgh, L
HI 1993-94-95

Roy, S (Needham)
VT 1973-75; HI 1969; 71 to 76; 83

Rusack, J
HI 1908

Singleton, B (Henderson)
HI 1939; 52 to 58; 60 to 65

Smith, J
HI 1999; ELTC 1999

Speir, Marigold
HI 1957-64-68-**(71)-(72)**

Stavert, M
HI 1979

Steel, Mrs DC
HI 1925

Stewart, Gillian
CC 1980-82; VT 1979-81-83; CT 1979-83; HI 1979 to 84; ELTC **1982-4**

Stewart, L (Scraggie)
HI 1921-22-23

Stirling, Heather
CC 2002; HI 1999-2000-01-02

Summers, M (Mackie)
HI 1986

Teacher, F
HI 1908-09-11-12-13

Thompson, M
HI 1949

Thomson, D
HI 1982-83-85-87

Thomson, M
HI 1907

Thomson, Muriel
CC 1978; VT 1977; HI 1974 to 78; ELTC 1978

Valentine, Jessie (Anderson)
CC 1938-48-50-52-54-56-58; CT 1959; HI 1934 to 39; 47; 49 to 55; **56**; 57-58

Veitch, F
HI 1912

Wallace-Williamson, Verona
CC **1938**; HI 1932

Wardlaw, Nan (Baird)
CC 1938; HI 1932; 35 to 39; 47-48

Wells, Laura
HI 2003

Wilson, A
HI 1973-74-**(85)**

Wood, S
HI 1999-2000

Wooldridge, W (Shaw)
HI 1982

Wright, Janette (Robertson)
CC 1954-56-58-60; VT 1959-61-63; CT 1959; HI 1952 to 61; 63-65-67-73; **(78)-(79)-(80)-(86)**; ELTC 1965

Wright, M
HI 1990-91-92; ELTC 1991

Wright, P
VT 1981; HI 1981 to 84; ELTC 1987

WALES

Allington-Hughes, Miss
HI 1908-09-10-12-14-22-25

Archer, L
HI 1999

Ashcombe, Lady
HI 1950 to 54

Aubertin, Mrs
HI 1908-09-10

Baker, J
HI 1990

Barron, M
HI 1929-30-31; 34 to 39; 47 to 58; 60 to 63

Bayliss, Mrs
HI 1921

Bloodworth, D (Lewis)
HI 1954 to 57; 60

Boyes, S
HI 1992

Bradley, K (Rawlings)
HI 1975 to 79; 82-83

Brearley, M
HI 1937-38

Brewerton, R (Becky)
CC 2000; ES 2002; VT 2001-03; HI 1997 to 2003; ELTC 1999-2001-03

Bridges, Mrs
HI 1933-38-39

Briggs, A (Brown)
VT 1971-75; HI 1969 to 80; **81-82-83**; 84; **93**; ELTC 1971-75

Bromley-Davenport, I (Rieben)
HI 1932 to 36; 48; 50 to 56

Brook, D
HI 1913

Brown, E (Jones)
HI 1947 to 50; 52-53; 57 to 66; 68-69-70

Brown, J
HI 1960-61-62-64-65; ELTC 1965-69

Brown, Mrs
HI 1924-25-27

Bryan-Smith, S
HI 1947 to 52; 56

Burrell, Mrs
HI 1939

Caryl, M
HI 1929

Chugg, Pam (Light)
HI 1973 to 78; 86-87-88; 96; (2002); ELTC 1975-87-(2001)

Clarkson, H (Reynolds)
HI 1935-38-39

Clay, E
HI 1912

Cole, C
HI 1998

Cowley, Lady
HI 1907-09

Cox, Margaret
HI 1924-25

Cox, Nell
HI 1954

Cross, M
HI 1922

Cunninghame, S
HI 1922-25-29-31

Dampney, S
HI 1924-25; 27 to 30

David, Mrs
HI 1908

Davies, Karen
CC 1986-88; VT 1987; CT 1987; HI 1981-82-83; ELTC 1987

Davies, P (Griffiths)
HI 1965 to 68; 70-71-73; ELTC 1971

Davis, Louise
HI 1997-98-2000-01-02; ELTC 1997-99

Deacon, Mrs
HI 1912-14

Dermott, Lisa
CC 1996; HI 1987-88-89; 91 to 96; ELTC 1991-93

Donne, A
HI 1993-94; ELTC 1993

Duncan, B
HI 1907 to 10; 12

Duncan, M
HI 1922-23-28-34

Edwards, E
HI 1949-50

Edwards, J
HI 1932-33-34-36-37

Edwards, J (Morris)
HI 1962-63; 66 to 70; (77)-(78)-(79); ELTC 1967-69-(93)

Ellis Griffiths, Mrs
HI 1907-08-09-12-13

Emery, MJ
HI 1928 to 38; 47

Evans, Kathryn
HI 1999-2000-01-02

Evans, N
HI 1908-09-10-13

Evans, Natalee
HI 1996 to 99;2003; ELTC 1997-99

Evans, Stephanie
HI 2002-03; ELTC 2003

Franklin Thomas, E
HI 1909

Freeguard, C
HI 1927

Garfield Evans, PR (Whittaker)
HI 1948 to 54; (55)-(56)-(57)-(58)

Gear Evans, A
HI 1932-33-34

Gethin Griffith, S
HI 1914-22-23-24; 28 to 31; 35

Gibbs, S
HI 1933-34-39

Griffith, W
HI 1981

Haig, J (Mathias Thomas)
HI 1938-39

Hartley, R
HI 1958-59-62

Hedley Hill, Miss
HI 1922

Highgate, Anna
CT 2003; HI 1999-2001-02-03; ELTC 2001-03

Hill, Mrs
HI 1924

Hort, K
HI 1929

Hughes, J
HI 1967-71-88-(89); ELTC 1971

Hughes, Miss
HI 1907

Humphreys, A (Coulman)
HI 1969-70-71

Hurst, Mrs
HI 1921-22-23-25-27-28

Inghram, E (Lever)
HI 1947 to 58; 64-65

Irvine, Miss
HI 1930

Isaac, Mrs
HI 1924

Isherwood, L
HI 1972-76-77-78-80-86; 88 to 91

Jenkin, B
HI 1959

Jenkins, J (Owen)
HI 1953-56

John, J
HI 1974

Johnson, A (Hughes)
HI 1964; 66 to 76; 78-79-85; (95); ELTC 1965-67-69-71

Johnson, J (Roberts)
HI 1955

Johnson, R
HI 1955

Jones, A (Gwyther)
HI 1959

Jones, B
HI 1994-95-96-98; ELTC 1993

Jones, K
HI (1959)-(60)-(61)

Jones, M (De Lloyd)
HI 1951

Jones, Sarah
CC 2002; HI 2000-01-02-03; ELTC 2001-03

Jones, Mrs
HI 1932-35

Justice, M
HI 1931-32

Laming Evans, Mrs
HI 1922-23

Langford, Mrs
HI 1937

Lawson, H
HI 1989 to 92; 97-98; ELTC 1991-93-97

Leaver, B
HI 1912-14-21

Llewellyn, Miss
HI 1912-13-14-21-22-23

Lloyd, J
HI 1988

Lloyd, P
HI 1935-36

Lloyd Davies, VH
HI 1913

Lloyd Roberts, V
HI 1907-08-10

Lloyd Williams, Miss
HI 1909-10-12-14

Lovatt, S
HI 1994-95

MacKean, Mrs
HI 1938-39-47

MacTier, Mrs
HI 1927

Magee, A-M
HI 1991 to 94

Marley, MV
HI 1921-22-23-30-37

Martin, P [Whitworth Jones] (Low)
HI 1948-50-56-59-60-61

Mason, Mrs
HI 1923

Matthews, Tegwen [Thomas] (Perkins)
CC 1974-76-78-80; ES 1974; VT 1973-75-77-79; CT 1975-79; HI 1972 to 84

Mills, I
HI 1935-36-37-39-47-48

Morgan, R [Becky]
CC 1998-2000; ES [1998]; VT 1997-99; CT 1999; HI 1996 to 99; ELTC 2001

Morgan, Miss
HI 1912-13-14

Mountford, Sara
HI 1989 to 92; ELTC 1991-2001

Musgrove, Mrs
HI 1923-24

Newman, L
HI 1927-31

Nicholls, M
HI (1962)

Nicholson, Jo
HI 2003

Oliver, M (Jones)
ES 1964; HI 1955; 60 to 66

Orr, Mrs
HI 1924

Owen, E
HI 1947

Perriam, A
HI 1988-90-91-92

Phelips, M
HI 1913-14-21

Phillips, Kate
CT 2003; HI 1999 to 2003; ELTC 2001-03

Phillips, Mrs
HI 1921

Pilgrim, Eleanor
HI 1995-97-2000-01; ELTC 1997-99-2001

Powell, M
HI 1908-09-10-12

Pritchard, Jo
HI 2002-03; ELTC 2003

Proctor, Mrs
HI 1907

Pyman, B
HI 1921-22-23-25; 28 to 39; 47 to 50; 52

Rawlings, M
VT 1981; HI 1979-80-81; 83 to 87

Rees, G
HI 1981

Rees, MB
HI 1927-31

Rhys, J
HI 1979

Richards, D
HI 1994-95-96

Richards, J
HI 1980-82-83-85

Richards, S
HI 1967

Rieben, Mrs
HI 1927 to 33

Roberts, B
HI (1984)-(85)-(86)

Roberts, G
HI 1949-52-53-54

Roberts, P
ES 1964; HI 1950-51-53; 55 to 63; (64)-(65)-(66)-(67); 68-69-70; ELTC 1965-67-69

Roberts, S
HI 1983 to 90; ELTC 1983-87

Rogers, J
HI 1972

Scott Chard, Mrs
HI 1928-30

Seddon, N
HI 1962-63; (74)-(75)-(76)

Selkirk, H
HI 1925-28

Shaw, P
HI 1913

Sheldon, A
HI 1981

Slocombe, E (Davies)
HI 1974-75

Smalley, Mrs A
HI 1924-25; 31 to 34

Sowter, Mrs
HI 1923

Stark, K
HI 1995-96

Stockton, Mrs
HI 1949

Storry, Mrs
HI 1910-14

Stroud, N
HI 1989

Thomas, C (Phipps)
HI 1959; 63 to 73; 76-77-80

Thomas, I
HI 1910

Thomas, J (Foster)
HI 1984 to 87; 92-93-95; ELTC 1987-89-91-93

Thomas, O
HI 1921

Thomas, S (Rowlands)
HI 1977-82-84-85

Thomas, Vicki (Rawlings)
CC 1982-84-86-88-90; ES 1990; VT 1979-83-85-87-89-91; CT 1979-83-87-91; HI 1971 to 98; ELTC 1973 to 83; 87-91-97-99

Thompson, M
HI 1937-38-39

Treharne, A (Mills)
HI 1952-61

Turner, S (Jump)
HI 1982-84-85-86-91-93

Valentine, P (Whitley)
HI 1973-74-75; 77 to 80; (90)

Wadsworth, Helen
CC 1984; HI 1987 to 90; ELTC 1987-90

Wakelin, H
HI 1955

Webster, S (Hales)
HI 1968-69-72; (91)

Wesley, N
HI 1986

Weston, R
HI 1927

Whieldon, Miss
HI 1908

Williams, M
HI 1936

Wilson Jones, D
HI 1952

Wright, N (Cook)
ES 1964; HI 1938-47-48-49; 51 to 54; 57 to 60; 62-63-64-66-67-68; (71)-(72)-(73); ELTC 1965; (71)

PART IX

Governing the Game

Rules get a major revision for the first time in 20 years   438
The Rules of Golf   441
Professional Governing Bodies   503
Amateur Governing Bodies   505
Championship and International Match Conditions   508
Golf Associations   513
Directory of Golfing Organisations Worldwide   515

Rules get major revision for first time in 20 years

Each of the thirty-four rules that govern play has been amended, with the emphasis put on making the rules easier to understand for everyone in the latest of the regular four-year revisions undertaken by the R&A and USGA coming into force in 2004.

Commenting on the changes R&A Rules Secretary David Rickman said: 'In an essentially self-regulating sport, players need the rules not only readily available but as simple to understand as we can make them. Our latest revision benefits from expert linguistic advice and players will see more plain language. This is the biggest change in content and presentation of the rules for 20 years and, whilst the rules remain detailed and precise, we have clarified and simplified them wherever possible.'

The R&A produces four million copies of the rule book in English and in audio CD format for visually impaired players. Golf Unions affiliated to the R&A, reproduce the Rules of Golf under licence in more than 20 other languages including Arabic, Chinese, Czech, Danish, Dutch, Farsi (Iran), French, German, Hebrew, Hungarian, Icelandic, Indonesian, Italian, Japanese, Korean, Norwegian, Portuguese, Russian, Spanish, siSwati (Swaziland) and Swedish.

Rolex, a patron of The Open Championship, are sponsoring the publication of the Rules of Golf booklet which means the R&A can make the rule books available free of charge to golfers around the world.

In addition to extensive language improvements other major changes include an expanded Etiquette section, with the ultimate sanction of disqualification for a serious breach; the dropping of Rule 18-2c covering the removal of loose impediments, which has stood for over 100 years; and a new ruling on club length and clubhead size, designed to draw a line in the sand for future technology developments.

Although there are non-conforming drivers being made around the world, the biggest clubhead made by a recognised manufacturer is the Redline driver which has a head measuring 460cc – 10cc within the new limit. Nike's biggest head is 450cc (Tiger Woods' newest driver the Igniter, is only 335cc), Taylormade's biggest clubhead is 440cc and Callaway's 385cc, although a larger-headed model is in production.

Although many players have questioned why more action has not been taken on ball flight – professional players are able to hit much further these days making the bunkering and hazards in some long-established courses obsolete – the R&A and USGA consider the discussion about limiting how far a ball can fly is still on-going.

The R&A and the USGA were jointly advised on the language used in the new Rules of Golf publication by Professor Kenneth Chapman, a linguistics expert and author of *The Rules of The Green*, a history of the rules of golf published by Virgin Books (1997).

Copies of the new R&A Rules of Golf will be distributed free of charge to golf clubs around the world and can be requested or downloaded from the R&A website at www.randa.org.

Two companion publications to the R&A Rules of Golf, entitled *Decisions on the Rules of Golf 2004–2005* and *Golf Rules Illustrated 2004* are additionally published by Hamlyn priced £14.99/ $21.50 from the R&A, high street and on-line bookstores.

The main rules changes are:

Rule 2 – Match Play

Definitions
All defined terms are in *italics* and are listed alphabetically in the Definitions section – see pages 448–451.

2-1. General
A match consists of one *side* playing against another over a *stipulated round* unless otherwise decreed by the *Committee*.

In match play the game is played by holes.

Except as otherwise provided in the *Rules*, a hole is won by the *side* that *holes* its ball in the fewer *strokes*. In a handicap match the lower net score wins the hole.

The state of the match is expressed by the terms: so many "holes up" or "all square", and so many "to play".

A *side* is "dormie" when it is as many holes up as there are holes remaining to be played.

2-2. Halved Hole
A hole is halved if each *side holes* out in the same number of *strokes*.

When a player has *holed* out and his opponent has been left with a *stroke* for the half, if the player subsequently incurs a penalty, the hole is halved.

2-3. Winner of Match
A match is won when one *side* leads by a number of holes greater than the number remaining to be played.

If there is a tie, the *Committee* may extend the *stipulated round* by as many holes as are required for a match to be won.

2-4. Concession of Next Stroke, Hole or Match
A player may concede his opponent's next *stroke* at any time provided the opponent's ball is at rest. The opponent is considered to have *holed* out with his next *stroke* and the ball may be removed by either *side*.

A player may concede a hole at any time prior to the start or conclusion of that hole.

A player may concede a match at any time prior to the start or conclusion of that match.

A concession may not be declined or withdrawn. (Ball overhanging hole – see Rule 16-2)

2-5. Doubt as to Procedure; Disputes and Claims
In match play, if a doubt or dispute arises between the players, a player may make a claim. If no duly authorised representative of the *Committee* is available within a reasonable time, the players must continue the match without delay. The *Committee* may consider a claim only if the player making the claim notifies his opponent (i) that he is making a claim, (ii) of the facts of the situation and (iii) that he wants a ruling. The claim must be made before any player in the match plays from the next *teeing ground* or, in the case of the last hole of the match, before all players in the match leave the *putting green*.

A later claim may not be considered by the *Committee* unless it is based on facts previously unknown to the player making the claim and he had been given wrong information (Rules 6-2a and 9) by an opponent.

Once the result of the match has been officially announced, a later claim may not be considered by the *Committee* unless it is satisfied that the opponent knew he was giving wrong information.

2-6. General Penalty
The penalty for a breach of a *Rule* in match play is loss of hole except when otherwise provided.

———————

The period a professional must wait to be re-instated an amateur has been reduced from three to two years and the waiting period for re-instatement after a minor rules breach has been cut from two years to one.

The maximum value of a prize that any player can accept without breaching amateur status has been increased by £200 to £500.

———————

The R&A will conduct a series of Rules of Golf seminars based on the revised rules of play, for national golf unions, in Japan, New Zealand and Australia, Argentina, Brazil and Ecuador and in several African and European countries.

The R&A, golf's world governing body with the USGA, operates with the consent of 127 golf-playing nations and on behalf of an estimated 26 million golfers in Europe, Africa, Asia and The Americas (outside the USA and Mexico). The United States Golf Association (USGA) is the game's governing body in the United States and Mexico.

Watson Wins Payne Stewart Award

Tom Watson is the latest recipient of the Payne Stewart Award presented annually by the US PGA Tour to perpetuate the memory of the former US Open and US PGA champion who died in an air accident in 1999.

It is presented annually to the player the selection panel believes shares Stewart's respect for the traditions of the game, his commitment to uphold the game's heritage of charitable support and his professional and meticulous presentation of himself and the sport through his dress and conduct.

'Tom Watson is a fine example of those attributes,' said PGA Tour commissioner Tim Finchem. 'He has always conducted himself on and off the course with style and grace and has fully embraced the philosophy of regularly giving back something to his community and to those less fortunate than himself.'

Watson won 39 Tour events including five Opens, two Masters and a US Open. Since joining the US Senior tour he has won two Senior majors. Since his long-time caddy Bruce Edwards was diagnosed with the neurological disease ALS in January 2003, Watson has taken on a visible role in helping raise public awareness for the disease through Driving 4 Life – a multi-million dollar fund-raising campaign supported by Watson, Edwards and another former Tour player Jeff Julian who has also contracted the disease.

When Watson won $1 million dollars in the Charles Schwab Cup at the end of the 2003 season he donated the annuity to ALS research and patient care and has established the Bruce Edwards Trust to help defray Edwards' medical bills

RULES
OF GOLF

As Approved by
R&A Rules Limited
and the
United States Golf Association

30th EDITION
EFFECTIVE 1st JANUARY 2004

HOW TO USE THE RULE BOOK

Understand the words

The Rules book is written in a very precise and deliberate fashion. You should be aware of and understand the following differences in word use.

may	=	optional
should	=	recommendation
shall/must	=	instruction (and penalty if not carried out)
a ball	=	you may substitute another ball (e.g. Rules 26, 27 or 28)
the ball	=	you may not substitute another ball (e.g. Rules 24-2 or 25-1)

Know the definitions

There are over sixty defined terms and these form the foundation around which the Rules of play are written. A good knowledge of the defined terms (which are italicised throughout the book) is very important to the correct application of the Rules.

Which rule applies?

The Contents pages may help you find the relevant Rule, alternatively there is an Index at the back of the book.

What is the ruling

To answer any question on the Rules you must first establish the facts of the case. To do so, you should identify:

1. The form of play (e.g. match play or stroke play, single, foursome or four-ball?)
2. Who is involved (e.g. the player, his partner or caddie, an outside agency?)
3. Where the incident occurred (e.g. on the teeing ground, in a bunker or water hazard, on the putting green or elsewhere on the course).

In some cases it might also be necessary to establish:

4. The player's intentions (e.g. what was he doing and what does he want to do?)
5. Any subsequent events (e.g. the player has returned his score card or the competition has closed).

Refer to the book

It is recommended that you carry a Rule book in your golf bag and use it whenever a question arises. If in doubt, play the course as you find it and play the ball as it lies. Once back in the Clubhouse, reference to Decisions on the Rules of Golf should help resolve any outstanding queries.

CONTENTS

Principal Changes..444
Section I. Etiquette 446
Section II. Definitions 448
Section III. The Rules of Play 452
  1. The Game...452
  2. Match Play 452
  3. Stroke Play 453
  4. Clubs 453
  5. The Ball 454
  6. The Player 455
  7. Practice...457
  8. Advice; Indicating Line of Play...457
  9. Information as to Strokes Taken 458
  10. Order of Play 458
  11. Teeing Ground 459
  12. Searching for and Identifying Ball...459
  13. Ball Played as It Lies 460
  14. Striking the Ball 461
  15. Substituted Ball; Wrong Ball 461
  16. The Putting Green 462
  17. The Flagstick 463
  18. Ball at Rest Moved..463
  19. Ball in Motion Deflected or Stopped 464
  20. Lifting, Dropping and Placing; Playing from Wrong Place....................465
  21. Cleaning Ball 467
  22. Ball Assisting or Interfering with Play...................................467
  23. Loose Impediments 468
  24. Obstructions 468
  25. Abnormal Ground Conditions, Embedded Ball and Wrong Putting
      Green 469
  26. Water Hazards (Including Lateral Water Hazards) 471
  27. Ball Lost or Out of Bounds; Provisional Ball 471
  28. Ball Unplayable 472
  29. Threesomes and Foursomes 472
  30. Three-Ball, Best-Ball and Four-Ball Match Play....................472
  31. Four-Ball Stroke Play..473
  32. Bogey, Par and Stableford Competitions.................................474
  33. The Committee..475
  34. Disputes and Decisions 476

  APPENDIX I   Contents 477
                         Part A Local Rules...................................477
                         Part B Specimen Local Rules 478
                         Part C Conditions of the Competition 482
  APPENDIX II   Design of Clubs 485
  APPENDIX III   The Ball 485

Handicaps 489
Rules of Amateur Status...489
Index 494

PRINCIPAL CHANGES

GENERAL

The entire Rule book has been redrafted for clarity, adopting a more modern style.

ETIQUETTE

Amended and expanded to give broader guidance on the etiquette of the game and to clarify that a Committee may disqualify a player for a serious breach of etiquette under Rule 33-7.

DEFINITIONS

Ball in Play
Expanded to clarify the status of a ball when played from outside the teeing ground.

Bunker
Amended to provide that a stacked turf face is not part of a bunker, whether grass-covered or earthen.

Lost Ball
Part b amended to state that a ball is lost if the player has made a stroke at a substituted ball, rather than simply having "put another ball into play".

Nearest Point of Relief
Amended for clarity.

Rule or Rules
Expanded to include Conditions of Competition and Decisions on the Rules of Golf.

Substituted Ball
A new Definition to clarify the distinction between a substituted ball and a wrong ball.

Tee
A new Definition to give specifications of a tee.

RULES

Rule 2-5. Doubt as to Procedure; Disputes and Claims
Expanded to clarify the procedure for making a valid claim.

Rule 3-3. Doubt as to Procedure
Amended to provide that the player must report to the Committee in all cases, including when he believes he has scored the same with both balls. The penalty for failure to do so is disqualification.

Rule 5-3. Ball Unfit for Play
Amended so that the procedures for lifting the ball under Rules 5-3 and 12-2 are more consistent.

Rule 6-4. Caddie
Penalty for having more than one caddie amended from disqualification to loss of hole in match play (adjustment to state of match) or two strokes in stroke play with a maximum of two holes in match play or four strokes in stroke play.

Rule 6-8d. Procedure When Play Resumed
Note added to provide that if the spot on which the ball is to be placed is not determinable, when resuming play it must be estimated and the ball is placed on the estimated spot (see corresponding Exception to Rule 20-3c).

Rule 7-1b. Practice Before or Between Rounds
Expanded to clarify what constitutes testing the surface prior to a round.

Rule 9-2. Information as to Strokes Taken; Match Play
Separated into two categories – information as to strokes taken and wrong information – and more explicit detail given on when a player is deemed to have given wrong information.

Rules 10-1b and 10-2b. Order of Play
Note introduced to clarify the order of play when a ball is not to be played as it lies (previously contained in Decisions 10/1, 10/2 and 10/3).

Rule 11-1. Teeing
Amended for clarity and to introduce a penalty of disqualification for use of a non-conforming tee.

Rule 12-2. Identifying Ball
Amended so that the procedures for lifting the ball under Rules 5-3 and 12-2 are more consistent.

Rule 13-2. Improving Lie, Area of Intended Stance or Swing, or Line of Play
Re-formatted for clarity.

Rule 13-4b. Ball in Hazard; Prohibited Actions
Amended to restrict penalty situations to touching ground in the hazard or water in the water hazard with a hand or a club.

Exception 2 to Rule 13-4. Ball in Hazard; Prohibited Actions
Amended so that the caddie is no longer permitted to smooth sand or soil in the hazard prior to the player making a stroke.

Rule 15. Substituted Ball; Wrong Ball
Re-formatted and amended for clarity.

Rule 16-1a. Touching Line of Putt
Amended to provide that the player may remove loose impediments on the putting green by any means, provided he does not press anything down.

Rule 17. The Flagstick
Amended for clarity.

Rule 18-6. Ball Moved in Measuring
Rule 10-4 has been withdrawn and new Rule 18-6 has been introduced to provide that no penalty is incurred if a ball or ball-marker is moved while proceeding under or in determining the application of a Rule.

Rule 20-3c. Placing and Replacing; Spot Not Determinable
Exception added to provide that a player resuming play under Rule 6-8d places the ball at the estimated spot if the exact spot is not determinable.

Rule 20-7. Playing from Wrong Place
Amended for clarity.

Rule 22. Ball Assisting or Interfering with Play
Amended for clarity.

Rule 23-1. Loose Impediments; Relief
Rule 18-2c has been withdrawn and Rule 23-1 has been amended to provide that a penalty for the player causing his ball, lying anywhere other than on a putting green, to move due to the removal of a loose impediment will be assessed under Rule 18-2a. There is no longer an automatic penalty if a ball moves after a loose impediment within one club-length of the ball is touched.

Rule 24-2b. Immovable Obstruction; Relief
Amended for clarity and to permit a player to take relief from an immovable obstruction in a bunker by dropping outside the bunker under penalty of one stroke.

Rule 24-3. Ball Lost in Obstruction
New Rule created to deal with a ball lost in a movable obstruction and a ball lost in an immovable obstruction (previously covered in Rule 24-2c).

Rule 25-1c. Ball Lost in Abnormal Ground Conditions
Amended to clarify the reference point for taking relief when a ball is lost in an abnormal ground condition (corresponding amendment made in new Rule 24-3b).

Rule 25-3b. Wrong Putting Green; Relief
Amended for clarity.

Rule 26-2a. Ball Played Within Water Hazard
Amended and expanded for clarity.

Rule 28. Ball Unplayable
Options b and c reversed in order to provide consistency with the construction of Rule 26-1.

Rule 34-1a. Claims and Penalties; Match Play
Amended by omitting the points already covered in Rule 2-5.

Rule 34-3. Committee's Decision
Reference to "Secretary" amended to "duly authorised representative of the Committee".

APPENDIX I

Table of Contents for Appendix I
Added for ease of reference.

Preferred Lies
Specimen Local Rule amended for clarity and to provide that the position of the ball must be marked when lifted to prefer the lie. The R&A will also now interpret this Local Rule.

Immovable Obstructions Close to Putting Green
Previous Local Rule for fixed sprinkler heads amended to allow for inclusion of any immovable obstructions within two club-lengths of the putting green.

APPENDIX II

Club Length
Clause 1c amended to include a new 48 inch limit. Putters are excepted.

Clubhead
Clause 4b amended to include new dimensional limit and a new maximum head size for woods of 470cc.

R&A Rules Limited

The Royal and Ancient Golf Club of St Andrews is transferring to R&A Rules Limited, with effect from 1st January 2004, the responsibilities and authority of The Royal and Ancient Golf Club of St Andrews in making, interpreting and giving decisions on the Rules of Golf and on the Rules of Amateur Status.

The new Rules of Golf and the new Rules of Amateur Status have, therefore, been approved by R&A Rules Limited.

As from 1st January 2004, the Rules of Golf and the Rules of Amateur Status shall be made, altered, interpreted and applied by R&A Rules Limited.

Gender

In the Rules of Golf, the gender used in relation to any person is understood to include both genders.

Golfers with Disabilities

The R&A publication entitled "A Modification of the Rules of Golf for Golfers with Disabilities", that contains permissible modifications of the Rules of Golf to accommodate disabled golfers, is available through the R&A.

SECTION I —
ETIQUETTE; BEHAVIOUR ON THE COURSE

INTRODUCTION

This section provides guidelines on the manner in which the game of golf should be played. If they are followed, all players will gain maximum enjoyment from the game. The overriding principle is that consideration should be shown to others on the course at all times.

THE SPIRIT OF THE GAME

Unlike many sports, golf is played, for the most part, without the supervision of a referee or umpire. The game relies on the integrity of the individual to show consideration for other players and to abide by the Rules. All players should conduct themselves in a disciplined manner, demonstrating courtesy and sportsmanship at all times, irrespective of how competitive they may be. This is the spirit of the game of golf.

SAFETY

Players should ensure that no one is standing close by or in a position to be hit by the club, the ball or any stones, pebbles, twigs or the like when they make a stroke or practice swing.

Players should not play until the players in front are out of range.

Players should always alert greenstaff nearby or ahead when they are about to make a stroke that might endanger them.

If a player plays a ball in a direction where there is a danger of hitting someone, he should immediately shout a warning. The traditional word of warning in such situations is "fore".

CONSIDERATION FOR OTHER PLAYERS

No Disturbance or Distraction

Players should always show consideration for other players on the course and should not disturb their play by moving, talking or making unnecessary noise.

Players should ensure that any electronic device taken onto the course does not distract other players.

On the teeing ground, a player should not tee his ball until it is his turn to play.

Players should not stand close to or directly behind the ball, or directly behind the hole, when a player is about to play.

On the Putting Green

On the putting green, players should not stand on another player's line of putt or, when he is making a stroke, cast a shadow over his line of putt.

Players should remain on or close to the putting green until all other players in the group have holed out.

Scoring

In stroke play, a player who is acting as a marker should, if necessary, on the way to the next tee, check the score with the player concerned and record it.

PACE OF PLAY

Play at Good Pace and Keep Up

Players should play at a good pace. The Committee may establish pace of play guidelines that all players should follow.

It is a group's responsibility to keep up with the group in front. If it loses a clear hole and it is delaying the group behind, it should invite the group behind to play through, irrespective of the number of players in that group.

Be Ready to Play

Players should be ready to play as soon as it is their turn to play. When playing on or near the putting green, they should leave their bags or carts in such a position as will enable quick movement off the green and towards the next tee. When the play of a hole has been completed, players should immediately leave the putting green.

Lost Ball

If a player believes his ball may be lost outside a water hazard or is out of bounds, to save time, he should play a provisional ball.

Players searching for a ball should signal the players in the group behind them to play through as soon as it becomes apparent that the ball will not easily be found. They should not search for five minutes before doing so. Having allowed the group behind to play through, they should not continue play until that group has passed and is out of range.

Priority on the Course

Unless otherwise determined by the Committee, priority on the course is determined by a group's pace of play. Any group playing a whole round is entitled to pass a group playing a shorter round.

CARE OF THE COURSE

Bunkers

Before leaving a bunker, players should carefully fill up and smooth over all holes and footprints made by them and any nearby made by others. If a rake is within reasonable proximity of the bunker, the rake should be used for this purpose.

Repair of Divots, Ball-Marks and Damage by Shoes

Players should carefully repair any divot holes made by them and any damage to the putting green made

by the impact of a ball (whether or not made by the player himself). On completion of the hole by all players in the group, damage to the putting green caused by golf shoes should be repaired.

Preventing Unnecessary Damage

Players should avoid causing damage to the course by removing divots when taking practice swings or by hitting the head of a club into the ground, whether in anger or for any other reason.

Players should ensure that no damage is done to the putting green when putting down bags or the flagstick.

In order to avoid damaging the hole, players and caddies should not stand too close to the hole and should take care during the handling of the flagstick and the removal of a ball from the hole. The head of a club should not be used to remove a ball from the hole.

Players should not lean on their clubs when on the putting green, particularly when removing the ball from the hole.

The flagstick should be properly replaced in the hole before the players leave the putting green.

Local notices regulating the movement of golf carts should be strictly observed.

CONCLUSION; PENALTIES FOR BREACH

If players follow the guidelines in this section, it will make the game more enjoyable for everyone.

If a player consistently disregards these guidelines during a round or over a period of time to the detriment of others, it is recommended that the Committee considers taking appropriate disciplinary action against the offending player. Such action may, for example, include prohibiting play for a limited time on the course or in a certain number of competitions. This is considered to be justifiable in terms of protecting the interest of the majority of golfers who wish to play in accordance with these guidelines.

In the case of a serious breach of etiquette, the Committee may disqualify a player under Rule 33-7.

SECTION II — DEFINITIONS

The Definitions are listed alphabetically and, in the *Rules* themselves, defined terms are in *italics*.

Abnormal Ground Conditions
An *"abnormal ground condition"* is any *casual water, ground under repair* or hole, cast or runway on the *course* made by a *burrowing animal*, a reptile or a bird.

Addressing the Ball
A player has *"addressed the ball"* when he has taken his *stance* and has also grounded his club, except that in a *hazard* a player has *addressed the ball* when he has taken his *stance*.

Advice
"Advice" is any counsel or suggestion that could influence a player in determining his play, the choice of a club or the method of making a *stroke*.
Information on the *Rules* or on matters of public information, such as the position of *hazards* or the *flagstick* on the *putting green*, is not *advice*.

Ball Deemed to Move
See *"Move or Moved"*.

Ball Holed
See *"Holed"*.

Ball Lost
See *"Lost Ball"*.

Ball in Play
A ball is *"in play"* as soon as the player has made a *stroke* on the *teeing ground*. It remains *in play* until it is *holed*, except when it is *lost, out of bounds* or lifted, or another ball has been *substituted* whether or not the substitution is permitted; a ball so *substituted* becomes the *ball in play*.
If a ball is played from outside the *teeing ground* when the player is starting play of a hole, or when attempting to correct this mistake, the ball is not *in play* and Rule 11-4 or 11-5 applies. Otherwise, *ball in play* includes a ball played from outside the *teeing ground* when the player elects or is required to play his next *stroke* from the *teeing ground*.
Exception in match play: *Ball in play* includes a ball played by the player from outside the *teeing ground* when starting play of a hole if the opponent does not require the *stroke* to be cancelled in accordance with Rule 11-4a.

Best-Ball
See *"Matches"*.

Bunker
A *"bunker"* is a *hazard* consisting of a prepared area of ground, often a hollow, from which turf or soil has been removed and replaced with sand or the like.
Grass-covered ground bordering or within a *bunker* including a stacked turf face (whether grass-covered or earthen), is not part of the *bunker*. A wall

or lip of the *bunker* not covered with grass is part of the *bunker*.
The margin of a *bunker* extends vertically downwards, but not upwards. A ball is in a *bunker* when it lies in or any part of it touches the *bunker*.

Burrowing Animal
A *"burrowing animal"* is an animal that makes a hole for habitation or shelter, such as a rabbit, mole, groundhog, gopher or salamander.
Note: A hole made by a non-burrowing animal, such as a dog, is not an *abnormal ground condition* unless marked or declared as *ground under repair*.

Caddie
A *"caddie"* is one who assists the player in accordance with the *Rules*, which may include carrying or handling the player's clubs during play.
When one *caddie* is employed by more than one player, he is always deemed to be the *caddie* of the player whose ball is involved, and *equipment* carried by him is deemed to be that player's *equipment*, except when the *caddie* acts upon specific directions of another player, in which case he is considered to be that other player's *caddie*.

Casual Water
"Casual water" is any temporary accumulation of water on the *course* that is visible before or after the player takes his *stance* and is not in a *water hazard*. Snow and natural ice, other than frost, are either *casual water* or *loose impediments*, at the option of the player. Manufactured ice is an *obstruction*. Dew and frost are not *casual water*. A ball is in *casual water* when it lies in or any part of it touches the *casual water*.

Committee
The *"Committee"* is the committee in charge of the competition or, if the matter does not arise in a competition, the committee in charge of the *course*.

Competitor
A *"competitor"* is a player in a stroke play competition. A *"fellow-competitor"* is any person with whom the *competitor* plays. Neither is *partner* of the other.
In stroke play *foursome* and *four-ball* competitions, where the context so admits, the word *"competitor"* or *"fellow-competitor"* includes his *partner*.

Course
The *"course"* is the whole area within any boundaries established by the *Committee* (see Rule 33-2).

Equipment
"Equipment" is anything used, worn or carried by or for the player except any ball he has played at the hole being played and any small object, such as a coin or a *tee*, when used to mark the position of a ball or the extent of an area in which a ball is to be dropped.

Equipment includes a golf cart, whether or not motorised. If such a cart is shared by two or more players, the cart and everything in it are deemed to be the *equipment* of the player whose ball is involved except that, when the cart is being moved by one of the players sharing it, the cart and everything in it are deemed to be that player's *equipment*.

Note: A ball played at the hole being played is *equipment* when it has been lifted and not put back into play.

Fellow-Competitor
See "*Competitor*".

Flagstick
The "*flagstick*" is a movable straight indicator, with or without bunting or other material attached, centered in the *hole* to show its position. It must be circular in cross-section. Padding or shock absorbent material that might unduly influence the movement of the ball is prohibited.

Forecaddie
A "*forecaddie*" is one who is employed by the *Committee* to indicate to players the position of balls during play. He is an *outside agency*.

Four-Ball
See "*Matches*".

Foursome
See "*Matches*".

Ground Under Repair
"*Ground under repair*" is any part of the *course* so marked by order of the *Committee* or so declared by its authorised representative. It includes material piled for removal and a hole made by a greenkeeper, even if not so marked.

All ground and any grass, bush, tree or other growing thing within the *ground under repair* is part of the *ground under repair*. The margin of *ground under repair* extends vertically downwards, but not upwards. Stakes and lines defining *ground under repair* are in such ground. Such stakes are *obstructions*. A ball is in *ground under repair* when it lies in or any part of it touches the *ground under repair*.

Note 1: Grass cuttings and other material left on the *course* that have been abandoned and are not intended to be removed are not *ground under repair* unless so marked.

Note 2: The *Committee* may make a Local Rule prohibiting play from *ground under repair* or an environmentally-sensitive area defined as *ground under repair*.

Hazards
A "*hazard*" is any *bunker* or *water hazard*.

Hole
The "*hole*" must be 4¼ inches (108 mm) in diameter and at least 4 inches (101.6 mm) deep. If a lining is used, it must be sunk at least 1 inch (25.4 mm) below the *putting green* surface unless the nature of the soil makes it impracticable to do so; its outer diameter must not exceed 4¼ inches (108 mm).

Holed
A ball is "*holed*" when it is at rest within the circumference of the *hole* and all of it is below the level of the lip of the *hole*.

Honour
The player who is to play first from the *teeing ground* is said to have the "*honour*".

Lateral Water Hazard
A "*lateral water hazard*" is a *water hazard* or that part of a *water hazard* so situated that it is not possible or is deemed by the *Committee* to be impracticable to drop a ball behind the *water hazard* in accordance with Rule 26-1b.

That part of a *water hazard* to be played as a *lateral water hazard* should be distinctively marked. A ball is in a *lateral water hazard* when it lies in or any part of it touches the *lateral water hazard*.

Note 1: Stakes or lines used to define a *lateral water hazard* must be red. When both stakes and lines are used to define *lateral water hazards*, the stakes identify the *hazard* and the lines define the *hazard* margin.

Note 2: The *Committee* may make a Local Rule prohibiting play from an environmentally-sensitive area defined as a *lateral water hazard*.

Note 3: The *Committee* may define a *lateral water hazard* as a *water hazard*.

Line of Play
The "*line of play*" is the direction that the player wishes his ball to take after a *stroke*, plus a reasonable distance on either side of the intended direction. The *line of play* extends vertically upwards from the ground, but does not extend beyond the *hole*.

Line of Putt
The "*line of putt*" is the line that the player wishes his ball to take after a *stroke* on the *putting green*. Except with respect to Rule 16-1e, the *line of putt* includes a reasonable distance on either side of the intended line. The *line of putt* does not extend beyond the *hole*.

Loose Impediments
"*Loose impediments*" are natural objects, including:
- stones, leaves, twigs, branches and the like,
- dung, and
- worms and insects and the casts and heaps made by them, provided they are not:
- fixed or growing,
- solidly embedded, or
- adhering to the ball.

Sand and loose soil are *loose impediments* on the *putting green*, but not elsewhere.

Snow and natural ice, other than frost, are either *casual water* or *loose impediments* at the option of the player.

Dew and frost are not *loose impediments*.

Lost Ball
A ball is deemed "*lost*" if:
a. It is not found or identified as his by the player within five minutes after the player's *side* or his or their *caddies* have begun to search for it; or

b. The player has made a *stroke* at a *substituted ball*; or

c. The player has made a *stroke* at a *provisional ball* from the place where the original ball is likely to be or from a point nearer the *hole* than that place.

Time spent in playing a *wrong ball* is not counted in the five-minute period allowed for search.

Marker
A *"marker"* is one who is appointed by the *Committee* to record a *competitor's* score in stroke play. He may be a *fellow-competitor*. He is not a *referee*.

Matches
Single: A match in which one plays against another.

Threesome: A match in which one plays against two, and each *side* plays one ball.

Foursome: A match in which two play against two, and each *side* plays one ball.

Three-Ball: A match play competition in which three play against one another, each playing his own ball. Each player is playing two distinct matches.

Best-Ball: A match in which one plays against the better ball of two or the best ball of three players.

Four-Ball: A match in which two play their better ball against the better ball of two other players.

Move or Moved
A ball is deemed to have *"moved"* if it leaves its position and comes to rest in any other place.

Nearest Point of Relief
The *"nearest point of relief"* is the reference point for taking relief without penalty from interference by an immovable *obstruction* (Rule 24-2), an *abnormal ground condition* (Rule 25-1) or a *wrong putting green* (Rule 25-3).

It is the point on the *course* nearest to where the ball lies:

(i) that is not nearer the *hole*, and

(ii) where, if the ball were so positioned, no interference by the condition from which relief is sought would exist for the *stroke* the player would have made from the original position if the condition were not there.

Note: In order to determine the *nearest point of relief* accurately, the player should use the club with which he would have made his next *stroke* if the condition were not there to simulate the *address* position, direction of play and swing for such a *stroke*.

Observer
An *"observer"* is one who is appointed by the *Committee* to assist a *referee* to decide questions of fact and to report to him any breach of a *Rule*. An *observer* should not attend the *flagstick*, stand at or mark the position of the *hole,* or lift the ball or mark its position.

Obstructions
An *"obstruction"* is anything artificial, including the artificial surfaces and sides of roads and paths and manufactured ice, except:

a. Objects defining *out of bounds*, such as walls, fences, stakes and railings;

b. Any part of an immovable artificial object that is *out of bounds*; and

c. Any construction declared by the *Committee* to be an integral part of the *course*.

An *obstruction* is a movable *obstruction* if it may be moved without unreasonable effort, without unduly delaying play and without causing damage. Otherwise it is an immovable *obstruction*.

Note: The *Committee* may make a Local Rule declaring a movable *obstruction* to be an immovable *obstruction*.

Out of Bounds
"Out of bounds" is beyond the boundaries of the *course* or any part of the *course* so marked by the *Committee*.

When *out of bounds* is defined by reference to stakes or a fence or as being beyond stakes or a fence, the *out of bounds* line is determined by the nearest inside points of the stakes or fence posts at ground level excluding angled supports.

Objects defining *out of bounds* such as walls, fences, stakes and railings, are not *obstructions* and are deemed to be fixed.

When *out of bounds* is defined by a line on the ground, the line itself is *out of bounds*.

The *out of bounds* line extends vertically upwards and downwards.

A ball is *out of bounds* when all of it lies *out of bounds*.

A player may stand *out of bounds* to play a ball lying within bounds.

Outside Agency
An *"outside agency"* is any agency not part of the match or, in stroke play, not part of the *competitor's side*, and includes a *referee*, a *marker*, an *observer* and a *forecaddie*. Neither wind nor water is an *outside agency*.

Partner
A *"partner"* is a player associated with another player on the same *side*.

In a *threesome, foursome, best-ball* or *four-ball* match, where the context so admits, the word "player" includes his *partner* or *partners*.

Penalty Stroke
A *"penalty stroke"* is one added to the score of a player or *side* under certain *Rules*. In a *threesome* or *foursome, penalty strokes* do not affect the order of play.

Provisional Ball
A *"provisional ball"* is a ball played under Rule 27-2 for a ball that may be *lost* outside a *water hazard* or may be *out of bounds*.

Putting Green
The *"putting green"* is all ground of the hole being played that is specially prepared for putting or otherwise defined as such by the *Committee*. A ball is on

the *putting green* when any part of it touches the *putting green*.

R&A

The "*R&A*" means R&A Rules Limited.

Referee

A "*referee*" is one who is appointed by the *Committee* to accompany players to decide questions of fact and apply the *Rules*. He must act on any breach of a *Rule* that he observes or is reported to him.

A *referee* should not attend the *flagstick*, stand at or mark the position of the *hole*, or lift the ball or mark its position.

Rub of the Green

A "*rub of the green*" occurs when a ball in motion is accidentally deflected or stopped by any *outside agency* (see Rule 19-1).

Rule or Rules

The term "*Rule*" includes:

a. The Rules of Golf and their interpretations as contained in Decisions on the Rules of Golf;

b. Any Conditions of Competition established by the *Committee* under Rule 33-1 and Appendix I;

c. Any Local Rules established by the *Committee* under Rule 33-8a and Appendix I; and

d. The specifications on clubs and the ball in Appendices II and III.

Side

A "*side*" is a player, or two or more players who are *partners*.

Single

See "*Matches*".

Stance

Taking the "*stance*" consists in a player placing his feet in position for and preparatory to making a *stroke*.

Stipulated Round

The "*stipulated round*" consists of playing the holes of the *course* in their correct sequence unless otherwise authorised by the *Committee*. The number of holes in a *stipulated round* is 18 unless a smaller number is authorised by the *Committee*. As to extension of *stipulated round* in match play, see Rule 2-3.

Stroke

A "*stroke*" is the forward movement of the club made with the intention of striking at and moving the ball, but if a player checks his downswing voluntarily before the clubhead reaches the ball he has not made a *stroke*.

Substituted Ball

A "*substituted ball*" is a ball put into play for the original ball that was either *in play, lost, out of bounds* or lifted.

Tee

A "*tee*" is a device designed to raise the ball off the ground. It must not be longer than 4 inches (101.6 mm) and it must not be designed or manufactured in such a way that it could indicate the *line of play* or influence the movement of the ball.

Teeing Ground

The "*teeing ground*" is the starting place for the hole to be played. It is a rectangular area two club-lengths in depth, the front and the sides of which are defined by the outside limits of two tee-markers. A ball is outside the *teeing ground* when all of it lies outside the *teeing ground*.

Three-Ball

See "*Matches*".

Threesome

See "*Matches*".

Through the Green

"*Through the green*" is the whole area of the *course* except:

a. The *teeing ground* and *putting green* of the hole being played; and

b. All *hazards* on the *course*.

Water Hazard

A "*water hazard*" is any sea, lake, pond, river, ditch, surface drainage ditch or other open water course (whether or not containing water) and anything of a similar nature on the *course*.

All ground or water within the margin of a *water hazard* is part of the *water hazard*. The margin of a *water hazard* extends vertically upwards and downwards. Stakes and lines defining the margins of *water hazards* are in the *hazards*. Such stakes are *obstructions*. A ball is in a *water hazard* when it lies in or any part of it touches the *water hazard*.

Note 1: Stakes or lines used to define a *water hazard* must be yellow. When both stakes and lines are used to define *water hazards*, the stakes identify the *hazard* and the lines define the *hazard* margin.

Note 2: The *Committee* may make a Local Rule prohibiting play from an environmentally-sensitive area defined as a *water hazard*.

Wrong Ball

A "*wrong ball*" is any ball other than the player's:

*   *ball in play*;
*   *provisional ball*; or
*   second ball played under Rule 3-3 or Rule 20-7c in stroke play;

and includes:

*   another player's ball;
*   an abandoned ball; and
*   the player's original ball when it is no longer *in play*.

Note: *Ball in play* includes a ball *substituted* for the *ball in play*, whether or not the substitution is permitted.

Wrong Putting Green

A "*wrong putting green*" is any *putting green* other than that of the hole being played. Unless otherwise prescribed by the *Committee*, this term includes a practice *putting green* or pitching green on the *course*.

SECTION III — THE RULES OF PLAY

THE GAME

Rule 1 – The Game

Definitions
All defined terms are in *italics* and are listed alphabetically in the Definitions section – see pages 448–451.

1-1. General
The Game of Golf consists of playing a ball with a club from the *teeing ground* into the *hole* by a *stroke* or successive *strokes* in accordance with the *Rules*.

1-2. Exerting Influence on Ball
A player or *caddie* must not take any action to influence the position or the movement of a ball except in accordance with the *Rules*.

(Removal of movable obstruction – see Rule 24-1)

PENALTY FOR BREACH OF RULE 1-2:
Match play – Loss of hole; Stroke play –
Two strokes.

Note: In the case of a serious breach of Rule 1-2, the *Committee* may impose a penalty of disqualification.

1-3. Agreement to Waive Rules
Players must not agree to exclude the operation of any *Rule* or to waive any penalty incurred.

PENALTY FOR BREACH OF RULE 1-3:
Match play – Disqualification of both sides;
Stroke play – Disqualification of competitors
concerned.

(Agreeing to play out of turn in stroke play – see Rule 10-2c)

1-4. Points Not Covered by Rules
If any point in dispute is not covered by the *Rules*, the decision should be made in accordance with equity.

Rule 2 – Match Play

Definitions
All defined terms are in *italics* and are listed alphabetically in the Definitions section – see pages 448–451.

2-1. General
A match consists of one *side* playing against another over a *stipulated round* unless otherwise decreed by the *Committee*.

In match play the game is played by holes.

Except as otherwise provided in the *Rules*, a hole is won by the *side* that *holes* its ball in the fewer *strokes*. In a handicap match the lower net score wins the hole.

The state of the match is expressed by the terms: so many "holes up" or "all square", and so many "to play".

A *side* is "dormie" when it is as many holes up as there are holes remaining to be played.

2-2. Halved Hole
A hole is halved if each *side holes* out in the same number of *strokes*.

When a player has *holed* out and his opponent has been left with a *stroke* for the half, if the player subsequently incurs a penalty, the hole is halved.

2-3. Winner of Match
A match is won when one *side* leads by a number of holes greater than the number remaining to be played.

If there is a tie, the *Committee* may extend the *stipulated round* by as many holes as are required for a match to be won.

2-4. Concession of Next Stroke, Hole or Match
A player may concede his opponent's next *stroke* at any time provided the opponent's ball is at rest. The opponent is considered to have *holed* out with his next *stroke* and the ball may be removed by either *side*.

A player may concede a hole at any time prior to the start or conclusion of that hole.

A player may concede a match at any time prior to the start or conclusion of that match.

A concession may not be declined or withdrawn.

(Ball overhanging hole – see Rule 16-2)

2-5. Doubt as to Procedure; Disputes and Claims
In match play, if a doubt or dispute arises between the players, a player may make a claim. If no duly authorised representative of the *Committee* is available within a reasonable time, the players must continue the match without delay. The *Committee* may consider a claim only if the player making the claim notifies his opponent (i) that he is making a claim, (ii) of the facts of the situation and (iii) that he wants a ruling. The claim must be made before any player in the match plays from the next *teeing ground* or, in the case of the last hole of the match, before all players in the match leave the *putting green*.

A later claim may not be considered by the *Committee* unless it is based on facts previously unknown to the player making the claim and he had been given wrong information (Rules 6-2a and 9) by an opponent.

Once the result of the match has been officially announced, a later claim may not be considered by the *Committee* unless it is satisfied that the opponent knew he was giving wrong information.

2-6. General Penalty
The penalty for a breach of a *Rule* in match play is loss of hole except when otherwise provided.

Rule 3 – Stroke Play

Definitions
All defined terms are in *italics* and are listed alphabetically in the Definitions section – see pages 448–451.

3-1. Winner
The *competitor* who plays the *stipulated round* or rounds in the fewest *strokes* is the winner.

In a handicap competition, the *competitor* with the lowest net score for the *stipulated round* or rounds is the winner.

3-2. Failure to Hole Out
If a *competitor* fails to hole out at any hole and does not correct his mistake before he makes a *stroke* on the next *teeing ground* or, in the case of the last hole of the round, before he leaves the *putting green*, he is disqualified.

3-3. Doubt as to Procedure
a. Procedure
In stroke play, if a *competitor* is doubtful of his rights or the correct procedure during play of a hole he may, without penalty, complete the hole with two balls.

After the doubtful situation has arisen and before taking further action, the *competitor* must announce to his *marker* or a *fellow-competitor* that he intends to play two balls and which ball he wishes to count if the *Rules* permit. If he fails to do so, the provisions of Rule 3-3b(ii) apply.

The *competitor* must report the facts of the situation to the *Committee* before returning his score card. If he fails to do so, he is disqualified.

b. Determination of Score for Hole
(i) If the ball that the *competitor* selected in advance to count has been played in accordance with the *Rules*, the score with that ball is the *competitor's* score for the hole. Otherwise, the score with the other ball counts if the *Rules* allow the procedure adopted for that ball.

(ii) If the *competitor* fails to announce in advance his decision to complete the hole with two balls, or which ball he wishes to count, the score with the original ball counts, provided it has been played in accordance with the *Rules*. If the original ball is not one of the balls being played, the first ball put into play counts, provided it has been played in accordance with the *Rules*. Otherwise, the score with the other ball counts if the *Rules* allow the procedure adopted for that ball.

Note 1: If a *competitor* plays a second ball under Rule 3-3, the *strokes* made after this Rule has been invoked with the ball ruled not to count and *penalty strokes* incurred solely by playing that ball are disregarded.

Note 2: A second ball played under Rule 3-3 is not a *provisional ball* under Rule 27-2.

3-4. Refusal to Comply with a Rule
If a *competitor* refuses to comply with a *Rule* affecting the rights of another *competitor*, he is disqualified.

3-5. General Penalty
The penalty for a breach of a *Rule* in stroke play is two strokes except when otherwise provided.

CLUBS AND THE BALL

The *R&A* reserves the right, at any time, to change the Rules relating to clubs and balls (see Appendices II and III) and make or change the interpretations relating to these Rules.

A player in doubt as to the conformity of a club should consult the *R&A*.

A manufacturer should submit to the *R&A* a sample of a club to be manufactured for a ruling as to whether the club conforms with the *Rules*. If a manufacturer fails to submit a sample or to await a ruling before manufacturing and/or marketing the club, the manufacturer assumes the risk of a ruling that the club does not conform with the *Rules*. Any sample submitted to the *R&A* becomes its property for reference purposes.

Rule 4 – Clubs

Definitions
All defined terms are in *italics* and are listed alphabetically in the Definitions section – see pages 448–451.

4-1. Form and Make of Clubs
a. General
The player's clubs must conform with this Rule and the provisions, specifications and interpretations set forth in Appendix II.

b. Wear and Alteration
A club that conforms with the *Rules* when new is deemed to conform after wear through normal use. Any part of a club that has been purposely altered is regarded as new and must, in its altered state, conform with the *Rules*.

4-2. Playing Characteristics Changed and Foreign Material
a. Playing Characteristics Changed
During a *stipulated round*, the playing characteristics of a club must not be purposely changed by adjustment or by any other means.

b. Foreign Material
Foreign material must not be applied to the club face for the purpose of influencing the movement of the ball.

PENALTY FOR BREACH OF RULE 4-1 or 4-2:
Disqualification.

4-3. Damaged Clubs: Repair and Replacement
a. Damage in Normal Course of Play
If, during a *stipulated round*, a player's club is damaged in the normal course of play, he may:
(i) use the club in its damaged state for the remainder of the *stipulated round*; or
(ii) without unduly delaying play, repair it or have it repaired; or

(iii) as an additional option available only if the club is unfit for play, replace the damaged club with any club. The replacement of a club must not unduly delay play and must not be made by borrowing any club selected for play by any other person playing on the *course*.

PENALTY FOR BREACH OF RULE 4-3a:
See Penalty Statement for Rule 4-4a or b, and c.

Note: A club is unfit for play if it is substantially damaged, e.g. the shaft is dented, significantly bent or breaks into pieces; the clubhead becomes loose, detached or significantly deformed; or the grip becomes loose. A club is not unfit for play solely because the club's lie or loft has been altered, or the clubhead is scratched.

b. Damage Other Than in Normal Course of Play
If, during a *stipulated round*, a player's club is damaged other than in the normal course of play rendering it non-conforming or changing its playing characteristics, the club must not subsequently be used or replaced during the round.

c. Damage Prior to Round
A player may use a club damaged prior to a round provided the club, in its damaged state, conforms with the *Rules*.

Damage to a club that occurred prior to a round may be repaired during the round, provided the playing characteristics are not changed and play is not unduly delayed.

PENALTY FOR BREACH OF RULE 4-3b or c:
Disqualification.

(Undue delay – see Rule 6-7)

4-4. Maximum of Fourteen Clubs
a. Selection and Addition of Clubs
The player must not start a *stipulated round* with more than fourteen clubs. He is limited to the clubs thus selected for that round except that, if he started with fewer than fourteen clubs, he may add any number provided his total number does not exceed fourteen.

The addition of a club or clubs must not unduly delay play (Rule 6-7) and the player must not add or borrow any club selected for play by any other person playing on the *course*.

b. Partners May Share Clubs
Partners may share clubs, provided that the total number of clubs carried by the *partners* so sharing does not exceed fourteen.

PENALTY FOR BREACH OF RULE 4-4a or b,
REGARDLESS OF NUMBER OF EXCESS
CLUBS CARRIED:
Match play – At the conclusion of the hole at which the breach is discovered, the state of the match is adjusted by deducting one hole for each hole at which a breach occurred. Maximum deduction per round: Two holes.
Stroke play – Two strokes for each hole at which any breach occurred; maximum penalty per round: Four strokes.

Bogey and par competitions – Penalties as in match play.
Stableford competitions – See Note 1 to Rule 32-1b.

c. Excess Club Declared Out of Play
Any club or clubs carried or used in breach of Rule 4-3a(iii) or Rule 4-4 must be declared out of play by the player to his opponent in match play or his *marker* or a *fellow-competitor* in stroke play immediately upon discovery that a breach has occurred. The player must not use the club or clubs for the remainder of the *stipulated round*.

PENALTY FOR BREACH OF RULE 4-4c:
Disqualification.

Rule 5 – The Ball

Definitions
All defined terms are in *italics* and are listed alphabetically in the Definitions section – see pages 448–451.

5-1. General
The ball the player plays must conform to requirements specified in Appendix III.
Note: The *Committee* may require, in the conditions of a competition (Rule 33-1), that the ball the player plays must be named on the current List of Conforming Golf Balls issued by the *R&A*.

5-2. Foreign Material
Foreign material must not be applied to a ball for the purpose of changing its playing characteristics.

PENALTY FOR BREACH OF RULE 5-1 or 5-2:
Disqualification.

5-3. Ball Unfit for Play
A ball is unfit for play if it is visibly cut, cracked or out of shape. A ball is not unfit for play solely because mud or other materials adhere to it, its surface is scratched or scraped or its paint is damaged or discoloured.

If a player has reason to believe his ball has become unfit for play during play of the hole being played, he may lift the ball without penalty to determine whether it is unfit.

Before lifting the ball, the player must announce his intention to his opponent in match play or his *marker* or a *fellow-competitor* in stroke play and mark the position of the ball. He may then lift and examine it provided that he gives his opponent, *marker* or *fellow-competitor* an opportunity to examine the ball and observe the lifting and replacement. The ball must not be cleaned when lifted under Rule 5-3. If the player fails to comply with all or any part of this procedure, he incurs a penalty of one stroke.

If it is determined that the ball has become unfit for play during play of the hole being played, the player may *substitute* another ball, placing it on the spot where the original ball lay. Otherwise, the original ball must be replaced. If a player *substitutes* a ball when not permitted and he makes a *stroke* at the

wrongly *substituted* ball, he incurs the general penalty for a breach of Rule 5-3, but there is no additional penalty under this Rule or Rule 15-1.

If a ball breaks into pieces as a result of a *stroke*, the *stroke* is cancelled and the player must play a ball without penalty as nearly as possible at the spot from which the original ball was played (see Rule 20-5).

*PENALTY FOR BREACH OF RULE 5-3:
Match play – Loss of hole; Stroke play – Two strokes.

*If a player incurs the general penalty for a breach of Rule 5-3, there is no additional penalty under this Rule.

Note: If the opponent, *marker* or *fellow-competitor* wishes to dispute a claim of unfitness, he must do so before the player plays another ball.

(Cleaning ball lifted from putting green or under any other Rule – see Rule 21)

PLAYER'S RESPONSIBILITIES

Rule 6 – The Player

Definitions
All defined terms are in *italics* and are listed alphabetically in the Definitions section – see pages 448–451.

6-1. Rules
The player and his *caddie* are responsible for knowing the *Rules*. During a *stipulated round*, for any breach of a *Rule* by his *caddie*, the player incurs the applicable penalty.

6-2. Handicap
a. Match Play
Before starting a match in a handicap competition, the players should determine from one another their respective handicaps. If a player begins a match having declared a handicap higher than that to which he is entitled and this affects the number of strokes given or received, he is disqualified; otherwise, the player must play off the declared handicap.

b. Stroke Play
In any round of a handicap competition, the *competitor* must ensure that his handicap is recorded on his score card before it is returned to the *Committee*. If no handicap is recorded on his score card before it is returned (Rule 6-6b), or if the recorded handicap is higher than that to which he is entitled and this affects the number of strokes received, he is disqualified from the handicap competition; otherwise, the score stands.

Note: It is the player's responsibility to know the holes at which handicap strokes are to be given or received.

6-3. Time of Starting and Groups
a. Time of Starting
The player must start at the time established by the *Committee*.

b. Groups
In stroke play, the *competitor* must remain throughout the round in the group arranged by the *Committee* unless the *Committee* authorises or ratifies a change.

PENALTY FOR BREACH OF RULE 6-3:
Disqualification.

(Best-ball and four-ball play – see Rules 30-3a and 31-2)

Note: The *Committee* may provide in the conditions of a competition (Rule 33-1) that, if the player arrives at his starting point, ready to play, within five minutes after his starting time, in the absence of circumstances that warrant waiving the penalty of disqualification as provided in Rule 33-7, the penalty for failure to start on time is loss of the first hole in match play or two strokes at the first hole in stroke play instead of disqualification.

6-4. Caddie
The player may be assisted by a *caddie*, but he is limited to only one *caddie* at any one time.

PENALTY FOR BREACH OF RULE 6-4:
Match play – At the conclusion of the hole at which the breach is discovered, the state of the match is adjusted by deducting one hole for each hole at which a breach occurred; maximum deduction per round – Two holes.
Stroke play – Two strokes for each hole at which any breach occurred; maximum penalty per round – Four strokes.
Match or stroke play – In the event of a breach between the play of two holes, the penalty applies to the next hole.

A player having more than one *caddie* in breach of this Rule must immediately upon discovery that a breach has occurred ensure that he has no more than one *caddie* at any one time during the remainder of the *stipulated round*. Otherwise, the player is disqualified.
Bogey and par competitions – Penalties as in match play.
Stableford competitions – See Note 2 to Rule 32-1b.

Note: The *Committee* may, in the conditions of a competition (Rule 33-1), prohibit the use of *caddies* or restrict a player in his choice of *caddie*.

6-5. Ball
The responsibility for playing the proper ball rests with the player. Each player should put an identification mark on his ball.

6-6. Scoring in Stroke Play
a. Recording Scores
After each hole the *marker* should check the score with the *competitor* and record it. On completion of the round the *marker* must sign the score card and hand it to the *competitor*. If more than one *marker* records the scores, each must sign for the part for which he is responsible.

b. Signing and Returning Score Card
After completion of the round, the *competitor* should check his score for each hole and settle any doubtful points with the *Committee*. He must ensure that the *marker* or *markers* have signed the score card, sign the score card himself and return it to the *Committee* as soon as possible.

PENALTY FOR BREACH OF RULE 6-6b:
Disqualification.

c. Alteration of Score Card
No alteration may be made on a score card after the *competitor* has returned it to the *Committee*.

d. Wrong Score for Hole
The *competitor* is responsible for the correctness of the score recorded for each hole on his score card. If he returns a score for any hole lower than actually taken, he is disqualified. If he returns a score for any hole higher than actually taken, the score as returned stands.

Note 1: The *Committee* is responsible for the addition of scores and application of the handicap recorded on the score card – see Rule 33-5.

Note 2: In *four-ball* stroke play, see also Rule 31-4 and -7a.

6-7. Undue Delay; Slow Play
The player must play without undue delay and in accordance with any pace of play guidelines that the *Committee* may establish. Between completion of a hole and playing from the next *teeing ground*, the player must not unduly delay play.

PENALTY FOR BREACH OF RULE 6-7:
Match play – Loss of hole; Stroke play – Two strokes.
Bogey and par competitions – See Note 3 to Rule 32-1a.
Stableford competitions – See Note 3 to Rule 32-1b.
For subsequent offence – Disqualification.

Note 1: If the player unduly delays play between holes, he is delaying the play of the next hole and, except for bogey, par and Stableford competitions (see Rule 32), the penalty applies to that hole.

Note 2: For the purpose of preventing slow play, the *Committee* may, in the conditions of a competition (Rule 33-1), establish pace of play guidelines including maximum periods of time allowed to complete a *stipulated round*, a hole or a *stroke*.

In stroke play only, the *Committee* may, in such a condition, modify the penalty for a breach of this Rule as follows:

First offence – One stroke;
Second offence – Two strokes.
For subsequent offence – Disqualification.

6-8. Discontinuance of Play; Resumption of Play
a. When Permitted
The player must not discontinue play unless:
(i) the *Committee* has suspended play;
(ii) he believes there is danger from lightning;

(iii) he is seeking a decision from the *Committee* on a doubtful or disputed point (see Rules 2-5 and 34-3); or
(iv) there is some other good reason such as sudden illness.

Bad weather is not of itself a good reason for discontinuing play.

If the player discontinues play without specific permission from the *Committee*, he must report to the *Committee* as soon as practicable. If he does so and the *Committee* considers his reason satisfactory, there is no penalty. Otherwise, the player is disqualified.

Exception in match play: Players discontinuing match play by agreement are not subject to disqualification unless by so doing the competition is delayed.

Note: Leaving the *course* does not of itself constitute discontinuance of play.

b. Procedure When Play Suspended by Committee
When play is suspended by the *Committee*, if the players in a match or group are between the play of two holes, they must not resume play until the *Committee* has ordered a resumption of play. If they have started play of a hole, they may discontinue play immediately or continue play of the hole, provided they do so without delay. If the players choose to continue play of the hole, they are permitted to discontinue play before completing it. In any case, play must be discontinued after the hole is completed.

The players must resume play when the *Committee* has ordered a resumption of play.

PENALTY FOR BREACH OF RULE 6-8b:
Disqualification.

Note: The *Committee* may provide in the conditions of a competition (Rule 33-1) that, in potentially dangerous situations, play must be discontinued immediately following a suspension of play by the *Committee*. If a player fails to discontinue play immediately, he is disqualified unless circumstances warrant waiving the penalty as provided in Rule 33-7.

c. Lifting Ball When Play Discontinued
When a player discontinues play of a hole under Rule 6-8a, he may lift his ball without penalty only if the *Committee* has suspended play or there is a good reason to lift it. Before lifting the ball the player must mark its position. If the player discontinues play and lifts his ball without specific permission from the *Committee*, he must, when reporting to the *Committee* (Rule 6-8a), report the lifting of the ball.

If the player lifts the ball without a good reason to do so, fails to mark the position of the ball before lifting it or fails to report the lifting of the ball, he incurs a penalty of one stroke.

d. Procedure When Play Resumed
Play must be resumed from where it was discontinued, even if resumption occurs on a subsequent day.

The player must, either before or when play is resumed, proceed as follows:

(i) if the player has lifted the ball, he must, provided he was entitled to lift it under Rule 6-8c, place a ball on the spot from which the original ball was lifted. Otherwise, the original ball must be placed on the spot from which it was lifted;

(ii) if the player entitled to lift his ball under Rule 6-8c has not done so, he may lift, clean and replace the ball, or *substitute* a ball on the spot from which the original ball was lifted. Before lifting the ball he must mark its position; or

(iii) if the player's ball or ball-marker is moved (including by wind or water) while play is discontinued, a ball or ball-marker must be placed on the spot from which the original ball or ball-marker was moved.

Note: If the spot where the ball is to be placed is impossible to determine, it must be estimated and the ball placed on the estimated spot. The provisions of Rule 20-3c do not apply.

*PENALTY FOR BREACH OF RULE 6-8c or d:
     Match play – Loss of hole; Stroke play –
          Two strokes.
*If a player incurs the general penalty for a breach
     of Rule
6-8d, there is no additional penalty under
          Rule 6-8c.

Rule 7 – Practice

Definitions
All defined terms are in *italics* and are listed alphabetically in the Definitions section – see pages 448–451.

7-1. Before or Between Rounds
a. Match Play
On any day of a match play competition, a player may practise on the competition *course* before a round.

b. Stroke Play
Before a round or play-off on any day of a stroke play competition, a *competitor* must not practise on the competition *course* or test the surface of any *putting green* on the *course* by rolling a ball or roughening or scraping the surface.

When two or more rounds of a stroke play competition are to be played over consecutive days, a *competitor* must not practise between those rounds on any competition *course* remaining to be played, or test the surface of any *putting green* on such *course* by rolling a ball or roughening or scraping the surface.

Exception: Practice putting or chipping on or near the first *teeing ground* before starting a round or play-off is permitted.

PENALTY FOR BREACH OF RULE 7-1b:
     Disqualification.

Note: The *Committee* may, in the conditions of a competition (Rule 33-1), prohibit practice on the competition *course* on any day of a match play competition or permit practice on the competition *course* or part of the *course* (Rule 33-2c) on any day of or between rounds of a stroke play competition.

7-2. During Round
A player must not make a practice *stroke* during play of a hole.

Between the play of two holes a player must not make a practice *stroke*, except that he may practise putting or chipping on or near:

(a) the *putting green* of the hole last played,

(b) any practice *putting green*, or

(c) the *teeing ground* of the next hole to be played in the round, provided a practice *stroke* is not made from a *hazard* and does not unduly delay play (Rule 6-7).

Strokes made in continuing the play of a hole, the result of which has been decided, are not practice *strokes*.

Exception: When play has been suspended by the *Committee*, a player may, prior to resumption of play, practise (a) as provided in this Rule, (b) anywhere other than on the competition *course* and (c) as otherwise permitted by the *Committee*.

PENALTY FOR BREACH OF RULE 7-2:
     Match play – Loss of hole; Stroke play –
          Two strokes.

In the event of a breach between the play of two holes, the penalty applies to the next hole.

Note 1: A practice swing is not a practice *stroke* and may be taken at any place, provided the player does not breach the *Rules*.

Note 2: The *Committee* may, in the conditions of a competition (Rule 33-1), prohibit:

(a) practice on or near the *putting green* of the hole last played, and

(b) rolling a ball on the *putting green* of the hole last played.

Rule 8 – Advice: Indicating Line of Play

Definitions
All defined terms are in *italics* and are listed alphabetically in the Definitions section – see pages 448–451.

8-1. Advice
During a *stipulated round*, a player must not:

(a) give *advice* to anyone in the competition playing on the *course* other than his *partner*, or

(b) ask for *advice* from anyone other than his *partner* or either of their *caddies*.

8-2. Indicating Line of Play
a. Other Than on Putting Green
Except on the *putting green*, a player may have the *line of play* indicated to him by anyone, but no one may be positioned by the player on or close to the line or an extension of the line beyond the *hole* while the *stroke* is being made. Any mark placed by the player or with his knowledge to indicate the line must be removed before the *stroke* is made.

Exception: *Flagstick* attended or held up – see Rule 17-1.

b. On the Putting Green
When the player's ball is on the *putting green*, the player, his *partner* or either of their *caddies* may, before but not during the *stroke*, point out a line for putting, but in so doing the *putting green* must not be touched. A mark must not be placed anywhere to indicate a line for putting.

PENALTY FOR BREACH OF RULE:
Match play – Loss of hole; Stroke play – Two strokes.

Note: The *Committee* may, in the conditions of a team competition (Rule 33-1), permit each team to appoint one person who may give *advice* (including pointing out a line for putting) to members of that team. The *Committee* may establish conditions relating to the appointment and permitted conduct of that person, who must be identified to the *Committee* before giving *advice*.

Rule 9 – Information as to Strokes Taken

Definitions
All defined terms are in *italics* and are listed alphabetically in the Definitions section – see pages 448–451.

9-1. General
The number of *strokes* a player has taken includes any *penalty strokes* incurred.

9-2. Match Play
a. Information as to Strokes Taken
An opponent is entitled to ascertain from the player, during the play of a hole, the number of *strokes* he has taken and, after play of a hole, the number of *strokes* taken on the hole just completed.

b. Wrong Information
A player must not give wrong information to his opponent. If a player gives wrong information, he loses the hole.

A player is deemed to have given wrong information if he:

(i) fails to inform his opponent as soon as practicable that he has incurred a penalty, unless (a) he was obviously proceeding under a *Rule* involving a penalty and this was observed by his opponent, or (b) he corrects the mistake before his opponent makes his next *stroke*; or

(ii) gives incorrect information during play of a hole regarding the number of *strokes* taken and does not correct the mistake before his opponent makes his next *stroke*; or

(iii) gives incorrect information regarding the number of *strokes* taken to complete a hole and this affects the opponent's understanding of the result of the hole, unless he corrects the mistake before any player makes a *stroke* from the next *teeing ground* or, in the case of the last hole of the match, before all players leave the *putting green*.

A player has given wrong information even if it is due to the failure to include a penalty that he did not know he had incurred. It is the player's responsibility to know the *Rules*.

9-3. Stroke Play
A *competitor* who has incurred a penalty should inform his *marker* as soon as practicable.

ORDER OF PLAY

Rule 10 – Order of Play

Definitions
All defined terms are in *italics* and are listed alphabetically in the Definitions section – see pages 448–451.

10-1. Match Play
a. When Starting Play of Hole
The *side* that has the *honour* at the first *teeing ground* is determined by the order of the draw. In the absence of a draw, the *honour* should be decided by lot.

The *side* that wins a hole takes the *honour* at the next *teeing ground*. If a hole has been halved, the *side* that had the *honour* at the previous *teeing ground* retains it.

b. During Play of Hole
After both players have started play of the hole, the ball farther from the *hole* is played first. If the balls are equidistant from the *hole* or their positions relative to the *hole* are not determinable, the ball to be played first should be decided by lot.

Exception: Rule 30-3c (*best-ball* and *four-ball* match play).

Note: When the original ball is not to be played as it lies and the player is required to play a ball as nearly as possible at the spot from which the original ball was last played (see Rule 20-5), the order of play is determined by the spot from which the previous *stroke* was made. When a ball may be played from a spot other than where the previous *stroke* was made, the order of play is determined by the position where the original ball came to rest.

c. Playing Out of Turn
If a player plays when his opponent should have played, there is no penalty, but the opponent may immediately require the player to cancel the *stroke* so made and, in correct order, play a ball as nearly as possible at the spot from which the original ball was last played (see Rule 20-5).

10-2. Stroke Play
a. When Starting Play of Hole
The *competitor* who has the *honour* at the first *teeing ground* is determined by the order of the draw. In the absence of a draw, the *honour* should be decided by lot.

The *competitor* with the lowest score at a hole takes the *honour* at the next *teeing ground*. The *competitor* with the second lowest score plays next and so on. If two or more *competitors* have the same score at

a hole, they play from the next *teeing ground* in the same order as at the previous *teeing ground*.

b. During Play of Hole
After the *competitors* have started play of the hole, the ball farthest from the *hole* is played first. If two or more balls are equidistant from the *hole* or their positions relative to the *hole* are not determinable, the ball to be played first should be decided by lot.

Exceptions: Rules 22 (ball assisting or interfering with play) and 31-5 (*four-ball* stroke play).

Note: When the original ball is not to be played as it lies and the player is required to play a ball as nearly as possible at the spot from which the original ball was last played (see Rule 20-5), the order of play is determined from which the previous *stroke* was made. When a ball may be played from a spot other than where the previous *stroke* was made, the order of play is determined by the position where the original ball came to rest.

c. Playing Out of Turn
If a *competitor* plays out of turn, there is no penalty and the ball is played as it lies. If, however, the *Committee* determines that *competitors* have agreed to play out of turn to give one of them an advantage, they are disqualified.

(Making stroke while another ball in motion after stroke from putting green – see Rule 16-1f)

(Incorrect order of play in threesomes and foursomes stroke play – see Rule 29-3)

10-3. Provisional Ball or Second Ball from Teeing Ground
If a player plays a *provisional ball* or a second ball from a *teeing ground*, he must do so after his opponent or *fellow-competitor* has played his first *stroke*. If a player plays a *provisional ball* or a second ball out of turn, Rule 10-1c or -2c applies.

TEEING GROUND

Rule 11 – Teeing Ground

Definitions
All defined terms are in *italics* and are listed alphabetically in the Definitions section – see pages 448–451.

11-1. Teeing
When the player's ball is to be teed within the *teeing ground*, it must be placed on:

- the surface of the *teeing ground*, including an irregularity of surface (whether or not created by the player), or
- a *tee* placed in or on the surface of the *teeing ground*, or
- sand or other natural substance placed on the surface of the *teeing ground*.

A player may stand outside the *teeing ground* to play a ball within it.

In teeing, if a player uses a non-conforming *tee* or any other object to raise the ball off the ground, he is disqualified.

11-2. Tee-Markers
Before a player makes his first *stroke* with any ball on the *teeing ground* of the hole being played, the tee-markers are deemed to be fixed. In these circumstances, if the player moves or allows to be moved a tee-marker for the purpose of avoiding interference with his *stance*, the area of his intended swing or his *line of play*, he incurs the penalty for a breach of Rule 13-2.

11-3. Ball Falling off Tee
If a ball, when not *in play*, falls off a *tee* or is knocked off a *tee* by the player in *addressing* it, it may be re-teed without penalty. However, if a *stroke* is made at the ball in these circumstances, whether the ball is moving or not, the *stroke* counts but there is no penalty.

11-4. Playing from Outside Teeing Ground
a. Match Play
If a player, when starting a hole, plays a ball from outside the *teeing ground* there is no penalty, but the opponent may immediately require the player to cancel the *stroke* and play a ball from within the *teeing ground*.

b. Stroke Play
If a *competitor*, when starting a hole, plays a ball from outside the *teeing ground*, he incurs a penalty of two strokes and must then play a ball from within the *teeing ground*.

If the *competitor* plays a *stroke* from the next *teeing ground* without first correcting his mistake or, in the case of the last hole of the round, leaves the *putting green* without first declaring his intention to correct his mistake, he is disqualified.

The *stroke* from outside the *teeing ground* and any subsequent *strokes* by the *competitor* on the hole prior to his correction of the mistake do not count in his score.

11-5. Playing from Wrong Teeing Ground
The provisions of Rule 11-4 apply.

PLAYING THE BALL

Rule 12 – Searching For and Identifying Ball

Definitions
All defined terms are in *italics* and are listed alphabetically in the Definitions section – see pages 448–451.

12-1. Searching for Ball; Seeing Ball
In searching for his ball anywhere on the *course*, the player may touch or bend long grass, rushes, bushes, whins, heather or the like, but only to the extent necessary to find and identify it, provided that this does not improve the lie of the ball, the area of his intended *stance* or swing or his *line of play*.

A player is not necessarily entitled to see his ball when making a *stroke*.

In a *hazard*, if a ball is believed to be covered by *loose impediments* or sand, the player may remove by probing or raking with a club or otherwise, as many *loose impediments* or as much sand as will enable him to see a part of the ball. If an excess is removed, there is no penalty and the ball must be re-covered so that only a part of it is visible. If the ball is *moved* during the removal, there is no penalty; the ball must be replaced and, if necessary, re-covered. As to removal of *loose impediments* outside a *hazard*, see Rule 23.

If a ball lying in an *abnormal ground condition* is accidentally *moved* during search, there is no penalty; the ball must be replaced, unless the player elects to proceed under Rule 25-1b. If the player replaces the ball, he may still proceed under Rule 25-1b if applicable.

If a ball is believed to be lying in water in a *water hazard*, the player may probe for it with a club or otherwise. If the ball is *moved* in probing, it must be replaced, unless the player elects to proceed under Rule 26-1. There is no penalty for causing the ball to *move* provided the movement of the ball was directly attributable to the specific act of probing. Otherwise, the player incurs a *penalty stroke* under Rule 18-2a.

PENALTY FOR BREACH OF RULE 12-1:
Match play – Loss of hole; Stroke play –
Two strokes.

12-2. Identifying Ball
The responsibility for playing the proper ball rests with the player. Each player should put an identification mark on his ball.

Except in a *hazard*, if a player has reason to believe a ball is his, he may lift the ball without penalty to identify it.

Before lifting the ball, the player must announce his intention to his opponent in match play or his *marker* or a *fellow-competitor* in stroke play and mark the position of the ball. He may then lift the ball and identify it provided that he gives his opponent, *marker* or *fellow-competitor* an opportunity to observe the lifting and replacement. The ball must not be cleaned beyond the extent necessary for identification when lifted under Rule 12-2. If the player fails to comply with all or any part of this procedure, or if he lifts his ball for identification in a *hazard*, he incurs a penalty of one stroke.

If the lifted ball is the player's ball he must replace it. If he fails to do so, he incurs the general penalty for a breach of Rule 12-2, but there is no additional penalty under this Rule.

*PENALTY FOR BREACH OF RULE 12-2:
Match play – Loss of hole; Stroke play –
Two strokes.
*If a player incurs the general penalty for a breach of Rule 12-2, there is no additional penalty under this Rule.

Rule 13 – Play Ball as it Lies

Definitions
All defined terms are in *italics* and are listed alphabetically in the Definitions section – see pages 448–451.

13-1. General
The ball must be played as it lies, except as otherwise provided in the *Rules*.
(Ball at rest moved – see Rule 18)

13-2. Improving Lie, Area of Intended Stance or Swing, or Line of Play
A player must not improve or allow to be improved:

- the position or lie of his ball,
- the area of his intended *stance* or swing,
- his *line of play* or a reasonable extension of that line beyond the *hole*, or
- the area in which he is to drop or place a ball,

by any of the following actions:

- moving, bending or breaking anything growing or fixed (including immovable *obstructions* and objects defining *out of bounds*),
- creating or eliminating irregularities of surface,
- removing or pressing down sand, loose soil, replaced divots or other cut turf placed in position, or
- removing dew, frost or water.

However, the player incurs no penalty if the action occurs:

- in fairly taking his *stance*,
- in making a *stroke* or the backward movement of his club for a *stroke* and the *stroke* is made,
- on the *teeing ground* in creating or eliminating irregularities of surface (Rule 11-1), or
- on the *putting green* in removing sand and loose soil or in repairing damage (Rule 16-1).

The club may be grounded only lightly and must not be pressed on the ground.
Exception: Ball in *hazard* – see Rule 13-4.

13-3. Building Stance
A player is entitled to place his feet firmly in taking his *stance*, but he must not build a *stance*.

13-4. Ball in Hazard; Prohibited Actions
Except as provided in the *Rules*, before making a *stroke* at a ball that is in a *hazard* (whether a *bunker* or a *water hazard*) or that, having been lifted from a *hazard*, may be dropped or placed in the *hazard*, the player must not:

a. Test the condition of the *hazard* or any similar *hazard*;

b. Touch the ground in the *hazard* or water in the *water hazard* with his hand or a club; or

c. Touch or move a *loose impediment* lying in or touching the *hazard*.

Exceptions:
1. Provided nothing is done that constitutes testing the condition of the *hazard* or improves the lie of the ball, there is no penalty if the player (a) touches the ground in any *hazard* or water in a *water hazard* as a

result of or to prevent falling, in removing an *obstruction*, in measuring or in retrieving, lifting, placing or replacing a ball under any *Rule* or (b) places his clubs in a *hazard*.

2. After making the *stroke*, the player or his *caddie* may smooth sand or soil in the *hazard*, provided that, if the ball is still in the *hazard* or has been lifted from the *hazard* and may be dropped or placed in the *hazard*, nothing is done that improves the lie of the ball or assists the player in his subsequent play of the hole.

Note: At any time, including at *address* or in the backward movement for the *stroke*, the player may touch with a club or otherwise any *obstruction*, any construction declared by the *Committee* to be an integral part of the *course* or any grass, bush, tree or other growing thing.

PENALTY FOR BREACH OF RULE:
Match play – Loss of hole; Stroke play – Two strokes.

(Searching for ball – see Rule 12-1)
(Relief for ball in water hazard – see Rule 26)

Rule 14 – Striking the Ball

Definitions
All defined terms are in *italics* and are listed alphabetically in the Definitions section – see pages 448–451.

14-1. Ball to be Fairly Struck At
The ball must be fairly struck at with the head of the club and must not be pushed, scraped or spooned.

14-2. Assistance
In making a *stroke*, a player must not:
a. accept physical assistance or protection from the elements; or
b. allow his *caddie*, his *partner* or his *partner's caddie* to position himself on or close to an extension of the *line of play* or the *line of putt* behind the ball.

PENALTY FOR BREACH OF RULE 14-1 or 14-2:
Match play – Loss of hole; Stroke play – Two strokes.

14-3. Artificial Devices and Unusual Equipment
The *R&A* reserves the right, at any time, to change the Rules relating to artificial devices and unusual equipment and make or change the interpretations relating to these Rules.

A player in doubt as to whether use of an item would constitute a breach of Rule 14-3 should consult the *R&A*.

A manufacturer may submit to the *R&A* a sample of an item to be manufactured for a ruling as to whether its use during a *stipulated round* would cause a player to be in breach of Rule 14-3. The sample becomes the property of the *R&A* for reference purposes. If a manufacturer fails to submit a sample before manufacturing and/or marketing the item, the manufacturer assumes the risk of a ruling that use of the item would be contrary to the *Rules*.

Except as provided in the *Rules*, during a *stipulated round* the player must not use any artificial device or unusual equipment:

a. That might assist him in making a *stroke* or in his play; or

b. For the purpose of gauging or measuring distance or conditions that might affect his play; or

c. That might assist him in gripping the club, except that:

(i) plain gloves may be worn;
(ii) resin, powder and drying or moisturising agents may be used; and
(iii) a towel or handkerchief may be wrapped around the grip.

PENALTY FOR BREACH OF RULE 14-3:
Disqualification.

14-4. Striking the Ball More than Once
If a player's club strikes the ball more than once in the course of a *stroke*, the player must count the *stroke* and add a *penalty stroke*, making two *strokes* in all.

14-5. Playing Moving Ball
A player must not make a *stroke* at his ball while it is moving.

Exceptions:
• Ball falling off *tee* – Rule 11-3
• Striking the ball more than once – Rule 14-4
• Ball moving in water – Rule 14-6

When the ball begins to *move* only after the player has begun the *stroke* or the backward movement of his club for the *stroke*, he incurs no penalty under this Rule for playing a moving ball, but he is not exempt from any penalty under the following *Rules*:
• Ball at rest *moved* by player – Rule 18-2a
• Ball at rest moving after *address* – Rule 18-2b

(Ball purposely deflected or stopped by player, partner or caddie – see Rule 1-2)

14-6. Ball Moving in Water
When a ball is moving in water in a *water hazard*, the player may, without penalty, make a *stroke*, but he must not delay making his *stroke* in order to allow the wind or current to improve the position of the ball. A ball moving in water in a *water hazard* may be lifted if the player elects to invoke Rule 26.

PENALTY FOR BREACH OF RULE 14-5
or 14-6:
Match play – Loss of hole; Stroke play – Two strokes.

Rule 15 – Substituted Ball; Wrong Ball

Definitions
All defined terms are in *italics* and are listed alphabetically in the Definitions section – see pages 448–451.

15-1. General

A player must hole out with the ball played from the *teeing ground* unless the ball is *lost, out of bounds* or the player *substitutes* another ball, whether or not substitution is permitted (see Rule 15-2). If a player plays a *wrong ball*, see Rule 15-3.

15-2. Substituted Ball

A player may *substitute* a ball when proceeding under a *Rule* that permits the player to play, drop or place another ball in completing the play of a hole. The *substituted ball* becomes the *ball in play*.

If a player *substitutes* a ball when not permitted to do so under the *Rules*, that *substituted ball* is not a *wrong ball*; it becomes the *ball in play*. If the mistake is not corrected as provided in Rule 20-6 and the player makes a *stroke* at a wrongly *substituted ball*, he incurs the penalty prescribed by the applicable Rule and, in stroke play, must play out the hole with the *substituted ball*.

(Playing from Wrong Place – see Rule 20-7)

15-3. Wrong Ball

a. Match Play

If a player makes a *stroke* at a *wrong ball* that is not in a *hazard*, he loses the hole.

There is no penalty if a player makes a *stroke* at a *wrong ball* in a *hazard*. Any *strokes* made at a *wrong ball* in a *hazard* do not count in the player's score.

If the *wrong ball* belongs to another player, its owner must place a ball on the spot from which the *wrong ball* was first played.

If the player and opponent exchange balls during the play of a hole, the first to make a *stroke* at a *wrong ball* that is not in a *hazard*, loses the hole; when this cannot be determined, the hole must be played out with the balls exchanged.

b. Stroke Play

If a *competitor* makes a *stroke* or *strokes* at a *wrong ball* that is not in a *hazard*, he incurs a penalty of two strokes.

There is no penalty if a *competitor* makes a *stroke* at a *wrong ball* in a *hazard*. Any *strokes* made at a *wrong ball* in a *hazard* do not count in the *competitor's* score.

The *competitor* must correct his mistake by playing the correct ball or by proceeding under the *Rules*. If he fails to correct his mistake before making a *stroke* on the next *teeing ground* or, in the case of the last hole of the round, fails to declare his intention to correct his mistake before leaving the *putting green*, he is disqualified.

Strokes made by a *competitor* with a *wrong ball* do not count in his score.

If the *wrong ball* belongs to another *competitor*, its owner must place a ball on the spot from which the *wrong ball* was first played.

(Lie of ball to be placed or replaced altered – see Rule 20-3b)

(Spot not determinable – see Rule 20-3c)

THE PUTTING GREEN

Rule 16 – The Putting Green

Definitions

All defined terms are in *italics* and are listed alphabetically in the Definitions section – see pages 448–451.

16-1. General

a. Touching Line of Putt

The *line of putt* must not be touched except:

(i) the player may remove *loose impediments*, provided he does not press anything down;

(ii) the player may place the club in front of the ball when *addressing* it, provided he does not press anything down;

(iii) in measuring – Rule 18-6;

(iv) in lifting the ball – Rule 16-1b;

(v) in pressing down a ball-marker;

(vi) in repairing old *hole* plugs or ball marks on the *putting green* – Rule 16-1c; and

(vii) in removing movable *obstructions* – Rule 24-1

(Indicating line for putting on putting green – see Rule 8-2b)

b. Lifting and Cleaning Ball

A ball on the *putting green* may be lifted and, if desired, cleaned. The position of the ball must be marked before it is lifted and the ball must be replaced (see Rule 20-1).

c. Repair of Hole Plugs, Ball Marks and Other Damage

The player may repair an old *hole* plug or damage to the *putting green* caused by the impact of a ball, whether or not the player's ball lies on the *putting green*. If a ball or ball-marker is accidentally *moved* in the process of the repair, the ball or ball-marker must be replaced. There is no penalty provided the movement of the ball is directly attributable to the specific act of repairing an old *hole* plug or damage to the *putting green* caused by the impact of a ball. Otherwise, the player incurs a *penalty stroke* under Rule 18-2a.

Any other damage to the *putting green* must not be repaired if it might assist the player in his subsequent play of the hole.

d. Testing Surface

During the play of a hole, a player must not test the surface of the *putting green* by rolling a ball or roughening or scraping the surface.

e. Standing Astride or on Line of Putt

The player must not make a *stroke* on the *putting green* from a *stance* astride, or with either foot touching, the *line of putt* or an extension of that line behind the ball.

f. Making Stroke While Another Ball in Motion

The player must not make a *stroke* while another ball is in motion after a *stroke* from the *putting green*, except that, if a player does so, there is no penalty if it was his turn to play.

(Lifting ball assisting or interfering with play while another ball in motion – see Rule 22)

PENALTY FOR BREACH OF RULE 16-1:
Match play – Loss of hole; Stroke play – Two strokes.

(Position of caddie or partner – see Rule 14-2)
(Wrong putting green – see Rule 25-3)

16-2. Ball Overhanging Hole
When any part of the ball overhangs the lip of the *hole*, the player is allowed enough time to reach the *hole* without unreasonable delay and an additional ten seconds to determine whether the ball is at rest. If by then the ball has not fallen into the *hole*, it is deemed to be at rest. If the ball subsequently falls into the *hole*, the player is deemed to have *holed* out with his last *stroke*, and must add a *penalty stroke* to his score for the hole; otherwise, there is no penalty under this Rule.

(Undue delay – see Rule 6-7)

Rule 17 – The Flagstick

Definitions
All defined terms are in *italics* and are listed alphabetically in the Definitions section – see pages 448–451.

17-1. Flagstick Attended, Removed or Held Up
Before making a *stroke* from anywhere on the *course*, the player may have the *flagstick* attended, removed or held up to indicate the position of the *hole*.

If the *flagstick* is not attended, removed or held up before the player makes a *stroke*, it must not be attended, removed or held up during the *stroke* or while the player's ball is in motion if doing so might influence the movement of the ball.

Note 1: If the *flagstick* is in the *hole* and anyone stands near it while a *stroke* is being made, he is deemed to be attending the *flagstick*.

Note 2: If, prior to the *stroke*, the *flagstick* is attended, removed or held up by anyone with the player's knowledge and he makes no objection, the player is deemed to have authorised it.

Note 3: If anyone attends or holds up the *flagstick* while a *stroke* is being made, he is deemed to be attending the *flagstick* until the ball comes to rest.

17-2. Unauthorised Attendance
If an opponent or his *caddie* in match play or a *fellow-competitor* or his *caddie* in stroke play, without the player's authority or prior knowledge, attends, removes or holds up the *flagstick* during the *stroke* or while the ball is in motion, and the act might influence the movement of the ball, the opponent or *fellow-competitor* incurs the applicable penalty.

*PENALTY FOR BREACH OF RULE 17-1 or 17-2:
Match play – Loss of hole; Stroke play – Two strokes.

*In stroke play, if a breach of Rule 17-2 occurs and the *competitor's* ball subsequently strikes the *flagstick*, the person attending or holding it or anything carried by him, the *competitor* incurs no penalty. The ball is played as it lies except that, if the *stroke* was made on the *putting green*, the *stroke* is cancelled and the ball must be replaced and replayed.

17-3. Ball Striking Flagstick or Attendant
The player's ball must not strike:
a. The *flagstick* when it is being attended, removed or held up;
b. The person attending or holding up the *flagstick*; or
c. The *flagstick* in the *hole*, unattended, when the *stroke* has been made on the *putting green*.

Exception: When the *flagstick* is attended, removed or held up without the player's authority – see Rule 17-2.

PENALTY FOR BREACH OF RULE 17-3:
Match play – Loss of hole; Stroke play – Two strokes and the ball must be played as it lies.

17-4. Ball Resting Against Flagstick
When the *flagstick* is in the *hole* and a player's ball when not *holed* rests against it, the player or another person authorised by him may move or remove the *flagstick* and if the ball falls into the *hole*, the player is deemed to have *holed* out with his last *stroke*; otherwise, the ball, if *moved*, must be placed on the lip of the *hole*, without penalty.

BALL MOVED, DEFLECTED OR STOPPED

Rule 18 – Ball at Rest Moved

Definitions
All defined terms are in *italics* and are listed alphabetically in the Definitions section – see pages 448–451.

18-1. By Outside Agency
If a ball at rest is *moved* by an *outside agency*, there is no penalty and the ball must be replaced.

(Player's ball at rest moved by another ball – see Rule 18-5)

18-2. By Player, Partner, Caddie or Equipment
a. General
When a player's ball is *in play*, if:
(i) the player, his *partner* or either of their *caddies* lifts or *moves* it, touches it purposely (except with a club in the act of *addressing* it) or causes it to *move* except as permitted by a *Rule*, or
(ii) *equipment* of the player or his *partner* causes the ball to *move*,
the player incurs a penalty of one stroke. If the ball is *moved*, it must be replaced unless the movement of the ball occurs after the player has begun the *stroke*

or the backward movement of the club for the *stroke* and the *stroke* is made.

Under the *Rules* there is no penalty if a player accidentally causes his ball to *move* in the following circumstances:

- In searching for a ball in a *hazard* covered by *loose impediments* or sand, for a ball in an *abnormal ground condition* or for a ball believed to be in water in a *water hazard* – Rule 12-1
- In repairing a *hole* plug or ball mark – Rule 16-1c
- In measuring – Rule 18-6
- In lifting a ball under a *Rule* – Rule 20-1
- In placing or replacing a ball under a *Rule* – Rule 20-3a
- In removing a *loose impediment* on the *putting green* – Rule 23-1
- In removing movable *obstructions* – Rule 24-1

b. Ball Moving After Address
If a player's *ball in play moves* after he has *addressed* it (other than as a result of a *stroke*), the player is deemed to have *moved* the ball and incurs a penalty of one stroke. The ball must be replaced unless the movement of the ball occurs after the player has begun the *stroke* or the backward movement of the club for the *stroke* and the *stroke* is made.

18-3. By Opponent, Caddie or Equipment in Match Play
a. During Search
If, during search for a player's ball, an opponent, his *caddie* or his *equipment moves* the ball, touches it or causes it to *move*, there is no penalty. If the ball is *moved*, it must be replaced.

b. Other Than During Search
If, other than during search for a player's ball, an opponent, his *caddie* or his *equipment moves* the ball, touches it or causes it to *move*, except as otherwise provided in the *Rules*, the opponent incurs a penalty of one stroke. If the ball is *moved*, it must be replaced.

(Playing a wrong ball – see Rule 15-3)
(Ball moved in measuring – see Rule 18-6)

18-4. By Fellow-Competitor, Caddie or Equipment in Stroke Play
If a *fellow-competitor*, his *caddie* or his *equipment moves* the player's ball, touches it or causes it to *move*, there is no penalty.

If the ball is *moved*, it must be replaced.
(Playing a wrong ball – see Rule 15-3)

18-5. By Another Ball
If a *ball in play* and at rest is *moved* by another ball in motion after a *stroke*, the *moved* ball must be replaced.

18-6. Ball Moved in Measuring
If a ball or ball-marker is *moved* in measuring while proceeding under or in determining the application of a *Rule*, the ball or ball-marker must be replaced. There is no penalty provided the movement of the ball or ball-marker is directly attributable to the specific act of measuring. Otherwise, the provisions of Rules 18-2a, 18-3b or 18-4 apply.

*PENALTY FOR BREACH OF RULE:
Match play – Loss of hole; Stroke play – Two strokes.

*If a player who is required to replace a ball fails to do so, he incurs the general penalty for breach of Rule 18. There is no additional penalty under Rule 18, except in the case of a wrongly *substituted* ball (Rule 15-2).

Note 1: If a ball to be replaced under this Rule is not immediately recoverable, another ball may be *substituted*.
Note 2: If the original lie of a ball to be placed or replaced has been altered, see Rule 20-3b.
Note 3: If it is impossible to determine the spot on which a ball is to be placed, see Rule 20-3c.

Rule 19 – Ball in Motion Deflected or Stopped

Definitions
All defined terms are in *italics* and are listed alphabetically in the Definitions section – see pages 448–451.

19-1. By Outside Agency
If a ball in motion is accidentally deflected or stopped by any *outside agency*, it is a *rub of the green*, there is no penalty and the ball must be played as it lies except:

a. If a ball in motion after a *stroke* other than on the *putting green* comes to rest in or on any moving or animate *outside agency*, the player must, *through the green* or in a *hazard*, drop the ball, or on the *putting green* place the ball, as near as possible to the spot where the *outside agency* was when the ball came to rest in or on it, and

b. If a ball in motion after a *stroke* on the *putting green* is deflected or stopped by, or comes to rest in or on, any moving or animate *outside agency* except a worm or an insect, the *stroke* is cancelled. The ball must be replaced and the *stroke* replayed.

If the ball is not immediately recoverable, another ball may be *substituted*.

(Player's ball deflected or stopped by another ball – see Rule 19-5)

Note: If the *referee* or the *Committee* determines that a player's ball has been purposely deflected or stopped by an *outside agency*, Rule 1-4 applies to the player. If the *outside agency* is a *fellow-competitor* or his *caddie*, Rule 1-2 applies to the *fellow-competitor*.

19-2. By Player, Partner, Caddie or Equipment
a. Match Play
If a player's ball is accidentally deflected or stopped by himself, his *partner* or either of their *caddies* or *equipment*, he loses the hole.

b. Stroke Play
If a *competitor's* ball is accidentally deflected or stopped by himself, his *partner* or either of their

caddies or *equipment*, the *competitor* incurs a penalty of two strokes. The ball must be played as it lies, except when it comes to rest in or on the *competitor's*, his *partner's* or either of their *caddies'* clothes or *equipment*, in which case the *competitor* must *through the green* or in a *hazard* drop the ball, or on the *putting green* place the ball, as near as possible to where the article was when the ball came to rest in or on it.

Exception: Dropped ball – see Rule 20-2a.

(Ball purposely deflected or stopped by player, partner or caddie – see Rule 1-2)

19-3. By Opponent, Caddie or Equipment in Match Play

If a player's ball is accidentally deflected or stopped by an opponent, his *caddie* or his *equipment*, there is no penalty. The player may, before another *stroke* is made by either side, cancel the *stroke* and play a ball without penalty as nearly as possible at the spot from which the original ball was last played (see Rule 20-5) or he may play the ball as it lies. However, if the player elects not to cancel the *stroke* and the ball has come to rest in or on the opponent's or his *caddie's* clothes or *equipment*, the player must *through the green* or in a *hazard* drop the ball, or on the *putting green* place the ball, as near as possible to where the article was when the ball came to rest in or on it.

Exception: Ball striking person attending *flagstick* – see Rule 17-3b.

(Ball purposely deflected or stopped by opponent or caddie – see Rule 1-2)

19-4. By Fellow-Competitor, Caddie or Equipment in Stroke Play

See Rule 19-1 regarding ball deflected by *outside agency*.

19-5. By Another Ball
a. At Rest

If a player's ball in motion after a *stroke* is deflected or stopped by a *ball in play* and at rest, the player must play his ball as it lies. In match play, there is no penalty. In stroke play, there is no penalty unless both balls lay on the *putting green* prior to the *stroke*, in which case the player incurs a penalty of two strokes.

b. In Motion

If a player's ball in motion after a *stroke* is deflected or stopped by another ball in motion after a *stroke*, the player must play his ball as it lies. There is no penalty unless the player was in breach of Rule 16-1f, in which case he incurs the penalty for breach of that Rule.

Exception: If the player's ball is in motion after a *stroke* on the *putting green* and the other ball in motion is an *outside agency* – see Rule 19-1b.

PENALTY FOR BREACH OF RULE:
Match play – Loss of hole; Stroke play – Two strokes.

Rule 20 – Lifting, Dropping and Placing; Playing from Wrong Place

Definitions
All defined terms are in *italics* and are listed alphabetically in the Definitions section – see pages 448–451.

20-1. Lifting and Marking

A ball to be lifted under the *Rules* may be lifted by the player, his *partner* or another person authorised by the player. In any such case, the player is responsible for any breach of the *Rules*.

The position of the ball must be marked before it is lifted under a *Rule* that requires it to be replaced. If it is not marked, the player incurs a penalty of one stroke and the ball must be replaced. If it is not replaced, the player incurs the general penalty for breach of this Rule but there is no additional penalty under Rule 20-1.

If a ball or ball-marker is accidentally *moved* in the process of lifting the ball under a *Rule* or marking its position, the ball or ball-marker must be replaced. There is no penalty provided the movement of the ball or ball-marker is directly attributable to the specific act of marking the position of or lifting the ball. Otherwise, the player incurs a penalty of one stroke under this Rule or Rule 18-2a.

Exception: If a player incurs a penalty for failing to act in accordance with Rule 5-3 or 12-2, there is no additional penalty under Rule 20-1.

Note: The position of a ball to be lifted should be marked by placing a ball-marker, a small coin or other similar object immediately behind the ball. If the ball-marker interferes with the play, *stance* or *stroke* of another player, it should be placed one or more clubhead-lengths to one side.

20-2. Dropping and Re-Dropping
a. By Whom and How

A ball to be dropped under the *Rules* must be dropped by the player himself. He must stand erect, hold the ball at shoulder height and arm's length and drop it. If a ball is dropped by any other person or in any other manner and the error is not corrected as provided in Rule 20-6, the player incurs a penalty of one stroke.

If the ball touches the player, his *partner*, either of their *caddies* or their *equipment* before or after it strikes a part of the *course*, the ball must be re-dropped, without penalty. There is no limit to the number of times a ball must be re-dropped in these circumstances.

(Taking action to influence position or movement of ball – see Rule 1-2)

b. Where to Drop

When a ball is to be dropped as near as possible to a specific spot, it must be dropped not nearer the *hole*

466 Governing the Game

than the specific spot which, if it is not precisely known to the player, must be estimated.

A ball when dropped must first strike a part of the *course* where the applicable *Rule* requires it to be dropped. If it is not so dropped, Rules 20-6 and -7 apply.

c. When to Re-Drop

A dropped ball must be re-dropped without penalty if it:

(i) rolls into and comes to rest in a *hazard*;

(ii) rolls out of and comes to rest outside a *hazard*;

(iii) rolls onto and comes to rest on a *putting green*;

(iv) rolls and comes to rest *out of bounds*;

(v) rolls to and comes to rest in a position where there is interference by the condition from which relief was taken under Rule 24-2b (immovable obstruction), Rule 25-1 (abnormal ground conditions), Rule 25-3 (wrong putting green) or a Local Rule (Rule 33-8a), or rolls back into the pitch-mark from which it was lifted under Rule 25-2 (embedded ball);

(vi) rolls and comes to rest more than two club-lengths from where it first struck a part of the *course*; or

(vii) rolls and comes to rest nearer the *hole* than:

(a) its original position or estimated position (see Rule 20-2b) unless otherwise permitted by the *Rules*; or

(b) the *nearest point of relief* or maximum available relief (Rule 24-2, 25-1 or 25-3); or

(c) the point where the original ball last crossed the margin of the *water hazard* or *lateral water hazard* (Rule 26-1).

If the ball when re-dropped rolls into any position listed above, it must be placed as near as possible to the spot where it first struck a part of the *course* when re-dropped.

If a ball to be re-dropped or placed under this Rule is not immediately recoverable, another ball may be *substituted*.

Note: If a ball when dropped or re-dropped comes to rest and subsequently *moves*, the ball must be played as it lies, unless the provisions of any other *Rule* apply.

20-3. Placing and Replacing
a. By Whom and Where

A ball to be placed under the *Rules* must be placed by the player or his *partner*. If a ball is to be replaced, the player, his *partner* or the person who lifted or *moved* it must place it on the spot from which it was lifted or *moved*. In any such case, the player is responsible for any breach of the *Rules*.

If a ball or ball-marker is accidentally *moved* in the process of placing or replacing the ball, the ball or ball-marker must be replaced. There is no penalty provided the movement of the ball or ball-marker is directly attributable to the specific act of placing or replacing the ball or removing the ball-marker. Oth-

erwise, the player incurs a *penalty stroke* under Rule 18-2a or 20-1.

b. Lie of Ball to be Placed or Replaced Altered

If the original lie of a ball to be placed or replaced has been altered:

(i) except in a *hazard*, the ball must be placed in the nearest lie most similar to the original lie that is not more than one club-length from the original lie, not nearer the *hole* and not in a *hazard*;

(ii) in a *water hazard*, the ball must be placed in accordance with Clause (i) above, except that the ball must be placed in the *water hazard*;

(iii) in a *bunker*, the original lie must be re-created as nearly as possible and the ball must be placed in that lie.

c. Spot Not Determinable

If it is impossible to determine the spot where the ball is to be placed or replaced:

(i) *through the green*, the ball must be dropped as near as possible to the place where it lay but not in a *hazard* or on a *putting green*;

(ii) in a *hazard*, the ball must be dropped in the *hazard* as near as possible to the place where it lay;

(iii) on the *putting green*, the ball must be placed as near as possible to the place where it lay but not in a *hazard*.

Exception: When resuming play (Rule 6-8d), if the spot where the ball is to be placed is impossible to determine, it must be estimated and the ball placed on the estimated spot.

d. Ball Fails to Come to Rest on Spot

If a ball when placed fails to come to rest on the spot on which it was placed, there is no penalty and the ball must be replaced. If it still fails to come to rest on that spot:

(i) except in a *hazard*, it must be placed at the nearest spot where it can be placed at rest that is not nearer the *hole* and not in a *hazard*;

(ii) in a *hazard*, it must be placed in the *hazard* at the nearest spot where it can be placed at rest that is not nearer the *hole*.

If a ball when placed comes to rest on the spot on which it is placed, and it subsequently *moves*, there is no penalty and the ball must be played as it lies, unless the provisions of any other *Rule* apply.

PENALTY FOR BREACH OF RULE 20-1,
20-2 or 20-3:
Match play – Loss of hole; Stroke play –
Two strokes.

20-4. When Ball Dropped or Placed is in Play

If the player's *ball in play* has been lifted, it is again in play when dropped or placed.

A *substituted ball* becomes the *ball in play* when it has been dropped or placed.

(Ball incorrectly substituted – see Rule 15-2)

(Lifting ball incorrectly substituted, dropped or placed – see Rule 20-6)

20-5. Making Next Stroke from Where Previous Stroke Made

When a player elects or is required to make his next *stroke* from where a previous *stroke* was made, he must proceed as follows:

a. **On the Teeing Ground:** The ball to be played must be played from within the *teeing ground*. It may be played from anywhere within the *teeing ground* and may be teed.

b. **Through the Green and in a Hazard:** The ball to be played must be dropped.

c. **On the Putting Green:** The ball to be played must be placed.

   PENALTY FOR BREACH OF RULE 20-5:
   Match play – Loss of hole; Stroke play –
   Two strokes.

20-6. Lifting Ball Incorrectly Substituted, Dropped or Placed

A ball incorrectly *substituted*, dropped or placed in a wrong place or otherwise not in accordance with the *Rules* but not played may be lifted, without penalty, and the player must then proceed correctly.

20-7. Playing from Wrong Place

a. General

A player has played from a wrong place if he makes a *stroke* with his *ball in play*:

(i) on a part of the *course* where the *Rules* do not permit a *stroke* to be played or a ball to be dropped or placed; or

(ii) when the *Rules* require a dropped ball to be re-dropped or a *moved* ball to be replaced.

Note: For a ball played from outside the *teeing ground* or from a wrong *teeing ground* – see Rule 11-4.

b. Match Play

If a player makes a *stroke* from a wrong place, he loses the hole.

c. Stroke Play

If a *competitor* makes a *stroke* from a wrong place, he incurs a penalty of two strokes under the applicable *Rule*. He must play out the hole with the ball played from the wrong place, without correcting his error, provided he has not committed a serious breach (see Note 1).

If a *competitor* becomes aware that he has played from a wrong place and believes that he may have committed a serious breach, he must, before making a *stroke* on the next *teeing ground*, play out the hole with a second ball dropped or placed in accordance with the *Rules*. If the hole being played is the last hole of the round, he must declare, before leaving the *putting green*, that he will play out the hole with a second ball dropped or placed in accordance with the *Rules*.

The *competitor* must report the facts to the *Committee* before returning his score card; if he fails to do so, he is disqualified. The *Committee* must determine whether the *competitor* has committed a serious breach of the applicable *Rule*. If he has, the score

with the second ball counts and the *competitor* must add two penalty strokes to his score with that ball. If the *competitor* has committed a serious breach and has failed to correct it as outlined above, he is disqualified.

Note 1: A *competitor* is deemed to have committed a serious breach of the applicable *Rule* if the *Committee* considers he has gained a significant advantage as a result of playing from a wrong place.

Note 2: If a *competitor* plays a second ball under Rule 20-7c and it is ruled not to count, *strokes* made with that ball and *penalty strokes* incurred solely by playing that ball are disregarded. If the second ball is ruled to count, the *stroke* made from the wrong place and any *strokes* subsequently taken with the original ball including *penalty strokes* incurred solely by playing that ball are disregarded.

Rule 21 – Cleaning Ball

Definitions

All defined terms are in *italics* and are listed alphabetically in the Definitions section – see pages 448–451.

A ball on the *putting green* may be cleaned when lifted under Rule 16-1b. Elsewhere, a ball may be cleaned when lifted except when it has been lifted:

a. To determine if it is unfit for play (Rule 5-3);

b. For identification (Rule 12-2), in which case it may be cleaned only to the extent necessary for identification; or

c. Because it is assisting or interfering with play (Rule 22).

If a player cleans his ball during play of a hole except as provided in this Rule, he incurs a penalty of one stroke and the ball, if lifted, must be replaced.

If a player who is required to replace a ball fails to do so, he incurs the penalty for breach of Rule 20-3a, but there is no additional penalty under Rule 21.

Exception: If a player incurs a penalty for failing to act in accordance with Rule 5-3, 12-2 or 22, there is no additional penalty under Rule 21.

Rule 22 – Ball Assisting or Interfering with Play

Definitions

All defined terms are in *italics* and are listed alphabetically in the Definitions section – see pages 448–451.

22-1. Ball Assisting Play

Except when a ball is in motion, if a player considers that a ball might assist any other player, he may:

a. lift the ball if it is his ball; or

b. have any other ball lifted.

A ball lifted under this Rule must be replaced (see Rule 20-3). The ball must not be cleaned unless it lies on the *putting green* (see Rule 21).

In stroke play, a player required to lift his ball may play first rather than lift the ball.

In stroke play, if the *Committee* determines that *competitors* have agreed not to lift a ball that might assist any other player, they are disqualified.

22-2. Ball Interfering with Play

Except when a ball is in motion, if a player considers that the ball of another player might interfere with his play, he may have it lifted.

A ball lifted under this Rule must be replaced (see Rule 20-3). The ball must not be cleaned unless it lies on the *putting green* (see Rule 21).

In stroke play, a player required to lift his ball may play first rather than lift the ball.

Note: Except on the *putting green*, a player may not lift his ball solely because he considers that it might interfere with the play of another player. If a player lifts his ball without being asked to do so, he incurs a penalty of one stroke for a breach of Rule 18-2a, but there is no additional penalty under Rule 22.

PENALTY FOR BREACH OF RULE:
Match play – Loss of hole; Stroke play –
Two strokes.

Rule 23 – Loose Impediments

Definitions
All defined terms are in *italics* and are listed alphabetically in the Definitions section – see pages 448–451.

23-1. Relief

Except when both the *loose impediment* and the ball lie in or touch the same *hazard*, any *loose impediment* may be removed without penalty.

If the ball lies anywhere other than on the *putting green* and the removal of a *loose impediment* by the player causes the ball to *move*, Rule 18-2a applies.

On the *putting green*, if the ball or ball-marker *moves* in the process of the player removing any *loose impediment*, the ball or ball-marker must be replaced. There is no penalty provided the movement of the ball or ball-marker is directly attributable to the removal of the *loose impediment*. Otherwise, if the player causes the ball to *move*, he incurs a penalty of one stroke under Rule 18-2a.

When a ball is in motion, a *loose impediment* that might influence the movement of the ball must not be removed.

Note: If the ball lies in a *hazard*, the player must not touch or move any *loose impediment* lying in or touching the same *hazard* – see Rule 13-4c.

PENALTY FOR BREACH OF RULE:
Match play – Loss of hole; Stroke play –
Two strokes.

(Searching for ball in hazard – see Rule 12-1)
(Touching line of putt – see Rule 16-1a)

Rule 24 – Obstructions

Definitions
All defined terms are in *italics* and are listed alphabetically in the Definitions section – see pages 448–451.

24-1. Movable Obstruction

A player may take relief without penalty from a movable *obstruction* as follows:

a. If the ball does not lie in or on the *obstruction*, the *obstruction* may be removed. If the ball *moves*, it must be replaced, and there is no penalty provided that the movement of the ball is directly attributable to the removal of the *obstruction*. Otherwise, Rule 18-2a applies.

b. If the ball lies in or on the *obstruction*, the ball may be lifted and the *obstruction* removed. The ball must *through the green* or in a *hazard* be dropped, or on the *putting green* be placed, as near as possible to the spot directly under the place where the ball lay in or on the *obstruction*, but not nearer the *hole*.

The ball may be cleaned when lifted under this Rule.

When a ball is in motion, an *obstruction* that might influence the movement of the ball, other than an attended *flagstick* or *equipment* of the players, must not be removed.

(Exerting influence on ball – see Rule 1-2)

Note: If a ball to be dropped or placed under this Rule is not immediately recoverable, another ball may be *substituted*.

24-2. Immovable Obstruction
a. Interference

Interference by an immovable *obstruction* occurs when a ball lies in or on the *obstruction*, or when the *obstruction* interferes with the player's *stance* or the area of his intended swing. If the player's ball lies on the *putting green*, interference also occurs if an immovable *obstruction* on the *putting green* intervenes on his *line of putt*. Otherwise, intervention on the *line of play* is not, of itself, interference under this Rule.

b. Relief

Except when the ball is in a *water hazard* or a *lateral water hazard*, a player may take relief from interference by an immovable *obstruction* as follows:

(i) Through the Green: If the ball lies *through the green*, the player must lift the ball and drop it without penalty within one club-length of and not nearer the *hole* than the *nearest point of relief*. The *nearest point of relief* must not be in a *hazard* or on a *putting green*. When the ball is dropped within one club-length of the *nearest point of relief*, the ball must first strike a part of the *course* at a spot that avoids interference by the immovable *obstruction* and is not in a *hazard* and not on a *putting green*.

(ii) In a Bunker: If the ball is in a *bunker*, the player must lift the ball and drop it either:

(a) Without penalty, in accordance with Clause (i) above, except that the *nearest point of relief* must be in the *bunker* and the ball must be dropped in the *bunker*; or

(b) Under penalty of one stroke, outside the *bunker* keeping the point where the ball lay directly between the *hole* and the spot on which the ball is dropped, with no limit to how far behind the *bunker* the ball may be dropped.

(iii) On the Putting Green: If the ball lies on the *putting green*, the player must lift the ball and place it without penalty at the *nearest point of relief* that is not in a *hazard*. The *nearest point of relief* may be off the *putting green*.

(iv) On the Teeing Ground: If the ball lies on the *teeing ground*, the player must lift the ball and drop it without penalty in accordance with Clause (i) above.

The ball may be cleaned when lifted under this Rule.

(Ball rolling to a position where there is interference by the condition from which relief was taken – see Rule 20-2c(v))

Exception: A player may not take relief under this Rule if (a) it is clearly unreasonable for him to make a *stroke* because of interference by anything other than an immovable *obstruction* or (b) interference by an immovable *obstruction* would occur only through use of an unnecessarily abnormal *stance*, swing or direction of play.

Note 1: If a ball is in a *water hazard* (including a *lateral water hazard*), the player may not take relief from interference by an immovable *obstruction*. The player must play the ball as it lies or proceed under Rule 26-1.

Note 2: If a ball to be dropped or placed under this Rule is not immediately recoverable, another ball may be *substituted*.

Note 3: The *Committee* may make a Local Rule stating that the player must determine the *nearest point of relief* without crossing over, through or under the *obstruction*.

24-3. Ball Lost in Obstruction

It is a question of fact whether a ball *lost* after having been struck toward an *obstruction* is *lost* in the *obstruction*. In order to treat the ball as *lost* in the *obstruction*, there must be reasonable evidence to that effect. In the absence of such evidence, the ball must be treated as a *lost ball* and Rule 27 applies.

a. Ball Lost in Movable Obstruction

If a ball is *lost* in a movable *obstruction*, a player may, without penalty, remove the *obstruction* and must *through the green* or in a *hazard* drop a ball, or on the *putting green* place a ball, as near as possible to the spot directly under the place where the ball last crossed the outermost limits of the movable *obstruction*, but not nearer the *hole*.

b. Ball Lost in Immovable Obstruction

If a ball is *lost* in an immovable *obstruction*, the spot where the ball last crossed the outermost limits of the *obstruction* must be determined and, for the purpose

of applying this Rule, the ball is deemed to lie at this spot and the player may take relief as follows:

(i) Through the Green: If the ball last crossed the outermost limits of the immovable *obstruction* at a spot *through the green*, the player may *substitute* another ball without penalty and take relief as prescribed in Rule 24-2b(i).

(ii) In a Bunker: If the ball last crossed the outermost limits of the immovable *obstruction* at a spot in a *bunker*, the player may *substitute* another ball without penalty and take relief as prescribed in Rule 24-2b(ii).

(iii) In a Water Hazard (including a Lateral Water Hazard): If the ball last crossed the outermost limits of the immovable *obstruction* at a spot in a *water hazard*, the player is not entitled to relief without penalty. The player must proceed under Rule 26-1.

(iv) On the Putting Green: If the ball last crossed the outermost limits of the immovable *obstruction* at a spot on the *putting green*, the player may *substitute* another ball without penalty and take relief as prescribed in Rule 24-2b(iii).

PENALTY FOR BREACH OF RULE:
Match play – Loss of hole; Stroke play – Two strokes.

Rule 25 – Abnormal Ground Conditions, Embedded Ball and Wrong Putting Green

Definitions

All defined terms are in *italics* and are listed alphabetically in the Definitions section – see pages 448–451.

25-1. Abnormal Ground Conditions

a. Interference

Interference by an *abnormal ground condition* occurs when a ball lies in or touches the condition or when the condition interferes with the player's *stance* or the area of his intended swing. If the player's ball lies on the *putting green*, interference also occurs if an *abnormal ground condition* on the *putting green* intervenes on his *line of putt*. Otherwise, intervention on the *line of play* is not, of itself, interference under this Rule.

Note: The *Committee* may make a Local Rule denying the player relief from interference with his *stance* by an *abnormal ground condition*.

b. Relief

Except when the ball is in a *water hazard* or a *lateral water hazard*, a player may take relief from interference by an *abnormal ground condition* as follows:

(i) Through the Green: If the ball lies *through the green*, the player must lift the ball and drop it without penalty within one club-length of and not nearer the *hole* than the *nearest point of relief*. The *nearest point of relief* must not be in a *hazard* or on a *putting green*. When the ball is dropped within one club-length of the *nearest point of relief*, the ball must first strike a part of the *course*

at a spot that avoids interference by the condition and is not in a *hazard* and not on a *putting green*.

(ii) **In a Bunker:** If the ball is in a *bunker*, the player must lift the ball and drop it either:

    (a) Without penalty, in accordance with Clause (i) above, except that the *nearest point of relief* must be in the *bunker* and the ball must be dropped in the *bunker*, or if complete relief is impossible, as near as possible to the spot where the ball lay, but not nearer the *hole*, on a part of the *course* in the *bunker* that affords maximum available relief from the condition; or

    (b) Under penalty of one stroke, outside the *bunker* keeping the point where the ball lay directly between the *hole* and the spot on which the ball is dropped, with no limit to how far behind the *bunker* the ball may be dropped.

(iii) **On the Putting Green:** If the ball lies on the *putting green*, the player must lift the ball and place it without penalty at the *nearest point of relief* that is not in a *hazard*, or if complete relief is impossible, at the nearest position to where it lay that affords maximum available relief from the condition, but not nearer the *hole* and not in a *hazard*. The *nearest point of relief* or maximum available relief may be off the *putting green*.

(iv) **On the Teeing Ground:** If the ball lies on the *teeing ground*, the player must lift the ball and drop it without penalty in accordance with Clause (i) above.

The ball may be cleaned when lifted under Rule 25-1b.

(Ball rolling to a position where there is interference by the condition from which relief was taken – see Rule 20-2c(v))

Exception: A player may not take relief under this Rule if (a) it is clearly unreasonable for him to make a *stroke* because of interference by anything other than an *abnormal ground condition* or (b) interference by an *abnormal ground condition* would occur only through use of an unnecessarily abnormal *stance*, swing or direction of play.

Note 1: If a ball is in a *water hazard* (including a *lateral water hazard*), the player is not entitled to relief without penalty from interference by an *abnormal ground condition*. The player must play the ball as it lies (unless prohibited by Local Rule) or proceed under Rule 26-1.

Note 2: If a ball to be dropped or placed under this Rule is not immediately recoverable, another ball may be *substituted*.

c. Ball Lost

It is a question of fact whether a ball *lost* after having been struck toward an *abnormal ground condition* is *lost* in such condition. In order to treat the ball as *lost* in the *abnormal ground condition*, there must be reasonable evidence to that effect. In the absence of such evidence, the ball must be treated as a *lost ball* and Rule 27 applies.

If a ball is *lost* in an *abnormal ground condition*, the spot where the ball last crossed the outermost limits of the condition must be determined and, for the purpose of applying this Rule, the ball is deemed to lie at this spot and the player may take relief as follows:

(i) **Through the Green:** If the ball last crossed the outermost limits of the *abnormal ground condition* at a spot *through the green*, the player may *substitute* another ball without penalty and take relief as prescribed in Rule 25-1b(i).

(ii) **In a Bunker:** If the ball last crossed the outermost limits of the *abnormal ground condition* at a spot in a *bunker*, the player may *substitute* another ball without penalty and take relief as prescribed in Rule 25-1b(ii).

(iii) **In a Water Hazard (including a Lateral Water Hazard):** If the ball last crossed the outermost limits of the *abnormal ground condition* at a spot in a *water hazard*, the player is not entitled to relief without penalty. The player must proceed under Rule 26-1.

(iv) **On the Putting Green:** If the ball last crossed the outermost limits of the *abnormal ground condition* at a spot on the *putting green*, the player may *substitute* another ball without penalty and take relief as prescribed in Rule 25-1b(iii).

25-2. Embedded Ball

A ball embedded in its own pitch-mark in the ground in any closely-mown area *through the green* may be lifted, cleaned and dropped, without penalty, as near as possible to the spot where it lay but not nearer the *hole*. The ball when dropped must first strike a part of the *course through the green*. "Closely-mown area" means any area of the *course*, including paths through the rough, cut to fairway height or less.

25-3. Wrong Putting Green

a. Interference

Interference by a *wrong putting green* occurs when a ball is on the *wrong putting green*.

Interference to a player's *stance* or the area of his intended swing is not, of itself, interference under this Rule.

b. Relief

If a player's ball lies on a *wrong putting green*, he must not play the ball as it lies. He must take relief, without penalty, as follows:

The player must lift the ball and drop it within one club-length of and not nearer the hole than the *nearest point of relief*. The *nearest point of relief* must not be in a *hazard* or on a *putting green*. When dropping the ball within one club-length of the *nearest point of relief*, the ball must first strike a part of the *course* at a spot that avoids interference by the *wrong putting green* and is not in a *hazard* and not on a *putting green*. The ball may be cleaned when lifted under this Rule.

PENALTY FOR BREACH OF RULE:
Match play – Loss of hole; Stroke play –
Two strokes.

Rule 26 – Winter Hazards (Including Lateral Water Hazards)

Definitions
All defined terms are in *italics* and are listed alphabetically in the Definitions section – see pages 448–451.

26-1. Relief for Ball in Water Hazard
It is a question of fact whether a ball *lost* after having been struck toward a *water hazard* is *lost* inside or outside the *hazard*. In order to treat the ball as *lost* in the *hazard*, there must be reasonable evidence that the ball lodged in it. In the absence of such evidence, the ball must be treated as a *lost ball* and Rule 27 applies.

If a ball is in or is *lost* in a *water hazard* (whether the ball lies in water or not), the player may under penalty of one stroke:

a. Play a ball as nearly as possible at the spot from which the original ball was last played (see Rule 20-5); or

b. Drop a ball behind the *water hazard*, keeping the point at which the original ball last crossed the margin of the *water hazard* directly between the *hole* and the spot on which the ball is dropped, with no limit to how far behind the *water hazard* the ball may be dropped; or

c. As additional options available only if the ball last crossed the margin of a *lateral water hazard*, drop a ball outside the *water hazard* within two club-lengths of and not nearer the *hole* than (i) the point where the original ball last crossed the margin of the *water hazard* or (ii) a point on the opposite margin of the *water hazard* equidistant from the *hole*.

The ball may be lifted and cleaned when proceeding under this Rule.

(Prohibited actions when ball is in a hazard – see Rule 13-4)

(Ball moving in water in a water hazard – see Rule 14-6)

26-2. Ball Played Within Water Hazard
a. Ball Comes to Rest in Same or Another Water Hazard

If a ball played from within a *water hazard* comes to rest in the same or another *water hazard* after the *stroke*, the player may:

(i) proceed under Rule 26-1a. If, after dropping in the *hazard*, the player elects not to play the dropped ball, he may:

  (a) with reference to this *hazard*, proceed under Rule 26-1b, or if applicable Rule 26-1c, adding the additional penalty of one stroke prescribed by that Rule; or

  (b) add an additional penalty of one stroke and play a ball as nearly as possible at the spot from which the last *stroke* from outside a *water hazard* was made (see Rule 20-5); or

(ii) proceed under Rule 26-1b, or if applicable Rule 26-1c; or

(iii) under penalty of one stroke, play a ball as nearly as possible at the spot from which the last *stroke* from outside a *water hazard* was made (see Rule 20-5).

b. Ball Lost or Unplayable Outside Hazard or Out of Bounds

If a ball played from within a *water hazard* is *lost* or declared unplayable outside the *hazard* or is *out of bounds*, the player may, after taking a penalty of one stroke under Rule 27-1 or 28a:

(i) play a ball as nearly as possible at the spot in the *hazard* from which the original ball was last played (see Rule 20-5); or

(ii) proceed under Rule 26-1b, or if applicable Rule 26-1c, adding the additional penalty of one stroke prescribed by the Rule and using as the reference point the point where the original ball last crossed the margin of the *hazard* before it came to rest in the *hazard*; or

(iii) add an additional penalty of one stroke and play a ball as nearly as possible at the spot from which the last *stroke* from outside the *hazard* was made (see Rule 20-5).

Note 1: When proceeding under Rule 26-2b, the player is not required to drop a ball under Rule 27-1 or 28a. If he does drop a ball, he is not required to play it. He may alternatively proceed under Rule 26-2b(ii) or (iii).

Note 2: If a ball played from within a *water hazard* is declared unplayable outside the *hazard*, nothing in Rule 26-2b precludes the player from proceeding under Rule 28b or c.

PENALTY FOR BREACH OF RULE:
Match play – Loss of hole; Stroke play –
Two strokes.

Rule 27 – Lost Ball or Ball Out of Bounds; Provisional Ball

Definitions
All defined terms are in *italics* and are listed alphabetically in the Definitions section – see pages 448–451.

27-1. Ball Lost or Out of Bounds
If a ball is *lost* or is *out of bounds*, the player must play a ball, under penalty of one stroke, as nearly as possible at the spot from which the original ball was last played (see Rule 20-5).

Exceptions:
1. If there is reasonable evidence that the original ball is *lost* in a *water hazard*, the player must proceed in accordance with Rule 26-1.

2. If there is reasonable evidence that the original ball is *lost* in an *obstruction* (Rule 24-3) or an *abnormal ground condition* (Rule 25-1c) the player may proceed under the applicable Rule.

PENALTY FOR BREACH OF RULE 27-1:
Match play – Loss of hole; Stroke play –
Two strokes.

27-2. Provisional Ball
a. Procedure

If a ball may be *lost* outside a *water hazard* or may be *out of bounds*, to save time the player may play another ball provisionally in accordance with Rule 27-1. The player must inform his opponent in match play or his *marker* or a *fellow-competitor* in stroke play that he intends to play a *provisional ball*, and he must play it before he or his *partner* goes forward to search for the original ball.

If he fails to do so and plays another ball, that ball is not a *provisional ball* and becomes the *ball in play* under penalty of stroke and distance (Rule 27-1); the original ball is *lost*.

(Order of play from teeing ground – see Rule 10-3)

Note: If a *provisional ball* played under Rule 27-2a might be *lost* outside a *water hazard* or *out of bounds*, the player may play another *provisional ball*. If another *provisional ball* is played, it bears the same relationship to the previous *provisional ball* as the first *provisional ball* bears to the original ball.

b. When Provisional Ball Becomes Ball in Play

The player may play a *provisional ball* until he reaches the place where the original ball is likely to be. If he makes a *stroke* with the *provisional ball* from the place where the original ball is likely to be or from a point nearer the *hole* than that place, the original ball is *lost* and the *provisional ball* becomes the *ball in play* under penalty of stroke and distance (Rule 27-1).

If the original ball is *lost* outside a *water hazard* or is *out of bounds*, the *provisional ball* becomes the *ball in play*, under penalty of stroke and distance (Rule 27-1).

If there is reasonable evidence that the original ball is *lost* in a *water hazard*, the player must proceed in accordance with Rule 26-1.

Exception: If there is reasonable evidence that the original ball is *lost* in an *obstruction* (Rule 24-3) or an *abnormal ground condition* (Rule 25-1c) the player may proceed under the applicable Rule.

c. When Provisional Ball to be Abandoned

If the original ball is neither *lost* nor *out of bounds*, the player must abandon the *provisional ball* and continue play with the original ball. If he makes any further *strokes* at the *provisional ball*, he is playing a *wrong ball* and the provisions of Rule 15 apply.

Note: If a player plays a *provisional ball* under Rule 27-2a, the *strokes* made after this Rule has been invoked with a *provisional ball* subsequently abandoned under Rule 27-2c and *penalty strokes* incurred solely by playing that ball are disregarded.

Rule 28 – Ball Unplayable

Definitions

All defined terms are in *italics* and are listed alphabetically in the Definitions section – see pages 448–451.

The player may deem his ball unplayable at any place on the *course* except when the ball is in a *water*

hazard. The player is the sole judge as to whether his ball is unplayable.

If the player deems his ball to be unplayable, he must, under penalty of one stroke:

a. Play a ball as nearly as possible at the spot from which the original ball was last played (see Rule 20-5); or

b. Drop a ball behind the point where the ball lay, keeping that point directly between the *hole* and the spot on which the ball is dropped, with no limit to how far behind that point the ball may be dropped; or

c. Drop a ball within two club-lengths of the spot where the ball lay, but not nearer the *hole*.

If the unplayable ball is in a *bunker*, the player may proceed under Clause a, b or c. If he elects to proceed under Clause b or c, a ball must be dropped in the *bunker*.

The ball may be lifted and cleaned when proceeding under this Rule.

> PENALTY FOR BREACH OF RULE:
> Match play – Loss of hole; Stroke play –
> Two strokes.

OTHER FORMS OF PLAY

Rule 29 – Threesomes and Foursomes

Definitions

All defined terms are in *italics* and are listed alphabetically in the Definitions section – see pages 448–451.

29-1. General

In a *threesome* or a *foursome*, during any *stipulated round* the *partners* must play alternately from the *teeing grounds* and alternately during the play of each hole. *Penalty strokes* do not affect the order of play.

29-2. Match Play

If a player plays when his *partner* should have played, his *side* loses the hole.

29-3. Stroke Play

If the *partners* make a *stroke* or *strokes* in incorrect order, such *stroke* or *strokes* are cancelled and the side incurs a penalty of two strokes. The *side* must correct the error by playing a ball in correct order as nearly as possible at the spot from which it first played in incorrect order (see Rule 20-5). If the *side* makes a *stroke* on the next *teeing ground* without first correcting the error or, in the case of the last hole of the round, leaves the *putting green* without declaring its intention to correct the error, the *side* is disqualified.

Rule 30 – Three-Ball, Four-Ball and Four-Ball Match Play

Definitions

All defined terms are in *italics* and are listed alphabetically in the Definitions section – see pages 448–451.

30-1. Rules of Golf Apply
The Rules of Golf, so far as they are not at variance with the following specific Rules, apply to *three-ball*, *best-ball* and *four-ball matches*.

30-2. Three-Ball Match Play
a. Ball at Rest Moved by an Opponent
Except as otherwise provided in the *Rules*, if the player's ball is touched or *moved* by an opponent, his *caddie* or *equipment* other than during search, Rule 18-3b applies. That opponent incurs a penalty of one stroke in his match with the player, but not in his match with the other opponent.

b. Ball Deflected or Stopped by an Opponent Accidentally
If a player's ball is accidentally deflected or stopped by an opponent, his *caddie* or *equipment*, there is no penalty. In his match with that opponent the player may play the ball as it lies or, before another *stroke* is played by either *side*, he may cancel the *stroke* and play a ball without penalty as nearly as possible at the spot from which the original ball was last played (see Rule 20-5). In his match with the other opponent, the ball must be played as it lies.

Exception: Ball striking person attending *flagstick* – see Rule 17-3b.

(Ball purposely deflected or stopped by opponent – see Rule 1-2)

30-3. Best-Ball and Four-Ball Match Play
a. Representation of Side
A *side* may be represented by one *partner* for all or any part of a match; all *partners* need not be present. An absent *partner* may join a match between holes, but not during play of a hole.

b. Maximum of Fourteen Clubs
The *side* is penalised for a breach of Rules 4-3a(iii) and 4-4 by any *partner*.

c. Order of Play
Balls belonging to the same *side* may be played in the order the *side* considers best.

d. Wrong Ball
If a player makes a *stroke* at a *wrong ball* that is not in a *hazard*, he is disqualified for that hole, but his *partner* incurs no penalty even if the *wrong ball* belongs to him. If the *wrong ball* belongs to another player, its owner must place a ball on the spot from which the *wrong ball* was first played.

e. Disqualification of Side
(i) A *side* is disqualified for a breach of any of the following by any *partner*:
- Rule 1-3   Agreement to Waive Rules
- Rule 4-1 or -2 Clubs
- Rule 5-1 or -2 The Ball
- Rule 6-2a   Handicap (playing off higher handicap)
- Rule 6-4   Caddie (having more than one caddie; failure to correct breach immediately)
- Rule 6-7   Undue Delay; Slow Play (repeated offence)

- Rule 14-3   Artificial Devices and Unusual Equipment

(ii) A *side* is disqualified for a breach of any of the following by all *partners*:
- Rule 6-3   Time of Starting and Groups
- Rule 6-8   Discontinuance of Play

(iii) In all other cases where a breach of a *Rule* would result in disqualification, the player is disqualified for that hole only.

f. Effect of Other Penalties
If a player's breach of a *Rule* assists his *partner's* play or adversely affects an opponent's play, the *partner* incurs the applicable penalty in addition to any penalty incurred by the player.

In all other cases where a player incurs a penalty for breach of a *Rule*, the penalty does not apply to his *partner*. Where the penalty is stated to be loss of hole, the effect is to disqualify the player for that hole.

g. Another Form of Match Played Concurrently
In a *best-ball* or *four-ball* match when another form of match is played concurrently, the above specific Rules apply.

Rule 31 – Four-Ball Stroke Play

Definitions
All defined terms are in *italics* and are listed alphabetically in the Definitions section – see pages 448–451.

31-1. General
In *four-ball* stroke play two *competitors* play as *partners*, each playing his own ball. The lower score of the *partners* is the score for the hole. If one *partner* fails to complete the play of a hole, there is no penalty.

The Rules of Golf, so far as they are not at variance with the following specific Rules, apply to *four-ball* stroke play.

31-2. Representation of Side
A *side* may be represented by either *partner* for all or any part of a *stipulated round*; both *partners* need not be present. An absent *competitor* may join his *partner* between holes, but not during play of a hole.

31-3. Maximum of Fourteen Clubs
The *side* is penalised for a breach of Rules 4-3a (iii) and 4-4 by either *partner*.

31-4. Scoring
The *marker* is required to record for each hole only the gross score of whichever *partner's* score is to count. The gross scores to count must be individually identifiable; otherwise the *side* is disqualified. Only one of the *partners* need be responsible for complying with Rule 6-6b.

(Wrong score – see Rule 31-7a)

31-5. Order of Play
Balls belonging to the same *side* may be played in the order the *side* considers best.

31-6. Wrong Ball
If a *competitor* makes a *stroke* at a *wrong ball* that is not in a *hazard*, he incurs a penalty of two strokes and must correct his mistake by playing the correct ball or by proceeding under the *Rules*. His *partner* incurs no penalty even if the *wrong ball* belongs to him.

If the *wrong ball* belongs to another *competitor*, its owner must place a ball on the spot from which the *wrong ball* was first played.

31-7. Disqualification Penalties
a. Breach by One Partner
A *side* is disqualified from the competition for a breach of any of the following by either *partner*:

• Rule 1-3	Agreement to Waive Rules
• Rule 3-4	Refusal to Comply with Rule
• Rule 4-1 or -2	Clubs
• Rule 5-1 or -2	The Ball
• Rule 6-2b	Handicap (playing off higher handicap; failure to record handicap)
• Rule 6-4	Caddie (having more than one caddie; failure to correct breach immediately)
• Rule 6-6b	Signing and Returning Score Card
• Rule 6-6d	Wrong Score for Hole, i.e. when the recorded score of the *partner* whose score is to count is lower than actually taken. If the recorded score of the *partner* whose score is to count is higher than actually taken, it must stand as returned
• Rule 6-7	Undue Delay; Slow Play (repeated offence)
• Rule 7-1	Practice Before or Between Rounds
• Rule 14-3	Artificial Devices and Unusual Equipment
• Rule 31-4	Gross Scores to Count Not Individually Identifiable

b. Breach by Both Partners
A *side* is disqualified:
(i) for a breach by both of Rule 6-3 (Time of Starting and Groups) or Rule 6-8 (Discontinuance of Play), or
(ii) if, at the same hole, each *partner* is in breach of a *Rule* the penalty for which is disqualification from the competition or for a hole.

c. For the Hole Only
In all other cases where a breach of a *Rule* would result in disqualification, the *competitor* is disqualified only for the hole at which the breach occurred.

31-8. Effect of Other Penalties
If a *competitor's* breach of a *Rule* assists his *partner's* play, the *partner* incurs the applicable penalty in addition to any penalty incurred by the *competitor*.

In all other cases where a *competitor* incurs a penalty for breach of a *Rule*, the penalty does not apply to his *partner*.

Rule 32 – Bogey; Par and Stableford Competitions

Definitions
All defined terms are in *italics* and are listed alphabetically in the Definitions section – see pages 448–451.

32-1. Conditions
Bogey, par and Stableford competitions are forms of stroke play in which play is against a fixed score at each hole. The *Rules* for stroke play, so far as they are not at variance with the following specific Rules, apply.

a. Bogey and Par Competitions
The scoring for bogey and par competitions is made as in match play. Any hole for which a *competitor* makes no return is regarded as a loss. The winner is the *competitor* who is most successful in the aggregate of holes.

The *marker* is responsible for marking only the gross number of *strokes* for each hole where the *competitor* makes a net score equal to or less than the fixed score.

Note 1: Maximum of Fourteen Clubs – Penalties as in match play – see Rule 4-4.

Note 2: One Caddie at Any One Time – Penalties as in match play – see Rule 6-4.

Note 3: Undue Delay; Slow Play (Rule 6-7) – The *competitor's* score is adjusted by deducting one hole from the overall result.

b. Stableford Competitions
The scoring in Stableford competitions is made by points awarded in relation to a fixed score at each hole as follows:

Hole Played In	Points
More than one over fixed score or no score returned	0
One over fixed score	1
Fixed score	2
One under fixed score	3
Two under fixed score	4
Three under fixed score	5
Four under fixed score	6

The winner is the *competitor* who scores the highest number of points.

The *marker* is responsible for marking only the gross number of *strokes* at each hole where the *competitor's* net score earns one or more points.

Note 1: Maximum of Fourteen Clubs (Rule 4-4) – Penalties applied as follows: From total points scored for the round, deduction of two points for each hole at which any breach occurred; maximum deduction per round: four points.

Note 2: One Caddie at Any One Time (Rule 6-4) – Penalties applied as follows: From the points scored for the round, deduction of two points for each hole at which any breach occurred; maximum deduction per round: four points.

Note 3: Undue Delay; Slow Play (Rule 6-7) – The *competitor's* score is adjusted by deducting two points from the total points scored for the round.

32-2. Disqualification Penalties

a. From the Competition

A *competitor* is disqualified from the competition for a breach of any of the following:

• Rule 1-3	Agreement to Waive Rules
• Rule 3-4	Refusal to Comply with Rule
• Rule 4-1 or -2	Clubs
• Rule 5-1 or -2	The Ball
• Rule 6-2b	Handicap (playing off higher handicap; failure to record handicap)
• Rule 6-3	Time of Starting and Groups
• Rule 6-4	Caddie (having more than one caddie; failure to correct breach immediately)
• Rule 6-6b	Signing and Returning Score Card
• Rule 6-6d	Wrong Score for Hole, i.e. when the recorded score is lower than actually taken, except that no penalty is incurred when a breach of this Rule does not affect the result of the hole
• Rule 6-7	Undue Delay; Slow Play (repeated offence)
• Rule 6-8	Discontinuance of Play
• Rule 7-1	Practice Before or Between Rounds
• Rule 14-3	Artificial Devices and Unusual Equipment

b. For a Hole

In all other cases where a breach of a *Rule* would result in disqualification, the *competitor* is disqualified only for the hole at which the breach occurred.

ADMINISTRATION

Rule 33 – The Committee

Definitions

All defined terms are in *italics* and are listed alphabetically in the Definitions section – see pages 448–451.

33-1. Conditions; Waiving Rule

The *Committee* must establish the conditions under which a competition is to be played.

The *Committee* has no power to waive a Rule of Golf.

Certain specific *Rules* governing stroke play are so substantially different from those governing match play that combining the two forms of play is not practicable and is not permitted. The results of *matches* played and the scores returned in these circumstances must not be accepted.

In stroke play the *Committee* may limit a *referee's* duties.

33-2. The Course

a. Defining Bounds and Margins

The *Committee* must define accurately:

(i) the *course* and *out of bounds*,

(ii) the margins of *water hazards* and *lateral water hazards*,

(iii) *ground under repair*, and

(iv) *obstructions* and integral parts of the *course*.

b. New Holes

New *holes* should be made on the day on which a stroke play competition begins and at such other times as the *Committee* considers necessary, provided all *competitors* in a single round play with each *hole* cut in the same position.

Exception: When it is impossible for a damaged *hole* to be repaired so that it conforms with the Definition, the *Committee* may make a new *hole* in a nearby similar position.

Note: Where a single round is to be played on more than one day, the *Committee* may provide in the conditions of a competition that the *holes* and *teeing grounds* may be differently situated on each day of the competition, provided that, on any one day, all *competitors* play with each *hole* and each *teeing ground* in the same position.

c. Practice Ground

Where there is no practice ground available outside the area of a competition *course*, the *Committee* should establish the area on which players may practise on any day of a competition, if it is practicable to do so. On any day of a stroke play competition, the *Committee* should not normally permit practice on or to a *putting green* or from a *hazard* of the competition *course*.

d. Course Unplayable

If the *Committee* or its authorised representative considers that for any reason the *course* is not in a playable condition or that there are circumstances that render the proper playing of the game impossible, it may, in match play or stroke play, order a temporary suspension of play or, in stroke play, declare play null and void and cancel all scores for the round in question. When a round is cancelled, all penalties incurred in that round are cancelled.

(Procedure in discontinuing and resuming play – see Rule 6-8)

33-3. Times of Starting and Groups

The *Committee* must establish the times of starting and, in stroke play, arrange the groups in which *competitors* must play.

When a match play competition is played over an extended period, the *Committee* establishes the limit of time within which each round must be completed. When players are allowed to arrange the date of their match within these limits, the *Committee* should announce that the match must be played at a stated time on the last day of the period unless the players agree to a prior date.

33-4. Handicap Stroke Table

The *Committee* must publish a table indicating the order of holes at which handicap *strokes* are to be given or received.

33-5. Score Card

In stroke play, the *Committee* must provide each *competitor* with a score card containing the date and the *competitor's* name or, in *foursome* or *four-ball* stroke play, the *competitors'* names.

In stroke play, the *Committee* is responsible for the addition of scores and application of the handicap recorded on the score card.

In *four-ball* stroke play, the *Committee* is responsible for recording the better-ball score for each hole and in the process applying the handicaps recorded on the score card, and adding the better-ball scores.

In bogey, par and Stableford competitions, the *Committee* is responsible for applying the handicap recorded on the score card and determining the result of each hole and the overall result or points total.

Note: The *Committee* may request that each *competitor* records the date and his name on his score card.

33-6. Decision of Ties

The *Committee* must announce the manner, day and time for the decision of a halved match or of a tie, whether played on level terms or under handicap.

A halved match must not be decided by stroke play. A tie in stroke play must not be decided by a match.

33-7. Disqualification Penalty; Committee Discretion

A penalty of disqualification may in exceptional individual cases be waived, modified or imposed if the *Committee* considers such action warranted.

Any penalty less than disqualification must not be waived or modified.

If a *Committee* considers that a player is guilty of a serious breach of etiquette, it may impose a penalty of disqualification under this Rule.

33-8. Local Rules

a. Policy

The *Committee* may establish Local Rules for local abnormal conditions if they are consistent with the policy set forth in Appendix I.

b. Waiving or Modifying a Rule

A Rule of Golf must not be waived by a Local Rule. However, if a *Committee* considers that local abnormal conditions interfere with the proper playing of the game to the extent that it is necessary to make a Local Rule that modifies the Rules of Golf, the Local Rule must be authorised by the *R&A*.

Rule 34 – Disputes and Decisions

Definitions

All defined terms are in *italics* and are listed alphabetically in the Definitions section – see pages 448–451.

34-1. Claims and Penalties

a. Match Play

If a claim is lodged with the *Committee* under Rule 2-5, a decision should be given as soon as possible so that the state of the match may, if necessary, be adjusted. If a claim is not made in accordance with Rule 2-5, it must not be considered by the *Committee*.

There is no time limit on applying the disqualification penalty for a breach of Rule 1-3.

b. Stroke Play

In stroke play, a penalty must not be rescinded, modified or imposed after the competition has closed. A competition is closed when the result has been officially announced or, in stroke play qualifying followed by match play, when the player has teed off in his first match.

Exceptions: A penalty of disqualification must be imposed after the competition has closed if a *competitor*:

(i) was in breach of Rule 1-3 (Agreement to Waive Rules); or

(ii) returned a score card on which he had recorded a handicap that, before the competition closed, he knew was higher than that to which he was entitled, and this affected the number of strokes received (Rule 6-2b); or

(iii) returned a score for any hole lower than actually taken (Rule 6-6d) for any reason other than failure to include a penalty that, before the competition closed, he did not know he had incurred; or

(iv) knew, before the competition closed, that he had been in breach of any other *Rule* for which the penalty is disqualification.

34-2. Referee's Decision

If a *referee* has been appointed by the *Committee*, his decision is final.

34-3. Committee's Decision

In the absence of a *referee*, any dispute or doubtful point on the *Rules* must be referred to the *Committee*, whose decision is final.

If the *Committee* cannot come to a decision, it may refer the dispute or doubtful point to the Rules of Golf Committee of the *R&A*, whose decision is final.

If the dispute or doubtful point has not been referred to the Rules of Golf Committee, the player or players may request that an agreed statement be referred through a duly authorised representative of the *Committee* to the Rules of Golf Committee for an opinion as to the correctness of the decision given. The reply will be sent to this authorised representative.

If play is conducted other than in accordance with the Rules of Golf, the Rules of Golf Committee will not give a decision on any question.

APPENDIX I – CONTENTS

Page

Part A   Local Rules 477
1. Defining Bounds and Margins 477
2. Water Hazards 477
   a. Lateral Water Hazards 477
   b. Provisional Ball 477
3. Areas of the Course Requiring Preservation;
   Environmentally-Sensitive Areas 477
4. Temporary Conditions – Mud, Extreme
   Wetness, Poor Conditions and Protection
   of the Course 477
   a. Lifting an Embedded Ball, Cleaning 477
   b. "Preferred Lies" and "Winter Rules" 477
5. Obstructions 478
   a. General 478
   b. Stones in Bunkers 478
   c. Roads and Paths 478
   d. Immovable Obstructions Close to
      Putting Green 478
   e. Protection of Young Trees 478
   f. Temporary Obstructions 478
6. Dropping Zones (Ball Drops) 478

Part B   Specimen Local Rules 478
1. Areas of the Course Requiring Preservation;
   Environmentally-Sensitive Areas 478
   a. Ground Under Repair; Play Prohibited 478
   b. Environmentally-Sensitive Areas 478
2. Protection of Young Trees 478
3. Temporary Conditions – Mud, Extreme
   Wetness, Poor Conditions and Protection
   of the Course 478
   a. Relief for Embedded Ball; Cleaning
      Ball 478
   b. "Preferred Lies" and "Winter Rules" 480
   c. Aeration Holes 480
4. Stones in Bunkers 480
5. Immovable Obstructions Close to Putting
   Green 480
6. Temporary Obstructions 480
   a. Temporary Immovable Obstructions 480
   b. Temporary Power Lines and Cables 482

Part C   Conditions of the Competition 482
1. Specification of the Ball 482
   a. List of Conforming Golf Balls 482
   b. One Ball Condition 482
2. Time of Starting 482
3. Caddie 482
4. Pace of Play 483
5. Suspension of Play Due to a Dangerous
   Situation 483
6. Practice 483
   a. General 483
   b. Practice Between Holes 483
7. Advice in Team Competitions 483
8. New Holes 483
9. Transportation 483
10. Anti-Doping 483
11. How to Decide Ties 483
12. Draw for Match Play 484

Part A – Local Rules

As provided in Rule 33-8a, the *Committee* may make and publish Local Rules for local abnormal conditions if they are consistent with the policy established in this Appendix. In addition, detailed information regarding acceptable and prohibited Local Rules is provided in "Decisions on the Rules of Golf" under Rule 33-8 and in "Guidance on Running a Competition".

If local abnormal conditions interfere with the proper playing of the game and the *Committee* considers it necessary to modify a Rule of Golf, authorisation from the *R&A* must be obtained.

1. Defining Bounds and Margins

Specifying means used to define *out of bounds*, *water hazards*, *lateral water hazards*, *ground under repair*, *obstructions* and integral parts of the *course* (Rule 33-2a).

2. Water Hazards
a. Lateral Water Hazards

Clarifying the status of *water hazards* that may be *lateral water hazards* (Rule 26).

b. Provisional Ball

Permitting play of a *provisional ball* under Rule 26-1 for a ball that may be in a *water hazard* of such character that if the original ball is not found, there is reasonable evidence that it is *lost* in the *water hazard* and it would be impracticable to determine whether the ball is in the *hazard* or to do so would unduly delay play. The ball is played provisionally under any of the available options under Rule 26-1 or any applicable Local Rule. In such a case, if a *provisional ball* is played and the original ball is in a *water hazard*, the player may play the original ball as it lies or continue with the *provisional ball* in play, but he may not proceed under Rule 26-1 with regard to the original ball.

3. Areas of the Course Requiring Preservation; Environmentally-Sensitive Areas

Assisting preservation of the *course* by defining areas, including turf nurseries, young plantations and other parts of the *course* under cultivation as "*ground under repair*" from which play is prohibited.

When the *Committee* is required to prohibit play from environmentally-sensitive areas that are on or adjoin the *course*, it should make a Local Rule clarifying the relief procedure.

4. Temporary Conditions – Mud, Extreme Wetness, Poor Conditions and Protection of Course
a. Lifting an Embedded Ball, Cleaning

Temporary conditions that might interfere with proper playing of the game, including mud and extreme wetness, warranting relief for an embedded ball anywhere *through the green* or permitting lifting, cleaning and replacing a ball anywhere *through the green* or on a closely-mown area *through the green*.

b. "Preferred Lies" and "Winter Rules"

Adverse conditions, including the poor condition of the *course* or the existence of mud, are sometimes so

general, particularly during winter months, that the *Committee* may decide to grant relief by temporary Local Rule either to protect the *course* or to promote fair and pleasant play. The Local Rule must be withdrawn as soon as the conditions warrant.

5. Obstructions
a. General
Clarifying status of objects that may be *obstructions* (Rule 24).

Declaring any construction to be an integral part of the *course* and, accordingly, not an *obstruction*, e.g., built-up sides of *teeing grounds*, *putting greens* and *bunkers* (Rules 24 and 33-2a).

b. Stones in Bunkers
Allowing the removal of stones in *bunkers* by declaring them to be "movable *obstructions*" (Rule 24-1).

c. Roads and Paths
(i) Declaring artificial surfaces and sides of roads and paths to be integral parts of the *course*, or
(ii) Providing relief of the type afforded under Rule 24-2b from roads and paths not having artificial surfaces and sides if they could unfairly affect play.

d. Immovable Obstructions Close to Putting Green
Providing relief from intervention by immovable *obstructions* on or within two club-lengths of the *putting green* when the ball lies within two club-lengths of the *obstruction*.

e. Protection of Young Trees
Providing relief for the protection of young trees.

f. Temporary Obstructions
Providing relief from interference by temporary *obstructions* (e.g., grandstands, television cables and equipment, etc).

6. Dropping Zones (Ball Drops)
Establishing special areas on which balls may or must be dropped when it is not feasible or practicable to proceed exactly in conformity with Rule 24-2b or 24-3 (Immovable Obstruction), Rule 25-1b or 25-1c (Abnormal Ground Conditions), Rule 25-3 (Wrong Putting Green), Rule 26-1 (Water Hazards and Lateral Water Hazards) or Rule 28 (Ball Unplayable).

Part B – Specimen Local Rules

Within the policy established in Part A of this Appendix, the *Committee* may adopt a Specimen Local Rule by referring, on a score card or notice board, to the examples given below. However, Specimen Local Rules 3a, 3b, 3c, 6a and 6b should not be printed or referred to on a score card as they are all of limited duration.

1. Areas of the Course Requiring Preservation; Environmentally-Sensitive Areas
a. Ground Under Repair; Play Prohibited
If the *Committee* wishes to protect any area of the *course*, it should declare it to be *ground under repair*

and prohibit play from within that area. The following Local Rule is recommended:

"The _____(defined by ___) is *ground under repair* from which play is prohibited. If a player's ball lies in the area, or if it interferes with the player's *stance* or the area of his intended swing, the player must take relief under Rule 25-1.

PENALTY FOR BREACH OF LOCAL RULE:
Match play – Loss of hole; Stroke play –
Two strokes."

b. Environmentally-Sensitive Areas
If an appropriate authority (i.e. a Government Agency or the like) prohibits entry into and/or play from an area on or adjoining the *course* for environmental reasons, the *Committee* should make a Local Rule clarifying the relief procedure.

The *Committee* has some discretion in terms of whether the area is defined as *ground under repair*, a *water hazard* or *out of bounds*. However, it may not simply define the area to be a *water hazard* if it does not meet the Definition of a "*Water Hazard*" and it should attempt to preserve the character of the hole.

The following Local Rule is recommended:

"I. Definition
An environmentally-sensitive area is an area so declared by an appropriate authority, entry into and/or play from which is prohibited for environmental reasons. These areas may be defined as *ground under repair*, a *water hazard*, a *lateral water hazard* or *out of bounds* at the discretion of the *Committee* provided that, in the case of an environmentally-sensitive area which has been defined as a *water hazard* or a *lateral water hazard*, the area is, by Definition, a *water hazard*.

Note: The *Committee* may not declare an area to be environmentally-sensitive.

II. Ball in Environmentally-Sensitive Area
a. Ground Under Repair
If a ball is in an environmentally-sensitive area that is defined as *ground under repair*, a ball must be dropped in accordance with Rule 25-1b.

If there is reasonable evidence that a ball is *lost* within an environmentally-sensitive area that is defined as *ground under repair*, the player may take relief without penalty as prescribed in Rule 25-1c.

b. Water Hazards and Lateral Water Hazards
If a ball is in or there is reasonable evidence that it is *lost* in an environmentally-sensitive area that is defined as a *water hazard* or *lateral water hazard*, the player must, under penalty of one stroke, proceed under Rule 26-1.

Note: If a ball, dropped in accordance with Rule 26 rolls into a position where the environmentally-sensitive area interferes with the player's *stance* or the area of his intended swing, the player must take relief as provided in Clause III of this Local Rule.

c. Out of Bounds
If a ball is in an environmentally-sensitive area that is defined as *out of bounds*, the player must play a ball, under penalty of one stroke, as nearly as possible at the spot from which the original ball was last played (see Rule 20-5).

III. Interference with Stance or Area of Intended Swing
Interference by an environmentally-sensitive area occurs when the condition interferes with the player's *stance* or the area of his intended swing. If interference exists, the player must take relief as follows:

(a) Through the Green: If the ball lies *through the green*, the point on the *course* nearest to where the ball lies must be determined that (a) is not nearer the *hole*, (b) avoids interference by the condition and (c) is not in a *hazard* or on a *putting green*. The player must lift the ball and drop it without penalty within one club-length of the point so determined on a part of the *course* that fulfils (a), (b) and (c) above.

(b) In a Hazard: If the ball is in a *hazard*, the player must lift the ball and drop it either:

(i) Without penalty, in the *hazard*, as near as possible to the spot where the ball lay, but not nearer the *hole*, on a part of the *course* that provides complete relief from the condition; or

(ii) Under penalty of one stroke, outside the *hazard*, keeping the point where the ball lay directly between the *hole* and the spot on which the ball is dropped, with no limit to how far behind the *hazard* the ball may be dropped. Additionally, the player may proceed under Rule 26 or 28 if applicable.

(c) On the Putting Green: If the ball lies on the *putting green*, the player must lift the ball and place it without penalty in the nearest position to where it lay that affords complete relief from the condition, but not nearer the *hole* or in a *hazard*.

The ball may be cleaned when lifted under Clause III of this Local Rule.

Exception: A player may not obtain relief under Clause III of this Local Rule if (a) it is clearly unreasonable for him to make a *stroke* because of interference by anything other than a condition covered by this Local Rule or (b) interference by the condition would occur only through use of an unnecessarily abnormal *stance*, swing or direction of play.

PENALTY FOR BREACH OF LOCAL RULE:
Match play – Loss of hole; Stroke play – Two strokes.

Note: In the case of a serious breach of this Local Rule, the *Committee* may impose a penalty of disqualification."

2. Protection of Young Trees
When it is desired to prevent damage to young trees, the following Local Rule is recommended:

"Protection of young trees identified by _____. If such a tree interferes with a player's *stance* or the area of his intended swing, the ball must be lifted, without penalty, and dropped in accordance with the procedure prescribed in Rule 24-2b (Immovable Obstruction). If the ball lies in a *water hazard*, the player must lift and drop the ball in accordance with Rule 24-2b(i) except that the *nearest point of relief* must be in the *water hazard* and the ball must be dropped in the *water hazard* or the player may proceed under Rule 26. The ball may be cleaned when lifted under this Local Rule.

Exception: A player may not obtain relief under this Local Rule if (a) it is clearly unreasonable for him to make a *stroke* because of interference by anything other than the tree or (b) interference by the tree would occur only through use of an unnecessarily abnormal *stance*, swing or direction of play.

PENALTY FOR BREACH OF LOCAL RULE:
Match play – Loss of hole; Stroke play – Two strokes."

3. Temporary Conditions – Mud, Extreme Wetness, Poor Conditions and Protection of the Course
a. Relief for Embedded Ball; Cleaning Ball
Rule 25-2 provides relief without penalty for a ball embedded in its own pitch-mark in any closely-mown area *through the green*. On the *putting green*, a ball may be lifted and damage caused by the impact of a ball may be repaired (Rules 16-1b and c). When permission to take relief for an embedded ball anywhere *through the green* would be warranted, the following Local Rule is recommended:

"*Through the green*, a ball that is embedded in its own pitch-mark in the ground, other than sand, may be lifted without penalty, cleaned and dropped as near as possible to where it lay but not nearer the *hole*. The ball when dropped must first strike a part of the *course through the green*.

Exception: A player may not obtain relief under this Local Rule if it is clearly unreasonable for him to make a *stroke* because of interference by anything other than the condition covered by this Local Rule.

PENALTY FOR BREACH OF LOCAL RULE:
Match play – Loss of hole; Stroke play – Two strokes."

Alternatively, conditions may be such that permission to lift, clean and replace the ball will suffice. In these circumstances, the following Local Rule is recommended:

"(Specify area) a ball may be lifted, cleaned and replaced without penalty.

Note: The position of the ball must be marked before it is lifted under this Local Rule – see Rule 20-1.

PENALTY FOR BREACH OF LOCAL RULE:
Match play – Loss of hole; Stroke play – Two strokes."

b. "Preferred Lies" and "Winter Rules"

Ground under repair is provided for in Rule 25 and occasional local abnormal conditions that might interfere with fair play and are not widespread should be defined as *ground under repair*.

However, adverse conditions, such as heavy snows, spring thaws, prolonged rains or extreme heat can make fairways unsatisfactory and sometimes prevent use of heavy mowing equipment. When such conditions are so general throughout a *course* that the *Committee* believes "preferred lies" or "winter rules" would promote fair play or help protect the course, the following Local Rule is recommended:

"A ball lying on a closely-mown area *through the green* [or specify a more restricted area, e.g. at the 6th hole] may be lifted without penalty and cleaned. Before lifting the ball, the player must mark its position. Having lifted the ball, he must place it on a spot within [specify area, e.g. six inches, one club-length, etc.] of and not nearer the *hole* than where it originally lay, that is not in a *hazard* and not on a *putting green*.

A player may place his ball only once, and it is in play when it has been placed (Rule 20-4). If the ball fails to come to rest on the spot on which it is placed, Rule 20-3d applies. If the ball when placed comes to rest on the spot on which it is placed and it subsequently *moves*, there is no penalty and the ball must be played as it lies, unless the provisions of any other *Rule* apply.

If the player fails to mark the position of the ball before lifting it or *moves* the ball in any other manner, such as rolling it with a club, he incurs a penalty of one stroke.

*PENALTY FOR BREACH OF LOCAL RULE:
Match play – Loss of hole; Stroke play –
Two strokes
*If a player incurs the general penalty for a breach of this Local Rule, no additional penalty under the Local Rule is applied."

c. Aeration Holes

When a *course* has been aerated, a Local Rule permitting relief, without penalty, from an aeration hole may be warranted. The following Local Rule is recommended:

"*Through the green*, a ball that comes to rest in or on an aeration hole may be lifted without penalty, cleaned and dropped, as near as possible to the spot where it lay but not nearer the *hole*. The ball when dropped must first strike a part of the *course through the green*.

On the *putting green*, a ball that comes to rest in or on an aeration hole may be placed at the nearest spot not nearer the *hole* that avoids the situation.

PENALTY FOR BREACH OF LOCAL RULE:
Match play – Loss of hole; Stroke play –
Two strokes."

4. Stones in Bunkers

Stones are, by definition, *loose impediments* and, when a player's ball is in a *hazard*, a stone lying in or

touching the *hazard* may not be touched or moved (Rule 13-4). However, stones in *bunkers* may represent a danger to players (a player could be injured by a stone struck by the player's club in an attempt to play the ball) and they may interfere with the proper playing of the game.

When permission to lift a stone in a *bunker* would be warranted, the following Local Rule is recommended:

"Stones in *bunkers* are movable *obstructions* (Rule 24-1 applies)."

5. Immovable Obstructions Close to Putting Green

Rule 24-2 provides relief without penalty from interference by an immovable *obstruction*, but it also provides that, except on the *putting green*, intervention on the *line of play* is not, of itself, interference under this Rule.

However, on some courses, the aprons of the *putting greens* are so closely mown that players may wish to putt from just off the green. In such conditions, immovable obstructions on the apron may interfere with the proper playing of the game and the introduction of the following Local Rule providing additional relief without penalty from intervention by an immovable *obstruction* would be warranted:

"Relief from interference by an immovable *obstruction* may be obtained under Rule 24-2. In addition, if a ball lies off the *putting green* but not in a *hazard* and an immovable *obstruction* on or within two club-lengths of the *putting green* and within two club-lengths of the ball intervenes on the *line of play* between the ball and the *hole*, the player may take relief as follows:

The ball must be lifted and dropped at the nearest point to where the ball lay that (a) is not nearer the *hole*, (b) avoids intervention and (c) is not in a *hazard* or on a *putting green*. The ball may be cleaned when lifted.

Relief under this Local Rule is also available if the player's ball lies on the *putting green* and an immovable *obstruction* within two club-lengths of the *putting green* intervenes on his *line of putt*. The player may take relief as follows:

The ball must be lifted and placed at the nearest point where the ball lay that (a) is not nearer the *hole*, (b) avoids intervention and (c) is not in a *hazard*. The ball may be cleaned when lifted.

PENALTY FOR BREACH OF LOCAL RULE:
Match play – Loss of hole; Stroke play –
Two strokes."

6. Temporary Obstructions

When temporary *obstructions* are installed on or adjoining the *course*, the *Committee* should define the status of such *obstructions* as movable, immovable or temporary immovable *obstructions*.

a. Temporary Immovable Obstructions

If the *Committee* defines such *obstructions* as temporary immovable *obstructions*, the following Local Rule is recommended:

"I. Definition
A temporary immovable *obstruction* is a non-permanent artificial object that is often erected in conjunction with a competition and is fixed or not readily movable.

Examples of temporary immovable *obstructions* include, but are not limited to, tents, scoreboards, grandstands, television towers and lavatories.

Supporting guy wires are part of the temporary immovable *obstruction* unless the *Committee* declares that they are to be treated as elevated power lines or cables.

II. Interference
Interference by a temporary immovable *obstruction* occurs when (a) the ball lies in front of and so close to the *obstruction* that the *obstruction* interferes with the player's *stance* or the area of his intended swing, or (b) the ball lies in, on, under or behind the *obstruction* so that any part of the *obstruction* intervenes directly between the player's ball and the *hole*; interference also exists if the ball lies within one club-length of a spot equidistant from the hole where such intervention would exist.

Note: A ball is under a temporary immovable *obstruction* when it is below the outer most edges of the *obstruction*, even if these edges do not extend downwards to the ground.

III. Relief
A player may obtain relief from interference by a temporary immovable *obstruction*, including a temporary immovable *obstruction* that is *out of bounds*, as follows:

(a) **Through the Green:** If the ball lies *through the green*, the point on the *course* nearest to where the ball lies must be determined that (a) is not nearer the *hole*, (b) avoids interference as defined in Clause II and (c) is not in a *hazard* or on a *putting green*. The player must lift the ball and drop it without penalty within one club-length of the point so determined on a part of the *course* that fulfils (a), (b) and (c) above.

(b) **In a Hazard:** If the ball is in a *hazard*, the player must lift and drop the ball either:

   (i) Without penalty, in accordance with Clause IIIa above, except that the nearest part of the *course* affording complete relief must be in the *hazard* and the ball must be dropped in the *hazard* or, if complete relief is impossible, on a part of the *course* within the *hazard* that affords maximum available relief; or

   (ii) Under penalty of one stroke, outside the *hazard* as follows: the point on the *course* nearest to where the ball lies must be determined that (a) is not nearer the *hole*, (b) avoids interference as defined in Clause II and (c) is not in a *hazard*. The player must drop the ball within one club-length of the point so determined on a part of the *course* that fulfils (a), (b) and (c) above.

The ball may be cleaned when lifted under Clause III.

Note 1: If the ball lies in a *hazard*, nothing in this Local Rule precludes the player from proceeding under Rule 26 or Rule 28, if applicable.

Note 2: If a ball to be dropped under this Local Rule is not immediately recoverable, another ball may be *substituted*.

Note 3: A *Committee* may make a Local Rule (a) permitting or requiring a player to use a dropping zone or ball drop when taking relief from a temporary immovable *obstruction* or (b) permitting a player, as an additional relief option, to drop the ball on the opposite side of the *obstruction* from the point established under Clause III, but otherwise in accordance with Clause III.

Exceptions: If a player's ball lies in front of or behind the temporary immovable *obstruction* (not in, on or under the *obstruction*) he may not obtain relief under Clause III if:

1. It is clearly unreasonable for him to make a *stroke* or, in the case of intervention, to make a *stroke* such that the ball could finish on a direct line to the *hole*, because of interference by anything other than the temporary immovable *obstruction*;

2. Interference by the temporary immovable *obstruction* would occur only through use of an unnecessarily abnormal *stance*, swing or direction of play; or

3. In the case of intervention, it would be clearly unreasonable to expect the player to be able to strike the ball far enough towards the *hole* to reach the temporary immovable *obstruction*.

Note: A player not entitled to relief due to these exceptions may proceed under Rule 24-2, if applicable.

IV. Ball Lost
If there is reasonable evidence that the ball is *lost* in, on or under a temporary immovable *obstruction*, a ball may be dropped under the provisions of Clause III or Clause V, if applicable. For the purpose of applying Clauses III and V, the ball is deemed to lie at the spot where it last crossed the outermost limits of the *obstruction* (Rule 24-3).

V. Dropping Zones (Ball Drops)
If the player has interference from a temporary immovable *obstruction*, the *Committee* may permit or require the use of a dropping zone or ball drop. If the player uses a dropping zone in taking relief, he must drop the ball in the dropping zone nearest to where his ball originally lay or is deemed to lie under Clause IV (even though the nearest dropping zone may be nearer the *hole*).

Note 1: A *Committee* may make a Local Rule prohibiting the use of a dropping zone or ball drop that is nearer the *hole*.

Note 2: If the ball is dropped in a dropping zone, the ball must not be re-dropped if it comes to rest within two club-lengths of the spot where it first struck a part of the *course* even though it may come to rest nearer the *hole* or outside the boundaries of the dropping zone.

PENALTY FOR BREACH OF LOCAL RULE:
Match play – Loss of hole; Stroke play –
Two strokes."

b. Temporary Power Lines and Cables

When temporary power lines, cables, or telephone lines are installed on the *course*, the following Local Rule is recommended:

"Temporary power lines, cables, telephone lines and mats covering or stanchions supporting them are *obstructions*:

1. If they are readily movable, Rule 24-1 applies.

2. If they are fixed or not readily movable, the player may, if the ball lies *through the green* or in a *bunker*, obtain relief as provided in Rule 24-2b. If the ball lies in a *water hazard*, the player may lift and drop the ball in accordance with Rule 24-2b(i) except that the *nearest point of relief* must be in the *water hazard* and the ball must be dropped in the *water hazard* or the player may proceed under Rule 26.

3. If a ball strikes an elevated power line or cable, the *stroke* must be cancelled and replayed, without penalty (see Rule 20-5). If the ball is not immediately recoverable another ball may be *substituted*.

Note: Guy wires supporting a temporary immovable *obstruction* are part of the temporary immovable *obstruction* unless the *Committee*, by Local Rule, declares that they are to be treated as elevated power lines or cables.

Exception: Ball striking elevated junction section of cable rising from the ground must not be replayed.

4. Grass-covered cable trenches are *ground under repair* even if not marked and Rule 25-1b applies."

Part C – Conditions of the Competition

Rule 33-1 provides, "The *Committee* must establish the conditions under which a competition is to be played." The conditions should include many matters such as method of entry, eligibility, number of rounds to be played, etc. which it is not appropriate to deal with in the Rules of Golf or this Appendix. Detailed information regarding these conditions is provided in "Decisions on the Rules of Golf" under Rule 33-1 and in "Guidance on Running a Competition".

However, there are a number of matters that might be covered in the Conditions of the Competition to which the *Committee's* attention is specifically drawn. These are:

1. Specification of the Ball (Note to Rule 5-1)

The following two conditions are recommended only for competitions involving expert players:

a. List of Conforming Golf Balls

The *R&A* periodically issues a List of Conforming Golf Balls which lists balls that have been tested and found to conform. If the *Committee* wishes to require players to play a brand of golf ball on the List, the List should be posted and the following condition of competition used:

"The ball the player plays must be named on the current List of Conforming Golf Balls issued by the *R&A*.

PENALTY FOR BREACH OF CONDITION:
Disqualification."

b. One Ball Condition

If it is desired to prohibit changing brands and types of golf balls during a *stipulated round*, the following condition is recommended:

"Limitation on Balls Used During Round: (Note to Rule 5-1)

(i) "One Ball" Condition
During a *stipulated round*, the balls a player plays must be of the same brand and type as detailed by a single entry on the current List of Conforming Golf Balls.

Note: If a ball of a different brand and/or type is dropped or placed it may be lifted, without penalty, and the player must then proceed by dropping or placing a proper ball (Rule 20-6).

PENALTY FOR BREACH OF CONDITION:
Match Play – At the conclusion of the hole at which the breach is discovered, the state of the match must be adjusted by deducting one hole for each hole at which a breach occurred; maximum deduction per round: Two holes.
Stroke Play – Two strokes for each hole at which any breach occurred; maximum penalty per round: Four strokes.

(ii) Procedure When Breach Discovered
When a player discovers that he has played a ball in breach of this condition, he must abandon that ball before playing from the next *teeing ground* and complete the round with a proper ball; otherwise, the player is disqualified. If discovery is made during play of a hole and the player elects to *substitute* a proper ball before completing that hole, the player must place a proper ball on the spot where the ball played in breach of the condition lay."

2. Time of Starting (Note to Rule 6-3a)

If the *Committee* wishes to act in accordance with the Note, the following wording is recommended:

"If the player arrives at his starting point, ready to play, within five minutes after his starting time, in the absence of circumstances that warrant waiving the penalty of disqualification as provided in Rule 33-7, the penalty for failure to start on time is loss of the first hole to be played in match play or two strokes in stroke play. Penalty for lateness beyond five minutes is disqualification."

3. Caddie (Note to Rule 6-4)

Rule 6-4 permits a player to use a *caddie* provided he has only one *caddie* at any one time. However, there may be circumstances where a *Committee* may wish to ban *caddies* or restrict a player in his choice of *caddie*, e.g. professional golfer, sibling, parent, another player in the competition, etc. In such cases, the following wording is recommended:

Use of Caddie Prohibited

"A player is prohibited from using a *caddie* during the *stipulated round*."

Restriction on Who May Serve as Caddie
"A player is prohibited from having _____ serve as his *caddie* during the *stipulated round*.

PENALTY FOR BREACH OF CONDITION:
Match play – At the conclusion of the hole at which the breach is discovered, the state of the match is adjusted by deducting one hole for each hole at which a breach occurred; maximum deduction per round – Two holes.
Stroke play – Two strokes for each hole at which any breach occurred; maximum penalty per round – Four strokes.
Match or stroke play – In the event of a breach between the play of two holes, the penalty applies to the next hole.
A player having a *caddie* in breach of this condition must immediately upon discovery that a breach has occurred ensure that he conforms with this condition for the remainder of the *stipulated round*. Otherwise, the player is disqualified.

4. Pace of Play (Note 2 to Rule 6-7)
The *Committee* may establish pace of play guidelines to help prevent slow play, in accordance with Note 2 to Rule 6-7.

5. Suspension of Play Due to a Dangerous Situation (Note to Rule 6-8b)
As there have been many deaths and injuries from lightning on golf courses, all clubs and sponsors of golf competitions are urged to take precautions for the protection of persons against lightning. Attention is called to Rules 6-8 and 33-2d. If the *Committee* desires to adopt the condition in the Note under Rule 6-8b, the following wording is recommended:
"When play is suspended by the *Committee* for a dangerous situation, if the players in a match or group are between the play of two holes, they must not resume play until the *Committee* has ordered a resumption of play. If they are in the process of playing a hole, they must discontinue play immediately and not resume play until the *Committee* has ordered a resumption of play. If a player fails to discontinue play immediately, he is disqualified unless circumstances warrant waiving the penalty as provided in Rule 33-7.
The signal for suspending play due to a dangerous situation will be a prolonged note of the siren."
The following signals are generally used and it is recommended that all *Committees* do similarly:
Discontinue Play Immediately: One prolonged note of siren
Discontinue Play: Three consecutive notes of siren, repeated
Resume Play: Two short notes of siren, repeated

6. Practice
a. General
The *Committee* may make regulations governing practice in accordance with the Note to Rule 7-1, Exception (c) to Rule 7-2, Note 2 to Rule 7 and Rule 33-2c.

b. Practice Between Holes (Note 2 to Rule 7)
It is recommended that a condition of competition prohibiting practice putting or chipping on or near the *putting green* of the hole last played be introduced only in stroke play competitions. The following wording is recommended:
"A player must not play any practice *stroke* on or near the *putting green* of the hole last played. If a practice *stroke* is played on or near the *putting green* of the hole last played, the player incurs a penalty of two strokes at the next hole, except that in the case of the last hole of the round, he incurs the penalty at that hole."

7. Advice in Team Competitions (Note to Rule 8)
If the *Committee* wishes to act in accordance with the Note under Rule 8, the following wording is recommended:
"In accordance with the Note to Rule 8 of the Rules of Golf, each team may appoint one person (in addition to the persons from whom *advice* may be asked under that Rule) who may give *advice* to members of that team. Such person (if it is desired to insert any restriction on who may be nominated insert such restriction here) must be identified to the *Committee* before giving *advice*."

8. New Holes (Note to Rule 33-2b)
The *Committee* may provide, in accordance with the Note to Rule 33-2b, that the *holes* and *teeing grounds* for a single round competition, being held on more than one day, may be differently situated on each day.

9. Transportation
If it is desired to require players to walk in a competition, the following condition is recommended:
"Players must walk at all times during a *stipulated round*.

PENALTY FOR BREACH OF CONDITION:
Match play – At the conclusion of the hole at which the breach is discovered, the state of the match must be adjusted by deducting one hole for each hole at which a breach occurred. Maximum deduction per round: Two holes.
Stroke play – Two strokes for each hole at which any breach occurred; maximum penalty per round: Four strokes. In the event of a breach between the play of two holes, the penalty applies to the next hole.
Match or stroke play – Use of any unauthorised form of transportation must be discontinued immediately upon discovery that a breach has occurred. Otherwise, the player is disqualified."

10. Anti-Doping
The *Committee* may require, in the Conditions of Competition, that players comply with an anti-doping policy.

11. How to Decide Ties
Rule 33-6 empowers the *Committee* to determine how and when a halved match or a stroke play tie is decided. The decision should be published in advance.

The *R&A* recommends:

Match Play

A match which ends all square should be played off hole by hole until one *side* wins a hole. The play-off should start on the hole where the match began. In a handicap match, handicap strokes should be allowed as in the prescribed round.

Stroke Play

(a) In the event of a tie in a scratch stroke play competition, a play-off is recommended. Such a play-off may be over 18 holes or a smaller number of holes as specified by the *Committee*. If that is not feasible or there is still a tie, a hole-by-hole play-off is recommended.

(b) In the event of a tie in a handicap stroke play competition, a play-off with handicaps is recommended. Such a play-off may be over 18 holes or a smaller number of holes as specified by the *Committee*. If the play-off is less than 18 holes the percentage of 18 holes to be played should be applied to the players' handicaps to determine their play-off handicaps. Handicap stroke fractions of one-half stroke or more should count as a full stroke and any lesser fraction should be disregarded.

(c) In either a scratch or handicap stroke play competition, if a play-off of any type is not feasible, matching score cards is recommended. The method of matching cards should be announced in advance. An acceptable method of matching cards is to determine the winner on the basis of the best score for the last nine holes. If the tying players have the same score for the last nine, determine the winner on the basis of the last six holes, last three holes and finally the 18th hole. If this method is used in a handicap stroke play competition, one-half, one-third, one-sixth, etc. of the handicaps should be deducted. Fractions should not be disregarded. If this method is used in a competition with a multiple tee start, it is recommended that the "last nine holes, last six holes, etc." is considered to be holes 10-18, 13-18, etc.

(d) If the conditions of the competition provide that ties are to be decided over the last nine, last six, last three and last hole, they should also provide what will happen if this procedure does not produce a winner.

12. Draw for Match Play

Although the draw for match play may be completely blind or certain players may be distributed through different quarters or eighths, the General Numerical Draw is recommended if matches are determined by a qualifying round.

General Numerical Draw

For purposes of determining places in the draw, ties in qualifying rounds other than those for the last qualifying place are decided by the order in which scores are returned, with the first score to be returned receiving the lowest available number, etc. If it is impossible to determine the order in which scores are returned, ties are determined by a blind draw.

UPPER HALF	LOWER HALF
64 QUALIFIERS	
1 vs. 64	2 vs. 63
32 vs. 33	31 vs. 34
16 vs. 49	15 vs. 50
17 vs. 48	18 vs. 47
8 vs. 57	7 vs. 58
25 vs. 40	26 vs. 39
9 vs. 56	10 vs. 55
24 vs. 41	23 vs. 42
4 vs. 61	3 vs. 62
29 vs. 36	30 vs. 35
13 vs. 52	14 vs. 51
20 vs. 45	19 vs. 46
5 vs. 60	6 vs. 59
28 vs. 37	27 vs. 38
12 vs. 53	11 vs. 54
21 vs. 44	22 vs. 43

UPPER HALF	LOWER HALF
32 QUALIFIERS	
1 vs. 32	2 vs. 31
16 vs. 17	15 vs. 18
8 vs. 25	7 vs. 26
9 vs. 24	10 vs. 23
4 vs. 29	3 vs. 30
13 vs. 20	14 vs. 19
5 vs. 28	6 vs. 27
12 vs. 21	11 vs. 22
16 QUALIFIERS	
1 vs. 16	2 vs.15
8 vs. 9	7 vs.10
4 vs. 13	3 vs.14
5 vs. 12	6 vs. 11
8 QUALIFIERS	
1 vs. 8	2 vs. 7
4 vs. 5	3 vs. 6

APPENDICES II AND III

Any design in a club or ball which is not covered by Rules 4 and 5 and Appendices II and III, or which might significantly change the nature of the game, will be ruled on by the *R&A*.

The dimensions contained in Appendices II and III are referenced in imperial measurements. A metric conversion is also referenced for information, calculated using a conversion rate of 1 inch = 25.4 mm. In the event of any dispute over the conformity of a club or ball, the imperial measurement takes precedence.

APPENDIX II – DESIGN OF CLUBS

A player in doubt as to the conformity of a club should consult the *R&A*.

A manufacturer should submit to the *R&A* a sample of a club, which is to be manufactured for a ruling as to whether the club conforms with the *Rules*. If a manufacturer fails to submit a sample or to await a ruling before manufacturing and/or marketing the club, the manufacturer assumes the risk of a ruling that the club does not conform with the *Rules*. Any sample submitted to the *R&A* becomes its property for reference purposes.

The following paragraphs prescribe general regulations for the design of clubs, together with specifications and interpretations. Further information relating to these regulations and their proper interpretation is provided in "A Guide to the Rules on Clubs and Balls".

Where a club, or part of a club, is required to have some specific property, this means that it must be designed and manufactured with the intention of having that property. The finished club or part must have that property within manufacturing tolerances appropriate to the material used.

1. Clubs
a. General

A club is an implement designed to be used for striking the ball and generally comes in three forms: woods, irons and putters distinguished by shape and intended use. A putter is a club with a loft not exceeding ten degrees designed primarily for use on the *putting green*.

The club must not be substantially different from the the traditional and customary form and make. The club must be composed of a shaft and a head. All parts of the club must be fixed so that the club is one unit, and it must have no external attachments except as otherwise permitted by the *Rules*.

b. Adjustability

Woods and irons must not be designed to be adjustable except for weight. Putters may be

designed to be adjustable for weight and some other forms of adjustability are also permitted. All methods of adjustment permitted by the *Rules* require that:

(i) the adjustment cannot be readily made;

(ii) all adjustable parts are firmly fixed and there is no reasonable likelihood of them working loose during a round; and

(iii) all configurations of adjustment conform with the *Rules*.

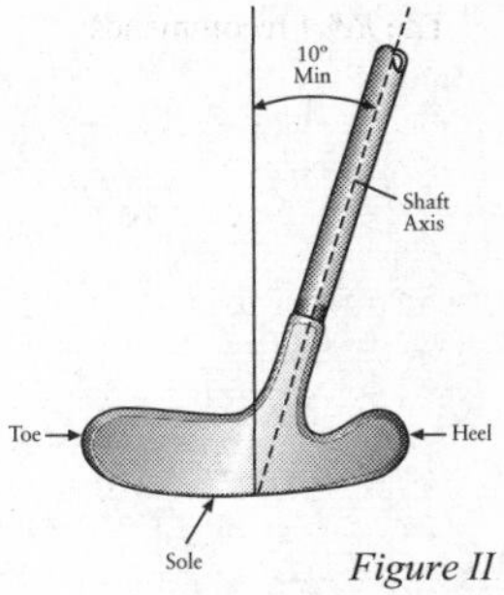

The disqualification penalty for purposely changing the playing characteristics of a club during a *stipulated round* (Rule 4-2a) applies to all clubs including a putter.

c. Length

The overall length of the club must be at least 18 inches (457.2 mm) and, except for putters, must not exceed 48 inches (1,219.2 mm). For woods and irons, the measurement of length is taken when the club is lying on a horizontal plane and the sole is set against a 60 degree plane as shown in Fig. I. The length is defined as the distance from the point of the intersection between the two planes to the top of the grip. For putters, the measurement of length is taken from the top of the grip along the axis of the shaft or a straight line extension of it to the sole of the club.

Note: Clubs in breach of the maximum length limit as specified in Appendix II, 1c, which were in use or marketed prior to 1st January 2004 and which otherwise conform to the *Rules*, may be used until 31st December 2004.

d. Alignment

When the club is in its normal address position the shaft must be so aligned that:

(i) the projection of the straight part of the shaft on to the vertical plane through the toe and heel must diverge from the vertical by at least 10 degrees (see Fig. II);

(ii) the projection of the straight part of the shaft on to the vertical plane along the intended line of play must not diverge from the verti-

Figure II

Figure III

Figure I

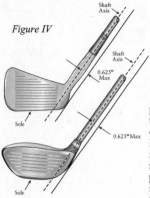

Figure IV

cal by more than 20 degrees forwards or 10 degrees backwards (see Fig. III).

Except for putters, all of the heel portion of the club must lie within 0.625 inches (15.88 mm) of the plane containing the axis of the straight part of the shaft and the intended (horizontal) line of play (see Fig. IV).

2. Shaft
a. Straightness
The shaft must be straight from the top of the grip to a point not more than 5 inches (127 mm) above the sole, measured from the point where the shaft ceases to be straight along the axis of the bent part of the shaft and the neck and/or socket (see Fig. V).

b. Bending and Twisting Properties
At any point along its length, the shaft must:

 (i) bend in such a way that the deflection is the same regardless of how the shaft is rotated about its longitudinal axis; and
 (ii) twist the same amount in both directions.

c. Attachment to Clubhead
The shaft must be attached to the clubhead at the heel either directly or through a single plain neck and/or socket. The length from the top of the neck and/or socket to the sole of the club must not exceed 5 inches (127 mm), measured along the axis of, and following any bend in, the neck and/or socket (see Fig. VI).

 Exception for Putters: The shaft or neck or socket of a putter may be fixed at any point in the head.

3. Grip (see Fig. VII)
The grip consists of material added to the shaft to enable the player to obtain a firm hold. The grip must

be straight and plain in form, must extend to the end of the shaft and must not be moulded for any part of the hands. If no material is added, that portion of the shaft designed to be held by the player must be considered the grip.

 (i) For clubs other than putters the grip must be circular in cross-section, except that a continuous, straight, slightly raised rib may be incorporated along the full length of the grip, and a slightly indented spiral is permitted on a wrapped grip or a replica of one.
 (ii) A putter grip may have a non-circular cross-section, provided the cross-section has no concavity, is symmetrical and remains generally similar through-out the length of the grip. (See Clause (v) overleaf).
 (iii) The grip may be tapered but must not have any bulge or waist. Its cross-sectional dimensions measured in any direction must not exceed 1.75 inches (44.45 mm).
 (iv) For clubs other than putters the axis of the grip must coincide with the axis of the shaft.
 (v) A putter may have two grips provided each is circular in cross-section, the axis of each coincides with the axis of the shaft, and they are separated by at least 1.5 inches (38.1 mm).

4. Clubhead
a. Plain in Shape
The clubhead must be generally plain in shape. All parts must be rigid, structural in nature and functional. It is not practicable to define plain in shape precisely and comprehensively but features which are deemed to be in breach of this requirement and are therefore not permitted include:

 (i) holes through the head,
 (ii) transparent material added for other than decorative or structural purposes,
 (iii) appendages to the main body of the head such as knobs, plates, rods or fins, for the purpose of meeting dimensional specifications, for aiming or for any other purpose. Exceptions may be made for putters.

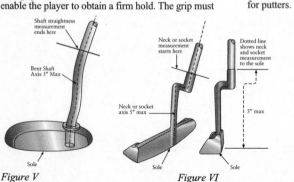

Figure V   *Figure VI*

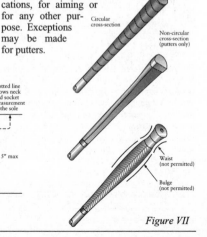

Figure VII

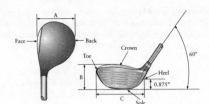

Figure VIII

Any furrows in or runners on the sole must not extend into the face.

b. Dimensions and Size
(i) Woods
When the club is in a 60 degree lie angle, the dimensions of the clubhead must be such that:

(a) the distance from the heel to the toe of the clubhead is greater than the distance from the face to the back;

(b) the distance from the heel to the toe of the clubhead is not greater than 5 inches (127 mm); and

(c) the distance from the sole to the crown of the clubhead is not greater than 2.8 inches (71.12 mm).

These dimensions are measured on horizontal lines between vertical projections of the outermost points of:

- the heel and the toe; and
- the face and the back (see Fig. VIII, dimension A);

and on vertical lines between the horizontal projections of the outermost points of the sole and the crown (see Fig. VIII, dimension B). If the outermost point of the heel is not clearly defined, it is deemed to be 0.875 inches (22.23 mm) above the horizontal plane on which the club is lying (see Fig. VIII, dimension C).

The size of the clubhead must not exceed 28.06 cubic inches (460 cubic centimetres), plus a tolerance of 0.61 cubic inches (10 cubic centimetres).

Note: Clubs in breach of the maximum size limit as specified in Appendix II, 4b (i), which were in use or marketed prior to 1st January 2004 and which otherwise conform to the *Rules*, may be used until 31st December 2004.

(ii) Irons and Putters
When the clubhead is in its normal address position the dimensions of the head must be such that the distance from the heel to the toe is greater than the distance from the face to the back. For traditionally shaped heads, these dimensions will be measured on horizontal lines between vertical projections of the outermost points of:

- the heel and the toe; and
- the face and the back.

For unusually shaped heads, the toe to heel dimension may be made at the face.

c. Striking Faces
The clubhead must have only one striking face, except that a putter may have two such faces if their characteristics are the same, and they are opposite each other.

5. Club Face   *Figure IX*
a. General
The material and construction of, or any treatment to, the face or clubhead must not have the effect at impact of a spring (test on file), or impart significantly more or less spin to the ball than a standard steel face, or have any other effect which would unduly influence the movement of the ball.

The face of the club must be hard and rigid (some exceptions may be made for putters) and, except for such markings listed below, must be smooth and must not have any degree of concavity.

b. Impact Area Roughness and Material
Except for markings specified in the following paragraphs, the surface roughness within the area where impact is intended (the "impact area") must not exceed that of decorative sandblasting, or of fine milling (see Fig. IX).

The whole of the impact area must be of the same material. Exceptions may be made for wooden clubs.

c. Impact Area Markings
Markings in the impact area must not have sharp edges or raised lips as determined by a finger test. Grooves or punch marks in the impact area must meet the following specifications:

(i) Grooves. A series of straight grooves with diverging sides and a symmetrical cross-section may be used (see Fig. X).

- The width and cross-section must be consistent across the face of the club and along the length of the grooves.
- Any rounding of groove edges must be in the form of a radius which does not exceed 0.020 inches (0.508 mm).
- The width of the grooves must not exceed 0.035 inches (0.9 mm), using the 30 degree method of measurement on file with the *R&A*.
- The distance between edges of adjacent grooves must not be less than three times the width of a groove, and not less than 0.075 inches (1.905 mm).

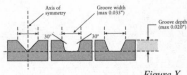

Figure X

- The depth of a groove must not exceed 0.020 inches (0.508 mm).

(ii) Punch Marks. Punch marks may be used.

- The area of any such mark must not exceed 0.0044 square inches (2.84 sq. mm).
- A mark must not be closer to an adjacent mark than 0.168 inches (4.27 mm) measured from centre to centre.
- The depth of a punch mark must not exceed 0.040 inches (1.02 mm).
- If punch marks are used in combination with grooves, a punch mark must not be closer to a groove than 0.168 inches (4.27 mm), measured from centre to centre.

d. Decorative Markings
The centre of the impact area may be indicated by a design within the boundary of a square whose sides are 0.375 inches (9.53 mm) in length. Such a design must not unduly influence the movement of the ball. Decorative markings are permitted outside the impact area.

e. Non-Metallic Club Face Markings
The above specifications apply to clubs on which the impact area of the face is of metal or a material of similar hardness. They do not apply to clubs with faces made of other materials and whose loft angle is 24 degrees or less, but markings which could unduly influence the movement of the ball are prohibited. Clubs with this type of face and a loft angle exceeding 24 degrees may have grooves of maximum width 0.040 inches (1.02 mm) and maximum depth 1½ times the groove width, but must otherwise conform to the markings specifications above.

f. Putter Face Markings
The specifications above with regard to roughness, material and markings in the impact area do not apply to putters.

APPENDIX III – THE BALL

1. Weight
The weight of the ball must not be greater than 1.620 ounces avoirdupois (45.93 gm).

2. Size
The diameter of the ball must not be less than 1.680 inches (42.67 mm). This specification will be satisfied if, under its own weight, a ball falls through a 1.680 inches diameter ring gauge in fewer than 25 out of 100 randomly selected positions, the test being carried out at a temperature of 23 +/- 1°C.

3. Spherical Symmetry
The ball must not be designed, manufactured or intentionally modified to have properties which differ from those of a spherically symmetrical ball.

4. Initial Velocity
The initial velocity of the ball must not exceed the limit specified (test on file) when measured on apparatus approved by the *R&A*.

5. Overall Distance Standard
The combined carry and roll of the ball, when tested on apparatus approved by the *R&A*, must not exceed the distance specified under the conditions set forth in the Overall Distance Standard for golf balls on file with the *R&A*.

HANDICAPS

The Rules of Golf do not legislate for the allocation and adjustment of handicaps. Such matters are within the jurisdiction of the National Union concerned and queries should be directed accordingly.

RULES OF AMATEUR STATUS
As approved by R&A Rules Limited
Effective from 1st January 2004

Preamble
The *R&A* reserves the right to change the *Rules* and to make and change the interpretations relating to Amateur Status at any time.

In the Rules of Amateur Status, the gender used in relation to any person is understood to include both genders.

DEFINITIONS
The Definitions are listed alphabetically and, in the *Rules* themselves, defined terms are in *italics*.

Amateur Golfer
An "Amateur Golfer" is one who plays the game as a non-remunerative and non-profit making sport and who does not receive remuneration for teaching golf or for other activities because of *golf skill or reputation*, except as provided in the *Rules*.

Committee
The "Committee" is the appropriate *Committee* of the *Governing Body*.

Golf Skill or Reputation
Generally, an *Amateur golfer* is only considered to have *golf skill* if he has gained representative honours at county or national level. *Golf reputation* can only be gained through *golf skill* and does not include prominence for service to the game of golf as an administrator. It is a matter for a *Governing Body* to decide whether a particular *Amateur golfer* has "golf skill or reputation".

Governing Body
The "Governing Body" for the Rules of Amateur Status in any country is the national union of that country.

Note: In Great Britain and Ireland, the *R&A* is the *Governing Body*.

Instruction
"Instruction" covers teaching the physical aspects of playing golf i.e. the actual mechanics of swinging a golf club and hitting a golf ball.

Junior Golfer
A "junior golfer" is an *Amateur golfer* who has not reached his 18th birthday in the year prior to the event, unless a different age is decided by the *Governing Body*.

Prize Voucher
A "prize voucher" is a voucher issued by the *Committee* in charge of a competition for the purchase of goods from a Professional's shop or other retail source.

R&A
The "R&A" means R&A Rules Limited.

Retail Value
The "retail value" of a prize is the normal recommended selling price at which merchandise is available to anyone at a retail source.

Rule or Rules
The term "Rule" or "Rules" refers to the Rules of Amateur Status as determined by the *Governing Body*.

Symbolic Prize
A "symbolic prize" is a trophy made of gold, silver, ceramic, glass or the like which is permanently and distinctively engraved.

Testimonial Award
A "testimonial award" relates to notable performances or contributions to golf as distinguished from competition prizes. A *testimonial award* may not be a monetary award.

Rule 1 – Amateurism

Definitions
All defined terms are in *italics* and are listed alphabetically in the Definitions section – see pages 448–451.

1-1. General
An *Amateur golfer* must play the game and conduct himself in accordance with the *Rules*.

1-2. Amateur Status

Amateur Status is a universal condition of eligibility for playing in golf competitions as an *Amateur golfer*. A person who acts contrary to the *Rules* may forfeit his status as an *Amateur golfer* and as a result will be ineligible to play in Amateur competitions.

1-3. Purpose and Spirit of the Rules

The purpose and spirit of the *Rules* is to maintain the distinction between Amateur golf and Professional golf and keep the Amateur game as free as possible from the abuses which may follow from uncontrolled sponsorship and financial incentive. It is considered necessary to safeguard Amateur golf, which is largely self-regulating with regard to the Rules of play and handicapping, so that it may be fully enjoyed by all *Amateur golfers*.

1-4. Doubt as to Rules

Any person who wishes to be an *Amateur golfer* and who is in doubt as to whether taking a proposed course of action is permitted under the *Rules* should consult the *Governing Body*.

Any organiser or sponsor of an Amateur golf competition or a competition involving *Amateur golfers*, who is in doubt as to whether a proposal is in accordance with the *Rules* should consult the *Governing Body*.

Rule 2 – Professionalism

Definitions

All defined terms are in italics and are listed alphabetically in the Definitions section – see pages 448–451.

2-1. General

An Amateur golfer must not take any action for the purpose of becoming a Professional golfer, including entering into an agreement, written or oral, with a sponsor or Professional agent.

Exception: Applying unsuccessfully for the position of an Assistant Professional.

Note: An Amateur golfer may enquire as to his likely prospects as a Professional and he may work in a Professional's shop and receive a salary, provided he does not infringe the Rules in any other way.

2-2. Professional Golfers' Associations

An Amateur golfer must not hold or retain membership of any Professional Golfers' Association.

2-3. Professional Tournament Players

An Amateur golfer must not hold or retain membership of a Professional Tour.

Note: If an Amateur golfer must compete in one or more qualifying competitions in order to be eligible for membership of a Professional Tour, he may enter and play in such qualifying competitions without forfeiting his Amateur Status, provided, in advance of play and in writing, he waives his right to any prize money in the competition.

Rule 3 – Prizes

Definitions

All defined terms are in *italics* and are listed alphabetically in the Definitions section – see pages 448–451.

3-1. Playing for Prize Money

An *Amateur golfer* must not play golf for prize money.

3-2. Prize Limits
a. General

An *Amateur golfer* must not accept a prize (other than a *symbolic prize*) or *prize voucher* of *retail value* in excess of £500 or the equivalent, or such a lesser figure as may be decided by the *Governing Body*. This limit applies to the total prizes or *prize vouchers* received by an *Amateur golfer* in any one competition or series of competitions, excluding any hole-in-one prize.

b. Hole-in-One Prizes

The limits prescribed in Rule 3-2a apply to a prize for a hole-in-one. However, such a prize may be accepted in addition to any other prize won in the same competition.

c. Exchanging Prizes

An *Amateur golfer* must not exchange a prize or *prize voucher* for cash.

Exception: An *Amateur golfer* may submit a *prize voucher* to a national or county union and thereafter be reimbursed from the value of that voucher for expenses incurred in participating in a golf competition, provided the reimbursement of such expenses is permitted under Rule 4-2.

Note 2: It is recommended that the total prize value of scratch prizes, or each division of handicap prizes, should not exceed twice the prescribed limit in an 18-hole competition, three times in a 36-hole competition, five times in a 54-hole competition and six times in a 72-hole competition.

3-3. Testimonial Awards
a. General

An *Amateur golfer* must not accept a *testimonial award* of *retail value* in excess of the limits prescribed in Rule 3-2a.

b. Multiple Awards

An *Amateur golfer* may accept more than one *testimonial award* from different donors, even though their total *retail value* exceeds the prescribed limit, provided they are not presented so as to evade the limit for a single award.

Rule 4 – Expenses

Definitions

All defined terms are in *italics* and are listed alphabetically in the Definitions section – see pages 448–451.

4-1. General

Except as provided in the *Rules*, an *Amateur golfer* must not accept expenses, in money or otherwise, from any source to play in a golf competition or exhibition.

4-2. Receipt of Expenses

An *Amateur golfer* may receive expenses, not exceeding the actual expenses incurred, to play in a golf competition or exhibition as follows:-

a. Family support

An *Amateur golfer* may receive expenses from a member of his family or a legal guardian.

b. Junior Golfers

A *junior golfer* may receive expenses when competing in a competition limited exclusively to *junior golfers*.

c. Team Events

(i) An *Amateur golfer*, who is representing his country, county or club (or similar body) in a team competition or at a training camp may receive expenses; and

(ii) An *Amateur golfer*, who is representing his country by taking part in a national championship abroad immediately before or after an international team competition may receive expenses.

The expenses must be paid by the body he represents or the body controlling golf in the country he is visiting.

d. Individual Events

An *Amateur golfer* may receive expenses when competing in individual events provided he complies with the following provisions:

(i) The player must be nominated to play in the competition by either his club, county or national union.

(ii) Where the competition is to take place in the player's own country and the nomination has been made by a club or county union, the approval of the national union, or the county union in the area in which the competition is to be staged, must first be obtained.

(iii) Where the competition is to take place in another country, the approval of the national union of the country in which the competition is to be staged and, if the nominating body is not the national union of the country from which the nomination is made, the approval of the national union must first be obtained by the nominating body.

(iv) The expenses must be paid only by the national union or county union responsible in the area from which the nomination is made or, subject to the approval of the nominating body, by the body controlling golf in the territory he is visiting.

(v) The expenses must be limited to a specific number of competitive days in any one calendar year as may be determined by the *Governing Body* in the country from which the nomination is made. The expenses are deemed to include reasonable travelling time and practice days in connection with the competitive days.

e. Celebrities, Business Associates, etc.

An *Amateur golfer* who is invited to take part in a competition for reasons unrelated to *golf skill* may receive expenses.

f. Exhibitions

An *Amateur golfer* who is participating in an exhibition in aid of a recognised charity may receive expenses, provided that the exhibition is not run in connection with another golfing event.

g. Sponsored Handicap Competitions

An *Amateur golfer* may receive expenses when competing in a sponsored handicap competition, provided the competition has been approved as follows:

(i) Where the competition is to take place in the player's own country, the annual approval of the *Governing Body* must first be obtained in advance by the sponsor; and

(ii) Where the competition is to take place in more than one country or involves golfers from another country, the approval of the two or more *Governing Bodies* must first be obtained in advance by the sponsor. The application for this approval should be sent to the *Governing Body* in the country where the competition commences.

Rule 5 – Instruction

Definitions

All defined terms are in *italics* and are listed alphabetically in the Definitions section – see pages 448–451.

5-1. General

Except as provided in the *Rules*, an *Amateur golfer* must not receive payment or compensation for giving *instruction* in playing golf.

5-2. Where Payment Permitted
a. Schools, Colleges, etc.

An *Amateur golfer*, who is an employee of an educational institution or system, may receive payment or compensation for golf *instruction* to students of the institution or system, provided that during a year the total time devoted to golf *instruction* comprises less than 50 percent of the time spent in the performance of all duties as such an employee.

b. Junior Golfers

An *Amateur golfer* may receive expenses, not exceeding the actual expenses incurred, for giving golf *instruction* to *junior golfers* as part of a programme which has been approved in advance by the *Governing Body*.

5-3. Instruction in Writing

An *Amateur golfer* may receive payment or compensation for *instruction* in writing, provided his ability or reputation as a golfer was not a major factor in his employment or in the commission or sale of his work.

Note: *Instruction* does not cover the many psychological aspects of the game or the Rules or Etiquette of Golf.

Rule 6 – Use of Golf Skill or Reputation

Definitions

All defined terms are in *italics* and are listed alphabetically in the Definitions section – see pages 448–451.

6-1. General

Except as provided in the *Rules*, an *Amateur golfer* of *golf skill or reputation* must not use that skill or reputation to promote, advertise or sell anything or for any financial gain.

6-2. Lending Name or Likeness

An *Amateur golfer* of *golf skill or reputation* must not use that skill or reputation to obtain payment, compensation, personal benefit or any financial gain for allowing his name or likeness to be used for the advertisement or sale of anything.

Note: An *Amateur golfer* may accept equipment from anyone dealing in such equipment provided no advertising is involved.

6-3. Personal Appearance

An *Amateur golfer* of *golf skill or reputation* must not use that skill or reputation to obtain payment, compensation, personal benefit or any financial gain for a personal appearance.

Exception: An *Amateur golfer* may receive actual expenses in connection with a personal appearance provided no golf competition or exhibition is involved.

6-4. Broadcasting and Writing

An *Amateur golfer* of *golf skill or reputation* must not use that skill or reputation to obtain payment, compensation, personal benefit or any financial gain for broadcasting concerning golf or writing golf articles or books.

Exception: An *Amateur golfer* may receive payment, compensation, personal benefit or any financial gain from broadcasting or writing provided:

(a) the player is actually the author of the commentary, article or books; and

(b) *instruction* in playing golf is not included.

6-5. Grants, Scholarships and Bursaries

An *Amateur golfer* of *golf skill or reputation* must not accept the benefits of a grant, scholarship or bursary, except one whose terms and conditions have been approved by the *Governing Body*.

6-6. Membership

An *Amateur golfer* of *golf skill or reputation* must not accept an offer of membership in a Golf Club without full payment for the class of membership if such an offer is made as an inducement to play for that Club.

Rule 7 – Other Conduct Incompatible with Amateurism

Definitions

All defined terms are in *italics* and are listed alphabetically in the Definitions section – see pages 448–451.

7-1. Conduct Detrimental to Amateurism

An *Amateur golfer* must not act in a manner which is considered detrimental to the best interests of the Amateur game.

7-2. Conduct Contrary to the Purpose and Spirit of the Rules

An *Amateur golfer* must not take any action, including actions relating to golf gambling, which is contrary to the purpose and spirit of the *Rules*.

Rule 8 – Procedure for Enforcement of the Rules

Definitions

All defined terms are in *italics* and are listed alphabetically in the Definitions section – see pages 448–451.

8-1. Decision on a Breach

If a possible breach of the *Rules* by a person claiming to be an *Amateur golfer* comes to the attention of the *Committee*, it is a matter for the *Committee* to decide whether a breach has occurred. Each case will be investigated to the extent deemed appropriate by the *Committee* and considered on its merits. The decision of the *Committee* shall be final, subject to an Appeal as provided in these *Rules*.

8-2. Enforcement

Upon a decision that a person has breached the *Rules*, the *Committee* may declare the Amateur Status of the person forfeited or require the person to refrain or desist from specified actions as a condition of retaining his Amateur Status.

The *Committee* must use its best endeavours to ensure that the person is notified and may notify any interested golf union of any action taken under Rule 8-2.

8-3. Appeals Procedure

Each *Governing Body* should put in place a procedure whereby any decision in respect of enforcement of these *Rules* may be appealed by the person affected by such decision.

Note: If a person, whose *Governing Body* is the *R&A*, is affected by a decision made by the Amateur Status Committee of the *R&A* in respect of the enforcement of these *Rules*, that person may raise an appeal of that decision with the Amateur Status Appeals Committee of the *R&A*.

Rule 9 – Reinstatement of Amateur Status

Definitions

All defined terms are in *italics* and are listed alphabetically in the Definitions section – see pages 448–451.

9-1. General

The *Committee* has sole power to reinstate a person to Amateur Status or to deny reinstatement, subject to an Appeal as provided in these *Rules*. Each application for reinstatement shall be considered on its merits.

9-2. Applications for Reinstatement

In considering an application for reinstatement, the *Committee* shall normally be guided by the following principles:

a. Awaiting Reinstatement

The Professional is considered to hold an advantage over the *Amateur golfer* by reason of having devoted himself to the game as his profession; other persons infringing the *Rules* also obtain advantages not available to the *Amateur golfer*. They do not necessarily lose such advantages merely by deciding to cease infringing the *Rules*. Therefore, an applicant for reinstatement to Amateur Status must undergo a period awaiting reinstatement as prescribed by the *Committee*.

The period awaiting reinstatement starts from the date of the person's last breach of the *Rules* unless the *Committee* decides that it starts from the date when the person's last breach became known to the *Committee*.

b. Period Awaiting Reinstatement

(i) Professionalism

The period awaiting reinstatement is normally related to the period the person was in breach. However, no applicant is normally eligible for reinstatement until he has conducted himself in accordance with the *Rules* for a period of at least one year.

It is recommended that the following guidelines on periods awaiting reinstatement are applied by the *Committee*:

Period of Breach: Period Awaiting Reinstatement:
under 5 years   1 year
5 years or more   2 years

The *Committee* reserves the right to extend or to shorten such a period. Players of national prominence who have been in breach for more than five years are not normally eligible for reinstatement.

(ii) Other Breaches of the Rules

The period awaiting reinstatement is normally related to the seriousness of the breach i.e. the value of the excessive prize, the amount of unauthorised expenses received, etc. However, no applicant is normally eligible for reinstatement until he has conducted himself in accordance with the Rules for a period of at least one year. It is recommended that the *Committee* extends the period awaiting reinstatement as the seriousness of the breach increases, with a period of up to five years applied for the most serious cases.

The Committee reserves the right to extend or shorten such a period.

c. Number of Reinstatements

A person is not normally reinstated more than twice.

d. Status While Awaiting Reinstatement

During the period awaiting reinstatement an applicant for reinstatement must comply with these *Rules* as they apply to an *Amateur golfer*.

He is not eligible to enter competitions as an *Amateur golfer*. However, he may enter competitions and win a prize solely among members of a Club of which he is a member, subject to the approval of the Club; but he may not represent such Club against other Clubs.

9-3. Procedure for Applications

Each application for reinstatement must be submitted to the *Committee*, in accordance with such procedures as may be laid down and it must include such information as the *Committee* may require.

9-4. Appeals Procedure

Each *Governing Body* should put in place a procedure whereby any decision in respect of reinstatement of Amateur Status may be appealed by the person affected by such decision.

Note: If a person, whose *Governing Body* is the *R&A*, is affected by a decision made by the Amateur Status Committee of the *R&A* in respect of reinstatement of Amateur Status, that person may raise an appeal of that decision with the Amateur Status Appeals Committee of the *R&A*.

Rule 10 – Committee Decision

Definitions

All defined terms are in *italics* and are listed alphabetically in the Definitions section – see pages 448–451.

10-1. Committee's Decision

The *Committee's* decision is final, subject to an Appeal as provided in Rules 8-3 and 9-4.

10-2. Doubt as to Rules

If the *Committee* considers the case to be doubtful or not covered by the *Rules*, it may, prior to making its decision, consult with the Amateur Status Committee of the *R&A*.

INDEX

The Rules of Golf are here indexed according to the
pertinant rule number, definition or appendix that has gone before.

Abnormal Ground Conditions   Def., 25
  Ball accidentally moved in   12-1
  Interference   25-1a
  Nearest point of relief   Def.
  Relief   25-1b
Address Position
  Determining nearest point of relief
Addressing the Ball   Def.   *See also* Stance
  Ball moving after address   18-2b
  Incurring penalty stroke   18-2b
  Line of putt touched   16-1a
Advice   Def.
  During stipulated round   8-1
  In team competitions   App. I
Aeration Holes
  Local rule   App. I
Animal, Burrowing, Hole By   Def.
  Ball moved in search   12-1
Artificial Devices
  Unusual equipment and   14-3
Artificial Objects
  Definition of obstruction
Assistance
  Penalty   14-2
Ball. *See also* Addressing the Ball; Dropped Ball;
  Lifting Ball; Lost Ball; Moved Ball; Out of
  Bounds; Placing Ball; Provisional Ball; Second
  Ball; Striking
  Assisting play   22-1
  In casual water   Def.
  Cleaning   21
  Damaged, unfit for play   5-3
  Deflected or stopped
    While at rest   18
    While in motion   19
  Embedded
    Local rule   App. I
    Relief   25-2
  Exchanging during play of hole   15-2
  Exerting influence on   1-2
  Fairly struck   14-1
  Falling off tee   11-3
  Foreign material applied   5-2
  Holed
    Definition
    Overhanging hole   16-2
  Holing out
    Ball played from teeing ground   1-1, 15-1
    Failure
      Match play   15-2
      Stroke play   3-2
  Identification
    Lifting for   12-2
    Mark   6-5, 12-2
  In ground under repair   Def.

In motion
  Deflected or stopped   19
  Removing loose impediment   23-1
  Removing obstruction   24-1
Influencing movement of   1-2
Interfering with play   22-2
Lie
  Altered   20-3b
  Improving   13-2
Played
  As it lies   13-1
  While moving   4-5, 14-6
  From wrong place, match play   20-7b
  From wrong place, stroke play   20-7c
Resting against flagstick   17-4
Searching for   12-1
Seeing when playing   12-1
Specifications
  Details   App. III
  General   5-1
Substituting
  Becoming ball in play   15-2, 20-4
  During play of hole   15-2
  If ball is not immediately recoverable   18 Note 1,
    19-1, 24-2b Note 2, 25-1b Note 2
  Incorrectly   20-6
  When lost in abnormal ground condition   25-1c
  When lost in obstruction   24-3
Touched
  By opponent   18-3
  By player, purposely   18-2a
Unplayable
  Damaged, unfit for play   5-3
  Procedure   28
In water hazard
  In moving water   14-6
  Played within, becomes lost or unplayable outside
    hazard   26-2b
  Played within, comes to rest in same hazard
    26-2a
  Relief   26-1
Wrong ball   Def.
  Four-ball, match play   30-3d
  Four-ball, stroke play   31-6
  Making stroke at   15-2
  Time spent in playing, definition of lost ball   Def.
Ball in Play   Def.   *See also* Ball, played; Moved
  Ball
  Provisional ball becoming   27-2b
  Substituted ball   20-4
Ball Marker
  Moved
    Accidentally   20-1
    After loose impediment touched   23-1
    In process of lifting ball   20-1

In process of repairing hole plugs or ball marks
16-3c
In process of replacing ball   20-3a
Best-Ball Match Play   Def.
Absent partner   30-3a
Maximum number of clubs   30-3b
Order of play   30-3c
Penalty
Disqualification penalties   30-3e
Effect of other penalties   30-3f
Blind Draw
Match-play draw   App. I
Bogey Competitions
Description of   32-1
Recording scores   32-1a
Scoring   32-1a
Bunkers   Def.   *See also* Hazards
Nearest point of relief   24-2b, 25-1b
Stones in, local rule   App. I
Unplayable ball in   28
Burrowing Animals   Def.
Hole made by   Def.
Ball moved in search   12-1
Relief   25-1
Caddie   Def.   *See also* Equipment
Attending the flagstick   17
Ball moved by   8-2, 18-3, 18-4
Breach of Rule by   6-4
One per player   6-4
Position of   14-2
Casual Water   Def.
Interference by and relief from   25-1
Chipping
Practice before round   7-1b
Practice during round   7-2
Claims
Match play
Claims and penalties   34-1a
Doubt or disputes   2-5
Stroke play, claims and penalties   34-1b
Cleaning Ball
When prohibited and permitted   21
On putting green   6-1b, 21, 22
Temporary conditions, relief   App. I
When taking relief from
Abnormal ground condition   25-1
Environmentally-sensitive area   App. I
Immovable obstruction   24-2
Movable obstruction   24-1
Temporary obstruction   App. I
Unplayable ball   28
Water hazard   26-1
Clubs
Adjustability   App. II
Borrowing or sharing   4-4b
Changing playing characteristics   4-2
Damaged
Other than in normal course of play   4-3b
In normal course of play   4-3a
Prior to round   4-3c
Declared out of play   4-4c
Design   App. II
Face   App. II

Grip
Artificial aid in gripping   14-3
Specifications   App. II
Grounding
In hazard   13-4
Lightly   13-2
Length   App. II
Maximum number allowed   4-4a
Penalties
Excess clubs   4-4
Foreign material applied   4-2b
Non-conforming clubs   4-1
Playing characteristics changed   4-2a
Replacement during round   4-3a
Samples submitted to the R&A   4
Shaft   App. II
Shared by partners   4-4b
Specifications   App. II
Unfit for play   4-3
Wear and alteration   4-1b
Committee   Def.   *See also* Conditions
Addition of scores and application of handicap
6-6d Note 1, 33-5
Construction declared as integral part of the course
definition of obstruction   33-2a
Decision
Final   34-3
Of ties   33-6, App. I
Defining
Bounds and margins of course   33-2, App. I
Movable obstructions to be immovable
Definition of obstruction   Def.
Practice ground   33-2c
Water hazards: definition of water hazard and
lateral water hazard   Def.
Duties and powers   33
Extending stipulated round in match play to settle a
tie   2-3
Handicap stroke table   33-4
Laying down conditions   33-1, App. I
Local rules made by   33-8a, App. I
Practice regulations   7-1, 7-2 Notes
Preventing slow play   6-7 Note 2
Setting times of starting and groups   6-3, 33-3
Suspension of play by   6-8b
Competitor   Def.   *See also* Fellow-Competitor
Ball in motion striking   19-2b
Doubt as to procedure   3-3a
Failure to hole out   3-2
Playing out of turn   10-2c
Playing outside teeing ground   11-4b
Playing strokes with wrong ball   15-3b
Refusal to comply with rules   3-4
Scoring responsibilities   6-6
Concession
Of next stroke, hole or match   2-4
Conditions
Advice in team competition   App. I
Committee to lay down   33-1
Decision of ties   App. I
New holes   App. I
Pace of play   App. I
Player responsible for knowing   6-1
Practice   App. I

Specifications of the ball
List of conforming golf balls   App. I
One ball condition   App. I
Suspension of play for dangerous situation   App. I
Temporary conditions   App. I
Time of starting   App. I
Transportation   App. I
Course   Def.   *See also* Ground Under Repair
Care of   Etiquette
Casual water on [definition of casual water]   Def.
Defining bounds and margins of   33-2a
Priority on   Etiquette
Unplayable   33-2d
Damaged Ball
Unfit for play   5-3
Decisions. *See also* Committee
Equity   1-4
Referee's final   34-2
Delay, Undue. *See* Slow Play
Discontinuance of Play
Conditions permitting   6-8a
Conditions requiring immediate discontinuance
6-8b Note, App. I
Lifting ball when play discontinued   6-8c
Procedure when play suspended by committee   6-8b
Disputes
Of claims   2-5, 34
Of points not covered by the Rules   1-4
Disqualification. *See under* Penalty
Distance
Gauging or measuring   14-3
Divots
Repair of divot hole   Etiquette
Replaced   13-2
Dormie
Definition   2-1
Doubt as to Procedure
Match play   2-5
Stroke play   3-3
Draw
General numerical   App. I
For match play   App. I
Dropped Ball. *See also* Through the Green
Dropping zones   App. I
In play   20-4
Lifting ball wrongly dropped   20-6
Near a specific spot   20-2b
Player must drop   20-2a
Playing dropped ball from wrong place   20-7
Re-dropping   20-2c
Rolling
Out of bounds, into a hazard, nearer hole, etc.
20-2c
To position, with interference by the condition
from which relief taken   20-2c
Touching player or equipment   20-2a
Embedded Ball
Local rule   App. I
Relief   25-2
Environmentally-Sensitive Areas
Committee decision on   App. I
Local rule   App. I
Equipment   Def.   *See also* Ball
Artificial devices   14-3
Ball moved by   8-2a, 18-3, 18-4

Ball moved by during search in match play
18-2a, 18-3b
Equity
Deciding disputes   1-4
Fellow-Competitor   Def.
Attending the flagstick   17
Ball in motion striking   19-4
Ball moved by   18-4
Disputing claim of unfit ball   5-3 Note
Doubt as to procedure   3-3a
Examining ball   5-3
Identifying ball   12-2
Flagstick   Def.
Attended, removed or held up   17-1
Replacing in the hole   Etiquette
Striking   17-3
Unauthorised attendance   17-2
Forecaddie   Def.
Definition of outside agency
Four-Ball Match Play   Def.
Absent partner   30-3a
Maximum number of clubs   30-3b
Order of play   30-3c
Penalty
Disqualification penalty   30-3e
Effect of other penalties   30-3f
Four-Ball Stroke Play   Def.
Absent partner   31-2
Order of play   31-5
Penalty
Disqualification penalties   31-7
Effect of other penalties   31-8
Recording scores   6-6d Note 2, 31-4, 31-7
Foursome   Def.
Match play   29-2
Order of play   29-1
Stroke play   29-3
Game of Golf
Definition   1-1
General Numerical Draw
Determining places in   App. I
General Penalty. *See under* Penalty
Golf Carts
Local regulations   Etiquette
Golf Shoe Spikes
Repairing damage by   Etiquette
Grass
Cuttings [definition of ground under repair]   Def.
In or bordering bunker, not hazard [definition of
bunker]   Def.
Touching
With club in hazard   13-4 Note
In finding and identifying ball   12-1
Green. *See* Putting Green
Greenkeeper
Hole made by, status of [definition of ground under
repair]   Def.
Grip. *See under* Clubs
Ground Under Repair   Def.
Ball within moved during search   12-1
Defined by committee   33-2a
Local Rule, dropping zones   App. I
Material piled for removal, status of [definition of
ground under repair]   Def.
Play prohibited   App. I

Relief   25-1
Groups. *See* Stroke Play
Halved Hole   2-2
Halved Match
  Committee decision of ties   33-6
Handicap
  Applying, committee's duty   33-5
  Match play   6-2a
  Player's duties   6-2
  Playing off wrong
    Knowingly in stroke play   34-1b
    Match play   6-2a
    Stroke play   6-2b
  Stroke table   33-4
Hazards   Def.   *See also* Obstructions
  Ball in
    Lifted may be dropped or placed back in   13-4
    Rolling into, nearer hole, etc. whether re-drop
      required   20-2c
  Bunkers [definition of bunker]   Def.
    Grounding club in   13-4
    Placing clubs in   13-4
    Practice prohibited from   7-2
    Previous stroke played from   20-5
    Relief from temporary obstructions   App. I
    Searching for covered ball in   12-1
    Strokes in, with wrong ball   15-3
  Water hazards
    Ball in, relief
    Dropping zones, Local Rule   App. I
    From abnormal ground condition prohibited
      25-1
    From immovable obstruction prohibited   24-2
    Options   26-1
  Ball moving in water played   14-6
  Ball played within becomes lost or unplayable
    outside hazard   26-2b
  Ball played within comes to rest in same hazard
    26-2a
  Casual water [definition of casual water]   Def.
  Definition
  Lateral water hazard [definition of lateral water
    hazard]   Def.
  Probing in water during search   12-1
  Provisional ball, Local Rule   App. I
Hole   Def.   *See also* Line of Play; Match Play
  Ball overhanging   16-2
  Conceding in match play   2-4
  Damaged   33-2b
  Determining score for   3-3b
  Halved   2-2
  Holing out
    Ball played from teeing ground   1-1, 15-1
    Failure, stroke play   3-2
  Made by burrowing animal [definition of burrowing
    animal]   Def.
  Made by greenkeeper [definition of ground under
    repair]   Def.
  New holes for competition   33-2b, App. I
  Number in a stipulated round [definition of
    stipulated round]   Def.
  Replacing flagstick in   Etiquette
  Testing putting green surface during play of   16-1d
  Time allowed to complete   6-7 Note 2
  Winner of   2-1

Wrong score   6-6d
Hole Plugs
  Repairing   16-1c
Honour   Def.
  Determining   0-1a, 10-2a
  Order of play   Etiquette
Identification of Ball. *See under* Ball, identification
Information as to Strokes Taken
  General   9-1
  In match play   9-2
  In stroke play   9-3
Irregularities of Surface   13-2
Lateral Water Hazard   Def.
  Committee decision on   App. I
  Relief   26-1
Lie of Ball. *See under* Ball
Lifting Ball. *See also* Cleaning Ball; Nearest Point
  of Relief
  Ball wrongly dropped   20-6
  Conditions permitting   22
  For identification   12-2
  From wrong place   20-6
  In a bunker   13-4, 24-2b(ii), 25-1b(ii)
  In or on movable obstruction   24-1
  In water hazard   26-1, 26-2
  Interference from temporary conditions   App. I
  Marking before   20-1
  On putting green   16-1b
  Penalty   5-3, 6-8c, 12-2, 18-2a, 20-1
  Through the green, without penalty   5-3, 6-8c,
    12-2, 22, 24-1, 24-2b, 25-1b
  To determine fitness   5-3
  When play discontinued   6-8c
Lightning
  Dangerous situation   App. I
  Discontinuance of play   6-8a
Line of Play   Def.   *See also* Line of Putt
  Avoiding interference with   11-2
  Improving   13-2
  Indicating
    Other than on putting green   8-2a
    On putting green   8-2b
  Intervention on   24-2a, 25-1a
  Intervention on, Local Rule
    Immovable obstructions close to putting
      green   App. I
    Temporary immovable obstructions   App. I
  Position of caddie or partner's caddie   14-2
Line of Putt   Def.   *See also* Line of Play
  Pointing out line for putting   8-2b
  Position of caddie or partner   14-2
  Removal of loose impediments   16-1a
  Repair of hole plugs, ball-marks and other damage
    16-1c
  Standing astride or on   16-1e
  Touching   16-1a
List of Conforming Golf Balls
  Conditions of competition   5-1, App. I
Local Rules. *See also* Specimen Local Rules
  Dropping zones, use of   App. I
  Committee responsibilities   33-8a, App. I
  Conflicting with the Rules of Golf   33-8
  Denying relief from interference with stance by
    abnormal ground condition   25-1a
  Nearest point of relief   24-2b Note 3

Preferred lies and winter rules   App. I
Prohibiting play
   From an environmentally-sensitive area
      [definition of ground under repair, definition of
      water hazard]   Def.
   From ground under repair [definition of ground
      under repair]   App. I
   Waiving penalty   33-8b
Loose Impediments   Def.   *See also* Hazards;
Obstructions
   Ball moving after touching   23-1
   Casual water [definition of casual water]   Def.
   On putting green [definition of loose impediment]
      Def.
   Relief   23-1
   Removal
      On line of putt   16-1a
      In hazard   13-4
      While ball in motion   23-1
   Stones in bunker, local rule   App. I
Lost Ball   Def.
   Abnormal ground conditions   25-1c
   Casual water, ground under repair, etc.   25-1c
   Obstruction   24-3
   Pace of play considerations   Etiquette
   Procedure   27-1
   In temporary immovable obstructions   App. I
   In water hazard   26-1
Marker   Def.
   Disputing claim of unfit ball   5-3
   Doubt as to procedure   3-3a
   Examining ball   5-3
   Identifying ball   12-2
   Outside agency [definition of outside agency]   Def.
   Recording scores
      Bogey and par competitions   32-1a
      Four-ball stroke play   31-4
      Competition   32-1b
      Stroke play   6-6a
   Reporting penalty to   9-3
Match   Def.   *See also* Sides
   Conceding   2-4
   Winner of   2-3
Match Play. *See also* Best-Ball Match Play; Four-Ball
Match Play; Penalties; Scores
   Ball moved by opponent
      Other than during search   18-3b
      During search   18-3a
   Ball moved by player   18-2
   Ball played from wrong place   20-7b
   Claims   2-5
   Combining with stroke play   33-1
   Concession of next stroke, hole or match   2-4
   Discontinuing play by agreement   6-8a
   Draw   App. I
   Flagstick, unauthorised attendance   17-2
   Halved hole   2-2
   Handicap   6-2a
   Information as to strokes taken   9-2
   Order of play   10-1a, 29-2, 30-3c
   Outside teeing ground   11-4a
   Pace of play   Etiquette
   Penalties
      Agreement.to waive   1-3

Claims   2-5
Disqualification, committee discretion   33-7
General penalty   2-6
Reporting to opponent   9-2
Time limit on imposition   34-1a
Practice
   Before or between rounds   7-1a
   During round   7-2
Reckoning of holes   2-1
Slow play   6-7
Stroke with wrong ball   15-3
Three-ball match, ball accidentally deflected or
   stopped by Opponent   30-2b
Ties, settling   2-3, App. I
Winner of
   Hole   2-1
   Match   2-3
Wrong information given as to strokes taken
   9-2
Material Piled for Removal [definition of ground
under repair]   Def.
Measuring
   Artificial device   14-3
   Ball moved in   18-6
Moved Ball   Def.   *See also* Lifting Ball
   After address   18-2b
   After loose impediment touched   23-1
   By another ball   18-5
   By fellow-competitor   18-4
   By opponent
      Not in search   18-3b
      In searching   18-3a
      In three-ball match   30-2a
   By outside agency   18-1
   By player
      Accidentally   18-2a
      After address   18-2b
      After loose impediment touched   23-1
      Purposely   1-2, 18-2a
      During search   18-1, 18-2a, 18-3a, 18-4
      In measuring   18-6
   In removing
      Ball-marker   20-1, 20-3a
      Loose impediment   23-1
      Movable obstruction   24-1
   In repairing hole plug or ball mark   16-1c
   In searching
      For ball in abnormal ground condition   12-1
      For covered ball in hazard   12-1
      In water in water hazard   2-1, 14-6
   Not immediately recoverable   18 Note 1, 19-1,
      20-2, 24-1, 24-2, 25-1, App.I
   Playing moving ball   14-5
Nearest Point of Relief   Def.
   In a bunker   4-2b, 25-1b
   On the putting green   24-2b, 25-1b
   Reference point for re-dropping   20-2c(vii)
   Through the green   24-2b, 25-1b
Numerical Draw
   Determining places in   App. I
Observer   Def.
   Outside agency [definition of outside agency]   Def.
Obstructions   Def.   *See also* Hazards; Loose
Impediments; Out of Bounds

Area of intended swing   4-1, 24-2a, App. I
Ball lost in   24-3
Committee decision on   App. I
Immovable   24-2, App. I
Immovable obstruction close to putting green
    App. I
Interference with lie of ball, stance, intervention on
    line of play or putt   24-1, 24-2a, App. I
Local Rule
    Dropping zones   App. I
    Immovable obstruction close to putting green
        App. I
    Stones in bunkers   App. I
    Temporary immovable obstructions   App. I
    Temporary power lines and cables   App. I
Movable   24-1
Removing   13-4
Touching   13-4 Note
One Ball Condition
Conditions of competition   App. I
Opponent
Attending flagstick without authority   17-2
Ball moved by   18-3
Reporting penalty to   9-2
Order of Play
Best-ball and four-ball match play   30-3c
Consideration for other players   Etiquette
Match play   10-1
Stroke play   10-2
Provisional or second ball played from teeing ground
    10-3
Out of Bounds   Def.   *See also* Obstructions
Committee decision on   App. I
Dropped ball rolling out of bounds   20-2c
Objects defining
    Fixed   13-2
    Not obstructions [definition of obstructions]   Def.
Pace of play considerations   Etiquette
Procedure   27-1
Stance out of bounds [definition of out of bounds]
    Def.
Outside Agency   Def.
Ball at rest moved by   18-1
Ball in motion deflected or stopped by   19-1
Forecaddie [definition of forecaddie]   Def.
Pace of Play
Preventing slow play   6-7 Note 2, App. I
When searching for ball   Etiquette
Par Competitions
Recording scores   32-1a
Scoring   32-1a
Partner   Def.
Absence
    Best-ball and four-ball match play   30-3a
    Four-ball stroke play   31-2
Position of during stroke   14-2
Requesting advice   8-1
Sharing clubs   4-4b
Penalty
Cancelled when round cancelled in stroke play
    33-2d
Disqualification penalty; waiving, modifying or
    imposing   33-7
General penalty

In match play   2-6
In stroke play   3-5
Reporting to opponent or marker   9-2, 9-3
Time limit on imposition
    Match play   34-1a
    Stroke play   34-1b
Waived
    By agreement   1-3
    By local rule   33-8b
Penalty Stroke   Def.
Physical Assistance   14-2
Placing Ball
If accidentally moved   20-3a
If ball dropped or placed is in play   20-4
If ball fails to come to rest on spot   20-3d
If incorrectly substituted, dropped or placed   20-6
If original lie is altered   20-3b
If spot is not determinable   20-3c
On the spot from which it was moved   20-3a
Procedure when play resumed   6-8d
Player
Ball moved
    Accidentally   18-2a
    After address   18-2b
    After loose impediment touched   23-1
    Purposely   1-2, 18-2a
Consideration for other players   Etiquette
Examining ball   5-3
Identifying ball   12-2
Making a claim   2-5
Responsibility for playing proper ball   6-5, 12-2
Practice Ground
Committee decision on   33-2c
Practice Swings
Avoiding damage to the course   Etiquette
Not a practice stroke   7-2 Note 1
Preferred Lies
Committee decision on   App. I
Local rule   App. I
Protection From the Elements   14-2
Provisional Ball   Def.
Abandoned   27-2c
Becoming ball in play [definition of lost ball]
    27-2b, Def
From teeing ground   10-3
Local rule permitting play of provisional when water
    hazard involved   App. I
Pace of play considerations   Etiquette
Putting Green   Def.   *See also* Hazards; Loose
Impediments; Obstructions
Aeration holes   App. I
Ball   Def.
    Cleaning   16-1b, 21, 22
    In abnormal ground conditions   25-1b
    Lifting   16-1b, 21
    Overhanging hole   16-2
Conceding opponent's next stroke   2-4
Failure to hole out in stroke play   3-2
Immovable obstruction close to putting green
    App. I
Indicating line for putting   8-2b
Leaving when hole is completed   Etiquette
Line of putt
    Position of caddie or partner   14-2

Standing astride or on   16-1e
Testing surface   16-1d
Touching   16-1a
Loose impediments on [definition of loose
impediments]   Def.
Making claim before leaving   2-5
Nearest point of relief   4-2b, 25-1b
Practice
Before or between rounds   7-1b
During round   7-2
Repairing damage to   Etiquette, Rule 16-1c
Testing surface   16-1d
Wrong putting green
Definition
Interference by   25-3a
Relief   25-3b
Referee   Def.
Decisions final   34-2
Limiting duties of by committee   33-1
Outside agency [definition of outside agency]   Def.
Rub of the Green   Def.
When ball is accidentally deflected or stopped by an
outside agency   19-1
Rules   Def.   *See also* Penalty
Applying in three-ball, best-ball and four-ball match
play   30-1
Authorisation to modify   App. I
Breached, general penalty
In match play   2-6
In stroke play   3-5
Local rules   33-8, App. I
Player responsibilities   6-1
Points not covered by   1-4
Refusal to comply, stroke play   3-4
Waiving
By agreement   1-3
Committee decision on   33-1
Safety
Considerations   Etiquette
Scorer. *See* Marker
Scores
Alteration prohibited after return   6-6c
Committee responsibilities   33-5
Competitor responsibilities   6-6b, 6-6d, 31-4
Determining for hole when second ball played,
stroke play   3-3b
Four-ball stroke play   31-4
Marker responsibilities   6-6a, 31-4, 32-1b
Wrong score   6-6d
Second Ball
Determining score for hole   3-3b
From teeing ground   10-3
Played when in doubt as to procedure   3-3
Sides   Def.   *See also* Matches
Disqualification of
Best-ball or four-ball match play   30-3e
Four-ball stroke play   31-7
Order of play
Best-ball or four-ball match play   30-3c
Four-ball stroke play   31-5
Honour on teeing ground   10-1a
Penalty, maximum of 14 clubs
Best-ball or four-ball match play   30-3b
Four-ball stroke play   31-3

Representation of
Best-ball, four-ball match play   30-3a
Four-ball stroke play   31-2
Single Matches   Def.
Slow Play
Penalty   6-7
Stroke play, condition modifying penalty   6-7
Note 2
Specimen Local Rules
Adopting   App. I, Part B
Aeration holes   App. I
Embedded ball   App. I
Environmentally-sensitive areas   App. I
Ground under repair, play prohibited   App. I
Immovable obstruction close to putting green
App. I
Preferred lies and winter rules   App. I
Protection of young trees   App. I
Stones in bunkers   App. I
Temporary obstructions   App. I
Temporary power lines   App. I
Spikes. *See* Golf Shoe Spikes
Stableford Competitions
Recording scores   32-1b
Scoring   32-1b
Stance   Def.   *See also* Stroke
Abnormal stance, interference with
By abnormal ground condition   25-1b
exception
By immovable obstruction   24-2b exception
Astride or touching line of putt   16-1e
Avoiding interference with tee markers   11-2
Building   13-3
Fairly taking   13-2
Interference with
By abnormal ground condition   25-1a
By immovable obstruction   24-2a
Local rule, denying relief from interference with
25-1a
Out of bounds [definition of out of bounds]   Def.
Outside teeing ground   11-1
Stipulated Round   Def.
Advice during   8-1
Artificial devices and unusual equipment, use of
during   14-3
Clubs
Damaged   4-3
Playing characteristics changed   4-2a
Extending to settle a tie in match play   2-3
Maximum clubs allowed   4-4a
Time allowed to complete   6-7 Note 2
Walking during, condition of competition   App. I
Striking
Fairly   14-1
Flagstick or attendant   17-3
More than once   14-4
Stroke   Def.   *See also* Stance
Assistance
Artificial devices   14-3
Physical assistance   14-2
Ball damaged as a result of   5-3
Best-ball or four-ball match play   30-3d
Cancelling   10-1c
Conceding   2-4

From outside teeing ground   11-4
Halved hole   2-2
Playing from where previous stroke played   20-5
Requesting advice   8-1
Safety considerations   Etiquette
Striking ball more than once   14-4
With provisional ball   27-2b
With wrong ball
    Best-ball or four-ball match play   30-3d
    Four-ball stroke play   31-6
    Match play   15-3a
    Stroke play   15-3b
Stroke Play. *See also* Four-Play Stroke Play; Penalties; Scores
    Agreeing to play out of turn   10-2c
    Ball played from outside teeing ground   11-4b
    Ball played from wrong place   20-7c
    Combining with match play   33-1
    Doubt as to procedure   3-3a
    Failure to hole out   3-2
    Flagstick, unauthorised attendance   17-2
    Groups
        Changing   6-3b
        Committee to arrange   33-3
    Handicap   6-2b
    Information as to strokes taken   9-3
    New holes   33-2b, App. I
    Order of play   10-2a, 10-2c, 29-3
    Penalties
        Agreement to waive   1-3
        Disqualification, committee discretion   33-7
        General penalty   3-5
        Reporting to marker   9-3
        Time limit on imposition   34-1b
    Playing out of turn   10-2c
    Refusal to comply with rules   3-4
    Second ball played   3-3b
    Slow play, modification of penalty   6-7
    Strokes with wrong ball   15-3
    Winner   3-1
Suspension of Play
    Committee decision   33-2d
    Procedure for players   6-8b
Tee Markers
    Status of   11-2
Teeing Ground   Def.   *See also* Honour
    Failure to hole out correction of error   3-2
    Holing out with ball played from tee   15-1
    Making claim before playing from next   2-5
    Order of play
        Match play   10-1a
        Stroke play   10-2a
        Threesome or foursome   29-1
    Playing outside   11-4
    Playing provisional or second ball from   10-3
    Practice on or near
        Before or between rounds   7-1b
        During round   7-2
    Previous stroke played from   20-5
    Standing outside to play ball within   11-1
    Teeing ball   11-1
    Wrong teeing ground   11-5

Tees
    Avoiding damage to   Etiquette
Temporary Conditions
    Committee decision on   App. I
Three-Ball Matches   Def.
    Ball accidentally deflected or stopped by opponent   30-2b
    Ball at rest moved by opponent   30-2a
Threesome   Def.
    Order of play   29-1
Through the Green   Def.
    Aeration holes   App. I
    Ball moved after loose impediment touched   23-1
    Nearest point of relief   24-2, 25-1
    Previous stroke played from   20-5
Ties
    Committee responsibilities   33-6
    Extending stipulated round to settle, match play   2-3
    Recommendation; options   App. I
Time of Starting
    Committee responsibilities   33-3, App. I
    Condition modifying penalty   6-3 Note, App. I
    Player responsibilities   6-3a
Touching Ball.   *See under* Ball
Transportation
    Walking during stipulated round, condition of competition   App. I
Turf
    Cut, placed in position   13-2
Undue Delay
    Penalty   6-7
Unplayable Ball
    Damaged, unfit for play   5-3
    Relief   28
Unplayable Course
    Committee decision   33-2d
Water Hazards   Def.   *See under* Hazards
Winter Rules
    Committee decision on   App. I
Wrong Ball   Def.
    Four-ball
        Match play   30-3d
        Stroke play   31-6
    Strokes with
        In match play   15-3a
        In stroke play   15-3b
    Time spent in playing, definition of lost ball   Def.
Wrong Information
    As to strokes taken in match play   9-2
    Voiding time limit for claim   2-5, 34-1
Wrong Place
    Ball played from
        In match play   20-7b
        In stroke play   20-7c
        General   20-7a
    Lifting ball dropped or placed at   20-6
Wrong Putting Green   Def.
    Nearest point of relief, definition of
    Relief   25-3
Wrong Score
    For hole   6-6d
Young Trees
    Protection of   App. I

R&A Contacts

The history of the Royal and Ancient Golf Club of St Andrews and up-to-date news of its activities worldwide can be found at the website
www.randa.org

Full details of the Open Championship can be found at
www.opengolf.com

R&A officials can be contacted on: Tel 01334 460000 Fax 01334 460001

Secretary: Peter Dawson

Assistant Secretary: Michael Tate

Championship Secretary: David Hill

Commercial Secretary: Angus Farquhar

Financial Secretary: Mark Dobell

Golf Development Secretary: Duncan Weir

Golf Heritage Secretary: Peter Lewis

Members' Secretary: Aubyn Stewart-Wilson

Projects Secretary: Lachlan McIntosh

Rules Secretary: David Rickman

Professional Governing Bodies

The Professional Golfers' Association

The Professional Golfers' Association was founded in 1901 to promote interest in the game of golf; to protect and advance the mutual and trade interests of its members; to arrange and hold meetings and tournaments periodically for the members; to institute and operate funds for the benefit of the members; to assist the members to obtain employment; and effect any other objects of a like nature as may be determined from time to time by the Association.

Classes of Membership

There shall be nine classes of membership:

(i)   **Class A** Members engaged as the nominated professional on a full-time basis at a PGA Club, PGA Course or PGA Driving Range in one of the seven Regions; and members engaged as the nominated professional on a full-time basis, at an establishment in one of the seven Regions at which the public can play and/or practise which, in the opinion of the Executive Committee does not qualify as a PGA Club, Course or Driving Range but does warrant Class A status. *Note:* Class A(T) – Class A members currently engaged at an establishment which has been inspected and approved as a PGA Training Establishment and currently holds that status will be identified where appropriate by the suffix (T) after their classification.

(ii) **Class B** Members engaged by a Class A or D member to assist the nominated professional at any PGA Establishment in one of the seven Regions on a full-time basis.

(iii) **Class C** Tournament playing members (men and women).

(iv) **Class D** Members engaged as the nominated professional on a full-time basis at a PGA Establishment within the seven Regions which does not qualify as a 'Class A' establishment, or engaged on a full-time basis within the seven Regions by any other Company or any other individual designated by the Executive Committee for this purpose. (Former Class G.)

(v)   **Class E** Honorary Associate Members (HAM). Those who in the opinion of the Executive Committee through their past or continuing membership justify retaining the full privileges of membership as Honorary Associate Members (HAM).

(vi) **Class F** Associate Members (AM). (a) Those who have ceased to be eligible for other categories of membership who in the opinion of the Executive Committee through their past membership justify retaining limited privileges of membership as Associate Members; and (b) Members of the PGA European Tour or WPGET who do not qualify for Class C membership but who in the opinion of the Executive Committee justify limited privileges of membership as Associate Members.

(vii) **Class G** Honorary Life Members (HLM). Those recommended by the Board to a Special General Meeting of the Association for election as Honorary Life Members. No form of application is needed nor need reference be made to the Regional Committee concerned.

(viii) **Class H** Members who are qualified members of the Association, and ineligible for any other class of membership, engaged on a full-time basis at an establishment acceptable to the Association outside the jurisdiction of the seven Regions. (Overseas)

(ix) **Class O** Members who have not qualified at the official training centre of the Association, who are ineligible for any other class of membership, and who are current members of another PGA approved by the Association and have held such member- ship for not less than two years.

The Management of the Association is under the overall direction and control of a Board. The Association is divided into seven Regions each of which employs a full-time secretary and runs tournaments for the benefit of members within its Region.

The Association is responsible for arranging and obtaining sponsorship of the Ryder Cup, Club Professionals' Championship, PGA Cup matches, Seniors' Championship, PGA Assistants' Championship, Assistants' Matchplay Championship and other National Championships.

Anyone who intends to become a club professional must serve a minimum of three years in registration and qualify at the PGA Training School before election as a full Member.

The Professional Golfers' Associations of Europe

The PGA of Europe was created in 1989 as an Association of national European PGAs to ensure uniformity of professional standards and objectives.

In its first ten years the PGAE grew to a body comprising 33 member PGAs, five of them Associate Members from outside the continent of Europe. These 33 PGAs are made up of a total of 12,000 professionals comprising Directors of Golf, Club Professionals, Teaching Professionals, all of whom provide a comprehensive service to the entire golfing community.

The purpose of the PGA or Europe is to:

(1) Unify and improve standards of education and qualification;

(2) Advise and assist golf professionals to achieve properly rewarded employment;

(3) Provide relevant playing opportunities;

(4) Be the central point of advice, information and support;

(5) Be a respected link with other golfing bodies throughout Europe and the rest of the world – all

for the benefit of its members and the enhancement of the sport.

PGA European Tour

To be eligible to become a member of the PGA European Tour a player must possess certain minimum standards which shall be determined by the Tournament Committee. In 1976 a Qualifying School for potential new members was introduced to be held annually. The leading players are awarded cards allowing them to compete in PGA European Tour tournaments.

In 1985 the PGA European Tour became ALL EXEMPT with no more Monday pre-qualifying. Full details can be obtained from the Wentworth Headquarters.

The Evian Tour (Ladies' European Tour)

The Evian Tour was founded in 1988 to further the development of women's professional golf throughout Europe and its membership is open to all nationalities. A qualifying school is held annually and an amateur wishing to participate must be 18 years of age and have a handicap of 1 or less. Full details can be obtained from the Tour Headquarters at Tytherington.

Entebbe course now has 18 holes

Daniel Nkata, the Ugandan journalist and golf course architect, has been involved in the extension of the Entebbe course from nine to 18-holes making it the fourth 18-hole course in the country. The other 10 courses are only nine holes. Golf in East Africa began in Entebbe where the original course was laid out at the end of the 19th century and was opened for play in 1902. The Tropic Inn GC, a nine-hole course which closed in 1972 is being re-opened and extended to 18 holes.

At a time when much is being done to encourage junior golf, architect Nkata has ensured there are so-called black tees on every hole – shortening them for use by children and the elderly. At another Ugandan course, Jinja, the club members can take advantage of a local rule which allows them to lift and place on the green no nearer the hole if the line to the hole is affected by a hippo footprint!

Golf is becoming much more popular in Uganda but that country is still well short of the number of 18-hole courses in Kenya where, Nkata reports, 20 per cent of the 50 courses are full length.

Amateur Governing Bodies

Home Unions

The English Golf Union

The English Golf Union was founded in 1924 and embraces 34 County Unions with 1895 affiliated clubs, 24 clubs overseas, and 500 Golfing Societies and Associations. Its objects are:

(1) To further the interests of Amateur Golf in England.
(2) To assist in maintaining a uniform system of handicapping.
(3) To arrange an English Championship; an English Strokeplay Championship; an English County Championship, International and other Matches and Competitions.
(4) To cooperate with the Royal & Ancient Golf Club of St Andrews and the Council of National Golf Unions.
(5) To cooperate with other National Golf Unions and Associations in such manner as may be decided.

The Scottish Golf Union

The Scottish Golf Union was founded in 1920 and embraces 695 clubs. Subject to the stipulation and declaration that the Union recognises the Royal & Ancient Golf Club of St Andrews as the Ruling Authority in the game of golf, the objects of the Union are:

(a) To foster and maintain a high standard of amateur golf in Scotland and to administer and organise and generally act as the governing body of amateur golf in Scotland.
(b) To institute and thereafter carry through annually a Scottish Amateur Championship, a Scottish Open Amateur Strokeplay Championship and other such competitions and matches as they consider appropriate.
(c) To administer and apply the rules of the Standard Scratch Score and Handicapping Scheme as approved by the Council of National Golf Unions from time to time.
(d) To deal with other matters of general or local interest to amateur golfers in Scotland.

The Union's organisation consists of Area Committees covering the whole of Scotland. There are 16 Areas, each having its own Association or Committee elected by the Clubs in that particular area and each Area Association or Committee elects one delegate to serve on the Executive of the Union.

Golfing Union of Ireland

The Golfing Union of Ireland, founded in 1891, embraces 398 Clubs. Its objects are:

(1) Securing the federation of the various Clubs.
(2) Arranging Amateur Championships, Inter-Provincial and Inter-Club Competitions, and International Matches.
(3) Securing a uniform standard of handicapping.
(4) Providing for advice and assistance, other than financial, to affiliated Clubs in all matters appertaining to Golf, and generally to promote the game in every way, in which this can be better done by the Union than by individual Clubs.

Its functions include the holding of the Close Championship for Amateur Golfers and Tournaments for Team Matches.

Its organisation consists of Provincial Councils in each of the four Provinces elected by the Clubs in the Province – each province electing a limited number of delegates to the Central Council which meets annually.

Welsh Golfing Union

The Welsh Golfing Union was founded in 1895 and is the second oldest of the four National Unions. Unlike the other Unions it is an association of Golf Clubs and Golfing Organisations. The present membership is 159. For the purpose of electing the Executive Council, Wales is divided into ten districts which between them return 22 members. The objects of the Union are:

(a) To take any steps which may be deemed necessary to further the interests of the amateur game in Wales.
(b) To hold a Championship Meeting or Meetings each year.
(c) To encourage, financially and/or otherwise, Inter-Club, Inter-County, and International Matches, and such other events as may be authorised by the Council.
(d) To assist in setting up and maintaining a uniform system of Handicapping.
(e) To assist in the establishment and maintenance of high standards of greenkeeping.

Note: The union recognises the Royal & Ancient Golf Club of St Andrews as the ruling authority.

The Council of National Golf Unions

At a meeting of Representatives of Golf Unions and Associations in Great Britain and Ireland, called at the

special request of the Scottish Golf Union, and held in York, on 14th February, 1924, resolutions were adopted from which the Council of National Golf Unions was constituted.

The Council holds an Annual Meeting in March, and such other meetings as may be necessary. Two representatives are elected from each national Home Union – England, Scotland, Ireland and Wales and one from the Royal and Ancient Golf Club of St Andrews – and hold office until the next Annual meeting when they are eligible for re-election.

The principal function of the Council, as laid down by the York Conference, was to formulate a system of Standard Scratch Scores and Handicapping, and to co-operate with the Royal & Ancient Championship Committee in matters coming under their jurisdiction. The responsibilities undertaken by the Council at the instance of the Royal & Ancient Golf Club or the National Unions are as follows:

1   The Standard Scratch Score and Handicapping Scheme, formulated in March, 1926, approved by the Royal & Ancient, and last revised in 2001.
2   The nomination of one member on the Board of Management of The Sports Turf Research Institute, with an experimental station at St Ives, Bingley, Yorkshire.
3   The management of the Annual Amateur International Matches between the four countries – England, Scotland, Ireland and Wales.

United States Golf Association

The USGA is the national governing body of golf in the United States, dedicated to promoting and conserving the best interests and true spirit of the game.

Founded on 22 December 1894 by representatives of five American golf clubs, the USGA was originally charged with conducting national championships, implementing a uniform code of rules, and maintaining a national system of handicapping.

Today, the principal functions of the association remain largely unchanged. Each year, the USGA conducts thirteen national championships for amateur and professional golfers; biennial competitions include State Team Championships for men and women, the Walker Cup, Curtis Cup, and World Amateur Team Championships. In cooperation with the Royal & Ancient Golf Club of St. Andrews, Scotland, the USGA continues to write and interpret the Rules of Golf, and oversees the standards regulating the equipment used to play the game. The association also maintains a national handicapping system, providing handicap computation services to state and regional golf associations through the Golf Handicap and Information Network.

Additional responsibilities assumed by the association encompass turfgrass and environmental research

conducted by the USGA Green Section; preservation and promotion of the game's rich history in the Museum and Archives; oversight of the Rules of Amateur Status; publication of *Golf Journal*, the USGA's official magazine; and direction of the USGA Members Program, with over 900,000 members globally. Since 1965, the USGA Foundation has functioned as the association's broad-based philanthropic arm, dedicated to maintaining and improving the opportunities for all individuals to participate fully in the game.

Tel: +1 908 234 2300\ Fax: +1 908 234 9687

Government of the Amateur and Open Golf Championship

In December 1919, on the invitation of the clubs who had hitherto controlled the Amateur and Open Golf Championships, the Royal & Ancient took over the government of those events. These two championships are now controlled by a committee appointed by the Royal & Ancient Golf Club of St Andrews. The Committee is called the Royal and Ancient Golf Club Championship Committee and consists of eight members of the Club elected by the Club.

Ladies' Golf Union (LGU)

The Ladies' Golf Union was founded in 1893 with the following objectives:

(1) To promote the interests of the game of Golf.
(2) To obtain a uniformity of the rules of the game by establishing a representative legislative authority.
(3) To establish a uniform system of handicapping.
(4) To act as a tribunal and court of reference on points of uncertainty.
(5) To arrange the Annual Championship Competition and obtain the funds necessary for that purpose.

After 100 years, only the language has changed, the present Constitution defines the objectives as:

(1) To uphold the rules of the game, to advance and safeguard the interests of women's golf and to decide all doubtful and disputed points in connection therewith.
(2) To maintain, regulate and enforce the LGU Handicapping System.
(3) To employ the funds of The Union in such a manner as shall be deemed best for the interests of women's golf, with power to borrow or raise money to use for the same purpose.
(4) To maintain and regulate International events, Championships and Competitions held under the LGU regulations and to promote the interests of Great Britain and Ireland in Ladies International Golf.

(5) To make, maintain and publish such regulations as may be considered necessary for the above purposes.

The constituents of the LGU are:

Home Countries. The English Ladies' Golf Association (founded 1952), the Irish Ladies' Golf Union (founded 1893), the Scottish Ladies' Golfing Association (founded 1904), the Welsh Ladies' Golf Union (founded 1904), plus ladies' societies, girls' schools and ladies' clubs affiliated to these organisations.

Overseas. Affiliated ladies' golf unions and golf clubs in the Commonwealth and any other overseas ladies' golfing organisation affiliated to the LGU.

Individual lady members of clubs within the above categories are regarded as members of the LGU.

The Rules of the Game and of Amateur Status, which the LGU is bound to uphold, are those published by the Royal & Ancient Golf Club of St Andrews.

In endeavouring to fulfil its responsibilities towards advancing and safeguarding women's golf, the LGU maintains contact with other golfing organisations – the Royal & Ancient Golf Club of St Andrews, the Council of National Golf Unions, the Golf Foundation, the Central Council of Physical Recreation, the Sports Council, the Women Professional Golfers' European Tour and the Women's Committee of the United States Golf Association. This contact ensures that the LGU is informed of developments and projected developments and has an opportunity to comment upon and to influence the future of the game for women.

Either directly or through its constituent national organisations the LGU advises and is the ultimate authority on doubts or disputes which may arise in connection with the handicapping system and regulations governing competitions played under LGU conditions.

The handicapping system, together with the system for assessment of Scratch Scores, is formulated and published by the LGU. Handicap Certificates are provided by the LGU and distributed through the National Organisations and appointed club officials to every member of every affiliated club which has fulfilled the requisite conditions for obtaining an LGU handicap.

The funds of the LGU are administered by the Hon. Treasurer on the authority of the Executive Council, and the accounts are submitted annually for adoption in General Meeting.

The Women's British Open Championship, Ladies' British Open Amateur Championship, Ladies' British Open Amateur Stroke Play Championship, Girls' British Open Amateur Championship, Senior Ladies' British Open Amateur Championship, Ladies British Open Mid-Amateur Championship and the Home International matches are organised annually by the LGU. International events involving a British or a combined British and Irish team are organised and controlled by the LGU

when held in this country and the LGU acts as the coordinating body for the Commonwealth Tournament in whichever of the five participating countries it is held, four-yearly, by rotation. The LGU selects and trains the teams, provides the uniforms and pays all the expenses of participation, whether held in this country or overseas. The LGU also maintains and regulates certain competitions played under handicap, such as Medal Competitions, Coronation Foursomes, Challenge Bowls, Australian Spoons and the LGU Pendant Competition.

The day-to-day administration of certain of the LGU responsibilities in the home countries is undertaken by the National Organisations, such as that concerned with handicapping regulations, Scratch Scores, and the organisation of Challenge Bowls and Australian Spoons Competitions.

Membership subscriptions to the LGU are assessed on a per capita basis of the club membership. To save unnecessary expense and duplication of administrative work in the home countries LGU subscriptions are collected by the National Organisations along with their own, and transmitted in bulk to the LGU.

Policy is determined and control over all the LGU's activities is exercised by an Executive Council of eight members – two each elected by the English, Irish, Scottish and Welsh national organisations. The Chairman is elected annually by the Councillors. During her chairmanship her place on the Council is taken by her Deputy and she has no vote other than a casting vote. The President and the Hon. Treasurer of the Union also attend and take part in Council meetings but with no vote. The Council meets five times a year.

The Annual General Meeting is held in January. The formal business includes presentation of the Report of the Executive Council for the previous year and of the Accounts for the last completed financial year, the election or re-election of President, Vice-Presidents, Hon. Treasurer and Auditors, and a report of the election of Councillors and their Deputies for the ensuing year and of the European Championship Committee representative. Voting is on the following basis: Executive Council, one each (8); members in the four home countries, one per national organisation (4) and in addition one per 100 affiliated clubs or part thereof; one per overseas Commonwealth Union with a membership of 50 or more clubs, and one per 100 individually affiliated clubs.

The Lady Golfer's Handbook is published annually by the LGU and is distributed free to all affiliated clubs and organisations and to appointed Handicap Advisers. It is also available for sale to anyone interested. It contains the regulations for British Championships and international matches (with results for the past twenty years) and for LGU competitions, and sets out the Rules of the Union. It also lists every affiliated organisation, with names and addresses of officials, and every affiliated club, with Scratch Score, county of affiliation, number of members, and other useful information.

Championship and International Match Conditions

Championship Conditions

Men

The Amateur Championship

The Championship, until 1982, was decided entirely by match play over 18 holes except for the final which was over 36 holes. Since 1983 the Championship has comprised two stroke play rounds of 18 holes each from which the leading 64 players and ties over the 36 holes qualify for the match play stages. Matches are over 18 holes except for the final which is over 36 holes. Full particulars can be obtained from the Championship Entries Department, Royal and Ancient Golf Club, St Andrews, Fife KY16 9JD. Tel: 01334 460000   Fax: 01334 460001

The Seniors Open Amateur Championship

The Championship consists of 18 holes on each of two days, the leading 50 players and ties over the 36 holes then playing a further 18 holes the following day. Entrants must have attained the age of 55 years prior to the first day of the Championship. Full particulars can be obtained from the Championship Entries Department, Royal and Ancient Golf Club, St Andrews, Fife KY16 9JD. Tel: 01334 460000 Fax: 01334 460001

National Championships

The English, Scottish, Irish and Welsh Amateur Championships are played by holes, each match consisting of one round of 18 holes except the final which is contested over 36 holes. Full particulars of conditions of entry and method of play can be obtained from the secretaries of the respective national Unions.

English Open Amateur Stroke Play Championship

The Championship consists of one round of 18 holes on each of two days after which the leading 40 and those tying for 40th place play a further two rounds. The remainder are eliminated.

Conditions for entry include: entrants must have a handicap not exceeding three; where the entries exceed 130, an 18-hole qualifying round is held the day before the Championship. Certain players are exempt from qualifying.

Full particulars of conditions of entry and method of play can be obtained from the Secretary, English Golf Union, National Golf Centre, The Broadway, Woodhall Spa, Lincs LN10 6PU. Tel: 01526 354500   Fax: 01526 354020

Scottish Open Amateur Stroke Play Championship

The Championship consists of one round of 18 holes on each of two days after which the leading 40 and those tying for 40th place play a further two rounds. The remainder are eliminated. Full particulars of conditions of entry and method of play can be obtained from the Scottish Golf Union, Scottish National Golf Centre, Drumoig, Leuchars, St Andrews, Fife KY 16 0DW. Tel: 01382 549500   Fax: 01382 549510

British Mid-Amateur Championship

The Championship comprises two stroke play rounds of 18 holes from which the leading 64 players over the 36 holes qualify for the match play stages. All matches including the final are over 18 holes. Entrants must have attained the age of 25 years prior to the first day of the Championship. Full particulars can be obtained from the Championship Entries Department, Royal and Ancient Golf Club, St Andrews, Fife KY16 9JD. Tel: 01334 460000   Fax: 01334 460001

Boys

Boys Amateur Championship

The Championship is played by match play, each match including the final consisting of one round of 18 holes. Entrants must be under 18 years of age at 00.00 hours on 1st January in the year of the Championship. Full particulars can be obtained from the Championship Entries Department, Royal and Ancient Golf Club, St Andrews, Fife KY16 9JD. Tel: 01334 460000 Fax: 01334 460001

Ladies

Ladies' British Open Amateur Championship

The Championship consists of one 18-hole qualifying round on each of two days. The players returning the 64 lowest scores over 36 holes shall qualify for match play. Ties for 64th place shall be decided by hole-by-hole play-off.

Ladies' British Open Amateur Stroke Play Championship

The Championship consists of 72 holes stroke play; 18 holes are played on each of two days after which the first 40 and all ties for 40th place qualify for a further 36 holes on the third day. Handicap limit is 6.4.

Ladies' British Open Championship

The Championship consists of 72 holes stroke play. 18 holes are played on each of four days, the field being reduced after the first 36 holes.

Entries accepted from lady amateurs with a handicap not exceeding scratch and from lady professionals. Full particulars for all three Championships can be obtained from the LGU, The Scores, St Andrews, Fife KY16 9AT. Tel: 01334 475811   Fax: 01334 472818

National Championships

Conditions of entry and method of play for the English, Scottish, Welsh and Irish Ladies' Close Championships can be obtained from the Secretaries of the respective associations.

Other championships organised by the respective national associations, from whom full particulars can be obtained, include English Ladies', Intermediate, English Ladies' Stroke Play, Scottish Girls' Open Amateur Stroke Play (under 21) and Welsh Ladies' Open Amateur Stroke Play.

Girls

Girls' British Open Amateur Championship

The Championship consists of two 18-hole qualifying rounds, followed by match play in two flights, the first of 32 and the second of 16 players.

Conditions of entry include:

Entrants must be under 18 years of age on the 1st January in the year of the Championship.

Competitors are required to hold a certified LGU international handicap not exceeding 12.4.

Full particulars can be obtained from the Administrator, LGU, The Scores, St Andrews, Fife KY16 9AT. Tel: 01334 475811   Fax: 01334 472818

National Championships

The English, Scottish, Irish and Welsh Girls' Close Championships are open to all girls of relevant nationality and appropriate age which may vary from country to country. A handicap limit may be set by some countries. Full particulars can be obtained via the secretaries of the respective associations.

International European Amateur Championships

Founded in 1986 by the European Golf Association, the International Amateur and Ladies Amateur Championships are held on an annual basis since 1990. These Championships consist of one round of 18 holes on each of three days after which the leading 70 and those tying for 70th place play one further round.

Full particulars of conditions of entry and method of play can be obtained from the European Golf Association.

Since 1991, the European Golf Association also holds an International Mid-Amateur Championship on an annual basis. The Championship consist of one round of 18 holes on each of two days after which the leading 90 and those tying for 90th place play one further round.

Full particulars of conditions of entry and method of play can be obtained from the European Golf Association.

Since 1996, the European Golf Association holds an International Seniors Championship for ladies and men on an annual basis.

The Championship consists of one round of 18 holes on each of two days after which there is a cut in both ladies and men categories. The competitors who pass the cut play one further round.

Additionally, a nation's cup is played within the tournament on the first two days. Teams are composed of three players. The two best gross scores out of three will count each day. The total aggregate of the four scores over two days will constitute the team's score.

Full particulars of conditions of entry and method of play can be obtained from the European Golf Association, Place de la Croix-Blanche 19, PO Box CH-1066 Epilanges, Switzerland. Tel: +41 21 784 32 32 Fax: +412 1 784 35 91

International Match Conditions

Men's Amateur Matches

Walker Cup – Great Britain and Ireland v United States of America

Mr GH Walker of the United States presented a Cup for international competition to be known as *The United States Golf Association International Challenge Trophy*, popularly described as *The Walker Cup*.

The Cup shall be played for by teams of amateur golfers selected from Clubs under the jurisdiction of the United States Golf Association on the one side and from England, Ireland, Scotland and Wales on the other.

The Walker Cup shall be held every two years in the United States of America and Great Britain and Ireland alternately.

The teams shall consist of not more than ten players and a captain.

The contest consists of four foursomes and eight singles matches over 18 holes on each of two days.

St Andrews Trophy – Great Britain and Ireland *v* Continent of Europe

First staged in 1956, the St Andrews Trophy is a biennial international match played between two selected teams of amateur golfers representing Great Britain and Ireland and the Continent of Europe. Each team consists of nine players and the match is played over two consecutive days with four morning foursomes followed each afternoon by eight singles. Selection of the Great Britain and Ireland team is carried out by the Selection Committee of The Royal and Ancient Golf Club. The European Golf Association select the Continent of Europe team.

Eisenhower Trophy – Men's World Team Championship

Founded in recognition of the need for an official world amateur team championship, the first event was played at St Andrews in 1958 and the Trophy has been played for every second year in different countries around the world.

Each country enters a team of four players who play strokeplay over 72 holes, the total of the three best individual scores to be counted for each round.

European Team Championship

Founded in 1959 by the European Golf Association for competition among member countries of the Association. The Championship is held biennially and played in rotation round the countries, which are grouped in four geographical zones.

Each team consists of six players who play two qualifying rounds of 18 holes, the five best scores of each round constituting the team aggregate. Flights for match play are then arranged according to qualifying rankings. The match play consists of two foursomes and five singles on each of three days.

A similar championship is held in alternate years for Youths teams, under 21 years of age and every year for Boys teams, under 18 years of age.

Raymond Trophy – Home Internationals

The first official International Match recorded was in 1902 at Hoylake between England and Scotland who won 32 to 25 on a holes up basis.

In 1932 International Week was inaugurated under the auspices of the British Golf Unions' Joint Advisory Council with the full approval of the four National Golf Unions. The Council of National Golf Unions is now responsible for running the matches. Teams of 11 players from England, Scotland, Ireland and Wales engage in matches consisting of five foursomes and ten singles over 18 holes, the foursomes being in the morning and the singles in the afternoon. Each team plays every other team.

The eligibility of players to play for their country shall be their eligibility to play in the Amateur Championship of their country.

Sir Michael Bonallack Trophy – Europe v Asia /Pacific

First staged in 1998, the Sir Michael Bonallack Trophy is a biennial international match played between two selected teams of amateur golfers representing Europe and Asia/Pacific. Each team consists of 12 players and the match is played over three days with five four balls in the morning and five foursomes in the afternoon of the first two days, followed by 12 singles on the last day. Selection of the European team is carried out by the European Golf Association. The Asia/Pacific Golf Confederation selects the Asia/Pacific team.

Men's Professional Matches

Ryder Cup – Europe v United States of America

This Cup was presented by Mr Samuel Ryder, St Albans, England (who died 2nd January, 1936), for competition between a team of British professionals and a team of American professionals. The trophy was first competed for in 1927. In 1929 the original conditions were varied to confine the British team to British-born professionals resident in Great Britain, and the American team to American-born professionals resident in the United States, in the year of the match. In 1979 the British team was extended to include European players. The matches are played

biennially, in alternate continents, in accordance with the conditions as agreed between the respective PGAs.

World Cup (formerly Canada Cup)

Founded in America by John Jay Hopkins in 1955 as a team event for professional golfers with the object of spreading international goodwill. Each country is represented by two players with the best team score over 72 holes producing the winners of the World Cup and the best individual score the winner of the International Trophy. Played for annually (but not in 1986) the event was run until 1999 by the International Gold Association but it is now organised as part of the new World Championship series of events by representatives of the leading professional golf tours.

Seve Ballesteros Trophy – Great Britain and Ireland v Continent of Europe

A match instituted in 2000 at Sunningdale and played along Ryder Cup lines in alternate years.

Llandudno Trophy (PGA Cup) – Great Britain and Ireland v United States of America

The Llandudno International Trophy was first awarded to England in 1939 after winning the first Home Tournament Series against Ireland, Scotland and Wales. With the outbreak of war the series was abolished and the Trophy formed part of Percy Alliss's personal collection. After Percy's death his son Peter donated the Llandudno Trophy to be awarded to the winner of the then annual PGA Cup Match. Now it is a biennial match played since 1973 in Ryder Cup format between Great Britain and Ireland and the United States of America involving top club professionals. No prize money is awarded to the competitors who compete solely for their country. Selection of the Great Britain and Ireland team is determined following completion of the Glenmuir PGA Club Professionals Championship.

Ladies Amateur Matches

Curtis Cup – Great Britain and Ireland v United States

For a trophy presented by the late Misses Margaret and Harriot Curtis of Boston, USA, for biennial competition between amateur teams from the United States of America and Great Britain and Ireland. The match is sponsored jointly by the United States Golf Association and the Ladies' Golf Union who may select teams of not more than eight players.

The match consists of three foursomes and six singles of 18 holes on each of two days, the foursomes being played each morning.

Vagliano Trophy – Great Britain and Ireland v Continent of Europe

For a trophy presented to the Comité des Dames de la Fédération Française de Golf and the Ladies' Golf Union by Monsieur AA Vagliano, originally for annual competition between teams of women amateur golfers from France and Great Britain and Ireland but, since 1959, by mutual agreement, for competition between teams from the Continent of Europe and Great Britain and Ireland.

The match is played biennially, alternately in Great Britain and Ireland and on the Continent of Europe, with teams of not more than nine players plus a non-playing captain. The match consists of four foursomes and eight singles, of 18 holes on each of two days. The foursomes are played each morning.

Espirito Santo Trophy – Women's World Team Championship

Presented by Mrs Ricardo Santo of Portugal for biennial competition between teams of not more than three women amateur golfers who represent a national association affiliated to the World Amateur Golf Council. First competed for in 1964. The Championship consists of 72 holes strokeplay, 18 holes on each of four days, the two best scores in each round constituting the team aggregate.

Lady Astor Trophy – Commonwealth Tournament

For a trophy presented by the late Viscountess Astor CH, and the Ladies' Golf Union for competition once in every four years between teams of women amateur golfers from Commonwealth countries.

The inaugural Commonwealth Tournament was played at St Andrews in 1959 between teams from Australia, Canada, New Zealand, South Africa and Great Britain and was won by the British team. The tournament is played in rotation in the competing countries, for the present Great Britain, Australia, Canada, and New Zealand, each country being entitled to nominate six players including a playing or non-playing captain.

Each team plays every other team and each team match consists of two foursomes and four singles over 18 holes. The foursomes are played in the morning and the singles in the afternoon.

European Team Championships

Founded in 19S9 by the European Golf Association for competition among member countries of the Association. The Championship is held biennially and played in rotation round the countries, which are grouped in four geographical zones.

Each team consists of six players who play two qualifying rounds of 18 holes, the five best scores of each round constituting the team aggregate. Flights for matchplay are then arranged according to qualifying rankings. The matchplay consists of two foursomes and five singles on each of three days.

A similar championship is held in alternate years for Lady Juniors teams, under 21 years of age and every year for Girls teams, under 18 years of age.

Home Internationals

Teams from England, Scotland, Ireland and Wales compete annually for a trophy presented to the LGU by the late Mr TH Miller. The qualifications for a player being eligible to play for her country are the same as those laid down by each country for its Close Championship.

Each team plays each other team. The matches consist of six singles and three foursomes, each of 18 holes. Each country may nominate teams of not more than eight players.

Ladies Professional Matches

Solheim Cup – Europe v United States

The Solheim Cup, named after Karsten Solheim who founded the sponsoring Ping company, is the women's equivalent of the Ryder Cup. In 1990 the inaugural competition between the top women professional golfers from Europe and America took place in Florida.

The matches are played biennially in alternate continents. The format is foursomes and fourball matches on the first two days, followed by singles on the third in accordance with the conditions as agreed between the Evian Tour and the United States LPGA Tour.

World Cup

Started in 2000 by the LPGA and the International Management Group, the event is held along similar lines to the men's World Cup with each country represented by two players. There is also an individual competiton incorporated in the regulations. It had been planned as an annual fixture but the 2001 Championship scheduled for Adelaide was cancelled. A new World Cup event is scheduled for South Africa in 2004.

Boys Matches

R & A Trophy – Home Internationals

Teams comprising 11 players from England, Scotland, Ireland and Wales compete against one another over three days in a single round robin format. Each fixture comprises five morning foursomes followed by ten afternoon singles.

To be eligible for selection, players must be under the age of 18 at 00.00 hours on 1st January in the year of the matches and have eligibility to play in their national championships

Jacques Léglise Trophy – Great Britain and Ireland v Continent of Europe

The Jacques Léglise Trophy is an annual international match played between two selected teams of amateur boy golfers representing Great Britain and Ireland and the Continent of Europe. Each team consists of nine players and the match is played over two consecutive days with four morning foursomes followed each afternoon by eight singles. Selection of the Great Britain and Ireland team is carried out by the Selection Committee of The Royal and Ancient Golf Club. The European Golf Association selects the Continent of Europe team

To be eligible for selection, players must be under the age of 18 at 00.00 hours on 1st January in the year of the matches.

Junior Ryder Cup

First staged in 1995, the Junior Ryder Cup is a biennial international match played between two selected teams of amateur golfers representing Europe and the USA, prior to the Ryder Cup. Each team consists of four girls and four boys under 16 as well as two girls and two boys under 18. The match is played over two consecutive days with six four balls on the first day and six mixed four balls on the second day.

Selection of the European team is carried out by the European Golf Association. Players and captains are then invited to watch the Ryder Cup.

Girls

Home Internationals

Teams from England, Scotland, Ireland and Wales compete annually for the Stroyan Cup. The qualifications for a player for the Girls' International Matches shall be the same as those laid down by each country for its Girls' Close Championship except that a player shall be under 18 years on the 1st January in the year of the Championship.

Each team, consisting of not more than eight players, plays each other team, a draw taking place to decide the order of play between the teams. The matches consist of three foursomes and six singles, each of 18 holes.

Golf Associations

The National Association of Public Golf Courses (Affiliated to English Golf Union)

The Association was founded in 1927 by golf course architect FG Hawtree and five-times Open Champion JH Taylor who saw the need for cohesion of private golf, public golf and the local councils. Until 1939 the Association was sustained by a small amount of financial support from the *News of the World*, which enabled the the Public Courses Championship of England, the so-called Unofficial Championship to be staged. After the War the Association was revitalised and the Championship was recognised by the National Union. Some 3500 public course golfers now try to qualify for the Unofficial Championship.

The success and importance of this prompted the inauguration of the Ladies' Championship and, subsequently, the Junior Championship. Various club team events came soon after, and these have now progressed to national level with a vast following from club members. Thus the Association now organises some 14 national events annually.

Many of the local councils' course management authorities (CMAs) are now full subscribing members, and many others permit the courtesy of the course for all the Association's national and zonal tournaments. Advice is offered to CMAs, when requested, on such matters as course construction, club formation and integration, establishment of Standard Scratch Score and par values, and many other topics concerned with the management of the game of golf. Overseas organisations and councils can seek advice and help in forming their own courses, clubs and associations.

The constitutional aims have not changed over the years, and the Association is proud to have maintained them. The aims are:

1. To unite the clubs formed on public courses in England and Wales, and their course managements in the furtherance of the interests of amateur golf.
2. To promote annual public course championships and such other matches, competitions and tournaments as shall be authorised by the executive of the Association.
3. To afford direct representation of public course interests in the National Union.

The organisation of the Association is wholly voluntary and honorary. Contact details p.514.

Association of Golf Club Secretaries

Membership is over 2,300, consisting of secretaries/managers and retired secretaries of clubs and golfing associations situated in the UK and Europe. The Association offers advice on all aspects of managing a golf club, including the use of an extensive information library, mainly available direct to members through its website. A national conference is held every three years. Potential and newly appointed secretaries can attend a residential training course while regular seminars are available to all members. The Association's journal, *Golf Club Management*, is published monthly and circulated to all members. The regular business of the Association is conducted from the 17 regions of the UK, along with a number of golf meetings. After five years members can apply for membership of the Institute of Golf Club Management, which is part of the Association. Contact details p.513.

The Association of Golf Writers

A group of 30 newspapermen attending the Walker Cup Match at St Andrews on 2 June 1938 decided there was a need for an organisation to 'protect the interests of golf writers'. Their main objective was to establish close liaison with the governing bodies and promoters of golf. Thus was born The Association of Golf Writers, now solidly established and rightly respected as the official negotiating body of the golfing press. The Association owes much to a membership which has included many internationally recognised names who have contributed to elevating the Association to a unique level among British sports writers' associations. Contact details p.513.

The Sports Turf Research Institute (STRI) (Bingley, West Yorkshire)

The STRI is officially recognised as the national centre for sports and amenity turf and is the official agronomist to the Championship Committee of the R&A. It is a non-profit distributing company limited by guarantee, its affairs managed by a small Executive Committee drawn from its Members Body comprising most sports controlling bodies. Golf is represented by the nominees of the R&A, the four home Golf Unions and the Council of National Golf Unions. The British Institute of Golf Course Architects, the British & International Greenkeepers Association and the PGA European Tour are also represented on its Members Body and Golf Committee.

STRI's mission is to carry out research and promote innovation; to provide advisory and consultancy services; and to provide education and publications for subscribing clubs, sports controlling bodies and the turfgrass industry at large. Contact details on p.514.

The European Institute of Golf Course Architects (EIGCA)

The European Institute of Golf Course Architects reprsents the vast majority of qualified and experienced golf course architects throughout Europe. EIGCA's goals include enhancing the professional status of the profession, developing the role of eduation and increasing the opportunities for its members to practise in countries throughout the world. EIGCA also provides educational courses to train future golf course architects and is the authoritative voice on all related matters, being recognised by the Royal and Ancient Golf Club of St Andrews. Contact details p.514.

The British Association of Golf Course Constructors

The BAGCC has always maintained its small though highly prestigious membership by 'invitation only', those selected proven by example to have performed work to the highest standard in every aspect of golf course construction: from initial consultation, survey, through design and construction to regular course maintenance. New members are admitted only if they satisfy the criteria of experience, professionalism and quality of workmanship set by the association. Membership remains an identity of considerable pride, worn in the same way, as, say, that of a qualified architect or surveyor. In simple terms it indicates that 'This organisation is skilled at its job, it is highly profesional and is recognised by its peers.' Contact details p.514.

British and International Golf Greenkeepers' Association (BIGGA)

Formed in 1987 from an amalgamation of the British, English and Scottish Associations. Objectives are to promote and advance all aspects of greenkeeping; to assist and encourage the proficiency of members; to arrange an international annual conference, educational seminars, functions and competitions; to collaborate with any body or organisation which may benefit the Association or its members or with which there may be a common interest; to carry out and perform any other duties which shall be in the general interests of the Association or its members. The Association has an official magazine, *Greenkeeping International,* which is issued free to all members. The Association also organised the annual BIGGA Turf Management Exhibition (BTME) which is Europe's largest indoor turf show. Currently the Association has over 7,300 members in the United Kingdom and world wide. Contact details p.514.

National Golf Clubs' Advisory Association

Founded in 1922, the Association's objectives are to protect the interests of golf clubs in general and to give legal advice and direction, under the opinion of Counsel, on the administrative and legal responsibilities of golf clubs. Financial assistance may sometimes be given in cases taken to the courts for decisions on points which, in the opinion of the Executive Committee, involve principles affecting the general interests of affiliated clubs. Contact details p.514.

European Golf Association
Association Européenne de Golf

Formed at a meeting held 20 November 1937 in Luxembourg, membership is restricted to European national amateur golf associations or unions. The Association concerns itself solely with matters of an international character. The association is presently composed of 30 member countries and is governed by the following committees:

• Executive Committee
• Championship Committee
• Professional Technical Committee
• EGA Handicapping & Course Rating Committee

Prime objectives are:

(a) To encourage international development of golf, to strengthen bonds of friendship existing between it members.

(b) To encourage the formation of new golf organisations representing the golf activities of European countries.

(c) To co-ordinate the dates of the Open and Amateur championships of its members and to arrange, in conjuction with host Federations, European champion-ships and specific matches of international character.

(d) To ratify and publish the calendar dates of the major Amateur and Professional championships and international matches in Europe.

(e) To create and maintain international relationships in the field of golf and undertake any action useful to the cause of golf on an international level.

The headquarters are situated in Epalinges, Switzerland. Contact details p.522.

Golf Club Stewards' Association

The Golf Club Stewards' Association was founded as early as 1912. Its members are Stewards in golf clubs throughout the UK and Ireland. It has a National Committee and Regional Branches in the South, North-West, Midlands, East Anglia, Yorkshire, Wales and the West, North-East Scotland and Ireland. The objectives of the Association are to promote the interests of members; to administer a Benevolent Fund for members in need; and to arrange golf competitions and matches. It also serves as an agency for the employment of Stewards in golf clubs. Contact details p.514.

Directory of Golfing Organisations Worldwide

National Associations

Great Britain and Ireland

The Royal and Ancient Golf Club of St Andrews
Sec, Peter Dawson, St Andrews, Fife KY16 9JD
Tel (01334) 460000   *Fax* (01334) 460001
E-mail thesecretary@randagc.org
Website www.randa.org

Council of National Golf Unions
Sec, Kevin McIntyre, Dromin, Dunleer, Co.Louth,
Ireland
Tel +353 41 686 1476
E-mail golfinmcinere@hotmail.com

Ladies European Tour
Ch Exec, I Randell,
The Tytherington Club, The Old Hall, Macclesfield,
Cheshire SK10 2LQ
Tel (01625) 611444   *Fax* (01625) 610406
E-mail mail@ladieseuropeantour.com
Website www.ladieseuropeantour.com

Ladies' Golf Union
Sec, Andy Salmon, The Scores, St Andrews, Fife
KY16 9AT
Tel (01334) 475811   *Fax* (01334) 472818
E-mail info@lgu.org
Website www.lgu.org

The Professional Golfers' Association
Ch Exec, Sandy Jones, Centenary House,
The De Vere Belfry, Sutton Coldfield, B76 9PT
Tel (01675) 470333   *Fax* (01675) 477888
Website www.pga.info

East Region: *Sec*, J Smith, Bishop's Stortford GC,
Dunmow, Bishop's Stortford, Herts CM23 5HP
Tel (01279) 652070   *Fax* (01279) 652732
E-mail john.smith@pga.org.uk

Midland Region: *Sec*, J Sewell, King's Norton GC,
Brockhill Lane, Weatheroak, Nr Alvechurch, Worcs
B48 7ED
Tel (01564) 824909
Fax (01564) 822805
E-mail jon.sewell@pga.org.uk

North Region: *Sec*, J Croxton, No 2 Cottage, Bolton
GC, Lostock Park, Chorley New Road, Bolton,
Lancs BL6 4AJ
Tel (01204) 496137   *Fax* (01204) 847959
E-mail jim.croxton@pga.org.uk

South Region: *Sec*, P Ward, Clandon Regis GC,
Epsom Road, West Clandon, Guildford, Surrey
GU4 7TT
Tel (01483) 224200   *Fax* (01483) 223224
E-mail peter.ward@pga.org.uk

West Region: *Sec*, R Ellis, Exeter G&CC, Topsham
Road, Countess Wear, Exeter EX2 7AE
Tel (01392) 877657   *Fax* (01392) 876382
E-mail ray.ellis@pga.org.uk

Irish Region: *Sec*, M McCumiskey, Dundalk GC,
Blackrock, Dundalk, Co Louth, Eire
Tel (00 353) 42 932 1193   *Fax* (00 353) 42 932 1899
E-mail michael.mccumiskey@pga.org.uk

Scottish Region: *Sec*, P Lloyd, King's Lodge,
Gleneagles, Auchterarder PH3 1NE
Tel (01764) 661840   *Fax* (01764) 661841
E-mail peter.lloyd@pga.org.uk

PGA European Tour
Exec Dir, KD Schofield CBE, PGA European Tour,
Wentworth Drive, Virginia Water, Surrey
GU25 4LX
Tel (01344) 840400   *Fax* (01344) 840451
E-mail kschofield@europeantour.com
Website www.europeantour.com

PGA of Europe
Sec, LE Thornton, Centenary House, The De Vere
Belfry, Sutton Coldfield, B76 9PT
Tel (01675) 477899   *Fax* (01675) 477890
E-mail info@pgae.com   *Website* www.pgae.com

Artisan Golfers' Association
Hon Sec, K Stevens, 85 The Avenue, Lightwater,
Surrey GU18 5RG
Tel (01276) 475103

Association of Golf Club Secretaries
National Sec, K Lloyd, 7a Beaconsfield Road,
Weston-super-Mare BS23 1YE
Tel (01934) 641166
Fax (01934) 644254
E-mail hq@agcs.org.uk
Website www.agcs.org.uk

Association of Golf Writers
Sec, Andrew Farrell, 1 Pilgrims Bungalow, Mulberry
Hill, Chilham, Kent CT4 8AH
Tel/Fax (01227) 732496
E-mail andyfarrell@compuserve.com

British Association of Golf Course Constructors
Sec, D White, Fore! The Dormy House, Cooden
Beach GC, Bexhill-on-Sea, TN39 4TR
Tel (01424) 842380   *Fax* (01424) 843375
E-mail mightyspyder@aol.com
Website www.bagcc.org.uk

British Golf Collectors' Society
Sec, CH Ibbetson, Apartado de Correos 215, 03180
Torrevieja, Alicante, Spain
E-mail bgcs@globalnet.co.uk
Website www.britgolfcollectors.wyenet.co.uk

The British Golf Museum
Dir, PN Lewis; *Curator*, Sam Groves, Bruce
Embankment, St Andrews, Fife KY16 9AB
Tel (01334) 460046   *Fax* (01334) 460064
E-mail alisonwood@randagc.org
Website www.britishgolfmuseum.co.uk

**British & International Golf Greenkeepers'
Association**
Exec Dir, N Thomas, Bigga House, Aldwark, Alne,
York Y061 1UF
Tel (01347) 833800   *Fax* (01347) 833801
E-mail reception@bigga.co.uk
Website www.bigga.org.uk

**British Turf & Landscape Irrigation
Association**
PO Box 709, Garstang PR3 1GT
Tel/Fax (07041) 363130
Website www.btlia.org.uk

**The European Institute of Golf Course Architects
(EIGCA)**
Sec, Chiddingford GC, Petworth Rd, Chiddingford,
GU8 4SL
Tel/Fax (01428) 68152
E-mail info@eigca.org
Website www.eigca.org

Golf Club Stewards' Association
Sec, Peter Payne, 3 St George's Drive,
Ickenham, Middx UB10 4HW
Tel (01895) 674325
E-mail golfclubstewards@aol.com

Golf Foundation
Ch. Exec, Michael Round, Foundation House, The
Spinney, Hoddesdon Rd, Stanstead Abbots, SG12 8GF
Tel (01920) 876200   *Fax* (01920) 876211
E-mail info@golf-foundation.org
Website www.golf-foundation.org

Golf Society of Great Britain
Sec, Mrs J Hesketh, Inglewood Farm, Minshull
Vernon, Middlewich, Cheshire CW10 0LS
Tel/Fax (01270) 522533
E-mail jackie@hesketh2000.freeserve.co.uk

National Association of Public Golf Courses
Hon Sec, E Mitchell, 12 Newton Close, Redditch
B98 7YR
Tel (01527) 542106   *Fax* (01527) 455320
E-mail eddiemitchell@blueyonder.co.uk

National Golf Clubs' Advisory Association
Sec, Michael Shaw LLM, Suite 16 Tranzart Business
Centre, Owl Gate, Roberts End, Hanley Swan
WR8 0DN
Tel (01684) 311353   *Fax* 311924
E-mail ngcaa@idealnet.co.uk
Website www.ngcaa.org.uk

Public Schools Old Boys Golf Association
Hon Sec, P de Pinna, Bruins, Wythwood,
Haywards Heath, West Sussex RH16 4RD
Tel (01444) 454883
Fax (01444) 415117

Public Schools' Golfing Society
Hon Sec, JNS Lowe, Merrow Cottage, The Street,
East Clandon, Surrey GU4 7RU
Tel (020) 7234 0007
Fax (020) 7234 0008
E-mail jeremy.lowe@solodigital.co.uk

The Sports Turf Research Institute (STRI)
Ch Exec; Dr IG McKillop; *Head Ext Affairs*,
Anne Wilson, St Ives Estate, Bingley, West Yorks
BD16 1AU.
Tel (01274) 565131   *Fax* (01274) 561891
E-mail info@stri.co.uk
Website www.stri.co.uk

Regional Associations

England

English Golf Union
Sec, PM Baxter, National Golf Centre, The
Broadway, Woodhall Spa, Lincs LN10 6PU
Tel (01526) 354500   *Fax* (01526) 354020
E-mail info@englishgolfunion.org
Website www.englishgolfunion.org

Midland Group: *Sec*, RJW Baldwin, Chantry
Cottage, Friar Street, Droitwich, Worcs WR9 8EQ
Tel (01905) 778560   *Fax* (01905) 795848
E-mail secretary@midlandgolfunion.co.uk
Website www.midlandgolfunion.co.uk

Northern Group: *Sec*, JE Allen, West Pines,
16 Macclesfield Rd, Prestbury, Cheshire
SK10 4BN
Tel/Fax (01625) 265373
E-mail jallen@onetel.net.uk

South Eastern Group: *Sec*, JW Gilding,
10 Mansion Lane, Iver, Bucks SL0 9RH
Tel (01753) 819686   *Fax* (01753) 771809
E-mail secretary@southeastgolfunion.co.uk

South Western Group: *Sec*, DR King, 41 West
Town Lane, Brislington, Bristol BS4 5DD
Tel/Fax (01179) 773330
E-mail davidswcga@btopenworld.com

English Men's County Unions

Bedfordshire CGU
Hon Sec, C Allen, West Grove, Wilden Rd, Renhold, MK41 0JJ
Tel (01234) 771047
E-mail bedsgus*ec*@ukonline.co.uk
Website www.bedsgolfunion.org

Berks, Bucks & Oxon UGC
Sec, PMJ York, Bridge House, Station Approach, Great Missenden, HP16 9AZ
Tel (01494) 867341   *Fax* (01494) 867342
E-mail secretary@bbogolf.com
Website www.bbogolf.com

Cambridgeshire Area GU
Sec, RAC Blows, 73 Pheasant Rise, Bar Hill, Cambridge CB3 8SB
Tel (01954) 780887

Cheshire UGC
Sec, SJ Foster, 15 Barley Croft, Boughton, Chester CH3 5SP
Tel/Fax (01244) 346662
E-mail sec*retary@cheshiregolf.org.uk
Website www.cheshiregolf.org.uk

Cornwall GU
Hon Sec, JG Rowe, 11 St Winnolls Park, Looe PL13 1DG
Tel/Fax (01503) 265814

Cumbria UGC
Hon Sec, W Ward, 10 The Hawthorns, Wigton, Cumbria CA7 9LE
Tel/Fax (01697) 342600

Derbyshire UGC
Hon Sec, CRJ Ibbotson, 4 The Spinney, Luke Lane, Brailsford, nr Ashbourne DE6 3BS
Tel (01335) 360889   *Fax* (01335) 361198
E-mail cliveibbotson@lineone.net
Website www.dugc.co.uk

Devon CGU
Sec, John Hirst, 20 Plymouth Rd, Tavistock PL19 8AY
Tel (01822) 610640   *Fax* (01822) 610540
E-mail info@devongolfunion.org.uk
Website www.devongolfunion.org.uk

Dorset CGU
Hon Sec, Douglas Pratt, 5 Farm Close, Southill, Weymouth DT4 0EG
Tel (01305) 786184   *Fax* (01305) 759134
E-mail douglas.pratt@virgin.net
Website www.dorsetgolfunion.com

Durham CGU
Sec, GP Hope, 7 Merrion Close, Moorside, Sunderland SR3 2QP
Tel/Fax (0191) 522 8605
E-mail secretary@durhamcountygolfunion.co.uk
Website www.durhamcountygolfunion.co.uk

Essex GU
Sec, AT Lockwood, 2d Maldon Road, Witham, Essex CM8 2AB
Tel (01376) 500998   *Fax* (01376) 500842
E-mail info@essexgolfunion.org
Website www.essexgolfunion.org

Gloucestershire GU
Sec, I Watkins, The Vyse, Olde Lane, Toddington, Glos GL54 5DQ
Tel/Fax (01242) 612476
E-mail secretary@gloucestershiregolfunion.co.uk
Website www.gloucestershiregolfunion.co.uk

Hampshire, Isle of Wight & Channel Islands GU
Sec, K Maplesden, c/o Liphook GC, Wheatsheaf Enclosure, Liphook, Hants GU30 7EH
Tel/Fax (01428) 725580
E-mail hgu@hampshiregolf.co.uk
Website www.hampshiregolf.org.uk

Hertfordshire GU
Hon Sec, JC Harkett, 5 Willow Way, Harpenden AL5 5JF
Tel (01582) 760841   *Fax* (01582) 462608
E-mail hertsgolfunionsec@lineone.net

Isle of Man GU
Hon Sec, Joe Boyd, Cheu-Ny-Hawiney, Phildraw Rd, Ballasalla, Isle of Man IM9 3EG
Tel/Fax (01624) 823098
E-mail joeboyd@manx.net

Kent CGU
Sec, SS Fullager, St Andrew's Road, Littlestone, New Romney, Kent TN28 8RB
Tel (01797) 367725   *Fax* (01797) 367726
E-mail kcgu@kentgolf.co.uk
Website www.kentgolf.org.uk

Lancashire UGC
Sec, AV Moss, 5 Dicconson Terrace, Lytham St Annes FY8 5JY
Tel (01253) 733323   *Fax* (01253) 795721
E-mail secretary@lancashiregolf.fsnet.co.uk

Leicestershire & Rutland GU
Hon Sec, C Chamberlain, 10 Shipton Close, The Meadows, Wigston Magna, Leicester LE18 3WL
Tel/Fax (0116) 288 9862
E-mail secretary@lrgu.co.uk
Website www.lrgu.co.uk

Lincolnshire UGC
Hon Sec, GH Moore OBE, Authorpe House, 36 Horncastle Road, Woodhall Spa LN10 6UZ
Tel/Fax (01526) 352792

Middlesex CGU
Sec, JAL Williams, Television House, Office no.6, 269 Field End Rd, Eastcote, Ruislip, HA4 9LS
Tel (0208) 429 9206
Fax (0208) 429 9156
E-mail mcgu@dial.pipex.com
Website www.mcgu.co.uk

Norfolk CGU
Hon Sec, RJ Trower, 12a Stanley Avenue, Thorpe, Norwich, Norfolk NR7 0BE
Tel/Fax (01603) 431026

Northamptonshire GU
Hon Sec, G Brooks, 17 Water Lane, Chelveston, Wellingborough NN9 6AP
Tel/Fax (01933) 625032
E-mail secretary@ngu.org.uk

Northumberland UGC
Hon Sec, WE Procter, 5 Oakhurst Drive, Kenton
Park, Gosforth, Newcastle-upon-Tyne NE3 4JS
Tel/Fax (0191) 285 4981
E-mail elliott.procter@ukonline.co.uk

Nottinghamshire UGC
Hon Sec, R Case, 68a Cropwell Rd, Radcliffe on
Trent, Nottingham NG12 2JG
Tel/Fax (0115) 933 4777

Shropshire & Herefordshire UGC
Hon Sec, JR Davies, 23 Poplar Crescent, Bayston
Hill, Shrewsbury SY3 0QB
Tel/Fax (01743) 872655
E-mail bdavies@blueyonder.co.uk

Somerset GU
Hon Sec, GA Yates, Little Manor, Greinton,
Nr Bridgwater TA7 9BW
Tel/Fax (01458) 210179
E-mail gyates@greinton.freeserve.co.uk
Website www.somerset.golfunion.com

Staffordshire UGC
Sec, MA Payne, 20 Kingsbrook Drive, Hillfield,
Solihull B91 3UU
Tel (0121) 704 4779

Suffolk CGU
Hon Sec, RA Kent, 77 Bennett Avenue, Bury St
Edmunds IP33 3JJ
Tel (01284) 705765   *Fax* (01284) 767607
E-mail golfsgu@aol.com

Surrey CGU
Sec, MW Ashton, Sutton Green GC, New Lane,
Sutton Green GU4 7QF
Tel (01483) 755788   *Fax* (01483) 751771
E-mail cgu@surreygolf.org
Website www.surreygolf.org

Sussex CGU
Sec, DJ Harmer, c/o Eastbourne Down GC, East
Dean Road, East Sussex BN20 8ES
Tel (01323) 746677   *Fax* (01323) 746777
E-mail info@sussexgolf.org
Website www.sussexgolf.org

Warwickshire UGC
Sec, J Stubbings, Quaker Cottage, Wiggins Hill
Road, Wishaw, Sutton Coldfield B76 9QE
Tel/Fax (01675) 470809
E-mail stubbings@wugc.fsnet.co.uk
Website www.warksgolf.co.uk

Wiltshire CGU
Sec, EK Hodges, 13 Elm Close, Boweshill,
Melksham, Wilts SN12 6SD
Tel/Fax (01225) 703255
E-mail keithhodges@tinyworld.co.uk

Worcestershire UGC
Hon Sec, A Boyd, The Bears Den, Upper Street,
Defford, Worcester WR8 9BG
Tel (01386) 750657
Fax (01386) 750472
E-mail aboydgolf@aol.com
Website www.wugc.co.uk

Yorkshire UGC
Hon Sec, KH Dowswell, 33 George Street,
Wakefield WF1 1LX
Tel (01924) 383869   *Fax* (01924) 383634
E-mail yorkshiregolf@lineone.net
Website www.yorkshireunionofgolf.co.uk

English Ladies' Golf Association
Sec, Mrs P Perla, Edgbaston GC,
Church Road, Birmingham B15 3TB
Tel (0121) 456 2088   *Fax* (0121) 454 5542
E-mail office@englishladiesgolf.org
Website www.englishladiesgolf.org
Northern Division: *Hon Sec*, Mrs R Horsfall, Rock
Bottom, Daisy Lea Lane, Edgerton, Huddersfield
HD3 3LL
Tel (01484) 533444
E-mail horsfall@rockbottom.fsnet.co.uk
Midlands Division: *Hon Sec*, Mrs J Latch,
3 The Barns, Soulbury Rd, Burcott, Leighton
Buzzard LU7 0JU
Tel (01296) 681214   *E-mail* jill.latch@talk21.com
South-Eastern Division: *Hon Sec*, Mrs R Wallis,
The Bungalow, The Green, Pirbright, Woking
GU24 0JE
Tel (01483) 476528
E-mail rhwallis@ukgateway.net
South-Western Division: *Hon Sec*, Mrs A Bates,
25 Brinsea Rd, Congresbury, nr Bristol BS49 5JF
Tel (01934) 833470
E-mail audreybates@fsmail.net

English Senior Ladies Golf Association
Hon Sec, Mrs J Buchanan, Bell House, Meonstoke,
Southampton SO32 3NJ
Tel (01489) 878228
E-mail jobuchanan@bellhouse71.fsnet.co.uk
Website www.eslga.org.uk

English Ladies' County Associations
Bedfordshire LCGA
Hon Sec, Mrs N Cole, 6 Church Lane, Eaton Bray,
Beds LU6 2DJ
Tel (01525) 220479
E-mail 8noreen.cole@ic24.net

Berkshire LCGA
Hon Sec, Mrs M Shepherd, 40 Florence Road,
College Town, Sandhurst GU47 0QD
Tel/Fax (01276) 35937

Buckinghamshire LCGA
Hon Sec, Mrs C Hawksworth, 8 White Hart Close,
Chalfont St Giles, HP8 4PH
Tel (01494) 870270

Cambs & Hunts LCGA
Hon Sec, Mrs S Ramsay, 11 Marriotts Yard,
Ramsey, Huntingdon PE26 1HN
Tel (01487) 710824

Cheshire CLGA
Hon Sec, Mrs L Lancely, 41 Croft Drive East, Caldy,
Wirral CH48 1LX
Tel (0151) 6250183

Cornwall LCGA
Hon Sec, Mrs C Penhale, 2 Scolars Close,
St Ives, Liskeard PL14 3UX
Tel (01579) 384595

Cumbria LCGA
Hon Sec, Mrs L Mayne, Jasmine Cottage, Stainton,
Nr Penrith CA11 0ES
Tel/Fax (01768) 865495

Derbyshire LCGA
Hon Sec, Mrs E Brammeld, 18 Cauldron Close, Leek
ST13 5SH
Tel (01538) 399553

Devon CLGA
Hon Sec, Mrs J Shayler, 2 Bystock Mews, Bystock,
Exmouth EX8 5EP
Tel (01395) 272801

Dorset LCGA
Hon Sec, Mrs A Michie, The Beagles, Cook Lane,
Axminster EX13 5SQ
Tel (01297) 35489

Durham CLGA
Hon Sec, Mrs E Whittle, 23 Kitswell Road,
Lanchester, Co Durham DH7 0JJ
Tel (01207) 520581

Essex LCGA
Hon Sec, Mrs M Low, 15 Rushdene Road,
Brentwood CM15 9ES
Tel (01277) 230849

Gloucestershire LCGA
Hon Sec, Mrs G Merry, Myles House,
Ashmead, Dursley GL11 3EN
Tel (01453) 542569

Hampshire LCGA
Sec, Mrs A Grosvenor, 16A Salterns Lane, Hayling
Island PO11 9PJ
Tel (023) 9246 5710

Hertfordshire CLGA
Hon Sec, Mrs M Broadbent, 6 Earlsmead,
Letchworth SG6 3UE
Tel (01462) 682767

Kent CLGA
Hon Sec, Mrs D Featherstone, 5 St Giles Close,
Farnborough BR6 7DT
Tel (01689) 858105

Lancashire LCGA
Hon Sec, Miss J Rogers, 19 Lonsdale Rd, Formby,
Liverpool L37 3HD
Tel (01704) 831009

Leicestershire & Rutland LCGA
Hon Sec, Mrs AL Adams, 23 Fisher Close,
Cossington, Leicester LE7 4US
Tel (01509) 812869

Lincolnshire LCA
Hon Sec, Mrs K Craigs, 11 Sylvan Avenue,
Woodhall Spa LN10 6SL
Tel (01526) 352293

Middlesex LCGA
Hon Sec, Mrs E Thomas, 62 Highview Avenue,
Edgware HA8 9UA
Tel (020) 8905 3631

Norfolk LCA
Hon Sec, Miss MA Fisher, 33 Brettingham Avenue,
Norwich NR4 6XQ
Tel (01603) 501181
E-mail fisher.m@btinternet.com

Northamptonshire LCGA
Hon Sec, Mrs SE Clark, The Leys, 32 West St, Earls
Barton, Northampton NN6 0EW
Tel (01604) 810257

Northumberland LCGA
Hon Sec, Mrs J McLane, 15 Whitebridge Park Way,
Newcastle upon Tyne NE3 5LU
Tel (0191) 213 1096

Nottinghamshire CLGA
Hon Sec, Mrs BA Patrick, 18 Delville Avenue,
Keyworth, Nottingham NG12 5JA
Tel (0115) 937 3237

Oxfordshire LCGA
Hon Sec, Mrs EA Sadler, 84 Mably Grove, Wantage,
Oxon OX12 9XN
Tel (01235) 760997

Shropshire LCGA
Hon Sec, Mrs HF Davies, Brooklands, Old Woods,
Bomere Heath, Shrewsbury SY4 3AX
Tel (01939) 290427

Somerset LCGA
Hon Sec, Mrs A Meek, The Old Barn, Woolverton,
Bath BA2 7QT
Tel (01373) 832828

Staffordshire LCGA
Hon Sec, Mrs PM Barrow, Heron's Pool, Roman Rd,
Little Aston, Sutton Coldfield B74 3AA
Tel/Fax (0121) 353 5753

Suffolk LCGA
Hon Sec, Mrs G Hughes, 142 Colneis Rd, Felixstowe
IP11 9QU
Tel (01394) 286329

Surrey LCGA
Sec, Mrs R Murray, , 14 Clifton Close, Boundstone,
Farnham, GU10 4TP
Tel (01252) 792987

Sussex CLGA
Hon Sec, Mrs JM Scott, Preferred Lie, Rufwood,
Crawley Down, West Sussex RH10 4HD
Tel (01342) 712213

Warwickshire LCGA
Hon Sec, Mrs I Howell, 7 Coppice Walk, Cheswick
Green, Solihull B90 4HY
Tel (01564) 200091

Wiltshire LCGA
Hon Sec, Mrs F Pinder, Pippins, Mill Orchard,
Fovant, Salisbury SP3 5JS
Tel (01722) 714767

Worcestershire CLGA
Hon Sec, Mrs J Purnell, 14 Bank Farm Close,
Pedmore, Stourbridge DY9 0TT
Tel (01562) 885043

Yorkshire LCGA
Hon Sec, Mrs A McMullen, 88 Ash Hill Drive,
Shadwell, Leeds LS17 8JR
Tel (0113) 273 7257

English County PGAs

Bedfordshire & Cambridgeshire PGA
Sec, B Wake, 6 Gazelle Close, Eaton Socon,
St Neots PE19 3QF
Tel (01480) 219760

Berks, Bucks & Oxon PGA
Hon Sec, Mrs M Green, Wayside, Aylesbury Road,
Monks Risborough, Princes Risborough
HP27 0JS
Tel (01844) 343012

Cheshire and North Wales PGA
Sec, J Croxton, No 2 Cottage, Bolton GC, Lostock
Park, Chorley New Road, Bolton
BL6 4AJ
Tel (01204) 496137   *Fax* (01204) 847959

Cornwall PGA
Sec, C Willis, Bowood Park GC, Camelford
PL32 9RF
Tel (01840) 213017   *Fax* (01840) 212622

Derbyshire PGA
Sec, F McCabe, Hillside, Lower Hall Close,
Holbrook, Derby DE56 0TN
Tel (01332) 880411

Devon PGA
Sec, I Marshall, Staddon Heights GC, Plymstock,
Plymouth PL9 9SP
Tel (01752) 492630

Dorset PGA
Sec/Treas, JM Nicholls, 230 St Michaels Avenue,
Yeovil, Somerset BA21 4LZ
Tel (01935) 472839
E-mail nicholls.john@lineone.net

Essex PGA
Sec, S Wooltorton, 27 Willowdene Court,
Brentwood, Essex CM14 5ET
Tel/Fax (01277) 223510
E-mail suzy@willowdene.fsnet.co.uk
Website www.essexpga.co.uk

Gloucestershire & Somerset PGA
Sec, E Goodwin, Cotswold Hills GC,
Ullenwood, Cheltenham GL53 9QT
Tel (01242) 515263

Hampshire PGA
Sec, DL Wheeler, South Winchester GC, Pitt,
Winchester SO22 5QW
Tel/Fax (01962) 860928
E-mail hampshirepga@yahoo.co.uk
Website www.hampshirepga.com

Hertfordshire PGA
Sec, Malcolm Plumbley, Stavonga Dell, Pasture Rd,
Letchworth SG6 3LP
Tel/Fax (01462) 485268
E-mail meplumbley@stavonga.co.uk
Website www.hertsgolf.org

Kent PGA
Sec, Miss K Page, Kent PGA Office, West Malling
GC, London Road, Addington, Maidstone
ME19 5AR
Tel/Fax (01732) 843420
E-mail karen@kpga.fsnet.co.uk
Website www.kentpga.co.uk

Lancashire PGA
Sec, J Croxton, No 2 Cottage, Bolton GC, Lostock
Park, Chorley New Road, Bolton BL6 4AJ
Tel (01204) 496137   *Fax* (01204) 847959

Leicestershire PGA
Sec, J Ashton, 2 Rose Tree Avenue, Birstall,
Leicester LE4 4CR
Tel (0116) 267 1316

Lincolnshire PGA
Sec, D Drake, Gainsborough GC, Thonock,
Gainsborough DN21 1PZ
Tel (01522) 703331

Middlesex PGA
Sec, B Eady, 8 Woodbank Drive, Chalfont
St Giles HP8 4RP
Tel (01494) 874487
E-mail brianeady@ukonline.co.uk

Norfolk PGA
Sec, R Evans, 4 Melton Drive, Thorpe Marriott,
Norwich NR8 6TT
Tel (01603) 868404
E-mail ronevans@supanet.com

North East & North West PGA
Hon Sec, R Sentance, 7 Larchlea, Ponteland,
Newcastle upon Tyne NE20 9LG
Tel/Fax (01661) 821336
E-mail ray@pgane.f9.co.uk

Northamptonshire PGA
Sec, c/o Midland Region, King's Norton GC,
Weatheroak, Nr Alvechurch, Worcs B48 7ED
Tel (016564) 824909
Fax (01564) 822805

Nottinghamshire PGA
Sec, Mrs Diane Ashley, The Old Dairy, Park Ligett,
Offington, Newark, Notts NG3 6LG
Tel (07937) 794903
E-mail diane@ashley2827.freeserve.co.uk

Shropshire & Hereford PGA
Sec, P Hinton, 1 Stanley Lane Cottages, Bridgnorth,
Shropshire
Tel (01746) 762045

Staffordshire PGA
Sec, D Unwin, 56 Sycamore Rd, Great Barr,
Birmingham B43 7SS
Tel (0121) 358 1053

Suffolk PGA
Sec, A Sleath, 21 Hasketon Road, Woodbridge
IP12 4LD
Tel (01394) 380011

Surrey PGA
Sec, K Parry, Clandon Regis GC, Epsom Road, West
Clandon, Guildford GU4 7TT
Tel (01483) 223031   *Fax* (01483) 223224
E-mail celia.shipp@pga.org.uk

Sussex PGU
Sec, C Pluck, 96 Cranston Avenue, Bexhill, East
Sussex TN39 3NL
Tel/Fax (01424) 221298
E-mail cliff@spgu.freeserve.co.uk
Website www.spgu.freeserve.co.uk

Warwickshire PGA
Sec, J Tunnicliff, 80 Wychwood Ave, Knowle,
Solihull B93 9DQ
Tel (01564) 773168

Wiltshire PGA
Sec, M Walters, Erlestoke Sands GC, Erlestoke,
Devizes SN10 5UB
Tel (01380) 831027

Worcestershire PGA
Sec, K Ball, 136 Alvechurch Road, West Heath,
Birmingham B31 3PW
Tel (0121) 475 7400

Yorkshire PGA
Sec, J Pape, 1 Summerhill Gardens, Leeds, Yorks
LS8 2EL
Tel (0113) 266 4746

English Blind Golf Association
Sec, N Baxter, 11 Higham View, North Weald,
Essex CM16 6DD
Tel/Fax (01992) 525172
Website www.englishblindgolf.co.uk

Ireland

Golfing Union of Ireland
Gen Sec, S Smith, Glencar House, 81 Eglinton Road,
Donnybrook, Dublin 4
Tel +353 1 269 4111   *Fax* +353 1 269 5368
E-mail gui@iol.ie   *Website* www.gui.ie

Irish Men's Branches

Connacht Branch: *Gen Sec*, E Lonergan,
2 Springfield Terrace, Castlebar, Mayo
Tel +353 94 28141   *Fax* +353 94 28143
E-mail guicb@eircom.net

Leinster Branch: *Exec Off*, P Smyth,
Unit 10, Block 8, Blanchardstown Corporate Park,
Dublin 15
Tel +353 1 882 9789   *Fax* +353 1 882 9804
E-mail guilb@indigo.ie

Munster Branch: *Hon Sec*, S MacMahon,
6 Town View, Mallow, Co Cork
Tel +353 22 21026   *Fax* +353 22 42373
E-mail guimb@iol.ie

Ulster Branch: *Sec*, BG Edwards, MBE,
58a High Street, Holywood, Co Down BT18 9AE
Tel (028) 9042 3708   *Fax* (028) 9042 6766
E-mail ulster.gui@virgin.net

Irish Ladies' Golf Union
Sec, Mrs T Thompson, 1 Clonskeagh Square,
Clonskeagh Road, Dublin 14
Tel +353 1 269 6244   *Fax* +353 1 283 8670
E-mail info@ilgu.ie   *Website* www.ilgu.ie

Irish Ladies' Districts

Eastern District: *Hon Sec*, Mrs T Morgan, Orchid
House, Station Road, Dunleer, Co.Louth
Tel +353 41 686 2857

Midland District: *Hon Sec*, Mrs B McTague,
Athlone Rd, Ferbane, Co Offaly
Tel +353 902 54961

Northern District: *Hon Sec*, Ms A Dickson, 12 The
Meadows, Strangford Road, Downpatrick, Co Down
BT20 6LN
Tel (028) 446 12286

Southern District: *Hon Sec*, Mrs M McMahon,
Ballysallach West, Newmarket-on-Fergus, Co.Clare
Tel +353 61 476 975

Western District: *Hon Sec*, Mrs K Reilly, Old
Church Street, Athenry, Co Galway
Tel +353 91 845417

Scotland

Scottish Golf Union
Sec, H Grey, Scottish National Golf Centre,
Drumoig, Leuchars, St Andrews, KY16 0DW
Tel (01382) 549500   *Fax* (01382) 549510
E-mail sgu@scottishgolf.com
Website www.scottishgolf.com

Scottish Men's Area Golf Associations

Angus: *Sec*, D Speed, 7 Eastgate, Friockheim,
Arbroath, DD11 4TG
Tel (01241) 828544   *Fax* (01241) 828455
E-mail david.speed2@btopenworld.com

Argyll & Bute: *Sec*, G Duncanson, 4 Shore Rd, Port
Bannatyne, Isle of Bute, PA20 0LQ
Tel (01700) 502468

Ayrshire: *Sec*, RL Crawford, 81 Connel Crescent,
Mauchline, Ayrshire KA5 5AU
Tel (01290) 551434   *Fax* (01290) 551078
E-mail secretaryaga@btinternet.com

Borders: *Sec*, RG Scott, 3 Whytbank Row,
Clovenfords, Galashiels, TD1 3NE
Tel/Fax (01896) 850570
E-mail ronscott@bordergolf.freeserve.co.uk

Clackmannanshire: *Sec*, T Johnson, 75 Dewar
Avenue, Kincardine on Forth, FK10 4RR
Tel/Fax (01259) 731168
E-mail thjohn01@aol.com

Dunbartonshire: *Sec*, AW Jones, 107 Larkfield Road, Lenzie, Glasgow G66 3AS
Tel/Fax (0141) 776 7430
E-mail alanjones@larky14.fsnet.co.uk

Fife: *Sec*, J Scott, Lauriston, East Links, Leven, KY8 4JL
Tel (01333) 423798 　*Fax* (01333) 439910
E-mail jscottga@blueyonder.co.uk

Glasgow: *Sec*, RJG Jamieson, 32 Eglinton Street, Beith, KA15 1AH
Tel/Fax (01505) 503000
E-mail r.jamieson-accountant@fsmail.net

Lanarkshire: *Sec*, T Logan, 41 Woodlands Drive, Coatbridge, ML5 1LB
Tel (01236) 428799 　*Fax* (01236) 429358
E-mail tlogan@btinternet.com

Lothians: *Sec*, A Shaw, 34 Caroline Terrace, Edinburgh EH12 8QX
Tel 0131 334 7291 　*Fax* 0131 334 9269
E-mail AllanGShaw@hotmail.com

North: *Sec*, AM Gartshore, 55 Holm Park, Inverness IV2 4XU
Tel (01463) 240727
E-mail agartshore@aol.com

North-East: *Sec*, G McIntosh, 35 School Road, Peterculter, AB14 0TB
Tel (01224) 733836
E-mail kayashish@msn.com

Perth & Kinross: *Sec*, DY Rae, 18 Carlownie Place, Auchterarder, PH3 1BT
Tel (01764) 662837 　*Fax* (01764) 662886

Renfrewshire: *Sec*, IJ Walker, 12 Langcraigs Drive, Glenburn, Paisley PA2 8JW
Tel (0141) 569 3515
E-mail walker.ian@ntlworld.com

South: *Sec*, J Burns, Glanavan, 14 Millfield Avenue, Stranraer, DG9 0EG
Tel/Fax (01776) 704778
E-mail glanavan@tesco.net

Stirlingshire: *Sec*, J Elliott, 65 Rosebank Avenue, Falkirk, FK1 5JR
Tel (01324) 634118
E-mail johnelliott65@aol.com

Scottish Blind Golf Society
Co.Sec, Jim Gales, 38 Crawley Crescent, Springfield, Cupar, KY15 5SF
Tel/Fax (01334) 653 767

Scottish Golfers' Alliance
Sec/Treas, Mrs MA Caldwell, 5 Deveron Avenue, Giffnock, Glasgow G46 6NH
Tel (0141) 638 2066

Scottish Ladies' Golfing Association
Sec, Dr Sheila Hartley, Scottish National Golf Centre, Drumoig, Leuchars, Fife KY16 0DW
Tel (01382) 549 502 　*Fax* (01382) 549 512
E-mail slga@scottishgolf.com
Website www.scottishgolf.com

Scottish Ladies County Golf Associations

Aberdeen LCGA
Hon Sec, Mrs M Robinson, 7 Carnegie Gardens, Aberdeen AB15 4AW
Tel (01224) 313582

Angus LCGA
Hon Sec, Mrs D Gordon, 11 Golf Avenue, Monifieth, DD5 4AS
Tel (01382) 532799

Ayrshire LCGA
Hon Sec, Miss AD Cree, 19 Woodfield Road, Ayr KA8 8LZ
Tel (01292) 260702

Border Counties' LGA
Hon Sec, Mrs B Cowe, Halfmyne, Smith's Road, Darnick TD6 9AT
Tel (01896) 826702

Dumfriesshire LCGA
Hon Sec, Miss MJ Greig, 10 Nelson Street, Dumfries DG2 9AY
Tel (01387) 254429

Dunbartonshire & Argyll LCGA
Hon Sec, Mrs M Johnston, Ardleish, 43 Hillside Road, Cardross, Dumbarton G82 5LU
Tel (01389) 841528

East Lothian LCGA
Hon Sec, Mrs R Thoresen, Westerlea, Abbotsford Rd, North Berwick EH39 5DB
Tel (01620) 892626

Fife CLGA
Hon Sec, Mrs A Robertson, 24 Abbey Court, St Andrews, KY16 9TL
Tel (01334) 473863

Galloway LCGA
Hon Sec, Mrs AM McClymont, Margleer, New Galloway DG7 3RT
Tel (01664) 420689

Lanarkshire LCGA
Hon Sec, Mrs M Heggie, 80 Weirwood Avenue, Garrowhill, Glasgow G69 6LN
Tel (0141) 771 3802

Midlothian CLGA
Hon Sec, Mrs A Leslie, 18 Swanston Grove, Edinburgh EH10 7BW
Tel (0131) 445 2411

Northern Counties' LGA
Hon Sec, Mrs M Vass, The Old Smithy, Tower St, Tain IV19 1DY
Tel (01862) 893731

Perth & Kinross LCGA
Hon Sec, Mrs D Butchart, 16 Airlie Street, Alyth, Blairgowrie PH11 8AJ
Tel (01828) 633000

Renfrewshire LCGA
Hon Sec, Mrs C Finlayson, Hazel Lodge, Hazelden Rd, Mearnskirk, Glasgow G77 6RR
Tel (0141) 639 5418

Stirling & Clackmannan LGA
Hon Sec, Mrs A Hunter, 22 Muirhead Road,
Stenhousemuir, FK5 4JA
Tel (01324) 554515

Scottish Veteran Ladies' Golfing Association
Hon Sec, Mrs I McDonald, 3A York Road, North
Berwick, East Lothian EH39 4LS
Tel (01620) 895 347

Wales

Welsh Golfing Union
Sec, R Dixon, Catsash, Newport, Gwent NP18 1JQ
Tel (01633) 430830   *Fax* (01633) 430843
E-mail wgu@welshgolf.org
Website www.welshgolf.org

Welsh Men's Golf Unions

Anglesey GU
Hon Sec, GP Jones, 20 Gwelfor Estate, Cemaes Bay,
Anglesey LL67 0NL
Tel (01407) 710755

Brecon & Radnor GU
Hon Sec, DJ Davies, Garden House, Howey,
Llandrindod Wells, Powys LD1 5PU
Tel (01597) 824316

Caernarfonshire & District GU
Hon Sec, RE Jones, 23 Bryn Rhos, Rhosbodrual,
Caernarfon, Gwynedd LL55 2BT
Tel (01286) 673486

Denbighshire GU
Hon Sec, EG Howells, 10 Lon Howell, Myddleton
Park, Dinbych, LL16 4AN, North Wales
Tel/Fax (01745) 813849

Dyfed GU
Hon Sec, AE Scott, 40 Clover Park, Haverfordwest,
Dyfed SA61 1UE
Tel (01437) 767578
E-mail ascott4347@aol.com

Union of Flintshire Golf Clubs
Hon Sec, JF Snead, 1 Cornist Cottages, Cornist Park,
Flint, Clwyd CH6 5RH, North Wales
Tel (01352) 733461

Glamorgan County GU
Hon Sec, P Austerberry, 10 Chestnut Tree Close,
Radyr, Cardiff CF4 8RY
Tel (02920) 419825

Gwent GU
Sec, G Harris, 4 Rolls Walk, Mount Pleasant,
Rogerstone, Gwent NP10 0AE
Tel (01633) 663750

North Wales PGA *see* Cheshire & North Wales
PGA

South Wales PGA
Sec, RC Thomas, 17 South Place, Porthcawl, Mid
Glamorgan CF36 3DB
Tel (01656) 783377

Welsh Ladies' Golf Union
Sec, Mrs Liz Edwards, Catsash, Newport NP18 1JQ
Tel (01633) 422 911
Fax (01633) 431106
E-mail wlgu@quinweb.net

Welsh Ladies' County Golf Associations

Caernarvonshire & Anglesey LCGA
Hon Sec, Mrs J Ellwood, Ty Ni, Wern-y-Wylan,
Morfa Nefyn, Pwllheli LL53 6DG
Tel (01758) 720193

Denbighshire & Flintshire LCGA
Hon Sec, Mrs K Harcombe, 6 Birch Drive, Gresford,
Wrexham LL12 8YZ
Tel (01978) 855933

Glamorgan LCGA
Hon Sec, Miss J Brown, Trefelin, 2 Windmill Lane,
Cowbridge, Vale of Glamorgan CF71 7HX
Tel (01446) 773292

Mid Wales LCGA
Hon Sec, Miss A James, Flat 4, Penbryn Court,
Lampeter, Ceredigion SA48 7EU
Tel (01570) 422463

Monmouthshire LCGA
Hon Sec, Mrs EL Davidson, Jon-Len, Goldcliff,
Newport NP18 2AU
Tel (01633) 274477

Overseas Associations

Europe

European Golf Association
Gen Sec, JC Storjohann, Place de la Croix Blanche
19, Case Postale CH-1066 Epalinges, Switzerland
Tel +41 21 784 35 32   *Fax* +41 21 784 35 91
E-mail info@ega-golf.ch
Website www.ega-golf.ch

Austrian Golf Association
Gen Sec, Mrs R Haderer, Haus des Sports,
Prinz-Eugen-Strasse 12, A-1040 Wien
Tel +43 1 505 3245   *Fax* +43 1 505 4962
E-mail oegv@golf.at
Website www.golf.at

Royal Belgian Golf Federation
Gen Sec, E Steghers, Chausée de la Hulpe 110,
B-1000 Brussels
Tel +32 2 672 2389   *Fax* +32 2 675 4619
E-mail info@golfbelgium.be
Website www.golfbelgium.be

Bulgarian Golf Association
Gen Sec, S Underwood , 66 Cherni Vrah Blvd, 1407
Sofia
Tel +359 268 1820   *Fax* +359 262 4226
E-mail s.underwood@golfbg.com

Croatian Golf Federation
Sec, D Kasapovic, Hotel Esplanade, Mihanoviceva
1, HR-10 000 Zagreb
Tel +385 1 456 6631   *Fax* +385 1 457 7907

Cyprus Golf Federation
Gen Sec, T Murray, PO Box 62085, 8062 Pafos
Tel +357 26 642 774   *Fax* +357 26 642 776
E-mail golfers2@cytanet.com.cy

Czech Golf Federation
Gen Sec, V Junek, Erpet Golf Centre, Strakonickà
2860, CZ-150 00 Prague 5-Smichov
Tel +420 2 5731 7865   *Fax* +420 2 5731 8618
E-mail cgf@cgf.cz
Website www.cgf.cz

Danish Golf Union
Gen Sec, K Thuen, Idraettens Hus, Brøndby Stadion
20, DK-2605 Brøndby
Tel +45 43 262 700   *Fax* +45 43 262 701
E-mail info@dgu-golf.dk
Website www.dgu-golf.dk

Estonian Golf Association
Sec Gen, M Schmidt, Narva mnt. 24, EE-10120
Tallinn
Tel +372 640 0450   *Fax* +372 631 2229
E-mail mait@eestiehitus.ee

Finnish Golf Union
Gen Sec, K Hagfors, Radiokatu 20,
FIN-00093 SLU
Tel +358 9 3481 2520   *Fax* +358 9 147 145
E-mail office@golf.slu.fi
Website www.golf.fi

French Golf Federation
Dir Gen, H Chesneau, 68 Rue Anatole France,
F-92309 Levallois-Perret Cedex
Tel +33 1 41 497 700   *Fax* +33 1 41 497 701
E-mail ffg@ffgolf.org   *Website* www.ffgolf.org

German Golf Association
Gen Sec, Ullrich Libor, Postfach 2106, D-65011
Wiesbaden
Tel +49 611 990 200   *Fax* +49 611 990 2040
E-mail info@dgv.golf.de   *Website* www.golf.de

Hellenic Golf Federation
Hon Sec, P Papalavrentis, PO Box 70003,
GR-166 10 Glyfada Athens
Tel +30 1 894 1933   *Fax* +30 1 894 5162
E-mail hgfederation@attglobal.net

Hungarian Golf Federation
Gen Sec, T Szlávy, Dózsa György út 1-3, H-1143
Budapest
Tel/Fax +36 1 221 5923
E-mail hungolf@hungolf.hu
Website: www.hungolf.hu

Golf Union of Iceland
Gen Sec, H Thorsteinsson, Sport Center,
Laugardal, IS-104 Reykjavik
Tel +354 514 4050   *Fax* +354 514 4051
E-mail gsi@isisport.is   *Website* www.golf.is

Italian Golf Federation
Sec Gen, S Manca, Viale Tiziano 74, I-00196 Roma
Tel +39 06 323 1825   *Fax* +39 06 322 0250
E-mail fig@federgolf.it
Website www.federgolf.it

Latvia Golf Federation
Gen Sec, N Mazjanis, Elizabetes Str.49 LV-1050 Riga
Tel +371 925 6220   *Fax* +371 782 8078
E-mail noris@navigators.lv

Lithuanian Golf Federation
Gen Sec, A Keseraukas, D Lapin km, Lapin Sen,
KUANO rajonas
Tel +370 687 81579

Luxembourg Golf Federation
Sec, Jules Heisbourg, 1 Route de Trèves,
L-2633 Senningerberg
Tel +352 34 00901   *Fax* +352 34 8391
E-mail flgsecretariat@flgolf.lu
Website www.flgolf.lu

Malta Golf Federation
Hon Sec, Alexander Mangion, c/o Royal Malta GC,
Marsa LQA 06, Malta
Tel +356 23 9302   *Fax* +356 22 7020
E-mail info@maltagolf.org
Website www.maltagolf.org

Netherlands Golf Federation
Gen Sec, HL Heyster, PO Box 221, NL-3454 ZL
De Meern.
Tel +31 30 242 6370   *Fax* +31 30 242 6380
E-mail golf@ngf.nl   *Website* www.golfsite.nl

Norwegian Golf Federation
Gen Sec, G Ove Berg, PO Box 163, Lilleaker,
N-0216 Oslo
Tel +47 22 73 6620   *Fax* +47 22 73 6621
E-mail ngf@ngf.golf.no

Polish Golf Union
Sec, J Czaplejewicz Centralny Osrodek Sportu, Ul.
Lazienkowska 6A, PL-00-449 Warszawa
Tel +48 22 5298 716   *Fax* +48 22 5298 916
E-mail pzg@pzg-golf.com.pl
Website www.golf.pl

Portuguese Golf Federation
Sec, J A Moreira, Av das Tulipas 6-17°, Miraflores,
P-1495-161 Algés
Tel +351 214 123 780   *Fax* +351 214 107 972
E-mail fpg@fpg.pt   *Website* www.fpg.pt

Russian Golf Association
Gen Sec, A Nikolov, Office 331, 8 Luzhnetskaya
emb, RU-119871 Moskow
Tel/Fax +7 095 725 4719
E-mail infor@rusgolf.ru   *Website* www.rusgolf.ru

San Marino Golf Federation
Gen Sec, F Sandro, Via XXV, Marzo 11, 47031
Domagnano
Tel +39 549 907 159   *Fax* +39 549 992 746

Slovak Golf Union
Gen Sec, J Kachlik, G&CC Bratislava, Bernolakovo,
Klobucnicka 7, SK-811 01 Bratislava
Tel/Fax +421 2 5443 3453   *Fax* +421 2 5443 2008
E-mail sgu@golfs.sk
Website www.sgu.sk

Slovenian Golf Association
Sec, M Ažman, Šmartinska 152, SLO-1000
Ljubljana
Tel +386 1 585 1753   *Fax* +386 1 585 1752
E-mail golfzveza@golfzveza-slovenije.si
Website www.golfzveza-slovenije.si

Royal Spanish Golf Federation
Sec, L Alvarez, Capitán Haya 9-5°, E-28020 Madrid
Tel +34 91 555 2682   *Fax* +34 91 556 3290
E-mail rfeg@golfspain.com
Website www.golfspainfederacion.com

Swedish Golf Federation
Gen Sec, Mats Enquist, PO Box 84, Kevinge Strand,
S-182 11 Danderyd
Tel +46 8 622 1500   *Fax* +46 8 755 8439
E-mail info@sgf.golf.se
Website www.sgf.golf.se

Swiss Golf Association
Sec, JC Storjohann, Place de la Croix Blanche 19,
Case Postale, CH-1066 Epalinges
Tel +41 21 784 3531   *Fax* +41 21 784 3536
E-mail info@asg.ch   *Website* www.asg.ch

Turkish Golf Federation
Co-ord, I Aktekin, GSGM Ulus Is Hani, A Blok 2
Kat, 205 Ulus 06050 Ankara
Tel +90 312 309 3945   *Fax* +90 312 309 1840
E-mail info@golfturk.org

Yugoslav Golf Federation
Pres, A Andjelkovic, Resavsla 2, Belgrade 11000

European Professional Associations

Austria PGA
Sec, R Hagan, A-8724 Spielberg,
Frauenbachstrasse 51
Tel +43 351 282 333   *Fax* +43 351 282 171
E-mail pga-austria@aon.at
Website www.apga.info.at

Belgian PGA
Sec, B De Bruyckere, Bergstraat 41, B-8790
Waregem
Tel +32 56 621 821   *Fax* +32 56 621 874
E-mail info@pga.be
Website www.pga.be

Denmark PGA
Sec, J Sunds, Centervej 1, Gatten 9640, Farso
Tel +45 98 662 235   *Fax* +45 98 662 236
E-mail pga@golfonline.dk
Website www.golfonline.dk.pga

Finland PGA
Sec, M Rantanen, Radiokatu 20, FIN-00093 SLU
Tel +358 9 3481 2377   *Fax* +358 9 3481 2378
E-mail mikko.rantanen@pga.fi
Website www.pga.fi

French PGA
Sec, A Vannier, National Golf Club, 2 Avenue du
Golf, 78 280 Guyancourt, France
Tel +33 1 34 52 0846   *Fax* +33 1 34 52 0548
E-mail pgafra@club-internet.fr
Website www.pgafrance.com

PGA of Germany
Sec, Rainer Goldrian, Arnulf Str 295, D-80639
München
Tel +49 8917 95880   *Fax* +49 8917 958829
E-mail info@pga.de   *Website* www.pga.de

Italy PGA
Sec, L Rendina, Via Marangoni 3, I-20124 Milano
Tel +39 02 670 5670   *Fax* +39 02 669 3600
E-mail pgaitaly@tin.it   *Website* www.pga.it

Netherlands PGA
Sec, Mrs R Vonk Mundt, Burg van der Borchlaan 1,
3722 GZ Bilthoven
Tel +31 30 228 7018   *Fax* +31 30 225 0261
E-mail npga@wxs.nl
Website www.pgaholland.com

Portugal PGA
Sec, David Silva, Apartado 1173, Vilamoura,
8125-914
Tel +351 289 300 120   *Fax* +351 289 300 128
E-mail pga.portugal@neto.pt
Website www.fpg.pt

Spain PGA
Sec, M Santamaría, c/o Capitán Haya 22-5C,
E-28020 Madrid
Tel +34 91 555 1393   *Fax* +34 91 597 0170
E-mail apge@wanadoo.es
Website www.pgaspain.com.es

Swedish PGA
Sec, M Sorling, Tylösand, S-302 73 Halmstad
Tel +46 35 320 30   *Fax* +46 35 320 25
E-mail pga@golf.se
Website www.pga.golf.se

Swiss PGA
Gen Sec, André Glauser, PO Box 107, CH-3177
Laupen
Tel +41 31 748 0312   *Fax* +41 31 748 0313
E-mail info@swisspga.ch
Website www.swisspga.ch

North America: Canada and USA

Royal Canadian Golf Association
Exec Dir, SD Ross, Golf House, Glen Abbey, 1333
Dorval Drive, Oakville, Ontario L6J 4Z3
Tel +1 905 849 9700   *Fax* +1 905 845 7040
E-mail golfhouse@rcga.org
Website www.rcga.org

Canadian Ladies' Golf Association
Exec Dir, Jeff Thompson, 1540 Cornwall Rd, Suite
215, Oakville, ON L6J 7W5
Tel +1 905 849 2542   *Fax* +1 905 849 0188
E-mail clga@clga.org
Website www.clga.org

Canadian PGA
Pres, Ch Exec, David J Colling, 13450 Dublin Line
RR#1, Acton, Ontario L7J 2W7
Tel +1 519 853 5450   *Fax* +1 519 853 5449
E-mail cpga@canadianpga.org
Website www.cpga.com

Canadian Tour
Comm, Ian Mansfield, 212 King Street West, Suite
203, Toronto, Ontario Canada M58 1K5
Tel +1 416 204 1564   *Fax* +1 416 204 1368
Website cantour.com

Ladies' Professional Golf Association
Pres, 100 International Golf Drive, Daytona Beach,
Florida 32124-1092
Tel +1 386 274 6200
Fax +1 386 274 1099
Website www.lpga.com

National Golf Foundation
Pres, 1150 South US Highway One, Jupiter,
Florida 33477
Tel +1 561 744 6006
Website www.ngf.org

PGA of America
Pres, Box 109601, 100 Avenue of the Champions,
Palm Beach Gardens, Florida 33418.
Tel +1 561 624 8400   *Fax* +1 561 624 8448
Website www.pgaonline.com

PGA Tour
Pres, The Commissioner, PGA Tour, 112 PGA Tour
Boulevard, Ponte Vedra Beach, Florida 32082
Tel +1 904 285 3700
Fax +1 904 285 7913
Website www.pgatour.com

United States Golf Association
Pres, Golf House, PO Box 708, Far Hills,
NJ 07931-0708
Tel +1 908 234 2300   *Fax* +1 908 234 9687
E-mail usga@usga.org   *Website* www.usga.org

The Caribbean and Central America

Caribbean Golf Association
Sec, David G Bird, PO Box 31329 SMB, Grand
Cayman, Cayman Islands
Tel +345 947 1903   *Fax* +345 947 3439
E-mail bird@candw.ky

Bahamas Golf Federation
Pres, Ambrose Gouthro, PO Box F-41790, Freeport,
Grand Bahama
Tel +242 373 7295   *Fax* +242 373 7926
E-mail agouthro@bgfnet.com
Website www.bgfnet.com

Barbados Golf Association
Pres, Birchmore Griffith, PO Box 585, Bridgetown,
Barbados
Tel +246 430 0808   *Fax* +246 437 7792
E-mail carib@caribsurf.com
Website www.barbadosgolfassociation.org

Bermuda Golf Association
Sec, Tom Smith, PO Box HM 433, Hamilton,
Bermuda HM-BX
Tel +1 441 238 1367   *Fax* +1 441 238 0983
E-mail bdagolf@ibl.bm

Cayman Islands Golf Association
Sec, David G Bird, PO Box 31329 SMB, Grand
Cayman
Tel +345 947 1903   *Fax* +345 947 3439
E-mail bird@candw.ky

National Golf Association of Costa Rica
Pres, F Solano, PO Box 10969, 1000 San Jose
Tel +506 221 8129   *Fax* +506 257 0439
E-mail fsolano@ rasca.co.cr
Website www.edenia.com/amagolf

Fedogolf (Dominican Republic)
Exec Dir, Rudys Soler, Campo Nacional de Golf,
Las Lagunas SA, Autopito Duarte Km 20, Santo
Domingo, Dominican Republic
Tel +809 231 4719
Fax +809 372 7406
E-mail fedogolf@hotmail.com
Website www.fedogolf.org

El Salvador Golf Federation
Sec, G Aceto Marini, Apartado Postal 631, San
Salvador C.A.
Tel +503 285 8503
Fax +503 289 1378
E-mail fesagolf@yahoo.com

Guatemalan Golf Federation
Exec *Sec*, Adolfo Ríos, Diagonal 6 10-76, Zona 10,
Guatemala
Tel +502 360 9435
Fax +502 360 9475

Hondurena Golf Association
Sec, LF Gutiérrez, Apartado Postal 3175,
Tegucigalpa, Honduras
Tel +504 37 2084   *Fax* +504 38 0456

Jamaica Golf Association
Pres, Gordon Hutchinson, PO Box 743, Kingston 8
Tel +1 876 925 2325   *Fax* +1 876 924 6330
E-mail jamgolf@n5.com.jm
Website www.jamaicagolfassociation.com

Mexican Golf Federation
Pres, Eugenio Eraña Av.Lomas de Sotelo No.1112
Despacho 103-104, Col.Lomas de Sotelo C.P.11200
Mexico DF
Tel +525 395 3245   *Fax* +525 580 2263
E-mail fedmexgolf@compuserve.com.mx
Website www.mexgolf.org

Nicaraguan Golf Association
Pres, Alfonso Llanes, Nicabox 538, PO Box 25640,
Miami, FL 33102, USA
Tel +350 441 7596   *Fax* +350 385 1464

OECS Golf Association
Sec, Joanna Paul, PO Box 456, Castries, St Lucia
Tel +758 452 3079   *Fax* +758 452 3885
E-mail joanpaul@candw.lc

Panama Golf Association
Pres, Anibal Galindo, PO Box 8613, Panama 5
Tel +507 266 7436   *Fax* +507 220 3994
E-mail master@pty.com

Puerto Rico Golf Association
Pres, Sidney Wolf, 58 Caribe St, San Juan, Puerto
Rico 00907-1909
Tel +787 721 7742   *Fax* +787 723 5760
E-mail golfpuertorico@prga.org
Website www.prga.org

Trinidad & Tobago Golf Association
Pres, Asraph Ali, c/o 36 Methuen St, Woodbrook,
Port of Spain, Trinidad
Tel +868 662 1047   *Fax* +868 662 5346
E-mail aali@trinidad.net
Website www.golftrinidad.com

Turks & Caicos Golf Association
Pres, John Phillips, PO Box 64, Suite C12,
Providenciales, Turks & Caicos Islands
Tel +649 946 4109   *Fax* +649 946 4939
E-mail claymore@tciway.tc

Virgin Islands Golfers' Federation
Pres, Bruce Streibich, PO Box 5187, Kingshill, St
Croix, US Virgin Islands 00851
Tel +340 779 2315   *Fax* +340 714 5393
E-mail bstreibich@vipowernet.net

South America

South American Golf Federation
Exec Sec, Rafael Enrique Otero D, Carrera 12 No
79-43 Of 704, Bogotá, Colombia
Tel +57 1 313 0624   *Fax* +57 1 313 0391
E-mail fedesud@007mundo.com

Argentine Golf Association
Exec Dir, Mark Lawrie, Corrientes 538-Pisos 11y12,
1043 Buenos Aires
Tel +54 11 4325 1113   *Fax* +54 11 4325 8660
E-mail golf@aag.com.ar
Website www.argengolf.org

Bolivian Golf Federation
Sec, Juan E Maclean, Ave.Mariscal Santa Cruz,
Edif.Camara de Comercio P6-of 604, C.P. 10217,
La Paz
Tel/Fax +591 02 315853
E-mail fbgolf@ceibo.entelnet.bo
Website www.bolivia-golf.com

Brasilian Golf Confederation
Sec, MA Aguiar Giusti, Rua Paes de Araujo 29cjs
42e43, CEP 04531 090 São Paulo SP.
Tel/Fax +55 11 3168
E-mail golfe@cbg.com.br
Website www.cbg.com.br

Chilean Golf Federation
Sec, Carlos Amenabar, Av el Golf 266, Las
Condes, Santiago
Tel +56 2 362 0777   *Fax* +56 2 362 0929
E-mail chilegolf@chilnet.cl
Website www.chilegolf.cl

Colombian Golf Federation
Sec, Jaime Rodríguez Posada, Carrera 7A, 72-64
Int 26, Apartado aéreo 88768, Bogotá
Tel +57 1 310 7664   *Fax* +57 1 235 5091
E-mail fedegolf@cable.net.co
Website www.federacioncolombianadegolf.com

Ecuador Golf Federation
Ex Dir, Patricia Pazmiño, Calle Rumihurco s/n,
Urbanización el Condado, C.P. 1701-2411 Quito
Tel + 593 22 491 512   *Fax* + 593 22 491 254
E-mail fedecuat@feg.org.ec
Website www.feg.org.ec

Guyana Golf Union
Sec, c/o Demerara Bauxite Co Ltd, Mackenzie,
Guyana

Paraguay Golf Association
Sec, Hugo H Troche, Manduriva 709, Casilla de
Correo No 76, Asunción
Tel +595 21 447 801   *Fax* +595 21 447 923
E-mail apg@mmail.com.py
Website www.apg.org.py

Peru Golf Federation
Sec, Juan Neira, Conde de la Monclova 315 Of 308,
San Isidro, Lima 27
Tel +51 1 441 1500
Fax +51 1 441 1992
E-mail fepegolf@terra.com,pe
Website www.fpg.org.pe

Uruguay Golf Association
Sec, Nelson Silva, Bulevar Artigas 379, Montevideo
Tel +598 2 7011 721
Fax +598 2 7115285
E-mail augolf@adinet.com.uy

Venezuela Golf Federation
Exec Dir, Julio L Torres, Av. Juan B Arismendi,
Unidad Comercial La Florida, Mezzanina, local 8,
La Florida, Caracas 1050
Tel +582 12 731 7662   *Fax* +582 12 730 2731
E-mail fvg@fvg.org   *Website* www.fvg.org

Africa

Algerian Golf Federation
Sec, Benmiloud Noureddine, rue Ahmed Ouaked,
Dely-Ibrahim
Tel +213 236 3059   *Fax* +213 261 4133

Botswana Golf Union
Sec, SE Palframan, PO Box 1033, Gaborone

Botswana Ladies Golf Union
Hon Sec, Mrs D Beesley, PO Box 1362, Gaborone

The Egyptian Golf Federation
Chair, Khaled Abou Taleb, 29 Abdel Moneim Hafaz
Street, Heliopolis, Cairo
Tel +202 291 9101   *Fax* +202 291 9102
E-mail attar@internetalex.com

Ghana Golf Association
Hon Sec, Col JA Kabore, PO Box 8, Achimota,
Accra
Tel/Fax 233-21-400221
E-mail vaghq@ghana.com

Ghana Ladies Golf Union
Hon Sec, Mrs M Amu, PO Box 8, Achimota, Accra

Côte d'Ivoire National Golf Federation
Sec, I Keita, O8 BP 1297, Abidjan 08
Tel +225 213 874   *Fax* +225 227 112

Kenya Golf Union
Chair, Vishy Talwas, PO Box 49609, Nairobi
Tel +254 2 763 898   *Fax* +254 2 765 118
E-mail kgu@connect.co.ke
Website www.kgu.org.ke

Kenya Ladies' Golf Union
Hon Sec, Mrs S Royle, PO Box 16751, Nairobi

KwaZulu-Natal Golf Union
Sec, RT Runge, PO Box 1939, Durban 4000
Tel +27 (0)31 202 7636   *Fax* +27 (0)31 202 1022
E-mail kzngu@kzngolf.co.za

Libyan Golf Federation
Pres, Mohamed El-Kheituni, PO Box 3674, Tripoli

Malawi Golf Union
Sec, J Hinde, PO Box 1198, Blantyre
Tel +265 643988   *Fax* +265 640135
E-mail jhinde@illovo.co.za

Malawi Ladies' Golf Union
Hon Sec, Mrs J Mullock, PO Box 30328, Lilongwe 3

Mauritius Golf Federation
Pres, Raj Ramlackhan, 42 Sir William Newton
Street, Port Louis
Tel +230 208 2440   *Fax* +230 208 2438
E-mail ramn@intnet.mu

The Royal Moroccan Golf Federation
Sec, Sad Benkirane, Royal Golf Rabat Dar-es-Salam,
Route des Zaers, Rabat
Tel +212 775 5636   *Fax* +212 775 1026

Namibian Golf Union
Treas, Hugh Mortimer, PO Box 2122, Windhoek,
Namibia
E-mail wcc@iafrica.com.na

Nigeria Golf Federation
Sec, Patrick Uwagbale, National Stadium Surulere,
PO Box 145, Lagos
Tel +234 1 545 6209   *Fax* +234 1 545 0530
E-mail nigeriagolffederation@yahoo.com

Nigerian Ladies Golf Union
Sec, Mrs OR Ogunleye, c/o Ikoyi GC, PO Box 239,
Ikoyi, Lagos

Sierra Leone Golf Federation
Pres, Freetown GC, PO Box 237, Lumley Beach,
Freetown

South Africa Sunshine Tour
Exec Dir, Louis Martin, 15 Postnet Suite #185,
Private Bag X15, Somerset West 7129
Tel +27 21 850 6500
Fax +27 21 852 8271

South African Golf Association
Exec Dir, BA Younge, PO Box 391994, Bramley,
South Africa 2018
Tel +27 11 442 3723   *Fax* +27 11 442 3753
E-mail sagolf@global.co.za
Website www.saga.co.za

South African Ladies' Golf Union
Hon Sec, Mrs V Horak, PO Box 209, Randfontein
1760, RSA
Tel/Fax +27 11 416 1263
E-mail salgu@global.co.za
Website www.salgu.co.za

South African PGA
Sec, Anne Du Toit, PO Box 949 Bedfordview 2008,
RSA
Tel +27 11 485 1370
Fax +27 11 640 4372
E-mail admin@pgasa.com
Website www.pgasa.com

South African Women's PGA
Sec, Mrs V Harrington, PO Box 781547, Sandton
2146
Tel/Fax +27 11 477 8606

Swaziland Golf Union
Sec, J Resting, PO Box 1739, Mbabane
Tel/Fax +268 404 2227
E-mail johnrest@realnet.co.sz

Tanzania Golf Union
Sec, PO Box 6018, Dar Es Salaam
Tel +255 22 215 1706
Fax +255 22 215 0626
E-mail tgu@tzgolfun.com
Website www.tzgolfun.com

Tanzania Ladies' Golf Union
Hon Sec, Mrs T Anthony, PO Box 286, Dar Es Salaam

Tunisian Golf Federation
Pres, Anror Atallah, Choutrana II, 2036 Soukra
Tel +216 1 865 745   *Fax* +216 1 865 700

Uganda Golf Union
Pres, GW Eggadu, Kitante Road, PO Box 2574, Kampala

Uganda Ladies Golf Union
Hon Sec, Mrs R Tumusiime, PO Box 624, Kampala

Zaire Golf Federation
Pres, Tshilombo Mwin Tshitol, BP 1648, Lubumbashi

Zambia Golf Union
Hon Sec, CH Chimuka, PO Box 31902, 8 Tito Rd, Rhodes Park, Lusaka
Tel +260 2 650697/621438   *Fax* +260 2 621834
E-mail collalum@coppernet.com

Zambia Ladies' Golf Union
Hon Sec, Mrs P Barker, PO Box 31051, Lusaka

Zimbabwe Golf Association
Sec, PO Box 3327, Harare
Tel +263 4 746 141   *Fax* +263 4 746 228

Zimbabwe Ladies' Golf Union
Hon Sec, Mrs JM Hall, PO Box HG 182, Highlands, Harare
E-mail benzon@africaonline.com.zw

Middle East

Bahrain Golf Committee
Gen Sec, Daij Khalifa, PO Box 38938, Riffa
Tel +973 778 620
Fax +973 778 595
E-mail bgcom@batelco.com.bh

The Golf Federation of the Islamic Republic of Iran
Sec Gen, Sayad Nasrolla Sadjadi, PO Box 15815-1881, Tehran
Tel +98 21 829 671
Fax +98 21 834 333

Israel Golf Federation
Sec, Gili Peleg, Gaash GC, Kibutz Gaash
E-mail golfgash@netvision.net.il

Lebanese Golf Federation
Pres, Faysal Alamldine, c/o GC of Lebanon, PO Box 11-3099, Beirut
Tel +961 1 822 470
Fax +961 1 822 474
E-mail info@golfclub.org.lb

Qatar Golf Association
Pres, Sheikh Abdullah Bin Ahmed Al Thani, PO Box 6177, Doha
Tel +974 454 284
Fax +974 430 132

Saudi Golf Committee
Sec Gen, Ali M.Al-Suhaim, PO Box 102201, Riyadh 11675, Saudi Arabia
Tel/Fax +966 1 402 1079

United Arab Emirates Golf Association
Sec Gen, Khalid Al Halyan, PO Box 31410, Dubai, UAE
Tel +971 4 295 6440   *Fax* +971 4 295 6026
E-mail uaegolf@emirates.net.ae
Website www.uaegolf.com

Asia

Asia-Pacific Golf Confederation
Sec Gen, Colin Phillips, Golf Australia House, 153–155 Cecil Street, South Melbourne, Victoria 3205
Tel +61 3 9699 7944   *Fax* +61 3 9690 8510
E-mail apgc@agu.org.au

Asian PGA
Sec, Ramlan Dato'harun, 415-417 Block A Kelana Business Centre, 97 Jalan SS 7/2 Kelana Jaya, Selangor, Malaysia
Tel +603 7492 0099   *Fax* +603 7492 0098
Website www.asianpgatour.com

Asia PGA Tour
Chief Exec Off, Justin Strachan, 15/F, One Harbourfront, 18 Tak Fung Street, Hunghom, Kowloon, Hong Kong
Tel +852 2330 8227   *Fax* +852 2801 5743
E-mail apgatour@asiaonline.net
Website www.asianpgatour.com

Cambodian Golf Association
Sec, Pok Yuthea, No 202 Norodom Blvd, Senak Building, Chamcar Morn, Phnom Penh

China Golf Association
Int Rel, Julia Wang, 5 Tiyuguan Rd, Beijing, China 100763
Tel +8610 858 18873
Fax +8610 858 25994
E-mail cga-cra@263.net

Golf Association of the Republic of China
Sec Gen, Lung-Kuo Chien, 12 F-1, 125 Nan-King East Road, Section 2, Taipei, Taiwan 104 R.O.C.
Tel +886 2 516 5611
Fax +886 2 516 3208

PGA Republic of China
2nd Floor 196 Cheng-Teh Road, Taipei, Taiwan
Tel +886 2 8220318
Fax +886 2 8229684

Hong Kong Golf Association Ltd
Ch Exec, David Roberts, Room 2003, Sports House, 1 Stadium Path, So Kon Po, Causeway Bay, Hong Kong
Tel +852 2522 8804
Fax +852 2845 1553
E-mail hkga@netvigator.com
Website www.hkga.com

Hong Kong PGA
Sec, Mr M Lai Wai Sing, Room 702 Landmark
North, Sheung Shui, NT Hong Kong
Tel +852 523 3171

Indian Golf Union
Sec, Mr PK Bhattacharyya, 'Sukh Sagar' 2nd Floor,
2/5 Sarat Bose Road, Calcutta 700 020
Tel +91 33 4745 795   *Fax* +91 33 4748 914
E-mail ingolf.union@gems.vsnl.net.in

Indonesian Golf Association
Sec Gen, Kusman Ismukanto, Rawamangun Muka
Raya, Jakarta 13220
Tel/Fax +62 21 470 1019
E-mail pgi@pgionline.org
Website www.pgionline.org

Japan Golf Association
Sec Gen, Ryo Shioda, Kyobashi ys Bldg 2nd Floor,
1-12-5 Kyobashi, Chuo-Ku, Tokyo 104-0031
Tel +81 3 3566 0003   *Fax* +81 3 3566 0101
E-mail info@jpa.org.jp

Japan Ladies PGA
7-16-3 Ginza, Nitetsu Kobiki Bldg 8F, Chuo-ku,
Tokyo 104-0061
Tel +81 3 3546 7801   *Fax* +81 3 3546 7805

Japan PGA
Int Com, Seien Kobayakawa, Top Hamamatsucho
Bldg, 1-5-12 Shiba.Minato-Ku, 8FL, Tokyo
105-0014
Tel +81 3 5419 2614   *Fax* +81 3 5419 2622
E-mail bp@pga.or.jp

Korean Golf Association
Sec Gen, Dong Wook Kim, 1318 Rm Manhattan
Bldg, 36-2 Yeo Eui Du-Dong, Yeong Deung Po Ku,
Seoul
Tel +82 2 783 4748   *Fax* +82 2 783 4747
E-mail kogolf@chollian.net
Website www.kgagolf.or.kr

Malaysian Golf Association
Sec, Tay Chong-Min, 12A Persiaran Ampang, 55000
Kuala Lumpur
Tel +60 3 4577931   *Fax* +60 3 4565596
E-mail mga@tm.net.my

PGA of Malaysia
Sec, Brig-Gen Mahendran, 1B Jalan Mamanda 7,
Ampang Point, 6800 Selangor Darul Ehsan,
Malaysia

Myanmar Golf Federation
Sec, U Aung Kyi, c/o Aung San Stadium, Rangoon
Tel +95 01 663 930   *Fax* +95 01 289 563

Pakistan Golf Federation
Hon Sec, W/Cdr Iftikhar A Khan (rtd), Jhelum Road,
PO Box No 1295, Rawalpindi
Tel +92 51 225 6995   *Fax* +92 51 228 0711

Philippines Golf Association
Sec Gen, Alfredo M Masigan, 209 Administration
Building, Rizal Memorial Sports Complex, Vito
Cruz, Manila-1000
Tel +63 2 588845   *Fax* +63 2 521 1587
E-mail rpgolf@pworld.net.ph

Singapore Golf Association
Sec, Dr Peter Tay, Tanglin Road Post Office, PO
Box 457, Singapore 912416
Tel +65 6 256 1318   *Fax* +65 6 256 1917
E-mail vanderlyn@sga.org.sg
Website www.sga.org.sg

Sri Lanka Golf Union
Hon Sec, AGG Punchihewa, PO Box 309, 223
Model Farm Road, Colombo 8, Sri Lanka

Thailand Golf Association
Sec Gen, Pongnat Vatanasak, Room 212/213
Rajmangala National Stadium, 2088 Ramkamhaeng
Rd, Hua Mark, Bangkapi, Bangkok 10240
Tel +66 2 369 3777   *Fax* +66 2 369 3776
E-mail pongnat_v@yahoo.com
Website www.tga.or.th

Australasia and the Pacific

Australian Golf Union
Sec, Colin Phillips, Golf Australia House, 153–155
Cecil Street, South Melbourne, Victoria 3205
Tel +61 3 9699 7944   *Fax* +61 3 9690 8510
E-mail agu@agu.org.au   *Website* www.agu.org.au

Women's Golf Australia
Exec Dir, Maisie Mooney, 355 Moray Street, South
Melbourne, Victoria 3205
Tel +61 3 9690 9344   *Fax* +61 3 9696 2060
E-mail info@womensgolfaus.org.au
Website www.womensgolfaus.org.au

Australian PGA
Ch Exec, Max Garske, PO Box 1314, Crows Nest,
New South Wales
Tel +61 2 9439 8111   *Fax* +61 2 9439 7888
E-mail maxgpga@oze-mail.com.au
Website www.pga.org.au

PGA Tour Australasia
Exec Dir, Andrew Georgiou, Suite 302, 77 Berry St,
North Sydney, NSW 2060
Tel +61 2 9956 0000   *Fax* +61 2 9956 0099
Website pgatour.com.au

Cook Islands Golf Association
Pres, Hugh M N Henry, Rarotonga GC, PO Box
151, Rarotonga, Cook Islands
Tel +682 27 360   *Fax* +682 25 420

National Golf Association of Fiji
Hon Sec, CM Lenz, GPO Box 13843, Suva, Fiji
Tel +679 301 897   *Fax* +679 301 647
E-mail fasanoc@is.com.fj

New Zealand Golf Association
Ch Exec, N Woodbury, PO Box 11842 Wellington
Tel +64 4 385 4330   *Fax* +64 4 385 4331
E-mail nzga@nzga.co.nz   *Website* www.nzga.co.nz

Womens' Golf New Zealand Inc
Exec Dir, Mrs J Mackay, PO Box 11187,
65 Victoria Street, Wellington
Tel +64 4 4726 733   *Fax* +64 4 4726 732
E-mail golf@womensgolf.org.nz
Website www.womensgolf.org.nz

New Zealand PGA
Exec Dir, PO Box 11-934, Wellington
Tel +64 4 4722 687   *Fax* +64 4 4712 152
E-mail postmaster@pga.org.nz
Website www.pga.org.nz

Papua New Guinea Golf Association
Hon Sec, c/o Lae G.C., PO Box 164, Lae MP, Papua
New Guinea
Tel +675 323 1120   *Fax* +675 323 1300

Papua New Guinea Ladies Golf Association
Hon Sec, Mrs L Illidge, PO Box 348,
Lae MP 411

Vanuatu Golf Association
Chairman, Bernie Cain, PO Box 358, Port Vila,
Vanuatu, Pacific Ocean
Tel +678 22178   *Fax* +678 25037
E-mail vilaref@vanuatu.com.vu

Websites

Royal and Ancient Golf Club	www.randa.org
Ladies Golf Union	www.lgu.org
United States Golf Association	www.usga.org
European Golf Association	www.ega-golf.ch
English Golf Union	www.englishgolfunion.org
English Ladies (ELGA)	www.englishladiesgolf.org
Golf Union of Ireland	www.gui.ie
Irish Ladies (ILGU)	www.ilgu.ie
Scottish Golf Union & Scottish Ladies (SLGA)	www.scottishgolf.com
Welsh Golfing Union	www.welshgolf.org
Professional Golfers Association	www.pga.org.uk
PGA of Europe	www.pgae.com
PGA of America	www.pga.com
PGA European Tour	www.europeantour.com
Evian Tour (Women's European)	www.eviantour.com
US PGA Tour	www.pgatour.com
US LPGA Tour	www.lpga.com
Asian Tour	www.asianpgatour.com
Australasian Tour	www.pgatour.com.au
South African Sunshine Tour	www.sunshinetour.com
Other tours via Golf Web	www.golfweb.com
BBC Online – Golf	www.bbc.co.uk/sport
The Golf Channel	www.thegolfchannel.com
Nick Faldo (Junior Series)	www.nickfaldo.org
Jack Nicklaus	www.nicklaus.com
Tiger Woods	www.tigerwoods.com

Royal Clubs

The following clubs are all from the UK and Commonwealth or former Commonwealth with the exception of Marianske Lazne GC which is in the Czech Republic and was granted the Royal title by Her Majesty Queen Elizabeth recently. The club opened in 1905 and Royal status was granted as a result of the strong connections King Edward VII had with the club.

Club	Year Founded	Year of Royal Patronage	Royal Patron
Duff House Royal Golf Club	1909	1925	Princess Louise, Dowager Duchess of Fife
Royal Ancient Golf Club, St Andrews	1745	1834	William IV
Royal Aberdeen	1780	1903	Edward VII (Leopold patron in 1872)
Royal Adelaide	1892	1923	George V
Royal Ascot	1887	1887	Victoria 1887; Elizabeth II 1977
Royal Ashdown Forest	1888	1893	Victoria
Royal Belfast	1881	1885	Edward, Prince of Wales
Royal Birkdale	1889	1951	George VI
Royal Blackheath	1766	1857	Not known
Royal Burgess	1773	1929	George V
Royal Calcutta	1829	1911	George V
Royal Canberra	1926	1933	George V
Royal Cape	1885	1910	George V
Royal Cinque Ports	1892	1910	George V
Royal Colombo	1879	1928	George V
Royal Colwood	1913	1931	George V
Royal County Down	1889	1908	Edward VII
Royal Cromer	1888	1887	Edward, Prince of Wales (later Edward VII)
Royal Dornoch	1877	1906	Edward VII
Royal Dublin	1885	1891	Victoria
Royal Durban	1892	1932	George V
Royal Eastbourne	1887	1887	Prince Albert Victor, Duke of Clarence; Victoria
Royal Epping Forest	1888	1888	Prince Arthur, Duke of Connaught
Royal Freemantle	—	1930	George V
Royal Guernsey	1890	1891	Victoria
Royal Harare	1898	1929	George V
Royal Hobart	—	1925	George V
Royal Jersey	1878	1879	Victoria
Royal Johannesburg	1890	1931	George V
Royal Liverpool	1869	1871	Prince Arthur, Duke of Connaught
Royal Lytham	1886	1926	George V
Royal Malta	1888	1888	Prince Alfred, Duke of Edinburgh
Royal Marianske Lazne	1905	2003	Elizabeth II
Royal Melbourne	1891	1895	Victoria
Royal Mid Surrey	1892	1926	George V
Royal Montreal	1873	1884	Victoria

Club	Year Founded	Year of Royal Patronage	Royal Patron
Royal Montrose	1810	1845	Prince Albert
Royal Musselburgh	1774	1876	Prince Arthur, Duke of Connaught
Royal Nairobi	1906	1935	George V
Royal North Devon	1864	1865	Edward, Prince of Wales
Royal Norwich	1893	1893	Duke of York (later George V)
Royal Ottawa	1891	1912	George V
Royal Perth	1824	1833	William IV
Royal Perth (Australia)	—	1937	George VI
Royal Port Alfred	—	1924	George V
Royal Porthcawl	1891	1909	Edward VII
Royal Portrush	1888	1892	Duke of York
Royal Quebec	1874	1934	George V
Royal Queensland	1920	1921	George V
Royal Regina	1899	1999	Elizabeth II
Royal Selangor	1893	1953	Elizabeth II
Royal St Davids	1894	1908	Edward VII
Royal St Georges	1887	1902	Edward VII
Royal Sydney	1893	1897	Victoria
Royal Tarlair	1925	1926	Princess Louise, Dowager Duchess of Fife
Royal Troon	1878	1978	Elizabeth II
Royal West Norfolk	1892	1892	Edward, Prince of Wales (later Edward VII)
Royal Wimbledon	1865	1882	Edward, Prince of Wales
Royal Winchester	1888	1913	Edward VII
Royal Worlington and Newmarket	1893	1895	Victoria

Three generations

Daniel Torrance, the 15-year-old son of 2002 Ryder Cup captain Sam Torrance whose father is highly respected golf coach Bob Torrance all pictured on the famous Swilcan Bridge at St Andrews. Sam and Daniel won the pro-am section of the Dunhill Links Championship after Daniel's father paid £7500 to allow him to play. The investment paid off – Sam made almost £40,000 as a result of the family success. Daniel, who plays off 3 at Sunningdale, has been taught by his grandfather and plans on turning professional next August when he turns 16 – the age his dad joined the paid ranks. 'Daniel is far better than I was at his age,' says Sam who now plays on the European Senior circuit.

PART X

Golf History

History of Championships and Team Events   536
Famous Personalities of the Past   542
Interesting Facts and Unusual Incidents   551
Record Scoring   579

History of Championships and Team Events run by the R&A

The following entries highlight the history of championship and team events that are organised by the Royal and Ancient Golf Club of St Andrews, or by the R&A in conjunction with other bodies.

Championships that come solely under the administration of the R&A are:
The Open Championship
The Amateur Championship
The Seniors Open Amateur Championship
The British Mid-Amateur Championship
The Boys Amateur Championship
The Junior Open Championships

Team events organised by the R&A and other bodies are:
The Walker Cup (R&A/USGA)
The Eisenhower Trophy (R&A/World Amateur Golf Council)
The St Andrews Trophy (R&A/EGA)
The Jacques Léglise Trophy (R&A/EGA)

Team events organised by the R&A are:
The Boys Home Internationals

The aim has been to focus on the origins and structural growth of each event, noting key changes in format and conditions. Current championship and international match conditions are defined elsewhere in the volume.

The Open Championship

The Open Championship began in 1860 at the Prestwick Golf Club and the original trophy was an ornate Challenge Belt, presented by the Earl of Eglinton. What is now recognised as the first Open Championship was played on October 17, 1860 at the end of the club's autumn meeting. A total of eight players competed in three rounds of the 12 hole course. No prize money for the Open was awarded until 1863, the winner simply received the Belt for a year. In 1863 it was decided to give money prizes to those finishing second, third and fourth but the winner still only received the Belt. It was not until 1864 that the winner received £6. The average field in the 1860s was only 12 players.

The original rules of the competition stated that the Belt 'becomes the property of the winner by being won

three years in succession.' In 1870 Tom Morris Junior won for the third year in a row and took possession of the Belt. He won £6 for his efforts out of a total prize fund of £12. No championship was held in 1871 whilst the Prestwick Club entered into discussions with the Royal and Ancient Golf Club and the Honourable Company of Edinburgh Golfers over the future of the event.

One of the key turning points in the history of the Open took place at the spring meeting of the Prestwick Club in April 1871. At that meeting it was proposed that 'in contemplation of St Andrews, Musselburgh and other clubs joining in the purchase of a Belt to be played for over four or more greens, it is not expedient for the Club to provide a Belt to be played solely for at Prestwick.' From that date onwards, the Open ceased to be under the sole control of the Prestwick Golf Club.

The Championship was played again under this new agreement in 1872 and the new trophy was the now famous Claret Jug. Until 1891, the host club remained responsible for all arrangements regarding the Championship, which continued to be played over 36 holes in one day.

In 1892, the Honourable Company of Edinburgh Golfers took four radical steps to transform the Open Championship. It expanded the Championship to 72 holes over two days, imposed an entrance charge for all competitors, moved the Championship to a new course at Muirfield and increased the total prize fund from £28 10s to £100. These actions were all taken unilaterally by the club, with the increased purse to counter a rival tournament held at Musselburgh.

A meeting was held between the three host clubs on June 9, 1893, for the purpose of 'placing the competition for the Open Championship on a basis more commensurate with its importance than had hitherto existed.' Three resolutions were agreed. Two English clubs, St George's, Sandwich and Royal Liverpool, would be invited to stage the Championship and join the rota, now of five clubs. Four rounds of 18 holes would be played over two days. Each of the five clubs would contribute £15 annually to the cost and the balance would come from an entry fee for all competitors. The prize money would total £100, with £30 for the winner. The date of each year's championship would be set by the host club, which would also bear

any additional necessary expenses. The representatives of the five clubs became known as the Delegates of the Associated Clubs.

The increasing number of entrants caused a cut to be introduced after two rounds in 1898 and between 1904 and 1906 the Championship was played over three days. It then reverted to two days in 1907 with the introduction of qualifying rounds. The entire field had to qualify and there were no exemptions.

On January 24, 1920, the Delegates of the Associated Clubs asked the R&A to take over 'the management of the Championship and the custody of the Challenge Cup.' The new Championship Committee was responsible for running both the Open and Amateur Championships and in 1922 it was decided that the Open should only be played over links courses. The venues included in today's circuit are: Carnoustie, Muirfield, Royal Birkdale, Royal Liverpool, Royal Lytham & St Annes, Royal St George's, Royal Troon, the Old Course, St Andrews and Turnberry.

Prestwick, birth place of the Open, played host to the Championship 24 times, the last in 1925. Other courses that have been used in the past are: Musselburgh (1874, 1877, 1880, 1883, 1886, 1889); Royal Cinque Ports, Deal (1909, 1920); Princes, Sandwich (1932); Royal Portrush (1951).

The Open was played regularly over three days starting in 1926, with a round on each of the first two days and two rounds on the final day, which from 1927 onwards was a Friday. The total prize money had reached £500 by 1939. The prize money was increased to £1000 in 1946 and reached £5000 in 1959.

As the Open went into its second century in the 1960s, it grew tremendously both as a championship and a spectator event. In 1963, exemptions from pre-qualifying were introduced for the leading players. Play was extended to four days in 1966, with the Championship finishing with a single round on the Saturday. In 1968, a second cut after 54 holes was introduced to further reduce the field on the final day and this remained in effect until 1985. To cope with the increasing spectator numbers, facilities were much improved. Grandstands were first introduced at the 1960 Open and they became a standard feature from 1963 onwards.

Regional qualifying had been tried as an experiment for one year in 1926, but did not become a regular feature until 1977. Some players were exempt but had to take part in final qualifying, while others were exempt from both regional and final qualifying.

Since 1980, the Championship has been scheduled to end on a Sunday instead of a Saturday. In the event of a tie for first place, play-offs took place over 36 holes up until 1963, when they were reduced to 18 holes. In 1985 a four-hole play-off, followed by sudden death, was introduced to guarantee a finish in four days.

The Open Championship was first televised by the BBC in 1955. The first live broadcast to America was in 1966 and was shown on ABC. In 1958, the television coverage lasted for a total of three hours, one and a half hours on each of the final two days. In 2001, the Open was broadcast for 1038 hours worldwide.

Admission charges to watch the Open were introduced in 1926. Paid admissions went over 50,000 for the first time in 1968 at Carnoustie and over 100,000 for the first time at St Andrews in 1978. The 200,000 attendance figure was reached for the first time at St Andrews in 1990. A new record was set at the Home of Golf in 2000 when 238,787 watched the Millennium Open.

Growth of prize money by decade

Year	Total Prize Money	First Prize
1862	£0	£0
1872	£20	£8
1882	£45	£12
1892	£100	£35
1902	£125	£50
1912	£135	£50
1922	£225	£75
1932	£500	£100
1946	£1000	£150
1952	£1700	£300
1962	£8500	£1400
1972	£50,000	£5500
1982	£250,000	£32,000
1992	£950,000	£95,000
2002	£3,800,000	£700,000
2003	£3,900,000	£730,000

Harry Vardon has scored most victories in the Open Championship. He won it six times between 1896 and 1914. J.H. Taylor, James Braid, Peter Thomson and Tom Watson have all won the Open five times each. Between 1860 and 1889, all the Open winners were Scottish. John Ball jr became the first Englishman and the first amateur to claim the title in 1890. Arnaud Massy from France was the first Continental winner in 1907.

Four players have completed a hat trick of Open wins: Tom Morris jr 1868–1870; Jamie Anderson 1877–1879; Bob Ferguson 1880–1882; Peter Thomson 1954–1956.

The Open has been won by an amateur six times – John Ball in 1890, Harold Hilton in 1892 and 1897 and Bobby Jones in 1926, 1927 and 1930. Walter Hagen was the first native born American to win the Open when he triumphed in 1922. Jock Hutchison, who had won the previous year, was resident in America at the time of his victory but was born in St Andrews.

The Amateur Championship

What became recognised at the first Amateur Championship was held at Hoylake in 1885, although earlier national amateur competitions had been played at St Andrews in 1857, 1858 and 1859. The R&A had considered holding a national amateur tournament in 1876 but decided not to proceed with the idea.

In December 1884, Thomas Owen Potter, the Secretary of Royal Liverpool Golf Club, proposed holding a championship for amateur players. The event was to be open to members of recognised clubs and it was hoped that it would make the game more popular and lead to improved standards of play.

A total of 44 players from 12 clubs entered the first championship. The format was matchplay, with the ruling that if two players tied they would both advance to the following round and play one another again. There were three semi-finalists: John Ball, Horace Hutchinson and Allan Macfie. After a bye to the final, Macfie beat Hutchinson 7 and 6.

Following the success of the first tournament, it was agreed that a championship open to all amateurs should be played at St Andrews, Hoylake and Prestwick in rotation.

A total of 24 golf clubs subscribed for the trophy, which was acquired in 1886. They were:

Alnmouth	Royal Aberdeen
Bruntsfield	Royal Albert (Montrose)
Dalhousie	Royal & Ancient
Formby	Royal Blackheath
Gullane	Royal Burgess
Honourable Company	Royal Liverpool
Innerleven	Royal North Devon
Kilspindie	Royal St George's
King James VI	Royal Wimbledon
New North Berwick	Tantallon
Panmure	Troon
Prestwick	West Lancashire

Representatives, known as Delegates of the Associated Clubs, were elected from these clubs to run the Championship and in 1919 they approached the R&A to accept future management. The Club agreed and in 1920 formed the Championship Committee. This committee became responsible for organising the Amateur and Open and for making decisions on the conditions of play. It was not until 1922, however, that the 1885 tournament was officially recognised as the first Amateur Championship and Allan Macfie the first winner.

The venue circuit gradually increased. Sandwich was added in 1892, Muirfield in 1897 and Westward Ho! in 1912. In its entire history the event has been to 22 locations throughout Britain. It first went to Ireland in 1949 (Portmarnock) and Wales in 1951 (Porthcawl).

Prior to 1930, only two non-British players won the Amateur Championship title, Walter Travis, who won in 1904, and Jesse Sweetser, who won in 1926. Both hailed from the United States, the former via Australia.

The Americans began to make their presence felt more strongly in the 1930s, with four Americans winning five Amateur Championships. Bobby Jones took the title at St Andrews 1930, the year in which he achieved the Grand Slam. Lawson Little won in 1934 and 1935, Robert Sweeney in 1937 and Charles Yates in 1938.

Following a break during World War II, the Amateur Championship resumed in 1946 at Birkdale when the handicap limit was raised from one to two as an encouragement to those amateurs who had been on war service.

Attempts were made during the 1950s and 1960s to control large numbers of entries. In 1956 the field was limited to 200 so that the quarter-final and semi-final matches and the final could be played over 36 holes.

This experiment lasted two years, when it was decided that only the semi-finals and final should be played over two rounds.

Regional qualifying over 36 holes was introduced in 1958 when 14 courses throughout the UK were selected. Using this method, the original entry of 500 was reduced to 200. Any player with a handicap of 5 or better could enter.

In 1961 regional qualifying was scrapped and the quarter-finals and semi-finals were played over 18 holes. Then in 1983 at Turnberry, 36 holes of stroke-play qualifying were introduced during the first two days. This format continues, with the leading 64 players and ties qualifying for the matchplay stages.

The Seniors Open Amateur Championship

The Seniors Open Amateur Championship was the first tournament to be initiated by the R&A. Prestwick Golf Club was responsible for starting the Open Championship, while Royal Liverpool Golf Club introduced the Amateur Championship. Other events, such as the Boys Amateur Championship and Boys Home Internationals were started by private individuals and then handed over, by agreement, to the R&A.

The Seniors Open Amateur Championship made its debut at Formby in 1969. It started as a means to help choose a Great Britain and Ireland team for the World Senior Amateur Team Championship which had begun in 1967 at Pinehurst, North Carolina, under the auspices of the World Amateur Golf Council.

Initially, the World Senior team event was to be played every two years, alternating with the competition for the Eisenhower Trophy, but it did not survive beyond 1969. The success of the Seniors Open Amateur Championship, however, was evident from the start and it became a popular event in its own right.

It began as a 36-hole strokeplay event, held over two days for players over the age of 55. The handicap limit was 5 and the field was restricted to 100. The winner was Reg Pattinson, who duly played his way onto the World Amateur Senior team. He was partnered by Alan Cave, A.L. Bentley and A.T. Kyle. The short-lived World Senior event was played in 1969 over the Old Course at St Andrews and was won for the second time by the United States. Great Britain and Ireland finished third out of an entry of only 13 teams.

Before the present format was introduced, various alternatives were tried, in order to satisfy increasing entry demands. Two courses were used in 1971, allowing an entry of 250 when the handicap limit was increased to 9. In 1974, a limit of 130 was imposed. Subsidiary competitions were introduced according to age group: 55–59, 60–64 and 65 and over. A fourth age group was added in 1975 for the over 70s and the entry limit was increased to 140. The special categories changed in 1999, to one only for the 65 and over age group.

Today, the Seniors Open Amateur Championship attracts a wide international field, the initial entry of

252 playing two rounds and the leading 50 and ties completing a further 18 holes. Scotland's Charlie Green is a multiple winner, having claimed the title six times between 1988 and 1994.

The British Mid-Amateur Championship

Introduced as recently as 1995, the British Mid-Amateur Championship does, in fact, have a longer history. In 1954, Sam Bunton founded the British Youths Open Championship for amateurs and assistant professionals under the age of 22. The aim was to provide a category for those players who were too old to compete in the Boys Championship, which catered for players under the age of 18, and who were too young to compete in major tournaments.

By the end of the 1950s, the British Youths had become a well established, popular event, with entries exceeding 200, but its future came under discussion in 1962 when the R&A Championship Committee was notified that the sponsor was anxious to hand over the event to another authority.

The R&A began its administration of the event in 1963. While it continued as an event for youths aged between 18 and 22, it was decided that professional entries should be excluded. The R&A also changed the title, renaming it the British Youths Open Amateur Championship.

The handicap limit, which was originally 6, was lowered in 1968 to 4. At the same time, the minimum age requirement was abolished and this format continued until 1994 when the Championship Committee decided to replace it with a new fixture. The British Mid-Amateur Championship made its debut at Sunningdale in 1995. Entries are accepted from competitors who have reached the age of 25 prior to the first day of the Championship. Gary Wolstenholme holds the record of most wins, claiming victory in 1995, 1996 and 1998.

The Boys Amateur Championship

The Boys Amateur Championship was introduced in 1921 for the under-16 age group. For the first two years it was played at Royal Ascot under the guidance of D.M. Mathieson and Colonel Thomas South. In 1948, Colonel South announced his intention to retire from his duties in connection with the event, declaring that 'nothing would give him greater pleasure than that the Royal and Ancient Golf Club should take over the conduct of the Championship.'

The venue for the first Boys Amateur Championship to be played under the administration of the R&A was the Old Course, St Andrews. A subcommittee ran the event until 1952 when it was finally handed over to the Championship Committee.

Since that year a prize has been presented to the best performing 16-year-old. This, the Peter Garner Bowl, commemorates the death of a competitor who was killed in a road accident while returning from the 1951 Championship.

Sir Michael Bonallack enjoyed early success in the Boys Amateur Championship. He won in 1952, and went on to win the Amateur Championship in 1961, 1965, 1968, 1969 and 1970.

Professionals who won the title earlier in their careers include Ronan Rafferty (1979), José María Olazábal (1983) and more recently Sergio García (1997).

The Junior Open Championships

Inaugurated in 1994, the Junior Open Championships came under the R&A's administrative control in 2000. All national golf unions and federations are invited to send their leading boy and girl under the age of 16 to compete in the three-day event. In previous years, only one player from each union or federation could enter. The biennial event is run on a course close to the Open Championship and in the same week so that all participants can spend time watching the world's finest players in action.

To encourage entries worldwide, there are three categories of competition defined by varying handicap limits. Gold is for those with a handicap of 3 and under, silver 4–9 and bronze 10–21.

The Walker Cup

The United States Golf Association International Challenge Trophy was originally intended to be presented to the winners of a contest to which all golf playing nations would be invited. However, as the R&A tactfully pointed out to their counterparts in the USGA in 1921, the only two countries capable of entering a team were Britain and America.

By this simple process of elimination the trophy presented by USGA President George Herbert Walker became the focal point of a biennial series between the finest amateur players of the two countries. The first unofficial match was played in 1921 on the eve of the Amateur Championship at Hoylake when 19-year-old Bobby Jones helped the American team to a 9–3 victory. For the next three years the event was played annually, but settled into its biennial pattern after 1924.

It was not until 1938 at St Andrews that Great Britain and Ireland recorded a first victory. In 1965 there was a 12–12 tie on American soil and St Andrews was again the venue for the next GB&I triumph in 1971.

Only after the first success in America, with a 12½–11½ victory at Peachtree in Georgia in 1989, did the GB&I team finally end American domination of the matches. In the years that followed there were home wins at Porthcawl in 1995 and Nairn in 1999. GB&I successfully defended the trophy two years later at Sea Island in Georgia by a convincing 15–9 margin. Under the captaincy of Garth McGimpsey, the Great Britain and Ireland golfers rallied on the final day at Ganton to win the Cup for a record third successive time in 2003. The next match is scheduled for the Chicago GC in Illinois in July 2005.

The man after whom the trophy and the matches are named has another claim to a place in world his-tory. His grandson, George Herbert Walker Bush and his great-grandson have both held office as President of the United States of America.

The Eisenhower Trophy

The United States Golf Association approached the R&A in 1958 with the proposal that the two bodies should sponsor a world-wide amateur golf event. The new competition was to take place biennially in non-Walker Cup years, and the first to be played at St Andrews in October 1958. All golfing bodies which observed the Rules of Golf and Amateur Status as approved by the R&A and the USGA were invited to send one representative to a meeting in Washington at which President Dwight D. Eisenhower presented a trophy to be awarded to the winning country. The controlling committee of the event was to be known as the World Amateur Golf Council.

The key objective of the new council was 'to foster friendship and sportsmanship among the peoples of the world through the conduct of an Amateur Team Championship for The Eisenhower Trophy.' In a meeting with the President in the Rose Garden of the White House, Eisenhower offered his advice to the delegates: 'I suggest, aside from the four hotshot golfers you bring, that you take along some high-handicap fellows and let them play at their full handicaps … This way golf doesn't become so important.' This observation led to the creation of a 'Delegates and Duffers Cup' for officials and non-playing captains.

The format decided for the Eisenhower Trophy was strokeplay. Each team consisted of four players who would play four rounds. The team score for each round was the three best individual scores. The first competition was held in St Andrews and attracted 29 teams. After 72 holes of golf, the American and Australian teams were both tied on an aggregate score of 918. A play-off was held and the Australian team won by two strokes. So far this has been the only play-off in the history of the event.

Australia went on to win the trophy twice more, in 1966 and 1996. However, the USA have dominated the event, winning it 11 times in total. The Great Britain and Ireland team won four times, in 1964, 1976, 1988 and 1998. In 2002 teams were reduced from four to three players with the best two scores counting in each round and for the first time England, Ireland, Scotland and Wales entered separate teams. In 2002 in Malaysia there was a field of 56 teams.

The St Andrews Trophy

In November 1955 the Championship Committee of The Royal and Ancient Golf Club put forward a recommendation that 'the European Golf Association should be approached with a view to arranging an international match between a Great Britain and Ireland and European side.'

The GB&I team, captained by Gerald Micklem, duly triumphed by a score of 12½ to 2½ in the first match played over the West Course at Wentworth in 1956. The event was so successful that it was immediately established as a biennial event in non-Walker Cup years and in 1964 the R&A donated the St Andrews Trophy to be presented to the winning team.

Although Great Britain and Ireland have dominated the match, winning 21 of the 24 encounters, the Continent of Europe had a convincing victory at Villa d'Este in Italy in 1998 and suffered only a narrow 13–11 defeat at Turnberry in 2000. GB&I won the event 14–10 in 2002.

The Jacques Léglise Trophy

The annual boys international match involving GB&I against a team from the Continent of Europe was introduced in 1958. This event was dominated originally by the British side, which won every match through 1966 prompting the match to be discontinued because it was a one-sided affair.

The match was revived in 1977 when the Continental team won by 7 points to 6. A new trophy, donated by Jean-Louis Dupont on behalf of Golf de Chantilly in memory of Jacques Léglise. a leading French golf administrator, was presented for the first time in 1978 when the Continental team again won. Since then the Continental players have triumphed in 1986 and again in 1996, 1997 and 2001. The match was played in conjunction with the Boys Amateur Championship and Home International events until 1996, since when it has been staged independently.

The Boys Home Internationals

Introduced at Dunbar in 1923, the Boys Home Internationals started off as a match played between England and Scotland. It was traditionally associated with the Boys Amateur Championship, being played the day before and acting as a prelude to the main event.

The R&A accepted responsibility for the Boys Amateur Championship in 1949 and with it the running of the England v Scotland match. The Championship Committee originally carried out team selection. Today, representatives from the four Home Unions select the teams.

In 1972, a team match between Ireland and Wales was added to the fixture and the current format was established in 1996. The four home countries compete against one another over three consecutive days in a round robin series. Each fixture comprises five morning foursomes, followed by the afternoon singles.

In 1997, there was a significant break with the past when, for the first time, the venue chosen for the Boys Home Internationals differed to that for the Boys Amateur Championship. This practice has remained, helping to shape the individual identity of the international matches. Since 1985, the R&A Trophy has been awarded to the winning team.

Important dates in the history of St Andrews, the Open and the R&A

1123   King David I grants links to powerful bishops of St Andrews.

1413   Evidence of golf being a regular pastime on the links.

1457   Golf so popular King James II of Scotland bans it.

1552   Archbishop Hamilton grants citizens rights to play games including golf on the links.

1744   First set of 13 rules laid out by golfers at Leith.

1754   22 noblemen and gentlemen of Kingdom of Fife form Society of St Andrews golfers.

1764   Golfers at St Andrews play over 18 instead of 22 holes – and set the standard for a round of golf.

1834   King William IV confers his patronage and the Society of St Andrews Golfers becomes the Royal and Ancient Golf Club.

1854   R&A Clubhouse completed and opened.

1860   First Open held at Prestwick.

1870   Tom Morris jr wins Open Belt for third time and gets to keep it.

1872   R&A, Prestwick and Honourable Company of Edinburgh Golfers take over running of the Open. Golfers play for Claret Jug.

1873   First Open at St Andrews.

1894   United States Golf Association responsible for rules in USA.

1897   Formation of Rules of Golf Committee. R&A becomes accepted authority for golf.

1904   Lost ball search time reduced from 10 to five minutes.

1919   R&A takes charge of Amateur Championship.

1920   R&A takes charge of Open Championship. First R&A–USGA rules conference.

1926   Open Championship first played over three days.

1929   USGA legitimises larger ball (1.68in.). Smaller ball (1.62in.) still used elsewhere.

1929   Steel shafts legalised for the first time.

1951   R&A and USGA meet to unify rules.

1952   R&A and USGA standardise rules except for ball size. Stymie abolished.

1955   First television coverage of the Open.

1956   First four-yearly rules revision.

1960   First grandstands erected at the Open.

1963   Last 36-hole play-off for Open Championship.

1966   First live coverage of Open Championship in America.

1966   Open played over four days for first time at Muirfield.

1974   Bigger American size ball (1.68in. compulsory in the Open for first time).

1980   Open Championship finished on a Sunday for the first time at Muirfield.

1985   R&A change play-off arrangements for Open to four holes.

1984   New dropping procedure at arms length from the shoulder.

1990   The American size 1.68in. ball becomes the only legal ball.

2004   Royal and Ancient Golf Club celebrates 250th anniversary.

Famous Personalities of the Past

In making the difficult choice of the names to be included, effort has been made to acknowledge the outstanding players and personalities of each successive era from the early pioneers to the stars of recent times.

Alliss, Percy   (1897–1975)

Finished in the top six in the Open Championship seven times, including joint third at Carnoustie in 1931, two strokes behind Tommy Armour. Twice winner of the Match Play Championship, five times German Open champion and twice winner of the Italian Open. Ryder Cup player in 1933–35–37, an international honour also gained by his son Peter. Spent much of his career as professional at the Wansee Club in Berlin.

Anderson, Jamie   (1842–1912)

Winner of three consecutive Open Championships – 1877–78–79. A native St Andrean, he once claimed to have played 90 consecutive holes on the Old Course without a bad or unintended shot. He was noted for his straight hitting and accurate putting.

Anderson, Willie   (1878–1910)

Took his typically Scottish flat swing to America where he won the US Open four times in a five year period from 1901. Only Bobby Jones, Ben Hogan and Jack Nicklaus have also won the US Open four times.

Armour, Thomas D.   (1896–1968)

Born in Edinburgh, he played for Britain against America as an amateur and, after emigrating, for America against Britain as a professional in the forerunners of the Walker and Ryder Cup matches. Won the US Open in 1927, the USPGA in 1930 and the 1931 Open at Carnoustie. Became an outstanding coach and wrote several bestselling instruction books.

Auchterlonie, William   (1872–1963)

Won the Open at Prestwick in 1893 at the age of 21 with a set of seven clubs he had made himself. Founded the famous family club-making business in St Andrews. He believed that golfers should master half, three-quarter and full shots with each club. Appointed Honorary Professional to the R&A in 1935.

Ball, John   (1861–1940)

Finished fourth in the Open of 1878 at the age of 16 and became the first amateur to win the title in 1890. He won the Amateur Championship eight times and shares with Bobby Jones the distinction of being the

winner of the Open and Amateur in the same year. He grew up on the edge of the links area which became the Royal Liverpool Golf Club and the birthplace of the Amateur. He was a master at keeping the ball low in the wind, but with the same straight-faced club could cut the ball up for accurate approach shots. His run of success could have been greater but for military service in the South African campaign and the First World War.

Barton, Pamela   (1917–1943)

At the age of 19 she held both the British and American Ladies Championships in 1936. She was French champion at 17, runner-up in the British in both 1934 and '35 and won the title again in 1939. A Curtis Cup team member in 1934 and '36 she was a Flight Officer in the WAAF when she was killed in a plane crash at an RAF airfield in Kent.

Boros, Julius   (1920–1994)

Became the oldest winner of a major championship when he won the USPGA in 1968 at the age of 48. He twice won the US Open, in 1952 and again 11 years later at Brookline when he was 43. In a play-off he

Pam Barton   Popperfoto

beat Jackie Cupit by three shots and Arnold Palmer by six. He played in four Ryder Cup matches between 1959–67, winning nine of his 16 matches and losing only three.

Bousfield, Kenneth (1919–2000)

Although a short hitter even by the standards of his era, he won five out of 10 matches in six Ryder Cup appearances from 1949–61. He captured the PGA Match Play Championship in 1955, one of eight tournament victories in Britain, and also won six European Opens. He represented England in the World Cup at Wentworth in 1956 and Tokyo in 1957.

Bradshaw, Harry (1913–1950)

One of Ireland's most loved golfers whose swing Bernard Darwin described as "rustic and rugged". With Christy O'Connor he won the Canadian Cup (World Cup) for Ireland in Mexico in 1958 but he is also remembered for losing the 1949 Open to Bobby Locke after having hit one shot out of a bottle at the fifth on the second day. That bit of bad luck, it was later considered, cost him £10,000.

Braid, James (1870–1950)

Together with Harry Vardon and J.H. Taylor he formed the Great Triumvirate and dominated the game for 20 years before the 1914–18 war. In a 10-year period from 1901 he became the first player in the history of the event to win the Open five times – and also finished second on three occasions. In that same period he won the Match Play Championship four times and the French Open. He was a tall, powerful player who hit the ball hard but always retained an appearance of outward calm. He was one of the founder members of the Professional Golfers' Association and did much to elevate the status of the professional golfer. He was responsible for the design of many golf courses and served as professional at Walton Heath for 45 years. He was an honorary member of that club for 25 years and became one of its directors. He was also an honorary member of the R&A.

Bruen, Jimmy (1920–1972)

Won the Irish Amateur at the age of 17 and defended his title the following year. At 18 he became the youngest ever Walker Cup player and in practice for the match at St Andrews in 1938 equalled the amateur course record of 68 set by Bobby Jones.

Campbell, Dorothy Iona (1883–1946)

One of only two golfers to win the British, American and Canadian Ladies titles. In total she won these three major championships seven times.

Compston, Archie (1893–1962)

Beat Walter Hagen 18 and 17 in a 72-hole challenge match at Moor Park in 1928 and tied for second place in the 1925 Open. Played in the Ryder Cup in 1927–29–31.

Cotton, Sir Henry (1907–1987)

The first player to be knighted for services to golf, he died a few days before the announcement of the award was made. He won the Open Championship three times, which included a round of 65 at Royal St George's in 1934 after which the famous Dunlop golf ball was named. His final 71 at Carnoustie to win the 1937 championship in torrential rain gave him great satisfaction and he set another record with a 66 at Muirfield on the way to his third triumph in 1948. He won the Match Play Championship three times and was runner-up on three occasions. He also won 11 Open titles in Europe, played three times in the Ryder Cup and was non-playing captain in 1953. Sir Henry worked hard to promote the status of professional golf and also championed the cause of young golfers, becoming a founder member of the Golf Foundation. He was a highly successful teacher, author and architect, spending much time at Penina, a course he created in southern Portugal. He was an honorary member of the R&A.

Crawley, Leonard (1903–1981)

Played four times in the Walker Cup in 1932–34–38–47 and won the English Amateur in 1931. He also played first-class cricket for Worcestershire and Essex and toured the West Indies with the MCC in 1936. After the Second World War he was golf correspondent for the *Daily Telegraph* for 30 years.

The Curtis sisters, Harriet (1878–1944) Margaret (1880–1965)

Donors of the Curtis Cup still contested biennially between the USA and GB&I. Harriet won the US Women's Amateur in 1906 and lost in the following year's final to her sister Margaret, who went on to win the championship three times.

Daly, Fred (1911–1990)

Daly won the Open at Royal Liverpool in 1947 and in four of the next five years was never out of the top four in the Championship. At Portrush, where he was born, he finished fourth to Max Faulkner in 1951, the only time the Open has been played in Northern Ireland. He was Ulster champion 11 times and three times captured the prestigious PGA Match Play Championship. He was a member of the Ryder Cup team four times, finishing on a high note at Wentworth in 1953 when he won his foursomes match in partnership with Harry Bradshaw and then beat Ted Kroll 9 and 7 in the singles.

Darwin, Bernard (1876–1961)

One of the most gifted and authoritative writers on golf, he was also an accomplished England international player for more than 20 years. While in America to report the 1922 Walker Cup match for *The Times*, he was called in to play and captain the side when Robert Harris became ill. A grandson of Charles Darwin, he was captain of the R&A in

1934–35. In 1937 he was awarded the CBE for services to literature.

Demaret, Jimmy (1910–1983)

Three times Masters champion, coming from five strokes behind over the final six holes to beat Jim Ferrier by two in 1950, he also won six consecutive tournaments in 1940 while still performing as a night club singer. He won all six Ryder Cup matches he played in the encounters of 1947–49–51.

Duncan, George (1884–1964)

Won the Open in 1920 by making up 13 shots on the leader over the last two rounds and came close to catching Walter Hagen for the title two years later. Renowned as one of the fastest players, his book was entitled *Golf at the Gallop*.

Ferguson, Bob (1848–1915)

The Open Championship winner three times in succession between 1880–82. He then lost a 36-hole play-off for the title by one stroke to Willie Fernie in 1883. At 18 he had won the Leith Tournament against the game's leading professionals.

Fernie, Willie (1851–1924)

In 1882 he was second to Bob Ferguson in the Open over his home course at St Andrews. The following year he beat the same player in a 36-hole play-off for the championship over Ferguson's home links at Musselburgh.

Hagen, Walter (1892–1969)

A flamboyant character who used a hired Rolls Royce as a changing room because professionals were not allowed in many clubhouses, he once gave his £50 cheque for winning the Open to his caddie. He won four consecutive USPGA Championships from 1924 when it was still decided by matchplay. He was four times a winner of the Open, in 1922–24–28–29 and captured the US Open title in 1914 and 1919. He captained and played in five Ryder Cup encounters between 1927–35, winning seven of his nine matches and losing only once. He was non-playing captain in 1937.

Herd, Alexander 'Sandy' (1868–1944)

When he first played in the Open at the age of 17 he possessed only four clubs. His only championship success came in the 1902 Open at Hoylake, the first player to capture the title using the new rubber-cored ball. He won the Match Play Championship at the age of 58 and took part in his last Open at St Andrews in 1939 at the age of 71.

Hilton, Harold (1869–1942)

Winner of the Amateur Championship four times between 1900 and 1913, he also became the first player and the only Briton to hold both the British and US

Amateur titles in the same year 1911. He won the Open in 1892 at Muirfield, the first time the championship was extended to 72 holes. A small but powerful player he was the first editor of *Golf Monthly*.

Hogan, Ben (1912–1997)

One of only five players to have won all four major championships, his record of capturing three in the same season has been matched by Tiger Woods. He dominated the golfing scene in America after the Second World War and in 1953 won the Masters, US Open and the Open Championship. A clash of dates between the Open and USPGA prevented an attempt on the Grand Slam, but his poor state of health after a near fatal car crash four years earlier would have made the matchplay format of 10 rounds in six days in the USPGA an impossibility. After his car collided with a Greyhound bus in fog, it was feared that Hogan might never walk again. He had won three majors before the accident and he returned to capture six more. His only appearance in the Open was in his tremendous season of 1953 and he recorded rounds of 73-71-70-68 to win by four strokes at Carnoustie. His dramatic life story was made into a Hollywood film entitled *Follow the Sun*.

Hutchinson, Horace (1859–1932)

Runner-up in the first Amateur Championship in 1885, he won the title in the next two years and reached the final again in 1903. Represented England from 1902–07. He was a prolific writer on golf and country life and became the first English captain of the R&A in 1908.

Jarman, Ted (1907–2003)

He competed in the 1935 Ryder Cup at Ridgewood, New Jersey, and until his death in 2003 he had been the oldest living Cup golfer. When he was 76 years and before he had to stop playing because of arthritis he shot a 75.

Jones, Bobby (1902–1971)

Always remembered for his incredible and unrepeatable achievement in 1930 of winning the Open and Amateur Championships of Britain and America in one outstanding season – the original and unchallenged Grand Slam. At the end of that year he retired from competitive golf at the age of 28. His victories included four US Opens, five US Amateur titles, three Opens in Britain and one Amateur Championship. Although his swing was stylish and fluent, he suffered badly from nerves and was often sick and unable to eat during championships.

He was also an accomplished scholar, gaining first-class honours degrees in law, English literature and mechanical engineering at three different universities. He subsequently opened a law practice in Atlanta and developed the idea of creating the Augusta National course and staging an annual invitation event which was to become known as the Masters.

Bobby Jones   Popperfoto

He was made an honorary member of the Royal and Ancient Golf Club in 1956 and two years later was given the freedom of the Burgh of St Andrews at an emotional ceremony. He died after many years of suffering from a crippling spinal disease and a hole on the Old Course bears his name.

King, Sam (1911–2003)

He played Ryder Cup golf immediately before and after World War II and came third in the 1939 Open behind Dick Burton at Royal St George's. In the 1947 Ryder Cup he prevented an American whitewash in the singles by beating Herman Kaiser. He was British Senior Champion in 1961 and 1962 and was often described as "the old master" – a golfer noted for his long, straight drives and superb putting.

Kirkaldy, Andrew (1860–1934)

First honorary professional appointed by the R&A, he lost a play-off for the Open Championship of 1889 to Willie Park at Musselburgh. He was second in the championship three times, a further three times finished third and twice fourth. A powerful player, he was renowned for speaking his mind.

Laidlay, John Ernest (1860–1940)

The man who first employed the overlapping grip which was later credited to Harry Vardon and universally known as the Vardon grip, Laidlay was a finalist in the Amateur Championship six times in seven years from 1888, winning the title twice at a time when John Ball, Horace Hutchinson and Harold Hilton were at their peak. He was runner-up in the Open to Willie Auchterlonie at Prestwick in 1893. Among the 130 medals he won, were the Gold Medal and Silver Cross in R&A competitions.

Leitch, 'Cecil' (1891–1977)

Christened Charlotte Cecilia, but universally known as Cecil, her list of international victories would undoubtedly have been greater but for the blank golfing years of the first world war. She first won the British Ladies Championship in 1908 at the age of 17. In 1914 she took the English, French and British titles and successfully defended all three when competition was resumed after the war. In all she won the French Championship five times, the British four times, the English twice, the Canadian once. Her total of four victories in the British has never been beaten and has been equalled only by her great rival Joyce Wethered. The victory in Canada was by a margin of 17 and 15 in the 36-hole final.

Lema, Tony (1934–1966)

His first visit to Britain, leaving time for only 27 holes of practice around the Old Course at St Andrews, culminated in Open Championship victory in 1964 by five shots over Jack Nicklaus. He had won three tournaments in four starts in America before arriving in Scotland and gave great credit for his Open success to local caddie Tip Anderson. He played in the Ryder Cup in 1963 and 1965 with an outstanding record. He lost only once in 11 matches, halved twice and won eight. Lema and his wife were killed when a private plane in which they were travelling to a tournament crashed in Illinois.

Little, Lawson (1910–1968)

Won the Amateur Championships of Britain and America in 1934 and successfully defended both titles the following year. He then turned his amateur form into a successful professional career, starting in 1936 with victory in the Canadian Open. He won the US Open in 1940 after a play-off against Gene Sarazen.

Locke, Bobby (1917–1987)

The son of Northern Irish emigrants to South Africa, Arthur D'Arcy Locke was playing off plus four by the age of 18 and won the South African Boys, Amateur and Open Championships. On his first visit to Britain in 1936 he was leading amateur in the Open Championship. Realising that his normal fade was leaving him well short of the leading players, he deliberately developed the hook shot to get more run

Bobby Locke   Popperfoto

on the ball. It was to become his trade-mark throughout a long career.

He was encouraged to try the American tour in 1947 and won five tournaments, one by the record margin of 16 shots. More successes followed and the USPGA framed a rule which banned him from playing in their events, an action described by Gene Sarazen as 'the most disgraceful action by any golf organisation'.

Disillusioned by the American attitude, Locke then played most of his golf in Europe, winning the Open four times. He shared a period of domination with Peter Thomson between 1949–1958 when they won the championship four times each, only Max Faulkner and Ben Hogan breaking the sequence. In his final Open victory at St Andrews in 1957 he failed to replace his ball in the correct spot on the 18th green after moving it from fellow competitor Bruce Crampton's line. The mistake, which could have led to disqualification, was only spotted on television replays. The R&A Championship Committee rightly decided that Locke, who had won by three strokes, had gained no advantage, and allowed the result to stand.

Following a career in which he won over 80 events around the world he was made an honorary member of the R&A in 1976.

Longhurst, Henry   (1909–1978)

Captain of Cambridge University golf team, runner-up in the French and Swiss Amateur Championships and winner of the German title in 1936, he became the most perceptive and readable golf corre-

spondent of his time and a television commentator who never wasted a single word. His relaxed, chatty style was based on the premise that he was explaining the scene to a friend in his favourite golf club bar. For 25 years his *Sunday Times* column ran without a break and became compulsory reading for golfers and non-golfers alike. He had a brief spell as a member of parliament and was awarded the CBE for services to golf.

McCormack, Mark   (1931–2003)

The Cleveland lawyer who created a golf management empire after approaching Arnold Palmer to look after his affairs. A keen golfer himself, he became one of the most influential and powerful men in sport, managing many golfing legends including Tiger Woods. He was responsible for the development of the modern game commercially and started the World Match Play Championship at Wentworth.

Mackenzie, Alister   (1870–1934)

A family doctor and surgeon, he became involved with Harry S. Colt in the design of the Alwoodley course in Leeds, where he was a founder member and honorary secretary and eventually abandoned his medical career and worked full time at golf course architecture. There are many outstanding examples of his work in Britain, Australia, New Zealand and America. His most famous creation, in partnership with Bobby Jones, is the Augusta National course in Georgia, home of the US Masters.

Massy, Arnaud   (1877–1958)

The first non-British player to win the Open Championship. Born in Biarritz, France, he defeated J.H. Taylor by two strokes at Hoylake in 1907. Four years later he tied for the title with Harry Vardon at Royal St George's, but conceded at the 35th hole when he was five strokes behind. He won the French Open four times, the Spanish on three occasions and the Belgian title once.

Micklem, Gerald   (1911–1988)

A pre-war Oxford Blue, he won the English Amateur Championship in 1947 and 1953 and played in the Walker Cup team four times between 1947 and 1955. He was non-playing captain in 1957 and 1959. In 1976 he set a record of 36 consecutive appearances in the President's Putter, an event that he won in 1953. In addition to his playing success he was a tireless administrator, serving as chairman of the R&A Rules, Selection and Championship Committees. He was president of the English Golf Union and the European Golf Association and captain of the R&A. In 1969 he received the Bobby Jones award for services to golf.

Middlecoff, Cary   (1921–1998)

Dentist turned golf professional, he became one of the most prolific winners on the US tour, with 37

victories that included two US Opens and a Masters victory. In the US Open of 1949 he beat Sam Snead and Clayton Heafner at Medinah, and seven years later recaptured the title by one shot ahead of Ben Hogan and Julius Boros at Oak Hill. His Masters success came in 1955 when he established a record seven-shot winning margin over Hogan.

Mitchell, Abe   (1897–1947)

Said by J.H. Taylor to be the finest player never to win an Open, he finished in the top six five times. He was more successful in the Match Play Championship, with victories in 1919, 1920 and 1929. He taught the game to St Albans seed merchant Samuel Ryder and is the figure depicted on top of the famous trophy.

Morgan, Wanda   (1910–1995)

Three-time English Amateur champion, in 1931–36–37, she also captured the British title in 1935 and played three times in the Curtis Cup from 1932–36.

Morris, Old Tom   (1821–1908)

Apprenticed as a feathery ball maker to Allan Robertson in St Andrews at the age of 18 he was one of the finest golfers of his day when he took up the position of Keeper of the Green at Prestwick, where he laid out the original 12-hole course. He was 39 when he finished second in the first Open in 1860, but subsequently won the title four times, and played in every Open until 1896 when he was 75. His success rate might have been much greater if he had been a better putter. His son once said: 'He would be a much better player if the hole was a yard closer.'

A man of fierce conviction, he returned to St Andrews to take up the duties of looking after the Old Course at a salary of £50 per year, paid by the R&A. He came to regard the course as his own property and was once publicly reprimanded for closing it without authority because he considered it needed a rest. A testimonial in 1896 raised £1,240 pounds towards his old age from golfers around the world and when he retired in 1903 the R&A continued to pay his salary. He died after a fall on the stairs of the New Club in 1908, having outlived his wife, his daughter and his three sons.

Morris, Young Tom   (1851–1875)

Born in St Andrews, but brought up in Prestwick, where his father had moved to become Keeper of the Green, he won a tournament against leading professionals at the age of 13. He was only 17 when he succeeded his father as Open champion in 1868 and then defended the title successfully in the following two years to claim the winner's belt outright. There was no championship in 1871, but when the present silver trophy became the prize in 1872, Young Tom's was the first name engraved on its base.

His prodigious talent was best demonstrated in his third successive Open victory in 1870 when he played 36 holes at Prestwick in 149 strokes, 12 shots ahead of his nearest rival, superb scoring given the equipment and the condition of the courses at that time.

He married in November 1874 and was playing with his father in a money match at North Berwick the following year when a telegram from St Andrews sent them hurrying back across the Firth of Forth in a private yacht. Young Tom's wife and baby had both died in childbirth. He played golf only twice after that, in matches that had been arranged long in advance, and fell into moods of deep depression. He died on Christmas morning of that same year from a burst artery in the lung. He was 24 years old. A public subscription paid for a memorial which still stands above his grave in the cathedral cemetery.

Ouimet, Francis   (1893–1967)

Regarded as the player who started the American golf boom after beating Harry Vardon and Ted Ray in a play-off for the 1913 US Open as a young amateur. Twice a winner of the US Amateur, he was a member of every Walker Cup team from 1922 to 1934 and non-playing captain from then until 1949. In 1951 he became the first non-British national to be elected captain of the R&A and was a committee member of the USPGA for many years.

Park, William   (1834–1903)

Winner of the first Open Championship in 1860. He won the title three more times, in 1863, 1866 and 1875, and was runner-up on four occasions. For 20 years he issued a standing challenge to play any man in the world for £100 a side. His reputation was built largely around a successful putting stroke and he always stressed the importance of never leaving putts short.

Park, Mungo   (1839–1904)

Younger brother to Willie Park, he spent much of his early life at sea, but won the Open Championship in 1874 at the age of 35, beating Young Tom Morris into second place by two shots on his home course at Musselburgh.

Park, William jr   (1864–1925)

Son of the man who won the first Open Championship, Willie Park jr captured the title twice – in 1887 and 1889 – and finished second to Harry Vardon in 1898. He was also an accomplished clubmaker who did much to popularise the bulger driver with its convex face and he patented the wry-neck putter in 1891. One of the first and most successful professionals to design golf courses, he was responsible for many layouts in Britain, Europe and America and also wrote two highly successful books on the game.

Philp, Hugh   (1782–1856)

One of the master craftsmen in St Andrews in the early days of the 19th century, he was renowned for his skill in creating long-nosed putters. After his death

Dai Rees   Popperfoto

his business was continued by Robert Forgan. Philp's clubs are much prized collector's items.

Picard, Henry   (1907–1997)

Winner of the 1938 US Masters and the 1939 USPGA Championship, where he birdied the final hole to tie with Byron Nelson and birdied the first extra hole for the title. Ill health cut short a career in which he won 27 tournaments.

Ray, Ted   (1877–1943)

Born in Jersey, his early years in golf were in competition with Channel Islands compatriot Harry Vardon and his fellow members of the Great Triumvirate, J.H. Taylor and James Braid. His only victory in the Open came in 1912, but he was runner-up to Taylor the following year and second again, to Jim Barnes of America, in 1925 when he was 48 years of age He claimed the US Open title in 1920 and remains one of only three British players to win the Open on both sides of the Atlantic. The others are Vardon and Tony Jacklin.

Rees, Dai   (1913–1983)

One of Britain's outstanding golfers for three decades, he played in nine Ryder Cup matches between 1937 and 1961 and was playing captain of the 1957 team which won the trophy for the first time since 1933. He was non-playing captain in 1967. He was runner-up in

the Open three times and won the PGA Match Play title four times. He was made an honorary member of the Royal and Ancient Golf Club in 1976.

Robertson, Allan   (1815–1858)

So fearsome was Robertson's reputation as a player that when the R&A staged an annual competition for local professionals, he was not allowed to take part so as to give the others a chance. A famous maker of feather golf balls, he strongly resisted the advance of the more robust gutta percha. Tom Morris senior was his apprentice and they were reputed never to have lost a foursomes match in which they were partners.

Ryder, Samuel   (1858–1936)

The prosperous seed merchant was so impressed with the friendly rivalry between British and American professionals at an unofficial match at Wentworth in 1926 that he donated the famous gold trophy for the first Ryder Cup match the following year. The trophy is still presented today for the contest between America and Europe.

Sarazen, Gene   (1902–1999)

Advised to find an outdoor job to improve his health, Sarazen became a caddie and then an assistant professional. At the age of 20 he became the first player to win the US Open and PGA titles in the same year. In claiming seven major titles he added the Open at Prince's in 1932 and when he won the second Masters tournament in 1935 he became the first of only five players to date who have won all four Grand Slam trophies during their careers. He played 'the shot heard around the world' on his way to Masters victory, holing a four-wood across the lake at the 15th for an albatross two. At the age of 71 he played in the Open at Troon and holed-in-one at the Postage Stamp eighth. The next day be holed from a bunker for a two at the same hole. He acted as an honorary starter at the Masters, hitting his final shot only a month before his death at the age of 97.

Sayers, Ben   (1857–1924)

A twinkling, elphin figure, the diminutive Sayers played a leading part in the game for more than four decades. He represented Scotland against England from 1903 to 1913 and played in every Open from 1880 to 1923.

Smith, Frances – *née* **Bunty Stephens** (1925–1978)

Dominated post-war women's golf, winning the British Ladies Championship in 1949 and 1954, was three times a winner of the English and once the victor in the French Championship. She represented Great Britain & Ireland in six consecutive encounters from 1950, losing only three of her 11 matches, and was non-playing captain of the team in 1962 and 1972. She was awarded the OBE for her services to golf.

Smith, Horton   (1908–1963)

In his first winter on the professional circuit as a 20-year-old in 1928–29 he won eight out of nine tournaments. He was promoted to that year's Ryder Cup team and played again in 1933 and 1935 and remained unbeaten He won the first Masters in 1934 and repeated that success two year's later. He received the Ben Hogan Award for overcoming illness or injury and the Bobby Jones Award for distinguished sportsmanship in golf.

Smith, Macdonald   (1890–1949)

Born into a talented Carnoustie golfing family, he was destined to become one of the finest golfers never to win the Open. He was second in 1930 and 1932, was twice third and twice fourth. His best chance came at Prestwick in 1925 when he led the field by five strokes with one round to play, but the enthusiastic hordes of Scottish supporters destroyed his concentration and he finished with an 82 for fourth place.

Snead, Samuel Jackson   (1912–2002)

Few would argue that 'Slammin' Sam Snead' possessed the sweetest swing in the history of the game. 'He just walked up to the ball and poured honey all over it', it was said. Raised during the Depression in Hot Springs, Virginia, he also died there on May 23 2002, four days short of his 90th birthday. His seven major titles comprised three Masters, three USPGA Championships and the 1946 Open at St Andrews, while he was runner-up four times in the US Open. But for the Second World War he would surely have added several more. He achieved a record 82 PGA Tour victories in America, the last of them at age 52, and was just as prolific round the world across six decades. He played in seven Ryder Cup matches, captained the 1969 United States team which tied at Royal Birkdale and after his retirement acted as honorary starter at the Masters until his death. Perhaps his greatest achievement came in the 1979 Quad Cities Open when he scored 67 and 66. He was 67 years of age at the time.

Solheim, Karsten   (1912–2000)

A golfing revolutionary who discovered the game at the age of 42 and, working in his garage, invented the Ping putter with its unique heel-toe weighting design, later adopted in his irons. A keen supporter of women's golf, he presented the Solheim Cup for a biennial competition between the American and European Ladies' Tours.

Stewart, Payne   (1957–1999)

Four months after winning his second US Open title Payne Stewart was killed in a plane crash. Only a month earlier he had been on the winning United States Ryder Cup team. His first major victory was in the 1989 USPGA Championship and he claimed his first US Open title two years later after a play-off against Scott Simpson. In 1999 he holed an 18-foot winning putt to beat Phil Mickleson for the US title he was never able to defend. In 1985 he finished a stroke behind Sandy Lyle in the Open at Royal St George's and five years later he shared second place as Nick Faldo won the Championship at St Andrews.

Tait, Freddie   (1870–1900)

In 1890 Tait set a new record of 77 for the Old Course, lowering that to 72 only four years later. He was three times the leading amateur in the Open Championship and twice won the Amateur Championship, in 1896 and 1898. The following year he lost at the 37th hole of an historic final to John Ball at Prestwick. He was killed while leading a charge of the Black Watch at Koodoosberg Drift in the Boer War.

Taylor, J.H.   (1871–1963)

Winner of the Open Championship five times between 1894 and 1913, Taylor was part of the Great Triumvirate with James Braid and Harry Vardon. He tied for the title with Vardon in 1896, but lost in the play-off and was runner-up another five times. He also won the French and German Opens and finished second in the US Open. A self-educated man, he was a thoughtful and compelling speaker and became the founding father of the Professional Golfers' Association. He was made an honorary member of the R&A in 1949.

Tolley, Cyril   (1896–1978)

Won the first of his two Amateur Championships in 1920 while still a student at Oxford and played in the unofficial match which preceded the Walker Cup a year later. He played in six Walker Cup encounters and was team captain in 1924. Tolley is the only amateur to have won the French Open, a title he captured in 1924 and 1928. After winning the Amateur for the second time in 1929 he was favourite to retain the title at St Andrews the following summer but was beaten by a stymie at the 19th hole in the fourth round by Bobby Jones in his Grand Slam year.

Travis, Walter   (1862–1925)

Born in Australia, he won the US Amateur Championship in 1900 at the age of 38, having taken up the game only four years earlier. He won again the following year and in 1903. He became the first overseas player to win the Amateur title in Britain in 1904, using a centre-shafted Schenectady putter he had just acquired. The club was banned a short time later. He was 52 years old when he last reached the semi-finals of the US Amateur in 1914.

Vardon, Harry   (1870–1937)

Still the only player to have won the Open Championship six times, Vardon, who was born in Jersey, won his first title in 1896, in a 36-hole play-off against J.H. Taylor and his last in 1914, this time beating Taylor by three shots. He won the US Open in 1900 and was beaten in a play-off by Francis Ouimet in 1913. He was one of the most popular of the play-

ers at the turn of the century and did much to popularise the game in America with his whistle-stop exhibition tours. He popularised the overlapping grip which still bears his name, although it was first used by Johnny Laidlay. He was also the originator of the modern upright swing, moving away from the flat sweeping action of previous eras. After his Open victory of 1903, during which he was so ill he thought he would not be able to finish, he was diagnosed with tuberculosis. His legendary accuracy and low scoring are commemorated with the award of the Vardon Trophy each year to the player on the European Tour with the lowest stroke average.

Vare, Glenna – *née* Collett (1903–1989)

Won the first of her six US Ladies Amateur titles at the age of 19 in 1922 and the last in 1935. A natural athlete, she attacked the ball with more power than was normal in the women's game. The British title eluded her, although at St Andrews in 1929 she was three-under par and five up on Joyce Wethered after 11 holes, but lost to a blistering counter-attack. She played in the first Curtis Cup match in 1932 and was a member of the team in 1936, 1938 and 1948 and was captain in 1934 and 1950.

Walker, George (1874–1953)

The President of the United States Golf Association who donated the trophy for the first match in 1922, at Long Island, New York, and which is still presented to the winning team in the biennial matches beteeen the USA and Great Britain & Ireland. His grandson and great grandson, George Walker Bush and George Bush jr have both become Presidents of the United States.

Ward, Charles Harold (1911–2001)

Charlie Ward played in three Ryder Cup matches from 1947–1951 and was twice third in the Open, behind Henry Cotton at Muirfield in 1948 and Max Faulkner at Royal Portrush in 1951.

Wethered, Joyce – Lady Heathcoat-Amory (1901–1997)

Entered her first English Ladies Championship in 1920 at the age of 18 and beat holder Cecil Leitch in the final. She remained unbeaten for four years, winning 33 successive matches. After they had played together at St Andrews, Bobby Jones remarked: 'I had never played golf with anyone, man or woman, amateur or professional, who made me feel so utterly outclassed.'

Wethered, Roger (1899–1983)

Amateur champion in 1923 and runner-up in 1928 and 1930, he played five times in the Walker Cup, acting as playing captain at Royal St George's in 1930, and represented England against Scotland every year from 1922 to 1930. In the Open Championship at St Andrews in 1921 he tied with Jock Hutchison despite incurring a penalty for treading on his own ball. Due to play in a cricket match in England the following day, he was persuaded to stay in St Andrews for the play-off, but lost by 150-159 over 36 holes.

Whitcombe, Ernest (1890–1971)
Charles (1895–1978)
Reginald (1898–1957)

The remarkable golfing brothers from Burnham, Somerset, were all selected for the Ryder Cup team of 1935. Charlie and Eddie were paired togther and won the only point in the foursomes in a heavy 9-3 defeat by the American team. Reg won the gale-lashed Open at Royal St George's in 1938, with a final round of 78 as the exhibition tent was blown into the sea. Ernest finished second to Walter Hagen in 1924 and Charlie was third at Muirfield in 1935.

Wilson, Enid (1910–1996)

Completed a hat-trick of victories in the Ladies British Amateur Championship from 1931–33. She was twice a semi-finalist in the American Championship, won the British Girls and English Ladies titles and played in the inaugural Curtis Cup match, beating Helen Hicks 2 and 1 in the singles. Retiring early from competitive golf, she was never afraid to express strongly held views on the game in her role as wormen's golf correspondent of the *Daily Telegraph*.

Wood, Craig (1901–1968)

Both Masters and US Open champion in 1941, Wood finally made up for a career of near misses, having lost play-offs for all four major championships between 1933 and 1939. He was three times a member of the American Ryder Cup team.

Zaharias, Mildred – *née* Didrickson (1915–1956)

As a 17-year-old, Babe, as she was universally known, broke three records in the 1932 Los Angeles Olympics – the javelin, 80 metres hurdles and high jump, but her high jump medal was denied her when judges decided her technique was illegal. Turning her attention to golf, she rapidly established herself as the most powerful woman golfer of the time and in 1945 played and made the cut in the LA Open on the men's PGA Tour. She won the final of the US Amateur by 11 and 9 in 1946, became the first American to win the British title the following year, then helped launch the women's professional tour. She won the US Women's Open in 1948, 1950 and 1954 and in 1950 won six of the nine events on the tour. In 1952 she had a major operation for cancer, but when she won her third and final Open two years later it was by the margin of 12 shots. She was voted Woman Athlete of the Year five times between 1932 and 1950 and Greatest Female Athlete of the Half-Century in 1949.

Interesting Facts and Unusual Incidents

Royal Golf Clubs

● The right to the designation *Royal* is bestowed by the favour of the Sovereign or a member of the Royal House. In most cases the title is granted along with the bestowal of royal patronage on the club. The Perth Golfing Society was the first to receive the designation *Royal*. That was accorded in June 1833. King William IV bestowed the honour on the Royal & Ancient Club in 1834. The most recent Club to be so designated is Royal Marianske Lazne in the Czech Republic. The club was granted Royal status in 2003 because of its association in the early part of the 20th century with King Edward VII. The next most recent was the Royal Regina Golf Club in 1999. A full list of Royal clubs can be found on pages 532–533.

Royal and Presidential Golfers

● In the long history of the Royal and Ancient game no reigning British monarch has played in an open competition. In 1922 the Duke of Windsor, when Prince of Wales, competed in the Royal & Ancient Autumn Medal at St Andrews. He also took part in competitions at Mid-Surrey, Sunningdale, Royal St George's and in the Parliamentary Handicap. He occasionally competed in American events, sometimes partnered by a professional. On a private visit to London in 1952, he competed in the Autumn competition of Royal St George's at Sandwich, scoring 97. As Prince of Wales he played on courses all over the world and, after his abdication, as Duke of Windsor he continued to enjoy the game for many years.

● King George VI, when still Duke of York, in 1930, and the Duke of Kent, in 1937, also competed in the Autumn Meeting of the Royal & Ancient, when they had formally played themselves into the Captaincy of the Club and each returned his card in the medal round. So too did Prince Andrew, the Duke of York, when he became captain in 2003. He also played in the medal and won the mixed foursomes the following day playing with former British ladies champion Julie Otto who works at the R&A.

● King Leopold of Belgium played in the Belgian Amateur Championship at Le Zoute, the only reigning monarch ever to have played in a national championship. The Belgian King played in many competitions subsequent to his abdication. In 1949 he reached the quarter-finals of the French Amateur Championship at St Cloud, playing as Count de Rethy.

● King Baudouin of Belgium in 1958 played in the triangular match Belgium-France-Holland and won his match against a Dutch player. He also took part in the Gleneagles Hotel tournament (playing as Mr B. de Rethy), partnered by Dai Rees in 1959.

● United States President George Bush accepted an invitation in 1990 to become an Honorary Member of the Royal & Ancient Golf Club of St Andrews. The honour recognised his long connection and that of his family with golf and the R&A. Both President Bush's father, Prescott Bush Sr, and his grandfather, George Herbert Walker – who donated the Walker Cup – were presidents of the United States Golf Association. Other Honorary Members of the R&A include Kel Nagle, Jack Nicklaus, Arnold Palmer, Gene Sarazen, Peter Thomson, Roberto de Vicenzo, Gary Player and five-times Open Championship winner Tom Watson, who was made an honorary member in 1999 on his 50th birthday.

● In September 1992, the Royal & Ancient Golf Club of St Andrews announced that His Royal Highness The Duke of York had accepted the Club's invitation of Honorary Membership. The Duke of York is the sixth member of the Royal Family to accept membership along with Their Royal Highnesses The Duke of Edinburgh and The Duke of Kent. He has since become a single handicapper, and has appeared in a number of pro-ams, partnering Open and Masters champion Mark O'Meara to victory in the Alfred Dunhill Cup pro-am at St Andrews in 1998. His Royal Highness is captain for 2003–2004 – the year the club celebrates its 250th anniversary.

First Lady Golfer

● Mary Queen of Scots, who was beheaded on 8th February, 1587, was probably the first lady golfer so mentioned by name. As evidence of her indifference to the fate of Darnley, her husband who was murdered at Kirk o' Field, Edinburgh, she was charged at her trial with having played at golf in the fields beside Seton a few days after his death.

Record Championship Victories

● In the Amateur Championship at Muirfield, 1920, Captain Carter, an Irish golfer, defeated an American entrant by 10 and 8. This is the only known instance where a player has won every hole in an Amateur Championship tie.

● In the final of the Canadian Ladies' Championship at Rivermead, Ottawa, in 1921, Cecil Leitch defeated

Mollie McBride by 17 and 15. Miss Leitch lost only 1 hole in the match, the ninth. She was 14 up at the end of the first round, making only 3 holes necessary in the second. She won 18 holes out of 21 played, lost 1, and halved 2.

● In the final of the French Ladies' Open Championship at Le Touquet in 1927, Mlle de la Chaume (St Cloud) defeated Mrs Alex Johnston (Moor Park) by 15 and 14, the largest victory in a European golf championship.

● At Prestwick in 1934, W. Lawson Little of Presidio, San Francisco, defeated James Wallace, Troon Portland, by 14 and 13 in the final of the Amateur Championship, the record victory in the Championship. Wallace failed to win a single hole.

Players who have won Two or More Majors in the Same Year

(The first Masters Tournament was played in 1934.)

1922 Gene Sarazen – USPGA, US Open
1924 Walter Hagen – USPGA, Open
1926 Bobby Jones – US Open, Open
1930 Bobby Jones – US Open, Open (Bobby Jones also won the US Amateur and British Amateur in this year.)
1932 Gene Sarazen – US Open, Open
1941 Craig Wood – Masters, US Open
1948 Ben Hogan – USPGA, US Open
1949 Sam Snead – USPGA, Masters
1951 Ben Hogan – Masters, US Open
1953 Ben Hogan – Masters, US Open, Open
1956 Jack Burke – USPGA, Masters
1960 Arnold Palmer – Masters, US Open
1962 Arnold Palmer – Masters, Open
1963 Jack Nicklaus – USPGA, Masters
1966 Jack Nicklaus – Masters, Open
1971 Lee Trevino – US Open, Open
1972 Jack Nicklaus – Masters, Open
1974 Gary Player – Masters, Open
1975 Jack Nicklaus – USPGA, Masters
1977 Tom Watson – Masters, Open
1980 Jack Nicklaus – USPGA, US Open
1982 Tom Watson – US Open, Open
1990 Nick Faldo – Masters, Open
1994 Nick Price – Open, US PGA
1998 Mark O'Meara – Masters, Open
2000 *Tiger Woods – US Open, Open, USPGA

*Woods also won the 2001 Masters to become the first player to hold all four Majors at the same time. He was 65-under-par for the four events.

Outstanding Records in Championships, International Matches and on the Professional Circuit

● The record number of victories in the Open Championship is six, held by Harry Vardon who won in 1896-98-99-1903-11-14.

● Five-time winners of the Championship are J.H. Taylor in 1894-95-1900-09-13; James Braid in 1901-

05-06-08-10; Peter Thomson in 1954-55-56-58-65 and Tom Watson in 1975-77-80-82-83. Thomson's 1965 win was achieved when the Championship had become a truly international event. In 1957 he finished second behind Bobby Locke. By winning again in 1958 Thomson was prevented only by Bobby Locke from winning five consecutive Open Championships.

● Four successive victories in the Open by *Young* Tom Morris is a record so far never equalled. He won in 1868-69-70-72. (The Championship was not played in 1871.) Other four-time winners are Bobby Locke in 1949-50-52-57, Walter Hagen in 1922-24-28-29, Willie Park 1860-63-66-75, and *Old* Tom Morris 1861-62-64-67.

● Since the Championship began in 1860, players who have won three times in succession are Jamie Anderson, Bob Ferguson, and Peter Thomson.

● Robert Tyre Jones won the Open three times in 1926-27-30; the Amateur in 1930; the American Open in 1923-26-29-30; and the American Amateur in 1924-25-27-28-30. In winning the four major golf titles of the world in one year (1930) he achieved a feat unlikely ever to be equalled. Jones retired from competitive golf after winning the 1930 American Open, the last of these Championships, at the age of 28.

● Jack Nicklaus has had the most wins (six) in the US Masters Tournament, followed by Arnold Palmer with four.

● In modern times there are four championships generally regarded as standing above all others – the Open, US Open, US Masters, and USPGA. Five players have held all these titles, Gene Sarazen, Ben Hogan, Gary Player, Jack Nicklaus and Tiger Woods in that order. In 1978 Nicklaus became the first player to have held each of them at least three times. His record in these events is: Open 1966-70-78; US Open 1962-67-72-80; US Masters 1963-65-66-72-75-86; USPGA 1963-71-73-75-80. His total of major championships is now 18. In 1998 at the age of 58, Nicklaus finished joint sixth in the Masters. By not playing in the Open Championship that year, he ended a run of 154 successive major championships for which he was eligible (stretching back to 1957).

In 1953 Ben Hogan won the Masters, US Open and Open, but did not compete in the USPGA because of a dates clash with the Open.

In 2000 Tiger Woods won the US Open by 15 strokes (a major championship record), the Open by eight strokes, and the USPGA in the play-off. In 2001 he then added the Masters winning by two shots to become the first player to hold all four major titles at the same time. He was 65-under-par for the four events.

● In the 1996 English Amateur Championship at Hollinwell, Ian Richardson (50) and his son, Carl, of Burghley Park, Lincolnshire, both reached the semi-finals. Both lost.

● The record number of victories in the US Open is four, held by Willie Anderson, Bobby Jones, Ben Hogan and Jack Nicklaus.

● Bobby Jones (amateur), Gene Sarazen, Ben Hogan, Lee Trevino, Tom Watson and Tiger Woods

are the only players to have won the Open and US Open Championships in the same year. Tony Jacklin won the Open in 1969 and the US Open in 1970 and for a few weeks was the holder of both.

● In winning the Amateur Championship in 1970 Michael Bonallack became the first player to win in three consecutive years.

● The English Amateur record number of victories is held by Michael Bonallack, who won the title five times.

● John Ball holds the record number of victories in the Amateur Championship, which he won eight times. Next comes Michael Bonallack (who was internationally known as *The Duke*) with five wins.

● Cecil Leitch and Joyce Wethered each won the British Ladies' title four times.

● The Scottish Amateur record was held by Ronnie Shade, who won five titles in successive years, 1963 to 1967. His long reign as Champion ended when he was beaten in the fourth round of the 1968 Championship after winning 44 consecutive matches.

● Joyce Wethered established an unbeaten record by winning the English Ladies' in five successive years from 1920 to 1924 inclusive.

● In winning the Amateur Championships of Britain and America in 1934 and 1935 Lawson Little won 31 consecutive matches. Other dual winners of these championships in the same year are R.T. Jones (1930) and Bob Dickson (1967).

● Peter Thomson's victory in the 1971 New Zealand Open Championship was his ninth in that championship.

● In a four-week spell in 1971, Lee Trevino won in succession the US Open, the Canadian Open and the Open Championships.

● Michael Bonallack and Bill Hyndman were the Amateur Championship finalists in both 1969 and 1970. This was the first time the same two players reached the final in successive years.

● On the US professional circuit the greatest number of consecutive victories is 11, achieved by Byron Nelson in 1945. Nelson also holds the record for most victories in one calendar year, again in 1945 when he won a total of 18 tournaments.

● Raymond Floyd, by winning the Doral Classic in March 1992, joined Sam Snead as the only winners of US Tour events in four different decades.

● Sam Snead won tournaments in six decades. His first win was the 1936 West Virginia PGA. In 1980 he won the *Golf Digest* Commemorative and in 1982 the Legends of Golf with Don January.

● Neil Coles has won official Tour events in six decades. His first victory was in 1958 and he was a winner on the European Senior Tour in June 2000 when he took the Microlease Jersey Senior Open. Coles still plays well enough to beat his age. Now 67, he shot a closing 64 in the final round of the 2003 Travis Perkins Senior Open over the Edinburgh course he helped design.

● Jack Nicklaus and the late Walter Hagen have had five wins each in the USPGA Championship. All

Hagen's wins were at match play; all Nicklaus's at stroke play.

● In 1953 Flory van Donck of Belgium had seven major victories in Europe, including the Open Championships of Switzerland, Italy, Holland, Germany and Belgium.

● Mrs Anne Sander won four major amateur titles each under a different name. She won the US Ladies' in 1958 as Miss Quast, in 1961 as Mrs Decker, in 1963 as Mrs Welts and the British Ladies' in 1980 as Mrs Sander.

● The highest number of appearances in the Ryder Cup matches is held by Nick Faldo who made his eleventh appearance in 1997.

● The greatest number of appearances in the Walker Cup matches is held by Irishman Joe Carr who made his tenth appearance in 1967.

● In the Curtis Cup Mary McKenna made her ninth consecutive appearance in 1986.

● Players who have represented their country in both Walker and Ryder Cup matches are: for the United States, Fred Haas, Ken Venturi, Gene Littler, Jack Nicklaus, Tommy Aaron, Mason Rudolph, Bob Murphy, Lanny Wadkins, Scott Simpson, Tom Kite, Jerry Pate, Craig Stadler, Jay Haas, Bill Rodgers, Hal Sutton, Curtis Strange, Davis Love III, Brad Faxon, Scott Hoch, Phil Mickelson, Corey Pavin, Justin Leonard, Tiger Woods and David Duval; and for Great Britain & Ireland, Norman Drew, Peter Townsend, Clive Clark, Peter Oosterhuis, Howard Clark, Mark James, Michael King, Gordon Brand Jr, Paul Way, Ronan Rafferty, Sandy Lyle, Philip Walton, David Gilford, Colin Montgomerie, Peter Baker, Padraig Harrington and Andrew Coltart.

Remarkable Recoveries in Matchplay

● There have been two remarkable recoveries in the Walker Cup Matches. In 1930 at Sandwich, J.A. Stout, Great Britain, round in 68, was 4 up at the end of the first round against Donald Moe. Stout started in the second round, 3, 3, 3, and was 7 up. He was still 7 up with 13 to play. Moe, who went round in 67, won back the 7 holes to draw level at the 17th green. At the 18th or 36th of the match, Moe, after a long drive placed his iron shot within three feet of the hole and won the match by 1 hole.

● In 1936 at Pine Valley, George Voigt and Harry Girvan for America were 7 up with 11 to play against Alec Hill and Cecil Ewing. The British pair drew level at the 17th hole, or the 35th of the match, and the last hole was halved.

● In the 1965 Piccadilly Match Play Championship Gary Player beat Tony Lema after being 7 down with 17 to play.

● Bobby Cruickshank, the old Edinburgh player, had an extraordinary recovery in a 36-hole match in a USPGA Championship for he defeated Al Watrous after being 11 down with 12 to play.

● In a match at the Army GC, Aldershot, on 5th July, 1974, for the Gradoville Bowl, M.C. Smart was 8 down with 8 to play against Mike Cook. Smart succeeded in winning all the remaining holes and the 19th for victory.

● In the 1982 Suntory World Match Play Championship Sandy Lyle beat Nick Faldo after being 6 down with 18 to play.

Oldest Champions

Open Championship: Belt Tom Morris in 1867 – 46 years 99 days. *Cup* Roberto de Vicenzo, 44 years 93 days, in 1967; Harry Vardon, 44 years 42 days, in 1914; J.H. Taylor, 42 years 97 days, in 1913.

Amateur Championship Hon. Michael Scot, 54, at Hoylake in 1933.

British Ladies Amateur Mrs Jessie Valentine, 43, at Hunstanton in 1958.

Scottish Amateur J.M. Cannon, 53, at Troon in 1969.

English Amateur Terry Shingler, 41 years 11 months at Walton Heath 1977; Gerald Micklem, 41 years 8 months, at Royal Birkdale 1947.

Welsh Amateur John Jermine, 56, at St David's, in 2000

US Open Hale Irwin, 45, at Medinah, Illinois, in 1990.

US Amateur Jack Westland, 47, at Seattle in 1952 (He had been defeated in the 1931 final, 21 years previously, by Francis Ouimet).

US Masters Jack Nicklaus, 46, in 1986.

European Tour Des Smyth, 48 years, 14 days, Madeira Open 1982; Neil Coles, 48 years 14 days, Sanyo Open 1982

European Senior Tour Neil Coles, 65, in 2000

USPGA Julius Boros, 48, in 1968. Lee Trevino, 44, in 1984.

USPGA Tour Sam Snead, 52, at Greensborough Open in 1965. Sam Snead, 61, equal second in Glen Campbell Open 1974.

Youngest Champions

Open Championship: Belt Tom Morris, Jr, 17 years 5 months, in 1868. *Cup* Willie Auchterlonie, 21 years 24 days, in 1893; Tom Morris, Jr, 21 years 5 months, in 1872; Severiano Ballesteros, 22 years 103 days, in 1979.

Amateur Championship J.C. Beharrell, 18 years 1 month, at Troon in 1956; R. Cole (SA) 18 years 1 month, at Carnoustie in 1966.

British Ladies Amateur May Hezlett, 17, at Newcastle, Co Down, in 1899; Michelle Walker, 18, at Alwoodley in 1971.

English Amateur Nick Faldo, 18, at Lytham St Annes in 1975; Paul Downes, 18, at Birkdale in 1978; David Gilford, 18, at Woodhall Spa in 1984; Ian Garbutt, 18, at Woodhall Spa in 1990; Mark Foster, 18, at Moortown in 1994.

English Amateur Strokeplay Ronan Rafferty, 16, at Hunstanton in 1980.

British Ladies Open Strokeplay Helen Dobson, 18, at Southerness in 1989.

British Boys Championship Mark Mouland (Wales) 15 years 120 days at Sunningdale in 1976; Pablo Martin (Spain) 15 years 120 days at Ganton 2001.

More records can be found on pages 579–588

Disqualifications

Disqualifications are now numerous, usually for some irregularity over signing a scorecard or for late arrival at the first tee. We therefore show here only incidents in major events involving famous players or players who were in a winning position or incidents which were in themselves unusual.

● J.J. McDermott, the American Open Champion 1911–12, arrived for the Open Championship at Prestwick in 1914 to discover that he had made a mistake of a week in the date the championship began. The American could not play, as the qualifying rounds were completed on the day he arrived.

● In the Amateur Championship at Sandwich in 1937, Brigadier-General Critchley, arriving at Southampton from New York on the *Queen Mary*, which had been delayed by fog, flew by specially chartered aeroplane to Sandwich. He circled over the clubhouse, so the officials knew he was nearly there, but he arrived six minutes late, and his name had been struck out. At the same championship a player, entered from Burma, who had travelled across the Pacific and the American Continent, and was also on the *Queen Mary*, travelled from Southampton by motor car and arrived four hours after his starting time to find after journeying more than halfway round the world he was *struck out*.

● An unprecedented disqualification was that of A. Murray in the New Zealand Open Championship, 1937. Murray, who was New Zealand Champion in 1935, was playing with J.P. Hornabrook, New Zealand Amateur Champion, and at the 8th hole in the last round, while waiting for his partner to putt, Murray dropped a ball on the edge of the green and made a practice putt along the edge. Murray returned the lowest score in the championship, but he was disqualified for taking the practice putt.

● At the Open Championship at St Andrews in 1946, John Panton, Glenbervie, in the evening practised putting on a green on the New Course, which was one of the qualifying courses. He himself reported his inadvertence to the Royal & Ancient and he was disqualified.

● At the Open Championship, Sandwich, 1949, C. Rotar, an American, qualified by four strokes to compete in the championship but he was disqualified because he had used a putter which did not conform to the accepted form and make of a golf club, the socket being bent over the centre of the club head. This is the only case where a player has been disqualified in the Open Championship for using an illegal club.

● In the 1957 American Women's Open Championship, Mrs Jackie Pung had the lowest score, 298 over four rounds, but lost the championship. The card she signed for the final round read *five* at the 4th hole instead of the correct *six*. Her total of 72 was correct but the error, under rigid rules, resulted in her disqualification. Betty Jameson, who partnered Mrs Pung and also returned a wrong score, was also disqualified.

● Mark Roe and Jesper Parnevik were disqualified in bizarre circumstances in the 2003 Open at Royal St George's, Sandwich. Roe had shot 67 to move into contention but it was discovered after they left the recorder's hut that they had not exchanged cards. Roe's figures were returned on a card with Parnevik's name on it and vice versa.

Longest Match

● W.R. Chamberlain, a retired farmer, and George New, a postmaster at Chilton Foliat, on 1st August, 1922, met at Littlecote, the 9-hole course of Sir Ernest Wills, and agreed to play every Thursday afternoon over the course. This continued until New's sudden death on 13th January, 1938. An accurate record of the match was kept, giving details of each round including wind direction and playing conditions. In the elaborate system nearly two million facts were recorded. They played 814 rounds, and aggregated 86,397 strokes, of which Chamberlain took 44,008 and New 42,371. New, therefore, was 1,637 strokes up. The last round of all was halved, a suitable end to such an unusual contest.

Longest Ties

● The longest known ties in 18-hole match play rounds in major events were in an early round of the News of the World Match Play Championship at Turnberry in 1960, when W.S. Collins beat W.J. Branch at the 31st hole and in the third round of the same tournament at Walton Heath in 1961 when Harold Henning beat Peter Alliss also at the 31st hole.
● In the 1970 Scottish Amateur Championship at Balgownie, Aberdeen, E. Hammond beat J. McIvor at the 29th hole in their second round tie.
● C.A. Palmer beat Lionel Munn at the 28th hole at Sandwich in 1908. This is the record tie of the British Amateur Championship. Munn has also been engaged in two other extended ties in the Amateur Championship. At Muirfield, in 1932, in the semi-final, he was defeated by John de Forest, the ultimate winner, at the 26th hole, and at St Andrews, in 1936, in the second round he was defeated by J.L. Mitchell, again at the 26th hole.

The following examples of long ties are in a different category for they occurred in competitions, either stroke play or match play, where the conditions stipulated that in the event of a tie, a further stated number of holes had to be played – in some cases 36 holes, but mostly 18. With this method a vast number of extra holes was sometimes necessary to settle ties.

● The longest known was between two American women in a tournament at Peterson (New Jersey) when 88 extra holes were required before Mrs Edwin Labaugh emerged as winner.
● In a match on the Queensland course, Australia, in October, 1933, H.B. Bonney and Col H.C.H. Robertson versus B.J. Canniffe and Dr Wallis Hoare required to play a further four 18-hole matches after being level at the end of the original 18 holes. In the fourth replay Hoare and Caniffe won by 3 and 2 which meant that 70 extra holes had been necessary to decide the tie.
● After finishing all square in the final of the Dudley GC's foursomes competition in 1950, F.W. Mannell and A.G. Walker played a further three 18-hole replays against T. Poole and E. Jones, each time finishing all square. A further 9 holes were arranged and Mannell and Walker won by 3 and 2 making a total of 61 extra holes to decide the tie.
● R.A. Whitcombe and Mark Seymour tied for first prize in the Penfold £750 Tournament at St Annes-on-Sea, in 1934. They had to play off over 36 holes and tied again. They were then required to play another 9 holes when Whitcombe won with 34 against 36. The tournament was over 72 holes. The first tie added 36 holes and the extra 9 holes made an aggregate of 117 holes to decide the winner. This is a record in first-class British golf but in no way compares with other long ties as it involved only two replays – one of 36 holes and one of 9.
● In the American Open Championship at Toledo, Ohio, in 1931, G. Von Elm and Billy Burke tied for the title. Each returned aggregates of 292. On the first replay both finished in 149 for 36 holes but on the second replay Burke won with a score of 148 against 149. This is a record tie in a national open championship.
● Cary Middlecoff and Lloyd Mangrum were declared co-winners of the 1949 Motor City Open on the USPGA Tour after halving 11 sudden death holes.
● Australian David Graham beat American Dave Stockton at the tenth extra hole in the 1998 Royal Caribbean Classic, a record on the US Senior Tour.
● Paul Downes was beaten by Robin Davenport at the 9th extra hole in the 4th round of the 1981 English Amateur Championship, a record marathon match for the Championship.
● Severiano Ballesteros was beaten by Johnny Miller at the 9th extra hole of a sudden-death play-off at the 1982 Million Dollar Sun City Challenge.
● José Maria Olazábal beat Ronan Rafferty at the 9th extra hole to win the 1989 Dutch Open on the Kennemer Golf and Country Club course. Roger Chapman had been eliminated at the first extra hole.

Long Drives

It is impossible to state with any certainty what is the longest ever drive. Many long drives have never been measured and many others have most likely never been brought to our attention. Then there are several outside factors which can produce freakishly long drives, such as a strong following wind, downhill terrain or bonehard ground. Where all three of these favourable conditions prevail outstandingly long drives can be achieved. Another consideration is that a long drive made during a tournament is a different proposition from one made for length alone, either on the practice ground, a long driving competition or in a game of no consequence. All this should be borne in mind when considering the long drives shown here.

● When professional Carl Hooper hit a wayward drive on the 3rd hole (456 yards) at the Oak Hills Country Club, San Antonio, during the 1992 Texas Open, he wrote himself into the record books but out of the tournament. The ball kept bouncing and rolling on a tarmac cart path until it was stopped by a fence – 787 yards away. It took Hooper two recovery shots with a 4-iron and then an 8-iron to return to the fairway. He eventually holed out for a double bogey six and failed to survive the half-way qualifying cut.

● Tommie Campbell of Portmarnock hit a drive of 392 yards at Dun Laoghaire GC in July 1964.

● Playing in Australia, American George Bayer is reported to have driven to within chipping distance of a 589 yards hole. *It was certainly a drive of over 500 yards,* said Bayer acknowledging the strong following wind, sharp downslope where his ball landed and the bone-hard ground.

● In September, 1934, over the East Devon course, T.H.V. Haydon, Wimbledon, drove to the edge of the 9th green which was a hole of 465 yards, giving a drive of not less than 450 yards.

● E.C. Bliss drove 445 yards at Herne Bay in August, 1913. The drive was measured by a government surveyor who also measured the drop in height from tee to resting place of the ball at 57 feet.

Long Carries

● At Sitwell Park, Rotherham, in 1935 the home professional, W. Smithson, drove a ball which carried a dyke at 380 yards from the 2nd tee.

● George Bell, of Penrith GC, New South Wales, Australia, using a number 2 wood drove across the Nepean River, a certified carry of 309 yards in a driving contest in 1964.

● After the 1986 Irish Professional Championship at Waterville, Co. Kerry, four long-hitting professionals tried for the longest-carry record over water, across a lake in the Waterville Hotel grounds. Liam Higgins, the local professional, carried 310 yards and Paul Leonard 311, beating the previous record by 2 yards.

● In the 1972 Algarve Open at Penina, Henry Cotton vouched for a carry of 305 yards over a ditch at the 18th hole by long-hitting Spanish professional Francisco Abreu. There was virtually no wind assistance.

● At the Home International matches at Portmarnock in 1949 a driving competition was held in which all the players in all four teams competed. The actual carry was measured and the longest was 280 yards by Jimmy Bruen.

● On 6th April, 1976, Tony Jacklin hit a number of balls into Vancouver harbour, Canada, from the 495-foot high roof of a new building complex. The longest carry was measured at 389 yards.

Long Hitting

There have been numerous long hits, not on golf courses, where an outside agency has assisted the length of the shot. Such an example was a 'drive' by

Liam Higgins in 1986, on the Airport runway at Baldonal, near Dublin, of 632 yards.

Longest Albatrosses

● The longest-known albatrosses (three under par) recorded at par 5 holes are:

● 647 yards-2nd hole at Guam Navy Club by Chief Petty Officer Kevin Murray of Chicago on 3rd January, 1982.

● 609 yards-15th hole at Mahaka Inn West Course, Hawaii, by John Eakin of California on 12th November, 1972.

● 602 yards-16th hole at Whiting Field Golf Course, Milton, Florida, by 27-year-old Bill Graham with a drive and a 3-wood, aided by a 25 mph tail wind.

● The longest-known albatrosses in open championships are: 580 yards 14th hole at Crans-sur-Sierre, by American Billy Casper in the 1971 Swiss Open; 558 yards 5th hole at Muirfield by American Johnny Miller in the 1972 Open Championship.

● In the 1994 German Amateur Championship at Wittelsbacher GC, Rohrenfield, Graham Rankin, a member of the visiting Scottish national team, had a two at the 592 yard 18th.

Eagles (Multiple and Consecutive)

● Wilf Jones scored three consecutive eagles at the first three holes at Moor Hall GC when playing in a competition there on August Bank Holiday Monday 1968. He scored 3, 1, 2 at holes measuring 529 yards, 176 yards and 302 yards.

● In a round of the 1980 Jubilee Cup, a mixed foursomes match play event of Colchester GC, Mrs Nora Booth and her son Brendan scored three consecutive gross eagles of 1, 3, 2 at the eighth, ninth and tenth holes.

● Three players in a four-ball match at Kington GC, Herefordshire, on 22nd July, 1948, all had eagle 2s at the 18th hole (272 yards). They were R.N. Bird, R. Morgan and V. Timson.

● Four Americans from Wisconsin on holiday at Gleneagles in 1977 scored three eagles and a birdie at the 300-yard par-4 14th hole on the King's course. The birdie was by Dr Kim Lulloff and the eagles by Dr Gordon Meiklejohn, Richard Johnson and Jack Kubitz.

● In an open competition at Glen Innes GC, Australia on 13th November, 1977, three players in a four-ball scored eagle 3s at the 9th hole (442 metres). They were Terry Marshall, Roy McHarg and Jack Rohleder.

● David McCarthy, a member of Moortown Golf Club, Leeds, had three consecutive eagles (3, 3, 2) on the 4th, 5th and 6th holes during a Pro-Am competition at Lucerne, Switzerland, on 7th August, 1992.

Speed of Golf Ball and Club Head and Effect of Wind and Temperature

● In *The Search for the Perfect Swing*, a scientific study of the golf swing, a first class golfer is said to

have the club head travelling at 100 mph at impact. This will cause the ball to leave the club at 135 mph. An outstandingly long hitter might manage to have the club head travelling at 130 mph which would produce a ball send-off speed of 175 mph. The resultant shot would carry 280 yards.

● According to Thomas Hardman, Wilson's director of research and development, wind will reduce or increase the flight of a golf ball by approximately $1\frac{1}{2}$ yards for every mile per hour of wind. Every two degrees of temperature will make a yard difference in a ball's flight.

Most Northerly Course

● Although the most northerly course used to be in Iceland, Björkliden Arctic Golf Club, Sweden, 250 km north of the Arctic Circle, has taken over that role. This may soon change, however, when a course opens in Narvic, Norway, which could be a few metres further north than Björkliden.

Most Southerly Course

● Golf's most southerly course is Scott Base Country Club, 13° north of the South Pole. The course is run by the New Zealand Antarctic Programme and players must be kitted in full survival gear. The most difficult aspect is finding the orange golf balls which tend to get buried in the snow. Other obstacles include penguins, seals and skuas. If the ball is stolen by a skua then a penalty of one shot is incurred; but if the ball hits a skua it counts as a birdie.

Highest Golf Courses

● The highest golf course in the world is thought to be the Tuctu GC in Peru which is 14,335 feet above sea-level. High courses are also found in Bolivia with the La Paz GC being about 13,500 feet. In the Himalayas, near the border with Tibet, a 9-hole course at 12,800 feet has been laid out by keen golfers in the Indian Army.

● The highest course in Europe is at Sestriere in the Italian Alps, 6,500 feet above sea-level.

● The highest courses in Great Britain are West Monmouthshire in Wales at 1,513 feet, Leadhills in Scotland at 1,500 feet and Church Stratton in England at 1,250 feet.

Longest Courses

● The longest course in the world is Dub's Dread GC, Piper, Kansas, USA measuring 8,101 yards (par 78).

● The longest course for the Open Championship was 7,361 yards at Carnoustie in 1999.

Longest Holes

● The longest hole in the world, as far as is known, is the 6th hole measuring 782 metres (860 yards) at Koolan Island GC, Western Australia. The par of the hole is 7. There are several holes over 700 yards throughout the world.

● The longest hole for the Open Championship is the 577 yards 6th hole at Royal Troon.

Longest Tournaments

● The longest tournament held was over 144 holes in the World Open at Pinehurst, N Carolina, USA, first held in 1973. Play was over two weeks with a cut imposed at the halfway mark.

● An annual tournament, played in Germany on the longest day of the year, comprises 100 holes' medal play. Best return, in 1995, was 399 strokes.

Largest Entries

● The Open – 2,477, St Andrews, 2000.

● The Amateur – 537, Muirfield, 1998.

● US Open – 8,457, Pebble Beach, 2000.

● The largest entry for a PGA European Tour event was 398 for the 1978 Colgate PGA Championship. Since 1985, when the all-exempt ruling was introduced, all PGA tournaments have had 144 competitors, slightly more or less.

● In 1952, Bobby Locke, the Open Champion, played a round at Wentworth against any golfer in Britain. Cards costing 2s. 6d. each (12½p), were taken out by 24,000 golfers. The challenge was to beat the local par by more than Locke could beat the par at Wentworth. 1,641 competitors, including women, succeeded in *beating* the Champion and each received a certificate signed by him. As a result of this challenge the British Golf Foundation benefited to the extent of £3,026, the proceeds from the sale of cards. A similar tournament was held in the US and Canada when 87,094 golfers participated; 14,667 players bettered Ben Hogan's score under handicap. The fund benefited by $80,024.

Largest Prize Money

● The Machrie Tournament of 1901 was the first tournament with a first prize of £100. It was won by J.H. Taylor, then Open Champion, who beat James Braid in the final.

● The richest event in the world (at time of writing) will be the American Express Championship scheduled for Mount Juliet in 2004. Total prize money will be $7 million. The richest first prize in Europe is the $1.3 million which goes to the winner of the Nedbank Golf Challenge at Sun City in South Africa.

Holing-in-One – Odds Against

● At the Wanderers Club, Johannesburg in January, 1951, forty-nine amateurs and professionals each played three balls at a hole 146 yards long. Of the 147 balls hit, the nearest was by Koos de Beer, professional at Reading Country Club, which finished $10\frac{1}{2}$ inches from the hole. Harry Bradshaw, the Irish professional who was touring with the British team in South Africa, touched the pin with his second shot, but the ball rolled on and stopped 3 feet 2 inches from the cup.

● A competition on similar lines was held in 1951 in New York when 1,409 players who had done a hole-in-one held a competition over several days at short holes on three New York courses. Each player was allowed a total of five shots, giving an aggregate of

7,045 shots. No player holed-in-one, and the nearest ball finished $3^{1}/_{2}$ inches from the hole.

● A further illustration of the element of luck in holing-in-one is derived from an effort by Harry Gonder, an American professional, who in 1940 stood for 16 hours 25 minutes and hit 1,817 balls trying to do a 160 yard hole-in-one. He had two official witnesses and caddies to tee and retrieve the balls and count the strokes. His 1,756th shot struck the hole but stopped an inch from the hole. This was his nearest effort.

● From this and other similar information an estimate of the odds against holing-in-one at any particular hole within the range of one shot was made at somewhere between 1,500 and 2,000 to 1 by a proficient player. Subsequently, however, statistical analysis in America has come up with the following odds: a male professional or top amateur 3,708 to 1; a female professional or top amateur 4,648 to 1; an average golfer 42,952 to 1.

Hole-in-One First Recorded

● Earliest recorded hole-in-one was in 1868 at the Open Championship when Tom Morris (Young Tom) did the 145-yard 8th hole Prestwick in one stroke. This was the first of four Open Championships won successively by Young Tom.

● The first hole-in-one recorded with the 1.66 in ball was in 1972 by John G. Salvesen, a member of the R&A Championship Committee. At the time this size of ball was only experimental. Salvesen used a 7-iron for his historical feat at the 11th hole on the Old Course, St Andrews.

Holing-in-One in Important Events

Since the day of the first known hole-in-one by Tom Morris Jr, at the 8th hole (145 yards) at Prestwick in the 1868 Open Championship, holes-in-one, even in championships, have become too numerous for each to be recorded. Only where other unusual or interesting circumstances prevailed are the instances shown here.

● All hole-in-one achievements are remarkable. Many are extraordinary. Among the more amazing was that of 2-handicap Leicestershire golfer Bob Taylor, a member of the Scraptoft Club. During the final practice day for the 1974 Eastern Counties Foursomes Championship on the Hunstanton Links, he holed his tee shot with a one-iron at the 188-yard 16th. The next day, in the first round of the competition, he repeated the feat, the only difference being that because of a change of wind he used a six-iron. When he stepped on to the 16th tee the following day his partner jokingly offered him odds of 1,000,000 to one against holing-in-one for a third successive time. Taylor again used his six-iron – and holed in one!

● 1878 – Jamie Anderson, competing in the Open Championship at Prestwick, holed the 17th hole in one. Anderson was playing the next to last hole, and though it seemed then that he was winning easily, it turned out afterwards that if he had not taken this hole in one stroke he would very likely have lost. Anderson was just about to make his tee shot when Andy Stuart (winner of the

first Irish Open Championship in 1892), who was acting as marker to Anderson, remarked he was standing outside the teeing ground, and that if he played the stroke from there he would be disqualified. Anderson picked up his ball and teed it in a proper place. Then he holed-in-one. He won the Championship by one stroke.

● On a Friday the 13th in 1990, Richard Allen holed-in-one at the 13th at the Barwon Heads Golf Club, Victoria, Australia, and then lost the hole. He was giving a handicap stroke to his opponent, brother-in-law Jason Ennels, who also holed-in-one.

● 1906 – R. Johnston, North Berwick, competing in the Open Championship, did the 14th hole at Muirfield in one. Johnston played with only one club throughout – an adjustable head club.

● 1959 – The first hole-in-one in the US Women's Open Championship was recorded. It was by Patty Berg on the 7th hole (170 yards) at Churchill Valley CC, Pittsburgh.

● 1962 – On 6th April, playing in the second round of the Schweppes Close Championship at Little Aston, H. Middleton of Shandon Park, Belfast, holed his tee shot at the 159-yard 5th hole, winning a prize of £1,000. Ten minutes later, playing two matches ahead of Middleton, R.A. Jowle, son of the professional, Frank Jowle, holed his tee shot at the 179-yard 9th hole. As an amateur he was rewarded by the sponsors with a £30 voucher.

● 1963 – By holing out in one stroke at the 18th hole (156 yards) at Moor Park on the first day of the Esso Golden round-robin tournament, H.R. Henning, South Africa, won the £10,000 prize offered for this feat.

● 1967 – Tony Jacklin in winning the Masters tournament at St George's, Sandwich, did the 16th hole in one. His ace has an exceptional place in the records for it was seen by millions on TV, the ball was in view in its flight till it went into the hole in his final round of 64.

● 1971 – John Hudson, 25-year-old professional at Hendon, achieved a near miracle when he holed two consecutive holes-in-one in the Martini Tournament at Norwich. They were at the 11th and 12th holes (195 yards and 311 yards respectively) in the second round.

● 1971 – In the Open Championship at Birkdale, Lionel Platts holed-in-one at the 212-yard 4th hole in the second round. This was the first instance of an Open Championship hole-in-one being recorded by television. It was incidentally Platts' seventh ace of his career.

● There have been four holes-in-one in the Ryder Cup: by Peter Butler at Muirfield in 1973, Nick Faldo at the Belfry in 1993, and by Costantino Rocca and Howard Clark at Oak Hill in 1995. No American has holed in one in the Cup competition.

● 1973 – In the 1973 Open Championship at Troon, two holes-in-one were recorded, both at the 8th hole, known as the Postage Stamp, in the first round. They were achieved by Gene Sarazen and amateur David Russell, who were by coincidence respectively the oldest and youngest competitors.

● Mrs Argea Tissies, whose husband Hermann took 15 at Royal Troon's Postage Stamp 8th hole in the 1950 Open, scored a hole-in-one at the 2nd hole at

Punta Ala in the second round of the Italian Ladies' Senior Open of 1978. Exactly five years later on the same date, at the same time of day, in the same round of the same tournament at the same hole, she did it again with the same club.

● In less than two hours play in the second round of the 1989 US Open at Oak Hill Country Club, Rochester, New York, four competitors – Doug Weaver, Mark Wiebe, Jerry Pate and Nick Price – each holed the 167-yard 6th hole in one. The odds against four professionals achieving such a record in a field of 156 are reckoned at 332,000 to 1.

● On 20th May, 1998, British golf journalist Derek Lawrenson, an eight-handicapper, won a Lamborghini Diablo car, valued at over £180,000, by holing his three-iron tee shot to the 175-yard 15th hole at Mill Ride, Berkshire. He was taking part in a charity day and was partnering England football stars Paul Ince and Steve McManaman.

● David Toms took the lead in the 2001 USPGA Championship at Atlanta Athletic Club with a hole-in-one at the 15th hole in the third round and went on to win. Nick Faldo (4th hole) and Scott Hoch (17th hole) also had holes-in-one during the event.

Holing-in-One – Longest Holes

● Bob Mitera, as a 21-year-old American student, standing 5 feet 6 inches and weighing under 12 stones, claimed the world record for the longest hole-in-one. Playing over the appropriately named Miracle Hill course at Omaha, on 7th October, 1965, Bob holed his drive at the 10th hole, 447 yards long. The ground sloped sharply downhill.

● Two longer holes-in-one have been achieved, but because they were at dog-leg holes they are not generally accepted as being the longest holes-in-one. They were 496 yards (17th hole, Teign Valley) by Shaun Lynch in July 1995 and 480 yards (5th hole, Hope CC, Arkansas) by L. Bruce on 15th November, 1962.

● In March, 1961, Lou Kretlow holed his tee shot at the 427-yard 16th hole at Lake Hefner course, Oklahoma City, USA.

● The longest known hole-in-one in Great Britain was the 393-yard 7th hole at West Lancashire GC, where in 1972 the assistant professional Peter Parkinson holed his tee shot.

● Paul Neilson, a 34-year-old golfer at South Winchester, holed in one at the club's par 4 fifth hole – 391 yards.

● Other long holes-in-one recorded in Great Britain have been 380 yards (5th hole at Tankersley Park) by David Hulley in 1961; 380 yards (12th hole at White Webbs) by Danny Dunne on 30th July, 1976; 370 yards (17th hole at Chilwell Manor, distance from the forward tee) by Ray Newton in 1977; 365 yards (10th hole at Harewood Downs) by K. Saunders in 1965; 365 yards (7th hole at Catterick Garrison GC) by Leslie Bruckner on 18th July, 1980.

● The longest-recorded hole-in-one by a woman was that accomplished in September, 1949 by Marie Robie – the 393-yard hole at Furnace Brook course, Wollaston, Mass, USA.

Holing-in-One – Greatest Number by One Person

59–Amateur Norman Manley of Long Beach, California.

50–Mancil Davis, professional at the Trophy Club, Forth Worth, Texas.

31–British professional C.T. le Chevalier who died in 1973.

22–British amateur, Jim Hay of Kirkintilloch GC.

At One Hole

13–Joe Lucius at 15th hole of Mohawk, Ohio.

5–Left-hander, the late Fred Francis at 7th (now 16th) hole of Cardigan GC.

Holing-in-One – Greatest Frequency

● The greatest number of holes-in-one in a calendar year is 11, by J.O. Boydstone of California in 1962.

● John Putt of Frilford Heath GC had six holes-in-one in 1970, followed by three in 1971.

● Douglas Porteous, of Ruchill GC, Glasgow, achieved seven holes-in-one in the space of eight months. Four of them were scored in a five-day period from 26th to 30th September, 1974, in three consecutive rounds of golf. The first two were achieved at Ruchill GC in one round, the third there two days later, and the fourth at Clydebank and District GC after another two days. The following May, Porteous had three holes-in-one, the first at Linn Park GC incredibly followed by two more in the one round at Clober GC.

● Mrs Kathleen Hetherington of West Essex has holed-in-one five times, four being at the 15th hole at West Essex. Four of her five aces were within seven months in 1966.

● Mrs Dorothy Hill of Dumfries and Galloway GC holed-in-one three times in 11 days in 1977.

● James C. Reid of Brodick, aged 59 and 8 handicap in 1987, achieved 14 holes-in-one, all but one on Isle of Arran courses. His success was in spite of severe physical handicaps of a stiff left knee, a damaged right ankle, two discs removed from his back and a hip replacement.

● Jean Nield, a member at Chorlton-cum-Hardy and Bramall Park, has had eleven holes-in-one and her husband Brian, who plays at Bramall Park, has had five – a husband and wife total of 16.

Holing Successive Holes-in-One

● Successive holes-in-one are rare; successive par 4 holes-in-one may be classed as near miracles. N.L. Manley performed the most incredible feat in September, 1964, at Del Valle Country Club, Saugus, California, USA. The par 4 7th (330 yards) and 8th (290 yards) are both slightly downhill, dog-leg holes. Manley had aces at both, en route to a course record of 61 (par 71).

● The first recorded example in Britain of a player holing-in-one stroke at each of two successive holes was achieved on 6th February, 1964, at the Walmer and Kingsdown course, Kent. The young assistant professional at that club, Roger Game (aged 17) holed out with a 4-wood at the 244-yard 7th hole, and repeated the feat at the 256-yard 8th hole, using a 5-iron.

● The first occasion of holing-in-one at consecutive holes in a major professional event occurred when John Hudson, 25-year-old professional at Hendon, holed-in-one at the 11th and 12th holes at Norwich during the second round of the 1971 Martini tournament. Hudson used a 4-iron at the 195-yard 11th and a driver at the 311-yard downhill 12th hole.

● Assistant professional Tom Doty (23 years), playing in a friendly match on a course near Chicago in October, 1971, had a remarkable four-hole score which included two consecutive holes-in-one, sandwiched either side by an albatross and an eagle: 4th hole (500 yards)-2; 5th hole (360 yards dog-leg)-1; 6th hole (175 yards)-1; 7th hole (375 yards)-2. Thus he was 10 under par for four consecutive holes.

● At the Standard Life Loch Lomond tournament on the European Tour in July 2000 Jarmo Sandelin holed-in-one at the 17th with the final shot there in the third round and fellow Swede Mathias Gronberg holed-in-one with the first shot there in the last round. A prize of $100,000 was only on offer in the last round.

Holing-in-One Twice (or More) in the Same Round by the Same Person

What might be thought to be a very rare feat indeed – that of holing-in-one twice in the same round – has in fact happened on many occasions as the following instances show. It is, nevertheless, compared to the number of golfers in the world, still something of an outstanding achievement. The first known occasion was in 1907 when J. Ireland playing in a three-ball match at Worlington holed the 5th and 18th holes in one stroke and two years later in 1909 H.C. Josecelyne holed the 3rd (175 yards) and the 14th (115 yards) at Acton on 24th November.

● The first mention of two holes-in-one in a round by a woman was followed later by a similar feat by another lady at the same club. On 19th May, 1942, Mrs W. Driver, of Balgowlah Golf Club, New South Wales, holed out in one at the 3rd and 8th holes in the same round, while on 29th July, 1948, Mrs F. Burke at the same club holed out in one at the second and eighth holes.

● The Rev Harold Snider, aged 75, scored his first hole-in-one on 9th June, 1976 at the 8th hole of the Ironwood course, near Phoenix. By the end of his round he had scored three holes-in-one, the other two being at the 13th (110 yards) and 14th (135 yards). Ironwood is a par-3 course, giving more opportunity of scoring holes-in-one, but, nevertheless, three holes-in-one in one round on any type of course is an outstanding achievement.

● When the Hawarden course in North Wales comprised only nine holes, Frank Mills in 1994 had two holes-in-one at the same hole in the same round. Each time, he hit a seven iron to the 134-yard 3rd and 12th.

● The youngest player to achieve two holes-in-one in the same round is thought to be Christopher Anthony Jones on 14 September, 1994. At the age of 14 years and 11 months he holed-in-one at the Sand Moor, Leeds, 137-yard 10th hole and then at the 156-yard 17th.

● The youngest woman to have performed the feat was a 17-year-old, Marjorie Merchant, playing at the Lomas Athletic GC, Argentina, at the 4th (170 yards) and 8th (130 yards) holes.

● Tony Hannam, left-handed, handicap 16 and age 71, followed a hole-in-one at the 142 yards 4th of the Bude and North Cornwall Golf Club course with another at the 143-yard 10th on Friday, 18th September, 1992.

● Brothers Eric and John Wilkinson were playing together at the Ravensworth Golf Club on Tyneside in 2001 and both holed-in-one at the 148 yards eighth. Eric (46) played first and then John to the hidden green but there is no doubting this unusual double ace. The club's vice-captain Dave Johnstone saw both balls go in! Postman Eric plays off 9. John, a county planner, has a handicap of 20. Next time they played the hole both missed the green.

Holes-in-One on the Same Day

● In July 1987, at the Skerries Club, Co Dublin, Rank Xerox sponsored two tournaments, a men's 18-hole four-ball with 134 pairs competing and a 9-hole mixed foursomes with 33 pairs. During the day each of the four par-3 holes on the course were holed-in-one: the 2nd by Noel Bollard, the 5th by Bart Reynolds, the 12th by Jackie Carr and the 15th by Gerry Ellis.

● Wendy Russell holed-in-one at the consecutive par threes in the first round of the British Senior Ladies' at Wrexham in 1989.

● Clifford Briggs, aged 65, holed-in-one at the 14th at Parkstone GC on the same day as his wife Gwen, 60, aced the 16th.

● In the final round of the 2000 Victor Chandler British Masters at Woburn Alastair Forsyth holed-in-one at the second. Playing partner Roger Chapman then holed-in-one at the eighth.

Two Holes-in-One at the Same Hole in the Same Game

● *First in World:* George Stewart and Fred Spellmeyer at the 18th hole, Forest Hills, New Jersey, USA in October 1919.

● *First in Great Britain:* Miss G. Clutterbuck and Mrs H.M. Robinson at the 15th hole (120 yards), St Augustine GC, Ramsgate, on 8th May, 1925.

● *First in Denmark:* In a Club match in August 1987 at Himmerland, Steffan Jacobsen of Aalborg and Peter Forsberg of Himmerland halved the 15th hole in one shot, the first known occasion in Denmark.

1–2–3 – now it's a record ...

Paul Neilson, a 34-year-old agent for a fruit farm, holed in one at the 391 yards par 4 fifth at the South Winchester Golf Club – two yards short of the British longest hole-in-one record set in 1972 by Peter Parkinson at the 393 yards seventh hole at West Lancashire GC where he was assistant professional. Then the head greenkeeper and the general manager at the South Winchester club discovered that Neilson had hit off from a point three yards behind the point on the tee from where the hole had been measured and claimed the record.

... and here's another one!

During the October monthly medal at Southport & Ainsdale Golf Club on Saturday October 18 2003, three holes-in-one were achieved at the 153-yard 8th by Stuart Fawcett (5 handicap), Brian Verinder (17 handicap) and junior member Andrew Kent (12 handicap). The players were not playing in the same group.

Two aces in two days

Ken Wilbraham, a 61-year-old member at the Bramley GC, had holes-in-one on consecutive days in the 2003 Johnny Williams Cup played at Maesdu GC and Conway GC. When playing with John Millington he aced the 140 yards first hole at Maesdu on April 10 and then holed-in-one again at Conway's 15th (147 yards) on April 11 when his playing partner was Richard Watson. Mr Wilbraham, who has been playing golf for 30 years, had his only other ace in 1993 at Goal Farm Golf Club, Pirbright, in the club's weekly medal.

Evans halve hole in one!

Richard Evans and Mark Evans may not be related but they have one thing in common – they both holed in one at the same hole when playing in a club competion – only the second report of that happening according to the Hole in One Society. The double ace occurred at Glynhir Golf Club's third hole which measures 189 yards. Thirty-seven-year-old surveyor Richard, who plays off 7, hit first and made his first hole-in-one in the 15 years he has played the game. His opponent, car worker Mark whose handicap is 12, then followed him in.

Double Ace for 76-year-old Mrs Sieghart

Having two holes-in-one in the same round is not unusual but what is rare is the feat being achieved by a 76-year-old lady golfer. The lady in question is Mrs Felicity Sieghart who achieved her two holes-in-one when playing in a club Stableford competition at the Aldeburgh club. Mrs Sieghart aced the 134 yards eighth and the 130 yards 17th – but sadly did not win the competition. She may, however, be the oldest lady golfer to ace two holes in one round.

Double Ace for Best Buddies

Richard Hall, who plays off 12, and high handicapper Peter McEvoy had never had a hole-in-one until one Saturday night at Shandon Park Golf Club in Belfast. Friends since their schooldays they play a lot of golf together so there was much excitement when Hall holed his 5-iron shot for an ace at the 180 yards eighth. Then he challenged McEvoy to match it. And he did! It was only the sixth recorded time of two players acing the same hole when playing together.

● *First in Australia:* Dr & Mrs B. Rankine, playing in a mixed 'Canadian foursome' event at the Osmond Club near Adelaide, South Australia in April 1987, holed-in-one in consecutive shots at the 2nd hole (162 metres), he from the men's tee with a 3-iron and his wife from the ladies' tee with a $1^1/_2$ wood.

● Jack Ashton, aged 76, holed-in-one at the 8th hole of the West Kent Golf Club at Downe but only got a half. Opponent Ted Eagle, in receipt of shot, made a 2, net 1.

● Dr Martin Pucci and Trevor Ironside will never forget one round at the Macdonald Club in Ellon last year. Playing in an open competition the two golfers with Jamie Cowthorne making up the three-ball reached the tee at the 169yards short 11th. Dr Pucci, with the honour, hit a 5-iron, Mr Ironside a 6-iron at the hole where only the top of the flag is visible. Both hit good shots but when they reached the green they could spot only one ball   and that was Mr Cowthorne's. Then they realised that something amazing might have happened. When they reached the putting surface they discovered that both Dr Pucci's and Mr Ironside's balls were wedged into the hole. Both had made aces. It was Dr Pucci's sixth and Mr Ironside's second.

● Eric and John Wilkinson went out for their usual weekly game at the Ravensworth Golf Club in Wrekenton on Tyneside in 2001 and both holed in one at the 148 yards eighth. Neither Eric, a 46-year-old 9-handicapper who has been playing golf since he was 14, nor John, who has been playing golf for ten years and has a handicap of 20, saw the balls go in because the green is over a hill but club vice-captain Dave Johnston did and described the incident as 'amazing' Next time the brothers played the hole both missed the green!

Holing-in-One – Youngest and Oldest players

● In January 1985 Otto Bucher of Switzerland holed-in-one at the age of 99 on La Manga's 130-yard 12th hole.

● Bob Hope had a hole-in-one at Palm Springs, California, at the age of 90.

● The youngest player ever to achieve a hole in one is now believed to be Matthew Draper, who was only five when he aced the 122-yard fourth hole at Cherwell Edge, Oxfordshire, in June 1997. He used a wood.

● Six-year-old Tommy Moore aced the 145-yard fourth hole at Woodbrier, West Virginia, in 1968. He had another at the same hole before his seventh birthday.

● Alex Evans, aged eight, holed-in-one with a 4-wood at the 136-yard 4th hole at Bromborough, Merseyside, in 1994.

Holing-in-One – Miscellaneous Incidents

● Chemistry student Jason Bohn, aged 19, of State College, Pennsylvania, supported a charity golf event at Tuscaloosa, Alabama, in 1992 when twelve competitors were invited to try to hole-in-one at the 135-yard second hole for a special prize covered by insurance. One attempt only was allowed. Bohn succeeded and was offered US$1m (paid at the rate of $5,000 a month for the next 20 years) at the cost of losing his amateur status. He took the money.

● The late Harry Vardon, who scored the greatest number of victories in the Open Championship, only once did a hole-in-one. That was in 1903 at Mundesley, Norfolk, where Vardon was convalescing from a long illness.

● In a guest day at Rochford Hundred, Essex, in 1994, there were holes-in-one at all the par threes. First Paul Cairns, of Langdon Hills, holed a 4-iron at the 205-yard 15th, next Paul Francis, a member of the home club, sank a 7-iron at the 156-yard seventh and finally Jim Crabb, of Three Rivers, holed a 9-iron at the 136-yard 11th.

● In April 1988, Mary Anderson, a bio-chemistry student at Trinity College, Dublin, holed-in-one at the 290-yard 6th hole at Island GC, Co Dublin.

● In April 1984 Joseph McCaffrey and his son, Gordon, each holed-in-one in the Spring Medal at the 164-yard 12th hole at Vale of Leven Club, Dunbartonshire.

● In 1977, 14-year-old Gillian Field after a series of lessons holed-in-one at the 10th hole at Moor Place GC in her first round of golf.

● When he holed-in-one at the second hole in a match against D. Graham in the 1979 Suntory World Match Play at Wentworth, Japanese professional Isao Aoki won himself a Bovis home at Gleneagles worth, inclusive of furnishings, £55,000. Brian Barnes has aced the short 10th and Thomas Bjørn won a car when he aced the short 14th in 2003

● On the morning after being elected captain for 1973 of the Norwich GC, J.S. Murray hit his first shot as captain straight into the hole at the 169-yard 1st hole.

● At Nuneaton GC in 1999 the men's captain and the ladies' captain both holed-in-one during their captaincies.

● Using the same club and ball, 11-handicap left-hander Christopher Smyth holed-in-one at the 2nd hole (170 yards) in two consecutive medal competitions at Headfort GC, Co Meath, in January, 1976.

● Playing over Rickmansworth course at Easter, 1960, Mrs A.E. (Paddy) Martin achieved a remarkable sequence of *aces*. On Good Friday she sank her tee shot at the 3rd hole (125 yards). The next day, using the same ball and the same 8-iron, at the same hole, she scored another *one*. And on the Monday (same ball, same club, same hole) she again holed out from the tee.

● At Barton-on-Sea in February 1989 Mrs Dorothy Huntley-Flindt, aged 91, holed-in-one at the par-3 13th. The following day Mr John Chape, a fellow member in his 80s, holed the par- 3 5th in one.

● In 1995 Roy Marsland of Ratho Park, Edinburgh, had three holes in one in nine days: at Prestonfield's 5th, at Ratho Park's 3rd and at Sandilands' 2nd.

● Michael Monk, age 82, a member of Tandridge Golf Club, Surrey, waited until 1992 to record his first hole-in-one. It continued a run of rare successes for his family. In the previous 12 months, Mr Monk's daughter,

Elizabeth, 52, daughter-in-law, Celia, 48, and grandson, Jeremy, 16, had all holed in one on the same course.

● Lou Holloway, a left-hander, recorded his second hole-in-one at the Mount Derby course in New Zealand 13 years after acing the same hole while playing right-handed.

● Ryan Procop, an American schoolboy, holed-in-one at a 168-yard par 3 at Glen Eagles GC, Ohio, with a putter. He confessed that he was so disgusted with himself after a 12 on the previous hole that he just grabbed his putter and hit from the tee.

● Ernie and Shirley Marsden, of Warwick Golf Club, are believed in 1993 to have equalled the record for holes-in-one by a married couple. Each has had three, as have another English couple, Mr and Mrs B.E. Simmonds.

● Russell Pugh, a 12-handicapper from Nottinghamshire, holed-in-one twice in three days at the 274-yard par-4 18th hole at Sidmouth in Devon in 1998. The hole has a blind tee shot.

Challenge Matches

One of the first recorded professional challenge matches was in 1843 when Allan Robertson beat Willie Dunn in a 20-round match at St Andrews over 360 holes by 2 rounds and 1 to play. Thereafter until about 1905 many matches are recorded, some for up to £200 a side – a considerable sum for the time. The Morrises, the Dunns and the Parks were the main protagonists until Vardon, Braid and Taylor took over in the 1890s. Often matches were on a home-and-away basis over 72 holes or more, with many spectators; Vardon and Willie Park Jr attracted over 10,000 at North Berwick in 1899.

Between the wars Walter Hagen, Archie Compston, Henry Cotton and Bobby Locke all played several such matches. Compston surprisingly beat Hagen by 18 up and 17 to play at Moor Park in 1928; yet typically Hagen went on to win the Open the following week at Sandwich. Cotton played classic golf at Walton Heath in 1937 when he beat Densmore Shute for £500-a-side at Walton Heath by 6 and 5 over 72 holes.

Curious and Large Wagers

(See also bets recorded under **Cross-Country Matches** *and in* **Challenge Matches***)*

● In the Royal and Ancient Club minutes an entry on 3rd November, 1870 was made in the following terms:

Sir David Moncrieffe, Bart, of Moncrieffe, backs his life against the life of John Whyte-Melville, Esq, of Strathkinnes, for a new silver club as a present to the St Andrews Golf Club, the price of the club to be paid by the survivor and the arms of the parties to be engraved on the club, and the present bet inscribed on it. No balls to be attached to it. In testimony of which this bet is subscribed by the parties thereto.

Thirteen years later, Mr Whyte-Melville, in a feeling and appropriate speech, expressed his deep regret at the lamented death of Sir Robert Moncrieffe, one of the most distinguished and zealous supporters of the club. Whyte-Melville, while lamenting the cause that led to it, had pleasure in fulfilling the duty imposed upon him by the bet, and accordingly delivered to the captain the silver putter. Whyte-Melville in 1883 was elected captain of the club a second time; he died in his eighty-sixth year in July, 1883, before he could take office and the captaincy remained vacant for a year. His portrait hangs in the Royal & Ancient clubhouse and is one of the finest and most distinguished pictures in the smoking room.

● In 1914 Francis Ouimet, who in the previous autumn had won the American Open Championship after a triangular tie with Harry Vardon and Ted Ray, came to Great Britain with Jerome D. Travers, the holder of the American amateur title, to compete in the British Amateur Championship at Sandwich. An American syndicate took a bet of £30,000 to £10,000 that one or other of the two United States champions would be the winner. It only took two rounds to decide the bet against the Americans. Ouimet was beaten by a then quite unknown player, H.S. Tubbs, while Travers was defeated by Charles Palmer, who was 56 years of age at the time.

● 1907 John Ball for a wager undertook to go round Hoylake during a dense fog in under 90, in not more than two and a quarter hours and without losing a ball. Ball played with a black ball, went round in 81, and also beat the time.

● The late Ben Sayers, for a wager, played the 18 holes of the Burgess Society course scoring a four at every hole. Sayers was about to start against an American, when his opponent asked him what he could do the course in. *Fours* replied Sayers, meaning 72, or an average of 4s for the round. A bet was made, then the American added, *Remember a three or a five is not a four.* There were eight bogey 5s and two 3s on the Burgess course at the time Old Ben achieved his feat.

Feats of Endurance

Although golf is not a game where endurance, in the ordinary sense in which the term is employed in sport, is required, there are several instances of feats on the links which demanded great physical exertion.

● Four British golfers, Simon Gard, Nick Harley, Patrick Maxwell and his brother Alastair Maxwell, completed 14 rounds in one day at Iceland's Akureyri Golf Club, the most northern 18-hole course in the world, during June 1991 when there was 24-hour daylight. It was claimed a record and £10,000 was raised for charity.

● In 1971 during a 24-hour period from 6 pm on 27th November until 5.15 pm on 28th November, Ian Colston completed 401 holes over the 6,061 yards Bendigo course, Victoria, Australia. Colston was a top marathon athlete but was not a golfer. However prior to his golfing marathon he took some lessons and became adept with a 6-iron, the only club he used throughout the 401 holes. The only assistance Colston had was a team of harriers to carry his 6-iron and look

for his ball, and a band of motor-cyclists who provided light during the night. This is, as far as is known, the greatest number of holes played in 24 hours on foot on a full-size course.

● In 1934 Col Bill Farnham played 376 holes in 24 hours 10 minutes at the Guildford Lake Course, Guildford, Connecticut, using only a mashie and a putter.

● To raise funds for extending the Skipton GC course from 12 to 18 holes, the club professional, 24-year-old Graham Webster, played 277 holes in the hours of daylight on Monday 20th June, 1977. Playing with nothing longer than a 5-iron he averaged 81 per 18-hole round. Included in his marathon was a hole-in-one.

● Michael Moore, a 7 handicap 26-year-old member of Okehampton GC, completed on foot 15 rounds 6 holes (276 holes) there on Sunday, 25th June, 1972, in the hours of daylight. He started at 4.15 am and stopped at 9.15 pm. The distance covered was estimated at 56 miles.

● On 21st June, 1976, 5-handicapper Sandy Small played 15 rounds (270 holes) over his home course Cosby GC, length 6,128 yards, to raise money for the Society of Physically Handicapped Children. Using only a 5-iron, 9-iron and putter, Small started at 4.10 am and completed his 270th hole at 10.39 pm with the aid of car headlights. His fastest round was his first (40 minutes) and slowest his last (82 minutes). His best round of 76 was achieved in the second round.

● During the weekend of 20th–21st June, 1970, Peter Chambers of Yorkshire completed over 14 rounds of golf over the Scarborough South Cliff course. In a non-stop marathon lasting just under 24 hours, Chambers played 257 holes in 1,168 strokes, an average of 84.4 strokes per round.

● Bruce Sutherland, on the Craiglockhart Links, Edinburgh, started at 8.15 pm on 21st June, 1927, and played almost continuously until 7.30 pm on 22nd June, 1927. During the night four caddies with acetylene lamps lit the way, and lost balls were reduced to a minimum. He completed fourteen rounds. Mr Sutherland, who was a physical culture teacher, never recovered from the physical strain and died a few years later.

● Sidney Gleave, motorcycle racer, and Ernest Smith, golf professional at Davyhulme Club, Manchester, on 12th June, 1939, played five rounds of golf in five different countries – Scotland, Ireland, Isle of Man, England and Wales. Smith had to play the five rounds under 80 in one day to win the £100 wager. They travelled by plane, and the following was their programme:

Start 3.40a.m. at Prestwick St Nicholas (Scotland), finished 1 hour 35 minutes later on 70.

2nd Course – Bangor, Ireland. Started at 7.15 a.m. and took 1 hour 30 minutes to finish on 76.

3rd Course – Castletown, Isle of Man. Started 10.15 am, scored 76 in 1 hour 40 minutes.

4th Course – Blackpool, Stanley Park, England. Started at 1.30 pm and scored 72 in 1 hour 55 minutes.

5th Course – Hawarden, Wales, started at 6 pm and finished 2 hours 15 minutes later with a score of 72.

● On 19th June, 1995, Ian Botham, the former England cricketer, played four rounds of golf in Ireland, Wales, Scotland and England. His playing companions were Gary Price, the professional at Branston, and Tony Wright, owner of Craythorne, Burton-on-Trent, where the last 18 holes were completed. The other courses were St Margaret's, Anglesey and Dumfries & Galloway. The first round began at 4.30 am and the last was completed at 8.30 pm.

● On Wednesday, 3rd July, 1974, E.S. Wilson, Whitehead, Co Antrim and Dr G.W. Donaldson, Newry, Co. Down, played a nine-hole match in each of seven countries in the one day. The first 9 holes was at La Moye (Channel Islands) followed by Hawarden (Wales), Chester (England), Turn-berry (Scotland), Castletown (Isle of Man), Dundalk (Eire) and Warrenpoint (N Ireland). They started their first round at 4.25 am and their last round at 9.25 pm. Wilson piloted his own plane throughout.

● In June 1986 to raise money for the upkeep of his medieval church, the Rector of Mark with Allerton, Somerset, the Rev Michael Pavey, played a sponsored 18 holes on 18 different courses in the Bath & Wells Diocese. With his partner, the well-known broadcaster on music, Antony Hopkins, they played the 1st at Minehead at 5.55 am and finished playing the 18th at Burnham and Berrow at 6.05 pm. They covered 240 miles in the 'round' including the distances to reach the correct tee for the 'next' hole on each course. Par for the 'round' was 70. Together the pair raised £10,500 for the church.

● To raise funds for the Marlborough Club's centenary year (1988), Laurence Ross, the Club professional, in June 1987, played eight rounds in 12 hours. Against a par of 72, he completed the 576 holes in 3 under par, playing from back tees and walking all the way.

● As part of the 1992 Centenary Celebrations of the Royal Cinque Ports Golf Club at Deal, Kent, and to support charity, a six-handicap member, John Brazell, played all 37 royal courses in Britain and Ireland in 17 days. He won 22 matches, halved three, lost 12; hit 2,834 shots for an average score of 76.6; lost 11 balls and made 62 birdies. The aim was to raise £30,000 for Leukaemia Research and the Spastics Society.

● To raise more than £500 for the Guide Dogs for the Blind charity in the summer of 1992, Mrs Cheryle Power, a member of the Langley Park Golf Club, Beckenham, Kent, played 100 holes in a day – starting at 5 am and finishing at 8.45 pm.

● David Steele, a former European Tour player, completed $17^{1}/_{2}$ rounds, 315 holes, between 6 am and 9.45 pm in 1993 at the San Roque club near Gibraltar in a total of 1,291 shots. Steele was assisted by a caddie cart and raised £15,000 for charity.

Fastest Rounds

● Dick Kimbrough, 41, completed a round on foot on 8th August, 1972, at North Platte CC, Nebraska (6,068 yards) in 30 minutes 10 seconds. He carried only a 3-iron.

● At Mowbray Course, Cape Town, November 1931, Len Richardson, who had represented South Africa in the Olympic Games, played a round which measured 6,248 yards in 31 minutes 22 seconds.

● The women's all-time record for the fastest round played on a course of at least 5,600 yards is held by Sue Ledger, 20, who completed the East Berks course in 38 minutes 8 seconds, beating the previous record by 17 minutes.

● In April, 1934, after attending a wedding in Bournemouth, Hants, Captain Gerald Moxom hurried to his club, West Hill in Surrey, to play in the captain's prize competition. With daylight fading and still dressed in his morning suit, he went round in 65 minutes and won the competition with a net 71 into the bargain.

● On 14th June, 1922, Jock Hutchison and Joe Kirkwood (Australia) played round the Old Course at St Andrews in 1 hour 20 minutes. Hutchison, out in 37, led by three holes at the ninth and won by 4 and 3.

● Fastest rounds can also take another form – the time taken for a ball to be propelled round 18 holes. The fastest known round of this type is 8 minutes 53.8 seconds on 25th August, 1979 by 42 members at Ridgemount CC Rochester, New York, a course measuring 6,161 yards. The Rules of Golf were observed but a ball was available on each tee; to be driven off the instant the ball had been holed at the preceding hole.

● The fastest round with the same ball took place in January 1992 at the Paradise Golf Club, Arizona. It took only 11 minutes 24 seconds; 91 golfers being positioned around the course ready to hit the ball as soon as it came to rest and then throwing the ball from green to tee.

● In 1992 John Daly and Mark Calcavecchia were both fined by the USPGA Tour for playing the final round of the Players' Championship in Florida in 123 minutes. Daly scored 80, Calcavecchia 81.

Curious Scoring

● C.W. Allen of Leek Golf Club chipped-in four times in a round in which he was partnered by K. Brint against G. Davies and R. Hollins. The shortest chip was a yard, the longest 20 yards.

● Tony Blackwell, playing off a handicap of four, broke the course record at Bull Bay, Anglesey, by four strokes when he had a gross 60 (net 56) in winning the club's town trophy in 1996. The course measured 6,217 yards.

● In the third round of the 1994 Volvo PGA Championship at Wentworth, Des Smyth, of Ireland, made birdie twos at each of the four short holes, the 2nd, 5th, 10th and 14th. He also had a two at the second hole in the fourth round.

● Also at Wentworth, in the 1994 World Match Play Championship, Seve Ballesteros had seven successive twos at the short holes – and still lost his quarter-final against Ernie Els.

● R.H. Corbett, playing in the semi-final of the Tangye Cup at Mullion in 1916, did a score of 27. The remarkable part of Corbett's score was that it was made up of nine successive 3s, bogey being 5, 3, 4, 4, 5, 3, 4, 4, 3.

● At Little Chalfont in June 1985 Adrian Donkersley played six successive holes in 6, 5, 4, 3, 2, 1 from the 9th to the 14th holes against a par of 4, 4, 3, 4, 3, 3.

● On 2nd September, 1920, playing over Torphin, near Edinburgh, William Ingle did the first five holes in 1, 2, 3, 4, 5.

● In the summer of 1970, Keith McMillan, on holiday at Cullen, had a remarkable series of 1, 2, 3, 4, 5 at the 11th to 15th holes.

● Marc Osborne was only 14 years of age when he equalled the Betchworth Park amateur course record with a 66 in July, 1993. He was playing in the Mortimer Cup, a 36-hole medal competition, and had at the time a handicap of 6.8.

● Playing at Addington Palace, July, 1934, Ronald Jones, a member of Hendon Club, holed five consecutive holes in 5, 4, 3, 2, 1.

● Harry Dunderdale of Lincoln GC scored 5, 4, 3, 2, 1 in five consecutive holes during the first round of his club championship in 1978. The hole-in-one was the 7th, measuring 294 yards.

● At the Open Amateur Tournament of the Royal Ashdown Forest in 1936 Bobby Locke in his morning round had a score of 72, accomplishing every hole in 4.

● George Stewart of Cupar had a four at every hole over the Queen's course at Gleneagles despite forgetting to change into his golf shoes and therefore still wearing his street shoes.

● Henry Cotton told of one of the most extraordinary scoring feats ever. With some other professionals he was at Sestrieres in the 30s for the Italian Open Championship and Joe Ezar, a colourful character in those days on both sides of the Atlantic, accepted a wager from a club official – 1,000 lira for a 66 to break the course record; 2,000 for a 65; and 4,000 for a 64. *I'll do 64*, said Ezar, and proceeded to jot down the hole-by-hole score figures he would do next day for that total. With the exception of the ninth and tenth holes where his predicted score was 3, 4 and the actual score was 4, 3, he accomplished this amazing feat exactly as nominated.

● Nick Faldo scored par figures at all 18 holes in the final round of the 1987 Open Championship at Muirfield to win the title.

● During the Colts Championship at Knowle Golf Club, Bristol, Chris Newman (Cotswold Hills) scored eight consecutive 3s with birdies at four of the holes.

● At the Toft Hotel Golf Club captain's day event L. Heffernan had an ace, D. Patrick a 2, R. Barnett a 3 and D. Heffernan a 4 at the 240 yard par-4 ninth.

● In the European Club Championship played at the Parco de Medici Club in Rome in 1998, Belgian

Dimitri van Hauwaert from Royal Antwerp had an albatross 2, Norwegian Marius Bjornstad from Oslo an eagle 3 and Scotsman Andrew Hogg from Turriff a birdie 4 at the 486 metre par-5 eighth hole.

High Scores

● In the qualifying competition at Formby for the 1976 Open Championship, Maurice Flitcroft, a 46-year-old crane driver from Barrow-in-Furness, took 121 strokes for the first round and then withdrew saying, *I have no chance of qualifying*. Flitcroft entered as a professional but had never before played 18 holes. He had taken the game up 18 months previously but, as he was not a member of a club, had been limited to practising on a local beach. His round was made up thus: 7, 5, 6, 6, 6, 6, 12, 6, 7-61; 11, 5, 6, 8, 4, 9, 5, 7, 5-60, total 121. After his round Flitcroft said, 'I've made a lot of progress in the last few months and I'm sorry I did not do better. I was trying too hard at the beginning but began to put things together at the end of the round.' R&A officials, who were not amused by the bogus professional's efforts, refunded the £30 entry money to Flitcroft's two fellow-competitors. Flitcroft has since tried to qualify for the Open under assumed names: Gerard Hoppy from Switzerland and Beau Jolley (as in the wine)!

● Playing in the qualifying rounds of the 1965 Open Championship at Southport, an American self-styled professional entrant from Milwaukee, Walter Danecki, achieved the inglorious feat of scoring a total of 221 strokes for 36 holes, 81 over par. His first round over the Hillside course was 108, followed by a second round of 113. Walter, who afterwards admitted he felt *a little discouraged and sad*, declared that he entered because he was *after the money*.

● The highest individual scoring ever known in the rounds connected with the Open Championship occurred at Muirfield, 1935, when a Scottish professional started 7, 10, 5, 10, and took 65 to reach the 9th hole. Another 10 came at the 11th and the player decided to retire at the 12th hole. There he was in a bunker, and after playing four shots he had not regained the fairway.

● In 1883 in the Open Championship at Musselburgh, Willie Fernie, the winner, had a 10, the only time double figures appeared on the card of the Open Champion of the year. Fernie won after a tie with Bob Ferguson, and his score for the last hole in the tie was 2. He holed from just off the green to win by one stroke.

● In the first Open Championship at Prestwick in 1860 a competitor took 21, the highest score for one hole ever recorded in this event. The record is preserved in the archives of the Prestwick Golf Club, where the championship was founded.

● In the first round of the 1980 US Masters, Tom Weiskopf hit his ball into the water hazard in front of the par-3 12th hole five times and scored 13 for the hole.

● In the French Open at St Cloud, in 1968, Brian Barnes took 15 for the short 8th hole in the second round. After missing putts at which he hurriedly snatched while the ball was moving he penalised himself further by standing astride the line of a putt. The amazing result was that he actually took 12 strokes from about three feet from the hole. The highest scores on the European Tour were also recorded in the French Open. Philippe Porquier had a 20 at La Baule in 1978 and Ian Woosnam a 16 at La Boulie in 1986.

● US professional Dave Hill 6-putted the fifth green at Oakmont in the 1962 US Open Championship.

● Many high scores have been made at the Road Hole at St Andrews. Davie Ayton, on one occasion, was coming in a certain winner of the Open Championship when he got on the road and took 11. In 1921, at the Open Championship, one professional took 13. In 1923, competing for the Autumn Medal of the Royal & Ancient, J.B. Anderson required a five and a four to win the second award, but he took 13 at the Road Hole. Anderson was close to the green in two, was twice in the bunkers in the face of the green, and once on the road. In 1935, R.H. Oppenheimer tied for the Royal Medal (the first award) in the Autumn Meeting of the Royal & Ancient. On the play-off he was one stroke behind Captain Aitken when they stood on the 17th tee. Oppenheimer drove three balls out of bounds and eventually took 11 to the Road Hole.

● British professional Mark James scored 111 in the second round of the 1978 Italian Open. He played the closing holes with only his right hand due to an injury to his left hand.

● In the 1927 Shawnee Open, Tommy Armour took 23 strokes to the 17th hole. Armour had won the American Open Championship a week earlier. In an effort to play the hole in a particular way, Armour hooked ball after ball out of bounds and finished with a 21 on the card. There was some doubt about the accuracy of this figure and on reaching the clubhouse Armour stated that it should be 23. This is the highest score by a professional in a tournament.

Freak Matches

● In 1912, the late Harry Dearth, an eminent vocalist, attired in a complete suit of heavy armour, played a match at Bushey Hall. He was beaten 2 and 1.

● In 1914, at the start of the First World War, J.N. Farrar, a native of Hoylake, was stationed at Royston, Herts. A bet was made of 10-1 that he would not go round Royston under 100 strokes, equipped in full infantry marching order, water bottle, full field kit and haversack. Farrar went round in 94. At the camp were several golfers, including professionals, who tried the same feat but failed.

● Captain Pennington took part in a match *from the air* against A.J. Young, the professional at Sonning. Captain Pennington, with 80 golf balls in the locker of his machine, had to find the Sonning greens by dropping the balls as he circled over the course. The balls were covered in white cloth to ensure that they did not bounce once they struck the ground. The airman completed the course in 40 minutes, taking 29 *strokes*,

while Young occupied two hours for his round of 68. Captain Pennington was eventually killed in an air crash in 1933.

● In April 1924, at Littlehampton, Harry Rowntree, an amateur golfer, played the better ball of Edward Ray and George Duncan, receiving an allowance of 150 yards to use as he required during the round. Rowntree won by 6 and 5 and had used only 50 yards 2 feet of his handicap. At one hole Duncan had a two – Rowntree, who was 25 yards from the hole, took this distance from his handicap and won the hole in one. Ray (died 1945) afterwards declared that, conceding a handicap of one yard per round, he could win every championship in the world. And he might, when reckoning is taken of the number of times a putt just stops an inch or two or how much difference to a shot three inches will make for the lie of the ball, either in a bunker or on the fairway. Many single matches on the same system have been played. An 18 handicap player opposed to a scratch player should make a close match with an allowance of 50 yards.

● The first known instance of a golf match by telephone occurred in 1957, when the Cotswold Hills Golf Club, Cheltenham, England, won a golf tournament against the Cheltenham Golf Club, Melbourne, Australia, by six strokes. A large crowd assembled at the English club to wait for the 12,000 miles telephone call from Australia. The match had been played at the suggestion of a former member of the Cotswold Hills Club, Harry Davies, and was open to every member of the two clubs. The result of the match was decided on the aggregate of the eight best scores on each side and the English club won by 564 strokes to 570.

Golf Matches Against Other Sports

● H.H. Hilton and Percy Ashworth, many times racket champion, contested a driving match, the former driving a golf ball with a driver, and the latter a racket ball with a racket. Best distances: Against breeze – Golfer 182 yards; Racket player 125 yards. Down wind – Golfer 230 yards; Racket player 140 yards. Afterwards Ashworth hit a golf ball with the racket and got a greater distance than with the racket ball, but was still a long way behind the ball driven by Hilton.

● In 1913, at Wellington, Shropshire, a match between a golfer and a fisherman casting a $2\frac{1}{2}$ oz weight was played. The golfer, Rupert May, took 87; the fisherman J.J.D. Mackinlay, in difficulty because of his short casts, 102. His longest cast, 105 yards, was within 12 yards of the world record at the time, held by French angler, Decautelle. When within a rod's length of a hole he ran the weight to the rod end and dropped into the hole. Five times he broke his line, and was allowed another shot without penalty.

● In December, 1913, F.M.A. Webster, of the London Athletic Club, and Dora Roberts, with javelins, played a match with the late Harry Vardon and Mrs

Gordon Robertson, who used the regulation clubs and golf balls. The golfers conceded two-thirds in the matter of distance, and they won by 5 up and 4 to play in a contest of 18 holes. The javelin throwers had a mark of two feet square in which to *hole out* while the golfers had to get their ball into the ordinary golf hole. Mr Webster's best throw was one of 160 feet.

● Several matches have taken place between a golfer on the one side and an archer on the other. The wielder of the bow and arrow has nearly always proved the victor. In 1953 at Kirkhill Golf Course, Lanarkshire, five archers beat six golfers by two games to one. There were two special rules for the match; when an archer's arrow landed six feet from the hole or the golfer's ball three feet from the hole, they were counted as holed. When the arrows landed in bunkers or in the rough, archers lifted their arrow and added a stroke. The sixth archer in this match called off and one archer shot two arrows from each of the 18 tees.

● In 1954, at the Southbroom Club, South Africa, a match over 9 holes was played between an archer and a fisherman against two golfers. The participants were all champions of their own sphere and consisted of Vernon Adams (archer), Dennis Burd (fisherman), Jeanette Wahl (champion of Southbroom and Port Shepstone), and Ron Burd (professional at Southbroom). The conditions were that the archer had holed out when his arrows struck a small leather bag placed on the green beside the hole and in the event of his placing his approach shot within a bow's length of the pin he was deemed to have 1-putted. The fisherman, to achieve a 1-putt, had to land his sinker within a rod's length of the pin. The two golfers were ahead for brief spells, but it was the opposition who led at the deciding 9th hole where *Robin Hood* played a perfect approach for a birdie.

● An *Across England* combined match was begun on 11th October, 1965, by four golfers and two archers from Crowborough Beacon Golf Club, Sussex, accompanied by *Penny*, a white Alsatian dog, whose duty it was to find lost balls. They teed off from Carlisle Castle via Hadrian's Wall, the Pennine Way, finally holing out in the 18th hole at Newcastle United GC in 612 teed shots. Casualties included 110 lost golf balls and 19 lost or broken arrows. The match took 5½ days, and the distance travelled was about 60 miles. The golfers were Miss P. Ward, K. Meaney, K. Ashdown and C.A. Macey; the archers were W.H. Hulme and T. Scott. The first arrow was fired from the battlements of Carlisle Castle, a distance of nearly 300 yards, by Cumberland Champion R. Willis, who also fired the second arrow right across the River Eden. R. Clough, president of Newcastle United GC, holed the last two putts. The match was in aid of *Guide Dogs for the Blind* and *Friends of Crowborough Hospital*.

Cross-country Matches

● Taking 1 year, 114 days, Floyd Rood golfed his way from coast to coast across the United States. He

took 114,737 shots including 3,511 penalty shots for the 3,397 mile course.

● Two Californian teenagers, Bob Aube (17) and Phil Marrone (18) went on a golfing safari in 1974 from San Francisco to Los Angeles, a trip of over 500 miles lasting 16 days. The first six days they played alongside motorways. Over 1,000 balls were used.

● In 1830, the Gold Medal winner of the Royal & Ancient backed himself for 10 sovereigns to drive from the 1st hole at St Andrews to the toll bar at Cupar, distance nine miles, in 200 teed shots. He won easily.

● In 1848, two Edinburgh golfers played a match from Bruntsfield Links to the top of Arthur's Seat – an eminence overlooking the Scottish capital, 822 feet above sea level.

● On a winter's day in 1898, Freddie Tait backed himself to play a gutta ball in 40 teed shots from Royal St George's Clubhouse, Sandwich, to the Cinque Ports Club, Deal. He was to hole out by hitting any part of the Deal Clubhouse. The distance as the crow flies was three miles. The redoubtable Tait holed out with his 32nd shot, so effectively that the ball went through a window.

● In 1900 three members of the Hackensack (NJ) Club played a game of four-and-a-half hours over an extemporised course six miles long, which stretched from Hackensack to Paterson. Despite rain, cornfields, and wide streams, the three golfers – J.W. Hauleebeek, Dr E.R. Pfaare, and Eugene Crassons – completed the round, the first and the last named taking 305 strokes each, and Dr Pfaare 327 strokes. The players used only two clubs, the mashie and the cleek.

● On 3rd December, 1920, P. Rupert Phillips and W. Raymond Thomas teed up on the first tee of the Radyr Golf Club and played to the last hole at Southerndown. The distance as the crow flies was 15½ miles, but circumventing swamps, woods, and plough, they covered, approximately, 20 miles. The wager was that they would not do the hole in 1,000 strokes, but they holed out at their 608th stroke two days later. They carried large ordnance maps.

● On 12th March, 1921, A. Stanley Turner, Macclesfield, played from his house to the Cat and Fiddle Inn, five miles distance, in 64 strokes. The route was broken and hilly with a rise of nearly 1,000 feet. Turner was allowed to tee up within two club lengths after each shot and the wagering was 6-4 against his doing the distance in 170 strokes.

● In 1919, a golfer drove a ball from Piccadilly Circus and, proceeding via the Strand, Fleet Street and Ludgate Hill, *holed out* at the Royal Exchange, London. The player drove off at 8 am on a Sunday, a time when the usually thronged thoroughfares were deserted.

● On 23rd April, 1939, Richard Sutton, a London stockbroker, played from Tower Bridge, London, to White's Club, St James's Street, in 142 strokes. The bet was he would not do *the course* in under 200 shots. Sutton used a putter, crossed the Thames at Southwark Bridge, and hit the ball short distances to keep out of trouble.

● Golfers produced the most original event in Ireland's three-week national festival of An Tostal, in 1953 – a cross-country competition with an advertised £1,000,000 for the man who could hole out in one. The 150 golfers drove off from the first tee at Kildare Club to hole out eventually on the 18th green, five miles away, on the nearby Curragh course, a distance of 8,800 yards. The unusual hazards to be negotiated included the main Dublin-Cork railway line and highway, the Curragh Racecourse, hoofprints left by Irish thoroughbred racehorses out exercising on the plains from nearby stables, army tank tracks and about 150 telephone lines. The Golden Ball Trophy, which is played for annually – a standard size golf ball in gold, mounted on a black marble pillar beside the silver figure of a golfer on a green marble base, designed by Captain Maurice Cogan, Army GHQ, Dublin – was for the best gross. And it went to one of the longest hitters in international golf – Amateur Champion, Irish internationalist and British Walker Cup player Joe Carr, with the remarkable score of 52.

● In 1961, as a University Charities Week stunt, four Aberdeen University students set out to golf their way up Ben Nevis (4,406 feet). About half-way up, after losing 63 balls and expending 659 strokes, the quartet conceded victory to Britain's highest mountain.

● Among several cross-country golfing exploits, one of the most arduous was faced by Iain Williamson and Tony Kent, who teed off from Cained Point on the summit of Fairfield in the Lake District. With the hole cut in the lawn of the Bishop of Carlisle's home at Rydal Park, it measured 7,200 yards and passed through the summits of Great Rigg Mann, Heron Pike and Nab Scar, descending altogether 1,900 feet. Eight balls were lost and the two golfers holed out in a combined total of 303 strokes.

Long-lived Golfers

● James Priddy, aged 80, played in the Seniors' Open at his home club, Weston-super-Mare, Avon, on 27th June, 1990, and scored a gross 70 to beat his age by ten shots.

● The oldest golfer who ever lived is believed to have been Arthur Thompson of British Columbia, Canada. He equalled his age when 103 at Uplands GC, a course of over 6,000 yards. He died two years later.

● Nathaniel Vickers celebrated his 103rd birthday on Sunday, 9th October, 1949, and died the following day. He was the oldest member of the United States Senior Golf Association and until 1942 he competed regularly in their events and won many trophies in the various age divisions. When 100 years old, he apologised for being able to play only nine holes a day. Vickers predicted he would live until 103 and he died a few hours after he had celebrated his birthday.

● American George Miller, who died in 1979 aged 102, played regularly when 100 years old.

● In 1999 94-year-old Mr W. Seneviratne, a retired schoolmaster who lived and worked in Malaysia, was

still practising every day and regularly competing in medal competitions at the Royal Colombo Golf Club which was founded in 1879.

● Phyllis Tidmarsh, aged 90, won a Stableford competition at Saltford Golf Club, near Bath, when she returned 42 points. Her handicap was cut from 28 to 27.

● George Swanwick, a member of Wallasey, celebrated his 90th birthday with a lunch at the club on 1st April, 1971. He played golf several times a week, carrying his own clubs, and had holed-in-one at the ages of 75 and 85. His ambition was to complete the sequence aged 95 … but he died in 1973 aged 92.

● The 10th Earl of Wemyss played a round on his 92nd birthday, in 1910, at Craigielaw. At the age of 87 the Earl was partnered by Harry Vardon in a match at Kilspindie, the golf course on his East Lothian estate at Gosford. After playing his ball the venerable earl mounted a pony and rode to the next shot. He died on 30th June, 1914.

● F.L. Callender, aged 78, in September 1932, played nine consecutive rounds in the Jubilee Vase, St Andrews. He was defeated in the ninth, the final round, by 4 and 2. Callender's handicap was 12. This is the best known achievement of a septuagenarian in golf.

● George Evans shot a remarkable one over par 71 at Brockenhurst Manor – remarkable because Mr Evans was 87 at the time. Playing with him that day was Hampshire, Isle of Wight and Channel Islands President John Nettell and former Ferndown pro Doug Sewell. 'It's good to shoot a score under your age, but when its 16 shots better that must be a record', said Mr Nettell. Mr Evans qualified for four opens while professional at West Hill, Surrey.

● Bernard Matthews, aged 82, of Banstead Downs Club, handicap 6, holed the course in 72 gross in August 1988. A week later he holed it in 70, twelve shots below his age. He came back in 31, finishing 4, 3, 3, 2, 3, against a par of 5, 4, 3, 3, 4. Mr Matthews's eclectic score at his Club is 37, or one over 2's.

Playing in the Dark

On numerous occasions it has been necessary to hold lamps, lighted candles, or torches at holes in order that players might finish a competition. Large entries, slow play, early darkness and an eclipse of the sun have all been causes of playing in darkness.

● Since 1972, the Whitburn Golf Club at South Shields, Tyne and Wear, has held an annual Summer Solstice Competition. All competitors, who draw lots for starting tees, must begin before 4.24 and 13 seconds am, the time the sun rises over the first hole on the longest day of the year.

● At the Open Championship in Musselburgh in November 1889 many players finished when the light had so far gone that the adjacent street lamps were lit. The cards were checked by candlelight. Several players who had no chance of the championship were paid small sums to withdraw in order to permit others who had a chance to finish in daylight. This was the last championship at Musselburgh.

● At the Southern Section of the PGA tournament on 25th September, 1907, at Burnham Beeches, several players concluded the round by the aid of torch lights placed near the holes.

● In the Irish Open Championship at Portmarnock in September, 1907, a tie in the third round between W.C. Pickeman and A. Jeffcott was postponed owing to darkness, at the 22nd hole. The next morning Pickeman won at the 24th.

● The qualifying round of the American Amateur Championship in 1910 could not be finished in one day, and several competitors had to stop their round on account of darkness, and complete it early in the morning of the following day.

● On 10th January, 1926, in the final of the President's Putter, at Rye, E.F. Storey and R.H. Wethered were all square at the 24th hole. It was 5 pm and so dark that, although a fair crowd was present, the balls could not be followed. The tie was abandoned and the Putter held jointly for the year. Each winner of the Putter affixes the ball he played; for 1926 there are two balls, respectively engraved with the names of the finalists.

● In the 1932 Walker Cup contest at Brooklyn, a total eclipse of the sun occurred.

● At Perth, on 14th September, 1932, a competition was in progress under good clear evening light, and a full bright moon. The moon rose at 7.10 and an hour later came under eclipse to the earth's surface. The light then became so bad that on the last three greens competitors holed out by the aid of the light from matches.

● At Carnoustie, 1932, in the competition for the *Craw's Nest Tassie* the large entry necessitated competitors being sent off in 3-ball matches. The late players had to be assisted by electric torches flashed on the greens.

● In February, 1950, Max Faulkner and his partner, R. Dolman, in a Guildford Alliance event finished their round in complete darkness. A photographer's flash bulbs were used at the last hole to direct Faulkner's approach. Several of the other competitors also finished in darkness. At the last hole they had only the light from the clubhouse to aim at and one played his approach so boldly that he put his ball through the hall doorway and almost into the dressing room.

● On the second day of the 1969 Ryder Cup contest, the last 4-ball match ended in near total darkness on the 18th green at Royal Birkdale. With the help of the clubhouse lights the two American players, Lee Trevino and Miller Barber, along with Tony Jacklin for Britain each faced putts of around five feet to win their match. All missed and their game was halved.

The occasions mentioned above all occurred in competitions where it was not intended to play in the dark. There are, however, numerous instances where players set out to play in the dark either for bets or for novelty.

● On 29th November, 1878, R.W. Brown backed himself to go round the Hoylake links in 150 strokes, starting at 11 pm. The conditions of the match were

that Mr Brown was only to be penalised *loss of distance* for a lost ball, and that no one was to help him to find it. He went round in 147 strokes, and won his bet by the narrow margin of three strokes.

● In 1876 David Strath backed himself to go round St Andrews under 100, in moonlight. He took 95, and did not lose a ball.

● In September 1928, at St Andrews, the first and last holes were illuminated by lanterns, and at 11 pm four members of the Royal and Ancient set out to play a foursome over the 2 holes. Electric lights, lanterns, and rockets were used to brighten the fairway, and the headlights of motor cars parked on Links Place formed a helpful battery. The 1st hole was won in four, and each side got a five at the 18th. About 1,000 spectators followed the freak match, which was played to celebrate the appointment of Angus Hambro to the captaincy of the club.

● In 1931, Rufus Stewart, professional, Kooyonga Club, South Australia, and former Australian Open Champion, played 18 holes of exhibition golf at night without losing a single ball over the Kooyonga course, and completed the round in 77.

● At Ashley Wood Golf Club, Blandford, Dorset, a night-time golf tournament was arranged annually with up to 180 golfers taking part over four nights. Over £6000 has been raised in four years for the Muscular Dystrophy Charity.

● At Pannal, 3rd July, 1937, R.H. Locke, playing in bright moonlight, holed his tee shot at the 15th hole, distance 220 yards, the only known case of holing-in-one under such conditions.

Fatal and Other Accidents on the Links

The history of golf is, unfortunately, marred by a great number of fatal accidents on or near the course. In the vast majority of such cases they have been caused either by careless swinging of the club or by an un-controlled shot when the ball has struck a spectator or bystander. In addition to the fatal accidents there is an even larger number on record which have resulted in serious injury or blindness. We do not propose to list these accidents except where they have some unusual feature. We would remind all golfers of the tragic consequences which have so often been caused by momentary carelessness. The fatal accidents which follow have an unusual cause and other accidents given may have their humorous aspect.

● English tournament professional Richard Boxall was three shots off the lead in the third round of the 1991 Open Championship when he fractured his left leg driving from the 9th tee at Royal Birkdale. He was taken from the course to hospital by ambulance and was listed in the official results as 'retired' which entitled him to a consolation prize of £3000.

A month later, Russell Weir of Scotland, was competing in the European Teaching Professionals' Championship near Rotterdam when he also fractured his left leg driving from the 7th tee in the first round.

● In July, 1971, Rudolph Roy, aged 43, was killed at a Montreal course; in playing out of woods, the shaft of his club snapped, rebounded off a tree and the jagged edge plunged into his body.

● Harold Wallace, aged 75, playing at Lundin Links with two friends in 1950, was crossing the railway line which separates the fifth green and sixth tee, when a light engine knocked him down and he was killed instantly.

● In the summer of 1963, Harold Kalles, of Toronto, Canada, died six days after his throat had been cut by a golf club shaft, which broke against a tree as he was trying to play out of a bunker.

● At Jacksonville, Florida, on 18th March, 1952, two women golfers were instantly killed when hit simultaneously by the whirling propeller of a navy fighter plane. They were playing together when the plane with a dead engine coming in out of control, hit them from behind.

● In May, 1993, at Ponoka Community GC, Alberta, Canada, Richard McCulough hit a poor tee shot on the 13th hole and promptly smashed his driver angrily against a golf cart. The head of the driver and six inches of shaft flew through the air, piercing McCulough's throat and severing his carotid artery. He died in hospital.

● Britain's first national open event for competitors aged over 80, at Moortown, Leeds in September, 1992, was marred when 81-year-old Frank Hart collapsed on the fourth tee and died. Play continued and Charles Mitchell, aged 80, won the Stableford competition with a gross score of 81 for 39 points.

● Playing in the 1993 Carlesburg-Tetley Cornish Festival at Tehidy Park, Ian Cornwell was struck on the leg by a wayward shot from a player two groups behind. Later, as he was leaving the 16th green, he was hit again, this time below the ear, by the same player, knocking him unconscious. This may be the first time that a player has been hit twice in the same round by the same player.

Lightning on the Links

There have been a considerable number of fatal and serious accidents through players and caddies having been struck by lightning on the course. The Royal & Ancient and the USGA have, since 1952, provided for discontinuance of play during lightning storms under the Rules of Golf (Rule 37, 6) and the United States Golf Association has given the following guide for personal safety during thunderstorms:

   (a) Do not go out of doors or remain out during thunderstorms unless it is necessary. Stay inside of a building where it is dry, preferably away from fireplaces, stoves, and other metal objects.

   (b) If there is any choice of shelter, choose in the following order:
      1. Large metal or metal-frame buildings.
      2. Dwellings or other buildings which are protected against lightning.
      3. Large unprotected buildings.
      4. Small unprotected buildings.

(c) If remaining out of doors is unavoidable, keep away from:
1. Small sheds and shelters if in an exposed location.
2. Isolated trees.
3. Wire fences.
4. Hilltops and wide open spaces.

(d) Seek shelter in:
1. A cave.
2. A depression in the ground.
3. A deep valley or canyon.
4. The foot of a steep or overhanging cliff.
5. Dense woods.
6. A grove of trees.

Note – Raising golf clubs or umbrellas above the head is dangerous.

● A serious incident with lightning involving well-known golfers was at the 1975 Western Open in Chicago when Lee Trevino, Jerry Heard and Bobby Nichols were all struck and had to be taken to hospital. At the same time Tony Jacklin had a club thrown 15 feet out of his hands.
● Two well-known competitors were struck by lightning in 1977. They were Mark James of Britain in the Swiss Open and Severiano Ballesteros of Spain in the Scandinavian Open. Fortunately neither appeared to be badly injured.
● Two spectators were killed by lightning in 1991: one at the US Open and the other at US PGA Championship.

Spectators Interfering with Balls

● Deliberate interference by spectators with balls in play during important money matches was not unknown in the old days when there was intense rivalry between the *schools* of Musselburgh, St Andrews, and North Berwick, and disputes arose in stake matches caused by the action of spectators in kicking the ball into either a favourable or an unfavourable position.
● Tom Morris, in his last match with Willie Park at Musselburgh, refused to go on because of interference by the spectators, and in the match on the same course about 40 years later, in 1895, between Willie Park Jr and J.H. Taylor, the barracking of the crowd and interference with play was so bad that when the Park-Vardon match came to be arranged in 1899, Vardon refused to accept Musselburgh as a venue.
● Even in modern times spectators have been known to interfere deliberately with players' balls, though it is usually by children. In the 1972 Penfold Tournament at Queen's Park, Bournemouth, Christy O'Connor Jr had his ball stolen by a young boy, but not being told of this at the time had to take the penalty for a lost ball. O'Connor finished in a tie for first place, but lost the play-off.
● In 1912 in the last round of the final of the Amateur Championship at Westward Ho! between Abe Mitchell and John Ball, the drive of the former to the short 14th

hit an open umbrella held by a lady protecting herself from the heavy rain, and instead of landing on the green the ball was diverted into a bunker. Mitchell, who was leading at the time by 2 holes, lost the hole and Ball won the Championship at the 38th hole.
● In the match between the professionals of Great Britain and America at Southport in 1937 a dense crowd collected round the 15th green waiting for the Sarazen-Alliss match. The American's ball landed in the lap of a woman, who picked it up and threw it so close to the hole that Sarazen got a two against Alliss' three.
● In a memorable tie between Bobby Jones and Cyril Tolley in the 1930 Amateur Championship at St Andrews, Jones' approach to the 17th green struck spectators massed at the left end of the green and led to controversy as to whether it would otherwise have gone on to the famous road. Jones himself had deliberately played for that part of the green and had requested stewards to get the crowd back. Had the ball gone on to the road, the historic Jones Quadrilateral of the year – the Open and Amateur Championships of Britain and the United States – might not have gone into the records.
● In the 1983 Suntory World Match Play Championship at Wentworth Nick Faldo hit his second shot over the green at the 16th hole into a group of spectators. To everyone's astonishment and discomfiture the ball reappeared on the green about 30ft from the hole, propelled there by a thoroughly misguided and anonymous spectator. The referee ruled that Faldo should play the ball where it lay on the green. Faldo's opponent, Graham Marsh, understandably upset by the incident, took three putts against Faldo's two, thus losing a hole he might well otherwise have won. Faldo won the match 2 and 1, but lost in the final to Marsh's fellow Australian Greg Norman by 3 and 2.

Golf Balls Killing Animals and Fish, and Incidents with Animals

● An astounding fatality to an animal through being hit by a golf ball occurred at St Margaret's-at-Cliffe Golf Club, Kent on 13th June, 1934, when W.J. Robinson, the professional, killed a cow with his tee shot to the 18th hole. The cow was standing in the fairway about 100 yards from the tee, and the ball struck her on the back of the head. She fell like a log, but staggered to her feet and walked about 50 yards before dropping again. When the players reached her she was dead.
● J.W. Perret, of Ystrad Mynach, playing with Chas R. Halliday, of Ralston, in the qualifying rounds of the Society of One Armed Golfers' Championship over the Darley course, Troon, on 27th August, 1935, killed two gulls at successive holes with his second shots. The *deadly* shots were at the 1st and 2nd holes.
● On the first day of grouse shooting of the 1975 season (12th August), 11-year-old schoolboy Willie Fraser, of Kingussie, beat all the guns when he killed a grouse with his tee shot on the local course.

● On 10th June, 1904, while playing in the Edinburgh High Constables' Competition at Kilspindie, Captain Ferguson sent a long ball into the rough at the Target hole, and on searching for it found that it had struck and killed a young hare.

● Playing in a mixed open tournament at the Waimairi Beach Golf Club in Christchurch, New Zealand, in the summer of 1961, Mrs R.T. Challis found her ball in fairly long spongy grass where a placing rule applied. She picked up, placed the ball and played her stroke. A young hare leaped into the air and fell dead at her feet. She had placed the ball on the leveret without seeing it and without disturbing it.

● In 1906 in the Border Championship at Hawick, a gull and a weasel were killed by balls during the afternoon's play.

● A golfer at Newark, in May, 1907, drove his ball into the river. The ball struck a trout 2lb in weight and killed it.

● On 24th April, 1975, at Scunthorpe GC, Jim Tollan's drive at the 14th hole, called *The Mallard*, struck and killed a female mallard duck in flight. The duck was stuffed and is displayed in the Scunthorpe Clubhouse.

● A. Samuel, Melbourne Club, at Sandringham, was driving with an iron club from the 17th tee, when a kitten, which had been playing in the long grass, sprang suddenly at the ball. Kitten and club arrived at the objective simultaneously, with the result that the kitten took an unexpected flight through the air, landing some 20 yards away.

● As Susan Rowlands was lining up a vital putt in the closing stages of the final of the 1978 Welsh Girls' Championship at Abergele, a tiny mouse scampered up her trouser leg. After holing the putt, the mouse ran down again. Susan, who won the final, admitted that she fortunately had not known it was there.

Interference by Birds and Animals

● Crows, ravens, hawks and seagulls frequently carry off golf balls, sometimes dropping the ball actually on the green, and it is a common incident for a cow to swallow a golf ball. A plague of crows on the Liverpool course at Hoylake are addicted to golf balls – they stole 26 in one day – selecting only new balls. It was suggested that members should carry shotguns as a 15th club!

● A match was approaching a hole in a rather low-lying course, when one of the players made a crisp chip from about 30 yards from the hole. The ball trickled slowly across the green and eventually disappeared into the hole. After a momentary pause, the ball was suddenly ejected on to the green, and out jumped a large frog.

● A large black crow named Jasper which frequented the Lithgow GC in New South Wales, Australia, stole 30 golf balls in the club's 1972 Easter Tournament.

● As Mrs Molly Whitaker was playing from a bunker at Beachwood course, Natal, South Africa, a large monkey leaped from a bush and clutched her round the neck. A caddie drove it off by clipping it with an iron club.

● In Massachusetts a goose, having been hit rather hard by a golf ball which then came to rest by the side of a water hazard, took revenge by waddling over to the ball and kicking it into the water.

● In the summer of 1963, S.C. King had a good drive to the 10th hole at the Guernsey Club. His partner, R.W. Clark, was in the rough, and King helped him to search. Returning to his ball, he found a cow eating it. Next day, at the same hole, the positions were reversed, and King was in the rough. Clark placed his woollen hat over his ball, remarking, *I'll make sure the cow doesn't eat mine.* On his return he found the cow thoroughly enjoying his hat; nothing was left but the pom-pom.

● On 5 August 2000 in the first round of the Royal Westmoreland Club Championship in Barbados, Kevin Edwards, a five-handicapper, hit a tee shot at the short 15th to a few feet of the hole. A monkey then ran onto the green, picked up the ball, threw it into the air a few times, then placed it in the hole before running off. Mr Edwards had to replace his ball, but was obliged afterwards to buy everyone a drink at the bar by virtue of a newly written rule.

Armless, One-armed, Legless and Ambidextrous Players

● In September, 1933, at Burgess Golfing Society of Edinburgh, the first championship for one-armed golfers was held. There were 43 entries and 37 of the competitors had lost an arm in the 1914-18 war. Play was over two rounds and the championship was won by W.E. Thomson, Eastwood, Glasgow, with a score of 169 (82 and 87) for two rounds. The Burgess course was 6,300 yards long. Thomson drove the last green, 260 yards. The championship and an international match are played annually.

● In the Boys' Amateur Championship 1923, at Dunbar and 1949 at St Andrews, there were competitors each with one arm. The competitor in 1949, R.P. Reid, Cupar, Fife, who lost his arm working a machine in a butcher's shop, got through to the third round.

● There have been cases of persons with no arms playing golf. One, Thomas McAuliffe, who held the club between his right shoulder and cheek, once went round Buffalo CC, USA, in 108.

● Group Captain Bader, who lost both legs in a flying accident prior to the World War 1939-45, took part in golf competitions and reached a single-figure handicap in spite of his disability.

● In 1909, Scott of Silloth, and John Haskins of Hoylake, both one-armed golfers, played a home and away match for £20-a-side. Scott started five up at Silloth. He was seven up and 14 to play at Hoylake but Haskins played so well that Scott eventually only won by 3 and 1. This was the first match between one-armed golfers. Haskins in 1919 was challenged by Mr Mycock, of Buxton, another one-armed player. The match was 36

holes, home and away. The first half was played over the Buxton and High Peak Links, and the latter half over the Liverpool Links, and resulted in a win for Haskins by 11 and 10. Later in the same year Haskins received another challenge to play against Alexander Smart of Aberdeen. The match was 18 holes over the Balgownie Course, and ended in favour of Haskins.

● In a match, November, 1926, between the Geduld and Sub Nigel Clubs – two golf clubs connected with the South African gold mines of the same names – each club had two players minus an arm. The natural consequence was that the quartet were matched. The players were – A.W.P. Charteris and E. Mitchell, Sub Nigel; and E.P. Coles and J. Kirby, Geduld. This is the first record of four one-armed players in a foursome.

● At Joliet Country Club, USA, a one-armed golfer named D.R. Anderson drove a ball 300 yards.

● Left-handedness, but playing golf right-handed, is prevalent and for a man to throw with his left hand and play golf right-handed is considered an advantage, for Bobby Jones, Jesse Sweetser, Walter Hagen, Jim Barnes, Joe Kirkwood and more recently Johnny Miller were eminent golfers who were left-handed and ambidextrous.

● In a practice round for the Open Championship in July, 1927, at St Andrews, Len Nettlefold and Joe Kirkwood changed sets of clubs at the 9th hole. Nettlefold was a left-handed golfer and Kirkwood right-handed. They played the last nine, Kirkwood with the left-handed clubs and Nettlefold with the right-handed clubs.

● The late Harry Vardon, when he was at Ganton, got tired of giving impossible odds to his members and beating them, so he collected a set of left-handed clubs, and rating himself at scratch, conceded the handicap odds to them. He won with the same monotonous regularity.

● Ernest Jones, who was professional at the Chislehurst Club, was badly wounded in the war in France in 1916 and his right leg had to be amputated below the knee. He persevered with the game, and before the end of the year he went round the Clacton course balanced on his one leg in 72. Jones later settled in the United States where he built fame and fortune as a golf teacher.

● Major Alexander McDonald Fraser of Edinburgh had the distinction of holding two handicaps simultaneously in the same club – one when he played left-handed and the other for his right-handed play. In medal competitions he had to state before teeing up which method he would use.

● Former England test cricketer Brian Close once held a handicap of 2 playing right-handed, but after retiring from cricket in 1977 decided to apply himself as a left-handed player. His left-handed handicap at the time of his retirement was 7. Close had the distinction of once beating Ted Dexter, another distinguished test cricketer and noted golfer twice in the one day, playing right-handed in the morning and left-handed in the afternoon.

Blind and Blindfolded Golf

● Major Towse, VC, whose eyes were shot out during the South African War, 1899, was probably the first blind man to play golf. His only stipulations when playing the game were that he should be allowed to touch the ball with his hands to ascertain its position, and that his caddie could ring a small bell to indicate the position of the hole. Major Towse, who played with considerable skill, was also an expert oarsman and bridge player. He died in 1945, aged 81.

● The United States Blind Golfers' Association in 1946 promoted an Invitational Golf Tournament for the blind at Inglewood, California, to be held annually. In 1953 there were 24 competitors, of which 11 completed the two rounds of 36 holes. The winner was Charley Boswell who lost his eyesight leading a tank unit in Germany in 1944.

● In July, 1954, at Lambton Golf and Country Club, Toronto, the first international championship for the blind was held. It resulted in a win for Joe Lazaro, of Waltham, Mass., with a score of 220 for the two rounds. He drove the 215-yard 16th hole and just missed an ace, his ball stopping 18 inches from the hole. Charley Boswell, who won the United States Blind Golfers' Association Tournament in 1953, was second. The same Charles Boswell, of Birmingham, Alabama, holed the 141-yard 14th hole at the Vestavia CC in one in October, 1970.

● Another blind person to have holed-in-one was American Ben Thomas while on holiday in South Carolina in 1978.

● Rick Sorenson undertook a bet in which, playing 18 holes blindfolded at Meadowbrook Course, Minneapolis, on 25th May, 1973, he was to pay $10 for every hole over par and receive $100 for every hole in par or better. He went round in 86 losing $70 on the deal.

● Alfred Toogood played blindfolded in a match against Tindal Atkinson at Sunningdale in 1912. Toogood was beaten 8 and 7. Previously, in 1908, I. Millar, Newcastle-upon-Tyne, played a match blindfolded against A.T. Broughton, Birkdale, at Newcastle, County Down.

● Wing-Commander *Laddie* Lucas, DSO, DFC, MP, played over Sandy Lodge golf course in Hertfordshire on 7th August, 1954, completely blindfolded and had a score of 87.

Trick Shots

● Joe Kirkwood, Australia, specialised in public exhibitions of trick and fancy shots. He played all kinds of strokes after nominating them, and among his ordinary strokes nothing was more impressive than those hit for low flight. He played a full drive from the face of a wrist watch, and the toe of a spectator's shoe, full strokes at a suspended ball, and played for slice and pull at will, and exhibited his ambidexterity by playing left-handed strokes with right-handed clubs. Holing six balls, stymieing, a full shot at a ball catching it as it descended, and hitting 12 full shots in rapid succession, with his face turned

away from the ball, were shots among his repertoire. In playing the last named Kirkwood placed the balls in a row, about six inches apart, and moved quickly along the line. Kirkwood, who was born in Australia lived for many years in America. He died in November, 1970 aged 73.

● On 2nd April, 1894, a 3-ball match was played over Musselburgh course between Messrs Grant, Bowden, and Waggot, the clubmaker, the latter teeing on the face of a watch at each tee. He finished the round in 41 the watch being undamaged in any way.

● In a match at Esher on 23rd November, 1931, George Ashdown, the professional, played his tee shot for each of the 18 holes from a rubber tee strapped to the forehead of Miss Ena Shaw.

● E.A. Forrest, a South African professional in a music hall turn of trick golf shots, played blindfolded shots, one being from the ball teed on the chin of his recumbent partner.

● The late Paul Hahn, an American trick specialist could hit four balls with two clubs. Holding a club in each hand he hit two balls, hooking one and slicing the other with the same swing. Hahn had a repertoire of 30 trick shots. In 1955 he flew round the world, exhibiting in 14 countries and on all five continents.

Balls Colliding and Touching

● Competing in the 1980 Corfu International Championship, Sharon Peachey drove from one tee and her ball collided in mid-air with one from a competitor playing another hole. Her ball ended in a pond.

● Playing in the Cornish team championship in 1973 at West Cornwall GC Tom Scott-Brown, of West Cornwall GC, and Paddy Bradley, of Tehidy GC, saw their drives from the fourth and eighth tees collide in mid-air.

● During a fourball match at Guernsey Club in June, 1966, near the 13th green from the tee, two of the players, D.G. Hare and S. Machin, chipped up simultaneously; the balls collided in mid-air and Machin's ball hit the green, then the flagstick, and dropped into the hole for a birdie 2.

● In May, 1926, during the meeting of the Army Golfing Society at St Andrews, Colonel Howard and Lieutenant-Colonel Buchanan Dunlop, while playing in the foursomes against J. Rodger and J. Mackie, hit full iron shots for the seconds to the 16th green. Each thought he had to play his ball first, and hidden by a bunker the players struck their balls simultaneously. The balls, going towards the hole about 20 yards from the pin and five feet in the air, met with great force and dropped either side of the hole five yards apart.

● In 1972, before a luncheon celebrating the centenary year of the Ladies' Section of Royal Wimbledon GC, a 12-hole competition was held during which two competitors, Mrs L. Champion and Mrs A. McKendrick, driving from the eighth and ninth tees respectively, saw their balls collide in mid-air.

● In 1928, at Wentworth Falls, Australia, Dr Alcorn and E.A. Avery, of Leura Club, were playing with professional E. Barnes. The tee shots of Avery and Barnes at the 9th hole finished on opposite sides of the fairway. Both players unknowingly hit their seconds (chip shots) at the same time. Dr Alcorn, standing at the pin, suddenly saw two balls approaching the hole from different angles. They met in the air and dropped into the hole.

● At Rugby, 1931, playing in a 4-ball match, H. Fraser pulled his drive from the 10th tee in the direction of the ninth tee. Simultaneously a club member, driving from the ninth tee, pulled his drive. The tees were about 350 yards apart. The two balls collided in mid-air.

● Two golf balls, being played in opposite directions, collided in flight over Longniddry Golf Course on 27th June, 1953. Immediately after Stewart Elder, of Longniddry, had driven from the third tee, another ball, which had been pulled off line from the second fairway, which runs alongside the third, struck his ball about 20 feet above the ground. S.J. Fleming, of Tranent, who was playing with Elder, heard a loud crack and thought Elder's ball had exploded. The balls were found undamaged about 70 yards apart.

Three and Two Balls Dislodged by One Shot

● In 1934 on the short 3rd hole (now the 13th) of Olton Course, Warwickshire, J.R. Horden, a scratch golfer of the club, sent his tee shot into long wet grass a few feet over the back of the green. When he played an *explosion* shot three balls dropped on to the putting green, his own and two others.

● A.M. Chevalier, playing at Hale, Cheshire, March, 1935, drove his ball into a grass bunker, and when he reached it there was only part of it showing. He played the shot with a niblick and to his amazement not one but three balls shot into the air. They all dropped back into the bunker and came to rest within a foot of each other. Then came another surprise. One of the *finds* was of the same manufacture and bore the same number as the ball he was playing with.

● Playing to the 9th hole, at Osborne House Club, Isle of Wight, George A. Sherman lost his ball which had sunk out of sight on the sodden fairway. A few weeks later, playing from the same tee, his ball again was plugged, only the top showing. Under a local rule he lifted his ball to place it, and exactly under it lay the ball he had lost previously.

Balls in Strange Places

● Playing at the John O' Gaunt Club, Sutton, near Biggleswade (Beds), a member drove a ball which did not touch the ground until it reached London – over 40 miles away. The ball landed in a vegetable lorry which was passing the golf course and later fell out of a package of cabbages when they were unloaded at Covent Garden, London.

● In the English Open Amateur Stroke Play at Moortown in 1974, Nigel Denham, a Yorkshire County

player, in the first round saw his overhit second shot to the 18th green bounce up some steps into the club-house. His ball went through an open door, ricocheted off a wall and came to rest in the men's bar, 20 feet from the windows. As the clubhouse was not out of bounds Denham decided to play the shot back to the green and opened a window 4 feet by 2 feet through which he pitched his ball to 12 feet from the flag. (Several weeks later the R&A declared that Denham should have been penalised two shots for opening the window. The clubhouse was an immovable obstruction and no part of it should have been moved.)

● In the Open Championship at Sandwich, 1949, Harry Bradshaw, Kilcroney, Dublin, at the 5th hole in his second round, drove into the rough and found his ball inside a beer bottle with the neck and shoulder broken off and four sharp points sticking up. Bradshaw, if he had treated the ball as in an unplayable lie might have been involved in a disqualification, so he decided to play it where it lay. With his blaster he smashed the bottle and sent the ball about 30 yards. The hole, a par 4, cost him 6.

● Kevin Sharman of Woodbridge GC hit a low, very straight drive at the club's 8th hole in 1979. After some minutes' searching, his ball was found embedded in a plastic sphere on top of the direction post.

● On the Dublin Course, 16th July, 1936, in the Irish Open Championship, A.D. Locke, the South African, played his tee shot at the 100-yard 12th hole, but the ball could not be found on arrival on the green. The marker removed the pin and it was discovered that the ball had been entangled in the flag. It dropped near the edge of the hole and Locke holed the short putt for a birdie two.

● While playing a round on the Geelong Golf Club Course, Australia, Easter, 1923, Captain Charteris topped his tee shot to the short 2nd hole, which lies over a creek with deep and steep clay banks. His ball came to rest on the near slope of the creek bank. He elected to play the ball as it lay, and took his niblick. After the shot, the ball was nowhere to be seen. It was found later embedded in a mass of gluey clay stuck fast to the face of the niblick. It could not be shaken off. Charteris did what was afterwards approved by the R&A, cleaned the ball and dropped it behind without penalty.

● In October, 1929, at Blackmoor Golf Club, Bordon, Hants, a player driving from the first tee holed out his ball in the chimney of a house some 120 yards distant and some 40 yards out of bounds on the right. The owner and his wife were sitting in front of the fire when they heard a rattle in the chimney and were astonished to see a golf ball drop into the fire.

● A similar incident occurred in an inter-club match between Musselburgh and Lothianburn at Preston-grange in 1938 when a member of the former team hooked his ball at the 2nd hole and gave it up for lost. To his amazement a woman emerged from one of the houses adjacent to this part of the course and handed back the ball which she said had come down the chimney and landed on a pot which was on the fire.

● In July, 1955, J. Lowrie, starter at the Eden Course, St Andrews, witnessed a freak shot. A visitor drove from the first tee just as a north-bound train was passing. He sliced the shot and the ball disappeared through an open window of a passenger compartment. Almost immediately the ball emerged again, having been thrown back on to the fairway by a man in the compartment, who waved a greeting which presumably indicated that no one was hurt.

● At Coombe Wood Golf Club a player hit a ball towards the 16th green where it landed in the vertical exhaust of a tractor which was mowing the fairway. The greenkeeper was somewhat surprised to find a temporary loss of power in the tractor. When sufficient compression had built up in the exhaust system, the ball was forced out with tremendous velocity, hit the roof of a house nearby, bounced off and landed some three feet from the pin on the green.

● When carrying out an inspection of the air conditioning system at St John's Hospital, Chelmsford, in 1993, a golf ball was found in the ventilator immediately above the operating theatre. It was probably the result of a hooked drive from the first tee at Chelmsford Golf Club, which is close by, but the ball can only have entered the duct on a rebound through a three-inch gap under a ventilator hood and then descended through a series of sharp bends to its final resting place.

● There have been many occasions when misdirected shots have finished in strange places after an unusual line of flight and bounce. At Ashford, Middlesex, John Miller, aged 69, hit his tee shot out of bounds at the 12th hole (237 yards). It struck a parked car, passed through a copse, hit more cars, jumped a canopy, flew through the clubhouse kitchen window, finishing in a cooking stock-pot, without once touching the ground. Mr Miller had previously done the hole in one on four occasions.

Balls Hit To and From Great Heights

● In 1798 two Edinburgh golfers undertook to drive a ball over the spire of St Giles' Cathedral, Edinburgh, for a wager. Mr Sceales, of Leith, and Mr Smellie, a printer, were each allowed six shots and succeeded in sending the balls well over the weather-cock, a height of more than 160 feet from the ground.

● Some years later Donald McLean, an Edinburgh lawyer, won a substantial bet by driving a ball over the Melville Monument in St Andrew Square, Edinburgh – height, 154 feet.

● Tom Morris in 1860, at the famous bridge of Ballochmyle, stood in the quarry beneath and, from a stick elevated horizontally, attempted to send golf balls over the bridge, 400 feet high, which was in itself a great feat with the gutta ball. He could raise them only to the pathway.

● Captain Ernest Carter, on 28th September, 1922, drove a ball from the roadway at the 1st tee on Harlech Links against the wall of Harlech Castle. The embattlements are 200 feet over the level of the roadway, and the point where the ball struck the

embattlements was 180 yards from the point where the ball was teed. Captain Carter, who was laid odds of £100 to £1, used a baffy.

● In 1896 Freddie Tait, then a subaltern in the Black Watch, drove a ball from the Rookery, the highest building on Edinburgh Castle, in a match against a brother officer to hole out in the fountain in Princes Street Gardens 350 feet below and about 300 yards distant.

● Prior to the 1977 Lancôme Tournament in Paris, Arnold Palmer hit three balls from the second stage of the Eiffel Tower, over 300 feet above ground. The longest was measured at 403 yards. One ball was hooked and hit a bus but no serious damage was done as all traffic had been stopped for safety reasons.

● Long drives have been made from mountain peaks, across the gorge at Victoria Falls, from the Pyramids, high buildings in New York, and from many other similar places. As an illustration of such freakish *drives* a member of the New York Rangers' Hockey Team from the top of Mount Edith Cavell, 11,033 feet high, drove a ball which struck the Ghost Glacier 5000 feet below and bounced off the rocky ledge another 1000 feet – a total drop of 2000 yards. Later, in June, 1968, from Pikes Peak, Colorado (14,110 feet), Arthur Lynskey hit a ball which travelled 200 yards horizontally but 2 miles vertically.

Remarkable Shots

● Remarkable shots are as numerous as the grains of sand; around every 19th hole, legends are recalled of astounding shots. One shot is commemorated by a memorial tablet at the 17th hole at the Lytham and St Annes Club. It was made by Bobby Jones in the final round of the Open Championship in 1926. He was partnered by Al Watrous, another American player. They had been running neck and neck and at the end of the third round, Watrous was just leading Jones with 215 against 217. At the 16th Jones drew level then on the 17th he drove into a sandy lie in broken ground. Watrous reached the green with his second. Jones took a mashie-iron (the equivalent to a 4-iron today) and hit a magnificent shot to the green to get his 4. This remarkable recovery unnerved Watrous, who 3-putted, and Jones, getting another 4 at the last hole against 5, won his first Open Championship with 291 against Watrous' 293. The tablet is near the spot where Jones played his second shot.

● Arnold Palmer (USA), playing in the second round of the Australian Wills Masters tournament at Melbourne, in October, 1964, hooked his second shot at the 9th hole high into the fork of a gum tree. Climbing 20 feet up the tree, Palmer, with the head of his 1-iron reversed, played a hammer stroke and knocked the ball some 30 yards forward, followed by a brilliant chip to the green and a putt.

● In the foursome during the Ryder Cup at Moortown in 1929, Joe Turnesa hooked the American side's second shot at the last hole behind the marquee adjoining the clubhouse, Johnny Farrel then pitched the ball over the marquee on to the green only feet away from the pin and Turnesa holed out for a 4.

Miscellaneous Incidents and Strange Golfing Facts

● Gary Player of South Africa was honoured by his country by having his portrait on new postage stamps which were issued on 12th December, 1976. It was the first time a specific golfer had ever been depicted on any country's postage stamps. In 1981 the US Postal Service introduced stamps featuring Bobby Jones and Babe Zaharias. They are the first golfers to be thus honoured by the United States.

● Gary Harris, aged 18, became the first player to make five consecutive appearances for England in the European Boys Team Championship at Vilamoura, Portugal, in 1994.

● In February, 1971, the first ever golf shots on the moon's surface were played by Captain Alan Shepard, commander of the Apollo 14 spacecraft. Captain Shepard hit two balls with an iron head attached to a makeshift shaft. With a one-handed swing he claimed he hit the first ball 200 yards aided by the reduced force of gravity on the moon. Subsequent findings put this distance in doubt. The second was a shank. Acknowledging the occasion the R&A sent Captain Shepard the following telegram: *Warmest congratulations to all of you on your great achievement and safe return. Please refer to Rules of Golf section on etiquette, paragraph 6, quote – before leaving a bunker a player should carefully fill up all holes made by him therein, unquote.* Shepard presented the club to the USGA Museum in 1974.

● Charles (Chick) Evans competed in every US Amateur Championship held between 1907 and 1962 by which time he was 72 years old. This amounted to 50 consecutive occasions discounting the six years of the two World Wars when the championship was not held.

● In winning the 1977 US Open at Southern Hills CC, Tulsa, Oklahoma, Hubert Green had to contend with a death threat. Coming off the 14th green in the final round, he was advised by USGA officials that a phone call had been received saying that he would be killed. Green decided that play should continue and happily he went on to win, unharmed.

● It was discovered at the 1977 USPGA Championship that the clubs with which Tom Watson had won the Open Championship and the US Masters earlier in the year were illegal, having grooves which exceeded the permitted specifications. The set he used in winning the 1975 Open Championship were then flown out to him and they too were found to be illegal. No retrospective action was taken.

● Mrs Fred Daly, wife of the former Open champion, saved the clubhouse of Balmoral GC, Belfast, from destruction when three men entered the professional's shop on 5th August, 1976, and left a bag containing a bomb outside the shop beside the clubhouse when refused money. Mrs Daly carried the bag over to a hedge some distance away where the bomb exploded

15 minutes later. The only damage was broken windows. On the same day several hours afterwards, Dungannon GC in Co. Tyrone suffered extensive damage to the clubhouse from terrorist bombs. Co. Down GC, proposed venue of the 1979 home international matches suffered bomb damage in May that year and through fear for the safety of team members the 1979 matches were cancelled.

● The Army Golfing Society and St Andrews on 21st April, 1934, played a match 200-a-side, the largest golf match ever played. Play was by foursomes. The Army won 58, St Andrews 31 and 11 were halved.

● Jamie Ortiz-Patino, owner of the Valderrama Golf Club at Sotogrande, Spain, paid a record £84,000 (increased to £92,400 with ten per cent buyers premium) for a late seventeenth- or early eighteenth-century rake iron offered at auction in Musselburgh in July, 1992. The iron, which had been kept in a garden shed, was bought to be exhibited in a museum being created in Valderrama.

● A Christie's golf auction during the week of the 1991 Open Championship created two world records. An American dealer bought a blacksmith-made iron club head dating from the seventeenth century for £44,000. It had been found 10 years before in a hedge near the North Berwick Golf Club in Scotland. Also, £165,000 was paid by a Japanese collector for an oil painting by Sir Francis Grant (1810–1878) of the 1823 Royal & Ancient captain, John Whyte-Melville, standing beside the Swilcan Burn at St Andrews. The same Japanese buyer successfully bid £35,200 for a rare gutty golf ball marking device from the workshops of Old Tom Morris in St Andrews, while an unused feathery golf ball by Allan Robertson fetched £11,000.

● In 1986 Alistair Risk and three colleagues on the 17th green at Brora, Sutherland, watched a cow giving birth to twin calves between the markers on the 18th tee, causing them to play their next tee shots from in front of the tee. Their application for a ruling from the R&A brought a Rules Committee reply that while technically a rule had been broken, their action was considered within the spirit of the game and there should be no penalty. The Secretary added that the Rules Committee hoped that mother and twins were doing well.

● In view of the increasing number of people crossing the road (known as Granny Clark's Wynd) which runs across the first and 18th fairways of the Old Course, St Andrews, as a right of way, the St Andrews Links committee decided in 1969 to control the flow by erecting traffic lights, with appropriate green for go, yellow for caution and red for stop. The lights are controlled from the starter's box on the first tee. Golfers on the first tee must wait until the lights turn to green before driving off and a notice has been erected at the Wynd warning pedestrians not to cross at yellow or stop.

● A traffic light for golfers was also installed in 1971 on one of Japan's most congested courses. After putting on the uphill 9th hole of the Fukuoka course in Southern Japan, players have to switch on a go-ahead signal for following golfers waiting to play their shots to the green.

● A 22-year-old professional at Brett Essex GC, Brentwood, David Moore, who was playing in the Mufulira Open in Zambia in 1976, was shot dead it is alleged by the man with whom he was staying for the duration of the tournament. It appeared his host then shot himself.

● Peggy Carrick and her daughter, Angela Uzielli, won the Mothers and Daughters Tournament at Royal Mid-Surrey in 1994 for the 21st time.

● Patricia Shepherd has won the ladies' club championship at Turriff GC Aberdeenshire 30 consecutive times from 1959 to 1988.

● Mrs Jackie Mercer won the South African Ladies' Championship in 1979, 31 years after her first victory in the event as Miss Jacqueline Smith.

● During the Royal & Ancient Golf Club of St Andrews' medal meeting on 25th September, 1907, a member of the Royal & Ancient drove a ball which struck the sharp point of a hatpin in the hat of a lady who was crossing the course. The ball was so firmly impaled that it remained in position. The lady was not hurt.

● John Cook, former English Amateur Champion, narrowly escaped death during an attempted coup against King Hassan of Morocco in July 1971. Cook had been playing in a tournament arranged by King Hassan, a keen golfer, and was at the King's birthday party in Rabat when rebels broke into the party demanding that the King give up his throne. Cook and many others present were taken hostage.

● When playing from the 9th tee at Lossiemouth golf course in June, 1971, Martin Robertson struck a Royal Navy jet aircraft which was coming in to land at the nearby airfield. The plane was not damaged.

● At a court in Inglewood, California, in 1978, Jim Brown was convicted of beating and choking an opponent during a dispute over where a ball should have been placed on the green.

● During the Northern Ireland troubles a home-made hand grenade was found in a bunker at Dungannon GC, Co. Tyrone, on Sunday, 12th September, 1976.

● Tiger Woods, 18, became both the youngest and the first black golfer to win the United States Amateur Championship at Sawgrass in 1994. He went on to win the title three years in a row and then won the first major championship he played as a professional, the 1997 Masters, by a record 12 strokes and with a record low aggregate of 270, 18 under par.

● To mark the centenary of the Jersey Golf Club in 1978, the Jersey Post Office issued a set of four special stamps featuring Jersey's most famous golfer, Harry Vardon. The background of the 13p stamp was a brief biography of Vardon's career reproduced from the *Golfer's Handbook*.

● Forty-one-year-old John Mosley went for a round of golf at Delaware Park GC, Buffalo, New York, in July, 1972. He stepped on to the first tee and was challenged over a green fee by an official guard. A scuffle

developed, a shot was fired and Mosley, a bullet in his chest, died on the way to hospital. His wife was awarded $131,250 in an action against the City of Buffalo and the guard. The guard was sentenced to 7¹/₂ years for second-degree manslaughter.

● When three competitors in a 1968 Pennsylvania pro-am event were about to drive from the 16th tee, two bandits (one with pistol) suddenly emerged from the bushes, struck one of the players and robbed them of wristwatches and $300.

● In the 1932 Walker Cup match at Brooklyn, Leonard Crawley succeeded in denting the cup. An errant iron shot to the 18th green hit the cup, which was on display outside the clubhouse.

● In Johannesburg, South Africa, three golf officials appeared in court accused of violating a 75-year-old Sunday Observance Law by staging the final round of the South African PGA championship on Sunday, 28th February, 1971. The Championship should have been completed on the Saturday but heavy rain prevented any play.

● In the Open Championship of 1876, at St Andrews, Bob Martin and David Strath tied at 176. A protest was lodged against Strath alleging he played his approach to the 17th green and struck a spectator. The Royal & Ancient ordered the replay, but Strath refused to play off the tie until a decision had been given on the protest. No decision was given and Bob Martin was declared the Champion.

● At Rose Bay, New South Wales, on 11th July, 1931, D.J. Bayly MacArthur, on stepping into a bunker, began to sink. MacArthur, who weighed 14 stone, shouted for help. He was rescued when up to the armpits. He had stepped on a patch of quicksand, aggravated by excess of moisture.

● The late Bobby Cruickshank was the victim of his own jubilation in the 1934 US Open at Merion. In the 4th round while in with a chance of winning he half-topped his second shot at the 11th hole. The ball was heading for a pond in front of the green but instead of ending up in the water it hit a rock and bounced on to the green. In his delight Cruickshank threw his club into the air only to receive a resounding blow on the head as it returned to earth.

● A dog with an infallible nose for finding lost golf balls was, in 1971, given honorary membership of the Waihi GC, Hamilton, New Zealand. The dog, called Chico, was trained to search for lost balls, to be sold back to the members, the money being put into the club funds.

● By 1980 Waddy, an 11-year-old beagle belonging to Bob Inglis, the secretary of Brokenhurst Manor GC, had found over 35,000 golf balls.

● Herbert M. Hepworth, Headingley, Leeds, Lord Mayor of Leeds in 1906, scored one thousand holes in 2, a feat which took him 30 years to accomplish. It was celebrated by a dinner in 1931 at the Leeds club. The first 2 of all was scored on 12th June, 1901, at Cobble Hall Course, Leeds, and the 1,000th in 1931 at Alwoodley, Leeds. Hepworth died in November, 1942.

● Fiona MacDonald was the first female to play in the Oxford and Cambridge University match at Ganton in 1986.

● Mrs Sara Gibbon won the Farnham (Surrey) Club's Grandmother's competition 48 hours after her first grand-child was born.

● At Carnoustie in the first qualifying round for the 1952 Scottish Amateur Championship a competitor drove three balls in succession out of bounds at the 1st hole and thereupon withdrew.

● In 1993, the Clark family from Hagley GC, Worcs, set a record for the county's three major professional events. The Worcestershire Stroke Play Championship was won by Finlay Clark, the eldest son, who beat his father Iain and younger brother Cameron, who tied second. In the Match Play Iain beat his son Finlay by 2 and 1 in the final; Cameron won the play-off for third place. Then in the Worcestershire Annual Pro-Am it was Cameron's turn to win, with his brother Finlay coming second and father Iain third. To add to the achievements of the family, Cameron also won the Midland Professional Match Play Championship.

● During a Captain–Pro foursomes challenge match at Chelmsford in 1993, Club Professional Dennis Bailey, put the ball into a hole only once in all 18 holes – when he holed-in-one at the fourth.

Strange Local Rules

● The Duke of Windsor, who played on an extraordinary variety of the world's courses, once took advantage of a local rule at Jinja in Uganda and lifted his ball from a hippo's footprint without penalty.

● At the Glen Canyon course in Arizona a local rule provides that *If your ball lands within a club length of a rattlesnake you are allowed to move the ball.*

● Another local rule in Uganda read: *If a ball comes to rest in dangerous proximity to a crocodile, another ball may be dropped.*

● The 6th hole at Koolan Island GC, Western Australia, also serves as a local air strip and a local rule reads: *Aircraft and vehicular traffic have right of way at all times.*

● A local rule at the RAF Waddington GC reads: *When teeing off from the 2nd, right of way must be given to taxiing aircraft.*

Record Scoring

In the Major Championships nobody has shot lower than 63. There have been seven 63s in the Open, four 63s in the US Open, two 63s in The Masters and eight 63s in the USPGA Championship. The lowest first 36 holes is 130 by Nick Faldo in the 1992 Open at Muirfield and the lowest 72 hole total is 265 by David Toms in the 2001 USPGA Championship at the Atlanta Athletic Club.

The Open Championship

Most times champions
6 Harry Vardon, 1896–98–99–1903–11–14
5 James Braid, 1901–05–06–08–10; J.H. Taylor, 1894–95–1900–09–13; Peter Thomson, 1954–55–56–58–65; Tom Watson, 1975–77–80–82–83

Most times runner-up
7 Jack Nicklaus, 1964–67–68–72–76–77–79
6 J.H. Taylor, 1896–1904–05–06–07–14

Oldest winner
Old Tom Morris, 46 years 99 days, 1867
Roberto De Vicenzo, 44 years 93 days, 1967

Youngest winner
Young Tom Morris, 17 years 5 months 8 days, 1868
Willie Auchterlonie, 21 years 24 days, 1893
Severiano Ballesteros, 22 years 3 months 12 days, 1979

Youngest and oldest competitor
Young Tom Morris, 15 years, 4 months, 29 days, 1866
Gene Sarazen, 71 years 4 months 13 days, 1973

Widest margin of victory
13 strokes Old Tom Morris, 1862
12 strokes Young Tom Morris, 1870
8 strokes J.H. Taylor, 1900 and 1913; James Braid, 1908; Tiger Woods, 2000
6 strokes Harry Vardon, 1903; J.H. Taylor, 1909; Bobby Jones, 1927; Walter Hagen, 1929; Arnold Palmer, 1962; Johnny Miller, 1976

Lowest winning aggregates
267 Greg Norman, 66-68-69-64, Sandwich, 1993
268 Tom Watson, 68-70-65-65, Turnberry, 1977; Nick Price, 69-66-67-66, Turnberry, 1994
269 Tiger Woods, 67-66-67-69, St Andrews, 2000
270 Nick Faldo, 67-65-67-71, St Andrews, 1990

Lowest in relation to par
19 under Tiger Woods, St Andrews, 2000
18 under Nick Faldo, St Andrews, 1990

Lowest aggregate by runner-up
269 (68-70-65-66), Jack Nicklaus, Turnberry, 1977; (69-63-70-67) Nick Faldo, Sandwich, 1993; (68-66-68-67) Jesper Parnevik, Turnberry, 1994

Lowest aggregate by an amateur
281 (68-72-70-71), Iain Pyman, Sandwich, 1993; (75-66-70-70), Tiger Woods, Royal Lytham, 1996

Lowest round
63 Mark Hayes, second round, Turnberry, 1977; Isao Aoki, third round, Muirfield, 1980; Greg Norman, second round, Turnberry, 1986; Paul Broadhurst, third round, St Andrews, 1990; Jodie Mudd,

fourth round, Royal Birkdale, 1991; Nick Faldo, second round, Payne Stewart, fourth round, Sandwich, 1993

Lowest round by an amateur
66 Frank Stranahan, fourth round, Troon, 1950; Tiger Woods, second round, Royal Lytham, 1996; Justin Rose, second round, Royal Birkdale, 1998

Lowest first round
64 Craig Stadler, Royal Birkdale, 1983; Christy O'Connor Jr, Royal St George's, 1985; Rodger Davis, Muirfield, 1987; Steve Pate, Ray Floyd, Muirfield, 1992

Lowest second round
63 Mark Hayes, Turnberry, 1977; Greg Norman, Turnberry, 1986; Nick Faldo, Sandwich, 1993

Lowest third round
63 Isao Aoki, Muirfield, 1980; Paul Broadhurst, St Andrews, 1990

Lowest fourth round
63 Jodie Mudd, Royal Birkdale, 1991; Payne Stewart, Sandwich, 1993

Lowest first 36 holes
130 (66-64), Nick Faldo, Muirfield, 1992
132 (67-65), Henry Cotton, Sandwich, 1934; Nick Faldo (67-65) and Greg Norman (66-66), St Andrews, 1990; Nick Faldo (69-63), Sandwich, 1993

Lowest second 36 holes
130 (65-65), Tom Watson, Turnberry, 1977; (64-66) Ian Baker-Finch, Royal Birkdale, 1991; (66-64) Anders Forsbrand, Turnberry, 1994

Lowest first 54 holes
198 (67-67-64) Tom Lehman, Royal Lytham, 1996
199 (67-65-67), Nick Faldo, St Andrews, 1990; (66-64-69) Nick Faldo, Muirfield, 1992

Lowest final 54 holes
199 (66-67-66) Nick Price, Turnberry, 1994
200 (70-65-65), Tom Watson, Turnberry, 1977; (63-70-67), Nick Faldo, Sandwich, 1993; (66-64-70), Fuzzy Zoeller, Turnberry, 1994; (66-70-64), Nick Faldo, Turnberry 1994

Lowest 9 holes
28 Denis Durnian, first 9, Royal Birkdale, 1983

Champions in three decades
Harry Vardon, 1986, 1903, 1911
J.H. Taylor, 1894, 1900, 1913
Gary Player, 1959, 1968, 1974

Biggest span between first and last victories
19 years, J.H. Taylor, 1894–1913
18 years, Harry Vardon, 1896–1914

15 years, Willie Park, 1860–75
15 years, Gary Player, 1959–74
14 years, Henry Cotton, 1934–48

Successive victories
4 Young Tom Morris, 1868–72 (no championship 1871)
3 Jamie Anderson, 1877–79; Bob Ferguson, 1880–82,
Peter Thomson, 1954–56
2 Old Tom Morris, 1861–62; J.H. Taylor, 1894–95;
Harry Vardon, 1898–99; James Braid, 1905–06; Bobby
Jones, 1926–27; Walter Hagen, 1928–29; Bobby Locke,
1949–50; Arnold Palmer, 1961–62; Lee Trevino,
1971–72; Tom Watson, 1982–83

Amateur champions
John Ball, 1890, Prestwick
Harold Hilton, 1892, Muirfield; 1897, Royal
Liverpool
Bobby Jones, 1926, Royal Lytham; 1927, St Andrews;
1930 Royal Liverpool

Highest number of top five finishes
16 J.H. Taylor and Jack Nicklaus
15 Harry Vardon and James Braid

Players with four rounds under 70
Greg Norman (66-68-69-64), Sandwich, 1993; Ernie Els
(68-69-69-68), Sandwich, 1993; Nick Price
(69-66-67-66), Turnberry, 1994; Jesper Parnevik
(68-66-68-67), Turnberry, 1994; Tiger Woods
(67-66-67-69), St Andrews, 2000

Highest number of rounds under 70

35 Nick Faldo	22 Ernie Els
33 Jack Nicklaus	21 Lee Trevino
28 Tom Watson	20 Severiano Ballesteros
25 Greg Norman	and Nick Price

**Outright leader after every round (since
Championship became 72 holes in 1892)**
James Braid, 1908; Ted Ray, 1912; Bobby Jones, 1927;
Gene Sarazen, 1932; Henry Cotton, 1934; Tom
Weiskopf, 1973

Record leads (since 1892)
After 18 holes: 4 strokes, Bobby Jones, 1927; Henry
Cotton, 1934; Christy O'Connor Jr, 1985
After 36 holes: 9 strokes, Henry Cotton, 1934
After 54 holes: 10 strokes, Henry Cotton, 1934;
7 strokes, Tony Lema, 1964; 6 strokes, James Braid,
1908; Tom Lehman, 1996; Tiger Woods, 2000

**Champions with each round lower than previous
one**
Jack White, 1904, Sandwich, 80-75-72-69
James Braid, 1906, Muirfield, 77-76-74-73
Ben Hogan, 1953, Carnoustie, 73-71-70-68
Gary Player, 1959, Muirfield, 75-71-70-68

Champion with four rounds the same
Densmore Shute, 1933, St Andrews, 73-73-73-73
(excluding the play-off)

Biggest variation between rounds of a champion
14 strokes, Henry Cotton, 1934, second round 65, fourth
round 79; 11 strokes, Jack White, 1904, first round 80,
fourth round 69; Greg Norman, 1986, first round 74,
second round 63, third round 74

Biggest variation between two rounds
20 strokes: R.G. French, 1938, second round 71, third
round 91; Colin Montgomerie, 2002, second round 64,

third round 84; 18 strokes: A. Tingey Jr, 1923, first
round 94, second 76; 17 strokes, Jack Nicklaus, 1981,
first round 83, second round 66; Ian Baker-Finch, 1986,
first round 86, second round 69

Best comeback by champions
After 18 holes: Harry Vardon, 1896, 11 strokes behind
the leader
After 36 holes: George Duncan, 1920, 13 strokes behind
leader
After 54 holes: Paul Lawrie, 1999, 10 strokes behind the
leader (won four-hole play-off)

Best comeback by non-champions
Of non-champions, Greg Norman, 1989, seven strokes
behind the leader and lost in a play-off

Best finishing round by a champion
64 Greg Norman, Sandwich, 1993
65 Tom Watson, Turnberry, 1977; Severiano
Ballesteros, Royal Lytham, 1988; Justin Leonard, Royal
Troon, 1997

Worst finishing round by a champion since 1920
79 Henry Cotton, Sandwich, 1934
78 Reg Whitcombe, Sandwich, 1938
77 Walter Hagen, Hoylake, 1924

Best opening round by a champion
66 Peter Thomson, Royal Lytham, 1958; NickFaldo,
Muirfield, 1992; Greg Norman, Sandwich, 1993
67 Henry Cotton, Sandwich, 1934; Tom Watson, Royal
Birkdale, 1983; Severiano Ballesteros,
Royal Lytham, 1988; Nick Faldo, St Andrews, 1990;
John Daly, St Andrews, 1995; Tom Lehman, Royal
Lytham, 1996, Tiger Woods, St Andrews, 2000

Worst opening round by a champion since 1919
80 George Duncan, Deal, 1920 (he also had a
second round of 80)
77 Walter Hagen, Hoylake, 1924

Biggest recovery in 18 holes by a champion
George Duncan, Deal, 1920, was 13 strokes behind the
leader, Abe Mitchell, after 36 holes and level after 54

Most consecutive appearances
47 Gary Player, 1955–2001

**Championship since 1946 with the fewest rounds
under 70**
St Andrews, 1946; Hoylake, 1947; Portrush, 1951;
Hoylake, 1956; Carnoustie, 1968. All had only two
rounds under 70

Longest course
Carnoustie, 1999, 7361 yds

Largest entries
2460 in 2000, St Andrews

Courses most often used
St Andrews, 26; Prestwick, 24 (but not since 1925);
Muirfield, 15; Sandwich, 12; Hoylake, 10; Royal
Lytham and St Annes, 10; Royal Birkdale, 8; Royal
Troon 7; Musselburgh, 6; Carnoustie, 6; Turnberry, 3;
Deal, 2; Royal Portrush and Prince's, 1

Albatrosses (Double-Eagles)
Both Jeff Maggert (6th hole, 2nd round) and Greg Owen
(11th hole, 3rd round) made albatrosses during the 2001
Open Championship at Royal Lytham and St Annes. No
complete record of albatrosses in the history of the event

Prize Money

Year	Total	First Prize £	Year	Total	First Prize £	Year	Total	First Prize £
1860	nil	nil	1959	5000	1,000	1985	530,000	65,000
1863	10	nil	1960	7000	1,250	1986	600,000	70,000
1864	16	6	1961	8500	1,400	1987	650,000	75,000
1876	20	20	1963	8500	1,500	1988	700,000	80,000
1889	22	8	1965	10,000	1,750	1989	750,000	80,000
1891	28.50	10	1966	15,000	2,100	1990	815,000	85,000
1892	110	(am)	1968	20,000	3,000	1991	900,000	90,000
1893	100	30	1969	30,000	4,250	1992	950,000	95,000
1910	125	50	1970	40,000	5,250	1993	1,000,000	100,000
1920	225	75	1971	45,000	5,500	1994	1,100,000	110,000
1927	275	100	1972	50,000	5,500	1995	1,250,000	125,000
1930	400	100	1975	75,000	7,500	1996	1,400,000	200,000
1931	500	100	1977	100,000	10,000	1997	1,586,300	250,000
1946	1000	150	1978	125,000	12,500	1998	1,774,150	300,000
1949	1700	300	1979	155,000	15,500	1999	2,029,950	350,000
1953	2450	500	1980	200,000	25,000	2000	2,722,150	500,000
1954	3500	750	1982	250,000	32,000	2001	3,229,748	600,000
1955	3750	1,000	1983	300,000	40,000	2002	3,880,998	700,000
1958	4850	1,000	1984	451,000	55,000	2003	3,931,000	700,000

is available but since 1980 there had been only three others – by Johnny Miller (Muirfield 5th hole) in 1980, Bill Rogers (Royal Birkdale 17th hole) 1983 and Manny Zerman (St Andrews) 2000.

US Open

Most times champion
4 Willie Anderson, 1901–03–04–05; Bobby Jones, 1923–26–29–30; Ben Hogan, 1948–50–51–53; Jack Nicklaus, 1962–67–72–80

Most times runner-up
4 Bobby Jones, 1922–24–25–28; Sam Snead, 1937–47–49–53; Arnold Palmer, 1962–63–66–67; Jack Nicklaus, 1960 (am)–68–71–82

Oldest winner
Hale Irwin, 45 years, 15 days, Medinah, 1990

Youngest winner
Johnny McDermott, 19 years, 10 months, 12 days, Chicago, 1911

Biggest winning margin
15 strokes Tiger Woods, Pebble Beach, 2000

Lowest winning aggregate
272 Jack Nicklaus, Baltusrol, 1980; Lee Janzen, Baltusrol, 1993; Tiger Woods, Pebble Beach, 2000

Lowest in relation to par
12 under Tiger Woods, Pebble Beach, 2000

Lowest round
63 Johnny Miller, fourth round, Oakmont, 1973; Jack Nicklaus, first round, Baltusrol, 1980; Tom Weiskopf, first round, Baltusrol, 1980; Vijay Singh, second round, Olympia Fields, 2003

Lowest 9 holes
29 Neal Lancaster, Shinnecock Hills, 1995, and Oakland Hills, 1996

Lowest first 36 holes
133 Jim Furyk, Vijay Singh, Olympia Fields, 2003

Lowest final 36 holes
132 Larry Nelson, Oakmont, 1983

Lowest first 54 holes
200 Jim Furyk, Olympia Fields, 2003

Lowest final 54 holes
204 Jack Nicklaus, Baltusrol, 1967; Raymond Floyd, Shinnecock Hills, 1986; Steve Jones, Oaklands Hills, 1996

Attendances

Year	Attendance	Year	Attendance	Year	Attendance	Year	Attendance
1962	37,098	1973	78,810	1984	193,126	1995	180,000
1963	24,585	1974	92,796	1985	141,619	1996	170,000
1964	35,954	1975	85,258	1986	134,261	1997	176,797
1965	32,927	1976	92,021	1987	139,189	1998	180,000
1966	40,182	1977	87,615	1988	191,334	1999	158,000
1967	29,880	1978	125,271	1989	160,639	2000	230,000
1968	51,819	1979	134,501	1990	207,000	2001	178,000
1969	46,001	1980	131,610	1991	192,154	2002	161,000
1970	82,593	1981	111,987	1992	150,100	2003	182,585
1971	70,076	1982	133,299	1993	140,100		
1972	84,746	1983	142,892	1994	128,000		

Most consecutive appearances
44 Jack Nicklaus 1957 to 2000

Successive victories
3 Willie Anderson, 1903–04–05

Players with four rounds under 70
Lee Trevino, 69-68-69-69, Oak Hill, 1968; Lee Janzen,
67-67-69-69, Baltusrol, 1993

Outright leader after every round
Walter Hagen, Midlothian, 1914; Jim Barnes,
Col-umbia, 1921; Ben Hogan, Oakmont, 1953; Tony
Jacklin, Hazeltine, 1970; Tiger Woods, Pebble Beach,
2000; Tiger Woods, Bethpage, 2002

Best opening round by a champion
63 Jack Nicklaus, Baltusrol, 1980

Worst opening round by a champion
91 Horace Rawlins, Newport, RI, 1895
Since World War II: 76 Ben Hogan, Oakland Hills,
1951; Jack Fleck, Olympic, 1955

Amateur champions
Francis Ouimet, Brookline, 1913; Jerome Travers,
Baltusrol, 1915; Chick Evans, Minikahda, 1916; Bobby
Jones, Inwood, 1923, Scioto, 1926, Winged Foot, 1929,
Interlachen, 1930; Johnny Goodman, North Shore, 1933

US Masters

Most times champion
6 Jack Nicklaus, 1963–65–66–72–75–86
4 Arnold Palmer, 1958–60–62–64

Most times runner-up
4 Ben Hogan, 1942–46–54–55; Jack Nicklaus,
1964–71–77–81

Oldest winner
Jack Nicklaus, 46 years, 2 months, 23 days, 1986

Youngest winner
Tiger Woods, 21 years, 3 months, 15 days, 1997

Biggest winning margin
12 strokes Tiger Woods, 1997

Lowest winning aggregate
270 Tiger Woods, 1997

Lowest in relation to par
18 under Tiger Woods, Augusta, 1997

Lowest aggregate by an amateur
281 Charles Coe, 1961 (joint second)

Lowest round
63 Nick Price, 1986; Greg Norman, 1996

Lowest 9 holes
29 Mark Calcavecchia, 1992; David Toms, 1998

Lowest first 36 holes
131 Raymond Floyd, 1976

Lowest final 36 holes
131 Johnny Miller, 1975

Lowest first 54 holes
201 Raymond Floyd, 1976; Tiger Woods, 1997

Lowest final 54 holes
200 Tiger Woods, 1997

Most appearances
49 Doug Ford 1952 to 2001

Successive victories
2 Jack Nicklaus, 1965–66; Nick Faldo, 1989–90; Tiger
Woods, 2001–02

Players with four rounds under 70
None

Outright leader after every round
Craig Wood, 1941; Arnold Palmer, 1960; Jack
Nicklaus, 1972; Raymond Floyd, 1976

Best opening round by a champion
65 Raymond Floyd, 1976

Worst opening round by a champion
75 Craig Stadler, 1982

Albatrosses
There have been three albatross twos in the Masters at
Augusta National: by Gene Sarazen at the 15th, 1935; by
Bruce Devlin at the eighth, 1967; and by Jeff Maggert at
the 13th, 1994.

USPGA Championship

Most times champion
5 Walter Hagen, 1921–24–25–26–27; Jack Nicklaus
1963–71–73–75–80

Most times runner-up
4 Jack Nicklaus, 1964–65–74–83

Oldest winner
Julius Boros, 48 years 4 months 18 days, Pecan Valley,
1968

Youngest winner
Gene Sarazen, 20 years 5 months 22 days, Oakmont,
1922

Biggest winning margin
7 strokes Jack Nicklaus, Oak Hill, 1980

Lowest winning aggregate
265 (-15) David Toms, Atlanta Athletic Club, 2001
267 Steve Elkington and Colin Montgomerie,
Riviera, 1995 – Montgomerie lost sudden death play-off

Lowest aggregate by runner-up
266 (-14) Phil Michelson, Atlanta Athletic Club, 2001

Lowest in relation to par
18 under Tiger Woods and Bob May, Valhalla, 2000
(May lost three-hole play-off)

Lowest round
63 Bruce Crampton, Firestone, 1975; Raymond Floyd,
Southern Hills, 1982; Gary Player, Shoal Creek, 1984;
Vijay Singh, Inverness, 1993; Michael Bradley and Brad
Faxon, Riviera, 1995; José Maria Olazábal, Valhalla,
2000; Mark O'Meara, Atlanta Athletic Club, 2001

Most successive victories
4 Walter Hagen, 1924–25–26–27

Lowest 9 holes
28 Brad Faxon, Riviera, 1995

Lowest first 36 holes
131 Hal Sutton, Riviera, 1983; Vijay Singh, Inverness, 1993; Ernie Els and Mark O'Meara, Riviera, 1995; Shingo Katayama and David Toms, Atlanta Athletic Club, 2001

Lowest final 36 holes
131 Mark Calcavecchia, Atlanta Athletic Club, 2001
132 Miller Barber, Dayton, 1969; Steve Elkington and Colin Montgomerie, Riviera, 1995

Lowest first 54 holes
196 David Toms, Atlanta Athletic Club, 2001

Lowest final 54 holes
199 Steve Elkington, Colin Montgomerie, Riviera, 1995; Mark Calcavecchia, David Toms, Atlanta Athletic Club, 2001

Most appearances
37 Arnold Palmer; Jack Nicklaus

Outright leader after every round
Bobby Nichols, Columbus, 1964; Jack Nicklaus, PGA National, 1971; Raymond Floyd, Southern Hills, 1982; Hal Sutton, Riviera, 1983

Best opening round by a champion
63 Raymond Floyd, Southern Hills, 1982

Worst opening round by a champion
75 John Mahaffey, Oakmont, 1978

European PGA Tour

Lowest 72-hole aggregate
258 (14 under par) David Llewellyn (Wal), AGF Biarritz Open, 1988; (18 under par) Ian Woosnam (Wal), Monte Carlo Open, 1990.
259 (29 under par) Ernie Els (RSA), Johnnie Walker Classic, Lake Karrinyup, 2003; (25 under par) Mark McNulty (Zim), German Open, Frankfurt, 1987; (21 under par) Tiger Woods (USA), NEC Invitational, 2000

Lowest 9 holes
27 (9 under par) José María Canizares (Esp), Swiss Open at Crans-sur-Sierre, 1978; (7 under par) Robert Lee (Eng), Johnnie Walker Monte Carlo Open at Mont Agel, 1985; (6 under par) Robert Lee, Portuguese Open at Estoril, 1987; (9 under par) Joakim Haeggman (Swe), Alfred Dunhill Cup at St Andrews, 1997

Lowest 18 holes
60 (-11) Baldovino Dassu (Ita), Swiss Open at Crans-sur-Sierre, 1971; David Llewellyn (Wal), AGF Biarritz Open, 1988; (-9) Ian Woosnam (Wal), Torras Monte Carlo Open at Mont Agel, 1990; (-12) Jamie Spence, Canon European Masters at Crans-sur-Sierre, 1992; (-10) Paul Curry, Bell's Scottish Open at Gleneagles, 1992; (-9) both Darren Clarke and Johan Rystrom, Monte Carlo Open at Mont Agel, 1992; (-12) Bernhard Langer (Ger), Linde German Masters at Motzener See, 1997; (-12) Darren Clarke, Smurfit European Open at K Club, 1999; (-10) Tobias Dier TNT Open, Hilversum, 2002; (-12) Fredrik Jacobson, Linde German Masters, Gut Larchenhof, 2003

Lowest 36 holes
124 (18 under par) Colin Montgomerie (Sco), Canon European Masters at Crans-sur-Sierre, 1996 (3rd and 4th rounds)

Lowest 54 holes
192 (18 under par) Tiger Woods, NEC Invitational, Firestone, Akron, Ohio, 2000 (first 3 rounds)
192 (24 under par) Anders Forsbrand (Swe), Ebel European Masters Swiss Open, Crans-sur-Sierre, 1987 (rounds 2-3-4)

Lowest first 36 holes
125 (15 under par) Tiger Woods, NEC Invitational World Championship, Firestone, Akron, Ohio, 2000
125 (17 under par) Frankie Minoza, Caltex Singapore Masters, Singapore Island, 2001

Largest winning margin
15 strokes Tiger Woods, United States Open, Pebble Beach, 2000 (**Note:** Bernhard Langer's 17-stroke victory in 1979 at Cacharel Under-25's Championship in Nîmes no longer counted a full European Tour event)

Highest winning score
306 Peter Butler (Eng), Schweppes PGA Close Championship at Royal Birkdale, 1963

Youngest winner
Dale Hayes, 18 years 290 days, Spanish Open, 1971

Oldest winner
Des Smyth (Ire), 48 years 34 days, Madeira Island Open, 2001

Most wins in one season
7 Norman von Nida (Aus), 1947

US Tour

Lowest 72-hole aggregate
254 (26 under par) Tommy Armour III, Valero Texas Open, 2003 (**Note:** Ernie Els' 261 at the 2003 Mercedes Championship was a record 31 under par)

Lowest 54 holes
189 (24 under par) Chandler Harper, Texas Open (last three rounds), 1954; John Cook, St Jude Classic (first three rounds), 1996; Mark Calcavecchia, Phoenix Open (first three rounds), 2001; (21 under par) Tommy Armour III, Valero Texas Open (first three rounds), 2003 (**Note:** Tim Herron's 190 at the 2003 Bob Hope Chrysler Classic (rounds 2-4) was a record 26 under par)

Lowest 36 holes
124 (18 under par) Mark Calcavecchia (USA), Phoenix Open, 2001 (2nd and 3rd rounds) (Note: Gay Brewer's 125 at the 1967 Pensacola Open (2nd and 3rd rounds), John Cook's 125 at the 1997 Bob Hope Chrysler Classic (last two rounds) and Tim Herron's 125 at the 2003 Bob Hope Chrysler Classic (2nd and 3rd rounds) were a record 19 under par)

Lowest 18 holes
59 Sam Snead, 3rd round, Greenbrier Open (Sam Snead Festival), White Sulphur Springs, West Virginia, 1959; Al Geiberger, 2nd round, Danny Thomas Memphis Classic, Colonial CC, 1977 (when preferred lies were in operation); (-13) Chip Beck on the 6,914-yards Sunrise GC course, Las Vegas, 3rd round, Las Vegas Invitational, 1991 (finished third but won a bonus prize of $500,000 and another $500,000 for charities; (-13) David Duval on 6,940-yd PGA West Arnold Palmer course, CA, final round, Bob Hope Chrysler Classic, 1999 (won tournament with last hole eagle)

Lowest 9 holes
27　(9 under par) Billy Mayfair, Buick Open, 2001; (8 under par) Mike Souchak, Texas Open, 1955; (7 under par) Andy North, BC Open, 1975

Lowest first 36 holes
125　(17 under par) Mark Calcavecchia (USA), Phoenix Open, 2001; (15 under par) Tiger Woods (USA), NEC Invitational World Championship, Firestone, Akron, Ohio, 2000

Largest winning margin
16 strokes J. Douglas Edgar, Canadian Open Championship, 1919; Bobby Locke, Chicago Victory National Championship, 1948

Youngest winner
Johnny McDermott, 19 years 10 months, US Open, 1911

Youngest to make cut
Bob Panasik, 15 years 8 months 20 days, Canadian Open, 1957

Oldest winner
Sam Snead, 52 years 10 months, Greater Greensboro Open, 1965

Most wins in one season
18　Byron Nelson, 1945

National opens – excluding Europe and USA

Lowest 72-hole aggregate
255　Peter Tupling, Nigerian Open, Lagos, 1981.

Lowest 36-hole aggregate
124　(18 under par) Sandy Lyle, Nigerian Open, Ikoyi GC, Lagos, 1978 (his first year as a professional)

Lowest 18 holes
59　Gary Player, second round, Brazilian Open, Gavea GC (6,185 yards), Rio de Janeiro, 1974.

Professional events – excluding Europe and USA

Lowest 72-hole aggregate
260　Bob Charles, Spalding Masters at Tauranga, New Zealand, 1969; Jason Bohn (USA), Bayer Classic, Huron Oaks, Canada, 2001.

Lowest 18-hole aggregate
58　(13 under par) Jason Bohn (USA), Bayer Classic, Huron Oaks, Canada, 2001 (**Note:** Miguel Angel Martin had round of 59 at South Argentine Open, 1987).

Lowest 9-hole aggregate
27　Bill Brask (USA) at Tauranga in the New Zealand PGA in 1976.

Amateur winners
Charles Evans, 1910 Western Open, Beverly, Illinois; John Dawson, 1942 Bing Crosby, Rancho Santa Fe, California; Gene Littler, 1954 San Diego Open, Rancho Santa Fe, California; Doug Sanders, 1956 Canadian Open, Beaconsfield, Quebec; Scott Verplank 1985 Western Open, Butler National, Illinois; Phil Mickelson 1991 Northern Telecom Open, Tucson, Arizona

Asian PGA Tour

Lowest 72 holes
259　(-29) Ernie Els, 2003 Johnnie Walker Classic

Lowest 54 holes
193　(-23) Ernie Els, 2003 Johnnie Walker Classic

Lowest 36 holes
125　(-17) Frankie Minoza, 2001 Caltex Singapore Masters

Lowest 18 holes
61　(-11) Chung Chun-hsing, 2001 Maekyung LG Fashion Open; Chanin Puntawong (amateur), 2003 Thailand Open

Lowest 9 holes
28　(-8) Chung Chun-hsing, 2001 Maekyung LG Fashion Open; (-7) Henrik Bjornstad, 2001 Omega Hong Kong Open

Biggest win
12　Bradley Hughes, 1996 Players Championship

Youngest winner
Kim Dae-sub (amateur), 17 years 83 days, 1998 Korean Open

Oldest winner
Mike Cunning, 44 years 243 days, 2003 Royal Challenge Indian Open

Most wins in a season
3　Lin Keng-chi 1995 (Tournament Players Championship, Singapore PGA Championship, Samsung Masters); Simon Dyson 2000 (Omega Hong Kong Open, Macau Open, Volvo China Open)

Highest winning score
293　(+5) Boonchu Ruangkit, 1996 Myanmar Open

Japan Golf Tour

Lowest 72 holes
260　(-20) Masashi 'Jumbo' Ozaki, 1995 Chunichi Crowns, Nagoya Wago
262　(-26) Masashi Ozaki, 1996 Japan Series, Tokyo Yomiuri
266　(-26) Brandt Jobe, 1995 Mitsubishi Gallant, Aso Prince Hotel

Lowest 54 holes
193　(-23) Masahiro Kuramoto, 1987 Maruman Open, Higashi Matsuyama; (-17) Masashi Ozaki, 1995 Chunichi Crowns, Nagoya Wago

Lowest 36 holes
126　(-18) Masahiro Kuramoto, 1987 Maruman Open, Higashi Matsuyama

Lowest 18 holes
59　(-12) Masahiro Kuramoto, 2003 Acom International

Lowest 9 holes
28　(-8) Isao Aoki, 1972 Kanto Pro, Isogo; Takashi Murakami, 1972 Kanto Pro, Isogo; Yoshinori Kaneko, 1994 Nikkei Open, Mitsui-kanko Tomakomai; Masayuki Kawamura, 1995 Gene Sarazen Jun Classic; Tsuyoshi Yoneyama, 1998 Sapporo Tokyu, Sapporo Kokusai; Toshimitsu Izawa, 2000 TPC Iiyama Cup, Horai

Largest winning margin
15 Masashi Ozaki, 1994 Daiwa International Hatoyama (pre-1973 tour formation: 19 Akira Muraki, 1930 Japan PGA Championship, Takarazuka)

Youngest winner
Seve Ballesteros, 20 years 5 months, 1977 Japan Open, Narashino (pre-1973 tour formation: Toichiro Toda, 18 years 6 months, 1933 Kansai Open)

Oldest winner
Masashi Ozaki, 55 years 8 months, 2002 ANA Open, Sapporo Wattsu

Most wins in a season
9 Tsuneyuki 'Tommy'Nakajima, 1983; Masashi Ozaki 1972 Masashi 'Jumbo' Ozaki

Highest winning score
298 (+10) Naomichi 'Joe' Ozaki, 1999 Japan Open, Otaru

South African Sunshine Tour

No records available at time of going to press

Australasian Tour

No records kept

Canadian Tour

Lowest 72 holes
260 (24 under par) Jason Bohn, 2001 Bayer Championship; (20 under par) Brian Kontak, 1998 Alberta Open (Note: Tim Clark's 261 at 1998 Royal Oaks New Brunswick Open was a record 27 under par)

Lowest 54 holes
194 Brian Kontak, 1999 Telus Henry Singer Alberta Open

Lowest 36 holes
126 Matt Cole, 1988 Windsor Charity Classic (first two rounds)

Lowest 18 holes
58 (13 under par) Jason Bohn, 2001 Bayer Championship

Lowest 9 holes
26 (9 under par) Jason Bohn, 2001 Bayer Championship

Largest winning margin
11 Arron Oberholser, 1999 Ontario Open Heritage Classic

Most wins in one season
4 Moe Norman, 1966 (Manitoba Open, CPGA Championship, Quebec Open, Alberta Open); Trevor Dodds, 1996 (Henry Singer Alberta Open, ED TEL Planet Open, Infiniti Championship, Canadian Masters)

LPGA Tour

Lowest 72 holes
261 (27 under par) Annika Sörenstam, Standard Register Ping, Moon Valley, Arizona, 2001; (23 under par) Se Ri Pak, Jamie Farr, Kroger Classic, Highland Meadows, Ohio, 1998

Lowest 54 holes
193 (23 under par) Karrie Webb, Oldsmobile Classic, Walnut Hills, Michigan, 2000; Annika Sörenstam, Standard Register Ping, Moon Valley, Arizona, 2001

Lowest 36 holes
124 (20 under par) Annika Sörenstam, Standard Register Ping, Moon Valley, Arizona, 2001; (16 under par) Meg Mallon, Welch's/Fry Championship, Dell Urich, Arizona, 2003

Lowest 18 holes
59 (13 under par) Annika Sörenstam, Standard Register Ping, Moon Valley, Arizona, 2001

Lowest 9 holes
28 (8 under par) Mary Beth Zimmerman, Rail Charity Classic, Springfield, Illinois, 1984; Annika Sörenstam, Standard Register Ping, Moon Valley, Arizona, 2001; (7 under par) Pat Bradley, Columbia Savings Classic, Green Gables, Colorado, 1984; Muffin Spencer-Devlin, MasterCard International Pro-am, Knollwood, New York, 1985; Peggy Kirsch, Phar-Mor Tournament, Squaw Creek, Ohio, 1991; Young Kim, Welch's/Fry Championship, Dell Urich, Arizona, 2003; (6 under par) Renee Heiken, Jamie Farr Kroger Classic, Highland Meadows, Ohio, 1996; Danielle Ammaccapane, Jamie Farr Kroger Classic, Highland Meadows, Ohio, 2002; Chris Johnson, Jamie Farr Kroger Classic, Highland Meadows, Ohio, 2003

Largest winning margin
14 strokes Cindy Mackey, MasterCard International Pro-am, Knollwood, New York, 1986

Youngest winner
Marlene Hagge, 18 years 14 days, Sarasota Open, 1952

Oldest winner
JoAnne Carner, 46 years 5 months 11 days, Safeco Classic, 1985

Most wins in a season
13 Mickey Wright, 1963

Ladies European Tour

Lowest 72 holes
267 Laura Davies, 1988 Biarritz Ladies Open, Biarritz; Laura Davies, 1995 Guardian Irish Holidays Open, St Margaret's; Juli Inkster, 2003 Evian Masters, Evian

Lowest 54 holes
198 Karrie Webb, 1997 Weetabix Women's British Open, Sunningdale

Lowest 36 holes
129 (-17) Sophie Gustafson, 2003 Ladies Irish Open, Killarney

Lowest 18 holes
62 (-11) Trish Johnson, 1996 Ladies French Open; (-10) Suzann Pettersen, 2003 HP Open

Lowest 9 holes
29 Kitrina Douglas, 1988 Italian Ladies Open, Cá Della Nave; Regine Lautens, 1988 Godiva European Masters, Royal Antwerp; Laura Davies, 1987 First Open de France, Feminin, Fourqueux; Anne Jones, 1990 Trophée International Coconut Skol, Fourqueux; Trish Johnson, 1999 Cantor Fitzgerald Laura Davies Invitational, Brocket Hall; Trish Johnson, 1999 Marrakech Palmeraie Open, Palmeraie Golf Palace; Rachel Hetherington, 2000 AAMI Women's Australian Open, Yarra Yarra; Federica Dassu, 2000 Chrysler Open, Halmstad; Susan Redman, 2000 Evian Masters, Evian

Largest winning margin
16 strokes Laura Davies, 1995 Guardian Irish Holidays Open, St Margaret's

Youngest winner
Florence Descampe, 19 years 74 days, 1988 Danish Ladies Open, Rungsted

Oldest winner
Federica Dassu, 46 years 105 days, 2003 Open de España Femenino, Campo De Golf De Salamanca

Most wins in a year
7 Marie-Laure de Lorenzi, 1988 (French Open, Volmac Open, Hennessy Cup, Gothenburg Open, Laing Charity Classic, Woolmark Matchplay, Qualitair Spanish Open)

Miscellaneous British

72-hole aggregate
Andrew Brooks recorded a 72-hole aggregate of 259 in winning the Skol (Scotland) tournament at Williamwood in 1974.

Lowest rounds
Playing on the ladies' course (4,020 yards) at Sunningdale on 26th September, 1961, Arthur Lees, the professional there, went round in 52, 10 under par. He went out in 26 (2, 3, 3, 4, 3, 3, 3, 3, 2) and came back in 26 (2, 3, 3, 3, 2, 3, 4, 3, 3).

On 1st January, 1936, A.E. Smith, Woolacombe Bay professional, recorded a score of 55 in a game there with a club member. The course measured 4,248 yards. Smith went out in 29 and came back in 26 finishing with a hole-in-one at the 18th.

Other low scores recorded in Britain are by C.C. Aylmer, an English International who went round Ranelagh in 56; George Duncan, Axenfels in 56; Harry Bannerman, Banchory in 56 in 1971; Ian Connelly, Welwyn Garden City in 56 in 1972; James Braid, Hedderwick near Dunbar in 57; H. Hardman, Wirral in 58; Norman Quigley, Windermere in 58 in 1937; Robert Webster, Eaglescliffe in 58, in 1970. Harry Weetman scored 58 in a round at the 6171 yards Croham Hurst on 30th January, 1956.

D. Sewell had a round of 60 in an Alliance Meeting at Ferndown, Bournemouth, a full-size course. He scored 30 for each half and had a total of 26 putts. In September 1986, Jeffrey Burn, handicap 1, of Shrewsbury GC, scored 60 in a club competition, made up of 8 birdies, an eagle and 9 pars. He was 30 out and 30 home and no. 5 on his card. Andrew Sherborne, as a 20-year-old amateur, went round Cirencester in 60 strokes. Dennis Gray completed a round at Broome Manor, Swindon (6906 yards, SSS 73) in the summer of 1976 in 60 (28 out, 32 in).

Playing over Aberdour on 13th June, 1936, Hector Thomson, British Amateur champion, 1936, and Jack McLean, former Scottish Amateur champion, each did 61 in the second round of an exhibition. McLean in his first round had a 63, which gave him an aggregate 124 for 36 holes.

Steve Tredinnick in a friendly match against business tycoon Joe Hyman scored a 61 over West Sussex (6211 yards) in 1970. It included a hole-in-one at the 12th (198 yards) and a 2 at the 17th (445 yards).

Another round of 61 on a full-size course was achieved by 18-year-old Michael Jones on his home course, Wor-

thing GC (6274 yards), in the first round of the President's Cup in May, 1974.

In the Second City Pro-Am tournament in 1970, at Handsworth, Simon Fogarty did the second 9 holes in 27 against the par of 36.

Miscellaneous USA

Lowest rounds
The lowest known scores recorded for 18 holes in America are 55 by E.F. Staugaard in 1935 over the 6419 yards Montebello Park, California, and 55 by Homero Blancas in 1962 over the 5002 yards Premier course in Longview, Texas. Staugaard in his round had 2 eagles, 13 birdies and 3 pars.

Equally outstanding is a round of 58 (13 under par) achieved by a 13-year-old boy, Douglas Beecher, on 6th July, 1976, at Pitman CC, New Jersey. The course measured 6180 yards from the back tees, and the middle tees, off which Douglas played, were estimated by the club professional to reduce the yardage by under 180 yards.

In 1941 at a 6100 yards course in Portsmouth, Virginia, Chandler Harper scored 58.

Jack Nicklaus in an exhibition match at Breakers Club, Palm Beach, California, in 1973 scored 59 over the 6200-yard course.

The lowest 9-hole score in America is 25, held jointly by Bill Burke over the second half of the 6384 yards Normandie CC, St Louis in May, 1970 at the age of 29; by Daniel Cavin, who had seven 3s and two 2s on the par 36 Bill Brewer Course, Texas, in September, 1959; and by Douglas Beecher over the second half of Pitman CC, New Jersey, on 6th July, 1976, at the amazingly young age of 13. The back 9 holes of the Pitman course measured 3150 yards (par 35) from the back tees, but even though Douglas played off the middle tees, the yardage was still over 3000 yards for the 9 holes. He scored 8 birdies and 1 eagle.

Horton Smith scored 119 for two consecutive rounds in winning the Catalina Open in California in December, 1928. The course, however, measured only 4700 yards.

Miscellaneous – excluding GB and USA
Tony Jacklin won the 1973 Los Lagartos Open with an aggregate of 261, 27 under par.

Henry Cotton in 1950 had a round of 56 at Monte Carlo (29 out, 27 in).

In a Pro-Am tournament prior to the 1973 Nigerian Open, British professional David Jagger went round in 59.

Max Banbury recorded a 9-hole score of 26 at Woodstock, Ontario, playing in a competition in 1952.

Women
The lowest score recorded on a full-size course by a woman is 59 by Sweden's Annika Sörenstam on the 6459 yards, par 72 Moon Valley course in Phoenix, Arizona. It broke by two the previous record of 61 by South Korean Se Ri Pak. Sörenstam began the tournament with a 65 and by adding rounds of 69 and 68 she equalled the LPGA record of 261 set by Pak (71-61-63-66) at Highland Meadows in Ohio in 1998. Sörenstam's score represents 27 under par, Pak's 23 under.

The lowest 9-hole score on the US Ladies' PGA circuit is 28, first achieved by Mary Beth Zimmerman in the 1984 Rail Charity Classic and since equalled

by Pat Bradley, Muffin Spencer-Devlin, Peggy Kirsch, Renee Heiken, Anika Sörenstam and Danielle Ammaccapane.

The Lowest 36-hole score is the 124 (20 under par) by Sörenstam at Moon Valley and the lowest 54-hole score 193 (23 under par) by Karrie Webb at Walnut Hills, Michigan, in the 2000 Oldsmobile Classic and equalled by Sörenstam at Moon Valley.

Patty Berg holds the record for the most number of women's majors with 15; Kathy Whitworth achieved a record number of tournament wins with 88; Mickey Wright's 13 wins in 1963 was the most in one season and the youngest and oldest winners of LPGA events were Marlene Hagge, 18 years and 14 days when she won the 1952 Sarasota Open and JoAnne Carner, 46 years 5 months 11 days when she won the 1985 Safeco Classic.

The lowest round on the European LPGA is 62 (11 under par) by Trish Johnson in the 1996 French Open. A 62 was also achieved by New Zealand's Janice Arnold at Coventry in 1990 during a Women's Professional Golfers' Association tournament.

The lowest 9-hole score on the European LPGA circuit is 29 by Kitrina Douglas, Regine Lautens, Laura Davies, Anne Jones and Trish Johnson.

In the Women's World Team Championship in Mexico in 1966, Mrs Belle Robertson, playing for the British team, was the only player to break 70. She scored 69 in the third round.

At Westgate-on-Sea GC (measuring 5002 yards), Wanda Morgan scored 60 in an open tournament in 1929.

Since scores cannot properly be taken in matchplay no stroke records can be made in matchplay events. Nevertheless we record here two outstanding examples of low scoring in the finals of national championships. Mrs Catherine Lacoste de Prado is credited with a score of 62 in the first round of the 36-hole final of the 1972 French Ladies' Open Championship at Morfontaine. She went out in 29 and came back in 33 on a course measuring 5933 yards. In the final of the English Ladies' Championship at Woodhall Spa in 1954, Frances Stephens (later Mrs Smith) did the first nine holes against Elizabeth Price (later Mrs Fisher) in 30. It included a hole-in-one at the 5th. The nine holes measured 3280 yards.

Amateurs

National championships

The following examples of low scoring cannot be regarded as genuine stroke play records since they took place in match play. Nevertheless they are recorded here as being worthy of note.

Michael Bonallack in beating David Kelley in the final of the English championship in 1968 at Ganton did the first 18 holes in 61 with only one putt under two feet conceded. He was out in 32 and home in 29. The par of the course was 71.

Charles McFarlane, playing in the fourth round of the Amateur Championship at Sandwich in 1914 against Charles Evans did the first nine holes in 31, winning by 6 and 5.

This score of 31 at Sandwich was equalled on several occasions in later years there. Then, in 1948, Richard Chapman of America went out in 29 in the fourth round eventually beating Hamilton McInally, Scottish Champion in 1937, 1939 and 1947, by 9 and 7.

In the fourth round of the Amateur Championship at Hoylake in 1953, Harvie Ward, the holder, did the first nine holes against Frank Stranahan in 32. The total yardage for the holes was 3474 yards and included one hole of 527 yards and five holes over 400 yards. Ward won by one hole.

Francis Ouimet in the first round of the American Amateur Championship in 1932 against George Voigt did the first nine holes in 30. Ouimet won by 6 and 5.

Open competitions

The 1970 South African Dunlop Masters Tournament was won by an amateur, John Fourie, with a score of 266, 14 under par. He led from start to finish with rounds of 65, 68, 65, 68, finally winning by six shots from Gary Player.

Jim Ferrier, Manly, won the New South Wales championship at Sydney in 1935 with 266. His rounds were: 67, 65, 70, 64, giving an aggregate 16 strokes better than that of the runner-up. At the time he did this amazing score Ferrier was 20 years old and an amateur.

Aaron Baddeley became the first amateur to win the Australian Open since Bruce Devlin in 1960 when he took the title at Royal Sydney in 1999. After turning pro he successfully defended the title the following year at Kingston Heath.

Holes below par

Most holes below par

E.F. Staugaard in a round of 55 over the 6419 yards Montbello Park, California, in 1935, had two eagles, 13 birdies and three pars.

American Jim Clouette scored 14 birdies in a round at Longhills GC, Arkansas, in 1974. The course measured 6257 yards.

Jimmy Martin in his round of 63 in the Swallow-Penfold at Stoneham in 1961 had one eagle and 11 birdies.

In the Ricarton Rose Bowl at Hamilton, Scotland, in August, 1981, Wilma Aitken, a women's amateur internationalist, had 11 birdies in a round of 64, including nine consecutive birdies from the 3rd to the 11th.

Mrs Donna Young scored nine birdies and one eagle in one round in the 1975 Colgate European Women's Open.

Jason Bohn had two eagles and 10 birdies in his closing 58 at the 2001 Bayer Classic on the Canadian Tour at the par 71 Huron Oaks.

Consecutive holes below par

Lionel Platts had ten consecutive birdies from the 8th to 17th holes at Blairgowrie GC during a practice round for the 1973 Sumrie Better-Ball tournament.

Roberto De Vicenzo in the Argentine Centre of the Republic Championship in April, 1974 at the Cordoba GC, Villa Allende, broke par at each of the first nine holes. (By starting his round at the 10th hole they were in fact the second nine holes played by Vicenzo.) He had one eagle (at the 7th hole) and eight birdies. The par for the 3,602 yards half was 37, completed by Vicenzo in 27.

Nine consecutive holes under par have been recorded by Claude Harmon in a friendly match over Winged Foot GC, Mamaroneck, NY, in 1931; by Les Hardie at Eastern GC, Melbourne, in April, 1934; by Jimmy Smith at McCabe GC, Nashville, Tenn, in 1969; by 13-year-old Douglas Beecher, in 1976, at Pitman CC, New Jersey; by Rick Sigda at Greenfield CC, Mass, in 1979; and by Ian Jelley at Brookman Park in 1994.

T.W. Egan in winning the East of Ireland Championship in 1962 at Baltray had eight consecutive birdies (2nd to 9th) in the third round.

On the United States PGA tour, eight consecutive holes below par have been achieved by three players – Bob Goalby in the 1961 St Petersburg Open, Fuzzy Zoeller in the 1976 Quad Cities Open and Dewey Arnette in the 1987 Buick Open.

Fred Couples set a PGA European Tour record with 12 birdies in a round of 61 during the 1991 Scandinavian Masters on the 72-par Drottningholm course. This has since been equalled by Ernie Els (1994 Dubai Desert Classic) and by Russell Claydon and Fredrik Lindgren (1995 German Masters). Ian Woosnam, Tony Johnstone, Severiano Ballesteros, John Bickerton, Mark O'Meara and Raymond Russell share another record with eight successive birdies.

The United States Ladies' PGA record is seven consecutive holes below par achieved by Carol Mann in the Borden Classic at Columbus, Ohio in 1975.

Miss Wilma Aitken recorded nine successive birdies (from the 3rd to the 11th) in the 1981 Ricarton Rose Bowl.

This has since been equalled by Ernie Els (1994 Dubai Desert Classic), Russell Claydon and Fredrik Lindgren (1995 Mercedes German Masters) and Darreb Clarke (1999 Smurfit European Open). Ian Woosnam, Tony Johnstone, Severiano Ballesteros, John Bickerton, Mark O'Meara, Raymond Russell, Darren Clarke and Marcello Santi and Marten Olander share another record with eight successive birdies.

Low scoring rarities

At Standerton GC, South Africa, in May 1937, F.F. Bennett, playing for Standerton against Witwaters-rand University, did the 2nd hole, 110 yards, in three 2s and a 1. Standerton is a 9-hole course, and in the match Bennett had to play four rounds.

In 1957 a fourball comprising H.J. Marr, E. Stevenson, C. Bennett and W.S. May completed the 2nd hole (160 yards) in the grand total of six strokes. Marr and Stevenson both holed in one while Bennett and May both made 2.

The old Meadow Brook Club of Long Island, USA, had five par 3 holes and George Low in a round there in the 1950s scored two at each of them.

In a friendly match on a course near Chicago in 1971, assistant professional Tom Doty (23 years) had a remarkable low run over four consecutive holes: 4th (350 yards) 2; 5th (360 yards, dogleg) 1; 6th (175 yards) 1; 7th (375 yards) 2.

R.W. Bishop, playing in the Oxley Park, July medal competition in 1966, scored three consecutive 2s. They occurred at the 12th, 13th and 14th holes which measured 151, 500 and 136 yards respectively.

In the 1959 PGA Close Championship at Ashburnham, Bob Boobyer scored five 2s in one of the rounds.

American Art Wall scored three consecutive 2s in the first round of the US Masters in 1974. They were at the 4th, 5th and 6th holes, the par of which was 3, 4 and 3.

Nine consecutive 3s have been recorded by R.H. Corbett in 1916 in the semi-final of the Tangye Cup; by Dr James Stothers of Ralston GC over the 2056 yards 9-hole course at Carradale, Argyll, during the summer of 1971; by Irish internationalist Brian Kissock in the Homebright Open at Carnalea GC, Bangor, in June, 1975; and by American club professional Ben Toski.

The most consecutive 3s in a British PGA event is seven by Eric Brown in the Dunlop at Gleneagles (Queen's Course) in 1960.

Hubert Green scored eight consecutive 3s in a round in the 1980 US Open.

The greatest number of 3s in one round in a British PGA event is 11 by Brian Barnes in the 1977 Skol Lager tournament at Gleneagles.

Fewest putts

The lowest known number of putts in one round is 14, achieved by Colin Collen-Smith in a round at Betchworth Park, Dorking, in June, 1947. He single-putted 14 greens and chipped into the hole on four occasions.

Professional Richard Stanwood in a round at Riverside GC, Pocatello, Idaho on 17th May, 1976 took 15 putts, chipping into the hole on five occasions.

Several instances of 16 putts in one round have been recorded in friendly games.

For 9 holes, the fewest putts is five by Ron Stutesman for the first 9 holes at Orchard Hills G&CC, Washington, USA in 1978.

Walter Hagen in nine consecutive holes on one occasion took only seven putts. He holed long putts on seven greens and chips at the other two holes.

In competitive stroke rounds in Britain and Ireland, the lowest known number of putts in one round is 18, in a medal round at Portpatrick Dunskey GC, Wilmslow GC professional Fred Taggart is reported to have taken 20 putts in one round of the 1934 Open Cham-pionship. Padraigh Hogan (Elm Park), when competing in the Junior Scratch Cup at Carlow in 1976, took only 20 putts in a round of 67.

The fewest putts in a British PGA event is believed to be 22 by Bill Large in a qualifying round over Moor Park High Course for the 1972 Benson and Hedges Match Play.

Overseas, outside the United States of America, the fewest putts is 19 achieved by Robert Wynn (GB) in a round in the 1973 Nigerian Open and by Mary Bohen (US) in the final round of the 1977 South Australian Open at Adelaide.

The USPGA record for fewest putts in one round is 18, achieved by Andy North (1990); Kenny Knox (1989); Mike McGee (1987) and Sam Trehan (1979). For 9 holes the record is eight putts by Kenny Knox (1989), Jim Colbert (1987) and Sam Trehan (1979).

The fewest putts recorded for a 72-hole US PGA Tour event is 93 by Kenny Knox in the 1989 Heritage Classic at Harbour Town Golf Links.

The fewest putts recorded by a woman is 17, by Joan Joyce in the Lady Michelob tournament, Georgia, in May, 1982.

PART XI

Guide to Golfing Services and Places to Stay in the British Isles and Ireland

Golf Club Facilities	590
Buyer's Guide	699
Golfing Hotel Compendium	616
Professional Associations	622

Golf Club Facilities

This section lists clubs which can offer hotel accommodation, and hotels which have their own golf facilities. They are able to provide for society or corporate days, and in some instances offer an extensive range of other sports and leisure activities.

Abbotsley Golf Hotel & Country Club
Eynesbury Hardwicke, St Neots, Cambridgeshire PE19 4XN
Tel: (01480) 474000 *Fax:* (01480) 471018
Set in 250 acres of idyllic countryside, offering two 18-hole courses, a par 3, driving range, squash courts, fitness centre and a 42-bedroom hotel. Golf breaks and residential packages available. Operated by American Golf (UK) Limited.

Beaufort Golf Course
Churchtown, Beaufort, Killarney, Co Kerry, Ireland
Tel: +353 64 44440 *Fax:* +353 64 44752
A traditional Kerry welcome awaits you at the *Friendliest Course in Kerry*. Challenging 18-hole par 71 championship course, buggies and caddies for hire, excellent golf shop, bar food and snacks. Tuition can be arranged with our golf professional. Societies and groups welcome. (*See advertisement on page 594 for further details.*)

Borth & Ynyslas Golf Club
Borth, Ceredigion SY24 5JS
Tel: (01970) 871202
*E-mail:*secretary@borthgolf.co.uk
18-hole links course adjoining Borth beach. Humps and hollows provide great variation, although the topography and springy turf make for easy walking. Professional's shop, practice area, modern clubhouse with bar and catering. Tuition available.

Burnham & Berrow Golf Club
St Christopher's Way, Burnham-on-Sea, Somerset TA8 2PE
Tel: (01278) 785760
E-mail: Secretary@BurnhamandBerrow .freeserve.co.uk
18-hole championship links golf course and 9-hole course. Dormy accommodation available. (*See advertisement on 596 page for further details.*)

Bushey Hall Golf Club
Bushey Hall Drive, Bushey, Hertfordshire WD23 2EP
Tel: (01923) 222253 (01923) 225802 (proshop)
*Website:*www.golfclubuk.co.uk

Established in 1890 Bushey Hall Golf Club has one of the oldest and best established courses in Hertfordshire. Facilities include a fully equipped pro shop, practice net, clubhouse restaurant and bar. Open for membership. Pay as you play operated. (*See advertisement on page 598 for further details.*)

Castletown Golf Links
Fort Island, Derbyhaven, Isle of Man IM9 1UA
Tel: (01624) 822220 *Fax:* (01624) 829661
E-mail: 1sttee@manx.net
Website: www.golfiom.com
An 18-hole links championship course voted number 82 in the UK by *Golf World* magazine. Measuring 6,707 yards SSS 72 established since 1892 it is set on the peninsula of Langness surrounded by sea on three sides and overlooking the Manx rolling hills. Accommodation is available twelve months of the year, three bars, excellent local cuisine, table d'hôte and à la carte in both restaurants. Visiting parties and non-members welcome.

Cave Castle Hotel & Country Club
South Cave, East Yorkshire HU15 2EU
Tel: (01430) 422245 *Fax:* (01430) 421118
Superb country manor house with 53 en suite bedrooms in tranquil 160-acre parkland setting with easy access to M62 motorway. Excellent, traditional cuisine is served in our character restaurant. 18-hole golf course with mix of park and meadowland providing good test of golf to all levels. Leisure facilities, including 19m indoor pool, gym, sauna, steam and spa. This is a Unique Leisure Experience not to be missed! Golf and leisure breaks, visiting parties and non-golfers welcome.

Charleville Golf Club
Charleville, Co Cork, Ireland.
Tel: +353 63 81257 *Fax:* +353 63 81274
E-mail: charlevillegolf@eircom.net
Website: www.charlevillegolf.com
Located in the foothills of Ballyhoura mountains enjoy uncrowded golf at our 27-hole championship parkland course renowned for its lush fairways and excellent greens. Driving range, full bar and catering facilities in our friendly clubhouse. Open from 7.30am to sunset.

Dalmunzie House Hotel

Spittal O'Glenshee, Blairgowrie, Perthshire
PH10 7QG
Tel: (01250) 885224
Fax: (01250) 885225

Set in the Highlands with our own 9-hole course. This friendly country house offers an ideal base for a golfing holiday with excellent local courses at Blairgowrie, Pitlochry, Alyth and many more. (*See advertisement page 608 for further details.*)

Edmondstown Golf Club

Rathfarnham, Dublin 16, Ireland.
Tel: +353 1493 1082
Fax: +353 1493 3152
*E-mail:*info@edmondstowngolfclub.ie
*Website:*www.edmondstowngolfclub.ie

Edmondstown Golf Club is situated amongst the most delightful surroundings on the foothills of the Dublin mountains, and only seven miles from Dublin City centre. A testing parkland course – it lends itself to the golfer who desires a socially enjoyable round of golf – on a well maintained and manicured golf course. (*See advertisement page 595 for further details.*)

The Grange & Links Hotel

Sea Lane, Sandilands, Sutton-on-Sea, Lincolnshire
LN12 2RA
Tel: (01507) 441334 *Fax:* (01507) 443033
E-mail: grangelinks@ic24.net
Website: www.grangeandlinkshotel.com

3-Star 30-bedroom hotel with own 18-hole links course. Two tennis courts, snooker and ballroom. Award-winning hotel renowned for superb cuisine, friendliness, comfort and service.

Harrogate Golf Club

Forest Lane Head, Harrogate, N. Yorkshire HG2 7TF
Tel: (01423) 862999 Fax:01423 860073

A long established 18-hole golf course set amongst mature trees formerly part of the Forest of Knaresborough. Visitors are assured of a warm reception in the extensively refurbished clubhouse and restaurant. (*See advertisement on page 598 for further details.*)

Howth Golf Club

St Fintan's, Carrickbrack Road, Sutton, Dublin 13, Ireland
Tel: +353 1 832 3055 *Fax:* +353 1 832 1793
E-mail: secretary@howthgolfclub.ie
Website: www.howthgolfclub.ie

Howth Golf Club is a long established heathland course located within ten miles of Dublin City centre and Dublin airport. The club boasts a fine clubhouse and enjoys panoramic views of land and sea scapes.

The Island Golf Club

Corballis, Donabate, Co Dublin, Ireland
Tel: +353 1 843 6205 *Fax:* +353 1 843 6860
E-mail: reservations@theislandgolfclub.com
Website: www.theislandgolfclub.com

Continuing a tradition of links golf since its inception in 1890. The magnificent splendour and solitude associated with the Island, is highlighted by undulating fairways rolling through majestic sand dunes. This classic championship links is less than 15 minutes from Dublin Airport and all visitors are ensured a warm welcome. Par 71, SSS 73, 6200 metres.

La Grande Mare Hotel Golf Club

La Grande Mare, Vazon, Castel, Guernsey
Tel: (01481) 256576 & 253544
Fax: (01481) 255194
Website: www.lgm.guernsey.net

Beautifully appointed luxury hotel with 18-hole golf course. Professional shop and tuition on-site. First class, well priced restaurant. 2-AA Rosettes. Beachside location. Golfing breaks catered for.

Linden Hall

Longhorsley, Morpeth, Northumberland NE65 8XF
Tel: (01670) 500011 *Fax:* (01670) 500001
Website: www.lindenhall.co.uk

Linden Hall golf course is located within the grounds of Linden Hall Hotel, a 3-Star, 52-bedroom luxury country house hotel, with swimming pool, health spa, gymnasium and conference facilities. An added facility is the 14-bedroom Linden Dormy House ideal for golfing parties. The 18-hole, 6,846 yard SSS 73 golf course completely surrounds the hotel and is set within mature woodland, rolling parkland with established burns and lakes amidst the stunning backdrop of the Cheviot hills and Northumbrian coastline.

Machrie Hotel & Golf Links

Port Ellen, Isle of Islay, Argyll PA42 7AN
Tel: (01496) 302310 *Fax:* (01496) 302404
E-mail: machrie@machrie.com
Website: www.machrie.com

Play a hidden gem of a course. Traditional 18-hole championship links course situated on the doorstep of the Machrie Hotel. Excellent accommodation, fine food and friendly service. Self-catering and golf packages also available.

Malone Golf Club

240 Upper Malone Road, Dunmurry, Belfast
BT17 9LB
Tel: 028 9061 2758 *Fax:* 028 9043 1394
E-mail: manager@malonegolfclub.co.uk
Website: www.malonegolfclub.co.uk

Superb 27-hole championship course set in 330 acres of rolling parkland. Five miles from Belfast city centre. Societies, groups and visitors welcome

592 Guide to Golfing Services

by arrangement. Full bar and catering facilities. (*See advertisement on page 596 for further details.*)

Mersey Valley Golf Club (1995)
Warrington Road, Bold Heath, Widnes, Cheshire
WA8 3XL
Tel: 0151-424 6060 *Fax:* 0151-257 9097

Conference facilities, corporate golf days and memberships, societies and visitors welcome. Buggy hire. We specialise in corporate golf days – easy walking course. 20 minutes from Liverpool and Manchester, two miles junction 7 on the M62. Superb bar and catering facilities.

North Shore Hotel Golf Club & Course
North Shore Road, Skegness PE25 1DN
Tel: (01754) 763298 *Fax:* (01754) 761902
E-mail: golf@north-shore.co.uk
Website: www.north-shore.co.uk

A mature and challenging 18-hole part parkland and part links course with sea views on the edge of Skegness. Good all year round climate. Rarely closed in winter with no winter greens. Rarely closed bars, superb bar food and à la carte restaurant. 36 bedrooms available.

Old Course Hotel – Golf Resort & Spa
St Andrews, Fife KY16 9SP
Tel: (01334) 474371 *Fax:* (01334) 477668

This luxury 134-bedroom hotel overlooks the 17th Road Hole of the Old Course and is a five minute walk to the beach and town. Facilities include health spa with swimming pool, whirlpool, fitness room and full range of massage and beauty treatments. The hotel has its own championship golf course, the Duke's Course. Open to non-residents, with residents enjoying guaranteed tee-times and reduced green fees.

Powerscourt Golf Club
Enniskerry, Co Wicklow, Ireland.
Tel: +353 1 204 6033 *Fax:* +353 1 276 1303
E-mail: golfclub@powerscourt.ie
Website: www.powerscourt.ie

Two Inspiring Courses in a Spectacular Location. The East and West courses at Powerscourt are both built to USGA specification. Free draining courses with links characteristics. The whole setting of Powerscourt Golf Club and the ambience is truly breathtaking. (*See advertisement page 594 for further details.*)

Prince's Golf Club
Sandwich Bay, Sandwich, Kent CT13 9QB
Tel: (01304) 611118 *Fax:* (01304) 612000
E-mail: hotel@princes-leisure.co.uk
Website: www.princes-leisure.co.uk

This previous Open Championship venue offers a challenging 27-hole course 6,690 yards par 71–72 and excellent driving range with friendly clubhouse

making visitors welcome. For overnight accommodation the Bell Hotel in Sandwich is within a ten minutes' drive where you can relax after a days golfing and enjoy imaginative cuisine and friendly service. (*See advertisement page 608 for further details.*)

Ramside Hall Hotel & Golf Club
Carrville, Durham DH1 1TD
Tel: 0191-386 5282 *Fax:* 0191-386 0399

Set in 220 acres on the outsksirts of the cathedral city of Durham and surrounded by a stimulating 27-hole golf course. 3-Star; 4-Crown Highly Commended. 80 luxury bedrooms, restaurant, grill room and carvery. Conference and banqueting facilities. Superb floodlit driving range and practice areas. (*See advertisement page 608 for further details.*)

Rosapenna Hotel & Golf Links
Rosapenna, Downings, Donegal, Ireland.
Tel: +353 74 55301 *Fax:* +353 74 55128

Rosapenna Hotel is set in the middle of its own 36-hole golf links course. Half a mile from the fishing village of Downings.

The Roxburghe Hotel & Golf Course
Heiton, By Kelso, Roxburghshire TD5 8JZ
Tel: (01573) 450331 *Fax:* (01573) 450611
E-mail: hotel@roxburghe.net
Website: www.roxburghe.net

A championship course, home to the Charles Church Scottish Seniors Open, owned by the Duke of Roxburghe set on the Roxburghe Estates. Designed by Dave Thomas at 7111 yards and par 72, the course record is 66 held by Sergio García. Currently the 5th best inland course in Scotland. Adjacent to the course is the four star, 22-bedroom country house hotel offering luxury accommodation and dining and the legendary Library offering an excellent selection of malt whiskies.

The Royal Dublin Golf Club
North Bull Island, Dollymount, Dublin 3, Ireland
Tel: +353 1 833 6346 *Fax:* +353 1 833 6504
E-mail: info@theroyaldublingolfclub.com
Website: www.theroyaldublingolfclub.com

The Royal Dublin Golf Club is Ireland's second oldest golf club and one of the country's premier sporting theatres. Royal Dublin provides visiting players with a combination of a superb championship links and a degree of hospitality that mirrors its historic development. (*See advertisement page on page 594 for further details.*)

Royal Lytham & St Anne's Golf Club
Links Gate, Lytham St Anne's, Lancashire
FY8 3LQ
Tel: (01253) 724206 *Fax:* (01253) 780946
*E-mail:*bookings@royallytham.org
*Website:*www.royallytham.org

Ideal for small parties wishing to play the championship course. Accommodation for men only.

THERE ARE MOMENTS

WHEN YOU REALISE YOU'VE JUST
BECOME PART OF SOMETHING BIGGER.

In 1894, Royal St. George's became the first club outside Scotland to host an Open Championship. Now, in 2003, the pursuit of the Claret Jug comes home to Royal St. George's for the 12th time. At Rolex, we are proud to be part of it. Because the perpetual quest for perfection is something we respect.

THE OPEN CHAMPIONSHIP, ROYAL ST. GEORGE'S.

ROLEX

OYSTER PERPETUAL DAY-DATE · WWW.ROLEX.COM

Apply to the assistant secretary. (*See advertisement
on this page for further details.*)

Rudding Park
Follifoot, Harrogate, North Yorkshire HG3 1DJ.
Tel: (01423) 872100 *Fax:* (01423) 873011
*E-mail:*sales@ruddingpark.com
*Website:*www.ruddingpark.com

Rudding Park, just two miles south of Harrogate
provides the complete golfing experience. The 18-
hole, par 72 Martin Hawtree designed parkland golf
course together with the award-winning hotel,
make for an enjoyable visit. The golf academy not
only boasts an 18-bay floodlit covered driving
range but also four PGA professionals. Corporate
and Society events welcome.

Sparkwell Golf Course
Blacklands, Sparkwell, Plymouth, Devon PL7 5DF
Tel/Fax: (01752) 837219

A testing 9-hole, pay as you play course and a par 3
course, set in 60 acres of parkland. Facilities
include a well equipped golf shop, excellent restaurant and friendly bar. Open to the public. Golf societies welcome.

St Helen's Bay Golf Resort
St Helens, Kilrane, Rosslare Harbour, Co Wexford,
Ireland
Tel: +353 53 33234
Fax: +353 53 33803

E-mail: sthelens@iol.ie
Website: www.sthelensbay.com

Superbly located championship 18-hole golf
course, which has blended the best of parkland
characteristics with a finish that is true links and
plenty of difficulty. Luxury on-site accommodation together with tennis courts. Full bar and
catering facilities available in the clubhouse.
Situated only five minutes from Rosslare ferryport. Green fee and society-friendly, playable all
year. With a new 9 holes opened in 2003, PGA
Teaching Professional & Teaching Academy, St
Helen's Bay is the ideal society play and stay
location.

Trevose Golf & Country Club
Constantine Bay, Padstow, North Cornwall
PL28 8JB
Tel: (01841) 520208 *Fax:* (01841) 521057
E-mail: reception@trevose-gc.co.uk
Website: www.trevose-gc.co.uk

Trevose offers not only great golf (championship
18-hole course, a 9-hole full length (3,100 yards)
par 35 plus a 9-hole short course) but also a first
class clubhouse and restaurant, three hard all-
weather tennis courts, a heated outdoor swimming
pool in the summer, a games room for the kids and
a boutique. Accommodation is available in bungalows, chalets, trehuel flats, dormy flats and cabins.
Send for our detailed colour brochure. Open all

year. Societies welcome. View website for latest special offers.

The Westin Turnberry Resort, Scotland

Turnberry, Ayrshire KA26 9LT
Tel: +44 (0) 1655 331000
Fax: +44 (0) 1655 331706
*E-mail:*turnberry@westin.com
*Website:*www.westin.com/turnberry

One of the finest golfing destinations in the world. Turnberry has two championship links courses, the legendary Ailsa (host to three Open's) and the highly acclaimed Kintyre. Whilst Colin Montgomerie Links Golf Academy offers world class teaching and practice facilities.

Wheathampstead Pay & Play Golf Course

Harpenden Road, St Albans, Hertfordshire AL4 8EZ
Tel/Fax: (01582) 833941

A 9-hole par 33 golf course and large practice area. Everyone is welcome. Doug Edgar, who built and designed the course, will help you with all your golfing needs. Telephone 01582 833941.

Whitefields Hotel Golf & Country Club

Coventry Road, Thurlaston, Nr Rugby, Warwickshire CV23 9JR
Tel: (01788) 521800 *Fax:* (01788) 521695
E-mail: mail@whitefields-hotel.co.uk
Website: www.whitefields-hotel.co.uk

18-hole course 6,289 yards. Floodlit driving range, putting green 18. Four conference rooms. 50 en suite rooms. Bars and à la carte restaurant. Pro – Mario Luca. Societies welcome seven days. Call the secretary on 01788 815555. Reservations 01788 521800.

Wicklow Golf Club

Dunbur Road, Wicklow, Ireland
Tel: +353 404 67379
Tel/Fax: +353 404 66122

A challenging and spectacular test of golf is promised here at Wicklow Golf Club. Par 71 SSS 70 5,720 metres featuring the natural contours of the terrain. Open from sunrise to sunset. Enjoy uncrowded golf and excellent clubhouse facilities. Visitors made very welcome.

Wokefield Park Golf Club

Mortimer, Reading, Berkshire RG7 3AE
Tel: 0118-933 4013
Fax: 0118-933 4031

Set amid the Berkshire countryside this challenging 7,000 yards golf course has mature trees, winding streams, nine lakes and large bunkers. Wokefield

The Open Championship
112,097 pars,
44,953 bogeys
or worse,
26,486 birdies,
644 eagles
23 years -
1 official scorer.

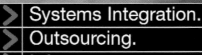

> Systems Integration.
> Outsourcing.
> Infrastructure.
> Server Technology.
> Consulting.

Imagine it:
31 ways to report scores in addition to the leaderboard. Plus pairings, tournament history - even weather conditions in real time. The R&A wanted a total scoring solution for this Open Championship

Done:
The R&A chose Unisys for all our abilities - and the comprehensive way we put them together to report scores accurately. As we do for all our clients, our competencies help realise a vision. In this case we developed The Open Championship scoring solution that's seamless, reliable and instantaneous. So the R&A can not only report a score for every kind of interest; it also has time to focus on what's even more important: the game.

Precision thinking, relentless execution to drive your vision forward.

UNISYS

Imagine it. Done.

unisys.com

also features 320 bedrooms, teaching academy and leisure facilities. Call the golf sales team on 0118-933 4013/4017.

Woodbury Park Golf & Country Club
Woodbury Castle, Woodbury, Exeter, Devon EX5 1JJ
Tel: (01395) 233382 *Fax:* (01395) 233384

Luxury 55-bedroom hotel with five superb lodges. The Nigel Mansell owned resort encompasses 27 holes, including the Oaks championship course, in addition to extensive leisure facilities. The ideal venue for your golfing break.

Buyer's Guide to Good Golfing and Golf Course Maintenance

This compact but informative guide to manufacturers and organisations offering services to golf clubs and individual golfers includes a wide number of categories, from services to personal accessories and golfing equipment to golf course maintenance.

Academic Qualifications 600
Agronomy 600
Architects and Consultants 600
Awards, Prizes and Trophies 602
Bag/Membership Tags 604
Bags/Golf Accessories 604
Ball Collectors 604
Book Sellers and Publishers 604
Carts, Trollies and Buggies 604
Computer Software/Systems 606
Corporate Gifts and Events 606
Course Construction and Upgrading 606
Course Measurement 607
Distributors and Wholesalers 607
Driving Range and Practice Equipment 609
Education 609
Electric Golf Cars 609
Electronic Point of Sale 609
Fixture Books 609
Gifts and Novelties .609
Golf Club Manufacturers/Suppliers 609
Golf Course Design Consultants 609
Golf Course Distance Guides 610
Golf Course Maintenance and Upgrading . . .610
Golf Development/Management 610
Golfing Aids/Practice Equipment 611
Greenkeeping and Driving Range Vehicles . . .611
Greenkeeping Information Service 611

Grips and Shafts 612
Insurance 612
Internet Tee-Time Booking 612
Irrigation Consultants/Design and
    Installation 612
Jewellery 613
Mail Order 613
Personal Equipment and Accessories 613
Personalised Products 613
Pictures and Prints .613
Practice Netting/Cages 613
Printing 613
Putters and Chippers: Manufacturers/
    Suppliers 613
Range Ball Manufacturers/Suppliers 613
Remote-Controlled Trollies 614
Ride-On Buggies 614
Scorecard and Planners 614
Simulator/Analysers 614
Tee Signs 614
Thermal Wear 614
Training and Teaching Aids 614
Trophies 614
Tuition 614
Water Features 615
Water Resources/Reservoir Design 615
Water Storage/Tanks 615
Weatherwear 615

ACADEMIC QUALIFICATIONS

Bournemouth University
School of Services Management, Fern Barrow,
Poole, Dorset BH12 5BB
Tel: (01202) 595146   *Fax:* (01202) 515707
E-mail: smu@bournemouth.ac.uk
Website: www.bournemouth.ac.uk
/services-management

The university has developed a unique degree for
those interested in a career in golf and/or sports
management. With the support of local golf clubs,
the BSc(Hons) in Sports Management (Golf) is a 4-
year sandwich degree which provides graduates
with the technical expertise as well as the manage-
rial skills necessary to succeed in this dynamic
industry. Contact: Programme Administrator,
School of Services Management.

AGRONOMY

British Rootzone & Topdressing Manufacturers Association
Federation House, NAC, Stoneleigh Park,
Warwickshire CV8 2RF
Tel: 024 7641 4999   *Fax:* 024 7641 4990
E-mail: brtma@sportslife.org.uk
Website: www.brtma.com

The Association is a collaboration of experience
and expertise in the manufacture of rootzone materials to offer architects, constructors and agronomists a recognised focal point for the industry.

PSD Agronomy Ltd
42 Garstang Road, Preston, Lancashire PR1 1NA
Tel: (01772) 884450   *Fax:* (01772) 884445
E-mail: psdgb@aol.com
Website: www.psdagronomy.com

A specialist team of golf course agronomists working throughout the UK and Europe. Whether building a new course, extending an existing one or just
making the best of what you have – we have the
technical expertise to help.

STRI – The Sports Turf Research Institute
St Ives Estate, Bingley, West Yorkshire BD16
1AU
Tel: (01274) 565131   *Fax:* (01274) 561891
E-mail: info@stri.co.uk
Website: www.stri.co.uk

Independent specialists offering you help and
advice for the design, construction, management
and maintenance, irrigation or renovation of your
golf course. Comprehensive in-house support services for ecology, testing, turf pathology and
research.

ARCHITECTS & CONSULTANTS

David Griffith
20 Clwyd Avenue, Dyserth, Denbighshire LL18 6HN
Tel: (01745) 570659   *Fax:* (01745) 571382
Mobile: 07778494123
E-mail: david@griffithgolf.co.uk

Golf course architect. Years of experience in a variety of golf projects ensures that no stone is left
unturned in fulfilling the potential of a site. A satisfaction guarantee is given to all projects.

David Williams Golf Design
187 Llanelian Road, Old Colwyn, Colwyn Bay,
North Wales LL29 8UW
Tel: (01492) 512070   *Fax:* (01492) 512077
E-mail: david@williamsgolf.co.uk
Website: www.williamsgolf.co.uk

Golf course architects and project managers. Fully
integrated service *from conception through construction to completion.* Over 20 new courses built
in Britain within the last ten years. Alterations,
improvements and upgrades undertaken through
the country. Member of the European Institute of
Golf Course Architects (EIGCA).

European Institute of Golf Course Architects – EIGCA
Chiddingfold Golf Club, Petworth Road,
Chiddingfold, Surrey GU8 4SL
Tel/Fax: +44 (0) 1428 681528
E-mail: info@eigca.org   *Website:* www.eigca.org

The EIGCA represents the vast majority of qualified and experienced golf course architects
throughout Europe. Our goals include enhancing
the professional status of the profession, developing the role of education and increasing the opportunities for its members to practice in countries
throughout the world. EIGCA also provides educational courses to train future golf course architects
and is an authoritative voice on all related matters,
being recognised by the R&A Golf Club of St
Andrews. Contact: Julia Green, Executive Officer.

Grassform Ltd – Golf Courses, Sports Grounds and Land Drainage Contractors
Dunsteads Farm, Trueloves Lane, Ingatestone,
Essex CM4 0NJ
Tel: (01277) 355500   *Fax:* (01277) 355504
E-mail: sales@grassform.co.uk
Website: www.grassform.co.uk

Grassform Limited undertakes all types of golf
course projects. From new build to re-construction of
tees, greens and bunkers. We also install land
drainage systems, sand banking, lakes, water features, footpaths, buggy paths and driving ranges. For
further information please contact Mark Dunning.

Make it a fourball

Make it happen

As one of the world's largest companies we continue
to take pride in our involvement with Scotland's greatest
home-grown game. From the world's oldest open competition
to the champions of tomorrow, we are dedicated to supporting all aspects of the game. We are delighted
to supply banking services to players, spectators, officials
and exhibitors as Patron to The Open Championship.

The Royal Bank of Scotland

www.rbs.co.uk

RBS

Hawtree Ltd – Golf Course Architects & Consultants

5 Oxford Street, Woodstock, Oxon OX20 1TQ
Tel: (01993) 811976 *Fax:* (01993) 812448
E-mail: mail@hawtree.co.uk
Website: www.hawtree.co.uk

Founded in 1912, Hawtree Limited is the longest continuous golf course practice, having designed and renovated over 800 golf courses worldwide. Just some of these include the renowned Birkdale, Portmarnock, Lahinch and Vilamoura golf courses.

J D Edgar – Golf Course Architect

Wheathampstead Pay & Play Golf Course,
Harpenden Road, St Albans, Hertfordshire AL4 8EZ
Tel/Fax: (01582) 833941

Doug Edgar the golf professional and golf course architect is a member of the PGA and PGAA. He designs and builds courses and can offer you a complete design consultancy service.

Philip Sparks Professional Golf Designs

Peak House, Hawksdown, Walmer, Deal, Kent
CT14 7PL
Tel: (01304) 374119 *Mobile:* 07957 862635
E-mail: manstongolf@hotmail.com

'*Creating future links with the Past*'. Specialising in golf course remodelling and renovation. Toro student architect of the year 2000. EIGCA professional diploma in golf course architecture (distinction).

Robin Hiseman Golf Course Design

Berrymeadow Cottage, 4 West Cairnbeg Cottages,
Laurencekirk, Aberdeenshire AU30 1SR
Tel/Fax: (01561) 320827
E-mail: info@robinhiseman.com
Website: www.robinhiseman.com

Scotland's EIGCA qualified golf architect provides a personal, professional and superior design service for existing clubs and new developers. A specialist in the alteration and extension of existing courses. Major projects completed for Royal Dornoch, Boat of Garten, Deeside, Nairn Dunbar and Cathcart Castle.

STRI – The Sports Turf Research Institute

See our main entry under AGRONOMY

Simon Gidman International Golf Course Architects

Wychwood House, 43 Shipton Road, Ascott Under
Wychwood, Oxon OX7 6AG.
Tel: (01993) 830441 *Fax:* (01993) 831860
Mobile: 07768600102
E-mail: srg@gidmangolf.co.uk
Website: www.gidmangolf.co.uk

A full member of the European Institute of Golf Course Architects (EIGCA), Simon Gidman has been involved with some 50 projects in Europe and throughout the world. The company also specialises in preparing reports and studies for the restoration and upgrading of existing golf courses.

Swan Golf Designs Ltd

Telfords Barn, Willingale, Ongar, Essex CM5 0QF
Tel: (01277) 896229 *Fax:* (01277) 896300
E-mail: swangolfdesigns@btinternet.com
Website: www.swangolfdesigns.com

Professional golf course architects with traditional values, offering initial appraisals, conceptual designs, detailed design work and construction management. Specialising in improvements of existing golf courses, extensions, re-design of greens and tees etc., including restorations of classic old courses.

York Martin International

PO Box 5498. Ringwood, Hants. BH24 3ZR
Tel: 0044 (0) 1425 477883 *Fax:* 0044 (0) 1425 482310
E-mail: info@yorkmartin.com
Website: www.yorkmartin.com

Independent irrigation consultants providing objective advice on all irrigation related matters including water sourcing, existing system evaluation, system designs and specifications, project supervision etc. Operating throughout the UK and mainland Europe.

AWARDS, PRIZES & TROPHIES

Bryants of Leeds

Speedwell Street, Meanwood Road, Leeds LS6 2TD
Tel: 0113-242 8330 *Fax:* 0113-242 6330
Website: www.dimplygolf.com

The leading supplier of personalised golf merchandise. Golf club membership tags and labels, green fee stationery. Captain's Day, Society events and Corporate Golf Day merchandise. Call for a free colour brochure or visit us on our website.

Derek Burridge (Wholesale) Ltd

Awards House, Unit 15, The Metro Centre,
Springfield Road, Hayes, Middlesex UB4 0LE
Tel: 020 8569 0123 *Fax:* 020 8569 0111

The country's leading suppliers of golf prizes, celebrating their 44th year. We offer a vast range of silverplate, crystal, china, clocks, leather goods and sporting trophies, all at trade prices. Glass and silverplate in-house engraving service. Next day delivery throughout the UK. Call for brochure. (*See advertisement page 605 for further details.*)

Galloway Crystal & Glass Ltd

Beeswing, by Dumfries DG2 8ED
Tel: 01387 760643   *Fax:* 01387 760537
E-mail: mccallum@gallowayglass.com
Websites: www.gallowayglass.com
         www.crystalforgolfers.com

Specialist plain and cut crystal suppliers and engravers. Many innovative golfing gift ideas through our special collections. Personalisation our speciality. Logos and crests engraved free-of-charge. Ask for our catalogue along with club and reseller price lists.

Richard Chorley Golf Art

See our main entry under PICTURES & PRINTS

Solent Souvenirs Ltd

Hamble Bank, 40 Newtown Road, Warsash, Southampton, Hampshire SO31 9FZ
Tel: (01489) 577985   *Fax:* (01489) 577886
E-mail: davinanunn@aol.com

Britain's premier supplier of specialised golf jewellery and quality gifts. Many items designed and manufactured exclusively for us and unobtainable elsewhere. Replace that traditional trophy with an elegant prize which will be both useful and cherished.

BAG/MEMBERSHIP TAGS

H M T Plastics Ltd

Fairway House, 31A Framfield Road, Uckfield, East Sussex TN22 5AH
Tel: (01825) 769393
Fax: (01825) 769494
E-mail: hmt@aol.com
Website: www.hmtplastics.com

Bag tags supplied in ten colours either round, pear shaped, shield maxi or sunrise to accommodate club logo, from a choice of print colours. Adhesive Year Stickers available in choice of ten colours and sold separately. (*See advertisement page 605 for further details.*)

BAGS/GOLF ACCESSORIES

Prosimmon Golf (UK) Ltd

21 Monkspath Business Park, Highlands Road, Shirley, Solihull, West Midlands B90 4NZ
Tel: 0121-744 9551
Fax: 0121-744 9541

Manufacturers of premier golf clubs, bags and accessories. Designers of unique *Matchplay* computerised custom club fitting system.

BALL COLLECTORS

European Golf Machinery – Rangeball UK Ltd

See our main entry under DRIVING RANGE & PRACTICE EQUIPMENT

BOOKSELLERS & PUBLISHERS

STRI – The Sports Turf Research Institute

See our main entry under AGRONOMY

Steve Schofield Golf Books

29 Nichols Way, Wetherby, West Yorkshire LS22 6AD
Tel/Fax: (01937) 581276
E-mail: golfbooks@steveschofield.com

Classic golf books for sale, new, old and antiquarian. Books on golf history, architecture, biography, club and ball collecting and instruction. Free catalogue on request.

CARTS, TROLLEYS & BUGGIES

A La Carts

Beechwood, Bakeham Lane, Englefield Green TW20 9TU
Tel/Fax: (01784) 472982
E-mail: jt@alacarts.co.uk
Website: www.fraser-products.co.uk

Manufacturers and distributors of single seater golf buggies. Also powered trolleys.

Middlemore Ltd

Sharrocks Street, Wolverhampton, West Midlands WV1 3RP
Tel: (01902) 870077   *Fax:* (01902) 455200
E-mail: electra-caddie@thama.co.uk
Website: www.thama.co.uk

European distributors of the world's foremost remote controlled powered golf trolley – the *LEC-TRONIC KADDY 'Dyna Steer 2000'*. Your hand held transmitter helps you to turn this amazing machine left to right and right to left with great ease. The original all-aluminium lightweight machine that helps you break par, not your back. Free colour brochure on request. (*See advertisement page 605 for further details.*)

Yamaha Motor (UK) Ltd

Sopwith Drive, Brooklands, Weybrldge, Surrey KTI3 0UZ
Tel: (0/932) 358096   *Fax:* (01932) 358099

Suppliers of petrol and electric golf cars for clubs and individuals. Fleet contracts with optional

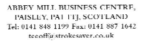

purchase and lease schemes, full maintenance and service support. On and off-course utility vehicles, multi-passenger cars and beverage units.

COMPUTER SOFTWARE/SYSTEMS

Euro Systems Projects (ESP)
See our main entry under ELECTRONIC POINT OF SALE

Links Software
6 Ascot Avenue, Westerlands Park, Glasgow G12 0AX
Tel/Fax: 0141-581 6759
E-mail: ac.provan@ntlworld.com
Website: www.linksgolf.co.uk
The complete software solution for golf clubs. Membership and subscriptions, handicaps, bookings (internet linked), EPOS and stock control. Compatible with most swipecards. Fully networkable. Modules start from £495.

Sports Coach Systems Ltd
Curtis Road, Dorking, Surrey RH4 1XD.
Tel: +44 (0) 1306 741888
Fax: +44 (0) 1306 877888
E-mail: sales@sports-coach.com
Website: www.sports-coach.com
Manufacturers of the world's finest range of golf electronics and software. Projected systems from under £6,000, club, ball and swing analysis, Links LS Simulators, Photographic Simulators and Driving Ranges. As well as digital firewire with the world famous Sports Coach 2004. Europe's largest manufacturer of golf mats, Portarange nets and cage nets.

CORPORATE GIFTS & EVENTS

Bryants of Leeds
See our main entry under AWARDS, PRIZES & TROPHIES

Derek Burridge (Wholesale) Ltd
See our main entry under AWARDS, PRIZES & TROPHIES

COURSE CONSTRUCTION & UPGRADING

MJ Abbott Ltd
Bratch Lane, Dinton, Salisbury, Wiltshire SP3 5EB
Tel: (01722) 716361 *Fax:* (01722) 716828
E-mail: enquiries@mjabbott.co.uk
Website: www.mjabbott.co.uk
MJ Abbott Limited offer a range of specialist services to the golf and leisure industry. Recognised as one of Britain's leading companies offering Rain Bird irrigation systems. Land drainage, golf course construction and maintenance are all undertaken by experienced employees utilising the company's own specially adapted machinery.

Brian D Pierson
32 New Road, Ringwood, Hampshire BH24 3AU
Tel: (01202) 822372 *Fax:* (01202) 826447
Mobile: 07768 170033
The Golf Course Builder – 35 years' experience on over 200 golf courses. New construction, alterations, project management. Contracts completed in USA, Canada, mainland Europe and British Isles. Work completed on seven Open Championship courses.

British Association of Golf Course Constructors – BAGCC
The Dormy House, Cooden Beach Golf Club, Bexhill-on-Sea TN39 4TR
Tel: (01424) 842380 *Fax:* (01424) 843375
E-mail: mightyspyder@aol.com
Website: www.bagcc.org.uk
Secretary: David White. Constructors who appear on the BAGCC membership roster qualify only by

passing a critical vetting process undertaken by their peers, who look for excellence in construction and a clear demonstration of skills pertinent only to the golf course industry. Utilising the services of a BAGCC member therefore ensures absolute professionalism.

David Williams Golf Design

See our main entry under ARCHITECTS & CONSULTANTS

Grassform Ltd – Golf Courses, Sports Grounds and Land Drainage Contractors

See our main entry under ARCHITECTS & CONSULTANTS

John Greasley Ltd

Ashfield House, 1154 Melton Road, Syston, Leicester LE7 2HB
Tel: 0116-269 6766 *Fax:* 0116-269 6866

John Greasley established his company in 1984 and has specialised in the construction of new courses, along with alterations, improvements and refurbishment on existing ones. Works have been completed on some of the countries oldest and most prestigious courses.

Land Unit Construction Ltd

Hanslope, Milton Keynes, Bucks MK19 7BX
Tel: (01908) 510414 *Fax:* (01908) 511056
E-mail: sales@landunitconstruction.co.uk
Website: www.landunitconstruction.co.uk

We have the knowledge and experience gained over 25 years in golf course construction and constantly work with many of the country's leading golf course architects to provide clients with unparalleled quality of service.

PSD Agronomy Ltd

See our main entry under AGRONOMY

STRI – The Sports Turf Research Institute

See our main entry under AGRONOMY

Simon Gidman International Golf Course Architects

See our main entry under ARCHITECTS & CONSULTANTS

Swan Golf Designs Ltd

See our main entry under ARCHITECTS & CONSULTANTS

COURSE MEASUREMENT

Eagle Promotions Ltd

See our main entry under SCORECARDS & PLANNERS

DISTRIBUTORS & WHOLESALERS

British Golf Industry Association

Federation House, Stoneleigh Park, Warwickshire CV8 2RF
Tel: 024 7641 7141 *Fax:* 024 7641 4990
E-mail: bgia@sportslife.org.uk

Trade association for manufacturers and distributors of golf equipment.

Eaton Ltd – Golf Pride Grips

See our main entry under GRIPS & SHAFTS

THE BELL HOTEL

Only a ten minute drive from some of the best golf in Kent. The Bell is the perfect golfers base and offers Special Inclusive Golf Breaks with The Prince's Golf Club. Situated in a delightful historic area The Bell offers comfort, relaxation and friendly service. All our rooms have private facilities. Choice of Continental or full English breakfast are served with our compliments to all hotel guests. Royal St George - Prince's - Royal Cinque Ports clubs.

The Bell Hotel,
The Quay, Sandwich,
Kent CT13 9EF

E-mail: hotel@princes-leisure.co.uk
Website: www.princes-leisure.co.uk

Tel: 01304 613388
Fax: 01304 615308

3-Star, 4-Crown
Highly Commended

THE NORTH EAST'S PREMIER PRIVATELY OWNED HOTEL
━━ WITH GOLF ━━

This marvellous 80-bedroom hotel, renowned for its popular bars and good food has 27 holes of golf, magnificent driving range, indoor golf academy incorporating computerised 'A Star' swing analyser and golf simulator. Recently opened clubhouse, sumptuous lounge, snooker room, steam, sauna and massage chair.

Ramside Hall Hotel
Carrville, Durham DH1 1TD
Tel: 0191-386 5282
Fax: 0191-386 0399

Dalmunzie House Hotel

the hotel in the hills

This family-run country house hotel has 17 bedrooms, 16 with private bathrooms, traditional Scottish cooking, open fires and personal service. On the doorstep is our own 9-hole golf course, and within an hour's drive are some of Scotland's finest courses.

For a brochure, please contact
Alexandra and Simon Winton,
Dalmunzie House,
Spittal O'Glenshee, Blairgowrie, Perthshire,
Scotland PH10 7QG.

Tel: Glenshee (01250) 885224 Fax: (01250) 885225

**AA - AA Rosette • TASTE OF SCOTLAND
STB 3-STAR

DRIVING RANGE & PRACTICE EQUIPMENT

European Golf Machinery – Rangeball UK Ltd.

Street Garage, Bucklesham, Ipswich, Suffolk IP10 0DN
Tel: (01473) 659815 *Fax:* (01473) 659045
E-mail: sales@golfmachinery.com
Website: www.golfmachinery.com
Manufacturers of driving range equipment including golf ball collectors, dispensers, ball washers and elevators. Kawasaki ATV and Mule distributors. (*See advertisement on page 606 for further details.*)

EDUCATION

Bournemouth University

See our main entry under ACADEMIC QUALIFICATIONS

ELECTRIC GOLF CARS

Yamaha Motor (UK) Ltd

See our main entry under CARTS, TROLLEYS & BUGGIES

ELECTRONIC POINT OF SALE

Euro Systems Projects (ESP)

Europa House, 1 Kimpton Link Business Park, Kimpton Road, Sutton, Surrey SM3 9QP
Tel: 020 8251 5100 *Fax:* 020 8251 5101
E-mail: enquiries@e-s-p.com
Website: www.e-s-p.com
ESP is universally recognised as the UK's market leader for the supply of integrated point of sale and management systems. Designed specifically for the golf industry their system incorporates modules to efficiently manage: membership; bookings; retail; food and beverage and access control and many others, and is used by over 200 clubs and courses throughout the UK and Europe.

FIXTURE BOOKS

Iain Crosbie Printers

Beechfield Road, Willowyard Industrial Estate, Beith, Ayrshire KA15 1LN
Tel: (01505) 504848
Fax: (01505) 504674
E-mail: crosbieprinters@dial.pipex.com

At Crosbie Printers we have over 20 years' experience in printing associated with golf and commerce. We manufacture scorecards (standard and bespoke), fixture books/diaries, green fee tickets, marketing brochures/leaflets and all associated printed stationery.

GIFTS & NOVELTIES

Derek Burridge (Wholesale) Ltd

See our main entry under AWARDS, PRIZES & TROPHIES

Solent Souvenirs Ltd

See our main entry under AWARDS, PRIZES & TROPHIES

GOLF CLUB MANUFACTURERS/ SUPPLIERS

Bronty Golf

3 Musgrave Mount, Eccleshill, Bradford, West Yorkshire BD2 3LA
Tel/Fax: +44 (0) 1274 773585
Mobile: +44 (0) 7950 397603
E-mail: brontygolf1@activemail.co.uk
Website: www.brontygolf.co.uk
Manufacturers of high quality British made custom golf clubs, putters and specialist clubs. Authentic replicas and hickory shafted putters etc.

Prosimmon Golf (UK) Ltd

See our main entry under BAGS/GOLF ACCESSORIES

True Temper UK/Europe c/o Tucker Fasteners

See our main entry under GRIPS & SHAFTS

GOLF COURSE DESIGN CONSULTANTS

David Griffith

See our main entry under ARCHITECTS & CONSULTANTS

David Williams Golf Design

See our main entry under ARCHITECTS & CONSULTANTS

European Institute of Golf Course Architects – EIGCA

See our main entry under ARCHITECTS & CONSULTANTS and in the Professional Associations Section.

Hawtree Ltd – Golf Course Architects & Consultants

See our main entry under ARCHITECTS & CONSULTANTS

Peter Alliss – Golf Ltd

25 St Johns Road, Farnham, Surrey GU9 8NV
Tel: (01252) 717711 *Fax:* (01252) 717722
E-mail: roy@allissgolf.demon.co.uk

Designers of golf courses and re-design of existing courses. Contact Peter Alliss or Roy Cooper.

Philip Sparks Professional Golf Designs

See our main entry under ARCHITECTS & CONSULTANTS

Robin Hiseman Golf Course Design

See our main entry under ARCHITECTS & CONSULTANTS

GOLF COURSE DISTANCE GUIDES

Strokesport

Abbey Mill Business Centre, Paisley PA1 1TJ
Tel: 0141-848 1199 *Fax:* 0141-887 1642

We are publishers of *Strokesaver Distance Guides* which are recognised as the most accurate and useful golf course management aids worldwide. *Strokesaver* provides professionals and clubs with a constant profit centre. Course measurement – measurement and survey to professional standard certification accepted by national golf unions. Leading specialists in course measurement. (*See advertisement page 605 for further details.*)

GOLF COURSE MAINTENANCE & UPGRADING

Arden Lea Irrigation Ltd

See our main entry under IRRIGATION CONSULTANTS/DESIGN & INSTALLATION

Brian D Pierson

See our main entry under COURSE CONSTRUCTION & UPGRADING

Glen Farrow (UK) Ltd

See our main entry under IRRIGATION CONSULTANTS/DESIGN & INSTALLATION

Grassform Ltd – Golf Courses, Sports Grounds and Land Drainage Contractors

See our main entry under ARCHITECTS & CONSULTANTS

Land Unit Construction Ltd

See our main entry under COURSE CONSTRUCTION & UPGRADING

Peter Alliss - Golf Ltd

See our main entry under GOLF COURSE DESIGN CONSULTANTS.

Toro Products – Lely (UK) Ltd

Station Road, St Neots, Huntingdon,
Cambridgeshire PE19 1QH
Tel: (01480) 226800 *Fax:* (01480) 226801
E-mail: toro.info@lely.co.uk
Website: www.toro.com

Toro offer an extensive range of professional turf maintenance equipment which includes: greens mowers, fairway mowers, triplex mowers, rotary mowers, aeration and utility vehicles. Also *Toro* irrigation and *Toro* consumer wheel horse range.

GOLF DEVELOPMENT/ MANAGEMENT

Association of Golf Club Secretaries

7A Beaconsfield Road, Weston-Super-Mare,
Somerset BS23 1YE
Tel: (01934) 641166 *Fax:* (01934) 644254
E-mail: hq@agcs.org.uk
Website: www.agcs.org.uk

Membership is available to golf secretaries, assistant secretaries and managers, course owners and others involved in golf club administration. The following services are available: monthly journal, information library, training courses, seminars, conferences, regional meetings and employment support.

Barrelfield Golf Ltd

302 Ewell Road, Surbiton, Surrey KT6 7AQ
Tel: 020 8390 6566 *Fax:* 020 8390 8830
Website: www.barrelfieldgolf.co.uk

Barrelfield Golf Limited has an unrivalled track record in the development, marketing, management and maintenance of profitable golf clubs in Britain. Other services include feasibility studies and arranging finance. For further information contact Melvin Thomas 020 8390 6566.

Bournemouth University

See our main entry under ACADEMIC QUALIFICATIONS

The Council of National Golf Unions

Dromin, Dunleer, Co Louth, Ireland
Tel/*Fax:* +353 41 6861476
E-mail: golfinmcinere@hotmail.com

The Council of National Golf Unions is the handicapping authority for Great Britain and Ireland. The Standard Scratch Score and handicapping Scheme has been in operation since March 1926. On 1st February 2004 a new Unified system for men and ladies will be introduced for the Home Counties. The CONGU Unified Handicapping System is the result of much work and consultation to produce a single handicapping system for men and ladies. With the introduction of the System the Council of National Golf Unions is to be re-constituted with a revised council consisting of an equal number of representatives from the English Golf Union, English Ladies' Golf Association, Golfing Union of Ireland, Irish Ladies' Golf Union, Scottish Golf Union, Scottish Ladies' Golf Association, Welsh Golfing Union, Welsh Ladies' Golf Union together with the Royal and Ancient Golf Club of St Andrews and the Ladies Golf Union.

English Golf Union – EGU

The National Golf Centre, The Broadway, Woodhall Spa, Lincolnshire LN10 6PU
Tel: (01526) 354500 *Fax:* (01526) 354020
E-mail: info@englishgolfunion.org
Website: www.englishgolfunion.org

As the governing body for men's amateur golf in England, the EGU organises championships and coaching for players and representative teams at all levels and offers an advisory service on all aspects of golf administration and management.

The Golf Foundation – Developing Junior Golf

Foundation House, The Spinney, Hoddesdon Road, Stanstead Abbotts, Hertfordshire SG12 8GF.
Tel: (01920) 876200
Fax: (01920) 876211
Website: www.golf-foundation.org

An organisation dedicated to the promotion and development of grass roots junior golf across the British Isles. *The Golf Foundation is a registered charity.*

National Association of Public Golf Courses – NAPGC

12 Newton Close, Redditch B98 7YR
Tel: (01527) 542106 *Fax:* (01527) 455320
E-mail: eddiemitchell@blueyonder.co.uk
Website: www.napgc.org.uk

The Association provides competition golf for men and lady players of all handicaps and age. It also offers help and advice to its member clubs – those playing over courses that they do not own.

National Golf Clubs' Advisory Association – NGCAA

Suite 16, Tranzart Business Centre, Owl Gate, Roberts End, Hanley Swan. Worcs. WR8 0DN
Tel: 01684 311353 *Fax:* 01684 311924
E-mail: ngcaa@idealnet.co.uk or
admin@ngcaa.org.uk
Website: www.ngcaa.org.uk

A non-profit making organisation providing legal advice and support to golf clubs throughout the UK. The Association is the only independent body supporting golf clubs in areas of activity other than those arising from playing the game.

GOLFING AIDS/PRACTICE EQUIPMENT

Pan European (Golf) 1973 (PEP)

Old Mill Works, High Street, Maldon, Essex CM9 5EH
Tel: (01621) 851700
Fax: (01621) 850417
E-mail: info@golfpep.co.uk
Website: www.golfpep.co.uk

Products include a wide range of practice nets and mats for beginners through to professionals. We also make a commercial range of nets and mats for clubs, stores and leisure centres. Worldwide export sales our speciality.

Sports Coach Systems Ltd

See our main entry under COMPUTER SOFTWARE/SYSTEMS

GREENKEEPING & DRIVING RANGE VEHICLES

European Golf Machinery – Rangeball UK Ltd

See our main entry under DRIVING RANGE & PRACTICE EQUIPMENT

Toro Products – Lely (UK) Ltd

See our main entry under GOLF COURSE MAINTENANCE & UPGRADING

GREENKEEPING INFORMATION SERVICE

British & International Golf Greenkeepers Association – BIGGA

BIGGA House, Aldwark, Alne, North Yorkshire YO61 1UF

Tel: (01347) 833800   *Fax:* (01347) 833801
E-mail: reception@bigga.co.uk
Website: www.bigga.org.uk

With over 7,000 members BIGGA is the largest European association for greenkeepers. These are based mainly in the UK, however it does have members in 32 countries worldwide. The Association provides extensive education and training programmes for its members as well as a wide range of benefits including the monthly publication *Greenkeeper International*. In January each year it organises a major fine turf and clubhouse exhibition incorporating a series of seminars. This is held in Harrogate, North Yorkshire and attracts visitors from all around the world.

GRIPS & SHAFTS

Eaton Ltd – Golf Pride Grips

Units 1 & 2 The Stirling Centre, Northfields Industrial Estate, Market Deeping, Nr Peterborough PE6 8EQ
Tel: (01778) 341555 *Fax:* (01778) 344025

Manufacturers of golf grips for over 50 years, Eaton have been the leader in golf grip technology and the leader in rubber and cord grip sales for both professional and amateur players alike.

True Temper UK/Europe c/o Tucker Fasteners

Walsall Road, Birmingham B42 1BP
Tel: 0121-331 2276 *Fax:* 0121-331 2286

Golf shaft manufacturer both steel and graphite. In 2003 achieved over 120 Tournament wins on PGA Tours. Dynamic Gold sill No.1 shaft used by Pro's and amateurs around the world.

INSURANCE

Golfplan – International Golf & Travel Insurance

Redcliffe House, Whitehouse Street, Bristol BS3 4AY
Tel: 0117-963 6198 *Fax:* 0117-923 1058
E-mail: info@golfplan.co.uk
Website: www.golfplan.co.uk

Golfplan, endorsed by the PGA, is Europe's largest specialist golf insurance provider. A Golfplan policy covers individual golfers against personal liability; accidental damage to third party property; golf equipment; personal effects; equipment hire charges; tournament entry fees; membership fees; personal accident; Hole-in-One. Contact your professional or call Golfplan quoting Ref: GHB8.

INTERNET TEE-TIME BOOKING

Links Software

See our main entry under COMPUTER SOFT-WARE/SYSTEMS

IRRIGATION CONSULTANTS/ DESIGN & INSTALLATION

MJ Abbott Ltd

See our main entry under COURSE CONSTRUC-TION & UPGRADING

Arden Lea Irrigation Ltd

160 Moss Lane, Hesketh Bank, Preston, Lancashire PR4 6AE
Tel: (01772) 812433 *Fax:* (01772) 815371
E-mail: alirrig@aol.com

Arden Lea Irrigation established nearly 30 years ago specialises in irrigation on golf courses and other leisure facilities. With our experienced staff we have completed work on many well known golf courses throughout the UK and Southern Ireland. We are an independent company and can supply any type of irrigation equipment. Full member of the British Turf and Landscape Irrigation Association.

Glen Farrow (UK) Ltd

Spalding Road, Pinchbeck, Spalding, Lincolnshire PE11 3UE
Tel: (01775) 722327 *Fax:* (01775) 725444
E-mail: info@glenfarrow.co.uk
Website: www.glenfarrow.co.uk

Glen Farrow are leading golf course irrigation specialists, providing state-of-the-art design, supply and installation service. Established for over 30 years and with an excellent reputation for quality and service, Glen Farrow will carefully assess your present and future water requirements, then design a water supply and irrigation system to maximise efficiency, reliability and future expansion potential. The result is a very cost-effective and low maintenance water solution for your golf course. In addition we offer full contract maintenance and emergency repair services. As BTLIA and UKIA members, Glen Farrow are a Company committed to delivering market leading water solutions to your business and raising standards within the irrigation industry.

Grassform Ltd – Golf Courses, Sports Grounds and Land Drainage Contractors

See our main entry under ARCHITECTS & CON-SULTANTS

L S Systems Ltd

188 Blackgate Lane, Tarleton, Preston, Lancashire
PR4 6UU.
Tel: (01772) 815080
Fax: (01772) 815417
E-mail: sales@lssystems.co.uk
Website: www.lssystems.co.uk

L S Systems are TORO Elite contractors. We provide a comprehensive design and installation service for complete irrigation solutions for all golf clubs. We are the largest stockist of TORO equipment in the north of England. Please call for a no obligation estimate.

Landline Ltd

See our main entry under WATER FEATURES

STRI – The Sports Turf Research Institute

See our main entry under AGRONOMY

Toro Irrigation Products – Lely (UK) Ltd

See our main entry under GOLF COURSE MAINTENANCE & UPGRADING

York Martin International

See our main entry under ARCHITECTS AND CONSULTANTS

JEWELLERY

Solent Souvenirs Ltd

See our main entry under AWARDS, PRIZES & TROPHIES

MAIL ORDER

Steve Schofield Golf Books

See our main entry under BOOKSELLERS & PUBLISHERS

PERSONAL EQUIPMENT & ACCESSORIES

Mycoal Warm Packs Ltd

See our main entry under THERMAL WEAR.

PERSONALISED PRODUCTS

Bryants of Leeds

See our main entry under AWARDS, PRIZES & TROPHIES

Derek Burridge (Wholesale) Ltd

See our main entry under AWARDS, PRIZES & TROPHIES

Galloway Crystal & Glass Ltd

See our main entry under AWARDS, PRIZES & TROPHIES

H M T Plastics Ltd

See our main entry under BAG/MEMBERSHIP TAGS

PICTURES & PRINTS

Richard Chorley Golf Art

159 Lonsdale Road, Stevenage, Hertfordshire
SG1 5DG
Tel/Fax: (01438) 727901

Richard Chorley, England's premier golf artist. Private commissions, original oil paintings, drawings and limited edition prints. Prints signed by the artist, numbered and embossed. Collection of classic courses and golfing greats. Ideal Corporate and captain's prizes gifts.

PRACTICE NETTING/CAGES

Pan European (Golf) 1973 (PEP)

See our main entry under GOLFING AIDS/PRACTICE EQUIPMENT

PRINTING

Iain Crosbie Printers

See our main entry under FIXTURE BOOKS

PUTTER & CHIPPERS MANUFACTURERS/ SUPPLIERS

Bronty Golf

See our main entry under GOLF CLUB MANUFACTURERS/SUPPLIERS

RANGE BALL MANUFACTURERS/SUPPLIERS

European Golf Machinery – Rangeball UK Ltd

See our main entry under DRIVING RANGE & PRACTICE EQUIPMENT

REMOTE CONTROLLED TROLLEYS

Middlemore Ltd
See our main entry under CARTS, TROLLEYS & BUGGIES

RIDE-ON BUGGIES

A La Carts
See our main entry under CARTS, TROLLEYS & BUGGIES

SCORECARDS & PLANNERS

Eagle Promotions Ltd
Eagle House, 1 Clearway Court, 139–141 Croydon Road, Caterham, Surrey CR3 6PF
Tel: (01883) 344244
Fax: (01883) 341777
E-mail: info@eaglepromotions.co.uk
Website: www.eaglepromotions.co.uk

Eagle Promotions offer a comprehensive range of products from certified course measurement and tee signs through to scorecards, yardage books, green fee tickets, members' tags, event and leader boards, honours boards, clubhouse and general course signage. For further information please contact Philip McInley on 01883 344244.

Iain Crosbie Printers
Beechfield Road, Willowyard Industrial Estate, Beith, Ayrshire KA15 1LN.
Tel: (01505) 504848 *Fax:* (01505) 504674
E-mail: crosbieprinters@dial.pipex.com

At Crosbie Printers we have over 20 years' experience in printing associated with golf and commerce. We manufacture scorecards (standard and bespoke), fixture books/diaries, green fee tickets, marketing brochures, leaflets and all associated printed stationery.

SIMULATORS/ANALYSERS

Sports Coach Systems Ltd
See our main entry under COMPUTER SOFTWARE/SYSTEMS

TEE SIGNS

Eagle Promotions Ltd
See our main entry under SCORECARDS & PLANNERS

THERMAL WEAR

Mycoal Warm Packs Ltd
Unit 1, Imperial Park, Empress Road, Southampton, Hampshire SO14 0JW
Tel: 023 8021 1068
Fax: 023 8023 1398
E-mail: sales@mycoal.co.uk
Website: www.mycoal.co.uk

Suppliers and manufacturers of the ever popular handwarmers and thermal mittens. All enquiries welcome – small or large.

TRAINING & TEACHING AIDS

STRI – The Sports Turf Research Institute
See our main entry under AGRONOMY

Sports Coach Systems Ltd
See our main entry under COMPUTER SOFTWARE/SYSTEMS

TROPHIES

Derek Burridge (Wholesale) Ltd
See our main entry under AWARDS, PRIZES & TROPHIES

Galloway Crystal & Glass Ltd
See our main entry under AWARDS, PRIZES & TROPHIES

TUITION

Beaufort Golf Course
Churchtown, Beaufort, Killarney, Co Kerry, Ireland
Tel: +353 64 44440 *Fax:* +353 64 44752

A traditional Kerry welcome awaits you at the *Friendliest Course in Kerry*. Challenging 18-hole par 71 championship course, buggies and caddies for hire, excellent golf shop, bar food and snacks. Tuition can be arranged with our golf professional. Societies and groups welcome. (*See advertisement page 594 for further details.*)

European Golf Teachers Federation – EGTF
5 Hastings Road, Bromley, Kent BR2 8NZ.
Tel: 020 8462 4120 *Fax:* 020 8462 3983
E-mail: egtf@dial.pipex.com
Website: www.egtf.co.uk

We offer intensive teaching courses for professionals and amateurs who would like to know how to

teach the game simply. The EGTF is the leader in the field of golf instruction.

Rodway Hill Golf Course

Newent Road, Highnam, Gloucestershire GL2 8DN
Tel: (01452) 384222

An 18-hole, par 70 course, open to the public, two miles south west of Gloucester, with panoramic views of the Cotswolds. It has a well stocked shop, practice and teaching facilities. Hire kit available. Bar and restaurant facilities. Societies welcome.

WATER FEATURES

Landline Ltd

1 Bluebridge Industrial Estate, Halstead, Essex CO9 2EX.
Tel: (01784) 476699 *Fax:* (01784) 472507
E-mail: info@landline.co.uk
Website: www.landline.co.uk

Landline are specialist suppliers, installers of lake, pond and irrigation reservoir linings. Free technical advisory service is available for all aspects of liner installation. We offer a complete service to customers backed by over 20 years' practical experience.

WATER RESOURCES/ RESERVOIR DESIGN

L S Systems Ltd

See our main entry under IRRIGATION CONSULTANTS/DESIGN & INSTALLATION

Landline Ltd

See our main entry under WATER FEATURES

WATER STORAGE/TANKS

Landline Ltd

See our main entry under WATER FEATURES

WEATHERWEAR

Mycoal Warm Packs Ltd

See our main entry under THERMAL WEAR.

Golfing Hotel Compendium

The Golfing Hotel Compendium is a comprehensive source of information for golfers wishing to find the most comfortable place to stay at or close to some of the finest courses in the country.

ENGLAND

South West

Burnham & Berrow – The Dormy
Burnham and Berrow Golf Club, St Christopher's Way, Burnham-on-Sea, Somerset TA8 2PE
Tel: (01278) 785760
E-mail: Secretary@BurnhamandBerrow
.freeserve.co.uk
18-hole championship links golf course and 9-hole course. Dormy accommodation available. (*See advertisement page 596 for further details.*)

Fircroft Hotel
Owls Road, Bournemouth, Dorset BH5 1AE
Tel: (01202) 309771 *Fax:* (01202) 395644
The hotel is situated close to sea and shops with many superb golf courses in the area. Fine restaurant with choice of menus. Large car park. Late bar. Free use of leisure club 9am to 6pm, with indoor pool, jacuzzi, sauna steam room and gym.
AA. RAC. ETC 2-Star. B&B from £30.00 daily.

Pines Hotel
Burlington Road, Swanage, Dorset BH19 1LT
Tel: (01929) 425211 *Fax:* (01929) 422075
E-mail: reservations@pineshotel.co.uk
Website: www.pineshotel.co.uk
50-bedroom family run 3-Star hotel. All bedrooms have private bathroom, telephone and colour TV. One and a half miles from Isle of Purbeck Golf Club. Within easy reach of all Dorset courses. Award-winning restaurant. Cliff top position with stunning sea views.

Trevose Golf & Country Club
Constantine Bay, Padstow, North Cornwall PL28 8JB
Tel: (01841) 520208 *Fax:* (01841) 521057

E-mail: info@trevose-gc.co.uk
Website: www.trevose-gc.co.uk
Trevose offers not only great golf (championship 18-hole course, a 9-hole full length (3,100 yards) par 35 plus a 9-hole short course) but also a first class clubhouse and restaurant, three hard all-weather tennis courts, a heated outdoor swimming pool in the summer, a games room for the kids and a boutique. Accommodation is available in bungalows, chalets, trehuel flats, dormy flats and cabins. Send for our detailed colour brochure. Open all year. Societies welcome. View website for latest special offers.

Woodbury Park Golf & Country Club
Woodbury Castle, Woodbury, Exeter, Devon EX5 1JJ
Tel: (01395) 233382 *Fax:* (01395) 233384
Luxury 56-bedroom hotel with five superb lodges. The Nigel Mansell owned resort encompasses 27 holes, including the Oaks championship course, in addition to extensive leisure facilities. The ideal venue for your golfing break.

South East

The Bell Hotel
The Quay, Sandwich, Kent CT13 9EF
Tel: (01304) 613388 *Fax:* (01304) 615308
E-mail: hotel@princes-leisure.co.uk
Website: www.princes-leisure.co.uk
The perfect base when playing Royal St Georges, Prince's and Royal Cinque Ports – all within ten minutes' drive. Relax in traditional comfort in historic surroundings. Individually designed rooms with en suite throughout. Special inclusive golf breaks with the Prince's Golf Club. (*See advertisement page 608 for further details.*)

Flackley Ash Hotel
Peasmarsh, Nr Rye, East Sussex TN31 6YH.
Tel: (01797) 230651 *Fax:* (01797) 230510
E-mail: enquiries@flackleyashhotel.co.uk
Website: www.flackleyashhotel.co.uk

3-Star Georgian country house hotel set in beautiful grounds with putting green. Indoor swimming pool, whirlpool spa, saunas, steam room, gym, massage and beauty treatments. Extensive wine list, good food and a friendly welcome.

East Anglia

Abbotsley Golf Hotel & Country Club
Eynesbury Hardwicke, St Neots, Cambridgeshire PE19 4XN
Tel: (01480) 474000 *Fax:* (01480) 471018

Set in 250 acres of idyllic countryside, offering two 18-hole courses, a par 3, driving range, squash courts, fitness centre and a 42-bedroom hotel. Golf breaks and residential packages available. Operated by American Golf (UK) Limited.

Beaumaris Hotel
15 South Street, Sheringham, Norfolk NR26 8LL.
Tel: (01263) 822370   *Fax:* (01263) 821421
E-mail: beauhotel@aol.com
Website: www.thebeaumarishotel.co.uk

Established and run by the same family for 57 years with a reputation for personal service and excellent English cuisine. 21 en suite bedrooms. AA 2-Star Ashley Courtenay Recommended; ETC 2-Star. Three minutes' walk Sheringham's exhilerating cliff top golf course.

Suffolk

Wentworth Hotel
Wentworth Road, Aldeburgh, Suffolk IP15 5BD
Tel: (01728) 452312 *Fax:* (01728) 454343
E-mail: stay@wentworth-aldeburgh.co.uk
Website: www.wentworth-aldeburgh.com

Country house hotel with sea views. Thirty-seven bedrooms, two comfortable, spacious lounges and Terrace Bar. AA Rosette restaurant serving local seafood. We know how to look after golfers. Visit our website for further information.

East Midlands

The Grange & Links Hotel
Sea Lane, Sandilands, Sutton-on-Sea, Lincolnshire LN12 2RA
Tel: (01507) 441334
Fax: (01507) 443033
E-mail: grangelinks@ic24.net
Website: www.grangeandlinkshotel.com

3-Star 30-bedroom hotel with own 18-hole links course. Two tennis courts, snooker and ballroom. Award-winning hotel renowned for superb cuisine, friendliness, comfort and service.

North Shore Hotel Golf Club & Course
North Shore Road, Skegness PE25 1DN
Tel: (01754) 763298
Fax: (01754) 761902
E-mail: golf@north-shore.co.uk
Website: www.north-shore.co.uk

A mature and challenging 18-hole part parkland and part links course with sea views on the edge of Skegness. Good all year round climate. Rarely closed in winter with no winter greens. Rarely closed bars, superb bar food and à la carte restaurant. 36 bedrooms available.

Petwood Hotel
Woodhall Spa, Lincolnshire LN10 6QF
Tel: (01526) 352411 *Fax:* (01526) 353473
Website: www.petwood.co.uk

Built in the early 1900s, this luxurious hotel is set in a 30-acre estate, close to Woodhall Spa's championship golf course. 50 en suite bedrooms and a popular restaurant specialising in local produce. Special golf packages available – ask for our golf brochure for further details.

West Midlands

Whitefields Hotel Golf & Country Club
Coventry Road, Thurlaston, Nr Rugby, Warwickshire CV23 9JR
Tel: (01788) 521800   *Fax:* (01788) 521695
E-mail: mail@whitefields-hotel.co.uk
Website: www.whitefields-hotel.co.uk

18-hole course 6,289 yards. Floodlit driving range, putting green 18. Four conference rooms. 50 en suite bedrooms. Bars and à la carte restaurant. Societies welcome seven days. Call the secretary on 01788 815555. Reservations 01788 521800. Pro – Mario Luca.

Yorkshire & Humberside

Cave Castle Hotel & Country Club
South Cave, East Yorkshire HU15 2EU
Tel: (01430) 422245 *Fax:* (01430) 421118
Superb country manor house with 53 en suite bedrooms in tranquil 160-acre parkland setting with easy access to M62 motorway. Excellent, traditional cuisine is served in our character restaurant. 18-hole golf course with mix of park and meadowland

providing good test of golf to all levels. Leisure facilities, including 19m indoor pool, gym, sauna, steam and spa. This is a Unique Leisure Experience not to be missed! Golf and leisure breaks, visiting parties and non-golfers welcome.

Hotel Majestic – Scarborough
57 Northstead Manor Drive, Scarborough, North Yorkshire YO12 6AG
Tel/*Fax:* (01723) 363806

ETB 2-Star. Privately owned hotel overlooking Peasholm Park. Minutes from Northcliffe Golf Course. All 19 bedrooms have en suite, double glazed, fully centrally heated. Cocktail bar. Draught beers. Golf parties welcomed. Flexible evening dinner times can be arranged.

Rudding Park Hotel & Golf
Follifoot, Harrogate, North Yorkshire HG3 1JH
Tel: (01423) 871350 *Fax:* (01423) 872286
E-mail: sales@ruddingpark.com
Website: www.ruddingpark.com
Rudding Park, just two miles south of Harrogate, is an ideal venue for the discerning golfer. The contemporary award-winning AA 4 Red Star hotel and AA 2-Rosette Clocktower Restaurant, coupled with the magnificent 18-hole, par 72, parkland golf course, ensures a relaxing break. Golfing packages and special seasonal offers are available.

Wrangham House Hotel
10 Stonegate, Hummanby, Nr Filey, North Yorkshire YO14 0NS
Tel: (01723) 891333 *Fax:* (01723) 892973
E-mail: mervynpoulter@lineone.net or
info@wranghamhouse.co.uk
Website: www.wranghamhouse.co.uk
Secluded Georgian country house hotel with 12 en suite rooms, dining room and bar. Ideally situated for golfers visiting Ganton, Filey, Scarborough and Bridlington courses.

North West

The Allerdale Court Hotel
Market Place, Cockermouth, Cumbria CA13 9NQ
Tel: (01900) 823654 *Fax:* (01900) 823033
Website: www.allerdalecourthotel.co.uk
2-Star Commended. Excellent restaurant, 24 en suite rooms, well stocked 19th hole. Two miles from Cockermouth Golf Club and near to Keswick and Silloth courses. Good value package deals for groups, societies and individuals.

Metropole Hotel
3 Portland Street, Southport, Merseyside PR8 1LL
Tel: (01704) 536836 *Fax:* (01704) 549041
E-mail: metropole.southport@btinternet.com
Website: www.btinternet.com
/-metropole.southport

RAC/AA 2-Star hotel. Centrally situated and close to Royal Birkdale and other championship courses. Fully licensed – late bar facilities for residents. Full size snooker table. Reduced rates for golfers. Golfing proprietors will assist with tee reservations.

Royal Lytham St Anne's – The Dormy House
Royal Lytham & St Anne's Golf Club Links Gate, Lytham St Anne's, Lancashire FY8 3LQ
Tel: (01253) 724206 *Fax:* (01253) 780946
E-mail: bookings@royallytham.org
Website: www.royallytham.org
Ideal for small parties wishing to play the championship course. Accommodation for men only. Apply to the assistant secretary. (*See advertisement page 595 for further details.*)

Isle of Man

Castletown Golf Links
Fort Island, Derbyhaven, Isle of Man IM9 1UA
Tel: (01624) 822220 *Fax:* (01624) 829661
E-mail: 1sttee@manx.net
Website: www.golfiom.com
An 18-hole links championship course voted number 82 in the UK by *Golf World* magazine. Measuring 6,707 yards SSS 72 established since 1892 is set on the peninsula of Langness surrounded by sea on three sides and overlooking the Manx rolling hills. Accommodation is available twelve months of the year, three bars, excellent local cuisine served in both the table d'hôte and à la carte restaurants. Visiting parties and non-members welcome.

North East

Linden Hall
Longhorsley, Morpeth, Northumberland NE65 8XF
Tel: (01670) 500011 *Fax:* (01670) 500001
Website: www.lindenhall.co.uk
Linden Hall golf course is located in the serene grounds of Linden Hall Hotel, a 3-Star, 52-bedroom luxury country house hotel with swimming pool, health spa, gymnasium and conference facilities. An added facility is the 14-bedroom, Linden Dormy House ideal for golfing parties. The 18-hole, 6,846 yard SSS 73 golf course completely surrounds the hotel and is set within mature woodland, rolling parkland with established burns and lakes amidst the stunning backdrop of the Cheviot hills and Northumbrian coastline.

Ramside Hall Hotel & Golf Club

Carrville, Durham DH1 1TD.
Tel: 0191-386 5282 *Fax:* 0191-386 0399
Set in 220 acres on the outsksirts of the cathedral city
of Durham and surrounded by a stimulating 27-hole
golf course. 3-Star; 4-Crown Highly Commended.
80 luxury bedrooms, restaurant, grill room and
carvery. Conference and banqueting facilities.
Superb floodlit driving range and practice areas. (*See
advertisement page 608 for futher details.*)

SCOTLAND

Scottish Borders

The Roxburghe Hotel & Golf Course

Heiton, By Kelso, Roxburghshire TD5 8JZ
Tel: (01573) 450331 *Fax:* (01573) 450611
E-mail: hotel@roxburghe.net
Website: www.roxburghe.net
A championship course, home to the Charles
Church Scottish Seniors Open, owned by the Duke
of Roxburghe set on the Roxburghe Estates.
Designed by Dave Thomas at 7111 yards and par
72, the course record is 66 held by Sergio García.
Currently the 5th best inland course in Scotland.
Adjacent to the course is the four star, 22-bedroom
country house hotel offering luxury accommoda-
tion and dining and the legendary Library offering
an excellent selection of malt whiskies.

Central & East

Ballathie House Hotel & Sportsman's Lodge

Kinclaven, Stanley, Perthshire PH1 4QN
Tel: (01250) 883268 *Fax:* (01250) 883396
E-mail: email@ballathiehousehotel.com
Website: www.ballathiehousehotel.com
STB 4-Star, AA 2-Rosettes, Taste of Scotland and
Thistle Award winner. Standing in its own grounds
overlooking the river Tay near Perth, Ballathie
House offers Scottish hospitality in a house of char-
acter and distinction. New Sportsman's Lodge
offers budget accommodation for our sporting
guests with all the advantages of a country hotel.
Fifteen minutes from Rosemount Golf Club and
many other courses.

Dalmunzie House Hotel

Spittal O'Glenshee, Blairgowrie, Perthshire
PH10 7QG
Tel: (01250) 885224 *Fax:* (01250) 885225
Set in the Highlands with our own 9-hole course.
This friendly country house offers an ideal base for
a golfing holiday with excellent local courses at
Blairgowrie, Pitlochry, Alyth and many more. (*See
advertisement page 608 for further details.*)

Goldenstones Hotel

Queens Road, Dunbar, East Lothian EH42 1LG
Tel: (01368) 862356 *Fax:* (01368) 865644
E-mail: info@goldenstones.co.uk
Website: www.goldenstones.co.uk
STB 2-Star. We can arrange tee-times for you at
some of the finest Scottish golf courses, including
Muirfield, Dunbar and North Berwick. There are
nineteen superb courses all within half an hour of
the hotel. £30.00 B&B.

Loch Monzievaird Chalets

Ochtertyre, Crieff, Perthshire PH7 4JR
Tel: (01764) 652586 *Fax:* (01764) 652555
Website: www.monzievaird.com
The beautiful grounds at Loch Monzievaird are
hidden away one mile from Crieff. Our Norwegian
and Danish chalets are laid out amongst ancient
oak, beech and scots pine. 20 golf courses within
half an hour's drive!

Old Course Hotel – Golf Resort & Spa

St Andrews, Fife KY16 9SP
Tel: (01334) 474371 *Fax:* (01334) 477668
E-mail: reservations@oldcoursehotel.co.uk
This luxury 134-bedroom hotel overlooks the 17th
Road Hole of the Old Course and is a five minute
walk to the beach and town. Facilities include
health spa with swimming pool, whirlpool, fitness
room and full range of massage and beauty treatments. The hotel has its own championship golf
course, the Duke's Course. Open to non-residents,
with residents enjoying guaranteed tee-times and
reduced green fees.

St Andrews Golf Hotel

St Andrews, Fife KY16 9AS
Tel: (01334) 472611 *Fax:* (01334) 472188
E-mail: reception@standrews-golf.co.uk
Website: www.standrews-golf.co.uk
AA 3-Star; (Top 200) 2-Rosettes; STB 4-Star.
Smart town house hotel offering great comfort and
traditional Scottish hospitality. Award-winning
restaurant and cellar. Two hundred yards from the
first tee of the Old Course. Let us take the hassle
out of arranging your golfing trip.

St Andrews Hazelbank Hotel
28 The Scores, St Andrews, Fife KY16 9AS.
Tel/Fax: (01334) 472466
Website: www.hazelbank.com
Situated 200 yards from the R&A Clubhouse overlooking St Andrews Bay, this family run hotel offers quality accommodation (STB 3-Star) at affordable prices. All rooms en suite. Rates for 2004 £37.50–£59.50 per person B&B, double/twin. Single supplement applies.

Highlands & Islands

Aurora Hotel – Italian Restaurant
2 Academy Street, Nairn, Inverness-shire IV12 4RJ
Tel: (01667) 453551 *Fax:* (01667) 456577
E-mail: aurorahotelnairn@aol.com
A family run 10-bedroomed hotel with traditional Italian restaurant offers a warm welcome and comfortable accommodation. Close to both of Nairn's championship courses, many more within 30 miles. Beautiful beaches, whisky and castle trails.

Machrie Hotel & Golf Links
Port Ellen, Isle of Islay, Argyll PA42 7AN
Tel: (01496) 302310 *Fax:* (01496) 302404
E-mail: machrie@machrie.com
Website: www.machrie.com
Play a hidden gem of a course. Traditional 18-hole championship links course situated on the doorstep of the Machrie Hotel. Excellent accommodation, fine food and friendly service. Self-catering and golf packages also available.

West

Dunduff House
Dunduff Farm, Dunure, Ayr KA7 4LH
Tel: (01292) 500225 *Fax:* (01292) 500222

Situated on the edge of Dunure overlooking Arran and Firth of Clyde. Golf courses include Royal Troon, Turnberry and many more interesting courses. All rooms have TV, radio, tea-making facilities, wash hand basin. Two double rooms have en suite facilities. STB 4-Star; AA/RAC 5-Diamonds. Self-catering cottage available – sleeps four.

Langley Bank Guest House
39 Carrick Road, Ayr KA7 2RD
Tel: (01292) 264246 *Fax:* (01292) 282628
Website: www.accommodation-ayr.co.uk
Langley Bank is an elegantly refurbished Victorian house offering quality accommodation at affordable prices. Centrally situated and in close proximity to all local golf courses. En suite facilities, direct dial telephone. Private car park.

Parkstone Hotel
Central Esplanade, Prestwick, Ayrshire KA9 1QN.
Tel: (01292) 477286 *Fax:* (01292) 477671
E-mail: info@parkstonehotel.co.uk
Website: www.parkstonehotel.co.uk
Seafront location adjacent to Prestwick Golf Club and close to town centre. 22 bedrooms all en suite AA 3-Star; AA Rosette. Special breaks available and all golfing arrangements can be made.

The Westin Turnberry Resort, Scotland
Turnberry, Ayrshire KA26 9LT
Tel: +44 (0) 1655 331000 *Fax:* +44 (0) 1655 331706
E-mail: turnberry@westin.com
Website: www.westin.com/turnberry
World renowned hotel located in spectacular coastal surroundings with unrivalled facilities. Savour the finest international cuisine, stay in luxuriously appointed hotel and lodge bedrooms, relax in the award-winning spa or enjoy a range of exciting outdoor pursuits.

WALES

Imperial Hotel – Llandudno
The Promenade, Llandudno, Gwynedd LL30 1AP
Tel: (01492) 877466
Fax: (01492) 878043
Website: www.theimperial.co.uk
100-bedroomed hotel with extensive leisure facilities including 45′ indoor swimming pool. Ideally situated for all North Wales' golf courses. Award-winning restaurant and private dining room for up to 30 available.

St Mary's Hotel Golf & Country Club
St Mary's Hill, Pencoed, Vale of Glamorgan CF35 5EA.
Tel: (01656) 861100   *Fax:* (01656) 863400
Website: www.stmaryshotel.com
24-bedroom hotel, 18-hole membership and pay course. 9-hole pay as you play, 15-bay floodlit driving range, clubhouse and restaurant conservatory and three bars. Fully stocked golf shop. Floodlit chipping and putting area and resident golf professional Mr John Peters.

CHANNEL ISLANDS

La Grande Mare Hotel Golf Club
La Grande Mare, Vazon, Castel, Guernsey.
Tel: (01481) 253544 *Fax:* (01481) 255194
Website: www.lgm.guernsey.net

Beautifully appointed luxury hotel with 18-hole golf course. Professional shop and tuition on-site. First class, well priced restaurant. 2-AA Rosettes, Beachside location. Golfing breaks catered for.

NORTHERN IRELAND

Bushmills Inn Hotel & Restaurant
9 Dunluce Road, Bushmills, Co Antrim
BT57 8QG
Tel: +44 (0) 28 2073 3000
Fax: +44 (0) 28 2073 2048
E-mail: rnail@bushmillsinn.com
Website: www.bushmillsinn.com

Just four scenic miles from Royal Portrush this multi award-winning hotel and restaurant has been outstandingly successful in recreating its origins as an old coaching inn. Turf fires, gas lights and stripped pine set the scene at this '*living museum of Ulster hospitality*'. Ireland's Golf Hotel of the Year 2003, A Perry Golf 'Partner'; Member of Ireland's Blue Book and Best-Loved Hotels of the World.

REPUBLIC OF IRELAND

Arnolds Hotel
Dunfanaghy, Co Donegal, Ireland
Tel: +353 74 9136208 *Fax:* +353 74 9136352
Website: www.arnoldshol.ie

Family hotel established since 1922 situated at the entrance to the village overlooking Horn Head and Sheephaven Bay. Ideal base to play the many scenic links of north west Donegal.

Bloomfield House Hotel & Leisure Club
Belvedere, Mullingar, Co Westmeath, Ireland.
Tel: +353 44 40894 *Fax:* +353 44 43767
E-mail: sales@bloomfieldhouse.com
Website: www.bloomfieldhouse.com

This beautifully appointed hotel boasts 65 en suite bedrooms. Leisure club and healing rooms offering a range of treatments. Adjacent to Mullingar's Championship Golf Course. Glasson, Esker Hills and Tullamore golf courses are also nearby.

Byrne's Mal Dua House
Clifden, Connemara, Co Galway, Ireland
Tel: +353 95 21171 *Fax:* +353 95 21739
UK Freefone: 08009047532
USA Toll Free: 1866 8919420
E-mail: info@maldua.com
Website: www.maldua.com

AA/RAC-5-Star; Bord Failte 4-Star. In the heart of Connemara, award-winning guesthouse, close to Connemara Golf Club, Byrne's Mal Dua House offers luxury in a relaxed atmosphere. Courtesy mini-bus. Bicycles for hire. Visit our website.

Casey's of Baltimore Hotel
Baltimore, Co Cork, Ireland
Tel: +353 28 20197 *Fax:* +353 28 20509

E-mail: caseys@eircom.net
Website: www.caseysofbaltimore.com

3-Star family run 14 en suite bedroom hotel. Seafood restaurant and traditional pub. Golf available at Skibbereen 18-hole golf course. Special rates for residents.

Inishowen Gateway Hotel Gateway Health & Fitness Club
Railway Road, Buncrana, Inishowen, Co Donegal, Ireland
Tel: 00353 74 9361144 *Fax:* 00353 74 9362278
E-mail: info@inishowengateway.com
Website: www.inishowengateway.com

Stylish hotel, 79 en suite bedrooms, with adjoining luxurious health and fitness club. Enjoying a delightful location on the white sandy shores of Lough Swilly. Ideal for golf at the championship Ballyliffin courses and North West Golf Club.

McEniff Ard Ri Hotel
Ferrybank, Waterford, Ireland
Tel: +353 51 832111 *Fax:* +353 51 832863

Situated on 38 acres of parkland and overlooking historic Waterford City, home to world renowned Waterford Crystal, this hotel has 98 bedrooms. Facilities include an extensive leisure centre, bar and restaurant. There are six 18-hole courses within a ten mile radius.

Rosapenna Hotel & Golf Links
Rosapenna, Downings, Donegal, Ireland
Tel: +353 74 9155301 *Fax:* +353 74 9155128

Rosapenna Hotel is set in the middle of its own 36-hole golf links course. Half a mile from the fishing village of Downings.

Professional Associations

Association of Golf Club Secretaries

7A Beaconsfield Road, Weston-Super-Mare, Somerset BS23 1YE
Tel: (01934) 641166   *Fax:* (01934) 644254
E-mail: hq@agcs.org.uk
Website: www.agcs.org.uk

Membership is available to golf secretaries and managers, course owners and others involved in golf club administration. The following services are available: monthly journal, information library, training courses. seminars, conferences, regional meetings and employment support.

British & International Golf Greenkeepers Association

BIGGA House, Aldwark, Alne, North Yorkshire YO61 1UF
Tel: (01347) 833800   *Fax:* (01347) 833801
E-mail: reception@bigga.co.uk
Website: www.bigga.org.uk

BIGGA

BIGGA has over 7,000 members and is the professional body that represents greenkeepers throughout the UK and has members in 32 countries worldwide. As well as providing extensive education and training programmes for its members, BIGGA produces a monthly magazine *Greenkeeper International*, and each January in Harrogate organises the BIGGA Turf Management Exhibition and the Clubhouse Exhibition. Contact Neil Thomas, Executive Director.

British Association of Golf Course Constructors

The Dormy House, Cooden Beach Golf Club, Bexhill-on-Sea TN39 4TR
Tel: (01424) 842380   *Fax:*(01424) 843375
E-mail: mightyspyder@aol.com
Website: www.bagcc.org.uk

Secretary: David White. Constructors who appear on the BAGCC membership roster qualify only by passing a critical vetting process undertaken by their peers, who look for excellence in construction and a clear demonstration of skills pertinent only to the golf course industry. Utilising the services of a BAGCC member therefore ensures absolute professionalism.

British Golf Industry Association – BGIA

Federation House, Stoneleigh Park, Warwickshire CV8 2RF.
Tel: 024 7641 7141   *Fax:* 024 7641 4990
E-mail: bgia@sportslife.org.uk

Trade association for manufacturers and distributors of golf equipment.

British Rootzone & Topdressing Manufacturers Association

Federation House, NAC, Stoneleigh Park, Warwickshire CV8 2RF
Tel: 024 7641 4999   *Fax:* 024 7641 4990
E-mail: brtma@sportslife.org.uk
Website: www.brtma.com

The Association is a collaboration of experience and expertise in the manufacture of rootzone materials to offer architects, constructors and agronomists a recognised focal point for the industry.

The Council of National Golf Unions

COUNCIL OF
NATIONAL
GOLF UNIONS

Dromin, Dunleer, Co Louth, Ireland.
Tel/Fax +35341 6861476
E-mail: golfinmcinere@hotmail.com

The Council of National Golf Unions is the handicapping authority for Great Britain and Ireland. The Standard Scratch Score and handicapping Scheme has been in operation since March 1926. On 1st February 2004 a new Unified system for men and ladies will be introduced for the Home Counties. The CONGU Unified Handicapping System is the result of much work and consultation to produce a single handicapping system for men and ladies. With the introduction of the System, the Council of National Golf Unions is to be re-constituted with a revised council consisting of an equal number of representatives from the English Golf Union, English Ladies' Golf Association, Golfing Union of Ireland, Irish Ladies' Golf Union, Scottish Golf Union, Scottish Ladies' Golf Association, Welsh Golfing Union, Welsh Ladies' Golf Union together with the Royal and Ancient Golf Club of St Andrews and the Ladies Golf Union.

English Golf Union – EGU

The National Golf Centre, The Broadway, Woodhall Spa, Lincolnshire LN10 6PU
Tel: (01526) 354500   *Fax:* (01526) 354020
E-mail: info@englishgolfunion.org
Website: www.englishgolfunion.org

As the governing body for men's amateur golf in England the EGU organises championships and coaching for players and representative teams at all levels and offers an advisory service on all aspects of golf administration and management.

European Golf Teachers Federation

5 Hastings Road, Bromley, Kent BR1 8NZ
Tel: 020 8462 4120   *Fax:* 020 8462 3983
E-mail: egtj@,dial.pipex.com
Website: www.egtf.co.uk

We offer intensive teaching courses for professionals and amateurs who would like to know how to teach the game simply. The EGTF is the leader in the field of golf instruction.

European Institute of Golf Course Architects

Chiddingfold Golf Club, Petworth Road, Chiddingfold, Surrey GU8 4SL
Tel/Fax +44 (0) 1428681528
E-mail: info@eigca.org
Website: www.eigca.org

EIGCA
EUROPEAN INSTITUTE OF
GOLF COURSE ARCHITECTS

The EIGCA represents the vast majority of qualified and experienced golf course architects throughout Europe. EIGCA's goals include enhancing the professional status of the profession, developing the role of education and increasing the opportunities for its members to practice in countries throughout the world. EIGCA also provides educational courses to train future golfcourse architects and is the authoritative voice on all related matters, being recognised by the R&A Golf Club of St Andrews. Contact: Julia Green, Executive Officer.

Golf Consultants Association

Federation House, Stoneleigh Park, Warwickshire CV5 2RF
Tel: (02476) 414999   *Fax:* (02476) 414990
E-mail: gca@spartslife.org.uk

The GCA provides a point of reference for those requiring independent, professional, golf consultancy services throughout the world.

The Golf Foundation – Developing Junior Golf

Foundation House, The Spinney, Hoddesdon Road,
Stanstead Abbotts, Hertfordshire S612 8GF.
Tel: (01920) 876200   *Fax:* (01920) 876211
Website: www.golf-foundation.org

An organisation dedicated to the promotion and development of grass
roots junior golf across the British Isles.
The Golf Foundation is a registered charity.

National Association of Public Golf Courses – NAPGC

12 Newton Close, Redditch 898 7YR
Tel: (01527) 542106   *Fax:* (01527) 455320
E-mail: eddiemitckel~blueyonder.co.uk
Website: www.napgc.org.uk

The Association provides competition golf for men and lady players of all
handicaps and age. It also offers help and advice to its member clubs – those
playing over courses that they do not own.

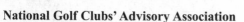

National Golf Clubs' Advisory Association

First Floor Chambers, 18–20 Stamford Street, Stalybridge, Cheshire SK15 2JZ.
Tel: 0161-338 8680   *Fax:* 0161-338 8408
E-mail: ngcaa@idealnet.co.uk
Website: www.ngcaa.org.uk

A non-profit making organisation providing legal advice and support to golf clubs
throughout the UK. The Association is the only independent body supporting golf
clubs in areas of activity other than those arising from playing the game.

STRI – The Sports Turf Research Institute

St Ives Estate, Bingley, West Yorkshire 8016 1AU.
Tel: (01274) 565131   *Fax:* (01274) 561891
E-mail: info@stri.co.uk
Website: www.stri.co.uk

Independent specialists offering you help and advice for the design, construction,
management and maintenance, irrigation or renovation of your golf course.
Comprehensive in-house support services for ecology, testing, turf pathology and
research.

PART XII

Clubs and Courses in the British Isles and Europe

Compiled by Shirley Card

Club Centenaries   626
Golf Clubs and Courses in the British Isles and Europe   627
Great Britain and Ireland County Index   628
Continent of Europe Country and Region Index   829

Club Centenaries

1904

Alness
Auchterderran
Bamburgh Castle
Blackpool North Shore
Blankney
Bonar Bridge/Ardgay
Coombe Wood
Erskine
Fereneze
Fintona
Flackwell Heath
Fulwell
Gifford
Haverfordwest
Highgate
Hindhead
Holywood
Hull
Isles of Scilly
Keighley
Kibworth
Kirkcaldy
Langland Bay
Lutterworth
Machynlleth
North Hants
Osborne
Piltdown
Pontefract & District
Ralston
Saddleworth
Saltford
Shirehampton Park
Spey Bay
Staddon Heights
Stand
Wath
Whitehead
Whiteleaf
Wolstanton
Wrexham
Yelverton

1905

Banchory
Bellshill
Blyth
Bramhall
Bridlington
Broomieknowe
Burley
Burnley
Caerphilly
Castle Douglas
Chapel-en-le-Frith
Clydebank & District
Colvend
Criccieth
Dunmurry
Ellesborough
Erewash Valley
Hindley Hall
Huyton & Prescot
Knighton
Knowle
Lee-on-the-Solent
Letchworth
Llandrindod Wells
Llanishen
Mannings Heath
Maryport
Morecambe
Mount Ellen
North Middlesex
Nuneaton
Old Ranfurly
Pontypridd
Porthmadog
Prenton
Prestatyn
Queens Park
 (Bournemouth)
Redditch
Sandyhills
Sleaford
Southerndown
St Medan
Stockport
Stranraer
Tenterden
The Dunnerholme
Verulam
Whitecraigs
Woodhall Hills
Worthing
Wrekin

1906

Allendale
Alston Moor
Bradford Moor
Brandhall
Carholme
Carradale
Chilwell Manor
Chipstead
Clayton
Cowglen
Deane
Dinsdale Spa
Dunstable Downs
Elgin
Enmore Park
Fulford
Glen (North Berwick)
Gorleston
Gosforth
Halesowen
Halifax West End
Hartlepool
Harwich & Dovercourt
Holywell
Knighton
Kyles of Bute
Leigh
Longcliffe
Matlock
Morpeth
Ormonde Fields
Otley
Outlane
Pannal
Prince's
Ravensworth
Serlby Park
Silverdale
South Bradford
South Leeds
Southport & Ainsdale
St Deiniol
Stafford Castle
Stanton-on-the-Wolds
The Dyke
Turnberry Hotel
Walmersley
West Byfleet
West Monmouthshire
Whitsand Bay Hotel
Whittaker
Williamwood
Wrotham

1907

Abersoch
Alderley Edge
Alnwick
The Alwoodley
Andover
Beckenham Place Park
Bishopbriggs
Blackley
Brampton (Talkin Tarn)
Burhill
Burslem
Caldy
Carmarthen
Carnwath
Colchester
Copt Heath
Ghyll
Halifax Bradley Hall
Harewood Downs
Headley
Ilford
Irvine Ravenspark
Kingsknowe
Lees Hall
Lightcliffe
Lymm
Mapperley
Merchants of Edinburgh
Mountain Ash
Nefyn & District
New Mills
Newton Green
North Oxford
North Worcestershire
Ogbourne Downs
Old Colwyn
Ripon City
Scrabo
The Spa
Seaford Head
Selby
Spalding
St Augustines
Tankersley park
Thorpe Hall
Troon St Meddans
Vale of Leven
Walsall
West Hill
Whiteleaf

Golf Clubs and Courses in the British Isles and Europe

How to use this section

Clubs in England, Ireland and Wales are listed in alphabetical order by country and county. Note that some clubs and courses are affiliated to a county different to that in which they are physically located. Clubs in Scotland are grouped under recognised administrative regions. The Great Britain and Ireland county index can be found on page 628.

European clubs are listed alphabetically by country and grouped under regional headings. The index for this can be found on page 829. In most European countries, only 18 hole courses are included.

All clubs and courses are listed in the the general index at the back of the book.

Club details (see Key to Symbols below)

The date after the name of the club indicates the year it was founded. Courses are private unless otherwise stated. Many public courses play host to members' clubs. Information on these can be obtained from the course concerned.

The address is the postal address.

Telephone: club telephone number for general use.

Membership: total number of playing members. The number of lady members (L) and juniors (J) is sometimes shown separately.

Secretary/Professional: telephone numbers for secretaries and professionals are shown separately.

Holes: the length of the course refers in most cases to the yardage from the medal tees.

Visitors: indicates the playing opportunities and restrictions for unaccompanied visitors.

Fees: green fees, the most up-to-date supplied, are quoted for visitors playing without a member. The basic cost per round or per day (D) is shown first, with the weekend rate in brackets. The cost of a weekly (W) ticket is sometimes shown.

Location: general location of club/course.

Miscellaneous: other golf facilities.

Architect: course architect/designer.

Abbreviations

WD	Weekdays.
WE	Weekends.
BH	Bank Holidays.
H	Handicap certificate required.
M	With a member, i.e. casual visitors are not allowed: only visitors playing with a member are permitted on the days stated.
NA	No visitors allowed.
SOC	Recognised Golfing Societies welcome if previous arrangements made with secretary.
U	Unrestricted.
CR	Course Rating (Europe)
SR	Slope Rating (Europe)

We are indebted to club secretaries in the British Isles and continental Europe for the information supplied.

Key to Symbols

☎ Telephone	✓ Professional	⊕ Miscellaneous
🖶 Fax	↦ Holes	⌂ Architect
✉ E-mail	👫 Visitors	■ Website
📖 Membership	£€ Fees	
✍ Secretary	⚓ Location	

Great Britain and Ireland County Index

England

Bedfordshire 629
Berkshire 630
Buckinghamshire 633
Cambridgeshire 636
Channel Islands 638
Cheshire 638
Cornwall 643
Cumbria 646
Derbyshire 648
Devon 650
Dorset 653
Durham 656
Essex 658
Gloucestershire 663
Hampshire 666
Herefordshire 670
Hertfordshire 671
Isle of Man 675
Isle of Wight 676
Kent 677
Lancashire 683
Leicestershire 689
Lincolnshire 691
London (list of
  clubs) 694

Manchester 694
Merseyside 696
Middlesex 699
Norfolk 702
Northamptonshire
  704
Northumberland 706
Nottinghamshire 708
Oxfordshire 710
Rutland 712
Shropshire 712
Somerset 714
Staffordshire 717
Suffolk 720
Surrey 722
Sussex (East) 731
Sussex (West) 733
Tyne & Wear 735
Warwickshire 737
Wiltshire 740
Worcestershire 741
Yorkshire (East) 745
Yorkshire (North) 746
Yorkshire (South) 750
Yorkshire (West) 752

Scotland

Aberdeenshire 784
  Aberdeen Clubs 786
  Aberdeen Courses
  786
Angus 787
  Carnoustie Clubs
  788
  Carnoustie Courses
  788
Argyll & Bute 788
Ayrshire 790
Borders 793
Clackmannanshire 794
Dumfries &
  Galloway 794
Dunbartonshire 796
Fife 797
  St Andrews Clubs
  800
  St Andrews Courses
  800

Glasgow 801
Highland
  Caithness &
    Sutherland 802
  Inverness 803
  Orkney & Shetland
    804
  West Coast 804
Lanarkshire 805
Lothians
  East Lothian 807
  Midlothian 808
  West Lothian 811
Moray 811
Perth & Kinross 812
Renfrewshire 814
Stirlingshire 816

Ireland

Co Antrim 758
Co Armagh 759
Belfast 760
Co Carlow 761
Co Cavan 761
Co Clare 761
Co Cork 762
Co Donegal 764
Co Down 765
Co Dublin 767
Dublin City 769
Co Fermanagh 770
Co Galway 770
Co Kerry 771
Co Kildare 773
Co Kilkenny 774
Co Laois 774

Co Leitrim 775
Co Limerick 775
Co Londonderry 775
Co Longford 776
Co Louth 776
Co Mayo 776
Co Meath 777
Co Monaghan 778
Co Offaly 778
Co Roscommon 779
Co Sligo 779
Co Tipperary 779
Co Tyrone 780
Co Waterford 781
Co Westmeath 781
Co Wexford 782
Co Wicklow 782

Wales

Cardiganshire 817
Carmarthenshire 817
Conwy 818
Denbighshire 818
Flintshire 819
Gwynedd 819
Isle of Anglesey 820

Mid Glamorgan 821
Monmouthshire 822
Pembrokeshire 824
Powys 824
South Glamorgan 825
West Glamorgan 826
Wrexham 827

England

Bedfordshire

Aspley Guise & Woburn Sands (1914)
West Hill, Aspley Guise, Milton Keynes, MK17 8DX
- ☎ **(01908) 583596**
- 📠 (01908) 583596
- 📖 590
- 🏌 Richard Norris (01908) 583596
- ⌛ C Clingan (01908) 582974
- ⏳ 18 L 6079 yds Par 71 SSS 70
- 👤 WD–H WE/BH–MH SOC–Wed & Fri
- £€ £28 (£38)
- 🏁 2 miles W of M1 Junction 13
- 🏠 Herd/Sandow

Aylesbury Vale (1991)
Wing, Leighton Buzzard, LU7 0UJ
- ☎ **(01525) 240196**
- 📠 (01525) 240848
- 📖 500
- 🏌 C Wright (Sec/Mgr)
- ⌛ J Pugh (01525) 240196
- ⏳ 18 L 6612 yds Par 72 SSS 72
- 👤 WD–U WE–U–phone first SOC–WD
- £€ £15 (£25)
- 🏁 3 miles W of Leighton Buzzard on Wing-Stewkley road
- ⊕ Driving range
- 🏠 Sq Ldr Don Wright

Beadlow Manor Hotel G&CC (1973)
Beadlow, Shefford, SG17 5PH
- ☎ **(01525) 860800**
- 📠 (01525) 861345
- 📖 700
- 🏌 R Tommey (01525) 843398
- ⌛ P Hetherington (01525) 861292
- ⏳ 18 L 6238 yds SSS 71
  18 L 6042 yds SSS 70
- 👤 U H SOC
- £€ On application
- 🏁 2 miles W of Shefford on A507
- ⊕ Driving range

The Bedford (1999)
Carnoustie Drive, Great Denham Golf Village, Biddenham, MK40 4FF
- ☎ **(01234) 320022**
- 📠 (01234) 320023
- 🏌 S Pepper (01234) 330559
- ⌛ M Litton
- ⏳ 18 L 6560 yds Par 72
- 👤 WD–U WE–U SOC–WD
- £€ £30 (£40)
- 🏁 2 miles W of Bedford (A428)
- ⊕ Driving range
- 🏠 David Pottage

Bedford & County (1912)
Green Lane, Clapham, Bedford, MK41 6ET
- ☎ **(01234) 352617**
- 📠 (01234) 357195
- ✉ olga@bedcounty.fsnet.co.uk
- 📖 600
- 🏌 RP Walker (Mgr), O Ebsworth (Asst Mgr)
- ⌛ R Tattersall (01234) 359189
- ⏳ 18 L 6420 yds SSS 70
- 👤 WD–U H SOC WE–M
- £€ D–£32
- 🏁 2 miles NW of Bedford on A6 (Clapham village)
- ■ www.bedfordandcountygolfclub.co.uk

Bedfordshire (1891)
Spring Lane, Stagsden, Bedford, MK43 8SR
- ☎ **(01234) 822555**
- 📠 (01234) 825052
- 📖 600
- 🏌 DE Romans (Gen Mgr)
- ⌛ D Armor (01234) 826100
- ⏳ 18 L 6565 yds SSS 72
- 👤 WD–U (phone first) WE–M before noon SOC–WD
- £€ On application
- 🏁 3 miles W of Bedford (A422). M1 Junction 14, 5 miles

Chalgrave Manor
Dunstable Road, Chalgrave, Toddington, LU5 6JN
- ☎ **(01525) 876556**
- 📠 (01525) 876556
- 📖 450
- 🏌 S Rumball
- ⌛ Geoff Swain
- ⏳ 18 L 6382 yds Par 72 SSS 70
- 👤 U SOC–WD
- £€ £20 (£30)
- 🏁 2 miles W of M1 J12 on A5120
- ⊕ Practice range
- 🏠 Mike Palmer

Colmworth (1992)
Proprietary
New Road, Colmworth, MK44 2NN
- ☎ **(01234) 378181**
- 📠 (01234) 376678
- ✉ julie@colmworthgc.fsnet.co.uk
- 📖 230
- 🏌 A Willis (01234) 402674
- ⌛ G Bithrey
- ⏳ 18 L 6435 yds Par 72 SSS 71
  9 hole Par 3 course
- 👤 U SOC
- £€ £13 (£20)
- 🏁 6 miles N of Bedford, off B660. 4 miles W of A1
- ⊕ Driving range Par 3. Self-catering cottages
- 🏠 John Glasgow
- ■ www.colmworthgolfclub.co.uk

Colworth (1985)
Unilever Research, Sharnbrook, Bedford, MK44 1LQ
- ☎ **(01933) 353269 (Sec)**
- 📖 405
- 🏌 E Thompson
- ⏳ 9 L 2626 yds Par 68 SSS 66
- 👤 M
- £€ D–£8
- 🏁 Sharnbrook, 10 miles N of Bedford, off A6

Dunstable Downs (1906)
Whipsnade Road, Dunstable, LU6 2NB
- ☎ **(01582) 604472**
- 📠 (01582) 478700
- ✉ ddgc@btconnect.com
- 📖 640
- 🏌 J Nolan (01582) 604472
- ⌛ M Weldon (01582) 662806
- ⏳ 18 L 5903 yds SSS 69
- 👤 WD–H WE–M SOC–WD exc Wed
- £€ £28.50 D–£40
- 🏁 2 miles SW of Dunstable on B4541. M1 Junction 11
- 🏠 James Braid
- ■ www.dunstable-golf.co.uk

Griffin (1985)
Chaul End Road, Caddington, LU1 4AX
- ☎ **(01582) 415573**
- 📠 (01582) 415314
- 📖 500
- 🏌 D Sweetman
- ⌛ D Marsden
- ⏳ 18 L 6240 yds Par 71 SSS 70
- 👤 WD–U WE/BH–phone first SOC
- £€ £14 Fri–£17 (£20)
- 🏁 3 miles W of Luton on A505 between Dunstable and Caddington. M1 Junction 10/11

Henlow (1985)
RAF Henlow, Henlow, SG16 6DN
- ☎ **(01462) 851515 Ext 7083**
- 📠 (01462) 816780
- 📖 250
- 🏌 A Smythe (01462) 851515 (Ext 7473)
- ⏳ 9 L 5618 yds SSS 67
- 👤 M
- £€ D–£10
- 🏁 3 miles SE of Shefford on A600
- ⊕ Driving range
- ■ www.henlowgolfclub.co.uk

John O'Gaunt (1948)
Sutton Park, Sandy, Biggleswade, SG19 2LY
- ☎ **(01767) 260360**
- 📠 (01767) 262834
- ✉ admin@johnogauntgolfclub.co.uk
- 📖 1450
- 🏌 SD Anthony
- ⌛ L Scarbrow (01767) 260094

⌐ John O'Gaunt 18 L 6513 yds
SSS 71 Par 71
Carthagena 18 L 5869 yds SSS 69
Par 69
🏌 H–phone first SOC–WD
£€ £50 (£60)
🚗 3 miles NE of Biggleswade on
B1040
🏰 Hawtree
■ www.johnogauntgolfclub.co.uk

Leighton Buzzard (1925)
*Plantation Road, Leighton Buzzard,
LU7 3JF*
☎ (01525) 244800
✉ secretary@leightonbuzzardgolf.net
🕮 650
🏌 D Mutton (01525) 244800
✓ M Campbell (01525) 244815
⌐ 18 L 6101 yds SSS 70
🏌 WD exc Tues–U H WE/BH–MH
£€ £34 D–£36
🚗 Heath and Reach, 1 mile N of
Leighton Buzzard. M1 Junction 12
■ www.leightonbuzzardgolf.net

The Millbrook (1980)
Ampthill, MK45 2JB
☎ (01525) 840252
🖥 (01525) 406249
✉ info@themillbrook.com
🕮 420
🏌 DC Cooke
✓ G Dixon (01525) 402269
⌐ 18 L 7021 yds SSS 73
🏌 WD–U WE after 12.00pm SOC
£€ £22 (£28)
🚗 4 miles from M1 Junctions 12 or 13
on A507
⊕ Practice range
🏰 W Sutherland
■ www.themillbrook.com

Mount Pleasant (1992)
Proprietary
*Station Road, Lower Stondon, Henlow,
SG16 6JL*
☎ (01462) 850999
🖥 (01462) 850257
✉ davidsimsmpgolf@aol.com
🕮 300
🏌 D Simkins (Prop) (01462) 850999
✓ M Roberts (01462) 850999
⌐ 9 L 6003 yds Par 70 SSS 69
🏌 U SOC–WD
£€ 9 holes–£8 (£10.50) 18 holes–£14
(£18)
🚗 4 miles N of Hitchin, off A600
🏰 Derek Young
■ www.mountpleasantgolfclub.co.uk

Mowsbury (1975)
Public
Kimbolton Road, Bedford, MK41 8DQ
☎ (01234) 216374/771041
🕮 484
🏌 BE Edwards
✓ M Summers
⌐ 18 L 6514 yds SSS 71
🏌 U
£€ £13.30 (£14)

🚗 2 miles N of Bedford on B660
⊕ Driving range
🏰 Hawtree

Pavenham Park (1994)
Pavenham, Bedford, MK43 7PE
☎ (01234) 822202
🖥 (01234) 826602
✉ kolvengolf@ukonline.co.uk
🕮 850
🏌 E Thompson
✓ ZL Thompson
⌐ 18 L 6353 yds SSS 71
🏌 WD–U WE–M SOC–WD
£€ £25 (£40)
🚗 4 miles NW of Bedford on A6
🏰 Zac Thompson
■ www.kolvengolf.com

South Beds (1892)
Warden Hill Road, Luton, LU2 7AE
☎ (01582) 575201
🖥 (01582) 495381
✉ office@southbedsgolfclub.co.uk
🕮 850
🏌 RJ Wright (01582) 591500
✓ E Cogle (01582) 591209
⌐ Galley 18 L 6438 yds SSS 71
Warden 9 L 4914 yds SSS 64
🏌 Galley WD–H (Ladies Day–Tues)
WE/BH–H exc comp days–NA
Warden–U
£€ Galley £23 D–£32 (£35 D–£44)
Warden £12 (£15)
🚗 3 miles N of Luton, E of A6
■ www.southbedsgolfclub.co.uk

Stockwood Park (1973)
Public
*Stockwood Park, London Rd, Luton,
LU1 4LX*
☎ (01582) 413704
🖥 (01582) 481001
✉ secretary@stockwoodparkgc
.freeserve.co.uk
🕮 750
🏌 Mrs B McMillan (01582) 431788
✓ G McCarthy
⌐ 18 L 6049 yds SSS 69
🏌 U
£€ £11.20 (£13.10)
🚗 1 mile S of Luton on A6. M1
Junction 10
⊕ Driving range

Tilsworth (1972)
Pay and play
*Dunstable Rd, Tilsworth, Dunstable,
LU7 9PU*
☎ (01525) 210721/210722
🖥 (01525) 210465
🕮 370
🏌 G Brandon-White
✓ N Webb (Mgr)
⌐ 18 L 5303 yds Par 69 SSS 67
🏌 U SOC
£€ £15 (£17.50)
🚗 2 miles N of Dunstable (A5)
⊕ Driving range
■ www.tilsworthgolf.co.uk

Wyboston Lakes (1978)
Public
Wyboston Lakes, Wyboston, MK44 3AL
☎ (01480) 223004
🖥 (01480) 407330
🕮 300
🏌 DJ Little (Mgr)
✓ P Ashwell (01480) 223004
⌐ 18 L 5995 yds Par 70 SSS 69
🏌 WD–U WE–booking SOC
£€ £15 (£20)
🚗 S of St Neots, off A1 and St Neots
by-pass
⊕ Driving range
🏰 Neil Ockden
■ www.wybostonlakes.co.uk

Berkshire

Bearwood (1986)
*Mole Road, Sindlesham, Wokingham,
RG41 5DB*
☎ (0118) 976 0060
🖥 (0118) 977 2687
🕮 500
🏌 BFC Tustin (Mgr)
(0118) 976 0060
✓ BJ Tustin (0118) 976 0156
⌐ 9 L 5614 yds SSS 68
🏌 WD–H before 4pm –M after 4pm
£€ 18 holes–£18 (£22)
9 holes–£10 (£12)
🚗 1 mile SW of Winnersh, on B3030.
M4 Junction 10
⊕ Driving range

Bearwood Lakes (1996)
*Bearwood Road, Sindlesham,
RG41 4SJ*
☎ (0118) 979 7900
🖥 (0118) 979 2911
✉ info@bearwoodlakes.co.uk
🕮 800
🏌 S Evans (Gen Mgr)
✓ T Waldron (0118) 978 3030
⌐ 18 L 6800 yds Par 72 SSS 72
🏌 M H
🚗 1 mile S of M4 Junction 10,
between Wokingham and
Sindlesham
🏰 Martin Hawtree
■ www.bearwoodlakes.co.uk

The Berkshire (1928)
Swinley Road, Ascot, SL5 8AY
☎ (01344) 621495
🖥 (01344) 623328
🕮 935
🏌 Lt Col JCF Hunt (01344) 621496
✓ P Anderson (01344) 622351
⌐ Red 18 L 6379 yds SSS 71
Blue 18 L 6260 yds SSS 71
🏌 WD–I WE/BH–M
£€ On application
🚗 3 miles from Ascot on A332. M3
Junction 3
🏰 Herbert Fowler

Billingbear Park
Pay and play
The Straight Mile, Wokingham,
RG40 5SJ
☎ **(01344) 869259**
🖀 (01344) 869259
📖 50
🏌 Mrs JR Blainey
✓ MW Blainey
🏳 9 L 5700 yds Par 68
9 hole Par 3 course
🏌 U
££ £8 (£10)
🚗 2 miles E of Wokingham via
B3034. M4 Junction 10

Bird Hills (1985)
Public
Drift Road, Hawthorn Hill, Maidenhead,
SL6 3ST
☎ **(01628) 771030**
🖀 (01628) 631023
📧 info@birdhills.co.uk
📖 400
🏌 S Farrin (Gen Mgr)
✓ N Slimming
🏳 18 L 6212 yds SSS 69
🏌 U SOC–WD
££ On application
🚗 4 miles S of Maidenhead on A330
⊕ Floodlit driving range
■ www.birdhills.co.uk

Blue Mountain Golf Centre (1993)
Pay and play
Wood Lane, Binfield, RG42 4EX
☎ **(01344) 300220**
🖀 (01344) 360960
📧 bluemountain@americangolf
.uk.com
📖 350
✓ I Looms (01344) 488858
🏳 18 L 6097 yds SSS 70
🏌 U SOC
££ Mon–Thur £18 Fri £20 (£25)
🚗 1 mile W of Bracknell on B3408.
M4 Junction 10
⊕ Driving range. Golf Academy

Calcot Park (1930)
Bath Road, Calcot, Reading, RG31 7RN
☎ **(0118) 942 7124**
🖀 (0118) 945 3373
📧 info@calcotpark.com
📖 550
🏌 Kim Brake
✓ IJ Campbell (0118) 942 7797
🏳 18 L 6216 yds SSS 70
🏌 WD–H WE/BH–M SOC–WD
££ £40 After 2pm–£25
🚗 3 miles W of Reading on A4. 1¹/₂
miles E of M4 Junction 12
🏠 HS Colt

Castle Royle (1994)
Knowl Hill, Reading, RG10 9XA
☎ **(01628) 825442**
🏌 Pam Sutcliffe

✓ R Watts
🏳 18 L 6828 yds Par 72 SSS 73
🏌 N/A
££ N/A
🚗 2 miles W of Maidenhead (A4). M4
Junction 8/9
🏠 Neil Coles

Caversham Heath (2000)
Chazey Heath, Mapledurham, Reading
RG4 7UT
☎ **0118 947 8600**
🖀 0118 947 8700
📧 robertclive@cavershamgolf.co.uk
🏌 Robert Clive
✓ Carl Rutherford (01189 479400)
🏳 18 7151 yds Par 73 SSS 74
🏌 UN restricted WD. WE–NA before
3.00 pm
££ £29 (£40)
🚗 3 miles N of Reading
🏠 David Williams

Datchet (1890)
Buccleuch Road, Datchet, SL3 9BP
☎ **(01753) 543887 (Clubhouse)**
🖀 (01753) 541872
📧 secretary@datchetgolfclub.co.uk
📖 435 60(L) 30(J)
🏌 KR Smith (01753) 541872
✓ I Godleman (01753) 545222
🏳 9 L 6087 yds SSS 69
🏌 WD–U M after 3pm WE–M SOC
££ £20 D–£27
🚗 Slough, Windsor 2 miles
🏠 JH Taylor
■ www.datchetgolfclub.co.uk

Deanwood Park (1995)
Pay and play
Stockcross, Newbury, RG20 8JS
☎ **(01635) 48772**
🖀 (01635) 48772
📧 deanwood@newburyweb.net
📖 400
🏌 J Bowness
✓ J Purton
🏳 9 L 4230 yds Par 64 SSS 60
🏌 U
££ £14.50 (£17.50)
🚗 2 miles W of Newbury (B4000).
M4 Junction 13, 2 miles
⊕ Driving range
■ www.newbury.net/deanwood

Donnington Valley (1985)
Snelsmore House, Snelsmore Common,
Newbury, RG14 3BG
☎ **(01635) 568140**
🖀 (01635) 568141
📖 550
🏌 LC Storey (01635) 568145
✓ M Balfour
🏳 18 L 6335 yds SSS 71
🏌 U
££ £22 (£28)
🚗 N of Newbury, off Old Oxford
road
■ www.donningtonvalley.co.uk

Downshire (1973)
Public
Easthampstead Park, Wokingham,
RG11 3DH
☎ **(01344) 302030**
🖀 (01344) 301020
🏌 P Stanwick (Golf Mgr)
✓ W Owers
🏳 18 L 6416 yds SSS 69
🏌 U SOC
££ £13.50 (£17)
🚗 Off Nine Mile Ride
⊕ Driving range. Pitch & putt

East Berkshire (1903)
Ravenswood Ave, Crowthorne, RG45
6BD
☎ **(01344) 772041**
🖀 (01344) 777378
📖 700
🏌 DP Kelly
✓ J Brant (01344) 774112
🏳 18 L 6345 yds SSS 70
🏌 WD–H WE/BH–M SOC
££ £40
🚗 Nr Crowthorne Station
🏠 P Paxton

Goring & Streatley (1895)
Rectory Road, Streatley-on-Thames,
RG8 9QA
☎ **(01491) 873229**
🖀 (01491) 875224
📖 740 115(L) 50(J)
🏌 Val Jones (Sec/Mgr)
✓ J Hadland (01491) 873715
🏳 18 L 6355 yds SSS 70
🏌 WD–U WE/BH–M SOC–WD
££ £30 D–£36 (£40)
🚗 10 miles NW of Reading on A417
🏠 Tom Dunne
■ www.goringgc.org

Hennerton (1992)
Crazies Hill Road, Wargrave, RG10 8LT
☎ **(0118) 940 1000/4778**
🖀 (0118) 940 1042
📖 450
✓ W Farrow (0118) 940 4778
🏳 9 L 2730 yds SSS 34
🏌 WD–U WE–pm only SOC
££ 18 holes–£17 (£20) 9 holes–£12
(£15)
🚗 Between Maidenhead and Reading
(A4/A321)
⊕ Driving range
🏠 Dion Beard
■ www.hennertongolfclub.co.uk

Hurst (1979)
Public
Sandford Lane, Hurst, Wokingham,
RG10 0SQ
☎ **(01734) 344355**
🏌 G Walters (Hon)
✓ Lee Newman
🏳 9 L 3016 yds SSS 71
££ On application
🚗 Reading 5 miles. Wokingham 3
miles

Maidenhead   (1896)

Shoppenhangers Road, Maidenhead,
SL6 2PZ
☎ **(01628) 624693**
✉ manager@maidenheadgolf.co.uk
☷ 600
♬ JR Maguire
✓ S Geary (01628) 624067
↣ 18 L 6360 yds SSS 70
👥 WD–H Fri–M after noon WE–M
£€ D–£35
🚗 Off A308, nr Maidenhead Station
■ www.maidenheadgolf.co.uk

Mapledurham   (1992)

Mapledurham, Reading, RG4 7UD
☎ **(0118) 946 3353**
☷ (0118) 946 3363
✉ d.reeves@clubhaus.com
☷ 750
♬ D Reeves
✓ D Boyce
↣ 18 L 5635 yds SSS 67
👥 WE–NA before 11am
£€ £19 (£24)
🚗 4 miles NW of Reading, off A4074
🏠 MRM Sandow

Mill Ride   (1990)

Mill Ride, Ascot, SL5 8LT
☎ **(01344) 886777**
☷ (01344) 886820
☷ 300
♬ G Irvine (Gen Mgr)
✓ M Palmer
↣ 18 L 6752 yds SSS 72
👥 H SOC
£€ On application
🚗 2 miles W of Ascot
⊕ www.mill-ride.com
🏠 Donald Steel

Newbury & Crookham

(1873)

Bury's Bank Road, Greenham Common,
Newbury, RG19 8BZ
☎ **(01635) 40035**
☷ (01635) 40045
✉ steve.myers@newburygolf.co.uk
☷ 626
♬ S Myers MBE (01635 40035)
✓ DW Harris (01635) 31201
↣ 18 L 5918 yds SSS 69
👥 WD–U H WE–M (recognised club members)
£€ £30 18 holes, £35 day
🚗 4 miles SE of Newbury. M4 Junction 13

Newbury Racecourse

(1994)

The Racecourse, Newbury, RG14 7NZ
☎ **(01635) 551464**
☷ (01635) 528354
☷ 300
♬ R Osgood (01635) 400015
✓ N Mitchell (01635) 551464
↣ 18 L 6311 yds Par 70 SSS 70
👥 U SOC
£€ £13 (£17)

🚗 4 miles S of M4 Junction 13 on A34/A39
⊕ Driving range
■ www.nrgc.co.uk

Parasampia G&CC

Donnington Grove, Grove Road,
Donnington, RG14 2LA
☎ **(01635) 581000**
☷ (01635) 552259
✉ enquiries@parasampia.com
☷ 450
♬ S Greenacre (Mgr)
✓ G Williams
↣ 18 L 7108 yds Par 72 SSS 74
👥 U SOC–WD/BH
£€ £35 D–£45 (£40 D–£55)
🚗 NW of Newbury, off old Oxford road (B4494). M4 J13, 3¹/₂ miles
🏠 Dave Thomas
■ www.parasampia.com

Reading   (1910)

17 Kidmore End Road, Emmer Green,
Reading, RG4 8SG
☎ **(0118) 947 2909**
☷ (0118) 946 4468
✉ secretaryt@readinggolfclub.com
☷ 600
♬ R Brown (0118) 947 2909
✓ S Fotheringham (0118) 947 6115
↣ 18 L 6251 yds SSS 70
👥 Mon–Thurs–UH Fri/WE/BH–M SOC–Tues–Thurs
£€ £30 D–£45
🚗 2 miles N of Reading, off Peppard Road (B481)
🏠 James Braid
■ www.readinggolfclub.com

Royal Ascot   (1887)

Winkfield Road, Ascot, SL5 7LJ
☎ **(01344) 625175**
☷ (01344) 872330
✉ golf@royalascotgc.fsnet.co.uk
☷ 600
♬ Mrs S Thompson (01344) 625175
✓ A White (01344) 624656
↣ 18 L 5716 yds SSS 68
👥 M SOC
£€ On application
🚗 On Ascot Heath, inside Ascot racecourse. Windsor 4 miles
🏠 JH Taylor

The Royal Household   (1901)

Crown Estates Office, Windsor
Castle, Windsor
☎ **(020) 7930 4832**
☷ (020) 7839 5950
☷ 200
♬ G Begley
↣ 9 L 4560 yds SSS 62
👥 Strictly by invitation
🚗 Home Park, Windsor Castle
🏠 Muir Ferguson

Sand Martins   (1993)

Finchampstead Road, Wokingham,
RG40 3RQ
☎ **(0118) 979 2711**

☷ (0118) 977 0282
☷ 750
♬ AJ Hall
✓ AJ Hall (0118) 977 0265
↣ 18 L 6204 yds Par 70 SSS 70
👥 WD–U WE–NA SOC
£€ £30
🚗 1 mile S of Wokingham. M4 Junction 10
⊕ Driving range
🏠 ET Fox
■ www.sandmartins.com

Sonning   (1911)

Duffield Road, Sonning, Reading,
RG4 6GJ
☎ **(0118) 969 3332**
☷ (0118) 944 8409
✉ secretary@sonning-golf-club.co.uk
☷ 750
♬ AJ Tanner
✓ RT McDougall (0118) 969 2910
↣ 18 L 6366 yds SSS 70
👥 WD–H WE–M
£€ On application
🚗 1¹/₂ miles E of A329(M). S of A4, nr Sonning

Swinley Forest   (1909)

Coronation Road, Ascot, SL5 9LE
☎ **(01344) 620197**
☷ (01344) 874733
✉ swinleyfgc@aol.com
☷ 350
♬ IL Pearce (01344) 874979
✓ S Hill (01344) 874811
↣ 18 L 6045 yds Par 69 SSS 70
👥 M
£€ £80
🚗 S of Ascot
🏠 HS Colt

Temple   (1909)

Henley Road, Hurley, Maidenhead,
SL6 5LH
☎ **(01628) 824795**
☷ (01628) 828119
☷ 566
♬ KGM Adderley (01628) 824795
✓ J Whiteley (01628) 824254
↣ 18 L 6248 yds SSS 70
👥 H SOC
£€ £36 (£44)
🚗 Between Maidenhead and Henley on A4130. M4 Junction 8/9. M40 Junction 4
🏠 Willie Park Jr

Theale

North Street, Theale, Reading, RG6 5EX
☎ **(01189) 305331**
☷ (01189) 305331
♬ M Lowe
✓ L Newman
↣ 18 L 6392 yds Par 72 SSS 71
👥 U SOC
£€ £16 (£23)
🚗 1 mile from M4 Junction 12
⊕ Driving range
🏠 M Lowe

West Berkshire   (1975)
Chaddleworth, Newbury, RG20 7DU
- ☎ **(01488) 638574**
- ☐ 700
- ♠ Mrs CM Clayton
- ✎ P Simpson (01488) 638851
- ▷ 18 L 7001 yds SSS 74
- ♟ WD–U WE–M SOC–WD
- ££ £25 D–£35 (£35)
- ⊕ Off A338 to Wantage. M4 Junction 14

Winter Hill   (1976)
Grange Lane, Cookham, SL6 9RP
- ☎ **(01628) 527613**
- ☐ 800
- ♠ M Goodenough
- ✎ R Frost (01628) 527610
- ▷ 18 L 6408 yds SSS 71
- ♟ WD–U WE–M SOC
- ££ D–£31 After 2pm–£21.50
- ⊕ Maidenhead 3 miles
- ♜ Charles Lawrie

Wokefield Park   (1998)
Mortimer, Reading, RG7 3AE
- ☎ **(0118) 933 4013/4018/4017**
- ☐ (0118) 933 4031
- ✉ wokefieldgolf@initialstyle.co.uk
- ♠ J Morgan (Hon), M Clark
- ✎ G Smith (0118) 933 4078
- ▷ 18 L 6961 yds Par 72 SSS 73
- ♟ WD–U WE–NA before 9.30am SOC
- ££ £30 (£45)
- ⊕ 8 miles SW of Reading, off A33. M4 Junction 11
- ⊕ Driving range
- ♜ Jonathan Gaunt
- ■ www.golf-isc.co.uk

Buckinghamshire

Abbey Hill   (1975)
Monks Way, Two Mile Ash, Milton Keynes, MK8 8AA
- ☎ **(01908) 563845**
- ☐ 300
- ♠ J Falconer
- ✎ G Woodham
- ▷ 18 L 6193 yds SSS 69
  Par 3 course
- ♟ U
- ££ On application
- ⊕ 2 miles S of Stony Stratford
- ⊕ Driving range

Aylesbury Golf Centre   (1992)
Public
Hulcott Lane, Bierton, HP22 5GA
- ☎ **(01296) 393644**
- ♠ K Partington (Mgr)
- ✎ R Wooster
- ▷ 18 L 5965 yds SSS 69
- ♟ U
- ££ £10 (£15)
- ⊕ 1 mile N of Aylesbury on A418

- ⊕ Driving range
- ♜ TS Benwell

Aylesbury Park   (1996)
Andrews Way, off Coldharbour Way, Osford Road, Aylesbury, HP17 8QQ
- ☎ **(01296) 399166/395381**
- ☐ (01296) 336830
- ☐ 360
- ♠ Carole Barnes (01296) 399196
- ✎ John Schell (01296) 399196
- ▷ 18 L 6150 yds SSS 69
  9-hole Par 3 short course
- ♟ U
- ££ 18: £16 (£21); 9: £5
- ⊕ SW of Aylesbury (A418). M40 Junction 8, 12 miles
- ⊕ Driving range
- ♜ Martin Hawtree

Beaconsfield   (1902)
Seer Green, Beaconsfield, HP9 2UR
- ☎ **(01494) 676545**
- ☐ (01494) 681148
- ✉ secretary@beaconsfieldgolfclub .co.uk
- ☐ 850
- ♠ KR Wilcox
- ✎ M Brothers (01494) 676616
- ▷ 18 L 6493 yds Par 72 SSS 71
- ♟ WD–H WE–M SOC
- ££ £35 D–£50
- ⊕ 2 miles E of Beaconsfield. M40 Junction 2
- ⊕ Driving range
- ♜ HS Colt

Buckingham   (1914)
Tingewick Road, Buckingham, MK18 4AE
- ☎ **(01280) 813282 (Clubhouse)**
- ☐ (01280) 821812
- ☐ 680
- ♠ T Gates (Gen Mgr) (01280) 815566
- ✎ G Hannah (01280) 815210
- ▷ 18 L 6082 yds SSS 69
- ♟ WD–U WE–M SOC–Tues & Thurs
- ££ £30
- ⊕ 2 miles SW of Buckingham on A421

Buckinghamshire   (1992)
Denham Court Mansion, Denham Court Drive, Denham, UB9 5PG
- ☎ **(01895) 835777**
- ☐ (01895) 835210
- ✉ golf@bucks.dircon.co.uk
- ☐ 650
- ♠ E Roca (01895) 836804
- ✎ J O'Leary (01895) 836814
- ▷ 18 L 6880 yds Par 72 SSS 73
- ♟ I or M SOC–WD exc Fri
- ££ £70 (£80)
- ⊕ Off A40(M). M25 Junction 16b/M40 Junction 1
- ⊕ Driving range (Members)
- ♜ John Jacobs
- ■ www.buckinghamshire-golfclub .co.uk

Burnham Beeches   (1891)
Green Lane, Burnham, Slough, SL1 8EG
- ☎ **(01628) 661448**
- ☐ (01628) 668968
- ✉ enquiries@bbgc.co.uk
- ☐ 670
- ♠ TP Jackson (Mgr) (01628) 661448
- ✎ R Bolton (01628) 661661
- ▷ 18 L 6449 yds SSS 71
- ♟ WD–I WE/BH–M H
- ££ £38 D–£56
- ⊕ 4 miles W of Slough
- ■ www.bbgc.co.uk

Chartridge Park   (1989)
Chartridge, Chesham, HP5 2TF
- ☎ **(01494) 791772**
- ☐ 700
- ♠ Mr & Mrs P Gibbins
- ✎ P Gibbins
- ▷ 18 L 5580 yds SSS 66
- ♟ U SOC
- ££ £25 (£30)
- ⊕ 2 miles NW of Chesham. 9 miles W of M25 Junction 18
- ♜ John Jacobs
- ■ www.cpgc.co.uk

Chesham & Ley Hill   (1900)
Ley Hill, Chesham, HP5 1UZ
- ☎ **(01494) 784541**
- ☐ (01494) 785506
- ✉ the.secretary@clhgolfclub.co.uk
- ☐ 322
- ♠ B Durand
- ▷ 9 L 5240 yds SSS 65
- ♟ WD–U exc Tues–NA before 3pm WE/BH–M SOC–Thurs & Fri
- ££ £13
- ⊕ Chesham 2 miles
- ⊕ Course closed Sun after 2pm from 1st Apr–30th Sept

Chiltern Forest
Aston Hill, Halton, Aylesbury, HP22 5NQ
- ☎ **(01296) 631267**
- ☐ (01296) 631267
- ✉ secretary@chilternforest.co.uk
- ☐ 650
- ♠ R Clift (01296) 631267
- ✎ A Lavers (01296) 631817
- ▷ 18 L 5765 yds Par 70 SSS 70
- ♟ WD–U WE–M SOC
- ££ £30
- ⊕ 5 miles SE of Aylesbury, off A4011
- ■ www.chilternforest.co.uk

Denham   (1910)
Tilehouse Lane, Denham, UB9 5DE
- ☎ **(01895) 832022**
- ☐ (01895) 835340
- ☐ 775
- ♠ MJ Miller
- ✎ S Campbell (01895) 832801
- ▷ 18 L 6462 yds SSS 71
- ♟ Mon–Thurs–I H Fri–Sun/BH–M
- ££ £55–£75
- ⊕ 2 miles NW of Uxbridge
- ♜ HS Colt

Ellesborough (1905)
Butlers Cross, Aylesbury, HP17 0TZ
- ☎ **(01296) 622114**
- ☐ (01296) 622114
- ✉ admin@ellesboroughgolf.co.uk
- ☐ 700
- ♖ B Weeds (Gen Mgr)
- ✎ M Squire (01296) 623126
- ⊳ 18 L 6283 yds SSS 71
- ♔ WE/BH–M WD–I or H SOC–Wed & Thurs only
- £€ On application
- ⊶ 1 mile W of Wendover
- ■ www.ellesboroughgolf.co.uk

Farnham Park (1974)
Public
Park Road, Stoke Poges, Slough, SL2 4PJ
- ☎ **(01753) 643332**
- ☐ 450
- ♖ Mrs M Brooker (01753) 647065
- ✎ P Warner
- ⊳ 18 L 6172 yds SSS 71
- ♔ U
- £€ £14.50
- ⊶ 2 miles N of Slough
- ♟ Hawtree

Flackwell Heath (1904)
Treadaway Road, Flackwell Heath, High Wycombe, HP10 9PE
- ☎ **(01628) 520929**
- ☐ (01628) 530040
- ☐ 700
- ♖ SJ Chandler
- ✎ P Watson (01628) 523017
- ⊳ 18 L 6211 yds SSS 70
- ♔ WD–H WE–M SOC–Wed & Thurs
- £€ £24
- ⊶ Between High Wycombe and Beaconsfield, off A40. M40 Junction 3/4
- ♟ J Turner

Gerrards Cross (1921)
Chalfont Park, Gerrards Cross, SL9 0QA
- ☎ **(01753) 883263**
- ☐ (01753) 883593
- ☐ 725
- ♖ Brian Cable
- ✎ M Barr (01753) 885300
- ⊳ 18 L 6212 yds SSS 70
- ♔ WD–H WE/BH–M SOC
- £€ £38 D–£52
- ⊶ 1 mile from Station, off A413
- ♟ B Pedlar

Harewood Downs (1907)
Cokes Lane, Chalfont St Giles, HP8 4TA
- ☎ **(01494) 762308**
- ☐ (01494) 766869
- ✉ secretary@hdgc.co.uk
- ☐ 700
- ♖ SJ Thornton (01494) 762184
- ✎ GC Morris (01494) 764102
- ⊳ 18 L 5958 yds SSS 69
- ♔ H
- £€ £33 (£38)
- ⊶ 2 miles E of Amersham, off A413
- ■ www.hdgc.co.uk

Harleyford (1996)
Harleyford Estate, Henley Road, Marlow, SL7 2SP
- ☎ **(01628) 402149**
- ☐ (01628) 478434
- ☐ 750
- ♖ Gary Ivory
- ✎ L Jackson
- ⊳ 18 L 6587 yds Par 72 SSS 72
- ♔ U SOC–WD after 10am SOC–WE after 1pm
- £€ £45 (£65)
- ⊶ 1 mile W of Marlow on A4155
- ⊕ Driving range
- ♟ Donald Steel

Hazlemere (1982)
Penn Road, Hazlemere, High Wycombe, HP15 7LR
- ☎ **(01494) 719300**
- ☐ (01494) 713914
- ☐ 500
- ♖ IJ Donnelly (01494) 719303
- ✎ P Harrison (01494) 719306
- ⊳ 18 L 5807 yds SSS 69
- ♔ WD–U WE–booking req SOC–WD
- £€ £20 (£30)
- ⊶ 3 miles NE of High Wycombe on B474
- ♟ Terry Murray

Huntswood (1996)
Taplow Common Road, Burnham, SL1 8LS
- ☎ **(01628) 667144**
- ☐ (01628) 663145
- ✉ chrislewis.huntswoodmembers .co.uk
- ☐ 450
- ♖ E Cottrell (01628) 810590
- ✎ N Pagett PGA (01628) 667144
- ⊳ 9 (18 Oct 2003) – Par/SSS not yet known
- ♔ U SOC WD WE
- £€ £16 (£19)
- ⊶ M4 Junction 7
- ■ www.huntswoodmembers.co.uk

Iver (1983)
Hollow Hill Lane, Iver, SL0 0JJ
- ☎ **(01753) 655615**
- ☐ (01753) 654225
- ☐ 500
- ♖ J Lynch (Golf Dir)
- ✎ J Lynch
- ⊳ 9 L 5146 yds SSS 66
  9 hole short course 1400 yds
- ♔ U SOC
- £€ 9 holes–£8 (£9.50) 18 holes–£14 (£17) 9 hole short course to be arranged
- ⊶ ¹/₂ mile from Langley station, off Langley Park Road. M4 J5, 2 miles

Ivinghoe (1967)
Wellcroft, Ivinghoe, Leighton Buzzard, LU7 9EF
- ☎ **(01296) 668696**
- ☐ (01296) 662755
- ☐ 250
- ♖ Mrs SE Garrad (01296) 662478

- ✎ PW Garrad (01296) 668696
- ⊳ 9 L 4508 yds SSS 62
- ♔ WD–U WE–U after 8am SOC
- £€ 18 holes–£9. 9 holes–£6
- ⊶ 3 miles N of Tring. M1 Junction 11, 5 miles
- ♟ R Garrad

Kingfisher CC (1995)
Proprietary
Buckingham Road, Deanshanger, Milton Keynes, MK19 6JY
- ☎ **(01908) 560354**
- ☐ (01908) 260857
- ✉ sales.kingfisher@tesco.net
- ☐ 110
- ♖ Roland Carlish (01908) 561505
- ✎ Brian Mudge (01604) 643555
- ⊳ 9 L 5034 yds Par 70 SSS 65 (18 tees)
- ♔ U SOC
- £€ 9: £8 (£11) 18: £12 (£15)
- ⊶ 10 min W central Milton Keynes, Junction 15
- ⊕ Driving range – phone for availability
- ♟ Donald Steele
- ■ www.kingfisher-hotelandgolf.co.uk

The Lambourne Club (1992)
Dropmore Road, Burnham, SL1 8NF
- ☎ **(01628) 666755**
- ☐ (01628) 663301
- ☐ 550
- ♖ B Sparks (Gen Mgr)
- ✎ D Hart (Golf Dir) (01628) 662936
- ⊳ 18 L 6771 yds SSS 73
- ♔ H
- £€ £50 (£75)
- ⊶ 1 mile N of Burnham. M40 Junction 2. M4 Junction 7
- ⊕ Driving range
- ♟ Donald Steel

Little Chalfont (1981)
Lodge Lane, Little Chalfont, Amersham, HP8 4AJ
- ☎ **(01494) 764877**
- ☐ (01494) 762860
- ☐ 400
- ♖ JM Dunne
- ✎ B Woodhouse (01494) 762942
- ⊳ 9 L 5752 yds SSS 68
- ♔ U SOC
- £€ £13 (£15)
- ⊶ Chalfont & Latimer Station ¹/₂ mile. M25 Junction 18, 1 mile
- ♟ JM Dunne

Magnolia Park
Arncott Road, Boarstall, HP18 9XX
- ☎ **(01844) 239700**
- ☐ (01844) 238991
- ☐ 300
- ♖ A Rutter (Gen Mgr)
- ✎ A Taylor (Golf Dir)
- ⊳ 18 holes Par 73 SSS 73
  9 hole course
- ♔ U SOC–WD
- £€ D–£40

⚑ 10 miles NW of Thame (B4011)
⊕ Golf Academy
⌂ Johnathan Gaunt

Mentmore G&CC (1992)
Mentmore, Leighton Buzzard, LU7 0UA
☎ (01296) 662020
⌨ (01296) 662592
✉ g.rayner@clubhaus.com
⌸ 1100
♠ Glenn Rayner
⌁ R Davies
⌐ Rothschild 18 L 6777 yds SSS 72;
   Rosebery 18 L 6850 yds SSS 73
♀♂ WD–U WE/BH–U after 11am SOC
£€ £30 (£40)
⚑ 4 miles S of Leighton Buzzard
⊕ Driving range
⌂ Bob Sandow
■ www.clubhaus.com

Oakland Park (1994)
Three Households, Chalfont St Giles, HP8 4LW
☎ (01494) 871277
⌨ (01494) 874692
⌸ 750
♠ SF Balmforth (Sec/Dir)
⌁ A Thatcher
⌐ 18 L 5246 yds Par 67 SSS 66
♀♂ U SOC–WD–WE
£€ £25
⚑ 3 miles N of M40 Junction 2
⊕ Driving range
⌂ Jonathan Gaunt

Princes Risborough (1990)
Lee Road, Saunderton Lee, Princes Risborough, HP27 9NX
☎ (01844) 346989 (Clubhouse)
⌨ (01844) 274938
⌸ 400
♠ JF Tubb (Man Dir)
⌁ S Lowry (01844) 274567
⌐ 9 L 5440 yds Par 68 SSS 67
♀♂ U SOC
£€ 18 holes–£15 (£20) 9 holes–£12 (£14)
⚑ 7 miles NW of High Wycombe on A4010
⌂ Guy Hunt
■ www.prgc.co.uk

Richings Park G&CC
(1996)
North Park, Iver, SL0 9DL
☎ (01753) 655352
⌨ (01753) 655409
⌸ 650
♠ A Garland (01753) 655370
⌁ S Kelly (01753) 655352
⌐ 18 L 6094 yds Par 70 SSS 69
   Par 3 Academy course
♀♂ WD–U WE–M
£€ £17
⚑ Nr M4 Junction 5
⊕ Driving range
⌂ Alan Higgins
■ www.richingspark.co.uk

Silverstone (1992)
Proprietary
Silverstone Road, Stowe, Buckingham, MK18 5LH
☎ (01280) 850005
⌨ (01280) 850156
✉ proshop@silverstonegolfclub.co.uk
⌸ 500
♠ B Major
⌁ R Holt
⌐ 18 L 6558 yds Par 72 SSS 71
♀♂ U–booking advisable SOC
£€ £18 (£25)
⚑ Opposite Silverstone Race Circuit, N of Buckingham
⊕ Driving range
⌂ David Snell

Stoke Poges (1908)
Park Road, Stoke Poges, SL2 4PG
☎ (01753) 717171
⌨ (01753) 717181
✉ info@stokeparkclub.com
⌸ 850
⌁ S Collier
⌐ 18 L 6721 yds SSS 72
   9 L 3074 yds
♀♂ U
£€ £125 (£200)
⚑ 5 miles N of Windsor
⌂ HS Colt

Stowe (1974)
Stowe, Buckingham, MK18 5EH
⌸ 300
♠ B Kemp (01280) 818282
⌐ 9 L 4472 yds SSS 62
♀♂ WD/WE 8am–1pm & after 7pm–M; School holidays–M SOC
£€ On application
⚑ M1 Junction 16. 4 miles NW of Buckingham

Thorney Park (1992)
Thorney Mill Lane, Iver, SL0 9AL
☎ (01895) 422095
⌨ (01895) 431307
⌸ 300
♠ A Killing
⌁ A Killing
⌐ 18 L 5731 yds Par 69 SSS 68
♀♂ U SOC
£€ £19.50 (£22)
⚑ 3 miles N of M4 Junction 5 (B470)
⌂ D Walker

Three Locks (1992)
Great Brickhill, Milton Keynes, MK17 9BH
☎ (01525) 270470
⌨ (01525) 270470
⌸ 300
♠ P Critchley
⌐ 18 L 6025 yds Par 70 SSS 68
♀♂ U SOC exc Sun
£€ £16.50 (£20)
⚑ N of Leighton Buzzard on A4146. M1 Junction 14
⌂ MRM Sandow

Wavendon Golf Centre (1990)
Lower End Road, Wavendon, Milton Keynes, MK17 8DA
☎ (01908) 281811
⌨ (01908) 281257
⌸ 250
♠ G Iron
⌁ G Iron
⌐ 18 L 5460 yds Par 67 SSS 66
   9 hole pitch & putt course
♀♂ U SOC
£€ £12.50 (£18)
⚑ 2 miles W of M1 Junction 13
⊕ Floodlit driving range

Weston Turville (1973)
New Road, Weston Turville, Aylesbury, HP22 5QT
☎ (01296) 424084
⌨ (01296) 395376
⌸ 600
♠ D Allen
⌁ G George (01296) 425949
⌐ 18 L 6008 yds SSS 69
♀♂ U
£€ £20 (£25)
⚑ 1½ miles SE of Aylesbury

Wexham Park (1979)
Pay and play
Wexham Street, Wexham, Slough, SL3 6ND
☎ (01753) 663271
⌨ (01753) 663318
⌸ 850
♠ J Dunne
⌁ J Kennedy (01753) 663425
⌐ 18 L 5251 yds SSS 66
   Green 9 L 2219 yds SSS 32
   Red 9 L 2727 yds SSS 34
♀♂ U SOC–WD/Sat pm
£€ 18: £13 (£17) 9: £8 (£9.50)
⚑ 2 miles N of Slough. M4 Junction 4
⊕ Driving range; practice area
⌂ David Morgan
■ www.wexhamparkgolfcourse.co.uk

Whiteleaf (1904)
Whiteleaf, Princes Risborough, HP27 0LY
☎ (01844) 343097/274058
⌨ (01844) 275551
✉ whiteleafgc@tiscali.co.uk
⌸ 300
♠ D Hill (01844) 274058
⌁ KS Ward (01844) 345472
⌐ 9 L 5391 yds SSS 66
♀♂ WD–U WE–M SOC
£€ £20
⚑ Princes Risborough 2 miles

Windmill Hill (1972)
Pay and play
Tattenhoe Lane, Bletchley, MK3 7RB
☎ (01908) 631113 (Bookings)
⌨ (01908) 630034
⌸ 130
♠ B Smith
⌁ C Clingan (01908) 378623

For list of abbreviations and key to symbols see page 627

18 L 6720 yds Par 73 SSS 72
U SOC after 11am
££ £11 (£15)
⊕ W of Milton Keynes on A421. M1 Junctions 13 & 14
⊕ Driving range
⌂ Sir Henry Cotton

Woburn   (1976)
Little Brickhill, Milton Keynes, MK17 9LJ
☎ (01908) 370756
⌨ (01908) 378436
✉ enquiries@woburngolf.com
📖 1400
✍ E Bullock (Man Dir) Glenna Beasley (Sec)
⚲ L Blacklock (01908) 626600
⊳ Duke's 18 L 6976 yds SSS 74
Duchess 18 L 6651 yds SSS 72
Marquess 18 L 7214 yds SSS 74
WD–H (by arrangement) WE–M
££ By arrangement
⊕ ½ mile E of A5. 4 miles W of M1 Junction 13
⌂ Charles Lawrie (Duke's/Duchess), Peter Alliss and Clive Clark, European Golf Design (Ross McMurray), Alex Hay (Marquess)
■ www.woburngolf.com

Wycombe Heights   (1991)
Public
Rayners Avenue, Loudwater, High Wycombe, HP10 9SZ
☎ (01494) 816686
⌨ (01494) 816728
✉ info@wycombeheightsgc.co.uk
📖 600
✍ P Talbot (01494) 816686
⚲ (01494) 812862
⊳ 18 L 6300 yds Par 70 SSS 72
18 hole Par 3 course
U SOC
££ £13 (£18.50)
⊕ ½ mile from M40 Junction 3, on A40 to Wycombe
⊕ Driving range
⌂ John Jacobs

Cambridgeshire

Abbotsley   (1986)
Proprietary
Eynesbury Hardwicke, St Neots, PE19 6XN
☎ (01480) 474000
⌨ (01480) 403280
✉ abbotsley@americangolf.uk.com
📖 500
✍ J Tubb (01480) 474000
⚲ S Connolly
⊳ 18 L 6311 yds SSS 72
WD/BH–U WE–M before 1pm –U after 1pm SOC
££ £20 (£30)
⊕ 2 miles SE of St Neots on B1046. M11 Junction 13 (A428)
⌂ Vivien Saunders

Bourn   (1991)
Toft Road, Bourn, Cambridge, CB3 7TT
☎ (01954) 718057
⌨ (01954) 718908
📖 600
⚲ C Watson (01954) 718958
⊳ 18 L 6417 yds SSS 71
WD–U WE–U after 1pm SOC–WD
££ On application
⊕ 8 miles W of Cambridge, off B1046. M11 Junction 12

Brampton Park   (1991)
Buckden Road, Brampton, Huntingdon, PE28 4NF
☎ (01480) 434700
⌨ (01480) 411145
✉ admin@bramptonparkgc.co.uk
📖 650
✍ RK Oakes (Gen Mgr)
⚲ A Currie (01480) 434705
⊳ 18 L 6300 yds SSS 72
U SOC
££ £25 (D–£35)
⊕ 3 miles W of Huntingdon, off A1/A604
⊕ Driving range
⌂ Simon Gidman
■ www.bramptonparkgc.co.uk

Cambridge
Station Road, Longstanton, Cambridge, CB4 5DR
☎ (01954) 789388
📖 300
✍ K Green
⚲ G Huggett, A Engleman
⊳ 18 L 6736 yds Par 72 SSS 74
U SOC
££ £10 (£13)
⊕ 5 miles NW of Cambridge, off A14 (B1050)
⊕ Floodlit driving range

Cambridge National
Proprietary
Comberton Road, Toft, Cambridge, CB3 7RY
☎ (01223) 264700
⌨ (01223) 264701
✉ meridian@golfsocieties.com
📖 500
✍ Ingrid van Rooyen, Vivien Saunders
⚲ J Saxon-Mills (01223) 264702
⊳ 18 L 6732 yds Par 73 SSS 72
U SOC
££ £15 (£20)
⊕ 3 miles SW of Cambridge on B1046. M11 Junction 12
⌂ Alliss/Clark
■ www.golfsocieties.com

Cambridgeshire Moat House   (1974)
Bar Hill, Cambridge, CB3 8EU
☎ (01954) 249988 (Hotel)
⌨ (01954) 780010
📖 650
✍ (01954) 249971

⚲ P Simpson (01954) 780098
⊳ 18 L 6734 yds Par 72 SSS 73
U SOC–WD
££ £20 (£30)
⊕ 5 miles NW of Cambridge on A14
■ www.cambridgeshiregolf.co.uk

Cromwell
Proprietary
Eynesbury Hardwicke, St Neots, PE19 6XN
☎ (01480) 215153
⌨ (01480) 406463
📖 300
✍ J Tubb (01480) 474000
⚲ S Connolly
⊳ 18 L 6087 yds SSS 69
9 hole Par 3 course
U SOC
££ £14 (£20)
⊕ 2 miles SE of St Neots on B1046. M11 Junction 13 (A428)
⊕ Floodlit driving range
⌂ Vivien Saunders

Elton Furze   (1993)
Bullock Road, Haddon, Peterborough, PE7 3TT
☎ (01832) 280118 (bar)
⌨ (01832) 280299
📖 540
✍ Helen Barron (01832) 280189
⚲ G Krause (01832) 280614
⊳ 18 L 6279 yds Par 70 SSS 71
WD–phone in advance SOC
££ £30 (£34)
⊕ 4 miles W of Peterborough on old A605
⊕ Driving range
⌂ Roger Fitton
■ www.eltonfurzegolfclub.co.uk

Ely City   (1961)
107 Cambridge Road, Ely, CB7 4HX
☎ (01353) 662751
⌨ (01353) 668636
✉ elygolf@lineone.net
📖 820
✍ MS Hoare (Mgr) (01353) 662751
⚲ A George (01353) 663317
⊳ 18 L 6627 yds SSS 72
WD–H WE–H SOC–Tues–Fri
££ £30 (£36)
⊕ 12 miles N of Cambridge
⌂ Henry Cotton
■ www.elygolf.co.uk

Girton   (1936)
Dodford Lane, Girton, CB3 0QE
☎ (01223) 276169
⌨ (01223) 277150
✉ secretary@girtongolfclub.co.uk
📖 800
✍ Miss VM Webb
⚲ S Thomson (01223) 276991
⊳ 18 L 6012 yds SSS 69
WD–U WE/BH–M SOC–WD
££ £20
⊕ 3 miles N of Cambridge (A14)
■ www.girtongolfclub.co.uk

The Gog Magog (1901)

Shelford Bottom, Cambridge, CB2 4AB
- ☎ **(01223) 247626**
- 🖳 (01223) 414990
- ✉ secretary@gogmagog.co.uk
- 📖 1300
- ✍ IM Simpson
- 🏌 I Bamborough (01223) 246058
- ▷ Old 18 L 6398 yds SSS 70
  Wandlebury 18 L 6735 yds SSS 72
- 👥 WD–I or H WE/BH–M SOC–Tues
  & Thurs
- £€ On application
- ⛳ 2 miles S of Cambridge on A1307
  (A604)
- ⛪ Hawtree
- ■ www.gogmagog.co.uk

Hemingford Abbots (1991)

Proprietary
*New Farm Lodge, Cambridge Road,
Hemingford Abbots, PE28 9HQ*
- ☎ **(01480) 495000**
- 🖳 (01480) 496000
- 📖 220
- ✍ RD Paton
- ▷ 9 L 5468 yds SSS 68
- 👥 U
- £€ On application
- ⛳ 2 miles S of Huntingdon on A14
- ⊕ Floodlit driving range
- ■ www.astroman.co.uk

Heydon Grange G&CC (1994)

Heydon, Royston, SG8 7NS
- ☎ **(01763) 208988**
- 🖳 (01763) 208926
- 📖 200
- ✍ S Akhtar
- ▷ 18 L 6512 yds SSS 72
  9 L 3249 yds SSS 36
- 👥 U SOC
- £€ £15 (£20)
- ⛳ 4 miles E of Royston on A505.
  M11 Junction 10
- ⊕ Driving range
- ⛪ Cameron Sinclair
- ■ www.heydongrange.co.uk

Lakeside Lodge (1992)

*Fen Road, Pidley, Huntingdon,
PE18 3DF*
- ☎ **(01487) 740540**
- 🖳 (01487) 740852
- 📖 1200
- ✍ Mrs J Hopkins
- 🏌 S Waterman (01487) 741541
- ▷ 18 L 6865 yds SSS 73
  9 L 2601 yds SSS 33
- 👥 U SOC
- £€ £14 (£22)
- ⛳ 4 miles N of St Ives on B1040
- ⊕ Driving range
- ⛪ A Headley

Malton (1993)

Pay and play
*Malton Lane, Meldreth, Royston,
SG8 6PE*
- ☎ **(01763) 262200**

- 🖳 (01763) 262209
- ✉ info@maltongolf.co.uk
- 📖 300
- ✍ A Boyce (01638) 751222
- 🏌 B Lyon
- ▷ 18 L 6708 yds Par 72 SSS 72
- 👥 U SOC–exc WE–NA before 11am
- £€ £10 (£16)
- ⛳ 8 miles SW of Cambridge, off A10.
  5 miles SW of M11 Junction 11
- ⊕ Driving range
- ⛪ Bruce Critchley
- ■ www.maltongolf.co.uk

March (1922)

*Frogs Abbey, Grange Rd, March,
PE15 0YH*
- ☎ **(01354) 652364**
- 📖 360
- ✍ Mrs J Gannaway
- 🏌 M Pond (01354) 657255
- ▷ 9 L 6210 yds SSS 70
- 👥 H SOC–WD
- £€ £17
- ⛳ 18 miles E of Peterborough on
  A141

Old Nene G&CC (1992)

*Muchwood Lane, Bodsey, Ramsey,
PE26 2XQ*
- ☎ **(01487) 813519/815622**
- 🖳 (01487) 813610
- 📖 200
- ✍ GHD Stoneman
- 🏌 N Grant (01487) 710122
- ▷ 9 L 5605 yds SSS 68
- 👥 U SOC
- £€ 18 holes–£12 (£17) 9 holes–£8
  (£12)
- ⛳ 1 mile N of Ramsey, towards
  Ramsey Mereside; 10 miles A1(M)
- ⊕ Floodlit driving range
- ⛪ Richard Edrich

Orton Meadows (1987)

Public
Ham Lane, Peterborough, PE2 5UU
- ☎ **(01733) 237478**
- 📖 450
- ✍ WL Stocks (01733) 234769
- 🏌 A Howard
- ▷ 18 L 5664 yds SSS 68
- 👥 U–phone Pro
- £€ £11.50 (£15.20)
- ⛳ 2 miles SW of Peterborough on old
  A605
- ⊕ 12 hole pitch & putt
- ⛪ D & R Fitton
- ■ www.ortonmeadowsgolfcourse
  .co.uk

Peterborough Milton (1937)

Milton Ferry, Peterborough, PE6 7AG
- ☎ **(01733) 380489**
- 🖳 (01733) 380489
- ✉ miltongolfclub@aol.com
- 📖 730
- ✍ AB Izod (01733) 380489
- 🏌 M Gallagher (01733) 380793
- ▷ 18 L 6505 yds SSS 72
- 👥 U SOC H

- £€ £30 (£40)
- ⛳ 4 miles W of Peterborough on A47
- ⛪ James Braid
- ■ www.club-noticeboard.co.uk

Ramsey (1964)

*4 Abbey Terrace, Ramsey, Huntingdon,
PE26 1DD*
- ☎ **(01487) 812600**
- 🖳 (01487) 815746
- ✉ admin@ramseyclub.co.uk
- 📖 750
- ✍ Mr Kjenstad
- 🏌 A Dyson (01487) 813022
- ▷ 18 L 6163 yds Par 71 SSS 70
- 👥 WD–H WE/BH–M SOC
- £€ £25
- ⛳ 12 miles SE of Peterborough
- ⛪ J Hamilton Stutt
- ■ www.ramseyclub.co.uk

St Ives (1923)

St Ives, Huntingdon, PE27 6DH
- ☎ **(01480) 464459**
- 🖳 (01480) 468392
- 📖 385
- ✍ BE Dunn (01480) 468392
- 🏌 D Glasby (01480) 466067
- ▷ 9 L 6180 yds SSS 70
- 👥 WD–U H WE–M
- £€ D–£20
- ⛳ 5 miles E of Huntingdon

St Neots (1890)

Crosshall Road, St Neots, PE19 7GE
- ☎ **(01480) 472363**
- 🖳 (01480) 472363
- ✉ office@stneots-golfclub.co.uk
- 📖 600
- ✍ J Howling (01480) 472363
- 🏌 J Boast (01480) 476513
- ▷ 18 L 6074 yds SSS 69
- 👥 WD–H WE–M
- £€ On application
- ⛳ By A1/B1048 Junction
- ⛪ Harry Vardon

Stilton Oaks (1997)

Proprietary
*High Street, Stilton, Peterborough,
PE7 3RA*
- ☎ **(01733) 245233**
- 📖 200
- ✍ Mrs M Smith
- 🏌 None
- ▷ 18 hole course
- 👥 U
- £€ £10 (£12)
- ⛳ 5 miles S of Peterborough. A1(M)
  Junction 16

Thorney Golf Centre (1991)

Public
*English Drove, Thorney, Peterborough,
PE6 0TJ*
- ☎ **(01733) 270570**
- 🖳 (01733) 270842
- 📖 400
- ✍ Jane Hind

✓ M Templeman
⊳ Fen 18 L 6104 yds SSS 69
   Lakes 18 L 6402 yds SSS 71
   9 hole Par 3 course
ⓜ Lakes WD–U SOC WE–M
££ Fen £7 (£9) Lakes £11.50 (£18.50)
⊷ 8 miles E of Peterborough, off A47
⊕ Floodlit driving range
ⓣ A Dow

Thorpe Wood   (1975)
Pay and play
Nene Parkway, Peterborough, PE3 6SE
☎ **(01733) 267701**
❏ (01733) 332774
✉ enquiries@thorpewoodgolfcourse
   .co.uk
✍ R Palmer
✓ R Fitton
⊳ 18 L 7086 yds SSS 74
ⓜ U–booking required SOC–WD
££ £11.50 (£15.20)
⊷ 3 miles W of Peterborough on A47
   (Junction 15)
ⓣ Alliss/Thomas
■ www.thorpewoodgolfcourse.co.uk

Waterbeach   (1968)
Waterbeach Barracks, Waterbeach,
Cambridge, CB5 9PA
☎ **(01223) 575260 (Sec)**
❏ (01223) 511525
✍ ES Rowlands (Hon)
⊳ 9 L 6236 yds Par 70 SSS 70
ⓜ M SOC–WD
££ £10
⊷ 6 miles NE of Cambridge, off A10

Channel Islands

Alderney
Route des Carrieres, Alderney,
GY9 3YD
☎ **(01481) 822835**
❏ (01481) 823609
▥ 420
✍ Ken Bithell (01481) 822835
⊳ 9 L 5006 yds Par 64 SSS 65
ⓜ U SOC H
££ D–£22 (D–£25)
⊷ 1 mile E of St Anne

La Grande Mare   (1994)
Vazon Bay, Castel, Guernsey, GY5 7LL
☎ **(01481) 255313**
❏ (01481) 253544
✉ lgmgolf@cwgsy.net
▥ 800
✍ J Vermeulen (01481) 253544
✓ M Groves (01481) 253432
⊳ 18 L 4596 yds SSS 64
ⓜ U–booking necessary SOC
££ D–£27 (£29)
⊷ Vazon Bay, W coast of Guernsey
ⓣ Hawtree
■ www.LGM.Guernsey.net

Les Mielles G&CC   (1994)
St Ouens Bay, Jersey, JE3 7FQ
☎ **(01534) 482787**
❏ (01534) 485414
▥ 1500
✍ J Le Brun (Golf
   Dir) (01534) 482787 Ext 4
✓ L Elstone (01534) 483699 W
   Osmand (01534) 483252
⊳ 18 L 5770 yds Par 70 SSS 69
ⓜ H or Green Card SOC
££ £22 (£25)
⊷ Five Mile Road, St Ouens Bay
⊕ Driving range
ⓣ Le Brun/Whitehead
■ www.lesmielles.com

La Moye   (1902)
La Moye, St Brelade, Jersey, JE3 8GQ
☎ **(01534) 743401,**
   (01534) 747166 (Bookings)
❏ (01534) 747289
▥ 1350
✍ CHM Greetham
✓ M Deeley (01534) 743130
⊳ 18 L 6664 yds SSS 73
ⓜ I H SOC–9.30–11am and 2.30–4pm
   WE–after 2.30pm
££ £45 D–£75 (£50)
⊷ 2 miles from Jersey Airport
⊕ Driving range
ⓣ James Braid

Les Ormes   (1996)
Pay and play
Mont à la Brune, St Brelade, Jersey,
JE3 8FL
☎ **(01534) 497000**
❏ (01534) 499122
▥ 1200
✍ M Graham (01534) 497002
✓ A Chamberlain (01534) 497000
⊳ 9 L 5018 yds Par 66 SSS 65
ⓜ U SOC
££ 9 holes–£13 (£16) 18 holes–£19.50
   (£24)
⊷ Mont à la Brune, nr Airport
⊕ Driving range

Royal Guernsey   (1890)
L'Ancresse, Guernsey, GY3 5BY
☎ **(01481) 247022**
❏ (01481) 243960
✉ bobby@rggc.fsnet.co.uk
▥ 1520
✍ M de Laune (01481) 246523
   R Eggo (Golf Mgr)
✓ N Wood (01481) 245070
⊳ 18 L 6215 yds SSS 70
ⓜ WD–H WE–M
££ £38
⊷ 3 miles N of St Peter Port
⊕ Driving range

Royal Jersey   (1878)
Grouville, Jersey, JE3 9BD
☎ **(01534) 854416**
❏ (01534) 854684
✉ thesecretary@royaljersey.com
▥ 1300

✍ DJ Attwood
✓ D Morgan (01534) 852234
⊳ 18 L 6100 yds SSS 70
ⓜ WD–H after 10am WE/BH–H after
   2.30pm
££ £50 (£50)
⊷ 4 miles E of St Helier
■ www.royaljersey.com

St Clements   (1925)
Public
St Clements, Jersey, JE2 6QN
☎ **(01534) 821938**
✓ R Marks
⊳ 9 L 3972 yds SSS 61
ⓜ U exc Sun am–NA
££ On application
⊷ 1 mile E of St Helier

St Pierre Park
Rohais, St Peter Port, Guernsey,
GY1 1FD
☎ **(01481) 727039**
▥ 290
✓ R Corbet (Mgr)
⊳ 9 hole Par 3 course
ⓜ U SOC
££ 18 holes–£15 (£17)
⊷ 1 mile W of St Peter Port
⊕ Driving range
ⓣ Tony Jacklin

Cheshire

Alder Root   (1993)
Alder Root Lane, Winwick, Warrington,
WA2 8RZ
☎ **(01925) 291919**
❏ (01925) 291961
▥ 450
✍ E Lander
✓ C McKevitt (01925) 291932
⊳ 10 L 5820 yds Par 69 SSS 68
ⓜ WD–U SOC
££ £12 (£20)
⊷ 4 miles N of Warrington (A49). M6
   Junction 22. M62 Junction 9
ⓣ Millington/Lander

Alderley Edge   (1907)
Brook Lane, Alderley Edge, SK9 7RU
☎ **(01625) 585583**
▥ 212 90(L) 40(J) 40(5)
✍ RC Harrison
✓ P Bowring (01625) 584493
⊳ 9 L 5823 yds SSS 68
ⓜ M or H SOC
££ £22 (£27.50); 2 for 1 scheme
⊷ 12 miles S of Manchester
■ www.aegc.co.uk

Aldersey Green
Aldersey, Chester, CH3 9EH
☎ **(01829) 782157**
✍ S Bradbury
✓ S Bradbury (01829) 782157
⊳ 18 L 6150 yds Par 70
ⓜ U SOC

For list of abbreviations and key to symbols see page 627

£€ £12 (£15)
⮂ 8 miles S of Chester, off A41

Altrincham Municipal
(1893)
Public
Stockport Road, Timperley, Altrincham,
WA15 7LP
☎ (0161) 928 0761
▦ 276
⚐ B Simpson
✎ S Partington
▷ 18 L 6385 yds Par 71 SSS 70
♟ U SOC
£€ £8.30 (£11.50)
⮂ 1 mile W of Altrincham (A560)
⊕ Driving range

Alvaston Hall   (1992)
Proprietary
Middlewich Road, Nantwich, CW5 6PD
☎ (01270) 628473
▤ (01270) 623395
▦ 340
⚐ N Perkins (01270) 760206
✎ K Valentine
▷ 9 L 3708 yds Par 64 SSS 59
♟ U
£€ £10 (£10)
⮂ 11 miles W of M6 Junction 16 on A530
⊕ Driving range
⛤ K Valentine

Antrobus
Foggs Lane, Antrobus, Northwich,
CW9 6JQ
☎ (01925) 730890
▤ (01925) 730100
▦ 550
⚐ Miss C Axford
✎ P Farrance (01925) 730900
▷ 18 L 6220 yds Par 71 SSS 72
♟ H SOC
£€ £22 (£25)
⮂ Nr M56 Junction 10, on A559 to Northwich
⊕ Driving range
⛤ Michael Slater
■ www.antrobusgolfclub.co.uk

Ashton-on-Mersey   (1897)
Church Lane, Sale, M33 5QQ
☎ (0161) 973 3220 (Clubhouse)
▤ (0161) 976 4390
✉ golf@aomgc.fsnet.co.uk
▦ 190 65(L) 40(J)
⚐ CW Hill (0161) 976 4390
✎ MJ Williams (0161) 962 3727
▷ 9 L 3073 yds SSS 69
♟ WD–U H exc Tues–NA before 3pm WE–M
£€ £20.50
⮂ 5 miles W of Manchester. M60 Junction 7, 1¹/₂ miles

Astbury   (1922)
Peel Lane, Astbury, Congleton,
CW12 4RE
☎ (01260) 272772

▦ 700
⚐ FM Reed (01260) 272772
✎ A Salt (01260) 272772
▷ 18 L 6296 yds SSS 70
♟ WD–H or M WE–M SOC–Thurs only
£€ £30 SOC–£25
⮂ 1 mile S of Congleton, off A34
■ www.astburygolfclub.com

Birchwood   (1979)
Kelvin Close, Birchwood, Warrington,
WA3 7PB
☎ (01925) 818819
▤ (01925) 822403
✉ birchwoodgolfclub.com@lineone.net
▦ 745
⚐ M Cullen
✎ P McEwan (01925) 825216
▷ 18 L 6727 yds Par 71 SSS 72
♟ U SOC–Mon/Wed/Thurs
£€ £12 D–£23 (£37)
⮂ M62 Junction 11, 2 miles. Signs to 'Science Park North'
⛤ TJA Macauley
■ www.birchwoodgolfclub.com

Bramall Park   (1894)
20 Manor Road, Bramhall, Stockport,
SK7 3LY
☎ (0161) 485 3119 (Clubhouse)
▤ (0161) 485 7101
▦ 400 160(L) 75(J)
⚐ CJ Shallcross (Hon) (0161) 485 7101
✎ M Proffit (0161) 485 2205
▷ 18 L 6214 yds SSS 70
♟ SOC–WD (enquire of Sec)
£€ £30 (£40)
⮂ 8 miles S of Manchester (A5102)
■ www.secppgc@hotmail.com

Bramhall   (1905)
Ladythorn Road, Bramhall, Stockport,
SK7 2EY
☎ (0161) 439 6092
▤ (0161) 439 0264
✉ office@bramhallgolfclub.com
▦ 325 155(L) 85(J)
⚐ B Hill (Hon) (0161) 439 6092
✎ R Green (0161) 439 1171
▷ 18 L 6300 yds SSS 70
♟ U H exc Thurs SOC–Wed
£€ £30 D–£35 (£37 D–£46)
⮂ S of Stockport, off A5102
■ www.bramhallgolfclub.com

Carden Park
Chester, CH3 9DQ
☎ (01829) 731600
▤ (01829) 731629
▦ 234
⚐ D Llewellyn
✎ S Edwards (01829) 731500
▷ Cheshire 18 L 6824 yds SSS 72;
Nicklaus 18 L 7045 yds Par 72
9 hole Par 3 course
♟ H SOC
£€ Cheshire–£40 Nicklaus–£60
⮂ 10 miles S of Chester on A534
⊕ Golf Academy. Driving range

Cheadle   (1885)
Shiers Drive, Cheadle Road, Cheadle,
SK8 1HW
☎ (0161) 491 4452
▦ 350
⚐ CT Openshaw
✎ S Booth (0161) 428 9878
▷ 9 L 4993 yds SSS 65
♟ H or I exc Tues & Sat–NA SOC
£€ £23 (£28)
⮂ 1 mile S of Cheadle. M63 Junction 11, 2 miles

Chester   (1901)
Curzon Park, Chester, CH4 8AR
☎ (01244) 675130
▤ (01244) 676667
✉ www@chestergolfclub.co.uk
▦ 840
⚐ VFC Wood (01244) 677760
✎ G Parton (01244) 671185
▷ 18 L 6461 yds SSS 71
♟ U H SOC
£€ £30 (£35)
⮂ Chester 1 mile
■ www.chestergolfclub.co.uk

Congleton   (1898)
Biddulph Road, Congleton, CW12 3LZ
☎ (01260) 273540
▤ (01260) 290902
✉ congletongolfclub@hotmail.com
▦ 440
⚐ R Brindley
✎ JA Colclough
▷ 12 L 5119 yds Par 68 SSS 65
♟ U H SOC
£€ £21 (£31)
⮂ 1¹/₂ miles E of Congleton on A527

Crewe   (1911)
Fields Road, Haslington, Crewe,
CW1 5TB
☎ (01270) 584227 (Steward)
▤ (01270) 256482
✉ secretary@crewegolfclub.co.uk
▦ 628
⚐ A Whittingham (01270) 584099
✎ D Wheeler (01270) 585032
▷ 18 L 6404 yds SSS 71
♟ WD–U WE/BH–M SOC
£€ £30 After 1pm–£24
⮂ Haslington, 2 miles NE of Crewe Station, off A534. 5 miles W of M6 Junction
■ www.crewegolfclub.co.uk

Davenport   (1913)
Worth Hall, Middlewood Road, Poynton,
SK12 1TS
☎ (01625) 876951
▤ (01625) 877489
▦ 650
⚐ JB Sandham (01625) 876951
✎ G Norcott (01625) 877319
▷ 18 L 6027 yds SSS 69
♟ U exc Wed & Sat–NA SOC–Tues & Thurs
£€ £30 (£40)
⮂ 5 miles S of Stockport. 7 miles N of Macclesfield

Delamere Forest (1910)

Station Road, Delamere, Northwich, CW8 2JE
☎ **(01606) 883264**
🖥 (01606) 889444
✉ delamere@btconnect.com
📖 400
🏌 JJ Mulder (01606) 883800
✎ EB Jones (01606) 883307
🏳 18 L 6328 yds SSS 71
👥 WD–U WE–2 ball only SOC
££ £35 D–£50 (£60)
🚗 10 miles E of Chester, off B5152
🏛 Herbert Fowler
■ www.dfgc.co.uk

Disley (1889)

Stanley Hall Lane, Disley, Stockport, SK12 2JX
☎ **(01663) 762071**
🖥 (01663) 762678
📖 500
🏌 Dianne Bradley (01663) 764001
✎ AG Esplin (01663) 762884
🏳 18 L 5942 yds Par 70
👥 WD–U exc Thurs WE/BH–M
££ £25 (£30)
🚗 6 miles S of Stockport on A6

Dukinfield (1913)

Yew Tree Lane, Dukinfield, SK16 5DB
☎ **(0161) 338 2340**
🖥 (0161) 303 0205
✉ dgc@telinco.co.uk
📖 300 80(L) 65(J)
🏌 K Marsh (0161) 368 6457
✎ A Jowett (0161) 338 2340
🏳 18 L 5338 yds SSS 66
👥 WD–U exc Wed pm WE–M SOC
££ £16.50
🚗 6 miles E of Manchester. M67 Junction 3
■ www.dukinfieldgolfclub.co.uk

Dunham Forest G&CC (1961)

Oldfield Lane, Altrincham, WA14 4TY
☎ **(0161) 928 2605**
🖥 (0161) 929 8975
✉ email@dunhamforestgolfclub.com
📖 600
🏌 Mrs S Klaus
✎ I Wrigley (0161) 928 2727
🏳 18 L 6636 yds SSS 72
👥 WD–U WE/BH–M SOC exc 12–1pm
££ £40 (£45)
🚗 1 mile SW of Altrincham. M56 Junction 7

Eaton (1965)

Guy Lane, Waverton, Chester, CH3 7PH
☎ **(01244) 335885**
🖥 (01244) 335782
✉ kerrybrown@eatongolfclub.co.uk
📖 550
🏌 K Brown
✎ W Tye (01244) 335826
🏳 18 L 6562 yds SSS 71
👥 H SOC

££ On application
🚗 3 miles SE of Chester, off A41
⊕ Driving range; chipping area
🏛 Donald Steel
■ www.eatongolfclub.co.uk

Ellesmere Port (1971)

Public
Chester Road, Childer Thornton, South Wirral, CH66 1QF
☎ **(0151) 339 7689**
📖 350
🏌 C Craggs
✎ T Roberts
🏳 18 L 6432 yds SSS 71
👥 WD–U WE–arrange with Pro SOC–WD
££ £6.70 (£7.40)
🚗 9 miles N of Chester on A41. M53 Junction 5

Frodsham (1990)

Simons Lane, Frodsham, WA6 6HE
☎ **(01928) 732159**
🖥 (01928) 734070
✉ office@frodshamgolfclub.co.uk
📖 600
🏌 El Roylance
✎ G Tonge (01928) 739442
🏳 18 L 6328 yds SSS 70
👥 WD–U WE/BH–M SOC–WD
££ £36
🚗 9 miles NE of Chester (A56). M56 Junction 12, 3 miles
🏛 John Day
■ www.frodshamgolfclub.co.uk

Gatley (1911)

Waterfall Farm, Styal Road, Heald Green, Cheadle SK8 3TW
☎ **(0161) 437 2091**
📖 450
🏌 RWR Salt
✎ J Matterson (0161) 436 2830
🏳 9 L 5934 yds SSS 68
👥 WD exc Tues–arrange with Pro WE/Tues–NA
££ £21
🚗 7 miles S of Manchester. Manchester Airport 2 miles

Hale (1903)

Rappax Road, Hale, WA15 0NU
☎ **(0161) 980 4225**
📖 350
🏌 JT Goodman
✎ A Bickerdike (0161) 904 0835
🏳 9 L 5780 yds SSS 68
👥 WD–U exc Thurs–NA before 5pm WE/BH–M SOC
££ D–£25
🚗 2 miles SE of Altrincham

Hazel Grove (1913)

Buxton Road, Hazel Grove, Stockport, SK7 6LU
☎ **(0161) 483 3217 (Clubhouse)**
📖 550
🏌 DJ Billington (0161) 483 3978
✎ J Hopley (0161) 483 7272
🏳 18 L 6263 yds SSS 70

👥 U SOC–Mon, Thurs & Fri
££ £25.50 D–£30.50 (£30.50 D–£35.50)
🚗 3 miles S of Stockport (A6)

Heaton Moor (1892)

Mauldeth Road, Heaton Mersey, Stockport, SK4 3NX
☎ **(0161) 432 2134**
🖥 (0161) 432 2134
✉ hmgc@ukgateway.net
📖 550
🏌 D Hudson (0161) 432 2134
✎ SJ Marsh (0161) 432 0846
🏳 18 L 5968 yds Par 70 SSS 69
👥 U SOC WD WE
££ £25 (£32)
🚗 2 miles from M60 J1, Stockport Town Centre

Helsby (1901)

Tower's Lane, Helsby, Frodsham, WA6 0JB
☎ **(01928) 722021**
🖥 (01928) 725384
✉ secathgc@aol.com
📖 620
🏌 LJ Norbury
✎ M Jones (01928) 725457
🏳 18 L 6265 yds SSS 70
👥 H WE–NA SOC–Tues & Thurs
££ £25 (£37)
🚗 1 mile SE of M56 Junction 14, off Primrose Lane
⊕ Driving range
🏛 James Braid
■ www.ukgolfer.org/clubs/helsby

Heyrose (1989)

Budworth Road, Tabley, Knutsford, WA16 0HZ
☎ **(01565) 733664**
🖥 (01565) 734578
✉ info@heyrosegolfclub.com
📖 600
🏌 Mrs E Bridge (Sec/Mgr) (01565) 733664
✎ P Affleck (01565) 734267
🏳 18 L 6499 yds SSS 71
👥 U SOC
££ £25 (£30)
🚗 3 miles W of Knutsford, off Pickmere Lane. M6 Junction 19, 1 mile
⊕ Driving range
🏛 CN Bridge
■ www.heyrosegolfclub.com

Houldsworth (1910)

Houldsworth Park, Houldsworth Street, Reddish, Stockport SK5 6BN
☎ **(0161) 442 1712**
🖥 (0161) 947 9678
📖 625
🏌 D Robertson (0161) 442 1712
✎ D Naylor (0161) 442 1714
🏳 18 L 6209 yds Par 70 SSS 70
👥 U SOC
££ £24 (£30)
🚗 4 miles S of Manchester, M60 J24

Knights Grange (1983)
Public
Grange Lane, Winsford, CW7 2PT
☎ **(01606) 552780**
⚑ Mrs P Littler (Mgr)
✇ G Moore (01606) 853564
▷ 18 L 6253 yds SSS 70
⚭ U SOC
£€ £8 (10)
⊕ Knights Grange Sports Complex. M6 Junctions 18 & 19

Knutsford (1891)
Mereheath Lane, Knutsford, WA16 6HS
☎ **(01565) 633355**
📖 250
⚑ DM Burgess
✇ G Ogden
▷ 9 L 6203 yds SSS 70
⚭ H exc Wed–NA SOC
£€ £25 (£30)
⊕ Knutsford ½ mile

Lymm (1907)
Whitbarrow Road, Lymm, WA13 9AN
☎ **(01925) 755020**
📠 (01925) 755020
✉ mail@lymmgolfclub.fsnet.co.uk
📖 400 100(L) 75(J) 50(5)
⚑ S Nash
✇ S McCarthy (01925) 755054
▷ 18 L 6341 yds SSS 70
⚭ WD–H WE–M SOC–Wed
£€ £26 (£32)
⊕ 5 miles SE of Warrington. M6 J20
■ www.lymm-golf-club.co.uk

Macclesfield (1889)
The Hollins, Macclesfield, SK11 7EA
☎ **(01625) 423227**
📠 (01625) 260061
✉ secretary@maccgolfclub.co.uk
📖 600
⚑ DJ English (01625) 615845
✇ T Taylor (01625) 616952
▷ 18 L 5714 yds SSS 68
⚭ WD/BH–H WE–M SOC–WD
£€ £30 (£40)
⊕ SE edge of Macclesfield, off A523
🏠 Hawtree
■ www.maccgolfclub.co.uk

Malkins Bank (1980)
Public
Betchton Road, Malkins Bank, Sandbach, CW11 4XN
☎ **(01270) 765931**
📠 (01270) 764730
⚑ P Pleasance (Mgr) (01270) 760233
✇ D Hackney
▷ 18 L 6071 yds SSS 69
⚭ U SOC
£€ £10 (£11.50)
⊕ 2 miles S of Sandbach via A534/A533. M6 Junction 17

Marple (1892)
Barnsfold Road, Hawk Green, Marple, Stockport SK6 7EL
☎ **(0161) 427 2311**

📠 (0161) 427 1125
📖 435 100(L) 60(J)
⚑ WM Buchanan (0161) 427 1125
✇ D Myers (0161) 427 1195
▷ 18 L 5552 yds SSS 67
⚭ WD–U exc Thurs–NA WE/BH–M SOC
£€ £20 (£30)
⊕ 2 miles from High Lane North, off A6

Mellor & Townscliffe (1894)
Tarden, Gibb Lane, Mellor, Stockport SK6 5NA
☎ **(0161) 427 9700 (Clubhouse)**
📠 (0161) 427 0103
📖 700
⚑ G Lee (0161) 427 2208
✇ G Broadley (0161) 427 5759
▷ 18 L 5925 yds SSS 69
⚭ WD–U WE–M SOC
£€ £22 (£31)
⊕ 7 miles SE of Stockport, off A626
■ www.mellorgolf.co.uk

Mere G&CC (1934)
Chester Road, Mere, Knutsford, WA16 6LJ
☎ **(01565) 830155**
📠 (01565) 830713
📖 375 200(L) 40(J)
✇ P Eyre (01565) 830219
▷ 18 L 6817 yds SSS 73
⚭ WE/BH–M Wed & Fri–M Mon/Tues/Thurs–H SOC
£€ D–£70
⊕ 1 mile E of M6 Junction 19. 2 miles W of M56 Junction 7
⊕ Driving range-members and green fees only
🏠 James Braid

Mersey Valley (1995)
Warrington Road, Bold Heath, Widnes, WA8 3XL
☎ **(0151) 424 6060**
📠 (0151) 257 9097
📖 550
⚑ A Stevenson
✇ A Stevenson
▷ 18 L 6300 yds SSS 70
⚭ U
£€ £18 (£20)
⊕ M62 Junction 7, 2 miles
🏠 RMR Bush

Mobberley
Burleyhurst Lane, Mobberley, Knutsford, WA16 7JZ
☎ **(01505) 880188**
📠 (01505) 880178
⚑ N Donaghy
✇ J Cheetham
▷ 9 L 5542 yds Par 67
⚭ U SOC
£€ £14.50 (£18)
⊕ Mobberley. M56 Junction 6

Mollington Grange (1999)
Townfield Lane, Mollington, Chester, CH1 6NJ
☎ **(01244) 851185**
📠 (01244) 851349
📖 500
⚑ MJ Olney-Smith
✇ L Corcoran
▷ 18 L 6696 yds Par 72 SSS 72
⚭ WD–U WE–NA before noon SOC–WD
£€ £25 (£30)
⊕ 2 miles N of Chester on A540. End of M56, 2 miles
⊕ Driving range
■ www.mollingtongolfclub.co.uk

Mottram Hall Hotel (1991)
Wilmslow Road, Mottram St Andrew, Prestbury, SK10 4QT
☎ **(01625) 828135**
📠 (01625) 829284
📖 500
⚑ M Turnock
✇ T Rastall
▷ 18 L 7006 yds SSS 74
⚭ U H
£€ £45 (£50)
⊕ 4 miles SE of Wilmslow
⊕ Driving range
🏠 Dave Thomas

Peover
Plumley Moor Road, Lower Peover, WA16 9SE
☎ **(01565) 723337**
📠 (01565) 723311
📖 350
⚑ PA Naylor
✇ Mike Grantham (07976) 894357
▷ 18 L 6702 yds Par 72
⚭ U SOC–WD
£€ £23 (£25)
⊕ 3 miles SW of Knutsford, off A556. M6 Junction 19
🏠 Peter Naylor

Portal G&CC (1992)
Cobblers Cross Lane, Tarporley, CW6 0DJ
☎ **(01829) 733933**
📠 (01829) 733928
✉ portalgolf@aol.com
📖 250
⚑ D Wills (Golf Dir)
✇ A Hill
▷ 18 L 7037 yds SSS 74
⚭ U H SOC
£€ £50
⊕ 11 miles SE of Chester on A51. M6 Junctions 16 or 19
⊕ Driving range
🏠 Donald Steel
■ www.portalgolf.co.uk

Portal Premier (1990)
Forest Road, Tarporley, CW6 0JA
☎ **(01829) 733884**
📠 (01829) 733666
📖 550
⚑ D Wills (Golf Dir)

✍ Miss J Statham (01829) 733703
🏴 18 L 6508 yds SSS 71
👥 U SOC–WD
££ £30 (£35)
🚗 1 mile N of Tarporley on A49
Warrington road
⊕ Driving range
🏛 Tim Rouse

Poulton Park   (1980)
Dig Lane, Cinnamon Brow, WA2 0SH
☎ (01925) 812034/822802
🖥 (01925) 822802
📖 360
✍ E Caise
✍ JJ Orrell (01925) 825220
🏴 9 L 4978 metres SSS 66
👥 WD–NA 5–6pm WE–NA
££ £15 (£17)
🚗 Off Crab Lane, Fearnhead

Prestbury   (1920)
Macclesfield Road, Prestbury,
Macclesfield, SK10 4BJ
☎ (01625) 828241
🖥 (01625) 828241
📧 office@prestburygolfclub.com
📖 700
✍ N Young (01625) 828241
✍ N Summerfield (01625) 828242
🏴 18 L 6359 yds SSS 71
👥 WD–I WE–M SOC–Thurs
££ £45
🚗 2 miles NW of Macclesfield
🏛 HS Colt
🌐 www.prestburygolfclub.com

Pryors Hayes   (1993)
Willington Road, Oscroft, Tarvin,
CH3 8NL
☎ (01829) 741250
🖥 (01829) 749077
📖 600
✍ JM Quinn
✍ M Redrup (01829) 740140
🏴 18 L 6054 yds Par 69 SSS 69
👥 U SOC
££ £20 (£30)
🚗 Tarvin, 5 miles E of Chester
🏛 John Day
🌐 www.pryors-hayes.co.uk

Queens Park   (1985)
Public
Queens Park Drive, Crewe, CW2 7SB
☎ (01270) 662378
📖 250
✍ TJ Weston (01270) 662887
🏴 9 L 4920 yds SSS 64
👥 WD–U WE–U after 12 noon SOC
££ £6.50 (£8.50)
🚗 2 miles from Crewe, off Victoria
Avenue

Reaseheath   (1987)
Reaseheath College, Reaseheath,
Nantwich, CW5 6DF
☎ (01270) 625131
🖥 (01270) 625665
📧 chrisb@reaseheath.ac.uk
📖 600

✍ CK Bishop (Hon)
🏴 9 L 3726 yds SSS 58
👥 M SOC–WD
££ £7
🚗 2 miles NW of Nantwich on
College campus
🏛 D Mortram

Reddish Vale   (1912)
Southcliffe Road, Reddish, Stockport,
SK5 7EE
☎ (0161) 480 2359
🖥 (0161) 477 8242
📧 admin@reddishvalegolfclub.co.uk
📖 550
✍ BJD Rendell JP
✍ RE Freeman (0161) 480 3824
🏴 18 L 6086 yds SSS 69
👥 WD–U exc 12.30–1.30pm–M
WE–M SOC–WD
££ £25
🚗 1 mile NNE of Stockport
🏛 Dr A MacKenzie
🌐 www.reddishvalegolfclub.co.uk

Ringway   (1909)
Hale Mount, Hale Barns, Altrincham,
WA15 8SW
☎ (0161) 904 9609
📧 enquiries@ringwaygolfclub.co.uk
📖 360 175(L) 60(J)
✍ A Scully (0161) 980 2630
✍ N Ryan (0161) 980 8432
🏴 18 L 6482 yds SSS 71
👥 Tues–NA before 3pm, Fri–M,
Sun–NA before 11am, SOC–Thurs
££ £35 (£45)
🚗 8 miles S of Manchester, off M56
Junction 6 (A538)
🏛 Harry Colt/James Braid
🌐 www.ringwaygolfclub.co.uk

Romiley   (1897)
Goosehouse Green, Romiley, Stockport,
SK6 4LJ
☎ (0161) 430 2392
🖥 (0161) 430 7258
📧 office@romileygolfclub.org
📖 625
✍ PR Trafford
✍ Lee Paul Sullivan
(0161) 430 7122
🏴 18 L 6412 yds Par 70 SSS 71
👥 U SOC
££ £30 (£40)
🚗 Station 3/4 mile (B6104)

Runcorn   (1909)
Clifton Road, Runcorn, WA7 4SU
☎ (01928) 572093 (Members)
🖥 (01928) 574214
📖 375 80(L) 80(J)
✍ BR Griffiths (01928) 574214
✍ D Ingman (01928) 564791
🏴 18 L 6035 yds SSS 69
👥 WD–U H exc comp days WE–M
SOC–Mon & Fri only
££ £24
🚗 Runcorn (A557). M56 Junction 12

Sale   (1913)
Sale Lodge, Golf Road, Sale,
M33 2XU
☎ (0161) 973 3404
🖥 (0161) 962 4217
📖 750
✍ IJ Vernon (Hon) (0161) 973 1638
✍ M Stewart (0161) 973 1730
🏴 18 L 6126 yds SSS 70
👥 U SOC–WD
££ £28 (£33)
🚗 N of Sale. M60 Junction 6
🌐 www.salegolfclub.com

Sandbach   (1895)
Middlewich Road, Sandbach,
CW11 1FH
☎ (01270) 762117
📖 240 115(L) 50(J)
✍ GF Wood
🏴 9 L 5598 yds SSS 67
👥 WD–U WE/BH–M
££ D–£20 (£10)
🚗 1 mile W of Sandbach (A533). M6
Junction 17

Sandiway   (1921)
Chester Road, Sandiway, CW8 2DJ
☎ (01606) 883247
🖥 (01606) 888548
📧 info@sandiwaygolf.fsnet.co.uk
📖 730
✍ RH Owens
✍ W Laird (01606) 883180
🏴 18 L 6435 yds SSS 72
👥 H SOC
££ £40 (£50)
🚗 15 miles E of Chester on A556
🏛 Ted Ray
🌐 www.sandiwaygolf.co.uk

Shrigley Hall Hotel & CC   (1989)
Shrigley Park, Pott Shrigley,
Macclesfield, SK10 5SB
☎ (01625) 575757
🖥 (01625) 575437
📖 500
✍ Louisa Lawton
✍ T Stevens (01625) 575626
🏴 18 L 6281 yds SSS 71
👥 U SOC
££ £36 (£41)
🚗 15 miles from centre of
Manchester. Airport 10 miles
🏛 Donald Steel

St Michaels Jubilee   (1977)
Public
Dundalk Road, Widnes, WA8 8BS
☎ (0151) 424 6230
📖 200
✍ KB Stevenson
✍ R Bilton (01295) 65241
🏴 18 L 5612 yds SSS 67
👥 U
££ On application
🚗 Widnes

Stamford (1901)

Oakfield House, Huddersfield Road, Stalybridge, SK15 3PY
- ☎ **(01457) 832126**
- 🕮 700
- ✍ BD Matthews
- ✏ B Badger (01457) 834829
- ⛳ 18 L 5701 yds SSS 68
- 🏌 WD–U WE comp days–after 2.30pm SOC–WD
- £€ £20 (£25)
- ⊶ NE boundary of Stalybridge on B6175

Stockport (1905)

Offerton Road, Offerton, Stockport, SK2 5HL
- ☎ **(0161) 427 2001 (Members)**
- 🖳 (0161) 449 8293
- ✉ stockportgolf@oz.co.uk
- 🕮 510
- ✍ JE Flanagan (0161) 427 8369
- ✏ M Peel (0161) 427 2421
- ⛳ 18 L 6326 yds SSS 71
- 🏌 SOC–WD
- £€ £40 (£50)
- ⊶ 4 miles SE of Stockport on A627
- ⌂ Herd/Hawtree

Styal (1994)

Station Road, Styal, SK9 4JN
- ☎ **(01625) 531359 (Bookings)**
- 🖳 (01625) 416373
- 🕮 850
- ✍ W Higham (01625) 530063
- ✏ S Forrest (01625) 528910
- ⛳ 18 L 6194 yds Par 70 SSS 70 9 hole Par 3 course
- 🏌 U SOC
- £€ 18 hole course £21 (£26)
- ⊶ 2 miles from M56 Junction 5. Manchester Airport 5 mins
- ⊕ Floodlit driving range
- ⌂ T Holmes
- ■ www.styalgolf.co.uk

Sutton Hall

Aston Lane, Sutton Weaver, Runcorn, WA7 3ED
- ☎ **(01928) 790747**
- 🖳 (01928) 759174
- 🕮 600 30(J)
- ✍ M Faulkner
- ✏ J Hope (01928) 714872
- ⛳ 18 L 6608 yds Par 72
- 🏌 U SOC–WD
- £€ £20 (£24)
- ⊶ 2 miles E of M56 Junction 12

The Tytherington Club (1986)

Macclesfield, SK10 2JP
- ☎ **(01625) 506000**
- 🖳 (01625) 506040
- 🕮 800
- ✍ To be appointed
- ✏ Gavin Beddow
- ⛳ 18 L 6737 yds SSS 73
- 🏌 U H SOC–WD
- £€ £28 D–£35 (£34 D–£45)

- ⊶ N of Macclesfield (A523)
- ⊕ Driving range
- ⌂ Thomas/Dawson

Upton-by-Chester (1934)

Upton Lane, Chester, CH2 1EE
- ☎ **(01244) 381183**
- 🖳 (01244) 376955
- 🕮 750
- ✍ F Hopley (01244) 381183
- ✏ S Dewhurst (01244) 381183
- ⛳ 18 L 5850 yds SSS 68
- 🏌 U SOC–WD
- £€ £20 D–£30 (£20 D–£30)
- ⊶ Off Liverpool road, near 'Frog' PH

Vale Royal Abbey (1998)

Whitegate, Northwich, CW8 2BA
- ☎ **(01606) 301291**
- 🖳 (01606) 301414
- 🕮 650
- ✏ R Stockdale (01606) 301702
- ⛳ 18 holes Par 71 SSS 71
- 🏌 U SOC
- £€ £35
- ⊶ 2 miles W of Hartford, off A556
- ⌂ Simon Gidman
- ■ www.crownsportsplc.com

Vicars Cross (1939)

Tarvin Road, Great Barrow, Chester, CH3 7HN
- ☎ **(01244) 335174**
- 🖳 (01244) 335686
- ✉ secretary@vcgc.fsnet.co.uk
- 🕮 800
- ✍ Mrs K Hunt
- ✏ JA Forsythe (01244) 335595
- ⛳ 18 L 6446 yds SSS 71
- 🏌 U SOC–Tues & Thurs
- £€ £30 (£30)
- ⊶ 3 miles E of Chester on A51
- ⊕ Driving range
- ⌂ E Parr
- ■ www.vicarscrossgc.co.uk

Walton Hall (1972)

Public
Warrington Road, Higher Walton, Warrington, WA4 5LU
- ☎ **(01925) 266775**
- 🕮 200
- ✍ D Johnson (01925) 266775
- ✏ J Jackson (01925) 263061
- ⛳ 18 L 6843 yds Par 72 SSS 73
- 🏌 U SOC
- £€ £13 (£15)
- ⊶ 2 miles S of Warrington. M56 Junctions 10/11
- ⌂ Thomas/Alliss

Warrington (1903)

Hill Warren, Appleton, WA4 5HR
- ☎ **(01925) 261620**
- 🖳 (01925) 265933
- 🕮 875
- ✍ NF Morrall (01925) 261775
- ✏ R Mackay (01925) 265431
- ⛳ 18 L 6210 yds SSS 70
- 🏌 U SOC–Wed
- £€ On application

- ⊶ 3 miles S of Warrington on A49. M56 Junction 10
- ■ www.warrington-golf-club.co.uk

Werneth Low (1912)

Werneth Low Road, Gee Cross, Hyde, SK14 3AF
- ☎ **(0161) 368 2503**
- 🖳 (0161) 320 0053
- 🕮 315 60(L) 40(J)
- ✍ M Gregg (0161) 336 9496
- ✏ T Bacchus (0161) 367 9376
- ⛳ 11 L 6113 yds Par 70 SSS 69
- 🏌 U exc Sun–NA Sat/BH–M SOC
- £€ £18
- ⊶ 2 miles SE of Hyde, nr Gee Cross. M67 Junction 4
- ⌂ Peter Campbell

Widnes (1924)

Highfield Road, Widnes, WA8 7DT
- ☎ **(0151) 424 2440**
- 🖳 (0151) 495 2849
- ✉ arudder.wgc@uhu.co.uk
- 🕮 600
- ✍ VA Rudder (0151) 424 2995
- ✏ J O'Brien (0151) 420 7467
- ⛳ 18 L 5729 yds SSS 68
- 🏌 WD–U WE–H NA on comp days SOC–Wed & Thurs
- £€ £18 (£24)
- ⊶ Station ½ mile. M62 Junction 7

Wilmslow

Great Warford, Mobberley, Knutsford, WA16 7AY
- ☎ **(01565) 872148**
- 🖳 (01565) 872172
- 🕮 855
- ✍ Mrs MI Padfield
- ✏ LJ Nowicki (01565) 873620
- ⛳ 18 L 6607 yds SSS 72
- 🏌 U H exc Wed–NA before 3pm
- £€ £45 (£55)
- ⊶ 3 miles W of Alderley Edge
- ■ www.wilmslowgolfclub.ukf.net

Woodside

Knutsford Road, Holmes Chapel, CW4 8HT
- ☎ **(01477) 532388**
- 🖳 (01477) 549207
- 🕮 350
- ✍ J Schneider
- ✏ Phil Bills (01477) 532388
- ⛳ 9 L 2944 yds Par 69 SSS 69
- 🏌 U
- ⊕ Floodlit driving range
- ■ www.woodsidegolf.co.uk

Cornwall

Bowood Park (1992)

Valley Truckle, Lanteglos, Camelford, PL32 9RF
- ☎ **(01840) 213017**
- 🖳 (01840) 212622
- ✉ golf@bowoodpark.com
- 🕮 300

For list of abbreviations and key to symbols see page 627

✓ J Phillips
▷ 18 L 6692 yds SSS 72
👥 H (phone first) SOC
££ £30
🚗 2 miles SW of Camelford, off A39, on to B3266
⊕ Driving range

Bude & North Cornwall (1891)

Burn View, Bude, EX23 8DA
☎ (01288) 352006
🖳 (01288) 356855
🕮 682 106(L) 38(J)
🖎 Mrs PM Ralph
✓ J Yeo (01288) 353635
▷ 18 L 6057 yds Par 71 SSS 70
👥 WD–U 9.30–12.30pm, 2–5pm and after 6.30pm WE–restricted
££ D–£27 (£32)
🚗 Bude town centre
■ www.budegolf.co.uk

Budock Vean Hotel (1922)

Mawnan Smith, Falmouth, TR11 5LG
☎ (01326) 252102
🖳 (01326) 250892
🖂 relax@budockvean.co.uk
🕮 150
🖎 RM Whitwam
✓ A Ramsden (Golf Mgr)
▷ 9 L 5153 yds SSS 65
👥 H
££ D–£18 (D–£20)
🚗 Falmouth 5 miles
🏠 James Braid

Cape Cornwall G&CC (1990)

St Just, Penzance, TR19 7NL
☎ (01736) 788611
🖳 (01736) 788611
🕮 450
🖎 M Waters
✓ M Atherton (01736) 788867
▷ 18 L 5650 yds SSS 68
👥 WD/Sat–U Sun–NA before noon SOC
££ £20 (£20)
🚗 1 mile W of St Just. 8 miles W of Penzance, off A3071
🏠 R Hamilton

Carlyon Bay (1926)

Carlyon Bay, St Austell, PL25 3RD
☎ (01726) 814250
🕮 500
🖎 P Clemo
✓ M Rowe (01726) 814228
▷ 18 L 6560 yds SSS 71
👥 U–book with Pro
££ £22–£39
🚗 2 miles E of St Austell
🏠 J Hamilton Stutt

China Fleet CC (1991)

Saltash, PL12 6LJ
☎ (01752) 848668
🖳 (01752) 848456
🖂 sales@china-fleet.co.uk

🕮 600
🖎 Mrs L Goddard
✓ N Cook
▷ 18 L 6551 yds SSS 72
👥 H–by arrangement SOC
££ On application
🚗 1 mile from Tamar Bridge, off A38
⊕ Floodlit driving range
🏠 Martin Hawtree

Culdrose

Royal Naval Air Station, Culdrose
☎ (01326) 574121 Ext 2413
🕮 173
🖎 VC Williams (01326) 572540
▷ 18 L 6432 yds Par 72 SSS 71
👥 M–play restricted to WE and evenings
££ D–£5 (D–£5)
🚗 Culdrose, 1 mile S of Helston on A3083

Falmouth (1894)

Swanpool Road, Falmouth, TR11 5BQ
☎ (01326) 311262/314296
🖳 (01326) 317783
🖂 falmouthgolfclub@freezone.co.uk
🕮 500
🖎 R Wooldridge (01326) 314296
✓ B Patterson (Golf Dir)
▷ 18 L 6037 yds Par 71 SSS 70
👥 U H SOC
££ On application
🚗 ¼ mile W of Swanpool Beach
⊕ Driving range
■ www.falmouthgolfclub.co.uk

Isles of Scilly (1904)

St Mary's, Isles of Scilly, TR21 0NF
☎ (01720) 422692
🖳 (01720) 423782
🕮 130
🖎 S Watt
▷ 9 L 6001 yds SSS 69
👥 U
££ £22
🚗 Hughtown 1½ miles
🏠 Horace Hutchinson

Killiow (1987)

Proprietary
Killiow, Kea, Truro, TR3 6AG
☎ (01872) 270246
🖳 (01872) 240915
🕮 500
🖎 J Crowson (01872) 266876
▷ 18 L 5274 yds Par 70 SSS 68
👥 U
££ £18.50
🚗 2½ miles S of Truro, off A39
⊕ Driving range

Lanhydrock (1991)

Lostwithiel Road, Bodmin, PL30 5AQ
☎ (01208) 73600
🖳 (01208) 77325
🖂 golfing@lanhydrock-golf.co.uk
🕮 300
🖎 G Bond (Gen Mgr)
✓ J Broadway
▷ 18 L 6100 yds Par 70 SSS 70

👥 U SOC
££ On application (see web page)
🚗 1 mile S of Bodmin, off B3268
⊕ Driving range
🏠 J Hamilton Stutt
■ www.lanhydrock-golf.co.uk

Launceston (1927)

St Stephen, Launceston, PL15 8HF
☎ (01566) 773442
🖳 (01566) 777506
🕮 900
🖎 C Hicks
✓ J Tozer
▷ 18 L 6415 yds SSS 71
👥 WD–U H WE–NA
££ D–£25
🚗 1 mile N of Launceston, off Bude road
🏠 J Hamilton Stutt
■ www.launcestongolfclub.com

Looe (1933)

Bin Down, Looe, PL13 1PX
☎ (01503) 240239
🖳 (01503) 240864
🕮 600
🖎 T Day (Hon)
✓ A MacDonald
▷ 18 L 5940 yds Par 70 SSS 69
👥 U SOC
££ On application
🚗 3 miles E of Looe
🏠 Harry Vardon

Lostwithiel G&CC (1990)

Lower Polscoe, Lostwithiel, PL22 0HQ
☎ (01208) 873550
🖳 (01208) 873479
🖂 reception@golf-hotel.co.uk
🕮 350
🖎 D Higman
✓ T Nash (01208) 873822
▷ 18 L 5984 yds Par 72
👥 U SOC
££ £25 (£29)
🚗 ½ mile E of Lostwithiel, off A390
⊕ Driving range
🏠 Stuart Wood
■ www.golf-hotel.co.uk

Merlin (1991)

Proprietary
Mawgan Porth, Newquay, TR8 4DN
☎ (01841) 540222
🖳 (01841) 541031
🖂 rossoliver@merlingolfcourse.co.uk
🖎 Mrs M Oliver
▷ 18 L 6210 yds Par 71 SSS 71
👥 U SOC
££ 18 holes–£16. 9 holes–£12
🚗 4 miles N of Newquay
⊕ Driving range
🏠 Ross Oliver
■ www.merlingolfcourse.co.uk

Mullion (1895)

Cury, Helston, TR12 7BP
☎ (01326) 240685
🖳 (01326) 240685
🕮 700

🖉 G Fitter
✎ P Blundell (01326) 241176
ᕓ 18 L 6037 yds SSS 70
👭 H (restricted comp days and open days) SOC–WD
££ D–£23 (£28)
⊶ 6 miles S of Helston
⊕ Golf academy
🏠 W Sich

Newquay   (1890)

Tower Road, Newquay, TR7 1LT
☎ (01637) 872091
📠 (01637) 874066
✉ newquaygolfclub@smartone.co.uk
📖 600
🖉 G Binney (01637) 874354
✎ M Bevan (01637) 874830
ᕓ 18 L 6151 yds SSS 69
👭 WD/Sat–H Sun–H SOC
££ £30 (£30) W–£90
⊶ Newquay town centre
🏠 HS Colt
🖥 www.newquaygolfclub.com

Perranporth   (1927)

Budnic Hill, Perranporth, TR6 0AB
☎ (01872) 572454
📠 (01872) 573701
📖 600
🖉 DC Mugford (01872) 573701
✎ DC Michell (01872) 572317
ᕓ 18 L 6252 yds SSS 72
👭 WD–U WE–H SOC
££ £25 (£30)
⊶ ¹/₂ mile NW of Perranporth
🏠 James Braid
🖥 www.perranporthgolfclub.com

Porthpean   (1992)

Porthpean, St Austell, PL26 6AY
☎ (01726) 64613
ᕓ 18 L 5210 yds Par 67 SSS 66
👭 U SOC
££ £14
⊶ 2 miles SE of St Austell on coast
⊕ Driving range

Praa Sands   (1971)

Praa Sands, Penzance, TR20 9TQ
☎ (01736) 763445
📠 (01736) 763399
📖 225
🖉 D & K Phillips (Props)
ᕓ 9 L 4122 yds Par 62 SSS 60
👭 U exc Sun am
££ £15 D–£20
⊶ 7 miles E of Penzance on A394 Penzance-Helston road
🏠 RA Hamilton

St Austell   (1911)

Tregongeeves, St Austell, PL26 7DS
☎ (01726) 74756
📖 780
🖉 K Trahair
✎ T Pitts (01726) 68621
ᕓ 18 L 6091 yds SSS 69
👭 SOC exc comp days
££ On application
⊶ 1¹/₂ miles W of St Austell

St Enodoc   (1890)

Rock, Wadebridge, PL27 6LD
☎ (01208) 863216
📠 (01208) 862976
✉ stenodocgolfclub@tiscali.co.uk
📖 1360
🖉 TD Clagett
✎ NJ Williams (01208) 862402
ᕓ Church 18 L 6243 yds SSS 70
    Holywell 18 L 4103 yds SSS 61
👭 Church H–max 24 SOC
    Holywell–U
££ Church £40 (£50) Holywell £15 (£15)
⊶ 6 miles NW of Wadebridge
🏠 James Braid

St Kew   (1993)

Proprietary
St Kew Highway, Wadebridge, Bodmin, PL30 3EF
☎ (01208) 841500
📠 (01208) 841500
✉ fjb@stkewgolf.fsnet.co.uk
📖 350
🖉 J Brown (Prop)
✎ N Rogers (01208) 841500
ᕓ 9 L 4543 yds SSS 62
👭 U SOC
££ 9 holes–£10. 18 holes–£15
⊶ 2¹/₂ miles N of Wadebridge on A39
⊕ Covered driving range
🏠 David Derry

St Mellion Hotel G&CC   (1976)

St Mellion, Saltash, PL12 6SD
☎ (01579) 351351
📠 (01579) 350537
📖 850
✎ D Moon
ᕓ Old 18 L 5782 yds SSS 68
    Nicklaus 18 L 6651 yds SSS 72
👭 U SOC
££ From £15
⊶ Tamar Bridge, 5 miles NW of Saltash
⊕ Driving range
🏠 Hamilton Stutt/Nicklaus
🖥 www.stmellion.co.uk

Tehidy Park   (1922)

Camborne, TR14 0HH
☎ (01209) 842208
📠 (01209) 843680
✉ secretary-manager@tehidyparkgolfclub.co.uk
📖 1000
🖉 R Parker (Sec/Mgr)
✎ J Dumbreck (01209) 842914
ᕓ 18 L 6241 yds SSS 71
👭 H
££ £25 (£30)
⊶ 3 miles N of Camborne
🖥 www.tehidyparkgolfclub.co.uk

Tregenna Castle Hotel   (1982)

St Ives, TR26 2DE
☎ (01736) 795254 Ext 121
📖 297

🖉 J Goodman
ᕓ 18 L 3549 yds SSS 57
👭 U SOC
££ On application
⊶ St Ives 1 mile, off A3074

Treloy   (1991)

Treloy, Newquay, TR7 4JN
☎ (01637) 878554
📖 145
🖉 J Paull
ᕓ 9 L 2143 yds SSS 31
👭 U SOC
££ 18 holes–£12.50 9 holes–£8
⊶ 2 miles E of Newquay on A3059
🏠 MRM Sandow

Trethorne

Kennards House, Launceston, PL15 8QE
☎ (01566) 86903
📠 (01566) 86929
✉ gen@trethornegolfclub.com
📖 450
🖉 M Boundy
✎ M Boundy
ᕓ 18 L 6188 yds Par 71 SSS 71
👭 U
££ £28
⊶ 2 miles SW of Launceston (A30)
⊕ Driving range; buggy hire
🏠 Frank Frayne

Trevose   (1924)

Constantine Bay, Padstow, PL28 8JB
☎ (01841) 520208
📠 (01841) 521057
📖 1500
🖉 P Gammon (Prop), N Gammon (Sec/Mgr)
✎ G Alliss (01841) 520261
ᕓ 18 L 6608 yds SSS 72
    9 L 3031 yds SSS 35
    9 L 1360 yds SSS 29
👭 H SOC
££ On application
⊶ 4 miles W of Padstow
⊕ 3 & 4 ball times restricted (phone first)
🏠 HS Colt
🖥 www.trevose-gc.co.uk

Truro   (1937)

Treliske, Truro, TR1 3LG
☎ (01872) 272640
📠 (01872) 278684
📖 1000
🖉 HWD Leicester (Sec/Mgr) (01872) 278684
✎ NK Bicknell (01872) 276595
ᕓ 18 L 5347 yds SSS 66
👭 U H SOC
££ £20 (£25)
⊶ 1 mile W of Truro on A390
🏠 Colt/Alison/Morrison
🖥 www.trurogolf.co.uk

West Cornwall   (1889)

Lelant, St Ives, TR26 3DZ
☎ (01736) 753401
📠 (01736) 753401
📖 825
🖉 IJ Veale

✓ P Atherton (01736) 753177
ᐅ 18 L 5884 yds SSS 69
☺ H SOC
££ £25 (£30)
⊶ 2 miles E of St Ives
■ www.westcornwallgolfclub.co.uk

Whitsand Bay Hotel (1906)

Portwrinkle, Torpoint, PL11 3BU
☎ **(01503) 230470 (Clubhouse)**
☐ (01503) 230329
▥ 320
✓ S Poole (01503) 230778
ᐅ 18 L 5953 yds Par 70 SSS 69
☺ U SOC
££ £15 (£18)
⊶ 6 miles W of Plymouth
⌂ Willie Fernie

Cumbria

Alston Moor (1906)

The Hermitage, Alston, CA9 3DB
☎ **(01434) 381675**
☐ (01434) 381675
▥ 180
✎ P Bell (01434) 382614
ᐅ 10 L 5380 yds SSS 66
☺ U SOC
££ D–£11 (D–£13)
⊶ 2 miles S of Alston on B6277
■ www.cybermoor.org.guest.golf

Appleby (1903)

Brackenber Moor, Appleby, CA16 6LP
☎ **(017683) 51432**
☐ (017683) 52773
▥ 736
✎ JMF Doig (Hon)
✓ J Taylor (017683) 52922
ᐅ 18 L 5901 yds SSS 68
☺ U H
££ £19 (£23)
⊶ 2 miles SE of Appleby. ¹/₂ mile N of A66
⌂ Willie Fernie
■ www.applebygolfclub.org.uk

Barrow (1921)

Rakesmoor Lane, Hawcoat, Barrow-in-Furness, LA14 4QB
☎ **(01229) 825444**
✉ barrowgolf@supanet.com
▥ 505 91(L) 67(J)
✎ J Slater (Hon)
ᐅ 18 L 6184 yds Par 71 SSS 70
☺ U H Ladies Day–Fri SOC
££ £20 W–£85
⊶ 2 miles E of Barrow, off A590

Brampton (Talkin Tarn) (1907)

Tarn Road, Brampton, CA8 1HN
☎ **(016977) 2255**
☐ (016977) 41487
✉ secretary@bramptongolfclub.com
▥ 750

✎ IJ Meldrum (01900) 827985
✓ S Wilkinson (016977) 2000
ᐅ 18 L 6407 yds Par 72 SSS 71
☺ U
££ D–£22 (D–£30)
⊶ B6413, 1 mile SE of Brampton
⊕ Driving range
⌂ James Braid
■ www.bramptongolfclub.com

Brayton Park (1986)

Pay and play
Lakeside Inn, Brayton Park, Aspatria, CA5 3TD
☎ **(016973) 20840**
▥ 60
✎ D Warwick
ᐅ 9 L 2521 yds SSS 65
☺ U
££ 9 holes–£5 (£6) 18 holes–£7 (£8)
⊶ 1 mile N of Aspatria. 10 miles N of Cockermouth

Carlisle (1908)

Aglionby, Carlisle, CA4 8AG
☎ **(01228) 513029**
☐ (01228) 513303
▥ 735
✎ JR Johnson
✓ Graeme Lisle (01228) 513241
ᐅ 18 L 6263 yds SSS 70
☺ WD–U exc Tues–NA Sat–M Sun–restricted SOC–Mon/Wed/Fri
££ £30 D–£45 (£40 D–£45)
⊶ ¹/₂ mile E of M6 Junction 43, on A69
⌂ Mackenzie Ross

Carus Green (1996)

Pay and play
Burneside Road, Kendal, LA9 6EB
☎ **(01539) 721097**
☐ (01539) 721097
▥ 520
✎ B Lumsden
✓ D Turner
ᐅ 18 L 5642 yds Par 70 SSS 68
☺ U SOC
££ £16 (£20)
⊶ 1 mile N of Kendal on Burneside Road
⊕ 16 bay driving range
■ www.carusgreen.co.uk

Casterton

Sedbergh Road, Casterton, Nr Kirkby Lonsdale, LA6 2LA
☎ **(015242) 71592**
☐ (015242) 74387
✉ castertongc@hotmail.com
▥ 300
✎ J & E Makinson (Props)
✓ R Williamson
ᐅ 9 L 3015 yds Par 35
☺ U SOC
££ £10 (£14)
⊶ 1 mile NE of Kirkby Lonsdale on A683. M6 Junction 36, 6 miles
⌂ Will Adamson
■ www.castertongc.co.uk

Cockermouth (1896)

Embleton, Cockermouth, CA13 9SG
☎ **(017687) 76223/76941**
☐ (017687) 76941
▥ 539
✎ RD Pollard (01900) 822650
✓ None
ᐅ 18 L 5496 yds SSS 67
☺ WD–U before 3.30pm exc Wed WE–restricted SOC
££ £18 (£22)
⊶ 4 miles E of Cockermouth
⌂ James Braid

Dalston Hall (1990)

Dalston Hall, Dalston, Carlisle, CA5 7JX
☎ **(01228) 710165**
▥ 270
✎ Jane Simpson
ᐅ 9 L 2700 yds SSS 67
☺ U
££ 9 holes–£6.50 (£7.50) 18 holes–£10 (£13)
⊶ 5 miles SW of Carlisle on B5299. 6 miles W of M6 Junction 42

The Dunnerholme (1905)

Duddon Road, Askam-in-Furness, LA16 7AW
☎ **(01229) 462675**
▥ 400
✎ LA Haines (01229) 826198
ᐅ 10 L 6138 yds SSS 70
☺ U
££ £15 any day
⊶ 6 miles N of Barrow on A595

Eden (1992)

Crosby-on-Eden, Carlisle, CA6 4RA
☎ **(01228) 573003**
☐ (01228) 818435
▥ 700
✓ S Harrison (01228) 573003
ᐅ 18 L 6368 yds SSS 72
☺ U SOC
££ £28 (£32)
⊶ 5 miles NE of Carlisle, off A689. M6 Junction 44
⊕ Driving range. Golf academy

Furness (1872)

Central Drive, Walney Island, Barrow-in-Furness, LA14 3LN
☎ **(01229) 471232**
▥ 625
✎ JW Anderson
✓ None
ᐅ 18 L 6363 yds SSS 71
☺ H SOC
££ £15 (£25)
⊶ Walney Island. M6 Junction 36

Grange Fell (1952)

Fell Road, Grange-over-Sands, LA11 6HB
☎ **(015395) 32536**
▥ 300
✎ M Higginson (015395) 34098
ᐅ 9 L 4840 metres SSS 66
☺ U

££ £15 (£20)
🚗 W of Grange-over-Sands, towards Cartmel

Grange-over-Sands (1919)

Meathop Road, Grange-over-Sands, LA11 6QX

☎ **(015395) 33180**
🖳 (015395) 33754
📖 430 170(L) 40(J)
🏌 SD Wright (015395) 33754
⛳ A Pickering (015395) 35937
▷ 18 L 5938 yds SSS 69
👥 H SOC
££ £20 D–£25 (£25 D–£30)
🚗 E of Grange, off B5277
🏠 A Mackenzie

Haltwhistle (1967)

Wallend Farm, Greenhead, Carlisle, CA8 7HN

☎ **(01697) 747367**
🖳 (01434) 344311
📖 300
🏌 KL Dickinson (Hon)
⛳ None
▷ 18 L 5532 yds Par 69 SSS 67
👥 U SOC
££ D–£14 (£17)
🚗 3 miles W of Haltwhistle on A69
🏠 Andrew Mair

Kendal (1891)

The Heights, Kendal, LA9 4PQ

☎ **(01539) 723499 (Bookings)**
🖳 (01539) 733708
📖 731
🏌 A Dunn (01539) 733708
⛳ P Scott (01539) 723499
▷ 18 L 5785 yds Par 70 SSS 68
👥 U H SOC
££ £22 (£27.50)
🚗 1 mile NW of Kendal
■ www.cumbria.com/kendalgcl

Keswick (1978)

Threlkeld Hall, Keswick, CA12 4SX

☎ **(017687) 79010 (Bookings)**
🖳 (017687) 79861
📖 900
🏌 RC Jackson (017687) 79324
⛳ G Watson (017687) 79010
▷ 18 L 6225 yds SSS 72
👥 U H–book with Pro SOC
££ D–£20 (£25)
🚗 4 miles E of Keswick (A66)
🏠 E Brown

Kirkby Lonsdale

Scaleber Lane, Barbon, Kirkby Lonsdale, LA6 2LJ

☎ **(015242) 76365**
🖳 (015242) 76503
📧 KLGolf@Dial/Pipex.com
📖 550 50(J)
🏌 G Hall (015242) 76365
⛳ C Barrett (015242) 76366
▷ 18 L 6538 yds SSS 72
👥 U SOC
££ £25 (£30)
🚗 3 miles N of Kirkby Lonsdale, off A683

🏠 W Squires
■ www.klgolf.dial.pipex.com

Maryport (1905)

Bankend, Maryport, CA15 6PA

☎ **(01900) 812605**
🖳 (01900) 815626
📖 430
🏌 Mrs M Skinner (01900) 815626
▷ 18 L 5982 yds SSS 70
👥 U SOC
££ D–£17 (£22)
🚗 1 mile N of Maryport, off B5300

Penrith (1890)

Salkeld Road, Penrith, CA11 8SG

☎ **(01768) 891919/865429**
📖 750
🏌 D Noble (01768) 891919
⛳ G Key (01768) 891919
▷ 18 L 6026 yds SSS 69
👥 WD–H WE/BH–H 10.06–11.30am & after 3pm
££ £24 D–£29 (£29 D–£34)
🚗 ¹/₂ mile E of Penrith

Seascale (1893)

Seascale, CA20 1QL

☎ **(019467) 28202/28800**
🖳 (019467) 28202
📖 570
🏌 JDH Stobart (019467) 28202
⛳ S Rudd (019467) 21779
▷ 18 L 6416 yds Par 71 SSS 71
👥 U SOC
££ £24 D–£29 (£27 D–£32)
🚗 15 miles S of Whitehaven
🏠 Campbell/Lowe

Sedbergh (1896)

Dent Road, Sedbergh, LA10 5SS

☎ **(015396) 21551**
🖳 (015396) 20993
📧 sedberghgc@btinternet.com
📖 200
🏌 AD Lord (015396) 20993
⛳ J Garner
▷ 9 L 5588 yds Par 70 SSS 68
👥 U–phone in advance SOC H
££ £18 D–£23 (£20 D–£25)
🚗 1 mile S of Sedbergh on Dent road. M6 Junction 37, 5 miles
🏠 WG Squires
■ www.sedberghgolfclub.co.uk

Silecroft (1903)

Silecroft, Millom, LA18 4NX

☎ **(01229) 774250**
🖳 (01229) 774342
📖 280
🏌 DLA MacLardie (01229) 774342
⛳ None
▷ 9 L 5877 yds Par 68 SSS 68
👥 WD–U WE/BH–restricted
££ D–£15 (£20)
🚗 3 miles W of Millom

Silloth-on-Solway (1892)

Silloth, Wigton, CA7 4BL

☎ **(016973) 31304**
🖳 (016973) 31782

📖 700
⛳ (016973) 32404
▷ 18 L 6618 yds SSS 73
👥 U H–booking advisable SOC
££ D–£32 (£43)
🚗 22 miles W of Carlisle (B5302). M6 Junction 43
🏠 David Grant

Silverdale (1906)

Red Bridge Lane, Silverdale, Carnforth, LA5 0SP

☎ **(01524) 701300**
🖳 (01524) 702074
📧 silverdalegolfclub@ecosse.net
📖 500
🏌 KD Smith (01524) 702074
▷ 18 L 5535 yds Par 70 SSS 68
👥 U exc Sun (Summer)–M
££ £20 (£25)
🚗 3 miles NW of Carnforth, by Silverdale Station
■ www.silverdalegolfclub.com

St Bees (1929)

Peckmill, Beach Road, St Bees, CA27 0EJ

☎ **(01946) 822515, (01946) 824300 (Clubhouse)**
📖 400
🏌 BG Ritson
▷ 9 L 5122 yds SSS 65
👥 WD–U exc Wed–NA after 4pm WE–NA before 3pm
££ £12 (£12)
🚗 4 miles S of Whitehaven

Stony Holme (1974)

Public
St Aidan's Road, Carlisle, CA1 1LS

☎ **(01228) 625511**
📖 375
🏌 WJ Hodgson (01228) 527112
⛳ S Ling (01228) 625511
▷ 18 L 5775 yds Par 69 SSS 68
👥 U SOC
££ £8.30 (£10.30)
🚗 1 mile E of Carlisle, off A69. M6 Junction 43
🏠 Frank Pennink

Ulverston (1895)

Bardsea Park, Ulverston, LA12 9QJ

☎ **(01229) 582824**
📧 ulverstongolf@bardseapark .freeserve.co.uk
📖 745
🏌 K Oliver
⛳ MR Smith (01229) 582806
▷ 18 L 6201 yds SSS 70
👥 H or I SOC
££ £28 D–£33 (£25 D–£33) Summer £15 D–£29 (£15 D–£20) Winter
🚗 1¹/₂ miles SW of Ulverston on A5087
🏠 Herd/Colt

Windermere (1891)

Cleabarrow, Windermere, LA23 3NB

☎ **(015394) 43123**
🖳 (015394) 43123

📖 700
🏌 KR Moffat
/ WSM Rooke (015394) 43550
🏴 18 L 5132 yds SSS 65
👥 H SOC
£€ £25 (£30)
🚗 1¹/₂ miles E of Bowness
🏠 George Lowe

Workington (1893)

Branthwaite Road, Workington, CA14 4SS
☎ **(01900) 603460**
🖥 (01900) 607122
✉ workingtongolf@aol.com
📖 600 110(L) 85(J)
🏌 TF Stout
/ A Drabble (01900) 67828
🏴 18 L 6252 yds SSS 70
👥 H SOC
£€ £22 (£25)
🚗 2 miles SE of Workington
🏠 James Braid
■ www.lakestay.co.uk /workingtongolf

Derbyshire

Alfreton (1892)

Oakerthorpe, Alfreton, DE55 7LH
☎ **(01773) 832070**
📖 350
🏌 E Brown
/ (01773) 831901
🏴 11 L 5393 yds SSS 66
👥 WD–U H before 4.30pm –M after 4.30pm WE–M SOC H
£€ £18
🚗 W of Alfreton (A38). M1 Junction 28

Allestree Park (1949)

Public
Allestree Hall, Allestree, Derby, DE22 2EU
☎ **(01332) 550616**
📖 200
🏌 A Maguire
/ L Woodward
🏴 18 L 5714 yds SSS 68
👥 WD–U WE–booking req SOC
£€ £11
🚗 2 miles N of Derby on A6

Ashbourne (1886)

Wyaston Road, Ashbourne, DE6 1NB
☎ **(01335) 342078**
🖥 (01335) 347937
✉ sec@ashbournegc.fsnet.co.uk
📖 600
🏌 (01335) 342078
/ A Smith (01335) 347960
🏴 18 L 6365 yds SSS 71
👥 WD–U SOC
£€ £20 (£30)
🚗 1¹/₂ miles SW of Ashbourne, off A52
⊕ Telephone to confirm green fee and starting time
🏠 David Hemstock
■ www.ashbournegolfclub.co.uk

Bakewell (1899)

Station Road, Bakewell, DE4 1GB
☎ **(01629) 812307**
📖 305 67(L) 25(J)
🏌 F Parker
/ None
🏴 9 L 5244 yds SSS 65
👥 WD–U WE/BH–by arrangement SOC
£€ £15 (£20)
🚗 ¹/₂ mile NE of Bakewell and A6

Birch Hall

Sheffield Road, Unstone, S18 5DH
☎ **(01246) 291979**
📖 300
🏌 G Jackson
/ None
🏴 18 L 6509 yds Par 73 SSS 71
👥 U
£€ On application
🚗 2 miles N of Chesterfield (B60557)
🏠 David Tucker

Blue Circle (1985)

Cement Works, Hope, S33 2RP
☎ **(01433) 622315**
📖 230
🏌 DS Smith
🏴 9 L 5350 yds SSS 66
👥 M
🚗 Hope Valley

Bondhay (1991)

Bondhay Lane, Whitwell, Worksop, S80 3EH
☎ **(01909) 723608**
🖥 (01909) 720226
✉ bondhay@aol.com
📖 520
🏌 H Hardisty
/ M Ramsden
🏴 18 L 6785 yds Par 72
9 hole course
👥 U SOC
£€ £18 (£23)
🚗 2 miles E of M1 Junction 30, off A619
⊕ Driving range
🏠 Donald Steel

Brailsford (1994)

Proprietary
Pools Head Lane, Brailsford, Ashbourne, DE6 3BU
☎ **(01335) 360096**
📖 131
🏌 K Wilson
/ D McCarthy
🏴 9 L 3148 yds Par 36 SSS 35
👥 U SOC
£€ 9 holes–£9 (£11.50) 18 holes–£13.50 (£16.50)
🚗 On A52 between Derby and Ashbourne
⊕ Driving range

Breadsall Priory Hotel G&CC (1976)

Moor Road, Morley, Derby, DE7 6DL
☎ **(01332) 832235**

🖥 (01332) 833509
📖 900
🏌 P Le Roi (Gen Mgr)
/ D Steels (01332) 834425
🏴 18 L 6201 yds SSS 70
18 L 6028 yds SSS 69
👥 WD–U SOC–WD only
£€ £25–£42
🚗 Morley, 5 miles N of Derby (A61). M1 Junction 25, 9 miles
⊕ Driving range

Broughton Heath

Bent Lane, Church Broughton, DE65 5BA
☎ **(01283) 521235**
🖥 (01283) 521235
📖 435
🏌 J Bentley
/ A Hyland
🏴 18 L 3087 yds Par 54 SSS 53
👥 WD–U WE–booking necessary SOC
£€ £8.50 (£11)
🚗 Church Broughton, 1 mile N of A516 at Hatton
🏠 K Tunnicliffe

Burton-on-Trent (1894)

43 Ashby Road East, Burton-on-Trent, DE15 0PS
☎ **(01283) 568708 (Clubhouse)**
🖥 (01283) 544551
✉ thesecretary@burtongolfclub.co.uk
📖 600
🏌 D Hartley (01283) 544551
/ G Stafford (01283) 562240
🏴 18 L 6579 yds SSS 71
👥 I H WD–NA before 9am or 1–2pm SOC
£€ £28 (£32)
🚗 3 miles E of Burton on A511
🏠 HS Colt

Buxton & High Peak (1887)

Townend, Buxton, SK17 7EN
☎ **(01298) 26263**
🖥 (01298) 26333
✉ secretary@bhpgc.fsnet.co.uk
📖 450
🏌 H Smith
/ G Brown (01298) 23112
🏴 18 L 5997 yds SSS 69
👥 U
£€ £24 (£30)
🚗 NE boundary of Buxton (A6)
⊕ Driving range adj. to course (separate business)
🏠 J Morris
■ www.buxtonandhighpeakgolfclub .co.uk

Carsington Water (1994)

Pay and play
Carsington, Wirksworth
☎ **(01629) 85650**
📖 300
🏌 GWR Coleman (Mgr) (01403) 784864
/ To be appointed
🏴 9 L 6000yds SSS
👥 U SOC

££ On application
⊕ 8 miles NE of Ashbourne, off B5035
🛆 John Ludlow

Cavendish (1925)
Gadley Lane, Buxton, SK17 6XD
☎ (01298) 23494
🖴 (01298) 79708
🕮 600
🏌 JD Rushton (01298) 79708
🏌 P Hunstone (01298) 25052
🏳 18 L 5833 yds SSS 68
🏌 U H SOC–by prior arrangement with Pro
££ £26 (£35)
⊕ ³/₄ mile W of Buxton Station. St John's Road (A53)
⊕ Driving range
🛆 Dr A Mackenzie

Chapel-en-le-Frith (1905)
The Cockyard, Manchester Road, Chapel-en-le-Frith, SK23 9UH
☎ (01298) 812118
🖴 (01298) 814990
🖂 info@chapelgolf.co.uk
🕮 640
🏌 J Hilton (01298) 813943
🏌 DJ Cullen (01298) 812118
🏳 18 L 6434 yds SSS 71
🏌 U
££ £27 (£38)
⊕ 13 miles SE of Stockport, off A6 (B5470)
■ www.chapelgolf.co.uk

Chesterfield (1897)
Walton, Chesterfield, S42 7LA
☎ (01246) 279256
🖴 (01246) 276622
🕮 600
🏌 BG Broughton
🏌 M McLean (01246) 276297
🏳 18 L 6281 yds Par 71 SSS 70
🏌 WD–U before 4.00pm WE–M SOC–WD
££ £28–£36
⊕ 2 miles SW of Chesterfield on A623

Chesterfield Municipal (1934)
Public
Murray House, Crow Lane, Chesterfield, S41 0EQ
☎ (01246) 273887, (01246) 239500 (Bookings)
🖴 (01246) 558024
🕮 350
🏌 J Hearnshaw
🏌 A Carnall (01246) 239500
🏳 18 L 6013 yds SSS 69
9 hole course
🏌 U
££ On application
⊕ ¹/₄ mile past Chesterfield station
⊕ Pitch & putt

Chevin (1894)
Duffield, Derby, DE56 4EE
☎ (01332) 841864
🖴 (01332) 844028
🖂 secretary@chevingolf.fsnet.co.uk
🕮 500 100(L) 80(J) 70(5D)
🏌 JA Milner
🏌 W Bird (01332) 841112
🏳 18 L 6057 yds SSS 69
🏌 WD–U WE–M SOC–WD H
££ £25 D–£30
⊕ 5 miles N of Derby on A6

Derby Sinfin (1923)
Public
Wilmore Road, Sinfin, Derby, DE24 9HD
☎ (01332) 766323
🏌 P Davidson
🏌 J Siddons (01332) 766462
🏳 18 L 6163 yds SSS 69
🏌 U SOC
££ On application
⊕ 1 mile S of Derby, off A52

Erewash Valley (1905)
Stanton-by-Dale, DE7 4QR
☎ (0115) 932 3258
🖴 (0115) 944 0061
🖂 secretary@erewashvalley.co.uk
🕮 675
🏌 JA Beckett (0115) 932 2984
🏌 MJ Ronan (0115) 932 4667
🏳 18 L 6547 yds SSS 71
🏌 WE/BH–NA before noon SOC–WD
££ £30 D–£40 (£40)
⊕ 10 miles E of Derby, off A52. M1 Junction 25, 3 miles
🛆 Hawtree
■ www.erewashvalley.co.uk

Glossop & District (1894)
Sheffield Road, Glossop, SK13 7PU
☎ (01457) 865247 (Clubhouse)
🕮 300
🏌 R Hargreaves
🏌 D Marsh (01457) 853117
🏳 11 L 5800 yds SSS 68
🏌 U SOC
££ £12.50 Mon £17.50 weekdays £20
⊕ 1 mile E of Glossop, off A57

Grassmoor Golf Centre
Proprietary
North Wingfield Road, Grassmoor, Chesterfield, S42 5EA
☎ (01246) 856044
🖴 (01246) 853486
🖂 enquiries@grassmoorgolf.co.uk
🕮 390
🏌 H Hagues
🏌 G Hagues
🏳 18 L 5721 yds Par 69
🏌 U–advance booking required SOC
££ £12 (£15)
⊕ 2 miles S of Chesterfield on B6038. M1 Junction 29, 3 miles
⊕ Floodlit driving range
🛆 Hawtree
■ www.grassmoorgolf.co.uk

Horsley Lodge (1992)
Smalley Mill Road, Horsley, DE21 5BL
☎ (01332) 780838
🖴 (01332) 781118
🕮 650
🏌 G Johnson
🏌 G Lyall (01332) 780838
🏳 18 L 6381 yds SSS 70
🏌 WD–U H
££ On application
⊕ 4 miles NE of Derby. M1 Junction 28
⊕ Driving range
🛆 GM White

Ilkeston (1929)
Public
Peewit West End Drive, Ilkeston, DE7 5GH
☎ (0115) 930 4550
🕮 100
🏌 M Ogden (0115) 944 2304
🏌 None
🏳 9 L 4116 yds Par 62 SSS 60
🏌 U SOC–WD
££ On application
⊕ ¹/₂ mile E of Ilkeston

Kedleston Park (1947)
Kedleston, Quarndon, Derby, DE22 5JD
☎ (01332) 840035
🖴 (01332) 840035
🕮 784
🏌 GR Duckmanton
🏌 P Wesselingh (01332) 841685
🏳 18 L 6675 yds SSS 72
🏌 WD–H
££ £35 (£45)
⊕ 4 miles N of Derby. National Trust signs to Kedleston Hall
🛆 James Braid
■ www.kedlestonparkgolf.co.uk

Matlock (1906)
Chesterfield Road, Matlock Moor, Matlock, DE4 5LZ
☎ (01629) 582191
🖴 (01629) 582135
🕮 496 78(L) 55(J)
🏌 J Odell (01629) 582191
🏌 M Whithorn (01629) 584934
🏳 18 L 5804 yds SSS 68
🏌 WD–U exc 12.30–1.30pm–NA WE/BH–M SOC–WD
££ D–£25
⊕ 1¹/₂ miles NE of Matlock (A632)

Maywood (1990)
Rushy Lane, Risley, Derby, DE7 3ST
☎ (0115) 939 2306
🕮 500
🏌 WJ Cockeram
🏌 S Sherratt (0115) 949 0043
🏳 18 L 6424 yds Par 72 SSS 71
🏌 WD–U before 4pm WE–restricted SOC
££ £15 (£20)
⊕ Between Nottingham and Derby. M1 Junction 25
🛆 P Moon

Mickleover (1923)
Uttoxeter Road, Mickleover, DE3 9AD
☎ **(01332) 513339 (Clubhouse)**
🖴 (01332) 516011
🕮 800
🏌 GW Finney (01332) 516011
⛳ T Coxon (01332) 518662
☞ 18 L 5708 yds SSS 68
👥 U SOC–Tues & Thurs
£€ £25 (£30)
⚐ 3 miles W of Derby on
A516/B5020

New Mills (1907)
*Shaw Marsh, New Mills, High Peak,
SK22 4QE*
☎ **(01663) 743485**
🕮 420
🏌 P Jenkinson (01663) 744305
⛳ C Cross (01663) 746161
☞ 18 L 5604 yds SSS 67
👥 WD–U WE–M SOC
£€ £15 (£20)
⚐ 8 miles SE of Stockport
🏠 David Williams

Ormonde Fields (1906)
*Nottingham Road, Codnor, Ripley,
DE5 9RG*
☎ **(01773) 742987**
🖴 (01773) 744848
🕮 660
🏌 K Constable
☞ 18 L 6504 yds SSS 72
👥 U SOC
£€ On application
⚐ A610 Ripley to Nottingham road.
M1 Junction 26, 5 miles
🏠 John Fearn

Pastures (1969)
*Pastures Hospital, Mickleover,
DE3 5DQ*
☎ **(01332) 521074**
🕮 320
🏌 S McWilliams
☞ 9 L 5095 yds SSS 65
👥 M SOC–WD
⚐ 4 miles W of Derby
🏠 JF Pennink

Shirland (1977)
Lower Delves, Shirland, DE55 6AU
☎ **(01773) 834935**
🕮 450
🏌 G Towle (01773) 874224
⛳ NB Hallam (01773) 834935
☞ 18 L 6072 yds SSS 70
👥 WD–U WE–U after 2pm SOC
£€ £18 (£25)
⚐ 1 mile N of Alfreton, off A61 by
Shirland Church

Sickleholme (1898)
Bamford, Sheffield, S33 0BH
☎ **(01433) 651306**
🕮 250 100(L) 72(J)
🏌 PH Taylor (Mgr)
⛳ PH Taylor
☞ 18 L 6064 yds SSS 69

👥 U exc Wed am
£€ £26 (£32)
⚐ W of Sheffield, between
Hathersage and Hope (A625)

Stanedge (1934)
*Walton Hay Farm, Chesterfield,
S45 0LW*
☎ **(01246) 566156**
🕮 325
🏌 W Tyzack (01246) 276568
☞ 9 L 5786 yds SSS 68
👥 WD–U before 2pm –M after 2pm
WE–M SOC
£€ £15
⚐ 5 miles SW of Chesterfield, off
B5057
■ www.ukgolfer.co.uk/stanedge

Devon

Ashbury (1991)
*Higher Maddaford, Okehampton,
EX20 4NL*
☎ **(01837) 55453**
🖴 (01837) 55468
🕮 100
🏌 N Agnew
⛳ R Cade
☞ 18 L 5374 yds SSS 66
  18 L 5628 yds SSS 67
  18 L 5351 yds SSS 66
👥 WD–U after 12 noon
£€ £20 (£25)
⚐ 4 miles W of Okehampton, off
A3079
🏠 DJ Fensom
■ www.ashburyhotel.co.uk

Axe Cliff (1894)
*Squires Lane, Axmouth, Seaton,
EX12 4AB*
☎ **(01297) 24371**
🕮 400
🏌 Mrs H Kenworthy
⛳ M Dack (01297) 21754
☞ 18 L 5969 yds SSS 70
👥 U H SOC
£€ £20 (£22)
⚐ Nr Yacht Club at Axmouth Bridge

Bigbury (1923)
Bigbury-on-Sea, TQ7 4BB
☎ **(01548) 810055 (Clubhouse)**
🖴 (01548) 810207
🕮 800
🏌 MJ Lowry (01548) 810557
⛳ S Lloyd (01548) 810412
☞ 18 L 6061 yds Par 70 SSS 69
👥 H SOC
£€ £27 (£30)
⚐ 15 miles SE of Plymouth on B3392
🏠 JH Taylor
■ www.bigburygolfclub.com

Chulmleigh (1976)
Pay and play
Leigh Road, Chulmleigh, EX18 7BL
☎ **(01769) 580519**

🖴 (01769) 580519
✉ chulmleighgolf@aol.com
🕮 100
🏌 RW Dow
☞ Summer 18 L 1450 yds SSS 54
  Winter 9 L 2309 yds SSS 54
👥 U
£€ £8.50 £7.50 before 10 am D–£15
⚐ 1 mile N of A377 at Chulmleigh
🏠 John Goodban
■ www.chulmleighgolf.co.uk

Churston (1890)
Churston, Brixham, TQ5 0LA
☎ **(01803) 842751**
🖴 (01803) 845738
✉ manager@churstongc.freeserve
.co.uk
🕮 983
🏌 SR Bawden (01803) 842751
⛳ N Holman (01803) 843442
☞ 18 L 6208 yds SSS 70
👥 H exc Tues am–NA
SOC–Mon/Thurs/Fri
£€ £30 (£35)
⚐ 5 miles S of Torquay
🏠 HS Colt
■ www.churstongolfclubunited.co.uk

Dainton Park (1993)
*Totnes Road, Ipplepen, Newton Abbot,
TQ12 5TN*
☎ **(01803) 815000**
🕮 600
🏌 M Penlington
⛳ M Tyson
☞ 18 L 6300 yds SSS 70
👥 U SOC
£€ £20 (£25)
⚐ 2 miles S of Newton Abbot on
A381
⊕ Driving range
🏠 Adrian Stiff

Dartmouth G&CC (1992)
Blackawton, Totnes, TQ9 7DE
☎ **(01803) 712686**
🖴 (01803) 712628
✉ info@dgcc.co.uk
🕮 800
🏌 J Waugh (Sec), R Clark (Asst. Sec)
⛳ S Dougan (01803) 712650
☞ Ch'ship 18 L 7191 yds SSS 74
  Dartmouth 18 L 4791 yds SSS 64
👥 WD–U phone first WE–H SOC
£€ Ch'ship £30 (£40). Dartmouth £16
(£17)
⚐ 4 miles NE of Dartmouth on A3122
⊕ Driving range
🏠 Jeremy Pern
■ www.dgcc.co.uk

Dinnaton (1989)
Ivybridge, PL21 9HU
☎ **(01752) 892512/892452**
🖴 (01752) 698334
🕮 300
🏌 B Rimes
⛳ D Ridyard (01752) 691288
☞ 9 L 4100 yds SSS 59
  9 hole course Par 64
👥 U SOC

££ D–£10 (D–£12.50)
⊕ 12 miles SE of Plymouth, off A38/B3213
🏠 Pink/Cotton

Downes Crediton (1976)
Hookway, Crediton, EX17 3PT
☎ (01363) 773025
🖳 (01363) 775060
✉ secretary@downescreditongc.co.uk
📖 700
🏌 PT Lee (01363) 773025
✓ S Macaskill (01363) 774464
🏴 18 L 5954 yds Par 70 SSS 69
👥 H SOC
££ £25 (£28)
⊕ 2 miles S of Crediton, off A377
■ www.downescreditongc.co.uk

East Devon (1902)
Links Road, Budleigh Salterton, EX9 6DG
☎ (01395) 443370
🖳 (01395) 445547
✉ secretary@edgc.co.uk
📖 850
🏌 R Burley (01395) 443370
✓ T Underwood (01395) 445195
🏴 18 L 6231 yds SSS 70
👥 H SOC–Thurs only
££ £30 (£40)
⊕ 12 miles SE of Exeter – M5 J30 – A376

Elfordleigh Hotel G&CC (1932)
Colebrook, Plympton, Plymouth, PL7 5EB
☎ (01752) 348425
🖳 (01752) 344581
✉ enquiries@elfordleigh.co.ul
📖 500
🏌 Mike Sheppard (01752) 348446
✓ Dominic Naughton (01752) 348425
🏴 18 L 5527 yds SSS 67
👥 U H–phone first SOC
££ £25 (£30)
⊕ 4 miles E of Plymouth, off Plympton road
🏠 JH Taylor

Exeter G&CC (1895)
Countess Wear, Exeter, EX2 7AE
☎ (01392) 874139
🖳 (01392) 874139
✉ golf@exetergcc.co.uk
📖 850
🏌 KJ Ham (Golf Mgr) (01392) 874639
✓ M Rowett (01392) 875028
🏴 18 L 5980 yds SSS 69
👥 WD–U H WE–I H SOC–Thurs
££ On application
⊕ 4 miles SE of Exeter
🏠 James Braid

Fingle Glen (1992)
Tedburn St Mary, Exeter, EX6 6AF
☎ (01647) 61817
🖳 (01647) 61135

📖 450
🏌 P Miliffe
✓ S Gould
🏴 18 L 5308 yds Par 68 SSS 66
👥 U SOC
££ £19 (£21)
⊕ 5 miles W of Exeter on A30
⊕ Driving range

Hartland Forest (1980)
Hartland Forest Golf & Leisure Parc, Woolsery, Biddeford, EX39 5RA
☎ (01237) 431442
🖳 (01237) 431734
✉ hartlandgoldsec@hotmail.com
📖 150
🏌 Kevin Murphy (01271) 343160
🏴 18 L 5870 yds Par 70 SSS 68
👥 U SOC
££ £15
⊕ 6 miles S of Clovelly, off A39
🏠 Alan Cartwright

Hele Park Golf Centre (1993)
Proprietary
Ashburton Road, Newton Abbot, TQ12 6JN
☎ (01626) 336060
🖳 (01626) 332661
✉ info@heleparkgolf.co.uk
📖 300
🏌 AJ Taylor (01626) 336060
✓ J Langmead
🏴 9 L 2584 yds SSS 65
👥 U SOC
££ £16 (£18)
⊕ W of Newton Abbot on A383
⊕ Driving range
🏠 M Craig
■ www.heleparkgolf.co.uk

Holsworthy (1937)
Kilatree, Holsworthy, EX22 6LP
☎ (01409) 253177
🖳 (01409) 253177
✉ hgcsecretary@aol.com
📖 450
🏌 B Megson
✓ G Webb (01409) 254771
🏴 18 L 6100 yds SSS 69
👥 WD–U Sun–U after 2.30pm
££ £25
⊕ 1 mile W of Holsworthy. 7 miles E of Bude (A3072)

Honiton (1896)
Middlehills, Honiton, EX14 9TR
☎ (01404) 44422
🖳 (01404) 46383
📖 800
🏌 BM Young
✓ A Cave (01404) 42943
🏴 18 L 5902 yds Par 69 SSS 68
👥 U (recognised club member) SOC
££ £24 (£30)
⊕ 2 miles S of Honiton towards Farway off A35

Hurdwick (1990)
Tavistock Hamlets, Tavistock, PL19 8PZ
☎ (01822) 612746

📖 175
🏌 Maj RW Cullen (Mgr)
R Hurle (Golf Sec)
🏴 18 L 5335 yds Par 67
👥 U SOC
££ £15 (£15)
⊕ 1 mile N of Tavistock, on Brentor Church road
🏠 Hawtree/Bartlett

Ilfracombe (1892)
Hele Bay, Ilfracombe, EX34 9RT
☎ (01271) 862176
🖳 (01271) 867731
✉ ilfracombe.golfclub@virgin.net
📖 500
🏌 J Hoskins
✓ M Davies (01271) 863328
🏴 18 L 5795 yds Par 69 SSS 68
👥 WD–H SOC WE/BH–U after 10am –NA 12–1pm
££ £22 (£27)
⊕ 2 miles E of Ilfracombe, towards Combe Martin
⊕ Driving range
🏠 TK Weir
■ www.ilfracombegolfclub.com

Libbaton (1988)
High Bickington, Umberleigh, EX37 9BS
☎ (01769) 560269
📖 475
🏌 Anne Fenge
✓ Andrew Norman
🏴 18 L 681 yds SSS 71
👥 U SOC
££ £20 (£24)
⊕ 1 mile S of High Bickington on B3217. M5 Junction 27
⊕ Floodlit driving range

Manor House Hotel (1929)
Moretonhampstead, TQ13 8RE
☎ (01647) 440998
🖳 (01647) 440961
✉ manortee@aol.com
📖 250
🏌 R Lewis
✓ R Lewis
🏴 18 L 6016 yds SSS 69
Par 3 course
👥 U H SOC
££ £30 (£35)
⊕ 15 miles SW of Exeter on B3212. M5 Junction 31
🏠 JF Abercromby

Mortehoe & Woolacombe (1992)
Easewell, Mortehoe, Ilfracombe, EX34 7EH
☎ (01271) 870225
📖 225
🏌 M Wilkinson (01271) 870745
🏴 9 L 4852 yds SSS 63
👥 U
££ 9 holes–£7 18 holes–£12
⊕ E of Mortehoe village
🏠 David Hoare

Newton Abbot (Stover)
(1930)
Bovey Road, Newton Abbot, TQ12 6QQ
☎ **(01626) 352460**
🖰 (01626) 330210
🖂 secretary@stovergc.tsnet.co.uk
🕮 750
🏌 GW Rees
✎ M Craig (01626) 362078
🏳 18 L 5764 yds SSS 68
👥 U H SOC
££ D–£28 (£32)
⛳ 3 miles N of Newton Abbot on A382. A38 Drumbridges Junction
🏠 James Braid
▇ www.stovergolfclub.com.uk

Okehampton (1913)
Okehampton, EX20 1EF
☎ **(01837) 52113**
🖰 (01837) 52734
🖂 okehamptongc@btconnect.com
🕮 500
🏌 C Yeo (Admin)
✎ A Moon (01837) 53541
🏳 18 L 5268 yds SSS 66 Par 68
👥 H SOC
££ On application
⛳ S boundary of Okehampton
🏠 JH Taylor
▇ www.okehamptongc.co.uk

Padbrook Park (1992)
Pay and play
Cullompton, EX15 1RU
☎ **(01884) 38286**
🖰 (01884) 34359
🕮 450
🏌 R Chard (Mgr)
✎ S Adwick (01884) 820805
🏳 9 L 6108 yds SSS 70
👥 U SOC–WD
££ 18 holes–£12 (£18). 9 holes–£10 (£15)
⛳ 10 miles E of Exeter. M5 Junction 28, 1 mile
🏠 Bob Sandow

Portmore Golf Park (1993)
Proprietary
Landkey Road, Barnstaple, EX32 9LB
☎ **(01271) 378378**
🖂 colin@portmoregolfpark.freeserve.co.uk
🕮 550
🏌 C Webber
✎ S Gould, D Everett
🏳 9 L 3048 yds Par 70
Further 9 due 2004 approx 6600 yds Par 71
9 hole Par 3 course
👥 U
££ 9 holes–£12.50. 18 holes–£18. Par 3 course–£7.50–£12.50
⛳ 1 mile E of Barnstaple, off A361
⊕ Floodlit driving rang; practice area
🏠 Hawtree

Royal North Devon (1864)
Golf Links Road, Westward Ho!, EX39 1HD
☎ **(01237) 473824 (Clubhouse)**

🖰 (01237) 423456
🖂 info@royalnorthdevongolfclub.co.uk
🕮 1100
🏌 R Fowler (01237) 473817
✎ R Herring (01237) 477598
🏳 18 L 6665 yds SSS 72
👥 U H
££ £32 D–£38 (£38 D–£42)
⛳ 2 miles N of Bideford (A39)
⊕ Golf Museum
🏠 Old Tom Morris
▇ www.royalnorthdevongolfclub.co.uk

Saunton (1897)
Saunton, Braunton, EX33 1LG
☎ **(01271) 812436**
🖰 (01271) 814241
🕮 1450
🏌 TC Reynolds
✎ AT Mackenzie (01271) 812013
🏳 East 18 L 6729 yds SSS 72
West 18 L 6403 yds SSS 71
👥 U H SOC
££ £50 D–£70 inc lunch
⛳ 6 miles W of Barnstaple
🏠 Fowler/Pennink
▇ www.sauntongolf.co.uk

Sidmouth (1889)
Cotmaton Road, Sidmouth, EX10 8SX
☎ **(01395) 513023**
🖰 (01395) 514661
🖂 secretary@sidmouthgolfclub.co.uk
🕮 850
🏌 IM Smith (01395) 513451
✎ Adrian Cave (01395) 516407
🏳 18 L 5068 yds SSS 65
👥 U SOC
££ £22 per round any day
⛳ ½ mile W of Sidmouth. 12 miles SE of M5 Junction 30
🏠 JH Taylor
▇ www.sidmouthgolfclub.co.uk

Sparkwell (1993)
Pay and play
Sparkwell, Plymouth, PL7 5DF
☎ **(01752) 837219**
🖰 (01752) 837219
🕮 108
🏌 G Adamson
✎ None
🏳 9 L 5772 yds SSS 68
👥 U SOC
££ 18 holes–£10 (£12) 9 holes–£6 (£7)
⛳ 8 miles NE of Plymouth. A38 Plympton Junction
⊕ 9 hole pitch & putt
🏠 J Gabb

Staddon Heights (1904)
Plymstock, Plymouth, PL9 9SP
☎ **(01752) 402475**
🖰 (01752) 401998
🕮 740
🏌 RW Brown
✎ I Marshall (01752) 492630
🏳 18 L 5845 yds SSS 70
👥 WE–H SOC–WD

££ D–£20 (D–£24)
⛳ SE Plymouth, via Plymstock

Tavistock (1890)
Down Road, Tavistock, PL19 9AQ
☎ **(01822) 612344**
🖰 (01822) 612344
🕮 700
🏌 MJ O'Dowd
✎ D Rehaag (01822) 612316
🏳 18 L 6250 yds SSS 70
👥 U SOC–WD
££ £24 (£30)
⛳ Whitchurch Down

Teign Valley (1995)
Christow, Exeter, EX6 7PA
☎ **(01647) 253026**
🖰 (01647) 253026
🖂 welcome@teignvalleygolf.co.uk
🕮 300
🏌 M Daniels (01647) 253026
✎ S Amiet (01647) 253127
🏳 18 L 5913 yds Par 70 SSS 68
👥 U SOC
££ £18.50 (£23)
⛳ SW of Exeter, via A38 (B3193)
🏠 Peter Nicholson

Teignmouth (1924)
Exeter Road, Teignmouth, TQ14 9NY
☎ **(01626) 777070**
🖰 (01626) 777304
🕮 900
🏌 W Hendry (01626) 777070
✎ P Ward, R Selley
🏳 18 L 6227 yds SSS 69
👥 WD–H (recognised club member) WE–by appointment SOC–WD
££ £27 (£29.50)
⛳ 2 miles N of Teignmouth on B3192
🏠 Dr A Mackenzie

Thurlestone (1897)
Thurlestone, Kingsbridge, TQ7 3NZ
☎ **(01548) 560405**
🖰 (01548) 562149
🕮 770
🏌 JR Scott (01548) 560405
✎ P Laugher (01548) 560715
🏳 18 L 6340 yds Par 71 SSS 70
👥 I or H
££ £32 W–£115
⛳ 5 miles W of Kingsbridge, off A379
🏠 HS Colt
▇ www.thurlestonegc.co.uk

Tiverton (1932)
Post Hill, Tiverton, EX16 4NE
☎ **(01884) 252114 (Clubhouse)**
🖰 (01884) 251607
🖂 tivertongolfclub@lineone.net
🕮 600 130(L) 45(J)
🏌 R Jessop (Sec/Mgr) (01884) 252187
✎ M Hawton (01884) 254836
🏳 18 L 6236 yds SSS 70
👥 H
££ On application

5 miles W of M5 Junction 27. 1¹/₂
miles E of Tiverton on B3391
Braid/Cotton

Torquay (1909)
Petitor Road, St Marychurch, Torquay,
TQ1 4QF
☎ (01803) 327471
🖫 (01803) 316116
📧 torquaygolfclub@skynow.net
📖 800
🏌 BG Long (01803) 314591
✒ M Ruth (01803) 329113
🏳 18 L 6198 yds Par 69 SSS 69
👫 H SOC
£€ £27.50 (£33)
🏵 2 miles N of Torquay
■ www.torquaygolfclub.org.uk

Torrington (1895)
Weare Trees, Torrington, EX38 7EZ
☎ (01805) 622229
🖫 (01805) 623878
📖 400
🏌 Mrs JM Cudmore
✒ None
🏳 9 L 4423 yds Par 64 SSS 62
👫 U exc Sun am–NA SOC–Tues/Wed
am
£€ D–£15
🏵 1 mile W of Torrington on Weare
Giffard road

Warren (1892)
Dawlish Warren, EX7 0NF
☎ (01626) 862255
🖫 (01626) 888005
📧 secretary@dwgc.co.uk
📖 600
🏌 T Aggett
✒ D Prowse (01626) 864002
🏳 18 L 5912 yds Par 69 SSS 68
👫 H SOC–Mon/Wed/Fri
£€ £25 (£28)
🏵 1¹/₂ miles E of Dawlish. M5
Junction 30
🏛 James Braid
■ www.dwgc.co.uk

Waterbridge (1992)
Pay and play
Down St Mary, Crediton, EX17 5LG
☎ (01363) 85111
🏌 G & A Wren (Props)
✒ D Ridyard (01837) 83406
🏳 9 L 1955 yds Par 32
👫 U
£€ 18 holes–£11.50 (£13.50)
9 holes–£7 (£8)
🏵 1 mile N of Copplestone on A337
🏛 David Taylor
■ www.waterbridge.business.co.uk

Willingcott Valley
Willingcott, Woolacombe, EX34 7HN
☎ (01271) 870173
🖫 (01271) 870800
📧 golf@willingcott.co.uk
📖 223

🏌 Andy Hodge (Mgr)
(01271) 870173
✒ David Elliott (01271) 8837801
Mobile: (07774) 211740
🏳 18 L 6205 SSS 70 Par 71 (White
tees)
18 L 5795 SSS 68 Par 71 (Yellow
tees)
18 L 5273 SSS 71 Par 72 (Red tees)
👫 U SOC
£€ £16 (£20)
🏵 Near Barnstaple, 45 min from M5
Junction 27
⊕ Practice facilities available
🏛 Hawtree (1st 9), Peter Lang (2nd 9)
■ www.willingcott.co.uk

Woodbury Park (1992)
Woodbury Castle, Woodbury, EX5 1JJ
☎ (01395) 233500
🖫 (01395) 233384
📖 720
🏌 A Richards (Mgr)
✒ A Richards
🏳 18 L 6870 yds SSS 73
9 L 4582 yds SSS 62
👫 U H
£€ 18 hole:£35 (£45) 9 hole:£11 (£12)
🏵 10 miles E of Exeter on A3052. M5
Junction 30, 6 miles
⊕ Driving range
🏛 J Hamilton Stutt

Wrangaton (1895)
Golf Links Road, Wrangaton, South
Brent, TQ10 9HJ
☎ (01364) 73229
🖫 (01364) 73229
📖 660
🏌 G Williams (01364) 73229
✒ G Richards (01364) 72161
🏳 18 L 6063 yds Par 70 SSS 69
👫 U SOC
£€ £20
🏵 Off A38 between South Brent and
Ivybridge
🏛 Donald Steel

Yelverton (1904)
Golf Links Road, Yelverton, PL20 6BN
☎ (01822) 852824
🖫 (01822) 854869
📧 secretary@yelvertongc.co.uk
📖 600
🏌 SM Barnes (01822) 852824
✒ T McSherry (01822) 853593
🏳 18 L 6353 yds Par 71 SSS 71
👫 H SOC
£€ D–£30 (£40)
🏵 6 miles N of Plymouth on A386
🏛 Herbert Fowler

Dorset

The Ashley Wood (1896)
Wimborne Road, Blandford Forum,
DT11 9HN
☎ (01258) 452253
🖫 (01258) 450590

📧 ashleywoodgolfclub@hotmail.com
📖 600
🏌 P Bodle
✒ J Shimmons
🏳 18 L 6270 yds Par 70 SSS 70
👫 WD after 10am WE–H after 1pm
£€ Phone in advance
🏵 1¹/₂ miles SE of Blandford on
B3082
🏛 Patrick Tallack

Bridport & West Dorset (1891)
Burton Road, Bridport, DT6 4PS
☎ (01308) 421095/422597
(Clubhouse)
🖫 (01308) 421095
📧 b_wdgc@btinternet.com
📖 600
🏌 PJ Ridler (01308) 421095
✒ D Parsons (01308) 421491
🏳 18 L 5729 yds Par 70 SSS 67
👫 WD/Sat–U after 9.30am Sun–U
after 1pm SOC
£€ £22. Afternoon–£16
🏵 1 mile E of A35 Bridport by-pass
on B3157
⊕ Driving range. 9 hole pitch & putt
course (Summer).
🏛 F Hawtree
■ www.bridportgolfclub.org.uk

Broadstone (Dorset) (1898)
Wentworth Drive, Broadstone,
BH18 8DQ
☎ (01202) 692595
🖫 (01202) 642520
📧 admin@broadstonegolfclub.com
📖 650
🏌 C Robinson (01202) 642521
✒ N Tokely (01202) 692835
🏳 18 L 6315 yds SSS 70
👫 WD–H from 9.30–11.30am and
2–4pm WE/BH–restricted
SOC–WD
£€ £40 (£55)
🏵 4 miles N of Poole, off A349
⊕ Incorporates The Dorset Golf Club
🏛 Dunn(1898)/Colt(1920)
■ www.broadstonegolfclub.com

Bulbury Woods (1989)
Bulbury Lane, Lytchett Minster, Poole,
BH16 6EP
☎ (01929) 459574
🖫 (01929) 459000
📧 enquiries@bulbury-woods.co.uk
📖 400
✒ D Adams
🏳 18 L 6002 yds Par 71 SSS 69
👫 U SOC–WD
£€ £16 (£21)
🏵 3 miles NW of Poole, off A35
■ www.bulbury-woods.co.uk

Came Down (1896)
Came Down, Dorchester, DT2 8NR
☎ (01305) 813494
🖫 (01305) 813494
📧 golf@camedowngolfclub.co.uk
📖 700

🏊 Mike Varney (Mgr)
  (01305) 813494
✓ N Rodgers (01305) 812670
▷ 18 L 6244 yds SSS 71 Par 70
🏌 U Sun am–NA SOC
££ £24 (£28)
🚗 2 miles S of Dorchester on A354
🏠 Harry S Colt
■ www.camedowngolfclub.co.uk

Canford Magna
Knighton Lane, Wimborne, BH21 3AS
☎ **(01202) 592552**
🖶 (01202) 592550
📖 1000
🏊 T Smith (Mgr) (01202) 592505
✓ M Cummins (01202) 591212
▷ Parkland 18 L 6495 yds Par 71
  SSS 71
  Riverside 18 L 6214 yds Par 70
  SSS 70
  Knighton 9 L 1377 yds Par 27
🏌 U
££ £7–£25
🚗 2 miles E of Wimborne on A341
⊕ Driving range. Golf Academy. 6
  holes pitch & putt course
🏠 Swan/Smith
■ www.canfordmagnagc.co.uk

Canford School
Canford School, Wimborne, BH21 3AD
☎ **(01202) 841254**
🖶 (01202) 881009
✉ msb@canford.com
📖 360
🏊 M Burley (Mgr)
▷ 9 L 5918 yds SSS 68
🏌 M SOC
££ £12
🚗 1 mile SE of Wimborne, off A341
🏠 P Boult

Charminster   (1998)
Proprietary
*Wolfedale Golf Course, Charminster,
Dorchester, DT2 7SG*
☎ **(01305) 260186**
🖶 (01305) 261376
📖 140
🏊 D Cox (Prop/Mgr) (01305) 260186
✓ T Lovegrove (01305) 260186
▷ 18 L 5467 yds Par 69 SSS 67
🏌 U
££ £11 (£11)
🚗 2 miles N of Dorchester

Chedington Court   (1991)
South Perrott, Beaminster, DT8 3HU
☎ **(01935) 891413**
🖶 (01935) 891217
📖 450
🏊 Ray Gudge (Gen Mgr)
✓ J lawrence
▷ 18 L 5950 yds SSS 70
🏌 U SOC
££ £18 (£22)
🚗 4 miles SE of Crewkerne on A356
⊕ 15 acre practice field; driving range
  planned
🏠 Chapman/Hemstock/Steel

Christchurch   (1977)
Pay and play
*Riverside Avenue, Bournemouth,
BH7 7ES*
☎ **(01202) 436436 (Bookings)**
📖 231
🏊 ME Harvey (01202) 436412
✓ L Moxon
▷ 18 L 6277 yds course
  9 hole short course
🏌 U SOC
££ 18 hole:£14.50 (£17.50) 9 hole:£10
  (£12)
🚗 Bournemouth/Christchurch
  boundary
⊕ Driving range

Crane Valley   (1992)
The Clubhouse, Verwood, BH31 7LE
☎ **(01202) 814088**
🖶 (01202) 813407
📖 600
🏊 D Ranson (Gen Mgr)
✓ D Ranson
▷ 18 L 6421 yds Par 72 SSS 71
  9 L 2030 yds Par 33 SSS 60
🏌 H SOC 9 hole–U
££ 18 hole: £25 (£35)
  9 hole: £5.50 (£6.50)
🚗 Nr Ringwood, on B3081 Verwood-
  Cranborne road
⊕ Floodlit driving range
🏠 Donald Steel

The Dorset G&CC   (1978)
Bere Regis, Wareham, BH20 7NT
☎ **(01929) 472244**
🖶 (01929) 471294
📖 850
🏊 G Packer (Gen Mgr)
✓ D Honan (Golf Dir)
▷ Lakeland 18 L 7027 yds SSS 72;
  Woodland 18 L 4887 yds SSS 64
🏌 U SOC
££ Lakeland–£33 (£38)
  Woodland–£23 (£26)
🚗 5 miles S of Bere Regis, off Wool
  road
⊕ Driving range, hotel
🏠 Martin Hawtree
■ www.dorsetgolfresort.com

Dudsbury   (1992)
Proprietary
*64 Christchurch Road, Ferndown,
BH22 8ST*
☎ **(01202) 593499**
🖶 (01202) 594555
✉ golf@dudsbury.demon.co.uk
🏊 GH Legg
✓ K Spurgeon (01202) 594488
▷ 18 L 6903 yds Par 71 SSS 73
🏌 U
££ £35 (£40)
🚗 3 miles N of Bournemouth (B3073)
⊕ Driving range. Academy course
🏠 Donald Steel
■ www.thedudsbury.co.uk

Ferndown   (1923)
*119 Golf Links Road, Ferndown,
BH22 8BU*
☎ **(01202) 874602**
🖶 (01202) 873926
📖 700
🏊 MC Davies (Mgr) (01202) 874602
✓ (01202) 873825
▷ 18 L 6452 yds SSS 71
  9 L 5604 yds SSS 68
🏌 WD–I H after 9.30am SOC–Tues &
  Fri
££ Old £45 (£60) President's £18
  (£20)
🚗 6 miles N of Bournemouth
🏠 Harold Hilton

Ferndown Forest   (1993)
*Forest Links Road, Ferndown,
BH22 9QE*
☎ **(01202) 876096**
🖶 (01202) 894095
📖 400
🏊 M Dodd
✓ M Dodd (01202) 894990
▷ 18 L 5200 yds Par 68 SSS 66
🏌 U SOC
££ £12 (£14)
🚗 5 miles N of Bournemouth. N of
  Ferndown Bypass
⊕ Floodlit driving range
🏠 Hunt/Grafham
■ www.ferndownforestgolf.co.uk

Halstock   (1988)
Pay and play
Common Lane, Halstock, BA22 9SF
☎ **(01935) 891689**
🖶 (01935) 891839
📖 200
🏊 LR Church (Mgr)
▷ 18 L 4481 yds Par 66 SSS 63
🏌 U SOC
££ £12 (£14)
🚗 6 miles S of Yeovil, off A37
⊕ Driving range

Highcliffe Castle   (1913)
*107 Lymington Road, Highcliffe-on-Sea,
Christchurch, BH23 4LA*
☎ **(01425) 272210/272953**
🖶 (01425) 272210
📖 350 100(L) 50(J)
🏊 G Fisher (01425) 272210
▷ 18 L 4776 yds Par 64 SSS 63
🏌 H SOC
££ £25.50 (£35.50)
🚗 8 miles E of Bournemouth

Isle of Purbeck   (1892)
Studland, BH19 3AB
☎ **(01929) 450361**
🖶 (01929) 450501
✉ bookings@purbeckgolf.co.uk
📖 400
🏊 Mrs J Robinson (Man Dir)
✓ I Brake (01929) 450354
▷ 18 L 6295 yds SSS 70
  9 L 2007 yds SSS 30
🏌 U SOC
££ £35 D–£45 (£40 D–£47.50)

🏌 3 miles N of Swanage on B3351.
Ferry from Sandbanks to Studland
🏠 HS Colt
⬛ www.purbeckgolf.co.uk

Knighton Heath   (1976)
Francis Avenue, West Howe,
Bournemouth, BH11 8NX
☎ **(01202) 572633**
🖳 (01202) 590774
📧 khgc@btinternet.com
📖 700
🏌 R Bestwick
⚲ P Brown (01202) 578275
🏴 18 L 6065 yds SSS 69
👥 WD–H after 9.30am WE–M
£€ On application
🏌 3 miles N of Poole, at junction of
A348/A3049

Lyme Regis   (1893)
Timber Hill, Lyme Regis, DT7 3HQ
☎ **(01297) 442963**
📧 secretarylymeregisgolfclub
@hotmail.co.uk
📖 750
🏌 S Wright (01297) 442963
⚲ D Driver (01297) 443822
🏴 18 L 6283 yds SSS 70
👥 H WD–U after 9.30am (2.30pm
Thurs) Sun–U after noon SOC
£€ £35 all day £30 am £25 after
2 pm
🏌 Between Lyme Regis and
Charmouth, off A3502/A35
⬛ www.lymeregisgolfclub.co.uk

Lyons Gate   (1991)
Proprietary
Lyons Gate Farm, Lyons Gate,
Dorchester, DT2 7AZ
☎ **(01300) 345239**
📖 80
🏌 NW Pires (01300) 345239
🏴 9 L 3834 yds Par 60 SSS 60
👥 U SOC
£€ 18 holes–£10 (£11)
9 holes–£6 (£7)
🏌 Middle Marsh, 12 miles N of
Dorchester (A352)
🏠 Ken Abel
⬛ www.lyonsgategolfclub.co.uk

Meyrick Park   (1890)
Pay and play
Central Drive, Meyrick Park,
Bournemouth, BH2 6LH
☎ **(01202) 786000,**
(01202) 786040 (Bookings)
📧 meyrickpark.lodge@clubhaus.com
📖 400
⚲ D Miles
🏴 18 L 5637 yds Par 69
👥 U
£€ £17 (£20)
🏌 ½ mile behind Town Hall,
Bournemouth
🏠 Dunn(1894)/Colt(1925)
⬛ www.clubhaus.com

Moors Valley   (1988)
Public
Horton Road, Ringwood, BH24 2ET
☎ **(01425) 480448**
🖳 (01425) 480799
📖 310
🏌 M Dean
⚲ M Torrens (01425) 479776
🏴 18 L 6270 yds SSS 70
4-hole short course
👥 U
£€ On application
🏌 4 miles SW of Ringwood, off A31
🏠 Martin Hawtree

Parkstone   (1910)
Links Road, Parkstone, Poole,
BH14 9QS
☎ **(01202) 707138**
🖳 (01202) 706027
📖 500 160(L) 75(J)
🏌 Christine Radford (Gen Mgr)
(01202) 707138
⚲ M Thompson (01202) 708092
🏴 18 L 6250 yds SSS 70
👥 H WD–NA before 9.38am and
12.30–2.10pm WE–NA before
9.45am and 12.30–2.30pm
£€ £40 D–£60 (£50 D–£70)
🏌 3 miles W of Bournemouth, off
A35
⊕ Practice range
🏠 W Park Jr/Braid

Parley Court
Proprietary
Parley Green Lane, Hurn, Christchurch,
BH23 6BB
☎ **(01202) 591600**
📧 info@parleygolf.co.uk
📖 200
🏌 Mrs SD Mitchell
🏴 9 L 2469 yds SSS 64
👥 U SOC
£€ 18 holes–£9 (£10). 9 holes–£6.50
(£7.50)
🏌 Nr Bournemouth Airport (B3073)
⬛ www.parleygolf.co.uk

Queens Park (Bournemouth)
(1905)
Public
Queens Park West Drive, Queens Park,
Bournemouth, BH8 9BY
☎ **(01202) 302611,**
(01202) 396198 (Bookings)
🖳 (01202) 302611
📧 dgibb@qbbgc.fsnet.co.uk
📖 350
🏌 R Polden (01202) 302611
⚲ R Hill (01202) 396817
🏴 18 L 6090 yds SSS 69
👥 U SOC
£€ £17 (£20)
🏌 2 miles NE of Bournemouth

Riversmeet Par Three
Stony Lane South, Christchurch,
BH23 1HW
☎ **(01202) 477987**

🖳 (01202) 470853
📖 250
🏌 N Williams
🏴 18 L 1650 yds Par 54
👥 U
£€ On application
🏌 2 miles W of Bournemouth

Sherborne   (1894)
Higher Clatcombe, Sherborne, DT9 4RN
☎ **(01935) 812274**
🖳 (01935) 814218
📖 700
🏌 P Gamble (01935) 814431
⚲ A Tresidder (01935) 812274
🏴 18 L 6415 yds Par 72 SSS 71
👥 H
£€ £25 (£36)
🏌 1 mile N of Sherborne, off B3145
🏠 James Braid

Solent Meads Par Three
Public
Rolls Drive, Southbourne, Bournemouth,
BA6 4NA
☎ **(01202) 420795**
📧 solentmeads@aol.com
🏌 Matt Steward (01202) 420795
⚲ Roddy Watkins (01202) 420795
🏴 18 L 2325 yds Par 54
👥 U
£€ £7.20
🏌 Hengistbury Head, S of
Christchurch
⊕ Driving range, 9 hole pitch and putt
course
⬛ www.solentmeads.co.uk

Sturminster Marshall
(1992)
Moor Lane, Sturminster Marshall,
BH21 4AH
☎ **(01258) 858444**
🖳 (01258) 858262
📖 490
🏌 DR Holdsworth
⚲ G Howell
🏴 9 L 5026 yds SSS 65
👥 U SOC
£€ 18 holes–£11. 9 holes–£8
🏌 8 miles N of Poole on A350
🏠 John Sharkey

Wareham   (1908)
Sandford Road, Wareham, BH20 4DH
☎ **(01929) 554147/557995**
🖳 (01929) 557993
📖 550
🏌 Peter McMullen
🏴 18 L 5753 yds SSS 68
👥 WD–after 9.30am WE–after 1pm
SOC–WD
£€ £22 D–£30 (£25)
🏌 N of Wareham on A351
🏠 C Whitcombe
⬛ www.warehamgolfclub.com

Weymouth   (1909)
Links Road, Weymouth, DT4 0PF
☎ **(01305) 773981**

☎ (01305) 788029
✉ weymouthgolfclub@aol.com
🏛 750
♣ BR Chatham
✓ D Lochrie (01305) 773997
▷ 18 L 5981 yds Par 70 SSS 69
♟ H SOC–WD
££ £24 (£30)
⛳ 1 mile from town centre (A354), off Manor roundabout
🏠 Braid/Hamilton Stutt
▪ www.weymouthgolfclub.co.uk

Durham

Barnard Castle (1898)
Harmire Road, Barnard Castle, DL12 8QN
☎ **(01833) 638355**
🖥 (01833) 695551
🏛 700
♣ J Kilgarriff
✓ D Pearce (01833) 631980
▷ 18 L 6406 yds SSS 71
♟ U SOC
££ £20 D–£26 (£27 D–£32)
⛳ N boundary of Barnard Castle on B6278
▪ www.barnardcastlegolfclub.org.uk

Beamish Park (1950)
Beamish, Stanley, DH9 0RH
☎ **(0191) 370 1382**
🖥 (0191) 370 2937
🏛 560
♣ G Cushlow (0191) 370 1382
✓ C Cole (0191) 370 1984
▷ 18 L 6205 yds SSS 70
♟ WD/Sat–U before 4pm Sun–NA SOC
££ £16 (£24)
⛳ Beamish, nr Stanley
🏠 Henry Cotton

Billingham (1967)
Sandy Lane, Billingham, TS22 5NA
☎ **(01642) 554494/533816**
🖥 (01642) 533816
✉ billingham@onetel.net.uk
🏛 850
♣ Peter B Hodgson (Sec/Mgr) (01642) 533816
✓ M Ure (01642) 557060
▷ 18 L 6333 yds SSS 70
♟ WD–H after 9am WE/BH–H after 10am SOC
££ D–£25 Reduction for parties
⛳ W boundary of Billingham by A19, E of bypass
🏠 Frank Pennink
▪ www.billinghamgolfclub.com

Bishop Auckland (1894)
High Plains, Durham Road, Bishop Auckland, DL14 8DL
☎ **(01388) 661618**
🖥 (01388) 607005
✉ enquiries@bagc.co.uk
🏛 860

♣ A Milne (01388) 661618
✓ D Skiffington (01388) 661618
▷ 18 L 6420 yds SSS 70
♟ H (closed Good Friday and Christmas Day)
££ £24 D–£30 (£30)
⛳ ¹/₂ mile NE of Bishop Auckland
🏠 James Kay
▪ www.bagc.co.uk

Blackwell Grange (1930)
Briar Close, Blackwell, Darlington, DL3 8QX
☎ **(01325) 464464**
🖥 (01325) 464458
✉ secretary@blackwellgrangegolf.com
🏛 700
♣ PB Burkill (Hon) (01325) 464458
✓ J Furby (01325) 462088
▷ 18 L 5621 yds Par 68 SSS 67
♟ U exc Wed 11am–2.30pm–NA Sat–booking req Sun–restricted SOC
££ £20 D–£25 (£30)
⛳ 1 mile S of Darlington on A66
🏠 Frank Pennink

Brancepeth Castle (1924)
The Clubhouse, Brancepeth Village, Durham, DH7 8EA
☎ **(0191) 378 0075**
🖥 (0191) 378 3835
🏛 768 68(L) 100(J)
♣ B Cullen
✓ D Howdon (0191) 378 0183
▷ 18 L 6400 yds SSS 70
♟ SOC–WD WE–by arrangement
££ £30 (£40) Society discounts
⛳ 4 miles W of Durham on A690
⊕ Practice area
🏠 HS Colt
▪ www.brancepeth-castle-golf.co.uk

Castle Eden & Peterlee (1927)
Castle Eden, Hartlepool, TS27 4SS
☎ **(01429) 836220**
🏛 650
♣ D Livingston (01429) 836510
✓ P Jackson (01429) 836689
▷ 18 L 6262 yds SSS 70
♟ U
££ £24 (£34)
⛳ 2 miles S of Peterlee
🏠 Henry Cotton
▪ www.ceden-golf.co.uk

Chester-Le-Street (1908)
Lumley Park, Chester-Le-Street, DH3 4NS
☎ **(0191) 388 3218**
🖥 (0191) 388 1220
🏛 435 130(L) 90(J)
♣ B Forster
✓ D Fletcher (0191) 389 0157
▷ 18 L 6437 yds SSS 71
♟ WD–H after 9.30am –NA 12–1pm WE–NA before 10.30am or 12–2pm
££ £22 (£27.50)

⛳ E of Chester-Le-Street
🏠 JH Taylor

Consett & District (1911)
Elmfield Road, Consett, DH8 5NN
☎ **(01207) 502186**
🖥 (01207) 505060
🏛 650
♣ IB Murray (01207) 529324
✓ J Ord (01207) 580210
▷ 18 L 6020 yds SSS 69
♟ WD–U SOC–exc Sat
££ £18 (£26)
⛳ 14 miles N of Durham on A691
🏠 Harry Vardon

Crook (1919)
Low Job's Hill, Crook, DL15 9AA
☎ **(01388) 762429/767926**
🏛 450
♣ JW Laing
✓ C Dilley (01388) 768145
▷ 18 L 6102 yds SSS 69
♟ U SOC
££ From £12
⛳ ¹/₂ mile E of Crook (A689)

Darlington (1908)
Haughton Grange, Darlington, DL1 3JD
☎ **(01325) 355324**
🖥 (01325) 488126
✉ darlington.golfclub@virgin.net
🏛 825
♣ GW Storey (Fax 01325 – 480668)
✓ C Dilley (01325) 484198
▷ 18 L 6181 yds Par 70 SSS 69
♟ WD–U from 10am–12 & 2–4pm WE–M
££ £25 D–£31
⛳ Off Salters Lane, NE of Darlington (A1150)
🏠 Dr Alistair Mackenzie

Dinsdale Spa (1906)
Middleton St George, Darlington, DL2 1DW
☎ **(01325) 332222**
🖥 (01325) 332222
🏛 875
♣ EP Davison (01325) 332297
✓ N Metcalfe (01325) 332515
▷ 18 L 6090 yds Par 71 SSS 69
♟ WD–U exc Tues–NA WE–M
££ D–£25
⛳ 5 miles SE of Darlington

Durham City (1887)
Littleburn, Langley Moor, Durham, DH7 8HL
☎ **(0191) 378 0069**
🖥 (0191) 378 4265
🏛 750
♣ LTI Wilson (0191) 386 4434
✓ S Corbally (0191) 378 0029
▷ 18 L 6326 yds SSS 70
♟ WD–U SOC
££ £24 (£30)
⛳ 1¹/₂ miles W of Durham, off A690
🏠 CC Stanton

Eaglescliffe (1914)

Yarm Road, Eaglescliffe, Stockton-on-Tees, TS16 0DQ
- ☎ **(01642) 780098 (Clubhouse)**
- ✉ egcsec@lineone.net
- 📖 835
- 🏌 MR Sample (01642) 780238
- ⚲ G Bell (01642) 790122
- ▷ 18 L 6275 yds SSS 70
- 👥 U SOC
- £€ £27 D–£37 (£36 D–£50)
- ⚘ 3 miles S of Stockton-on-Tees on A135
- 🏠 Braid/Cotton
- ■ www.eaglescliffegolfclub.co.uk

Hartlepool (1906)

Hart Warren, Hartlepool, TS24 9QF
- ☎ **(01429) 274398**
- 📠 (01429) 274129
- 📖 700
- 🏌 LG Gordon (01429) 261723
- ⚲ G Laidlaw (01429) 267473
- ▷ 18 L 6255 yds SSS 70
- 👥 WD–U SOC
- £€ £26 (£38)
- ⚘ N boundary of Hartlepool
- ■ www.hartlepoolgolfclub.co.uk

High Throston (1997)

Hart Lane, Hartlepool, TS26 0UG
- ☎ **(01429) 275325**
- 📖 240
- 🏌 Mrs J Sturrock (01429) 268071
- ⚲ None
- ▷ 18 L 6247 yds Par 71 SSS 70
- 👥 U SOC
- £€ £16 (£19)
- ⚘ 2 miles NW of Hartlepool (A179)
- 🏠 Jonathan Gaunt

Hobson (1978)

Hobson, Burnopfield, Newcastle-upon-Tyne, NE16 6BZ
- ☎ **(01207) 271605**
- 🏌 RJ Handrick (01207) 270941
- ⚲ J Ord
- ▷ 18 L 6403 yds SSS 71
- 👥 U SOC
- £€ £15 (£18)
- ⚘ Between Gateshead and Consett on A692

Knotty Hill Golf Centre

(1992)
Pay and play
Sedgefield, Stockton-on-Tees, TS21 2BB
- ☎ **(01740) 620320**
- 📠 (01740) 622227
- ✉ khgc21@btinternet.com
- 🏌 D Craggs (Mgr)
- ▷ Princes 18 L 6577 yds Par 72 SSS 71
  Bishops 18 L 5886 yds Par 70
- 👥 U SOC
- £€ £12 (£13)
- ⚘ 1 mile N of Sedgefield on A177. A1(M) Junction 60, 2 miles
- ⊕ Floodlit driving range
- 🏠 Chris Stanton

Mount Oswald (1924)

South Road, Durham City, DH1 3TQ
- ☎ **(0191) 386 7527**
- 📠 (0191) 386 0975
- ✉ info@mountoswald.co.uk
- 📖 200
- 🏌 N Galvin
- ▷ 18 L 5984 yds SSS 69
- 👥 U SOC
- £€ £12.50 D–£22 (£15 D–£25)
- ⚘ SW of Durham on A177
- ■ www.mountoswald.co.uk

Norton (1989)

Pay and play
Junction Road, Norton, Stockton-on-Tees, TS20 1SU
- ☎ **(01642) 676385**
- 📠 (01642) 608467
- ▷ 18 L 5870 yds SSS 71
- 👥 U SOC
- £€ £11.50 (£13.50)
- ⚘ 1 mile E of A177 on B1274
- 🏠 Tim Harper

Oakleaf Golf Complex

(1993)
Pay and play
School Aycliffe Lane, Newton Aycliffe, DL5 6QZ
- ☎ **(01325) 310820**
- 📠 (01325) 300873
- 🏌 A Bailey (Mgr) (01325) 300700
- ⚲ A Waites
- ▷ 18 L 5821 yds SSS 68
- 👥 WD–U WE–booking necessary
- £€ £7.80 (£8.85)
- ⚘ 1 mile W of Aycliffe on A6072, from A68
- ⊕ Floodlit driving range

Ramside (1995)

Ramside Hall Hotel, Carrville, Durham, DH1 1TD
- ☎ **(0191) 386 9514**
- 📠 (0191) 386 9519
- 📖 400
- 🏌 MJ Davis
- ⚲ R Lister (0191) 386 9514
- ▷ 27 holes:
  6217-6851 yds SSS 70-73
- 👥 U SOC Soft spikes only
- £€ £30 (£37)
- ⚘ 2 miles NE of Durham on A690. A1(M) Junction 62
- ⊕ Driving range. Golf Academy
- 🏠 J Gaunt

Roseberry Grange (1986)

Public
Grange Villa, Chester-Le-Street, DH2 3NF
- ☎ **(0191) 370 0670**
- 📠 (0191) 370 2047
- 📖 500
- 🏌 R McDermott (Hon)
- ⚲ C Jones (0191) 370 0660
- ▷ 18 L 5892 yds SSS 68
- 👥 U SOC
- £€ £12 (£15)

- ⚘ 3 miles W of Chester-Le-Street on A693
- ⊕ Driving range

Ryhope (1992)

Public
Leechmere Way, Hollycarrside, Ryhope, Sunderland SR2 0DH
- ☎ **(0191) 523 7333**
- 📠 (0191) 521 3811
- 📖 300
- 🏌 A Brown
- ⚲ None
- ▷ 18 L 4601 yds SSS 65
- 👥 U
- £€ £6 (£6)
- ⚘ 2 miles SW of Sunderland, off A1018
- 🏠 Jonathan Gaunt

Seaham (1911)

Shrewsbury Street, Dawdon, Seaham, SR7 7RD
- ☎ **(0191) 581 2354**
- 📖 550
- 🏌 V Smith (0191) 581 1268
- ⚲ G Jones (0191) 513 0837
- ▷ 18 L 5972 yds SSS 69
- 👥 U SOC
- £€ On application
- ⚘ Dawdon, 2 miles NE of A19

Seaton Carew (1874)

Tees Road, Hartlepool, TS25 1DE
- ☎ **(01429) 266249/261040**
- 📖 650
- 🏌 J Hall (01429) 296496
- ⚲ M Rogers (01429) 890660
- ▷ Old 18 L 6613 yds SSS 72
  Brabazon 18 L 6855 yds SSS 73
- 👥 U SOC
- £€ On application
- ⚘ Hartlepool 2 miles
- 🏠 Dr A Mackenzie
- ■ www.seatoncarewgolfclub.org.uk

South Moor (1923)

The Middles, Craghead, Stanley, DH9 6AG
- ☎ **(01207) 232848/283525**
- 📠 (01207) 284616
- ✉ bryandavison@southmoorgc.freeserve.co.uk
- 📖 520
- 🏌 B Davison (0191) 388 4523
- ⚲ S Cowell (01207) 283525
- ▷ 18 L 6271 yds Par 72 SSS 70
- 👥 WD WE/BH SOC–WD/Sat
- £€ £15 (£26)
- ⚘ 6 miles W of Chester-le-Street
- 🏠 Dr A Mackenzie
- ■ www.southmoorgolfclub.com

Stressholme (1976)

Public
Snipe Lane, Darlington, DL2 5SA
- ☎ **(01325) 461002**
- 📠 (01325) 461002
- 🏌 R Givens
- ⚲ R Givens
- ▷ 18 L 6511 yds SSS 71

For list of abbreviations and key to symbols see page 627

🖑 U
£€ On application
⊶ 2 miles S of Darlington on A66
⊕ Floodlit driving range

Woodham G&CC   (1983)
Proprietary
Burnhill Way, Newton Aycliffe, DL5 4PN
☎ (01325) 320574
🖥 (01325) 315254
📖 610
🏌 JD Jenkinson
⤸ Peter Kelly (01325) 315257
🏵 18 L 6688 yds Par 73 SSS 72
🖑 WD–SOC–U
£€ £18 (£29)
⊶ 1 mile N of Newton Aycliffe. 6 miles from A1 (A689)
🏠 J Hamilton Stutt

The Wynyard Club
Wellington Drive, Wynyard Park, Billingham, TS22 5QJ
☎ (01740) 644399
🖥 (01740) 644599
🏌 C Mounter (Golf Dir)
⤸ C Mounter
🏵 18 holes Par 72 SSS 73
🖑 M SOC–H
£€ On application
⊶ 5 miles E of Sedgefield, between A1 and A19
⊕ Floodlit driving range. Golf Academy
🏠 Hawtree

Essex

Abridge G&CC   (1964)
Epping Lane, Stapleford Tawney, RM4 1ST
☎ (01708) 688396
🖥 (01708) 688550
📧 info@abridgegolf.com
📖 650
🏌 Michael Gottlieb (01708) 688396
⤸ S Layton (01708) 688333
🏵 18 L 6703 yds SSS 72
🖑 WD–H WE/BH–NA
£€ £35 (£45)
⊶ Theydon Bois/Epping Stations 3 miles
⊕ Driving range & full practice facilities
🏠 Henry Cotton
■ www.abridgegolf.com

Ballards Gore G&CC
(1980)
Gore Road, Canewdon, Rochford, SS4 2DA
☎ (01702) 258917
🖥 (01702) 258571
📖 600
🏌 A Hall
⤸ R Emery
🏵 18 L 6874 yds SSS 73
🖑 WD–U WE–M after 12.30pm (summer) 11.30am (winter) SOC

£€ £30
⊶ 1½ miles NE of Rochford

Basildon   (1967)
Public
Clayhill Lane, Kingswood, Basildon, SS16 5JP
☎ (01268) 533297
🖥 (01268) 284163
📧 basildongc@onetel.net
📖 300
🏌 A Merrington
⤸ M Oliver (01268) 533532
🏵 18 L 6236 yds Par 72 SSS 70
🖑 U SOC
£€ £10.80 (£17.50)
⊶ 1 mile S of Basildon, off A176 at Kingswood roundabout
■ www.basgolfclub.fsnet.co.uk

Belfairs   (1926)
Public
Eastwood Road North, Leigh-on-Sea, SS9 4LR
☎ (01702) 525345 (Starter)
🏵 18 L 5802 yds SSS 68
🖑 WD–U exc Thurs am. Booking necessary
£€ £11 (£16)
⊶ Between A127 and A13

Belhus Park G&CC   (1972)
Pay and play
Belhus Park, South Ockendon, RM15 4QR
☎ (01708) 854260
📖 280
🏌 J Cleary
⤸ G Lunn
🏵 18 L 5188 yds SSS 68
🖑 U
£€ £10 (£15)
⊶ 1 mile N of A13/M25 Dartford Tunnel
⊕ Floodlit driving range; leisure centre

Bentley G&CC   (1972)
Ongar Road, Brentwood, CM15 9SS
☎ (01277) 373179
🖥 (01277) 375097
📖 550
🏌 JA Vivers
⤸ N Garrett (01277) 372933
🏵 18 L 6709 yds SSS 72
🖑 WD–UH WE–M afternoon BH–after 11am SOC–WD
£€ £22 D–£30
⊶ 18 miles E of London. M25 Junction 28, 3 miles

Benton Hall   (1993)
Wickham Hill, Witham, CM8 3LH
☎ (01376) 502454
🖥 (01376) 521050
📧 g.barre@clubhaus.com
🏌 D Reeves
⤸ C Fairweather
🏵 18 L 6570 yds SSS 72
9 hole Par 3 course
🖑 U SOC–WD

£€ £20–£30
⊶ Witham, 8 miles NE of Chelmsford, off A12
⊕ Driving range
🏠 Walker/Cox
■ www.clubhaus.com

Birch Grove   (1970)
Layer Road, Colchester, CO2 0HS
☎ (01206) 734276
🖥 (01206) 734276
📖 280
🏌 Mrs M Marston
🏵 9 L 4532 yds SSS 63
🖑 U exc Sun–U after 1pm SOC
£€ D–£12
⊶ 3 miles S of Colchester on B1026

Boyce Hill   (1921)
Vicarage Hill, Benfleet, SS7 1PD
☎ (01268) 793625
🖥 (01268) 750497
📧 secretary@boycehillgolfclub.co.uk
📖 700
🏌 PD Keeble
⤸ G Burroughs (01268) 752565
🏵 18 L 6003 yds SSS 69
🖑 WD–UH WE/BH–MH SOC–Thurs only
£€ D–£25
⊶ 4 miles W of Southend
🏠 James Braid

Braintree   (1891)
Kings Lane, Stisted, Braintree, CM77 8DD
☎ (01376) 346079
🖥 (01376) 348677
📖 700
🏌 N Wells
⤸ T Parcell (01376) 343465
🏵 18 L 6228 yds SSS 70
🖑 WD–U H SOC
£€ £25 (£42)
⊶ 1 mile E of Braintree, off A120 towards Stisted
🏠 Hawtree

Braxted Park   (1953)
Braxted Park, Witham, CM8 3EN
☎ (01376) 572372
🖥 (01621) 892840
📖 100
🏌 Mrs V Keeble
⤸ J Hudson
🏵 9 L 5704 yds Par 70 SSS 68
🖑 WD–U SOC–WD
£€ 18 holes–£12.50 9 holes–£9.50
⊶ 1½ miles off A12, nr Kelvedon
🏠 Sir Allen Clark

Bunsay Downs   (1982)
Public
Little Baddow Road, Woodham Walter, Maldon, CM9 6RW
☎ (01245) 412648/412369
🏌 MFL Durham
⤸ H Roblin (01245) 222648
🏵 9 L 2913 yds SSS 68
9 hole Par 3 course
🖑 WD–U WE/BH–book in advance SOC–WD

££   On application
⊕   7 miles E of Chelmsford, off A414
⊕   Indoor driving range

Burnham-on-Crouch   (1923)
Ferry Road, Creeksea, Burnham-on-Crouch, CM0 8PQ
☎   (01621) 782282/785508
🖂   (01621) 784489
⊞   600
🏌   Mrs D Evers
✓   S Cardy (01621) 782282
▷   18 L 6056 yds SSS 69
🏌   WD–H
££   £26
⊕   1½ miles W of Burnham
⋔   D Swan

The Burstead   (1995)
Tye Common Road, Little Burstead, Billericay, CM12 9SS
☎   (01277) 631171
🖂   (01277) 632766
⊞   800
🏌   L Mence
✓   K Bridges
▷   18 L 6275 yds SSS 70
🏌   WD–U H WE–NA pm SOC
££   £25 (£30)
⊕   2 miles S of Billericay, off A176
⋔   Patrick Tallack

Canons Brook   (1962)
Elizabeth Way, Harlow, CM19 5BE
☎   (01279) 421482
🖂   (01279) 626393
⊞   700
🏌   Mrs SJ Langton
✓   A McGinn (01279) 418357
▷   18 L 6763 yds SSS 73
🏌   WD–U WE/BH–M
££   £25 D–30
⊕   25 miles N of London
⋔   Henry Cotton
■   www.canonsbrook.com

Castle Point   (1988)
Public
Waterside Farm, Somnes Avenue, Canvey Island, SS8 9FG
☎   (01268) 510830
⊞   240
🏌   Mrs J Worthington
✓   S Richardson
▷   18 L 6153 yds SSS 69
🏌   U SOC
££   £9 (£13)
⊕   On A130 to Canvey Island, off A13 Eastbound
⊕   Driving range
⋔   Golf Landscapes

Channels   (1974)
Belsteads Farm Lane, Little Waltham, Chelmsford, CM3 3PT
☎   (01245) 440005
🖂   (01245) 442032
🖂   info@channelsgolf.co.uk
⊞   650
🏌   AM Squire
✓   IB Sinclair (01245) 441056

▷   18 L 6402 yds Par 71 SSS 71
     18 L 4779 yds Par 67 SSS 63
🏌   WD–U WE–M SOC
££   £32 D–£45
⊕   3 miles NE of Chelmsford on A130
⊕   Pitch & putt course. Driving range
■   www.channelsgolf.co.uk

Chelmsford   (1893)
Widford Road, Chelmsford, CM2 9AP
☎   (01245) 256483
🖂   (01245) 256483
🖂   office@chelmsfordgc.co.uk
⊞   650
🏌   G Winckless (01245) 256483
✓   M Welch (01245) 257079
▷   18 L 5981 yds SSS 69
🏌   WD–H WE/BH–M SOC
££   £37 D–£47
⊕   Off A414 at Widford roundabout
⋔   HS Colt
■   www.chelmsfordgc.co.uk

Chigwell   (1925)
High Road, Chigwell, IG7 5BH
☎   (020) 8500 2059
🖂   (020) 8501 3410
⊞   780
🏌   RH Danzey
✓   R Beard (020) 8500 2384
▷   18 L 6279 yds SSS 70
🏌   WD–H WE/BH–M
££   £35 D–£45
⊕   13 miles NE of London (A113)
⋔   Hawtree/Taylor

Chingford   (1923)
158 Station Road, Chingford, London E4
☎   (0208) 529 2107
🏌   B Sinden
✓   A Trainor (0208) 529 5708
▷   18 L 6342 yds Par 71 SSS 70
🏌   U
££   £12 (£16)

Clacton-on-Sea   (1892)
West Road, Clacton-on-Sea, CO15 1AJ
☎   (01255) 421919
🖂   (01255) 424602
🖂   clactongolfclub@btclick.com
⊞   650
🏌   JH Wiggam (01255) 421919
✓   SJ Levermore (01255) 426304
▷   18 L 6532 yds SSS 71
🏌   H WE/BH–H after 11am SOC–WD
££   £20 (£30)
⊕   On Clacton sea front. 13 miles E of Colchester (A120)

Colchester GC   (1907)
21 Braiswick, Colchester, CO4 5AU
☎   (01206) 853396
🖂   (01206) 852698
🖂   colchester.golf@btinternet.com
⊞   756
🏌   WM Beckett
✓   M Angel (01206) 853920
▷   18 L 6347 yds SSS 70
🏌   WD/WE–H BH–NA SOC
££   £30 D–£40 (£40)

⊕   ¾ mile NW of Colchester North Station, towards West Berholt on B1508
⊕   Driving range
⋔   James Braid

Colne Valley   (1991)
Station Road, Earls Colne, CO6 2LT
☎   (01787) 224343
🖂   (01787) 224126
⊞   500
🏌   T Smith (01787) 224343
✓   P Garlick (01787) 220770
▷   18 L 6301 yds SSS 70
🏌   WD–U WE/BH–after 11am SOC
££   £25 (£30)
⊕   12 miles W of Colchester (A1124)
⋔   Howard Swann

Crondon Park   (1994)
Proprietary
Stock Road, Stock, CM4 9DP
☎   (01277) 841115
🖂   (01277) 841356
⊞   875
🏌   P Cranwell
✓   P Barham (01277) 841887
▷   18 L 6585 yds SSS 71
     9 hole course
🏌   WD–U WE–M SOC–WD
££   £20 (£30)
⊕   5 miles S of Chelmsford on B1007. M25 Junction 28
⊕   Driving range
⋔   Martin Gillett
■   www.crondon.com

Elsenham Golf Centre (1997)
Hall Road, Elsenham, Bishop's Stortford, CM22 6DH
☎   (01279) 812865
🖂   (01279) 816970
🖂   golfacad@compuserve.com
🏌   O McKenna (Prop)
✓   O McKenna
▷   9 L 5854 yds Par 70
🏌   U
££   9 holes–£12 (£14) 18 holes–£16 (£18)
⊕   Off M11, by Stansted Airport
⊕   Driving range
■   www.egcltd.co.uk

Essex G&CC   (1990)
Earls Colne, Colchester, CO6 2NS
☎   (01787) 224466
🖂   (01787) 224410
⊞   600
🏌   J Gathercole (Mgr)
✓   L Cocker
▷   18 L 7019 yds Par 73
     9 L 2190 yds Par 34
🏌   WD–U WE–U after 11am SOC
££   £25 (£30)
⊕   2 miles N of A120 at Coggeshall on B1024
⊕   Floodlit driving range.
⋔   Reg Plumbridge
■   www.clubhaus.com

Essex Golf Centres, Hainault Forest (1912)

Public
Romford Road, Chigwell Row, IG7 4QW
☎ (020) 8500 2131
   (Proshop/Reception)
✉ info@essexgolfcentre.com
▥ 630
♟ Ben Jones (020) 8500 2131
✓ CS Hope (0181) 500 2131
⊱ No 1 18 L 5754 yds SSS 67
   No 2 18 L 6600 yds SSS 71
♙ U
£€ From £16 (£21)
⌗ Hog Hill, Redbridge. M25/A12
⊕ 22 bay driving range
⌂ James Braid
■ www.essexgolfcentre.com

The Essex Golf Complex (1993)

Pay and play
Garon Park, Eastern Avenue, Southend-on-Sea, SS9 4PT
☎ (01702) 601701
▤ (01702) 601033
▥ 700
♟ Mrs J Jacom
✓ G Jacom
⊱ 18 L 6237 yds SSS 70
   9 hole Par 3 course
♙ U SOC
£€ £17 (£23)
⌗ E side of Southend-on-Sea. M25 Junction 29
⊕ Floodlit driving range
⌂ Walker/Cox

Fairlop Waters (1987)

Public
Forest Road, Barkingside, Ilford, IG6 3JA
☎ (020) 8500 9911
▥ 135
♟ L Quinn
✓ B Preston (0181) 501 1881
⊱ 18 L 6288 yds SSS 72
   9 hole Par 3 course
♙ U
£€ £7.50 (£11)
⌗ 2 miles from S end of M11, by Fairlop underground station
⊕ Driving range

Five Lakes Hotel G&CC (1974)

Colchester Road, Tolleshunt Knights, Maldon, CM9 8HX
☎ (01621) 868888 (Hotel),
   (01621) 862307 (Bookings)
▤ (01621) 869696
▥ 600
♟ N Popper
✓ G Carter (01621) 862326
⊱ Links 18 L 6250 yds SSS 70
   Lakes 18 L 6765 yds SSS 72
♙ U BH–U after 1pm SOC
£€ Links £22 (£28). Lakes £29 (£38)
⌗ 8 miles S of Colchester, off B1026
⊕ Driving range
⌂ Neil Coles

Forrester Park (1975)

Beckingham Road, Great Totham, Maldon, CM9 8EA
☎ (01621) 891406
▤ (01621) 891406
▥ 900
♟ T Forrester-Muir
✓ G Pike (01621) 893456
⊱ 18 L 6073 yds SSS 69
♙ WD–U WE–NA before noon SOC–WD
£€ £19 (£21)
⌗ 3 miles NE of Maldon on B1022
⌂ Everett/Forrester-Muir

Frinton (1895)

1 The Esplanade, Frinton-on-Sea, CO13 9EP
☎ (01255) 674618
▤ (01255) 682450
✉ frintongolf@lineone.net
▥ 850
♟ Lt Col RW Attrill
✓ P Taggart (01255) 671618
⊱ 18 L 6259 yds SSS 70
   9 L 2508 yds SSS 33
♙ 18 hole:H WE/BH–NA before 11.30am SOC
£€ 18 hole: D–£30. 9 hole: £10
⌗ 18 miles E of Colchester
⌂ W Park Jr/HS Colt
■ www.frintongolfclub.com

Gosfield Lake (1986)

The Manor House, Gosfield, Halstead, CO9 1SE
☎ (01787) 474747
▤ (01787) 476044
✉ gosfieldlakegc@btconnect.com
▥ 800
♟ JA O'Shea (Sec/Mgr)
✓ R Wheeler (01787) 474488
⊱ Lakes 18 L 6756 yds Par 72 SSS 72
   Meadows 9 L 4180 yds Par 66
♙ Lakes WD–H WE(pm)–H by arrangement SOC. Meadows–U
£€ Lakes £30 D–£35. Meadows £15 D–£18
⌗ 7 miles N of Braintree (A1017)
⌂ Sir H Cotton/Swann
■ www.gosfield-lake-golf-club.co.uk

Hanover G&CC (1991)

Owned privately
Hullbridge Road, Rayleigh, SS6 9QS
☎ (01702) 232377
▤ (01702) 231811
▥ 700
♟ T Harrold
✓ A Blackburn
⊱ Georgian 18 L 6669 yds SSS 73 Regency 18 L 3700 yds SSS 58
♙ Georgian:WD–H WE–M SOC Regency:U SOC
£€ Georgian £25 D–£35. Regency £12.50 (£15)
⌗ 3 miles NW of Southend
⌂ Reg Plumbridge

Hartswood (1967)

Pay and play
King George's Playing Fields, Brentwood, CM14 5AE
☎ (01277) 214830 (Bookings)
▥ 270
♟ D Mancey (01227) 218850
✓ S Cole (01277) 218714
⊱ 18 L 6192 yds SSS 70
♙ WD–U after 10am SOC
£€ £11 (£16)
⌗ E of Brentwood on A128

Harwich & Dovercourt (1906)

Station Road, Parkeston, Harwich, CO12 4NZ
☎ (01255) 503616
▤ (01255) 503323
▥ 400
♟ AR Boddy
✓ None
⊱ 9 L 2950 yds SSS 69
♙ WD–H WE–M SOC
£€ £20
⌗ A120 to roundabout to Parkstone Village & Golf Club (first exit)

Ilford (1907)

291 Wanstead Park Road, Ilford, IG1 3TR
☎ (020) 8554 2930
▤ (020) 8554 0822
▥ 500
♟ GH Smith
✓ S Dowsett (020) 8554 0094
⊱ 18 L 5299 yds SSS 66
♙ WD–U WE–phone Pro SOC
£€ £16 (£20)
⌗ S end of M11, off A406

Langdon Hills (1991)

Lower Dunton Road, Bulphan, RM14 3TY
☎ (01268) 548444/544300
▤ (01268) 490084
▥ 800
♟ B Hardie
✓ T Moncur (01268) 544300
⊱ 27 holes:
   Langdon 9 L 3111 yds Par 35
   Bulphan 9 L 3351 yds Par 37
   Horndon 9 L 3028 yds Par 36
♙ U SOC WD WE after 2.00
£€ £17.75 (£25)
⌗ SW of Basildon between A127 and A13. M25 Junction 29, 8 miles
⊕ Floodlit driving range
⌂ MRM Sandow

Lexden Wood (1993)

Pay and play
Bakers Lane, Colchester, CO3 4AU
☎ (01206) 843333
▤ (01206) 854775
▥ 850
♟ L Cole
✓ P Grice
⊱ 18 L 5160 yds Par 67 SSS 65
♙ U SOC

££ £20 (£24)
⊕ NW of Colchester, off A12
⊕ Driving range. Pitch & putt course
🏠 Jon Johnson

Loughton (1981)
Public
*Clays Lane, Debden Green, Loughton,
IG10 2RZ*
☎ (020) 8502 2923
📖 100
🗐 A Day
🏴 9 L 4735 yds SSS 63
👥 U–booking required SOC
££ 18 holes–£12 (£14) 9 holes–£7.50
(£8.50)
⊕ M25 Junction 26

Maldon (1891)
Beeleigh Langford, Maldon, CM9 6LL
☎ (01621) 853212
🖳 (01621) 855232
✉ maldon.golf@virgin.net
📖 380
🗐 D Kelly
🏴 9 L 6253 yds Par 71 SSS 70
👥 WD–U H WE–M SOC
££ £15 D–£20
⊕ 3 miles NW of Maldon on B1019

Maylands (1936)
Harold Park, Romford, RM3 0AZ
☎ (01708) 341777
🖳 (01708) 343777
📖 650
🗐 (01708) 341777
🗐 D Parker (017083) 46466
🏴 18 L 6361 yds SSS 70
👥 WD–H WE/BH–M SOC H
££ £25 (£40)
⊕ 2 miles E of Romford on A12. M25
Junction 28, half mile
🏠 HS Colt

Nazeing (1992)
Middle Street, Nazeing, EN9 2LW
☎ (01992) 893798/893915
🖳 (01992) 893882
📖 350
🗐 J Speller (01992) 893915
🗐 R Green (01992) 893798
🏴 18 L 6598 yds SSS 71
👥 WD–H WE/BH–H after 11am
SOC
££ £20 (£28)
⊕ 3 miles SW of Harlow. M11
Junction 7
⊕ Open air driving range
🏠 Martin Gillett

North Weald (1996)
*Rayley Lane, North Weald, Epping,
CM16 6AR*
☎ (01992) 522118
🖳 (01992) 522881
📖 500
🗐 PH Newson
🗐 D Rawlings (01992) 524725
🏴 18 L 6311 yds Par 71 SSS 70
👥 U SOC–WD
££ £20 (£27.50)

⊕ 1½ miles E of M11 J7 on A414
⊕ Driving range
🏠 David Williams

The Notleys (1995)
*The Green, Black Notley, Witham,
CM8 1RG*
☎ (01376) 329328
📖 300
🗐 R Mortier
🗐 D Bugg
🏴 18 L 6022 yds Par 71
9 hole Par 3 course
👥 U SOC
££ £12 (£17)
⊕ Black Notley, S of Braintree, off
A120
⊕ Driving range
🏠 John Day

Orsett (1899)
Brentwood Road, Orsett, RM16 3DS
☎ (01375) 891352
🖳 (01375) 892471
📖 700
🗐 (01375) 893409
🗐 P Joiner (01375) 891797
🏴 18 L 6614 yds SSS 72
👥 WD–H WE–M SOC–WD exc
Thurs & Fri
££ £35–£50
⊕ 4 miles NE of Grays on A128. M25
Junction 30/31
🏠 James Braid

The Priors (1992)
*Horseman's Side, Tysea Hill, Stapleford
Abbotts, RM4 1JU*
☎ (01708) 381108,
(01708) 373344 (Bookings)
🖳 (01708) 386345
🗐 D Eagle (Gen Mgr)
🗐 J Stanion
🏴 18 L 5720 yds SSS 68
👥 U SOC
££ £11–£15
⊕ 3 miles N of Romford. M25 J8
🏠 Howard Swann

Regiment Way Golf Centre (1995)
Pay and play
*Back Lane, Little Waltham, Chelmsford,
CM3 3PR*
☎ (01245) 361100
🖳 (01245) 442032
🗐 R Pamphilon
🗐 D Marsh
🏴 9 L 4887 yds Par 65 SSS 64
👥 U
££ 9 holes–£10 (£11) 18 holes–£14
(£16)
⊕ 3 miles NE of Chelmsford (A130)
⊕ Floodlit driving range
■ www.channelgolf.co.uk

Risebridge (1972)
Pay and play
*Risebridge Chase, Lower Bedfords Road,
Romford, RM1 4DG*
☎ (01708) 741429

📖 175
🗐 L Bushell
🗐 P Jennings (01708) 741429
🏴 18 L 6394 yds SSS 71
9 hole Par 3 course
👥 U
££ £13.50 (£15.50)
⊕ 2 miles from M25 Junction 28, off
A12
⊕ Driving range
🏠 F Hawtree

Rivenhall Oaks (1994)
Pay and play
Forest Road, Witham, Essex, CM8 2PS
☎ (01376) 510222
📖 200
🗐 S Brice
🗐 J Hudson
🏴 9 L 3128 yds Par 36
9 hole Par 3 course
👥 U
££ £8 (£11)
⊕ 4 miles E of Witham, off A12
⊕ Floodlit driving range
🏠 Alan Walker

Rochford Hundred (1893)
*Rochford Hall, Hall Road, Rochford,
SS4 1NW*
☎ (01702) 544302
🖳 (01702) 541343
📖 375 90(L) 60(J)
🗐 WJ Collantine
🗐 GS Hill
🏴 18 L 6256 yds SSS 70
👥 WD–U H WE–M
££ On application
⊕ 4 miles N of Southend-on-Sea
🏠 James Braid

Romford (1894)
*Heath Drive, Gidea Park, Romford,
RM2 5QB*
☎ (01708) 740007 (Members)
🖳 (01708) 752157
📖 680
🗐 Mrs H Robinson (01708) 740986
🗐 C Goddard (01708) 749393
🏴 18 L 6410 yds SSS 71
👥 WD–I WE–NA SOC
££ £27.50 D–£37.50
⊕ 1 mile E of Romford. 3 miles W of
M25 Junction 29
🏠 HS Colt

Royal Epping Forest (1888)
*Forest Approach, Station Road,
Chingford, London E4 7AZ*
☎ (020) 8529 6407
🖳 (020) 8559 4664
✉ office@refgc.co.uk
📖 300 50(L) 25(J)
🗐 R Bright-Thomas (0181) 529 2195
🗐 A Traynor (0181) 529 5708
🏴 18 L 6342 yds Par 71 SSS 70
👥 U–booking necessary SOC
££ £12 (£16.50)
⊕ Nr Chingford station. M25 Junction
26
⊕ Red coats or trousers compulsory

Saffron Walden (1919)

Windmill Hill, Saffron Walden,
CB10 1BX
☎ **(01799) 522786**
🖵 (01799) 520313
✉ office@swgc.com
📖 950
🏌 C Charlton (01799) 522786
⚲ P Davis (01799) 527728
🇫 18 L 6606 yds SSS 72
👥 WD–U H WE/BH–M SOC
💶 £35
⛳ Saffron Walden, on B184

South Essex G&CC

Herongate, Brentwood, CM13 3LW
☎ **(01277) 811289**
🖵 (01277) 811304
✉ southessex@americangolf.uk.com
📖 600
🏌 R Brewer (Gen Mgr)
⚲ G Stewart
🇫 18 L 6851 yds Par 72 SSS 73
   9 L 3102 yds Par 35
👥 U SOC
💶 £18 (£24)
⛳ 4 miles E of M25 Junction 29
   (A127/A128)
⊕ Driving range. Golf Academy
🏠 Reg Plumbridge
■ www.americangolf.com

St Cleres

St Cleres Hall, Stanford-le-Hope,
SS17 0LX
☎ **(01375) 361565**
📖 500
🏌 D Wood (01375) 361565
⚲ D Wood (01375) 361565
🇫 18 holes Par 72 SSS 71
👥 U H SOC
💶 £17 (£23)
⛳ 5 miles E of M25 Junction 30/31
   (A13)
⊕ Driving range
🏠 Adrian Stiff

Stapleford Abbotts (1989)

Horseman's Side, Tysea Hill, Stapleford
Abbotts, RM4 1JU
☎ **(01708) 381108**
🖵 (01708) 386345
📖 750
🏌 G Ivory
⚲ J Cornish (01708) 381108
🇫 18 L 6501 yds SSS 71
   9 hole Par 3 course
👥 WD–U WE–H SOC
💶 £25–£45
⛳ 3 miles N of Romford. M25
   Junction 28
🏠 Howard Swann

Stock Brook Manor (1992)

Queen's Park Avenue, Stock, Billericay,
CM12 0SP
☎ **(01277) 653616**
🖵 (01277) 633063
📖 850
🏌 C Laurence (Golf Dir)
⚲ C Laurence

🇫 18 L 6905 yds SSS 73
   9 L 2952 yds SSS 69
👥 H–booking necessary
💶 £25 (£30)
⛳ 5 miles S of Chelmsford on B1007
⊕ Driving range. Par 3 course
🏠 Martin Gillett

Theydon Bois (1897)

Theydon Road, Theydon Bois, Epping,
CM16 4EH
☎ **(01992) 813054**
🖵 (01992) 815602
✉ theydonboisgolf@btconnect.com
📖 600
🏌 MC Slatter (01992) 813054
⚲ RJ Hall (01992) 812460
🇫 18 L 5480 yds SSS 68
👥 U exc Thurs am–restricted SOC
💶 £26 After 2pm–£22
⛳ 1 mile S of Epping. M25 Junction
   26
🏠 James Braid

Thorndon Park (1920)

Ingrave, Brentwood, CM13 3RH
☎ **(01277) 810345**
🖵 (01277) 810645
✉ tpgc@btclick.com
📖 415 140(L) 45(J)
🏌 Lt Col RM Estcourt
⚲ BV White (01277) 810736
🇫 18 L 6492 yds SSS 71
👥 WD–I WE/BH–M
💶 £45 D–£60
⛳ 2 miles SE of Brentwood on A128
🏠 HS Colt
■ www.thorndonparkgolfclub.com

Thorpe Hall (1907)

Thorpe Hall Avenue, Thorpe Bay,
SS1 3AT
☎ **(01702) 582205**
🖵 (01702) 584498
📖 1000
🏌 GW Smith
⚲ WJ McColl (01702) 588195
🇫 18 L 6319 yds SSS 71
👥 WD–H SOC–Fri only
💶 On application
⛳ E of Southend-on-Sea

Three Rivers (1973)

Stow Road, Purleigh, Chelmsford,
CM3 6RR
☎ **(01621) 828631**
🖵 (01621) 828060
📖 800
🏌 J Martin (Gen Mgr)
⚲ S Clark
🇫 Kings 18 L 6449 yds Par 72 SSS 71
   Jubilee 18 L 4501 yds Par 64
   SSS 62
👥 WD–U exc Mon & Wed–NA
   before 11.30am WE–U after
   1.30pm SOC
💶 Kings £20 (£25) Jubilee £10
   (£12.50)
⛳ Cold Norton, 5 miles S of Maldon
🏠 Hawtree
■ www.clubhaus.com

Toot Hill (1991)

School Road, Toot Hill, Ongar,
CM5 9PU
☎ **(01277) 365747**
🖵 (01277) 364509
📖 400
🏌 Mrs Cameron
⚲ M Bishop
🇫 18 L 6053 yds Par 70 SSS 69
👥 H WE–NA before 1pm SOC–WD
💶 £25 (£30)
⛳ 2 miles W of Ongar
⊕ Practice range
🏠 Martin Gillett

Top Meadow (1986)

Fen Lane, North Ockendon, RM14 3PR
☎ **(01708) 852239 (Clubhouse)**
✉ info@topmeadow.co.uk
🏌 D Stock
⚲ R Porter (01708) 859545
🇫 18 L 6227 yds Par 72
👥 WD–U WE–M SOC
💶 £12
⛳ N Ockendon, off B186
⊕ Driving range
■ www.topmeadow.co.uk

Towerlands (1985)

Panfield Road, Braintree, CM7 5BJ
☎ **(01376) 326802**
🖵 (01376) 552487
📖 250
🏌 Brian Clark
⚲ (01376) 347951
🇫 9 L 5559 yds Par 68
👥 WD–U exc Wed & Fri–NA after
   4.30pm WE–NA before 1pm SOC
💶 18 holes–£10 (£12) 9 holes–£8
⛳ 1 mile NW of Braintree (B1053)

Upminster (1928)

114 Hall Lane, Upminster, RM14 1AU
☎ **(01708) 222788**
🖵 (01708) 222484
📖 1070
🏌 GW Scott
⚲ S Cipa (01708) 220000
🇫 18 L 6031 yds SSS 69
👥 WD–U H exc Tues am Ladies Day
   WE/BH–NA SOC
💶 £26 D–£31
⛳ Station 3/4 mile

Wanstead (1893)

Wanstead, London, E11 2LW
☎ **(020) 8989 0604**
🖵 (020) 8532 9138
✉ wgclub@aol.com
📖 650
🏌 K Jones (020) 8989 3938
⚲ D Hawkins (020) 8989 9876
🇫 18 L 6262 yds SSS 69
👥 WD–H WE/BH–M
💶 D–£30
⛳ Off A12, nr Wanstead station
🏠 James Braid
■ www.wansteadgolf.org.uk

For list of abbreviations and key to symbols see page 627

Warley Park   (1975)

Magpie Lane, Little Warley, Brentwood, CM13 3DX

☎ **(01277) 224891**
🖥 (01277) 200679
📖 800
🏌 K Regan
⚐ K Smith (01277) 200441
🏴 27 hole course
👤 WD–H
£€ £30
⛳ 2 miles S of Brentwood. M25 Junction 29
�🏼 Reg Plumbridge

Warren   (1932)

Woodham Walter, Maldon, CM9 6RW

☎ **(01245) 223258/223198**
🖥 (01245) 223989
📖 800
🏌 MFL Durham (01245) 223258
⚐ D Brooks (01245) 224662
🏴 18 L 6211 yds SSS 69
👤 WD–H WE–M SOC
£€ £30 D–£35
⛳ 7 miles E of Chelmsford, off A414
⊕ Golf Academy (01245) 223198
■ www.warrengolfclub.co.uk

Weald Park   (1994)

Coxtie Green Road, South Weald, Brentwood, CM14 5RJ

☎ **(01277) 375101**
🖥 (01277) 374888
📖 600
🏌 M Orwin (Gen Mgr)
⚐ K Clark
🏴 18 L 6612 yds SSS 72
👤 U–booking necessary WE–U after 11am SOC
£€ £18 (£24)
⛳ 3 miles from M25 Junction 28 (A1023)
⊕ Driving range
�🏼 Reg Plumbridge
■ www.americangolf.com

West Essex   (1900)

Bury Road, Sewardstonebury, Chingford, London E4 7QL

☎ **(020) 8529 7558**
🖥 (020) 8524 7870
📖 720
🏌 D Wilson
⚐ R Joyce (020) 8529 4367
🏴 18 L 6289 yds SSS 70
👤 WD–U H WE/BH–M H SOC–Mon/Wed/Fri
£€ £35 D–£40
⛳ 2 miles N of Chingford BR station. M25 Junction 26
⊕ Driving range
�🏼 James Braid

Woodford   (1890)

2, Sunset Avenue, Woodford Green, IG8 0ST

☎ **(020) 8504 0553 (Clubhouse)**
🖥 (020) 8559 0504
📖 400
🏌 FR Wolstenholme (020) 8504 3330

⚐ R Layton (020) 8504 4254
🏴 9 L 5867 yds SSS 68
👤 WD–U exc Tues am–NA Sat–M Sun–NA before noon SOC
£€ £9–£15
⛳ 11 miles NE of London
⊕ Major item of red clothing to be worn on course
�🏼 Tom Dunn

Woolston Manor   (1994)

Woolston Manor, Abridge Road, Chigwell, IG7 6BX

☎ **(020) 8500 2549**
🖥 (020) 8501 5452
📖 650
🏌 P Spargo
⚐ P Eady (0181) 559 8272
🏴 18 L 6408 yds SSS 71
👤 H SOC–WD
£€ £35 (£45)
⛳ 1 mile from M11 Junction 5
⊕ Floodlit driving range
�🏼 Neil Coles

Gloucestershire

Brickhampton Court

Proprietary
Cheltenham Road, Churchdown, GL2 9QF

☎ **(01452) 859444**
🖥 (01452) 859333
📧 info@brickhampton.co.uk
🏌 R East
⚐ C Gillick
🏴 Spa 18 L 6449 yds Par 71 SSS 71 Glevum 9 L 1859 yds Par 31
👤 U SOC–WD
£€ Spa £21 Mon–Thur £23 Fri (£27. Glevum 9 holes £7.50 (£9.50) 18 holes £13 (£15)
⛳ Between Cheltenham and Gloucester on B4063. M5 Junction 11, 3 miles
⊕ 26-bay floodlit driving range
�🏼 Simon Gidman
■ www.brickhampton.co.uk

Bristol & Clifton   (1891)

Beggar Bush Lane, Failand, Clifton, Bristol BS8 3TH

☎ **(01275) 393474/393117**
🖥 (01275) 394611
📖 650
🏌 CR Vane Percy (01275) 393474
⚐ P Mitchell (01275) 393031
🏴 18 L 6316 yds SSS 70
👤 WD–UH WE/BH–UH after 11am SOC
£€ On request
⛳ 2 miles W of suspension bridge. 4 miles S of M5 Junction 19
⊕ Driving range
■ www.bristolgolf.co.uk

Broadway   (1895)

Willersey Hill, Broadway, Worcs, WR12 7LG

☎ **(01386) 858997**

🖥 (01386) 858643
📖 515 165(L) 75(J)
🏌 B Carnie (Sec/Mgr) (01386) 853683
⚐ M Freeman (01386) 853275
🏴 18 L 6228 yds Par 72 SSS 70
👤 H exc Sat–M SOC
£€ £30 (£38)
⛳ 1½ miles E of Broadway (A44)
�🏼 James Braid

Canons Court   (1982)

Bradley Green, Wotton-under-Edge, GL12 7PN

☎ **(01453) 843128**
📖 200
⚐ I Watts
🏴 9 L 5724 yds SSS 65
👤 U
£€ £10
⛳ 3 miles E of M5 Junction 14, off B4058

Chipping Sodbury

Chipping Sodbury, Bristol, BS37 6PU

☎ **(01454) 312024 (Members)**
🖥 (01454) 320052
📖 750
🏌 R Wilmott (01454) 319042
⚐ M Watts (01454) 314087
🏴 18 L 6786 yds SSS 73
👤 WD–U WE–pm only Sat/Sun am–XL SOC
£€ £22 (£27)
⛳ 12 miles NE of Bristol. M4 Junction 18, 5 miles. M5 Junction 14, 9 miles.
⊕ Driving range
�🏼 Fred Hawtree
■ www.chippingsodburygolfclub.co.uk

Cirencester   (1893)

Cheltenham Road, Bagendon, Cirencester, GL7 7BH

☎ **(01285) 653939**
🖥 (01285) 650665
📧 info@cirencestergolfclub.co.uk
📖 800
🏌 IA Gray (01285) 652465
⚐ P Garratt (01285) 656124
🏴 18 L 6055 yds Par 70 SSS 69
👤 H SOC–WD
£€ £25 (£30)
⛳ 1½ miles N of Cirencester on A435
�🏼 James Braid
■ www.cirencestergolfclub.co.uk

Cleeve Hill   (1892)

Pay and play
Cleeve Hill, Cheltenham, GL52 3PW

☎ **(01242) 672025**
📧 golf@cleevehill.com
🏌 S Gilman (Mgr)
⚐ D Finch (01242) 672592
🏴 18 L 6496 yds Par 72 SSS 71
👤 U exc Sat 11–3pm/Sun dawn–11.00 am SOC
£€ £15 (£18)
⛳ 3 miles N of Cheltenham on A46 to Winchcombe
⊕ Tee booking 7 days in advance
■ www.clevehill.com

Cotswold Edge (1980)
Upper Rushmire, Wotton-under-Edge, GL12 7PT
- ☎ **(01453) 844167**
- 🖳 (01453) 845120
- 📖 800
- 🏌 NJ Newman
- ✓ R Hibbitt (01453) 844398
- ⛳ 18 L 5816 yds SSS 69
- 👥 WD–U WE–M
- ££ £15 (£20)
- ⛳ 2 miles NE of Wotton-under-Edge on B4058 Tetbury road. M5 Junction 14

Cotswold Hills (1902)
Ullenwood, Cheltenham, GL53 9QT
- ☎ **(01242) 515264**
- 🖳 (01242) 515317
- ✉ golf@chgc.freeserve.co.uk
- 📖 750
- 🏌 P Burroughes (Gen Mgr) (01242) 515264
- ✓ J Latham (01242) 515263
- ⛳ 18 L 6849 yds Par 72 SSS 72
- 👥 U–recognised club members SOC
- ££ £32 D–£36 (£37 D–£40)
- ⛳ 3 miles S of Cheltenham. M5 Junction 11A
- 🏠 MD Little
- 🖥 www.cotswoldhills-golfclub.com

Dymock Grange (1995)
The Old Grange, Leominster Road, Dymock, GL18 2AN
- ☎ **(01531) 890840**
- 🖳 (01531) 890852
- 📖 180
- 🏌 BA Crossman (Gen Mgr)
- ✓ None
- ⛳ 9 L 2696 yds Par 36
  9 L 1695 yds Par 30
- 👥 U
- ££ £12 (£15)
- ⛳ 14 miles NW of Gloucester (B4215)

Filton (1909)
Golf Course Lane, Bristol, BS34 7QS
- ☎ **(0117) 969 2021**
- 🖳 (0117) 931 4359
- ✉ thesecretary@filtongolfclub.co.uk
- 📖 700
- 🏌 Mrs E Mannering (0117) 969 4169
- ✓ D Robinson (0117) 969 6968
- ⛳ 18 L 6208 yds SSS 70
- 👥 WD–U WE/BH–M SOC–WD
- ££ £22 D–£27
- ⛳ 4 miles N of Bristol
- 🏠 Hawtree

Forest Hills (1992)
Proprietary
Mile End Road, Coleford, GL16 7BY
- ☎ **(01594) 810620**
- 🖳 (01594) 810823
- 📖 550
- 🏌 D Bowen (01594) 837134
- ✓ R Ballard (01594) 810620
- ⛳ 18 L 6300 yds SSS 72
- 👥 U SOC
- ££ £17 (£22)

- ⛳ 1 mile E of Coleford (B4028)
- ⊕ Driving range
- 🏠 Adrian Stiff
- 🖥 www.fweb.org.uk/forestgolf

Forest of Dean (1973)
Lords Hill, Coleford, GL16 8BE
- ☎ **(01594) 832583**
- 🖳 (01594) 832584
- ✉ enquiries@bellshotel.co.uk
- 📖 500
- 🏌 R Sanzen-Baker
- ✓ A Gray (01594) 833689
- ⛳ 18 L 5682 yds SSS 69
- 👥 U SOC
- ££ £18 (£25)
- ⛳ ¹/₂ mile SE of Coleford on Parkend road. M50, 10 miles
- 🏠 John Day

The Gloucestershire (1976)
Tracy Park Estate, Bath Road, Wick, Bristol BS30 5RN
- ☎ **(0117) 937 2251**
- 🖳 (0117) 937 4288
- ✉ golf@thegloucestershire.com
- 📖 700
- 🏌 D Knipe (Dir)
- ✓ D Morgan
- ⛳ Crown 18 L 6252 yds SSS 70
  Cromwell 18 L 6246 yds SSS 70
- 👥 U–phone first SOC
- ££ £30 (£38)
- ⛳ 3 miles NW of Bath, off A420. M4 Junction 18
- ⊕ Driving range
- 🖥 www.thegloucestershire.com

Gloucester Hotel (1976)
Matson Lane, Gloucester, GL4 9EA
- ☎ **(01452) 525653**
- 📖 500
- ✓ S Harrison (Mgr) (01452) 411311
- ⛳ 18 L 6127 yds SSS 69
  9 L 1980 yds SSS 27
- 👥 U
- ££ £19 (£25)
- ⛳ 2 miles S of Gloucester, off Painswick road. M5 Junction 11
- ⊕ Driving range

Henbury (1891)
Westbury-on-Trym, Bristol, BS10 7QB
- ☎ **(0117) 950 0660**
- 🖳 (0117) 959 1928
- 📖 760
- 🏌 (0117) 950 0044
- ✓ N Riley (0117) 950 2121
- ⛳ 18 L 6007 yds SSS 70
- 👥 WD–H WE–M SOC–Tues & Fri
- ££ £25
- ⛳ 3 miles N of Bristol, off A4018. M5 Junction 17
- 🖥 www.henburygolfclub.co.uk

Hilton Puckrup Hall Hotel (1992)
Puckrup, Tewkesbury, GL20 6EL
- ☎ **(01684) 296200/271591**
- 🖳 (01684) 850788

- 📖 500
- 🏌 G Spring
- ✓ N Whitton
- ⛳ 18 L 6189 yds SSS 70
- 👥 WD–H SOC WE–residents
- ££ £25 (£30)
- ⛳ 2 miles N of Tewkesbury on A38. M50 Junction 1. M5 Junction 8
- 🏠 Simon Gidman

The Kendleshire
Henfield Road, Coalpit Heath, Bristol, BS36 2TUY
- ☎ **(0117) 956 7007**
- 🖳 (0117) 957 3433
- ✉ info@kendleshire.co.uk
- 📖 750
- 🏌 P Murphy
- ✓ M Bessell (0117) 956 7000
- ⛳ 27 L 6249-6544 yds Par 70-71
- 👥 U SOC
- ££ £28 (£35)
- ⛳ 1 mile NE of Bristol. M32 J1
- ⊕ Driving range. Golf Academy
- 🏠 Adrian Stiff/Peter McEvoy

Knowle (1905)
Fairway, West Town Lane, Brislington, Bristol BS4 5DF
- ☎ **(0117) 977 6341**
- 🖳 (0117) 972 0615
- 📖 700
- 🏌 MJ Harrington (0117) 977 0660
- ✓ R Hayward (0117) 977 9193
- ⛳ 18 L 6006 yds SSS 69
- 👥 WD exc Thurs–H WE/BH–H SOC–Thurs
- ££ £22 D–£27 (£27 D–£32)
- ⛳ Brislington Hill, 3 miles S of Bristol, off A4
- 🏠 JH Taylor

Lilley Brook (1922)
Cirencester Road, Charlton Kings, Cheltenham, GL53 8EG
- ☎ **(01242) 526785**
- 🖳 (01242) 256880
- ✉ secretary@lilleybrookgc.fsnet.co.uk
- 📖 900
- 🏌 MF Jordan (Gen Mgr)
- ✓ K Hayler (01242) 525201
- ⛳ 18 L 6226 yds SSS 70
- 👥 WD–H or I (recognised club members) WE–M SOC–WD
- ££ £25 D–£30 (£30 D–£35)
- ⛳ 3 miles SE of Cheltenham on A435. M5 Junction 11 or 11A

Long Ashton (1893)
Clarken Coombe, Long Ashton, Bristol, BS41 9DW
- ☎ **(01275) 392229**
- 🖳 (01275) 394395
- ✉ info@longashtongolfclub.co.uk
- 📖 750
- 🏌 R Williams (01275) 392229
- ✓ M Hart (01275) 392229
- ⛳ 18 L 6077 yds SSS 70
- 👥 WD–U H WE/BH–I H SOC–Wed & Fri
- ££ £30 (£35)

---

3 miles S of Bristol on B3128
JH Taylor
www.longashtongolfclub.co.uk

Lydney (1909)

The Links, Off Lakeside Avenue, Lydney,
GL15 5QA
☎ (01594) 842614
🏕 300
🏌 J Mills (01594) 841186
🏳 9 L 5430 yds SSS 66
👤 U SOC
££ £10
⛳ 20 miles SW of Gloucester
■ www.members.tripod.co.uk/kenfar
/lgc

Mangotsfield (1975)

Carsons Road, Mangotsfield, Bristol,
BS17 3LW
☎ (0117) 956 5501
🏕 600
🏌 C Main
🏌 C Trewin
🏳 18 L 5337 yds SSS 66
👤 U
££ On application
⛳ 6 miles NE of Bristol

Minchinhampton (1889)

Minchinhampton, Stroud, GL6 9BE
☎ (01453) 832642 (Old),
    (01453) 833840 (New)
🏕 (01453) 837360
🏕 1860
🏌 P Keeling (01453) 833866
🏌 C Steele (01453) 837351
🏳 Old 18 L 6019 yds SSS 69;
    Avening 18 L 6263 yds SSS 70;
    Cherington 18 L 6430 yds SSS 71
👤 H SOC
££ Old–£12 (£15). New–£30 (£34)
⛳ Old-3 miles E of Stroud. New-5
    miles E of Stroud
🏠 Old: R Wilson. Avening:
    F Hawtree. Cherington: M Hawtree

Naunton Downs (1993)

Naunton, Cheltenham, GL54 3AE
☎ (01451) 850090
🏕 (01451) 850091
🏕 750
🏌 Janette Knight
🏌 N Ellis (01451) 850092
🏳 18 L 6135 yds Par 71 SSS 69
👤 WD–U–by arrangement WE–NA
    before 11am
££ £19 (£27.50)
⛳ 5 miles SW of Stow-on-the-Wold,
    on B4068
🏠 Jacob Pott
■ www.nauntondowns.co.uk

Newent (1994)

Pay and play
Coldharbour Lane, Newent, GL18 1DJ
☎ (01531) 820478
🏕 (01531) 820478
🏕 50
🏌 W Russell
🏌 T Brown

🏳 9 L 2100 yds Par 33 SSS 59
👤 U SOC
££ 9 holes–£6 (£7) 18 holes–£10 (£12)
⛳ 10 miles NW of Gloucester on
    B4215. M50 Junction 3, 4 miles

Painswick (1891)

Painswick, Stroud, GL6 6TL
☎ (01452) 812180
🏕 (01452) 814423
🏕 430
🏌 AB Layton-Smith (01452) 612622
🏌 None
🏳 18 L 4780 yds SSS 63
👤 WD/Sat–U Sun–M SOC
££ £17.50 Sat–£22.50
⛳ ¹/₂ mile N of Painswick on A46
🏠 David Brown

Rodway Hill (1991)

Pay and play
Newent Road, Highnam, GL2 8DN
☎ (01452) 384222
🏕 (01452) 313814
🏕 350
🏌 R Howe
🏌 T Grubb
🏳 18 L 6040 yds Par 70 SSS 69
👤 U SOC
££ 18 holes–£12 (£14). 9 holes–£8
    (£9)
⛳ 2 miles W of Gloucester (B4215)
🏠 J Gabb

Sherdons Golf Centre (1993)

Pay and play
Tredington, Tewkesbury, GL20 7BP
☎ (01684) 274782
🏕 (01684) 275358
🏕 300
🏌 R Chatham
🏌 P Clark, J Parker
🏳 9 L 2654 yds Par 34 SSS 66
👤 U
££ 18 holes–£11 (£14) 9 holes–£7 (£8)
⛳ 2 miles S of Tewkesbury, off A38
⊕ Driving range

Shirehampton Park (1904)

Park Hill, Shirehampton, Bristol,
BS11 0UL
☎ (0117) 982 2083
🏕 (0117) 982 5280
📧 info@shirehamptonparkgolfclub
    .co.uk
🏕 600
🏌 A Hobbs (0117) 982 2083
🏌 B Ellis (0117) 982 2488
🏳 18 L 5430 yds Par 67 SSS 66
👤 WD–H WE–M SOC
££ £20 (£17)
⛳ 2 miles E of M5 Junction 18, on
    B4054

Stinchcombe Hill (1889)

Stinchcombe Hill, Dursley, GL11 6AQ
☎ (01453) 542015
🏕 (01453) 549545
📧 stinchcombehill@golfers.net

🏕 550
🏌 PH Jones
🏌 P Bushell (01453) 543878
🏳 18 L 5734 yds SSS 68
👤 U–phone Pro SOC
££ £24 (£30)
⛳ 1 mile W of Dursley. M5 J14
🏠 A Hoare

Tewkesbury Park Hotel (1976)

Lincoln Green Lane, Tewkesbury,
GL20 7DN
☎ (01684) 295405 (Hotel)
🏕 (01684) 292386
📧 golfsec.tewkesburypark
    @corushotels.com
🏕 600
🏌 RH Love (01684) 272322
🏌 C Boast (01684) 272320
🏳 18 L 6533 yds Par 73 SSS 71
    6 hole Par 3 course
👤 WD–U H WE–restricted SOC–WD
££ £25 (£35)
⛳ ¹/₂ mile S of Tewkesbury on A38.
    M5 Junction 9, 2 miles
⊕ Driving range
■ www.corushotels.com
    /tewkesburypark

Thornbury Golf Centre (1992)

Bristol Road, Thornbury
☎ (01454) 281144
🏕 (01454) 281177
🏕 500
🏌 I Gibson
🏌 S Hubbard
🏳 18 L 6207 yds SSS 69 Par 71
    18 L 2195 yds Par 54
👤 U SOC–WD
££ £17 (£21.50)
⛳ 10 miles N of Bristol, off A38
⊕ Driving range
🏠 Hawtree

Westonbirt (1971)

Westonbirt, Tetbury, GL8 8QG
☎ (01666) 880242
🏕 200
🏌 Bursar, Westonbirt School
🏳 9 L 4504 yds SSS 61
👤 U SOC–WD
££ On application
⛳ 3 miles S of Tetbury, off A433

Woodlands G&CC (1989)

Pay and play
Woodlands Lane, Almondsbury, Bristol,
BS32 4JZ
☎ (01454) 619319
🏕 (01454) 619397
📧 golf@woodlands-golf.com
🏌 I Knipe
🏌 L Riddiford
🏳 18 L 6100 yds SSS 70
👤 U SOC
££ £13 (£15)
⛳ Nr M5 Junction 16
■ www.woodlands-golf.com

For list of abbreviations and key to symbols see page 627

Woodspring G&CC (1994)
Yanley Lane, Long Ashton, Bristol, BS41 9LR
- ☎ **(01275) 394378**
- 🖥 (01275) 394473
- ♠ M Pierce (Gen Mgr)
- ✓ N Beer
- ⮡ 27 holes:
  6209-6587 yds Par 71 SSS 70-71
- 👥 W–H SOC
- £€ £25 (£28.50)
- ⛳ 2 miles S of Bristol on A38.
- ⊕ Floodlit driving range
- ⌂ Allis/Clark

Hampshire

Alresford (1890)
Cheriton Road, Alresford, SO24 0PN
- ☎ **(01962) 733746**
- 🖥 (01962) 736040
- ✉ secretary@alresfordgolf.co.uk
- 📖 625
- ♠ T Adams
- ✓ M Scott (01962) 733998
- ⮡ 18 L 5905 yds Par 69 SSS 68
- 👥 U H SOC–WD
- £€ £25 D–£35 (£40)
- ⛳ 1 mile S of Alresford on B3046
- ⌂ Scott Webb Young
- ■ www.alresfordgolf.com

Alton (1908)
Old Odiham Road, Alton, GU34 4BU
- ☎ **(01420) 82042**
- 📖 370
- ♠ R Keeling
- ✓ R Keeling (01420) 86518
- ⮡ 9 L 5744 yds SSS 68
- 👥 WD–U WE–H or M SOC–WD
- £€ 18 holes–£15 D–£20 9 holes–£10
- ⛳ 2 miles N of Alton. 6 miles S of Odiham, off B3349
- ⌂ James Braid

Ampfield Par Three (1963)
Winchester Road, Ampfield, Romsey, SO51 9BQ
- ☎ **(01794) 368480**
- 📖 500
- ♠ Joyce Cantrell
- ✓ R Benfield (01794) 368750
- ⮡ 18 L 2478 yds SSS 53
- 👥 WD–U WE/BH (phone first) SOC
- £€ £10 (£12)
- ⛳ 5 miles E of Romsey on A31
- ⌂ Henry Cotton

Andover (1907)
51 Winchester Road, Andover, SP10 2EF
- ☎ **(01264) 323980**
- 🖥 (01264) 358040
- ✉ play@andovergolfclub.fsnet.co.uk
- 📖 455 48(L) 80(J)
- ♠ G Daws (01264) 358040
- ✓ D Lawrence (01264) 324151
- ⮡ 9 L 6096 yds SSS 69
- 👥 U H SOC
- £€ £20 (£25)

- ⛳ ½ mile S of Andover on A3057
- ⌂ JH Taylor

Army (1883)
Laffan's Road, Aldershot, GU11 2HF
- ☎ **(01252) 336776**
- 🖥 (01252) 337562
- ✉ agc@ic24.net
- 📖 750
- ♠ Maj (Retd) JWG Douglass (01252) 337272
- ✓ G Cowley (01252) 336722
- ⮡ 18 L 6579 yds SSS 71
- 👥 WD–H–contact Sec/Mgr SOC
- £€ Special rates for Forces
- ⛳ Between Aldershot and Farnborough
- ■ www.whichgolfclub.com/army

Barton-on-Sea (1897)
Milford Road, New Milton, BH25 5PP
- ☎ **(01425) 615308**
- 🖥 (01425) 621457
- 📖 1000
- ♠ G Prince
- ✓ P Rodgers (01425) 611210
- ⮡ 27 holes:
  L 6289-6505 yds Par 72
- 👥 H NA before 9am SOC–WD exc Tues
- £€ D–£36 (D–£41)
- ⛳ 1 mile from New Milton, off B3058. M27 Junction 1
- ⌂ J Hamilton Stutt
- ■ www.barton-on-sea-golf.co.uk

Basingstoke (1928)
Kempshott Park, Basingstoke, RG23 7LL
- ☎ **(01256) 465990**
- 🖥 (01256) 331793
- ✉ enquiries@basingstokegolfclub.co.uk
- 📖 700
- ♠ WA Jefford
- ✓ G Shoesmith (01256) 351332
- ⮡ 18 L 6350 yds SSS 70
- 👥 WD–H WE–M SOC–Wed & Thurs
- £€ £32 D–£42
- ⛳ 3 miles W of Basingstoke on A30. M3 Junction 7
- ⌂ James Braid
- ■ www.basingstokegolfclub.co.uk

Bishopswood (1978)
Proprietary
Bishopswood Lane, Tadley, Basingstoke, RG26 4AT
- ☎ **(0118) 981 2200/5213**
- 🖥 (0118) 940 8606
- 📖 400
- ♠ Mrs J Jackson-Smith (0118) 982 0312
- ✓ S Ward
- ⮡ 9 L 6474 yds Par 72 SSS 71
- 👥 WD–U WE–M SOC
- £€ 9 holes–£12. 18 holes–£18
- ⛳ 6 miles N of Basingstoke, off A340
- ⊕ 12- bay floodlit driving range
- ⌂ Blake/Phillips
- ■ www.bishopswoodgolfcourse.co.uk

Blackmoor (1913)
Whitehill, Bordon, GU35 9EH
- ☎ **(01420) 472775**
- 🖥 (01420) 487666
- ✉ admin@blackmoorgolf.co.uk
- 📖 680 100(L) 70(J)
- ♠ AN Harris
- ✓ S Clay (01420) 472345
- ⮡ 18 L 6213 yds SSS 70
- 👥 WD–H SOC–WD
- £€ £35 D–£47
- ⛳ ½ mile W of Whitehill on A325
- ⌂ HS Colt
- ■ www.blackmoorgolf.co.uk

Blacknest (1993)
Blacknest, GU34 4QL
- ☎ **(01420) 22888**
- 🖥 (01420) 22001
- ✉ info@huntswoodgolf.com
- 📖 420
- ✓ T Cook
- ⮡ 18 L 5938 yds SSS 69
  9 hole Par 3 course
- 👥 U SOC
- £€ £20 (£25)
- ⛳ 7 miles SW of Farnham, off A325
- ⊕ Driving range
- ■ www.huntswoodgolf.com

Blackwater Valley
Chandlers Lane, Yateley, Surrey, GU46 7SZ
- ☎ **(01252) 874725**
- 🖥 (01252) 874725
- 📖 50
- ✓ J Rodger
- ⮡ 9 L 2365 yds Par 66
- 👥 U SOC
- £€ £7 (£9)
- ⛳ 5 miles W of Camberley (B3272)
- ⊕ Floodlit driving range
- ⌂ HJ Allenby

Botley Park Hotel G&CC (1989)
Winchester Road, Boorley Green, Botley, SO3 2UA
- ☎ **(01489) 780888 Ext 451**
- 🖥 (01489) 789242
- 📖 700
- ♠ James Leeming (Mgr)
- ✓ Kevin Caplehorn (01489) 789771
- ⮡ 18 L 6389 yds SSS 70
- 👥 H SOC
- £€ £30 (£45) SOC on request
- ⛳ 6 miles E of Southampton on B3354. M27 Junction 7. 8 miles SE of M3 Junction 11
- ⊕ Driving range; leisure club; swimming pool; squash courts; tennis courts
- ⌂ Potterton/Murray

Bramshaw (1880)
Brook, Lyndhurst, SO43 7HE
- ☎ **(023) 8081 3433**
- 🖥 (023) 8081 3460
- 📖 1200
- ♠ RD Tingey

✓ C Bonner (023) 8081 3434
⚑ Forest 18 L 5774 yds SSS 68
Manor 18 L 6517 yds SSS 71
👥 U H
££ Forest–£30. Manor–£35
🚗 10 miles SW of Southampton. M27
Junction 1, 1 mile
■ www.bramshaw.co.uk

Brokenhurst Manor (1919)
Sway Road, Brockenhurst, SO42 7SG
☎ (01590) 623332
📠 (01590) 624140
✉ secretary@brokenhurst-
manor.org.uk
🏠 800
✍ PE Clifford
✓ B Parker (01590) 623092
⚑ 18 L 6222 yds SSS 70
👥 WD–H after 9.30am exc
Tues–Ladies' Day SOC–Thurs only
££ £48 D–£58 (£58 D–£73)
🚗 1 mile SW of Brockenhurst on
B3055
⛳ HS Colt

Burley (1905)
*Cott Lane, Burley, Ringwood,
BH24 4BB*
☎ (01425) 403737 (Clubhouse)
📠 (01425) 404168
✉ secretary@burleygolfclub.fsnet
.co.uk
🏠 520
✍ GJ Stride (01425) 402431
⚑ 9 L 6149 yds Par 71 SSS 69
👥 Bona fide club members only – H
preferred
££ £16 (£20) W–£75
🚗 4 miles SE of Ringwood

Cams Hall Estate
Cams Hall Estate, Fareham, PO16 8UP
☎ (01329) 827222
📠 (01329) 827111
🏠 950
✍ S Wright (Sec/Mgr)
✓ J Neve (01329) 837732
⚑ 27 L 6244-6477 yds SSS 70-71
👥 U SOC
££ £24 (£32)
🚗 8 miles W of Portsmouth. M27
Junction 11
⛳ Alliss/Clarke

Chilworth (1989)
*Main Road, Chilworth, Southampton,
SO16 7JP*
☎ (023) 8074 0544
📠 (023) 8073 3166
🏠 650
✍ F Bendall
✓ D Newing
⚑ 18 L 5837 yds SSS 68
👥 U
££ £12 (£15)
🚗 Between Romsey and Southampton
on A27
⊕ Floodlit driving range

Corhampton (1891)
Corhampton, Southampton, SO32 3LP
☎ (01489) 877279
📠 (01489) 877680
✉ secretary@corhamptongc.co.uk
🏠 800
✍ Mrs L Collins
✓ I Roper (01489) 877638
⚑ 18 L 6444 yds SSS 71
👥 WD–U H WE/BH–M SOC–Mons
& Thurs
££ £30 D–£40
🚗 9 miles S of Winchester
■ www.corhamptongc.co.uk

Dibden Golf Centre (1974)
Public
*Main Road, Dibden, Southampton,
SO45 5TB*
☎ (023) 8020 7508 (Bookings)
🏠 700
✓ P Smith (023) 8084 5596
⚑ 18 L 5986 yds SSS 69
9 hole course
👥 U
££ £12.50 (£14.60)
🚗 10 miles W of Southampton, off
A326 at Dibden roundabout
⊕ Floodlit driving range
■ www.nfdc.gov.uk/golf

Dummer (1993)
Dummer, Basingstoke, RG25 2AR
☎ (01256) 397888
📠 (01256) 397889
✉ golf@dummergc.co.uk
🏠 600
✍ R Corkhill
✓ A Fannon (01256) 397950
⚑ 18 L 6403 yds SSS 71
👥 U SOC
££ £30 (£34)
🚗 4 miles SW of Basingstoke, by M3
Junction 7
⊕ Covered driving range
⛳ Alliss/Clark
■ www.dummergc.co.uk

Dunwood Manor (1969)
*Danes Road, Awbridge, Romsey,
SO51 0GF*
☎ (01794) 340549
📠 (01794) 341215
✉ admin@dunwood-golf.co.uk
🏠 600
✍ JR Basford
✓ H Teschner (01794) 340663
⚑ 18 L 5767 yds SSS 69
👥 WE/BH–restricted SOC–WD
££ £25 (£37)
🚗 Romsey 4 miles, off A27
■ www.dunwood-golf.co.uk

Fareham Woods (1997)
*Skylark Meadows, Whiteley, Fareham,
PO15 6RS*
☎ (01329) 844441
📠 (01329) 844442
🏠 600
✍ M Woodman
✓ S Edwards

⚑ 18 L 5622 yds Par 70 SSS 67
👥 WD–U WE–M SOC–WD
££ £15
🚗 6 miles W of Fareham. M27
Junction 9

Fleetlands (1961)
Fareham Road, Gosport, PO13 0AW
☎ (023) 9254 4492
🏠 140
✍ M Barnes (023) 9254 4592
⚑ 9 L 4852 yds SSS 64
👥 M at all times
🚗 2 miles S of Fareham on A32
Gosport road. M27 Junction 12

Fleming Park (1973)
Public
*Fleming Park, Magpie Lane, Eastleigh,
SO50 9LH*
☎ (023) 8061 2797
✍ A Wheavil
✓ C Strickett
⚑ 18 L 4436 yds SSS 62
👥 U SOC–WD
££ On application
🚗 6 miles N of Southampton

Four Marks (1994)
*Headmore Lane, Four Marks, Alton,
GU34 3ES*
☎ (01420) 587214
📠 (01420) 587313
✉ fourmarksgolf@btopenworld.com
🏠 238
✍ W Falloon
✓ P Chapman (01420) 587214
⚑ 9 L 2077 yds Par 62 SSS 61
👥 U SOC
££ 9 holes–£8 (£9) 18 holes–£10.90
(£11.90)
🚗 6 miles SW of Alton (A31)
⛳ Wright/Falloon/Wrigglesworth

Furzeley (1993)
Pay and play
Furzeley Road, Denmead, PO7 6TX
☎ (023) 9223 1180
📠 (023) 9223 0921
✍ T Brown
✓ D Brown
⚑ 18 L 4363 yds Par 62 SSS 61
👥 U SOC
££ £11 (£12.50)
🚗 2 miles NW of Waterlooville

Gosport & Stokes Bay (1885)
Fort Road, Haslar, Gosport, PO12 2AT
☎ (023) 9258 1625
📠 (023) 9252 7941
🏠 450
✍ B Gibson (023) 9252 7941
⚑ 9 L 5995 yds SSS 69
👥 U exc Sun am–NA
SOC–Mon/Tues/Wed/Fri
££ £15 (£20)
🚗 S boundary of Gosport

The Hampshire
Winchester Road, Goodworth Clatford, Andover, SP11 7TB
☎ **(01264) 357555**
🖳 (01264) 356606
📖 735
🏌 T Fiducia
✓ I Powell
⊳ 18 L 6442 yds Par 72
   9 hole Par 3 course
👥 U SOC
££ £17 (£25)
🚗 1 mile SW of Andover (A3057)
⊕ Covered driving range
🏠 T Fiducia

Hartley Wintney   (1891)
London Road, Hartley Wintney, Hook, RG27 8PT
☎ **(01252) 844211**
🖳 (01252) 844211
✉ office@hartleywintneygolfclub
   .com
📖 750
🏌 MG Bryant (01252) 844211
✓ M Smith (01252) 843779
⊳ 18 L 6240 yds SSS 71
👥 Wed–Ladies Day
   WE/BH–restricted SOC
££ £30 (£35)
🚗 A30 between Camberley and
   Basingstoke
■ www.hartleywintneygolfclub.com

Hayling   (1883)
Links Lane, Hayling Island, PO11 0BX
☎ **(023) 9246 3712**
🖳 (023) 9246 1119
✉ hgcltd@aol.com
📖 1020
🏌 CJ Cavill (023) 9246 4446
✓ R Gadd (023) 9246 4491
⊳ 18 L 6531 yds SSS 71
👥 H WE/BH–after 10am SOC–Tues
   & Wed
££ £40 (£48)
🚗 5 miles S of Havant on A3023
🏠 Taylor(1905)/Simpson(1933)

Hockley   (1915)
Twyford, Winchester, SO21 1PL
☎ **(01962) 713165**
🖳 (01962) 713612
✉ hockleygolfclub@aol.com
📖 750
🏌 Mrs L Dyer
⊳ 18 L 6336 yds SSS 70
👥 U H SOC
££ On application
🚗 2 miles S of Winchester on B3335
🏠 James Braid
■ www.hockleygolfclub.org.uk

Leckford   (1929)
Leckford, Stockbridge, SO20 6JS
☎ **(01264) 810320**
🖳 (01264) 810439
📖 400
🏌 J Wood
✓ T Ashton (01264) 338175
⊳ Old 9 L 3251 yds SSS 71
   New 9 L 2281 yds SSS 62

👥 M
££ £10 (£14)
🚗 5 miles W of Andover

Lee-on-the-Solent   (1905)
Brune Lane, Lee-on-the-Solent, PO13 9PB
☎ **(023) 9255 0207**
🖳 (023) 9255 4233
✉ enquiries@leeonthesolentgolfclub
   .co.uk
📖 700
🏌 M Topper (Mgr) (023) 9255 1170
✓ R Edwards (023) 9255 1181
⊳ 18 L 5926 yds SSS 69
👥 WD–U H WE–M H SOC–Thurs
££ D–£36 (£40)
🚗 3 miles S of Fareham. M27
   Junction 11
■ www.leeonthesolentgolfclub.co.uk

Liphook   (1922)
Liphook, GU30 7EH
☎ **(01428) 723271/723785**
🖳 (01428) 724853
✉ liphookgolfclub@btconnect.com
📖 700
🏌 Maj JB Morgan MBE
   (01428) 723785/723271
✓ I Mowbray
⊳ 18 L 6167 yds SSS 69
👥 I H (max 24) Sun–NA before 1pm
   SOC
££ £39 D–£46 (D–£55)
🚗 1 mile S of Liphook on B2070 (old
   A3)
🏠 ACG Groome

Marriott Meon Valley Hotel   (1977)
Sandy Lane, Shedfield, Southampton, SO32 2HQ
☎ **(01329) 833455**
🖳 (01329) 834411
📖 730
🏌 GF McMenemy (Golf Dir)
✓ R Cameron
⊳ 18 L 6520 yds SSS 71
   9 L 2885 yds SSS 68
👥 H SOC
££ 18 hole: £36 (£45) 9 hole: £12
🚗 2 miles NW of Wickham. N off
   A334
⊕ Driving range
🏠 J Hamilton Stutt

New Forest   (1888)
Southampton Road, Lyndhurst, SO43 7BU
☎ **(023) 8028 2752**
✉ barbara@nfgc.sagehost.co.uk
📖 500
🏌 Mrs B Shaw, R Macdonald
   (Prop) (023) 8028 2484
✓ C Murray
⊳ 18 L 5742 yds SSS 68
👥 U exc Sun am SOC–WD
££ £12 (£15)
🚗 8 miles W of Southampton on A35
■ www.nfgc.sageweb.co.uk

North Hants   (1904)
Minley Road, Fleet, GU51 1RF
☎ **(01252) 616443**
🖳 (01252) 811627
📖 550
🏌 G Hogg
✓ S Porter (01252) 616655
⊳ 18 L 6519 yds Par 71 SSS 72
👥 WD–H by prior arrangement
   WE/BH–MH SOC–Tues & Wed
££ On application
🚗 3 miles W of Farnborough on
   B3013. M3 Junction 4A
🏠 James Braid

Old Thorns   (1982)
Pay and play
Longmoor Road, Griggs Green, Liphook, GU30 7PE
☎ **(01428) 724555**
🖳 (01428) 725036
🏌 GM Jones (Gen Mgr)
✓ K Stevenson
⊳ 18 L 6533 yds SSS 71
👥 U SOC
££ £35 (£45)
🚗 Griggs Green exit off A3
⊕ Driving range
🏠 Cdr John Harris

Otterbourne Golf Centre   (1995)
Poles Lane, Otterbourne, Winchester, SO21 2EL
☎ **(01962) 775225**
🏌 JM Garner (Mgr)
⊳ 9 L 1939 yds Par
👥 U
££ £4 (£5)
🚗 On A31 between Otterbourne and
   Hursley
⊕ Driving range

Park   (1995)
Pay and play
Avington, Winchester, SO21 1DA
☎ **(01962) 779945 (Clubhouse)**
🖳 (01962) 779530
📖 350
🏌 R Stent (Prop) (01962) 779955
✓ None
⊳ 9 L 1907 yds Par 61 SSS 58
👥 U SOC
££ 9 holes–£8 (£11). 18 holes–£12
   (£16.50)
🚗 4 miles E of Winchester. M3
   Junction 9

Paultons Golf Centre
Pay and play
Old Salisbury Road, Ower, Romsey, SO51 6AN
☎ **(023) 8081 3992**
🖳 (023) 8081 3993
🏌 R Pilbury
✓ (023) 8081 4626
⊳ 18 L 6238 yds SSS 71
   9 hole Academy course
👥 U SOC
££ 18 holes–£16 (£20) 9 holes–£6 (£6)

⚬ Nr M27 Junction 2, at Ower
⊕ Driving range

Petersfield (1892)
Tankerdale Lane, Liss, GU33 7QY
☎ (01730) 895165
🖷 (01730) 894713
▥ 730
♠ RR Hine
✓ G Hughes (01730) 895216
⊱ 18 L 6450 yds Par 72 SSS 71
♔ WD–U WE/BH–NA before noon
SOC–Mon/Wed/Fri
£€ £25 (£30)
⚬ Off A3, at Liss exit (B3006)
⌂ Hawtree

Petersfield Sussex Road
Pay and play
Sussex Road, Petersfield
☎ (01730) 267732
♠ RR Hine
✓ G Hughes
⊱ 9 L 3005 yds
♔ U
£€ 9 holes–£7 (£9)
18 holes–£11 (£13)
⚬ Petersfield

Portsmouth (1926)
Public
Crookhorn Lane, Widley, Waterlooville,
PO7 5QL
☎ (023) 9237 2210
🖷 (023) 9220 0766
▥ 650
♠ D Houlihan (023) 9220 1827
ext 21
✓ J Banting (023) 9237 2210 ext 24
⊱ 18 L 6139 yds SSS 70
♔ U SOC–arrange with Pro
£€ £9–£12
⚬ 1 mile N of Portsmouth, on B2177
⊕ Practice area, putting green,
practice nets
⌂ Hawtree
■ www.portsmouthgc.com

Romsey (1900)
Nursling, Southampton, SO16 0XW
☎ (023) 8073 2218
🖷 (023) 8074 1036
▥ 655
♠ MR Batty (023) 8073 4637
✓ M Desmond (023) 8073 6673
⊱ 18 L 5856 yds SSS 68
♔ WD–H WE/BH–M H
£€ £27.50 D–£33
⚬ 2 miles SE of Romsey on A3057.
M27/M271 Junction 3
■ www.romseygolfclub.com

Rowlands Castle (1902)
Links Lane, Rowlands Castle,
PO9 6AE
☎ (023) 9241 2216
🖷 (023) 9241 3649
▨ manager@rowlandscastlegolfclub
.co.uk
▥ 800 150(L) 50(J)
♠ KD Fisher (023) 9241 2784

✓ P Klepacz (023) 9241 2785
⊱ 18 L 6618 yds Par 72 SSS 72
♔ WD–U H exc Wed am–restricted
WE–phone first Sat–M SOC–Tues
& Thurs
£€ £34 (£38)
⚬ 9 miles S of Petersfield, off A3(M).
3 miles N of Havant
⌂ HS Colt

Royal Winchester (1888)
Sarum Road, Winchester, SO22 5QE
☎ (01962) 852462
🖷 (01962) 865048
▥ 750
♠ A Buck
✓ S Hunter (01962) 862473
⊱ 18 L 6216 yds SSS 70
♔ WD–U H WE/BH–M
SOC–Mon/Tues/Wed
£€ On application
⚬ W of Winchester. M3 Junction 11
⌂ JH Taylor

Sandford Springs (1988)
Wolverton, Tadley, RG26 5RT
☎ (01635) 296800
🖷 (01635) 296801
▨ garye@leaderboardgolf.co.uk
▥ 700
♠ G Edmunds
✓ G Edmunds (01635) 296808
⊱ 27 L 6100 yds SSS 70
♔ WD–prior booking WE–M
SOC–WD
£€ £28 D–£37
⚬ 8 miles N of Basingstoke on A339
⌂ Hawtree

Somerley Park (1995)
Somerley, Ringwood, BH24 3PL
☎ (01425) 655538
▥ 169
♠ P Kinnison
✓ J Waring (01202) 821703
⊱ 9 L 2155 yds Par 33 SSS 62
♔ M SOC
£€ £10
⚬ 5 miles W of Ringwood
⌂ John Jacobs OBE

South Winchester
Romsey Road, Pitt, Winchester,
SO22 5QX
☎ (01962) 877800
🖷 (01962) 877900
▨ winchester-sales@crown-golf.co.uk
▥ 750
♠ L Ross (Gen Mgr)
(01962) 877800
✓ R Adams (01962) 840469
⊱ 18 L 7086 yds SSS 74
♔ H SOC
£€ £25 (£40)
⚬ S side of Winchester, M3 J11
⊕ Driving range
⌂ Dave Thomas/Peter Alliss
■ www.crown-golf.co.uk

Southampton Municipal
(1935)
Public
1 Golf Course Road, Bassett,
Southampton, SO16 7AY
☎ (023) 8076 8407
▨ donaldcampbell
@southamptongolfclub.fsnet.co.uk
♠ D Campbell (07720) 846713
✓ L Walsh
⊱ 18 L 6218 yds SSS 70
9 L 2391 yds SSS 33
♔ U
£€ On application
⚬ 2 miles N of Southampton
⌂ JH Taylor
■ www.southamptongolfclub.co.uk

Southsea (1914)
Public
The Clubhouse, Burrfields Road,
Portsmouth, PO3 5JJ
☎ (023) 9266 4549
🖷 (023) 9265 0525
▥ 350
♠ K Parker (023) 9266 8667
✓ T Healy
⊱ 18 L 5970 yds SSS 68
♔ U SOC
£€ £11 (£13)
⚬ 1 mile off M27 on A2030
⊕ Driving range

Southwick Park (1977)
Pinsley Drive, Southwick, PO17 6EL
☎ (023) 9238 0131
🖷 (023) 9221 0289
▥ 650 80(L)
♠ NW Price
✓ J Green (023) 9238 0442
⊱ 18 L 5884 yds SSS 69
♔ WD–U booking necessary WE–NA
before 2pm SOC
£€ On application. Service Personnel
reduced rate
⚬ 5 miles N of Portsmouth, off B2177

Southwood (1977)
Public
Ively Road, Farnborough, GU14 0LJ
☎ (01252) 548700
🖷 (01252) 549091
▥ 480
♠ MJ Pettifor
✓ M Robbins
⊱ 18 L 5738 yds Par 69 SSS 68
♔ U
£€ £15.90 (£18.50)
⚬ 1 mile W of Farnborough, off
A325; 2 miles from M3 J4A
⌂ M Hawtree

Stoneham (1908)
Monks Wood Close, Bassett,
Southampton, SO16 3TT
☎ (023) 8076 9272
🖷 (023) 8076 6320
▨ richard.penley-
martin@stonehamgolfclub.org.uk
▥ 600

For list of abbreviations and key to symbols see page 627

⚭ R Penley-Martin (Mgr)
(023) 8076 9272
⚐ I Young (023) 8076 8397
⚒ 18 L 6387 yds SSS 70
⚶ H SOC–Mon/Thurs/Fri
£€ £35 D–£40 (£45 D–£57)
⚭ 2 miles N of Southampton on A27
♟ Willie Park

Test Valley (1992)
Micheldever Road, Overton,
Basingstoke, RG25 3DS
☏ **(08707) 459020**
⚐ (08707) 459023
♭ 550
⚭ A Briggs (Mgr) (08707) 459021
⚐ A Briggs
⚒ 18 L 6897 yds SSS 73
⚶ U SOC
£€ £18 (£24)
⚭ 2 miles S of Overton on
Micheldever road. M3 Junction 8
(A303)
♟ Wright/Darcy

Tournerbury Golf Centre (1993)
Pay and play
Tournerbury Road, Hayling Island,
PO11 9DL
☏ **(023) 9246 2266**
⚐ R Brown
⚒ 9 L 2956 yds SSS 35
⚶ U SOC
£€ 9 holes–£7 (£8.30)
⚭ E coast of Hayling Island. 3 miles S
of Havant
⊕ Driving range

Tylney Park (1973)
Rotherwick, Basingstoke, RG27 9AY
☏ **(01256) 762079**
⚐ (01256) 763079
♭ 700
⚭ MR Alcock
⚐ C de Bruin (Mgr)
⚒ 18 L 6108 yds SSS 69
⚶ WD–U WE–M or H SOC
£€ On application
⚭ 2 miles NW of Hook. M3 J5

Waterlooville (1907)
Cherry Tree Ave, Cowplain,
Waterlooville, PO8 8AP
☏ **(023) 9226 3388**
⚐ (023) 9224 2980
✉ secretary@waterloovillegolfclub
.co.uk
♭ 800
⚭ D Nairne
⚐ J Hay (023) 9225 6911
⚒ 18 L 6602 yds SSS 72
⚶ WD/WE–M H (Sun am–XL) SOC
£€ £30 D–£35
⚭ 10 miles N of Portsmouth on A3
♟ Henry Cotton
■ www.waterloovillegolfclub.co.uk

Wellow (1991)
Ryedown Lane, East Wellow, Romsey,
SO51 6BD
☏ **(01794) 322872**

⚐ (01794) 323832
♭ 600
⚭ Mrs C Gurd
⚐ N Bratley (01794) 323833
⚒ 27 L 6000 yds SSS 69
⚶ U SOC–WD
£€ £17 (£21)
⚭ 2 miles W of Romsey. M27
Junction 2, via A36
♟ W Wiltshire

Weybrook Park (1971)
Rooksdown Lane, Basingstoke,
RG24 9NT
☏ **(01256) 320347**
⚐ (01256) 812973
✉ office_weybrookpark@barbox.net
♭ 600
⚭ A Dillon (Mgr)
⚐ A Dillon (01256) 333232
⚒ 18 L 6468 yds SSS 71
⚶ WD–U WE–contact Mgr SOC
£€ £21.50 (£28)
⚭ 1¹/₂ miles N of Basingstoke

Wickham Park
Titchfield Lane, Wickham, Fareham,
PO17 5PJ
☏ **(01329) 833342**
⚐ (01329) 834798
✉ i.yates@crown-golf.co.uk
⚭ I Yates (Mgr)
⚐ S Edwards
⚒ 18 L 5737 yds Par 69 SSS 67
⚶ U SOC–WD
£€ £14 (£17)
⚭ 2 miles N of Fareham. M27
Junction 10
♟ Jon Payn
■ www.grown-golf.co.uk

Worldham Park (1993)
Pay and play
Cakers Lane, Worldham, Alton,
GU34 3AG
☏ **(01420) 543151/544606**
♭ 500
⚭ NV Harvey (01420) 544606
⚐ J Le Roux (01420) 543151
⚒ 18 L 6196 yds SSS 70
⚶ WD–U WE–U after 11am
SOC–WD
£€ £12 (£15)
⚭ ¹/₂ mile E of Alton on B3004 to
Bordon
⊕ Driving range
♟ Troth/Whidborne

Herefordshire

Belmont Lodge (1983)
Belmont, Hereford, HR2 9SA
☏ **(01432) 352666**
⚐ (01432) 358090
✉ info@belmont-hereford.co.uk
♭ 500
⚭ B Macaskill (Mgr)
⚐ M Welsh (01432) 352717
⚒ 18 L 6511 yds SSS 71

⚶ U SOC
£€ On application
⚭ 1¹/₂ miles S of Hereford on A465
♟ B Sandow
■ www.belmont-hereford.co.uk

Burghill Valley (1991)
Tillington Road, Burghill, Hereford,
HR4 7RW
☏ **(01432) 760456**
⚐ (01432) 761654
✉ golf@bvgc.co.uk
⚭ K Smith (Mgr)
⚐ N Clarke (01432) 760808
⚒ 18 L 6239 yds SSS 70
⚶ U SOC
£€ £20 (£25)
⚭ 3 miles N of Hereford, off A4110
■ www.bvgc.co.uk

Cadmore Lodge (1990)
Pay and play
Berrington Green, Tenbury Wells,
Worcester, WR15 8TQ
☏ **(01584) 810044**
⚐ (01584) 810044
♭ 150
⚭ RV Farr
⚐ None
⚒ 9 L 5129 yds Par 68 SSS 65
⚶ U
£€ D–£10 (D–£14)
⚭ 2 miles S of Tenbury Wells on
A4112
■ www.cadmorelodge.demon.co.uk

Hereford Municipal (1983)
Public
Holmer Road, Hereford, HR4 9UD
☏ **(01432) 344376**
⚐ (01432) 266281
♭ 200
⚭ G Morgan (Mgr)
⚐ G Morgan (01432) 344376
⚒ 9 L 3060 yds Par 70 SSS 69
⚶ U SOC
£€ 18 holes–£7.50 9 holes–£5
⚭ Hereford Leisure Centre, A49
Leominster road
⊕ Practice area and putting green

Herefordshire (1896)
Raven's Causeway, Wormsley, Hereford,
HR4 8LY
☏ **(01432) 830219**
⚐ (01432) 830095
♭ 770 150(L) 55(J)
⚭ B Maggs
⚐ D Hemming (01432) 830465
⚒ 18 L 6031 yds SSS 69
⚶ U–phone first SOC
£€ £20 D–£25 (£25 D–£32)
⚭ 6 miles NW of Hereford

Kington (1926)
Bradnor Hill, Kington, HR5 3RE
☏ **(01544) 230340**
⚐ (01544) 340270
♭ 500
⚭ GR Wictome (01544) 340270
⚐ A Gealy (01544) 231320

18 L 5840 yds SSS 68
WE–NA before 10.15am –restricted
1.30–2.45pm SOC
£€ £16 D–£21 (£22 D–£27)
1 mile N of Kington
CK Hutchinson

Leominster (1967)

Ford Bridge, Leominster, HR6 0LE
☎ **(01568) 612863 (Clubhouse)**
(01568) 610055
leominstergolf@freeuk.com
450
L Green (01568) 610055
A Ferriday (01568) 611402
18 L 6026 yds SSS 69
U SOC
£€ £15.50 D–£19 (£22 D–£25)
3 miles S of Leominster on A49
(Leominster By-pass)
R Sandow

Ross-on-Wye (1903)

*Two Park, Gorsley, Ross-on-Wye,
HR9 7UT*
☎ **(01989) 720267**
(01989) 720212
secretary@therossonwyegolfclub
.co.uk
760
Peter Plumb
N Catchpole (01989) 720439
18 L 6500 yds Par 72 SSS 71
U SOC–Wed–Fri (min 16 players)
£€ £36–£46 SOC–£28–£40
5 miles N of Ross-on-Wye, by M50
Junction 3
Parkland driving range
CK Cotton
www.rossonwyegolfclub.co.uk

Sapey (1991)

Proprietary
Upper Sapey, Worcester, WR6 6XT
☎ **(01886) 853288**
(01886) 853485
anybody@sapeygolf.co.uk
450
Miss L Stevenson
C Knowles
18 L 5939 yds SSS 68
9 hole Par 3 course
WD–U WE–NA before 10am SOC
£€ £18 (£23)
6 miles N of Bromyard on B4203.
M5 Junction 5
www.sapeygolf.co.uk

South Herefordshire (1992)

*Twin Lakes, Upton Bishop, Ross-on-Wye,
HR9 7UA*
☎ **(01989) 780535**
(01989) 780535
300
RLA Lee (Mgr)
E Litchfield
18 L 6672 yds Par 71 SSS 72
9 hole Par 3 course
U SOC
£€ £15 (£20)
3 miles NE of Ross-on-Wye. M50
Junction 4

Floodlit driving range
John Day

Hertfordshire

Aldenham G&CC (1975)

*Church Lane, Aldenham, Watford,
WD25 8NN*
☎ **(01923) 853929**
(01923) 858472
info@aldenhamgolfclub.co.uk
500
Mrs J Phillips
T Dunstan (01923) 857889
18 L 6456 yds SSS 71
9 L 2350 yds
WD–U WE–U after 12.30pm
£€ 18 hole: £26 (£35). 9 hole: £10
(£12)
3 miles E of Watford, off B462. M1
Junction 5

Aldwickbury Park (1995)

*Piggottshill Lane, Wheathampstead
Road, Harpenden, AL5 1AB*
☎ **(01582) 765112**
(01582) 760113
enquiries
@aldwickburyparkgolfclub.com
700
A Knott
P Toyer (01582) 760112
18 L 6032 yds Par 71 SSS 69
9 hole Par 3 course
WD–U booking necessary WE–U
after 12.00 SOC–WD
£€ £26 (£32)
E of Harpenden on
Wheathampstead road. M1 Junction
9. A1(M) Junction 4
Gillett/Brown
www.aldwickburyparkgolfclub.com

Arkley (1909)

Rowley Green Road, Barnet, EN5 3HL
☎ **(020) 8449 0394**
(020) 8440 5214
secretary@arkleygolfclub.co.uk
350
DDR Campbell
M Porter (020) 8440 8473
9 L 6046 yds SSS 69 – 18 tees
WD–U WE–M SOC–Wed–Fri
£€ £25
NW of Barnet, off A1(M)
James Braid
www.arkleygolfclub.co.uk

Ashridge (1932)

*Little Gaddesden, Berkhamsted,
HP4 1LY*
☎ **(01442) 842244**
(01442) 843770
info@ashridgegolfclub.ltd.uk
700
MS Silver
A Ainsworth (01442) 842307
18 L 6580 yds SSS 71
WD only–phone Sec

£€ On application
5 miles N of Berkhamsted on
B4506
Campbell/Hutchison/Hotchkin
www.ashridgegolfclub.ltd.uk

Barkway Park (1992)

*Nuthampstead Road, Barkway, Royston,
SG8 8EN*
☎ **(01763) 849070**
285
GS Cannon
J Bates (01763) 848215
18 L 6997 yds SSS 74
U
£€ £10 (£15)
5 miles SE of Royston, on B1368
Vivien Saunders

Batchwood Hall (1935)

Pay and play
Batchwood Drive, St Albans, AL3 5XA
☎ **(01727) 833349**
(01582) 833530
425
B Hudson
18 L 6487 yds SSS 71
WD–U WE–NA before 10am
£€ £10.80 (£13.90)
NW of St Albans on A5081. 5
miles S of M1 Junction 9
JH Taylor

Batchworth Park (1996)

London Road, Rickmansworth, WD3 1JS
☎ **(01923) 711400**
(01923) 710200
750
S Proudfoot (01923) 714922
18 L 6723 yds Par 72 SSS 72
M
£€ N/A
1 mile SE of Rickmansworth on
A404. M25 Junction 18
Indoor Academy. Practice range
Dave Thomas

Berkhamsted (1890)

The Common, Berkhamsted, HP4 2QB
☎ **(01442) 865832**
(01442) 863730
barryh@berkhamstedgc.co.uk
450 120(L) 50(J)
BJ Hill
J Clarke (01442) 865851
18 L 6605 yds Par 71 SSS 72
U H WD after 8.30am WE after
11.30am SOC Mon–Wed–Fri
£€ On application
1 mile N of Berkhamsted. M25
Junction 21 (A41). M1 Junction 8
HS Colt/James Braid

Bishop's Stortford (1910)

*Dunmow Road, Bishop's Stortford,
CM23 5HP*
☎ **(01279) 654715**
(01279) 655215
office@bsgc.co.uk
900
B Collins

✔ SM Bryan (01279) 651324
⊳ 18 L 6404 yds SSS 71
🏌 WD–U H WE–M SOC–WD exc
Tues
££ £30 D–£39
⛳ E of Bishop's Stortford on A1250.
M11 Junction 8, ¹/₂mile
🏠 James Braid
■ www.bsgc.co.uk

Boxmoor   (1890)
*18 Box Lane, Hemel Hempstead,
HP3 0DJ*
☎ **(01442) 242434 (Clubhouse)**
📖 290
⚲ CJ Horsted (07976) 747567
✔ None
⊳ 9 L 4854 yds SSS 64
🏌 U exc Sun–NA
££ £12 Sat–£14
⛳ 1 mile W of Hemel Hempstead on
B4505 to Chesham
■ www.boxmoorgolfclub.co.uk

Brickendon Grange
(1964)
*Pembridge Lane, Brickendon, Hertford,
SG13 8PD*
☎ **(01992) 511258**
🖄 (01992) 511411
✉ play@brickendongrangegc.co.uk
📖 700
⚲ Martin Bennet
✔ G Tippett (01992) 511218
⊳ 18 L 6420 yds SSS 71
🏌 WD–U H WE/BH–M SOC
££ £33 D–£45
⛳ Bayford, 3 miles S of Hertford
🏠 CK Cotton
■ www.brickendongrangegc.co.uk

Bridgedown   (1994)
St Albans Road, Barnet, EN5 4RE
☎ **(020) 8440 4120**
🖄 (020) 8441 7649
📖 400
⚲ Mrs A Menai-Davis (020) 8441
7649
✔ L Jones
⊳ 18 L 6626 yds Par 72 SSS 72
🏌 U
££ £15 (£17)
⛳ 1 mile S of South Mimms on
A1081. M25 Junction 23
⊕ Practice range
🏠 Howard Swann

Briggens House Hotel
(1988)
*Briggens Park, Stanstead Road,
Stanstead Abbotts, SG12 8LD*
☎ **(01279) 793742**
🖄 (01279) 793685
📖 280
⚲ A Battle (Mgr)
⊳ 9 L 5825 yds SSS 69
🏌 U SOC
££ 9 holes–£10 (£12)
⛳ 4 miles E of Hertford, off A414

Brocket Hall   (1992)
Welwyn, AL8 7XG
☎ **(01707) 368808**
✉ paulden@brocket-hall.co.uk
📖 850
⚲ P Densham (01707) 368808
✔ K Wood (01707) 390063
⊳ Melbourne 18 L 6616 yds SSS 72;
Palmerston 18 L 7061 yds SSS 73
🏌 M H
⛳ On B653 to Wheathampstead.
A1(M) Junction 4
⊕ Driving range. Nick Faldo Golf
Institute
🏠 Melbourne-Alliss/Clark.
Palmerston-Steel

Brookmans Park   (1930)
Brookmans Park, Hatfield, AL9 7AT
☎ **(01707) 652487**
🖄 (01707) 661851
📖 800
⚲ PA Gill
✔ I Jelley (01707) 652468
⊳ 18 L 6473 yds SSS 71
🏌 WD–UH WE/BH–M SOC
££ £32
⛳ 3 miles S of Hatfield, off A1000
🏠 Hawtree/Taylor

Bushey G&CC   (1980)
High Street, Bushey, WD2 1BJ
☎ **(020) 8950 2283**
🖄 (020) 8386 1181
📖 446
⚲ B Worthington
✔ G Atkinson (020) 8950 2215
⊳ 9 L 3030 yds SSS 70
🏌 WD–U before 6pm WE/BH–U after
3.30pm Wed–closed SOC–WD exc
Wed
££ 18 holes–£18 (£21). 9 holes–£12
(£14)
⛳ 2 miles S of Watford on A4008
⊕ Driving range

Bushey Hall   (1890)
Bushey Hall Drive, Bushey, WD23 2EP
☎ **(01923) 222253**
🖄 (01923) 229759
✉ roy@golfclubuk.co.uk
📖 460
⚲ R Penman
✔ K Wickham (01923) 225802
⊳ 18 L 6055 yds SSS 69
🏌 U SOC–WD WE–NA before 11.00
££ £25 (£32)
⛳ 1 mile SE of Watford. M1 Junction
5
🏠 James Braid
■ www.golfclubuk.co.uk

Chadwell Springs   (1974)
Hertford Road, Ware, SG12 9LE
☎ **(01920) 463647**
📖 350
⚲ M Scott (01920) 461447
✔ M Wall (01920) 462075
⊳ 9 L 3021 yds SSS 69
🏌 WD–U WE–M
££ £20

⛳ Between Ware and Hertford on
A119

Chesfield Downs   (1991)
Pay and play
*Jack's Hill, Graveley, Stevenage,
SG4 7EQ*
☎ **(08707) 460020**
🖄 (08707) 460021
📖 550
⚲ P Barnfather
✔ K Bond
⊳ 18 L 6646 yds SSS 71
9 holes Par 3 course
🏌 U SOC
££ 18 hole:£20 (£28). 9 hole:£5.50
(£6.50)
⛳ B197, N of Stevenage. A1(M)
Junctions 8 or 9
⊕ Driving range
🏠 Jonathan Gaunt

Cheshunt   (1976)
Public
Park Lane, Cheshunt, EN7 6QD
☎ **(01992) 29777**
📖 280
⚲ B Furne
✔ D Banks (01992) 24009
⊳ 18 L 6608 yds SSS 71
🏌 U–booking required
££ £12 (£16.50)
⛳ Off A10 at Church Lane, Cheshunt.
M25 Junction 25, 3 miles
🏠 Hawtree

Chorleywood   (1890)
Common Road, Chorleywood, WD3 5LN
☎ **(01923) 282009**
🖄 (01923) 286739
✉ chorleywood.gc@btclick.com
📖 320
⚲ RA Botham
✔ RM Mandeville
⊳ 9 L 2856 yds SSS 67
🏌 WD–U exc Tues am WE–U after
11.30am SOC
££ £20 (£25)
⛳ 3 miles N of Rickmansworth, off
A404. M25 Junction 18

Danesbury Park   (1991)
Codicote Road, Welwyn, AL6 9SD
☎ **(01438) 840100**
🖄 (01727) 840768
✉ d.s@snowdongolf.com
📖 300
⚲ D Snowdon (01438) 840100
✔ Carl Duke (01438) 840100
⊳ 9 L 4150 yds SSS 60
🏌 U WD WE after 11pm
££ £10 (£12)
⛳ ³/₄ mile from A1(M) Junction 6 on
B656 Hitchin road
🏠 Derek Snowdon

Dyrham Park CC   (1963)
Galley Lane, Barnet, EN5 4RA
☎ **(020) 8440 3361**
🖄 (020) 8441 9836
📖 600

🖉 K Sutton
✓ W Large (020) 8440 3904
🏳 18 L 6422 yds SSS 71
👭 M SOC–Wed
🚗 10 miles N of London. M25
Junction 23
🏠 CK Cotton

East Herts   (1899)
Hamels Park, Buntingford, SG9 9NA
☎ (01920) 821923
🖥 (01920) 823700
📧 secretary@ehgc.fsnet.co.uk
📖 700
🖉 C Day (01920) 821978
✓ G Culmer (01920) 821922
🏳 18 L 6456 yds SSS 71
👭 WD–H exc Wed–NA before 1pm
WE–M
£€ £30 (£40)
🚗 ¼ mile N of Puckeridge on A10
📶 www.ehgc.co.uk

Elstree   (1984)
Watling Street, Elstree, WD6 3AA
☎ (020) 8238 6947 (Clubhouse)
🖥 (020) 8207 6390
📧 admin@elstree-golf.co.uk
📖 400
🖉 K Roberts (020) 8238 6942
✓ M Warwick (020) 8238 6941
🏳 18 L 6556 yds Par 73 SSS 72
👭 U SOC
£€ On application
🚗 A5183, 1 mile N of Elstree. M1
Junction 4
⊕ Floodlit driving range
🏠 Donald Steel
📶 www.elstree-golfclub.co.uk

Forest Hills   (1994)
Newgate Street, SG13 8EW
☎ (01707) 876825
🖥 (01707) 876825
📖 170
🖉 G Spearpoint
✓ C Easton
🏳 9 L 3220 yds Par 72 SSS 71
👭 WD–U WE/BH–by arrangement
£€ £15 (£20)
🚗 3 miles W of Cheshunt. M25
Junction 25
🏠 Mel Flannagan

Great Hadham   (1993)
*Great Hadham Road, Bishop's Stortford,
SG10 6JE*
☎ (01279) 843558
🖥 (01279) 842122
📖 700
🖉 I Bailey
✓ K Lunt (01279) 843888
🏳 18 L 6854 yds Par 72 SSS 73
👭 WD–U WE/BH–NA before 12
noon SOC
£€ £20 (£27)
🚗 3 miles SW of Bishops Stortford
(B1004). M11 Junction 8
⊕ Driving range

The Grove   (2003)
*Chandler's Cross, Rickmansworth,
WD3 4TG*
☎ (01923) 807807
🖥 (01923) 294268
📧 golf@thegrove.co.uk
🖉 Blyth Reid (Dir. of Golf)
✓ Spencer Schaub
🏳 18 L 6766 yds
👭 U
£€ £60–£130 depending on time of year
🚗 2 miles S of M25 (J20) on the A411
🏠 Kyle Phillips
📶 www.thegrove.co.uk

Hadley Wood   (1922)
*Beech Hill, Hadley Wood, Barnet,
EN4 0JJ*
☎ (020) 8449 4328
🖥 (020) 8364 8633
📧 gen.mgr@hadleywoodgc.com
📖 635
🖉 CS Silcox (Gen Mgr)
✓ P Jones (020) 8449 3285
🏳 18 L 6514 yds SSS 71
👭 WD–H WE/BH–M SOC
£€ On application
🚗 10 miles N of London, off A111
between Potters Bar and
Cockfosters. 2 miles S of M25 J4
⊕ Practice range
🏠 Dr A Mackenzie
📶 www.hadleywoodgc.com

Hanbury Manor G&CC
(1990)
Ware, SG12 0SD
☎ (01920) 487722
🖥 (01920) 487692
📧 golf.hanbury@marriotthotels.co.uk
📖 400
🖉 Iain McInally (Dir. of Golf)
✓ D Ingram
🏳 18 L 7016 yds SSS 74
👭 M H + Hotel guests SOC
£€ £85
🚗 8 miles N of M25 Junction 25 on
A10 at Thundridge
🏠 Jack Nicklaus II
📶 www.hanbury-manor.com

Harpenden   (1894)
Hammonds End, Harpenden, AL5 2AX
☎ (01582) 712580
🖥 (01582) 712725
📧 office@harpendengolfclub.co.uk
📖 800
🖉 FLK Clapp (Gen Mgr)
✓ P Cherry (01582) 767124
🏳 18 L 6377 yds SSS 70
👭 WD–U exc Thurs WE/BH–M
SOC–WD exc Thurs
£€ £30 D–£40
🚗 6 miles N of St Albans on B487
🏠 Hawtree/Taylor

Harpenden Common   (1931)
East Common, Harpenden, AL5 1BL
☎ (01582) 711320
🖥 (01582) 711321
📧 admin@hcgc.co.uk

📖 740
🖉 PJ Clarke (01582) 711320
✓ D Fitzsimmon (01582) 460655
🏳 18 L 6214 yds SSS 70
👭 WD–U H WE–M SOC
£€ £25 (£30)
🚗 4 miles N of St Albans, on A1081
M1, J9
🏠 K Brown (1995)

Hartsbourne G&CC   (1946)
*Hartsbourne Avenue, Bushey Heath,
WD23 1JW*
☎ (020) 8421 7272
🖥 (020) 8950 5357
📖 750
🖉 I Thomas
✓ R Weedon (020) 8421 7266
🏳 18 L 6385 yds SSS 70
9 L 5773 yds SSS 68
👭 NA SOC
🚗 5 miles SE of Watford, off A4008
🏠 Hawtree/Taylor

Hatfield London CC   (1976)
*Bedwell Park, Essendon, Hatfield,
AL9 6HN*
☎ (01707) 260360
🖥 (01707) 278475
📧 hlccgolf@aol.com
📖 260
🖉 H Takeda
✓ N Greer (01707) 650431
🏳 18 L 6808 yds SSS 72
18 L 6938 yds SSS 73
36 hole course
👭 U SOC
£€ £22 (£31)
🚗 4 miles E of Hatfield on B158. M25
Junction 24. A1(M) Junction 4
⊕ 9 hole pitch & putt course
🏠 Fred Hawtree

The Hertfordshire   (1995)
Proprietary
*Broxbournebury Mansion, White Stubbs
Lane, Broxbourne, EN10 7PY*
☎ (01992) 466666
🖥 (01992) 470326
📧 hertfordshire@americangolf.co.uk
📖 690
🖉 J Hetherington
✓ D Smith
🏳 18 L 6400 yds Par 70 SSS 70
👭 U H SOC
£€ £30
🚗 8 miles N of M25 J25, off A10
⊕ Floodlit driving range
🏠 Jack Nicklaus II

Kingsway Golf Centre
(1991)
*Cambridge Road, Melbourn, Royston,
SG8 6EY*
☎ (01763) 262727
🖥 (01763) 263298
📖 200
🖉 B Smith
✓ S Brown
🏳 9 L 2500 yds Par 33
9 hole Par 3 course
👭 U SOC

£€ 9 holes–£5.50 (£7.50). 18 holes–£9 (£12)
⛳ N of Royston on A10
⊕ Driving range

Knebworth (1908)

Deards End Lane, Knebworth, SG3 6NL
☎ **(01438) 812752 (Clubhouse)**
🖥 (01438) 815216
📧 knebworthgolf@virgin.net
💻 1000
🏌 M Parsons MBE (01438) 812752
⛳ G Parker (01438) 812757
🏴 18 L 6492 yds SSS 71
👥 WD–U H WE–M SOC–Mon/Tues/Thurs
£€ £35
⛳ 1 mile S of Stevenage on B197. A1(M) Junction 7
⛩ Willie Park

Lamerwood (1996)

Codicote Road, Wheathampstead, AL4 8GB
☎ **(01582) 833013**
🖥 (01582) 832604
📧 lamerwood.cc@virgin.net
🏌 S Takabatake (Golf Dir)
⛳ M Masters (01582) 833013
🏴 18 L 6953 yds Par 72
9 hole Par 3 course
👥 U
£€ £25 (£40)
⛳ 5 miles W of A1(M) J4 on B653
⊕ Driving range
⛩ Cameron Sinclair

Letchworth (1905)

Letchworth Lane, Letchworth Garden City, SG6 3NQ
☎ **(01462) 683203**
🖥 (01462) 484567
📧 letchworthgolfclub@uk2.net
💻 900
🏌 C Allen
⛳ (01462) 682713
🏴 18 L 6459 yds SSS 71
👥 WD–H WE–M SOC–Wed–Fri
£€ £30
⛳ S of Letchworth, off A505. A1(M) Junction 9
⊕ Driving range
⛩ Harry Vardon

Little Hay Golf Complex (1977)

Pay and play
Box Lane, Bovingdon, Hemel Hempstead, HP3 0DQ
☎ **(01442) 833798**
🖥 (01442) 831399
🏌 C Gordon (Golf Mgr)
⛳ N Allen and M Perry
🏴 18 L 6592 yds SSS 71
👥 U SOC
£€ £13 (£17)
⛳ 2 miles W of Hemel Hempstead, on B4505 to Chesham
⊕ Driving range. Pitch & putt
⛩ Hawtree

Manor of Groves G&CC (1991)

High Wych, Sawbridgeworth, CM21 0JU
☎ **(01279) 600777**
🖥 (01279) 600374
💻 650
🏌 R Walker (01279) 722247
⛳ R Hurd
🏴 18 L 6227 yds par 71 SSS 70
👥 WD–U WE–NA before noon SOC
£€ On application
⛳ 1 mile N of Harlow (M11 J7)

Mid Herts (1892)

Gustard Wood, Wheathampstead, AL4 8RS
☎ **(01582) 832242**
🖥 (01582) 834834
📧 secretary@mid-hertsgolfclub.co.uk
💻 500(M) 125(L)
🏌 RJH Jourdan
⛳ B Puttick (01582) 832788
🏴 18 L 6060 yds SSS 69
👥 WD–UH exc Tues & Wed pm WE/BH–M SOC
£€ On application
⛳ 6 miles N of St Albans on B651
■ www.mid-hertsgolfclub.co.uk

Mill Green (1994)

Gypsy Lane, Mill Green, Welwyn Garden City, AL7 4TY
☎ **(01707) 276900**
🖥 (01707) 276898
🏌 Tim Hudson
⛳ I Parker (01707) 270542
🏴 18 L 6615 yds Par 72 SSS 72
Par 3 course
👥 U SOC–WD
£€ £25 (£30)
⛳ S of Welwyn Garden City, off A414. A1 Junction 4
⛩ Clark/Alliss

Moor Park (1923)

Rickmansworth, WD3 1QN
☎ **(01923) 773146**
🖥 (01923) 777109
💻 1700
🏌 JM Moore (01923) 773146
⛳ L Farmer (01923) 774113
🏴 High 18 L 6713 yds SSS 72
West 18 L 5823 yds SSS 68
👥 WD–H WE/BH–M SOC
£€ High £69. West £42.50
⛳ 1 mile SE of Rickmansworth, off Batchworth roundabout (A4145). M25 Junction 18, 2 miles
⛩ HS Colt
■ www.moorparkgc.co.uk

Old Fold Manor (1910)

Old Fold Lane, Hadley Green, Barnet, EN5 4QN
☎ **(020) 8440 9185**
🖥 (020) 8441 4863
📧 manager@oldfoldmanor.co.uk
💻 550
🏌 B Cullen (Mgr)
⛳ P McEvoy (020) 8440 7488
🏴 18 L 6466 yds SSS 71

👥 WD–H WE–M SOC–Thurs & Fri
£€ £25 D–£35
⛳ 1 mile N of Barnet on A1000
■ www.oldfoldmanor.co.uk

Oxhey Park

Prestwick Road, South Oxhey, Watford, WD19 7EX
☎ **(01923) 248213/210118**
💻 110
🏌 AT Duggan (Prop)
⛳ J Wright
🏴 9 L 1637 yds Par 58
👥 U
£€ 9 holes–£6 (£8). 18 holes–£8 (£10)
⛳ 2 miles SW of Watford. M1 J5
⊕ Driving range

Panshanger Golf Complex (1976)

Old Herns Lane, Welwyn Garden City, AL7 2ED
☎ **(01707) 333312/333350 (Bookings)**
🏴 18 L 6167 yds SSS 70
9 hole Par 3 course
👥 U
£€ On application
⛳ 2 miles off A1, via B1000 to Hertford

Porters Park (1899)

Shenley Hill, Radlett, WD7 7AZ
☎ **(01923) 854127**
🖥 (01923) 855475
💻 850
🏌 P Marshall
⛳ D Gleeson (01923) 854366
🏴 18 L 6313 yds SSS 70
👥 WD–H (phone first) WE/BH–M SOC–Wed & Thurs
£€ £40–£55
⛳ E of Radlett on Shenley road. M25 Junction 22

Potters Bar (1923)

Darkes Lane, Potters Bar, EN6 1DE
☎ **(01707) 652020**
🖥 (01707) 655051
💻 600
🏌 PK Watson (Mgr)
⛳ G A'ris, J Harding (01707) 652987
🏴 18 L 6279 yds SSS 70
👥 WD–H WE/BH–M SOC–WD exc Wed
£€ £25 D–£35
⛳ 1 mile N of M25 J24, off A1000
⛩ James Braid
■ www.pottersbargolfclub.com

Redbourn (1970)

Kinsbourne Green Lane, Redbourn, St Albans, AL3 7QA
☎ **(01582) 793493**
🖥 (01582) 794362
📧 enquiries@redbourngolfclub.com
🏌 S Hatch (01582) 794888
⛳ S Hunter
🏴 18 L 6506 yds SSS 71
9 hole Par 3 course
👥 WD–U booking necessary WE/BH–H SOC–WD

£€ 18 hole: £26 (£32) 9 hole: £6 (£7)
⬥ 4 miles N of St Albans, off A5. 1
mile S of M1 Junction 9
⊕ Target golf range
■ www.redbourngolfclub.com

Rickmansworth (1937)
Public
Moor Lane, Rickmansworth, WD3 1QL
☎ (01923) 775278
🖳 (01923) 775278
📖 250
✎ A Dobbins (01923) 775278
⮕ 18 L 4493 yds SSS 62
9 hole Par 3 course
👤 U
£€ £12.50 (£17.50)
⬥ ¹/₂ mile SE of Rickmansworth, off
Batchworth roundabout (A4145).
M25 Junction 18, 2 miles
🏠 HS Colt

Royston (1892)
Baldock Road, Royston, SG8 5BG
☎ (01763) 242696
🖳 (01763) 246910
📧 roystongolf@btconnect.com
📖 660
✎ J Beech (01763) 242696
✎ S Clark (01763) 243476
⮕ 18 L 6086 yds SSS 70
👤 WD–H WE–M SOC–WD
£€ £25 D–£30
⬥ SW of Royston on A505
🏠 H Vardon
■ www.roystongolfclub.co.uk

Sandy Lodge (1910)
*Sandy Lodge Lane, Northwood, Middx,
HA6 2JD*
☎ (01923) 825429
🖳 (01923) 824319
📖 700
✎ JC Coombes
✎ J Pinsent (01923) 825321
⮕ 18 L 6328 yds SSS 71
👤 H or M SOC
£€ On application
⬥ Adjacent Moor Park Station
🏠 Harry Vardon

Shendish Manor (1988)
Pay and play
*Shendish Manor, London Road, Apsley,
HP3 0AA*
☎ (01442) 251806
🖳 (01442) 230683
📧 golf@shendish-manor.com
✎ T Concannon
⮕ 18 L 5660 yds Par 70 SSS 68
👤 U SOC
£€ £15 (£25)
⬥ S of Hemel Hempstead, off A41.
M25 Junction 20
🏠 Cotton/Steel
■ www.shendish-manor.com

South Herts (1899)
*Links Drive, Totteridge, London,
N20 8QU*
☎ (020) 8445 0117
🖳 (020) 8445 7569

📖 850
✎ KA Bravant (020) 8445 2035
✎ RY Mitchell (020) 8445 4633
⮕ 18 L 6470 yds SSS 71
9 L 1581 yds
👤 WD–IH WE/BH–M
£€ On application
⬥ Totteridge Lane
🏠 Harry Vardon

Stevenage (1980)
Public
Aston Lane, Stevenage, SG2 7EL
☎ (01438) 880424
📖 450
✎ Mrs S Elwin (01438) 880322
✎ S Barker (01438) 880424
⮕ 18 L 6451 yds SSS 71
9 hole Par 3 course
👤 U
£€ £14 (£18)
⬥ Off A602 to Hertford. A1(M) J7
⊕ Driving range
🏠 John Jacobs

Stocks Hotel G&CC (1994)
Stocks Road, Aldbury, Tring, HP23 5RX
☎ (01442) 851341
🖳 (01442) 851253
📖 440
✎ R Darling (Golf Mgr)
✎ PR Lane (Ext 311)
⮕ 18 L 7016 yds SSS 74
👤 H SOC
£€ £30 (£40)
⬥ Aldbury, 2 miles E of Tring.
A41(T), 2 miles
⊕ Practice range
🏠 M Billcliffe

Verulam (1905)
226 London Road, St Albans, AL1 1JG
☎ (01727) 853327
🖳 (01727) 812201
📖 712
✎ B Kelly
✎ N Burch (01727) 861401
⮕ 18 L 6448 yds Par 72 SSS 71
👤 WD–H exc Mon–U WE/BH–M
SOC–Tues & Thurs
£€ £25 Mon–£20
⬥ 1 mile SE of St Albans on A1081.
M25 Junction 21A or 22. M1
Junction 6
⊕ Practice range
🏠 Braid/Steel
■ www.verulamgolf.co.uk

Welwyn Garden City (1922)
*Mannicotts, High Oaks Road, Welwyn
Garden City, AL8 7BP*
☎ (01707) 325243
🖳 (01707) 393213
📖 900
✎ R Blower (Gen Mgr)
(01707) 325243
✎ R May (01707) 325525
⮕ 18 L 6100 yds SSS 69
👤 WD–H WE/BH–NA
£€ On application
⬥ 1 mile N of Hatfield. A1(M)
Junction 4 – B197 to Valley Road
🏠 Hawtree

West Herts (1890)
Cassiobury Park, Watford, WD3 3GG
☎ (01923) 236484
🖳 (01923) 222300
📖 700
✎ CC Dodman
✎ CS Gough (01923) 220352
⮕ 18 L 6488 yds SSS 71
👤 WD–U WE/BH–M SOC–Wed &
Fri
£€ £35 (£45)
⬥ Off A412, between Watford and
Rickmansworth
🏠 Morris/Mackenzie

Wheathampstead (2001)
Pay and play
*Harpenden Road, Wheathampstead, St
Albans, AL4 8EZ*
☎ (01582) 833941
🖳 (01582) 833941
✎ JD Edgar
✎ JD Edgar
⮕ 9 L 2100 yds Par 31 SSS 31
👤 U SOC
£€ £13 (£14). 9 holes–£8.50
⬥ 1 mile W of Wheathampstead
(B653)
⊕ Driving range
🏠 JD Edgar

Whipsnade Park (1974)
Studham Lane, Dagnall, HP4 1RH
☎ (01442) 842330
🖳 (01442) 842090
📧 whipsnadeparkgolfc@btopenworld
.com
📖 600
✎ Andrea King
✎ D Turner
⮕ 18 L 6812 yds SSS 72
👤 WD–U WE–M SOC–WD
£€ £28 D–£38
⬥ 8 miles N of Hemel Hempstead, off
A4147
■ www.whipsnadeparkgolf.co.uk

Whitehill (1990)
Dane End, Ware, SG12 0JS
☎ (01920) 438495
🖳 (01920) 438891
📧 whitehillgolfcentre@btinternet.com
📖 550
✎ Mr & Mrs A Smith (Props)
✎ M Belsham
⮕ 18 L 6802 yds SSS 72
👤 U
£€ £21 (£25.50)
⬥ 4 miles N of Ware (A10)
⊕ Floodlit driving range

Isle of Man

Castletown Golf Links
(1892)
Fort Island, Derbyhaven, IM9 1UA
☎ (01624) 822220
🖳 (01624) 829661

📧 1sttee@manx.net
📖 500
⛳ B Watts (Hon)/Mrs D Barron
✓ M Crowe (01624) 822211
� 18 L 6707 yds SSS 72
👥 U SOC
££ £35 (£40)
🚗 1 mile E of Castletown. 3 miles from Airport
🏠 Old Tom Morris
■ www.golfiom.com

Douglas Municipal (1927)

Public

Pulrose Park, Douglas, IM2 1AE

☎ **(01624) 675952 (Clubhouse)**
📖 300
⛳ Mrs E Vincent (01624) 616865
✓ M Vipond/P O'Reilly (01624) 661558
� 18 L 5922 yds Par 69 SSS 69
👥 U
££ £8.50 (£10.50)
🚗 Douglas Pier 2 miles
🏠 Dr A Mackenzie

King Edward Bay (1893)

Groudle Road, Onchan, IM3 2JR

☎ **(01624) 620430/673821**
📠 (01624) 676794
📖 400
⛳ C Kelly (01624) 836556
✓ D Jones (01624) 672709
⏯ 18 L 5457 yds SSS 65
👥 U SOC
££ £10 (£12)
🚗 1 mile N of Douglas
🏠 Tom Morris (1893 course)

Mount Murray G&CC (1994)

Santon, IM4 2HT

☎ **(01624) 661111**
📠 (01624) 611116
📖 360
⛳ AD Dyson (Ext 3023)
✓ AD Dyson (Ext 3023)
⏯ 18 L 6664 yds SSS 72
👥 U H SOC
££ £18 (£24)
🚗 3 miles SW of Douglas
⊕ Driving range

Peel (1895)

Rheast Lane, Peel, IM5 1BG

☎ **(01624) 842227**
📠 (01624) 843456
📧 peelgc@manx.net
📖 600
⛳ MND Robinson (01624) 843456
✓ M Crowe
⏯ 18 L 5874 yds SSS 69
👥 WD–U WE/BH–NA before 10.30am SOC
££ £20 (£28)
🚗 10 miles W of Douglas via A1
🏠 James Braid

Port St Mary (1936)

Public

Kallow Road, Port St Mary, IM9 5EJ

☎ **(01624) 834932**

⛳ T Boyle (Hon)
✓ M Crowe (01624) 822221
⏯ 9 L 2711 yds SSS 66
👥 WD–U WE–NA before 10.30am SOC
££ On application
🚗 6 miles S of Castletown via A5
🏠 George Duncan

Ramsey (1891)

Brookfield, Ramsey, IM8 2AH

☎ **(01624) 813365/812244**
📠 (01624) 815833
📖 700
⛳ Mr M Horton (01624) 812244
✓ A Dyson (01624) 814736
⏯ 18 L 5982 yds Par 71 SSS 70
👥 WD–U after 10am WE–M SOC
££ £20 (£28)
🚗 N of Douglas via A18. W boundary of Ramsey
🏠 James Braid

Rowany (1895)

Rowany Drive, Port Erin, IM9 6LN

☎ **(01624) 834108**
📠 (01624) 834072
📧 rowany@iommail.net
📖 500
⛳ CA Corrin (Mgr) (01624) 834072
⏯ 18 L 5774 yds SSS 69
👥 U SOC
££ £15 (£20)
🚗 6 miles W of Castletown via A5

Isle of Wight

Cowes (1909)

Crossfield Avenue, Cowes, PO31 8HN

☎ **(01983) 280135**
📖 300
⛳ D Weaver (01983) 292303; Members (01983) 280135
⏯ 9 L 5878 yds SSS 68
👥 H Thurs–NA before 3pm (Ladies Day) Sun am–NA
££ £15 (£18)
🚗 Nr Cowes High School
🏠 J Hamilton Stutt

Freshwater Bay (1894)

Afton Down, Freshwater, PO40 9TZ

☎ **(01983) 752955**
📠 (01983) 752955
📧 tr.fbgc@btopenworld.com
📖 550
⛳ T Riddett (01983) 752955
⏯ 18 L 5725 yds SSS 68
👥 H–NA before 9.30am SOC
££ £22 (£26)
🚗 400 yds off Military Road (A3055)
■ www.isle-of-wight.uk.com/golf

Newport (1896)

St George's Down, Shide, Newport, PO30 3BA

☎ **(01983) 525076**
📖 350
⛳ C Bradshaw (01983) 525076

⏯ 9 L 5674 yds SSS 68
👥 WD–U exc Wed–NA 12–2.30pm Sat–NA before 3.30pm Sun–NA before noon SOC
££ £15 (£17.50)
🚗 1 mile SE of Newport
🏠 Guy Hunt

Osborne (1904)

Osborne House Estate, East Cowes, PO32 6JX

☎ **(01983) 295421**
📖 260 90(L)
⛳ RS Jones
⏯ 9 L 6372 yds SSS 70
👥 WD–U exc Ladies Day (Tues) 9am–1pm–NA WE–NA before noon SOC
££ £20 (£22) 5D–£65
🚗 S of East Cowes in grounds of Osborne House

Ryde (1895)

Binstead Road, Ryde, PO33 3NF

☎ **(01983) 614809**
📠 (01983) 567418
📧 secretary@rydegolfclub.co.uk
📖 450
⛳ RA Dean
✓ None
⏯ 9 L 772 yds Par 70 SSS 68
👥 WD–U exc Wed Sat–NA before 10.30am Sun–NA before noon
££ £18 (£20)
🚗 On main Ryde/Newport road
🏠 J Hamilton Stutt
■ www.rydegolf.co.uk

Shanklin & Sandown (1900)

The Fairway, Lake, Sandown, PO36 9PR

☎ **(01983) 403217**
📠 (01983) 403007
📖 650
⛳ AC Creed
✓ P Hammond (01983) 404424
⏯ 18 L 6062 yds SSS 69
👥 WD–U WE–NA before 12 noon
££ £27.50 (£33) 3WD–£66
🚗 1 mile off A3055 in Lake
🏠 James Braid

Ventnor (1892)

Steephill Down Road, Ventnor, PO38 1BP

☎ **(01983) 853326**
📧 ventnorgolf@lineone.net
📖 250
⛳ S Blackmore
⏯ 12 L 5767 yds Par 70 SSS 68
👥 WD–U exc Mon Sun–NA before 1pm SOC
££ On application
🚗 NW boundary of Ventnor
■ www.ventnorgolfclub.co.uk

Westridge

Brading Road, Ryde, PO33 1QS

☎ **(01983) 613131**
⏯ 9 L 3225 yds Par
👥 U
££ £10 (£11)

⛴ 2 miles S of Ryde (A3054)
⊕ Driving range

Kent

Aquarius (1911)
Marmora Rd, Honor Oak, London, SE22 0RY
☎ (020) 8693 1626
📖 400
🏌 J Halliday
✓ F Private
🏳 9 L 5246 yds SSS 66
🏃 M
£€ On application
■ aquariusgolfclub@btopenworld.com

Ashford (1903)
Sandyhurst Lane, Ashford, TN25 4NT
☎ (01233) 620180
📞 (01233) 622655
📖 650
🏌 AH Story (01233) 622655
✓ H Sherman (01233) 629644
🏳 18 L 6284 yds SSS 70
🏃 WD–H WE/BH–H SOC
£€ £28 D–£38 (£35)
⛴ Ashford 1¹/₂ miles (A20)
🏠 Cotton

Austin Lodge (1991)
Upper Auston Lodge Road, Eynsford, Swanley, DA4 0HU
☎ (01322) 863000
📞 (01322) 862406
📖 600
🏌 G Haenen (Mgr)
✓ G Haenen
🏳 18 L 6600 yds Par 73 SSS 71
🏃 WD–U WE–NA before noon SOC
£€ £22 (£30)
⛴ Off A225, nr Eynsford Station. M25 Junction 3, 3 miles
⊕ Driving range for members and guests
🏠 Peter Bevan

Barnehurst (1903)
Public
Mayplace Road East, Bexley Heath, DA7 6JU
☎ (01322) 523746
📞 (01322) 554612
📖 300
🏳 9 L 5448 yds SSS 69
🏃 U SOC
£€ £9.25 (£12.60)
⛴ Between Crayford and Bexleyheath
🏠 James Braid

Bearsted (1895)
Ware Street, Bearsted, Maidstone, ME14 4PQ
☎ (01622) 738389
📞 (01622) 735608
📖 780
🏌 Mrs LM Siems (01622) 738198
✓ T Simpson (01622) 738024

🏳 18 L 6253 yds SSS 70
🏃 WD–I H WE–H M (recognised GC members) SOC
£€ £32–£42 (£37)
⛴ 2¹/₂ miles E of Maidstone; J7 off M20

Beckenham Place Park (1907)
Public
Beckenham Hill Road, Beckenham, BR3 2BP
☎ (020) 8650 2292
📞 (020) 8663 1201
✓ H Davies-Thomas
🏳 18 L 5722 yds SSS 68
🏃 U
£€ £7.60 (£12.40) WE–booking fee
⛴ Off A21 on A222

Bexleyheath (1907)
Mount Road, Bexleyheath, DA6 8JS
☎ (020) 8303 6951
📖 350
🏌 Mrs J Smith
🏳 9 L 5239 yds SSS 66
🏃 WD–H before 4pm
£€ £20
⛴ Station 1 mile

Birchwood Park (1990)
Birchwood Road, Wilmington, Dartford, DA2 7HJ
☎ (01322) 662038
📞 (01322) 667283
📖 690
🏌 Mrs SA Morley (Mgr) (01322) 662038
✓ S Cranfield (01322) 615209
🏳 18 L 6364 yds Par 71 SSS 70 9 hole course
🏃 U SOC
£€ £18 (£23)
⛴ 2 miles S of A2/A2018 Junction
⊕ Driving Range & Health Club
🏠 Howard Swann
■ www.birchwoodparkgc.co.uk

Boughton (1993)
Pay and play
Brickfield Lane, Boughton, Faversham, ME13 9AJ
☎ (01227) 752277
📞 (01227) 752361
📖 300
🏌 G Haenen (Mgr)
✓ T Dungate
🏳 18 L 6452 yds SSS 71
🏃 U SOC–WD
£€ £19 (£25)
⛴ NE of Boughton, nr M2/A2 interchange. 6 miles W of Canterbury
⊕ Driving range
🏠 Philip Sparks

Broke Hill (1993)
Sevenoaks Road, Halstead, TN14 7HR
☎ (01959) 533225
📞 (01959) 532680

🏌 C Winning (Gen Mgr)
✓ C McKillop (01959) 533810
🏳 18 L 6374 yds Par 72 SSS 71
🏃 WD–U before 5pm WE–NA SOC–WD
£€ £35
⛴ 4 miles S of Bromley on A21. M25 Junction 4
🏠 David Williams
■ www.brokehillgolf.co.uk

Bromley (1948)
Public
Magpie Hall Lane, Bromley, BR2 8JF
☎ (020) 8462 7014
📞 (020) 8462 6916
📖 100
✓ A Hodgson
🏳 9 L 5538 yds SSS 66
🏃 U
£€ £6 (£7.85)
⛴ Off Bromley Common (A21)

Broome Park (1981)
Broome Park Estate, Barham, Canterbury, CT4 6QX
☎ (01227) 830728
📞 (01227) 832591
📖 600
🏌 G Robins
✓ T Britz (01227) 831126
🏳 18 L 6580 yds SSS 71
🏃 H WE–NA before noon SOC–WD
£€ £40 (£50)
⛴ M2/A2-A260 Folkestone road, 1¹/₂ miles on RH side
⊕ Driving range
🏠 Donald Steel
■ www.broomepark.co.uk

Canterbury (1927)
Scotland Hills, Littlebourne Road, Canterbury, CT1 1TW
☎ (01227) 453532
📞 (01227) 784277
📧 cgc@freeola.com
📖 680
✓ P Everard (01227) 462865
🏳 18 L 6272 yds SSS 70
🏃 WD–U H WE–NA before 11.30am SOC–Tues/Thurs/Fri
£€ £36 D–£36 (£40)
⛴ 1 mile E of Canterbury on A257
🏠 HS Colt
■ www.canterburygolfclub.org.uk

Chart Hills (1993)
Weeks Lane, Biddenden, Ashford, TN27 8JX
☎ (01580) 292222
📞 (01580) 292233
📖 495
✓ D French (Golf Mgr) (01580) 292148
🏳 18 L 7135 yds SSS 74
🏃 U exc Mon/Wed/Sat–NA SOC
£€ On application
⛴ 12 miles W of Ashford (A262)
⊕ Golf Academy
🏠 Nick Faldo

Chelsfield Lakes Golf Centre (1992)
Pay and play
Court Road, Orpington, BR6 9BX
☎ (01689) 896266
🖬 (01689) 824577
📖 650
🏌 P Smith (Mgr)
✓ N Lee, B Hodkin
⊮ 18 L 6077 yds Par 71 SSS 69
9 hole Par 3 course
👥 U–booking required
🚗 1 mile from M25 Junction 4 (A224)
⊕ Target golf range
🏠 MRM Sandow
■ www.clubhaus.com

Cherry Lodge (1969)
Jail Lane, Biggin Hill, Westerham, TN16 3AX
☎ (01959) 572250
🖬 (01959) 540672
🖂 info@cherrylodgegc.co.uk
📖 650
🏌 W Tambling
✓ N Child (01959) 572989
⊮ 18 L 6593 yds SSS 73
👥 WD–U WE–M SOC–WD before 3pm
£€ £35 D–£50
🚗 3 miles N of Westerham, off A233
⊕ Driving range
🏠 John Day
■ www.cherrylodgegc.co.uk

Chestfield (1925)
103 Chestfield Road, Whitstable, CT5 3LU
☎ (01227) 794411
🖬 (01227) 794454
🖂 secretary@chestfield-golfclub.co.uk
📖 600
🏌 Alan Peel (01227) 794411
✓ J Brotherton (01227) 793563
⊮ 18 L 6208 yds SSS 70
👥 WD–U WE–NA before noon SOC
£€ £25 (£28)
🚗 ¹/₂ mile S of A2990 and Chestfield Station
🏠 Donald Steel
■ www.chestfield-golfclub.co.uk

Chislehurst (1894)
Camden Place, Camden Park Road, Chislehurst, BR7 5HJ
☎ (020) 8467 3055
🖬 (020) 8295 0874
📖 740
🏌 P Foord (020) 8467 2782
✓ J Bird (020) 8467 6798
⊮ 18 L 5128 yds SSS 65
👥 WD–H WE–M SOC
£€ £30
🚗 M25 Junction 3/A20/A222

Cobtree Manor Park (1984)
Public
Chatham Road, Boxley, Maidstone, ME14 3AZ
☎ (01622) 753276

🏌 A Ferras
⊮ 18 L 5716 yds SSS 68
👥 WD–U WE/BH–(book 1 wk in advance) SOC–WD
£€ £10 (£18)
🚗 3 miles N of Maidstone on A229
🏠 F Hawtree

Cray Valley (1972)
Pay and play
Sandy Lane, St Paul's Cray, Orpington, BR5 3HY
☎ (01689) 837909
🖬 (01689) 891428
📖 600
🏌 J Scappatura (01689) 839677
✓ G Sheriff (01689) 837909
⊮ 18 L 5624 yds SSS 67
9 L 2100 yds SSS 60
👥 U
£€ £13 (£19)
🚗 Off A20 Ruxley roundabout at Sidcup

Darenth Valley (1973)
Pay and play
Station Road, Shoreham, Sevenoaks, TN14 7SA
☎ (01959) 522944 (Clubhouse), (01959) 522922 (Bookings)
🖬 (01959) 525089
🖂 darenthvalleygolfcourse @shoreham2000.fsbusiness.co.uk
🏌 JR Cooper (Mgr)
✓ D Copsey (01959) 522922
⊮ 18 L 6258 yds Par 72 SSS 71
👥 U–booking required SOC
£€ £17.50 (£23)
🚗 3 miles N of Sevenoaks, off A225. M25 Junctions 3 or 5

Dartford (1897)
Heath Lane, Dartford, DA1 2TN
☎ (01322) 223616
🖂 dartfordgolf@hotmail.com
📖 750
🏌 KJ Rawlins (01322) 226455
✓ J Gregory (01322) 226409
⊮ 18 L 5909 yds Par 69 SSS 69
👥 WD–I WE–M H
£€ £22.50
🚗 Dartford 2 miles. Dartford Heath turn off A2
🏠 James Braid

Deangate Ridge (1972)
Public
Duxcourt Road, Hoo, Rochester, ME3 8RZ
☎ (01634) 251950
📖 560
🏌 Mrs CJ Williams (01634) 251950
✓ R Fox (01634) 251180
⊮ 18 L 6300 yds SSS 70
👥 U SOC
£€ On application
🚗 7 miles NE of Rochester on A228. M2, 5 miles
⊕ Driving range. Pitch & putt

Edenbridge G&CC (1973)
Crouch House Road, Edenbridge, TN8 5LQ
☎ (01732) 867381
🖬 (01732) 867029
📖 800
🏌 Mrs C Lloyd (Gen Mgr)
✓ K Burkin (01732) 865202
⊮ 18 L 6577 yds SSS 72
18 L 5605 yds SSS 67
9 hole course
👥 WD/WE–booking necessary
£€ £20 (£27.50)
🚗 2 miles W of Edenbridge. M25 Junction 6
⊕ Floodlit driving range
🏠 David Williams

Eltham Warren (1890)
Bexley Road, Eltham, London, SE9 2PE
☎ (020) 8850 1166
🖂 secretary@elthamwarren.tdps.co.uk
📖 430
🏌 DJ Clare (020) 8850 4477
✓ G Brett (020) 8859 7909
⊮ 9 L 5850 yds SSS 68
👥 WD–I WE/BH–M SOC–Thurs only
£€ D–£28 (£14)
🚗 ¹/₂ mile from Eltham station on A210
🏠 James Braid
■ www.elthamwarrengolfclub.co.uk

Etchinghill (1995)
Pay and play
Canterbury Road, Etchinghill, Folkestone, CT18 8FA
☎ (01303) 863863
🖬 (01303) 863210
📖 550
🏌 B Barnes (01303) 269143
✓ C Hodgson (01303) 863966
⊮ Valley: 18 L 6101 Par 70 SSS 69
Leas: 18 L 5824 Par 70 SSS 69
9 hole Par 3 course
👥 WD–U WE–NA 7am–11am
£€ £19 (£25) Leas; £14 (£21) Vall
🚗 1 mile N of M20 Junction 12 on B2065
⊕ Driving range
🏠 John Sturdy

Faversham (1902)
Belmont Park, Faversham, ME13 0HB
☎ (01795) 890561
🖬 (01795) 890760
📖 850
🏌 J Edgington
✓ S Rokes (01795) 890275
⊮ 18 L 5965 yds Par 70 SSS 69
👥 WD–I or H WE–M
£€ £30
🚗 Faversham and M2, 2 miles

Fawkham Valley (1987)
Gay Dawn Farm, Fawkham, Dartford, DA3 8LZ
☎ (01474) 707144
🖬 (01474) 707911
📖 350
🏌 J Marchant

For list of abbreviations and key to symbols see page 627

✔ N Willis
▶ 9 L 6547 yds Par 72 SSS 72
👥 WD–U H WE/BH–NA before 1pm
SOC
££ £20 (£27.50)
⊕ 4 miles S of Dartford Tunnel. E of
Brands Hatch along Fawkham
Valley road
■ www.fawkhamvalleygolf.com

Gillingham (1905)
Woodlands Road, Gillingham, ME7 2AP
☎ (01634) 850999
🖥 (01634) 574749
📖 700
✍ Mr C Cooper (01634) 853017
✔ S Green (01634) 855862
▶ 18 L 5495 yds SSS 66
👥 WD–I H WE/BH–M
££ £20 D–£28
⊕ A2/M2, 2 miles
🏠 Braid/Steel

Hawkhurst (1968)
High Street, Hawkhurst, TN18 4JS
☎ (01580) 754074/752396
🖥 (01580) 754074
📧 hawkhurstgolfclub@tiscali.co.uk
📖 450
✍ B Morrison (Gen Mgr)
✔ J Walpole (01580) 754088
▶ 9 L 5751 yds Par 70 SSS 68
👥 WD–U WE–M SOC
££ 18 holes–£20 (£24) 9 holes–£12
⊕ 14 miles S of Tunbridge Wells on
A268
■ HawkhurstGolfClub.org.uk

Hemsted Forest (1969)
Golford Road, Cranbrook, TN17 4AL
☎ (01580) 712833
🖥 (01580) 714274
✍ K Stevenson
▶ 18 L 6305 yds SSS 70
👥 WD–U WE/BH–restricted SOC
££ £30 (£40)
⊕ 15 miles S of Maidstone. M25
Junction 5-A21/A262
🏠 Cdr J Harris

Herne Bay (1895)
Eddington, Herne Bay, CT6 7PG
☎ (01227) 374097
📖 500
✍ B Warren (01227) 373964
✔ S Dordoy (01227) 374727
▶ 18 L 5567 yds SSS 68
👥 WD–U WE/BH–H after noon
SOC–WD
££ £18 D–£25 (£25)
⊕ A2299 Thanet road

Hever (1993)
Hever Road, Hever, TN8 7NP
☎ (01732) 700771
🖥 (01732) 700775
📖 700
✔ R Tinworth
▶ 18 L 7002 yds SSS 75
9 L 2784 yds
👥 H SOC

££ £35 (£55)
⊕ 2 miles E of Edenbridge
⊕ Driving range
🏠 Peter Nicholson
■ www.hever.com

High Elms (1969)
Public
*High Elms Road, Downe, Orpington,
BR6 7SZ*
☎ (01689) 858175
🖥 (01689) 856326
✍ Mrs P O'Keeffe (Hon)
✔ P Remy
▶ 18 L 6221 yds Par 71 SSS 70
👥 U
££ On application
⊕ Off A21 via Shire Lane

Hythe Imperial (1950)
Prince's Parade, Hythe, CT21 6AE
☎ (01303) 233745
🖥 (01303) 267554
📖 445
✍ B Duncan (01303) 267554
✔ G Ritchie (01303) 233745
▶ 9 L 5560 yds SSS 67
👥 H SOC
££ £15 (£20)
⊕ On coast, 4 miles W of Folkestone

Kings Hill (1996)
Kings Hill, West Malling, ME19 4AF
☎ (01732) 875040/842121
(Bookings)
🖥 (01732) 875019
📖 530
✍ Margaret Gilbert (Mgr)
✔ D Hudspith (01732) 842121
▶ 18 L 6622 yds Par 72 SSS 72
👥 WD–U SOC–WD
££ £30
⊕ 3 miles from M20 Junction 4, off
A228
🏠 David Williams

Knole Park (1924)
Seal Hollow Road, Sevenoaks, TN15 0HJ
☎ (01732) 452150
🖥 (01732) 463159
📖 700
✍ AP Mitchell (01732) 452150
✔ P Sykes (01732) 451740
▶ 18 L 6266 yds SSS 70
👥 WD–restricted WE/BH–M H SOC
££ £40 D–£50
⊕ ¹/₂ mile from Sevenoaks centre
🏠 JF Abercromby
■ www.knoleparkgolfclub.co.uk

Lamberhurst (1890)
Church Road, Lamberhurst, TN3 8DT
☎ (01892) 890241
🖥 (01892) 891140
📧 secretary@lamberhurstgolfclub
.com
📖 600
✍ RJ Walden (01892) 890591
✔ BM Impett (01892) 890552
▶ 18 L 6364 yds SSS 70
👥 WD–U H WE–NA before noon

££ £26 D–£36 (£41)
⊕ 5 miles SE of Tunbridge Wells, off
A21
■ www.lamberhurstgolfclub.com

Langley Park (1910)
*Barnfield Wood Road, Beckenham,
BR3 6SZ*
☎ (020) 8650 6849
🖥 (020) 8658 6310
📧 manager@langleyparkgolf.co.uk
📖 750
✍ R Pollard (Gen Mgr) (020) 8658
6849
✔ C Staff (020) 8650 1663
▶ 18 L 6488 yds SSS 71
👥 WD–H WE–M SOC–WD
££ £25 D–£35
⊕ Bromley South Station 1 mile. M25
Junction 4
🏠 JH Taylor
■ www.langleyparkgolf.co.uk

Leeds Castle (1928)
Pay and play
*Leeds Castle, Hollingbourne, Maidstone,
ME17 1PL*
☎ (01622) 880467/767828
🖥 (01622) 735616
✔ S Purves
▶ 9 L 2451 yds Par 33
👥 U SOC–WD
££ 9 holes–£11 (£13)
⊕ 4 miles E of Maidstone (A20). M20
Junction 8, 1 mile
⊕ 6-day advance booking
🏠 Neil Coles
■ www.leeds-castle.com

Littlestone (1888)
*St Andrews Road, Littlestone, New
Romney, TN28 8RB*
☎ (01797) 362310
🖥 (01797) 362740
📧 secretary@littlestonegolfclub
.org.uk
📖 550
✍ Col C Moorhouse (01797) 363355
✔ A Jones (01797) 362231
▶ 18 L 6676 yds Par 71 SSS 73
👥 WD–H WE–by arrangement SOC
££ £38 (£55)
⊕ 2 miles E of New Romney. 15
miles SE of Ashford. M20 Junction
10
🏠 W Laidlaw Purves/Dr A Mackenzie
■ www.littlestonegolfclub.org.uk

London Beach (1998)
Pay and play
*Ashford Road, St Michaels, Tenterden,
TN30 6SP*
☎ (01580) 766279
🖥 (01580) 763884
📧 enquiries@londonbeach
✍ P Edmonds
✔ M Chilcott (01580) 764135
▶ 9 L 5860 yds
👥 U SOC
££ 9 holes–£18 (£20). 18 holes–£20
(£25)
⊕ 2 miles out of Tenterden

⊕ Driving range. Pitch & putt
■ www.londonbeach.com

The London Golf Club
(1993)
*South Ash Manor Estate, Stansted Lane,
Ash, TN15 7EN*
☎ **(01474) 879899**
⌨ (01474) 879912
▭ 550
✍ D Loh
✓ B Longmuir
☞ Heritage 18 L 7208 yds Par 72
SSS 74;
International 18 L 7005 yds Par 72
SSS 74
♟ M I SOC–WD
£€ On application
⛳ Off A20, nr Brands Hatch
⊕ Driving range. Academy
⛩ Nicklaus/Kirby
■ www.londongolf.co.uk

Lullingstone Park (1967)
Public
*Parkgate Road, Chelsfield, Orpington,
BR6 7PX*
☎ **(01959) 533793**
✍ CJ Pocock (0208) 303 9545
✓ M Watt
☞ 18 L 6779 yds SSS 72
9 L 2445 yds Par 33
♟ U
£€ On application
⛳ Off Orpington by-pass (A224)
towards Well Hill. M25 Junction 4
⊕ Driving range. 9 hole pitch & putt
course

Lydd
*Romney Road, Lydd, Romney Marsh,
TN29 9LS*
☎ **(01797) 320808**
⌨ (01797) 321482
✉ info@lyddgolfclub.co.uk
▭ 576
✍ BM Evans, S Balcomb (Gen Mgr)
✓ Richard Perkins (01797) 321201
☞ 18 L 6517 yds Par 71 SSS 71
Driving range
♟ U SOC
£€ £17 (£25)
⛳ 15 miles SE of Ashford, by Lydd
Airport (B2075). M20 Junction 10
⊕ Driving range
⛩ M Smith
■ www.lyddgolfclub.co.uk

Mid Kent (1908)
Singlewell Road, Gravesend, DA11 7RB
☎ **(01474) 568035**
⌨ (01474) 564218
▭ 870
✍ P Gleeson (01474 568035
✓ M Foreman (01474) 332810
☞ 18 L 6106 yds Par 70 SSS 69
♟ WD–H WE–M
£€ £25/£35 weekdays only
⛳ SE of Gravesend, nr A2
⊕ Practice range – irons only
⛩ Frank Pennink

Moatlands (1993)
*Watermans Lane, Brenchley, Tonbridge,
TN12 6ND*
☎ **(01892) 724400**
⌨ (01892) 723300
✉ moatlandsgolf@btconnect.com
▭ 600
✍ K Wiley
✓ J Eldridge (01892) 724252
☞ 18 L 7060 yds Par 72 SSS 74
♟ WD–U H WE–H NA before noon
SOC–WD exc Wed
£€ £29 (£39)
⛳ Between Matfield and Paddock
Wood, off B2160
⊕ Driving range
⛩ T Saito
■ www.moatlands.com

Nizels (1992)
*Nizels Lane, Hildenborough, Tonbridge,
TN11 8NU*
☎ **(01732) 833833**
⌨ (01732) 835492
✉ nizels@clubhaus.com
▭ 700
✍ J Martin (Gen Mgr)
✓ N Thirkell (01732) 833833
☞ 18 L 6297 yds SSS 71
♟ WD–U SOC
£€ £30 (£40)
⛳ 4 miles from M25 on B245. A21
Tonbridge North Junction
⛩ Lennan/Purnell
■ www.clubhaus.com

North Foreland (1903)
*Convent Road, Broadstairs, Thanet,
CT10 3PU*
☎ **(01843) 862140**
⌨ (01843) 862663
✉ office@northforeland.co.uk
▭ 1100
✍ AJ Adams (01843) 862140
✓ D Parris (01843) 604471
☞ 18 L 6430 yds SSS 71
18 hole Par 3 course
♟ WD–H WE–NA am –H pm
£€ £35 (£50)
⛳ B2052, 1½ miles N of Broadstairs
⛩ Fowler/Simpson

Oastpark (1992)
Malling Road, Snodland, ME6 5LG
☎ **(01634) 242661**
⌨ (01634) 240744
▭ 300
✍ Lesley Murrock (01634) 242818
✓ D Porthouse (01634) 242661
☞ 9 L 2850 yds Par 34 SSS 34
♟ U SOC
£€ 9 holes–£7 (£8) 18 holes–£12 (£14)
⛳ 1 mile E of M20 Junction 4
⊕ Driving range

Park Wood (1994)
Proprietary
*Chestnut Avenue, Tatsfield, Westerham,
TN16 2EG*
☎ **(01959) 577744**
⌨ (01959) 572702

✉ mail@parkwoodgolf.co.uk
▭ 450
✍ Miss RLR Gold Smith (Man Dir)
✓ N Terry (01959) 577177
☞ 18 L 6573 yds Par 72 SSS 72
♟ U SOC
£€ £22.50–£25 (£27.50)
⛳ Tatsfield, nr Westerham. M25
Junction 4
■ www.parkwoodgolf.co.uk

Poult Wood (1974)
Public
Higham Lane, Tonbridge, TN11 9QR
☎ **(01732) 364039 (Bookings),
(01732) 366180 (Clubhouse)**
▭ 481
✍ S Taylor
✓ C Miller
☞ 18 L 5524 yds Par 68 SSS 66
9 L 2562 yds Par 28
♟ U–booking required SOC–WD
£€ £12.50 (£18)
⛳ 1 mile N of Tonbridge, off A227
⛩ Hawtree

Prince's (1906)
Proprietary
Sandwich Bay, Sandwich, CT13 9QB
☎ **(01304) 611118**
⌨ (01304) 612000
✉ golf@princes-leisure.co.uk
▭ 250
✍ WM Howie (Dir) (01304) 626909
✓ D Barbour (01304) 613797
☞ 27 hole course (3 x 9 holes):
Dunes/Himalayas/Shore
Length 6813-7145 yds
Par 71-72 SSS 72-73
♟ U SOC
£€ On application
⛳ Sandwich Bay (A256)
⊕ Driving range
⛩ Morrison/Campbell
■ www.princes-leisure.co.uk

Redlibbets
*West Yoke, Ash, Nr Sevenoaks,
TN15 7HT*
☎ **(01474) 879190**
⌨ (01474) 879290
✉ redlibbets@golfandsport.co.uk
▭ 500
✍ J Potter
✓ R Taylor (01474) 872278
☞ 18 L 6651 yds Par 72
♟ WD SOC
£€ £40
⛳ Off A20 between Fawkham and
Ash. M20 Junction 2. M25 Junction
3
⛩ Jonathan Gaunt
■ www.golfandsport.co.uk

The Ridge (1993)
*Chartway Street, East Sutton, Maidstone,
ME17 3JB*
☎ **(01622) 844382**
⌨ (01622) 844168
✍ C Harrandine (Gen Mgr)
✓ J Cornish (01622) 844243

▷ 18 L 6254 yds SSS 72
ᨢ U SOC
££ £16 (£22)
⊶ 3 miles E of Maidstone, off A274.
M20 Junction 8
⊕ Driving range
⚐ Patrick Dawson

Riverside (1991)

Pay and play
Summerton Way, Thamesmead, London,
SE28 8PP
☎ (020) 8310 7975
▷ 9 L 5485 yds Par 66
ᨢ U SOC–WD
££ £7 (£9)
⊶ Woolwich

Riverside Golf Centre (1991)

Pay and play
Fairway Drive, Summerton Way,
Thamesmead, London SE28 8PP
☎ (020) 8310 7975
🖳 (020) 8312 3441
🏌 BD Jarrett
⚲ Sarah Jarrett
▷ 9 L 5462 yds Par 70 SSS 66
ᨢ U SOC
££ 18 holes–£10.50 (£12) 9
holes–£6.50 (£8.50)
⊕ Floodlit driving range
■ www.riversidegolf.co.uk

Rochester & Cobham Park (1891)

Park Pale, by Rochester, ME2 3UL
☎ (01474) 823411
🖳 (01474) 824446
🕮 605
🏌 DW Smith (Mgr)
⚲ I Higgins (01474) 823658
▷ 18 L 6597 yds SSS 71
ᨢ WD–U H WE–M before 5pm
SOC–Tues & Thurs. Soft spikes
only
££ £35
⊶ 3 miles E of Gravesend exit (A2)
⊕ Full practice facilities
⚐ D Steel
■ www.rochesterandcobhamgc.co.uk

Romney Warren (1993)

Pay and play
St Andrews Road, Littlestone, New
Romney, TN28 8RB
☎ (01797) 362231
🖳 (01797) 362740
🕮 250
🏌 E Purkiss (Hon)
⚲ S Watkins
▷ 18 L 5126 yds SSS 65
ᨢ U SOC
££ £13 (£18)
⊶ 2 miles E of New Romney. 15
miles SE of Ashford
⚐ Evans/Lewis
■ www.romneywarrengolfclub.co.uk

Royal Blackheath (1608)

Court Road, Eltham, London, SE9 5AF
☎ (020) 8850 1795
🖳 (020) 8859 0150
✉ secretary@rbgc.com
🕮 700
🏌 AG Dunlop
⚲ R Harrison (020) 8850 1763
▷ 18 L 6219 yds SSS 70
ᨢ WD–I or H WE/BH–M SOC
££ £45 D–£65
⊶ 5 miles W of M25 Junction 3
⊕ Golf Museum
⚐ James Braid
■ www.rbgc.com

Royal Cinque Ports (1892)

Golf Road, Deal, CT14 6RF
☎ (01304) 374007 (Office),
(01304) 374328 (Clubhouse)
🖳 (01304) 379530
🕮 650
🏌 Ian Symington (01304) 374007
⚲ A Reynolds (01304) 374170
▷ 18 L 6899 yds SSS 73
ᨢ WD–H after 9.30am SOC
££ On application
⊶ A258, N of Deal
⊕ Driving range
■ www.royalcinqueports.com

Royal St George's (1887)

Sandwich, CT13 9PB
☎ (01304) 613090
🖳 (01304) 611245
✉ secretary@royalstgeorges.com
🕮 775
🏌 HCG Gabbey
⚲ A Brooks (01304) 615236
▷ 18 L 7102 yds Par 70 SSS 74
ᨢ WD–I H WE–M SOC–WD
££ £95 D–£130
⊶ 1 mile E of Sandwich
⚐ Dr Laidlaw Purves
■ www.royalstgeorges.com

Ruxley Park (1975)

Pay and play
Sandy Lane, St Paul's Cray, Orpington,
BR5 3HY
☎ (01689) 871490
🖳 (01689) 891428
🕮 500
🏌 J Scappatura
⚲ A Langoon
▷ 18 L 6027 yds SSS 69
9 hole Par 3 course
ᨢ U
££ £11 (£18)
⊶ Off A20 Ruxley roundabout at
Sidcup
⊕ Floodlit driving range

Sene Valley (1888)

Sene, Folkestone, CT18 8BL
☎ (01303) 268513
🖳 (01303) 237513
✉ svgc@svgc.freeserve.co.uk
🕮 650
🏌 G Sykes (Mgr)
⚲ N Watson (01303) 268514

▷ 18 L 6196 yds SSS 70
ᨢ H SOC
££ £25 (£30)
⊶ 2 miles N of Hythe on B2065
⚐ Henry Cotton
■ www.sceneatsene.co.uk

Sheerness (1909)

Power Station Road, Sheerness,
ME12 3AE
☎ (01795) 662585
🖳 (01795) 668100
✉ thesecretary@sheernessgc
.freeserve.co.uk
🕮 600
🏌 AF Jones
⚲ L Stanford (01795) 583060
▷ 18 L 6460 yds SSS 71
ᨢ WD–U SOC
££ £20
⊶ 9 miles N of Sittingbourne. M20,
M2 or A2 to A249

Shooter's Hill (1903)

Lowood, Eaglesfield Road, London,
SE18 3DA
☎ (020) 8854 1216
🖳 (020) 8854 0469
🕮 596 69(L) 46(J)
🏌 M Bond (020) 8854 6368
⚲ D Brotherton (020) 8854 0073
▷ 18 L 5721 yds SSS 68
ᨢ WD–I WE/BH–M SOC–Tues &
Thurs only
££ £22 D–£27
⊶ Off A207 nr Blackheath
⚐ Willie Park

Shortlands (1894)

Meadow Road, Shortlands, Bromley,
BR2 0DX
☎ (020) 8460 2471
🖳 (020) 8460 8828
🕮 525
🏌 PS May (020) 8460 8828
⚲ R Latham (020) 8464 6182
▷ 9 L 5261 yds SSS 66
ᨢ M
££ 18 holes–£15. 9 holes–£10
⊶ Ravensbourne Ave, Shortlands

Sidcup (1891)

7 Hurst Road, Sidcup, DA15 9AE
☎ (020) 8300 2864
🖳 (020) 8300 2150
✉ sidcupgolfclub@tiscali.co.uk
🕮 400
🏌 J Auchterlony (020) 8300 2150
⚲ J Auchterlony (020) 8309 0679
▷ 9 L 5571 yds Par 68 SSS 68
ᨢ WD–H WE/BH–M SOC–WD
££ £18
⊶ On A222. A2/A20, 2 miles

Sittingbourne & Milton Regis (1929)

Wormdale, Newington, Sittingbourne,
ME9 7PX
☎ (01795) 842261
🖳 (01795) 844117

✉ sittingbourne@golfclub.totalserve.co.uk
☎ 725
♣ HDG Wylie
✓ JR Hearn (01795) 842775
⊳ 18 L 6291 yds SSS 70
👤 WD–H Sat–NA Sun–M SOC–Tues & Thurs
£€ £28
⚘ N of M2 Junction 5, towards Danaway

Southern Valley (1999)
Pay and play
Thong Lane, Shorne, Gravesend, DA12 4LF
☎ **(01474) 740026, (01474) 568568 (Bookings)**
📠 (01474) 360366
✉ info@southernvalley.co.uk
☎ 410
♣ Anne Green
✓ L Batchelor
⊳ 18 L 6100 yds Par 69 SSS 69
👤 U SOC
£€ 9 holes–£10 (£12.50). 18 holes–£16.50 (£19)
⚘ S of Gravesend, off A2
🏠 Weller/Richardson

St Augustines (1907)
Cottington Road, Cliffsend, Ramsgate, CT12 5JN
☎ **(01843) 590333**
📠 (01843) 590444
✉ sagc@ic24.net
☎ 650 55(J)
♣ LP Dyke
✓ DB Scott (01843) 590222
⊳ 18 L 5254 yds SS 66
👤 H SOC–WD
£€ £18 (£19.50)
⚘ 2 miles SW of Ramsgate from A253 or A256. Signs to St Augustines Cross
🏠 Tom Vardon

Staplehurst Golf Centre
Cradducks Lane, Staplehurst, TN12 0DR
☎ **(01580) 893362**
♣ C Jenkins
✓ C Jenkins
⊳ 9 L 6114 yds Par 72 SSS 70
👤 U
£€ £12 (£13)
⚘ 8 miles S of Maidstone on A229
⊕ Driving range
🏠 Sayner/Jenkins

Sundridge Park (1901)
Garden Road, Bromley, BR1 3NE
☎ **(020) 8460 0278**
📠 (020) 8289 3050
✉ secretary@spgc.co.uk
☎ 1200
♣ C Winning (020) 8460 0278
✓ S Dowsett (020) 8460 5540
⊳ East 18 L 6538 yds SSS 71
   West 18 L 6019 yds SSS 69
👤 H SOC–WD
£€ D–£55

⚘ 1 mile N of Bromley, by Sundridge Park Station. M25 Junctions 3/4

Sweetwoods Park (1994)
Cowden, Edenbridge, TN8 7JN
☎ **(01342) 850729**
📠 (01342) 850866
✉ danhowe@sweetwoodspark.com
☎ 750
♣ D Howe (01342) 850942
✓ P Lyons (01342) 850729
⊳ 18 L 5299-6610 yds Par 72 S SS 69-73
👤 U SOC
£€ £24 (£32)
⚘ 5 miles E of E Grinstead on A264
⊕ Driving range
🏠 P Strand
■ www.sweetwoodspark.com

Tenterden (1905)
Woodchurch Road, Tenterden, TN30 7DR
☎ **(01580) 763987**
📠 (01580) 763987
☎ 650
♣ N Taylor (Sec/Mgr)
✓ K Kelsall (01580) 762409
⊳ 18 L 6050 yds Par 70 SSS 69
👤 WD–U WE/BH–M Sun–NA before noon SOC–WD
£€ On application
⚘ 1 mile E of Tenterden on B2067
■ www.tenterdengolfclub.co.uk

Tudor Park (1988)
Proprietary
Ashford Road, Bearsted, Maidstone, ME14 4NQ
☎ **(01622) 734334**
📠 (01622) 735360
☎ 750
♣ J Ladbrook (01622) 737119
✓ N McNally (01622) 739412
⊳ 18 L 6085 yds SSS 69
👤 H SOC WE–NA before 11am
£€ £35 (£40)
⚘ 3 miles E of Maidstone on A20. M20 Junction 8
⊕ Driving range
🏠 Donald Steel

Tunbridge Wells (1889)
Langton Road, Tunbridge Wells, TN4 8XH
☎ **(01892) 523034**
📠 (01892) 536918
☎ 220 48(L) 54(J)
♣ RF Mealing (01892) 536918
✓ M Barton (01892) 541386
⊳ 9 L 4725 yds SSS 62
👤 U H SOC
£€ £14 (£20)
⚘ Tunbridge Wells, next to Spa Hotel

Upchurch River Valley (1991)
Pay and play
Oak Lane, Upchurch, Sittingbourne, ME9 7AY
☎ **(01634) 360626**

☎ (01634) 387784
☎ 652
♣ D Candy (01634) 260594
✓ R Cornwell (01634) 379592
⊳ 18 L 6237 yds SSS 70
   9 hole course
👤 U SOC–WD
£€ 18 hole: £12.95 (£16.45)
   9 hole: £6.75 (£7.75)
⚘ 3 miles NE of Rainham, off A2. M2 J4
⊕ Floodlit driving range
🏠 David Smart

Walmer & Kingsdown (1909)
The Leas, Kingsdown, Deal, CT14 8EP
☎ **(01304) 373256**
📠 (01304) 382336
☎ 627
♣ J Morgan
✓ M Paget (01304) 363017
⊳ 18 L 6444 yds Par 72 SSS 71
👤 WD–H WE–after noon SOC
£€ D–£25 (£30)
⚘ 2½ miles S of Deal on clifftop
🏠 James Braid

Weald of Kent (1992)
Pay and play
Maidstone Road, Headcorn, TN27 9PT
☎ **(01622) 890866**
📠 (01622) 890070
☎ 500
♣ K Brown (Golf Dir)
✓ P Foston (01622) 890866
⊳ 18 L 6289 yds SSS 70
👤 U–booking 5 days in advance SOC
£€ £16 (£20)
⚘ 5 miles S of Maidstone on A274. M20 Junction 8
🏠 John Millen

West Kent (1916)
West Hill, Downe, Orpington, BR6 7JJ
☎ **(01689) 851323**
📠 (01689) 858693
✉ golf@wkgc
☎ 750
♣ AP Barclay
✓ RS Fidler (01689) 856863
⊳ 18 L 6385 yds Par 70 SSS 70
👤 WD–H or I–phone to arrange WE/BH–M
£€ On application
⚘ 5 miles S of Orpington
■ www.wkgc.co.uk

West Malling (1974)
Addington, Maidstone, ME19 5AR
☎ **(01732) 844785**
📠 (01732) 844795
☎ 900
♣ MR Ellis
✓ D Lambert
⊳ Spitfire 18 L 6142 yds Par 70
   Hurricane 18 L 6240 yds Par 70
👤 WD–U WE–U H after noon
£€ £25 (£35)
⚘ 12 miles W of Maidstone (A20)
⊕ Driving range

⬆ Max Faulkner
■ www.westmallinggolf.com

Westerham
Valence Park, Brasted Road, Westerham, TN16 1LJ
☎ **(01959) 567100**
🖳 (01959) 567101
📖 700
✍ R Sturgeon (Gen Mgr)
🏌 J Marshal
▶ 18 L 6272 yds Par 72
👥 WD–U WE–after 12.00pm
££ £29 (£36)
🚗 E of Westerham (A25), off M25 Junction 5
⊕ Driving range
⬆ David Williams
www.westerhamgc.co.uk

Westgate & Birchington
(1893)
176 Canterbury Road, Westgate-on-Sea, CT8 8LT
☎ **(01843) 831115/833905**
📖 350
✍ TJ Sharp
🏌 R Game
▶ 18 L 4889 yds SSS 64
👥 WD–NA before 10am WE–NA before 11am SOC
££ £20 (£18)
🚗 1 mile W of Birchington (A28)

Whitstable & Seasalter
(1911)
Collingwood Road, Whitstable, CT5 1EB
☎ **(01227) 272020**
🖳 (01227) 280822
📖 350
✍ C Chapman
▶ 9 L 5357 yds Par 63 SSS 63
👥 U
££ 18 holes–£15
🚗 1 mile W of Whitstable

Wildernesse (1890)
Seal, Sevenoaks, TN15 0JE
☎ **(01732) 761526**
📖 700
✍ RA Foster (01732) 761199
🏌 CA Walker (01732) 761527
▶ 18 L 6482 yds Par 72 SSS 71
👥 WD–I H SOC–Mon/Thurs/Fri
££ £40 D–£60
🚗 2 miles E of Sevenoaks (A25). M25 Junction 5

Woodlands Manor (1928)
Woodlands, Tinkerpot Lane, Sevenoaks, TN15 6AB
☎ **(01959) 523806**
🖳 (01959) 524398
📖 650
✍ CG Robins (01959) 523806
🏌 P Womack (01959) 524161
▶ 18 L 6000 yds SSS 69
👥 WD–U WE–H NA before noon SOC–WD
££ On application

🚗 4 miles S of M25 Junction 3. Off A20 between West Kingsdown and Otford
⊕ Driving range
⬆ Coles/Lyons

Wrotham Heath (1906)
Seven Mile Lane Comp, Sevenoaks, TN15 8QZ
☎ **(01732) 884800**
📖 424 75(L) 50(J)
✍ LJ Byrne
🏌 H Dearden (01732) 883854
▶ 18 L 5954 yds SSS 69
👥 WD–H WE/BH–M SOC–Thurs & Fri
££ £30 D–£40
🚗 8 miles W of Maidstone on B2016. M26/A20 Junction, 1 mile
⬆ Donald Steel

Lancashire

Accrington & District
(1893)
West End, Oswaldtwistle, Accrington, BB5 4LS
☎ **(01254) 381614**
🖳 (01254) 233273
✉ info@accrington-golf-club.fsnet.co.uk
📖 350
✍ GA Dixon (01254) 381614
🏌 W Harling (01254) 231091
▶ 18 L 6044 yds SSS 69
👥 WD/WE–U H SOC–H
££ On application
🚗 3 miles SW of Accrington. M65 Junctions 6/7
■ www.accrington-golf-club.fsnet.co.uk

Ashton & Lea (1913)
Tudor Ave, Off Blackpool Rd, Lea, Preston PR4 0XA
☎ **(01772) 735282**
🖳 (01772) 735762
✉ ashtonleagolf@supanet.com
📖 750
✍ I Hulley (01772) 735282
🏌 M Greenough (01772) 720374
▶ 18 L 6334 yds SSS 71
👥 U SOC
££ £26 (£30)
🚗 3 miles W of Preston, off A5085. Nr M6, M55 and M65
⬆ J Steer

Ashton-in-Makerfield
(1902)
Garswood Park, Liverpool Road, Ashton-in-Makerfield, WN4 0YT
☎ **(01942) 727267**
🖳 (01942) 719330
📖 675
✍ HG Williams (01942) 719330
🏌 P Allan (01942) 724229
▶ 18 L 6212 yds SSS 70
👥 WD–U exc Wed WE/BH–M SOC

££ £28
🚗 1 mile W of Ashton-in-Makerfield on A58. M6 Junction 23/24

Ashton-under-Lyne (1912)
Gorsey Way, Hurst, Ashton-under-Lyne, OL6 9HT
☎ **(0161) 330 1537**
🖳 (0161) 330 6673
📖 600
✍ A Jackson (0161) 330 1537
🏌 C Boyle (0161) 308 2095
▶ 18 L 6209 yds SSS 70
👥 WD–U WE/BH–M SOC
££ On application
🚗 8 miles E of Manchester. M60 Junction 23

Bacup (1910)
Maden Road, Bankside Lane, Bacup, OL13 8HN
☎ **(01706) 873170**
🖳 (01706) 867726
✉ bacup@onetel.net.uk
✍ T Leyland (01706) 879644
▶ 9 L 6018 yds SSS 69
👥 U
££ On application
🚗 Bankside Lane

Baxenden & District (1913)
Top o' th' Meadow, Baxenden, Accrington, BB5 2EA
☎ **(01254) 234555**
📖 400
✍ N Turner (01706) 225423
▶ 9 L 5702 yds SSS 68
👥 WD–U WE/BH–M
££ £15
🚗 2 miles SE of Accrington
■ www.baxendengolf.co.uk

Beacon Park (1982)
Public
Beacon Lane, Dalton, Up Holland, WN8 7RU
☎ **(01695) 625551**
📖 250
✍ T Harris
🏌 G Nelson (01695) 622700
▶ 18 L 6155 yds SSS 70
👥 U–book 6 days in advance SOC
££ On application
🚗 Nr Ashurst Beacon and M58/M6 Junction 26
⊕ Driving range

Blackburn (1894)
Beardwood Brow, Blackburn, BB2 7AX
☎ **(01254) 51122**
🖳 (01254) 665578
📖 476 65(L) 104(J)
✍ K Taylor (01254) 51122
🏌 A Rodwell (01254) 55942
▶ 18 L 6144 yds SSS 70
👥 U SOC–WD WE/BH–restricted
££ £26 (£30)
🚗 1 mile NW of Blackburn (A677). M6 Junction 31

Blackpool North Shore
(1904)
Devonshire Road, Blackpool, FY2 0RD
☎ (01253) 352054
🖥 (01253) 591240
✉ office@bnsgc.com
📖 750
🏌 JW Morris (01253) 352054 ext 6
⚐ B Ward (01253) 354640
🏳 18 L 6443 yds SSS 71
👫 WD–U WE–restricted SOC
£€ £35 (£38)
🏌 ½ mile E of Queens Promenade (B5124)
🏠 HS Colt

Blackpool Park   (1925)
Public
North Park Drive, Blackpool, FY3 8LS
☎ (01253) 397916
🖥 (01253) 397916
📖 650
🏌 D Stones (01253) 397916
⚐ B Purdie (01253) 391004
🏳 18 L 6192 yds SSS 69
👫 U–no telephone booking
£€ £13 (£15)
🏌 2 miles E of Blackpool, signposted off M55
🏠 Dr A Mackenzie

Bolton   (1891)
Lostock Park, Bolton, BL6 4AJ
☎ (01204) 843278
🖥 (01204) 843067
✉ boltongolf@lostockpark.fsbusiness .co.uk
📖 600
🏌 Mrs HM Stuart (01204) 843067
⚐ R Longworth (01204) 843073
🏳 18 L 6237 yds Par 70 SSS 70
👫 U SOC
£€ £32 D–£38 (£35 D–£42)
🏌 3 miles W of Bolton. M61 Junction 6, 2 miles

Bolton Old Links   (1891)
Chorley Old Road, Montserrat, Bolton, BL1 5SU
☎ (01204) 840050
🖥 (01204) 842307
✉ mail@boltonoldlinks.co.uk
📖 600
🏌 Mrs J Boardman (01204) 842307
⚐ P Horridge (01204) 843089
🏳 18 L 6469 yds SSS 71
👫 U H exc comp Sats SOC
£€ £30 (£40)
🏌 3 miles NW of Bolton on B6226
🏠 Dr A Mackenzie
■ www.boltonoldlinks.co.uk

Bolton Open Golf Course
Pay and play
Longsight Park, Longsight Lane, Harwood, BL2 4JX
☎ (01204) 597659/309778
📖 250
🏌 H Swindells (Sec/Mgr) (01204) 597659

⚐ Tolly Howarth (01204) 309778
🏳 18 holes Par 70 SSS 68
👫 WD–U WE–booking necessary SOC
£€ £10 (£12)
🏌 2 miles NE of Bolton (A666)
⊕ Driving range

Brackley Municipal   (1977)
Public
Bullows Road, Little Hulton, Worsley, M38 9TR
☎ (0161) 790 6076
⚐ S Lomax (Mgr)
🏳 9 L 3003 yds SSS 69
👫 U
£€ On application
🏌 2 miles NW of Walkden, off A6

Breightmet   (1911)
Red Bridge, Ainsworth, Bolton, BL2 5PA
☎ (01204) 399275
📖 280
🏌 ID Cooke
🏳 9 L 6416 yds SSS 71
👫 WD–H WE–NA SOC–WD
£€ £15 (£20)
🏌 3 miles E of Bolton

Brookdale   (1896)
Medlock Road, Woodhouses, Failsworth, M35 9WQ
☎ (0161) 681 4534
🖥 (0161) 688 6872
📖 725
🏌 MJ Chadwick
⚐ T Cuppello (0161) 681 2655
🏳 18 L 5841 yds SSS 68
👫 WD–U SOC–WD
£€ £26
🏌 5 miles NE of Manchester, M60 Junction 22
■ www.brookdalegolfclub.co.uk

Burnley   (1905)
Glen View, Burnley, BB11 3RW
☎ (01282) 451281
🖥 (01282) 451281
✉ burnleygolfclub@onthegreen.co.uk
📖 600
🏌 RDM Wills (01282) 451281
⚐ P McEvoy (01282) 455266
🏳 18 L 5939 yds SSS 69
👫 H SOC
£€ £20 (£25)
🏌 Via Manchester Rd to Glen View Rd
■ www.burnleygolfclub.org.uk

Bury   (1890)
Unsworth Hall, Blackford Bridge, Bury, BL9 9TJ
☎ (0161) 766 4897
🖥 (0161) 796 3480
📖 650
🏌 R Adams
⚐ D Procter (0161) 766 2213
🏳 18 L 5927 yds SSS 69
👫 SOC WD WE
£€ £28 (£32)
🏌 A56, 5 miles N of Manchester. 3 miles N of M62 Junction 17

Castle Hawk   (1975)
Chadwick Lane, Castleton, Rochdale, OL11 3BY
☎ (01706) 640841
🖥 (01706) 860587
✉ teeoff@castlehawk.co.uk
📖 200
🏌 L Entwistle
⚐ A Duncan
🏳 18 L 5398 yds SSS 68
9 L 3158 yds SSS 55
👫 U SOC
£€ WD/Sat D–£9 Sun D–£11
🏌 Castleton Station 1 mile. M62 Junction 20
⊕ Driving range

Chorley   (1897)
Hall o' th' Hill, Heath Charnock, Chorley, PR6 9HX
☎ (01257) 480263
🖥 (01257) 480722
✉ secretary@chorleygolfclub .freeserve.co.uk
📖 550
🏌 Mrs A Allen (01257) 480263
⚐ M Bradley (01257) 481245
🏳 18 L 6240 yds SSS 70
👫 WD–I or H WE–NA SOC
£€ On application
🏌 1 mile S of Chorley at junction A6/A673
🏠 JA Steer
■ www.chorleygolfclub.co.uk

Clitheroe   (1891)
Whalley Road, Clitheroe, BB7 1PP
☎ (01200) 422618 (Clubhouse)
🖥 (01200) 422292
✉ secretary@clitheroegolfclub.com
📖 700
🏌 T Ashton (01200) 422292
⚐ J Twissell (01200) 424242
🏳 18 L 6326 yds SSS 71
👫 WD–U H SOC
£€ £32 D–£38 (£45)
🏌 2 miles S of Clitheroe
⊕ Range
🏠 James Braid
■ www.clitheroegolfclub.com

Colne   (1901)
Law Farm, Skipton Old Road, Colne, BB8 7EB
☎ (01282) 863391
📖 354
🏌 JT Duerden (Hon)
⚐ None
🏳 9 L 5961 yds SSS 69
👫 U exc comp days SOC–WD
£€ £16 (£20)
🏌 1½ miles N of Colne. From end of M65, signs to Keighley and then Lothersdale

Crompton & Royton   (1914)
High Barn, Royton, Oldham, OL2 6RW
☎ (0161) 624 2154
🖥 (0161) 652 4711
✉ secretary @cromptonandroytongolfclub.co.uk

For list of abbreviations and key to symbols see page 627

620
✏ S Porter (0161) 624 0986
✓ DA Melling (0161) 624 2154
▷ 18 L 6186 yds SSS 70
⋔ U SOC–WD
££ £25 (£35)
⊶ 3 miles NW of Oldham
■ www.cromptonandroytongolfclub
.co.uk

Darwen (1893)

*Winter Hill, Duddon Avenue, Darwen,
BB3 0LB*
☎ (01254) 701287
▭ (01254) 773833
▥ 375 70(L) 60(J)
✏ JR Lawson (01254) 704367
✓ W Lennon (01254) 776370
▷ 18 L 5863 yds Par 69 SSS 68
⋔ U exc Tues & Sat–NA
££ £25 (£30)
⊶ Darwen 1¹/₂ miles. M65 Junction 4

Dean Wood (1922)

*Lafford Lane, Up Holland, Skelmersdale,
WN8 0QZ*
☎ (01695) 622219
▭ (01695) 622245
✉ office@dwgc.fsnet.co.uk
▥ 750
✏ A McGregor
✓ S Danchin
▷ 18 L 6148 yds SSS 70
⋔ WD–U WE/BH–M SOC
££ £30 (£33)
⊶ 4 miles W of Wigan (A577)
⌂ James Braid

Deane (1906)

*Off Junction Road, Deane, Bolton,
BL3 4NS*
☎ (01204) 61944
▥ 490
✏ DA Thompson (01204) 651808
✓ D Martindale
▷ 18 L 5652 yds SSS 67
⋔ WD–U WE–restricted
SOC–Tues/Thurs/Fri
££ £24 (£28)
⊶ 2 miles W of Bolton. M61 Junction
5, 1 mile

Dunscar (1908)

*Longworth Lane, Bromley Cross, Bolton,
BL7 9QY*
☎ (01204) 598228
▭ (01204) 303321
✉ secretary@dunscargolfclub.fsnet
.co.uk
▥ 600
✏ JW Jennings (01204) 303321
✓ G Treadgold (01204) 592992
▷ 18 L 6085 yds Par 71 SSS 69
⋔ WD–U WE–restricted SOC
££ £20 (£30)
⊶ 3 miles N of Bolton, off A666

Duxbury Park (1975)

Public
*Duxbury Hall Road, Duxbury Park,
Chorley, PR7 4AS*
☎ (01257) 265380

▭ (01257) 241378
✏ PA Smith
✓ D Clarke
▷ 18 L 6270 yds SSS 70
⋔ U
££ £8 (£10.50)
⊶ 1¹/₂ miles S of Chorley, off Wigan
Lane

Fairhaven (1895)

*Oakwood Avenue, Ansdell, Lytham St
Annes, FY8 4JU*
☎ (01253) 736741
▭ (01253) 731461
▥ 900
✏ S Last
✓ (01253) 736976
▷ 18 L 6883 yds SSS 73
⋔ WD–U WE–NA before 9am
SOC–WD
££ £40 (£50)
⊶ Lytham 2 miles. St Annes 2 miles.
M55 Junction 4

Fishwick Hall (1912)

*Glenluce Drive, Farringdon Park,
Preston, PR1 5TD*
☎ (01772) 798300
▭ (01772) 704600
▥ 750
✏ JP Davis
✓ M Watson (01772) 795870
▷ 18 L 6045 yds Par 70 SSS 69
⋔ Apply to Sec SOC
££ £20 (£32)
⊶ 1 mile E of Preston, nr junction of
A59 and M6 Junction 31

Fleetwood (1932)

*Golf House, Princes Way, Fleetwood,
FY7 8AF*
☎ (01253) 873114 (Clubhouse)
▭ (01253) 773573
✉ fleetwoodgc@aol.com
▥ 548
✏ N Robinson (01253) 773573
✓ S McLaughlin (01253) 873661
▷ L 18 L 6308 yds SSS 70
⋔ U H exc Tues SOC
££ £30 (£40)
⊶ 1 mile W of Fleetwood centre
⌂ A Steer
■ www.fleetwoodgolfclub.org.uk

Gathurst (1913)

*Miles Lane, Shevington, Wigan,
WN6 8EW*
☎ (01257) 252861 (Clubhouse)
▭ (01257) 255953
✉ gathurst.golfclub@02.co.uk
▥ 675
✏ Mrs I Fyffe (01257) 255235
✓ D Clarke (01257) 255882
▷ 18 L 6089 yds Par 70 SSS 69
⋔ WD–U before 5pm
WE/BH/Wed–M SOC–WD
££ £27
⊶ 4 miles W of Wigan. 1 mile S of
M6 Junction 27
⌂ N Pearson-ADAS

Ghyll (1907)

*Ghyll Brow, Barnoldswick, Colne,
BB18 6JH*
☎ (01282) 842466
✉ secretary@ghyllgc.freeserve.com
▥ 310
✏ JL Gill (01524) 412958
▷ 9 L 5708 yds SSS 68
⋔ U exc Sun–NA
££ D–£15 (D–£18)
⊶ 7 miles N of Colne, off A56
(B6252)
■ www.ghyllgc.co.uk

Great Harwood (1896)

Harwood Bar, Great Harwood, BB6 7TE
☎ (01254) 884391
▭ (01254) 879495
▥ 195 65(L) 45(J)
✏ J Spibey (01254) 879494
▷ 9 L 6404 yds SSS 71
⋔ U SOC
££ £16 (£22)
⊶ 5 miles NE of Blackburn. M65
Junction 7

Green Haworth (1914)

Green Haworth, Accrington, BB5 3SL
☎ (01254) 237580
▭ (01254) 396176
▥ 250
✏ W Halstead
▷ 9 L 5556 yds SSS 67
⋔ WD–U exc Wed–Ladies only after
5pm WE/BH–M SOC
££ On application
⊶ Willows Lane

Greenmount (1920)

Greenmount, Bury, BL8 4LH
☎ (01204) 883712
▥ 220
✏ MD Barron (Hon)
✓ C Maloney
▷ 9 L 5874 yds SSS 69
⋔ WD–U exc Tues WE–M
££ £15
⊶ 3 miles N of Bury

Haigh Hall (1972)

Public
*Haigh Hall Country Park, Haigh, Wigan,
WN2 1PE*
☎ (01942) 833337 (Clubhouse)
▭ (01942) 831417
▥ 300
✏ W Fleetwood
✓ I Lee (01942) 831107
▷ 9 L 1446 yds
18 L 6350 yds (open June 2002)
⋔ U
££ £3.60 (£4.60)
⊶ 2 miles NW of Wigan. M6 Junction
27. M61 Junction 6
⌂ Gaunt/Marnoch

Hart Common (1995)

Proprietary
*Westhoughton Golf Centre, Wigan Road,
Westhoughton, BL5 2BX*
☎ (01942) 813195

✉ hartcommon@ukgolfer.org
🚵 B Hill (01942) 813195
✓ G Benson (01942) 813195
▷ 18 L 6243 yds (white) Par 72
  SSS 70
  L 5719 yds (yellow) Par 71 SSS 68
  9 L 694 yds Par 27
👥 U SOC
£€ 18: £10 (£15); 9: £3.50 (£3.50
🚵 In-between Bolton and Wigan on
  A58, M51 J5
⊕ 27 bay driving range
■ www.ukgolfer.org/courses
  /hartcommon

Harwood (1926)

Roading Brook Road, Bolton, BL2 4JD
☎ **(01204) 522878**
🖥 (01204) 524233
✉ secretary@harwoodgolfclub.co.uk
🚵 IW Lund (01204) 524233
✓ (01204) 362834
▷ 18 L 5786 yds SSS 68
👥 WD–H WE–M SOC
£€ £20
🚵 4 miles NE of Bolton (B6391)
🏠 J Shuttleworth
■ www.harwoodgolfclub.co.uk

Heysham (1910)

*Trumacar Park, Middleton Road,
Heysham, Morecambe LA3 3JH*
☎ **(01524) 851011**
🖥 (01524) 853030
📖 685
🚵 FA Bland (Sec/Mgr)
✓ R Dône (01524) 852000
▷ 18 L 6258 yds SSS 70
👥 U H SOC
£€ £30 (£40)
🚵 2 miles S of Morecambe. M6
  Junction 34, 5 miles
🏠 A Herd

Hindley Hall (1905)

Hall Lane, Hindley, Wigan, WN2 2SQ
☎ **(01942) 255131**
🖥 (01942) 253871
✉ sechindley@aol.com
📖 430
🚵 Louise Hedley (01942) 255131
✓ D Clarke (01942) 255991
▷ 18 L 5913 yds SSS 68
👥 U SOC
£€ £20 (£27)
🚵 2 miles S of Wigan. M61 Junction 6

Horwich (1895)

Victoria Road, Horwich, BL6 5PH
☎ **(01204) 696980**
🖥 (01942) 205316
📖 300
✓ C Sherborne
✓ B Sharrock
▷ 9 L 5404 yds SSS 66
👥 U SOC–WD
£€ £16
🚵 5 miles W of Bolton
🏠 George Lowe

Hurlston Hall (1994)

*Hurlston Lane, Southport Road,
Scarisbrick, L40 8HB*
☎ **(01704) 840400**
🖥 (01704) 841404
✉ hurlston_hall@btinternet.com
📖 650
🚵 M Atherton
✓ J Esclapez (01704) 841120
▷ 18 L 6746 yds SSS 72
👥 H SOC
£€ £35 (£40)
🚵 2 miles NW of Ormskirk (A570).
  M58 Junction 3
⊕ Floodlit driving range
🏠 Donald Steel
■ www.hurlstonhall.co.uk

Ingol (1981)

*Tanterton Hall Road, Ingol, Preston,
PR2 7BY*
☎ **(01772) 734556**
📖 700
🚵 H Parker
✓ S Laycock
▷ 18 L 5868 yds SSS 68
👥 U SOC–WD
£€ £15 (£25)
🚵 1¹/₂ miles NW of Preston (A6). M6
  Junction 32

Knott End (1910)

*Wyreside, Knott End-on-Sea, Poulton-le-
Fylde, FY6 0AA*
☎ **(01253) 810254 (Clubhouse)**
🖥 (01253) 813446
✉ knottendgolfclub@btinternet.com
📖 660
🚵 A Crossley (01253) 810576
✓ P Walker (01253) 811365
▷ 18 L 5849 yds SSS 68
👥 WD–U WE/BH–by arrangement
  SOC–WD/WE
£€ D–£26 (£31)
🚵 Over Wyre, 12 miles NE of
  Blackpool (A588)
⊕ Practice ground/net
🏠 James Braid

Lancaster (1932)

*Ashton Hall, Ashton-with-Stodday,
Lancaster, LA2 0AJ*
☎ **(01524) 752090 (Clubhouse)**
🖥 (01524) 752742
📖 530 170(L) 62(J)
🚵 PJ Irvine (01524) 751247
✓ DE Sutcliffe (01524) 751802
▷ 18 L 6500 yds SSS 71
👥 WD–H SOC–WD
£€ £35
🚵 2 miles S of Lancaster (A588)
⊕ Dormy House
🏠 James Braid

Lansil (1947)

Caton Road, Lancaster, LA4 3PE
☎ **(01524) 39269**
📖 450
🚵 J Ollerton (01995) 601451
▷ 9 L 5608 yds Par 70 SSS 67
👥 WD–U Sun–U after 1pm

£€ £12 (£12)
🚵 A683, 2 miles E of Lancaster

Leyland (1924)

Wigan Road, Leyland, PR25 5UD
☎ **(01772) 436457**
🖥 (01772) 435605
✉ manager@leylandgolfclub.com
📖 750
🚵 J Ross
✓ C Burgess (01772) 423425
▷ 18 L 6298 yds SSS 70
👥 WD–U WE–M SOC–WD
£€ £25
🚵 M6 Junction 28, ¹/₂mile
■ www.leylandgolfclub.com

Lobden (1888)

Whitworth, Rochdale, OL12 8XJ
☎ **(01706) 343228**
🖥 (01706) 343228
✉ lobdengc@hotmail.com
📖 220
🚵 J Keate (01706) 345598
▷ 9 L 5697 yds Par 70 SSS 68
👥 U
£€ £12 (£15)
🚵 4 miles N of Rochdale

Longridge (1877)

*Fell Barn, Jeffrey Hill, Longridge,
Preston PR3 2TU*
☎ **(01772) 783291**
🖥 (01772) 783022
📖 700
🚵 DC Wensley
✓ S Taylor (01772) 783291
▷ 18 L 5969 yds SSS 69
👥 U
£€ £15 (£20)
🚵 8 miles NE of Preston, off B6243

Lowes Park (1915)

Hilltop, Lowes Road, Bury, BL9 6SU
☎ **(0161) 764 1231**
🖥 (0161) 763 9503
✉ lowes@parkgc.fsnet.co.uk
📖 400
🚵 J Entwistle
▷ 9 L 6006 yds Par 70 SSS 69
👥 WD–U exc Wed–NA WE/BH–by
  arrangement
£€ Summer £10 (£15) Winter £5 (£10)
🚵 1 mile NE of Bury, off A56

Lytham Green Drive (1922)

Ballam Road, Lytham, FY8 4LE
☎ **(01253) 734782**
🖥 (01253) 731350
✉ sec@greendrive.fsnet.co.uk
📖 700
🚵 S Higham (01253) 737390
✓ A Lancaster (01253) 737379
▷ 18 L 6163 yds SSS 69
👥 WD–U H WE–NA SOC–WD
£€ £32 (£40)
🚵 Lytham St Annes. M55 Junction 4
🏠 JA Steer
■ www.ukgolfer.org

Marland (1928)
Public
Springfield Park, Bolton Road,
Rochdale, OL11 4RE
- ☎ **(01706) 649801**
- 📠 (01706) 523082
- 📖 300
- 🏌 J Wallis
- ⚲ D Wills
- ▷ 18 L 5237 yds SSS 66
- 👥 WD–U WE–booking necessary
- £€ £7.50 (£9.50)
- ⚙ W of Rochdale (A58). M62
  Junctions 19/20, 2 miles

Marsden Park (1969)
Public
Townhouse Road, Nelson, BB9 8DG
- ☎ **(01282) 661912**
- 🏌 N Standage (01282) 701249
- ▷ 18 L 5813 yds Par 70 SSS 68
- 👥 U SOC
- £€ On application
- ⚙ M65 Junction 13, signposted
  Walton Lane

Morecambe (1905)
Bare, Morecambe, LA4 6AJ
- ☎ **(01524) 418050**
- 📠 (01524) 400088
- ✉ morecambegolf@btconnect.com
- 📖 850
- 🏌 Mrs J Atkinson (01524) 412841
- ⚲ S Fletcher (01524) 415596
- ▷ 18 L 5750 yds SSS 69
- 👥 U H SOC
- £€ On application
- ⚙ On coast road towards Carnforth
  (A5105)

Mossock Hall (1996)
Liverpool Road, Bickerstaffe, L39 0EE
- ☎ **(01695) 421717**
- 📠 (01695) 424961
- 📖 600
- 🏌 G Brown
- ⚲ P Atkis (01695) 424969
- ▷ 18 L 6375 yds Par 71 SSS 71
- 👥 U exc comp days SOC
- £€ £30 (£35)
- ⚙ 4 miles S of Ormskirk
- 🏠 Steve Marnoch

Mytton Fold Hotel & Golf Complex (1994)
Proprietary
Whalley Road, Langho, BB6 8AB
- ☎ **(01254) 240662 (Hotel)**
- 📠 (01254) 248119
- ✉ golfshop@myttonfold.co.uk
- 📖 350
- 🏌 D Woodburn
- ⚲ A Twist (01254) 245392
- ▷ 18 L 6155 yds SSS 69
- 👥 U SOC
- £€ £16 (£16)
- ⚙ 6 miles N of Blackburn, off A59.
  M6 Junction 31
- 🏠 F Hargreaves
- ■ www.myttonfold.co.uk

Nelson (1902)
Kings Causeway, Brierfield, Nelson,
BB9 0EU
- ☎ **(01282) 614583**
- 📠 (01282) 606226
- 📖 550
- 🏌 BR Thomason (01282) 611834
- ⚲ N Reeves (01282) 617000
- ▷ 18 L 6006 yds Par 70 SSS 69
- 👥 WD–U H exc Thurs–NA WE–U
  exc Sat before 4pm SOC
- £€ £30 D–£35
- ⚙ 2 miles N of Burnley. M65 Junction
  12
- 🏠 Dr A MacKenzie

Oldham (1892)
Lees New Road, Oldham, OL4 5PN
- ☎ **(0161) 624 4986**
- 📖 230 45(L) 20(J)
- 🏌 J Brooks
- ⚲ R Heginbotham (0161) 626 8346
- ▷ 18 L 5045 yds SSS 65
- 👥 U SOC
- £€ On application
- ⚙ Off Oldham-Stalybridge road

Ormskirk (1899)
Cranes Lane, Lathom, Ormskirk,
L40 5UJ
- ☎ **(01695) 572112**
- 📖 300
- 🏌 RDJ Lawrence (01695) 572227
- ⚲ J Hammond (01695) 572074
- ▷ 18 L 6358 yds SSS 71
- 👥 I exc Sat–NA SOC
- £€ £40 Wed–£45 Sun–£45 D–£55
- ⚙ 2 miles E of Ormskirk

Pennington
Pennington Country Park, Leigh,
WN7 3PA
- ☎ **(01942) 682852**
- 📖 122
- 🏌 BW Lythgoe
- ⚲ T Kershaw (01942) 682852
- ▷ 9 L 5521 yds Par 70 SSS 67
- 👥 U SOC
- £€ £3.80 (£4.80)
- ⚙ ¹/₂ mile off A580, on Leigh By-
  Pass. Follow signs for Pennington
  Flash

Penwortham (1908)
Blundell Lane, Penwortham, Preston,
PR1 0AX
- ☎ **(01772) 744630**
- 📠 (01772) 740172
- ✉ penworthamgolfclub@supanet.com
- 📖 820
- 🏌 N Annandale
- ⚲ D Hopwood (01772) 742345
- ▷ 18 L 5877 yds SSS 69
- 👥 WD–U WE–no parties
- £€ £25 (£33)
- ⚙ 1¹/₂ miles W of Preston (A59)

Pleasington (1891)
Pleasington, Blackburn, BB2 5JF
- ☎ **(01254) 202177**
- 📠 (01254) 201028
- ✉ jean@pleasington-golf.co.uk
- 📖 545
- 🏌 M Trickett
- ⚲ GJ Furey (01254) 201630
- ▷ 18 L 6445 yds SSS 71
- 👥 H
- £€ £38 (£42)
- ⚙ 3 miles SW of Blackburn

Poulton-le-Fylde (1982)
Public
Myrtle Farm, Breck Road, Poulton-le-
Fylde, FY6 7HJ
- ☎ **(01253) 892444**
- 📖 250
- 🏌 P Drew
- ⚲ J Greenwood
- ▷ 9 L 2979 yds SSS 69
- 👥 U
- £€ On application
- ⚙ 3 miles NE of Blackpool
- ⊕ Indoor driving range

Preston (1892)
Fulwood Hall Lane, Fulwood, Preston,
PR2 8DD
- ☎ **(01772) 700011**
- 📠 (01772) 794234
- ✉ prestongolfclub@btinternet.com
- 📖 800
- 🏌 SH Newland (01772) 700011
- ⚲ A Greenbank (01772) 700022
- ▷ 18 L 6312 yds SSS 71
- 👥 WD–U H WE–M SOC–WD
- £€ D–£40
- ⚙ 1¹/₂ miles W of M6 Junction 32
- ⊕ Driving range. Golf academy
- 🏠 James Braid
- ■ www.prestongolfclub.com

Regent Park (Bolton) (1931)
Public
Links Road, Chorley New Road, Bolton,
BL6 4AF
- ☎ **(01204) 844170**
- 📖 260
- 🏌 J Rogers
- ⚲ B Longworth (01204) 842336
- ▷ 18 L 6221yds Par 70 SSS 69
- 👥 U SOC–WD
- £€ £8 (£10)
- ⚙ A673, 3 miles W of Bolton. M61
  Junction 6

Rishton (1927)
Eachill Links, Hawthorn Drive, Rishton,
BB1 4HG
- ☎ **(01254) 884442**
- 📠 (01254) 887701
- ✉ rishtongc@onetel.net
- 📖 302
- 🏌 T Charnock
- ▷ 9 L 6097 yds SSS 69
- 👥 WD–U WE–M
- £€ £17 without member (£10 with
  member only)
- ⚙ 3 miles E of Blackburn
- 🏠 Thomas/Alliss
- ■ www.rishton-golf-club.co.uk

Rochdale   (1888)

Edenfield Road, Bagslate, Rochdale, OL11 5YR

☎ **(01706) 646024 (Clubhouse)**
🖳 (01706) 861113
📖 750
🏌 P Chappell (01706) 643818
🏑 A Laverty (01706) 522104
🏴 18 L 6031 yds SSS 69
👥 U
£€ £20 (£25)
🚗 3 miles from M62 Junction 20 on A680
🏠 George Lowe

Rossendale   (1903)

Ewood Lane Head, Haslingden, Rossendale, BB4 6LH

☎ **(01706) 831339**
🖳 (01706) 228669
📖 713
🏌 AV Townsend
🏑 SJ Nicholls (01706) 213616
🏴 18 L 6293 yds SSS 71
👥 WD/Sun–U Sat–M
£€ £25 (£30) (1999)
🚗 7 miles N of Bury, nr end of M66

Royal Lytham & St Annes   (1886)

Links Gate, Lytham St Annes, FY8 3LQ

☎ **(01253) 724206**
🖳 (01253) 780946
✉ bookings@royallytham.org
📖 600
🏌 RJG Cochrane
🏑 E Birchenough (01253) 720094
🏴 18 L 6685 yds SSS 73
👥 WD–I H
£€ £105 (£155) 2003 rates – may increase in 2004
🚗 St Annes 1 mile (A584)
⊕ Dormy House

Saddleworth   (1904)

Mountain Ash, Uppermill, Oldham, OL3 6LT

☎ **(01457) 873653**
🖳 (01457) 820647
✉ secretary@saddleworthgolfclub .org.uk
📖 700
🏌 AE Gleave
🏑 RI Johnson
🏴 18 L 6118 yds SSS 69
👥 U
£€ £23 (£30)
🚗 Uppermill, 5 miles E of Oldham
🏠 Mackenzie/Leaver

Shaw Hill Hotel G&CC   (1925)

Preston Road, Whittle-le-Woods, Chorley, PR6 7PP

☎ **(01257) 269221**
🖳 (01257) 261223
✉ info@shaw-hill.co.uk
📖 500
🏌 DFW Dimsdale
🏑 D Clarke (01257) 279222
🏴 18 L 6246 yds Par 73 SSS 70

👥 WD–U H SOC
£€ £30 (£40)
🚗 A6, 1¹/₂ miles N of Chorley. M61 Junction 8. M6 Junction 28

St Annes Old Links   (1901)

Highbury Road East, Lytham St Annes, FY8 2LD

☎ **(01253) 723597**
🖳 (01253) 781506
✉ secretary@coastalgolf.co.uk
📖 945
🏌 New appointment awaited
🏑 D Webster (01253) 722432
🏴 18 L 6684 yds SSS 72
👥 WD–NA before 9.30am and 12–1.30pm WE/BH–arrange with Sec SOC
£€ £45 am £30 pm (£50)
🚗 Between St Annes and Blackpool, off A584
🏠 Herd
■ www.coastalgolf.co.uk

Standish Court   (1995)

Rectory Lane, Standish, Wigan, WN6 0XD

☎ **(01257) 425777**
🖳 (01257) 425888
📖 300
🏌 G O'Neill
🏑 B Toone
🏴 18 L 5266 yds Par 68 SSS 66
👥 U SOC
£€ £10 (£15)
🚗 M6 Junction 27, 2 miles
🏠 Patrick Dawson
■ www.standishgolf.co.uk

Stonyhurst Park   (1980)

Stonyhurst, Hurst Green, Clitheroe, BB7 9QB

☎ **(01254) 826478**
📖 380
🏌 JM Aitken (01254) 823666
🏴 9 L 5572 yds SSS 67
👥 WD–U WE–NA
£€ £15
🚗 5 miles SW of Clitheroe (B6243)
⊕ Green fees payable at Bayley Arms, Hurst Green

Towneley   (1932)

Public

Towneley Park, Todmorden Road, Burnley, BB11 3ED

☎ **(01282) 451636**
📖 280
🏌 N Clark (01282) 414555
🏑 (01282) 438473
🏴 18 L 5811 yds Par 70 SSS 68
   9 hole course
👥 U
£€ £9.55 (£10.60)
🚗 1¹/₂ miles E of Burnley

Tunshill   (1901)

Kiln Lane, Milnrow, Rochdale, OL16 3TS

☎ **(01706) 342095**
📖 300

🏌 P Lowthian (01706) 357037
🏴 9 L 5745 yds SSS 68
👥 WD–U WE–M SOC
£€ £16
🚗 2 miles E of Rochdale. M62 Junction 21

Turton   (1908)

Wood End Farm, Chapeltown Road, Bromley Cross, Bolton BL7 9QH

☎ **(01204) 852235**
📖 300 56(L) 51(J)
🏌 MJ McNeill (01204) 306971
🏑 Mark Saunders (01204) 853576
🏴 18 L 6124 yds Par 70 SSS 69
👥 WD–U exc Wed–NA 10.00–2.30pm WE/BH–M U H SOC
£€ £20 (£25)
🚗 3¹/₂ miles N of Bolton, nr Last Drop Village

De Vere Herons Reach   (1993)

Pay and play

East Park Drive, Blackpool, FY3 8LL

☎ **(01253) 766156**
🖳 (01253) 798800
📖 550
🏌 P Heaton
🏑 R Bowman (01253) 766156
🏴 18 L 6461 yds SSS 72
👥 U H SOC
£€ £40 (£45)
🚗 M55 Junction 4. Follow signs to Blackpool Zoo
⊕ Floodlit driving range
🏠 Alliss/Clark

Walmersley   (1906)

Garrett's Close, Walmersley, Bury, BL9 6TE

☎ **(0161) 764 1429**
🖳 (0161) 764 7770
📖 450
🏌 RO Goldstein (0161) 764 7770
🏑 P Thorpe (0161) 763 9050
🏴 18 L 5341 yds SSS 67
👥 WD–U exc Tues–NA Sat–NA Sun–M SOC–Wed–Fri
£€ D–£20
🚗 2 miles N of Bury (A56). S of M66 Junction 1
🏠 SG Marnoch

Werneth   (1908)

Green Lane, Garden Suburb, Oldham, OL8 3AZ

☎ **(0161) 624 1190**
📖 400
🏌 JH Barlow
🏑 R Penny
🏴 18 L 5363 yds SSS 66
👥 WD–U WE–M SOC
£€ D–£16.50
🚗 2 miles S of Oldham
🏠 Sandy Herd

Westhoughton   (1929)

Long Island, Westhoughton, Bolton, BL5 2BR

☎ **(01942) 811085/608958**

☉ 230
✏ F Donohue
ⅲ 9 L 5834 yds SSS 68
☺ WD–U WE/BH–M
££ D–£18
↷ 4 miles SW of Bolton on A58

Whalley (1912)

Long Leese Barn, Clerkhill Road, Whalley, BB7 9DR
☎ **(01254) 822236**
⎅ (01254) 824760
☉ 350
✏ P Lord (01282) 779167
✓ J Hunt (01254) 822236
ⅲ 9 L 6258 yds Par 72 SSS 71
☺ U exc Sat (Apr–Oct) SOC–WD
££ £20 (£25)
↷ 7 miles NE of Blackburn off A59
■ www.whalleygolfclub.co.uk

Whittaker (1906)

Littleborough, OL5 0LH
☎ **(01706) 378310**
✏ S Noblett (01706) 842541
ⅲ 9 L 5666 yds SSS 67
☺ WD/Sat–U Sun–NA
££ £14 (£18)
↷ 1¹/₂ miles N of Littleborough, off A58. M62 Junction 21
☗ NP Stott

Wigan (1898)

Arley Hall, Haigh, Wigan, WN1 2UH
☎ **(01257) 421360**
☉ 300
✏ E Walmsley
ⅲ 18 L 6008 yds SSS 70
☺ U exc Tues & Sat
££ £30 (£40)
↷ 4 miles N of Wigan, off A5106/B5239. M6 Junction 27
☗ Gaunt/Marnoch

Wilpshire (1890)

72 Whalley Road, Wilpshire, Blackburn, BB1 9LF
☎ **(01254) 248260**
⎅ (01254) 248260
☉ 650
✏ HE Aspden
✓ W Slaven (01254) 249558
ⅲ 18 L 5911 yds SSS 69
☺ WD–U WE/BH–on request
££ £25 (£40)
↷ 3 miles NE of Blackburn, off A666

Leicestershire

Beedles Lake (1993)

170 Broome Lane, East Goscote, LE7 3WQ
☎ **(0116) 260 6759/7086**
☉ 336
✏ L Emery (Gen Mgr) (0116) 260 4414
✓ S Byrne
ⅲ 18 L 6732 yds Par 72 SSS 71
☺ U SOC WD (WE restricted)

££ £12 (£16)
↷ 4 miles N of Leicester on B5328, off A46. M1, 8 miles
⊕ Driving range
☗ D Tucker

Birstall (1900)

Station Road, Birstall, Leicester, LE4 3BB
☎ **(0116) 267 4450**
⎅ (0116) 267 4322
✉ suechilton@btconnect.com
☉ 400 80(L) 50(J)
✏ Mrs SE Chilton (0116) 267 4322
✓ D Clark (0116) 267 5245
ⅲ 18 L 6213 yds SSS 70
☺ WD–I WE–M SOC
££ £25 D–£40
↷ 3 miles N of Leicester (A6)
■ www.birstallgolfclub.co.uk

Blaby (1991)

Pay and play
Lutterworth Road, Blaby, LE8 3DB
☎ **(0116) 278 4804**
✓ B Morris
ⅲ 9 L 2600 yds SSS 68
☺ U
££ 18 holes–£6 (£8)
↷ S of Blaby village
⊕ Driving range

Breedon Priory (1990)

Green Lane, Wilson, Derby, DE73 1LG
☎ **(01332) 863081**
⎅ (01332) 865319
✉ bpgc@barbox.net
☉ 500
✏ M Mayfield
✓ L Sheldon
ⅲ 18 L 5777 yds Par 69 SSS 68
☺ WD–U WE–NA before 2pm (phone first) SOC–WD
££ £20 (£25)
↷ 3¹/₂ miles W of M1 Junction 23A on A453
☗ Snell/Ashton

Charnwood Forest (1890)

Breakback Road, Woodhouse Eaves, Loughborough, LE12 8TA
☎ **(01509) 890259**
⎅ (01509) 890925
✉ secretary@charnwoodforestgc.co.uk
☉ 330
✏ Mrs J Bowler
ⅲ 9 L 5960 yds SSS 69
☺ WD–H WE/BH–NA SOC–Wed–Fri
££ £20 (£25)
↷ M1 Junction 22/23, 3 miles

Cosby (1895)

Chapel Lane, Broughton Road, Cosby, Leicester LE9 1RG
☎ **(0116) 286 4759**
⎅ (0116) 286 4484
✉ secretary@cosby-golf-club.co.uk
☉ 690
✏ DC Jones (0116) 286 4759

✓ M Wing (0116) 284 8275
ⅲ 18 L 6417 yds Par 71 SSS 71
☺ WD–U H before 4pm WE/BH–M H SOC–WD–H
££ £24 D–£35
↷ ¹/₂ mile S of Cosby. 7 miles S of Leicester
■ www.cosby-golf-club.co.uk

Enderby (1986)

Public
Mill Lane, Enderby, Leicester, LE19 4LX
☎ **(0116) 284 9388**
✓ C D'Araujo
ⅲ 9 L 5712 yds Par 72 SSS 71
☺ U
££ 18 holes–£6.75 (£9)
↷ Enderby 2 miles. M1 Junction 21

Forest Hill (1991)

Markfield Lane, Botcheston, LE9 9FJ
☎ **(01455) 824800**
⎅ (01455) 828522
✉ gerry@hyde14.fsnet.co.uk
☉ 650
✏ GD Hyde
✓ G Quilter
ⅲ 18 L 6126 yds Par 71 SSS 69
☺ WD–U WE–M
££ On application
↷ 6 miles W of Leicester. M1 Junction 22, 4 miles
⊕ Driving range, putting green
☗ York/Fixter

Glen Gorse (1933)

Glen Road, Oadby, Leicester, LE2 4RF
☎ **(0116) 271 4159**
⎅ (0116) 271 4159
✉ secretary@gggc.co.uk
☉ 440 115(L) 60(J)
✏ Mrs J James (0116) 271 4159
✓ D Fitzpatrick (0116) 271 3748
ⅲ 18 L 6648 yds SSS 72
☺ WD–U WE/BH–M SOC–WD
££ £25 D–£30
↷ 3 miles S of Leicester on A6

Hinckley (1894)

Leicester Road, Hinckley, LE10 3DR
☎ **(01455) 615124**
⎅ (01455) 890841
☉ 650
✏ D Gray (Sec), L Jackson (Finance & Admin)
✓ R Jones (01455) 615014
ⅲ 18 L 6527 yds SSS 71
☺ WD–U exc Tues Sat–NA before 4pm Sun–M after 11am SOC
££ £30 D–£35
↷ NE of Hinckley on B4668, nr M69
■ www.hinckleygolfclub.com

Humberstone Heights (1978)

Public
Gipsy Lane, Leicester, LE5 0TB
☎ **(0116) 299 5570/1**
⎅ (0116) 299 5569
☉ 350

🔗 B Tuttle
✓ P Highfield (0116) 299 5570
ᐟ 18 L 6343 yds SSS 70
👥 U SOC
£€ On application
⛳ 3 miles E of Leicester, off A47
⊕ Driving range. Pitch & putt course
🏠 Hawtree

Kibworth   (1904)

Weir Road, Kibworth Beauchamp,
Leicester, LE8 0LP
☎ **(0116) 279 2301**
📠 (0116) 279 6434
🖩 700
🔗 J Noble (Mgr)
✓ (0116) 279 2283
ᐟ 18 L 6354 yds SSS 71
👥 WD–U WE–M SOC–WD
£€ £25
⛳ 9 miles SE of Leicester, off A6
⊕ Driving range

Kilworth Springs   (1993)

South Kilworth Road, North Kilworth,
Lutterworth, LE17 6HJ
☎ **(01858) 575082**
📠 (01858) 575078
📧 kilworthsprings@ukonline.co.uk
🖩 816
🔗 Ann Vicary
✓ A Mankert
ᐟ 18 L 6718 yds SSS 72
👥 U SOC
£€ £20 (£22)
⛳ 4 miles E of M1 Junction 20
⊕ Driving range

Kirby Muxloe   (1893)

Station Road, Kirby Muxloe, Leicester,
LE9 2EP
☎ **(0116) 239 3457**
📠 (0116) 239 3457
🖩 630
🔗 GB Woodcock (0116) 239 3457
✓ B Whipham (0116) 239 2813
ᐟ 18 L 6307 yds Par 71 SSS 70
👥 WD–U before 3.45pm exc
    Tues–NA WE–Captain's
    permission only SOC–H
£€ £25 D–£30
⛳ 3 miles W of Leicester. M1
    Junctions 21 or 21A
⊕ Driving range for members and
    green fees only

Langton Park G&CC   (1994)

Langton Hall, Leicester, LE16 7TY
☎ **(01858) 545374**
📠 (01858) 545358
🖩 200
🔗 J Window
ᐟ 18 L 6724 yds SSS 72
👥 H or I SOC
£€ On application
⛳ 12 miles SE of Leicester, off A6. 2
    miles N of Market Harborough
🏠 Hawtree

Leicestershire   (1890)

Evington Lane, Leicester, LE5 6DJ
☎ **(0116) 273 8825**
📠 (0116) 273 1900
📧 enquiries@thelgc.co.uk
🖩 750
🔗 CR Chapman
✓ DT Jones (0116) 273 6730
ᐟ 18 L 6329 yds SSS 71
👥 U H SOC–arrange with Sec or Pro
£€ £24 (£29)
⛳ 2 miles E of Leicester
■ www.thelgc.co.uk

Lingdale   (1967)

Joe Moore's Lane, Woodhouse Eaves,
Loughborough, LE12 8TF
☎ **(01509) 890703**
📠 (01509) 890703
🖩 659
🔗 M Green
✓ P Sellears (01509) 890684
ᐟ 18 L 6545 yds SSS 71
👥 U SOC
£€ D–£30 (£40)
⛳ 6 miles S of Loughborough. M1
    Junction 23, 4 miles

Longcliffe   (1906)

Snells Nook Lane, Nanpantan,
Loughborough, LE11 3YA
☎ **(01509) 216321**
📧 longcliffegolf@btconnect.com
🖩 650
🔗 Mrs E Mackenzie (01509) 239129
✓ DC Mee (01509) 231450
ᐟ 18 L 6695 yds SSS 72
👥 WD–H WE–M
£€ £30
⛳ 3 miles SW of Loughborough. M1
    Junction 23

Lutterworth   (1904)

Rugby Road, Lutterworth, LE17 4HN
☎ **(01455) 552532**
📠 (01455) 553586
🖩 753
🔗 J Faulks (01455) 552532
✓ R Tisdall (01455) 557199
ᐟ 18 L 6226 yds SSS 70
👥 WD–U WE–M SOC–WD
£€ £22 D–£30
⛳ By M1 Junction 20 and M6
    Junction 1

Market Harborough   (1898)

Great Oxendon Road, Market
Harborough, LE16 8NF
☎ **(01858) 463684**
📠 (01858) 432906
🖩 650
🔗 AP Price-Jones
✓ FJ Baxter (01858) 463684
ᐟ 18 L 6022 yds Par 70 SSS 69
👥 WD–U WE–M SOC–WD
£€ £25 D–£30
⛳ 1 mile S of Market Harborough on
    A508
🏠 Howard Swan

Melton Mowbray   (1925)

Waltham Rd, Thorpe Arnold, Melton
Mowbray, LE14 4SD
☎ **(01664) 562118**
📠 (01664) 562118
📧 mmgc@LE144SD.fsbusiness.co.uk
🖩 660
✓ N Curtis (01664) 569629
ᐟ 18 L 6222 yds SSS 70
👥 U H before 3pm –M after 3pm SOC
£€ £25 (£30)
⛳ 2 miles NE of Melton Mowbray on
    A607
■ www.mmgc.org

Oadby   (1974)

Public
Leicester Road, Oadby, Leicester,
LE2 4AJ
☎ **(0116) 270 9052/270 0215**
🖩 350
🔗 (0116) 270 3828
✓ A Wells (0116) 270 9052
ᐟ 18 L 6311 yds Par 72 SSS 70
👥 WD–U WE/BH–book with Pro
    SOC–WD
£€ £10 (£13)
⛳ Leicester Racecourse, 2 miles SE of
    Leicester (A6)

Park Hill   (1994)

Park Hill, Seagrave, LE12 7NG
☎ **(01509) 815454**
📠 (01509) 816062
📧 mail@parkhillgolf.co.uk
🖩 500
🔗 JP Hutson
✓ M Ulyett (01509) 815775
ᐟ 18 L 7219 yds Par 73 SSS 74
👥 U SOC
£€ £22 D–£30 (£26 D–£38)
⛳ 6 miles N of Leicester on A46. M1
    Junction 21A
⊕ Driving range (20 bay), grass tees
■ www.parkhillgolf.co.uk

Rothley Park   (1911)

Westfield Lane, Rothley, Leicester,
LE7 7LH
☎ **(0116) 230 2019**
📠 (0116) 230 2809
📧 secretary@rothleypark.co.uk
🔗 SG Winterton (0116) 230 2809
✓ D Spillane (0116) 230 3023
ᐟ 18 L 6487 yds SSS 71
👥 WD–H exc Tues–NA WE/BH–NA
    SOC
£€ £25 D–£30
⛳ 6 miles N of Leicester, W of A6
■ www.rothleypark.com

Scraptoft   (1928)

Beeby Road, Scraptoft, Leicester,
LE7 9SJ
☎ **(0116) 241 9000**
📠 (0116) 241 9000
📧 info@scraptoft-golf.co.uk
🖩 600
🔗 Paul Henry (0116) 241 9000
✓ Simon Wood (0116) 241 9138
ᐟ 18 L 6151 yds Par 70 SSS 70

WD–U WE–M SOC–WD
£€ £24 D–£29 (£29 after noon)
⟅ 3 miles E of Leicester
■ www.scraptoft-golf.co.uk

Six Hills
Pay and play
Six Hills, Melton Mowbray, LE14 3PR
☎ (01509) 881225
⌨ (01509) 889090
▥ 100
⟅ Mrs J Showler
✓ T Westwood
▷ 18 L 5758 yds Par 71 SSS 69
♙♙ U
£€ £12 (£15)
⟅ 10 miles N of Leicester, off A46
⊕ Driving range

Ullesthorpe Court Hotel
(1976)
*Frolesworth Road, Ullesthorpe,
Lutterworth, LE17 5BZ*
☎ (01455) 209023
⌨ (01455) 202537
▥ 600
⟅ PE Woolley
✓ D Bowring (01455) 209150
▷ 18 L 6650 yds SSS 72
♙♙ U SOC–WD
£€ £20 D–£35
⟅ 3 miles NW of Lutterworth, off
B577. M1 Junction 20, 5 miles
■ www.ullesthorpecourt.co.uk

Western Park   (1920)
Public
Scudamore Road, Leicester, LE3 1UQ
☎ (0116) 287 2339/287 6158
▥ 300
⟅ IA Nicholson
✓ BN Whipham (0116) 287 2339
▷ 18 L 6532 yds SSS 71
♙♙ U
£€ On application
⟅ 4 miles W of Leicester. M1
Junction 21, 3 miles

Whetstone   (1965)
*Cambridge Road, Cosby, Leicester,
LE9 5SH*
☎ (0116) 286 1424
⌨ (0116) 286 1424
▥ 550
⟅ D Dalby
✓ D Raitt
▷ 18 L 5795 yds Par 68 SSS 68
♙♙ U SOC
£€ £15 (£16)
⟅ S boundary of Leicester
⊕ Driving range
🏠 E Callaway

Willesley Park   (1921)
*Measham Road, Ashby-de-la-Zouch,
LE65 2PF*
☎ (01530) 414596
⌨ (01530) 564169
✉ info@willesleypark.com
▥ 760 103(L) 38(J)

⟅ RE Brown (01530) 414596
✓ BJ Hill (01530) 414820
▷ 18 L 6304 yds SSS 70
♙♙ WD–H WE/BH–H after 9.30am
SOC
£€ £28 (£35)
⟅ 2 miles S of Ashby on B5006. M1
Junctions 22/23/24. A42(M)
Junction 12
🏠 James Braid
■ www.willesleypark.com

Lincolnshire

Ashby Decoy   (1936)
*Ashby Decoy, Burringham Road,
Scunthorpe, DN17 2AB*
☎ (01724) 842913
⌨ (01724) 271708
✉ ashby.decoy@btclick.com
▥ 520 130(L) 65(J)
⟅ Mrs J Harrison (01724) 866561
✓ A Miller (01724) 868972
▷ 18 L 6281 yds SSS 71
♙♙ WD–H Sat–M SOC–WD exc Tues
£€ £18 (£23)
⟅ 2 miles SW of Scunthorpe
■ www.ashbydecoy.co.uk

Belton Park   (1890)
*Belton Lane, Londonthorpe Road,
Grantham, NG31 9SH*
☎ (01476) 567399
⌨ (01476) 592078
▥ 900
⟅ T Ireland
✓ B McKee (01476) 563911
▷ 27 holes:
Brownlow L 6452 yds SSS 71
Ancaster L 6305 yds SSS 70
Belmont L 6075 yds SSS 69
♙♙ U H SOC–WD exc Tues
£€ £30 (£36)
⟅ 2 miles N of Grantham
🏠 T Williamson
■ www.beltonpark.co.uk

Belton Woods Hotel   (1991)
Belton, Grantham, NG32 2LN
☎ (01476) 593200
⌨ (01476) 574547
▥ 350
⟅ A Ozolins (01636) 672305
✓ S Sayers
▷ Lakes 18 L 6831 yds SSS 73
Woodside 18 L 6623 yds SSS 72
9 hole Par 3 course
♙♙ U SOC
£€ £27 D–£45 (£30 D–£50)
⟅ 2 miles N of Grantham on A607
towards Lincoln
⊕ Driving range
🏠 Cayford

Blankney   (1904)
Blankney, Lincoln, LN4 3AZ
☎ (01526) 320263
⌨ (01526) 322521
▥ 664 138(L) 50(J)

⟅ DA Priest
✓ G Bradley (01526) 320202
▷ 18 L 6638 yds SSS 73
♙♙ U H SOC
£€ £24 (£30)
⟅ 10 miles SE of Lincoln on B1188
🏠 Cameron Sinclair
■ www.blankneygolf.co.uk

Boston   (1902)
*Cowbridge, Horncastle Road, Boston,
PE22 7EL*
☎ (01205) 350589
⌨ (01205) 367526
▥ 650 115(L) 60(J)
⟅ SP Shaw (01205) 350589
✓ N Hiom (01205) 362306
▷ 18 L 6483 yds Par 72 SSS 71
♙♙ WD–U WE/BH–U H
£€ £22.50 (£27.50)
⟅ 2 miles N of Boston on B1183

Boston West   (1995)
Hubbert's Bridge, Boston, PE20 3QX
☎ (01205) 290670
⌨ (01205) 290725
✉ info@bostonwestgolfclub.co.uk
▥ 650
⟅ MJ Couture (01205) 290670
✓ P Creasey (01205) 290540
▷ 18 L 6333 yds Par 72 SSS 70
6 hole Par 3 course
♙♙ U
£€ £15 (£18)
⟅ 2 miles W of Boston on B1192
⊕ Floodlit driving range
🏠 Michael Zara
■ www.bostonwestgolfclub.co.uk

Burghley Park   (1890)
St Martin's, Stamford, PE9 3JX
☎ (01780) 753789
⌨ (01780) 753789
✉ burghley.golf@lineone.net
▥ 750 140(L) 100(J)
⟅ PH Mulligan
(Sec/Mgr) (01780) 753789
✓ G Davies (01780) 762100
▷ 18 L 6236 yds SSS 70
♙♙ WD–I or H WE/BH–M SOC–WD
£€ £28
⟅ 1 mile S of Stamford, off A1 to
B1081
🏠 Rev JD Day

Canwick Park   (1893)
*Canwick Park, Washingborough Road,
Lincoln, LN4 1EF*
☎ (01522) 542912/522166
⌨ (01522) 526997
✉ manager@canwickpark.co.uk
▥ 650
⟅ P Roberts (01522) 542912
✓ S Williamson (01522) 536870
▷ 18 L 6150 yds SSS 69
♙♙ WD–U WE–M before 2.30pm
SOC–WD
£€ £17 (£21)
⟅ 1 mile SE of Lincoln
🏠 Hawtree
■ www.canwickpark.co.uk

Carholme (1906)

Carholme Road, Lincoln, LN1 1SE
☎ **(01522) 523725**
🖥 (01522) 533733
📧 info@carholme-golf-club.co.uk
🏠 600
♣ J Lammin
✓ M Ross (01522) 536811
↳ 18 L 6215 yds Par 71 SSS 70
👤 WD–U WE–U after 2pm BH–SOC
££ £18 (£22)
🚗 Lincoln 1 mile (A57)
■ www.carholme-golf-club.co.uk

Cleethorpes (1894)

Kings Road, Cleethorpes, DN35 0PN
☎ **(01472) 814060 (Pro)**
📧 seccleethorpesgc@btconnect.com
🏠 650
♣ AJ Thompson (01472) 816110
✓ P Davies (01472) 814060
↳ 18 L 6351 yds SSS 70
👤 WD–U exc Tues am Wed pm
    SOC–exc Tues/Wed/Sat
££ D–£20 (D–£25)
🚗 1 mile S of Cleethorpes
■ www.cleethorpesgolfclub.co.uk

Elsham (1900)

Barton Road, Elsham, Brigg, DN20 0LS
☎ **(01652) 680291**
🖥 (01652) 680308
📧 elshamgolfclub@lineone.net
🏠 650
♣ T Hartley (Mgr) (01652) 680291
✓ S Brewer (01652) 680432
↳ 18 L 6426 yds SSS 71
👤 H SOC–WD
££ £24 D–£30
🚗 3 miles N of Brigg. M180 Junction
    5
■ www.elshamgolfclub.co.uk

Forest Pines (1996)

Ermine Street, Brigg, DN20 0AQ
☎ **(01652) 650756**
🖥 (01652) 650495
🏠 400
♣ D Edwards (Golf Dir)
✓ D Edwards
↳ 27 holes: 6393-6859 yds
    Par 71-73 SSS 70-73
👤 U SOC
££ £35 D–£45
🚗 M180 Junction 4, on A15 to
    Scunthorpe
⊕ Golf range, hotel and leisure
    facilities
🏠 John Morgan
■ www.forestpines.co.uk

Gainsborough (1894)

Thonock, Gainsborough, DN21 1PZ
☎ **(01427) 613088**
🖥 (01427) 810172
🏠 600
♣ D Bowers
✓ S Cooper
↳ 18 L 6266 yds Par 70 SSS 70
    18 L 6724 yds Par 72 SSS 72
👤 U

££ £30 D–£40
🚗 N of Gainsborough
⊕ Floodlit driving range
🏠 Neil Coles

Gedney Hill (1991)

Public
West Drove, Gedney End Hill, PE12 0NT
☎ **(01406) 330922**
🏠 400
♣ M Page
✓ D Hutton
↳ 18 L 5450 yds SSS 66
👤 U SOC–WD
££ £6.50 (£11)
🚗 4 miles from A47 on B1166
⊕ Driving range
🏠 C Britton

Grange Park (1992)

Pay and play
Butterwick Road, Messingham,
Scunthorpe, DN17 3PP
☎ **(01724) 762945**
♣ I Cannon (Mgr)
✓ J Drury
↳ 13 L 6180 yds Par 70
    9 hole Par 3 course
👤 U
££ £10.50 (£12.50)
🚗 5 miles from Scunthorpe. M180
    Junction 3
⊕ Floodlit driving range
🏠 RW Price

Grimsby (1922)

Littlecoates Road, Grimsby, DN34 4LU
☎ **(01472) 342823 (Clubhouse)**
🖥 (01472) 342630
🏠 720 150(L) 70(J)
♣ K Skingle (01472) 342630
✓ R Smith (01472) 356981
↳ 18 L 6057 yds Par 70 SSS 69
👤 WD–U Sat pm/Sun am–XL
    SOC–Mon & Fri
££ £22 D–£28
🚗 1 mile W of Grimsby, off A46. 1
    mile from A180
🏠 HS Colt

Hirst Priory Park

Crowle, Scunthorpe, DN17 4BU
☎ **(07715) 420519**
🏠 400
♣ M Thompson
✓ (01724) 711619
↳ 18 L 6199 yds Par 71 SSS 69
👤 U SOC
££ £13.75 (£17.50)
🚗 ³/₄ mile N of M180 Junction 2, on
    A161 to Crowle
🏠 David Baxter

Holme Hall (1908)

Holme Lane, Bottesford, Scunthorpe,
DN16 3RF
☎ **(01724) 862078**
🖥 (01724) 862078
📧 tracey.curtis@btconnect.com
🏠 470 90(L) 30(J)
♣ Miss TL Curtis

✓ R McKiernan (01724) 851816
↳ 18 L 6404 yds SSS 71
👤 WD–U WE–M H SOC–WD
££ £27 D–£35
🚗 4 miles SE of Scunthorpe. M180
    Junction 4

Horncastle (1990)

West Ashby, Horncastle, LN9 5PP
☎ **(01507) 526800**
🏠 300
♣ D Hardy
✓ EC Wright
↳ 18 L 5717 yds SSS 70
👤 U SOC
££ £15 D–£20
🚗 1 mile N of Horncastle, off A158
🏠 EC Wright

Humberston Park

Humberston Avenue, Humberston,
DN36 4SJ
☎ **(01472) 210404**
🏠 230
♣ R Bean (01472) 690361
↳ 9 L 3670 yds Par 60 SSS 57
👤 U exc Wed pm/Thurs am/Sun am
    SOC
££ £10 (£12)
🚗 Humberston, 3 miles S of Grimsby
    (A1031)
🏠 T Barraclough

Immingham (1975)

St Andrews Lane, Off Church Lane,
Immingham, DN40 2EU
☎ **(01469) 575298**
🖥 (01469) 577636
🏠 650
✓ N Harding (01469) 575493
↳ 18 L 6215 yds SSS 70
👤 WD–U WE–restricted (ring for
    details) SOC–WD
££ £15 D–£20
🚗 N of St Andrew's Church,
    Immingham
🏠 Hawtree/Pennink
■ www.immgc.com

Kenwick Park (1992)

Kenwick, Louth, LN11 8NY
☎ **(01507) 605134**
🖥 (01507) 606556
📧 golfatkenwick@nascr.net
♣ PG Shillington
✓ E Sharp (01507) 607161
↳ 18 L 6815 yds Par 72 SSS 73
👤 U SOC
££ D–£27(£35)
🚗 1 mile SE of Louth
⊕ Teaching Academy. Driving range
🏠 Patrick Tallack
■ www.louthnet.co.uk

Kingsway (1971)

Public
Kingsway, Scunthorpe, DN15 7ER
☎ **(01724) 840945**
♣ C Mann
✓ C Mann
↳ 9 L 1915 yds SSS 59

☺ U
£€ On application
⌚ ¾ mile W of Scunthorpe, off A18

Kirton Holme (1992)
Pay and play
Holme Road, Kirton Holme, Boston,
PE20 1SY
☏ (01205) 290669
□ 320
⌚ Mrs T Welberry (01205) 290560
℣ 9 L 2884 yds SSS 68
☺ U SOC–WD
£€ D–£9 (£10)
⌚ 3 miles W of Boston, off A52
⌂ DW Welberry

Lincoln (1891)
Torksey, Lincoln, LN1 2EG
☏ (01427) 718721
□ (01427) 718721
✉ info@lincolngc.co.uk
□ 700
⌚ DB Linton
✓ A Carter (01427) 718273
℣ 18 L 6438 yds SSS 71
☺ WD–H SOC
£€ £28 D–£35 (£30 D–40)
⌚ 12 miles NW of Lincoln, off A156
■ www.lincolngc.co.uk

Louth (1965)
Crowtree Lane, Louth, LN11 9LJ
☏ (01507) 603681
□ (01507) 608501
✉ louthgolfclub1992@btinternet.com
□ 700
⌚ (01507) 603681
✓ AJ Blundell (01507) 604648
℣ 18 L 6436 yds SSS 71
☺ WD U SOC WE – not Sat/Sun after 11
£€ £20 D–£26 (£30 D–£35)
⌚ W side of Louth
■ www.louthgolfclub.com

Manor (Laceby) (1992)
Laceby Manor, Laceby, Grimsby,
DN37 7EA
☏ (01472) 873468
□ (01472) 276706
□ 550
⌚ Mrs J Mackay, G Mackay (Mgr)
℣ 18 L 6354 yds SSS 70
☺ U SOC
£€ D–£18 (£22)
⌚ 5 miles W of Grimsby at Barton Street (A18)
⌂ Nicholson/Rushton

Market Rasen & District (1912)
Legsby Road, Market Rasen, LN8 3DZ
☏ (01673) 842319
□ 600
⌚ JA Brown
✓ AM Chester (01673) 842416
℣ 18 L 6209 yds SSS 70
☺ WD–I WE/BH–M SOC
£€ £20 D–£30
⌚ 1 mile E of Market Rasen

Market Rasen Racecourse
Legsby Road, Market Rasen, LN8 3EA
☏ (01673) 843434
□ (01673) 844532
✉ marketrasen@rht.net
℣ 9 L 2350 yds
☺ U
£€ On application
⌚ Market Rasen Racecourse
■ www.marketrasenraces.co.uk

Martin Moor
Martin Road, Blankney, LN4 3BE
☏ (01526) 378243
□ 150
⌚ M Lovett
℣ 9 L 6325 yds Par 72 SSS 70
☺ U
£€ £8.50 (£10)
⌚ 3 miles E of Metheringham (B1189)
⌂ Harrison/Lovett

Millfield (1985)
Laughterton, Lincoln, LN1 2LB
☏ (01427) 718473
□ (01427) 718473
□ 500
⌚ P Grey-Guthrie
℣ 18 L 6004 yds SSS 69
18 L 4585 yds
9 hole Par 3 course
☺ U
£€ £5 – £8
⌚ 9 miles W of Lincoln, nr Torksey (B1133)
⊕ Driving range
⌂ C Watson

Normanby Hall (1978)
Public
Normanby Park, Scunthorpe, DN15 9HU
☏ (01724) 280444 Ext 852 (Bookings)
□ 850
⌚ P McNicholas (01724) 853212
✓ C Mann (01724) 720226
℣ 18 L 6548 yds SSS 71
☺ U SOC–WD
£€ £11.50 D–£16 (£13.50)
⌚ 5 miles N of Scunthorpe
⌂ Hawtree

North Shore (1910)
North Shore Road, Skegness, PE25 1DN
☏ (01754) 763298
□ (01754) 761902
□ 450
⌚ B Howard (01754) 763298
✓ J Cornelius (01754) 764822
℣ 18 L 6254 yds SSS 71
☺ H–soft spikes only Apr–Oct SOC–WD
£€ £24 D–£35 (£33 D–£43)
⌚ 1 mile N of Skegness
⊕ 36 en-suite bedroom hotel on site
⌂ James Braid
■ www.north-shore.co.uk

Pottergate
Moor Lane, Branston, Lincoln
☏ (01522) 794867
□ 300
⌚ G McFee
✓ L Tasker
℣ 9 L 5164 yds Par 68 SSS 65
☺ U
£€ £8 (£9.50)
⌚ 3 miles SE of Lincoln (B1188)
⌂ WT Bailey

RAF Coningsby (1972)
RAF Coningsby, Lincoln, LN4 4SY
☏ (01526) 342581 Ext 6828
□ 220
⌚ S Ellis (01526) 347640
℣ 9 L 5354 yds Par 68 SSS 66
☺ WD–U before 5pm SOC–WD
£€ £8
⌚ Between Woodhall Spa and Coningsby on B1192

RAF Waddington
Waddington, Lincoln, LN5 9NB
☏ (01522) 720271 Ext 7958
□ 90
⌚ D Bennett
℣ 9 L 5519 yds SSS 69
☺ By prior arrangement
£€ On application
⌚ 4 miles S of Lincoln (A607)

Sandilands (1901)
Sandilands, Sutton-on-Sea, LN12 2RJ
☏ (01507) 441432
□ (01507) 441617
□ 300
⌚ C Carpenter (01507) 441432
℣ 18 L 6068 yds SSS 69
☺ U SOC
£€ £18 (£20)
⌚ 1 mile S of Sutton-on-Sea, off A52

Seacroft (1895)
Drummond Road, Seacroft, Skegness,
PE25 3AU
☏ (01754) 763020
□ (01754) 763020
✉ enquiries@seacroft-golfclub.co.uk
□ 328 107(L) 87(J)
⌚ R England (Sec/Mgr)
✓ R Lawie (01754) 769624
℣ 18 L 6479 yds SSS 71
☺ U H SOC
£€ £30 (£35)
⌚ S boundary of Skegness, nr Nature Reserve
⌂ Willie Fernie
■ www.seacroft-golfclub.co.uk

Sleaford (1905)
Willoughby Road, South Rauceby,
Sleaford, NG34 8PL
☏ (01529) 488273
□ (01529) 488326
✉ sleafordgolfclub@btinternet.com
□ 630
⌚ TE Gibbons
✓ J Wilson (01529) 488644

⊳ 18 L 6503 yds SSS 71
⋔ U H exc Sun–NA (Winter)
SOC–WD
£€ £22 (£36)
⊶ 1 mile W of Sleaford on A153
⋔ Tom Williamson

South Kyme   (1990)
Skinners Lane, South Kyme, Lincoln,
LN4 4AT
☎ (01526) 861113
🖥 (01526) 861080
✉ southkymegc@hotmail.com
🖉 P Chamberlain (Golf Dir)
⫽ P Chamberlain
⊳ 18 L 6597 yds SSS 71
⋔ U SOC
£€ £20 (£24)
⊶ 2 miles from A17 on B1395
⊕ 6 hole practice course
⋔ Graham Bradley
■ www.skgc.co.uk

Spalding   (1907)
Surfleet, Spalding, PE11 4EA
☎ (01775) 680386
🖥 (01775) 680988
📖 750
🖉 BW Walker (01775) 680386
⫽ J Spencer (01775) 680474
⊳ 18 L 6483 yds SSS 71
⋔ U H SOC–Tues after 2pm & Thurs
£€ £25 (£30)
⊶ 4 miles N of Spalding, off A16
⊕ Driving range
⋔ Spencer/Ward/Price

Stoke Rochford   (1924)
Great North Rd, Grantham, NG33 5EW
☎ (01476) 530275
📖 570
🖉 J Martindale (01572) 756305
⫽ A Dow (01476) 530218
⊳ 18 L 6252 yds SSS 70
⋔ WD–U WE/BH–U after 10.30am
£€ On application
⊶ 6 miles S of Grantham (A1)
⋔ Maj Hotchkin (1935)

Sudbrook Moor   (1991)
Public
Charity Street, Carlton Scroop,
Grantham, NG32 3AT
☎ (01400) 250796
🖉 Judith Hutton
⫽ T Hutton (01400) 250796
⊳ 9 L 4827 yds Par 66 SSS 64
⋔ U–phone first
£€ D–£7 (D–£9)
⊶ Carlton Scroop, 6 miles NE of
Grantham (A607)
⋔ Tim Hutton
■ www.sudbrookmoor.co.uk

Sutton Bridge   (1914)
New Road, Sutton Bridge, Spalding,
PE12 9RQ
☎ (01406) 350323 (Clubhouse)
📖 320
🖉 NE Davis (01945) 582447
⫽ Simon Dicksee (01406) 351422

⊳ 9 L 5820 yds SSS 68
⋔ WD–H WE–M SOC
£€ £20
⊶ 8 miles N of Wisbech (A17)
⊕ Driving range

Tetney
Station Road, Tetney, Grimsby,
DN36 5HY
☎ (01472) 211644
🖥 (01472) 211644
📖 425
🖉 J Abrams
⫽ J Abrams
⊳ 18 L 6100 yds Par 71 SSS 69
⋔ U SOC
£€ £10 (£11)
⊶ 5 miles S of Grimsby, off A16
⊕ Driving range

Toft Hotel   (1988)
Proprietary
Toft, Bourne, PE10 0JT
☎ (01778) 590616
🖥 (01778) 590264
📖 500
🖉 R Morris (01778) 590654
⫽ M Jackson
⊳ 18 L 6486 yds Par 72 SSS 71
⋔ U
£€ £25 (£35)
⊶ 8 miles from Stamford on A6121
⋔ D & R Fitton
■ www.thetofthotelgolfclub.com

Waltham Windmill   (1997)
Proprietary
Cheapside, Waltham, Grimsby,
DN37 0HT
☎ (01472) 824109
🖥 (01472) 828391
📖 600
🖉 GW Fielding (01472) 824109
⫽ N Burkitt (01472) 823963
⊳ 18 L 6400 yds Par 71 SSS 71
⋔ WD–U SOC
£€ £20 (£27)
⊶ 2 miles S of Grimsby, off A16
⋔ Fox/Payne

Welton Manor   (1995)
Proprietary
Hackthorn Road, Welton, LN2 3PD
☎ (01673) 862827
🖥 (01673) 860917
✉ golf@weltonmanorgolfcentre.co.uk
📖 650
🖉 J Barlow
⫽ G Leslie (01673) 862827
⊳ 18 L 5703 yds SSS 67
⋔ U SOC
£€ £12 (£15)
⊶ Off A46 Lincoln to Grimsby road
⊕ Driving range
■ www.weltonmanorgolfcentre.co.uk

Woodhall Spa   (1891)
Woodhall Spa, LN10 6PU
☎ (01526) 351835,
(01526) 352511 (Bookings)
🖥 (01526) 352778

📖 525
🖉 M Underwood
⫽ S Williams (01526) 351831
⊳ Hotchkin 18 L 7047 yds SSS 75;
Bracken 18 L 6735 yds SSS 74
⋔ Booking essential SOC
£€ Hotchkin–£60 D–£100
Bracken–£40 D–£65
⊶ 19 miles SE of Lincoln (B1191)
⊕ Driving range. Teaching Academy
⋔ Hotchkin/Steel

Woodthorpe Hall   (1986)
Woodthorpe, Alford, LN13 0DD
☎ (01507) 450000
🖥 (01507) 450000
✉ secretary@woodthorpehallgolfclub
.fsnet.co.uk
📖 200
🖉 Joan Smith (01507) 450000
⊳ 18 L 5140 yds Par 67 SSS 65
⋔ U SOC
£€ £10 D–£15
⊶ 3 miles N of Alford, off B1373. 8
miles SE of Louth
■ www.woodthorpehall.co.uk

London Clubs

Aquarius *Kent*
Beckenham Place Park *Kent*
Central London Golf Centre *Surrey*
Dulwich & Sydenham Hill *Surrey*
Eltham Warren *Kent*
Finchley *Middlesex*
Hampstead *Middlesex*
Hendon *Middlesex*
Highgate *Middlesex*
Lee Valley *Middlesex*
London Scottish *Surrey*
Mill Hill *Middlesex*
Muswell Hill *Middlesex*
North Middlesex *Middlesex*
Richmond Park *Surrey*
Roehampton *Surrey*
Royal Blackheath *Kent*
Royal Epping Forest *Essex*
Royal Wimbledon *Surrey*
Shooter's Hill *Kent*
South Herts *Hertfordshire*
Trent Park *Middlesex*
Wanstead *Essex*
West Essex *Essex*
Wimbledon Common *Surrey*
Wimbledon Park *Surrey*

Manchester

Blackley   (1907)
Victoria Avenue East, Manchester,
M9 7HW
☎ (0161) 643 2980
✉ office@blackleygolfclub.com
📖 800
🖉 S Mainwaring (0161) 654 7770
⫽ C Gould (0161) 643 3912

🏴 18 L 6235 yds SSS 70
👤 WD–U WE–M SOC–WD exc
Thurs/Fri
💷 £24
🚗 North Manchester
🏠 Gaunt and Marnoch

Boysnope Park (1998)
Proprietary
Liverpool Road, Barton Moss, Eccles,
M30 7RF
☎ **(0161) 707 6125**
🖥 (0161) 707 3622
📠 Jean Stringer (0161) 707 6125
✓ S Currie (0161) 787 8687
🏴 18 L 3506 yds Par 72 SSS 71
👤 U SOC
💷 £12 (£14)
🚗 SW of Manchester on A57. M60
Junction 11, 1 mile
⊕ Driving range
◼ www.boysnopegolfclub.co.uk

Chorlton-cum-Hardy
(1902)
Barlow Hall, Barlow Hall Road,
Manchester, M21 7JJ
☎ **(0161) 881 3139**
🖥 (0161) 881 4532
📧 chorltongolf@hotmail.com
📖 600
📠 IR Booth (0161) 881 5830
✓ DR Valentine (0161) 881 9911
🏴 18 L 5980 yds SSS 69
👤 U H SOC–Thurs & Fri
💷 £25 (£30)
🚗 4 miles S of Manchester
(A5103/A5145)
◼ www.chorltoncumhardygolfclub
.sagenet.co.uk

Davyhulme Park (1911)
Gleneagles Road, Davyhulme,
Manchester, M41 8SA
☎ **(0161) 748 2260**
🖥 (0161) 747 4067
📖 700
📠 GR Swarbrick
✓ D Butler (0161) 748 3931
🏴 18 L 6237 yds SSS 70
👤 WD–H exc Wed & Fri–NA
Sat–NA Sun–M
SOC–Mon/Tues/Thurs
💷 £24. 27 holes–£30
🚗 7 miles SW of Manchester

Denton (1909)
Manchester Road, Denton, Manchester,
M34 2GG
☎ **(0161) 336 3218**
🖥 (0161) 336 4751
📖 686
📠 EW Tewson
✓ M Hollingworth (0161) 336 2070
🏴 18 L 6496 yds SSS 71
👤 WD–U WE/BH–NA before 3pm
SOC
💷 £25 (£30)
🚗 M60 J24, A57 to Manchester

Didsbury (1891)
Ford Lane, Northenden, Manchester,
M22 4NQ
☎ **(0161) 998 9278**
🖥 (0161) 902 3060
📧 golf@didsburygolfclub.com
📖 760
📠 AL Watson (Mgr)
✓ P Barber (0161) 998 2811
🏴 18 L 6210 yds SSS 70
👤 WD–U H exc 9–10am &
12–1.30pm–NA WE–U H
10.30–11.30am & after 4pm
💷 £28 (£32)
🚗 6 miles S of Manchester. M60
Junction 5
◼ www.didsburygolfclub.com

Ellesmere (1913)
Old Clough Lane, Worsley, Manchester,
M28 7HZ
☎ **(0161) 790 2122**
📧 honsec@ellesmeregolf.fsnet.co.uk
📖 380 80(L) 75(J)
📠 A Chapman (0161) 799 0554
✓ T Morley (0161) 790 8591
🏴 18 L 6238 yds SSS 70
👤 U exc comp days (check with Pro)
SOC–WD
💷 £22 (£28)
🚗 6 miles W of Manchester, nr
junction of M60/A580

Fairfield Golf & Sailing
Club (1892)
Booth Road, Audenshaw, Manchester,
M34 5GA
☎ **(0161) 301 4528**
📧 secretary@fairfieldgolf.co.uk
📖 550
📠 H Jagger (Sec/Mgr) (0161) 370
2808
✓ SA Pownell (0161) 370 2292
🏴 18 L 5664 yds SSS 68
👤 WD–U WE–NA before noon
SOC–WD
💷 £20 (£25)
🚗 5 miles E of Manchester on A635

Flixton (1893)
Church Road, Flixton, Urmston,
Manchester M41 6EP
☎ **(0161) 748 2116**
🖥 (0161) 748 2116
📖 400
📠 P Gollaglee (0161) 748 2116
✓ GP Coope (0161) 746 7160
🏴 9 L 6410 yds SSS 71
👤 WD–U exc Wed SOC
💷 £16
🚗 6 miles SW of Manchester on
B5213. M60 Junction 10

Great Lever & Farnworth
(1901)
Plodder Lane, Farnworth, Bolton,
BL4 0LQ
☎ **(01204) 656493**
🖥 (01204) 656137
📖 600

📠 MJ Ivill (01204) 656137
✓ T Howarth (01204) 656650
🏴 18 L 6064 yds SSS 69
👤 H SOC–WD
💷 £20 (£27)
🚗 2 miles S of Bolton. M61 Junction
4

Heaton Park Golf Centre
(1912)
Public
Heaton Park, Middleton Road,
Prestwich, M25 2SW
☎ **(0161) 654 9899**
📠 JK Mort (Mgr)
🏴 18 L 5755 yds SSS 68
18 hole Par 3 course
👤 U SOC
💷 £10 (£12.50)
🚗 North Manchester, via M60
Junction 19 to Middleton Road
⊕ Bar, restaurant, club & trolley hire
🏠 JH Taylor

Manchester (1882)
Hopwood Cottage, Rochdale Road,
Middleton, Manchester M24 6QP
☎ **(0161) 643 2718,**
(0161) 643 0023 (Bookings)
🖥 (0161) 643 9174
📖 700
📠 KG Flett (0161) 643 3202
✓ B Connor (0161) 643 2638
🏴 18 L 6450 yds SSS 72
👤 WD–H WE–NA SOC
💷 D–£25 (£40)
🚗 7 miles N of Manchester. M62
Junction 20
⊕ Driving range-members and green
fees only
🏠 HS Colt
◼ www.mangc.co.uk

New North Manchester
(1894)
Rhodes House, Manchester Old Road,
Middleton, M24 4PE
☎ **(0161) 643 9033**
🖥 (0161) 643 7775
📧 secretary@nmgc.co.uk
📖 650
📠 D Parkinson
✓ J Peel (0161) 643 7094
🏴 18 L 6598 yds SSS 72
👤 H WD
💷 £28
🚗 5 miles N of Manchester. M60
Junction 19
🏠 A Compston
◼ www.nmgc.co.uk

Northenden (1913)
Palatine Road, Manchester, M22 4FR
☎ **(0161) 998 47079**
🖥 (0161) 945 5592
📧 northenden.golfclub@btopenworld
.com
📖 700
📠 Francesca Woodworth
(Sec/Mgr) (0161) 998 4738
✓ J Curtis (0161) 945 3386

For list of abbreviations and key to symbols see page 627

▷ 18 L 6503 yds SSS 71
ⓜ U SOC
££ £28 (£32)
⊶ 5 miles S of Manchester. M60 Junction 5

Old Manchester (1818)

Club
c/o 9 Ashbourne Grove, Whitefield, M45 7NJ
☎ (0161) 766 4157
✍ PT Goodall
▷ Club without a course

Pike Fold (1909)

Hills Lane, Pole Lane, Unsworth, Bury BL9 8QP
☎ (0161) 766 3561
🖳 (0161) 796 3569
▥ 250
✍ J O'Donnell
✓ A Cory
▷ 9 L 6312 yds Par 72 SSS 71
ⓜ WD–U WE/BH–M
££ On application
⊶ 8 miles N of Manchester, by M66

Prestwich (1908)

Hilton Lane, Prestwich, M25 9XB
☎ (0161) 772 0700
🖳 (0161) 772 0700
📧 1908@prestwichgc.fsnet.co.uk
▥ 500
✍ R Mason
✓ S Wakefield (0161) 773 1404
▷ 18 L 5103 yds SSS 64
ⓜ WD–H WE–NA before 3pm SOC
££ £20 (£20)
⊶ 2½ miles N of Manchester, off A56. M60 Junction 17

Stand (1904)

The Dales, Ashbourne Grove, Whitefield, Manchester M45 7NL
☎ (0161) 766 2388
🖳 (0161) 796 3234
▥ 600
✍ TE Thacker (0161) 766 3197
✓ M Dance (0161) 766 2214
▷ 18 L 6411 yds SSS 71
ⓜ U SOC–WD
££ £30
⊶ 5 miles N of Manchester. M60 Junction 17
🏠 Alex Herd

Swinton Park (1926)

East Lancashire Road, Swinton, Manchester, M27 5LX
☎ (0161) 794 1785
🖳 (0161) 281 0698
▥ 450 120(L) 50(J)
✍ TH Glover (0161) 794 0861
✓ J Wilson (0161) 793 8077
▷ 18 L 6726 yds SSS 72
ⓜ WD–U WE–M SOC–not Thur/Sat/Sun/Bank Hols
££ On application
⊶ On A580, 5 miles NW of Manchester

Whitefield (1932)

Higher Lane, Whitefield, Manchester, M45 7EZ
☎ (0161) 351 2700
🖳 (0161) 351 2712
▥ 538
✍ Mrs A Schofield
✓ P Reeves (0161) 351 2709
▷ 18 L 6063 yds SSS 69
18 L 5793 yds SSS 68
ⓜ U SOC–WD
££ £30 (£45)
⊶ 4 miles N of Manchester. M60 Junction 17

William Wroe (1973)

Public
Pennybridge Lane, Flixton, Manchester, M31 3DL
☎ (0161) 748 8680
✓ B Parkinson
▷ 18 L 4395 yds SSS 61
ⓜ U–booking necessary
££ On application
⊶ 6 miles SW of Manchester, by M63 Junction 4

Withington (1892)

243 Palatine Road, West Didsbury, Manchester, M20 2UE
☎ (0161) 445 9544
🖳 (0161) 445 5210
📧 withingtongc@lineone/net
▥ 600
✍ B Grundy (0161) 445 9544
✓ RJ Ling (0161) 445 4861
▷ 18 L 6410 yds SSS 70
ⓜ WD–H exc Thurs SOC
££ On application
⊶ 6 miles S of Manchester on B5166
■ www.withingtongolfclub.co.uk

Worsley (1894)

Stableford Avenue, Monton Green, Eccles, Manchester M30 8AP
☎ (0161) 789 4202
🖳 (0161) 789 3200
▥ 625
✍ R Hamlett (Hon)
✓ C Cousins
▷ 18 L 6217 yds SSS 70
ⓜ H SOC
££ £30 (£35)
⊶ 5 miles W of Manchester

Merseyside

Allerton Municipal (1934)

Public
Allerton Road, Liverpool, L18 3JT
☎ (0151) 428 1046
✓ B Large
▷ 18 L 5494 yds SSS 65
9 hole course
ⓜ U SOC
££ On application
⊶ 5 miles S of Liverpool

Arrowe Park (1931)

Public
Arrowe Park, Woodchurch, Birkenhead, CH49 5LW
☎ (0151) 677 1527
✍ C Jones
✓ C Disbury
▷ 18 L 6396 yds SSS 70
ⓜ U
££ £7.70 (£7.70)
⊶ 3 miles S of Birkenhead on A552. M53 Junction 3, 1 mile

Bidston (1913)

Bidston Link Road, Wallasey, Wirral, CH44 2HR
☎ (0151) 638 3412
▥ 550
✍ JR Whitton (Hon)
✓ Mark Eagles (0151) 638 3412
▷ 18 L 6207 yds SSS 70
ⓜ WD–U WE–U after 3pm SOC
££ £18 (£25)
⊶ Off Bidston Link Road. M53 Junction 1
■ www.bidstongolf.co.uk

Blundells Hill

Blundells Lane, Rainhill, L35 6NA
☎ (0151) 430 0100
🖳 (0151) 426 5256
▥ 600
✍ A Roberts
✓ R Burbidge
▷ 18 L 6347 yds Par 71
ⓜ U SOC
££ £25 (£30)
⊶ 2 miles SW of St Helens. M62 Junction 7
⊕ Driving range
🏠 Steve Marnoch
■ www.blundellshill.co.uk

Bootle (1934)

Dunnings Bridge Road, Litherland, L30 2PP
☎ (0151) 928 6196
▥ 400
✍ J Morgan
✓ A Bradshaw (0151) 928 1371
▷ 18 L 6362 yds SSS 70
ⓜ U–book by phone SOC
££ £7.70 (£9.80)
⊶ 5 miles N of Liverpool (A565)
🏠 Fred Stevens

Bowring (1913)

Public
Bowring Park, Roby Road, Huyton, L36 4HD
☎ (0151) 489 1901
✓ D Weston
▷ 9 L 5592 yds SSS 66
ⓜ U
££ On application
⊶ 6 miles N of Liverpool. M62 Junction 5

Brackenwood (1933)

Public
Bracken Lane, Bebington, Wirral, L63 2LY
- ☎ **(0151) 608 3093**
- ✓ K Lamb
- ⮞ 18 L 6232 yds SSS 70
- 👥 U SOC
- ££ On application
- ⛳ Nr M53 Junction 4

Bromborough (1903)

Raby Hall Road, Bromborough, CH63 0NW
- ☎ **(0151) 334 2155**
- 🖥 (0151) 334 7300
- 📖 800
- ♫ (0151) 334 2155
- ✓ G Berry (0151) 334 4499
- ⮞ 18 L 6547 yds SSS 72
- 👥 U–contact Pro in advance
- ££ £40 (£40)
- ⛳ Mid Wirral, M53 Junction 4
- ■ www.bromborough-golf-club.freeserve.co.uk

Caldy (1907)

Links Hey Road, Caldy, Wirral, CH48 1NB
- ☎ **(0151) 625 5660**
- 🖥 (0151) 625 7394
- ✉ gail@caldygolfclub.fsnet.co.uk
- 📖 900
- ♫ Gail Copple
- ✓ K Jones (0151) 625 1818
- ⮞ 18 L 6601 yds SSS 72
- 👥 WD–U exc before 9.30am and from 1–2pm (booking necessary) SOC
- ££ On application
- ⛳ 1¹/₂ miles S of West Kirby

Childwall (1913)

Naylors Road, Gateacre, Liverpool, L27 2YB
- ☎ **(0151) 487 0654**
- 🖥 (0151) 487 0882
- 📖 650
- ✓ N Parr (0151) 487 9871
- ⮞ 18 L 6470 yds SSS 71
- 👥 WD–Tues–restricted. WE/BH–restricted SOC
- ££ £35 (£45)
- ⛳ 7 miles E of Liverpool. M62 Junction 6, 2 miles
- ⛳ James Braid

Eastham Lodge (1973)

117 Ferry Road, Eastham, Wirral, CH62 0AP
- ☎ **(0151) 327 1483 (Clubhouse)**
- 🖥 (0151) 327 7574
- 📖 750
- ♫ CS Camden (0151) 327 3003
- ✓ N Sargent (0151) 327 3008
- ⮞ 18 L 5706 yds SSS 68
- 👥 WD–U WE/BH–M SOC
- ££ £23.50
- ⛳ 6 miles S of Birkenhead, off A41. M53 Junction 5. Signs to Eastham Country Park
- ⛳ Hawtree/Hemstock

Formby (1884)

Golf Road, Formby, Liverpool, L37 1LQ
- ☎ **(01704) 872164**
- 🖥 (01704) 833028
- ✉ info@formbygolfclub.co.uk
- 📖 690
- ♫ CCH Barker (01704) 872164
- ✓ GH Butler (01704) 873090
- ⮞ 18 L 7024 yds SSS 74
- 👥 WD–I H SOC
- ££ £80 (£90)
- ⛳ By Freshfield Station, Formby
- ⛳ Willie Park
- ■ www.formbygolfclub.co.uk

Formby Hall

Southport Old Road, Formby, L37 0AB
- ☎ **(01704) 875699**
- ✓ D Lloyd
- ⮞ 18 L 6875 yds Par 73
- 👥 WD–U SOC
- ££ On application
- ⛳ Off Formby by-pass
- ⊕ Floodlit driving range

Formby Ladies' (1896)

Golf Road, Formby, Liverpool, L37 1YH
- ☎ **(01704) 873493**
- 🖥 (01704) 873493
- ✉ secretary@formbyladiesgolfclub.co.uk
- ♫ Mrs J Houghton (01704) 873493
- ✓ G Butler (01704) 873090
- ⮞ 18 L 5374 yds SSS 71
- 👥 U–phone first SOC
- ££ £40 (£45)
- ⛳ Formby, off A565
- ■ www.formbyladiesgolfclub.co.uk

Grange Park (1891)

Prescot Road, St Helens, WA10 3AD
- ☎ **(01744) 22980 (Members)**
- 🖥 (01744) 26318
- 📖 730
- ♫ I Fisher (01744) 26318
- ✓ P Roberts (01744) 28785
- ⮞ 18 L 6446 yds SSS 71
- 👥 I SOC–WD exc Tues
- ££ £26 (£33)
- ⛳ 1¹/₂ miles W of St Helens on A58
- ■ www.ukgolfer.org

Haydock Park (1877)

Golborne Park, Newton Lane, Newton-le-Willows, WA12 0HX
- ☎ **(01925) 224389**
- 🖥 (01925) 224984
- ✉ secretary@haydockparkgc@onetel.net.uk
- 📖 400 120(L)
- ♫ Mrs V Wiseman (01925) 228525
- ✓ PE Kenwright (01925) 226944
- ⮞ 18 L 6058 yds SSS 69
- 👥 H or I SOC–WD exc Tues
- ££ £30
- ⛳ 1 mile E of M6 Junction 23

Hesketh (1885)

Cockle Dick's Lane, Cambridge Road, Southport, PR9 9QQ
- ☎ **(01704) 530226**

- 🖥 (01704) 539250
- ✉ hesketh@ukgolfer.org /clubs/hesketh
- 📖 650
- ♫ MG Senior (01704) 536897
- ✓ J Donoghue (01704) 530050
- ⮞ 18 L 6655 yds SSS 72
- 👥 WD–U WE/BH–restricted SOC
- ££ £50 D–£60 (£60)
- ⛳ 1 mile N of Southport (A565)
- ⛳ JOF Morris
- ■ www.ukgolfer.org

Heswall (1902)

Cottage Lane, Gayton, Heswall, CH60 8PB
- ☎ **(0151) 342 1237**
- 🖥 (0151) 342 6140
- ✉ dawn@eswallgolfclub.com
- 📖 902
- ♫ A Brooker
- ✓ AE Thompson (0151) 342 7431
- ⮞ 18 L 6492 yds SSS 72
- 👥 U H BH–NA SOC–Wed & Fri
- ££ £35 (£40)
- ⛳ 8 miles NW of Chester off A540. M53 Junction 4
- ■ www.heswallgolfclub.com

Hillside (1911)

Hastings Road, Hillside, Southport, PR8 2LU
- ☎ **(01704) 569902**
- 🖥 (01704) 563192
- ✉ secretary@hillside-golfclub.co.uk
- 📖 800
- ♫ JG Graham (01704) 567169
- ✓ B Seddon (01704) 568360
- ⮞ 18 L 6850 yds SSS 74
- 👥 By arrangement with Sec
- ££ £60 D–£75
- ⛳ Southport
- ⛳ Hawtree

Houghwood (1996)

Billinge Hill, Crank Road, Crank, St Helens WA11 8RL
- ☎ **(01744) 894754**
- 🖥 (01744) 894754
- 📖 630
- ♫ B Haigh
- ✓ P Dickenson (01744) 894444
- ⮞ 18 L 6268 yds SSS 70
- 👥 WD–U SOC–WD
- ££ £19.50 (£27.50)
- ⛳ 3 miles N of St Helens, off A580 (B5201). M6 Junctions 23 or 26
- ⛳ N Pearson

Hoylake Municipal (1933)

Public
Carr Lane, Hoylake, Wirral, L47 4BG
- ☎ **(0151) 632 2956/4883 (Bookings)**
- ♫ ME Down (0151) 632 6823
- ✓ S Hooton
- ⮞ 18 L 6330 yds SSS 70
- 👥 WD–U WE–phone booking 1 week in advance SOC
- ££ £8
- ⛳ 4 miles W of Birkenhead
- ⛳ James Braid

For list of abbreviations and key to symbols see page 627

Huyton & Prescot   (1905)
Hurst Park, Huyton Lane, Huyton,
L36 1UA
- ☎ **(0151) 489 1138**
- 🖥 (0151) 489 0797
- 📖 700
- 🏌 D Hughes (0151) 489 3948
- 🏌 J Fisher (0151) 489 2022
- ⛳ 18 L 5839 yds SSS 68
- 👤 WD–U WE–H SOC–WD
- ££ On application
- 🚗 7 miles E of Liverpool. 1 mile S of Prescot on B5199. M57 Junction 2

Leasowe   (1891)
Leasowe Road, Moreton, Wirral,
CH46 3RD
- ☎ **(0151) 677 5852**
- 🖥 (0151) 641 8519
- 📖 610
- 🏌 L Jukes (0151) 677 5852
- 🏌 AJ Ayre (0151) 678 5460
- ⛳ 18 L 6263 yds SSS 70
- 👤 U SOC–H
- ££ D–£25.50 (D–£30.50)
- 🚗 1 mile N of Queensway Tunnel. M53 Junction 1
- 🏛 John Ball Jr

Lee Park   (1954)
Childwall Valley Road, Gateacre,
Liverpool, L27 3YA
- ☎ **(0151) 487 9861 (Clubhouse)**
- 📖 580
- 🏌 A Fagan (0151) 487 3882
- ⛳ 18 L 6108 yds Par 72 SSS 70
- 👤 U SOC
- ££ On application
- 🚗 7 miles SE of Liverpool (B5171)

Liverpool Municipal   (1967)
Public
Ingoe Lane, Kirkby, Liverpool, L32 4SS
- ☎ **(0151) 546 5435**
- 🏌 D Weston
- ⛳ 18 L 6571 yds SSS 71
- 👤 U WE–booking required SOC
- ££ On application
- 🚗 M57 Junction 6 to B5192

Prenton   (1905)
Golf Links Road, Prenton, Birkenhead,
CH42 8LW
- ☎ **(0151) 608 1461**
- 🖥 (0151) 608 4659
- 📖 470 100(L) 80(J)
- 🏌 N Brown (0151) 608 1053
- 🏌 R Thompson (0151) 608 1636
- ⛳ 18 L 6429 yds SSS 71
- 👤 U SOC–Mon/Wed/Fri
- ££ £35 (£40)
- 🚗 Outskirts of Birkenhead. M53 Junction 3
- 🌐 www.prentongolfclub.co.uk

RLGC Village Play   (1895)
Club
c/o 18 Waverley Road, Hoylake, Wirral,
CH47 3DD
- 📖 40

- 🏌 PD Williams (0151) 632 5156
- ⛳ Play over Royal Liverpool, Hoylake

Royal Birkdale   (1889)
Waterloo Road, Birkdale, Southport,
PR8 2LX
- ☎ **(01704) 567920**
- 🖥 (01704) 562327
- ✉ secretary@royalbirkdale.com
- 🏌 MC Gilyeat
- 🏌 B Hodgkinson (01704) 568857
- ⛳ 18 L 6703 yds SSS 73
- 👤 I H SOC
- ££ £122 D–£147 (£137)
- 🚗 1½ miles S of Southport (A565)
- 🏛 George Lowe
- 🌐 www.royalbirkdale.com

Royal Liverpool   (1869)
Meols Drive, Hoylake, CH47 4AL
- ☎ **(0151) 632 3101/3102**
- 🖥 (0151) 632 6737
- ✉ sec@royal-liverpool-golf.com
- 📖 810
- 🏌 Gp Capt CT Moore CBE
- 🏌 J Heggarty (0151) 632 5868
- ⛳ 18 L 7165 yds SSS 74
- 👤 H SOC
- ££ On application
- 🚗 On A553 from M53 Junction 2
- 🌐 www.royal-liverpool-golf.com

Sherdley Park Municipal
Public
Sherdley Park, St Helens
- ☎ **(01744) 813149**
- 🖥 (01744) 817967
- 🏌 B Collins (Mgr)
- ⛳ 18 L 5974 yds SSS 69
- 👤 U SOC
- ££ £7.20 (£8.50)
- 🚗 2 miles E of St Helens (A570). M62 Junction 7, 2 miles
- ⊕ Driving range

Southport & Ainsdale   (1906)
Bradshaws Lane, Ainsdale, Southport,
PR8 3LG
- ☎ **(01704) 578000**
- 🖥 (01704) 570896
- ✉ secretary@sandagolfclub.co.uk
- 📖 452 94(L) 51(J)
- 🏌 CA Birrell
- 🏌 J Payne (01704) 577316
- ⛳ 18 L 6687 yds Par 72 SSS 73
- 👤 WD–H WE–NA before noon
- ££ £60 D–£75 (£75)
- 🚗 3 miles S of Southport on A565
- 🏛 James Braid
- 🌐 www.sandagolfclub.co.uk

Southport Municipal   (1914)
Public
Park Road West, Southport, PR9 0JS
- ☎ **(01704) 535286**
- 🏌 W Fletcher
- ⛳ 18 L 6253 yds SSS 69
- 👤 U SOC

- ££ On application
- 🚗 N end of Southport promenade

Southport Old Links   (1926)
Moss Lane, Southport, PR9 7QS
- ☎ **(01704) 228207**
- 🖥 (01704) 505353
- ✉ secretary@solgc.freeserve.co.uk
- 📖 450
- 🏌 BE Kenyon
- 🏌 Gary Copeman (07802) 65309
- ⛳ 9 L 6349 yds Par 72 SSS 71
- 👤 U exc Wed & Sun/H/BH NA
- ££ £22 (£30)
- 🚗 Churchtown, 3 miles NE of Southport

Wallasey   (1891)
Bayswater Road, Wallasey, CH45 8LA
- ☎ **(0151) 691 1024**
- 🖥 (0151) 638 8988
- ✉ wallaseygc@aol.com
- 📖 459 70(L) 45(J)
- 🏌 JT Barraclough (0151) 691 1024
- 🏌 M Adams (0151) 638 3888
- ⛳ 18 L 6503 yds SSS 72
- 👤 H SOC
- ££ £50 (£65)
- 🚗 M53–signs to New Brighton
- 🏛 Tom Morris
- 🌐 www.wallaseygolfclub.com

Warren   (1911)
Public
Grove Road, Wallasey, Wirral,
CH45 0JA
- ☎ **(0151) 639 8323 (Clubhouse)**
- 🏌 KE McCormack (0151) 678 0330
- 🏌 M Eagles (0151) 639 5730
- ⛳ 9 L 5914 yds SSS 68
- 👤 U except Sun a.m.
- ££ On application
- 🚗 Wallasey
- 🌐 www.warrengc.freeserve.co.uk

West Derby   (1896)
Yew Tree Lane, Liverpool, L12 9HQ
- ☎ **(0151) 228 1540**
- 🖥 (0151) 259 0505
- 📖 550
- 🏌 AP Milne (0151) 254 1034
- 🏌 A Witherup (0151) 220 5478
- ⛳ 18 L 6277 yds SSS 70
- 👤 SOC–WD after 9.30am
- ££ £28.50 (£37)
- 🚗 2 miles E of Liverpool, off A580–West Derby Junction

West Lancashire   (1873)
Hall Road West, Blundellsands,
Liverpool, L23 8SZ
- ☎ **(0151) 924 1076**
- 🖥 (0151) 931 4448
- ✉ sec@westlancashiregolf.co.uk
- 📖 700
- 🏌 S King (0151) 924 1076
- 🏌 G Edge (0151) 924 5662
- ⛳ 18 L 6767 yds SSS 73
- 👤 H SOC–WD exc Tues

For list of abbreviations and key to symbols see page 627

££ £60 D–£75 (£85)
⊕ Between Liverpool and Southport, off A565
🏠 CK Cotton
🌐 www.westlancashiregolf.co.uk

Wirral Ladies (1894)

93 Bidston Road, Birkenhead, Wirral, CH43 6TS
☎ **(0151) 652 1255**
🖂 (0151) 653 4323
✉ wirralladies@tiscali.co.uk
🏛 450
🏌 Mrs SA Headford
✓ A Law (0151) 652 2468
🏳 18 L 4948 yds SSS 69 (Ladies)
  18 L 5185 yds SSS 65 (Men)
♟ U H SOC–WD
££ £25 (£25)
⊕ Birkenhead ¹/₂ mile. M53, 2 miles

Woolton (1900)

Doe Park, Speke Road, Woolton, Liverpool L25 7TZ
☎ **(0151) 486 1601**
🖂 (0151) 486 1664
✉ keith@wooltongolf.co.uk
🏛 750
🏌 K Hamilton (0151) 486 2298
✓ D Thompson (0151) 486 1298
🏳 18 L 5706 yds SSS 68
♟ U exc comp days
££ £24 (£35)
⊕ SE Liverpool. End of M62/M57

Middlesex

Airlinks (1984)

Public
Southall Lane, Hounslow, TW5 9PE
☎ **(020) 8561 1418**
🖂 (020) 8813 6284
🏌 S Brewster
✓ T Martin
🏳 18 L 6001 yds SSS 69
♟ U
££ £10 (£16)
⊕ Just off M4 Junction 3
⊕ Floodlit driving range
🏠 Alliss/Taylor

Ashford Manor (1898)

Fordbridge Road, Ashford, TW15 3RT
☎ **(01784) 424644**
🖂 (01784) 424649
✉ ashfordmanorgolfclub@fsnet.co.uk
🏛 700
🏌 I Buchan (Gen Mgr) (01784) 424644
✓ I Partington (01784) 255940
🏳 18 L 6352 yds SSS 71
♟ WD–U WE–H
££ £35 WD
⊕ A308 Ashford. M25 Junction 13
🏠 T Hogg

Brent Valley (1938)

Public
Church Road, Hanwell, London, W7 3BE
☎ **(020) 8567 4230 (Clubhouse),**
  (020) 8567 1287 (Bookings)
🏛 195
🏌 Ms M Griffin
✓ P Bryant (020) 8567 1287
🏳 18 L 5426 yds SSS 66
♟ U SOC
££ On application

Bush Hill Park (1895)

Bush Hill, Winchmore Hill, London, N21 2BU
☎ **(020) 8360 5738**
🖂 (020) 8360 5583
🏛 630
🏌 Miss R Meade
✓ A Andrews (020) 8360 4103
🏳 18 L 5825 yds SSS 68
♟ WD–H WE–NA SOC
££ £28.50
⊕ S of Enfield
🌐 www.bushhillparkgolfclub.co.uk

C & L Country Club (1991)

West End Road, Northolt UB5 6RD
☎ **(020) 8845 5662**
🏳 9 L 4440 yds SSS 62
♟ U SOC
££ £10
⊕ A40, opp Northolt Airport
🏠 Patrick Tallack

Crews Hill (1920)

Cattlegate Road, Crews Hill, Enfield, EN2 8AZ
☎ **(020) 8363 6674**
🖂 (020) 8363 2343
🏛 600
🏌 AD Stewart (020) 8363 6674
✓ N Wichelow (020) 8366 7422
🏳 18 L 6273 yds SSS 70
♟ WD–I H WE/BH–M SOC
££ On application
⊕ 2¹/₂ miles N of Enfield. M25 Junction 24
🏠 HS Colt

Ealing (1898)

Perivale Lane, Greenford, UB6 8SS
☎ **(020) 8997 0937**
🖂 (020) 8998 0756
🏛 600
🏌 June Mackison (Gen Mgr)
✓ D Barton (020) 8997 3959
🏳 18 L 6216 yds SSS 70
♟ WD–U H WE/BH–M
££ On application
⊕ Marble Arch 6 miles on A40–Perivale junction
🏠 HS Colt

Enfield (1893)

Old Park Road South, Enfield, EN2 7DA
☎ **(020) 8363 3970**
🖂 (020) 8342 0381
🏛 625
🏌 JA North

✓ L Fickling (020) 8366 4492
🏳 18 L 6154 yds SSS 70
♟ WD–H WE/BH–M SOC–WD
££ £25 D–£30
⊕ 1 mile NE of Enfield. M25 Junction 24-A1005
🏠 James Braid
🌐 www.enfieldgolfclub.co.uk

Finchley (1929)

Nether Court, Frith Lane, London, NW7 1PU
☎ **(020) 8346 2436**
🖂 (020) 8343 4205
✉ secretary@finchleygolfclub.co.uk
🏛 550
🏌 JM Seatter
✓ DM Brown (020) 8346 5086
🏳 18 L 6356 yds SSS 71
♟ WD–U WE–pm only SOC
££ On application
⊕ M1 Junction 2
🏠 James Braid
🌐 www.finchleygolfclub.co.uk

Fulwell (1904)

Wellington Road, Hampton Hill, TW12 1JY
☎ **(020) 8977 2733**
🖂 (020) 8977 7732
✉ secretary@fulwellgolfclub.co.uk
🏛 750
🏌 PF Butcher
✓ N Turner (020) 8977 3844
🏳 18 L 6544 yds SSS 71
♟ WD–I WE–M SOC
££ £30 (£35)
⊕ Opposite Fulwell Station

Grim's Dyke (1910)

Oxhey Lane, Hatch End, Pinner, HA5 4AL
☎ **(020) 8428 4539**
🖂 (020) 8421 5494
🏛 600
🏌 R Millard (020) 8428 4539
✓ L Curling (020) 8428 7484
🏳 18 L 5600 yds SSS 67
♟ WD–U H WE–M SOC exc BH–NA
££ £30 D–£35
⊕ 2 miles NW of Harrow (A4008). M1 Junctions 4/5
🏠 James Braid

Hampstead (1893)

Winnington Road, London, N2 0TU
☎ **(020) 8455 0203**
🖂 (020) 8731 6194
🏛 450
🏌 ACM Harris
✓ PJ Brown (020) 8455 7089
🏳 9 L 5812 yds SSS 68
♟ H–phone Pro first
££ £30 (£35)
⊕ 1 mile from Hampstead, nr Spaniards Inn
🏠 Tom Dunn

Harrow School (1978)

High Street, Harrow-on-the-Hill, HA1 3HW
🏛 440 100(L) 10(J)

🏌 CV Davies (020) 8872 8232
🏴 9 L 3690 yds SSS 57
👤 M H
🚗 Harrow School, NW London
🏠 Donald Steel

Haste Hill   (1933)

Public
The Drive, Northwood, HA6 1HN
☎ (01923) 825224
📠 (01923) 826485
📖 250
🏌 M Devereaux
🏴 C Smilie
🏴 18 L 5736 yds SSS 68
👤 U SOC
££ £13.50 (£19.50)
🚗 Northwood-Hillingdon

Heath Park   (1975)

Stockley Road, West Drayton
☎ (01895) 444232
📠 (01895) 444232
📧 heathparkgolf@yahoo.co.uk
📖 180
🏌 B Sharma (Prop)
🏴 9 L 3236 yds SSS 56
👤 WD–U Sun–NA before 11am SOC
££ £8 (£9)
🚗 Crowne Plaza Hotel, Heathrow
🏠 Neil Coles
■ www.hpgc.co.uk

Hendon   (1903)

*Ashley Walk, Devonshire Road, London,
NW7 1DG*
☎ (020) 8346 6023
📠 (020) 8343 1974
📖 560
🏌 DE Cooper
🏴 M Deal (020) 8346 8990
🏴 18 L 6289 yds Par 70 SSS 70
👤 WD–U WE/BH–bookings SOC
££ £30 D–£35 (£35)
🚗 M1 Junction 2, on to Holders Hill Road
🏠 HS Colt

Highgate   (1904)

*Denewood Road, Highgate, London,
N6 4AH*
☎ (020) 8340 1906 (Clubhouse)
📠 (020) 8348 9152
📧 secretary@highgategolfclub
   .freeserve.co.uk
📖 700
🏌 NA Challis (020) 8340 3745
🏴 R Turner (020) 8340 5467
🏴 18 L 5964 yds SSS 69
👤 WD–U exc Wed–NA before noon
   WE/BH–M SOC
££ £30
🚗 Off Sheldon Avenue/Hampstead Lane
🏠 Cuthbert Butchart
■ www.highgategolfclub.freeserve
   .co.uk

Hillingdon   (1892)

*18 Dorset Way, Hillingdon, Uxbridge,
UB10 0JR*
☎ (01895) 239810

🏠 (01895) 233956
📖 375
🏌 KJ Newton (01895) 233956
🏴 PCR Smith (01895) 460035
🏴 9 L 5459 yds SSS 67
👤 WD–U exc Thurs 12–4pm WE
   pm–M H SOC–WD
££ £15 D–£27
🚗 Off Uxbridge Road, opposite St John's Church

Horsenden Hill   (1935)

Public
Woodland Rise, Greenford, UB6 0RD
☎ (020) 8902 4555
📖 84
🏌 AK Witte
🏴 J Quarshie
🏴 9 L 3264 yds SSS 56
👤 U
££ 9 holes–£4.40 (£6.40)
🚗 Greenford, near Sudbury Town tube station

Hounslow Heath   (1979)

Public
Staines Road, Hounslow, TW4 5DS
☎ (020) 8570 5271
📖 130
🏌 R Mulford
🏴 18 L 5901 yds Par 69 SSS 68
👤 WD–U WE–booking essential
££ £9.25 (£13.40)
🚗 Opposite Green Lane, Staines Road (A315)
🏠 Fraser

Leaside GC   (1974)

Pay and play
*Lee Valley Leisure, Picketts Lock Lane,
Edmonton, London N9 0AS*
☎ (020) 8803 3611
🏴 RG Gerken
🏴 18 L 4974 yds SSS 64
👤 WD–U WE–booking advisable
££ £12 (£16)
🚗 1 mile N of north Circular Road, Edmonton on Meridian Way
⊕ Floodlit driving range

London Golf Centre   (1984)

Public
Ruislip Road, Northolt, UB5 6QZ
☎ (020) 8841 6162/845 2332
📠 (020) 8842 2097
🏌 JP Clifford (Gen Mgr)
🏴 G Newall (020) 8845 3180
🏴 9 L 5838 yds SSS 69
👤 U SOC
££ 9 holes–£5. 18 holes–£9
🚗 Off A40, nr Polish war memorial
⊕ Driving range

Mill Hill   (1925)

*100 Barnet Way, Mill Hill, London,
NW7 3AL*
☎ (020) 8959 2282
📠 (020) 8906 0731
📧 haslehurstd@aol.com
📖 570
🏌 RE Haslehurst (020) 8959 2339

🏴 D Beal (020) 8959 7261
🏴 18 L 6309 yds SSS 70
👤 WD–U H WE/BH–U H after
   11.30am SOC–WD
££ £25 (£30)
🚗 1/2 mile N of Apex Corner, nr A1/A41 junction
🏠 Abercromby/Colt

Muswell Hill   (1893)

*Rhodes Avenue, Wood Green, London,
N22 7UT*
☎ (020) 8888 2044
📠 (020) 8889 9380
📖 600
🏌 J Underhill (020) 8888 1764
🏴 D Wilton (020) 8888 8046
🏴 18 L 6474 yds SSS 71
👤 WD–U WE–book with Pro SOC
££ £30 D–£40 (£35)
🚗 1 mile from Bounds Green Station.
   Central London 7 miles
🏠 Braid/Wilson

North Middlesex   (1905)

*The Manor House, Friern Barnet Lane,
Whetstone, London N20 0NL*
☎ (020) 8445 1732
📠 (020) 8445 5023
📧 office@northmiddlesexgc.co.uk
📖 500
🏌 Ms A McDonald (Mgr) (020) 8445 1604
🏴 (020) 8445 3060
🏴 18 L 5594 yds SSS 67
👤 WE/BH–restricted SOC–WD
££ £25 (£30)
🚗 5 miles S of M25 Junction 23, between Barnet and Finchley
🏠 Willie Park Jr
■ www.northmiddlesexgc.co.uk

Northolt   (1991)

Pay and play
Huxley Close, Northolt, UB5 5UL
☎ (020) 8841 5550
📖 250
🏌 L Gribben
🏴 I Godleman
🏴 9 hole course Par 56 SSS 55
👤 U SOC
££ £5
🚗 Nr M40 Target roundabout
⊕ Driving range

Northwood   (1891)

*Rickmansworth Road, Northwood,
HA6 2QW*
☎ (01923) 825329
📠 (01923) 840150
📧 secretary@northwoodgolf.co.uk
📖 560
🏌 T Collingwood (01923) 821384
🏴 CJ Holdsworth (01923) 820112
🏴 18 L 6553 yds Par 71 SSS 71
👤 WD–H WE/BH–NA SOC
££ £36
🚗 3 miles SE of Rickmansworth (A404)
🏠 James Braid

Perivale Park   (1932)

Public
Stockdove Way, Argyle Road, Greenford,
UB6 8EN
☎ **(020) 8575 7116**
📖 140
🖉 P Smith
✒ P Bryant (020) 8575 7116
🏌 9 L 5296 yds SSS 67
👥 U
£€ 9 holes–£4.40 (£6.50) 18
    holes–£11.50
🚗 1 mile E of Greenford, off A40

Pinner Hill   (1927)

Southview Road, Pinner Hill, HA5 3YA
☎ **(020) 8866 0963**
🖥 (020) 8868 4817
📧 pinnerhillgc.@uk2.net
📖 770
🖉 IN Prentice (020) 8866 0963
✒ M Grieve (020) 8866 2109
🏌 18 L 6392 yds SSS 71
👥 WD–H exc Wed & Thurs–U
    Sun/BH–M SOC
£€ £33 (£33) exc Wed & Thurs–£16.
🚗 1 mile W from Pinner Green
🏠 JH Taylor
■ www.pinnerhillgc.co.uk

Ruislip   (1936)

Public
Ickenham Road, Ruislip, HA4 7DQ
☎ **(01895) 638835**
🖥 (01895) 622172
📖 201
🖉 PC Thornton (01895) 638835
✒ P Glozier
🏌 18 L 5571 yds Par 69 SSS 67
👥 U SOC
£€ £13.50 (£19.50)
🚗 W Ruislip BR/LTE Station
⊕ Driving range
🏠 A Herd

Stanmore   (1893)

29 Gordon Avenue, Stanmore, HA7 2RL
☎ **(020) 8954 2599**
🖥 (020) 8954 2599
📧 secretary@stanmoregolfclub.co.uk
📖 500
🖉 Maria Bateman (020) 8954 2599
✒ J Reynolds (020) 8954 2599
🏌 18 L 5885 yds SSS 68
👥 WD–H WE/BH–M SOC
£€ £15 – £22 (£30)
🚗 Between Stanmore and Belmont,
    off Old Church Lane
■ www.stanmoregolfclub.co.uk

Stockley Park   (1993)

Pay and play
The Clubhouse, Stockley Park, Uxbridge,
UB11 1AQ
☎ **(020) 8813 5700/561 6339**
    (Bookings)
🖥 (020) 8813 5655
🖉 C Kennedy
✒ A Knox
🏌 18 L 6548 yds SSS 71
👥 U SOC

£€ £25 (£35)
🚗 Heathrow Airport, 1 mile. M4
    Junction 4, 1 mile
🏠 Robert Trent Jones Sr

Strawberry Hill   (1900)

Wellesley Road, Strawberry Hill,
Twickenham, TW2 5SD
☎ **(020) 8894 0165**
🖥 (020) 8898 0786
📖 350
🖉 Paul Astbury (020) 8894 0165
✒ P Buchan (020) 8898 2082
🏌 9 L 2381 yds Par 64 SSS 62
👥 WD–U WE–M
£€ £20
🚗 Strawberry Hill Station
🏠 JH Taylor

Sudbury   (1920)

Bridgewater Road, Wembley,
HA0 1AL
☎ **(020) 8902 3713 (office),**
    (020) 8902 7910 (bookings)
🖥 (020) 8903 2966
📧 enquiries@sudburygolfclubltd
    .co.uk
📖 640
🖉 N Cropley (Gen Mgr)
✒ N Jordan (020) 8902 7910
🏌 18 L 6282 yds SSS 70
👥 WD–H WE–M SOC–Tues–Fri
£€ On application
🚗 Junction of A4005/A4090
■ www.sudburygolfclubltd.co.uk

Sunbury   (1993)

Proprietary
Charlton Lane, Shepperton, TW17 8QA
☎ **(01932) 770298**
🖥 (01932) 789300
📖 350
🖉 J Wright (Gen Mgr)
    (01932) 770298
✒ A Hardaway (01932) 772898
🏌 18 L 5103 yds Par 68 SSS 65
    9 L 2444 yds Par 33
👥 U–phone Pro SOC
£€ £15 (£22)
🚗 SE of Queen Mary Reservoir, nr
    Chalton. M3 Junction 1, 2 miles
⊕ Floodlit driving range

Trent Park   (1973)

Public
Bramley Road, Southgate, London,
N14 4UW
☎ **(020) 8367 4653**
🖥 (020) 8366 4581
✒ R Stocker
🏌 18 L 6008 yds SSS 69
👥 WD–U SOC WE–NA before 11am
£€ £13.50 (£17)
🚗 Nr Oakwood Tube station
⊕ Driving range

Twickenham   (1977)

Pay and play
Staines Road, Twickenham, TW2 5JD
☎ **(020) 8783 1698**
🖥 (020) 8941 9134

🖉 Suzy Watt (020) 8783 1698
🏌 9 L 6014 yds SSS 69
👥 U
£€ £6.50 (£7)
🚗 2 miles NW of Hampton Court, nr
    end of M3
⊕ Floodlit driving range

Uxbridge   (1947)

Public
The Drive, Harefield Place, Uxbridge,
UB10 8AQ
☎ **(01895) 231169**
🖥 (01895) 810262
🖉 T Atkins (01895) 272457
✒ (01895) 237287
🏌 18 L 5711 yds SSS 68
👥 U SOC
£€ £12.50 (£18.50)
🚗 2 miles N of Uxbridge. B467 off
    A40 towards Ruislip. M25 Junction
    16, 3 miles

West Middlesex   (1891)

Greenford Road, Southall, UB1 3EE
☎ **(020) 8574 3450**
🖥 (020) 8574 2383
📧 westmid.gc@virgin.net
📖 650
🖉 E Marper
✒ T Talbot (020) 8574 1800
🏌 18 L 6119 yds SSS 69
👥 WD–U WE–NA before 3pm (phone
    Pro) SOC–Tues/Thurs/Fri
£€ Mon–£13 Tues/Thurs/Fri–£24
    Wed–£15 WE–£30
🚗 Junction of Uxbridge Road and
    Greenford Road
🏠 James Braid
■ www.westmiddxgolfclub.co.uk

Whitewebbs   (1932)

Public
Beggars Hollow, Clay Hill, Enfield,
EN2 9JN
☎ **(020) 8363 2951**
📖 200
🖉 IF Forsyth
✒ P Garlick (020) 8363 4454
🏌 18 L 5863 yds SSS 68
👥 U
£€ £10 (£12)
🚗 1 mile N of Enfield

Wyke Green   (1928)

Syon Lane, Isleworth, Osterley,
TW7 5PT
☎ **(020) 8560 8777**
🖥 (020) 8569 8392
📧 office@wykegreengolfclub.co.uk
📖 700
🖉 D Pearson
✒ N Smith (020) 8847 0685
🏌 18 L 6182 yds SSS 70
👥 WD–U exc Fri–NA WE/BH–H
    after 4pm SOC
£€ £28 D–£40 After 5pm–£20
🚗 ¹/₂ mile from Gillette Corner (A4)
⊕ Practice range
🏠 Hawtree/Taylor

Norfolk

Barnham Broom Hotel

(1977)

Honingham Road, Barnham Broom,
Norwich, NR9 4DD

☎ (01603) 759393 (Hotel),
(01603) 759552 (Golf Shop)
🖵 (01603) 758224
📖 500
🖉 P Ballingall (Golf Dir)
(01603) 759393 Ext 278
🏌 A Rudge
🏴 Valley 18 L 6483 yds Par 72
SSS 71
Hill 18 L 6495 yds Par 71 SSS 71
🕴 U SOC
💷 £40 (£50)
🔗 10 miles SW of Norwich, off A47.
5 miles NW of Wymondham, off
A11
⊕ 3 Academy holes
🏠 Pennink/Steel
■ www.barnham-broom.co.uk

Bawburgh   (1978)

Glen Lodge, Marlingford Road,
Bawburgh, Norwich NR9 3LU

☎ (01603) 740404
🖵 (01603) 740403
🖂 info@bawburgh.com
📖 650
🖉 I Ladbrooke (Golf Dir), J Barnard
🏌 C Potter (01603) 742323
🏴 18 L 6209 yds SSS 70
🕴 U–phone first SOC
💷 £25 (£34)
🔗 2 miles W of Norwich, off A47
Norwich Southern Bypass
⊕ Floodlit driving range. Golf
Academy
🏠 Shaun Manser
■ www.bawburgh.com

Caldecott Hall

Caldecott Hall, Beccles Road, Fritton,
NR31 9EY

☎ (01493) 488488
🖵 (01493) 488561
📖 600
🖉 R Beales
🏌 S Shulver
🏴 18 L 6685 yds Par 73 SSS 73
9 hole Par 3 course
🕴 H SOC
💷 £20 (£26)
🔗 5 miles SW of Gt Yarmouth on
A413
⊕ Floodlit driving range. 9 holes pitch
& putt course
■ www.caldecotthall.co.uk

Costessey Park   (1983)

Costessey Park, Costessey, Norwich,
NR8 5AL

☎ (01603) 746333
🖵 (01603) 746185
📖 600
🖉 GC Stangoe
🏌 A Young (01603) 747085

🏴 18 L 5900 yds Par 71 SSS 69
🕴 U SOC–WD
💷 On application
🔗 3 miles W of Norwich, off A47 at
Round Well PH

Dereham   (1934)

Quebec Road, Dereham, NR19 2DS

☎ (01362) 695900
🖵 (01362) 695904
🖂 derehamgolfclub@dgolfclub
.freeserve.co.uk
📖 400
🖉 S Kaye
🏌 N Allsebrook (01362) 695631
🏴 9 L 6225 yds SSS 70
🕴 H
💷 £17.50 D–£22.50
🔗 Dereham ¹/₂ mile

Dunham   (1979)

Proprietary
Little Dunham, Swaffham, PE32 2DF

☎ (01328) 701906
🖂 info@dunhamgolfclub.com
📖 120
🖉 G & S Potter (Props)
(01328) 701906
🏌 G Potter (01328) 701906
🏴 9 L 2560 yds Par 66 SSS 64
🕴 Pay and Play
💷 From £10 (18 holes)
🔗 4 miles NE of Swaffham, off A47.
Signs from Necton
🏠 Cecil Denny
■ www.dunhamgolfclub.com

Eagles   (1990)

39 School Road, Tilney All Saints, Kings
Lynn, PE34 4RS

☎ (01553) 827147
🖵 (01553) 829777
📖 200
🖉 D Horn (Prop)
🏌 N Pickerell
🏴 9 L 2142 yds SSS 61
9 hole Par 3 course
🕴 U
💷 9 holes–£ 7.95 (£8.95)
🔗 5 miles W of Kings Lynn on A47
⊕ Driving range
🏠 David Horn
■ www.eagles-golf-tennis.co.uk

Eaton   (1910)

Newmarket Road, Norwich, NR4 6SF

☎ (01603) 451686
🖵 (01603) 451686
🖂 administrator@eatongc.co.uk
📖 640 135(L) 70(J)
🖉 Mrs LA Bovill
🏌 M Allen (01603) 452478
🏴 18 L 6114 yds SSS 70
🕴 H WE–NA before noon SOC–WD
💷 £30 (£40)
🔗 S Norwich, off A11
■ www.eatongc.co.uk

Fakenham   (1973)

The Race Course, Fakenham, NR21 7NY

☎ (01328) 862867

📖 510
🖉 G Cocker (01328) 855665
🏌 C Williams (01328) 863534
🏴 9 L 6174 yds SSS 69
🕴 WD–U WE–NA before 12 noon
SOC
💷 £14 (£18)
🔗 Fakenham racecourse

Feltwell   (1976)

Thor Ave, Wilton Road, Feltwell,
IP26 4AY

☎ (01842) 827644
🖵 (01842) 827644
🖂 secretary@feltwellgolfclub.force9
.co.uk
📖 400
🖉 Linda Ball (01842) 827644
🏌 C Puttock (01842) 829089
🏴 9 L 6488 yds Par 72 SSS 71
🕴 U SOC–WD
💷 £16 (£25)
🔗 1 mile S of Feltwell on B1112
⊕ Former Feltwell aerodrome
■ www.clubnoticeboard.co.uk

Gorleston   (1906)

Warren Road, Gorleston, Gt Yarmouth,
NR31 6JT

☎ (01493) 661911
🖵 (01493) 661911
🖂 manager@gorlestongolfclub.co.uk
📖 900
🖉 JE Woodhouse (01493) 661911
🏌 N Brown (01493) 662103
🏴 18 L 6391 yds SSS 71
🕴 U H SOC
💷 £25 (£30) W–£85
🔗 S of Gorleston, off A12
🏠 JH Taylor

Great Yarmouth & Caister

(1882)

Beach House, Caister-on-Sea, Gt
Yarmouth, NR30 5TD

☎ (01493) 728699
🖵 (01493) 728831
📖 700
🖉 HJ Harvey
🏌 M Clarke (01493) 720421
🏴 18 L 6330 yds SSS 70
🕴 WE–NA before noon SOC
💷 £30 (£35)
🔗 Caister-on-Sea
■ www.caistergolf.com

Hunstanton   (1891)

Golf Course Road, Old Hunstanton,
PE36 6JQ

☎ (01485) 532811
🖵 (01485) 532319
🖂 hunstanton.golf@eidosnet.co.uk
📖 660 125(L) 77(J)
🖉 DP Thomson
🏌 J Dodds (01485) 532751
🏴 18 L 6759 yds SSS 73
🕴 WD–H after 9.30am WE–H after
10.30am SOC
💷 D–£60 (£70)
🔗 1¹/₂ miles NE of Hunstanton

⊕ 2-ball play only
🏠 George Fernie

King's Lynn (1923)
Castle Rising, King's Lynn, PE31 6BD
☎ (01553) 631654
🖥 (01553) 631036
✉ klgc@eidosnet.co.uk
📖 910
🏌 MP Sackrée (01553) 633000
⛳ J Reynolds (01553) 631655
🏴 18 L 6609 yds SSS 73
👥 U H SOC
££ £40 (£50)
🎣 4 miles NE of King's Lynn, off A149
🏠 Alliss/Thomas
■ www.club-noticeboard.co.uk

Links Country Park Hotel & Golf Club (1903)
West Runton, Cromer, NR27 9QH
☎ (01263) 838383
🖥 (01263) 838264
✉ sales@links-hotel.co.uk
📖 300
🏌 CB Abbott
⛳ J Tuck (01263) 838215
🏴 9 L 4814 yds Par 66 SSS 64
👥 U
££ £30 (£35)
🎣 3 miles W of Cromer (A149)
🏠 JH Taylor
■ www.links-hotel.co.uk

Marriott Sprowston Manor Hotel (1980)
Wroxham Road, Sprowston, Norwich, NR7 8RP
☎ (01603) 254290
🖥 (01603) 788884
📖 680
🏌 J O'Malley (Golf Dir) (01603) 254294
⛳ G Ireson (01603) 254290
🏴 18 L 5982 yds SSS 70
👥 U SOC
££ £30 (£38)
🎣 4 miles NE of Norwich on A1151
⊕ Floodlit driving range
■ www.marriott.co.uk/nwigs

Mattishall (1990)
South Green, Mattishall, Dereham
☎ (01362) 850464
📖 180
🏌 B Hall
🏴 9 L 6170 yds Par 70 SSS 69
👥 WD–U WE–U before noon SOC
££ £8 (£12)
🎣 6 miles E of Dereham (B1063)
⊕ 9 hole pitch & putt
🏠 BC Todd

Middleton Hall (1989)
Proprietary
Middleton, King's Lynn, PE32 1RH
☎ (01553) 841800
🖥 (01553) 841800
✉ middleton-hall@btclick.com

📖 600
🏌 J Holland
⛳ S White (01553) 841801
🏴 18 L 5756 yds Par 71 SSS 68
👥 U SOC
££ £25 (£30)
🎣 2 miles SE of King's Lynn on A47
⊕ Driving range
🏠 D Scott
■ www.middletonhall.co.uk

Mundesley (1901)
Links Road, Mundesley, NR11 8ES
☎ (01263) 720095
🖥 (01263) 720279
📖 500
🏌 TE Duke (Gen Mgr) (01263) 720095
⛳ TG Symmons (01263) 720279
🏴 9 L 5377 yds SSS 66
👥 WD–U H exc Wed 10.30–3.30pm WE–NA before 3.30pm
££ £20 (£25)
🎣 5 miles SE of Cromer

The Norfolk G&CC (1993)
Hingham Road, Reymerston, Norwich, NR9 4QQ
☎ (01362) 850297
🖥 (01362) 850614
📖 530
🏌 M de Boltz
⛳ T Varney (01362) 850297
🏴 18 L 6609 yds SSS 72
👥 WD–U before 4pm –M after 4pm WE/BH–NA before noon SOC
££ £22 (£27)
🎣 14 miles W of Norwich, off B1135 Dereham to Wymondham road
⊕ Driving range. 9 hole pitch & putt course
■ www.thenorfolk.co.uk

RAF Marham (1974)
RAF Marham, Kings Lynn, PE33 9NP
📖 290
🏌 WR Benton (01760) 337261 (Ext 6507)
🏴 9 L 5244 yds SSS 66
👥 By prior arrangement–U exc Sun am
🎣 11 miles SE of King's Lynn, nr Narborough
⊕ Course situated on MOD land, and may be closed without prior notice

Richmond Park (1990)
Saham Road, Watton, IP25 6EA
☎ (01953) 881803
🖥 (01953) 881817
📖 600
🏌 A Hemsley
⛳ A Hemsley
🏴 18 L 6300 yds SSS 70
👥 WD–U WE–H before noon SOC
££ £22 (£30)
🎣 ½ mile NW of Watton
⊕ Driving range
🏠 Scott/Jessup

Royal Cromer (1888)
Overstrand Road, Cromer, NR27 0JH
☎ (01263) 512884
🖥 (01263) 512430
✉ general.manager@royal-cromer.co.uk
📖 700
🏌 Mrs DC Hopkins
⛳ L Patterson (01263) 512267
🏴 18 L 6508 yds SSS 72
👥 H SOC–WD
££ D–£37 (D–£50)
🎣 1 mile E of Cromer on B1159
🏠 Morris/Taylor/Braid/Pennink
■ www.royal-cromer.com

Royal Norwich (1893)
Drayton High Road, Hellesdon, Norwich, NR6 5AH
☎ (01603) 425712
🖥 (01603) 417945
✉ mail@royalnorwichgolf.co.uk
📖 700
🏌 J Meggy (Mgr) (01603) 429928
⛳ D Futter (01603) 408459
🏴 18 L 6506 yds Par 72 SSS 72
👥 WE/BH–restricted SOC
££ D–£38 (£46)
🎣 ½ mile W of Norwich ring road, on Fakenham road (A1067)
🏠 James Braid
■ www.royalnorwichgolf.co.uk

Royal West Norfolk (1892)
Brancaster, King's Lynn, PE31 8AX
☎ (01485) 210223
🖥 (01485) 210087
📖 800
🏌 Maj NA Carrington Smith (01485) 210087
⛳ S Rayner (01485) 210616
🏴 18 L 6427 yds SSS 71
👥 M No four balls allowed Mid July–mid Sept WE–NA before 10am SOC
££ £65 (£75)
🎣 7 miles E of Hunstanton on A419
🏠 Holcombe Ingleby

Ryston Park (1932)
Ely Road, Denver, Downham Market, PE38 0HH
☎ (01366) 382133
🖥 (01366) 383834
✉ rystonparkgc.fsnet.co.uk
📖 320
🏌 WJ Flogdell
⛳ None
🏴 9 L 6310 yds SSS 70
👥 WD–H WE/BH–M SOC
££ £20 D–£25
🎣 1 mile S of Downham Market on A10
🏠 James Braid
■ www.club-noticeboard.co.uk

Sheringham (1891)
Sheringham, NR26 8HG
☎ (01263) 822038 (Clubhouse)
🖥 (01263) 825189
✉ sgc.sec@care4free.net

☐ 700
✍ PJ Mounfield (01263) 823488
✓ MW Jubb (01263) 822980
🏴 18 L 6456 yds SSS 71
👥 WD & WE NA before 9–30am H
  SOC
£€ £45 (£60)
⊕ ¹/₂ mile W of Sheringham (A149)
🏠 Tom Dunn
■ www.sheringhamgolfclub.co.uk

Swaffham (1922)

Cley Road, Swaffham, PE37 8AE
☎ (01760) 721621
🖥 (01760) 721621
☐ 500
✍ MA Rust
✓ P Field (01760) 721611
🏴 18 L 6554 yds SSS 71
👥 WD–U WE–M exc Sun am–NA
£€ £35/day, £25/half day, £15 country
  cards, £6 juniors.
⊕ 1¹/₂ miles SW of Swaffham
■ www.swaffhamgc.supanet.com

Thetford (1912)

Brandon Road, Thetford, IP24 3NE
☎ (01842) 752258 (Clubhouse)
🖥 (01842) 766212
📧 sally@thetfordgolfclub.co.uk
☐ 700
✍ Mrs SA Redpath (01842) 752169
✓ G Kitley (01842) 752662
🏴 18 L 6879 yds SSS 73
👥 H SOC–Wed–Fri
£€ £38
⊕ 2 miles W of Thetford (B1107), off
  A11 By-pass
🏠 CH Mayo

De Vere Dunston Hall
(1994)

Pay and play
Ipswich Road, Dunston, Norwich,
NR14 8PQ
☎ (01508) 470178
🖥 (01508) 471499
☐ 400
✍ P Briggs
✓ P Briggs
🏴 18 L 6200 yds Par 71 SSS 70
👥 U
£€ £25 (£30)
⊕ 5 miles S of Norwich on A140
⊕ Floodlit driving range
🏠 John Glasgow

Wensum Valley (1990)

Beech Avenue, Taverham, Norwich,
NR8 6HP
☎ (01603) 261012
🖥 (01603) 261664
☐ 850
✍ Mrs B Hall
✓ P Whittle
🏴 18 L 6223 yds SSS 70
  18 L 6037 yds SSS 69
👥 U SOC
£€ £20
⊕ 4 miles NW of Norwich on A1067
⊕ Floodlit driving range

🏠 BC Todd
■ www.wensumvalleyhotel.co.uk

Weston Park (1993)

Weston Longville, Norwich, NR9 5JW
☎ (01603) 872363
🖥 (01603) 873040
📧 golf@weston-park.co.uk
☐ 450
✍ RR Wright
✓ MR Few (01603) 872998
🏴 18 L 6603 yds SSS 72
👥 WD–U H
£€ £30 (£38)
⊕ 7 miles NW of Norwich, off A1067
🏠 John Glasgow
■ www.weston-park.co.uk

Northamptonshire

Brampton Heath

Sandy Lane, Church Brampton,
NN6 8AX
☎ (01604) 843939
🖥 (01604) 843885
📧 slawrence@bhgc.co.uk
☐ 500
✍ (01604) 843939
✓ R Hudson (01604) 843939
🏴 18 L 6450 yds Par 72 SSS 71
  9 hole short course
👥 U SOC
£€ £17 (£21)
⊕ 4 miles N of Northampton between
  A508 and A428
⊕ Driving range
■ www.bhgc.co.uk

Cold Ashby (1974)

Stanford Road, Cold Ashby,
Northampton, NN6 6EP
☎ (01604) 740548
🖥 (01604) 740548
📧 coldashby.golfclub@virgin.net
☐ 600 40(L) 40(J)
✍ DA Croxton (Prop) (01604) 740548
✓ S Rose (01604) 740099
🏴 27 L 6308 yds Par 72 SSS 71
👥 WD–U WE–U after 12 noon (if
  booked) SOC
£€ £16 (£18.50)
⊕ 11 miles N of Northampton, nr
  A5199/A14 Junction 1. 7 miles E of
  M1 Junction 18
⊕ Driving range
🏠 David Croxton
■ www.coldashbygolfclub.com

Collingtree Park (1990)

Windingbrook Lane, Northampton,
NN4 0XN
☎ (01604) 700000
🖥 (01604) 702600
☐ 900
✍ J Hammond (Gen Mgr)
✓ G Pook
🏴 18 L 6776 yds SSS 72
👥 H SOC
£€ £25 (£30)

⊕ ¹/₂ mile E of M1 Junction 15
⊕ Floodlit driving range
🏠 Johnny Miller
■ www.collingtreeparkgolf.com

Daventry & District (1911)

Norton Road, Daventry, NN11 5LS
☎ (01327) 702829
☐ 350
✍ E Smith
✓ None
🏴 9 L 5812 yds Par 69 SSS 68
👥 WD–U Sun–NA before 11am
  SOC–phone Sec
£€ £10 (£15)
⊕ ¹/₂ mile E of Daventry

Delapre (1976)

Public
Eagle Drive, Nene Valley Way,
Northampton, NN4 7DU
☎ (01604) 764036/763957
🖥 (01604) 706378
📧 delapre@btinternet.com
☐ 350
✍ R Wilson (Mgr) (01604) 764036
✓ J Corby, J Cuddihy (01604) 764036
🏴 Oaks 18 L 6293 yds SSS 70
  Hardingstone 9 L 2146 yds SSS 32
  2 x 9 holes Par 3 courses
👥 U SOC
£€ £12 (£17.50)
⊕ 3 miles from M1 Junction 15, on
  A508/A45
⊕ Pitch & putt. Driving range
🏠 Jacobs/Corby
■ www.jackbarker.com

Embankment (1975)

The Embankment, Wellingborough,
NN8 1LD
☎ (01933) 228465
☐ 175
✍ JB Andrew, E Walden (Mgr)
🏴 9 L 3400 yds SSS 56
👥 WD–M
£€ £4
⊕ 1 mile SE of Wellingborough
🏠 TH Neal

Farthingstone Hotel (1974)

Farthingstone, Towcester, NN12 8HA
☎ (01327) 361291
🖥 (01327) 361645
📧 interest@farthingstone.co.uk
☐ 400
✍ DC Donaldson (Prop/Mgr)
✓ L Brockway (01327) 361533
🏴 18 L 6003 yds SSS 70
👥 U SOC
£€ £17 D–£25 (£25 D–£35) SOC–£20
⊕ 4 miles W of A5 on Farthingstone-
  Everdon road. M1 Junction 16, 6
  miles
■ www.farthingstone.co.uk

Hellidon Lakes Hotel
G&CC (1991)

Hellidon, Daventry, NN11 6GG
☎ (01327) 262550

☎ (01327) 262559
⌂ 500
♠ MA Thomas
✐ G Wills (01327) 262551
↱ 18 L 6700 yds SSS 72
 9 L 5582 yds SSS 67
♙ U H SOC
£€ £20 (£30)
♣ 7 miles SW of Daventry, via A361.
 M40 Junction 11 and M1 Junction
 16
♙ David Snell
■ www.hellidon.co.uk

Kettering (1891)

Headlands, Kettering, NN15 6XA
☎ **(01536) 511104**
⌂ (01536) 511104
✉ secretary@kettering-golf.co.uk
⌂ 700 100(L) 50(J)
♠ NA Sandell (01536) 511104
✐ K Theobald (01536) 481014
↱ 18 L 6057 yds SSS 69
♙ WD–U WE/BH–M SOC
£€ D–£35
♣ S boundary of Kettering
♙ Tom Morris
■ www.kettering-golf.co.uk

Kingfisher Hotel

Proprietary
Buckingham Road, Deanshanger, Milton Keynes, MK19 6JY
☎ **(01908) 560354/562332**
⌂ (01908) 260857
⌂ 98
♠ Roland Carlish
✐ B Mudge
↱ 9 L 5690 yds Par 70 SSS 67
♙ U exc Sun–restricted SOC
£€ 9 holes–£8 (£12). 18 holes–£11
 (£15)
♣ NW of Milton Keynes on A422 to
 Buckingham. M1 Junction 15
⊕ Driving range
♙ Donald Steel
■ www.kingfisher-hotelandgolf.co.uk

Kingsthorpe (1908)

Kingsley Road, Northampton, NN2 7BU
☎ **(01604) 711173**
⌂ (01604) 710610
✉ secretary@kingsthorpe-golf.co.uk
⌂ 650
♠ JE Harris (01604) 710610
✐ P Armstrong (01604) 719602
↱ 18 L 5918 yds SSS 69
♙ WD–U WE/BH–M H SOC–WD
£€ D–£25
♣ 2 miles N of Northampton centre,
 off A508
♙ Alison /Colt
■ www.kingsthorpe-golf.co.uk

Northampton (1893)

Harlestone, Northampton, NN7 4EF
☎ **(01604) 845102 (Clubhouse)**
⌂ (01604) 820262
✉ golf@northamptongolfclub.co.uk
⌂ 700
♠ S Malherbe (01604) 845155
✐ B Randall (01604) 845167

↱ 18 L 6615 yds Par 72 SSS 72
♙ H WD–U (except Weds) WE–M
 SOC–WD (except Weds)
£€ £40
♣ 4 miles NW of Northampton, on
 A428 beyond Harlestone
♙ Donald Steel
■ www.northamptongolfclub.co.uk

Northamptonshire County (1909)

Church Brampton, Northampton, NN6 8AZ
☎ **(01604) 843025**
⌂ (01604) 843463
⌂ 650
♠ Peter Walsh (01604) 843025
✐ T Rouse (01604) 842226
↱ 18 L 6505 yds SSS 72
♙ H SOC
£€ Summer–£45 (£45) Winter–£30
 (£30)
♣ 5 miles NW of Northampton,
 between A428 and A50
♙ HS Colt

Oundle (1893)

Benefield Road, Oundle, PE8 4EZ
☎ **(01832) 273267**
⌂ (01832) 273267
✉ oundlegc@btopenworld.com
⌂ 630
♠ D Foley (01832) 273267
✐ R Keys (01832) 272273
↱ 18 L 6265 yds Par 72 SSS 70
♙ WD–U H WE–M before 10.30am
 –U H after 10.30am SOC
£€ £23 D–£30 (£40)
♣ 1½ miles W of Oundle on A427
■ www.oundlegolfclub.com

Overstone Park (1994)

Watermark Leisure, Billing Lane, Northampton, NN6 0AP
☎ **(01604) 647666**
⌂ (01604) 642635
✉ enquiries@overstonepark.co.uk
⌂ 450
♠ D Jones
✐ B Mudge (01604) 643555
↱ 18 L 6602 yds SSS 72
♙ WD–U SOC
£€ £26 (£30)
♣ 4 miles E of Northampton, off A45.
 M1 Junction 15
⊕ Driving range
♙ Donald Steel
■ www.overstonepark.co.uk

Priors Hall (1965)

Public
Stamford Road, Weldon, Corby, NN17 3JH
☎ **(01536) 260756**
⌂ (01536) 260756
⌂ 400
♠ T Arnold
✐ G Bradbrook
↱ 18 L 6631 yds SSS 72
♙ U SOC–WD
£€ On application

♣ 4 miles E of Corby (A43)
♙ Hawtree

Rushden (1919)

Kimbolton Road, Chelveston, Wellingborough, NN9 6AN
☎ **(01933) 418511**
⌂ 400
♠ DL Waite
↱ 10 L 6335 yds Par 71 SSS 70
♙ WD–U exc Wed pm WE/BH–M
 SOC
£€ £18
♣ On B645, 2 miles E of Higham
 Ferrers

Staverton Park (1977)

Staverton Park, Staverton, Daventry, NN11 6JT
☎ **(01327) 302000/302118**
⌂ (01327) 311428
♠ I Conder (Gen Mgr), Mrs A
 Radford (Sec)
✐ R Mudge (01327) 705506
↱ 18 L 6602 yds SSS 72
♙ U SOC
£€ On application
♣ 1 mile SW of Daventry, off A425.
 M1 Junctions 16/18. M40 Junction
 11
⊕ Driving range

Stoke Albany (1995)

Ashley Road, Stoke Albany, Market Harborough, LE16 8PL
☎ **(01858) 535208**
⌂ (01858) 535505
⌂ 450
♠ R Want
✐ A Clifford
↱ 18 L 6132 yds Par 71 SSS 69
♙ U SOC
£€ £17 (£20)
♣ Between Market Harborough and
 Corby (A427)
♙ Hawtree

Wellingborough (1893)

Harrowden Hall, Great Harrowden, Wellingborough, NN9 5AD
☎ **(01933) 677234/673022**
⌂ (01933) 679379
✉ info@wellingboroughgolfclub.org
⌂ 850
♠ R Tomlin (01933) 677234
✐ D Clifford (01933) 678752
↱ 18 L 6651 yds SSS 72
♙ WD–U H exc Tues WE–M
 SOC–WD exc Tues
£€ D–£40
♣ 2 miles N of Wellingborough on
 A509
♙ Hawtree

Whittlebury Park G&CC (1992)

Whittlebury, Towcester, NN12 8WP
☎ **(01327) 858092**
⌂ (01327) 858009
✉ enquiries@whittlebury.com

⌂ 500
✓ S Hallock (01327 858588)
↦ 36 holes:
5000-7000 yds SSS 68-72
⚇ U SOC
£€ £10 D–£30 (£20 D–£35)
🚗 4 miles S of Towcester on A413.
M1 J15a. M40 J10
⊕ Driving range
⌂ Cameron Sinclair
▪ www.whittlebury.com

Northumberland

Allendale (1906)
High Studdon, Allenheads Road, Allendale, Hexham NE47 9DH
☎ **(01434) 683926**
⌨ (01434) 683926
⌂ 145 26(L) 35(J)
✍ TS Norton (Hon)
↦ 9 L 4501 yds Par 66 SSS 64
⚇ U
£€ D–£12
🚗 1¹/₂ miles S of Allendale on B6295
▪ www.allendale-golf.org

Alnmouth (1869)
Foxton Hall, Alnmouth, NE66 3BE
☎ **(01665) 830231**
⌨ (01665) 830922
✉ secretary@alnmouthgolfclub.com
⌂ 750
✍ P Simpson
✓ Shop (01665) 830043
↦ 18 L 6484 yds SSS 71
⚇ Mon/Tues/Thurs–H (restricted) SOC
£€ £27 D–£32
🚗 5 miles SE of Alnwick
⊕ Dormy House
⌂ HS Colt

Alnmouth Village (1869)
Marine Road, Alnmouth, NE66 2RZ
☎ **(01665) 830370**
✉ golf@alnmouth-village.fsnet.co.uk
⌂ 340
✍ JE Clark (01665) 603797
↦ 9 L 6020 yds SSS 70
⚇ H
£€ £15 (£20)
🚗 Alnmouth

Alnwick (1907)
Swansfield Park, Alnwick, NE66 1AB
☎ **(01665) 602632**
✉ mail@alnwickgolfclub.co.uk
⌂ 450
✍ LE Stewart (01665) 602499
↦ 18 L 6250 yds SSS 70
⚇ U
£€ D–£20 (D–£25)
🚗 Alnwick, off A1
⌂ Rochester/Rae
▪ www.alnwickgolfclub.co.uk

Arcot Hall (1909)
Dudley, Cramlington, NE23 7QP
☎ **(0191) 236 2794**
⌨ (0191) 217 0370
⌂ 700
✍ F Elliott (0191) 236 2794
✓ J Metcalfe (0191) 236 2794
↦ 18 L 6389 yds SSS 70
⚇ WD–H WE/BH–M SOC
£€ D–£26 (£30) After 3pm–£21
🚗 7 miles N of Newcastle, off A1
⌂ James Braid
▪ www.arcothallgolfclub.com

Bamburgh Castle (1904)
The Club House, 40 The Wynding, Bamburgh, NE69 7DE
☎ **(01668) 214378**
⌨ (01668) 214607
⌂ 730
✍ RA Patterson (01668) 214321
↦ 18 L 5621 yds Par 68 SSS 67
⚇ WD–U H WE/BH–M SOC
£€ D–£30 (£30 D–£35)
🚗 5 miles E of A1, via B1341 or B1342
⌂ George Rochester

Bedlingtonshire (1972)
Acorn Bank, Hartford Road, Bedlington, NE22 6AA
☎ **(01670) 822457**
⌨ (01670) 823048
✉ secretary@bedlingtongolfclub.com
⌂ 820
✍ FM Hanson (01670) 822457
✓ M Webb (01670) 822457
↦ 18 L 6224 metres SSS 73
⚇ U SOC
£€ £18 (£26)
🚗 12 miles N of Newcastle (A1068)
⌂ Frank Pennink
▪ www.bedlingtongolfclub.com

Belford (1993)
South Road, Belford, NE70 7HY
☎ **(01668) 213433**
⌨ (01668) 213919
✉ belfordgoldclub@tiscali.co.uk
⌂ 200
✍ AM Gilhome
✓ None
↦ 9 L 6304 yds SSS 70
⚇ U SOC
£€ On application
🚗 15 miles N of Alnwick, off A1
⊕ Driving range
⌂ Nigel Williams

Bellingham (1893)
Boggle Hole, Bellingham, NE48 2DT
☎ **(01434) 220530/220152**
⌨ (01434) 220160
✉ admin@bellinghamgolfclub.com
⌂ 420
✍ P Cordiner (01434) 220182
↦ 18 L 6093 yds Par 70 SSS 70
⚇ U SOC
£€ £20 (£25)
🚗 15 miles N of Hexham, off B6320
⊕ Driving range
⌂ I Wilson

Berwick-upon-Tweed (1890)
Goswick, Berwick-upon-Tweed, TD15 2RW
☎ **(01289) 387256**
⌨ (01289) 387334
✉ goswickgc@btconnect.com
⌂ 600
✍ D Wilkinson
✓ P Terras (01289) 387380
↦ 18 L 6686 yds SSS 72
⚇ WD–U 9.30–11.30am & after 2pm
WE–U 10–11.30am & after 2.30pm
SOC
£€ £27 (£32)
🚗 5 miles S of Berwick, off A1
⌂ James Braid
▪ www.goswicklinksgc.co.uk

Blyth (1905)
New Delaval, Blyth, NE24 4DB
☎ **(01670) 540110**
⌨ (01670) 540134
✉ clubmanager@blythgolf.co.uk
⌂ 800
✍ J Wright (01670) 540110
✓ A Brown (01670) 356514
↦ 18 L 6456 yds SSS 71
⚇ WD–U before 4pm WE/BH–U after 2pm SOC
£€ £21 D–£26 (£25)
🚗 10 miles NE of Newcastle. Close to Northumberland Spine Road A189
⌂ J Hamilton Stutt
▪ www.blythgolf.co.uk

Burgham Park (1994)
Felton, Morpeth, NE65 8QP
☎ **(01670) 787898**
⌨ (01670) 787164
⌂ 570
✍ J Carr
✓ A Hartley (01670) 787898
↦ 18 L 6751 yds SSS 72
⚇ U SOC
£€ £15 (£18)
🚗 5 miles N of Morpeth on A1
⊕ Pitch & putt course
⌂ Andrew Mair

Close House (1968)
Close House, Heddon-on-the-Wall, Newcastle-upon-Tyne, NE15 0HT
☎ **(01661) 852953**
⌂ 900
✍ ME Pearse (0191) 488 6515
↦ 18 L 5671 yds SSS 67
⚇ SOC–WD H–WD June–Aug 9am–3pm
£€ SOC D–£15
🚗 9 miles W of Newcastle on A69
⌂ Hawtree

Dunstanburgh Castle (1900)
Embleton, NE66 3XQ
☎ **(01665) 576562**
⌂ 396
✍ PFC Gilbert (Mgr)
↦ 18 L 6298 yds SSS 70
⚇ U
£€ £16 (£20)
🚗 7 miles NE of Alnwick on B1339
⌂ James Braid

Hexham (1892)

Spital Park, Hexham, NE46 3RZ
☎ **(01434) 603072**
📠 (01434) 601865
📖 750
🏌 Dawn Wylie (01434) 603072
🏌 MW Forster (01434) 604904
🏳 18 L 6272 yds SSS 70
👥 U
£€ £30 (£40)
⛳ 21 miles W of Newcastle (A69)
🏠 Vardon/Caird
■ www.hexhamgolfclub.ntb.org.uk

Linden Hall (1997)

Longhorsley, Morpeth, NE65 8XF
☎ **(01670) 500011**
📠 (01670) 500001
📧 golf@lindenhall.co.uk
📖 350
🏌 D Curry (Sec/Mgr)
🏌 D Curry (01670) 500011
🏳 18 L 6846 yds Par 72 SSS 73
👥 U H SOC WD WE
£€ £25 (£30)
⛳ 8 miles NW of Morpeth, off A697
⊕ Driving range
🏠 Jonathan Gaunt

Longhirst Hall Golf Course (1997)

Longhirst Hall, Longhirst, NE61 3LL
☎ **(01670) 791505 (Clubhouse), (01670) 858519 (Admin)**
📠 (01670) 818309
📧 enquiries@longhirstgolf.co.uk
📖 1700
🏌 c/o Dawson & Sanderson (01670) 858519
🏌 G Cant
🏳 Championship 18 L 6101 yds White tees Par 70
Leisure 18 L 6713 yds White tees Par 72
Winter (Nov–Mar tee mats in use) 18 L 6572 yds
👥 U SOC
£€ £2, £16, £12 (depending on tee
⛳ 4 miles NE of Morpeth, via A197/B1337
⊕ Driving range
🏠 B Poole
■ www.longhirstgolf.co.uk

Magdalene Fields (1903)

Pay and play
Magdalene Fields, Berwick-upon-Tweed, TD15 1NE
☎ **(01289) 306384**
📖 330
🏌 MJ Lynch
🏳 18 L 6407 yds SSS 71
👥 U SOC
£€ £20 (£22)
⛳ Berwick-upon-Tweed 1 mile
🏠 Park/Jefferson/Thompson
■ www.magdalene-fields.co.uk

Matfen Hall Hotel (1994)

Matfen, Hexham, NE20 0RH
☎ **(01661) 886500 (Hotel), (01661) 886400 (Bookings)**

📠 (01661) 886055
📧 golf@matfenhall.fsnet.co.uk
📖 500
🏌 D Burton
🏌 J Harrison
🏳 18 L 6569 yds Par 72
9 hole Par 3 course
👥 WD–U WE–U after 10am
£€ £30 (£35)
⛳ 12 miles W of Newcastle, off B6318
⊕ Driving range
🏠 Mair/James/Gaunt
■ www.matfenhall.com

Morpeth (1906)

The Clubhouse, Morpeth, NE61 2BT
☎ **(01670) 504942**
📠 (01670) 504918
📖 700
🏌 KD Cazaly (01670) 504942
🏌 MR Jackson (01670) 515675
🏳 18 L 5671 metres SSS 69
👥 H SOC
£€ £25 (£30)
⛳ 1 mile S of Morpeth on A197

Newbiggin (1884)

Newbiggin-by-the-Sea, NE64 6DW
☎ **(01670) 817344 (Clubhouse)**
📠 (01670) 520236
📖 500
🏌 GW Beattie (01670) 852959
🏳 18 L 6516 yds SSS 71
👥 U after 10am exc comp days–NA SOC
£€ D–£20 (D–£25)
⛳ Newbiggin, nr Church Point
🏠 Willie Park

Ponteland (1927)

53 Bell Villas, Ponteland, Newcastle-upon-Tyne, NE20 9BD
☎ **(01661) 822689**
📠 (01661) 860077
📧 secretary@thepontelandgolfclub.co.uk
📖 480 170(L) 115(J)
🏌 JN Dobson
🏌 A Robson-Crosby
🏳 18 L 6524 yds SSS 71
👥 WD–U SOC–Tues & Thurs
£€ £25
⛳ 6 miles NW of Newcastle on A696, nr Airport
■ www.thepontelandgolfclub.co.uk

Prudhoe (1930)

Eastwood Park, Prudhoe-on-Tyne, NE42 5DX
☎ **(01661) 832466**
📠 (01661) 830710
📖 450
🏌 ID Pauw
🏌 J Crawford (01661) 836188
🏳 18 L 5839 yds SSS 69
👥 WD–U WE–NA before 3pm SOC
£€ £20 (£25)
⛳ 12 miles W of Newcastle (A1/A695 junction)

Rothbury (1891)

Old Race Course, Rothbury, Morpeth, NE65 7TR
☎ **(01669) 621271**
📖 300
🏌 DA Woolley (01669) 630378
🏌 None
🏳 9 L 5779 yds Par 68 SSS 67
👥 WD–U exc Tues after 4pm & Wed am WE–by arrangement
£€ D–£13 (D–£18)
⛳ 15 miles N of Morpeth on A697. W side of Rothbury
🏠 JB Radcliffe
■ www.rothburygolfclub.com

Seahouses (1913)

Beadnell Road, Seahouses, NE68 7XT
☎ **(01665) 720794**
📠 (01665) 721994
📧 secretary@seahousesgolf.co.uk
📖 600
🏌 JA Gray
🏳 18 L 5542 yds SSS 67
👥 U SOC
£€ £25 (£30+Bank Hols)
⛳ 14 miles N of Alnwick. 9 miles E of A1 on B1340
■ www.seahousesgolf.co.uk

Stocksfield (1913)

New Ridley, Stocksfield, NE43 7RE
☎ **(01661) 843041**
📠 (01661) 843046
📖 426 100(L) 75(J)
🏌 B Slade
🏌 S Cowell
🏳 18 L 5998 yds SSS 69
👥 U SOC–exc Wed & Sat
£€ £20 (£25)
⛳ 2 miles S of Stocksfield. 3 miles E of A68
🏠 F Pennink
■ www.sgcgolf.co.uk

Swarland Hall (1993)

Coast View, Swarland, Morpeth, NE65 9JG
☎ **(01670) 787940 (Clubhouse)**
🏌 K Rutter (01670) 787010
🏌 Shop (01670) 787010
🏳 18 L 6628 yds SSS 72
👥 U
£€ £15 (£20)
⛳ 8 miles S of Alnwick, 1 mile W of A1

Tynedale (1908)

Public
Tyne Green, Hexham, NE46 3HQ
☎ **(01434) 608154**
🏌 J McDiarmid
🏌 Mrs C Brown
🏳 9 L 5706 yds SSS 68
👥 U exc Sun–booking necessary
£€ £10 (£12) (1993)
⛳ S side of Hexham

De Vere Slaley Hall   (1988)
Slaley, Hexham, NE47 0BY
- ☎ **(01434) 673154**
- 🖂 (01434) 673152
- 📖 350
- ✍ M Stancer (Golf Mgr)
- ✓ M Stancer (01434) 673154
- ⊳ Hunting 18 L 7073 yds Par 72
  SSS 71-74;
  Priestman 18 L 7010 Par 72
  SSS 71-74
- 👥 U SOC
- £€ Hunting–£70. Priestman–£42.50
- 🚗 20 miles W of Newcastle. 7 miles S
  of Corbridge, off A68
- ⊕ Driving range. Golf Academy
- ♔ Hunting-Dave Thomas. Priestman-
  Neil Coles
- ■ www.deveregolf.go.uk

Warkworth   (1891)
The Links, Warkworth, Morpeth,
NE65 0SW
- ☎ **(01665) 711596**
- 📖 400
- ✍ M Rowe
- ⊳ 9 L 5986 yds SSS 69
- 👥 U exc Tues & Sat SOC
- £€ D–£12 (D–£20)
- 🚗 9 miles SE of Alnwick (A1068)
- ♔ Old Tom Morris

Wooler   (1975)
Dod Law, Doddington, Wooler,
NE71 6EA
- ☎ **(01668) 282135**
- 📖 250
- ✍ S Lowrey (01668) 281631
- ✓ None
- ⊳ 9 L 6372 yds SSS 70
- 👥 U SOC
- £€ £15 (£20) £10 for 9 holes
- 🚗 3 miles N of Wooler on B6525

Nottinghamshire

Beeston Fields   (1923)
Beeston, Nottingham, NG9 3DD
- ☎ **(0115) 925 7062**
- 🖂 (0115) 925 4280
- 📖 510 148(L) 58(J)
- ✍ J Lewis
- ✓ A Wardle (0115) 925 7062
- ⊳ 18 L 6404 yds SSS 71
- 👥 U H SOC
- £€ £26 (£32)
- 🚗 4 miles W of Nottingham. M1
  Junction 25
- ♔ Tom Williamson
- ■ www.beestonfields.co.uk

Brierley Forest   (1993)
Main Street, Huthwaite, Sutton-in-
Ashfield, NG17 2LG
- ☎ **(01623) 550761**
- 🖂 (01623) 550761
- 📖 130
- ✍ D Crafts
- ⊳ 18 L 6008 yds Par 72 SSS 69

- 👥 WD–U bookings only WE–NA
  before noon
- £€ £11 (£13)
- 🚗 W of Sutton-in-Ashfield. M1
  Junction 28, 2 miles

Bulwell Forest   (1902)
Public
Hucknall Road, Bulwell, Nottingham,
NG6 9LQ
- ☎ **(0115) 977 0576 (Clubhouse)**
- 🖂 (0115) 976 3172 (Pro)
- 📖 350
- ✍ D Waddilove (Hon)
  (0115) 960 8435
- ✓ L Rawlings (0115) 976 3172
- ⊳ 18 L 5746 yds Par 68 SSS 67
- 👥 U SOC
- £€ £12 (£15). 4 ball–£44 (£48)
- 🚗 4 miles N of Nottingham. M1
  Junction 26, 3 miles

Chilwell Manor   (1906)
Meadow Lane, Chilwell, Nottingham,
NG9 5AE
- ☎ **(0115) 925 8958**
- 🖂 (0115) 922 0575
- 🖂✉ chilwellmanorgolfclub@barbox.net
- 📖 700
- ✍ RA Westcott
- ✓ P Wilson (0115) 925 8993
- ⊳ 18 L 6255 yds Par 70 SSS 71
- 👥 U SOC
- £€ £20 (£20)
- 🚗 4 miles W of Nottingham on A6005
- ♔ Tom Williamson

College Pines   (1994)
Worksop College Drive, Sparken Hill,
Worksop, S80 3AP
- ☎ **(01909) 501431**
- 🖂 (01909) 481227
- 📖 550
- ✍ C Snell (Golf Dir)
- ✓ C Snell (01909) 501431
- ⊳ 18 L 6801 yds SSS 73
- 👥 U–phone first SOC
- £€ £13 (£19)
- 🚗 1 mile SE of Worksop on B6034,
  off Worksop Bypass
- ⊕ Driving range
- ♔ David Snell

Cotgrave Place G&CC
(1991)
Owned privately
Stragglethorpe, Nr Cotgrave Village,
Cotgrave, NG12 3HB
- ☎ **(0115) 933 3344**
- 🖂 (0115) 933 4567
- 🖂✉ cotgrave@americangolf.com
- 📖 780
- ✍ M Evans
- ✓ R Smith
- ⊳ Open 18 L 6302 yds SSS 70
  Masters 18 L 5933 yds SSS 69
- 👥 U SOC
- £€ Open £22 (£25). Masters £21 (£25)
- 🚗 4 miles SE of Nottingham, off A52
- ⊕ Driving range
- ♔ Small/Glasgow/Alliss
- ■ www.americangolf.com

Coxmoor   (1913)
Coxmoor Road, Sutton-in-Ashfield,
NG17 5LF
- ☎ **(01623) 557359**
- 🖂 (01623) 557359
- 🖂✉ coxmoor@freeuk.com
- 📖 650
- ✍ P Snow
- ✓ D Ridley (01623) 559906
- ⊳ 18 L 6501 yds SSS 72
- 👥 H exc Ladies Day–Tues WE–NA
  SOC
- £€ £40/round £50/day
- 🚗 1¹/₂ miles S of Mansfield. 4 miles
  NE of M1 Junction 27 on A611
- ■ www.coxmoor.freeuk.com

Edwalton   (1982)
Public
Edwalton, Nottingham, NG12 4AS
- ☎ **(0115) 923 4775**
- 📖 700
- ✍ Mrs DJ Parkes (Hon)
- ✓ J Staples
- ⊳ 9 L 3336 yds SSS 36
  9 hole Par 3 course
- 👥 U
- £€ On application
- 🚗 2 miles S of Nottingham (A606)

Kilton Forest   (1978)
Public
Blyth Road, Worksop, S81 0TL
- ☎ **(01909) 486563**
- 📖 340
- ✍ A Mansbridge (Hon)
  (01909) 486269
- ✓ S Betteridge (01909) 486563
- ⊳ 18 L 6424 yds Par 72 SSS 71
- 👥 WD–U WE–booking nec. SOC
- £€ £12 (£15)
- 🚗 1 mile NE of Worksop on B6045

Leen Valley Golf Centre
(1994)
Pay and play
Wigwam Lane, Hucknall, NG15 7TA
- ☎ **(0115) 964 2037**
- 🖂 (0115) 964 2724
- 📖 350
- ✍ BR Goodman (Gen Mgr)
- ✓ J Lines (01623) 422764
- ⊳ 18 L 6521 yds Par 72 SSS 70
  9 hole Par 3 course
- 👥 U SOC
- £€ £10 (£15)
- 🚗 ¹/₂ mile from Hucknall town centre
- ♔ Tom Hodgetts

Mansfield Woodhouse
(1973)
Public
Mansfield Woodhouse, NG19 9EU
- ☎ **(01623) 23521**
- ✍ M Stuart
- ✓ L Highfield Jr
- ⊳ 9 L 2411 yds SSS 65
- 👥 U
- £€ £3
- 🚗 2 miles N of Mansfield (A60)

For list of abbreviations and key to symbols see page 627

Mapperley (1907)

Central Avenue, Plains Road,
Mapperley, Nottingham NG3 5RH
☎ **(0115) 955 6672**
▢ (0115) 955 6670
✉ mapperleygc@onetel.net.uk
▥ 650
♟ A Newton
✑ J Barker (0115) 955 6673
ⱶ 18 L 6307 yds SSS 70
♛♛ U SOC
££ £20 D–£25
♣ 3 miles NE of Nottingham, off
B684
♠ J Mason
■ www.mapperleygolfclub.org

Newark (1901)

Coddington, Newark, NG24 2QX
☎ **(01636) 626282**
▢ (01636) 626497
✉ secretary@newark-golf-club.co.uk
▥ 650
♟ DA Collingwood (01636) 626282
✑ PA Lockley (01636) 626492
ⱶ 18 L 6458 yds SSS 71
♛♛ H SOC
££ £24 (£30)
♣ 4 miles E of Newark on A17
⊕ Driving range on site
■ www.newark-golf-club.co.uk

Norwood Park (1999)

Norwood Park, Southwell, NG25 0PF
☎ **(01636) 816626**
▢ (01636) 815756
✉ mail@norwoodgolf.co.uk
▥ 515
♟ R Beckett (01636) 813226
✑ P Thornton (01636) 816626
ⱶ 18 L 6805 yds Par 72 SSS 72
♛♛ U SOC
££ £16 D–£28 (£22 D–£36)
♣ ¹/₂ mile W of Southwell, off
Kirklington road. Nearest road
A617/612
⊕ Driving range
♠ Clyde Johnston
■ www.norwoodpark.org.uk

Nottingham City (1910)

Public
Lawton Drive, Bulwell, Nottingham,
NG6 8BL
☎ **(0115) 927 8021**
▢ (0115) 927 6916
▥ 460
♟ (0115) 927 6916
✑ CR Jepson (0115) 927 2767
ⱶ 18 L 6218 yds SSS 70
♛♛ WD–U WE–NA before noon SOC
££ £12 (£15)
♣ 5 miles N of Nottingham. M1
Junction 26

Notts (1887)

Hollinwell, Kirkby-in-Ashfield,
NG17 7QR
☎ **(01623) 753225**
▢ (01623) 753655
▥ 330

♟ JB Noble
✑ A Thomas (01623) 753087
ⱶ 18 L 7103 yds Par 72 SSS 75
♛♛ WD–H WE/BH–M
££ On application
♣ 4 miles S of Mansfield on A611.
M1 Junction 27
⊕ Driving range-green fees only
♠ Willie Park Jr

Oakmere Park (1974)

Oaks Lane, Oxton, NG25 0RH
☎ **(0115) 965 3545**
▢ (0115) 965 5628
▥ 450
♟ D St-John Jones
✑ D St-John Jones (0115) 965 3545
ⱶ 18 L 6617 yds SSS 72
9 L 3495 yds SSS 37
♛♛ WD–U WE/BH–arrange times with
Mgr SOC
££ 18 hole: £18 (£25) 9 hole: £6 (£8)
♣ 8 miles NE of Nottingham on A614
⊕ Floodlit driving range
♠ F Pennink
■ www.oakmerepark.co.uk

Radcliffe-on-Trent (1909)

Dewberry Lane, Cropwell Road,
Radcliffe-on-Trent, NG12 2JH
☎ **(0115) 933 3000**
▢ (0115) 911 6991
✉ les.rotgc@talk21.com
▥ 700
♟ L Wake
✑ C George (0115) 933 2396
ⱶ 18 L 6381 yds Par 70 SSS 71
♛♛ H SOC–Wed only
££ £23 (£28)
♣ 6 miles E of Nottingham, off A52
♠ Tom Williamson
■ www.radcliffeontrentgc.co.uk

Ramsdale Park Golf Centre (1992)

Pay and play
Oxton Road, Calverton, NG14 6NU
☎ **(0115) 965 5600**
▢ (0115) 965 4105
✉ info@ramsdaleparkgc.co.uk
♟ N Birch (Mgr)
✑ R Macey
ⱶ 18 L 6546 yds SSS 71
18 hole Par 3 course
♛♛ U SOC–WD
££ £17 (£22)
♣ 5 miles NE of Nottingham on
B6386. M1 Junction 27
⊕ Floodlit driving range
♠ Hawtree
■ www.ramsdaleparkgc.co.uk

Retford (1921)

Brecks Road, Ordsall, Retford,
DN22 7UA
☎ **(01777) 703733**
▢ (01777) 710412
✉ retfordgolfclub@lineone.net
▥ 700
♟ Linda Colclough (01777) 711188
✑ C Morris

ⱶ 18 L 6370 yds SSS 70
♛♛ WD–U WE–after 2pm SOC–WD
££ £22 D–£30 (£28)
♣ 2 miles SW of Retford, off A638 or
A620. M1 Junction 30

Ruddington Grange (1988)

Wilford Road, Ruddington, Nottingham,
NG11 6NB
☎ **(0115) 984 6141**
▢ (0115) 940 5165
✉ info@ruddingtongrange.com
▥ 600
♟ A Johnson
✑ R Simpson (0115) 921 1951
ⱶ 18 L 6490 yds SSS 72
♛♛ WD–U SOC
££ D–£17.50 (£25)
♣ 3 miles S of Nottingham
♠ J Small

Rufford Park G&CC

Rufford Lane, Rufford, Newark,
NG22 9DG
☎ **(01623) 825253**
▢ (01623) 825254
✉ enquiries@ruffordpark.co.uk
▥ 500
♟ Mrs K Whitehead (01623) 825253
✑ J Vaughan, J Thompson
ⱶ 18 L 6286 yds Par 70 SSS 70
♛♛ U–booking necessary
SOC–WD/WEpm
££ £19 (£25)
♣ Nr Rufford Abbey on A614. 8
miles S of A1/A614 junction
⊕ Floodlit driving range
■ www.ruffordpark.co.uk

Rushcliffe (1909)

Stocking Lane, East Leake,
Loughborough, LE12 5RL
☎ **(01509) 852959**
▢ (01509) 852688
✉ secretary.rushcliffegc
@btopenworld.com
▥ 704
♟ KW Hodkinson
✑ C Hall (01509) 852701
ⱶ 18 L 6090 yds SSS 69
♛♛ SOC–WD
££ £25 (£30)
♣ 9 miles S of Nottingham. M1
Junction 24

Serlby Park (1906)

Serlby, Doncaster, DN10 6BA
☎ **(01777) 818268**
▥ 250
♟ KJ Crook (01302) 742280
ⱶ 9 L 5370 yds SSS 66
♛♛ M SOC–WD
££ £20
♣ 12 miles S of Doncaster, between
A614 and A638

Sherwood Forest (1895)

Eakring Road, Mansfield, NG18 3EW
☎ **(01623) 626689**
▢ (01623) 420412
▥ 648

For list of abbreviations and key to symbols see page 627

🖎 Ms A Miles (01623) 626689
✓ K Hall (01623) 627403
🏳 18 L 6843 yds SSS 74
👭 H SOC–WD
££ On application to Professional
🚵 2 miles E of Mansfield (A617)
🏠 HS Colt/James Braid

Southwell   (1993)
Proprietary
Southwell Racecourse, Rolleston,
Newark, NG25 0TS
☎ (01636) 816501/816795
📠 (01636) 812271
🖎 info@southwellgolfclub.com
📖 450
🖎 M Harness (01636) 821651
✓ (01636) 813706
🏳 18 L 5767 yds Par 69 SSS 68
👭 U SOC
££ £15 (£18)
🚵 6 miles W of Newark on A617.
   Course adjacent to racetrack
🏠 RA Muddle
■ www.southwellgolfclub.com

Springwater   (1991)
Proprietary
Moor Lane, Calverton, Nottingham,
NG14 6FZ
☎ (0115) 965 4946
🖎 springwater@rapidial.co.uk
📖 400
🖎 W Turner (0115) 965 2565
✓ P Drew (0115) 965 4946
🏳 18 L 6262 yds Par 71
👭 U SOC WD WE after 12.30pm
££ £18 (£23)
🚵 Off A6097 between Lowdham and
   Oxton
⊕ Driving range
🏠 N Foott/P Wharmsby
■ www.springwatergolfclub.co.uk

Stanton-on-the-Wolds
(1906)
Golf Road, Stanton-on-the-Wolds,
Nottingham, NG12 5BH
☎ (0115) 937 2044
📠 (0115) 937 4885
📖 500 167(L) 100(J)
🖎 AR Evans (0115) 937 4885
✓ N Hernon ((0115) 937 2390
🏳 18 L 6421 yds SSS 71
👭 WD–U exc comp days WE–M SOC
££ £23 D–£31 SOC–£25–£30
🚵 9 miles S of Nottingham

Trent Lock Golf Centre
(1991)
Lock Lane, Sawley, Long Eaton,
NG10 2FY
☎ (0115) 946 4398
📠 (0115) 946 1183
🖎 emccausland@aol.com
📖 550
🖎 R Gregory
✓ M Taylor
🏳 18 L 5730 yds Par 69 SSS 68
   9 L 2908 yds Par 36
👭 U SOC

££ £15 (£17.50) 9 hole: £6
🚵 S of Long Eaton. M1 Junction 25
⊕ Driving range, 24 bays; power tees
   (floodlit)
🏠 E McCausland
■ www.trenlock.co.uk

Wollaton Park   (1927)
Wollaton Park, Nottingham, NG8 1BT
☎ (0115) 978 7574
📠 (0115) 970 0736
🖎 wollatonparkgc@aol.com
📖 700
🖎 MT Harvey
✓ J Lower (0115) 978 4834
🏳 18 L 6445 yds SSS 71
👭 U SOC
££ On application
🚵 2 miles SW of Nottingham. M1
   Junction 25, 5 miles
🏠 T Williamson

Worksop   (1911)
Windmill Lane, Worksop, S80 2SQ
☎ (01909) 472696
📠 (01909) 477731
🖎 worksopgolfclub@worksop.co.uk
📖 500
🖎 DA Dufall (01909) 477731
✓ C Weatherhead (01909) 477732
🏳 18 L 6660 yds Par 72 SSS 73
👭 WD–H (phone first) WE/BH–M
   SOC
££ On application
🚵 1 mile SE of Worksop, off A6034
   via by-pass (A57). M1 Junction 30,
   9 miles
■ www.worksopgolfclub.com

Oxfordshire

Aspect Park   (1988)
Remenham Hill, Henley-on-Thames,
RG9 3EH
☎ (01491) 578306
📠 (01491) 578306
📖 600
🖎 T Notley (Mgr) (01491) 578306
✓ T Notley (01491) 577562
🏳 18 L 6559 yds Par 72 SSS 71
👭 WD–U WE–restricted before noon
   SOC
££ £20 (£25)
🚵 1 mile E of Henley. M40 Junction
   4, 8 miles
⊕ Driving range. Pitch & putt
🏠 T Winsland

Badgemore Park   (1972)
Proprietary
Henley-on-Thames, RG9 4NR
☎ (01491) 637300
📠 (01491) 576899
🖎 info@badgemorepark.com
📖 600
🖎 J Connell (Mgr) (01491) 637300
✓ J Dunn (01491) 574175
🏳 18 L 6129 yds SSS 69
👭 WD–U exc Tues am–NA WE–U
   after 11am SOC–Wed to Fri

££ £24 (£36)
🚵 1 mile NW of Henley on
   Rotherfield Greys road
🏠 B Sandow
■ www.badgemorepark.com

Banbury Golf Centre   (1993)
Aynho Road, Adderbury, Banbury,
OX17 3NT
☎ (01295) 810419
📠 (01295) 810056
🖎 office@banburygolfcentre.co.uk
📖 300
🖎 MA Reed (Prop)
✓ S Kier (01295) 812880
🏳 27 holes :
   L 5766-6706 yds Par 72 SSS 72
👭 U SOC
££ £17 (£27)
🚵 6 miles S of Banbury on B4100.
   M40 Junction 10/11
🏠 Reed/Payn
■ www.banburygolfcentre.co.uk

Bicester G&CC   (1973)
Chesterton, Bicester, OX26 1TE
☎ (01869) 241204
🖎 bicestergolf@ukonline.co.uk
📖 650
🖎 P Fox (01869) 241204
✓ J Goodman (01869) 242023
🏳 18 L 6013 yds SSS 70
👭 U SOC–WD
££ £20 (£27.50)
🚵 2 miles SW of Bicester. M40
   Junction 9
■ www.bicestergolf.co.uk

Brailes   (1992)
Sutton Lane, Lower Brailes, Banbury,
OX15 5BB
☎ (01608) 685336
📠 (01608) 685205
🖎 office@brailes-golf-club.co.uk
📖 580
🖎 RAS Malir
✓ A Brown (01608) 685633
🏳 18 L 6310 yds Par 71 SSS 70
👭 U SOC–WD
££ £20 (£30)
🚵 3 miles E of Shipston-on-Stour on
   B4035. M40 Junction 11, 10 miles
⊕ Driving range
🏠 BA Hull
■ www.brailes-golf-club.co.uk

Burford   (1936)
Burford, OX18 4JG
☎ (01993) 822583
📠 (01993) 822801
📖 760
🖎 RP Thompson
✓ M Ridge (01993) 822344
🏳 18 L 6432 yds SSS 71
👭 WD–H SOC
££ On application
🚵 19 miles W of Oxford on A40

Carswell CC   (1993)
Carswell, Faringdon, SN7 8PU
☎ (01367) 870422

☎ (01367) 870592
✉ info@carswellgolfandcountryclub
.co.uk
🛏 500
🔑 G Lisi (Prop)
✓ S Parker
🏌 18 L 6133 yds Par 72
👥 U SOC–WD
££ £18 (£25)
🚗 12 miles W of Oxford on A420
⊕ Floodlit driving range

Cherwell Edge (1980)
Chacombe, Banbury, OX17 2EN
☎ (01295) 711591
🛏 (01295) 712404
🛏 462
🔑 RA Beare
✓ J Kingston
🏌 18 L 5947 yds SSS 68
👥 U SOC–WD
££ £12 (£16)
🚗 3 miles E of Banbury on B4525
⊕ Driving range

Chipping Norton (1890)
Southcombe, Chipping Norton,
OX7 5QH
☎ (01608) 642383
🛏 (01608) 645422
✉ chippingnortongc@virgin.net
🛏 900
🔑 S Chislett
✓ N Rowlands (01608) 643356
🏌 18 L 6280 yds Par 71 SSS 70
👥 WD–U WE–M
££ £32
🚗 1 mile E of Chipping Norton on
A44

Drayton Park (1992)
Pay and play
Steventon Road, Drayton, Abingdon,
OX14 2RR
☎ (01235) 550607/528989
🛏 (01235) 525731
✉ admin@draytonparkgc.co.uk
🛏 400
🔑 (01235) 528989
✓ M Morbey (01235) 550607
🏌 18 L 5535 yds SSS 67
9 hole Par 3 course
👥 U SOC
££ £36
🚗 5 miles S of Oxford on A34. M4
Junction 13. 5 miles from The
Belfry
⊕ Floodlit driving range
🏠 Hawtree
■ www.draytonparkgc.co.uk

Frilford Heath (1908)
Frilford Heath, Abingdon, OX13 5NW
☎ (01865) 390864
🛏 (01865) 390823
🛏 1250 210(L)
🔑 S Styles
✓ DC Craik (01865) 390887
🏌 Red 18 L 6884 yds SSS 73
Green 18 L 6006 yds SSS 69
Blue 18 L 6728 yds SSS 72
👥 H SOC

££ £55 (£70)
🚗 3 miles W of Abingdon on A338
🏠 Blue-Simon Gidman

Hadden Hill (1990)
Wallingford Road, Didcot, OX11 9BJ
☎ (01235) 510410
🛏 (01235) 511260
🛏 420 52(L)
🔑 MV Morley
✓ I Mitchell
🏌 18 L 6563 yds SSS 71
👥 WD–U SOC–WD
££ £17 (£22)
🚗 E of Didcot on A4130
⊕ Floodlit driving range
🏠 MV Morley
■ www.haddenhillgolf.co.uk

Henley (1907)
Harpsden, Henley-on-Thames, RG9 4HG
☎ (01491) 575781
🛏 (01491) 412179
✉ henleygolfclub@btinternet.com
🛏 750
🔑 AM Chaundy (01491) 575742
✓ M Howell (01491) 575710
🏌 18 L 6329 yds SSS 70
👥 WD–H WE–M SOC
££ D–£33
🚗 1 mile S of Henley (A4155)
🏠 James Braid
■ www.henleygc.com

Hinksey Heights (1995)
South Hinksey, Oxford, OX1 5AB
☎ (01865) 327775
🛏 (01865) 736930
✉ play@oxford-golf.co.uk
🛏 360
🔑 K Martin (Gen Mgr)
✓ D Bolton (01865) 327775
🏌 18 L 6936 yds Par 74 SSS 73
9 hole Par 3 course
👥 U SOC
££ £17.50 (£25)
🚗 W of Oxford, off A34 at South
Hinksey, between Oxford and
Abingdon
⊕ Practice range. Golf academy
🏠 D Heads
■ www.oxford-golf.co.uk

Huntercombe (1901)
Nuffield, Henley-on-Thames, RG9 5SL
☎ (01491) 641207
🛏 (01491) 642060
✉ office@huntercombegolfclub.co.uk
🛏 800
🔑 KS McCrea
✓ D Reffin (01491) 641241
🏌 18 L 6271 yds SSS 70
👥 H–by appointment only SOC–WD
££ D–£46 (D–£60)
🚗 6 miles W of Henley on A4130
⊕ Foursomes and singles only;
practice ground
🏠 Willie Park Jr
■ www.huntercombegolfclub.co.uk

Kirtlington (1995)
Kirtlington, OX5 3JY
☎ (01869) 351133
🛏 (01869) 331143
✉ info@kirtlingtongolfclub.co.uk
🛏 450
🔑 P Smith (Sec/Mgr)
✓ Andy Taylor (0800) 587 2489
🏌 18 holes Par 70 SSS 69
9 hole Par 30
👥 U SOC
££ £20 (£25)
🚗 1 mile from Kirtlington on A4095.
M40 Junction 9
⊕ Driving range
🏠 G Webster
■ www.kirtlingtongolfclub.co.uk

North Oxford (1907)
Banbury Road, Oxford, OX2 8EZ
☎ (01865) 554415
🛏 (01865) 515921
✉ secretary@nogc.co.uk
🛏 701
🔑 GW Pullin (01865) 554924
✓ R Harris (01865) 553977
🏌 18 L 5805 yds SSS 67
👥 WD–U SOC–WD exc Thurs
££ £18 D–£25 After 5pm–£14
🚗 4 miles N of Oxford, off A4260 to
Kidlington
■ www.nogc.co.uk

The Oxfordshire (1993)
Rycote Lane, Milton Common, Thame,
OX9 2PU
☎ (01844) 278300
🛏 (01844) 278003
✉ info@theoxfordshiregolfclub.com
🛏 600
🔑 R Moan
✓ N Pike
🏌 18 L 7187 yds Par 72 SSS 75
👥 I H WE–NA before noon
££ On application
🚗 1¹/₂ miles W of Thame on A329.
M40 Junction 7, 1¹/₂ miles. M40
Junction 8, 4 miles
⊕ Driving range
🏠 Rees Jones
■ www.theoxfordshiregolfclub.com

RAF Benson (1975)
Royal Air Force, Benson, Wallingford,
OX10 6AA
☎ (01491) 837766 Ext 7322
🛏 200
🔑 M Bickley (01491) 833689
🏌 9 L 4412 yds Par 63 SSS 61
👥 M
££ £7
🚗 3¹/₂ miles NE of Wallingford

Rye Hill
Milcombe, Banbury, OX15 4RU
☎ (01295) 721818
🛏 (01295) 720089
✉ tony@pennock20.freeserve.co.uk
✓ T Pennock (01295) 721818
🏌 18 L 6919 yds Par 72
👥 U–booking necessary SOC

£€ £17 (£22)
⌒ 5 miles SW of Banbury, off A361.
   M40 Junction 11
⊕ 3 x Par 3 holes
■ www.ryehill.co.uk

Southfield   (1875)

Hill Top Road, Oxford, OX4 1PF
☎ (01865) 242158
⌨ (01865) 242158
⌑ 700
⌁ A Rees (01865) 244258
⊩ 18 L 6230 yds SSS 70
⚇ WD–U WE/BH–M H SOC
£€ £25
⌒ 2 miles E of Oxford
⌂ HS Colt

The Springs Hotel   (1998)

Wallingford Road, North Stoke,
Wallingford, OX10 6BE
☎ (01491) 827310
⌨ (01491) 827312
✉ thespringsproshop@hotmail.com
⌑ 550
⌁ D Allen (01491) 827307
⌁ P Ivil (01491) 827310
⊩ 18 L 6470 yds Par 72 SSS 71
⚇ By arrangement SOC
£€ £29 (£35)
⌒ 2 miles SW of Wallingford on
   B4009. M40 Junction 6
⌂ Brian Huggett
■ www.thespringsgc.com

Studley Wood   (1996)

The Straight Mile, Horton-cum-Studley,
Oxford, OX33 1BF
☎ (01865) 351144
⌨ (01865) 351166
✉ admin@swgc.co.uk
⌑ 650
⌁ R Booth (01865) 351144
⌁ T Williams (01865) 351122
⊩ 18 L 6722 yds Par 73 SSS 72
⚇ WD–U WE–NA before noon
   SOC
£€ £34 (£44)
⌒ 4 miles NE of Oxford. M40
   Junction 8
⊕ Driving range. Golf academy
⌂ Simon Gidman
■ www.studleywoodgolf.co.uk

Tadmarton Heath   (1922)

Wigginton, Banbury, OX15 5HL
☎ (01608) 737278
⌨ (01608) 730548
✉ thgc@btinternet.com
⌑ 650
⌁ J Cox
⌁ T Jones (01608) 730047
⊩ 18 L 5917 yds SSS 69
⚇ WD–H by appointment WE–M
   SOC–WD
£€ £39 (£43). After 2pm–£30
⌒ 5 miles SW of Banbury, off B4035
⌂ Maj CJ Hutchison
■ www.thgc.btinternet.com

Waterstock   (1994)

Pay and play
Thame Road, Waterstock, Oxford,
OX33 1HT
☎ (01844) 338093
⌨ (01844) 338036
⌑ 500
⌁ AJ Wyatt
⌁ P Bryant
⊩ 18 L 6535 yds Par 73
⚇ U SOC
£€ £18.50 (£20)
⌒ E of Oxford on A418. M40
   Junction 8
⊕ Floodlit driving range
⌂ Donald Steel

Witney Lakes   (1994)

Downs Road, Witney, OX8 5SY
☎ (01993) 893010
⌨ (01993) 778866
⌑ 450
⌁ M Percival
⌁ A South, A Campbell
⊩ 18 L 6460 yds SSS 71
⚇ U
£€ £16 (£22)
⌒ 2 miles W of Witney on B4047
⊕ Floodlit driving range
⌂ Simon Gidman
■ www.witney-lakes.co.uk

The Wychwood   (1992)

Proprietary
Lyneham, Chipping Norton, OX7 6QQ
☎ (01993) 831841
⌨ (01993) 831775
✉ golf@wychwoodgc.freeserve.co.uk
⌑ 750
⌁ CJT Howkins
⌁ J Fincher
⊩ 18 L 6669 yds SSS 72
⚇ WD–U WE–U after 11am SOC
£€ £23 (£28)
⌒ 4 miles W of Chipping Norton, off
   A361
⊕ Driving range
⌂ D Carpenter
■ www.golf@lynehamgc.freeserve
   .co.uk

Rutland

Greetham Valley   (1992)

Greetham, Oakham, LE15 7NP
☎ (01780) 460004
⌨ (01780) 460623
✉ gvgc@webleicester.co.uk
⌑ 1000
⌁ FE Hinch
⌁ J Pengelly (01780) 460666
⊩ 18 holes SSS 71
   18 holes SSS 68
   9 hole Par 3 course
⚇ U SOC–WD
£€ £28 (£32)
⌒ 5 miles NE of Oakham (B668), nr
   A1
⊕ Floodlit driving range

Luffenham Heath   (1911)

Ketton, Stamford, PE9 3UU
☎ (01780) 720205
⌨ (01780) 722146
✉ jringleby@theluffenhamheathgc
   .co.uk
⌑ 555
⌁ JR Ingleby
⌁ I Burnett (01780) 720298
⊩ 18 L 6315 yds SSS 70
⚇ U H SOC–WD
£€ £40 D–£50 (£40 D–£50)
⌒ 5 miles W of Stamford on A6121
⌂ James Braid
■ www.luffenhamheath.co.uk

RAF Cottesmore   (1982)

Oakham, Leicester, LE15 7BL
☎ (01572) 812241 Ext 6706
⌑ 150
⌁ GA Lawrence
⊩ 9 L 5767 yds SSS 67
⚇ By arrangement
£€ £10
⌒ RAF Cottesmore

RAF North Luffenham   (1975)

RAF North Luffenham, Oakham,
LE15 8RL
☎ (01780) 720041 Ext 7523
⌑ 350 62(L) 25(J)
⌁ S Nicholson
⊩ 9 L 6048 yds Par 70 SSS 69
⚇ U SOC
£€ D–£8
⌒ 1/2 mile from S shore of Rutland
   Water

Rutland County   (1991)

Great Casterton, Stamford, PE9 4AQ
☎ (01780) 460239/460330
⌨ (01780) 460437
✉ info@rutlandcountygolf.co.uk
⌁ S Lowe (Golf Dir)
⌁ Fred Fearn
⊩ 18 L 6401 yds SSS 71
   9 hole Par 3 course
⚇ U H SOC
£€ £25 (£30)
⌒ 3 miles N of Stamford on A1
⊕ Driving range
⌂ Cameron Sinclair
■ www.rutlandcountygolf.co.uk

Shropshire

Aqualate

Proprietary
Stafford Road, Newport, TF10 9JT
☎ (01952) 811699
⌨ (01952) 825343
⌑ 160
⌁ HB Dawes (Mgr) (01952) 825343
⌁ K Short (01952) 811699
⊩ 18 L 5659 yds Par 69 SSS 67
⚇ U
£€ £10 (£13)

⊕ 1 mile E of Newport (A518/A41 junction)
⊕ Floodlit driving range
■ www.aqualategolf.f2s.com

Arscott (1992)
Arscott, Pontesbury, Shrewsbury, SY5 0XP
☎ (01743) 860114
🖳 (01743) 860114
✉ argoco@tiscali.co.uk
☐ 550
🏌 BK Harper
✓ (01743) 860881
🏴 18 L 6112 yds SSS 69
👥 WD–U WE/BH–M before 2pm SOC
£€ £18 (£22)
⊕ 5 miles SW of Shrewsbury, off A488
🏠 Martin Hamer
■ www.arscottgolfclub.co.uk

Bridgnorth (1889)
Stanley Lane, Bridgnorth, WV16 4SF
☎ (01746) 763315
🖳 (01746) 761381
✉ bridgnorth-golf@supanet.com
☐ 690
🏌 GC Kelsall
✓ P Hinton (01746) 762045
🏴 18 L 6582 yds SSS 72
👥 H SOC WD
£€ £26 (£32)
⊕ 1 mile N of Bridgnorth
■ www.bridgnorthgolfclub.co.uk

Chesterton Valley
Chesterton, Worfield, Bridgnorth, WV15 5NX
☎ (01746) 783682
☐ 350
🏌 P Hinton
✓ P Hinton
🏴 18 L 5860 yds Par 69 SSS 67
👥 U–phone first SOC
£€ £14.50 (£15.50)
⊕ 10 miles W of Wolverhampton on B4176

Church Stretton (1898)
Trevor Hill, Church Stretton, SY6 6JH
☎ (01694) 722281
✉ secretary@churchstrettongolfclub.co.uk
☐ 410
🏌 John Povall (01743) 860679
✓ J Townsend (01694) 722281
🏴 18 L 5020 yds SSS 65
👥 U WE–NA before 10.30am SOC
£€ £18 (£26)
⊕ ¹/₂ mile W of Church Stretton, off A49
🏠 James Braid
■ www.churchstrettongolfclub.co.uk

Cleobury Mortimer (1993)
Wyre Common, Cleobury Mortimer, DY14 8HQ
☎ (01299) 271112 (Clubhouse)
🖳 (01299) 271468

✉ enquiries@cleoburygolfclub.com
☐ 704
🏌 G Pain (Gen Mgr)
✓ J Jones, M Payne
🏴 27 holes:
L 6147-6438 yds SSS 69-71
👥 WD–U H WE–M H SOC
£€ £20 (£30)
⊕ 10 miles SW of Kidderminster on A4117
⊕ Driving range and short game practice area
■ www.cleoburygolfclub.com

Hawkstone Park (1920)
Weston-under-Redcastle, Shrewsbury, SY4 5UY
☎ (01939) 200611
🖳 (01939) 200311
✉ info@hawkstone.co.uk
☐ 700
🏌 T Harrop
✓ S Leech
🏴 Hawkstone 18 L 6491 yds SSS 72
Windmill 18 L 6764 yds SSS 72
Academy 6 holes Par 3 course
👥 U
£€ £30 D–£44 (£36 D–£50)
⊕ 10 miles S of Whitchurch. 14 miles N of Shrewsbury on A49
⊕ Driving range
🏠 Braid/Huggett
■ www.hawkstone.co.uk

Hill Valley G&CC (1975)
Terrick Road, Whitchurch, SY13 4JZ
☎ (01948) 663584
🖳 (01948) 665927
☐ 600
🏌 JS Pickering
✓ AR Minshall, CT Burgess
🏴 Emerald 18 L 6628 yds Par 73
Sapphire 18 L 4801 yds Par 66
👥 U
£€ Emerald £20 (£25) Sapphire £11 (£15)
⊕ 1 mile N of Whitchurch, off A41/A49 Bypass
⊕ 6-bay practice range
🏠 Alliss/Thomas

Horsehay Village Golf Centre (1999)
Pay and play
Wellington Road, Horsehay, Telford, TF4 3BT
☎ (01952) 632070
🖳 (01952) 632074
✉ horsehayvillagegolfcentre@belford.gov.uk
☐ 350
🏌 M Morgan
✓ D Thorp & M Lea (01952) 632070
🏴 18 L 5929 yds Par 70 SSS 69
👥 U SOC
£€ £12 (£14)
⊕ Nr M54 Junction 6
⊕ Driving range. Pitch & putt course
🏠 Howard Swan

Lilleshall Hall (1937)
Abbey Road, Lilleshall, Newport, TF10 9AS
☎ (01952) 604776
🖳 (01952) 604776
☐ 600
🏌 EM Grimshaw (01952) 604776
✓ S McKane (01952) 604104
🏴 18 L 5813 yds SSS 68
👥 WD–U WE–M SOC
£€ £25
⊕ 3 miles S of Newport between Lilleshall and Sheriffhales. M54 Junction 4
🏠 HS Colt

Llanymynech (1933)
Pant, Oswestry, SY10 8LB
☎ (01691) 830542
☐ 760
🏌 DR Thomas (01691) 830983
✓ A Griffiths (01691) 830879
🏴 18 L 6114 yds Par 70 SSS 69
👥 U before 4.30pm –M after 4.30pm SOC–WD
£€ £20 (£25)
⊕ 5 miles S of Oswestry on A483
■ www.llanymynechgolfclub.co.uk

Ludlow (1889)
Bromfield, Ludlow, SY8 2BT
☎ (01584) 856285
🖳 (01584) 856366
✉ ludlowgo@barbox.net
☐ 550
🏌 RJ Heath (01584) 856285 (am)
✓ R Price (01584) 856366
🏴 18 L 6277 yds SSS 70
👥 H SOC–WD
£€ £22 (£25)
⊕ 2 miles N of Ludlow (A49)

Market Drayton (1926)
Sutton, Market Drayton, TF9 2HX
☎ (01630) 652266
☐ 550
🏌 DB Palmer
✓ R Clewes (01630) 656237
🏴 18 L 6290 yds SSS 71
👥 WD–U WE–NA
£€ £26
⊕ 1 mile S of Market Drayton off A41

Meole Brace (1976)
Public
Meole Brace, Shrewsbury SY2 6QQ
☎ (01743) 364050
🖳 (01743) 364050
🏌 N Bramall
🏴 9 L 2915 yds SSS 68
👥 WD–U WE–book in advance
£€ On application
⊕ 1 mile S of Shrewsbury, off A49

Mile End (1992)
Proprietary
Mile End, Oswestry, SY11 4JF
☎ (01691) 671246
🖳 (01691) 670580
✉ mileendgc@aol.com

For list of abbreviations and key to symbols see page 627

🏌 R Thompson
🏌 S Carpenter (01691) 671246
🏳 18 L 6292 yds SSS 70
👥 U SOC
£€ £16 D–£24 (£22 D–£30)
🚗 1 mile SE of Oswestry, off
A5/A483
⊕ Driving range, PGA tuition
🏠 Price/Gough
■ www.mileendgolfclub.co.uk

Oswestry (1903)

Aston Park, Oswestry, SY11 4JJ
☎ (01691) 610221
🖥 (01691) 610535
📖 880
🏌 PB Turner (01691) 610535
🏌 D Skelton (01691) 610448
🏳 18 L 6038 yds SSS 69
👥 M or H SOC–WD
£€ £25 (£31)
🚗 3 miles SE of Oswestry on A5
🏠 James Braid

Patshull Park Hotel G&CC
(1980)

Pattingham, WV6 7HR
☎ (01902) 700100
🖥 (01902) 700874
📖 395
🏌 M Ellam
🏌 R Bissell (01902) 700342
🏳 18 L 6412 yds SSS 71
👥 U H SOC
£€ £40
🚗 7 miles W of Wolverhampton, off
A41. M54 Junction 3, 5 miles
⊕ Practice facilities, putting green,
on-site hotel
🏠 John Jacobs
■ www.patshull-park.co.uk

Severn Meadows (1990)

Pay and play
Highley, Bridgnorth, WV16 6HZ
☎ (01746) 862212
📖 190
🏌 C Harrison
🏌 None
🏳 18 L 6357 yds Par 72 SSS 70
👥 WD–U WE–booking required
£€ £12 (£14)
🚗 8 miles S of Bridgnorth on B4555

Shifnal (1929)

Decker Hill, Shifnal, TF11 8QL
☎ (01952) 460467/460330
🖥 (01952) 461127
📧 secretary@shifnalgolfclub.co.uk
📖 700
🏌 M Vanner (01952) 460330
🏌 J Flanaghan (01952) 460457
🏳 18 L 6422 yds SSS 71
👥 WD–phone first WE/BH–M
£€ £25
🚗 1 mile NE of Shifnal. M54 Junction
4, 2 miles
🏠 Pennink
■ www.shifnalgolfclub.co.uk

Shrewsbury (1891)

Condover, Shrewsbury, SY5 7BL
☎ (01743) 872976
🖥 (01743) 874647
📧 info@shrewsbury-golf-club.co.uk
📖 525 184(L) 70(J)
🏌 Mrs SM Kenny (01743) 872977
🏌 P Seal (01743) 874581
🏳 18 L 6178 yds Par 70 SSS 69
👥 H SOC
£€ £22 (£25)
🚗 4 miles S of Shrewsbury
■ www.club-
noticeboard.co.uk/shrewsbury

The Shropshire (1992)

Muxton, Telford, TF2 8PQ
☎ (01952) 677866/677800
🖥 (01952) 677622
📖 300
🏌 Steve Whiting
🏌 Rob Grier
🏳 27 L 6589-6637 yds SSS 70-72
👥 U SOC WD WE
£€ £18 (£24)
🚗 3 miles NW of Telford (B5060).
M54 Junction 4
⊕ Floodlit driving range. Pitch & putt
course
🏠 Martin Hawtree
■ www.theshropshire.co.uk

Telford (1976)

Great Hay Drive, Sutton Heights,
Telford, TF7 4DT
☎ (01952) 429977
🖥 (01952) 586602
📧 ibarklem@aol.com
📖 400
🏌 I Lucas (01952) 422960
🏌 D Bateman (01952) 586052
🏳 18 L 6741 yds SSS 72
👥 H SOC
£€ On application
🚗 4 miles SE of Telford, off A442
⊕ Driving range
🏠 John Harris
■ www.telford-golfclub.co.uk

Worfield (1991)

Worfield, Bridgnorth, WV15 5HE
☎ (01746) 716541
🖥 (01746) 716302
📖 500
🏌 W Weaver (Gen Mgr)
(01746) 716372
🏌 S Russell (01746) 716541
🏳 18 L 6660 yds SSS 72
👥 U SOC
£€ £20 (£25)
🚗 7 miles W of Wolverhampton on
A454
🏠 Gough/Williams

Wrekin (1905)

Wellington, Telford, TF6 5BX
☎ (01952) 244032
🖥 (01952) 252906
📧 wrekingolfclub@lineone.net
📖 400 100(L) 90(J)
🏌 D Briscoe

🏌 K Housden (01952) 223101
🏳 18 L 5657 yds SSS 67
👥 WD–U before 5pm –M after 5pm
SOC
£€ £22 (£30)
🚗 Wellington, off B5061

Somerset

Bath (1880)

Sham Castle, North Road, Bath,
BA2 6JG
☎ (01225) 425182
🖥 (01225) 331027
📧 enquiries@bathgolfclub.org.uk
📖 730
🏌 SP Watkins (01225) 463834
🏌 P Hancox (01225) 466953
🏳 18 L 6442 yds SSS 71
👥 H SOC
£€ £30 (£36)
🚗 1¹/₂ miles SE of Bath, off A36. M4
Junction 18 (A46)
🏠 HS Colt
■ www.bathgolfclub.org.uk

Brean (1973)

Coast Road, Brean, Burnham-on-Sea,
TA8 2QY
☎ (01278) 752111
🖥 (01278) 752111
📧 golf@brean.com
📖 400
🏌 I Ross (Hon)
🏌 D Haines (01278) 752111
🏳 18 L 5565 yds SSS 67
👥 WD–U WE–pm only SOC
£€ £18 (£20)
🚗 4 miles N of Burnham-on-Sea. M5
Junction 22, 6 miles

Burnham & Berrow (1890)

St Christopher's Way, Burnham-on-Sea,
TA8 2PE
☎ (01278) 783137
🖥 (01278) 795440
📧 secretary@burnhamandberrow
.freeserve.co.uk
📖 800
🏌 PE Ware (01278) 785760
🏌 M Crowther-Smith (01278) 784545
🏳 18 L 6606 yds SSS 73
9 L 6332 yds SSS 72
👥 I H SOC
£€ 18: £45 (£60) 9: £15
🚗 1 mile N of Burnham-on-Sea on
B3140. M5 Junction 22
⊕ Dormy House

Cannington (1993)

Pay and play
Cannington College, Bridgwater,
TA5 2LS
☎ (01278) 655050
🖥 (01278) 652479
📖 200
🏌 R Macrow (Mgr)
🏌 R Macrow
🏳 9 L 6072 yds Par 68 SSS 70

For list of abbreviations and key to symbols see page 627

U exc Wed eve–restricted
18 holes–£14 (£18.50) 9 holes–£9 (£12.50)
4 miles NW of Bridgwater on A39. M5 Junction 24
Driving range
Hawtree

Clevedon (1891)
Castle Road, Clevedon, BS21 7AA
(01275) 874057
(01275) 341228
800
J Cunning (01275) 874057
R Scanlan (01275) 874704
18 L 6557 yds Par 72 SSS 72
WD–U H exc Wed am WE/BH–U H (phone first) SOC–WD
£25 (£40)
Off Holly Lane, Walton, Clevedon. M5 Junction 20
JH Taylor

Enmore Park (1906)
Enmore, Bridgwater, TA5 2AN
(01278) 671244 (Members)
(01278) 671740
golfclub@enmore.fsnet.co.uk
780
D Weston (01278) 671481
N Wixon (01278) 671519
18 L 6411 yds SSS 71
U SOC–WD
£25 (£35)
3 miles W of Bridgwater, off Durleigh road. M5 Junctions 23/24
Hawtree
www.golfdirector.com/enmore

Entry Hill (1985)
Public
Entry Hill, Bath, BA2 5NA
(01225) 834248
J Sercombe
T Tapley
9 L 4206 yds SSS 61
WD/WE–booking only
18 holes–£10.50. 9 holes–£6.85
1 mile S of Bath, off A367

Farrington (1992)
Marsh Lane, Farrington Gurney, Bristol, BS39 6TS
(01761) 451596
(01761) 451021
info@farringtongolfclub.net
620
SG Cook (01761) 451596
J Cowgill (01761) 451046
18 L 6716 yds Par 72 SSS 72
9 L 3002 yds Par 54 SSS 53
WD–U H SOC–WD
18 hole: £20 (£30). 9 hole: £6 (£8)
12 miles S of Bristol (A37). 10 miles S of Bath (A39)
Floodlit driving range
Peter Thompson

Fosseway CC (1970)
Charlton Lane, Midsomer Norton, Radstock, BA3 4BD
(01761) 412214

(01761) 418357
270
PJ Jordan (Mgr)
9 L 4565 yds SSS 63
WD–U exc Wed–M after 5pm WE–NA before 1.30pm
£15
10 miles SW of Bath on A367

Frome (1994)
Proprietary
Critchill Manor, Frome, BA11 4LJ
(01373) 453410
(01373) 453410
fromegolfclub@yahoo.co.uk
400
Mrs S Austin
T Issacs
18 hole course Par 69 SSS 67
U
£14 D–£19 (£16 D–£20)
12 miles S of Bath
Driving range
www.fromegolf.fsnet.co.uk

Isle of Wedmore (1992)
Lineage, Lascots Hill, Wedmore, BS28 4QT
(01934) 712452
(01934) 713696
670
AC Edwards (01934) 712222
G Coombe (01934) 712452
18 L 6006 yds Par 70 SSS 69
U SOC–WD
£20 (£20)
¾ mile N of Wedmore. M5 Junction 22
Terry Murray

Kingweston (1983)
(Sec) Mead Run, Compton Street, Compton Dundon, Somerton TA11 6PP
(01458) 43921
200
JG Willetts
9 L 4516 yds SSS 62
M exc Wed & Sat 2–5pm–NA
NA
1 mile SE of Butleigh. 2 miles SE of Glastonbury

Lansdown (1894)
Lansdown, Bath, BA1 9BT
(01225) 422138
(01225) 339252
admin@lansdowngolfclub.co.uk
750
Mrs E Bacon
T Mercer (01225) 420242
18 L 6316 yds SSS 70
H SOC
£23 (£29)
2 miles NW of Bath, by racecourse. M4 Junction 18, 6 miles
HS Colt
www.lansdowngolfclub.co.uk

Long Sutton (1991)
Pay and play
Long Load, Langport, TA10 9JU
(01458) 241017
(01458) 241022
reservations@longsuttongolf.com
700
T Tulk
A Hayes
18 L 6367 yds SSS 71
WD–U WE–booking required SOC
£18 (£22)
3 miles E of Langport
Floodlit driving range
Patrick Dawson
www.longsuttongolf.com

The Mendip (1908)
Gurney Slade, Radstock, BA3 4UT
(01749) 840570
(01749) 841439
secretary@mendipgolfclub.co.uk
800
J Scott
A Marsh (01749) 840793
18 L 6383 yds SSS 71
WD–U WE–H SOC–WD
£24 (£35)
3 miles N of Shepton Mallet (A37)
CK Cotton
www.mendipgolfclub.co.uk

Mendip Spring (1992)
Honeyhall Lane, Congresbury, BS49 5JT
(01934) 853337/852322
(01934) 853021
500
A Melhuish
J Blackburn
18 L 6352 yds SSS 70
9 L 4784 yds SSS 66
U
18 hole: £25 (£34). 9 hole: £8.50 (£9)
Congresbury. M5 Junction 21.
Driving range
Langholt

Minehead & West Somerset (1882)
The Warren, Minehead, TA24 5SJ
(01643) 702057
(01643) 705095
secretary@mineheadgolf.co.uk
604
RAJ Rayner
I Read (01643) 704378
18 L 6228 yds SSS 70
U after 9.30am SOC
£26 (£30) W–£100
E end of sea front
www.mineheadgolf.co.uk

Oake Manor (1993)
Oake, Taunton, TA4 1BA
(01823) 461993
(01823) 461995
600
R Gardner (Golf Mgr)
R Gardner

18 L 6109 yds Par 70 SSS 69
U–phone first SOC
£€ £19 (£25)
⊕ 4 miles W of Taunton, off B3227.
M5 Junctions 25/26 onto A38
⊕ Driving range. Academy course
♔ Adrian Stiff
■ www.oakemanor.com

Orchardleigh   (1996)
Frome, BA11 2PH
☎ (01373) 454200/454206
(Bookings)
▭ (01373) 454202
▯ 500
⚐ T Atkinson (Mgr)
✎ I Ridsdale
▷ 18 L 6810 yds Par 72 SSS 73
♔ WD/BH–U WE–U after 11am SOC
£€ £30 (£40)
⊕ 2 miles NW of Frome on A362. 12
miles S of Bath
⊕ Practice range
♔ Brian Huggett

Puxton Park   (1992)
Pay and play
Puxton, Weston-super-Mare, BS24 6TA
☎ (01934) 876942
✎ C Ancsell
▷ 18 L 6600 yds Par 72
♔ U SOC
£€ £8 (£10)
⊕ A370, 2 miles E of M5 Junction 21

Saltford   (1904)
*Golf Club Lane, Saltford, Bristol,
BS31 3AA*
☎ (01225) 873220
▭ (01225) 873525
▯ 650
⚐ V Radnedge (01225) 873513
✎ D Millensted (01225) 872043
▷ 18 L 6225 yds SSS 70
♔ WD–U SOC–Mon & Thurs
£€ £24
⊕ 7 miles SE of Bristol

Stockwood Vale   (1991)
Public
*Stockwood Lane, Keynsham, Bristol,
BS31 2ER*
☎ (0117) 986 6505
▭ (0117) 986 8974
✉ stockwoodvale@aol.com
▯ 650
⚐ M Edenborough
✎ J Richards
▷ 18 L 6031 yds SSS 71
♔ U SOC–WD
£€ £15.50 (£18)
⊕ 1 mile SE of Bristol, off A4174
⊕ Driving range
♔ Ramsay
■ www.stockwoodvale.com

Tall Pines   (1991)
*Cooks Bridle Path, Downside, Backwell,
Bristol BS48 3DJ*
☎ (01275) 472076
▭ (01275) 474869

▯ 500
⚐ T Murray
✎ A Murray
▷ 18 L 6100yds Par 70 SSS 69
♔ U SOC
£€ £18 (£18)
⊕ 8 miles SW of Bristol (A470/A38)
♔ Terry Murray

Taunton & Pickeridge   (1892)
Corfe, Taunton, TA3 7BY
☎ (01823) 421876
▭ (01823) 421742
✉ sec@taunt-
pickgolfclub.sagehost.co.uk
▯ 660
⚐ MPD Walls (01823) 421537
✎ G Milne (01823) 421790
▷ 18 L 6015 yds SSS 69
♔ H SOC
£€ £24 (£35)
⊕ 5 miles S of Taunton on B3170
♔ Hawtree

Taunton Vale   (1991)
Creech Heathfield, Taunton, TA3 5EY
☎ (01823) 412220
▭ (01823) 413583
✉ tvgc@easynet.co.uk
▯ 750
⚐ Mrs J Wyatt
✎ M Keitch (01823) 412880
▷ 18 L 6167 yds Par 70 SSS 69
9 L 2004 yds Par 64 SSS 60
♔ U SOC
£€ 18: £20 (£25). 9: £10 (£12)
⊕ 3 miles N of Taunton, off A361.
M5 Junctions 24/25
⊕ Floodlit driving range
♔ John Pyne
■ www.tauntonvalegolf.co.uk

Tickenham   (1994)
*Clevedon Road, Tickenham, Bristol,
BS21 6RY*
☎ (01275) 856626
▯ 1250
✎ A Sutcliffe
▷ 9 L 2000 yds
♔ U–phone first SOC
£€ 18 holes–£11 (£14)
⊕ 2 miles E of M5 Junction 20 on
B3130, nr Nailsea
⊕ Floodlit driving range
♔ Andrew Sutcliffe
■ www.tickenhamgolf.co.uk

Vivary   (1928)
Public
Vivary Park, Taunton, TA1 3JW
☎ (01823) 289274 (Clubhouse)
▯ 300
⚐ Christine Miller
✎ D Hawker (01823) 333875
▷ 18 L 4620 yds SSS 63
♔ U SOC–WD
£€ £8.40
⊕ Centre of Taunton
♔ Herbert Fowler

Wells   (1893)
East Horrington Road, Wells, BA5 3DS
☎ (01749) 675005
▭ (01749) 683170
▯ 750
✎ A Bishop (01749) 679059
▷ 18 L 6053 yds SSS 69
♔ WD–U WE–H SOC–WD
£€ £24 (£30)
⊕ 1½ miles E of Wells, off Bath road
(B3139)
⊕ Floodlit driving range

Weston-super-Mare   (1892)
*Uphill Road North, Weston-super-Mare,
BS23 4NQ*
☎ (01934) 626968
▭ (01934) 621360
✉ karen@wsmgolfclub.fsnet.co.uk
▯ 752
⚐ Mrs K Drake (01934) 626968
✎ M La Band (01934) 633360
▷ 18 L 6251 yds SSS 70
♔ H SOC
£€ £36 D–£49 (£54 D–£60)
⊕ Weston-super-Mare
♔ T Dunn – redesigned A Mackenzie

Wheathill   (1993)
Wheathill, Somerton, TA11 7HG
☎ (01963) 240667
▭ (01963) 240230
▯ 400
⚐ A Lyddon (Sec/Mgr)
✎ A England
▷ 18 L 5362 yds SSS 66
4 holes Par 3 course
♔ U SOC
£€ £15 (£20)
⊕ 3 miles W of Castle Cary on B3153

Windwhistle   (1932)
Cricket St Thomas, Chard TA20 4DG
☎ (01460) 30231
▭ (01460) 30055
✉ info@windwhistlegolf.co.uk
▯ 550
⚐ IN Dodd
✎ P Deeprose
▷ 18 L 6510 yds SSS 71
♔ U–phone first SOC
£€ On application
⊕ Windwhistle, 3 miles E of Chard on
A30. M5 Junction 25, 12 miles
⊕ Driving range
♔ JH Taylor/L Fisher
■ www.windwhistlegolf.co.uk

Worlebury   (1908)
*Monks Hill, Worlebury, Weston-super-
Mare, BS22 9SX*
☎ (01934) 625789
▭ (01934) 621935
✉ secretary@worleburyg.c.co.uk
▯ 640
⚐ MW Wake
✎ G Marks (01934) 418473
▷ 18 L 5963 yds SSS 69
♔ H SOC–WD
£€ £25 (£30)
⊕ 2 miles NE of Weston, off A370

⛳ H Vardon
⬛ www.worlebury.g.c.co.uk

Yeovil (1919)

Sherborne Road, Yeovil, BA21 5BW
☎ **(01935) 475949 (Clubhouse)**
🖬 (01935) 411283
🕮 710 122(L) 101(J)
🏌 GR Dodd (01935) 422965
🏌 G Kite (01935) 473763
➢ 18 L 6144 yds SSS 70
   9 L 4876 yds SSS 65
👫 WD–U H WE/BH–H
   (WD/WE–phone Pro) SOC
££ 18: £25 (£30). 9: £18 (£20)
🚗 1 mile from Yeovil on A30 to
   Sherborne
⊕ 20-bay floodlit driving range open
   7am-9pm WD, 7am-6pm WE
⛳ Fowler/Alison

Staffordshire

Alsager G&CC (1992)

Audley Road, Alsager, Stoke-on-Trent,
ST7 2UR
☎ **(01270) 875700**
🖬 (01270) 882207
🕮 660
🏌 M Davenport
🏌 R Brown
➢ 18 L 6225 yds SSS 70
👫 WD–U before 5pm –M after 5pm
   SOC
££ £25
🚗 5 miles W of Crewe. M6 Junction
   16
⬛ www.alsagergolfclub.com

Aston Wood (1994)

Blake Street, Sutton Coldfield, B74 4EU
☎ **(0121) 580 7803**
🖬 (0121) 353 0354
🖂 enquiries@astonwoodgolfclub
   .co.uk
🕮 850
🏌 K Heathcote (0121) 580 7803
🏌 S Smith (0121) 580 7801
➢ 18 holes Par 71 SSS 71
👫 WD–M before 5pm WE–M SOC
££ £22 (£33)
🚗 3 miles NE of Sutton Coldfield on
   A4026. M6 Junct. 7. M42 Junct. 9
⊕ Driving range
⛳ Alliss/Clarke
⬛ www.astonwoodgolfclub.co.uk

Barlaston (1987)

Meaford Road, Stone, ST15 8UX
☎ **(01782) 372867**
🖬 (01782) 372867
🖂 barlaston.gc@virgin.net
🕮 650
🏌 W Thompson (01782 372867)
🏌 I Rogers (01782) 372795
➢ 18 L 5800 yds SSS 68
👫 WD–U WE–NA before 10am
££ On application
🚗 ¹/₂ mile S of Barlaston. M6 Junction
   14/15

⛳ P Aliss
⬛ www.bgc.everplay.net

Beau Desert (1921)

Hazel Slade, Cannock, WS12 0PJ
☎ **(01543) 422626/422773**
🖬 (01543) 451137
🖂 bdgc@btconnect.com
🕮 650
🏌 John Bradbury (01543) 422626
🏌 Barrie Stevens (01543) 422492
➢ 18 L 6310 yds Par 70 SSS 71
👫 WD–U WE–phone in advance
   BH–NA SOC
££ £40 (£50)
🚗 4 miles NE of Cannock, off A460
⊕ Driving range
⛳ WH Fowler
⬛ www.bdgc.co.uk

Bloxwich (1924)

136 Stafford Road, Bloxwich, WS3 3PQ
☎ **(01922) 476593**
🖬 (01922) 493449
🖂 bloxwich.golf-club@virgin.net
🕮 700
🏌 DA Frost (01922) 476593
🏌 RJ Dance (01922) 476889
➢ 18 L 6257 yds SSS 71
👫 WD–U WE–M SOC
££ £30 (£35)
🚗 N of Walsall on A34

Branston G&CC (1975)

Burton Road, Branston, Burton-on-
Trent, DE14 3DP
☎ **(01283) 543207**
🖬 (01283) 566984
🖂 sales@branston-golf-club.co.uk
🕮 800
🏌 G Pyle (Golf Mgr)
🏌 J Sture
➢ 18 L 6697 yds Par 72 SSS 72
   9 L 1856 yds Par 30
👫 WD–U WE–M before noon SOC
££ £30 (£40)
🚗 ¹/₂ mile S of Burton (A38)
⊕ Driving range
⛳ G Hamshall

Brocton Hall (1894)

Brocton, Stafford, ST17 0TH
☎ **(01785) 662627**
🖬 (01785) 661591
🕮 500
🏌 G Ashley (01785) 661901
🏌 N Bland (01785) 661485
➢ 18 L 6095 yds SSS 69
👫 I H SOC
££ £33 (£40)
🚗 4 miles SE of Stafford, off A34
⛳ Harry Vardon

Burslem (1907)

Wood Farm, High Lane, Stoke-on-Trent,
ST6 7JT
☎ **(01782) 837006**
🕮 300
🏌 B Bavington (01782) 784063
➢ 9 L 5274 yds SSS 66
👫 WD–U WE–NA

££ £16
🚗 Burslem 2 miles

Calderfields (1983)

Aldridge Road, Walsall, WS4 2JS
☎ **(01922) 646888 (Clubhouse),**
   (01922) 632243 (Bookings)
🖬 (01922) 640540
🕮 750
🏌 Mrs K Williams
🏌 I Roberts (01922) 613675
➢ 18 L 6636 yds SSS 72
👫 U SOC
££ £18 peak, £12 off-peak
🚗 1 mile N of Walsall (A454). M6
   Junction 10
⊕ 27 bay floodlit driving range
⬛ www.calderfieldsgolf.com

Cannock Park (1993)

Public
Stafford Road, Cannock, WS11 2AL
☎ **(01543) 578850**
🖬 (01543) 578850
🕮 230
🏌 CB Milne (01543) 571091
🏌 D Dunk
➢ 18 L 5149 yds SSS 65
👫 U SOC–WD
££ £9 (£11)
🚗 ¹/₂ mile N of Cannock on A34. M6
   Junction 11, 2 miles
⛳ John Mainland

The Chase (1999)

Pottal Pool Road, Penkridge, ST19 5RN
☎ **(01785) 712191**
🖬 (01785) 712692
🖂 chase-sales@crowngolf.co.uk
🕮 600
🏌 M Clarke (01785) 712888
🏌 R Stockdale (01785) 712191
➢ 18 L 6354 yds Par 72 SSS 72
👫 U H
££ £20 (£25)
🚗 10 miles S of Stafford, off A449.
   M6 Junctions 12 & 13
⊕ Driving range (20 bays)

The Craythorne (1972)

Craythorne Road, Stretton, Burton-on-
Trent, DE13 0AZ
☎ **(01283) 564329**
🖬 (01283) 511908
🖂 admin@craythorne.co.uk
🕮 450
🏌 AA Wright (Man Dir)
🏌 S Hadfield (01283) 533745
➢ 18 L 5556 yds Par 68 SSS 68
   Pitch & putt course
👫 WD–U SOC
££ £24 (£30)
🚗 Stretton, 1¹/₂ miles N of Burton.
   A38/A5121 Junction
⊕ Floodlit driving range
⬛ www.craythorne.co.uk

Dartmouth (1910)

Vale Street, West Bromwich, B71 4DW
☎ **(0121) 588 2131**
🖬 (0121) 588 5746

For list of abbreviations and key to symbols see page 627

📖 350
🏌 CF Wade (0121) 532 4070
⛳ G Kilminster (0121) 588 2131
🏴 9 L 6036 yds SSS 71
👥 WD–U WE–M after 1pm
    SOC–Tues & Thurs
💶 D–£25 (£17)
🚗 1 mile from W Bromwich, behind
    site of new estate. M5 J1, M6 J7
⬛ www.dartmouth-golf-club.co.uk

Denstone College

Denstone, Uttoxeter, ST14 5HN
☎ **(01889) 590484**
🏌 M Raisbeck (Mgr)
⛳ None
🏴 9 L 4404 yds Par 64 SSS 62
👥 M SOC
💶 £6
🚗 Grounds of Denstone College. 6
    miles N of Uttoxeter
🏠 MP Raisbeck

Drayton Park (1897)

Drayton Park, Tamworth, B78 3TN
☎ **(01827) 251139**
📠 (01827) 284035
📖 650
🏌 DO Winter
⛳ MW Passmore (01827) 251478
🏴 18 L 6473 yds SSS 71
👥 WD–H WE/BH–NA SOC–Tues &
    Thurs
💶 £34 D–£34
🚗 2 miles S of Tamworth (A4091)
🏠 James Braid

Druids Heath (1974)

Stonnall Road, Aldridge, WS9 8JZ
☎ **(01922) 455595**
📠 (01922) 452887
📖 539 80(L) 50(J)
🏌 KI Taylor
⛳ G Williams (01922) 459523
🏴 18 L 6661 yds Par 72 SSS 73
👥 WD–U WE–NA before 2pm
    SOC–WD
💶 £30 (£38)
🚗 6 miles NW of Sutton Coldfield, off
    A452

Enville (1935)

Highgate Common, Enville, Stourbridge,
DY7 5BN
☎ **(01384) 872074**
📠 (01384) 873396
📧 secretary@envillegolfclub.com
📖 900
🏌 JJ Bishop (Sec/Mgr)
    (01384) 872074
⛳ S Power (01384) 872585
🏴 Highgate 18 L 6531 yds SSS 72;
    Lodge 18 L 6290 yds SSS 70
👥 WD–U WE/BH–M H SOC
💶 £30–£40
🚗 6 miles W of Stourbridge
⬛ www.envillegolfclub.com

Goldenhill (1983)

Public
Mobberley Road, Goldenhill, Stoke-on-
Trent, ST6 5SS
☎ **(01782) 784715**
📠 (01782) 775940
📖 600
🏌 P Jones
⛳ A Clingan
🏴 18 L 5957 yds SSS 68
👥 U SOC–book with Pro
💶 £6 (£7)
🚗 Between Tunstall and Kidsgrove,
    off A50

Great Barr (1961)

Chapel Lane, Birmingham, B43 7BA
☎ **(0121) 357 1232**
📖 600
🏌 Mrs HK Devey (0121) 358 4376
⛳ R Spragg (0121) 357 5270
🏴 18 L 6459 yds SSS 72
👥 WD–U WE–I (h'cap max 18) SOC
💶 £32
🚗 6 miles NW of Birmingham. M6
    Junction 7

Greenway Hall (1908)

Stockton Brook, Stoke-on-Trent, ST9 9LJ
☎ **(01782) 503158**
📧 jackbarker_greenwayhallgolfclub
    @hotmail.com
📖 300
🏌 M Armitage
⛳ M Armitage
🏴 18 L 5676 yds SSS 67
👥 U SOC
💶 £10 (£13.50)
🚗 5 miles N of Stoke, off A53
⬛ www.jackbarker.com

Handsworth (1895)

11 Sunningdale Close, Handsworth
Wood, Birmingham, B20 1NP
☎ **(0121) 554 3387**
📠 (0121) 554 6144
📧 info@handsworthgolfclub.net
📖 850
🏌 PS Hodnett (Hon)
⛳ L Bashford (0121) 523 3594
🏴 18 L 6267 yds SSS 70
👥 WD–U WE/BH–M SOC
💶 £35
🚗 3 miles NW of Birmingham. M5
    Junction 1. M6 Junction 7

Himley Hall (1980)

Pay and play
Himley Hall Park, Dudley, DY3 4DF
☎ **(01902) 895207**
📖 300
🏌 M Harris
⛳ J Nicholls (01902) 895207
🏴 9 L 3145 yds SSS 36
    9 hole short course
👥 WD–U WE/BH–restricted
💶 18 holes–£11. 9 holes–£7.50
🚗 Grounds of Himley Hall Park.
    B4176, off A449
🏠 A & K Baker

Ingestre Park (1977)

Ingestre, Stafford, ST18 0RE
☎ **(01889) 270061**
📠 (01889) 271434
📧 ipgc@lineone.net
📖 740
🏌 CJ Radmore (Mgr) (01889) 270845
⛳ D Scullion (01889) 270304
🏴 18 L 6352 yds SSS 71
👥 WD–H before 3.30pm WE/BH–M
    SOC–WD exc Wed
💶 £25 D–£30
🚗 6 miles E of Stafford, off Tixall
    Road. M6 Junctions 13/14
🏠 Hawtree

Izaak Walton

Cold Norton, Stone, ST15 0NS
☎ **(01785) 760900**
📖 425
🏌 TT Tyler
⛳ J Brown
🏴 18 L 6398 yds SSS 72
👥 U SOC
💶 £15 (£20)
🚗 7 miles NW of Stafford on B5026.
    M6 Junction 14
⊕ Driving range

Keele Golf Centre (1973)

Public
Keele Road, Newcastle-under-Lyme,
ST5 5AB
☎ **(01782) 717417**
📠 (01782) 712972
🏌 GA Bytheway
⛳ C Smith
🏴 18 L 5822 metres SSS 70
👥 U
💶 £6.50 (£8.40)
🚗 2 miles W of Newcastle on A525,
    opposite University. M6 Junction
    15
⊕ Floodlit driving range
🏠 Hawtree

Lakeside (1969)

Rugeley Power Station, Rugeley,
WS15 1PR
☎ **(01889) 575667**
📖 550
🏌 T Moore
🏴 18 L 5765 yds Par 71 SSS 69
👥 M
🚗 2 miles SE of Rugeley on A513

Leek (1892)

Big Birchall, Leek, ST13 5RE
☎ **(01538) 385889**
📠 (01538) 384535
📖 520 135(L) 65(J)
🏌 JB Cooper (01538) 384779
⛳ I Benson (01538) 384767
🏴 18 L 6218 yds SSS 70
👥 U H before 3pm –M after 3pm
    SOC–Wed only
💶 £26 (£32)
🚗 1 mile S of Leek on A520

Little Aston (1908)

Streetly, Sutton Coldfield, B74 3AN
☎ (0121) 353 2066
🖥 (0121) 580 8387
📖 250
🐦 G Ridley (Mgr) (0121) 353 2942
✒ (0121) 353 0330
🏌 18 L 6670 yds SSS 73
👫 H WE–by prior arrangement
   SOC–WD
££ £50 D–£60
⛳ 4 miles NW of Sutton Coldfield, off
   A454
🏠 Harry Vardon
■ www.littleastongolf.co.uk

Manor (Kingstone) (1991)

*Leese Hill, Kingstone, Uttoxeter,
ST14 8QT*
☎ (01889) 563234
🖥 (01889) 563234
📖 300
🐦 A Campbell
🏌 18 hole course
👫 U
££ £12 (£20)
⛳ 4 miles W of Uttoxeter on A518
🏠 E Anderson

Newcastle-under-Lyme (1908)

*Whitmore Road, Newcastle-under-Lyme,
ST5 2QB*
☎ (01782) 616583
🖥 (01782) 617531
📖 575
🐦 KP Geddes (Sec/Mgr)
   (01782) 617006
✒ P Symonds (01782) 618526
🏌 18 L 6317 yds SSS 71
👫 WD–U H WE/BH–M SOC
££ On application
⛳ 2 miles SW of Newcastle-under-
   Lyme on A53

Onneley (1968)

Onneley, Crewe, Cheshire, CW3 5QF
☎ (01782) 750577
📖 410
🐦 P Ball (01782) 846759
✒ None
🏌 13 L 5781 yds SSS 68
👫 WD–U Sat/BH–M Sun–NA
   SOC–Thurs
££ D–£20
⛳ 8 miles W of Newcastle, off A525
🏠 A Benson

Oxley Park (1913)

*Stafford Road, Bushbury,
Wolverhampton, WV10 6DE*
☎ (01902) 425892
🖥 (01902) 773981
✉ secretary@oxleyparkgolfclub.fsnet
   .co.uk
📖 550
🐦 RJ Wormstone (01902) 425892
✒ LA Burlison (01902) 425445
🏌 18 L 6226 yds SSS 71
👫 U SOC
££ £25 (£25)

Parkhall (1989)

Public
*Hulme Road, Weston Coyney, Stoke-on-
Trent, ST3 5BH*
☎ (01782) 599584
🐦 N Worrall (Mgr) (01831) 456409
✒ A Clingan
🏌 18 L 2335 yds Par 54
👫 WE–booking necessary SOC
££ On application
⛳ 3 miles E of Stoke. Longton 1 mile

Penn (1908)

*Penn Common, Wolverhampton,
WV4 5JN*
☎ (01902) 341142
🖥 (01902) 620504
✉ secretary@penn-
   golf.freeserve.co.uk
📖 650
🐦 MH Jones
✒ B Burlison (01902) 330472
🏌 18 L 6487 yds SSS 72
👫 WD–U WE–M SOC
££ £23. Nov–Feb £15
⛳ 2 miles SW of Wolverhampton, off
   A449

Perton Park (1990)

*Wrottesley Park Road, Perton,
Wolverhampton, WV6 7HL*
☎ (01902) 380103/380073
🖥 (01902) 326219
📖 300
🐦 E Greenway (Mgr)
✒ J Harrold (01902) 380073
🏌 18 L 6520 yds SSS 72
👫 U SOC
££ £12 (£18)
⛳ 6 miles W of Wolverhampton, off
   A454
⊕ Driving range

Sandwell Park (1895)

*Birmingham Road, West Bromwich,
B71 4JJ*
☎ (0121) 553 4637
🖥 (0121) 525 1651
✉ secretary@sandwellparkgolfclub
   .co.uk
📖 600
🐦 DA Paterson (0121) 553 4637
✒ N Wylie (0121) 553 4384
🏌 18 L 6468 yds SSS 73
👫 WD–U WE–MH SOC–WD
££ £30–£40
⛳ West Bromwich/Birmingham
   boundary. By M5 Junction 1
🏠 HS Colt
■ www.sandwellparkgolfclub.co.uk

Sedgley (1992)

Pay and play
*Sandyfields Road, Sedgley, Dudley,
DY3 3DL*
☎ (01902) 880503
✉ info@sedgleygolf.co.uk

📖 150
🐦 JA Cox
✒ G Mercer
🏌 9 L 3150 yds SSS 71
👫 U
££ 9 holes–£7. 18 holes–£9.50
⛳ ½ mile from Sedgley, off A463
   between Dudley and
   Wolverhampton
⊕ Driving range
🏠 WG Cox
■ www.sedgleygolf.co.uk

Seedy Mill (1991)

Pay and play
Elmhurst, Lichfield, WS13 8HE
☎ (01543) 417333
🖥 (01543) 418098
✉ k.denver@clubhaus.com
📖 1100
🐦 R Gee
✒ C Stanley
🏌 18 L 6305 yds SSS 70
   9 hole Par 3 course
👫 WD–U WE–U after 12 noon SOC
££ £23 (£28)
⛳ 2 miles N of Lichfield on A515
⊕ Floodlit driving range
🏠 Hawtree
■ www.clubhaus.com

South Staffordshire (1892)

*Danescourt Road, Tettenhall,
Wolverhampton, WV6 9BQ*
☎ (01902) 754406
🖥 (01902) 741753
✉ manager@ssgc.fsnet.co.uk
📖 550
🐦 WR Benton (Mgr) (01902) 751065
✒ M Sparrow (01902) 754816
🏌 18 L 6500 yds SSS 71
👫 WD–U WE/BH–M or by
   arrangement SOC
££ £36 D–£42 (£50)
⛳ 3 miles W of Wolverhampton, off
   A41
🏠 Harry Vardon

St Thomas's Priory (1995)

*Armitage Lane, Armitage, Rugeley,
WS15 1ED*
☎ (01543) 491116
🖥 (01543) 492244
📖 500
🐦 J Bissell
✒ RMR O'Hanlon (01543) 492096
🏌 18 L 5969 yds SSS 70
👫 H SOC–WD
££ £20 (£25)
⛳ 1 mile SE of Rugeley on A513, opp
   Ash Tree Inn
🏠 Paul Mulholland
■ www.st-thomass-golfclub.com

Stafford Castle (1906)

Newport Road, Stafford, ST16 1BP
☎ (01785) 223821
📖 440
🐦 Mrs S Calvert
🏌 9 L 638e yds Par 71 SSS 70
👫 WD–U WE–after 1pm
££ £16 (£20)
⛳ ½ mile W of Stafford

Stone   (1896)
The Fillybrooks, Stone, ST15 0NB
- ☎ **(01785) 813103**
- ✉ stonegolfc@onetel.net
- 📖 314
- 🏌 PR Farley (01785) 284875
- ⛳ 9 L 6299 yds Par 71 SSS 70
- 👥 WD–U WE/BH–M SOC–WD
- ££ £20
- 🚗 ¹/₂ mile W of Stone on A34

Swindon   (1976)
Bridgnorth Road, Swindon, Dudley, DY3 4PU
- ☎ **(01902) 897031**
- 📠 (01902) 326219
- ✉ golf@swindonperton.fsbusiness .co.uk
- 📖 500
- 🏌 E Greenway (Mgr)
- ✍ P Lester (01902) 896191
- ⛳ 18 L 6121 yds SSS 70
  9 hole Par 3 course
- 👥 U SOC–WD
- ££ £20 (£30)
- 🚗 5 miles SW of Wolverhampton on B4176
- ⊕ Driving range
- 🌐 www.swindongolfclub.co.uk

Tamworth   (1976)
Public
Eagle Drive, Amington, Tamworth, B77 4EG
- ☎ **(01827) 709303**
- 📠 (01827) 709304
- 📖 500
- ✍ W Allcock
- ⛳ 18 L 6695 yds SSS 72
- 👥 U SOC–WD
- ££ £13
- 🚗 2¹/₂ miles E of Tamworth on B5000. M42, 3 miles
- ⊕ Driving range

Trentham   (1894)
14 Barlaston Old Road, Trentham, Stoke-on-Trent, ST4 8HB
- ☎ **(01782) 642347**
- 📠 (01782) 644024
- ✉ secretary@trenthamgolf.org
- 📖 420
- 🏌 RN Portas (01782) 658109
- ✍ S Wilson (01782) 657309
- ⛳ 18 L 6644 yds SSS 72
- 👥 WD–U H WE/BH–M (or enquire Sec) SOC–WD
- ££ £40 (£50)
- 🚗 3 miles S of Newcastle-under-Lyme on A5305, off A34. M6 Junction 15
- 🌐 www.trenthamgolf.org

Trentham Park   (1936)
Trentham Park, Stoke-on-Trent, ST4 8AE
- ☎ **(01782) 642245**
- 📠 (01782) 658800
- ✉ trevor.berrisford@barbox.net
- 📖 500 100(L) 50(J)
- 🏌 T Berrisford (01782) 658800
- ✍ S Lynn (01782) 642125
- ⛳ 18 L 6425 yds SSS 71

- 👥 H SOC–Wed & Fri
- ££ £30 (£35)
- 🚗 4 miles S of Newcastle on A34. M6 Junction 15, 1 mile

Uttoxeter   (1970)
Wood Lane, Uttoxeter, ST14 8JR
- ☎ **(01889) 566552**
- 📠 (01889) 567501
- 📖 700
- 🏌 A Griffiths
- ✍ AD McCandless (01889) 564884
- ⛳ 18 L 5801 yds Par 70 SSS 69
- 👥 WD–U WE–by arrangement SOC
- ££ D–£22 (£30)
- 🚗 Close to A50, by Uttoxeter racecourse

Walsall   (1907)
Broadway, Walsall, WS1 3EY
- ☎ **(01922) 613512**
- 📠 (01922) 616460
- 📖 600
- 🏌 JK Harding (01922) 613512
- ✍ R Lambert (01922) 626766
- ⛳ 18 L 6259 yds SSS 71
- 👥 WD–U WE–M SOC
- ££ £33
- 🚗 1 mile S of Walsall, off A34. M6 Junction 7
- 🏗 McKenzie

Wergs   (1990)
Pay and play
Keepers Lane, Tettenhall, WV6 8UA
- ☎ **(01902) 742225**
- 📠 (01902) 744748
- 📖 150
- 🏌 Mrs G Parsons
- ✍ S Weir (07973) 899607
- ⛳ 18 L 6949 yds Par 72 SSS 73
- 👥 U
- ££ D–£15 (£20)
- 🚗 3 miles W of Wolverhampton on A41
- 🏗 CW Moseley

Westwood   (1923)
Newcastle Road, Wallbridge, Leek, ST13 7AA
- ☎ **(01538) 398385**
- 📠 (01538) 382485
- 📖 800
- 🏌 Ms C Povey
- ✍ D Squire
- ⛳ 18 L 6207 yds SSS 70
- 👥 U SOC–WD
- ££ WD–£20
- 🚗 W boundary of Leek on A53

Whiston Hall   (1971)
Whiston, Cheadle, ST10 2HZ
- ☎ **(01538) 266260**
- 📖 500
- 🏌 LC & RM Cliff (Mgr)
- ⛳ 18 L 5742 yds SSS 69
- 👥 U SOC
- ££ £10
- 🚗 8 miles NE of Stoke-on-Trent on A52, nr Alton Towers

Whittington Heath   (1886)
Tamworth Road, Lichfield, WS14 9PW
- ☎ **(01543) 432317 (Admin)**
  (01543) 432212 (Steward)
- 📠 (01543) 433962
- ✉ info@whgcgolf.freeserve.co.uk
- 📖 670
- 🏌 Mrs JA Burton
- ✍ AR Sadler (01543) 432261
- ⛳ 18 L 6490 yds SSS 71
- 👥 WD–H or I WE/BH–M SOC–Wed & Thurs
- ££ £35 D–£50
- 🚗 2¹/₂ miles E of Lichfield on Tamworth road (A51)

Wolstanton   (1904)
Dimsdale Old Hall, Hassam Parade, Wolstanton, Newcastle ST5 9DR
- ☎ **(01782) 616995**
- 📖 625
- 🏌 Mrs VJ Keenan (01782) 622413
- ✍ S Arnold (01782) 622718
- ⛳ 18 L 5533 yds SSS 68
- 👥 WD–H WE–M SOC–WD
- ££ £25
- 🚗 1¹/₂ miles NW of Newcastle (A34)

Suffolk

Aldeburgh   (1884)
Aldeburgh, IP15 5PE
- ☎ **(01728) 452890**
- 📠 (01728) 452937
- 📖 879
- 🏌 GM Gadney
- ✍ K Preston (01728) 453309
- ⛳ 18 L 6323 yds Par 68 SSS 71
  9 L 2114 yds SSS 64
- 👥 H–2 ball play only SOC
- ££ On application
- 🚗 6 miles E of A12 (A1094)
- 🏗 W Fernie/J Thompson
- 🌐 www.aldeburghgolfclub.co.uk

Beccles   (1899)
The Common, Beccles, NR34 9BX
- ☎ **(01502) 712244**
- 📖 150
- 🏌 DW Trunks (01502) 714616
- ⛳ 9 L 2696 yds SSS 67
- 👥 WD–U Sun–M SOC
- ££ £5 (£10)
- 🚗 10 miles W of Lowestoft (A146)

Brett Vale   (1992)
Noakes Road, Raydon, Ipswich, IP7 5LR
- ☎ **(01473) 310718**
- 📖 620
- 🏌 JS Reid
- ✍ P Bate, R Taylor
- ⛳ 18 L 5797 yds Par 70 SSS 67
- 👥 U–booking advisable. Soft spikes only. SOC–WD
- ££ £20 (£25)
- 🚗 5 miles N of Colchester, off A12 (B1070), towards Hadleigh
- ⊕ Driving range. 3 x 3 Par 3 holes
- 🏗 Howard Swan
- 🌐 www.brettvale.com

For list of abbreviations and key to symbols see page 627

Bungay & Waveney Valley
(1889)
Outney Common, Bungay, NR35 1DS
☎ **(01986) 892337**
🖥 (01986) 892222
📖 673
✍ JR Lunniss
✒ AR Collison
▷ 18 L 6044 yds Par 69 SSS 69
👥 WD–U WE–M SOC–WD
££ £24 D–£30
🚗 ¹/₂ mile W of Bungay, on N side of A143
🏠 James Braid

Bury St Edmunds   (1922)
Tut Hill, Bury St Edmunds, IP28 6LG
☎ **(01284) 755979**
🖥 (01284) 763288
📧 john@burygolf.co.uk
📖 750 180(L)
✍ JF Taylor
✒ M Jillings (01284) 755978
▷ 18 L 6675 yds Par 72 SSS 72
9 L 2217 yds Par 31 SSS 31
👥 WD/BH–U WE–M SOC–WD
££ 18: D–£30 9: £13 (£15.50)
🚗 2 miles W of Bury St Edmunds on B1106, off A14
🏠 Ted Ray
■ www.club-noticeboard.co.uk /burystedmunds

Cretingham   (1984)
Grove Farm, Cretingham, Woodbridge, IP13 7BA
☎ **(01728) 685275**
🖥 (01728) 685488
📖 400
✍ Mrs K Jackson
✒ N Jackson
▷ 18 L 4969 yds
9 L 4969 yds Par 33
9 hole short course
👥 U SOC
££ 18 holes–£14 (£16)
🚗 2 miles SE of Earl Soham. 11 miles N of Ipswich
⊕ Practice range
🏠 J Austin

Diss   (1903)
Stuston Common, Diss, IP21 4AA
☎ **(01379) 641025**
🖥 (01379) 644586
📧 sec.dissgolf@virgin.net
📖 750
✍ Chris Wellstead (01379) 641025
✒ Nigel Taylor (01379) 644399
▷ 18 L 6206 yds Par 70 SSS 69
👥 WD–UH WE–phone first SOC
££ £25 PR £30 PD
🚗 1 mile SE of Diss, off A140
⊕ Driving range 1 miles from clubhouse on A143/A140 junction
■ www.club-noticeboard.co.uk

Felixstowe Ferry   (1880)
Ferry Road, Felixstowe, ID11 9RY
☎ **(01394) 283060**
🖥 (01394) 273679

📧 secretary@felixstowegolf.co.uk
📖 1000
✍ R Tibbs (01394) 286834
✒ I Macpherson (01394) 283975
▷ 18 L 6308 yds SSS 70
9 L 2986 yds Par 35
👥 WD–H after 9am WE–H after 2.30pm SOC. 9 hole course–U
££ 18 hole: £25 (£35) day 9 hole: £19 (£15) day
🚗 2 miles NE of Felixstowe, towards Ferry
🏠 Henry Cotton (1947)
■ www.felixstowegolf.co.uk

Flempton   (1895)
Bury St Edmunds, IP28 6EQ
☎ **(01284) 728291**
📖 260
✍ MS Clark
✒ M Jillings
▷ 9 L 6240 yds Par 70 SSS 70
👥 WD–H WE/BH–M
££ D–£30 (£30)
🚗 4 miles NW of Bury St Edmunds on A1101
🏠 JH Taylor

Fynn Valley   (1991)
Proprietary
Witnesham, Ipswich, IP6 9JA
☎ **(01473) 785267**
🖥 (01473) 785632
📧 enquiries@fynn-valley.co.uk
📖 650
✍ AR Tyrrell (01473) 785267
✒ K Vince (01473) 785463
▷ 18 L 6361 yds Par 70 SSS 71
9 hole Par 3 course
👥 U exc Sun am SOC
££ £22 (£25)
🚗 2 miles N of Ipswich on B1077
⊕ Driving range; restaurant; conference facilities
🏠 Antonio Primavera
■ www.fynn-valley.co.uk

Halesworth   (1990)
Bramfield Road, Halesworth, IP19 9XA
☎ **(01986) 875567**
🖥 (01986) 874565
📖 400
✒ S Harrison
▷ 18 L 6506 yds SSS 72
9 L 2280 yds SSS 33
👥 U
££ 18: £18 D–£22 (£25) 9: £5
🚗 1 mile S of Halesworth, off A144
⊕ Floodlit driving range

Haverhill   (1974)
Coupals Road, Haverhill, CB9 7UW
☎ **(01440) 761951**
🖥 (01440) 761951
📧 haverhillgolf@coupalsroad.fsnet .co.uk
📖 700
✍ Mrs J Edwards, D Renyard (Mgr)
✒ N Duc (01440) 712628
▷ 18 L 5929 yds SSS 70
👥 U–phone Pro SOC–WD
££ £25 (£34)

🚗 1 mile E of Haverhill, off A1107
🏠 Lawrie/Pilgrem
■ www.club-noticeboard.co.uk

Hintlesham Hall   (1991)
Hintlesham, Ipswich, IP8 3NS
☎ **(01473) 652761**
🖥 (01473) 652750
📧 office@hintleshamhallgolfclub.com
📖 475
✍ I Procter (Mgr)
✒ A Spink
▷ 18 L 6638 yds SSS 72
👥 WD–U after 10.30am WE–NA SOC
££ £36 (£46)
🚗 4 miles W of Ipswich on A1071
🏠 Hawtree

Ipswich (Purdis Heath)
(1895)
Purdis Heath, Bucklesham Road, Ipswich, IP3 8UQ
☎ **(01473) 727474 (Steward)**
🖥 (01473) 715236
📖 740
✍ NM Ellice (01473) 728941
✒ SJ Whymark (01473) 724017
▷ 18 L 6435 yds Par 71 SSS 71
9 L 1930 yds Par 31
👥 18 hole: H SOC 9 hole: U
££ 18 hole: £40 (£45) 9 hole: £10 (£12.50)
🚗 3 miles E of Ipswich
🏠 James Braid
■ www.ipswichgolfclub.com

Links (Newmarket)   (1902)
Cambridge Road, Newmarket, CB8 0TG
☎ **(01638) 663000**
🖥 (01638) 661476
📧 secretary@linksgc.fsbusiness.co.uk
📖 750
✍ ML Hartley
✒ J Sharkey (01638) 662395
▷ 18 L 6424 yds SSS 72
👥 H exc Sun–M before 11.30am SOC
££ £24 D–£32 (£28 D–£36)
🚗 1 mile SW of Newmarket

Newton Green   (1907)
Newton Green, Sudbury, CO10 0QN
☎ **(01787) 377217**
🖥 (01787) 377549
📧 info@newtongreengolfclub.co.uk
📖 650
✍ R Baines (01787) 377217
✒ T Cooper (01787) 313215
▷ 18 L 5893 yds SSS 69
👥 WD–U WE SOC
££ £22
🚗 4 miles S of Sudbury on A134
■ www.newtongolfclub.co.uk

Rookery Park   (1891)
Beccles Road, Carlton Colville, Lowestoft, NR33 8HJ
☎ **(01502) 509190**
🖥 (01502) 509191

⌨ office@rookeryparkgolfclub.co.uk
🏛 1000
✍ T Atkinson
✓ M Elsworthy (01502) 515103
⮞ 18 L 6714 yds Par 72 SSS 72
   9 hole Par 3 course
👥 WD–U Sat/BH–after 11am
   Sun–NA SOC H
£€ £20 (£25)
🚗 3 miles W of Lowestoft (A146)
■ www.club-noticeboard.co.uk

Royal Worlington & Newmarket   (1893)
Golf Links Road, Worlington, Bury St Edmunds, IP28 8SD
☎ (01638) 712216 (Clubhouse)
🖳 (01638) 717787
🏛 325
✍ Sqn-Ldr KJ Weston
   (01638) 717787
✓ M Hawkins (01638) 715224
⮞ 9 L 6210 yds SSS 70
👥 I or H–phone first (2 ball or
   foursomes only) WE–NA
£€ D–£55. After 2pm–£40
🚗 6 miles NE of Newmarket, off A11
🏠 Tom Dunn

Rushmere   (1927)
Rushmere Heath, Ipswich, IP4 5QQ
☎ (01473) 725648
🖳 (01473) 273852
⌨ rushmeregolfclub@talk21.com
🏛 770
✍ RWG Tawell (01473) 725648
✓ NTJ McNeill (01473) 728076
⮞ 18 L 6262 yds SSS 70
👥 WD–H WE/BH–H after 2.30pm
£€ £30
🚗 3 miles E of Ipswich, off
   Woodbridge road (A1214)
🏠 David Williams (1999)
■ www.club-
   noticeboard.co.uk/rushmere

Seckford   (1991)
Seckford Hall Road, Great Bealings, Woodbridge, IP13 6NT
☎ (01394) 388000
🖳 (01394) 382818
⌨ info@seckfordgolf.co.uk
🏛 400
✍ N Gruntvig (Sec/Mgr)
✓ S Jay
⮞ 18 L 4936 yds Par 67 SSS 64
👥 U–booking necessary SOC WD
   WE after 12
£€ £20 (£30, £20, £15)
🚗 SW of Woodbridge, off A12
⊕ Driving range, practice green,
   practice bunker
■ www.seckfordgolf.co.uk

Southwold   (1884)
The Common, Southwold, IP18 6TB
☎ (01502) 723234
🏛 450
✍ PJ Obern (01502) 723248
✓ B Allen (01502) 723790
⮞ 9 L 6050 yds SSS 69

👥 U (subject to fixtures)
£€ £26 (£28)
🚗 35 miles NE of Ipswich

Stoke-by-Nayland   (1972)
Keepers Lane, Leavenheath, Colchester, CO6 4PZ
☎ (01206) 262836
🖳 (01206) 263356
⌨ info@golf-club.co.uk
🏛 1400
✍ PG Barfield (01206) 265815
✓ K Lovelock (01206) 262769
⮞ Gainsborough 18 L 6498 yds
   SSS 71
   Constable 18 L 6544 yds SSS 71
👥 WD–U WE/BH–H after 10am SOC
£€ £25 (£35)
🚗 Off A134 Colchester-Sudbury road
   on B1068
⊕ Driving range
■ www.stokebynaylandclub.co.uk

Stowmarket   (1962)
Lower Road, Onehouse, Stowmarket, IP14 3DA
☎ (01449) 736473
🖳 (01449) 736826
🏛 600
✍ GR West (01449) 736473
✓ D Burl
⮞ 18 L 6119 yds SSS 69
👥 H SOC–Thurs & Fri
£€ £31 (£37)
🚗 2¹/₂ miles SW of Stowmarket
⊕ Driving range
■ www.club-noticeboard.co.uk
   /stowmarket

The Suffolk G&CC   (1974)
Fornham St Genevieve, Bury St Edmunds, IP28 6JQ
☎ (01284) 706777
🖳 (01284) 706721
⌨ the-lodge@the-suffolk.co.uk
🏛 652
✍ P Thorpe
✓ S Hall
⮞ 18 L 6376 yds SSS 71
👥 U SOC
£€ £25 (£30)
🚗 2 miles NW of Bury St Edmunds,
   off B1106
■ www.the-suffolk.co.uk

Thorpeness Hotel   (1923)
Thorpeness, Leiston, IP16 4NH
☎ (01728) 452176
🖳 (01728) 453868
🏛 520
✍ Charlie Damonsing (01728) 452176
✓ (01728) 454926
⮞ 18 L 6281 yds SSS 71
👥 H
£€ £33 (£38)
🚗 2 miles N of Aldeburgh
🏠 James Braid
■ www.thorpeness.co.uk

Ufford Park Hotel   (1992)
Yarmouth Road, Ufford, Woodbridge, IP12 1QW
☎ (01394) 382836
🖳 (01394) 383582
🏛 350
✍ B Tidy
✓ S Robertson
⮞ 18 L 6485 yds SSS 71
👥 U H SOC
£€ £25 (£30)
🚗 2 miles N of Woodbridge, off A12
⊕ Golf Academy
🏠 P Pilgrim
■ www.uffordpark.co.uk

Waldringfield   (1983)
Newbourne Road, Waldringfield, Woodbridge, IP12 4PT
☎ (01473) 736768
🖳 (01473) 736793
🏛 520
✍ Pat Witham
✓ Rex Osman (Golf Mgr)
   (01473) 736417
⮞ 18 L 6141 yds SSS 69
👥 WD–U WE/BH–M before noon
   SOC–WD
£€ £22 (£26)
🚗 3 miles E of Ipswich, off A12
🏠 P Pilgrem

Woodbridge   (1893)
Bromeswell Heath, Woodbridge, IP12 2PF
☎ (01394) 382038
🖳 (01394) 382392
⌨ woodbridgegc@anglianet.co.uk
🏛 925
✍ A Theunissen
✓ C Elliott (01394) 383213
⮞ 18 L 6299 yds SSS 70
   9 L 6382 yds SSS 70
👥 WD–H WE/BH–M SOC
£€ 18 hole: £40. 9 hole: £18
🚗 2 miles E of Woodbridge on A1152
   towards Orford
🏠 F Hawtree

Surrey

Abbey Moor   (1991)
Pay and play
Green Lane, Addlestone, KT15 2XU
☎ (01932) 570741/570765
🏛 300
✍ T Stannard (01932) 561313
✓ P Trigwell (01932) 570741
⮞ 9 L 5277 yds Par 68
👥 U
£€ £9.50 (£11)
🚗 Nr M25 Junction 11, off A318
🏠 D Walker

The Addington   (1913)
205 Shirley Church Road, Croydon, CR0 5AB
☎ (020) 8777 1055
🖳 (020) 8777 1701

✉ theaddgc@dialstart.net
🖊 RAR Hill
▷ 18 L 6338 yds SSS 71
👥 H SOC–WD
££ £55 (£80)
🚗 E Croydon 2¹/₂ miles
🏠 JF Abercromby

Addington Court (1931)

Pay and play
*Featherbed Lane, Addington, Croydon,
CR0 9AA*
☎ (020) 8657 0281 (Bookings)
📠 (020) 8651 0282
✉ addington@americangolf.uk.com
📖 600
🖊 T O'Keefe (020) 8651 5270
✍ T O'Keefe (020) 8657 0281
▷ Championship 18 L 5577 yds
   SSS 67
   Falconwood 18 L 5472 yds SSS 67
   9 L 1804 yds SSS 62
   18 hole pitch & putt course
👥 U SOC
££ Championship £16.35 (£19.60)
   Falconwood £14.35 (£17.60)
   9 hole: £9 (£10)
🚗 3 miles SE of Croydon
⊕ Driving range
🏠 F Hawtree Sr

Addington Palace (1923)

*Addington Park, Gravel Hill, Addington,
CR0 5BB*
☎ (020) 8654 3061
📠 (020) 8655 3632
📖 700
🖊 DMG Monk
✍ R Williams (020) 8654 1786
▷ 18 L 6410 yds SSS 71
👥 WD–H WE/BH–M
££ £35 D–£40
🚗 2 miles E of Croydon Station

Banstead Downs (1890)

*Burdon Lane, Belmont, Sutton,
SM2 7DD*
☎ (020) 8642 2284
📠 (020) 8642 5252
📖 700
🖊 G Oatham (Mgr)
✍ I Golding (020) 8642 6884
▷ 18 L 6194 yds SSS 69
👥 WD–H WE/BH–M SOC–Thurs
££ £35 After 12 noon–£25
🚗 6 miles north of M25 J8

Barrow Hills (1970)

Longcross, Chertsey, KT16 0DS
☎ (01344) 635770
📖 230
🖊 R Hammond (01483) 234807
▷ 18 L 3090 yds SSS 53
👥 M
££ On application
🚗 4 miles W of Chertsey

Betchworth Park (1911)

Reigate Road, Dorking, RH4 1NZ
☎ (01306) 882052
📠 (01306) 877462

✉ manager@betchworthparkgc.co.uk
📖 725
🖊 J Holton (Mgr)
✍ A Tocher (01306) 884334
▷ 18 L 6266 yds SSS 70
👥 WD–by arrangement exc Tues &
   Wed am WE–NA exc Sun pm
   SOC–Mon & Thurs
££ £34 (£45)
🚗 1 mile E of Dorking on A25
🏠 HS Colt

Bletchingley (1993)

Proprietary
Church Lane, Bletchingley, RH1 4LP
☎ (01883) 744666
📠 (01883) 744284
📖 500
🖊 R Borer (Mgr)
✍ A Dyer (01883) 744848
▷ 18 L 6504 yds Par 72 SSS 71
👥 WD–U WE–M before 2.15pm SOC
££ £28 (£38)
🚗 1 mile S of M25 Junction 6 on A25
🏠 Paul Wright
⬛ www.bletchingleygolf.co.uk

Bowenhurst Golf Centre

*Mill Lane, Crondall, Farnham,
GU10 5RP*
☎ (01252) 851695
📠 (01252) 852039
📖 202
🖊 GL Corbey (01252) 851695
✍ Geoff Lee (01252) 851344
▷ 9 L 2007 yds Par 62 SSS 60
👥 U SOC
££ 18 holes–£11 (£14). 9 holes–£8
   (£9.50)
🚗 2 miles SW of Farnham on A287.
   M3 Junction 5
⊕ Driving range
🏠 G Finn, N Finn

Bramley (1913)

Bramley, Guildford, GU5 0AL
☎ (01483) 892696
📠 (01483) 894673
✉ secretary@bramleygolfclub.co.uk
📖 900
🖊 Gary Peddie (Gen Mgr)
   (01483) 892696
✍ G Peddie (01483) 893685
▷ 18 L 5990 yds SSS 69
👥 WD–U WE–M SOC–WD
££ £35 D–£40
🚗 3 miles S of Guildford on A281
⊕ Driving range – members and green
   fees only
🏠 Mayo/Braid

Broadwater Park

*Guildford Road, Farncombe,
Godalming, GU7 3BU*
☎ (01483) 429955
📖 126
🖊 MJ Winwright (Dir)
✍ KD Milton
▷ 9 L 1301 yds Par 27
👥 U
££ £5.25 (£6)
🚗 1 mile SE of Godalming (A3100)
🏠 KD Milton

Burhill (1907)

*Burwood Road, Walton-on-Thames,
KT12 4BL*
☎ (01932) 227345
📠 (01932) 267159
📖 1100
🖊 D Cook (Gen Mgr)
✍ L Johnson (01932) 221729
▷ Old 18 L 6479 yds SSS 71
   New 18 L 6597 yds SSS 71
👥 WD–H WE/BH–M
££ On application
🚗 Between Walton-on-Thames and
   Cobham, off Burwood Road
⊕ Game Improvement Centre
🏠 Willie Park/Gidman

Camberley Heath (1912)

Golf Drive, Camberley, GU15 1JG
☎ (01276) 23258
📠 (01276) 692505
📖 725
🖊 M Harris
✍ G Ralph (01276) 27905
▷ 18 L 6326 yds SSS 71
👥 WD–H WE–M SOC H
££ £52 (£68)
🚗 1¹/₂ miles S of Camberley on A325
⊕ Driving range
🏠 HS Colt

Central London Golf Centre (1992)

Public
*Burntwood Lane, Wandsworth, London,
SW17 0AT*
☎ (020) 8871 2468
📠 (020) 8874 7447
📖 200
🖊 J Robson
✍ J Robson
▷ 9 L 4658 yds SSS 62
👥 U SOC
££ £9 (£11)
🚗 Off Burntwood Lane SW17
⊕ Driving range
🏠 Patrick Tallack
⬛ www.clgc.co.uk

Chessington Golf Centre (1983)

Pay and play
Garrison Lane, Chessington KT9 2LW
☎ (020) 8391 0948
📠 (020) 8397 2068
✉ info@chessingtongolf.co.uk
📖 85
🖊 M Bedford
✍ M Janes
▷ 9 L 1679 yds Par 60 SSS 55
👥 U
££ £8.50 (£10)
🚗 Off A243, opp Chessington South
   Station. M25 Junction 9
⊕ Driving range

Chiddingfold (1994)

Petworth Road, Chiddingfold, GU8 4SL
☎ (01428) 685888
📠 (01428) 685939

⊞ · 400
✍ Miss C Mentz (Gen Mgr)
✓ G Wallis ⟍
▷ 18 L 5482 yds Par 70 SSS 67
⚅ U SOC
££ £16 (£22)
⊕ On A283 between Petworth and Guildford
⌂ Johnathan Gaunt

Chipstead (1906)
How Lane, Chipstead, Coulsdon, CR5 3LN
☎ (01737) 555781
⌨ (01737) 555404
✉ office@chipsteadgolf.co.uk
⊞ 600
✍ Mrs SA Wallace (Admin) (01737) 555781
✓ G Torbett (Golf Dir) (01737) 554939
▷ 18 L 5450 yds SSS 67
⚅ WD–U WE/BH–M
££ £30. After 4pm–£20
⊕ M25 Junction 8 (A217)
■ www.chipsteadgolf.co.uk

Chobham (1994)
Chobham Road, Knaphill, Woking, GU21 2TZ
☎ (01276) 855584
⌨ (01276) 855663
⊞ 750
✍ T Pond (Gen Mgr)
✓ T Coombes (01276) 855748
▷ 18 L 5959 yds Par 69 SSS 69
⚅ M H–restricted SOC
££ £36
⊕ 3 miles E of M3 Junction 3 between Chobham and Knaphill (A3046)
⌂ Alliss/Clark
■ www.chobhamgolfclub.co.uk

Clandon Regis (1994)
Epsom Road, West Clandon, GU4 7TT
☎ (01483) 224888
⌨ (01483) 211781
✉ office@clandonregis-golfclub.co.uk
⊞ 650
✍ Paul Napier (Gen Mgr)
✓ S Lloyd (01483) 223922
▷ 18 L 6419 yds Par 72 SSS 71
⚅ WD–U WE–NA before 10.30am SOC–WD
££ £30 (£40)
⊕ 3 miles E of Guildford on A246
⌂ David Williams
■ www.clandonregis-golfclub.co.uk

Coombe Hill (1911)
Golf Club Drive, Coombe Lane West, Kingston, KT2 7DF
☎ (020) 8336 7600
⌨ (020) 8336 7601
⊞ 544
✍ Mrs C De Foy
✓ C De Foy (020) 8949 3713
▷ 18 L 6293 yds SSS 71
⚅ WD–I or H WE–NA SOC
££ £80 D–£100
⊕ 1 mile W of New Malden on A238
⌂ JF Abercromby
■ www.coombehillgolfclub.com

Coombe Wood (1904)
George Road, Kingston Hill, Kingston-upon-Thames, KT2 7NS
☎ (020) 8942 3828 (Clubhouse)
⌨ (020) 8942 0388
✉ cwoodgc@ukonline.co.uk
⊞ 600
✍ MT Newley (020) 8942 0388
✓ P Wright (020) 8942 6764
▷ 18 L 5299 yds SSS 66
⚅ WD–U WE–NA before 3pm SOC–WD
££ £28 (£36)
⊕ 1 mile E of Kingston-upon-Thames, off A3 at Robin Hood roundabout or Coombe junction
⌂ Williamson
■ www.combewoodgolf.com

Coulsdon Manor (1937)
Pay and play
Coulsdon Court Road, Old Coulsdon, Croydon, CR5 2LL
☎ (020) 8660 6083
⌨ (020) 8668 3118
✓ James Leaver (020) 8660 6083
▷ 18 L 6037 yds SSS 70
⚅ U
££ £15.95 (£19.95)
⊕ 5 miles S of Croydon on B2030. M25 Junction 7
⌂ HS Colt
■ www.marstonhotels.com

The Cranleigh (1985)
Barhatch Lane, Cranleigh, GU6 7NG
☎ (01483) 268855
⌨ (01483) 267251
⊞ 650
✍ MG Kateley
✓ T Longmuir (01483) 277188
▷ 18 L 5648 yds SSS 67
⚅ WD–U WE/BH–pm only SOC–WD
££ £24 (£26)
⊕ 1 mile from Cranleigh, off A281
⊕ Driving range

Croham Hurst (1911)
Croham Road, South Croydon, CR2 7HJ
☎ (020) 8657 5581
⌨ (020) 8657 3229
✉ secretary@chgc.co.uk
⊞ 515 110(L) 50(J)
✍ DS Free
✓ M Pagett (020) 8657 7705
▷ 18 L 6290 yds SSS 70
⚅ WD–I WE/BH–M
££ £40 (£50)
⊕ 1 mile from S Croydon. M25 Junction 6-A22-B270-B269
⌂ Braid/Hawtree
■ www.chgc.co.uk

Cuddington (1929)
Banstead Road, Banstead, SM7 1RD
☎ (020) 8393 0951
⌨ (020) 8786 7025
✉ ds@cuddingtongc.com
⊞ 760
✍ DM Scott (020) 8393 0952

✓ M Warner (020) 8393 5850
▷ 18 L 6614 yds SSS 71
⚅ WD–I WE–M
££ £45 (£55)
⊕ Nr Banstead Station
⌂ HS Colt
■ www.cuddingtongc.com

Dorking (1897)
Deepdene Avenue, Chart Park, Dorking, RH5 4BX
☎ (01306) 886917
⌨ (01306) 886917
⊞ 360
✍ A Smeal (Mgr)
✓ A Smeal
▷ 9 L 5163 yds SSS 65
⚅ WD–U WE/BH–M SOC–WD
££ £15
⊕ 1 mile S of Dorking on A24
⌂ James Braid

Drift (1976)
The Drift, East Horsley, KT24 5HD
☎ (01483) 284641
⌨ (01483) 284642
✉ info@driftgolfclub.com
⊞ 700
✍ L Greasley (Sec/Mgr)
✓ M Smith (01483) 284772
▷ 18 L 6425 yds SSS 72
⚅ WD–U WE–U after 12.00 SOC
££ £30 (£45)
⊕ 2 miles off A3 (B2039). M25 Junction 10
⊕ Driving range
⌂ Sir Henry Cotton & Robert Sandow
■ www.driftgolfclub.com

Dulwich & Sydenham Hill (1894)
Grange Lane, College Road, London, SE21 7LH
☎ (020) 8693 3961
⌨ (020) 8693 2481
✉ secretary@dulwichgolf.co.uk
⊞ 850
✍ BW O'Farrell
✓ D Baillie (020) 8693 8491
▷ 18 L 6051 yds SSS 69
⚅ WD–H WE/BH–M SOC
££ £30

Dunsfold Aerodrome (1965)
Dunsfold Aerodrome, Godalming, GU8 4BS
☎ (01483) 265403
⌨ (01483) 265670
⊞ 270
✍ F Tuck
✓ None
▷ 9 L 6236 yds Par 72 SSS 70
⚅ M
££ £6 (£6)
⊕ 10 miles S of Guildford, off A281
⌂ Sharkey/Hayward

Effingham (1927)
Guildford Road, Effingham, KT24 5PZ
☎ (01372) 452203

⌨ (01372) 459959
✉ secretary@effinghamgolfclub.com
📖 980
✎ Simon Sheppard
✓ Steve Hoatson (01372) 452606
▷ 18 L 6524 yds SSS 71
♔ WD–H WE/BH–M
££ £35 – £50
⚙ 8 miles E of Guildford on A246.
M25 Junctions 9 or 10
⊕ Practice facilities available
⌂ HS Colt
■ www.effinghamgolfclub.com

Epsom (1889)
Longdown Lane South, Epsom Downs, Epsom, KT17 4JR
☎ **(01372) 721666**
⌨ (01372) 817183
📖 800
✎ LR Anderson
✓ R Goudie (01372) 741867
▷ 18 L 5658 yds SSS 68
♔ WD–U exc Tues am WE/BH–NA before noon SOC
££ £29 (£32)
⚙ ¾ mile NE of Epsom Racecourse

Farleigh Court (1997)
Proprietary
Old Farleigh Road, Farleigh, CR6 9PX
☎ **(01883) 627733 (Bookings)**
⌨ (01883) 627722
✎ C Dryden (Mgr) (01883) 627711
✓ S Graham (01883) 627733
▷ 18 hole course Par 72 SSS 71
9 hole course par 36
♔ WD–U after 10am WE–U after 12 noon
££ 18 hole: £30 (£40) 9 hole: £14 (£17)
⚙ 5 miles SE of Croydon. M25 Junction 6
⊕ Driving range
⌂ John Jacobs

Farnham (1896)
The Sands, Farnham, GU10 1PX
☎ **(01252) 783163**
⌨ (01252) 781185
✉ info@farnhamgolfclub.com
📖 750
✎ Judy Elliott (01252) 782109
✓ G Cowlishaw (01252) 782198
▷ 18 L 6447 yds SSS 71
♔ WD–H WE–M
SOC–Wed/Thurs/Fri
££ £40 D–£45
⚙ 1 mile E of Farnham, off A31

Farnham Park Par Three (1966)
Pay and play
Farnham Park, Farnham, GU9 0AU
☎ **(01252) 715216**
⌨ (01252) 718246
📖 75
✎ A Curtis
✓ A Curtis
▷ 9 L 1163 yds Par 54
♔ U
££ £4.50 (£5)

⚙ By Farnham Castle
⌂ Henry Cotton

Foxhills (1975)
Stonehill Road, Ottershaw, KT16 0EL
☎ **(01932) 872050**
⌨ (01932) 874762
📖 975
✎ A Laking (Mgr)
✓ E Summerscales (01932) 873961
▷ 18 L 6680 yds SSS 73
18 L 6547 yds SSS 72
9 hole course
♔ WD–U WE–NA before noon SOC–WD am
££ £60 D–£80 (£70)
⚙ 2 miles SW of Chertsey on B386
⊕ Driving range
⌂ FW Hawtree
■ www.foxhills.co.uk

Gatton Manor Hotel G&CC (1969)
Standon Lane, Ockley, Dorking, RH5 5PQ
☎ **(01306) 627555**
⌨ (01306) 627713
✉ gattonmanor@enterprise.net
📖 250
✎ LC Heath
✓ R Sargent (01306) 627557
▷ 18 L 6653 yds SSS 72
♔ U exc Sun before 1 pm–NA SOC–WD
££ £23 (£30)
⚙ 1½ miles SW of Ockley, off A29. M25 Junction 9, S on A24
⊕ Driving range
⌂ Henry Cotton
■ www.gattonmanor.co.uk

Goal Farm Par Three
Proprietary
Gole Road, Pirbright, GU24 0PZ
☎ **(01483) 473183/473205**
✎ GJ Williams
▷ 9 hole Par 3 course
♔ Sat/Thurs am–restricted SOC–WD
££ £4.90 (£5.20)
⚙ 7 miles NW of Guildford

Guildford (1886)
High Path Road, Merrow, Guildford, GU1 2HL
☎ **(01483) 563941**
⌨ (01483) 453228
📖 600
✎ BJ Green
✓ PG Hollington (01483) 566765
▷ 18 L 6090 yds SSS 70
♔ WD–U WE–M SOC–WD
££ £35
⚙ 2 miles E of Guildford on A246
⌂ Taylor/Hawtree

Hampton Court Palace (1895)
Hampton Wick, Kingston-upon-Thames, KT1 4AD
☎ **(020) 8977 2423**

⌨ (020) 8977 5938
📖 650
✓ A Smith (020) 8977 2658
▷ 18 L 6513 yds SSS 71
♔ WD–U WE–U after 2.30pm
££ Mon–Thur £30 Fri £40 (£50)
⚙ 1 mile W of Kingston
⌂ Willie Park

Hankley Common (1896)
Tilford, Farnham, GU10 2DD
☎ **(01252) 792493**
⌨ (01252) 795699
📖 700
✎ JSW Scott
✓ P Stow (01252) 793761
▷ 18 L 6438 yds SSS 71
♔ WD–U WE–H at discretion of Sec SOC
££ £55 (£70)
⚙ 3 miles SE of Farnham on Tilford road
■ www.hankley.co.uk

Hazelwood Golf Centre
Pay and play
Croysdale Avenue, Green Street, Sunbury-on-Thames, TW16 6QU
☎ **(01932) 770932**
⌨ (01932) 770933
📖 94
✎ P Framrose
✓ F Sheridan (01932) 770932
▷ 9 L 5660 yds Par 35 SSS 67
♔ U SOC
££ £7.50 (£9.50)
⚙ M3 Junction 1, 1 mile
⊕ Driving range. Golf academy
⌂ Jonathan Gaunt

Hersham Village
Assher Road, Hersham, Walton-on-Thames, KT12 4RA
☎ **(01932) 267666**
⌨ (01932) 240975
✎ R Hutton (Golf Dir)
✓ R Hutton
▷ 9 L 3097 yds Par 36
♔ U
££ 18 holes–£15
⚙ 5 miles N of M25 Junction 10 (B365)
⊕ Floodlit driving range

The Hindhead (1904)
Churt Road, Hindhead, GU26 6HX
☎ **(01428) 604614**
⌨ (01428) 608508
✉ secretary@the-hindhead-golf-club .co.uk
📖 500 76(L) 81(J)
✎ JA Davies
✓ I Benson (01428) 604458
▷ 18 L 6356 yds SSS 70
♔ WD–U WE–by arrangement H SOC–Wed & Thurs
££ £40 (£50)
⚙ 1½ miles N of A3 on A287. M25 Junction 10, 25 miles

For list of abbreviations and key to symbols see page 627

Hoebridge Golf Centre
(1982)

Public
Old Woking Road, Old Woking,
GU22 8JH
☎ **(01483) 722611**
📠 (01483) 740369
🏠 480
♠ P Dawson (Mgr)
/ TD Powell
ᐟ 18 L 6587 yds SSS 71
Inter 9 L 2294 yds Par 33
18 hole Par 3 course
👥 U SOC–WD
££ 18 hole: £18.75 (£24.75) Inter: £10.
Par 3: £8
♠♠ Between Old Woking and West
Byfleet on B382
⊕ Floodlit driving range
🏠 Jacobs/Hawtree
■ www.hoebridge.co.uk

Horne Park
Croydon Barn Lane, Horne, South
Godstone, RH9 8JP
☎ **(01342) 844443**
📠 (01342) 841828
🖂 hornepark@pncl.co.uk
🏠 360
♠ Derek Shield
/ Neil Burke (01342) 844715
ᐟ 9 L 2718 yds Par 34
👥 U
££ 9 holes–£9.50 (£10.50)
♠♠ Off A22. M25 Junction 6
⊕ Driving range
🏠 Howard Swann
■ www.horneparkgolf.co.uk

Horton Park G&CC   (1987)

Pay and play
Hook Road, Epsom, KT19 8QG
☎ **(020) 8393 8400 (Enquiries),**
(020) 8394 2626 (Bookings)
📠 (020) 8394 1369
🖂 hortonparkgc@aol.com
🏠 450
/ M Hirst (020) 8394 2626
ᐟ 18 L 5728 yds SSS 70
9 L 3274 yds Par 60
👥 U SOC
££ £16 (£18)
♠♠ 1 mile from A3, W of Epsom. M25
Junction 9
⊕ Driving range
🏠 P Nicholson

Hurtmore   (1992)

Pay and play
Hurtmore Road, Hurtmore, Godalming,
GU7 2RN
☎ **(01483) 426492**
📠 (01483) 426121
🏠 200
♠ Maxine Burton (01483) 426492
/ Maxine Burton (01483) 424440
ᐟ 18 L 5530 yds Par 70 SSS 67
👥 U SOC
££ £12.50 (£18)
♠♠ 6 miles S of Guildford on A3. M25
Junction 10

⊕ Practice nets and putting green
🏠 Alliss/Clark

Kingswood   (1928)
Sandy Lane, Kingswood, Tadworth,
KT20 6NE
☎ **(01737) 833316**
📠 (01737) 833920
🏠 770
♠ L Andrews (Admin)
(01737) 832188
/ T Sims (01737) 832334
ᐟ 18 L 6904 yds SSS 73
👥 U SOC
££ £40 (£55)
♠♠ 5 miles S of Sutton on A217. M25
Junction 8, 2 miles
⊕ Driving range
🏠 James Braid

Laleham   (1903)
Laleham Reach, Chertsey KT16 8RP
☎ **(01932) 564211**
📠 (01932) 564448
🖂 sec@laleham-golf.co.uk
🏠 600
♠ Mrs PA Kennett
/ H Stott (01932) 562877
ᐟ 18 L 6203 yds SSS 70
👥 WD–U 9.30–4.30pm WE–M
SOC–Mon–Wed
££ £25 – £30
♠♠ 2 miles S of Staines, opp Thorpe
Park
■ www.laleham-golf.co.uk

Leatherhead   (1903)
Proprietary
Kingston Road, Leatherhead, KT22 0EE
☎ **(01372) 843966**
📠 (01372) 842241
🖂 secretary@lgc-golf.co.uk
🏠 600
♠ A Norman (01372) 843966
/ S Norman (01372) 843956
ᐟ 18 L 6203 yds Par 71 SSS 70
👥 WD–U WE–NA before 2pm SOC
££ £37.50 (£47.50)
♠♠ On A243 to Chessington. M25
Junction 9
■ www.lgc-golf.co.uk

Limpsfield Chart   (1889)
Westerham Road, Limpsfield, RH8 0SL
☎ **(01883) 723405/722106**
🏠 300
♠ MA Baker
/ None
ᐟ 9 L 5718 yds SSS 68
👥 WD–U exc Thurs (Ladies Day)
WE–M or by appointment SOC
££ £20 (£22)
♠♠ 1 mile E of Oxted on A25

Lingfield Park   (1987)
Racecourse Road, Lingfield, RH7 6PQ
☎ **(01342) 834602**
📠 (01342) 836077
🖂 cmorley@lingfieldpark.co.uk
🏠 700
♠ C Morley

/ C Morley (01342) 832659
ᐟ 18 L 6500 yds SSS 72
👥 WD–U WE/BH–M SOC–WD
££ £40 (£50)
♠♠ Next to Lingfield racecourse. M25
Junction 6
⊕ Driving range

London Scottish   (1865)
Windmill Enclosure, Wimbledon
Common, London, SW19 5NQ
☎ **(020) 8788 0135**
📠 (020) 8789 7517
🖂 secretary.lsgc@virgin.net
🏠 250
♠ S Barr (020) 8789 7517
/ S Barr (020) 8789 1207
ᐟ 18 L 5458 yds Par 68 SSS 66
👥 WD–U WE/BH–NA SOC
££ £15 Mon–£10
♠♠ Wimbledon Common
⊕ Red upper garment must be worn
🏠 Willie Dunn/Tom Dunn

Malden   (1893)
Traps Lane, New Malden, KT3 4RS
☎ **(020) 8942 0654**
📠 (020) 8336 2219
🖂 maldengolfclub@lwcdial.net
🏠 800
♠ Mrs A Besant (Mgr)
/ R Hunter (Golf Mgr) (020) 8942
6009
ᐟ 18 L 6295 yds SSS 70
👥 WD–U WE–restricted
SOC–Wed–Fri
££ On application
♠♠ Off A3, between Wimbledon and
Kingston
■ www.maldengolfclub.com

Merrist Wood   (1997)
Coombe Lane, Worplesdon, Guildford,
GU3 3PE
☎ **(01483) 238890**
📠 (01483) 238896
🏠 700
♠ P Flavin
/ C Connell (01483) 238894
ᐟ 18 L 6575 yds Par 72 SSS 71
👥 H–soft spikes only SOC
££ £30 D–£45
♠♠ 2 miles W of Guildford, off A323
⊕ Driving range
🏠 David Williams
■ www.merristwood-golfclub.co.uk

Milford
Proprietary
Station Lane, Milford, GU8 5HS
☎ **(01483) 419200**
📠 (01483) 419199
🖂 milford@americangolf.uk.com
🏠 750
♠ R Griffiths (Mgr)
/ P Creamer (01483) 416291
ᐟ 18 L 5960 yds Par 69 SSS 68
👥 WD–U WE–after 12 noon SOC
££ £25 (£30)
♠♠ 3 miles SW of Guildford, off A3
🏠 Alliss/Clark

Mitcham (1924)

Carshalton Road, Mitcham Junction,
CR4 4HN
☎ **(020) 8648 1508,**
   (020) 8640 4280 (Bookings)
📠 (020) 8648 4197
📖 500
🏌 WJ Dutch (020) 8648 4197
🏌 JA Godfrey (020) 8640 4280
🏴 18 L 5931 yds SSS 68
👥 WD–U WE–NA before 1.30pm
   SOC
£€ £18 (£20)
🚃 Mitcham Junction Station

Moore Place (1926)

Public
Portsmouth Road, Esher, KT10 9LN
☎ **(01372) 463533**
📠 (01372) 463533
📖 80
🏌 J Darby (01931) 880186
🏌 N Gadd
🏴 9 L 2078 yds SSS 61
👥 U
£€ £7 (£9)
🚗 Centre of Esher
🏚 D Allen
■ www.moore-place.co.uk

New Zealand (1895)

Woodham Lane, Addlestone, KT15 3QD
☎ **(01932) 345049**
📠 (01932) 342891
✉ roger.marrett@nzgc.org
📖 300
🏌 RA Marrett (01932) 342891
🏌 VR Elvidge (01932) 349619
🏴 18 L 6075 yds SSS 69
👥 By request
£€ On application
🚗 Woking 3 miles. West Byfleet 1
   mile. Weybridge 5 miles
🏚 Simpson/Fergusson

North Downs (1899)

Northdown Road, Woldingham,
Caterham, CR3 7AA
☎ **(01883) 652057**
📠 (01883) 652832
✉ info@northdownsgolfclub.co.uk
📖 550
🏌 DM Sinden (Sec/Mgr)
   (01883) 652057
🏌 MJ Homewood (01883) 653004
🏴 18 L 5857 yds Par 69 SSS 68
👥 WD–U WE–NA before 3pm
   (summer), 12 noon (winter)
   SOC–WD
£€ £30 (£25)
🚗 3 miles E of Caterham. M25
   Junction 6
🏚 JF Pennink
■ www.northdownsgolfclub.co.uk

Oak Park (1984)

Heath Lane, Crondall, Farnham,
GU10 5PB
☎ **(01252) 850850**
📠 (01252) 850851
📖 550

🏌 D Maskery
🏌 (01252) 850066
🏴 Woodland 18 L 6352 yds Par 70
   SSS 70;
   Village 9 L 3279 yds Par 36
👥 U SOC
£€ Woodland £22 (£32) Village £10
   (£13.50)
🚗 Off A287 Farnham-Odiham road.
   M3 Junction 5, 4 miles
⊕ Driving range; teaching academy
🏚 Patrick Dawson

Oaks Sports Centre (1973)

Public
Woodmansterne Road, Carshalton,
SM5 4AN
☎ **(020) 8643 8363**
📠 (020) 8770 7303
✉ golf@oaks.sagehost.co.uk
📖 1000
🏌 G Horley
🏴 18 L 6033 yds SSS 69
   9 hole course
👥 U
£€ 18 hole: £17.40 (£21.00)
   9 hole: £8.70 (£10.50)
🚗 2 miles from Sutton on B278
⊕ Floodlit driving range
■ www.oakssportscentre.co.uk

Pachesham Park Golf Centre (1990)

Pay and play
Oaklawn Road, Leatherhead, KT22 0BT
☎ **(01372) 843453**
📠 (01372) 844076
✉ info@pacheshamgolf.co.uk
📖 250
🏌 P Taylor
🏌 P Taylor
🏴 9 L 2804 yds Par 35
👥 U SOC
£€ 9 holes–£9 (£10.50)
🚗 NW of Leatherhead, off A244. M25
   Junction 9
⊕ Driving range
🏚 P Taylor
■ www.pacheshamgolf.co.uk

Pine Ridge (1992)

Pay and play
Old Bisley Road, Frimley, Camberley,
GU16 9NX
☎ **(01276) 20770**
📠 (01276) 678837
✉ enquiry@pineridgegolf.co.uk
🏌 CD Smith (Sec/Mgr)
   (01276) 675444
🏌 P Sefton
🏴 18 L 6458 yds SSS 71
👥 U SOC
£€ £22.50 (£29)
🚗 Off Maultway, between Lightwater
   and Frimley. M3 Junction 3, 2
   miles
⊕ Floodlit driving range
🏚 Clive D Smith
■ www.pineridgegolf.co.uk

Purley Downs (1894)

106 Purley Downs Road, South Croydon,
CR2 0RB
☎ **(020) 8657 8347**
📠 (020) 8651 5044
✉ info@purleydowns.co.uk
📖 660
🏌 Mrs SJ Burr
🏌 G Wilson (020) 8651 0819
🏴 18 L 6275 yds SSS 70
👥 WD–I WE–M SOC–WD exc Tues
   am & Fri
£€ On application
🚗 3 miles S of Croydon (A235)
■ www.purleydowns.co.uk

Puttenham (1894)

Puttenham, Guildford, GU3 1AL
☎ **(01483) 810498**
📠 (01483) 810988
✉ enquiries@puttenhamgolfclub
   .co.uk
📖 600
🏌 G Simmons
🏌 D Lintott (01483) 810277
🏴 18 L 6220 yds SSS 71
👥 WD–by prior appointment
   WE/BH–M SOC–Wed, Thurs &
   Fri
£€ On application
🚗 Between Guildford and Farnham on
   B3000, just off Hog's Back
⊕ Driving range for green fee/society
   visitors & members
■ www.puttenhangolfclub.co.uk

Pyrford (1993)

Warren Lane, Pyrford, GU22 8XR
☎ **(01483) 723555**
📠 (01483) 729777
✉ pyrford@americangolf.uk.com
📖 650
🏌 D Brewer (01483) 751070
🏴 18 L 6256 yds SSS 70
👥 WD–U WE–M before noon
   SOC–WD
£€ £40 (£45)
🚗 2 miles from A3 at Ripley
🏚 Alliss/Clark

Redhill (1993)

Pay and play
Canada Avenue, Redhill, RH1 5BF
☎ **(01737) 770204**
📠 (01737) 760046
📖 90
🏌 S Furlonger
🏌 J Edgar
🏴 9 L 1903 yds Par 31 SSS 59
👥 U SOC
£€ 9 holes–£4.95 (£5.95)
🚗 1½ miles S of Redhill on A23, off
   Three Arch Road
⊕ Floodlit driving range

Redhill & Reigate (1887)

Clarence Lodge, Pendleton Road,
Redhill, RH1 6LB
☎ **(01737) 244626/244433**
📠 (01737) 242117
📖 500

🖉 W Pike (01737) 240777
✒ W Pike (01737) 244433
▶ 18 L 5272 yds SSS 68
👥 WD–U WE–phone first SOC
££ £20 (£30)
🚗 1 mile S of Redhill on A23

Reigate Heath (1895)

The Club House, Reigate Heath, RH2 8QR

☎ (01737) 242610
🖥 (01737) 249226
📖 330 80(L) 60(J)
🖉 RJ Perkins (01737) 226793
✒ B Davies
▶ 9 L 5658 yds SSS 67
👥 WD–U Sun/BH–M SOC–Wed & Thurs
££ On application
🚗 W boundary of Reigate Heath

Reigate Hill

Gatton Bottom, Reigate, RH2 0TU

☎ (01737) 645577
🖥 (01737) 642650
📖 550
✒ C Forsyth (01737) 646070
▶ 18 L 6175 yds Par 72 SSS 70
👥 WD–U WE–M SOC
££ £30 (£40)
🚗 1 mile from M25 Junction 8, off A217
🏛 David Williams

The Richmond (1891)

Sudbrook Park, Richmond, TW10 7AS

☎ (020) 8940 1463
🖥 (020) 8332 7914
📧 generalmanager.rgc@tiscali.co.uk
📖 600
🖉 DR Cromie (020) 8940 4351
✒ N Job (020) 8940 7792
▶ 18 L 6100 yds SSS 70
👥 WD–H
££ £40
🚗 Between Richmond and Kingston-upon-Thames
⊕ Driving range
🏛 T Dunn

Richmond Park (1923)

Public
Roehampton Gate, Richmond Park, London, SW15 5JR

☎ (020) 8876 3205/1795
🖥 (020) 8878 1354
📧 info@richmondparkgolf.co.uk
🖉 AJ Gourvish
✒ D Bown, A Ocana, A Morgan, S Hill
▶ Dukes 18 L 6036 yds SSS 68
   Princes 18 L 5868 yds SSS 67
👥 WD–U WE–booking necessary SOC–WD
££ On application
🚗 In Richmond Park
⊕ Driving range
🏛 Hawtree
■ www.richmondparkgolf.co.uk

Roehampton Club (1901)

Roehampton Lane, London, SW15 5LR

☎ (020) 8480 4200
🖥 (020) 8480 4265
📧 admin@roehamptonclub.co.uk
📖 2500
🖉 M Wilson (Chief Exec) (020) 8480 4200
✒ AL Scott (020) 8876 3858
▶ 18 L 6065 yds Par 71
👥 WD/WE–Introduced by member
££ On application
🚗 1 mile W of Putney, off South Circular
■ www.roehamptonclub.co.uk

Roker Park (1993)

Pay and play
Holly Lane, Aldershot Road, Guildford, GU3 3PB

☎ (01483) 236677
📖 200
🖉 C Tegg
✒ A Carter (01483) 236677
▶ 9 L 3037 yds SSS 72
👥 U SOC
££ £8.50 (£10)
🚗 2 miles W of Guildford on A323
⊕ Driving range
🏛 Alan Helling

Royal Automobile Club (1913)

Woodcote Park, Epsom, KT18 7EW

☎ (01372) 276311
🖥 (01372) 276117
🖉 D Adams (01372) 273091
✒ I Howieson (01372) 279514
▶ Old 18 L 6709 yds SSS 72
   Coronation 18 L 6223 yds SSS 70
👥 M SOC
🚗 Epsom Station 2 miles
🏛 Fowler/Myddleton

Royal Mid-Surrey (1892)

Old Deer Park, Richmond, TW9 2SB

☎ (020) 8940 1894
🖥 (020) 8332 2957
📧 secretary@rmsgc.co.uk
📖 1420
✒ P Talbot (020) 8940 0459
▶ Outer 18 L 6385 yds SSS 70
   Inner 18 L 5446 yds SSS 67
👥 WD–H or M WE/BH–M SOC
££ D–£68
🚗 Nr Richmond roundabout, off A316
🏛 JH Taylor
■ www.rmsgc.co.uk

Royal Wimbledon (1865)

29 Camp Road, Wimbledon Common, London, SW19 4UW

☎ (020) 8946 2125
🖥 (020) 8944 8652
📧 secretary@rwgc.co.uk
📖 800
🖉 NI Smith
✒ DR Jones (020) 8946 4606
▶ 18 L 6348 yds SSS 70
👥 WD–H by arrangement

🚗 Wimbledon Common, 2 miles S of A23 Tibbets Corner
🏛 HS Colt
■ www.rwgc.co.uk

Rusper (1992)

Rusper Road, Newdigate, RH5 5BX

☎ (01293) 871456,
   (01293) 871871 (Bookings)
🖥 (01293) 871456
📧 jill@ruspergolfclub.co.uk
📖 302
🖉 Mrs J Thornhill
✒ Janice Arnold (01293) 871871
▶ 18 L 6724 yds SSS 72
👥 U SOC
££ 18 holes–£17.50 (£20). 9 holes–£12 (£15) Prices subject to alteration
🚗 5 miles S of Dorking, off A24
⊕ Driving range
🏛 AW Blunden

Sandown Park Golf Centre (1970)

Public
More Lane, Esher, KT10 8AN

☎ (01372) 461234
🖥 (01372) 461203
📖 500
🖉 D Parr (Mgr)
✒ J Skinner (01372) 461282
▶ 9 L 5658 yds SSS 67
   9 hole Par 3 course
👥 U–closed on race days
££ £6.75 (£8.50)
🚗 Sandown Park Racecourse
⊕ Floodlit driving range
🏛 John Jacobs
■ www.sandown.co.uk

Selsdon Park Hotel (1929)

Addington Road, Sanderstead, South Croydon, CR2 8YA

☎ (020) 8657 8811
🖥 (020) 8657 3401
🖉 Mrs C Screene
✒ M Churchill (020) 8657 4129
▶ 18 L 6473 yds SSS 71
👥 U SOC (min 12 golfers)
££ £20 (£30)
🚗 3 miles S of Croydon on A2022 Purley-Addington road
⊕ Driving range
🏛 JH Taylor

Shirley Park (1914)

194 Addiscombe Road, Croydon, CR0 7LB

☎ (020) 8654 1143
🖥 (020) 8654 6733
📖 600
🖉 D Roy
✒ Michael Taylor (020) 8654 8767
▶ 18 L 6210 yds SSS 69
👥 WD–U WE/BH–M SOC
££ £38 (£45)
🚗 On A232, 1 mile E of East Croydon Station
🏛 Simpson/Fowler
■ www.shirleyparkgolfclub.co.uk

Silvermere (1976)
Pay and play
Redhill Road, Cobham, KT11 1EF
- ☎ **(01932) 584300**
- 📠 (01932) 584301
- ✉ sales@silvermere.freeserve.co.uk
- 🏠 750
- ♣ Mrs P Devereux
- ✓ D McClelland
- ▷ 18 L 6027 yds SSS 71
- 🚹 WD–U WE–NA before 11am SOC
- ££ £22.50 (£35)
- ⚬ ½ mile from M25 Junction 10 on B366 to Byfleet
- ⊕ Floodlit driving range
- ■ www.crowngolf.co.uk

St George's Hill (1912)
Golf Club Road, St George's Hill, Weybridge, KT13 0NL
- ☎ **(01932) 847758**
- 📠 (01932) 821564
- ✉ admin@stgeorgeshillgolfclub.co.uk
- 🏠 600
- ♣ J Robinson
- ✓ AC Rattue (01932) 843523
- ▷ 27 L 6097-6496 yds SSS 69-71
- 🚹 WD–I H WE/BH–M SOC–Wed–Fri
- ££ £80 – £105
- ⚬ 2 miles N of M25/A3 Junction, on B374
- ⛳ HS Colt
- ■ www.stgeorgeshillgolfclub.co.uk

Sunningdale (1900)
Ridgemount Road, Sunningdale, Berks, SL5 9RR
- ☎ **(01344) 621681**
- 📠 (01344) 624154
- 🏠 900
- ♣ S Zuill
- ✓ K Maxwell (01344) 620128
- ▷ Old 18 L 6581 yds SSS 72 New 18 L 6617 yds SSS 73
- 🚹 Mon–Thurs–I Fri/WE–M
- ££ Old–£125 New–£95
- ⚬ Sunningdale Station ¼ mile, off A30
- ⛳ Willie Park/HS Colt

Sunningdale Ladies (1902)
Cross Road, Sunningdale, SL5 9RX
- ☎ **(01344) 620507**
- ✉ slgolfclub@tiscali.co.uk
- 🏠 400
- ♣ Mr SP Harris
- ▷ 18 L 3616 yds SSS 60
- 🚹 H WD/WE–by appointment. No 3 or 4 balls before 10.30am
- ££ £22 (£25)
- ⚬ Sunningdale Station ¼ mile
- ⛳ HS Colt

Surbiton (1895)
Woodstock Lane, Chessington, KT9 1UG
- ☎ **(020) 8398 3101**
- 📠 (020) 8399 0992
- ✉ surbitongolfclub@btconnect.com
- 🏠 800
- ♣ CJ Cornish

- ✓ P Milton (020) 8398 6619
- ▷ 18 L 6055 yds SSS 69
- 🚹 WD–H WE/BH–M
- ££ £30 D–£45
- ⚬ 2 miles E of Esher

Surrey Downs (2001)
Proprietary
Outwood Lane, Kingswood, KT20 6JS
- ☎ **(01737) 839090**
- 📠 (01737) 839080
- ✉ booking@surreydownsgc.co.uk
- ♣ Marc Osborne
- ✓ S Blacklee (01737) 832726
- ▷ 18 L 6356 yds Par 71 SSS 70
- 🚹 U SOC
- ££ £25 (£37)
- ⚬ N of Kingswood, off A217/B2032. M25 Junction 8
- ⊕ Golf academy and range
- ⛳ Peter Alliss
- ■ www.surreydownsgc.co.uk

Surrey National (1999)
Rook Lane, Chaldon, Caterham, CR3 5AA
- ☎ **(01883) 344555**
- 📠 (01883) 344422
- 🏠 550
- ♣ S Hodsdon (Gen Mgr) (01883) 334962
- ✓ D Kent
- ▷ 18 L 6858 yds Par 72 SSS 73
- 🚹 WD–U WE–NA before 11.00am SOC
- ££ £25 (£28)
- ⚬ 5 miles S of Croydon. M25 Junction 7
- ⊕ Driving range, function room
- ⛳ David Williams
- ■ www.surreynational.co.uk

Sutton Green (1994)
New Lane, Sutton Green, Guildford, GU4 7QF
- ☎ **(01483) 747898**
- 📠 (01483) 750289
- ✉ admin@suttongreengc.co.uk
- 🏠 600
- ♣ J Buchanan
- ✓ P Tedder (01483) 766849
- ▷ 18 L 6300 yds Par 71 SSS 70
- 🚹 WD–U WE–U after 2pm
- ££ £40 (£50)
- ⚬ 2 miles S of Woking, just off A3, M25 J10
- ⛳ Walker/Davies
- ■ www.suttongc.co.uk

Tandridge (1925)
Oxted, RH8 9NQ
- ☎ **(01883) 712273 (Clubhouse)**
- 📠 (01883) 730537
- ✉ info@tandridge.fsnet.co.uk
- 🏠 750
- ♣ Lt Cdr SE Kennard RN (01883) 712274
- ✓ C Evans (01883) 713701
- ▷ 18 L 6250 yds SSS 70
- 🚹 Mon/Wed/Thurs only–H SOC–Mon/Wed/Thurs

- ££ On application
- ⚬ 5 miles E of Redhill, off A25. M25 Junction 6
- ⛳ HS Colt
- ■ www.tandridgegolfclub.com

Thames Ditton & Esher (1892)
Portsmouth Road, Esher, KT10 9AL
- ☎ **(020) 8398 1551**
- 🏠 150
- ♣ A Barry
- ✓ R Jones
- ▷ 9 L 5419 yds SSS 65
- 🚹 WD–U WE–by arrangement
- ££ £10 (£12)
- ⚬ Esher

Tyrrells Wood (1924)
Tyrrells Wood, Leatherhead, KT22 8QP
- ☎ **(01372) 376025 (2 lines)**
- 📠 (01372) 360836
- 🏠 744
- ♣ CGR Kydd
- ✓ S DeFoy (01372) 375200
- ▷ 18 L 6282 yds SSS 70
- 🚹 WD–I BH/Sat–NA Sun–NA before noon SOC
- ££ £35 (£45)
- ⚬ 2 miles SE of Leatherhead, off A24 nr Headley. M25 Junction 9, 1 mile
- ■ www.tyrrellswood-golfclub.co.uk

Walton Heath (1903)
Deans Lane, Walton-on-the-Hill, Tadworth, KT20 7TP
- ☎ **(01737) 812060**
- 📠 (01737) 814225
- ✉ secretary@whgc.co.uk
- 🏠 900
- ♣ MW Bawden (01737) 812380
- ✓ K Macpherson (01737) 812152
- ▷ Old 18 L 6836 yds SSS 73 New 18 L 6613 yds SSS 72
- 🚹 WD–H booking necessary WE/BH–M SOC–WD
- ££ On application
- ⚬ 18 miles S of London on A217/B2032. 2 miles N of M25 Junction 8
- ⛳ WH Fowler
- ■ www.whgc.co.uk

Wentworth Club (1924)
Wentworth Drive, Virginia Water, GU25 4LS
- ☎ **(01344) 842201**
- 📠 (01344) 842804
- ♣ S Christie (Admin)
- ✓ D Rennie (01344) 846306
- ▷ West 18 L 7047 yds SSS 74 East 18 L 6201 yds SSS 74 Edinburgh 18 L 7004 yds SSS 74 Executive 9 L 1902 yds Par 27
- 🚹 WD–H by prior arrangement WE–M SOC–WD
- ££ On application
- ⚬ 21 miles SW of London at A30/A329 junction. M25 Junction 13, 3 miles
- ⊕ Driving range

⋔ HS Colt (East/West). Jacobs/Player
(Edinburgh)
▮ www.wentworthclub.com

West Byfleet   (1906)
Sheerwater Road, West Byfleet,
KT14 6AA
☎ (01932) 345230
▯ (01932) 340667
✉ admin@wbgc.co.uk
▥ 550
🏌 DG Lee (Gen Mgr) (01932) 343433
✓ D Regan (01932) 346584
🏴 18 L 6211 yds SSS 70
👥 WD–U WE/BH–M SOC
££ £50 D–£75
🚗 West Byfleet ½ mile on A245.
M25 Junction 10 or 11
⋔ CS Butchart

West Hill   (1907)
Bagshot Road, Brookwood, GU24 0BH
☎ (01483) 474365/472110
▯ (01483) 474252
▥ 550
🏌 IM McColl
✓ JA Clements (01483) 473172
🏴 18 L 6322 yds Par 69 SSS 71
👥 WD–H WE–M SOC
££ £55 D–£75
🚗 5 miles W of Woking on A322
⋔ CS Butchart
▮ www.westhill-golfclub.co.uk

West Surrey   (1910)
Enton Green, Godalming, GU8 5AF
☎ (01483) 421275
▯ (01483) 415419
▥ 750
🏌 RT Crabb
✓ A Tawse (01483) 417278
🏴 18 L 6479 yds SSS 71
👥 H SOC–Wed/Thurs/Fri
££ £36 (£40)
🚗 ½ mile SE of Milford Station
⋔ Herbert Fowler

Wildwood CC   (1992)
Horsham Road, Alfold, GU6 8JE
☎ (01403) 753255
▯ (01403) 752005
✉ wayne@wildwoodgolf.co.uk
▥ 640
🏌 W Berry (Gen Mgr)
✓ S Andrews
🏴 18 L 6655 yds SSS 73
Par 3 course
👥 WE–NA before noon SOC
££ £30 (£45)
🚗 10 miles S of Guildford on A281
⊕ Driving range
⋔ Hawtree
▮ www.wildwoodgolf.co.uk

Wimbledon Common
(1908)
19 Camp Road, Wimbledon Common,
London, SW19 4UW
☎ (020) 8946 0294
▯ (020) 8947 8697

▥ 275
🏌 RJW Pierce (020) 8946 7571
✓ JS Jukes
🏴 18 L 5438 yds SSS 66
👥 WD–U WE–M SOC
££ WD–£15 exc Mon–£10
🚗 Wimbledon Common
⊕ Pillarbox red outer garment must be
worn. London Scottish play here
⋔ Willie Dunn/Tom Dunn

Wimbledon Park   (1898)
Home Park Road, London, SW19 7HR
☎ (020) 8946 1250
▯ (020) 8944 8688
✉ secretary@wpgc.co.uk
▥ 800
🏌 Mrs E Inwood (020) 8946 1250
✓ D Wingrove (020) 8946 4053
🏴 18 L 5492 yds SSS 66
👥 WD–H I WE/BH–after 3pm SOC
££ D–£50 (£50)
🚗 2 miles from A3 at Tibbets Corner
▮ www.wpgc.co.uk

Windlemere   (1978)
Pay and play
Windlesham Road, West End, Woking,
GU24 9QL
☎ (01276) 858727
▯ (01276) 678837
🏌 CD Smith
✓ D Thomas
🏴 9 L 5346 yds SSS 66
👥 M
££ 9 holes–£9 (£10.50)
🚗 A319 at Lightwater/West End
⊕ Floodlit driving range
⋔ Clive D Smith

Windlesham   (1994)
Grove End, Bagshot, GU19 5HY
☎ (01276) 452220
▯ (01276) 452290
✉ admin@windleshamgolf.com
▥ 800
🏌 R Park
✓ L Mucklow (01276) 472323
🏴 18 L 6650 yds SSS 72
👥 H–phone first WE–pm only
SOC–WD
££ £25 (£35)
🚗 ½ mile N of M3 Junction 3, off
A30/A322
⊕ Driving range
⋔ Tommy Horton
▮ www.windleshamgolf.com

The Wisley   (1991)
Ripley, Woking, GU23 6QU
☎ (01483) 211022
▯ (01483) 211662
✉ reception@wisleygc.com
▥ 700
🏌 AD Lawrence (Gen Mgr)
✓ D Pugh (01483) 211213
🏴 27 holes SSS 73:
Church 9 L 3356 yds
Garden 9 L 3385 yds
Mill 9 L 3473 yds
👥 M

🚗 1 mile S of M25 J10
⊕ Driving range
⋔ Robert Trent Jones Jr
▮ www.wisleygc.com

Woking   (1893)
Pond Road, Hook Heath, Woking,
GU22 0JZ
☎ (01483) 760053
▯ (01483) 772441
✉ woking.golf@btconnect.com
▥ 500
🏌 G Ritchie
✓ C Bianco (01483) 769582
🏴 18 L 6340 yds SSS 70
👥 WD–H WE/BH–M SOC–WD
££ £45/round £60/day
🚗 W of Woking in St John's / Hook
Heath area
⋔ Tom Dunn

The Woldingham   (1996)
Halliloo Valley Road, Woldingham,
CR3 7HA
☎ (01883) 653501
▯ (01883) 653502
▥ 650
🏌 P Harrison
✓ N Carter (01883) 653541
🏴 18 L 6322 yds Par 71 SSS 70
👥 WD–U WE–NA before noon SOC
££ £25 (£40)
🚗 2½ miles N of M25 Junction 6, off
A22
⊕ Practice range
⋔ Bradford Benz

Woodcote Park   (1912)
Meadow Hill, Bridle Way, Coulsdon,
CR5 2QQ
☎ (020) 8668 2788
▯ (020) 8660 0918
✉ info@woodcotepgc.com
▥ 630
🏌 AP Dawson
✓ W Grant (020) 8668 1843
🏴 18 L 6680 yds Par 71 SSS 72
👥 WD–H WE–M
££ £35
🚗 Purley 2 miles. M25 Junction 7
⋔ HS Colt

Worplesdon   (1908)
Heath House Road, Woking, GU22 0RA
☎ (01483) 472277
▯ (01483) 473303
▥ 600
🏌 JT Christine
✓ JT Christine (01483) 473287
🏴 18 L 6440 yds SSS 71
👥 WD–H WE–M
££ On application
🚗 E of Woking, off A322. 6 miles N
of Guildford (A3). 6 miles S of M3
Junction 3

Sussex (East)

Brighton & Hove (1887)
Devils Dyke Road, Brighton,
BN1 8YJ
- ☎ **(01273) 556482**
- 🖨 (01273) 554247
- 🏛 320
- ✍ P Bonsall (Golf Dir)
- ✓ P Bonsall (01273) 556686
- ⛳ 9 L 5704 yds SSS 68
- 👤 U SOC Sun–NA before noon
- £€ £18 (£25)
- ⊶ 4 miles N of Brighton
- ⌂ James Braid

Cooden Beach (1912)
Cooden Beach, Bexhill-on-Sea,
TN39 4TR
- ☎ **(01424) 842040**
- 🖨 (01424) 842040
- ✉ manager@coodenbeachgc/force9
  .co.uk
- 🏛 700
- ✍ KP Wiley (01424) 842040
- ✓ J Sim (01424) 843938
- ⛳ 18 L 6504 yds Par 72 SSS 71
- 👤 H SOC
- £€ £32 (£35)
- ⊶ W boundary of Bexhill
- ⊕ Full practice facility (inc driving
  range)
- ⌂ Herbert Fowler
- ■ www.coodenbeach.com

Crowborough Beacon
(1895)
Beacon Road, Crowborough, TN6 1UJ
- ☎ **(01892) 661511**
- 🖨 (01892) 611988
- ✉ cbgc@eastsx.fsnet.co.uk
- 🏛 700
- ✍ Mrs V Harwood (01892) 661511
- ✓ D Newnham (01892) 653877
- ⛳ 18 L 6273 yds SSS 70
- 👤 WD–H WE/BH–H after 2.30pm
  SOC
- £€ £32/£40
- ⊶ 9 miles S of Tunbridge Wells on
  A26
- ■ www.crowboroughbeacongolfclub
  .co.uk

Dale Hill Hotel (1973)
Ticehurst, Wadhurst, TN5 7DQ
- ☎ **(01580) 200112**
- 🖨 (01580) 201249
- 🏛 1000
- ✍ Ms M Harris (Sec/Mgr)
  (01580) 201800
- ✓ M Woods (01580) 201090
- ⛳ 18 L 5856 yds SSS 69
  Woosnam 18 L 6512 yds SSS 71
- 👤 U SOC
- £€ £25 (£35) Woosnam–£55 (£65)
- ⊶ B2087, off A21 at Flimwell
- ⊕ Driving range
- ■ www.dalehill.co.uk

Dewlands Manor (1992)
Cottage Hill, Rotherfield, TN6 3JN
- ☎ **(01892) 852266**
- 🖨 (01892) 853015
- ✍ T Robins
- ✓ N Godin
- ⛳ 9 L 3186 yds Par 36
- 👤 U–phone first
- £€ 9 holes–£15 (£17). 18 holes–£25
  (£30) 15 minute tee times
- ⊶ ¹/₂ mile S of Rotherfield, off
  A267/B2101. 10 miles S of
  Tunbridge Wells. M25 Junction 5
- ⌂ Reg Godin

The Dyke (1906)
Devil's Dyke, Devil's Dyke Road,
Brighton, BN1 8YJ
- ☎ **(01273) 857296**
- 🖨 (01273) 857078
- ✉ secretary@dykegolfclub.org.uk
- 🏛 750
- ✍ MD Harrity (Sec/Mgr)
- ✓ R Arnold (01273) 857260
- ⛳ 18 L 6627 yds SSS 72
- 👤 WD–U H WE–U H after noon
  SOC–WD
- £€ £28 D–£38 (£35)
- ⊶ 4 miles N of Brighton
- ⌂ Fred Hawtree
- ■ www.dykegolfclub.co.uk

East Brighton (1893)
Roedean Road, Brighton, BN2 5RA
- ☎ **(01273) 604838**
- 🖨 (01273) 680277
- ✉ msw@ebgc.co.uk
- 🏛 650
- ✍ ME Page
- ✓ M Stuart-William (Golf Mgr)
  (01273) 603989
- ⛳ 18 L 6346 yds SSS 70
- 👤 WD–U H after 9am WE–NA before
  11am SOC
- £€ £27.50 D–£37.50 (£32.50)
- ⊶ 1¹/₂ miles E of Town Centre,
  overlooking Marina
- ⌂ James Braid
- ■ www.ebgc.co.uk

East Sussex National
(1989)
Little Horsted, Uckfield, TN22 5ES
- ☎ **(01825) 880088**
- 🖨 (01825) 880066
- ✉ golf@eastsussecnational.co.uk
- 🏛 770
- ✍ DT Howe M.Inst, GCM (Gen Mgr)
- ✓ S MacLennan (01825) 880088
- ⛳ East 18 L 7138 yds SSS 74
  West 18 L 7154 yds SSS 74
- 👤 U on one course
- £€ Summer–£45 (£55). Winter–£40
  (£45)
- ⊶ 2 miles S of Uckfield, on A22
- ⊕ Driving range; golf academy;
  hotel
- ⌂ Bob Cupp
- ■ www.eastsussexnational.co.uk

Eastbourne Downs (1908)
East Dean Road, Eastbourne, BN20 8ES
- ☎ **(01323) 720827**
- 🖨 (01323) 412506
- 🏛 550
- ✍ AJ Reeves
- ✓ T Marshall (01323) 732264
- ⛳ 18 L 6601 yds SSS 72
- 👤 WD–U WE–NA before 11am
- £€ D–£23
- ⊶ ¹/₂ mile W of Eastbourne on A259
- ⌂ JH Taylor

Eastbourne Golfing
Park (1992)
Pay and play
Lottbridge Drove, Eastbourne,
BN23 6QJ
- ☎ **(01323) 520400**
- 🖨 (01323) 520400
- 🏛 250
- ✍ J Plumley
- ✓ B Finch
- ⛳ 9 L 5046 yds SSS 65
- 👤 U
- £€ £9 (£10)
- ⊶ ¹/₂ mile S of Hampden Park
- ⊕ All weather floodlit driving range
- ⌂ David Ashton

Hastings G&CC (1973)
Beauport Park, Battle Road, St
Leonards-on-Sea, TN37 7BP
- ☎ **(01424) 854243**
- 🖨 (01424) 854244
- 🏛 300
- ✍ M Strevett
- ✓ C Giddins (01424) 852981
- ⛳ 18 L 6180 yds SSS 71
- 👤 U–booking necessary SOC
- £€ £14 (£17.50)
- ⊶ 3 miles N of Hastings, off A2100
  Battle road
- ⊕ Driving range
- ■ www.hastingsgolfclub.com

Highwoods (1925)
Ellerslie Lane, Bexhill-on-Sea, TN39 4LJ
- ☎ **(01424) 212625**
- 🖨 (01424) 216866
- ✉ secretary@highwoodsgolfclub
  .co.uk
- 🏛 800
- ✍ LM Dennis-Smither
- ✓ MJ Andrews (01424) 212770
- ⛳ 18 L 6218 yds SSS 70
- 👤 WD/Sat–H Sun am–M Sun pm–H
- £€ £30 (£35)
- ⊶ 2 miles N of Bexhill
- ⌂ JH Taylor

Hollingbury Park (1908)
Public
Ditchling Road, Brighton, BN1 7HS
- ☎ **(01273) 552010**
- 🖨 (01273) 552010
- 🏛 300
- ✍ Mrs M Bailey
- ✓ G Crompton (01273) 500086
- ⛳ 18 L 6415 yds SSS 71
- 👤 U SOC

££   £14 (£19)
⊸   1 mile NE of Brighton
■   www.hollingburygolfclub.co.uk

Holtye   (1893)
Holtye, Cowden, Nr Edenbridge,
TN8 7ED
☎   **(01342) 850635**
📠   (01342) 850576
✉   secretary@holtye.com
📖   390
🏌   Mrs DM Botham (01342) 850576
⚲   K Hinton (01342) 850957
🏴   9 L 5325 yds SSS 66
👥   WD–U exc Wed/Thurs am–NA
      WE–NA before noon SOC–Tues &
      Fri
££   D–£18 (£20)
⊸   4 miles E of E Grinstead on A264
■   www.holtye.com

Horam Park   (1985)
Pay and play
Chiddingly Road, Horam, TN21 0JJ
☎   **(01435) 813477**
📠   (01435) 813677
✉   angie@horamgolf.freeserve.co.uk
📖   400
🏌   Mrs A Briggs
⚲   G Velvick
🏴   9 L 6128 yds SSS 70
👥   U SOC
££   18 holes–£16.50 (£18) 9 holes–£11
      (£11.50)
⊸   ¹/₂ mile S of Horam towards
      Chiddingley. 12 miles N of
      Eastbourne on A267
⊕   Floodlit driving range; pitch & putt
      course; putting green
🏠   Glen Johnson
■   www.horamparkgolf.co.uk

Lewes   (1896)
Chapel Hill, Lewes, BN7 2BB
☎   **(01273) 473245**
📠   (01273) 483474
📖   650
🏌   Miss J Raffety (01273) 483474
⚲   P Dobson (01273) 483823
🏴   18 L 6190 yds Par 71 SSS 70
👥   WD–U WE–NA before 2pm SOC
££   £28 (£36)
⊸   ¹/₂ mile from Lewes at E end of
      Cliffe High Street

Mid Sussex   (1995)
Proprietary
Spatham Lane, Ditchling, BN6 8XJ
☎   **(01273) 846567**
📠   (01273) 845767
✉   admin@midsussexgolfclub.co.uk
📖   600
🏌   A McNiven (Golf Dir)
⚲   N Plimmer
🏴   18 L 6450 yds Par 71 SSS 71
👥   WD–U WE–pm only SOC–WD
££   £25 (£25)
⊸   1 mile E of Ditchling
⊕   Driving range
🏠   David Williams
■   www.midsussexgolfclub.co.uk

Nevill   (1914)
Benhall Mill Road, Tunbridge Wells,
TN2 5JW
☎   **(01892) 525818**
📠   (01892) 517861
✉   manager@nevillgolfclub.co.uk
📖   800
🏌   TJ Fensom
⚲   P Huggett (01892) 532941
🏴   18 L 6349 yds SSS 70
👥   WD–H WE/BH–M
££   £30 D–£45
⊸   Tunbridge Wells 1 mile

Peacehaven   (1895)
Brighton Road, Newhaven, BN9 9UH
☎   **(01273) 514049**
📠   (01273) 512571
✉   golf@peacehavengc.freeserve.co.uk
📖   290
🏌   Mrs D Corke (01273) 512571
⚲   I Pearson (01273) 512602
🏴   9 L 5488 yds SSS 67
👥   WD–U WE/BH–after 11am SOC
££   £15 (£20)
⊸   8 miles E of Brighton on A259
🏠   James Braid

Piltdown   (1904)
Piltdown, Uckfield, TN22 3XB
☎   **(01825) 722033**
📠   (01825) 724192
✉   piltdowngolf@lineone.net
📖   400
🏌   Peter de Pinna (Hon)
⚲   J Partridge (01825) 722389
🏴   18 L 6076 yds SSS 69
👥   I or H exc BH/Tues am/Thurs
      am/Sun am SOC
££   £30 D–£40
⊸   1 mile W of Maresfield, off A272
      towards Isfield

Royal Ashdown Forest
(1888)
*Chapel Lane, Forest Row, East
Grinstead, RH18 5LR*
☎   **(01342) 822018 (Old),**
      (01342) 824866 (West)
📠   (01342) 825211
📖   450
🏌   DED Neave
⚲   MA Landsborough (01342) 822247
🏴   Old 18 L 6477 yds SSS 71
      West 18 L 5606 yds SSS 67
👥   On application–phone first
££   Old–£45 D–£55 (£60 R) West £22
      (£32)
⊸   4 miles S of E Grinstead on B2110
      Hartfield road. M25 Junction 6
■   www.royalashdown.co.uk

Royal Eastbourne   (1887)
Paradise Drive, Eastbourne, BN20 8BP
☎   **(01323) 729738**
📠   (01323) 729738
📖   850
🏌   David Lockyer (01323) 729278
⚲   A Harrison (01323) 736986
🏴   Devonshire 18 L 6131 yds SSS 69
      Hartington 9 L 2147 yds SSS 61

👥   U H SOC–WD
££   Devonshire–£25 (£30)
      Hartington–£15 (£15)
⊸   ¹/₂ mile from Town Hall

Rye   (1894)
Camber, Rye, TN31 7QS
☎   **(01797) 225241**
📠   (01797) 225460
📖   1000 125(L) 100(J)
🏌   JAL Smith
⚲   MP Lee (01797) 225218
🏴   18 L 6308 yds SSS 71
      9 L 6141 yds SSS 70
👥   M
⊸   3 miles E of Rye on B2075
🏠   HS Colt

Seaford   (1887)
East Blatchington, Seaford, BN25 2JD
☎   **(01323) 892442**
📠   (01323) 894113
📖   420 110(L) 37(J)
🏌   PAA Court (Gen Mgr)
⚲   (01323) 894160
🏴   18 L 6233 yds SSS 70
👥   WD–U after 10am exc Tues WE–M
      SOC
££   D–£30 (£35)
⊸   1 mile N of Seaford (A259)
⊕   Driving range
🏠   JH Taylor
■   www.seafordgolfclub.co.uk

Seaford Head   (1907)
Public
Southdown Road, Seaford, BN25 4JS
☎   **(01323) 890139**
🏌   I Perkins (01323) 894843
⚲   AJ Lowles (01323) 890139
🏴   18 L 5812 yds SSS 68
👥   U
££   £15 (£18)
⊸   8 miles W of Eastbourne. ³/₄ mile S
      of A259

Sedlescombe   (1990)
Kent Street, Sedlescombe, TN33 0SD
☎   **(01424) 871700**
📠   (01424) 871712
✉   golf@golfschool.co.uk
📖   380
🏌   Dan Gale
⚲   J Andrews
🏴   18 L 6269 yds Par 72 SSS 70
👥   U SOC
££   On application
⊸   5 miles N of Hastings
⊕   Floodlit driving range + golf
      school
🏠   Glen Johnson

Waterhall   (1923)
Public
Waterhall Road, Brighton, BN1 8YR
☎   **(01273) 508658**
📖   300
🏌   LB Allen
⚲   P Charman
🏴   18 L 5775 yds SSS 68
👥   WD–U WE–U after 8am

Wellshurst G&CC (1992)

North Street, Hellingly, BN27 4EE
- ☎ **(01435) 813636**
- 🖳 (01435) 812444
- ✉ info@wellshurst.com
- 📖 400
- 🏌 M Adams (Man Dir)
- ✎ M Jarvis (01435) 813456
- ⏢ 18 L 5992 yds SSS 69
- 👥 U SOC
- ££ £18 (£22)
- ⛳ 2 miles N of Hailsham on A267
- ⊕ Driving range

West Hove (1910)

Church Farm, Hangleton, Hove, BN3 8AN
- ☎ **(01273) 413411 (Clubhouse)**
- 🖳 (01273) 439988
- 📖 600
- 🏌 Megan Bibby (Mgr) (01273) 419738
- ✎ D Cook (01273) 413494
- ⏢ 18 L 6226 yds SSS 70 Par 71
- 👥 U–phone first SOC
- ££ On application
- ⛳ N of Brighton By-pass. 2nd junction W from A23 flyover
- ⊕ Practice driving range
- 🏠 Hawtree
- ▇ www.westhovegolfclubinfo

Willingdon (1898)

Southdown Road, Eastbourne, BN20 9AA
- ☎ **(01323) 410981**
- 🖳 (01323) 411510
- 📖 550
- 🏌 Mrs J Packham (01323) 410981
- ✎ T Moore (01323) 410984
- ⏢ 18 L 6049 yds SSS 69
- 👥 WD–U H WE–MH exc Sun am–NA SOC–H
- ££ D–£25 (£28)
- ⛳ ½ mile N of Eastbourne, off A2200
- 🏠 JH Taylor/Dr A Mackenzie

Sussex (West)

Bognor Regis (1892)

Downview Road, Felpham, Bognor Regis, PO22 8JD
- ☎ **(01243) 865867**
- 🖳 (01243) 860719
- ✉ sec@bognorgolfclub.co.uk
- 📖 750
- 🏌 PD Badger (01243) 821929
- ✎ S Bassil (01243) 865209
- ⏢ 18 L 6121 yds Par 70 SSS 69
- 👥 WD–I or H after 9.30am WE/BH–M (Apr–Sept) –I H (Oct–Mar) SOC–WD
- ££ £25 (£35)
- ⛳ 2 miles E of Bognor Regis, off A259
- 🏠 James Braid
- ▇ www.bognorgolfclub.co.uk

Brinsbury College (1991)

North Heath, Pulborough, RH20 1DZ
- ☎ **(01798) 872218**
- 🖳 (01798) 875222
- 📖 200
- 🏌 S Hall (01798) 877421
- ✎ S Hall (01798) 877421
- ⏢ 9 holes Par 62 SSS 57
- 👥 WD–U WE–U exc Sun am–NA SOC–WD
- ££ £8 (£12)
- ⛳ 2 miles N of Pulborough on A29
- ⊕ Driving range

Burgess Hill Golf Centre

Pay and play
Cuckfield Road, Burgess Hill
- ☎ **(01444) 258585**
- 🖳 (01444) 247318
- 🏌 CJ Collins (Mgr)
- ✎ M Groombridge
- ⏢ 9 hole Par 3 course
- 👥 U
- ££ On application
- ⛳ N of Burgess Hill
- ⊕ Floodlit driving range
- 🏠 Steel/Collins
- ▇ www.golfsussex.co.uk

Chartham Park (1993)

Proprietary
Felcourt, East Grinstead, RH19 2JT
- ☎ **(01342) 870340**
- 🖳 (01342) 870719
- ✉ b.smith@clubhaus.com
- 🏌 P Ferguson
- ✎ D Hobbs (01342) 870008
- ⏢ 18 L 6688 yds Par 72 SSS 72
- 👥 WD–U WE–U after 2pm
- ££ £35 (£40)
- ⛳ 2 miles N of East Grinstead, off A22. M25 Junction 6
- ⊕ Driving range
- 🏠 Neil Coles
- ▇ www.clubhaus.com

Chichester (1990)

Hunston Village, Chichester, PO20 6AX
- ☎ **(01243) 533833**
- 🖳 (01243) 539922
- ✉ enquiries@chichestergolf.com
- 📖 575
- 🏌 J Slinger
- ⏢ 18 L 6442 yds SSS 71 / 18 L 6109 yds SSS 69 / 9 hole Par 3 course
- 👥 U SOC
- ££ £16–£21 (£18–£29)
- ⛳ 2 miles S of A27 on B2145 to Selsey
- ⊕ Driving range
- 🏠 Phillip Sanders
- ▇ www.chichestergolf.com

Copthorne (1892)

Borers Arm Road, Copthorne, RH10 3LL
- ☎ **(01342) 712508**
- 🖳 (01342) 717682
- ✉ info@copthornegolfclub.co.uk
- 📖 565
- 🏌 JP Pyne (01342) 712033
- ✎ J Burrell (01342) 712405
- ⏢ 18 L 6435 yds SSS 71
- 👥 WD–U WE/BH–after 1pm SOC
- ££ £32 (£40)
- ⛳ 1 mile E of M23 Junction 10, on A264
- 🏠 James Braid
- ▇ www.copthornegolfclub.co.uk

Cottesmore (1975)

Proprietary
Buchan Hill, Pease Pottage, Crawley, RH11 9AT
- ☎ **(01293) 528256**
- 🖳 (01293) 522819
- ✉ cottesmore@americangolf.uk.com
- 📖 800
- 🏌 RG Nipper
- ✎ C Callan (01293) 535399
- ⏢ Griffin 18 L 6248 yds Par 71 SSS 70 / Phoenix 18 L 5514 yds Par 69 SSS 67
- 👥 U SOC
- ££ Griffin–£24 (£32). Phoenix–£13 (£17)
- ⛳ 4 miles S of Crawley, off M23 Junction 11
- 🏠 MD Rogerson

Cowdray Park (1920)

Petworth Road, Midhurst, GU29 0BB
- ☎ **(01730) 813599**
- 🖳 (01730) 815900
- ✉ cowdray-golf@lineone.net
- 📖 700
- 🏌 P Fairminer
- ✎ R Gough (01730) 813599
- ⏢ 18 L 6212 yds SSS 70
- 👥 H U SOC Mon–Thur
- ££ £40
- ⛳ 1 mile E of Midhurst on A272
- ⊕ Driving range on site
- 🏠 T Simpson
- ▇ www.cowdraygolf.co.uk

Effingham Park (1980)

Proprietary
West Park Road, Copthorne, RH10 3EU
- ☎ **(01342) 716528**
- 🖳 (0870) 890 0215
- ✉ mark.root@mill-cop/com
- 📖 300
- 🏌 IWB McRobbie (Hon)
- ✎ M Root
- ⏢ 9 L 1822 yds Par 30 SSS 57
- 👥 WD–U exc Wed & Thurs before 12 noon WE–I after 11.30am
- ££ £10 D–£15 (£12 D–£17)
- ⛳ B2028/B2039. M23 Junction 10
- ⊕ Golf academy
- 🏠 Francisco Escario
- ▇ www.crown-golf.co.uk

Foxbridge (1993)

Foxbridge Lane, Plaistow, RH14 0LB
- ☎ **(01403) 753303 (Bookings)**
- 🖳 (01403) 753303
- 📖 300
- 🏌 PA Clark
- ✎ S Hall
- ⏢ 9 L 3118 yds SSS 70

ⓦ U SOC
£€ £24 (£30)
⊕ 15 miles S of Guildford, off B2133
🏠 Paul Clark

The Goodwood Club
(1892)
Kennel Hill, Goodwood, Chichester,
PO18 0PN
☎ (01243) 755130
🖥 (01243) 755135
▦ 900
✍ Carole Davison (01243) 755130
✓ D Allard (01243) 755133
▷ 18 L 6401 yds SSS 71
ⓦ WD–H after 9am WE–H after
   10am SOC–Wed & Thurs
£€ £32 (£42)
⊕ 3 miles NE of Chichester, on road
   to racecourse
🏠 James Braid

Goodwood Park G&CC
(1989)
Goodwood, Chichester, PO18 0QB
☎ (01243) 520117
▦ 700
✍ M Pierce
✓ A Wratting
▷ 18 L 6530 yds SSS 72
ⓦ WD–H WE/BH–NA before noon H
   SOC
£€ £28 (£35)
⊕ 4 miles N of Chichester
⊕ Driving range
🏠 Donald Steel

Ham Manor   (1936)
West Drive, Angmering, Littlehampton,
BN16 4JE
☎ (01903) 783288
🖥 (01903) 850886
▦ 860
✍ VJ Chaszczewski
✓ S Buckley (01903) 783732
▷ 18 L 6216 yds SSS 70
ⓦ WD/WE–H
£€ On application
⊕ Between Worthing and
   Littlehampton
🏠 HS Colt
■ www.hammanor.co.uk

Hassocks   (1995)
Pay and play
London Road, Hassocks, BN6 9NA
☎ (01273) 846990
🖥 (01273) 846070
▦ 350
✍ Mrs J Brown (Gen Mgr)
   (01273) 846630
✓ C Ledger (01273) 846990
▷ 18 L 5754 yds Par 70 SSS 68
ⓦ U
£€ £15 (£19.95)
⊕ 1 mile S of Burgess Hill on A273.
   7 miles N of Brighton
🏠 Paul Wright
■ www.hassocksgolfclub.co.uk

Haywards Heath   (1922)
High Beech Lane, Haywards Heath,
RH16 1SL
☎ (01444) 414457
🖥 (01444) 458319
▦ 771
✍ GB Kullner
✓ M Henning (01444) 414866
▷ 18 L 6248 yds SSS 70
ⓦ WD/WE–H–restricted SOC–Wed
   & Thurs
£€ £26 (£36)
⊕ 2 miles N of Haywards Heath, off
   B2112

Hill Barn   (1935)
Public
Hill Barn Lane, Worthing, BN14 9QE
☎ (01903) 237301
✉ info@hillbarn.com
✍ Simon Blanshard (01903) 237301
✓ F Morley
▷ 18 L 6224 yds SSS 70
ⓦ U
£€ £15 (£17.50)
⊕ NE of A27 at Warren Road
   roundabout
🏠 Hawtree

Hilton Avisford Park
(1990)
Pay and play
Yapton Lane, Walberton, Arundel,
BN18 0LS
☎ (01243) 554611
▦ 240
✍ N Upjohn
✓ C Rota
▷ 18 L 5390 yds Par 67 SSS 66
ⓦ U SOC
£€ £15 (£18)
⊕ 4 miles W of Arundel on A27

Horsham   (1993)
Pay and play
Worthing Road, Horsham, RH13 7AX
☎ (01403) 271525
🖥 (01403) 274528
▦ 300
✍ E Purton (01403) 271525
✓ Alex Paterson
▷ 9 L 2061 yds Par 33 SSS 30
ⓦ U SOC
£€ 9 holes–£7 (£8)
⊕ 1 mile S of Horsham, off A24

Ifield   (1927)
Rusper Road, Ifield, Crawley, RH11 0LN
☎ (01293) 520222
🖥 (01293) 612973
▦ 875
✍ J Earl
✓ J Earl (01293) 523088
▷ 18 L 6319 yds SSS 70
ⓦ WD–H WE–M SOC
£€ £30 D–£40 (£35 Sun NA before 2
⊕ W of Crawley. M23 Junction 11
🏠 Hawtree/Taylor

Littlehampton   (1889)
170 Rope Walk, Littlehampton,
BN17 5DL
☎ (01903) 717170
🖥 (01903) 726629
✉ lgc@talk21.com
▦ 650
✍ S Graham (01903) 717170
✓ G McQuitty (01903) 716369
▷ 18 L 6244 yds SSS 70
ⓦ WD–U after 9.30am WE/BH–NA
   before noon SOC
£€ £30 (£38)
⊕ W bank of River Arun,
   Littlehampton
🏠 Hawtree

Mannings Heath   (1905)
Fullers, Hammerpond Road, Mannings
Heath, Horsham RH13 6PG
☎ (01403) 210228
🖥 (01403) 270974
▦ 730
✍ S Kershaw
✓ C Tucker (01403) 210228
▷ Waterfall 18 L 6378 yds Par 73
   SSS 70
   Kingfisher 18 L 6217 yds Par 70
   SSS 70
ⓦ U H SOC
£€ From £42
⊕ 3 miles SE of Horsham (A281).
   M23 Junction 11
⊕ Driving range; steam room
🏠 Kingfisher-David Williams
■ www.exclusivehotels.co.uk

Paxhill Park   (1990)
East Mascalls Lane, Lindfield,
RH16 2QN
☎ (01444) 484467
🖥 (01444) 482709
✉ johnbowen@paxhillpark.fsnet
   .co.uk
▦ 540
✍ JD Bowen
✓ M Green
▷ 18 L 6196 yds SSS 68
ⓦ WD–U WE–U
£€ £15 (£20)
⊕ 1 mile N of Lindfield, off B2028. 4
   miles NE of Haywards Heath
⊕ Driving range
🏠 Patrick Tallack

Pease Pottage   (1986)
Horsham Road, Pease Pottage, Crawley,
RH11 9AP
☎ (01293) 521706
🖥 (01293) 521706
▦ 56
✍ A Venn (01293) 521766
✓ D Blair (01293) 521706
▷ 9 L 3511 yds SSS 57
ⓦ U
£€ £8.50 (£11)
⊕ S of Crawley, off A23. M23
   Junction 11
⊕ 20 bay floodlit driving range

Petworth   (1989)
Pay and play
London Road, Petworth, GU28 9LX
☎ **(01798) 344097/(07932) 163941**
🖷 (01798) 344097
📖 105
🖎 D Windows (01730) 817707
✒ A Long (01798) 344097
🏱 18 L 6191 yds Par 71 SSS 69
🎎 U SOC
£€ £11 any time 18 holes; £17.50
🕳 2½ miles N of Petworth on A283
⊕ Practice net/green
🕆 C & T Duncton

Pyecombe   (1894)
Clayton Hill, Pyecombe, Brighton, BN45 7FF
☎ **(01273) 845372**
🖷 (01273) 843338
🖎 pycombegc@btopenworld.com
📖 650
🖎 IR Bradbery
✒ CR White (01273) 845398
🏱 18 L 6278 yds SSS 70
🎎 WD–U exc Tues after 9.15am
    WE–U after 2pm
    SOC–Mon/Wed/Thurs
£€ £25 (£30)
🕳 6 miles N of Brighton on A273

Rustington   (1992)
Public
Golfers Lane, Angmering, BN16 4NB
☎ **(01903) 850790**
🖷 (01903) 850982
🖎 SP Langmead
✒ (01903) 850790
🏱 18 L 5735 yds Par 70 SSS 68
    9 hole Par 3 course
🎎 U SOC
£€ On application
🕳 On A259 between Worthing and
    Littlehampton
⊕ Floodlit driving range
🕆 David Williams
■ www.rgcgolf.com

Selsey   (1908)
Golf Links Lane, Selsey, PO20 9DR
☎ **(01243) 605176 (Members)**
🖷 (01243) 602203
📖 400
🖎 P Carter (01243) 602203
✒ P Grindley
🏱 9 L 5834 yds SSS 68
🎎 U
£€ 18 holes–£11 (£18). 9 holes–£10
    (£14)
🕳 7 miles S of Chichester

Shillinglee Park   (1980)
Pay and play
Chiddingfold, Godalming, GU8 4TA
☎ **(01428) 653237**
🖷 (01428) 644391
📖 400
🖎 G Baxter (Prop)
✒ M Dowdell
🏱 9 L 2516 yds Par 32
🎎 U SOC exc Sat am

£€ 18 holes–£13 (£15) 9 holes–£8.50
    (£9.50)
🕳 2½ miles SE of Chiddingfold
⊕ Pitch & putt course
🕆 Roger Mace

Singing Hills   (1992)
Proprietary
Albourne, Brighton, BN6 9EB
☎ **(01273) 835353**
🖷 (01273) 835444
📖 400
🖎 DO Weston
✒ W Street
🏱 27 holes SSS 69-72:
    River 9 L 2826 yds
    Valley 9 L 3348 yds
    Lakes 9 L 3253 yds
🎎 U SOC
£€ £23 (£31)
🕳 6 miles N of Brighton, off B2117
⊕ Driving range
🕆 MRM Sandow

Slinfold Park   (1993)
Stane Street, Slinfold, Horsham, RH13 7RE
☎ **(01403) 791154 (Clubhouse)**
🖷 (01403) 791465
📖 600
🖎 S Blake (Gen Mgr)
✒ T Clingan (01403) 791555
🏱 18 L 6450 yds SSS 71
    9 hole course
🎎 U SOC
£€ £25 (£30)
🕳 3 miles W of Horsham (A29)
⊕ Driving range; academy course
🕆 John Fortune
■ www.slinfoldpark.co.uk

Tilgate Forest   (1982)
Public
Titmus Drive, Tilgate, Crawley, RH10 5EU
☎ **(01293) 530103**
🖷 (01293) 523478
📖 320
🖎 J MacDonnell
✒ S Trussell, D McClelland
🏱 18 L 6359 yds SSS 70
    9 hole Par 3 course
🎎 U SOC–Mon–Thurs
£€ 18 hole: £14.80 (£19.60)
    9 hole: £4.40 (£5.40)
🕳 1½ miles SE of Crawley. M23
    Junction 11
⊕ Driving range

West Chiltington   (1988)
Proprietary
Broadford Bridge Road, West Chiltington, RH20 2YA
☎ **(01798) 813574**
🖷 (01798) 812631
🖎 cottongolf@westchiltington
    .fsbusiness.co.uk
📖 500
🖎 G McKay
✒ Lorraine Cousins (01798) 812115
🏱 18 L 5969 yds Par 70 SSS 68
    9 hole Par 3 course

🎎 U SOC
£€ £19 (£23.50)
🕳 2 miles E of Pulborough
⊕ Driving range
🕆 Faulkner/Barnes

West Sussex   (1930)
Golf Club Lane, Wiggonholt, Pulborough, RH20 2EN
☎ **(01798) 872563**
🖷 (01798) 872033
🖎 secretary@westsussexgolf.co.uk
📖 800
🖎 CP Simpson
✒ T Packham (01798) 872426
🏱 18 L 6223 yds SSS 70
🎎 WD–I H after 9.30am exc Fri–M
    SOC–Wed & Thurs
£€ On application
🕳 1½ miles E of Pulborough on A283
⊕ Driving range
🕆 Campbell/Hutcheson
■ www.westsussexgolf.co.uk

Worthing   (1905)
Links Road, Worthing, BN14 9QZ
☎ **(01903) 260801**
🖷 (01903) 694664
📖 1000
🖎 IJ Evans (01903) 260801
✒ S Rolley (01903) 260718
🏱 Lower 18 L 6530 yds Par 71
    SSS 72
    Upper 18 L 5243 yds Par 66 SSS 66
🎎 WD–U H WE–confirm in advance
    with Pro
£€ On application
🕳 Central Station 1½ miles (A27), nr
    A24 Junction
🕆 HS Colt
■ www.worthinggolf.co.uk

Tyne & Wear

Backworth   (1937)
The Hall, Backworth, Shiremoor, Newcastle-upon-Tyne NE27 0AH
☎ **(0191) 268 1048**
📖 400
🖎 GM Sales
✒ None
🏱 9 L 5930 yds SSS 69
🎎 Mon & Fri–U Tues–Thurs–M after
    5pm WE–after 12.30pm exc comp
    Sats–after 6pm
£€ On application
🕳 Off Tyne Tunnel link road,
    Holystone roundabout

Birtley   (1922)
Birtley Lane, Birtley, DH3 2LR
☎ **(0191) 410 2207**
📖 230
🖎 RC Landells
🏱 9 L 5660 yds SSS 67
🎎 WD–U exc Fri pm–M WE/BH–M
    SOC
£€ £14.50
🕳 3 miles from Birtley service area on
    A1(M)

Boldon (1912)

Dipe Lane, East Boldon, NE36 0PQ
- ☎ **(0191) 536 4182 (Clubhouse)**
- 🖥 (0191) 537 2270
- ✉ info@boldongolfclub.co.uk
- 🛏 700
- 🏌 RW Benton (0191) 536 5360
- ⚐ Phipps Golf (0191) 536 5835
- ⏚ 18 L 6348 yds SSS 70
- 🏌 WD–U WE/BH–NA before 3.30pm
- ££ £20 (£24)
- ⚒ 8 miles SE of Newcastle
- ⊕ Driving range
- ⛳ H Vardon
- ■ www.boldongolfclub.co.uk

City of Newcastle (1891)

Three Mile Bridge, Gosforth, Newcastle-upon-Tyne, NE3 2DR
- ☎ **(0191) 285 1775**
- 🖥 (0191) 284 0700
- 🛏 400 110(L) 60(J)
- 🏌 AJ Matthew (Mgr)
- ⚐ S McKenna (0191) 285 5481
- ⏚ 18 L 6523 yds SSS 71
- 🏌 U SOC
- ££ £25 D–£32 (£30)
- ⚒ B1318, 3 miles N of Newcastle
- ⛳ Harry Vardon

Garesfield (1922)

Chopwell, NE17 7AP
- ☎ **(01207) 561309**
- 🖥 (01207) 561309
- 🛏 700
- 🏌 Mrs J Barclay
- ⚐ D Race (01207) 563082
- ⏚ 18 L 6458 yds SSS 72
- 🏌 U (NA Wed, Sat)
- ££ On application
- ⚒ On B6315 to High Spen off A694 from A1 at Rowlands Gill
- ⛳ William Woodend

Gosforth (1906)

Broadway East, Gosforth, Newcastle upon Tyne, NE3 5ER
- ☎ **(0191) 285 6710**
- 🖥 (0191) 284 6274
- 🛏 380 100(L) 60(J)
- 🏌 B Pluse (0191) 285 3495
- ⚐ G Garland (0191) 285 0553
- ⏚ 18 L 6024 yds SSS 69
- 🏌 U SOC
- ££ £25 (£25)
- ⚒ 3 miles N of Newcastle, off A6125
- ■ www.gosforthgolfclub.co.uk

Hetton-le-Hole

Pay and play
Elemore Golf Course, Elemore Lane, DH5 0QB
- ☎ **(0191) 517 3057**
- 🖥 (0191) 517 3054
- 🏌 E Booth
- ⏚ 18 L 5950 yds Par 69
- 🏌 U SOC
- ££ £10 (£13)
- ⚒ 4 miles E of A1(M)/A690 junction

Heworth (1912)

Gingling Gate, Heworth, Gateshead, NE10 8XY
- ☎ **(0191) 469 4424**
- ✉ theheworthgolfclub@supanet.com
- 🛏 800
- 🏌 G Holbrow
- ⚐ A Marshall
- ⏚ 18 L 6404 yds SSS 71
- 🏌 WD–U WE–NA before noon
- ££ £18
- ⚒ SE boundary of Gateshead

Houghton-le-Spring (1908)

Copt Hill, Houghton-le-Spring, DH5 8LU
- ☎ **(0191) 584 1198**
- 🛏 600
- 🏌 N Wales (0191) 584 0048
- ⚐ (0191) 584 7421
- ⏚ 18 L 6416 yds Par 72 SSS 71
- 🏌 U SOC
- ££ £20 (£27)
- ⚒ 3 miles SW of Sunderland

Newcastle United (1892)

Ponteland Road, Cowgate, Newcastle-upon-Tyne, NE5 3JW
- ☎ **(0191) 286 9998 (Clubhouse)**
- ✉ info@nugc.co.uk
- 🛏 700
- 🏌 S Darbyshire (Hon)
- ⚐ (0191) 286 9998
- ⏚ 18 L 6617 yds SSS 72
- 🏌 WD–U WE/BH–M
- ££ On application
- ⚒ Nuns Moor, 2 miles W of city centre
- ■ www.nugc.co.uk

Northumberland (1898)

High Gosforth Park, Newcastle-upon-Tyne, NE3 5HT
- ☎ **(0191) 236 2498 / 2009**
- 🖥 (0191) 236 2036
- 🛏 500
- 🏌 JM Forteath QGM
- ⚐ None
- ⏚ 18 L 6680 yds SSS 72
- 🏌 WD–I BH–M
- ££ £40 (£50)
- ⚒ 5 miles N of Newcastle
- ⛳ HS Colt/James Braid

Parklands (1971)

High Gosforth Park, Newcastle-upon-Tyne, NE3 5HQ
- ☎ **(0191) 236 4480**
- 🛏 600
- 🏌 B Woof
- ⚐ B Rumney
- ⏚ 18 L 6013 yds Par 71 SSS 69
- 🏌 U
- ££ £15 (£18)
- ⚒ 5 miles N of Newcastle
- ⊕ 9 hole pitch & putt course; driving range

Ravensworth (1906)

Angel View, Long Bank, Gateshead, NE9 7NE
- ☎ **(0191) 487 6014/2843**

- 🛏 550
- 🏌 RW Hill (091) 442 1042
- ⚐ S Cowell (0191) 491 3475
- ⏚ 18 L 5872 yds SSS 68
- 🏌 U H SOC
- ££ £20 (£27)
- ⚒ 3 miles S of Newcastle on B1296

Ryton (1891)

Doctor Stanners, Clara Vale, Ryton, NE40 3TD
- ☎ **(0191) 413 3253**
- 🖥 (0191) 413 1642
- ✉ secretary@rytongolfclub.co.uk
- 🛏 600
- 🏌 S Dix
- ⏚ 18 L 5499 metres SSS 69
- 🏌 WD–U WE–M SOC
- ££ £16 (£21)
- ⚒ 7 miles W of Newcastle, off A695

South Shields (1893)

Cleadon Hills, South Shields, NE34 8EG
- ☎ **(0191) 456 0475**
- ✉ thesecretary@south-shields-golf.freeserve.co.uk
- 🛏 700
- 🏌 R Stanness (0191) 456 8942
- ⚐ G Parsons (0191) 456 0110
- ⏚ 18 L 6221 yds SSS 70
- 🏌 U SOC
- ££ On application
- ⚒ Cleadon Hills

Tynemouth (1913)

Spital Dene, Tynemouth, North Shields, NE30 2ER
- ☎ **(0191) 257 4578**
- 🖥 (0191) 259 5193
- 🛏 855
- 🏌 TJ Scott (0191) 257 3381
- ⚐ J McKenna (0191) 258 0728
- ⏚ 18 L 6359 yds SSS 70
- 🏌 WD–U 9.30am–5pm –NA before 9.30am and after 5pm WE/BH–M
- ££ £22.50 D–£25.50
- ⚒ 8 miles E of Newcastle
- ⛳ Willie Park

Tyneside (1879)

Westfield Lane, Ryton, NE40 3QE
- ☎ **(0191) 413 2177**
- 🖥 (0191) 413 2742
- 🛏 660
- 🏌 E Stephenson (0191) 413 2742
- ⚐ M Gunn (0191) 413 1600
- ⏚ 18 L 6009 yds SSS 69
- 🏌 WD–U exc 11.30–1.30pm Sat–NA Sun–NA before 3pm SOC
- ££ £22 (£30)
- ⚒ 7 miles W of Newcastle. S of river, off A695
- ⛳ HS Colt

Wallsend (1973)

Public
Rheydt Avenue, Bigges Main, Wallsend, NE28 8SU
- ☎ **(0191) 262 1973**
- 🏌 D Souter
- ⚐ K Phillips (0191) 262 4231

▷ 18 L 6608 yds SSS 72
ᛤ U
£€ £15.50 (£17.50)
⛳ Between Newcastle and Wallsend on coast road
⊕ Driving range
🏠 G Showball

Washington (1979)

Stone Cellar Road, High Usworth, District 12, Washington NE37 1PH
☎ (0191) 417 8346
📠 (0191) 415 1166
🏠 600
🖊 G Robinson
✓ D Patterson
▷ 18 L 6604 yds SSS 72
9 hole Par 3 course
ᛤ WD–U WE–after 10.30am SOC
£€ £20 (£25)
⛳ Off A1(M), on A195
⊕ Driving range
🌐 www.corushotels.com/hotels/wasgeo

Wearside (1892)

Coxgreen, Sunderland, SR4 9JT
☎ (0191) 534 2518
📠 (0191) 534 6186
🏠 800
🖊 M Gowland
✓ D Brolls (0191) 534 4269
▷ 18 L 6315 yds SSS 70
Par 3 course
ᛤ H SOC
£€ £20 (£26)
⛳ 2 miles W of Sunderland, off A183, by A19

Westerhope (1941)

Whorlton Grange, Westerhope, Newcastle-upon-Tyne, NE5 1PP
☎ (0191) 286 9125
📠 (0191) 214 6287
🏠 778
🖊 B Bell (0191) 286 7636
✓ N Brown (0191) 286 0594
▷ 18 L 6407 yds SSS 71
ᛤ WD–U
£€ £20
⛳ 5 miles W of Newcastle

Whickham (1911)

Hollinside Park, Fellside Road, Whickham, Newcastle-upon-Tyne NE16 5BA
☎ (0191) 488 7309 (Clubhouse)
📠 (0191) 488 1577
🏠 650
🖊 Mrs J Miller (0191) 488 1576
✓ A Hall (0191) 488 8591
▷ 18 L 5878 yds Par 68 SSS 68
ᛤ U SOC–WD
£€ £20 (£25)
⛳ 5 miles SW of Newcastle

Whitburn (1931)

Lizard Lane, South Shields, NE34 7AF
☎ (0191) 529 2144
📠 (0191) 529 4944
✉ wgsec@ukonline.co.uk

🏠 580 73(L) 85(J)
🖊 Mr A Atkinson (0191) 529 4944
✓ D Stephenson (0191) 529 4210
▷ 18 L 5899 yds Par 70 SSS 68
ᛤ U SOC–WD exc Tues
£€ £23 (£27)
⛳ 2 miles N of Sunderland on coast
🏠 Colt/Alison/Morrison
🌐 www.golf-whitburn.co.uk

Whitley Bay (1890)

Claremont Road, Whitley Bay, NE26 3UF
☎ (0191) 252 0180
📠 (0191) 297 0030
✉ secretary@whitleybaygolfclub.co.uk
🏠 700
🖊 H Hanover (0191) 252 0180
✓ G Shipley (0191) 252 5688
▷ 18 L 6579 yds SSS 71
ᛤ WD–U WE–M
£€ £22 D–£24
⛳ 10 miles E of Newcastle
🌐 www.whitleybaygolfclub.co.uk

Warwickshire

Ansty (1992)

Brinklow Road, Ansty, Coventry, CV7 9JL
☎ (024) 7662 1341/7660 2568
📠 (024) 7660 2568
🏠 375
🖊 W Britton
✓ S Firkins
▷ 18 L 6079 yds Par 71 SSS 69
Par 3 course
ᛤ U SOC
£€ £11 (£16)
⛳ Between Ansty and Brinklow (B4029). M6 Junction 2, 1 mile.
⊕ Driving range
🏠 D Morgan

Atherstone (1894)

The Outwoods, Coleshill Road, Atherstone, CV9 2RL
☎ (01827) 713110
📠 (01827) 715686
🏠 400 40(L) 40(J)
🖊 VA Walton (01827) 892568
▷ 18 L 6012 yds Par 72 SSS 70
ᛤ WD–U BH/Sat–M Sun–M after 5pm SOC–WD
£€ D–£25
⛳ ¼ mile from Atherstone on Coleshill road

The Belfry (1977)

Public
Wishaw, B76 9PR
☎ (01675) 470301
📠 (01675) 470174
🖊 R Maxfield
✓ P McGovern
▷ Brabazon 18 L 7118 yds SSS 74
Derby 18 L 6009 yds SSS 69
PGA National 18 L 6737 yds SSS 72

ᛤ H SOC
£€ Brabazon £70–£135. PGA National £40–£70. Derby £20–£35
⛳ 2 miles N of M42 Junc 9, off A446
⊕ Driving range
🏠 Brabazon & Derby-Alliss/Thomas; PGA National-Thomas

Bidford Grange (1992)

Stratford Road, Bidford-on-Avon, B50 4LY
☎ (01789) 490319
📠 (01789) 778184
🏠 310
🖊 M Smith (Mgr)
✓ D Webber
▷ 18 L 7233 yds Par 72 SSS 74
ᛤ U SOC
£€ £12 (£15)
⛳ 5 miles W of Stratford-on-Avon on B439
🏠 Swann/Tillman/Granger

Boldmere (1936)

Public
Monmouth Drive, Sutton Coldfield, Birmingham, BJ3 6JR
☎ (0121) 354 3379
✉ boldmeregolfclub@hotmail.com
🏠 300
🖊 R Leeson
✓ T Short
▷ 18 L 4463 yds SSS 62
ᛤ U
£€ £9 (£11)
⛳ By Sutton Park, 1 mile W of Sutton Coldfield

Bramcote Waters

Pay and play
Bazzard Road, Bramcote, Nuneaton, CV11 6QJ
☎ (01455) 220807
📠 (01203) 388775
✓ N Gilks
▷ 9 L 4995 yds Par 66 SSS 64
ᛤ U
£€ £12 (£13)
⛳ 4 miles SE of Nuneaton, off B4114
🏠 David Snell

City of Coventry (Brandon Wood) (1977)

Public
Brandon Lane, Coventry, CV8 3GQ
☎ (024) 7654 3141
📠 (024) 7654 5108
🏠 400
🖊 C Gledhill
✓ C Gledhill
▷ 18 L 6521 yds SSS 71
ᛤ U SOC
£€ On application
⛳ 6 miles SE of Coventry, off A45(S)
⊕ Floodlit driving range

Copt Heath (1907)

1220 Warwick Road, Knowle, Solihull, B93 9LN
☎ (01564) 772650

☎ (01564) 771022
✉ golf@copt-heath.co.uk
🕮 700
✍ CV Hadley
✓ BJ Barton (01564) 776155
🏴 18 L 6517 yds SSS 71
👥 WD/WE–H BH–M SOC
££ £40 – £50
⛳ 2 miles S of Solihull on A4141.
M42 J5, half a mile
■ www.coptheathgolf.co.uk

Coventry (1887)

*St Martins Road, Finham Park, Coventry,
CV3 6RJ*
☎ (024) 7641 1123
☎ (024) 7669 0131
✉ coventrygolfclub@hotmail.com
🕮 750
✍ A Smith (024) 7641 4152
✓ P Weaver (024) 7641 1298
🏴 18 L 6601 yds SSS 73
👥 WD–H
££ £35
⛳ 2 miles S of Coventry on
A444/B4113
🏠 Vardon/Hawtree
■ www.coventrygolfcourse.co.uk

Coventry Hearsall (1894)

Beechwood Avenue, Coventry, CV5 6DF
☎ (024) 7671 3470
☎ (024) 7669 1534
✉ secretary
@coventry hearsallgolfclub.co.uk
🕮 600
✍ Mrs ME Hudson
✓ M Tarn (024) 7671 3156
🏴 18 L 6005 yds SSS 69
👥 WD–U WE–M
££ D–£30
⛳ 1¹/₂ miles S of Coventry, off A45
■ www.hearsallgolfclub.co.uk

Harborne (1893)

*40 Tennal Road, Harborne, Birmingham,
B32 2JE*
☎ (0121) 427 1728
☎ (0121) 427 4039
🕮 600
✍ GA Tozer (0121) 427 3058
✓ P Johnson (0121) 427 3512
🏴 18 L 6210 yds SSS 70
👥 WD–U WE/BH–M SOC
££ £30 D–£35
⛳ 3 miles SW of Birmingham. M5
Junction 3
🏠 HS Colt

Harborne Church Farm
(1926)

Public
*Vicarage Road, Harborne, Birmingham,
B17 0SN*
☎ (0121) 427 1204
☎ (0121) 428 3126
🕮 180
✍ B Flanagan
✓ P Johnson
🏴 9 L 4882 yds Par 66 SSS 64
👥 U

££ 18 holes–£9 (£10.50) 9 holes–£6
(£7)
⛳ 3 miles SW of Birmingham
■ www.learnaboutgolf.co.uk

Hatchford Brook (1969)

Public
*Coventry Road, Sheldon, Birmingham,
B26 3PY*
☎ (0121) 743 9821
☎ (0121) 743 3420
✉ idt@hbgc.freeserve.co.uk
🕮 400
✍ ID Thomson (0121) 742 6643
✓ M Hampton
🏴 18 L 6137 yds Par 70 SSS 69
👥 U SOC
££ £9.50 (£11)
⛳ City boundary close to airport.
A45/M42 Junction
■ www.golfpro-direct.co.uk/hbgc

Henley G&CC (1994)

*Birmingham Road, Henley-in-Arden,
B95 5QA*
☎ (01564) 793715
☎ (01564) 795754
✉ enquiries@henleygcc.co.uk
🕮 600
✍ E Wright (Ch Exec)
✓ N Hyde
🏴 18 L 6933 yds SSS 73
9 hole Par 3 course
👥 U–booking required SOC
££ £25 (£30)
⛳ N of Stratford-on-Avon on A3400.
M40 Junction 16, 3 miles
⊕ Driving range
🏠 N Selwyn-Smith

Hilltop (1979)

Public
*Park Lane, Handsworth, Birmingham,
B21 8LJ*
☎ (0121) 554 4463
✍ K Highfield (Mgr)
✓ K Highfield
🏴 18 L 6114 yds SSS 69
👥 U
££ £9.50 (£11)
⛳ Sandwell Valley. M5 Junction 1

Ingon Manor (1993)

*Ingon Lane, Snitterfield, Stratford-on-
Avon, CV37 0QE*
☎ (01789) 731857
✉ info@ingonmanor.co.uk
🕮 350
✓ P Taylor (01789) 731938
🏴 18 L 6575 yds Par 73 SSS 71
👥 U H SOC
££ £25 (£30)
⛳ 3 miles N of Stratford-on-Avon, off
A461. M40 Junction 15
⊕ Driving range
🏠 David Hemstock
■ www.ingonmanor.co.uk

Kenilworth (1889)

Crewe Lane, Kenilworth, CV8 2EA
☎ (01926) 854296

☎ (01926) 864453
✉ secretary@kenilworthgolfclub.co.uk
🕮 750
✍ John McTavish (01926) 858517
✓ Steve Yates (01926) 512732
🏴 18 L 6400 yds SSS 71
👥 U H BH–M SOC–WD
££ £35 (£45) per round/day
⛳ 1¹/₂ miles E of Kenilworth. 5 miles
S of Coventry
🏠 Hawtree
■ www.kenilworthgolfclub.co.uk

Ladbrook Park (1908)

*Poolhead Lane, Tanworth-in-Arden,
Solihull, B94 5ED*
☎ (01564) 742264
☎ (01564) 742909
🕮 700
✍ Mrs SE Burrows (Admin)
✓ R Mountford (01564) 742581
🏴 18 L 6427 yds SSS 71
👥 WD–U H WE/BH–M H
££ On application
⛳ 12 miles S of Birmingham. M42
Junction 3
🏠 HS Colt

Leamington & County
(1908)

*Golf Lane, Whitnash, Leamington Spa,
CV31 2QA*
☎ (01926) 425961
☎ (01926) 425961
✉ secretary@leamingtongolf.co.uk
🕮 650
✍ David M Beck
✓ J Mellor (01926) 428014
🏴 18 L 6439 yds SSS 71
👥 U SOC
££ £35 (£40)
⛳ 1¹/₂ miles S of Leamington Spa
🏠 HS Colt

Marconi (Grange GC)

Copsewood, Coventry, CV3 1HS
☎ (024) 7656 3339
🕮 370
✍ REC Jones (Hon)
🏴 9 L 6048 yds SSS 71
👥 WD–U before 2.30pm exc Wed–NA
Sat–NA Sun–NA before noon
££ £15 (£20)
⛳ 2¹/₂ miles E of Coventry on A428
🏠 TJ McAuley

Marriott Forest of Arden
Hotel (1970)

*Maxstoke Lane, Meriden, Coventry,
CV7 7HR*
☎ (01676) 522335
☎ (01676) 523711
🕮 650
✍ S Follett (Golf Dir)
✓ P Hoye
🏴 Arden 18 L 6707 yds Par 72 SSS 73
Aylesford 18 L 5801 yds Par 69
SSS 68
👥 WD–U SOC–WD
££ Arden–£80 (£90). Aylesford–£40
(£50)

🏌 9 miles W of Coventry, off A45.
M6 Junction 4
⊕ Driving range
⌂ Donald Steel

Maxstoke Park (1898)

Castle Lane, Coleshill, Birmingham,
B46 2RD
☎ (01675) 466743
🖳 (01675) 466185
✉ @maxstokepark.fsnet.co.uk
🏛 780
⚲ GE Crawford
✓ N McEwan (01675) 464915
🏴 18 L 6442 yds SSS 71
👥 WD–U H WE–M
££ £27.50
🏌 3 miles SE of Coleshill. M6
Junction 6

Moor Hall (1932)

Moor Hall Drive, Four Oaks, Sutton
Coldfield, B75 6LN
☎ (0121) 308 6130
🖳 (0121) 308 8560
✉ manager@moorhallgolfclub.fsnet
.co.uk
🏛 668
⚲ DJ Etheridge
✓ (0121) 308 5106
🏴 18 L 6249 yds SSS 70
👥 WD–U H exc Thurs–U after 1pm
WE/BH–M
££ £33 D–£44
🏌 1 mile E of Sutton Coldfield

Newbold Comyn (1973)

Public
Newbold Terrace East, Leamington Spa,
CV32 4EW
☎ (01926) 421157
🏛 191
⚲ CV Baker (01926) 887220
✓ R Carvell
🏴 18 L 6315 yds SSS 70
👥 WD–U WE–booking 1 week in
advance SOC
££ £8.30 (£12.70)
🏌 Off Willes Road (B4099)

North Warwickshire (1894)

Hampton Lane, Meriden, Coventry,
CV7 7LL
☎ (01676) 522464 (Clubhouse)
🖳 (01676) 523004
🏛 450
⚲ Mrs A Dicks (Hon) (01676) 522915
✓ A Bownes (01676) 522259
🏴 9 L 6374 yds SSS 71
👥 WD–U WE/BH–M SOC
££ £20
🏌 6 miles W of Coventry, off A45

Nuneaton (1905)

Golf Drive, Whitestone, Nuneaton,
CV11 6QF
☎ (024) 7634 7810
🖳 (024) 7632 7563
🏛 650
⚲ P Smith
✓ J Salter (024) 7634 0201

🏴 18 L 6412 yds SSS 71
👥 WD–U H WE–M SOC
££ £24 D–£35
🏌 2 miles S of Nuneaton, off
Lutterworth road

Oakridge

Arley Lane, Ansley Village, Nuneaton,
CV10 9PH
☎ (01676) 541389
🖳 (01676) 542709
🏛 500
⚲ Mrs S Lovric (Admin)
🏴 18 L 6242 yds Par 72 SSS 70
👥 U SOC–WD
££ £16
🏌 B4112 from Nuneaton. M6
Junction 3
⌂ Algie Jayes

Olton (1893)

Mirfield Road, Solihull, B91 1JH
☎ (0121) 705 1083
🖳 (0121) 711 2010
✉ mailbox@oltongolfclub.fsnet.co.uk
🏛 600
⚲ R Weatherley (0121) 704 1936
✓ C Haynes (0121) 705 7296
🏴 18 L 6232 yds SSS 71
👥 WD–U exc Wed am WE–M
SOC–WD
££ £40
🏌 7 miles SE of Birmingham (A41)
◼ www.oltongolf.co.uk

Purley Chase (1980)

Pipers Lane, Ridge Lane, Nuneaton,
CV10 0RB
☎ (024) 7639 3118
✉ enquiries@purley-chase.co.uk
🏛 660
⚲ Linda Jackson
🏴 18 L 6772 yds SSS 72
👥 WD/BH–U WE–U after 2.30pm
SOC
££ On application
🏌 4 miles WNW of Nuneaton on
B114 (A47). A5 Mancetter Island

Pype Hayes (1932)

Public
Eachelhurst Road, Walmley, Sutton
Coldfield, B76 8EP
☎ (0121) 351 1014
🖳 (0121) 313 0206
🏛 320
⚲ L Brogan
✓ J Kelly
🏴 18 L 5996 yds SSS 69
👥 U
££ On application
🏌 5 miles NE of Birmingham

Robin Hood (1893)

St Bernards Road, Solihull, B92 7DJ
☎ (0121) 706 0061
🖳 (0121) 706 0061
🏛 650
✓ A Harvey (0121) 706 0806
🏴 18 L 6635 yds SSS 72
👥 WD–U WE/BH–M SOC–WD H

££ £30 D–£35
🏌 7 miles S of Birmingham
⌂ HS Colt

Rugby (1891)

Clifton Road, Rugby, CV21 3RD
☎ (01788) 544637 (Clubhouse)
🖳 (01788) 542306
✉ golf@rugbygc.fsnet.co.uk
🏛 750
⚲ N Towler (01788) 542306
✓ N Summers (01788) 575134
🏴 18 L 5614 yds SSS 67
👥 WD–U WE/BH–M SOC
££ On application
🏌 1 mile N of Rugby on B5414

Shirley (1956)

Stratford Road, Monkspath, Shirley,
Solihull B90 4EW
☎ (0121) 744 6001
🖳 (0121) 746 5645
✉ shirleygolfclub@btclick.com
🏛 650
⚲ R Maclean (0121) 744 6001
✓ S Bottrill (0121) 746 5646
🏴 18 L 6524 yds SSS 71
👥 WD–U M WE–M SOC (Thur)
££ £25 D–£35
🏌 8 miles S of Birmingham, nr M42
Junction 4
⌂ John Morrison

Sphinx (1948)

Sphinx Drive, Coventry, CV3 1WA
☎ (024) 7645 1361
🏛 300
⚲ GE Brownbridge (024) 7659 7731
🏴 9 L 4262 yds SSS 60
👥 Fri/WE–M after 4.30pm SOC
££ £8 (£10)
🏌 Nr Binley Road, Coventry

Stonebridge Golf Centre

Somers Road, Meriden, CV7 7PL
☎ (01676) 522442
🖳 (01676) 522447
🏛 400
⚲ R Grier
✓ R Grier
🏴 18 L 6250 yds Par 70
👥 U
££ £15.50 (£18.50)
🏌 2 miles E of M42 Junction 6
⊕ Driving range

Stoneleigh Deer Park (1992)

The Old Deer Park, Coventry Road,
Stoneleigh, CV8 3DR
☎ (024) 7663 9991
🖳 (024) 7651 1533
🏛 800
⚲ C Reay
✓ M McGuire/Sarah Perkins
🏴 18 L 6023 yds SSS 71
9 hole Par 3 course
👥 WD–U WE–NA before 2pm SOC
££ On application
🏌 ½ mile E of Stoneleigh

Stratford Oaks (1991)

Bearley Road, Snitterfield, Stratford-on-Avon, CV37 0EZ
- ☎ **(01789) 731980**
- ☐ (01789) 731981
- ✉ admin@stratfordoaks.co.uk
- ☐ 700
- ⚐ ND Powell (Golf Dir)
- ✓ A Dunbar
- ⊳ 18 L 6100 yds SSS 71
- 👫 WD–U WE–U booking necessary
- ££ £23 (£28)
- ⊕ 4 miles NE of Stratford-on-Avon
- ⊕ Driving range
- ⌂ Howard Swann

Stratford-on-Avon (1894)

Tiddington Road, Stratford-on-Avon, CV37 7BA
- ☎ **(01789) 205749**
- ☐ (01789) 414909
- ✉ sec@stratford.co.uk
- ☐ 770
- ⚐ NS Dodd (01789) 205749
- ✓ D Sutherland (01789) 205677
- ⊳ 18 L 6374 yds SSS 70
- 👫 U H SOC
- ££ £40 (£50)
- ⊕ ¹/₂ mile E of Stratford-on-Avon on B4086
- ⌂ JH Taylor
- ■ www.stratfordgolf.co.uk

Sutton Coldfield (1889)

110 Thornhill Road, Sutton Coldfield, B74 3ER
- ☎ **(0121) 580 7878**
- ☐ (0121) 353 5503
- ✉ sc.golf@virgin.net
- ☐ 600
- ⚐ RG MItchell, KM Tempest (0121) 353 9633
- ✓ JK Hayes (0121) 580 7878
- ⊳ 18 L 6541 yds SSS 71
- 👫 U H SOC
- ££ £30 D–£40 (£40)
- ⊕ 9 miles N of Birmingham, off B4138
- ■ www.suttoncoldfieldgc.com

Tidbury Green (1994)

Pay and play
Tilehouse Lane, Shirley, Solihull, B90 1HP
- ☎ **(01564) 824460**
- ☐ 300
- ⚐ Lucy Broadhurst
- ✓ R Thompson
- ⊳ 9 L 2473 yds Par 34
- 👫 U SOC
- ££ 18 holes–£9 (£9) 9 holes–£6 (£6)
- ⊕ 2 miles from M42 Junction 4, nr Earlswood Lakes
- ⊕ Driving range
- ⌂ Derek Stevenson

Walmley (1902)

Brooks Road, Wylde Green, Sutton Coldfield, B72 1HR
- ☎ **(0121) 373 0029**
- ☐ (0121) 377 7272
- ✉ walmleygolfclub@aol.com
- ☐ 750
- ⚐ Mrs AM Clibbery
- ✓ CJ Wicketts (0121) 373 0029 ext 5
- ⊳ 18 L 6585 yds SSS 72
- 👫 WD–U WE–M SOC
- ££ £30 D–£35
- ⊕ N boundary of Birmingham

Warwick (1971)

Public
Warwick Racecourse, Warwick, CV34 6HW
- ☎ **(01926) 494316**
- ⚐ Mrs R Dunkley
- ✓ P Sharp (01926) 491284
- ⊳ 9 L 2682 yds SSS 66
- 👫 U exc while racing in progress & Sun am
- ££ £11 (£12)
- ⊕ Centre of Warwick Racecourse
- ⊕ Driving range
- ⌂ DG Dunkley

The Warwickshire (1993)

Proprietary
Leek Wootton, Warwick, CV35 7QT
- ☎ **(01926) 409409**
- ☐ (01926) 408409
- ☐ 1100
- ⚐ B Fotheringham (Golf Mgr)
- ✓ M Dulson
- ⊳ 18 L 7178 yds SSS 74
  18 L 7154 yds SSS 74
  9 hole Par 3 course
- 👫 H SOC
- ££ £39 (£49)
- ⊕ 1 mile N of Warwick, off A46. M40 Junction 15
- ⊕ Driving range
- ⌂ Karl Litton

Welcombe Hotel

Warwick Road, Stratford-on-Avon, CV37 0NR
- ☎ **(01789) 413800**
- ☐ (01789) 414666
- ☐ 200
- ⚐ N Price (01789) 295252
- ✓ K Hayler (01789) 413800
- ⊳ 18 L 6294 yds SSS 70
- 👫 U H
- ££ D–£40 (D–£50)
- ⊕ 1¹/₂ miles NE of Stratford-on-Avon on A439 towards Warwick. M40 Junction 15
- ⊕ Driving range
- ⌂ T McAuley

West Midlands (2003)

Marsh House Farm Lane, Barston, Solihull B92 0LB
- ☎ **(01675) 444890**
- ☐ (01675) 444891
- ⊳ 18 L 6624 yds Par 72 SSS 72
- 👫 WD–U WE–M before 10am
- ££ £19.95 (£24.95)
- ⊕ 10 min from Birminghm and Coventry, 5 min from NEC
- ⌂ Nigel Harrhy, Mark Harrhy, David Griffith
- ■ www.wmgc.co.uk

Whitefields Hotel (1992)

Coventry Road, Thurlaston, Rugby, CV23 9JR
- ☎ **(01788) 815555**
- ☐ (01788) 521695/817777
- ✉ mail@whitefields-hotel.co.uk
- ☐ 400
- ⚐ B Coleman (01788) 815555
- ✓ Austin Curtis (01788) 815555
- ⊳ 18 L 6289 yds Par 71 SSS 70
- 👫 U SOC WE
- ££ £20 (£30)
- ⊕ 3 miles SW of Rugby at A45/M45 Junction
- ⊕ Driving range (floodlit)
- ■ www.whitefields-hotel.co.uk

Widney Manor (1993)

Pay and play
Saintbury Drive, Widney Manor, Solihull, B91 3SZ
- ☎ **(0121) 704 0704**
- ☐ (0121) 704 7999
- ☐ 503
- ⚐ R Guthrie (Sec/Mgr)
- ✓ T Atkinson
- ⊳ 18 L 5654 yds Par 71
- 👫 U–booking 7 days in advance SOC
- ££ £10.95 (£15.95)
- ⊕ 3 miles from M42 Junction 4, off A34
- ⊕ Driving range

Windmill Village (1990)

Birmingham Road, Allesley, Coventry, CV5 9AL
- ☎ **(024) 7640 4041**
- ☐ (024) 7640 4042
- ✉ leisure@windmillvillagehotel.co.uk
- ☐ 450
- ⚐ M Hartland (Mgr)
- ✓ R Hunter (024) 7640 4041
- ⊳ 18 L 5213 yds Par 70
- 👫 U SOC
- ££ £14.50 (£17.95)
- ⊕ 3 miles W of Coventry on A45
- ⌂ Hunter/Harrhy

Wishaw (1995)

Proprietary
Bulls Lane, Wishaw, Sutton Coldfield, B76 9QW
- ☎ **(0121) 313 2110**
- ☐ 306
- ⚐ PM Lewington
- ⊳ 18 L 5680 yds Par 70 SSS 66 8
- 👫 U SOC
- ££ £12 (£20)
- ⊕ 3 miles NW of M42 Junction 9
- ⌂ RS Wallis

Wiltshire

Bowood G&CC (1992)

Proprietary
Derry Hill, Calne, SN11 9PQ
- ☎ **(01249) 822228**
- ☐ (01249) 822218

✉ golfclub@bowood.org
📖 450
🏌 Karen Elson (Mgr)
✓ M Taylor
🏳 18 L 7317 yds Par 72 SSS 73
👥 U–booking required WE–M before noon SOC
££ £38 (£40)
🚗 3 miles SE of Chippenham on A342. M4 Junction 14 (A4)
⊕ Driving range; 3 Academy holes
🏠 David Thomas
■ www.bowood.org

Bradford-on-Avon (1991)

Trowbridge Road, Bradford-on-Avon
☎ (01225) 868268
✓ G Sawyer
🏳 9 L 2100 metres SSS 61
👥 WD–U WE–pm only
££ 9 holes–£6.50. 18 holes–£10
🚗 SE of Bradford, nr River Avon

Brinkworth (1984)

Longmans Farm, Brinkworth, Chippenham, SN15 5DG
☎ (01666) 510277
📖 250
🏌 J Sheppard
🏳 18 L 5900 yds SSS 69
👥 U SOC
££ On application
🚗 2 miles from Brinkworth (B4042). 12 miles NE of Chippenham

Broome Manor (1976)

Public
Pipers Way, Swindon, SN3 1RG
☎ (01793) 532403
📠 (01793) 433255
✉ bmgc.sec@eclipse.co.uk
📖 800
🏌 JE Poolman (01793) 823462
✓ B Sandry (01793) 532403
🏳 18 L 6283 yds SSS 70
   9 L 2690 yds SSS 67
👥 U
££ 18 hole: £19.10. 9 hole: £11.60
🚗 Swindon 2 miles. M4 Junction 15
⊕ Floodlit driving range
🏠 F Hawtree
■ www.bmgc.co.uk

Chippenham (1896)

Malmesbury Road, Chippenham, SN15 5LT
☎ (01249) 652040
📠 (01249) 446681
✉ chippenhamgc@onetel.co.uk
📖 650
🏌 B Cook
✓ W Creamer (01249) 655519
🏳 18 L 5602 yds SSS 67
👥 U WE–M SOC
££ £22 (£27)
🚗 1 mile N of Chippenham, off A350. Near M4 Junction 17
■ www.chippenhamgolfclub.co.uk

Cricklade Hotel (1992)

Common Hill, Cricklade SN6 6HA
☎ (01793) 750751
📠 (01793) 751767
📖 70
🏌 C Withers
✓ I Bolt
🏳 9 L 1830 yds Par 62 SSS 58
👥 WD–U SOC–WD
££ £16 D–£25
🚗 ¹/₂ mile W of Cricklade on B4040. M4 Junctions 15/16
🏠 Bolt/Smith

Cumberwell Park (1994)

Bradford-on-Avon, BA15 2PQ
☎ (01225) 863322
📠 (01225) 868160
✉ enquiries@cumberwellpark.com
📖 1250
✓ J Jacobs (Golf Dir)
🏳 27 hole course
👥 U SOC
££ £26 (£32)
🚗 Between Bradford-on-Avon and Bath on A363. M4 Junction 18
⊕ Driving range
🏠 Adrian Stiff
■ www.cumberwellpark.com

Defence Academy (1953)

Shrivenham, Swindon, SN6 8LA
☎ (01793) 785725
📖 500
🏌 A Willmett (Mgr)
🏳 18 L 5684 yds SSS 69
👥 M SOC
££ £10 (£10)
🚗 Grounds of Defence Academy. Entry must be arranged with Mgr

Erlestoke Sands (1992)

Erlestoke, Devizes, SN10 5UB
☎ (01380) 831069
📠 (01380) 831284
✉ info@erlestokesands.co.uk
📖 620
🏌 M Pugsley
✓ M Walters (01380) 831027
🏳 18 L 6406 yds Par 73 SSS 71
👥 U–book with Pro SOC
££ £25 (£30)
🚗 6 miles E of Westbury on B3098
⊕ Driving area; 3 Academy holes
🏠 Adrian Stiff

Hamptworth G&CC (1994)

Elmtree Farmhouse, Hamptworth Road, Landford, SP5 2DU
☎ (01794) 390155
📠 (01794) 390022
🏌 P Stevens
✓ M White
🏳 18 L 6516 yds SSS 71
👥 H
££ £25 D–£30
🚗 10 miles SE of Salisbury, off A36/B3079. M27 Junc 2, 6 miles
⊕ Driving range, croquet lawns & fitness centre
■ www.hamptworthgolf.co.uk

High Post (1922)

Great Durnford, Salisbury, SP4 6AT
☎ (01722) 782356
📠 (01722) 782674
📖 625
🏌 P Grimes (01722) 782356
✓ T Isaacs (01722) 782219
🏳 18 L 6305 yds Par 70 SSS 70
👥 WD–U WE/BH–H SOC
££ £30 D–£40 (£40 D–£50) SOC–£40
🚗 4 miles N of Salisbury on A345
🏠 Hawtree

Highworth (1990)

Swindon Road, Highworth, SN6 7SJ
☎ (01793) 766014
🏌 KW Loveday
🏳 9 L 3220 yds SSS 70
👥 U
££ £7.90
🚗 5 miles N of Swindon (A361). M4 Junction 15
⊕ 9 hole pitch & putt course

Kingsdown (1880)

Kingsdown, Corsham, SN13 8BS
☎ (01225) 742530
📖 640 105(L) 45(J)
🏌 JE Elliott (01225) 743472
✓ A Butler (01225) 742634
🏳 18 L 6445 yds SSS 71
👥 WD–H WE–M
££ £27
🚗 5 miles E of Bath

Manor House (1992)

Proprietary
Castle Combe, SN14 7JW
☎ (01249) 782982
📠 (01249) 782992
✉ enquiries@manorhousegolfclub.com
📖 400
🏌 Susan Auld (Gen Mgr)
✓ P Green
🏳 18 L 6286 yds SSS 71
👥 U H–booking necessary SOC
££ £50 Fri/WE–£60
🚗 N of Castle Combe, off B4039. M4 Junction 17, 4 miles
⊕ Driving range
🏠 Alliss/Clarke
■ www.manorhousegolfclub.com

Marlborough (1888)

The Common, Marlborough, SN8 1DU
☎ (01672) 512147
📠 (01672) 513164
✉ contactus@marlboroughgolfclub.co.uk
📖 750
🏌 JAD Sullivan
✓ S Amor (01672) 512493
🏳 18 L 6514 yds SSS 71
👥 WD/WE–H SOC
££ £27 D–£36 (£33 D–£45)
🚗 ¹/₂ mile N of Marlborough (A346). 7 miles S of M4 Junction 15
■ www.marlboroughgolfclub.co.uk

Monkton Park Par Three
(1965)
Pay and play
Chippenham, SN15 3PP
- ☎ **(01249) 653928**
- 🖱 (01249) 653928
- 🕮 100
- ✍ MR & BJ Dawson (Props)
- ⊳ 9 hole Par 3 course
- 👤 U
- ££ 18 holes–£6.90 9 holes–£4.80
- ⛳ Centre of Chippenham. M4 Junction 17
- ⌂ M Dawson
- ■ www.pitchandputtgolf.com

North Wilts   (1890)
Bishops' Cannings, Devizes, SN10 2LP
- ☎ **(01380) 860257**
- 🖱 (01380) 860877
- 🖂 secretary@northwiltsgolf.com
- 🕮 625 105(L) 90(J)
- ✍ Mrs P Stephenson (01380) 860627
- ✎ GJ Laing (Golf Mgr) (01380) 860330
- ⊳ 18 L 6414 yds SSS 71
- 👤 U exc Xmas Day–Jan 31–M SOC
- ££ D–£30 (£35/round)
- ⛳ 1 mile from A4, E of Calne
- ■ www.northwiltsgolf.com

Oaksey Park   (1991)
Pay and play
Oaksey, Malmesbury, SN16 9SB
- ☎ **(01666) 577995**
- 🖱 (01666) 577174
- ⊳ 9 L 2900 yds SSS 68
- 👤 U SOC
- ££ £10 (£15)
- ⛳ 8 miles NE of Malmesbury, off A429
- ⊕ Driving range
- ⌂ Chapman/Warren

Ogbourne Downs   (1907)
Ogbourne St George, Marlborough, SN8 1TB
- ☎ **(01672) 841327**
- 🖱 (01672) 841101
- 🕮 700
- ✍ Miss M Green (01672) 841327
- ✎ A Kirk (01672) 841287
- ⊳ 18 L 6363 yds Par 71 SSS 70
- 👤 WD–H WE–M SOC–WD
- ££ £30
- ⛳ 5 miles S of M4 Junction 15, on A346
- ⌂ JH Taylor

Rushmore Golf Club
Tollard Royal, Salisbury, SP5 5QB
- ☎ **(01725) 516326**
- 🖱 (01725) 516437
- 🖂 rushmoregolf@btinternet.com
- 🕮 508
- ✍ Andrea Cooper (01725 516391)
- ✎ S McDonagh (01725 516326)
- ⊳ 18 L 6131 yds Par 71 SSS 68
- 👤 U SOC
- ££ £20 (£25)
- ⛳ 8 miles SE of Shaftesbury (B3081)

- ⊕ Driving range
- ⌂ D Pottage
- ■ www.rushmoregolfclub.co.uk

Salisbury & South Wilts
(1888)
Netherhampton, Salisbury, SP2 8PR
- ☎ **(01722) 742645**
- 🖱 (01722) 742676
- 🖂 mail@salisburygolf.co.uk
- 🕮 1100
- ✍ Pat Clash (Gen Mgr)
- ✎ J Cave (01722) 742929
- ⊳ 18 L 6485 yds SSS 71
   9 hole course Par 34
- 👤 WD–U SOC–WD
- ££ £25 (£40 – £30 after 2.30)
- ⛳ Wilton, 3 miles SW of Salisbury on A3094
- ⌂ Taylor/Gidman
- ■ www.sswgc.com

Shrivenham Park   (1967)
Pay and play
Penny Hooks Lane, Shrivenham, Swindon, SN6 8EX
- ☎ **(01793) 783853**
- 🕮 140
- ✍ S Ash (01793) 783853
- ✎ T Pocock (01793) 783853
- ⊳ 18 L 5769 yds SSS 69
- 👤 U SOC
- ££ £14 (£18)
- ⛳ 4 miles E of Swindon, off A420. M4 Junction 15

Thoulstone Park   (1992)
Chapmanslade, Westbury, BA13 4AQ
- ☎ **(01373) 832825**
- 🖱 (01373) 832821
- ✍ Mrs J Pearce
- ✎ T Isaacs (01373) 832808
- ⊳ 18 L 6300 yds Par 71 SSS 70
- 👤 U SOC–WD
- ££ £18 (£24)
- ⛳ 12 miles S of Bath, off A36
- ⊕ Driving range
- ⌂ MRM Sandow

Tidworth Garrison   (1908)
Bulford Road, Tidworth, SP9 7AF
- ☎ **(01980) 842321 (Clubhouse)**
- 🖱 (01980) 842301
- 🖂 tidworth@garrison-golfclub.fsnet.co.uk
- 🕮 800
- ✍ T Harris (01980) 842301
- ✎ T Gosden (01980) 842393
- ⊳ 18 L 6320 yds Par 70 SSS 70
- 👤 WD–U H SOC–Tues & Thurs
- ££ £32
- ⛳ 1 mile SW of Tidworth on Bulford road (A338)
- ⌂ Donald Steel
- ■ www.tidworthgolfclub.co.uk

Upavon   (1918)
Douglas Avenue, Upavon, SN9 6BQ
- ☎ **(01980) 630787,**
   (08712) 300 800 daily course info line

- 🖱 (01980) 635419
- 🖂 play@upavongolfclub.co.uk
- 🕮 550
- ✍ L Mitchell
- ✎ R Blake (01980) 630281
- ⊳ 18 L 6415 yds SSS 71
- 👤 WD–U WE–M before noon –U after noon SOC–WD
- ££ £26 D–£26 (£36)
- ⛳ 1.5 miles SE of Upavon on A342, Andover road
- ⌂ R Blake
- ■ www.upavongolfclub.co.uk

West Wilts   (1891)
Elm Hill, Warminster, BA12 0AU
- ☎ **(01985) 213133**
- 🖱 (01985) 219809
- 🖂 westwiltsgc@btopenworld.com
- 🕮 570 70(L) 50(J)
- ✍ GN Morgan
- ✎ S Swales (01985) 212110
- ⊳ 18 L 5754 yds SSS 68
- 👤 WD–U H WE–M H
- ££ £25 D–£35 (£30 D–£45)
- ⛳ 1 mile off A350, on Westbury to Warminster road
- ⌂ JH Taylor
- ■ www.westwiltsgolfclub.co.uk

Whitley   (1993)
Pay and play
Corsham Road, Whitley, Melksham, SN12 7QE
- ☎ **(01225) 790099**
- 🕮 250
- ✍ C Tomkins (01225) 790099
- ✎ None
- ⊳ 9 L 2200 yds Par 33 SSS 61
- 👤 U
- ££ 18 holes–£9. 9 holes–£7
- ⛳ 1 mile N of Melksham on B3553
- ⊕ Driving range
- ⌂ Laurence Ross

The Wiltshire golf & Country Club
Vastern, Wootton Bassett, Swindon, SN4 7PB
- ☎ **(01793) 849999**
- 🖱 (01793) 849988
- 🕮 600
- ✍ Mr E Shah (Gen Mgr); Mrs T Lee (Club Mgr)
- ✎ Kevin Pickett
- ⊳ 18 L 6519 yds SSS 72
- 👤 U SOC
- ££ £25 (£35)
- ⛳ 1 mile S of Wootton Bassett on A3102. M4 Junction 16
- ⌂ Alliss/Clark

Wrag Barn G&CC   (1990)
Shrivenham Road, Highworth, Swindon, SN6 7QQ
- ☎ **(01793) 861327**
- 🖱 (01793) 861325
- 🕮 600
- ✍ M Betteridge
- ✎ B Loughrey (01793) 766027
- ⊳ 18 L 6633 yds SSS 72

For list of abbreviations and key to symbols see page 627

👫 WD–U WE–NA before noon
SOC–WD
££ £30 (£35)
⛳ 6 miles NE of Swindon on B4000.
M4 Junction 15, 8 miles
⊕ Driving range; 6-hole Academy course
🏠 Hawtree
■ www.wragbarn.com

Worcestershire

Abbey Hotel G&CC (1985)
Dagnell End Road, Redditch, B98 7BE
☎ **(01527) 406600**
📠 (01527) 406514
✉ info@theabbeyhotel.co.uk
📖 400
🏌 R Davies (01527) 406500
🏳 18 L 6499 yds SSS 72
👫 WD–U SOC
££ £17 (£23)
⛳ B4101, off A441 Birmingham road. M42 Junction 2
⊕ Driving range
🏠 Donald Steel

Bank House Hotel G&CC (1992)
Bransford, Worcester, WR6 5JD
☎ **(01886) 833551**
📠 (01886) 832461
📖 350
🏌 PAD Holmes
🏌 Scot Fordyce
🏳 18 L 6204 yds SSS 71
👫 U SOC
££ £20 (£30)
⛳ 3 miles SW of Worcester on A4103 Hereford road. M5 Junction 7
⊕ Driving range
🏠 Bob Sandow
■ www.bankhousehotel.com

Blackwell (1893)
Blackwell, Bromsgrove, Worcestershire, B60 1PY
☎ **(0121) 445 1994**
📠 (0121) 445 4911
📖 291 65(L) 10(J)
🏌 JT Mead
🏌 N Blake (0121) 445 3113
🏳 18 L 6260 yds SSS 71
👫 WD–U H WE/BH–M
££ £50 D–£60
⛳ 3 miles E of Bromsgrove. M42 Junction 1 (South)
⊕ Practice area
🏠 Herbert Fowler/Tom Simpson

Brandhall (1906)
Public
Heron Road, Oldbury, Warley, B68 8AQ
☎ **(0121) 552 7475**
📖 300
🏌 C Yates (0121) 552 2195
🏳 18 L 5813 yds Par 71 SSS 68
👫 U exc first 1¹/₂ hrs Sat/Sun
££ £11

⛳ 6 miles NW of Birmingham. M5 Junction 2, 1¹/₂ miles

Bromsgrove Golf Centre (1992)
Proprietary
Stratford Road, Bromsgrove, B60 1LD
☎ **(01527) 575886**
📠 (01527) 570964
✉ enquiries@bromsgrovegolf.f9.co.uk
📖 900
🏌 D Went
🏌 G Long (01527) 575886
🏳 18 L 5969 yds SSS 69
👫 U SOC
££ £15.50 (£20.50)
⛳ Junction of A38/A448. M42 Junction 1. M5 Junction 4/5
⊕ Driving range
🏠 Hawtree
■ www.bromsgrovegolfcentre.co.uk

Churchill & Blakedown (1926)
Churchill Lane, Blakedown, Kidderminster, DY10 3NB
☎ **(01562) 700018**
📖 380
🏌 P Bailey
🏳 9 L 6472 yds Par 72 SSS 71
👫 WD–U WE–M
££ £25
⛳ 3 miles N of Kidderminster on A456

Cocks Moor Woods (1926)
Public
Alcester Road, South King's Heath, Birmingham, B14 4ER
☎ **(0121) 464 3584**
🏌 S Ellis
🏳 18 L 5769 yds Par 69 SSS 68
👫 U
££ On application
⛳ 6 miles S of Birmingham (A435)

Droitwich G&CC (1897)
Ford Lane, Droitwich, WR9 0BQ
☎ **(01905) 774344**
📠 (01905) 797290
📖 782
🏌 M Ashton (01905) 774344
🏌 CS Thompson (01905) 770207
🏳 18 L 6058 yds SSS 69
👫 WD–U WE/BH–M SOC–Wed & Fri
££ £18 – £26
⛳ 1 mile N of Droitwich, off A38. M5 Junction 5

Dudley (1893)
Turners Hill, Rowley Regis, B65 9DP
☎ **(01384) 253719**
📠 (01384) 233177
✉ info@dudleygc.fsnet.co.uk
📖 320
🏌 RP Fortune (01384) 233877
🏌 G Dean (01384) 254020
🏳 18 L 5730 yds SSS 68
👫 WD–U WE–M

££ On application
⛳ 2 miles S of Dudley

Evesham (1894)
Craycombe Links, Fladbury, Pershore, WR10 2QS
☎ **(01386) 860395**
📠 (01386) 861356
✉ eveshamgolf@btopenworld.com
📖 360
🏌 Mr J Dale (01386) 860395
🏌 D Cummins (01386) 861144
🏳 9 L 6415 yds SSS 71
👫 WD–H WE–M NA on comp/match days SOC
££ D–£20
⛳ Fladbury, 4 miles W of Evesham (A4538)

Fulford Heath (1933)
Tanners Green Lane, Wythall, Birmingham, B47 6BH
☎ **(01564) 822806 (Clubhouse)**
📠 (01564) 822629
✉ secretary@fulfordheath.co.uk
📖 750
🏌 Mrs MA Tuckett (01564) 824758
🏌 R Dunbar (01564) 822930
🏳 18 L 6179 yds SSS 70
👫 WD–H WE/BH–M SOC–Tues & Thurs
££ On application
⛳ 8 miles S of Birmingham. M42 Junction 3
🏠 Braid/Hawtree

Gay Hill (1913)
Hollywood Lane, Birmingham, B47 5PP
☎ **(0121) 430 6523/7077**
📠 (0121) 436 7796
✉ secretary@ghgc.org.uk
📖 700
🏌 Mrs J Morris (0121) 430 8544
🏌 A Potter (0121) 474 6001
🏳 18 L 6406 yds SSS 72
👫 WD–U H WE–U SOC
££ £32.00 (round/day ticket)
⛳ 7 miles S of Birmingham on A435. M42 Junction 3, 3 miles
■ www.ghgc.org.uk

Habberley (1924)
Low Habberley, Kidderminster, DY11 5RG
☎ **(01562) 745756**
📠 (01562) 745756
📖 170
🏌 B Blakeway
🏳 9 L 5401 yds SSS 67
👫 WD–U WE–M SOC
££ £12 (£15)
⛳ 3 miles NW of Kidderminster

Hagley (1980)
Proprietary
Wassell Grove, Hagley, Stourbridge, DY9 9JW
☎ **(01562) 883701**
📠 (01562) 887518
📖 750
🏌 GF Yardley (01562) 883701

✓ I Clark (01562) 883852
➤ 18 L 6376 yds SSS 72
👥 WD–U WE–M after 10am
SOC–WD
££ £26 D–£31
⛳ 5 miles SW of Birmingham on
A456. M5 Junction 3
■ www.hagleygolfandcountryclub
.co.uk

Halesowen (1906)
The Leasowes, Halesowen, B62 8QF
☎ (0121) 501 3606
🖷 (0121) 501 3606
📖 680
✍ P Crumpton
✓ J Nicholas (0121) 503 0593
➤ 18 L 5754 yds SSS 69
👥 WD–U WE–M SOC–WD exc Wed
££ £26 D–£31
⛳ M5 Junction 3, 2 miles

Kidderminster (1909)
Russell Road, Kidderminster, DY10 3HT
☎ (01562) 822303
🖷 (01562) 827866
📖 900
✍ Alan Biggs
✓ NP Underwood (01562) 740090
➤ 18 L 6405 yds SSS 71
👥 WD–H WE–M SOC–Thurs
££ £30 D–£35
⛳ Signposted off A449
Wolverhampton-Worcester road

Kings Norton (1892)
*Brockhill Lane, Weatheroak, Alvechurch,
Birmingham B48 7ED*
☎ (01564) 826789
🖷 (01564) 826955
📖 1050
✍ T Webb (Mgr)
✓ K Hayward (01564) 822822
➤ 9 L 3382 yds SSS 36
9 L 3372 yds SSS 36
9 L 3290 yds SSS 36
👥 WD–U WE–NA SOC
££ £32 D–£40
⛳ 7 miles S of Birmingham. 1 mile N
of M42 Junction 3
⊕ 12 hole short course
🏌 Fred Hawtree
■ www.kingsnortongolfclub.co.uk

Lickey Hills (1927)
Public
*Lickey Hills, Rednal, Birmingham,
B45 8RR*
☎ (0121) 453 3159
📖 260
✍ AG Cushing (07976) 793698
✓ Mark Toombs
➤ 18 L 6010 yds SSS 69
👥 U
££ On application
⛳ 10 miles SW of Birmingham. M5
J4. M42 J2

Little Lakes (1975)
*Lye Head, Bewdley, Worcester,
DY12 2UZ*
☎ (01299) 266385

🖷 (01299) 266398
📖 400 50(L)
✍ J Dean (01562) 741704
✓ M Laing
➤ 18 L 6278 yds SSS 71
👥 U SOC
££ £18 (£22)
⛳ 3 miles W of Bewdley, off A456

Moseley (1892)
*Springfield Road, Kings Heath,
Birmingham, B14 7DX*
☎ (0121) 444 2115
🖷 (0121) 441 4662
📖 600
✍ AM Sanders (0121) 444 4957
✓ M Griffin (0121) 444 2063
➤ 18 L 6315 yds SSS 71 Par 70
👥 WD–H or M
££ £37
⛳ 2 miles S of Birmingham off A435.
5 miles N of M42 J3
🏌 HS Colt

North Worcestershire
(1907)
*Frankley Beeches Road, Northfield,
Birmingham, B31 5LP*
☎ (0121) 475 1047
🖷 (0121) 476 8681
📖 550
✍ D Wilson
✓ IF Clark (0121) 475 5721
➤ 18 L 5907 yds SSS 69
👥 WD–U WE/BH–M
££ £25 D–£35
⛳ 7 miles SW of Birmingham, off
A38
🏌 James Braid

Ombersley (1991)
*Bishopswood Road, Ombersley,
Droitwich, WR9 0LE*
☎ (01905) 620747
🖷 (01905) 620047
✉ enquiries@ombersleygolfclub
.co.uk
📖 750
✍ G Glenister (Gen Mgr)
✓ G Glenister
➤ 18 L 6139 yds SSS 69
👥 U
££ £16.20 (£22.50)
⛳ 6 miles N of Worcester, off A449
⊕ Driving range
🏌 David Morgan
■ www.ombersleygolfclub.co.uk

Perdiswell Park
Pay and play
Bilford Road, Worcester, WR3 8DX
☎ (01905) 754668
🖷 (01905) 756608
📖 286
✍ R Gardner
✓ M Woodward (01905) 754668
➤ 18 L 5297 yds SSS 68
👥 U
££ 9 holes–£6.25 (£8.00) 18
holes–£9.50 (£13.00)
⛳ Worcester. M5 Junction 6

Pitcheroak (1973)
Public
Plymouth Road, Redditch, B97 4PB
☎ (01527) 541054
📖 148
✍ R Barnett
✓ D Stewart
➤ 9 L 4561 yds Par 65 SSS 62
👥 U
££ 18 holes–£11.55 (£10.35) 9
holes–£8.00 (£8.55)
⛳ Redditch

Ravenmeadow
*Hindlip Lane, Clanes, Worcester,
WR3 8SA*
☎ (01905) 757525
🖷 (01905) 458876
📖 300
✍ T Senter (Mgr) (01905) 458876
✓ M Slater (01905) 756665
➤ 9 L 5440 yds 18 tees Par 68 SSS 68
👥 U–SOC WD WE
££ £8–£12 (£10–£15)
⛳ 3 miles N of Worcester, off A38.
M5 Junction 6
⊕ Driving range; chipping greens;
putting greens; 9 hole par 3 pitch &
putt course
🏌 R Baldwyn

Redditch (1913)
*Lower Grinsty, Green Lane, Callow Hill,
Redditch B97 5PJ*
☎ (01527) 543079
🖷 (01527) 547413
✉ redditchgolfclub@btconnect.com
📖 883
✍ TJ Sheldon
✓ D Down (01527) 546372
➤ 18 L 6494 yds SSS 72
👥 WD–U SOC
££ £35
⛳ 3 miles SW of Redditch, off A441
🏌 F Pennink
■ www.redditchgolfclub.com

Stourbridge (1892)
*Worcester Lane, Pedmore, Stourbridge,
DY8 2RB*
☎ (01384) 393062
🖷 (01384) 444660
📖 820
✍ Mrs MA Betts (01384) 395566
✓ M Male (01384) 393129
➤ 18 L 6231 yds SSS 70
👥 WD–U exc Wed before 1.30pm–M
WE/BH–M
££ £30
⛳ 1 mile S of Stourbridge on
Worcester road. M5 Junctions 3/4
■ www.stourbridge-golf-club.co.uk

Tolladine (1898)
*The Fairway, Tolladine Road,
Worcester, WR4 9BA*
☎ (01905) 21074 (Clubhouse)
📖 270
✍ D Turner
✓ M Slater
➤ 9 L 5174 yds SSS 67

WD–U before 4pm –M after 4pm
WE/BH–M SOC
£€ On application
M5 Junction 6, 1 mile

The Vale (1991)
Bishampton, Pershore, WR10 2LZ
☎ (01386) 462781
🖫 (01386) 462597
📖 850
✍ R Griffiths (Gen Mgr)
✓ Caroline Griffiths (01386) 462520
⊳ 18 L 6644 yds SSS 72
9 L 2628 yds SSS 65
WD–U WE–U after 1pm SOC–WD
£€ On application
6 miles NW of Evesham, off A44.
M5 Junction 6, 12 miles
⊕ Driving range
M Sandow
■ www.crown-golf.co.uk

Warley (1921)
Public
Lightwoods Hill, Warley, B67 5EQ
☎ (0121) 429 2440
✍ A Woolridge
✓ D Ashington
⊳ 9 L 2606 yds SSS 64
U SOC
£€ On application
5 miles W of Birmingham, off A456

Wharton Park (1992)
Longbank, Bewdley, DY12 2QW
☎ (01299) 405222
🖫 (01299) 405121
✉ enquiries@wharton park.co.uk
📖 550
✓ A Hoare (01299) 405163
⊳ 18 L 6435 yds Par 72 SSS 71
U SOC–WD
£€ £20 (£25)
Bewdley By-pass on A456
⊕ Practice ground
Howard Swann

Worcester G&CC (1898)
Boughton Park, Worcester, WR2 4EZ
☎ (01905) 421132 (Clubhouse)
🖫 (01905) 749090
📖 1005
✍ DG Bettsworth (01905) 422555
✓ C Colenso (01905) 422044
⊳ 18 L 6251 yds SSS 70
WD–H WE–M SOC
£€ £30
1 mile W of Worcester on B4485
(formerly A4103)
Dr A Mackenzie (1926)/C Colenso
(1991)

Worcestershire (1879)
*Wood Farm, Malvern Wells,
WR14 4PP*
☎ (01684) 575992
🖫 (01684) 893334
✉ secretary
@theworcestershiregolfclub
.co.uk
📖 770

✍ Mrs JP Howe (Sec/Mgr)
(01684) 575992
✓ RAF Lewis (01684) 564428
⊳ 18 L 6449 yds SSS 71
WD–H WE–H after 10am
£€ £25 (£34)
2 miles S of Gt Malvern, off
A449/B4209
■ www.theworcestershiregolfclub
.co.uk

Wyre Forest Golf Centre
Pay and play
*Zortech Avenue, Kidderminster,
DY11 7EX*
☎ (01299) 822682
🖫 (01299) 879433
✉ simonprice@wyreforestgolf.com
📖 363
✍ S Price (Mgr)
✓ S Price
⊳ 18 L 5790 yds Par 70 SSS 68
U SOC
£€ £12 (£16)
18 miles S of Birmingham on
A451, between Kidderminster and
Stourport
⊕ Floodlit driving range

Yorkshire (East)

Allerthorpe Park
Allerthorpe, York, YO42 4RL
☎ (01759) 306686
🖫 (01759) 304308
📖 520
✍ JD Atkinson (Sec/Mgr)
✓ (01759) 306686
⊳ 18 L 5506 yds Par 67 SSS 66
U SOC
£€ £18 (£18)
2 miles W of Pocklington, off
A1079
JG Hatcliffe & Partners

Beverley & East Riding
(1889)
The Westwood, Beverley, HU17 8RG
☎ (01482) 867190
🖫 (01482) 868757
📖 550
✍ M Drew (01482) 868757
✓ A Ashby (01482) 869519
⊳ 18 L 5972 yds SSS 69
U SOC
£€ £15 (£20)
Beverley-Walkington road (B1230)

Boothferry Park (1982)
*Spaldington Lane, Spaldington, Nr
Howden, DN14 7NG*
☎ (01430) 430364
🖫 (01430) 430567
✓ James Major (01430) 430364
⊳ 18 L 6651 yds SSS 72 Par 73
U SOC
£€ £10 (£14)
3 miles N of Howden on B1288.
M62 Junction 37, 2 miles
Donald Steel

Bridlington (1905)
Belvedere Road, Bridlington, YO15 3NA
☎ (01262) 672092/606367
🖫 (01262) 606367
✉ enquiries@bridlingtongolfclub
.co.uk
📖 623
✍ CB Rhodes (01262) 606367
✓ ARA Howarth (01262) 674721
⊳ 18 L 6638 yds Par 72 SSS 72
U exc Sun–NA
£€ £20 D–£30 (£35)
1¹/₂ miles S of Bridlington, off
A165
James Braid
■ www.bridlingtongolfclub.co.uk

The Bridlington Links
(1993)
Pay and play
*Flamborough Road, Marton,
Bridlington, YO15 1DW*
☎ (01262) 401584
🖫 (01262) 401702
📖 300
✍ PM Hancock (Gen Mgr)
✓ S Raybould
⊳ 18 L 6720 yds SSS 72
9 hole course
U
£€ £12 (£15)
2 miles N of Bridlington on B1255
⊕ Floodlit driving range; 3 Academy
holes
Howard Swann

Brough (1893)
Cave Road, Brough, HU15 1HB
☎ (01482) 667374
🖫 (01482) 669873
📖 700
✍ GW Townhill (Golf Dir)
(01482) 667291
✓ GW Townhill (01482) 667483
⊳ 18 L 6075 yds SSS 69
WD–U exc Wed–NA
£€ ˙£32
10 miles W of Hull on A63
■ www.brough-golfclub.co.uk

Cave Castle (1989)
South Cave, Nr Brough, HU15 2EU
☎ (01430) 421286
🖫 (01430) 421118
✍ C Welton (Admin)
✓ S MacKinder (01430) 421286
⊳ 18 L 6409 yds SSS 71
U SOC
£€ £12.50 (£18)
10 miles W of Hull. Junction of
A63/M62

Cherry Burton (1993)
Pay and play
*Leconfield Road, Cherry Burton,
Beverley, HU17 7RB*
☎ (01964) 550924
📖 220
✍ JK Walmsley (01182) 587877

✔ J Calam (01964) 550924
☞ 9 L 3290 yds Par 36 SSS 71
☖ U SOC
££ £15 for 18, £12 for 9
⛳ 2 miles N of Beverley, off Malton road
⊕ Floodlit driving range
⛫ Will Adamson
■ cherryburtongolfclub.co.uk

Cottingham   (1984)

Woodhill Way, Cottingham, Hull, HU16 5RZ
☎ **(01482) 842394**
☖ (01482) 845932
☐ 600
✍ RJ Wiles (01482) 846030
✔ CW Gray (01482) 842394
☞ 18 L 6459 yds Par 72 SSS 71
☖ WD–U WE/BH–restricted SOC after 2pm
££ £16 D–£24 (£24 D–£36)
⛳ 3 miles N of Hull, off A164
⊕ Driving range
⛫ Wiles/Litten
■ www.golf-in-england.co.uk/cottingham

Driffield   (1923)

Sunderlandwick, Driffield, YO25 9AD
☎ **(01377) 240448 (Clubhouse),**
(01377) 253116 (Office)
☖ (01377) 240599
✉ info@driffieldgolfclub.co.uk
☐ 670
✍ JR Nicholson, M.Inst.GCM
✔ K Wright (01377) 241224
☞ 18 L 6212 yds SSS 70
☖ H I SOC
££ £24 D–£30 (£30 D–£40)
⛳ S of Driffield on A164
■ www.driffieldgolfclub.co.uk

Flamborough Head   (1932)

Lighthouse Road, Flamborough, Bridlington, YO15 1AR
☎ **(01262) 850333/850417**
☖ (01262) 850279
✉ secretary
@flamboroughheadgolfclub.co.uk
☐ 400
✍ GS Thornton
✔ P Harrison (01262) 850222
☞ 18 L 6189 yds Par 71 SSS 69
☖ U
££ £20 (£25) 5D–£80
⛳ 5 miles NE of Bridlington
■ www.flamboroughheadgolfclub.co.uk

Ganstead Park   (1976)

Longdales Lane, Coniston, Hull, HU11 4LB
☎ **(01482) 811280 (Steward)**
☖ (01482) 817754
✉ secretary@gansteadpark.co.uk
☐ 700
✍ G Drewery (01482) 817754
✔ M Smee (01482) 811121
☞ 18 L 6801 yds SSS 73
☖ U H WE–NA before noon SOC

££ On application
⛳ 5 miles E of Hull on A165
⛫ Peter Green
■ www.gansteadpark.co.uk

Hainsworth Park   (1983)

Brandesburton, Driffield, YO25 8RT
☎ **(01964) 542362**
☖ (01964) 542362
☐ 550
✍ R Hounsfield, BW Atkin (Prop)
✔ PR Binnington (01964) 542362
☞ 18 L 6362 yds SSS 71
☖ SOC
££ £20 (£24)
⛳ 6 miles NW of Beverley, off A165 at Brandesburton roundabout

Hessle   (1898)

Westfield Road, Raywell, Cottingham, HU16 5YL
☎ **(01482) 650171**
☖ (01482) 652679
☐ 680
✍ D Pettit
✔ G Fieldsend (01482) 650190
☞ 18 L 6604 yds SSS 72
☖ WD–U exc Tues 9am–1pm WE–NA before 11.30am
££ £25 (£32)
⛳ 3 miles SW of Cottingham
⛫ Thomas/Alliss

Hornsea   (1898)

Rolston Road, Hornsea, HU18 1XG
☎ **(01964) 532020**
☖ (01964) 532020
☐ 600
✍ David Crossley (01964) 532020
✔ S Wright (01964) 534989
☞ 18 L 6661 yds SSS 72
☖ WD–U WE–restricted SOC
££ £24 D–£32
⛳ 300 yds past Hornsea Free Port
⛫ Mackenzie/Braid

Hull   (1904)

The Hall, 27 Packman Lane, Kirk Ella, Hull HU10 7TJ
☎ **(01482) 653026/658919**
☖ (01482) 658919
☐ 821
✍ Mrs C Toffolo (01482) 658919
✔ D Jagger (01482) 653074/658919
☞ 18 L 6246 yds SSS 70
☖ WD–U WE–by arrangement
££ £26.50 D–£32
⛳ 5 miles W of Hull
⛫ James Braid

Kilnwick Percy   (1995)

Pocklington, York, East Yorkshire, YO42 1UF
☎ **(01759) 303090**
☐ 350
✍ Mrs A Clayton (Sec/Mgr)
✔ J Townhill
☞ 18 L 6214 yds Par 70 SSS 70
☖ U SOC
££ £18 (£20)
⛳ 1 mile E of Pocklington, off B1246

⛫ John Day
■ www.kilnwickpercygolfclub.co.uk

Springhead Park   (1930)

Public
Willerby Road, Hull, HU5 5JE
☎ **(01482) 656309**
✍ Mrs R Taylor (01482) 654875
☞ 18 L 6402 yds SSS 71
☖ U SOC–WD
££ £10.50 (£12.50)
⛳ 4 miles W of Hull

Sutton Park   (1935)

Public
Salthouse Road, Hull, HU8 9HF
☎ **(01482) 374242**
☖ (01482) 701428
☐ 300
✍ CR Alsop
✔ (01482) 711450
☞ 18 L 6251 yds SSS 70
☖ U SOC–exc Sun
££ £10.00 (£12.50)
⛳ 3 miles E of Hull on A165

Withernsea   (1909)

Chestnut Avenue, Withernsea, HU19 2PG
☎ **(01964) 612258 (Clubhouse)**
☐ 329 30(L) 36(J)
✍ K Purdue (Admin) (01694) 612078
☞ 9 L 6207 yds Par 72 SSS 70
☖ WD–U WE/BH–M before 1pm SOC
££ £10
⛳ 17 miles E of Hull on A1033. S side of Withernsea

Yorkshire (North)

Aldwark Manor   (1978)

Aldwark, Alne, York, YO61 1UF
☎ **(01347) 838353**
☖ (01347) 833991
☐ 400
✍ GF Platt (Mgr) (01347) 838353
☞ 18 L 6187 yds Par 72 SSS 70
☖ U SOC
££ £25 D–£35 (£30 D–£40)
⛳ 5 miles SE of Boroughbridge, off A1. 13 miles NW of York, off A19

Ampleforth College   (1972)

Castle Drive, Gilling East, York, YO62 4HP
☎ **(01439) 788212**
✉ golf@michaelwilson.plus.com
☐ 260
✍ Dr M Wilson (01904) 768861
☞ 9 L 5567 yds Par 69 SSS 69
☖ U exc 2–4pm during term time
££ £12 (£12)
⛳ Gilling East, 18 miles N of York (B1363)
⊕ Green fees payable at Fairfax Arms, Gilling East
⛫ Rev Jerome Lambert OSB
■ www.ampleforthgolf.co.uk

Bedale (1894)
Leyburn Road, Bedale, DL8 1EZ
- ☎ **(01677) 422568**
- ✉ bedalegolfclub@aol.com
- 📖 600 76(J)
- ⚐ Mrs G Brown (01677) 422451
- ⚑ AD Johnson (01677) 422443
- ⚐ 18 L 6610 yds SSS 72
- 👘 U SOC
- £€ £23 D–£28 (£30 D–£35)
- 🚗 N boundary of Bedale

Bentham (1922)
Robin Lane, Bentham, Lancaster, LA2 7AG
- ☎ **(015242) 62455**
- (015242) 62470
- ✉ secretary@benthamgolfclub.co.uk
- 📖 450
- ⚐ J Mann (015242) 62455
- ⚐ 18 L 6000 yds SSS 68
- 👘 U SOC
- £€ D–£25
- 🚗 NE of Lancaster on B6480 towards Settle. 13 miles E of M6 Junction 34
- ■ www.benthamgolfclub.co.uk

Catterick (1930)
Leyburn Road, Catterick Garrison, DL9 3QE
- ☎ **(01748) 833268**
- (01748) 833268
- 📖 600
- ⚐ G McDonnell (Sec/Mgr)
- ⚑ A Marshall (01748) 833671
- ⚐ 18 L 6329 yds SSS 71
- 👘 H WE–NA before 10am SOC
- £€ £27 (£33)
- 🚗 6 miles SW of Scotch Corner, via A1
- 🏠 Arthur Day
- ■ www.catterickgolfclub.co.uk

Cleveland (1887)
Majuba Road, Redcar, TS10 5BJ
- ☎ **(01642) 471798**
- (01642) 471798
- 📖 800
- ⚐ JA Moran (01642) 471798
- ⚑ (01642) 483462
- ⚐ 18 L 6696 yds SSS 72
- 👘 WD–U WE/BH–by arrangement SOC
- £€ £25 (£28)
- 🚗 S bank of River Tees
- ■ www.clevelandgolfclub.co.uk

Cocksford (1992)
Stutton, Tadcaster, LS24 9NG
- ☎ **(01937) 834253**
- (01937) 834253
- ⚐ F Judson
- ⚑ G Thompson
- ⚐ 18 L 5570 yds Par 71 SSS 69
- 👘 WD–U WE–by arrangement SOC
- £€ £19 D–£25 (£25 D–£28)
- 🚗 1½ miles S of Tadcaster
- ■ www.cocksfordgolfclub.freeserve.co.uk

Crimple Valley (1976)
Pay and play
Hookstone Wood Road, Harrogate, HG2 8PN
- ☎ **(01423) 883485**
- (01423) 881018
- 📖 200
- ⚐ P Lumb
- ⚑ P Lumb
- ⚐ 9 L 2500 yds SSS 33
- 👘 U
- £€ 9 holes–£7 (£8) 18 holes–£11 D–£15
- 🚗 1 mile S of Harrogate, off A61, by Yorkshire Showground
- 🏠 R Lumb

Drax (1989)
Drax, Selby, YO8 8PQ
- ☎ **(01757) 618041**
- 📖 450
- ⚐ K Onions (01405) 860872
- ⚐ 9 L 5434 yds Par 68 SSS 66
- 👘 M SOC
- £€ £10 (£18)
- 🚗 5 miles S of Selby, off A1041
- 🏠 JM Scott

Easingwold (1930)
Stillington Road, Easingwold, York, YO61 3ET
- ☎ **(01347) 821486**
- (01347) 822474
- ✉ brian@easingwold-golf-club.fsnet.co.uk
- 📖 690
- ⚐ DB Stockley (01347) 822474
- ⚑ J Hughes (01347) 821964
- ⚐ 18 L 6717 yds Par 73 SSS 72
- 👘 U
- £€ D–£28 D–£30 (£35) – £8 junior
- 🚗 12 miles N of York on A19. S end of Easingwold
- ⊕ Target golf
- 🏠 Hawtree/OCM
- ■ www.easingwold-golf-club.co.uk

Filey (1897)
West Ave, Filey, YO14 9BQ
- ☎ **(01723) 513293**
- (01723) 514952
- ✉ secretary@fileygolfclub.com
- 📖 768
- ⚐ Mrs DA Willis
- ⚑ GM Hutchinson (01723) 513134
- ⚐ 18 L 6112 yds SSS 69
  9 L 1513 yds Par 30
- 👘 U H SOC
- £€ £25 (£30) Summer. £20 (£25) Winter
- 🚗 1 mile S of Filey centre
- 🏠 James Braid

Forest of Galtres (1993)
Moorlands Road, Skelton, York, YO32 2RF
- ☎ **(01904) 766198**
- (01904) 769400
- 📖 450
- ⚐ Mrs SJ Procter
- ⚑ P Bradley
- ⚐ 18 L 6412 yds Par 72 SSS 70
- 👘 U SOC–WD/Sun
- £€ £20 (£27)
- 🚗 Skelton, 4 miles N of York. 1½ miles off A19
- ⊕ Driving range
- 🏠 Simon Gidman
- ■ www.forestofgaltres.co.uk

Forest Park (1991)
Stockton-on Forest, York, YO32 9UW
- ☎ **(01904) 400425**
- ✉ admin@forestparkgolfclub.co.uk
- 📖 650
- ⚐ N Crossley (01904) 400688
- ⚑ M Winterburn (01904) 400425
- ⚐ 18 L 6660 yds Par 71 SSS 72
  9 L 3186 yds Par 70 SSS 70
- 👘 U SOC
- £€ £18 D–£24 (£23 D–£32) 9 hole: £8 (£10)
- 🚗 1½ miles from E end of A64 York By-pass
- ⊕ Driving range + new undercover driving range
- ■ www.forestparkgolfclub.co.uk

Fulford (1906)
Heslington Lane, York, YO10 5DY
- ☎ **(01904) 413579**
- (01904) 416918
- 📖 750
- ⚐ I Mackland
- ⚑ M Brown (01904) 412882
- ⚐ 18 L 6775 yds SSS 72
- 👘 By arrangement with Mgr
- £€ £40 D–£48 (£48)
- 🚗 2 miles S of York (A64)
- 🏠 Major C McKenzie

Ganton (1891)
Station Road, Ganton, Scarborough, YO12 4PA
- ☎ **(01944) 710329**
- (01944) 710922
- ✉ secretary@gantongolfclub.com
- 📖 550
- ⚐ Maj RG Woolsey
- ⚑ G Brown (01944) 710260
- ⚐ 18 L 6734 yds SSS 73
- 👘 By prior arrangement
- £€ On application
- 🚗 11 miles SW of Scarborough on A64
- 🏠 Dunn/Vardon/Braid/Colt
- ■ www.gantongolfclub.com

Harrogate (1892)
Forest Lane Head, Harrogate, HG2 7TF
- ☎ **(01423) 863158 (Clubhouse)**
- (01423) 860073
- 📖 700
- ⚐ (01423) 862999
- ⚑ P Johnson (01423) 862547
- ⚐ 18 L 6241 yds SSS 70
- 👘 WD–U WE/BH–enquire first SOC–WD exc Tues
- £€ £36 (£40)
- 🚗 2 miles E of Harrogate on Knaresborough road (A59)
- 🏠 Sandy Herd
- ■ www.harrogate-gc.co.uk

Heworth (1911)

Muncaster House, Muncastergate, York,
YO31 9JY

- ☎ **(01904) 424618**
- 🖳 (01904) 426156
- ✉ golf@heworth-gc.fsnet.co.uk
- 📖 345 80(L) 50(J)
- ♣ RJ Hunt (01904) 426156
- ✓ S Burdett (01904) 422389
- ▷ 12 L 6141 yds Par 70 SSS 69
- ♟ U
- ££ £15 (£20)
- ⛳ NE boundary of York (A1036)

Hunley Hall (1993)

Brotton, Saltburn, TS12 2QQ

- ☎ **(01287) 676216**
- 🖳 (01287) 678250
- ✉ enquiries@hunleyhall.co.uk
- 📖 500
- ♣ E Lillie (01287) 676216
- ✓ A Brook (01287) 677444
- ▷ 27 holes:
  5948-6918 yds Par/SSS 68-73
- ♟ U SOC–exc Sun
- ££ £25 (£30)
- ⛳ 15 miles SE of Middlesbrough on A174
- ⊕ Floodlit driving range; hotel
- 🏠 John Morgan
- ■ www.hunleyhall.co.uk

Kirkbymoorside (1951)

Manor Vale, Kirkbymoorside, York,
YO62 6EG

- ☎ **(01751) 431525**
- 🖳 (01751) 433190
- ✉ enqs@kmsgolf.fsnet.co.uk
- 📖 630
- ♣ RJ Butter
- ✓ J Hinchliffe (01751) 430402
- ▷ 18 L 6047 yds SSS 69
- ♟ U after 9am
- ££ £22 (£32)
- ⛳ A170 between Helmsley and Pickering
- ■ www.kirkbymoorsidegolf.co.uk

Knaresborough (1920)

Boroughbridge Road, Knaresborough,
HG5 0QQ

- ☎ **(01423) 864865**
- 🖳 (01423) 869345
- ✉ knaresboroughgolfclub
  @btopenworld.com
- 📖 795
- ♣ JL Hall (Mgr) (01423) 862690
- ✓ GJ Vickers (01423) 864865
- ▷ 18 L 6354 yds Par 70 SSS 70
- ♟ U SOC
- ££ £28.50 (£35.50)
- ⛳ 1¹/₂ miles N of Knaresborough on A6055
- 🏠 Hawtree

Malton & Norton (1910)

Welham Park, Welham Road, Norton,
Malton YO17 9QE

- ☎ **(01653) 697912**
- 🖳 (01653) 697912
- 📖 820

- ♣ E Harrison (01653) 697912
- ✓ SI Robinson (01653) 693882
- ▷ 27 holes:
  Welham L 6456 yds SSS 71
  Park L 6242 yds SSS 70
  Derwent L 6286 yds SSS 70
- ♟ WD–U WE–restricted on match days H SOC
- ££ £25 (£30)
- ⛳ 18 miles NE of York (A64)
- ⊕ Driving range

Masham (1895)

Burnholme, Swinton Road, Masham,
Ripon HG4 4HT

- ☎ **(01765) 689379**
- 📖 327
- ♣ Mrs J McGee (01765) 688054
- ▷ 9 L 6088 yds SSS 69
- ♟ WD–U before 5pm WE–M BH–NA
- ££ D–£20 £16 (18 holes)
- ⛳ 10 miles N of Ripon, off A6108

Middlesbrough (1908)

Brass Castle Lane, Marton,
Middlesbrough, TS8 9EE

- ☎ **(01642) 311515**
- 🖳 (01642) 319607
- ✉ enquiries@brasscastle.net
- 📖 975
- ♣ PM Jackson
- ✓ DJ Jones (01642) 311766
- ▷ 18 L 6278 yds SSS 70
- ♟ WD–U exc Tues–H Sat–NA SOC
- ££ D–£35 (£40)
- ⛳ 3 miles S of Middlesbrough
- 🏠 James Braid
- ■ www.middlesbroughgolfclub.co.uk

Middlesbrough Municipal (1977)

Public
Ladgate Lane, Middlesbrough, TS5 7YZ

- ☎ **(01642) 315533**
- 🖳 (01642) 300726
- 📖 625
- ♣ JC Taylor (Hon)
- ✓ A Hope (01642) 300720
- ▷ 18 L 6333 yds SSS 70
- ♟ U
- ££ £11 (£14)
- ⛳ 2 miles S of Middlesbrough on A174
- ⊕ Floodlit driving range

Oakdale (1914)

Oakdale, Harrogate, HG1 2LN

- ☎ **(01423) 567162**
- 🖳 (01423) 536030
- ✉ sec@oakdale-golfclub.com
- 📖 775
- ♣ MJ Cross
- ✓ C Dell (01423) 560510
- ▷ 18 L 6456 yds SSS 71
- ♟ WD–U 9.30–12.30 and after 2pm SOC–WD
- ££ £30 D–£45
- ⛳ ¹/₂ mile NE of Royal Hall, Harrogate
- 🏠 Dr A Mackenzie
- ■ www.oakdale-golfclub.com

The Oaks (1996)

Aughton Common, Aughton, York,
YO42 4PW

- ☎ **(01757) 288001 (Clubhouse),**
  (01757) 288007 (Bookings)
- 🖳 (01757) 289029
- 📖 675
- ♣ Mrs S Nutt (01757) 288577
- ✓ J Townhill
- ▷ 18 L 6743 yds Par 72 SSS 72
- ♟ WD–U WE–M SOC–WD
- ££ £22 D–£35
- ⛳ 1 mile N of Bubwith on B1228. 14 miles SE of York. M62 Junction 37
- ⊕ Driving range
- 🏠 Julian Covey
- ■ www.theoaksgolfclub.co.uk

Pannal (1906)

Follifoot Road, Pannal, Harrogate,
HG3 1ES

- ☎ **(01423) 871641**
- 🖳 (01423) 870043
- ✉ secretary@pannalgc.co.uk
- 📖 780
- ♣ R Braddon (01423) 872628
- ✓ D Padgett (01423) 872620
- ▷ 18 L 6622 yds SSS 72
- ♟ WD–H 9.30–12 and after 1.30pm WE–H 11–12 and after 2.30pm SOC
- ££ £41 D–£51 (£51)
- ⛳ 2¹/₂ miles S of Harrogate, on A61
- 🏠 Herd/Mackenzie

Pike Hills (1904)

Tadcaster Road, Askham Bryan, York,
YO23 3UW

- ☎ **(01904) 700797**
- 🖳 (01904) 700797
- 📖 750
- ♣ L Hargrave
- ✓ I Gradwell (01904) 708756
- ▷ 18 L 6146 yds SSS 70
- ♟ WD–U H before 4.30pm –M after 4.30pm SOC–WD
- ££ £22 D–£26
- ⛳ 3 miles SW of York on A64

Richmond (1892)

Bend Hagg, Richmond, DL10 5EX

- ☎ **(01748) 825319**
- 🖳 (01748) 821709
- 📖 600
- ♣ BD Aston (01748) 823231
- ✓ P Jackson (01748) 822457
- ▷ 18 L 5886 yds SSS 68
- ♟ U
- ££ £22 D–£24 (£25 D–£30)
- ⛳ 3 miles SW of Scotch Corner
- 🏠 Frank Pennink

Ripon City (1907)

Palace Road, Ripon, HG4 3HH

- ☎ **(01765) 603640**
- 🖳 (01765) 692880
- ✉ office@ripongolf.com
- 📖 650 100(L) 45(J)
- ♣ CJ Webb
- ✓ T Davis (01765) 600411
- ▷ 18 L 6084 yds SSS 69

👥 U SOC
£€ £23 (£30)
🚗 1 mile N of Ripon on A6108
⊕ Driving range
🏠 ADAS
■ www.ripongolf.com

Romanby (1993)

Pay and play
Yafforth Road, Northallerton, DL7 0PE
☎ (01609) 779988
🖥 (01609) 779084
📖 550
🏌 G McDonnell (01609) 778855
⛳ T Jenkins
🏳 18 L 6663 yds SSS 72
👥 U SOC
£€ £25 (£30)
🚗 1 mile W of Northallerton on B6271
⊕ Floodlit driving range
🏠 Will Adamson

Rudding Park (1995)

Pay and play
Rudding Park, Harrogate, HG3 1DJ
☎ (01423) 872100
🖥 (01423) 873011
📖 500
🏌 J Watson
⛳ M Moore (01423) 873400
🏳 18 L 6871 yds SSS 72
👥 U H SOC
£€ £22.50. Fri/WE–£27.50
🚗 2 miles S of Harrogate (A658)
⊕ Driving range; Golf Academy
🏠 Hawtree
■ www.ruddingpark.com

Saltburn (1894)

Hob Hill, Saltburn-by-the-Sea, TS12 1NJ
☎ (01287) 622812
🖥 (01287) 625988
✉ info@saltburngolf.co.uk
📖 900
⛳ N Whinham (01287) 624653
🏳 18 L 5897 yds Par 70 SSS 68
👥 U H SOC
£€ £24 (£30)
🚗 1 mile S of Saltburn
■ www.saltburngolf.co.uk

Scarborough North Cliff (1909)

North Cliff Avenue, Burniston Road, Scarborough, YO12 6PP
☎ (01723) 360786
🖥 (01723) 362134
📖 860
🏌 JR Freeman
⛳ SN Deller (01723) 365920
🏳 18 L 6425 yds Par 71 SSS 71
👥 U H exc Sat am/Sun before 10am and comp days SOC
£€ £24 D–£30 (£28 D–£34)
🚗 2 miles N of Scarborough on coast road
🏠 James Braid
■ www.ncgc.co.uk

Scarborough South Cliff (1902)

Deepdale Avenue, Scarborough, YO11 2UE
☎ (01723) 374737
🖥 (01723) 374737
✉ secretary@scarboroughgolfclub.co.uk
📖 700
🏌 D Roberts
⛳ T Skingle (01723) 365150
🏳 18 L 6405 yds SSS 71
👥 U H
£€ £25 (£30)
🚗 1 mile S of Scarborough, off A165
🏠 Dr A Mackenzie
■ www.scarboroughgolfclub.co.uk

Scarthingwell (1993)

Scarthingwell, Tadcaster, LS24 9DG
☎ (01937) 557878
🖥 (01937) 557909
📖 400
⛳ S Footman (01937) 557864
🏳 18 L 6642 yds Par 71 SSS 72
👥 U SOC
£€ £16 (£20)
🚗 4 miles S of Tadcaster on A162

Selby (1907)

Mill Lane, Brayton, Selby, YO8 9LD
☎ (01757) 228622
🖥 (01757) 228785
📖 749
🏌 JN Proctor
⛳ N Ludwell (01757) 228785
🏳 18 L 6374 yds SSS 71
👥 WD–H WE–NA SOC–WD
£€ £30 D–£35
🚗 3 miles SW of Selby, off A19 at Brayton. 5 miles N of M62 Junction 34
🏠 JH Taylor/Hawtree
■ www.selbygolfclub.co.uk

Settle (1895)

Giggleswick, Settle, BD24 0DH
☎ (01729) 825288
📖 250
🏌 J Ketchell (01729) 823727
🏳 9 L 6089 yds SSS 72
👥 U exc Sun–restricted SOC
£€ D–£15
🚗 1 mile N of Settle on A65
🏠 Tom Vardon

Skipton (1893)

Short Lee Lane, Skipton, BD23 3LF
☎ (01756) 793922
🖥 (01756) 796665
📖 720
🏌 TH Newman (01756) 795657
⛳ P Robinson (01756) 793257
🏳 18 L 6076 yds SSS 70
👥 U SOC
£€ £24 (£26)
🚗 1 mile N of Skipton on A59

Teesside (1901)

Acklam Road, Thornaby, TS17 7JS
☎ (01642) 676249
🖥 (01642) 676252
✉ teessidegolfclub@btconnect.com
📖 730
🏌 M Fleming (01642) 616516
⛳ K Hall (01642) 673822
🏳 18 L 6535 yds Par 72 SSS 71
👥 WD–U before 4.30pm WE–U after 11am BH–M before 11am SOC
£€ D–£26 (£30)
🚗 2 miles S of Stockton on A1130. ¹/₂ mile from A19 on A1130
🏠 Makepeace/Summerville
■ www.teessidegolfclub.com

Thirsk & Northallerton (1914)

Thornton-le-Street, Thirsk, YO7 4AB
☎ (01845) 522170
🖥 (01845) 525115
📖 500
🏌 GS Batterbee (01845) 525115
⛳ R Garner (01845) 526216
🏳 18 L 6495 yds SSS 71
👥 WD/Sat–U H Sun–M SOC
£€ £22 D–£28 Sat/BH–£28 D–£33
🚗 2 miles N of Thirsk, nr A19 and A168 roundabout
🏠 ADAS

Whitby (1892)

Sandsend Road, Low Straggleton, Whitby, YO21 3SR
☎ (01947) 600660
🖥 (01947) 600660
📖 650
🏌 (01947) 600660
⛳ T Mason (01947) 602719
🏳 18 L 6134 yds SSS 69
👥 U H SOC
£€ £22 (£28)
🚗 2 miles N of Whitby on A174

Wilton (1952)

Wilton, Redcar, Cleveland, TS10 4QY
☎ (01642) 465265/465886
🖥 (01642) 465463
✉ secretary@wiltongolfclub.co.uk
📖 863
🏌 R Douglas (01642) 465265
⛳ Pat Smillie (01642) 452730
🏳 18 L 6145 yds Par 70 SSS 69
👥 WD–U after 10am Sat–NA Sun/BH–U after 10am SOC–WD exc Tues & Thurs
£€ D–£23 (D–£26)
🚗 3 miles W of Redcar on A174–signs to Wilton Castle
■ www.wiltongolfclub.co.uk

York (1890)

Lords Moor Lane, Strensall, York, YO32 5XF
☎ (01904) 491840
🖥 (01904) 491852
📖 400 129(L) 78(J)
🏌 SG Watson
⛳ AP Hoyles (01904) 490304

18 L 6301 yds SSS 70
U–phone Sec SOC
£€ £32–£40 (£42–£46)
⌖ 4 miles N of York ring road
(A1237)
🏠 JH Taylor

Yorkshire (South)

Abbeydale   (1895)
*Twentywell Lane, Dore, Sheffield,
S17 4QA*
☎ **(0114) 236 0763**
🖳 (0114) 236 0762
📖 650
⌨ GL Lord
✎ N Perry (0114) 236 5633
⏱ 18 L 6261 yds SSS 71
U SOC–H by arrangement
£€ £30 (£45)
⌖ 5 miles S of Sheffield, off A621
🏠 Herbert Fowler
▪ www.abbeydalegolf.co.uk

Barnsley   (1925)
Public
*Wakefield Road, Staincross, Barnsley,
S75 6JZ*
☎ **(01226) 382856**
📖 550
⌨ B Caunt
✎ S Wyke (01226) 380358
⏱ 18 L 5951 yds Par 69 SSS 69
U
£€ £10.50 (£12.50)
⌖ 4 miles N of Barnsley on A61

Bawtry G&CC   (1974)
*Cross Lane, Austerfield, Doncaster,
DN10 6RF*
☎ **(01302) 710841**
📖 490 25(L) 20(J)
⌨ PD Ludbrook
✎ H Selby-Green
⏱ 18 L 6900 yds Par 73 SSS 73
U SOC
£€ £14 (£18)
⌖ 2 miles NE of Bawtry, on A614
⊕ Driving range
🏠 E & M Baker

Beauchief   (1925)
Public
*Abbey Lane, Beauchief, Sheffield,
S18 0DB*
☎ **(0114) 236 7274**
📖 450
⏱ 18 L 5452 yds SSS 66
U
£€ £8.50 – £10
⌖ A621 Sheffield

Birley Wood   (1974)
Public
Birley Lane, Sheffield, S12 3BP
☎ **(0114) 264 7262**
🖂 birleysec@hotmail.com
📖 258
⌨ P Renshaw (0114) 265 3784
✎ P Ball

18 L 5734 yds Par 69 SSS 67
U
£€ £9 (£11)
⌖ 4 miles S of Sheffield on A616. M1
Junction 30
▪ www.birleywood.free-online.co.uk

Concord Park   (1952)
Pay and play
Shiregreen Lane, Sheffield, S5 6AE
☎ **(0114) 257 7378**
🖳 (0114) 234 7792
🖂 concordparkgc@tiscali.co.uk
⌨ PJ Wilson (0114) 234 7792
✎ W Allcroft (0114) 257 7378
⏱ 18 L 4872 yds Par 67 SSS 64
U
£€ £8 (£10)
⌖ M1 Junction 34, 1 mile
⊕ Driving range

Crookhill Park   (1974)
Public
Conisborough, Doncaster, DN12 2AH
☎ **(01709) 862979**
📖 50
⌨ TA Cusack
⏱ 18 L 5860 yds SSS 68
U
£€ £9.95 (£11.30)
⌖ 3 miles W of A1(M)/A630 junction

Doncaster   (1894)
*Bawtry Road, Bessacarr, Doncaster,
DN4 7PD*
☎ **(01302) 865632**
🖳 (01302) 865994
🖂 doncastergolf@aol.com
📖 576
⌨ GJ Needham
✎ G Bailey (01302) 868404
⏱ 18 L 6220 yds SSS 70
WD–U H WE/BH–NA before
11.30am SOC–WD
£€ £30 D–£36 (£15)
⌖ 4¹/₂ miles S of Doncaster on A638
🏠 Mackenzie/Hawtree

Doncaster Town Moor
(1895)
*Bawtry Road, Belle Vue, Doncaster,
DN4 5HU*
☎ **(01302) 533778**
📖 540
⌨ J Stoddart
✎ S Shaw (01302) 535286
⏱ 18 L 6001 yds SSS 69
U exc Sun–NA before 3.30pm SOC
£€ £20 (£22)
⌖ Inside racecourse; clubhouse on
A638

Dore & Totley   (1913)
*Bradway Road, Bradway, Sheffield,
S17 4QR*
☎ **(0114) 236 0492**
🖳 (0114) 235 3436
📖 580
⌨ JR Johnson (0114) 236 9872
✎ G Roberts (0114) 236 6844

18 L 6265 yds Par 70 SSS 70
WD–restricted Sat–NA
Sun–restricted before 1pm
SOC–Tues & Thurs
£€ £26 (£30) Sun–£15 after 2pm
⌖ 5 miles SW of Sheffield, off A61

Grange Park   (1972)
Pay and play
*Upper Wortley Road, Kimberworth,
Rotherham, S61 2SJ*
☎ **(01709) 558884**
📖 150
⌨ RP Townley (01709) 558884
✎ E Clark (01709) 559497
⏱ 18 L 6461 yds SSS 71
U SOC–phone Pro
£€ £10.20 (£12.75)
⌖ 2 miles W of Rotherham on A629
⊕ Driving range

Hallamshire   (1897)
Sandygate, Sheffield, S10 4LA
☎ **(0114) 230 1007**
🖳 (0114) 230 2153
📖 600
⌨ Mrs KE Renshaw (0114) 230 2153
✎ G Tickell (0114) 230 5222
⏱ 18 L 6333 yds SSS 71
H SOC–WD
£€ £39 (£43)
⌖ W boundary of Sheffield

Hallowes   (1892)
Dronfield, Sheffield, S18 1UR
☎ **(01246) 413734**
🖳 (01246) 413753
📖 597
⌨ T Marshall
✎ P Dunn (01246) 411196
⏱ 18 L 6342 yds SSS 71
WD–U WE–M
£€ £30 D–£35
⌖ 6 miles S of Sheffield on B6057

Hickleton   (1909)
Hickleton, Doncaster, DN5 7BE
☎ **(01709) 896081**
🖳 (01709) 896083
📖 525
⌨ JA Mills
✎ PJ Audsley (01709) 888436
⏱ 18 L 6208 yds SSS 71
WD–U WE–NA before noon SOC
£€ £20 (£27)
⌖ On A635 3 miles A1(M) J37
🏠 Huggett/Coles
▪ www.hickleongc.co.uk

Hillsborough   (1920)
Worrall Road, Sheffield, S6 4BE
☎ **(0114) 234 9151 (Secretary)**
🖳 (0114) 229 4105
🖂 admin@hillsboroughgolfclub.co.uk
📖 534
⌨ TC Pigott (0114) 234 9151
✎ L Horsman (0114) 229 4100
⏱ 18 L 6035 yds SSS 70
H SOC
£€ £30 (£35)
⌖ Wadsley, Sheffield

Lees Hall   (1907)

Hemsworth Road, Norton, Sheffield,
S8 8LL
- ☎ **(0114) 255 4402**
- ⌨ (0114) 255 2900
- 📖 550
- ✍ JW Poulson (0114) 255 2900
- ⛏ S Berry
- ⛳ 18 L 6171 yds SSS 70
- 🏌 U SOC
- ££ £20 (£30)
- ⛴ 3 miles S of Sheffield. E of A61

Lindrick   (1891)

Lindrick Common, Worksop, Notts,
S81 8BH
- ☎ **(01909) 485802**
- ⌨ (01909) 488685
- 📖 500
- ✍ J Armitage (01909) 475282
- ⛏ JR King (01909) 475820
- ⛳ 18 L 6486 yds Par 71 SSS 71
- 🏌 U H–by prior arrangement exc Tues
  SOC–WD
- ££ £50 (£55)
- ⛴ 4 miles W of Worksop on A57. M1
  Junction 31
- ■ www.lindrickgolf.com

Owston Park   (1988)

Public
Owston Lane, Owston, Carcroft,
DN6 8EP
- ☎ **(01302) 330821**
- ✍ MT Parker
- ⛳ 9 L 6148 yds SSS 71
- 🏌 U
- ££ On application
- ⛴ 5 miles N of Doncaster on A19
- ⛏ Michael Parker

Phoenix   (1932)

Pavilion Lane, Brinsworth, Rotherham,
S60 5PA
- ☎ **(01709) 363788**
- ⌨ (01709) 363788
- 📖 700
- ✍ A Webb (01709) 365905
- ⛏ M Roberts (01709) 382624
- ⛳ 18 L 6181 yds SSS 70
- 🏌 U
- ££ £18 D–£24 (£24 D–£32)
- ⛴ 2 miles S of Rotherham. M1
  Junction 34
- ⊕ Driving range
- ⛏ H Cotton

Renishaw Park   (1911)

Golf House, Mill Lane, Renishaw,
Sheffield S21 3UZ
- ☎ **(01246) 432044**
- 📖 450
- ✍ TJ Childs
- ⛏ J Oates (01246) 435484
- ⛳ 18 L 6262 yds SSS 70
- 🏌 H SOC
- ££ £28 D–£37.50 (£42)
- ⛴ 7 miles SE of Sheffield. 2 miles W
  of M1 Junction 30

Owston Hall (the Robin Hood golf course)   (1996)

Owston Hall Hotel & Golf Club, Owston,
Doncaster, DN6 9JF
- ☎ **(01302) 722800**
- ⌨ (01302) 728885
- 📖 200
- ✍ C Tanswell
- ⛏ J Laszkowicz (01302) 722231
- ⛳ 18 L 6937 yds Par 72 SSS 73
- 🏌 U SOC
- ££ £16 (£22)
- ⛴ 5 miles N of Doncaster on A19
  (B1220)
- ⛏ Will Adamson

Rother Valley Golf Centre   (1997)

Mansfield Road, Wales Bar, Sheffield,
S26 5PQ
- ☎ **(0114) 247 3000**
- ⌨ (0114) 247 6000
- ✉ rother-jackbarker@btinternet.com
- 📖 300
- ✍ Mrs M Goodman
- ⛏ JK Ripley
- ⛳ 18 L 6602 yds Par 72 SSS 72
  9 hole Par 3 course
- 🏌 U SOC
- ££ £12 (£17.50)
- ⛴ Rother Valley Country Park, 2
  miles S of M1 Junction 31
- ⊕ Floodlit driving range
- ⛏ Shattock/Roe

Rotherham   (1902)

Thrybergh Park, Rotherham, S65 4NU
- ☎ **(01709) 850466**
- ⌨ (01709) 859517
- 📖 400
- ✍ G Smalley (01709) 850466
- ⛏ S Thornhill (01709) 850480
- ⛳ 18 L 6324 yds SSS 70
- 🏌 WD–U SOC
- ££ £38 (£40)
- ⛴ 4 miles E of Rotherham on A630

Roundwood   (1976)

Green Lane, Rawmarsh, Rotherham,
S62 6LA
- ☎ **(01709) 523471**
- 📖 700
- ✍ M Pantry (01709) 527583
- ⛳ 18 L 5620 yds Par 67 SSS 67
- 🏌 WE–NA before 5pm on comp days
  SOC–WD
- ££ £15 (£18)
- ⛴ 2 miles N of Rotherham on A633

Sandhill   (1993)

Pay and play
Little Houghton, Barnsley, S72 0HW
- ☎ **(01226) 753444**
- ⌨ (01226) 753444
- 📖 420
- ✍ BD Murray
- ⛳ 18 L 6250 yds SSS 70
- 🏌 U SOC
- ££ £11 (£15)
- ⛴ 6 miles E of Barnsley, off A635

- ⊕ Driving range
- ⛏ John Royston

Sheffield Transport   (1923)

Meadow Head, Sheffield, S8 7RE
- ☎ **(0114) 237 3216**
- 📖 125
- ✍ AE Mason
- ⛳ 18 L 3966 yds SSS 62
- 🏌 M
- ⛴ S of Sheffield on A61

Silkstone   (1893)

Field Head, Elmhirst Lane, Silkstone,
Barnsley S75 4LD
- ☎ **(01226) 790328**
- ⌨ (01226) 792653
- 📖 600
- ✍ Alan Butcher
- ⛏ K Guy (01226) 790128
- ⛳ 18 L 6069 yds SSS 70
- 🏌 WD–U SOC–WD
- ££ £24 D–£30 SOC(12+)–£40
- ⛴ 1 mile W of M1 Junction 37 on
  A628

Sitwell Park   (1913)

Shrogs Wood Road, Rotherham,
S60 4BY
- ☎ **(01709) 541046**
- ⌨ (01709) 703637
- 📖 500
- ✍ KT Salvin
- ⛏ N Taylor (01709) 540961
- ⛳ 18 L 6250 yds SSS 70
- 🏌 WD–U Sat–M Sun–NA before
  11.30am SOC
- ££ £25 D–£30 (£30)
- ⛴ 2½ miles E of Rotherham on A631.
  M18 Junction 1
- ⛏ Dr A Mackenzie

Stocksbridge & District   (1924)

Royd Lane, Deepcar, Sheffield, S36 2RZ
- ☎ **(0114) 288 7479**
- ⌨ (0114) 288 2003
- ✉ secretary@stocksbridgeand
  districtgolfclub.com
- 📖 300
- ✍ R Milnes (0114) 288 2003
- ⛏ R Broad (0114) 288 2779
- ⛳ 18 L 5200 yds Par 65 SSS 65
- 🏌 U SOC
- ££ £21 (£31)
- ⛴ 9 miles W of Sheffield (A616)
- ■ www.stocksbridgeand
  districtgolfclub.com

Styrrup Hall   (2000)

Main Street, Styrrup, Doncaster
DN11 8NB
- ☎ **(01302) 751122 (Golf)**
  (01302) 759933 (Clubhouse)
- 📖 350
- ✍ P Ramsey (Prop.)
- ⛏ Richard Allen
- ⛳ 18 L 6745 yds SSS 72
- 🏌 SOC
- ££ £13 (£18 + Bank Hols)

For list of abbreviations and key to symbols see page 627

⊶ 2 miles from Blyth Services on
A1M
⊕ Driving range

Tankersley Park (1907)
Park Lane, High Green, Sheffield,
S35 4LG
☎ (0114) 246 8247
🖥 (0114) 245 7818
📖 574
🏌 A Brownhill (0114) 246 8247
✓ I Kirk (0114) 245 5583
🏴 18 L 6212 yds Par 69 SSS 70
🚶 WD–U WE–M SOC–WD
££ £27 D–£36 (£36)
⊶ Chapeltown, 7 miles N of Sheffield.
M1 Junctions 35A/36
🏠 Hawtree

Thorne (1980)
Pay and play
Kirton Lane, Thorne, Doncaster,
DN8 5RJ
☎ (01405) 812084
🖥 (01405) 741899
📖 120
🏌 R Highfield
✓ ED Highfield (01405) 812084
🏴 18 L 5294 yds SSS 66
🚶 U
££ £9.50 (£10.50)
⊶ 10 miles NE of Doncaster. M18
Junction 5/6
🏠 RD Highfield

Tinsley Park (1920)
Public
High Hazels Park, Darnall, Sheffield,
S9 4PE
☎ (0114) 203 7435
📖 500
🏌 ML Shillito
✓ AP Highfield (0114) 203 7435
🏴 18 L 6084 yds SSS 69
🚶 WD–U WE–by arrangement SOC
££ £10
⊶ M1 Junction 33, 3 miles (A6102)

Wath (1904)
Abdy Rawmarsh, Rotherham, S62 7SJ
☎ (01709) 878609
🖥 (01709) 877097
📧 wathgolf@aol.com
📖 680
🏌 M Godfrey (01709) 583174
✓ C Bassett (01709) 878609
🏴 18 L 6123 yds SSS 69
🚶 WD–U WE/BH–M SOC
££ £24 D–£29
⊶ Abdy Farm, 1½ miles S of Wath-
upon-Dearne. M1 junction 36.

Wheatley (1913)
Armthorpe Road, Doncaster,
DN2 5QB
☎ (01302) 831655
🖥 (01302) 812736
📧 wheatleygolfclub@route56.co.uk
📖 385 100(L) 50(J)
🏌 RTJ Bruno
✓ S Fox (01302) 834085

🏴 18 L 6405 yds SSS 71
🚶 U SOC
££ £27 (£33)
⊶ 3 miles NE of Doncaster

Wombwell Hillies (1989)
Public
Wentworth View, Wombwell, Barnsley,
S73 0LA
☎ (01226) 754433
🖥 (01226) 758635
🏌 J Hayes (01226) 756761
🏴 9 L 2095 yds SSS 60
🚶 U
££ On application
⊶ 4 miles SE of Barnsley

Wortley (1894)
Hermit Hill Lane, Wortley, Sheffield,
S35 7DF
☎ (0114) 288 8469
🖥 (0114) 288 8488
📧 wortleygolfclub@virgin.net
📖 500
🏌 Dr FA Wilson
✓ I Kirk (0114) 288 6490
🏴 18 L 6035 yds SSS 69
🚶 WD–U WE–NA before 10.30am
SOC
££ £28 (£35)
⊶ 2 miles W of M1 Junc 36, off A629

Yorkshire (West)

The Alwoodley (1907)
Wigton Lane, Alwoodley, Leeds,
LS17 8SA
☎ (0113) 268 1680
🖥 (0113) 293 9458
📧 via website
📖 450
🏌 CD Wilcher
✓ JR Green (0113) 268 9603
🏴 18 L 6785 yds SSS 73
🚶 U SOC–WD
££ £60 (£75)
⊶ 5 miles N of Leeds on A61
🏠 Dr A Mackenzie
◼ www.alwoodley.co.uk

Bagden Hall Hotel (1993)
Wakefield Road, Scissett, HD8 9LE
☎ (01484) 865330
🖥 (01484) 861001
📖 175
🏌 J Rinder
✓ N Hirst (Golf Dir)
🏴 9 L 3022 yds Par 56 SSS 55
🚶 U
££ £10 (£13)
⊶ On A636 between Derby Dale and
Scissett. M1 Junction 39
🏠 F O'Donnell

Baildon (1896)
Moorgate, Baildon, Shipley, BD17 5PP
☎ (01274) 584266
📧 sec@baildongolf.freeserve
.co.uk

📖 750
🏌 JA Cooley (01274) 584266
✓ R Masters (01274) 595162
🏴 18 L 6231 yds par 70 SSS 70
🚶 WD–U before 5pm (restricted
Tues) WE/BH–restricted
££ £20 (£24)
⊶ 5 miles N of Bradford, off A6038
🏠 Tom Morris/James Braid
◼ www.baildongolfclub.com

Ben Rhydding (1947)
High Wood, Ben Rhydding, Ilkley,
LS9 8SB
☎ (01943) 608759
📧 secretary@benrhyddinggc
.freeserve.co.uk
📖 195 60(L) 45(J)
🏌 S Brown
🏴 9 L 4611 yds SSS 63
🚶 WD–U exc Wed pm & Thurs am
WE–M
££ £12 (£17)
⊶ 2 miles SE of Ilkley

Bingley St Ives (1931)
St Ives Estate, Bingley, BD16 1AT
☎ (01274) 562436
🖥 (01274) 511788
🏌 Mr S Axford
✓ R Firth (01274) 562506
🏴 18 L 6480 yds SSS 71
🚶 WD–U before 4pm
££ £25 D–£30
⊶ 6 miles NW of Bradford, off
A650

Bracken Ghyll (1993)
Skipton Road, Addingham, Ilkley,
LS29 0SL
☎ (01943) 831207
📧 office@brackenghyll.co.uk
📖 400
🏌 JW Williams
✓ None
🏴 18 L 5600 yds Par 69 SSS 67
🚶 WD/BH–U WE–NA before 11am
on comp days SOC
££ £20 (£24)
⊶ 3 miles W of Ilkley on old A65 to
Addingham
⊕ Indoor practice area
◼ 222.brackenghyll.co.uk

Bradford (1891)
Hawksworth Lane, Guiseley, Leeds,
LS20 8NP
☎ (01943) 875570
🖥 (01943) 875570
📖 700
🏌 T Eagle
✓ S Weldon (01943) 873719
🏴 18 L 6259 yds SSS 71
🚶 WD–U WE–NA before noon
SOC–WD
££ On application
⊶ 8 miles N of Bradford, off A6038.
10 miles N of Leeds on A650

Bradford Moor   (1906)
Scarr Hall, Pollard Lane, Bradford, BD2 4RW
☎ **(01274) 771716**
📖 350
✍ CP Bedford (01274) 771693
⌇ 9 L 5854 yds SSS 68
👤 WD–U
£€ £10
⛳ 2 miles N of Bradford

Bradley Park   (1978)
Public
Bradley Road, Huddersfield, HD2 1PZ
☎ **(01484) 223772**
📞 (01484) 451613
📖 300
✍ K Blackwell
⌁ PE Reilly
⌇ 18 L 6202 yds SSS 70
9 hole Par 3 course
👤 WE–NA
£€ £15.50 (£17.50)
⛳ 2 miles N of Huddersfield, off A6107, M62 Junction 25
⊕ Floodlit driving range

Branshaw   (1912)
Branshaw Moor, Oakworth, Keighley, BD22 7ES
☎ **(01535) 643235**
📞 (01535) 648011
📧 branshaw@golfclub.fslife.co.uk
📖 525
✍ T O'Hara
⌁ S Jowitt (01535) 647441
⌇ 18 L 5858 yds SSS 68
👤 WD–U SOC–WD
£€ D–£20 (D–£30)
⛳ 2 miles SW of Keighley on B6143
🏠 James Braid/Dr A Mackenzie

Calverley   (1984)
Woodhall Lane, Pudsey, LS28 5QY
☎ **(0113) 256 9244**
📞 (0113) 256 4362
📖 600
✍ N Wendel-Jones (Mgr)
⌁ N Wendel-Jones
⌇ 18 L 5527 yds SSS 67
9 L 2137 yds Par 33
👤 WD–U WE–pm only
£€ £12 (£15)
⛳ 4 miles NE of Bradford
⊕ Driving range

Castlefields   (1903)
Rastrick Common, Brighouse, HD6 3HL
☎ **(01484) 713276**
📖 180
✍ FC Tolley
⌇ 6 L 2406 yds Par 54 SSS 50
👤 M
£€ £6 (£8)
⛳ 1 mile S of Brighouse

City of Wakefield   (1936)
Public
Lupset Park, Horbury Road, Wakefield, WF2 8QS
☎ **(01924) 367442**

⌁ R Holland (01924) 360282
⌇ 18 L 6319 yds SSS 70
👤 U SOC–WD
£€ On application
⛳ A642, 2 miles W of Wakefield. 2 miles E of M1 Junction 39/40
🏠 JSF Morrison

Clayton   (1906)
Thornton View Road, Clayton, Bradford, BD14 6JX
☎ **(01274) 880047**
📖 170 26(L) 54(J)
✍ DA Smith (01274) 572311
⌇ 9 L 5515 yds SSS 67
👤 WD–U Sat–U Sun–after 4pm
£€ £12 D–£14 (£14)
⛳ 3 miles W of Bradford, off A647

Cleckheaton & District   (1900)
483 Bradford Road, Cleckheaton, BD19 6BU
☎ **(01274) 874118 (Clubhouse)**
📞 (01274) 871382
📧 info@cleckheatongolf.fsnet.co.uk
📖 572
✍ Mrs R Newsholme (Asst Sec) (01274) 851266
⌁ M Ingham (01274) 851267
⌇ 18 L 5860 yds SSS 69
👤 U SOC
£€ £25 D–£30 (£30)
⛳ Nr M62 Junction 26–A638
■ www.cleckheatongolfclub.fsnet .co.uk

Cookridge Hall
Cookridge Lane, Cookridge, Leeds, LS16 7NL
☎ **(0113) 230 0641**
📞 (0113) 203 0198
📧 cookridgehall@americangolf.uk .com
📖 650
✍ W Carr (Gen Mgr) (0113) 230 0641
⌁ M Pearson
⌇ 18 L 6788 yds Par 72 SSS 72
👤 WD–U Sat–U after 2pm Sun–U after 12 noon SOC
£€ £19 (£24)
⛳ 5 miles NW of Leeds, via A660
⊕ Driving range; Golf Academy
🏠 Karl Litten

Crosland Heath   (1914)
Felks Stile Road, Crosland Heath, Huddersfield, HD4 7AF
☎ **(01484) 653216**
📞 (01484) 461079
📖 600
✍ D Walker (Sec/Mgr) (01484) 653216
⌁ J Eyre (01484) 653877
⌇ 18 L 6004 yds SSS 70
👤 U SOC
£€ On application
⛳ 3 miles W of Huddersfield, off A62

Crow Nest Park   (1994)
Coach Road, Hove Edge, Brighouse, HD6 2LN
☎ **(01484) 401121**
📞 (01484) 720975
📧 crownest@btconnect.com
📖 300
✍ A Naylor
⌁ P Everitt (01484) 401121
⌇ 9 L 6020 yds Par 70 SSS 69
👤 WD–U WE–U before noon
£€ 18 holes–£24. 9 holes–£12
⛳ 5 miles E of Halifax. M62 Junction 25
⊕ Driving range
🏠 Will Adamson
■ www.crownestgolf.co.uk

Dewsbury District   (1891)
The Pinnacle, Sands Lane, Mirfield, WF14 8HJ
☎ **(01924) 492399**
📧 dewsburygolf@btconnect.com
📖 650
✍ DM Ellis
⌁ N Hirst (01924) 496030
⌇ 18 L 6360 yds SSS 71
👤 WD–U WE–M –U after 3pm SOC
£€ £18 (£15)
⛳ 2 miles W of Dewsbury, off A644
🏠 Tom Morris/Alliss/Thomas
■ www.dewsburygolf.co.uk

East Bierley   (1928)
South View Road, Bierley, Bradford, BD4 6PP
☎ **(01274) 681023**
📧 rjwelch@ebgc.fsnet.co.uk
📖 156 47(L) 30(J)
✍ RJ Welch (01274) 683666
⌁ J Whittam (07904) 141248
⌇ 9 L 4692 yds SSS 63
👤 U exc Mon–NA after 4pm Sun–NA
£€ £14 (£16)
⛳ 4 miles SE of Bradford. M62-M606

Fardew   (1993)
Pay and play
Nursery Farm, Carr Lane, East Morton, Keighley BD20 5RY
☎ **(01274) 561229**
📞 (01274) 561229
📧 fardew@dial.pipex.com
📖 100
✍ GA Richardson
⌁ I Bottomley
⌇ 9 L 3104 yds Par 72 SSS 70
👤 U SOC
£€ 9 holes–£8 (£9) 18 holes–£12 (£14)
⛳ 2 miles W of Bingley on A650
🏠 Will Adamson

Ferrybridge 'C'   (1976)
PO Box 39, Stranglands Lane, Knottingley, WF11 8SQ
☎ **(01977) 884165**
📖 305
✍ TD Ellis
⌇ 9 L 5137 yds SSS 65
👤 M
£€ D–£6 (D–£7)

For list of abbreviations and key to symbols see page 627

⊶ ¹/₂ mile off A1, on B6136
🏠 NE Pugh

Fulneck (1892)
Fulneck, Pudsey, LS28 8NT
☎ **(0113) 256 5191**
📖 290
✍ Mrs P Warburton (0113) 256 2606
▷ 9 L 5456 yds SSS 67
👥 WD–U WE/BH–M SOC
££ £15
⊶ 5 miles W of Leeds

Garforth (1913)
Long Lane, Garforth, Leeds, LS25 2DS
☎ **(0113) 286 2021**
🖥 (0113) 286 3308
📖 619
✍ NG Douglas (0113) 286 3308
✓ K Findlater (0113) 286 2063
▷ 18 L 6304 yds SSS 70
👥 WD–U H WE/BH–M SOC
££ £34 D–£40
⊶ 9 miles E of Leeds, between Garforth and Barwick-in-Elmet
⊕ Driving range
🏠 Dr A Mackenzie
■ www.garforthgolfclub.co.uk

Gotts Park (1933)
Public
Armley Ridge Road, Armley, Leeds, LS12 2QX
☎ **(0113) 234 2019**
📖 300
✍ M Gill (0113) 256 2994
✓ J Marlor
▷ 18 L 4960 yds SSS 64
👥 U
££ On application
⊶ 2 miles W of Leeds

Halifax (1895)
Union Lane, Ogden, Halifax, HX2 8XR
☎ **(01422) 244171**
🖥 (01422) 241459
📖 450
✓ M Allison (01422) 240047
▷ 18 L 6037 yds SSS 69
👥 U WD–parties welcome SOC
££ £20 (£25)
⊶ 4 miles N of Halifax on A629
🏠 Alex Herd/James Braid

Halifax Bradley Hall (1907)
Holywell Green, Halifax, HX4 9AN
☎ **(01422) 374108**
📖 608
✍ M Dredge (01484) 374108
✓ P Wood (01422) 370231
▷ 18 L 6138 yds SSS 70
👥 U SOC
££ £25 (£30)
⊶ S of Halifax on A6112

Halifax West End (1906)
Paddock Lane, Highroad Well, Halifax, HX2 0NT
☎ **(01422) 341878**
🖥 (01442) 341878

📧 info@westend.co.uk
📖 340 100(L) 60(J)
✍ G Gower (01422) 341878
✓ D Rishworth (01422) 363293
▷ 18 L 5951 yds SSS 69
👥 U SOC
££ £25 (£30)
⊶ 2 miles NW of Halifax
■ www.westend.co.uk

Hanging Heaton (1922)
Whitecross Road, Bennett Lane, Dewsbury, WF12 7DT
☎ **(01924) 461606**
🖥 (01924) 430100
📧 ken.wood@hhgc.org
📖 400
✍ K Wood (01924) 430100
✓ (01924) 467077
▷ 9 L 2923 yds SSS 68
👥 WD–U WE–M
££ £16
⊶ Dewsbury ³/₄ mile (A653)

Headingley (1892)
Back Church Lane, Adel, Leeds, LS16 8DW
☎ **(0113) 267 3052 (Clubhouse)**
🖥 (0113) 281 7334
📖 675
✍ JR Burns JP (Mgr) (0113) 267 9573
✓ NM Harvey (0113) 267 5100
▷ 18 L 6298 yds SSS 70
👥 WD–U before 3.30pm SOC
££ £30 D–£35 (£40)
⊶ 5 miles NW of Leeds, off A660
🏠 Dr A MacKenzie

Headley (1907)
Headley Lane, Thornton, Bradford, BD13 3LX
☎ **(01274) 833481**
🖥 (01274) 833481
📖 270 35(L) 35(J)
✍ A Goodman
▷ 9 L 4914 yds SSS 64
👥 WD–U WE–M SOC
££ On application
⊶ 5 miles W of Bradford (B6145)

Hebden Bridge (1930)
Great Mount, Wadsworth, Hebden Bridge, HX7 8PH
☎ **(01422) 842896**
📖 300
✍ R Priestley (01422) 842896
▷ 9 L 5242 yds Par 68 SSS 67
👥 WD–U
££ £10–£12 (£15)
⊶ 1 mile N of Hebden Bridge

Horsforth (1906)
Layton Rise, Layton Road, Horsforth, Leeds LS18 5EX
☎ **(0113) 258 6819**
🖥 (0113) 258 9336
📧 secretary@horsforthgolfclubltd.co.uk
📖 365 90(L) 85(J)
✍ Mrs LA Harrison

✓ Simon Booth & Dean Stokes (0113) 258 5200
▷ 18 L 6293 yds SSS 70
👥 WD–U WD–SOC WE–after 2.30 (contact Pro)
££ D–£26 (£36)
⊶ M62 – follow signs for Leeds Bradford Airport
🏠 Dr Alistair Mackenzie
■ www.horsforthgolfclubltd.co.uk

Howley Hall (1900)
Scotchman Lane, Morley, Leeds, LS27 0NX
☎ **(01924) 350100**
🖥 (01924) 350104
📧 office@howleyhall.co.uk
📖 492
✍ D Jones (01924) 350100
✓ G Watkinson (01924) 350102
▷ 18 L 6058 yds Par 71 SSS 69
👥 U SOC–WD/Sun before 5pm
££ £29 D–£35 (£39)
⊶ 4 miles SW of Leeds on B6123

Huddersfield (1891)
Fixby Hall, Lightridge Road, Huddersfield, HD2 2EP
☎ **(01484) 420110**
🖥 (01484) 424623
📖 656
✍ Mrs S Dennis (Gen Mgr), Mrs D Lockett (01484) 426203
✓ P Carman (01484) 426463
▷ 18 L 6432 yds SSS 71
👥 U SOC–WD
££ £37 D–£47 (£47 D–£57)
⊶ 2 miles N of Huddersfield, off A6107. M62 Junction 24
⊕ Driving range
■ www.huddersfield-golf.co.uk

Ilkley (1890)
Myddleton, Ilkley, LS29 0BE
☎ **(01943) 607277**
🖥 (01943) 816130
📧 honsec@ilkleygolfclub.co.uk
📖 530
✍ PG Richardson (01943) 600214
✓ JL Hammond (01943) 607463
▷ 18 L 6260 yds SSS 70
👥 U–H
££ £40 (£45)
⊶ NW of Ilkley, off A65

Keighley (1904)
Howden Park, Utley, Keighley, BD20 6DH
☎ **(01535) 604778**
🖥 (01535) 610572
📧 manager@keighleygolfclub.com
📖 600
✍ G Cameron Dawson
✓ M Bradley (01535) 665370
▷ 18 L 6141 yds SSS 70
👥 WD–NA before 9.30am & 12–1.30pm Sat–NA Sun/BH–NA before 2pm
££ £28 D–£32 (£32 D–£38)
⊶ 1 mile W of Keighley on A629

Leeds (1896)

Elmete Road, Roundhay, Leeds, LS8 2LJ
- ☎ **(0113) 265 8775**
- ☐ (0113) 232 3369
- ✉ secretary@leedsgolfclub.com
- ☐ 545
- ✍ SJ Clarkson (0113) 265 9203
- ✓ S Longster (0113) 265 8786
- ⊳ 18 L 6092 yds SSS 69
- ⋔ WD–U WE–M SOC
- £€ £25 D–£32
- ⬡ 4 miles NE of Leeds, off A58
- ■ www.leedsgolfclub.com

Leeds Golf Centre (1994)

Pay and play
Wike Ridge Lane, Shadwell, Leeds, LS17 9JW
- ☎ **(0113) 288 6000**
- ☐ (0113) 288 6185
- ☐ 500
- ✍ D Dourambeis
- ✓ M Pinkett
- ⊳ 18 L 6800 yds SSS 72
- 12 hole Par 3 course
- ⋔ U SOC
- £€ £14.50 (£18)
- ⬡ NE of Leeds, between A58 and A61
- ⊕ Driving range; Golf Academy
- ⌂ Donald Steel
- ■ www.leedsgolfcentre.com

Lightcliffe (1907)

Knowle Top Road, Lightcliffe, HX3 8SW
- ☎ **(01422) 202459**
- ☐ 180 95(L) 84(J)
- ✍ CCD Balaam (01422) 201650
- ✓ R Kershaw
- ⊳ 9 L 5368 metres SSS 68
- ⋔ U H–exc Wed Sun am–M SOC
- £€ £16 (£20)
- ⬡ 3 miles E of Halifax (A58)

Lofthouse Hill

Leeds Road, Lofthouse Hill, Wakefield, WF3 3LR
- ☎ **(01924) 823703**
- ☐ (01924) 823703
- ✍ N Todd
- ✓ B Janes (01924) 820048
- ⊳ 9 L 3167 yds Par 35
- ⋔ M SOC
- £€ 18 holes–£17.50 9 holes–£10
- ⬡ Between Leeds and Wakefield
- ⊕ Driving range

Longley Park (1910)

Maple Street, Huddersfield, HD5 9AX
- ☎ **(01484) 426932**
- ☐ 400
- ✓ N Leeming (01484) 422304
- ⊳ 9 L 5212 yds Par 66 SSS 66
- ⋔ WD–U exc Thurs WE–restricted
- £€ £13.50 (£16)
- ⬡ Huddersfield ¹/₂ mile

Low Laithes (1925)

Park Mill Lane, Flushdyke, Ossett, WF5 9AP
- ☎ **(01924) 273275**

- ☐ (01924) 266067
- ✉ info@low-laithes-golf-club.co.uk
- ☐ 610
- ✍ P Browning (Sec/Mgr)
- (01924) 266067
- ✓ P Browning (01924) 274667
- ⊳ 18 L 6468 yds SSS 71
- ⋔ U WE–no parties SOC–WD
- £€ £22 D–£25 (£36)
- ⬡ 2 miles W of Wakefield. M1 Junction 40
- ⌂ Dr A Mackenzie

The Manor

Bradford Road, Drighlington, Bradford, BD11 1AB
- ☎ **(0113) 285 2644**
- ☐ 300
- ✍ J Crompton (Sec/Mgr)
- ✓ J Crompton
- ⊳ 18 L 6508 yds Par 72 SSS 71
- ⋔ U SOC–exc Sat
- £€ £15 (£15)
- ⬡ 1 mile from M62 Junction 27, off A650
- ⊕ Floodlit driving range. 6 holes pitch & putt course
- ⌂ David Hemstock

Marriott Hollins Hall Hotel (1999)

Hollins Hill, Baildon, Shipley, BD17 7QW
- ☎ **(01274) 534212**
- ☐ (01274) 534220
- ☐ 300
- ✍ Gary Pearce (01274) 534250
- ✓ Gordon Brand Jr, Mark Wood
- ⊳ 18 L 6700 yds Par 71 SSS 72
- ⋔ H
- £€ £35 (£50)
- ⬡ 6 miles N of Bradford on A6038
- ⊕ Driving range, leisure facilities, 4-star hotel
- ⌂ Ross McMurray

Marsden (1921)

Hemplow, Marsden, Huddersfield, HD7 6NN
- ☎ **(01484) 844253**
- ☐ 200 50(L) 50(J)
- ✍ SJ Boustead (01457) 874158
- ✓ R Johnson
- ⊳ 9 L 5702 yds SSS 68
- ⋔ WD–U Sat–NA before 4pm Sun–M SOC
- £€ £12
- ⬡ 8 miles W of Huddersfield, off A62
- ⌂ Dr A Mackenzie

Meltham (1908)

Thick Hollins Hall, Meltham, Huddersfield, HD9 4DQ
- ☎ **(01484) 850227**
- ☐ (01484) 859051
- ✉ melthamgolf@supanet.com
- ☐ 700
- ✍ CJ Naylor (Hon)
- ✓ PF Davies (01484) 851521
- ⊳ 18 L 6396 yds SSS 70
- ⋔ H

- £€ £25 (£35)
- ⬡ 5 miles SW of Huddersfield (B6107)
- ■ www.meltham-golf.co.uk

Mid Yorkshire (1993)

Havercroft Lane, Darrington, Pontefract, WF8 3BP
- ☎ **(01977) 704522**
- ☐ (01977) 600823
- ☐ 600
- ✍ Linda Darwood
- ✓ Michael Hessay (01977) 704522
- ⊳ 18 L 6340 yds SSS 71
- ⋔ U H SOC
- £€ £15 (£25)
- ⬡ Nr A1/M62 junction
- ⊕ Floodlit driving range
- ⌂ Steve Marnoch

Middleton Park (1933)

Public
Ring Road, Beeston Park, Middleton, LS10 3TN
- ☎ **(0113) 270 0449**
- ✉ lynn@ratcliffel.fsnet.co.uk
- ☐ 250
- ✍ Mrs L Ratcliffe (01132) 777715
- ✓ None
- ⊳ 18 L 5233 yds SSS 66
- ⋔ U
- £€ On application
- ⬡ 3 miles S of Leeds

Moor Allerton (1923)

Coal Road, Wike, Leeds, LS17 9NH
- ☎ **(0113) 266 1154**
- ☐ (0113) 237 1124
- ☐ 800
- ✍ N Lomas
- ✓ R Lane (0113) 266 5209
- ⊳ 27 L 6470-6843 yds SSS 73-74
- ⋔ WD/Sat–U Sun–NA SOC
- £€ £45 D–£50 (£60 D–£65)
- ⬡ 5¹/₂ miles N of Leeds, off A61
- ⊕ Driving range
- ⌂ Robert Trent Jones Sr

Moortown (1909)

Harrogate Road, Leeds, LS17 7DB
- ☎ **(0113) 268 6521**
- ☐ (0113) 268 0986
- ☐ 600
- ✍ KC Bradley
- ✓ Martin Heggie (0113) 268 3636
- ⊳ 18 L 6995 yds SSS 74
- ⋔ H
- £€ £60 (£70)
- ⬡ 5¹/₂ miles N of Leeds on A61
- ⌂ Dr A Mackenzie

Normanton (1903)

Hatfeild Hall, Aberford Road, Stanley, Wakefield WF3 4JP
- ☎ **(01924) 377943**
- ☐ (01924) 200777
- ☐ 800
- ✍ RJ Metcalfe
- ✓ F Houlgate (01924) 200900
- ⊳ 18 L 6191 yds Par 72 SSS 69
- ⋔ WD SOC

££ £26
🚗 3 miles N of Wakefield (A642).
M62 Junction 30
🛖 Patrick Dawson
■ www.normantongolf.co.uk

Northcliffe (1921)
High Bank Lane, Shipley, Bradford,
BD18 4LJ
☎ (01274) 584085
🖳 (01274) 584148
✉ northcliffe@bigfoot.com
📖 867
🏌 I Collins (01274) 596731
🏌 M Hillas (01274) 587193
🏳 18 L 6113 yds SSS 71
👥 U SOC
££ £25 (£30)
🚗 3 miles NW of Bradford, off A650
Keighley road
🛖 James Braid
■ www.northcliffegolfclubshipley
.co.uk

Otley (1906)
West Busk Lane, Otley, LS21 3NG
☎ (01943) 465329
🖳 (01943) 850387
✉ office@otley-golfclub.co.uk
📖 700
🏌 PJ Clarke Ext 202
🏌 S Tomkinson Ext 203
🏳 18 L 6245 yds SSS 70
👥 U exc Sat–NA SOC
££ £29 (£36)
🚗 1 mile W of Otley, off A6038
■ www.otley-golfclub.co.uk

Oulton Park (1990)
Public
Oulton, Rothwell, Leeds, LS26 8EX
☎ (0113) 282 3152
🖳 (0113) 282 6290
📖 390
🏌 A Cooper (Mgr)
🏌 S Gromett
🏳 18 L 6479 yds SSS 71
9 L 3287 yds SSS 35
👥 U SOC–WD
££ 18 hole: £10.15 (£13.15) 9 hole:
£5.95 (£6.95)
🚗 5 miles SE of Leeds, off A642. N of
M62 Junction 30
⊕ Driving range
🛖 Alliss/Thomas

Outlane (1906)
Slack Lane, New Hey Road, Outlane,
HD3 3YL
☎ (01422) 374762
🖳 (01422) 311789
📖 500
🏌 P Jackson
🏌 D Chapman
🏳 18 L 6010 yds SSS 69
👥 U SOC
££ £19 (£29)
🚗 4 miles W of Huddersfield, off
A640. M62 Junction 23

Painthorpe House (1961)
Painthorpe Lane, Crigglestone,
Wakefield, WF4 3HE
☎ (01924) 255083
🖳 (01924) 252022
📖 180
🏌 TJ Mead (01924) 254737
🏳 9 L 4520 yds SSS 62
👥 U
££ £6 (£7)
🚗 1 mile SE of M1 Junction 39

Phoenix Park (1922)
Dick Lane, Thornbury, Bradford,
BD3 7AT
☎ (01274) 667573
📖 180
🏌 C Lally (01274) 668218
🏌 None
🏳 9 L 4982 yds SSS 64
👥 WD/BH–U WE–NA
££ On application
🚗 Thornbury Roundabout (A647)

Pontefract & District (1904)
Park Lane, Pontefract, WF8 4QS
☎ (01977) 792241
🖳 (01977) 792241
✉ manager@pdgc.co.uk
📖 841
🏌 RE Guiver (Mgr)
🏌 NJ Newman (01977) 706806
🏳 18 L 6227 yds SSS 70
👥 WD–I WE–after 3pm SOC–WD
exc Wed & WE
££ £22 (£32)
🚗 Pontefract 1 mile on B6134. M62
Junction 32
🛖 Alistair Mackenzie
■ www.pdgc.co.uk

Pontefract Park (1973)
Public
Park Road, Pontefract, WF8
☎ (01977) 702799
🏳 18 L 4068 yds SSS 62
👥 U
££ On application
🚗 Between Pontefract and M62
roundabout, nr racecourse

Queensbury (1923)
Brighouse Road, Queensbury, Bradford,
BD13 1QF
☎ (01274) 882155
🖳 (01274) 882155
✉ queensburygc@btconnect.com
📖 400 48(L) 47(J)
🏌 B Cox
🏌 D Delaney (01274) 816864
🏳 9 L 5008 yds SSS 65
👥 U
££ £15 (£30)
🚗 4 miles SW of Bradford (A647)
■ www.queensburygc.co.uk

Rawdon (1896)
Buckstone Drive, Micklefield Lane,
Rawdon, LS19 6BD
☎ (0113) 250 6040

📖 220 55(L) 50(J)
🏌 RA Adams (0113) 250 6064
🏌 (0113) 250 5017
🏳 9 L 5982 yds SSS 69
👥 WD–H WE/BH–M SOC
££ £16
🚗 6 miles NW of Leeds nr A65/A658
junction

Riddlesden (1927)
Howden Rough, Riddlesden, Keighley,
BD20 5QN
☎ (01535) 602148
📖 400
🏌 M Nield (01535) 602148
🏳 18 L 4295 yds Par 63 SSS 61
👥 U exc Sun–NA before 2pm
££ £16 (£21)
🚗 1 mile from Riddlesden, off Scott
Lane West. 3 miles N of Keighley,
off A650

Roundhay (1923)
Public
Park Lane, Leeds, LS8 2EJ
☎ (0113) 266 2695
📖 230
🏌 RH McLauchlan
🏌 JA Pape (0113) 266 1686
🏳 9 L 5322 yds SSS 65
👥 U
££ On application
🚗 N of Leeds, off Moortown Ring
Road

Ryburn (1910)
Norland, Sowerby Bridge, Halifax,
HX6 3QP
☎ (01422) 831355
📖 300
🏌 J Hoyle (01422) 843070
🏳 9 L 5127 yds SSS 65
👥 U
££ £15 (£20)
🚗 3 miles S of Halifax

Sand Moor (1926)
Alwoodley Lane, Leeds, LS17 7DJ
☎ (0113) 268 5180
🖳 (0113) 266 1105
📖 540
🏌 I Kerr
🏌 P Tupling (0113) 268 3925
🏳 18 L 6429 yds SSS 71
👥 WD–H by arrangement WE–NA
££ £40 (£50)
🚗 5 miles N of Leeds, off A61
⊕ Driving Range
🛖 Dr A Mackenzie

Scarcroft (1937)
Syke Lane, Leeds, LS14 3BQ
☎ (0113) 289 2311
🖳 (0113) 289 3835
✉ scarcroftgc@btconnect.com
📖 580
🏌 D Tear (Gen Mgr) (0113) 289 2311
🏌 D Tear (0113) 289 2780
🏳 18 L 6426 yds SSS 71
👥 WD–U WE/BH–M or by
arrangement SOC–WD

£€ £32 D–£40 (£40)
⛳ 7 miles N of Leeds, off A58
🖥 www.scarcroftgc.co.uk

Shipley (1896)
Beckfoot Lane, Cottingley Bridge,
Bingley, BD16 1LX
☎ (01274) 563212
🖳 (01274) 567739
🏠 600
🏌 Mrs MJ Bryan (01274) 568652
✓ JR Parry (01274) 563674
🏴 18 L 6235 yds SSS 70
🕴 WD–U exc Tues–NA before 2pm
  Sat–NA before 4pm
£€ D–£35 (D–£40)
⛳ 6 miles N of Bradford on A650
🏔 Colt/Alison/Mackenzie/Braid
🖥 www.shipleygc.co.uk

Silsden (1913)
Brunthwaite Lane, Brunthwaite, Silsden,
BD20 0ND
☎ (01535) 652998
🖳 (01535) 654273
🖂 info@silsdengolfclub.co.uk
🏠 300
🏌 J Bellerby
🏴 18 L 5259 yds Par 67 SSS 64
🕴 Sat–restricted Sun–U after 1pm
£€ £18 (£23)
⛳ 5 miles N of Keighley, off A6034
🖥 www.silsdengolfclub.co.uk

South Bradford (1906)
Pearson Road, Odsal, Bradford,
BD6 1BH
☎ (01274) 679195
🏠 200
🏌 B Broadbent (01274) 690643
✓ P Cooke (01274) 673346
🏴 9 L 6076 yds SSS 69
🕴 WD–U WE–M
£€ On application
⛳ Bradford 2 miles, nr Odsal Stadium

South Leeds (1906)
Gipsy Lane, Ring Road, Beeston, Leeds
LS11 5TU
☎ (0113) 270 0479
🖂 sec@slgc.freeserve.co.uk
🏠 450
🏌 J Neal (0113) 277 1676
✓ L Turner (0113) 270 2598
🏴 18 L 5865 yds SSS 68
🕴 WD–U WE–M SOC
£€ £14 (£20)
⛳ 4 miles S of Leeds. 2 miles from
  M62 and M1

Temple Newsam (1923)
Public
Temple Newsam Road, Halton, Leeds,
LS15 0LN
☎ (0113) 264 5624
🏠 500
🏌 G Hollins
✓ J Pape (0113) 264 7362
🏴 Lord Irwin 18 L 6448 yds SSS 71
  Lady Dorothy Wood 18 L 6229 yds
  SSS 70

🕴 U SOC
£€ £7.50 (£9) Summer £7 (£8.50)
  Winter
⛳ 5 miles E of Leeds, off A63

Todmorden (1894)
Rive Rocks, Cross Stone, Todmorden,
0L14 8RD
☎ (01706) 812986
🏠 165 43(L) 24(J)
🏴 9 L 5902 yds SSS 68
🕴 WD/BH–U WE–M SOC–WD
£€ £15 (£20)
⛳ 1 mile N of Todmorden, off A646

Wakefield (1891)
28 Woodthorpe Lane, Sandal, Wakefield,
WF2 6JH
☎ (01924) 255104
🖳 (01924) 242752
🖂 wakefieldgolfclub
  @woodthorpelane-freeserve.co.uk
🏠 500
🏌 AJ McVicar (01924) 258778
✓ IM Wright (01924) 255380
🏴 18 L 6653 yds SSS 72
🕴 U H SOC–Wed–Fri
£€ On application
⛳ 3 miles S of Wakefield on A61. M1
  Junction 39
🏔 Alex Herd

Waterton Park (1995)
The Balk, Walton, Wakefield, WF2 6QL
☎ (01924) 259525
🖳 (01924) 256969
🏠 650
🏌 L Lammas
✓ N Wood (01924) 255557
🏴 18 L 6843 yds Par 72 SSS 73
🕴 WD–H SOC
£€ D–£30
⛳ 4 miles SE of Wakefield centre
⊕ Driving range
🏔 Simon Gidman

West Bowling (1898)
Newall Hall, Rooley Lane, Bradford,
BD5 8LB
☎ (01274) 724449
🖳 (01274) 393207
🏠 500
🏌 IW Brogden (01274) 393207
✓ IA Marshall (01274) 728036
🏴 18 L 5769 yds SSS 68
🕴 WD–U H SOC
£€ £24 (£30)
⛳ Junction of M606 and Bradford
  Ring Road East

West Bradford (1900)
Chellow Grange Road, Haworth Road,
Bradford, BD9 6NP
☎ (01274) 542767
🖳 (01274) 482079
🏠 450
🏌 IP Milnes (Hon) (01274) 542767
✓ NM Barber (01274) 542102
🏴 18 L 5738 yds SSS 68 Par 69
🕴 WD–U WE–U after 3.00 pm
£€ £21 (£21)
⛳ 3 miles NW of Bradford (B6144)

Wetherby (1910)
Linton Lane, Linton, Wetherby,
LS22 4JF
☎ (01937) 580089
🖳 (01937) 581915
🖂 info@wetherbygolfclub.fsnet.co.uk
🏠 630
🏌 L McGrae (Mgr) (01937) 580089
✓ M Daubney (01937) 580089
🏴 18 L 6235 yds SSS 70
🕴 WE–U after 10am SOC–WD H
£€ £28 (£40)
⛳ ³/₄ mile W of Wetherby. A1
  Wetherby roundabout
⊕ Driving range

Whitwood (1987)
Public
Altofts Lane, Whitwood, Castleford,
WF10 5PZ
☎ (01977) 512835
🏌 D Everitt (Hon) (01977) 557703
✓ R Holland
🏴 9 L 6176 yds SSS 69
🕴 WD–U WE–booking necessary
£€ On application
⛳ 2 miles SW of Castleford (A655).
  M62 Junction 31

Willow Valley (1993)
Pay and play
Clifton, Brighouse, HD6 4JB
☎ (01274) 878624
🖂 sales@wvgc.co.uk
🏠 350
🏌 H Butterfield
✓ J Haworth
🏴 South 18 L 7076 Par 72 SSS 74
  Fountain 9 L 2039 Par 60 SSS 60
🕴 U
£€ 18 hole: £23 (£28). 9 hole: £7
  (£8.50)
⛳ SW of Leeds, M62 Junction 25
⊕ Driving range (floodlit)
🏔 Jonathan Gaunt
🖥 www.wvgc.co.uk

Woodhall Hills (1905)
Woodhall Road, Calverley, Pudsey,
LS28 5UN
☎ (0113) 256 4771 (Clubhouse)
🖳 (0113) 295 4594
🏠 550
🏌 J Armitage (0113) 255 4594
✓ W Lockett (0113) 256 2857
🏴 18 L 6184 yds SSS 70
🕴 WD–U Sat–U after 4.30pm Sun–U
  after 9.30am
£€ £20.50 (£25.50)
⛳ 4 miles E of Bradford, off A647,
  past Calverley GC

Woodsome Hall (1922)
Woodsome Hall, Fenay Bridge,
Huddersfield, HD8 0LQ
☎ (01484) 602971
🖳 (01484) 608260
🏠 279 130(L) 85(J)
🏌 TJ Mee (01484) 602739
  RB Shaw (Hon)

✓ M Higginbottom (01484) 602034
ⱶ 18 L 6080 yds SSS 69
🕴 U H exc Tues–NA before 4pm
SOC
£€ £30 D–£40 (£50 D–£60)
🚗 6 miles SE of Huddersfield on
A629 Penistone road
■ www.woodsomehall.co.uk

Woolley Park (1995)
Woolley, Wakefield, WF4 2JS
☎ **(01226) 380144 (Bookings)**
🖥 (01226) 390295
📖 500
✍ D Rowbottom
(Prop) (01226) 382209

✓ J Baldwin
ⱶ 18 L 6636 yds Par 71 SSS 72
🕴 WD–U WE–restricted SOC
£€ £16 (£24)
🚗 5 miles S of Wakefield on A61. M1
Junction 38, 2 miles
⛨ M Shattock
■ www.woolleypark.co.uk

Ireland

Co Antrim

Antrim (1997)
Allen Park Golf Centre, 45 Castle Road,
Antrim, BT41 4NA
☎ **(028) 9442 9001**
🖥 (028) 9442 9001
📧 allenpark@antrim.gov.uk
📖 500
✍ Marie Agnew (Mgr)
✓ P Russell
ⱶ 18 L 6110 m Par 72 SSS 72
🕴 U
£€ £15.50 (£17.50)
🚗 Antrim
⊕ Driving range

Ballycastle (1890)
Cushendall Road, Ballycastle, BT64 6QP
☎ **(028) 2076 2536**
🖥 (028) 2076 9909
📖 920
✍ BJ Dillon (Hon)
✓ I McLaughlin (028) 2076 2506
ⱶ 18 L 5927 yds SSS 70
🕴 U H SOC
£€ £20 (£30)
🚗 Between Portrush and Cushendall
(A2)

Ballyclare (1923)
25 Springvale Road, Ballyclare,
BT39 9JW
☎ **(028) 9334 2352 (Clubhouse)**
🖥 (028) 9332 2696
📧 ballyclaregolfclub@supanet.com
📖 440
✍ H McConnell (028) 9332 2696
ⱶ 18 L 5840 yds SSS 71
🕴 WD–U WE–NA before 4pm
£€ £20 (£25)
🚗 1¹/₂ miles N of Ballyclare. 14 miles
N of Belfast
⛨ T McAuley

Ballymena (1903)
128 Raceview Road, Ballymena,
BT42 4HY
☎ **(028) 2586 1207/1487**
🖥 (028) 2586 1487
📖 940
✍ S Crummey (Hon)
✓ K Revie

ⱶ 18 L 5299 m Par 68 SSS 67
🕴 WD/Sun–U SOC
£€ £17 (£22)
🚗 2 miles E of Ballymena on A42

Bentra
Public
Slaughterford Road, Whitehead,
BT38 9TG
☎ **(028) 9337 8996**
✍ N Houston (028) 9335 1711
ⱶ 9 L 3155 yds Par 36 SSS 34
🕴 U
£€ £8 (£11)
🚗 4 miles N of Carrickfergus on A2
Larne road
⛨ James Braid

Burnfield House
10 Cullyburn Road, Newtownabbey,
BT36 5BN
☎ **(028) 9083 8737**
📧 michaelhj@ntlworld.com
✍ MH Jackson (028) 9038 6652
ⱶ 9 L 2751 yds Par 35 SSS 39
🕴 U
£€ £10 (£14)
🚗 10 miles N of Belfast (A2)
■ www.burnfieldhousegolfclub.co.uk

Bushfoot (1890)
50 Bushfoot Road, Portballintrae,
BT57 8RR
☎ **(028) 2073 1317**
🖥 (028) 2073 1852
📧 bushfootgolfclub@btinternet.com
📖 860
✍ J Knox Thompson (Sec/Mgr)
ⱶ 9 L 6001 yds SSS 68
🕴 U Sat–NA after noon SOC
£€ £15 (£19)
🚗 1 mile N of Bushmills. 4 miles E of
Portrush

Cairndhu (1928)
192 Coast Road, Ballygally, Larne,
BT40 2QC
☎ **(028) 2858 3324**
🖥 (028) 2858 3324
📖 875
✍ N Moore (028) 2858 3324
✓ R Walker (028) 2858 3417
ⱶ 18 L 6112 yds SSS 69
🕴 U exc Sat–NA

£€ £20 (£25)
🚗 4 miles N of Larne
⛨ JSF Morrison

Carrickfergus (1926)
35 North Road, Carrickfergus, BT38 8LP
☎ **(028) 9336 3713**
🖥 (028) 9336 3023
📧 carrickfergusgc@talk21
📖 967
✍ I McLean (Hon Sec)
✓ Gary Mercer
ⱶ 18 L 5713 yds SSS 68
🕴 U SOC
£€ £19.50 (£26.50)
🚗 7 miles E of Belfast via M5

Cushendall (1937)
21 Shore Road, Cushendall, BT44 0NG
☎ **(028) 2177 1318**
📖 834
✍ S McLaughlin (028) 2175 8366
ⱶ 9 L 4834 m SSS 63
🕴 WE–restricted SOC
£€ £13 (£18)
🚗 Cushendall, 25 miles N of Larne

Down Royal (1990)
Dungarton Road, Maze, Lisburn,
BT27 5RT
☎ **(028) 9262 1339**
🖥 (028) 9262 1339
📖 52
✍ J Tinnion (Mgr)
✓ C Calder
ⱶ 18 L 7071 yds Par 72 SSS 73 72 69
🕴 U
£€ £12 D–£17 (£24)
🚗 Lisburn, W of Belfast City (M1)
⛨ Stewart Assoc

Galgorm Castle (1997)
200 Galgorm Road, Ballymena,
BT42 1HL
☎ **(028) 2565 0210**
🖥 (028) 2565 1151
📧 golf@galgormcastle.com
📖 500
✍ B McGrown (Mgr)
✓ P Collins
ⱶ 18 L 6724 yds Par 72 SSS 72
🕴 U SOC
£€ £25 (£30)
🚗 Ballymena

⊕ Driving range
⚏ Simon Gidmon
■ www.galgormcastle.com

Gracehill (1995)
Proprietary
141 Ballinlea Road, Stranocum,
Ballymoney, BT53 8PX
☎ (028) 2075 1209
⚏ (028) 2075 1074
✉ info@gracehillgolfclub.co.uk
▥ 360
✍ M McClure (Mgr)
✓ None
ⵒ 18 L 6600 yds Par 72
⚏ U
££ £15–£20 (£25)
⚘ 6 miles N of Ballymoney (B66)
⚏ Frank Ainsworth
■ www.gracehillgolfclub.co.uk

Greenacres (1996)
153 Ballyrobert Road, Ballyclare,
BT39 9RT
☎ (028) 9335 4111
⚏ (028) 9335 4166
▥ 357
✍ Thomas Pollock
ⵒ 18 L 5802 yds Par 70 SSS 68
⚏ U
££ £14 (£20)
⚘ 3 miles from Corrs Corner on B56
⊕ Floodlit driving range
■ www.greenacresgolfclub.co.uk

Greenisland (1894)
156 Upper Road, Greenisland,
Carrickfergus, BT38 8RW
☎ (028) 9086 2236
✉ greenisland.golf@virgin.net
▥ 740
✍ WJ McLaughlin (Hon) (028) 9086 3232
ⵒ 9 L 6045 metres Par 71 SSS 69
⚏ WD–U Sat–NA before 5pm SOC–exc Sat
££ £12 (£18)
⚘ 9 miles NE of Belfast
⚏ H Middleton

Hilton Templepatrick
Castle Upton Estate, Paradise Walk,
Templepatrick, BT39 0DD
☎ (028) 9443 5542
⚏ (028) 9443 5511
✉ bill_donald@hilton.com
▥ 350
✍ W Donald (Mgr)
✓ E Logue and L McCool
ⵒ 18 L 7300 yds Par 71 SSS 71
⚏ U H
££ £40 (£45)
⚘ 12 miles N of Belfast. M2 Junction 5. Belfast Airport 6 miles
⊕ Driving range
⚏ Jones/Feherty

Lambeg (1986)
Bells Lane, Lambeg, Lisburn, BT27 4QH
☎ (028) 9266 2738
⚏ (028) 9260 3432

▥ 200
✍ B Jackson (Hon)
✓ I Murdock
ⵒ 18 L 4139 m Par 66 SSS 62
⚏ U SOC
££ £7.40 (£9.40)
⚘ SW of Belfast, off Lisburn road

Larne (1894)
54 Ferris Bay Road, Islandmagee,
Larne, BT40 3RJ
☎ (028) 9338 2228
⚏ (028) 9338 2088
✉ info@larnegolfclub.co.uk
▥ 420
✍ RI Johnston
ⵒ 9 L 6288 yds SSS 70
⚏ WD–U WE–M after 5pm SOC–WD/Sun
££ £10 (£18)
⚘ 6 miles N of Whitehead on Browns Bay road
⚏ George Baillie

Lisburn (1891)
68 Eglantine Road, Lisburn, BT27 5RQ
☎ (028) 9267 7216
⚏ (028) 9260 3608
▥ 1421
✍ GE McVeigh (Sec/Mgr)
✓ BR Campbell (028) 9267 7217
ⵒ 18 L 6647 yds Par 72 SSS 72
⚏ WD–U WE–M SOC–Mon & Thurs
££ £25 (£30)
⚘ 3 miles S of Lisburn on A1
⚏ Hawtree

Mallusk (1992)
Antrim Road, Glengormley,
Newtownabbey, BT36 4RF
☎ (028) 9084 3799
▥ 75
✍ J Patterson
ⵒ 9 L 4444 m SSS 62
⚏ U
££ £6.50 (£8.75)
⚘ 4 miles NW of Newtownabbey (B95)

Massereene (1895)
51 Lough Road, Antrim, BT41 4DQ
☎ (028) 9442 9293
⚏ (028) 9448 7661
✉ massereenegc@utvinternet.com
▥ 850
✍ K Stevens (028) 9442 8096
✓ J Smyth (028) 9446 4074
ⵒ 18 L 6602 yds SSS 72
⚏ U SOC
££ £20 (£25)
⚘ 1 mile S of Antrim
⚏ Howard Swann Golf Designs
■ www.massereenegolfclub1895.com

Rathmore
Bushmills Road, Portrush, BT56 8JG
☎ (028) 7082 2996
✍ DR Williamson (Mgr)
ⵒ 18 L 6304 yds Par 70
⚏ U
££ £30 (£35)
⚘ Portrush

Royal Portrush (1888)
Dunluce Road, Portrush, BT56 8JQ
☎ (028) 7082 2311
⚏ (028) 7082 3139
✉ info@royalportrushgolfclub.com
▥ 997 297(L)
✍ Miss W Erskine
✓ G McNeill (028) 7082 3335
ⵒ Dunluce 18 L 6772 yds SSS 73 Valley 18 L 6273 yds SSS 70 Skerries-9 hole course
⚏ WD–I H exc Wed & Fri pm–NA Sat–NA before 3pm Sun–NA before 10.30am SOC
££ Dunluce £85 (£95) Valley £30 (£37.50)
⚘ Portrush Coastal Rd ¹/₂ mile
⊕ Driving range
⚏ HS Colt
■ www.royalportrushgolfclub.com

Whitehead (1904)
McCrae's Brae, Whitehead,
Carrickfergus, BT38 9NZ
☎ (028) 9337 0820
⚏ (028) 9337 0825
✉ robin@whiteheadgc.fsnet.co.uk
▥ 1076
✍ RA Patrick (Hon)
✓ C Farr (028) 9337 0821
ⵒ 18 L 6050 yds SSS 69
⚏ WD–U WE–M SOC–exc Sat
££ £15 (£20)
⚘ ¹/₂ mile from Whitehead, off road to Island Magee
⚏ AB Armstrong

Co Armagh

Ashfield (1990)
Freeduff, Cullyhanna, Newry, BT35 0JJ
☎ (028) 3086 8180
▥ 100
✍ J Quinn (Sec/Mgr)
✓ E Maney
ⵒ 18 L 5110 m Par 69 SSS 67
⚏ U
££ £10 (£12)
⚘ 6 miles S of Newtownhamilton (B135)
⊕ Driving range
⚏ Frank Ainsworth

Cloverhill
Lough Road, Mullaghbawn, BT35 9XP
☎ (028) 3088 9374
✍ Joe Pilkinton
ⵒ 18 L 5496 yds par 69
⚏ U
££ £10
⚘ W of Newry
■ www.cloverhillgc.com

County Armagh (1893)
Newry Road, Armagh, BT60 1EN
☎ (028) 3752 2501
⚏ (028) 3752 5861
✉ june@golfarmagh.co.uk
▥ 1350

🏌 P McNaney (028) 3752 5861
✓ A Rankin (028) 3752 5864
⊩ 18 L 6184 yds SSS 69
👤 SOC
££ £15 (£20)
🚗 40 miles SW of Belfast by M1

Edenmore (1992)
*Drumnabreeze Road, Magheralin,
Craigavon, BT67 0RH*
☎ **(028) 9261 1310**
🖥 (028) 9261 3310
✉ edenmoregc@aol.com
📖 620
🏌 K Logan (Sec/Mgr)
⊩ 18 L 6244 yds Par 71 SSS 70
👤 U SOC
££ £14 (£18)
🚗 4 miles E of Lurgan (A3)
🎯 F Ainsworth

Loughgall
11-14 Main Street, Loughgall
☎ **(028) 3889 2900**
🖥 (028) 3889 2902
🏌 G Ferson (Mgr)
⊩ 18 L 6229 yds Par 72
👤 U SOC
££ £14 (£16)
🚗 8 miles W of Portadown (B77)
🎯 Don Patterson
■ www.armagh.gov.uk

Lurgan (1893)
The Demesne, Lurgan, BT67 9BN
☎ **(028) 3832 2087 (Clubhouse)**
🖥 (028) 3831 6166
📖 918
🏌 Mrs M Sharpe
✓ D Paul (028) 3832 1068
⊩ 18 L 6257 yds SSS 70
👤 U SOC–Mon/Thurs/Fri am/Sun am
££ £15 (£20)
🚗 Nr Brownlow Castle, Lurgan
🎯 Frank Pennink

Portadown (1902)
192 Gilford Road, Portadown, BT63 5LF
☎ **(028) 3835 5356**
🖥 (028) 3839 1394
📖 959
🏌 Mrs ME Holloway
✓ P Stevenson (028) 3833 4655
⊩ 18 L 5794 yds SSS 70
👤 WD–U exc Tues
££ £18 (£23)
🚗 3 miles S of Portadown, towards
   Gilford

Silverwood (1983)
*Turmoyra Lane, Silverwood, Lurgan,
BT66 6NG*
☎ **(028) 3832 6606**
🖥 (028) 3834 7272
📖 280
🏌 K Devlin
✓ D Paul (028) 3832 6606
⊩ 18 L 6459 yds Par 72 SSS 71
👤 U
££ £12 (£15)
🚗 Lurgan 1 mile. M1 Junction 10
⊕ Floodlit driving range

Tandragee (1922)
Markethill Road, Tandragee, BT62 2ER
☎ **(028) 3884 0727 (Clubhouse)**
🖥 (028) 3884 0664
✉ office@tandragee.co.uk
📖 1205
🏌 D Clayton (028) 3884 1272
✓ D Keenan (028) 3884 1761
⊩ 18 L 5754 m Par 71 SSS 70
👤 U SOC
££ £15 (£20)
🚗 5 miles S of Portadown on A27
🎯 F Hawtree
■ www.tandragee.co.uk

Belfast

Ballyearl Golf Centre
Public
*585 Doagh Road, Newtownabbey,
BT36 5RZ*
☎ **(028) 9084 8287**
🖥 (028) 9084 4896
✓ J Robinson (028) 9084 0899
⊩ 9 L 2362 yds Par 3 course
👤 U
££ £4.90 (£5.70)
🚗 N of Mossley on B59, via A8
⊕ Floodlit driving range

Balmoral (1914)
518 Lisburn Road, Belfast, BT9 6GX
☎ **(028) 9038 1514**
🖥 (028) 9066 6759
📖 925
🏌 RC McConkey (Mgr)
✓ G Bleakley (028) 9066 7747
⊩ 18 L 5909 m SSS 70
👤 U exc Sat SOC–Mon & Thurs
££ £20 (£30)
🚗 2 miles S of Belfast by Kings Hall

Belvoir Park (1927)
*73 Church Road, Newtownbreda,
Belfast, BT8 4AN*
☎ **(028) 9049 1693**
🖥 (028) 9064 6113
📖 1100
🏌 Ann Vaughan (028) 9049 1693
✓ GM Kelly
⊩ 18 L 6501 yds SSS 71
👤 U–booking necessary
££ £33 (£38)
🚗 3 miles S of Belfast centre, off
   Newcastle road
🎯 HS Colt

Cliftonville (1911)
Westland Road, Belfast, BT14 6NH
☎ **(028) 9074 4158**
📖 429
🏌 JM Henderson (Hon) (028) 9074
   6595
⊩ 9 L 6242 yds SSS 70
👤 U exc Sat
££ £13 (£16)
🚗 Belfast

Dunmurry (1905)
*91 Dunmurry Lane, Dunmurry, Belfast,
BT17 9JS*
☎ **(028) 9061 0834**
🖥 (028) 9060 2540
✉ dunmurrygc@hotmail.com
📖 493 127(L) 117(J)
🏌 T Cassidy (Golf Mgr)
✓ J Dolan (028) 9062 1314
⊩ 18 L 6096 yds Par 70 SSS 69
👤 Tues & Thurs–NA after 5pm
   Sat–NA before 5pm SOC
££ £27 (£37) SOC–£23
🚗 Belfast 5 miles
🎯 T McAuley

Fortwilliam (1891)
Downview Avenue, Belfast, B15 4EZ
☎ **(028) 9037 0770**
🖥 (028) 9078 1891
✉ michael@fortwilliam.co.uk
📖 1100
🏌 M Purdy
✓ P Hanna (028) 9077 0980
⊩ 18 L 6030 yds SSS 69
👤 U SOC
££ £22 (£29)
🚗 2 miles N of Belfast on M2
■ www.fortwilliam.co.uk

Gilnahirk (1983)
*Manns Corner, Upper Braniel Road,
Belfast, BT5 7TX*
☎ **(028) 9044 8477**
📖 200
🏌 A Carson
✓ K Gray
⊩ 9 L 2699 m SSS 68
👤 U
££ £9
🚗 3 miles SE of Belfast, off A23

The Knock Club (1895)
*Summerfield, Dundonald, Belfast,
BT16 2QX*
☎ **(028) 9048 2249**
🖥 (028) 9048 7277
📖 900
🏌 Anne Armstrong (028) 9048 3251
✓ G Fairweather (028) 9048 3825
⊩ 18 L 6407 yds SSS 71
👤 U SOC–Mon & Thurs
££ D–£25 (£40)
🚗 4 miles E of Belfast on the Upper
   Newtownards Road
🎯 Colt/Mackenzie/Alison

Malone (1895)
*240 Upper Malone Road, Dunmurry,
Belfast, BT17 9LB*
☎ **(028) 9061 2758**
🖥 (028) 9043 1394
✉ manager@malonegolfclub.co.uk
📖 759 379(L) 211(J)
🏌 JNS Agate (028) 9061 2758
✓ M McGee (028) 9061 4917
⊩ 18 L 6599 yds SSS 71
   9 L 3160 yds SSS 36
👤 Tues/Wed pm–NA Sat–NA before
   3.30pm SOC–Mon & Thurs
££ £40 (£45)

6 miles S of Belfast
J Harris/CK Cotton
www.malonegolfclub.co.uk

Ormeau (1893)
50 Park Road, Belfast, BT7 2FX
☎ **(028) 9064 1069 (Members)**
🖳 (028) 9064 6250
📖 280 70(L) 45(J)
✍ R Barnes (028) 9064 0700
✓ (028) 9064 0999
🏴 9 L 5308 yds SSS 65
👥 U SOC
💷 £14 (£16.50)
⛳ 2 miles S of Belfast

Shandon Park (1926)
73 Shandon Park, Belfast, BT5 6NY
☎ **(028) 9079 3730**
🖳 (028) 9040 2773
📖 1100
✍ DG Jenkins (Mgr) (028) 9040 1856
✓ B Wilson (028) 9079 7859
🏴 18 L 6261 yds SSS 70
👥 WD–U Sat–NA before 5pm SOC
💷 £22 (£27)
⛳ 3 miles E of Belfast on the Knock road

Co Carlow

Borris (1907)
Deerpark, Borris
☎ **(0503) 73310**
🖳 (0503) 73750
📖 475
✍ Nollaig Lucas (Sec/Mgr) (0503) 73310
🏴 9 L 5680 m Par 70 SSS 69
👥 WD–U Sun–M SOC–WD/Sat
💷 €20
⛳ Borris

Carlow (1899)
Deer Park, Dublin Road, Carlow
☎ **(0503) 31695**
🖳 (0503) 40065
✉ carlowgolfclub@eircom.net
📖 1300
✍ Dr Donald MacSweeney (Sec/Mgr)
✓ A Gilbert (0503) 41745
🏴 18 L 5844 m Par 70 SSS 71
👥 U SOC–WD
💷 €42 (€54)
⛳ 2 miles N of Carlow (N9) 50 miles S of Dublin (N7)
🏗 Tom Simpson
■ www.carlowgolfclub.com

Mount Wolseley (1996)
Tullow
☎ **(059) 915 1674**
🖳 (059) 915 2123
✉ wolseley@iol.ie
📖 250
✍ D Morrissey (Mgr)
🏴 18 L 6497 m Par 72 SSS 74
👥 U SOC
💷 €50 (€70)

15 miles E of Carlow (R275)
Christy O'Connor Jr
www.mountwolseley.ie

Co Cavan

Belturbet (1950)
Erne Hill, Belturbet
☎ **(049) 952 2287**
📖 110
✍ PF Coffey (049) 22498
✓ None
🏴 9 L 6118 m Par 72
👥 U SOC
💷 €13
⛳ 1 mile E of Belturbet

Blacklion (1962)
Toam, Blacklion, via Sligo
☎ **(072) 53024**
📖 250
✍ P Maguire (Hon)
🏴 9 L 5716 m SSS 69
👥 U SOC
💷 D–€10 (D–€12)
⛳ 12 miles SW of Enniskillen on A4 to N16
🏗 Eddie Hackett

Cabra Castle (1978)
Kingscourt
☎ **(042) 966 7030**
🖳 (042) 966 7039
📖 160
✍ Tom Lynch
🏴 9 L 5261 m Par 70
👥 U exc Sun–NA SOC
💷 €15
⛳ 2 miles E of Kingscourt

County Cavan (1894)
Arnmore House, Drumelis, Cavan
☎ **(049) 433 1541**
🖳 (049) 433 1541
✉ info@cavangolf.ie
📖 800
✍ B Fitzsimons
✓ B Noble
🏴 18 L 5519 m SSS 69
👥 U
💷 On application
⛳ 2 miles W of Cavan on Killeshandra road
⊕ Driving range
🏗 Eddie Hackett

Slieve Russell G&CC (1994)
Ballyconnell
☎ **(049) 952 6458**
✉ slieve-russell@quinn-hotels.com
📖 500
✍ I Hewson (049) 952 5090
✓ L McCool (049) 952 5090
🏴 18 L 7053 yds Par 72 SSS 74
   9 hole Par 3 course
👥 U SOC
💷 €50 Sat–€65
⛳ 15 miles N of Cavan Town
⊕ Driving range
🏗 Paddy Merrigan

Virginia (1945)
Park Hotel, Virginia
☎ **(049) 854 8066**
📖 570
✍ S MacGabhann
🏴 9 L 4139 m Par 64 SSS 62
👥 U
💷 €12
⛳ 35 miles SE of Cavan, nr Lough Ramor (N3)

Co Clare

Clonlara (1993)
Clonlara
☎ **(061) 354141**
📖 85
✍ M Morris
🏴 12 L 5289 m Par 70 SSS 69
👥 U
💷 €9
⛳ 8 miles NE of Limerick

Dromoland Castle (1964)
Newmarket-on-Fergus
☎ **(061) 368444**
🖳 (061) 368498
📖 400
✍ J O'Halloran
✓ P Murphy
🏴 18 L 6098 yds SSS 71
👥 U SOC
💷 D–€36 (€42)
⛳ 18 miles NW of Limerick. Shannon Airport 4 miles
■ www.dromoland.ie

East Clare (1992)
Bodyke
☎ **(061) 921322**
📖 700
✍ Michael O'Hanlon
🏴 18 L 5922 m Par 71 SSS 69
👥 U
💷 €25 (€30)
⛳ 20 miles E of Ennis (R352)

Ennis (1907)
Drumbiggle, Ennis
☎ **(065) 682 4074**
🖳 (065) 684 1848
📖 1246
✍ N O'Donnell (Gen Mgr)
✓ M Ward (065) 682 0690
🏴 18 L 5592 m Par 71 SSS 69
👥 U SOC
💷 €30
⛳ ¹/₂ mile NW of Ennis, off N18
■ www.ennisgolfclub.com

Kilkee (1896)
East End, Kilkee
☎ **(065) 905 6048**
🖳 (065) 905 6977
✉ kilkeegolfclub@eircom.net
📖 704
✍ M Culligan (Sec/Mgr)
🏴 18 L 555 m Par 70 SSS 69

※ U SOC
£€ €24
∞ End of Kilkee Promenade. 10 miles NW of Kilrush
⌂ Eddie Hackett

Kilrush (1934)

Parknamoney, Kilrush
☎ (065) 905 1138
⌨ (065) 905 2633
▥ 338
✍ DF Nagle (Sec/Mgr) M Cody (Hon)
⤴ J McDermott
ℙ 18 L 5986 yds Par 70 SSS 69
※ U SOC
£€ €21 (€25)
∞ 25 miles SW of Ennis on Lahinch-Ballybunion road
⌂ Arthur Spring
▮ www.kilrushgolfclub.com

Lahinch (1892)

Lahinch
☎ (065) 708 1003
⌨ (065) 708 1592
✉ info@lahinchgolf.com
▥ 1250
✍ A Reardon (Sec/Mgr)
⤴ R McCavery (065) 708 1408
ℙ Old 18 L 6950 yds SSS 74
    Castle 18 L 5620 yds SSS 69
※ WD–U WE–NA 9–10.30am and 1–2pm SOC
£€ Old–€110. Castle–€50
∞ 20 miles NW of Ennis on T69
⌂ Old – Morris/Gibson/Mackenzie/Hawtree, Castle – Harris

Shannon (1966)

Shannon
☎ (061) 471020
⌨ (061) 471507
▥ 1050
✍ M Corry (061) 471849
⤴ A Pike (061) 471551
ℙ 18 L 6515 yds Par 72 SSS 72
※ WD–U SOC
£€ €35
∞ Shannon Airport

Spanish Point (1915)

Spanish Point, Miltown Malbay
☎ (065) 708 4219
▥ 200
✍ D Fitzgerald
ℙ 9 L 4624 m Par 64 SSS 63
※ U
£€ €35
∞ 2 mile S of Miltown Malbay (N67). 20 miles W of Ennis
▮ www.spanish-point.com

Woodstock (1993)

Shanaway Road, Ennis
☎ (065) 682 9463
⌨ (065) 682 0304
✉ woodstock.ennis@eircom.net
▥ 400
✍ Avril Guerin (Sec/Mgr)
ℙ 18 L 5879 m SSS 71

※ U
£€ €40
∞ Ennis, 18 miles from Shannon Airport
⌂ Arthur Spring
▮ www.woodstockgolfclub.com

Co Cork

Bandon (1909)

Castlebernard, Bandon
☎ (023) 41111
⌨ (023) 44690
▥ 800
✍ N O'Sullivan (Hon)
⤴ P O'Boyle (023) 42224
ℙ 18 L 5663 m Par 70 SSS 69
※ U
£€ On application
∞ Bandon 1½ miles. 18 miles SW of Cork

Bantry Bay (1975)

Donemark, Bantry, West Cork
☎ (027) 50579/53773
⌨ (027) 53790
✉ info@bantrygolf.com
▥ 650
✍ J O'Sullivan (Mgr)
ℙ 18 L 5914 m Par 71 SSS 72
※ WD–U before 4.30 pm
    WE/BH–booking necessary SOC
£€ €40 (€40)
∞ 1 mile N of Bantry on Glengarriff road (N71)
⌂ E Hackett/C O'Connor jr
▮ www.bantrygolf.com

Berehaven (1902)

Millcove, Castletownbere
☎ (027) 70700
⌨ (027) 71957
✉ bearagolfglub@aircom.net
▥ 208
✍ B Twomey (Hon)
ℙ 9 L 5114 m SSS 67 (ladies), SSS 65 (men)
※ U SOC
£€ €20 (€25)
∞ 2 miles E of Castletownbere on Glengarriff road
⌂ James Healy
▮ www.bearagolf.com

Charleville (1909)

Charleville
☎ (063) 81257
⌨ (063) 81274
✉ charlevillegolf@eircom.net
▥ 1250
✍ P Nagle (Sec/Mgr)
⤴ D Keating
ℙ 18 L 6430 yds SSS 69
    9 L 6750 yds SSS 72
※ WD–U WE–book in advance SOC
£€ €35 (€40) SOC–€28 (€35)
∞ 35 miles N of Cork on Limerick road
⊕ Driving range
▮ www.charlevillegolf.com

Cobh (1987)

Ballywilliam, Cobh
☎ (021) 812399
⌨ (021) 812615
▥ 120
✍ H Cunningham
ℙ 9 L 4576 m SSS 64
※ WD–U WE–NA
£€ €11
∞ 1 mile N of Cobh. 16 miles SE of Cork
⌂ Eddie Hackett

Coosheen (1989)

Coosheen, Schull
☎ (028) 28182
▥ 200
✍ L Morgan
ℙ 9 L 4001 m Par 60 SSS 61
※ U
£€ €14 (€14)
∞ 15 miles S of Bantry

Cork (1888)

Little Island, Cork
☎ (021) 435 3451/3037
⌨ (021) 435 3410
✉ corkgolfclub@eircom.net
▥ 366 176 (L)
✍ M Sands (021) 435 3451
⤴ P Hickey (021) 435 3421
ℙ 18 L 6065 m SSS 72
※ WD–U H exc 12–2pm –M after 4pm Thurs–(Ladies Day)–phone in advance WE–NA before 2.30pm H
£€ €75 (€85)
∞ 5 miles E of Cork, off N25
⌂ Dr A Mackenzie
▮ www.corkgolfclub.ie

Doneraile (1927)

Doneraile
☎ (022) 24137
▥ 750
✍ J O'Leary (022) 24379
ℙ 9 L 5528 yds SSS 67
※ WD/Sat–U
£€ €20
∞ 8 miles NW of Mallow

Douglas (1909)

Douglas, Cork
☎ (021) 489 1086
⌨ (021) 489 5297
✉ admin@douglasgolfclub.ie
▥ 839
✍ B Kiely (Mgr) (021) 489 5297
⤴ GS Nicholson (021) 436 2055
ℙ 18 L 5972 m SSS 71
※ WD–U exc Tues WE–NA before 2pm SOC–WD
£€ €50 (€60)
∞ Cork 3 miles
⌂ P McEvoy
▮ www.douglasgolfclub.ie

Dunmore (1967)

Muckross, Clonakilty
☎ (023) 34644
▥ 430

For list of abbreviations and key to symbols see page 627

L O'Donovan
9 L 4464 yds SSS 61
WD–U exc Wed WE–M SOC–Sat
€20
3 miles S of Clonakilty
Eddie Hackett

East Cork   (1971)

Gortacrue, Midleton

(021) 463 1687
(021) 461 3695
eastcorkgolfclub@eircom.net
600
M Moloney (Sec/Mgr)
D MacFarlane
18 L 5207 m SSS 67
WD–U WE–NA before noon
BH–U
€25
2 miles N of Midleton on L35
Driving range
Eddie Hackett

Fermoy   (1892)

Corrin, Fermoy

(025) 32694
(025) 33072
1000
K Murphy
B Moriarty (025) 31472
18 L 5847 m SSS 70
U SOC
€20 (€30)
2 miles S of Fermoy, off N8
Cdr John Harris

Fernhill   (1994)

Carrigaline

(021) 437 2226
(021) 437 1011
fernhill@iol.ie
120
A Bowes (Mgr)
W Callaghan (087) 284 1365
18 L 5766 m Par 70 SSS 67
U
€20 Mon–Thur (€30 Fri–Sun)
7 miles SE of Cork (R609), nr
Ringskiddy
ML Bowes
www.fernhillgolfhotel.com

Fota Island   (1993)

Carrigtwohill, Cork

(021) 488 3710
(021) 453 2047
reservations@fotaisland.ie
650
Jonathon Woods
K Morris
18 L 6927 yds Par 71 SSS 73
U
€62–€83 (€75–€98)
8 miles E of Cork on N25
Driving range
O'Connor Jr/McEvoy/Howes

Frankfield   (1984)

Frankfield, Douglas

(021) 363124
320

A MacFarlane
D Whyte, M Ryan
9 L 4621 m SSS 65
U SOC
€6
S of Cork
Driving range

Glengarriff   (1935)

Glengarriff

(027) 63150
(027) 63575
250
N Deasy (Hon)
9 L 4094 m SSS 66
U
D–€14 (€18)
1 mile E of Glengarriff (N71)

Harbour Point   (1991)

Clash, Little Island

(021) 353094
(021) 354408
300
Mrs N Dwyer (Sec/Mgr)
M O'Donovan (021) 353719
18 L 6063 yds SSS 72
U SOC
€20–€32
5 miles E of Cork
Floodlit driving range
Paddy Merrigan

Kanturk   (1971)

Fairyhill, Kanturk

(029) 50534
410
T McAuliffe
None
18 L 6262 yds Par 72 SSS 70
U
€15
2 miles SW of Kanturk (R579)
R Barry

Kinsale Farrangalway
(1993)

Farrangalway, Kinsale

(021) 477 4722
(021) 477 3114
kinsaleg@indigo.ie
740
G Broderick (021) 477 3258
18 L 6609 yds SSS 72
WD–U WE–NA SOC
€35 (€50)
3 miles NW of Kinsale. 18 miles S
of Cork
Jack Kenneally

Kinsale Ringenane   (1912)

Ringenane, Belgooly, Kinsale

(021) 477 2197
740
None
9 L 5332 yds SSS 68
U SOC
€18
2 miles E of Kinsale (R600). 16
miles S of Cork

Lee Valley G&CC   (1993)

Clashanure, Ovens, Cork

(021) 733 1721
(021) 733 1695
450
C Nylan
J Savage (021) 733 1758
18 L 6800 yds SSS 72
U SOC
€41
8 miles W of Cork (N22)
Floodlit driving range
C O'Connor Jr

Macroom   (1924)

Lackaduve, Macroom

(026) 41072
(026) 41391
mcroomgc@iol.com
725
C O'Sullivan (Mgr)
None
18 L 5574 m Par 72 SSS 70
U SOC
€25 (€30)
Macroom Town, through Castle
Arch. 25 miles W of Cork
Jack Kenneally

Mahon   (1980)

Clover Hill, Blackrock, Cork

(021) 294280
450
T O'Connor
T O'Connor
18 L 4818 m SSS 66
U
€15
SE of Cork City

Mallow   (1948)

Ballyellis, Mallow

(022) 21145
(022) 42501
golfmall@gofree.indigo.ie
1500
D Curtin (Sec/Mgr)
S Conway (022) 43424
18 L 6559 yds SSS 72
WD–U before 5pm SOC
€35 (€40)
1 mile SE of Mallow Bridge on
Killavullen road
J Harris

Mitchelstown   (1908)

Gurrane, Mitchelstown

(025) 24072
500
T Lewis
18 L 5157 m Par 67
U SOC
€25
30 miles NE of Cork
David Jones

Monkstown   (1908)

Parkgarriffe, Monkstown

(021) 484 1376
(021) 484 1722

✉ office@monkstowngolfclub.com
🏛 900
✍ H Madden (Sec/Mgr)
✓ B Murphy (021) 486 3912
🏌 18 L 5669 m SSS 69
👥 U SOC
£€ €37 (€44)
⛳ 7 miles SE of Cork
■ www.monkstowngolfclub.com

Muskerry　(1907)
Carrigrohane
☎ **(021) 438 5297**
📠 (021) 451 6860
🏛 803
✍ H Gallagher
✓ WM Lehane (021) 438 1445
🏌 18 L 5786 m SSS 71
👥 Restricted at certain times–phone first SOC
£€ €35
⛳ 7 miles NW of Cork. 2 miles W of Blarney

Old Head Golf Links　(1997)
Kinsale
☎ **(021) 477 8444**
📠 (021) 477 8022
✉ info@oldheadgolf.ie
✍ J O'Brien (Gen Mgr)
🏌 18 L 7300 yds SSS 72
👥 U H
£€ €250
⛳ 7 miles S of Kinsale
⊕ Driving range
🏠 Carr/Merrigan/Kirby/Hackett
■ www.oldheadgolflinks.com

Raffeen Creek　(1989)
Ringaskiddy
☎ **(021) 437 8430**
🏛 530
✍ J Kiely
🏌 9 L 5098 m Par 70 SSS 67
👥 WD–U WE–U after noon
£€ €18
⛳ 1 mile from Ringaskiddy Ferryport
🏠 Eddie Hackett

Skibbereen　(1931)
Licknavar, Skibbereen
☎ **(028) 21227**
📠 (028) 22994
✉ bookings@skibbgolf.com
🏛 580
✍ S Brett (Mgr)
✓ None
🏌 18 L 5474 m Par 71 SSS 69
👥 U SOC–Sat
£€ €30
⛳ 1 mile W of Skibbereen. 52 miles SW of Cork
🏠 Eddie Hackett
■ www.skibbgolf.com

Youghal　(1898)
Knockaverry, Youghal
☎ **(024) 92787/92861**
📠 (024) 92641
✉ youghalgolfclub@eircom.net

🏛 827
✍ Margaret O'Sullivan
✓ L Burns (024) 92590
🏌 18 L 5646 m SSS 70
👥 U
£€ €25 (€32)
⛳ 30 miles E of Cork on N25 from Rosslare
🏠 Cdr Harris
■ www.youghalgolfclub.net

Co Donegal

Ballybofey & Stranorlar　(1957)
The Glebe, Stranorlar
☎ **(074) 31093**
📠 (074) 31058
🏛 655
✍ John McCaughan (074) 31377
✓ (074) 31093 (shop)
🏌 18 L 5922 yds Par 68 SSS 68
👥 U SOC
£€ €20 (€25)
⛳ Stranorlar ¹/₂ mile
🏠 PC Carr

Ballyliffin　(1947)
Ballyliffin, Inishowen
☎ **(077) 76119**
📠 (077) 76672
🏛 828
✍ C Doherty (Sec/Mgr)
✓ None
🏌 Old 18 L 6611 yds SSS 72
　　Glashedy 18 L 6837 yds Par 72
👥 U SOC–WD
£€ Old €30 Glashedy €44
⛳ 8 miles N of Buncrana. 15 miles N of Londonderry
🏠 Glashedy-Craddock/Ruddy
■ www.ballyliffingolfclub.com

Buncrana　(1951)
Buncrana
☎ **(077) 62279/20749**
✉ buncranagc@eircom.net
🏛 300
✍ F McGrory (Hon) (077) 20749
✓ J Doherty
🏌 9 L 4250 m SSS 62
👥 U
£€ €8 – €13
⛳ S of Buncrana, nr Gateway Hotel

Bundoran　(1894)
Bundoran
☎ **(072) 41302**
📠 (072) 42014
✉ bundorangolfclub@eircom.net
🏛 620
✍ J McGagh (Sec/Mgr)
✓ D Robinson
🏌 18 L 5688 m Par 70 SSS 70
👥 WD–U WE–restricted SOC
£€ €35 (€45)
⛳ E boundary of Bundoran. 20 miles S of Donegal
🏠 H Vardon

Cruit Island　(1985)
Kincasslagh, Dunglow
☎ **(075) 43296**
📠 (075) 48028
🏛 350
✍ T Gallagher
✓ None
🏌 9 L 5297 yds Par 68 SSS 64
👥 U SOC
£€ €12 (€18)
⛳ 5 miles N of Dunglow, off R259
■ www.homepage.eircom.net /~cruitisland

Donegal　(1960)
Murvagh, Laghey
☎ **(073) 34054**
📠 (073) 34377
🏛 650
✍ J Nixon (073) 22166
　　P Nugent (Gen Mgr)
🏌 18 L 7271 yds SSS 73
👥 H SOC–exc Sun
£€ €40 (€55)
⛳ 7 miles S of Donegal, off N15
🏠 Eddie Hackett
■ www.donegalgolfclub.ie

Dunfanaghy　(1906)
Kill, Dunfanaghy, Letterkenny
☎ **(074) 36335**
📠 (074) 36335
🏛 390
✍ J Moffitt
🏌 18 L 5350 m Par 68 SSS 66
👥 U SOC
£€ €22 (€27)
⛳ 25 miles NW of Letterkenny on N56
⊕ Driving range
🏠 Harry Vardon
■ www.golfdunfanaghy.com

Greencastle　(1892)
Greencastle
☎ **(074) 93 81013**
📠 (074) 93 81015
🏛 750
✍ HM Morris
✓ None
🏌 18 L 5211 m SSS 67
👥 WD–U WE–restricted SOC
£€ €25 (€35)
⛳ 21 miles NE of Londonderry, nr Moville
🏠 Eddie Hackett

Gweedore　(1926)
Magheragallon, Derrybeg, Letterkenny
☎ **(075) 31140**
🏛 250
✍ S McGowan
🏌 9 L 6201 yds SSS 69
👥 U
£€ €13 (€15)
⛳ 3 miles N of Gweedore, off R257

Letterkenny　(1913)
Barnhill, Letterkenny
☎ **(074) 21150**

☎ (074) 21175
▥ 790
✍ B Ramsay (074) 24491
► 18 L 6239 yds SSS 71
※ U–booking necessary SOC
£€ €25 (€35)
⛳ 1 mile E of Letterkenny
⌂ Eddie Hackett

Narin & Portnoo (1931)
Narin, Portnoo
☎ **(075) 45107**
▤ (074) 45107
✉ narinportnoo@eircom.net
▥ 835
✍ E Bonner (Hon)
✓ None
► 18 L 5950 yds Par 69 SSS 68
※ WD/Sat–U H Sun–NA before 2pm SOC
£€ €26 (€32) SOC–€21 (€27)
⛳ 6 miles N of Ardara. West Donegal

North West (1891)
Lisfannon, Fahan
☎ **(077) 61027**
▤ (077) 63284
▥ 555
✍ D Coyle (Hon)
✓ S McBriarty (077) 61715
► 18 L 6239 yds SSS 70
※ U
£€ €25 (€30)
⛳ 2 miles S of Buncrana. 12 miles N of Londonderry

Otway (1893)
Saltpans, Rathmullan, Letterkenny
☎ **(074) 58319**
✉ gmcgivern@ntlworld.com
▥ 97
✍ G McGivern (Hon)
► 9 L 4234 yds SSS 60
※ U
£€ €13
⛳ 15 miles NE of Letterkenny, by Lough Swilly

Portsalon (1891)
Portsalon, Fanad
☎ **(074) 915 9459**
▤ (074) 915 9919
▥ 550
✍ P Doherty
► 18 L 6185m Par 72SSS 72
※ U–phone in advance
£€ €21 (€26)
⛳ 20 miles N of Letterkenny (R246)
⌂ Pat Ruddy

Redcastle (1983)
Redcastle, Moville
☎ **(077) 82073**
▥ 120
✍ D McCartney (Hon)
► 9 L 6046 yds Par 72
※ U
£€ €13
⛳ 15 miles N of Londonderry, by Lough Foyle (R238)

Rosapenna (1894)
Downings, Rosapenna
☎ **(074) 55301**
▤ (074) 55128
✉ rosapenna@eircom.net
▥ 250
✍ N McManus
► 18 L 6254 yds Par 70 SSS 71
※ U
£€ €40 (€45)
⛳ 20 miles N of Letterkenny
⊕ Golf academy; driving range
⌂ Morris/Vardon/Braid/Ruddy
■ www.rosapenna.ie

St Patricks Courses (1994)
Carrigart
☎ **(074) 55114**
▤ (074) 55250
✍ D Walsh (Mgr)
► 18 L 7108 yds Par 72 SSS 73
  18 L 5822 yds Par 71 SSS 71
※ U
£€ €42 (€54)
⛳ 2 miles from Carrigart on Creeslough road
⌂ Hackett/O'Haire

Co Down

Ardglass (1896)
Castle Place, Ardglass, BT30 7PP
☎ **(028) 4484 1219**
▤ (028) 4484 1841
▥ 901
✍ Miss D Polly
✓ P Farrell (028) 4484 1022
► 18 L 5776 yds Par 70 SSS 69
※ U SOC
£€ £28 (£40)
⛳ 7 miles SE of Downpatrick on B1

Ardminnan (1995)
15 Ardminnan Road, Portaferry, BT22 1QJ
☎ **(028) 4277 1321**
▤ (028) 4277 1321
▥ 170
✍ E McGrattan
✓ T McCartney
► 9 L 2766 m Par 70
※ U
£€ £10 (£15)
⛳ 10 miles E of Downpatrick via ferry. 18 miles SE of Newtownards (A20)
⌂ Frank Ainsworth

Banbridge (1912)
116 Huntly Road, Banbridge, BT32 3UR
☎ **(028) 4066 2342 (restaurant)**
▤ (028) 4066 9400
▥ 850
✍ Mrs J Anketell (028) 4066 2211
► 18 L 5590 m SSS 69
※ U SOC
£€ £17 (£22)
⛳ 1 mile W of Banbridge
⌂ F Ainsworth
■ www.banbridgegolf.freeserve.co.uk

Bangor (1903)
Broadway, Bangor, BT20 4RH
☎ **(028) 9127 0922**
▤ (028) 9145 3394
✉ bgcsecretary@aol.com
▥ 1100
✍ DJ Ryan (Sec/Mgr)
✓ M Bannon
► 18 L 6424 yds SSS 71
※ WD–U exc –M 1–2pm Wed–U before 4.45pm Sat–NA SOC
£€ £25 Sun–£30
⛳ 1 mile S of Bangor, off Donaghadee road
⌂ James Braid

Blackwood (1995)
150 Crawfordsburn Road, Bangor, BT19 1GB
☎ **(028) 9185 2706**
▤ (028) 9185 3785
▥ 265
✍ James Kennedy
✓ Debbie Hanna
► 18 L 6392 yds SSS 70
※ U
£€ On application
⛳ W of Bangor
⊕ Driving range

Bright Castle (1970)
14 Coniamstown Road, Bright, Downpatrick, BT30 8LU
☎ **(028) 4484 1319**
▥ 100
✍ J McCawl (Hon)
► 18 L 6700 yds Par 73 SSS 72
※ U SOC
£€ £12 (£14)
⛳ 5 miles S of Downpatrick, off Killough road (B176)

Carnalea (1927)
Station Road, Bangor, BT19 1EZ
☎ **(028) 9146 5004**
▤ (028) 9127 3989
▥ 800
✍ GY Steele (028) 9127 0368
✓ T Loughran (028) 9127 0122
► 18 L 5647 yds SSS 67
※ U SOC–WD
£€ £17.50 (£22)
⛳ By Carnalea Station, Bangor

Clandeboye (1933)
Conlig, Newtownards, BT23 7PN
☎ **(028) 9127 1767 (office), (028) 9147 3706 (bar)**
▤ (028) 9147 3711
✉ contact@cgc-ni.com
▥ 1456
✍ R Eddis (Admin Mgr) (028) 9127 1767
✓ P Gregory (028) 9127 1750
► Dufferin 18 L 6559 yds SSS 71
  Ava 18 L 5755 yds SSS 68
※ WD–U WE–M SOC
£€ Dufferin–£27.50 (£33) Ava–£22
⛳ Conlig, off A21 Bangor-Newtownards road
⌂ Von Limburger/Alliss/Thomas
■ www.cgc-ni.com

Crossgar (1993)

231 Derryboye Road, Crossgar,
BT30 9DL
☎ **(028) 4483 1523**
▥ 105
✍ D Myles (Sec/Mgr)
ᛈ 9 L 4170 m Par 64 SSS 63
ᛘ U
£€ £10 (£10)
⊶ 6 miles N of Downpatrick (A7)

Donaghadee (1899)

84 Warren Road, Donaghadee,
BT21 0PQ
☎ **(028) 9188 3624**
▯ (028) 9188 8891
✉ deegolf@freenet.co.uk
▥ 1135
✍ JRW Thomas
✓ G Drew (028) 9188 2392
ᛈ 18 L 5614 m Par 71
ᛘ U exc Sat–NA SOC–exc Sat
£€ £22 (£25)
⊶ 6 miles S of Bangor on coast road.
18 miles E of Belfast

Downpatrick (1930)

Saul Road, Downpatrick, BT30 6PA
☎ **(028) 4461 5947/2152**
▯ (028) 4461 7502
▥ 960
✍ BA Hitchens (028) 4461 5947
✓ (028) 4461 5167
ᛈ 18 L 5702 m SSS 69
ᛘ U SOC
£€ £20 (£24)
⊶ 25 miles SE of Belfast (A1).
Downpatrick 1¹⁄₂ miles
♛ Hawtree
▆ www.downpatrickgolfclub.com

Helen's Bay (1896)

Golf Road, Helen's Bay, Bangor,
BT19 1TL
☎ **(028) 9185 2601 (Clubhouse)**
▯ (028) 9185 2660
▥ 700
✍ PB Clarke (028) 9185 2815
ᛈ 9 L 5261 m Par 68 SSS 67
ᛘ WD/Sun–U
Tues/Thurs/Sat–restricted
SOC–WD
£€ On application
⊶ 9 miles E of Belfast, off A2

Holywood (1904)

Nuns Walk, Demesne Road, Holywood,
BT18 9LE
☎ **(028) 9042 2138**
▯ (028) 9042 5040
▥ 1000
✍ GA Fyfe (Gen Mgr)
(028) 9042 3135
✓ P Gray (028) 9042 5503
ᛈ 18 L 5885 yds SSS 68
ᛘ WD–U exc 1.30–2.15pm Sat–after
5pm
£€ £16 (£25)
⊶ 5 miles E of Belfast on Bangor road
▆ www.holywoodgolfclub.co.uk

Kilkeel (1948)

Mourne Park, Kilkeel, BT34 4LB
☎ **(028) 4176 2296/5095**
▯ (028) 4176 5579
▥ 720
✍ SC McBride (Hon)
(028) 4176 5095
✓ None
ᛈ 18 L 6579 yds SSS 72
ᛘ U SOC–exc Sat
£€ £20 (£25)
⊶ 3 miles W of Kilkeel on Newry
road
♛ Badington/Hackett

Kirkistown Castle (1902)

142 Main Road, Cloughey,
Newtownards, BT22 1JA
☎ **(028) 4277 1233**
▯ (028) 4277 1699
▥ 948
✍ R Coulter (028) 4277 1233
✓ J Peden (028) 4277 1004
ᛈ 18 L 5616 m Par 69 SSS 70
ᛘ WD/Sun–U Sat–NA before 2.30pm
£€ £20.75 (£27.75)
⊶ 25 miles SE of Belfast
♛ James Braid
▆ www.kcgc.org

Mahee Island (1930)

Comber, Belfast, BT23 6ET
☎ **(028) 9754 1234**
▥ 500
✍ M Marshall (Hon)
✓ A McCracken
ᛈ 9 L 5822 yds Par 71 SSS 70
ᛘ U exc Sat–NA before 5pm
SOC–WD exc Mon
£€ £10 (£15)
⊶ Strangford Lough, 14 miles SE of
Belfast
♛ Mr Robinson

Mount Ober G&CC (1985)

Ballymaconaghy Road, Knockbracken,
Belfast, BT8 6SB
☎ **(028) 9079 2108 (Bookings)**
▯ (028) 9070 5862
▥ 500
✍ D McNamara (Sec/Mgr)
✓ S Rourke (028) 9070 1648
ᛈ 18 L 5436 yds SSS 68
ᛘ WD–U Sat–NA before 3pm
Sun–NA before 10.30am SOC
£€ £14.50 (£16.50)
⊶ 2 miles SW of Belfast, nr Four
Winds
⊕ Floodlit driving range
▆ www.mountober.com

Mourne (1946)

Club
36 Golf Links Road, Newcastle,
BT33 0AN
☎ **(028) 4372 3218**
▯ (028) 4372 2575
✉ secretary@mourne.freeserve.co.uk
▥ 385
✍ P Keown (Hon)
ᛈ Play over Royal Co Down
▆ www.mournegc.freeserve.co.uk

Ringdufferin (1993)

Ringdufferin Road, Toye, Downpatrick,
BT30 9PH
☎ **(028) 4482 8812**
▥ 260
✍ M Dallas (Hon)
ᛈ 18 L 4652 m Par 68 SSS 66
ᛘ U
£€ £9 (£10)
⊶ 2 miles N of Killyleagh, off A22

Rockmount (1995)

28 Drumalig Road, Carryduff, Belfast,
BT8 8EQ
☎ **(028) 9081 2279**
▯ (028) 9081 5851
✉ d.patterson@btconnect.com
▥ 700
✍ D Patterson (Mgr)
ᛈ 18 L 6373 yds Par 72 SSS 71
ᛘ U
£€ £20 (£24)
⊶ 8 miles S of Belfast (A24)
▆ www.rockmountgolfclub.co.uk

Royal Belfast (1881)

Holywood, Craigavad, BT18 0BP
☎ **(028) 9042 8165**
▯ (028) 9042 1404
▥ 1200
✍ Mrs SH Morrison
✓ C Spence (028) 9042 8586
ᛈ 18 L 6184 yds SSS 70
ᛘ I Sat–NA before 4.30pm
£€ £40 (£50)
⊶ E of Belfast on A2

Royal County Down (1889)

Newcastle, BT33 0AN
☎ **(028) 4372 3314**
▯ (028) 4372 6281
✉ golf@royalcountydown.org
▥ 450
✍ JH Laidler
✓ KJ Whitson (028) 4372 2419
ᛈ Ch'ship 18 L 7065 yds SSS 74
Annesley 18 L 4708 yds SSS 63
ᛘ Contact Sec
£€ Ch'ship–£95 (£105) Annesley–£18
(£28)
⊶ 30 miles S of Belfast
♛ Tom Morris

Scrabo (1907)

233 Scrabo Road, Newtownards,
BT23 4SL
☎ **(028) 9181 2355**
▯ (028) 9182 2919
▥ 958
✍ Mr JW Thomson (Gen Mgr)
✓ P McCrystal (028) 9181 7848
ᛈ 18 L 5699 m SSS 71
ᛘ WD–U WE–after 5pm SOC
£€ £18 (£23)
⊶ 2 miles W of Newtownards, by
Scrabo Tower

The Spa (1907)

Grove Road, Ballynahinch, BT24 8BR
☎ **(028) 9756 2365**

☎ (028) 9756 4158
📖 920
✍ TG Magee
🏌 18 L 6003 m SSS 72
👥 U exc Wed–NA after 3pm Sat–NA
££ £16 (£20)
⛳ 1 mile S of Ballynahinch. 15 miles
S of Belfast

Temple   (1994)
60 Church Road, Boardmills, Lisburn,
BT27 6UP
☎ **(028) 9263 9213**
🖥 (028) 9263 8637
📖 300
✍ D Kinnear (Sec/Mgr)
🏌 9 L 5451 yds Par 68 SSS 66
👥 U
££ £10 (£14)
⛳ 5 miles S of Belfast on
Ballynahinch road

Warrenpoint   (1893)
Lower Dromore Rd, Warrenpoint,
BT34 3LN
☎ **(028) 4175 2219 (Clubhouse)**
🖥 (028) 4175 2918
✉ warrenpointgolfclub@talk21.com
📖 1575
✍ M Trainor (028) 4175 3695
✓ N Shaw (028) 4175 2371
🏌 18 L 5628 m SSS 70
👥 U SOC
££ £22 (£28)
⛳ 5 miles S of Newry
🏠 Tom Craddock
■ www.warrenpointgolf.com

Co Dublin

Balbriggan   (1945)
Blackhall, Balbriggan
☎ **(01) 841 2229**
🖥 (01) 841 3927
📖 600
✍ M O'Halloran (Sec/Mgr)
(01) 841 2229
✓ None
🏌 18 L 5881 m SSS 71
👥 WD–U WE–M SOC
££ €4 (€37)
⛳ 1 mile S of Balbriggan on N1. 18
miles N of Dublin
🏠 Paramour/Stillwell/Ruddy
■ www.balbriggangolfclub.com

Balcarrick   (1972)
Corballis, Donabate
☎ **(01) 843 6228**
🖥 (01) 843 6957
📖 880
✓ S Rayfus
🏌 18 L 5940 m Par 73 SSS 71
👥 WD–U Sat–NA before 10am
Sun–NA SOC
££ €32
⛳ 2km E of Donabate. 18km N of
Dublin

Ballinascorney   (1971)
Ballinascorney, Tallaght, Dublin
☎ **(01) 451 6430**
📖 500
🏌 18 L 5464 m Par 71 SSS 67
👥 WD–U
££ On application
⛳ 8 miles SW of Dublin

Beaverstown   (1985)
Beaverstown, Donabate
☎ **(01) 843 6439/6721**
🖥 (01) 843 5059
✉ manager@beaverstown.com
📖 935
✍ D Monaghan (Sec/Mgr)
(01) 843 6439
🏌 18 L 5972 m Par 72 SSS 72
👥 WD–U WE–phone first SOC
££ €52 (€68)
⛳ 4 miles N of Dublin Airport
🏠 Hackett/McEvoy
■ www.beaverstown.com

Beech Park   (1983)
Johnstown, Rathcoole
☎ **(01) 458 0522**
🖥 (01) 458 8365
📖 550
✍ E Mooney (Hon), P Muldowney
(Mgr)
✓ None
🏌 18 L 5730 m SSS 70
👥 WD–U exc Tues/Wed–M WE–M
BH–NA
££ €38
⛳ Rathcoole 2 miles on Kilteel road.
SW of Dublin
🏠 Eddie Hackett

Coldwinters   (1994)
Newtown House, St Margaret's
☎ **(01) 864 0324**
🖥 (01) 834 1400
📖 375
✍ Mrs K Yates
✓ W Noble
🏌 18 L 5973 m SSS 71
9 L 3133 m SSS 31
👥 U
££ €13 (€20)
⛳ NW of Dublin. Airport 2 miles
⊕ Driving range; Golf Academy
🏠 Martin Hawtree

Corrstown   (1993)
Corrstown, Killsallaghan
☎ **(01) 864 0533**
🖥 (01) 864 0537
📖 1050
✍ J Kelly
✓ P Gittens (01) 864 3322
🏌 River 18 L 6077 m Par 72 SSS 71
Orchard 9 L 2792 m Par 35 SSS 69
👥 Booking necessary
££ €13
⛳ Dublin Airport 6 miles
🏠 E Connaughton
■ www.corrstown.com

Donabate   (1925)
Balcarrick, Donabate
☎ **(01) 843 6345**
🖥 (01) 843 4488
✉ marie@donabategolfclub.com
📖 913
✍ Betty O'Connor (01) 843 6346
Brian Hay (01) 843 6346 (Golf
Administrator)
✓ H Jackson
🏌 18 L 6670 yds SSS 73
9 L 3200 yds Par 36
👥 U (booking system)
££ €45 (€55), €25 (€35) before 10
⛳ 6 miles N of Dublin Airport on N1
⊕ Practice range, putting green, buggy
hire

Dublin Mountain   (1993)
Gortlum, Brittas
☎ **(01) 458 2570**
🖥 (01) 458 2503
📖 430
✍ F Carolan
🏌 18 L 5433 m Par 71
👥 U
££ €9
⛳ SW of Dublin

Dun Laoghaire   (1910)
Eglinton Park, Tivoli Road,
Dun Laoghaire
☎ **(01) 280 3916**
🖥 (01) 280 4868
📖 880
✍ DA Peacock (Gen Mgr)
(01) 280 3916
✓ V Carey (01) 280 1694
🏌 18 L 5478 m SSS 69
👥 WD–U exc 12–1.30pm SOC
££ €42
⛳ 7 miles S of Dublin. Ferry Port 1
mile
🏠 HS Colt
■ www.dunlaoghairegolfclub.ie

Finnstown
Finnstown House Hotel, Lucan
☎ **(01) 628 0644**
🖥 (01) 628 1088
📖 300
✍ M Doyle (01) 836 3423
🏌 9 L 5172 yds SSS 64
👥 H SOC
££ €14 (€19)
⛳ 7 miles W of Dublin
🏠 B Browne

Forrest Little   (1940)
Forrest Little, Cloghran
☎ **(01) 840 1763**
🖥 (01) 840 1000
✉ forrestlittle@eircom.net
📖 1000
✍ T Judd (01) 840 7670
🏌 18 L 5900 m Par 72 SSS 72
👥 WD–U WE–NA
££ €45
⛳ Approx. 1/2 mile from Dublin
Airport
🏠 F Hawtree
■ www.forrestlittle.com

Glencullen

Glencullen, Co Dublin, IRELAND
- ☎ **(01) 295 2895**
- ✍ G Davy
- ✒ R Lucy
- ⊁ 9 L 4705 m Par 69
- 👥 U
- ££ €15
- ⚸ 12 miles S of Dublin
- ■ www.glencullengc.ie

Hermitage   (1905)

Lucan
- ☎ **(01) 626 5396**
- ✉ hermitagegolf@eircom.net
- ▥ 1153
- ✍ P Maguire (01) 626 8491
- ✒ S Byrne (01) 626 8072
- ⊁ 18 L 6032 m SSS 71
- 👥 U SOC–WD
- ££ €75 (€85)
- ⚸ Lucan 2 miles. 8 miles W of Dublin

Hibernian   (1994)

City West Hotel, Saggert
- ☎ **(01) 851 0565**
- ☐ (01) 831 5779
- ▥ 270
- ✍ B Cooling (Mgr)
- ⊁ 18 L 6441 yds Par 70
- 👥 U
- ££ €32
- ⚸ 10 miles SW of Dublin, off N7
- ■ www.hiberniangolf.com

Hollywood Lakes   (1992)

Ballyboughal
- ☎ **(01) 843 3406/7**
- ☐ (01) 843 3002
- ✉ hollywoodlakes.gc@eircom.net
- ▥ 750
- ✍ AC Brogan (Sec/Mgr)
- ✒ None
- ⊁ 18 L 6834 yds Par 72 SSS 72
- 👥 WD–U WE/BH–U after noon
- ££ €30 (€35)
- ⚸ 10 miles N of Dublin Airport
- ⌂ Mel Flanagan

The Island   (1890)

Corballis, Donabate
- ☎ **+353 1843 6205**
- ☐ +353 1843 6860
- ✉ reservations@theislandgolfclub .com
- ▥ 1000
- ✍ P McDunphy (01) 843 6205
- ✒ K Kelliher (01) 843 5005
- ⊁ 18 L 6205 m SSS 73
- 👥 WD/WE–some restrictions, please enquire
- ££ €110
- ⚸ 14 miles N of Dublin, 15 min from airport
- ⌂ Hawtree
- ■ www.theislandgolfclub.com

Killiney   (1903)

Ballinclea Road, Killiney
- ☎ **(01) 285 2823**
- ☐ (01) 285 2861
- ▥ 520
- ✍ MF Walsh
- ✒ P O'Boyle (01) 285 6294
- ⊁ 9 L 6220 yds SSS 70
- 👥 WD
- ££ €50
- ⚸ 8 miles S of Dublin
- ⌂ E Connaughton

Kilternan   (1987)

Kilternan
- ☎ **(01) 295 5559**
- ☐ (01) 295 5670
- ▥ 906
- ✍ J Kinsella
- ✒ Shop (01) 295 2986
- ⊁ 18 L 5413 yds SSS 67
- 👥 U SOC
- ££ €21 (€26)
- ⚸ 12 miles S of Dublin
- ⌂ Eddie Connaughton

Lucan   (1897)

Celbridge Road, Lucan
- ☎ **(01) 628 2106**
- ☐ (01) 628 2929
- ✉ lucangolf:eircom.net
- ▥ 840
- ✍ T O'Donnell (Sec/Mgr) (01) 628 2106
- ⊁ 18 L 5958 m Par 71 SSS 70
- 👥 WD–U WE/BH–M SOC–WD exc Thurs
- ££ €45
- ⚸ 14 miles W of Dublin, nr Lucan on N4
- ⌂ Eddie Hackett

Luttrellstown Castle G&CC   (1993)

Castleknock, Dublin 15
- ☎ **(353) 1 808 9988**
- ☐ (353) 1 808 9989
- ✉ golf@luttrellstown.ie
- ▥ 400
- ✒ E Doyle (353) 1 808 9980
- ⊁ 18 L 6384 m Par 72 SSS 73
- 👥 U–soft spikes only SOC
- ££ €85 (€95)
- ⚸ 7 miles W of Dublin
- ⊕ Driving range
- ⌂ Bielenberg/Connaughton
- ■ www.luttrellstown.ie

Malahide   (1892)

Beechwood, The Grange, Malahide
- ☎ **(01) 846 1611**
- ☐ (01) 846 1270
- ✉ malgc@clubi.ie
- ▥ 850
- ✍ J McCormack (Sec/Mgr)
- ✒ J Murray
- ⊁ 27 L 6257-6633 yds SSS 70-72
- 👥 WD–U WE–by arrangement SOC
- ££ €50 (€85)
- ⚸ 1½ miles S of Malahide. 10 miles N of Dublin, nr Airport
- ⌂ Eddie Hackett
- ■ www.malahidegolfclub.ie

Milltown   (1907)

Lower Churchtown Road, Milltown, Dublin 14
- ☎ **(01) 497 6090**
- ☐ (01) 497 6008
- ✉ reception@milltowngolfclub.ie
- ▥ 1432
- ✍ E Lawless (Gen Mgr)
- ✒ J Harnett (01) 497 7072
- ⊁ 18 L 5638 m Par 71 SSS 69
- 👥 WD–U exc Tues & Wed pm Fri/WE–M BH–NA SOC–Mon & Thurs before 3.45pm
- ££ €80
- ⚸ 4 miles S of Dublin centre
- ⌂ Freddie Davis

Portmarnock   (1894)

Portmarnock
- ☎ **(01) 846 2794 (Clubhouse)**
- ☐ (01) 846 2601
- ▥ 971
- ✍ JJ Quigley (01) 846 2968
- ✒ J Purcell (01) 846 2634
- ⊁ 27 holes: 6997-7400 yds SSS 72-74
- 👥 I WE–XL
- ££ €165 (€190)
- ⚸ 8 miles NE of Dublin

Portmarnock Hotel   (1995)

Proprietary
Strand Road, Portmarnock
- ☎ **(01) 846 1800**
- ☐ (01) 846 1077
- ✉ golf@portmarnock.com
- ✍ Moira Cassidy (Golf Dir) (01) 846 1800
- ⊁ 18 L 6260 m Par 71 SSS 73
- 👥 U H
- ££ €110 Residents–€80
- ⚸ 8 miles NE of Dublin. Airport 15 mins
- ⌂ Bernhard Langer
- ■ www.portmarnock.com

Rush   (1943)

Rush
- ☎ **(01) 843 8177**
- ☐ (01) 843 8177
- ✉ info@rushgolfclub.com
- ▥ 450
- ✍ Noeline Quirile (Sec/Mgr)
- ⊁ 9 L 5639 m Par 69 SSS 68
- 👥 WD–U WE–M
- ££ €29
- ⚸ 16 miles N of Dublin, off N1
- ■ www.rushgolfclub.com

Silloge Park

Ballymun Road, Swords, Co Dublin, IRELAND
- ☎ **(01) 862 0464**
- ✍ D D'Arcy
- ✒ P O'Connor
- ⊁ 18 L 5905 m Par 70
- 👥 U
- ££ €13
- ⚸ Swords, N of Dublin

Skerries   (1905)
Hacketstown, Skerries
☎ **(01) 849 1204 (Clubhouse)**
🖂 (01) 849 1591
✉ skerriesgolfclub@eircom.net
📖 1060
🖊 A Burns (01) 849 1567
✓ J Kinsella (01) 849 0925
⊱ 18 L 6107 m Par 73 SSS 72
👥 U SOC
£€ €50 (€60)
⛳ 20 miles N of Dublin
■ www.skerriesgolfclub.ie

Slade Valley   (1970)
Lynch Park, Brittas
☎ **(01) 458 2739**
🖂 (01) 458 2784
📖 800
🖊 (01) 458 2183
✓ J Dignam
⊱ 18 L 5337 m SSS 68
👥 WD–U am WE–M
£€ €20
⛳ 8 miles W of Dublin, off N4
🏠 Sullivan/O'Brien

The South County
Lisheen Road, Brittas, Co Dublin
☎ **(01) 458 2965**
✉ info@southcountygolf.ie
⊱ 18 L 7013 yds Par 72
👥 U H
£€ On application
⛳ SW of Dublin (N81)
■ www.southcountygolf.com

St Margaret's G&CC   (1993)
St Margaret's, Dublin
☎ **(01) 864 0400**
🖂 (01) 864 0289
📖 260
🖊 B Begley (Chief Exec)
⊱ 18 L 6900 yds SSS 73
👥 U SOC
£€ €60–€80
⛳ 3 miles NW of Dublin Airport, between N1/N2
⊕ Driving range
🏠 Craddock/Ruddy
■ www.st-margarets.net

Swords   (1996)
Balheary Avenue, Swords
☎ **(01) 840 9819**
🖂 (01) 840 9819
📖 485
🖊 O McGuinness (Mgr)
⊱ 18 L 5631 m Par 71 SSS 69
👥 U
£€ €15 (€22)
⛳ 10 miles N of Dublin, nr Airport
🏠 T Halpin

Turvey   (1994)
Turvey Avenue, Donabate
☎ **(01) 843 5169**
📖 335
🖊 R Martin (Mgr)

⊱ 18 hole course
👥 U
£€ €24 (€29)
⛳ Donabate
🏠 Paddy McGuirk

Westmanstown   (1988)
Clonsilla, Dublin 15
☎ **(01) 820 5817**
🖂 (01) 820 5858
📖 1000
🖊 JA Joyce (Hon)
⊱ 18 L 5819 m SSS 70
👥 U SOC
£€ €30 (€36)
⛳ 5 miles W of Dublin, nr Lucan
🏠 Eddie Hackett

Woodbrook   (1926)
Dublin Road, Bray
☎ **(01) 282 4799**
🖂 (01) 282 1950
✉ woodbrook@internet-ireland.ie
📖 1100
🖊 PF Byrne (Gen Mgr) (01) 282 4799
✓ W Kinsella (01) 282 0205
⊱ 18 L 6221 m SSS 72
👥 WD–U WE–phone Sec SOC
£€ €80 (€90)
⛳ 11 miles SE of Dublin on N11
🏠 P McEvoy
■ www.woodbrook.ie

Dublin City

Carrickmines   (1900)
Golf Lane, Carrickmines, Dublin 18
☎ **(01) 295 5972**
📖 650
🖊 TJB Webb (Hon)
⊱ 9 L 6303 yds Par 71 SSS 69
Alternate fees make 18 holes
👥 U exc Wed/Sat–NA
£€ €33 Sun–€38
⛳ 6 miles S of Dublin

Castle   (1913)
Woodside Drive, Rathfarnham, Dublin 14
☎ **(01) 490 4207**
🖂 (01) 492 0264
📖 1400
🖊 John McCormack (Gen Mgr)
✓ D Kinsella (01) 492 0272
⊱ 18 L 6270 yds SSS 70
👥 Mon/Thurs/Fri–U Wed–U before 12.30pm WE/BH–M SOC
£€ €60
⛳ 5 miles S of Dublin

Clontarf   (1912)
Donnycarney House, Malahide Road, Dublin 3
☎ **(01) 833 1892**
🖂 (01) 833 1933
✉ info.cgc@indigo.ie
📖 1137
🖊 A Cahill (Mgr)
✓ M Callan (01) 833 1877

⊱ 18 L 5317 m SSS 68
👥 U SOC
£€ €38 (€50)
⛳ 2 miles NE of Dublin city centre
🏠 HS Colt
■ www.clontarfgolfclub.ie

Deer Park   (1974)
Deer Park Hotel, Howth
☎ **(01) 832 6039**
📖 340
🖊 BM Dunne (Hon)
✓ None
⊱ 18 L 6781 yds Par 72 SSS 71
18 L 6475 yds Par 72 SSS 70
12 hole Par 3 course
👥 U SOC
£€ €13
⛳ 8 miles NE of Dublin
🏠 F Hawtree

Edmondstown   (1944)
Rathfarnham, Dublin 16
☎ **(01) 493 2461**
🖂 (01) 493 3152
✉ info@edmondstowngolfclub.ie
📖 600
🖊 SS Davies (01) 493 1082
✓ A Crofton (01) 494 1049
⊱ 18 L 6011 m Par 71 SSS 73
👥 WD/BH–U SOC
£€ €55 (€65)
⛳ 5 miles S of Dublin. M50 Junction 12
🏠 McEvoy/Cooke
■ www.edmondstowngolfclub.ie

Elm Green   (1996)
Castleknock, Dublin 15
☎ **(01) 820 0797**
🖂 (01) 822 6668
📖 500
🖊 G Carr (Sec/Mgr)
✓ A O'Connor
⊱ 18 L 5300 m Par 71 SSS 66
👥 U
£€ €14 (€21)
⛳ NW Dublin
⊕ Floodlit driving range
🏠 Eddie Hackett

Elm Park   (1927)
Nutley House, Donnybrook, Dublin 4
☎ **(01) 269 3438/269 3014**
🖂 (01) 269 4505
✉ office@elmparkgolfclub.ie
📖 1750
🖊 A McCormack (01) 269 3438
✓ S Green (01) 269 2650
⊱ 18 L 5374 m SSS 69
👥 U–phone Pro
£€ €70 (€80)
⛳ 3 miles S of Dublin

Foxrock   (1893)
Torquay Road, Foxrock, Dublin 18
☎ **(01) 289 5668**
🖂 (01) 289 4943
📖 660
🖊 WM Daly (01) 289 3992
✓ D Walker (01) 289 3414

P 9 L 5667 m Par 70 SSS 68
WD/BH/Sun–M Tues & Sat–NA
€€ €36
6 5 miles S of Dublin

Grange (1911)

Whitechurch Road, Rathfarnham, Dublin 14
☎ (01) 493 2889
⌨ (01) 493 9490
💻 1050 235(L) 210(J)
🏌 JA O'Donoghue (01) 493 2889
⛳ B Hamill (01) 493 2299
P 18 L 5517 m SSS 69
WD–U exc Tues/Wed pm–NA
WE–M
€€ €51
6 Rathfarnham, 5 miles from centre of Dublin

Hazel Grove (1988)

Mount Seskin Road, Jobstown, Dublin 24
☎ (01) 452 0911
💻 400 175(L)
🏌 J Matthews
⛳ None
P 9 L 5300 m SSS 67
Mon/Wed/Fri–U Sun–NA
Tues/Thurs/Sat–restricted
€€ €15
6 3 miles from Tallaght, off Blessington road
🏠 Eddie Hackett

Howth (1916)

Carrickbrack Road, Sutton, Dublin 13
☎ (01) 832 3055
⌨ (01) 832 1793
✉ secretary@howthgolfclub.ie
💻 1200
🏌 Ms A MacNeice (01) 832 3055
⛳ JF McGuirk (01) 839 3895
P 18 L 5672 m SSS 69
WD–U exc Wed WE–M
€€ €50
6 9 miles NE of Dublin, nr Sutton Cross
🏠 James Braid
■ www.howthgolfclub.ie

Kilmashogue (1994)

St Columba's College, Whitechurch, Dublin 16
☎ (087) 274 9844
💻 260 200(L)
🏌 H Farrell
P 9 L 5320 m Par 70
M
6 Dublin

Newlands (1926)

Clondalkin, Dublin 22
☎ (01) 459 2903
⌨ (01) 459 3498
💻 1086
🏌 AT O'Neill (01) 459 3157
⛳ K O'Donnell (01) 459 3538
P 18 L 6184 yds SSS 70
WD–U am WE/BH–NA SOC
€€ €42

6 6 miles SW of Dublin at Newlands Cross (N7)
🏠 James Braid

Rathfarnham (1899)

Newtown, Dublin 16
☎ (01) 493 1201/493 1561
⌨ (01) 493 1561
💻 561
🏌 C McInerney (01) 493 1201
⛳ B O'Hara
P 14 L 5424 m SSS 70
U exc Tues & Sat–NA
€€ €38
6 6 miles S of Dublin
🏠 John Jacobs

Royal Dublin (1885)

North Bull Island Nature Reserve, Dollymount, Dublin 3
☎ (01) 833 6346/1262
⌨ (01) 833 6504
✉ jlambe@theroyaldublingolfclub.com
💻 1150
🏌 JA Lambe (01) 833 1262
⛳ L Owens (01) 833 6477 (Senior Pro C O'Connor Sr)
P 18 L 6925 yds SSS 73
U H exc Wed Sat–NA before 4pm Sun–NA exc 10.30–12 noon SOC–WD
€€ €110 (€125)
6 3 miles NE of Dublin, on coast road to Howth
⊕ Practice range
🏠 HS Colt
■ www.theroyaldublingolfclub.com

St Anne's (1921)

North Bull Island, Dollymount, Dublin 5
☎ (01) 833 6471
⌨ (01) 833 4618
💻 636
🏌 Shirley Sleator
⛳ P Skerritt
P 18 L 5669 m Par 70 SSS 70
WE/BH–NA SOC
€€ €36 (€48)
6 Dublin 5 miles. M50, 5 miles
🏠 Eddie Hackett
■ www.stanneslinksgolf.com

Stackstown (1975)

Kellystown Road, Rathfarnham, Dublin 16
☎ (01) 494 2338
⌨ (01) 493 3934
✉ stackstowngolfclub@eircom.net
💻 1300
🏌 P Kennedy (Sec/Mgr) (01) 494 1993
⛳ M Kavanagh (01) 494 4561
P 18 L 6494 m SSS 70
WD Mon/Thur/Fri; WE Sun 12–2.00
€€ €35 (€45)
6 7 miles SE of Dublin. M50 junction 13, 2 miles

Sutton (1890)

Cush Point, Sutton, Dublin 13
☎ (01) 832 3013
⌨ (01) 832 1603
✉ info@suttongolfclub.org
💻 625
🏌 S Carroll (Hon)
⛳ N Lynch (01) 832 1703
P 9 L 5624 m Par 70 SSS 67
Tues–NA Sat–NA before 5.30pm
€€ €25 (€35)
6 7 miles E of Dublin
■ www.suttongolfclub.org

Co Fermanagh

Castle Hume

Belleek Road, Enniskillen, BT93 7ED
☎ (028) 6632 7077
⌨ (028) 6632 7076
💻 270
🏌 Wilma Connor (Admin)
⛳ S Donnelly (028) 6632 7077
P 18 L 5932 m Par 72 SSS 71
U
€€ £20/€35 (£25/€40). Special rates for groups of 12
6 Enniskillen (A46)
⊕ 5-tier driving range
🏠 Tony Carroll
■ www.castlehumegolf.com

Enniskillen (1896)

Castlecoole, Enniskillen, BT74 6HZ
☎ (028) 6632 5250
⌨ (028) 6632 5250
✉ enquiries@enniskillengolfclub.com
💻 480
🏌 R Ferguson
⛳ None
P 18 L 5574 m Par 71 SSS 69
U SOC
€€ D–£18 (£22)
6 1 mile SE of Enniskillen, on Castlecoole Estate
🏠 TJ McAuley
■ www.enniskillengolfclub.com

Co Galway

Ardacong

Milltown Road, Tuam, Co Galway, IRELAND
☎ (093) 25525
🏌 Catherine Hahessy
P 18 L 6002 yds Par 70
€€ €10
6 25 miles N of Galway

Athenry (1902)

Palmerstown, Oranmore
☎ (091) 794466
⌨ (091) 794971
✉ athenrygc@eircom.net
💻 800
🏌 P Flattery (Sec/Mgr) (086) 825 4454

✓ R Ryan (091) 790599
🏳 18 L 6300 yds Par 70 SSS 70
🏌 WD/Sat–U Sun–NA SOC
£€ €30 (€35)
🚗 10 miles E of Galway on Athenry road (R348), off N6
⊕ Driving range
🏠 Eddie Hackett

Ballinasloe   (1894)
Rosgloss, Ballinasloe
☎ (0905) 42126
🖥 (0905) 42538
📖 925
🏌 M Kelly
✓ None
🏳 18 L 5865 m Par 72 SSS 70
🏌 U SOC
£€ €18 (€21)
🚗 Ballinasloe 2 miles
🏠 Hackett/Connaughton

Bearna   (1996)
Corboley, Bearna
☎ (091) 592677
🖥 (091) 592674
✉ info@bearnagolfclub.com
📖 500
🏳 18 L 5746 m Par 72 SSS 72
🏌 U
£€ €32 (€40)
🏠 RJ Browne
■ www.bearnagolfclub.com

Connemara   (1973)
Ballyconneely, Clifden
☎ (095) 23502/23602
🖥 (095) 23662
✉ links@iol.ie
📖 900
🏌 R Flaherty (Sec/Mgr)
✓ H O'Neill (095) 23502
🏳 27 L 6560 m SSS 72
🏌 U H SOC
£€ €50 – €55
🚗 8 miles SW of Clifden
🏠 Eddie Hackett

Connemara Isles
Annaghvane, Lettermore, Connemara
☎ (091) 572498
🖥 (091) 572498
📖 114
🏌 J Lynch
🏳 9 L 5168 yds Par 70 SSS 67
🏌 U SOC
£€ €15 (€20)
🚗 3 miles W of Costello
🏠 Craddock/Ruddy

Curra West   (1996)
Curra, Kylebrack, Loughrea
☎ (091) 45121
📖 60
🏳 18 L 4546 m Par 67
🏌 U
£€ €13
🚗 8 miles SE of Loughrea

Galway   (1895)
Blackrock, Salthill, Galway
☎ (091) 522033
🖥 (091) 529783
📖 1020
🏌 P Fahy
✓ D Wallace (091) 523038
🏳 18 L 5828 m SSS 70
🏌 Restricted Tues & Sun
£€ €30 (€36)
🚗 3 miles W of Galway City

Galway Bay G&CC   (1993)
Renville, Oranmore
☎ (091) 790500
🖥 (091) 792510
📖 425
🏌 Ann Hanley (Golf Dir)
✓ E O'Connor (091) 790503
🏳 18 L 6350 m SSS 73
🏌 U H SOC
£€ €42–€48
🚗 10 miles E of Galway City (N18)
⊕ Driving range. Golf Academy
🏠 C O'Connor Jr
■ www.gbaygolf.com

Glenlo Abbey
Glenlo Abbey Hotel, Bushy Park, Galway
☎ (091) 519698
🖥 (091) 519699
🏌 P Murphy (Sec/Mgr)
✓ P Murphy
🏳 9 L 5943 m Par 71
🏌 U
£€ €15
🚗 Galway Town
■ www.glenlo.com

Gort   (1924)
Castlequarter, Gort
☎ (091) 632244
🖥 (091) 632387
✉ info@gortgolf.com
📖 840
🏌 J Hannigan (Hon) (091) 631486
✓ None
🏳 18 L 5974 m Par 71
🏌 U exc Sun am SOC
£€ €22 (€26)
🚗 20 miles S of Galway
🏠 C O'Connor Jr
■ www.gortgolf.com

Loughrea   (1924)
Graigue, Loughrea
☎ (091) 841049
🖥 (091!) 847472
📖 400
🏌 M Hawkins (Mgr)
🏳 18 L 5261 m Par 69
🏌 U SOC
£€ €15
🚗 1 mile N of Loughrea, off Dublin-Galway road. 20 miles E of Galway
🏠 Eddie Hackett

Mountbellew   (1929)
Shankill, Mountbellew, Ballinasloe
☎ (0905) 79259
🖥 (0905) 79274
📖 380
🏌 M Meehan (Mgr)
🏳 9 L 5214 m Par 69
🏌 U SOC
£€ €13
🚗 50km NE of Galway on N63

Oughterard   (1973)
Gortreevagh, Oughterard
☎ (091) 552131
🖥 (091) 552733
📖 1000
🏌 J Waters
✓ M Ryan (Ext 201)
🏳 18 L 6752 yds SSS 69
🏌 U SOC
£€ €24
🚗 15 miles NW of Galway on N59
🏠 Harris/Merrigan

Portumna   (1913)
Ennis Road, Portumna
☎ (0509) 41059
📖 600
🏌 D Frawley (Hon)
✓ R Clarke
🏳 18 L 5474 m Par 72 SSS 71
🏌 U H SOC
£€ €25
🚗 40 miles SE of Galway on Lough Derg
🏠 E Connaughton

Tuam   (1904)
Barnacurragh, Tuam
☎ (093) 28993
🖥 (093) 26003
📖 700
🏌 V Gaffney (Sec/Mgr)
✓ L Smyth (093) 24091
🏳 18 L 5944 m Par 72 SSS 71
🏌 Sun–NA SOC–WD
£€ €23
🚗 20 miles N of Galway
🏠 Eddie Hackett

Co Kerry

Ardfert   (1993)
Sackville, Ardfert, Tralee
☎ (066) 713 4744
🖥 (066) 713 4744
📖 171
🏌 T Lawlor
✓ N Cassidy
🏳 9 L 4754 m Par 66
🏌 U
£€ €22
🚗 60 miles NW of Tralee (R551)
⊕ Driving range
🏠 James Healy

Ballybeggan Park
Ballybeggan, Tralee, Co Kerry
☎ (066) 712 6188

☒ P Colleran
➤ 9 L 6278 m Par 70
♟ U
£€ €19
🚗 Tralee

Ballybunion (1893)

Sandhill Road, Ballybunion
☎ (068) 27146
🖳 (068) 27387
🎫 648
☒ J McKenna (Sec/Mgr)
✓ B O'Callaghan
➤ Old 18 L 6542 yds SSS 72
    Cashen 18 L 6477 yds SSS 70
♟ U SOC
£€ Phone for 2004 rates
🚗 2 miles S of Ballybunion. 50 miles
    W of Limerick, via Tarbert
⊕ Driving range

Ballyheigue Castle (1995)

Ballyheigue, Tralee
☎ (066) 713 3555
🖳 (066) 713 3934
🎫 350
☒ J Casey (Sec/Mgr) (01) 713 3555
➤ 9 L 6292 m Par 72 SSS 74
♟ U
£€ €15 (€15)
🚗 11 miles NW of Tralee (R551)
🏛 Roger Jones

Beaufort (1994)

Churchtown, Beaufort, Killarney
☎ (064) 44440
🖳 (064) 44752
☒ beaufortgc@eircom.net
🎫 300
☒ C Kelly
✓ H Duggan
➤ 18 L 6605 yds Par 71 SSS 72
♟ WD–H SOC WE
£€ €45 (€55)
🚗 7 miles W of Killarney, off N72
🏛 Dr Arthur Spring
■ www.beaufortgolfclub.com

Castlegregory

Stradbally, Castlegregory
☎ (066) 39444
🎫 296
☒ G O'Connor (Sec/Mgr)
➤ 9 L 5340 m SSS 68
♟ U SOC
£€ €21
🚗 18 miles W of Tralee
🏛 Arthur Spring

Ceann Sibeal (1924)

Ballyferriter
☎ (066) 915 6255/6408
🖳 (066) 915 6409
☒ dinglegc@iol.ie
🎫 460
☒ S Fahy (Mgr)
➤ 18 L 6690 yds SSS 71
♟ U SOC
£€ €55 – €75
🚗 Dingle Peninsula, W of Tralee
🏛 Hackett/O'Connor Jr
■ www.dinglelinks.com

Dooks (1889)

Glenbeigh
☎ (066) 976 8205
🖳 (066) 976 8476
☒ office@dooks.com
🎫 900
☒ D Mangan
➤ 18 L 5346 m Par 70 SSS 68
♟ WD–U H before 5pm
    WE/BH–phone first SOC
£€ €48
🚗 3 miles N of Glenbeigh, on Ring of
    Kerry (N70)
🏛 M Hawtree
■ www.dooks.com

Dunloe

Dunloe, Beaufort, Co Kerry
☎ (064) 44578
☒ K Crehan
✓ K Crehan
➤ 9 L 4706 m Par 68
♟ U
£€ €20
🚗 8 miles W of killarney

Kenmare (1903)

Kenmare
☎ (064) 41291
🖳 (064) 42061
☒ info@kenmaregolfclub.com
🎫 600
☒ S Duffield
✓ None
➤ 18 L 5441 m SSS 69
♟ U SOC
£€ €40
🚗 20 miles S of Killarney on Cork
    road
🏛 Eddie Hackett

Kerries (1995)

Tralee
☎ (066) 712 2112
🎫 280
☒ H Barrett
➤ 9 L 2718 m Par 70
♟ U
£€ €19
🚗 Tralee

Killarney (1893)

Mahoney's Point, Killarney
☎ (064) 31034
🖳 (064) 33065
☒ reservations@killarney-golf.com
🎫 1500
☒ T Prendergast
✓ T Coveney (064) 31615
➤ Mahoney's Point 18 L 6164 m
    SSS 72
    Killeen 18 L 6475 m SSS 73
    Lackabane 18 L 6410 m SSS 73
♟ H SOC
£€ On application
🚗 3 miles W of Killarney (N72)
⊕ Driving range
🏛 Mahoney's Point-Longhurst;
    Campbell; Killeen-Hackett/
    O'Sullivan;Lackabane-Steel
■ www.killarney-golf.com

Killorglin (1992)

Stealroe, Killorglin
☎ (669) 761 979
🖳 (669) 761 437
☒ kilgolf@iol.ie
🎫 230
☒ B Dodd
✓ None
➤ 18 L 6464 yds SSS 72
♟ U SOC
£€ €25 (€30)
🚗 1 mile from Killorglin on Tralee
    road (N70). 12 miles W of
    Killarney
🏛 Eddie Hackett
■ www.killorglingolf.ie

Listowel (1993)

Pay and play
Feale View, Listowel
☎ (068) 21592
🖳 (068) 23387
☒ Caroline Barrett
➤ 9 L 5728 yds Par 70 SSS 68
♟ U SOC
£€ 9 holes–€12 18 holes–€18
🚗 Nr Listowel on N69
🏛 Eddie Hackett

Parknasilla (1974)

Parknasilla, Sneem
☎ (064) 45122
🖳 (064) 45323
🎫 230
☒ M Walsh (Mgr) (064) 45233
➤ 12 L 5284 m Par 69 SSS 67
♟ U SOC
£€ €30
🚗 Great Southern Hotel, 2 miles E of
    Sneem on Ring of Kerry
🏛 Arthur Spring

Ring of Kerry G&CC (1998)

Templenoe, Kenmare
☎ (064) 42000
🖳 (064) 42533
☒ reservations@ringofkerrygolf.com
🎫 212
☒ E Edwards (Gen Mgr)
✓ D O'Sullivan
➤ 18 L 6869 yds Par 72 SSS 73
♟ U H SOC
£€ €80
🚗 4 miles W of Kenmare on N70
⊕ Driving range
🏛 Eddie Hackett
■ www.ringofkerrygolf.com

Ross (1995)

Ross Road, Killarney
☎ (064) 31125
🖳 (064) 31860
🎫 280
☒ A O'Meara
✓ A O'Meara
➤ 9 L 5674 m Par 72 SSS 72
♟ U
£€ 18 holes–€21 9 holes–€14
🚗 In Killarney
🏛 Rodger Jones

Tralee (1896)

West Barrow, Ardfert
- ☎ (066) 713 6379
- 🖁 (066) 713 6008
- ✉ info@traleegolfclub.com
- ⌑ 1241
- ✍ A Byrne (Gen Mgr)
- ✓ D Power
- ▷ 18 L 6252 m SSS 71
- ♙ WD–U H before 4.30pm exc
  Wed–restricted Sat/BH–NA exc
  11–1pm–H Sun–NA SOC–WD
- ££ €130
- ⇔ 8 miles NW of Tralee, off Spa/Fenit
  road in Barrow
- 🛅 Arnold Palmer
- ■ www.traleegolfclub.com

Waterville (1889)

*Waterville Golf Links, Ring of
Kerry, Waterville*
- ☎ (353) 66 947 4102
- 🖁 (353) 6 947 4482
- ⌑ 466
- ✍ N Cronin
- ✓ L Higgins
- ▷ 18 L 7280 yds SSS 74
- ♙ U H SOC
- ££ €150 (Mon–Thur before 8 am &
  after 4 pm excl. Bank Hols, €105)
- ⇔ 1 mile N of Waterville on Ring of
  Kerry
- ⊕ Practice range
- 🛅 Hackett/Mulcahy/Fazio

Co Kildare

Athy (1906)

Geraldine, Athy
- ☎ (0507) 31729
- 🖁 (0507) 34710
- ✉ info@athygolfclub.com
- ⌑ 525
- ✍ P Fleming (Hon)
- ✓ None
- ▷ 18 L 6308 yds Par 71 SSS 69
- ♙ WD–U Sat–M SOC
- ££ €20 (€30)
- ⇔ 1 mile N of Athy on Kildare road
- ■ www.athygolfclub.com

Bodenstown (1983)

Bodenstown, Sallins
- ☎ (045) 897096
- ⌑ 650
- ✍ J Hughes
- ▷ Bodenstown 18 L 6132 m SSS 71
  Ladyhill 18 L 5278 m SSS 68
- ♙ U exc WE–NA (Old course)
- ££ €18
- ⇔ 4 miles N of Naas on Clane road.
  18 miles W of Dublin, off N7

Carton House

Carton House, Maynooth, Co Kildare
- ☎ (01) 628 6271
- ✉ sales@carton.ie
- ✍ David Fleming (Dir. of Golf)

- ▷ 36 holes
- ££ From €75 – €125
- ⇔ Maynooth, W of Dublin (N4)
- 🛅 Mark O'Meara/Colin Montgomerie
- ■ www.carton.ie

Castlewarden G&CC (1989)

Straffan
- ☎ (01) 458 9254
- 🖁 (01) 458 8972
- ⌑ 565 225(L)
- ✍ J McGowan (Hon)
- ✓ G Egan (01) 458 8219
- ▷ 18 L 6624 yds Par 72 SSS 71
- ♙ WD–U WE–M SOC
- ££ €28–€37 (€38)
- ⇔ 13 miles W of Dublin, off N7
- 🛅 Halpin/Browne
- ■ www.castlewardengolfclub.com

Celbridge Elm Hall

Elmhall, Celbridge, Ci Kildare
- ☎ (01) 628 8208
- ✍ S Lawless
- ▷ 9 L 5415 m Par 70
- ♙ U
- ££ €19
- ⇔ 15 miles W of Dublin

Cill Dara (1920)

Little Curragh, Kildare Town
- ☎ (045) 521433
- ⌑ 400
- ✍ F Curran (Hon)
- ✓ M O'Boyle
- ▷ 9 L 5842 m SSS 70
- ♙ WD–U before 2pm exc Wed–NA
  Sat–NA after noon Sun/BH–NA
  SOC
- ££ €13
- ⇔ 1 mile W of Kildare town

Craddockstown (1991)

Blessington Road, Naas
- ☎ (045) 897610
- 🖁 (045) 896968
- ⌑ 580
- ✍ L Watson
- ▷ 18 L 6134 m Par 71 SSS 70
- ♙ U
- ££ €23
- ⇔ Naas
- 🛅 Arthur Spring

The Curragh (1883)

Curragh
- ☎ (045) 441238/441714
- 🖁 (045) 442476
- ✉ curraghgolf@eircom.net
- ⌑ 500 176(L)
- ✓ Ann Culleton (045) 441714
- ✓ G Burke (045) 441896
- ▷ 18 L 6035 m SSS 71
- ♙ WD–U exc Tues–phone Sec
- ££ €32 (€37)
- ⇔ 3 miles S of Newbridge via M7
  from Dublin
- ■ www.curraghgolf-club.com

Highfield (1992)

Highfield House
- ☎ (046) 973 1021
- 🖁 (046) 973 1021
- ⌑ 550
- ✍ P Duggan (Sec/Mgr)
- ▷ 18 L 5707 m SSS 69
- ♙ WD–U WE–U after 12 noon
- ££ €25 (€35)
- ⇔ 32 miles W of Dublin off N4
- ⊕ Driving range
- 🛅 Alan Duggan
- ■ www.highfield-golf.ie

The K Club (1991)

Straffan
- ☎ (01) 601 7300
- 🖁 (01) 601 7399
- ✉ golf@kclub.ie
- ⌑ 527
- ✍ P Crowe (Golf Dir)
- ✓ E Jones, J McHenry
- ▷ 18 L 7227 yds SSS 72
- ♙ U H SOC–WD
- ££ €275
- ⇔ 18 miles SW of Dublin (N7)
- ⊕ Driving range
- 🛅 Arnold Palmer

Kilkea Castle (1995)

Castledermot
- ☎ (0503) 45555
- 🖁 (0503) 45505
- ▷ 18 L 6200 m Par 71 SSS 71
- ♙ U
- ££ €36 (€42)
- ⇔ 7 miles N of Castledermot (R418)
- 🛅 David Cassidy

Killeen (1986)

Killeenbeg, Kill
- ☎ (045) 866003
- 🖁 (045) 875881
- ⌑ 170
- ✍ M Kelly
- ✓ None
- ▷ 18 L 5815 m Par 71 SSS 71
- ♙ WD–U WE–NA before 10am
- ££ €25
- ⇔ 2 miles off N7 on Sallins road
- 🛅 Ruddy/Craddock

Knockanally (1985)

Donadea, North Kildare
- ☎ (045) 869322
- 🖁 (045) 869322
- ✉ golf@knockanally.com
- ⌑ 500
- ✍ N Lyons
- ✓ M Darcy
- ▷ 18 L 6424 yds SSS 71
- ♙ U
- ££ €30 (€50)
- ⇔ 20 miles W of Dublin on Galway
  road (M4)
- 🛅 N Lyons

For list of abbreviations and key to symbols see page 627

Leixlip (1994)

Leixlip
- ☎ **(01) 624 4978**
- 🖥 (01) 624 6185
- 📖 200
- ✏ J McKone
- ⮞ 9 L 6030 yds Par 72 SSS 70
- 👥 U
- £€ €15 (€18)
- 🚗 10 miles W of Dublin on N4
- 🛡 Eddie Hackett

Naas (1896)

Kerdiffstown, Naas
- ☎ **(045) 874644**
- 🖥 (045) 896109
- 📖 1000
- ✏ M Conway
- ⮞ 18 L 6232 m SSS 69
- 👥 U SOC
- £€ €21 (€29)
- 🚗 2 miles N of Naas
- 🛡 Arthur Spring

Newbridge (1997)

Tankardsgarden, Newbridge
- ☎ **(045) 486110**
- 🖥 (045) 431289
- 📖 220
- ✏ D Neylon (Hon)
- ⮞ 18 L 5960 m Par 72 SSS 72
- 👥 U
- £€ €16 (€19)
- 🚗 30 mins from Dublin on M7
- 🛡 Pat Suttle

Woodlands (1985)

Coolereagh, Coill Dubh
- ☎ **(045) 860777**
- 🖥 (045) 860988
- 📖 615
- ✏ J Russell
- ⮞ 18 L 6020 m Par 72 SSS 71
- 👥 U
- £€ €14 (€18)
- 🚗 Naas
- 🛡 Tommy Halpin

Co Kilkenny

Callan (1929)

Geraldine, Callan
- ☎ **(056) 25136/25949**
- 🖥 (056) 55155
- 📖 750
- ✏ M Duggan (Hon)
- ✓ J O'Dwyer (086) 817 2464
- ⮞ 18 L 6422 yds Par 72 SSS 70
- 👥 U SOC
- £€ €25
- 🚗 1 mile SE of Callan. 10 miles SW of Kilkenny
- 🛡 Bryan Moor

Castlecomer (1935)

Dromgoole, Castlecomer
- ☎ **(056) 4441139**
- 🖥 (056) 4441139
- ✉ castlecomergolf@eircom.net
- 📖 700
- ✏ M Dooley (Hon)
- ⮞ 18 L 6175 m Par 72 SSS 72
- 👥 U SOC–WD WE
- £€ €50
- 🚗 11 miles N of Kilkenny on N7
- 🛡 Pat Ruddy
- ⬛ www.castlecomergolfclub.com

Kilkenny (1896)

Glendine, Kilkenny
- ☎ **(056) 65400**
- 🖥 (056) 23593
- 📖 950
- ✏ A O'Neill (056) 776 5400
- ✓ J Bolger (056) 776 1730
- ⮞ 18 L 6500 yds SSS 70
- 👥 U
- £€ €35 (€40)
- 🚗 1 mile N of Kilkenny, off N77

Mount Juliet (1991)

Thomastown
- ☎ **(056) 73000**
- 🖥 (056) 73019
- ✏ Kim Thomas
- ✓ K Morris
- ⮞ 18 L 7299 yds Par 72 SSS 74
- 👥 U
- £€ €104 (€120)
- 🚗 10 miles S of Kilkenny, off Dublin-Waterford road.
- ⊕ Driving range-residents and green fees. Golf Academy
- 🛡 Jack Nicklaus
- ⬛ www.mountjuliet.com

Mountain View (1997)

Kiltorcan, Ballyhale
- ☎ **(056) 68122**
- 🖥 (056) 24655
- 📖 300
- ✏ M Kelly
- ⮞ 9 L 5025 m Par 70
- 👥 U
- £€ €13 (€13)
- 🚗 12 miles S of Kilkenny
- 🛡 John O'Sullivan

Co Laois

Abbeyleix (1895)

Rathmoyle, Abbeyleix
- ☎ **(0502) 31450**
- 📖 601
- ✏ M Martin (Hon)
- ⮞ 18 L 6031 yds Par 72 SSS 70
- 👥 WD–U WE–NA SOC–WD/WE
- £€ €15 (€25)
- 🚗 10 miles S of Portlaoise. 60 miles SW of Dublin on Cork road
- 🛡 Mel Flanagan

The Heath (1930)

The Heath, Portlaoise
- ☎ **(0502) 46533**
- 🖥 (0502) 46566
- ✉ info@theheathgc.ie

- 📖 830
- ✏ J McNamara (Hon)
- ✓ (0502) 46622
- ⮞ 18 L 5873 m Par 71 SSS 70
- 👥 U
- £€ €16 (€30)
- 🚗 4 miles E of Portlaoise
- ⊕ Floodlit driving range

The Heritage G&CC

Proprietary
The Heritage Golf & Country Club, Killenard
- ☎ **(0502) 45994**
- 🖥 (0502) 45052
- ✉ info@theheritagegolf.com
- 📖 200
- ✏ Joe McNamara (Dir of Golf) (0502) 45994
- ✓ Eddie Doyle – head pro (0502) 45994 Eamonn O'Flanagan – teaching pro (0502) 45052
- ⮞ 18 L 7345 m Par 72
- 👥 H SOC WD WE
- £€ €80 (€100)
- 🚗 2 miles off N7 – 40 miles S of Dublin
- ⊕ Driving range, Seve Ballesteros Natural Golf School, Spa Leisure Centre, bowling greens and hotel
- 🛡 Seve Ballesteros/Jeff Howes
- ⬛ www.theheritagegolf.com

Mountrath (1929)

Knockanina, Mountrath
- ☎ **(0502) 32558/32643**
- 🖥 (0502) 32643
- ✉ mountrathgolfclub.eircom.net
- 📖 800
- ✏ D Kingsley (0502) 22782
- ⮞ 18 L 5643 m Par 71 SSS 69
- 👥 U
- £€ €20
- 🚗 10 miles W of Portlaoise. Mountrath 2 miles

Portarlington (1908)

Garryhinch, Portarlington
- ☎ **(0502) 23115**
- 🖥 (0502) 23044
- ✉ portarlingtongc@eircom.net
- 📖 646
- ✏ J Cannon
- ⮞ 18 L 5906 m Par 71 SSS 71
- 👥 WD–U WE–restricted SOC WD+WE Sat before 1pm
- £€ €20 (€25)
- 🚗 Between Portarlington and Mountmellick on L116
- 🛡 Eddie Hackett
- ⬛ www.portarlingtongolf.com

Rathdowney (1930)

Coulnaboul West, Rathdowney
- ☎ **(0505) 46170**
- 🖥 (0505) 46065
- ✉ rathdowneygolf@eircom.net
- 📖 700
- ✏ S Bolger (Hon) (0505) 46233
- ⮞ 18 L 5864 m Par 71 SSS 70
- 👥 U exc Sun–NA SOC
- £€ €20 (€25)

æ Half mile S of Rathdowney. 20
   miles SW of Portlaoise
⌂ Hackett/Suttle
■ www.rathdowneygolfclub.com

Co Leitrim

Ballinamore (1941)
Creevy, Ballinamore
☎ **(078) 44346**
▦ 120
✍ J Cryan
⮡ 9 L 5514 m Par 70 SSS 68
♟ U SOC
æ 2 miles N of Ballinamore. 20 miles
   NE of Carrick-on-Shannon
⌂ Arthur Spring

Carrick-on-Shannon (1910)
Woodbrook, Carrick-on-Shannon
☎ **(079) 67015**
▦ 210
✍ HP Gralton (Sec/Mgr)
⮡ 9 L 5584 yds SSS 68
♟ U
£€ €14
æ 4 miles W of Carrick-on- Shannon
   on N4

Co Limerick

Abbeyfeale (1993)
Dromtrasna, Collins Abbeyfeale
☎ **(068) 32033**
▦ 85
✍ M O'Riordan (Mgr)
✓ C Ahern
⮡ 9 L 4004 yds Par 61
♟ U
£€ €10
æ 12 miles SW of Newcastle West

Adare Manor (1900)
Adare
☎ **(061) 396204**
🖥 (061) 396800
✉ info@adaremanorgolfclub.com
▦ 750
✍ P O'Brien
✓ J Coyle
⮡ 18 L 5764 yds SSS 69
♟ WD–U WE–M
£€ €35
æ 10 miles SW of Limerick (N21)
⌂ Sayers/Hackett
■ www.adaregolfclub.com

Castletroy (1937)
Castletroy, Limerick
☎ **(061) 335261**
🖥 (061) 335373
▦ 940
✍ L Hayes (061) 335753
✓ Shop (061) 330450
⮡ 18 L 5802 m SSS 71
♟ WD–U Sat am–U Sat pm/Sun–M
   SOC–Mon/Wed/Fri

£€ €27 (€36)
æ 2 miles N of Limerick on Dublin
   road

Limerick (1891)
Ballyclough, Limerick
☎ **(061) 414083**
🖥 (061) 319219
▦ 1325
✍ P Murray (061) 415146
✓ L Harrington (061) 412492
⮡ 18 L 6479 yds SSS 71
♟ WD–U before 5pm exc Tues
   WE–M SOC–WD
£€ €50
æ 3 miles S of Limerick

Limerick County G&CC
Ballyneety
☎ **(061) 351881**
🖥 (061) 351384
✉ lcgolf@iol.ie
▦ 800
✍ Gerry McKeon (Mgr)
✓ Donal McSweeney
⮡ 18 L 6137 m Par 72 SSS 74
♟ U SOC
£€ €37 (€50)
æ 5 miles S of Limerick (R512)
⊕ Driving range
⌂ Des Smyth
■ www.limerickcounty.com

Newcastle West (1938)
Ardagh
☎ **(069) 76500**
🖥 (069) 76511
✉ n.c.w.golf@aircom.net
▦ 950
✍ P Lyons (Sec/Mgr) acting
✓ Tom Murphy (069) 76599
⮡ 18 L 6141 m Medal 6444 m
   Championship SSS 72
♟ U exc Sun–U after 4pm SOC
£€ €30 (€35)
æ 6 miles N of Newcastle West, off
   N21
⊕ Floodlit driving range
⌂ Arthur Spring

Rathbane
Rathbane, Crossagalla, Limerick
☎ **(061) 313655**
✍ Joh O'Sullivan
✓ N Cassidy
⮡ 18 L 5671 m Par 70
♟ U
£€ €17 (€20)
æ Limerick

Co Londonderry

Benone Par Three
*53 Benone Avenue, Benone, Limavady,
BT49 0LQ*
☎ **(028) 7775 0555**
✍ MI Clark
⮡ 9 L 1427 yds Par 3 course

♟ U
£€ On application
æ 12 miles N of Limavady on A2
   coast road

Brown Trout (1984)
*209 Agivey Road, Aghadowey,
Coleraine, BT51 4AD*
☎ **(028) 7086 8209**
🖥 (028) 7086 8878
✉ bill@browntroutinn.com
▦ 150
✍ B O'Hara (Sec/Mgr)
✓ K Revie
⮡ 9 L 2800 yds SSS 68
♟ U SOC
£€ £10 (£15)
æ 8 miles S of Coleraine at junction
   of A54/B66
⌂ W O'Hara Sr
■ www.browntroutinn.com

Castlerock (1901)
65 Circular Road, Castlerock, BT51 4TJ
☎ **(028) 7084 8314**
🖥 (028) 7084 9440
✉ info@castlerockgc.co.uk
▦ 1150
✍ M Steen (Sec/Mgr)
✓ Ian Blair (028) 7084 9424
⮡ 18 L 6121 m SSS 72
   9 L 2457 m SSS 34
♟ WD–U exc Fri SOC
£€ 18 hole: £35 (£60)
   9 hole: £12 (£15)
æ 5 miles W of Coleraine on A2
⌂ Ben Sayers
■ www.castlerockgc.co.uk

City of Derry (1912)
*49 Victoria Road, Londonderry,
BT47 2PU*
☎ **(028) 7134 6369**
🖥 (028) 7131 0008
✉ info@cityofderrygolfclub.com
▦ 775
✍ M Doherty (028) 7131 1610
⮡ Prehen 18 L 6487 yds SSS 71
   Dunhugh 9 L 4708 yds SSS 63
♟ WD–U before 4pm –M after 4pm
   WE–UH SOC
£€ £15 (£20)
æ 3 miles from E end of Craigavon
   Bridge, towards Strabane
⌂ Harry S Colt
■ www.cityofderrygolfclub.com

Foyle (1994)
12 Alder Road, Londonderry, BT48 8DB
☎ **(028) 7135 2222**
🖥 (028) 7135 3967
✉ mail@foylegolf.club24.co.uk
▦ 265
✍ M Lapsley (028) 7135 2222
✓ K McLaughlin
⮡ 18 L 6678 m SSS 72
   9 hole course
♟ U
£€ £12 (£15)
æ Londonderry
⊕ Driving range

For list of abbreviations and key to symbols see page 627

⛫ Frank Ainsworth
■ www.foylegolfcentre.co.uk

Kilrea (1920)
47a Lisnagrot Road, Kilrea
☎ (028) 295 40044
▯ 310
✍ K McWilliams (028) 295 40044
► 9 L 5494 yds Par 68 SSS 68
♟ U SOC Tues & Wed–NA after 5pm
Sat–NA before 4pm
££ £12.50 (£15)
♣ Kilrea, 15 miles S of Coleraine

Moyola Park (1976)
15 Curran Road, Castledawson,
Magherafelt, BT45 8DG
☎ (028) 7946 8468
▯ (028) 7946 8468
✉ moyolapark@btconnect.com
▯ 940
✍ LWP Hastings (Hon)
✎ Bob Cockcroft (028) 7946 8830
► 18 L 6519 yds Par 71
♟ U SOC exc Sat
££ £18 (£30)
♣ 40 miles NW of Belfast by M2. 35
miles S of Coleraine
⛫ Don Patterson

Portstewart (1894)
117 Strand Road, Portstewart,
BT55 7PG
☎ (028) 7083 2015
▯ (028) 7083 4097
✉ info@portstewartgc.co.uk
▯ 1588
✍ M Moss BA (028) 7083 3839
✎ A Hunter (028) 7083 2601
► Strand 18 L 6784 yds SSS 73
Riverside 9 L 2662 yds Par 32
Old 18 L 4733 yds SSS 62
♟ SOC–by arrangement
££ Strand–£60 (£80). Riverside–£12
(£17). Old £10 (£14)
■ W boundary of Portstewart
■ www.portstewartgc.co.uk

Roe Park (1993)
Roe Park Hotel, Limavady, BT49 9LB
☎ (028) 7776 0105
▯ 500
✍ D Brockerton
✎ S Duffy
► 18 L 6318 yds Par 70 SSS 71
♟ U
££ £20 (£25)
♣ Limavady
⊕ Driving range

Traad Ponds
Shore Road, Magherafelt, BT45 6LR
☎ (028) 7941 8865
✍ R Gribben
► 9 L 4888 m Par 66
♟ U
££ £10
♣ Magherafelt

Co Longford

County Longford (1900)
Glack, Dublin Road, Longford
☎ (043) 46310
▯ (043) 47082
▯ 800
✍ D Rooney
✎ D Keenaghan
► 18 L 6008 yds SSS 69
♟ U SOC
££ On application
♣ Longford ¹/₂ mile on Dublin road
⛫ Eddie Hackett

Co Louth

Ardee (1911)
Town Parks, Ardee
☎ (041) 685 3227
▯ (041) 685 6137
✉ ardeegolf@oceanfree.net
▯ 700
✍ MP Conoulty (Sec/Mgr)
✎ S Kirkpatrick
► 18 L 6348 yds SSS 71
♟ U SOC
££ £35 (€50)
♣ ¹/₂ mile N of Ardee
⊕ Driving range
⛫ Eddie Hackett

Carnbeg
Carnbeg, Dundalk, Co Louth
☎ (042) 933 2518
✍ P Kirk
✎ J Frawley
► 18 L 6000 m Par 72
♟ U
££ €18
♣ Dundalk

County Louth (1892)
Baltray, Drogheda
☎ (041) 988 15309
▯ (041) 988 1531
✉ michael@countylouthgolfclub.com
▯ 1055
✍ M Delany
✎ P McGuirk (041) 988 1536
► 18 L 6965 yds SSS 73
♟ By prior arrangement
££ €100
♣ 3 miles NE of Drogheda
⛫ Tom Simpson
■ www.countylouthgolfclub.com

Dundalk (1904)
Blackrock, Dundalk
☎ (042) 932 1731
▯ (042) 932 2022
✉ dkgc@iol.ie
▯ 850
✍ T Sloane (Sec/Mgr)
✎ Leslie Walker (042) 932 2102
► 18 L 6028 m Par 72
♟ U SOC
££ €55

♣ 3 miles S of Dundalk
■ www.eiresoft.com/dundalkgc

Greenore (1896)
Greenore
☎ (042) 937 3212/3678
▯ (042) 937 3678
▯ 1100
✍ Linda Clarke
✎ Robert Coles (042) 938 3718
► 18 L 6514 yds Par 71 SSS 71
♟ WD–U before 5pm WE/BH–by
arrangement SOC
££ €32 (€45)
♣ 15 miles E of Dundalk on
Carlingford Lough
⛫ Eddie Hackett

Killinbeg (1991)
Killin Park, Dundalk
☎ (042) 933 9303
▯ (042) 933 4320
▯ 175
✍ T Bell (Sec/Mgr)
✎ None
► 18 L 4717 m Par 69 SSS 64
♟ U SOC
££ €15
♣ 2 miles NW of Dundalk on
Castletown road

Seapoint (1993)
Termonfeckin, Drogheda
☎ (041) 982 2333
▯ (041) 982 2331
✉ golflinks@seapoint.ie
▯ 530
✍ K Carrie
✎ D Carroll (041) 988 1066
► 18 L 6420 m Par 72 SSS 74
♟ U SOC
££ €40 – €50 (€60)
♣ 5 miles NE of Drogheda (R166)
⛫ Des Smyth
■ www.seapointgolfclub.com

Townley Hall (1994)
Tullyallen, Drogheda
☎ (041) 984 2229
▯ (041) 984 2229
✉ townleyhall@oceanfree.net
▯ 250
✍ M Foley (Hon)
✎ Kevin Beirth (087) 281 1202
► 9 L 5221 m Par 71 SSS 69
♟ U
££ €12 (€15)
♣ 5 miles NW of Drogheda, off M1
⊕ Driving range

Co Mayo

Achill (1951)
Keel, Achill
☎ (098) 43456
▯ 100
✍ DT Vesey
► 9 L 2689 m Par 70 SSS 67

👥 U H SOC
£€ €13
⚬ 50 miles NW of Westport, on Achill Island
🏠 P Skerritt

Ashford Castle
Cong
☎ (092) 46003
🏴 9 L 4500 yds SSS 68
👥 U SOC
£€ €18
⚬ 25 miles N of Galway on Lough Corrib
🏠 Eddie Hackett

Ballina (1910)
Mossgrove, Shanaghy, Ballina
☎ (096) 21050
🖥 (096) 21050
📖 460
✎ P Connolly
🏴 18 L 6103 yds Par 71
👥 WD–U Sun–NA before noon SOC–WD
£€ €20
⚬ 1 mile E of Ballina
■ www.ballinagolfclub.com

Ballinrobe (1895)
Clooncastle, Ballinrobe
☎ (04) 954 1118
🖥 (094) 954 1889
📧 bgcgolf@iol.ie
📖 700
✎ T Moran (Sec/Mgr)
🏴 18 L 6043 m Par 73 SSS 72
👥 U exc Sun–NA SOC
£€ €30
⚬ 2 miles NW of Ballinrobe on R331
⊕ Driving range
🏠 Eddie Hackett

Ballyhaunis (1929)
Coolnaha, Ballyhaunis
☎ (0907) 30014
📖 300
✎ J Mooney (Hon)
🏴 9 L 5413 m Par 70 SSS 68
👥 U exc Thurs (Ladies Day)–M Sun–NA SOC–WD
£€ €13
⚬ 2 miles N of Ballyhaunis

Carne Golf Links (1995)
Carne, Belmullet
☎ (097) 82292
🖥 (097) 81477
📧 carnegolf@iol.ie
📖 350
✎ J O'Hara (Sec/Mgr)
🏴 18 L 6119 m SSS 72
👥 U SOC
£€ €40 W–€200
⚬ 2 miles W of Belmullet. 40 miles W of Ballina
🏠 Eddie Hackett
■ www.carnegolflinks.com

Castlebar (1910)
Hawthorn Avenue, Rocklands, Castlebar
☎ (094) 21649
🖥 (094) 26088
📖 950
✎ EJ Lonergan (086) 837 3944
🏴 18 L 6500 yds Par 71 SSS 72
👥 WD/Sat–U Sun–NA
£€ €24 (€30)
⚬ 1 mile S of Castlebar, on Galway road
🏠 P McEvoy (1999)
■ www.castlebar.ie/golf

Claremorris (1917)
Castlemacgarrett, Claremorris
☎ (094) 71527
📖 500
✎ A Finn (Hon)
🏴 18 L 5827 yds Par 73 SSS 71
👥 WD–U before noon Sat–U before noon SOC
£€ €23 (€25)
⚬ 2 miles S of Claremorris (N17)
🏠 Tom Craddock

Mulranny (1968)
Mulranny, Westport
☎ (098) 36262
📖 100
✎ C Moran (Hon)
🏴 9 L 6255 yds Par 71 SSS 69
👥 U
£€ €13
⚬ 20 miles NW of Castlebar

Swinford (1922)
Brabazon Park, Swinford
☎ (094) 51378
📖 300
✎ T Regan (094) 51502
🏴 9 L 5901 yds SSS 68
👥 U SOC–exc Sun
£€ €13
⚬ S of Swinford, off Kiltimagh road

Westport (1908)
Carrowholly, Westport
☎ (098) 28262/27070
🖥 (098) 27217
📖 850
✎ M Walsh
✎ A Mealia
🏴 18 L 6653 yds SSS 72
👥 U SOC
£€ €38 (€47)
⚬ 2 miles W of Westport
🏠 F Hawtree
■ www.golfwestport.com

Co Meath

Ashbourne (1991)
Archerstown, Ashbourne
☎ (01) 835 2005
🖥 (01) 835 2561
📖 700
✎ J Clancy

✎ J Dwyer
🏴 18 L 5778 m Par 71 SSS 70
👥 WD–U WE–NA before 1pm SOC
£€ €35 (€45)
⚬ 12 miles N of Dublin, off N2
🏠 Des Smyth

Black Bush (1987)
Thomastown, Dunshaughlin
☎ (01) 825 0021
🖥 (01) 825 0400
📧 golf@blackbush.iol.ie
📖 1050
✎ Kate O'Rourke (Admin) (01) 825 0021
✎ S O'Grady (01) 825 0793
🏴 18 L 6930 yds SSS 73
9 L 2800 yds SSS 35
👥 WD–U WE–NA before 4pm SOC
£€ €30 (€35)
⚬ 1 mile E of Dunshaughlin, off N3. 20 miles NW of Dublin
⊕ Driving range for members and green fees
🏠 Robert J Browne

County Meath (1898)
Newtownmoynagh, Trim
☎ (046) 9431463
🖥 (046) 9437554
📖 800
✎ J Kearney (086) 274 9859
✎ R Machin
🏴 18 L 6720 yds SSS 72
👥 WD–U WE–restricted SOC–exc Sun
£€ €30 (€35)
⚬ 2 miles SW of Trim. 25 miles NW of Dublin
🏠 Hackett/Craddock
■ www.trimgolf.net

Gormanston College (1961)
Franciscan College, Gormanston
☎ (01) 841 2203
📖 160
✎ Br Laurence Brady
✎ B Browne
🏴 9 L 1973 m Par 32
👥 NA
⚬ 22 miles N of Dublin

Headfort (1928)
Kells
☎ (046) 924 0146
🖥 (046) 924 9282
📖 1100
✎ Nora Murphy (Admin) (046) 924 0146
✎ B McGovern (046) 924 0639
🏴 New 18 L 6164 m SSS 73
Old 18 L 5973 m SSS 71
👥 U before 4pm exc NA 12.30–2pm SOC
£€ New–€50. Old–€35 (€40)
⚬ 65km NW of Dublin on N3
🏠 Christy O'Connor Jr

Kilcock (1985)
Gallow, Kilcock
☎ (01) 628 7592

☎ (01) 628 7283
💻 650
🖉 S Kelly (Sec/Mgr)
🏌 18 L 5794 m SSS 71
👥 U SOC
£€ €25 Fri/WE–€30
⛳ 20 miles W of Dublin (N4)
🏠 E Hackett

Laytown & Bettystown (1909)

Bettystown
☎ (041) 982 7170/7534
💻 (041) 982 8506
📧 bettystowngolfclub@utvinternet.com
💻 850
🖉 Helen Finnegan (041) 982 7170
🖊 RJ Browne (041) 982 8793
🏌 18 L 6454 yds SSS 72
👥 U SOC–WD
£€ €45 (€55) – 2003 prices
⛳ 25 miles N of Dublin

Moor Park (1993)

Moortown, Navan
☎ (046) 27661
💻 180
🖉 M Fagan (Mgr)
🏌 18 L 5600 m Par 72 SSS 69
👥 U
£€ €10
⛳ Navan

Royal Tara (1906)

Bellinter, Navan
☎ (046) 902 5244/902 5508/902 5584
💻 (046) 9026684
📧 info@royaltaragolfclub.com
💻 1000
🖉 Damian Usher (Hon), L Clarke (Gen Mgr)
🖊 A Whiston (046) 26009
🏌 18 L 5757 yds Par 71
    9 L 3184 yds Par 35
👥 U
£€ €35 (€40)
⛳ 25 miles N of Dublin, off N3
■ www.royaltaragolfclub.com

South Meath

Longwood Road, Trim, Co Meath
☎ (046) 31471
🖉 D Durney (Hon)
🏌 9 L 5612 m Par 70
👥 U
£€ €10
⛳ S of Trim (R160)

Summerhill

Agher, Rathmoylan, Co Meath, IRELAND
☎ (046) 9557857
🖉 M Nangle
🏌 9 L 6037 m Par 72
👥 U
£€ €15 (€20)
⛳ 8 miles S of Trim (R159)

Co Monaghan

Castleblayney (1985)

Onomy, Castleblayney
☎ (042) 974 9485
💻 275
🖉 R Kernan (042) 974 0451
🏌 9 L 2678 yds SSS 66
👥 U SOC
£€ €10 (€12)
⛳ Castleblayney town centre. 18 miles SE of Monaghan
🏠 R Browne

Clones (1913)

Hilton Demesne, Clones
☎ (047) 56017/56913
💻 (047) 56017
📧 clonesgolfclub@eircom.net
💻 400
🖉 M Taylor (049) 555 2354
🏌 18 L 6100 yds SSS 69
👥 WD–U WE–book in advance
£€ €25
⛳ Hilton Park, 3km from Clones on Scotshouse Road
⊕ Practice putting area; practice ground
🏠 Dr Arthur Spring

Mannan Castle (1993)

Donaghmoyne, Carrickmacross
☎ (042) 966 3308
💻 (042) 966 3195
💻 600
🖉 R Howell (042) 966 2531
🏌 18 L 6020 yds Par 70 SSS 69
👥 U
£€ €18
⛳ 4 miles N of Carrickmacross

Nuremore (1964)

Nuremore, Carrickmacross
☎ (042) 966 4016
📧 nuremore@eircom.net
💻 260
🖉 A Capaldi
🖊 M Cassidy
🏌 18 L 5870 m Par 71 SSS 69
👥 U
£€ €30 (€40)
⛳ 1 mile S of Carrickmacross on Dublin road
🏠 Eddie Hackett
■ www.nuremore-hotel.ie

Rossmore (1916)

Rossmore Park, Monaghan
☎ (047) 81316
💻 750
🖉 J McKenna (Hon)
🖊 Gareth McShea (047) 71222
🏌 18 L 6082 yds Par 70 SSS 69
👥 WD–U WE/BH–U SOC
£€ €25 (€35 – inc Bank Hols)
⛳ 2 miles S of Monaghan on Cootehill road
🏠 Des Smyth

Co Offaly

Birr (1893)

The Glenns, Birr
☎ (0509) 20082
💻 (0509) 22155
💻 750
🖉 Mary O'Gorman (Hon)
🖊 S O'Grady (0509) 21606
🏌 18 L 6216 yds SSS 70
👥 U SOC–exc Sun–NA 11.30–12
£€ €14 (€17)
⛳ 2 miles W of Birr
⊕ Driving range
🏠 Eddie Connaughton

Castle Barna (1992)

Castlebarnagh, Daingean
☎ (0506) 53384
💻 (0506) 53077
📧 info@castlabarna.ie
💻 600
🖉 E Mangan
🏌 18 L 5595 m Par 72 SSS 69
👥 U
£€ €18 (€25)
⛳ 10 miles E of Tullamore (R402)
🏠 Alan Duggan
■ www.castlebarna.ie

Edenderry (1910)

Kishawanny, Edenderry
☎ (046) 973 1072
💻 (046) 973 3911
📧 enquiries@edenderrygolfclub.com
💻 1000
🖉 P O'Connell (044) 22211
🏌 18 L 6121 m Par 72 SSS 72
👥 WD–U exc Thurs (Ladies Day) WE–restricted SOC
£€ On application
⛳ 1 mile E of Edenderry town
🏠 Havers/Hackett
■ www.edenderrygolfclub.com

Esker Hills G&CC

Proprietary
Tullamore, Co Offaly
☎ (0506) 55999
💻 (0506) 55021
💻 200
🖉 C Guinan
🏌 18 L 6669 yds Par 71
👥 U
£€ €35 (€45)
⛳ Tullamore
🏠 Christy O'Connor Jr
■ www.eskerhillsgolf.com

Tullamore (1896)

Brookfield, Tullamore
☎ (0506) 21439
💻 (0506) 41806
📧 tullamoregolfclub@eircom.net
💻 1000
🖉 J Barber-Loughnane
🖊 D McArdle (0506) 51757
🏌 18 L 6428 yds Par 70 SSS 71
👥 WD exc Tues–U Sat–restricted Sun–NA SOC

£€ €39 (€48)
⊕ 2¹/₂ miles S of Tullamore, off N52
🏠 Braid/Merrigan
■ www.tullamoregolfclub.com

Co Roscommon

Athlone (1892)
Hodson Bay, Athlone
☎ (0902) 92073/92235
🖵 (0902) 94080
🕮 1000
🏌 I Dockery
✓ M Quinn
🏴 18 L 5854 m SSS 71
🏌 U SOC
£€ D–€21 (€24)
⊕ 3 miles N of Athlone on Roscommon road
🏠 F Hawtree

Ballaghaderreen (1937)
Aughalustia, Ballaghaderreen
☎ (0907) 60295
🕮 350
🏌 J Corcoran (Hon)
🏴 9 L 5663 yds Par 70 SSS 66
🏌 U SOC
£€ €15
⊕ Ballaghaderreen 3 miles
🏠 P Skerritt

Boyle (1911)
Knockadoo, Brusna, Boyle
☎ (079) 62192/62594
🕮 145
🏌 J Mooney (Hon) (087) 776 0161
🏴 9 L 4914 m Par 67 SSS 64
🏌 U SOC
£€ D–€15
⊕ 1¹/₂ miles S of Boyle
🏠 Eddie Hackett

Castlerea (1905)
Clonallis, Castlerea
☎ (0907) 21214
🕮 200
🏌 V Rabitte
🏴 9 L 5466 yds Par 68
🏌 WD/Sat–U Sun–by arrangement
£€ €13
⊕ Knock Road, Castlerea

Roscommon (1904)
Moate Park, Roscommon
☎ (0903) 26382
🖵 (0903) 26043
🖂 rosgolf@eircom.net
🕮 720
🏌 N O'Grady (0903) 25998
🏴 18 L 6059 m Par 72 SSS 71
🏌 WD–U WE/BH–restricted SOC
£€ €25 (€30)
⊕ 1 mile S of Roscommon
🏠 Eddie Connaughton

Strokestown (1995)
Strokestown
🕮 350
🏌 L Glover (Hon) (078) 33528
🏴 9 L 5230 m Par 68 SSS 67
🏌 U
£€ €15
⊕ 15 miles N of Roscommon (R368). N5 to Longford/Westport

Co Sligo

Ballymote (1943)
Ballinascarrow, Ballymote
☎ (071) 83504
🕮 250
🏌 J O'Connor
🏴 9 L 5302 m Par 68
🏌 U
£€ €13
⊕ 15 miles S of Sligo

County Sligo (1894)
Rosses Point
☎ (071) 77134/77186
🖵 (071) 77460
🖂 cosligo@iol.ie
🕮 1169
🏌 J Ironside (Mgr) (071) 77134
✓ J Robinson (071) 77171
🏴 18 L 6037 m SSS 72
    9 L 2795 m SSS 35
🏌 U H–booking required SOC
£€ €60 Fri/WE–€75
⊕ 5 miles NW of Sligo
🏠 Colt/Allison
■ www.countysligogolfclub.ie

Enniscrone (1931)
Ballina Road, Enniscrone
☎ (096) 36297
🖵 (096) 36657
🕮 740
🏌 M Staunton (Sec/Mgr)
✓ C McGoldrick (096) 36666
🏴 18 L 6671 yds SSS 72
    9 L 3364 yds Par 72
🏌 WD–U WE/BH–phone first SOC
£€ €45 (€60)
⊕ S of Enniscrone. Ballina 13 km
⊕ Driving range
🏠 Hackett/Steel
■ www.homepage.eircom.net /~enniscronegolf

Strandhill (1932)
Strandhill
☎ (071) 68188
🖵 (071) 68811
🕮 450
🏌 Sandra Corcoran
✓ Golf Shop
🏴 18 L 6032 yds Par 69 SSS 68
🏌 WD–U WE/BH–restricted SOC
£€ €30 (€36)
⊕ 6 miles W of Sligo

Tubbercurry (1990)
Ballymote Road, Tubbercurry
☎ (071) 85849
🖂 contact@tubbercurrygolfclub.com
🕮 300
🏌 F Kelly (071) 85124
🏴 9 L 5478 m SSS 69
🏌 U
£€ €15 (€15)
⊕ 20 miles S of Sligo/15 miles off motorway
🏠 Eddie Hackett
■ www.tubbercurrygolfclub.com

Co Tipperary

Ballykisteen (1994)
Ballykisteen, Limerick Junction
☎ (062) 33333
🕮 260
🏌 J Ryan
✓ D Reddan
🏴 18 L 5765 yds Par 72
🏌 U SOC–book in advance
£€ €25
⊕ 3 miles NW of Tipperary town
⊕ Driving range
🏠 Des Smyth

Cahir Park (1968)
Kilcommon, Cahir
☎ (052) 41474
🖵 (052) 42717
🕮 575
🏌 J Costigan (052) 41146
✓ M Joseph (052) 43944
🏴 18 L 6351 yds Par 71 SSS 71
🏌 U SOC–WD/Sat
£€ €21 (€24)
⊕ 1 mile S of Cahir
⊕ Driving range
🏠 Eddie Hackett

Carrick-on-Suir (1939)
Garravoone, Carrick-on-Suir
☎ (051) 640047
🖵 (051) 640558
🕮 500
🏌 A Murphy (Sec/Mgr)
🏴 18 L 6061 m Par 72 SSS 70
🏌 U exc Sun–NA before 11am SOC–WD/Sat
£€ €22
⊕ 2 miles S of Carrick on Dungarvan road
🏠 Eddie Hackett

Clonmel (1911)
Lyreanearla, Mountain Road, Clonmel
☎ (052) 21138/24050
🖵 (052) 83349
🖂 cgc@indigo.ie
🕮 820
🏌 A Myles-Keating (052) 24050
✓ R Hayes (052) 24050
🏴 18 L 6347 yds SSS 71
🏌 WD–U WE–SOC M
£€ €30 (Fri/WE–€35) €25 with memb
⊕ 2 miles SW of Clonmel

⌂ Eddie Hackett
■ www.clonmelgolfclub.com

County Tipperary (1993)
Dundrum, Cashel
☎ (062) 71717
🖳 (062) 71718
📖 380
🏌 W Crowe (Mgr) (062) 71717
🏳 18 L 6955 yds SSS 73
👫 U SOC
💶 €45 (€55)
🚗 6 miles W of Cashel
⌂ Philip Walton
■ www.dundrumhousehotel.com

Nenagh (1929)
Beechwood, Nenagh
☎ (067) 31476
🖳 (067) 34808
📧 nenaghgolfclub@eircom.net
📖 1200
🏌 T Murphy (Hon)
✎ R Kelly (067) 33242
🏳 18 L 6009 m Par 72 SSS 72
👫 U SOC
💶 €30
🚗 3 miles NE of Nenagh on old Birr road
⌂ Patrick Merrigan
■ www.nenaghgolfclub.com

Roscrea (1892)
Derryvale, Roscrea
☎ (0505) 21130
🖳 (0505) 23410
📖 500
🏌 S Crofton (Hon)
🏳 18 L 5782 m SSS 71
👫 U
💶 €20 (€25)
🚗 2 miles E of Roscrea on Dublin road (N7)
⌂ Arthur Spring

Slievenamon
Clonacody, Lisronagh, Co Tipperary
☎ (052) 32213
🖳 (052) 38025
📧 info@slievnamongolfclub.com
🏌 B Kenny (052) 32213
✎ D Kiely (087) 238 8856
🏳 18 L 5000 m Par 67
👫 U
💶 €10 (€15)
🚗 4 miles N of Clonmel off Fethard Road
⊕ Practice area
■ www.slievnamongolfclub.com

Templemore (1970)
Manna South, Templemore
☎ (0504) 32923/31400
📧 johnkm@tinet.ie
📖 350
🏌 John Hackett
🏳 9 L 5442 yds SSS 67
👫 U exc Sun SOC
💶 €15 (€20)
🚗 ¼ mile S of Templemore

Thurles (1909)
Turtulla, Thurles
☎ (0504) 21983/24599
🖳 (0504) 24647
📖 850
🏌 C Murphy (Admin)
✎ S Hunt
🏳 18 L 5904 m Par 72 SSS 71
👫 U
💶 €25
🚗 1 mile S of Thurles
⊕ Driving range
⌂ Lionel Hewson

Tipperary (1896)
Rathanny, Tipperary
☎ (062) 51119
🖳 (062) 52132
📧 tipperarygolfclub@eircom.net
📖 550
🏌 J Considine (Sec/Mgr)
✎ Ger Jones
🏳 18 L 5843 m Par 72 SSS 71
👫 U SOC
💶 €25 (€30)
🚗 Tipperary 1 mile
⊕ Driving range on site

Co Tyrone

Auchnacloy (1995)
99 Tullyvar Road, Auchnacloy
☎ (028) 8255 7050
📖 180
🏌 S Houston
🏳 9 L 5017 m Par 70 SSS 68
👫 U
💶 €10 (€12)
🚗 12 miles SW of Dungannon (B35)
⊕ Driving range

Benburb Valley
Maydown Road, Benburb, BT71 7LJ
☎ (028) 3754 9868
🏌 T McKillion
🏳 9 L 6408 m Par 72
👫 U SOC
💶 €10 (€14)
🚗 8 miles S of dungannon
⊕ Buggy & trolley hire
⌂ R Irwin

Dungannon (1890)
34 Springfield Lane, Mullaghmore, Dungannon, BT70 1QX
☎ (028) 8772 2098
🖳 (028) 8772 7338
📧 info@dungannongolfclub.com
📖 840
🏌 ST Hughes, Brenda McKenna (Sec/Mgr)
✎ Vivian Teague
🏳 18 L 6046 yds SSS 69
👫 U
💶 €18 (€22)
🚗 ½ mile NW of Dungannon on Donaghmore road

Fintona (1904)
Eccleville Desmesne, 1 Kiln Street, Fintona, BT78 2BJ
☎ (028) 8284 1480
🖳 (028) 8284 1480
📖 400
🏌 V McCarney (028) 8284 0777
✎ P Leonard (028) 8284 1480
🏳 9 L 5765 m Par 72 SSS 70
👫 U exc comp days SOC
💶 €10 (€15)
🚗 8 miles S of Omagh

Killymoon (1889)
200 Killymoon Road, Cookstown, BT80 8SD
☎ (028) 8676 3762
🖳 (028) 8676 3762
📧 kgcl@btopenworld.com
📖 950
🏌 V Wilson
✎ G Chambers
🏳 18 L 5488 m SSS 69
👫 U H SOC
💶 €14 (€18)
🚗 1 mile S of Cookstown, off A29

Newtownstewart (1914)
38 Golf Course Road, Newtownstewart, BT78 4HU
☎ (028) 8166 1466
🖳 (028) 8166 2506
📧 newtown.stewart@lineone.net
📖 700
🏌 JE Mackin (028) 8167 1487
✎ None
🏳 18 L 5341 m Par 70 SSS 69
👫 WD–U WE–NA after noon SOC
💶 €12 (€17)
🚗 2 miles SW of Newtownstewart on B84
⌂ Frank Pennink
■ www.globalgolf.com /newtownstewart

Omagh (1910)
83A Dublin Road, Omagh, BT78 1HQ
☎ (028) 8224 3160/1442
🖳 (028) 8224 3160
📖 817
🏌 Mrs F Caldwell
✎ None
🏳 18 L 5364 m SSS 68
👫 U SOC
💶 €15 (€20)
🚗 1 mile from Omagh on Belfast-Dublin road

Strabane (1908)
Ballycolman, Strabane, BT82 9PH
☎ (028) 7138 2271/2007
🖳 (028) 7188 6514
📖 800
🏌 G Glover (028) 7138 2007
✎ None
🏳 18 L 5552 m SSS 69
👫 WD–U WE–by arrangement SOC
💶 €12 (€15)
🚗 ½ mile from Strabane, nr Fir Trees Hotel

Co Waterford

Dungarvan   (1924)
Knocknagranagh, Dungarvan
☎ **(058) 43310/41605**
🖱 (058) 44113
✉ dungarvangc@eircom.net
📖 900
✍ Irene Howell (Mgr) (058) 43310
⛳ D Hayes (058) 44707
🏁 18 L 6134 m Par 72 SSS 73
👤 U SOC
£€ €35 (€45)
🚗 2 miles E of Dungarvan on N25. 25 miles W of Waterford
🏠 Maurice Fives
■ www.dungarvangolfclub.com

Dunmore East   (1993)
Dunmore East
☎ **(051) 383151**
🖱 (051) 383151
📖 300
✍ M Skehan
🏁 18 L 6655 yds Par 72 SSS 70
👤 U
£€ €14 (€21)
🚗 10 miles S of Waterford (R684)
🏠 J O'Riordan
■ www.dunmore-golf.com

Faithlegg   (1993)
Faithlegg House, Faithlegg
☎ **(051) 382241**
🖱 (051) 382664
📖 260
✍ J Santry (Hon)
⛳ Daragh Tighe
🏁 18 L 6690 yds SSS 72
👤 U SOC
£€ €40 (€55)
🚗 6 miles E of Waterford City on Dunmore East road
🏠 Patrick Merrigan

Gold Coast   (1993)
Ballinacourty, Dungarvan
☎ **(058) 42249/44055**
🖱 (058) 43378
📖 600
✍ T Considine (058) 44055
⛳ None
🏁 18 L 6171 m Par 72 SSS 72
👤 U SOC
£€ €35 (€45)
🚗 E of Dungarvan, off R675
🏠 M Fives
■ www.goldcoastgolfclub.com

Lismore   (1965)
Ballyin, Lismore
☎ **(058) 54026**
🖱 (058) 53338
📖 450
✍ S Hales
🏁 9 L 5291 m Par 69 SSS 67
👤 WD–U before 5pm –M after 5pm
   WE–phone first SOC–exc Sun
£€ €14 (€18)
🚗 1 mile N of Lismore, off N72

Tramore   (1894)
Newtown Hill, Tramore
☎ **(051) 386170/381247**
🖱 (051) 390961
📖 1396
✍ J Cox (Sec/Mgr)
⛳ D Kiely
🏁 18 L 6055 m SSS 73
👤 U
£€ €40 (€45)
🚗 7 miles S of Waterford
🏠 Capt Tippett
■ www.tramoregolfclub.com

Waterford   (1912)
Newrath, Waterford
☎ **(051) 874182 (public/bar)**
🖱 (051) 853405
📖 961
✍ J Condon (Sec/Mgr) (051) 876748
⛳ J Condon
🏁 18 L 5722 m Par 71 SSS 70
👤 U
£€ €35 (€45)
🚗 1 mile N of Waterford (N25)
🏠 Willie Park/James Braid

Waterford Castle   (1991)
The Island, Ballinakill, Waterford
☎ **(051) 871633**
🖱 (051) 871634
📖 550
✍ M Garland (Dir. of Golf)
⛳ None
🏁 18 L 6231 m Par 72 SSS 71
👤 U H SOC
£€ €49 (€59)
🚗 2 miles E of Waterford, off R683. Island in River Suir
⊕ Driving range
🏠 Des Smyth
■ www.waterfordcastle.com

West Waterford G&CC   (1993)
Dungarvan
☎ **(058) 43216/41475**
🖱 (058) 44343
✉ info@westwaterfordgolf.com
📖 350
✍ T Whelan (Sec/Mgr)
🏁 18 L 6712 yds Par 72
👤 U SOC
£€ €29 (€38)
🚗 4km W of Dungarvan, off N25
⊕ Practice range
🏠 Eddie Hackett
■ www.westwaterfordgolf.com

Co Westmeath

Ballinlough Castle
Clonmellon, Co Westmeath
☎ **(044) 64544**
✍ T Brady
🏁 9 L 6114 m Par 70
👤 U
£€ €13
🚗 25 miles NE of Mullingar

Delvin Castle   (1992)
Clonyn, Delvin
☎ **(044) 64315**
📖 330
✍ F Dillon
⛳ D Keenaghan
🏁 18 L 5818 m Par 70 SSS 68
👤 U
£€ €20
🚗 15 miles NE of Mullingar (N52)

Glasson Hotel   (1993)
Glasson, Athlone
☎ **(090) 648 5120**
🖱 (090) 648 5444
✉ info@glassongolf.ie
📖 170
✍ F Reid
⛳ None
🏁 18 L 7120 yds Par 72 SSS 72
👤 U
£€ €55 (€70)
🚗 6 miles NE of Athlone (N55)
⊕ Golf Academy
🏠 C O'Connor Jr
■ www.glassongolf.ie

Moate   (1900)
Aghanargit, Moate
☎ **(0902) 81271**
🖱 (0902) 81267
📖 600
✍ A O'Brien
🏁 18 L 6294 yds SSS 70
👤 U SOC–WD
£€ €15
🚗 Moate town centre
🏠 Bobby Browne

Mount Temple   (1991)
Proprietary
Mount Temple, Moate
☎ **(0902) 81841**
🖱 (0902) 81957
📖 150
✍ M Dolan
⛳ None
🏁 18 L 6500 yds SSS 71
👤 U H SOC
£€ €23
🚗 3 miles N of N6, between Athlone and Moate
🏠 Michael Dolan

Mullingar   (1894)
Belvedere, Mullingar
☎ **(044) 48366**
🖱 (044) 41499
📖 560
✍ Ann Scully
⛳ J Burns
🏁 18 L 6370 yds SSS 71
👤 U SOC
£€ €32
🚗 3 miles S of Mullingar (M52)
🏠 James Braid

Co Wexford

Courtown (1936)

Kiltennel, Gorey
- ☎ **(055) 25166**
- 📠 (055) 25553
- ✉ courtown@aol.ie
- 📖 1600
- ✍ S O'Hara
- ⚲ J Coone (055) 25860
- ⊵ 18 L 6398 yds SSS 71
- 👥 U SOC
- ££ €37 (€42)
- ⛳ 2 miles SE of Gorey
- 🏠 Harris
- ■ www.courtowngolfclub.com

Enniscorthy (1908)

Knockmarshall, Enniscorthy
- ☎ **(054) 33191**
- 📖 830
- ✍ J Maguire
- ⚲ M Sludds (054) 37600
- ⊵ 18 L 6115 m Par 72 SSS 72
- 👥 U exc Tues & Sun–phone first SOC
- ££ €25 (€34)
- ⛳ 1¹/₂ miles SW of Enniscorthy on New Ross road
- ⊕ Driving range
- 🏠 Eddie Hackett

New Ross (1905)

Tinneranny, New Ross
- ☎ **(051) 421433**
- 📠 (051) 420098
- 📖 700
- ✍ Kathleen Daly (Sec/Mgr) (051) 421433
- ⊵ 18 L 5751 m SSS 70
- 👥 U exc Sun SOC
- ££ €20 (€30)
- ⛳ 1 mile W of New Ross

Rosslare (1905)

Rosslare Strand, Rosslare
- ☎ **(053) 32113 (Clubhouse),
  (053) 32203 (Bookings)**
- 📠 (053) 32263
- ✉ office@rosslaregolf.com
- 📖 1000
- ✍ JP Hanrick (Gen Mgr)
- ⚲ J Young (053) 32032
- ⊵ 18 L 6782 yds Par 72 SSS 72
  12 L 3887 yds Par 46
- 👥 U SOC
- ££ 18 hole: €35 (€50) 12 hole: €20
- ⛳ 10 miles S of Wexford. Rosslare Ferry 6 miles
- 🏠 Hawtree/Taylor/O'Connor Jr
- ■ www.rosslaregolf.com

St Helen's Bay (1993)

St Helen's, Kilrane, Rosslare Harbour
- ☎ **(053) 33234**
- 📠 (053) 33803
- ✉ sthelens@iol.ie
- 📖 604
- ✍ S Hession
- ⚲ L Bowler
- ⊵ 18 L 6091 m SSS 72

- 👥 U SOC
- ££ €25 (€32)
- ⛳ Nr Rosslare Ferry terminal
- 🏠 Philip Walton
- ■ www.sthelensbay.com

Tara Glen (1993)

Ballymoney, Gorey
- ☎ **(055) 25413**
- 📠 (055) 25612
- ✍ D Popplewell
- ⊵ 9 L 5826 m Par 72 SSS 70
- 👥 U
- ££ €18
- ⛳ 4 miles E of Gorey. 12 miles S of Arklow

Wexford (1960)

Mulgannon, Wexford
- ☎ **(053) 42238**
- 📠 (053) 42243
- ✉ info@wexfordgolfclub.ie
- 📖 805
- ✍ P Daly (Hon)
- ⚲ D McGrane (053) 46300
- ⊵ 18 L 6338 yds Par 72 SSS 70
- 👥 U SOC
- ££ €28 (€32)
- ⛳ Wexford ¹/₂ mile
- ■ www.wexfordgolfclub.ie

Co Wicklow

Arklow (1927)

Abbeylands, Arklow
- ☎ **(0402) 32492**
- 📠 (0402) 91604
- ✉ arklowgolflinks@eircom.net
- 📖 500
- ✍ B Timmons (Hon)
- ⚲ None
- ⊵ 18 L 6475 yds Par 69 SSS 67
- 👥 WD–U Sat–U after 5pm Sun–NA SOC
- ££ €40
- ⛳ 1 mile from Arklow
- 🏠 Hawtree/Taylor/Hackett/ Connaughton
- ■ www.arklowgolfclublinks.ie

Baltinglass (1928)

Baltinglass
- ☎ **(059) 648 1350**
- 📠 (059) 648 2842
- ✉ baltinglassgc@eircom.net
- 📖 550
- ✍ O Cooney (Hon)
- ⊵ 18 L 5912 Par 71
- 👥 U SOC
- ££ Contact office
- ⛳ 38 miles S of Dublin (N81)
- 🏠 Eddie Connaughton
- ■ www.baltinglassgc.com

Blainroe (1978)

Blainroe
- ☎ **(0404) 68168**
- 📠 (0404) 69369
- 📖 1100

- ✍ W O'Sullivan (Sec/Mgr)
- ⚲ J McDonald
- ⊵ 18 L 6175 m SSS 72
- 👥 U
- ££ €48 (€63)
- ⛳ 3 miles S of Wicklow on coast
- 🏠 FW Hawtree

Boystown

Baltyboys, Blessington, Co Wicklow
- ☎ **(045) 867146**
- ✍ D McEvoy
- ⊵ 9 L 6950 yds Par 72
- 👥 U
- ££ €16
- ⛳ Blessington, 15 miles SW of Dublin

Bray (1897)

Greystones Road, Bray
- ☎ **(01) 286 2484/2092**
- 📠 (01) 286 2484
- ✉ braygolfclub@aircom.net
- 📖 530
- ✍ G Montgomery (Sec/Mgr)
- ⚲ Ciaron Carroll
- ⊵ Men: Blue tees 18 L 5869 m Par 71 SSS 72
  White tees 18 L 5533 m Par 71 SSS 71
  Yellow tees 18 L 5198 m Par 71 SSS 69
  Ladies: Red tees 18 L 4983 m Par 72 SSS 72
- 👥 U before 6pm SOC–WD
- ££ €45 (€55 Sat/Bank Hol) winter €60 (€70 Sat/Bank Hol) summer
- ⛳ 12 miles S of Dublin
- 🏠 Des Smyth/Declan Brannigan
- ■ www.braygolfclub.com

Charlesland G&CC (1993)

Greystones
- ☎ **(01) 287 4350**
- 📠 (01) 287 4360
- ✉ teetimes@charlesland.com
- 📖 830
- ✍ P Bradshaw (Gen Mgr)
- ⚲ P Duignan
- ⊵ 18 L 6739 yds Par 72 SSS 71
- 👥 U SOC
- ££ €45 (€60)
- ⛳ 18 miles SE of Dublin
- ⊕ Full practice ground/range facilities; hotel on site
- 🏠 Eddie Hackett

Coollattin (1960)

Coollattin, Shillelagh
- ☎ **(055) 29125**
- 📠 (055) 29125
- 📖 950
- ✍ D Byrne (Hon)
- ⚲ P Jones
- ⊵ 18 L 6148 yds Par 70 SSS 69
- 👥 U
- ££ €35 (€45)
- ⛳ 50 miles S of Dublin on Wicklow/Carlow border
- 🏠 Peter McEvoy

Delgany (1908)
Delgany
☎ **(01) 287 4536**
🖬 (01) 287 3977
🗐 994
🖎 Peter Ribeiro (Gen Mgr)
🏌 G Kavanagh (01) 287 4697
🏳 18 L 6025 yds SSS 69
🎎 U exc comp days
SOC–Mon/Thurs/Fri am
🎇 €40 (€50)
🚗 18 miles S of Dublin, nr
Greystones, off N11
🏠 H Vardon

Djouce (1995)
Roundwood
☎ **(01) 281 8585**
🖬 (01) 281 8522
🗐 250
🖎 D McGillycuddy (Mgr)
🏳 9 L 6296 yds Par 71 SSS 70
🎎 U SOC
🎇 €15 (€20)
🚗 15 miles NW of Wicklow (R764),
off N11 at Kilmacanogue
🏠 Eddie Hackett

Druid's Glen (1995)
Newtownmountkennedy
☎ **(01) 287 3600**
🖬 (01) 287 3699
🗐 200
🖎 D Flinn (Gen Mgr)
🏌 E Darcy
🏳 18 L 7026 yds Par 71 SSS 74
🎎 U SOC
🎇 €104
🚗 20 miles S of Dublin (N11)
⊕ Golf Academy
🏠 Craddock/Ruddy

The European Club (1989)
Brittas Bay, Wicklow
☎ **(0404) 47415**
🖬 (0404) 47449
🖂 info@theeuropeanclub.com
🗐 120
🖎 P Ruddy
🏌 None
🏳 18 L 7323 yds SSS 71
🎎 H SOC
🎇 €75 – €100
🚗 30 miles S of Dublin, off N11
⊕ Large practice area, pitching green,
3 putting greens
🏠 Pat Ruddy

Glen of the Downs
Coolnaskeagh, Delgany, Co Wicklow
☎ **(01) 287 6240**
🖬 (01) 287 0063
🖂 info@glenofthedowns.com
🗐 650
🖎 Gavin Hunt
🏳 18 L 5891 m Par 71
🎎 U
🎇 Summer €65 (€80) – early bird
rates also avail. Winter €65 (€50)

🚗 Off N11, nr Delgany
🏠 Peter McEvoy
🖥 www.glenofthedowns.com

Glenmalure (1993)
Greenane, Rathdrum
☎ **(0404) 46679**
🖬 (0404) 46783
🗐 300
🏳 18 L 5237 m Par 71 SSS 66
🎎 U SOC
🎇 €18 (€21)
🚗 2 miles SW of Rathdrum on
Glenmalure road

Greystones (1895)
Greystones
☎ **(01) 287 6624/4136**
🖬 (01) 287 3749
🖂 secretary@greystonesgc.com
🗐 850
🖎 J Melody (01) 287 4136
🏌 K Holmes (01) 287 5308
🏳 18 L 5322 m SSS 69
🎎 WD–U
🎇 €45
🚗 Greystones, 18 miles S of Dublin
🖥 www.greystonesgc.com

Kilcoole (1992)
Kilcoole
☎ **(01) 287 2066**
🖬 (01) 201 0497
🖂 adminkg@eircom.net
🗐 400
🖎 E Lonergan
🏌 Seamus Clinton
🏳 9 L 5506 m Par 70 SSS 69
🎎 WD–U WE–NA before noon
SOC–WD
🎇 €30 (€35)
🚗 S of Kilcoole on Newcastle road,
off N11
🏠 Brian Williams
🖥 www.kilkoolegolfclub.com

Old Conna (1987)
Ferndale Road, Bray
☎ **(01) 282 6055**
🖬 (01) 282 5611
🗐 1000
🖎 Tom Sheridan (Gen Mgr)
🏌 P McDaid (01) 272 0022
🏳 18 L 6551 yds SSS 72
🎎 WD–U before 4pm WE/BH–NA
SOC
🎇 €45
🚗 2 miles N of Bray. 12 miles S of
Dublin
🏠 Eddie Hackett
🖥 www.oldconna.com

Powerscourt (East) (1996)
Powerscourt Estate, Enniskerry
☎ **(01) 204 6033**
🖬 (01) 276 1303
🖂 golfclub@powerscourt.ie
🗐 627
🖎 B Gibbons (Mgr)
🏌 P Thompson

🏳 18 L 5858 m Par 72 SSS 72
🎎 U
🎇 €100
🚗 Enniskerry, 5 miles W of Bray
⊕ Driving range, putting green,
chipping area, apartments,
conference facilities
🏠 Peter McEvoy
🖥 www.powerscourt.ie

Powerscourt (West) (2003)
Powerscourt Estate, Enniskerry
☎ **(01) 204 6033**
🖬 (01) 276 1303
🖂 golfclub@powerscourt.ie
🖎 B Gibbons (Mgr)
🏌 P Thompson
🏳 18 L 5906 m Par 72 SSS 72
🎎 U
🎇 €100
🚗 Enniskerry, 5 miles W of Bray
🏠 David McLay Kidd
🖥 www.powerscourt.ie

Rathsallagh (1993)
Dunlavin
☎ **(045) 403316**
🖬 (045) 403295
🖂 info@rathsallagh.com
🗐 290
🖎 J O'Flynn (045) 403316
🏌 B McDaid (045) 403316
🏳 18 L 5943 m Par 72 SSS 72
🎎 U
🎇 €75
🚗 14 miles S of Naas (R412)
⊕ Driving range
🏠 McEvoy/O'Connor Jr
🖥 www.rathsallagh.com

Roundwood (1995)
Ballinahinch, Newtownmountkennedy
☎ **(01) 281 8488**
🖬 (01) 284 3642
🖎 M McGuirk
🏳 18 L 6685 yds Par 72 SSS 72
🎎 U
🎇 €41
🚗 15 miles NW of Wicklow (R764)

Tulfarris (1987)
Blessington Lakes
☎ **(045) 867644**
🖬 (045) 867000
🗐 200
🖎 A Williams (Mgr)
🏌 AV Williams
🏳 18 L 7172 m SSS 74
🎎 U SOC
🎇 €65 (€80)
🚗 30 miles S of Dublin, off N81
⊕ Driving range
🏠 Patrick Merrigan

Vartry Lakes (1997)
Proprietary
Roundwood
☎ **(01) 281 7006**
🖬 (01) 281 7006
🗐 242
🖎 J & A McDonald

For list of abbreviations and key to symbols see page 627

◢ None
⊵ 9 L 5276 m Par 70 SSS 70
👯 U SOC–WD/Sat
£€ €15 (€22)
⛳ Roundwood village. SW of Bray, off N11
■ www.wicklow.ie

Wicklow   (1904)
Dunbur Road, Wicklow
☎ (0404) 67379
🕮 450

◢ J Kelly (Hon)
◢ D McLoughlin (0404) 66122
⊵ 18 L 5695 m SSS 70
👯 SOC–WD/Sat
£€ €35
⛳ 32 miles S of Dublin, in Wicklow town
🏠 Craddock/Ruddy

Woodenbridge   (1884)
Vale of Avoca, Arklow
☎ (0402) 35202

🖳 (0402) 35754
✉ wgc@eircom.net
🕮 750
◢ H Crummy
⊵ 18 L 6400 yds Par 71 SSS 70
👯 U exc Sat & Thurs
£€ €51 (€63)
⛳ 4 miles W of Arklow. 45 miles S of Dublin
⊕ Practice ground
🏠 Patrick Merrigan
■ www.woodenbridgegolfclub.com

Scotland

Aberdeenshire

Aboyne   (1883)
Formaston Park, Aboyne, AB34 5HP
☎ (013398) 86328
🖳 (013398) 87078
✉ aboynegolf@btinternet.com
🕮 725 180(J)
◢ Mrs M MacLean (013398) 87078
◢ S Moir (013398) 86328
⊵ 18 L 5910 yds SSS 68
👯 U
£€ On application
⛳ E end of Aboyne. 30 miles W of Aberdeen (A93)

Alford
Montgarrie Road, Alford, AB33 8AE
☎ (019755) 62178
🖳 (019755) 64910
🕮 560
◢ Mrs Irene Currie
◢ None
⊵ 18 L 5483 yds Par 69 SSS 66
👯 WD–U WE–restricted on comp days SOC
£€ £13 (£20)
⛳ 25 miles W of Aberdeen on A944
■ www.golfalford.co.uk

Auchenblae   (1894)
Pay and play
Auchenblae, Laurencekirk, AB30 1TX
☎ (01561) 320002 (Bookings)
🕮 450
◢ J Thomson (Treas) (01561) 320245
⊵ 9 L 2217 yds Par 64 SSS 61
👯 U exc Wed & Fri 5.30–9pm Apr–Aug only
£€ £9 (£12)
⛳ 11 miles SW of Stonehaven. 3 miles W of A90

Ballater   (1892)
Victoria Road, Ballater, AB35 5QX
☎ (013397) 55567
🖳 (013397) 55057
🕮 670

◢ AE Barclay
◢ W Yule (013397) 55658
⊵ 18 L 6094 yds SSS 69
👯 U
£€ On application
⛳ 42 miles W of Aberdeen on A93
■ www.ballatergolfclub.co.uk

Banchory   (1905)
Kinneskie Road, Banchory, AB31 5TA
☎ (01330) 822365
🖳 (01330) 822491
✉ info@banchorygolfclub.co.uk
🕮 1000
◢ W Crighton
◢ D Naylor (01330) 822447
⊵ 18 L 5781 yds SSS 68
👯 WD–U WE–restricted
£€ £20 (£23)
⛳ W of Banchory, off A93

Braemar   (1902)
Cluniebank Road, Braemar, AB35 5XX
☎ (013397) 41618
🕮 300
◢ J Pennet (01224) 704471
⊵ 18 L 4916 yds SSS 64
👯 U SOC
£€ £13 D–£17 (£17 D–£23) W–£60
⛳ Braemar ½ mile. 17 miles W of Ballater
🏠 J Anderson

Cruden Bay   (1899)
Cruden Bay, Peterhead, AB42 0NN
☎ (01779) 812285
🖳 (01779) 812945
✉ cbaygc@aol.com
🕮 1070
◢ Mrs R Pittendrigh (Sec/Mgr)
◢ RG Stewart (01779) 812414
⊵ 18 L 6395 yds SSS 72
   9 L 5106 yds SSS 65
👯 WD–U WE–H exc comp days
£€ £55 D–£75 (£65)
⛳ 22 miles NE of Aberdeen (A90)
⊕ Driving range
🏠 Thomas Simpson
■ www.crudenbaygolfclub.co.uk

Cullen   (1879)
The Links, Cullen, Buckie, AB56 4WB
☎ (01542) 840685
✉ cullengolfclub@btinternet.com
🕮 625
◢ Mrs JM James (01542) 840174
◢ None
⊵ 18 L 4610 yds Par 63 SSS 62
👯 U SOC
£€ £14 D–£20 (£18 D–£24)
⛳ 5 miles E of Buckie, off A98 between Aberdeen and Inverness
🏠 Tom Morris
■ www.cullen-golf-club.co.uk

Duff House Royal   (1910)
The Barnyards, Banff, AB45 3SX
☎ (01261) 812062
🖳 (01261) 812224
🕮 547 167(L) 132(J)
◢ Mrs J Corbett
◢ RS Strachan (01261) 812075
⊵ 18 L 6161 yds SSS 70
👯 WD–U H WE–H 8.30–11am and 12.30–3pm
£€ £18–£24 (£24–£30)
⛳ Moray Firth coast, between Buckie and Fraserburgh
🏠 Dr A & Maj CA Mackenzie

Dunecht House   (1925)
Dunecht, Skene, AB3 7AX
🕮 300
◢ B McIntosh (01330) 860223
⊵ 9 L 3135 yds SSS 70
👯 M
£€ £8
⛳ 12 miles W of Aberdeen on A944

Fraserburgh   (1881)
Philorth, Fraserburgh, AB43 8TL
☎ (01346) 516616
🖳 (01346) 516616
🕮 642 56(L) 119(J)
◢ J Mollison
⊵ 18 L 6308 yds SSS 70
   9 L 2400 yds Par 64
👯 U SOC
£€ £17 D–£22 (£22 D–£27)

⌚ 1 mile SE of Fraserburgh
⌂ James Braid
■ www.fraserburghgolfclub.net

Huntly (1892)

Cooper Park, Huntly, AB54 4SH
☏ **(01466) 792643**
⌂ (01466) 792643
⌂ 800
✎ EA Stott (01466) 792360
✓ (01466) 794181 (Shop)
※ 18 L 5399 yds SSS 66
☺ U SOC
£€ £12 D–£18 (£18 D–£24) W–£65
⌚ N side of Huntly. 38 miles NW of Aberdeen, off A96
■ www.huntlygc.com

Inchmarlo (1995)

Glassel Road, Banchory, AB31 4BQ
☏ **(01330) 826424**
✎ HG Emslie (Sales & Marketing Dir) (01330) 822557 Ext 11
Andrew Shinie (Sec)
✓ P Lovie (01330) 826422 Ext 20
※ 18 L 6218 yds Par 71 SSS 70
9 L 4300 yds Par 64 SSS 62
☺ U SOC–WD
£€ 18 hole: £25 (£30) 9 hole: £10 (£11)
⌚ ¹/₂ mile W of Banchory on A93
⊕ 30 bay floodlit driving range
⌂ Graeme Webster
■ www.inchmarlo.com

Insch

Golf Terrace, Insch, AB52 6JY
☏ **(01464) 820363**
⌂ (01464) 820363
✎ C McLachlan
※ 18 L 5350 yds SSS 67
☺ U
£€ On application
⌚ 28 miles NW of Aberdeen, off A96

Inverallochy

Public
Whitelink, Inverallochy, Fraserburgh, AB43 8XY
☏ **(01346) 582000**
⌂ 400
✎ GM Young
✓ None
※ 18 L 5300 yds SSS 66
☺ U
£€ D–£12 (£15)
⌚ 4 miles E of Fraserburgh, off A92

Inverurie (1923)

Blackhall Road, Inverurie, AB51 5JB
☏ **(01467) 620207**
⌂ (01467) 621051
✉ administrator@inveruriegc.co.uk
⌂ 780
✎ A Angus (01467) 624080
✓ J Logue (01467) 620193
※ 18 L 5711 yds SSS 68
☺ U SOC
£€ £16 D–£20 (£20 D–£26)
⌚ Off the A96 at the Blackhall roundabout
■ www.inveruriegc.co.uk

Keith (1963)

Mar Court, Fife Keith, Keith, AB55 5GF
☏ **(01542) 882469**
⌂ (01542) 888176
⌂ 250
※ 18 L 5802 yds SSS 68
☺ U
£€ £15 (£20)
⌚ Fife Park, W side of Keith

Kemnay (1908)

Monymusk Road, Kemnay, AB51 5RA
☏ **(01467) 642060 (Clubhouse),
(01467) 643746 (Office)**
⌂ (01467) 643746
⌂ 820
✎ Y Moir
✓ R McDonald (01647) 642225
※ 18 L 6362 yds Par 71 SSS 71
☺ U
£€ £20 D–£26 (£24 D–£30)
⌚ 15 miles W of Aberdeen (B994, off A96)
■ www.kemnaygolfclub.co.uk

Kintore (1911)

Balbithan Road, Kintore, AB51 0UR
☏ **(01467) 632631**
⌂ (01467) 632995
✉ kintoregolfclub@lineone.net
⌂ 700
✎ J Black
※ 18 L 6019 yds SSS 69
☺ U
£€ £15 (£20)
⌚ 12 miles NW of Aberdeen on A96

Longside

West End, Longside, Peterhead, AB42 7XJ
☏ **(01779) 821558**
⌂ (01779) 821564
⌂ 569
✎ K Allan (01771) 622424
✓ None
※ 18 L 5225 yds Par 66 SSS 66
☺ U exc Sun–NA before 10.30am SOC
£€ £10 D–£14 Sun–£15 D–£20
⌚ 5 miles W of Peterhead on A590

Lumphanan (1924)

10 Main Road, Lumphanan, Banchory, AB31 4PY
☏ **(013398) 83480**
✉ lumphanan.golf.club@lineone.net
✎ Mrs PA Thorn (013398) 83589
※ 9 L 3718 yds Par 62 SSS 62
☺ U
£€ £8 D–£12 (£10 D–£15)
⌚ 25 miles W of Aberdeen on A980
■ www.lineone.net/~lumphanan.golf.club

McDonald (1927)

Hospital Road, Ellon, AB41 9AW
☏ **(01358) 720576**
⌂ (01358) 720001
✉ mcdonald.golf@virgin.net
⌂ 750

✎ IA Shaw
✓ R Urquhart (01358) 722891
※ 18 L 5991 yds Par 70 SSS 70
☺ U
£€ On application
⌚ 15 miles N of Aberdeen, off A90
■ www.freespace.virgin.net/mcdonald.golf

Meldrum House (1998)

Meldrum House Estate, Oldmeldrum, AB51 0AE
☏ **(01651) 873553**
⌂ (01651) 873635
⌂ 400
✎ J Caven (Golf Dir)
✓ N Marr
※ 18 L 6379 yds Par 70 SSS 72
☺ M
£€ N/A
⌚ 11 miles N of Aberdeen on A947
⌂ Graeme Webster
■ www.meldrumhouse.co.uk

Newburgh-on-Ythan (1888)

Newburgh, AB41 6BE
☏ **(01358) 789058**
✉ secretary@newburgh-on-ythan.co.uk
⌂ 540 60(L) 80(J)
✎ RV Bruce (01358) 789084
✓ None
※ 18 L 6162 yds SSS 71
☺ U exc Tues after 3pm & Sat before 1pm–NA
£€ £20 (£25)
⌚ 12 miles N of Aberdeen (A975)
⊕ Driving range
■ www.newburgh-on-ythan.co.uk

Newmachar (1989)

Swailend, Newmachar, Aberdeen, AB21 7UU
☏ **(01651) 863002**
⌂ (01651) 863055
✉ info@newmachargolfclub.co.uk
⌂ 1040
✎ DS Wade
✓ G Simpson (01651) 862127
※ 18 L 6659 yds Par 72 SSS 74
18 L 6388 yds Par 72 SSS 71
☺ H SOC
£€ Hawkshill £30 (£40) Swailend £15 (£20)
⌚ 12 miles N of Aberdeen on A947
⊕ Driving range
⌂ Dave Thomas
■ www.newmachargolfclub.co.uk

Oldmeldrum (1885)

Kirk Brae, Oldmeldrum, AB51 0DJ
☏ **(01651) 872648/873555**
⌂ (01651) 873555
⌂ 800
✎ J Page (01651) 872315
✓ H Love (01651) 873555
※ 18 L 5988 yds Par 70 SSS 69
☺ WD–U before 5pm WE–phone first
£€ £14 (D–£24)
⌚ 17 miles N of Aberdeen on A947

Peterhead   (1841)

Craigewan Links, Peterhead, AB42 1LT
- ☎ **(01779) 472149/480725**
- ⌨ (01779) 480725
- ✉ phdgc@freenetname.co.uk
- ☖ 500 45(L)
- ↦ 18 L 6173 yds SSS 71
  9 L 2237 yds SSS 62
- 👥 U exc Sat–restricted
- ££ On application
- ⊕ 1 mile N of Peterhead
- ↟ Willie Park Jr/James Braid

Rosehearty

c/o Mason's Arms Hotel, Rosehearty, Fraserburgh, AB43 7JJ
- ☎ **(01346) 571250 (Capt)**
- ⌨ (01346) 571306
- ☖ 220
- ⚐ S Hornal
- ↦ 9 L 2197 yds SSS 62
- 👥 U
- ££ D–£10 (D–£12)
- ⊕ 4 miles W of Fraserburgh (B9031)

Rothes   (1990)

Blackhall, Rothes, Aberlour, AB38 7AN
- ☎ **(01340) 831443**
- ⌨ (01340) 831443
- ☖ 340
- ✓ None
- ↦ 9 L 4972 yds Par 68 SSS 64
- 👥 U
- ££ £12 (£15)
- ⊕ ¹/₂ mile SW of Rothes. 10 miles S of Elgin on A941
- ↟ John Souter

Royal Tarlair   (1926)

Buchan Street, Macduff, AB44 1TA
- ☎ **(01261) 832897**
- ⌨ (01261) 833455
- ✉ info@royaltarlair.co.uk
- ☖ 520
- ⚐ Mrs C Davidson
- ↦ 18 L 5866 yds SSS 68
- 👥 U
- ££ £15 D–£20
- ⊕ Macduff, 4 miles E of Banff. 45 miles E of Aberdeen
- ■ www.royaltarlair.co.uk

Stonehaven   (1888)

Cowie, Stonehaven, AB39 3RH
- ☎ **(01569) 762124**
- ⌨ (01569) 765973
- ✉ stonehaven.golfclub@virgin.net
- ☖ 500
- ⚐ WA Donald
- ✓ None
- ↦ 18 L 5128 yds Par 66 SSS 65
- 👥 Sat–NA before 3.45pm Sun–NA before 10.45am
- ££ £16 (£22)
- ⊕ 1 mile N of Stonehaven
- ↟ A Simpson

Strathlene   (1877)

Portessie, Buckie, AB56 2DJ
- ☎ **(01542) 831798**

- ⌨ (01542) 831798
- ☖ 400
- ⚐ G Jappy
- ↦ 18 L 5977 yds SSS 69
- 👥 U SOC
- ££ D–£15 (D–£15)
- ⊕ ¹/₂ mile E of Buckie
- ↟ G Smith
- ■ www.scottishholidays.net/strathlene

Tarland   (1908)

Aberdeen Road, Tarland, AB34 4TB
- ☎ **(013398) 81000**
- ⌨ (013398) 81000
- ☖ 360
- ⚐ Mrs L Ward (013398) 81000
- ↦ 9 L 5875 yds SSS 68
- 👥 WD–U WE–enquiry advisable SOC–WD only
- ££ £15 (£20)
- ⊕ 5 miles NW of Aboyne. 30 miles W of Aberdeen
- ↟ Tom Morris

Torphins   (1896)

Bog Road, Torphins, AB31 4JU
- ☎ **(013398) 82115**
- ⌨ (013398) 82402
- ✉ stuart@macgregor5.fsnet.co.uk
- ☖ 370
- ⚐ S MacGregor (013398) 82402
- ↦ 9 L 4738 yds SSS 64
- 👥 U SOC
- ££ £13 (£14)
- ⊕ 1¹/₂ miles W of Torphins towards Lumphanan

Turriff   (1896)

Rosehall, Turriff, AB53 4HD
- ☎ **(01888) 562982**
- ⌨ (01888) 568050
- ✉ grace@turriffgolf.scl.co.uk
- ☖ 794
- ⚐ B Cook
- ✓ JR Black (01888) 563025
- ↦ 18 L 6145 yds SSS 69
- 👥 H WE–NA before 10am SOC
- ££ £18 D–£22 (£22 D–£28)
- ⊕ 35 miles N of Aberdeen (A947)
- ↟ GM Fraser
- ■ www.turriffgolfclub.free-online.co.uk

Aberdeen Clubs

Bon Accord   (1872)

Club
19 Golf Road, Aberdeen, AB2 1QB
- ☎ **(01224) 633464**
- ☖ 450
- ⚐ FN Shand
- ↦ Play over King's Links

Caledonian   (1899)

Club
20 Golf Road, Aberdeen, AB2 1QB
- ☎ **(01224) 632443**
- ☖ 620
- ⚐ JA Bridgeford
- ↦ Play over King's Links

Northern   (1897)

Public
22 Golf Road, Aberdeen, AB24 5QB
- ☎ **(01224) 636440**
- ⌨ (01224) 622679
- ☖ 561
- ⚐ AW Garner
- ↦ Play over King's Links

Aberdeen Courses

Auchmill   (1975)

Bonnyview Road, West Heatheryfold, Aberdeen, AB2 7FQ
- ☎ **(01224) 715214**
- ☖ 300
- ⚐ G Adams (01224) 715214
- ✓ None
- ↦ 18 L 5883 yds Par 70 SSS 68
- 👥 U
- ££ On application
- ⊕ 3 miles NW of Aberdeen city centre
- ↟ Coles/Huggett

Balnagask   (1955)

Public
St Fitticks Road, Aberdeen
- ☎ **(01224) 871286**
- ⌨ (01224) 873418
- ⚐ A Fraser
- ✓ None
- ↦ 18 L 5472 metres SSS 69
- 👥 U SOC
- ££ £9 (£11.25)
- ⊕ 1¹/₂ miles SE of Aberdeen

Deeside   (1903)

Golf Road, Bieldside, Aberdeen, AB15 9DL
- ☎ **(01224) 869457**
- ⌨ (01224) 869457
- ✉ admin@deesidegolfclub.com
- ☖ 1100
- ⚐ JW Keepe (Sec/Mgr) (01224) 869457
- ✓ FJ Coutts (01224) 861041
- ↦ 18 L 6264 yds SSS 70
  9 L 3316 yds SSS 36
- 👥 H
- ££ £45 (£60)
- ⊕ 3 miles SW of Aberdeen on A93

Hazlehead   (1927)

Public
Hazlehead Park, Aberdeen, AB15 8BD
- ☎ **(01224) 321830**
- ✓ I Smith
- ↦ 18 L 5673 metres SSS 70
  18 L 5303 metres SSS 68
  9 L 2531 metres SSS 34
- 👥 U
- ££ £9 (£11.25)
- ⊕ 4 miles W of Aberdeen

King's Links

Public
Golf Road, King's Links, Aberdeen, AB24 5QB
- ☎ **(01224) 632269**

⌇ B Davidson (01224) 641577
�ℙ 18 L 5838 metres SSS 71
👥 U
£€ £9.50 (£11.50)
⊶ 1 mile E of Aberdeen
⊕ Driving range. Bon Accord, Caledonian and Northern Clubs play here

Murcar (1909)
Bridge of Don, Aberdeen, AB23 8BD
☎ (01224) 704354
⌨ (01224) 704354
✉ golf@murcar.co.uk
📖 850
♫ Barbara Rogerson (01224) 704354
⌇ G Forbes (01224) 704370
ℙ 18 L 6287 yds SSS 71
   9 L 5369 yds SSS 67
👥 H
£€ £50 (£60)
⊶ 5 miles N of Aberdeen, off A90
⊕ Driving range; practice facilities
🏛 A Simpson
■ www.murcar.co.uk

Peterculter (1989)
Oldtown, Burnside Road, Peterculter, AB14 0LN
☎ (01224) 735245
⌨ (01224) 735580
✉ info@petercultergolfclub.co.uk
📖 925
♫ D Vannet (Mgr)
⌇ D Vannet (01224) 734994
ℙ 18 L 6207 yds SSS 70
👥 WD–U before 4pm WE–U SOC
£€ £20–£27 (£24–£30)
⊶ 8 miles W of Aberdeen on A93
■ www.petercultergolfclub.co.uk

Portlethen (1983)
Badentoy Road, Portlethen, Aberdeen, AB12 4YA
☎ (01224) 781090
⌨ (01224) 781090
📖 1100
⌇ Muriel Thomson (01224) 782571
ℙ 18 L 6670 yds SSS 72
👥 WD–U exc Wed after 2pm Sat–NA before 4pm Sun–NA before 1pm
£€ £15 D–£22 (£22)
⊶ 6 miles S of Aberdeen on A90
🏛 Donald Steel

Royal Aberdeen (1780)
Links Road, Bridge of Don, Aberdeen, AB23 8AT
☎ (01224) 702571
⌨ (01224) 826591
✉ admin@royalaberdeengolf.com
📖 350 100(J)
⌇ GF Webster
⌇ R MacAskill (Golf Dir)
   (01224) 702221
ℙ 18 L 6415 yds SSS 73
   18 L 4066 yds SSS 60
👥 I H SOC
£€ £65 D–£90 (£75)
⊶ 2 miles N of Aberdeen on A90
🏛 Simpson/Braid
■ www.royalaberdeengolf.com

Westhill (1977)
Westhill Heights, Westhill, AB32 6RY
☎ (01224) 742567
⌨ (01224) 749124
✉ wgolfclub@aol.com
📖 900
♫ Amelia Burt (Admin)
⌇ G Bruce (01224) 740159
ℙ 18 L 5849 yds SSS 69
👥 WD–U before 4.30pm Sat–M Sun–U
£€ £14 D–£20 (£20 D–£25)
⊶ 8 miles W of Aberdeen, off A944
🏛 Charles Lawrie
■ www.westhillgolfclub.com

Angus

Arbroath Artisan (1903)
Public
Elliot, Arbroath, DD11 2PE
☎ (01241) 872069,
   (01241) 875837 (Bookings)
⌨ (01241) 875837
📖 650
♫ RA Atkinson
⌇ L Ewart (01241) 875837
ℙ 18 L 6185 yds Par 70 SSS 69
👥 WD–U SOC WE–NA before 10am
£€ £18 D–£24 (£24 D–£32)
⊶ 1 mile SW of Arbroath on A92
🏛 James Braid

Brechin (1893)
Trinity, Brechin, DD9 7PD
☎ (01356) 622383
⌨ (01356) 626925
📖 750
♫ IA Jardine
⌇ S Rennie (01356) 625270
ℙ 18 L 6200 yds SSS 70
👥 U exc Wed SOC
£€ £20 D–£28 (£25 D–£33)
⊶ 1 mile N of Brechin on B90

Caird Park (1926)
Public
Mains Loan, Caird Park, Dundee, DD4 9BX
☎ (01382) 453606,
   (01382) 438871 (Starter)
📖 350
♫ G Martin (01382) 461460
⌇ J Black (01382) 459438
ℙ 18 L 6303 yds SSS 70
   Yellow 9 L 1692 yds SSS 29
   Red 9 L 1983 yds SSS 29
👥 U SOC
£€ Contact Starter
⊶ Off Kingsway by-pass, N of Dundee

Camperdown (1960)
Public
Camperdown Park, Dundee, DD2 4TF
☎ (01382) 623398
📖 200
♫ T Finegan (01382) 459524
⌇ R Brown (01382) 623398

ℙ 18 L 6561 yds SSS 72
👥 U
£€ £18 (£18)
⊶ 2 miles NW of Dundee (A923)

Downfield (1932)
Turnberry Ave, Dundee, DD2 3QP
☎ (01382) 825595
⌨ (01382) 813111
✉ downfieldgc@aol.com
📖 750
♫ Mrs M Stewart
⌇ KS Hutton (01382) 889246
ℙ 18 L 6822 yds SSS 73
👥 WD–U 9.30–noon and 2.18–3.42pm WE–limited access after 2pm
£€ 18 holes: £34 D–£45 36 hole package £49
⊶ N of Dundee, off A923
🏛 James Braid, CK Cotton
■ www.downfieldgolf.co.uk

Edzell (1895)
High St, Edzell, DD9 7TF
☎ (01356) 647283
⌨ (01356) 648094
✉ mail@edzellgolfclub.net
📖 885
♫ IG Farquhar (01356) 647283
⌇ AJ Webster (01356) 648462
ℙ 18 L 6367 yds SSS 71
   9 L 2057 yds Par 32
   West Water 9 hole course
   9 holes £10, 18 holes £15
👥 WD–NA 4.45–6.15pm WE–NA 7.30–10am & 12–2pm SOC
£€ £25 D–£35 (£31 D–£45)
⊶ 6 miles N of Brechin on B966
⊕ Driving range
🏛 Bob Simpson

Forfar (1871)
Cunninghill, Arbroath Road, Forfar, DD8 2RL
☎ (01307) 462120
⌨ (01307) 468495
✉ forfargolfclub@uku.co.uk
📖 535 150(L) 100(J)
♫ W Baird (01307) 463773
⌇ P McNiven (01307) 465683
ℙ 18 L 6066 yds Par 69 SSS 70
👥 U exc Sat SOC
£€ £24 (£35)
⊶ 1½ miles E of Forfar on A932
🏛 Tom Morris/James Braid
■ www.forfargolfclub.com

Kirriemuir (1884)
Northmuir, Kirriemuir, DD8 4PN
☎ (01575) 572144 (Clubhouse),
   (01575) 573317 (Starter)
⌨ (01575) 574608
📖 850
♫ C Gowrie
⌇ Mrs K Dallas (01575) 573317
ℙ 18 L 5510 yds SSS 67
👥 WD–U WE–by arrangement SOC
£€ £20 D–£26 (£25 D–£32)
⊶ NE outskirts of Kirriemuir. 17 miles N of Dundee
🏛 James Braid

Letham Grange (1987)
Letham Grange, Colliston, Arbroath, DD11 4RL
- ☎ **(01241) 890377**
- ☐ (01241) 890725
- ☐ 780
- ✍ D Speed
- ✎ Shop (01241) 890377
- ⊳ Old 18 L 6968 yds SSS 73
  Glens 18 L 5528 yds SSS 68
- ♟ WD–U WE–U after 10.30am SOC
- ££ Old £35 D–£40 (£35 D–£55) Glens
  £18 D–£20 (£20 D–£30)
- ⊶ 4 miles NW of Arbroath on A993
- ⌂ Old-Steel/Smith. New-T MacAuley

Monifieth Golf Links
Medal Starter's Box, Princes Street, Monifieth, DD5 4AW
- ☎ **(01382) 532767 (Medal)**
  (01382) 532967 (Ashludie)
- ☐ (01382) 535816
- ☐ 1450
- ✍ S Fyffe (01382) 535553
- ✎ I McLeod (01382) 532945
- ⊳ Medal 18 L 6650 yds SSS 72
  Ashludie 18 L 5123 SSS 66
- ♟ WD–U Sat–NA before 2pm
  Sun–NA before 10am SOC
- ££ Medal £35 (£45). Ashludie £17
  Medal + Ashludie £55 (incl
  catering)
- ⊶ 6 miles E of Dundee
- ⊕ Abertay, Broughty, Grange/Dundee
  and Monifieth clubs play here
- ■ www.monifiethgolf.co.uk

Montrose (1562)
Public
Traill Drive, Montrose, DD10 8SW
- ☎ **(01674) 672932**
- ☐ (01674) 671800
- ✉ secretary@montroselinks.co.uk
- ☐ 1300
- ✍ Mrs M Stewart
- ✎ J Boyd (01674) 672634
- ⊳ Medal 18 L 6544 yds SSS 72
  Broomfield 18 L 4830 yds SSS 63
- ♟ Medal–WD–U Sat–NA before
  2.30pm Sun–NA before 10am
  Broomfield–U
- ££ Medal £32 (£36) Broomfield £16
  (£18)
- ⊶ 1 mile from Montrose centre, off
  A92
- ⊕ Royal Montrose, Caledonia and
  Mercantile clubs play here
- ⌂ Willie Park (1903)
- ■ www.montroselinks.co.uk

Montrose Caledonia (1896)
Club
Dorward Road, Montrose, DD10 8SW
- ☎ **(01674) 672313**
- ✍ M Watson (01674) 672891
- ⊳ Play over Montrose courses

Montrose Mercantile
Club
East Links, Montrose, DD10 8SW
- ☎ **(01674) 672408**

- ☐ 980
- ✍ R Alexander (01674) 675716
- ⊳ Play over Montrose courses

Panmure (1845)
Barry, Carnoustie, DD7 7RT
- ☎ **(01241) 853120**
- ☐ (01241) 859737
- ☐ 500
- ✍ Maj (Retd) GW Paton
  (01241) 855120
- ✎ N Mackintosh (01241) 852460
- ⊳ 18 L 6317 yds Par 70 SSS 71
- ♟ WD/Sun–U Sat–NA
- ££ On application
- ⊶ 2 miles W of Carnoustie, off A930

Royal Montrose (1810)
Club
Dorward Road, Montrose, DD10 8SW
- ☎ **(01674) 672376**
- ☐ 650
- ✍ JD Sykes (01674) 672785
- ⊳ Play over Montrose courses

Carnoustie Clubs

Carnoustie (1842)
Club
3 Links Parade, Carnoustie, DD7 7JE
- ☎ **(01241) 852480**
- ☐ (01241) 856459
- ✉ admin@carnoustiegolfclub.com
- ☐ 900
- ✍ WH Law
- ⊳ Play over Carnoustie courses
- ■ www.carnoustiegolfclub.com

Carnoustie Caledonia (1887)
Club
Links Parade, Carnoustie, DD7 7JF
- ☎ **(01241) 852115**
- ☐ 640
- ✍ JSB Robinson
- ⊳ Play over Carnoustie courses

Carnoustie Ladies (1873)
Club
12 Links Parade, Carnoustie, DD7 7JF
- ☎ **(01241) 855252**
- ☐ 96
- ✍ Mrs JM Mitchell (01241) 855035
- ⊳ Play over Carnoustie courses

Carnoustie Mercantile (1896)
Club
Links Parade, Carnoustie, DD7 7JE
- ☐ 30
- ✍ DG Ogilvie
- ⊳ Play over Carnoustie courses

Dalhousie (1868)
Club
c/o Glencoe Hotel, Links Parade, Carnoustie, DD7 7JF
- ☎ **(01241) 853273**

- ☐ 150
- ✍ WM Osler
- ⊳ Play over Carnoustie courses

Carnoustie Courses

Buddon Links (1981)
Public
Links Parade, Carnoustie, DD7 7JE
- ☎ **(01241) 853249 (Starter),**
  (01241) 853789 (Bookings)
- ☐ (01241) 853720
- ✍ G Duncan
- ⊳ 18 L 5420 yds SSS 66
- ♟ WD–U WE–U after 11am
- ££ £20
- ⊶ 12 miles E of Dundee, by A92 or
  A930

Burnside (1914)
Public
Links Parade, Carnoustie, DD7 7JE
- ☎ **(01241) 855344 (Starter)**
  (01241) 853789 (Bookings)
- ☐ (01241) 853720
- ✍ G Duncan
- ⊳ 18 L 6020 yds SSS 69
- ♟ WD–U Sat–U after 2pm Sun–U
  after 11.30am
- ££ £25
- ⊶ 12 miles E of Dundee, by A92 or
  A930

Carnoustie Championship (16th)
Public
Links Parade, Carnoustie, DD7 7JE
- ☎ **(01241) 853249 (Starter)**
  (01241) 853789 (Bookings)
- ☐ (01241) 853720
- ✍ G Duncan
- ⊳ 18 L 6941 yds SSS 75
- ♟ WD–H Sat–H after 2pm Sun–H
  after 11.30am
- ££ £80
- ⊶ 12 miles E of Dundee, by A92 or
  A930

Argyll & Bute

Blairmore & Strone (1896)
High Road, Strone, Dunoon, PA23 8JJ
- ☎ **(01369) 840676**
- ☐ 120
- ✍ JC Fleming (01369) 860307
- ⊳ 9 L 2122 yds SSS 62
- ♟ Mon–NA after 6pm Sat–NA
  12–4pm
- ££ D–£10
- ⊶ Strone, 8 miles N of Dunoon
- ⌂ James Braid

Bute (1888)
32 Marine Place, Ardbeg, Rothesay, Isle of Bute PA20 0LF
- ✉ secretary@butegolfclub.com

⌂ 234
🏌 F Robinson (01700) 502158
� 9 L 2497 yds SSS 64
👥 U Sat–U after 11.30am
££ D–£8
⛳ Stravanan Bay, 6 miles S of
Rothesay, off A845
🖥 www.butegolfclub.com

Carradale (1906)
Carradale, Campbeltown, PA28 6SA
☎ (01583) 431321
⌂ 260
🏌 Dr RJ Abernethy
✓ None
▷ 9 L 2370 yds SSS 64
👥 U
££ D–£12
⛳ Carradale, 15 miles N of
Campbeltown (B842)

Colonsay
Owned privately
Isle of Colonsay, PA61 7YP
☎ (019512) 316
⌂ 100
🏌 K Byrne
▷ 18 L 4775 yds Par 72
👥 U
££ On application
⛳ W coast of Colonsay, at Machrins

Cowal (1891)
Ardenslate Road, Dunoon, PA23 8LT
☎ (01369) 705673
🖥 (01369) 705673
✉ info@cowalgolfclub.co.uk
⌂ 900
🏌 Mrs W Fraser (01369) 705673
✓ RD Weir (01369) 702395
▷ 18 L 6063 yds SSS 70
👥 U
££ £15 (£25)
⛳ NE boundary of Dunoon
⛳ James Braid (1928)

Craignure (1895)
*Scallastle, Craignure, Isle of Mull,
PA65 6BA*
☎ (01680) 300402
✉ Mullair@btinternet.com
⌂ 102
🏌 DS Howitt
▷ 9 L 5357 yds SSS 66
👥 U
££ D–£15
⛳ 1 mile N of Craignure Ferry
Terminal (Oban 40mins)

Dalmally (1986)
Old Saw Mill, Dalmally, PA33 1AS
☎ (01838) 200370
⌂ 120
🏌 AJ Burke (01838) 200370
✓ None
▷ 9 L 2277 yds Par 64 SSS 63
👥 U SOC
££ R/D–£10
⛳ 1 mile W of Dalmally on A85
🖥 www.loch-awe.com/golfclub

Dunaverty (1889)
Southend, Campbeltown, PA28 6RW
☎ (01586) 830677
🖥 (01586) 830677
✉ dunavertygc@aol.com
⌂ 430
🏌 B Brannigan (Hon)
▷ 18 L 4799 yds SSS 63
👥 U
££ £15 (£18)
⛳ 10 miles S of Campbeltown

Gigha (1992)
Isle of Gigha, Kintyre, PA41 7AA
☎ (01583) 505242
⌂ 30
🏌 J Bannatyne
▷ 9 L 5042 yds SSS 65
👥 U
££ D–£10
⛳ Off W coast of Kintyre

Glencruitten (1908)
Glencruitten Road, Oban, PA34 4PU
☎ (01631) 562868
⌂ 400
🏌 AG Brown (01631) 564604
✓ Shop (01631) 564115
▷ 18 L 4452 yds SSS 63
👥 U
££ £17 (£20)
⛳ Oban 1 mile
⛳ James Braid

Helensburgh (1893)
*25 East Abercromby Street,
Helensburgh, G84 9HZ*
☎ (01436) 674173
🖥 (01436) 671170
✉ thesecretary@helensburghgolfclub
.org.uk
⌂ 863
🏌 K Print (01436) 674173
✓ D Fotheringham (01436) 675505
▷ 18 L 6104 yds Par 69 SSS 70
👥 WD–U WE–NA
££ £25 D–£35
⛳ N of Helensburgh and A814. 8
miles W of Dumbarton
⛳ Tom Morris

Innellan (1891)
Knockamillie Road, Innellan, Dunoon
☎ (01369) 830242
⌂ 200
🏌 A Wilson (01369) 702573
▷ 9 L 4878 yds SSS 64
👥 U SOC
££ 18 holes–£12. 9 holes–£8
⛳ 4 miles S of Dunoon (A815)

Inveraray (1893)
North Cromalt, Inveraray, Argyll
☎ (01499) 302079
⌂ 175
🏌 A McIntosh
▷ 9 L 5600 yds SSS 68
👥 U SOC
££ D–£15
⛳ 1 mile S of Inveraray on A83

Islay (1891)
*25 Charlotte St, Port Ellen, Isle of Islay,
PA42 7DF*
☎ (01496) 300094
⌂ 400
🏌 T Dunn
▷ 18 L 6226 yds SSS 70
👥 U SOC
££ £35
⛳ Machrie, 5 miles N of Port Ellen
⊕ Driving range
⛳ Willie Campbell
🖥 www.islay.golf.btinternet.co.uk

Isle of Seil (1996)
Pay and play
Balvicar, Isle of Seil, PA34 4TL
☎ (01852) 300348
🖥 (01852) 300392
✉ b.r.m@tesco.net
⌂ 80
🏌 B Mitchell
✓ None
▷ 9 L 2335 yds Par 32
👥 U
££ D–£8
⛳ 13 miles S of Oban on B844
⛳ Donald Campbell

Kyles of Bute (1906)
Tighnabruaich, PA21 2EE
☎ (01700) 811603
⌂ 160
🏌 Dr J Thomson
▷ 9 L 2389 yds SSS 32
👥 U
££ D–£10
⛳ 26 miles W of Dunoon

Lochgilphead (1963)
Blarbuie Road, Lochgilphead, PA31 8LE
☎ (01546) 602340
⌂ 250
🏌 D MacVicar (01546) 602659
▷ 9 L 4484 yds SSS 63
👥 U SOC
££ D–£10 (D–£10)
⛳ ¹/₂ mile N of Lochgilphead by
Hospital

Lochgoilhead (1994)
*Drymsynie Estates, Lochgoilhead,
PA24 8AD*
☎ (01301) 703247
🖥 (01301) 703538
✓ None
▷ 9 L 1900 yds Par 60
👥 N of Lochgoilhead, off Rest & Be
Thankful Road
££ On application

Machrihanish (1876)
Machrihanish, Campbeltown, PA28 6PT
☎ (01586) 810213
🖥 (01586) 810221
⌂ 742 152(L) 178(J)
🏌 Mrs A Anderson
✓ K Campbell (01586) 810277
▷ 18 L 6225 yds SSS 71
9 hole course

For list of abbreviations and key to symbols see page 627

👥 U
£€ £30 D–£50 exc Sat £40 D–£60
🚗 5 miles W of Campbeltown

Millport (1888)
Millport, Isle of Cumbrae, KA28 0HB
☎ (01475) 530311
🖥 (01475) 530306
🖩 288 120(L) 78(J)
✍ Janette Frazer (01475) 530306
⛳ (01475) 530305
🏁 18 L 5828 yds SSS 69
👥 U SOC
£€ £20 D–£25 (£25 D–£31) W–£60
🚗 W of Millport (Largs car ferry)
🏠 James Braid

Port Bannatyne (1912)
Bannatyne Mains Road, Port Bannatyne, Isle of Bute, PA20 0PH
☎ (01700) 504544
🖩 150
✍ Mrs BK Burnett (01700) 505142
🏁 13 L 5085 yds Par 68 SSS 65
👥 U
£€ £11 (£16)
🚗 2 miles N of Rothesay
🏠 Peter Morrison

Rothesay (1892)
Canada Hill, Rothesay, Isle of Bute, PA20 9HN
☎ (01700) 503554
🖥 (01700) 503554
📧 pro@rothesaygolfclub.com
🖩 500
⛳ J Dougal (01700) 503554
🏁 18 L 5395 yds SSS 66
👥 WD–U WE–book with Pro SOC
£€ On application
🚗 1 mile E of Rothesay
⊕ Practice range
🏠 Braid/Sayers
🌐 www.rothesaygolfclub.com

Tarbert (1910)
Kilberry Road, Tarbert, PA29 6XX
☎ (01880) 820565
🖩 101
✍ P Cupples
🏁 9 L 4460 yds SSS 63
👥 U SOC
£€ D–£10 W–£30
🚗 1 mile W of Tarbert on B8024, off A83

Taynuilt (1987)
Taynuilt, PA35 1JE
☎ (01866) 822429
🖥 (01866) 822255 (phone first)
📧 michael.urwin@which.net
✍ MJP Urwin (Hon) (01866) 833341
🏁 9 L 4510 yds Par 64 SSS 63
👥 U
£€ D–£10
🚗 12 miles E of Oban on A85

Tobermory (1896)
Erray Road, Tobermory, Isle of Mull, PA75 6PS
🖥 (01688) 302140

📧 secretary@tobermorygolfclub.com
🖩 180
✍ J Weir (01688) 302338
🏁 9 L 2492 yds SSS 64
👥 U
£€ D–£15 W–£60
🚗 Tobermory, Isle of Mull
⊕ Tickets from Western Isles Hotel, Brown's shop and Fairways Lodge + clubhouse (Apr–Sep); practice ground and net
🏠 David Adams
🌐 www.tobermorygolfclub.com

Vaul (1920)
Scarinish, Isle of Tiree, PA77 6TP
🖩 130
✍ S Sweeney (01879) 220729
🏁 9 L 2837 yds Par 72 SSS 68
👥 U
£€ £10 (9 holes) D–£15
🚗 3 miles E of Scarinish, E end of Tiree. 40 min flight from Glasgow

Ayrshire

Annanhill (1957)
Public
Irvine Road, Kilmarnock, KA3 2RT
☎ (01563) 521512 (Starter)
🖩 350
✍ T Denham (01563) 521644/525557
🏁 18 L 6270 yds SSS 70
👥 WD/Sun–U Sat–NA SOC–exc Sat
£€ On application
🚗 1 mile N of Kilmarnock
🏠 J McLean

Ardeer (1880)
Greenhead Avenue, Stevenston, KA20 4LB
☎ (01294) 464542/465316
🖥 (01294) 465316
🖩 700
✍ P Watson (01294) 465316
⛳ R Summerfield (Starter) (01294) 601327
🏁 18 L 6409 yds SSS 71
👥 U exc Sat–NA SOC–WD
£€ £22 D–£35 Sun–£30 D–£45
🚗 ½ mile N of Stevenston, off A78
🏠 H Stutt

Auchenharvie (1981)
Public
Moor Park Road, West Brewery Park, Saltcoats, KA20 3HU
☎ (01294) 603103
🖩 50
✍ W White (01294) 603775
⛳ R Rodgers
🏁 9 L 5300 yds Par 66 SSS 65
👥 WD–U WE–U after 9.30am
£€ £5.50 (£7.30)
🚗 Low road between Saltcoats and Stevenston
⊕ Driving range

Ballochmyle (1937)
Ballochmyle, Mauchline, KA5 6LE
☎ (01290) 550469
🖥 (01290) 553657
🖩 750
✍ RL Crawford
⛳ None
🏁 18 L 5952 yds SSS 69
👥 WD/WE–U BH–M SOC exc Sat
£€ On application
🚗 1 mile S of Mauchline on B705, off A76

Beith (1896)
Threepwood Road, Beith, KA15 2JR
☎ (01505) 503166 (Clubhouse)
🖥 (01505) 506814
🖩 400
✍ M Murphy (01505) 506814 (am only)
🏁 18 L 5625 yds SSS 68
👥 WD–U exc Tues 9–10.30am/4.30–6.30pm; Thur 9–10.30am;Sat–NA before 2pm; Sun–NA 2.30pm
£€ £20 (£25)
🚗 Off Beith By-pass on A737
🌐 www.beithgolfclub.co.uk

Belleisle (1927)
Public
Bellisle Park, Doonfoot Road, Ayr, KA7 4DU
☎ (01292) 441258
🖥 (01292) 442632
⛳ D Gemmell (01292) 441314
🏁 18 L 6477 yds SSS 72
👥 U SOC
£€ £18 (£25)
🚗 S of Ayr in Belleisle Park
🏠 James Braid
🌐 www.golfsouthayrshire.com

Brodick (1897)
Brodick, Isle of Arran, KA27 8DL
☎ (01770) 302349
🖥 (01770) 302349
📧 secretary@brodickgolfclub.org
🖩 525
✍ Doug McVitie ⛳ PS McCalla (01770) 302349
🏁 18 L 4747 yds SSS 64
👥 U SOC
£€ £18 D–£25 (£20 D–£30)
🚗 Brodick Pier ½ mile
🌐 www.brodickgolfclub.org

Brunston Castle (1992)
Golf Course Road, Dailly, Girvan, KA26 9GD
☎ (01465) 811471
🖥 (01465) 811545
🖩 350
✍ P Muirhead
⛳ A Reid
🏁 18 L 6792 yds SSS 72
👥 U–booking necessary SOC
£€ £26 D–£45
🚗 4 miles E of Girvan
⊕ Driving range
🏠 Donald Steel
🌐 www.brunstoncastle.co.uk

Caprington

Public
Ayr Road, Caprington, Kilmarnock,
KA1 4UW
☎ **(01563) 521915 (Starter)**
🖥 400
🖈 G Bray (01563) 520566
🏌 18 L 5810 yds SSS 68
   9 hole course
👤 U
££ On application
⛳ 1 mile S of Kilmarnock (B7038)

Corrie (1892)

Corrie, Sannox, Isle of Arran, KA27 8JD
☎ **(01770) 810223/810606**
🖥 270
🖈 C Bell (01770) 600613
🏌 9 L 1948 yds SSS 61
👤 U exc Thurs 12–2.30pm & Sat–NA
££ D–£14 W–£56
⛳ 6 miles N of Brodick

Dalmilling (1961)

Public
Westwood Avenue, Ayr, KA8 0QY
☎ **(01292) 263893**
🖥 (01292) 610543
🖊 P Cheyney (Golf Mgr)
🏌 18 L 5724 yds SSS 68
👤 U
££ £13 D–£21 (£16.50 D–£29)
⛳ NE boundary of Ayr, nr Ayr
   racecourse

Doon Valley (1927)

1 Hillside, Patna, Ayr, KA6 7JT
☎ **(01292) 531607**
🖥 (01292) 532489
🖥 90
🖈 H Johnstone
🖊 None
🏌 9 L 5858 yds SSS 70
👤 U
££ £10 (£15)
⛳ 8 miles SE of Ayr (A713)

Girvan (1860)

Public
Golf Course Road, Girvan, KA26 9HW
☎ **(01465) 714272/714346 (Starter)**
🖥 (01465) 714346
🖥 170
🖈 WB Tait
🏌 18 L 5095 yds SSS 64
👤 U
££ £13–£25
⛳ N side of Girvan (A77). 22 miles S
   of Ayr
🏛 James Braid

Glasgow GC Gailes (1892)

Gailes, Irvine, KA11 5AE
☎ **(01294) 311258**
🖥 (01294) 279366
📧 secretary@glasgow-golf.com
🖥 1200
🖈 DW Deas (0141) 942 2011
   Fax (0141) 942 0770
🖊 J Steven (01294) 311561
🏌 18 L 6535 yds Par 71 SSS 72

👤 WD WE/BH–NA before 2.30pm
   SOC
££ £45 D–£60 (£58)
⛳ 1 mile S of Irvine, off A78
🏛 Willie Park Jr
🖥 www.glasgowgailes-golf.com

Irvine (1887)

Bogside, Irvine, KA8 8SN
☎ **(01294) 275979**
🖥 450
🖈 W McMahon
🖊 J McKinnon (01294) 275626
🏌 18 L 6408 yds SSS 71
👤 U SOC–WD
££ On application
⛳ 1 mile N of Irvine towards
   Kilwinning

Irvine Ravenspark (1907)

Public
Kidsneuk Lane, Irvine, KA12 8SR
☎ **(01294) 271293**
📧 secretary@irgc.co.uk
🖥 400
🖈 S Howie (01294) 553904
   mobile (07050) 351758
🖊 P Bond (01294) 276467
🏌 18 L 6429 yds SSS 71
👤 U exc Sat–U after 2.30pm Apr–Sep
   only
££ £14 D–£25
⛳ N side of Irvine, off A737. 7 miles
   N of Troon
🖥 www.irgc.co.uk

Kilbirnie Place (1922)

Largs Road, Kilbirnie, KA25 7AT
☎ **(01505) 683398**
🖥 450
🖈 Mrs C McGurk
🖊 None
🏌 18 L 5411 yds SSS 67
👤 WD/Sun–U
££ On application
⛳ ¹/₂ mile W of Kilbirnie, S of A760.
   15 miles SW of Paisley

Kilmarnock (Barassie)

(1887)
29 Hillhouse Road, Barassie, Troon,
KA10 6SY
☎ **(01292) 313920/311077**
🖥 (01292) 318300
📧 barassiegc@lineone.net
🖥 600
🖈 D Wilson (01292) 313920
🖊 G Howie (01292) 311322
🏌 18 L 6484 yds SSS 74
   9 L 2888 yds SSS 34
👤 WD–U WE–Na before 3pm
   SOC–Mon/Tues & Thurs
££ £58 (£60)
⛳ Opp Barassie Railway Station
🏛 Theodore Moone
🖥 www.kbgc.co.uk

Lamlash (1889)

Lamlash, Isle of Arran, KA27 8JU
☎ **(01770) 600296 (Clubhouse)**
   (01770) 600196 (Starter)

🖥 (01770) 600296
📧 lamlashgolfclub@connectfree.co.uk
🖥 450
🖈 J Henderson
🖊 None
🏌 18 L 4640 yds SSS 64
👤 U SOC
££ On application
⛳ 3 miles S of Brodick on A841
🏛 Auchterlonie/Fernie
🖥 www.arrangolf.co.uk
   www.lamashgolfclub.co.uk

Largs (1891)

Irvine Road, Largs, KA30 8EU
☎ **(01475) 674681 (Clubhouse)**
🖥 (01475) 673594
🖥 800
🖈 J Callaghan (01475) 673594
🖊 K Docherty (01475) 686192
🏌 18 L 6115 yds Par 70 SSS 71
👤 U SOC–WD
££ £30 D–£40 (£40)
⛳ 1 mile S of Largs on A78
🏛 JH Stutt
🖥 www.largsgolfclub.co.uk

Lochranza (1991)

Pay and play
Lochranza, Isle of Arran, KA27 8HL
☎ **(0177083) 0273**
🖥 (0177083) 0600
📧 golf@lochgolf.co.uk
🖈 IM Robertson
🏌 18 L 5470 yds SSS 70
👤 U SOC–Apr–Oct
££ £15
⛳ 14 miles N of Brodick
🏛 IM Robertson
🖥 www.lochgolf.co.uk

Loudoun Gowf (1909)

Galston, KA4 8PA
☎ **(01563) 821993/820551**
🖥 (01563) 820011
📧 secretary@loudoungowf.sol.uk
🖥 850
🖈 L Gilliland (01563) 821993
🏌 18 L 6016 yds SSS 69
👤 WD–U WE–M
££ £21 D–£31
⛳ 5 miles E of Kilmarnock on A71
🖥 www.loudoungowfclub.biz

Machrie Bay (1900)

Machrie Bay, Brodick, Isle of Arran,
KA27 8DZ
☎ **(01770) 850232**
🖥 (01770) 850247
🖥 160
🖈 J Milesi
🖊 None
🏌 9 L 2200 yds Par 66 SSS 62
👤 U
££ D–£10 W–£35
⛳ 10 miles W of Brodick
🏛 William Fernie

Maybole (1970)

Public
Memorial Park, Maybole, KA19
☎ **(01655) 889770**

⮞ 9 L 2635 yds SSS 65
👤 U
£€ £8 (£9)
⛳ S of Maybole, off A77. 8 miles S of Ayr

Muirkirk (1991)

Pay and play
c/o 65 Main Street, Muirkirk, KA18 3QR
☎ (01290) 660184
📖 100
✍ R Bradford
⮞ 9 L 5366 yds SSS 67
👤 U SOC
£€ £9
⛳ 12 miles W of M74 Junction 12 on A70

New Cumnock (1902)

Lochill, Cumnock Road, New Cumnock, KA18 4BQ
☎ (01290) 423659
📖 250
✍ D Scott
⮞ 9 L 2588 yds SSS 65
👤 U exc Sun am–NA
£€ £5 D–£8
⛳ 1 mile W of New Cumnock
🏠 William Fernie

Prestwick (1851)

2 Links Road, Prestwick, KA9 1QG
☎ (01292) 477404
🖥 (01292) 477255
📧 bookings@prestwickgc.co.uk
📖 580
✍ IT Bunch
✓ FC Rennie (01292) 479483
⮞ 18 L 6668 yds SSS 73
👤 WD/Sun–I on application only
£€ £90 D–£130 (2003)
⛳ Prestwick Airport 1 mile, nr Railway Station
🏠 Tom Morris
■ www.prestwickgc.co.uk

Prestwick St Cuthbert (1899)

East Road, Prestwick, KA9 2SX
☎ (01292) 477101
🖥 (01292) 671730
📖 865
✍ JC Rutherford
⮞ 18 L 6470 yds SSS 71
👤 WD–U WE/BH–M SOC–WD
£€ £24 D–£32
⛳ ¹/₂ mile E of Prestwick
■ www.stcuthbert.co.uk

Prestwick St Nicholas (1851)

Grangemuir Road, Prestwick, KA9 1SN
☎ (01292) 477608
🖥 (01292) 473900
📧 secretary@prestwickstnicholas.com
📖 600 155(L) 68(J)
✍ Tom Hepburn
✓ Starter (01292) 473904
⮞ 18 L 5952 yds SSS 69
👤 WD–U WE–NA exc Sun pm

£€ £36 D–£56 Sun pm–£41
⛳ Prestwick
🏠 C Hunter
■ www.prestwickstnicholas.com

Routenburn (1914)

Greenock Road, Largs, KA30 9AH
☎ (01475) 673230 – public,
(01475) 686475 – steward
📖 350
✍ RB Connal (Mgr) (01475) 672757
✓ G McQueen (01475) 687240
⮞ 18 L 5650 yds SSS 68
👤 U–phone Pro SOC–WD
£€ £14.50
⛳ N of Largs, off A78
🏠 James Braid

Royal Troon (1878)

Craigend Road, Troon, KA10 6EP
☎ (01292) 311555
🖥 (01292) 318204
📧 admin@royaltroon.com
📖 800
✍ JW Chandler
✓ RB Anderson (01292) 313281
⮞ Old 18 L 7150 yds SSS 74
Portland 18 L 6289 yds SSS 75
👤 Booking required – h/cap limit: men 20, ladies 30. Mon/Tues/Thurs only–H
£€ Old + Portland D–£180 (incl Lunch). Portland D–£100 (inc Lunch)
⛳ SE of Troon (B749). Prestwick Airport 3 miles
⊕ Practice range
🏠 W Fernie
■ www.royaltroon.com

Seafield (1930)

Public
Belleisle Park, Doonfoot Road, Ayr, KA7 4DU
☎ (01292) 441258
🖥 (01292) 442632
✓ D Gemmell (Golf Mgr) (01292) 441314
⮞ 18 L 5498 yds SSS 66
👤 U
£€ £13–£25
⛳ S of Ayr in Belleisle Park

Shiskine (1896)

Shiskine, Blackwaterfoot, Isle of Arran, KA27 8HA
☎ (01770) 860226
🖥 (01770) 860205
📖 550 154(L) 42(J)
✍ Mrs F Crawford (Mgr) (01770) 860548
⮞ 12 L 2990 yds SSS 42
👤 U SOC
£€ £15 (£19)
⛳ 11 miles SW of Brodick
🏠 Willie Fernie
■ www.shiskinegolf.com

Skelmorlie (1891)

Skelmorlie, PA17 5ES
☎ (01475) 520152

📖 429
✍ Mrs J Campbell (Hon)
⮞ 18 L 5030 yds SSS 65
👤 U exc Sat (Apr–Oct)
£€ D–£20 Sun–£25
⛳ Wemyss Bay Station 1¹/₂ miles
🏠 James Braid
■ www.skelmorliegolf.co.uk

Troon Municipal

Public
Harling Drive, Troon, KA10 6NF
☎ (01292) 312464
🖥 (01292) 312578
✓ G McKinlay
⮞ Lochgreen 18 L 6785 yds SSS 73
Darley 18 L 6501 yds SSS 72
Fullarton 18 L 4822 yds SSS 63
👤 U SOC
£€ Lochgreen £19–£31. Darley £15–£29. Fullarton £13–£25
⛳ 4 miles N of Prestwick at Station Brae

Troon Portland (1894)

Club
1 Crosbie Road, Troon KA10
☎ (01292) 313488
📖 120
✍ G Clark (01292) 317367
⮞ Play over Portland at Royal Troon

Troon St Meddans (1907)

Club
Harling Drive, Troon, KA10 6NF
📧 troonstmeddans@btinternet.com
📖 264
✍ G Hope (01560) 482748
⮞ Play over Troon Municipal courses Lochgreen and Darley

Turnberry Hotel (1906)

Turnberry, KA26 9LT
☎ (01655) 331000
🖥 (01655) 331069
📖 380
✍ P Burley (Golf Dir) (01655) 334000
✓ P Burley (01655) 334000
⮞ Ailsa 18 L 6976 yds SSS 72
Kintyre 18 L 6719 yds SSS 71
Arran 9 L 1996 yds Par 31
👤 On application
£€ On application
⛳ 18 miles S of Ayr on A77
⊕ Golf Academy. Driving range
🏠 Ailsa-Mackenzie Ross. Kintyre-Donald Steel
■ www.westin.com/turnberry

West Kilbride (1893)

Fullerton Drive, Seamill, West Kilbride, KA23 9HT
☎ (01294) 823911
🖥 (01294) 829573
📖 900
✍ H Armour
✓ G Ross (01294) 823042
⮞ 18 L 6452 yds SSS 71
👤 WD–U WE–M BH–NA SOC
£€ On application

  West Kilbride
  Old Tom Morris/James Braid

Western Gailes (1897)
Gailes, Irvine, KA11 5AE
☎ **(01294) 311649**
📠 (01294) 312312
✉ secretary@westerngailes.com
📖 450
⚲ AM McBean, DJ Lithgow (Mgr)
🏴 18 L 6639 yds SSS 74
👥 WD–H Mon/Wed/Fri only
  (booking necessary) Sun pm
££ £90 D–£125 Sun pm–£90 (2003
  tariff)
⛳ 3 miles N of Troon (A78), Marine
  Drive
■ www.westerngailes.com

Whiting Bay (1895)
Golf Course Road, Whiting Bay, Isle of Arran, KA27 8PR
☎ **(01770) 700775**
📖 290
⚲ Mrs M Auld (01770) 820208
🏴 18 L 4405 yds SSS 63
👥 U
££ On application
⛳ 8 miles S of Brodick

Borders

Duns (1894)
Hardens Road, Duns, TD11 3NR
☎ **(01361) 882194**
📠 (01361) 883599
✉ secretary@dunsgolfclub.com
📖 410
⚲ A Preston (01361) 882194
✓ None
🏴 18 L 6209 yds SSS 70
👥 U SOC
££ £22 (£25)
⛳ 1 mile W of Duns, off A6105
■ www.dunsgolfclub.com

Eyemouth (1894)
Gunsgreen House, Eyemouth, TD14 5DX
☎ **(018907) 50551 (Clubhouse)**
📖 400
⚲ M Gibson (018907) 50004
✓ P Terras (018907) 50004 C
  Maltman (Touring)
🏴 18 L 6520 yds SSS 72
👥 U SOC
££ £20 (£25)
⛳ 6 miles N of border, off A1
⛳ JR Bain

Galashiels (1884)
Ladhope Recreation Ground, Galashiels, TD1 2NJ
☎ **(01896) 753724**
📖 366
⚲ R Gass (01896) 755307
🏴 18 L 5309 yds SSS 67
👥 U SOC
££ £20 D–£25 (£25 D–£30)
⛳ ¼ mile NE of Galashiels, off A7
⛳ James Braid

Hawick (1877)
Vertish Hill, Hawick, TD9 0NY
☎ **(01450) 372293**
✉ thesecretary@hawickgolfclub
  .fsnet.co.uk
📖 600
⚲ J Reilly
🏴 18 L 5929 yds SSS 69
👥 U
££ £21 D–£26
⛳ ½ mile S of Hawick
■ www.ukgolfer.com/hawick

The Hirsel (1948)
Kelso Road, Coldstream, TD12 4NJ
☎ **(01890) 882678**
📠 (01890) 882233
✉ bookings@hirselgc.co.uk
📖 800
⚲ SA Galbraith (01890) 882678
🏴 18 L 6111 yds SSS 70
👥 U SOC
££ £24 (£30)
⛳ ½ mile W of Coldstream (A697)
■ www.hirsel.co.uk

Innerleithen (1886)
Leithen Water, Leithen Road, Innerleithen, EH44 6NL
☎ **(01896) 830951**
📖 175
⚲ S Wyse (01896) 830071
🏴 9 L 6066 yds SSS 69
👥 U
££ £11 (£13)
⛳ 1 mile N of Innerleithen on Heriot
  road
⛳ Willie Park

Jedburgh (1892)
Dunion Road, Jedburgh, TD8 6LA
☎ **(01835) 863587**
📠 (01835) 862360
📖 300
⚲ K Swailes (01830) 520818
🏴 9 L 5600 yds Par 68 SSS 67
👥 U
££ £18 (£18)
⛳ Jedburgh 1 mile (signposted from
  centre)
⛳ Willie Park
■ www.tweeddalepress.co.uk

Kelso (1887)
Golf Course Road, Kelso, TD5 7SL
☎ **(01573) 223009**
📠 (01573) 228490
✉ golf@kelsogc.fsnet.co.uk
📖 400
⚲ DR Jack
🏴 18 L 6066 yds SSS 69
👥 U SOC
££ £18 (£22)
⛳ 1 mile N of Kelso, inside
  racecourse
⛳ James Braid

Langholm (1892)
Langholm, DG13 0JR
☎ **(013873) 81408/81247**

📖 150
⚲ WT Goodfellow
🏴 9 L 3090 yds SSS 70
👥 U
££ £10 (£10)
⛳ 21 miles N of Carlisle on A7
■ www.langholmgolfclub.co.uk

Lauder (1896)
Pay and play
Galashiels Road, Lauder, TD2 6QD
☎ **(01578) 722526**
✉ djdfamily@aol.com
📖 250
⚲ D Dickson (01578) 722526
🏴 9 L 6050 yds Par 72 SSS 69
👥 U SOC
££ £10 (£10)
⛳ ½ mile W of Lauder
⛳ W Park Jr

Melrose (1880)
Dingleton Road, Melrose, TD6 9HS
☎ **(01896) 822855**
📠 (01896) 822855
📖 340
⚲ J Orrett (01896) 822788
🏴 9 L 5562 yds Par 70 SSS 68
👥 U exc during competitions
££ £20 D–£26
⛳ S boundary of Melrose, off A68

Minto (1928)
Denholm, Hawick, TD9 8SH
☎ **(01450) 870220**
📠 (01450) 870126
✉ pat@mintogolfclub.freeserve.co.uk
📖 600
⚲ P Brown
✓ None
🏴 18 L 5542 yds SSS 67
👥 H SOC
££ £25 (£30)
⛳ Denholm, 6 miles E of Hawick

Newcastleton (1894)
Holm Hill, Newcastleton, TD9 0QD
☎ **(013873) 75608**
⚲ GA Wilson
✓ None
🏴 9 L 5491 yds Par 69 SSS 70
👥 U SOC
££ £10
⛳ W of Newcastleton, off B6357 (via
  A7). M6 Junction 44
⛳ John Shade

Peebles (1892)
Kirkland Street, Peebles, EH45 8EU
☎ **(01721) 720197**
📖 650
⚲ H Gilmore
✓ C Imlah
🏴 18 L 6160 yds SSS 70
👥 H SOC
££ £30 D–£45
⛳ 23 miles S of Edinburgh, via A703
⛳ James Braid/HS Colt
■ www.peeblesgolfclub.co.uk

The Roxburghe Hotel
(1997)
Heiton, Kelso, TD5 8JZ
☎ (01573) 450331
🖳 (01573) 450611
📧 golf@roxburghe.net
📖 300
🏌 Jeannette Thomson (Bookings)
⛳ C Montgomerie (01573) 450333
🏴 18 L 6925 yds Par 72 SSS 73
👤 By arrangement SOC
££ £50 (£70)
🚗 On A698 between Jedburgh and Kelso
⊕ Driving range
🏠 Dave Thomas
■ www.roxburghe.net

Selkirk   (1883)
The Hill, Selkirk, TD7 4NW
☎ (01750) 20621
📖 363
🏌 A Wilson
🏴 9 L 5560 yds SSS 68
👤 WD–U exc Mon pm WE–phone first SOC
££ D–£20 (£20)
🚗 1 mile S of Selkirk on A7
🏠 Willie Park

St Boswells   (1899)
St Boswells, Melrose, TD6 0DE
☎ (01835) 823527
📖 320
🏌 JG Phillips
🏴 9 L 5274 yds SSS 66
👤 U SOC
££ D–£18 (D–£20)
🚗 Off A68 at St Boswells Green, by River Tweed
🏠 Willie Park/Shade

Torwoodlee   (1895)
Edinburgh Road, Galashiels, Torwoodlee, TD1 2NE
☎ (01896) 752260
🖳 (01896) 752260
📧 thesecretary@torwoodleegolfclub .org.uk
📖 550
🏌 A Owenson
🏴 18 L 6021 yds Par 69 SSS 70
👤 WD–U from 9.30am–12.30pm and after 1.30pm exc Thurs–NA from 4–6pm WE–by arrangement SOC
££ £26 D–£36 (£32 D–£42)
🚗 1 mile N of Galashiels on A7
🏠 Willie Park
■ www.torwoodleegolfclub.org.uk

Woll   (1993)
Proprietary
New Woll Estate, Ashkirk, Selkirkshire, TD7 4PE
☎ (01750) 32711
📧 wollgolf@btinternet.com
📖 360
🏌 Nicholas Brown (01750) 32711
🏴 9 L 6408 yds Par 72 SSS 71
👤 U SOC

££ £18 (£18)
🚗 Ashkirk, just off A7
⊕ Driving range nearby; accommodation on site
■ www.wollgolf.co.uk

Clackmannanshire

Alloa   (1891)
Schawpark, Sauchie, Alloa, FK10 3AX
☎ (01259) 722745
🖳 (01259) 218796
📖 550 80(L) 130(J)
🏌 T Crampton (Admin)
⛳ W Bennett (01259) 724476
🏴 18 L 6229 yds Par 70 SSS 71
👤 WD–U WE–parties restricted
££ £26 D–£30 (£36 D–£40)
🚗 Sauchie, N of Alloa on A908
🏠 James Braid

Alva
Beauclerc Street, Alva, FK12 5LH
☎ (01259) 760431
📖 320
🏴 9 L 2423 yds SSS 64
👤 U
££ On application
🚗 Back Road, Alva, on A91 Stirling-St Andrews road. Signs to Alva Glen

Braehead   (1891)
Cambus, Alloa, FK10 2NT
☎ (01259) 725766
🖳 (01259) 214070
📧 braehead.gc@btinternet.com
📖 800
🏌 Anne Nash
⛳ Jamie Stevenson (01259) 722078
🏴 18 L 6086 yds SSS 69
👤 U–booking necessary SOC
££ £20 D–£30 (£30 D–£40)
🚗 2 miles W of Alloa (A907)
⊕ Small practice area
🏠 Robert Tait
■ www.braehead.gc.co.uk

Dollar   (1890)
Brewlands House, Dollar, FK14 7EA
☎ (01259) 742400
🖳 (01259) 743497
📧 dollar.g.c@brewlandshouse .freeserve.co.uk
📖 375
🏌 T Young
🏴 18 L 5242 yds SSS 66
👤 U SOC
££ £13.50 D–£17.50 (£22)
🚗 Dollar, off A91
🏠 Ben Sayers
■ http://.mysite.freeserve.com /dollargolfclub

Tillicoultry   (1899)
Alva Road, Tillicoultry, FK13 6BL
☎ (01259) 750124
🖳 (01259) 750124
📖 400

🏌 M Todd
🏴 9 L 2761 yds SSS 67
👤 WD/WE–U SOC
££ £12 (£17)
🚗 9 miles E of Stirling

Tulliallan   (1902)
Kincardine, Alloa, FK10 4BB
☎ (01259) 730396
🖳 (01259) 733950
📧 enquiries@tulliallangc.f9.co.uk
📖 550 71(L) 100(J)
🏌 D Berry
⛳ S Kelly (01259) 730798
🏴 18 L 5982 yds SSS 69
👤 U exc comp days
££ £16.50 (£21)
🚗 5 miles SE of Alloa
■ www.tulliallan-golf-club.co.uk

Dumfries & Galloway

Brighouse Bay   (1999)
Pay and play
Borgue, Kirkcudbright, DG6 4TS
☎ (01557) 870409
🖳 (01557) 870409
📧 brighousebayglfclub@tiscali.co.uk
🏌 E Diamond (Sec) (01557) 870509
D Sutton (Golf Coordinator) (01557) 870509
🏴 18 L 6366 yds Par 73 SSS 72
👤 WD–U WE–booking advisable
££ £22 (£26)
🚗 6 miles SW of Kirkcudbright, off B727
⊕ Driving range; short game area
🏠 Duncan Gray
■ www.brighousebay-golfclub.co.uk

Castle Douglas   (1905)
Abercromby Road, Castle Douglas, DG7 1BA
☎ (01556) 502801
📖 510
🏌 AD Millar (01556) 502099
🏴 9 L 5400 yds SSS 66
👤 U
££ £12
🚗 Off A75/A713, NE of Castle Douglas

Colvend   (1905)
Sandyhills, Dalbeattie, DG5 4PY
☎ (01556) 630398
🖳 (01556) 630495
📧 sec.@colvendgolfclub.co.uk
📖 500
🏌 JB Henderson
🏴 18 L 5200 yds SSS 67
👤 U
££ D–£22
🚗 6 miles S of Dalbeattie on A710
🏠 Fernie/Soutar

Crichton   (1884)
Bankend Road, Dumfries, DG1 4TH
☎ (01387) 247894/702221
🖳 (01387) 702223
📖 600

For list of abbreviations and key to symbols see page 627

9 L 3084 yds SSS 69
WD–U before 3pm SOC
£€ £15 D–£28
1 mile from Dumfries, nr Hospital

Dalbeattie   (1894)
60 Maxwell Park, Dalbeattie,
DG5 4LS
☎ **(01556) 611421/610311**
✉ ArthurHowatson@aol.com
📖 400
A Howatson (01556) 610311
None
9 L 5710 yds SSS 68
U SOC
£€ £16 D–£20
14 miles SW of Dumfries on
A711/B794
■ www.dalbeattiegc.co.uk

Dumfries & County   (1912)
Nunfield, Edinburgh Road, Dumfries,
DG1 1JX
☎ **(01387) 253585**
📞 (01387) 253585
✉ dumfriesc@aol.com
📖 600 100(J)
BRM Duguid (01387) 253585
S Syme (01387) 268918
18 L 5918 yds SSS 69
WD–U exc 11.30–2pm–NA
Sat–NA Sun–NA before 10am
£€ £24.50 D–£33.50
1 mile NE of Dumfries, on A701
W Fernie
■ www.dumfriesandcounty-gc
.fsnet.co.uk

Dumfries & Galloway
(1880)
2 Laurieston Avenue, Maxwelltown,
Dumfries, DG2 7NY
☎ **(01387) 253582**
📞 (01387) 263848
✉ info@dggc.co.uk
📖 750
TM Ross (01387) 263848
J Fergusson (01387) 256902
18 L 6325 yds SSS 70
U
£€ £27 (£33)
Dumfries
Willie Fernie

Gatehouse   (1921)
'Innisfree', Laurieston, Castle Douglas,
DG7 2PW
☎ **(01557) 814766 (Clubhouse)**
  (01644) 450260 (Bookings)
📞 (01644) 450260
✉ gatehousegolf@sagainternet.co.uk
📖 300
KA Cooper (01644) 450260
9 L 2521 yds SSS 66
WD–U WE–not before noon Sun
£€ D–£12 (D–£12)
¾ mile N of Gatehouse, off A75. 9
miles NW of Kirkcudbright

Gretna   (1991)
Kirtle View, Gretna, DG16 5HD
☎ **(01461) 338464**
RM & VA Birnie (Props)
Gareth Dick PGA (01461) 204642
9 L 6430 yds SSS 71
U SOC
£€ 9 holes–£5. 18 holes–£10
1 mile W of Gretna, off A75
⊕ Driving range
Nigel Williams

Hoddom Castle   (1973)
Pay and play
Hoddom Bridge, Ecclefechan, DG11 1AS
☎ **(01576) 300251**
📞 (01576) 300757
G Condron
9 L 2274 yds SSS 33
U
£€ £7 (£11)
2 miles SW of Ecclefechan on
B725. M74 Junction 6

Kirkcudbright   (1893)
Stirling Crescent, Kirkcudbright,
DG6 4EZ
☎ **(01557) 330314**
✉ david@kirkcudbrightgolf.co.uk
📖 500
DA MacKenzie
18 L 5739 yds SSS 69
U H–phone first SOC
£€ £20 D–£25
½ mile from Kirkcudbright town
centre

Lochmaben   (1926)
Castlehill Gate, Lochmaben, DG11 1NT
☎ **(01387) 810552**
✉ lochmabengc@aol.com
📖 670
JM Dickie
18 L 5927 yds SSS 70
WD–U before 5pm WE–U exc
comp days SOC
£€ £20 D–£25 (£25 D–£30)
4 miles W of Lockerbie on A709. 8
miles NE of Dumfries
James Braid

Lockerbie   (1889)
Corrie Road, Lockerbie, DG11 2ND
☎ **(01576) 203363**
📞 (01576) 203363
✉ enquiries@lockerbiegolf
📖 530
J Thomson
18 L 5418 yds SSS 67
U exc Sun–NA before 11.30am
£€ £18 (£20)
½ mile NE of Lockerbie, on Corrie
road
James Braid

Moffat   (1884)
Coatshill, Moffat, DG10 9SB
☎ **(01683) 220020**
📞 (01683) 221802
✉ moffatgolfclub@onetel.net.uk

📖 380
JW Mein (01683) 220020
None
18 L 5259 yds Par 69 SSS 67
U exc Wed–NA after 3pm SOC
£€ £19.50 D–£24 (£27 D–£33)
A74(M) Junction 15. Follow signs
to Moffat
Ben Sayers
■ www.moffatgolfclub.co.uk

New Galloway   (1902)
New Galloway, Dumfries, DG7 3RN
☎ **(01644) 450685**
📖 280
NE White
9 L 5006 yds Par 68 SSS 67
U
£€ D–£13
S of New Galloway on A762. 20
miles N of Kirkcudbright
Baillie

Newton Stewart   (1981)
Kirroughtree Avenue, Minnigaff, Newton
Stewart, DG8 6PF
☎ **(01671) 402172**
📖 380
M Large
18 L 5903 yds Par 69 SSS 70
U H
£€ £22 D–£25 (£23 D–£27)
N of Newton Stewart, off A75

Pines Golf Centre
Pay and play
Lockerbie Road, Dumfries, DG1 3PF
☎ **(01387) 247444**
📞 (01387) 249600
✉ admin@pinesgolf.com
📖 160
G Gray (Sec/Mgr)
B Gemmell, B Gray (01387) 247444
18 L 5870 yds Par 68 SSS 69
U SOC
£€ £14 D–£21
By A75 Dumfries by-pass. M74
Junctions 15 or 17
⊕ Driving range
Duncan Gray
■ www.pinesgolf.com

Portpatrick   (1903)
Golf Course Road, Portpatrick,
DG9 8TB
☎ **(01776) 810273**
📞 (01776) 810811
✉ enquiries@portpatrickgolfclub.com
📖 550
J McPhail
Dunskey 18 L 5913 yds SSS 69
Dinvin 9 L 1504 yds Par 27
U H SOC
£€ £25 D–£35 (£30 D–£40) W–£120
Dinvin £10 D–£15
8 miles SW of Stranraer
CW Hunter

Powfoot   (1903)
Cummertrees, Annan, DG12 5QE
☎ **(01461) 700276 (Bookings)**

☎ (01461) 700276
📖 920
🖊 CL McDairmant (Mgr)
✈ S Smith (01461) 700327 (also for bookings)
🏳 18 L 6266 yds SSS 71
👤 WD–U Sat–NA Sun–NA before 1pm
££ Winter £15 D–£20 Summer £28 D–£35 (£30)
⛳ 4 miles W of Annan. 15 miles SE of Dumfries, off B724
🏠 James Braid

Sanquhar (1894)
Blackaddie Road, Sanquhar, Dumfries, DG4 6JZ
☎ (01659) 50577
🖂 tich@rossirene.fsnet.co.uk
📖 180
🖊 Ian Macfarlane
🏳 9 L 5630 yds SSS 68
👤 U–parties welcome
££ D–£10 (D–£12); parties of 12 and over £20 for
⛳ ¹/₂ mile W of Sanquhar (A76). 30 miles N of Dumfries
🏠 W Fernie
■ www.scottishgolf.com

Southerness (1947)
Southerness, Dumfries, DG2 8AZ
☎ (01387) 880677
🖶 (01387) 880644
📖 800
🖊 IA Robin
✈ None
🏳 18 L 6566 yds SSS 73
👤 H–phone first SOC
££ D–£38 (D–£48)
⛳ 16 miles S of Dumfries, off A710
🏠 Mackenzie Ross
■ www.southernessgolfclub.com

St Medan (1905)
Monreith, Newton Stewart, DG8 8NJ
☎ (01988) 700358
📖 150
🖊 DR Graham (01988) 840214
🏳 9 L 2277 yds SSS 63
👤 U SOC
££ £15 (£15)
⛳ 3 miles S of Port William, off A747
🏠 James Braid

Stranraer (1905)
Creachmore, Leswalt, Stranraer, DG9 0LF
☎ (01776) 870245
🖶 (01776) 870445
🖂 stranraergolf@btclick.com
📖 700
🖊 BC Kelly
🏳 18 L 6308 yds SSS 72
👤 WE–NA before 9.30am and 11.45am–1.45pm
££ £24 (£30)
⛳ 2 miles NW of Stranraer on A718
🏠 James Braid
■ www.stranraergolfclub.net

Thornhill (1893)
Blacknest, Thornhill, DG3 5DW
☎ (01848) 330546
🖂 coordinatorthornhillgc@btinternet.com
📖 535
🖊 J Tait
🏳 18 L 6085 yds SSS 70
👤 U
££ On application
⛳ 14 miles N of Dumfries (A76)

Wigtown & Bladnoch (1960)
Lightlands Terrace, Wigtown, DG8 9EF
☎ (01988) 403354
📖 170
🖊 B Wilson
🏳 9 L 2731 yds SSS 67
👤 U SOC
££ £15 (£15)
⛳ Between Wigtown and Bladnoch, off A714
🏠 J Muir

Wigtownshire County (1894)
Mains of Park, Glenluce, Newton Stewart, DG8 0NN
☎ (01581) 300420
🖂 enquiries @wigtownshirecountygolfclub.com
📖 420
🖊 R McKnight
✈ None
🏳 18 L 5843 yds SSS 68
👤 U exc Wed–NA after 6pm
££ £21 D–£27 (£23 D–£29)
⛳ 8 miles E of Stranraer on A75
🏠 W Gordon Cunningham
■ www.wigtownshirecountygolfclub.com

Dunbartonshire

Balmore (1894)
Balmore, Torrance, G64 4AW
☎ (01360) 620284
🖶 (01360) 622742
📖 750
🖊 SB Keir (01360) 620284
✈ K Craggs (01360) 620123
🏳 18 L 5584 yds SSS 67
👤 WD–U SOC
££ On application
⛳ 4 miles N of Glasgow, off A807
🏠 Harry Vardon

Bearsden (1891)
Thorn Road, Bearsden, Glasgow, G61 4BP
☎ (0141) 856 5300
📖 600
🖊 Iain Inglis
🏳 9 L 6014 yds SSS 69
👤 By arrangement
⛳ 6 miles NW of Glasgow

Cardross (1895)
Main Road, Cardross, Dumbarton, G82 5LB
☎ (01389) 841213 (Clubhouse)

🖶 (01389) 842162
🖂 golf@cardross.com
📖 850
🖊 IT Waugh (01389) 841754
✈ R Farrell (01389) 841350
🏳 18 L 6469 yds SSS 72
👤 WD–U WE–M SOC
££ £30 D–£45
⛳ 4 miles W of Dumbarton on A814
🏠 Fernie (1904)/Braid(1921)
■ www.cardross.com

Clober (1951)
Craigton Road, Milngavie, Glasgow, G62 7HP
☎ (0141) 956 1685
🖶 (0141) 955 1416
📖 700
🖊 B Davidson
✈ (0141) 956 6963 (Golf Shop)
🏳 18 L 4963 yds SSS 65
👤 WD–U before 4pm WE–M BH–NA SOC–WD
££ £16
⛳ 7 miles NW of Glasgow
■ www.clober.com

Clydebank & District (1905)
Hardgate, Clydebank, G81 5QY
☎ (01389) 383833
🖶 (01389) 383831
📖 780
🖊 Mrs K Stoddart (01389) 383831
✈ PR Jamieson (01389) 383835
🏳 18 L 5823 yds SSS 68
👤 WD–H
££ On application
⛳ 2 miles N of Clydebank

Clydebank Municipal (1927)
Public
Overtoun Road, Dalmuir, Clydebank, G81 3RE
☎ (0141) 952 8698 (Starter)
🖶 (0141) 952 6372
✈ R Bowman (0141) 952 6372
🏳 18 L 5349 yds SSS 66
👤 U exc Sat–NA 11am–2.30pm
££ On application
⛳ 8 miles W of Glasgow

Dougalston (1977)
Strathblane Road, Milngavie, Glasgow, G62 8HJ
☎ (0141) 955 2434
🖶 (0141) 955 2406
📖 770
🖊 Mrs H Everett
✈ C Everett
🏳 18 L 6225 yds SSS 71
👤 WD–U SOC
££ £22 (£28)
⛳ 7 miles N of Glasgow on A81
🏠 J Harris

Douglas Park (1897)
Hillfoot, Bearsden, Glasgow, G61 2TJ
☎ (0141) 942 2220 (Clubhouse)
🖶 (0141) 942 0985
🖂 secretary@douglasparkgolfclub.net
📖 470 270(L) 120(J)

✎ JG Fergusson (0141) 942 0985
✓ D Scott (0141) 942 1482
♭ 18 L 5962 yds SSS 69
♙ M SOC
££ WD–£23
⌖ 6 miles NW of Glasgow, nr Hillfoot Station
⌂ Willie Fernie

Dullatur (1896)

1a Glendouglas Drive, Craigmarloch, Cumbernauld, G68 0DW

☎ (01236) 723230
✆ (01236) 727271
☐ 580 64(L)
✎ Carol Millar (01236) 723230
✓ D Sinclair (01236) 794721
♭ 18 L 6312 yds SSS 70
   18 L 5875 yds SSS 68
♙ WD–U WE SOC
££ £20 (£30)
⌖ 3 miles N of Cumbernauld

Dumbarton (1888)

Broadmeadow, Dumbarton, G82 2BQ

☎ (01389) 732830
✆ (01389) 765995
✉ golf@dumbartongolfclub.co.uk
☐ 500
✎ DM Mitchell
♭ 18 L 6018 yds SSS 69
♙ WD–U WE–NA
££ D–£25
⌖ 1 mile N of Dumbarton
■ www.dumbartongolfclub.co.uk

Hayston (1926)

Campsie Road, Kirkintilloch, Glasgow, G66 1RN

☎ (0141) 776 1244
✆ (0141) 776 9030
✉ secretary@haystongolf.com
☐ 440 70(L) 60(J)
✎ JV Carmichael (0141) 775 0723
✓ S Barnett (0141) 775 0882
♭ 18 L 6042 yds SSS 70
♙ WD–I before 4.30pm –M after 4.30pm WE–M
££ £25
⌖ 1 mile N of Kirkintilloch
⌂ James Braid
■ www.haystongolf.com

Hilton Park (1927)

Auldmarroch Estate, Stockiemuir Road, Milngavie, G62 7HB

☎ (0141) 956 5124/1215
✆ (0141) 956 4657
✉ info@hiltonparkgolfclub.fsnet.co.uk
☐ 1200
✎ Mrs JA Dawson (0141) 956 4657
✓ W McCondichie (0141) 956 5125
♭ Hilton 18 L 6054 yds SSS 70
   Allander 18 L 5374 yds SSS 69
♙ WD–U before 4pm
££ On application
⌖ 8 miles NW of Glasgow on A809
⌂ James Braid

Kirkintilloch (1895)

Todhill, Campsie Road, Kirkintilloch, G66 1RN

☎ (0141) 776 1256
☐ 450 100(L) 100(J)
✎ IM Gray (0141) 775 2387
♭ 18 L 5860 yds SSS 69
♙ M SOC
££ SOC–On application
⌖ 7 miles N of Glasgow

Lenzie (1889)

19 Crosshill Road, Lenzie, G66 5DA

☎ (0141) 776 1535
✆ (0141) 777 7748
☐ 501 125(L) 125(J)
✎ SM Davidson (0141) 812 3018
✓ J McCallum (0141) 777 7748
♭ 18 L 5984 yds SSS 69
♙ M SOC
££ £24 D–£30
⌖ 6 miles NE of Glasgow
■ www.lenziegolfclub.co.uk

Loch Lomond

Rossdhu House, Luss, G83 8NT

☎ (01436) 655555
✆ (01436) 655500
✎ K Williams
✓ C Campbell
♭ 18 L 7095 yds Par 71
♙ NA
⌖ 20 miles NW of Glasgow on A82
⌂ Weiskopf/Morrish
■ www.lochlomond.com

Milngavie (1895)

Laighpark, Milngavie, Glasgow, G62 8EP

☎ (0141) 956 1619
✆ (0141) 956 4252
✉ secretary@milngaviegc.fsnet.co.uk
☐ 390
✎ S McInnes
✓ None
♭ 18 L 5818 yds SSS 68
♙ M SOC
££ On application
⌖ 7 miles NW of Glasgow

Palacerigg (1975)

Public

Palacerigg Country Park, Cumbernauld, G67 3HU

☎ (01236) 734969
✆ (01236) 721461
✉ palacerigg-golfclub@lineone.net
☐ 320
✎ DSA Cooper
♭ 18 L 6444 yds Par 72 SSS 71
♙ U SOC
££ £8 (£10)
⌖ 3 miles SE of Cumbernauld, off A80
⌂ Henry Cotton
■ www.palaceriggolfclub.co.uk

Ross Priory

Ross Loan, Gartocharn, Alexandria, G83 8NL

☎ (01389) 830398

☐ (01389) 830357
☐ 800
✎ R Cook
✓ None
♭ 9 L 5758 yds Par 70 SSS 68
♙ M
££ N/A
⌖ Off A881 at Gartocharn
⌂ George Campbell

Vale of Leven (1907)

Northfield Road, Bonhill, Alexandria, G83 9ET

☎ (01389) 752351
✆ (08707) 498950
✉ clubadministrator @valeoflevengolfclub.org.uk
☐ 600
✎ R Barclay
✓ B Campbell (08707) 498914
♭ 18 L 5167 yds Par 67 SSS 66
♙ U H exc Sat (Apr–Sept) SOC (max 36 members)
££ £16 D–£24 (£20 D–£30)
⌖ Bonhill, 3 miles N of Dumbarton, off A82
■ www.valeoflevengolfclub.org.uk

Westerwood Hotel G&CC (1989)

St Andrews Drive, Cumbernauld, G68 0EW

☎ (01236) 725281
✆ (01236) 860730
✉ alantait@morton-hotels.com
☐ 250
✎ A Tait
✓ A Tait
♭ 18 L 6616 yds SSS 72
♙ U SOC
££ £27.50 (£30)
⌖ 13 miles NE of Glasgow, off A80
⌂ Thomas/Ballesteros

Windyhill (1908)

Windyhill, Bearsden, G61 4QQ

☎ (0141) 942 2349
✆ (0141) 942 5874
✉ secretary@windyhill.co.uk
☐ 650
✎ W Proven
✓ C Duffy (0141) 942 7157
♭ 18 L 6254 yds SSS 70
♙ WD–U Sun–M SOC–WD
££ £25
⌖ 8 miles NW of Glasgow
⌂ James Braid
■ www.windyhill.co.uk

Fife

Aberdour (1896)

Seaside Place, Aberdour, KY3 0TX

☎ (01383) 860080
✆ (01383) 860050
✉ aberdourgc@aol.com
☐ 670
✎ (01383) 860080
✓ D Gemmell (01383) 860256

☞ 18 L 5460 yds Par 67 SSS 66
👥 WD–book with Pro Sat–NA SOC
£€ £20 (£35)
🚗 8 miles SE of Dunfermline, on coast
🏠 Robertson/Anderson

Anstruther   (1890)
Marsfield Shore Road, Anstruther, KY10 3DZ
☎ **(01333) 310956**
🖴 (01333) 312283
📖 500
🏌 J Boal
☞ 9 L 4504 yds SSS 63
👥 U SOC
£€ £12 (£15)
🚗 9 miles S of St Andrews

Auchterderran   (1904)
Public
Woodend Road, Cardenden, KY5 0NH
☎ **(01592) 721579**
📖 70
🏌 C Taylor (01592 720080)
☞ 9 L 5400 yds SSS 66
👥 U SOC
£€ £8 (£11)
🚗 1 mile N of Cardenden. 6 miles W of Kirkcaldy, off A910

Balbirnie Park   (1983)
Balbirnie Park, Markinch, Glenrothes, KY7 6NR
☎ **(01592) 612095**
🖴 (01592) 612383
📖 800
🏌 S Oliver (Admin)
✓ C Donnelly (01592) 752006
☞ 18 L 6210 yds SSS 70
👥 WE–booking essential
£€ £27 D–£35 (£33 D–£45)
🚗 2 miles E of Glenrothes
🏠 Fraser Middleton

Ballingry
Pay and play
Lochore Meadows Country Park, Crosshill, Lochgelly, KY5 8BA
☎ **(01592) 860086**
📖 150
☞ 9 L 6482 yds SSS 71
👥 U
£€ On application
🚗 2 miles N of Lochgelly (B920)

Burntisland   (1797)
Club
51 Craigkennochie Terrace, Burntisland, KY3 9EN
☎ **(01592) 872728**
📖 90
🏌 AD McPherson
☞ Play over Dodhead Course, Burntisland
■ www.burntislandgolfclub.co.uk

Burntisland Golf House Club   (1898)
Dodhead, Burntisland, KY3 9LQ
☎ **(01592) 874093**

🖴 (01592) 874093
📖 800
🏌 WK Taylor (Mgr) (01592) 874093
✓ P Wytrazek (01592) 872116
☞ 18 L 5965 yds SSS 70
👥 U H SOC
£€ £20 D–£30 (£30 D–£40)
🚗 1 mile E of Burntisland on B923
🏠 Willie Park Jr/James Braid

Canmore   (1897)
Venturefair Avenue, Dunfermline, KY12 0PE
☎ **(01383) 724969**
🖴 (01383) 731649
📖 547 70(L) 85(J)
🏌 C Stuart (01383) 513604
✓ G Cook (01383) 728416
☞ 18 L 5437 yds SSS 66
👥 WD–U WE–restricted
£€ £16 D–£22 (£21 D–£32)
🚗 1 mile N of Dunfermline on A823
🏠 Ben Sayers

Charleton   (1994)
Pay and play
Charleton, Colinsburgh, KY9 1HG
☎ **(01333) 340505**
🖴 (01333) 340583
✉ clubhouse@charleton.co.uk
🏌 P Griffiths
✓ A Hutton (01333) 330009
☞ 18 L 6149 yds SSS 70
👥 U SOC
£€ £22 (£25)
🚗 1 mile W of Colinsburgh, off B492
⊕ Driving range. 9 holes pitch & putt course. Drive-on buggies
🏠 John Salvesen
■ www.charleton.co.uk

Cowdenbeath   (1991)
Public
Seco Place, Cowdenbeath, KY4 8PD
☎ **(01383) 511918**
📖 400
🏌 D Ferguson
☞ 18 L 6100 yds SSS 69
👥 U
£€ On application
🚗 In Cowdenbeath, signposted from A909/A92

Crail Golfing Society   (1786)
Balcomie Clubhouse, Fifeness, Crail, KY10 3XN
☎ **(01333) 450686**
🖴 (01333) 450416
📖 1800
🏌 A Busby (01333) 450686
✓ G Lennie (01333) 450960/450967
☞ Balcomie 18 L 5922 yds SSS 69
   Craighead 18 L 6728 yds Par 71 SSS 73
👥 U
£€ £32 (£40)
🚗 11 miles SE of St Andrews
🏠 Balcomie-Tom Morris. Craighead-Gil Hanse
■ www.crailgolfingsociety.co.uk

Cupar   (1855)
Hilltarvit, Cupar, KY15 5JT
☎ **(01334) 653549**
✉ secretary@cupargolfclub.freeserve .co.uk
📖 350
🏌 JM Houston (01334) 654101
☞ 9 L 5153 yds SSS 65
👥 WD–U Sat–NA SOC–WD/Sun
£€ D–£15
🚗 10 miles W of St Andrews
■ www.cupargolfclub.co.uk

Drumoig
Leuchars, St Andrews, KY16 0DW
☎ **(01382) 541144**
🖴 (01382) 541133
🏌 N Simpson (Gen Mgr)
✓ JM Farmer (Golf Mgr) (01382) 541144
☞ 18 hole course
👥 U
£€ On application
🚗 7 miles NW of St Andrews on A919
⊕ Driving range
🏠 Dave Thomas

Dunfermline   (1887)
Pitfirrane, Crossford, Dunfermline, KY12 8QW
☎ **(01383) 723534**
✉ pitfarrane@aol.com
📖 690
🏌 R De Rose
✓ C Nugent (01383) 729061
☞ 18 L 6121 yds SSS 70
👥 WD–U 10–12 & 2–4pm WE–M SOC–WD
£€ £25 D–£35
🚗 2 miles W of Dunfermline on A994
🏠 JR Stutt

Dunnikier Park   (1963)
Public
Dunnikier Way, Kirkcaldy, KY1 3LP
☎ **(01592) 261599**
🖴 (01592) 642541
✉ raynondjohnston@blueyonder.com
📖 600 35(L) 75(J)
🏌 R Johnston
✓ G Whyte (01592) 642121
☞ 18 L 6601 yds SSS 72
👥 U SOC
£€ £11.50 (£15.50)
🚗 N boundary of Kirkcaldy
🏠 R Stutt
■ www.dunnikierparkgolfclub.com

Earlsferry Thistle   (1875)
Club
Melon Park, Elie, KY9 1AS
📖 60
🏌 A Muir (01333) 330363
☞ Play over Golf House Club Course

Elmwood
Pay and play
Stratheden, Nr Cupar, KY15 8RS
☎ **(01334) 658780**

☎ (01334) 658781
✉ clubhouse@elmwoodgc.co.uk
🖊 Sharif Sulaiman (Golf Admin) (01334) 658780
🏌 Graeme McDowall (01334) 658780
► 18 L 5600 yds SSS 69
👥 U SOC
££ £18 (£22)
🚗 M90 J7 (southbound)/J8 (northbound). A91 to St Andrews
⊕ Practice area
■ www.elmwoodgc.co.uk

Falkland (1976)
The Myre, Falkland, KY15 7AA
☎ (01337) 857404
📖 350
🖊 Mrs L Henry
► 9 L 2384 metres SSS 66
👥 WD WE restricted on comp. days SOC
££ On application
🚗 5 miles N of Glenrothes on A912

Glenrothes (1958)
Public
Golf Course Road, Glenrothes, KY6 2LA
☎ (01592) 754561/758686
✉ secretary@glenrothesgolf.org.uk
📖 600 35(L) 50(J)
🖊 Miss C Dawson
► 18 L 6444 yds SSS 71
👥 U
££ £13 (£17)
🚗 Glenrothes West, off A92. M90 Junction 29
🏠 JR Stutt

Golf House Club (1875)
Elie, Leven, KY9 1AS
☎ (01333) 330327
📠 (01333) 330895
🖊 A Sneddon (01333) 330301
🏌 R Wilson (01333) 330955
► 18 L 6273 yds SSS 70
9 L 2277 yds SSS 32
👥 July–Sept ballot. WE–no party bookings. WE–NA before 3pm (May–Sept)
££ £40 D–£55 (£50 D–£65)
🚗 12 miles S of St Andrews

Kinghorn Ladies (1894)
Club
Golf Clubhouse, McDuff Crescent, Kinghorn, KY3 9RE
☎ (01592) 890345
📖 38
► Play over Kinghorn Municipal

Kinghorn Municipal (1887)
Public
McDuff Crescent, Kinghorn, KY3 9RE
☎ (01592) 890345
📖 200
🖊 I Gow (01592) 265445
🏌 None
► 18 L 5629 yds SSS 67
👥 U SOC
££ £11 (£16)
🚗 3 miles S of Kirkcaldy (A921)

⊕ Kinghorn and Kinghorn Thistle Clubs play here
🏠 Tom Morris

Kingsbarns Links
Kingsbarns, Fife, KY16 8QD
☎ (01334) 460860
📠 (01334) 460877
✉ info@kingsbarns.com
🖊 D Scott (Golf Dir)
🏌 D Scott
► 18 hole course
👥 U
££ £135 D–£200
🚗 Between St Andrews and Crail on coast road (A917)
⊕ Driving range
🏠 Phillips/Parsinen
■ www.kingsbarns.com

Kirkcaldy (1904)
Balwearie Road, Kirkcaldy, KY2 5LT
☎ (01592) 205240
📠 (01592) 205240
✉ enquiries@kirkcaldygolfclub.sol.co.uk
📖 600
🖊 AC Thomson (01592) 205240
🏌 A Caira (01592) 203258
► 18 L 6040 yds SSS 69
👥 U exc Sat–NA
££ £24–£30 Sun–£30–£38
🚗 S end of Kirkcaldy

Ladybank (1879)
Annsmuir, Ladybank, KY15 7RA
☎ (01337) 830814
📠 (01337) 830725 (Starter)
📠 (01337) 831505
📖 1000
🖊 D Allan
🏌 MJ Gray (01337) 830725
► 18 L 6601 yds SSS 72
👥 WD–U 9.30am–4pm M–after 4pm WE–NA
££ £40 (£45)
🚗 6 miles SW of Cupar, off A92 from Melville Lodges roundabout
■ www.ladybankgolf.co.uk

Leslie (1898)
Balsillie Laws, Leslie, Glenrothes, KY6 3EZ
☎ (01592) 620040
📖 300
🖊 G Lewis
► 9 L 4940 yds SSS 64
👥 U
££ £5 (£8)
🚗 3 miles W of Glenrothes. M90 Junction 5/7, 11 miles

Leven Golfing Society (1820)
Club
Links Road, Leven, KY8 4HS
☎ (01333) 426096/424229
📠 (01333) 424229
✉ LGS@bosinternet.com
📖 500

🖊 AJ McDonald (01333) 424229
► Play over Leven Links

Leven Links (1846)
The Promenade, Leven, KY8 4HS
☎ (01333) 421390 (Starter)
📠 (01333) 428859
✉ secretary@leven-links.com
📖 1200
🖊 (01333) 428859 (Links Committee)
► 18 L 6427 yds SSS 71
👥 WD–U before 5pm Sat–no parties Sun–NA before 10.30am SOC
££ £30 (£35)
🚗 E of Leven, on promenade. 12 miles SW of St Andrews

Leven Thistle (1867)
Club
Balfour Street, Leven, KY8 4JF
☎ (01333) 426397
📠 (01333) 439910
✉ secretary@leventhistlegolfclub.fsnet.co.uk
📖 500
🖊 J Scott (01333) 426333
► Play over Leven Links

Lochgelly (1895)
Cartmore Road, Lochgelly, Kirkcaldy, KY5 9PB
☎ (01592) 780174
📖 450
🖊 RF Stuart (01383) 512238
🏌 None
► 18 L 5454 yds SSS 66
👥 U
££ £12 (£17)
🚗 NW edge of Lochgelly. 5 miles W of Kirkcaldy

Lundin (1868)
Golf Road, Lundin Links, KY8 6BA
☎ (01333) 320202
📠 (01333) 329743
✉ secretary@lundingolfclub.co.uk
📖 850
🖊 DR Thomson
🏌 DK Webster (01333) 320051
► 18 L 6371 yds SSS 71
👥 WD–U Sat–NA before 2.30pm Sun–restricted
££ £40 D–£50 (£50)
🚗 3 miles E of Leven
🏠 James Braid
■ www.lundingolfclub.co.uk

Lundin Ladies (1891)
Woodielea Road, Lundin Links, KY8 6AR
☎ (01333) 320022 (Starter), (01333) 320832 (Sec)
✉ secretary@lundinladies.co.uk
✉ lundinladies@madasafish.com
📖 375
🖊 Marion Mitchell
► 9 L 2365 yds SSS 67 Par 68
👥 U
££ On application
🚗 3 miles E of Leven

Methil (1892)

Club
Links House, Links Road, Leven,
KY8 4HS
☎ (01333) 425535
▭ (01333) 425187
▭ 50
♫ ATJ Traill
⊳ Play over Leven Links

Pitreavie (1922)

Queensferry Road, Dunfermline,
KY11 8PR
☎ (01383) 722591
▭ (01383) 722591
▭ 800
♫ E Comerford
✓ P Brookes (01383) 723151
⊳ 18 L 6031 yds SSS 69
♦ U–phone Pro SOC (Parties–max
   36–must be booked in advance)
££ £19 D–£26 (£38)
⊖ 2 miles off M90 Junction 2,
   between Rosyth and Dunfermline
⌂ Dr A Mackenzie

Saline (1912)

Kinneddar Hill, Saline, KY12 9LT
☎ (01383) 852591
▭ 400
♫ P Bridson (01383) 851040
⊳ 9 L 5302 yds SSS 66
♦ U exc medal Sat
££ £10 (£12)
⊖ 5 miles NW of Dunfermline

Scoonie (1951)

Public
North Links, Leven, KY8 4SP
☎ (01333) 307007
▭ (01333) 307008
♫ S Kuczerepa
✓ None
⊳ 18 L 4979 metres SSS 65
♦ U SOC
££ On application
⊖ Adjoins Leven Links

Scotscraig (1817)

Golf Road, Tayport, DD6 9DZ
☎ (01382) 552515
▭ (01382) 553130
▭ 900
♫ BD Liddle
✓ SJ Campbell
⊳ 18 L 6550 yds SSS 72
♦ WD–U WE–by prior arrangement
   SOC
££ On application
⊖ 10 miles N of St Andrews

St Michaels (1903)

Leuchars, St Andrews, KY16 0DX
☎ (01334) 839365 (Clubhouse)
▭ (01334) 838789
✉ stmichaelsgc@btclick.com
▭ 550
♫ WA Spong (01334) 838666
⊳ 18 L 5802 yds SSS 68
♦ Sun am–NA (Mar–Oct) SOC

££ D–£22 (£30)
⊖ 5 miles N of St Andrews on
   Dundee road (A919)
■ www.stmichaelsgc.co.uk

Thornton (1921)

Station Road, Thornton, KY1 4DW
☎ (01592) 771173 (Starter)
▭ (01592) 774955
▭ 700
♫ BSL Main (01592) 771111
⊳ 18 L 6155 yds Par 70 SSS 69
♦ U
££ £15 D–£25 (£22 D–£32)
⊖ 5 miles N of Kirkcaldy, off A92
■ www.thorntongolfclubfife.co.uk

St Andrews Clubs

New (1902)

Club
3-5 Gibson Place, St Andrews, KY16 9JE
☎ (01334) 473426
▭ (01334) 477570
✉ golf@standrewsnewgolfclub.co.uk
▭ 1700
♫ H Campbell Graham (Sec/Mgr)
⊳ Play over St Andrews Links
   courses
■ www.standrewsnewgolfclub.com

The Royal and Ancient
(1754)

Club
St Andrews, KY16 9JD
☎ (01334) 460000
▭ (01334) 460001
✉ thesecretary@randagc.org
▭ 1800
♫ P Dawson
⊳ Play over St Andrews Links
■ www.randa.org
   www.opengolf.com

St Andrews (1843)

Club
Links House, 13 The Links, St Andrews,
KY16 9JB
☎ (01334) 479799
▭ (01334) 479577
✉ sec@thestandrewsgolfclub.co.uk
▭ 1600
♫ T Gallacher (01334) 479799
⊳ Play over St Andrews Links
■ www.thestandrewsgolfclub.co.uk

St Andrews Thistle (1817)

Club
18 Morton Crescent, St Andrews,
KY16 8RA
▭ 180
♫ JD Gray (01334) 474668
⊳ Play over St Andrews Links

St Regulus Ladies' (1913)

Club
9 Pilmour Links, St Andrews, KY16 9JG
✉ admin@st-regulus-lgc.fsnet.co.uk

▭ 273
♫ Mrs J Lumsden (01334) 472249
⊳ Play over St Andrews Links

The St Rule Club (1898)

Club
12 The Links, St Andrews, KY16 9JB
☎ (01334) 472988
▭ (01334) 472988
✉ strule.club@virgin.net
▭ 284
♫ Mrs J Allan
⊳ Play over St Andrews Links

St Andrews Courses

Balgove Course (1993)

Public
St Andrews Links Trust, Pilmour House,
St Andrews, KY16 9SF
☎ (01334) 466666
▭ (01334) 479555
♫ AJR McGregor (Gen Mgr)
⊳ 9 L 1520 yds Par 30
♦ U
££ £7 – £10
⊖ St Andrews Links, on A91
⊕ Driving range
⌂ Donald Steel
■ www.standrews.org.uk

Duke's (1995)

Craigtoun, St Andrews, KY16 8NS
☎ (01334) 474371
▭ (01334) 477668
✉ reservations@oldcoursehotel.co.uk
▭ 350
♫ S Toon (01334) 470214
✓ R Walker (01334) 470214
⊳ 18 L 7271 yds Par 72 SSS 75
♦ U H SOC
££ £65 (£75)
⊖ 3 miles S of St Andrews on
   Pitscottie road
⊕ Golf academy
⌂ Peter Thomson CBE
■ www.oldcoursehotel.co.uk

Eden Course (1914)

Public
St Andrews Links Trust, Pilmour House,
St Andrews, KY16 9SF
☎ (01334) 466666
▭ (01334) 479555
♫ AJR McGregor (Gen Mgr)
⊳ 18 L 6195 yds Par 70 SSS 70
♦ U SOC
££ £22 – £30
⊖ St Andrews Links, on A91
⊕ 3D–£65–£120 W–£130–£240
   (unlimited play over Jubilee, New,
   Eden and Strathtyrum courses).
   Driving range
⌂ HS Colt
■ www.standrews.org.uk

Jubilee Course (1897)

Public
St Andrews Links Trust, Pilmour House,
St Andrews, KY16 9SF
☎ **(01334) 466666**
⌨ (01334) 479555
🖎 AJR McGregor (Gen Mgr)
⊩ 18 L 6742 yds Par 72 SSS 73
👥 U SOC
££ £32 –£50
🚗 St Andrews Links, on A91. Signs to
    West Sands
⊕ 3D-£65-£120 W-£130-£240
    (unlimited play over Jubilee,
    Strathtyrum, Eden & New courses).
    Driving range
🏠 Angus/Steel
▪ www.standrews.org.uk

New Course (1895)

Public
St Andrews Links Trust, Pilmour House,
St Andrews, KY16 9SF
☎ **(01334) 466666**
⌨ (01334) 479555
🖎 AJR McGregor (Gen Mgr)
⊩ 18 L 6604 yds Par 71 SSS 73
👥 U SOC
££ £38 – £55
🚗 St Andrews Links, on A91. Signs to
    West Sands
⊕ 3D-£65-£120 W-£130-£240
    (unlimited play over Jubilee, New,
    Eden and Strathtyrum courses).
    Driving range
🏠 Old Tom Morris
▪ www.standrews.org.uk

Old Course (15th Century)

Public
St Andrews Links Trust, Pilmour House,
St Andrews, KY16 9SF
☎ **(01334) 466666**
⌨ (01334) 479555
🖎 linkstrust@standrews.org.uk
🖎 AJR McGregor (Gen Mgr)
⊩ 18 L 6566 yds Par 72 SSS 72
👥 H I No Sun play
££ £75 – £110
🚗 St Andrews Links, on A91. Signs to
    West Sands
⊕ Driving range
▪ www.standrews.org.uk

Strathtyrum Course (1993)

Public
St Andrews Links Trust, Pilmour House,
St Andrews, KY16 9SF
☎ **(01334) 466666**
⌨ (01334) 479555
🖎 AJR McGregor (Gen Mgr)
⊩ 18 L 5094 yds Par 69 SSS 65
👥 U SOC
££ £16 – £20
🚗 St Andrews Links, on A91
⊕ 3D-£65-£120 W-£130-£240
    (unlimited play over Jubilee, New,
    Eden and Strathtyrum courses).
    Driving range
🏠 Donald Steel
▪ www.standrews.org.uk

Glasgow

Alexandra Park (1880)

Public
Alexandra Park, Dennistoun, Glasgow,
G31 8SE
☎ **(0141) 556 1294**
⌨ 250
🖎 G Campbell
⊩ 9 L 4562 yds Par 62
👥 U
££ On application
🚗 ¹/₂ mile E of Glasgow, nr M8
🏠 Graham McArthur

Bishopbriggs (1907)

Brackenbrae Road, Bishopbriggs,
Glasgow, G64 2DX
☎ **(0141) 772 1810**
⌨ (0141) 762 2532
🖎 bgcsecretary@dial.pipex.com
⌨ 400 150(A) 120(J)
🖎 A Smith (0141) 772 8938
⊩ 18 L 6041 yds SSS 69
👥 H SOC–WD
££ £22.50 D–£32.50
🚗 6 miles N of Glasgow on A803
🏠 James Braid
▪ www.thebishopbriggsgolfclub.com

Cathcart Castle (1895)

Mearns Road, Clarkston, G76 7YL
☎ **(0141) 638 0082**
⌨ (0141) 638 1201
⌨ 950
🖎 IG Sutherland (0141) 638 9449
🖎 S Duncan (0141) 638 3436
⊩ 18 L 5832 yds SSS 68
👥 M SOC
££ £28 D–£40
🚗 1 mile from Clarkston on B767

Cawder (1933)

Cadder Road, Bishopbriggs, Glasgow,
G64 3QD
☎ **(0141) 761 1281**
⌨ (0141) 761 1285
🖎 secretary@cawdergolfclub.org.uk
⌨ 1400
🖎 (0141) 761 1282
🖎 K Stevely (0141) 772 7102
⊩ Cawder 18 L 6279 yds SSS 71
    Keir 18 L 5880 yds SSS 68
👥 WD–U SOC–WD
££ £30
🚗 N of Glasgow, off A803
    Kirkintilloch Road
🏠 Braid/Steel
▪ www.cawdergolfclub.org.uk

Cowglen (1906)

301 Barrhead Road, Glasgow, G43 1EU
☎ **(0141) 632 0556**
⌨ 485
🖎 RJG Jamieson (01505) 503000
🖎 S Payne (0141) 649 9401
⊩ 18 L 6079 yds SSS 69
👥 WD–by arrangement with Sec
    WE–M
££ £25.50 D–£35

🚗 3 miles SW of Glasgow (B762)
🏠 James Braid

Glasgow (1787)

Killermont, Bearsden, Glasgow,
G61 2TW
☎ **(0141) 942 1713**
⌨ (0141) 942 0770
🖎 secretary@glasgow-golf.com
⌨ 800
🖎 DW Deas (0141) 942 2011
🖎 J Steven (0141) 942 8507
⊩ 18 L 5977 yds Par 70 SSS 69
👥 M
🚗 4 miles NW of Glasgow
🏠 Tom Morris Sr

Haggs Castle (1910)

70 Dumbreck Road, Dumbreck,
Glasgow, G41 4SN
☎ **(0141) 427 0480**
⌨ (0141) 427 1157
🖎 haggscastlegc@lineone.net
⌨ 900
🖎 A Williams (0141) 427 1157
🖎 C Elliott (0141) 427 3355
⊩ 18 L 6426 yds SSS 71
👥 WD–H SOC–Weds only
££ SOC–£40
🚗 SW Glasgow (B768). M77 Junct 1
🏠 Dave Thomas (1998)

King's Park (1934)

Public
150A Croftpark Avenue, Croftfoot,
Glasgow, G54
☎ **(0141) 630 1597**
🖎 PJ King
⊩ 9 L 4236 yds Par 64 SSS 60
👥 U
££ On application
🚗 Croftfoot, 3¹/₂ miles S of Glasgow

Knightswood (1929)

Public
Knightswood Park, Lincoln Avenue,
Glasgow, G13 3DN
☎ **(0141) 959 6358**
⌨ 40
🖎 D Gardner (0141) 959 8158
🖎 None
⊩ 9 L 2793 yds Par 68 SSS 67
👥 U exc Wed & Fri before 9am and
    10–11am–NA
££ £7.80
🚗 4 miles NW of Glasgow, S of A82

Lethamhill (1933)

Public
Cumbernauld Road, Glasgow,
G33 1AH
☎ **(0141) 770 6220**
⌨ (0141) 770 0520
⊩ 18 L 5836 yds SSS 68
👥 U
££ £7.85
🚗 3 miles NE of Glasgow (A80)

Linn Park (1924)
Public
Simshill Road, Glasgow, G44 5TA
☎ (0141) 633 0377
🏳 18 L 4592 yds SSS 65
👥 U–phone 1 day in advance
££ £7.30 (£7.30)
🚗 4 miles S of Glasgow, W of B766

Littlehill (1926)
Public
Auchinairn Road, Glasgow, G64 1UT
☎ (0141) 772 1916
🏳 18 L 6228 yds SSS 70
👥 U
££ On application
🚗 3 miles NE of Glasgow, E of A803

Pollok (1892)
90 Barrhead Road, Glasgow, G43 1BG
☎ (0141) 632 1080
🖳 (0141) 649 1398
✉ pollok.gc@lineone.net
📖 500
🖊 I Cumming (0141) 632 4351
✓ None
🏳 18 L 6358 yds SSS 70
👥 WD–I XL WE–NA SOC–WD
££ £35 D–£45 (£40)
🚗 3 miles SW of Glasgow (B762). M77 Junction 2

Ralston (1904)
Strathmore Avenue, Ralston, Paisley, PA1 3DT
☎ (0141) 882 1349
🖳 (0141) 883 9837
📖 440 165(L) 100(J)
🖊 J Pearson
✓ C Munro (0141) 810 4925
🏳 18 L 6100 yds SSS 69
👥 M SOC
🚗 2 miles E of Paisley (A761)

Rouken Glen (1922)
Public
Stewarton Road, Thornliebank, Glasgow, G46 7UZ
☎ (0141) 638 7044
🏳 18 L 4800 yds SSS 63
👥 U SOC
££ On application
🚗 5 miles S of Glasgow, W of A77
⊕ Driving range

Ruchill (1928)
Public
Ruchil Park, Brassey Street, Maryhill, Glasgow G20
📖 60
🏳 9 L 2240 yds SSS 31
👥 U
££ On application
🚗 2 miles N of Glasgow, W of A879

Sandyhills (1905)
223 Sandyhills Road, Glasgow, G32 9NA
☎ (0141) 778 1179
📖 700

🖊 CJ Wilson
🏳 18 L 6253 yds SSS 71
👥 M SOC
££ £17.50
🚗 4 miles SE of Glasgow, N of A74

Williamwood (1906)
Clarkston Road, Netherlee, Glasgow, G44 3YR
☎ (0141) 637 1783
🖳 (0141) 571 0166
📖 911
🖊 RJ Templeton
✓ S Marshall (0141) 637 2715
🏳 18 L 5878 yds SSS 69
👥 WD–H
££ £27
🚗 5 miles S of Glasgow
🏠 James Braid

Highland

Caithness & Sutherland

Bonar Bridge/Ardgay (1904)
Bonar-Bridge, Ardgay, IV24 3EJ
☎ (01863) 766199 (Clubhouse)
✉ bonarardgaygolf@aol.com
📖 250
🖊 J Reid (01863) 766750
🏳 9 L 5162 yds SSS 65 Par 68
👥 U
££ D–£14 (£14)
🚗 ½ mile N of Bonar-Bridge on A836. 12 miles W of Dornoch

Brora (1891)
Public
Golf Road, Brora, KW9 6QS
☎ (01408) 621417/621911
🖳 (01408) 622157
✉ secretary@broragolf.co.uk
🖊 J Fraser
🏳 18 L 6110 yds SSS 69
👥 U exc comp days –H for open comps SOC
££ £27 D–£35 (£32 D–£40)
🚗 18 miles N of Dornoch (A9)
🏠 James Braid
■ www.broragolf.co.uk

The Carnegie Club (1995)
Skibo Castle, Dornoch, Sutherland, IV25 3RQ
☎ (01862) 881 260
🖳 (01862) 881 260
✉ sharon.stewart@carnegieclubs.com
📖 500
🖊 Sharon Stewart
✓ D Thomson (Dir of Golf)
🏳 18 L 6671 yds Par 71 SSS 72
👥 H–booking required WD only
££ £100
🚗 3 miles SW of Dornoch
🏠 Donald Steel
■ www.carnegieclubs.com

Durness (1988)
Pay and play
Balnakeil, Durness, IV27 4PN
☎ (01971) 511364
🖳 (01971) 511321
✉ lucy@durnessgolfclub.org
📖 150
🖊 Mrs L Mackay (01971) 511364
🏳 9 L 5555 yds SSS 67
👥 U
££ D–£15 W–£50
🚗 57 miles NW of Lairg on A838

Golspie (1889)
Ferry Road, Golspie, KW10 6ST
☎ (01408) 633266
🖳 (01408) 633393
✉ info@golspie-golf-club.co.uk
📖 315
✓ None
🏳 18 L 5990 yds SSS 68
👥 U SOC
££ £25 D–£35
🚗 11 miles N of Dornoch
🏠 James Braid
■ www.golspie-golf-club.co.uk

Helmsdale (1895)
Golf Road, Helmsdale, KW8 6JA
📖 50
🖊 R Sutherland
🏳 9 L 3720 yds SSS 61
👥 U
££ £5 D–£10 W–£25
🚗 30 miles N of Dornoch (A9)

Lybster (1926)
Main Street, Lybster, KW1 6BL
📖 100
🖊 AG Calder (01595) 721316
🏳 9 L 1896 yds SSS 61
👥 U
££ D–£10
🚗 13 miles S of Wick on A99

Reay (1893)
Reay, Thurso, Caithness, KW14 7RE
☎ (01847) 811288
🖳 (01847) 894189
✉ info@reaygolfclub.co.uk
📖 300
🖊 W McIntosh
✓ None
🏳 18 L 5831 yds Par 69 SSS 69
👥 U SOC
££ D–£20 W–£60
🚗 11 miles W of Thurso
🏠 James Braid
■ www.reaygolfclub.co.uk

Royal Dornoch (1877)
Golf Road, Dornoch, IV25 3LW
☎ (01862) 810219
🖳 (01862) 810792
✉ bookings@royaldornoch.com
📖 1127 220(L) 72(J) 300 (Struie)
🖊 JS Duncan (Sec/Mgr) (01862) 811220
✓ A Skinner (01862) 810902
🏳 C'ship 18 L 6514 yds SSS 73 Struie 18 L 6276 yds SSS 70

C'ship–H Struie–U
£€ £66 (£76)
⛳ 45 miles N of Inverness, off A9, N of Dornoch
⊕ Helipad by clubhouse. Airstrip nearby. Practice ground nearby
🖥 www.royaldornoch.com

Thurso (1893)
Newlands of Geise, Thurso, KW14 7XD
☎ (01847) 893807
🏠 300
✍ RM Black (01847) 892575
🏌 18 L 5828 yds SSS 69
👥 U
£€ £20 (£20)
⛳ 2 miles SW of Thurso

Ullapool
North Road, Ullapool, IV26 2TH
☎ (01854) 613323
🏠 (01854) 613133
📧 info@ullapool-golf.co.uk
🏠 220
✓ None
🏌 9 L 5338 yds Par 70 SSS 66 (18 tees)
👥 U
£€ D–£17 (£17) W–£60
⛳ Ullapool
🖥 www.ullapool-golf.co.uk

Wick (1870)
Reiss, Wick, KW1 5LJ
☎ (01955) 602726
📧 wickgolfclub@hotmail.com
🏠 320
✍ D Shearer (01955) 602935
🏌 18 L 6123 yds SSS 71
👥 U
£€ £20 (£20)
⛳ 3 miles N of Wick on A99
🖥 www.wickgolfclub.fsnet.co.uk

Inverness

Abernethy (1893)
Nethy Bridge, PH25 3EB
☎ (01479) 821305
🏠 (01479) 821305
📧 info@abernethygolfclub.com
🏠 450
✍ RH Robbie
🏌 9 L 2520 yds SSS 66
👥 U SOC
£€ £13 (£16)
⛳ 5 miles S of Grantown (B970)
🖥 www.abernethygolfclub.com

Alness (1904)
Ardross Rd, Alness, Ross-shire, IV17 0QA
☎ (01349) 883877
📧 info@alnessgolfclub.co.uk
🏠 300
✍ Mrs M Rogers
🏌 18 L 4886 yds Par 67 SSS 64
👥 U SOC
£€ £13 (£15)
⛳ ¼ mile N of Alness. 20 miles N of Inverness

🏠 I Scott Taylor
🖥 www.alness.com

Boat-of-Garten (1898)
Boat-of-Garten, PH24 3BQ
☎ (01479) 831282
🏠 (01479) 831523
📧 boatgolf@enterprise.net
🏠 650
✍ P Smyth
🏌 18 L 5967 yds SSS 69
👥 U–booking advisable
£€ £29 D–£34 (£34 D–£39)
⛳ 27 miles SE of Inverness (A95)
🏠 James Braid
🖥 www.boatgolf.com

Carrbridge (1980)
Carrbridge, PH23 3AU
☎ (01479) 841623 (Clubhouse)
📧 enquiries@carrbridgegolf
🏠 550
✍ Gordon Calmer
🏌 9 L 2623 yds Par 71 SSS 68
👥 U exc comp days–NA
£€ D–£16 (D–£18)
⛳ 20 miles SE of Inverness, off A9
🖥 www.carrbridgegolf.com

Fort Augustus (1926)
Pay and play
Markethill, Fort Augustus, PH32 4AU
📧 info@fagc.co.uk
🏠 110
✍ J Morgan (01320) 366758
🏌 9 L 5454 yds SSS 67
👥 U
£€ £12 D–£15
⛳ W end of Fort Augustus on A82
🏠 Harry S Colt
🖥 www.fagc.co.uk

Fort William (1974)
North Road, Fort William, PH33 6SN
☎ (01397) 704464
🏠 430
✍ R Macintyre
🏌 18 L 5686 metres SSS 71
👥 U
£€ £22
⛳ 3 miles N of Fort William (A82)
🏠 JR Stutt

Fortrose & Rosemarkie (1888)
Ness Road East, Fortrose, IV10 8SE
☎ (01381) 620529
🏠 (01381) 621328
📧 secretary@fortrosegolfclub.co.uk
🏠 830
✍ M MacDonald
🏌 18 L 5885 yds Par 71 SSS 69
👥 U SOC
£€ £25 (£30)
⛳ Black Isle, 12 miles N of Inverness
⊕ Driving range; 2 putting greens
🏠 James Braid
🖥 www.fortrosegolfclub.co.uk

Grantown-on-Spey (1890)
Golf Course Road, Grantown-on-Spey, PH26 3HY
☎ (01479) 872079
🏠 (01479) 873725
📧 secretary @grantownonspeygolfclub.co.uk
🏠 800
✍ JS Macpherson
🏌 18 L 5710 yds Par 70 SSS 68
👥 WD–U WE–U after 10am SOC
£€ £20 D–£25 (£25 D–£30)
⛳ E side of Grantown (A95)
🏠 Park/Braid/Brown
🖥 www.grantownonspeygolfclub.co.uk

Invergordon (1893)
King George Street, Invergordon, IV18 0BD
☎ (01349) 852715
🏠 170 30(L) 50(J)
🏌 18 L 6030 yds Par 69 SSS 69
👥 U SOC
£€ £20
⛳ 15 miles NE of Dingwall (A9/B817)
🏠 A Rae (1994)

Inverness (1883)
Culcabock Road, Inverness, IV2 3XQ
☎ (01463) 239882
🏠 (01463) 239882
🏠 1100
✍ JS Thomson
✓ AP Thomson (01463) 231989
🏌 18 L 6226 yds SSS 70
👥 WE/BH–restricted SOC
£€ £29 D–£39 (£29 D–£39)
⛳ 1 mile S of Inverness
🏠 James Braid
🖥 www.invernessgolfclub.co.uk

Kingussie (1891)
Gynack Road, Kingussie, PH21 1LR
☎ (01540) 661374 (Clubhouse)
🏠 (01540) 662066
🏠 800
✍ ND MacWilliam (01540) 661600
✓ None
🏌 18 L 5555 yds SSS 68
👥 U
£€ £20 D–£25 (£25 D–£28)
⛳ Kingussie (A9)
🏠 H Vardon
🖥 www.kingussie-golf.co.uk

Loch Ness (1996)
Castle Heather, Inverness, IV2 6AA
☎ (01463) 713334/5
🏠 (01463) 712695
📧 info@golflochness.com
🏠 600
✍ ND Hampton (01463) 713335
✓ M Piggot (01463) 713334
🏌 18 L 6772 yds Par 73 SSS 72
👥 U SOC
£€ D–£25 (D–£30)
⛳ Culduthel, SW Inverness (A9)
⊕ Floodlit driving range
🖥 www.golflochness.com

Muir of Ord (1875)

Great North Road, Muir of Ord, IV6 7SX
☎ **(01463) 870825**
📠 (01463) 871867
✉ muirgolf@supanet.com
🏛 700
♘ Mrs J Gibson
⚒ Shop (01463) 871311
⛳ 18 L 5557 yds SSS 68
👥 U SOC
💶 D–£16 (£20) WD–£50 WE £20 (£25)
🚗 15 miles N of Inverness (A862)
🏚 James Braid

Nairn (1887)

Seabank Road, Nairn, IV12 4HB
☎ **(01667) 453208**
📠 (01667) 456328
✉ bookings@nairngolfclub.co.uk
🏛 1330
♘ D Corstorphine (01667) 453208
⚒ R Fyfe (01667) 452787
⛳ 18 L 6705 yds Par 72 SSS 74
9 hole course
👥 U SOC
💶 On application
🚗 Nairn West Shore (A96). 15 miles E of Inverness
🏚 Old Tom Morris/Braid/Simpson
■ www.nairngolfclub.co.uk

Nairn Dunbar (1899)

Lochloy Road, Nairn, IV12 5AE
☎ **(01667) 452741**
📠 (01667) 456897
✉ secretary@nairndunbar.com
🏛 900
♘ JS Falconer
⚒ DH Torrance (01667) 453964
⛳ 18 L 6765 yds SSS 74 SR 139
👥 U
💶 £37.50 D–£50 (£45 D–£60)
🚗 In Nairn
■ www.nairndunbar.com

Newtonmore (1893)

Golf Course Road, Newtonmore, PH20 1AT
☎ **(01540) 673878**
📠 (01540) 670147
✉ secretary@newtonmoregolf.com
🏛 450
♘ C Bisset
⚒ R Henderson (01540) 673611
⛳ 18 L 6029 yds SSS 69
👥 U SOC
💶 £18 D–£22 (£20 D–£27)
🚗 4 miles W of Kingussie. 46 miles S of Inverness
■ www.newtonmoregolf.com

Spean Bridge

Spean Bridge, Fort William, PH33
🏛 65
⚒ K Dalziel (01397) 703907
⛳ 9 hole course SSS 63
👥 U
💶 D–£12
🚗 9 miles N of Fort William on A82

Strathpeffer Spa (1888)

Golf Course Road, Strathpeffer, IV14 9AS
☎ **(01997) 421011/421219**
📠 (01997) 421011
🏛 360 50(L) 85(J)
♘ Gayle Anderson (01997) 421011
⛳ 18 L 4792 yds SSS 64
👥 U SOC
💶 £18 D–£23
🚗 ¼ mile N of Strathpeffer. 5 miles W of Dingwall
⊕ Putting green + small practice area
🏚 Willie Park/Tom Morris
■ www.strathpeffergolf.co.uk

Tain (1890)

Chapel Road, Tain, IV19 1JE
☎ **(01862) 892314**
📠 (01862) 892099
✉ info@tain-golfclub.co.uk
🏛 500
♘ Mrs KD Ross
⚒ None
⛳ 18 L 6404 yds SSS 71
👥 U
💶 £33 D–£40 (£40 D–£50)
🚗 35 miles N of Inverness (A9). 8 miles S of Dornoch
🏚 Tom Morris
■ www.tain-golfclub.co.uk

Tarbat (1909)

Portmahomack, Tain, IV20 1YB
☎ **(01862) 871486**
📠 (01862) 871598
🏛 240
♘ Christina Ince
⛳ 9 L 2568 yds SSS 65
👥 U SOC
💶 D–£12
🚗 10 miles E of Tain

Torvean (1962)

Public
Glenurquhart Road, Inverness, IV3 8JN
☎ **(01463) 711434 (Starter)**
📠 (01463) 225651 (Sec)
✉ info@torveangolfclub.com
🏛 750
♘ Atholl S Menzies (Mgr) (01463) 225651
⚒ None
⛳ 18 L 5784 yds SSS 68
👥 U
💶 £15 (£18)
🚗 SW of Inverness on A82 1 mile from city centre

Orkney & Shetland

Orkney (1889)

Grainbank, Kirkwall, Orkney, KW15 1RD
☎ **(01856) 872457**
📠 (01856) 872457
🏛 415
♘ GR Donaldson (01856) 877533
⛳ 18 L 5411 yds SSS 67
👥 U

💶 D–£15 W–£50
🚗 1 mile W of Kirkwall
■ www.orkneygc.co.uk

Sanday (1977)

Sanday, Orkney, KW17 2BW
☎ **(01857) 600341**
📠 (01857) 600341
🏛 20
♘ R Thorne
⛳ 9 L 2600 yds Par 35 SSS 36
👥 U
💶 £15 per annum
🚗 2 miles N of Lady on B9069

Shetland (1891)

Dale, Gott, Shetland, ZE2 9SB
☎ **(01595) 840369**
📠 (01595) 840369
🏛 400
♘ E Groat
⛳ 18 L 5776 yds SSS 68
👥 U
💶 D–£15
🚗 3 miles N of Lerwick (A907)
🏚 Fraser Middleton
■ www.shetlandgolfclub.co.uk

Stromness (1890)

Stromness, Orkney, KW16 3DU
☎ **(01856) 850772**
🏛 250
♘ GA Bevan (01856) 850885
⛳ 18 L 4762 yds SSS 63
👥 U
💶 D–£15
🚗 Stromness, 16 miles W of Kirkwall on Hoy Sound
■ www.stromnessgc.co.uk

Whalsay (1976)

Skaw Taing, Whalsay, Shetland, ZE2 9AL
☎ **(01806) 566450/566481**
🏛 100
♘ C Hutchison
⚒ None
⛳ 18 L 6009 yds Par 70 SSS 68
👥 U SOC
💶 £10
🚗 5 miles N of Symbister Ferry

West Coast

Askernish (1891)

Lochboisdale, Askernish, South Uist, HS81 5ST
☎ **(01878) 710312**
🏛 50
♘ A MacIntyre
⛳ 18 L 5114 yds SSS 67
👥 U
💶 £10
🚗 5 miles NW of Lochboisdale
🏚 Tom Morris Sr

Barra

Cleat, Castlebay, Isle of Barra, HS9 5XX
☎ **(01871) 810591**

☎ (01871) 810418
▷ 9 L 2396 yds
👥 U
££ D–£5
⛳ 6 miles N of Castlebay

Gairloch (1898)

Gairloch, IV21 2BQ
☎ (01445) 712407
✉ secretary@gairlochgc.freeserve
.co.uk
🏠 285
🖊 A Shinkins
▷ 9 L 2281 yds SSS 64
👥 U–phone first
££ D–£15 W–£55
⛳ 60 miles W of Dingwall in Wester
Ross
■ www.gairlochgolfclub.co.uk

Isle of Harris

Scarista, Isle of Harris, HS5 3HX
☎ (01859) 520331
✉ harrisgolf@ic24.net
🏠 72
🖊 J MacLean
✔ None
▷ 9 L 2442 yds Par 68 SSS 64
👥 U
££ £10 (£10)
⛳ 13 miles S of Tarbert on W coast
■ www.harrisgolf.com

Isle of Skye (1964)

Sconser, Isle of Skye, IV48 8TD
☎ (01478) 650414
🏠 250
🖊 I Macmillan
▷ 9 L 4798 yds Par 66 SSS 64
👥 U
££ D–£15
⛳ Between Broadford and Sligachan

Lochcarron (1908)

Lochcarron, Strathcarron, IV54 8YU
🏠 124
🖊 AG Beattie ((01520) 766211
▷ 9 L 3575 yds Par 60 SSS 60
👥 U exc Sat 2–5pm–NA
££ D–£10 W–£40
⛳ ¹/₂ mile E of Lochcarron in Wester
Ross
■ www.lochcarrongolf.co.uk

Skeabost (1982)

Skeabost Bridge, Isle of Skye, IV51 9NP
☎ (01470) 532202
🏠 (01470) 532454
🏠 80
🖊 DJ Matheson (01470) 532319
(Skeabost House Hotel)
▷ 9 L 3224 yds SSS 59
👥 U
££ D–£13
⛳ 6 miles NW of Portree on
Dunvegan road

Stornoway (1890)

*Lady Lever Park, Stornoway, Isle of
Lewis, HS2 0XP*
☎ (01851) 702240

🏠 400
🖊 KW Galloway (01851) 702533
▷ 18 L 5252 yds Par 68 SSS 67
👥 U exc Sun–NA SOC
££ D–£15 W–£45
⛳ Off A857 in Lews Castle, Isle of
Lewis
■ www.stornowaygolfclub.co.uk

Traigh (1947)

Arisaig, Inverness-shire, PH39 4NT
☎ (01687) 450337
🏠 160
🖊 A Macintyre (01687) 462431
✔ None
▷ 9 L 2456 yds Par 68 SSS 65
👥 U
££ D–£14
⛳ 2 miles N of Arisaig off A830 Fort
William-Mallaig road
🏛 John Salvesen; redesigned and
enlarged 1995
■ www.traighgolf.co.uk

Lanarkshire

Airdrie (1877)

Rochsoles, Airdrie, ML6 0PQ
☎ (01236) 762195
🏠 (01236) 760584
✉ airdrie.golfclub@virgin.net
🏠 450
🖊 DM Hardie
✔ J Carver (01236) 754360
▷ 18 L 6004 yds SSS 69
👥 M I WE/BH–NA SOC
££ £20 D–£25
⛳ Airdrie 1 mile
🏛 James Braid

Bellshill (1905)

*Community Road, Orbiston, Bellshill,
ML4 2RZ*
☎ (01698) 745124
🏠 680
🖊 T McLaughlin
▷ 18 L 5900 yds Par 69 SSS 69
👥 WD–U Sun–NA before 1.30pm
SOC
££ D–£24 (£30)
⛳ 30 miles W (A725) M74 Junction 5

Biggar (1895)

Public
*The Park, Broughton Road, Biggar,
ML12 6AH*
☎ (01899) 220618 (Clubhouse)
(01899) 220319 (Bookings)
🏠 140
🖊 T Rodger (01698) 382311
✔ None
▷ 18 L 5537 yds SSS 67
👥 U–booking recommended
££ £10 (£12)
⛳ 12 miles SE of Lanark (A702)
🏛 Willie Park

Blairbeth (1910)

*Burnside, Rutherglen, Glasgow,
G73 4SF*
☎ (0141) 634 3355 (Clubhouse)

🏠 450
🖊 TI Whyte (0141) 634 3325
▷ 18 L 5518 yds SSS 68
👥 SOC–WD
££ On application
⛳ 1 mile S of Rutherglen

Bothwell Castle (1922)

*Blantyre Road, Bothwell, Glasgow,
G71 8PJ*
☎ (01698) 853177
🏠 (01698) 854052
🏠 1000
🖊 DA McNaught (01698) 854052
✔ A McCloskey (01698) 852052
▷ 18 L 6225 yds SSS 70
👥 WD–U 9.30–10.30am &
2.30–3.30pm
££ £24 D–£32
⛳ 2 miles N of Hamilton. M74
Junction 5

Calderbraes (1891)

*57 Roundknowe Road, Uddingston,
G71 7TS*
☎ (01698) 813425
🏠 300
🖊 S McGuigan (0141) 773 2287
▷ 9 L 5046 yds Par 66 SSS 67
👥 WD–U WE–M
££ D–£12
⛳ Start of M74

Cambuslang (1892)

*30 Westburn Drive, Cambuslang,
G72 7NA*
☎ (0141) 641 3130
🏠 200 100(L) 75(J)
🖊 RM Dunlop
▷ 9 L 5942 yds SSS 69
👥 M
££ On application
⛳ Cambuslang Station ³/₄ mile

Carluke (1894)

*Hallcraig, Mauldslie Road, Carluke,
ML8 5HG*
☎ (01555) 770574/771070
🏠 (01555) 770574
🏠 460 100(L)
🖊 T Pheely (01555) 770574
✔ C Ronald (01555) 751053
▷ 18 L 5805 yds SSS 68
👥 WD–U before 4pm WE/BH–NA
SOC
££ £23 D–£28
⛳ 20 miles SE of Glasgow

Carnwath (1907)

1 Main Street, Carnwath, ML11 8JX
☎ (01555) 840251
🏠 (01555) 841070
🏠 582
🖊 Mrs L McPate
✔ None
▷ 18 L 5955 yds SSS 69
👥 WD–U before 4pm Sat–NA
Sun–restricted
££ £18 D–£28 Sun–£24 D–£34
⛳ 7 miles E of Lanark

For list of abbreviations and key to symbols see page 627

Cathkin Braes   (1888)

Cathkin Road, Rutherglen, Glasgow,
G73 4SE
- ☎ (0141) 634 6605
- ☏ (0141) 630 9186
- ✉ golf@cathkinbraes.freeserve.co.uk
- 🏠 930
- ♘ DE Moir
- ✒ S Bree (0141) 634 0650
- ⛳ 18 L 6208 yds SSS 71
- 👥 WD–I
- £€ £25
- 🚗 5 miles S of Glasgow (B759)
- ⛴ James Braid
- ■ www.cathkinbraesgolfclub.co.uk

Coatbridge Municipal (1971)

Public
Townhead Road, Coatbridge, ML52 2HX
- ☎ (01236) 28975
- ⛳ 18 L 6020 yds SSS 69
- 👥 U
- £€ On application
- 🚗 Townhead, E of Glasgow. ¹/₂ mile E of M73
- ⊕ Driving range

Colville Park   (1923)

Jerviston Estate, Motherwell, ML1 4UG
- ☎ (01698) 263017
- ☏ (01698) 230418
- 🏠 900 64(L) 140(J)
- ♘ L Innes (01698) 262808
- ✒ J Stark (01698) 265779
- ⛳ 18 L 6301 yds Par 71 SSS 70
- 👥 WD–U 11am–3pm (exc Fri–NA) WE–NA SOC–WD
- £€ £15 D–£25
- 🚗 1 mile NE of Motherwell on A723
- ⛴ James Braid

Crow Wood   (1925)

Cumbernauld Road, Muirhead, Glasgow,
G69 9JF
- ☎ (0141) 799 2011
- ☏ (0141) 779 9148
- 🏠 700
- ♘ FM Davidson (0141) 779 4954
- ✒ B Moffat (0141) 779 1943
- ⛳ 18 L 6168 yds Par 71 SSS 70
- 👥 WD–H (prior notice required) SOC
- £€ £23 D–£34
- 🚗 5 miles NE of Glasgow, off A80
- ⛴ James Braid

Dalziel Park   (1997)

100 Hagen Drive, Motherwell, ML1 5RZ
- ☎ (01698) 862862
- ☏ (01698) 862863
- 🏠 400
- ♘ I Donnachie
- ✒ None
- ⛳ 18 L 6137 yds Par 70
- 👥 WD–U SOC
- £€ £20
- 🚗 5 miles E of Motherwell via A723 and B7029
- ⊕ Driving range
- ⛴ Nigel Williams

Douglas Water   (1922)

Rigside, Lanark, ML11 9NB
- ☎ (01555) 880361
- 🏠 190
- ♘ D Hogg
- ⛳ 9 L 2916 yds SSS 69
- 👥 U exc Sat–restricted
- £€ £8 (£10)
- 🚗 7 miles S of Lanark. M74 Junctions 11 & 12

Drumpellier   (1894)

Drumpellier Ave, Coatbridge, ML5 1RX
- ☎ (01236) 424139/428723
- ☏ (01236) 428723
- ✉ administrator@drumpelliergc .freeserve.co.uk
- 🏠 500
- ♘ JM Craig
- ✒ JM Carver (01236) 432971
- ⛳ 18 L 6227 yds SSS 70
- 👥 I
- £€ £30 D–£40
- 🚗 8 miles E of Glasgow
- ⛴ James Braid
- ■ www.drumpellier.com

East Kilbride   (1900)

Chapelside Road, Nerston, East Kilbride,
G74 4PH
- ☎ (01355) 220913 (Clubhouse)
- 🏠 850
- ♘ WG Gray (01355) 247728
- ✒ P McKay (01355) 222192
- ⛳ 18 L 6402 yds SSS 71
- 👥 M SOC–WD
- £€ £25 D–£35
- 🚗 8 miles S of Glasgow

Easter Moffat   (1922)

Mansion House, Plains, Airdrie,
ML6 8NP
- ☎ (01236) 842878
- ☏ (01236) 842904
- ✉ secretary@emgc.org.uk
- 🏠 500
- ♘ G Miller (01236) 620972
- ✒ G King (01236) 843015
- ⛳ 18 L 6221 yds SSS 70
- 👥 WD only
- £€ £20 D–£30
- 🚗 3 miles E of Airdrie

Hamilton   (1892)

Riccarton, Ferniegair, Hamilton,
ML3 7UE
- ☎ (01698) 282872
- 🏠 500
- ♘ GM Chapman (01698) 459537
- ✒ R Forrest (01698) 282324
- ⛳ 18 L 6255 yds SSS 71
- 👥 M or by arrangement with Sec
- £€ On application
- 🚗 1¹/₂ miles S of Hamilton
- ⛴ James Braid

Hollandbush   (1954)

Public
Acre Tophead, Lesmahagow, Coalburn,
ML11 0JS
- ☎ (01555) 893484

- 🏠 420
- ♘ R Lynch
- ✒ I Rae (01555) 893646
- ⛳ 18 L 6246 yds SSS 70
- 👥 U
- £€ £8.20 (9.50)
- 🚗 10 miles SW of Lanark, off A74, between Lesmahagow and Coalburn

Kirkhill   (1910)

Greenlees Road, Cambuslang, Glasgow,
G72 8YN
- ☎ (0141) 641 3083 (Clubhouse)
- ☏ (0141) 641 8499
- 🏠 570
- ♘ C Downes (0141) 641 8499
- ✒ D Williamson (0141) 641 7972
- ⛳ 18 L 6030 yds SSS 70
- 👥 WD–by prior arrangement WE/BH–NA SOC
- £€ On application
- 🚗 Cambuslang, SE Glasgow
- ⛴ James Braid

Lanark   (1851)

The Moor, Lanark, ML11 7RX
- ☎ (01555) 663219
- ☏ (01555) 663219
- ✉ lanarkgolfclub@talk21.com
- 🏠 520 130(L) 150(J)
- ♘ GH Cuthill
- ✒ A White (01555) 661456
- ⛳ 18 L 6306 yds SSS 71 9 hole course
- 👥 WD–U until 4pm WE–M
- £€ 18 hole: £30 D–£40 9 hole: £7
- 🚗 30 miles S of Glasgow, off A74
- ⛴ Tom Morris

Langlands   (1985)

Public
Langlands Road, East Kilbride,
G75 0QQ
- ☎ (01355) 248173
- ☎ (01355) 224685 (Starter)
- ☏ (01355) 248121
- 🏠 350
- ♘ A Craik (01355) 248401
- ⛳ 18 L 6201 yds Par 70 SSS 70
- 👥 U
- £€ £8.70 (£10.10)
- 🚗 2 miles SE of East Kilbride, off Strathaven Road
- ⛴ F Hawtree

Larkhall

Public
Burnhead Road, Larkhall, Glasgow
- ☎ (01698) 881113
- 🏠 150
- ♘ M Mallinson
- ⛳ 9 L 6234 yds SSS 70
- 👥 U exc Tues 5–8pm & Sat 7am–5pm
- £€ On application
- 🚗 SW of Larkhall on B7109. 10 miles SE of Glasgow

Leadhills   (1935)

2 Gowan Bank, Leadhills, ML16 6YB
- ☎ (01654) 74356

For list of abbreviations and key to symbols see page 627

☎ (01654) 74356
🏫 40
🏌 N Davies
➢ 9 L 2177 yds SSS 64
👥 U
£€ D–£5 (£5)
🏌 6 miles S of Abington, off A74

Mount Ellen (1905)

Lochend Road, Gartcosh, Glasgow, G69 9EY
☎ (01236) 872277
🖥 (01236) 872249
🏫 480
🏌 WJ Dickson
✍ G Reilly
➢ 18 L 5525 yds SSS 68
👥 WD–U from 9am–4pm WE–NA
£€ On application
🏌 8 miles NE of Glasgow, W of M73

Mouse Valley (1993)

East End, Cleghorn, Lanark, ML11 8NR
☎ (01555) 870015
🖥 (01555) 870022
📧 info@kames-golf-club.com
🏫 300
➢ 18 L 6300 yds SSS 72
9 L 2200 yds SSS 65
👥 U
£€ 18 hole: £15 (£20) 9 hole: £8 (£11)
🏌 2 miles W of Carnwath on A721
⛳ Graham Taylor
■ www.kames-golf-club.com

Shotts (1895)

Blairhead, Benhar Road, Shotts, ML7 5BJ
☎ (01501) 820431
🏫 700
🏌 GT Stoddart (01501) 825868
✍ J Strachan (01501) 822658
➢ 18 L 6205 yds SSS 70
👥 WD–U Sat–NA before 4.30pm
£€ £18 (£26)
🏌 18 miles E of Glasgow on B7057. M8 Junction 5, 1¹/₂ miles
⛳ James Braid

Strathaven (1908)

Glasgow Road, Strathaven, ML10 6NL
☎ (01357) 520421
🖥 (01357) 520539
📧 manager@strathavengolfclub .fsbusiness.co.uk
🏫 1000
🏌 AW Wallace
✍ S Kerr (01357) 521812
➢ 18 L 6226 yds SSS 71
👥 WD–I before 4pm WE–NA
£€ £26 D–£36
🏌 N of Strathaven, off Glasgow road (A726)

Strathclyde Park

Public
Mote Hill, Hamilton, ML3 6BY
☎ (01698) 429350
🏫 200
🏌 K Will
✍ W Walker (01698) 285511

➢ 9 L 6350 yds SSS 70
👥 U exc medal days (phone booking)
£€ 18 holes: £7 (£8.20) – adult; 9 holes: £1.75 (£2.05) – junior
🏌 Hamilton. M74 Junction 5
⊕ Driving range

Torrance House (1969)

Public
Strathaven Road, East Kilbride, Glasgow, G75 0QZ
☎ (01355) 248638
🏫 650
🏌 JB Asher (01355) 249720
✍ J Dunlop (013552) 33451
➢ 18 L 6415 yds SSS 71
👥 U
£€ £16
🏌 S of East Kilbride, off Strathaven road (A726)

Wishaw (1897)

55 Cleland Road, Wishaw, ML2 7PH
☎ (01698) 372869 (Clubhouse)
🖥 (01698) 357480
📧 jwdouglas@btconnect.com
🏫 475 100(L)
🏌 JW Douglas (01698) 357480
✍ S Adair (01698) 358247
➢ 18 L 5999 yds SSS 69
👥 WD–U until 4pm NA–sat WE–Sun
£€ £20 D–£30 Sun–£25 D–£35
🏌 N of Wishaw town centre
⛳ James Braid

Lothians

East Lothian

Aberlady (1912)

Club
Aberlady, EH32 0RB
📧 ithomps3@aol.com
🏫 43
🏌 I Thompson (01875) 870029
➢ Play over Kilspindie course

Bass Rock (1873)

Club
22 Smileyknowes Court, North Berwick, EH39 4RG
📧 andelsthor@lineone.net
🏫 110
🏌 A Thorburn (01620) 893391
➢ Play over North Berwick

Castle Park (1994)

Pay and play
Gifford, Haddington, EH41 4PL
☎ (01620) 810733
🖥 (01620) 810723
📧 stuartfortune@aol.com
🏫 375
🏌 S Fortune (01620) 810733
✍ D Small (01368) 862872
➢ 18 L 6121 yds Par 72 SSS 70
👥 U SOC
£€ £20 D–£28 (£25 D–£35)

🏌 2 miles S of Gifford on Longyester road
⊕ Driving range
■ www.castleparkgolfclub.co.uk

Dirleton Castle (1854)

Club
15 The Pines, Gullane, EH31 2DT
☎ (01620) 843591
🏫 100
🏌 J Taylor
➢ Play over Gullane courses

Dunbar (1856)

East Links, Dunbar, EH42 1LL
☎ (01368) 862317
🖥 (01368) 865202
📧 secretary@dunbargolfclub.co.uk
🏫 998
🏌 Liz Thom
✍ J Montgomery (01368) 862086
➢ 18 L 6404 yds Par 71 SSS 71
👥 U SOC–exc Thurs
£€ £40 D–£55 (£50 D–£70)
🏌 ¹/₂ mile E of Dunbar. 30 miles E of Edinburgh, off A1
⛳ Tom Morris
■ www.dunbar-golfclub.co.uk

Gifford (1904)

Edinburgh Road, Gifford, EH41 4JE
☎ (01620) 810591 (Starter)
📧 thesecretary@giffordgolfclub.fsnet .co.uk
🏫 570
🏌 G MacColl (01620) 810267
➢ 9 L 6050 yds SSS 69
👥 U–booking required
£€ 18 holes–£15 D–£25
🏌 4 miles S of Haddington. 20 miles SE of Edinburgh (B6355)
⛳ Willie Watt

Glen (North Berwick) (1906)

East Links, Tantallon Terrace, North Berwick, EH39 4LE
☎ (01620) 892726
🖥 (01620) 895447
📧 secretary@glengolfclub.co.uk
🏫 650
🏌 K Fish
✍ Shop (01620) 894596
➢ 18 L 6243 yds SSS 70
👥 U–booking recommended
£€ £28 D–£38 (£38 D–£50)
🏌 20 miles E of Edinburgh, off A198
⛳ Braid/Sayers/Mackenzie Ross
■ www.glengolfclub.co.uk

Gullane (1882)

Gullane, EH31 2BB
☎ (01620) 842255 (Starter)
🖥 (01620) 842327
📧 manager@gullanegolfclub.com
🏫 870 300(L) 60(J)
🏌 SC Owram (01620) 842255
✍ AL Good (01620) 843111
➢ No 1 18 L 6466 yds SSS 72
No 2 18 L 6244 yds SSS 71
No 3 18 L 5252 yds SSS 66
6 hole children's course

♀️ No 1–H Nos 2/3–U
£€ No 1 £72 D–£95 (£87) No 2 £30
    D–£41 (£36) No 3 £18 D–£25 (£25)
    Children's course free
⊶ 18 miles E of Edinburgh on A198
⊕ Advance booking advisable
■ www.gullanegolfclub.com

Haddington (1865)
Amisfield Park, Haddington, EH41 4PT
☎ **(01620) 823627**
🖵 (01620) 826580
✉ hadd.golf1@tesco.net
📖 650
♪ DM Swarbrick (Mgr)
✏ J Sandilands (01620) 822727
ℙ 18 L 6317 yds SSS 70
♀️ WD–U WE–U 10am–12 & 2–4pm
£€ £20 (£30)
⊶ 17 miles E of Edinburgh on A1. ³/4
    mile E of Haddington

The Honourable Company of Edinburgh Golfers
(1744)
Muirfield, Gullane, EH31 2EG
☎ **(01620) 842123**
🖵 (01620) 842977
📖 625
♪ Gp Capt JA Prideaux
ℙ 18 L 6673 yds SSS 73
    (Championship L 7034 yds)
♀️ WD–Tues & Thurs I H
    WE/BH–NA SOC
£€ 1 round £100, 2 rounds £130
⊶ NE outskirts of Gullane, opposite
    sign for Greywalls Hotel on A198

Kilspindie (1867)
Aberlady, EH32 0QD
☎ **(01875) 870358**
🖵 (01875) 870358
✉ kilspindie@btconnect.com
📖 400 150(L) 70(J)
♪ PB Casely
✏ GJ Sked (01875) 870695
ℙ 18 L 5012 m SSS 66
♀️ Phone Sec in advance WD–U after
    9.45am WE–U after 11am SOC
£€ £28.50 D–£45 (£35 D–£57)
⊶ Aberlady, 17 miles E of Edinburgh
♠ Ross/Sayers

Longniddry (1921)
Links Road, Longniddry, EH32 0NL
☎ **(01875) 852141**
🖵 (01875) 853371
✉ secretary@longniddrygolfclub
    .co.uk
📖 1100
♪ N Robertson
✏ WJ Gray (01875) 852228
ℙ 18 L 6260 yds SSS 70
♀️ WD–U H SOC–WD after 9.18am
£€ £35 D–£50 (£45)
⊶ 13 miles E of Edinburgh, off A1
♠ HS Colt
■ www.longniddrygolfclub.co.uk

Luffness New (1894)
Aberlady, EH32 0QA
☎ **(01620) 843114**
🖵 (01620) 842933
✉ lngc@talk21.com
📖 700
♪ Gp Capt AG Yeates
    (01620) 843336
✏ None
ℙ 18 L 6122 yds SSS 70
♀️ H or I XL before 10am
    WE/BH–NA SOC
£€ £45 D–£65
⊶ 1 mile W of Gullane (A198)
♠ Morris/Braid

Musselburgh (1938)
Monktonhall, Musselburgh, EH21 6SA
☎ **(0131) 665 2005**
✉ secretary@themusselburghgolfclub
    .com
📖 1000
♪ P Millar
✏ F Mann (0131) 665 7055
ℙ 18 L 6725 yds SSS 73
♀️ WD–U before 4.30pm WE–NA
    before 10am
£€ £25 (£30)
⊶ 1 mile S of Musselburgh on B6415
♠ James Braid
■ www.themusselburghgolfclub.com

Musselburgh Old Course
Public
*10 Balcarres Road, Musselburgh,
EH21 7SD*
☎ **(0131) 665 6981**
    (0131) 665 5438 (Starter)
✉ mocgc@breathemail.net
📖 200
♪ L Freedman (0131) 665 4861
✏ None
ℙ 9 L 5748 yds SSS 69
♀️ WD/BH–U WE–U after 1pm
£€ 9 holes–£8
⊶ 7 miles E of Edinburgh on A1
■ www.musselburgholdlinks.co.uk

North Berwick (1832)
*West Links, Beach Road, North Berwick,
EH39 4BB*
☎ **(01620) 895040**
🖵 (01620) 893274
✉ northberwickgc@aol.com
📖 324
♪ NA Wilson (01620) 895040
✏ D Huish (01620) 893233
ℙ 18 L 6420 yds SSS 71
♀️ U H
£€ £45 D–£70 (£70) Winter–£25
    D–£25 (£30)
⊶ Centre of North Berwick. 24 miles
    E of Edinburgh (A198)

Royal Musselburgh (1774)
*Prestongrange House, Prestonpans,
EH32 9RP*
☎ **(01875) 810276**
    (advance bookings)
🖵 (01875) 810276
✉ royalmusselburgh@btinternet.com

📖 800
♪ TH Hardie (Sec/Mgr) J Hanratty
    (Golf Sec) (01875) 819000
✏ J Henderson (01875) 810139
ℙ 18 L 6237 yds SSS 70
♀️ U SOC
£€ £25 D–£35 (£35)
⊶ 8 miles E of Edinburgh on B1361
    North Berwick road
♠ James Braid
■ www.royalmusselburgh.co.uk

Tantallon (1853)
Club
32 Westgate, North Berwick, EH39 4AH
☎ **(01620) 892114**
🖵 (01620) 894399
📖 300
♪ DA Leckie
ℙ Play over North Berwick West
    Links

Thorntree (1856)
Club
*Prestongrange House, Prestonpans,
EH32 9RP*
☎ **(01875) 810139**
📖 100
♪ C Mackie
ℙ Play over Royal
    Musselburgh course

Whitekirk (1995)
Whitekirk, North Berwick, EH39 5PR
☎ **(01620) 870300**
🖵 (01620) 870330
✉ countryclub@whitekirk.com
📖 400
♪ D Brodie
✏ P Wardell
ℙ 18 L 6526 yds Par 72 SSS 72
♀️ U SOC
£€ £20 (£30)
⊶ 3 miles SE of North Berwick
    (A198)
⊕ Practice range
♠ Cameron Sinclair
■ www.whitekirk.com

Winterfield (1935)
Public
*St Margarets, North Road, Dunbar,
EH42 1AU*
☎ **(01368) 862280**
✉ kevinphillips@tiscali.co.uk
📖 350
✏ K Phillips (01368) 863562
ℙ 18 L 5053 yds SSS 65
♀️ U
£€ On application–phone Pro
⊶ W side of Dunbar. 28 miles E of
    Edinburgh (A1)

Midlothian

Baberton (1893)
*50 Baberton Avenue, Juniper Green,
Edinburgh, EH14 5DU*
☎ **(0131) 453 4911**
🖵 (0131) 453 4678

babertongolfclub@btinternet.com
900
BM Flockhart (0131) 453 4911
K Kelly (0131) 453 3555
18 L 6129 yds SSS 70
WD–U Sun – 2–4pm
££ £25 D–£35 (£28 D–£38)
5 miles SW of Edinburgh (A70)
Willie Park Jr
www.baberton.co.uk

Braid Hills (1893)
Public
Braid Hills Road, Edinburgh, EH10 6JY
☎ (0131) 447 6666 (Starter)
No 1 18 L 5731 yds Par 71 SSS 68
No 2 18 L 4832 yds Par 66 SSS 64
U–phone Starter. No 2 course
closed Sun
££ £11 (£14)
3 miles S of Edinburgh (A702)
⊕ No 2 course open Apr-Oct
Ferguson/McEwan

Braids United (1897)
Club
22 Braid Hills Approach, Edinburgh,
EH10 6JY
☎ (0131) 452 9408
60
WJ Mitchell (0131) 476 2238
Play over Braids 1

Broomieknowe (1905)
36 Golf Course Road, Bonnyrigg,
EH19 2HZ
☎ (0131) 663 9317
(0131) 663 2152
500
JD Fisher
M Patchett (0131) 660 2035
18 L 6200 yds Par 70
WD–U WE/BH–NA
££ £19 D–£25 (£25)
7 miles SE of Edinburgh
Braid/Hawtree
www.broomieknowe.com

Bruntsfield Links Golfing Society (1761)
The Clubhouse, 32 Barnton Avenue,
Edinburgh, EH4 6JH
☎ (0131) 336 2006
(0131) 336 5538
secretary@bruntsfield.sol.co.uk
1130
Cdr DM Sandford (0131) 336 1479
B Mackenzie (0131) 336 4050
18 L 6407 yds SSS 71
WD–U WE–apply to Sec SOC–H
££ £42 D–£60 (£47 D–£65)
3 miles NW of Edinburgh, off A90
at Davidson Mains
Willie Park/Mackenzie/Hawtree

Carrick Knowe (1930)
Public
Glendevon Park, Edinburgh, EH12 5VZ
☎ (0131) 337 1096 (Starter)
18 L 6184 yds SSS 68

U–phone Starter
££ £12.50
3 miles W of Edinburgh centre

Craigentinny (1891)
Public
Fillyside Road, Edinburgh EH7
☎ (0131) 554 7501 (Starter)
18 L 5418 yds SSS 66
U–phone Starter
££ £8.80–£9.65
2½ miles NE of Edinburgh

Craigmillar Park (1895)
1 Observatory Road, Edinburgh,
EH9 3HG
☎ (0131) 667 2837
craigmillarparkgc@lineone.net
440 120(L) 70(J)
B Knowles (0131) 667 0047
B McGhee (0131) 667 2850
18 L 5859 yds SSS 69
WD–I or H before 3.30pm
WE/BH–NA
££ On application
Blackford, S of Edinburgh
James Braid

Duddingston (1895)
Duddingston Road West, Edinburgh,
EH15 3QD
☎ (0131) 661 7688
(0131) 652 6057
generalmanager@duddingston-
golf-club.com
600
IF Sproule (0131) 661 7688
A McLean (0131) 661 4301
18 L 6473 yds SSS 72
WD–U WE–phone Pro SOC–Tues
& Thurs
££ £35 D–£45 SOC–£25 D–£35
SE Edinburgh
www.duddingston-golf-club.com

Glencorse (1890)
Milton Bridge, Penicuik, EH26 0RD
☎ (01968) 677177
(01968) 674399
700
W Oliver (01968) 677189
C Jones (01968) 676481
18 L 5217 yds Par 64 SSS 66
WD–U SOC–WD/Sun pm
££ £25 (£32)
8 miles S of Edinburgh (A701)
Willie Park

Kings Acre (1997)
Pay and play
Lasswade, EH18 1AU
☎ (0131) 663 3456
(0131) 663 7076
info@kings-acregolf.com
Lizzie King
A Murdoch (0131) 663 3456
18 L 6031 yds Par 70
Junior Par 3 course
U SOC
££ £19 (£26)
3 miles S of Edinburgh, off A720

⊕ Floodlit driving range
Graeme Webster
www.kings-acregolf.com

Kingsknowe (1907)
326 Lanark Road, Edinburgh,
EH14 2JD
☎ (0131) 441 1144
(0131) 441 2079
819
LI Fairlie (0131) 441 1145
C Morris (0131) 441 4030
18 L 5981 yds SSS 69
WD–U before 4pm WE–phone Pro
SOC–WD before 4pm
££ £20 (£30)
SW Edinburgh
Herd/Braid

Liberton (1920)
297 Gilmerton Road, Edinburgh,
EH16 5UJ
☎ (0131) 664 3009
(0131) 666 0853
797
I Seath (0131) 664 1056
18 L 5170 yds SSS 65
WD–U before 5pm WE–NA before
2pm
££ £20 (£30)
3 miles S of Edinburgh

Lothianburn (1893)
106a Biggar Road, Edinburgh,
EH10 7DU
☎ (0131) 445 2206
lothianburngc@golfers.net
600 75(L) 100(J)
WFA Jardine (0131) 445 5067
K Mungall (0131) 445 2288
18 L 5662 yds SSS 68 Par 71
WD–U before 4.30pm –M after
4.30pm WE–NA SOC–H
££ £16.50 D–£22.50 (£22.50
D–£27.50)
S of Edinburgh, on A702.
Lothianburn exit from Edinburgh
by-pass
⊕ Motorised buggies for hire
James Braid (1928)
www.lothianburngolfclub.com

Marriott Dalmahoy Hotel & CC
Dalmahoy, Kirknewton, EH27 8EB
☎ (0131) 335 8010
(0131) 335 3577
I Burns (Golf Dir),
Mrs JM Bryans (Sec)
N Graham
East 18 L 6677 yds SSS 72
West 18 L 5185 yds SSS 66
WD–U H SOC–WD
££ East–£65 (£80) West–£45 (£55)
7 miles W of Edinburgh on A71
⊕ Floodlit driving range
James Braid

Melville Golf Centre   (1995)

Proprietary
Lasswade, Edinburgh, EH18 1AN
☎ (0131) 663 8038 (range, shop, tuition), (0131) 654 0224 (course)
📠 (0131) 654 0814
✉ golf@melvillegolf.co.uk
🔲 60
♠ Mr & Mrs MacFarlane (Props)
✓ G Carter (0131) 663 8038
▷ 9 L 4604 yds Par 66 SSS 62
👥 U SOC
££ £9–£16 (£11–£20)
⛳ 7 miles S of Edinburgh, signposted off city by-pass on A7 (South)
⊕ Floodlit golf range, practice bunker, Pay & Play 9-hole course
🏠 G Webster
■ www.melvillegolf.co.uk

Merchants of Edinburgh (1907)

10 Craighill Gardens, Morningside, Edinburgh, EH10 5PY
☎ (0131) 447 1219
📠 (0131) 446 9833
✉ admin@merchantsgolf.com
🔲 983
♠ J Elvin
✓ NEM Colquhoun (0131) 447 8709
▷ 18 L 4889 yds SSS 64
👥 WD–U before 4pm –M after 4pm WE–M SOC–WD
££ £16
⛳ SW of Edinburgh, off A701
🏠 Braid/Letters
■ www.merchantsgolf.com

Mortonhall   (1892)

231 Braid Road, Edinburgh, EH10 6PB
☎ (0131) 447 2411
📠 (0131) 447 8712
✉ clubhouse@mortonhallgc.co.uk
🔲 1000
♠ Ms BM Giefer (0131) 447 6974
✓ MT Leighton (0131) 447 5185
▷ 18 L 6502 yds SSS 72
👥 SOC WE–NA before 10.30
££ £35 (£45)
⛳ 2 miles S of Edinburgh on A702
🏠 James Braid/FW Hawtree
■ www.mortonhallgc.co.uk

Murrayfield   (1896)

43 Murrayfield Road, Edinburgh, EH12 6EU
☎ (0131) 337 1009
📠 (0131) 313 0721
🔲 815
♠ Mrs MK Thomson (0131) 337 3478
✓ Kieron Stevenson (0131) 337 3479
▷ 18 L 5794 yds Par 70 SSS 69
👥 WD–I WE–M
££ £30 (£35)
⛳ 2 miles W of Edinburgh centre

Newbattle   (1896)

Abbey Road, Eskbank, Dalkeith, EH22 3AD
☎ (0131) 663 2123

📠 (0131) 654 1810
✉ newbattlegolf@freeuk.com
🔲 600
♠ HG Stanners (0131) 663 1819
✓ S McDonald (0131) 660 1631
▷ 18 L 6025 yds SSS 70
👥 WD–U before 4pm WE–M
££ £20 D–£30
⛳ 6 miles S of Edinburgh on A7 and A68
🏠 HS Colt

Portobello   (1853)

Public
Stanley Street, Portobello, Edinburgh, EH15 1JJ
☎ (0131) 669 4361 (Starter)
▷ 9 L 2405 yds SSS 64
👥 U–phone Starter
££ £8.80–£9.65
⛳ 4 miles E of Edinburgh

Prestonfield   (1920)

6 Priestfield Road North, Edinburgh, EH16 5HS
☎ (0131) 667 9665
📠 (0131) 667 9665
✉ prestonfield@btclick.com
🔲 900
♠ AS Robertson
✓ J Macfarlane (0131) 667 8597
▷ 18 L 6214 yds SSS 70 Par 70
👥 WD–U WE–Sun after 3.00pm SOC–WD
££ £22 D–£33
⛳ 2 miles SE of Edinburgh, off A7 Dalkeith Road
🏠 Peter Robertson
■ www.prestonfieldgolfclub.co.uk

Ratho Park   (1928)

Ratho, Edinburgh, EH28 8NX
☎ (0131) 335 0069
📠 (0131) 333 1752
✉ secretary.rpgc@btinternet.com
🔲 550 106(L) 72(J)
♠ JS Yates (0131) 335 0068
✓ A Pate (0131) 333 1406
▷ 18 L 5932 yds SSS 68
👥 U SOC–Tues/Wed/Thurs
££ £25 D–£35 (£35)
⛳ 8 miles W of Edinburgh centre (A71)
🏠 James Braid
■ www.rathoparkgolfclub.com

Ravelston   (1912)

24 Ravelston Dykes Road, Edinburgh, EH4 3NZ
☎ (0131) 315 2486
🔲 610
♠ Jim Lowrie
▷ 9 L 5218 yds SSS 66
👥 WD–H
££ WD–£15
⛳ Off Queensferry Road (A90). Turn S at Blackhall
🏠 James Braid

Royal Burgess Golfing Society of Edinburgh   (1735)

181 Whitehouse Road, Barnton, Edinburgh, EH4 6BU
☎ (0131) 339 2075
📠 (0131) 339 3712
✉ secretary@royalburgess.co.uk
🔲 635 60(J)
♠ G Seeley (0131) 339 2075
✓ S Brian (0131) 339 6474
▷ 18 L 6486 yds Par 71 SSS 71
👥 I SOC
££ £40 D–£55 (£75)
⛳ Queensferry Road (A90)
🏠 Tom Morris
■ www.royalburgess.co.uk

Silverknowes   (1947)

Public
Silverknowes Parkway, Edinburgh, EH4 5ET
☎ (0131) 336 3843 (Starter)
▷ 18 L 6214 yds SSS 70
👥 U–phone Starter
££ £11 (£13.50)
⛳ 4 miles N of Edinburgh

Swanston   (1927)

111 Swanston Road, Fairmilehead, Edinburgh, EH10 7DS
☎ (0131) 445 2239
📠 (0131) 445 2239
🔲 500
♠ J Allan
✓ S Pardoe (0131) 445 4002
▷ 18 L 5004 yds SSS 65
👥 U exc comp days–NA WE–NA after 1pm
££ £15 D–£20 (£20 D–£25)
⛳ S of Edinburgh, off Biggar road (A702) Edinburgh By-pass
■ www.swanstongolfclub.com

Torphin Hill   (1895)

Torphin Road, Edinburgh, EH13 0PG
☎ (0131) 441 1100
📠 (0131) 441 7166
🔲 450
♠ AJ Hepburn
✓ J Browne
▷ 18 L 5230 yds SSS 66
👥 WD–U WE–U exc comp days SOC
££ D–£14 (D–£20)
⛳ SW boundary of Edinburgh

Turnhouse   (1897)

154 Turnhouse Road, Corstorphine, Edinburgh, EH12 0AD
☎ (0131) 339 1014
📠 (0131) 339 1844
🔲 640
♠ DEJ Cullum (0131) 441 5119
✓ J Murray (0131) 339 7701
▷ 18 L 6153 yds SSS 70
👥 WD WE
££ On application
⛳ W of Edinburgh (A9080)
■ www.turnhousegc.com

For list of abbreviations and key to symbols see page 627

Vogrie   (1990)

Pay and play
*Vogrie Estate Country Park, Gorebridge,
EH23 4NU*
☎ **(01875) 821716**
ⱶ 9 hole course Par 66
⋔ U
£€ £5.70
♣ SE of Edinburgh, off A68 (B6372)

West Lothian

Bathgate   (1892)

Edinburgh Road, Bathgate, EH48 1BA
☎ **(01506) 652232**
⎙ (01506) 636775
▦ 580
✍ WA Osborne (01506) 630505
⌁ S Strachan (01506) 630553
ⱶ 18 L 6328 yds SSS 70
⋔ U
£€ £20 (£25)
♣ 15 miles W of Edinburgh. M8
Junction 4
🛉 Wm Park Sr

Bridgend & District   (1994)

*Willowdean, Bridgend, Linlithgow,
EH49 6NW*
☎ **(01506) 834140**
⎙ (01506) 834706
✍ Linda Dalgliesh
ⱶ 9 L 5192 yds Par 68 SSS 67
⋔ U
£€ £10 (£12)
♣ Nr Linlithgow
■ www.bridgendgolfclub.co.uk

Deer Park CC   (1978)

*Golf Course Road, Knightsridge,
Livingston, EH54 8AB*
☎ **(01506) 446699**
⎙ (01506) 435608
✉ deerpark@muir-group.co.uk
▦ 850
⌁ B Dunbar
ⱶ 18 L 6688 yds SSS 72
⋔ U SOC
£€ £26 (£38)
♣ N of Livingston. M8 Junction 3

Dundas Parks   (1957)

South Queensferry, EH30 9SS
▦ 550
✍ Mrs C Wood (0131) 319 1347
ⱶ 9 L 6056 yds SSS 70
⋔ M I SOC
£€ D–£12
♣ Dundas Estate (Private). 1 mile S of
Queensferry (A8000)
■ www.dundasparks.co.uk

Greenburn   (1953)

*6 Greenburn Road, Fauldhouse,
EH47 9HG*
☎ **(01501) 770292**
✉ secretary@greenburngolfclub
.fsnet.co.uk
▦ 500

✍ Alan Harris (Club Admin)
⌁ Scott Catlin (01501) 771187
ⱶ 18 L 6210 yds SSS 71
⋔ U
£€ On application
♣ 4 miles S of M8 Junction 4
(East)/Junction 5 (West)

Harburn   (1933)

West Calder, EH55 8RS
☎ **(01506) 871256**
⎙ (01506) 870286
▦ 600 80(L) 120(J)
✍ J McLinden (01506) 871131
⌁ S Mills (01506) 871582
ⱶ 18 L 5921 yds SSS 69
⋔ U
£€ £20 (£27)
♣ 2 miles S of W Calder on B7008,
via A70 or A71

Linlithgow   (1913)

Braehead, Linlithgow, EH49 6QF
☎ **(01506) 842585**
⎙ (01506) 842764
▦ 430
✍ WS Christie
⌁ S Rosie (01506) 844356
ⱶ 18 L 5729 yds SSS 68
⋔ U exc Sat–NA SOC
£€ £20 D–£25 Sun–£25 D–£30
♣ SW of Linlithgow, off M9
🛉 Robert Simpson

Niddry Castle   (1983)

Castle Road, Winchburgh, EH52 2RQ
☎ **(01506) 891097**
▦ 500
✍ G McLeod
ⱶ 9 L 5914 yds SSS 69
⋔ U
£€ £13 (£19)
♣ 10 miles W of Edinburgh (B9080)

Polkemmet   (1981)

Public
Whitburn, Bathgate, EH47 0AD
☎ **(01501) 743905**
ⱶ 9 L 2967 metres SSS 37
⋔ U
£€ £5.10 (£5.95)
♣ Between Whitburn and Harthill on
B7066. M8 Junctions 4/5
⊕ Driving range

Pumpherston   (1895)

*Drumshoreland Road, Pumpherston,
EH53 0LH*
☎ **(01506) 432869/433336**
⎙ (01506) 438250
▦ 533 29(L) 126(J)
✍ I McArthur (01506) 854584
⌁ R Fyvie (01506) 433337
ⱶ 18 L 6006 yds Par 70 SSS 69
⋔ WD–U SOC–WD
£€ On application
♣ 14 miles W of Edinburgh. M8
Junction 3
🛉 Glen Andrews
■ www.pumpherstongolfclub.com

Rutherford Castle   (1998)

West Linton, EH46 7AS
☎ **(01968) 661233**
⎙ (01968) 661233
✉ info@ruth-castlegc.co.uk
▦ 150
⌁ None
ⱶ 18 L 6558 yds Par 72 SSS 71
⋔ U SOC
£€ £15 (£25)
♣ 10 miles S of Edinburgh on A702
🛉 Bryan Moor
■ www.ruth-castlegc.co.uk

Uphall   (1895)

Houston Mains, Uphall, EH52 6JT
☎ **(01506) 856404**
⎙ (01506) 855358
✉ uphallgolfclub@business-
unmetered.com
▦ 650
✍ WA Crighton
⌁ G Law (01506) 855553
ⱶ 18 L 5588 yds Par 69 SSS 67
⋔ U
£€ £15 D–£20 (£20 D–£30)
♣ 7 miles W of Edinburgh Airport
(A8). M8 Junction 3

West Linton   (1890)

Medwun Road, West Linton, EH46 7HN
☎ **(01968) 660970**
⎙ (01968) 660970
▦ 750 100 (J)
✍ JS Macnab (01968) 660970
⌁ I Wright (01968) 660256
ⱶ 18 L 6132 yds SSS 70
⋔ WD–U WE–phone Pro
£€ £25 D–£40 (£40)
♣ 18 miles S of Edinburgh on A702.

West Lothian   (1892)

Airngath Hill, Linlithgow, EH49 7RH
☎ **(01506) 826030**
⎙ (01506) 826462
▦ 850
✍ I Osborough
⌁ I Taylor (01506) 825060
ⱶ 18 L 6249 yds SSS 70
⋔ WD–NA after 4pm WE–by
arrangement
£€ On application
♣ 1 mile N of Linlithgow, towards
Bo'ness
⊕ Buggies for hire
🛉 W Park Jr/Adams/Middleton
■ www.thewestlothiangolfclub.co.uk

Moray

Buckpool   (1933)

Barhill Road, Buckie, AB56 1DU
☎ **(01542) 832236**
⎙ (01542) 832236
✉ golf@buckpoolgolf.com
▦ 500
✍ Miss M Coull
ⱶ 18 L 6257 yds SSS 70
⋔ U

££   £13 D–£15 (£20 D–£25)
⚭   W end of Buckpool, ¹/₂ mile off
A98
🖥   www.buckpoolgolf.com

Dufftown   (1896)

Tomintoul Road, Dufftown, AB55 4BS
☎   **(01340) 820325**
🖳   (01340) 820325
📖   310
🏌   Mrs M Swann (Admin)
✓   None
🏴   18 L 5308 yds SSS 67
👤   U
££   £12 D–£15
⚭   1 mile SW of Dufftown on B9009
🖥   www.dufftowngolfclub.com

Elgin   (1906)

Hardhillock, Birnie Road, Elgin,
IV30 8SX
☎   **(01343) 542338**
🖳   (01343) 542341
📖   854 113(L) 150(J)
🏌   DF Black
✓   K Stables (01343) 542884
🏴   18 L 6411 yds SSS 71
👤   WD–U after 9.30am WE–U after
10am SOC–WD SOC–WE by
arrangement
££   £28 D–£38
⚭   1 mile S of Elgin on A941
⊕   Driving range
🏠   John MacPherson
🖥   www.elgingolfclub.com

Forres   (1889)

Muiryshade, Forres, IV36 2RD
☎   **(01309) 672949**
📖   950 150(J)
🏌   David Mackintosh
✓   S Aird (01309) 672250
🏴   18 L 6141 yds SSS 70
👤   U SOC
££   £24 (£22)
⚭   1 mile SE of Forres, off B9010

Garmouth & Kingston   (1932)

Garmouth, Fochabers, IV32 7NJ
☎   **(01343) 870388**
🖳   (01343) 870388
📖   600
🏌   A Robertson (01343) 870231
🏴   18 L 5935 yds SSS 69
👤   U SOC
££   £18 D–£18 (£22 D–£25)
⚭   8 miles NE of Elgin

Hopeman   (1909)

Hopeman, Moray, IV30 5YA
☎   **(01343) 830578**
🖳   (01343) 830152
📧   hopemangc@aol.com
📖   700
🏌   J Fraser (01343) 835068
🏴   18 L 5590 yds SSS 67
👤   WD–U Sat–NA before 10am and
12.30–2pm Sun–NA before 9am
SOC

££   £16 (£21)
⚭   7 miles NW of Elgin on B9012
🏠   J McKenzie
🖥   www.hopeman-golf-club.co.uk

Moray   (1889)

Stotfield Road, Lossiemouth,
IV31 6QS
☎   **(01343) 812018**
🖳   (01343) 815102
📧   secretary@moraygolf.co.uk
📖   1500
🏌   SM Crane
✓   A Thomson (01343) 813330
🏴   Old 18 L 6643 yds SSS 73
New 18 L 6005 yds SSS 69
👤   U H SOC
££   On application
⚭   6 miles N of Elgin
⊕   Practice range
🏠   Old Tom Morris
🖥   www.moraygolf.co.uk

Spey Bay   (1904)

Spey Bay Hotel, Spey Bay, Fochabers,
IV32 7PJ
☎   **(01343) 820424**
🖳   (01343) 829282
📧   info@speybay.com
📖   200
🏌   I Ednie (Gen Mgr)
🏴   18 L 6092 yds Par 70 SSS 70
👤   U
££   £20 (£25)
⚭   7 miles W of Buckie, off A96
(B9104)
⊕   Driving range
🏠   Ben Sayers
🖥   www.speybay.com

Perth & Kinross

Aberfeldy   (1895)

Taybridge Road, Aberfeldy, PH15 2BH
☎   **(01887) 820535**
🖳   (01887) 820535
📖   200
🏌   AR Menzies (01887) 820535
🏴   18 L 5600 yds Par 68 SSS 66
👤   U
££   £18 (£23)
⚭   10 miles W of Ballinluig, off A9
🏠   Souters

Alyth   (1894)

Pitcrocknie, Alyth, PH11 8HF
☎   **(01828) 632268**
🖳   (01828) 633491
📖   850
🏌   J Docherty
✓   T Melville (01828) 632411
🏴   18 L 6205 yds SSS 70
👤   U SOC
££   On application
⚭   16 miles NW of Dundee (A91)
🏠   Tom Morris/James Braid
🖥   www.alythgolfclub.co.uk

Auchterarder   (1892)

Ochil Road, Auchterarder, PH3 1LS
☎   **(01764) 662804**
🖳   (01764) 664423
📧   secretary@auchterardergolf.co.uk
📖   820
🏌   WM Campbell
✓   G Baxter (01764) 663711
🏴   18 L 5757 yds SSS 68
👤   U SOC
££   £22 D–£33 (£27 D–£43)
⚭   1 mile SW of Auchterarder
🖥   www.auchterardergolf.co.uk

Bishopshire   (1903)

Pay and play
Kinnesswood, Kinross, KY13
📖   150
🏌   J Proudfoot (01592) 780203
🏴   10 L 4700 metres SSS 64
👤   U
££   £5 (£10)
⚭   3 miles E of Kinross (A911). M90
Junction 7
🏠   W Park

Blair Atholl   (1896)

Invertilt Road, Blair Atholl, PH18 5TG
☎   **(01796) 481407**
🖳   (01796) 481751
📖   445
🏌   T Boon
🏴   9 L 5816 yds SSS 68
👤   U
££   £16 (£18)
⚭   35 miles N of Perth, off A9

Blairgowrie   (1889)

Rosemount, Blairgowrie, PH10 6LG
☎   **(01250) 872594**
🖳   (01250) 875451
📧   office@theblairgowriegolfclub
.co.uk
📖   1200
🏌   JN Simpson (Managing Sec)
(01250) 872622
✓   C Dernie (01250) 873116
🏴   Rosemount 18 L 6588 yds SSS 72
Landsdowne 18 L 6895 yds
SSS 73; Wee 9 L 4614 yds SSS 63
👤   Mon/Tues/Thurs–U H 8am–12 &
2–3.30pm Wed/Fri/WE–restricted
££   On application
⚭   1 mile S of Blairgowrie, off A93.
15 miles N of Perth
🏠   Rosemount-Braid; Lansdowne-
Alliss/Thomas; Wee-Old Tom
Morris
🖥   www.theblairgowriegolfclub.co.uk
www.blairgowrie.golf.co.uk

Callander   (1890)

Aveland Road, Callander, FK17 8EN
☎   **(01877) 330090**
🖳   (01877) 330062
📧   callandergc@nextcall.net
📖   500
🏌   Mrs S Smart
✓   A Martin (01877) 330975
🏴   18 L 5185 yds SSS 65
👤   U SOC

£€ £20 (£30)
⬦ Off A84, E end of Callander
🏠 Tom Morris
◼ www.callander.co.uk

Comrie (1891)
Laggan Braes, Comrie, PH6 2LR
☎ (01764) 670055
✉ enquiries@comriegolf.co.uk
🛏 400
🎁 S van der Walt (01764) 670055
↦ 9 L 3020 yds Par 70 SSS 70
👤 U exc Mon & Tues
£€ £16 (£20)
⬦ 7 miles W of Crieff (A85)
◼ www.comriegolf.co.uk

Craigie Hill (1911)
Cherrybank, Perth, PH2 0NE
☎ (01738) 620829
📠 (01738) 620829
✉ CGCH@fairieswell.freeserve.co.uk
🛏 625
🎁 A Tunnicliffe (01738) 620829
✔ I Muir (01738) 622644
↦ 18 L 5386 yds SSS 67
👤 U exc Sat
£€ £18 (£25)
⬦ W boundary of Perth
🏠 Fernie/Anderson
◼ www.craigiehill.scottishgolf.com

Crieff (1891)
Perth Road, Crieff, PH7 3LR
☎ (01764) 652909 (Bookings)
📠 (01764) 655096
✉ secretary@crieffgolf.co.uk
🛏 735
🎁 JS Miller (01764) 652397
✔ DJW Murchie
↦ Ferntower 18 L 6402 yds SSS 72
     Dornock 9 L 4772 yds SSS 63
👤 U H NA–12–2pm or after 5pm
     SOC
£€ Ferntower £28 (£38) Dornock £15
⬦ 1 mile NE of Crieff (A85). 17 miles
     W of Perth
🏠 James Braid
◼ www.crieffgolf.co.uk

Dalmunzie (1948)
Glenshee, Blairgowrie, PH10 7QG
☎ (01250) 885226
📠 (01250) 885225
🛏 80
🎁 S Winton (Mgr)
↦ 9 L 2099 yds SSS 60
👤 U
£€ D–£12.50
⬦ 22 miles N of Blairgowrie on A93.
     (Dalmunzie Hotel sign)

Dunkeld & Birnam (1892)
Fungarth, Dunkeld, PH8 0HU
☎ (01350) 727524
📠 (01350) 728660
✉ richbrrnc@aol.com
🛏 550
🎁 RD Barrance
✔ None
↦ 18 L 5511 yds SSS 70

👤 WD–U WE–phone first
£€ On application
⬦ Dunkeld 1 mile, off A923. 15 miles
     N of Perth
◼ www.dunkeldandbirnamgolfclub
     .co.uk

Dunning (1953)
Rollo Park, Dunning, PH2 0QX
☎ (01764) 684747
🛏 580
🎁 R Weetman (01764) 684897
↦ 9 L 4894 yds Par 66 SSS 63
👤 WD–U Sat–NA before 4pm
£€ £14 (£16)
⬦ 9 miles SW of Perth, off A9 on
     B9141

Foulford Inn (1995)
Pay and play
Crieff, PH7 3LN
☎ (01764) 652407
📠 (01764) 652407
✉ foulford@btconnect.com
🎁 M Beaumont
↦ 9 hole Par 3 course
👤 U
£€ £4 D–£6
◼ www.foulfordinn.co.uk

The Gleneagles Hotel
Auchterarder, PH3 1NF
☎ (01764) 694360 (Golf)
     (01764) 662231 (Hotel)
✉ golf.gleneagles@gleneagles.com
🎁 G Marchbank (Golf Dir)
✔ S Smith (01764) 694343
↦ King's 18 L 6471 yds SSS 71
     Queen's 18 L 5965 yds SSS 69
     PGA Centenary 18 L 7081 SSS 74
     9 hole Par 3 course
👤 U
£€ May–Sept £110
⬦ 16 miles SW of Perth on A9
⊕ Driving range. Golf academy
🏠 Braid/Nicklaus
◼ www.gleneagles.com

Glenisla (1998)
Proprietary
Pitcrocknie Farm, Alyth, PH11 8JJ
☎ (01828) 632445
📠 (01828) 633749
🛏 300
🎁 E Wilson (Admin)
↦ 18 L 6402 yds Par 71 SSS 72
👤 U H
£€ £22 (£26)
⬦ Nr Alyth (B954)
◼ www.golf-glenisla.co.uk

Green Hotel Golf Courses (1900)
2 The Muirs, Kinross, KY13 8AS
☎ (01577) 863407
📠 (01577) 863180
✉ golf@green-hotel.com
🛏 450
🎁 Eileen Gray
↦ Red 18 L 6257 yds SSS 70
     Blue 18 L 6456 yds SSS 71

👤 U
£€ £15 D–£25 (£25 D–£35)
⬦ Half mile from M90 J7
◼ www.green-hotel.com

Kenmore (1992)
Pay and play
*Mains of Taymouth, Kenmore, Aberfeldy,
PH15 2HN*
☎ (01887) 830226
📠 (01887) 829059
✉ golf@taymouth.co.uk
🛏 120
🎁 R Menzies (Mgr)
✔ None
↦ 9 L 6052 yds SSS 69
👤 U SOC
£€ 9 holes–£10 (£11) 18 holes–£15
     (£16)
⬦ Kenmore, 6 miles W of Aberfeldy
     on A827
🏠 D Menzies & Partners
◼ www.taymouth.co uk

Killin (1911)
Killin, FK21 8TX
☎ (01567) 820312
📠 (01567) 820312
✉ info@killingolfclub.co.uk
🛏 253
🎁 TL Taylor (01764) 683778
↦ 9 L 5016 yds Par 66 SSS 65
👤 U SOC–Apr–Oct
£€ £15 (£15)
⬦ Killin, W end of Loch Tay
🏠 John Duncan
◼ www.killingolfclub.co.uk

King James VI (1858)
Moncreiffe Island, Perth, PH2 8NR
☎ (01738) 625170
     (01738) 632460 (Starter)
📠 (01738) 445132
✉ info@kjvigc.fsnet.co.uk
🛏 675
🎁 Mrs H Blair (01738) 445132
✔ A Crerar (01738) 632460
↦ 18 L 5664 yds SSS 69
👤 U exc Sat Sun–by reservation
£€ £18 D–£25 Sun D–£30
⬦ Island in River Tay, Perth
🏠 Tom Morris
◼ www.kingjamesvi.co.uk

Milnathort (1910)
*South Street, Milnathort, Kinross,
KY13 9XA*
☎ (01577) 864069
✉ milnathortgolf@ukgateway.net
🛏 575
🎁 K Dziennik (Admin. Mgr)
↦ 9 L 5985 yds SSS 69
👤 U SOC
£€ £13 D–£19 (£15 D–£21)
⬦ 1 mile N of Kinross. M90 Junction
     6/7

Muckhart (1908)
*Drumburn Road, Muckhart, Dollar,
FK14 7JH*
☎ (01259) 781423

For list of abbreviations and key to symbols see page 627

☎ (01259) 781544
✉ enquiries@muckhartgolf.com
📖 550 125(L) 100(J)
✍ CA Page
✓ K Salmoni (01259) 781493
⊳ 27 L 5895-6174 yds SSS 70-72
👤 U SOC
££ £20 D–£30 (£25 D–£35)
🚗 A91, 3 miles E of Dollar, towards
  Rumbling Bridge
■ www.muckhartgolf.com

Murrayshall (1981)
Murrayshall, New Scone, Perth,
PH2 7PH
☎ (01738) 554804
🖷 (01738) 552595
✉ info@murrayshall.co.uk
📖 300
✍ A Bryan (Mgr)
✓ AT Reid (01738) 552784
⊳ Murrayshall 18 L 6441 yds SSS 72
  Lynedoch 18 L 5362 yds SSS 69
👤 U SOC
££ Murrayshall £30 D–£45 Lynedoch
  £20 D–£35
🚗 3 miles NE of Perth, off A94
⊕ Driving range
🏠 Hamilton Stutt

Muthill (1911)
Peat Road, Muthill, PH5 2DA
☎ (01764) 681523
🖷 (01764) 681557
✉ muthillgolfclub@lineone.com
📖 350
✍ J Elder (01764) 681523
⊳ 9 L 2371 yds SSS 63
👤 U SOC
££ £15 (£18)
🚗 3 miles S of Crieff on A822
■ www.muthillgolfclub.co.uk

North Inch
Public
c/o Perth & Kinross Council, 5 High
Street, Perth, PH1 5JS
☎ (01738) 636481 (Starter)
✍ G Harbut (01738) 475215
⊳ 18 L 4340 metres SSS 65
👤 U SOC
££ On application
🚗 Nr Perth and A9, by River Tay.
  Signs to Bell's Sports Centre

Pitlochry (1909)
Pitlochry Estate Office, Pitlochry,
PH16 5NE
☎ (01796) 472792 (Bookings)
🖷 (01796) 473947 (bookings)
📖 498
✍ DCM McKenzie JP
  (01796) 472114
✓ M Pirie (01796) 472792
⊳ 18 L 5811 yds SSS 69
👤 U SOC
££ On application
🚗 N side of Pitlochry (A9). 28 miles
  NW of Perth
🏠 Fernie/Hutchison

Royal Perth Golfing Society (1824)
Club
1/2 Atholl Crescent, Perth, PH1 5NG
☎ (01738) 622265
🖷 (01764) 664049
📖 250
✍ DP McDonald (Gen Sec)
  (01738) 622265, L Rutherford
  (Golf Sec) (01764) 664049
⊳ Play over North Inch, Perth &
  Strathmore courses

St Fillans (1903)
South Lochearn Rd, St Fillans,
PH26 2NJ
☎ (01764) 685312
✉ stfillansgolf@aol.com
📖 400
✍ J Stanyon (01764) 685300
⊳ 9 L 6054 yds SSS 69
👤 U SOC
££ £15 (£20)
🚗 12 miles W of Crieff, on A85
🏠 W Auchterlonie
■ www.st-fillans-golf.com

Strathmore Golf Centre (1995)
Pay and play
Leroch, Alyth, Blairgowrie, PH11 8NZ
☎ (01828) 633322
🖷 (01828) 633533
📖 350
✍ C Spencer
✓ A Lamb
⊳ 18 L 6454 yds Par 72 SSS 72
  9 L 1666 yds Par 29 SSS 58
👤 U SOC
££ Prices on application
🚗 5 miles E of Blairgowrie, off A926
⊕ Floodlit driving range
🏠 John Salvesen

Strathtay (1909)
Lyon Cottage, Strathtay, Pitlochry,
PH9 0PG
☎ (01887) 840211
📖 237
✍ IA Ramsay
⊳ 9 L 4082 yds SSS 63
👤 U exc Thurs–NA after 5pm Sat–NA
  10–10.30am Sun–NA 1–4pm SOC
££ D–£10
🚗 4 miles W of Ballinluig (A827),
  towards Aberfeldy

Taymouth Castle (1923)
Kenmore, Aberfeldy, PH15 2NT
☎ (01887) 830228
🖷 (01887) 830228
📖 200
✍ AA MacTaggart (Golf Dir)
✓ G Dott
⊳ 18 L 6066 yds SSS 69
👤 U WE–booking essential SOC
££ £22 D–£32 (£26 D–£40)
🚗 6 miles W of Aberfeldy (A827)
🏠 James Braid

Whitemoss (1994)
Whitemoss Road, Dunning, Perth,
PH2 0QX
☎ (01738) 730300
📖 500
✍ S Gaden
✓ None
⊳ 18 L 6200 yds Par 69 SSS 69
👤 U SOC
££ £15 (£15)
🚗 Aberuthven, 10 miles SW of Perth,
  off A9

Renfrewshire

Barshaw (1927)
Public
Barshaw Park, Glasgow Road,
Paisley PA2
☎ (0141) 889 2908
🖷 (0141) 840 2148
📖 60
✍ W Collins (0141) 884 2533
⊳ 18 L 5711 yds SSS 68
👤 U M
££ £8
🚗 1 mile E of Paisley Cross, off A737

Bonnyton (1957)
Eaglesham, Glasgow, G76 0QA
☎ (01355) 302781
🖷 (01355) 303151
📖 950
✍ A Hughes
✓ K McWade (01355) 302256
⊳ 18 L 6255 yds SSS 71
👤 I SOC–WD
££ £40
🚗 2 miles W of Eaglesham. 6 miles S
  of Glasgow

Caldwell (1903)
Caldwell, Uplawmoor, G78 4AU
☎ (01505) 850329
🖷 (01505) 850604
✉ CaldwellGolfClub@aol.com
📖 450
✍ HIF Harper (01505) 850366
✓ S Forbes (01505) 850616
⊳ 18 L 6195 yds SSS 70
👤 WD–booking before 4pm–M after
  4pm WE–M
££ On application
🚗 5 miles SW of Barrhead on A736
  Glasgow-Irvine road
■ www.caldwellgolfclub.i8.com

Cochrane Castle (1895)
Scott Avenue, Craigston, Johnstone,
PA5 0HF
☎ (01505) 320146
🖷 (01505) 325338
✉ secretary@cochranecastle.sol.co.uk
📖 425
✍ Mrs PIJ Quin
✓ A Logan (01505) 328465
⊳ 18 L 6194 yds Par 71 SSS 71
👤 WD–U WE–M
££ £22 (£30)

⚬ ¹/₂ mile S of Beith Road, Johnstone
⌂ Charles Hunter

East Renfrewshire (1922)
Pilmuir, Newton Mearns, G77 6RT
☎ (01355) 500256
⌨ (01355) 500323
⌸ 450
♫ DS McKenzie (Mgr)
☑ S Russell (01355) 500206
▷ 18 L 6097 yds SSS 70
♕ On application
££ £30 D–£40
⚬ 2 miles SW of Newton Mearns
⌂ James Braid

Eastwood (1893)
Muirshield, Loganswell, Newton Mearns, Glasgow G77 6RX
☎ (01355) 500261
⌸ 900
♫ VE Jones (01355) 500280
☑ I Darroch (01355) 500285
▷ 18 L 6071 yds SSS 69
♕ WD SOC
££ £24 D–£30
⚬ 9 miles SW of Glasgow
⌂ Theodore Moone

Elderslie (1908)
63 Main Road, Elderslie, PA5 9AZ
☎ (01505) 323956
⌨ (01505) 340346
⌸ 450
♫ Mrs A Anderson
☑ R Bowman (01505) 320032
▷ 18 L 6165 yds SSS 70
♕ M SOC–WD
££ £24.50 D–£32.50
⚬ 2 miles SW of Paisley

Erskine (1904)
Bishopton, PA7 5PH
☎ (01505) 862302
⌸ 400 140(L)
♫ TA McKillop
☑ P Thomson (01505) 862108
▷ 18 L 6287 yds SSS 70
♕ WD–I WE–M
££ £31
⚬ 5 miles NW of Paisley

Fereneze (1904)
Fereneze Avenue, Barrhead, G78 1HJ
☎ (0141) 881 1519
⌸ 700
♫ G McCreadie (0141) 881 7149
☑ H Lee (0141) 880 7058
▷ 18 L 5962 yds SSS 70
♕ M SOC–WD
££ D–£22
⚬ 9 miles SW of Glasgow

Gleddoch (1974)
Langbank, PA14 6YE
☎ (01475) 540304
⌨ (01475) 540459
⌸ 600
♫ DW Tierney
☑ K Campbell (01475) 540704

▷ 18 L 6375 yds SSS 71
♕ WD–U WE–restricted SOC
££ £30
⚬ 16 miles W of Glasgow (M8/A8)
⌂ J Hamilton Stutt

Gourock (1896)
Cowal View, Gourock, PA19 1HD
☎ (01475) 631001
⌨ (01475) 638307
☑ secretary@gourockgolfclub.com
⌸ 538 98(L) 86(J)
♫ AD Taylor
☑ J Mooney (01475) 636834
▷ 18 L 6408 yds SSS 72
♕ WD–I before 4.30pm SOC
££ £20 (£27)
⚬ 3 miles SW of Greenock, off A770. 7 miles W of Port Glasgow

Greenock (1890)
Forsyth Street, Greenock, PA16 8RE
☎ (01475) 720793
⌨ (01475) 791912
⌸ 500 111(L) 110(J)
♫ EJ Black (01475) 791912
☑ JH Duncan (Starter) (01475) 787236
▷ 18 L 5888 yds SSS 69
9 L 2149 yds SSS 32
♕ WD–U WE/BH–M
££ D–£25 (£30)
⚬ 1 mile SW of Greenock on A8
⌂ James Braid
■ www.greenockgolfclub.co.uk

Kilmacolm (1891)
Porterfield Road, Kilmacolm, PA13 4PD
☎ (01505) 872139
⌨ (01505) 874007
⌸ 888
♫ R Weldin
☑ I Nicholson (01505) 872695
▷ 18 L 5960 yds SSS 69
♕ WD–U WE–M
££ £25 (£30)
⚬ 10 miles W of Paisley (A761)

Lochwinnoch (1897)
Burnfoot Road, Lochwinnoch, PA12 4AN
☎ (01505) 842153
⌨ (01505) 843668
⌸ 600
♫ RJG Jamieson
☑ G Reilly (01505) 843029
▷ 18 L 6243 yds SSS 71
♕ WD–U before 4.30pm SOC–WD
££ £22
⚬ 9 miles SW of Paisley
■ www.lochwinnochgolf.co.uk

Old Ranfurly (1905)
Ranfurly Place, Bridge of Weir, PA11 3DE
☎ (01505) 613612 (Clubhouse)
⌨ (01505) 613214
⌸ 817
♫ QJ McClymont (01505) 613214
☑ D McIntosh
▷ 18 L 6089 yds SSS 70

♕ WD–I WE–M SOC
££ On application
⚬ 7 miles W of Paisley, off A761

Paisley (1895)
Braehead Road, Paisley, PA2 8TZ
☎ (0141) 884 2292 (Clubhouse)
⌨ (0141) 884 3903
☑ paisleygc@onetel.net.uk
⌸ 805
♫ J Hillis (0141) 884 3903
☑ G Stewart (0141) 884 4114
▷ 18 L 6466 yds Par 71 SSS 72
♕ WD–H SOC
££ £24 D–£32
⚬ Glenburn, S of Paisley
⌂ John H Stutt
■ www.paisleygc.com

Port Glasgow (1895)
Devol Farm, Port Glasgow, PA14 5XE
☎ (01475) 704181
☑ honorarysecretary@portglasgowgolfclub.com
⌸ 265
♫ A Hughes (01475) 791214
▷ 18 L 5712 yds SSS 68
♕ WD–U before 5pm –M after 5pm WE–NA SOC
££ £15 D–£20 (£20 D–£30)
⚬ 1 mile S of Port Glasgow

Ranfurly Castle (1889)
Golf Road, Bridge of Weir, PA11 3HN
☎ (01505) 612609
⌨ (01505) 610406
☑ secranfur@aol.com
⌸ 400 160(A) 120(J)
♫ J King
☑ T Eckford (01505) 614795
▷ 18 L 6284 yds SSS 71
♕ WD–H WE–M SOC–WD
££ £25 D–£35
⚬ 7 miles W of Paisley (A761)
⌂ Kirkcaldy/Auchterlonie
■ www.ranfurlycastle.com

Renfrew (1894)
Blythswood Estate, Inchinnan Road, Renfrew, PA4 9EG
☎ (0141) 886 6692
⌨ (0141) 886 1808
☑ secretary@renfrew.scottishgolf.com
⌸ 465 110(L) 80(J)
♫ G Tennant
☑ D Grant (0141) 885 1754
▷ 18 L 6818 yds SSS 73
♕ WD–H WE–M SOC–WD
££ £30
⚬ 3 miles N of Paisley, nr Airport. M8 Junctions 26 or 27
⌂ Cdr JD Harris
■ www.renfrew.scottishgolf.com

Whinhill (1911)
Beith Road, Greenock, PA16
☎ (01475) 24694
⌸ 250
♫ R Kirkpatrick (01475) 719260

✓ None
🏳 18 L 5504 yds SSS 68
👤 U
££ On application
🚗 Upper Greenock-Largs road
🏠 W Fernie

Whitecraigs (1905)

72 Ayr Road, Giffnock, Glasgow, G46 6SW

☎ **(0141) 639 4530**
📠 (0141) 616 3648
📧 wcraigsgc@aol.com
🏢 1150
🏌 AG Keith CA
✓ A Forrow (0141) 639 2140
🏳 18 L 6013 yds SSS 70
👤 WD–U before 5pm WE–M SOC–WD
££ £40
🚗 6 miles S of Glasgow (A77), nr Whitecraigs Station
■ www.thewhitecraigsgolfclub.co.uk

Stirlingshire

Aberfoyle (1890)

Braeval, Aberfoyle, FK8 3UY

☎ **(01877) 382493**
🏢 600
🏌 EJ Barnard (01630) 550847
🏳 18 L 5218 yds SSS 66
👤 WD–U WE–NA before 11.30am
££ £15 D–£20 (£20 D–£28)
🚗 Braeval, 18 miles NW of Stirling (A81)

Balfron (1992)

Kepculloch Road, Balfron, G63 0QP

📧 golfbalfron@aol.com
🏢 475
🏌 I Rubython (01360) 440915
✓ None
🏳 18 L 5903 yds Par 72 SSS 70
👤 WD–U before 4pm WE–restricted SOC
££ £15 (£15)
🚗 18 miles NW of Glasgow, off A81
■ www.balfrongolfsociety.homepage.com

Bonnybridge (1925)

Larbert Road, Bonnybridge, Falkirk, FK4 1NY

☎ **(01324) 812822**
📧 bonnybridgegolfclub@hotmail.com
🏢 425
🏌 J Mullen (01324) 812323
🏳 9 L 6058 yds SSS 70
👤 WD–I SOC
££ £16 D–£20
🚗 3 miles W of Falkirk. M876 Junction 1

Bridge of Allan (1895)

Sunnylaw, Bridge of Allan, Stirling

☎ **(01786) 832332**
🏢 513
🏌 AA Blackstock

🏳 9 L 4932 yds SSS 66
👤 U exc Sat SOC (by arrangement)
££ £14 (£18)
🚗 4 miles N of Stirling, off A9
🏠 Tom Morris Sr
■ bridgeofallangolfclub.com

Buchanan Castle (1936)

Proprietary
Drymen, G63 0HY

☎ **(01360) 660307**
📠 (01360) 660993
🏢 730
🏌 R Kinsella
✓ K Baxter (01360) 660330
🏳 18 L 6047 yds SSS 69
👤 By arrangement with Sec SOC
££ £34 D–£44 (£34 D–£44)
🚗 18 miles NW of Glasgow. 25 miles W of Stirling, off A811
🏠 James Braid

Campsie (1897)

Crow Road, Lennoxtown, Glasgow, G66 7HX

☎ **(01360) 310244**
📧 campsiegolfclub@aol.com
🏢 650
🏌 NP Darroch (01360) 312249
✓ M Brennan (01360) 310920
🏳 18 L 5517 yds SSS 68
👤 WD–U before 4.30pm SOC
££ £20 D–£25 (£25)
🚗 N of Lennoxtown on B822 Fintry road
🏠 Auchterlonie/Stark

Dunblane New (1923)

Perth Road, Dunblane, FK15 0LJ

☎ **(01786) 821521**
📠 (01786) 821522
📧 secretary@dngc.co.uk
🏢 700
🏌 JH Dunsmore
✓ RM Jamieson
🏳 18 L 5930 yds SSS 69
👤 WD–U WE–M SOC
££ £25 (£35)
🚗 E side of Dunblane. 6 miles N of Stirling
🏠 James Braid

Falkirk (1922)

Stirling Road, Camelon, Falkirk, FK2 7YP

☎ **(01324) 611061/612219**
📠 (01324) 639573
📧 carmuirs.fgc@virgin.net
🏢 700
🏌 J Elliott
🏳 18 L 6282 yds SSS 70
👤 WD–U until 4pm Sat–NA SOC–exc Sat
££ £20 D–£30 Sun–£40
🚗 1¹/₂ miles W of Falkirk on A9
🏠 James Braid
■ www.falkirkcarmuirsgolfclub.co.uk

Falkirk Tryst (1885)

86 Burnhead Road, Larbert, FK5 4BD

☎ **(01324) 562415**

📠 (01324) 562054
📧 falkirktrystgc@tiscali.co.uk
🏢 800
🏌 RC Chalmers (01324) 562054
✓ S Dunsmore (01324) 562091
🏳 18 L 6053 yds SSS 69
👤 WD–U WE–M SOC–WD
££ £22 D–£30
🚗 3 miles NW of Falkirk on A88

Glenbervie (1932)

Stirling Road, Larbert, FK5 4SJ

☎ **(01324) 562605**
📠 (01324) 551054
🏢 600
🏌 Donald McKellar
✓ David Ross (01324) 562725
🏳 18 L 6423 yds Par 71 SSS 71
👤 WD–U before 4pm WE–M SOC–Tues & Thurs
££ £30 D–£40
🚗 1 mile N of Larbert on A9. M876 Junction 2
🏠 James Braid

Grangemouth (1973)

Public
Polmonthill, Polmont, FK2 0YA

☎ **(01324) 711500**
📠 (01324) 717087
🏢 700
🏌 I Hutton (Hon)
✓ G McFarlane (01324) 503840
🏳 18 L 6527 yds SSS 70
👤 U–book with Pro SOC
££ £12.50 D–£18 (£16 D–£21.50)
🚗 3 miles NE of Falkirk. M9 Junct 4

Kilsyth Lennox (1900)

Tak-Ma-Doon Road, Kilsyth, G65 0RS

☎ **(01236) 824115 (Bookings)**
📠 (01236) 823089
📧 info@klgs.co.uk
🏢 250
🏌 AG Stevenson (01236) 823213
🏳 18 L 5515 yds Par 68
Temp. layout during major course reconstruction
👤 WD–U until 5pm –M after 5pm Sat–NA before 4pm Sun–NA before 2pm SOC
££ On application
🚗 N of Kilsyth and A803. 12 miles NE of Glasgow

Polmont (1901)

Manuel Rigg, Maddiston, Falkirk, FK2 0LS

☎ **(01324) 711277 (Clubhouse)**
📠 (01324) 712504
🏢 300
🏌 P Lees (01324) 713811
🏳 9 L 3044 yds SSS 70
👤 U exc Sat–NA
££ £8 Sun–£15
🚗 4 miles SE of Falkirk on B805

Stirling (1869)

Queen's Road, Stirling, FK8 3AA

☎ **(01786) 464098**
📠 (01786) 460090

✉ enquiries@stirlinggolfclub.tv
☐ 1000
✍ AMS Rankin (01786) 464098
✓ I Collins (01786) 471490
⊳ 18 L 6409 yds SSS 71
♔ WD–U SOC WE–NA
££ £28 D–£40
⛳ ¹/₂ mile from Stirling centre. M9 Junction 10

⌂ Braid/Cotton
■ www.stirlinggolfclub.tv

Strathendrick   (1901)
Glasgow Road, Drymen, G63 0AA
☎ **(01360) 660695**
☐ 480
✍ M Quyn (01360) 660733

⊳ 9 L 4982 yds SSS 64
♔ WD–U SOC–WD before 5pm
££ £14
⛳ 25 miles W of Stirling, off A811
⌂ W Fernie

Wales

Cardiganshire

Aberystwyth   (1911)
Bryn-y-Mor, Aberystwyth, SY23 2HY
☎ **(01970) 615104**
☐ (01970) 626622
✉ aberystwythgolf@talk21.com
☐ 390
✓ (01970) 625301
⊳ 18 L 6119 yds SSS 71
♔ U SOC
££ £20 (£25)
⛳ Aberystwyth ¹/₂ mile
⌂ H Varden
■ www.aberystwythgolfclub.com

Borth & Ynyslas   (1885)
Borth, Ceredigion, SY24 5JS
☎ **(01970) 871202**
☐ (01970) 871202
☐ 550
✍ GJ Pritchard
✓ JG Lewis (01970) 871557
⊳ 18 L 6100 yds SSS 70
♔ WD–U WE/BH–by prior arrangement SOC
££ £28
⛳ 8 miles N of Aberystwyth (B4353), off A487

Cardigan   (1895)
Gwbert-on-Sea, Cardigan, SA43 1PR
☎ **(01239) 612035/621775**
☐ (01239) 621775
✉ golf@cardigan.fsnet.co.uk
☐ 600
✍ JJ Jones (01239) 621775
✓ C Parsons (01239) 615359
⊳ 18 L 6687 yds SSS 73
♔ H SOC
££ D–£20 (£25) W–£80
⛳ 3 miles N of Cardigan
⌂ Grant/Hawtree
■ www.cardigangolf.co.uk

Cilgwyn   (1977)
Llangybi, Lampeter, SA48 8NN
☎ **(01570) 493286**
☐ 290
✍ JD Morgan
⊳ 9 L 5327 yds SSS 67

♔ U SOC
££ £10 (£15) W–£60
⛳ 5 miles NE of Lampeter, off A485 at Llangybi

Penrhos G&CC   (1991)
Llanrhystud, Aberystwyth, SY23 5AY
☎ **(01974) 202999**
☐ (01974) 202100
✉ info@Penrhosgolf.co.uk
☐ 300
✍ R Rees-Evans
✓ P Diamond
⊳ 18 L 6641 yds SSS 73 · 9 hole Par 3 course
♔ U SOC
££ £20 (£30)
⛳ 9 miles S of Aberystwyth, signposted off A487
⊕ Driving range
⌂ Jim Walters
■ www.Penrhosgolf.co.uk

Carmarthenshire

Ashburnham   (1894)
Cliffe Terrace, Burry Port, SA16 0HN
☎ **(01554) 832466**
☐ (01554) 832466
☐ 725
✍ DK Williams (01554) 832269
✓ RA Ryder (01554) 833846
⊳ 18 L 6916 yds SSS 72
♔ H
££ £27 D–£32 (£32 D–£42)
⛳ 5 miles W of Llanelli (A484)

Carmarthen   (1907)
Blaenycoed Road, Carmarthen, SA33 6EH
☎ **(01267) 281214**
☐ 700
✍ (01267) 281588
✓ P Gillis (01267) 281493
⊳ 18 L 6245 yds SSS 71
♔ H SOC
££ £20 (£25)
⛳ 4 miles NW of Carmarthen
⌂ JH Taylor

Derllys   (1993)
Derllys Court, Llysonnen Road, Carmarthen, SA33 5DT
☎ **(01267) 211575/211309**
☐ (01267) 211575
☐ 48
✍ R Walters
⊳ 18 L 5610 yds Par 70 SSS 68
   9 L 2859 yds Par 70 SSS 66
♔ U
⛳ 4 miles W of Carmarthen, off A40
⌂ P Johnson/S Finney

Garnant Park
Garnant, Ammanford, SA18 1NP
☎ **(01269) 826472**
☐ (01269) 823365
☐ 320
✍ Mrs R Liles (01639) 844357
✓ Gethin Collins
⊳ 18 L 6163 yds Par 72 SSS 72
♔ U SOC
££ £11.50 (£16.50)
⛳ On A474, between Ammanford and Pontardawe. M4 Junction 45
⌂ Roger Jones

Glyn Abbey   (1992)
Proprietary
Trimsaran, SA17 4LB
☎ **(01554) 810278**
☐ (01554) 810889
☐ 300
✍ M Lane (Man Dir) (01554) 810304
✓ Darren Griffiths (01554) 810278
⊳ 18 L 6173 yds Par 70 SSS 70
♔ U SOC
££ £14 (£17)
⛳ 4 miles NW of Llanelli, between Trimsaran and Carway
⊕ Driving range, gym
⌂ Hawtree
■ www.glynabbey.co.uk

Glynhir   (1909)
Glynhir Road, Llandybie, Ammanford, SA18 2TF
☎ **(01269) 850472**
☐ (01269) 851365
☐ 700
✍ D Kenchington, K Williams (01269) 851365

D Prior (01269) 851010
18 L 6006 yds SSS 70
WD/Sat–H Sun–NA SOC–WD
Winter £10 (£12) 5D–£45 Summer £16 (£22) 5D–£70
3½miles N of Ammanford
Hawtree

Saron Golf Course
Pay and play
Penwern, Saron, Llandysul, SA44 4EL
(01559) 370705
9 L 2091 yds Par 32
U
9 holes–£7. 18 holes–£10
On A484 Newcastle Emlyn to Carmarthen road

Conwy

Abergele (1910)
Tan-y-Gopa Road, Abergele, LL22 8DS
(01745) 824034
(01745) 824772
secretary@abergelegolfclub.freeserve.co.uk
1250
CP Langdon
I Runcie (01745) 823813
18 L 6520 yds SSS 71
U SOC
On application
Abergele Castle Grounds
David Williams
www.abergelegolfclub.co.uk

Betws-y-Coed (1977)
Clubhouse, Betws-y-Coed, LL24 0AL
(01690) 710556
info@golfbetws-y-coed.co.uk
350
Mrs P Rowley
9 L 4996 yds SSS 64
U SOC
£16 (£22)
¼ mile off A5, in Betws-y-Coed

Conwy (Caernarvonshire) (1890)
Morfa, Conwy, LL32 8ER
(01492) 593400
(01492) 593363
secretary@conwygolfclub.co.uk
1000
DL Brown (01492) 592423
JP Lees (01492) 593225
18 L 6936 yds SSS 74
H WE–restricted SOC
£35 (£40)
½ mile W of Conway, off A55
www.conwygolfclub.co.uk

Llandudno (Maesdu) (1915)
Hospital Road, Llandudno, LL30 1HU
(01492) 876450
(01492) 871570
george@maesdugolfclub.freeserve.co.uk
1109

G Dean
S Boulden (01492) 875195
18 L 6513 yds SSS 72
U H–recognised GC members SOC
£25 (£30)
1 mile S of Llandudno Station, nr Hospital

Llandudno (North Wales) (1894)
72 Bryniau Road, West Shore, Llandudno, LL30 2DZ
(01492) 875325
(01492) 873355
691
Gordon Downs (01492) 875325
RA Bradbury (01492) 876878
18 L 6247 yds Par 71 SSS 71
U SOC–phone Sec
£25 (£30)
¾ mile from Llandudno on West Shore
www.northwalesgolfclub.co.uk

Llanfairfechan (1971)
Llannerch Road, Llanfairfechan, LL33 0EB
(01248) 680144
352
MJ Charlesworth (01248) 680524
9 L 3119 yds SSS 57
U
£10 (£10)
7 miles E of Bangor on A55

Old Colwyn (1907)
Woodland Avenue, Old Colwyn, LL29 9NL
(01492) 515581
250
DA Jones
9 L 5243 yds SSS 66
WD–U WE–by arrangement SOC
£10 (£15)
2 miles E of Colwyn Bay, off A55 Chester-Holyhead road

Penmaenmawr (1910)
Conway Old Road, Penmaenmawr, LL34 6RD
(01492) 623330
(01492) 622105
600
Mrs JE Jones
9 L 5143 yds SSS 66
U SOC
£12 (£18)
4 miles W of Conway

Rhos-on-Sea (1899)
Penrhyn Bay, Llandudno, LL30 3PU
(01492) 549641
(01492) 549100
600
JM Bray
J M Macara
18 L 6064 yds SSS 69
U
£22 (£30)
On coast at Rhos-on-Sea. 4 miles E of Llandudno
Simpson

Denbighshire

Bryn Morfydd Hotel (1982)
Llanrhaeadr, Denbigh, LL16 4NP
(01745) 890280
(01745) 890488
250
IP Jones
18 L 5800 yds Par 70 SSS 67
9 hole Par 3 course
U SOC
£15 (£20)
2½ miles SE of Denbigh on A525
Duchess-Alliss/Thomas. Dukes-Muirhead/Henderson
www.bryn-morfydd.co.uk

Denbigh (1922)
Henllan Road, Denbigh, LL16 5AA
(01745) 814159
(01745) 814888
550
Mrs C Hewitt (01745) 816669
M Jones (01745) 814159
18 L 5712 yds SSS 69
U SOC
On application
1 mile NW of Denbigh (B5382)

Kinmel Park (1989)
Pay and play
Bodelwyddan, LL18 5SR
(01745) 833548
(01745) 833502
Mrs Fetherstonhaugh
9 L 1550 yds Par 29
U
£4 (£5)
Off A55, between Abergele and St Asaph
Driving range
Peter Stebbings

Prestatyn (1905)
Marine Road East, Prestatyn, LL19 7HS
(01745) 854320
(01745) 888327
prestatyngcmanager@freenet.co.uk
680
GB Palfrey (Mgr) (01745) 888353
D Ames (01745) 852083
18 L 6825 yds SSS 73
H SOC WD WE
£25 (£30)
1 mile E of Prestatyn
S Collins
www.prestatyngc.co.uk

Rhuddlan (1930)
Meliden Road, Rhuddlan, LL18 6LB
(01745) 590217
(01745) 590472
560 136(L) 104(J)
BP Jones
A Carr (01745) 590898
18 L 6473 yds SSS 70
H Sun–M SOC–WD
£25 (£30)
2 miles N of St Asaph, J27 off A55
F Hawtree
www.rhuddlangolfclub.co.uk

Rhyl (1890)

Coast Road, Rhyl, LL18 3RE
- ☎ **(01745) 353171**
- 🖥 (01745) 353171
- 📖 600
- ✍ Tim Metcalfe
- ⌁ T Leah
- ⊱ 9 L 6220 yds SSS 70
- 👥 U SOC
- ££ £20 (£25)
- ⊶ On A548 between Rhyl and Prestatyn
- ⛪ James Braid
- ■ www.rhylgolfclub.com

Ruthin-Pwllglas (1920)

Pwllglas, Ruthin, LL15 2PE
- ☎ **(01824) 702296**
- 🖥 (01978) 790692
- 📖 360
- ✍ Eric Owen (01824) 702383
- ⌁ Michael Jones
- ⊱ 10 L 5362 yds SSS 66
- 👥 U SOC
- ££ £14 (£20)
- ⊶ 2¹/₂ miles S of Ruthin

St Melyd (1922)

The Paddock, Meliden Road, Prestatyn, LL19 8NB
- ☎ **(01745) 854405**
- 🖥 (01745) 856908
- 📖 400
- ✍ KJ Woodward, Mrs A Thompson
- ⊱ 9 L 5857 yds SSS 68
- 👥 U SOC
- ££ £18 (£22)
- ⊶ S of Prestatyn on A547
- ■ www.stmelydgolf.co.uk

Vale of Llangollen (1908)

Holyhead Road, Llangollen, LL20 7PR
- ☎ **(01978) 860613**
- 🖥 (01978) 860906
- 📖 850
- ✍ AD Bluck (01978) 860906
- ⌁ DI Vaughan (01978) 860040
- ⊱ 18 L 6656 yds Par 72 SSS 73
- 👥 U H SOC
- ££ £30 (£40)
- ⊶ 1¹/₂ miles E of Llangollen on A5

Flintshire

Caerwys (1989)

Pay and play
Caerwys, Mold, CH7 5AQ
- ☎ **(01352) 721222**
- 📖 210
- ✍ G Nicholls (01352) 720692
- ⊱ 9 L 3080 yds SSS 60
- 👥 U SOC
- ££ £7 (£9)
- ⊶ SW of Caerwys. 1¹/₂ miles S of A55 Express Way, between Holywell and St Asaph
- ⛪ Eleanor Barlow

DeVere Northop Country Park (1994)

Northop, Chester, CH7 6WA
- ☎ **(01352) 840440**
- 🖥 (01352) 840445
- ✍ M Pritchard
- ⌁ M Pritchard
- ⊱ 18 L 6802 yds Par 72
- 👥 U–phone first SOC
- ££ £40
- ⊶ 3 miles S of Flint, off A55
- ⊕ Driving range
- ⛪ John Jacobs

Flint (1966)

Cornist Park, Flint, CH6 5HJ
- ☎ **(01352) 732327, (01244) 812974**
- 🖥 (01244) 811885
- 📖 390
- ✍ TE Owens
- ⊱ 9 L 5953 yds SSS 69
- 👥 WD–U before 5pm SOC–WD
- ££ D–£10 (£10)
- ⊶ 1 mile SW of Flint. End of M56, 8 miles

Hawarden (1911)

Groomsdale Lane, Hawarden, Deeside, CH5 3EH
- ☎ **(01244) 531447**
- 🖥 (01244) 536901
- ✉ secretary@hawardengolfclub.co.uk
- 📖 480
- ✍ MB Coppack
- ⌁ A Rowlands (01244) 520809
- ⊱ 18 L 5809 yds SSS 69
- 👥 H SOC–WD
- ££ £19 (£25)
- ⊶ 6 miles W of Chester, off A55
- ■ www.hawardengolfclub.co.uk

Holywell (1906)

Brynford, Holywell, CH8 8LQ
- ☎ **(01352) 710040/713937**
- 🖥 (01352) 713937
- 📖 375 60(L)
- ✍ JF Snead (01352) 713937
- ⌁ M Parsley (01352) 710040
- ⊱ 18 L 6100 yds Par 70 SSS 70
- 👥 WD–U WE–SOC
- ££ £18 (£23)
- ⊶ 2 miles S of Holywell, off A5026

Kinsale

Pay and play
Llanerchymor, Holywell, CH8 9DX
- ☎ **(01745) 561080**
- 🖥 (01745) 561079
- 📖 85
- ✍ A Backhurst (Golf Dir)
- ⌁ A Backhurst
- ⊱ 9 holes Par 71 SSS 70
- 👥 U
- ££ 9 holes–£6.60. 18 holes–£9.90
- ⊶ 4 miles N of Holywell on A548
- ⊕ Floodlit driving range
- ⛪ K Smith

Mold (1909)

Cilcain Road, Pantymwyn, Mold, CH7 5EH
- ☎ **(01352) 740318/741513**
- 🖥 (01352) 741517
- 📖 450 90(L) 95(J)
- ✍ P Mather (01352) 741513
- ⌁ M Jordan (01352) 740318
- ⊱ 18 L 5512 yds Par 67 SSS 67
- 👥 U SOC
- ££ £18 (£25)
- ⊶ 3 miles W of Mold
- ⛪ Hawtree

Old Padeswood (1978)

Station Road, Padeswood, Mold, CH7 4JL
- ☎ **(01244) 547701 (Clubhouse)**
- 📖 500
- ✍ B Slater (Hon) (01244) 816753
- ⌁ A Davies (01244) 547401
- ⊱ 18 L 6728 yds SSS 72
- 👥 U exc comp days SOC–WD
- ££ £18 D–£25 (£20)
- ⊶ 2 miles from Mold on A5118
- ■ www.oldpadeswoodgolfclub.co.uk

Padeswood & Buckley (1933)

The Caia, Station Lane, Padeswood, Mold CH7 4JD
- ☎ **(01244) 550537**
- 🖥 (01244) 541600
- 📖 592
- ✍ JM Conway
- ⌁ D Ashton (01244) 543636
- ⊱ 18 L 5982 yds Par 70 SSS 69
- 👥 WD–U 9am–4pm –M after 4pm Sat–U Sun–NA SOC–WD Ladies Day–Wed
- ££ £20 (£25)
- ⊶ 8 miles W of Chester, off A5118. 2nd golf club on right
- ⛪ D Williams

Pennant Park

Proprietary
Whitford, Holywell, CH8 9EP
- ☎ **(01745) 560000**
- ✍ P Roberts, R Jones
- ⊱ 18 holes Par 72
- 👥 U SOC
- ££ £14 (£18)
- ⊶ Nr North Wales Expressway (A55)
- ⊕ Driving range. Academy course
- ⛪ Roger Jones
- ■ www.pennant-park.co.uk

Gwynedd

Aberdovey (1892)

Aberdovey, LL35 0RT
- ☎ **(01654) 767210**
- 🖥 (01654) 767027
- 📖 800
- ✍ JM Griffiths (01654) 767493
- ⌁ J Davies (01654) 767602
- ⊱ 18 L 6445 yds SSS 71
- 👥 NA–8–9.30am & 1–2pm

££   On application
⌖   ¹/₂ mile W of Aberdovey (A493)
🏠   Braid/Fowler/Swan
■   www.aberdoveygolf.co.uk

Abersoch   (1907)

Golf Road, Abersoch, LL53 7EY
☎   (01758) 712636
⛾   (01758) 712777
⛁   700
🖉   A Drosinos Jones (01758) 712622
✓   A Drosinos Jones
🏌   18 L 5819 yds SSS 69
👥   U H SOC
££   £18 (£20)
⌖   ¹/₂ mile S of Abersoch (A55). 7
     miles S of Pwllheli
🏠   Harry Vardon
■   www.abersochgolf.co.uk

Bala   (1973)

Penlan, Bala, LL23 7YD
☎   (01678) 520359
⛾   (01678) 521361
⛁   340
🖉   G Rhys Jones
✓   T Davies
🏌   10 L 4962 yds SSS 64
👥   WD–U WE–NA pm SOC
££   £15 (£20) W–£40
⌖   ¹/₂ mile SW of Bala, off A494 to
     Dolgellau

Bala Lake Hotel

Bala, LL23 7YF
☎   (01678) 520344/520111
⛾   (01678) 521193
⛁   50
🖉   D Pickering
🏌   9 L 4280 yds SSS 61
👥   U
££   On application
⌖   1¹/₂ miles S of Bala on B4403

Criccieth   (1905)

Ednyfed Hill, Criccieth, LL52
☎   (01766) 522154
⛁   200
🖉   MG Hamilton (01766) 522697
🏌   18 L 5755 yds SSS 68
👥   U
££   £12 Sun–£15
⌖   4 miles W of Portmadoc

Dolgellau   (1911)

*Hengwrt Estate, Pencefn Road,
Dolgellau, LL4 0SE*
☎   (01341) 422603
⛁   300
🖉   Ms JM May
✓   H Jones Davies
🏌   9 L 4671 yds Par 66 SSS 63
👥   U
££   £15 (£20)
⌖   ¹/₂ mile N of Dolgellau
🏠   J Medway

Ffestiniog   (1893)

Y Cefn, Ffestiniog
☎   (01766) 762637 (Clubhouse)

⛁   138
🖉   A Roberts (01766) 831829
🏌   9 L 4570 metres Par 68 SSS 66
👥   U
££   £10 (£10)
⌖   1 mile E of Ffestiniog on Bala road
     (B4391)

Nefyn & District   (1907)

Morfa Nefyn, Pwllheli, LL53 6DA
☎   (01758) 720218 (Clubhouse)
⛾   (01758) 720476
🖂   nefyngolf@tesco.net
⛁   880
🖉   JB Owens (01758) 720966
✓   J Froom (01758) 720102
🏌   18 L 6548 yds SSS 71
     9 L 2618 yds SSS 34
👥   U SOC
££   £27 D–£33 (£32 D–£36)
⌖   1¹/₂ miles W of Nefyn. 20 miles W
     of Caernarfon

Porthmadog   (1905)

*Morfa Bychan, Porthmadog,
LL49 9UU*
☎   (01766) 512037 (Clubhouse)
⛾   (01766) 514638
⛁   920
🖉   Mrs A Richardson (Office
     Mgr) (01766) 514124
✓   P Bright (01766) 513828
🏌   18 L 6363 yds Par 71 SSS 71
👥   U H SOC
££   D–£25 (D–£30)
⌖   2 miles S of Porthmadog, towards
     Black Rock Sands
🏠   James Braid
■   www.porthmadog-golf-club.co.uk

Pwllheli   (1900)

Golf Road, Pwllheli, LL53 5PS
☎   (01758) 701644
⛾   (01758) 701644
⛁   820
🖉   Mrs M Nash (Gen Mgr)
✓   S Pilkington (01758) 612520
🏌   18 L 6091 yds SSS 70
👥   U
££   £25 (£30) – 2003 fees
⌖   ¹/₂ mile SW of Pwllheli
🏠   James Braid
■   www.pwllheligolfclub.co.uk

Royal St David's   (1894)

Harlech, LL46 2UB
☎   (01766) 780203
⛾   (01766) 781110
🖂   secretary@royalstdavids.co.uk
⛁   880
🖉   DL Morkill (01766) 780361
✓   J Barnett (01766) 780857
🏌   18 L 6571 yds SSS 73
👥   U H–booking necessary SOC
££   £40 (£50)
⌖   W of Harlech on A496
🏠   H Finch-Hatton
■   www.royalstdavids.co.uk

Royal Town of Caernarfon   (1909)

*Aberforeshore, LLanfaglan, Caernarfon,
LL54 5RP*
☎   (01286) 673967
⛾   (01286) 672535
🖂   caerngc@talk21.com
⛁   735
🖉   G Jones (01286) 673783
✓   A Owen (01286) 678359
🏌   18 L 5941 yds SSS 68
👥   U SOC
££   £22 Sat–£28 Sun–£25
⌖   2¹/₂ miles SW of Caernarfon
■   www.caernarfongolfclub.co.uk

St Deiniol   (1906)

Penybryn, Bangor, LL57 1PX
☎   (01248) 353098
⛾   (01248) 370792
🖂   secretary@stdeiniol.fsbusiness
     .co.uk
⛁   300
🖉   RD Thomas MBE (01248) 353098
🏌   18 L 5654 yds SSS 67
👥   U SOC
££   £16 (£20)
⌖   Off A5/A55 Junction 11, 1 mile E
     of Bangor on A5122
🏠   James Braid
■   www.st-deiniol.co.uk

Isle of Anglesey

Anglesey   (1914)

Station Road, Rhosneigr, LL64 5QX
☎   (01407) 810219 (Clubhouse)
⛾   (01407) 811127
🖂   info@theangleseygolfclub.com
⛁   450
🖉   VB Musgrave (Mgr)
     (01407) 811127
✓   M Parry (01407)811202
🏌   18 L 6330 yds SSS 70
👥   U H SOC
££   £20
⌖   8 miles SE of Holyhead, off
     A4080
🏠   H Hilton
■   www.theangleseygolfclub.com

Baron Hill   (1895)

Beaumaris, LL58 8YW
☎   (01248) 810231
🖂   golf@baronhill.co.uk
⛁   360
🖉   A Pleming
🏌   9 L 5062 metres SSS 68
👥   U exc comp days SOC–WD & Sat
     (apply Sec)
££   £15 W–£45
⌖   1 mile SW of Beaumaris

Bull Bay   (1913)

Bull Bay Road, Amlwch, LL68 9RY
☎   (01407) 830213
⛾   (01407) 832612
⛁   700

✍ I Furlong (Sec/Mgr)
(01407) 830960
✓ J Burns (01407) 831188
↦ 18 L 6276 yds SSS 70
👥 U SOC WD WE
££ £22 (£27)
🚗 ¹/₂ mile W of Amlwch on A5025
🏠 WH Fowler
■ www.bullbaygc.co.uk

Henllys Hall
Llanfaes, Beaumaris, LL58 8HU
☎ (01248) 811717
🖳 (01248) 811511
✓ P Maton
↦ 18 L 6062 yds Par 72
👥 U SOC
££ £20 (£25)
🚗 2 miles N of Beaumaris (B5109)
🏠 Roger Jones

Holyhead   (1912)
Trearddur Bay, Holyhead, LL65 2YL
☎ (01407) 763279/762119
🖳 (01407) 763279
📧 mgrsec@aol.com
🖳 790 396(L)
✍ JA Williams
✓ S Elliott (01407) 762022
↦ 18 L 5540 metres SSS 70
👥 H SOC
££ £20 (£29)
🚗 2 miles S of Holyhead
🏠 James Braid
■ www.holyheadgolfclub.co.uk

Llangefni   (1983)
Public
Llangefni, LL77 8YQ
☎ (01248) 722193
✓ P Lovell
↦ 9 L 1467 yds Par 28
👥 U
££ £3.30 (£3.50)
🚗 ¹/₂ mile S of Llangefni, off A5111
🏠 Hawtree

RAF Valley
Anglesey, LL65 3NY
☎ (01407) 762241
🖳 150
✍ MJ Constable (Mgr)
↦ 9 L 5604 yards SSS 68
👥 U – booking necessary
££ D–£6 (£6)
🚗 RAF Valley base, off A55

Storws Wen   (1996)
Proprietary
Brynteg, Benllech, LL78 8JY
☎ (01248) 852673
🖳 (01248) 853843
🖳 260
✍ CS Henderson (Gen Mgr)
✓ J Kelly
↦ 9 L 5002 yds Par 68 SSS 64
👥 U SOC
££ £15 (£18)
🚗 2 miles from Benllech on B5108
🏠 K Jones

Mid Glamorgan

Aberdare   (1921)
Abernant, Aberdare, CF44 0RY
☎ (01685) 871188 (Clubhouse)
🖳 (01685) 872797
🖳 500
✍ T Mears (01685) 872797
✓ AW Palmer (01685) 878735
↦ 18 L 5875 yds SSS 69
👥 H SOC
££ £17 (£21)
🚗 ¹/₂ mile E of Aberdare. 12 miles
NW of Pontypridd

Bargoed   (1913)
Heolddu, Bargoed, CF81 9GF
☎ (01443) 830143
🖳 548
✍ G Williams (01443) 830608
✓ Craig Easton (01443) 836179
↦ 18 L 6233 yds SSS 70
👥 WD–U WE–M SOC–WD
££ £15
🚗 NW boundary of Bargoed. 8 miles
N of Caerphilly (A469)

Bryn Meadows Golf Hotel   (1973)
The Bryn, Hengoed, CF8 7SM
☎ (01495) 225590/224103
🖳 (01495) 228272
🖳 550
✍ B Mayo
✓ B Hunter (01495) 221905
↦ 18 L 6156 yds SSS 69
👥 U
££ £17.50 (£22.50)
🚗 6 miles N of Caerphilly (A469)
🏠 Mayo/Jefferies

Caerphilly   (1905)
Pencapel, Mountain Road, Caerphilly, CF83 1HJ
☎ (029) 2088 3481
🖳 (029) 2086 3441
🖳 650
✍ (029) 2086 3441
✓ J Hill (029) 2086 9104
↦ 13 L 5728 yds SSS 69
👥 WD–U H WE–M
££ £24 W–£50
🚗 7 miles N of Cardiff, off A469

Castell Heights   (1982)
Pay and play
Blaengwynlais, Caerphilly, CF8 1NG
☎ (029) 2088 6666 (Bookings)
🖳 (029) 2086 9030
🖳 600
✓ S Bebb
↦ 9 L 2688 yds SSS 66
👥 U
££ 9 holes–£4.50 (£5.50)
🚗 4 miles from M4 Junction 32
⊕ Driving range
🏠 J Page

Coed-y-Mwstwr   (1994)
Coychurch, Bridgend, CF35 6TN
☎ (01656) 864934
🖳 (01656) 864934
📧 secretary@coed-y-mwstrw.co.uk
🖳 260
✍ JR North (Sec/Mgr)
↦ 12 L 6144 yds Par 70 SSS 70
👥 U H Sat–M SOC–WD
££ £17.50 (£19.50)
🚗 2 miles W of M4 Junction 35
■ www.coed-y-mstwr.co.uk

Creigiau   (1921)
Creigiau, Cardiff, CF15 9NN
☎ (029) 2089 0263
🖳 (029) 2089 0706
🖳 700
✍ AJ Greedy
✓ I Luntz (029) 2089 1909
↦ 18 L 6063 yds SSS 70
👥 WD–U WE/BH–M SOC–WD
££ £30
🚗 5 miles NW of Cardiff. M4
Junction 34

Grove
South Cornelly, Bridgend, CF33 4RP
☎ (01656) 788771
🖳 540
✍ M Thomas (01656) 788771
✓ L Warne (01656) 788300
↦ 18 L 5884 yds Par 70 SSS 70
👥 WD–U WE–NA before 3pm
££ £18 (£20)
■ www.grovegolf.com

Llantrisant & Pontyclun   (1927)
Ely Valley Road, Talbot Green, Llantrisant, CF72 8AL
☎ (01443) 222148
📧 lpgc@barbox.net
🖳 600
✍ RW Rowsell (01443) 224601
✓ M Phillips (01443) 228169
↦ 18 L 5328 yds SSS 66
👥 WD–H WE/BH–M SOC–WD
££ On application
🚗 10 miles NW of Cardiff. 2 miles N
of M4 Junction 34

Maesteg   (1912)
Mount Pleasant, Neath Road, Maesteg, CF34 9PR
☎ (01656) 734102
🖳 (01656) 731822
🖳 614
✍ Ian McBride (01656) 734106
↦ 18 L 5929 yds SSS 69
👥 WD–H SOC
££ £17 (£20)
🚗 1 mile W of Maesteg on B4282. M4
Junctions 36 or 40

Merthyr Tydfil   (1909)
Cilsanws Mountain, Cefn Coed, Merthyr Tydfil, CF48 2NU
☎ (01685) 723308
🖳 200

🖉 V Price
✓ None
▷ 18 L 5622 yds SSS 68
👭 U SOC–WD
££ £10 (£15)
🕸 2 miles N of Merthyr Tydfil, off A470 at Cefn Coed
🕾 Viv Price/Richard/Mathias

Morlais Castle   (1900)
Pant, Dowlais, Merthyr Tydfil, CF48 2UY
☎ **(01685) 722822**
✉ meurig.price@lineone.net
🏠 600
🖉 M Price
✓ H Jarrett (01685) 388700
▷ 18 L 6320 yds SSS 71
👭 WD–U Sat–NA 12–4pm Sun–NA 8am–12noon SOC
££ £16 (£20)
🕸 3 miles N of Merthyr Tydfil, nr Mountain Railway

Mountain Ash   (1907)
Cefnpennar, Mountain Ash, CF45 4DT
☎ **(01443) 472265 (Clubhouse)**
📠 (01443) 479628
🏠 530
🖉 G Matthews (01443) 479459
✓ D Clark (01443) 478770
▷ 18 L 5535 yds SSS 67
👭 WD–U H WE–M
££ £20
🕸 9 miles NW of Pontypridd

Mountain Lakes   (1988)
Heol Penbryn, Blaengwynlais, Caerphilly, CF83 1NG
☎ **(029) 2086 1128**
📠 (029) 2086 3243
🏠 480
🖉 DC Rooney (Hon)
▷ 18 L 6300 yds SSS 72
👭 U SOC
££ £18 (£18)
🕸 4 miles from M4 Junction 32
🕾 R Sandow

Pontypridd   (1905)
Ty Gwyn Road, Pontypridd, CF37 4DJ
☎ **(01443) 402359**
📠 (01443) 491622
🏠 850
🖉 Vikki Hooley (01443) 409904
✓ W Walters (01443) 491210
▷ 18 L 5725 yds SSS 68
👭 WD–U H WE/BH–M H SOC–WD H
££ On application
🕸 E of Pontypridd, off A470. 12 miles NW of Cardiff

Pyle & Kenfig   (1922)
Waun-y-Mer, Kenfig, Bridgend, CF33 4PU
☎ **(01656) 783093**
📠 (01656) 772822
✉ secretary@pyleandkenfiggolfclub.co.uk
🏠 860

🖉 DA Fallowes (01656) 771613
✓ R Evans (01656) 772446
▷ 18 L 6741 yds Par 71 SSS 73
👭 WD–U WE (Sun) H WE–M SOC
££ D–£40
🕸 2 miles NW of Porthcawl. M4 Junction 37
🕾 HS Colt
■ www.pyleandkenfiggolfclub.co.uk

Rhondda   (1910)
Penrhys, Ferndale, Rhondda, CF43 3PW
☎ **(01443) 433204**
📠 (01443) 441384
🏠 500
🖉 Mrs P Norman (01443) 441384
✓ G Bebb (01443) 441385
▷ 18 L 6428 yds SSS 71
👭 U H SOC
££ £15 (£20)
🕸 6 miles W of Pontypridd

Ridgeway   (1997)
Caerphilly Mountain, Caerphilly, CF83 1LY
☎ **(029) 2088 2255**
🖉 R Jones
✓ Jack Taylor/Steve Bowen
▷ 9 L 4800 yds SSS 68 (18 tees)
👭 U H
££ £15 (£18)
🕸 3 miles from M4 J32 at top of Caerphilly Mountain on A469
⊕ 18 bay driving range

Royal Porthcawl   (1891)
Rest Bay, Porthcawl, CF36 3UW
☎ **(01656) 782251**
📠 (01656) 771687
🏠 800
🖉 JV Dinsdale
✓ P Evans (01656) 773702
▷ 18 L 6673 yds SSS 74
👭 WD–I or H WE/BH–M SOC–H
££ On application
🕸 22 miles W of Cardiff. M4 Junction 37
⊕ Driving range. Dormy House
🕾 Charles Gibson
■ www.royalporthcawl.com

Southerndown   (1905)
Ogmore-by-Sea, Bridgend, CF32 0QP
☎ **(01656) 880476/880326**
📠 (01656) 880317
✉ southerndowngolf@btconnect.com
🏠 700
🖉 AJ Hughes (01656) 880476
✓ DG McMonagle
▷ 18 L 6449 yds SSS 72
👭 U H
££ £40 (£50)
🕸 3 miles S of Bridgend, nr Ogmore Castle ruins
🕾 W Fernie

Virginia Park   (1993)
Pay and play
Virginia Park, Caerphilly, CF83 3SW
☎ **(029) 2086 3919**
🏠 200

🖉 Mrs C Lewis
✓ P Clark (029) 2085 0650
▷ 9 L 4661 yds Par 66 SSS 63
👭 U SOC
££ On application
🕸 Caerphilly, 7 miles N of Cardiff
⊕ Driving range

Whitehall   (1922)
The Pavilion, Nelson, Treharris, CF46 6ST
☎ **(01443) 740245**
✉ mark@wilde6755.freeserve.co.uk
🏠 300
🖉 PM Wilde
▷ 9 L 5666 yds SSS 68
👭 WD–U WE–M SOC
££ £18 (£12 with member)
🕸 15 miles NW of Cardiff

Monmouthshire

Alice Springs   (1989)
Keneys Commander, Usk, NP15 1JY
☎ **(01873) 880708**
📠 (01873) 881075
🏠 350
🖉 KR Morgan
✓ M Davies (01873) 880914
▷ Red 18 L 5870 yds SSS 69
    Green 18 L 6438 yds SSS 72
👭 U SOC
££ £16 (£20)
🕸 3 miles N of Usk on B4598
⊕ Driving range
🕾 Keith Morgan

Blackwood   (1914)
Cwmgelli, Blackwood, NP12 1BR
☎ **(01495) 223152**
🏠 300
🖉 AD Watkins
✓ None
▷ 9 L 5304 yds SSS 66
👭 WD–I SOC WE/BH–M
££ £14
🕸 ¹⁄₄ mile N of Blackwood

Caerleon   (1974)
Pay and play
Broadway, Caerleon, NP6 1AY
☎ **(01633) 420342**
🏠 150
🖉 P John
✓ A Campbell
▷ 9 L 3092 yds SSS
👭 U
££ 18 holes–£5 9 holes–£3.30
🕸 M4 Junction 25, 3 miles
⊕ Driving range
🕾 Donald Steel

The Celtic Manor Resort   (1995)
Coldra Woods, Newport, NP6 1JQ
☎ **(01633) 413000**
📠 (01633) 410309
🏠 450

🏌 S Wesson (01633) 413000
✓ S Patience (01633) 413000
▷ 18 L 7001 yds Par 70 SSS 74
 18 L 4094 yds Par 61 SSS 60
 18 L 7403 yds Par 72 SSS 77
👥 H SOC
£€ On application
🚗 E of Newport on A48. M4 Junction 24
⊕ Golf Academy. Driving range
🏠 Robert Trent Jones Sr

Dewstow (1988)
Proprietary
Caerwent, NP26 5AH
☎ (01291) 430444
🖥 (01291) 425816
✉ info@dewstow.com
📖 850
🏌 D Bradbury (01291) 430444
✓ J Skuse (01291) 430444
▷ Valley 18 L 6091 yds Par 72 SSS 70
 Park 18 L 6226 yds Par 69 SSS 69
👥 U SOC
£€ £16 (£20)
🚗 Caerwent, 5 miles W of old Severn Bridge, off A48
⊕ Driving range
■ www.dewstow.com

Greenmeadow G&CC (1979)
Treherbert Road, Croesyceiliog, Cwmbran, NP44 2BZ
☎ (01633) 869321
🖥 (01633) 868430
✉ info@greenmeadowgolf.com
📖 430
🏌 PJ Richardson (01633) 869321
✓ D Woodman (01633) 862626
▷ 18 L 6078 yds Par 70 SSS 70
👥 WD–U WE–NA before 11am SOC
£€ On application
🚗 4 miles N of Newport on A4042. M4 Junction 26
⊕ Floodlit driving range
■ www.greenmeadowgolf.com

Llanwern (1928)
Tennyson Avenue, Llanwern, Newport, NP18 2DW
☎ (01633) 412380
🖥 (01633) 412029
📖 776
🏌 MW Penny (01633) 412029
✓ S Price (01633) 413233
▷ 18 L 6115 yds SSS 69
👥 WD–U WE–restricted I H SOC
£€ WD–£20
🚗 1 mile S of M4 Junction 24

Marriott St Pierre Hotel & CC (1962)
St Pierre Park, Chepstow, NP16 6YA
☎ (01291) 625261
🖥 (01291) 629975
📖 840
🏌 Mr Arnie Pidgeon
✓ Craig Dun (01291) 635205
▷ Old 18 L 6818 yds SSS 74; Mathern 18 L 5732 yds SSS 68

👥 H SOC–WD
£€ On application
🚗 2 miles W of Chepstow (A48)
⊕ Driving range
🏠 CK Cotton

Monmouth (1896)
Leasbrook Lane, Monmouth, NP25 3SN
☎ (01600) 712212
🖥 (01600) 772399
✉ sec.mongc@barbox.net
📖 500
🏌 P Tully (01600) 712212
✓ Mike Waldron (01600) 712212
▷ 18 L 5698 yds SSS 69
👥 U SOC WD WE (Sun only after 11.30am)
£€ £19 (£22)
🚗 Signposted ¼ mile along A40 Monmouth-Ross road
🏠 George Walden
■ www.monmouthgolfclub.co.uk

Monmouthshire (1892)
Llanfoist, Abergavenny, NP7 9HE
☎ (01873) 852606
🖥 (01873) 850470
✉ secretary@mgcabergavenny.fsnet.co.uk
📖 520 103(L) 49(J)
🏌 R Bradley
✓ (01873) 852532
▷ 18 L 5978 yds SSS 70
👥 WD–H SOC
£€ D–£30 (D–£35)
🚗 2 miles SW of Abergavenny
🏠 James Braid
■ www.monmouthshiregolfclub.co.uk

Newport (1903)
Great Oak, Rogerstone, Newport, NP10 9FX
☎ (01633) 892643/894496
🖥 (01633) 896676
✉ newportgolfclub.gwent@euphony.net
📖 800
🏌 (01633) 892643
✓ PM Mayo (01633) 893271
▷ 18 L 6453yds SSS 71
👥 WD–H
£€ £30 (£35)
🚗 3 miles W of Newport on B4591. M4 Junction 27, 1 mile
🏠 Ross/Fernie

Oakdale (1990)
Pay and play
Llwynon Lane, Oakdale, NP2 0NF
☎ (01495) 220044
🏌 M Lewis (Dir)
✓ (01495) 220440
▷ 9 L 1344 yds Par 28
👥 U SOC
£€ On application
🚗 15 miles NW of Newport via A467/B4251. M4 Junction 28
⊕ Driving range
🏠 Ian Goodenough

Parc (1990)
Pay and play
Church Lane, Coedkernew, Newport, NP1 9TU
☎ (01633) 680933
🖥 (01633) 681011
📖 450
🏌 C Hicks (Mgr), M Cleary (Sec)
✓ J Skuse (01633) 680955
▷ 18 L 5512 yds SSS 67
👥 U SOC
£€ £11 (£13)
🚗 2 miles W of Newport on A48. M4 Junction 28
⊕ Floodlit driving range
🏠 B Thomas

Pontnewydd (1875)
Maesgwyn Farm, Upper Cwmbran, NP44 1AB
☎ (01633) 482170
🖥 (01633) 838598
✉ ctphillips@virgin.net
📖 250
🏌 CT Phillips (01633) 484447
▷ 11 L 5278 yds SSS 67
👥 WD–U WE–M SOC
£€ £15 (£15)
🚗 W outskirts of Cwmbran

Pontypool (1903)
Lasgarn Lane, Trevethin, Pontypool, NP4 8TR
☎ (01495) 763655
✉ pontypoolgolf@btconnect.com
📖 581 41(L) 80(J)
🏌 L Dodd
✓ J Howard (01495) 755544
▷ 18 L 5712 yds SSS 69
👥 U H SOC
£€ £20 (£24)
🚗 1 mile N of Pontypool (A4042). M4 Junction 26
■ www.pontypoolgolf.co.uk

Raglan Parc
Parc Lodge, Raglan, NP5 2ER
☎ (01291) 690077
📖 380
🏌 S Dobney
✓ G Gage
▷ 18 L 6604 yds Par 73
👥 U
£€ £15 (£15)
🚗 Nr A40/A449 junction

The Rolls of Monmouth (1982)
The Hendre, Monmouth, NP25 5HG
☎ (01600) 715353
🖥 (01600) 713115
📖 200
🏌 Mrs SJ Orton
✓ None
▷ 18 L 6733 yds SSS 73
👥 U SOC
£€ £36 (£40)
🚗 3½ miles W of Monmouth on B4233

Shirenewton (1995)
Shirenewton, Chepstow, NP16 6RL
☎ **(01291) 641642**
📠 (01291) 641472
🖉 T Morgan (Mgr)
✒ T Morgan (01291) 641471
🏳 18 L 6607 yds Par 72 SSS 72
🕴 U SOC
£€ £16 (£18)
⛳ 5 miles W of Chepstow, off A48.
M4 Junction 22

Tredegar & Rhymney (1921)
Tredegar, Rhymney, NP2 3BQ
☎ **(07944) 843400**
📖 180
🖉 P Kenealy (07944) 843400
🏳 18 L 5564 yds SSS 68
🕴 U
£€ £10
⛳ 1¹/₂ miles W of Tredegar (B4256)

Tredegar Park (1923)
Parc-y-Brain Road, Rogerstone,
Newport, NP10 9TG
☎ **(01633) 895219**
📠 (01633) 897152
📧 tpgh@btinternet.com
📖 800
🖉 AJ Trickett (01633) 894433
✒ Lee Pagett (01633) 894517
🏳 18 L 6564 yds SSS 72
🕴 H SOC–WD
£€ D–£18 (£25)
⛳ W of Newport, off M4 Junction 27
🏛 R Sandow

Wernddu Golf Centre
Old Ross Road, Abergavenny, NP7 8NG
☎ **(01873) 856223**
📠 (01873) 852177
📖 520
🖉 L Turvey
✒ Tina Tetley
🏳 18 L 5500 yds Par 68 SSS 67
🕴 U
£€ 9 holes–£10. 18 holes–£15
⛳ 1¹/₂ miles NE of Abergavenny on
B4521
⊕ Floodlit driving range
■ www.wernddugolfclub.co.uk

West Monmouthshire
(1906)
Golf Road, Pond Road, Nantyglo, Ebbw
Vale, NP23 4QT
☎ **(01495) 310233/311361**
📠 (01495) 311361
📖 300
🖉 SE Williams (01495) 310233
🏳 18 L 6118 yds SSS 69
🕴 WD/Sat–U Sun–M SOC–WD
£€ £15
⛳ Nr Dunlop Semtex, off Brynmawr
Bypass, towards Winchestown
🏛 Ben Sayers

Woodlake Park (1993)
Glascoed, Usk, NP4 0TE
☎ **(01291) 673933**

📠 (01291) 673811
📧 golf@woodlake.co.uk
📖 500
🖉 D Hawker
✒ L Lancey (01291) 671135
🏳 18 L 6300 yds Par 71 SSS 72
🕴 H SOC WD WE
£€ Summer–£22.50 (£30) Winter–£15
(£20)
⛳ 3 miles W of Usk, nr Llandegfedd
reservoir
■ www.woodlake.co.uk

Pembrokeshire

Haverfordwest (1904)
Arnolds Down, Haverfordwest,
SA61 2XQ
☎ **(01437) 763565**
📠 (01437) 764143
📖 800
🖉 P Lewis (01437) 764523
✒ A Pile (01437) 768409
🏳 18 L 5966 yds SSS 69
🕴 U SOC
£€ £20 (£25)
⛳ 1 mile E of Haverfordwest on A40
■ www.hwestgolf.homestead.com

Milford Haven (1913)
Hubberston, Milford Haven, SA72 3RX
☎ **(01646) 697762**
📠 (01646) 697870
📖 380 65(L) 90(J)
🖉 WS Brown
✒ M Stimson (01646) 697762
🏳 18 L 6071 yds SSS 71
🕴 U SOC
£€ £17.50 (£22.50)
⛳ W boundary of Milford Haven
■ www.mhgc.co.uk

Newport (Pembs) (1925)
Newport, SA42 0NR
☎ **(01239) 820244**
📠 (01239) 820085
📧 newportgc@lineone.net
📖 500
🖉 Mrs A Payne (Mgr)
✒ Mr J Noott
🏳 9 L 3089 yds SSS 68
🕴 U SOC
£€ £20 (£24)
⛳ 2¹/₂ miles NW of Newport, towards
Newport Beach
⊕ Driving range
🏛 James Braid
■ www.newportgc.sagenet.co.uk

Priskilly Forest (1992)
Castle Morris, Haverfordwest,
SA62 5EH
☎ **(01348) 840276**
📠 (01348) 840276
📧 jevans@priskilly-forest.co.uk
🖉 P Evans
🏳 9 L 5874 yds Par 70 SSS 69
🕴 U SOC
£€ 18 holes–£16 D–£18 9 holes–£12

⛳ 2 miles off A40 at Letterston
🏛 J Walters
■ www.priskilly-forest.co.uk

South Pembrokeshire (1970)
Military Road, Pembroke Dock,
SA72 6SE
☎ **(01646) 621453**
📖 350
🖉 WD Owen (01646) 621453/621804
✒ None
🏳 18 L 5638 yds SSS 69
🕴 U before 4.30pm SOC
£€ On application
⛳ Pembroke Dock

St Davids City (1903)
Whitesands Bay, St Davids, SA62 6PT
☎ **(01437) 721751 (Clubhouse)**
📧 wjwilcox@hotmail.com
📖 200
🖉 J Wilcox (01437) 720058
🏳 9 L 6117 yds SSS 70
🕴 U SOC
£€ D–£15
⛳ 2 miles W of St Davids. 15 miles
NW of Haverfordwest

Tenby (1888)
The Burrows, Tenby, SA70 7NP
☎ **(01834) 842978**
📠 (01834) 842978
📖 800
🖉 DJ Hancock (01834) 842978
✒ M Hawkey (01834) 844447
🏳 18 L 6450 yds SSS 71
🕴 H SOC
£€ £30 D–£45 (£35 D–£52.50))
⛳ Tenby, South Beach
🏛 James Braid
■ www.tenbygolf.co.uk

Trefloyne (1996)
Trefloyne Park, Penally, Tenby,
SA70 7RG
☎ **(01834) 842165**
📖 250
✒ S Laidler (01834) 842165
🏳 18 L 6635 yds Par 71
🕴 U SOC
£€ £22 (£26)
⛳ 1¹/₂ miles W of Tenby, off A4139
Pembroke road
🏛 FH Gilman
■ www.trefloynegolfcourse.co.uk

Powys

Brecon (1902)
Newton Park, Llanfaes, Brecon,
LD3 8PA
☎ **(01874) 622004**
📖 330
🏳 9 L 5256 yds Par 68 SSS 66
🕴 U SOC
£€ £12 (£15)

🖁 ¹/₂ mile W of Brecon on A40
🛉 James Braid

Builth Wells (1923)
Golf Club Road, Builth Wells, LD2 3NF
☎ **(01982) 553296**
📠 (01982) 551064
📧 builthwellsgolfclub1@btinternet
.com
💷 400
♬ JN Jones
√ S Edwards
🏌 18 L 5376 yds SSS 67
🙋 U H SOC
£€ £17 D–£22 (£23 D–£28)
🚗 W of Builth Wells on Llandovery
road (A483)
■ www.builthwellsgolfclub.co.uk

Cradoc (1967)
Penoyre Park, Cradoc, Brecon, LD3 9LP
☎ **(01874) 623658**
📠 (01874) 611711
📧 secretary@cradoc.co.uk
💷 750
♬ Mrs EG Price (01874) 623658
√ R Davies (01874) 625524
🏌 18 L 6331 yds Par 72 SSS 72
🙋 U SOC
£€ £22 (£28)
🚗 2 miles NW of Brecon, off B4520
⊕ Driving range
🛉 CK Cotton
■ www.cradoc.co.uk

Knighton (1906)
Ffrydd Wood, Knighton, LD7 1EF
☎ **(01547) 528646**
📠 (01547) 529284
💷 150
♬ DB Williams (Hon)
🏌 9 L 5362 yds Par 68 SSS 66
🙋 U SOC
£€ £10 (£12)
🚗 SW of Knighton. 20 miles NE of
Llandrindod Wells
🛉 H Vardon

Llandrindod Wells (1905)
Llandrindod Wells, LD1 5NY
☎ **(01597) 823873**
📠 (01597) 823873
📧 secretary@lwgc.co.uk
💷 400
♬ R Southcott (01597) 823873
√ P Davies (01597) 822247
🏌 18 L 5759 yds Par 69 SSS 69
🙋 U SOC
£€ £17 (£22)
🚗 ¹/₂ mile E of Llandrindod Wells
centre
⊕ Driving range
🛉 Harry Vardon
■ www.lwgc.co.uk

Machynlleth (1904)
*Ffordd Drenewydd, Machynlleth,
SY20 8UH*
☎ **(01654) 702000**
💷 250
♬ Margaret Vince (01654) 702928

🏌 9 L 5726 yds SSS 67
🙋 U Sun–NA before 11.30am SOC
£€ (£15)
🚗 1 mile E of Machynlleth, off A489

Rhosgoch (1991)
Rhosgoch, Builth Wells, LD2 3JY
☎ **(01497) 851251**
💷 150
♬ C Dance
🏌 9 L 5078 yds SSS 65
🙋 U SOC
£€ £7 (£10)
🚗 5 miles N of Hay-on-Wye

St Giles Newtown (1895)
Pool Road, Newtown, SY16 3AJ
☎ **(01686) 625844**
💷 350
√ DP Owen
🏌 9 L 6012 yds SSS 70
🙋 U SOC
£€ £13.50 (£16)
🚗 1 mile E of Newtown (A483). 14
miles SW of Welshpool

St Idloes (1920)
Owned privately
Penrhallt, Llanidloes, SY18 6LG
☎ **(01686) 412559**
📠 (01926) 889536
💷 292
♬ JC Green
√ P Parkin
🏌 9 L 5510 yds SSS 66
🙋 U H Sun–restricted SOC
£€ £10 (£12) W–£45
🚗 ¹/₂ mile from Llanidloes on
Trefeglwys road (B4569)

Welsh Border Golf Complex
(1991)
*Bulthy Farm, Bulthy, Middletown,
SY21 8ER*
☎ **(01743) 884247**
💷 200
♬ J Watt
√ A Griffiths
🏌 9 L 3050 yds SSS 69
9 hole course
🙋 U SOC
£€ £14
🚗 Between Shrewsbury and
Welshpool on A458
⊕ Driving range
🛉 A Griffiths

Welshpool (1929)
Golfa Hill, Welshpool, SY21 9AQ
☎ **(01938) 850249**
📧 welshpool.golfclub@virgin.net
💷 400
♬ D Lewis (01938) 810757
√ None
🏌 18 L 5708 yds Par 70 SSS 68
🙋 U
£€ £12.50 D–£20.50 Winter–£15.50
🚗 4¹/₂ miles W of Welshpool, on
Dolgellau road (A458)
🛉 James Braid
■ www.welshpoolgolfclub.co.uk

South Glamorgan

Brynhill (1921)
Port Road, Barry, CF62 8PN
☎ **(01446) 720277**
💷 700
♬ R Cook/S Clarke (01446) 720277
√ M Herbert (01446) 740004
🏌 18 L 6352 yds SSS 71
🙋 WD/Sat–H Sun–NA SOC–WD
£€ £20 Sat–£25 SOC–£17
🚗 A4050, 8 miles SW of Cardiff

Cardiff (1921)
*Sherborne Avenue, Cyncoed, Cardiff,
CF23 6SJ*
☎ **(029) 2075 3067**
📠 (029) 2068 0011
💷 930
♬ Mrs K Newling (029) 2075 3320
√ T Hanson (029) 2075 4772
🏌 18 L 6015 yds SSS 70
🙋 WD–H WE–M SOC–Thurs
£€ £35 (£40)
🚗 3 miles N of Cardiff. 2 miles W of
Pentwyn exit of A48(M). M4
Junction 29

Cottrell Park (1996)
St Nicholas, Cardiff, CF5 6JY
☎ **(01446) 781781**
📠 (01446) 781187
📧 admin@cottrell-park.co.uk
💷 1050
♬ DW Marchant
√ S Birch
🏌 18 L 6606 yds Par 72 SSS 72
18 L 6156 yds Par 71 SSS 68
🙋 U SOC–WD–WE
£€ 18 hole: £25 (£35)
🚗 4 miles W of Cardiff on A48. M4
Junction 33
⊕ Driving range
🛉 Bob Sandow
■ www.cottrell-park.co.uk

Dinas Powis (1914)
Old Highwalls, Dinas Powis, CF64 4AJ
☎ **(029) 2051 2727**
📠 (029) 2051 2727
💷 490
♬ Ginny Golding
√ G Bennett (029) 2051 3682
🏌 18 L 5486 yds SSS 68
🙋 H SOC
£€ D–£25 (£30)
🚗 3 miles SW of Cardiff (A4055)

Glamorganshire (1890)
Lavernock Road, Penarth, CF64 5UP
☎ **(029) 2070 1185**
📠 (029) 2070 1185
📧 glamgolf@btconnect.com
💷 1100
♬ BM Williams (029) 2070 1185
√ A Kerr-Smith (029) 2070 7401
🏌 18 L 6181 yds SSS 70
🙋 WD/WE–H SOC
£€ £35 (£40)
🚗 5 miles SW of Cardiff, M4 J33
■ www.glamorganshiregolfclub.co.uk

Llanishen (1905)

Heol Hir, Cardiff, CF14 9UD
- ☎ **(029) 2075 5078**
- 📠 (029) 2075 5078
- 🔢 850
- ✍ Mrs A Gregory (029) 2075 5078
- ⟋ RA Jones (029) 2075 5076
- ⊳ 18 L 5338 yds SSS 67
- ❀ WD–U WE–M H SOC–Thurs & Fri
- ££ £32
- ⊕ 5 miles N of Cardiff

Peterstone Lakes

Peterstone, Wentloog, Cardiff, CF3 2TN
- ☎ **(01633) 680009**
- 📠 (01633) 680563
- ✉ peterstone_lakes@yahoo.com
- 🔢 600
- ✍ P Millar
- ⟋ P Glynn (01633) 680075
- ⊳ 18 L 6555 yds Par 72 SSS 72
- ❀ U SOC
- ££ £18 (£25)
- ⊕ 3 miles S of Castleton, off A48. M4 Junction 28
- ⋔ Robert Sandow

Radyr (1902)

Drysgol Road, Radyr, Cardiff, CF15 8BS
- ☎ **(029) 2084 2408**
- 📠 (029) 2084 3914
- ✉ manager@radyrgolf.co.uk
- 🔢 915
- ✍ AM Edwards (Mgr) (029) 2084 2408
- ⟋ R Butterworth (029) 2084 2476
- ⊳ 18 L 6053 yds SSS 70
- ❀ SOC–Wed/Thurs/Fri
- ££ D–£38
- ⊕ 5 miles NW of Cardiff, off A470. M4 Junction 32
- ⊕ Large practice area
- ⋔ Braid/Holt
- ■ www.radyrgolf.co.uk

RAF St Athan (1977)

St Athan, Barry, CF62 4WA
- ☎ **(01446) 751043**
- 📠 (01446) 751862
- 🔢 450
- ✍ PF Woodhouse (01446) 797186
- ⊳ 9 L 6452 yds SSS 72
- ❀ U exc Sun am–NA
- ££ £12 (£17)
- ⊕ 2 miles E of Llantwit Major. 10 miles S of Bridgend

St Andrews Major (1993)

Coldbrook Road, Cadoxton, Barry, CF6 3BB
- ☎ **(01446) 722227**
- 🔢 350
- ✍ N Edmunds
- ⊳ 9 L 2931 yds
- ❀ U SOC
- ££ 9 holes–£8. 18 holes–£13
- ⊕ Barry Docks Link road. M4 Junction 33
- ⋔ MRM Leisure

St Mary's Hotel G&CC (1990)

Pay and play
St Mary's Hill, Pencoed, CF35 5EA
- ☎ **(01656) 861100**
- 📠 (01656) 863400
- 🔢 800
- ✍ Kay Brazell
- ⟋ J Peters (01656) 861599
- ⊳ 18 L 5291 yds Par 69 SSS 66
  9 L 2426 yds Par 35
- ❀ H SOC–WD
- ££ 18 hole: £15 (£17) 9 hole:£5 (£6)
- ⊕ Off M4 Junction 35
- ⊕ Floodlit driving range

St Mellons (1937)

St Mellons, Cardiff, CF3 2XS
- ☎ **(01633) 680408**
- 📠 (01633) 681219
- 🔢 550 89(L) 67(J)
- ✍ RH Boyce (01633) 680408
- ⟋ B Thomas (01633) 680101
- ⊳ 18 L 6225 yds SSS 70
- ❀ U exc Sat–NA SOC
- ££ £27.50
- ⊕ 4 miles E of Cardiff on A48. M4 Junction 28

Vale of Glamorgan Hotel G&CC

Hensol Park, Hensol, CF7 8JY
- ☎ **(01443) 665899**
- 📠 (01443) 222220
- 🔢 900
- ✍ Mrs L Edwards
- ⟋ P Johnson
- ⊳ Lake 18 L 6507 yds Par 72
  Hensol 9 L 3115 yds Par 36
- ❀ H SOC
- ££ £25 (£30)
- ⊕ 1 mile from M 4 Junction 34
- ⊕ Driving range. Golf Academy
- ⋔ Peter Johnson

Wenvoe Castle (1936)

Wenvoe, Cardiff, CF5 6BE
- ☎ **(029) 205 94371**
- 📠 (029) 205 94371
- ✉ wenvoe-castlegc@virgin.net
- 🔢 600
- ✍ N Sims (029) 2059 4371
- ⟋ J Harris (029) 2059 3649
- ⊳ 18 L 6422 yds SSS 71
- ❀ WD–H WE/BH–M SOC–WD
- ££ £32
- ⊕ 4 miles W of Cardiff, off A4050
- ■ www.wenvoecastlegolfclub.com

Whitchurch (1915)

Pantmawr Road, Whitchurch, Cardiff, CF4 6XD
- ☎ **(029) 2062 0125**
- 📠 (029) 2052 9860
- 🔢 780
- ✍ (029) 2062 0985
- ⟋ (029) 2061 4660
- ⊳ 18 L 6212 yds Par 71 SSS 71
- ❀ U H SOC–Thurs
- ££ £35 (£40)

- ⊕ 3 miles NW of Cardiff on A470. M4 Junction 32

West Glamorgan

Allt-y-Graban (1993)

Allt-y-Graban Road, Pontlliw, Swansea, SA4 1DT
- ☎ **(01792) 885757**
- 🔢 154
- ✍ Mrs GM Head
- ⟋ S Rees
- ⊳ 9 L 2480 yds Par 64 SSS 64
- ❀ U SOC
- ££ 18 holes–£11 (£11) 9 holes–£7 (£7)
- ⊕ 3 miles of M4 Junction 47, on A48
- ⋔ FG Thomas

Clyne (1920)

120 Owls Lodge Lane, Mayals, Swansea, SA3 5DP
- ☎ **(01792) 401989**
- 📠 (01792) 401078
- 🔢 900
- ✍ RH Thompson FCA (Mgr)
- ⟋ J Clewett (01792) 402094
- ⊳ 18 L 6323 yds SSS 72
- ❀ U H SOC
- ££ £26 (£32)
- ⊕ 3 miles SW of Swansea
- ⊕ Driving range
- ⋔ Colt/Harris

Earlswood (1993)

Pay and play
Jersey Marine, Neath, SA10 6JP
- ☎ **(01792) 321578**
- ✍ Mrs D Goatcher (01792) 812198
- ⟋ M Day
- ⊳ 18 L 5174 yds SSS 68
- ❀ U SOC
- ££ £8
- ⊕ 5 miles E of Swansea, off A483 (B4290)

Fairwood Park (1969)

Blackhills Lane, Upper Killay, Swansea, SA2 7JN
- ☎ **(01792) 203648**
- 📠 (01792) 297849
- 🔢 650
- ✍ D Giltrap, J Pettifer (Mgr)
- ⟋ G Hughes (01792) 299194
- ⊳ 18 L 6650 yds SSS 73
- ❀ U SOC
- ££ £25 (£30)
- ⊕ 4 miles W of Swansea (A4118)
- ⋔ Hawtree

Glynneath (1931)

Penygraig, Pontneathvaughan, Glynneath, SA11 5UH
- ☎ **(01639) 720452**
- 📠 (01639) 720452
- ✉ glynneathgolf@tiscali.co.uk
- 🔢 644
- ✍ DA Fellowes
- ⟋ N Evans
- ⊳ 18 L 5656 yds SSS 68

U H SOC
£€ £17 (£22)
⊶ 2 miles NW of Glynneath on
B4242. 15 miles NE of Swansea
⌂ Cotton/Pennink/Lawrie

Gower
Cefn Goleu, Three Crosses, Gowerton,
Swansea SA4 3HS
☎ (01792) 872480
🖳 (01792) 872480
✉ adrian.richards@gowergolf.co.uk
📖 600
♟ JD Morgan (01792) 872480
✓ A Williamson (01792) 879905
🏳 18 L 6450 yds Par 71 SSS 72
👫 H
£€ £20
⊶ 5 miles W of Swansea, off B4295
⌂ Donald Steele
■ www.gowergolf.co.uk

Inco (1965)
Clydach, Swansea, SA6 5QR
☎ (01792) 841257
📖 600
♟ DE Jones (01792) 842929
🏳 18 L 6064 yds Par 70 SSS 69
👫 U
£€ £18 (£23)
⊶ N of Swansea (A4067)

Lakeside (1992)
Pay and play
Water Street, Margam, Port Talbot,
SA13 2PA
☎ (01639) 899959
📖 150
♟ B Channell
✓ M Wootton
🏳 18 L 4550 yds Par 63 SSS 63
👫 U SOC
£€ £10
⊶ Nr M4 Junction 38
⊕ Driving range
⌂ M Wootton

Langland Bay (1904)
Langland Bay Road, Langland, Swansea,
SA3 4QR
☎ (01792) 366023
🖳 (01792) 361082
✉ golf@langlandbay.sagehost.co.uk
📖 800
♟ Mrs L Coleman (01792) 361721
✓ M Evans (01792) 366186
🏳 18 L 5857 yds SSS 69
👫 H SOC
£€ £28 (£30)
⊶ 6 miles S of Swansea (A4067). M4
Junction 45
■ www.langlandbaygolfclub.com

Morriston (1919)
160 Clasemont Road, Morriston,
Swansea, SA6 6AJ
☎ (01792) 771079
🖳 (01792) 796528
📖 585
♟ KJ Hackford (Sec/Mgr)
(01792) 796528

✓ (01792) 772335
🏳 18 L 5785 yds SSS 68
👫 U H SOC–WD
£€ £18 (£30)
⊶ 4 miles N of Swansea on A48. M4
Junction 46, 1 mile

Neath (1934)
Cadoxton, Neath, SA10 8AH
☎ (01639) 643615
🖳 (01639) 632759
📖 750
♟ DM Hughes (01639) 632759
✓ EM Bennett (01639) 633693
🏳 18 L 6500 yds SSS 72
👫 WD–U WE–M SOC
£€ Summer–£20 (£20) Winter £12
(£12)
⊶ 2 miles NE of Neath (B4434)
⌂ James Braid

Palleg (1930)
Palleg Road, Lower Cwmtwrch, Swansea
Valley, SA9 2QQ
☎ (01639) 842193
🖳 (01639) 845661
✉ palleg@golf-club.freeserve.co.uk
📖 250
♟ C Percival
✓ Sharon Roberts (01639) 842193
🏳 9 L 3209 yds SSS 72
18 holes open May 2004
👫 WD–U Sat–NA Sun/BH–phone
first SOC
£€ On application
⊶ 15 miles NE of Swansea (A4067).
M4 Junction 45

Pennard (1896)
2 Southgate Road, Southgate, Swansea,
SA3 2BT
☎ (01792) 233131
🖳 (01792) 234797
✉ pigeon01@globalnet.co.uk
📖 775
♟ EM Howell (01792) 233131
✓ MV Bennett (01792) 233451
🏳 18 L 6265 yds SSS 72
👫 U H SOC–WD only
£€ £27 (£35) W–£90
⊶ 8 miles W of Swansea, by A4067
and B4436
■ www.golfagent.com/clubsites
/pennard

Pontardawe (1924)
Cefn Llan, Pontardawe, Swansea,
SA8 4SH
☎ (01792) 863118
🖳 (01792) 830041
✉ pontardawe@btopenworld.com
📖 574
♟ K Davey (Hon), Mrs M Griffiths
(Admin)
✓ G Hopkins (01792) 830977
🏳 18 L 6101 yds SSS 70
👫 H SOC–WD
£€ £18
⊶ 5 miles N of M4 Junction 45, off
A4067
■ www.pontardawegc.co.uk

Swansea Bay (1892)
Jersey Marine, Neath, SA10 6JP
☎ (01792) 812198
📖 400
♟ Mrs D Goatcher (01792) 814153
✓ M Day (01792) 816159
🏳 18 L 6256 yds SSS 71
👫 U SOC
£€ £17 (£24)
⊶ 5 miles E of Swansea, off A483
(B4290). M4 Junction 42

Wrexham

Chirk (1990)
Chirk, Wrexham, LL14 5AD
☎ (01691) 774407
🖳 (01691) 773878
✉ chirk-jackbarker@btinternet.com
📖 300
♟ MCA Moss
✓ M Maddison
🏳 18 L 7045 yds Par 72 SSS 73
9 hole Par 3 course
👫 U after 10am SOC
£€ £18 D–£25 (£19 D–£25)
⊶ 8 miles S of Wrexham on A483
⊕ Driving range
■ www.jackbarker.com

Clays (1992)
Bryn Estyn Road, Wrexham, LL13 9UB
☎ (01978) 661406
🖳 (01978) 661417
✉ clays@wrexhamgolf.fsnet.co.uk
📖 500
✓ D Larvin
🏳 18 L 6000 yds Par 69
Par 3 short course
👫 U SOC
£€ £14 (£19)
⊶ Wrexham, off A534
⊕ 16 bay floodlit driving range

Moss Valley (1990)
Pay and play
Moss Road, Wrexham, LL11 6HA
☎ (01978) 720518
🖳 (01978) 720518
📖 100
♟ J Parry, J Lloyd (Mgr)
🏳 9 L 2641 yds Par 68 SSS 67
👫 U
£€ 9 holes–£6 (£8) 18 holes–£9 (£12)
⊶ N of Wrexham, off A541
■ www.mossvalleygolf.com

Pen-y-Cae (1993)
Ruabon Road, Pen-y-Cae, Wrexham,
LL14 1TW
☎ (01978) 810108
📖 100
♟ G Williams (Mgr)
🏳 9 L 4280 yds Par 64 SSS 62
👫 U SOC–WD
£€ 9 holes–£5 (£6) 18 holes–£7.50
(£9.50)
⊶ 6 miles S of Wrexham, via
A483/A539
⌂ John Day

Plassey   (1992)
Eyton, Wrexham, LL13 0SP
☎ **(01978) 780020**
🖥 (01978) 781397
📖 165
✍ J Taylor (01978) 780020
✓ S Ward (01978) 780020
🏴 9 L 4962 yds Par 66 SSS 64
👥 U SOC

£€ £14 (£16)
⛳ 2 miles SW of Wrexham, off A483
⊕ 9 hole pitch & putt course
🏠 K Williams
◼ www.plasseygolf.co.uk

Wrexham   (1904)
Holt Road, Wrexham, LL13 9SB
☎ **(01978) 261033**

🖥 (01978) 364268
✉ info@wrexhamgolfclub.co.uk
📖 650
✍ J Johnson (01978) 364268
✓ P Williams (01978) 351476
🏴 18 L 6233 yds Par 70 SSS 70
👥 H SOC–WD
£€ £25 (£30)
⛳ 2 miles NE of Wrexham on A534
🏠 James Braid

Continent of Europe – Country and Region Index

Austria
Innsbruck & Tirol 830
Klagenfurt & South 830
Linz & North 830
Salzburg Region 831
Steiermark 832
Vienna & East 833
Vorarlberg 834

Belgium
Antwerp Region 834
Ardennes & South 834
Brussels & Brabant 835
East 836
West & Oost Vlaanderen 836

Czech Republic 837

Denmark
Bornholm Island 837
Funen 837
Greenland 838
Jutland 838
Zealand 840

Finland
Central 842
Helsinki & South 842
North 843
South East 844
South West 844

France
Bordeaux & South West 844
Brittany 846
Burgundy & Auvergne 847
Centre 848
Channel Coast & North 850
Corsica 851
Ile de France 852
Languedoc-Roussillon 853
Loire Valley 854
Normandy 855
North East 856
Paris Region 858
Provence & Côte d'Azur 858
Rhône-Alps 860
Toulouse & Pyrenees 862

Germany
Berlin & East 863
Bremen & North West 863

Central North 864
Central South 865
Hamburg & North 866
Hanover & Weserbergland 868
Munich & South Bavaria 869
Nuremberg & North Bavaria 871
Rhineland North 872
Rhineland South 875
Saar-Pfalz 876
Stuttgart & South West 876

Greece 878

Hungary 878

Iceland 879

Italy
Como/Milan/Bergamo 879
Elba 881
Emilia Romagna 881
Gulf of Genoa 881
Lake Garda & Dolomites 882
Naples & South 882
Rome & Centre 882
Sardinia 883
Sicily 883
Turin & Piemonte 883
Tuscany & Umbria 884
Venice & North East 885

Luxembourg 886

Malta 886

Netherlands
Amsterdam & Noord Holland 886
Breda & South West 887
East Central 887
Eindhoven & South East 888
Limburg Province 889
North 889
Rotterdam & The Hague 889
Utrecht & Hilversum 890

Norway 891

Poland 892

Portugal
Algarve 892
Azores 893

Lisbon & Central Portugal 893
Madeira 894
North 894

Slovenia 895

Spain
Alicante & Murcia 895
Almería 896
Badajoz & West 896
Balearic Islands 896
Barcelona & Cataluña 897
Burgos & North 898
Canary Islands 899
Córdoba 899
Galicia 899
Granada 899
Madrid Region 900
Málaga Region 900
Marbella & Estepona 901
Seville & Gulf of Cádiz 902
Valencia & Castellón 903
Valladolid 903
Zaragoza 903

Sweden
East Central 903
Far North 905
Gothenburg 906
Malmö & South Coast 907
North 908
Skane & South 909
South East 910
South West 912
Stockholm 913
West Central 915

Switzerland
Bern 916
Bernese Oberland 916
Lake Geneva & South West 916
Lugano & Ticino 917
St Moritz & Engadine 917
Zürich & North 917

Turkey 918

Austria

Innsbruck & Tirol

Achensee   (1934)
6213 Pertisau/Tirol
☎ (05243) 5377
🖥 (05243) 6202
📧 golfclub-achensee@tirol.com
⊳ 9 L 5501 m SSS 70
👭 U H
££ €38 (€43)
👬 Pertisau, 50km NE of Innsbruck
🖥 www.golfclub-achensee.com

Innsbruck-Igls   (1935)
Oberdorf 11, 6074 Rinn
☎ (05223) 78177
🖥 (05223) 78177-77
📧 office@golfclub-innsbruck-igls.at
⊳ Rinn 18 L 6055 m Par 71 CR 71.3
    SR 129
    Lans 9 L 4597 m Par 66 CR 64.3
👭 H–booking necessary
££ €44 (€53)
👬 Rinn, 10km E of Innsbruck. Lans,
    8km from Innsbruck
🖥 www.golfclub-innsbruck-igls.at

Kaiserwinkl GC Kössen
(1988)
6345 Kössen, Mühlau 1
☎ (05375) 2122
🖥 (05375) 2122-13
📧 club@golf-koessau.at
⊳ 18 L 5645 m CR 70.7 SR 127
👭 H
££ €52 (€55)
👬 30km N of Kitzbühel, nr German
    border
🏛 Donald Harradine
🖥 www.golf-koessen.at

Kitzbühel   (1955)
Schloss Kaps, 6370 Kitzbühel
☎ (05356) 63007
🖥 (05356) 63007-7
⊳ 9 hole reconstruction open July
    2004
👭 H
👬 Kitzbühel
🏛 Max Lamberg
🖥 www.golf.at.gckitzbuehel

Kitzbühel-Schwarzsee (1988)
6370 Kitzbühel, Golfweg Schwarzsee 35
☎ (05356) 71645
🖥 (05356) 72785
⊳ 18 L 6247 m SSS 72
👭 H–booking necessary
££ €47–€55
👬 4km from Kitzbühel
🏛 G Hauser

Seefeld-Wildmoos   (1968)
6100 Seefeld, Postfach 22
☎ (0699) 1-606606-0

🖥 (0699) 4-606606-3
⊳ 18 L 5894 m CR 72 SR 130
👭 H–booking necessary
££ €40–€55
👬 7 km W of Seefeld. 24 km W of
    Innsbruck
🏛 Donald Harradine
🖥 www.seefeldgolf.com

Klagenfurt & South

Austria-Wörther See
9062 Moosburg, Golfstr 2
☎ (04272) 83486
🖥 (04272) 82055
📧 moosburg@golfktn.at
⊳ 18 L 6011 m SSS 72
    9 L 2341 m SSS 35
👭 U
££ €50
👬 3km N of Wörther See/Pörtschach
🏛 G Hauser
🖥 www.moosburg.golfktn.at

Bad Kleinkirchheim-
Reichenau   (1977)
9564 Padergassen, Plass 19
☎ (04275) 594
🖥 (04275) 594-4
⊳ 18 L 6074 m Par 72 SSS 72
👭 H
££ €434 (€53)
👬 Kleinkirchheim, 50 km NW of
    Klagenfurt, via Route 95
🏛 Donald Harradine

Kärntner   (1927)
Dellach, 9082 Maria Wörth, Golfstr 3
☎ (04273) 2515
🖥 (04273) 2514-20
⊳ 18 L 5778 m Par 71
👭 H
££ €60
👬 Dellach, S side of Wörther See.
    15km W of Klagenfurt
🖥 www.kgcdellach.at

Klopeiner See-Turnersee
(1988)
9122 St Kanzian, Grabelsdorf 94
☎ (04239) 3800-0
🖥 (04239) 3800-18
⊳ 18 L 6114 m Par 72
👭 U
££ €44
👬 25km E of Klagenfurt
🏛 Donald Harradine

Wörther See/Velden   (1988)
9231 Köstenberg, Golfweg u1
☎ (04274) 7045/7087
🖥 (04274) 708715
🖩 330
⊳ 18 L 6081 m SSS 72
👭 H
££ €54
👬 30km W of Klagenfurt. 12km from
    Velden

🏛 Erhardt/Rossknecht
🖥 www.golfk+n.at

Linz & North

Amstetten-Ferschnitz   (1972)
3325 Ferschnitz, Gut Edla 18
☎ (07473) 8293
🖥 (07473) 82934
📧 office@golfclub-amstetten.at
⊳ 18 holes Par 71
👭 U H
££ €45 (€50)
👬 70km E of Linz
🏛 F Bouchard
🖥 www.golfclub-amstetten.at

Böhmerwald GC
Ulrichsberg   (1990)
4161 Ulrichsberg, Seitelschlag 50
☎ (07288) 8200
🖥 (07288) 8422
⊳ 18 L 6240 m SSS 73
    9 hole Par 3 course
👭 U H
££ €35 (€41)
👬 65km NW of Linz
🏛 Rossknecht/Erhardt

Haugschlag
3874 Haugschlag 160
☎ (02865) 8441
🖥 (02865) 8441-22
⊳ 18 L 6140 m SSS 72
    18 L 6448 m SSS 74
    18 hole Par 3 course
👭 H
££ €46 (€62)
👬 25km N of Gmund. 140km NW of
    Vienna
🖥 www.golfresort.at

Herzog Tassilo   (1991)
Blankenbergerstr 30, 4540 Bad Hall
☎ (07258) 5480
🖥 (07258) 5480-11
⊳ 18 L 5710 m SSS 70
👭 U
££ €35 (€50)
👬 30km SW of Linz
🏛 Peter Mayerhofer
🖥 www.golf.at

PGC Kremstal   (1989)
Schachen 20, 4531 Kematen/Krems
☎ (07228) 7644-0
🖥 (07228) 7644-7
⊳ 18 L 5763 m Par 70
👭 H
££ €40/€50 (€50)
👬 20km W of Linz
🏛 Peter Mayerhofer
🖥 www.pgckremstal.at

Linz-St Florian   (1960)
4490 St Florian, Tillysburg 28
☎ (07223) 828730
🖥 (07223) 828737

℗ 18 L 5864 m Par 72 SSS 72
👥 H
£€ €51 (€62)
⛳ St Florian, 15km SE of Linz
🏠 Hanz Georg Erhardt

Linzer Luftenberg (1990)
4222 Luftenberg, Am Luftenberg 1a
☎ (07237) 3893
🖥 (07237) 3893-40
📧 gclinz-luftenberg@golf.at
℗ 18 L 5862 m CR 69.9 SR 119
👥 U H
£€ €45 (€50)
⛳ 15km NE of Linz
🏠 Keith Preston

Maria Theresia (1989)
Letten 5, 4680 Haag am Hausruck
☎ (07732) 3944
🖥 (07732) 3944-9
℗ 18 L 6055 m Par 72 SSS 72
👥 H
£€ €36 (€44)
⛳ Between Passau and Wels. A8 exit Haag
🏠 Angst/Stärk
🖥 www.members.eunet.at /gcmariatheresia

Ottenstein (1988)
3532 Niedergrünbach 60
☎ (02826) 7476
🖥 (02826) 7476-4
℗ 18 L 6129 m CR 71.9 SR 125
👥 U
£€ €40 (€50)
⛳ 90km NE of Linz. 100km NW of Vienna
🏠 Preston/Zinterl/Erhardt
🖥 www.golfclub-ottenstein.at

St Oswald-Freistadt (1988)
Promenade 22, 4271 St Oswald
☎ (07945) 7938
🖥 (07945) 79384
℗ 9 L 5888 m Par 72
👥 WD–UH WE–U H restricted
£€ €26 (€33)
⛳ 40km N of Linz
🏠 Mel Flanegan

St Pölten Schloss Goldegg (1989)
3100 St Pölten Schloss Goldegg
☎ (02741) 7360/7060
🖥 (02741) 73608
℗ 18 L 6249 m SSS 73
👥 H or I
£€ €29 (€36)
⛳ 8km NW of St Pölten. 60km W of Vienna

Schärding-Pramtal (1994)
Maad 2, 4775 Taufkirchen/Pram
☎ (07719) 8110
🖥 (07719) 8110 15
℗ 18 L 6386 m CR 72.2 SR 119
👥 H
£€ €38 (€43)

⛳ 10km S of Schärding on B137
🖥 www.gcschaerding.at

Schloss Ernegg (1973)
3261 Steinakirchen, Schloss Ernegg
☎ (07488) 76770
🖥 (07488) 76771/71171
℗ 18 L 5803 m SSS 71 9 L 2076 m SSS 62
👥 U
£€ €33 (€40)
⛳ Steinakirchen, 80km SE of Linz. 125km W of Vienna
🏠 Tucker/Day
🖥 www.ernegg.at

Traunsee Kircham
4656 Kircham, Kampesberg 38
☎ (07619) 2576
🖥 (07619) 2576-11
℗ 18 L 5725 m Par 70 SSS 70
👥 U
£€ €36 (€44)
⛳ 10km E of Gmunden. 50km SW of Linz

Weitra (1989)
3970 Weitra, Hausschachen
☎ (02856) 2058
🖥 (02856) 2058-4
℗ 18 L 5916 m Par 72
👥 WD–U WE–H
£€ €33 (€40)
⛳ 75km NE of Linz, nr Czech border
🏠 M Gansdorfer

Wels (1981)
4616 Weisskirchen, Weyerbach 37
☎ (07243) 56038
🖥 (07243) 56685
℗ 18 L 6098 m Par 72
👥 H
£€ €36 (€44)
⛳ 5 km from Salzburg-Vienna highway. 8km SE of Wels
🏠 Hauser/Hunt Hastings

Salzburg Region

Bad Gastein (1960)
5640 Bad Gastein, Golfstrasse 6
☎ (06434) 2775
🖥 (06434) 2775-4
℗ 18 L 5639 m Yellow Par 71 CR 69.4 SR 125 Red Par 71 CR 70.8 SR 122
👥 H
£€ €49
⛳ Bad Gastein 2 km. Salzburg 100km
🏠 B von Limburger

Goldegg
5622 Goldegg, Postfach 6
☎ (06415) 8585
🖥 (06415) 8585-4
℗ 18 L 4693 m Par 70
👥 U
£€ €40 (€45)
⛳ 60km SW of Salzburg

Gut Altentann (1989)
Hof 54, 5302 Henndorf am Wallersee
☎ (06214) 6026-0
🖥 (06214) 6105-81
℗ 18 L 6103 m CR 70 SR 125
👥 H (max 34) – booking necessary
£€ €56–€67
⛳ Henndorf, 16km NE of Salzburg
🏠 Jack Nicklaus
🖥 www.gutaltentann.com

Gut Brandlhof G&CC (1983)
5760 Saalfelden am Steinernen Meer, Hohlwegen 4
☎ (06582) 7800-555
🖥 (06582) 7800-529
℗ 18 L 6218 m SSS 72
👥 I H
£€ €40 (€47)
⛳ Saalfelden, 70km SW of Salzburg towards Zell am See
🏠 Kofler

Kobernausserwald
Strass 1, A-5241 Höhnart
☎ (07743) 20066
🖥 (07743) 20077
📧 office@gckobernausserwald.at
👤 E Reinhard (Mgr)
℗ Men: 18 L 5200 m Par 70 Ladies: 18 L 4750 m par 70
👥 M
£€ Mon–Fri 9 €19, 18 €38 Fri–Sun 9 €22, 18 €43
⛳ 50km from Salzburg, 120km from Linz, 150km from Munich
🏠 Heinz Schmidbauer
🖥 www.gckobernausserwald.at

Lungau (1991)
5582 St Michael, Feldnergasse 165
☎ (06477) 7448
🖥 (06477) 7448-4
℗ 18 L 6438 m CR 72.4 SR 121 9 L 2502 m Par 56
👥 U – soft spikes only
£€ €46 (€54)
⛳ St Michael, 120km S of Salzburg
🏠 Keith Preston
🖥 www.golfclub-lungau.at

Am Mondsee (1986)
St Lorenz 400, 5310 Mondsee
☎ (06232) 3835-0
🖥 (06232) 3835-83
℗ 18 L 6036 m SSS 72
👥 H
£€ €40 (€47)
⛳ Mondsee, 25km E of Salzburg
🏠 Marc Miller

Radstadt Tauerngolf (1991)
Römerstrasse 18, 5550 Radstadt
☎ (06452) 5111
🖥 (06452) 7336
📧 info@radstadtgolf.at
℗ 18 L 6023 m Par 71 Men: CR 70.5 SR 127. Women: CR 72.5 SR 127 9 hole Par 3 course

👥 U
£€ €41 (€58)
🚗 70km NW of Salzburg
💻 www.radstatdgolf.at

Salzburg Fuschl (1995)

5322 Hof/Salzburg
☎ (06229) 2390
🖥 (06229) 2390
🏴 9 L 3650 m Par 62
9 hole Par 3 course
👥 U
£€ €22–€29
🚗 Hof, 12km E of Salzburg

Salzburg G&CC (1955)

Schloss Klessheim, 5071 Wals
☎ (0662) 850851
🖥 (0662) 857925
📧 gccsalzburg@golf.at
🏴 9 L 5700 m SSS 70
👥 U H–max M36 W36
£€ €40 (€48) 9 holes €25 (€25)
🚗 5km N of Salzburg
🏠 Robert Trent Jones Jr

Salzkammergut (1933)

4820 Bad Ischl, Postfach 506
☎ (06132) 26340
🖥 (06132) 26708
🏴 18 L 5673 m Par 71
👥 U H
£€ €40 (€50)
🚗 6 km W of Bad Ischl, nr Strobl. 50 km E of Salzburg
💻 www.salzkammergut-golf.at

Urslautal (1991)

Schinking 1, 5760 Saalfelden
☎ (06584) 2000
🖥 (06584) 7475-10
🏴 18 L 6030 m SSS 71
👥 U H
£€ €50 (€55)
🚗 80km SW of Salzburg
🏠 Keith Preston
💻 www.golf-urslautal.at

Zell am See-Kaprun (1983)

5700 Zell am See-Kaprun, Golfstr 25
☎ (06542) 56161
🖥 (06542) 56161-16
📧 gc.zellamsee-kaprun@telecom.at
🏴 18 L 5980 m CR 71.2 SR 122
18 L 6003 m CR 70.5 SR 125
👥 H
£€ €57 (€65)
🚗 Zell am See, 80km SW of Salzburg
🏠 Harradine/Schauer
💻 www.europasportregion.at/golfclub

Steiermark

Bad Gleichenberg (1984)

Am Hoffeld 3, 8344 Bad Gleichenberg
☎ (03159) 3717
🖥 (03159) 3065
📧 gcgleichenberg@golf.at

🏴 9 L 5422 m CR 69.5 SR 129
👥 M
£€ €30 (€36)
🚗 60km SE of Graz
🏠 Hauser
💻 www.murhofgrieppe.at

Dachstein Tauern (1990)

8967 Haus/Ennstal, Oberhaus 59
☎ (03686) 2630
🖥 (03686) 2630-15
🏴 18 L 5910 m SSS 71
👥 U
£€ €60
🚗 2km from Schladming. 100km SE of Salzburg
🏠 Bernhard Langer
💻 www.schladming-golf.at

Ennstal-Weissenbach G&LC (1978)

8940 Liezen, Postfach 193
☎ (03612) 24821
🖥 (03612) 24821-4
🏴 18 L 5655 m SSS 70
👥 U H I
£€ €33 (€36)
🚗 100km SE of Salzburg. 100km NW of Graz
🏠 Gert Aigner

Furstenfeld (1984)

8282 Loipersdorf, Gillersdorf 50
☎ (03382) 8533
🖥 (03382) 8533-33
🏴 18 L 6192 m SSS 72
👥 U
£€ €36 (€44)
🚗 70km E of Graz

Graz (1989)

8051 Graz-Thal, Windhof 137
☎ (0316) 572867
🖥 (0316) 572867-4
🏴 9 L 5102 m CR 67 SR 112
👥 U
£€ €33–€40 (€45)
🚗 10km W of Graz
🏠 Herwig Zisser

Gut Murstätten (1989)

8403 Lebring, Oedt 14
☎ (03182) 3555
🖥 (03182) 3688
🏴 18 L 6238 m CR 70.5 SR 122
9 L 5990 m CR 70.4 SR 116
👥 H
£€ €46 (€55)
🚗 25km S of Graz
🏠 J Dudok van Heel
💻 www.gcmurstaetten.at

Maria Lankowitz (1992)

Puchbacher Str 109, 8591 Maria Lankowitz
☎ (03144) 6970
🖥 (03144) 6970-4
🏴 18 L 6121 m SSS 72
👥 U
£€ €33 (€40)

🚗 40km W of Graz
🏠 Herwig Zisser

Murhof (1963)

8130 Frohnleiten, Adriach 53
☎ (03126) 3010
🖥 (03126) 3000-29
🏴 18 L 6198 m Par 72
👥 U H
£€ €48 (€63)
🚗 Frohnleiten, 25km N of Graz. 150km S of Vienna
🏠 B von Limburger

Murtal (1995)

Frauenbachstr 51, 8724 Spielberg
☎ (03512) 75213
🖥 (03512) 75213
🏴 18 L 5951 m Par 72
👥 H I
£€ €40 (€44)
🚗 Knittelfeld, 80km NW of Graz, via Route S36
🏠 Jeff Howes
💻 www.gcmurtal.at

Reiting G&CC (1990)

8772 Traboch, Schulweg 7
☎ (0663) 833308/(03847) 5008
🖥 (03847) 5682
🏴 9 L 6300 m Par 73 SSS 72
👥 U
£€ €26 (€30)
🚗 60km N of Graz

St Lorenzen (1990)

8642 St Lorenzen, Gassing 22
☎ (03864) 3961
🖥 (03864) 3961-2
🏴 9 L 5374 m Par 70 SSS 70
👥 U
£€ €26 (€30)
🚗 60km N of Graz, nr Kapfenberg
🏠 Manfred Flasch

Schloss Frauenthal (1988)

8530 Deutschlandsberg, Ulrichsberg 7
☎ (03462) 5717
🖥 (03462) 5717-5
📧 office@gcfrauenthal.at
🏴 18 L 5447 m SSS 70
👥 U H
£€ €45 (€50)
🚗 30km SW of Graz
🏠 Stephan Breisach
💻 www.gcfrauenthal.at

Schloss Pichlarn (1972)

8952 Irdning/Ennstal, Gatschen 28
☎ (03682) 22841-540
🖥 (03682) 22841-580
🏴 18 L 5863 m CR 70.7 SR 125
👥 U
£€ €43 (€51)
🚗 2km E of Irdning, off Salzburg-Graz road. 120km SE of Salzburg
🏠 Donald Harradine
💻 www.pichlarn.at

Vienna & East

Adamstal   (1994)
Gaupmannsgraben 21, 3172 Ramsal
☎ **(02764) 3500**
🖳 (02764) 3500-15
🏌 18 L 5514 m CR 70 SR 128
👥 U
£€ €45 (€60)
🚗 65km SW of Vienna
🏠 Jeff Howes
🖥 www.adamstal.at

Bad Tatzmannsdorf G&CC (1991)
Am Golfplatz 2, 7431 Bad Tatzmannsdorf
☎ **(03353) 8282-0**
🖳 (03353) 8282-1735
🏌 18 L 6180m Par 73 CR 72.7 SR 129
    9 L 3660 m Par 60 CR 60.2 Slope 103
👥 U H
£€ 18: €43 (€55) 9: €30 (€35)
🚗 120km SE of Vienna
🏠 Rossknecht/Erhardt

Brunn G&CC   (1988)
2345 Brunn/Gebirge, Rennweg 50
☎ **(02236) 33711**
🖳 (02236) 33863
🖂 club@gccbrunn.at
🏌 18 L 5749 m Par 70 CR 70 SR 121
👥 H – soft spikes only
£€ €45 (€55)
🚗 10km S of Vienna
🏠 G Hauser
🖥 www.golf.at

Colony Club Gutenhof (1988)
2325 Himberg, Gutenhof
☎ **(02235) 87055-0**
🖳 (02235) 87055-14
🏌 East 18 L 6335 m SSS 73
    West 18 L 6397 m SSS 73
👥 H
£€ €36 (€55)
🚗 7km SE of Vienna
🏠 Rossknecht/Erhardt

Danube Golf-Wien   (1995)
Weingartenallee 22, 1220 Wien
☎ **(0222) 25072**
🖳 (0222) 25072-44
🏌 18 L 6130 m SSS 72
👥 H
£€ €40 (€40)
🚗 15km NE of Vienna
🏠 Rossknecht/Erhardt

Eldorado Bucklige Welt (1990)
Golfplatz 1, 2871 Zöbern
☎ **(02642) 8451**
🖳 (02642) 8451-52
🏌 18 L 4029m CR 64.5 SR 118

👥 H–max 45
£€ €32 (€50)
🚗 90km S of Vienna via A2 Exit 80
🏠 DI Anton P Reithofer
🖥 WWW.golf1.at

Enzesfeld   (1970)
2551 Enzesfeld
☎ **(02256) 81272**
🖳 (02256) 81272-4
🖂 gcenzesfeld@golf.at
🏌 18 L 6061 m Par 72 CR 72.3 SR 129
👥 H
£€ €52 (€70)
🚗 32km S of Vienna. A2 Junction 29 (Leobersdorf)
🏠 Cdr John D Harris

Föhrenwald   (1968)
2700 Wiener Neustadt, Postfach 105
☎ **(02622) 29171**
🖳 (02622) 29171-4
🖂 gcfoehrenwald@golf.at
🏌 18 L 6317 m SSS 72
👥 H
£€ €45 (€60)
🚗 5 km S of Wiener Neustadt on Route B54
🏠 Jeff Howes
🖥 www.gcf.at

Fontana   (1996)
Fontana Allee 1, 2522 Oberwaltersdorf
☎ **(02253) 606401**
🖳 (02253) 606403
🏌 18 L 6088 m Par 72
👥 U–booking necessary. Soft spikes only
£€ €73 (€99)
🚗 20km S of Vienna
🏠 Carrick/Erhardt

Hainburg/Donau   (1977)
2410 Hainburg, Auf der Heide 762
☎ **(02165) 62628**
🖳 (02165) 626283
🏌 18 L 6064 m SSS 72
👥 H
£€ €30 (€50)
🚗 50km E of Vienna
🏠 G Hauser

Lengenfeld   (1995)
Am Golfplatz 1, 3552 Lengenfeld
☎ **(02719) 8710**
🖳 (02719) 8738
🏌 18 L 6130 m Par 72
👥 U
£€ €29 (€36)
🚗 80km W of Vienna. Krems 8km

Neusiedlersee-Donnerskirchen (1988)
7082 Donnerskirchen
☎ **(02683) 8171**
🖳 (02683) 817231
🏌 18 L 5937 m SSS 72
👥 U
£€ €36 (€36)

🚗 45km SE of Vienna
🏠 Rossknecht-Erhardt

Schloss Ebreichsdorf   (1988)
2483 Ebreichsdorf, Schlossallee 1
☎ **(02254)73888**
🖳 (02254) 73888-13
🖂 office@gcebreichsdorf.at
🏌 18 L 6161 m Par 72 SSS 73
👥 WD–H WE–on request
£€ €48 (€65)
🚗 28km S of Vienna
🏠 Keith Preston
🖥 www.golf.at

Schloss Schönborn   (1987)
2013 Schönborn 4
☎ **(02267) 2863/2879**
🖳 (02267) 2879-19
🏌 27 L 6265-6474 m Par 72-73
👥 U H
£€ €44 (€58)
🚗 40km N of Vienna

Schönfeld   (1989)
A-2291 Schönfeld, Am Golfplatz 1
☎ **+44 (02213) 2063**
🖳 +43 (02213) 20631
🖂 gcschoenfeld@golf.at
🏌 18 L 6089 m Par 72
    CR 71.9 SR 123 (white)
    CR 70.7 SR 121 (yellow)
    CR 74.1 SR 127 (black)
    CR 72.4 SR 124 (red)
    9 hole Par 3 course
👥 H
£€ 18 hole: €36 (€50) 9 hole: €22 (€30)
🚗 35km E of Vienna
🏠 G Hauser
🖥 www.golf.at
    /clubdetail.asp?clubnr=315

Semmering   (1926)
2680 Semmering
☎ **(02664) 8154**
🖳 (02664) 2114
🏌 9 L 3786 m SSS 60
👥 H
£€ €26 (€33)
🚗 30km SW of Vienna Neustadt

Thayatal Drosendorf   (1994)
Autendorf 18, 2095 Drosendorf
☎ **(02915) 62625**
🖳 (02915) 62625
🏌 18 L 4289 m CR 64.4 SR 110
👥 U
£€ €18 (€29)
🚗 100km NW of Vienna, nr Czech border (B4)
🏠 Rudolf Schedl

Wien   (1901)
1020 Wien, Freudenau 65a
☎ **(0222) 728 9564 (Clubhouse)**
    (0222) 728 9667 (Caddymaster)
🖳 (0222) 728 9564-20
🏌 18 L 5861 m SSS 71
👥 WE–NA
£€ €58
🚗 10 mins SE of Vienna

Wienerberg   (1989)
1100 Wien, Gutheil Schoder 9
- ☎ **(0222) 66123-7000**
- ⌨ (0222) 66123-7789
- ✆ 9 L 5710 m SSS 70
- 👥 H
- £€ €36
- ⛳ Vienna District 10
- 🏠 G Hauser

Wienerwald   (1981)
1130 Wien, Altgasse 27
- ☎ **(0222) 877 3111 (Sec)**
- ✆ 9 L 4652 m SSS 65
- 👥 H
- £€ €22 (€36)
- ⛳ Laaben, 35km W of Vienna
- 🏠 Herbert Illo Holy

Vorarlberg

Bludenz-Braz   (1996)
Oberradin 60, 6751 Braz bei Bludenz
- ☎ **(05552) 33503**
- ⌨ (05552) 33503-3
- ✆ 12 L 5259 m Par 69 SSS 69
- 👥 M H
- £€ D–€32 (D–€35)
- ⛳ 5km E of Bludenz
- 🏠 Maurice O'Fives

Bregenzerwald   (1997)
Unterlitten 3a, 6943 Riefensberg
- ☎ **(05513) 8400**
- ⌨ (05513) 8400-4
- ✆ 18 L 5702 m Par 71
- 👥 U I
- £€ €34 (€43)
- ⛳ 32km E of Bregenz. 150km E of Zürich
- 🏠 Kurt Rossknecht

Montafon   (1992)
6774 Tschagguns, Zelfenstrasse 110
- ☎ **(05556) 77011**
- ⌨ (05556) 77045
- ✉ info@golfclub-montafon.at
- ✆ 9 L 3708 m Par 62
  CR 61.9 SR 106 (men)
  CR 62.6 SR 100 (women)
- 👥 U H
- £€ €34 Mon–Thur (€38 Fri–Sun)
- ⛳ 60km S of Lake Constance
- 🏠 Stefan Breisach
- ■ www.golfclub-montafon.at

Belgium

Antwerp Region

Bossenstein   (1989)
Moor 16, Bossenstein Kasteel, 2520 Broechem
- ☎ **(03) 485 64 46**
- ⌨ (03) 485 78 41
- ✆ 18 L 6203 m SSS 72
  9 hole course
- 👥 H
- £€ €35 (€45)
- ⛳ 15km E of Antwerp. 5km N of Lier
- 🏠 Paul Rolin

Cleydael   (1988)
Kasteel Cleydael, 2630 Aartselaar
- ☎ **(03) 887 00 79/887 18 74**
- ⌨ (03) 887 00 15
- ✆ 18 L 6059 m SSS 72
- 👥 H WE–NA before 2pm
- £€ €37 (€60)
- ⛳ 8km S of Antwerp. 40km N of Brussels
- 🏠 Paul Rolin

Inter-Mol   (1984)
Goorstraat, 2400 Mol
- ☎ **(011) 39 17 80/60 02 46**
- ✆ 9 L 1557 m Par 29
- 👥 H
- £€ €12 (€17)
- ⛳ Mol, 60km E of Antwerp

Kempense   (1986)
Kiezelweg 78, 2400 Mol
- ☎ **(014) 81 46 41 (Clubhouse)**
- ⌨ (014) 81 62 78
- ✆ 18 L 5904 m Par 72
- 👥 H
- £€ €30 (€42)
- ⛳ 60km E of Antwerp
- 🏠 Marc de Keyser

Lilse   (1988)
Haarlebeek 3, 2275 Lille
- ☎ **(014) 55 19 30**
- ⌨ (014) 55 19 31
- ✆ 9 L 2007 m Par 64
- 👥 U
- £€ €15 (€20)
- ⛳ Lille, 10km SW of Turnhout, nr E7. 25km E of Antwerp

Rinkven G&CC   (1980)
Sint Jobsteenweg 120, 2970 Schilde
- ☎ **(03) 380 12 85**
- ⌨ (03) 384 29 33
- ✆ 27 hole course
- 👥 H–phone before visit
- £€ €47 (€50)
- ⛳ 17 km NE of Antwerp, off E19

Royal Antwerp   (1888)
Georges Capiaulei 2, 2950 Kapellen
- ☎ **(03) 666 84 56**
- ⌨ (03) 666 44 37
- ✆ 18 L 6140 m SSS 73
  9 L 2655 m SSS 34
- 👥 WD–H (phone first)
- £€ €60–€75
- ⛳ Kapellen, 20km N of Antwerp
- 🏠 Willie Park/T Simpson
- ■ www.ragc.be

Steenhoven   (1985)
Steenhoven 89, 2400 Postel-Mol
- ☎ **(014) 37 36 61**
- ⌨ (014) 37 36 62
- ✆ 18 L 5950 m SSS 71
- 👥 H–booking necessary
- £€ €55 (€65)
- ⛳ 30 mins W of Antwerp
- 🏠 Pierre de Broqueville

Ternesse G&CC   (1976)
Uilenbaan 15, 2160 Wommelgem
- ☎ **(03) 355 14 30**
- ⌨ (03) 355 14 35
- ✆ 18 L 5829 m Par 71
  9 L 1981 m Par 33
- 👥 H–30
- £€ €50 (€62.50)
- ⛳ 5km E of Antwerp on E313
- 🏠 HJ Baker

Ardennes & South

Andenne   (1988)
Ferme du Moulin 52, Stud, 5300 Andenne
- ☎ **(085) 84 34 04**
- ⌨ (085) 84 34 04
- ✆ 9 L 2447 m SSS 66
- 👥 U
- £€ €12 (€17)
- ⛳ Andenne, 20km E of Namur
- 🏠 C Bertier

Château Royal d'Ardenne
Tour Léopold, Ardenne 6, 5560 Houyet
- ☎ **(082) 66 62 28**
- ⌨ (082) 66 74 53
- ✆ 18 L 5363 m SSS 71
- 👥 H
- £€ €30 (€45)
- ⛳ 9km SE of Dinant on Rochefort road

Falnuée   (1987)
Rue E Pirson 55, 5032 Mazy
- ☎ **(081) 63 30 90**
- ⌨ (081) 63 37 64
- ✆ 18 L 5700 m SSS 70
- £€ €30 (€45)
- ⛳ 18km NW of Namur. Mons-Liège highway Junction 13
- 🏠 J Jottrand
- ■ www.falnuee.be

Five Nations C C   (1990)
Ferme du Grand Scley, 5372 Méan (Havelange)
- ☎ **(086) 32 32 32**
- ⌨ (086) 32 30 11
- ✆ 18 L 6066 m Par 72
- 👥 WD–U WE–H
- £€ €35 (€45)
- ⛳ 30km S of Liège
- 🏠 Gary Player

Mont Garni (1989)

*Rue du Mont Garni 3, 7331
Saint Ghislain*
- ☎ **(065) 62 27 19**
- 🖬 (065) 62 34 10
- ⊳ 18 L 6353 m Par 74
- ⚥ H
- ££ €30 (€45)
- 🏌 St Ghislain, 15km W of Mons. 65km SW of Brussels
- ⭐ T Macauley
- ■ www.golfmontgarni.be

Rougemont

Chemin du Beau Vallon 45, 5170 Profondeville
- ☎ **(081) 41 14 18**
- 🖬 (081) 41 21 42
- ⊳ 18 L 5645 m Par 72
- ⚥ U
- ££ €30 (€40)
- 🏌 Profondeville, 10km S of Namur
- ■ www.golfderougemont.be

Royal GC du Hainaut
(1933)

Rue de la Verrerie 2, 7050 Erbisoeul
- ☎ **(065) 22 96 10 (Clubhouse)**
- **(065) 22 02 00 (Sec)**
- 🖬 (065) 22 02 09
- ⊳ 9 L 3117 m Par 36
- 9 L 2925 m Par 36
- 9 L 3218 m Par 36
- ⚥ U H (max 36)
- ££ €37 (€50)
- 🏌 6km NW of Mons towards Ath on N56. Paris-Brussels motorway Junction 23
- ⭐ Martin Hawtree
- ■ www.viewgolf.net/RGCH

Brussels & Brabant

Bercuit (1965)

Les Gottes 3, 1390 Grez-Doiceau
- ☎ **(010) 84 15 01**
- 🖬 (010) 84 55 95
- ⊳ 18 L 5931 m Par 72 SSS 72
- ⚥ U H
- ££ €50 (€100)
- 🏌 Grez-Doiceau, 27km SE of Brussels. Brussels-Namur highway exit 8
- ⭐ Robert Trent Jones Sr
- ■ www.golfdubercuit.be

Brabantse (1982)

Steenwagenstraat 11, 1820 Melsbroek
- ☎ **(02) 751 82 05**
- 🖬 (02) 751 84 25
- ✉ brabantse.golf@skynet.be
- ⊳ 18 L 5905 m Par 72
- ⚥ H
- ££ €35 (€45)
- 🏌 10km NE of Brussels, nr airport
- ⭐ Paul Rolin
- ■ www.golf.be/brabantse

La Bruyère (1988)

Rue Jumerée 1, 1495 Sart-Dames-Avelines
- ☎ **(071) 87 72 67**
- 🖬 (071) 87 43 38
- ⊳ 18 L 5937 m SSS 71
- ⚥ U
- ££ €27.5 (€50)
- 🏌 40km S of Brussels towards Charleroi
- ⭐ Theys

Château de la Bawette
(1988)

Chaussée du Chateau Bawette 5, 1300 Wavre
- ☎ **(010) 22 33 32**
- 🖬 (010) 22 90 04
- ⊳ Parc 18 L 6076 m SSS 72
- Champs 9 L 2146 m SSS 63
- ⚥ H–booking required
- ££ €30–€44 (€40–€66)
- 🏌 1km N of Wavre. 15km S of Brussels. E411 Exit 5
- ⭐ Tom Macauley
- ■ www.golfduchateaudelabawette.be

Château de la Tournette

Chemin de Baudemont 23, 1400 Nivelles
- ☎ **(067) 89 42 66/89 42 68**
- 🖬 (067) 21 95 17
- ✉ info@tournette.com
- ⊳ 18 L 6031 m Par 72
- 18 L 6024 m Par 71
- ⚥ U
- ££ €41 (€66)
- 🏌 29km S of Brussels (E19)
- ⭐ Alliss/Clark
- ■ www.tournette.com

L'Empereur (1989)

Rue Emile François 9, 1474 Ways (Genappe)
- ☎ **(067) 77 15 71**
- 🖬 (067) 77 18 33
- ⊳ 18 L 6157 m Par 72
- 9 L 1660 m Par 31
- ⚥ U H
- ££ 18 hole:€35 (€65) 9 hole:€20 (€35)
- 🏌 25km S of Brussels
- ⭐ Marcel Vercruyce
- ■ www.golfempereur.com

Hulencourt (1989)

Bruyère d'Hulencourt 15, 1472 Vieux Genappe
- ☎ **(067) 79 40 40**
- 🖬 (067) 79 40 48
- ⊳ 18 L 6215 m Par 72
- 9 hole Par 3 course
- ⚥ H–max 36
- ££ €55 (€80)
- 🏌 30km SE of Brussels
- ⭐ JM Rossi

Kampenhout (1989)

Wildersedreef 56, 1910 Kampenhout
- ☎ **(016) 65 12 16**
- 🖬 (016) 65 16 80
- ⊳ 18 L 6142 m SSS 72

- ⚥ H
- ££ €35 (€45)
- 🏌 15km NE of Brussels (E19)
- ⭐ R de Vooght

Keerbergen (1968)

Vlieghavelaan 50, 3140 Keerbergen
- ☎ **(015) 23 49 61**
- 🖬 (015) 23 57 37
- ✉ keerbergen.golfclub@skynet.be
- ⊳ 18 L 5503 m SSS 70
- ⚥ H
- ££ €40 (€50)
- 🏌 30km NE of Brussels
- ⭐ Frank Pennink
- ■ www.golf.be/keerbergen

Louvain-la-Neuve

Rue A Hardy 68, 1348 Louvain-la-Neuve
- ☎ **(010) 45 05 15**
- 🖬 (010) 45 44 17
- ⊳ 18 L 6226 m Par 72
- ⚥ U
- ££ €30 (€50)
- 🏌 20km SE of Brussels, off E411
- ⭐ J Dudok van Heel

Overijse (1986)

Gemslaan 55, 3090 Overijse
- ☎ **(02) 687 50 30**
- 🖬 (02) 687 37 68
- ⊳ 9 L 5723 m Par 71
- ⚥ H
- ££ €20 (€37)
- 🏌 10km S of Brussels
- ⭐ Rossi

Pierpont (1992)

1 Grand Pierpont, 6210 Frasnes-lez-Gosselies
- ☎ **(071) 85 17 75/85 14 19**
- 🖬 (071) 85 15 43
- ⊳ 18 L 6257 m Par 72
- 5 hole Par 3 course
- ⚥ U
- ££ €30 (€60)
- 🏌 30km S of Brussels via N5
- ⭐ J Dudok van Heel
- ■ www.pierpont.be

Rigenée (1981)

Rue de Châtelet 62, 1495 Villers-la-Ville
- ☎ **(071) 87 77 65**
- 🖬 (071) 87 77 83
- ✉ golf@rigence.be
- ⊳ 18 L 6031 m SSS 73
- ⚥ H
- ££ €30 (€50)
- 🏌 35km S of Brussels towards Charleroi
- ⭐ Rolin/Descampe

Royal Amicale
Anderlecht (1987)

Rue Scholle 1, 1070 Bruxelles
- ☎ **(02) 521 16 87**
- 🖬 (02) 521 51 56
- ⊳ 18 L 5037 m Par 70 CR 68.7 SR 123
- ⚥ WD–U H WE–booking required

£€ €30 (€45)
⟷ SW Brussels

Royal Golf Club de Belgique (1906)

Château de Ravenstein, 3080 Tervuren
☎ (02) 767 58 01
⌨ (02) 767 28 41
⊳ 18 L 6033 m SSS 72
9 L 1960 m Par 32
👥 WD–H–max 20(men) 24(ladies)–phone first. Course closed Mon
£€ €90
⟷ Tervuren, 10km E of Brussels
⌂ Simpson

Royal Waterloo (1923)

Vieux Chemin de Wavre 50, 1380 Ohain
☎ (02) 633 18 50
⌨ (02) 633 28 66
⊳ 18 L 6211 m SSS 72
18 L 6224 m SSS 73
9 L 2143 m SSS 33
👥 WD–H
£€ €90
⟷ 22km SE of Brussels
⌂ Hawtree/Rolin

Sept Fontaines (1987)

1021, Chaussée d'Alsemberg, 1420 Braine L'Alleud
☎ (02) 353 02 46/353 03 46
⌨ (02) 354 68 75
⊳ 18 L 6047 m Par 72 SSS 72
18 L 4870 m Par 69 SSS 67
9 hole short course
👥 U H
£€ €40 (€70)
⟷ Braine L'Alleud, 15km S of Brussels. Motorway exit 15
⌂ Rossi
🖥 www.golf7fontaines.be

Winge G&CC (1988)

Leuvensesteenweg 252, 3390 Sint Joris Winge
☎ (016) 63 40 53
⌨ (016) 63 21 40
⊳ 18 L 6049 m Par 72 CR 72.4
👥 H
£€ €35 (€50)
⟷ 35km E of Brussels via Leuven
⌂ P Townsend
🖥 www.golf.be/winge

East

Avernas

Route de Grand Hallet 19A, 4280 Hannut
☎ (019) 51 30 66
⌨ (019) 51 53 43
⊳ 9 L 2674 m SSS 68
👥 H
£€ €17 (€22)
⟷ 40km W of Liège. Brussels 50km
⌂ Hawtree/Cappart

Durbuy (1991)

Route d'Oppagne 34, 6940 Barvaux-su-Ourthe
☎ (086) 21 44 54
⊳ 18 L 5963 m SSS 72
9 hole Par 3 course
👥 U
£€ €32 (€45)
⟷ 45km S of Liège
⌂ Martin Hawtree

Flanders Nippon Hasselt (1988)

Vissenbroekstraat 15, 3500 Hasselt
☎ (011) 26 34 82
⌨ (011) 26 34 83
⊳ 18 L 5966 m SSS 72
9 L 1750 m SSS 32
👥 U H
£€ €35 (€45)
⟷ 5km E of Hasselt. 85km E of Brussels
⌂ Rolin/Wirtz
🖥 www.golf.be/flandersnippon

Henri-Chapelle (1988)

Rue du Vivier 3, 4841 Henri-Chapelle
☎ (087) 88 19 91
⌨ (087) 88 36 55
⊳ 18 L 6040 m SSS 72
9 L 2168 m SSS 34
6 hole Par 3 course
👥 18 hole: WE–H
£€ 18 hole: €39–€49 9 hole: €19 – €29
⟷ 15km NE of Liège. Aachen 10km
⌂ Steensels/Dudok van Heel

International Gomze (1986)

Sur Counachamps 8, 4140 Gomze Andoumont
☎ (041) 360 92 07
⌨ (041) 360 92 06
⊳ 18 L 5918 m SSS 72
👥 U H
£€ On application
⟷ 15km S of Liège. Spa 20km
⌂ Paul Rolin

Limburg G&CC (1966)

Golfstraat 1, 3530 Houthalen
☎ (089) 38 35 43
⌨ (089) 84 12 08
✉ limburggolf@wanadoo.be
⊳ 18 L 6049 m SSS 72
👥 WD WE H
£€ €45 (€55)
⟷ Houthalen, 15km N of Hasselt
⌂ Hawtree
🖥 www.golf.be

Royal GC du Sart Tilman (1939)

Route du Condroz 541, 4031 Liège
☎ (041) 336 20 21
⌨ (041) 337 20 26
⊳ 18 L 6002 m SSS 72
👥 H–booking required
£€ D–€38 (€50)
⟷ 10km S of Liège on Route 620 (N35), towards Marche
⌂ T Simpson

Royal Golf des Fagnes (1930)

1 Ave de l'Hippodrome, 4900 Spa
☎ (087) 79 30 30
⌨ (087) 79 30 39
⊳ 18 L 6010 m Par 72
👥 H–booking required
£€ €37–50 (€45–55)
⟷ 5km N of Spa. 35km SE of Liège
⌂ T Simpson

Spiegelven GC Genk (1988)

Wiemesmeerstraat 109, 3600 Genk
☎ (0032) 89 359616
⌨ (0032) 90 364184
✉ spiegelven@advalas.be
⊳ 18 L 6198 m SSS 72
9 hole Par 3 course
👥 H
£€ €40 (€50)
⟷ Genk, 18km E of Hasselt. 20km N of Maastricht
⌂ Ron Kirby
🖥 www.spiegelven.be

West & Oost Vlaanderen

Damme G&CC (1987)

Doornstraat 16, 8340 Damme-Sijsele
☎ (050) 35 35 72
⌨ (050) 35 89 25
✉ damme.gcc@skynet.be
⊳ 18 L 6046 m SSS 72
9 hole short course
👥 H 35
£€ €48 (€60)
⟷ 7km E of Bruges. Knokke 15km
⌂ J Dudok van Heel
🖥 www.golf.be/damme

Oudenaarde G&CC (1975)

Kasteel Petegem, Kortrykstraat 52, 9790 Wortegem-Petegem
☎ (055) 33 41 61
⌨ (055) 31 98 49
⊳ 18 L 6172 m Par 72
9 L 2492 m Par 34
👥 H
£€ €50 (€65)
⟷ 3 km SW of Oudenaarde
⌂ HJ Baker
🖥 www.golf.be/oudenaarde

De Palingbeek (1991)

Eekhofstraat 14, 8902 Hollebeke-Ieper
☎ (057) 20 04 36
⌨ (057) 21 89 58
⊳ 18 L 6165 m Par 72
👥 H
£€ €40 (€50)
⟷ 5km SE of Ieper, nr Hollebeke
⌂ HJ Baker
🖥 www.golfpalingbeek.com

Royal Latem (1909)

9830 St Martens-Latem
☎ (092) 82 54 11

☎ (092) 82 90 19
✉ latem@golf.be
☞ 18 L 5767 m Par 72 SR 123
👥 H
£€ €50 (€65)
⛳ 10 km SW of Ghent on route N43
Ghent-Deinze
■ www.golf.be/latem

Royal Ostend (1903)

Koninklijke Baan 2, 8420 De Haan
☎ (059) 23 32 83
☎ (059) 23 37 49
☞ 18 L 5618 m CR 70.1 SR 123
👥 H–max 34
£€ €40–€50 (€50–€60)
⛳ 8km N of Ostend towards De Haan
🏚 M Hawtree (1993/4)
■ www.golfoostende.be

Royal Zoute (1899)

Caddiespad 14, 8300 Knokke-le-Zoute
☎ (050) 60 16 17 (Clubhouse),
(050) 60 37 81 (Starter)
☎ (050) 62 30 29
☞ No 1 18 L 6172 m Par 72
No 2 18 L 3607 m Par 64
👥 H No 1 course–max 20
WE–restricted
£€ €85
⛳ Knokke-Heist
🏚 HS Colt

Waregem (1988)

Bergstraat 41, 8790 Waregem
☎ (056) 60 88 08
☎ (056) 62 18 23
☞ 18 L 6038 m SSS 72
👥 H Sun–NA before 1pm
£€ €38 (€50)
⛳ 30km SW of Ghent (E17)
🏚 Paul Rolin
■ www.golf.be/waregem

Czech Republic

Karlovy Vary (1904)

Prazska 125, PO Box 67, 360 01 Karlovy Vary
☎ (017) 333 1001-2
☎ (017) 333 1101
☞ 18 L 6226 m SSS 72
👥 H
£€ 1100czk (1300czk)
⛳ 8km from Karlovy Vary (Road 6)
🏚 Noskowski

Lísnice (1928)

252 10 Mnísek pod Brdy
☎ (0318) 599 151
☎ (0318) 599 151
☞ 9 L 4948 m CR 66 SR 135
👥 H
£€ 800czk (1000czk)

⛳ 30km from Prague towards Dobrís
■ www.gkl.cz

Lokomotiva-Brno (1967)

c/o Chlupova 7, 602 00 Brno
☎ (05) 744615
☎ (05) 759309
☞ 9 L 4632 m SSS 68
👥 H
£€ 100czk (180czk)
⛳ Svratka, 80km NW of Brno. 100km SE of Prague
🏚 Chocholac

Mariánské Lázne (1905)

PO Box 267, 353 01 Mariánské Lázne
☎ (0165) 4300
☎ (0165) 625195
☞ 18 L 6195 m SSS 72
👥 H
£€ D–1000czk
⛳ 2km NE of Mariánské Lázne, opposite Golf Hotel

Park GC Ostrava (1968)

Dolni 412, 747 15 Silherovice
☎ (0420) 595 054 144
☎ (0420) 595 054 144
✉ office@golf-ostrava.cz
📧 Michal Navrat (Mgr)
☞ 18 L 5593 m CR 70.3 SR 125
👥 H
£€ 1000czk (1200czk)
⛳ 15km N of Ostrava
🏚 Jan Cieslar
■ www.golf-ostrava.cz

Podebrady (1964)

Na Zalesi 530, 29080 Podebrady
☎ (0324) 610928
☎ (0324) 610981
☞ 18 L 5790 m CR 70.3 SR 114
👥 U H
£€ 600czk (800czk)
⛳ E side of Podebrady
🏚 Wagner/Havelka/Kodes
■ www.golfpodebrady.cz

Praha (1926)

Na Morani 4, 128 00 Praha 2
☎ (02) 292828/644 3828
☎ (02) 292828
☞ 9 L 5960 m SSS 72
👥 U
⛳ Prague-Motol, towards Plzen

Semily (1970)

Bavlnarska 521, 513 01 Semily
☎ (0431) 622443/624428
☎ (0431) 623000
☞ 9 L 4176 m Par 64
👥 WD–U WE–NA
£€ 400czk (600czk)
⛳ 2km from Semily. 100km NE of Prague
🏚 Schovánek/Janata
■ www.semily.cz

Denmark

Bornholm Island

Bornholm (1972)

Plantagevej 3B, 3700 Rønne
☎ 56 95 68 54
☎ 56 95 68 53
☞ 18 L 4819 m Par 68
9 hole Par 3 course
👥 H
£€ 180kr
⛳ 4km E of Rønne, off Route 38 towards Aakirkeby
🏚 Frederik Dreyer
■ www.hjem.get2net.dk/bgk

Nexø

Dueodde Golfbane, Strandmarksvejen 14, 3730 Nexø
☎ 56 48 89 87
☎ 56 48 89 69
☞ 18 L 5470 m CR 69.4 SR 124
👥 H
£€ 200kr (200kr)
⛳ 12km S of Nexø, nr Dueodde beach
🏚 Frederik Dreyer
■ www.dueodde-golf.dk

Nordbornholm-Rø (1987)

Spellingevej 3, Rø, 3760 Gudhjem
☎ 56 48 40 50
☎ 56 48 40 52
☞ 18 L 5369 m SSS 71
👥 WD–U WE–H
£€ D–200kr
⛳ Rø, 8km W of Gudhjem. 22km NE of Rønne
🏚 Anders Amilon
■ www.roegolfbane.dk

Funen

Faaborg (1989)

Dalkildegards Allee 1, 5600 Faaborg
☎ 62 61 77 43
☎ 62 61 79 34
☞ 18 L 5715 m Par 72
👥 U H
£€ D–200kr
⛳ 35km S of Odense
🏚 Frederik Dreyer

Lillebaelt (1990)

O.Hougvej 130, 5500 Middelfart
☎ 64 41 80 11
☎ 64 41 14 11
✉ gkl@posf10.tele.dk
☞ 18 L 5586 m Par 71 CR 69.9
👥 H
£€ D–200kr (D–250kr)
⛳ 2km from Middelfart. 45km W of Odense
🏚 Malling Petersen
■ www.gkl.dk

Odense (1927)

Hestehaven 200, 5220 Odense SØ
- ☎ 65 95 90 00
- 🖥 65 95 90 88
- ⛳ 18 L 6098 m CR 71
  9 L 4044 m CR 61
- 👥 U H
- £€ 250kr (300kr)
- ⚲ SE outskirts of Odense
- �’ Jan Sederholm
- ■ www.odensegolfklub.dk

Odense Eventyr (1993)

Falen 227, 5250 Odense SV
- ☎ 6565 2020
- 🖥 6562 2021
- ✉ oegc@golfin.dk
- ⛳ 18 hole course Par 72
  9 hole course
- 👥 H
- £€ 260kr (300kr)
- ⚲ 5km SW of Odense
- �’ Michael Møller
- ■ www.golfin.dk

SCT Knuds (1954)

Slipshavnsvej 16, 5800 Nyborg
- ☎ 65 31 12 12
- 🖥 65 30 28 04
- ✉ mail@sct-knuds.dk
- ⛳ 18 L 5810 m CR 72
- 👥 H
- £€ 250kr D–300kr (D–500kr)
- ⚲ 3km SE of Nyborg
- �’ Cotton/Dreyer
- ■ www.sct-knuds.dk

Svendborg (1970)

*Tordensgaardevej 5, Sørup,
5700 Svendborg*
- ☎ 62 22 40 77
- 🖥 62 20 29 77
- ⛳ 18 L 5490 m CR 70.2 SR 127
- 👥 H–max 36
- £€ 225kr (275kr)
- ⚲ 4km NW of Svendborg
- �’ Frederik Dreyer
- ■ www.svendborg-golf.dk

Vestfyns (1974)

*Rønnemosegård, Krengerupvej 27,
5620 Glamsbjerg*
- ☎ 63 72 19 20
- 🖥 63 72 19 27
- ⛳ 18 L 5629 m Par 71 CR 71
- 👥 H–max 48 (WE–max 36)
- £€ 200kr (300kr)
- ⚲ Glamsbjerg, 25km SW of Odense
- ■ www.golfonline.dk/klub/vestfyn

Greenland

Sondie Arctic Desert (1990)

Box 58, 3910 Kangerlussuaq, Greenland
- ☎ 29 91 14 13
- 🖥 29 91 11 74
- ⛳ 18 L 5521 m SSS 72
- 👥 U

- ⚲ 2km E of Kangerlussuaq Airport,
  Greenland
- �’ Ulf Larson

Jutland

Aalborg (1908)

*Jaegersprisvej 35, Restrup Enge,
9000 Aalborg*
- ☎ 98 34 14 76
- 🖥 98 34 15 84
- ⛳ 18 L 6081 m CR 73.4
- 👥 H (max 36)
- £€ D–300kr (D–300kr)
- ⚲ 7 km SW of Aalborg
- �’ R Harris
- ■ www.aalborggk.dk

Aarhus (1931)

Ny Moesgaardvej 50, 8270 Hojbjerg
- ☎ 86 27 63 22
- 🖥 86 27 63 21
- ⛳ 18 L 5725 m Par 72 CR 71
- 👥 H
- £€ D–250kr (D–300kr)
- ⚲ 6km S of Aarhus, Route 451
- �’ Brian Huggett
- ■ www.aarhusgolf.dk

Blokhus Klit (1993)

Hunetorpvej 115, Box 37, 9490 Pandrup
- ☎ 98 20 95 00
- 🖥 98 20 95 01
- ⛳ 18 L 5584 m CR 70.5
- 👥 U H
- £€ 230kr (300kr)
- ⚲ 35km NW of Aalborg
- �’ Frederik Dreyer

Breinholtgård (1992)

Koksspangvej 17-19, 6710 Esbjerg V
- ☎ 75 11 57 00
- 🖥 75 11 55 12
- ⛳ 27 holes Par 71
- 👥 U H
- £€ 250kr
- ⚲ 11km N of Esbjerg
- �’ Gaunt/Trådsdahl

Brønderslev (1971)

PO Box 94, 9700 Brønderslev
- ☎ 98 82 32 81
- 🖥 98 82 45 25
- ⛳ 18 L 5683 m CR 71
  9 hole short course
- 👥 H WE–booking necessary
- £€ 180kr (200kr)
- ⚲ 3km W of Brønderslev
- �’ Erik Schnack

Brundtlandbanen (2000)

*Ostergade 63, 6520
Toftlund, DENMARK*
- ☎ 73 83 16 00
- 🖥 73 83 16 19
- 🖩 600
- ⛳ 18 L 5890 m Par 73
  9 L 1255 m Par 29

- 👥 H
- £€ 200kr (250kr)
- ⚲ Toftlund, central Jutland
- �’ Henrik Jacobsen
- ■ www.brundtlandbanen.dk

Dejbjerg (1966)

Letagervej 1, Dejbjerg, 6900 Skjern
- ☎ 97 35 00 09
- 🖥 96 80 11 18
- ✉ dejbjerggk@mail.tele.dk
- ⛳ 18 L 5078 m Par 69
  CR 67.0 SR 122 (men)
  CR 67.3 SR 117 (women)
- 👥 U
- £€ D–200kr (D–220kr)
- ⚲ 6km N of Skjern. 25km from W
  coast on Skjern-Ringkøbing road
  (Route 28)
- �’ Schnack/Dreyer
- ■ www.dejbjerggk.dk

Ebeltoft (1966)

Strandgårdshøj 8a, 8400 Ebeltoft
- ☎ 86 34 47 87/86 34 01 40
- ⛳ 18 L 5027 m Par 68 CR 67.6
- 👥 U
- £€ D–200kr
- ⚲ 1km N of Ebeltoft
- �’ Frederik Dreyer

Esbjerg (1921)

*Sønderhedevej 11, Marbaek,
6710 Esbjerg*
- ☎ 75 26 92 19
- 🖥 75 26 94 19
- ✉ esbjerg@golfonline.dk
- ⛳ 18 L 6434 m CR 71
  9 L 5520 m CR 70
- 👥 U H
- £€ 300kr
- ⚲ 15km N of Esbjerg
- �’ Frederik Dreyer
- ■ www.esbjerg-golfklub.dk

Fanø Golf Links (1901)

Golfvejen 5, 6720 Fanø
- ☎ 76 66 00 77
- 🖥 76 66 00 44
- ⛳ 18 L 5080 m CR 68.7
- 👥 U
- £€ D–250kr
- ⚲ W side of Fanø Island. Ferry from
  Esbjerg 15 mins
- ■ www.fanoe-golf-links.dk

Grenaa (1981)

Vestermarken 1, 8500 Grenaa
- ☎ (86) 32 79 29
- ⛳ 18 L 5782 m Par 70
- 👥 U
- £€ 150kr
- ⚲ 1km W of Grenaa. 60km NE of
  Aarhus
- �’ Dreyer/Sommer

Gyttegård (1974)

Billundvej 43, 7250 Hejnsvig
- ☎ 75 33 63 82
- 🖥 75 33 68 20

ᛒ 18 L 5548 m SSS 70
🏌 H
££ 200kr (250kr)
🚗 2km NE of Hejnsvig. 5km SW of
Billund
🛏 Amilon/Bossen

Haderslev (1971)
Viggo Carstensvej 7, 6100 Haderslev
☎ 74 52 83 01
🖥 74 53 36 01
ᛒ 18 L 5233 m CR 69
🏌 H
££ 220kr
🚗 2km NW of Haderslev

Han Herreds
Starkaervej 20, 9690 Fjerritslev
☎ 98 21 26 66
🖥 98 21 24 44
ᛒ 18 L 5359 m CR 70.5
🏌 H
££ 150kr
🚗 1km N of Fjerritslev. 40km W of
Aalborg

Henne (1989)
Hennebysvej 30, 6854 Henne
☎ 75 25 56 10
🖥 75 25 56 30
📧 post@hennegolfklub.dk
ᛒ 18 L 5998 m Par 71 CR 72.5
9 hole Par 3 course
🏌 U H
££ 200kr
🚗 19km NW of Varde. 35km N of
Esbjerg
🛏 Frederik Dreyer
🖥 www.hennegolf.dk

Herning (1964)
Golfvej 2, 7400 Herning
☎ 97 21 00 33
🖥 97 21 00 34
ᛒ 18 L 5571 m CR 71.8
🏌 H
££ 150kr (200kr)
🚗 2km E of Herning on Route 15
🛏 Dreyer/Baekgaard

Himmerland G&CC (1979)
Centervej 1, Gatten, 9640 Farsö
☎ 96 49 61 00
🖥 98 66 14 56
📧 hgcc@himmerlandgolf.dk
ᛒ Old 18 L 5422 m CR 68.5/70 SR
124/121 Par 70
New 18 L 6102 m CR 73/74.9 SR
129/129 Par 73
18 hole Par 3 course
🏌 H
££ 275kr D–400kr (375kr D–550kr)
🚗 Gatten, 35km NW of Hobro
towards Løgstør (Route 29)
🛏 Jan Sederholm
🖥 www.himmerlandgolf.dk

Hirtshals (1990)
Kjulvej 10, PO Box 51, 9850 Hirtshals
☎ 98 94 94 08

🖥 98 94 19 35
ᛒ 18 L 5620 m Par 72
🏌 U H max 48 WE–NA 10–12 noon
££ 200kr
🚗 12km N of Hjørring
🛏 Erik Nielsen

Hjarbaek Fjord (1992)
Lynderup, 8832 Skals
☎ 86 69 62 88
🖥 86 69 62 68
ᛒ 27 L 8595 m SSS 72
🏌 H
££ 220kr (300kr)
🚗 17km NW of Viborg
🛏 Henrik Jacobsen

Hjorring (1985)
Vinstrupvej, PO Box 215, 9800 Hjorring
☎ 98 91 18 28
🖥 98 90 31 00
ᛒ 18 L 5945 m SSS 72
🏌 H WE–NA 9–11am & 1.30–2.30pm
££ 200kr (220kr)
🚗 N of Hjorring. 50km N of Aalborg
🛏 Erik Schnack
🖥 www.hjoerringgolf.dk

Holmsland Klit
Klevevej 19, Søndervig, 6950 Ringkøbing
☎ 97 33 88 00
🖥 97 33 86 80
ᛒ 18 L 5611 m SSS 69
🏌 H
££ 175kr
🚗 10km W of Ringkøbing
🛏 Leif Baekgaard

Holstebro (1970)
Råsted, 7570 Vemb
☎ 97 48 51 55
ᛒ 18 L 5856 m CR 71.5
9 L 2510 m
🏌 H
££ 250kr (300kr)
🚗 13km W of Holstebro (Route 16)
🛏 Erik Schnack

Horsens (1972)
Silkeborgvej 44, 8700 Horsens
☎ 75 61 51 51
🖥 75 61 40 51
ᛒ 18 L 6020 m CR 72.4
9 hole Par 3 course
££ 220kr (250kr)
🚗 1 km W of Horsens towards
Silkeborg
🛏 Jan Sederholm
🖥 www.horsensgolf.dk

Hvide Klit (1972)
Hvideklitvej 28, 9982 Aalbaek
☎ 98 48 90 21/48 84 26
🖥 98 48 91 12
ᛒ 18 L 5875 m SSS 72
🏌 H
££ 250kr (300kr)
🚗 3km N of Aalbaek. 24km N of
Frederikshavn
🛏 Anders Amilon

Juelsminde (1973)
Bobroholtvej 11a, 7130 Juelsminde
☎ 75 69 34 92
🖥 75 69 46 11
📧 golf@juelsmindegolf.dk
ᛒ 18 L 5680 m SSS 72
🏌 U H
££ 250kr
🚗 20 km S of Horsens on coast. 2km
N of Juelsminde
🛏 Mehlsen/Jacobsen/Møller
🖥 www.juelsmindegolf.dk

Kaj Lykke (1988)
Kirkebrovej 5, 6740 Bramming
☎ 75 10 22 46
🖥 75 10 26 68
ᛒ 18 L 5975 m CR 72.3 SR 131
Par 3 course
🏌 H
££ 200kr
🚗 18km E of Esbjerg
🛏 Bent Nielsen
🖥 www.kaj-lykke-golfklub.dk

Kalo (1992)
Aarhusvej 32, 8410 Rønde
☎ 86 37 36 00
🖥 86 37 36 46
ᛒ 18 L 5936 m CR 72.2
🏌 U
££ 220kr (250kr)
🚗 20km E of Aarhus
🛏 Frederik Dreyer

Kolding (1933)
Egtved Alle 10, 6000 Kolding
☎ 75 52 37 93
🖥 75 52 42 42
📧 kgc@koldinggolfclub.dk
ᛒ 18 L 5373 m Par 69 SSS 69 SR 123
9 L 2065 m Par 31 SSS 62 SR 101
🏌 U
££ 250kr (300kr)
🚗 3km N of Kolding
🛏 Jan Sederholm
🖥 www.koldinggolfclub.dk

Lemvig (1986)
Søgårdevejen 6, 7620 Lemvig
☎ 97 81 09 20
🖥 97 81 09 20
ᛒ 18 L 5890 m CR 72
🏌 H
££ 200kr (200kr)
🚗 2km N of Lemvig. 35km NE of
Holsterbro
🛏 Frederik Dreyer
🖥 www.home11.inet.tele.dk/lemviggk

Løkken (1990)
*Vrenstedvej 226, PO Box 43,
9480 Løkken*
☎ 98 99 26 57
🖥 98 99 26 58
ᛒ 18 L 5902 m CR 72.3 SR 127
9 L 2964 m Par 29
🏌 U H
££ 200kr (200kr)
🚗 45km NW of Aalborg

For list of abbreviations and key to symbols see page 627

⌂ Kaj Andersen
■ www.loekken-golfklub.dk

Nordvestjysk (1971)
Nystrupvej 19, 7700 Thisted
☎ 97 97 41 41
▷ 18 L 5675 m CR 72
⑨ H
£€ 150kr (150kr)
⬤ 17km NW of Thisted
⌂ Schnack/Jacobsen

Odder (1990)
Akjaervej 200, Postbox 46, 8300 Odder
☎ 86 54 54 51
▷ 18 L 5428 m Par 70 CR 70
⑨ U
£€ 200kr (250kr)
⬤ 4km SW of Odder, off Route 451
⌂ Frederik Dreyer

Randers (1958)
Himmelbovej 22, Fladbro, 8900 Randers
☎ 86 42 88 69
⌸ 86 40 88 69
✉ postmaster@randersgolf.dk
▷ 18 L 5453 m SSS 70
9 hole Par 3 course
£€ 225kr (275kr)
⬤ 5km W of Randers towards Langå
⌂ Mogens Harbo
■ www.randersgolf.dk

Ribe (1979)
Rønnehave, Snepsgårdevej 14, 6760 Ribe
☎ 30 73 65 18
▷ 18 L 5430 m CR 69
⑨ U
£€ 150kr
⬤ 8 km SE of Ribe on Haderslev road
⌂ Frederik Dreyer

Rold Skov
Golfvej 1, 9520 Skørping
☎ 96 82 8300
⌸ 96 82 8309
▷ 18 L 5850 m SSS 72
⑨ U H
£€ 250kr (300kr)
⬤ 30km S of Aalborg
⌂ Henrik Jacobsen

Royal Oak (1992)
Golfvej, Jels, 6630 Rødding
☎ 74 55 32 94
⌸ 74 55 32 95
▷ 18 L 5967 m Par 72
⑨ H–booking necessary. Soft spikes only
£€ 300kr
⬤ 25km SW of Kolding
■ www.royal-oak.dk

Saeby
Vandløsvej 50, 9300 Saeby
☎ 98 46 76 77
⌸ 98 46 11 24
▷ 18 L 5944 m SSS 72
⑨ U

£€ 200kr (200kr)
⬤ Saeby, 12km S of Fredrikshavn
⌂ Anders Amilon

Silkeborg (1966)
Sensommervej 15C, 8600 Silkeborg
☎ 86 85 33 99
⌸ 86 85 35 22
▷ 18 L 5975 m SSS 72
⑨ H
£€ 275kr (350kr)
⬤ 5km E of Silkeborg
⌂ Frederik Dreyer
■ www.silkeborggolf.dk

Sønderjyllands (1968)
Uge Hedegård, 6360 Tinglev
☎ 74 68 75 25
⌸ 74 68 75 05
▷ 18 L 5856 m Par 71
⑨ H
£€ 200kr (260kr)
⬤ 9km NE of Tinglev. 9km S of Abenraa
⌂ Erik Schnack
■ www.sdj-golfklub.dk

Varde (1991)
Gellerupvej 111b, 6800 Varde
☎ 75 22 49 44
⌸ 75 22 48 35
▷ 18 L 6104 m Par 71
⑨ H
£€ 200kr (300kr)
⬤ 20km N of Esbjerg
⌂ Erik Fauerholt

Vejle (1970)
Faellessletgard, Ibaekvej, 7100 Vejle
☎ 75 85 81 85
⌸ 75 85 83 01
✉ vejle@golfonline.dk
▷ 27 holes:
5677-6148 m Par 71-73
9 hole Par 3 course
⑨ H
£€ 250kr (300kr)
⬤ 5 km SE of Vejle
⌂ J Malling Pedersen
■ www.veijlegolfclub.com

Viborg (1973)
Spangsbjerg Alle 50,’ Overlund, 8800 Viborg
☎ 86 67 30 10
⌸ 86 67 34 15
▷ 18 L 5767 m CR 72
⑨ WD–H 48 WE–H 36
£€ 200kr (225kr)
⬤ 2 km E of Viborg
⌂ Frederik Dreyer
■ www.viborggolfklub.dk

Zealand

Asserbo (1946)
Bødkergaardsvej, 3300 Frederiksvaerk
☎ 47 72 14 90

⌸ 47 72 14 26
▷ 18 L 5851 m Par 72
⑨ H
£€ 300kr (350kr)
⬤ 3km from Frederiksvaerk towards Liseleje
⌂ Ross/Samuelsen
■ www.agc.dk

Copenhagen (1898)
Dyrehaven 2, 2800 Kgs. Lyngby
☎ 39 63 04 83
⌸ 39 63 46 83
✉ info@kghgolf.dk
▷ 18 L 5761 m SSS 71
⑨ WD–U WE–NA after 13.00
£€ 350kr (400kr)
⬤ 13 km N of Copenhagen, in deer park
■ www.kghgolf.dk

Dragør
Kalvebodvej 100, 2791 Dragør
☎ 32 53 89 75
⌸ 32 53 88 09
▷ 18 L 5864 m SSS 71
6 hole Par 3 course
⑨ WD–U WE–U H
£€ 200kr (300kr)
⬤ 15km SE of Copenhagen centre, nr Airport
⌂ Henning Jensen/Kierkegaard
■ www.dragor-golf.dk

Falster (1994)
Virketvej 44, 4863 Eskilstrup, Falster Island
☎ 54 43 81 43
⌸ 54 43 81 23
▷ 18 L 5912 m Par 72
⑨ H
£€ 250kr (300kr)
⬤ 20km NE of Nykøbing (Route 271)
⌂ Anders Amilon

Frederikssund (1974)
Egelundsgården, Skovnaesvej 9, 3630 Jaegerspris
☎ 47 31 08 77
⌸ 47 31 21 88
▷ 18 L 5868 m SSS 71
⑨ WD–U H WE–H 30
£€ 250kr (300kr)
⬤ 3km S of Frederikssund towards Skibby (Route 53)
⌂ Dreyer/Samuelsen

Furesø (1974)
Hestkøbgård, Hestkøb Vaenge 4, 3460 Birkerød
☎ 45 81 74 44
⌸ 45 82 02 24
▷ 27 holes:
5328-5641 m CR 70-71
⑨ H WD–NA before 11am WE–NA before noon
£€ 300kr (400kr)
⬤ 25 km N of Copenhagen
⌂ Jan Sederholm
■ www.furesoegolfklub.dk

Gilleleje (1970)
Ferlevej 52, 3250 Gilleleje
☎ 49 71 80 56
📠 49 71 80 86
📏 18 L 6641 yds Par 72 CR 71
⛳ H–max 32
££ 300kr (400kr)
🚗 62km N of Copenhagen
🏠 Jan Sederholm
■ www.gillelejegolfklub.dk

Hedeland (1980)
Staerkendevej 232A, 2640 Hedehusene
☎ 46 13 61 88/46 13 61 69
📠 46 13 62 78
📏 18 L 6070 m Par 72
9 hole Par 3 course
⛳ H WE–NA before noon
££ 200kr (250kr)
🚗 7km SE of Roskilde. 20km SW of
Copenhagen
🏠 Jan Sederholm

Helsingør
GL Hellebaekvej, 3000 Helsingør
☎ 49 21 29 70
📠 49 21 09 70
📏 18 L 5612 m Par 71 CR 71
⛳ U H
££ 275–400kr (350–500kr)
🚗 2km N of Helsingør

Hillerød (1966)
*Nysøgårdsvej 9, Ny Hammersholt,
3400 Hillerød*
☎ 48 26 50 46/48 25 40 30 (Pro)
📠 48 25 29 87
📏 18 L 5255 m CR 70
⛳ H WE–NA before noon
££ 350kr (400kr)
🚗 3 km S of Hillerød
🏠 Sederholm/Knudsen

Holbaek (1964)
Dragerupvej 50, 4300 Holbaek
☎ 59 43 45 79
📠 59 44 51 61
📏 18 L 5290 m Par 70
⛳ U H
££ 240kr (280kr)
🚗 Kirsebaerholmen, 2km E of
Holbaek
🏠 Dreyer/Sederholm
■ www.holbakgolfklub.dk

Køge (1970)
Gl.Hastrupvej12, 4600 Køge
☎ 56 65 10 00
📠 56 65 13 45
📧 admin@kogegolf.dk
📏 18 L 6042 m Par 72
9 L 3659 m Par 62
⛳ WE–H max 27 WD max 48
££ 270kr (320kr)
🚗 3km S of Køge. Copenhagen
38 km
■ www.kogegolf.dk

Kokkedal (1971)
Kokkedal Alle 9, 2970 Horsholm
☎ 45 76 99 59
📠 45 76 99 03
📏 18 L 5936 m Par 72
⛳ H–WE pm only
££ 300kr (350kr)
🚗 Hørsholm, 30 km N of Copenhagen
🏠 Frank Pennink
■ www.kokkedalgolf.dk

Korsør (1996)
Ornumvej 8, Postbox 53, 4220 Korsør
☎ 58 37 18 36
📠 58 37 18 39
📧 golf@korsoergolf.dk
📏 18 L 5752 m CR 71.1 SR 130
⛳ H–NA before 9am
££ 250 (300kr)
🚗 1km E of Korsør, on Korsør Bay
■ www.korsoergolf.dk

Mølleåens (1970)
*Stenbaekgård, Rosenlundvej 3,
3540 Lynge*
☎ 48 18 86 31/48 18 86 36 (Pro)
📠 48 18 86 43
📏 18 L 5494 m SSS 69
⛳ H
££ 200kr (250kr)
🚗 32 km NW of Copenhagen
🏠 Jan Sederholm

Odsherred (1967)
4573 Hojby
☎ 59 30 20 76
📠 59 30 36 76
📏 18 L 5536 m Par 71
⛳ H
££ 200kr (240kr)
🚗 5km SW of Nykøbing
🏠 Amilon/Dreyer

Roskilde (1973)
*Gedevad, Kongemarken 34,
4000 Roskilde*
☎ 46 37 01 81
📠 46 32 85 79
📏 18 L 5700 m CR 71
⛳ U H WE–NA before 10am
££ 250kr (300kr)
🚗 5km W of Roskilde
🏠 Jan Sederholm

Rungsted (1937)
*Vestre Stationsvej 16, 2960
Rungsted Kyst*
☎ 45 86 34 44
📠 45 86 57 70
📧 rungsted-golf@webpartner.dk
📏 18 L 5981 m Par 72 CR 71.0 SR
128 (yellow tee-men)
⛳ H–max 26 (WE–21) WE–NA
before noon
££ 450kr (500kr)
🚗 Rungsted, 24km N of Copenhagen
🏠 Maj CA Mackenzie
■ www.rungstedgolfklub.dk

Simon's (1993)
Nybovej 5, 3490 Kvistgaard
☎ 49 19 14 78
📠 49 19 14 70
📏 18 L 6401 m SSS 75
⛳ H–max 36
££ 450kr (600kr)
🚗 10km S of Helsingør. 35km N of
Copenhagen
🏠 Martin Hawtree

Skjoldenaesholm (1992)
skjoldenawsvej 101, 4174 Jystrup
☎ 57 53 87 00
📠 57 53 87 15
📧 sgc@golfin.dk
📏 18 L 5958 m Par 71
⛳ H–max 36
££ 280kr (330kr)
🚗 10km N of Ringsted. 60km SW of
Copenhagen
🏠 Otto Bojesen
■ www.golfin.dk/sgc

Skovlunde Herlev (1980)
Syvendehusvej 111, 2730 Herlev
☎ 44 68 90 09
📠 44 68 90 04
📏 18 L 5125 m CR 67.8 SR 122
9 hole Par 3 course
⛳ H
££ 250kr (300kr)
🚗 Herlev/Ballerup, 15km NW of
Copenhagen
🏠 Torben Starup
■ www.shgk.dk

Søllerød
Brillerne 9, 2840 Holte
☎ 45 80 17 84, 45 80 18 77
📠 45 80 70 08
📏 18 L 5952 m SSS 72
⛳ U
££ 280kr (350kr)
🚗 19km N of Copenhagen
■ www.sollerodgolf.dk

Sorø (1979)
Suserupvej 7a, 4180 Sorø
☎ 57 84 93 95
📠 57 84 85 58
📏 18 L 5693 m Par 71 CR 71
⛳ H–max 42
££ 250kr (300kr)
🚗 6km S of Sorø. 15km W of
Ringsted
🏠 Jan Sederholm
■ www.soroegolf.dk

Sydsjaellands (1974)
*Borupgården, Mogenstrup,
4700 Naestved*
☎ 55 76 15 55
📠 55 76 15 88
📏 18 L 5663 m CR 70.5
⛳ H
££ 240kr (300kr)
🚗 10km SE of Naestved towards
Praestø
🏠 Dreyer/Amillon

Vaerlose Golfklub   (1993)

Christianshovej 22, 3500 Vaerlose
☎ (+45) 4447 2124
📠 (+45) 4447 2128
📧 mail@vaerloese-golfklub.dk
⊳ 18 L 5800 m Par 72 CR 71.3 SR 128
👥 H WD WE
££ £38
🏠 Sederholm
■ www.vaerloese-golfklub.dk

Vallensbaek   (1985)

Golfsvinget 12, 2625 Vallensbaek
☎ 43 62 18 99
📠 43 62 18 33
⊳ 18 L 5965 m Par 71 CR 72 SR 123
👥 H
££ 220kr (260kr)
🚴 15km W of Copenhagen
🏠 Frederik Dreyer

Finland

Central

Etelä-Pohjanmaan   (1986)

P O Box 136, 60101 Seinäjoki
☎ (06) 423 4545
📠 (06) 423 4547
⊳ 18 L 5806 m CR 71.9
👥 U
££ €34
🚴 5km E of Seinäjoki. 300km NW of Helsinki
🏠 Robert Trent Jones Jr
■ www.ruuhikoskigolf.fi

Karelia Golf   (1987)

Vaskiportintie, 80780 Kontioniemi
☎ (013) 732411
📠 (013) 732472
⊳ 18 L 5619 m CR 71
👥 U H
££ €31
🚴 18km N of Joensuu. 460km NE of Helsinki
🏠 Kosti Kuronen

Kokkolan   (1957)

P O Box 164, 67101 Kokkola
☎ (06) 822 1636
📠 (06) 822 1630
⊳ 18 L 5572 m SSS 71
👥 U H
££ €30
🚴 3km S of Kokkola. 500km N of Helsinki
🏠 KJ Indola

Laukaan Peurunkagolf   (1989)

Valkolantie 68, 41530 Laukaa
☎ (014) 3377 300
📠 (014) 3377 305
⊳ 18 L 5547 m CR 71
👥 H
££ €40
🚴 28km NE of Jyväskylä. 300km N of Helsinki
🏠 Ronald Fream
■ www.golfpiste.com/lpg

Tarina Golf   (1988)

Golftie 135, 71800 Siilinjärvi
☎ (017) 462 5299
📠 (017) 462 5269
⊳ Old 18 L 5593 m CR 70.2 SR 130
   New 18 L 5866 m CR 71.5 SR 128
👥 U H
££ €34 (€43)
🚴 21km N of Kuopio (Route 5)
🏠 Kuronen/Sederholm

Vaasan   (1969)

Golfkenttätie 61, 65380 Vaasa
☎ (06) 356 9989
📠 (06) 356 9091
⊳ 18 L 5602 m Par 72
👥 H or Green card
££ €24
🚴 Kraklund, 6km SE of Vaasa on Route 724. 417km NW of Helsinki
🏠 Björn Eriksson

Helsinki & South

Aura Golf   (1958)

Ruissalon Puistotie 536, 20100 Turku
☎ (02) 258 9201/9221
📠 (02) 258 9121
⊳ 18 L 5843 m SSS 71
👥 H–max 30 (men) 36 (women)
££ €50 (€55)
🚴 Ruissalo Island, 9km W of Turku
🏠 Pekka Sivula
■ www.auragolf.fi

Espoo Ringside Golf   (1990)

Niipperintie 20, 02920 Espoo
☎ (09) 849 4940
📠 (09) 853 7132
⊳ 18 L 5855 m SSS 72
👥 H
££ €34 (€40)
🚴 20km NW of Helsinki
🏠 Kosti Kuronen

Espoon Golfseura   (1982)

Mynttiläntie 1, 02780 Espoo
☎ (09) 8190 3444
📠 (09) 8190 3434
⊳ 18 L 5920 m CR 72.3
👥 H
££ €45
🚴 Espoo, 24km W of Helsinki
🏠 Jan Sederholm
■ www.espoongolfseura.fi

Harjattula G&CC   (1989)

Harjattulantie 84, 20960 Turku
☎ (02) 276 2180
📠 (02) 258 7218
⊳ 18 L 6348 m Par 72 SSS 75
👥 H–max 36
££ €35 (€43)
🚴 22km S of Turku
🏠 Kosti Kuronen
■ www.harjattula.fi

Helsingin Golfklubi   (1932)

Talin Kartano, 00350 Helsinki
☎ (09) 2252 3710
📠 (09) 2252 3732
⊳ 18 L 5486 m CR 68.7 SR 120
👥 H–max 24
££ €45 (€50)
🚴 7km W of Helsinki
🏠 Kosti Kuronen
■ www.helsingingolfklubi.fi

Hyvinkään   (1989)

Golftie 63, 05880 Hyvinkää
☎ (019) 489390
📠 (019) 489392
⊳ 18 L 5457 m CR 72.1
👥 U H
££ €29
🚴 3km N of Hyvinkää. 50km N of Helsinki
🏠 Kosti Kuronen

Keimola Golf   (1988)

Kirkantie 32, 01750 Vantaa
☎ (09) 276 6650
📠 (09) 896790
⊳ 27 L 5870-5924 m SSS 71-74
👥 WD–U before 3pm –M after 3pm WE–M H
££ €27
🚴 15km N of Helsinki
🏠 Pekka Wesamaa

Kurk Golf   (1985)

02550 Evitskog
☎ (09) 819 0480
📠 (09) 819 04810
📧 kurk@kurkgolf.fi
⊳ 18 L 5848 m Par 72
   9 hole course
👥 H
££ €45 (€55)
🚴 40km W of Helsinki
🏠 Reijo Hillberg, Peter Fjallman
■ www.kurkgolf.fi

Master Golf   (1988)

Bodominkuja 7, 02940 Espoo
☎ (09) 849 2300
📠 (09) 849 23011
⊳ 18 L 5708 m CR 71.2 SR 128
   18 L 5553 m CR 70.7 SR 124
👥 WD before 2pm H–max 30 (M) 36 (L)
££ €60 (€60)
🚴 24km NW of Helsinki
🏠 Kuronen/Persson
■ www.mastergolf.fi

Meri-Teijo (1990)
Mathildedalin Kartano,
25660 Mathildedal
☎ **(02) 736 3955**
🖳 (02) 736 3945
🏳 18 L 5842 m CR 70.7
👫 U
£€ €19 (€24)
⛳ 20km S of Salo. 70km E of Turku

Messilä (1988)
Messiläntie 240, 15980 Messilä
☎ **(03) 753 8171**
🖳 (03) 753 8174
🏳 18 L 6013 m Par 73
👫 WD–U before 3pm
£€ D–€30
⛳ 8km W of Lahti. 100km N of Helsinki
🏳 Kosti Kuronen

Nevas Golf (1988)
01190 Box
☎ **(09) 272 6313**
🖳 (09) 272 6345
🏳 18 L 5267 m CR 68.5
👫 U
£€ €35
⛳ 30km E of Helsinki
🏳 Kosti Kuronen

Nordcenter G&CC (1988)
10410 Aminnefors
☎ **(019) 2766850**
🖳 (019) 238871
🏳 18 L 6375 m SSS 77
18 L 6069 m SSS 72
👫 H
£€ €67 (€75)
⛳ 80km W of Helsinki
🏳 Fream/Benz
🖳 www.nordcenter.com

Nurmijärven (1990)
Ratasillantie, 05100 Röykkä
☎ **(09) 276 6230**
🖳 (09) 276 62330
🏳 27 L 6002-6214 m SSS 73-75
👫 H
£€ €20–€30
⛳ 23km W of Klaukkala. 50km NW of Helsinki

Peuramaa
02400 Kirkkonummi
☎ **(09) 295 588**
🖳 (09) 2955 8210
🏳 36 holes
👫 H
£€ €30 (€40)
⛳ 27km W of Helsinki
🏳 Kuronen/Persson
🖳 www.peuramaagolf.com

Pickala Golf (1986)
Golfkuja 5, 02580 Siuntio
☎ **(09) 221 9080**
🖳 (09) 221 90899
🏳 Seaside 18 L 5820 m SSS 72
Park 18 L 5897 m SSS 72

H
£€ €40 (€60)
⛳ 42km W of Helsinki, on South coast
🏳 Reijo Hillberg
🖳 www.pickalagolf.fi

Ruukkigolf (1986)
Brödtorp, 10420 Skuru
☎ **(019) 245 4485**
🖳 (019) 245 4285
🏳 18 L 6165 m Par 72
👫 U
£€ €20 (€29)
⛳ 85km W of Helsinki
🏳 Lasse Heikkinen

Sarfvik (1984)
P O Box 27, 02321 Espoo
☎ **(09) 221 9000**
🖳 (09) 297 7134
🏳 18 L 5690 m CR 70.5
18 L 5399 m CR 69.8
👫 WD–U H
£€ €67
⛳ 20km W of Helsinki
🏳 Jan Sederholm

Sea Golf Rönnäs (1989)
Rönnäs, 07750 Isnäs
☎ **+358 (0) 19 634 434**
🖳 +358 (0) 19 634 458
✉ seagolf@co.inet.fi
🏳 27: Old Course: White: CR 71.6 SR 126 (men)
Yellow: 69.6/125 (m), 75.3/128 (w)
Red: 65.8/118 (m), 70.6/118 (w)
New: Yelllow: 65.3/113 (m), 70.0/122 (w)
Red: 62.0/106 (m), 66.6/114 (w)
👫 U
£€ €32 (€40) inc. trolleys
⛳ 27km SE of Porvoo. 80km E of Helsinki (1 hour)
🏳 Kosti Kuronen
🖳 www.ronnas.net

St Laurence (1989)
Kaivurinkatu, 08200 Lohja
☎ **(019) 357821**
🖳 (019) 386666
🏳 18 L 6240 m CR 71.5 SR 128
18 L 6340 m CR 70.7 SR 120
👫 WD–H WE–M H
£€ €50
⛳ 50km W of Helsinki
🏳 Kosti Kuronen

Suur-Helsingin (1965)
Rinnekodintie 29, 02980 Espoo
☎ **(09) 855 8687**
🖳 (09) 855 0648
🏳 Lakisto 18 L 5551 m SSS 71
Luukki 18 L 5085 m SSS 70
👫 U
£€ €25
⛳ 25km N of Helsinki

Golf Talma (1989)
Nygårdintie 115-6, 04240 Talma
☎ **(09) 274 6540**
🖳 (09) 274 65432
✉ golftalma@golftalma.fi
🏳 18 L 5809 m SSS 72
18 L 5758 m SSS 72
9 hole Par 3 course
👫 WD–H WE–M H
£€ €50 (€60)
⛳ 35km N of Helsinki
🏳 Henrik Wartiainen
🖳 www.golftalma.fi

Tuusula (1983)
Kirkkotie 51, 04301 Tuusula
☎ **(042) 410241**
🖳 (09) 274 60860
🏳 18 L 5626 m CR 71
👫 H
£€ €37
⛳ 30km N of Helsinki, nr airport
🏳 Henrik Wartiainen
🖳 www.golfpiste.com/tgk

Virvik Golf (1981)
Virvik, 06100 Porvoo
☎ **(915) 579292**
🖳 (915) 579292
🏳 18 L 5855 m SSS 72
👫 H
£€ €20 (€24)
⛳ 18km SE of Porvoo. 66km E of Helsinki
🏳 Reijo Louhimo

North

Green Zone Golf (1987)
Näräntie, 95400 Tornio
☎ **(016) 431711**
🖳 (016) 431710
🏳 18 L 5870 m SSS 73
👫 U
£€ €20
⛳ 2km N of Tornio. 140km N of Oulu, on Finnish/Swedish border
🏳 Ake Persson

Katinkulta (1990)
88610 Vuokatti
☎ **(08) 669 7488**
🖳 (08) 669 7480
🏳 18 L 6000 m Par 72
👫 H
£€ €49
⛳ 36km E of Kajaani. 600km N of Helsinki
🏳 Jan Sederholm

Oulu (1964)
peltolantie 8A, 90230ulu
☎ **(08) 531 5222**
🖳 (08) 531 5129
✉ oulun.golf@kolumbus.fi
🏳 18 L 6160 m SSS 73
9 L 2990 m SSS 73
👫 H

£€ €45–€50
⚭ Sanginsuu, 18km E of Oulu
⌂ Ronald Fream
▪ www.golfpiste.com/ogk

South East

Imatran Golf   (1986)
Golftie 11, 55800 Imatra
☎ (05) 473 4954
🖳 (05) 473 4953
⊳ 18 L 5738 m CR 71.4
👫 U
£€ €29 (€29)
⚭ 6km N of Imatra. 270km E of Helsinki
⌂ Kosti Kuronen

Kartano Golf   (1988)
P O Box 60, 79601 Joroinen
☎ (017) 572257
🖳 (017) 572263
⊳ 18 L 5597 m CR 71
👫 U
£€ €22 (€29)
⚭ 20km S of Varkaus. 330km NE of Helsinki
⌂ Ake Persson

Kerigolf   (1990)
Kerimantie 65, 58200 Kerimäki
☎ (015) 252600
🖳 (015) 252606
✉ clubhouse@kerigolf.fi
⊳ 18 L 6218 m Par 72 SSS 75
👫 H
£€ €35
⚭ 15km E of Savonlinna. 350km NE of Helsinki
⌂ Ronald Fream
▪ www.kerigolf.fi

Koski Golf   (1987)
Eerolan Golfkeskus, 45700 Kuusankoski
☎ (05) 864 4600
🖳 (05) 864 4644
⊳ 18 L 6375 m Par 73
👫 H I
£€ €35 (€40)
⚭ 3km E of Kuusankoski. 70km E of Lahti
⌂ Kosti Kuronen
▪ www.koskigolf.com

Kymen Golf   (1964)
Mussalo Golfcourse, 48310 Kotka
☎ (05) 210 3700
🖳 (05) 210 3730
⊳ 18 L 5672 m CR 70.6 SR 129
👫 H
£€ €35
⚭ 5km W of Kotka, Mussalo Island. 130km E of Helsinki
⌂ Kosti Kuronen
▪ www.kymengolf.fi

Lahden Golf   (1959)
Takkulantie, 15230 Lahti
☎ (03) 784 1311

🖳 (03) 784 1311
⊳ 18 L 5547 m CR 71.7
👫 U H
£€ €32 (€40)
⚭ 6km NE of Lahti. 110km NE of Helsinki

Porrassalmi   (1989)
Annila, 50100 Mikkeli
☎ (015) 335518/335446
🖳 (015) 335446
⊳ 18 L 5430 m CR 69.8
👫 H
£€ €30–€35
⚭ 5km S of Mikkeli

Vierumäen Golfseura   (1988)
Suomen Urheiluopisto, 19120 Vierumäki
☎ (03) 842 4501
🖳 (03) 842 4630
⊳ 18 L 5580 m CR 71.1
👫 U
£€ €29
⚭ 25km NE of Lahti

South West

Porin Golfkerho   (1939)
P O Box 25, 28601 Pori
☎ (02) 630 3888
🖳 (02) 630 38813
⊳ 18 L 6160 m SSS 74
👫 H
£€ €34
⚭ 5km NW of Pori, at Kalafornia
⌂ Reijo Louhimo

River Golf   (1988)
Taivalkunta, 37120 Nokia
☎ (03) 340 0234
🖳 (03) 340 0235
⊳ 18 L 5616 m CR 70.8
👫 U
£€ €25
⚭ Nokia, 20km W of Tampere
⌂ Kosti Kuronen

Salo Golf   (1988)
Liikuntapuisto 8, 24100 Salo
☎ (02) 731 7321
🖳 (02) 731 5600
⊳ 18 L 5447 m CR 69
👫 U
£€ €20 (€25)
⚭ 110km W of Helsinki

Tammer Golf   (1965)
Toimelankatu 4, 33560 Tampere
☎ (03) 261 3316
🖳 (03) 261 3130
⊳ 18 L 5717 m CR 70
👫 U
£€ €25
⚭ Ruotula, 5km NE of Tampere

Tawast Golf   (1987)
Tawastintie 48, 13270 Hämeenlinna
☎ (03) 630 610
🖳 (03) 630 6120
⊳ 18 L 6063 m Par 72
👫 WD–H–max 30 WE–M
£€ €42
⚭ 5km E of Hämeenlinna
⌂ Reijo Hillberg
▪ www.tawastgolf.fi

Vammala   (1991)
38100 Karkku
☎ (03) 513 4070
🖳 (03) 513 90711
⊳ 18 L 5522 m CR 69.2
👫 H
£€ €20 (€27)
⚭ 11km N of Vammala. 210km NW of Helsinki
⌂ Kosti Kuronen

Wiurila G&CC   (1990)
Viurilantie 126, 24910 Halikko
☎ (02) 737 1400
🖳 (02) 737 1404
⊳ 18 L 5584 m CR 71.7
👫 U
£€ €22 (€27)
⚭ 5km W of Salo. 115km W of Helsinki

Yyteri Golf   (1988)
Karhuluodontie 85, 28840 Pori
☎ (02) 638 0380
🖳 (02) 638 0385
⊳ 18 L 5738 m Par 72
👫 H
£€ €34–€42
⚭ 20km W of Pori
⌂ Reijo Louhimo
▪ www.yyterilinks.com

France

Bordeaux & South West

Albret   (1986)
Le Pusocq, 47230 Barbaste
☎ 05 53 65 53 69
🖳 05 53 65 61 19
⊳ 18 L 5911 m SSS 71
👫 U
£€ €21 (€26)
⚭ Barbaste, 30km W of Agen
⌂ JL Pega

Arcachon   (1955)
35 Bd d'Arcachon, 33260 La Teste De Buch
☎ 05 56 54 44 00
🖳 05 56 66 86 32
⊳ 18 L 5930 m SSS 71
👫 U H

££ €28.30–€41.20
🚗 60km SW of Bordeaux
🏠 CR Blandford

Arcangues (1991)
64200 Arcangues
☎ 05 59 43 10 56
🖥 05 59 43 12 60
🏌 18 L 6142 m Par 72
👥 U
££ On application
🚗 3km SE of Biarritz
🏠 Ronald Fream

Biarritz (1888)
Ave Edith Cavell, 64200 Biarritz
☎ 05 59 03 71 80
🖥 05 59 03 26 74
📧 golf.biarritz@wanadoo.fr
🏌 18 L 5376 m:
White CR 69.0 SR 121
Yellow CR 67.2 SR 118
Blue CR 69.8 SR 116
Red CR 68.8 SR 113
👥 U H36 WD WE
££ €40.50 (€50)
🚗 400 m from the town
🏠 Willie Dunn
■ www.golf-biarritz.com

Biscarrosse (1989)
Route d'Ispe, 40600 Biscarrosse
☎ 05 58 09 84 93
🖥 05 58 09 84 50
🏌 Lake 9 L 2172 m SSS 32
Forest 9 L 3030 m SSS 36
👥 U
££ €16–€42
🚗 80km SW of Bordeaux
🏠 Brizon/Veyssieres

Blue Green-Artiguelouve (1986)
Domaine St Michel, Pau-Artiguelouve, 64230 Artiguelouve
☎ 05 59 83 09 29
🖥 05 59 83 14 05
🏌 18 L 6063 m Par 71
👥 U
££ €29 (€36)
🚗 8km NW of Pau, off Bayonne road
🏠 J Garaialde

Blue Green-Seignosse
(1989)
Avenue du Belvédère, 40510 Seignosse
☎ 05 58 41 68 30
🖥 05 58 41 68 31
🏌 18 L 6124 m Par 72
👥 U
££ €40–€60
🚗 30km N of Biarritz, nr Airport
🏠 Robert von Hagge
■ www.golfseignosse.com

Bordeaux-Cameyrac (1972)
33450 St Sulpice-et-Cameyrac
☎ (+33) (0)5 56 72 96 79
🖥 (+33) (0)5 56 72 86 56

📧 contact@golf-bordeaux-cameyrac.com
🏌 18 L 5777 m Par 72 CR 72.3 SR 132
9 L 1188 m Par 28
👥 U
££ €26 (€36)
🚗 15 min drive from Bordeaux and Saint Emillion between the wine fields
🏠 Jacques Quenot
■ www.golf-bordeaux-cameyrac.com

Bordeaux-Lac (1977)
Public
Avenue de Pernon, 33300 Bordeaux
☎ 05 56 50 92 72
🖥 05 56 29 01 84
🏌 18 L 6156 m SSS 72
18 L 6159 m SSS 72
👥 U
££ €23 (€33)
🚗 2km N of Bordeaux
🏠 Jean Bourret
■ www.golfbordeauxlac.com

Bordelais (1900)
Domaine de Kater, Allee F Arago, 33200 Bordeaux-Caudéran
☎ 05 56 28 56 04
🖥 05 56 28 59 71
🏌 18 L 4727 m SSS 67
👥 H–restricted Tues
££ €35 (€45)
🚗 3km NW of Bordeaux

Casteljaloux (1989)
Route de Mont de Marsan, 47700 Casteljaloux
☎ 05 53 93 51 60
🖥 05 5320 90 98
📧 golfdecasteljaloux@tiscali.fr
🏌 18 L 5916 m SSS 72
👥 U
££ €25 (€30)
🚗 60km SW of Agen
🏠 Michel Gayon
■ www.golfdecasteljaloux.com

Castelnaud (1987)
'La Menuisière', 47290 Castelnaud de Gratecambe
☎ 05 53 01 74 64
🖥 05 53 01 78 99
🏌 18 L 6322 m SSS 73
9 L 2184 m SSS 27
🚗 10km N of Villeneuve on N21. 40km N of Agen

Chantaco (1928)
Route d'Ascain, 64500 St Jean-de-Luz
☎ 05 59 26 14 22/05 59 26 19 22
🖥 05 59 26 48 37
🏌 18 L 5833 m SSS 70
👥 U H
££ €45–€56
🚗 2km S of St Jean-de-Luz, on Route d'Ascain
🏠 HS Colt
■ www.golfdechantaco.com

Château des Vigiers (1992)
24240 Monestier
☎ 05 53 61 50 33
🖥 05 53 61 50 31
📧 reserve@vigiers.com
🏌 18 L 6003 m Par 72
6 hole Academy course
👥 H
££ €35–€55
🚗 15km SW of Bergerac. 75km E of Bordeaux
🏠 Donald Steel
■ www.vigiers.com

Chiberta (1926)
Boulevard des Plages, 64600 Anglet
☎ 05 59 63 83 20
🖥 05 59 63 30 56
🏌 18 L 5650 m SSS 70
👥 H–booking required
🚗 3km N of Biarritz. Airport 5km
🏠 T Simpson

Domaine de la Marterie
(1987)
St Felix de Reillac, 24260 Le Bugue
☎ 05 53 05 61 00
🖥 05 53 05 61 01
🏌 18 L 6130 m Par 73
👥 U
££ €26 (€36)
🚗 30km S of Perigueux, between La Douze and Le Bugue (D710)
🏠 Martine Lacroix
■ www.marterie.fr

Graves et Sauternais (1989)
St Pardon de Conques, 33210 Langon
☎ 05 56 62 25 43
🏌 18 L 5810 m SSS 71
👥 U
🚗 5km from Langon. 45km SW of Bordeaux via A62

Gujan (1990)
Route de Souguinet, 33470 Gujan Mestras
☎ 05 57 52 73 73
🖥 05 56 66 10 93
🏌 18 L 6225 m SSS 72
9 L 2635 m SSS 35
👥 U
££ 18 holes: €27–43 9 holes: €21–26
🚗 12km E of Arcachon on RN 250. 40km W of Bordeaux
🏠 Alain Prat

Hossegor (1930)
333 Ave du Golf, 40150 Hossegor
☎ 05 58 43 56 99
🖥 05 58 43 98 52
📧 golf.hossegor@wanadoo.fr
🏌 18 L 6001 m SSS 71
👥 H–max 35
££ €42–€57
🚗 15km N of Bayonne, on coast
🏠 J Morrison
■ www.golfhossegor.asso.fr

Lacanau Golf & Hotel (1980)

Domaine de l'Ardilouse,
33680 Lacanau-Océan
☎ (+33) 5560 39292
🖳 (+33) 5562 63057
➢ 18 L 5932 m SSS 72
👥 H
⊛ 45km W of Bordeaux
🏠 John Harris

Makila

Route de Cambo, 64200 Bassussarry
☎ 05 59 58 42 42
🖳 05 59 58 42 48
➢ 18 L 6176 m SSS 72
👥 H
£€ €34–€46
⊛ 5km SE of Biarritz. Airport 2km
🏠 R Roquemore

Médoc

Chemin de Courmateau, Louens, 33290
Le Pian Médoc
☎ 05 56 70 11 90
🖳 05 56 70 11 99
➢ Chateaux 18 L 6316 m SSS 73
  Vignes 18 L 6220 m SSS 73
👥 H
£€ €35 (€46)
⊛ 20km NW of Bordeaux
🏠 Coore/Whitman

Moliets (1989)

Public
Rue Mathieu Desbieys, 40660 Moliets
☎ 05 58 48 54 65
🖳 05 58 48 54 88
➢ 18 L 6172 m SSS 73
  9 hole course
👥 U H–max 30
£€ €40–€58
⊛ Moliets, 40km N of Bayonne. 40km
  W of Dax
🏠 Robert Trent Jones Sr
■ www.golfmoliets.com

La Nivelle (1907)

Place William Sharp, 64500 Ciboure
☎ 05 59 47 18 99/05 59 47 19 72
➢ 18 L 5570 m SSS 69
👥 U
⊛ 2km S of St Jean-de-Luz

Pau (1856)

Rue de Golf, 64140 Pau-Billère
☎ 05 59 13 18 56
🖳 05 59 13 18 57
➢ 18 L 5312 m SSS 69
👥 H
£€ €35–€43
⊛ 2km S of Pau. Bordeaux 200km
🏠 Willie Dunn

Périgueux (1980)

Public
Domaine de Saltgourde, 24430 Marsac
☎ 05 53 53 02 35
🖳 05 53 09 46 29
➢ 18 L 6120 m SSS 72

👥 U
⊛ 3km W of Périgueux, via
  Angoulême-Riberac road
🏠 Robert Berthet

Pessac (1989)

Rue de la Princesse, 33600 Pessac
☎ 05 57 26 03 33
🖳 05 56 36 52 89
➢ 18 L 5567-5935 m SSS 72
  9 L 2911 m SSS 36
  9 hole Par 3 course
👥 U
£€ €35 (€45)
⊛ 4km W of Bordeaux
🏠 Olivier Brizon

Stade Montois (1993)

Pessourdat, 40090 Saint Avit
☎ 05 58 75 63 05
🖳 05 58 06 80 72
➢ 18 L 5944 m Par 71
👥 U
£€ €27 (€27)
⊛ Pau 80km. Biarritz 100km
🏠 J Garaialde

Brittany

Ajoncs d'Or (1976)

Kergrain Lantic, 22410 Saint-
Quay Portrieux
☎ 02 96 71 90 74
🖳 02 96 71 40 83
➢ 18 L 6125 m SSS 72
👥 U
£€ €23–€34 (€30–€34)
⊛ 17km N of Saint-Brieuc. 6km W of
  Étables-sur-Mer
🏠 Carlian-Des Heulles

Baden

Kernic, 56870 Baden
☎ 02 97 57 18 96
🖳 02 97 57 22 05
➢ 18 L 6145 m SSS 73
👥 U
⊛ 12km SW of Vannes
🏠 Yves Bureau

Belle Ile en Mer (1987)

Les Poulins, 56360 Belle-Ile-en-Mer
☎ 02 97 31 64 65
➢ 18 L 5820 m Par 72
👥 U
⊛ Island off S coast of Brittany, near
  Quiberon
🏠 Yves Bureau

Brest Les Abers (1990)

Kerhoaden, 29810 Plouarzel
☎ 02 98 89 68 33
➢ 18 L 5060 m Par 71
👥 U
£€ €31
⊛ 15km W 0f Brest (D5)
🏠 Ch Dunoyer

Brest-Iroise (1976)

Parc de Lann-Rohou, Saint-Urbain,
29800 Landerneau
☎ 02 98 85 16 17
🖳 02 98 85 19 39
➢ 18 L 5672 m Par 71
  9 L 3329 m Par 37
👥 U
£€ €32 (€35)
⊛ 25km E of Brest
🏠 M Fenn

Cicé-Blossac (1992)

Domaine de Cicé-Blossac, 35170 Bruz
☎ 02 99 52 79 79
🖳 02 99 57 93 60
➢ 18 L 6343 m SSS 72
👥 U
⊛ Bruz, SW of Rennes (N177)
🏠 Macauley/Quenouille

Dinard (1890)

35800 St-Briac-sur-Mer
☎ 02 99 88 32 07
🖳 02 99 88 04 53
➢ 18 L 5137 m Par 68
⊛ 8km W of Dinard. 15km W of
  Saint-Malo

La Freslonnière (1989)

Le Bois Briand, 35650 Le Rheu
☎ 02 99 14 84 09
🖳 02 99 14 94 98
➢ 18 L 5756 m SSS 72 SR 125
👥 U
£€ €31–€42
⊛ 4km SW of Rennes, off N24
🏠 A du Bouexic

L'Odet (1987)

Clohars-Fouesnant, 29950 Benodet
☎ 02 98 54 87 88
🖳 02 98 54 61 40
➢ 18 L 5843 m SSS 72
  9 hole Par 3 course
👥 U H
£€ €27–€44
⊛ 6km S of Benodet. 15km SE of
  Quimper
🏠 Robert Berthet

Les Ormes (1988)

Château des Ormes, Epiniac, 35120 Dol-
de-Bretagne
☎ 02 99 73 54 44
🖳 02 99 73 53 65
➢ 18 L 5801 m SSS 72
👥 H
£€ €31–€41
⊛ 8km S of Dol, off D795
🏠 A d'Ormesson

Pléneuf-Val André

Rue de la Plage des Vallées, 22370
Pléneuf-Val André
☎ 02 96 63 01 12
🖳 02 96 63 01 06
➢ 18 L 6052 m Par 72
👥 U

££ €24–€41
⌖ 30km E of St Brieuc on coast.
60km W of St Malo
⌂ Alain Prat

Ploemeur Océan (1990)

Kerham Saint-Jude, 56270 Ploemeur
☎ **02 97 32 81 82**
⌨ 02 97 32 80 90
⌖ 18 L 5957 m SSS 72 SR 126
👥 U H
££ €25 (€39)
⌖ 10km from Lorient-Brest road, exit
Ploemeur
⌂ Macauley/Quenouille
■ www.formule-golf.com

Quimper-Cornouaille (1959)

Manoir du Mesmeur, 29940 La Forêt-Fouesnant
☎ **02 98 56 97 09**
⌨ 02 98 56 86 81
⌖ 18 L 5451 m CR 69.6 SR 124
👥 U
££ €47 (€47)
⌖ 15km SE of Quimper
⌂ F Hawtree
■ www.golfdecornouaille.com

Rennes Saint Jacques

B P 1117, 37136 St-Jacques-de-la-Lande
☎ **02 99 30 18 18**
⌨ 02 99 31 51 04
⌖ 18 L 6135 m Par 72
9 L 2100 m Par 32
9 hole short course
👥 U
££ €37
⌖ 5km SW of Rennes
⌂ Robert Berthet

Rhuys-Kerver (1988)

Public
Formule Golf, Domaine de Kerver, 56730 St-Gildas-de-Rhuys
☎ **02 97 45 30 09**
⌨ 02 97 45 36 58
⌖ 18 L 6197 m SSS 73
👥 U
££ €35
⌖ 30km S of Vannes
⌂ Olivier Brizon

Les Rochers (1989)

Route d'Argentré du Plessis 3, 35500 Vitré
☎ **02 99 96 52 52**
⌨ 02 99 96 79 34
⌖ 18 L 5721 m Par 72
👥 U
££ €24 (€24)
⌖ Vitré, 30km E of Rennes
⌂ JC Varro

Sables-d'Or-les-Pins (1925)

22240 Fréhel
☎ **02 96 41 42 57**

⌨ 02 96 41 51 44
⌖ 18 L 5586 m SSS 71
👥 U
££ €27–€34
⌖ 6km SW of Fréhel. 30km W of
Dinard

St Cast Pen Guen (1926)

22380 Saint-Cast-le-Guildo
☎ **02 96 41 91 20**
⌨ 02 96 41 77 62
⌖ 18 L 4967m SSS 68
👥 U
££ €30–€36
⌖ 25km W of Dinard. 30km W of
Saint-Malo

St Laurent (1975)

Ploemel, 56400 Auray
☎ **02 97 56 85 18**
⌨ 02 97 56 89 99
✉ golf.stlaurent@wanadoo.fr
♟ 6
⌖ 18 L 6128 m SSS 72
9 L 2705 m SSS 35
👥 U
££ €38 (€47); 9 hole: €28
⌖ Ploemel, 30km SW of Auray
⌂ Fenn/Bureau
■ www.formuli-golf.com

St Malo-Le Tronchet (1986)

Le Tronchet, 35540 Miniac-Morvan
☎ **02 99 58 96 69**
⌨ 02 99 58 10 39
⌖ 18 L 5936 m SSS 72
9 L 2684 m SSS 36
👥 U
££ D–€40
⌖ 23km S of St Malo, off RN 137
⌂ Hubert Chesneau

St Samson (1965)

Route de Kérénoc, 22560 Pleumeur-Bodou
☎ **02 96 23 87 34**
⌨ 02 96 23 84 59
⌖ 18 L 5807 m Par 71
👥 U
££ €32 (€58)
⌖ 7km N of Lannion on Tregastel
road
⌂ Hawtree

Val Queven (1990)

Public
Kerruisseau, 56530 Queven
☎ **02 97 05 17 96**
⌨ 02 97 05 19 18
⌖ 18 L 6127 m SSS 72 SR 118
👥 U Sun–restricted
££ €30–€44
⌖ 10km W of Lorient
⌂ Yves Bureau
■ www.formule-golf.com

Burgundy & Auvergne

Aubazine (1977)

Public
19190 Aubazine
☎ **03 55 27 25 66**
⌨ 03 55 27 29 33
⌖ 18 L 5400 m Par 70
👥 U
⌖ 15km E of Brive
⌂ Hubert Chesneau

Beaune-Levernois (1990)

21200 Levernois
☎ **03 80 24 10 29**
⌨ 03 80 24 03 78
⌖ 18 L 6129 m Par 72
9 L 1316 m Par 29
👥 U
££ €31 (€40)
⌖ 5km SE of Beaune (D470/D111)
⌂ Christian Piot

Chalon-sur-Saône (1976)

Parc de Saint Nicolas, 71380 Chatenoy-en-Bresse
☎ **03 85 93 49 65**
⌨ 03 85 93 56 95
⌖ 18 L 5859 m SSS 71
👥 U
££ €25
⌖ 3km SE of Chalon. 125km N of
Lyon
⌂ Michel Rio
■ www.golf_chalon_sur_saone.com

Chambon-sur-Lignon (1986)

*Riondet, La Pierre de la Lune, 43400
Le Chambon-sur-Lignon*
☎ **04 71 59 28 10**
⌨ 04 71 65 87 14
⌖ 18 L 6110 m Par 72
👥 U
££ On application
⌖ 60km NW of Saint Etienne. 120km
NW of Lyon
⌂ Michel Gayon
■ www.golf-chambon.com

Château d'Avoise (1992)

9 Rue de Mâcon, 71210 Montchanin
☎ **03 85 78 19 19**
⌨ 03 85 78 15 16
⌖ 18 L 6350 m Par 72
👥 WD–U WE–H
⌖ 25km W of Chalon
⌂ Martin Hawtree

Château de Chailly (1990)

Chailly-sur-Armançon, 21320 Pouilly-en-Auxois
☎ **03 80 90 30 40**
⌨ 03 80 90 30 05
✉ reservation@chailly.com
⌖ 18 L 6146 m SSS 72
SR 130 (White), 124 (Yellow), 126
(Blue), 195 (Red)
👥 U

£€ €40 (€55)
⇔ A6 motorway, Pouilly-en-Auxois exit, 45km SW of Dijon, 40km NW of Beau
↟ Sprecher/Watine

Dijon-Bourgogne (1972)
Bois des Norges, 21490 Norges-la-Ville
☎ 03 80 35 71 10
⌨ 03 80 35 79 27
↣ 18 L 6179 m SSS 72
👥 U
£€ €29 (€38)
⇔ 7km N of Dijon towards Langres
↟ Fenn/Radcliffe

Domaine de Roncemay (1989)
89110 Chassy
☎ 03 86 73 50 50
⌨ 03 86 73 69 46
↣ 18 L 6401 m Par 72 SSS 73
👥 H WE–restricted
£€ €31 (€43)
⇔ 15km W of Auxerre
↟ Jeremy Pern

Limoges-St Lazare (1976)
Public
Avenue du Golf, 87000 Limoges
☎ 05 55 28 30 02
↣ 18 L 6238 m SSS 73
👥 U
⇔ 2km S of Limoges on RN20
↟ Hubert.Chesneau

Mâcon La Salle (1989)
La Salle-Mâcon Nord, 71260 La Salle
☎ 03 85 36 09 71
⌨ 03 85 36 06 70
↣ 18 L 6024 m Par 71
👥 H or green card
£€ €29 (€36)
⇔ 5km N of Mâcon (A6)
↟ Robert Berthet
■ www.golfmacon.com

Le Nivernais
Public
Le Bardonnay, 58470 Magny Cours
☎ 03 58 18 30
⌨ 03 58 04 04
↣ 18 L 5670 m Par 71
👥 U
⇔ 12km S of Nevers on N7. 50km N of Moulins
↟ Alain Prat

La Porcelaine
Célicroux, 87350 Panazol
☎ 05 55 31 10 69
⌨ 05 55 31 10 69
✉ golf@golf.porcelaine.com
↣ 18 L 6035 m SSS 72
👥 U
£€ €35–€40
⇔ 6km NE of Limoges
↟ Jean Garaialde
■ www.golf-porcelaine.com

St Junien (1997)
Les Jouberties, 87200 Saint Junien
☎ 05 55 02 96 96
⌨ 05 55 02 32 52
↣ 18 L 5677 m Par 72 SSS 69.9
9 hole course
👥 U
£€ €22 (€25)
⇔ 30km W of Limoges (N141)
■ www.golfdesaintjunien.com

Sporting Club de Vichy (1907)
Allée Baugnies, 03700 Bellerive/Allier
☎ 04 70 32 39 11
⌨ 04 70 32 00 54
↣ 18 L 5463 m SSS 70
👥 H
⇔ In Vichy
↟ Arnaud Massy

Val de Cher (1975)
03190 Nassigny
☎ 04 70 06 71 15
↣ 18 L 5450 m Par 70
👥 U
£€ €31
⇔ 20km N of Montluçon on N144
↟ Bourret/Vigand

Les Volcans (1984)
La Bruyère des Moines, 63870 Orcines
☎ 04 73 62 15 51
⌨ 04 73 62 26 52
✉ golfdesvolcans@nat.fr
↣ 18 L 6286 m SSS 73
9 L 1377 m SSS 29
👥 U H
£€ €37 (€43)
⇔ 12km W of Clermont-Ferrand on RN41
↟ Lucien Roux
■ www.golfdesvolcans.com

Centre

Les Aisses (1992)
RN20 Sud, 45240 La Ferté St Aubin
☎ 02 38 64 80 87
⌨ 02 38 64 80 85
↣ 27 L 6200 m Par 72
👥 U
£€ €48
⇔ 30km S of Orléans. 140km S of Paris
↟ Olivier Brizon

Ardrée (1988)
37360 St Antoine-du-Rocher
☎ 02 47 56 77 38
⌨ 02 47 56 79 96
↣ 18 L 5758 m Par 70
👥 U
⇔ 10km N of Tours
↟ Olivier Brizon

Les Bordes (1987)
41220 Saint Laurent-Nouan
☎ 02 54 87 72 13
⌨ 02 54 87 78 61
↣ 18 L 6412 m Par 72
👥 U
£€ €150
⇔ 30km SW of Orléans
↟ Robert van Hagge
■ www.lesbordes.com

Château de Cheverny
La Rousselière, 41700 Cheverny
☎ 02 54 79 24 70
⌨ 02 54 79 25 52
↣ 18 L 6276 m Par 71
👥 U
£€ €40
⇔ 15km S of Blois. 200km SW of Paris, via A10
↟ O Van der Vynckt
■ www.golf-cheverny.com

Château de Maintenon (1988)
Route de Gallardon, 28130 Maintenon
☎ 02 37 27 18 09
⌨ 02 37 27 10 12
↣ 18 L 6393 m SSS 74
9 L 1541 m SSS 30
👥 WD–U WE–restricted
⇔ 20km W of Rambouillet (D906). 70km SW of Paris
↟ Michel Gayon

Château des Sept Tours (1989)
Le Vivier des Landes, 37330 Courcelles de Touraine
☎ 02 47 24 69 75
⌨ 02 47 24 23 74
↣ 18 L 6194 m Par 72
👥 U
£€ €31 (€38)
⇔ 35km NW of Tours
↟ Donald Harradine

Cognac (1987)
Saint-Brice, 16100 Cognac
☎ 05 45 32 18 17
⌨ 05 45 35 10 76
↣ 18 L 6142 m SSS 72
👥 H
⇔ 5km E of Cognac
↟ Jean Garaialde

Le Connétable (1987)
Parc Thermal, 86270 La Roche Posay
☎ 05 49 86 25 10
⌨ 05 49 19 48 40
↣ 18 L 6014 m SSS 72
👥 U
£€ €23 (€27)
⇔ La Roche-Posay, 20km E of Châtellerault. 40km NE of Poitiers
↟ J Garaialde

Domaine de Vaugouard
(1987)
Chemin des Bois, Fontenay-sur-Loing,
45210 Ferrières
☎ 02 38 89 79 00
🖳 02 38 89 79 01
ᚺ 18 L 5914 m SSS 72
🙎 U
€€ €30–€40 (€40–€55)
ᚙ 10km N of Montargis. 100km S of Paris
⌂ Fromanger/Adam

Les Dryades (1987)
36160 Pouligny-Notre-Dame
☎ 02 54 30 28 00
🖳 02 54 30 10 24
ᚺ 18 L 6120 m SSS 72
🙎 U
€€ €31 (€38)
ᚙ 10km S of La Châtre (D940). 60km SW of Bourges
⌂ Michel Gayon

Ganay (1991)
Prieuré de Ganay, 41220 St Laurent-Nouan
☎ 02 54 87 26 24
🖳 02 54 87 72 50
ᚺ 27 hole course
🙎 U
€€ €15 (€21)
ᚙ 130km S of Paris
⌂ Jim Shirley

Haut-Poitou (1987)
86130 Saint-Cyr
☎ 05 49 62 53 62
🖳 05 49 88 77 14
ᚺ 18 L 6590 m SSS 75
9 L 1800 m Par 31
🙎 U
€€ 9 holes: €14; 18 holes: €24–€3
ᚙ 20km N of Poitiers. 70km S of Tours
⌂ HG Baker

Loudun-Roiffe (1985)
Domaine St Hilaire, 86120 Roiffe
☎ 05 49 98 78 06
🖳 05 49 98 72 57
ᚺ 18 L 6343 m Par 72
🙎 U
€€ €24–€36
ᚙ 18km N of Loudun. 15km S of Saumur
⌂ Hubert Chesneau
▣ www.golf-loudun.com

Marcilly (1986)
Domaine de la Plaine, 45240 Marcilly-en-Villette
☎ 02 38 76 11 73
🖳 02 38 76 18 73
ᚺ 18 L 6324 m SSS 73
9 hole course
🙎 U
€€ €26 (€34)
ᚙ 20km SE of Orléans
⌂ Olivier Brizon

Niort
Chemin du Grand Ormeau, 79000 Niort Romagne, FRANCE
☎ 05 49 09 01 41
🖳 05 49 73 41 53
ᚺ 18 L 5865 m Par 71
🙎 U
€€ €27 (€35)
ᚙ 80km W of Poitiers

Orléans Donnery
Château de la Touche, 45450 Donnery
☎ 02 38 59 25 15
🖳 02 38 57 01 98
ᚺ 18 L 5771 m SSS 71
🙎 U
ᚙ 16km E of Orléans
⌂ Trent Jones/Van der Vinckt

Golf du Perche (1987)
La Vallée des Aulnes, 28400 Souancé au Perche
☎ 02 37 29 17 33
🖳 02 37 29 12 88
ᚺ 18 L 6073 m Par 72
🙎 U
€€ €27 (€38)
ᚙ 60km SW of Chartres (D9). 130km SW of Paris
⌂ Laurent Heckly

Petit Chêne (1987)
Le Petit Chêne, 79310 Mazières-en-Gâtine
☎ 05 49 63 20 95
🖳 05 49 63 33 75
ᚺ 18 L 6060 m SSS 72
🙎 U
€€ €25 (€33)
ᚙ 15km SW of Parthenay. 25km NE of Niort
⌂ Robert Berthet

La Picardière
Chemin de la Picardière, 18100 Vierzon
☎ 02 48 75 21 43
🖳 02 48 71 87 61
ᚺ 18 L 6077 m Par 72
🙎 U
€€ €29 (€34)
ᚙ 75km S of Orléans, off A71
⌂ JL Pega

Poitiers
Domaine de Beauvoir, 86550 Mignaloux Beauvoir
☎ 05 49 46 70 27
🖳 05 49 55 31 95
ᚺ 18 L 6032 m SSS 71
🙎 WD–U WE–H
€€ €26–€31
ᚙ 6km SE of Poitiers (RN147)
⌂ Olivier Brizon

Poitou (1991)
Domaine des Forges, 79340 Menigoute
☎ 05 49 69 91 77
ᚺ 18 L 6400 m Par 74
9 L 3200 m Par 37
🙎 U

€€ €29 (€35)
ᚙ 30km W of Poitiers
⌂ Bjorn Eriksson

La Prée-La Rochelle
(1990)
Marsilly, 17137 Nieul-sur-Mer
☎ 05 46 01 24 42
🖳 05 46 01 25 84
ᚺ 18 L 6012 m SSS 72
🙎 U
€€ €32–€45
ᚙ 6km N of La Rochelle
⌂ Olivier Brizon
▣ www.golflarochelle.com

Royan (1977)
Maine-Gaudin, 17420 Saint-Palais
☎ 05 46 23 16 24
🖳 05 46 23 23 38
ᚺ 18 L 5970 m SSS 71
6 hole short course
🙎 U
€€ €25–€45
ᚙ Saint-Palais, 7km W of Royan
⌂ Robert Berthet

Saintonge (1953)
Fontcouverte, 17100 Saintes
☎ 05 46 74 27 61
🖳 05 46 92 17 92
ᚺ 18 L 4971 m Par 68 SR 130
🙎 H
€€ €23–€32.50
ᚙ 2km NE of Saintes
⌂ Hervé Bertrand

Sancerrois (1989)
St Thibault, 18300 Sancerre
☎ 02 48 54 11 22
🖳 02 48 54 28 03
ᚺ 18 L 5820 m SSS 71
🙎 U
€€ €22–€35 (€30–€39)
ᚙ 45km NE of Bourges
⌂ Didier Fruchet
▣ www.sancerre.net/golf

Sully-sur-Loire (1965)
L'Ousseau, 45600 Viglain
☎ 02 38 36 52 08
ᚺ 18 L 6154 m Par 72
9 L 3155 m Par 36
ᚙ 3km SW of Sully-sur-Loire

Touraine (1971)
Château de la Touche, 37510 Ballan-Miré
☎ 02 47 53 20 28
🖳 02 47 53 31 54
ᚺ 18 L 5671 m SSS 71
🙎 WE–H
€€ D–€35 (D–€46)
ᚙ Ballan-Miré, 10km SW of Tours
⌂ Michael Fenn

Val de l'Indre (1989)
Villedieu-sur-Indre, 36320 Tregonce
☎ 02 54 26 59 44

☐ 02 54 26 06 37
⌖ 18 L 6250 m SSS 72
👥 U
££ €27 (€35)
🚗 12km NW of Chateauroux. 80km SE of Tours on RN 143
🏠 Yves Bureau

Channel Coast & North

Abbeville　(1989)

Route du Val, 80132 Grand-Laviers
☎ 03 22 24 98 58
☐ 03 22 24 49 61
⌖ 18 L 6080 m Par 73
👥 U
££ €23 (€27)
🚗 3km NW of Abbeville
🏠 Didier Fruchet

L'Ailette

02000 Laon
☎ 23 24 83 99
☐ 23 24 84 66
⌖ 18 L 6127 m Par 72
　 9 hole short course
👥 WD–H WE–H restricted
££ €28 (€37)
🚗 13km S of Laon. 45km NW of Reims
🏠 Michel Gayon

Amiens　(1925)

80115 Querrieu
☎ 03 22 93 04 26
☐ 03 22 93 04 61
⌖ 18 L 6114 m SSS 72
👥 U
££ €22–30 (€32–40)
🚗 7km NE of Amiens (D929)
🏠 Ross/Pennink

Apremont　(1992)

60300 Apremont
☎ 03 44 25 61 11
☐ 03 44 25 11 72
⌖ 18 L 6395 m SSS 73 SR 134
👥 H
££ €40 (€75)
🚗 45km N of Paris
🏠 John Jacobs
⬛ www.apremont-golf.com

Arras　(1989)

Rue Briquet Taillandier, 62223 Anzin-St-Aubin
☎ 03 21 50 24 24
☐ 03 21 50 29 71
⌖ 18 L 6150 m SSS 72
　 9 L 1656 m SSS 31
👥 U
££ €23 (€45)
🚗 50km S of Lille. 110km SE of Calais
🏠 JC Cornillot
⬛ www.arras-golfclub.com

Belle Dune

Promenade de Marquenterre, 80790 Fort-Mahon-Plage
☎ 03 22 23 45 50
☐ 03 22 23 93 41
⌖ 18 L 5909 m Par 72 SSS 71
👥 H or Green card
🚗 25km S of Le Touquet on coast
🏠 JM Rossi

Bois de Ruminghem　(1991)

1613 Rue St Antoine, 62370 Ruminghem
☎ 03 21 85 30 33
☐ 03 21 36 38 38
⌖ 18 L 6115 m Par 73
👥 U
££ €38 (€42)
🚗 20km NE of Calais
🏠 Bill Baker

Bondues　(1968)

Château de la Vigne, BP 54, 59587 Bondues Cedex
☎ 03 20 23 20 62
☐ 03 20 23 24 11
✉ golfebondues@nordnet.fr
⌖ 18 L 6163 m SSS 73 SR 130
　 18 L 6009 m SSS 72 SR 127
👥 H–max 30. Closed Tues
££ €48 (€72 – no green fee July/August)
🚗 10km NE of Lille
🏠 Hawtree/Trent Jones

Brigode　(1970)

36 Avenue de Golf, 59650 Villeneuve D'Ascq
☎ 03 20 91 17 86
☐ 03 20 05 96 36
⌖ 18 L 6182 m SSS 72
👥 WD–H
🚗 8km NE of Lille
🏠 HJ Baker

Champagne　(1986)

02130 Villers-Agron
☎ 03 23 71 62 08
☐ 03 23 71 50 40
⌖ 18 L 5760 m SSS 72
££ €30 (€40)
🚗 25km SW of Reims, via E50
🏠 JC Cornillot
⬛ www.golf-de-champagne.com

Chantilly　(1909)

Allée de la Ménagerie, 60500 Chantilly
☎ 03 44 57 04 43
☐ 03 44 57 26 54
✉ golfchan@club-internet.fr
⌖ Vineuil 18 L 6597 m SSS 71
　 Longeres 18 L 6378 m SSS 72
👥 WE–NA
££ WD–€80
🚗 45km N of Paris
🏠 Tom Simpson

Château de Raray

4 Rue Nicolas de Lancy, 60810 Raray
☎ 03 44 54 70 61
☐ 03 44 54 74 97
⌖ 18 L 6455 m Par 72
　 9 L 2921 m Par 35
👥 H
££ €23–€34 (€38–€53)
🚗 60km N of Paris (A1)
🏠 Patrick Leglise

Chaumont-en-Vexin　(1963)

Château de Bertichère, 60240 Chaumont-en-Vexin
☎ 03 44 49 00 81
☐ 03 44 49 32 71
⌖ 18 L 6195 m SSS 72
👥 H
££ €23 (€46)
🚗 65km NW of Paris
🏠 Donald Harradine

Compiègne　(1896)

Ave Royale, 60200 Compiègne
☎ 03 44 38 48 00
☐ 03 44 40 23 59
⌖ 18 L 6015 m Par 71
👥 U
££ €23 (€38)
🚗 80km NE of Paris
🏠 W Freemantel

Deauville l'Amiraute　(1992)

CD 278, Tourgéville, 14800 Deauville
☎ 02 31 14 42 00
☐ 02 31 88 32 00
⌖ 18 L 6055 m Par 73
👥 U
££ €43–€61 (€53–€64)
🚗 4km S of Deauville
🏠 Bill Baker
⬛ www.amiraute-resort.com

Domaine du Tilleul　(1984)

Landouzy-la-Ville, 02140 Vervins
☎ 03 23 98 48 00
☐ 03 23 98 46 46
⌖ 18 L 5203 m SSS 71
👥 Groups 10+ welcome
££ €15–€23 (€23–€27)
🚗 7km S of Hirson. 65km N of Reims

Dunkerque　(1991)

Public
Fort Vallières, Coudekerque-Village, 59380 Bergues
☎ 03 28 61 07 43
☐ 03 28 60 05 93
✉ golf@golf-dk.com
⌖ 18 L 5710 m Par 71
££ €40 (€50)
🚗 5km E of Dunkerque
🏠 Robert Berthet
⬛ www.golf-dk.com

Golf Dolce Chantilly　(1991)

Route d'Apremont, 60500 Vineuil St-Firmin
☎ 03 44 58 47 74

☐ 03 44 58 50 28
✉ golf.dolce.chantilly@wanadoo.fr
↦ 18 L 6209 m SSS 73
👫 U
££ €29 (€50)
🚗 40km N of Paris (A1)
🏠 Huau/Nelson
⬛ www.dolce.com/chantilly

Hardelot Dunes Course
(1991)
Ave du Golf, 62152 Hardelot
☎ **03 21 83 73 10**
☐ 03 21 83 24 33
↦ 18 L 5713 m SSS 72
👫 U H
££ €37–€61 (€49–€89)
🚗 15km S of Boulogne
🏠 JP Cornillot

Hardelot Pins Course
Ave du Golf, 62152 Hardelot
☎ **03 21 83 73 10**
☐ 03 21 83 24 33
↦ 18 L 5926 m SSS 73
👫 U
££ €37–€46 (€55 D–€84)
🚗 15km S of Boulogne
🏠 Tom Simpson (1931)

International Club du Lys
(1929)
Rond-Point du Grand Cerf,
60260 Lamorlaye
☎ **03 44 21 26 00**
☐ 03 44 21 35 52
↦ 18 L 6022 m Par 71
   18 L 4770 m Par 66
👫 WD–H WE–H (booking necessary)
££ WD–€46
🚗 5km S of Chantilly. 40km N of
   Paris
🏠 Tom Simpson
⬛ www.golf-lys-chantilly.com

Morfontaine *(1907)*
60128 Mortefontaine
☎ **03 44 54 68 27**
☐ 03 44 54 60 57
↦ 18 L 5803 m SSS 70.9
   9 L 2526 m Par 36
👫 Members' guests only
££ NA
🚗 10km S of Senlis. N of Paris
🏠 Tom Simpson

Mormal *(1991)*
Bois St Pierre, 59144 Preux-au-Sart
☎ **03 27 63 07 00**
☐ 03 27 39 93 62
✉ info@golf-mormal.com
↦ 18 L 6022 m Par 72
👫 H
££ €29 (€39)
🚗 15km E of Valenciennes, off RN49
🏠 JC Cornillot
⬛ www.golf-mormal.com

Nampont-St-Martin *(1978)*
Maison Forte, 80120 Nampont-St-Martin
☎ **03 22 29 92 90/03 22 29 89 87**
☐ 03 22 29 97 54
↦ Cygnes 18 L 6051 m SSS 72
   Belvédère 18 L 5145 m SSS 72
👫 U
££ €20–€23 (€31–€37)
🚗 50km S of Boulogne. Motorway
   A16 Junction 25
🏠 Thomas Chatterton

Rebetz *(1988)*
Route de Noailles, 60240 Chaumont-en-Vexin
☎ **03 44 49 15 54**
☐ 03 44 49 14 26
↦ 18 L 6409 m SSS 73
👫 H
££ €23 (€53)
🚗 Chaumont-en-Vexin, 65km NW of
   Paris, via D43
🏠 J-P Fourès
⬛ www.rebetz.com

Saint-Omer
Chemin des Bois, Acquin-Westbécourt,
62380 Lumbres
☎ **03 21 38 59 90**
☐ 03 21 93 02 47
↦ 18 L 6294 m Par 73
   9 L 2038 m Par 31
👫 U
££ €26–€40 (€34–€49)
🚗 10km W of Saint-Omer. 40km S of
   Calais
🏠 J Dudok van Heel

Le Sart *(1910)*
5 Rue Jean-Jaurès, 59650
Villeneuve D'Ascq
☎ **03 20 72 02 51**
☐ 03 20 98 73 28
↦ 18 L 5721 m SSS 71
👫 H
££ €38 (€46 D–€76)
🚗 5km E of Lille. Motorway Lille-
   Gand Junction 9 (Breucq-Le Sart)
🏠 Allan Macbeth

Thumeries *(1935)*
Bois Lenglart, 59239 Thumeries
☎ **03 20 86 58 98**
☐ 03 20 86 52 66
↦ 18 L 5933 m SSS 72
👫 U
££ €27 (€38)
🚗 10km N of Douai. 15km S of Lille
🏠 Boomer/Rossi

Le Touquet 'La Forêt'
(1904)
Ave du Golf, BP 41, 62520 Le Touquet
☎ **03 21 06 28 00**
☐ 03 21 06 28 01
↦ 18 L 5659 m CR 69.8 SR 123
👫 U H
££ €48 (€58)
🚗 2km S of Le Touquet. 30km S of
   Boulogne

🏠 H Hutchinson
⬛ www.opengolfclub.com

Le Touquet 'La Mer' *(1930)*
Ave du Golf, BP 41, 62520 Le Touquet
☎ **03 21 06 28 00**
☐ 03 21 06 28 01
↦ 18 L 6275 m CR 74.9 SR 131
👫 U H
££ €54 (€64)
🚗 As 'La Forêt'
🏠 HS Colt

Le Touquet 'Le Manoir'
(1994)
Ave du Golf, BP 41, 62520 Le Touquet
☎ **03 21 06 28 00**
☐ 03 21 06 28 01
↦ 9 L 2817 m Par 35 SR 118
👫 U
££ €32 (€38)
🚗 As 'La Forêt'
🏠 HJ Baker

Val Secret *(1984)*
Brasles, 02400 Château Thierry
☎ **03 23 83 07 25**
☐ 03 23 83 92 73
✉ accueil@golfvalsecret.com
↦ 18 L 5540 m Par 70 SR 135
👫 U
££ €26.50 (€42.50)
🚗 58km W of Reims via A4. Paris
   89km
⬛ www.golfvalsecret.com

Vert Parc *(1991)*
3 Route d'Ecuelles, 59480 Illies
☎ **03 20 29 37 87**
☐ 03 20 49 76 39
↦ 18 L 6328 m SSS 73
👫 U
🚗 18km SW of Lille
🏠 Patrice Simon

Wimereux *(1901)*
Route d'Ambleteuse, 62930 Wimereux
☎ **03 21 32 43 20**
☐ 03 21 33 62 21
↦ 18 L 6150 m Par 72
👫 U
££ €25–€40 (€35–€50)
🚗 6km N of Boulogne on D940. 30km
   S of Calais
🏠 Campbell/Hutchinson

Corsica

Spérone *(1990)*
Domaine de Spérone, 20169 Bonifacio
☎ **04 95 73 17 13**
☐ 04 95 73 17 85
↦ 18 L 6106 m SSS 73
👫 H–max 28
££ €50–75 W–€230–435
🚗 S point of Corsica, SE of Bonifacio.
   25km S of Airport
🏠 Robert Trent Jones Sr

Ile de France

Ableiges (1989)
95450 Ableiges
- ☎ **01 30 27 97 00**
- 🖳 01 30 27 97 10
- ⮞ 18 L 6261 m Par 72
- 9 L 2137 m Par 33
- ⚇ 18 holes:U H (max 30)
- ££ 18 holes: €23 (€38) 9 holes: €18 (€23)
- ⛳ 40km NW of Paris, nr Cergy Pontoise
- ⛾ Pern/Garaialde

Bellefontaine (1987)
95270 Bellefontaine
- ☎ **01 34 71 05 02**
- 🖳 01 34 71 90 90
- ⮞ 27 holes:
- 6098-6306 m Par 72
- ⚇ U
- ££ €31 (€53)
- ⛳ 27km N of Paris
- ⛾ Michel Gayon

Bondoufle (1990)
Departmentale 31, 91070 Bondoufle
- ☎ **01 60 86 41 71**
- 🖳 01 60 86 41 56
- ⮞ 18 L 6161 m SSS 73
- ⚇ U H
- ⛳ 30km S of Paris
- ⛾ Michel Gayon

Bussy-St-Georges (1988)
Promenade des Golfeurs, 77600 Bussy-St-Georges
- ☎ **01 64 66 00 00**
- 🖳 01 64 66 22 92
- ⮞ 18 L 5890 m SSS 72
- ⚇ U
- ££ On application
- ⛳ 20km E of Paris. Motorway A4 Junction 12
- ⛾ Rolin/Cornillot

Cély (1990)
Le Château, Route de Saint-Germain, 77930 Cély-en-Bière
- ☎ **01 64 38 03 07**
- 🖳 01 64 38 08 78
- ⮞ 18 L 5874 m SSS 72
- ⚇ U
- ££ €34 (€53)
- ⛳ Fontainebleau 15km
- ⛾ Adam/Fromanger
- ■ www.celygolf.com

Cergy Pontoise (1988)
2 Allee de l'Obstacle d'Eau, 95490 Vaureal
- ☎ **01 34 21 03 48**
- 🖳 01 34 21 03 34
- ⮞ 18 L 6100 m SSS 72
- ⚇ WD–U WE–U H
- ⛳ 30km NW of Paris. A15 Junction 12
- ⛾ Michel Gayon

Chevannes-Mennecy (1994)
91750 Chevannes
- ☎ **01 64 99 88 74**
- 🖳 01 64 99 88 67
- ✉ legolfchevannes@wanadoo.fr
- ⮞ 18 L 6137 m Par 72 SR 123 men, 117 women
- ⚇ U
- ££ €25 (€42)
- ⛳ 45km S of Paris
- ⛾ A d'Ormesson

Clement Ader (1990)
Domaine Château Pereire, 77220 Gretz
- ☎ **01 64 07 34 10**
- 🖳 01 64 07 82 10
- ⮞ 18 L 6350 m CR 73.9 SR 145
- ⚇ U
- ££ On application
- ⛳ 30km SE of Paris
- ⛾ Saito/Gayon
- ■ www.golfclementader.com

Coudray (1960)
Ave du Coudray, 91830 Le Coudray-Montceaux
- ☎ **01 64 93 81 76**
- 🖳 01 64 93 99 95
- ⮞ 18 L 5761 m Par 71
- 9 L 1350 m Par 29
- ⚇ H
- ££ €30 (€50)
- ⛳ 35km S of Paris on A6 (Junction 11)
- ⛾ CK Cotton

Courson Monteloup (1991)
91680 Bruyères-le-Chatel
- ☎ **01 64 58 80 80**
- 🖳 01 64 58 83 06
- ⮞ 36 hole course:
- 6171-6520 m SSS 72-75
- ⚇ WD–U WE–M exc Jul/Aug
- ££ €38 (€61)
- ⛳ 35km SW of Paris, off Route D3
- ⛾ Robert von Hagge
- ■ www.golf-stadefrancais.com

Crécy-la-Chapelle (1987)
Ferme de Monpichet, 77580 Crécy-la-Chapelle
- ☎ **01 64 04 70 75**
- ⮞ 18 L 6211 m SSS 72
- ⚇ U
- ⛳ 20km E of Paris by A4

Disneyland Golf (1992)
1 Allee de la Mare Houleuse, 77700 Magny-le-Hongre
- ☎ **01 60 45 68 90**
- 🖳 01 60 45 68 33
- ✉ dlp.nwy.golf@disney.com
- ⮞ 18 L 6221 m Par 72
- 9 L 2905 m Par 36
- ⚇ U
- ££ On application
- ⛳ 32km E of Paris via A4
- ⛾ Ronald Fream
- ■ www.disneylandparis.com

Domaine de Belesbat (1989)
Courdimanche-sur-Essonne, 91820 Boutigny-sur-Essonne
- ☎ **01 69 23 19 10**
- 🖳 01 69 23 19 01
- ⮞ 18 L 6033 m SSS 72 SR 138
- ⚇ U–Booking required
- ££ €50 (€85)
- ⛳ 50km S of Paris, between Etampes and Fontainebleau
- ⛾ Fromanger/Adam
- ■ www.belesbat.com

Domont-Montmorency
Route de Montmorency, 95330 Domont
- ☎ **01 39 91 07 50**
- 🖳 01 39 91 25 70
- ⮞ 18 L 5775 m SSS 71
- ⚇ H
- ££ €38 (€73)
- ⛳ 18km N of Paris
- ⛾ Hawtree

Étiolles (1990)
Vieux Chemin de Paris, 91450 Étiolles
- ☎ **01 69 89 59 59**
- 🖳 01 69 89 59 60
- ⮞ 18 L 6239 m Par 74
- 9 L 2665 m SSS 36
- ⚇ U
- ££ €42 (€62.50)
- ⛳ 30km S of Paris
- ⛾ Michel Gayon

Fontainebleau (1909)
Route d'Orleans, 77300 Fontainebleau
- ☎ **01 64 22 22 95**
- 🖳 01 64 22 63 76
- ⮞ 18 L 6074 m SSS 72
- ⚇ WD–U WE–Jul/Aug only
- ££ WD–€53
- ⛳ 1km SW of Fontainebleau. 60km SE of Paris
- ⛾ Simpson/M Hawtree

Fontenailles (1991)
Domaine de Bois Boudran, 77370 Fontenailles
- ☎ **01 64 60 51 00**
- 🖳 01 60 67 52 12
- ⮞ 18 L 6256 m SSS 74
- 9 L 2870 m
- ⚇ WD–U WE–H
- ££ €27–€31 (€49–€69)
- ⛳ 60km SE of Paris
- ⛾ Michel Gayon

Forges-les-Bains (1989)
Rue du Général Leclerc, 91470 Forges-les-Bains
- ☎ **01 64 91 48 18**
- 🖳 01 64 91 40 52
- ⮞ 18 L 6167 m SSS 72
- ⚇ H or Green card
- ££ €30 (€50)
- ⛳ 35km S of Paris, off A10
- ⛾ JM Rossi
- ■ www.golf-forgelesbains.com

La Forteresse (1989)

Domaine de la Forteresse,
77940 Thoury-Ferrottes
- ☎ (+33) 01 60 96 95 10
- ☐ (+33) 01 60 96 01 41
- ⊁ 18 L 5888 m Par 72
- ♟ H or Green card
- ££ €30 (€55)
- ⬡ 25km SE of Fontainebleau
- ♜ Fromanger/Adam
- ■ www.golf-forteresse.com

Greenparc (1993)

Route de Villepech, 91280 St Pierre-du-
Perray
- ☎ 01 60 75 40 60
- ☐ 01 60 75 40 04
- ⊁ 18 L 5839 m SSS 71
- ♟ U
- ££ €18 (€38)
- ⬡ 30km SW of Paris
- ♜ Robin Nelson

L'Isle Adam (1995)

1 Chemin des Vanneaux, 95290
L'Isle Adam
- ☎ 01 34 08 11 11
- ☐ 01 34 08 11 19
- ⊁ 18 L 6230 m Par 72
- ♟ U
- ££ €23–€38 (€42–€57)
- ⬡ 30km N of Paris
- ♜ Ronald Fream

Marivaux (1992)

Bois de Marivaux, 91640 Janvry
- ☎ 01 64 90 85 85
- ☐ 01 64 90 82 22
- ⊁ 18 L 6116 m Par 72
- ♟ U H–max 36
- ££ €23–€27 (€38–€53)
- ⬡ 25km SW of Paris
- ♜ Macauley/Quenouille

Meaux-Boutigny (1985)

Rue de Barrois, 77470 Boutigny
- ☎ 01 60 25 63 98
- ☐ 01 60 25 60 58
- ⊁ 18 L 5981 m SSS 72
- 9 L 1499 m SSS 30
- ♟ U
- ££ €27 (€46)
- ⬡ 45km E of Paris-Highway 4
- ♜ Michel Gayon

Mont Griffon

RD 909, 95270 Luzarches
- ☎ 01 34 68 10 10
- ☐ 01 34 68 04 10
- ✉ golf.mont.griffon@wanadoo.fr
- ⊁ 18 L 5897 m CR 70.8 SR 132
- ♟ U
- ££ €37 (€58)
- ⬡ 27km N of Paris, nr Chantilly
- ♜ Nelson/Huau/Dongradi
- ■ www.golfhotelparis.com

Ormesson (1969)

Chemin du Belvedère, 94490 Ormesson-
sur-Marne
- ☎ 01 45 76 20 71

- ☐ 01 45 94 86 85
- ⊁ 18 L 6130 m SSS 72
- ♟ H
- ££ €31 (€53)
- ⬡ 21km SE of Paris
- ♜ Harris/CK Cotton

Ozoir-la-Ferrière (1926)

Château des Agneaux, 77330 Ozoir-la-
Ferrière
- ☎ 01 60 02 60 79
- ☐ 01 64 40 28 20
- ⊁ 18 L 5859 m Par 71
- 9 L 2700 m Par 35
- ♟ U H
- ££ 18 holes: €32 (€61) 9 holes: €21 (€31)
- ⬡ 25km SE of Paris via A4 (Porte de Bercy)
- ♜ Sir Henry Cotton

Paris International (1991)

18 Route du Golf, 95560 Baillet-en-
France
- ☎ 01 34 69 90 00
- ☐ 01 34 69 97 15
- ⊁ 18 L 6319 m SSS 74
- ♟ Members and guests only
- ££ €75 (€100)
- ⬡ 24km NW of Paris
- ♜ Jack Nicklaus

St Aubin (1976)

Public
Route du Golf, 91190 St Aubin
- ☎ 01 69 41 25 19
- ☐ 01 69 41 02 25
- ⊁ 18 L 5971 m SSS 71
- 9 L 1918 m SSS 31
- ♟ U
- ⬡ 30km SW of Paris
- ♜ Berthet/Rio

St Germain-les-Corbeil

6 Ave du Golf, 91250 St Germain-les-
Corbeil
- ☎ 01 60 75 81 54
- ☐ 01 60 75 52 89
- ⊁ 18 L 5800 m SSS 71
- ⬡ 30km S of Paris

Seraincourt (1964)

Gaillonnet-Seraincourt, 95450 Vigny
- ☎ 01 34 75 47 28
- ☐ 01 34 75 75 47
- ⊁ 18 L 5760 m SSS 70
- ♟ WD–U WE–H
- ⬡ 35km NW of Paris

Villarceaux (1971)

Château du Couvent, 95710 Chaussy
- ☎ 01 34 67 73 83
- ☐ 01 34 67 72 66
- ⊁ 18 L 6059 m Par 72
- ♟ H
- ££ €34 (€53)
- ⬡ 60km NW of Paris
- ♜ M Backer

Villeray (1974)

Public
Melun-Sénart, St Pierre du Perray,
91100 Corbeil
- ☎ 01 60 75 17 47
- ☐ 01 69 89 00 73
- ⊁ 18 L 6169 m SSS 72
- ♟ U
- ££ £15 (£28)
- ⬡ 30km SE of Paris, off N6
- ♜ Hubert Chesneau

Languedoc-Roussillon

Cap d'Agde (1989)

Public
4 Ave des Alizés, 34300 Cap d'Agde
- ☎ 04 67 26 54 40
- ☐ 04 67 26 97 00
- ⊁ 18 L 6160 m SSS 72
- ♟ U
- ⬡ 25km E of Béziers
- ♜ Ronald Fream

Carcassonne (1988)

Route de Ste-Hilaire,
11000 Carcassonne
- ☎ 06 13 20 85 43
- ☐ 04 68 72 57 30
- ⊁ 18 L 5758 m Par 71
- ♟ U
- ££ €27 (€34)
- ⬡ 2km SW of Carcassonne
- ♜ J-P Basurco

Coulondres (1984)

72 Rue des Erables, 34980 Saint-Gely-
du-Fesc
- ☎ 04 67 84 13 75
- ☐ 04 67 84 06 33
- ⊁ 18 L 6175 m SSS 73
- ♟ U
- ££ €23 (€31)
- ⬡ 10km N of Montpellier towards Ganges
- ♜ Donald Harradine
- ■ www.coulondres.com

Domaine de Falgos (1992)

BP 9, 66260 St Laurent-de-Cerdans
- ☎ 04 68 39 51 42
- ☐ 04 68 39 52 30
- ✉ contact@falgos.com
- ⊁ 18 L 5177 m SSS 69
- ♟ U
- ££ €50
- ⬡ 60km S of Perpignan, nr Spanish border (D115)
- ■ www.falgos.com

Fontcaude (1991)

Route de Lodève, Domaine de
Fontcaude, 34990 Juvignac
- ☎ 04 67 45 90 10
- ☐ 04 67 45 90 20

☞ 18 L 6992 m SSS 72
9 hole short course
㋡ U
££ €38–€46
♨ 6km W of Montpellier
⌂ C Pitman

La Grande-Motte (1987)

Clubhouse du Golf, 34280 La Grande-Motte
☎ 04 67 56 05 00
⌨ 04 67 29 18 84
☞ 18 L 6161 m CR 73.3 SR 133
18 L 3076 m Par 58
6 hole short course
㋡ U
££ €38 (€46)
♨ 18km E of Montpellier
⌂ Robert Trent Jones Sr

Montpellier Massane (1988)

Domaine de Massane, 34670 Baillargues
☎ 04 67 87 87 87
⌨ 04 67 87 87 90
☞ 18 L 6231 m Par 72
9 hole Par 3 course
㋡ U
££ €40 (€48)
♨ 9km E of Montpellier. A9 Junction 28
⌂ Ronald Fream

Nîmes Campagne (1968)

Route de Saint Gilles, 30900 Nîmes
☎ 04 66 70 17 37
⌨ 04 66 70 03 14
☞ 18 L 6135 m SSS 72
㋡ H
££ €38 (€46)
♨ 7km S of Nîmes, by Airport
⌂ Morandi/Harradine

Nîmes-Vacquerolles (1990)

Route de Sauve, 30900 Nîmes
☎ 04 66 23 33 33
⌨ 04 66 23 94 94
☞ 18 L 6300 m SSS 72
㋡ U
££ €35.50 (€44.50)
♨ W of Nîmes centre (D999)
⌂ W Baker

St Cyprien (1974)

Le Mas D'Huston, 66750 St Cyprien Plage
☎ 04 68 37 63 63
⌨ 04 68 37 64 64
☞ 18 L 6480 m SSS 73
9 L 2724 m SSS 35
㋡ U H
££ €38 (€51)
♨ 15km SE of Perpignan
⌂ Wright/Tomlinson

St Thomas (1992)

Route de Bessan, 34500 Béziers
☎ 04 67 39 03 09
⌨ 04 67 39 10 65
☞ 18 L 6130 m Par 72
㋡ U

££ On application
♨ 7km NE of Béziers (RN 113)
⌂ Patrice Lambert

Loire Valley

Angers (1963)

Moulin de Pistrait, 49320 St Jean des Mauvrets
☎ 02 41 91 96 56
☞ 18 L 5460 m Par 70
££ €26 (€34)
♨ 14km SE of Angers. Right bank of Loire.

Anjou G&CC (1990)

Route de Cheffes, 49330 Champigné
☎ 02 41 42 01 01
⌨ 02 41 42 04 37
☞ 18 L 6227 m SSS 72
6 hole short course
㋡ U H
££ €29 (€34)
♨ 23km N of Angers
⌂ F Hawtree
▦ www.anjougolf.com

Avrillé (1988)

Château de la Perrière, 49240 Avrillé
☎ 02 41 69 22 50
⌨ 02 41 34 44 60
✍ J Goudard (Dir)
☞ 18 L 6116 m SSS 71
9 hole Par 3 course
㋡ U
££ €27 (€33)
♨ 5km N of Angers
⌂ Robert Berthet

Baugé-Pontigné (1994)

Public
Route de Tours, 49150 Baugé
☎ 02 41 89 01 27
⌨ 02 41 89 05 50
☞ 18 L 5558 m Par 72
㋡ U
££ €20 (€29)
♨ 45km E of Angers. 70km SW of Tours
⌂ M Prat

La Bretesche (1967)

Domaine de la Bretesche, 44780 Missillac
☎ 02 51 76 86 86
⌨ 02 40 88 36 28
☞ 18 L 6080 m SSS 72
㋡ U
££ €40 (€60)
♨ 8km NW of Pontchâteau, between Nantes and Vannes
⌂ Cotton/Baker

Carquefou (1991)

Boulevard de l'Epinay, 44470 Carquefou
☎ 02 40 52 73 74
⌨ 02 40 52 73 20
☞ 18 L 5790 m SSS 71

㋡ U
££ €26 (€35)
♨ NE of Nantes
⌂ M Hawtree

Cholet (1989)

Allée du Chêne Landry, 49300 Cholet
☎ 02 41 71 05 01
⌨ 02 41 56 06 94
☞ 18 L 5792 m Par 71
㋡ WD–U WE–H
♨ 2km N of Cholet. 52km SE of Nantes
⌂ Olivier Brizon

La Domangère

La Roche-sur-Yon, Route de la Rochelle, 85310 Nesmy
☎ 02 51 07 65 90
⌨ 02 51 07 65 95
☞ 18 L 6480 m SSS 72 SR 143
㋡ U
££ €27.50–€41
♨ 6km S of La Roche-sur-Yon. 70km S of Nantes
⌂ Michel Gayon
▦ www.golfdomangere.free.fr

Fontenelles

Public
Saint-Gilles-Croix-de-Vie, 85220 Aiguillon-sur-Vie
☎ 02 51 54 13 94
⌨ 02 51 55 45 77
☞ 18 L 6185 m Par 72
㋡ U
££ €21–39
♨ 6km E of St-Gilles-Croix-de-Vie. 75km SW of Nantes
⌂ Yves Bureau

Ile d'Or (1988)

BP 10, 49270 La Varenne
☎ 02 40 98 58 00
⌨ 02 40 98 51 62
☞ 18 L 6292 m Par 72
9 L 1217 m Par 27
㋡ U H
♨ 30km NE of Nantes
⌂ Michel Gayon

International Barriere-La Baule (1976)

44117 Saint-André-des Eaux
☎ 02 40 60 46 18
⌨ 02 40 60 41 41
✉ golfinterlabaule@lucienbarriere.com
☞ 18 L 6055 m Par 72 SSS 73
18 L 6301 m Par 72 SSS 74
9 L 2969 m Par 36
㋡ H
££ €40.62. 9 hole :€21.35
♨ Avrillac, 3km NE of La Baule
⌂ Alliss/Thomas/Gayon
▦ www.lucienbarriere.com

Laval-Changé (1972)

Le Jariel, 53000 Changé-les-Laval
☎ 02 43 53 16 03

🖧 02 43 49 35 15
🏴 18 L 6068 m Par 72 SSS 72
9 L 3388 m
👥 U
££ €27
🚗 5km N of Laval. 60km E of Rennes
🏠 JP Foures

Le Mans Mulsanne (1961)

Route de Tours, 72230 Mulsanne
☎ 02 43 42 00 36
🖧 02 43 42 21 31
🏴 18 L 5821 m SSS 71
👥 H
££ €31–€55 (€37–€61)
🚗 Mulsanne, 12km S of Le Mans

Nantes

44360 Vigneux de Bretagne
☎ 02 40 63 25 82
🖧 02 40 63 64 86
🏴 18 L 5940 m SSS 72
👥 H
££ €26 (€38)
🚗 12km NW of Nantes
🏠 Frank Pennink

Nantes Erdre (1990)

Chemin du Bout des Landes, 44300 Nantes
☎ 02 40 59 21 21
🖧 02 51 84 94 50
🏴 18 L 5876 m SSS 71
👥 U
££ €26 (€34)
🚗 Nantes
🏠 Yves Bureau
◼ www.ngc-nantes.fr

Les Olonnes

Gazé, 85340 Olonne-sur-Mer
☎ 02 51 33 16 16
🖧 02 51 33 10 45
🏴 18 L 6109 m Par 72
👥 U
££ €24–€37
🚗 3km N of Les Sables d'Olonne
🏠 Bruno Parpoil

Pornic (1912)

49 Boulevard de l'Océan, Sainte-Marie/Mer, 44210 Pornic
☎ 02 40 82 06 69
🖧 02 40 82 80 65
🏴 18 L 6119 m Par 72
👥 U
££ €23–€38
🚗 1km E of Pornic. 30km S of La Baule
🏠 Michel Gayon

Port Bourgenay (1990)

Avenue de la Mine, Port Bourgenay, 85440 Talmont-St-Hilaire
☎ 02 51 23 35 45
🖧 02 51 23 35 48
🏴 18 L 5800 m SSS 72
👥 U
££ €17–€41

🚗 10km SE of Sables d'Olonne.
100km S of Nantes
🏠 Pierre Thevenin

Sablé-Solesmes

Domaine de l'Outinière, Route de Pincé, 72300 Sablé-sur-Sarthe
☎ 02 43 95 28 78
🖧 02 43 92 39 05
🏴 27 holes SSS 72:
Forêt 9 L 3197 m
Rivière 9 L 2992 m
Cascade 9 L 3069 m
👥 U
££ €40–€49
🚗 40km SW of Le Mans
🏠 Michel Gayon

St Jean-de-Monts (1988)

Ave des Pays de la Loire, 85160 Saint Jean-de-Monts
☎ 02 51 58 82 73
🖧 02 51 59 18 32
🏴 18 L 5962 m SSS 72
👥 U
🚗 60km SW of Nantes on coast

Sargé-Le-Mans (1990)

Rue de Bonnétable, 72190 Sargé-les Le Mans
☎ 02 43 76 25 07
🖧 02 43 76 45 25
🏴 18 L 6054 m SSS 72
👥 U
££ €21 (€31)
🚗 6km NE of Le Mans
🏠 Antoine d'Ormesson

Savenay (1990)

44260 Savenay
☎ 02 40 56 88 05
🖧 02 40 56 89 04
🏴 18 L 6335 m Par 73
9 L 1122 m Par 30
👥 U
££ €24–€36
🚗 36km W of Nantes. 30km E of La Baule
🏠 Michel Gayon

Normandy

Bellême-St-Martin (1988)

Les Sablons, 61130 Bellême
☎ 02 33 73 00 07
🖧 02 33 73 00 17
🏴 18 L 6011 m SSS 72
👥 U
££ €26 (€38)
🚗 40km NE of Le Mans
🏠 Eric Vialatel

Cabourg-Le Home (1907)

38 Av Président Réné Coty, Le Home Varaville, 14390 Cabourg
☎ 02 31 91 25 56
🖧 02 31 91 18 30
🏴 18 L 5234 m SSS 68

👥 H
££ €20–€40
🚗 4km W of Cabourg
🏠 Jackson/Brizon

Caen (1990)

Le Vallon, 14112 Bieville-Beuville
☎ 02 31 94 72 09
🖧 02 31 47 45 30
🏴 18 holes SSS 72 Par 72
9 hole course
👥 U
🚗 5km N of Caen (D60)
🏠 F Hawtree

Champ de Bataille

Château du Champ de Bataille, 27110 Le Neubourg
☎ 02 32 35 03 72
🖧 02 32 35 83 10
🏴 18 L 6575 m SSS 72
👥 U
🚗 28km NW of Evreux. 45km SW of Rouen
🏠 Nelson/Huau

Clécy (1988)

Manoir de Cantelou, 14570 Clécy
☎ 02 31 69 72 72
🖧 02 31 69 70 22
✉ golf-de-clecy@golf-de-clecy.com
🏴 18 L 5965 m Par 72
👥 U
££ €23–€40
🚗 30km S of Caen, via D562
🏠 W Baker
◼ www.golf-de-clecy.com

Coutainville (1925)

Ave du Golf, 50230 Agon-Coutainville
☎ 02 33 47 03 31
🖧 02 33 47 38 42
🏴 18 L 5045 m SSS 68
👥 H
££ €31
🚗 12km W of Coutances. 75km S of Cherbourg

Dieppe-Pourville (1897)

51 Route de Pourville, 76200 Dieppe
☎ 02 35 84 25 05
🖧 02 35 84 97 11
🏴 18 L 5780 m Par 70
👥 U
££ €25–€42 (€42–€45)
🚗 2km W of Dieppe towards Pourville
🏠 Willie Park Jr
◼ www.golf-dieppe.com

Étretat (1908)

BP No 7, Route du Havre, 76790 Étretat
☎ 02 35 27 04 89
🏴 18 L 5994 m SSS 72
👥 H
🚗 25km N of Le Havre. Étretat 1km
🏠 Chantepie/Fruchet

Forêt Verte
Bosc Guerard, 76710 Montville
- ☎ **02 35 33 62 94**
- ⊫ 18 L 7000 yds SSS 72
- ⋒ U
- ⊷ 10km N of Rouen
- ⋔ Thierry Huau

Granville   (1912)
Bréville, 50290 Bréhal
- ☎ **02 33 50 23 06**
- ⊟ 02 33 61 91 87
- ⊫ 18 L 5854 m Par 71
  9 L 2323 m Par 33
- ⋒ U
- ££ 18 holes: €24 (€35) 9 holes: €15
  (€20)
- ⊷ 5km N of Granville
- ⋔ Colt/Allison/Hawtree

Le Havre   (1933)
Hameau Saint-Supplix, 76930 Octeville-sur-Mer
- ☎ **02 35 46 36 50**
- ⊟ 02 35 46 32 66
- ✉ golf.le-havre@wanadoo.fr
- ⊫ 18 L 5955 m SSS 72
- ⋒ H
- ££ €40 (€60)
- ⊷ 10km N of Le Havre

Houlgate   (1981)
Route de Gonneville, 14510 Houlgate
- ☎ **02 31 24 80 49**
- ⊟ 02 31 28 04 48
- ⊫ 18 L 5558 m SSS 72
- ⋒ U
- ££ €20–€37
- ⊷ 2km S of Houlgate. 15km SW of
  Deauville
- ⋔ Alliss/Thomas

Léry Poses   (1989)
BP 7, 27740 Poses
- ☎ **02 32 59 47 42**
- ⊫ 18 L 6242 m SSS 73
  9 hole Par 3 course
- ⋒ U
- ⊷ 25km SE of Rouen
- ⋔ J Baker

New Golf Deauville   (1929)
14 Saint Arnoult, 14800 Deauville
- ☎ **02 31 14 24 24**
- ⊟ 02 31 14 24 25
- ⊫ 18 L 5933 m SSS 71
  9 L 3033 m SSS 72
- ⋒ U–booking required
- ££ €46–€76
- ⊷ 3km S of Deauville
- ⋔ Simpson/Cotton

Omaha Beach   (1986)
Ferme St Sauveur, 14520 Port-en-Bessin
- ☎ **02 31 22 12 12**
- ⊟ 02 31 22 12 13
- ⊫ 18 L 6216 m SSS 72
  9 L 2693 m SSS 35
- ⋒ U H

- ££ €24–€43
- ⊷ 8km N of Bayeux
- ⋔ Yves Bureau
- ■ www.best-channel-golfs.com

Parc de Brotonne   (1991)
Jumièges, 76480 Duclair
- ☎ **02 35 05 32 97**
- ⊟ 02 35 37 99 97
- ⊫ 18 L 6040 m SSS 72
- ⋒ U
- ££ €19 (€28.50)
- ⊷ 20km W of Rouen
- ⋔ JP Fourès

Rouen-Mont St Aignan
(1911)
*Rue Francis Poulenc, 76130 Mont
St Aignan*
- ☎ **02 35 76 38 65**
- ⊟ 02 35 75 13 86
- ⊫ 18 L 5522 m SSS 70
- ⋒ H WE–H after 4pm
- ££ €23–€30 (€30–€46)
- ⊷ 4km N of Rouen

St Gatien Deauville   (1987)
14130 St Gatien-des-Bois
- ☎ **02 31 65 19 99**
- ⊟ 02 31 65 11 24
- ⊫ 18 L 6272 m Par 72
  9 L 3035 m Par 36
- ⋒ U
- ££ €31 (€46)
- ⊷ 8km E of Deauville
- ⋔ Olivier Brizon

St Saëns   (1987)
Domaine du Vaudichon, 76680 St Saëns
- ☎ **02 35 34 25 24**
- ⊟ 02 35 34 43 33
- ⊫ 18 L 6009 m SSS 71
- ⋒ U
- ££ €34 (€46)
- ⊷ 30km NE of Rouen
- ⋔ D Robinson
- ■ www.golfstsaens.com

St Julien
*St Julien-sur-Calonne, 14130 Pont-
l'Évêque*
- ☎ **02 31 64 30 30**
- ⊟ 02 31 64 12 43
- ⊫ 18 L 6035 m SSS 72
  9 L 2275 m SSS 64
- ⋒ U
- ££ €21–€29 (€31–€38)
- ⊷ 3km SE of Pont l'Évêque
- ⋔ Prat/Baker

Le Vaudreuil   (1962)
27100 Le Vaudreuil
- ☎ **02 32 59 02 60**
- ⊟ 02 32 59 43 88
- ⊫ 18 L 6320 m SSS 74
- ⋒ H
- ££ €27 (€42)
- ⊷ 6km NE of Louviers. 25km SE of
  Rouen
- ⋔ F Hawtree

North East

Ammerschwihr
*BP 19, Route des Trois Épis,
68770 Ammerschwihr*
- ☎ **03 89 47 17 30**
- ⊟ 03 89 47 17 77
- ⊫ 18 L 5795 m Par 70
  9 hole short course
- ⋒ U
- ££ €31 (€38)
- ⊷ 8km W of Colmar. 70km S of
  Strasbourg
- ⋔ Robert Berthet

Bâle G&CC   (1926)
*Rue de Wentzwiller, 68220 Hagenthal-le-
Bas*
- ☎ **03 89 68 50 91**
- ⊟ 03 89 68 55 66
- ✉ gccbasel@wanadoo.fr
- ⊫ 18 L 6255 m Par 72 SSS 73
- ⋒ WD–H (max 28) WE–M
- ££ €70
- ⊷ 15km SW of Bâle
- ⋔ B von Limburger
- ■ www.swissgolfnetwork.ch

Besançon   (1968)
La Chevillotte, 25620 Mamirolle
- ☎ **03 81 55 73 54**
- ⊟ 03 81 55 88 64
- ⊫ 18 L 6070 m SSS 73
- ⋒ H
- ££ €35 (€41)
- ⊷ 12km E of Besançon
- ⋔ Michael Fenn
- ■ www.golfbesancon.com

Bitche   (1988)
Rue des Prés, 57230 Bitche
- ☎ **03 87 96 15 30**
- ⊟ 03 87 96 08 04
- ⊫ 18 L 6082 m SSS 72
  9 L 2293 m SSS 34
- ⋒ U
- ⊷ 75km NW of Strasbourg. 55km SE
  of Saarbrücken
- ⋔ Fromanger

Château de Bournel   (1990)
25680 Cubry
- ☎ **03 81 86 00 10**
- ⊟ 03 81 86 01 06
- ✉ info@bournel.com
- ⊫ 18 L 5767 m Par 71 CR 71.6 SR
  133
- ⋒ H
- ££ €35 (€50)
- ⊷ 50km NE of Besançon
- ⋔ Robert Berthet
- ■ www.bournel.com

Combles-en-Barrois   (1948)
*14 Rue Basse, 55000 Combles-en-
Barrois*
- ☎ **03 29 45 16 03**
- ⊟ 03 29 45 16 06
- ⊫ 18 L 6100 m Par 72

U
£€ €34 (€39)
🚗 80km W of Nancy, nr Bar-le-Duc
🏠 Michel Gayon

Épinal (1985)
Public
Rue du Merle-Blanc, 88001 Épinal
☎ 03 29 34 65 97
🏴 18 L 5700 m SSS 70
U
H
🚗 Épinal, 70km S of Nancy
🏠 Michel Gayon

Faulquemont-Pontpierre (1993)
Rue du Golf, 57380 Faulquemont
☎ 03 87 29 21 21
🖥 03 87 90 76 25
🏴 18 L 6000 m SSS 72
   9 hole par 3 course
U
🚗 30km E of Metz
🏠 Flipo/Fourès

Forêt d'Orient
BP13 Rouilly-Sacey, 10220 Piney
☎ 03 25 46 37 78
🏴 18 L 6120 m Par 72
U
🚗 20km E of Troyes
🏠 E Rossi

Grande Romanie (1988)
La Grande Romanie, 51460 Courtisols
☎ 06 61 50 01 00
🖥 03 26 66 65 97
🏴 18 L 6578 m SSS 76
U
£€ €31–€38
🚗 St Etienne-au-Temple, 6km from
   A4 Junction 28
🏠 Alain Tribout

La Grange aux Ormes
La Grange aux Ormes, 57155 Marly
☎ 03 87 63 10 62
🖥 03 87 55 01 77
🏴 18 L 6200 m Par 72
   9 L 2001 m Par 31
U
£€ €26–€35 (€29–€45)
🚗 3km S of Metz
🏠 Philippe Gourdon
🌐 www.grange-aux-ormes.com

Kempferhof (1988)
Golf-Hôtel-Academie, 67115 Plobsheim
☎ 0033 (0) 3 88 98 72 72
🖥 0033 (0) 3 88 98 74 76
📧 info@golf-kempferhof.com
🏴 18 L 6024 m SSS 73 SR 145
H
£€ €35 (€95)
🚗 15km S of Strasbourg
🏠 Bob von Hagge
🌐 www.golf-kempferhof.com

La Largue G&CC (1988)
Rue du Golf, 68580 Mooslargue
☎ 03 89 07 67 67
🖥 03 89 25 62 83
📧 lalargue@golf-lalargue.com
🏴 18 L 6142 m SSS 72
WD–H WE before 10.00 or after
   13.00 H
£€ €77 (€100)
🚗 25km W of Basle
🏠 Jean Garaialde

Les Rousses (1986)
*1305 Route du Noirmont, 39220
Les Rousses*
☎ 03 84 60 06 25
🖥 03 84 60 01 73
🏴 18 L 5388 m Par 71
U
£€ €27 (€38)
🚗 30km N of Geneva (N5)

Metz Technopole
*Rue Félix Savart, 57070 Metz
Technopole 2000*
☎ 03 87 39 95 95
🏴 18 L 5774 m SSS 71
   6 hole Par 3 course
H or Green card
🚗 SE of Metz centre
🏠 Robert Berthet

Metz-Cherisey (1963)
Château de Cherisey, 57420 Cherisey
☎ 03 87 52 70 18
🖥 03 87 52 42 44
🏴 18 L 6172 m SSS 72
H
£€ €31 (€38)
🚗 15km SE of Metz
🏠 Donald Harradine

Nancy-Aingeray (1962)
Aingeray, 54460 Liverdun
☎ 03 83 24 53 87
🏴 18 L 5577 m SSS 69
H
£€ €31 (€38)
🚗 17km NW of Nancy
🏠 Michael Fenn

Nancy-Pulnoy (1993)
10 Rue du Golf, 54425 Pulnoy
☎ 03 83 18 10 18
🖥 03 83 18 10 19
🏴 18 L 6000 m SSS 72
   9 hole Par 3 course
WD–U WE–H
£€ €26 (€38)
🚗 10km E of Nancy
🏠 Hawtree/Flipo

Prunevelle (1930)
*Ferme des Petits-Bans,
25420 Dampierre-sur-le-Doubs*
☎ 03 81 98 11 77
🖥 03 81 90 28 65
🏴 18 L 6281 m SSS 73
🚗 10km S of Montbéliard, on D126

Reims-Champagne (1928)
*Château des Dames de France,
51390 Gueux*
☎ 03 26 05 46 10
🖥 03 26 05 46 19
🏴 18 L 6026 m SSS 72
U
£€ €31 (€43)
🚗 10km W of Reims
🏠 Michael Fenn

Rhin Mulhouse (1969)
Ile du Rhin, 68490 Chalampe
☎ 03 89 83 28 32
🖥 03 89 83 28 42
🏴 18 L 5991 m SSS 72
WE–M
£€ €44 (€56)
🚗 20km E of Mulhouse
🏠 Donald Harradine

Rougemont-le-Château (1990)
*Route de Masevaux, 90110 Rougemont-
le-Château*
☎ 03 84 23 74 74
🖥 03 84 23 03 15
🏴 18 L 6002 m SSS 72
U H
£€ €37 (€49)
🚗 18km NE of Belfort. 25km NW of
   Mulhouse
🏠 Robert Berthet

Strasbourg (1934)
Route du Rhin, 67400 Illkirch
☎ 03 88 66 17 22
🖥 03 88 65 05 67
🏴 27 holes:
   6105-6138 m SSS 72-73
WD–H (max 35)
£€ WD only–€35
🚗 10km S of Strasbourg
🏠 Donald Harradine

Troyes-Cordelière (1957)
*Château de la Cordelière,
10210 Chaource*
☎ 03 25 40 18 76
🖥 03 25 40 13 66
🏴 18 L 6154 m SSS 72
H
£€ €27 (€38)
🚗 NE of Chaource on N443. 30km SE
   of Troyes
🏠 P Hirigoyen

Val de Sorne
*Domaine de Val de Sorne,
39570 Vernantois*
☎ 03 84 43 04 80
🖥 03 84 47 31 21
🏴 18 L 6000 m SSS 72
H
£€ €31–€43
🚗 5km SE of Lons-le-Saunier,
   between Geneva and Lyon
🏠 Hugues Lambert
🌐 www.valdesorne.com

For list of abbreviations and key to symbols see page 627

Vittel

BP 122, 88804 Vittel-Cedex
☎ **03 29 08 18 80**
➤ St Jean 18 L 6326 m SSS 72
Peulin 18 L 6100 m SSS 72
9 hole course
⚬ Vittel, 70km S of Nancy
🏛 Allison/Morrison/Begin

La Wantzenau   (1991)

C D 302, 67610 La Wantzenau
☎ **03 88 96 37 73**
▢ 03 88 96 34 71
➤ 18 L 6400 m SSS 72
👥 H
£€ €43 (€61)
⚬ 12km N of Strasbourg
🏛 Pern/Garaialde

Paris Region

Béthemont-Chisan CC

(1989)
12 Rue du Parc de Béthemont,
78300 Poissy
☎ **01 39 75 51 13**
▢ 01 39 75 49 90
➤ 18 L 6035 m SSS 72
👥 U
£€ €38 (€76)
⚬ 30km W of Paris
🏛 Bernhard Langer

La Boulie

La Boulie, 78000 Versailles
☎ **01 39 50 59 41**
➤ 18 L 6055 m SSS 71
18 L 6206 m SSS 72
9 hole course
👥 H WE–M
⚬ 15km SW of Paris

Feucherolles   (1992)

78810 Feucherolles
☎ **01 30 54 94 94**
▢ 01 30 54 92 37
➤ 18 L 6358 m Par 72
👥 U
£€ €46–€53 (€58–€75)
⚬ 23km W of Paris
🏛 JM Poellot

Fourqueux   (1963)

Rue Saint Nom 36, 78112 Fourqueux
☎ **01 34 51 41 47**
▢ 01 39 21 00 70
➤ 18 L 5578 m CR 70.5 SR 132
9 L 2564 m CR 67.2 SR 126
👥 WD–U WE–M
⚬ 4km SW of St Germain-en-Laye, W of Paris

Isabella   (1969)

RN12, Sainte-Appoline, 78370 Plaisir
☎ **01 30 54 10 62**
▢ 01 30 54 67 58
➤ 18 L 5629 m SSS 71
👥 WD–H WE–NA

⚬ 28km W of Paris (RN12)
🏛 Paul Rolin

Joyenval   (1992)

Chemin de la Tuilerie,
78240 Chambourcy
☎ **01 39 22 27 50**
▢ 01 39 79 12 90
✉ joyenval@wanadoo.fr
➤ Retz 18 L 6211 m Par 72
Marly 18 L 6249 m Par 72
👥 M
⚬ 25km N of Paris, nr St Germain-en-Laye
🏛 Robert Trent Jones Sr
■ www.joyenval.com

National   (1990)

2 Avenue du Golf, 78280 Guyancourt
☎ **01 30 43 36 00**
▢ 01 30 43 85 58
➤ Albatros 18 L 6495 m Par 72
Aigle 18 L 5936 m Par 71
Oiselet 9 L 2010 m Par 32
👥 H or Green card
£€ €18–€47 (€18–€75)
⚬ St Quentin-en-Yvelines, SW of Paris (D36)
🏛 Chesneau/Von Hagge
■ www.golf-national.com

Rochefort   (1964)

78730 Rochefort-en-Yvelines
☎ **01 30 41 31 81**
▢ 01 30 41 94 01
➤ 18 L 5735 m SSS 71
👥 U
£€ €38–€69
⚬ 45km SW of Paris
🏛 Hawtree

St Cloud   (1911)

60 Rue du 19 Janvier, Garches 92380
☎ **01 47 01 01 85**
▢ 01 47 01 19 57
➤ 18 L 5939 m SSS 72
18 L 4823 m SSS 67
👥 H
£€ €76 (€92)
⚬ Porte Dauphine, 9km W of Paris
🏛 HS Colt

St Germain   (1922)

Route de Poissy, 78100 St Germain-en-Laye
☎ **01 39 10 30 30**
▢ 01 39 10 30 31
✉ golfstgermain@nerim.net
➤ 18 L 6117 m SSS 72
9 L 2030 m SSS 33
👥 WD–H WE–M
£€ €75
⚬ 20km W of Paris
🏛 HS Colt
■ www.golfstgermain.org

St Quentin-en-Yvelines

Public
RD 912, 78190 Trappes
☎ **01 30 50 86 40**

➤ 18 L 5900 m SSS 71
18 L 5753 m SSS 70
👥 H
⚬ 20km SW of Paris
🏛 Hubert Chesneau

St Nom-La-Bretêche   (1959)

Hameau Tuilerie-Bignon, 78860 St Nom-La-Bretêche
☎ **01 30 80 04 40**
▢ 01 34 62 60 44
➤ 18 L 6685 yds SSS 72
18 L 6712 yds SSS 72
👥 H
£€ WD only–€80
⚬ 24km W of Paris on A-13
🏛 F Hawtree

La Vaucouleurs   (1987)

Rue de l'Eglise, 78910 Civry-la-Forêt
☎ **01 34 87 62 29**
▢ 01 34 87 70 09
✉ vaucouleurs@vaucouleurs.fr
🖉 J Pelard
➤ Rivière 18 L 6138 m CR 73.2 SR 138
Vallons 18 L 5553 m Par 70 CR 68.6 SR 115
👥 H or Green card
£€ €40 (€65)
⚬ 50km W of Paris, between Mantes and Houdan
🏛 Michel Gayon
■ www.vaucouleurs.fr

Les Yvelines

Château de la Couharde, 78940 La-Queue-les-Yvelines
☎ **01 34 86 48 89**
▢ 01 34 86 50 31
➤ 18 L 6344 m Par 72
9 L 2065 m Par 31
👥 U
£€ €26 (€44)
⚬ Montfort-l'Amaury, 45km W of Paris
🏛 HJ Baker

Provence & Côte d'Azur

Aix Marseille   (1935)

13290 Les Milles
☎ **04 42 24 40 41/04 42 24 23 01**
▢ 04 42 39 97 48
✉ golfaixmarseille@aol.com
➤ 18 L 6291 m SSS 73
👥 H
£€ €42 (€58)
⚬ 7km SW of Aix-en-Provence. 30km N of Marseille
🏛 Peter Cannon

Barbaroux   (1989)

Route de Cabasse, 83170 Brignoles
☎ **04 94 69 63 63**
▢ 04 94 59 00 93
➤ 18 L 6367 m SSS 72

Les Baux de Provence
(1989)
Domaine de Manville, 13520 Les Baux-de-Provence
☎ 04 90 54 40 20
🖳 04 90 54 40 93
↦ 9 L 2812 m SSS 36
👥 U H
£€ €23 (€29)
⊕ 15km NE of Arles. 15km S of Avignon. 80km W of Marseilles
🏠 Martin Hawtree
■ www.golfsprovence.com

Beauvallon-Grimaud
Boulevard des Collines, 83120 Sainte-Maxime
☎ 04 94 96 16 98
↦ 9 L 2503 m SSS 34
👥 H
⊕ 3km SW of Sainte Maxime

Biot (1930)
La Bastide du Roy, 06410 Biot
☎ 04 93 65 08 48
🖳 04 93 65 05 63
↦ 18 L 4511 m CR 62.7 SR 94
👥 U
£€ €40 (€45)
⊕ Antibes 5km. Nice 15km

Cannes Mandelieu (1891)
Route de Golf, 06210 Mandelieu
☎ 04 92 97 32 00
🖳 04 93 49 92 90
↦ 18 L 5871 m SSS 71
  9 L 2852 m SSS 33
👥 U H
£€ €50 (€50)
⊕ Mandelieu, 7km W of Cannes

Cannes Mandelieu Riviera
(1990)
Avenue des Amazones, 06210 Mandelieu
☎ 04 92 97 49 49
🖳 04 92 97 49 42
↦ 18 L 5736 m SSS 71
👥 U H–max 36
£€ €40 (€44)
⊕ 10km SW of Cannes, off A8
🏠 Robert Trent Jones

Cannes Mougins (1925)
175 Route d'Antibes, 06250 Mougins
☎ 04 93 75 79 13
🖳 04 93 75 27 60
↦ 18 L 6263 m SSS 72
👥 H–max 28
£€ €100
⊕ 8km NE of Cannes (D35)
🏠 Colt/Simpson (1925).
  Alliss/Thomas (1977)

👥 H
£€ €55
⊕ Brignoles, 50km E of Aix. 40km N of Toulon
🏠 Pete Dye/PB Dye
■ www.barbaroux.com

Châteaublanc
Les Plans, 84310 Morières-les-Avignon
☎ 04 90 33 39 08
🖳 04 90 33 43 24
↦ 18 L 6141 m SSS 72
  9 L 1267 m Par 28
👥 H
£€ €31 (€38)
⊕ 5km SE of Avignon, nr Airport
🏠 Thierry Sprecher
■ www.golfchateaublanc.com

Digne-les-Bains (1990)
Public
4 Route du Chaffaut, 0400 Digne-les-Bains
☎ 04 92 30 58 00
🖳 04 92 30 58 13
↦ 18 L 5210 m SSS 68
👥 U
⊕ 100km NE of Aix-en-Provence
🏠 Robert Berthet
■ www.golfdigne.com

Estérel Latitudes (1989)
Ave du Golf, 83700 St Raphaël
☎ 04 94 52 68 30
🖳 04 94 52 68 31
↦ 18 L 5921 m SSS 71
  9 L 1392 m Par 29
👥 U H
£€ €41–€46
⊕ 3km N of St-Raphaël
🏠 Robert Trent Jones

Frégate (1992)
Dolce Frégate, RD 559, 83270 St Cyr-sur-Mer
☎ 04 94 29 38 00
🖳 04 94 29 96 94
✉ golf-fregate@wanadoo.fr
↦ 18 L 6210 m SSS 72
  9 hole short course
👥 U
£€ €50 (Jan–Mar, Nov/Dec) €55 (Apr/May & Oct) €60 (Jun–Sep)
⊕ 25km W of Toulon on coast
🏠 Ronald Fream
■ www.fregate.dolce.com

Gap-Bayard (1988)
Centre d'Oxygénation, 05000 Gap
☎ 04 92 50 16 83
🖳 04 92 50 17 05
✉ gap-bayard@wanadoo.fr
↦ 18 L 6023 m SSS 72
👥 U
£€ €33 (€38)
⊕ 7km N of Gap. 80km S of Grenoble
🏠 Hugues Lambert
■ www.ville-gap.fr

Grand Avignon (1989)
BP 121, Les Chênes Verts, 84270 Vedene
☎ 04 90 31 49 94
🖳 04 90 31 01 21
↦ 18 L 6046 m Par 72
  9 hole short course
👥 U
£€ €32 (€38)

⊕ Vedene, 10km NE of Avignon
🏠 Georges Roumeas

La Grande Bastide (1990)
Chemin des Picholines, 06740 Châteauneuf de Grasse
☎ 04 93 77 70 08
🖳 04 93 77 72 36
↦ 18 L 6105 m SSS 72
👥 U H
£€ €44 (€49)
⊕ Grasse, 17km N of Cannes
🏠 Cabell Robinson

Grasse CC (1992)
1 Route des Trois Ponts, 06130 Grasse
☎ 04 93 60 55 44
🖳 04 93 60 55 19
↦ 18 L 6021 m SSS 72
👥 U
£€ €46 (€49)
⊕ 18km N of Cannes
🏠 JP Fourès

Luberon (1986)
La Grande Gardette, 04860 Pierrevert
☎ 04 92 72 17 19
🖳 04 92 72 59 12
↦ 18 L 6040 m SSS 72
👥 U
£€ €42
⊕ 5km SW of Manosque. 45km NE of Aix-en-Provence
🏠 Artea
■ www.golf-du-luberon.com

Marseille La Salette (1988)
65 Impasse des Vaudrans, 13011 La Valentine Marseille
☎ 04 91 27 12 16
🖳 04 91 27 21 33
✉ lasalette@opengolfclub.com
↦ 18 L 5539 m CR 71.2 SR 142
👥 H
£€ €38 (€48)
⊕ Nr centre of Marseilles
🏠 Michel Gayon
■ www.opengolfclub.com

Miramas (1993)
Mas de Combe, 13140 Miramas
☎ 04 90 58 56 55
🖳 04 90 17 38 73
↦ 18 L 5670m Par 72
👥 H or Green card
£€ €17–€23 (€23–€31)
⊕ 50km S of Avignon. 50km NW of Marseilles
🏠 Serge Giraud

Monte Carlo (1910)
Route du Mont-Agel, 06320 La Turbie
☎ 04 92 41 50 70
🖳 04 93 41 09 55
↦ 18 L 5679 m SSS 71
👥 H
£€ €85 (€100)
⊕ Mont Agel, La Turbie, 10km N of Monte Carlo

For list of abbreviations and key to symbols see page 627

Opio-Valbonne   (1966)

Route de Roquefort-les-Pins, 06650 Opio
- ☎ **04 93 12 00 08**
- 📞 04 93 12 26 00
- ⛳ 18 L 5892 m SSS 72 SR 123
- 👤 H
- ££ €65
- ⊶ 15km N of Cannes
- ⌂ Donald Harradine
- ■ www.opengolfclub.com

Pont Royal   (1992)

Pont Royal, 13370 Mallemort
- ☎ **04 90 57 40 79**
- 📞 04 90 57 50 19
- ⛳ 18 L 6303 m SSS 72
- 👤 H
- ££ €45–€60
- ⊶ 35km SE of Avignon on N7, between Avignon and Aix en Provence
- ⌂ Severiano Ballesteros

Provence G&CC   (1991)

Route de Fontaine de Vaucluse, L'Isle sur la Sorgue, 84800 Saumane
- ☎ **04 90 20 20 65**
- 📞 04 90 20 32 01
- ⛳ 18 L 6045 m SSS 72
  9 hole short course
- 👤 U
- ⊶ 20km E of Avignon
- ⌂ Jean Garaialde

Roquebrune   (1989)

CD 7, 83520 Roquebrune-sur-Argens
- ☎ **04 94 82 92 91**
- 📞 04 94 82 94 74
- ⛳ 18 L 6031 m SSS 71
- 👤 H
- ££ €40
- ⊶ 35km N of Saint-Tropez. 40km SW of Cannes
- ⌂ Udo Barth

Royal Mougins   (1993)

424 Avenue du Roi, 06250 Mougins
- ☎ **04 92 92 49 69, 04 92 92 49 79**
- 📞 04 92 92 49 70
- ⛳ 18 L 6004 m SSS 72
- 👤 H
- ££ €150 (inc lunch)
- ⊶ 5km N of Cannes
- ⌂ Robert von Hagge
- ■ www.royalmougins.fr

St Endreol   (1992)

Route de Bagnols-en-Forêt, 83920 La Motte
- ☎ **04 94 51 89 89**
- 📞 04 94 51 89 90
- ⛳ 18 L 6219 m Par 72 CR 72.4
- 👤 U H
- ££ €68
- ⊶ 30km N of St Tropez. 40km W of Cannes
- ⌂ Michel Gayon
- ■ www.st-endreol.com

Sainte Victoire   (1985)

Domaine de Château L'Arc, 13710 Fuveau
- ☎ **04 42 53 89 09**
- 📞 04 42 53 89 08
- ⛳ 18 L 6300 m SSS 71
- 👤 U
- ££ €38
- ⊶ 15km SE of Aix-en-Provence
- ⌂ Michel Gayon
- ■ www.golfchateaularc.com

La Sainte-Baume   (1988)

Golf Hotel, Domaine de Châteauneuf, 83860 Nans-les-Pins
- ☎ **04 94 78 60 12**
- 📞 04 94 78 63 52
- ⛳ 18 L 6062 m SSS 72
- 👤 U
- ££ €40–€55 (€41)
- ⊶ 30km SE of Aix-en-Provence, via A8 (exit Saint-Maximin)
- ⌂ Robert Berthet

Sainte-Maxime

Route de Débarquement, 83120 Sainte-Maxime
- ☎ **04 94 55 02 02**
- 📞 04 94 55 02 03
- ⛳ 18 L 6155 m SSS 71
- 👤 H
- ⊶ 15km N of Saint Tropez. 80km W of Nice (RN98)
- ⌂ Donald Harradine

Servanes   (1989)

Domaine de Servanes, 13890 Mouriès
- ☎ **04 90 47 59 95**
- 📞 04 90 47 52 58
- ⛳ 18 L 6100m SSS 72
- 👤 H
- ££ €31 (€38)
- ⊶ 35km S of Avignon
- ⌂ Sprecher/Watine

Taulane

Domaine du Château de Taulane, RN 85, 83840 La Martre
- ☎ **04 93 60 31 30**
- 📞 04 93 60 33 23
- ⛳ 18 L 6250 m Par 72
- 👤 H
- ££ €31–€46 (€53)
- ⊶ 55km N of Cannes on N85 (Route Napoleon)
- ⌂ Gary Player

Valcros   (1964)

Domaine de Valcros, 83250 La Londe-les-Maures
- ☎ **04 94 66 81 02**
- 📞 04 94 66 90 48
- ⛳ 18 L 5274 m SSS 69
- 👤 H
- ££ €45
- ⊶ 10km W of Le Lavandou
- ⌂ F Hawtree

Valescure   (1895)

BP 451, 83704 St-Raphaël Cedex
- ☎ **04 94 82 40 46**
- 📞 04 94 82 41 42
- ⛳ 18 L 5067 m Par 68
- 👤 U H
- ££ €50 (€60)
- ⊶ 5km E of St-Raphaël
- ⌂ Lord Ashcombe

Rhone-Alps

Aix-les-Bains   (1913)

Avenue du Golf, 73100 Aix-les-Bains
- ☎ **04 79 61 23 35**
- 📞 04 79 34 06 01
- ⛳ 18 L 5519 m Par 70 SR 124
- 👤 H
- ££ €46 (€52)
- ⊶ 3km S of Aix
- ■ www.golf-aixlesbains.com

Albon   (1989)

Domaine de Senaud, Albon, 26140 St Rambert d'Albon
- ☎ **04 75 03 03 90**
- 📞 04 75 03 11 01
- ✉ golf.albon@wanadoo.fr
- ⛳ 18 L 6108 m CR 70.4 SR 125
  9 L 1260 m Par 29
- 👤 U
- ££ €40–€46
- ⊶ 60km S of Lyon, motorway exit Chanas
- ⌂ Antoine d'Ormesson
- ■ www.golf-albon.com

Annecy   (1953)

Echarvines, 74290 Talloires
- ☎ **04 50 60 12 89**
- 📞 04 50 60 08 80
- ✉ golflocannecy@wanadoo.fr
- ⛳ 18 L 5017 m SSS 68
- 👤 H
- ⊶ 13km E of Annecy
- ⌂ Cecil Blandford
- ■ www.golf-locannecy.com

Annonay-Gourdan   (1988)

Domaine de Gourdan, 07430 Saint Clair
- ☎ **04 75 67 03 84**
- 📞 04 75 67 79 50
- ⛳ 18 L 5900 m SSS 71
- 👤 U
- ⊶ 35km SE of St Etienne. 50km SW of Lyon
- ⌂ Sprecher/Watine

Les Arcs

B P 18, 73706 Les Arcs Cedex
- ☎ **04 79 07 43 95**
- 📞 04 79 07 47 65
- ⛳ 18 L 5547 m SSS 70
- 👤 H
- ⊶ 90 km E of Chambery on N90

For list of abbreviations and key to symbols see page 627

Le Beaujolais (1991)
69480 Lucenay-Anse
- ☎ **04 74 67 04 44**
- 🖂 04 74 67 09 60
- ⊳ 18 L 6137 m SSS 72
- ⚇ U H
- ⊶ 25km N of Lyon

Bossey G&CC (1985)
Château de Crevin, 74160 Bossey
- ☎ **04 50 43 95 50**
- 🖂 04 50 95 32 57
- ⊳ 18 L 5954 m Par 71
- ⚇ WD–U WE–NA
- £€ €70
- ⊶ 6km S of Geneva
- 🏠 Robert Trent Jones Jr

La Bresse
Domaine de Mary, 01400 Condessiat
- ☎ **04 74 51 42 09**
- 🖂 04 74 51 40 09
- ⊳ 18 L 6217 m Par 72
- ⚇ WD–U WE–H
- £€ €34 (€45)
- ⊶ 15km SW of Bourg-en-Bresse, via RN73
- 🏠 Jeremy Pern

Chamonix (1934)
35 Route du Golf, 74400 Chamonix
- ☎ **04 50 53 06 28**
- 🖂 04 50 53 38 69
- ✉ info@golfdechamonix.com
- ⊳ 18 L 6087 m SSS 72
- ⚇ H
- £€ €33–€68 (€38–€60)
- ⊶ 3km N of Chamonix (RN 506). Geneva 80km
- 🏠 Robert Trent Jones Sr
- ■ www.golfdechamonix.com

Le Clou (1985)
01330 Villars-les-Dombes
- ☎ **04 74 98 19 65**
- 🖂 04 74 98 15 15
- ✉ golfduclou.fr@freesbee.fr
- ⊳ 18 L 5000 m SSS 67
- ⚇ WD–U WE–H
- ⊶ 30km NE of Lyon
- ■ www.golfduclou.com

La Commanderie (1964)
L'Aumusse-Crottet, 01290 Pont-de-Veyle
- ☎ **04 85 30 44 12**
- 🖂 04 85 30 55 02
- ⊳ 18 L 5560 m SSS 69
- ⚇ H
- ⊶ 7km E of Mâcon on RN 79

Corrençon-en-Vercors (1987)
Les Ritons, 38250 Corrençon-en-Vercors
- ☎ **04 76 95 80 42**
- 🖂 04 76 95 84 63
- ⊳ 18 L 5550 m Par 71
- ⚇ U
- ⊶ 35km S of Grenoble, off D531
- 🏠 Hugues Lambert

Divonne (1931)
Ave des Thermes, 01220 Divonne-les-Bains
- ☎ **04 50 40 34 11**
- 🖂 04 50 40 34 25
- ⊳ 18 L 5858 m SSS 72
- ⚇ H–max 30
- £€ €46 (€77)
- ⊶ Divonne ¹/₂ km. 18km N of Geneva
- 🏠 Nakowski

Esery (1990)
Esery, 74930 Reignier
- ☎ **04 50 36 58 70**
- 🖂 04 50 36 57 62
- ✉ info@golf-club-esery.com
- ⊳ 18 L 6350 m SSS 73
     9 L 2024 m SSS 31
- ⚇ WD–H WE–NA
- £€ €60
- ⊶ 10km S of Geneva
- 🏠 Michel Gayon
- ■ www.golf-club-esery.com

Evian Masters (1904)
Rive Sud du lac de Genève, 74500 Évian
- ☎ **04 50 26 85 00**
- 🖂 04 50 75 65 54
- ⊳ 18 L 6006 m SSS 72
- ⚇ H
- £€ €32–€53 (€45–€64)
- ⊶ 2km W of Évian. 40km NE of Geneva Airport
- 🏠 Cabell Robinson
- ■ www.royalparcevian.com

Giez (1991)
Lac d'Annecy, 74210 Giez
- ☎ **04 50 44 48 41**
- 🖂 04 50 32 55 93
- ⊳ 18 L 5820 m Par 72
     9 L 2250 m Par 33
- ⚇ H or Green card
- £€ €38–€46
- ⊶ 20km SE of Annecy
- 🏠 Didier Fruchet

Le Gouverneur
Château du Breuil, 01390 Monthieux
- ☎ **04 72 26 40 34**
- 🖂 04 72 26 41 61
- ⊳ 18 L 6477 m Par 72
     18 L 5959 m Par 72
     9 L 2365 m Par 34
- ⚇ H or green card
- £€ €45
- ⊶ NE of Lyon, off A46
- 🏠 Fruchet/Sprecher

Grenoble-Bresson (1990)
Route de Montavie, 38320 Eybens
- ☎ **04 76 73 65 00**
- 🖂 04 76 73 65 51
- ⊳ 18 L 6343 m SSS 72
- ⚇ U
- £€ €35 (€41)
- ⊶ 10km SE of Grenoble
- 🏠 Robert Trent Jones Jr

Grenoble-Charmeil (1988)
38210 St Quentin-sur-Isère
- ☎ **04 76 93 67 28**
- 🖂 04 76 93 62 04
- ⊳ 18 L 5733 m Par 73
- ⚇ U
- £€ €31 (€40)
- ⊶ 15km NW of Grenoble, off A49
- 🏠 Perl/Garaialde
- ■ www.bluegreen.com

Grenoble-Uriage (1921)
Les Alberges, 38410 Uriage
- ☎ **04 76 89 03 47**
- 🖂 04 76 73 15 80
- ⊳ 9 L 2004 m Par 64
- ⚇ U
- £€ €23 (€27)
- ⊶ 15km E of Grenoble
- 🏠 Watine/Sprecher

Lyon (1921)
38280 Villette-d'Anthon
- ☎ **04 78 31 11 33**
- 🖂 04 72 02 48 27
- ⊳ 18 L 6229 m SSS 72
     18 L 6727 m SSS 74
- ⚇ U H
- £€ €34 (€50)
- ⊶ 20km E of Lyon
- 🏠 Fenn/Lambert

Lyon-Chassieu
Route de Lyon, 69680 Chassieu
- ☎ **04 78 90 84 77**
- 🖂 04 78 90 88 85
- ⊳ 18 L 5941 m Par 70
- ⚇ H
- ⊶ 10km E of Lyon
- 🏠 Chris Pittman

Lyon-Verger (1977)
69360 Saint-Symphorien D'Ozon
- ☎ **04 78 02 84 20**
- 🖂 04 78 02 08 12
- ⊳ 18 L 5800 m SSS 69
- ⚇ U
- £€ €27 (€38)
- ⊶ 14km S of Lyon on A7, or RN7
     2km S of Feyzin

Maison Blanche G&CC (1991)
01170 Echenevex
- ☎ **04 50 42 44 42**
- 🖂 04 50 42 44 43
- ⊳ 18 L 6246 m SSS 72
     9 L 1757 m Par 31
- ⚇ WD–U H–max 30
- ⊶ 15km from Geneva
- 🏠 Harradine/Dongradi

Méribel (1973)
BP 54, 73553 Méribel Cedex
- ☎ **04 79 00 52 67**
- 🖂 04 79 00 38 85
- ⊳ 18 L 5319 m SSS 70
- ⚇ H
- £€ €41

  ↦ 15km S of Moutiers. 35km S of
Albertville
⌂ Sprecher/Watine

Mionnay La Dombes (1986)
Chemin de Beau-Logis, 01390 Mionnay
☎ 04 78 91 84 84
▯ 04 78 91 02 73
↦ 18 L 5763 m SSS 71
Ⅲ U
££ €36 (€47.10)
↦ 20km N of Lyon towards Bourg
⌂ Jacques Vouilloux

Mont-d'Arbois (1964)
74120 Megève
☎ 04 50 21 29 79
▯ 04 50 93 02 63
↦ 18 L 6100 m SSS 72
Ⅲ WE–restricted. Booking required
Jul/Aug
££ €31–€46
↦ 3km SE of Megève
⌂ Henry Cotton

Pierre Carée (1984)
74300 Flaine
☎ 04 50 90 85 44
▯ 04 50 90 88 21
↦ 18 L 3693 m Par 63
Ⅲ U
↦ 4km N of Flaine. 60km SE of
Geneva Airport
⌂ Robert Berthet

St Etienne (1989)
62 Rue St Simon, 42000 St Etienne
☎ 04 77 32 14 63
▯ 04 77 33 61 23
↦ 18 L 5700 m Par 72
6 hole Par 3 course
Ⅲ U
££ €27 (€35)
↦ Nr centre of St Etienne. Lyon 60km
⌂ Thierry Sprecher

Salvagny
*100 Rue des Granges, 69890 La Tour
de Salvagny*
☎ 04 78 48 83 60
▯ 04 78 48 00 16
↦ 18 L 6300 m SSS 73 Par 72
Ⅲ U
↦ Lyon 20km
⌂ Drancourt

La Sorelle (1991)
*Domaine de Gravagnieux,
01320 Villette-sur-Ain*
☎ 04 74 35 47 27
▯ 04 74 35 44 51
↦ 18 L 6100 m SSS 72
Ⅲ U
££ €28 (€37)
↦ 50km NE of Lyon

Tignes (1968)
Val Claret, 73320 Tignes
☎ 04 79 06 37 42 (Summer)

▯ 04 79 06 35 64
↦ 18 L 4810 m SSS 68
Ⅲ H–max 35
££ €32
↦ 50km E of Moutiers, off D902, nr
Italian border. 90km S of Chamonix

Valdaine (1989)
*Domaine de la Valdaine,
Montboucher/Jabron,
26740 Montelimar-Montboucher*
☎ 04 75 00 71 33
▯ 04 75 01 24 49
↦ 18 L 5631 m SSS 71
Ⅲ U
££ €31 (€43)
↦ 4km E of Montelimar. 50km S of
Valence
⌂ TJ Macauley
■ www.domainedelavaldaine.com

Valence St Didier (1983)
26300 St Didier de Charpey
☎ 04 75 59 67 01
▯ 04 75 59 68 19
↦ 18 L 5807 m SSS 71
Ⅲ U
££ €24 (€31)
↦ 12km E of Valence
⌂ Thierry Sprecher

Toulouse & Pyrenees

Albi Lasbordes (1989)
Château de Lasbordes, 81000 Albi
☎ 05 63 54 98 07
▯ 05 63 47 21 55
↦ 18 L 6200 m SSS 72
Ⅲ U
££ €26 (€35)
↦ 70km NE of Toulouse
⌂ Garaialde/Pern

Ariège (1986)
Unjat, 09240 La Bastide-de-Serou
☎ 05 61 64 56 78
▯ 05 61 64 57 99
↦ 18 L 6000 m SSS 71
Ⅲ H
££ €22 (€30)
↦ Unjat, 20km NW of Foix
⌂ Michel Gayon

La Bigorre (1992)
Pouzac, 65200 Bagnères de Bigorre
☎ 05 62 91 06 20
▯ 05 62 91 06 20
↦ 18 L 5909 m SSS 72
Ⅲ U
↦ 18km S of Tarbes. 150km W of
Toulouse
⌂ Olivier Brizon

Embats
Route de Montesquiou, 32000 Auch
☎ 05 62 05 20 80/05 62 61 10 11
▯ 05 62 05 92 55
↦ 18 L 4751 m SSS 65

Ⅲ U
££ €23 (€26)
↦ 4km W of Auch. 80km W of
Toulouse
⌂ André Migret

Étangs de Fiac (1987)
Brazis, 81500 Fiac
☎ 05 63 70 64 70
▯ 05 63 75 32 91
↦ 18 L 5800 m SSS 71
Ⅲ U
££ €26–€34
↦ 45km NE of Toulouse
⌂ M Hawtree

Florentin-Gaillac (1990)
*Le Bosc, Florentin, 81150 Marssac-sur-
Tarn*
☎ 05 63 55 20 50
▯ 05 63 53 26 41
↦ 18 L 6150 m SSS 71
Ⅲ U
↦ 10km W of Albi. 70km NE of
Toulouse
⌂ Robert Berthet

Golf de tarbes (1987)
1 Rue du Bois, 65310 Laloubère
☎ 05 62 45 14 50
▯ 05 62 45 11 78
✉ golf.des.tumulus@wanadoo.fr
↦ 18 L 5050 m Par 70 CR 69.2 SR
127
Ⅲ U
££ €29
↦ 2km S of Tarbes, towards Bagnères
⌂ Charles de Ginestet
■ www.perso.wanadoo.fr/tumulus

Guinlet (1986)
32800 Eauze
☎ 05 62 09 80 84
▯ 05 62 09 84 50
↦ 18 L 5565 m Par 71
Ⅲ U
££ €27 (€30)
↦ 60km SW of Agen. 150km SE of
Bordeaux
⌂ M Larrouy
■ www.guinlet.fr

Lannemezan
La Demi-Lune, 65300 Lannemezan
☎ 05 62 98 01 01
↦ 18 L 5872 m Par 70
Ⅲ H
↦ 38km SE of Tarbes
⌂ Hirigoyen/Laserre

Lourdes (1988)
Chemin du Lac, 65100 Lourdes
☎ 05 62 42 02 06
▯ 05 62 42 02 06
↦ 18 L 5372 m Par 71 CR 70.6
Ⅲ U
££ €23–€27 (€26–€31)
↦ 4km W of Lourdes, off D940
⌂ Olivier Brizon

For list of abbreviations and key to symbols see page 627

Luchon   (1908)
BP 40, 31110 Bagnères de Luchon
☎   **05 61 79 03 27**
🖅   9 L 2375 m SSS 66
👥   H
⛳   Luchon, 90km SE of Tarbes.
145km S of Toulouse
🏠   Fenn/Hawtree

Mazamet-La Barouge
(1956)
81660 Pont de l'Arn
☎   **05 63 61 08 00/05 63 67 06 72**
🖅   05 63 61 13 03
🖅   18 L 5623 m SSS 70
👥   U
£€   €27 (€36)
⛳   2km N of Mazamet. 80km E of
Toulouse. 80km W of Béziers
🏠   Mackenzie Ross/Hawtree

Toulouse   (1951)
31320 Vieille-Toulouse
☎   **05 61 73 45 48**
🖅   05 62 19 04 67
🖅   18 L 5602 m Par 69
👥   U
£€   €38
⛳   8km S of Toulouse
🏠   Hawtree

Toulouse-La Ramée
Ferme Cousturier, 31170 Tournefeuille
☎   **05 61 07 09 09**
🖅   05 61 07 15 93
🖅   18 L 5605 m SSS 69
9 hole short course
👥   H
⛳   SW of Toulouse
🏠   Hawtree

Toulouse-Palmola   (1974)
Route d'Albi, 31660 Buzet-sur-Tarn
☎   **05 61 84 20 50**
🖅   05 61 84 48 92
🖅   18 L 6156 m SSS 73
👥   H
£€   €38 (€53)
⛳   18km NE of Toulouse. A68
Junction 4
🏠   Michael Fenn

Toulouse-Seilh
Route de Grenade, 31840 Seilh
☎   **05 61 42 59 30**
🖅   05 61 42 34 17
🖅   Red 18 L 6122 m SSS 72
Yellow 18 L 4202 m SSS 64
👥   H
£€   €31–€36
⛳   15km N of Toulouse. Blagnac
Airport 5km
🏠   Jean Garaialde

Toulouse-Teoula
*71 Avenue des Landes, 31830 Plaisance
du Touch*
☎   **05 61 91 98 80**
🖅   05 61 91 49 66

🖅   18 L 5500 m Par 69
👥   H or green card
£€   €31
⛳   15km W of Toulouse
🏠   Martin Hawtree

Germany

Berlin & East

Balmer See   (1995)
Drewinscher Weg 1, 17429 Neppermin
☎   **(038379) 28199**
🖅   (038379) 28200
✉   info@golfhotel-usedom.de
🖅   27 L 5662-6090 m Par 71-73
👥   U H
£€   €36 (€46)
⛳   Usedom, 50km E of Greifswald
🏠   M Skeide
■   www.golfhotel-usedom.de

Berlin Motzener See   (1991)
Am Golfplatz 5, 15741 Motzen
☎   **(033769) 50130**
🖅   (033769) 50134
✉   info@golfclubmotzeen.de
🖅   18 L 6330 m Par 73
9 L 2756 m Par 54
👥   H–max 45. Booking necessary
£€   €35–€45 (€75)
⛳   30km S of Berlin
🏠   Kurt Rossknecht
■   www.golfclubmotzen.de

Berlin Wannsee   (1895)
Golfweg 22, 14109 Berlin
☎   **(030) 806 7060**
🖅   (030) 806 706-10
🖅   18 L 6088 m SR 127
9 L 4442 m SR 102
👥   WD–U H WE–M
£€   €55
⛳   Berlin (SW)
🏠   Harris Brothers (1925)
■   www.glcbw.de

Elbflorenz GC
Dresden   (1992)
*Ferdinand von Schillstr 4a,
01728 Possendorf*
☎   **(035206) 2430**
🖅   (035206) 24317
🖅   18 L 5902 m Par 72
£€   €35 (€40)
⛳   Dresden 12km
🏠   Dieter Sziedat
■   www.dresdnergolfclub.de

Palmerston Golf Resort
(1991)
Parkallee 1, 15526 Bad Sarrow
☎   **(033631) 63300**
🖅   (033631) 63310

🖅   18 L 6118 m Par 72
18 L 6084 m Par 72
18 L 5593 m Par 71
9 hole course
👥   U
£€   €18 (€35)
⛳   70km SE of Berlin
Palmer/Faldo/Eby/McEwan
■   www.palmerston.de

Potsdamer GC   (1990)
*Tremmener Landstrasse,
14641 Tremmen*
☎   **(033233) 80244**
🖅   (033233) 80957
✉   potsdammer.golfclub@berlin.de
🖅   18 L 5162 m CR 72.6 SR 124
(ladies)
18 L 5758 m CR 70.2 SR 121
(men)
👥   H
£€   €30 (€40)
⛳   W of Berlin
🏠   Graf T.6 Oxenstierna
■   www.pgc.de

Schloss Meisdorf   (1996)
Petersberger Trift 33, 06463 Meisdorf
☎   **(034743) 98450**
🖅   (034743) 98499
🖅   18 L 6236 m Par 72
👥   U H
£€   €20 (€30)
⛳   70km S of Magdeburg
🏠   Gerd Osterkamp

Seddiner See   (1993)
Zum Weiher 44, 14552 Wildenbruch
☎   **(033205) 7320**
🖅   (033205) 73229
🖅   North 18 L 6259 m Par 72
South 18 L 6486 m Par 72
👥   North–U H   South–M H
£€   North €35 (€45) South €50 (€60)
⛳   40km SW of Berlin
North-Preissman. South-Trent
Jones Jr

Semlin am See   (1992)
Ferchesarerstrasse 8b, 14712 Semlin
☎   **(03385) 5540**
🖅   (03385) 554400
🖅   18 L 6348 m SSS 73
👥   H
£€   €30 (€50)
⛳   75km W of Berlin (B5/B188)
🏠   Christoph Städler
■   www.golfhotelsemlin.de

Bremen & North West

Bremer Schweiz   (1991)
Wölpscherstr 4, 28779 Bremen
☎   **(0421) 609 5331**
🖅   (0421) 609 5333
🖅   18 L 5865 m Par 72
👥   H

£€ €20
⊷ N of Bremen
⌂ Wolfgang Siegmann
■ www.golfclub-bremerschweiz.de

Club Zur Vahr (1905)
Bgm-Spitta-Allee 34, 28329 Bremen
☎ **Bremen (0421) 204480,**
Garlstedt (04795) 417
⌨ (0421) 244 9248
⊳ Garlstedt 18 L 6408 m CR 73.6 SR 136
Bremen 9 L 5777 m CR 68.5 SR 111
⚇ WD–H WE–M
£€ Garlstedt–€45 Bremen–€30
⊷ Garlstedt-30km N of Bremen. Vahr-Bremen
⌂ B von Limburger

Herzogstadt Celle (1985)
Beukenbusch 1, 29229 Celle
☎ (05086) 395
⌨ (05086) 8288
⊳ 18 L 5915 m SSS 71
⚇ H
⊷ 6km NE of Celle, towards Lüneburg. 40km NE of Hanover
⌂ Wolfgang Siegmann

Küsten GC Hohe Klint (1978)
Hohe Klint, 27478 Cuxhaven
☎ (04723) 2737
⌨ (04723) 5022
⊳ 18 L 6047 m SSS 72
⚇ U H
£€ €25 (€35)
⊷ 12km SW of Cuxhaven on Route 6, nr Oxstedt
■ www.golf-cuxhaven.de

Münster-Wilkinghege (1963)
Steinfurterstr 448, 48159 Münster
☎ (0251) 214090
⌨ (0251) 261518
⊳ 18 L 5990 m SSS 71
⚇ WD–H WE–I
£€ €30 (€40)
⊷ 2km N of Münster
⌂ W Siegmann

Oldenburgischer (1964)
Am Golfplatz 1, 26180 Rastede
☎ (04402) 7240
⌨ (04402) 70417
⊳ 18 L 6109 m SSS 72
⚇ WD–U WE–U H
£€ €35 (€40)
⊷ 10km N of Oldenburg, nr Rastede
⌂ Von Limburger/Schnatmeyer

Ostfriesland (1980)
Postbox 1220, 26634 Wiesmoor
☎ (04944) 6440
⌨ (04944) 6441
⊳ 18 L 6183 m CR 72.7 SR 124
⚇ U

£€ €30 (€35)
⊷ 25km SW of Wilhelmshaven
⌂ Frank Pennink
■ www.golfclub-ostfriesland.de

Soltau (1982)
Hof Loh, 29614 Soltau
☎ (05191) 967 63 33
⌨ (05191) 967 63 34
⊳ 18 L 6011 m SSS 73
9 L 2340 m SSS 54
⚇ H
£€ €25 (€30)
⊷ Tetendorf, S of Soltau

Syke (1989)
Schultenweg 1, 28857 Syke-Okel
☎ (04242) 8230
⌨ (04242) 8255
⊳ 18 L 6266 m Par 73
⚇ U H
£€ €25 (€30)
⊷ 20km S of Bremen

Tietlingen (1979)
29683 Fallingbostel
☎ (05162) 3889
⌨ (05162) 7564
⊳ 18 L 6193 m Par 72 SSS 73
⚇ H
£€ €25 (€30)
⊷ 65km N of Hanover, between Walsrode and Fallingbostel
⌂ Bruns/Chadwick

Verden (1988)
Holtumer Str 24, 27283 Verden
☎ (04230) 1470
⌨ (04230) 1550
⊳ 18 hole course Par 72 SSS 72
⚇ U
£€ €25 (€30)
⊷ 30km E of Bremen, nr Walle

Worpswede (1974)
Giehlermühlen, 27729 Vollersode
☎ (04763) 7313
⌨ (04763) 6193
⊳ 18 L 6200 m SSS 72
⚇ WD–U H WE–M H
£€ €25 (€30)
⊷ Giehlermuhlen, 20km N of Bremen, off B74

Central North

Dillenburg
Auf dem Altscheid, 35687 Dillenburg
☎ (02771) 5001
⌨ (02771) 5002
✉ info@gc-dillenburg.de
⊳ 18 L 6115 m Par 72
Yellow: CR 71.2 SR 127
Blue: CR 69.4 SR 124
Red: CR 73.0 SR 122
⚇ U H
£€ Mon €32 Tues/Fri €35 (€40)
⊷ 30km S of Siegen. 100km N of Frankfurt
■ www.gc-dillenburg.de

Hofgut Praforst (1992)
Postfach 1137, 36081 Hünfeld
☎ (06652) 9970
⌨ (06652) 99755
⊳ 18 hole course
9 hole course
⚇ H–54 max
£€ €36 (€46)
⊷ Hünfeld, 10km N of Fulda, off Route 27
⌂ Deutsche Golf Consult
■ www.praforst.de

Kassel-Wilhelmshöhe (1958)
Ehlenerstr 21, 34131 Kassel
☎ (0561) 33509
⌨ (0561) 37729
⊳ 18 L 5586 m SSS 70
⚇ U H
£€ €30 (€40)
⊷ Wilhelmshöhe, 5km W of Kassel
⌂ Donald Harradine

Kurhessischer GC Oberaula (1987)
Postfach 31, 36278 Oberaula
☎ (06628) 1573
⌨ (06628) 919456
⊳ 18 L 6050 m SSS 72
⚇ U H
£€ €25 (€35)
⊷ 50km S of Kassel, nr Kircheim
⌂ Deutsche Golf Consult

Licher GC (1992)
35423 Lich
☎ (06404) 91071
⌨ (06404) 91072
⊳ 18 L 6065m SSS 72
⚇ H–booking necessary Sun–M
£€ €35 (€60)
⊷ 45km N of Frankfurt
⌂ Heinz Fehring

Rhoen (1971)
Am Golfplatz, 36145 Hofbieber
☎ (06657) 1334
⌨ (06657) 914809
⊳ 18 L 5686 m CR 68.5 SR 127
⚇ H
£€ €26 (€36)
⊷ Hofbieber, 11km E of Fulda
⌂ Kurt Peters
■ www.golfclub-fulda.de

Schloss Braunfels (1970)
Homburger Hof, 35619 Braunfels
☎ (06442) 4530
⌨ (06442) 6683
⊳ 18 L 6085 m Par 73
⚇ WD–H (max 36) WE–H NA 10am–2pm
£€ D–€35 (€45)
⊷ 70km N of Frankfurt
⌂ Bernhard von Limburger

For list of abbreviations and key to symbols see page 627

Schloss Sickendorf   (1990)

Schloss Sickendorf, 36341 Lauterbach
- ☎ **(06641) 96130**
- 🖵 (06641) 961335
- ⟟ 18 L 6045 m Par 72 SSS 72
- 👥 H
- ££ €25 (€35)
- ⛳ 30km W of Fulda. 120km E of Frankfurt
- ⌂ Spangemacher

Winnerod

Parkstr 22, 35447 Reiskirchen
- ☎ **(06408) 9513-0**
- 🖵 (06408) 9513-13
- ⟟ 18 L 6069 m Par 72
  9 hole Par 3 course
- 👥 U H
- ££ €25 (€45)
- ⛳ Hessen, 30km N of Frankfurt/Main
- ⌂ Michael Pinner

Zierenberg Gut Escheberg (1995)

Gut Escheberg, 34289 Zierenberg
- ☎ **(05606) 2608**
- 🖵 (05606) 2609
- ⟟ 18 L 6122 m Par 72
- 👥 U H WE–booking necessary
- ££ €34 (€46)
- ⛳ 20km NW of Kassel
- ⌂ Volker Püschel
- 🖳 www.golfclub-escheberg.de

Central South

Bad Kissingen   (1910)

Euerdorferstr 11, 97688 Bad Kissingen
- ☎ **(0971) 3608**
- 🖵 (0971) 60140
- ⟟ 18 L 5699 m SSS 70
- 👥 U H
- ££ €35 (€40)
- ⛳ Bad Kissingen 2km. 65km N of Würzburg

Frankfurter   (1913)

Golfstrasse 41, 60528 Frankfurt/Main
- ☎ **(069) 666 2318**
- 🖵 (069) 666 7018
- ⟟ 18 L 6769 yds CR 72.5 SR 129
- 👥 H–32 max
- ££ €60 (€70)
- ⛳ 6km SW of Frankfurt, nr Airport
- ⌂ HS Colt
- 🖳 www.fgc.de

Hanau-Wilhelmsbad   (1958)

Wilhelmsbader Allee 32, 63454 Hanau
- ☎ **(06181) 82071**
- 🖵 (06181) 86967
- ⟟ 18 L 6110 m Par 73
- 👥 WD–H WE–M H
- ££ €46 (€56)
- ⛳ 4km NW of Hanau on B8-40/AB66. Frankfurt 15km

Hof Trages

Hofgut Trages, 63579 Freigericht, GERMANY
- ☎ **(06055) 91380**
- 🖵 (06055) 913838
- ⟟ 18 L 5940 m CR 71.3 SR 127
- 👥 WD–H WE–M
- ££ €50 (€60)
- ⛳ 60km E of Frankfurt/Main
- ⌂ Kurt Rossknecht
- 🖳 www.hoftrages.de

Homburger   (1899)

Saalburgchaussee 2, 61350 Bad Homburg
- ☎ **(06172) 306808**
- 🖵 (06172) 32648
- ⟟ 10 holes Par 70 SSS 69
- 👥 H
- ££ €25 (€35)
- ⛳ On B456 to Usingen

Idstein   (2001)

Am Nassen Berg, 65510 Idstein
- ☎ **(06126) 9322-13**
- 🖵 (06126) 9322-33
- ⟟ 18 L 6255 m Par 72
- 👥 U
- ££ €15
- ⛳ 25km N of Wiesbaden
- ⌂ Siegfried Heinz
- 🖳 www.golfpark-idstein.de

Idstein-Wörsdorf   (1989)

Gut Henriettenthal, 65510 Idstein
- ☎ **(06126) 9322-0**
- 🖵 (06126) 9322-22
- ⟟ 18 L 6140 m Par 72
- 👥 WD–H WE–M
- ££ €25 (€35)
- ⛳ 25km N of Wiesbaden
- ⌂ Siegfried Heinz
- 🖳 www.golfpark-idstein.de

Kitzingen   (1980)

Larson Barracks, 97318 Kitzingen
- ☎ **(09321) 4956**
- 🖵 (09321) 21936
- ⟟ 18 L 5956 m (men) 5262 m (ladies)
  Par 71 CR 70.3 SR 119
- 👥 U H WD/WE
- ££ €25 (€30)
- ⛳ 20km E of Würzburg
- ⌂ Greens of Scotland
- 🖳 www.golf.de/kitzingen

Kronberg G&LC   (1954)

Schloss Friedrichshof, Hainstr 25, 61476 Kronberg/Taunus
- ☎ **(06173) 1426**
- 🖵 (06173) 5953
- ⟟ 18 L 4941 m SSS 68
- 👥 WD–U H WE–M H
- ££ €45 (€55)
- ⛳ 16km NW of Frankfurt
- ⌂ Harder/Harris

Main-Spessart   (1990)

Postfach 1204, 97821 Marktheidenfeld-Eichenfürst
- ☎ **(09391) 8435**

- 🖵 (09391) 8816
- ⟟ 18 holes Par 72
  6 hole short course
- 👥 H–max 36
- ££ €26 (€36)
- ⛳ 80km E of Frankfurt/Main
- ⌂ Harradine
- 🖳 www.main-spessart-golf.de

Main-Taunus   (1979)

Lange Seegewann 2, 65205 Wiesbaden
- ☎ **(06122) 52550/52208(Sec)**
- ⟟ 18 L 6045 m SSS 72
- 👥 H
- ⛳ 15km NW of Frankfurt Airport

Mannheim-Viernheim (1930)

Alte Mannheimer Str 3, 68519 Viernheim
- ☎ **(06204) 607020**
- 🖵 (06204) 607044
- ⟟ 18 L 6060 m SSS 72
- 👥 WD–H WE–M H (Summer)
- ⛳ 10km NE of Mannheim

Maria Bildhausen

Rindhof 1, 97702 Münnerstadt
- ☎ **(09766) 1601**
- 🖵 (09766) 1602
- ⟟ 18 L 6047 m Par 72
  6 hole short course
- 👥 U
- ££ €31 (€40)
- ⛳ 80km NE of Wurzburg
- ⌂ Christian Habeck

Neuhof

Hofgut Neuhof, 63303 Dreieich
- ☎ **(06102) 327927/327010**
- 🖵 (06102) 327012
- ⟟ 18 L 6151 m SSS 72
- 👥 WD–H WE–M
- ££ €50
- ⛳ Hofgut Neuhof, S of Frankfurt, off A3
- ⌂ Patrick Merrigan

Rhein Main   (1977)

Steubenstrasse 9, 65189 Wiesbaden
- ☎ **(0611) 373014**
- ⟟ 18 L 6116 m SSS 71
- 👥 M
- ⛳ Wiesbaden 6km

Rheinblick

Weisser Weg, 65201 Wiesbaden-Frauenstein
- ☎ **(0611) 420675**
- 🖵 (0611) 941 0434
- ⟟ 18 L 6604 yds SSS 70
- 👥 Monday play only
- ⛳ 2km from Wiesbaden at Hessen

Rheintal   (1971)

An der Bundesstrr 291, 68723 Oftersheim
- ☎ **(06202) 56390**
- ⟟ 18 L 5840 m SSS 71
- ££ On application
- ⛳ Oftersheim, SE of Mannheim

For list of abbreviations and key to symbols see page 627

St Leon-Rot (1996)

Opelstrasse 30, 68789 St Leon-Rot
- ☎ **(06227) 86080**
- 💻 (06227) 860888
- ⓟ Rot: 18 L 6047 m Par 72 SR133
  St Leon: 18 L 6178 m Par 72 SR
  139
- ⚇ WD–U before 2pm WE–M
- £€ €70 (€85)
- ♠ 20km S of Heidelberg
- ♙ Hannes Schreiner (Rot), Dave
  Thomas (St Leon)

Spessart (1972)

*Golfplatz Alsberg, 63628 Bad Soden-
Salmünster*
- ☎ **(06056) 91580**
- 💻 (06056) 915820
- ⓟ 18 L 5956 m Par 72 SR 135
- ⚇ H
- £€ €35 (€48) W–€135
- ♠ 70km NE of Frankfurt, via A66
  towards Fulda
- ♙ Elliot Rowan
- ■ www.gc-spessart.de

Taunus Weilrod (1979)

*Merzhäuser Strasse, 61276 Weilrod-
Altweilnau*
- ☎ **(06083) 95050**
- 💻 (06083) 950515
- ✉ golfclub-taunus-weilrod.de
- ⓟ 18 L 5981 m
  Yellow – men: Par 72 CR 71.4
  SR 126
  Blue – men: Par 72 CR 69.2 SR 121
  Red – women: PAR 72 CR 72.6
  SR 124
- ⚇ H WD 54 WE 36
- £€ €33 (€46)
- ♠ 25km NW of Bad Homburg
- ♙ Donald Harradine
- ■ www.golfclub@taunus-weilrod.de

Wiesbadener (1893)

Chausseehaus 17, 65199 Wiesbaden
- ☎ **(0611) 460238**
- 💻 (0611) 463251
- ⓟ 9 L 5172 m
  Par 68 CR 68.6 SR 124 (men)
  Par 68 CR 70.2 SR 125 (ladies)
- ⚇ WD–H (max 36) WE–H (max 28)
- £€ €35 (€45)
- ♠ 8km NW of Wiesbaden, towards
  Schlangenbad
- ♙ Hirsch

Wiesloch-Hohenhardter
Hof (1983)

*Hohenhardter Hof, 69168 Wiesloch-
Baiertal*
- ☎ **(06222) 78811-0**
- 💻 (06222) 78811-11
- ⓟ 18 L 5885 m SSS 72
- ⚇ WD–H WE–M
- £€ €32 (€45)
- ♠ 17km S of Heidelberg
- ♙ Harradine/Weishaupt
- ■ www.golfclub-wiesloch.de

Hamburg & North

Altenhof (1971)

Eckernförde, 24340 Altenhof
- ☎ **(04351) 41227,**
  (04351) 45800 (Pro)
- 💻 (04351) 41227
- ⓟ 18 L 6066 m SSS 72
- ⚇ H
- £€ €25 (€35)
- ♠ 3km S of Eckernförde. 25km NW
  of Kiel
- ♙ Donald Harradine

Berhinderten (1994)

Gustav-Delle Str 18a, 22926 Ahrensburg
- ☎ **(04102) 41544**
- 💻 (04102) 44516
- ⓟ 18 hole course
- ⚇ U
- £€ On application
- ♠ 20km NE of Hamburg

Brodauer Mühle (1986)

Baumallee 14, 23730 Gut Beusloe
- ☎ **(04561) 8140**
- 💻 (04561) 407397
- ⓟ 18 L 6113 m Par 72 SSS 72
- ⚇ U H–36
- £€ €25 (€40)
- ♠ 30km N of Lübeck
- ♙ Siegmann/Osterkamp

Buchholz-Nordheide

An der Rehm 25, 21244 Bucholz
- ☎ **(04181) 36200**
- 💻 (04181) 97294
- ⓟ 18 L 6130 m SSS 72
- ⚇ WD–U H WE–H I before 10am
- £€ €35 (€40)
- ♠ 30km S of Hamburg

Buxtehude (1982)

Zum Lehmfeld 1, 21614 Buxtehude
- ☎ **(04161) 81333**
- 💻 (04161) 87268
- ⓟ 18 L 6480 m CR 73.6 SR 132
- ⚇ H
- £€ €30 (€40)
- ♠ 30km SW of Hamburg on Route 73
  from Harburg
- ♙ Wolfgang Siegmann
- ■ www.golfclubbuxtehude.de

Deinster Mühle (1994)

Im Mühlenfeld 30, 21717 Deinste
- ☎ **(04149) 925112**
- 💻 (04149) 925111
- ⓟ 18 L 5918 m CR 70.9 SR 123
- ⚇ U H
- £€ €31 (€41)
- ♠ 50km SW of Hamburg
- ♙ David Krause

Föhr (1966)

25938 Nieblum
- ☎ **(04681) 580455**
- 💻 (04681) 580456
- ⓟ 18 L 5894 m CR 71.3 SR 120

- ⚇ H
- £€ €35 (€40)
- ♠ 1km SW of Wyk (Island of Föhr)

Gut Apeldör (1996)

Gut Apeldör, 25779 Hennstedt
- ☎ **(04836) 8408**
- 💻 (04836) 8409
- ⓟ 18 L 6048 m Par 72
  6 hole short course
- ⚇ U H
- £€ €30 (€40)
- ♠ 11km W of Heide. 110km N of
  Hamburg
- ♙ DJ Krause
- ■ www.apeldoer.de

Gut Grambek (1981)

Schlosstr 21, 23883 Grambek
- ☎ **(04542) 841474**
- 💻 (04542) 841476
- ⓟ 18 L 5877 m SSS 71
- ⚇ H
- £€ €25 (€45)
- ♠ 30km S of Lübeck. 50km E of
  Hamburg
- ■ www.gcgrambek.de

Gut Kaden (1984)

Kadenerstrasse 9, 25486 Alveslohe
- ☎ **(04193) 9929-0**
- 💻 (04193) 992919
- ⓟ 18 L 6076 m Par 72
  9 hole course
- ⚇ U H
- £€ €40 (€55)
- ♠ Alveslohe, 30km N of Hamburg

Gut Uhlenhorst (1989)

24229 Uhlenhorst
- ☎ **(04349) 91700**
- 💻 (04349) 919400
- ✉ E-mail:golf@gut-uhlenhorst.de
- ⓟ 27 L 6195 m SSS 72
- ⚇ U
- £€ €20 (€40)
- ♠ 8km N of Kiel
- ♙ Donald Harradine
- ■ E-mail:golf@gut-uhlenhorst.de

Gut Waldhof (1969)

Am Waldhof, 24629 Kisdorferwohld
- ☎ **(04194) 99740**
- 💻 (04194) 1251
- ⓟ 18 L 5939 m CR 71.3 SR 128
- ⚇ WD–H WE–M
- £€ €35 (€45)
- ♠ 34km N of Hamburg via A7 to
  Kaltenkirchen or B432
- ■ www.gut-waldhof.de

Gut Waldshagen (1996)

24306 Gut Waldshagen
- ☎ **(04522) 766766**
- 💻 (04522) 766767
- ⓟ 18 L 6372 m CR 73.1 SR 129
  6 hole short course
- ⚇ U
- £€ €35 (€45)

🚗 35km S of Kiel. 91km NE of Hamburg
■ www.gut-golf.de

Hamburg (1906)

In de Bargen 59, 22587 Hamburg
☎ (040) 812177
🖳 (040) 817315
🏷 18 L 5749 m CR 70.1 SR 126
👥 H WE–M
€€ €40 (€45)
🚗 Blankenese, 14km W of Hamburg
🏠 Colt/Allison/Morrison

Hamburg Ahrensburg (1964)

Am Haidschlag 39-45, 22926 Ahrensburg
☎ (04102) 51309
🖳 (04102) 81410
🏷 18 L 5782 m SSS 71
👥 WD–U WE–M only
🚗 20km NE of Hamburg. Motorway exit Ahrensburg

Hamburg Hittfeld (1957)

Am Golfplatz 24, 21218 Seevetal
☎ (04105) 2331
🖳 (04105) 52571
🏷 18 L 5903 m SSS 71
👥 WD–U WE–M
€€ €30 (€40)
🚗 25km S of Hamburg
🏠 Morrison/Gärtner

Hamburg Holm (1993)

Haverkamp 1, 25488 Holm
☎ (04103) 91330
🖳 (04103) 913313
🏷 27 holes CR 72.3 SR 124
👥 WD–U WE–M
€€ €40 (€45)
🚗 20km W of Hamburg
🏠 Harradine/Rossknecht
■ www.gchh.de

Hamburg Walddörfer (1960)

Schevenbarg, 22949 Ammersbek
☎ (040) 605 1337
🖳 (040) 605 4879
📧 info@gchw.de
🏷 18 L 6093 m CR 72.5 SR 131
   18 hole pitch & putt course
👥 WD–U H WE–M H
€€ €40 (€50)
🚗 20km N of Hamburg
🏠 B von Limburger
■ www.gchw.de

Hoisdorf (1977)

Hof Bornbek/Hoisdorf, 22952 Lütjensee
☎ (04107) 7831
🖳 (04107) 9934
🏷 18 L 5958 m Par 71
👥 WD–U WE–M only
€€ €35 (€40)
🚗 25km NE of Hamburg

Jersbek (1986)

GolfClub Jersbek e.V., Oberteicher Weg, 22941 Jersbek
☎ (040) 20950
🖳 (040) 24779
📧 gcjersbek@t-online.de
🏷 18 L 5921 m (men) 5220 (ladies) SSS 71
   CR 70.7 (men) 72.2 (ladies) SR 125
👥 U H36 WD WE
€€ €35 (€40)
🚗 20km N of Hamburg
🏠 Von Schinkel
■ www.golfclub-jersbek.de

Kieler GC Havighorst (1988)

Havighorster Weg 20, 24211 Havighorst
☎ (04302) 965980
🖳 (04302) 965981
📧 golfclub.havighorst@t-online.de
🏷 18 L 6234 m Par 72 CR 73.9 SR 130
👥 WD–U H WE–H
€€ €35 (€40)
🚗 7km S of Kiel. 85km N of Hamburg
🏠 Udo Barth

Lübeck-Travemünder (1921)

Kowitzberg 41, 23570 Lübeck-Travemünde
☎ (04502) 74018
🖳 (04502) 72182
📧 info@ltgk.de
🏷 27 L 6063 – 6152 m CR 72.7 – 74.5 SR 125 – 134
👥 H
€€ €35 (€50)
🚗 18km NE of Lübeck. 70km NE of Hamburg
■ www.ltgk.de

Maritim Timmendorfer Strand (1973)

Am Golfplatz 3, 23669 Timmendorfer Strand
☎ (04503) 5152
🖳 (04503) 86344
🏷 North 18 L 6065 m SSS 72
   South 18 L 3755 m SSS 60
👥 WE–booking required
€€ North D–€30 (D–€45) South D–€25 (D–€35)
🚗 15km N of Lübeck
🏠 B von Limburger

Mittelholsteinischer Aukrug (1969)

Zum Glasberg 9, 24613 Aukrug-Bargfeld
☎ (04873) 595
🖳 (04873) 1698
🏷 18 L 6140 m SSS 72
👥 WD–H WE–H booking necessary
🚗 10km W of Neumunster. Mitte exit on Route 430

Peiner Hof

Peiner Hag, 25497 Prisdorf
☎ (04101) 73790
🖳 (04101) 76640
🏷 18 holes CR 69.9 SR 126
👥 U
€€ €35 (€45)
🚗 20km NW of Hamburg
■ www.peinerhof.de

An der Pinnau (1982)

Pinnebergerstr 81a, 25451 Quickborn-Rensel
☎ (04106) 81800
🖳 (04106) 82003
🏷 18 L 6023 m Par 72 SR 127
   18 L 5231 m Par 72 SR 127
👥 H or I
€€ €35 (€45)
🚗 25km NW of Hamburg, nr Quickborn
🏠 David Krause
■ www.pinnau.de

Am Sachsenwald (1985)

Am Riesenbett, 21521 Dassendorf
☎ (04104) 6120
🖳 (04104) 6551
🏷 18 L 6118 m SSS 72
👥 H
€€ €25 (€30)
🚗 20km SE of Hamburg
🏠 Deutsche Golf Consult

St Dionys (1972)

Widukindweg, 21357 St Dionys
☎ (04133) 213311
🖳 (04133) 213313
🏷 18 L 6125 m SSS 72
👥 By appointment only
€€ €40 (€50)
🚗 10km N of Lüneburg

Schloss Breitenburg

25524 Breitenburg
☎ (04828) 8188
🖳 (04828) 8100
🏷 27 hole course
👥 H
€€ €32 (€40)
🚗 50km N of Hamburg
🏠 Osterkamp/Krause
■ www.golfclubschlossbreitenberg.de

Schloss Lüdersburg (1985)

Lüdersburger Strasse 21, 21379 Lüdersburg
☎ (04139) 6970-0
🖳 (04139) 6970 70
🏷 18 L 6568 m SSS 73
   18 L 6169 m SSS 72
   4 hole par 3 course
👥 U H
€€ €30 (€47)
🚗 12km E of Lüneburg. 55km SE of Hamburg
🏠 Wolfgang Siegmann
■ www.luedersburg.de

Sylt
Am Golfplatz, 25996 Wenningstedt
- ☎ **(04651) 99598-0**
- 🖳 (04651) 99598-19
- ▷ 18 L 6200 m Par 72
- ⚇ H–max 36
- ££ €55
- ⊶ Sylt Island, 75km W of Flensburg
- ⋔ D Harradine

Treudelberg G&CC   (1990)
Lemsahler Landstr 45, 22397 Hamburg
- ☎ **(040) 608 22500**
- 🖳 (040) 608 22444
- ▷ 18 L 6182 m SSS 72
- 9 hole pitch & putt
- ⚇ U H
- ££ €35 (€45)
- ⊶ N of Hamburg centre
- ⋔ Donald Steel
- ■ www.treudelberg.com

Auf der Wendlohe
Oldesloerstr 251, 22457 Hamburg
- ☎ **(040) 550 5014/5**
- 🖳 (040) 550 3668
- ▷ 27 holes:
  5675-6050 m SSS 72
- ⚇ WD–U WE–M
- ⊶ 15km N of Hamburg
- ⋔ Ernst-Dietmar Hess

Wentorf-Reinbeker   (1901)
Golfstrasse 2, 21465 Wentorf
- ☎ **(040) 72 97 80 68**
- 🖳 (040) 72 97 80 67
- ▷ 18 L 5821 m CR 72.2 SR 127
- ⚇ WD–U H WE–M
- ££ €40
- ⊶ 20km SE of Hamburg
- ⋔ Ernst Hess

Hanover & Weserbergland

Bad Salzuflen G&LC
(1956)
Schwaghof 4, 32108 Bad Salzuflen
- ☎ **(05222) 10773**
- 🖳 (05222) 13954
- ▷ 18 L 6138 m Par 72
- ⚇ H
- ££ €30 (€35)
- ⊶ 3km NE of Bad Salzuflen
- ⋔ B von Limburger

Braunschweig   (1926)
Schwartzkopffstr 10,
38126 Braunschweig
- ☎ **(0531) 691369**
- ▷ 18 L 5893 m SSS 71
- ⊶ Braunschweig 5km

Burgdorf   (1970)
Waldstr 15, 31303 Burgdorf-
Ehlershausen
- ☎ **(05085) 7628**

- 🖳 (05085) 6617
- ▷ 18 L 6426 m SSS 74
- ⚇ H
- ⊶ Burgdorf-Ehlershausen, 20km NE
  of Hanover

Gifhorn   (1982)
Wilscher Weg 69, 38518 Gifhorn
- ☎ **(05371) 16737**
- 🖳 (05371) 51092
- ▷ 18 L 5972 m SSS 72
- ⚇ H
- ££ €30 (€40)
- ⊶ 30km N of Braunschweig

Gütersloh Garrison
Princess Royal Barracks, BFPO 47
- ☎ **(05241) 842606**
- ▷ 9 L 5761 yds SSS 68
- ££ £11
- ⊶ 5km W of Gütersloh

Hameln   (1985)
Schloss Schwöbber, 31855 Aerzen
- ☎ **(05154) 9870**
- 🖳 (05154) 9871-11
- ▷ 18 L 6222 m Par 73
  18 hole short course
- ⊶ 10km SW of Hameln. 60km SW of
  Hanover

Hannover   (1923)
Am Blauen See, 30823 Garbsen
- ☎ **(05137) 73235**
- ▷ 18 L 5855 m SSS 71
- ⊶ 15km NW of Hanover

Hardenberg   (1969)
Gut Levershausen, 37154 Northeim
- ☎ **(05551) 61915**
- 🖳 (05551) 61863
- ▷ 18 L 5970 m SSS 72
- ⚇ H
- ££ €32 (€42)
- ⊶ 20km N of Göttingen, towards
  Northeim
- ⋔ Dr Siegmann
- ■ www.gchardenberg.de

Isernhagen   (1983)
Auf Gut Lohne 22, 30916 Isernhagen
- ☎ **(05139) 893185**
- 🖳 (05139) 27033
- ▷ 18 L 6118 m SSS 72
- ⚇ H–max 34
- ⊶ Gut Lohne, 12km NE of Hanover
- ■ www.golfclub-isernhagen.de

Langenhagen   (1989)
Hainhaus 22, 30688 Langenhagen
- ☎ **(0511) 736832**
- 🖳 (0511) 726 1990
- ▷ 27 L 6161 m Par 72
- ⚇ H
- ££ €25 (€35)
- ⊶ 25km N of Hannover
- ⋔ Siegmann

Lipperland zu Lage
Ottenhauserstr 100, 32791 Lage/Lippe
- ☎ **(05232) 66829**
- 🖳 (05232) 18165
- ▷ 18 L 6260 m SSS 73
- ⚇ H
- ⊶ 22km E of Bielefeld
- ⋔ Heinz Wolters

Lippischer   (1980)
Huxoll 14, 32825 Blomberg-Cappel
- ☎ **(05231) 459**
- 🖳 (05236) 8102
- ▷ 18 L 5990 m CR 71.5 SR 126
- ⚇ H
- ££ €30 (€40)
- ⊶ 12km E of Detmold
- ■ www.lippischergc.de

Marienfeld   (1986)
Remse 27, 33428 Marienfeld
- ☎ **(05247) 8880**
- 🖳 (05247) 80386
- ▷ 18 L 5830 m CR 71.3 SR 132
- ⚇ U H
- ££ €30 (€40)
- ⊶ Gütersloh 10km
- ⋔ Spangemacher
- ■ www.gc-marienfeld.de

Paderborner Land   (1983)
Wilseder Weg 25, 33102 Paderborn
- ☎ **(05251) 4377**
- ▷ 18 L 5670 m SSS 68
- ⚇ U
- ⊶ Salzkotten/Thule, between B-1 and
  B-64

Pyrmonter   (1961)
Postfach 100 828, 31758 Hameln
- ☎ **(05281) 8196**
- 🖳 (05281) 8196
- ▷ 18 L 5775 m SSS 70
- ⚇ H
- ££ €25 (€30)
- ⊶ 4km S of Bad Pyrmont. 20km SW
  of Hameln
- ⋔ Donald Harradine

Ravensberger Land
Sudstrasse 96, 32130 Enger-
Pödinghausen
- ☎ **(09224) 79751**
- 🖳 (09224) 699446
- ▷ 18 hole course SSS 72
  6 hole pitch & putt
- ⚇ WD–H WE–M
- ££ €20 (€25)
- ⊶ 25km NE of Bielefeld towards
  Herford
- ⋔ Heinz Wolters

Senne GC Gut Welschof
(1992)
Augustdorferstr 72, 33758 Schloss Holte-
Stukenbrock
- ☎ **(05207) 920936**
- 🖳 (05207) 88788
- ▷ 18 L 6246 m SSS 72

👔 U H
£€ €30 (€40)
⛳ 20km S of Bielefeld
🏠 Christoph Städler

Sennelager (British Army) (1963)

Bad Lippspringe, BFPO 16
☎ (05252) 53794
🖳 (05252) 53811
↦ 18 L 5658 m SSS 72
    9 L 5214 m SSS 68
👔 H
£€ (Forces) €20 (€25) (Civilians) €30
    (€40)
⛳ 9km E of Paderborn, off Route 1

Sieben-Berge Rheden (1965)

Postfach 1152, 31021 Gronau
☎ (05182) 52336
🖳 (05182) 52336
↦ 18 L 5856 m SSS 71
👔 U H
£€ €25 (€30)
⛳ 35km S of Hanover
🏠 B von Limburger

Weserbergland (1982)

Weissenfelder Mühle, 37647 Polle
☎ (05535) 8842
🖳 (05535) 1225
↦ 18 holes SSS 72
👔 H
⛳ 35km S of Hameln

Westfälischer Gütersloh

Gütersloher Str 127, 33397 Rietberg
☎ (05244) 2340/10528
🖳 (05244) 1388
↦ 18 L 6135 m CR 71.6 SR 124
👔 U H
£€ €30 (€40)
⛳ 8km SE of Gütersloh, nr
    Neuenkirchen
🏠 B von Limburger
■ www.golf-gt.de

Widukind-Land (1985)

Auf dem Stickdorn 63, 32584 Löhne
☎ (05228) 7050
🖳 (05228) 1039
↦ 18 hole course
👔 U H
£€ €30 (€35)
⛳ 30km NE of Bielefeld
🏠 Dahlmeier/Brinkmeier

Munich & South Bavaria

Allgäuer G&LC (1984)

Hofgut Boschach, 87724 Ottobeuren
☎ (08332) 1310
🖳 (08332) 5161
↦ 18 L 6096 m CR 71.1 SR 123
    6 hole short course

👔 H
£€ €40 (€50)
⛳ 2km S of Ottobeuren. 20km N of
    Kempten

Altötting-Burghausen (1986)

Piesing 4, 84533 Haiming
☎ (08678) 986903
🖳 (08678) 986905
↦ 18 L 5948 m Par 70 CR 70.7 SR
    122 (men)
    18 L 5376 m Par 72 CR 73.2 SR
    123 (ladies)
    18 L 6028 m Par 72 CR 71.6 SR
    124 (men)
    18 L 5319 m Par 72 CR 73.6
    SR125 (ladies)
👔 U
£€ €35 (€45)
⛳ Schloss Piesing, 4km N of
    Burghausen
🏠 G von Mecklenberg
■ www.gc-altoetting-burghausen.de

Augsburg (1959)

Engelshofer Str 2, 86399 Bobingen-Burgwalden
☎ (08234) 5621
🖳 (08234) 7855
↦ 18 L 6077 m CR 72.1 SR 133
👔 H—max 34
£€ €40 (€55)
⛳ 18km SW of Augsburg
🏠 Kurt Rossknecht
■ www.golfclub-augsburg.de

Bad Tölz (1973)

83646 Wackersberg
☎ (08041) 9994
🖳 (08041) 2116
↦ 9 L 2886 m SSS 71
👔 WD–H WE–M
£€ €25 (€30)
⛳ 5km W of Bad Tölz. 55km S of
    Munich

Bad Wörishofen

Schlingenerstr 9, 87668 Rieden
☎ (08346) 777
↦ 18 L 6318 m SSS 71
⛳ 10km S of Bad Wörishofen

Beuerberg (1982)

Gut Sterz, 82547 Beuerberg
☎ (08179) 671/728
🖳 (08179) 5234
↦ 18 L 6250 m SL 132 CR 72.6
👔 WD–H WE–M H
£€ €55 (€65)
⛳ Beuerberg, 45km SW of Munich
🏠 Donald Harradine

Im Chiemgau (1982)

Kötzing 1, 83339 Chieming
☎ (08669) 87330
🖳 (08669) 87333
↦ 18 L 6221 m SSS 72
    9 hole Par 3 course
👔 WD–H

£€ €40 (€55)
⛳ 40km W of Salzburg. Munich
    100km
🏠 J Dudok van Heel
■ www.Golfchieming.de

Donauwörth (1995)

Lederstatt 1, 86609 Donauwörth
☎ (0906) 4044
🖳 (0906) 999 8164
↦ 18 L 5939 m Par 72
👔 U H
£€ €30 (€40)
⛳ 45km N of Augsburg
🏠 Peter Harradine

Ebersberg (1988)

Postfach 1351, 85554 Ebersberg
☎ (08094) 8106
🖳 (08094) 8386
↦ 18 L 5907 m Par 72
    6 hole Par 3 course
👔 U H
£€ €35 (€45)
⛳ Zaissing, 35km E of Munich
🏠 Thomas Himmel

Erding-Grünbach (1973)

Am Kellerberg, 85461 Grünbach
☎ (08122) 49650
🖳 (08122) 49684
↦ 18 L 6109 m SSS 72
👔 WD–H (max 35) WE–H (max 28)
£€ €35 (€45)
⛳ 40km NE of Munich

Eschenried (1983)

Kurfürstenweg 10, 85232 Eschenried
☎ (08131) 567410/56740
🖳 (08131) 567418/567410
↦ Eschenried 18 L 5935 m Par 72
    SR 124
    Eschenhof 18 L 5550 m Par 70
    SR 124
    Gut Häsern 18 L 6104 m Par 72
    SR 125
    Gut Häsern 6 L 680 m
    Gröbenbach 9 L 1810 m Par 32
👔 U H
£€ Eschenried €45 (€55) Eschenhof
    €40 (€50) Gut Hausern 18: €50
    (€60); 6: Gröbenbach €25 (€32)
⛳ 8km NW of Munich
🏠 G von Mecklenburg/P Haradine
■ www.gc-eschenried.de

Feldafing (1926)

Tutzinger Str 15, 82340 Feldafing
☎ (08157) 9334-0
🖳 (08157) 9334-99
📧 info@golfclub-Feldafing.de
↦ 18 L 5738 m Par 71 SSS 71 CR
    70.2 SR 128
👔 WD–H WE–M
£€ €60 (€70)
⛳ 32km S of Munich
🏠 B von Limburger
■ www.golfclub-Feldafing.de

Garmisch-Partenkirchen
(1928)
Gut Buchwies, 82496 Oberau
☎ **(08824) 8344**
🖥 (08824) 8344
🏳 18 L 6210 m Par 72
👥 U H
££ €35 (€45)
🚗 10km N of Garmisch-Partenkirchen

Gut Ludwigsberg   (1989)
Augsburgerstr 51, 86842 Turkheim
☎ **(08245) 3322**
🖥 (08245) 3789
🏳 18 L 6078 m Par 72
   9 hole Par 3 course
👥 U
££ €35 (€45)
🚗 50km SW of Munich
🏠 Kurt Rossknecht

Gut Rieden
Gut Rieden, 82319 Starnberg
☎ **(08151) 90770**
🖥 (08151) 907711
🏳 18 L 6046 yds SSS 72
👥 H WE–M
££ €40 (€50)
🚗 25km S of Munich

Hohenpähl   (1988)
82396 Pähl
☎ **(08808) 9202-0**
🖥 (08808) 9202-22
📧 info@gchp.de
📧 Gabriele Gestner, Susanne Ott
🏳 18 L 5692 m Par 71 SR 126
👥 H36
££ €50 (€65)
🚗 40km S of Munich on B2 (km 41)
🏠 Kurt Rossknecht
🖥 www.golfclub-hohenpaehl.de

Holledau
Weihern 3, 84104 Rudelzhausen
☎ **(08756) 96010**
🖥 (08756) 815
🏳 18 L 6085 m SSS 72
   9 hole course
👥 U H
££ €25 (€40)
🚗 55km N of Munich

Höslwang im Chiemgau
(1975)
Kronberg 3, 83129 Höslwang
☎ **(08075) 714**
🖥 (08075) 8134
🏳 18 L 6049 m Par 72 SSS 72
👥 H
££ €40 (€50)
🚗 80km S of Munich
🏠 Thomas Himmel
🖥 www.golfclub-hoeslwang.de

Iffeldorf
Gut Rettenberg, 82393 Iffeldorf
☎ **(08856) 925555**
🖥 (08856) 925559

🏳 18 L 5904 m CR 70.6 SR 122
👥 U
££ €40–€50 (€60)
🚗 45km S of Munich
🏠 Hery Beer

Landshut   (1989)
Oberlippach 2, 84095 Furth-Landshut
☎ **(08704) 8378**
🖥 (08704) 8379
🏳 18 L 6251 m SSS 73
👥 H
££ €35 (€45)
🚗 65 km E of Munich
🏠 Kurt Rossknecht

Mangfalltal G&LC
Oed 1, 83620 Feldkirchen-Westerham
☎ **(08063) 6300**
🖥 (08063) 6958
🏳 18 L 5742 m CR 70.4 SR 125
👥 WD–U WE–M
🚗 40km SE of Munich
🖥 www.glcm.de

Margarethenhof   (1982)
Gut Steinberg,
83666 Waakirchen/Marienstein
☎ **(08022) 7506-0**
🖥 (08022) 74818
🏳 18 L 5730 m Par 71
👥 WD–H WE–before 10am
££ €70 (€90)
🚗 Tegernsee, 45km S of Munich
🏠 Frank Pennink
🖥 www.margarethenhof.com

Memmingen Gut Westerhart
(1994)
Westerhart 1b, 87740 Buxheim
☎ **(08331) 71016**
🖥 (08331) 71018
🏳 18 hole course
👥 U H
££ €40 (€50)
🚗 120km W of Munich. Memmingen
   5km

München Nord-Eichenried
(1989)
Münchnerstr 57, 85452 Eichenried
☎ **(08123) 93080**
🖥 (08123) 930893
🏳 18 L 6318 m Par 73
👥 WD–U WE–M
££ €50 (€80)
🚗 19km NE of Munich
🏠 Kurt Rossknecht
🖥 www.gc-eichenried.de

München West-Odelzhausen
(1988)
Gut Todtenried, 85235 Odelzhausen
☎ **(08134) 1618**
🖥 (08134) 7623
🏳 18 L 6169 m Par 72 SSS 72
👥 I
££ €30 (€45)
🚗 35km NW of Munich

München-Riedhof
82544 Egling-Riedhof
☎ **(08171) 7065**
🖥 (08171) 72452
🏳 18 L 6216 m SSS 72
👥 WD–U H
🚗 25km S of Münich
🏠 Heinz Fehring

Münchener   (1910)
Tölzerstrasse 95, 82064 Strasslach
☎ **(08170) 450**
🖥 (08170) 611
🏳 Strasslach 27 L 6177 m SSS 72
   Thalkirchen 9 L 2528 m SSS 69
👥 WD–H WE–M
££ WD–€60
🚗 Strasslach: 10km from Munich.
   Thalkirchen: Munich

Olching   (1980)
Feursstrasse 89, 82140 Olching
☎ **(08142) 48290**
🖥 (08142) 482914
🏳 18 L 6028 m Par 72
👥 H WE–NA
££ €45 (€60)
🚗 15km W of Munich
🏠 J Dudok van Heel

Pfaffing Wasserburger
Golfclub Pfaffing München-Ost e.V, wsw
Golf AG, Köckmühle 132, 83539 Pfaffing
☎ **(08076) 91650**
🖥 (08076) 916514
📧 info@golfclub-pfaffing.de
🏳 18 L 6123 m SSS 73 CR 72.3 SR
   133
   9 hole course
👥 U H
££ €50 (€65)
🚗 50km E of Münich
🏠 Kurt Rossknecht
🖥 www.golfclub-pfaffing.de

Reit im Winkl-Kössen   (1986)
Postfach 1101, 83237 Reit im Winkl
☎ **(05375) 628535**
🖥 (05375) 628537
🏳 18 L 5221 m Par 70
👥 U
££ €30 (€40)
🚗 100km SE of Munich
🏠 Georg Böhm

Rottaler G&CC   (1972)
Am Fischgartl 2, 84332 Herbertsfelden
☎ **(08561) 5969**
🖥 (08561) 2646
🏳 18 L 6105 m Par 72 SSS 72
👥 U
££ €45
🚗 5km W of Pfarrkirchen on B388.
   120km E of Munich
🏠 Donald Harradine

Rottbach   (1995)
Weiherhaus 5, 82216 Rottbach
☎ **(08135) 93290**

☎ (08135) 932911
▷ 18 L 6409 m Par 72
👥 U
£€ €35 (€45)
⊶ 20km NW of Munich
🏠 Thomas Himmel

St Eurach G&LC (1973)
Eurach 8, 82393 Iffeldorf
☎ (08801) 1332
🖥 (08801) 2523
▷ 18 L 6509 m SSS 74
👥 H exc Wed & Fri pm–NA WE–NA
£€ €50
⊶ 40km S of Munich
🏠 Donald Harradine

Schloss Maxlrain
Freiung 14, 83104 Maxlrain-Tuntenhausen
☎ (08061) 1403
🖥 (08061) 30146
▷ 18 L 6083 m CR 73 SR 129
  9 hole Par 3 course
👥 U H
£€ €46 (€60)
⊶ 40km S of Munich
🏠 Paul Krings

Sonnenalp (1976)
Hotel Sonnenalp, 87527 Ofterschwang
☎ (08321) 272181 (Sec)
🖥 (08321) 272242
▷ 18 L 5938 m SSS 71
⊶ 4km W of Sonthofen
🏠 Donald Harradine

Starnberg (1986)
Uneringerstr, 82319 Starnberg
☎ (08151) 12157
🖥 (08151) 29115
▷ 18 L 6057 m Par 72
👥 WD–H WE–M
£€ €50 (€65)
⊶ 30km S of Munich
🏠 Kurt Rossknecht
🖳 www.gcstarnberg.de

Tegernseer GC Bad Wiessee (1958)
Robognerhof, 83707 Bad Wiessee
☎ (08022) 8769
🖥 (08022) 82747
▷ 18 L 5459 m CR 68.6 SR 130
👥 WD–H WE–H before 9.30am
£€ €55 (€65)
⊶ Tegernsee, 50km S of Munich
🏠 D Harradine

Tutzing (1983)
82327 Tutzing-Deixlfurt
☎ (08158) 3600
🖥 (08158) 7234
▷ 18 L 6159 m SSS 72
👥 U H
£€ €50
⊶ Starnberger See, 30km SW of Munich

Waldegg-Wiggensbach (1988)
Hof Waldegg, 87487 Wiggensbach
☎ (08370) 93073
🖥 (08370) 93074
🖂 info@golf-wiggensbach.com
▷ 18 L 5373 m CR 68.6 SR 132
👥 H–max 54
£€ €40 (€50)
⊶ 10km W of Kempten, nr Swiss/Austrian border
🏠 H Jersombek
🖳 www.golf-wiggensbach.com

Wittelsbacher GC Rohrenfeld-Neuburg (1988)
Rohrenfeld, 86633 Neuburg/Donau
☎ (08431) 44118
🖥 (08431) 41301
▷ 18 L 6350 m SSS 73
👥 U H
£€ €40 (€50)
⊶ 7km E of Neuburg. 70km NW of Munich
🏠 J Dudok van Heel
🖳 www.wittelbacher-golf.de

Wörthsee (1982)
Gut Schluifeld, 82237 Wörthsee
☎ (08153) 93477-0
🖥 (08153) 93477-40
▷ 18 L 5913 m CR 70.2 SR 118
👥 WD–H WE–M
£€ €60 (€75)
⊶ Wörthsee, 20km W of Munich
🏠 Kurt Rossknecht
🖳 www.golfclub-woerthsee.de

Nuremberg & North Bavaria

Abenberg (1988)
Am Golfplatz 19, 91183 Abenberg
☎ (09178) 98960
🖥 (09178) 989696
▷ 18 holes CR 72.3 SR 131
👥 WD–H
£€ €35 (€45)
⊶ 10km S of Schwabach. 30km S of Nuremberg

Bad Griesbach
Holzhäuser 8, 94086 Bad Griesbach
☎ (08532) 790-0
🖥 (08532) 790-45
▷ Uttlau 18 L 6115 m SSS 72
  Lederbach 18 L 5998 m SSS 71
  Brunnwies 18 L 6029 m SSS 72
  Beckenbauer 18 L 6500 m SSS 72
👥 I H
£€ €36 (€72)
⊶ 28km SW of Passau
🏠 Kurt Rossknecht
🖳 www.hartl.de

Bad Windsheim (1992)
Am Weinturm 2, 91438 Bad Windsheim
☎ (09841) 5027
🖥 (09841) 3448
🖂 gcbadwindsheim@t-online.de
▷ 18 L 6198 m Par 73 SR 125 (men)
  18 L 5494 m Par 73, SR 124 (women)
👥 H
£€ €30 (€45)
⊶ 40km from Nuremberg
🖳 www.golf-bw.de

Bamberg (1973)
Postfach 1525, 96006 Bamberg
☎ (09547) 7212/7109
🖥 (09547) 7817
▷ 18 L 6175 m SSS 72
👥 H
£€ €30 (€40)
⊶ Gut Leimershof, 16km N of Bamberg
🏠 Dieter Sziedat

Donau GC Passau-Rassbach (1986)
Rassbach 8, 94136 Thyrnau-Passau
☎ (08501) 91313
🖥 (08501) 91314
🖂 info@golf-passau.de
▷ 18 L 5877 m Par 72
👥 U
£€ €36 (€41)
⊶ 10km E of Passau
🏠 Götz Mecklenburg
🖳 www.golf-passau.de

Fränkische Schweiz (1974)
Kanndorf 8, 91316 Ebermannstadt
☎ (09194) 4827
🖥 (09194) 5410
▷ 18 L 6050 m SSS 72
👥 H
£€ €30 (€40)
⊶ 5km E of Ebermannstadt. 40km N of Nuremberg

Fürth (1951)
Vacherstrasse 261, 90768 Fürth
☎ (0911) 757522
🖥 (0911) 973 2989
▷ 18 L 6478 yds SSS 71
👥 H
£€ €25 (€40)
⊶ 20km W of Nuremburg
🏠 C Wagner (1992)

Gäuboden (1992)
Gut Fruhstorf, 94330 Aiterhofen
☎ (09421) 72804
🖥 (09421) 72804
▷ 18 L 6233 m Par 72
👥 U H
£€ €30 (€35)
⊶ 40km SE of Regensburg, nr Straubing
🏠 Prof Schmidt

Hof (1985)

Postfach 1324, 95012 Hof
☎ (09281) 43749
🖥 (09821) 60318/709999
▷ 18 L 6040 m SSS 72
⚭ H
££ €25 (€35)
⟋ 2km NE of Hof (B173)
⋔ Dieter Sziedat

Lauterhofen (1987)

Ruppertslohe 18, 92283 Lauterhofen
☎ (09186) 1574
🖥 (09186) 1527
▷ 18 L 6054 m SSS 72
⚭ H
££ €35 (€45)
⟋ 25km SE of Nuremberg
⋔ Dillschnitter

Lichtenau-Weickershof (1980)

Weickershof 1, 91586 Lichtenau
☎ (09827) 92040
🖥 (09827) 9204-44
▷ 18 L 6218 m SSS 72
⚭ WD–H (max 35) WE–M
££ €30 (€40)
⟋ 10km E of Ansbach
⋔ Dieter Sziedat

Oberfranken Thurnau (1965)

Postfach 1349, 95304 Kulmbach
☎ (09228) 319
🖥 (09228) 7219
▷ 18 L 6152 m SSS 72
⚭ I H
⟋ Thurnau, 18km NW of Bayreuth. 14km SW of Kulmbach
⋔ Donald Harradine

Oberpfälzer Wald G&LC (1977)

Ödengrub, 92431 Kemnath bei Fuhrn
☎ (09439) 466
🖥 (09439) 1247
▷ 18 L 5799 m SSS 71
⚭ I
££ €25 (€30)
⟋ 10km E of Schwarzenfeld, towards Neunburg
⋔ Max Haseneder

Oberzwieselau (1990)

94227 Lindberg
☎ (01049) 9922/2367
🖥 (01049) 9922/2924
▷ 18 L 5949 m SSS 72
⚭ U H
££ €40 (€50)
⟋ 170km NE of Munich
■ www.golfpark-oberzwieselau.de

Regensburg (1966)

93093 Jagdschloss Thiergarten
☎ (09403) 505
🖥 (09403) 4391

▷ 18 L 5734 m CR 70.2 SR 131
⚭ U
££ €35 (€50)
⟋ 14km E of Regensburg, nr Walhalla
⋔ Harradine/Himmel

Regensburg-Sinzing

Minoritenhof 1, 93161 Sinzing
☎ (0941) 32504
🖥 (0941) 36299
▷ 18 L 5984 m SSS 72
     6 hole short course
⚭ U H
££ €30 (€35)
⟋ 7km SW of Regensburg

Am Reichswald (1960)

Schiestlstr 100, 90427 Nürnberg
☎ (0911) 305730
🖥 (0911) 301200
▷ 18 L 6041 m CR 71.8 SR 129
⚭ U H
££ €50 (€65)
⟋ 10km N of Nuremberg

Sagmühle (1984)

Golfplatz Sagmühle 1, 94086
Bad Griesbach
☎ (08532) 2038
🖥 (08532) 3165
▷ 18 L 6168 m SSS 72
⚭ H
££ €35 (€40)
⟋ 25km SW of Passau
⋔ Kurt Rossknecht

Schloss Fahrenbach (1993)

95709 Tröstau
☎ (09232) 882-256
🖥 (09232) 882-345
▷ 18 L 5858 m Par 72 SSS 72
⚭ U
££ €30 (€35)
⟋ 15km W of Marktredwitz. 40km E of Bayreuth
⋔ Deutsche Golf Consult
■ www.golfhotel-fahrenbach.de

Schloss Reichmannsdorf (1991)

Schlosshof 4, 96132 Schlüsselfeld
☎ ()9546) 9215-10
🖥 (09546) 9215-20
▷ 18 L 5800 m CR 70.8 SR 128
⚭ H
££ €30 (€35)
⟋ 7km from Schlüsselfeld
■ www.golfanlage-reichmannsdorf.de

Schlossberg (1985)

Grünbach 8, 94419 Reisbach
☎ (08734) 7035
🖥 (08734) 7795
▷ 18 L 6070 m SSS 72
⚭ U
££ €35
⟋ Sommershausen, 15km from Dingolfing. 100km NE of Munich, off Route 11

Schmidmühlen G&CC (1968)

Am Theilberg, 92287 Schmidmühlen
☎ (09474) 701
🖥 (09474) 8236
▷ 18 L 5946 m Par 72
⟋ 35km NW of Regensburg

Schwanhof (1994)

Klaus Conrad Allee 1, 92706 Luhe-Wildenau
☎ (09607) 92020
🖥 (09607) 920248
▷ 18 hole course SSS 72
⚭ U H
££ €35 (€45)
⟋ 80km N of Regensburg
⋔ Pate/Weisshaupt

Die Wutzschleife (1997)

Hillstedt 40, 92444 Rötz
☎ (09976) 18460
🖥 (09976) 18180
▷ 18 L 4728 m Par 65
⚭ U
££ €25–€30 (€30–€35)
⟋ 70km N of Regensburg. 180km NE of Munich
⋔ Deutsche Golf Consult

Rhineland North

Aachen (1927)

Schurzelter Str 300, 52074 Aachen
☎ (0241) 12501
🖥 (0241) 171075
▷ 18 L 6063 m Par 72
⚭ H
££ €40 (€50)
⟋ Seffent, 5km NW of Aachen
⋔ Murray/Morrison/Pennink

Ahaus

Schmäinghook 36, 48683 Ahaus-Alstätte
☎ (02567) 405
🖥 (02567) 3524
▷ 18 hole course SSS 72
     9 hole course
⚭ U H
££ €50 (€70)
⟋ 60km W of Münster
⋔ Deutsche Golf Consult
■ www.glc-ahaus.de

Alten Fliess (1995)

Am Alten Fliess 66, 50129 Bergheim
☎ (02238) 94410
🖥 (02238) 944119
▷ 27 holes:
     6050–6075 m Par 72
⚭ U H–36 max
££ €22–€25 (€30–€60)
⟋ 12km W of Cologne
⋔ Kurt Rossknecht

Artland   (1988)
Westerholte 23, 49577 Ankum
☎ **(05466) 301**
🖳 (05466) 91081
🏴 18 holes Par 72
👥 U H – booking required
£€ €32 (€42)
🚗 Ankum, 30km N of Osnabrück
🏠 Udo Schmidt
◼ www.artlandgolf.de

Bergisch-Land
Siebeneickerst 386, 42111 Wuppertal
☎ **(02053) 7177**
🖳 (02053) 7303
🏴 18 L 6037 m SSS 72
👥 WD–H WE–M
£€ €40
🚗 Elberfeld, 8km W of Wuppertal

Bochum   (1982)
Im Mailand 127, 44797 Bochum
☎ **(0234) 799832**
🖳 (0234) 795775
🏴 18 L 5300 m SSS 68
👥 WD–H
🚗 Bochum-Stiepel, 7km S of Bochum

Castrop-Rauxel
Dortmunder Str 383, 44577 Castrop-Rauxel
☎ **(02305) 62027**
🖳 (02305) 61410
🏴 18 L 6181 m SSS 72
👥 U
🚗 10km W of Dortmund

Dortmund   (1956)
Reichmarkstr 12, 44265 Dortmund
☎ **(0231) 774133/774609**
🖳 (0231) 774403
🏴 18 L 6174 m SSS 72
👥 WE–M
£€ €30 (€40)
🚗 8km S of Dortmund
🏠 B von Limburger

Düsseldorf   (1961)
Rommerljansweg 12, 40882 Ratingen
☎ **(02102) 81092**
🖳 (02102) 81782
🏴 18 L 5905 m SSS 71
👥 WD–U WE–M
🚗 11km N of Düsseldorf

Düsseldorf Hösel
In den Höfen 32, 40883 Ratingen
☎ **(02102) 68629**
🏴 18 L 6160 m SSS 72
👥 U
🚗 Hösel, 15km NE of Düsseldorf

Elfrather Mühle   (1991)
An der Elfrather Mühle 145, 47802 Krefeld
☎ **(02151) 4969-0**
🖳 (02151) 477459
🏴 18 L 6125 m Par 72 SSS 72
👥 H–max 36

£€ €35 (€45)
🚗 Krefeld 7km. Düsseldorf 25km
🏠 Ron Kirby

Erftaue   (1991)
Zur Mühlenerft 1, 41517 Grevenbroich
☎ **(02181) 280637**
🖳 (02181) 280639
🏴 18 L 6003 m Par 72 CR 71.5 SR 127
👥 WD–H WE–H after 1pm
£€ €35 (€45)
🚗 25km SW of Düsseldorf
🏠 Karl Grohs
◼ www.golf-erftaue.de

Essen Haus Oefte   (1959)
Laupendahler Landstr, 45219 Essen-Kettwig
☎ **(02054) 83911**
🖳 (02054) 83850
🏴 18 L 6011 m CR 71.7 SR 126
👥 U H
🚗 14km SW of Essen

Essen-Heidhausen   (1970)
Preutenborbeckstr 36, 45239 Essen
☎ **(0201) 404111**
🏴 18 L 5937 m SSS 71
👥 U H
🚗 10km S of Essen on B224, nr Werden

Euregio Bad Bentheim   (1987)
Postbox 1205, Am Hauptelick 8, 48443 Bad Bentheim
☎ **(05922) 7776-0**
🖳 (05922) 7776-18
🏴 18 L 5780 m CR 70.4 SR 130
👥 WD H WE (inc. Bank Hol.) H
£€ €54 (€32–men, €35–ladies)
🚗 55km N of Münster
🏠 Prof Schmidt
◼ www.golfclub-euregio.de

Grevenmühle Ratingen   (1988)
Grevenmühle, 40882 Ratingen-Homberg
☎ **(02102) 9595-0**
🖳 (02102) 959515
🏴 18 L 6023 m Par 72
👥 WD–H WE–M
£€ €40 (€50)
🚗 10km N of Düsseldorf
🏠 Peter Drecker

Haus Bey   (1992)
An Haus bey 16, 41334 Nettetal
☎ **(02153) 9197-0**
🖳 (02153) 919750
🏴 18 L 5948 m CR 71.8 SR 122
👥 U H
🚗 40km NW of Düsseldorf
🏠 Paul Krings
◼ www.hausbey.de

Haus Kambach   (1989)
Kambachstrasse 9-13, 52249 Eschweiler-Kinzweiler
☎ **(02403) 37615**
🖳 (02403) 21270
🏴 18 L 6178 m SSS 72
👥 U
£€ €35 (€45)
🚗 20km E of Aachen
🏠 Dieter Sziedat

Hubbelrath   (1961)
Bergische Landstr 700, 40629 Düsseldorf
☎ **(02104) 72178/71848**
🖳 (02104) 75685
🏴 East 18 L 6208 m SSS 72
West 18 L 4325 m SSS 62
👥 WD–U WE–M H–max 28 East, 36 West
£€ East €50 (€60) West €40 (€50)
🚗 Hubbelrath, 13km E of Düsseldorf, on Route B7
🏠 B von Limburger

Hummelbachaue Neuss   (1987)
Norfer Kirchstrasse, 41469 Neuss
☎ **(02137) 91910**
🖳 (02137) 4016
🏴 18 L 6091 m Par 73
👥 WD–H WE–M
£€ €20–€40 (€40)
🚗 5km W of Düsseldorf
🏠 Udo Barth

Issum-Niederrhein   (1973)
Pauenweg 68, 47661 Issum 1
☎ **(02835) 92310**
🖳 (02835) 9231-20
🏴 18 L 5769 m CR 70.6 SR 125
👥 H
£€ €40 (€50)
🚗 10km E of Geldern

Juliana   (1979)
Frielinghausen 1, 45549 Sprockhövel
☎ **(0202) 647070/648220**
🖳 (0202) 649891
🏴 18 L 6100 m SSS 71
👥 H
🚗 30km E of Düsseldorf
🏠 De Buer

Köln G&LC
Golfplatz 2, 51429 Bergisch Gladbach
☎ **0049 (0) 2204-9276-0**
🖳 0049 (0) 2204-9276-15
✉ info@glckoeln.de
✍ Iris Sahre
🏴 18 L Men 5988 m Ladies 5281 m
Men: white Par 72 CR 72.8 SR 133
yellow Par 72 CR 71.7 SR 132
Ladies: black Par 72 CR 74.1 SR 136
red Par 72 CR 73.3 SR 135
👥 WD–H WE–M
£€ €65
🚗 15km from Cologne
◼ www.glckoeln.de

Kosaido International
Am Schmidtberg 11, 40629 Düsseldorf
☎ **(02104) 77060**
📞 (02104) 770611
🖰 18 L 5562 m CR 70 SR 132
👥 WD–U WE–NA before 2.30pm
££ €45 (€60)
🚗 10km NE of Düsseldorf
🏠 Tomizawa/Preissmann
■ www.kosaido.de

Krefeld (1930)
Eltweg 2, 47809 Krefeld
☎ **(02151) 570071/72**
🖰 18 L 6082 m SSS 72
👥 WD–U H–max 28
££ €45 (€55)
🚗 7km SE of Krefeld. Düsseldorf 16km
🏠 B von Limburger

Mühlenhof (1990)
Mühlenhof, 47546 Kalkar
☎ **(02824) 924040**
📞 (02824) 924093
🖂 info@muehlenhof.net
🖰 18 L 6103 m Par 72
👥 U
££ €30 (€40)
🚗 80km N of Düsseldorf (B57)
🏠 Hans Herkberger
■ www.muehlenhof.net

Nordkirchen (1974)
Am Golfplatz 6, 59394 Nordkirchen
☎ **(02596) 9191**
📞 (02596) 9195
🖰 18 L 5828 m SSS 71
👥 WD–I WE–H
££ €35 (€40)
🚗 30km S of Münster
🏠 Christoph Städtler
■ www.glc-nordkirchen.de

Op de Niep (1995)
Bergschenweg 71, 47506 Neukirchen-Vluyn
☎ **(02845) 28051**
📞 (02845) 28052
🖰 18 L 6374 m CR 72.8 SR 130
  9 L 3926 m Par 66 CR 61.8
👥 WD–U H WE–M
££ 18 holes: €25 (€40) 9 holes: €17 (€22)
🚗 20km W of Duisburg. 30km NW of Düsseldorf
🏠 Heinz Wolters

Osnabrück (1955)
Karmannstr 1, 49084 Osnabrück
☎ **(05402) 5636**
📞 (05402) 5257
🖰 18 L 5731 m Par 71
👥 U
££ €35 (€50)
🚗 13km SE of Osnabrück
■ www.ogc.de

Rheine/Mesum (1998)
Wörstr 201, 48432 Rheine
☎ **(05975) 9490**
📞 (05975) 9491
🖂 info@golfclub-rheine.de
🖰 18 L 6036 m Par 72 SSS 72
  9 L 4442 m Par 68 SSS 64
👥 U H–max 36
££ €15–€36 (€20–€46)
🚗 Rheine/Mesum, 40km W of Münster
🏠 Christoph Städler
■ www.golfclub-rheine.de

Rittergut Birkhof (1996)
Rittergut Birkhof, 41352 Korschenbroich
☎ **(02131) 510660**
📞 (02131) 510616
🖰 18 L 6037 m Par 73
  9 hole Par 3 course
👥 I H
££ €35 (€45)
🚗 20km W of Düsseldorf
🏠 Kurt Rossknecht

St Barbara's Royal Dortmund (1969)
Hesslingweg, 44309 Dortmund
☎ **(0231) 202551**
📞 (0231) 259183
🖰 18 L 5967 m SSS 73
👥 H–by prior arrangement
££ €30 (€40)
🚗 Dortmund Brackel
🏠 Brig Jones/Maj Coleman

Schloss Georghausen (1962)
Georghausen 8, 51789 Lindlar-Hommerich
☎ **(02207) 4938**
📞 (02207) 81230
🖰 18 L 6045 m SSS 72
👥 H
££ €35 (€45)
🚗 30km E of Cologne

Schloss Haag (1996)
Bartelter Weg 8, 47608 Geldern
☎ **(02831) 94777**
📞 (02831) 94778
🖰 18 L 6193 m Par 73
👥 H or I
££ €25 (€30)
🚗 60km NW of Düsseldorf (Route 9)
🏠 W Hardes

Schloss Myllendonk (1965)
Myllendonkerstr 113, 41352 Korschenbroich 1
☎ **(02161) 641049**
📞 (02161) 648806
🖰 18 L 6120 m CR 71.3 SR 128
👥 H
££ €48 (€55)
🚗 Korschenbroich, 5km E of Mönchengladbach
■ www.gc-schloss-myllendonk.de

Schmitzhof (1975)
Arsbeckerstr 160, 41844 Wegberg
☎ **(02436) 39090**
📞 (02436) 390915
🖰 18 L 6115 m CR 71.6 SR 132
👥 H
££ €35 (€45)
🚗 Wegberg-Merbeck, 20km SW of Mönchengladbach
■ www.golfclubschmitzhof.de

Schwarze Heide
Gahlenerstrasse 44, 46244 Bottrop-Kirchellen
☎ **(02045) 82488**
📞 (02045) 83077
🖰 18 L 6051 m SSS 72
👥 I H
££ €25 (€35)
🚗 55km N of Düsseldorf
🏠 Peter Drecker

Siegen-Olpe (1966)
Am Golfplatz, 57482 Wenden
☎ **(02762) 9762-0**
📞 (02762) 9762-12
🖰 18 L 5959 m CR 71.1 SR 127
👥 U H–max 36
££ €40 (€45)
🚗 20km NW of Siegen

Siegerland (1993)
Berghäuser Weg, 57223 Kreuztal-Mittelhees
☎ **(02732) 59470**
📞 (02732) 594724
🖰 18 Par 72
  Men: L 5865 m CR 71.0 SR 129
  Ladies: L 5162 m CR 72.9 SR 125
👥 H
££ €35 (€45)
🚗 15km N of Siegen
🏠 Spangemacher

Unna-Fröndenberg (1985)
Schwarzer Weg 1, 58730 Fröndenberg
☎ **(02373) 70068**
📞 (02373) 70069
🖂 golf-club-unf@t-online.de
🖰 18 L 6061 m CR 71.2 SR 123
  9 hole Par 3 course
👥 M H (max 34)
££ €35 (€45)
🚗 25km W of Dortmund
🏠 Karl Grohs
■ www.gcuf.de

Vechta-Welpe (1989)
Welpe 2, 49377 Vechta
☎ **(04441) 5539/82168**
📞 (04441) 852480
🖰 18 L 5957 m Par 72 CR 72.0 SR 133
👥 H
££ €25 (€35)
🚗 50km SW of Bremen
🏠 Rainer Preissmann
■ www.golfclub-vechta.de

For list of abbreviations and key to symbols see page 627

Velbert – Gut Kuhlendahl

Kuhlendahler Str 283, 42553 Velbert
☎ (02053) 923290
🖥 (02053) 923291
📋 18 L 5608 m CR 70.4 SR 130
🏌 H
💶 €35 (€45)
⛳ Between Düsseldorf and Wuppertal
🏠 Grohs/Preissmann
💻 www.gcvelbert.de

Vestischer GC
Recklinghausen (1974)

Bockholterstr 475,
45659 Recklinghausen
☎ (02361) 93420
🖥 (02361) 934240
📧 vest.golfclub@t-online.de
📋 18 L 5934 m CR 71.0 SR 126
🏌 WD–H exc Mon–NA WE–H
💶 €40 (€50)
⛳ Nr Loemühle Airport, N of
   Recklinghausen
🏠 Donald Harradine
💻 www.gc-recklinghausen.de

Wasserburg Anholt (1972)

Schloss 3, 46419 Isselburg Anholt
☎ (02874) 915120
🖥 (02874) 915128
📧 sekretariat@golfclub-anholt.de
📋 18 L 6115 m SSS 72
🏌 WD–U WE–H
💶 €35 (€50)
⛳ Parkhotel, Wasserburg Anholt. 15
   km W of Bocholt
💻 www.golfclub-anholt.de

West Rhine (1956)

Javelin Barracks, BFPO 35
☎ (02163) 974463
🖥 (02163) 80049
📋 18 L 6522 yds SSS 71
🏌 WD–U WE–M
💶 €30
⛳ On B230, 1km from Dutch/German
   border. 25km W of
   Mönchengladbach

Westerwald (1979)

Steinebacherstr, 57629 Dreifelden
☎ (02666) 8220
🖥 (02666) 8493
📋 18 holes SSS 72
🏌 H
💶 €30 (€40)
⛳ Hachenburg, 60km E of Bonn

Rhineland South

Bad Neuenahr
G&LC (1979)

Remagener Weg, 53474 Bad Neuenahr-Ahrweiler
☎ (02641) 950950
🖥 (02641) 950 9595
📋 18 L 6060 m SSS 72

🏌 WD–H WE–H before 10am & after
   4pm
💶 €40 (€50)
⛳ Bad Neuenahr, 40km S of Bonn
🏠 Grohs/Preismann

Bitburger Land (1994)

Zur Weilersheck 1,
54636 Wissmannsdorf
☎ (06527) 9272-0
🖥 (06527) 9272-30
📋 18 L 6168 m Par 72 SR 128
🏌 H
💶 €36 (€46)
⛳ 25km NE of Trier
🏠 Karl Grohs
💻 www.bitgolf.de

Bonn-Godesberg in
Wachtberg (1960)

Landgrabenweg, 53343 Wachtberg-Niederbachen
☎ (0228) 344003
🖥 (0228) 340820
📋 18 L 5700 m Par 71
🏌 WD–H WE–M
💶 €35 (€45)
⛳ Niederbachem, 4km from Bad
   Godesberg
🏠 M Harris

Burg Overbach (1984)

Postfach 1213, 53799 Much
☎ (02245) 5550
🖥 (02245) 8247
📋 18 L 6056 m SSS 72
🏌 H
💶 €30 (€40)
⛳ Much, 45km E of Cologne, off A4
🏠 Deutsch Golf Consult
💻 www.golfclub-burg-overbach.de

Burg Zievel (1994)

Burg Zievel, 53894 Mechernich
☎ (02256) 1651
🖥 (02256) 3479
📋 18 L 6143 m Par 72
🏌 H
💶 €15–€35
⛳ 30km S of Cologne
🏠 G Knappertz

Eifel (1977)

Kölner Str, 54576 Hillesheim
☎ (06593) 1241
🖥 (06593) 9421
📋 18 L 6017 m Par 72
🏌 H–phone before play
💶 €30 (€40)
⛳ 70km S of Cologne
🏠 Grohs/Preismann

Gut Heckenhof (1993)

53783 Eitorf
☎ (02243) 9232310
🖥 (02243) 923299
📋 27 L 6214 m SSS 72
🏌 H
💶 On request
⛳ 40km SE of Cologne
🏠 William Amick

Internationaler GC
Bonn (1992)

Gut Grossenbusch, 53757 St Augustin
☎ (02241) 39880
🖥 (02241) 398888
📋 18 L 5927 m Par 72
🏌 U H
💶 €35 (€50)
⛳ 6km E of Bonn
💻 www.golf-course-bonn.de

Jakobsberg (1990)

Im Tal der Loreley, 56154 Boppard
☎ (06742) 808491
🖥 (06742) 808493
📋 18 L 5950 m Par 72 SSS 72
🏌 U
💶 €35 (€45)
⛳ 80km N of Mainz
🏠 Wolfgang Jersombek
💻 www.jakobsberg.de

Kyllburger Waldeifel

Lietzenhof, 54597 Burbach
☎ (06553) 961039
🖥 (06553) 3282
📋 18 hole course
💶 On application
⛳ 15km S of Siegen
💻 www.golf-lietzenhof.de

Mittelrheinischer Bad Ems
(1938)

Denzerheide, 56130 Bad Ems
☎ (02603) 6541
🖥 (02603) 13995
📋 18 L 6050 m SSS 72
🏌 H
💶 €40 (€55)
⛳ 13km E of Koblenz, nr Bad Ems
   (6km)
🏠 Karl Hoffmann

Nahetal (1971)

Drei Buchen, 55583 Bad Münster
am Stein
☎ (06708) 2145
🖥 (06708) 1731
📋 18 L 5883 m Par 72 SSS 72
🏌 H
💶 €40 (€50)
⛳ 6 km S of Bad Kreuznach. 70km
   SW of Frankfurt
🏠 Armin Keller
💻 www.golfclub-nahetal.de

Rhein Sieg (1971)

Postfach 1216, 53759 Hennef
☎ (02242) 6501
📋 18 L 6081 m Par 72
⛳ Hennef, 30km SE of Cologne

Stromberg-Schindeldorf
(1987)

Park Village Golfanlagen, Buchenring 6,
55442 Stromberg
☎ (06724) 93080
🖥 (06724) 930818

🏳 18 L 5161 Par 68 SSS 68
👥 U H–booking necessary
££ €30 (€42)
🚗 5km from A61 exit Stromberg

Trier   (1977)
54340 Ensch-Birkenheck
☎ **(06507) 993255**
🖳 (06507) 993257
📧 info@golf-club-trier-de
🏳 18 L 6069 m Par 72
👥 H–max 36
££ €35 (€45)
🚗 Trier 20km. Koblenz 80km
■ www.golf-club-trier.de

Waldbrunnen   (1983)
Brunnenstr 11, 53578 Windhagen
☎ **(02645) 8041**
🖳 (02645) 8042
📧 info@golfclub-waldbrunnen.de
🏳 18 L 5787 m Par 71
👥 U
££ €33 (€45)
🚗 30km S of Bonn
🏠 Donald Harradine
■ www.golfclub-waldebrunnen.de

Wiesensee   (1992)
Am Wiesensee, 56459 Westerburg-
Stahlhofen
☎ **(02663) 991192**
🖳 (02663) 991193
🏳 18 L 5917 m Par 72
     9 hole Par 3 course
👥 H
££ €40 (€45)
🚗 100km NW of Frankfurt. Cologne
     80KM
🏠 E Bensing

Saar-Pfalz

Pfalz Neustadt   (1971)
Im Lochbusch, 67435 Neustadt-
Geinsheim
☎ **(06327) 97420**
🖳 (06327) 974218
🏳 18 L 6180 m CR 72.1 SR 130
👥 U H WE–NA
££ €40 (€55)
🚗 Geinsheim, 15km SE of Neustadt
     towards Speyer
🏠 B von Limburger

Saarbrücken   (1961)
Oberlimbergerweg, 66798 Wallerfangen-
Gisingen
☎ **(06837) 91800/1584**
🖳 (06837) 91801
🏳 18 L 5971 m CR 71.9 SR 130
👥 H
££ €40 (€50)
🚗 B406 towards Wallerfangen. 8km
     N of Saarlouis
🏠 Donald Harradine
■ www.golfclub-saarbruecken.de

Websweiler Hof   (1991)
Websweiler Hof, 66424 Homburg/Saar
☎ **(06841) 7777-60**
🖳 (06841) 7777-666
🏳 18 L 6188 m Par 72 SSS 74
👥 U H
££ €30 (€40)
🚗 35km E of Saarbrücken
■ www.golf-saar.de

Westpfalz Schwarzbachtal
(1988)
66509 Rieschweiler
☎ **(06336) 6442**
🖳 (06336) 6408
🏳 18 L 5740 m Par 70
👥 H
🚗 40km E of Saarbrücken

Woodlawn
6792 Ramstein Flugplatz
☎ **(06371) 476240**
🖳 (06371) 42158
🏳 18 L 6225 yds Par 70
👥 Military GC–visitors restricted
££ $16
🚗 Ramstein 3km. Kaiserlautern 10km
■ www.ramsteingolf.com

Stuttgart & South West

Bad Liebenzell
Golfplatz 1-9, 75378 Bad Liebenzell
☎ **(07052) 9325-0**
🖳 (07052) 9325-25
🏳 18 L 6113 m Par 72 SSS 72
     18 L 5853 m Par 72 SSS 71
👥 H–max 33 WE–M 10.30am–2pm
££ €40 (€50)
🚗 35km W of Stuttgart
🏠 Elger/Mühl

Bad Rappenau   (1989)
Ehrenbergstrasse 25a, 74906
Bad Rappenau
☎ **(07264) 3666**
🖳 (07264) 3838
🏳 18 L 6103 m SSS 72
👥 U H
££ €30 (€40)
🚗 10km NW of Heilbronn
🏠 Karl Gross

Bad Salgau   (1995)
Koppelweg 103, 88348 Bad Salgau
☎ **(07581) 527459**
🖳 (07581) 527487
🏳 18 L 6190 m CR 71.8 SR 126
👥 U
££ €35 (€45)
🚗 5km SW of Bad Salgau

Baden Hills GC Rastatt
(1982)
Cabot Trail G208, 77836 Rheinmünster
☎ **(07229) 661501**

🖳 (07229) 661509
🏳 18 L 5906 m Par 72
👥 H–booking necessary
££ D–€30 (D–€40)
🚗 10km W of Baden-Baden. 50km N
     of Strasbourg

Baden-Baden   (1901)
Fremersbergstr 127, 76530 Baden-
Baden
☎ **(07221) 23579**
🖳 (07221) 3025659
🏳 18 L 4282 m Par 64
👥 U
££ €35 (€50)
🚗 Baden-Baden
🏠 Harry Vardon

GC Bodensee Weissenberg
eV   (1986)
Lampertsweiler 51, 88138 Weissensberg
☎ **(08389) 89190**
🖳 (08389) 923907
🏳 18 L 6112 m CR 72.1 SR 141
👥 H
££ €50 (€65)
🚗 5km NE of Lindau/Bodensee
🏠 Robert Trent Jones Sr
■ www.gcbw.de

Freiburg   (1970)
Krüttweg 1, 79199 Kirchzarten
☎ **(07661) 9847-0**
🖳 (07661) 984747
🏳 18 L 5945 m CR 71.8 SR 127
👥 H
££ €40 (€45)
🚗 Freiburg-Kappel/Kirchzarten
🏠 B von Limburger

Fürstlicher Golfclub
Waldsee   (1998)
Hopfenweiler, 88339 Bad Waldsee
☎ **(07524) 4017 200**
🖳 (07524) 4017 100
🏳 18 L 6474 m Par 72
     (CR 71.5 SR 130 men;
     CR 73.2 SR 129 ladies)
     9 hole Par 3 course
👥 U
££ 18 holes: €50 (€65) 9 holes: €20
     (€26)
🚗 60km SW of Ulm (Route 30)
🏠 Knauss/Himmel

Hechingen Hohenzollern
(1955)
Postfach 1124, 72379 Hechingen
☎ **(07471) 6478**
🏳 18 holes SSS 72
👥 WE–M
££ On application
🚗 Hechingen, 50km S of Stuttgart

Heidelberg-Lobenfeld
(1968)
Biddersbacherhof, 74931 Lobbach-
Lobenfeld
☎ **(06226) 952110**

☎ (06226) 952111
✉ golf@gc-heidelberg-lobenfeld.de
⊵ 18 L 5989 m SSS 72
⚇ WD–H WE–M H
£€ €40 (€50)
⛳ 20km E of Heidelberg
⌂ Donald Harradine
■ www.gc-heidelberg-lobenfeld.de

Heilbronn-Hohenlohe
(1964)
Hofgasse, 74639 Zweiflingen-Friedrichsruhe
☎ (07941) 920810
✉ (07941) 920819
⊵ 18 L
  Ladies: 5169 m CR 73.2 SR 128
  Men: 5852 m CR 71.4 SR 125
⚇ H
£€ €30 (€50)
⛳ 25km W of Heilbronn, nr Öhringen
■ www.friedrichsruhe.de

Hetzenhof
Hetzenhof 7, 73547 Larch
☎ (07172) 9180-0
✉ (07172) 9180-30
⊵ 18 Holes Par 72 SR 131
  6 hole short course
⚇ WD–H WE–M
£€ €40
⛳ 35km E of Stuttgart Airport, via B29 and B297
■ www.golfclub-hetzenhof.de

Hohenstaufen (1959)
Unter den Ramsberg, 73072 Donzdorf-Reichenbach
☎ (07162) 27171/20050
⊵ 18 L 6540 yds SSS 72
⛳ 15km E of Goppingen. 45km E of Stuttgart

Kaiserhöhe (1995)
Im Laber 4a, 74747 Ravenstein
☎ (06297) 399
✉ (06297) 599
⊵ 18 L 6049 m CR 71.3 SR 122
  (men)
  18 L 5196 m CR 73.0 SR 121
  (women)
  9 hole Par 3 course
⚇ U H
£€ €30 (€45)
⛳ 60km S of Würzburg
⌂ Kurt Rossknecht
■ www.gck.geoid.de

Konstanz (1965)
Langenrain, Kargegg, 78476 Allensbach
☎ (07533) 5124
✉ (07533) 4897
⊵ 18 L 6058 m SSS 72
⚇ WD–I WE–H max 28
⛳ 15km NW of Konstanz, nr Langenrain

Lindau-Bad Schachen
(1954)
Am Schönbühl 5, 88131 Lindau
☎ (08382) 96170
✉ (08382) 961750
⊵ 18 L 5871 m Par 71 SSS 71
£€ €45 (€55)
⛳ Nr Lindau, Bodensee

Markgräflerland
Kandern (1984)
Feuerbacher Str 35, 79400 Kandern
☎ (07626) 97799-0
✉ (07626) 97799-22
✉ info@gcmkandern.de
⊵ 18 L 5931 m CR 71.5 SR 131
⚇ WD–U WE–M
£€ €50 (€60)
⛳ Kandern, 10km N of Lörrach. 14km NW of Basle
⌂ Grohs/Benz
■ www.swissgolfnetwork.de

Neckartal (1974)
Aldingerstr, Gebäude 975, 70806 Kornwestheim
☎ (07141) 871319
✉ (07141) 81716
✉ info@gc-neckartal.de
⊵ 18 L 6162 m Par 72, CR 71.5 SR 124
⚇ WD–U WE–M
£€ €34 (€40)
⛳ 5km NE of Stuttgart, nr Kornwestheim
⌂ B von Limburger
■ www.golf.de/gcneckartal

Nippenburg (1993)
Nippenburg 21, 71701 Schwieberdingen
☎ (07150) 39530
✉ (07150) 353518
⊵ 18 L 5866 m Par 71
⚇ H
£€ €35 (€50)
⛳ 16km NW of Stuttgart
⌂ Bernhard Langer

Obere Alp (1989)
Am Golfplatz 1-3, 79780 Stühlingen
☎ (07703) 9203-0
✉ (07703) 9203-18
⊵ 18 L 6147 m SSS 72 SR 128
  9 L 3522 m SSS 60
⚇ H
£€ 18 hole: €40 (€50) 9 hole: €25 (€35)
⛳ 40km N of Zürich, nr Swiss border
⌂ Karl Grohs
■ www.golf-oberealp.de

Oberschwaben-Bad
Waldsee (1968)
Hopfenweiler 2d, 88339 Bad Waldsee
☎ (07524) 5900
✉ (07524) 6106
⊵ 18 L 5986 m CR 72.1 SR 133
⚇ H–(max 34)
£€ €50 (€60)
⛳ Bad Waldsee, 60km SW of Ulm
⌂ Donald Harradine

Oeschberghof L & GC
(1976)
Golfplatz 1, 78166 Donaueschingen
☎ (0771) 84525
✉ (0771) 84540
⊵ 18 L 6580 m SSS 74
  9 L 4120 m SSS 62
⚇ H
£€ 18 hole: €52 (€67) 9 hole: €31 (€47)
⛳ Donaueschingen, 60km E of Freiburg
⌂ Deutsche Golf Consult

Owingen-Überlingen
Alte Owinger Str, 88696 Owingen
☎ (07551) 83040
✉ (07551) 830422
⊵ 18 L 6148 m SSS 72
⚇ H
£€ €30 (€45)
⛳ 5km N of Überlingen, nr Lake Konstanz

Pforzheim Karlshäuser
Hof (1987)
Karlshäuser Weg, 75248 Ölbronn-Dürrn
☎ (07237) 9100
✉ (07237) 5161
✉ info@gc-pf.de
⊵ 18 hole course SSS 72
⚇ H–max 36
£€ €35 (€45)
⛳ 6km N of Pforzheim. 30km E of Karlsruhe
⌂ Reinhold Weishaupt
■ www.gc-pf.de

Reischenhof (1987)
Industriestrasse 12, 88489 Wain
☎ (07353) 1732
✉ (07373) 3824
⊵ 27 L 5998 m CR 71.9 SR 129
⚇ M H
£€ €45 (€60)
⛳ 30km S of Ulm
⌂ Wolfgang Jersombeck
■ www.golf.de/gc-reischenhof

Reutlingen-Sonnenbühl
(1987)
Im Zerg, 72820 Sonnenbühl
☎ (07128) 92660
✉ (07128) 926692
⊵ 18 L 6085 m SSS 72
⚇ H
£€ €30 (€40)
⛳ 40km S of Stuttgart

Rhein Badenweiler (1971)
79401 Badenweiler
☎ (07632) 7970
✉ (07632) 797150
⊵ 18 L 6134 m SSS 72
⚇ WD–H WE–M
⛳ 16km W of Badenweiler. 30km SW of Freiburg
⌂ Donald Harradine

Rickenbach   (1979)

Hennematt 20, 79736 Rickenbach
- ☎ **(07765) 777**
- 🖳 (07765) 544
- ⊳ 18 L 5544 m CR 71 SR 134
- 👤 WD/Sat–U H exc Tues/Thurs am Sun–NA before 3pm
- ££ €50 (€60)
- ⊷ 20km N of Bad Säckingen
- 🏠 Dudok van Heel/Himmel
- ■ www.golfclub-rickenbach.de

Schloss Klingenburg-Günzburg   (1978)

Schloss Klingenburg, 89343 Jettingen-Scheppach
- ☎ **(08225) 3030**
- 🖳 (08225) 30350
- ⊳ 18 L 6237 m SSS 72
- 👤 H
- ££ €35 (€50)
- ⊷ 40km W of Augsburg. 5km from Stuttgart-Munich motorway, exit Burgau
- 🏠 Harradine/Sziedat

Schloss Langenstein   (1991)

Schloss Langenstein, 78359 Orsingen-Nenzingen
- ☎ **(07774) 50651**
- 🖳 (07774) 50699
- ⊳ 18 L 6341 m CR 73.3 SR 124 9 hole course
- 👤 WD–H WE–H (restricted)
- ££ €42 (€62)
- ⊷ 120km S of Stuttgart. 75km NE of Zürich
- 🏠 Rod Whitman
- ■ www.schloss-langenstein.com

Schloss Liebenstein   (1982)

Postfach 27, 74380 Neckarwestheim
- ☎ **(07133) 9878-0**
- 🖳 (07133) 9878-18
- ⊳ 27 L 5890-6361 m SSS 71-73
- 👤 U
- ££ €30 (€40)
- ⊷ 35km N of Stuttgart
- 🏠 Donald Harradine

Schloss Weitenburg   (1984)

Sommerhalde 11, 72181 Starzach-Sulzau
- ☎ **(07472) 15050**
- 🖳 (07472) 15051
- ⊳ 18 L 5978 m CR 71.3 SR 123 9 hole course
- 👤 I or U
- ££ 18 holes: €40 (€60) 9 holes: €15
- ⊷ 50km SW of Stuttgart in Neckar Valley
- 🏠 Heinz Fehring

Sinsheim

Buchenauerhof 4, 74889 Sinsheim
- ☎ **(07265) 7258**
- 🖳 (07265) 7379
- ⊳ 18 hole course
- 👤 H
- ££ €35 (€45)
- ⊷ 35km S of Heidelberg

- 🏠 Georg Boehm
- ■ www.golfclubsinsheim.de

Steisslingen   (1991)

Brunnenstr 4b, 78256 Steisslingen-Wiechs
- ☎ **(07738) 7196**
- 🖳 (07738) 923297
- ⊳ 18 L 6145 m Par 72 6 hole course
- 👤 U
- ££ €38 Sun–€55
- ⊷ 30km N of Konstanz
- 🏠 Dave Thomas
- ■ www.golfclub-steisslingen.de

Stuttgarter Solitude   (1927)

71297 Mönsheim
- ☎ **(07044) 911 0410**
- 🖳 (07044) 911 0420
- ⊳ 18 L 6045 m Par 72
- 👤 WD–H max 28 WE–M (phone first)
- ££ €45 (€65)
- ⊷ 30km W of Stuttgart
- 🏠 B von Limburger
- ■ www.golfclub-stuttgart.com

Ulm/Neu-Ulm   (1963)

Wochenauer Hof 2, 89186 Illerrieden
- ☎ **(07306) 929500**
- 🖳 (07306) 9295025
- ⊳ 18 L 6076 m SSS 72
- 👤 H–max 36
- ££ €45 (€60)
- ⊷ 15km S of Ulm
- 🏠 Deutsche Golf Consult

Greece

Afandou   (1973)

Afandou, Rhodes
- ☎ **(0241) 51255**
- ⊳ 18 L 6060 m Par 72
- 👤 U
- ⊷ Afandou, 20km S of Rhodes town

Corfu   (1972)

PO Box 71, Ropa Valley, 49100 Corfu
- ☎ **(0661) 94220**
- 🖳 (0661) 94220
- ⊳ 18 L 6183 m SSS 72
- 👤 U
- ££ €25–€50
- ⊷ Ermones Bay, 16km W of Corfu town
- 🏠 Donald Harradine
- ■ www.corfugolfclub.com

Glyfada   (1962)

PO Box 70116, 166-10 Glyfada, Athens
- ☎ **(01) 894 6459**
- 🖳 (01) 894 6834
- ⊳ 18 L 6189 m Par 72
- 👤 H
- ££ €70 (€82)

- ⊷ 12km S of Athens
- 🏠 Donald Harradine
- ■ www.athensgolfclub.com

Porto Carras G&CC   (1979)

Porto Carras, Halkidiki
- ☎ **(0375) 71381/71221**
- ⊳ 18 L 6086 m SSS 72
- 👤 U
- ⊷ Sithonia Peninsula, 100km SE of Thessaloniki

Hungary

Birdland G&CC   (1991)

Thermal krt.10, 9740 Bükfürdö
- ☎ **(94) 358060**
- 🖳 (94) 359000
- ⊳ 18 L 6459 m Par 72 SSS 71-75 9 hole Par 3 course
- 👤 U H
- ££ £33
- ⊷ 120km SE of Vienna
- 🏠 G Hauser
- ■ www.birdland.hu

Budapest G&CC

Becsi u.5, 2024 Kisoroszi
- ☎ **(1) 317 6025**
- 🖳 (1) 317 2749
- ⊳ 18 L 6089 m SSS 72
- 👤 U
- ££ €25 (€30)
- ⊷ 35km N of Budapest via Highway 11
- 🏠 D Hajnal

European Lakes

Kossuth u.3, 7232 Hencse
- ☎ **(82) 481245**
- 🖳 (82) 481248
- ⊳ 18 L 6231 m Par 72
- 👤 U
- ££ €55 (package €80)
- ⊷ 20km from Kaposvar (SW Hungary)
- 🏠 J Dudok van Heel
- ■ www.europeanlakes.com

Old Lake

PO Box 127, 2890 Tata-Remeteségpuszta
- ☎ **(34) 587620**
- 🖳 (34) 587623
- ⊳ 18 L 5915 m Par 72
- 👤 U H
- ££ £17 (£27)
- ⊷ 5km from Tata. 60km W of Budapest (M1)
- 🏠 Lázló Soproni
- ■ www.oldlakegolf.com

Pannonia G&CC

Alcsútdoboz, 8087 Mariavölgy
- ☎ **(22) 594200**
- 🖳 (22) 594205
- ✉ info@golfclub.hu

18 L 5659 m CR 71.3 SR 123
U
€45 (€62)
Budapest 30km
H-G Erhardt
www.pannonia-golf.hu

St Lorence G&CC
Pellérdi ut 55, 7634 Pécs
☎ (72) 252844/252142
🖳 (72) 252844/252173
🏌 18 holes Par 72
👥 U
⛳ Szentlörinc, 11km W of Pécs

Iceland

Akureyri (1935)
PO Box 317, 602 Akureyri
☎ (462) 2974
🖳 (461) 1755
🏌 18 L 5783 m Par 71
👥 U H
€€ 2500 Ikr
⛳ 1km from Akureyri (N coast)
🏠 Solnes/Gudmundsson
■ www.nett.is/ga

Borgarness (1973)
Hamar, 310 Borgarnes
☎ (345) 437 1663
✉ hamar@gbborgarnes.net
🏌 9 L 2857 m SSS 72 SR 134 (yellow tees)
👥 U
€€ 2000 Ikr (1500 Ikr before 2pm)
⛳ 4km N of Borgarnes. 83km N of Reykjavik (tunnel) (Ringroad#1)
🏠 Torvaldur Asgeirsson & Hannes Torsteinsson
■ www.golf.is/gb
www.gbborgarnes.net

Eskifjördar (1976)
735 Eskifjördur
🏌 9 L 4418 m Par 66
€€ 1000 Ikr
⛳ 3km W of Eskifjördur (E coast)

Húsavík (1967)
PO Box 23, Kötlum, 640 Húsavík
☎ (464) 1000
🖳 (464) 1678
🏌 9 L 2460m Par 70
👥 U
€€ 1000 Ikr
⛳ 2km from Húsavík (N coast)
🏠 Nils Skjöld

Isafjördar (1978)
PO Box 367, 400 Isafjördur
☎ (456) 5081
🖳 (456) 4547
🏌 9 L 4980 m Par 70
👥 U
€€ 1000Ikr
⛳ 3km W of Isafjördur (NW coast)

Jökull (1973)
Postholf 67, 355 Olafsvík
☎ (436) 1666
🏌 9 L 4598 m Par 68
👥 U
€€ 1000 Ikr
⛳ 5km SE of Olafsvík (W coast)

Keilir (1967)
Box 148, 222 Hafnarfjördur
☎ (565) 3360
🖳 (565) 2560
🏌 18 L 5449 m Par 71
9 L 2748 m Par 36
👥 U
€€ 18 holes: 2000 Ikr 9 holes: 1000 Ikr
⛳ Hafnarfjördur, 10km S of Reykjavik
🏠 Hannes Thorsteinsson

Kopavogs og Gardabaejar (1994)
Postholf 214, 212 Gardabaer
☎ (565) 7373
🖳 (565) 9190
🏌 18 L 5437 m Par 70
👥 U
€€ 1700 Ikr
⛳ Gardabaer, S of Reykjavik

Leynir (1965)
PO Box 9, 300 Akranes
☎ (431) 2711
🖳 (431) 3711
🏌 18 L 5959 m Par 72
👥 U
€€ 2000Ikr
⛳ 2km from Akranes (SW coast)
🏠 H Thorsteinsson
■ www.leynir@aknet.is

Ness-Nesklúbburinn (1964)
PO Box 66, 172 Seltjarnarnes
☎ (561) 1930
🖳 (561) 1966
🏌 9 L 5374 m Par 72
👥 U
€€ 1500 Ikr
⛳ 3km W of Reykjavík

Oddafellowa (1990)
Urridavatnsdölum, 210 Gardabaer
☎ (565) 9094
🖳 (565) 9074
🏌 18 L 5830 m Par 71
👥 U
€€ 2500 Ikr
⛳ Gardabaer, S of Reykjavík
■ www.oddur.is

Olafsfjördar (1968)
Skeggjabrekku, 625 Olafsfjördur
☎ (466) 2611
🖳 (466) 2611
🏌 9 L 4570 m Par 66
👥 U
€€ 1000 Ikr
⛳ 60 km NW of Akureyri (N coast)

Reykjavíkur (1934)
Grafarholt, 112 Reykjavík
☎ (585) 0200/0210
🖳 (585) 0201
🏌 18 L 6075 m Par 71
18 L 6188 m Par 72
9 L 1761 m Par 32
👥 U H
€€ 4000–4800 Ikr
⛳ 10km E of Reykjavík
🏠 Skjold/Thorsteinsson
■ www.grgolf.is

Saudárkróks (1970)
Hlidarendi, Postholf 56, 550 Saudárkrókur
☎ (453) 5075
🏌 9 L 5902 m Par 72
👥 U
€€ 1000 Ikr
⛳ 2km W of Saudárkrókur (N coast)

Sudurnesja (1964)
PO Box 112, 232 Keflavik
☎ (421) 4100
🖳 (421) 5981
🏌 18 L 5861 m Par 72
👥 U
€€ 4000 Ikr
⛳ N of Keflavik (SW coast). Airport 5 km

Vestmannaeyja (1938)
Postholf 168, 902 Vestmannaeyar
☎ (481) 2363
🖳 (481) 2362
🏌 18 L 5322 m Par 70
👥 U
€€ 1500 Ikr
⛳ 2km W of Vestmannaeyar. Island off S coast – 20 min flight from Reykjavík

Italy

Como/Milan/ Bergamo

Ambrosiano (1994)
Cascina Bertacca, 20080 Bubbiano-Milan
☎ (0290) 840820
🖳 (0290) 849365
✉ gcambros@tin.it
🏌 18 L 6047 m Par 72
👥 U
€€ €37 (€58)
⛳ 25km SW of Milan
🏠 Cornish/Silva
■ www.k-grm.com

Barlassina CC (1956)
Via Privata Golf 42, 20030 Birago di Camnago (MI)
- ☎ **(0362) 560621/2**
- 🖵 (0362) 560934
- ⟝ 18 L 6197 m SSS 72
- 👥 WD–U
- €€ €56.80 (€80)
- 🖘 22km N of Milan
- 🏠 D Harradine

Bergamo L'Albenza (1961)
Via Longoni 12, 24030 Almenno S. Bartolomeo (BG)
- ☎ **(035) 640028**
- 🖵 (035) 643066
- ⟝ 27 L 6129-6253 m SSS 72
- 👥 U–book by fax
- €€ €40 (€60)
- 🖘 13km NW of Bergamo. Milan 45 km
- 🏠 Cotton/Sutton

Bogogno (1996)
Via Sant'Isidoro 1, 28010 Bogogno
- ☎ **(0322) 863794**
- 🖵 (0322) 863798
- ✉ info@circologolfbogogno.com
- ✍ Tiziano Capello
- ⟝ 18 L 6171 m Par 72
- 👥 H
- €€ €57–€96
- 🖘 Bogogno, 25km N of Novara
- 🏠 Robert von Hagge
- ■ www.circolo9golfbogogno.com

Brianza (1996)
Cascina Cazzu, 20040 Usmate Velate (Mi)
- ☎ **(039) 682 9089/079**
- 🖵 (039) 682 9059
- ✉ brianzagolf@tin.it
- ⟝ 18 L 5709 m Par 72 SSS 71
- 👥 U
- €€ €42 (€55)
- 🖘 24km NE of Milan. Monza 6km
- 🏠 Marco Croze

Carimate (1962)
Via Airoldi 2, 22060 Carimate (CO)
- ☎ **(031) 790226**
- 🖵 (031) 791927
- ✉ golfcarimate@virgilio.it
- ⟝ 18 L 6021 m SSS 71 SR 1290
- 👥 U H
- €€ €45 (€65)
- 🖘 15km from Como. 20 km from Milan
- 🏠 Piero Mancinelli
- ■ www.golfcarimate.it

Castelconturbia (1984)
Via Suno, 28010 Agrate Conturbia
- ☎ **(0322) 832093**
- 🖵 (0322) 832428
- ✉ castelconturbia@tin.it
- ⟝ Red 9 L 3330 m Par 36
  Yellow 9 L 3070 m Par 36
  Blue 9 L 3210 m Par 36
- 👥 WD–H WE–M H

- €€ €66 (€102)
- 🖘 23km N of Novara. Milan 60 km
- 🏠 Robert Trent Jones Sr

Castello di Tolcinasco (1993)
20090 Pieve Emanuele (MI)
- ☎ **(02) 9046 7201**
- ⟝ 27 L 6253-6322 m Par 72
  9 hole Par 3 course
- 👥 U
- €€ €40 (€50)
- 🖘 12km S of Milan
- 🏠 Arnold Palmer

Franciacorta (1986)
Via Provinciale 34b, 25040 Nigoline di Corte Franca, (Brescia)
- ☎ **(030) 984167**
- 🖵 (030) 984393
- ⟝ 18 L 5924 m Par 72 SSS 72
  9 hole Par 3 course
- 👥 WD–U WE–NA before 2pm
- €€ €35 (€50)
- 🖘 Nigoline, 25km E of Bergamo. Autostrada A4 exit Rovato
- 🏠 Dye/Croze

Lanzo Intelvi (1962)
22024 Lanzo Intelvi (CO)
- ☎ **(031) 840169**
- 🛏 241
- ⟝ 9 L 2438 m SSS 66
- 👥 U
- 🖘 32km NW of Como

Menaggio & Cadenabbia (1907)
Via Golf 12, 22010 Grandola E Uniti
- ☎ **(0344) 32103**
- 🖵 (0344) 30780
- ✉ segretaria@golfclubmenaggio.it
- ⟝ 18 L 5455 m Par 70 CR 68.8 SR 122
- 👥 WD–H WE–H restricted
- €€ €50 (€65)
- 🖘 5km W of Menaggio. 40km N of Como
- 🏠 John Harris
- ■ www.menaggio.it

Milano (1928)
20052 Parco di Monza (MI)
- ☎ **(039) 303081/2/3**
- 🖵 (039) 304427
- ⟝ 18 L 6414 m SSS 73
  9 L 2976 m SSS 36
- 👥 WD–H WE–by appointment
- €€ €48 (€72)
- 🖘 6km N of Monza. 18km NE of Milan
- 🏠 Gannon/Blandford

Molinetto CC (1982)
SS Padana Superiore 11, 20063 Cernusco S/N (MI)
- ☎ **(02) 9210 5128/9210 5983**
- 🖵 (02) 9210 6635
- ⟝ 18 L 6010 m Par 71

- 👥 WD–H WE–restricted
- 🖘 Cernusco, 10km E of Milan

Monticello (1975)
Via Volta 4, 22070 Cassina Rizzardi
- ☎ **(031) 928055**
- 🖵 (031) 880207
- ⟝ 18 L 6413 m SSS 72
  18 L 6056 m SSS 72
- 👥 WD–H WE–NA
- €€ €40 (€50)
- 🖘 10km SE of Como
- 🏠 Jim Fazio

La Pinetina (1971)
Via al Golf 4, 22070 Carbonate (CO)
- ☎ **(031) 933202**
- 🖵 (031) 890342
- ✉ info@golfpinetina.it
- ⟝ 18 L 5754 m Par 70
  Men: white CR70.8; yellow CR 69.6
  Women: white CR 72.5; yellow CR 70.9
- 👥 WD–U WE–booking necessary – H
- €€ €54 (€78)
- 🖘 12km SW of Como. Milan 25km
- 🏠 Harris/ Albertini
- ■ www.golfpinetine.it

Le Robinie (1992)
Via per Busto Arsizio 9, 21058 Solbiate Olona (VA)
- ☎ **(039) 331 329260**
- 🖵 (039) 331 329266
- ⟝ 18 L 6250 m Par 72 SSS 74
- 👥 WD–U WE–H
- €€ €45 (€65)
- 🖘 25km NW of Milan. Malpensa Airport 6km
- 🏠 Jack Nicklaus
- ■ www.lerobinie.com

La Rossera (1970)
Via Montebello 4, 24060 Chiuduno
- ☎ **(035) 838600**
- 🖵 (035) 442 7047
- ✉ golfrossera@libero.it
- ⟝ 9 L 2510 m SSS 68
- 👥 U
- €€ €25 (€40)
- 🖘 2km from Chiuduno. 18km SE of Bergamo

Le Rovedine (1978)
Via Karl Marx, 20090 Noverasco di Opera (Mi)
- ☎ **(02) 5760 6420**
- 🖵 (02) 5760 6405
- ✉ info@rovedine.com
- ⟝ 18 L 6259 m CR 72.8 SR 126
- 👥 U
- €€ €31 (€55)
- 🖘 4km S of Milan
- 🏠 Croze/Cavalsani/Piras
- ■ www.rovedone.com

Varese (1934)
Via Vittorio Veneto 32, 21020 Luvinate (VA)
- ☎ **(0332) 227394/229302**

- (0332) 222107
- 18 L 5936 m SSS 72
- WD–U H
- €40 (€60)
- 5km NW of Varese
- Gannon/Blandford

Vigevano (1974)

Via Chitola 49, 27029 Vigevano (PV)
- **(0381) 346628/346077**
- (0381) 346091
- 18 L 5678 m SSS 72
- 25km SE of Novara. 35km SW of Milan

Villa D'Este (1926)

Via Cantù 13, 22030 Montorfano (CO)
- **(031) 200200**
- (031) 200786
- golf.villadeste@tin.it
- 18 L 5727 m Par 69
  White CR 71.0 SR 130
  Yellow CR 70.0 SR 129
  Black CR 72.2 SR 124
  Red CR 71.3 SR 123
- I H
- €55 Italian, €65 foreign
- Montorfano, 7km SE of Como
- Peter Gannon

Zoate

20067 Zoate di Tribiano (MI)
- **(02) 9063 2183/9063 1861**
- (02) 9063 1861
- 18 L 6122 m Par 72
- WD–U H
- €35 (€50)
- Zoate, 17km SE of Milan
- Marmori

Elba

Acquabona (1971)

57037 Portoferraio, Isola di Elba (LI)
- **(0565) 940066**
- (0565) 933410
- 9 L 5144 m SSS 67
- U
- €27–€32
- 5km NW of Porto Azzurro. 6km NW of Porto Ferraio
- Gianni Albertini

Emilia Romagna

Adriatic GC Cervia (1985)

Via Jelenia Gora No 6, 48016 Cervia-Milano Marittima
- **(0544) 992786**
- (0544) 993410
- 18 L 6246 m SSS 72
- U H
- €42 (€50)
- 20km SE of Ravenna
- Marco Croze

Bologna (1959)

Via Sabattini 69, 40050 Monte San Pietro (BO)
- **(051) 969100**
- (051) 672 0017
- 18 L 6171 m SSS 72
- U
- €40 (€50)
- 20km W of Bologna
- Harris/Cotton

Croara (1976)

29010 Croara di Gazzola
- **(0523) 977105/977148**
- (0523) 977100
- 18 L 6065 m SSS 72
- H
- 16km SW of Piacenza. 84km SE of Milan
- Buratti/Croze

Matilde di Canossa (1987)

Via Casinazzo 1, 42100 San Bartolomeo
- **(0522) 371295**
- (0522) 371204
- 18 L 6231 m SSS 72
- U
- €30 (€40)
- 50km NW of Bologna
- Marco Croze

Modena G&CC (1987)

Via Castelnuovo Rangone 4, 41050 Colombaro di Formigine (MO)
- **(059) 553482**
- (059) 553696
- segretaria@modenagolf.it
- 18 L 6423 m Par 72 SSS 74
  Men: CR 73.6 SR 131 (champ.)
  72.2/128 (am)
  Ladies: CR 74.9 SR 130 (champ.)
  74.9/127 (am)
  9 hole Par 3 course
- H
- €40 (€60)
- Formigine, 10km SW of Modena
- Bernhard Langer
- www.modenagolf.it

La Rocca (1985)

Via Campi 8, 43038 Sala Baganza (PR)
- **(0521) 834037**
- (0521) 834575
- 18 L 6076 m SSS 71
- U
- €30 (€40)
- 8km S of Parma
- Marco Croze
- www.officeitalia.it/golflarocca

La Torre (1992)

Via Limisano 10, Riolo Terme (RA)
- **(0546) 74035**
- (0546) 74076
- 18 L 6350 m Par 72
- H
- €20 (€25)
- 30km SW of Bologna
- Alberto Croze

Gulf of Genoa

Degli Ulivi (1932)

Via Campo Golf 59, 18038 Sanremo
- **(0184) 557093**
- (0184) 557388
- 18 L 5203 m SSS 67
- U
- €37 (€55)
- 5km N of Sanremo
- Peter Gannon
- www.sanremogolf.it

Garlenda (1965)

Via Golf 7, 17033 Garlenda
- **(0182) 580012**
- (0182) 580561
- info@garlendagolf.it
- 18 L 6085 m Par 72 SSS 72
- H
- €50 (€70)
- 15km N of Alassio. Genoa 90km
- John Harris
- www.garlendagolf.it

Marigola (1975)

Via Vallata 5, 19032 Lerici (SP)
- **(0187) 970193**
- (0187) 970193
- 9 L 2116 m Par 49
- U
- 6km SE of La Spezia
- Franco Marmori

Pineta di Arenzano (1959)

Piazza del Golf 3, 16011 Arenzano (GE)
- **(010) 911 1817**
- (010) 911 1270
- 9 L 5527 m SSS 70
- H
- €30 (€42)
- Arenzano Pineta, 20km W of Genoa
- Donald Harradine

Rapallo (1930)

Via Mameli 377, 16035 Rapallo (GE)
- **(0185) 261777**
- (0185) 261779
- 18 L 5638 m Par 70
- Tue–NA H WE–NA before noon
- €58 – WE p.m. only
- 25km SE of Genoa. A12 motorway exit Rapallo
- Cabell Robinson

Versilia (1990)

Via Sipe 100, 55045 Pietrasanta (LU)
- **(0584) 88 15 74**
- (0584) 75 22 72
- 18 L 5873 m Par 71
- U H
- €52–€80
- 30km N of Pisa on coast, nr Forte dei Marmi
- Marco Croze

Lake Garda & Dolomites

Asiago   (1967)
Via Meltar 2, 36012 Asiago (VI)
☎ **(0424) 462721**
🖥 (0424) 465133
▷ 18 L 6005 m Par 70 SSS 71
👭 U H
£€ €40 (€55)
⊙ 3km N of Asiago. 50km N of Vicenza
🏠 Peter Harradine
■ www.golfasiago.it

Bogliaco   (1912)
Via Golf 21, 25088 Toscolano-Maderno
☎ **(0365) 643006**
🖥 (0365) 643006
✉ golfbogliaco@tin.it
▷ 18 L 4600 m Par 72
👭 H
£€ €40 (€50)
⊙ Lake Garda, 40km NE of Brescia
■ www.bogliaco.com

Ca' degli Ulivi   (1988)
Via Ghiandare 2, 37010 Marciaga di Costermano (VR)
☎ **(045) 725 6463/725 6485**
🖥 (045) 725 6876
▷ 18 L 6000 m SSS 72
   9 hole course
⊙ Above village of Garda. Verona Airport 35km

Campo Carlo Magno   (1922)
Golf Hotel, 38084 Madonna di Campiglio (TN)
☎ **(0465) 440622**
🖥 (0465) 440298
▷ 9 L 5148 m SSS 67
👭 H
£€ €37–€50
⊙ Madonna di Campiglio 1 km. 74km NW of Trento
🏠 Henry Cotton

Folgaria   (1987)
Loc Costa di Folgaria, 38064 Folgaria (TN)
☎ **(0464) 720480**
🖥 (0464) 720480
▷ 9 L 2582 m SSS 70
👭 H
£€ €30 (€35)
⊙ 30km S of Trento, off A22
🏠 Marco Croze

Gardagolf CC   (1985)
Via Angelo Omodeo 2, 25080 Soiano Del Lago (BS)
☎ **(0365) 674707 (Sec)**
🖥 (0365) 674788
✉ info@gardagolf.com
▷ 18 L 6505 m SSS 74
   Men: CR 75.9 SR 139
   Women: CR 77.3 SR 140
   9 L 2635 m Par 35

👭 H (min 36)
£€ €60 (€70)
⊙ Lake Garda, 30 km NE of Brescia.
🏠 Cotton/Pennink/Steel
■ www.gardagolf.com

Karersee-Carezza
Loc Carezza 171, 39056 Welschofen-Nova Levante
☎ **(0471) 612200**
🖥 (0471) 612200
▷ 9 L 5340 m SSS 68
👭 H
£€ €30 (€35)
⊙ 30km S of Bolzano
🏠 Marco Croze

Petersberg   (1987)
Unterwinkel 5, 39040 Petersberg (BZ)
☎ **(0471) 615122**
🖥 (0471) 615229
✉ info@golfclubpetersberg.it
▷ 18 L 5800 m Par 72 SSS 71
👭 U
£€ €46 (€58)
⊙ 35km SE of Bolzano, nr Nova Ponente
🏠 Marco Croze
■ www.golfclubpetersberg.it

Ponte di Legno   (1980)
Corso Milano 36, 25056 Ponte di Legno (BS)
☎ **(0364) 900306**
🖥 (0364) 900555
▷ 9 L 4803 m SSS 68
👭 U
£€ €25 (€35)
⊙ 90km W of Trento, nr San Michele
🏠 Caremoli

Verona   (1963)
Ca' del Sale 15, 37066 Sommacampagna
☎ **(045) 510060**
🖥 (045) 510242
▷ 18 L 6054 m SSS 72
👭 H
£€ €50 (€60)
⊙ 7km W of Verona
🏠 John Harris

Naples & South

Napoli   (1983)
Via Campiglione 11, 80072 Arco Felice (NA)
☎ **(081) 526 4296**
▷ 9 L 4776 m SSS 68
👭 M
⊙ Pozzuoli, 10 km W of Naples

Porto d'Orra   (1977)
PB 102, 88063 Catanzaro Lido
☎ **(0961) 791045**
🖥 (0961) 791444
▷ 9 L 5686 m SSS 70
👭 U
⊙ 9km N of Catanzaro Lido on coast

Riva Dei Tessali   (1971)
74011 Castellaneta
☎ **(099) 843 9251**
🖥 (099) 843 9255
▷ 18 L 5960 m SSS 71
👭 U
£€ €30
⊙ 34km SW of Taranto
🏠 Marco Croze

San Michele
Loc Bosco 8/9, 87022 Cetraro (CS)
☎ **(0982) 91012**
🖥 (0982) 91430
▷ 9 L 2760 m SSS 70
👭 U H
£€ €15 (€17)
⊙ Cetraro, 50km N of Cosenza. 250km SE of Naples
🏠 Piero Mancinelli

Rome & Centre

Castelgandolfo   (1987)
Via Santo Spirito 13, 00040 Castelgandolfo
☎ **(06) 931 2301/931 3084**
🖥 (06) 931 2244
▷ 18 L 6025 m SSS 72
👭 U H Sun–restricted
£€ €30 (€50)
⊙ 22km SE of Rome
🏠 Robert Trent Jones

Eucalyptus   (1988)
Via Cogna 5, 04011 Aprilia (Roma)
☎ **(06) 927 46252**
🖥 (06) 926 8502
▷ 18 L 6310 m Par 72 SSS 73
👭 WD–U WE–U H
£€ €25 (€30) low season €30 (€35) high season (Easter, June/July)
⊙ 20km S of Rome on Aprilia-Anzio road
🏠 D'Onofrio
■ www.eucalyptusgolfclub.it

Fioranello
CP 96, 00134 Roma (RM)
☎ **(06) 713 8080**
🖥 (06) 713 8212
▷ 18 L 5360 m Par 70
👭 U
£€ €36 (€42)
⊙ Santa Maria, 17km SE of Rome
🏠 David Mezzacane

Fiuggi   (1928)
Superstrada Anticolana 1, 03015 Fiuggi (FR)
☎ **(0775) 55250**
🖥 (0775) 506742
▷ 9 L 5697 m SSS 70
👭 U
⊙ 60km SE of Rome

Marco Simone   (1989)
*Via di Marco Simone, 00012
Guidonia (RM)*
- ☎ **(0774) 366469**
- ⌨ (0774) 366476
- ⤳ 18 L 6317 m SSS 73
  18 hole course Par 64
- ⋔ U
- ⛳ 17km NE of Rome
- ⌂ Fazio/Mezzacane

Nettuno
*Via della Campana 18, 00048
Nettuno (RM)*
- ☎ **(06) 981 9419**
- ⌨ (06) 989 88142
- ⤳ 18 L 6260 m SSS 72
- ⋔ U H
- £€ €25 (€35)
- ⛳ 60km S of Rome on coast
- ⌂ Marco Croze

Olgiata   (1961)
Largo Olgiata 15, 00123 Roma
- ☎ **(06) 308 89141**
- ⌨ (06) 308 89968
- ⤳ 18 L 6347 m
  9 L 2947 m
- ⋔ WE–H
- £€ €50 (€65)
- ⛳ 19km NW of Rome, nr La Storta
- ⌂ CK Cotton

Parco de' Medici   (1989)
*Viale Parco de' Medici 165,
00148 Roma*
- ☎ **(06) 655 3477**
- ⌨ (06) 655 3344
- ⤳ 18 L 6303 m Par 71 SSS 71
  Yellow tees CR 70.7 SR 174
  9 L 2620 m Par 34 SSS 68
- ⋔ U
- £€ €60 (€72)
- ⛳ 15km SW of Rome, nr Airport
- ⌂ Mezzacane/Rebecchini
- ■ www.sheraton.com

Pescara   (1992)
*Contrado Cerreto 58, 66010
Miglianico (CH)*
- ☎ **(0871) 959566**
- ⌨ (0871) 950363
- ⤳ 18 L 6184 m Par 72 SSS 72
- ⋔ U
- £€ €25 (€35)
- ⛳ S of Pescara (Adriatic coast)

Le Querce
San Martino, 01015 Sutri (VT)
- ☎ **(0761) 68789**
- ⌨ (0761) 68142
- ⤳ 18 L 6433 m SSS 72
- ⋔ U
- £€ €35
- ⛳ 42km N of Rome
- ⌂ Fazio/Mezzacane

Roma   (1903)
Via Appia Nuova 716A, 00178 Roma
- ☎ **(06) 780 3407**
- ⌨ (06) 783 46219
- ⤳ 18 L 5854 m Par 71 SSS 70
- ⋔ WD–H WE–M H
- £€ €35 (€50)
- ⛳ 7km SE of Rome towards
  Ciampino

Tarquinia
*Loc Pian di Spille, Via degli Alina 271,
01016 Marina Velca/Tarquinia (VT)*
- ☎ **(0766) 812109**
- ⤳ 9 L 5442 m SSS 69
- ⛳ 80km N of Rome on coast

Torvaianica
Via Enna 30, 00040 Marina di Ardea
- ☎ **(06) 913 3250**
- ⌨ (06) 913 3592
- ⤳ 9 L 4416 m SSS 64
- ⋔ H
- ⛳ 30km S of Rome
- ⌂ Leonardo Basili

Sardinia

Is Molas   (1975)
CP 49, 09010 Pula
- ☎ **(070) 924 1013/4**
- ⌨ (070) 924 2121
- ⤳ 18 L 6383 m SSS 72
  9 L 2966 m SSS 36
- £€ €60 (€70)
- ⛳ Pula, 32km S of Cagliari
- ⌂ Cotton/Pennink/Lurie

Pevero GC Costa Smeralda
(1972)
07020 Porto Cervo
- ☎ **(0789) 96072/96210/96211**
- ⌨ (0789) 96572
- ⤳ 18 L 6186 m SSS 72
- ⋔ U H
- £€ €40–€100
- ⛳ Porto Cervo, 30km N of Olbia, on
  Costa Smeralda
- ⌂ Robert Trent Jones

Sicily

Il Pìcciolo   (1988)
*Via Picciolo 1, 95030 Castiglione
di Sicilia*
- ☎ **(0942) 986252**
- ⌨ (0942) 986252
- ✉ segretia@ilpicciologolf.com
- ⤳ 18 L 5810 m Par 72 SSS 71
- ⋔ H
- £€ €42 (€52)
- ⛳ 18km E of Taormina
- ⌂ Rota Caremoli
- ■ www.ilpicciologolf.com

Turin & Piemonte

Alpino Di Stresa   (1924)
*Viale Golf Panorama 49, 28839
Vezzo (VB)*
- ☎ **(0323) 20642/20101**
- ⌨ (0323) 20642
- ⤳ 9 L 5397 m Par 69 SSS 68
- ⋔ WE–U WE–restricted
- £€ 18 holes: €25 (€35) 9 holes: €17
  (€25)
- ⛳ 7km W of Stresa. Milan 80km
- ⌂ Peter Gannon

Biella Le Betulle   (1958)
Valcarozza, 13887 Magnano (BI)
- ☎ **(015) 679151**
- ⌨ (015) 679276
- ✉ golf@lebetulle.com
- ⤳ 18 L 6427 m CR 73.1 SR 141
- ⋔ H
- £€ €60 (€96)
- ⛳ 17km SW of Biella
- ⌂ John Morrison
- ■ www.lebetulle.com

Cervino   (1955)
11021 Cervinia-Breuil (AO)
- ☎ **(0166) 949131**
- ⌨ (0116) 949131
- ⤳ 9 L 4796 m SSS 66
- ⋔ U
- £€ €25–€35
- ⛳ 53km NE of Aosta
- ⌂ Donald Harradine

Cherasco CC   (1982)
Via Fraschetta 8, 12062 Cherasco (CN)
- ☎ **(0172) 489772/488489**
- ⌨ (0172) 488304
- ⤳ 18 L 6041 m Par 72 SSS 72
- ⋔ H
- £€ €32 (€45)
- ⛳ Cherasco, 45km S of Turin
- ⌂ Gianmarco Croze
- ■ www.golfcherasco.com

Claviere   (1923)
*Strada Nazionale 45, 10050
Claviere (TO)*
- ☎ **(0122) 878917**
- ⤳ 9 L 4650 m SSS 65
- ⋔ U
- ⛳ 96km W of Turin
- ⌂ Luzi

Courmayeur
11013 Courmayeur (AO)
- ☎ **(0165) 89103**
- ⤳ 9 L 2650 m SSS 67
- ⛳ 5km NE of Courmayeur

Cuneo   (1990)
*Via degli Angeli 3, 12012 Mellana-
Bóves (CN)*
- ☎ **(0171) 387041**
- ⌨ (0171) 390763
- ⤳ 18 L 5851 m Par 71 SSS 70
- ⋔ U H

For list of abbreviations and key to symbols see page 627

€€　€35 (€45)
🏌　80km S of Turin, nr Cúneo
🏠　Graham Cooke

Le Fronde　(1973)

Via Sant-Agostino 68, 10051
Avigliana (TO)
☎　(011) 932 8053/0540
🖥　(011) 932 0928
🏳　18 L 5976 m SSS 71
🏌　WD–U WE–H max 34
€€　€30 (€40)
🏌　Avigliana, 20km W of Turin
🏠　John Harris

I Girasoli　(1991)

Via Pralormo 315, 10022
Carmagnola (TO)
☎　(011) 979 5088
🖥　(011) 979 5228
🏳　18 L 4585 m Par 65
🏌　H
€€　€20 (€30)
🏌　25km S of Turin
◼　www.girasoligolf.it

Iles Borromees

Loc Motta Rossa, 28833 Brovello
Carpugnino (VB)
☎　(0323) 929285
🖥　(0323) 929190
📧　info@golfdeslesborromees.it
🏳　18 L 6445 m SSS 72
🏌　U
€€　€40 (€65)
🏌　5km S of Stresa. 80km NW of
　　Milan
🏠　Marco Croze
◼　www.golfdesilesborromees.it

Golf dei Laghi　(1993)

Via Trevisani 6, 21028 Travedona
Monate (VA)
☎　(0332) 978101
🖥　(0332) 977532
🏳　18 L 6400 m Par 72 SSS 73
🏌　H
€€　€30 (€50)
🏌　30km SW of Varese. 50km NW of
　　Milan
🏠　Piero Mancinelli

Margara　(1975)

Via Tenuta Margara 5, 15043
Fubine (AL)
☎　(0131) 778555
🖥　(0131) 778772
🏳　18 L 6045 m SSS 72
🏌　U
🏌　15km NW of Alessandria

La Margherita

Strada Pralormo 29, Carmagnola (TO)
☎　(011) 979 5113
🖥　(011) 979 5204
📧　golf.lamargherita@libero.it
🏳　18 L 6114 Par 72 SR 136 (men)/124
　　(ladies)
🏌　U
€€　€40 (€55 with reservation)

🏌　20km S of Turin
🏠　Croze/Ferraris
◼　www.golfclubmargherita.com

Piandisole　(1964)

Via Pineta 1, 28057 Premeno (NO)
☎　(0323) 587100
🏳　9 L 2830 m SSS 67
🏌　U
🏌　Premeno, 30km N of Stresa

I Roveri　(1971)

Rotta Cerbiatta 24, 10070 Fiano (TO)
☎　(011) 923 5719/923 5667
🖥　(011) 923 5668
🏳　18 L 6218 m SSS 72
　　9 L 3107 m SSS 36
🏌　WE–NA
🏌　16km NW of Turin. Caselle Airport
　　10km
🏠　Robert Trent Jones

La Serra　(1970)

Via Astigliano 42, 15048 Valenza (AL)
☎　(0131) 954778
🖥　(0131) 928294
🏳　9 L 2820 m SSS 70
🏌　H
€€　€20 (€35)
🏌　4km W of Valenza. 7km N of
　　Alessandria
🏠　Migliorini

Sestrieres　(1932)

Piazza Agnelli 4, 10058 Sestrieres (TO)
☎　(0122) 755170/76243
🖥　(0122) 76294
🏳　18 L 4598 m Par 67 SSS 65
🏌　U H
€€　€27 (€40)
🏌　Sestrieres, 96km W of Turin

Stupinigi　(1972)

Corso Unione Sovietica 506,
10135 Torino
☎　(011) 347 2640
🖥　(011) 397 8038
🏳　9 L 2175 m SSS 63
🏌　Mirafiore, Turin

Torino　(1924)

Via Agnelli 40, 10070 Fiano Torinese
☎　(011) 923 5440/923 5670
🖥　(011) 923 5886
📧　info@circologolftorino.it
🏳　18 L 6216 m SSS 72
　　18 L 6214 m SSS 72
🏌　U H
€€　€60 (€90)
🏌　23km NW of Turin
🏠　Morrison/Croze/Cooke
◼　www.circologolftorino.it

Vinovo　(1986)

Via Stupinigi 182, 10048 Vinovo (TO)
☎　(011) 965 3880
🖥　(011) 962 3748
🏳　9 L 5732 m Par 72 SSS 71
🏌　U

€€　€25 (€30)
🏌　Vinovo, 3km SW of Turin
🏠　Croce/Chiaravigcio

Tuscany & Umbria

Casentino　(1985)

Via Fronzola, 6 Loc Palazzo, 52014
Poppi (Arezzo)
☎　(0575) 529810
🖥　(0575) 520167
📧　golfc@lina.it
🏠　Luca Alterini
🏳　9 L 5550 m Par 72 SSS 69 SR 130
🏌　WD–U WE–H
€€　€25 (€31)
🏌　Poppi, 50km SE of Florence, 35km
　　N of Arezzo
🏠　Brami/Baracchi
◼　www.casentino.net/golf

Castelfalfi G&CC

50050 Montaione (FI)
☎　(0571) 698093/4
🖥　(0571) 698098
🏳　18 L 6095 m SSS 73
🏌　H
🏌　45km SW of Florence
🏠　Pier Mancinelli

Circolo Golf Ugolino　(1933)

Strada Chiantigiana 3, 50015 Grassina
☎　(055) 230 1009/1085
🖥　(055) 230 1141
🏳　18 L 5676 m CR 70.6 SR 131
🏌　WD–H WD–NA
€€　€60 (€80)
🏌　Grassina, 10km S of Florence
🏠　Blandford/Gannon

Conero GC Sirolo　(1987)

Via Betellico 6, 60020 Sirolo (AN)
☎　(071) 736 0613
🖥　(071) 736 0380
🏳　18 L 6185 m Par 72
　　9 hole course Par 29
🏌　U
🏌　Sirolo, 20km SE of Ancona.
　　Falconara Airport 25km
🏠　Marco Croze

Cosmopolitan G&CC　(1992)

Viale Pisorno 60, 56018 Tirrenia
☎　(050) 33633
🖥　(050) 384707
🏳　18 L 6291 m Par 73
🏌　U
€€　€30
🏌　15km SW of Pisa
🏠　David Mezzacane

Lamborghini-Panicale　(1992)

Loc Soderi 1, 06064 Panicale (PG)
☎　(075) 837582
🖥　(075) 837582
🏳　9 L 5872 m Par 72 SSS 70
🏌　U H

€€ €25 (€30)
🚗 30km W of Perugia, nr Lake Trasimeno
🏠 Ferruccio Lamborghini
⬛ www.lamborghinionline.it

Montecatini (1985)

Via Dei Brogi 5, Loc Pievaccia, 51015 Monsummano Terme
☎ **(0572) 62218,**
    (+39) 3291 790808 (mobile)
🖵 (0572) 617435
▷ 18 L 5857 m Par 72 CR 71.2 SR 129 (men)
    18 L 5127 m Par 72 CR 73.4 SR 121 (women)
👥 WD–U H
🚗 8km SE of Montecatini Terme. 50 km SW of Florence (A11)
🏠 Marco Croze

Le Pavoniere (1986)

Via Traversa Il Crocifisso, 59100 Prato
☎ **(0574) 620855**
🖵 (0574) 624558
▷ 18 L 6137 m Par 72 CR 72.4 SR 137
👥 H
€€ €60 (€75)
🚗 Prato 7km, Florence 20km
🏠 Arnold Palmer

Perugia (1959)

06074 Santa Sabina-Ellera
☎ **(075) 517 2204**
🖵 (075) 517 2370
▷ 18 L 5735 m Par 70 SSS 70
👥 U
€€ €42 (€52)
🚗 6km NW of Perugia
🏠 David Mezzacane
⬛ www.golfclubperugia.it

Poggio dei Medici (1995)

Via S Gavino 27 – Loc. Cingano, I-50038 Scarperia
☎ **(055) 843 0436**
🖵 (055) 843 0439
✉ info@poggiodeimedici.com
✍ Cristiano Bevilacqua (Mgr)
▷ 18 L 6060-6338 m CR 73.0-74.3 SR 131-136 (men)
    18 L 5364-5660 m CR 74.6-75.8 SR 131-132 (ladies)
👥 H WD WE
€€ 18: €80 (€80); 9: €50 (€50)
🚗 27km from Florence (highway exit 'Barberino di Mugello')
🏠 Fioravanti/Dassù
⬛ www.poggiodeimedici.com

Punta Ala (1964)

Via del Golf 1, 58040 Punta Ala (GR)
☎ **(0564) 922121/922719**
🖵 (0564) 920182
▷ 18 L 6168 m SSS 72
👥 U
€€ €50–€80
🚗 40km NW of Grosseto. Siena 90km. Florence 180km
⬛ www.puntaAla.net/golf

Tirrenia (1968)

Viale San Guido, 56018 Tirrenia (PI)
☎ **(050) 37518**
🖵 (050) 33286
▷ 9 L 3065 m SSS 72
🚗 15km SW of Pisa on coast

Venice & North East

Albarella

Isola di Albarella, 45010 Rosolina (RO)
☎ **(0426) 330124**
🖵 (0426) 330628
▷ 18 L 6100 m SSS 72
👥 H
€€ €40 (€50)
🚗 80km S of Venice
🏠 Harris/Croze

Ca' della Nave (1986)

Piazza Vittoria 14, 30030 Martellago
☎ **(041) 540 1555**
🖵 (041) 540 1926
▷ 18 L 6380 m SSS 73
    9 L 1240 m Par 28
👥
🚗 Martellago, 12km NW of Venice
🏠 Arnold Palmer

Cansiglio (1956)

CP 152, 31029 Vittorio Veneto
☎ **(0438) 585398**
🖵 (0438) 585398
▷ 18 L 6007 m SSS 71
👥 WD–U WE–H
€€ €40 (€50)
🚗 21km NE of Vittorio Veneto. 80km NE of Venice
🏠 Trent Jones/Croze

Colli Berici (1986)

Strada Monti Comunali, 36040 Brendola (VI)
☎ **(0444) 601780**
🖵 (0444) 400777
▷ 18 L 5798 m SSS 71
👥 U
€€ €40 (€50)
🚗 Vicenza 10km. Venice 70km
🏠 Marco Croze

Frassanelle (1990)

35030 Frassanelle di Rovolon (PD)
☎ **(049) 991 0722**
🖵 (049) 991 0722
✉ info@golffrassanelle.it
▷ 18 L 6180 m SSS 72
👥 H
€€ €58 (€65)
🚗 20km S of Padova, nr Via dei Colli
🏠 Marco Croze
⬛ www.golffrassanelle.it

Lignano

Via Bonifica 3, 33054 Lignano Sabbiadoro (UD)
☎ **(0431) 428025**

🖵 (0431) 423230
▷ 18 L 6069 m Par 72
👥 H
€€ €54 (€64)
🚗 90km E of Venice on coast
🏠 Marco Croze
⬛ www.golflignano.it

La Montecchia (1989)

Via Montecchia 12, 35030 Selvazzano (PD)
☎ **(049) 805 5550**
🖵 (049) 805 5737
▷ 18 L 6318 m SSS 73
    9 L 3012 m Par 36
👥 U H
€€ €50 (€55)
🚗 8km W of Padova. 40km W of Venice
🏠 T Macauley

Padova (1964)

35050 Valsanzibio di Galzigano (PD)
☎ **(049) 913 0078**
🖵 (049) 913 1193
✉ info@golfpadova.it
▷ 18 L 6053 m SSS 72
    8 L 3000 m SSS 36
👥 H WD–U WE–M
€€ €48 (€55) Low season €56 (€65) High season
🚗 Valsanzibio, 20km S of Padua
🏠 John D Harris (18), Marco Crozo (9)
⬛ www.golfpadova.it

San Floriano-Gorizia (1987)

Castello di San Floriano, 34070 San Floriano del Collio (GO)
☎ **(0481) 884252/884234**
🖵 (0481) 884252/884052
▷ 9 L 3810 m Par 62
👥 U
€€ €25
🚗 6km NW of Gorizia. 50km SE of Udine, nr Slovenian border
🏠 Pellicciari

Trieste (1954)

Via Padriciano 80, 34012 Trieste
☎ **(040) 226159/226270**
🖵 (040) 226159
▷ 18 L 5883 m SSS 72
👥 U–closed Tues
€€ €35 (€50)
🚗 Padriciano, 7km E of Trieste

Udine (1971)

Via dei Faggi 1, Località Villaverde, 33034 Fagagna (UD)
☎ **(0432) 800418**
🖵 (0432) 801312
✉ golfudine@libero.it
▷ 18 L 6088 m Par 72 CR 72.1 SR 129
👥 H
€€ €50 (€65)
🚗 15km NW of Udine
🏠 Marco Croze
⬛ www.golfudine.com

Venezia (1928)

Via del Forte, 30011 Alberoni (Venezia)
- ☎ **(041) 731015/731333**
- 🖳 (041) 731339
- ✉ info@circologolfvenezia.it
- ⮡ 18 L 6199 m SSS 72
- 👥 U H
- £€ €55 (€65)
- ⛳ Venice Lido
- ⌂ Cruickshank/Cotton/Croze
- ■ www.circologolfvenezia.it

Villa Condulmer (1960)

Via della Croce 3, 31021 Zerman di Mogliano Veneto
- ☎ (041) 457062
- 🖳 (041) 457202
- ⮡ 18 L 5995 m SSS 71
- 9 hole short course
- 👥 H
- £€ €50 (Sun–€60)
- ⛳ Mogliano Veneto, 17km N of Venice
- ⌂ Harris/Croze

Luxembourg

Christnach (1993)

Am Lahr, 7641 Christnach
- ☎ **87 83 83**
- 🖳 87 95 64
- ✉ gcc@gms.lu
- ⮡ 18 L 6210 m CR 71 SR 124
- 9 L 1241 m Par 72 SSS 71
- 👥 Greencard
- £€ 18 €30 (€35) 9 €20 (€25)
- ⛳ 25km N of Luxembourg city
- ■ www.golfclubchristnach.lu

Clervaux (1992)

Mecherwee, 9748 Eselborn
- ☎ **92 93 95**
- 🖳 92 94 51
- ⮡ 18 L 6144 m Par 72
- 👥 H
- £€ €26 (€28)
- ⛳ 3km from Clervaux, North Luxembourg

Gaichel

Rue de Eischen, 8469 Gaichel
- ☎ **39 71 08**
- 🖳 39 00 75
- ⮡ 9 L 5155 m Par 70
- 👥 U H
- £€ €17 (€23)
- ⛳ 10km W of Mersch on Belgian border

Golf de Luxembourg (1993)

Domaine de Belenhaff, L-6141 Junglinster
- ☎ **(00252) 78 00 68-1**
- 🖳 (00352) 78 71 28
- ✉ info@golfdeluxembourg.lu
- ⮡ 18 L 6068 m Par 72 CR 73.2 SR 131

- 👥 U–unrestricted (Green card)
- £€ €50 except Tues (€60)
- ⛳ 17km NE of Luxembourg City
- ⌂ Green Concept, Lyon, Frnce
- ■ www.golfdeluxembourg.lu

Grand-Ducal de Luxembourg (1936)

1 Route de Trèves, 2633 Senningerberg
- ☎ **34 00 90-1**
- 🖳 34 83 91
- ⮡ 18 L 5765 m SSS 71
- 👥 H
- £€ €50 (€60)
- ⛳ 7km N of Luxembourg
- ⌂ Maj Simpson

Kikuoka Country Club (1991)

Scheierhaff, L-5412 Canach
- ☎ **+352 35 61 35**
- 🖳 +352 35 74 50
- ✉ playgolf@kikuoka.lu
- ⮡ 18 L 6444 m SSS 73.4 SR 128
- 👥 H 35
- £€ €45–€55 Oct–April, (€55–€70) May–Aug
- ⛳ 15 km from Luxembourg Airport
- ⌂ Iwao Uematsu
- ■ www.kikuoka.lu

Malta

Royal Malta (1888)

Marsa LQA 06, Malta
- ☎ **(356) 21 23 93 02**
- 🖳 (356) 21 22 70 20
- ✉ info@maltagolf.org
- ⮡ 18 L 5020 m SSS 67
- 👥 U exc Thurs–NA before 11am Sat–NA before noon
- £€ £M12–£M15
- ⛳ Marsa, 3 miles from Valetta
- ■ www.maltagolf.org

Netherlands

Amsterdam & Noord Holland

Amsterdam Old Course (1990)

Zwarte Laantje 4, 1099 CE Amsterdam
- ☎ **(020) 694 3650**
- 🖳 (020) 663 4621
- ⮡ 9 L 5264 m SSS 68
- 👥 WE–H
- £€ €41
- ⛳ 5km SE of Amsterdam

Amsterdamse (1934)

Bauduinlaan 35, 1047 HK Amsterdam
- ☎ **(020) 497 7866**
- 🖳 (020) 497 5966
- ⮡ 18 L 6124 m CR 73.1
- 👥 WD–H WE–M
- £€ €55–€65
- ⛳ 10km W of Amsterdam
- ⌂ Rolin/Jol

BurgGolf Purmerend (1989)

Westerweg 60, 1445 AD Purmerend
- ☎ **(+31) 299 689160**
- 🖳 (+31) 299 647081
- ✉ purmerend@burggolf.nl
- ⮡ 18 L 5556 m Par 72
- 18 L 5593 m Par 71
- 9 L 5656 m par 72
- 👥 H
- £€ €42.50 (€52.50)
- ⛳ 16km N of Amsterdam
- ⌂ Tom McAuley & Bruno Steensels
- ■ www.burggolf.nl

Haarlemmermeersche

Spieringweg 745, 2142 ED Cruquius
- ☎ **(023) 558 9000**
- 🖳 (023) 558 9009
- ⮡ 27: 18 L 5868 m Par 73, 9 L 2472 m par 34
- + 9 hole short course
- 👥 H
- £€ €45 (€52.50)
- ⛳ Haarlemmermeer, W of Amsterdam
- ⌂ O'Connor Jr/Rijks

Heemskerkse (1998)

Communicatieweg 18, 1967 PR Heemskerk
- ☎ **(0251) 250088**
- 🖳 (0251) 241627
- ⮡ 18 L 6138 m CR 71.9 SR 127
- 👥 WD
- £€ €46
- ⛳ 25km NW of Amsterdam

Kennemer G&CC (1910)

Kennemerweg 78, 2042 XT Zandvoort
- ☎ **(023) 571 2836/8456**
- 🖳 (023) 571 9520
- ⮡ 27 holes CR 71.5-73.2
- Van Hengel 9 L 2951 m
- Pennink 9 L 2916 m
- Colt 9 L 2942 m
- 👥 H WE–NA before 3pm
- £€ €75
- ⛳ Zandvoort, 6km W of Haarlem
- ⌂ Colt/Pennink/Van Hengel

De Noordhollandse (1982)

Sluispolderweg 6, 1817 BM Alkmaar
- ☎ **(072) 515 6807**
- 🖳 (072) 520 9918
- ⮡ 18 L 5865 m CR 70.6
- 👥 H
- £€ €39 (€50)
- ⛳ 2km N of Alkmaar
- ⌂ Ryks/Dudok van Heel
- ■ www.dnhgc.nl

Olympus (1976)
Abcouderstraatweg 46, 1105 AA
Amsterdam Zuid-Oost
☎ **(0294) 281241**
📠 (0294) 286347
🏌 18 L 5722 m SSS 71
   9 hole par 3/4
👥 U–phone first
£€ €37 (€42)
⊕ SE of Amsterdam, nr A2 and AMC
   Hospital
🏠 Dudok van Heel/Jol

Spaarnwoude (1977)
Het Hoge Land 5, 1981 LT Velsen-Zuid
☎ **(023) 538 2708 (club)**
   (023) 538 5599 (5) (reservations)
📠 (023) 538 7274
🏌 18 L 5682 m Par 71
   9 L 3075 m Par 36
👥 U
£€ €26
⊕ 14km W of Amsterdam. 10km NE
   of Haarlem
🏠 Pennink/Jol
■ www.golfbaanspaarnwoude.nl

Waterlandse (1990)
Buikslotermeerdijk 141, 1027
AC Amsterdam
☎ **(020) 632 5650**
📠 (0200 634 3506
🏌 18 L 5156 m Par 71
£€ €23
⊕ 10km N of Amsterdam

Zaanse (1988)
Zuiderweg 68, 1456 NH Wijdewormer
☎ **(0299) 438199**
📠 (0299) 438199
🏌 9 L 5282 m Par 70
👥 WD–H WE–M
£€ €40 (€45)
⊕ 15km NE of Amsterdam
🏠 Gerard Jol
■ www.zaansegolfclub.com

Breda & South West

Brugse Vaart (1993)
Brugse Vaart 10, 4501 NE Oostburg
☎ **(0117) 453410**
📠 (0117) 455511
🏌 18 L 6409 m SSS 73
👥 H
£€ €40 (€50)
⊕ 15km N of Bruges, nr Knokke,
   Belgium
🏠 Alexander de Vos

Domburgsche (1914)
Schelpweg 26, 4357 BP Domburg
☎ **(0118) 586106**
📠 (0118) 586109
✉ golfdgc@zeelandnet.nl
🏌 9 L 5435 m CR 69 SR 127
👥 H
£€ €42.50 (€47.50)

⊕ 15km NW of Middelburg
■ www.domburgschegolfclub.nl

Efteling (1994)
Veldstraat 6, 5176 NB Kaatsheuvel
☎ **(0416) 288399**
📠 (0416) 288439
🏌 18 L 5896 m Par 72
👥 H
£€ €41 (€50)
⊕ 20km NE of Breda
■ www.efteling.com

Grevelingenhout (1988)
Oudendijk 3, 4311 NA Bruinisse
☎ **(0111) 482650**
📠 (0111) 481566
🏌 18 L 6151 m CR 72.0
   9 hole Par 3 course
👥 H
£€ €50–€55
⊕ 55km SW of Rotterdam
🏠 Donald Harradine

Oosterhoutse (1985)
Dukaatstraat 21, 4903 RN Oosterhout
☎ **(0162) 458759**
📠 (0162) 433285
🏌 18 L 5908 m CR 71 SR 126
👥 WD–H WE–M
£€ €60
⊕ 10km NE of Breda
🏠 J Dudok van Heel
■ www.ogcgolf.nl

Princenbosch (1991)
Bavelseweg 153, 5126 PX Molenschot
☎ **(0161) 431811**
📠 (0161) 434254
✉ info@princenbosch.net
🏌 27 Par 70/72
👥 H–max 32
£€ €45
⊕ 10km SW of Breda
🏠 Alan Rÿks
■ www.princenbosch.net

Reymerswael (1986)
Grensweg 21, 4411 ST Rilland Bath
☎ **(0113) 551265**
📠 (0113) 551264
✉ golf@reymerswael.nl
🏌 9 L 5866 m CR 71.4 SR 126
   6 hole course
👥 H
£€ €30 (€35)
⊕ 20km W of Bergen op Zoom. 50km
   W of Breda, off A58
🏠 Dudok van Heel/Rijks
■ www.reymerswael.nl

Toxandria (1928)
Veenstraat 89, 5124 NC Molenschot
☎ **(0161) 411200**
📠 (0161) 411715
🏌 18 L 5834 m Par 72
👥 WD–I Phone first
£€ €50 (€70)
⊕ 8km E of Breda
🏠 Morrison/Dudok van Heel
■ www.Toxandria.nl

De Woeste Kop (1986)
Justaasweg 4, 4571 NB Axel
☎ **(0115) 564467/564831 (Pro)**
📠 (0115) 564851
✉ woestekop@de-man.com
🏌 18 L 5473 m Par 71 SSS 71
👥 U
£€ €30 (€35)
⊕ 45km W of Antwerp
🏠 Paneels/Bosch
■ www.dewoestekop.nl

Wouwse Plantage (1981)
Zoomvlietweg 66, 4624 RP Bergen
op Zoom
☎ **(0165) 377100**
📠 (0165) 377101
🏌 18 L 6162 m CR 72.1 SR 131
👥 H WE–M
£€ €50
⊕ 10km E of Bergen-op-Zoom, nr
   Roosendaal
🏠 Pennink/Rolin
■ www.golfwouwseplantage.nl

East Central

Breuninkhof
Bussloselaan 6, 7383 RP Bussloo
☎ **(0571) 261955**
📠 (0571) 262089
🏌 9 L 6178 m SSS 72
👥 H
£€ €25 (€30)
⊕ 100km E of Amsterdam
🏠 Eschauzier

Edese (1978)
Papendallaan 22, 6816 VD Arnhem
☎ **(026) 482 1985**
📠 (026) 482 1348
🏌 18 L 5740 m SSS 70
👥 H
£€ €27 (€36)
⊕ National Sportcentrum Papendal.
   NW of Arnhem, towards Ede
🏠 Pennink/Dudok van Heel

De Graafschap (1987)
Sluitdijk 4, 7241 RR Lochem
☎ **(0573) 254323**
📠 (0573) 258450
🏌 18 L 6059 m CR 71.6
👥 H–booking necessary
£€ €41 (€45)
⊕ Lochem, 35km NW of Arnhem
■ www.lochemsegolfclub.nl

Hattemse G&CC (1930)
Veenwal 11, 8051 AS Hattem
☎ **(038) 444 1909**
🏌 9 L 5808 yds SSS 68
👥 WD–H WE–M+H
£€ €18 (€23)
⊕ Hattem, 5km S of Zwolle
🏠 Del Court van Krimpen

For list of abbreviations and key to symbols see page 627

Keppelse   (1926)
Burg Kehrerstraat 52, 7002
LD Doetinchem
☎ **(0314) 343662**
📠 (0314) 366523
🏌 9 L 5360 m Par 70
👥 H
£€ €35 (€40)
⛳ Laag-Keppel, 25km E of Arnhem
🏠 JP Eschauzier

De Koepel   (1983)
Postbox 88, 7640 AB Wierden
☎ **(0546) 576150/574070**
📠 (0546) 578109
🏌 9 L 2863 m SSS 70
👥 WE–H
£€ €23 (€27)
⛳ 7km W of Almelo
🏠 F Pennink

Nunspeetse G&CC   (1987)
Public
Plesmanlaan 30, 8072 PT Nunspeet
☎ **(0341) 255255**
📠 (0341) 255285
🏌 27 L 6100 m Par 72
👥 U
£€ €50 (€57.50)
⛳ Nunspeet, 80km E of Amsterdam
🏠 Paul Rolin
■ www.nunspeetsegolf.nl

Rosendaelsche   (1895)
Apeldoornseweg 450, 6816 SN Arnhem
☎ **(026) 442 1438**
📠 (026) 351 1196
🏌 18 L 6057 m CR 72.3 SR 132
👥 WD–H WE–NA
£€ €55
⛳ 5km N of Arnhem on Route N50
🏠 Frank Pennink

Sallandsche De Hoek   (1934)
PO Box 24, 7430 AA Diepenveen
☎ **(0570) 593269**
📠 (0570) 590102
🏌 18 L 5889 m SSS 71
👥 WD–H WE–M H
£€ €55
⛳ 6km N of Deventer
🏠 Pennink/Steel

Sybrook   (1992)
Veendijk 100, 7525 PZ Enschede
☎ **(0541) 530331**
📠 (0541) 531690
🏌 18 L 5878 m Par 71
👥 WD–H WE–M
£€ €36
⛳ 10km N of Enschede
🏠 Rolin/Rijks

Twentsche   (1926)
Almelosestraat 17, 7495 TG
Ambt Delden
☎ **(074) 384 1167**
📠 (074) 384 1067
🏌 18 L 6178 m SSS 72

👥 H
£€ €45 (€50)
⛳ 4km N of Delden
🏠 TJ McAuley
■ www.twentschegolfclub.nl

Veluwse   (1957)
Nr 57, 7346 AC Hoog Soeren
☎ **(055) 519 1275**
📠 (055) 519 1275
🏌 9 L 6264 yds SSS 70
👥 WD–U WD–H
£€ €27 (€32)
⛳ 5km W of Apeldoorn

Welderen   (1994)
Grote Molenstraat 173, 6661 NH Elst
☎ **(0481) 376591**
📠 (0481) 377055
🏌 18 L 6015 m Par 72
👥 WD–H WE–M
£€ €36
⛳ Elst, S of Arnhem via A325 or A15
🏠 JE Eschauzier
■ www.welderen.nl

Eindhoven & South East

De Berendonck   (1985)
Public
Weg Door de Berendonck 40, 6603
LP Wijchen
☎ **(024) 642 0039**
📠 (024) 641 1254
🏌 18 L 5671 m Par 71 SSS 70
👥 WE–restricted
£€ €25 (€30)
⛳ 5km SW of Nijmegen
🏠 J Dudok van Heel

Best G&CC
Golflaan 1, 5683 RZ Best
☎ **(0499) 391443**
📠 (0499) 393221
🏌 18 L 6079 m CR 71.7 SR 131
👥 H
£€ €45 (€55)
⛳ Best, 5km NW of Eindhoven
🏠 J Dudok van Heel

Crossmoor G&CC   (1986)
Laurabosweg 8, 6006 VR Weert
☎ **(0495) 518438**
📠 (0495) 518709
🏌 18 L 6043 m Par 72
9 hole Par 3 course
👥 H
£€ €45 (€55)
⛳ Weert/Altweertheide, 30km SE of Eindhoven
🏠 J Dudok van Heel

De Dommel   (1928)
Zegenwerp 12, 5271 NC
St Michielsgestel
☎ **(073) 551 9168**

📠 (073) 551 9441
✉ info@gcdedommel.nl
🏌 18 L 5607 m CR 69.7 SR 122
👥 WD–H WE–NA
£€ €45 (€45)
⛳ 10km S of Hertogenbosch
🏠 Colt/Steel
■ www.gcdedommel.nl

Eindhovensche Golf   (1930)
Eindhovenseweg 300, 5553
VB Valkenswaard
☎ **(040) 201 4816**
📠 (040) 207 6177
🏌 18 L 5923 CR 71.9 SR130/6223
CR 72.6 SR 135
👥 H
£€ €60
⛳ 8km S of Eindhoven
🏠 HS Colt

Geijsteren G&CC   (1974)
Het Spekt 2, 5862 AZ Geijsteren
☎ **(0478) 531809/532592**
📠 (0478) 532963
🏌 18 L 6090 m Par 72
👥 U but phone first
£€ €45 (€50)
⛳ Off A73 Junction 9, N270 to Wanssum. 25km N of Venlo
🏠 Pennink/Steel

Gendersteyn   (1994)
Locht 140, 5504 RP Veldhoven
☎ **(040) 253 4444**
📠 (040) 254 9747
🏌 18 L 5770 m Par 72
£€ €30 (€36)
⛳ 10km SW of Eindhoven

Havelte   (1977)
Postbus 29, Kolonieweg 2, 7970
AA Havelte
☎ **(0521) 342200**
📠 (0521) 343134
🏌 18 L 6243 m CR 72.7 SR 135
👥 H
£€ €35 (€45)
⛳ 30km SW of Assen (N371)
🏠 Donald Steel

Haviksoord   (1976)
Maarheezerweg Nrd 11, 5595 XG
Leende (NB)
☎ **(040) 206 1818**
📠 (040) 206 2761
🏌 9 L 5948 m CR 71.1 SR 136
👥 H
£€ €35 (€40)
⛳ 10km S of Eindhoven

Herkenbosch   (1991)
Stationsweg 100, 6075 CD Herkenbosch
☎ **(0475) 529529**
📠 (0475) 533580
🏌 18 L 5758 m Par 72
👥 U WD + WE H
£€ €50 (€60)
⛳ 20km S of Venlo, nr German border
■ www.gccherkenbosch.nl

Het Rijk van Nijmegen
(1985)
Postweg 17, 6561 KJ Groesbeek
☎ **(024) 397 6644**
📠 (024) 397 6942
🏌 18 L 6010 m CR 70.7
18 L 5717 m CR 69.1
👥 H
£€ €32 (€39)
🏁 5km E of Nijmegen
🏚 Paul Rolin
■ www.golfbaanhetrijkvannijmegen
.nl

De Peelse Golf (1991)
Maasduinenweg 1, 5977 NP Eversoord-Sevenum
☎ **(077) 467 8030**
📠 (077) 467 8031
🏌 18 L 6047 m Par 72
👥 U H
£€ €40 (€50) – 2003 rates
🏁 20km W of Venlo
🏚 Alan Rijks

De Schoot (1973)
Schootsedijk 18, 5491 TD
Sint Oedenrode
☎ **(04134) 73011**
📠 (04134) 71358
🏌 9 L 2886 m Par 72
👥 U
£€ €27 (€32)
🏁 20km N of Eindhoven
🏚 A Rijks

Tongelreep G&CC (1984)
Charles Roelslaan 15, 5644
HX Eindhoven
☎ **(040) 252 0962**
📠 (040) 293 2238
🏌 9 L 5345 m CR 69.2 SR 122
👥 WD–H WE–H by introduction only
£€ €17.50–€30
🏁 Eindhoven
🏚 J van Rooy

Welschap (1993)
Welschapsedijk 164, 5657 BB Eindhoven
☎ **(040) 251 5797**
📠 (040) 252 9297
📧 secretariaat@golfclubwelschap.nl
🏌 18 L 5208 m Par 70
£€ €42.50 (€47.50)
🏁 Eindhoven
■ www.golfclubwelschap.nl

Limburg Province

Brunssummerheide (1985)
Rimburgerweg 50, Brunssum
☎ **(045) 527 0968**
📠 (045) 527 3939
🏌 27 L 5933 m Par 72
9 hole Par 3 course
👥 U H
£€ €36 (€45)
🏁 25km NE of Maastricht

Hoenshuis G&CC (1987)
Hoensweg 17, 6367 GN Voerendaal
☎ **(045) 575 3300**
📠 (045) 575 0900
🏌 18 L 6074 m CR 71.2
👥 WE–NA 10am–2pm
£€ €30 (€43)
🏁 Limburg, 10km NE of Maastricht
🏚 Paul Rolin

De Zuid Limburgse G&CC
(1956)
Dalbissenweg 22, 6281 NC Mechelen
☎ **(043) 455 1397/1254/3958**
📠 (043) 455 1576/3958
📧 zlgolf@wanadoo/nl
🏌 18 L 5904 m Par 71
👥 WD–H WE–H28 before 10am –
after 3pm
£€ €40 (€50)
🏁 Mechelen, 25km SE of Maastricht
🏚 Hawtree/Snelder/Rolin
■ www.zlgolf.nl

North

Gelpenberg (1970)
Gebbeveenweg 1, 7854 TD Aalden
☎ **(0591) 371929**
📠 (0591) 372422
🏌 18 L 6031 m Par 71
👥 H
£€ €45 (€55)
🏁 16km W of Emmen
🏚 Pennink/Steel

Holthuizen (1985)
Oosteinde 7a, 9301 ZP Roden
☎ **(050) 501 5103**
📠 (050) 501 3685
📧 golfclub.holthuizen@planet.nl
🏌 9 L 6079 m SSS 72
👥 H
£€ €25 (€35)
🏁 10km S of Groningen
🏚 Rijks/Eschauzier
■ www.gc-holthuizen.nl

Lauswolt G&CC (1964)
Van Harinxmaweg 8A, PO Box 36, 9244
ZN Beetsterzwaag
☎ **(0512) 383590/382594**
📠 (0512) 383739
📧 algemeenbn@golfclublauswolt.nl
🏌 18 L 6087 m CR 71.5
👥 H
£€ €50 (€70)
🏁 Beetsterzwaag, 5km S of Drachten
🏚 Pennink/Steel

Noord Nederlandse G&CC
(1950)
Pollselaan 5, 9756 CJ Glimmen
☎ **(050) 406 2004**
📠 (050) 406 1922
📧 info@hngcc.nl
🏌 18 L 5755 m CR 70.2 Par 71
👥 H

£€ €60
🏁 12km S of Groningen, off A28
🏚 Campbell (1950), Pennick/Steel
(1987)
■ www.nngcc.nl

De Semslanden (1986)
Nieuwe Dijk 1, 9514
BX Gasselternijveen
☎ **(0599) 564661/565531**
📠 (0599) 565594
🏌 18 L 5973 m CR 127
👥 H
£€ €27 (€32)
🏁 25km E of Assen
🏚 Eschauzier/Thate/Jol

Vegilinbosschen
Legemeersterweg 18, 8527 DS Legemeer
☎ **(0513) 499466**
📠 (0513) 499777
🏌 18 L 5765 m SSS 71
👥 H
£€ €36 (€41)
🏁 120km NE of Amsterdam
🏚 Allen Rijks

Rotterdam & The Hague

Broekpolder (1981)
Watersportweg 100, 3138
HD Vlaardingen
☎ **(010) 249 5566,**
(010) 249 5555/249 5577
📠 (010) 249 5579
🏌 18 L 6048 m SSS 72
👥 H
£€ €75 (€100)
🏁 15km W of Rotterdam, off A20
🏚 Frank Pennink/Gerard Jol

Capelle a/d IJssel (1977)
Gravenweg 311, 2905 LB Capelle
a/d IJssel
☎ **(010) 442 2485**
📠 (010) 284 0606
📧 info@golfclubcapelle.nl
🏌 18 L 5220 m CR 68.0 SR 110
👥 WD–U WE–M
£€ €45
🏁 5km S of Rotterdam
🏚 Donald Harradine
■ www.golfclubcapelle.nl

Cromstrijen (1989)
Veerweg 26, 3281 LX Numansdorp
☎ **(0186) 654455**
📠 (0186) 654681
📧 g.c.cromstrijen@hetnet.nl
🏌 18 L 6099 m Par 72
9 L 3800 m Par 62
👥 H–max 28 (men) 34 (ladies)
£€ €60 (€70)
🏁 30km S of Rotterdam (A29)
🏚 Tom McAuley

De Hooge Bergsche (1989)

Rottebandreef 40, 2661
JK Bergschenhoek
☎ **(010) 522 0052/522 0703**
✉ secretariaat@hoogebergsche.nl
ⓟ 18 L 5370 m Par 71 SR 116
👥 U
£€ €40 (€50)
⛳ Bergschenhoek, 2km NE of Rotterdam
� Gerard Jol
■ www.hoogebergsche.nl

Koninklijke Haagsche G&CC (1893)

Groot Haesebroekeseweg 22, 2243
EC Wassenaar
☎ **(070) 517 9607**
📞 (070) 514 0171
ⓟ 18 L 5674 m Par 72 SR 129
👥 WD–H (max 24) WE–M
£€ €120
⛳ 6km N of The Hague
🏠 Allison/Colt

Kralingen

Kralingseweg 200, 3062 CG Rotterdam
☎ **(010) 452 2283**
ⓟ 9 L 5220 yds CR 66.6
👥 H
£€ €35 (€40)
⛳ 5km from centre of Rotterdam
🏠 Copijn/Cotton

Leidschendamse Leeuwenbergh (1988)

Elzenlaan 31, 2495 AZ Den Haag
☎ **(070) 395 4556**
📞 (070) 399 8615
ⓟ 18 L 5461 m Par 70
£€ €55
⛳ E side of The Hague

De Merwelanden (1985)

Public
Golfbaan Crayestein, Baanhoekweg 50, 3313 LP Dordrecht
☎ **(078) 621 1221**
📞 (078) 616 1036
ⓟ 18 L 5722 m Par 71
👥 U
£€ €35 (€42.50)
⛳ 20km SE of Rotterdam
🏠 H & C Kuijsters

Noordwijkse (1915)

Randweg 25, PO Box 70, 2200
AB Noordwijk
☎ **(0252) 373761**
📞 (0252) 370044
✉ noordwijkse.gc@worldonline.nl
ⓟ 18 L 5823 m CR 71.9 SR 135 (men)
  18 L 5002 m CR 73.0 SR 126 (women)
👥 WD–H before noon and after 3pm
£€ €80
⛳ 5km N of Noordwyk. 15 km NW of Leiden

🏠 Frank Pennink
■ www.noordwijksegolfclub.nl

Oude Maas (1975)

Veerweg 2a, 3161 EX Rhoon
☎ **(010) 501 5135**
📞 (010) 501 5604
ⓟ 18 L 5471 m Par 71
👥 H
£€ €40 (€45)
⛳ Rhoon, 10km S of Rotterdam via A15
🏠 Pennink/Jol/Rijks
■ www.golfcluboudemaas.nl

Rijswijkse (1987)

Delftweg 58, 2289 AL Rijswijk
☎ **(070) 395 4864**
📞 (070) 399 5040
✉ secretariaat@rijswijksegolf.nl
ⓟ 18 L 5722 m Par 71 CR 69.5
👥 H
£€ €45 (€58)
⛳ 5km SE of The Hague
🏠 Steel/Rijks

Wassenaarse Rozenstein (1984)

Dr Mansveltkade 15, 2242
TZ Wassenaar
☎ **(070) 511 7846**
📞 (070) 511 9302
ⓟ 18 L 5820 m SSS 70
👥 H
£€ €50 (€60)
⛳ 14km NE of The Hague
🏠 Dudok van Heel/Jol
■ www.rozenstein.nl

Westerpark Zoetermeer (1985)

Heuvelweg 3, 2716 DZ Zoetermeer
☎ **(079) 351 7283**
📞 (079) 352 1335
ⓟ 18 L 5891 m Par 71
£€ €32 (€36)
⛳ 10km E of The Hague (A12)

Zeegersloot (1984)

Kromme Aarweg 5, PO Box 190, 2400
AD Alphen a/d Rijn
☎ **(0172) 474567**
📞 (0172) 494660
ⓟ 18 L 5793 m SSS 70
  9 hole Par 3 course
👥 U H
£€ 18 hole: €38 (€52) 9 hole: €16.50 (€21)
⛳ Alphen, 15km N of Gouda. 20km S of Amsterdam
🏠 Gerard Jol

Utrecht & Hilversum

Almeerderhout (1986)

Watersnipweg 19-21, 1341 AA Almere
☎ **(036) 521 9130**

📞 (036) 521 9131
ⓟ 27 L 6004-6046 m CR 71.9-72.2
  9 hole Par 3 course
👥 WD–U WE–M (Max h'cap 28)
£€ €40 (€57.50)
⛳ 30km N of Hilversum
🏠 Dudok van Heel/Ryks

Anderstein

Woudenbergseweg 13a, 3953
ME Maarsbergen
☎ **(0343) 431330**
📞 (0343) 432062
ⓟ 18 L 6048 m CR 72
👥 WD–U WE–M only
£€ €36–50
⛳ 20km E of Utrecht
🏠 Jol/Dudok van Heel

De Batouwe (1990)

Oost Kanaalweg 1, 4011 LA Zoelen
☎ **(0344) 624370**
📞 (0344) 613096
ⓟ 18 L 5717 m Par 72 SSS 70
  9 hole Par 3 course
👥 U H–booking necessary
£€ €43 (€57)
⛳ Tiel, 25km SE of Utrecht
🏠 Alan Rijks

Flevoland (1979)

Bosweg 98, 8231 DZ Lelystad
☎ **(0320) 230077**
📞 (0320) 230932
ⓟ 18 L 5836 m Par 71
👥 WD–U H WE–M+H
£€ €27 (€34)
⛳ Island of Flevoland. 1km NW of Lelystad. 45km N of Hilversum
🏠 JS Eschauzier

De Haar (1974)

PO Box 104, Parkweg 5, 3450
AC Vleuten
☎ **(030) 677 2860**
📞 (030) 677 3903
ⓟ 9 L 6650 yds SSS 71
👥 WD–H WE–NA
£€ €60
⛳ 10km NW of Utrecht
🏠 F Pennink

Hilversumsche (1910)

Soestdijkerstraatweg 172, 1213
XJ Hilversum
☎ **(035) 685 7060**
📞 (035) 685 3813
ⓟ 18 L 5859 m Par 72 CR 71.2 SR 135
👥 Phone booking necessary
£€ €75
⛳ 3km E of Hilversum, nr Baarn
🏠 Burrows/Colt

De Hoge Kleij (1985)

Appelweg 4, 3832 RK Leusden
☎ **(033) 461 6944**
📞 (033) 465 2921
ⓟ 18 L 6046 m SSS 72
👥 WD–H

1km SE of Amersfoort 20km NE of Utrecht via A28
Donald Steel

Nieuwegeinse (1985)
Postbus 486, 3437 AL Nieuwegein
(030) 604 2192
(030) 636 9410
9 L 5208 m Par 70
WD–U WE–NA before 4pm
€40
7km S of Utrecht
Alan Rÿks

Utrechtse 'De Pan' (1894)
Amersfoortseweg 1, 3735 LJ Bosch en Duin
(030) 695 6427
(030) 696 3769
18 L 5694 m Par 72 CR 70.1
WD–M WE–NA
€75
10km E of Utrecht, off A28
HS Colt

Zeewolde
Golflaan 1, 3896 LL Zeewolde
(036) 522 2103
(036) 522 4100
27 L 6259 m Par 72
9 hole course Par 58
H
€50
20km N of Hilversum. 60km NE of Amsterdam
A Rijks
www.golfclub-zeewolde.nl

Norway

Arendal og Omegn (1986)
Nes Verk, 4900 Tvedestrand
37 19 90 30
37 16 02 11
post@arendalgk.no
18 L 5528 m Par 72
9 hole course
U
300kr (350kr)
Nes Verk, 20km E of Arendal (E18). 95km NE of Kristiansand
www.arendalgk.no

Baerum (1972)
Hellerudveien 26, 1350 Lommedalen
67 87 67 00
67 87 67 20
18 L 5300 m Par 71
9 hole short course
H–restricted. Max 28 (men) 32 (ladies). Booking advisable
375kr (425kr)
10km W of Oslo. 10km N of Sandvika
Jeremy Turner

Bergen (1937)
Erikveien 120, 5080 Eidsvåg
05 18 20 77
9 L 4461 m Par 67
U
150kr
8km N of Bergen

Borre (1991)
Semb Hovedgaard, 3186 Horten
33 07 15 15
33 07 15 16
borregb@online.no
18 L 6120 m Par 73 – 27 from summer 2004
H
400kr (400kr)
In Horten, 50km S of Drammen. 100km SW of Oslo
T Nordström
wwww.borregb.no

Borregaard (1927)
PO Box 348, 1702 Sarpsborg
69 12 15 00
69 15 74 11
borregaardgk@golf.no
9 L 4500 m SSS 65
H
200kr
Opsund, 1km N of Sarpsborg
www.borregaardgk.no

Drøbak (1988)
Belsjøveien 50, 1440 Drøbak
64 93 16 80
64 93 39 80
18 L 5089 m Par 70
H
325kr (375kr)
40km SE of Oslo
Hauser

Elverum (1980)
PO Box 71, 2401 Elverum
62 41 35 88
62 41 55 13
18 L 5845 m Par 72
H
200kr (220kr)
Starmoen Fritidspark, 10km E of Elverum. 35km E of Hamar. 150km N of Oslo

Grenland (1976)
Luksefjellvn 578, 3721 Skien
35 59 07 03
35 59 06 10
18 L 5777 m Par 72
U
250kr
6km from Skien
Jan Sederholm

Groruddalen (1988)
Postboks 37, Stovner, 0913 Oslo
22 79 05 60
22 79 05 79
9 L 2844 m CR 58.2 SR 102
U–before 3pm
150kr
15km N of Oslo
Leif Nilsson
www.grorudgk.no

Hemsedal (1994)
3560 Hemsedal
32 06 23 77
32 06 00 84
9 L 4816 m Par 68
U H
180kr (240kr)
40km N of Gol. 380km NW of Oslo
Leif Nilsson

Kjekstad (1976)
PO Box 201, 3440 Royken
31 29 79 90
31 29 79 99
18 L 5100 m SSS 67
H
250kr (300kr)
12km SE of Drammen on Route 282. 40km SW of Oslo
Jan Sederholm

Kristiansand (1973)
PO Box 6090, Søm, 4602 Kristiansand
38 04 35 85
38 04 34 15
9 L 2485 m SSS 70
U
D–150kr
8 km E of Kristiansand (E18)

Larvik (1989)
Fritzøe Gård, 3267 Larvik
33 14 01 45
33 14 01 49
18 L 6147 m Par 72
H
350kr (400kr)
3km S of Larvik on R301 to Stavern
Jan Sederholm
www.larvikgolf.no

Narvik (1992)
8523 Elvegard
76 95 12 01
76 95 12 06
18 L 5890 m Par 72
U H
250kr
30km S of Narvik
Jan Sederholm
www.narvikgolf.no

Nes (1988)
Rommen Golfpark, 2160 Vormsund
63 91 20 30
63 91 20 31
18 L 5962 m CR 71.5 SR 128
H or Green card
280kr (340kr)
50km NE of Oslo, via E6/RV2
Hauser/own design

Onsøy (1987)
Golfveien, 1626 Manstad
☎ **69 33 91 50**
🖳 69 33 35 24
▷ 18 L 5600 m Par 72
👥 WD–U WE–H
£€ 300kr
⛳ 10km W of Fredrikstad. Oslo 80km
🏠 Andersen/Mejstedt

Oppdal (1987)
PO Box 19, 7340 Oppdal
☎ **72 42 25 10**
▷ 9 L 2621 m Par 72
👥 U
£€ 150kr
⛳ 120km S of Trondheim
🏠 Jan Sederholm

Oppegård (1985)
Kongeveien 198, PO Box 50,
1416 Oppegård
☎ **66 81 59 90**
🖳 66 81 59 91
▷ 18 L 5280 m Par 71
👥 U H
£€ 250kr (350kr)
⛳ 22km S of Oslo
■ www.oppegardgk.no

Oslo (1924)
Bogstad, 0757 Oslo
☎ **22 51 05 60**
🖳 22 51 05 61
▷ 18 L 6719 yds SSS 72
👥 H–Max 20 (men) 28 (ladies)
   WD–restricted before 2pm
   WE–restricted after 2pm
£€ 400kr (400kr)
⛳ 8km NW of Oslo. Signs to
   'Bogstad Camping'.

Ostmarka (1989)
Postboks 63, 1914 Ytre Enebakk
☎ **64 92 38 40**
🖳 64 92 47 55
▷ 18 L 5640 m
👥 H
£€ 200kr (300kr)
⛳ 35km E of Oslo

Oustoen CC (1965)
PO Box 100, 1330 Fornebu
☎ **67 83 23 80/22 56 33 54**
🖳 67 53 95 44/22 59 91 83
✉ occ@occ.no
▷ 18 L 5626 m SSS 72
👥 M H
£€ 500kr
⛳ Small island in Oslofjord, 10km W
   of Oslo
■ www.occ.no

Skjeberg (1986)
PO Box 528, 1701 Sarpsborg
☎ **69 16 63 10**
▷ 18 L 5500 m Par 72
👥 U
£€ 150kr (200kr)

⛳ Hevingen, 2km N of Sarpsborg
🏠 Jan Sederholm

Sorknes (1990)
Sorknes Gaard, 2450 Rena
☎ **62 44 18 70**
🖳 62 44 00 27
✉ post@sorknes.no
▷ 18 L 6150 m SSS 72
👥 U
£€ 270kr (380kr)
⛳ 170km N of Oslo
🏠 Juul Soegaard
■ www.sorknes.no

Stavanger (1956)
Longebakke 45, 4042 Hafrsfjord
☎ **51 55 54 31**
🖳 51 55 73 11
▷ 18 L 5751 m Par 71
👥 H
£€ 250kr
⛳ 6km SW of Stavanger
🏠 F Smith

Trondheim (1950)
PO Box 169, 7401 Trondheim
☎ **73 53 18 85**
🖳 73 52 75 05
▷ 9 L 5513 m SR 136
👥 H
£€ 250kr
⛳ Trondheim 3 km
■ www.golfklubben.no

Tyrifjord (1982)
Postboks 91, 3529 Røyse
☎ **32 16 13 30**
🖳 32 16 13 40
▷ 18 L 5747 m Par 72 SR 140
👥 H
£€ 350kr (400kr)
⛳ 40km NW of Oslo (E16)
🏠 Sederholm/Eia
■ www.tyrifjord-golfklubb.no

Vestfold (1958)
PO Box 64, 3108 Vear
☎ **33 36 25 00**
🖳 33 36 25 01
✉ v6k@vestfoldgolfclubb.no
▷ 18 L 6414 / 5979 / 4877 m SSS 72
   9 hole course Par 64
👥 H
£€ 350kr
⛳ Tønsberg 8km
🏠 Smith/Turner
■ www.vestfoldgolfklubb.no

Poland

Amber Baltic (1993)
Baltycka Street 13, 72-514 Kolczewo
☎ **(091) 32 65 110/120**
🖳 (091) 32 65 333
▷ 18 L 5802 m Par 72
   9 L 1307 m Par 28

👥 U
£€ €27 (€40)
⛳ 80km N of Szczecin
🏠 H-G Erhardt

Portugal

Algarve

Alto G&CC (1991)
Quinta do Alto do Poço, P O Box 1, 8501
906 Alvor
☎ **(0282) 460870**
🖳 (0282) 460879
✉ golf@altoclub.com
▷ 18 L 6125 m SSS 73 SR 120
👥 U H
£€ €56–€70
⛳ 2km W of Portimão
🏠 Sir Henry Cotton
■ www.altoclub.com

Floresta Parque (1987)
Vale do Poço, Budens, 8650 Vila
do Bispo
☎ **(0282) 695333**
🖳 (0282) 695157
▷ 18 L 5787 m SSS 72
👥 U
£€ €40
⛳ 16km W of Lagos, nr Salema
🏠 Pepe Gancedo

Palmares (1975)
Apartado 74, Meia Praia, 8600
901 Lagos
☎ **(0282) 790500**
🖳 (0282) 790509
▷ 18 L 5961 m Par 71 SSS 72
👥 U H
£€ €45–€70
⛳ Meia Praia, 5km E of Lagos
🏠 Frank Pennink
■ www.palmaresgolf.com

Penina (1966)
PO Box 146, Penina, 8502 Portimao
☎ **(0282) 420200**
🖳 (0282) 420300
▷ Ch'ship 18 L 6343 m SSS 73
   Resort 9 L 3987 m SSS 71
   Academy 9 L 1851 m Par 30
👥 H–max 28 (M) or 36 (L) – soft
   spikes only
£€ Ch'ship €65–90 Resort €37
   Academy €33
⛳ 5km W of Portimao. 12km E of
   Lagos
🏠 Sir Henry Cotton

Pestana (1991)
Apartado 1011, 8400-908 Carvoeiro Lga
☎ **(0282) 340900**
🖳 (0282) 340901

▷ Gramacho 18 L 5919 m Par 72
   SSS 71
   Pinta 18 L 6727 m Par 71 SSS 72
👤 U
£€ Garmacho €37–€50 Pinta €50–€70
🚗 10km E of Portimão. 54km W of
   Faro Airport
🏠 Ronald Fream
■ www.pestana.com

Pine Cliffs G&CC   (1991)
Pinhal do Concelho, 8200 Albufeira
☎ **(0289) 500100/501999**
🖵 (0289) 501950
▷ 9 L 2324 m Par 66 SSS 67
👤 U H
£€ 9 hole: €27
🚗 7km W of Vilamoura
🏠 Martin Hawtree

Pinheiros Altos   (1992)
Quinta do Lago, 8135 Almancil
☎ **(0289) 359910**
🖵 (0289) 394392
▷ 18 L 6236 m Par 72
👤 H–phone first. Soft spikes only
£€ €100
🚗 Quinta do Lago, 15km W of Faro
🏠 Ronald Fream

Quinta do Lago   (1974)
Quinta Do Lago, 8135 Almancil
☎ **(0289) 390700/9**
🖵 (0289) 394013
▷ Quinta do Lago 18 L 6488 m
   SSS 72
   Ria Formosa 18 L 6205 m SSS 72
👤 H–by prior arrangement
£€ €65
🚗 15km W of Faro. Airport 20km
🏠 Mitchell/Lee

Salgados
*Apartado 2362, Vale do Rabelho, 8200
917 Albufeira*
☎ **(0289) 583030**
🖵 (0289) 591112
▷ 18 L 6080 m Par 72
👤 U
£€ On application
🚗 W of Albufeira
🏠 P de Vasconcelos

San Lorenzo   (1988)
Quinta do Lago, 8135 Almancil
☎ **(289) 396522**
🖵 (289) 396908
▷ 18 L 6238 m SSS 73
👤 H–restricted
£€ €150
🚗 16km W of Faro
🏠 Joseph Lee

Vale de Milho   (1990)
*Apartado 1273, Praia do Carvoeiro,
8401-911 Carvoeiro Lga*
☎ **(282) 358502**
🖵 (282) 358497
▷ 9 hole Par 3 course
👤 U

£€ 18 holes: €34 9 holes: €21.50 Up to
   30% discount with season
🚗 2¹/₂ km E of Carvoeiro
🏠 Dave Thomas

Vale do Lobo   (1968)
*Vale Do Lobo, 8135-864 Vale do Lobo-
Almançil*
☎ **(0289) 353535**
🖵 (0289) 353003
▷ Ocean 18 L 5424 m Par 71
   Royal 18 L 6050 m Par 72
👤 H
£€ Ocean €90 Royal €110
🚗 19km W of Faro. Airport 19km
🏠 Cotton/Roquemore

Vila Sol   (1991)
*Alto do Semino, Vilamoura,
8125 Quarteira*
☎ **(0289) 300505**
🖵 (0289) 316499
▷ 27 L 6335 m Par SSS 72
👤 U H
£€ €90
🚗 5km E of Vilamoura. Faro Airport
   10km
🏠 Donald Steel

Vilamoura Laguna   (1990)
8125-507 Vilamoura, Algarve
☎ **(0289) 310180**
🖵 (0289) 310183
▷ 18 L 6133 m CR 71.1 SR 126
👤 H–max 28(M) 36(L)
£€ €60
🚗 As Vilamoura Old
🏠 Joseph Lee
■ www.vilamoura.net

Vilamoura Millennium
(2000)
8125-507 Vilamoura, Algarve
☎ **(0289) 310188**
🖵 (0289) 310183
▷ 18 L 6143 m CR 69.2 SR 113
👤 H–max 28(M) 36(L). Soft spikes
   only
£€ €60
🚗 As Vilamoura Old
🏠 Martin Hawtree
■ www.vilamoura.net

Vilamoura Old   (1969)
8125-507 Vilamoura, Algarve
☎ **(0289) 310341**
🖵 (0289) 310321
▷ 18 L 6254 m CR 70.9 SR 124
👤 H–max 24(M) 28(L) Soft spikes
   only
£€ €110
🚗 Quarteira, 25km W of Faro
🏠 Frank Pennink
■ www.vilamoura.net

Vilamoura Pinhal   (1976)
8125-507 Vilamoura, Algarve
☎ **(0289) 310390**
🖵 (0289) 310393
▷ 18 L 6206 m CR 70.4 SR 122

👤 H–max 28(M) 36(L)
£€ €75
🚗 As Vilamoura Old
🏠 Pennink/Trent Jones
■ www.vilamoura.net

Azores

Batalha   (1995)
*Rua do Bom Jesus, Aflitos, 9545-234
Fenais da Luz (Açores)*
☎ **(0296) 298559/498560**
🖵 (0296) 498284
▷ 18 L 6435 m CR 72.8 SR 131
👤 H
£€ €40
🚗 Sao Miguel Island. Ponta Delgada
   10km
🏠 Cameron/Powell
■ www.virtualazores.com/verdegolf

Furnas   (1939)
*Rua do Bom Jesus, Aflitos Furnas, 9545
Fenais da Luz (Açores)*
☎ **(0296) 498559/584341**
🖵 (0296) 498284/584651
▷ 18 L 6232 m SSS 72
👤 H
£€ €40
🚗 São Miguel Island. Furnas Villa
   5km
🏠 Mackenzie Ross/Cameron/Powell
■ www.virtualazores.com/verdegolf

Terceira Island   (1954)
*Caixa Postal 15, 9760 909 Praia da
Victória (Açores)*
☎ **(0295) 902444**
🖵 (0295) 902445
▷ 18 L 5790 m Par 72 SSS 70
👤 U H
£€ €30
🚗 10km NW of Praia da Victoria

Lisbon & Central Portugal

Aroeira   (1972)
*Herdade da Aroeira, 2815-207 Charneca
da Caparica*
☎ **(+351) 212 979 110/1**
🖵 (+351) 212 979 119
✉ fpleite/aroeira@clix.pt
▷ 18 L 6044 m CR 71.0 SR 123
   18 L 6367 m CR 72.3 SR 130
👤 U H
£€ €46 (€65)
🚗 20km S of Lisbon, off
   Setúbal/Costa da Caparica road
🏠 Pennink/Steel
■ www.aroeira.com

Belas
Alameda do Aqueducto, 2605-199 Belas
☎ **(021) 962 6600**
🖵 (021) 962 6601

☘ 18 L 6200 m Par 72
☠ U
✈ W of Lisbon (N117)

Estoril   (1945)
Avenida da República, 2765-273 Estoril
☏ (021) 466 0367
⌨ (021) 468 2796
✉ reserva@golfestoril.com
☘ 18 L 5313 m Par 69 CR 67.9 SR
125
9 L 2350 m SSS 65
☠ WD–U WE–M
££ €54 (€58)
✈ N of Estoril on Sintra road. 30km
W of Lisbon
⌂ Mackenzie Ross

Estoril-Sol Golf Academy
(1976)
Quinta do Outeira, Linhó, 2710 Sintra
☏ (01) 923 2461
⌨ (01) 923 2461
☘ 9 L 4118 m Par 66 SSS 66
☠ U
✈ 7km N of Estoril. Lisbon 35km
⌂ Harris/Fream

Lisbon Sports Club   (1922)
Casal da Carregueira, 2745 Belas
☏ (01) 431 0077
⌨ (01) 431 2482
☘ 18 L 5216 m Par 69 SSS 69
☠ U
££ D–€37 (D–47)
✈ Belas, 20km NW of Lisbon
⌂ Hawtree

Marvao
*Estrada do Monte Pobre, Sao Salvador
do d'Aramanha, 7330 Marvao*
☏ (045) 93755
⌨ (045) 93805
☘ 18 holes Par 72
☠ U
✈ 25km N of Portalegre, nr Spanish
border (N118/N246)

Montado
Apartado 40, Algeruz, 2950 Palmela
☏ (065) 706648
⌨ (065) 706775
☘ 18 L 6060 m SSS 72
☠ U
££ €42
✈ 5km E of Setúbal. 40km S of
Lisbon
⌂ Duarte Sottomayor

Penha Longa   (1992)
*Estrada da Lagoa Azul, Linhó, 2714-
511 Sintra*
☏ (021) 924 9011
⌨ (021) 924 9024
✉ golf@penhalonga.com
☘ 18 L 6290 m CR 70.2 SR 120
9 L 2588 m Par 35
☠ U H
££ 18 hole:€89 (€110) 9 hole :€33
(€43)

✈ 8km N of Estoril. 17km W of
Lisbon
⌂ Robert Trent Jones Jr
■ www.penhalonga.com

Quinta da Beloura   (1994)
Estrada de Albarraque, 2710 444 Sintra
☏ (021) 910 6350
⌨ (021) 910 6359
✉ belouragolf@mail.telopac.pt
☘ 18 L 5774 m Par 73 CR 71.2 SR
128
☠ U
££ D–€45 (D–€60)
✈ Between Estoril and Sintra, off N9.
Lisbon 34km
⌂ Rocky Roquemore
■ www.pestana.com

Quinta da Marinha   (1984)
Quinta da Marinha, 2750 Cascais
☏ (021) 486 0180
⌨ (021) 486 9032
☘ 18 L 6014 m CR 68.5 SR 114
☠ U
££ €61 (€76)
✈ 2km W of Cascais. 32km W of
Lisbon
⌂ Robert Trent Jones
■ www.quintadamarinha.com

Quinta do Perú
*Alameda da Serra 2, 2975-666 Quinta
do Conde*
☏ (021) 213 4320
⌨ (021) 213 4321
✉ play@golfquintadoperu.com
☘ 18 L 6036 m CR 72 SR 137
☠ H
££ €58 (€88)
✈ E of Lisbon, off EN10
⌂ Rocky Roquemore
■ www.golfquintadoperu.com

Tróia Golf Championship
Course   (1980)
Tróia, 7570-789 Carvalhal
☏ (265) 494 112
⌨ (265) 494 315
✉ triogolf@sonae.pt
☘ 18 L 6320 m Par 72 CR 74.8 (white
tees)
SR 124 (white tees)
☠ U H
££ €57 (€68.50)
✈ On Tróia Peninsula, 42km S of
Lisbon. From Lisbon take A2/A12
to Setubal then follow signs for
Tróia to ferry. In Tróia follow EN
234-1 to Comporta
⌂ Robert Trent Jones sr
■ www.troiagolf.com

Vimeiro
*Praia do Porto Novo, Vimeiro, 2560
Torres Vedras*
☏ (061) 984157
⌨ (061) 984621
☘ 9 L 4781 m Par 68 SSS 67
☠ U

££ €25
✈ Vimeiro, 20km N of Torres Vedras.
65km N of Lisbon
⌂ Frank Pennink

Madeira

Madeira   (1991)
*Sto Antonio da Serra, 9200
Machico, Madeira*
☏ (091) 552345/552356
⌨ (091) 552367
☘ 18 L 6040 m Par 72
☠ U
££ €40
✈ 25km E of Funchal. Airport 3km
⌂ Robert Trent Jones

Palheiro   (1993)
*Sitio do Balancal, Sao Gonçalo, 9050-
296 Funchal, Madeira*
☏ (00351) 291 792 116,
(00351) 291 790 125 (Bookings)
⌨ (00351) 291 792 456
✉ reservations@palheirogolf.com
☘ 18 L 6086 m Par 72 CR 71.6 SR
130
☠ May–Sept–U Oct–April–H
££ €77
✈ 5km from Funchal, off Airport road
to Camacha
⌂ Cabell Robinson
■ www.palheirogolf.com

North

Amarante   (1997)
*Quinta da Deveza, Fregim, 4600-
593 Amarante*
☏ (0255) 446060
⌨ (0255) 446202
☘ 18 L 5085 m CR 65.4 SR 114
☠ H
££ €36.80 (€47.30)
✈ 50km E of Oporto, off A4
⌂ J Santana da Silva

Golden Eagle G&CC
Quinta do Brincal, 2040 Rio Maior
☏ (0243) 908148
⌨ (0243) 908149
☘ 18 L 6021 m Par 72
☠ H
££ €50 (€60)
✈ 55km N of Lisbon, off N1 towards
Leiria
⌂ R Roquemore

Miramar   (1932)
*Av Sacadura Cabral, Miramar, 4405-
0013 Arcozelo*
☏ (022) 762 2067
⌨ (022) 762 7859
☘ 9 L 2655 m Par 70 SSS 69
☠ H WD WE
££ €40 (€60)
✈ 8km S of Oporto
⌂ Swan/Gordon

Montebelo

Farminhão, 3510 Viseu
☎ **(032) 856464**
📠 (032) 856401
► 18 L 6300 m Par 72 SSS 72
🚶 U
⛳ 75km NE of Coimbra

Oporto   (1890)

Sisto-Paramos, 4500 Espinho
☎ **(022) 734 2008**
📠 (022) 734 6895
► 18 L 5780 m Par 71 SSS 70
🚶 H WE–restricted
££ €50
⛳ Espinho, 15km S of Oporto

Ponte de Lima

Quinta de Pias, Fornelos, 4490 Ponte de Lima
☎ **(058) 43414**
📠 (058) 743424
► 18 L 6005 m Par 71 SSS 70
🚶 U
⛳ 75km N of Oporto (N201)

Praia d'el Rey G&CC

(1997)
Vale de Janelas, Apartado 2, 2510 Obidos
☎ **(+351) 262 905005**
📠 (+351) 262 905009
✉ golf@praia-del-rey.com
► 18 L 6467 m Par 72 CR 71.7 SR 122
🚶 U H
££ €75 (€95)
⛳ 65km N of Lisbon, nr Obidos (Motorway A 8)
🏠 Cabell Robinson
■ www.praia-del-rey.com

Golfe Quinta da Barca

(1997)
Barca do Lago, 4740-476 Esposende
☎ **(+351) 2539 66723**
📠 (+351) 2539 969068
✉ lcatarino@quintabarca.com
► 9 L 1927 m Par 62 CR 61.0 SR 104
🚶 H
££ 18: €30 (€40); 9: €23 (€40)
⛳ 50km N of Oporto
🏠 Jorge Santana da Silva
■ www.quintabarca.com

Vidago

Pavilhão do Golfe, 5425 Vidago
☎ **(076) 907356**
📠 (076) 996622
► 9 L 2256m Par 66 SSS 64
⛳ 50km N of Vila Real. 130km NE of Oporto
🏠 Mackenzie Ross

Slovenia

G&CC Bled   (1937)

Public
Kidričeva 10 c, 4260 Bled
☎ **(04) 753 777 11**
📠 (04) 53 777 22
► 18 L 6325 m SSS 73
9 L 3092 m SSS 72
🚶 H–36 max
££ £4 (£7)
⛳ 3km W of Bled. 50km NW of Ljubljana, nr Austro-Italian border
🏠 Donald Harradine
■ www.golf.bled.si

Castle Mokrice   (1992)

Terme Catez, Topliska Cesta 35, 8250 Brezice
☎ **(00386) 7 457 4260**
📠 (00386) 7 495 7007
► 18 L 5835 m Par 71 SSS 73 (men)
18 L 5235 m Par 71 SSS 73 (women)
🚶 U
££ €37 (€43)
⛳ 30km N of Zagreb
🏠 Donald Harradine
■ www.terme-catez.si

Lipica   (1989)

Lipica 5, 66210 Sezana
☎ **(067) 31580**
📠 (067) 72818
► 9 L 6240 m SSS 71
🚶 U
££ £2 (£8)
⛳ 11km NE of Trieste. 85km SW of Ljubljana
🏠 Donald Harradine

Spain

Alicante & Murcia

Alicante   (1998)

Av. Locutor Vicente Hipolito 37, Playa San Juan, 03540 Alicante
☎ **(96) 515 37 94/515 20 43**
📠 (96) 516 37 07
► 18 L 6236 m Par 72
🚶 U H
££ €54 (€65 buggy inc)
⛳ Playa San Juan, N of Alicante
🏠 Severiano Ballesteros
■ www.alicantegolf.com

Altorreal   (1994)

Urb Altorreal, 30500 Molina de Segura (Murcia)
☎ **(968) 64 81 44**
📠 (986) 64 82 48
► 18 L 6239 m Par 72 SSS 73
🚶 H

££ €30 (€36)
⛳ 10km from Murcia on Madrid road
🏠 Dave Thomas

Bonalba   (1993)

Partida de Bonalba, 03110 Mutxamiel (Alicante)
☎ **(96) 595 5955**
► 18 L 6190m Par 72 SSS 73
🚶 U
££ €48
⛳ 10km N of Alicante. A7 Junction 67
🏠 Ramón Espinosa
■ www.golfbonalba.com

Don Cayo   (1974)

Apartado 341, 0359 Altea La Vieja (Alicante)
☎ **(96) 584 80 46**
📠 (96) 584 11 88
► 9 L 6156 m SSS 72
🚶 U H
⛳ 4km N of Altea, nr Callosa
🏠 Barber/Sanz

Ifach   (1974)

Crta Moraira-Calpe Km 3, Apdo 28, 03720 Benisa (Alicante)
☎ **(96) 649 71 14**
📠 (96) 649 71 14
► 9 L 3408 m SSS 59
🚶 U
££ D–€19
⛳ 9km N of Calpe, towards Moraira
🏠 Javier Arana

Jávea   (1981)

Apartado 148, 03730 Jávea, (Alicante)
☎ **(96) 579 25 84**
📠 (96) 646 05 54
► 9 L 6070 m SSS 71
🚶 H
££ D–€33
⛳ Lluca, Jávea. 90km NE of Alicante
🏠 Francisco Moreno

La Manga   (1971)

Los Belones, 30385 Cartagena (Murcia)
☎ **(968) 13 72 34**
📠 (968) 15 72 72
► North 18 L 5780 m SSS 70
South 18 L 6259 m SSS 73
Princesa 18 L 5971 m SSS 72
🚶 U
⛳ 30km NE of Cartagena, nr Murcia airport
🏠 RD Putman

La Marquesa   (1989)

Ciudad Quesada II, 03170 Rojales, (Alicante)
☎ **(+34) 96 671 42 58**
📠 (+34) 96 671 42 67
✉ golflamarquesa@ctv.es
► 18 L 6111Par 72 CR 72.5 SR 132
🚶 U
££ D–€50
⛳ Rojales, 40km S of Alicante
🏠 Justo Quesada Samper

For list of abbreviations and key to symbols see page 627

Las Ramblas (1991)

Crta Alicante-Cartagena Km48, 03189
Urb Villamartin, Orihuela (Alicante)
- ☎ **(96) 532 20 11**
- 🖥 (96) 532 21 59
- ⏞ 18 L 5770 m SSS 71
- 👫 U H
- ££ €42
- 🏌 9km S of Torrevieja
- 🏠 José Gancedo

Real Campoamor (1989)

Crta Cartagena-Alicante Km48, Apdo
17, 03189 Orihuela-Costa (Alicante)
- ☎ **(96) 532 13 66**
- 🖥 (96) 532 24 54
- ⏞ 18 L 6203 m Par 72 SSS 73
- 👫 U H
- ££ €30
- 🏌 Torrevieja 9km (N332)
- 🏠 C Gracia Caselles

La Sella (1991)

Ctra La Xara-Jesús Pobre, 03749 Jesús
Pobre (Alicante)
- ☎ **(96) 645 42 52/645 41 10**
- 🖥 (96) 645 42 01
- ⏞ 18 L 6289 m CR 73.3 SR 136
- 👫 U H (36 max)
- ££ €56
- 🏌 Denia 5km
- 🏠 Juan de la Cuadra, José Maria Olazabal

Villamartin (1972)

Crta Alicante-Cartagena Km50, 03189
Urb Villamartin, Orihuela (Alicante)
- ☎ **(96) 676 51 27/676 51 60**
- 🖥 (96) 676 51 70
- ⏞ 18 L 6132 m SSS 72
- 👫 U H
- ££ €48
- 🏌 8km S of Torrevieja
- 🏠 Paul Putman

Almería

Almerimar (1976)

Urb Almerimar, 04700 El
Ejido (Almería)
- ☎ **(950) 48 02 34**
- 🖥 (950) 49 72 33
- ⏞ 18 L 6111 m SSS 72
- 👫 U
- 🏌 35km W of Almería
- 🏠 Gary Player

Cortijo Grande (1976)

Apdo 2, Cortijo Grande, 04639
Turre (Almería)
- ☎ **(951) 47 91 76**
- ⏞ 18 L 6024 m Par 72 SSS 71
- 👫 U
- 🏌 20km W of Turre. 85km N of Almería, nr Mojácar
- 🏠 PJ Polansky

La Envia (1993)

Apdo 51, 04720 Aguadulce (Almería)
- ☎ **(950) 55 96 41**
- ⏞ 18 L 5810 m Par 72 SSS 70
- 👫 U
- 🏌 10km from Almería
- 🏠 F Mendoza

Playa Serena (1979)

Urb Playa Serena, 04740 Roquetas de
Mar (Almería)
- ☎ **(950) 33 30 55**
- 🖥 (950) 33 30 55
- ⏞ 18 L 6301 m Par 72
- 👫 H
- ££ €30–€39
- 🏌 20km S of Almería
- 🏠 Gallardo/Alliss

Badajoz & West

Guadiana (1992)

Crta Madrid-Lisboa Km 393, Apdo 171,
06080 Badajoz
- ☎ **(924) 44 81 88**
- ⏞ 18 L 6381 m Par 72 SSS 73
- 👫 U
- 🏌 Badajoz
- 🏠 Daniel Calero

Norba (1988)

Apdo 880, 10080 Cáceres
- ☎ **(927) 23 14 41**
- 🖥 (927) 23 14 80
- ⏞ 18 L 6422 m Par 72 SSS 74
- 👫 U
- ££ €24 (€36)
- 🏌 4km S of Cáceres
- 🏠 Carlos Corsini

Salamanca (1988)

Monte de Zarapicos, 37170
Zarapicos (Salamanca)
- ☎ **(923) 32 91 02**
- ⏞ 18 L 6267 m Par 72 SSS 72
- 👫 U
- 🏌 W of Salamanca,nr Parada de Arriba (C-517)
- 🏠 Manuel Piñero

Balearic Islands

Canyamel

Urb Canyamel, Crta de Cuevas, 07580
Capdepera, (Mallorca)
- ☎ **(971) 56 44 57**
- 🖥 (971) 56 53 80
- ⏞ 18 L 6115 m SSS 72
- 👫 H
- 🏌 70km NE of Palma, nr Cala Ratjada
- 🏠 José Gancedo

Capdepera (1989)

Apdo 6, 07580 Capdepera, Mallorca
- ☎ **(971) 56 58 75/56 58 57**

- 🖥 (971) 56 58 74
- ⏞ 18 L 6284 m SSS 72
- 👫 U H
- 🏌 71km E of Palma, between Artá and Capdepera
- 🏠 Maples/Pape

Club Son Parc (1977)

Urb Son Parc, Mercadel (Menorca)
- ☎ **(971) 18 88 75**
- 🖥 (971) 35 95 91
- ⏞ 9 L 2791 m SSS 69
- 👫 U H
- ££ 18 holes: €42–€54 9 holes: €24–€33
- 🏌 Mercadal, 18km N of Mahón
- 🏠 JF Martínez
- ■ www.clubsonparc.com

Ibiza (1990)

Apdo 1270, 07840 Santa Eulalia, (Ibiza)
- ☎ **(971) 19 61 18**
- 🖥 (971) 19 60 51
- ⏞ 18 L 6083 m SSS 72
- 9 L 5867 m SSS 70
- 👫 H
- ££ €36–€72
- 🏌 7km N of Ibiza town
- 🏠 Thomas/Rivero

Pollensa (1986)

Ctra Palma-Pollensa Km 49, 07460
Pollensa, (Mallorca)
- ☎ **(971) 53 32 16**
- 🖥 (971) 53 32 65
- ✉ rec@golfpollensa.com
- ⏞ 9 L 5304 m Par 70 SSS 70
- 👫 U H
- ££ 9: €52; 18: €55
- 🏌 Pollensa, 45km N of Palma
- 🏠 José Gancedo
- ■ www.golfpollensa.com

Poniente (1978)

Costa de Calvia, 07181
Calvia (Mallorca)
- ☎ **(971) 13 01 48**
- 🖥 (971) 13 01 76
- ⏞ 18 L 6430 m SSS 72
- 👫 U H
- ££ €65
- 🏌 12km SW of Palma towards Cala Figuera
- 🏠 John Harris
- ■ www.ponientegolf.com

Pula Golf (1995)

Ctra. Son Servera-Capdepera, E-07550
Son Servera-Mallorca
- ☎ **(971) 81 70 34**
- 🖥 (971) 81 70 35
- ✉ pulagolf@eresmas.com
- 🔑 Rahel Wanke
- ⏞ 18 L 5758 m Par 72 CR 70.5 SR 132
- 👫 U H
- ££ 18: €84; 9: €42
- 🏌 70km NE of Palma

Real Golf Bendinat (1986)

C. Campoamor, 07015
Calviá, (Mallorca)
- ☎ **(971) 40 52 00**

For list of abbreviations and key to symbols see page 627

☎ (971) 70 07 86
🏳 18 L 5768 m SSS 71
👥 U H
🚗 7km W of Palma
🏛 Martin Hawtree

Santa Ponsa (1976)

Santa Ponsa, 07180 Calvia (Mallorca)
☎ **(971) 69 02 11/69 08 00**
🖥 (971) 69 33 64
📧 golf1@habitatgolf.es
🏳 18 L 6520 m
18 L 6053 m
SR White tees 124
Yellow tees 123
👥 No 1–U H No 2–NA
££ €69
🚗 18km W of Palma
🏛 Folco Nardi
■ www.habitatgolf.es

Son Antem (1993)

Apartado 102, 07620 Llucmajor, Mallorca
☎ **(971) 12 92 00**
🖥 (971) 12 92 01
🏳 East 18 L 6327 m CR 73.9 SR 134
West 18 L 6293 m CR 74 SR 137
👥 U–East H–West
££ €64
🚗 20km E of Palma (Route 717)
🏛 F López Segales

Son Servera (1967)

Costa de Los Pinos, 07759 Son Servera, (Mallorca)
☎ **(971) 84 00 96**
🖥 (971) 84 01 60
🏳 9 L 5956 m SSS 72
👥 H
££ D–€42
🚗 Son Servera, 64km E of Palma
🏛 John Harris

Son Vida (1964)

Urb Son Vida, 07013 Palma (Mallorca)
☎ **(971) 79 12 10**
🖥 (971) 79 11 27
🏳 18 L 5740 m SSS 71
👥 U H
££ €66
🚗 3km NW of Palma
🏛 FW Hawtree

Vall d'Or (1985)

Apdo 23, 07660 Cala D'Or, (Mallorca)
☎ **(971) 83 70 68/83 70 01**
🖥 (971) 83 72 99
📧 valldorgolf@valldorgolf.com
🏳 18 L 5602 m SSS 71
👥 H
££ €69
🚗 60km E of Palma, between Cala d'Or and Porto Colóm
🏛 Benz/Bendly
■ www.valldorgolf.com

Barcelona & Cataluña

Aro-Mas Nou (1990)

Apdo 429, 17250 Playa de Aro
☎ **(972) 82 69 00,**
(972) 81 67 27 (Bookings)
🖥 (972) 82 69 06
🏳 18 L 6218 m Par 72
9 holes Par 3 course
👥 U H
££ €53 (€57)
🚗 35km SE of Gerona on coast. A7 Junction 9 Barcelona Airport 100km
🏛 Ramón Espinosa

Bonmont Terres Noves (1990)

Urb Terres Noves, 43300 Montroig (Tarragona)
☎ **(977) 81 81 40**
🖥 (977) 81 81 46
🏳 18 L 6371 m SSS 72
👥 U H
££ €33 (€48)
🚗 S of Tarragona. 130km S of Barcelona
🏛 Robert Trent Jones Jr
■ www.bonmont.com

Caldes Internacional (1992)

Apdo 200, 08140 Caldes de Montbui (Barcelona)
☎ **(93) 865 38 28**
🏳 18 L 6258 m Par 72 SSS 73
👥 U
🚗 28km from Barcelona
🏛 Ramón Espinosa

Can Bosch (1984)

Trav de les Corts 322, 08029 Barcelona
☎ **(93) 405 04 22/866 25 71**
🖥 (93) 419 9659
🏳 9 L 3027 m SSS 71
👥 U H
🚗 35km NE of Barcelona
🏛 Ramon Espinosa

Costa Brava (1962)

La Masia, 17246 Sta Cristina d'Aro (Gerona)
☎ **(972) 83 71 50**
🖥 (972) 83 72 72
🏳 18 L 5573 m SSS 70
👥 H
££ €36–57
🚗 Playa de Aro 5km. 30km SE of Gerona
🏛 J Hamilton Stutt
■ www.golfcostabrava.com

Costa Dorada (1983)

Apartado 600, 43080 Tarragona
☎ **(977) 65 33 61**
🏳 18 L 6223 m SSS 73
🚗 Tarragona
🏛 José Gancedo

Empordà (1990)

Crta Torroella de Montgri, 17257 Gualta (Gerona)
☎ **(972) 76 04 50/76 01 36**
🖥 (972) 75 71 00
🏳 27 L 5855-6112 m SSS 70-71
👥 U H
££ €33 (€51)
🚗 35km E of Gerona, nr Pals. 130km N of Barcelona
🏛 Robert von Hagge

Fontanals de Cerdanya (1994)

Fontanals de Cerdanya, 17538 Soriguerola (Girona)
☎ **(972) 14 43 74**
🏳 18 L 6454 m Par 72 SSS 74
👥 U
🚗 2km from Alp de Puigcerdá

Girona (1992)

Urb Golf Girona, 17481 Sant Juliá de Ramis, (Girona)
☎ **(972) 17 16 41**
🖥 (972) 17 16 82
🏳 18 L 6100 m CR 72 SR 133
👥 H–booking required
££ €38 (€52)
🚗 Sant Juliá de Ramis, 4km from Girona. Barcelona 98km
🏛 Hawtree
■ www.golfgirona.com

Llavaneras (1945)

Camino del Golf, 08392 San Andres de Llavaneras, (Barcelona)
☎ **(93) 792 60 50**
🖥 (93) 795 25 58
🏳 18 L 4644 m SSS 66
👥 U H
££ €36 (€72)
🚗 4km N of Mataró. 34km N of Barcelona (A19)
🏛 Hawtree/Espinosa

Masia Bach (1990)

Ctra Martorell-Capellades, 08781 Sant Esteve Sesrovires
☎ **(93) 772 8800**
🖥 (93) 772 8810
🏳 18 L 6039 m SSS 72
9 L 3578 m SSS 62
👥 H
££ €54 (€120)
🚗 30km NW of Barcelona
🏛 JM Olazábal

Osona Montanya (1988)

Masia L'Estanyol, 08553 El Brull (Barcelona)
☎ **(93) 884 01 70**
🖥 (93) 884 04 07
🏳 18 L 6036 m Par 72
👥 U H
🚗 60km NE of Barcelona
🏛 Dave Thomas

Golf Platja de Pals   (1966)
Pay and play
Ctra. Del Golf, s/n, 17256 Pals, Gerona
- ☎ (+34) 972 66 77 39
- 📞 (+34) 972 63 67 99
- 📧 cial@golfplatjedepals.com
- 🖊 Alexandra Reig (Mgr)
- ▷ 18 Par 73 SSS 72
  White: L 6222 m CR 72.0 SR 127
  Yellow: L 5940 m CR 70.5 SR 122
  Blue: L 5360 m CR 72.9 SR 123
  Red: L 5089 m CR 71.2 SR 120
- 👥 H–WD/WE
- ££ Low season: 18 €45 9 €35 Mid
  Season: 18 €50 9 €40 High Season
  & WE: 18 €68 9 €48
- 🚗 40km E of Gerona, 135km NE of
  Barcelona
- 🏠 FW Hawtree
- ■ www.golfplatjedepals.com

Peralada Golf   (1993)
La Garriga, 17491 Peralada, Girona
- ☎ (972) 53 82 87
- 📞 (972) 53 82 36
- ▷ 18 L 5990 m SSS 71
  9 holes Par 3
- 👥 H
- ££ €46 low season, €52 mid season,
  €68 high season
- 🚗 Costa Brava, on French border.
  40km S of Perpignan Airport, nr
  Figueres
- 🏠 Jorge Soler
- ■ www.golfperalada.com

Platja de Pals   (1966)
Pay and play
Ctra. Del Golf, s/n, 17256, Pals
(Costa Brava)
- ☎ (34) 972 66 77 39
- 📞 (34) 972 63 67 99
- 📧 cial@golfplatjadepals.com
- 🖊 Alexandra Reig (Mgr)
- ▷ 18 Par 73 SSS 72
  White L 6222 m CR 72.0 SR 127
  Yellow L 5950 m CR 70.5 SR 122
  Blue L 5630 m CR 72.9 SR 123
  Red L 5089 m CR 71.2 SR 120
- 👥 H (36)
- ££ 18: €45 (low season), €50 (mid &
  high season) €68 (weekends)
  9: €35 / €40 / €48
- 🚗 A7 exit 6 Girona Nord. Follow
  Bisbap-Palamós route. 6 km past la
  Bisbal to Torrent-Pals roundabout
- 🏠 FW Hawtree
- ■ www.golfplatjadepals.com

Real Cerdaña   (1929)
Apdo 63, Puigcerdá, (Gerona)
- ☎ (972) 88 13 38
- ▷ 18 L 5735 m SSS 70
- 🚗 Cerdaña, 1km from Puigcerdá
- 🏠 Javier Arana

Real Golf El Prat   (1956)
- 🚗 The club is moving to a new site
  in Terrassa (Barcelona) in 2004
  Please see website for details
- ■ www.realclubdegolfelprat.com

Reus Aiguesverds   (1989)
Crta Cambrils, Mas Guardiá,
43206 Reus
- ☎ (977) 75 27 25
- 📞 (977) 75 19 38
- ▷ 18 L 6905 yds SSS 72
- 👥 U
- ££ €42
- 🚗 10km W of Tarragona. 100km S of
  Barcelona

Sant Cugat   (1914)
08190 Sant Cugat del Valles
- ☎ (93) 674 39 08/674 39 58
- ▷ 18 L 5209 m SSS 68
- 🚗 20km NW of Barcelona

Sant Jordi
Urb Sant Jordi d'Alfama, 43860 Ametlla
de Mar, (Tarragona)
- ☎ (977) 49 34 57
- 📞 (977) 49 32 77
- ▷ 9 L 5696 m SSS 70
- 👥 U H
- 🚗 50km S of Tarragona
- 🏠 Lauresno Nomen

Terramar   (1922)
Apdo 6, 08870 Sitges
- ☎ (93) 894 05 80/894 20 43
- 📞 (93) 894 70 51
- ▷ 18 L 5878 m Par 72
- 👥 H
- ££ €42 (€66)
- 🚗 Sitges, 37km S of Barcelona
- 🏠 Hawtree/Piñero/Fazio

Torremirona   (1994)
Ctra N260 Km46, 17744
Navata (Girona)
- ☎ (972) 55 37 37
- 📞 (972) 55 37 16
- ▷ 18 L 6184 m Par 72
- 👥 U
- ££ €47 (€63)
- 🚗 30km from Girona. A7 Junction 4
- 🏠 Joan Anglada

Vallromanes   (1972)
C/Afveras, 08188
Vallromanes, (Barcelona)
- ☎ (93) 572 90 64
- 📞 (93) 572 93 30
- ▷ 18 L 6038 m Par 72
- 👥 H
- 🚗 23km N of Barcelona between
  Alella and Granollers. A7 Junct 13
- 🏠 FW Hawtree

Burgos & North

Barganiza   (1982)
Apartado 277, 33080 Oviedo, Asturias
- ☎ (985) 74 24 68
- ▷ 18 L 5549 m SSS 70
- 🚗 12km N of Oviedo on Gijon old
  road
- 🏠 Victor García

Castillo de Gorraiz   (1993)
Urb Castillo de Gorraiz, 31620 Valle de
Egues (Navarra)
- ☎ (948) 33 70 73
- 📞 (948) 33 73 15
- 📧 administracion@golfgorraiz.com
- ▷ 18 L 6321 m CR 73.1 SR 130
- 👥 U
- ££ €47 (€50 inc public hols)
- 🚗 4km from Pamplona, 5 min from
  Pamplona
- 🏠 Cabell B Robinson
- ■ www.golfgorraiz.com

La Cuesta
Apdo 40, 33500 Llanes
- ☎ (98) 541 7084
- 📞 (98) 540 1973
- ▷ 9 L 5456 m SSS 69
- 👥 U
- 🚗 3km from Llanes (N-634)

Izki Golf   (1992)
01119 Urturi (Alava)
- ☎ (945) 37 82 62
- 📞 (945) 37 82 66
- ▷ 18 L 6576 m Par 73
- 👥 U
- ££ €40
- 🚗 Urturi, 39km from Vitoria
- 🏠 Severiano Ballesteros

Larrabea   (1989)
Crta de Landa, 01170 Legutiano, (Alava)
- ☎ (945) 46 58 44/46 58 41
- 📞 (945) 46 57 25
- ▷ 18 L 5991 m Par 72
- 👥 U
- ££ €30 (€36)
- 🚗 14km N of Vitoria, nr Villareal de
  Alava
- 🏠 José Gancedo

Laukariz   (1976)
Laukariz-Munguía, (Viscaya)
- ☎ (94) 674 08 58/674 04 62
- ▷ 18 L 6112 m SSS 72
- 👥 U
- 🚗 15km N of Bilbao towards Mungía
- 🏠 RD Putman

Lerma   (1991)
Ctra Madrid-Burgos Km195, 09340
Lerma (Burgos)
- ☎ (947) 17 12 14/17 12 16
- 📞 (947) 17 12 16
- 📧 golflerma@csa.es
- ▷ 18 L 6235 m SSS 72
- 👥 H
- ££ €37 (€50)
- 🚗 30km S of Burgos, nr Villa Ducal
  de Lerma – 196km
- 🏠 Pepe Gancedo

La Llorea   (1994)
Crta Nacional 632, Km 62, 33394
Lloreda (Gijón)
- ☎ (985) 18 10 30
- 📞 (985) 36 47 26

18 L 5971 m Par 72
H
£€ €34.80 (€41.10)
⊕ 10km E of Gijón
⌂ Roland Fabret
■ www.golflallorea.com

Real Golf Castiello (1958)
Apdo Correos 161, 33200 Gijón
☎ (985) 36 63 13
⌨ (985) 13 18 00
18 L 4817 m Par 70
WE–restricted
£€ €48
⊕ 5km S of Gijón

Real Golf Neguri (1911)
Apdo Correos 9, 48990 Algorta
☎ (94) 469 02 00/04/08
18 L 6319 m SSS 72
6 hole Par 3 course
⊕ La Galea, 20km N of Bilbao
⌂ Javier Arana

Real Golf Pedreña (1928)
Apartado 233, Santander
☎ (942) 50 00 01/50 02 66
⌨ (942) 50 04 21
18 L 5745 m SSS 70
9 L 2740 m SSS 36
H
£€ €34 (€54)
⊕ 20km from Santander, on Bay of Santander
⌂ Colt/Ballesteros

Real San Sebastián (1910)
PO Box 6, Fuenterrabia, (Guipúzcoa)
☎ (943) 61 68 45/61 68 46
⌨ (943) 61 14 91
18 L 6020 m SSS 71
WD–U H from 9–12 noon WE–NA
£€ €60–€90
⊕ Jaizubia Valley, 14km NE of San Sebastián
⌂ P Hirigoyen

Real Zarauz (1916)
Apartado 82, Zarauz, (Guipúzcoa)
☎ (943) 83 01 45
9 L 5184 m SSS 68
⊕ Zarauz, 25km W of San Sebastián

Ulzama (1965)
31779 Guerendiain (Navarra)
☎ (948) 30 51 62
⌨ (948) 30 54 71
18 L 6246 m Par 72
U
£€ On application
⊕ 20km N of Pamplona
⌂ Javier Arana

Canary Islands

Amarilla (1988)
Urb Amarilla Golf, San Miguel de Abona, 38630 Santa Cruz de Tenerife
☎ (922) 73 03 19

⌨ (922) 73 00 85
18 L 6077 m Par 72
H
£€ €60
⊕ 6km SW of South Airport. 12km from Playa de las Americas
⌂ Donald Steel

Costa Teguise (1978)
Apdo 170, 35080 Arrecife de Lanzarote
☎ (928) 59 05 12
⌨ (928) 59 04 90
18 L 5853 m SSS 72
U
£€ Summer €33 Winter €42
⊕ 4km N of Arrecife
⌂ John Harris

Maspalomas (1968)
Av de Neckerman, Maspalomas, 35100 Gran Canaria
☎ (928) 76 25 81/76 73 43
⌨ (928) 76 82 45
18 L 6216 m SSS 72
H
£€ €36–€72
⊕ Maspalomas, S coast of Gran Canaria
⌂ Mackenzie Ross
■ www.maspalomasgolf.net

Real Club de Golf de Tenerife (1932)
Campo de Golf No.1 38350, Tacoronte, Tenerife
☎ (922) 63 66 07
⌨ (922) 63 64 80
✉ director.golf@interbook.net
18 L 5750 m Par 71
WD except hols 8–12.30 H (24 men; 28 ladies)
£€ €75
⊕ 20km N of Santa Cruz. Puerto Cruz 15km
⌂ J Laynez and others
■ www.realgolfdetenerife.com (Spanish only)

Real Golf Las Palmas (1891)
PO Box 93, 35380 Santa Brigida, Gran Canaria
☎ (928) 35 10 50/35 01 04
⌨ (928) 35 01 10
18 L 5690 m SSS 71
WD–U WE–NA
£€ €48–€73
⊕ Bandama, Las Palmas 14km
⌂ Mackenzie Ross

Golf del Sur (1987)
San Miguel de Abona, 38620 Tenerife (Canarias)
☎ (922) 73 81 70
⌨ (922) 78 82 72
North 9 L 2913 m SSS 36
Links 9 L 2469 m SSS 34
South 9 L 2957 m SSS 36
H
£€ €67

⊕ Airport 3km. Playa de las Américas 12km
⌂ Pepe Gancedo
■ www.golfdelsur.net

Cordoba

Córdoba (1976)
Apartado 436, 14080 Córdoba
☎ (957) 35 02 08
18 L 5964 m Par 72 SSS 73
U
⊕ 9km N of Córdoba, towards Obejo

Pozoblanco (1984)
Apdo 118, 14400 Pozoblanco, (Córdoba)
☎ (957) 33 91 71
⌨ (957) 33 91 71
9 L 3020 m Par 72
U
⊕ Pozoblanco 3km
⌂ Carlos Luca

Galicia

Aero Club de Santiago (1976)
General Pardiñas 34, Santiago de Compostela (La Coruña)
☎ (981) 59 24 00
9 L 5816 m SSS 70
⊕ Santiago Airport

Aero Club de Vigo (1951)
Reconquista 7, 36201 Vigo
☎ (986) 48 66 45/48 75 09
9 L 5622 m SSS 60
⊕ Peinador Airport, 8km from Vigo

Domaio (1993)
San Lorenzo-Domaio, 36950 Moaña (Pontevedra)
☎ (986) 32 70 50
18 L 6110 m Par 72 SSS 73
U
⌂ Ramón Espinosa

La Toja (1970)
Isla de La Toja, El Grove, Pontevedra
☎ (986) 73 01 58/73 08 18
⌨ (986) 73 31 22
9 L 5178 m SSS 72
H
£€ €36–€57
⊕ La Toja island. 30km W of Pontevedra
⌂ Ramón Espinosa

Granada

Granada
Avda de los Corsarios, 18110 Las Gabias (Granada)
☎ (958) 58 44 36

18 L 6037 m Par 71 SSS 73
U
Las Gabias, 8km from Granada
Ramón Espinosa

Madrid Region

Barberán (1967)
Apartado 150.239, Cuatro Vientos,
28080 Madrid
☎ (91) 509 00 59/509 11 40
🖳 (91) 706 2174
📴 9 L 6042 m SSS 72
M H
10km SW of Madrid

La Dehesa (1991)
Calle Real 19, 28691 Villanueva
La Canada
☎ (91) 815 70 22/815 70 37
🖳 (91) 815 54 68
📴 18 L 6456 m SSS 72
35km NW of Madrid
Manuel Piñero

Herreria (1966)
PO Box 28200, San Lorenzo del
Escorial, (Madrid)
☎ (91) 890 51 11
📴 18 L 6050 m SSS 72
Escorial, 50km W of Madrid
Antonio Lucena

Jarama R.A.C.E. (1967)
Urb Ciudalcampo, 28707 San Sebastian
de los Reyes, (Madrid)
☎ (91) 657 00 01
🖳 (91) 657 04 62
📴 18 L 6505 m Par 72
9 hole Par 3 course
28km N of Madrid on Burgos road
Javier Arana

Lomas-Bosque (1973)
Urb El Bosque, 28670 Villaviciosa de
Odón, (Madrid)
☎ (91) 616 75 00
🖳 (91) 616 73 93
📴 18 L 6075 m SSS 72
9 hole Par 3 course
WD–U H WE–M H
€€ €25–€78
20km SW of Madrid
RD Putman

La Moraleja (1976)
La Moraleja, Alcobendas (Madrid)
☎ (91) 650 07 00
📴 18 L 6016 m SSS 72
M
9km N of Madrid on Burgos road
Jack Nicklaus

Nuevo De Madrid (1972)
Las Matas (Madrid)
☎ (91) 630 08 20
📴 18 L 5647 m SSS 70

U H
25km NW of Madrid on La Coruña
road

Olivar de la Hinojosa (1995)
Avda de Dublin, Campo de las Naciones,
28042 Madrid
☎ (91) 721 18 89
📴 18 L 6163 m Par 72 SSS 72
U
Nr Madrid Airport M40

Puerta de Hierro (1896)
Avda de Miraflores, Ciudad Puerta de
Hierro, 28035 Madrid
☎ (91) 316 1745
🖳 (91) 373 8111
📴 High 18 L 6375 m CR 72.5 SR 124
   Low 18 L 6504 m CR 73.9 SR 130
M only
€€ €78 (€162)
4km N of Madrid (Route VI)
Harris/Simpson/Trent Jones

Los Retamares (1991)
Crta Algete-Alalpardo Km 2300, 28130
Valdeolmos (Madrid)
☎ (91) 620 25 40
📴 18 L 6238 m Par 72 SSS 73
9 hole Par 3 course
U
25km N of Madrid via N-1

Somosaguas (1971)
Avda de la Cabaña, 28223 Pozuelo de
Alarcón, (Madrid)
☎ (91) 352 16 47
🖳 (91) 352 00 30
📴 9 L 6054 m Par 72
Somosaguas
John Harris

Valdeláguila (1975)
Apdo 9, Alcalá de Henares, (Madrid)
☎ (91) 885 96 59
🖳 (91) 885 96 59
📴 9 L 5724 m Par 72
WD–U WE–NA
Villalbilla, 10km S of Alcalá

Villa de Madrid CC (1932)
Crta Castilla, 28040 Madrid
☎ (91) 357 21 32
🖳 (91) 549 07 97
📴 27 L 5900-6321 m SSS 73-74
U H
€€ €40 (€77)
4km NW of Madrid, in the Casa del
Campo
Javier Arana

Malaga Region

Alhaurín (1994)
Crta 426 Km15, Alhaurín el Grande
☎ (952) 59 59 70
🖳 (952) 59 45 86

18 L 6221 m Par 72
18 hole Par 3 course
9 hole Par 3 course
U
€€ €36
6km from Mijas
Severiano Ballesteros

Añoreta (1989)
Avenida del Golf, 29730 Rincón de la
Victoria, (Málaga)
☎ (952) 40 40 00
🖳 (952) 40 40 50
📴 18 L 5976 m SSS 71
U
€€ €15 (€18)
12km E of Málaga
JM Canizares

La Cala Resort (1991)
La Cala de Mijas, 29649 Mijas-
Costa (Málaga)
☎ (952) 66 90 00, (952) 66 90 33
🖳 (952) 66 90 34
📴 North 18 L 6187 m Par 73
   South 18 L 5966 m Par 72
6 hole Par 3 course
U H
€€ €66
6km from Cala de Mijas, between
Fuengirola and Marbella
Cabell B Robinson
◼ www.lacala.com

El Candado (1965)
Urb El Candado, El Palo, 29018 Málaga
☎ (952) 29 93 40/1
📴 9 L 4676 m SSS 66
El Palo, 5km E of Málaga on Route
N340
Carlos Fernández

El Chaparral
Urb El Chaparral, Mijas-Costa
☎ (952) 49 38 00
🖳 (952) 49 40 51
📴 18 L 5700 m SSS 71
U H
5km W of Fuengirola on N340
Pepe Gancedo

Guadalhorce (1988)
Crtra de Cártama Km7, Apartado 48,
29590 Campanillas (Málaga)
☎ (952) 17 93 78
🖳 (952) 17 93 72
📴 18 L 6194 m SSS 72
9 hole Par 3 course
WD–H before 1pm (booking
necessary) WE–M
€€ €24–€30
8km W of Málaga
Kosti Kuronen

Lauro (1992)
Los Caracolillos, 29130 Alhaurín de la
Torre, (Málaga)
☎ (95) 241 27 67
🖳 (95) 241 47 57
📴 27 L 6067 m Slope 135

U
£€ €50
⬥ Drive west from Málaga airport.
Take exit 'Coín' onto A-366
towards 'Alhourin el Grande,
Coín'. Lauro Golf is 77km
⛳ Folco Nardi, Mariano Benitee
■ www.laurogolf.com

Málaga Club de Campo
(1925)

Parador de Golf, Apdo 324,
29080 Málaga
☎ (952) 38 12 55
⬛ (952) 38 21 41
▷ 18 L 6249 m SSS 72
👥 U
⬥ Torremolinos 4km. 12km S of
Málaga, nr Airport
⛳ Tom Simpson

Mijas (1976)

Apartado 145, Fuengirola, Málaga
☎ (952) 47 68 43
⬛ (952) 46 79 43
▷ Lagos 18 L 6548 m Par 71 SSS 74;
Olivos 18 L 6009 m Par 72 SSS 72
👥 H–booking required Oct–Apr
£€ €37
⬥ 4km NW of Fuengirola (Mijas
Valley)
⛳ Robert Trent Jones

Miraflores (1989)

Urb Riviera del Sol, 29647 Mijas-Costa
☎ (952) 93 19 60
⬛ (952) 93 19 42
▷ 18 L 5113 m SSS 71
👥 U H
£€ €59
⬥ 15km E of Marbella
⛳ Folco Nardi

Los Moriscos (1974)

Costa Granada, Motril (Granada)
☎ (958) 82 55 27
⬛ (958) 25 52 51
▷ 9 L 5689 m SSS 72 Par 70
👥 U
⬥ 8km W of Motril, nr Salobrena.
80km E of Málaga
⛳ Ibergolf

Torrequebrada (1976)

Public
Apdo 120, Crta de Cadiz Km 220,
29630 Benalmadena
☎ (95) 244 27 42
⬛ (95) 256 11 29
✉ torrequebrada@grn.es
▷ 18 L 5806 m Par 72 SSS 71
👥 H (men 27, ladies 35 max)
£€ €90
⬥ Benalmadena, 25km S of Málaga
Airport
⛳ Pepe Gancedo
■ www.golftorrequebrada.com

Marbella &
Estepona

Alcaidesa Links (1992)

CN-340 Km124.6, 11315 La
Linea (Cádiz)
☎ (956) 79 10 40
⬛ (956) 79 10 41
▷ 18 L 5766 m Par 72 SSS 71
👥 U–booking advised
£€ €54
⬥ 15km E of Gibraltar. San Roque
3km
⛳ Alliss/Clark

Aloha (1975)

Nueva Andalucía, 29660 Marbella
☎ (952) 81 37 50/90 70 85/86,
(952) 81 23 88 (Caddymaster)
⬛ (952) 81 23 89
▷ 18 L 6261 m SSS 72
9 hole short course
👥 H–booking necessary
£€ €108
⬥ 8km W of Marbella, nr Puerto
Banus
⛳ Javier Arana

Los Arqueros (1991)

Crta de Ronda Km43, 29679
Benahavis (Málaga)
☎ (952) 78 46 00
⬛ (952) 78 67 07
▷ 18 L 6130 m SSS 72
👥 H
£€ €27
⬥ 5km N of San Pedro de Alcántara
⛳ Severiano Ballesteros

Atalaya G&CC (1968)

Crta Benahavis 7, 29688 Málaga
☎ (952) 88 28 12
⬛ (952) 88 78 97
▷ 18 L 5856 m Par 72
18 L 5217 m Par 72
👥 U H
£€ On application
⬥ 12km S of Marbella. 60km SW of
Málaga
⛳ Von Limburger/Krings

Las Brisas (1968)

Apdo 147, 29660 Nueva
Andalucía, (Málaga)
☎ (952) 81 08 75/81 30 21
⬛ (952) 81 55 18
▷ 18 L 6094 m SSS 72
👥 H–restricted
£€ €120
⬥ 8km S of Marbella, nr Puerto Banus
⛳ Robert Trent Jones

La Cañada (1982)

Ctra Guadiaro Km 1, 11311
Guadiaro (Cádiz)
☎ (956) 79 41 00
⬛ (956) 79 42 41
▷ 18 L 5235 m SSS 71
👥 U

⬥ Guadiaro, 1km from Sotogrande
⛳ Dave Thomas 1st 9, Robert Trent
Jones 2ne 9

La Duquesa G&CC (1987)

Urb El Hacho, 29691 Manilva (Málaga)
☎ (952) 89 04 25/89 04 26
⬛ (952) 89 00 57
▷ 18 L 6142 m SSS 72
👥 U
⬥ 10km S of Estepona
⛳ Robert Trent Jones

Estepona (1989)

Arroyo Vaquero, Apartado 532, 29680
Estepona (Málaga)
☎ (952) 11 30 81
⬛ (952) 11 30 80
▷ 18 L 5610 m Par 72 SSS 70
👥 U
£€ €55
⬥ 5km W of Estepona (CN340)
⛳ Luis López
■ www.esteponagolf.com

Guadalmina (1959)

Guadalmina Alta, San Pedro de
Alcántara, 29678 Marbella (Málaga)
☎ (952) 88 65 22
⬛ (952) 88 34 83
▷ North 18 L 5825 m SSS 70
South 18 L 6075 m SSS 72
9 hole Par 3 course
👥 H (max 27M/35L)
£€ €45
⬥ San Pedro, 12km W of Marbella
⛳ Arana/Nardi

Marbella (1994)

CN 340 Km 188, 29600
Marbella (Málaga)
☎ (952) 83 05 00
▷ 18 L 5864 m Par 71 SSS 72
👥 U
⬥ Marbella
⛳ Robert Trent Jones

Monte Mayor (1989)

PO Box 962, 29679 Benahavis (Málaga)
☎ (+34) 95 293 7111
⬛ (+35) 95 293 7112
▷ 18 L 5652 m Par 71 SSS 71
👥 H
£€ €90 high season, €70 mid season
€50 low season
⬥ Exit on N340 at km 165.5
Cancelada
⛳ Jose Gancedo

Los Naranjos (1977)

Apdo 64, 29660 Nueva
Andalucía, Marbella
☎ (952) 81 52 06/81 24 28
⬛ (952) 81 14 28
▷ 18 L 6484 m SSS 72
👥 U H
⬥ 8km S of Marbella, nr Puerto Banus
⛳ Robert Trent Jones Sr

El Paraiso (1974)

Ctra Cádiz-Málaga Km 167, 29680
Estepona (Málaga)
☎ **(95) 288 38 35/288 38 46**
🖥 (95) 288 58 27
🏱 18 L 6116 m SSS 72
👥 U
££ €65
🕰 14km S of Marbella
🏠 Player/Kirby

La Quinta G&CC (1989)

Urb La Quinta, 29660 Nueva Andalucía
☎ **(952) 76 23 90**
🖥 (952) 76 23 99
🖂 depcom@laquintagolf.com
🏱 27 L 5797-5945 m SSS 71-72
👥 U H
££ €72
🕰 3km N of San Pedro de Alcántara
🏠 Piñero/García-Garrido
■ www.laquintagolf.com

Rio Real (1965)

Urb Rio Real, PO Box 82, 29600
Marbella (Málaga)
☎ **(95) 277 95 09**
🖥 (95) 277 21 40
🏱 18 L 6130 m SSS 72
👥 U
🕰 5km E of Marbella. Málaga Airport
　　50km
🏠 Javier Arana

San Roque (1990)

CN 340 Km 126, San Roque,
11360 Cádiz
☎ **(956) 61 30 30/60/90**
🖥 (956) 61 30 12/61 30 13
🏱 18 L 6440 m SSS 74
👥 U H
££ €42
🕰 3km W of Sotogrande. 15km E of
　　Gibraltar
🏠 Dave Thomas
■ www.sanroque.com

Santa María G&CC

Urb. Elviria, Crta N340 Km 192, 29600
Marbella (Málaga)
☎ **(952) 83 03 86/83 03 88/83 10 36**
🖥 (952) 83 08 70 / 83 47 97
🏱 18 L 5586 m Par 70
👥 U
🕰 10km E of Marbella, opp Hotel
　　Don Carlos
🏠 A García Garrido (1st 9 holes),
　　Santa Maria's Technical Team (2nd
　　9 holes)

Sotogrande (1964)

Paseo del Parque, Apartado 14,
Sotogrande (Cádiz)
☎ **(956) 79 50 50/79 50 51**
🖥 (956) 79 50 29
🏱 18 L 6224 m SSS 74
　　9 L 1299 m Par 29
👥 U
🕰 30km N of Gibraltar, nr Guadiaro
🏠 Robert Trent Jones

Valderrama (1985)

Avenida de los Cortjos S/N, 11310
Sotogrande (Cadiz)
☎ **(956) 79 12 00**
🖥 (956) 79 60 28
🏱 18 L 6952 yds Par 71 SSS 72 CR
　　76.0 SR 146
　　9 hole Par 3 course
👥 H–12–2pm
££ €250 (€275)
🕰 18km N of Gibraltar
🏠 Robert Trent Jones Sr
■ www.valderrama.com

La Zagaleta (1994)

Crta San Pedro-Ronda Km 9,
29679 Benahavis
☎ **(95) 285 54 53**
🏱 18 L 6039 m Par 72 SSS 72
👥 U
🕰 S of Marbella on Ronda road
🏠 Bradford Benz

Seville & Gulf of Cádiz

Bellavista (1976)

Crta Huelva-Punta Umbría, Apdo
335, Huelva
☎ **(955) 31 90 17**
🖥 (955) 31 90 25
🏱 9 L 6270 m SSS 73
👥 U
🕰 Aljaraque, 6km SW of Huelva,
　　towards Punta Umbria

Costa Ballena (1997)

Crta Sta Maria-Chipiona, 11520 Rota
☎ **(956) 84 70 70**
🏱 18 L 6187 m Par 72 SSS 72
👥 U
🏠 J-M Olazábal

Isla Canela (1993)

Crta de la Playa, 21400
Ayamonte (Huelva)
☎ **(959) 47 72 63**
🖥 (959) 47 72 71
🏱 18 L 5937 m Par 72
👥 U H
££ €42
🕰 Ayamonte, 4km from Portuguese
　　border
🏠 Juan Caterineu

Islantilla (1993)

Urb Islantilla, Apdo 52, 21410 Isla
Cristina (Huelva)
☎ **(959) 48 60 39/48 60 49**
🖥 (959) 48 61 04
🏱 27 L 5926-6142 m SSS 72-73
👥 U H
££ €51
🕰 30km W of Huelva, nr Portuguese
　　border
🏠 Canales/Recasens

Montecastillo (1992)

Carretera de Arcos, 11406 Jérez
☎ **(956) 15 12 00**
🖥 (956) 15 12 09
🏱 18 L 6494 m SSS 72
👥 H
££ €90
🕰 10km NE of Jérez. 75km S of
　　Seville
🏠 Jack Nicklaus

Montenmedio G&CC (1996)

CN 340 Km42.5, 11150 Vejer-
Barbate (Cádiz)
☎ **(956) 45 12 16**
🖥 (956) 45 12 95
🏱 18 L 5897 m Par 72 SSS 72
👥 H
££ €75
🕰 Cádiz-Algeciras road (CN 340)
🏠 A Maldonado
■ www.monteenmedio.com

Novo Sancti Petri (1990)

Urb Novo Sancti Petri, Playa de la
Barrosa, 11139 Chiclana de la Frontera
☎ **(956) 49 40 05**
🖥 (956) 49 43 50
🏱 18 L 6071 m Par 72
　　18 L 6476 m Par 72
👥 U H
££ €58
🕰 La Barrosa, 24km SE of Cádiz.
　　Jérez Airport 50km
🏠 Severiano Ballesteros
■ www.golf-novosancti.es

Pineda De Sevilla (1939)

Apartado 1049, 41080 Sevilla
☎ **(954) 61 14 00**
🏱 18 L 6120 m SSS 72
👥 U
🕰 3km S of Seville on Cádiz road
🏠 R & F Medina

Real Sevilla (1992)

Autovía Sevilla-Utrera, 41089
Montequinto (Sevilla)
☎ **(954) 12 43 01**
🖥 (954) 12 42 29
🏱 18 L 6321 m SSS 73
👥 U H WE–booking necessary
££ €39
🕰 3km S of Seville
🏠 José María Olazabal
■ www.sevillagolf.com

Sevilla Golf (1989)

Hacienda Las Minas, Ctra de Isla
Mayor, Aznalcazar (Sevilla)
☎ **(955) 75 04 14**
🏱 9 L 5910 m Par 71
👥 U
🕰 15km W of Seville
🏠 A García Garrido

Vista Hermosa (1975)

Apartado 77, Urb Vista Hermosa, 11500
Puerto de Santa María, Cádiz
☎ **(956) 87 56 05**

▷ 9 L 5614 m Par 70
⮀ 25km W of Cádiz

Zaudin
Crta Tomares-Mairena, 41940
Tomares (Sevilla)
☎ **(954) 15 41 59,**
  (954) 15 25 52 (reservations)
⌨ (954) 15 33 44
▷ 18 L 6192 m Par 71 SSS 72
👤 U
£€ €46 (€66) Jan–Sep Dec €55.20
  (€78) Oct–Nov
⮀ Cornisa del Aljarafe, 3km from
  Seville
🏠 Gary Player

Valencia & Castellón

El Bosque (1989)
Crta Godelleta, 46370 Chiva-Valencia
☎ **(96) 180 41 42**
⌨ (96) 180 40 09
▷ 18 L 6384 m SSS 74
👤 U
⮀ Nr Chiva, 24km W of Valencia, off
  Madrid road
🏠 Robert Trent Jones Sr

Costa de Azahar (1960)
Ctra Grao-Benicasim, Castellón de
la Plana
☎ **(964) 22 70 64**
▷ 9 L 2724 m SSS 70
⮀ 5km NE of Castellón, on coast
🏠 Angel Pérez

Escorpión (1975)
Apartado Correos 1, Betera (Valencia)
☎ **(96) 160 12 11**
⌨ (96) 169 01 87
▷ 27 L 6081-6383 m Par 71-73
👤 WD–H
£€ €60
⮀ Betera, 20km N of Valencia
🏠 Kirby/Vidaor

Manises (1964)
Apartado 22.029, Manises (Valencia)
☎ **(96) 152 18 71**
▷ 9 L 6094 m Par 73
⮀ 8km W of Valencia
🏠 Javier Arana

Mediterraneo CC (1978)
Urb La Coma, 12190
Borriol, (Castellón)
☎ **(964) 32 12 27**
⌨ (964) 65 77 34
✉ club@ccmediterraneo.com
▷ 18 L 6227 m Par 72
👤 H
£€ €42 (€48)
⮀ Borriol, 4km NW of Castellón
🏠 Ramón Espinosa
■ www.ccmediterraneo.com

Oliva Nova (1995)
46780 Oliva (Valencia)
☎ **(096) 285 76 66**
⌨ (096) 285 76 67
▷ 18 L 6270m Par 72
  5 hole Par 3 course
👤 H
£€ €65
⮀ 15km N of Denia on N332. A7
  Junction 61
🏠 Severiano Ballesteros
■ www.olivanovagolf.com

Panorámica (1995)
Urb Panorámica, 12320 San
Jorge (Castellón)
☎ **(964) 49 30 72**
▷ 18 L 6429 m Par 72 SSS 74
👤 U
⮀ A7 Junction 42 towards Vinaroz
🏠 Bernhardt Langer

El Saler (1968)
Parador Luis Vives, 46012 El
Saler (Valencia)
☎ **(96) 161 11 86**
⌨ (96) 162 70 16
▷ 18 L 6485 m SSS 75
👤 U
⮀ Oliva, 18km S of Valencia, towards
  Cullera
🏠 Javier Arana

Valladolid

Entrepinos (1990)
Avda del Golf 2, Urb Entrepinos, 47130
Simancas (Valladolid)
☎ **(983) 59 05 11/59 05 61**
⌨ (983) 59 07 65
▷ 18 L 5215 m Par 69 SSS 69
👤 U H
£€ €32 (€45)
⮀ 15km SW of Valladolid
🏠 Manuel Piñero

Zaragoza

Aero Club de Zaragoza (1966)
Coso 34, 50004 Zaragoza
☎ **(976) 21 43 78**
▷ 9 L 5042 m SSS 67
⮀ 12km SW of Zaragoza, by airbase

La Penaza (1973)
Apartado 3039, Zaragoza
☎ **(976) 34 28 00/34 22 48**
⌨ (976) 34 28 00
▷ 18 L 6122 m SSS 72
👤 H
⮀ 15km SW of Zaragoza on Madrid
  road, nr airbase
🏠 FW Hawtree

Sweden

East Central

Ängsö (1979)
Björnövägen 2, 721 30 Västerås
☎ **(0171) 441012**
⌨ (0171) 441049
▷ 18 hole course Par 72 SR 130
👤 H
£€ 240kr (340kr)
⮀ 15km E of Västerås
🏠 Åke Hultström
■ www.angsogolf.org

Arboga
PO Box 263, 732 25 Arboga
☎ **(0589) 402 35**
⌨ (0589) 701 90
✉ arbogagk@arbogagk.nu
🔑 Gun Peterson
▷ 18 L 5890 m Par 72
👤 U
£€ 220kr (280kr)
⮀ 5km S of Arboga
🏠 Sune Linde
■ www.arbogagk.nu

Ärila (1951)
Nicolai, 611 92 Nyköping
☎ **(0155) 216617**
⌨ (0155) 267657
▷ 18 L 5826 m Par 72
👤 H
£€ 200kr (270kr)
⮀ 5km SE of Nyköping
🏠 Sköld/Linde

Askersund (1980)
Box 3002, 696 03 Ammeberg
☎ **(0583) 34943**
⌨ (0583) 34945
▷ 18 L 5835 m CR 71.2 SR 133
👤 H
£€ 220kr (280kr)
⮀ 10km SE of Askersund towards
  Ammeberg. 1km on road to Kärra
🏠 Ronald Fream
■ www.golf.se/askersundsgk

Burvik
Burvik, 740 12 Knutby
☎ **(0174) 43060**
⌨ (0174) 43062
✉ info:burvik.se
▷ 18 L 5785 m SSS 72
👤 U
£€ On application
⮀ 45km E of Uppsala. 70km N of
  Stockholm
🏠 Bengt Lorichs
■ www.burvik.se

Edenhof (1991)
740 22 Bälinge
☎ **(018) 334185**
⌨ (018) 334186

☞ 18 L 5898 m SSS 72
※ H
££ 180kr (240kr)
⇔ 17km NW of Uppsala
⋔ Sune Linde

Enköping (1970)

Box 2006, 745 02 Enköping
☎ (0171) 20830
⌨ (0171) 20823
☞ 18 L 5660 m Par 71
※ H
££ 220kr (300kr)
⇔ 1km E of Enköping, off E18
■ www.enkopinggolf.se

Eskilstuna (1951)

Strängnäsvägen, 633 49 Eskilstuna
☎ (016) 142629
⌨ (016) 148729
✉ info@eskilstungagk.golf.se
☞ 18 L 5610 m SSS 70
※ H
££ 220kr (320kr)
⇔ 2km E of Eskilstuna. 20km E of Örebro
⋔ Douglas Brasier

Fagersta (1970)

Box 2051, 737 02 Fagersta
☎ (0223) 54060
⌨ (0223) 54000
☞ 18 L 5775 m Par 71
※ U
££ 140kr (180kr)
⇔ 7km W of Fagersta (Route 65). 70km N of Västerås

Frösåker (1989)

Frösåker Gård, Box 17015, 720 17 Västerås
☎ (021) 25401
⌨ (021) 25485
☞ 18 L 5820 m Par 72
※ U H
££ 200kr (250kr)
⇔ 15km SE of Västerås
⋔ Sune Linde

Fullerö (1988)

Jotsberga, 725 91 Västerås
☎ (021) 50132
⌨ (021) 50431
☞ 18 L 5633 m SSS 71
※ H
££ 200kr (280kr)
⇔ 6km SW of Västerås
⋔ Hultström/Sjöberg
■ www.golf.se/fullerogk

Gripsholm (1991)

Box 133, 647 32 Mariefred
☎ (0159) 350050
⌨ (0159) 350059
☞ 18 L 6203 m Par 73 SR 128
※ H
££ 300kr (400kr)
⇔ Mariefred, 70km SW of Stockholm
⋔ Bengt Lorichs
■ www.golf.se/gripsholmsgk

Grönlund (1989)

PO Box 38, 740 10 Almunge
☎ (0174) 20670
⌨ (0174) 20455
☞ 18 L 5865 m SSS 71
※ H
££ 250kr (340kr)
⇔ 20km E of Uppsala. 25km NE of Arlanda Airport
⋔ Åke Persson

Gustavsvik

Box 22033, 702 02 Örebro
☎ (019) 244486
⌨ (019) 246490
☞ 18 holes SSS 72
※ H
££ 200kr
⇔ 1km S of Örebro
⋔ Turner/Wirhed

Katrineholm (1959)

Jättorp, 641 93 Katrineholm
☎ (0150) 39270
⌨ (0150) 39011
☞ 18 L 5850 m SSS 72
   9 L 2850 m
※ U
££ 250kr (300kr)
⇔ 7km E of Katrineholm
⋔ Skjöld/Lorichs

Köping (1963)

Box 278, 731 26 Köping
☎ (0221) 81090
⌨ (0221) 81277
☞ 18 L 5636 m Par 71
※ U
££ 200kr (250kr)
⇔ 3km N of Köping (E18)
⋔ Brasier/Sederholm

Kumla (1987)

Box 46, 692 21 Kumla
☎ (019) 577370
⌨ (019) 577373
☞ 18 L 5845 m SSS 72
※ U
££ 200kr
⇔ 8km E of Kumla. 20km SE of Örebro
⋔ Jan Sederholm

Linde (1984)

Dalkarlshyttan, 711 31 Lindesberg
☎ (0581) 13960
⌨ (0581) 12936
☞ 18 L 5539 m Par 71
※ H
££ 180kr (180kr)
⇔ 42km N of Örebro on R60. Lindesberg 2km
⋔ Jan Sederholm

Mosjö (1989)

Mosjö Gård, 705 94 Örebrö
☎ (019) 225780
⌨ (019) 225045
☞ 18 L 6160 m Par 72

※ WD–U WE–H
££ 200kr (200kr)
⇔ 10km S of Örebrö
⋔ Åke Persson

Nora (1988)

Box 108, 713 23 Nora
☎ (0587) 311660
⌨ (0587) 15050
☞ 18 L 5865 m Par 72
※ U
££ 200kr (240kr)
⇔ 33km N of Örebro
⋔ Jeremy Turner

Örebro (1939)

Lanna, 719 93 Vintrosa
☎ (019) 291065
⌨ (019) 291055
☞ 18 L 5870 m Par 71
※ H–max 36
££ 260kr (320kr)
⇔ 18km W of Örebro on Route E18
⋔ Sköld/Sundblom/Berglund
■ www.golf.se/golfklubbar/orebrogk

Roslagen

Box 110, 761 22 Norrtälje
☎ (0176) 237194
⌨ (0176) 237103
☞ 18 L 5614 m SSS 72
   9 L 2888 m SSS 36
※ H
££ 18 holes: 250kr (300kr)
   9 holes: 150kr
⇔ 7km N of Norrtälje
⋔ TG Oxenstierna

Sala (1970)

Norby Fallet 100, 733 92 Sala
☎ (0224) 53077/53055/53064
⌨ (0224) 53143
✉ kansli@salagk.nu
☞ 27 L 5895 m SSS 72
※ U
££ 220kr (270kr)
⇔ 11km E of Sala towards Uppsala, Route 67/72
⋔ Tedrup/Linde/Turner

Sigtunabygden (1961)

Box 89, 193 22 Sigtuna
☎ (08) 592 54012
⌨ (08) 592 54167
☞ 18 L 5710 m SSS 72
※ H
££ 300kr (380kr)
⇔ Sigtuna, 50km N of Stockholm
⋔ Nils Sköld

Skepptuna

Skepptuna, 195 93 Märsta
☎ (08) 512 93069
⌨ (08) 512 93163
☞ 18 L 5745 m CR 71.4 SR 131
※ U H
££ 260kr (350kr)
⇔ 50km N of Stockholm, via Route 273
⋔ Jan Sederholm
■ www.skepptunagk.nu

For list of abbreviations and key to symbols see page 627

Södertälje (1952)

Box 9074, 151 09 Södertälje
- ☎ **(08) 550 91995**
- 📠 (08) 550 62549
- ᛒ 18 L 5875 m SSS 72
- ⚇ H WE–NA before 1pm
- ££ 300kr (350kr)
- ⚷ 4km W of Södertälje
- 🛖 Nils Sköld

Strängnäs (1968)

Kilenlundavägen, 645 91 Strängnäs
- ☎ **(0152) 14731**
- 📠 (0152) 14716
- ᛒ 18 L 5625 m SSS 72
- ⚇ H
- ££ 240kr (300kr)
- ⚷ 3km S of Strängnäs
- 🛖 Anders Amilon

Torshälla (1960)

Box 128, 64422 Torshälla
- ☎ **(016) 358722**
- 📠 (016) 357491
- ᛒ 18 L 5934 m Par 72
- ⚇ H
- ££ 200kr (250kr)
- ⚷ 5km N of Eskilstuna
- 🛖 Brasier/Linde

Tortuna

Nicktuna, Tortuna, 725 96 Västerås
- ☎ **(021) 65300**
- 📠 (021) 65302
- ᛒ 18 L 5750 m SSS 72
- ⚇ U
- ££ 150kr (180kr)
- ⚷ 10km N of Västerås
- 🛖 Husell/Hultström

Trosa (1972)

Box 80, 619 22 Trosa
- ☎ **(0156) 22458**
- 📠 (0156) 22454
- ᛒ 18 L 5727 m Par 72
- ⚇ U
- ££ 200kr
- ⚷ 5km W of Trosa, towards Uttervik
- 🛖 P Chamberlain

Upsala (1937)

Håmö Gård, Läby, 755 92 Uppsala
- ☎ **(018) 460120**
- 📠 (018) 461205
- ✉ info@upsalagk.golf.se
- ᛒ 18 L 5818 m SSS 72 CR 72.0
  SR 128
  9 L 2674 m SSS 70 CR 68.1
  SR 112
  9 L 1673 m SSS 58 CR 58.7 SR 96
- ⚇ H
- ££ 300kr (350kr)
- ⚷ 10km W of Uppsala
- 🛖 Greger Paulsson/Peter
  Nordwall/Nils Nyberg/Einar
  Jansson
- ▦ www.upsalagk.com

Vassunda (1989)

Smedby Gård, 741 91 Knivsta
- ☎ **(018) 381230/381235**
- 📠 (018) 381416
- ᛒ 18 L 6141 m Par 72
- ⚇ H
- ££ 240kr (340kr)
- ⚷ 45km N of Stockholm
- 🛖 Sune Linde

Västerås (1931)

Bjärby, 724 81 Västerås
- ☎ **(021) 357543**
- 📠 (021) 357573
- ᛒ 18 L 5250 m SSS 69
- ⚇ U
- ££ 200kr (250kr)
- ⚷ 2km N of Västerås
- 🛖 Nils Sköld

Far North

Boden (1946)

Tallkronsvägen 2, 961 51 Boden
- ☎ **(0921) 72051**
- 📠 (0921) 72047
- ᛒ 18 L 5495 m SSS 72
- ⚇ H
- ££ 250kr
- ⚷ 7km S of Boden
- 🛖 Björn Eriksson

Funäsdalsfjällen (1972)

Box 66, 840 95 Funäsdalen
- ☎ **(0684) 21100**
- 📠 (0684) 21142
- ᛒ 18 L 5300 m SSS 72
- ⚇ U
- ££ 180kr
- ⚷ Funäsdalen, nr Norwegian border
- 🛖 Sköld/Linde

Gällivare-Malmberget (1973)

Box 35, 983 21 Malmberget
- ☎ **(0970) 20770**
- 📠 (0970) 20776
- ᛒ 18 L 5528 m Par 71
- ⚇ H
- ££ 200kr
- ⚷ 4km NW of Gällivare, towards
  Malmberget
- 🛖 Jan Sederholm
- ▦ www.gellivare/forening/golf

Haparanda (1989)

Mattila 140, 953 35 Haparanda
- ☎ **(0922) 10660**
- 📠 (0922) 15040
- ᛒ 18 L 6230 m SSS 73
- ⚇ H
- ££ 250kr
- ⚷ 3kn N or Haparanda
- 🛖 Peter Chamberlain

Härnösand (1957)

Box 52, 871 22 Härnösand
- ☎ **(0611) 67000**
- 📠 (0611) 66165
- ᛒ 18 L 5819 m SSS 72
- ⚇ H
- ££ D–200kr (250kr)
- ⚷ Vägnön, 16km N of Härnösand on
  E4, towards Hemsö Island
- 🛖 Sköld/Turner
- ▦ www.harnosand.gk.just.nu

Kalix (1990)

Box 32, 952 21 Kalix
- ☎ **(0923) 15945/15935**
- 📠 (0923) 77735
- ᛒ 18 L 5700m SSS 71
- ⚇ U
- ££ 160kr
- ⚷ 80km N of Luleå
- 🛖 Jan Sederholm

Luleå (1955)

Golfbaneväg 80, 975 96 Luleå
- ☎ **(0920) 256300**
- 📠 (0920) 256362
- ᛒ 18 L 5675 m Par 72
- ⚇ H
- ££ 250kr (250kr)
- ⚷ Rutvik, 12km E of Luleå
- 🛖 Skjöld/Tideman

Norrmjöle (1992)

905 82 Umeå
- ☎ **(090) 81581**
- 📠 (090) 81565
- ᛒ 18 L 5619 m Par 72
- ⚇ U
- ££ 200kr (220kr)
- ⚷ 19km S of Umeå
- 🛖 Acke Lundgren

Östersund-Frösö (1947)

Kungsgården 205, 832 96 Frösön
- ☎ **(063) 576030**
- 📠 (063) 43765
- ᛒ 18 L 6005 m Par 73
  9 hole Par 3 course
- ⚇ H
- ££ 250kr (270kr)
- ⚷ Island of Frösön, 8km from
  Ostersund
- 🛖 Nils Sköld
- ▦ www.ofg.nu

Öviks GC Puttom (1967)

Ovansjö 1970, 891 95 Arnäsvall
- ☎ **(0660) 254001**
- 📠 (0660) 254040
- ᛒ 18 L 5795 m SSS 72
- ⚇ H
- ££ 180kr
- ⚷ 15km N of Örnsköldsvik on E4
- 🛖 Nils Sköld

Piteå (1960)

Nötöv 119, 941 41 Piteå
- ☎ **(0911) 14990**
- 📠 (0911) 14960
- ᛒ 18 L 5325 m Par 69

H
££ 160kr
⛳ 2km SE of Piteå
🏁 Jan Sederholm

Skellefteå (1967)
Rönnbäcken, 931 92 Skellefteå
☎ (0910) 779333
📠 (0910) 779777
🏳 27 L 6135 m SSS 72
Par 3 course
U H
££ 250kr (300kr)
⛳ Skellefteå 5km
🏁 Sköld/Carlsson/Larsson

Sollefteå (1970)
Box 213, 881 25 Sollefteå
☎ (0620) 21477/12670
📠 (0620) 21477/12670
🏳 18 L 5770 m SSS 72
H
££ 180kr
⛳ Österforse, 15km SW of Sollefteå (Route 89)
🏁 Nils Sköld

Sundsvall (1952)
Golfvägen 5, 862 00 Kvissleby
☎ (060) 561056
📠 (060) 561909
🏳 18 L 5885 m SSS 72
WD–H before noon WE–H after 10am
££ 180kr (200r)
⛳ Skottsund, 15km S of Sundsvall

Timrå
Golfbanevägen 2, 860 32 Fagervik
☎ (060) 570153
📠 (060) 578136
🏳 18 L 5715 m Par 72
H
££ 180kr (200kr)
⛳ 1km S of Sundsvall airport
🏁 Sune Linde

Umeå (1954)
Lövön, 913 35 Holmsund
☎ (090) 41071/41066
📠 (090) 149120
🏳 18 L 5751 m SSS 72
9 L 2688 m SSS 70
U
££ 200kr
⛳ 16km SE of Umeå
🏁 Bo Engdahl

Gothenburg

Albatross (1973)
Lillhagsvägen, 422 50 Hisings-Backa
☎ (031) 551901/550500
📠 (031) 555900
🏳 18 L 6020 m SSS 72
££ 220kr (250kr)
⛳ 10km N of Gothenburg on Hising Island

Chalmers
PO Box 40, 438 21 Landvetter
☎ (031) 918430
📠 (031) 916338
🏳 18 L 5560 m SSS 71
WD–U H before 4pm –M H after 4pm WE–M H before 2pm –U H after 2pm
££ 200kr (200kr)
⛳ 20km E of Gothenburg. 2km from Landvetter airport
🏁 Gyllenhammar/Henrikson

Delsjö (1962)
Kallebäck, 412 76 Göteborg
☎ (031) 406959
📠 (031) 703 0431
🏳 18 L 5703 m Par 71
H WE–NA before 1pm
££ 400kr
⛳ 5km E of Gothenburg (Route 40)
🏁 Douglas Brasier
🖥 www.degk.se

Forsgårdens (1982)
Gamla Forsv 1, 434 47 Kungsbacka
☎ (0300) 566350
📠 (0300) 566351
🏳 18 L 6110 m SSS 72
9 L 2915 m
WD–U WE–NA before 2pm
££ 350kr (400kr)
⛳ 1km SE of Kungsbacka. 20km S of Gothenburg
🏁 Sune Linde
🖥 www.forsgardensgk.org

Göteborg (1902)
Box 2056, 436 02 Hovås
☎ (031) 282444
📠 (031) 685333
🏳 18 L 5935 yds SSS 70
WD–U H–max 28(M) 32 (L) WE–M before 2pm
££ 350kr (400kr)
⛳ 11km S of Gothenburg (Route 158)

Gullbringa (1968)
442 95 Kungälv
☎ (0303) 227161
📠 (0303) 227778
🏳 18 L 5775 m Par 70
U
££ 220kr
⛳ 14km W of Kungälv, towards Marstrand
🏁 Douglas Brasier

Kungälv-Kode
Ö Knaverstad 140, 442 97 Kode
☎ (0303) 51300
📠 (0303) 50205
🏳 18 L 5984 m Par 72
U
££ 200kr
⛳ 30km N of Gothenburg
🏁 Lars Andreasson

Kungsbacka (1971)
Hamra Gård 515, 429 44 Särö
☎ (031) 936277
📠 (031) 935085
🏳 18 L 5855 m SSS 72
9 L 2880 m SSS 36
WD–U WE–NA before 2pm
££ 250kr (300kr)
⛳ 7km N of Kungsbacka on Route 158
🏁 Pennink/Davidsson/Nordström

Lysegården (1966)
Box 532, 442 15 Kungälv
☎ (0303) 223426
📠 (0303) 223075
🏳 18 L 5670 m SSS 71
9 L 5444 m SSS 70
H
££ 200kr
⛳ 10km N of Kungälv
🏁 Röhss/Engström

Mölndals (1979)
Box 77, 437 21 Lindome
☎ (031) 993030
📠 (031) 994901
🏳 18 L 5625 m SSS 73
H WE–NA before 11am
££ 270kr (320kr)
⛳ Lindome, 20km S of Gothenburg
🏁 Ronald Fream
🖥 www.molndalsgk.se

Öijared (1958)
Pl 1082, 448 92 Floda
☎ (0302) 30604
📠 (0302) 35370
🏳 18 L 5875 m Par 72
18 L 5655 m Par 71
H WE–NA before 1pm
££ 250kr (250kr)
⛳ 35km NE of Gothenburg (E20), nr Nääs
🏁 Brasier/Amilon
🖥 www.oijaredgk.o.se

Partille (1986)
Box 234, 433 24 Partille
☎ (031) 987043
📠 (031) 987757
🏳 18 L 5475 m Par 70
WD–H WE–NA before 1pm
££ 220kr (220kr)
⛳ Öjersjö, 10km E of Gothenburg
🏁 Jan Sederholm
🖥 www.golf.se/partillegk

Sjögärde
430 30 Frillesås
☎ (0340) 657860
📠 (0340) 657861
🏳 18 L 5723 m SSS 72
6 hole short course
H
££ 220kr (250kr)
⛳ 20km S of Kungsbacka
🏁 Lars Andreasson

Stenungsund (1993)
Lundby Pl 7480, 444 93 Spekeröd
- ☎ **(0303) 778470**
- 📠 (0303) 778350
- ⊳ 18 L 6245 m Par 72
- 👥 WD–H WE–NA 10–12
- ££ 240kr (300kr)
- 🚗 40km N of Gothenburg
- 👤 Peter Nordwall
- ■ www.golf.se/golfklubbar
  /stenungsundgk

Stora Lundby (1983)
Valters Väg 2, 443 71 Grabo
- ☎ **(0302) 44200**
- 📠 (0302) 44125
- ⊳ 18 L 6040 m Par 72
- 9 hole Par 3 course
- 👥 H
- ££ 180kr (220kr)
- 🚗 25km NE of Gothenburg
- 👤 Frank Pennink
- ■ www.storalundbygk.o.se

Malmö & South Coast

Abbekas (1989)
Kroppsmarksvagen, 274 56 Abbekas
- ☎ **(0411) 533233**
- 📠 (0411) 533419
- ⊳ 18 L 5817 m Par 72
- 👥 U H
- ££ 220kr (260kr)
- 🚗 20km W of Ystad
- 👤 Tommy Nordström

Barsebäck G&CC (1969)
246 55 Löddeköpinge
- ☎ **(046) 776230**
- 📠 (046) 772630
- ⊳ Old 18 L 5910 m Par 72
- New 18 L 6025 m Par 72
- 👥 WD–H booking necessary
- ££ D–360kr
- 🚗 35km N of Malmö
- 👤 Bruce/Steel

Bokskogen (1963)
Torupsvägen 408-140, 230 40 Bara
- ☎ **(040) 406900**
- 📠 (040) 406929
- ⊳ Old 18 L 6054 m Par 72
- New 18 L 5552 m Par 71
- 👥 H WE–after 1pm Old course
- ££ 400kr (400kr)
- 🚗 15km SE of Malmö, off E65
- 👤 Amilon/Sederholm/Lorichs/Brasier/
  Pennink/Nyquist/nordstrøum

Falsterbo (1909)
Fyrvägen, 239 40 Falsterbo
- ☎ **(040) 470078/475078**
- 📠 (040) 472722
- ✉ info@falsterbogk.golf.se
- ⊳ 18 L 6577 yds Par 71 CR 73.2
- SR 129
- 👥 H

Flommens (1935)
239 40 Falsterbo
- ☎ **(040) 475016**
- 📠 (040) 473157
- ⊳ 18 L 5735 m SSS 72
- 👥 U H
- ££ 260kr–320kr
- 🚗 35km SW of Malmö
- 👤 Bergendorff/Kristersson
- ■ www.flommensgk.com

Kävlinge (1989)
Box 138, 244 22 Kävlinge
- ☎ **(046) 736270**
- 📠 (046) 728486
- ⊳ 18 L 5800 m SSS 72
- 👥 H
- ££ 250kr (300kr)
- 🚗 12km N of Lund
- 👤 Rolf Collijn

Ljunghusen (1932)
Kinellsvag, Ljunghusen, 236 42 Höllviken
- ☎ **(040) 450384**
- 📠 (040) 454265
- ⊳ 27 holes:
  L 5455-5895 m SSS 70-73
- 👥 WD–U H WE–M before noon
- ££ 350kr (500kr)
- 🚗 Falsterbo Peninsula. 30km SW of Malmö
- 👤 Douglas Brasier
- ■ www.ljgk.se

Lunds Akademiska (1936)
Kungsmarken, 225 92 Lund
- ☎ **(046) 99005**
- 📠 (046) 99146
- ⊳ 18 L 5780 m
- 👥 H
- ££ 300kr (350kr)
- 🚗 5km E of Lund
- 👤 Boström/Morrison

Malmö
Segesvängen, 212 27 Malmö
- ☎ **(040) 292535/292536**
- 📠 (040) 292228
- ⊳ 18 L 5750 m SSS 71
- 👥 H
- ££ 320kr
- 🚗 NE of Malmö
- 👤 Jan Sederholm
- ■ www.malmogolfklubb.com

Örestad (1986)
Golfvägen, Habo Ljung, 234 22 Lomma
- ☎ **(040) 410580**
- 📠 (040) 416320
- ⊳ 18 L 6036 m Par 73
- 9 L 2923 m Par 35
- 18 hole Par 3 course
- 👥 H
- ££ 250kr (300kr)

Österlen (1945)
Lilla Vik, 272 95 Simrishamn
- ☎ **(0414) 412550**
- 📠 (0414) 412551
- ⊳ 18 L 5835 m CR 69.8
- 18 L 5741 m CR 71.3
- 👥 H
- ££ 300kr
- 🚗 Vik, 8km N of Simrishamn
- 👤 Tommy Nordström
- ■ www.osterlensgk.com

Romeleåsen (1969)
Kvarnbrodda, 240 14 Veberöd
- ☎ **(046) 82012**
- 📠 (046) 82113
- ⊳ 18 L 5783 m Par 72
- 👥 H
- ££ 280kr (350kr)
- 🚗 6km S of Veberöd. 25km E of Malmö
- 👤 Douglas Brasier
- ■ www.golf.romeleasensgk.com

Söderslätts
Ellaboda Grevier 260, 235 94 Vellinge
- ☎ **(040) 429680**
- 📠 (040) 429684
- ⊳ 18 L 5800 m SSS 72
- 9 hole Par 3 course
- 👥 WD–H WE–M H before noon
- ££ 250kr
- 🚗 15km SE of Malmö
- 👤 Sune Linde

Tegelberga (1988)
Alstad Pl 140, 231 96 Trelleborg
- ☎ **(040) 485690**
- 📠 (040) 485691
- ⊳ 27 L 6011 m CR 73.5
- 👥 U H
- ££ 250kr (300kr)
- 🚗 11km N of Trelleborg. 25km E of Malmö
- 👤 Peter Chamberlain
- ■ www.golf.se/tegelbergagk

Tomelilla
Ullstorp, 273 94 Tomelilla
- ☎ **(0417) 13420**
- 📠 (0417) 13657
- ⊳ 18 L 6455 m Par 73 SSS 75
- 👥 H
- ££ 240kr (240kr)
- 🚗 15km N of Ystad. 60km E of Malmö
- 👤 Tommy Nordström
- ■ www.tomelillagolfklubb.com

Trelleborg (1963)
Maglarp, Pl 431, 231 93 Trelleborg
- ☎ **(0410) 330460**
- 📠 (0410) 330281
- ⊳ 18 L 5278 m Par 70
- 👥 U H
- ££ 200kr

D–400kr–500kr
- 🚗 30km SW of Malmö
- 👤 Gunnar Bauer
- ■ www.falsterbogk.com

15km N of Malmö
- 👤 Åke Persson
- ■ www.orestadsgk.com

5km W of Trelleborg
Brasier/Chamberlain
www.trelleborgsgk.com

Vellinge (1991)
Toftadals Gård, 235 41 Vellinge
☎ (040) 443255
📞 (040) 443179
🏌 18 L 5766 m SSS 72
6 hole short course
👥 WD–U WE–U H
££ 200kr (250kr)
🚗 10km SE of Malmö
🏠 Tommy Nordström

Ystad (1930)
Långrevsvägen, 270 22 Köpingebro
☎ (0411) 550350
📞 (0411) 550392
🏌 18 L 5800 m Par 72
👥 U
££ 200kr–250kr
🚗 7km E of Ystad, towards
Simrishamn
🏠 Thure Bruce

North

Alvkarleby
Västanåvägen 5, 814 94 Alvkarleby
☎ (026) 72757
📞 (026) 82307
✉ info@alvkarlebygk.se
🏌 18 L 5420 m Par 70
👥 H
££ £15 (£20)
🚗 25km from Gävle (Route 76)
🏠 Jan Sederholm
www.alvkarlebygk.com

Avesta (1963)
Åsbo, 774 61 Avesta
☎ (0226) 55913/10866/12766
📞 (0226) 12578
🏌 18 L 5560 m SSS 71
👥 H
££ 220kr (280kr)
🚗 3km NE of Avesta
🏠 Sune Linde
www.golf.se/golfklubbar/avestagk

Bollnäs (1963)
Norrfly 4526, 823 91 Kilafors
☎ (0278) 650540
📞 (0278) 651220
✉ info@bollnasgk.com
🏌 18 L 5870 m Par 72
👥 H
££ 200kr (250kr)
🚗 15km S of Bollnäs (Route 83)

Dalsjö (1989)
Dalsjö 3, 781 94 Borlänge
☎ (0243) 220080
📞 (0243) 220140
✉ dgolf@dalsjo-golf.se
🏌 18 L 5715 m Par 72
👥 H

££ 300kr
🚗 5km NE of Borlänge
🏠 Jeremy Turner
www.dalsjo-golf.se

Falun-Borlänge (1956)
Storgarden 10, 791 93 Falun
☎ (023) 31015
📞 (023) 31072
🏌 18 L 6085 m Par 72
👥 U
££ 280kr (340kr)
🚗 Aspeboda, 8km N of Borlänge
🏠 Nils Sköld

Gävle (1949)
Bönavägen 23, 805 95 Gävle
☎ (026) 120333/120338
📞 (026) 516468
🏌 18 L 5735 m SSS 73
££ 200kr (250kr)
🚗 3km N of Gävle

Hagge (1963)
Hagge, 771 90 Ludvika
☎ (0240) 28087/28513
📞 (0240) 28515
🏌 18 L 5519 m SSS 71
👥 H
££ D–150kr
🚗 7km S of Ludvika
🏠 Sune Linde

Hofors (1965)
Box 117, 813 22 Hofors
☎ (0290) 85125
📞 (0290) 85101
🏌 18 L 5400 m Par 70
👥 U
££ 180kr (200kr)
🚗 5km SE of Hofors
🏠 Sune Linde

Högbo (1962)
Daniel Tilas Väg 4, 811 92 Sandviken
☎ (026) 215015
📞 (026) 215322
🏌 18 L 5760 m Par 72
9 L 2590 m Par 35
👥 U
££ 220kr (300kr)
🚗 6km N of Sandviken (Route 272)
🏠 Sköld/Linde

Hudiksvall (1964)
Tjuvskär, 824 01 Hudiksvall
☎ (0650) 15930
📞 (0650) 18630
🏌 18 L 5665 m SSS 72
👥 U
££ 160kr
🚗 4km SE of Hudiksvall
🏠 Linde/Sköld

Leksand (1977)
Box 25, 793 21 Leksand
☎ (0247) 14640
📞 (0247) 14157
🏌 18 L 5263 m Par 70

👥 U
££ 120kr (180kr)
🚗 2km N of Leksand
🏠 Nils Sköld

Ljusdal (1973)
Svinhammarsv.2, 827 23 Ljusdal
☎ (0651) 16883, (0651) 12566 (shop)
📞 (0651) 16883
🏌 18 L 5920 m Par 72
👥 U
££ 200kr
🚗 2km E of Ljusdal
🏠 Eriksson/Skjöld
www.golfiljusdal.nu

Mora (1980)
Box 264, 792 24 Mora
☎ (0250) 10182
📞 (0250) 10306
📖 1100
🏌 18 L 5600 m Par 72
££ 150kr
🚗 1km N of Mora. 40km NW of
Rättvik
🏠 Sune Linde

Rättvik (1954)
Box 29, 795 21 Rättvik
☎ (0248) 51030
📞 (0248) 12081
🏌 18 L 5375 m SSS 70
👥 U
££ 200–300kr
🚗 2km N of Rättvik

Sälenfjallens (1991)
Box 20, 780 67 Sälen
☎ (0280) 20670
📞 (0280) 20670
🏌 18 L 5710 m Par 72
👥 U H
££ 220kr
🚗 230km NW of Borlänge. 400km
NW of Stockholm
🏠 Sune Linde
www.golf.se/salenfjallensgk

Säter (1984)
Box 89, 783 22 Säter
☎ (0225) 50030
📞 (0225) 51424
🏌 18 L 5781 m Par 72
👥 U
££ 160kr
🚗 25km SE of Borlänge. 180km NW
of Stockholm
🏠 Sune Linde

Snöå (1990)
Snöå Bruk, 780 51 Dala-Järna
☎ (0281) 24072
📞 (0281) 24009
🏌 18 L 5738 m SSS 73
👥 H
££ 200kr
🚗 80km W of Borlänge, nr Dala-Järna
(Route 71)
🏠 Åke Persson
www.snoabruk.se/snoagk

For list of abbreviations and key to symbols see page 627

Söderhamn (1961)

Box 117, 826 23 Söderhamn
☎ **(0270) 281300**
🖥 (0270) 281003
➪ 18 L 5940 m Par 72
👥 H
£€ 200–220kr
⛳ 8km N of Söderhamn
🚶 Nils Sköld
■ www.soderhamnsgk.com

Sollerö (1991)

Levsnäs, 79290 Sollerön
☎ **(0250) 22236**
🖥 (0250) 22854
➪ 18 L 7226 yds Par 72
👥 H
£€ 160kr
⛳ 14km from Mora on Island of Sollerön in Siljan
🚶 JR Turner

Skane & South

Allerum (1992)

Pl 7592, 260 35 Ödåkra
☎ **(042) 93051**
🖥 (042) 93045
➪ 18 L 6201 m SSS 73
👥 U
£€ 250kr–300kr
⛳ 9km NE of Helsingborg
🚶 Hans Fock
■ www.golf.se/golfklubbar/allerumgk

Ängelholm (1973)

Box 1117, 262 22 Ängelholm
☎ **(0431) 430260/431460**
🖥 (0431) 431568
➪ 18 L 5760 m Par 72
👥 H (max 36)
£€ 200kr–250kr
⛳ 10km E of Ängelholm on route 114
🚶 Jan Sederholm
■ www.golf.se/golfklubbar/angelholmsgk

Araslöv

Starvägen 1, 291 75 Färlöv
☎ **(044) 71600**
🖥 (044) 71575
➪ 18 L 5817 m Par 72
👥 H or Green card
£€ 160kr (220kr)
⛳ 9km NW of Kristianstad (Route 19)
🚶 Sune Linde

Båstad (1929)

Box 1037, 269 21 Båstad
☎ **(0431) 78370**
🖥 (0431) 73331
➪ 18 L 5632 m Par 71
18 L 6163 m Par 72
👥 H
£€ 450kr
⛳ 4km W of Båstad (Route 115)
🚶 Hawtree/Taylor/Nordström

Bedinge (1931)

Golfbanevägen, 231 76 Beddingestrand
☎ **(0410) 25514**
🖥 (0410) 25411
➪ 18 L 5444 m Par 70
👥 H
£€ 120 (160kr)
⛳ Beddingestrand, 20km E of Trelleborg
🚶 Åke Persson

Bjäre

Salomonhög 3086, 269 93 Båstad
☎ **(0431) 361053**
🖥 (0431) 361764
➪ 18 L 5550 m SSS 71
👥 H
£€ 350kr
⛳ 2km E of Båstad. 60km N of Helsingborg
🚶 Svante Dahlgren

Bosjökloster (1974)

243 95 Höör
☎ **(0413) 25858**
🖥 (0413) 25895
➪ 18 L 5890 m Par 72
👥 H
£€ 240kr (280kr)
⛳ 7km S of Höör. 50km NE of Malmö
🚶 Douglas Brasier

Carlskrona (1949)

PO Almö, 370 24 Nättraby
☎ **(0457) 35123**
🖥 (0457) 35090
➪ 18 L 5485 m Par 70
👥 U
£€ D–220kr
⛳ 18km SW of Karlskrona
🚶 Jan Sederholm
■ www.carlskronagk.com

Degeberga-Widtsköfle

Box 71, 297 21 Degeberga
☎ **(044) 355035**
🖥 (044) 355075
➪ 18 L 6129 m SSS 72
9 hole Par 3 course
👥 U
£€ 100kr–170kr
⛳ 20km S of Kristianstad

Eslöv (1966)

Box 150, 241 22 Eslöv
☎ **(0413) 18610**
🖥 (0413) 18613
➪ 18 L 5610 m CR 70.7 SR 133
👥 H
£€ 260kr (300kr)
⛳ 4km S of Eslöv (Route 113)
🚶 Thure Bruce
■ www.golf.se/golfklubbar/eslovsgk

Hässleholm (1978)

Skyrup, 282 95 Tyringe
☎ **(0451) 53111**
🖥 (0451) 53138

➪ 18 L 5830 m SSS 72
👥 U
£€ 280kr
⛳ 15km NW of Hässleholm
🚶 Persson/Bruce/Jensen

Helsingborg (1924)

260 40 Viken
☎ **(042) 236147**
➪ 9 L 4578 m Par 68
👥 U
£€ 180kr (200kr)
⛳ 15km NW of Helsingborg
🚶 W Hester

Karlshamn (1962)

Box 188, 374 23 Karlshamn
☎ **(0454) 50085**
🖥 (0454) 50160
➪ 18 L 5861 m SSS 72
18 holes SSS 72
👥 H
£€ D–220kr (250kr)
⛳ Morrum, 10 km W of Karlshamn
🚶 Brasier/Victorsson/Sederholm

Kristianstad (1924)

Box 41, 296 21 Åhus
☎ **(044) 247656**
🖥 (044) 247635
➪ 18 L 5810 m SSS 72
9 L 2945 m SSS 36
👥 H
£€ D–300kr (D–350kr)
⛳ 18km SE of Kristianstad. Airport 20km
🚶 Brasier/Nordström

Landskrona (1960)

Erikstorp, 261 61 Landskrona
☎ **(0418) 446260**
🖥 (0418) 446262
➪ Old 18 L 5700 m SSS 71
New 18 L 4300 m SSS 64
👥 U
£€ 300kr (320kr)
⛳ 4km N of Landskrona, towards Borstahusen

Mölle (1943)

260 42 Mölle
☎ **(042) 347520**
🖥 (042) 347523
➪ 18 L 5292 m Par 70
👥 H–max 36
£€ 320kr
⛳ Mölle, 35km NW of Helsingborg
🚶 Thure Bruce
■ www.mollegk.m.se

Örkelljunga

Rya 472, 286 91 Örkelljunga
☎ **(0435) 53690/53640**
🖥 (0435) 53670
➪ 18 L 5700 m SSS 72
👥 H
£€ 200kr (240kr)
⛳ 8km S of Örkelljunga. 40km NE of Helsingborg (E4)
🚶 Hans Fock

Östra Göinge   (1981)

Box 114, 289 21 Knislinge
☎ **(044) 60060**
📠 (044) 69060
📏 18 L 5898 m Par 72
👥 H
🚗 20km N of Kristianstad
🏠 T Nordström
■ www.golf.se/ostragoingegk

Perstorp   (1964)

Gustavsborg 501, 284 91 Perstorp
☎ **(0435) 35411**
📠 (0435) 35959
📏 18 L 5675 m Par 71
6 hole short course
👥 H 36
€€ 150kr (300kr)
🚗 1km S of Perstorp. 45km E of Helsingborg
🏠 Amilon/Bruce/Persson

Ronneby   (1963)

Box 26, 372 21 Ronneby
☎ **(0457) 10315**
📠 (0457) 10412
📏 18 L 5323 m Par 72
👥 U
€€ 250kr
🚗 3km S of Ronneby
■ www.golf.se/ronnebygk

Rya   (1934)

PL 5500, 255 92 Helsingborg
☎ **(042) 220182**
📠 (042) 220394
📏 18 L 5599 m Par 72
👥 H
€€ 260kr
🚗 10km S of Helsingborg
🏠 Petterson/Sundblom

St Arild   (1987)

Golfvagen 48, 260 41 Nyhamnsläge
☎ **(042) 346860**
📠 (042) 346042
📏 18 L 5805 m Par 72
👥 H
€€ 260kr (260kr)
🚗 50km N of Helsingborg
🏠 Jan Sederholm
■ www.starild.se

Skepparslov   (1984)

Udarpssäteri, 291 92 Kristianstad
☎ **(044) 229508**
📠 (044) 229503
📏 18 L 5996 m SSS 73
👥 U
€€ 180kr (250kr)
🚗 7km W of Kristianstad
🏠 Rolf Collijn
■ www.golf.se/golfklubbar /skepparslovsgk

Söderåsen   (1966)

Box 41, 260 50 Billesholm
☎ **(042) 73337**
📠 (042) 73963

✉ info@soderasensgk.golf.se
📏 18 L 5657 m Par 71
👥 U H
€€ 300kr (330kr)
🚗 20km E of Helsingborg
🏠 Thure Bruce
■ www.golf.se

Sölvesborg

Box 63, 294 22 Sölvesborg
☎ **(0456) 70650**
📠 (0456) 70650
📏 18 L 5900 m Par 72
👥 U
€€ 240kr
🚗 30km E of Kristianstad
🏠 Sune Linde

Svalöv   (1989)

Månstorp Pl 1365, 268 90 Svalöv
☎ **(0418) 662462**
📠 (0418) 663284
📏 18 L 5874 m SSS 73
👥 U
€€ 230kr (280kr)
🚗 20km E of Landskrona
🏠 Tommy Nordström
■ www.golf.se/golfklubbar/svalovsgk

Torekov   (1924)

Råledsu 31, 260 93 Torekov
☎ **(0431) 449840**
📠 (0431) 364916
📏 18 L 5701 m Par 72
👥 Jun–Aug–H WE–M before noon
€€ 350kr (350kr)
🚗 3km N of Torekov
🏠 Nils Sköld

Trummenas

373 02 Ramdala
☎ **(0455) 60505**
📠 (0455) 60571
📏 18 L 5600 m Par 72
9 hole course
👥 H
€€ 200kr
🚗 15km SE of Karlskrona, off Route 22
🏠 Ingmar Ericsson

Vasatorp   (1973)

Box 13035, 250 13 Helsingborg
☎ **(042) 235058**
📠 (042) 235135
📏 18 L 5775 m SSS 72
36 hole course
👥 H–max 36
€€ 350kr (400kr) – 18 hole
🚗 9km E of Helsingborg
🏠 Bruce/Persson

Wittsjö   (1962)

Ubbaltsgården, 280 22 Vittsjö
☎ **(0451) 22635**
📠 (0451) 22567
📏 18 L 5461 m Par 71
👥 U
€€ 160kr (200kr)
🚗 2km SE of Vittsjö
🏠 Sköld/Amilon

South East

A 6 Golfklubb

Centralvägen, 553 05 Jönköping
☎ **(036) 308130**
📠 (036) 308140
📏 27 hole course:
9 L 3185 m Par 38
9 L 3115 m Par 37
9 L 2935 m Par 36
👥 U H
€€ 250kr–300kr
🚗 2km SE of Jönköping
🏠 Peter Nordwall

Älmhult   (1975)

Pl 1215, 343 90 Älmhult
☎ **(0476) 14135**
📠 (0476) 16565
📏 18 L 5407 m SSS 71
👥 U H
€€ D–200kr
🚗 2km E of Älmhult on Route 23
🏠 Persson/Söderberg

Åtvidaberg   (1954)

Västantorp, 597 41 Åtvidaberg
☎ **(0120) 35425**
📠 (0120) 13502
📏 18 L 5570 m Par 71
👥 H
€€ 300kr (350kr)
🚗 30km SE of Linköping
🏠 Brasier/Nordvall

Ekerum

387 92 Borgholm, Öland
☎ **(0485) 80000**
📠 (0485) 80010
📏 18 L 5975 m Par 73
18 L 5862 m Par 72
👥 U H
€€ 270kr–390kr
🚗 12km S of Borgholm. 25km N of Öland bridge
🏠 Peter Nordwall

Eksjö   (1938)

Skedhult, 575 96 Eksjö
☎ **(0381) 13525**
📏 18 L 5930 m SSS 72
👥 WD–U WE–H
€€ 300kr
🚗 6km W of Eksjö on Nässjö road
🏠 Anders Amilon

Emmaboda   (1976)

Kyrkogatan, 360 60 Vissefjärda
☎ **(0471) 20505/20540**
📠 (0471) 20440
📏 18 L 6165 m SSS 72
👥 H
€€ 200kr
🚗 12km S of Emmaboda. 50km N of Karlskrona
■ www.golf.se/golfklubbar /emmabodagk

Finspång (1965)
Viberga Gård, 612 92 Finspång
- ☎ **(0122) 13940**
- 📠 (0122) 18888
- ⌖ 27 L 5800 m SSS 72
- ⚭ U
- €€ 250kr (300kr)
- ⛳ 2km E of Finspång, Route 51. Norrköping 25km.
- ♟ Sköld/Linde/Chamberlain

Gotska (1986)
Box 1119, 621 22 Visby, Gotland
- ☎ **(0498) 215545**
- 📠 (0498) 256332
- ⌖ 18 L 5202 m Par 69
  9 L 5414 m Par 72
- ⚭ U H
- €€ 18 holes: 250kr; 9 holes: 120kr
- ⛳ N outskirts of Visby
- ♟ Jack Wenman

Grönhögen (1996)
PL 1270, 380 65 Öland
- ☎ **(0485) 665995**
- 📠 (0485) 665999
- ⌖ 18 L 5100 m Par 70
- ⚭ H
- €€ 120kr–180kr (140kr–280kr)
- ⛳ 45km S of Öland Bridge
- ♟ Kenneth Nilsson
- ◼ www.gronhogen.se

Gumbalde
Box 35, 620 13 Ståga, Gotland
- ☎ **(0498) 482880**
- 📠 (0498) 482884
- ⌖ 18 L 5600 m SSS 71
- ⚭ U
- €€ 200kr–240kr
- ⛳ 50km SE of Visby, Gotland island
- ♟ Lars Lagergren

Hooks
560 13 Hok
- ☎ **(0393) 21420**
- 📠 (0393) 21379
- ⌖ 18 L 5758 m SSS 72
  18 L 5750 m SSS 73
  9 hole Par 3 course
- ⚭ H
- €€ 300kr (350kr)
- ⛳ Hok, 30km SE of Jönköping, towards Växjö
- ♟ Edberg/Bruce/Sederholm
- ◼ www.hooksgk.com

Isaberg (1968)
Nissafors Bruk, 330 27 Hestra
- ☎ **(0370) 336330**
- 📠 (0370) 336325
- ⌖ East 18 L 5823 m CR 71.8
  West 18 L 5568 m CR 70.0
- ⚭ H
- €€ 250kr (300kr)
- ⛳ Nissafors, 18km N of Gislaved. 60km S of Jönköping
- ♟ Amilon/Bruce/Persson

Jönköping (1936)
Kettilstorp, 556 27 Jönköping
- ☎ **(036) 76567**
- 📠 (036) 76511
- ⌖ 18 L 5313 m Par 70
- ⚭ Phone in advance H–max 30
- €€ 300kr (350kr)
- ⛳ Kettilstorp, 3km S of Jönköping
- ♟ Frank Dyer
- ◼ www.golf.se/jonkopingsgk

Kalmar (1947)
Box 278, 391 23 Kalmar
- ☎ **(0480) 472111**
- 📠 (0480) 472314
- ⌖ Blue 18 L 5700 m SSS 72
  Red 18 L 5634 m SSS 72
- ⚭ H
- €€ 300kr (350kr)
- ⛳ 9km N of Kalmar via E22
- ♟ Brasier/Sköld/Linde
- ◼ www.golf.se/golfklubbar/kalmargk

Lagan (1966)
Box 63, 340 14 Lagan
- ☎ **(0372) 30450/35460**
- 📠 (0372) 35307
- ⌖ 18 L 5539 m SSS 70
  9 L 2419 m Par 34
- ⚭ U
- €€ 160kr
- ⛳ Lagan, 10km N of Ljungby, on Route E4
- ♟ Amilon/Persson/Magnusson

Landeryd (1987)
Bogestad Gård, 585 93 Linköping
- ☎ **(013) 362200**
- 📠 (013) 362208
- ⌖ North 18 L 5675 m SSS 72
  South 18 L 5085 m SSS 68
  9 hole short course
- ⚭ U
- €€ 220kr (240kr)
- ⛳ 7km SE of Linköping
- ♟ Nordström/Persson

Lidhems (1988)
360 14 Väckelsång
- ☎ **(0470) 33660**
- 📠 (0470) 33761
- ⌖ 18 L 5755 m Par 72
- ⚭ H
- €€ 200kr
- ⛳ 30km S of Växjo (Road 30)
- ♟ Ingmar Eriksson
- ◼ www.golf.se/lidhemsgk

Linköping (1945)
Box 15054, 580 15 Linköping
- ☎ **(013) 120646**
- 📠 (013) 140769
- ⌖ 18 L 5659 m SSS 71
- ⚭ H
- €€ 250kr (300kr)
- ⛳ 3km SW of Linköping
- ♟ Sundblom/Brasier

Mjölby (1986)
Blixberg, Miskarp, 595 92 Mjölby
- ☎ **(0142) 12570**
- 📠 (0142) 16553
- ⌖ 18 L 5485 m SSS 71
- ⚭ H
- €€ 230kr (260kr)
- ⛳ 35km WSW of Linköping (E4)
- ♟ Åke Persson
- ◼ www.mjolbygk.com

Motala (1956)
PO Box 264, 591 23 Motala
- ☎ **(0141) 50840**
- 📠 (0141) 208990
- ⌖ 18 L 5905 m Par 72
- ⚭ U
- €€ 220kr (300kr)
- ⛳ 3km S of Motala via Route 50 or 32
- ♟ Sköld/Sederholm

Nässjö (1988)
Box 5, 571 21 Nässjö
- ☎ **(0380) 10022**
- 📠 (0380) 12082
- ⌖ 18 L 5783 m Par 72
- ⚭ U H
- €€ 170kr
- ⛳ 40km E of Jönköping
- ♟ Bjorn Magnusson

Norrköping (1928)
Borg, 605 97 Norrköping
- ☎ **(011) 335235/183654**
- 📠 (011) 335014
- ✉ info@ngk.nu
- ⌖ 18 L 5860 m SSS 73
- ⚭ U H
- €€ 250kr (300kr)
- ⛳ Klinga, 9km S of Norrköping on E4
- ♟ Nils Sköld
- ◼ www.ngk.nu

Oskarshamn (1972)
Box 148, 572 23 Oskarshamn
- ☎ **(0491) 94033**
- 📠 (0491) 94038
- ⌖ 18 L 5545 m SSS 71
- ⚭ H
- €€ 220kr (250kr)
- ⛳ 10km SW of Oskarshamn, nr Forshult
- ♟ Nils Sköld

Skinnarebo
Skinnarebo, 555 93 Jönköping
- ☎ **(036) 69075**
- 📠 (036) 362975
- ⌖ 18 L 5686 m SSS 71
  9 hole Par 3 course
- ⚭ H
- €€ 180kr
- ⛳ 14km SW of Jönköping
- ♟ Björn Magnusson

Söderköping (1983)
Hylinge, 605 96 Norrköping
- ☎ **(011) 70579**
- ⌖ 18 L 5730 m SSS 72

🏵 U
£€ 300kr
⛳ Västra Husby, 9km W of
Söderköping
🏚 Ronald Fream, Peta Ejellmann

Tobo (1971)
Fredensborg 133, 598 91 Vimmerby
☎ (0492) 30346
📠 (0492) 30871
🏌 18 L 5720 m Par 72
🏵 U
£€ 200kr (240kr)
⛳ 10km S of Vimmerby, nr Storebro.
60km SW of Västervik
🏚 Brasier/Jensen
🌐 www.tbgk.h.se

Tranås (1952)
Box 430, 573 25 Tranås
☎ (0140) 311661
📠 (0140) 16161
🏌 18 L 5830 m SSS 72
🏵 U
£€ 240kr (280kr)
⛳ 2km N of Tranås

Vadstena (1957)
Hagalund, Box 122, 592 33 Vadstena
☎ (0143) 12440
📠 (0143) 12709
🏌 18 L 5486 m Par 71
🏵 U
£€ 220kr (300kr)
⛳ 3km S of Vadstena, towards
Vaderstad

Värnamo (1962)
Box 146, 331 21 Värnamo
☎ (0370) 23123
📠 (0370) 23216
🏌 18 L 6253 m SSS 72
🏵 U
£€ 200kr
⛳ 8km E of Värnamo on Route 127
🏚 Nils Sköld

Västervik (1959)
Box 62, Ekhagen, 593 22 Västervik
☎ (0490) 32420
📠 (0490) 32421
🏌 18 L 5760 m Par 72
🏵 U
£€ 200kr (250kr)
⛳ 1km E of Västervik
🏚 Sune linde

Växjö (1959)
Box 227, 351 05 Växjö
☎ (0470) 21515
📠 (0470) 21557
🏌 18 L 5860 m Par 71
🏵 H
£€ 250kr
⛳ 5km NW of Växjö
🏚 Douglas Brasier
🖥 www.vaxjogk.com

Vetlanda (1983)
Box 249, 574 23 Vetlanda
☎ (0383) 18310
📠 (0383) 19278
🏌 18 L 5552 m SSS 71
🏵 U
£€ 160kr
⛳ Östanå, 3km W of Vetlanda. 80km
SE of Jönköping
🏚 Jan Sederholm

Visby
*Kronholmen Västergarn, 620 20
Klintehamn, Gotland*
☎ (0498) 245058
📠 (0498) 245240
🏌 18 L 5765 m Par 72
9 hole course
🏵 Jun–Aug–H
£€ 300kr
⛳ Kronholmen, 25km S of Visby,
Gotland island
🏚 Nordwall/Sköld
🖥 www.golf.se/visbygk

Vreta Kloster
Box 144, 590 70 Ljungsbro
☎ (013) 169700
📠 (013) 169707
🏌 18 L 5666 m Par 72
🏵 H
£€ 250kr (300kr)
⛳ 15km N of Linköping
🏚 Sune Linde

South West

Alingsås (1985)
Hjälmared 4050, 441 95 Alingsås
☎ (0322) 52421
🏌 18 L 5735 m SSS 72
🏵 U
£€ 240kr
⛳ 5km SE of Alingsås towards
Borås

Bäckavattnet (1977)
Marbäck, 305 94 Halmstad
☎ (035) 162040
📠 (035) 162049
🏌 18 L 5740 m Par 71
🏵 H
£€ 250kr (320kr)
⛳ 13km E of Halmstad (RD25)
🖥 www.backavattnetsgk.com

Billingen (1949)
St Kulhult, 540 17 Lerdala
☎ (0511) 80291
📠 (0511) 80244
🏌 18 L 5470 m Par 71
🏵 H
£€ 180kr
⛳ 20km NW of Skövde
🏚 Douglas Brasier

Borås (1933)
Östra Vik, Kråkered, 504 95 Borås
☎ (033) 250250
📠 (033) 250176
🏌 North 18 L 6005 m Par 72
South 18 L 5085 m Par 69
🏵 H–booking necessary
£€ 200kr (200kr)
⛳ 6km S of Borås, on Route 41
towards Varberg
🏚 Brasier/Persson

Ekarnas (1970)
Balders Väg 12, 467 31 Grästorp
☎ (0514) 12061
📠 (0514) 12062
📧 info@ekarnasgk.golf.se
🏌 18 L 5501 m SSS 71
🏵 H
£€ 200kr (220kr)
⛳ 25km E of Trollhättan. Lidköping
35km
🏚 Jan Andersson
🖥 www.golf.se/golfklubbar/ekarnasgk

Falkenberg (1949)
Golfvägen, 311 72 Falkenberg
☎ (0346) 50287
📠 (0346) 50997
🏌 27 L 5575-5680 m SSS 72
🏵 H
£€ 250–280kr
⛳ 5km S of Falkenberg

Falköping (1965)
Box 99, 521 02 Falköping
☎ (0515) 31270
📠 (0515) 31389
🏌 18 L 5835 m Par 72
🏵 H
£€ 220kr
⛳ 7km E of Falköping on Route 46
towards Skovde
🏚 Nils Sköld

Halmstad (1930)
302 73 Halmstad
☎ (035) 176800/176801
📠 (035) 176820
🏌 18 L 5955 m CR 72.4
18 L 5542 m CR 69.9
🏵 H WE–M before 1pm
£€ 480kr
⛳ Tylosand, 9km W of Halmstad
🏚 Sundblom/Sköld/Pennink

Haverdals (1988)
Slingervägen 35, 31042 Haverdal
☎ (035) 144990
📠 (035) 53890
🏌 18 L 5840 m Par 72
🏵 H
£€ 320kr
⛳ 11km NW of Halmstad
🏚 Anders Amilon/Bjorn Magnusson

Hökensås (1962)
PO Box 116, 544 22 Hjo
☎ (0503) 16059

(0503) 16156
18 L 5540 m Par 72
9 hole course
U
200kr (200kr)
8km S of Hjo on Route 195
Sune Linde

Holms (1990)

Nannarp, 305 92 Halmstad
- **(035) 38189**
- (035) 38488
- 18 L 5782 m Par 72
- H–max 36
- £24 (£30)
- 15km from Halmstad
- Peter Nordvall
- www.holmsgk.com

Hulta (1972)

Box 54, 517 22 Bollebygd
- **(033) 204340**
- (033) 204345
- 18 L 6000 m SSS 72
- H
- 260kr
- Bollebygd, 35km E of Gothenburg
- Jan Sederholm

Knistad G&CC

541 92 Skövde
- **(0500) 463170**
- (0500) 463075
- 18 L 5790 m SSS 72
- H
- 200kr
- 10km NE of Skövde
- Jeremy Turner

Laholm (1964)

Box 101, 312 22 Laholm
- **(0430) 30601**
- (0430) 30891
- 18 L 5430 m Par 70 CR 69.5 SR 128
- 9 L 2660 m Par 72 CR 71.0 SR 135
- U H
- 280kr (300kr)
- 5 miles E of Laholm on Route 24
- Jan Sederholm

Lidköping (1967)

Box 2029, 531 02 Lidköping
- **(0510) 546144**
- (0510) 546495
- 18 L 5382 m CR 68.6
- H
- 180kr
- 5km E of Lidköping
- Douglas Brasier

Mariestad (1975)

Gummerstadsvägen 45, 542 94 Mariestad
- **(0501) 47147**
- (0501) 78117
- 18 L 5970 m SSS 73
- H
- 250kr

4km W of Mariestad, at Lake Vänern
www.mariestadsgk.com

Marks (1962)

Brättingstorpsvägen 28, 511 58 Kinna
- **(0320) 14220**
- (0320) 12516
- 18 L 5530 m Par 70
- H
- 160kr (200kr)
- Kinna, 30km S of Borås
- Sköld/Sederholm

Onsjö (1974)

Box 6331 A, 462 42 Vänersborg
- **(0521) 68870**
- (0521) 17106
- 18 L 5730 m SSS 72
- U
- 220kr (270kr)
- 3km S of Vänersborg. 80km N of Gothenburg
- Sköld/Linde
- www.golf.se/golfklubbar/onsjogk

Ringenäs (1987)

Strandlida, 305 91 Halmstad
- **(035) 161590**
- (035) 161599
- 27 L 5395-5615 m Par 71-72
- H
- 200kr–300kr (320kr)
- 10km NW of Halmstad
- Sune Linde
- www.ringenasgolfbana.com

Skogaby (1988)

312 93 Laholm
- **(0430) 60190**
- (0430) 60225
- skogaby.gk@telia.com
- 18 L 5555 m Par 71
- U H
- 270kr
- 10km E of Laholm. 30km SE of Halmstad
- J Rosengren

Sotenas Golfklubb (1988)

Pl Onna, 450 46 Hunnebostrand
- **(0523) 52302**
- (0523) 52390
- 18 L 5695 m CR 71.1 SR 123
- H–max 33
- 250kr (300kr)
- 100km N of Gothenburg via E6
- Jan Sederholm
- www.sotenasgolf.com

Töreboda (1965)

Box 18, 545 21 Töreboda
- **(0506) 12305**
- (0506) 12305
- 18 L 5355 m SSS 70
- U
- 200kr
- 7km E of Töreboda

Trollhättan (1963)

Stora Ekeskogen, 466 91 Sollebrunn
- **(0520) 441000**
- (0520) 441049
- 18 L 6200 m SSS 73
- U
- 200kr
- Koberg, 20km SE of Trollhättan
- Nils Sköld

Ulricehamn (1947)

523 33 Ulricehamn
- **(0321) 10021**
- (0321) 16004
- 18 L 5509 m Par 71
- WD–H
- 160kr (200kr)
- Lassalyckan, 2km E of Ulricehamn

Vara-Bjertorp

Bjertorp, 535 91 Kvänum
- **(0512) 20261**
- (0512) 20261
- 18 L 6005 m Par 72
- H
- 150kr (220kr)
- 10km N of Vara. 110km NE of Gothenburg (E20)
- Jan Sederholm
- www.golf.se/golfklubbar /varabjertorpgk

Varberg (1950)

430 10 Tvååker
- **(0340) 43446/37496**
- (0340) 43447
- East 18 L 5440 m Par 71 CR 71
- West 18 L 6435 m Par 72 CR 76
- H
- 30kr–370kr
- East:15km E of Varberg. West: 8km S of Varberg, nr E6
- Sköld/Nordström
- www.varbergsgk.com

Vinberg (1992)

Sannagård, 311 95 Falkenberg
- **(0346) 19020**
- (0346) 19042
- 18 L 4050 m Par 65
- U
- 160kr (180kr)
- 5km E of Falkenberg on coast
- Nilsson/Haglund

Stockholm

Ågesta (1958)

123 52 Farsta
- **(08) 447 3330**
- (08) 447 3337
- 18 L 5632 m SSS 72
- 9 L 3404 m SSS 62
- WD–U
- 400kr
- Farsta, 15km S of Stockholm
- Sköld/Sederholm

Botkyrka
Malmbro Gård, 147 91 Grödinge
- ☎ **(08) 530 29650**
- 📞 (08) 530 29409
- ▷ 18 holes Par 73
  9 hole Par 3 course
- 👥 WD–U H WE–H after 1pm
- ££ 250kr (300kr)
- 🚗 30km S of Stockholm
- ▩ www.golf.se/botkyrkagk

Bro-Bålsta (1978)
Ginnlögs Väg, 197 91 Bro
- ☎ **(08) 582 41310**
- 📞 (08) 582 40006
- ▷ 18 L 6505 m Par 73
  9 L 1715 m Par 31
- 👥 WD–H (max 30) TH–NA
- ££ 400kr
- 🚗 40 km NW of Stockholm
- 🏛 Peter Nordwall

Djursholm (1931)
Hagbardsvägen 1, 182 63 Djursholm
- ☎ **(08) 5449 6451**
- 📞 (08) 5449 6456
- ✉ robert@dgk.nu
- ▷ 18 L 5569 m SSS 71
  9 L 2135 m SSS 34
- 👥 WD–U H before 5pm –M after 5pm
  WE–M before noon –U H after
  noon
- ££ 450kr (450kr)
- 🚗 12km N of Stockholm
- ▩ www.dkg.nu (Swedish only)

Drottningholm (1958)
PO Box 183, 178 93 Drottningholm
- ☎ **(08) 759 0085**
- 📞 (08) 759 0851
- ▷ 18 L 5745 m SSS 71
- 👥 WD–U H before 3pm –M after 3pm
  WE–M before 3pm –U H after 3pm
- ££ 450kr
- 🚗 16km W of Stockholm
- 🏛 Sundblom/Sköld

Fågelbro G&CC
Fågelbro Säteri, 139 60 Värmdö
- ☎ **(08) 571 41800**
- 📞 (08) 571 40671
- ✉ info.fagelbro@telia.com
- ▷ 18 L 5522 m Par 71
- 👥 WD–H WE–M
- ££ 500kr (600kr)
- 🚗 35km E of Stockholm
- 🏛 Eriksson/Oredsson

Haninge (1983)
Årsta Slott, 136 91 Haninge
- ☎ **(08) 500 32850**
- 📞 (08) 500 32851
- ▷ 27 L 5930 m Par 73
- 👥 WD–U before 1pm –M after 1pm
  WE–M before 1pm –U after 1pm
- ££ 400kr (450kr)
- 🚗 30km S of Stockholm towards
  Nynäshamn
- 🏛 Jan Sederholm
- ▩ www.haningegk.se

Ingarö (1962)
Fogelvik, 134 64 Ingarö
- ☎ **(08) 570 28244**
- 📞 (08) 570 28379
- ▷ Old 18 L 5024 m SSS 71
  New 18 L 5203 m SSS 70
- 👥 WD–U H WE–NA before 3pm
- ££ 350kr (400kr)
- 🚗 30km E of Stockholm via Route
  222
- 🏛 Sköld/Eriksson
- ▩ www.igk.se

Kungsängen (1992)
Box 133, 196 21 Kungsängen
- ☎ **(08) 584 50730**
- 📞 (08) 581 71002
- ▷ Kings 18 L 6100 m Par 71
  Queens 18 L 5300 m Par 69
- 👥 U H
- ££ Kings–600kr. Queens–400kr
- 🚗 25km W of Stockholm via E18 to
  Brunna
- 🏛 Anders Forsbrand

Lidingö (1933)
Box 1035, 181 21 Lidingö
- ☎ **(08) 765 7911**
- 📞 (08) 765 5479
- ▷ 18 L 5647 m SSS 72
- 👥 WD–U H before 3pm –NA after
  3pm Sat–NA Sun–NA before 1pm
- ££ 400kr
- 🚗 6km NE of Stockholm
- 🏛 MacDonald/Sundblom

Lindö (1978)
186 92 Vallentuna
- ☎ **(08) 511 72260**
- 📞 (08) 511 74122
- ▷ 18 L 2850 m Par 71
- 👥 U
- ££ 300kr (400kr)
- 🚗 Vallentuna, 20 km N of Stockholm
- 🏛 Åke Persson

Lindo Park
Lindö Park, 186 92 Vallentuna
- ☎ **(08) 511 70055 (Bookings)**
- 📞 (08) 511 70613
- ▷ 18 L 5800 m SSS 72
  18 L 5795 m SSS 72
- 👥 U H–book day before play
- ££ 300kr (400kr)
- 🚗 30km N of Stockholm
- 🏛 Persson/Bruce/Eriksson
- ▩ www.lindopark.se

Nya Johannesberg G&CC (1990)
762 95 Rimbo
- ☎ **(08) 514 50000**
- 📞 (08) 512 92390
- ▷ 18 L 6328 m SSS 74
  9 hole course
- 👥 H
- ££ 250kr (350kr)
- 🚗 55km N of Stockholm
- 🏛 Donald Steel
- ▩ www.golf.se/golfklubbar
  /johannesberggcc

Nynäshamn (1977)
Korunda 40, 148 91 Ösmo
- ☎ **(08) 524 30590/524 30599**
- 📞 (08) 524 30598
- ▷ 27 L 5690 m SSS 72
- 👥 H–phone first
- ££ 340kr (390kr)
- 🚗 Ösmo, 40km S of Stockholm
- 🏛 Sune Linde
- ▩ www.nynashamnsgk.a.se

Österakers
Hagby 1, 184 92 Akersberga
- ☎ **(08) 540 85165**
- 📞 (08) 540 66832
- ▷ 18 L 5792 m Par 72
  18 L 5780 m Par 72
- 👥 H WE–NA after 2pm
- ££ 320kr–380kr (380kr–450kr)
- 🚗 30km NE of Stockholm
- 🏛 Sederholm/Tumba

Österhaninge (1992)
Husby, 136 91 Haninge
- ☎ **(08) 500 32077**
- 📞 (08) 500 32293
- ▷ 18 L 5600 m Par 70
- 👥 H
- ££ 240kr (300kr)
- 🚗 35km S of Stockholm
- 🏛 Bengt Lorichs

Saltsjöbaden (1929)
Box 51, 133 21 Saltsjöbaden
- ☎ **(08) 717 0125**
- 📞 (08) 5561 6739
- ▷ 18 L 5436 m SSS 71
  9 L 3756 m SSS 64
- 👥 WD–U WE–M H before 2pm
- ££ 18 holes: D–420kr 9 holes: D–240kr
- 🚗 15km E of Stockholm city, via
  Route 228

Sollentuna (1967)
Skillingegården, 192 77 Sollentuna
- ☎ **(08) 594 70995**
- 📞 (08) 594 70999
- ▷ 18 L 5895 m SSS 72
- 👥 WD–H before 3pm WE–H after
  3pm
- ££ 400kr
- 🚗 19km N of Stockholm. 1km W of
  E4 (Rotebro)
- 🏛 Nils Sköld

Stockholm (1904)
Kevingestrand 20, 182 57 Danderyd
- ☎ **(08) 544 90710**
- 📞 (08) 544 90712
- ▷ 18 L 5180 m SSS 69
- 👥 WD–M after 3pm WE–M before
  3pm
- ££ 340kr (420kr)
- 🚗 7km NE of Stockholm via Route
  E18

Täby (1968)
Skålhamra Gård, 187 70 Täby
- ☎ **(08) 510 23261**

☎ (08) 510 23441
↦ 18 L 5776 m SSS 73
👥 WD–H
£€ 350kr–450kr
🚗 15km N of Stockholm
🛎 Nils Sköld

Troxhammar
179 75 Skå
☎ **(08) 564 20610**
📠 (08) 560 24870
↦ 27 holes Par 72
👥 H–max 34
£€ £30
🚗 15km W of Stockholm, nr Drottningholm Castle
🛎 Jan Sederholm
■ www.golf.se/troxhammargk

Ullna (1981)
Rosenkälla, 184 94 Åkersberga
☎ **(08) 514 41230**
📠 (08) 510 26068
↦ 18 L 5825 m Par 72
👥 H
£€ 600kr
🚗 20km N of Stockholm via Route E18
🛎 Sven Tumba
■ www.ullnagolf.se

Ulriksdal
Box 8033, 171 08 Solna
☎ **(08) 857931**
↦ 18 L 3900 m SSS 61
👥 H
£€ 130kr (160kr)
🚗 8km N of Stockholm
🛎 Alec Backhurst

Vallentuna (1989)
Box 266, 186 24 Vallentuna
☎ **(08) 514 30560/1**
📠 (08) 514 30569
↦ 18 L 5700 m SSS 72
👥 WD–U WE–U after 1pm
£€ 300kr (400kr)
🚗 35km N of Stockholm
🛎 Sune Linde
■ www.vallentunagk.nu

Viksjö (1969)
Fjällens Gård, 175 45 Järfälla
☎ **(08) 580 31300/31310**
📠 (08) 580 31340
↦ 18 L 5930 m SSS 73
9 L 1830 m Par 30
👥 U
£€ 9 holes: 150kr (150kr)
18 holes: 300kr (300kr)
🚗 18km NW of Stockholm
■ www.golf.se/viksjogk

Wäsby
Box 2017, 194 02 Upplands Väsby
☎ **(08) 514 103 50**
📠 (08) 514 103 55
↦ 18 L 6170 m SSS 72
9 hole course
👥 WD–H WE–H

£€ 350kr (400kr)
🚗 20km N of Stockholm. 20km S of Airport
🛎 Björn Eriksson

Wermdö G&CC (1966)
Torpa, 139 40 Värmdö
☎ **(08) 574 60700**
📠 (08) 574 60729
↦ 18 L 5555 m Par 72
👥 H WE–NA before 3pm
£€ 450kr (450kr)
🚗 25km E of Stockholm via Route 222
🛎 Nils Sköld

West Central

Arvika (1974)
Box 197, 671 25 Arvika
☎ **(0570) 54133**
📠 (0570) 54233
↦ 18 L 5815 m Par 72
👥 U
£€ 200kr
🚗 11km E of Arvika (Route 61)
🛎 Nils Sköld
■ www.arvikagk.nu

Billerud (1961)
Valnäs, 660 40 Segmon
☎ **(0555) 91313**
📠 (0555) 91306
↦ 18 L 5874 m SSS 72
👥 H
£€ 180kr
🚗 Valnäs, 15km N of Säffle
🛎 Brasier/Sköld

Eda (1992)
Noresund, 670 40 Åmotfors
☎ **(0571) 34101**
📠 (0571) 34191
↦ 18 L 5575 m Par 72
👥 U
£€ 230kr (260kr)
🚗 30km W of Arvika
🛎 Leif Nilsson
■ www.edagk.com

Färgelanda
Box 23, 458 21 Färgelanda
☎ **(0528) 20385**
📠 (0528) 20045
↦ 18 L 6000 m SSS 71
👥 U
£€ 160kr
🚗 23km N of Uddevalla. 100km N of Gothenburg
🛎 Åke Persson

Fjällbacka (1965)
450 71 Fjällbacka
☎ **(0525) 31150**
📠 (0525) 32122
↦ 18 L 5850 m SSS 72
👥 H
£€ 250kr (350kr)
🚗 2km N of Fjällbacka (Route 163)

Forsbacka (1969)
Box 136, 662 23 Åmål
☎ **(0532) 43073**
📠 (0532) 43116
↦ 18 L 5860 m SSS 72
👥 H
£€ 250kr (300kr)
🚗 6km W of Åmål (Route 164)
🛎 Nils Sköld
■ www.golf.se/golfklubbar /forsbackagk/

Hammarö (1991)
Sätter Tallbacken, 663 91 Hammarö
☎ **(054) 521621**
📠 (054) 521863
↦ 18 L 6200 m Par 72
👥 H
£€ 240kr (300kr)
🚗 11km S of Karlstad
🛎 Sune Linde
■ www.golf.se/hammarogk

Karlskoga (1975)
Bricketorp 647, 691 94 Karlskoga
☎ **(0586) 728190**
📠 (0586) 728417
↦ 18 L 5705 m Par 72
£€ 180kr
🚗 Valåsen, 5km E of Karlskoga via Route E18
🛎 Sköld/Sederholm/Engdahl

Karlstad (1957)
Höja 510, 655 92 Karlstad
☎ **(054) 866353**
📠 (054) 866478
↦ 18 L 5970 m Par 72
9 L 2875 m Par 36
👥 H
£€ 280 kr (320kr)
🚗 8km N of Karlstad (Route 63)
🛎 Sköld/Linde
■ www.golf.se/karlstadgk

Kristinehamn (1974)
Box 337, 681 26 Kristinehamn
☎ **(0550) 82310**
📠 (0550) 19535
↦ 18 L 5800 m SSS 72
👥 H
£€ 250kr–300kr
🚗 3km N of Kristinehamn
🛎 Sune Linde
■ www.golf.se/golfklubbar /kristinehamnsgk

Lyckorna (1967)
Box 66, 459 22 Ljungskile
☎ **(0522) 20176**
📠 (0522) 22304
↦ 18 L 5820 m SSS 72
👥 H
£€ 200kr
🚗 20km S of Uddevalla
🛎 Anders Amilon

For list of abbreviations and key to symbols see page 627

Orust (1981)

Morlanda 9404, 474 93 Ellös
- ☎ **(0304) 53170**
- 📠 (0304) 53174
- ⏸ 18 L 5770 m SSS 72
- 👥 H
- ££ 220kr–350kr
- ⛳ Ellös, 10km from Henån. 80km N of Gothenburg
- ⌂ Lars Andreasson
- ⬛ www.orustgk.org

Saxå (1964)

Saxån, 682 92 Filipstad
- ☎ **(0590) 24070**
- 📠 (0590) 24101
- ⏸ 18 L 5680 m Par 72
- 👥 U
- ££ 160kr
- ⛳ 20km NE of Filipstad (Route 63)
- ⌂ Sköld/Bäckman

Skaftö (1963)

Röd PL 4476, 450 34 Fiskebäckskil
- ☎ **(0523) 23211**
- 📠 (0523) 23215
- ⏸ 18 L 4831 m SSS 69
- 👥 WD–H
- ££ 150kr–300kr
- ⛳ 40km W of Uddevalla, through Fiskebäckskil
- ⌂ Sköld/Sederholm

Strömstad (1967)

Golfbanevägen, 452 90 Strömstad 1
- ☎ **(0526) 61788**
- 📠 (0526) 14766
- ⏸ 18 L 5615 m SSS 71
- 👥 H
- ££ 250kr (300kr)
- ⛳ 6km N of Strömstad
- ⌂ Sköld/Sederholm
- ⬛ www.golf.se/stromstadgk

Sunne (1970)

Box 108, 686 23 Sunne
- ☎ **(0565) 14100/14210**
- 📠 (0565) 14855
- ⏸ 18 hole course SSS 72
- 👥 H
- ££ 200kr
- ⛳ 2km S of Sunne. 60km N of Karlstad on Route 45
- ⌂ Jan Sederholm

Torreby (1961)

Torreby Slott, 455 93 Munkedal
- ☎ **(0524) 21365/21109**
- 📠 (0524) 21351
- ⏸ 18 L 5885 m Par 72
- 👥 H
- ££ 200kr
- ⛳ Munkedal 8km. Uddevalla 30km.
- ⌂ Douglas Brasier

Uddeholm (1965)

Risäter 20, 683 93 Råda
- ☎ **(0563) 60564**
- 📠 (0563) 60017

- ⏸ 18 L 5830 m SSS 72
- 👥 U H
- ££ D–160kr
- ⛳ Lake Råda, 80km N of Karlstad, via RD62

Switzerland

Bern

G&CC Blumisberg (1959)

3184 Wünnewil
- ☎ **(026) 496 34 38**
- 📠 (026) 496 35 23
- ⏸ 18 L 6048 m Par 72
- 👥 WD–U H WE–M
- ££ 80fr (80fr)
- ⛳ Wünnewil, 16km SW of Bern
- ⌂ B von Limburger

Les Bois (1988)

Case Postale 26, 2336 Les Bois
- ☎ **(032) 961 10 03**
- 📠 (032) 961 10 17
- ⏸ 9 L 3000 m Par 72
- 👥 WD–U WE–M
- ££ 75fr (90fr)
- ⛳ 12km NE of La Chaux-de-Fonds, on Basel road
- ⌂ Jeremy Pern

Neuchâtel (1928)

Hameau de Voëns, 2072 Saint-Blaise
- ☎ **(032) 753 55 50**
- 📠 (032) 753 29 40
- ✉ golf.ne@bluewin.ch
- ⏸ 18 L 5913 m SSS 71
- 👥 H
- ££ 80fr (100fr)
- ⛳ Voëns/Saint-Blaise, 5km E of Neuchâtel. 30km W of Bern

Payerne (1996)

Public
Domaine des Invuardes, 1530 Payerne
- ☎ **(026) 662 4220**
- 📠 (026) 662 4221
- ⏸ 18 L 5450 m Par 70
- 👥 U H
- ££ 80fr (100fr)
- ⛳ 50km W of Bern. 50km NE of Lausanne
- ⌂ Yves Bureau

Wallenried (1992)

1784 Wallenried
- ☎ **(026) 684 84 80**
- 📠 (026) 684 84 90
- ✉ info@golf-wollenreid.ch
- ⏸ 18 L 6000 m Par 72
- 👥 WD–U H WE–U H
- ££ 80fr (100fr)
- ⛳ 6km W of Fribourg
- ⌂ Ruzzo Reuss
- ⬛ www.swissgolfnetwork.ch

Wylihof (1994)

4542 Luterbach
- ☎ **(032) 682 28 28**
- 📠 (032 682 65 17
- ⏸ 18 L 6580 yds Par 73
- 👥 WD–U H–max 36 WE–M H
- ££ 100fr (100fr)
- ⛳ 40km N of Bern. 90km W of Zürich
- ⌂ Ruzzo Reuss von Plauen
- ⬛ www.golf.ch

Bernese Oberland

Interlaken-Unterseen (1964)

Postfach 110, 3800 Interlaken
- ☎ **(033) 823 60 16**
- 📠 (033) 823 42 03
- ⏸ 18 L 5980 m Par 72
- 👥 H
- ££ 90fr (105fr)
- ⛳ Interlaken 3km
- ⌂ Donald Harradine
- ⬛ www.interlakengolf.ch

Riederalp (1986)

3987 Riederalp
- ☎ **(027) 927 29 32**
- 📠 (027) 927 29 32
- ⏸ 9 L 3066 m SSS 55
- 👥 U
- ££ 45fr
- ⛳ 10km NE of Brig
- ⌂ Donald Harradine

Lake Geneva & South West

Bonmont (1983)

Château de Bonmont, 1275 Chéserex
- ☎ **(022) 369 99 00**
- 📠 (022) 369 99 09
- ⏸ 18 L 6080m CR 71.6 SR 126
- 👥 WD–restricted WE–M
- ££ WD–100fr
- ⛳ 3km from Nyon. 30km NE of Geneva
- ⌂ Donald Harradine

Les Coullaux (1989)

1846 Chessel
- ☎ **(024) 481 22 46**
- 📠 (024) 481 66 46
- ⏸ 9 L 2940 m Par 58
- 👥 U
- ££ 9 holes: 30fr (45fr) 2x9 holes: 35fr (55fr)
- ⛳ Chessel, between Evian and Montreux
- ⌂ Donald Harradine

Crans-sur-Sierre (1906)

C P 112, 3963 Crans-sur-Sierre
- ☎ **(027) 485 97 97**
- 📠 (027) 485 97 98

▷ 18 L 6341 m SSS 72
9 L 2729 m SSS 35
9 hole Par 3 course
ᛈ H
£€ On application
⛳ 20km E of Sion. Geneva 2 hrs

Domaine Impérial (1987)
Villa Prangins, 1196 Gland
☎ (022) 999 06 00
▯ (022) 999 06 06
▷ 18 L 6297 m SSS 74
ᛈ WD–H exc Mon am
£€ WD–150fr
⛳ Nyon, 20km N of Geneva
⌂ Pete Dye

Geneva (1923)
70 Route de la Capite, 1223 Cologny
☎ (+41) 22 707 48 00
▯ (+41) 22 707 48 20
✉ secretariat@golfgeneve.ch
▷ 18 L 6150 m Par 72
ᛈ WD–am only Tues–Fri WE–M
£€ 150fr
⛳ 4km from centre of Geneva
⌂ Robert Trent Jones Sr

Lausanne (1921)
Route du Golf 3, 1000 Lausanne 25
☎ (021) 784 84 84
▯ (021) 784 84 80
✉ golf.lausanne@bluewin.ch
▷ 18 L 6295 m SSS 74
ᛈ H
£€ 90fr (110fr)
⛳ 7km N of Lausanne towards Le
Mont
⌂ Narbel/Harradine/Pern

Montreux (1898)
54 Route d'Evian, 1860 Aigle
☎ (024) 466 46 16
▯ (024) 466 60 47
✉ gcmtx@swissonline.ch
▷ 18 L 6143 m Par 72 SSS 73
ᛈ H
£€ 80fr (100fr)
⛳ Aigle, 15km S of Montreux
⌂ Donald Harradine
■ www.swissgolfnetwork.ch

Sion (1995)
CP 639, Rte Vissigen 150, 1951 Sion
☎ (+41) (0) 027 203 79 00
▯ (+41) (0) 02 203 79 01
✉ info@golfclubsion.ch
✍ Guy Reynard
▷ 18 L 5543 m Par 70 SR 120 (men
champion)
18 L 5095 m Par 70 SR 118 (men)
18 L 4859 m Par 70 SR 123 (ladies
champion)
18 L 4423 m Par 70 SR 119 (ladies)
ᛈ H–booking necessary
£€ 90 fr (100 fr)
⛳ Sion, 80km SE of Montreux
⌂ JL Tronchet
■ www.golfclubsion.ch

Verbier (1970)
1936 Verbier
☎ (027) 771 53 14
▯ (027) 771 60 93
▷ 18 L 4880 m Par 69
ᛈ U
£€ 50fr–70fr (80fr)
⛳ Centre of Verbier
⌂ Donald Harradine
■ www.verbiergolf.com

Villars (1922)
C P 152, 1884 Villars
☎ (024) 495 42 14
▯ (024) 495 42 18
✍ Eric Krol (Mgr)
▷ 18 L 5250 m SSS 70
ᛈ U
£€ 60fr (80fr)
⛳ 5km E of Villars towards Les
Diablerets
⌂ Thierry Sprecher
■ www.golf-villars.ch

Lugano & Ticino

Lugano (1923)
6983 Magliaso
☎ (091) 606 15 57
▯ (091) 606 65 58
▷ 18 L 5575 m Par 70
ᛈ H–max 36
£€ 90fr (110fr)
⛳ 8km W of Lugano towards Ponte
Tresa
⌂ Harradine/Robinson
■ www.golflugano.ch

Patriziale Ascona (1928)
Via al Lido 81, 6612 Ascona
☎ (091) 791 21 32
▯ (091) 791 07 06
▷ 18 L 5933 m Par 71
ᛈ H–max 30
£€ 100fr (100fr)
⛳ 5km W of Locarno
⌂ CK Cotton
■ www.golf.ascona.ch

St Moritz & Engadine

Arosa (1944)
Postfach 95, 7050 Arosa
☎ (081) 377 42 42
▯ (081) 377 46 77
▷ 18 L 4340 m Par 66
ᛈ U
£€ 70fr
⛳ 30km S of Chur
⌂ D Harradine/P Harradine
■ www.arosa.ch/golf

Bad Ragaz (1957)
Hans Albrecht Strasse, 7310 Bad Ragaz
☎ (081) 303 37 17
▯ (081) 303 37 27

▷ 18 L 5750 m Par 70
ᛈ H
£€ D–120fr
⛳ 20km N of Chur. 100km SE of
Zürich
⌂ Donald Harradine
■ www.resortragaz.ch

Davos (1929)
Postfach, 7260 Davos Dorf
☎ (081) 46 56 34
▯ (081) 46 25 55
▷ 18 L 5208 yds Par 68
ᛈ WD–U
£€ On application
⛳ 1km outside Davos
⌂ Donald Harradine

Engadin (1893)
7503 Samedan
☎ (081) 851 04 66
▯ (081) 851 04 67
▷ 18 L 6350 m SSS 73
ᛈ H
£€ 90fr
⛳ Samedan, 6km NE of St Moritz
⌂ M Verdieri

Lenzerheide Valbella (1950)
7078 Lenzerheide
☎ (081) 385 13 13
▯ (081) 385 13 19
▷ 18 L 5269 m SSS 69
ᛈ H
£€ 60fr–80fr
⛳ 20km S of Chur towards St Moritz
⌂ Donald Harradine

Vulpera (1923)
7552 Vulpera Spa
☎ (081) 864 96 88
▯ (081) 864 96 89
▷ 9 L 1982 m SSS 62
ᛈ H
£€ 60fr (70fr) W–290fr
⛳ Tarasp, nr Vulpera. 60km NE of St
Moritz
⌂ Dell/Spencer
■ www.swissgolfnetwork.ch-9holes-
vulpera

Zürich & North

Breitenloo (1964)
8309 Oberwil b. Bassersdorf
☎ (01) 836 40 80
▯ (01) 837 10 85
▷ 18 L 6125 m Par 72 SSS 72
ᛈ WD–H by appointment WE–M H
£€ 100fr
⛳ 10km NE of Zürich Airport
⌂ Harradine/Pennink

Bürgenstock (1928)
6363 Bürgenstock
☎ (041) 610 2434
▯ (041) 610 3761
✉ club@buergenstock-hotels.ch

For list of abbreviations and key to symbols see page 627

9 L 2200 m Par 33
H
40fr (50fr) Season May–October
15km S of Lucerne
Fritz Frey
www.buergenstock-hotels.com

Dolder (1907)
Kurhausstrasse 66, 8032 Zürich
- **(01) 261 50 45**
- (01) 261 53 02
- 9 L 1735 m SSS 58
- WD–H WE–M
- WD–70fr
- Zürich

Entfelden (1988)
Postfach 230, Muhenstrasse 52, 5036 Oberentfelden
- **(062) 723 89 84**
- (062) 723 84 36
- 9 L 3960 m SSS 60
- H
- 50fr (70fr)
- 50km W of Zürich
- Donald Harradine

Erlen (1988)
Schlossgut Eppishausen, Schlossstr 7, 8586 Erlen
- **(071) 648 29 30**
- (071) 648 29 40
- 18 L 5913 m SSS 71
- H
- 80fr (110fr)
- 30km NW of St Gallen. 60km W of Zürich
- Deutsche Golfconsult

Hittnau-Zürich G&CC (1964)
8335 Hittnau
- **(01) 950 24 42**
- (01) 951 01 66
- 18 L 5519 m CR 69.4 SR 127
- WD–U WE–M
- WD–110fr
- Hittnau, 30km E of Zürich

Küssnacht (1994)
Sekretariat/Grossarni, 6403 Küssnacht am Rigi
- **(041) 850 70 60**
- (041) 850 70 41
- 18 L 5397 m Par 68
- WD–U H WE–M H
- 100fr (120fr)
- 20km NE of Lucerne
- Peter Harradine
- www.golfkuessnacht.ch

Lucerne (1903)
Dietschiberg, 6006 Luzern
- **(041) 420 97 87**
- (041) 420 82 48
- 18 L 6082 m Par 72 SSS 71-73
- H
- 80fr (100fr)
- Lucerne 2km

Ostschweizerischer (1948)
Club
9246 Niederbüren
- **(071) 422 18 56**
- (071) 422 18 25
- 18 L 5920 m SSS 71
- WD–H
- D–90fr
- Niederbüren, 25km NW of St Gallen
- Donald Harradine
- www.osgc.ch

Schinznach-Bad (1929)
5116 Schinznach-Bad
- **(056) 443 12 26**
- (056) 443 34 83
- 9 L 5670 m Par 71
- WD–U
- 70fr
- 6km S of Brugg. 35km W of Zürich

Schönenberg (1967)
8824 Schönenberg
- **(01) 788 90 40**
- (01) 788 90 45
- 18 L 6205 m CR 73.4 SR 137
- WD–H–by appointment WE–M H
- 120fr
- 20km S of Zürich
- Donald Harradine
- www.swissgolfnetwork.ch

Sempachersee (1996)
6024 Hildisrieden, Lucerne
- **(041) 462 71 71**
- (041) 462 71 72
- 18 L 6161 m Par 72 SR 107
  9 L 3890 m Par 31
- WD–U H WE–M H
- 90fr (90fr)
- 13km NW of Lucerne
- Kurt Rossknecht
- www.golf-sempachersee.ch

Zürich-Zumikon (1929)
Weid 9, 8126 Zumikon
- **(043) 288 1088**
- (043) 288 1078
- gcc2.2vmikon@ggaweb.ch
- 18 L 6350 m Par 72 CR 73 SR 130
- WD–H by appointment WE–M
- WD–150fr
- 10km SE of Zürich
- Donald Harradine
- www.swissgolfnetwork.ch

Turkey

Gloria Golf
Acisu Mevkii PK27 Belek, Serik, Antalya
- **(242) 715 15 20**

(242) 715 15 25
18 holes Par 72
9 hole Academy course
U
Antalya
Michel Gayon

Kemer G&CC
Goturk Koyu Mevkii Kemerburgaz, Eyup, Istanbul
- **(212) 239 70 10**
- (212) 239 73 76
- 18 holes Par 73
- U–phone for booking
- $50 ($90)
- 30km from Istanbul
- J Dudok van Heel

Klassis G&CC
Silivri, Istanbul
- **(212) 748 46 00**
- (212) 748 46 43
- 18 L 6200 m Par 73
  9 hole Par 3 course
- U
- Istanbul
- Tony Jacklin

National Golf Club, Antalya
Belek Turizm Merkezi, 07500 Serik, Antalya
- **(242) 725 46 20**
- (242) 725 46 23
- 18 L 6232 m Par 72 SSS 72
  9 L 1547 m Par 29
- H
- £50
- Belek, 30km from Antalya
- Feherty/Jones
- www.nationalturkey.com

Robinson Golf Club Nobilis (1998)
Acisu Mevkii, Belek, 07500 Serik/Antalya, Antalya
- **(+90) 242 715 1491**
- (+90) 242 715 1985
- golf.nobilis@robinson.de
- Gents: 18 L 5743 m Par 71 CR 70.6 SR 121
  Ladies: 18 L 5037 m Par 71 CR 72.3 SR 124
- H gents 28, ladies 36
- €74
- 35km E of Antalya on Mediterranean coast
- Dave Thomas
- www.robinson.de

Tat Golf International
Belek International Golf, Kum Tepesi Belek, 07500 Serik, Antalya
- **(242) 725 53 03**
- (242) 725 52 99
- 27 holes Par 72
- U
- Antalya
- Hawtree

General Index

84 Lumber Classic of Pennsylvania, 145

A 6 Golfklubb, 910
Aa St Omer Open, 122
Aachen, 872
Aalborg, 838
AAMI Australian Women's Open, 196, 214
Aarhus, 838
Abbekas, 907
Abbeville, 850
Abbey Hill, 633
Abbey Hotel G & CC, 743
Abbeyleix, 774
Abbey Moor, 722
Abbeydale, 750
Abbeyfeale, 775
Abbotsley, 636
Abenberg, 871
Aberconwy Trophy, 257
Aberdare, 821
Aberdeenshire Ladies', 331
Aberdour, 797
Aberdovey, 819
Aberfeldy, 812
Aberfoyle, 816
Abergele, 818
Aberlady, 807
Abernethy, 803
Abersoch, 820
Aberystwyth, 817
Ableiges, 852
Aboyne, 784
Abridge G & CC, 658
Accenture Match Play Championship, 160
Accrington & District, 683
Achensee, 830
Achill, 776
Acquabona, 881
Adamstal, 833
Adare Manor, 775
The Addington, 722
Addington Court, 723
Addington Palace, 723
Adriatic GC Cervia, 881
Aero Club de Santiago, 899
Aero Club de Vigo, 899
Aero Club de Zaragoza, 903
Afandou, 878
Ågesta, 913
Ahaus, 872
L'Ailette, 850
Airdrie, 805
Airlinks, 699
Les Aisses, 848
Aix-les-Bains, 860
Aix Marseille, 858
Ajoncs d'Or, 846
Akureyri, 879

Albarella, 885
Albatross, 906
Albi Lasbordes, 862
Albon, 860
Albret, 844
Alcaidesa Links, 901
Aldeburgh, 720
Aldenham G & CC, 671
Alder Root, 638
Alderley Edge, 638
Alderney, 638
Aldersey Green, 638
Aldwark Manor, 746
Aldwickbury Park, 671
Alexandra Park, 801
Alford, 784
Alfred Dunhill Championship, 115
Alfred Dunhill Cup, 182
Alfreton, 648
Algarve Open de Portugal, 117
Alhaurín, 900
Alicante, 895
Alice Springs, 822
Alingsås, 912
Allendale, 706
Allerthorpe Park, 745
Allerton Municipal, 696
Allerum, 909
Allestree Park, 648
Allgäuer G & LC, 869
Alloa, 794
Allt-y-Graban, 826
Almeerderhout, 890
Almerimar, 896
Älmhult, 910
Alness, 803
Alnmouth, 706
Alnmouth Village, 706
Alnwick, 706
Aloha, 901
Alpino Di Stresa, 883
Alresford, 666
Alsager G & CC, 717
Alston Moor, 646
Alten Fliess, 872
Altenhof, 866
Alto G & CC, 892
Alton, 666
Altorreal, 895
Altötting-Burghausen, 869
Altrincham Municipal, 639
Alva, 794
Alvaston Hall, 639
Alvkarleby, 908
Alwoodley, 752
Alyth, 812
Amarante, 894
Amarilla, 899
Amateur Championship, 218
Amber Baltic, 892
Ambrosiano, 879

American Express Challenge, 163
Amiens, 850
Ammerschwihr, 856
Ampfield Par Three, 666
Ampleforth College, 746
Amsterdam Old Course, 886
Amsterdamse, 886
Amstetten-Ferschnitz, 830
Andenne, 834
Anderstein, 890
Andover, 666
Ängelholm, 909
Angers, 854
Anglesey, 285, 820
Ängsö, 903
Angus, 283
Angus Ladies', 331
Anjou G & CC, 854
Annanhill, 790
Annecy, 860
Annonay-Gourdan, 860
Añoreta, 900
Anstruther, 798
Ansty, 737
Antlers, The, 273
Antrim, 758
Antrobus, 639
The ANZ Championship, 115
ANZ Ladies Masters, 196
Appleby, 646
Apremont, 850
Aqualate, 712
Aquarius, 677
Araslöv, 909
Arboga, 903
Arbroath Artisan, 787
Arcachon, 844
Arcangues, 845
Arcot Hall, 706
Les Arcs, 860
Ardacong, 769
Ardee, 776
Ardeer, 790
Ardfert, 771
Ardglass, 765
Ardminnan, 765
Ardrée, 848
Arendal og Omegn, 891
Argyll and Bute, 283
Ariège, 862
Ärila, 903
Arkley, 671
Arklow, 782
Army, 666
Arnold Palmer Award, 364
Aro-Mas Nou, 897
Aroeira, 893
Arosa, 917
Los Arqueros, 901
Arras, 850
Arras Open de France Dames, 197

Arrowe Park, 696
Arscott, 713
Artland, 873
Arvika, 915
Asahi Ruokuken International
    Championship, 201
Ashbourne, 648, 777
Ashburnham, 817
Ashbury, 650
Ashby Decoy, 691
Ashfield, 759
Ashford, 677
Ashford Castle, 777
Ashford Manor, 699
The Ashley Wood, 653
Ashridge, 671
Ashton & Lea, 683
Ashton-in-Makerfield, 683
Ashton-on-Mersey, 639
Ashton-under-Lyne, 683
Asiago, 882
Asian PGA Tour, 154
Askernish, 804
Askersund, 903
Aspect Park, 710
Aspley Guise & Woburn Sands, 629
Asserbo, 840
Association of Golf Writers' Trophy,
    362
Astbury, 639
Aston Wood, 717
AT&T Pebble Beach National
    Pro-Am, 139
Atalaya G & CC, 901
Athenry, 769
Atherstone, 737
Athlone, 779
Athy, 773
Åtvidaberg, 910
Aubazine, 847
Auchenblae, 784
Auchenharvie, 790
Auchmill, 786
Auchnacloy, 780
Auchterarder, 812
Auchterderran, 798
Augsburg, 869
Aura Golf, 842
Austin Lodge, 677
Australasian Tour, 155
Australian Amateur Championship,
    286
Australian Ladies' Masters, 214
Australian Open, 191
Austria-Wörther See, 830
Austrian Open, 191
Avernas, 836
Avesta, 908
Avrillé, 854
Axe Cliff, 650
Aylesbury Golf Centre, 633
Aylesbury Park, 633
Aylesbury Vale, 629
Ayrshire, 283
Ayrshire Ladies', 331

Baberton, 808
Bäckavattnet, 912
Backworth, 735

Bacup, 683
Bad Gleichenberg, 832
Bad Griesbach, 871
Bad Kissingen, 865
Bad Kleinkirchheim-Reichenau, 830
Bad Liebenzell, 876
Bad Neuenahr G & LC, 875
Bad Ragaz, 917
Bad Rappenau, 876
Bad Salgau, 876
Bad Salzuflen G & LC, 868
Bad Tatzmannsdorf G & CC, 833
Bad Tölz, 869
Bad Windsheim, 871
Bad Wörishofen, 869
Baden, 846
Baden Hills GC Rastatt, 876
Baden-Baden, 876
Bad Gastein, 831
Badgemore Park, 710
Baerum, 891
Bagden Hall Hotel, 752
Baildon, 752
Bakewell, 648
Bala, 820
Bala Lake Hotel, 820
Balbirnie Park, 798
Balbriggan, 767
Balcarrick, 767
Bâle G & CC, 856
Balfron, 816
Balgove Course, 800
Ballaghaderreen, 779
Ballards Gore G & CC, 658
Ballater, 784
Ballina, 777
Ballinamore, 775
Ballinascorney, 767
Ballinasloe, 771
Ballingry, 798
Ballinlough Castle, 781
Ballinrobe, 777
Ballochmyle, 790
Ballybeggan Park, 771
Ballybofey & Stranorlar, 764
Ballybunion, 772
Ballycastle, 758
Ballyclare, 758
Ballyearl Golf Centre, 760
Ballyhaunis, 777
Ballyheigue Castle, 772
Ballykisteen, 779
Ballyliffin, 764
Ballymena, 758
Ballymote, 779
Balmer See, 863
Balmoral, 760
Balmore, 796
Balnagask, 786
Baltinglass, 782
Bamberg, 871
Bamburgh Castle, 706
Banbridge, 765
Banbury Golf Centre, 710
Banchory, 784
Bandon, 762
Bangor, 765
Bank House Hotel G & CC, 743
Bank of America Colonial, 142

Bank of Scotland Junior Masters
    (Boys), 346
Bank of Scotland Junior Masters
    (Girls), 355
Banstead Downs, 723
Bantry Bay, 762
Barbaroux, 858
Barberán, 900
Barganiza, 898
Bargoed, 821
Barkway Park, 671
Barlassina CC, 880
Barlaston, 717
Barnard Castle, 656
Barnehurst, 677
Barnham Broom Hotel, 702
Barnsley, 750
Baron Hill, 820
Barra, 804
Barrow, 646
Barrow Hills, 723
Barsebäck G & CC, 907
Barshaw, 814
Barton-on-Sea, 666
Basildon, 658
Basingstoke, 666
Bass Rock, 807
Båstad, 909
Batalha, 893
Batchwood Hall, 671
Batchworth Park, 671
Bath, 714
Bathgate, 811
De Batouwe, 890
Baugé-Pontigné, 854
Les Baux de Provence, 859
Bawburgh, 702
Bawtry G & CC, 750
Baxenden & District, 683
Bay Hill Invitational, 140
BC Open, 143
Beacon Park, 683
Beaconsfield, 633
Beadlow Manor Hotel G & CC, 629
Beamish Park, 656
Bearna, 771
Bearsden, 796
Bearsted, 677
Bearwood, 630
Bearwood Lakes, 630
Beau Desert, 717
Beauchief, 750
Beaufort, 772
Le Beaujolais, 861
Beaune-Levernois, 847
Beauvallon-Grimaud, 859
Beaverstown, 767
Beccles, 720
Beckenham Place Park, 677
Bedale, 747
Bedford, 629
Bedford & County, 629
Bedford & Cambridge PGA, 188
Bedfordshire, 281, 629
Bedfordshire Ladies', 328
Bedinge, 909
Bedlingtonshire, 706
Beech Park, 767
Beedles Lake, 689

Beeston Fields, 708
Berhinderten, 866
Beith, 790
Belas, 893
Belfairs, 658
Belford, 706
The Belfry, 737
Belhus Park G & CC, 658
Bell Canadian Open, 144
Bellavista, 902
Belle Dune, 850
Bellefontaine, 852
Belleisle, 790
Bellême-St-Martin, 855
Bellingham, 706
Bellshill, 805
BellSouth Classic, 141
Belmont Lodge, 670
Belton Park, 691
Belton Woods Hotel, 691
Belturbet, 761
Belvoir Park, 760
Ben Rhydding, 752
Benone Par Three, 775
Benson and Hedges International
    Open, 119
Bentham, 747
Bentley G & CC, 658
Benton Hall, 658
Bentra, 758
Bercuit, 835
Berehaven, 762
De Berendonck, 888
Bergamo L'Albenza, 880
Bergen, 891
Bergisch-Land, 873
Berkhamsted, 671
Berkhamsted Trophy, 268
Berks, Bucks and Oxon, 188, 281
The Berkshire, 630
Berkshire Ladies', 328
Berkshire Trophy, 257
Berlin Motzener See, 863
Berlin Wannsee, 863
Berwick-upon-Tweed, 706
Besançon, 856
Best G & CC, 888
Betchworth Park, 723
Béthemont-Chisan CC, 858
Betws-y-Coed, 818
Beuerberg, 869
Beverley & East Riding, 745
Bexleyheath, 677
Biarritz, 845
Biarritz Ladies Classic, 198
Bicester G & CC, 710
Bidford Grange, 737
Bidston, 696
Biella Le Betulle, 883
Bigbury, 650
Biggar, 805
La Bigorre, 862
Bill Johnson Trophy, 363
Billerud, 915
Billingbear Park, 631
Billingen, 912
Billingham, 656
Bingley St Ives, 752
Biot, 859

Birch Grove, 658
Birch Hall, 648
Birchwood, 639
Birchwood Park, 677
Bird Hills, 631
Birdland G & CC, 878
Birley Wood, 750
Birr, 778
Birstall, 689
Birtley, 735
Biscarrosse, 845
Bishop Auckland, 656
Bishop's Stortford, 671
Bishopbriggs, 801
Bishopshire, 812
Bishopswood, 666
Bitburger Land, 875
Bitche, 856
Bjäre, 909
Blaby, 689
Black Bush, 777
Blackburn, 683
Blackley, 694
Blacklion, 761
Blackmoor, 666
Blacknest, 666
Blackpool North Shore, 684
Blackpool Park, 684
Blackwater Valley, 666
Blackwell, 743
Blackwell Grange, 656
Blackwood, 765, 822
Blainroe, 782
Blair Atholl, 812
Blairbeth, 805
Blairgowrie, 812
Blairmore & Strone, 788
Blankney, 691
G & CC Bled, 895
Bletchingley, 723
Blokhus Klit, 838
Bloxwich, 717
Bludenz-Braz, 834
Blue Circle, 648
Blue Green-Artiguelouve, 845
Blue Green-Seignosse, 845
Blue Mountain Golf Centre, 631
G & CC Blumisberg, 916
Blundells Hill, 696
Blyth, 706
BMO Financial Group Canadian
    Women's Open, 202
BMW Asian Open, 114
BMW International Open, 126
BMW Russian Open, 125
Boat-of-Garten, 803
Bob Hope Chrysler Classic, 139
Bobby Jones Award, 366
Bochum, 873
Boden, 905
Bodenstown, 773
Bogliaco, 882
Bognor Regis, 733
Bogogno, 880
Böhmerwald GC Ulrichsberg, 830
Les Bois, 916
Bois de Ruminghem, 850
Bokskogen, 907
Boldmere, 737

Boldon, 736
Bollnäs, 908
Bologna, 881
Bolton, 684
Bolton Old Links, 684
Bolton Open Golf Course, 684
Bon Accord, 786
Bonalba, 895
Bonar Bridge/Ardgay, 802
Bondhay, 648
Bondoufle, 852
Bondues, 850
Bonmont, 916
Bonmont Terres Noves, 897
Bonn-Godesberg in Wachtberg,
    875
Bonnybridge, 816
Bonnyton, 814
Boothferry Park, 745
Bootle, 696
Borås, 912
Bordeaux-Cameyrac, 845
Bordeaux-Lac, 845
Bordelais, 845
Border Counties Ladies', 331
Border Golfers' Association, 283
Les Bordes, 848
Borgarness, 879
Bornholm, 837
Borre, 891
Borregaard, 891
Borris, 761
Borth & Ynyslas, 817
Bosjökloster, 909
El Bosque, 903
Bossenstein, 834
Bossey G & CC, 861
Boston, 691
Boston West, 691
Bothwell Castle, 805
Botkyrka, 914
Botley Park Hotel G & CC, 666
Boughton, 677
La Boulie, 858
Bourn, 636
Bowenhurst Golf Centre, 723
Bowood G & CC, 740
Bowood Park, 643
Bowring, 696
Boxmoor, 672
Boyce Hill, 658
Boyd Quaich, 279
Boyle, 779
Boys' Amateur Championship, 338
Boys' Home Internationals (R&A
    Trophy), 349
Boysnope Park, 695
Boystown, 782
Brabantse, 835
Bracken Ghyll, 752
Brackenwood, 697
Brackley Municipal, 684
Bradford, 752
Bradford Moor, 753
Bradford-on-Avon, 741
Bradley Park, 753
Braehead, 794
Braemar, 784
Braid Hills, 809

Braids United, 809
Brailes, 710
Brailsford, 648
Braintree, 658
Bramall Park, 638
Bramcote Waters, 737
Bramhall, 638
Bramley, 723
Brampton (Talkin Tarn), 646
Brampton Heath, 704
Brampton Park, 636
Bramshaw, 666
Brancepeth Castle, 656
Brandhall, 743
Branshaw, 753
Branston G & CC, 717
Braunschweig, 868
Braxted Park, 658
Bray, 782
Brayton Park, 646
Breadsall Priory Hotel G & CC, 648
Brean, 714
Brechin, 787
Brecon, 824
Brecon & Radnor, 285
Breedon Priory, 689
Bregenzerwald, 834
Breightmet, 684
Breinholtgård, 838
Breitenloo, 917
Bremer Schweiz, 863
Brent Valley, 699
La Bresse, 861
Brest Les Abers, 846
Brest-Iroise, 846
La Bretesche, 854
Brett Vale, 720
Breuninkhof, 887
Brianza, 880
Brickendon Grange, 672
Brickhampton Court, 663
Bridge of Allan, 816
Bridgedown, 672
Bridgend & District, 811
Bridget Jackson Bowl, 324
Bridgnorth, 713
Bridlington, 745
The Bridlington Links, 745
Bridport & West Dorset, 653
Brierley Forest, 708
Briggens House Hotel, 672
Brighouse Bay, 794
Bright Castle, 765
Brighton & Hove, 731
Brigode, 850
Brinkworth, 741
Brinsbury College, 733
Las Brisas, 901
Bristol & Clifton, 663
British Mid-Amateur Championship, 221
British Seniors' Open Amateur Championship, 220
British Youths Open Amateur Championship, 339
Bro-Bålsta, 914
Broadstone, 653
Broadwater Park, 723
Broadway, 663

Brocket Hall, 672
Brocton Hall, 717
Brodauer Mühle, 866
Brodick, 790
Broekpolder, 889
Broke Hill, 677
Brokenhurst Manor, 667
Bromborough, 697
Bromley, 677
Bromsgrove Golf Centre, 743
Brønderslev, 838
Brookdale, 684
Brookmans Park, 672
Broome Manor, 741
Broome Park, 677
Broomieknowe, 809
Brora, 802
Brough, 745
Broughton Heath, 648
Brown Trout, 775
Brugse Vaart, 887
Brundtlandbanen, 838
Brunn G & CC, 833
Brunssummerheide, 889
Brunston Castle, 790
Bruntsfield Links Golfing Society, 809
La Bruyère, 835
Bryn Meadows Golf Hotel, 821
Bryn Morfydd Hotel, 818
Brynhill, 825
BT Ladies Open, 197
Buchanan Castle, 816
Buchholz-Nordheide, 866
Buckingham, 633
Buckinghamshire, 633
Buckinghamshire Ladies', 328
Buckpool, 811
Budapest G & CC, 878
Buddon Links, 788
Bude & North Cornwall, 644
Budock Vean Hotel, 644
Buick Classic, 142
Buick Invitational, 139
Buick Open, 143
Builth Wells, 825
Bulbury Woods, 653
Bull Bay, 820
Bulwell Forest, 708
Buncrana, 764
Bundoran, 764
Bungay & Waveney Valley, 721
Bunsay Downs, 658
Burford, 710
Burg Overbach, 875
Burg Purmerend, 886
Burg Zievel, 875
Burgdorf, 868
Bürgenstock, 917
Burgess Hill Golf Centre, 733
Burgham Park, 706
Burghill Valley, 670
Burghley Park, 691
Burhill, 723
Burhill Family Foursomes, 273
Burley, 667
Burnfield House, 758
Burnham & Berrow, 714
Burnham Beeches, 633

Burnham-on-Crouch, 659
Burnley, 684
Burnside, 788
Burntisland, 798
Burntisland Golf House Club, 798
Burslem, 717
The Burstead, 659
Burton-on-Trent, 648
Burvik, 903
Bury, 684
Bury St Edmunds, 721
Bush Hill Park, 699
Bushey G & CC, 672
Bushey Hall, 672
Bushfoot, 758
Bussy-St-Georges, 852
Bute, 788
Buxtehude, 866
Buxton & High Peak, 648

C & L Country Club, 699
Ca' degli Ulivi, 882
Ca' della Nave, 885
Cabourg-Le Home, 855
Cabra Castle, 761
Cadmore Lodge, 670
Caen, 855
Caerleon, 822
Caernarfon and District, 285
Caernarfonshire and Angelsey Ladies', 332
Caernarfonshire Cup, 285
Caerphilly, 821
Caerwys, 819
Cahir Park, 779
Caird Park, 787
Cairndhu, 758
La Cala, 900
Calcot Park, 631
Caldecott Hall, 702
Calderbraes, 805
Calderfields, 717
Caldes Internacional, 897
Caldwell, 814
Caldy, 697
Caledonian, 786
Callan, 774
Callander, 812
Caltex Singapore Masters, 115
Calverley, 753
Camberley Heath, 723
Cambridge, 636
Cambridge National, 636
Cambridgeshire, 281
Cambridgeshire and Huntingdonshire Ladies', 328
Cambridgeshire Moat House, 636
Cambuslang, 805
Came Down, 653
Cameron Corbett Vase, 258
Camperdown, 787
Campo Carlo Magno, 882
Campsie, 816
Cams Hall Estate, 667
Can Bosch, 897
La Cañada, 901
Canadian Amateur Championship, 286
Canadian Open, 191

Canadian Tour 2002, 158
Canarias Open de España, 117
El Candado, 900
Canford Magna, 654
Canford School, 654
Canmore, 798
Cannes Mandelieu, 859
Cannes Mandelieu Riviera, 859
Cannes Mougins, 859
Cannington, 714
Cannock Park, 717
Canons Brook, 659
Canons Court, 663
Cansiglio, 885
Canterbury, 677
Canwick Park, 691
Canyamel, 896
Cap d'Agde, 853
Capdepera, 896
Cape Cornwall G & CC, 644
Capelle a/d IJssel, 889
Caprington, 791
Carad Trophy, 258
Carcassonne, 853
Carden Park, 638
Cardiff, 825
Cardigan, 817
Cardross, 796
Carholme, 692
Caribbean Open, 192
Carimate, 880
Carlisle, 646
Carlow, 761
Carlsberg Malaysian Open, 116
Carlskrona, 909
Carluke, 805
Carlyon Bay, 644
Carmarthen, 817
Carnalea, 765
Carnbeg, 776
Carne Golf Links, 777
The Carnegie Club, 802
Carnoustie, 788
Carnoustie Caledonia, 788
Carnoustie Championship, 788
Carnoustie Ladies, 788
Carnoustie Mercantile, 788
Carnwath, 805
Carquefou, 854
Carradale, 789
Carrbridge, 803
Carrick Knowe, 809
Carrick-on-Shannon, 775
Carrick-on-Suir, 779
Carrickfergus, 758
Carrickmines, 769
Carsington Water, 648
Carswell CC, 710
Carton House, 773
Carus Green, 646
Casentino, 884
Castelconturbia, 880
Castelfalfi G & CC, 884
Castelgandolfo, 882
Casteljaloux, 845
Castell Heights, 821
Castello di Tolcinasco, 880
Castelnaud, 845
Casterton, 646

Castillo de Gorraiz, 898
Castle, 769
Castle Barna, 778
Castle Douglas, 794
Castle Eden & Peterlee, 656
Castle Hawk, 684
Castle Hume, 770
Castle Mokrice, 895
Castle Park, 807
Castle Point, 659
Castle Royle, 631
Castlebar, 777
Castleblayney, 778
Castlecomer, 774
Castlefields, 753
Castlegregory, 772
Castlerea, 779
Castlerock, 775
Castletown Golf Links, 675
Castletroy, 775
Castlewarden G & CC, 773
Castrop-Rauxel, 873
Cathcart Castle, 801
Cathkin Braes, 806
Catterick, 747
Cave Castle, 745
Cavendish, 649
Caversham Heath, 631
Cawder, 801
Ceann Sibeal, 772
Celbridge Elm Hall, 773
The Celtic Manor Hotel Resort, 822
Cély, 852
Central London Golf Centre, 723
Cergy Pontoise, 852, 852
Cervino, 883
Chadwell Springs, 672
Chalgrave Manor, 629
Chalmers, 906
Chalon-sur-Saône, 847
Chambon-sur-Lignon, 847
Chamonix, 861
Champ de Bataille, 855
Champagne, 850
Channel Islands, 281
Channels, 659
Chantaco, 845
Chantilly, 850
El Chaparral, 900
Chapel-en-le-Frith, 649
Charlesland G & CC, 782
Charleton, 798
Charleville, 762
Charminster, 654
Charnwood Forest, 689
Chart Hills, 677
Chartham Park, 733
Chartridge Park, 633
The Chase, 717
Château d'Avoise, 847
Château de la Bawette, 835
Château de Bournel, 856
Château de Chailly, 847
Château de Cheverny, 848
Château de Maintenon, 848
Château de Raray, 850
Château de la Tournette, 835
Château des Forges, 848
Château des Sept Tours, 848

Château des Vigiers, 845
Château Royal d'Ardenne, 834
Châteaublanc, 859
Chaumont-en-Vexin, 850
Cheadle, 638
Chedington Court, 654
Chelmsford, 659
Chelsfield Lakes Golf Centre, 678
Cherasco CC, 883
Cherry Burton, 745
Cherry Lodge, 678
Cherwell Edge, 711
Chesfield Downs, 672
Chesham & Ley Hill, 633
Cheshire, 281
Cheshire Ladies', 328
Cheshire & North Wales, 188
Cheshunt, 672
Chessington Golf Centre, 723
Chester, 638
Chester-Le-Street, 656
Chesterfield, 649
Chesterfield Municipal, 649
Chesterton Valley, 713
Chestfield, 678
Chevannes-Mennecy, 852
Chevin, 649
Chiberta, 845
Chichester, 733
Chick-fil-A Charity Championship, 201
Chiddingfold, 723
Im Chiemgau, 869
Chigwell, 659
Childwall, 697
Chiltern Forest, 633
Chilwell Manor, 708
Chilworth, 667
China Fleet CC, 644
Chingford, 659
Chippenham, 741
Chipping Norton, 711
Chipping Sodbury, 663
Chipstead, 724
Chirk, 827
Chislehurst, 678
Chobham, 724
Cholet, 854
Chorley, 684
Chorleywood, 672
Chorlton-cum-Hardy, 695
Christchurch, 654
Christnach, 886
Chrysler Classic, 140
Chrysler Classic of Greensboro, 145
Chulmleigh, 650
Church Stretton, 713
Churchill & Blakedown, 743
Churston, 650
Cicé-Blossac, 846
Cilgwyn, 817
Cill Dara, 773
Circolo Golf Ugolino, 884
Cirencester, 663
Cisco World Ladies' Match Play Championship, 205
City of Coventry (Brandon Wood), 737
City of Derry, 775

City of Newcastle, 736
City of Wakefield, 753
Clackmannanshire, 284
Clacton-on-Sea, 659
Clandeboye, 765
Clandon Regis, 724
Claremorris, 777
Claviere, 883
Clays, 827
Clayton, 753
Cleckheaton & District, 753
Clécy, 855
Cleethorpes, 692
Cleeve Hill, 663
Clement Ader, 852
Cleobury Mortimer, 713
Clervaux, 886
Clevedon, 715
Cleveland, 747
Cleydael, 834
Cliftonville, 760
Clitheroe, 684
Clober, 796
Clones, 778
Clonlara, 761
Clonmel, 779
Clontarf, 769
Close House, 706
Le Clou, 861
Cloverhill, 759
Club Son Parc, 896
Club Zur Vahr, 864
Clwyd Open, 258
Clydebank & District, 796
Clydebank Municipal, 796
Clyne, 826
Coatbridge Municipal, 806
Cobh, 762
Cobtree Manor Park, 678
Cochrane Castle, 814
Cockermouth, 646
Cocks Moor Woods, 743
Cocksford, 747
Coed-y-Mwstwr, 821
Cognac, 848
Colchester, 659
Cold Ashby, 704
Coldwinters, 767
College Pines, 708
Colli Berici, 885
Collingtree Park, 704
Colmworth, 629
Colne, 684
Colne Valley, 659
Colonsay, 789
Colony Club Gutenhof, 833
Colvend, 794
Colville Park, 806
Colworth, 629
Combles-en-Barrois, 856
La Commanderie, 861
Commonwealth Tournament, 319
Compiègne, 850
Comrie, 813
Conagra LPGA Skins Game, 200
Concord Park, 750
Conero GC Sirolo, 884
Congleton, 638
Connaught Ladies, 327

Connemara, 771
Connemara Isles, 771
Le Connétable, 848
Consett & District, 656
Conwy (Caernarvonshire), 818
Cooden Beach, 731
Cookridge Hall, 753
Coollattin, 782
Coombe Hill, 724
Coombe Wood, 724
Coosheen, 762
Copa de las Americas, 251
Copenhagen, 840
Copt Heath, 737
Copthorne, 733
Córdoba, 899
Corfu, 878
Corhampton, 667
Cork, 762
Cornwall, 281
Cornwall Ladies', 328
Corrençon-en-Vercors, 861
Corrie, 791
Corrstown, 767
Cortijo Grande, 896
Cosby, 689
Cosmopolitan G & CC, 884
Costa Ballena, 902
Costa Brava, 897
Costa de Azahar, 903
Costa Dorada, 897
Costa Teguise, 899
Costessey Park, 702
Cotgrave Place G & CC, 708
Cotswold Edge, 664
Cotswold Hills, 664
Cottesmore, 733
Cottingham, 746
Cottrell Park, 825
Coudray, 852
Les Coullaux, 916
Coulondres, 853
Coulsdon Manor, 724
County Armagh, 759
County Cavan, 761
County Longford, 776
County Louth, 776
County Meath, 777
County Sligo, 779
County Tipperary, 780
Courmayeur, 883
Courson Monteloup, 852
Courtown, 782
Coutainville, 855
Coventry, 738
Coventry Hearsall, 738
Cowal, 789
Cowdenbeath, 798
Cowdray Park, 733
Cowes, 676
Cowglen, 801
Coxmoor, 708
Craddockstown, 773
Cradoc, 825
Craigentinny, 809
Craigie Hill, 813
Craigielaw Classic, 187
Craigmillar Park, 809
Craigmillar Park Open, 258

Craignure, 789
Crail Golfing Society, 798
Crane Valley, 654
The Cranleigh, 724
Crans-sur-Sierre, 916
Cray Valley, 678
The Craythorne, 717
Crécy-la-Chapelle, 852
Creigiau, 821
Cretingham, 721
Crewe, 638
Crews Hill, 699
Criccieth, 820
Crichton, 794
Cricklade Hotel, 741
Crieff, 813
Crimple Valley, 747
Critchley Salver, 324
Croara, 881
Croham Hurst, 724
Crompton & Royton, 684
Cromstrijen, 889
Cromwell, 636
Crondon Park, 659
Crook, 656
Crookhill Park, 750
Crosland Heath, 753
Crossgar, 766
Crossmoor G & CC, 888
Crow Nest Park, 753
Crow Wood, 806
Crowborough Beacon, 731
Cruden Bay, 784
Cruit Island, 764
Cuddington, 724
La Cuesta, 898
Culdrose, 644
Cullen, 784
Cumberwell Park, 741
Cumbria, 281
Cumbria Ladies', 328
Cuneo, 883
Cupar, 798
Curra West, 771
The Curragh, 773
Curtis Cup Individual Records, 315
Cushendall, 758

Dachstein Tauern, 832
Daily Telegraph Damovo British
    Masters, 121
Daily Telegraph Woman Golfer of the
    Year, 362
Dainton Park, 650
Dalbeattie, 795
Dale Hill Hotel, 731
Dalhousie, 788
Dalmally, 789
Dalmilling, 791
Dalmunzie, 813
Dalsjö, 908
Dalston Hall, 646
Dalziel Park, 806
Damme G & CC, 836
Danesbury Park, 672
Danish Open, 192
Danube Golf-Wien, 833
Darenth Valley, 678
Darlington, 656

Dartford, 678
Dartmouth, 717
Dartmouth G & CC, 650
Darwen, 685
Datchet, 631
Davenport, 638
Daventry & District, 704
Davos, 917
Davyhulme Park, 695
The De Vere PGA Seniors'
    Championship, 183
Dean Wood, 685
Deane, 685
Deangate Ridge, 678
Deanwood Park, 631
Deauville l'Amiraute, 850
Deer Park, 769
Deer Park CC, 811
Deeside, 786
Defence Academy, 741
Degeberga-Widtsköfle, 909
Degli Ulivi, 881
La Dehesa, 900
Deinster Mühle, 866
Dejbjerg, 838
Delamere Forest, 640
Delapre, 704
Delgany, 783
Delsjö, 906
Delvin Castle, 781
Denbigh, 818
Denbighshire and Flintshire Ladies',
    332
Denham, 633
Denstone College, 718
Denton, 695
Derby Sinfin, 649
Derbyshire, 281
Derbyshire Ladies', 328
Derbyshire Professionals', 188
Dereham, 702
Derllys, 817, 817
Deutsche Bank — SAP Open TPC of
    Europe, 119
Deutsche Bank US Championship,
    144
DeVere Northop Country Park, 819
Devon, 281
Devon Ladies', 328
Devon Open, 188
Dewlands Manor, 731
Dewsbury District, 753
Dewstow, 823
Diageo Championship, 122
Dibden Golf Centre, 667
Didsbury, 695
Dieppe-Pourville, 855
Digne-les-Bains, 859
Dijon-Bourgogne, 848
Dillenburg, 864
Dinard, 846
Dinas Powis, 825
Dinnaton, 650
Dinsdale Spa, 656
Dirleton Castle, 807
Disley, 640
Disneyland Golf, 852
Diss, 721
Divonne, 861

Djouce, 783
Djursholm, 914
Dolder, 918
Dolgellau, 820
Dollar, 794
Domaine de Belesbat, 852
Domaine de Falgos, 853
Domaine de la Marterie, 845
Domaine de Roncemay, 848
Domaine du Tilleul, 850
Domaine de Vaugouard, 849
Domaine Impérial, 917
Domaio, 899
La Domangère, 854
Domburgsche, 887
De Dommel, 888
Domont-Montmorency, 852
Don Cayo, 895
Donabate, 767
Donaghadee, 766
Donau GC Passau-Rassbach, 871
Donauwörth, 869
Doncaster, 750
Doncaster Town Moor, 750
Donegal, 764
Doneraile, 762
Donnington Valley, 631
Dooks, 772
Doon Valley, 791
Dore & Totley, 750
Dorking, 724
Dorset, 281
The Dorset G & CC, 654
Dorset Ladies', 328
Dortmund, 873
Dougalston, 796
Douglas, 762
Douglas Municipal, 676
Douglas Park, 796
Douglas Water, 806
Down Royal, 758
Downes Crediton, 651
Downfield, 787
Downpatrick, 766
Downshire, 631
Dragør, 840
Drax, 747
Drayton Park, 711, 718
Driffield, 746
Drift, 724
Drøbak, 891
Droitwich G & CC, 743
Dromoland Castle, 761
Drottningholm, 914
Druid's Glen, 783
Druids Heath, 718
Drumoig, 798
Drumpellier, 806
Les Dryades, 849
du Maurier Classic, 106
Dubai Desert Classic, 116
Dublin Mountain, 767
Duddingston, 809
Dudley, 743
Dudsbury, 654
Duff House Royal, 784
Dufftown, 812
Duke of York Trophy Winners, 358
Duke's Course, 800

Dukinfield, 640
Dullatur, 797
Dulwich & Sydenham Hill, 724
Dumbarton, 797
Dumfries & County, 795
Dumfries & Galloway, 795
Dumfriesshire Ladies', 331
Dummer, 667
Dun Laoghaire, 767
Dunaverty, 789
Dunbar, 807
Dunbartonshire, 284
Dunbartonshire and Argyll Ladies',
    331
Dunblane New, 816
Duncan Putter, 259
Dundalk, 776
Dundas Parks, 811
Dunecht House, 784
Dunfanaghy, 764
Dunfermline, 798
Dungannon, 780
Dungarvan, 781
Dunham, 702
Dunham Forest G & CC, 640
dunhill links championship, 127
Dunkeld & Birnam, 813
Dunkerque, 850
Dunloe, 772
Dunmore, 762
Dunmore East, 781
Dunmurry, 760
The Dunnerholme, 646
Dunnikier Park, 798
Dunning, 813
Duns, 793
Dunscar, 685
Dunsfold Aerodrome, 724
Dunstable Downs, 629
Dunstanburgh Castle, 706
Dunwood Manor, 667
La Duquesa G & CC, 901
Durbuy, 836
Durham, 281
Durham City, 656
Durham Ladies', 328
Durness, 802
Düsseldorf, 873
Düsseldorf Hösel, 873
Dutch Open, 127
Duxbury Park, 685
Dyfed, 285
The Dyke, 731
Dymock Grange, 664
Dynasty Cup, 182
Dyrham Park CC, 672

Eagles, 702
Eaglescliffe, 657
Ealing, 699
Earlsferry Thistle, 798
Earlswood, 826
Easingwold, 747
East Anglian Open, 188
East Berkshire, 631
East Bierley, 753
East Brighton, 731
East Clare, 761
East Cork, 763

East Devon, 651
East Herts, 673
East Kilbride, 806
East Lothian Ladies', 331
East of Ireland Open Amateur, 265
East of Scotland Open Stroke Play
  Amateur, 266
East Region PGA, 188
East Renfrewshire, 815
East Sussex National, 731
Eastbourne Downs, 731
Eastbourne Golfing Park, 731
Easter Moffat, 806
Eastern Division Ladies' (Scotland),
  331
Eastham Lodge, 697
Eastwood, 815
Eaton, 640, 702
Ebeltoft, 838
Ebersberg, 869
Eda, 915
Eden, 646
Eden Course, 800
Edenbridge G & CC, 678
Edenderry, 778
Edenhof, 903
Edenmore, 760
Edese, 887
Edmondstown, 769
Edwalton, 708
Edzell, 787
Effingham, 724
Effingham Park, 733
Efteling, 887
Eifel, 875
Eindhovensche Golf, 888
Ekarnas, 912
Ekerum, 910
Eksjö, 910
Elbflorenz GC Dresden, 863
Elderslie, 815
Eldorado Bucklige Welt, 833
Elfordleigh Hotel G & CC, 651
Elfrather Mühle, 873
Elgin, 812
Ellesborough, 634
Ellesmere, 695
Ellesmere Port, 640
Elm Green, 769
Elm Park, 769
Elmwood, 793
Elsenham Golf Centre, 659
Elsham, 692
Elstree, 673
Eltham Warren, 678
Elton Furze, 636
Elverum, 891
Ely City, 636
Embankment, 704
Embats, 862
Emmaboda, 910
L'Empereur, 835
Empordà, 897
Enderby, 689
Enfield, 699
Engadin, 917
England and Wales Ladies' County
  Championship, 322
English Amateur Championship, 221

English Boys' County Finals, 349
English Boys' Stroke Play
  Championship, 340
English Boys' Under-16
  Championship (McGregor
  Trophy), 340
English Club Championship, 254
English County Champions'
  Tournament, 224
English County Championship, 254
English Girls Close Championship,
  351
English Ladies' Close Amateur
  Championship, 297
English Ladies' Close Amateur Stroke
  Play Championship, 299
English Ladies' Open Intermediate
  Championship, 300
English Ladies' Under-23
  Championship, 299
English Open Amateur Stroke Play
  Championship (Brabazon Trophy),
  222
English Open Mid-Amateur
  Championship (Logan Trophy),
  223
English Senior Ladies Close Amateur
  Championship, 300
English Senior Ladies' Match Play
  Championship, 300
English Senior Ladies' Stroke Play
  Championship, 300
English Seniors' Amateur
  Championship, 223
Enköping, 904
Enmore Park, 715
Ennis, 761
Enniscorthy, 782
Enniscrone, 779
Enniskillen, 770
Ennstal-Weissenbach G & LC, 832
Entfelden, 918
Entrepinos, 903
Entry Hill, 715
La Envia, 896
Enville, 718
Enzesfeld, 833
Épinal, 857
Epsom, 725
Erding-Grünbach, 869
Erewash Valley, 649
Erftaue, 873
Erlen, 918
Erlestoke Sands, 741
Erskine, 815
Esbjerg, 838
Eschenried, 869
Escorpión, 903
Esery, 861
Esker Hills G & CC, 778
Eskifjardar, 879
Eskilstuna, 904
Eslöv, 909
Espoo Ringside Golf, 842
Espoon Golfseura, 842
Essen Haus Oefte, 873
Essen-Heidhausen, 873
Essex, 281
Essex G & CC, 659

The Essex Golf Complex, 660
Essex Ladies', 328
Essex Open, 188
Essex Professionals, 188
Estepona, 901
Estérel Latitudes, 859
Estoril, 894
Estoril-Sol Golf Academy, 894
Étangs de Fiac, 862
Etchinghill, 678
Etelä-Pohjanmaan, 842
Étiolles, 852
Étretat, 855
Eucalyptus, 882
Euregio Bad Bentheim, 873
Europe v Asia Pacific (Bonallack
  Cup), 251
European Amateur Championship,
  233
European Amateur Team
  Championship, 252
European Boys' Team Championship,
  347
European Challenge Tour, 2003, 134
The European Club, 783
European Club Cup (Albacom
  Trophy), 252
European Club Cup, 321
European Girls' Team Championship,
  356
European Lady Juniors' Team
  Championship, 356
European Lakes, 878
European Mid-Amateur
  Championship, 233
European Senior Ladies'
  Championship, 308
European Senior Tour, 2003, 131
European Seniors' Championship, 233
European Tour 2003 and Past Results,
  111
European Young Masters (Boys), 347
European Young Masters (Girls), 356
European Youths' Team
  Championship, 347
Evesham, 743
Evian Ladies' European Tour, 2003,
  195
Evian Masters, 197, 203, 861
Evian Tour Order of Merit, 363
Evian Tour Stroke Average Winners,
  365
Exeter G & CC, 651
Eyemouth, 793

Faaborg, 837
Fågelbro G & CC, 914
Fagersta, 904
Fairfield Golf & Sailing Club, 695
Fairhaven, 685
Fairlop Waters, 660
Fairwood Park, 826
Faithlegg, 781
Fakenham, 702
Falkenberg, 912
Falkirk, 816
Falkirk Tryst, 816
Falkland, 799
Falköping, 912

Falmouth, 644
Falnuée, 834
Falster, 840
Falsterbo, 907
Falun-Borlänge, 908
Fanø Golf Links, 838
Fardew, 753
Fareham Woods, 667
Färgelanda, 915
Farleigh Court, 725
Farnham, 725
Farnham Park, 634
Farnham Park Par Three, 725
Farrington, 715
Farthingstone Hotel, 704
Fathers and Sons Foursomes, 274
Faulquemont-Pontpierre, 857
Faversham, 678
Fawkham Valley, 678
FBR Capital Open, 142
FedEx St Jude Classic, 142
Feldafing, 869
Felixstowe Ferry, 721
Feltwell, 702
Fereneze, 815
Fermoy, 763
Ferndown, 654
Ferndown Forest, 654
Fernhill, 763
Ferrybridge "C", 753
Feucherolles, 858
Ffestiniog, 820
Fife, 284
Fife County Ladies', 331
Filey, 747
Filton, 664
Finchley, 699
Fingle Glen, 651
Finnish Open, 192
Finnstown, 767
Finspång, 911
Fintona, 780
Fioranello, 882
First Lady of Golf Award, 364
Fishwick Hall, 685
Fiuggi, 882
Five Lakes Hotel G & CC, 660
Five Nations C C, 834
Fjällbacka, 915
Flackwell Heath, 634
Flamborough Head, 746
Flanders Nippon Hasselt, 836
Fleetlands, 667
Fleetwood, 685
Fleming Park, 667
Flempton, 721
Flevoland, 890
Flint, 819
Flintshire, 285
Flixton, 695
Flommens, 907
Florentin-Gaillac, 862
Floresta Parque, 892
Föhr, 866
Föhrenwald, 833
Folgaria, 882
Fontainebleau, 852
Fontana, 833
Fontanals de Cerdanya, 897

Fontcaude, 853
Fontenailles, 852
Fontenelles, 854
Ford Championship, 140
Forest Hill, 689
Forest Hills, 664, 673
Forest of Dean, 664
Forest of Galtres, 747
Forest Park, 747
Forest Pines, 692
Forêt d'Orient, 857
Forêt Verte, 856
Forfar, 787
Forges-les-Bains, 852
Formby, 697
Formby Hall, 697
Formby Ladies', 697
Forres, 812
Forrest Little, 767
Forrester Park, 660
Forsbacka, 915
Forsgårdens, 906
Fort Augustus, 803
Fort William, 803
La Forteresse, 853
Fortrose & Rosemarkie, 803
Fortwilliam, 760
Fosseway CC, 715
Fota Island, 763
Foulford Inn, 813
Four Marks, 667
Fourqueux, 858
Foursomes Events, 273
Foxbridge, 733
Foxhills, 725
Foxrock, 769
Foyle, 775
Frame Trophy, 269
Franciacorta, 880
Frankfield, 763
Frankfurter, 865
Fränkische Schweiz, 871
Fraserburgh, 784
Frassanelle, 885
Frederikssund, 840
Frégate, 859
Freiburg, 876
French Ladies Open, 214
French Open, 192
Freshwater Bay, 676
La Freslonnière, 846
Frilford Heath, 711
Frinton, 660
Frodsham, 640
Frome, 715
Le Fronde, 884
Frösåker, 904
Fulford, 747
Fulford Heath, 743
Fullerö, 904
Fulneck, 754
Fulwell, 699
Funai Classic, 187
Funäsdalsfjällen, 905
Furesø, 840
Furnas, 893
Furness, 646
Furstenfeld, 832
Fürstlicher Waldsee, 876

Fürth, 871
Furzeley, 667
Futures Tour, 2003, 206
Fynn Valley, 721

Gaichel, 886
Gainsborough, 692
Gairloch, 805
Galashiels, 793
Galgorm Castle, 758
Gällivare-Malmberget, 905
Galloway Ladies', 331
Galway, 771
Galway Bay G & CC, 771
Ganay, 849
Ganstead Park, 746
Ganton, 747
Gap-Bayard, 859
Gardagolf CC, 882
Garesfield, 736
Garforth, 754
Garlenda, 881
Garmisch-Partenkirchen, 870
Garmouth & Kingston, 812
Garnant Park, 817
Gatehouse, 795
Gathurst, 685
Gatley, 640
Gatton Manor Hotel G & CC, 725
Gäuboden, 871
Gävle, 908
Gay Hill, 743
GC Bodensee Weissenberg eV, 876
Gedney Hill, 692
Geijsteren G & CC, 888
Gelpenberg, 889
Gendersteyn, 888
Geneva, 917
Gerrards Cross, 634
Ghyll, 685
Giant Eagle LPGA Classic, 202
Giez, 861
Gifford, 807
Gifhorn, 868
Gigha, 789
Gilleleje, 841
Gillingham, 679
Gilnahirk, 760
Girvan, 791
I Girasoli, 884
Girls' British Open Championship, 350
Girls' Home International (Stroyan Cup), 356
Girona, 897
Girton, 636
Girvan, 791
Glamorgan, 285
Glamorgan County Ladies', 332
Glamorganshire, 825
Glasgow, 284, 801
Glasgow GC Gailes, 791
Glasson Hotel, 781
Gleddoch, 815
Glen (North Berwick), 807
Glen Gorse, 689
Glen of the Downs, 783
Glenbervie, 816
Glencorse, 809
Glencruitten, 789

Glencullen, 768
The Gleneagles Hotel, 813
Glengarriff, 763
Glenisla, 813
Glenlo Abbey, 771
Glenmalure, 783
Glenmuir Club Professionals'
    Championship, 184
Glenrothes, 799
Gloria Golf, 918
Glossop & District, 649
Gloucester Hotel, 664
Gloucestershire, 282
The Gloucestershire, 664
Gloucestershire Ladies', 329
Glyfada, 878
Glyn Abbey, 817
Glynhir, 817
Glynneath, 826
Goal Farm Par Three, 725
The Gog Magog, 637
Gold Coast, 781
Goldegg, 831
Golden Eagle G & CC, 894
Goldenhill, 718
Golf de Luxembourg, 886
Golf de tarbes, 832
Golf Dolce Chantilly, 850
Golf Foundation Award Winners, 359
Golf Foundation Schools' Team
    Championship for the R&A
    Trophy, 348
Golf House Club, 799
Golf Illustrated Gold Vase, 269
Golf Platja de Pals, 898
Golf Weekly World Ranking for
    Women's Professional Golf, 194
Golfe Quinta da Barca, 895
Golspie, 802
Goodwood, 734
Goodwood Park G & CC, 734
Goring & Streatley, 631
Gorleston, 702
Gormanston College, 777
Gort, 771
Gosfield Lake, 660
Gosforth, 736
Gosport & Stokes Bay, 667
Göteborg, 906
Gotska, 911
Gotts Park, 754
Gourock, 815
Le Gouverneur, 861
Gower, 827
De Graafschap, 887
Gracehill, 759
Grafton Morrish Trophy, 277
Granada, 899
Grand Avignon, 859
Grand-Ducal de Luxembourg, 886
La Grande Bastide, 859
La Grande Mare, 638
Grande Romanie, 857
La Grande-Motte, 854
Grange, 770
La Grange aux Ormes, 857
Grange Fell, 646
Grange Park, 692, 697, 750
Grange-over-Sands, 647

Grangemouth, 816
Grantown-on-Spey, 803
Granville, 856
Grasse CC, 859
Grassmoor Golf Centre, 649
Graves et Sauternais, 845
Graz, 832
Great Barr, 718
Great Britain & Ireland v USA for the
    Curtis Cup, 309
Great Britain and Ireland v Continent
    of Europe (Jacques Léglise
    Trophy), 348
Great Hadham, 673
Great Harwood, 685
Great Lever & Farnworth, 695
Great Yarmouth & Caister, 702
Greater Hartford Open, 143
Greater Milwaukee Open, 143
Green Haworth, 685
Green Hotel, 813
Green Zone Golf, 843
Greenacres, 759
Greenburn, 811
Greencastle, 764
Greenisland, 759
Greenmeadow G & CC, 823
Greenmount, 685
Greenock, 815
Greenore, 776
Greenparc, 853
Greenway Hall, 718
Greetham Valley, 712
Grenaa, 838
Grenland, 891
Grenoble-Bresson, 861
Grenoble-Charmeil, 861
Grenoble-Uriage, 861
Gretna, 795
Grevelingenhout, 887
Grevenmühle Ratingen, 873
Greystones, 783
Griffin, 629
Grim's Dyke, 699
Grimsby, 692
Gripsholm, 904
Grönhögen, 911
Grönlund, 904
Groruddalen, 891
Grove, 821
The Grove, 673
Guadalhorce, 900
Guadalmina, 901
Guadiana, 896
Guildford, 725
Guinlet, 862
Gujan, 845
Gullane, 807
Gullbringa, 906
Gumbalde, 911
Gustavsvik, 904
Gut Altentann, 831
Gut Apeldör, 866
Gut Brandlhof G & CC, 831
Gut Grambek, 866
Gut Heckenhof, 875
Gut Kaden, 866
Gut Ludwigsberg, 870
Gut Murstätten, 832

Gut Rieden, 870
Gut Uhlenhorst, 866
Gut Waldhof, 866
Gut Waldshagen, 866
Gütersloh Garrison, 868
Gweedore, 764
Gwent, 285
Gyttegård, 838

De Haar, 890
Haarlemmermeersche, 886
Habberley, 743
Hadden Hill, 711
Haddington, 808
Haderslev, 838
Hadley Wood, 673
Hagge, 908
Haggs Castle, 801
Hagley, 743
Haigh Hall, 685
Hainault Forest, 660
Hainburg/Donau, 833
Hainsworth Park, 746
Hale, 640
Halesowen, 744
Halesworth, 721
Halford-Hewitt Cup, 276
Halifax, 754
Halifax Bradley Hall, 754
Halifax West End, 754
Hallamshire, 750
Hallowes, 750
Halmstad, 912
Halstock, 654
Haltwhistle, 647
Ham Manor, 734
Hamburg, 867
Hamburg Ahrensburg, 867
Hamburg Hittfeld, 867
Hamburg Holm, 867
Hamburg Walddörfer, 867
Hameln, 868
Hamilton, 806
Hammarö, 915
The Hampshire, 668
Hampshire Hog, 269
Hampshire, Isle of Wight and Channel
    Islands, 282
Hampshire, Isle of Wight and Channel
    Islands Open, 188
Hampshire Ladies', 329
Hampshire Match Play, 188
Hampshire PGA, 188
Hampshire Rose, 325
Hampshire Salver, 259
Hampstead, 699
Hampton Court Palace, 725
Hamptworth G & CC, 741
Han Herreds, 838
Hanau-Wilhelmsbad, 865
Hanbury Manor G & CC, 673
Handsworth, 718
Hanging Heaton, 754
Haninge, 914
Hankley Common, 725
Hannover, 868
Hanover G & CC, 660
Haparanda, 905
Harborne, 738

Harborne Church Farm, 738
Harbour Point, 763
Harburn, 811
Hardelot Dunes Course, 851
Hardelot Pins Course, 851
Hardenberg, 868
Harewood Downs, 634
Harjattula G & CC, 842
Harleyford, 634
Härnösand, 905
Harpenden, 673
Harpenden Common, 673
Harrogate, 747
Harrow School, 699
Harry Vardon Trophy, 366
Hartland Forest, 651
Hartlepool, 657
Hartley Wintney, 668
Hartsbourne G & CC, 673
Hartswood, 660
Harwich & Dovercourt, 660
Harwood, 686
Hassan II Trophy, 167
Hässleholm, 909
Hassocks, 734
Haste Hill, 700
Hastings G & CC, 731
Hatchford Brook, 738
Hatfield London CC, 673
Hattemse G & CC, 887
Haugschlag, 830
Haus Bey, 873
Haus Kambach, 873
Haut-Poitou, 849
Havelte, 888
Haverdals, 912
Haverfordwest, 824
Haverhill, 721
Haviksoord, 888
Le Havre, 856
Hawarden, 819
Hawick, 793
Hawkhurst, 679
Hawkstone Park, 713
Haydock Park, 697
Hayling, 668
Hayston, 797
Haywards Heath, 734
Hazel Grove, 640, 770
Hazelwood Golf Centre, 725
Hazlehead, 786
Hazlemere, 634
Headfort, 777
Headingley, 754
Headley, 754
The Heath, 774
Heath Park, 700
Heaton Moor, 640
Heaton Park Golf Centre, 695
Hebden Bridge, 754
Hechingen Hohenzollern, 876
Hedeland, 841
Heemskerkse, 886
Heidelberg-Lobenfeld, 876
Heilbronn-Hohenlohe, 877
Heineken Classic, 115
Hele Park Golf Centre, 651
Helen's Bay, 766
Helensburgh, 789

Hellidon Lakes Hotel G & CC, 704
Helmsdale, 802
Helsby, 640
Helsingborg, 909
Helsingin Golfklubi, 842
Helsingør, 841
Hemingford Abbots, 637
Hemsedal, 891
Hemsted Forest, 679
Henbury, 664
Hendon, 700
Henley, 711
Henley G & CC, 738
Henllys Hall, 821
Henlow, 629
Henne, 838
Hennerton, 631
Henri-Chapelle, 836
Hereford Municipal, 670
Herefordshire, 670
The Heritage G&CC, 774
Herkenbosch, 888
Hermitage, 768
Herne Bay, 679
Herning, 838
Herreria, 900
Hersham Village, 725
Hertfordshire, 282
The Hertfordshire, 673
Hertfordshire Ladies', 329
Herts Professionals, 188
Herzog Tassilo, 830
Herzogstadt Celle, 864
Hesketh, 697
Hessle, 746
Heswall, 697
Het Rijk van Nijmegen, 889
Hetton-le-Hole, 736
Hetzenhof, 877
Hever, 679
Heworth, 736, 748
Hexham, 707
Heydon Grange G & CC, 637
Heyrose, 640
Heysham, 686
Hibernian, 768
Hickleton, 750
High Elms, 679
High Post, 741
High Throston, 657
Highcliffe Castle, 654
Highfield, 773
Highgate, 700
Highwoods, 731
Highworth, 741
Hill Barn, 734
Hill Valley G & CC, 713
Hillerød, 841
Hillingdon, 700
Hills Wiltshire Pro Champ, 190
Hillsborough, 750
Hillside, 697
Hilltop, 738
Hilton Avisford Park, 734
Hilton Park, 797
Hilton Puckrup Hall Hotel, 664
Hilton Templepatrick, 759
Hilversumsche, 890
Himley Hall, 718

Himmerland G & CC, 838
Hinckley, 689
Hindhead, 725
Hindley Hall, 686
Hinksey Heights, 711
Hintlesham Hall, 721
The Hirsel, 793
Hirst Priory Park, 692
Hirtshals, 839
Hittnau-Zürich G & CC, 918
Hjarbaek Fjord, 839
Hjorring, 839
Hobson Municipal, 657
Hockley, 668
Hoddom Castle, 795
Hoebridge Golf Centre, 726
Hoenshuis G & CC, 889
Hof, 872
Hof Trages, 865
Hofgut Praforst, 864
Hofors, 908
Högbo, 908
De Hoge Kleij, 890
Hohenpähl, 870
Hohenstaufen, 877
Hoisdorf, 867
Hökensås, 912
Holbaek, 841
Hollandbush, 806
Holledau, 870
Hollingbury Park, 731
Hollywood Lakes, 768
Holme Hall, 692
Holms, 913
Holmsland Klit, 839
Holstebro, 839
Holsworthy, 651
Holthuizen, 889
Holtye, 732
Holyhead, 821
Holywell, 819
Holywood, 766
Homburger, 865
Home Internationals, 253
Honda Classic, 140
Hong Kong Open, 192
Honiton, 651
The Honourable Company of
    Edinburgh Golfers, 808
De Hooge Bergsche, 890
Hooks, 911
Hopeman, 812
Horam Park, 732
Horncastle, 692
Horne Park, 726
Hornsea, 746
Horsehay Village, 713
Horsenden Hill, 700
Horsens, 839
Horsforth, 754
Horsham, 734
Horsley Lodge, 649
Horton Park G & CC, 726
Horwich, 686
Höslwang im Chiemgau, 870
Hossegor, 845
Houghton-le-Spring, 736
Houghwood, 697
Houldsworth, 640

Houlgate, 856
Hounslow Heath, 700
Howley Hall, 754
Howth, 770
Hoylake Municipal, 697
HP Classic of New Orleans, 141
HP Open, 197
HSBC World Match Play
  Championship, 128
Hubbelrath, 873
Huddersfield, 754
Hudiksvall, 908
Hulencourt, 835
Hull, 746
Hulta, 913
Humberston Park, 692
Humberstone Heights, 689
Hummelbachaue Neuss, 873
Hunley Hall, 748
Hunstanton, 702
Huntercombe, 711
Huntly, 785
Huntwood, 634
Hurdwick, 651
Hurlston Hall, 686
Hurst, 631
Hurtmore, 726
Húsavík, 879
Huyton & Prescot, 698
Hvide Klit, 839
Hythe Imperial, 679
Hyvinkään, 842

Ibiza, 896
Idstein, 865
Idstein-Wörsdorf, 865
Ifach, 895
Iffeldorf, 870
Ifield, 734
Ile d'Or, 854
Iles Borromees, 884
Ilford, 660
Ilfracombe, 651
Ilkeston, 649
Ilkley, 754
Imatran Golf, 844
Immingham, 692
IMSL Irish Boys' Championship,
  341
Inchmarlo, 785
Inco, 827
Indian Open, 192
Ingarö, 914
Ingestre Park, 718
Ingol, 686
Ingon Manor, 738
Innellan, 789
Innerleithen, 793
Innsbruck-Igls, 830
Insch, 785
Inter-Mol, 834
Interlaken-Unterseen, 916
The International, 144
International Barriere-La Baule, 854
International Club du Lys, 851
International Gomze, 836
Internationaler GC Bonn, 875
Inverallochy, 785
Inveraray, 789

Invergordon, 803
Inverness, 803
Inverurie, 785
Ipswich (Purdis Heath), 721
Irish Amateur Close Championship,
  225
Irish Amateur Open Championship,
  224
Irish Club Professionals'
  Championship, 186
Irish Girls' Championship, 352
Irish Ladies' Close Amateur
  Championship, 301
Irish Ladies' Open Amateur Stroke
  Play Championship, 303
Irish Senior Ladies' Amateur
  Championship, 303
Irish Seniors' Open Amateur
  Championship, 227
Irish Youth's Open Amateur
  Championship, 341
Irvine, 791
Irvine Ravenspark, 791
Is Molas, 883
Isabella, 858
Isaberg, 911
Isafjördar, 879
Isernhagen, 868
Isla Canela, 902
The Island, 768
Islantilla, 902
Islay, 789
L'Isle Adam, 853
Isle of Harris, 805
Isle of Man, 282
Isle of Purbeck, 654
Isle of Seil, 789
Isle of Skye, 805
Isle of Wedmore, 715
Isles of Scilly, 644
Issum-Niederrhein, 873
Italian Ladies' Open, 214
Italian Open, 192
Italian Open Telecom Italia, 118
Iver, 634
Ivinghoe, 634
Izaak Walton, 718
Izki Golf, 898

Jack Nicklaus Award, 364
Jakobsberg, 875
Jamie Farr Kroger Classic, 203
Japan LPGA Tour, 2003, 207
Japan PGA Tour, 152
Japanese Open, 192
Jarama R.A.C.E., 900
Jávea, 895
Jedburgh, 793
Jersbek, 867
John Cross Bowl, 268
John Deere Classic, 145
John O'Gaunt, 629
John Q Hammons Hotel Classic, 204
Johnnie Walker Classic, 115
Jökull, 879
Jönköping, 911
Joyce Wethered Trophy, 362
Joyenval, 858
Jubilee Course, 801

Juelsminde, 839
Juliana, 873
Junior Ryder Cup (Boys), 349

The K Club, 773
Kaiserhöhe, 877
Kaiserwinkl GC Kössen, 830
Kaj Lykke, 839
Kalix, 905
Kalmar, 911
Kalo, 839
Kampenhout, 835
Kanturk, 763
Karelia Golf, 842
Karersee-Carezza, 882
Karlovy Vary, 837
Karlshamn, 909
Karlskoga, 915
Karlstad, 915
Kärntner, 830
Kartano Golf, 844
Kassel-Wilhelmshöhe, 864
Katinkulta, 843
Katrineholm, 904
Kävlinge, 907
Kedleston Park, 649
Keele Golf Centre, 718
Keerbergen, 835
Keighley, 754
Keilir, 879
Keimola Golf, 842
Keith, 785
Kellogg-Keebler Classic, 201
Kelso, 793
Kemer G & CC, 918
Kemnay, 785
Kempense, 834
Kempferhof, 857
Kendal, 647
Kendleshire, 664
Kenilworth, 738
Kenmare, 772
Kenmore, 813
Kennemer G & CC, 886
Kent, 282
Kent Ladies', 329
Kent Open, 188
Kent Professionals, 188
Kenwick Park, 692
Kenyan Open, 192
Keppelse, 888
Kerigolf, 844
Kerries, 772
Keswick, 647
Kettering, 705
Kibworth, 690
Kidderminster, 744
Kieler GC Havighorst, 867
Kikuoka CC Chant Val, 886
Kilbirnie Place, 791
Kilcock, 777
Kilcoole, 783
Kilkea Castle, 773
Kilkee, 761
Kilkeel, 766
Kilkenny, 774
Killarney, 772
Killeen, 773
Killin, 813

Killinbeg, 776
Killiney, 768
Killiow, 644
Killorglin, 772
Killymoon, 780
Kilmacolm, 815
Kilmarnock (Barassie), 791
Kilmashogue, 770
Kilnwick Percy, 746
Kilrea, 776
Kilrush, 762
Kilspindie, 808
Kilsyth Lennox, 816
Kilternan, 768
Kilton Forest, 708
Kilworth Springs, 690
King Edward Bay, 676
King George V Coronation Cup, 270
King James VI, 813
King's Links, 786
King's Lynn, 703
King's Park, 801
Kingfisher CC, 634
Kingfisher Hotel, 705
Kinghorn Ladies, 799
Kinghorn Municipal, 799
Kings Acre, 809
Kings Hill, 679
Kings Norton, 744
Kingsbarns Links, 799
Kingsdown, 741
Kingsknowe, 809
Kingsthorpe, 705
Kingsway, 692
Kingsway Golf Centre, 673
Kingswood, 726
Kington, 670
Kingussie, 803
Kingweston, 715
Kinmel Park, 818
Kinsale, 819
Kinsale Farrangalway, 763
Kinsale Ringenane, 763
Kintore, 785
Kirby Muxloe, 690
Kirkby Lonsdale, 647
Kirkbymoorside, 748
Kirkcaldy, 799
Kirkcudbright, 795
Kirkhill, 806
Kirkintilloch, 797
Kirkistown Castle, 766
Kirriemuir, 787
Kirtlington, 711
Kirton Holme, 693
Kitzbühel, 830
Kitzbühel-Schwarzsee, 830
Kitzingen, 865
Kjekstad, 891
Klassis G & CC, 918
Klopeiner See-Turnersee, 830
Knaresborough, 748
Knebworth, 674
Knighton, 825
Knighton Heath, 655
Knights Grange, 641
Knightswood, 801
Knistad G & CC, 913
The Knock Club, 760

Knockanally, 773
Knole Park, 679
Knott End, 686
Knotty Hill Golf Centre, 657
Knowle, 664
Knutsford, 641
Kobernausserwald, 831
De Koepel, 888
Køge, 841
Kokkedal, 841
Kokkolan, 842
Kolding, 839
Köln G & LC, 873
Koninklijke Haagsche G & CC, 890
Konstanz, 877
Kopavogs og Gardabaejar, 879
Köping, 904
Korean Open, 192
Korsør, 841
Kosaido International, 874
Koski Golf, 844
Kraft Nabisco Championship, 200
Kralingen, 890
Krefeld, 874
Kremstal, 830
Kristiansand, 891
Kristianstad, 909
Kristinehamn, 915
Kronberg G & LC, 865
Kumla, 904
Kungälv-Kode, 906
Kungsängen, 914
Kungsbacka, 906
Kurhessischer GC Oberaula, 864
Kurk Golf, 842
Küssnacht, 918
Küsten GC Hohe Klint, 864
Kyles of Bute, 789
Kyllburger Waldeifel, 875
Kymen Golf, 844

La Perla Italian Open, 196
Lacanau Golf & Hotel, 846
Ladbrook Park, 738
Ladies British Open Mid-Amateur
    Championship, 297
Ladies Open of Costa Azul, 196
Ladies' British Amateur
    Championship, 294
Ladies' British Open Amateur Stroke
    Play Championship, 296
Ladies' European Open Amateur
    Championship, 308
Ladies' Irish Open, 197
Lady Astor Salver, 324
Ladybank, 799
Lagan, 911
Golf dei Laghi, 884
Lagonda Trophy, 260
Lahden Golf, 844
Lahinch, 762
Laholm, 913
Lakeside, 718, 827
Lakeside Lodge, 637
Laleham, 726
Lambeg, 759
Lamberhurst, 679
Lamborghini-Panicale, 884
The Lambourne Club, 634

Lamerwood, 674
Lamlash, 791
Lanark, 806
Lanarkshire, 284
Lanarkshire Ladies' County, 331
Lancashire, 282
Lancashire Ladies', 329
Lancashire Open, 189
Lancaster, 686
Landeryd, 911
Landshut, 870
Landskrona, 909
Langdon Hills, 660
Langenhagen, 868
Langholm, 793
Langland Bay, 827
Langlands, 806
Langley Park, 679
Langton Park G & CC, 690
Lanhydrock, 644
Lannemezan, 862
Lansdown, 715
Lansil, 686
Lanzo Intelvi, 880
Largs, 791
La Largue G & CC, 857
Larkhall, 806
Larne, 759
Larrabea, 898
Larvik, 891
Las Vegas Invitational, 145
Lauder, 793
Laukaan Peurunkagolf, 842
Laukariz, 898
Launceston, 644
Lauro, 900
Lausanne, 917
Lauswolt G & CC, 889
Lauterhofen, 872
Laval-Changé, 854
Laytown & Bettystown, 778
Leadhills, 806
Leamington & County, 738
Leaside GC, 700
Leasowe, 698
Leatherhead, 726
Leckford, 668
Lee-on-the-Solent, 668
Lee Park, 698
Lee Valley G & CC, 763
Leeds, 755
Leeds Castle, 679
Leeds Golf Centre, 755
Leek, 718
Leen Valley Golf Centre, 708
Lees Hall, 751
Leicestershire, 690
Leicestershire and Rutland, 282
Leicestershire and Rutland Ladies',
    329
Leicestershire and Rutland Open, 189
Leidschendamse Leeuwenbergh, 890
Leighton Buzzard, 630
Leinster Ladies, 327
Leixlip, 774
Leksand, 908
Lemvig, 839
Lengenfeld, 833
Lenzerheide Valbella, 917

Lenzie, 797
Leominster, 671
Lerma, 898
Léry Poses, 856
Les Rousses, 857
Leslie, 799
LET Players' Player of the Year, 362
Letchworth, 674
Letham Grange, 788
Lethamhill, 801
Letterkenny, 764
Leven Golfing Society, 799
Leven Links, 799
Leven Thistle, 799
Lewes, 732
Lexden Wood, 660
Lexus European Under-21
   Championship, 308
Leyland, 686
Leynir, 879
Libbaton, 651
Liberton, 809
Licher Golf, 864
Lichtenau-Weickershof, 872
Lickey Hills, 744
Lidhems, 911
Lidingö, 914
Lidköping, 913
Lightcliffe, 755
Lignano, 885
Lillebaelt, 837
Lilleshall Hall, 713
Lilley Brook, 664
Lilse, 834
Limburg G & CC, 836
Limerick, 775
Limerick County G & CC, 775
Limoges-St Lazare, 848
Limpsfield Chart, 726
Lincoln, 693
Lincolnshire, 282
Lincolnshire Ladies', 329
Lincolnshire Open, 189
Lindau-Bad Schachen, 877
Linde, 904
Linde German Masters, 127
Linden Hall, 707
Lindö, 914
Lindo Park, 914
Lindrick, 751
Lingdale, 690
Lingfield Park, 726
Linköping, 911
Links (Newmarket), 721
Links Country Park Hotel, 703
Linlithgow, 811
Linn Park, 802
Linz-St Florian, 830
Linzer Luftenberg, 831
Liphook, 668
Liphook Scratch Cup, 325
Lipica, 895
Lipperland zu Lage, 868
Lippischer, 868
Lisbon Sports Club, 894
Lisburn, 759
Lismore, 781
Lisnice, 837
Listowel, 772

Little Aston, 719
Little Chalfont, 634
Little Hay Golf Complex, 674
Little Lakes, 744
Littlehampton, 734
Littlehill, 802
Littlestone, 679
Liverpool Municipal, 698
Ljunghusen, 907
Ljusdal, 908
Llandrindod Wells, 825
Llandudno (Maesdu), 818
Llandudno (North Wales), 818
Llanfairfechan, 818
Llangefni, 821
Llanishen, 826
Llantrisant & Pontyclun, 821
Llanwern, 823
Llanymynech, 713
Llavaneras, 897
La Llorea, 898
Lobden, 686
Loch Lomond, 797
Loch Ness, 803
Lochcarron, 805
Lochgelly, 799
Lochgilphead, 789
Lochgoilhead, 789
Lochmaben, 795
Lochranza, 791
Lochwinnoch, 815
Lockerbie, 795
Lofthouse Hill, 755
Løkken, 839
Lokomotiva-Brno, 837
Lomas-Bosque, 900
London Beach, 679
London Golf Centre, 700
The London Golf Club, 680
London Ladies' Foursomes, 327
London Scottish, 726
Long Ashton, 664
Long Sutton, 715
Longcliffe, 690
Longhirst Hall, 707
Longley Park, 755
Longniddry, 808
Longridge, 686
Longs Drugs Challenge, 204
Longside, 785
Looe, 644
Lostwithiel G & CC, 644
Lothianburn, 809
Lothians, 284
Loudoun Gowf, 791
Loudun-Roiffe, 849
Loughall, 760
Loughrea, 771
Loughton, 661
Lourdes, 862
Louth, 693
Louvain-la-Neuve, 835
Low Laithes, 755
Lowes Park, 686
LPGA Corning Classic, 201
LPGA Takefuji Classic, 200
Lübeck-Travemünder, 867
Luberon, 859
Lucan, 768

Lucerne, 918
Luchon, 863
Ludlow, 713
Luffenham Heath, 712
Luffness New, 808
Lugano, 917
Luleå, 905
Lullingstone Park, 680
Lumphanan, 785
Lundin, 799
Lundin Ladies, 799
Lunds Akademiska, 907
Lungau, 831
Lurgan, 760
Lutterworth, 690
Luttrellstown Castle G & CC, 768
Lybster, 802
Lyckorna, 915
Lydd, 680
Lydney, 665
Lyme Regis, 655
Lymm, 641
Lyon, 861
Lyon-Chassieu, 861
Lyon-Verger, 861
Lyons Gate, 655
Lysegården, 906
Lytham Green Drive, 686
Lytham Trophy, 261

Macclesfield, 641
Machrie Bay, 791
Machrihanish, 789
Machynlleth, 825
Mackie Trophy, 326
Mâcon La Salle, 848
Macroom, 763
Madeira, 894
Madeira Island Open, 117
Maesteg, 821
Magdalene Fields, 707
Magnolia Park, 634
Mahee Island, 766
Mahon, 763
Maidenhead, 632
Main-Spessart, 865
Main-Taunus, 865
Maison Blanche G & CC, 861
Makila, 846
Málaga Club de Campo, 901
Malahide, 768
Malden, 726
Maldon, 661
Malkins Bank, 641
Mallow, 763
Mallusk, 759
Malmö, 907
Malone, 760
Malton, 637
Malton & Norton, 748
Manchester, 695
La Manga, 895
Mangfalltal G & LC, 870
Mangotsfield, 665
Manises, 903
Mannan Castle, 778
Mannheim-Viernheim, 865
Mannings Heath, 734
The Manor, 755

Manor (Kingstone), 719
Manor (Laceby), 693
Manor House, 741
Manor House Hotel, 651
Manor of Groves G & CC, 674
Le Mans Mulsanne, 855
Mansfield Woodhouse, 708
Mapledurham, 632
Mapperley, 709
Marbella, 901
March, 637
Marcilly, 849
Marco Simone, 883
Marconi (Grange GC), 738
Margara, 884
Margarethenhof, 870
La Margherita, 884
Maria Bildhausen, 865
Maria Lankowitz, 832
Maria Theresia, 831
Mariánské Lázne, 837
Marienfeld, 868
Mariestad, 913
Marigola, 881
Maritim Timmendorfer Strand, 867
Marivaux, 853
Market Drayton, 713
Market Harborough, 690
Market Rasen & District, 693
Market Rasen Racecourse, 693
Markgräflerland Kandern, 877
Marks, 913
Marland, 687
Marlborough, 741
Marple, 641
La Marquesa, 895
Marriott Dalmahoy Hotel & CC, 809
Marriott Forest of Arden Hotel, 738
Marriott Hollins Hall Hotel, 755
Marriott Meon Valley Hotel, 668
Marriott Sprowston Manor Hotel, 703
Marriott St Pierre Hotel & CC, 823
Marsden, 755
Marsden Park, 687
Marseille La Salette, 859
Martin Moor, 693
Marvao, 894
Mary McCallay Trophy, 326
Maryport, 647
Masham, 748
Masia Bach, 897
Maspalomas, 899
Massereene, 759
Master Golf, 842
Masters, The, 60, 117, 141
Matfen Hall Hotel, 707
Matilde di Canossa, 881
Matlock, 649
Mattishall, 703
Maxstoke Park, 739
Maybole, 791
Maylands, 661
Maywood, 649
Mazamet-La Barouge, 863
McDonald, 785
McDonald's LPGA Championship,
    91, 201
MCI Heritage, 141
Meaux-Boutigny, 853

Mediterraneo CC, 903
Médoc, 846
Meldrum House, 785
Mellor & Townscliffe, 641
Melrose, 793
Meltham, 755
Melton Mowbray, 690
Melville Golf Centre, 810
Memmingen Gut Westerhart, 870
Memorial Tournament, 142
Men's Major Title Table, 75
Menaggio & Cadenabbia, 880
The Mendip, 715
Mendip Spring, 715
Mentmore G & CC, 635
Meole Brace, 713
Mercedes Championship, 139
Merchants of Edinburgh, 810
Mere G & CC, 641
Meri-Teijo, 843
Méribel, 861
Merlin, 644
Merrist Wood, 726
Mersey Valley, 641
Merthyr Tydfil, 821
De Merwelanden, 890
Messilä, 843
Methil, 800
Metz Technopole, 857
Metz-Cherisey, 857
Meyrick Park, 655
Michelob Light Open, 201
Mickleover, 650
Mid Herts, 674
Mid Kent, 680
Mid Sussex, 732
Mid Yorkshire, 755
Middlesbrough, 748
Middlesbrough Municipal, 748
Middlesex, 282
Middlesex Ladies', 329
Middlesex Open, 189
Middlesex PGA, 190
Middleton Hall, 703
Middleton Park, 755
Midland Boys' Amateur
    Championship, 345
Midland Ladies (Ireland), 327
Midland Open, 264
Midland Professionals, 189
Midlothian Ladies', 331
Mid-Wales Ladies', 332
Les Mielles G & CC, 638
Mijas, 901
Milano, 880
Mile End, 713
Milford, 726
Milford Haven, 824
Mill Green, 674
Mill Hill, 700
Mill Ride, 632
Millbrook, 630
Millfield, 693
Millport, 790
Milltown, 768
Milnathort, 813
Milngavie, 797
Minchinhampton, 665
Minehead & West Somerset, 715

Minto, 793
Mionnay La Dombes, 862
Miraflores, 901
Miramar, 894
Miramas, 859
Mitcham, 727
Mitchelstown, 763
Mittelholsteinischer Aukrug, 867
Mittelrheinischer Bad Ems, 875
Mizuno Classic, 204
Mjölby, 911
Moate, 781
Moatlands, 680
Mobberley, 641
Modena G & CC, 881
Moffat, 795
Mold, 819
Moliets, 846
Molinetto CC, 880
Mölle, 909
Mølleåens, 841
Mollington Grange, 641
Mölndals, 906
Am Mondsee, 831
Monifieth Golf Links, 788
Monkstown, 763
Monkton Park Par Three, 742
Monmouth, 823
Monmouthshire, 823
Monmouthshire Ladies', 332
Mont Garni, 835
Mont Griffon, 853
Mont-d'Arbois, 862
Montado, 894
Montafon, 834
Monte Carlo, 859
Monte Mayor, 901
Montebelo, 895
Montecastillo, 902
Montecatini, 885
La Montecchia, 885
Montenmedio G & CC, 902
Monticello, 880
Montpellier Massane, 854
Montreux, 917
Montrose, 788
Montrose Caledonia, 788
Montrose Mercantile, 788
Moor Allerton, 755
Moor Hall, 739
Moor Park, 674, 778
Moore Place, 727
Moors Valley, 655
Moortown, 755
Mora, 908
La Moraleja, 900
Moray, 812
Morecambe, 687
Morfontaine, 851
Los Moriscos, 901
Morlais Castle, 822
Mormal, 851
Morpeth, 707
Morriston, 827
Mortehoe & Woolacombe, 651
Mortonhall, 810
Moseley, 744
Mosjö, 904
Moss Valley, 827

Mossock Hall, 687
Motala, 911
Mothers and Daughters Foursomes, 327
Mottram Hall Hotel, 641
Mount Ellen, 807
Mount Juliet, 774
Mount Murray G & CC, 676
Mount Ober G & CC, 766
Mount Oswald, 657
Mount Pleasant, 630
Mount Temple, 781
Mount Wolseley, 761
Mountain Ash, 822
Mountain Lakes, 822
Mountain View, 774
Mountbellew, 771
Mountrath, 774
Mourne, 766
Mouse Valley, 807
Mowsbury, 630
La Moye, 638
Moyola Park, 776
Muckhart, 813
Mühlenhof, 874
Muir of Ord, 804
Muirkirk, 792
Mullingar, 781
Mullion, 644
Mulranny, 777
München Nord-Eichenried, 870
München West-Odelzhausen, 870
München-Riedhof, 870
Münchener, 870
Mundesley, 703
Munross Trophy, 326
Munster Ladies, 327
Münster-Wilkinghege, 864
Murcar, 787
Murhof, 832
Murrayfield, 810
Murrayshall, 814
Murtal, 832
Muskerry, 764
Musselburgh, 808
Musselburgh Old Course, 808
Muswell Hill, 700
Muthill, 814
Mytton Fold Hotel, 687

Naas, 774
Nabisco Dinah Shore, 99
Nahetal, 875
Nairn, 804
Nairn Dunbar, 804
Nampont-St-Martin, 851
Nancy-Aingeray, 857
Nancy-Pulnoy, 857
Nantes, 855
Nantes Erdre, 855
Napoli, 882
Los Naranjos, 901
Narin & Portnoo, 765
Narvik, 891
Nässjö, 911
National Amateur Orders of Merit, 234
National Antalya, 918
National, 858

Nations Cup (Asia), 183
Nations Cup (Latin America), 183
Naunton Downs, 665
Nazeing, 661
Neath, 827
NEC Invitational, 161
Neckartal, 877
Nedbank Golf Challenge, 167
Nefyn & District, 820
Nelson, 687
Nenagh, 780
Nes, 891
Ness Open, 326
Ness-Nesklúbburinn, 879
Nettuno, 883
Neuchâtel, 916
Neuhof, 865
Neusiedlersee-Donnerskirchen, 833
Nevas Golf, 843
Nevill, 732
New Course, 801
New Cumnock, 792
New Forest, 668
New Galloway, 795
New, 800
New Golf Deauville, 856
New Mills, 650
New North Manchester, 695
New Ross, 782
New Zealand, 727
New Zealand Amateur Championship, 287
New Zealand Open, 192
Newark, 709
Newbattle, 810
Newbiggin, 707
Newbold Comyn, 739
Newbridge, 774
Newburgh-on-Ythan, 785
Newbury & Crookham, 632
Newbury Racecourse, 632
Newcastle United, 736
Newcastle West, 775
Newcastle-under-Lyme, 719
Newcastleton, 793
Newent, 665
Newlands, 770
Newmachar, 785
Newport, 676, 823
Newport (Pembs), 824
Newquay, 645
Newton Abbot (Stover), 652
Newton Green, 721
Newton Stewart, 795
Newtonmore, 804
Newtownstewart, 780
Nexø, 837
Nick Faldo Junior Series, 345
Nick Faldo Junior Series (Girls), 355
Nick Faldo Junior Series (International Trophy), 345
Niddry Castle, 811
Nieuwegeinse, 891
Nîmes Campagne, 854
Nîmes-Vacquerolles, 854
Niort, 849
Nippenburg, 877
Nissan Irish Open, 124

Nissan Open, 140
La Nivelle, 846
Le Nivernais, 848
Nizels, 680
Noord Nederlandse G & CC, 889
De Noordhollandse, 886
Noordwijkse, 890
Nora, 904
Norba, 896
Nordbornholm-Rø, 837
Nordcenter G & CC, 843
Nordic Open, 125
Nordkirchen, 874
Nordvestjysk, 840
Norfolk, 282
The Norfolk G & CC, 703
Norfolk Ladies', 329
Norfolk Open, 189
Norfolk Professionals, 189
Normanby Hall, 693
Normanton, 755
Norrköping, 911
Norrmjöle, 905
North Berwick, 808
North Downs, 727
North-East (Scotland), 284
North Foreland, 680
North Hants, 668
North Inch, 814
North Middlesex, 700
North of Ireland Open Amateur, 265
North of Scotland Open Stroke Play Amateur, 267
North Oxford, 711
North (Scotland), 284
North Shore, 693
North Warwickshire, 739
North Weald, 661
North West, 765
North Wilts, 742
North Worcestershire, 744
North-East Scotland District Championship, 267
Northampton, 705
Northamptonshire, 282
Northamptonshire County, 705
Northamptonshire Ladies', 329
Northcliffe, 756
Northenden, 695
Northern, 786
Northern Counties (Scotland) Ladies', 331
Northern Division Ladies (Scotland), 331
Northern Ladies Close (ELGA), 329
Northern Ladies Counties Championship, 329
Northern Open, 189
Northern Region PGA, 189
Northolt, 700
Northumberland, 282, 736
Northumberland and Durham Open, 189
Northumberland Ladies', 329
Northwood, 700
Norton, 657
Norwood Park, 709
The Notleys, 661

Nottingham City, 709
Nottinghamshire, 282
Nottinghamshire Ladies', 330
Notts, 709
Novo Sancti Petri, 902
Nuevo De Madrid, 900
Nuneaton, 739
Nunspeetse G & CC, 888
Nuremore, 778
Nurmijärven, 843
Nya Johannesberg G & CC, 914
Nynäshamn, 914

Oadby, 690
Oak Park, 727
Oakdale, 748, 823
Oake Manor, 715
Oakland Park, 635
Oakleaf Golf Complex, 657
Oakmere Park, 709
Oakridge, 739
The Oaks, 748
Oaks Sports Centre, 727
Oaksey Park, 742
Oastpark, 680
Obere Alp, 877
Oberfranken Thurnau, 872
Oberpfälzer Wald G & LC, 872
Oberschwaben-Bad Waldsee, 877
Oberzwieselau, 872
Oddafellowa, 879
Odder, 840
Odense, 838
Odense Eventyr, 838
L'Odet, 846
Odsherred, 841
Oeschberghof L & GC, 877
Office Depot Championship, 200
Official World Golf Ranking, Top 50
    (at end 2003 Season), 110
Ogbourne Downs, 742
Öijared, 906
Okehampton, 652
Olafsfjrödar, 879
Olching, 870
Old Colwyn, 818
Old Conna, 783
Old Course (15th Century), 801
Old Fold Manor, 674
Old Head Golf Links, 764
Old Lake, 878
Old Manchester, 696
Old Nene G & CC, 637
Old Padeswood, 819
Old Ranfurly, 815
Old Thorns, 668
Oldenburgischer, 864
Oldham, 687
Oldmeldrum, 785
Olgiata, 883
Oliva Nova, 903
Olivar de la Hinojosa, 900
Les Olonnes, 855
Olton, 739
Olympus, 887
Omagh, 780
Omaha Beach, 856
Ombersley, 744
Omega European Masters, 126

Omega Hong Kong Open, 114
Onneley, 719
Onsjö, 913
Onsøy, 892
Oosterhoutse, 887
Op de Niep, 874
Open Championship, 42, 124, 143
Open de España Femenino, 196
Open de France, 123
Opio-Valbonne, 860
Oporto, 895
Oppdal, 892
Oppegård, 892
Orchardleigh, 715
Örebro, 904
Örestad, 907
Örkelljunga, 909
Orkney, 804
Orléans Donnery, 849
Ormeau, 761
Les Ormes, 638, 846
Ormesson, 853
Ormonde Fields, 650
Ormskirk, 687
Orsett, 661
Orton Meadows, 637
Orust, 916
Osborne, 676
Oskarshamn, 911
Oslo, 892
Osnabrück, 874
Osona Montanya, 897
Österakers, 914
Österhaninge, 914
Österlen, 907
Östersund-Frösö, 905
Ostfriesland, 864
Ostmarka, 892
Östra Göinge, 910
Ostschweizerischer, 918
Oswestry, 714
Otley, 756
Ottenstein, 831
Otterbourne Golf Centre, 668
Otway, 765
Oude Maas, 890
Oudenaarde G & CC, 836
Oughterard, 771
Oulton Park, 756
Oulu, 843
Oundle, 705
Oustoen CC, 892
Outlane, 756
Overijse, 835
Overseas Amateur Championships,
    286
Overstone Park, 705
Öviks GC Puttom, 905
Owingen-Überlingen, 877
Owston Hall, 751
Owston Park, 751
Oxford and Cambridge Golfing
    Society for the President's Putter,
    278
Oxford v Cambridge Varsity Match,
    277
The Oxfordshire, 711
Oxfordshire Ladies', 330
Oxhey Park, 674

Oxley Park, 719
Ozoir-la-Ferrière, 853

Pachesham Park Golf Centre, 727
Padbrook Park, 652
Paderborner Land, 868
Padeswood & Buckley, 819
Padova, 885
Painswick, 665
Painthorpe House, 756
Paisley, 815
Palacerigg, 797
Palheiro, 894
De Palingbeek, 836
Palleg, 827
Palmares, 892
Palmer Cup, 279
Palmerston Golf Resort, 863
Panmure, 788
Pannal, 748
Pannonia G & CC, 878
Panorámica, 903
Panshanger Golf Complex, 674
El Paraiso, 902
Parasampia G & CC, 632
Parc, 823
Parc de Brotonne, 856
Parco de' Medici, 883
Paris International, 853
Park, 668
Park GC Ostrava, 837
Park Hill, 690
Park Wood, 680
Parkhall, 719
Parklands, 736
Parknasilla, 772
Parkstone, 655
Parley Court, 655
Partille, 906
Pastures, 650
Patriziale Ascona, 917
Patshull Park Hotel G & CC, 714
Pau, 846
Paultons Golf Centre, 668
Pavenham Park, 630
Le Pavoniere, 885
Paxhill Park, 734
Payerne, 916
Payne Stewart Award, 364
Peacehaven, 732
Pease Pottage, 734
Peebles, 793
Peel, 676
De Peelse Golf, 889
Peiner Hof, 867
Pen-y-Cae, 827
La Penaza, 903
Penha Longa, 894
Penina, 892
Penmaenmawr, 818
Penn, 719
Pennant Park, 819
Pennard, 827
Pennington, 687
Penrhos G & CC, 817
Penrith, 647
Penwortham, 687
Peover, 641
Peralada, 897

Golf du Perche, 849
Perdiswell Park, 744
Périgueux, 846
Perivale Park, 701
Perranporth, 645
Perstorp, 910
Perth and Kinross, 284
Perth and Kinross Ladies', 332
Perton Park, 719
Perugia, 885
Pescara, 883
Pessac, 846
Pestana, 892
Peter McEvoy Trophy, 345
Peterborough Milton, 637
Peterculter, 787
Peterhead, 786
Petersberg, 882
Petersfield, 669
Petersfield Sussex Road, 669
Peterstone Lakes, 826
Petit Chêne, 849
Petworth, 735
Peuramaa, 843
Pevero GC Costa Smeralda, 883
Pfaffing Wasserburger, 870
Pfalz Neustadt, 876
Pforzheim Karlshäuser Hof, 877
PGA British Assistants
   Championship, 185
PGA Cup, 181
PGA of Europe Championship, 187
PGA of Europe Team Championship,
   187
Phoenix, 751
Phoenix Open, 139
Phoenix Park, 756
Piandisole, 884
La Picardière, 849
Il Picciolo, 883
Pickala Golf, 843
Pierpont, 835
Pierre Carée, 862
Pike Fold, 696
Pike Hills, 748
Piltdown, 732
Pine Cliffs G & CC, 893
Pine Ridge, 727
Pineda De Sevilla, 902
Pines Golf Centre, 795
Pineta di Arenzano, 881
La Pinetina, 880
Pinheiros Altos, 893
An der Pinnau, 867
Pinner Hill, 701
Pitcheroak, 744
Piteå, 905
Pitlochry, 814
Pitreavie, 800
Plassey, 828
Platja de Pals, 898
Playa Serena, 896
Players Championship, 140
Pleasington, 687
Pléneuf-Val André, 846
Ploemeur Océan, 847
Podebrady, 837
Poggio dei Medici, 885
Poitiers, 849

Poitou, 849
Polkemmet, 811
Pollensa, 896
Pollok, 802
Polmont, 816
Poniente, 896
Pont Royal, 860
Pontardawe, 827
Ponte de Lima, 895
Ponte di Legno, 882
Pontefract & District, 756
Pontefract Park, 756
Ponteland, 707
Pontnewydd, 823
Pontypool, 823
Pontypridd, 822
La Porcelaine, 848
Porin Golfkerho, 844
Pornic, 855
Porrassalmi, 844
Port Bannatyne, 790
Port Bourgenay, 855
Port Glasgow, 815
Port St Mary, 676
Portadown, 760
Portal G & CC, 641
Portal Premier, 641
Portarlington, 774
Porters Park, 674
Porthmadog, 820
Porthpean, 645
Portlethen, 787
Portmarnock, 768
Portmarnock Hotel Links, 768
Portmore Golf Park, 652
Porto Carras G & CC, 878
Porto d'Orra, 882
Portobello, 810
Portpatrick, 795
Portsalon, 765
Portsmouth, 669
Portstewart, 776
Portuguese Open, 192
Portumna, 771
Potsdamer Tremmen, 863
Pottergate, 693
Potters Bar, 674
Poult Wood, 680
Poulton Park, 642
Poulton-le-Fylde, 687
Powerscourt (East), 783
Powerscourt (West), 783
Powfoot, 795
Pozoblanco, 899
Praa Sands, 645
Praha, 837
Praia d'el Rey G & CC, 895
Praia d'el Rey Rover European Cup,
   182
La Prée-La Rochelle, 849
Prenton, 698
Presidents Cup, 181
Prestatyn, 819
Prestbury, 642
Preston, 687
Prestonfield, 810
Prestwich, 696
Prestwick, 792
Prestwick St Cuthbert, 792

Prestwick St Nicholas, 792
Prince of Wales Challenge Cup,
   270
Prince's, 680
Princenbosch, 887
Princes Risborough, 635
The Priors, 661
Priors Hall, 705
Priskilly Forest, 824
Provence G & CC, 860
Prudhoe, 707
Prunevelle, 857
Pryors Hayes, 642
Puerta de Hierro, 900
Pula Golf, 896
Pumpherston, 811
Punta Ala, 885
Purley Chase, 739
Purley Downs, 727
Puttenham, 727
Puxton Park, 715
Pwllheli, 820
Pyecombe, 735
Pyle & Kenfig, 822
Pype Hayes, 739
Pyrford, 727
Pyrmonter, 868

Qatar Masters, 116
Queen Elizabeth Coronation Schools
   Trophy, 280
Queens Park (Bournemouth), 655
Queens Park, 642
Queensbury, 756
Le Querce, 883
Quimper-Cornouaille, 847
La Quinta G & CC, 902
Quinta da Beloura, 894
Quinta da Marinha, 894
Quinta do Lago, 893
Quinta do Perú, 894

R&A Junior Open, 346
Radcliffe-on-Trent, 709
Radstadt Tauerngolf, 831
Radyr, 826
RAF Benson, 711
RAF Coningsby, 693
RAF Cottesmore, 712
RAF Marham, 703
RAF North Luffenham, 712
RAF St Athan, 826
RAF Valley, 821
RAF Waddington, 693
Raffeen Creek, 764
Raglan Parc, 823
Ralston, 802
Las Ramblas, 896
Ramsdale Park Golf Centre, 709
Ramsey, 637, 676
Ramside, 657
Randers, 840
Ranfurly Castle, 815
Rapallo, 881
Rathbane, 775
Rathdowney, 774
Rathfarnham, 770
Rathmore, 759
Ratho Park, 810

Rathsallagh, 783
Rättvik, 908
Ravelston, 810
Ravenmeadow, 744
Ravensberger Land, 868
Ravensworth, 736
Rawdon, 756
Reading, 632
Real Campoamor, 896
Real Golf Castiello, 899
Real Cerdaña, 897
Real Golf El Prat, 897
Real Golf Las Palmas, 899
Real Golf Neguri, 899
Real Golf Pedreña, 899
Real San Sebastián, 899
Real Sevilla, 902
Real Tenerife, 899
Real Zarauz, 899
Reaseheath, 642
Reay, 802
Rebetz, 851
Redbourn, 674
Redcastle, 765
Reddish Vale, 642
Redditch, 744
Redhill, 727
Redhill & Reigate, 727
Redlibbets, 680
Regensburg, 872
Regensburg-Sinzing, 872
Regent Park (Bolton), 687
Regiment Way Golf Centre, 661
Am Reichswald, 872
Reigate Heath, 728
Reigate Hill, 728
Reims-Champagne, 857
Reischenhof, 877
Reit im Winkl-Kössen, 870
Reiting G & CC, 832
Renfrew, 815
Renfrewshire, 284
Renfrewshire Ladies', 332
Renishaw Park, 751
Rennes Saint Jacques, 847
Reno-Tahoe Open, 144
Los Retamares, 900
Retford, 709
Reus Aiguesverds, 897
Reutlingen-Sonnenbühl, 877
Reykjavíkur, 879
Reymerswael, 887
Rhein Badenweiler, 877
Rhein Sieg, 875
Rhein Main, 865
Rheinblick, 865
Rheine/Mesum, 874
Rheintal, 865
Rhin Mulhouse, 857
Rhoen, 864
Rhondda, 822
Rhos-on-Sea, 818
Rhosgoch, 825
Rhuddlan, 819
Rhuys-Kerver, 847
Rhyl, 819
Ribe, 840
Riccarton Rosse Bowl, 326
Richings Park G & CC, 635

Richmond, 728, 748
Richmond Park, 703, 728
Rickenbach, 878
Rickmansworth, 675
Riddlesden, 756
The Ridge, 680
Ridgeway, 822
Riederalp, 916
Rigenée, 835
Rijswijkse, 890
Ring of Kerry G & CC, 772
Ringdufferin, 766
Ringenäs, 913
Ringway, 642
Rinkven G & CC, 834
Rio Real, 902
Ripon City, 748
Risebridge, 661
Rishton, 687
Rittergut Birkhof, 874
Riva Dei Tessali, 882
Rivenhall Oaks, 661
River Golf, 844
Riverside, 681
Riverside Golf Centre, 681
Riversmeet Par Three, 655
RLGC Village Play, 698
Robin Hood, 739
Le Robinie, 880
Robinson Golf Club Nobilis, 918
La Rocca, 881
Rochdale, 688
Rochefort, 858
Les Rochers, 847
Rochester & Cobham Park, 681
Rochford Hundred, 661
Rockmount, 766
Rodway Hill, 665
Roe Park, 776
Roehampton Club, 728
Roehampton Gold Cup, 325
Roker Park, 728
Rold Skov, 840
The Rolls of Monmouth, 823
Roma, 883
Romanby, 749
Romeleåsen, 907
Romford, 661
Romiley, 642
Romney Warren, 681
Romsey, 669
Ronneby, 910
Rookery Park, 721
Roquebrune, 860
Rosapenna, 765
Roscommon, 779
Roscrea, 780
Roseberry Grange, 657
Rosebery Challenge Cup, 271
Rosehearty, 786
Rosendaelsche, 888
Roskilde, 841
Roslagen, 904
Ross, 772
Ross Priory, 797
Ross-on-Wye, 671
Rossendale, 688
La Rossera, 880
Rosslare, 782

Rossmore, 778
Rothbury, 707
Rother Valley Golf Centre, 751
Rotherham, 751
Rothes, 786
Rothesay, 790
Rothley Park, 690
Rottaler G & CC, 870
Rottbach, 870
Rouen-Mont St Aignan, 856
Rougemont, 835
Rougemont-le-Château, 857
Rouken Glen, 802
Roundhay, 756
Roundwood, 751, 783
Routenburn, 792
Le Rovedine, 880
I Roveri, 884
Rowany, 676
Rowlands Castle, 669
The Roxburghe Hotel, 794
The Royal & Ancient, 800
Royal Aberdeen, 787
Royal Amicale Anderlecht, 835
Royal Antwerp, 834
Royal Ascot, 632
Royal Ashdown Forest, 732
Royal Automobile Club, 728
Royal Belfast, 766
Royal Bendinat, 896
Royal Birkdale, 698
Royal Blackheath, 681
Royal Burgess Golfing Society of
   Edinburgh, 810
Royal Cinque Ports, 681
Royal County Down, 766
Royal Cromer, 703
Royal Dornoch, 802
Royal Dublin, 770
Royal Eastbourne, 732
Royal Epping Forest, 661
Royal GC du Hainaut, 835
Royal GC du Sart Tilman, 836
Royal Golf Club de Belgique, 836
Royal Golf des Fagnes, 836
Royal Guernsey, 638
The Royal Household, 632
Royal Jersey, 638
Royal Latem, 836
Royal Liverpool, 698
Royal Lytham & St Annes, 688
Royal Malta, 886
Royal Mid-Surrey, 728
Royal Montrose, 788
Royal Mougins, 860
Royal Musselburgh, 808
Royal North Devon, 652
Royal Norwich, 703
Royal Oak, 840
Royal Ostend, 837
Royal Perth Golfing Society, 814
Royal Porthcawl, 822
Royal Portrush, 759
Royal St David's, 820
Royal St George's, 681
Royal Tara, 778
Royal Tarlair, 786
Royal Town of Caernarfon, 820
Royal Troon, 792

Royal Waterloo, 836
Royal West Norfolk, 703
Royal Wimbledon, 728
Royal Winchester, 669
Royal Worlington & Newmarket, 722
Royal Zoute, 837
Royan, 849
Royston, 675
Ruchill, 802
Rudding Park, 749
Ruddington Grange, 709
Rufford Park Golf Centre, 709
Rugby, 739
Ruislip, 701
Runcorn, 642
Rungsted, 841
Rush, 768
Rushcliffe, 709
Rushden, 705
Rushmere, 722
Rushmore Park, 742
Rusper, 728
Russian Open, 192
Rustington, 735
Rutherford Castle, 811
Ruthin-Pwllglas, 819
Rutland County, 712
Ruukkigolf, 843
Ruxley Park, 681
Rya, 910
Ryburn, 756
Ryde, 676
Ryder Cup, 168
Ryder Cup — Individual Records, 176
Rye, 732
Rye Hill, 711
Ryhope, 657
Ryston Park, 703
Ryton, 736

Saarbrücken, 876
Sables-d'Or-les-Pins, 847
Sablé-Solesmes, 855
Am Sachsenwald, 867
Saddleworth, 688
Saeby, 840
Safeway Classic, 204
Safeway PING, 200
Saffron Walden, 662
Sagmühle, 872
St Andrews, 800
St Andrews Links Trophy, 261
St Andrews Major, 826
St Andrews Thistle, 800
St Andrews Trophy, 252
St Anne's, 770
St Annes Old Links, 688
St Aubin, 853
St Augustines, 682
St Austell, 645
St Bees, 647
St Boswells, 794
St Clements, 638
St Cleres, 662
St Cloud, 858
St Cyprien, 854
St David's Gold Cross, 261
St Davids City, 824
St Deiniol, 820

St Endreol, 860
St Enodoc, 645
St Etienne, 862
St Fillans, 814
St Gatien Deauville, 856
St George's Grand Challenge Cup, 271
St George's Hill, 729
St Germain, 858
St Germain-les-Corbeil, 853
St Giles Newtown, 825
St Helen's Bay, 782
St Idloes, 825
St Ives, 637
St Jean-de-Monts, 855
St Julien, 856
St Junien, 848
St Kew, 645
St Laurence, 843
St Laurent, 847
St Malo-Le Tronchet, 847
St Margaret's G & CC, 769
St Mary's Hotel G & CC, 826
St Medan, 796
St Mellion Hotel G & CC, 645
St Mellons, 826
St Melyd, 819
St Michaels, 800
St Michaels Jubilee, 642
St Neots, 637
St Nom-La-Bretêche, 858
Saint-Omer, 851
St Patricks Courses, 765
St Pierre Park, 638
St Quentin-en-Yvelines, 858
St Regulus Ladies', 800
The St Rule Club, 800
St Rule Trophy, 326
St Saëns, 856
St Samson, 847
St Thomas, 854
St Thomas's Priory, 719
La Sainte-Baume, 860
Sainte-Maxime, 860
Saintonge, 849
Sala, 904
Salamanca, 896
Sale, 642
Sälenfjallens, 908
El Saler, 903
Salgados, 893
Saline, 800
Salisbury & South Wilts, 742
Sallandsche De Hoek, 888
Salo Golf, 844
Saltburn, 749
Saltford, 715
Saltsjöbaden, 914
Salvagny, 862
Salzburg Fuschl, 832
Salzburg G & CC, 832
Salzkammergut, 832
Samsung World Championship, 204
San Floriano-Gorizia, 885
San Lorenzo, 893
San Michele, 882
San Roque, 902
Sancerrois, 849
Sand Martins, 632

Sand Moor, 756
Sanday, 804
Sandbach, 642
Sandford Springs, 669
Sandhill, 751
Sandilands, 693
Sandiway, 642
Sandown Park Golf Centre, 728
Sandwell Park, 719
Sandy Lodge, 675
Sandyhills, 802
St Arild, 910
St Barbara's Royal Dortmund, 874
St Dionys, 867
St Eurach G & LC, 871
St Leon-Rot, 866
St Lorence G & CC, 879
St Lorenzen, 832
St Oswald-Freistadt, 831
St Pölten Schloss Goldegg, 831
Sanquhar, 796
Sant Cugat, 897
Sant Jordi, 897
Santa María G & CC, 902
Santa Ponsa, 897
Sapey, 671
Sarfvik, 843
Sargé-Le-Mans, 855
Saron Golf Course, 818
Le Sart, 851
Säter, 908
Saudárkróks, 879
Saunton, 652
Savenay, 855
Saxå, 916
Scandic Carlsberg Scandinavian Masters, 125
Scarborough North Cliff, 749
Scarborough South Cliff, 749
Scarcroft, 756
Scarthingwell, 749
Schärding-Pramtal, 831
Schinznach-Bad, 918
Schloss Braunfels, 864
Schloss Breitenberg, 867
Schloss Ebreichsdorf, 833
Schloss Ernegg, 831
Schloss Fahrenbach, 872
Schloss Frauenthal, 832
Schloss Georghausen, 874
Schloss Haag, 874
Schloss Klingenburg-Günzburg, 878
Schloss Langenstein, 878
Schloss Liebenstein, 878
Schloss Lüdersburg, 867
Schloss Maxlrain, 871
Schloss Meisdorf, 863
Schloss Myllendonk, 874
Schloss Pichlarn, 832
Schloss Reichmannsdorf, 872
Schloss Schönborn, 833
Schloss Sickendorf, 865
Schloss Weitenburg, 878
Schlossberg, 872
Schmidmühlen G & CC, 872
Schmitzhof, 874
Schönenberg, 918
Schönfeld, 833
De Schoot, 889

Schwanhof, 872
Schwarze Heide, 874
Scoonie, 800
Scotscraig, 800
Scottish Amateur Championship, 227
Scottish Area Team Championship,
    255
Scottish Boys' Championship, 341
Scottish Boys' Stroke Play
    Championship, 342
Scottish Boys' Team Championship,
    349
Scottish Boys' Under-16 Stroke Play
    Championship, 343
Scottish Champion of Champions,
    230
Scottish Club Championship, 255
Scottish Clubs Handicap
    Championship, 256
Scottish Foursomes Tournament
    (*Glasgow Evening Times* Trophy),
    256
Scottish Girls' Close Championship,
    353
Scottish Ladies' Close Amateur
    Championship, 303
Scottish Ladies' County
    Championship, 323
Scottish Ladies' Foursomes, 323
Scottish Ladies' Junior Open Stroke
    Play Championship, 353
Scottish Ladies' Open Stroke Play
    Championship (Helen Holm
    Trophy), 305
Scottish Match Play Championship,
    186
Scottish Mid-Amateur Championship,
    230
The Scottish Open, 124
Scottish Open Amateur Stroke Play
    Championship, 229
Scottish Professionals' Championship,
    256
Scottish Senior Championship, 229
Scottish Senior Ladies' Amateur
    Championship, 305
Scottish Youths' Stroke Play
    Championship, 343
Scrabo, 766
Scraptoft, 690
SCT Knuds, 838
Sea Golf Rönnäs, 843
Seacroft, 693
Seafield, 792
Seaford, 732
Seaford Head, 732
Seaham, 657
Seahouses, 707
Seapoint, 776
Seascale, 647
Seaton Carew, 657
Seckford, 722
Sedbergh, 647
Seddiner See, 863
Sedgley, 719
Sedlescombe, 732
Seedy Mill, 719
Seefeld-Wildmoos, 830
Selborne Salver, 272

Selby, 749
Selkirk, 794
La Sella, 896
Selsdon Park Hotel, 728
Selsey, 735
Semily, 837
Semlin am See, 863
Semmering, 833
Sempachersee, 918
De Semslanden, 889
Sene Valley, 681
Senior Halford-Hewitt Competitions,
    276
Senior Home Internationals, 254, 322
Senior Ladies' British Open Amateur
    Stroke Play Championship, 297
Senne GC Gut Welschof, 868
Sennelager (British Army), 869
Sept Fontaines, 836
Seraincourt, 853
Serlby Park, 709
La Serra, 884
Servanes, 860
Sestrieres, 884
Settle, 749
Seve Trophy, 130, 181
Severn Meadows, 714
Sevilla Golf, 902
Shandon Park, 761
Shanklin & Sandown, 676
Shannon, 762
Shaw Hill Hotel G & CC, 688
Sheerness, 681
Sheffield Transport, 751
Shell Houston Open, 141
Shendish Manor, 675
Sherborne, 655
Sherdley Park Municipal, 698
Sherdons Golf Centre, 665
Sheringham, 703
Sherry Cup, 262, 326
Sherwood Forest, 709
Shetland, 804
Shifnal, 714
Shillinglee Park, 735
Shipley, 757
Shirehampton Park, 665
Shirenewton, 824
Shirland, 650
Shirley, 739
Shirley Park, 728
Shiskine, 792
Shooter's Hill, 681
Shoprite LPGA Classic, 202
Shortlands, 681
Shotts, 807
Shrewsbury, 714
Shrigley Hall Hotel & CC, 642
Shrivenham Park, 742
The Shropshire, 714
Shropshire and Hertfordshire, 282
Shropshire Ladies', 330
Sickleholme, 650
Sidcup, 681
Sidmouth, 652
Sieben-Berge Rheden, 869
Siegen-Olpe, 874
Siegerland, 874
Sigtunabygden, 904

Silecroft, 647
Silkeborg, 840
Silkstone, 751
Silloge Park, 768
Silloth-on-Solway, 647
Silsden, 757
Silverdale, 647
Silverknowes, 810
Silvermere, 729
Silverstone, 635
Silverwood, 760
Simon's, 841
Singapore Open, 192
Singing Hills, 735
Sinsheim, 878
Sion, 917
Sir Henry Cotton European Rookie of
    the Year, 365
Sittingbourne & Milton Regis, 681
Sitwell Park, 751
Six Hills, 691
Sjögärde, 906
Skaftö, 916
Skeabost, 805
Skellefteå, 906
Skelmorlie, 792
Skepparslov, 910
Skepptuna, 904
Skerries, 769
Skibbereen, 764
Skinnarebo, 911
Skipton, 749
Skjeberg, 892
Skjoldenaesholm, 841
Skogaby, 913
Skovlunde Herlev, 841
Slade Valley, 769
Sleaford, 693
Slieve Russell G & CC, 761
Slievenamon, 780
Slinfold Park, 735
Smurfit European Open, 123
Smurfit Irish PGA Championship, 185
Snöå, 908
Söderåsen, 910
Söderhamn, 909
Söderköping, 911
Söderslätts, 907
Södertälje, 905
Solent Meads Par Three, 655
Solheim Cup, 198, 204, 209
Solheim Cup — Individual Records,
    212
Sollefteå, 906
Sollentuna, 914
Sollerö, 909
Søllerød, 841
Soltau, 864
Sölvesborg, 910
Somerley Park, 669
Somerset, 283
Somerset Ladies', 330
Somosaguas, 900
Son Antem, 897
Son Servera, 897
Son Vida, 897
Sønderjyllands, 840
Sondie Arctic Desert, 838
Sonnenalp, 871

Sonning, 632
Sony Open, 139
La Sorelle, 862
Sorknes, 892
Sorø, 841
Sotenas Golfklubb, 913
Sotogrande, 902
South African Amateur
    Championship, 287
South African Airways Open, 114
South African Open, 192
South African Stroke Play, 288
South African Sunshine Tour, 156
South Beds, 630
South Bradford, 757
The South County, 769
South-East Scotland Championship,
    284
South-Eastern Ladies', 330
South Essex G & CC, 662
South Herefordshire, 671
South Herts, 675
South Kyme, 694
South Leeds, 757
South Meath, 778
South Moor, 657
South of Ireland Open Amateur, 266
South of Scotland Ladies', 332
South Pembrokeshire, 824
South Shields, 736
South Staffordshire, 719
South West PGA, 189
South Winchester, 669
South-East Scotland District
    Championship, 267
Southampton Municipal, 669
Southern Assistants, 189
Southern Assistants Match Play, 189
Southern Division Ladies' (Scotland),
    332
Southern Farm Bureau Classic, 145
Southern Professionals, 189
Southern Valley, 682
Southerndown, 822
Southerness, 796
Southfield, 712
Southport & Ainsdale, 698
Southport Municipal, 698
Southport Old Links, 698
Southsea, 669
Southwell, 710
Southwick Park, 669
Southwold, 722
Southwood, 669
The Spa, 766
Spaarnwoude, 887
Spalding, 694
Spanish Open, 192
Spanish Point, 762
Sparkwell, 652
Spean Bridge, 804
Spérone, 851
Spessart, 866
Spey Bay, 812
Sphinx, 739
Spiegelven GC Genk, 836
Sporting Club de Vichy, 848
Sports Today CJ Nine Bridges
    Classic, 204

Springhead Park, 746
The Springs Hotel, 712
Springwater, 710
St Cast Pen Guen, 847
Stackstown, 770
Staddon Heights, 652
Stade Montois, 846
Stafford Castle, 719
Staffordshire, 283
Staffordshire and Shropshire Stroke
    Play, 190
Staffordshire Ladies', 330
Staffordshire Open, 189
Stamford, 643
Stand, 696
Standard Life Leven Gold Medal,
    260
Standish Court, 688
Stanedge, 650
Stanmore, 701
Stanton-on-the-Wolds, 710
Stapleford Abbotts, 662
Staplehurst Golf Centre, 682
Starnberg, 871
State Farm Classic, 203
Stavanger, 892
Staverton Park, 705
Steenhoven, 834
Steisslingen, 878
Stenungsund, 907
Stevenage, 675
Stilton Oaks, 637
Stinchcombe Hill, 665
Stirling, 816
Stirling and Clackmannan County
    Ladies', 332
Stirlingshire, 284
Stock Brook Manor, 662
Stockholm, 914
Stockley Park, 701
Stockport, 643
Stocks Hotel G & CC, 675
Stocksbridge & District, 751
Stocksfield, 707
Stockwood Park, 630
Stockwood Vale, 715
Stoke Albany, 705
Stoke Poges, 635
Stoke Rochford, 694
Stoke-by-Nayland, 722
Stone, 720
Stonebridge Golf Centre, 739
Stoneham, 669
Stonehaven, 786
Stoneleigh Deer Park, 739
Stony Holme, 647
Stonyhurst Park, 688
Stora Lundby, 907
Stornoway, 805
Storws Wen, 821
Stourbridge, 744
Stowe, 635
Stowmarket, 722
Strabane, 780
Strandhill, 779
Strängnäs, 905
Stranraer, 796
Strasbourg, 857
Stratford Oaks, 740

Stratford-on-Avon, 740
Strathaven, 807
Strathclyde Park, 807
Strathendrick, 817
Strathlene, 786
Strathmore Golf Centre, 814
Strathpeffer Spa, 804
Strathtay, 814
Strathtyrum Course, 801
Strawberry Hill, 701
Stressholme, 657
Strokestown, 779
Stromberg-Schindeldorf, 875
Stromness, 804
Strömstad, 916
Studley Wood, 712
Stupinigi, 884
Sturminster Marshall, 655
Stuttgarter Solitude, 878
Styal, 643
Styrrup Hall, 751
Sudbrook Moor, 694
Sudbury, 701
Sudurnesja, 879
Suffolk, 283
The Suffolk G & CC, 722
Suffolk Ladies', 330
Suffolk Open, 190
Suffolk Professionals, 190
Sully-sur-Loire, 849
Sunbury, 701
Sundridge Park, 682
Sundsvall, 906
Sunne, 916
Sunningdale, 729
Sunningdale Foursomes, 274
Sunningdale Ladies, 729
Golf del Sur, 899
Surbiton, 729
Surrey, 283
Surrey Downs, 729
Surrey Ladies', 330
Surrey Open, 190
Surry National, 729
Sussex, 283
Sussex Ladies', 330
Sussex Open, 190
Sutherland Chalice, 262
Sutton, 770
Sutton Bridge, 694
Sutton Coldfield, 740
Sutton Green, 729
Sutton Hall, 643
Sutton Park, 746
Suur-Helsingin, 843
Svalöv, 910
Svendborg, 838
Swaffham, 704
Swansea Bay, 827
Swanston, 810
Swarland Hall, 707
Sweetwoods Park, 682
Swindon, 720
Swinford, 777
Swinley Forest, 632
Swinton Park, 696
Swords, 769
Sybase Big Apple Classic, 202
Sybrook, 888

Sydsjaellands, 841
Syke, 864
Sylt, 868

Täby, 914
Tadmarton Heath, 712
Tain, 804
Taiwan Open, 191
Tall Pines, 716
Golf Talma, 843
Tammer Golf, 844
Tamworth, 720
Tandragee, 760
Tandridge, 729
Tankersley Park, 752
Tantallon, 808
Tara Glen, 782
Tarbat, 804
Tarbert, 790
Tarina Golf, 842
Tarland, 786
Tarquinia, 883
Tat Golf International, 918
Taulane, 860
Taunton & Pickeridge, 716
Taunton Vale, 716
Taunus Weilrod, 866
Tavistock, 652
Tawast Golf, 844
Taymouth Castle, 814
Taynuilt, 790
Teesside, 749
Tegelberga, 907
Tegernseer GC Bad Wiessee, 871
Tehidy Park, 645
Teign Valley, 652
Teignmouth, 652
Telefonica Open de Madrid, 129
Telford, 714
Temple, 632, 767
Temple Newsam, 757
Templemore, 780
Tenby, 824
Tenerife Ladies Open, 196
Tennant Cup, 262
Tenterden, 682
Terceira Island, 893
Ternesse G & CC, 834
Terramar, 897
Test Valley, 670
Tetney, 694
Tewkesbury Park Hotel, 665
Thames Ditton & Esher, 729
Thayatal Drosendorf, 833
Theale, 632
Thetford, 704
Theydon Bois, 662
Thirsk & Northallerton, 749
Thornbury Golf Centre, 665
Thorndon Park, 662
Thorne, 752
Thorney Golf Centre, 637
Thorney Park, 635
Thornhill, 796
Thornton, 800
Thorntree, 808
Thorpe Hall, 662
Thorpe Wood, 638
Thorpeness Hotel, 722

Thoulstone Park, 742
Three Locks, 635
Three Rivers, 662
Thumeries, 851
Thurles, 780
Thurlestone, 652
Thurso, 803
Tickenham, 716
Tidbury Green, 740
Tidworth Garrison, 742
Tietlingen, 864
Tignes, 862
Tilgate Forest, 735
Tillicoultry, 794
Tillman Trophy, 263
Tilsworth, 630
Timrå, 906
Tinsley Park, 752
Tipperary, 780
Tirrenia, 885
Tiverton, 652
Tobermory, 790
Tobo, 912
Todmorden, 757
Toft Hotel, 694
La Toja, 899
Tolladine, 744
Tomelilla, 907
Tongelreep G & CC, 889
Toot Hill, 662
Top Meadow, 662
Töreboda, 913
Torekov, 910
Torino, 884
Torphin Hill, 810
Torphins, 786
Torquay, 653
Torrance House, 807
La Torre, 881
Torreby, 916
Torremirona, 897
Torrequebrada, 901
Torrington, 653
Torshälla, 905
Tortuna, 905
Torvaianica, 883
Torvean, 804
Torwoodlee, 794
Toulouse, 863
Toulouse-La Ramée, 863
Toulouse-Palmola, 863
Toulouse-Seilh, 863
Toulouse-Teoula, 863
Le Touquet "La Forêt", 851
Le Touquet "La Mer", 851
Le Touquet "Le Manoir", 851
Tour Championship, The, 146
Tour de las Americas, 159
Touraine, 849
Tournerbury Golf Centre, 670
Towerlands, 662
Towneley, 688
Towneley Hall, 776
Toxandria, 887
Toyota World Junior Team
   Championship, 347
Traigh, 805
Tralee, 773
Tramore, 781

Tranås, 912
Traunsee Kircham, 831
Tredegar & Rhymney, 824
Tredegar Park, 824
Trefloyne, 824
Tregenna Castle Hotel, 645
Trelleborg, 907
Treloy, 645
Trent Lock Golf Centre, 710
Trent Park, 701
Trentham, 720
Trentham Park, 720
Trethorne, 645
Treudelberg G & CC, 868
Trevose, 645
Trier, 876
Trieste, 885
Tróia Golf, 894
Trollhättan, 913
Trondheim, 892
Troon Municipal, 792
Troon Portland, 792
Troon St Meddans, 792
Trophée Lancôme, 127
Trosa, 905
Troxhammar, 915
Troyes-Cordelière, 857
Trubshaw Cup, 263
Trummenas, 910
Truro, 645
Tuam, 771
Tubbercurry, 779
Tucker Trophy, 263
Tudor Park, 682
Tulfarris, 783
Tullamore, 778
Tulliallan, 794
Tunbridge Wells, 682
Tunshill, 688
Turespaña Mallorca Classic, 129
Turnberry Hotel, 792
Turnhouse, 810
Turriff, 786
Turton, 688
Turvey, 769
Tutzing, 871
Tuusula, 843
Twentsche, 888
Twickenham, 701
Tylney Park, 670
Tynedale, 707
Tynemouth, 736
Tyneside, 736
Tyrifjord, 892
Tyrrells Wood, 729
The Tytherington Club, 643

UBS Cup, 183
Uddeholm, 916
Udine, 885
Ufford Park Hotel, 722
Ullapool, 803
Ullesthorpe Court Hotel, 691
Ullna, 915
Ulm/Neu-Ulm, 878
Ulricehamn, 913
Ulriksdal, 915
Ulster Open Ladies, 327
Ulster Professionals, 190

Ulverston, 647
Ulzama, 899
Umeå, 906
United States Amateur Championship, 288
United States Ladies' Amateur Championship, 333
University and School Events, 276
Unna-Fröndenberg, 874
Upavon, 742
Upchurch River Valley, 682
Uphall, 811
Upminster, 662
Upsala, 905
Upton-by-Chester, 643
Urslautal, 832
US Champions Tour, 2003, 147
US LPGA Rolex Player of the Year, 363
US LPGA Rookie of the Year, 363
US LPGA Tour, 2003, 199
US LPGA Vare Trophy, 364
US Nationwide Tour, 2002, 150
US Open Championship, 52
US Open Championship, 122
US Open Championship, 142
US PGA Championship, 67, 125, 144
US PGA Player of the Year, 365
US PGA Tour, 2003, 136
US Vardon Trophy, 365
US Women's Open, 202
US Women's Open Championship, 83
USPGA Rookie of the Year, 365
Utrechtse "De Pan", 891
Uttoxeter, 720
Uxbridge, 701

Vaasan, 842
Vadstena, 912
Vaerlose Golfklub, 842
Vagliano Trophy — Great Britain & Ireland v Continent of Europe, 320
Val de l'Indre, 849
Val de Sorne, 857
Val Queven, 847
Val Secret, 851
Val de Cher, 848
Valcros, 860
Valdaine, 862
Valdeláguila, 900
Valderrama, 902
The Vale, 745
Vale de Milho, 893
Vale do Lobo, 893
Vale of Glamorgan Hotel G & CC, 826
Vale of Leven, 797
Vale of Llangollen, 819
Vale Royal Abbey, 643
Valence St Didier, 862
Valero Texas Open, 145
Valescure, 860
Vall d'Or, 897
Vallensbaek, 842
Vallentuna, 915
Vallromanes, 897
Vammala, 844
Vara-Bjertorp, 913

Varberg, 913
Varde, 840
Varese, 880
Värnamo, 912
Vartry Lakes, 783
Vasatorp, 910
Vassunda, 905
Västerås, 905
Västervik, 912
La Vaucouleurs, 858
Le Vaudreuil, 856
Vaul, 790
Växjö, 912
Vechta-Welpe, 874
Vegilinbosschen, 889
Vejle, 840
Velbert – Gut Kuhlendahl, 875
Vellinge, 908
Veluwse, 888
Venezia, 886
Ventnor, 676
Verbier, 917
Verden, 864
De Vere Dunston Hall, 704
De Vere Herons Reach, 688
De Vere Slaley Hall, 708
The De Vere PGA Seniors Championship, 184
Verizon Byron Nelson Classic, 142
Verona, 882
Versilia, 881
Vert Parc, 851
Verulam, 675
Vestfold, 892
Vestfyns, 838
Vestischer GC Recklinghausen, 875
Vestmannaeyja, 879
Vetlanda, 912
Viborg, 840
Vicars Cross, 643
Vidago, 895
Vierumäen Golfseura, 844
Vigevano, 881
Viksjö, 915
Vila Sol, 893
Vilamoura Laguna, 893
Vilamoura Millennium, 893
Vilamoura Old, 893
Vilamoura Pinhal, 893
Villa Condulmer, 886
Villa D'Este, 881
Villa de Madrid CC, 900
Villamartin, 896
Villarceaux, 853
Villars, 917
Villeray, 853
Vimeiro, 894
Vinberg, 913
Vinovo, 884
Virginia, 761
Virginia Park, 822
Virvik Golf, 843
Visby, 912
Vista Hermosa, 902
Vittel, 858
Vivary, 716
Vivien Saunders Trophy, 363
Vogrie, 811
Les Volcans, 848

Volvo Masters Andalucia, 129
Volvo order of merit, 111
Volvo PGA Championship, 120
Vreta Kloster, 912
Vulpera, 917

Wachovia Championship, 141
Wachovia LPGA Classic, 203
Wakefield, 757
Waldbrunnen, 876
Waldegg-Wiggensbach, 871
Waldringfield Heath, 722
The Wales Open, 121
Wales WPGA Championship of Europe, 198
Walker Cup, 235
Walker Cup — Individual Records, 244
Wallasey, 698
Wallenried, 916
Wallsend, 736
Walmer & Kingsdown, 682
Walmersley, 688
Walmley, 740
Walsall, 720
Waltham Windmill, 694
Walton Hall, 643
Walton Heath, 729
Wanstead, 662
La Wantzenau, 858
Waregem, 837
Wareham, 655
Warkworth, 708
Warley, 745
Warley Park, 663
Warren, 653, 663, 698
Warrenpoint, 767
Warrington, 643
Warwick, 740
Warwickshire, 283
The Warwickshire, 740
Warwickshire Ladies', 330
Warwickshire Open, 190
Warwickshire Professional, 190
Wäsby, 915
Washington, 737
Wassenaarse Rozenstein, 890
Wasserburg Anholt, 875
Waterbeach, 638
Waterbridge, 653
Waterford, 781
Waterford Castle, 781
Waterhall, 732
Waterlandse, 887
Waterlooville, 670
Waterstock, 712
Waterton Park, 757
Waterville, 773
Wath, 752
Wavendon Golf Centre, 635
Weald of Kent, 682
Weald Park, 663
Wearside, 737
Websweiler Hof, 876
Weetabix Age Goup Championships, 357
Weetabix Challenge, 323
Weetabix Women's British Open Championship, 76

Weetabix Women's British Open, 197, 203
Wegman's Rochester International, 202
Weitra, 831
Welch's/Fry's Championship, 200
Welcombe Hotel, 740
Welderen, 888
Wellingborough, 705
Wellow, 670
Wells, 716
Wellshurst G & CC, 733
Wels, 831
Welschap, 889
Welsh Amateur Championship, 230
Welsh Open Amateur Stroke Play Championship, 232
Welsh Border Golf Complex, 825
Welsh Boys' Stroke Play Championship, 344
Welsh Boys' Championship, 343
Welsh Boys' Under-15 Championship, 344
Welsh Girls' Championship, 354
Welsh Inter-Counties Championship, 256
Welsh Ladies' Amateur Championship, 305
Welsh Ladies' Open Amateur Stroke Play Championship, 307
Welsh Ladies' Team Championship, 323
Welsh Nationals Championship, 186
Welsh Open Youths' Championship, 345
Welsh Senior Ladies' Championship, 307
Welsh Seniors' Amateur Championship, 232
Welsh Team Championship, 256
Welsh Tournament of Champions, 233
Welshpool, 825
Welton Manor, 694
Welwyn Garden City, 675
Auf der Wendlohe, 868
Wendy's Championship for Children, 202
Wensum Valley, 704
Wentorf-Reinbeker, 868
Wentworth Club, 729
Wenvoe Castle, 826
Wergs, 720
Wermdö G & CC, 915
Wernddu Golf Centre, 824
Werneth, 688
Werneth Low, 643
Weserbergland, 869
West Berkshire, 633
West Bowling, 757
West Bradford, 757
West Byfleet, 730
West Chiltington, 735
West Cornwall, 645
West Derby, 698
West Essex, 663
West Herts, 675
West Hill, 730
West Hove, 733

West Kent, 682
West Kilbride, 792
West Lancashire, 698
West Linton, 811
West Lothian, 811
West Malling, 682
West Middlesex, 701
West Midlands, 740
West Monmouthshire, 824
West of England Open Match Play Amateur, 264
West of England Open Stroke Play Amateur, 265
West of Ireland Open Amateur, 266
West of Scotland Open Amateur, 267
West Region PGA, 190
West Rhine, 875
West Surrey, 730
West Sussex, 735
West Waterford G & CC, 781
West Wilts, 742
Westerham, 683
Westerhope, 737
Western Division Ladies' (Scotland), 332
Western Gailes, 793
Western Open, 143
Western Park, 691
Westerpark Zoetermeer, 890
Westerwald, 875
Westerwood Hotel G & CC, 797
Westfälischer Gütersloh, 869
Westgate & Birchington, 683
Westhill, 787
Westhoughton, 688
Westmanstown, 769
Weston Park, 704
Weston Turville, 635
Weston-super-Mare, 716
Westonbirt, 665
Westpfalz Schwarzbachtal, 876
Westport, 777
Westridge, 676
Westwood, 720
Wetherby, 757
Wexford, 782
Wexham Park, 635
Weybrook Park, 670
Weymouth, 655
WGC Accenture Match Play, 116, 140
WGC: American Express Stroke Play Championship, 127
WGC America Express Championship, 127, 145
WGC: NEC Invitational, 125, 144
Whalley, 689
Whalsay, 804
Wharton Park, 745
Wheathampstead, 675
Wheathill, 716
Wheatley, 752
Whetstone, 691
Whickham, 737
Whinhill, 815
Whipsnade Park, 675
Whiston Hall, 720
Whitburn, 737
Whitby, 749

Whitchurch, 826
Whitecraigs, 816
Whitefield, 696
Whitefields Hotel, 740
Whitehall, 822
Whitehead, 759
Whitehill, 675
Whitekirk, 808
Whiteleaf, 635
Whitemoss, 814
Whitewebbs, 701
Whiting Bay, 793
Whitley, 742
Whitley Bay, 737
Whitsand Bay Hotel, 646
Whitstable & Seasalter, 683
Whittaker, 689
Whittington Heath, 720
Whittlebury Park G & CC, 705
Whitwood, 757
Wick, 803
Wickham Park, 670
Wicklow, 784
Widnes, 643
Widney Manor, 740
Widukind-Land, 869
Wien, 833
Wienerberg, 834
Wienerwald, 834
Wiesbadener, 866
Wiesensee, 876
Wiesloch-Hohenhardter Hof, 866
Wigan, 689
Wigtown & Bladnoch, 796
Wigtownshire County, 796
Wildernesse, 683
Wildwood CC, 730
Willesley Park, 691
William Wroe, 696
Williamwood, 802
Willingcott Valley, 655
Willingdon, 733
Willow Valley, 757
Wilmslow, 643
Wilpshire, 689
Wilton, 749
Wiltshire, 283
The Wiltshire, 742
Wiltshire Ladies', 330
Wimbledon Common, 730
Wimbledon Park, 730
Wimereux, 851
Windermere, 647
Windlemere, 730
Windlesham, 730
Windmill Hill, 635
Windmill Village, 740
Windwhistle, 716
Windyhill, 797
Winge G & CC, 836
Winnerod, 865
Winter Hill, 633
Winterfield, 808
Wirral Ladies, 699
Wishaw, 740, 807
The Wisley, 730
Withernsea, 746
Withington, 696
Witney Lakes, 712

Wittelsbacher GC Rohrenfeld-Neuburg, 871
Wittsjö, 910
Wiurila G & CC, 844
Woburn, 636
De Woeste Kop, 887
Wokefield Park, 633
Woking, 730
The Woldingham, 730
Woll, 794
Wollaton Park, 710
Wolstanton, 720
Wombwell Hillies, 752
Women's European Amateur Team Championship, 320
Women's Home Internationals, 321
Women's Major Title Table, 107
Women's World Amateur Team Championship (Espirito Santo Trophy), 319
Woodbridge, 722
Woodbrook, 769
Woodbury Park, 653
Woodcote Park, 730
Woodenbridge, 784
Woodford, 663
Woodhall Hills, 757
Woodhall Spa, 694
Woodham G & CC, 658
Woodlake Park, 824
Woodlands, 774
Woodlands G & CC, 665
Woodlands Manor, 683
Woodlawn, 876
Woodside, 643

Woodsome Hall, 757
Woodspring G & CC, 666
Woodstock, 762
Woodthorpe Hall, 694
Wooler, 708
Woolley Park, 758
Woolston Manor, 663
Woolton, 699
Worcester G & CC, 745
Worcestershire, 283, 745
Worcestershire Ladies', 330
Worcestershire Open, 190
Worcestershire PGA, 190
Worfield, 714
Workington, 648
Worksop, 710
World Amateur Team Championship (Eisenhower Trophy), 251
World Championship Events, 160
World Cup of Golf, 164
Worldham Park, 670
Worlebury, 716
Worplesdon, 730
Worplesdon Mixed Foursomes, 275
Worpswede, 864
Worsley, 696
Wörther See/Velden, 830
Worthing, 735
Wörthsee, 871
Wortley, 752
Wouwse Plantage, 887
Wrag Barn G & CC, 742
Wrangaton, 653
Wrekin, 714
Wrexham, 828

Wrotham Heath, 683
Die Wutzschleife, 872
Wyboston Lakes, 630
Wychwood, 712
Wycombe Heights, 636
Wyke Green, 701
Wylihof, 916
The Wynyard Club, 658
Wyre Forest Golf Centre, 745

Yelverton, 653
Yeovil, 717
York, 749
Yorkshire, 283
Yorkshire Ladies', 330
Yorkshire Professionals, 190
Youghal, 764
Young Professionals Scottish Championship, 186
Ystad, 908
Les Yvelines, 858
Yyteri Golf, 844

Zaanse, 887
La Zagaleta, 902
Zambian Open, 192
Zaudin, 903
Zeegersloot, 890
Zeewolde, 891
Zell am See-Kaprun, 832
Zierenberg Gut Escheberg, 865
Zoate, 881
De Zuid Limburgse G & CC, 889
Zürich-Zumikon, 918

Contributors: Articles in the 2004 edition were provided by John Hopkins (*The Times*), David Davies (*The Guardian*), Mark Garrod (Press Association), Furman Bisher (*Atlanta Journal–Constitution*), Lewine Mair (*Daily Telegraph*), Ian Wooldridge (*Daily Mail*), Mike Aitken (*The Scotsman*) and Keith Mackie.

Mick Card was in charge of design and typesetting, Shirley Card handled the clubs section and proof reading and Alan and Heather Elliott supervised the collection of results and the address section of the book.

Natasha Martin was managing editor for the 2004 edition. Most pictures were provided by Phil Sheldon with others from IMG, David Phillips, the R&A and GSR Photographic.

To all involved – grateful thanks.

Renton Laidlaw, Editor.